THE DICTIONARY OF BIOGRAPHICAL QUOTATION

THE DICTIONARY OF BIOGRAPHICAL QUOTATION

OF BRITISH AND AMERICAN SUBJECTS

Edited by

Richard Kenin and Justin Wintle

Dorset Press

New York

This edition published by Dorset Press,
a division of Marboro Books Corporation,
by arrangement with Alfred A. Knopf, Inc.
1989 Dorset Press

ISBN 0-88029-344-6
(Formerly ISBN 0-394-50027-x)

Printed in the United States of America
M 9 8 7 6 5 4 3 2 1

Since this page cannot accommodate the
permission acknowledgments, they appear
on pages x-xii inclusive.

For our parents

Contents

Research Team   ix

Acknowledgments   x

Guidelines   xiii

Introduction   xv

Quotations   1

Index of Persons Quoted   828

Research Team

Julian Barnes   John Baxter   Dr Joan Hart   Amy Henderson

Robert Hewison   Dr May Hofman   Sally Issler

Jonathan Keates   Sarah Maitland   Deirdre McKenna

Ivan Pichardo   Martha Sandweiss   Basil Thesiger

Giles Waterfield   William Waterfield   Charlotte Willson-Pepper

Peter Yapp

Acknowledgments

The editors are entirely indebted to the industry and enthusiasm of each member of the research team which produced a mountain of biographical quotation from which the final selection was made. In addition, the editors wish to express their gratitude to the following: Mrs. Anne Francis, Harriett Gilbert, Sebastian Lucas, Jennifer Martin, Claudia Still, Christopher and Sarah Wintle, and the staff of the London Library.

Where they have drawn extensively from works which are still in copyright the Editors would like to make the following acknowledgments:

For excerpts from Lloyd Morris, *Not So Long Ago*, used by permission of Random House Inc.; for excerpts from Wolcott Gibbs, *Season in the Sun and Other Pleasures*, used by permission of Random House, Inc.; for excerpts from W. H. Auden, *The Dyer's Hand and other Essays*, used by permission of Random House, Inc. and Faber and Faber Ltd; from Ezra Pound, *Personae* (Copyright 1926 by Ezra Pound), reprinted by permission of New Directions and of Faber and Faber Ltd; from *Selected Letters 1907–1941 of Ezra Pound*, ed. D. G. Paige (Copyright 1950 by Ezra Pound), reprinted by permission of New Directions and of Faber and Faber Ltd; from *Selected Letters of Dylan Thomas* ed. Constantine Fitzgibbon (Copyright 1965, 1966 by the Trustees for the Copyrights of Dylan Thomas), reprinted by permission of New Directions and of J. M. Dent and Sons Ltd; from William Carlos Williams, *Collected Later Poems* (Copyright 1944 by William Carlos Williams), reprinted by permission of New Directions; from *Agee on Film, Volume I* by James Agee (Copyright © 1946, 1949, 1958 by the James Agee trust), used by permission of Grosset and Dunlap, Inc. and of Peter Owen Ltd, London; from *It All Started With Columbus* by Richard Armour (Copyright 1961 by Richard Armour), used by permission of McGraw-Hill Book Company; for six lines from 'Frederick Douglas' from *The Complete Poems of Paul Laurence Dunbar*, reprinted by permission of Dodd, Mead & Company, Inc.; for four lines from Olive Dargan, *To William Blake*, reprinted by permission of Charles Scribner's Sons; for excerpts from T. S. Eliot, *Murder in the Cathedral* (Copyright 1935 by Harcourt Brace Jovanovich, Inc., renewed 1963 by T. S. Eliot), reprinted by permission of Harcourt Brace Jovanovich, Inc. and of Faber and Faber Ltd; from Carl Sandburg, *The People, Yes* (Copyright 1936 by Harcourt Brace Jovanovich, Inc., renewed 1964 by Carl Sandburg), reprinted by permission of the publishers; from Edgar Lee Masters, 'At Sagamore Hill' from *Starved Rook*, published by the Macmillan Publishing Company, Inc., reprinted by the permission of Ellen C. Masters; for four lines from 'Blood and the Moon' and sixteen lines from 'In Memory of Major Robert Gregory' from W. B. Yeats, *Collected Poems* (Copyright the Macmillan Publishing Company 1919, 1933, renewed by Bertha Georgie Yeats 1961 and 1947 respectively), reprinted with the permission of the Macmillan Publishing Company and of A. P. Watt Ltd; for eighteen lines from 'Bryan, Bryan, Bryan, Bryan' from Vachel Lindsay, *Collected Poems* (Copyright the Macmillan

Publishing Company, Inc. 1920, renewed 1948 by Elizabeth C. Lindsay), reprinted with permission of the Macmillan Publishing Company; for nine lines from 'The Raft', twelve lines from 'Our Mother Pocahontas', eight lines from 'The Knight in Disguise' and eleven lines from 'General William Booth Enters into Heaven' from Vachel Lindsay, *Collected Poems* (Copyright by the Macmillan Publishing Company, Inc. 1917, renewed 1945 by Elizabeth C. Lindsay), reprinted by permission of the Macmillan Publishing Company, Inc.; from Eleanor Ruggles, *Prince of Players, Edwin Booth* (Copyright 1953 by W. W. Norton & Company, Inc. Copyright renewed 1981 by Eleanor Ruggles O'Leary), reprinted with permission of W. W. Norton & Company Inc.; from Stephen Vincent Benét, *John Brown's Body* (published by Holt, Rinehart and Winston, Inc., copyright 1927, 1928 by Stephen Vincent Benét, renewed 1955, 1956 by Rosemary Carr Benét), reprinted with permission of Brandt & Brandt, Literary Agency, Inc.; from Stephen Vincent Benét, *Roosevelt* (Copyright by Stephen Vincent Benét), reprinted by permission of Brandt & Brandt, Literary Agents, Inc.; from 'Captain Kidd, Thomas Jefferson, Daniel Boone, John James Audubon and Cotton Mather' from Rosemary and Stephen Vincent Benét, *A Book of Americans* (published by Holt, Rinehart and Winston Inc., copyright 1933 by Stephen Vincent Benét, renewed 1961 by Rosemary Carr Benét), reprinted by permission of Brandt & Brandt, Literary Agency, Inc.; from Otis Ferguson, *The Film Criticism of Otis Ferguson*, edited by Robert Wilson (Copyright 1971), reproduced by permission of Temple University Press; from Harold Nicolson: *Diaries and Letters*, 3 vols., edited by Nigel Nicolson (Copyright © 1966, 1967, 1968 by William Collins Sons & Co. Ltd.), reprinted by permission of Atheneum Publishers, an imprint of Macmillan Publishing Company, and William Collins Sons & Co., Ltd.; for nine lines from 'H. L. Mencken Meets a Poet in the West Side YMCA' from E. B. White, *The Fox of Peapack and Other Poems* (Copyright 1936 by E. B. White), reprinted by permission of Harper & Row, Publishers, Inc.; for excerpts from T. S. Eliot, *The Sacred Wood*, reproduced by permission of Barnes & Noble Books; from Janet Flanner, *Paris Was Yesterday*, 1925–9 (Copyright 1925–1939 (inclusive) © 1972 by the New Yorker Magazine Inc.), used by permission of the Viking Press and of Angus and Robertson (UK) Ltd; from Malcolm Cowley, *The Second Flowering* (Copyright © 1956, 1967, 1968, 1970, 1973 by Malcolm Cowley), used by permission of the Viking Press; for four lines from "Jonathan Edwards in Western Massachusetts" from *For the Union Dead* by Robert Lowell (Copyright © 1956, 1959, 1960, 1961, 1962, 1963, 1964 by Robert Lowell), reprinted by permission of Farrar, Straus & Giroux, Inc.; and of Faber and Faber Ltd; for eight lines from Dorothy Parker, *Sunset Gun*, used by permission of the Viking Press, and of Gerald Duckworth & Co.; from 'Steiglitz' by Gertrude Stein from *America and Alfred Steiglitz* (Copyright 1934 by Doubleday & Company, Inc.), used by permission of the publisher; from Adela Rogers St. John, *The Honeycomb* (Copyright 1969 by Adela Rogers St. John), used by permission of Doubleday and Company, Inc.; for five Clerihews from W. H. Auden, *Academic Grafitti* (Copyright W. H. Auden), used by permission of Random House, Inc. and of Faber and Faber Ltd; for ten lines from 'New Year Letter' from W. H. Auden, *Collected Poems* ed. Edward Mendelson, used by permission of Random House Inc. and of Faber and Faber Ltd; for eight lines from 'To T. S. Eliot on His Sixtieth Birthday' from W. H. Auden,

ACKNOWLEDGMENTS

Collected Poems ed. Edward Mendelson, used by permission of Random House Inc. and of Faber and Faber Ltd; from Eero Saarinen, *Eero Saarinen, on His Work* ed. Aline Saarinen (Copyright © 1962, 1968 Yale University Press), used by permission of Yale University; from 'Elegaics for T. S. Eliot' from George Barker, *Dreams of a Summer Night*, used by permission of Faber and Faber Ltd; for seven lines from 'Five-finger Exercises' and eight lines from 'Whispers of Immortality' from T. S. Eliot, *Collected Poems 1909–1962*, Copyright, 1936 by Harcourt Brace Jovanovich, Inc., Copyright © 1963, 1964 by T. S. Eliot, used by permission of Faber and Faber Ltd and of Harcourt Brace Jovanovich, Inc.; from Walter de la Mare, *Epitaph for William Blake*, used by permission of The Literary Trustees of Walter de la Mare and the Society of Authors as their representatives; from Leo Sherley-Price's translation of Bede's *A History of the English Church and People* (Copyright © Leo Sherley-Price 1955, 1968), used by permission of Penguin Books Ltd; from A. P. Herbert, *To B-P*, used by permission of The Estate of the Late Sir Alan Herbert; from G. K. Chesterton, *Ballad of the White Horse*, reprinted by permission of The Estate of the Late G. K. Chesteron; from Brendan Kennelly: *Yeats*, used by permission of Brendan Kennelly, and for excerpts from *On Native Grounds*, Copyright 1942, 1970 by Alfred Kazin, reprinted by permission of Harcourt Brace Jovanovich, Inc.

Guidelines

They only who live with a man can write his life with any genuine exactness and discrimination, and few people who have lived with a man know what to remark about him.

James Boswell, *Life of Johnson.*

A biography, at best, is a series of photographs, taken from a limited number of positions, on a selectively sensitive plate, by a photographer whose presence affects the expression of the sitter in a characteristic way.

C. D. Broad, *Ethics and the History of Philosophy.*

I wonder how the deuce any body could make such a world; for what purpose Dandies, for instance, were ordained — and kings — and fellows of colleges — and women of 'a certain age' — and many men of any age — and myself, most of all.

Lord Byron, Journal, 14 February 1814 — Midnight.

History is the essence of innumerable biographies.

Thomas Carlyle, *Essay on History.*

There is nothing more unfair to persons of mark than the attempts of those who know them but slightly to portray their characters or descant on their manners. Few men are to be seen through at a single or even a double glance, particularly those who are observed and waylaid, so to say, by the professional sketchers, who lie in wait for, and suddenly pounce upon them. The 'Eminent Individuals' soon acquire a knack of keeping on their guard, of almost sleeping with their eyes open. They learn to assume a conventional air, adopt certain set phrases, sometimes lay themselves out for effect, and too often display but a 'counterfeit resemblance' of their real nature. The lion-hunters teach the lions how to baffle them, and the latter shake the mane, or lash the tail, or growl or grin, according to a regular stereotyped plan for deceiving the tribe they are beset by.

Thomas Colley Grattan, *Beaten Paths and Those Who Trod Them.*

History may be formed from permanent monuments and records; but Lives can only be written from personal knowledge, which is growing every day less and in a short time is lost for ever. What is known can seldom be immediately told; and when it might be told, it is no longer known. The delicate features of the mind, the nice discriminations of character, and the minute peculiarities of conduct, are soon obliterated; and it is surely better that caprice, obstinacy, frolic and folly, however they might delight in the description, should be silently forgotten, than that, by wanton merriment, and unseasonable detection, a pang should be given to a widow, a daughter, a brother, or a friend.

Samuel Johnson, *Lives of the Poets*: 'Addison'.

The remedies of all our diseases will be discovered long after we are dead; and the world will be made a fit place to live in, after the death of most of those by whose exertions it will have been made so. It is to be hoped that those who live in those days will look back with sympathy to their known and unknown benefactors.

John Stuart Mill, Diary, 15 April 1854.

The man who makes no mistakes does not usually make anything.

E. J. Phelps, Speech at Mansion House, 1899.

One cannot define in a sentence a man whom it has taken God several millions of years to make.

Arthur Ransome, *Oscar Wilde, A Critical Study*.

A Character differeth from a Picture only in this, every Part of it must be like, but it is not necessary that every Feature should be comprehended in it as in a Picture, only some of the most remarkable.

George Savile, Marquis of Halifax, *A Character of King Charles the Second*.

Every great man nowadays has his disciples, and it is usually Judas who writes the biography.

Oscar Wilde, in the *Court and Society Review,* 20 April 1887.

Most people are other people. Their thoughts are someone else's opinions, their life a mimicry, their passions a quotation.

Oscar Wilde, Letter to Lord Alfred Douglas, in *De Profundis*.

When we meet, all the world to nothing we shall laugh; and, in truth Sir this world is worthy of nothing else.

Sir Henry Wotton, Letter to Sir Edmund Bacon, 21 March 1614.

Introduction

Somewhere between Alexander Pope's dictum that 'The Proper study of Mankind is Man' and the popular adage 'there's nowt so queer as folk' lies the key to the world's most intriguing subject: the individual.

The idea of 'Proper study' implies method, and there has never been a shortage of invented means for dealing systematically with human character. If today we are mildly incredulous of Good and Bad Angels, of the Four Humours or the Ruling Passions; or if perhaps we smile at the alchemical endeavours of Physiognomy, or Astrology, that is because we have, in modern psychology and psychoanalysis, our own interpretative devices. But method is predisposed toward finding stereotypes, toward reducing its materials to instances of common rules, and is often impervious to the essential queerness, the unclassifiable peculiarities of the individual personality. We adopt method in our search for similarities in human behaviour, forgetting that what originally attracts us to the task are the differences.

This book, *The Dictionary of Biographical Quotation*, has been compiled to keep the differences alive, to give an impression of the rich diversity of the things people have written and said about one another. First and foremost we hope that, in this respect, it is a repository of linguistic use. But it has also been our intention that it should have a practical value, as a source of reference for students of all disciplines that are concerned with human endeavour. For this reason the compilation has been made according to historical principles.

Millions of observations have been made about millions of people. Somehow we had to impose some limitations on the undertaking if it was to have any coherent, feasible shape. We began therefore by restricting ourselves for our subjects to those deceased Britons and Americans whose contributions to their respective cultures (and sometimes to both) have, over the years, attracted most attention, be it fame or notoriety; while for quotations about them we decided that both contemporaneous and post-contemporaneous sources should be used, so that each individual might appear in the lights of his or her own times, as well as under the scrutiny of posterity. We considered including living subjects as well, but felt this would not have been entirely ethical.

When preparing our lists of subjects we aimed to represent all walks of life, without any bias toward one particular group, although we later discovered natural biases in the sense that poets, for example, have tended to attract rather more lively comment than, say, scientists. To do this we used such standard authorities as the *Dictionary of National Biography* and the *Dictionary of American Biography*. But we had to be careful. The *DNB* is unduly strong on staunch Victorian clerics and pedagogues, and somewhat less accommodating toward women. The *DAB* shares these prejudices, and is perhaps over-hospitable to soldiers. Where we were aware of this kind of weighting, we tried to redress the imbalance. This said, it would be presumptuous for us to claim that this Dictionary is without its contours. As Britain is an older nation than the United States, there are inevitably more British names, particularly from the period when Great Britain was the world power; but as we move into the twentieth century, the proportion changes in favour of the Americans.

The overwhelming advantage of these parameters was that they ensured the Dictionary would have the right balance between cultural unity and cultural diversity. The contrasting histories of Britain and the United States are indissolubly linked, and their shared language, English, has been modified by each without becoming incomprehensible to the other.

There were also disadvantages. Mainly it meant excluding such figures as Jesus Christ, Napoleon and others whose influence on English and American communities is obvious. But to have made any exceptions would simply have been to further involve ourselves in decisions of an arbitrary nature. To have included Napoleon would have entailed including Hitler; but would it have entailed including Bismarck? Our list of subjects, itself an arbitrary selection, threatened to over-extend, and so we chose to stick by our guns.

Having thus established our boundaries, we then sought ways of achieving flexibility within them. There was the question of what kind of quotation should find its way into the Dictionary, and our answer was: every kind. This included criticism of our subjects' achievements. 'Every man's work', wrote Samuel Butler in *The Way of All Flesh,* 'whether it be literature or music or portraits or architecture or anything else, is always a portrait of himself.' And, still bearing with the generous spirit of this remark, we also extended the brief to our researchers to cover autobiographical quotations.

These were the principles by which we measured and cast our net. When, more than a year later, we examined the landed catch, we discovered there was no necessary correlation between, on the one hand, the quality and quantity of comment about a given individual, and, on the other, his or her received stature. For this reason we do not pretend that *The Dictionary of Biographical Quotation,* through the number of quotations pertaining to each subject, provides a gauge to the subject's relative importance; although we do content ourselves that the hundred or so indisputably major figures have been accorded justice. Certain persons, not of the first rank, but still of acknowledged significance, have been omitted altogether for want of appealing material. Conversely, when irresistably attractive material relating to acknowledged insignificants surfaced during the research our inclination was not to exclude it. It would, for example, have been unforgivable to have overlooked Pope's caricature of Lord Hervey ('Let Sporus tremble'), even though other, more important courtiers of Hervey's generation have not been so fortunate in their condemnations. We would have been unduly fastidious had we said No Butts.

In making a final selection of quotations we were concerned, wherever possible, with exhibiting a balance of views relating to each subject, so that the insights of both a man's detractors and his admirers might be shown side-by-side. But even these, when they are plentiful on both sides, do not constitute a balanced portrait of a personality, and we should emphasize that *The Dictionary of Biographical Quotation* offers no short cuts to the understanding of historical and cultural figures, which can only be attained through detailed study of their lives and achievements. But having studied, the quotations here should oil the shift from knowledge to interpretation.

There is, of course, one crucial complexity. When one person evaluates another, he inevitably reveals something of his own values. Of this we were mindful, and we very often included a quotation precisely on account of what it seemed to be telling us about its author. Thus William Hone, the Regency propagandist, is represented by two comments reflecting the diametrically opposed reactions to his trial on the parts of John Keats and William Wordsworth. To get the best out of this book we suggest that the reader who is anxious to find out about, for instance, Lord Byron, should first turn to the quotations about him, and then see what he has said about other subjects. To this end we have provided an index of authors. Those marked q.v. are also featured in the main body of the Dictionary, which is arranged alphabetically according to subject.

However, our principal criteria for selection lay in the quotations themselves. The qualities we looked for were critical or psychological acuity, lively satire, ingenious wit or good humour, articulate calumny or delicious malice, transparent flattery or veiled defamation, for fine reflection and original perspective. Most of all we sought the magic that comes when insight and expression are married into a new amalgam of content and form. This is the *raison d'être* of all books of quotations. But because we had an overall purpose, the specifically biographical quest, we have been able to take some liberties with tradition. It will be seen that whereas many entries are succinct and concise, thereby conforming to the normal concept of a 'good quote', others are longer, more passage-like. These we opted to keep for two reasons. First, to have performed pruning operations on what are often classic statements of character analysis would have been a travesty, while to have excluded them altogether would have been a denial of our aims. Second, there was a tendency, though by no means absolute, for the seriousness of a comment to increase in proportion to its length, and we were determined that there should be an equal distribution of fun and thoughtfulness. Again, we have sometimes incorporated two- or three-word phrases which would not stand up as quotations elsewhere; but taken in context with the other quotations relating to the same subject they met our purposes. And the same is true of course of some of the longer quotations as well.

Finally, our materials have been drawn from a great number of sources: not only from the standard lives, biographies and biographical collections, but also from anecdotes, epigrams, epitaphs, eulogies, obituaries, reminiscences, memoirs, reviews, essays, critical works, letters, diaries, volumes of poetry, verse, ballads and songs, pamphlets, tracts, broadsheets, sermons, newspapers, broadcasts, institutional reports, chronicles, histories, as well as from entendus, slogans, graffitti, and from at least one horoscope. Out of this diversity we hope we have been able to assemble a representative reflection of the many aspects of the human character as mirrored by itself.

Justin Wintle, London
Richard Kenin, Washington

A

ABERDEEN, EARL OF (GEORGE HAMILTON GORDON)

1784–1860 Statesman

His grief was such that at times he felt as if every drop of blood that would be shed would rest upon his head.
> On himself, concerning the Crimean war, in conversation with John Bright, 22 March 1854, Bright, Diary.

You complain'd of Lord Aberdeen's unceasing conversation, but with his knowledge and cleverness it was not such a bad substitute for a book.
> Lady Beesborough, Letter to Lord Granville Leveson-Gower, November 1812.

His temper naturally morose, has become licentiously peevish. Crossed in his Cabinet, he insults the House of Lords, and plagues the most eminent of his colleagues with the crabbed malice of a maundering witch.
> Benjamin Disraeli, Letter to the Press, 1853.

See also Lord Russell, Queen Victoria

ABERNETHY, JOHN

1764–1831 Surgeon

He had none of the chivalrous and grand spirit of Cooper. With all his eccentricities and his studied profession of ignoring 'gain', he was thoroughly a selfish man.
> J. F. Clarke, *Autobiographical Recollections of the Medical Profession.*

You, who never knew Mr. Abernethy, have no conception of his powers as a lecturer. He so eloquently expounded some of the highest truths; he so nicely disentangled the perplexities of many abstruse subjects; he made that so easy which was before so difficult, that every man who heard him feels perhaps to this day, that, for some important portion of his knowledge, he is indebted to Mr. Abernethy. But he reserved all his enthusiasm for his peculiar doctrine; he so reasoned it, so acted it, so dramatized it (those who have heard him will know what I mean): and then in his own droll way he so disparaged the more laborious searchers after truth, calling them contemptuously 'the Doctors', and so disported himself with ridicule of every system but his own, that we accepted the doctrine in all its fulness. We should have been ashamed to do otherwise. We accepted it with acclamation, and voted ourselves by acclamation the profoundest of medical philosophers, at the easy rate of one half hour's instruction.
> P. M. Latham, *Lectures on Subjects Connected with Clinical Medicine.*

One of the brightest points in Abernethy's character, was, that, however he might sometimes forget the courtesy due to his private patients, he was never unkind to those whom charity had confided to his care. One morning, leaving home for the hospital, when some one was desirous of detaining him, he said: 'Private patients, if they do not like me, can go elsewhere; but the poor devils in the hospital I am bound to take care of'.
> George Macilwain, *Memoirs of John Abernethy, F.R.S.*

Many years after this, I met him coming into the hospital one day, a little before two (the hour of lecture), and seeing him rather smartly dressed, with a white waistcoat, I said:
'You are very gay to-day, Sir?'
'Ay,' said he; 'one of the girls was married this morning'.
'Indeed, Sir,' I said. 'You should have given yourself a holiday on such an occasion, and not come down to lecture'.
'Nay,' returned he. 'Egad! I came down to lecture the day I was married myself!'
> *Ibid.*

He is reported to have been consulted by the late Duke of York; and he stood before his royal highness, whistling, with his hands in his breeches-pockets, as usual. The duke, astonished at his conduct, said, 'I suppose you know who I am?' 'Suppose I do,' said he, 'what of that?' And his advice to his royal highness was given thus: 'Cut off the *supplies*, as the Duke of Wellington did in his campaigns, and the enemy will leave the citadel.'
> Thomas Joseph Pettigrew, *Medical Portrait Gallery.*

ACHESON, DEAN

A man of rank consulted Mr. Abernethy, and was received by him with remarkable rudeness. Upon some severe remark being made, the patient lost his temper, and told Mr. A. he would make him *eat his words*. 'It will be of no use', said Mr. A., coolly, 'for they will be sure to come up again!'
> *Ibid.*

John Abernethy ... developed the physiological side of surgery and investigated the causes of disease and its non-operative treatment, for he took little pleasure in the manipulative part of his profession.
> Sir D'Arcy Power, The Hunterian Oration, 14 February 1925.

When Abernethy was canvassing for the office of surgeon to St. Bartholomew Hospital, he called upon such a person, — a rich grocer, one of the governors. The great man behind the counter seeing the great surgeon enter, immediately assumed the grand air towards the supposed suppliant for his vote. 'I presume, sir, you want my vote and interest at this momentous epoch of your life'. Abernethy, who hated humbugs, and felt nettled at the tone, replied: 'No, I don't: I want a pennyworth of figs; come, look sharp and wrap them up: I want to be off!'
> Samuel Smiles, *Self-help.*

ACHESON, DEAN G.

1893–1971 Government Official

I am something of a stoic both by nature and by inheritance. And I learned from the example of my father that the manner in which one endures what must be endured is more important than the thing that must be endured.
> On himself, in Merle Miller, *Plain Speaking, An Oral Biography of Harry S. Truman.*

I will undoubtedly have to seek what is happily known as gainful employment, which I am glad to say does not describe holding public office.
> On himself, on leaving his post as Secretary of State, in *Time*, 22 December 1952.

His career was a text book example of the rise of a patrician in the snug embrace of the American establishment.
> Anon., in *Time*, 25 October 1971.

I watch his smark-aleck manner and his British clothes and that New Dealism, everlasting New Dealism in everything he says and does, and I want to shout 'Get out, get out. You stand for every-thing that has been wrong with the United States for years.'
> Senator Hugh Butler, in Merle Miller, *Plain Speaking, An Oral Biography of Harry S. Truman.*

Acheson found it difficult to conceal his contempt for the contemptible.
> Douglas Southall Freeman, in *ibid.*

Not only did he not suffer fools gladly, he did not suffer them at all.
> Lester Pearson, in *Time*, 25 October 1971.

See also Adlai Stevenson, Harry S. Truman

ACTON, LORD, JOHN EMERICH EDWARD DALBERG

1834–1902 Historian

I think our studies ought to be all but purposeless. They want to be pursued with chastity like mathematics. This ... is my profession of faith.
> On himself, Letter to Richard Simpson, 19 January 1859.

I am afraid I am a partisan of sinking ships, and I know none more ostensibly sinking just now than St Peter's....
> On himself, Letter to Richard Simpson, 7 December 1859.

... such men [as Acton] are all vanity: they have the inflation of German professors, and the ruthless talk of undergraduates.
> Cardinal Manning, comment, 1870, in Lytton Strachey, *Eminent Victorians.*

Somebody said of Hallam that he was the magistrate of history. In a far deeper sense it was true of Acton.
> Lord John Morley, *Recollections.*

... He is thoroughly eclectic in his friendships, and when he is in London he flits from Lady Hayter's tea-table to Mr Goschen's bureau, analyses at the Athenaeum the gossip which he acquired at Brooks's, and by dinner-time is able, if only he is willing, to tell you what Spain intends and what America; the present relations between the Curia and the Secret Societies ... and the latest theory about the side of Whitehall on which Charles I was beheaded.
> G. W. E. Russell, *Collections and Recollections.*

... a historian to whom learning and judgment had not been granted in equal proportions ... that laborious and scrupulous scholar, that life-long

enthusiast for liberty, that almost hysterical reviler of priestcraft and persecution, trailing his learning so discrepantly along the dusty Roman way . . . there are some who know how to wear their Rome with a difference; and Lord Acton was one of these.
Lytton Strachey, *Eminent Victorians.*

ADAM, ROBERT

1728—92 Architect

I am a very promising young man.
On himself, Letter to his family, 1756.

Mr. Adam's success arose chiefly from his knowledge of detail and his minute and elaborate taste — but he was not an artist of any force nor of very sound judgement — he began with details and adapted them to the necessary lines. I am sure his ideas first assembled in ornament & decorations — his plans are a labyrinth . . .
C. R. Cockerell, Diary, July 1821.

. . . in the obvious & palpable disposition of the house your way is never direct, sometimes sideways like a crab, sometimes thro' alcove or corner you come into a magnificent room you know not how.
Ibid

The chief merit of the Adam variation of the classical style was its recognition of the ancillary trades and crafts. It had, moreover, the attraction of being economical while retaining the appearance of being costly.
Sir Albert Richardson, *An Introduction to Georgian Architecture.*

Adam, our most admired [architect], is all gingerbread, filigraine, and fan-painting.
Horace Walpole, Letter to Sir Horace Mann, 22 April 1775.

Mr. Adam has published the first number of his Architecture. In it is a magnificent gateway and screen for the Duke of Northumberland at Sion, which I see erecting every time I pass. It is all lace and embroidery, and as croquant as his frames for tables; consequently most improper to be executed in the high road to Brentford. From Kent's mahogany we are dwindled to Adam's filigree. Grandeur and simplicity are not yet in fashion. In his Preface he seems to tax Wyatt with stealing from him; but Wyatt has employed the antique with more judgement, and the 'Pantheon' is still the most beautiful edifice in England. What are the Adelphi Buildings? warehouses laced down the seams, like a

soldier's trull in a regimental lace coat.
Horace Walpole, Letter to the Rev. W. Mason, 29 July 1773.

ADAMS, ABIGAIL

1744—1818 Letter writer

She is a farmer cultivating the land, and discussing the weather and the crops; a merchant reporting prices-current and the rates of exchange, and directing the making up of invoices; a politician speculating upon the probabilities of peace or war; and a mother writing the most exalted sentiments to her son. All of these pursuits she adopts together; some from choice, the rest from the necessity of the case; and in all she appears equally well.
Charles Francis Adams, *Familiar Letters of John Adams and His Wife During the Revolution.*

The central and conspicuous fact about Abigail Adams' letters is that she hardly knew how to write a full paragraph.
L. H. Butterfield, *The Book of Abigail and John.*

Mrs. President not of the United States but of a faction.
Albert Gallatin, in *Dictionary of American Biography,* I.

ADAMS, FRANKLIN PIERCE

1881—1960 Journalist

As I often have said, I am easily influenced. Compared with me a weather vane is Gibraltar.
On himself, in Robert E. Drennan ed., *Wit's End.*

ADAMS, HENRY BROOKS

1838—1918 Historian

I want to look like an American Voltaire or Gibbon, but am slowly settling down to be a third-rate Boswell hunting for a Dr Johnson.
On himself, in Ernest Samuels, *Henry Adams, The Major Phase.*

I have no object but a superficial one as far as history is concerned. To me, accuracy is relative. I care very little whether my details are exact, if only my *ensemble* is in scale. . . .
On himself, in an undated letter to Henry Osborn Taylor, in George Hochfield, *Henry Adams, An Introduction and Interpretation.*

So far as [I] had a function in life, it was as stable-companion to statesmen.
    On himself, in James D. Hart, *The Oxford Companion to American Literature*.

Adams is like a fish in the hand, one is no sooner conscious of having him than he is gone; he can never be held for good without impairing that essential stuff of complexity with which Nature so richly endowed him.
    Harold Dean Cater, 'Biographical Introduction', in Harold Dean Cater ed., *Henry Adams and His Friends*.

. . . with the wings of a beautiful but ineffectual conscience beating vainly in a vacuum jar.
    T. S. Eliot, in J. C. Levenson, *The Mind and Art of Henry Adams*.

When I happened to fall in with him on the street, he could be delightful, but when I called at his house and he was posing to himself as the old cardinal he would turn everything to dust and ashes. After a tiresome day's work one didn't care to have one's powers of resistance taxed by discourse of that sort, so I called rarely.
    Justice Oliver Wendell Holmes, in Ernest Samuels, *Henry Adams, The Major Phase*.

. . . the only man in America who could sit on a fence and see himself go by.
    Ed Howe, in *ibid.*

In these great stresses, friendship reaches out to the making of an image of the friend who has suffered assault — and I make one of you thus according to my sense of your rich and ingenious mind and your great resources of contemplation, speculation, resignation — a curiosity in which serenity is yet at home.
    Henry James, in a 1912 letter to Adams after the latter's stroke, in J. C. Levenson, *The Mind and Art of Henry Adams*.

Henry Adams, snob, scholar, and misanthrope. . . .
    Alfred Kazin, *On Native Grounds*.

Henry Adams offers to his fellow Americans the richest and most challenging image of what they are, what they have been, and what they may be.
    J. C. Levenson, *The Mind and Art of Henry Adams*.

Adams' gift and his flaw was pride. His saving was the transcendence of that personal pride into humanity's. His thought is most valuable as a leaven. Deposited among the over-complacent truths of the democratic society, it preserves and transforms them into a better kind of bread.
    Elizabeth Stevenson, *Henry Adams*.

He was a seismograph recording earthquakes of the future. We are engulfed in them now, having traveled far along the road he foresaw. We can read him with more appreciation than his own generation could.
    Ibid.

Adams, in brief, did not care for truth, unless it was amusing; for he was a modern nihilist, and hence a hedonist or nothing.
    Yvor Winters, *The Anatomy of Nonsense*.

ADAMS, JOHN

1735—1826 Second United States President

Vanity, I am sensible, is my cardinal vice and cardinal folly.
    On himself, in J. T. Morse, *John Adams*.

Siste, Viator
With much delight these pleasing hills you view,
Where Adams from an envious world withdrew,
Where sick of glory, faction, power, and pride,
Sure judge how empty all, who had all tried,
Beneath his shades the weary chief repos'd,
And life's great scene in quiet virtue clos'd.
    On himself, proposed inscription for his tomb, 25 November 1808, in Gilbert Chinard, *Honest John Adams*.

See Johnny at the helm of State,
Head itching for a crowny,
He longs to be like Georgy, great,
And pull Tom Jeffer downy.
    Anon., in Arthur Styron, *The Last of the Cocked Hats*.

To A Would-Be Great Man
Daddy vice, Daddy vice
One may see in a trice
The drift of your fine publication
As sure as a gun
The thing was done
To secure you — a pretty station.
    Anon. rhyme 1789, in Gilbert Chinard, *Honest John Adams*.

Be grateful then, YE CHOSEN! mod'rate wise,
Nor stretch your claims to such preposterous size,
Lest your too partial country — wiser grown —
Shou'd on your native dunghills set you down.
Ape not the fashions of the foreign great,
Nor make your betters at your levees wait —

Resign your awkward pomp, parade and pride,
And lay that useless *etiquette* aside;
The unthinking laugh, but all the thinking hate
Such vile, abortive mimickry of State;
Those idle lackeys, saunt'ring at your door,
But ill become *poor servants* of the POOR.
    Anon., in Page Smith, *John Adams,
    1784—1826.*

Although Adams was the second president, he was the first vice-president, and this was some consolation.
    Richard Armour, *It All Started With Columbus.*

Ali Baba among his Forty Thieves is no more deserving of sympathy than John Adams shut up within the seclusion of his Cabinet room with his official family of secret enemies.
    Claude G. Bowers, *Jefferson and Hamilton.*

. . . he was the founder of a dynasty and belonged to his descendants rather than to his ancestors.
    Gilbert Chinard, *Honest John Adams.*

. . . of a restless and irritable temperament, jealous of others' praise and suspicious of their influence; obstinate and yet fickle . . . vain to a degree approaching insanity; he was himself incapable alike of conceiving or of acting upon a settled system of policy, and was to others as easy a subject for indirect management as he was impracticable to a more legitimate approach. . . .
    George Gibbs, in Arthur Styron, *The Last of the Cocked Hats.*

. . . an imagination sublimated and eccentric, propitious neither to the regular display of sound judgment nor to steady perseverance in a systematic plan of conduct.
    Alexander Hamilton, in Page Smith, *John Adams, 1784—1826.*

Adams was in a very real sense Washington's creator.
    Rupert Hughes, *George Washington.*

He is vain, irritable, and a bad calculator of the force and probable effect of the motives which govern men. This is all the ill which can possibly be said of him. He is as disinterested as the Being who made him.
    Thomas Jefferson, Letter to James Madison, 1787.

His Rotundity.
    William Maclay, in Page Smith, *John Adams, 1784—1826.*

It has been the political career of this man to begin with hypocrisy, proceed with arrogance, and finish with contempt.
    Tom Paine, *Open Letter To The Citizens Of The United States*, 22 November 1802.

He was *terribly* open, earnest, and direct, and could not keep his mouth shut.
    Theodore Parker, in James B. Peabody ed., *John Adams, A biography in his own words.*

He can't dance, drink, game, flatter, promise, dress, swear with the gentlemen, and small talk and flirt with the ladies — in short, he has none of the essential *arts* or *ornaments* which make up a courtier — there are thousands who with a tenth part of his understanding, and without a spark of his honesty, would distance him infinitely in any court in Europe.
    Jonathan Sewall, 1787, in Page Smith, *John Adams, 1784—1826.*

See also John Quincy Adams

ADAMS, JOHN QUINCY
1767—1848 Sixth United States President

I am a man of reserved, cold, austere, and forbidding manners: my political adversaries say, a gloomy misanthropist, and my personal enemies, an unsocial savage.
    On himself, Diary, 4 June 1819.

He that played Sir Pander
    While wages were to be had,
And saved slave-trading Andrew,
    Now rails at them like mad;
And turning to him he modestly says
    'Your language is too bad.'
    Anon. (John Quincy Adams though an abolitionist had antagonized the radicals in the movement.) In Marie B. Hecht, *John Quincy Adams, A Personal History of an Independent Man.*

Asked by the Nation's chief to take my tea,
    I hastened to him in surprising glee,
But when I got there, all my treat, by God,
    Is just to watch His Excellency's Nod.
    Anon. contemporary, in S. F. Bemis, *John Quincy Adams and the Union.*

Well has he been called 'The Massachusettes Madman.' He boasts that he places all his glory in independence. If independence is synonymous with obstinacy, he is the most independent statesman living.

Anon., in *New York Times* on the Emancipation debates, in L. Falkner, *The President Who Wouldn't Retire.*

Quiet is not his sphere. And when a legitimate scene of action does not present itself, it is much to be feared that he will embrace an illegitimate one.
  Charles Francis Adams, in Marie B. Hecht, *John Quincy Adams, A Personal History of an Independent Man.*

John Quincy Adams was the second Adams to become president. He is not to be confused with his father, John Adams, who was the first Adams but the second president, or with his Uncle Sam Adams (who was not the real Uncle Sam, except to his nieces and nephews). It was fortunate for us, if not for the second John Adams, that he had the Quincy, which the first John did not.
  Richard Armour, *It All Started With Columbus.*

Like George Washington he did not believe in parties or in sections, the essential realities of American politics — and they did not believe in him.
  S. F. Bemis, *John Quincy Adams and the Union.*

Punctual to every duty, death found him at the post of duty; and where else could it have found him, at any stage of his career, for the fifty years of his illustrious public life.
  Thomas Hart Benton, in B. C. Clark, *John Quincy Adams.*

In politics he was an apostate, and in private life a pedagogue, and in everything but amiable and honest.
  De Witt Clinton, in R. V. Remini, *Martin Van Buren and the Making of the Democratic Party.*

When they talk about his old age and venerableness and nearness to the grave, he knows better. He is like one of those old cardinals, who as quick as he is chosen Pope, throws away his crutches and his crookedness, and is as straight as a boy. He is an old roué, who cannot live on slops, but must have sulphuric acid in his tea.
  Ralph Waldo Emerson, *Journals.*

Mr. Adams belongs to no local district, to no political party, but to the Nation and to the people; he is elected by his district in Massachusetts, comes here with his family during the sessions of Congress, and keeps house by himself, while in the House of Representatives he consults with no one, takes the advice of no one, and holds himself accountable to no one but the Nation.
  Joshua R. Giddings, in Walter Buell, *Joshua Giddings.*

. . . in many respects the most wonderful man of the age, certainly the greatest in the United States — perfect in knowledge but deficient in practical results. As a statesman he was pure and incorruptible, but too irascible to lead men's judgment.
  Philip Hone on the death of John Quincy Adams, 24 February 1848, in S. F. Bemis, *John Quincy Adams and the Union.*

Of all the men, whom it was ever my lot to accost and to waste civilities upon, [he] was the most doggedly and systematically repulsive. With a vinegar aspect, cotton in his leathern ears, and hatred of England in his heart, he sat in the frivolous assemblies of Petersburg like a bull-dog among spaniels; and many were the times that I drew monosyllables and grim smiles from him and tried in vain to mitigate his venom.
  Hon. W. H. Lyttleton, Letter to Charles Bagot, 22 January 1827.

To him, who alike inherits
The *Name*, and the *place*, of his Sire;—
Who has *won* the rank he merits,
By vigor that cannot tire.
  J. Percival, *Ode*, 4 March 1825 (verse to be sung at dinner in celebration of John Quincy Adams' election), in Marie B. Hecht, *John Quincy Adams, A Personal History of an Independent Man.*

The cub is a greater bear than the old one.
  John Randolph of Roanoke, in Alfred Steinberg, *The First Ten.*

John Quincy Adams was a short, stout, bald, brilliant and puritanical twig off a short, stout, bald, brilliant, and puritanical tree. Little wonder, then, that he took the same view of the office of President as had his father.
  Alfred Steinberg, in *ibid.*

He loved country, desired to serve it, and was properly conscious of the honor of doing so.
  Martin Van Buren, in S. F. Bemis, *John Quincy Adams and the Union.*

Sedate, circumspect and cautious; reserved, but not distant; grave but not repulsive. He receives but seldom communicates, and discerns with great quickness motives, however latent, and intentions, however concealed . . . Mr. Adams has more capacity than genius; he can comprehend better than he can invent; and execute nearly as rapidly as he can design.
  George Waterton, in Marie B. Hecht, *John Quincy Adams, A Personal History of an Independent Man.*

See also Henry Clay, Robert A. Taft, John Tyler

ADAMS, SAMUEL

1722–1803 Revolutionary Statesman

Lo Adams rose, in warfare nobly try'd
His country's saviour, Father shield & Guide,
Urg'd by her wrongs, he wag'd ye: glorious strife
Nor paus'd to waste a Coward Thought on Life.
  Anon. verse on a mezzotint, John Mitchell after
  John Singleton Copley, 1775.

The whole continent is ensnared by that Machiavel
of chaos.
  Anon. Letter to Governor Thomas Hutchinson,
  14 September 1776.

. . . a grief and distress to his family, a weeping,
helpless object of compassion for years.
  John Adams, *Works,* vol. X.

Sam Adams was born with a silver spoon in his
mouth, but once it was removed he became a fine
orator.
  Richard Armour, *It All Started With Columbus.*

No man contributed more towards our revolution,
& no man left behind him less, distinctly to mark
his resolutions, his peculiar genius & communications.
He was feared by his enemies, but too secret to be
loved by his friends. He did not put confidence in
them, while he was of importance to them. He was
not known till he acted & how far he was to act was
unknown.
  Reverend William Bentley, Diary, 3 October 1803.

Every dip of his pen stung like a horned snake.
  Governor Sir Francis Bernard, in J. C. Miller,
  Samuel Adams, Pioneer in Propaganda.

A man, who though by no means remarkable for
brilliant abilities, yet is equal to most men in popular
intrigue, and the management of a faction. He eats
little, drinks little, sleeps little, thinks much, and is
most decisive and indefatigable in the pursuit of his
objects. It was this man, who by his superior
application managed at once the faction in Congress
at Philadelphia, and the factions in New England.
Whatever these patriots in Congress wished to have
done by their colleagues without . . . Mr. Adams
advised and directed to be done.
  Joseph Galloway, *Historical and Political
  Reflections.*

Mr Samuel Adams, although not fluent of elocution,
was so rigorously logical, so clear in his views,
abundant in good sense, and master always of his
subject, that he commanded the most profound
attention whenever he arose in an assembly by
which the froth of declamation was heard with
the most sovereign contempt.
  Thomas Jefferson, in Stewart Beach, *Samuel
  Adams, The Fateful Years, 1764–1776.*

Truly the Man of the Revolution.
  Thomas Jefferson, in John C. Miller, *Sam Adams,
  Pioneer in Propaganda.*

Although Sam Adams was expert in overturning
governments, he knew nothing of rebuilding them.
His weaknesses are most apparent in his attempts to
control the American army during the war and the
protracted feuds he carried on with his political
enemies in Congress.
  John C. Miller, in *ibid.*

I shall . . . give you a sketch of some of Mr. Samuel
Adams' features, and I do not know how to de-
lineate them stronger than by the observation made
by a celebrated painter in America, viz., 'That if he
wished to draw the picture of the devil, that he
would get Sam Adams to sit for him.' . . . He understood human nature, in low life, so well that he
could turn the minds of the great vulgar as well as
the small into any course he might choose.
  Peter Oliver, *Origins and Progress of the
  American Revolution: A Tory View.*

He possessed a quick understanding, a cool head,
stern manners, a smooth address, and Roman-like
firmness, united with that sagacity and penetration
that would have made a figure in a conclave. He was
at the same time liberal in opinion and uniformly
devout; social with men of all denominations, grave
in deportment, placid, yet sober and indefatigable;
calm in seasons of difficulty, tranquil and unruffled
in the vortex of political altercation; too firm to be
intimidated, too haughty for condescension, his
mind was replete with resources that dissipated fear,
and extricated in the greatest emergencies. Thus
qualified, he stood forth early and continued firm
through the great struggle.
  Mrs Mercy Otis Warren, 1805, in Stewart Beach,
  Samuel Adams, The Fateful Years, 1764–1776.

See also John Quincy Adams

ADDAMS, JANE

1860–1935 Social Reformer

It was only when a great war raged in the world,
tremendous international emotions were let loose,
that this good woman essayed a task beyond her,
and in excess of zeal and shocked horror, stood
forth for peace where there was no peace, and

made public utterances from a full heart that were better left unsaid.

Anon., in *Los Angeles Times*, March 1918, in Allen F. Davis, *American Heroine, The Life and Legend of Jane Addams.*

Jane Addams is to Chicago what Joan of Arc was to her people, she is sacrificing all for the masses.

Anon., in *Springfield Caxton*, August 1910, in *ibid.*

It is a breed of little blinded men
And wanton women who would laugh at her
Because in time of war she sets astir
Against the sword the legions of the pen
To write the name of Jesus Christ again
And on this page, a swarming broken blur,
Restore the word of the Deliverer
Above the words of little blinded men.

Anon., in *Harper's Weekly*, August 1915.

One wrote of Filomena, saint of old,
Who bore a lamp in dark and lonesome place;
And with like blesses charity and grace
Wrought England's Florence with her heart of gold.

Now comes another who with courage bold
Dark pathways of sad souls with love doth trace,
Light comes to all who look upon her face
Transfigured with the faith of martyrs old.

O'er sorrowing hearts her loving heart doth yearn.
Deep grief to allay and to assuage the pain;
Great wrongs to right her eager soul doth burn,
And always from the false the true discern.
Be this her joy, her work is not in vain,
In loyal hearts enshrined, our own Saint Jane.

Florence Holbrook, 8 October 1923, in Allen F. Davis, *American Heroine, The Life and Legend of Jane Addams.*

She simply inhabits reality, and everything she says necessarily expresses its nature. *She can't help writing truth.*

William James, in *American Journal of Sociology*, 1909.

She had compassion without condescension. She had pity without retreat into vulgarity. She had infinite sympathy for common things without forgetfulness of those that are uncommon.
That, I think, is why those who have known her say she was not only good, but great.

Walter Lippmann, 23 May 1935, in Allen F. Davis, *American Heroine, The Life and Legend of Jane Addams.*

Remember Botticelli's Fortitude
In the Uffizi? — The worn, waiting face;

The pale, fine-fibred hands upon the mace;
The brow's serenity, the lips that brood,
The vigilant, tired patience of her mood?
There was a certain likeness I could trace
The day I heard her in a country place,
Talking to knitting women about Food.
Through cool statistics glowed the steady gleam
Of that still undismayed, interned desire;
But — strength and stay, and deeper than the dream —
The two commands that she is pledged to keep
In the red welter of a world on fire,
Are, 'What is that to thee?' and 'Feed my sheep!'

Ruth Comfort Mitchell, 'Jane Addams', in *Atlantic Monthly*, November 1918.

The crowning irony of Jane Addams' life ... was that she compromised her intellect for the sake of human experiences which her nature prevented her from having. Life, as she meant the term, forever eluded her.

William L. O'Neill, *Everyone was brave.*

ADDINGTON, HENRY, VISCOUNT SIDMOUTH

1757–1844 Statesman, Prime Minister

I stand before your Lordships charged with having used my best endeavours to stop the progress of blasphemy and sedition. To that charge I plead guilty, and while I live I shall be proud to have such a charge brought against me.

On himself, on his action to curb the cheap Press, House of Lords debate, 12 May 1817.

I hate liberality . . . nine times out of ten it is cowardice, and the tenth time lack of principle.

On himself, in John Mitford's MS notebook, 'Sayings of Lord Sidmouth'.

This is the true and lamentable story of the rise and progress of the Doctor and Co., who, like Bazilio in the Barbier de Seville, works his way in and then, piano, piano, spreads and dilates and gathers strength from the weakness or necessities of those around him.

Lady Bessborough, Letter to Lord Granville Leveson-Gower, 27 September 1806.

I am afraid of this damned Addington being bullied out of his pacific disposition. He will be most cursedly run at, and he has neither talents to command open coadjutors, nor sufficient skill in intriguing to acquire new ones.

Thomas Creevey, Letter to Dr Currie, 8 November 1802.

Am I to be the only man in England who cannot lay his head on his pillow without the painful consciousness of having rather injured than benefited the fortunes of the best friend he has in the world? Why is Mr Addington too proud to accept a proof of friendship from the King? I am a proud man too, and is *that* the situation in which the King of England ought to be placed?
George III's exclamation to Addington, May 1804, noted in Mary Anne Addington's Notebook.

The Duke of Wellington upon home service.
George IV, comment on Addington's conduct of the Cato Street operation, in Sir Benjamin Bloomfield, Letter to Addington, 12 March 1820.

The King has two favourites; the War and the Doctor. But the doctor has at present preference; and even the war would be given up for him.
Francis Horner, writing in 1802, in Harriet Martineau, *History of England 1800–1815*.

The indefinable air of a village apothecary inspecting the tongue of the State.
Lord Rosebery, *Life of Pitt*.

[Pitt] exclaiming, 'I am delighted to have got amongst you, for we have had the Doctor travelling with his own horses for the last hour and a half, and we thought he would never arrive at the end of the stage.' In those days gentlemen's postillions used to drive with long whips and velvet caps with silver tassels to them, which played up and down in conformity with the measured and slow action of the postillions on their horses. And one can conceive Addington's pompous delivery, measured phraseology, and monotonous intonation, affording a capital likeness of a gentleman's own horses during a long stage.
The Duke of Rutland, Letter to John Wilson Croker, 2 March 1847.

Clothed with the Bible, as with light,
And the shadows of the night,
Like Sidmouth, next Hypocrisy
On a crocodile rode by.
Percy Bysshe Shelley, *The Mask of Anarchy*.

. . . two vultures sick for battle,
Two scorpions under one wet stone,
Two bloodless wolves whose dry throats rattle,
Two crows perched on the murrained cattle,
Two vipers tangled into one.
Percy Bysshe Shelley, *Similes for two Political Characters*.

ADDISON, JOSEPH
1672–1719 Poet, Statesman

Thus I live in the world rather as a Spectator of mankind, than as one of the species, by which means I have made myself a speculative statesman, soldier, merchant, and artisan, without ever meddling with any practical part of life.
On himself, in *Spectator*, no. 1, March 1711.

Addison was responsible for many of the evils from which English prose has since suffered. He made prose artful and whimsical, he made it sonorous when sonority was not needed, affected when it did not require affectation. . . . He was the first Man of Letters. Addison had the misuse of an extensive vocabulary and so was able to invalidate a great number of words and expressions; the quality of his mind was inferior to the language which he used to express it.
Cyril Connolly, *Enemies of Promise*.

In him
Humour in holiday and slightly trim
Sublimity and Attic taste, combin'd,
To polish, furnish, and delight the mind.
William Cowper, *Table-Talk*.

As a teacher of wisdom, he may be confidently followed. His religion has nothing in it enthusiastic or superstitious: he appears neither weakly credulous, nor wantonly sceptical; his morality is neither dangerously lax, nor impracticably rigid. All the enchantment of fancy, and all the cogency of argument, are employed to recommend to the reader his real interest, the care of pleasing the Author of his being.
Samuel Johnson, *Lives of the Poets*.

No whiter page than Addison remains.
He from the taste obscene reclaims our youth,
And sets the passions on the side of Truth,
Forms the soft bosom with the gentlest Art,
And pours each human virtue in the heart.
Alexander Pope, *Imitations of Horace: Epistles; Book II, epistle i*.

Statesman, yet friend to truth! of soul sincere,
In action faithful, and in honour clear;
Who broke no promise, served no private end,
Who gained no title, and who lost no friend.
Alexander Pope, *Moral Essays, epistle* vii 'To Mr Addison'.

Blest with each talent and each art to please,
And born to write, converse, and live with ease:
Should such a man, too fond to rule alone,
Bear, like the Turk, no brother near the throne;

View him with scornful, yet with jealous eyes,
And hate for arts that caus'd himself to rise;
Damn with faint praise, assent with civil leer,
And without sneering, teach the rest to sneer;
Willing to wound, and yet afraid to strike,
Just hint a fault, and hesitate dislike;
Alike reserv'd to blame, or to commend,
A tim'rous foe, and a suspicious friend;
Dreading ev'n fools, by Flatterers besieg'd,
And so obliging, that he ne'er oblig'd;
Like *Cato*, give his little Senate laws,
And sit attentive to his own applause;
While Wits and Templars ev'ry sentence raise,
And wonder with a foolish face of praise: —
Who must but laugh, if such a man there be?
Who would not weep, if ATTICUS were he?
    Alexander Pope, *Epistle to Dr Arbuthnot.*

Mr. Addison could not give out a common order in
writing, from his endeavouring always to word it
too finely. — He had too beautiful an imagination to
make a man of business.
    Alexander Pope, in Joseph Spence, *Anecdotes.*

Whan panting Virtue her last efforts made,
You brought your Clio to the virgin's aid.
    William Somerville (referring to the fact that
    Addison signed his paper in the *Spectator* with one
    or other of the letters of Clio's name), *Poetical
    Address to Mr Addison.*

If business calls, or crowded courts invite,
Th' unblemished statesman seems to strike my sight;
If in the stage I seek to soothe my care,
I meet his soul which breathes in Cato there;
If pensive to the rural shades I rove,
His shape o'ertakes me in the lonely grove;
'Twas there of just and good he reason'd strong,
Clear'd some great truth, or rais'd some serious song:
There patient show'd us the wise course to steer,
A candid censor and a friend sincere.
    Thomas Tickell, *To the Earl of Warwick, on the
    Death of Addison.*

There still remains the fact that the essays of
Addison are perfect essays. . . . Whether it was a
high thing, or whether it was a low thing, whether
an epic is more profound or a lyric more passionate,
undoubtedly it is due to Addison that prose is now
prosaic — the medium which makes it possible for
people of ordinary intelligence to communicate
their ideas to the world.
    Virginia Woolf, *The Common Reader.*

See also Henry Fielding, Samuel Johnson,
Alexander Pope

ADRIAN IV (NICHOLAS BREAKSPEAR)
d. 1159 Pope

He held his place four years, *eight months,* and
eight and twenty dayes: and Anno 1158 [sic], as
he was drinking, was choakt with a *Fly*: which in
the large Territory of St. *Peters patrimony* had no
place but his Throat to get into. . . .
    Thomas Fuller, *The History of the Worthies of
    England.*

It was in acquiescence to my petitions that Adrian
granted and entrusted Ireland to the illustrious king
of the English, Henry II, to be possessed by him and
his heirs, as the papal letters still give evidence. This
was by virtue of the fact that all islands are said to
belong to the Roman Church, by an ancient right,
based on the Donation of Constantine, who established and conceded this privilege.
    John of Salisbury, *Metalogicon,* translated by
    D. D. McGarry.

AELFRIC
— d. 1005 Archbishop of Canterbury

I, Aelfric, monk and priest, though meaner than is
fitting for that order, was sent in the reign of King
Ethelred by Bishop Aelfheah, Aethelwold's
successor, to a monastery which is called Cerne, at
the request of the thegn Aethelmaer — his rank and
virtue are known everywhere. It then entered my
mind, by the grace of God, I trust, to turn this book
from the Latin language into the English tongue,
not from confidence of great learning, but because I
saw and heard much error in many English books,
which unlearned men in their simplicity accounted
great wisdom; and I was sorry that they did not
know nor possess the evangelical teaching among
their books, except for those men alone who knew
Latin, and except for the books which King Alfred
wisely translated from Latin into English, which
are obtainable.
    On himself, Preface to the first volume of his
    Catholic Homilies, translated by B. Thorpe.

In connection with Aelfric having made translations
of books of the Bible for laymen, it has been well
remarked that he had evidently no aversion such as
prevailed among the clergy later on, to the Scriptures
being read by the laity; and he desired only to
suppress those parts of the Old Testament which
might perplex them by encouraging polygamy, or
which were less profitable as regards their practical
lessons.
    S. H. Gem, *An Anglo-Saxon Abbot.*

AGASSIZ, JEAN LOUIS RODOLPHE

1807—73 Geologist

Agassiz was born a naturalist as Raphael was born a painter. Nature was his first and last love; to live with her and study her was his life. His allegiance to her was unreserved. To be false to nature, or to belittle her — to warp her teachings, or to set them aside — was an offense which he resented almost as a personal one to himself. One of his last sayings (in the *Atlantic Monthly*) was that 'philosophers and theologians have still to learn that a physical fact is as sacred as a moral principle.'
     Arnold Guyot, in *Biographical Memoirs*,
     National Academy of Sciences.

This is perhaps the place to notice a faculty of Agassiz, which was one of the secrets of his success as a naturalist. He was endowed with a most exquisite sense of form. At a glance he perceived, as by intuition, the characteristic form of an animal as well as its minute details. This once vividly impressed on his plastic imagination would never be forgotten. It was astonishing to see how, in passing his eye over a large collection, he would at once detect the new forms which he had not seen before and add them to his treasure of mental photographs.
     Ibid.

AIDAN, SAINT

— d. 651 First Bishop of Lindisfarne

King Oswin . . . had given Aidan a very fine horse, in order that he could ride whenever he had to cross a river or undertake any difficult or urgent journey, although the bishop ordinarily travelled on foot. Not long afterwards, when a poor man met the bishop and asked for alms, the bishop immediately dismounted and ordered the horse with all its royal trappings to be given to the beggar; for he was most compassionate, a protector of the poor and a father to the wretched. When this action came to the king's ears, he asked the bishop as they were going in to dine; 'My lord bishop, why did you give away the royal horse which was necessary for your own use?' . . . The bishop at once answered, 'What are you saying, Your Majesty? Is this child of a mare more valuable to you than this child of God?' . . . As he stood by the fire, the king turned over in his mind what the bishop had said; then suddenly un-buckling his sword and handing it to a servant, he impulsively knelt at the bishop's feet and begged his forgiveness. At the bishop's request, the king sat down and began to be merry; but Aidan on the contrary grew so sad that he began to shed tears. His chaplain asked him in his own language, which the king and his servants did not understand, why he wept. Aidan replied: 'I know that the king will not live very long; for I have never before seen a humble king.' . . . Not very long afterwards, as I have related, the bishop's foreboding was borne out by the king's death.
     Bede, *Ecclesiastical History of the English People*,
     translated by Leo Sherley-Price.

AIKIN, LUCY

1781—1864 Author

Nor are the immunities of sex the only immunities which Miss Aikin may rightfully plead. Several of her works . . . have fully entitled her to the privileges enjoyed by good writers. One of those privileges we hold to be this, that such writers, when either from the unlucky choice of a subject or from the indolence too often produced by success they happen to fail, shall not be subjected to the severe discipline which it is sometimes necessary to inflict upon dunces and imposters, but shall merely be reminded by a gentle touch, like that with which the Laputan flapper roused his dreaming lord, that it is high time to wake.
     T. B. Macaulay, *Essays*: Review of Aikin's
     Life of Addison.

Miss Lucy Aikin . . . pert as a pear-monger.
     Robert Southey, Letter to Caroline Bowles,
     8 February 1835.

AILRED OF RIEVAULX, SAINT

1109—66 Cistercian Abbot

I shall not omit to tell how he had built a small chamber of brick under the floor of the novice house, like a little tank, into which water flowed from hidden rills. Its opening was shut by a very broad stone in such a way that nobody would notice it. Ailred would enter this contrivance, when he was alone and undisturbed, and immerse his whole body in the icy cold water, and so quench the heat in himself of every vice.
     Walter Daniel, *The Life of Ailred of Rievaulx*,
     translated from the Latin by F. M. Powicke.

Perfect in every part of his body, the dead father shone like a carbuncle, was fragrant as incense, pure and immaculate in the radiance of his flesh as a child. I was not able to restrain the kisses which I gave his feet, although I chose his feet lest feeling rather than pure affection should reproach me; the

AITKEN, WILLIAM MAXWELL

beauty of one who sleeps rather than the love of
one who lies as he lay.
   Ibid.

AITKEN, WILLIAM MAXWELL,
see BEAVERBROOK, LORD

AKENSIDE, MARK

1721—70 Poet

His diction is certainly poetical as it is not prosaick,
and elegant as it is not vulgar. He is to be commended as having fewer artifices of disgust than
most of his brethren of the blank song. He rarely
either recalls old phrases or twists his metre into
harsh inversions. The sense, however, of his words
is strained . . . and the pedant surely intrudes — but
when was blank verse without pedantry?
   Samuel Johnson, *Lives of the Poets.*

I see they have published a splendid edition of
Akenside's words. One bad Ode may be suffered,
but a number of them together makes one sick.
   Samuel Johnson, in James Boswell, *Life of
Johnson.*

Another of these tame genius's, a Mr Akinside.
   Horace Walpole, Letter to Sir Horace Mann,
   29 March 1745.

ALBERT FRANCIS CHARLES AUGUSTUS

1819—61 Prince Consort to Victoria

I do not cling to life. You do: but I set no store by
it . . . I am sure that if I had a severe illness I should
give up at once, I should not struggle for life. I have
no tenacity of life.
   On himself, in conversation with Queen Victoria,
   circa November 1861.

I have had wealth, rank and power, but, if these
were all I had, how wretched I should be.
   On himself, attributed last words.

. . . When in doubt about 'who's to blame', play
Prince Albert, it is always a trump card, and ten to
one it takes the trick.
   'F. Airplay Esq.', *Prince Albert: Why is he
unpopular?*

. . . His Royal Highness ought to be considered . . .
as an Alter Ego, and not as a Privy Councillor, and

[that] this communication was the inevitable result
of a female being on the throne.
   Lord Campbell, Statement to the Lords, 1854.

The Queen talked freely of the Prince: he *would*
die: he seemed not to care to live. Then she used
these words 'He died from want of what they call
pluck'.
   Benjamin Disraeli, *Reminiscences.*

The Prince had wit. There was a picture at Balmoral;
all the children introduced, game birds &c: one said
where is Princess Helena; reply, there with a King-
fisher. 'A very proper bird for a Princess', said Albert.
   Ibid.

. . . His character always comes out *honest.* I take it
that he governs us really, in everything.
   Emily Eden, Letter to Mrs Drummond,
   January 1848.

He has, I think, that average stock of energy, which
enables men to do that which they cannot well
avoid doing, or that which is made ready to their
hands: but he has not the rare supply of it, which
enables a man to make duty, and so win honour and
confidence.
   W. E. Gladstone, Letter to Earl Granville,
   December 1870.

The Prince is become so identified with the Queen,
that they are one person, and as He likes and She
dislikes business, it is obvious that while she has the
title he is really discharging the functions of the
Sovereign. He is King to all intents and purposes.
   Charles Greville, *Memoirs.*

As for his sense of fun . . . I never could discover it.
He went into immoderate fits of laughter at anything like a practical joke; for instance, if anyone
caught his foot in a mat, or nearly fell into the fire
. . . the mirth of the whole Royal Family, headed by
the Prince, knew no bounds. His original jokes were
heavy and lumbered.
   M. Ponsonby, *Mary Elizabeth, Lady Ponsonby,
A Memoir . . . .*

. . . she is inclined to think it will be better for her,
instead of attempting an Enactment by Parliament,
with its attendant discussions, to do merely as much
as her Prerogative will enable her . . . and to content
herself by simply giving her husband by Letters
Patent the title of 'Prince Consort' which can injure
no one while it will give him an *English title* consistent with his position, & avoid his being treated
by Foreign Courts as a *junior Member* of the house
of *Saxe Coburg.*
   Queen Victoria, Letter to Lord Palmerston,
   15 March 1857.

None of you can *ever* be proud enough of being the *child* of SUCH a Father who has not his *equal* in this world — so great, so good, so faultless. Try, all of you to follow in his footsteps and don't be discouraged, for to be *really* in everything like him *none* of you, I am sure, will ever be. Try, therefore, to be like him in *some* points, and you will have *acquired a great deal.*
    Queen Victoria, Letter to the Prince of Wales, 26 August 1857.

See also Queen Victoria, Duke of Wellington

ALCOTT, AMOS BRONSON

1799—1888 Educator, Author, Mystic

. . . [a] man up in a balloon, with his family and friends holding the ropes which confine him to earth, and trying to haul him down. . . .
    Louisa May Alcott, in Marjorie Worthington, *Miss Alcott of Concord.*

. . . like a venerable Don Quixote, whom nobody can laugh at without loving.
    Thomas Carlyle, in James D. Hart, *The Oxford Companion to American Literature.*

The good Alcott, with his long, lean face and figure, with his grey worn temples and mild radiant eyes; all bent on saving the world by a return to acorns and the golden age.
    Thomas Carlyle, in Marjorie Worthington, *Miss Alcott of Concord.*

The tedious archangel.
    Ralph Waldo Emerson, in Florence Whiting Brown, *Alcott and the Concord School of Philosophy.*

He is a philosopher worthy of the palmy times of ancient Greece, — a man whom the worldings of Boston hold in as much horror as the worldings of ancient Athens held Socrates.
    Margaret Fuller, in F. B. Sandborn and William T. Harris, *A. Bronson Alcott, His Life and Philosophy.*

As for Alcott particularly, he was a singular person, a natural Levite, a priest forever after the order of Melchizedek, whom all good persons would readily combine to maintain as a priest to live in his own cottage — literary, spiritual, and choosing his own methods of teaching and action.
    Hubert H. Hoeltje, *Sheltering Tree.*

He was an air plant, which put out no roots, but could readily and without ill results be transported anywhere. He was always quite ready to abandon his present ways to put into practice any new dream that bubbled up in the effervescence of discourse.
    Ibid.

Most spectral-like was the apparition of Bronson Alcott, a man born in the wrong century, a reincarnation, it would seem, of Old Platinus or Diogenes.
    Fred Lewis Pattee, *The First Century of American Literature, 1770—1870.*

A blue-robed man, whose fittest roof is the overarching sky, which reflects his serenity. I do not see how he can ever die. Nature cannot spare him.
    Henry Thoreau, in Odell Shepard, *Pedlar's Progress.*

ALCOTT, LOUISA MAY

1832—88 Author

Now I am beginning to live a little and feel less like a sick oyster at low tide.
    On herself, in Ednah D. Cheney, *Louisa May Alcott, Her Life, Letters and Journals.*

When I don't look like the tragic muse, I look like a smoky relic of the great Boston Fire.
    On herself, in Katharine Anthony, *Louisa May Alcott.*

If I think of my woes I fall into a vortex of debts, dishpans, and despondency awful to see.
    On herself, in Gamaliel Bradford, *Portraits and Personalities.*

Louisa is a guideless creature, the child of instinct yet unenlightened by love. On the impetuous stream of instinct she has set sail and regardless alike of the quick-sand and the rocks, of the careering winds and winter currents that oppose the course, she looks only towards the objects of her desire and steers proudly, adventurously . . . toward the heaven of her hopes.
    Amos Bronson Alcott, in Katharine Anthony, *Louisa May Alcott.*

[She] resolved to take fate by the throat and shake a living out of her.
    Ednah D. Cheney, *Louisa May Alcott, Her Life, Letters and Journals.*

If Miss Alcott's experience of human nature has been small, as we should suppose, her admiration of it is nevertheless great.
    Henry James, in Katharine Anthony, *Louisa May Alcott.*

Living almost always among intellectuals, she preserved to the age of fifty-six that contempt for ideas which is normal among boys and girls of fifteen.

Odell Shepard, 'Mother of Little Women', in *North American Review.*

ALDRICH, THOMAS BAILEY

1836–1907 Poet, Editor

His writing was undoubtedly distinguished. It was lucid, skillful, crisp and fresh; and the neat-handed Aldrich, who was very seldom commonplace, always knew when to stop, an unusual virtue. The fluent elder poets had not possessed it; and Aldrich's flute-like note was exceedingly pleasant in a world that was used to poets who went on and on.

Van Wyck Brooks, *New England: Indian Summer 1865–1915.*

His language is so clean, so free from vulgar suggestion, that one almost sees the author wearing gloves as he writes.

Alexander Cowie, *The Rise of the American Novel.*

Witty, charming in manners, in love with art and devoted to a painstaking craftsmanship, he was a hollow reed through which blew into flawless form the refinements of his world and group.

Vernon Louis Parrington, *Main Currents in American Thought, Vol. III.*

When it came to making fun of a folly, or silliness, a windy pretense, a wild absurdity, Aldrich the brilliant, Aldrich the sarcastic, Aldrich the ironical, Aldrich the merciless, was a master.

Mark Twain, in Bernard De Voto ed., *Mark Twain in Eruption.*

Aldrich was always brilliant, he couldn't help it; he is a fire-opal set round with rose diamonds; when he is not speaking, you know that his dainty fancies are twinkling and glimmering around in him; when he speaks, the diamonds flash.

Mark Twain, in Charles E. Samuels, *Thomas Bailey Aldrich.*

ALEXANDER II OF SCOTLAND

1198–1249

Quhen Alysandyr oure Kyng wes dede,

Dat Scotland led in Luwe and Le,
Away wes sons of Ale and Brede
Of Wyne and Wax, of Gamyn and Gle:
Oure Gold wes changyd in-to Lede.
Cryst, borne in-to Virgynytè,
Succour Scotland, and remede,
Dat stad is in perplexytè.

Andrew Wyntoun, *De Orygynale Cronykil of Scotland*, Book VII.

ALEXANDER, HAROLD RUPERT LEOFRIC GEORGE, EARL ALEXANDER OF TUNIS

1891–1969 Soldier

I have had a good weathering in this war, and I am going to get the fruits of it if I can. You can bet your life that I shall have a good try.

On himself, Letter to his Aunt Margaret, 22 November 1918.

He did not issue an order. He sold the . . . general the idea, and made him think that he had thought of it all himself. This system, which he invariably pursued, made Alexander particularly fit to command an Allied army . . . in the Italian campaign controlling the troops of many countries, he developed this method into a remarkable technique. If Montgomery was the Wellington, Alexander was certainly the Marlborough of this war.

Harold Macmillan, *The Blast of War, 1939–45.*

He had almost every quality you could wish to have, except that he had the average brain of an average English gentleman. He lacked that little extra cubic centimetre which produces genius. If you recognise that, it's perhaps a greater tribute to what he did achieve by leadership, courage and inspiring devotion in those who served under him.

Earl Mountbatten, in Nigel Nicolson, *Alex.*

Alex wouldn't do any work, except when he had to, and when he had to, it was on big exercises . . . He was ambitious to do his duty. He was lazy, but not over the essentials. He relied on his staff. If they did something wrong he would pull them up. His laziness was a virtue. It meant a capacity to delegate, and in wartime it became a tremendous asset, because it meant that he could relax and unhook.

Field Marshal Sir Gerald Templer, in *ibid.*

The Dominion's most industrious gadabout. . . .
Time, October 1946.

ALEXANDER, SIR WILLIAM, EARL OF STIRLING

1567?—1640 Poet, Statesman

His minor pieces are elegant and musical. There is less of conceit in the merely conceitful sense than was common with contemporaries, and if you only persevere, opalescent hues edge long passages otherwise comparable with mist and fog.

Alexander Balloch Grosart, in *Dictionary of National Biography*.

ALEXANDRA CAROLINE MARY CHARLOTTE LOUISE JULIA

1844—1925 Queen Consort to Edward VII

I may be pale, but it is from anger at being obliged to see the King of Prussia, and not from cold.

On herself, retort to Sir William Knollys, 11 October 1867, in Philip Magnus, *King Edward the Seventh*.

Alex, good as she is, is not worth the price we have to pay for her in having such a family connection [the Queen of Denmark].

Queen Victoria, Letter to her daughter, the Crown Princess of Prussia, 11 October 1864.

ALFRED

849—901 King of England

Then king Alfred ordered warships to be built to meet the Danish ships: they were almost twice as long as the others, some had sixty oars, some more; they were both swifter, steadier, and with more freeboard than the others; they were built neither after the Frisian design nor after the Danish, but as it seemed to himself that they could be most serviceable.

Anglo-Saxon Chronicle, translated by G. N. Garmonsway

And from his cradle a longing for wisdom before all things and among all the pursuits of this present life, combined with his noble birth, filled the noble temper of his mind; but alas, by the unworthy carelessness of his parents and tutors he remained ignorant of letters until his twelfth year, or even longer. But he listened attentively to Saxon poems day and night, and hearing them often repeated by others committed them to his retentive memory. . . . When therefore, his mother one day was showing him and his brothers a certain book of Saxon poetry which she held in her hand she said: 'I will give this book to whichever of you can learn it most quickly.' And moved by these words, or rather by divine inspiration, and attracted by the beauty of the initial letter of the book, Alfred said in reply to his mother, forestalling his brothers, his elders in years though not in grace: 'Will you really give this book to one of us, to the one who can soonest understand and repeat it to you?' And, smiling and rejoicing she confirmed it. . . . Then taking the book from her hand he immediately went to his master, who read it. And when it was read, he went back to his mother and repeated it.

Asser, *Life of King Alfred*, translated by L. C. Jane

He often affirmed with frequent laments and sighs from the bottom of his heart, that among all his difficulties and hindrances in this present life this was the greatest: that during the time when he had youth and leisure and aptitude for learning, he had no teachers; but when he was more advanced in years, he did have teachers and writers to some extent, when he was not able to study because he was harrassed, nay rather disturbed, day and night both with illnesses unknown to all physicians of this island, and with the cares of the royal office at home and abroad, and also with the invasions of pagans by land and sea.

Ibid.

Viewed in retrospect, and seeing what Alfred had to put up with — as if the Danes weren't enough, he was also up against the witenagemot *and* the British working carl — his achievements were pretty terrific. For which reason posterity has nicknamed him Alfred the Great. The name is also applied to the manager of England's team, Sir Alf Ramsay.

Nicolas Bentley, *Golden Sovereigns*.

There was not English Armour left,
Nor any English thing,
When Alfred came to Athelney
To be an English King.

G. K. Chesterton, *Ballad of the White Horse*, Book I.

There is a story that King Arthur once burnt some cakes belonging to Mrs. Girth, a great lady of the time, at a place called Atheling. As, however, Alfred could not have been an Incendiary King *and* a Good King, we may dismiss the story as absurd, and in any case the event is supposed to have occurred in a marsh where the cakes would not have burnt properly. Cf. the famous lines of poetry about King Arthur and the cakes: 'Then slowly answered Alfred from the marsh —' *Arthur, Lord Tennyson*.

W. C. Sellar and R. J. Yeatman, *1066 and All That*.

Truth-teller was our England's Alfred named.
>   Alfred, Lord Tennyson, *Ode on the Death of the Duke of Wellington.*

Thus cruel ages pass'd; and rare appear'd
White mantled Peace, exulting o'er the vale,
As when, with Alfred, from the wilds she came
To policed cities and protected plains.
>   James Thomson, *Liberty: Britain.*

Not long after venturing from his concealment, he hazarded an experiment of consummate art. Accompanied only by one of his most faithful adherents, he entered the tent of the Danish King under the disguise of a minstrel; and being admitted as a professor of the mimic art, to the banqueting room, there was no object of secrecy that he did not minutely attend to both with eyes and ears. Remaining there several days, till he had satisfied his mind on every matter which he wished to know, he returned to Ethelingai: and assembling his companions, pointed out the insolence of the enemy and the easiness of their defeat.
>   William of Malmesbury, *History of the Kings of England*, translated by J. Sharpe.

See also Hengist and Horsa

ALGER, HORATIO

1834—99 Author

He helped make success a quasi-religious moral idea that leaves people who fail (whether in spelling or in something bigger) with the conviction they are unloved. He stands for trying harder, wanting more, and contributing to the community chest. The people who want to distribute Sears, Roebuck catalogs to Russians to persuade them of America's superiority are his disciples, too.
>   Richard Fink, in John Tebbel, *From Rags to Riches.*

Horatio Alger wrote the same novel 135 times and never lost his audience.
>   George Juergens, *Joseph Pulitzer and the New York World.*

In his books he has captured the spirit of reborn America. The turmoil of the city streets is in them. You can hear the rattle of pails on the farms. Above all, you can hear the cry of triumph of the oppressed over the oppressor. What Alger has done is to portray the soul — the ambitious soul — of the country.
>   A. K. Loring, in Ralph D. Gardner, *Horatio Alger, or The American Hero Era.*

All of Horatio Alger's heroes started poor and ended up well-to-do. All of them were in search of money. Everybody could understand their motives. There in is the main reason for Alger's literary leadership for thirty years . . . Alger's heroes never slew dragons. But they lifted mortgages.
>   Herbert Mayes, in John Tebbel, *From Rags to Riches.*

See also Jo Davidson

ALLEN, ETHAN

1737/8—89 Revolutionary Soldier

. . . that his name was Ethan Allen Captain of that Mob, and that his authority was his arms, pointing to his gun, that he and his companions were a Lawless Mob there [sic] Law being Mob Law . . . that he had run these woods in the same manner these seven years past and never were catched yet . . . and that if any of Colo Reid's settlers offered hereafter to Build any house & keep Possession the Green Mountain Boys as they call themselves would burn their houses and whip them in the Bargain.
>   On himself, as reported by James Henderson, in J. Pell, *Ethan Allen.*

Ever since I arrived at the state of manhood and acquainted myself with the general history of mankind, I have felt a sincere passion for liberty. The history of nations, doomed to perpetual slavery, in consequence of yielding up to tyrants their natural-born liberties, I read with a sort of philosophical horror; so that the first systematical and bloody attempt, at Lexington, to enslave America, thoroughly electrified my mind and fully determined me to take part with my country.
>   *Ibid.*

Sr. You have heard many Accounts of my Conduct Called by the Name of Riatous Disorderly &ce and it is probable before Next Campaign is out You may hear more Such Sort of News. I am Informed Governour Tryon has Advertised me and some Others and Offered Considerable Reward to have us Delivered at New York. But a Late account from there Informs me by Virtue of a Late Law in Province they are Not Allowed to hang any man before they have ketched him. . . .
>   On himself, Letter of March 1772, in *ibid.*

His spirit tried the
Mercies of his God
In Whom he firmly trusted.
>   *Epitaph* on the first stone marking Allen's grave.

Old Ethan once said over a full bowl of grog
Though I believe not in Jesus, I hold to a God,
There is also a devil — you will see him one day
In a whirlwind of fire take Levi away.
Levi Allen, attributed in J. Pell, *Ethan Allen*.

I have seldom met with a man, possessing, in my
opinion, a stronger mind, or whose mode of
expression was more vehement and oratorical. His
style was a singular compound of local barbarisms,
scriptural phrases, and oriental wildness; and though
unclassic and sometimes ungrammatical, it was
highly animated and forcible. . . .
Alexander Graydon, *Memoirs*.

I have taken much pains, by prisoners and intelligent
Loyalists to discover if anything might be effected
with Allen, and the people of Vermont — I was
assured by all, that no dependence can be had in
him — his character is well known, and his Followers,
or dependents, are a collection of the most
abandoned wretches that ever lived, to be bound by
no Laws or Ties.
General Sir Frederick Haldimand, Letter to
General Sir Henry Clinton, in J. Pell, *Ethan Allen*.

Allen is really an original; at least I never met a genius
like him. Had his natural talents been cultivated by
a liberal education, he would have made no bad
figure among the sons of science; but perhaps his
want of such an education is not to be lamented, as
unless he had more grace it would make him a
dangerous member of society.
Ebenezer Hazard, Letter to Jeremy Belknap,
in *ibid*.

Died in Vermont the profane and
impious Deist Gen. Ethan Allen. . . .
And in Hell he lift up his eyes, being in
Torments.
Ezra Stiles, Diary entry, 28 February 1789.

ALLEN, FRED (JOHN FLORENCE SULLIVAN)

1894–1956 Comedian

Eventually I have high hopes I'll be able to retire
from the human race.
On himself, in Maurice Zolotow, *No People
Like Show People*.

I don't have to look up my family tree, because I
know that I'm the sap.
On himself, *Much Ado About Me*.

Fred Allen delivers [his jokes] in a flat voice like
the wit of the senior dormitories. He is not merely
an ingratiating comedian, but a deft one, with an
extraordinary talent for making his points at a
skimming pace.
Brooks Atkinson, Review of *The Little Show*,
in *New York Times*, 1 May 1929.

You can count on the thumb of one hand the
American who is at once a comedian, a humorist, a
wit and a satirist, and his name is Fred Allen.
James Thurber, in Joe McCarthy ed., *Fred
Allen's Letters*.

ALLEN, THOMAS

1542–1632 Mathematician

In those dark times, Astrologer, Mathematician,
and Conjurer were accounted the same things; and
the vulgar did verily beleeve him to be a Conjurer.
He had a great many Mathematicall Instruments
and Glasses in his Chamber, which did also con-
firme the ignorant in their opinion, and his servitor
(to impose on Freshmen and simple people) would
tell them that sometimes he should meet the Spirits
comeing up his staires like Bees. Now there is to
some men a great Lechery in Lying, and imposing
on the understandings of beleeving people, and he
thought it for his credit to serve such a Master.
John Aubrey, *Brief Lives*.

ALLEN, WILLIAM

1770–1843 Philanthropist

All the world is a little queer save thee and me, and
even thou art a little queer.
Robert Owen, attributed, 1828.

ALLENBY, EDMUND HENRY HYNMAN, VISCOUNT

1861–1936 Soldier

The last of the Paladins.
Sir Ronald Storrs, *Orientations*.

See also T. E. Lawrence

ALLEYN, EDWARD

1566–1626 Actor

The Tradition concerning the Occasion of the
Foundation [of Dulwich College], runs thus; that

17

Mr. *Alleyne*, being a Tragedian, and one of the Original Actors in many of the celebrated *Shakespear*'s Plays, in one of which he played a Daemon, with six others, and was in the midst of the Play surpriz'd by an *Apparition* of the *Devil*. which so worked on his Fancy, that he made a Vow, which he perform'd at this place.

John Aubrey, *The Natural History and Antiquities of the County of Surrey.*

Alleyne's fortune proceeded no doubt from marrying three wives, each of whom brought a handsome fortune, partly from the success of his theatre, partly from his being keeper of the King's wild beasts, and master of the Royal Bear Garden, and partly from his being a most rigid and penurious economist, which character he so strictly enjoined himself, that he was the first pensioner in his own charity.

C. Dibdin, in Clark Russell, *Representative Actors.*

He was bred a stage-player; a calling which many have condemned, more have questioned, some few have excused, and far fewer conscientious people have commended. He was the Roscius of our age, so acting to the life, that he made any part (especially a majestick one) to become him. He got a very great estate, and in his old age, following Christ's counsel (on what forcible motive belongs not to me to inquire), 'he made friends of his unrighteous Mammon,' building therewith a fair college at Dulwich in Kent, for the relief of poor people.

Some I confess count it built on a foundered foundation, seeing in a spiritual sense none is good and lawful money, save what is honestly and industriously gotten. But perchance such who condemn Master Allin herein, have as bad shillings in the bottom of their own bags, if search was made therein. Sure I am, no hospital is tied with better or stricter laws, that it may not *sagg* from the intention of the founder. The poor of his native parish, Saint Boltolph, Bishopsgate, have a privilege to be provided for therein, before others. Thus he, who out-acted others in his life, out-did himself before his death, which happened Anno Domini 1626.

Thomas Fuller, *The History of the Worthies of England.*

. . . th'other wan
The attributes of peerlesse, being a man
Whom we may ranke with (doing no one wrong)
Proteus for Shapes, and *Roscius* for a Tongue,
So could he speake, so vary.

Thomas Heywood, *The Prologue to the Stage, at the Cocke-pit, to the Jew of Malta.*

Edward Allen, alias Allein, of Dull-wich, Esquire, at this time built a very faire Hospitall at Dulwich, in *Surrey*, for six poore men and six poore women, and for 12 poore children from the age of 4 or 6 yeares, to be there kept, maintained and taught, untill they come to the age of 14 or 16 yeares: their schoolemaster to have his diet, lodging, and a competent stipend. He intends also to have a Master to reside in the same Hospitall, whose name shall be Allen or Alleyne, and by that name to be chosen to that Government of his Hospitall for ever, as the place shall grow vacant.

Edmund Howe, *Continuation of Stow's Annales or Generall Chronicle.*

Weare this renowne. 'Tis just, that who did give
So many *Poets* life, by one should live.
Ben Jonson, *Epigrammes.*

ALLSTON, WASHINGTON

1779—1843 Artist, Author

I cannot but think that the life of an artist, whether poet or painter, depends much on a happy youth; I do not mean as to outward circumstances, but as to his inward being; in my own case, at least, I feel the dependence; for I seldom step into the ideal world but I find myself going back to the age of first impressions. The germs of our best thoughts are certainly often to be found there; sometimes, indeed (though rarely) we find them in full flower, and when so, how beautiful to us these flowers seem through an atmosphere of thirty years.

On himself, in E. P. Richardson, *Washington Allston.*

And now you have already learned that Allston is dead, — the solitary link as it seemed between America and Italy. Not strange that he should die, but that he should have lived sixty-four years. I never heard of his being younger, or a beginner, and suppose that his first strokes were masterly. He was like one of those boulders which geologists sometimes find a thousand or two miles from the mountain from which they were detached, and science cannot show how they were conveyed. A little sunshine of his own has this man of Beauty made in the American forest, and who has not heard of his veiled picture, which now alas must be veiled.

Ralph Waldo Emerson, Letter to Margaret Fuller, 11 July 1843.

The calm and meditative ease of these pictures, the ideal beauty that shone *through* rather than *in* them, and the harmony of coloring were as unlike anything else I saw, as the Vicar of Wakefield to Cooper's novels. I seemed to recognise in painting

that self-possessed elegance, that transparent depth, which I most admired in literature; I thought with delight that such a man as this had been able to grow up in our bustling, reasonable community, that he had kept his foot upon the ground, yet never lost sight of the rose-clouds of beauty floating above him. I saw, too, that he had not been troubled, but possessed his own soul with the blandest patience; and I hoped, I scarce know what, probably the *mot d'enigme* for which we are all looking. How the poetical mind can live and work in peace and good faith! how it may unfold to its due perfection in an unpoetical society!
Margaret Fuller, in *Dial*, 1839.

One man may sweeten a whole town. I never pass through Cambridge Port without thinking of Allston. His memory is the quince in the drawer, and perfumes the atmosphere.
Henry Wadsworth Longfellow, in Longfellow MSS.

I go to Allston as a comet goes to the sun, not to add to his material, but to imbibe light from him.
Samuel F. B. Morse, in Harry B. Wehle, *Samuel F. B. Morse*.

. . . he believed that our powers are very limited in contrast with the vastness of the universe; that there is and must always be a realm of mystery beyond our knowledge, yet in this realm is to be found the supreme reality. The sense of mystery runs through all his art.
For who shall hope the mystery to scan
Of that dark being symbolized in *Man*?
he wrote in his sonnet, 'On a Word, Man.' This was the theme of his dramatic early compositions, whose subjects lie upon the border line between human life and the supernatural or the divine.
E. P. Richardson, *Washington Allston*.

To express the intense, violent, and tragic moods of romanticism, painting had to be given a more eloquent and moving style. This was where Allston was to surpass [Benjamin] West, for he not only mastered significant movement but saw the expressive nature of the movement of light, the resonance of tone, and the radiance of color.
Ibid.

ALTGELD, JOHN PETER
1847—1902 Politician

Where is Altgeld, brave as the truth,
Whose name the few still say with tears?
Gone to join the ironies with Old John Brown

Whose fame rings loud for a thousand years.
Vachel Lindsay, *Bryan, Bryan, Bryan, Bryan*.

ALVANLEY, LORD, see ARDEN, RICHARD PEPPER

AMES, FISHER
1758—1808 Statesman

These gifts were thine immortal AMES
Of motive pure, of life sublime!
Their loss our flowing sorrow claims;
Their praise survives the wrecks of time.
Ode to Mr Ames by Mr Gardiner, sung at his funeral, *Columbian Centinel* (Boston), 9 July 1808.

Mr. Ames's friends treated his *memory* as they did his *body*.
John Quincy Adams, *Mr. Adams's Review. Remarks on the Hon. John Q. Adams's Review of Mr. Ames's Works, with some strictures on the views of the author.*

ANDERSON, ELIZABETH GARRETT
1836—1917 Doctor

I was a young woman living at home with nothing to do in what authors call 'comfortable circumstances.' But I was wicked enough not to be comfortable. I was full of energy and vigour and of the discontent that goes with unemployed activities. Everything seemed wrong to me.
On herself, MS draft for a speech.

'Why not be a nurse?' said the doctor. 'Because I prefer to earn a thousand rather than twenty pounds a year.'
On herself, in Louisa Garrett Anderson, *Dr. Elizabeth Garrett Anderson*.

But for Miss Garrett, I must say of her that I gained more from her than from any other doctor, for she not only repeated what all of the others had said, but entered much more into my mental state and way of life than they could do, because I was able to *tell* her so much more than I ever could or would tell to any *man*.
Josephine Butler, in E. M. Bell, *Josephine Butler*.

She was neither a brilliant nor a born doctor. She made no outstanding contribution to medical science; although she read widely her temperament was not suited to laboratory work and she had neither time nor ambition to undertake original research. If one regards medicine as a pure science her claims to distinction are not high. If one regards it as a skilled exercise in personal relationships one must rate her very high indeed. It was as a general practitioner that she excelled, with all the qualities of character that calling demands — courage, sense of duty, good judgement and warm humanity. By these she disarmed a hostile profession and won the trust of a whole generation of women patients.

Naomi Mitchison, *Revaluations — Studies in Biography*.

I am much pleased at Miss Garrett's success. She ought to have a vote for Westminster, but not to sit in Parliament. It would make too much confusion.

Lord John Russell, Letter to Lord Amberley, 1870.

Mrs. Anderson was not the woman to let the grass grow under her feet, nor was she one to consider unduly the effects of overwork or fatigue on herself and her colleagues. She was a persistent, shameless and highly successful beggar.

Mary Scharlieb, *Reminiscences*.

See also Dame Millicent Fawcett

ANDERSON, MAXWELL

1888—1959 Author, Playwright

He has brought verse and the form of verse back to the American stage — not as an experiment, not as an oddity, but as an essential of the later plays he had written. And because of it, he has opened a shut door.

Stephen Vincent Benét, in Jean Gould, *Modern American Playwrights*.

Maxwell Anderson is a dramatist to be respected even if he is not always one who can be enjoyed or understood. He has courage, a mind of his own — rarest of all — he has ears which he likes to bathe in sound.

John Mason Brown, *Dramatis Personae*.

Only Mr Maxwell Anderson has written plays in verse which seemed to fit easily into the pattern of the contemporary stage, which attract in large numbers the regular patrons of the theater and which seem natural outgrowths of contemporary dramatic writing rather than protests against it.

Joseph Wood Krutch, *The American Drama Since 1918*.

ANDERSON, SHERWOOD

1876—1941 Author

And so in my inner self I have accepted my own Mid-American as a walled-in place. There are walls everywhere, about individuals, about groups. The houses are mussy. People die inside the walls without ever having seen the light. I want the houses cleaned, the doorsteps washed, the walls broken away. That can't happen in my time. Culture is a slow growth.

On himself, in a letter to Paul Rosenfeld, 24 October 1921, in Mark Schorer, *Sherwood Anderson*.

For all my egotism I know I am but a minor figure.

On himself, in Irving Howe, *Sherwood Anderson*.

I'm for anything crooked but like to be approached as a fellow crook.

On himself, in a letter to Ben Hecht, in Ben Hecht, *Letters from Bohemia*.

Anderson, his life and his writings, epitomize for me the pilgrimage of a poet and dreamer across this limited stage called life, whose reactions to the mystery of our being and doings here . . . involved tenderness, love and beauty, delight in the strangeness of our will-less reactions as well as pity, sympathy and love for all things both great and small.

Theodore Dreiser, Sherwood Anderson, in Paul P. Appel ed., *Homage to Sherwood Anderson*.

As a matter of fact Anderson is a man of practically no ideas — *but he is one of the very best and finest writers in the English language today*. God, he can write.

F. Scott Fitzgerald, in a letter to Maxwell Perkins, 1 June 1925, in Andrew Turnbull ed., *The Letters of F. Scott Fitzgerald*.

Intoxication with the wine of creativity and not the leisurely tasting of its less heady moments was his obsession.

Julius W. Friend, 'The Philosophy of Sherwood Anderson', in Paul P. Appel ed., *Homage to Sherwood Anderson*.

Adopting a naturalistic interpretation of American life, he believed that the primal forces of human behavior are instinctive and not to be denied, as he supposed they are, by the standardization of a machine age. His characters are puzzled, grasping, baffled, and possess no vision of order or channel for directing their energies against the frustrations of contemporary existence.

James D. Hart, *The Oxford Companion to American Literature*.

If a girl was with us, I was sure to hear Swatty open up as a searcher for deep truths. You could tell how smitten he was with a girl by how ardently he started praising himself. He called it self-revelation.
Ben Hecht, *Letters from Bohemia.*

Anderson seemed the archetype of all those writers who were trying to raise themselves to art by sheer emotion and sheer will, who suspected intellect as a cosmopolitan snare that would destroy their gift for divining America's mystic essence, and who abominated the society which had formed them but knew no counterpoise of value by which to escape its moral dominion.
Irving Howe, *Sherwood Anderson.*

Anderson more than others, in fact, gave to a younger generation growing up in the twenties a sense of curiosity, an unashamed acceptance of their difficulties and yearnings, that was to remain with them long after he had come to seem a curiously repetitive and even confused figure.
Alfred Kazin, *On Native Grounds.*

He seemed to have the real, the authentic American voice. The style was as free and natural, I thought then, as the glass of ice water which stands on every table in every home and restaurant. Later I learned that it was not so free and natural, that it had been acquired through long apprenticeship.
Henry Miller, 'Anderson the Storyteller', in Paul P. Appel ed., *Homage to Sherwood Anderson.*

His imagination was ceaselessly occupied in trying to penetrate into the hidden life that throbbed somewhere behind the masks that people offered to the world. Hence many of his stories are focused on almost intangible perceptions, moments of intensity or understanding, casual actions that reveal the soul's leanings, or the rising to the surface of some monstrous creation from the subconscious world.
Arthur Hobson Quinn ed., *The Literature of the American People.*

Anderson, like Thoreau, refused to bow down before the god of progress. He could not see any virtue in the roaring bustle of American commerce, in its shallow intellectuality and blind disregard of human values. He was under no illusions.
Ibid.

... On November 27, 1912, a successful manufacturer in the town of Elyria, Ohio, dreaming of becoming a great benevolent tycoon, chafing more often at the stultifying routines of promotion and salesmanship, Sherwood Anderson, aged thirty-six, walked out of his office and away from his wife and family into the freedom of a wandering literary life, never to return to business.
Mark Schorer, 'Sherwood Anderson', in Perry Miller ed., *Major Writers of America,* vol. 2.

At his best, Sherwood Anderson functions with a natural ease and beauty on a plane in the depths of life — as if under a diving-bell submerged in the human soul — which makes the world of the ordinary novelist seem stagy and superficial.
Edmund Wilson, *The Shores of Light.*

ANDREWES, LANCELOT
1555—1626 Bishop of Winchester

His sermons are too well built to be readily quotable; they stick too closely to the point to be entertaining. Yet they rank with the finest English prose of their time, of any time . . . The most conspicuous qualities of the style are three: ordonnance, or arrangement and structure, precision in the use of words, and relevant intensity . . . Andrewes takes a word and derives the world from it; squeezing and squeezing the word until it yields a full juice of meaning which we should never have supposed any word to possess. . . . When Andrewes begins his sermon, from beginning to end you are sure that he is wholly in his subject, unaware of anything else, that his emotion grows as he penetrates more deeply into his subject, that he is finally 'alone with the Alone', with the mystery which he is seeking to grasp more and more firmly . . . Andrewes's emotion is purely contemplative; it is not personal, it is wholly evoked by the object of contemplation, to which it is adequate; his emotions wholly contained in, and explained by its object.
T. S. Eliot, *Lancelot Andrewes.*

The world, Wanted Learning to know how learned this man was, so skilled in all (especially oriental) languages, that some conceived he might (if then living) have almost served as an interpreter-general at the Confusion of Tongues.
Thomas Fuller, *Church History of Britain.*

Truth however, compels us to add, that in some points Andrewes was not in advance of his age.
John Henry Overton, in *Dictionary of National Biography.*

ANNE
1665—1714 Queen of England

. . . as long as I live it shall be my endeavour to

make my country and my friends easy and though those that come after me may be more capable of so great a trust as it has pleased God to put into my hands, I am sure they can never discharge it more faithfully than her that is sincerely your humble servant.

On herself, Letter to Sidney Godolphin, 1707.

I believe sleep was never more welcome to a weary traveller than death was to her.

Dr John Arbuthnot, Letter to Jonathan Swift, 12 August 1713.

Queen Anne was one of the smallest people ever set in a great place.

Walter Bagehot, *The English Constitution*.

I have tried here to render comprehensible some of the Inarticulates of this world by setting down my own reading of that Queen of Inarticulates — Anne Stuart.

Beatrice Curtis Brown, *Anne Stuart, Queen of England*.

If it were in my power, I would not be a favourite, which few will believe . . . as fond as people are of power, I fancy that anybody that had been shut up so many tedious hours as I have been, with a person that had no conversation, and yet must be treated with respect, would feel something of what I did, and be very glad, when their circumstances did not want it, to be freed from such a slavery, which must be uneasy at all times, though I do protest that upon the account of her loving me and trusting me so entirely as she did, I had a concern for her which was more than you will easily believe, and I would have served her with the hazard of my life upon any occasion; but after she put me at liberty by using me ill, I was very easy, and liked better that anybody should have her favour than myself at the price of flattery, without which I believe nobody can be well with a King or a Queen.

Sarah Churchill, Duchess of Marlborough, Letter, 23 April 1711.

Queen Anne had a person and appearance not at all ungraceful, till she grew exceeding gross and corpulent. There was something of Majesty in her look, but mixed with a sullen and constant frown, that plainly betrayed a gloominess of soul and a cloudiness of disposition within. She seemed to inherit a good deal of her father's moroseness which naturally produced in her the same sort of stubborn positiveness in many cases, both ordinary and extraordinary, as well as the same sort of bigotry in religion.

Sarah Churchill, *Character of Queen Anne*.

It was a sort of unhappiness to her that she naturally loved to have a great crowd come to her; for when they were come to Court, she never cared to have them come in to her, nor to go out herself to them, having little to say to them but that it was either hot or cold; and little to enquire of them, but how long they had been in town, or the like weighty matters. She never discovered any readiness of parts either in asking questions, or in giving answers. In matters of ordinary moment, her discourse had nothing of brightness or wit: and in weightier matters she never spoke but in a hurry, and had a certain knack of sticking to what had been dictated to her, to a degree often very disagreeable, and without the least sign of understanding or judgement.

Ibid.

Her friendships were flames of extravagant passion ending in aversion.

Ibid.

She moved on broad, homely lines. She was devoted to her religion, to her husband, and to friends whose fidelity she had proved. It cannot be doubted at all that she would have faced poverty, exile, imprisonment, or even death with placid, unconquerable resolution for the sake of any of them. Once she got set, it took years to alter her. She was not very wise, nor clever, but she was very like England.

Winston Churchill, *Marlborough, His Life and Times*.

Being asked if he could remember Queen Anne, 'He had (he said) a confused, but somehow a sort of solemn recollection of a lady in diamonds and a long black hood.'

Samuel Johnson, in James Boswell, *Life of Johnson*.

Anne . . . when in good humour, was meekly stupid, and when in bad humour, was sulkily stupid.

T. B. Macaulay, *History of England*.

Nature had made her a bigot. Such was the constitution of her mind that to the religion of her nursery she could not but adhere, without examination and without doubt, till she was laid in her coffin. In the Court of her father she had been deaf to all that could be urged in favour of transubstantiation and auricular confession. In the Court of her brother in law, she was equally deaf to all that could be urged in favour of a general union among Protestants. This slowness and obstinacy made her important. It was a great thing to be the only member of the Royal Family who regarded Papist and Presbyterians with impartial aversion.

Ibid.

In religion narrow, constant, and sincere, she gave the rest of her small mind to determining the rival claims of her favourites upon her preference and her affections. If she had been born to a private station, she would have passed almost unnoticed as a good woman and a regular churchgoer, with a singular incapacity for rearing the numerous children to whom she gave birth. The tempests that rocked the world in which, from no choice of her own, she played a conspicuous, if not an important part, scarcely stirred the dull shallows of her soul.
    Herbert Paul, *Queen Anne.*

Close by those meads, for ever crowned with flowers,
Where Thames with pride surveys his rising towers,
There stands a structure of majestic frame,
Which from the neighb'ring Hampton takes it name.
Here Britain's statesmen oft the fall foredoom
Of foreign tyrants and of nymphs at home;
Here thou, great *Anna*! whom three realms obey,
Dost sometimes counsel take — and sometimes tea.
    Alexander Pope, *The Rape of the Lock*, canto iii.

The Queen, from the Variety of Hands she had employed and Reasonings she had heard since her coming to the Crown, was grown very fond of moderating Scheams, which, as things then stood, were by no means reduceable to Practice. She had likewise a good Share of that Adherence to her Own Opinions which is usually charged upon her Sex. And lastly . . . having received some Hints that she had formerly been too much governed, she grew very difficult to be advised . . . The Queen was by no means inclined to make many changes in Employments, she was positive in her Nature, and extremely given to Delay.
    Jonathan Swift, *Enquiry into the Behaviour of the Queen's last Ministry.*

It was with the utmost Difficulty that she could ever be persuaded to dismiss any Person upon the Score of Party.
    Ibid.

She has been called stupid: she was not stupid in the policies she adopted, but there is a certain stupidity in her personal relations with anyone against whom she had taken umbrage. She could not rise out of the circumstances of the moment as poor mortals should when saying a long farewell.
    G. M. Trevelyan, *England in the Reign of Queen Anne.*

For all her simplicity the wisest and most triumphant of her race.
    Ibid.

The Church's wet-nurse, Goody Anne.
    Horace Walpole, Letter to William Mason, 1778.

See also John Arbuthnot, William III

ANSELM, SAINT

1033—1109 Archbishop of Canterbury, Statesman

In truth, had your divine Anselm, your divine Pope Gregory have had their way, the results had been very notable. Our Western World had all become a European Thibet, with one Grand Lama sitting at Rome; our one honourable business that of singing mass, all day and night. Which would not in the least have suited us!
    Thomas Carlyle, *Past and Present.*

In so far as Anselm lived in yesterday, Anselm was what we now call a liberal and even a freethinker.
    G. K. Chesterton, Introduction to Carlyle's *Past and Present.*

This Riculfus, whom I have mentioned, held the office of sacrist in the monastery. One night, when he was walking through the cloister waiting for the moment when he would waken the brethren for vigils, he happened to pass the door of the chapter house. He looked in and saw Anselm standing in prayer in the midst of a great ball of blazing light.
    Eadmer, *Life of St. Anselm*, translated by R. W. Southern.

Secular business however was something which he could not patiently abide, and he used every pretext to withdraw himself from it so far as he could. . . . When useless uproars, controversies and altercations arose, as sometimes happens, he tried either to stem them, or to get out as quickly as possible. For unless he did this, he was immediately overcome with weariness; his spirits drooped, and he even ran the risk of serious illness. When long experience had taught us this tendency of his, we drew him out of the crowd when such an occasion arose and put to him some question of Holy Scripture; and so we brought his body and mind back to their accustomed state, restored to health by this sort of wholesome antidote.
    Ibid.

See also William II

ANSON, GEORGE, LORD

1697—1762 Voyager

Stay, traveller, awhile and view

One who has travelled more than you.
Quite round the globe, through each degree,
Anson and I have ploughed the sea,
Torrid and frigid zones have passed,
And safe ashore arriv'd at last.
In ease, with dignity, appear
He in the House of Lords, I here.
>Inscription on the pedestal of the figurehead of
>Anson's flagship *Centurion*.

His popularity among the settlers of South Carolina
was very great. They gave his name to districts,
towns and mines; and we still find, on our maps,
Anson County, Anson Ville, Anson's Mines.
>Sir John Barrow, *Life of Admiral Lord Anson.*

It was a melancholy day for human nature when
that stupid Lord Anson, after beating about for
three years, found himself again at Greenwich. The
circumnavigation of our globe was accomplished,
but the illimitable was annihilated & a fatal blow
dealt to all imagination.
>Benjamin Disraeli, *Reminiscences.*

Lord Anson was reserved and proud, and so ignorant
of the world, that Sir Charles Williams said he had
been round it, but never in it. He had been strictly
united with the Duke of Bedford and Lord
Sandwich, but not having the same command of his
ambition that he had of his other passions, he had
not been able to refuse the offer of the Chancellor's
daughter nor the direction of the Admiralty.
>Horace Walpole, *Memoirs.*

ANTHONY, SUSAN BROWNELL

1820—1906 Suffragette

Miss Anthony is one of the most remarkable women
of the Nineteenth Century — remarkable for the
purity of her life, the earnestness with which she
promulgates her peculiar views, and the indomitable
courage with which she bears defeat and misfortune.
No longer in the bloom of youth — if she ever had
any bloom — hard-featured, guileless, cold as an
icicle, fluent and philosophical, she wields today
tenfold more influence than all the beautiful and
brilliant female lecturers that ever flaunted upon
the platform as preachers of social impossibilities.
>Anon., in *St. Louis Globe-Democrat,* early
>1870s, in Rheta Claude Dorr, *Susan B. Anthony,*
>*The Woman who Changed the Mind of a Nation.*

Along the city's thoroughfare,
A grim Old Gal with manly air
Strode amidst the noisy crowd,

Tooting her horn both shrill and loud;
Till e'en above the city's roar,
Above its din and discord, o'er
All, was heard, 'Ye tyrants, fear!
The dawn of freedom's drawing near —
>Woman's Rights and Suffrage!'

A meek old man, in accents wild,
Cried, 'Sal! turn back and nurse our child!'
She bent on him a withering look,
Her bony fist at him she shook,
And screeched, 'Ye brute! ye think I'm flat
To mend your clothes and nurse your brat?
Nurse it yourself, I'll change the plan,
When I am made a congressman —
>Woman's Rights and Suffrage!'
>Anon., in *Herald,* Albany, Oregon, 1871,
>in Ida Husted Harper, *Life and Work of*
>*Susan B. Anthony,* vol. 1.

Susan is lean, cadaverous and intellectual, with the
proportions of a file and the voice of a hurdy-gurdy.
>Anon., in *New York World,* 1866, in *ibid.*

She is the Bismarck; she plans the campaigns, provides the munitions of war, organizes the raw
recruits, sets the squadrons in the field. Indeed,
in the presence of a timid lieutenant, she sometimes heads the charge; but she is a quick, bright,
nervous, alert woman of fifty or so — not at all
inclined to embonpoint — sharp-eyed, even behind
her spectacles. She presides over the treasury, cuts
the Gordian knots, and when the uncontrollables
get by the ears at the conventions, she is the one
who straightway drags them asunder and turns
chaos to order again.
>Anon., in *Photographs of Our Agitators.*

. . . who does not feel sympathy for Susan Anthony?
She has striven long and earnestly to become a
man. She has met with some rebuffs, but has never
succumbed. She has never done any good in the
world, but then she doesn't think so. She is sweet
in the eyes of her own mirror, but her advanced age
and maiden name deny that she has been so in the
eyes of others.
>Anon., in *Utica Herald,* 1870, in Ida Husted
>Harper, *Life and Work of Susan B. Anthony,*
>vol. 1.

The press sneers at Miss Anthony, men tell her she is
out of her proper sphere, people call her a scold,
good women call her masculine, a monstrosity in
petticoats; but if one-half of her sex possessed one-
half of her acquirements, her intellectual culture,
her self-reliance and independence of character, the
world would be better for it.
>Anon., in *Denver News,* in *ibid.*

People went there to see Susan B. Anthony, who has achieved an evanescent reputation by her strenuous endeavours to defy nature. Not one woman in a hundred cares to vote, cares ought for the ballot, would take it with the degrading influences it would surely bring. . . . Old, angular, sticking to black stockings, wearing spectacles, a voice highly suggestive of midnight caudleism at poor Anthony, if he ever comes around, though he never will. If all woman's righters look like that, the theory will lose ground like a darkey going through a cornfield in a light night. If she had come out and plainly said, 'see here, ladies, see me, I am the result of twenty years of constant howling at man's tyranny,' there would never have been another 'howl' uttered in Detroit.
Anon., in *Free Press*, Detroit, 1870, in *ibid*.

Imagine her then in a full black satin frock cut off at the knee, with Turkish trousers of the same material, her wrap a double broche shawl, and on her head the hideous great bonnet then in fashion. I have seen scarecrows that did credit to farmers' boys' ingenuity, but never one better calculated to scare all birds, beasts and human beings.
Mary Bull, in Andrew Sinclair, *The Better Half*.

We touch our caps, and place to night
   The visitor's wreath upon her,
The woman who outranks us all
   In courage and in honor.

While others in domestic broils
   Have proved by word and carriage,
That one of the United States
   Is not the state of marriage.

She caring not for loss of men,
   Nor for the world's confusion,
Has carried on a civil war
   And made a 'Revolution.'
Phoebe Cary, in Ida Husted Harper, *Life and Work of Susan B. Anthony*, vol. 1.

In thought and sympathy we were one, and in the division of labor we exactly complemented each other. In writing we did better work together than either could do alone. While she is slow and analytical in composition, I am rapid and synthetic. I am the better writer, she the better critic, she supplied the facts and statistics, I the philosophy and rhetoric, and together we made arguments which have stood unshaken by the storms of nearly fifty long years.
Elizabeth Cady Stanton, *Reminiscences*.

In ancient Greece she would have been a Stoic; in the era of the Reformation, a Calvinist; in King Charles' time a Puritan; but in the Nineteenth Century, by the very laws of her being, she is a reformer.
Elizabeth Cady Stanton, in Rheta Claude Dorr, *Susan B. Anthony, The Woman who Changed the Mind of a Nation.*

ARBUCKLE, ROSCOE CONKLING 'FATTY'

1887—1933 Actor

Roscoe had been a poor boy, abandoned as a kid by his father, who was an alcoholic. So I guess he had to make up for his impoverished childhood. He spent money wildly. He was the first star to have the entourage. Roscoe bought me a Rolls-Royce, the first one in Hollywood with a genuine silver radiator. And jewels, my darling, like you've never seen. He was the most generous man on earth. I never knew a man as generous as he was, not only to me but to everybody. He couldn't say no to anyone. Roscoe used to give me all the money he didn't spend himself. My dear, I've sat with thousands and thousands of dollars in my purse. Roscoe always said 'I'll make it, darlin', and you spend it'.
Minta Durfee Arbuckle, in Walter Wagner, *You Must Remember This.*

As a comedy star, Fatty Arbuckle had contributed nothing but laughter, maybe a little comfort to those others who had been told that nobody loves a fat man. But my father [lawyer Earl Rogers] had said at once that, though he was innocent, beyond question he would be publicly castigated because it was repulsive to think of a fat man in the role of a rapist.
Adela Rogers St Johns, *The Honeycomb.*

In spite of his suet [Arbuckle] was an agile man — the kind of fat man known as light on his feet -- [and] became a superb pie pitcher. Arbuckle was ambidextrous and had double vision like a T-formation quarterback. He could throw two pies at once in different directions, but he was not precise in this feat.
Mack Sennett, *King of Comedy.*

ARBUTHNOT, JOHN

1667—1735 Physician, Wit

He never rails at a great man but to his face; which I can assure you, he has both the opportunity and licence to do. He has some few weak friends, and fewer enemies; if any, he is low enough to be rather despised than pushed at by them.
On himself, Letter to Jonathan Swift, November 1723.

The disinterestedness of modern science, its emancipation from a narrow range of fact, was his. Such disinterestedness is enriching; it exposes the mind to swarms of minutiae. On the other hand, it entails the danger of a mechanical level of values, of undue dissociation, dispersion, and incoherence.

    Lester M. Beattie, *John Arbuthnot*.

His imagination was almost inexhaustible . . . it was at anybody's service, for as soon as he was exonerated he did not care what became of it; insomuch that his sons, when young, have frequently made kites of his scattered papers of hints, which would have furnished good matter for folios.

    Lord Chesterfield, *Letters*, Mahon, ed., 1845.

This leach Arbuthnot was yclept,
Who many a night not once had slept,
But watch'd our gracious Sovereign still;
For who could rest when she was ill?
Oh, mayst thou henceforth sweetly sleep.
Shear, swains, oh shear your softest sheep
To swell his couch; for well I ween,
He saved the Realm who saved the Queen.

    John Gay, Prologue to *The Shepherd's Week*.

He has shewed himself equal to any of his contemporaries in humour and vivacity; and he was superior to most men in acts of humanity and benevolence; his very sarcasms are the satirical strokes of good nature; they are like flaps of the face given in jest, the effects of which may raise blushes, but no blackness after the blows. . . .

    Lord Orrery, in G. A. Aitken, *Life and Works of John Arbuthnot*.

. . . a man who during a long life . . . while classic-serving, antiquarianising, science-seeking, satire-writing, wit-making, and fun-distributing, managed, by hook or by crook, to write prescriptions, the physic of which the people and even royalty swallowed . . . with infinitely more faith in its efficacy than ever satisfied the conscience of the renowned prescriber.

    Sir B. W. Richardson, *Disciples of Aesculapius*.

The grating scribbler! Whose untuned Essays
Mix the Scotch Thistle with the English Bays;
By either Phoebus preordained to ill,
The hand prescribing, or the flattering quill,
Who doubly plagues, and boasts two Arts to kill.

    James Moore Smythe, *One Epistle to Mr Alexander Pope, occasion'd by Two Epistles lately published*.

The Doctor is the King of Inattention!
    Jonathan Swift, Letter to John Gay, 10 July 1732.

See also Jonathan Swift

ARDEN, RICHARD PEPPER, LORD ALVANLEY

1745—1804 Beau, Wit

The Chancellor was fond of snubbing Mr Arden, and one day the latter having in the excitement of his argument, in a cause in which the age of a woman was in dispute, said to the opposing counsel, 'I'll lay you a bottle of wine she is more than forty-five,' — at once seeing the indecency, apologised to the Chancellor, declaring that he forgot where he was. Thurlow growled forth, 'I suppose you thought you were in your own court,' alluding to the free and easy manner in which the proceedings in the Welsh courts were then conducted.

    Edward Foss, *The Judges of England*.

ARKWRIGHT, SIR RICHARD

1732—92 Inventor

The fact is too strikingly characteristic not to be mentioned, that he separated from his wife not many years after their marriage, because she, convinced that he would starve his family by scheming when he should have been shaving, broke some of his experimental models of machinery.

    Edward Baines, *History of the Cotton Manufacture in Great Britain*.

Arkwright was a tremendous worker, and a man of marvellous energy, ardor, and application in business. At one period of his life he was usually engaged, in the severe and continuous labors involved by the organization and conduct of his numerous manufactories, from four in the morning until nine at night. At fifty years of age he set to work to learn English grammar, and improve himself in writing and orthography. When he travelled, to save time, he went at great speed, drawn by four horses. Be it for good or for evil, Arkwright was the founder in England of the modern factory system, a branch of industry which has unquestionably proved a source of immense wealth to individuals and to the nation.

    Samuel Smiles, *Self-help*.

See also Samuel Crompton

ARLEN, MICHAEL

1895—1956 Novelist

Arlen, for all his reputation, is not a bounder. He is

every other inch a gentleman.
Alexander Woollcott, in Robert E. Drennan ed., *Wit's End*.

ARLINGTON, EARL OF (HENRY BENNETT)

1618—85 Statesman

. . . the inkhorn Lord.
John Ayloffe, *The Dream of the Cabal*.

He had learned during a life passed in travelling and negotiating, the art of accommodating his language and deportment to the society in which he found himself. His vivacity in the closet amused the King; his gravity in debates and conferences imposed on the public; and he had succeeded in attaching to himself, partly by services and partly by hopes, a considerable number of personal retainers.
T. B. Macaulay, *History of England*.

On the 14 of Mar. 1664 Sir Henry Benet, sometimes student of Ch. Ch. was created 'lord Arlington of Arlington', and the reason why he would not be called 'lord Benet' was, as 'tis said, 1, because the name did not sound well, and 2dly, because there was an old bawd at Westminster called 'lady Benet.'
Anthony à Wood, *Life and Times*, 14 March 1663/4.

ARLISS, GEORGE

1868—1946 Actor

How skeletal his face was, I thought, The skin was drawn so tightly that I imagined there would have to be a knot somewhere in the back of his head. His small dark eyes held an ancient sadness; but his taut, triangular mouth seemed always to be repressing an irrepressible mirth . . . There was a gentleness in his face that warmed me. I couldn't help thinking that now he looked like an inhibited satyr — a satyr who had materialized at Eton and then Oxford, a civilized gnome as misplaced in this Hollywood world as I seemed to be.
Bette Davis, *The Lonely Life*.

This time he is an Eastern Rajah, but who can change the sly soft episcopal speech, the long upper-lip, like that of a well-bred horse, the general tone of a good club?
Graham Greene, reviewing *East Meets West*, in *Spectator*, 18 September 1936.

George Arliss was a man of such dignity, such *sang froid*, that he became typecast as a historical figure,

and a school superintendent expressed anxiety that a whole generation of schoolchildren might grow up believing that all great men of the past looked like George Arliss. He outmanoeuvred Gladstone, outwitted D'Artagnan and the Three Musketeers, and outspent the rest of the Rothschild brothers. Arliss left audiences feeling euphoric.
William Manchester, *The Glory and the Dream*.

With his countenance at once gentle and diabolic, with his cat-like tread and with his uneasy but sinister hands, he seems to have been roaming our stage all his days in wistful quest of a play about a rajah with richly encrusted garments, a sardonic humor and an evil heart. Now he has found it, and it has the look and sound of a vehicle likely to trundle him as far and as comfortably as did *Disraeli*.
Alexander Woollcott, reviewing 'The Green Goddess', in *New York Times*, 19 January 1921.

ARMOUR, PHILIP DANFORTH

1832—1901 Captain of Industry

I like to turn bristles, blood, and the inside and out-side of pigs and bullocks into revenue. . . .
On himself, in Matthew Josephson, *The Robber Barons*.

. . . the premier 'pork baron' who taught mankind how to use 'all the pig but the squeal.'
Harper Leech and John Charles Carroll, *Armour and His Times*.

ARMSTRONG, LOUIS DANIEL

1900—71 Musician

To me wherever you go — even behind the Iron Curtain — it's just another city. All hotels are alike — bed, bureau, two pillows. Maybe after a show, you try to make one or two joints, have a ball, get stoned, and that's it for the night. That's my life.
On himself, in Richard Merryman, *Louis Armstrong — A Self-Portrait*.

He does not know it. He just blows his trumpet, as he used to deliver milk. He has given a new form of art to his people and a new kind of music to his country. Yet not very long ago Louis Armstrong, unable to find a good hotel in Boston willing to accommodate him, was forced to lodge in a hovel. And in a Southern city recently, without a word of protest, he meekly took a seat in the colored section of a bus.
'How can you stand it, Pops?' asked a friend.

'It's my country, and I love it. If we don't love it an' fight for it, we'll never be free and equal!'
    Richard Goffin, *Horn of Plenty: The Story of Louis Armstrong*, translated from the French by James F. Bezon.

ARNE, THOMAS AUGUSTINE

1710—78 Composer

Hark! Hark! What notes enchant my Ears
Sweet as the musick of the Spheres?
'Tis ARNE — the Gods' Viceregent comes,
Now vanish Rackets, Routs, and Drums;
And with him come the Muses Hand in Hand,
To see fulfilled Apollo's great command.

See Taste with Joy its Head uprears,
Rais'd by Arne's heav'nly Airs;
Skill'd with equal Pow'r t'inspire
Irene's youth with martial Fire,
And lull to Rest, with Soul-delighting Sounds,
The Pains of Grief, and heal Love's bleeding Wounds.

Not he that charm'd the Thracians' Plains,
E'er tun'd his Lyre to softer strains;
Nor does the warbling Bird of Night
More than his sweet-song'd Spouse delight.
O say! What Price or Gifts can both engage
Here to remain, to save a sinking age?
    Anon., in *Faulkner's Journal*, January 1756.

During his residence at Ditton, near Hampton Court, he received a visit from Mr Garrick ... 'Tommy (said he, in his usual familiar way), you should consider that music is, at best, but pickle to my roast-beef.' 'By ————, Davy (replied the Doctor, in a strain of equal jocularity), your beef shall be well pickled before I have done.'
    Biographia Dramatica.

Dr Arne died on the 5th of March 1778, of a spasm on his lungs; retaining his faculties to the last moment of his existence. He had originally been instructed in the principles of the Romish Church: these however he had for many years wholly neglected, as inconsistent with a life of ease and gallantry, in which he indulged to the full extent of his purse and constitution. In his last stage, the dormant seeds of early maxims and prejudices (as is usually the case) revived in his bosom, too strong to be checked, or perhaps discriminated by sound reason. The complicated train of doubts, hopes and fears, operated so forcibly on the Doctor's feelings, at this awful period, that a priest was sent for, by whom he was soon awed into a state of most submissive repentance. In thus renewing the duties of a Christian, those of his professional line were not

forgotten: for about an hour before his death, he sung an harmonious Halleluja; a flight of fancy calculated, as it were, to usher him into the other world.
    Ibid.

Thoughtless, dissipated and careless, he neglected or rather scoffed at all other but musical reputation. And he was so little scrupulous in his ideas of propriety, that he took pride, rather than shame in being publicly classed, even in the decline of life, as a man of pleasure. Such a character was ill qualified to form or protect the morals of a youthful pupil, and it is probable that not a notion of duty occurred to Dr. Arne, so happy was his self-complacency in the fertility of his invention and the ease of his compositions, and so dazzled by the brilliancy of his success in the powers of melody — which, in truth, for the English stage, were in sweetness and variety unrivalled — that, satisfied and flattered by the practical exertions and the popularity of his fancy, he had no ambition, or rather, no thought concerning the theory of his art.
    Fanny Burney, *A Memoir of Dr. Burney.*

Let Tommy Arne, with usual pomp of style,
Whose chief, whose only merit's to compile,
Who, meanly pilfering here and there a bit,
Deals music out, as Murphy deals out wit;
Publish proposals, laws for taste prescribe,
And chaunt the praise of an Italian tribe;
Let him reverse Kind Nature's first decrees,
And teach e'en Brent a method not to please:
But never shall a truly British age
Bear a vile race of eunuchs on the stage:
The boasted work's called national in vain
If one Italian voice pollute the strain....
    Charles Churchill, *The Rosciad.*

He further managed to acquire some proficiency on the violin, and soon contrived to get some lessons from the accomplished and eminent violinist, Michael Festing ... Calling in King Street one day for this purpose, Festing found Arne diligently practising with his music supported on the lid of a coffin. Horrified with the sight, he declared he could not play under such circumstances, as he would be constantly imagining there might be a corpse in the coffin beneath. 'So there is,' said Arne, and gave proof by removing the lid.
    W. H. Cummings, *Dr. Arne and Rule, Britannia.*

I have read your play and rode your horse, and do not approve of either. They both want particular spirit which alone can give pleasure to the reader and the rider. When the one wants wits, and the other the spur, they both jog on very heavily. I must keep the horse, but I have returned you the play. I pretend to some little knowledge of the last; but as I am no jockey, they cannot say that the knowing one is taken in.

David Garrick, undated letter endorsed 'Designed for Dr. Arne, who sold me a horse, a very dull one; and sent me a comic opera, ditto.'

He carries light armour: he wins by readiness of attack and dexterity of movement: he is less at his ease in the larger and more stately exercises of art than in those of the pleasaunce and the playing ground: but his sentiment, if a little shallow, is always sincere and his melody is delightfully fresh and spontaneous. In an age when our music had become dull and academic he lightened it with a native wood-note of genuine sweetness and charm.

Sir Henry Hadow, *English Music*.

ARNOLD, BENEDICT

1741—1801 Revolutionary Soldier

Our troops by Arnold thoroughly were bang'd
  And poor St. André was by Arnold hang'd.
To George a Rebel, to the Congress traitor,
  Pray what can make the name of Arnold greater?
By one bold treason more to gain his ends.
  Let him betray his new adopted friends.
Anon., in Charles Coleman Sellers, *Benedict Arnold: The Proud Warrior*.

Base Arnold's head by luck was saved,
  Poor André was gibbeted.
Arnold's to blame for André's fame
  And André's to be pitied.
  Ibid.

To North with Lean said George the Wise,
  'Here's with one Arnold much ado;'
The drowsy Premier, starting, cries,
  ''Tis well, my liege, there are not two.'
  Ibid.

And why, sweet Minstrel, from the harp of fame
Withhold so long that once resounding name?
The chief who, steering by that boreal star,
O'er wild Canadia led our infant war,
In desperate straits superior powers display'd
Burgoyne's dread scourge, Montgomery's ablest aid;
Ridgefield and Campo saw his valorous might
With ill-arm'd swains put veteran troops to flight.
The treason foul hath since absorb'd his soul,
Bade waves of dark oblivion round him roll,
Sunk his proud heart, abhorrent and aborr'd
Effaced his memory and defiled his sword;
Yet then untarnished roll'd his conquering car,
The famed and foremost in the ranks of war

Brave Arnold trod; high valor warm'd his breast
And beams of glory play'd around his crest.
  Joel Barlow, *The Columbiad*.

A name scented with powder smoke, the man whose wild adventures added the thrill of glory to defeat, in his uniform of buff and blue, his scarlet sash and shining epaulettes, this stocky, florid-faced war-hawk. . . .
  Charles Coleman Sellers, *Benedict Arnold: The Proud Warrior*.

With Benedict Arnold honor was not a character neatly defined or conveniently abstract, as with most of us. It was his peace of mind, it was his sense of superiority over other men. It was his instinct to command, and when he felt that it was not respected he was hostile or aloof. He saw the world in terms of this domineering self. When he embraced a cause he did so vigorously, whole-heartedly, with no sense of duty or submission to a higher self, higher than his personal ambition.
  Ibid.

The merit of this gentleman is certainly great, and I heartily wish that fortune may distinguish him as one of her favorites. I am convinced that he will do everything that his prudence and valor shall suggest to add success to our arms.
  George Washington, in *ibid.*

From some traits of his character which have lately come to my knowledge, he seems to have been so hackneyed in villainy, and so lost to all sense of honor and shame that while his facilities will enable him to continue his sordid pursuits there will be no time for remorse.
  George Washington, Letter to John Laurens, 13 October 1780.

See also Nathan Hale

ARNOLD, MATTHEW

1822—88 Poet, Critic

My poems represent, on the whole, the main movement of mind of the last quarter of a century, and thus they will probably have their day as people become conscious to themselves of what that movement of mind is, and interested in the literary productions which reflect it. It might be fairly urged that I have less poetical sentiment than Tennyson, and less intellectual vigour and abundance than Browning; yet, because I have perhaps more of a fusion of the two than either of them . . . I am likely enough to have my turn, as they have had theirs.

On himself, Letter to his Mother, 5 June 1869.

Mr Arnold, to those who cared for him at all, was the most *useful* poet of his day. He lived much nearer us than poets of his distinction usually do. He was neither a prophet nor a recluse. He lived neither above us nor away from us. There are two ways of being a recluse — a poet may live remote from men, or he may live in a crowded street but remote from their thoughts. Mr Arnold did neither, and consequently his verse tells and tingles. None of it is thrown away. His readers feel that he bore the same yoke as themselves.

Augustine Birrell, in *Scribner's Magazine*, November 1888.

'Is there a God?' asks the reader. 'Oh yes,' replies Mr Arnold, 'and I can verify him in experience.' 'And what is he then?' cries the reader. 'Be virtuous, and as a rule you will be happy,' is the answer. 'Well, and God?' 'That is God,' says Mr Arnold; 'there is no deception, and what more do you want?' I suppose we do want a good deal more. Most of us, certainly the public which Mr Arnold addresses, want something they can worship; and they will not find that in any hypostasized copybook heading, which is not much more adorable than 'Honesty is the best policy', or 'Handsome is that handsome does', or various other edifying maxims, which have not yet come to an apotheosis.

F. H. Bradley, *Ethical Studies*.

There is a power & nobility of thought surrounded by a chrystalline atmosphere in Arnold's poetry. He wants vital heat, passion & imagination, & these are great wants. ... He is an admirable poet in one sense — an admirable *poetical writer*. But he must break up all his ice of meditation, & consent to feel like a child & attain to seeing like a seer, before we call him a poet in the absolute sense.

Elizabeth Barrett Browning, Letter to Mrs David Ogilvy, 19 February 1854.

You are a fortunate man. The young men read you; they no longer read me. And you have invented phrases which everyone quotes — such as 'Philistinism' and 'Sweetness and Light'.

Benjamin Disraeli, to Arnold, *circa* 1880, in G. W. E. Russell, *Collections and Recollections*.

Mat Arnold when at college bathed in a river in front of a village. The clergyman came to remonstrate. Mat quite naked waved the towel gracefully and with quiet seriousness said, Is it possible that you see anything indelicate in the human form divine?

George Eliot, Diary, 10 April 1878.

Arnold is a poet to whom one readily returns. It is a pleasure, certainly after associating with the riff-raff of the early part of the century, to be in the company of a man *qui sait se conduire*; but Arnold is something more than an agreeable Professor of Poetry. With all his fastidiousness and superciliousness and officiality, Arnold is more intimate with us than Browning, more intimate than Tennyson. ... He is the poet and critic of a period of false stability ... but his poetry, the best of it, is too honest to employ any but his genuine feelings of unrest, loneliness and dissatisfaction.

T. S. Eliot, *The Use of Poetry and the Use of Criticism*.

In a society in which the arts were seriously studied, in which the art of writing was respected, Arnold might have become a critic ... Arnold was not so much occupied in establishing a criticism as in attacking the uncritical. The difference is that while in constructive work something can be done, destructive work must incessantly be repeated; and furthermore Arnold, in his destruction, went for game outside of the literary preserve altogether, much of it political game untouched and inviolable by ideas ... Arnold is not to be blamed: he wasted his strength, as men of superior ability sometimes do, because he saw something to be done and no one else to do it. The temptation, to any man who is interested in ideas and primarily in literature, to put literature into the corner until he has cleaned up the whole country first, is almost irresistible.

T. S. Eliot, *The Sacred Wood*.

Other poets say anything — say everything that is in them ... Matthew Arnold alone says only what is worth saying. In other words, he selects: from his matter whatever is impertinent is eliminated and only what is vital is permitted to remain.

W. E. Henley, in *Athenaeum*, 22 August 1885.

I met Matthew Arnold and had a few words with him. He is not as handsome as his photographs — or as his poetry.

Henry James, Letter to Charles Eliot Norton, 31 March 1873.

In his absence the whole tone of discussion would have seemed more stupid, more literal. Without his irony to play over its surface, to clip it here and there of its occasional fustiness, the life of our Anglo-Saxon race would present a much greater appearance of insensibility.

Henry James, in *English Illustrated Magazine*, January 1884.

Finally, we take leave of Mr Arnold, with his cleverness and his scholarship, his somewhat super-

ciliously announced theories of poetry, his attachment to ancient models, and his echoes (for all that) of the Tennysonian cadences, in the conviction that, although he has written no common verses ... he was not born a poet, and therefore never can be one. Many claim the rank; few show claims so plausible as his, because of the superiority of his general talents and culture; but his claims also want the genuine stamp. We say so, not without pain, but distinctly.
  Harriet Martineau, in *Daily News*, 26 December 1853.

Arnold gives distinction to everything he touches. His style reminds one of a very well-bred and cultured lady, somewhat advanced in years so that the passions of life are more than half forgotten, and of such exquisite manners as to suggest a bygone day, yet with humour and vivacity such that the thought never occurs to one that she belongs to an older generation.
  Somerset Maugham, *A Writer's Notebook*.

Admirably as I think Matthew Arnold's style was suited to his particular purposes, I must admit that his mannerisms are often irritating. His style was an instrument that he had forged once for all; it was not like the human hand capable of performing a variety of actions.
  Somerset Maugham, *The Summing Up*.

Arnold is a dandy Isaiah, a poet without passion, whose verse, written in a surplice, is for freshmen and for gentle maidens who will be wooed to the arms of these future rectors.
  George Meredith, in *Fortnightly Review*, July 1909.

'When Abraham Lincoln was murdered
The one thing that interested Matthew
    Arnold
Was that the assassin shouted in Latin
As he leapt from the stage.
This convinced Matthew
There was still hope for America.
  Christopher Morley, *Point of View*.

Of all the variously horrid forms in which sentence of annihilation has been passed on famous writers, none seems more unjust than that reserved for Matthew Arnold, who, during the spring of 1888, fell dead in a Liverpool street while running for a tramcar. The background, the occasion, the haste, the lack of dignity — all might have been contrived to make an inappropriate ending. It was as if the spirit of the 19th century, symbolised by a noisy mechanical juggernaut grinding towards the docks between shabby prosperous warehouses, had finally

vanquished the gallant exponent of a less inharmonious order.
  Peter Quennell, *The Singular Preference*.

The exquisite poet who so soon abandoned poetry; the supreme critic whose best criticism is so scanty; the great writer who wasted his best years in dull official routine; the advocate of Hellenism and sweet reasonableness who soon gave himself up to angry recrimination, and who, whether owing to exasperation with his contemporaries or to some arrogant streak in his own nature, more and more abandoned that serene aloofness from contemporary conflicts which had been his ideal, and adopted a pose of aggressive, self-satisfied contempt, and a harsh browbeating style full of derisive catchwords.
  Logan Pearsall Smith, *Unforgotten Years*.

Poor Matt, he's gone to Heaven, no doubt — but he won't like God.
  Robert Louis Stevenson, on hearing of Arnold's death.

[Wordsworth's] Immortality Ode ... is no more than moderately good ... I put by its side the poems of Matthew Arnold, and think what a delightfully loud splash the two would make if I dropped them into a river.
  Dylan Thomas, Letter to Pamela Hansford Johnson, 1933.

An English saint in side whiskers.
  Oscar Wilde, in L. Lévinson ed., *Bartlett's Unfamiliar Quotations*.

See also Phineas Barnum, John Dryden

ARNOLD, THOMAS

1795—1842 Headmaster

My love for any place, or person, or institution, is exactly the measure of my desire to reform them; a doctrine which seems to me as natural now, as it seemed strange when I was a child.
  On himself. Letter to Dean Stanley, 4 March 1835.

My object will be, if possible, to form Christian men, for Christian boys I can scarcely hope to make.
  On himself, Letter written at the time of his appointment to the Headship of Rugby, 1828.

Dr Arnold was almost indisputably an admirable master for a common English boy, — the small, apple eating animal whom we know. He worked, he pounded, if the phrase may be used, into the boy a belief, or at any rate a floating, confused conception, that there are great subjects, that there are strange problems, that knowledge has an indefinite value, that life is a serious and solemn thing. The influence of Arnold's teaching on the majority of his pupils was probably very vague, but very good. To impress on the ordinary Englishman a general notion of the importance of what is intellectual and the reality of what is supernatural, is the greatest benefit which can be conferred upon him. ... But there are a few minds which are very likely to think too much of such things. A susceptible, serious, intellectual boy may be injured by the incessant inculcation of the awfulness of life and the magnitude of great problems. It is not desirable to take this world too much *au serieux*; most persons will not; and the one in a thousand who will, should not.

Walter Bagehot, *Essay on Clough*.

There are men — such as Arnold — too intensely, fervidly practical to be literally, accurately, consistently theoretical; too eager to be observant, too royal to be philosophical, too fit to head armies and rule kingdoms to succeed in weighing words and analysing emotions; born to do, they know not what they do.

A. H. Clough, *Poems and Prose Remains*.

Despite his high seriousness, Arnold had never gone through the process of growing up. At the age of ten he was already as great a prig as during his headmastership. His moral philosophy was evolved not as the outcome of experience, but through a fear of the deep springs of emotion which he so successfully damped down. He embraced this philosophy with a desperate passion.

Michael Holroyd, *Lytton Strachey*.

Most educated men are agreed that the Arnold system is inferior to that obtaining in Scotland, where social snobbery (the bane of the Arnold system) scarcely exists at all.

Percy Wyndham Lewis, Letter to John Slocum, 21 November 1940.

He was the first Englishman who drew attention in our public schools to the historical, political and philosophical value of philology and of the ancient writers, as distinguished from the mere verbal criticism and elegant scholarship of the last century. And besides the general impulse which he gave to miscellaneous reading, both in the regular examinations and by encouraging the tastes of particular boys for geology or other like pursuits, he incorporated the study of Modern History, Modern Languages and Mathematics into the work of the school, which attempt, as it was the first of its kind,

so it was at one time the chief topic of blame and praise in his system of instruction.

A. P. Stanley, *Life of Arnold*.

See also A. H. Clough

ARTHUR, PRINCE OF WALES

1486—1502

Robert viscount Fitzwater deposed, the prince was then about 15, and queen Catherine elder; and that, the next day after being in bed together (which he remembered after they entered to be solemnly blessed) he waited at breakfast on prince Arthur, where Maurice St. John did carve, and he the lord Fitzwater give drink; at which time the said Maurice demanding of the prince how he had done that night? The prince answered, I have been in Spain this night . . . Anthony Willoughby, knight, deposed that being the morrow after the Marriage in the prince's privy-chamber, the said prince spake afore divers witnesses these words, 'Willoughby, give me a cup of ale, for I have been this night in the midst of Spain.' After which he said, 'Masters, it is a good pastime to have a wife'. . . .

William Cobbett, *State Trials* (the evidence at a divorce hearing between Henry VIII and Catherine of Aragon that her marriage with Prince Arthur had been consummated).

See also Thomas Linacre

ARTHUR, CHESTER ALAN

1830—86 Twenty-First United States President

First in ability on the list of second rate men.
Anon., in *New York Times*, 20 February 1872.

. . . a creature for whose skin the romancist ought to go with carving knife.
Henry Adams, in George Frederick Howe, *Chester Arthur: A Quarter of a Century of Machine Politics*.

. . . Chester A. Arthur, who became honest after becoming president.
Richard Armour, *It All Started With Columbus*.

I have but one annoyance with the administration of President Arthur, and that is, that, in contrast with it, the Administration of Hayes becomes respectable, if not heroic.
Roscoe Conkling, in George Frederick Howe, *Chester Arthur: A Quarter of a Century of Machine Politics*.

I am but one in 55,000,000; still, in the opinion of this one-fifty-five millionth of the country's population, it would be hard to better President Arthur's Administration. But don't decide till you hear from the rest.
    Mark Twain, in *The American Heritage Pictorial History of the Presidents*, vol. 2.

A non entity with side whiskers.
    Attrib. Woodrow Wilson, in Marcus Cunliffe, *American Presidents and the Presidency*.

ASCH, SHOLEM

1880–1957 Author

I am not a Yiddish artist, I am a universal artist.
    On himself, in Charles A. Madison, *Yiddish Literature*.

Simultaneously a pagan poet who sees things through the prism of earthly beauty and a passionate Jew who must cry out when his people are in pain, he again and again submits to his conscience – to the detriment of his sensuous imagination.
    Charles A. Madison, 'Sholem Asch' in *Poet Lore*, Winter 1940.

... the Jewish Dickens.
    Louis Nizer, *Between You and Me*.

ASHMOLE, ELIAS

1617–92 Antiquary

Born in Litchfield, critically skilled in ancient coins, chemistry, heraldry, mathematicks, and what not?
    Thomas Fuller, *The History of the Worthies of England*.

ASQUITH, HERBERT HENRY, EARL OF OXFORD AND ASQUITH

1852–1928 Prime Minister

You were, in the world above, almost a classical example of *Luck*. You were endowed at birth with brains above the average. You had, further, some qualities of temperament which are exceptionally useful for mundane success – energy under the guise of lethargy; a faculty for working quickly, which is more effective in the long run than plodding perseverance; patience (which is one of the rarest of human qualities); a temperate but persistent ambition; a clear mind, a certain quality and lucidity of speech; intellectual, but not moral, irritability; a natural tendency to understand & appreciate the opponent's point of view: and, as time went on, & your nature matured, a growing sense of proportion, which had its effect upon both friends and foes, and which, coupled with detachment from any temptation to intrigue, and, in regard to material interests & profits, an unaffected indifference, secured for you the substantial advantage of personality and authority ... you were what is called in the slang vocabulary of your time a 'good get out'.
    On himself, from his private sketch imagining the assessment of the Judge of the Infernal Tribunal, March 1915, in Roy Jenkins, *Asquith*.

For twenty years he has held a season ticket on the line of least resistance, and gone wherever the train of events has carried him, lucidly justifying his position at whatever point he has happened to find himself.
    L. S. Amery, in the House of Commons, *circa* 1916.

... black and wicked and with only a nodding acquaintance with the truth.
    Lady Cunard, in Henry Channon, Diary, 7 January 1944.

Asquith's mind is a perfect instrument, and he takes points after the manner of a trained lawyer. But he lacks some element of character; perhaps hardiness, I should say he was a soft man; and his chin *recedes* when an attack is possible or imminent.
    Lord Esher, Diary, 28 November 1907.

My colleagues tell military secrets to their wives, except X who tells them to other people's wives.
    Lord Kitchener, in Philip Magnus, *Kitchener*.

The criticism which is directed against the govt. and against yourself is chiefly based on this – that as Prime Minister you have not devoted yourself absolutely to co-ordinating all the moves of the war because so much of your time and energy has been devoted to control of the political machine.
    Andrew Bonar Law, Letter to Asquith, 2 November 1915.

Asquith worries too much about small points. If you were buying a large mansion he would come to you and say 'Have you thought that there is no accommodation for the cat.'
    David Lloyd George, Letter to Lord Riddell, 1915.

... A forensic gladiator who never made a heart beat quicker by his words, and who never by any

possibility brought a lump into his hearers' throats.
W. T. Stead, in *Review of Reviews*, January 1906.

... the P.M. is absolutely devoid of all principles
except one — that of retaining his position as Prime
Minister. He will sacrifice everything except No. 10
Downing St. D[avid Lloyd George] says he is for all
the world like a Sultan with his harem of 23, using
all his skill and wiles to prevent one of them from
eloping.
Frances Stevenson, Diary, 30 November 1916.

His public career suggests a parallel with Walpole.
But one gathers that under all Sir Robert's low-
minded opportunism there was a certain grandeur,
and that his actual capacity was supreme. In
Asquith's case the inveterate lack of ideals and
imagination seems really unredeemed; when one has
peeled off the brown-paper wrapping of phrases and
compromises, one finds — just nothing at all.
Lytton Strachey, in M. Holroyd, *Lytton
Strachey*.

See also Bonar Law

ASQUITH, EMMA ALICE MARGARET (MARGOT), COUNTESS OF OXFORD AND ASQUITH

1864—1945 Society Woman

The affair between Margot Asquith and Margot
Asquith will live as one of the prettiest love stories
in all literature.
Dorothy Parker, in Robert Drennan ed.,
Wit's End.

ASTON, SIR ARTHUR

— d. 1649 Soldier

September 1644. — Sir Arthur Aston was governour
of Oxon at what time it was garrison'd for the king,
a testy, forward, imperious and tirannical person,
hated in Oxford and elsewhere by God and Man.
Who kervetting on horseback in Bullington green
before certaine ladies, his horse flung him and broke
his legge: so that it being cut off and he therupon
rendred useless for employment, one coll. Legge
succeeded him. Soon after the country people
coming to market would be ever and anon asking
the sentinell, 'who was governor of Oxon?' They
answered 'one Legge.' Then replied they: 'A pox
upon him! Is he governor still?'
Anthony à Wood, *Life and Times*.

ASTOR, JOHN JACOB

1763—1848 Capitalist, Fur-Trader

At his most detestable, he was no hypocrite, but
rather his own worst enemy, prey to a moral blindness which was instinctive rather than reasoned.
How he would have hated himself had he been able
to view some of his acts objectively....
Kenneth W. Porter, *John Jacob Astor*.

An arrant individualist, selfish, narrow-minded,
quite blandly antisocial, he went after whatever he
sought and took it by fair means or foul — and
whoever didn't like it was welcome to a battle.
Ibid.

ASTOR, NANCY WITCHER, VISCOUNTESS

1879—1964 First Woman Member of Parliament

The Wait and See Policy has changed me into a
fighting woman.
On herself, Sentence omitted from the final
version of a Letter to Margot Asquith, 1915.

I am a Virginian, so naturally I am a politician.
On herself, Acceptance speech, Autumn 1919.

Nobody wants me as a Cabinet Minister and they
are perfectly right. I am an agitator, not an
administrator.
On herself, Address to a women's luncheon,
circa 1929.

Am I dying or is this my birthday?
On herself, at the sight of all her children
assembled in her last illness, April 1964.

Nancy: Winston, if I were married to you, I'd put
poison in your coffee.
Churchill: Nancy, if you were my wife, I'd drink it.
Exchange at Blenheim Palace, *circa* 1912, in
Elizabeth Langhorne, *Nancy Astor and her
friends*.

When I married Nancy, I hitched my wagon to a
star and when I got into the House of Commons in
1910, I found that I had hitched my wagon to a
shooting star. In 1919 when she got into the House,
I found that I had hitched my wagon to a sort of
V-2 rocket.
Viscount Astor, Speech to a women's organization
dinner, December 1944.

Here England buries her grudge against Columbus.
Kensal Green (Colin Hurry), *Premature Epitaphs.*

Viscount Waldorf Astor owned Britain's two most influential newspapers, *The Times* and the *Observer,* but his American wife, Nancy, had a wider circulation than both papers put together.
Emery Kelen, *Peace in Their Time.*

I shall not soon forget the sight of Lady Astor's trim little figure dressed in appropriate black, advancing from the bar of the House of Commons flanked by Mr Balfour and Mr Lloyd George. . . . That was your second conquest of Britain.
Lord Lothian, British Ambassador, to the Virginia Legislature, 1939.

Nannie was a devout Christian Scientist, but not a good one. She kept confusing herself with God. She didn't know when to step aside and give God a chance.
Mrs Gordon Smith, in Elizabeth Langhorne, *Nancy Astor and her friends.*

ATTERBURY, FRANCIS

1662—1732 Bishop of Rochester

. . . a mind inexhaustibly rich in all the resources of controversy, and familiar with all the artifices which make falsehood look like truth and ignorance like knowledge.
T. B. Macaulay, *Life of Atterbury.*

His devotion to the Protestant faith was warm and pure; his labours for the Established Church no less praiseworthy; but his defence was of somewhat too fierce and turbulent a character; he thought less of personal worth than of party principles in others; and he was one of whom it has been wittily said that out of their zeal for religion they never have time to say their prayers. . . . On the whole, he would have made an admirable Bishop had he been a less good partisan.
Lord Mahon, *History of England, 1713—1783.*

Atterbury goes before, and sets everything on fire. I come after him with a bucket of water.
George Smalridge, Bishop of Bristol, in T. B. Macaulay, *Life of Atterbury.*

He never attempts your passions until he has convinced your reason. All the objections which he can form are laid open and dispersed, before he uses the least vehemence in his sermon; but when he thinks he has your head, he very soon wins your heart; and never pretends to show the beauty of holiness, until he hath convinced you of the truth of it.
Richard Steele, in *Tatler,* no. 66.

ATTLEE, CLEMENT RICHARD, EARL ATTLEE

1883—1967 Prime Minister

I am a very diffident man. I find it hard to carry on a conversation. But if any of you wish to come and see me, I will welcome you.
On himself, speaking to junior Labour ministers, June 1945.

I have none of the qualities which create publicity.
On himself, in Harold Nicolson, Diary, 14 January 1949.

He seems determined to make a trumpet sound like a tin whistle. . . . He brings to the fierce struggle of politics the tepid enthusiasm of a lazy summer afternoon at a cricket match.
Aneurin Bevan, in *Tribune,* 1945.

[*As it Happened*] is a good title. Things happened to him. He never *did* anything.
Aneurin Bevan, on Attlee's *Autobiography,* in Michael Foot, *Aneurin Bevan.*

He is a sheep in sheep's clothing.
Winston Churchill, attributed, 1945.

Anyone can respect him, certainly, but admire — no!
Winston Churchill, in Henry Channon, Diary, 20 July 1948.

We all understand his position. 'I am their leader, I must follow them'.
Winston Churchill, attributed.

A modest little man with much to be modest about.
Winston Churchill, in Michael Foot, *Aneurin Bevan.*

Attlee is a charming and intelligent man, but as a public speaker he is, compared to Winston [Churchill], like a village fiddler after Paganini.
Harold Nicolson, Diary, 10 November 1947.

See also Winston Churchill

AUBREY, JOHN

1626—97 Antiquary, Biographer

My Memoires of Lives is now a booke of 2 quires,

close written: and after I had begun it I had such an impulse in my spirit that I could not be at quiet till I had done it. I Beleeve never any in England were delivered so faithfully and with so good authority.

On himself, Letter to Anthony à Wood.

Mild of spirit; mightily susceptible of Fascination. My Idea very cleer; Phansie like a Mirrour, pure chrystal water which the least wind does disorder and unsmooth. Never riotous or prodigall; but (as Sir E. Leech said) Sloath and carelessness are equivalent to all other vices.

On himself, his schooldays, *Brief Lives*.

About as credulous an old goose as one could hope to find out of Gotham.

B. G. Johns, 'John Aubrey of Wilts', in *Gentleman's Magazine*, 1893.

His insatiable passion, for singular odds and ends had a meaning in it; he was groping towards a scientific ordering of phenomena; but the twilight of his age was too confusing, and he could rarely distinguish between a fact and a fantasy. He was clever enough to understand the Newtonian system, but he was not clever enough to understand that a horoscope was an absurdity; and so, in his crowded curiosity shop of a brain, astronomy and astrology both found a place, and were given equal values.

Lytton Strachey, *John Aubrey*.

He was a shiftless person, roving and magotis-headed, and sometimes little better than crased. And being exceedingly credulous, would stuff his many letters sent to A.W. with fooleries, and misinformations, which sometimes would guid him into the paths of errour.

Anthony à Wood, *Life and Times*.

AUDEN, WYSTAN HUGH

1907—73 Poet

It is a sad fact about our culture that a poet can earn much more money writing or talking about his art than he can by practicing it. All the poems I have written were written for love; naturally, when I have written one, I try to market it, but the prospect of a market played no role in its writing. On the other hand, I have never written a line of criticism except in response to a demand by others for a lecture, an introduction, a review, etc.; though I hope that some love went into their writing, I wrote them because I needed the money.

On himself, Foreword to *The Dyer's Hand*.

Most people enjoy the sight of their own hand-writing as they enjoy the smell of their own farts. Much as I loathe the typewriter, I must admit that it is a help in self-criticism. Typescript is so impersonal and hideous to look at that, if I type out a poem, I immediately see defects which I missed when I looked through it in manuscript.

On himself, *The Dyer's Hand*.

The son of book-loving, Anglo-Catholic parents of the professional class ... I was ... mentally precocious, physically backward, shortsighted, a rabbit at all games, very untidy and grubby, a nail-biter, a physical coward, dishonest, sentimental, with no community sense whatever, in fact a typical little highbrow and difficult child.

On himself, in Dennis Davison, *W. H. Auden*.

A face like a wedding cake left out in the rain.

Anon., in L. Levinson, *Bartlett's Unfamiliar Quotations*.

In a century of the symbolist, surreal, and absurd, W. H. Auden is essentially a poet of the reasonable.

James D. Brophy, *W. H. Auden*.

Later, standing in the wings,
I heard you read: no dramatics,
More interested in what you said
Than how you said it;
Airless Stateside vowels
Ricocheting off the kippered panelling
Like custard pies, yet more telling
Than bullets or blood transfusions.

Charles Causley, *Letter from Jericho*.

Poetry is highly explosive, but no good poet since Eliot can but perceive the extreme difficulty of writing good poetry ... We have one poet of genius in Auden, who is able to write prolifically, carelessly, and exquisitely, nor does he seem to have to pay any price for his inspiration. It is as if he worked under the influence of some mysterious drug which presents him with a private vision, a mastery of form and of vocabulary.

Cyril Connolly, *Enemies of Promise*.

The youthful Auden ... was tall and slim, with a mole on his upper lip, rather untidy tow-coloured hair in a loop over his forehead, with extraordinary greenish eyes suggesting that iceberg glare he liked to claim from his Norse ancestors ... My feelings towards him were entirely platonic ... but my subconscious demanded more and I was put out by a dream (based on his ballad) in which, stripped to the waist beside a basin ('O plunge your hands in water') he indicated to me two small firm breasts: 'Well, Cyril, how do you like my lemons?'

Cyril Connolly, in *Encounter*, March 1975.

Auden is . . . something of an intellectual jackdam, picking up bright pebbles of ideas so as to fit them into exciting conceptual patterns.

Richard Hoggart, *W. H. Auden*.

Auden is, and always has been, a most prolific writer. Problems of form and technique seem to bother him very little. You could say to him: 'Please write me a double ballade on the virtues of a certain brand of toothpaste, which also contains at least ten anagrams on the names of well-known politicians, and of which the refrain is as follows . . .' Within twenty-four hours your ballade would be ready — and it would be good.

Christopher Isherwood, in *New Verse*, November 1937.

One never steps twice into the same Auden.

Randall Jarrell, *The Third Book of Criticism*.

. . . an engaging, bookish, American talent, too verbose to be memorable and too intellectual to be moving.

Philip Larkin, in George T. Wright, *W. H. Auden*.

He is all ice and woodenfaced acrobatics.

Percy Wyndham Lewis, *Blasting and Bombardiering*.

[At Oxford] Auden, then as always, was busy getting on with the job. Sitting in a room all day with the blinds down, reading very fast and very widely — psychology, ethnology, *Arabia Deserta*. He did not seem to *look* at anything, admitted he hated flowers and was very free with quasi-scientific jargon, but you came away from his presence always encouraged; here at· least was someone to whom ideas were friendly — they came and ate out of his hand — who would always have an interest in the world and always have something to say.

Louis MacNeice, *The Strings are False*.

Wystan Auden reads us some of his new poem in the evening. . . . It interests me particularly as showing, at last, that I belong to an older generation. I follow Auden in his derision of patriotism, class distinctions, comfort, and all the ineptitudes of the middle-classes. But when he also derides the other soft little harmless things which make my life comfortable, I feel a chill autumn wind. I feel that were I a communist the type of person whom I should most wish to attack would not be the millionaire or the imperialist, but the soft, reasonable, tolerant, secure, self-satisfied intellectual like Vita and myself. A man like Auden with his fierce repudiation of half-way houses and his gentle integrity makes one feel terribly discontented with one's own smug successfulness. I go to bed feeling terribly Edwardian and

back-number, and yet, thank God, delighted that people like Wystan Auden should actually exist.

Harold Nicolson, Diary, 4 August 1933.

Mr Auden's brand of amoralism is only possible if you are the kind of person who is always somewhere else when the trigger is pulled. So much of left-wing thought is a kind of playing with fire by people who don't even know that fire is hot.

George Orwell, *Inside the Whale*.

I personally do *not* share the Auden craze, it isn't as much as a craze anyhow; it is merely that Auden is so large a part of what little they've got. Mutatis mutandis, another J. E. Flecker, I mean about that general mule-power.

Ezra Pound, Letter to Harriet Monroe, 27 March 1931.

Surely, at some deep level . . . Auden's notorious rudeness and his despotic directives — go easy with the lavatory paper; bring your own cigarettes — were efforts to be *interesting*. Lurking somewhere was the demand for love, and the fear of being boring. Somehow, though, in later life, he was less and less able to work the trick to his own satisfaction. His many friends went on loving him in spite of his cantankerous behaviour: Auden evidently wished to be loved because of it. At the touch of pity he withdrew inside the famous carapace.

Craig Raine, in *New Statesman*, 28 March 1975.

People sometimes divide others into those you laugh at and those you laugh with. The young Auden was someone you could laugh-at-with.

Stephen Spender, *Valedictory Address*, 27 October 1973, at Auden's memorial service at Christ Church, Oxford.

Few understand the works of Cummings,
And few James Joyce's mental slummings,
And few young Auden's coded chatter;
But then it is the few that matter.

Dylan Thomas, Letter to Pamela Hansford Johnson, 1933.

I sometimes think of Mr Auden's poetry as a hygiene, a knowledge and practice, based on a brilliantly prejudiced analysis of contemporary disorders, relating to the preservation and promotion of health, a sanitary science and a flusher of melancholies. I sometimes think of his poetry as a great war, admire intensely the mature, religious, and logical fighter, and deprecate the boy bushranger.

Dylan Thomas, in *New Verse*, November 1937.

Auden often writes like Disney. Like Disney, he knows the shape of beasts (and incidentally he, too,

might have a company of artists producing his lines) ; unlike Lawrence, he does not know what shapes or motivates those beasts. He's a naturalist who looks for beasts that resemble himself, and, failing that, he tries to shape them in his own curious image. The true naturalist, like Gilpin, offers his toe to the vampire bat; Auden would suck the bat off.
Dylan Thomas, Letter to Henry Treece, 1938.

It is interesting to go back over Auden's books and to try to trace the effect on his work of his residence in the United States. . . . This influence of America does not seem to me in the least to have diluted the Englishness of Auden or to have changed its essential nature. Auden's genius is basically English — though in ways which, in the literary world, seem at present rather out of fashion. He is English in his toughness, his richness, his obstinacy, his adventurousness, his eccentricity. What America has done for Auden is to help him to acquire what is certainly today one of the best things an American can hope to have: a mind that feels itself at the center of things. It has given him a point of view that is inter- or super-national.
Edmund Wilson, The Bit Between My Teeth.

Mr Auden himself has presented the curious case of a poet who writes an original poetic language in the most robust English tradition, but who seems to have been arrested at the mentality of an adolescent schoolboy. His technique has seemed to mature, but he has otherwise not grown up. His mind has always been haunted, as the minds of boys at prep school still are, by parents and uncles and aunts. His love poems seem unreal and ambiguous as if they were the products of adolescent flirtations and prep-school homosexuality. . . . The seizure of power he dreams of is an insurrection in the schoolroom.
Edmund Wilson, The Shores of Light.

See also Edith Sitwell

AUDUBON, JOHN JAMES LEFOREST

1785—1851 Artist, Ornithologist

Some men live for warlike deeds,
Some for women's words.
John James Audubon
Lived to look at birds . . .

Colored them and printed them
In a giant book
'Birds of North America' —
All the world said, 'Look!'
Stephen Vincent Benét, John James Audubon.

Call Audubon vain, call him in some things selfish, call him flighty, and inconsequential in his worldly conduct, — all these qualities are palpable in every page of the diary. He was handsome, and he knew it; he was elegant, and he prided himself upon it. He was generous in most things, but he did not love his rivals. He prattled about himself like an infant, gloried in his long hair, admired the fine curve of his nose, thought 'blood' a great thing, and reverenced the great. Well, happy is the man who has no greater errors than these.
Robert Buchanan, Life and Adventures of Audubon the Naturalist.

AUSTEN, JANE

1775—1817 Novelist

What dreadful hot weather we have! It keeps me in a continual state of inelegance.
On herself, Letter, September 1796.

I think I may boast myself to be, with all possible vanity, the most unlearned and uninformed female who ever dared to be an authoress.
On herself, Letter to the Rev. James Clarke, 1815.

The little bit (two inches wide) of Ivory on which I work with so fine a Brush, as produces little effect after much labour.
On herself, describing her own work, Letter to Edward Austen, 1816.

What became of that Jane Austen (if she ever existed) who set out bravely to correct conventional notions of the desirable and virtuous? From being their critic (if she ever was) she became their slave. That is another way of saying that her judgement and her moral sense were corrupted. Mansfield Park is the witness of that corruption.
Kingsley Amis, What Became of Jane Austen?

Beside her Joyce seems innocent as grass.
It makes me most uncomfortable to see
An English spinster of the middle class
Describe the amorous effects of 'brass',
Reveal so frankly and with such sobriety
The economic basis of society.
W. H. Auden, Letter to Lord Byron, part 1.

She supported, during two months, all the varying pain, irksomeness, and tedium, attendant on decaying nature, with more than resignation, with a truly elastic cheerfulness. She retained her faculties, her memory, her fancy, her temper, and her affections, warm, clear, and unimpaired, to the last

. . . She wrote whilst she could hold a pen, and with a pencil when a pen was become too laborious. The day preceding her death she composed some stanzas replete with fancy and vigour. Her last voluntary speech conveyed thanks to her medical attendant; and to the final question asked of her, purporting to know her wants, she replied, 'I want nothing but death.'

Henry Austen, *Biographical Notice.*

I had not seen *Pride and Prejudice* till I read that sentence of yours, and then I got the book. And what did I find? An accurate daguerreotyped portrait of a commonplace face; a carefully fenced, highly cultivated garden, with neat borders and delicate flowers; but no glance of a bright, vivid physiognomy, no open country, no fresh air, no blue hill, no bonny beck. I should hardly like to live with her ladies and gentlemen, in their elegant but confined houses.

Charlotte Brontë, Letter to G. H. Lewes, 12 January 1848.

Her business is not half so much with the human heart as with the human eyes, mouth, hands, and feet; what sees keenly, speaks aptly, moves flexibly, it suits her to study; but what throbs fast and full, though hidden, what the blood rushes through, what is the unseen seat of Life and the sentient target of death — *this* Miss Austen ignores . . . Jane Austen was a complete and most sensible lady, but a very incomplete and rather insensible (*not senseless*) woman. If this is heresy, I cannot help it.

Charlotte Brontë, Letter to W. S. Williams, 1850.

Jane Austen is slandered if she is called either a miniaturistic or a naturalistic novelist. Her books are domestic in the sense that *Oedipus Rex* is domestic. Her moral dilemmas are often drawn in precisely oedipal terms.

Brigid Brophy, *Don't Never Forget.*

Too washy; water-gruel for mind and body at the same time were too bad.

Jane Welsh Carlyle (anticipating her uncle's reply if offered a novel by Jane Austen to read), Letter to Helen Walsh, March 1843.

My uncle Southey and my father had an equally high opinion of her merits, but Mr Wordsworth used to say that though he admitted that her novels were an admirable copy of life, he could not be interested in productions of that kind; unless truth to nature were presented to him clarified, as it were, by the pervading light of imagination, it had scarce any attractions in his eyes.

Sara Coleridge, Letter to Emily Trevenen, August 1834.

I am at a loss to understand why people hold Miss Austen's novels at so high a rate, which seem to me vulgar in tone, sterile in artistic invention, imprisoned in the wretched conventions of English society, without genius, wit, or knowledge of the world. Never was life so pinched and narrow. The one problem in the mind of the writer in both the stories I have read . . . is marriageableness. All that interests in any character introduced is still this one, Has he or [she] the money to marry with, and conditions conforming? 'Tis the 'nympholepsy of a fond despair', say, rather, of an English boarding-house. Suicide is more respectable.

Ralph Waldo Emerson, *Journal,* 1861.

Scott misunderstood it when he congratulated her for painting on a square of ivory. She is a miniaturist, but never two-dimensional. All her characters are round, or capable of rotundity.

E. M. Forster, *Aspects of the Novel.*

I am amusing myself with Miss Austin's novels. She has great power and discrimination in delineating common-place people; and her writings are a capital picture of real life, with all the little wheels and machinery laid bare like a patent clock. But she explains and fills out too much. Those who have not power to fill up gaps and bridge over chasms as they read, must therefore take particular delight in such minuteness of detail.

Henry Wadsworth Longfellow, Journal, 23 May 1839.

She has given us a multitude of characters, all in a certain sense, common-place, all such as we meet every day. Yet they are all as perfectly discriminated from each other as if they were the most eccentric of human beings.

T. B. Macaulay, in *Edinburgh Review*, January 1843.

Nothing very much happens in her books, and yet, when you come to the bottom of a page, you eagerly turn it to learn what will happen next. Nothing very much does and again you eagerly turn the page. The novelist who has the power to achieve this has the most precious gift a novelist can possess.

Somerset Maugham, *Ten Novels and Their Authors.*

I have discovered that our great favourite, Miss Austen, is my countrywoman . . . with whom mamma before her marriage was acquainted. Mamma says that she was then the prettiest, silliest, most affected, husband-hunting butterfly she ever remembers.

Mary Russell Mitford, Letter to Sir William Elford, 3 April 1815.

... A friend of mine, who visits her now, says that she has stiffened into the most perpendicular, taciturn piece of single-blessedness that ever existed, and that, till *Pride and Prejudice* showed what a precious gem was hidden in that unbending case, she was no more regarded in society than a poker or fire-screen ... She is still a poker, but a poker of whom everybody is afraid.

    Mary Russell Mitford, *Life of Mary Russell Mitford*.

I have been reading *Emma*. Everything Miss Austen writes is clever, but I desiderate something. There is a want of *body* to the story. The action is frittered away in over-little things ... Miss Austen has no romance — none at all. What vile creatures her parsons are!

    John Henry Newman, Letter to Mrs John Mozley, 10 January 1837.

Read again, and for the third time at least, Miss Austen's very finely written novel of *Pride and Prejudice*. ... The Big Bow-wow strain I can do myself like any now going; but the exquisite touch, which renders ordinary commonplace things and characters interesting, from the truth of the description and the sentiment, is denied to me.

    Sir Walter Scott, *Journal*, 14 March 1826.

I have finished the novel called *Pride and Prejudice*, which I think a very superior work. It depends not on any of the common resources of novel-writers, no drownings, no conflagrations, nor runaway horses, nor lap-dogs and parrots, nor chambermaids and milliners, nor rencontres and disguises. I really think it is the *most probable* I have ever read. It is not a crying book, but the interest is very strong.

    Charlotte Smith, Letter to her Mother, 1 May 1813.

When I take up one of Jane Austen's books ... I feel like a barkeeper entering the kingdom of heaven. I know what his sensation would be and his private comments. He would not find the place to his taste, and he would probably say so.

    Mark Twain, in Q. D. Leavis, *Fiction & the Reading Public*.

See also William Dean Howells, Henry James, Rudyard Kipling, Thomas Rowlandson, Virginia Woolf

AUSTIN, ALFRED

1835—1913 Poet Laureate

Mr Alfred Austin has a clearly-defined talent, the limits of which are by this time generally recognized.

    Anon., in *Daily Telegraph*, 22 May 1908.

Mr Austin is neither an Olympian nor a Titan, and all the puffing in Paternoster Row cannot set him on Parnassus.

    Oscar Wilde, in *Pall Mall Gazette*, 1887.

AUSTIN, JAMES LANGASHAW

1911—60 Philosopher

You are like a greyhound who doesn't want to run himself, and bites the other greyhounds, so they cannot run either.

    A. J. Ayer, in Sir Isaiah Berlin, 'Austin and the Early Beginnings of Oxford Philosophy', in Berlin *et al.*, *Essays on J. L. Austin*.

He wanted us to think of philosophy as more like a science than an art, as a matter of finding things out and getting things settled, not of creating a certain individual effect. And certainly not as one of the *performing* arts; once, when I saw him in the audience of a very distinguished philosophical performer, he found the spectacle so manifestly intolerable to him that he had to go away — and was not himself play-acting in doing so. He could not bear histrionics.

    G. J. Warnock, 'Saturday Mornings', in *ibid*.

B

BABBAGE, CHARLES

1792—1871 Mathematician

He once tried to investigate statistically the credibility of the biblical miracles. In the course of his analysis he made the assumption that the chance of a man rising from the dead is 1 in 10^{12}
  B. V. Bowden, *Faster than Thought.*

Shortly before his death he told a friend that he could not remember a single completely happy day in his life: 'He spoke as if he hated mankind in general, Englishmen in particular, and the English Government and Organ Grinders most of all'.
  Ibid.

I remember a funny dinner at my brother's, where, amongst a few others, were Babbage and Lyell, both of whom liked to talk. Carlyle, however, silenced every one by haranguing during the whole dinner on the advantages of silence. After dinner, Babbage, in his grimmest manner, thanked Carlyle for his very interesting lecture on silence.
  Charles Darwin, *Autobiography.*

I knew Mr. Babbage, and am quite sure that he was not the man to say anything on the topic of calculating machines which he could not justify.
  T. H. Huxley, in L. Huxley, *Life and Letters of Thomas Henry Huxley.*

BACKUS, ISAAC

1724—1806 Clergyman

Greater men than he expressed the theological, the political, the Enlightenment views of the latter part of the eighteenth century. . . . But few men expressed so well in thought and action that vigorous, fervent, conscientious, experimental pietism which constituted the fundamental spirit of the new nation and which made its experiment in freedom unique.
  William G. McLoughlin, *Isaac Backus and the American Pietistic Tradition.*

BACON, FRANCIS, VISCOUNT ST ALBANS

1561—1626 Philosopher, Statesman

Lastly, I confess that I have as vast contemplative ends, as I have moderate civil ends: for I have taken all knowledge to be my province; . . .
  On himself, Letter to Lord Burghley, 1591.

It is my act, my hand, my heart: I beseech your lordships to be merciful to a broken reed.
  On himself, identifying his confession at his Trial, 1621.

He had a delicate, lively, hazel Eie; Dr. Harvey tolde me it was like the Eie of a viper.
  John Aubrey, *Brief Lives.*

I remember Sir John Danvers told me, that his Lordship much delighted in his curious pretty garden at Chelsey, and as he was walking there one time he fell downe in a dead-sowne. My Lady Denvers rubbed his face, temples, etc., and gave him cordiall water, as soon as he came to himselfe, sayde he, *Madam, I am no good footman.*
  Ibid.

Mr. Hobbs told me that the cause of his Lordship's death was trying an experiment; viz. as he was taking the aire in a Coach with Dr. Witherborne . . . towards High-gate, snow lay on the ground, and it came into my Lord's thoughts, why flesh might not be preserved in snow, as in Salt. They were resolved they would try the Experiment presently. They alighted out of the Coach and went into a poore woman's house at the bottom of Highgate hill, and bought a Hen, and made the woman exenterate it, and then stuffed the body with Snow, and my Lord did help to doe it himselfe. The Snow so chilled him that he immediately fell so extremely ill, that he could not returne to his Lodging . . . but went to the Earle of Arundel's house at High-gate, where they putt him in a good bed warmed with a Panne, but it was a damp bed that had not been layn-in in about a yeare before, which gave him such a colde that in 2 or 3 days as I remember Mr. Hobbes told me, he dyed of Suffocation.
  Ibid.

When their lordships asked Bacon
How many bribes he had taken

He had at least the grace
To get very red in the face.
    Edmund Clerihew Bentley, *Baseless Biography*.

In Bacon see the culminating prime
Of British intellect and British crime.
He died, and Nature, settling his affairs,
Parted his powers among us, his heirs:
To each a pinch of common-sense for seed,
And, to develop it, a pinch of greed.
Each frugal heir, to make the gift suffice,
Buries the talent to manure the vice.
    Ambrose Bierce, 'Sir Francis Bacon', in
    Lantern, 1874.

An Atheist pretending to talk against Atheism!
    William Blake, *Annotations to Bacon*.

It is evident that he was a sincere if unenthusiastic
Christian of that sensible school which regards the
Church of England as a branch of the Civil Service,
and the Archbishop of Canterbury as the British
Minister for Divine Affairs.
    C. D. Broad, *Ethics and the History of
    Philosophy*.

There is a skeleton in the cupboard of Inductive
Logic, which Bacon never suspected and Hume first
exposed to view. . . . May we venture to hope that
when Bacon's next centenary is celebrated the great
work which he set going will be completed; and that
Inductive Reasoning, which has long been the glory
of Science, will have ceased to be the scandal of
Philosophy?
    Ibid.

Lord Bacon could as easily have created the planets
as he could have written *Hamlet*.
    Thomas Carlyle, in A. K. Adams, *The Home
    Book of Humorous Quotations*.

Bacon, like Moses, led us forth at last;
    The barren Wilderness he past,
    Did on the very Border stand
    Of the blest promis'd Land,
And from the mountan's Top of his Exalted Wit
    Saw it himself, and shew'd us it.
    Abraham Cowley, *To the Royal Society*.

The word *wisdom* characterises him more than any
other. It was not that he did so much himself to
advance the knowledge of man or nature, as that he
saw what others had done to advance it, and what
was still wanting to its full accomplishment . . . He
was master of the comparative anatomy of the mind
of man, of the balance of power among the different
faculties.
    William Hazlitt, *Lectures on the Age of Elizabeth:
    Character of Lord Bacon's Works*.

His strength was in reflection, not in production: he
was the surveyor, not the builder of science.
    Ibid.

It is not easy to make room for him and his reputation together. This great and celebrated man in
some of his works recommends it to pour a bottle
of claret into the ground of a morning, and to stand
over it inhaling the perfumes. So he sometimes
enriched the dry and barren soil of speculation with
the fine aromatic spirit of his genius.
    William Hazlitt, Footnote to 'On Persons one
    Would Wish to have Seen', in *New Monthly
    Magazine*, January 1826.

He not only made a scientific philosophy out of the
practice of artisans: he also secularized their age-old
chiliastic dreams, and suggested the possibility of
getting back behind the Fall on earth before the
millennium. This made possible new attitudes
towards history — progress without chiliasm, change
without apocalypse, reformation without tarrying
for the Second Coming.
    Christopher Hill, *Intellectual Origins of the
    English Revolution*.

In his adversity I ever prayed, that God would give
him strength; for greatness he could not want.
    Ben Jonson, *Timber, or Discoveries*.

Some people think that physics was invented by Sir
Francis Bacon, who was hit by an apple when he
was sitting under a tree one day writing Shakespeare.
    Eric Larrabee, *Humor from Harper's*.

His faults were — we write it with pain — coldness
of heart, and meanness of spirit. He seems to have
been incapable of feeling strong affection, of facing
great dangers, of making great sacrifices. His desires
were set on things below, titles, patronage, the
mace, the seals, the coronet, large houses, fair
gardens, rich manors, many services of plate, gay
hangings, curious cabinets, had as great attraction
for him as for any of the courtiers who dropped on
their knees in the dirt when Elizabeth went by, and
then hastened home to write to the King of Scots
that her Grace seemed to be breaking fast.
    T. B. Macaulay, *Essays*: 'Lord Bacon'.

The difference between the soaring angel and the
creeping snake was but a type of the difference
between Bacon the philosopher and Bacon the
Attorney-General, Bacon seeking for truth, and
Bacon seeking for the Seals.
    Ibid.

In Plato's opinion man was made for philosophy; in
Bacon's opinion philosophy was made for man.
    Ibid.

Lo! Rome herself, proud mistress now no more
Of arts, but thund'ring against heathen lore;
Her grey-hair's Synods damning books unread,
And Bacon trembling for his brazen head.
Alexander Pope, *The Dunciad*, book 3.

If Parts allure thee, think how Bacon shin'd,
The wisest, brightest, meanest of mankind.
Alexander Pope, *Essay on Man*, epistle 4.

We ought, he says, to be neither like spiders, which
spin things out of their own insides, nor like ants,
which merely collect, but like bees, which both
collect and arrange. This is somewhat unfair to the
ants, but it illustrates Bacon's meaning.
Bertrand Russell, *History of Western Philosophy*.

Lord Bacon was a poet. His language has a sweet
and majestic rhythm, which satisfies the sense, no
less than the almost superhuman wisdom of his
philosophy satisfies the intellect; it is a strain which
distends, and then bursts the circumference of the
reader's mind, and pours itself forth together with it
into the universal element with which it has
perpetual sympathy.
Percy Bysshe Shelley, *A Defence of Poetry*.

Francis Bacon has been described more than once
with the crude vigour of antithesis; but in truth
such methods are singularly inappropriate to his
most unusual case. It was not by the juxtaposition
of a few opposites, but by the infiltration of a
multitude of highly varied elements, that his mental
composition was made up. He was not striped
frieze; he was shot silk.
Lytton Strachey, *Elizabeth and Essex*.

The great Secretary of Nature and all learning, Sir
Francis Bacon.
Izaak Walton, *Life of Herbert*.

. . . . It was a misfortune to the world, that my Lord
Bacon was not skilled in Mathematicks, which made
him jealous of their Assistance in naturall Enquiries;
when the operations of nature shall be followed to
their Staticall (and Mechanicall) causes, the use of
Induction will cease, and Sylogisme succeed in the
place of it, in the interim we are to desire that men
have patience not to lay aside Induction before they
have reason.
Seth Ward, *Vindiciae Academiarum*.

Bacon's task, it may be said, was to prove that natural
science was Promethean and not Mephisthophelean.
Basil Willey, *The Seventeenth Century
Background*.

Sir Francis Bacon, in Parliament, after a very fair
speech made, said: I should willingly assent to your
former speech, if we were not come hither rather
for physic, than music.
Sir Henry Wotton, *Table Talk*.

The splendid fault of Lord Bacon . . . is being too
beautiful and too entertaining, in points that require
reasoning alone.
Edward Young, in Joseph Spence, *Anecdotes*.

See also Roger Bacon, Samuel Taylor Coleridge,
James I, Samuel Johnson, George Washington

BACON, ROGER

1214?—94 Scientist

He speculated on lenses which would focus the sun
and so burn up enemies at long range, 'for the
perfect experimenter could destroy any hostile
force by this combustion', and he foresaw that
'machines for navigating rivers' were 'possible without rowers.' 'Likewise,' he wrote, 'cars may be made
so that without a draft animal they may be moved
with inestimable impetus. . . . And flying machines
are possible so that a man may sit in the middle
turning some device by which artificial wings may
beat the air in the manner of a flying bird.'
John Bowle, *England, A Portrait.*

The neglect of observation and experiment, the
abuse of syllogistic reasoning, the blind deference
to authority in science and philosophy as well as in
religion — on all these points Roger Bacon, writing
in the thirteenth century, is as vigorous a censor of
the ordinary, scholastic methods as Francis Bacon
in the seventeenth, even though he sometimes
illustrates the very defects which he condemns.
H. Rashdall, *The Universities of Europe in the
Middle Ages*.

BADEN-POWELL, ROBERT STEPHENSON SMYTH

1857—1941 Soldier, Founder of the Boy Scouts and
Girl Guides

I know my weak points and am only thankful that I
have managed to get along in spite of them! I think
that's the policy for this world: Be glad of what you
have got, and not miserable about what you would
like to have had, and not over-anxious about what
the future will bring.
On himself, Letter to Mrs Juliette Low, 4 July
1911.

Man, matron, maiden
Please call it Baden.
Further for Powell,
Rhyme it with Noel.
    On himself, in William Hillcourt, *Baden-Powell: the two lives of a hero.*

Chief Scout of the World.
    Title awarded by the boy scouts assembled at the first Boy Scout International Jamboree, 7 August 1920.

Few pioneers live long enough to see
    what they have done;
Most men are glad if they can leave
    the world a single son;
Did ever man, before he died, see
    such a dream come true?
Did any leave so many living
    monuments as you?
    A. P. Herbert, *To B-P, 12 January 1941.*

BAGEHOT, WALTER

1826–77 Economist, Journalist

He had a very fine skin, very white near where the hair started, and a high colour ... Such a colour is associated with soft winds and a moist air, cider-growing orchards, and very green, wet grass. His eyelids were thin, and of singularly delicate texture, and the white of his eyeballs was a blue white. He would pace a room when talking, and, as the ideas framed themselves in words, he would throw his head back as some animals do when sniffing the air.
    Mrs Russell Barrington, *Life of Bagehot.*

More than any of his contemporaries he excelled in the art of informal criticism — of what it would be tempting to call talkative criticism, if that didn't suggest the maundering velvet-jacketed causerie of a later date. His occasional excursions into the uplands of literary theory, such as his well-known tripartite division of poetry into the Pure, the Ornate, the Grotesque, are the least rewarding part of his work. Luckily they *are* only occasional. For the rest, he generalizes cheerfully but undogmatically: he is a master of the disposable aphorism, the working classification which he knows when to jettison.
    John Gross, *The Rise and Fall of the Man of Letters.*

Walter Bagehot defies classification. He was not a literary critic in the academic sense of the term, nor a political economist, nor an historian. He was all of these and none of them. He was in fact an amateur of genius with that breadth of mind and wide range of interests which to us looking back seems one of the most valuable and agreeable characteristics of the Victorian age.
    Norman St John-Stevas, Introduction to Bagehot's *Works.*

BAILLIE, JOANNA

1762–1851 Dramatist, Poet

She is a little, quiet, feminine woman, who you would think might shrink from grappling with the horrors of a tragedy, and whom it would be possible to mistake for the maiden sister of the curate, bent only on her homely duties. Notwithstanding this simplicity, however, there was a deeply seated earnestness about her, that bespoke the good faith and honesty of the higher impulses within.
    James Fenimore Cooper, *England with Sketches of Life in the Metropolis.*

Both Joanna and her sister have most agreeable and new conversation, not old, trumpery literature over again and reviews, but new circumstances worth telling, apropos to every subject that is touched upon; frank observations on character, without either ill nature, or the fear of committing themselves; no blue-stocking tittle-tattle, or habits of worshiping or being worshiped.
    Maria Edgeworth, *Life and Letters of Maria Edgeworth.*

North: James, who is the best female poet of the age?
Shepherd: Female what?
Tickler: Poet.
Shepherd: Mrs John Biley. In her *Plays on the Passions* she has a' the vigor o' a man, and a' the delicacy o' a woman. And Oh, Sire, but her Lyrics are gems, and she wears them gracefully, like diamond drops danglin' frae the ears o' Melpomene. The very worst play she ever wrote is better than the best o' any ither body's that hasna kickt the bucket.
    J. Wilson, *Noctes Ambrosianae.*

If I had to present any one to a foreigner as model of an English Gentlewoman, it would be Joanna Baillie.
    William Wordsworth, in Henry Crabb Robinson, *Reminiscences and Correspondence.*

BAILY, FRANCIS

1774–1844 Astronomer

To term Mr. Baily a man of brilliant genius or great

invention, would in effect be doing him wrong. His talents *were* great, but rather solid and sober than brilliant, and such as seized their subject rather with a tenacious grasp than with a sudden pounce. His mind, though, perhaps, not excursive, was yet always in progress, and by industry, activity, and using to advantage every ray of light as it broke upon his path, he often accomplished what is denied to the desultory efforts of more imaginative men. Whatever he knew he knew thoroughly, and enlarged his frontier by continually stepping across the boundary and making good a new and well-marked line between the cultivation within and the wilderness without.

> Sir J. F. W. Herschel, in *Monthly Notices of the Royal Astronomical Society*, November 1844

BALDWIN, STANLEY, EARL OF BEWDLEY

1867—1947 Prime Minister

I speak not as the man in the street even, but as a man in a field-path, a much simpler person steeped in tradition and impervious to new ideas.

> On himself, speaking during his first ministry, in *Dictionary of National Biography*.

He is the grandson of a blacksmith. . . . It is an instinct of the blood to protect the offspring of our kind. Baldwin talks a lot about pigs, but he really means pig-iron.

> Lord Beaverbrook, Letter to Lord Melchett, 11 November 1930.

He is an incorruptible Walpole.

> Lord Beaverbrook, Letter to [? S. Samuel], 2 November 1935.

The Flying Scotsman is no less splendid a sight when it travels north to Edinburgh than when it travels south to London. Mr Baldwin denouncing sanctions was as dignified as Mr Baldwin imposing them. At times it seemed that there were two Mr Baldwins on the stage, a prudent Mr Baldwin, who scented the danger in foolish projects, and a reckless Mr Baldwin, who plunged into them head down, eyes shut. But there was, in fact, only one Mr Baldwin, a well-meaning man of indifferent judgement, who, whether he did right or wrong, was always sustained by a belief that he was acting for the best.

> Lord Beaverbrook, in *Daily Express*, 29 May 1937.

It is medicine man talk. It lifts the discussion on to so abstract a plane that minds of the hearers are relieved of the effort of considering the details of the immediate problems. It imposes no intellectual strain because thought drifts into thought, assembling and dissolving like clouds in the upper air, having no connection with earthly obstacles. It flatters, because it appears to offer intimate companionship with a rare and noble spirit. It pleases the unsceptical, because it blurs the outline of unpleasant fact in a maze of meaningless generalities. Over and over again I have been amazed by the ease with which even Labour members are deceived by this nonsense. Murmurs of admiration break out as this second-rate orator trails his tawdry wisps of mist over the parliamentary scene.

> Aneurin Bevan, in *Tribune*, 1937.

I see no point in swapping donkeys when crossing a stream.

> Lord Birkenhead, comment to F. W. Hirst on a pre-election proposal to replace Baldwin.

I think Baldwin has gone mad. He simply takes one jump in the dark; looks round; and then takes another.

> Lord Birkenhead, Letter to Austen Chamberlain, August 1923.

. . . Not dead. But the candle in that great turnip has gone out.

> Winston Churchill, on Baldwin's retirement, in Harold Nicolson, Diary, 17 August 1950.

Not even a public figure.

> Lord Curzon, in Harold Nicolson, *Curzon*.

Had he been a greater man, either he would have been all right, or so unpopular that he could have been soon defeated; had he been completely incompetent, he could never have kept his high position; it was that fatal touch of talent . . . and England and the Empire and the world are suffering now in consequence.

> J. L. Garvin, in Henry Channon, Diary, 24 March 1942.

His fame endures; we shall not forget
The name of Baldwin until we're out of debt.

> Kensal Green (Colin Hurry), *Premature Epitaphs*.

The conspirators got, instead of him [Lord Curzon] Stanley Baldwin, the Prime Minister they preferred. And that might have been possible to bear, had it not been for the fact that the people — who had played no part in this squalid comedy — got Stanley Baldwin too.

> Leonard Mosley, *The Glorious Fault*.

See also John Locke

BALFE, MICHAEL WILLIAM

1808—70 Composer

... when the day's allowance of stiff 'collar work' was accomplished, which was always by an early hour in the day, he delighted to be the gentleman at large, scouting with the frankest contempt the puppyism of appearing overdone with work — a hollow-cheeked devotee at the inexorable shrine of Art. Equally did he avoid the contrary affectation of treating production as the result of a divine afflatus — a gift of the gods costing nothing but the trouble of transcribing the heavenly inspiration.
> Charles Lamb Kenney, *A Memoir of Michael William Balfe.*

Macfarren, Glover, Wallace — Balfe's countrymen whom the critics loved to pit against him and endow with heaven knows what depths of science to his confusion — passed over the arena like fugitive shadows to return to their profound abysms of fugue and counterpoint, leaving their shallow-brained compeer sole, substantial flesh-and-blood occupant of the point of sight.
> *Ibid.*

BALFOUR, ARTHUR JAMES, EARL

1848—1930 Prime Minister

You put a pistol to my head — yes.
> On himself, remark on Lloyd George's offer of the foreign secretaryship, December 1916.

The difference between Joe [Chamberlain] and me is the difference between youth and age: I am age.
> On himself, in Denis Judd, *Balfour and the British Empire.*

We are none of us infallible — not even the youngest of us.
> Dr W. H. Thompson, Master of Trinity, in G. W. E. Russell, *Collections and Recollections.*

See also Nancy Astor

BANCROFT, GEORGE

1800—91 Historian, Diplomat

He crystallized all the hero worship of the old Fourth-of-July school into a large work written in a style acceptable to the time.
> John Spencer Bassett, *The Middle Group of American Historians.*

Still, one wonders a little why a Harvard man with sufficient independence to become a Jacksonian democrat, should not have realized that a 'style' suitable for telling the story of the Trojan War or the Fall of Lucifer is not the best for relating the history of the United States.
> Carl Becker, in Harvey Wish, *The American Historian.*

... a tough Yankee man, of many worthy qualities more tough than musical. ...
> Thomas Carlyle, in Richard Hofstadter, *The Progressive Historians.*

He needs a great deal of cutting and pruning, but we think him an infant Hercules.
> Ralph Waldo Emerson, in Michael Kraus, 'George Bancroft' in *New England Quarterly,* December 1934.

Bancroft has simply taken phrases and sentences here and there from a long document and re-arranged, combined, and in some cases, actually paraphrased them in his own way. Logically and rhetorically, the work is his own. Like Thucydides he composed speeches for his heroes, but unlike the Greek historian he did not have the privilege of participating in the events described.
> Thomas Wentworth Higginson, in Harvey Wish, *The American Historian.*

The secret of Bancroft's success is that by aid of a vigorous imagination and a crisp, nervous style, he has been enabled, by a few sudden strokes, to reveal startling and brilliant pictures, over which the dust had collected and hardened, as it seemed, forever. It is a work rather of genius than of laborious detail.
> John Lothrop Motley, in *ibid.*

BANCROFT, RICHARD

1544—1610 Archbishop of Canterbury

... Dr. Bancroft, that metropolitan who understood the church excellently, and had almost rescued it out of the hands of the Calvinian party, and very much subdued the unruly spirit of the non-conformists, by and after the conference at Hampton-court; countenanced men of the greatest parts in learning, and disposed the clergy to a more solid course of study, than they had been accustomed to; and, if he had lived, would quickly have extinguished all that fire in England which had been kindled at Geneva. ...
> Edward Hyde, Earl of Clarendon, *History of the Rebellion.*

BANKHEAD, TALLULAH BROCKMAN

1903—68 Actress

I'm as pure as driven slush.
> On herself, in *Observer*, 24 February 1957.

A day away from Tallulah Bankhead is like a month in the country.
> Anon., in *Show Business Illustrated*, 17 October 1961.

Watching Tallulah Bankhead on the stage is like watching somebody skating over very thin ice — and the English want to be there when she falls through.
> Mrs Patrick Campbell, in Gavin Lambert, *On Cukor*.

Dorothy Parker gave a party one night at the Algonquin, and guest Tallulah Bankhead, slightly inebriated, carried on in a wild indecorous manner. After Miss Bankhead had been escorted out, Mrs Parker called in from an adjoining room, 'Has Whistler's Mother left yet?'
The next day at lunch Tallulah took out a pocket mirror, examined herself painfully, and said, with a glance at Mrs Parker, 'The less I behave like Whistler's Mother the night before, the more I look like her the morning after.'
> Robert E. Drennan, *Wit's End*.

Tallulah was crowding seventeen when she arrived from Alabama, stage-struck, sultry-voiced, and brimming with a roseleaf beauty which she determinedly hid under the then-fashionable mask of white powder, blue eye-shadow, and beef-coloured lipstick. She fondly believed that this made her look like Ethel Barrymore, who was her idol.
> Margaret Case Harriman, *The Vicious Circle*.

And of the many 'images' which have since fascinated the public, Tallulah's was archetypally modern. She informed people, through her own projectile, that she was an open, wayward, free, cosmopolitan, liberated, sensuous human being. In thus systematically invading her own privacy, she was the first of the modern personalities.
> Lee Israel, *Miss Tallulah Bankhead*.

BANKS, SIR JOSEPH

1743—1820 President of the Royal Society

Sir Joseph was so exceedingly shy that we made no sort of acquaintance at all. If instead of going round the world he had only fallen from the moon, he could not appear less versed in the usual modes of a tea-drinking party. But what, you will say, has a tea-drinking party to do with a botanist, a man of science, a president of the Royal Society?
> Fanny Burney, Diary, March 1788.

The Great Southern Caterpillar transformed into a Bath Butterfly — This insect first crawled into notice from among the weeds and mud of the Southern Seas and being afterwards placed in a warm situation by the Royal Society was changed by the heat of the sun into its present form. It is noticed and valued solely on account of the powerful red which encircles its body and the shining spot on its breast, a distinction which never fails to render caterpillars valuable.
> James Gillray, in H. C. Cameron, *Sir Joseph Banks*.

I passed 3 days at Stamford Rivers last week. There was nobody there but Lord Chas. Somerset. He told a good story. Sir Joseph Bankes was desirous of being civil to a painter who had executed some work for him, and invited him to his house in the country. He excused himself because he had a naval gentleman with him. Sir J. begged he would bring his Friend with him, who was the captain of an Irish Merchantman employed on the Eastern Coast, but whom Sir J. imagined to be a Captain in the navy. He received them very politely and asked the Irishman 'where he had principally served?' — 'In the East, Sir Joseph.' — 'In the East, then doubtless, sir, you must have seen a variety of very curious objects. Pray Sir allow me to ask you if you ever happened to see a black Cockatoo?' — 'A Black Cockatoo, no, Sir Joseph, I never happened to see a Black Cockatoo, but I'll tell you what Sir Joseph I have very frequently seen a black c——— or two'.
> Charles Greville, Diary, 30 July 1820.

Sir Joseph Banks himself was necessarily a very conspicuous personage in these parties at his house. Seated and wheeled about in his armchair — his limbs helplessly knotted with gouty tumours — speaking no other language than English — and carrying his scientific knowledge little beyond the domain of Natural History, he nevertheless looked the governing power of the Royal Society, and was such in reality.
> Sir Henry Holland, *Recollections of Past Life*.

He was not himself a genius who, by his discoveries, astonished and enlightened mankind, but he was one who in his early youth, without a guide, discovered the path that led to Science, and from that moment never deviated from it till the end of his life.
> Sir Everard Home, in the Hunterian Oration for 1822.

To give a breakfast in Soho,
Sir Joseph's very bitterest foe
   Must certainly allow him peerless merit;
Where, on a wagtail and tomtit,
He shines, and sometimes on a nit,
   Displaying powers few Gentlemen inherit.

I grant he is no intellectual lion
Subduing everything he darts his eye on;
   Rather, I ween, an intellectual flea,
Hopping on Science's broad, bony back
Poking its pert proboscis of attack,
   Drawing a drop of blood, and fancying it a sea!
   Peter Pindar (John Wolcot), *On A Report in the Newspapers that Sir Joseph Banks was made A Privy Counsellor.*

Lord, that's Sir Joseph Banks! — how grand his look!
Who sail'd all round the world with Captain Cook.
   Peter Pindar, *Peter's Prophecy.*

      Lord Paramount of Moth Debate . . .
Ibid.

Butler, the author of *Hudibras,* might as well be employed to describe a solemn funeral, in which there was nothing ridiculous. This, however, is better than his going to draw naked savages, and be scalped, with that wild man Banks, who is poaching in every ocean for the fry of little islands that escaped the drag-net of Spain.
   Horace Walpole, Letter to Sir Horace Mann, 20 September 1772.

BANNISTER, JOHN ('JACK')

1760—1836 Comedian

The most mortifying infirmity in human nature, to feel in ourselves, or to contemplate in another, is, perhaps, cowardice. To see a coward *done to the life* upon a stage, would produce anything but mirth. Yet we most of us remember Jack Bannister's cowards. Could anything be more agreeable, more pleasant? We loved the rogues. How was this effected but by the exquisite art of the actor in a perpetual subinsinuation to us, the spectators, even in the extremity of the shaking fit, that he was not half such a coward as we took him for? We saw all the common symptoms of the malady upon him; the quivering lip, the cowering knees, the teeth chattering; and could have sworn 'that man was frightened.' But we forgot all the while — or kept it almost a secret to ourselves — that he never once lost his self-possession; that he let out by a thousand droll looks and gestures — meant *at* us, and not at all supposed to be visible to his fellows in the scene, that his confidence in his own resources had never once deserted him. Was this a genuine picture of a coward? or not rather a likeness which the clever artist contrived to palm upon us instead of an original; while we secretly connived at the delusion for the purpose of greater pleasure, than a more genuine counterfeiting of the imbecility, helplessness, and utter self-desertion, which we knew to be concomitants of cowardice in real life, could have given us.
   Charles Lamb, 'Stage Illusion', *London Magazine,* August 1825.

BARA, THEDA

1890—1955 Actress

Theda Bara was another dream-world figure. Surrounded by potted palms, silken hangings and blackamoors and other dust collectors, Miss Bara was Pestilence herself, her monumental wickedness would not have been tolerated by Caligula in his beatnik depths for one moment. She was divinely, hysterically, insanely malevolent. The public fell at Miss Bara's feet. She climbed from option to option while thousands cheered.
   Bette Davis, *The Lonely Life.*

In the minds of millions she became the 'fascinating and the unfathomable whose passion is touched with death.' Her staring, sensual face, with exotic heavy-lidded eyes, was photographed with skull and a crossbones and was described as 'the wickedest face in the world, dark, brooding, beautiful and heartless.' Theda Bara was indeed set up as the embodiment of evil. She brought to the screen a voluptuousness and sophistication not there before. . . . She . . . frankly admits her desire for and her right to love and luxury.
   Lewis Jacobs, *The Rise of the American Film.*

By 1920 Bara's screen career was at an end. Her contribution to the art of the film was negligible, but her contribution to the making of the sex symbol — a major figure in screen history — was considerable. Bara laid most of the ground rules. She was the first popular star whose primary attraction was her sexuality. She proved conclusively that audiences paid vast sums of money to see women projecting a highly sexual image. She showed the industry that a star can be built from the publicity man's head and through the media. She showed that *true* sex symbols have a bisexual appeal in that they attract equally the fantasies of the opposite sex and the vanity of their own. Men adored, women emulated.
   Clyde Jeavons and Jeremy Pascall, *A Pictorial History of Sex in the Movies.*

Miss Bara was a more memorable creation than any of the sermons she illustrated. She was, so to speak, an industrial product, as artfully designed to whet the popular appetite as any automobile. A brilliant staff of experts gave her a personality, equipped her with a legend, and made the nation aware of her with so stupefying a campaign of publicity that it might appropriately have been described as a barrage.

Lloyd Morris, *Not So Long Ago*.

Miss Bara made voluptuousness a common American commodity, as accessible as chewing gum.

Ibid.

White-faced, with brooding, heavy-lidded eyes, and a dark cloud of hair, her columbrine body sheathed in low-cut gowns of glistening satin, Miss Bara was exotic, voluptuous and ... irresistibly though fatally alluring. She typified the power that can be exercised by a woman adept in sensuality, coldly selfish, bent upon luxury and the satisfaction of her physical passions. She opened fresh vistas to decorous American matrons, and introduced some disturbing notions into the domestic attitudes of the American male. . . .

Ibid.

. . . a pyrogenic half pint . . . who immortalized the vamp just as Little Egypt, at the World's Fair of 1893, had the hoochie-coochie.

S. J. Perelman, 'Cloudland Revisited: The Wickedest Woman in Larchmont', in *The Most of S. J. Perelman*.

This deadly Arab girl was a crystal-gazing seeress of profoundly occult powers, wicked as fresh red paint and poisonous as dried spiders. The stronger the copy grew, the more it was printed. Little girls read it and swallowed their gum with excitement.

Terry Ramsaye, *A Million and One Nights*.

Theda Bara vamped at a rate that makes the mind boggle. She made dotty pictures in which she seduced unwitting men, her ample bosom heaving, her curvaceous figure draped with semi-transparent silks, her undulating walk an invitation to unbridled passion. Once the men were won away from wives or lovers and completely under Theda's spell, she began to reverse her course, scorning the advances of her conquests, driving them mad with frustration. Daggers, poison, fire and flame — by one device or another their lives came to an end. As one observer put it, an enterprising undertaker could have made a fortune simply by camping on her trail.

Norman Zierold, *The Moguls*.

See also Marilyn Monroe

BARBER, MARY

1690—1757 Poet

I have read most of her poems; and believe your Lordship will observe, that they generally contain something new and useful, tending to the Reproof of some Vice or Folly, and recommending some Virtue. ... In short, she seemeth to have a true poetical Genius, better cultivated than could well be expected, either from her Sex, or the Scene she hath acted in, as the Wife of a Citizen. Yet I am assured, that no Woman was ever more useful to her Husband in the Way of Business. Poetry hath only been her favourite Amusement.

Jonathan Swift, Letter to the Earl of Orrery, 20 August 1733.

BARBIROLLI, SIR JOHN

1899—1970 Conductor

If you want a cure for a cold, put on two pullovers, take up a baton, poker or pencil, tune the radio to a symphony concert, stand on a chair, and conduct like mad for an hour or so and the cold will have vanished. It never fails. You know why conductors live so long? Because we perspire so much.

On himself, in Leslie Ayre, *The Wit of Music*.

I prefer to face the wrath of the police rather than the wrath of Sir John Barbirolli.

A member of the Hallé Orchestra, to a magistrate, on being fined for parking his car outside Huddersfield Town Hall in order not to be late for rehearsal.

BARING, EVELYN, EARL OF CROMER

1841—1917 Statesman

His temperament, all in monochrome, touched in with cold blues and indecisive greys, was eminently unromantic. He had a steely colourlessness, and a steely pliability, and a steely strength. Endowed beyond most men with the capacity of foresight, he was endowed as very few men have ever been with that staying-power which makes the fruit of foresight attainable. His views were long, and his patience was even longer. He progressed imperceptibly; he constantly withdrew; the art of giving way he practised with the refinement of a virtuoso. But, though the steel recoiled and recoiled, in the end it would spring forward.

Lytton Strachey, *Eminent Victorians*.

His ambition can be stated in a single phrase; it was, to become an institution; and he achieved it.
Ibid.

BARKER, HARLEY GRANVILLE

1877—1946 Actor, Dramatist

He extended the format of the well-made drawing-room play to attack drawing-room values; he brought hard-headed political debate onto the English stage; and he championed female independence with unstrident sympathy. Combining radical ideas with a feeling of upholstered solidity, his plays are rather like time-bombs secreted on a luxury liner.
Michael Billington, in *Guardian*, 3 October 1975.

Oh G.B. you are a very clever and interesting youth of 30; but you are an atrocious manager. You don't know where to put your high light and where to put your smudge.
George Bernard Shaw, Letter to Granville Barker, 18 September 1907.

When will you understand that what has ruined you as a manager is your love for people who are 'a little weak perhaps, but just the right tone'. The right tone is never a little weak perhaps; it is always devastatingly strong. Keep your worms for your own plays; and leave me the drunken, stagey, brassbowelled barnstormers my plays are written for.
George Bernard Shaw, Letter to Granville Barker, 19 January 1908.

BARLOW, JOEL

1754—1812 Poet, Statesman

. . . a compound of Milton, Rousseau, and the Duke of Bridgewater.
Henry Adams, in J. C. Levenson, *The Mind and Art of Henry Adams*.

It is time that historians of American literature should more generally recognize Joel Barlow as something more than a writer of good doggerel and the author of a turgid epic couched in 'gaudy and inane phraseology'.
M. Ray Adams, 'Joel Barlow, Political Romanticist', in *American Literature*, May 1937.

A thoroughgoing radical in economics and politics, Barlow was no innovator in polite literature. He had

pulled himself out of many a Connecticut provincialism, but he stuck fast in the bog of provincial poetry.
Vernon Louis Parrington, *Main Currents in American Thought*, vol. 1.

No poet with so little of poetry ever received so much of glory.
Fred Lewis Pattee, *The First Century of American Literature, 1770—1870*.

BARNARD, HENRY

1811—1900 Pedagogue

It was as if he lived far above the world and could see enormous amounts of territory at a glance, and then kept coming down from his vantage point in the educational heavens to jot down what he saw.
Ralph Jenkins and Gertrude Chandler Warner, *Henry Barnard, An Introduction*.

BARNUM, PHINEAS TAYLER

1810—91 Impresario

You and I, Mr. Arnold, ought to be acquainted. You are a celebrity, I am a notoriety.
On himself, Letter to Matthew Arnold, in R. Werner, *Barnum*.

I am not in the show business alone to make money. I feel it my mission, as long as I live, to provide clean, moral, and healthful recreation for the public to which I have so long catered.
On himself, in Neil Harris, *Humbug*.

This is a trading world and men, women and children, who cannot live on gravity alone, need something to satisfy their gayer, lighter moods and hours, and he who ministers to this want is in a business established by the Author of our nature. If he worthily fulfills his mission and amuses without corrupting, he need never feel that he has lived in vain.
On himself, in Irving Wallace, *The Fabulous Showman*.

He will ultimately take his stand in the social rank . . . among the swindlers, blacklegs, pickpockets, and thimble-riggers of his day.
Anon., in *Tait's Edinburgh Magazine*, 1855.

Barnum is gone. That fine flower of Western civilization, that *arbiter elegantiarum* to Demos . . . gave, in the eyes of the seekers after amusement, a lustre to America. . . . He created the *métier* of showman on a grandiose scale, worthy to be professed by a man of genius. He early realized that essential feature of a modern democracy, its readiness to be led to what will amuse and instruct it. He knew that 'the people' means crowds, paying crowds; that crowds love the fashion and will follow it; and that the business of the great man is to make and control the fashion. To live on, by, and before the public was his ideal. For their sake and his own, he loved to bring the public to see, to applaud, and to pay. . . . His name is a proverb already, and a proverb it will continue.

Anon., Obituary in *The Times*.

Barnum was not simply the Prometheus of the Pleasure Principle, as his admirers portrayed him. Nor was he a 'damaged soul' as some of his detractors argued. He began his career, as his society began its own existence, as an act of criticism; he ended it as a yea-sayer. If the transformation was inevitable, few carried it off with so much enjoyment, or demonstrated so conclusively the involvement of the politics of entertainment with the politics of life.

Neil Harris, *Humbug*.

Of all the men whom I met in those days in the way of business, Mr. Barnum, the great American humbug, was by far the honestest and freest from guile or deceit or 'ways that were dark, or tricks that were vain.' He was very kind-hearted and benevolent and gifted with a sense of fun which was even stronger than his desire for dollars. . . . He was a genius like Rabelais, but one who employed business and humanity for material instead of literature, just as Abraham Lincoln, who was a brother of the same band, employed patriotism and politics. All three of them expressed vast problems, financial, intellectual or natural by the brief arithmetic of a joke.

Charles Godfrey Leland, in Irving Wallace, *The Fabulous Showman*.

Barnum believed that amusement and sensation were the natural prerogatives of the masses, who had little else, and that those who deprived them of pleasure were evil. As a showman, he could give New York, and then America, and finally the world, the gift of enjoyment. So, against all odds, he fought to make entertainment and amusement respectable. That he succeeded is evident with every circus, concert, legitimate play, motion picture, and television program that we, his heirs, freely and guiltlessly attend.

Ibid.

What was it, after all, that made Barnum a showman? We know, of course, what made him óne of the *greatest* showmen in history. This was talent, or a kind of genius, if you will — the gift of chromosomes or his Maker — the instinctive understanding of what startled, amazed, astonished, titillated, thrilled, the special extra sense of knowing what Everyman was curious about and finding the means by which to exploit this curiosity.

Ibid.

See also Aimee Semple McPherson, James McNeill Whistler

BARRETT, LAWRENCE

1838—91 Actor

His face with its craggy Celtic cheekbones and bulging forehead looked like a monk's, but the hunger in his unhappy eyes was not for God. Fate was unjust, for [Edwin] Booth, who had been born to fame, could have been happy if the world had never heard of him, and here was Barrett whose unique desire was to be recognized by the world as a great, a *great* actor.

Eleanor Ruggles, *Prince of Players: Edwin Booth*.

In the bosom of his home Barrett was relaxed and loving. But the fire that is never quenched burned in him still, and one afternoon as he and [Edwin] Booth sat gossiping with friends, Barrett said intensely that he would be willing to act without making any money *for fifty years* if by then he would be considered the head of his profession. Booth . . . asked 'Well, Larry, after you get this leadership, what do you think it's worth?' Barrett snapped back: 'You ought to know. You have it'. Booth shook his head. 'Leadership has its thorns'. The brooding Barrett's fingers itched to feel those thorns.

Ibid.

When the toga'd Barrett stalked into the Forum he was Cassius to the core. Cassius whether he would or no, for the same nature was in him. He too was the lean and hungry one: gloomy, combative, suspicious, intellectual, grudging in tendency, yet capable of generous deeds and with a streak of nobility.

Ibid., on Barrett in Booth's 1871 production of *Julius Caesar*.

It is a fact that great tragedians generally look as if Nature had molded them for the express purpose of playing tragedy. Of all of them, Lawrence Barrett was the most tragedian-like in appearance. He had a classic face, somewhat Milesian, and his deep-set

melancholy eyes suggested *Hamlet* about to begin a soliloquy.
  Harry B. Smith. *First Nights and First Editions.*

BARRIE, SIR JAMES MATTHEW

1860–1937 Playwright, Novelist

I am not young enough to know everything.
  On himself, in A. K. Adams, *The Home Book of Humorous Quotations.*

A little child whom the Gods have whispered to.
  Mrs Patrick Campbell, Letter to Bernard Shaw, January 1913.

The cheerful clatter of Sir James Barrie's cans as he went round with the milk of human kindness.
  Philip Guedella, *Some Critics.*

Barrie struck twelve once — with *Peter Pan* — a subtly unwholesome sweetmeat, like most of his books.
  Florence Becker Lennon, *Lewis Carroll.*

Mr Barrie is a born storyteller; and he sees no further than his stories — conceives any discrepancy between them and the world as a shortcoming on the world's part, and is only too happy to be able to re-arrange matters in a pleasanter way. The popular stage, which was a prison to Shakespeare's genius, is a playground to Mr Barrie's. At all events he does the thing as if he liked it, and does it very well. He has apparently no eye for human character; but he has a keen sense of human qualities, and he produces highly popular assortments of them. He cheerfully assumes, as the public wish him to assume, that one endearing quality implies all endearing qualities, and one repulsive quality, all repulsive qualities; the exceptions being comic characters, who are permitted to have 'weaknesses' or stern and terrible souls who are at once understood to be saving up some enormous sentimentality for the end of the last act but one.
  George Bernard Shaw, in *Saturday Review*, 13 November 1897.

I like Barrie and his work; but someday a demon in the shape of Alice will sit by the fire in hell and poke up the flames in which he is consuming.
  George Bernard Shaw, Letter to Ellen Terry, November 1905.

See also H. G. Wells

52

BARRINGTON, GEORGE

b. 1755 Pickpocket, Author

From distant climes, o'er widespread seas we come
Tho' not with much *éclat* or beat of drum;
True Patriots we, for be it understood,
We left our country for our country's good.
No private views disgraced our generous zeal,
What urged our travels was our country's weal;
And none will doubt but that our emigration
Has proved most useful to the British nation.
  On himself, writing from Australia, Prologue to *Dr Young's Revenge,* January 1796.

The ignominy of being thus mingled with felons of all descriptions, many scarce a degree above the brute creation, intoxicated with liquor, and shocking the ears of those they passed with blasphemy, oaths, and songs, the most offensive to modesty, inflicted a punishment more severe than the sentence of my country, and fully avenged that society I had so much wronged.
  On himself, *A Voyage to New South Wales.*

The coarse, incompetent, and generally cowardly highwaymen of the early part of the eighteenth century have undeservedly become the heroes of schoolboys, and the lay-figures of romance-makers. But here we have a veritable villain who disdained force, and practised to perfection urbanity and refinement; who penetrated the society of princes and peers, and was accepted as their companion and equal; who pursued theft with the same persistence and versatility as another man might pursue trade; and who never made an enemy, and never admitted defeat.
  Richard S. Lambert, *The Prince of Pickpockets.*

BARRY, ELIZABETH

1658–1713 Actress

This fine Creature was not handsome, her Mouth opening most on the Right side, which she strove to draw t'other Way, and at Times, composing her Face, as if sitting to have her Picture drawn, — Mrs *Barry* was middle-sized, and had darkish Hair, light Eyes, dark Eye-brows, and was indifferently plump: — Her Face somewhat preceded her Action, as the latter did her Words, her Face ever expressing the Passions; not like the Actresses of late Times, who are afraid of putting their Faces out of the Forms of Non-meaning, lest they should crack the Cerum, Whitewash, or other Cosmetic, trowe'd on.
  Antony Aston, *A Brief Supplement to Colley Cibber's Lives.*

This great Actress dy'd of a Fever towards the latter end of Queen *Anne*; the year I have forgot; but perhaps you will recollect it by an Expression that fell from her in blank Verse, in her last Hours, when she was delirious, *viz.*

Ha, ha! and so they make us Lords, by Dozens!
Colley Cibber, *Apology for the Life of Colley Cibber.*

BARRY, JAMES

1741—1806 Painter

Barry would not dine at the table of a private friend without leaving two shillings upon the cloth, the price, whatever the entertainment, set upon it by his own arbitrary valuation.
H. Angelo, *Reminiscences.*

Barry was another instance of those who scorn nature, and are scorned by her. He could not make a likeness of any one object in the universe: when he attempted it, he was like a drunken man on horse-back; his eye reeled, his hand refused its office, — and accordingly he set up for an example of the *great style* in art, which, like charity, covers all other defects.
William Hazlitt, in *Edinburgh Review*, August 1820.

BARRYMORE, ETHEL

1879—1959 Actress

For an actress to be a success she must have the face of Venus, the brains of Minerva, the grace of Terpsichore, the memory of Macaulay, the figure of Juno, and the hide of a rhinoceros.
On herself, in George Jean Nathan, *The Theatre in the Fifties.*

Miss Barrymore . . . did what came naturally to her; took the stage, filled it, and left the rest of us to stage rear.
Edward G. Robinson, *All My Yesterdays.*

BARRYMORE, JOHN

1882—1942 Actor

My only regret in the theatre is that I could never sit out front and watch me.
On himself, in Eddie Cantor, *The Way I See It.*

John Barrymore was Icarus who flew so close to the sun that the wax on his wings melted and he plunged back to earth — from the peak of classical acting to the banalities of show business.
Brooks Atkinson, *Broadway.*

Excepting Sothern and Marlowe, whose romantic Shakespeare had given me pleasant though vague impressions for years, Barrymore was the first actor to cut neat and deep into a somewhat sluggish consciousness. Other actors had more surface as I watched their playing from the balcony, but Barrymore cut through the darkness of the theatre like a sharp, glittering penknife.
Brooks Atkinson, in Alma Power-Waters, *John Barrymore.*

In some paradoxical fashion, the very manner in which Barrymore seemed almost to revel in his disintegration convinced people who had never seen him in *Hamlet* and *The Jest* that he must have been among the giants. For even when he showed signs of physical and spiritual collapse he did not enter into any kind of ordinary decline. Everything he did was in an epic way, and, even when he appeared to be making an embarrassing clown of himself, he did so on a grand and whole-sale scale, coming apart with boisterous gargantuan humor and a sardonic air of self-criticism.
Gene Fowler, *Good Night, Sweet Prince.*

The death of John Barrymore made us think again for a minute of F. Scott Fitzgerald. They were very different men; a lot alike. Undoubtedly they both worked hard, but there was the same sense of a difficult technique easily mastered (too easily, perhaps); there was the same legend of great physical magnetism, working incessantly for its own destruction; there was the same need for public confession, either desperate or sardonic; and there was always a good deal of time wasted, usually accompanied by the sweet smell of grapes. We have seen Scott Fitzgerald when everything he said was a childish parody of his own talent, and the last time we saw John Barrymore he was busy with a sick and humiliating parody of his. The similarity probably ends there. Up to the day he died, we believe, Fitzgerald still kept his original and eager devotion to his profession, along, we like to think, with the confidence that he might still achieve the strict perfection that was so often almost his. Barrymore, on the other hand, had given up long ago. It is absurd, of course, to say that a man was never gifted on the ground that he has lent himself to a savage burlesque of his own gifts, but it is a good deal easier to accept his death. We mourned Scott Fitzgerald with a sense of waste and loss because, in spite of everything, he must have died with some

BARRYMORE, LIONEL

hope still bright in his heart. We are going to miss John Barrymore, but it is hard to regret what surely must have remained of his career — a few more foolish jokes to be made over the radio, a few more cheap paragraphs to be written in the gossip columns, just a little while longer to pull down what was left of the hateful and magnificent past.

Wolcott Gibbs, *Season in the Sun.*

There can scarcely be an adult in North America who doesn't know Mr. Barrymore almost as intimately as the family doctor knows his oldest and most bothersome patient. The great man comes on the stage of the Belasco trailing a thousand anecdotes, familiar from Bangor to Pasadena. He is love, alcohol, beauty, and the heir of a dramatic tradition going back, it often seems, to the Old Testament. He can (and does) act in a way that appears to be a vicious parody of Mr. Walter Hampden, and the audience watches him with boundless delight. Half of this effect lies in simply being a Barrymore and therefore presumably engaged in something supernatural; the other half lies in a very carefully fostered reputation for doing the unexpected.

Wolcott Gibbs, reviewing *My Dear Children,* in *ibid.*

At all moments Barrymore was the artist. He created out of his own texture. He borrowed nothing. He copied nothing. His whole search was within himself. His wine was from his own vine. Whatever jewels adorned his final creation were brought from his own inner contact with the deep richness that is hidden in all men but found by so few. It is the finding that makes the true artist brother to all mankind. In revealing himself he reveals others to themselves.

Arthur Hopkins, in Toby Cole and Helen Krich Chinoy, *Actors on Acting.*

His rich imagination seemed to find its most arresting conjurings in ribaldry. There was constantly being unrolled before him a series of hilarious pictures, for which he knew the precise and shattering words. One realized that it was no easy task for a mind so engrossingly inhabited to avoid all pleasant wanderings and really confine itself to the painful creation of an entirely new picture, the picture of a proud, human soul in turmoil and death. . . . Rehearsals for him were a ceaseless quest. This was not externalized by a conscious seeking for the impressive pose or the embroidered reading. He weaved himself into the complete texture, leaving no bright threads lying to emphasize his presence. He was the director's dream, an actor who asked no special emphasis.

Ibid.

Here is a great actor who did not want to act, but to paint pictures, an idol of the people who on that very account hates flattery; an artist who appraises his own merits as nil.

Alma Power-Waters, *John Barrymore.*

See also Lionel Barrymore, Errol Flynn, Edward G. Robinson

BARRYMORE, LIONEL
1878—1954 Actor

Neither Jack nor myself . . . preferred the stage. . . . Yet it seemed that we had to be actors. It was as if our father had been a street cleaner, and had dropped dead near a fire hydrant, and we went out to pick up the shovel and broom and continue his work.

On himself, in Toby Cole and Helen Krich Chinoy, *Actors on Acting.*

Of the three Barrymores, Lionel was the one most at odds with the theater. His attitude towards it amounted to a psychosis. He needed it; he had plenty of talent for it. But he was not a public person. He was happier — though less successful — in private occupations like painting, sculpting, etching, composing music, and writing. John Barrymore's conflict was more flamboyant and in the open where everyone could see it. Lionel's conflict was internal — private, wounding, elusive.

Brooks Atkinson, *Broadway.*

With Lionel Barrymore on the set, you have to stretch yourself, do better than you thought you could do. I've never played with him that I didn't envy him his consummate art. One thing I envy him in particular is his uncanny ability to lose himself instantly in a character. Most of us have to get up steam before we can throw ourselves into a part. I don't need the wail of violins to urge me to tears, but I confess I do like a few minutes to myself before I am required to weep my heart out on the screen. Not so Lionel. One moment he is chatting pleasantly with a fellow actor; the next he does a vanishing act before your very eyes. The director calls, 'Let 'er roll!' and presto! Barrymore is gone. Another ego has taken possession of his body; another man stands in his shoes, using the eloquent Barrymore voice and the more eloquent Barrymore hands. And yet, the second the camera stops grinding, there Lionel is back again, taking up the conversation where he left it. The change is instant, complete. No acting off the set for him.

Marie Dressler, *My Own Story.*

54

BARTON, ELIZABETH, 'MAID OF KENT'

1506?—34 Heretic

Now began Elizabeth Barton to play her tricks, commonly called 'the holy maid of Kent'; though at this day OF KENT alone is left unto her, as whose *maidenship* is vehemently suspected, and *holiness* utterly denied.

Thomas Fuller, *Church History of Britain.*

BARUCH, BERNARD MANNES

1870—1965 Financier

I'm not smart. I try to observe. Millions saw the apple fall but Newton was the one who asked why.

On himself, in *New York Post*, 24 June 1965.

We can't always cross a bridge until we come to it; but I always like to lay down a pontoon ahead of time.

On himself, in A. K. Adams, *The Home Book of Humorous Quotations.*

BASKERVILLE, JOHN

1706—75 Printer

O BASKERVILLE! the anxious wish was thine
Utility with beauty to combine;
To bid the O'erweening thirst of gain subside;
Improvement all thy care and all thy pride;
When Birmingham — for riots and for crimes
Shall meet the long reproach of future times,
Then shall she find amongst our honour'd race,
One name to save her from entire disgrace.

Anon., in J. H. Benton, *Baskerville.*

Although constructed with the light timber of a frigate, his movement was solemn as a ship of the line.

William Hutton, in *European Magazine*, November 1785.

BASS, SAM

1851—78 Desperado

I've lived a dog's life, Parson. And I'll die a dog's death.

On himself (as he lay dying), in Harold Preece, *Lone Star Man: Ira Aten, Last of the Old Texas Rangers.*

As a mawkish ballad testifies, Sam Bass called Indiana his 'native home.' In Texas, he had progressed from cotton picker to cowhand to race track gambler, and finally to leadership of mounted rowdies whose reward was much more notoriety than it ever was tangible loot. His forebears were of those semi-derelict wanderers who lived by luck and scrapings on the thin margins of every frontier society during America's periods of pioneer expansion.

Harold Preece, in *ibid.*

BAXTER, RICHARD

1615—91 Presbyterian Divine

I was but a pen, and what praise is due to a pen?

On himself, *Reliquiae Baxterianae.*

I had rather to be a Martyr for love, than for any other article of the Christian Creed.

Ibid.

Another time, as I sat in my study, the weight of my greatest folio books brake down three or four of the highest shelves, when I sat close under them, and they fell down on every side of me, and not one of them hit me, save one upon the arm; whereas, the place, the weight, and greatness of the books was such, and my head just under them, that it was a wonder they had not beaten out my brains, one of the shelves right over my head having the six volumes of Dr Walton's Oriental Bible, and all Austin's Works, and the Biblioteca Patrum.

Ibid.

As to myself, my faults are no disgrace to any university; for I was of none. I have little but what I had out of books, and inconsiderable helps of country tutors. Weakness and pain helped me to study how to die; that set me on studying how to live; and that on studying the doctrine from which I must fetch my motives and comforts. Beginning with necessities I proceeded by degrees, and now am going to see that for which I have lived and studied.

On himself, Letter to Anthony à Wood, in *Athenae Oxonienses.*

He had a very moving and pathetical way of writing, and was his whole life long a man of great zeal and much simplicity; but was most unhappily subtle and metaphysical in every thing.

Gilbert Burnet, *History of His Own Time.*

Baxter often expresses himself so as to excite a suspicion that he was inclined to Sabellianism.

Samuel Taylor Coleridge, *Notes on English Divines.*

Baxter, like most scholastic logicians, had a sneaking affection for Puns. The cause is: the necessity of attending to the primary sense of words, i.e. the visual image or general relation expresst, & which remains common to all the after-senses, however widely or even incongruously different from each other in other respects. . . .
Ibid.

I may not unfrequently doubt Baxter's memory, or even his competence, in consequence of his particular modes of thinking; but I could almost as soon doubt the Gospel verity as his veracity.
Ibid.

I can deal with saints as well as sinners. There stands Oates on one side of the pillory; and, if Baxter stood on the other, the two greatest rogues in the kingdom would stand together. . . . This is an old rogue, a schismatical knave, a hypocritical villain. He hates the Liturgy. He would have nothing but longwinded cant without book: . . . Richard, thou art an old knave. Thou hast written books enough to load a cart, and every book as full of sedition as an egg is full of meat.
Judge Jeffreys, at Baxter's Trial, 1685.

There he stands, an intellectual giant as he was, playing with his quill as Hercules with the distaff, his very sport a labour under which anyone but himself would have staggered.
Sir James Stephen, *Essays on Ecclesiastical Biography.*

BEACONSFIELD, see under DISRAELI, BENJAMIN

BEARDSLEY, AUBREY VINCENT

1872–98 Artist, Author

My favourite authors are Balzac, Voltaire, and Beardsley.
On himself, from an interview with him in *Idler*, March 1897.

I have one aim — the grotesque. If I am not grotesque I am nothing.
On himself, in Stanley Weintraub, *Aubrey Beardsley.*

I make a blot upon the paper and begin to shove the ink about and something comes.
Ibid.

Awfully Weirdly.
Popular nickname, quoted in Stanley Weintraub, *Aubrey Beardsley.*

B is for Beardsley, the idol supreme,
Whose drawings are not half so bad as they seem.
Gelett Burgess, *Our Clubbing List,* an alphabetical guide to the nineties, 1896.

A peal of morning dew.
Roy Campbell, *Flowering Rifle,* part 2.

The Fra Angelico of Satanism.
Roger Fry, in Stanley Weintraub, *Aubrey Beardsley.*

It was an inner existence that Beardsley had put down on paper, of sexual images and fantastic literary reveries. He had a sort of innocent familiarity with evil, he communed with the leering dwarfs, the bloated, epicene figures that peopled the depraved landscapes and grotesque interiors designed by his pen, as a child might talk with fairies.
William Gaunt, *The Aesthetic Adventure.*

Beardsley was incapable of creating anything belonging to a higher and a better art. His influence lowered taste and did not elevate it. His influence was only a passing one. Already his work is well-nigh forgotten . . . A coming age will wonder why there was any brief interest taken in Beardsley's work. It was a passing fad, a little sign of decadence and nothing more.
New York Times editorial, a fortnight after Beardsley's death in 1898.

Beware the Yallerbock, my son!
The aims that rile, the art that racks,
Beware the Aub-Aub bird, and shun
The stumious Beerbomax!
Mostyn Piggott, burlesque of Lewis Carroll's *Jabberwock,* in Haldane MacFall, *Aubrey Beardsley.*

With the art of Beardsley we enter the realm of pure intellect; the beauty of the work is wholly independent of the appearance of the thing portrayed.
Ezra Pound, in *Forum,* April 1912.

Daubaway Weirdsley.
Punch, February 1895.

Beardsley was an impassioned worker, and his hand was unerringly skilful. But for all his craftsmanship there was something hard and insensitive in his line, and narrow and small in his design, which affected me unsympathetically. He, too, remarkable boy as

he was, had something harsh, too sharply defined in his nature — like something seen under an arc-lamp.
William Rothenstein, *Men and Memories.*

He is the satirist of essential things; it is always the soul, and not the body's discontent only, which cries out of these insatiable eyes, that have looked on all their lusts, and out of these bitter mouths, that have eaten the dust of all their sweetnesses, and out of these hands, that have laboured delicately for nothing, and out of these feet, that have run after vanities. They are so sorrowful because they have seen beauty, and because they have departed from the line of beauty.
Arthur Symons, *Aubrey Beardsley.*

There were great possibilities always in the cavern of his soul, and there is something macabre and tragic in the fact that one who added another terror to life should have died at the age of a flower.
Oscar Wilde, Letter to Leonard Smithers, March 1898.

Absinthe is to all other drinks what Aubrey's drawings are to other pictures; it stands alone; it is like nothing else; it shimmers like southern twilight in opalescent colouring; it has about it the seduction of strange sins. It is stronger than any other spirit and brings out the subconscious self in man. It is just like your drawings, Aubrey; it gets on one's nerves and is cruel.
Oscar Wilde, in conversation, reported in Frank Harris, *Oscar Wilde.*

A monstrous orchid.
Oscar Wilde, in conversation, quoted in Stanley Weintraub, *Aubrey Beardsley.*

I invented Aubrey Beardsley.
Ibid.

. . . a face like a silver hatchet, with grass-green hair.
Oscar Wilde, in Richard Le Gallienne, *The Romantic '90s.*

BEAUFORT, HENRY

— d. 1447 Bishop of Winchester

Beaufort himself stands depicted in the strangest colours as at once the greatest ecclesiastic, and the most grasping usurer of his day; who struggled with the equal tenacity for his see and for his money; and exhibits all the contradictions of his nature in the petition containing in incongruous juxtaposition, — prayers that he might have good security for his loans, and might be allowed before he died to go a pilgrimage.
A. V. Dicey, *The Privy Council.*

BEAUMONT, FRANCIS
1584—1616 Dramatist

They [Beaumont and Fletcher] lived together on the Banke side, not far from the Play-house, both batchelors; lay together; had one Wench in the house between them, which they did so admire; the same cloathes and cloake, &c.; betweene them.
John Aubrey, *Brief Lives.*

On Death, thy murderer, this revenge I take:
I slight his terror, and just question make
Which of us two the best precedence have,
Mine to this wretched world, thine to the grave.
Thou should'st have followed me, but Death, to
       blame,
Miscounted years, and measured age by fame.
Sir John Beaumont, *Epitaph on His Brother.*

In Shakespeare the mere generalities of sex, mere words oftenest, seldom or never distinct images — all head-work, and fancy-drolleries — no sensation supposed in the Speaker, no itchy wriggling. In B. and F. the minutiae of a lecher.
Samuel Taylor Coleridge, Annotation to Stockdale's edition of Beaumont and Fletcher's Works, 1811.

B. & F. always write as if Virtue or Goodness were a sort of Talisman or Strange Something that might be lost without the least fault on the part of the Owner. In short, their chaste Ladies value their Chastity as a material thing, not as an act or state of being — and this mere *thing* being merely imaginary, no wonder that all his [sic] Women are represented with the minds of Strumpets, except a few irrational Humorists far less capable of exciting our sympathy than a Hindoo, who had had a basin of Cow-broth thrown over him — for this, though a debasing superstition is still real, and we might pity the poor wretch, though we cannot help despising him. But B & F's Lucinas are clumsy *Fictions.* It is too plain that the authors had no one idea of Chastity as a virtue — but only such a conception as a blind man might have of the power of seeing by handling an Ox's Eye.
Ibid.

I have never been able to distinguish the presence of Fletcher during the life of Beaumont, nor the absence of Beaumont during the survival of Fletcher.
Samuel Taylor Coleridge, *Notes for Lecture on Beaumont and Fletcher.*

Their plots were generally more regular than Shakespeare's . . . and they understood and imitated the conversation of gentlemen much better; whose wild debaucheries, and quickness of wit in repartees, no poet can ever paint as they have done. Humour, which Ben Jonson derived from particular persons, they made it not their business to describe; they represented all the passions very lively, but above all, love. I am apt to believe that the English language in them arrived to its highest perfection.

> John Dryden, *An Essay of Dramatic Poesy*.

The blossoms of Beaumont and Fletcher's imagination draw no sustenance from the soil, but are cut and slightly withered flowers stuck into sand ... The evocative quality of the verse of Beaumont and Fletcher during the life of Beaumont, nor the and associations which they have not themselves grasped; it is hollow. It is superficial with a vacuum behind it.

> T. S. Eliot, *Essays*: 'Ben Jonson'.

They are not safe teachers of morality; they tamper with it, like an experiment tried *in corpore vili*; and seem to regard the decomposition of the common affections, and the dissolution of the strict bonds of society, as an agreeable study, and a careless pastime.

> William Hazlitt, *Lectures on the Age of Elizabeth: On Beaumont and Fletcher*.

How I doe love thee *Beaumont*, and thy *Muse*
   That unto me dost such religion use!
How I doe feare my selfe, that am not worth
   The least indulgent thought thy pen drops forth!
At once thou mak'st me happie, and unmak'st;
   And giving largely to me, more thou tak'st.
What fate is mine, that so it selfe bereaves?
   What art is thine, that so thy friend deceives?
When even there, where most thou praysest mee,
   For writing better, I must envie thee.

> Ben Jonson, *Epigrammes*.

Bards of Passion and of Mirth
Ye have left your souls on earth!
Have ye souls in heaven too,
Double lived in regions new?

> John Keats, *Ode* inscribed in his copy of *The Fair Maid of the Inn*.

... Beaumont and Fletcher so aim at getting the maximum of poetic thrill out of each incident in turn irrespective of the rest that no reservoir of significance can accumulate and even the finest separate pieces fail of a maximum effect. Power leaks out into the wide areas of second-rate event and sentiment.

> G. Wilson Knight, *The Crown of Life*.

I confess to a condescending tolerance for Beaumont and Fletcher. ... The pair wrote a good deal that

was pretty disgraceful; but at all events they had been educated out of the possibility of writing Titus Andronicus.

> George Bernard Shaw, in *Saturday Review*, 19 February 1898.

Would thy melancholy have a cure? thou shalt laugh at Democritus himself, and but reading one piece of this comic variety, find thy exalted fancy in Elysium; and when thou art sick of this cure (for the excess of delight may too much dilate thy soul) thou shalt meet almost in every leaf a soft purling passion, or spring of sorrow, so powerfully wrought high by the tears of innocence and wronged lovers, it shall persuade thy eyes to weep into the stream, and yet smile when they contribute to their own ruins.

> James Shirley, Address to the Reader, in the Folio of Beaumont and Fletcher's *Works*.

Beaumont bringing the Ballast of Judgement, *Fletcher* the Sail of Phantasie, but compounding a Poet to admiration. ... It is reported of them, that meeting once in a tavern, to contrive the rude Draught of a Tragedy, *Fletcher* undertook to *kill the King* therein, whose words being overheard by a Listener (though his loyalty was not to be blamed herein) he was accused of High Treason, till the Mistake soon appearing, that the Plot was only against a Dramatick and Scenicall King, all wound off in Merriement.

> William Winstanley, *Lives of the Most Famous English Poets*.

See also John Fletcher, Philip Massinger, Shakespeare

BEAVERBROOK, LORD (WILLIAM MAXWELL AITKEN)

1879—1964 Newspaper Magnate

My principle is — take a trick while you can and go on with the game.

> On himself, Letter to F. B. Edwards, 6 March 1930.

I learnt one thing from father, and that was, to hate! to hate!

> On himself, to Lloyd George, in Frances Stevenson, Diary, 10 January 1935.

I can give it and I can take it.

> On himself, Letter to Tom Driberg, 3 December 1952.

... a Maxi-millionaire.

> On himself, comment to William Gerhardie, in A. J. P. Taylor, *Beaverbrook*.

... there are many other people to whom it will be easy to talk. Chief among these is Beaverbrook. He is a magnet to all young men, and I warn you if you talk to him no good will come of it. Beware of flattery.

> Clement Attlee, speaking to junior Labour ministers, June 1945.

Beaverbrook is so pleased to be in the Government that he is like the town tart who has finally married the Mayor!

> Beverley Baxter, in Henry Channon, Diary, 12 June 1940.

... he likes me and I like him, but that would not prevent him doing me in.

> David Lloyd George, in A. J. Sylvester, Diary, 2 January 1932.

... so long as there is a battle on, B[eaverbrook] will behave as a great and loyal fighter. But once the battle is over and victory is assured, B. will get bored and will create battles, if necessary in his own party. His pugnacity destroys both his judgment and his decent feeling. If they ally themselves with B. they must think of some bone to give him later which will keep him busy. He lives only by opposition: if he cannot find an opposition he creates one.

> Harold Nicolson, advice to Sir Oswald Mosley, Diary, 6 November 1930.

... He is first, second & third 'a Bonar Law man'.

> Frances Stevenson, Diary, 18 November 1916.

Lord Beaverbrook seemed to create an atmosphere of confusion, because it could be amusing, or because it could be confusing or startling to others.

> C. M. Vines, A Little Nut-Brown Man: my three years with Lord Beaverbrook.

If Max gets to Heaven he won't last long. He will be chucked out for trying to pull off a merger between Heaven and Hell ... after having secured a controlling interest in key subsidiary companies in both places, of course.

> H. G. Wells, in A. J. P. Taylor, Beaverbrook.

BECKER, CARL LOTUS

1873–1945 Historian

As for you, I have heard on good authority that you are no Historian; nothing except a Man of Letters. It makes me jealous.

> Charles Beard, undated letter to Becker in Cushing Strout, 'The Pragmatic Revolt' in American History: Carl Becker and Charles Beard.

Becker ... embodies all the honest hesitancies and doubts of that vast group of American literate and trained white-collar workers who have at one and the same time always insisted upon their intellectual and professional independence and identified themselves economically with the middleclass.

> Louis Hacker, in Charlotte Watkins Smith, Carl Becker: On History & The Climate of Opinion.

BECKET, see under THOMAS À BECKET

BECKFORD, WILLIAM

1759–1844 Novelist, Art Collector

... On Hartford Bridge, we changed horses at an Inn where the great Apostle of Paederasty Beckford! sojourned for the night, we tried in vain to see the Martyr of Prejudice, but could not.

> Lord Byron, Letter to Francis Hodgson, 25 June 1809.

Restless, half-sincere charlatans, like d'Annunzio, have an undying attraction for those whose daydreams need stimulating; and myth always gathers round very rich men. Beckford has both appeals, and it is not surprising that fascinated historians have made him an influence on the Gothic Revival. This suggestion was made in Beckford's day, and was not well received. 'No,' he said, 'I have enough sins to answer for without having that laid to my charge.'

> Kenneth Clark, The Gothic Revival.

Mr Beckford has undoubtedly shown himself an industrious bijoutier, a prodigious virtuoso, an accomplished patron of unproductive labour, an enthusiastic collector of expensive trifles. ... The author of Vathek is a scholar; the proprietor of Fonthill has travelled abroad, and has seen all the finest remains of antiquity and boasted specimens of modern art. Why not lay his hands on some of these? He had power to carry them away ... Hardly an article of any consequence that does not seem to be labelled to the following effect — 'This is mine, and there is no one else in the whole world in whom it can inspire the least interest, or any feeling beyond a momentary surprise!'

> William Hazlitt, Fonthill Abbey.

A male Horace Walpole.

> J. G. Lockhart, in Quarterly Review, June 1834.

He lived a strictly secluded life. A wall twelve feet high surrounded his estate [at Fonthill], and, at the heavy double gates, servants were stationed with orders to exclude strangers. It was a rare mark of favour to be invited inside the entrance, and it is said that even George IV was denied a sight of the Abbey. Strange stories began to circulate of what went on there, but the truth is that Beckford lived absorbed in his books and his building, with only his doctor and one or two artists for company, and an Italian dwarf as his personal attendant. We are told that the sight of this hideous little creature opening the Abbey doors, thirty feet high, provided another of those contrasts that so delighted his master.

Osbert Sitwell and Margaret Barton, *Sober Truth.*

See also James Wyatt

BEDE, THE 'VENERABLE'

673—735 Historian

Northumbria was fortunate ... in having in this twilight scene a chronicler ... whose words have descended to us out of the long silence of the past. Bede, a monk of high ability, working unknown in the recesses of the Church, now comes forward as the most effective and almost the only audible voice from the British islands in these dim times. ... He alone attempts to paint for us, and, so far as he can, explain the spectacle of Anglo-Saxon England in its first phase.

Winston Churchill, *History of the English-Speaking People.*

O venerable Bede!
The saint, the scholar from a circle freed
Of toil stupendous, in a hallowed seat
Of learning where thou heard'st the billows beat
On a wild coast, rough monitors to feed
Perpetual industry. Sublime Recluse!
The recreant soul, that dares to shun the debt
Imposed on human kind, must first forget
Thy diligence, thy unrelaxing use
Of a long life; and in the hour of death,
The last dear service of thy passing breath!

William Wordsworth, *Ecclesiastical Sonnets.*

BEDLOE, WILLIAM

1650—80 Perjurer

The Lord is pleased when Man does cease to sin;
The Divil is pleased when he a soul does win;
The World is pleased when every Rascal dies:
So all are pleased, for here Will Bedloe lies.

Anon., *Epitaph.*

Sad fate! our valiant Captain Bedloe
In earth's cold bed lies with his head low;
Who to his last made out the Plot
And swearing, di'd upon the spot.
Sure Death was Popishly affected
She had our witness else protected;
Or downright Papist, or the jade
A Papist is in masquerade.

Richard Duke, *Funeral Tears upon the Death of Captain William Bedloe.*

One *Bedlow,* a man of inferior note.

John Evelyn, Diary, 18 July 1679.

BEECHAM, THOMAS

1820—1907 Industrialist

Hark! the Herald Angels sing,
Beecham's Pills are just the thing.

Anon., *circa* 1892, subsequently used by Beecham in his advertising campaigns.

There is a small house next to the stables on the Lawn Farm, Cropredy, where Thomas Beecham of Beecham's Pill Fame, used to live as a shepherd, and where he used to make the knitting sheaths that he gave to some of his old friends. ... According to the old tales he experimented while he was there, and when he got on in the world a bit, he used to send some of the old people in the village a box of his famous pills with a guinea at the bottom. That is how they came to be known to 'be worth a guinea a box.'

Anon., in *Banbury Guardian,* 29 December 1932.

It seems he owed his success to a single phrase. As he stood in the market place at St. Helens selling his pills, a woman came to him to buy, saying they were worth a guinea a box.

Anon., in *Witney Gazette,* 13 April 1907.

BEECHAM, SIR THOMAS

1879—1961 Conductor

Indeed I was the most ordinary and, in some ways, the most satisfactory kind of youngster any parents could wish to have. I disliked noise of any sort, never indulged in it myself, was a model of taciturnity and gentle melancholy, and altogether an embryonic hero for a Bulwer-Lytton novel.

On himself, *A Mingled Chime.*

I have always been noted for my instability. I am a very, very low brow.

On himself, reported by Adam Bell, in *Evening Standard*, 8 March 1961.

I am not the greatest conductor in this country. On the other hand I'm better than any damned foreigner.

On himself, as reported by Noel Goodwin, in *Daily Express*, 9 March 1961.

At a rehearsal I let the orchestra play as they like. At the concert I make them play as *I* like.

On himself, in Neville Cardus, *Sir Thomas Beecham*.

He conducted like a dancing dervish.

Sir John Barbirolli, in Charles Reid, *John Barbirolli*.

One day there was a face strange to him among the woodwind. 'Er, Mr.–?' 'Ball' came the reply. 'I beg your pardon?' 'Ball, Sir Thomas.' 'Ball? Ah – *Ball*. Very singular.'

Neville Cardus, *Sir Thomas Beecham*.

. . . I never heard him refer to religion. To women he referred once, saying that none of them was worth the loss of a night's sleep.

Ibid.

'Have you ever been at a loss for a word?' I asked him, 'ever been unable to cope with a situation at any time of your life?' He thought about it for a few moments. 'Yes,' he replied. 'Once . . . I was rehearsing *Tristan*. And that glorious singer Walter Widdop was Tristan. I was obliged to pull him up – no small act of courage, for Walter, an intrepid Yorkshireman, feared nobody. "Walter," I said, "you are singing divinely. But really, you must carry yourself with more dignity, more pride of carriage. Don't you know who Tristan is supposed to be?" And Walter answered, "E's only a sailor, isn't he?" I was rendered speechless, entirely speechless.'

Ibid.

Occasionally his conducting was as slapdash as well could be; to such a level of unconscious bluff on the rostrum could he descend that often I have blushed for him. The finale of the Seventh Symphony of Beethoven acted on him as red rag to a bull.

Ibid.

. . . For the impish joy he brought to music, the martinet Arturo Toscanini dismissed him as *pagliaccio* – 'buffoon'.

Gerald Jackson, in *Reader's Digest*, July 1972.

He would address a choir: 'Ladies and gentlemen, if you will make a point of singing *All we, like sheep, have gone astray* with a little less satisfaction, we shall meet the aesthetical as well as the theological requirements.'

Liverpool Echo and Evening Express, 8 March 1961.

At a dinner given in honour of his seventieth birthday, when messages of congratulation from great musicians all over the world were being read out, he was heard to murmur: 'What, nothing from Mozart?'

Patricia Young, *Great Performers*.

See also Frederick Delius, Edward Elgar

BEECHER, CATHERINE ESTHER

1800–78 Educator, Reformer

I am so much engaged in moulding, correcting, and inspecting the characters of others that I sometimes fear that my own will be a 'cast away'. . . .

On herself, in Kathryn Kish Sklar, *Catherine Beecher*.

Catherine's life had been a rich mixture of affirmation and denial. Her own attitude toward her abilities alternated between a desire to succeed and a will to fail.

Kathryn Kish Sklar, *ibid*.

Catherine has been here and we have all been pretty thoroughly metaphysicated.

Harriet Beecher Stowe, in *ibid*.

BEECHER, HENRY WARD

1813–87 Clergyman, Abolitionist

Mr. Beecher is a real humorist; his satire burns, but it does not harden; he will laugh men out of their sins if he cannot otherwise persuade them, and he will show how very ridiculous an action may be, when he feels that no other kind of denunciation is likely to affect his hearers.

H. R. Haves, in *Contemporary Review*, vol. 14, 1872.

The Reverend Henry Ward Beecher
Called a hen a most elegant creature.
   The hen, pleased with that,
   Laid two eggs in his hat.
And thus did the hen reward Beecher.

Oliver Wendell Holmes, attrib., *An Eggstravagance*.

The movement of his thoughts is that of the chopping sea, rather than the long, rolling, rhythmical wave-procession of phrase-balancing rhetoricians.

Oliver Wendell Holmes, in *Atlantic Monthly*, January 1864.

Henry Ward Beecher was born in a Puritan penitentiary, of which his father was one of the wardens — a prison with very narrow and closely-grated windows. . . . In this prison the creed and catechism were primers for children, and from a pure sense of duty their loving hearts were stained and scarred with the religion of John Calvin.

Robert G. Ingersoll, in Paxton Hibben, *Henry Ward Beecher: An American Portrait*.

He slapped the backs of all men, he tickled the ribs of almost all the current ideas, and he kissed a surprising proportion of the women.

Sinclair Lewis, Introduction to Paxton Hibben, *Henry Ward Beecher: An American Portrait*.

He came out for the right side of every question — always a little too late.

Ibid.

As a preacher he is a landscape painter of Christianity.

Sen. Oliver H. Smith, *Early Indiana Trials and Reminiscences.*

In Boston the human race is divided into 'the Good, the Bad, and the Beechers.'

The Rev. W. M. Taylor, in *Scottish Review*, October 1859.

BEERBOHM, SIR HENRY MAXIMILIAN (MAX)

1872—1956 Author, Cartoonist

I was a modest, good-humoured boy. It is Oxford that has made me insufferable.

On himself, *More.*

If one compares two drawings or two books of his, it is almost impossible, on the evidence of the works themselves, to date them. Despite this lack of development, his work doesn't 'date', as one would expect, and as the work of so many of his contemporaries does. If one asks why this should be so, the answer is, I believe, that in him the aesthetic sensibility was never divorced, as it was in many of his colleagues, from the moral feelings. Fashions in what is considered beautiful or interesting are always changing, but the difference between a man of honour and a scoundrel is eternal.

W. H. Auden, *Forewords and Afterwords.*

Very little gold has come the way of Sir Max. Although few writers have acquired his réclame — he has since his first success had a legendary quality — yet his books were sold in very small quantities and today are out of print. It is rather terrible to know that the successful Somerset Maugham criticized Max as being someone whose shirt-cuffs were generally dirty.

Cecil Beaton, *The Strenuous Years.*

Max's attitude to his public reputation was complex. It was not a matter of supreme importance to him. On the other hand, he disliked people getting a wrong impression of him; and took pains to avoid this happening. The fact was that he — it was one of the paradoxes of his character — had always been both showman and recluse, desirous to escape from the world yet enjoying cutting a figure in it.

David Cecil, *Max Beerbohm.*

It always makes me cross when Max is called 'The Incomparable Max'. He is not incomparable at all, and in fact compares very poorly with Harold Nicolson, as a stylist, a wit, and an observer of human nature. He is a shallow, affected, self-conscious fribble — so there.

Vita Sackville-West, Letter to Harold Nicolson, 9 December 1959.

He has the most remarkable and seductive genius — and I should say about the smallest in the world.

Lytton Strachey, Letter to Clive Bell, 4 December 1917.

According to the analyses of humour prepared by the humourless, Max Beerbohm was impossible. He could not have existed. He laughed where he loved; and loved where he laughed; but he neither beamed nor sniggered. By the annotated laws of laughter, no man could behave so anomalously. The question arises whether there was ever a real Max Beerbohm or whether he invented himself as he invented Enoch Soames and extra-illustrated the books in his library, for his own secret entertainment.

Frank Swinnerton, *The Georgian Literary Scene.*

We went to tea with Max Beebohm who is in a little house near Stroud. A delicious little old dandy, very quick in mind still. A touch of Ronnie Knox and of Harold Acton. 'The tongue has, correct me if I am wrong, seven follicles in adult life.' Much of what he said would have been commonplace but for his exquisite delivery.

Evelyn Waugh, Diary, 17 May 1947.

Tell me, when you are alone with Max, does he take off his face and reveal his mask?

Oscar Wilde, in W. H. Auden, *Forewords and Afterwords.*

The Gods bestowed on Max the gift of perpetual old age.

> Oscar Wilde, in Vincent O'Sullivan, *Aspects of Wilde*.

His hands were quite astonishing — they seemed unlike any others I had ever seen. Instead of being slender with tapering fingers, the fingers were long and of uniform thickness, almost like the legs of a spider crab, and they were sharpened at the ends like pencils. It was as if they were very large engraver's tools, the instruments of a formidable craftsman.

> Edmund Wilson, *The Bit Between my Teeth*.

Max like a Cheshire cat. Orbicular. Jowled. Blue eyed . . . all curves.

> Virginia Woolf, *A Writer's Diary*, 1 November 1928.

See also Aubrey Beardsley, Aldous Huxley, Rudyard Kipling

BELL, ALEXANDER GRAHAM

1847—1922 Inventor

Mr. Thomas A. Watson, Bell's assistant, relates that it was on March 10, 1876, over a line extending between two rooms in a building at No. 5 Exeter Place, Boston, that the first complete sentence was ever spoken by Bell and heard by Watson, who recorded it in his notebook at the time. It consisted of these words: 'Mr. Watson, come here; I want you.' Thus the telephone was born.

> John J. Carty, in *The Smithsonian Report for 1922*.

BELLOC, JOSEPH HILAIRE PIERRE RENÉ

1870--1953 Author, Historian

Gentlemen, I am a Catholic. As far as possible, I go to Mass every day. . . . As far as possible, I kneel down and tell these beads every day. If you reject me on account of my religion, I shall thank God that He has spared me the indignity of being your representative.

> On himself, in a speech to the electors of South Salford in 1906, after being warned to avoid the religious question.

When I am dead, I hope it may be said:
'His sins were scarlet, but his books were read.'

> On himself, *On His Books*.

Mr Hilaire Belloc
Is a case for legislation ad hoc.
He seems to think nobody minds
His books being all of different kinds.

> E. C. Bentley, *Biography for Beginners*.

You, Mister Belloc, thought it fine
To put one's faith in God and Wine;
You see the Pickle I am in
Who put my faith in Men and Gin.

> W. Bridges-Adams, *Reproach*.

In so far as he is a traditionalist, he is an English traditionalist. But when he was specially a revolutionist, he was in the very exact sense a French Revolutionist. And it might be roughly symbolised by saying that he was an English poet but a French soldier.

> G. K. Chesterton, *Autobiography*.

The respectable and the middle generation, illustrious punks and messers, . . . all degrading the values . . . Belloc pathetic in that he had *meant* to do the fine thing and been jockeyed into serving, at least to some extent, a — — — — order of a pewked society.

> Ezra Pound, Letter to Michael Roberts, July 1937.

Wells and I, contemplating the Chesterbelloc, recognize at once a very amusing pantomime elephant, the front legs being that very exceptional and unEnglish individual Hilaire Belloc, and the hind legs that extravagant freak of French nature, G. K. Chesterton.

> George Bernard Shaw, 'The Chesterbelloc', in *New Age*, 15 February 1908.

Poor Mr Belloc looked as though the grave were the only place for him. He has grown a splendid white beard and in his cloak, which with his hat he wore indoors and always, he seemed an archimandrite. He lost and stole and whatever went into his pockets, toast, cigarettes, books never appeared, like the reverse of a conjuror's hat. He talked incessantly, proclaiming with great clarity the grievances of 40 years ago. . . . At times he was coaxed by the women to sing and then with face alight with simple joy and many lapses of memory, he quavered out old French marching songs and snatches from the music halls of his youth. He is conscious of being decrepit and forgetful, but not of being a bore.

> Evelyn Waugh, Diary, 1 May 1945.

See also G. K. Chesterton, P. G. Wodehouse

BELLOWS, GEORGE

1882—1925 Painter, Lithographer

All civilization and culture are the results of the creative imagination or artist quality in man. The artist is the man who makes life more interesting or beautiful, more understandable or mysterious, or probably, in the best sense, more wonderful. His trade is to deal in illimitable experience. It is therefore only of importance that the artist discover whether he be an artist, and it is for society to discover what return it can make to its artists.

On himself, *The Paintings of George Bellows*.

The ideal artist is he who knows everything, feels everything, experiences everything and retains his experience in a spirit of wonder and feeds upon it with creative lust. He is therefore best able to select and order the components best suited to fulfill any given desire. The ideal artist is the superman. He uses every possible power, intellectual, spiritual, emotional, consciously and subconsciously to arrive at his ends.

Ibid.

It is a misfortune not only for his many friends but for America and art that George Bellows should have died before his work was done. He had the experimental temper from the first to last. He was continually seeking new solutions of the ancient problems with which every artist is confronted, continually interested in and hospitable to fresh theory, and in all his ventures and speculations he was consistently himself. He was a valuable driving force in art and his talent was great. Time can only enhance the effect of his sound craftsmanship and personal vision.

Anon., in *New York Times*, 10 January 1925.

He has contrived to combine the drastic energy of Courbet with the clear palette of the neo-impressionists, though, like Manet, he fears not black when he needs it.

Anon., in *New York Evening Post*, 11 December 1909.

But Bellows became the most characteristically 'native' of our painters, not because he avoided Cubism and the movements that came with it, nor because he lived in America, but because his emotions, tastes and personal quality remained so purely and so completely American. If we, as a people, are restive, conglomerate, incautious, humorous, intolerant of prescriptions, inclined to bravura, so, also, are the paintings of George Bellows.

Frank Crowninshield, Introduction to *Memorial Exhibition of the Work of George Bellows*.

As time went on Bellows began more and more to embody the geography and democracy of our country. For one thing, he never set foot in Europe. All of his reactions, all of his emotional qualities, were derived from America; from the soil, sky, wind and water which he knew and observed so well. Many explanations have been offered for his continued refusal to leave America, the simple truth being that the call to leave was too faint, the need to stay too strong.

Ibid.

He was perhaps the first of our painters — as Whitman had been the first of our writers — to pay anything like inspired attention to the city or the crowd, ... The universe, to him, was distinctly a peopled vision. Man was always the primary datum or unit. From that unit he proceeded rapidly, in human multiples, to the group or crowd.

Ibid.

Perhaps the ingredients of his art can best be suggested by the story told of his small daughter Anne, who, at the age of four, was serving tea with a set of child's china to three invisible guests. Asked who they were, she replied solemnly, 'God, Rembrandt, and Emma Goldman.'

Charles H. Morgan, *George Bellows*.

George was six feet tall and weighed around one hundred and eighty pounds; he looked and moved like an athlete, which he was. He had a rich baritone voice, took vocal lessons, and liked to sing for his friends. He had a wonderful sense of humor and a quick wit as demonstrated in his already well-known retort to Joseph Pennell. When the latter accused him of being a slacker for having painted the execution of Edith Cavell without having witnessed it, Bellows replied that, though he had not witnessed the execution, neither had Leonardo da Vinci been present at the Last Supper! He was impressionable and enthusiastic; a warm sympathetic human being with a great heart and a touch of the romantic.

Eugene Speicher, *A Personal Reminiscence*.

BENCHLEY, ROBERT CHARLES

1889—1945 Humorist, Critic, Actor

I do most of my work sitting down; that's where I shine.

On himself, in *The Treasury of Humorous Quotations*.

I haven't been abroad in so long that I almost speak English without an accent.

On himself, in Robert E. Drennan ed., *Wit's End*.

A friend once told Benchley that a particular drink he was drinking was slow poison, to which Benchley replied, 'So who's in a hurry?'
Ibid.

It took me fifteen years to discover that I had no talent for writing, but I couldn't give it up because by that time I was too famous.
Ibid.

Drawing on my fine command of language I said nothing.
On himself, in A. K. Adams, *The Home Book of Humorous Quotations.*

Merely as an observer of natural phenomena, I am fascinated by my own personal appearance. This does not mean that I am pleased with it, mind you, or that I can even tolerate it. I simply have a morbid interest in it.
On himself, in Nathaniel Benchley ed., *The Benchley Roundup.*

Arriving home with a group of friends one rainy evening Benchley suggested (though some have attributed the remark to Aleck Woollcott), 'Let's get out of these wet clothes and into a dry martini.'
Robert E. Drennan ed., *Wit's End.*

Robert Benchley has a style that is weak and lies down frequently to rest.
Max Eastman, *Enjoyment of Laughter.*

The most finished master of the technique of literary fun in America.
Stephen Leacock, in Nathaniel Benchley, *The Benchley Roundup.*

He *was* Humor, with his instinctive humanity, toleration, wisdom, non-competitiveness, non-aggressiveness, democracy (not in the political sense). I warmed myself at that fire and what I wrote always was, unconsciously, for his approval. It still is.
Donald Ogden Stewart, in James Thurber, 'The Incomparable Mr. Benchley', in *Credos and Curios*

When he died, one of them said, 'They're going to have to stay up late in heaven now.'
James Thurber, *Credos and Curios.*

I was always looking for his stuff, and thought he was wonderful, and still think he was wonderful. He was certainly wonderfully kind, and he slayed his dragons with the minimum of pain. He had the gift of brevity, of course, and I was impressed by that, and I'm sure I imitated Benchley and kept trying to do what he was succeeding in doing. The day

[Harold] Ross told me Benchley had praised something I had written was one of the big days of the twenties for me.
E. B. White, in *ibid.*

Benchley, as I first knew him, had the manner of a quiet and modest young Harvard graduate, with whom it was pleasant and easy to deal. Later, when he went to Hollywood, where he had some success doing comic shorts, he seemed to have become transformed. He was florid and self-assertive. He at one time became obsessed by an unimportant girl on the stage, whom Dorothy [Parker] thought to be very inferior. I remember this girl's saying once that she had to leave us to try out for 'a leg and fanny show'; but he used to insist to Dorothy that she entered a room with the presence 'of a queen'. He got to drinking heavily and died of cirrhosis of the liver. I used, in the days I first knew him, to urge him to do serious satire, but he proved to be incapable of this. His usual character for himself was that of an unsure suburban duffer who was always being frightened and defeated, and this, even in his Hollywood shorts, seemed to be the only role in which he was able to appear. He lived out of town with his family in a perfectly conventional way, and I believe that his rather obnoxious phase was an attempt to counteract this. Dorothy regarded him as a kind of saint, and he did have some admirable qualities. He testified in court at the Sacco-Vanzetti case that Judge Thayer had shown his prejudice at the golf club by threatening 'to get those anarchist bastards' or something of the kind.
Edmund Wilson, *The Twenties.*

BENJAMIN, JUDAH PHILIP

1811—84 Confederate Politician, Lawyer

Mr. Benjamin was a brilliant lawyer, but he knew as much about war as an Arab knows of the Sermon on the Mount.
Anon. Confederate soldier, in Alexander Hunter, *Johnny Reb and Billy Yank.*

Judah P. Benjamin, the dapper Jew,
Seal-sleek, black-eyed, lawyer and epicure,
Able, well-hated, face alive with life,
Looked round the council-chamber with the slight
Perpetual smile he held before himself
Continually like a silk-ribbed fan.
Behind the fan, his quick, shrewd fluid mind
Weighed Gentiles in an old balance. . . .
The mind behind the silk-ribbed fan
Was a dark prince, clothed in an Eastern stuff,
Whose brown hands cupped about a crystal egg

That filmed with coloured cloud. The egg stared
                                              searching.
  Stephen Vincent Benét, *John Brown's Body*.

. . . the Mephistopheles of the Southern Confederacy.
  James G. Blaine, in S. I. Nieman, *Judah Benjamin*.

One ubiquitous and most acceptable social factor of the official circle, that smooth brevet bachelor, Hon. Judah P. Benjamin, Attorney General with the plus sign. There was no circle, official or otherwise, that missed his soft, purring presence, or had not regretted in so doing. He was always expected, almost always found time to respond, and was inevitably compensating. He moved into and through the most elegant or the simplest assemblage on natural rubber tires and well-oiled bearings, a smile of recognition for the mere acquaintance, a reminiscent word for the intimate, and a general diffusion of placid bonhommie.
  T. C. De Leon, in *ibid*.

BENNETT, ENOCH ARNOLD
1867–1931 Novelist

I cannot conceive that any author should write, as the de Goncourts say they wrote, 'for posterity' . . . I would not care a bilberry for posterity. I should be my own justest judge, from whom there would be no appeal; and having satisfied him (whether he was right or wrong) I should be content — as an artist. As a *man*, I should be disgusted if I could not earn plenty of money and the praise of the discriminating.
  On himself, *Journal*, 28 January 1897.

I have written between seventy and eighty books. But I have also written only four: *The Old Wives' Tale, The Card, Clayhanger*, and *Riceyman Steps*.
  On himself, in Frank Swinnerton, *Arnold Bennett*.

The best books I think are very fine indeed, on the highest level, deeply moving, original, and dealing with material that I had never before encountered in fiction, but only in life . . . I don't expect everybody will share my affection for some of his fantasies, though plenty did in the past, but I've found it to be undiminished by familiarity. Some of his silliest jokes make me laugh, and his manuals on self-improvement still make me want to improve myself. I find his impact undiminished by time.
  Margaret Drabble, *Arnold Bennett*.

When Arnold Bennett lay dying in his luxury flat at Chiltern Court, with the straw spread lavishly across the width of Marylebone Road, I reflected, as sadly I stood and looked up at his windows, that the astute A.B., were he conscious, would have been the first to point out how obsolete in our day of pneumatic tyres and smooth roads, with no sound but the hooting of horns and the changing of gear, is a custom designed to deaden the noise of wooden wheel and iron hoof on cobblestones. Presently, I hoped, he would come to and expose the archaism in an article in the *Evening Standard*. When I passed again the straw had been removed, and Arnold Bennett was dead.
  William Gerhardie, *Memoirs of a Polyglot*.

'Twas Arnold Bennett's habit to deplore
That younger writers did not publish more
And yet it would be easier to assess
His own position had he written less.
  Kensal Green (Colin Hurry), *Premature Epitaphs*.

It is a neat piece of inadvertent symbolism, as Walter Allen has pointed out, that Bennett should have made his journalistic début by winning a competition in *Tit-Bits*, and then followed this up by publishing a short story in the *Yellow Book*; from the very outset he was disconcertingly ready to switch roles, to appear now as a tradesman, now as a dedicated artist.
  John Gross, *The Rise and Fall of the Man of Letters*.

The psychology of an artist cannot be reduced to the simple contrasts of a morality play. Bennett's naked careerism may have done him lasting damage as a writer, yet without it, would he have had any career at all? *Psychologiser, c'est tout pardonner* — but there is surely a very good case for supposing that Bennett's cruder ambitions were bound up with his stamina, his curiosity, his appetite for experience, with qualities which were indispensable to him as a novelist.
  Ibid.

Bennett — sort of pig in clover.
  D. H. Lawrence, Letter to Aldous Huxley, 27 March 1928.

The Hitler of the book-racket.
  Percy Wyndham Lewis (on Bennett's powers as literary editor of *Evening Standard*), *Blasting and Bombardiering*.

I remember that once, beating his knee with his clenched fist to force the words from his writhing lips, he said: 'I am a nice man.' He was.
  Somerset Maugham, *The Vagrant Mood*.

I am going to show you how Arnold Bennett writes

66

all his books. ... First he takes a sheet of paper. And then he takes a pen and he dips the pen in the ink and then he writes the title of the book on one sheet, and the numbers of the chapters on another sheet. Then he writes 'Chapter I', at the top of a page and begins with the first line, and then he writes the rest of the book straight through, to the very end, until he has finished it. *I cannot write like that!*

> George Moore, in Nancy Cunard, *Memories of George Moore*.

1908 saw a stirring. By 1912 it was established, at least in Ormond St., that Arnold Bennett was inadequate, that British impressionism was too soft.

> Ezra Pound, in *Criterion*, 1937.

Arnold Bennett knew his eggs. Whatever his interest in good writing, he never showed the public anything but his AVARICE. Consequently they adored him.

> Ezra Pound, Letter to Laurence Pollinger, May 1936.

Nickel cash-register Bennett.

> Ezra Pound, Letter to Michael Roberts, July 1937.

Never have I known anyone else so cheerfully objective as Bennett. His world was as bright and hard surfaced as crockery — his *persona* was, as it were, a hard, definite china figurine. What was not precise, factual and contemporary, could not enter into his consciousness. He was friendly and self-assured; he knew quite clearly that we were both on our way to social distinction and incomes of several thousands a year. ... He had a through ticket and a time-table — and he proved to be right.

> H. G. Wells, *Experiment in Autobiography*.

The trouble is, whenever I do a thing, Arnold does it too, but twice as posh.

> H. G. Wells, in Osbert Sitwell, *Noble Essences*.

I enjoy meeting authors tremendously, but more on my own level. I got the impression that Arnold Bennett was awfully pretentious. I don't know why, I suppose it was just his manner. They all seemed to be priding themselves on being terribly great authors.

> P. G. Wodehouse, in an interview in *Radio Times*, 1974.

'Art is long, life is short,' save when it
is applied to Arnold Bennett,
whose Art was aimed (unless we wrong her)
to prove that life's a d———d sight longer.

> Humbert Wolfe, *Lampoons*.

We had hardly met Bennett before, and I felt rather overwhelmed ... Bennett did not put me at my ease. I had reviewed his novel, *Lord Raingo*, rather critically in the *Nation*. When we sat down to dinner ... Bennett fixed me with his eye, leant across, and said, 'W-w-woolf d-d-does not l-l-like my novels.' I tried to expostulate that this was not the case, but several times during the dinner the minute gun was fired at me across the table: 'W-w-woolf d-d-does not l-l-like my novels.'

> Leonard Woolf, *Beginning Again*.

He can make a book so well constructed and solid in its craftmanship that it is difficult for the most exacting of critics to see through what chink or crevice decay can creep in. And yet — if life should refuse to live there?

> Virginia Woolf, *The Common Reader*.

Arnold Bennett died last night, which leaves me sadder than I should have supposed. A loveable genuine man: impeded, somehow a little awkward in life; well meaning; ponderous; kindly; coarse; knowing he was coarse; dimly floundering and feeling for something else; glutted with success; wounded in his feelings.... Some real understanding power, as well as gigantic absorbing power. Queer how one regrets the dispersal of anybody who seemed — as I say — genuine: who had direct contact with life — for he abused me; and yet I rather wished him to go on abusing me; and me abusing him.

> Virginia Woolf, *A Writer's Diary*, 28 March 1931.

See also Virginia Woolf

BENNETT, HENRY, see under ARLINGTON

BENNETT, JAMES GORDON

1795—1872 Editor

I tell the honest truth in my paper, and leave the consequences to God. Could I leave them in better hands?

> On himself, *New York Morning Herald*, 10 May 1836.

BENNETT, JAMES GORDON JR

1841—1918 Editor

He was too-many-sided; of more phases than the eight moons of Saturn. In modern times, at least, there have been none like him; the mold was broken and the age is gone that made him possible. Even in his day he robbed fiction of an almost incredible character.

Albert Stevens Crockett, *When James Gordon Bennett was Caliph of Bagdad*.

He knew how to make news, not by the simple and unsatisfying process of creating it out of whole cloth, but by starting something that would find an echo in the popular imagination and stimulate a demand for more.

Albert Stevens Crockett, in Richard O'Connor, *The Scandalous Mr Bennett*.

He strides up Broadway with the step of an athlete, dons his navy blue and commands his yacht, shoots pigeons, and prefers the open air of Newport to the confinement of the *Herald* office.

Charles Anderson Dana, in Frank M. O'Brien, *The Story of the Sun*.

By nature and training he is too suspicious to trust his friends, and he makes enemies unconsciously of those who would be, and have been, most truly devoted to him, by regarding all mankind as a band of conspirators organized to influence the *Herald* for their own purposes.

Stephen Fiske, in Richard O'Connor, *The Scandalous Mr Bennett*.

... a low-mouthed, blatant, witless, brutal scoundrel.

Horace Greeley, in Peter Allen Isely, *Horace Greeley and the Republican Party, 1853–1861*.

... Bennett calmly waited for death, certain he would die on his seventy-seventh birthday. He did. The commodore liked to have his own way, even with death.

Richard O'Connor, *The Scandalous Mr Bennett*.

He is a human paradox. Always a patrician, he is frequently a buffoon. To him the whole world is a joke, but to no one else will he permit the privilege of looking upon it in any but a serious manner.

Leo L. Redding, 'Bennett of the Herald', in *Everybody's Magazine*, June 1914.

He it was who originated the definition of a great editor as one who knows where hell is going to break loose next and how to get a reporter first on the scene — a definition attributed to various others, but belonging to him and reflecting some light upon his methods of thought.

Ibid.

Under the tigerish proprietor Bennett, with his fickleness and brutality, men were unjustly fired or demoted. Even the most deserving staff members were reduced in rank or in pay through young Bennett's erratic and contemptible conduct. Serving his evil system of ill-usage was as desperate as serving in the French Foreign Legion....

R. W. Stallman, *Stephen Crane*.

He liked the novel and the bizarre and he did not mind if people ridiculed him and the *Herald*; what he dreaded was their not talking about his papers.

Oswald Garrison Villard, 'The James Gordon Bennetts and their Newspaper', in *Nation*, 25 May 1918.

BENNY, JACK (Benjamin Kubelsky)

1894–1974 Comedian

I was born in Waukegan a long, long *long* time ago. As a matter of fact, our rabbi was an Indian ... he used a tomahawk ... I was eight days old ... what did I know?

On himself in Irving A. Fein, *Jack Benny*

I'm not able to sleep any more. You probably ask, 'Why can't he sleep? He has money, beauty, talent, vigor and many teeth' — but the possession of all these riches has nothing to do with it. I see Bund members dropping down my chimney, Comrades under my bed, Fifth Columnists in my closets, a bearded dwarf, called Surtax, doing a gavotte on my desk with a little lady known as Confiscation. I'm setting aside a small sum for poison which I'm secreting in a little sack under my mattress.

On himself in a letter to Arthur Sheekman, 12 June 1940.

I don't want to say that Jack Benny is cheap, but he's got short arms and carries his money low in his pockets.

Fred Allen in Irving A. Fein, *Jack Benny*

When Jack Benny plays the violin, it sounds as if the strings are still back in the cat.

Ibid.

Is Mr Benny tight. Well, a little snug, perhaps. ... If he can't take it with him, he ain't gonna go.

Eddie 'Rochester' Anderson in *ibid*.

You know, Jack's show did a lot for the image of black people in America. You ready? Before Jack came along, everybody thought blacks were only fit to be shoeshine boys and railroad porters. The Jack Benny program proved to America that they could also be chauffeurs, dishwashers, houseboys!

Demond Wilson, on *Dean Martin's Comedy Hour Celebrity Roast*, February 1974.

BENTHAM, JEREMY
1748—1832 Political Theorist

It seems to me, all deniers of Godhood, and all lip-believers of it, are bound to be Benthamites, if they have courage and honesty. Benthamism is an *eyeless* Heroism: the Human Species, like a hapless blinded Samson grinding in the Philistine Mill, clasps convulsively the pillars of its Mill; brings huge ruin down, but ultimately deliverance withal.
Thomas Carlyle, *On Heroes and Hero Worship.*

Hunt told me after of the prodigious power of Bentham's mind. 'He proposed,' said Hunt, 'a reform in the handle of battledores!' 'Did he?' said I with awful respect. 'He did,' said Hunt, 'taking in everything, you see, like the elephant's trunk, which lifts alike a pin or twelve hundredweight. Extraordinary mind!'
Benjamin Haydon, *Autobiography and Memoirs.*

His eye is quick and lively, but it glances not from object to object, but from thought to thought. He is evidently a man occupied with some train of fine and inward association. He regards people as no more than flies of a summer. He meditates the coming age. He hears and sees only what suits his purpose, or some 'foregone conclusion'; and looks out for facts and passing occurrences in order to put them into his logical machinery and grind them into the dust and powder of some subtle theory, as the miller looks out for grist to his mill.
William Hazlitt, *The Spirit of the Age.*

Mr. Bentham is not the first writer (by a great many) who has assumed the principle of UTILITY as the foundation of just laws, and of all moral and political reasoning: — his merit is, that he applied this principle more closely and literally; that he has brought all the objections and arguments, more distinctly labelled and ticketted, under this one head, and made a more constant and explicit reference to it at every step of his progress, than any other writer.
Ibid.

It is not that you can be said to see his favourite doctrine of Utility glittering everywhere through his system, like a vein of rich, shining ore (that is not the nature of the material) — but it might be plausibly objected that he had struck the whole mass of fancy, prejudice, passion, sense, whim, with his petrific, leaden mace, that he had 'bound volatile Hermes', and reduced the theory and practice of human life to a *caput mortuum* of reason, and dull, plodding, technical calculation.
Ibid.

The universal admission of Mr. Bentham's great principle would, as far as we can see, produce no other effect than those orators who, while waiting for a meaning, gain time (like bankers paying in sixpences during a run) by uttering words that mean nothing, would substitute 'the greatest happiness', or rather, as the longer phrase, 'the greatest happiness of the greatest number', for 'under existing circumstances', — 'now that I am on my legs', — and 'Mr. Speaker, I, for one, am free to say'. In fact principles of this sort resemble those forms which are sold by law-stationers, with blanks for the names of parties, and for special circumstances of every case — mere customary headings and conclusions which are equally at the command of the most honest and of the most unrighteous claimant.
T. B. Macaulay, *Miscellaneous Writings*: 'Westminster Reviewer's Defence of Mill'.

The arch-philistine Jeremy Bentham was the insipid, pedantic, leather-tongued oracle of the bourgeois intelligence of the Nineteenth Century.
Karl Marx, *Das Kapital.*

It is by the influence of the modes of thought with which his writings inoculated a considerable number of thinking men, that the yoke of authority has been broken, and innumerable opinions, formerly received on traditions as incontestable, are put upon their defence, and required to give account of themselves.
John Stuart Mill, *Dissertations*: 'Bentham'.

The father of English innovation, both in doctrines and in institutions, is Bentham: he is the great *subversive*, or, in the language of continental philosophers, the great *critical*, thinker of his age and country.
Ibid.

It is the introduction into the philosophy of human conduct, of this method of detail — of this practice of never reasoning about wholes till they have been resolved into their parts, nor about abstractions till they have been translated into realities — that constitutes the originality of Bentham in philosophy, and makes him the great reformer of the moral and political branch of it.
Ibid.

In many of the most natural and strongest feelings of human nature he had no sympathy; from many of its greater experiences he was altogether cut off; and the faculty by which one mind understands a mind different from itself, and throws itself into the feelings of that other mind, was denied him by his deficiency of Imagination.
Ibid.

No one need feel any delicacy in canvassing his opinions in my presence.

John Stuart Mill, in Caroline Fox, *Journals*, May 1840.

Bentham and the utilitarians interpret 'justice' as 'equality': when two men's interests clash, the right course is that which produces the greatest total of happiness, regardless of which of the two enjoys it, or how it is shared among them. If more is given to the better man than to the worse, that is because, in the long run, the general happiness is increased by rewarding virtue and punishing vice, not because of an ultimate ethical doctrine that the good deserve more than the bad.

Bertrand Russell, *History of Western Philosophy*.

Bentham's adoption of the principle of 'the greatest happiness of the greatest number' was no doubt due to democratic feeling, but it involved opposition to the doctrine of the rights of man, which he bluntly characterized as 'nonsense'.

Ibid.

To Bentham, determinism in psychology was important, because he wished to establish a code of laws — and more generally, a social system — which would automatically make men virtuous. His second principle, that of the greatest happiness, became necessary at this point in order to define 'virtue'.

Ibid.

There is an obvious lacuna in Bentham's system. If every man always pursues his own pleasure, how are we to secure that the legislator shall pursue the pleasure of mankind in general? Bentham's own instinctive benevolence (which his psychological theories prevented him from noticing) concealed the problem from him.

Ibid.

Apparently Bentham thought that human beings had but two desires, gain and pleasure, and he accepted those desires as the facts of our condition (he hated St. Paul) and tried to make of them a philosophy whose keystone was an eloquent defence of usury. He would have been at home in New York.

Gore Vidal, *Burr*.

See also James Mill, John Stuart Mill

BENTINCK, WILLIAM, EARL OF PORTLAND

1649–1709 Politician

At Paris he was shewn, in the royal palace, Le Brun's series of paintings, illustrative of Louis the Fourteenth's victories, and was asked whether William's were to be seen in his residence. 'No,' replied Bentinck, 'the monuments of my master's actions are to be seen everywhere but in his palace.'

Gilbert Burnet, *A History of My Own Time*.

The Earl of Sunderland had a very mean opinion of the Earl of Portland; and said, upon Keppel's being sent to him by the king upon some business, 'This young man brings and carries a message well; but Portland is so dull an animal that he can neither fetch nor carry.'

Speaker Arthur Onslow, note in the Oxford edition of Burnet, *A History of My Own Time*.

BENTLEY, RICHARD

1662–1742 Scholar

The special glory of England in classical scholarship.

G. N. Clark, *The Seventeenth Century*.

Once, and only once, I recollect his giving me a gentle rebuke for making a most outrageous noise in the room over his library and disturbing him in his studies; I had no apprehension of anger from him, and confidently answered that I could not help it, as I had been at battledore and shuttlecock with Master Gooch, the Bishop of Ely's son. 'And I have been at this sport with his father,' he replied, 'but thine has been the more amusing game; so there's no harm done.'

Richard Cumberland, *Memoirs*.

There is the story of the dinner party at Bishop Stillingfleet's, at which the guest, who had been sitting next Bentley, said to the Bishop after dinner, 'My Lord, that chaplain of yours is certainly a very extraordinary man. . . .' 'Yes,' said Stillingfleet, 'had he but the gift of humility, he would be the most extraordinary man in Europe.'

R. C. Jebb, *Bentley*, 1822.

While Bentley, long to wrangling schools confin'd,
And, but by books, acquainted with mankind,
Dares, in the fulness of the pedant's pride,
Rhyme, tho' no genius; though no judge, decide;
Yet he, prime pattern of the captious arts,
Out-tibbalding poor Tibbald, tops his parts,
Holds high the scourge o'er each fam'd author's
                                        head;
Nor are their graves a refuge for the dead.

David Mallet, *On Verbal Criticism*.

As many quit the streams that murm'ring fall
To lull the sons of Marg'ret and Clare-hall,

Where Bentley late tempestuous wont to sport
In troubled waters, but now sleeps in Port.
Before them march'd that awful Aristarch;
Plough'd was his front with many a deep Remark:
His Hat, which never vail'd to human pride,
Walker with rev'rence took, and laid aside.
Low bow'd the rest: He, kingly, did but nod,
So upright Quakers please both Man and God.
Mistress! dismiss that rabble from your throne:
Avaunt — is Aristarchus yet unknown?
Thy mighty Scholiast, whose unweary'd pains
Made Horace dull, and humbled Milton's strains.
    Alexander Pope, *The Dunciad*, Book IV.

Tall, but without Shape and Comeliness; Large, but without strength or Proportion. His Armour was patch'd up of a thousand incoherent Pieces; and the Sound of it, as he march'd, was loud and dry, like that made by the Fall of a Sheet of Lead, which an *Etesian* Wind blows suddenly down from the Roof of some Steeple. His Helmet was of old rusty Iron, but the Vizard was Brass, which tainted by his Breath, corrupted into Copperas, nor wanted Gall from the same Fountain; so that whenever provoked by Anger or Labour, an atramentous Quality, of most malignant Nature, was seen to distil from his Lips.
    Jonathan Swift, *Battle of the Books*.

BENTON, THOMAS HART

1792—1858 Politician

Mr. President, sir . . . I never quarrel, sir. But sometimes I fight, sir; and whenever I fight, sir, a funeral follows, sir.
    On himself, in John F. Kennedy, *Profiles in Courage.*

A house lamb and a street lion.
    On himself, in William M. Meigs, *The Life of Thomas Hart Benton.*

They'll elect him, they'll elect him, and then if they
                       can,
They'll a President make of 'that dangerous man.'
    Anon., in *Argus*, 1838, on Benton's re-election to the Senate, in *ibid.*

A caricature likeness of Louis Philippe (the 'Bourgeois' King of France) — the same rotundity, the same pear-shaped head. . . . His lower features are drilled into imperturbable suavity, while the eye, that undrillable tale-teller, twinkles of inward slyness.
    Anon., in William Nisbet Chambers, *Old Bullion Benton: Senator from the New West.*

Colonel Benton has read a good deal; but his mind is like a baggage wagon, full of all kinds of lumber. . . . His imagination is a sort of Cyclops' great sledge hammer, heavy, weighty, crushing, iron-wrought.
    Ibid.

With a readiness that was often surprising, he could quote from a Roman Law or a Greek Philosopher, from Virgil's Georgics, The Arabian Nights, Herodotus or Sancho Panza, from the Sacred Carpets, the German Reformers or Adam Smith, from Fénelon or Hudibras, from the financial reports of Necca or the doings of the Council of Trent, from the debates on the adoption of the Constitution or the intrigues of the Kitchen Cabinet or from some forgotten speech of a deceased member of Congress.
    Anon., Obituary, in L. A. Harris, *The Fine Art of Political Wit.*

. . . the doughty knight of the stuffed cravat.
    John Quincy Adams, in Alfred Steinberg, *The First Ten.*

. . . a liar of magnitude.
    John Quincy Adams, in L. Falkner, *The President Who Wouldn't Retire.*

That he was the inferior to Mr. Webster as a close, logical reasoner; that he was not the equal of Mr. Clay as an orator; and that Mr. Calhoun surpassed him in the power and condensation of language, all must admit. But in depth of mind, originality of thought, and power to conceive and execute any great measure of public welfare, he was the equal of either, and in some respects the superior of all.
    W. V. N. Bay, *The Bench and Bar of Missouri.*

If he ever forgot or gave an intended injury, only his creator knew it.
    Mr Birch, in William M. Meigs, *The Life of Thomas Hart Benton.*

. . . the greatest of all humbugs, and could make more out of nothing than any other man in the world. He ought to have gone about all his life with quack doctors, and written puffs for their medicines. Had he done so, he might have made a fortune.
    John C. Calhoun, in Charles Sellers, *James K. Polk — Continentalist, 1834—46.*

. . . in physique, temper and ferocity he was a Roman gladiator, who somehow had become imbedded in the nineteenth century.
    Oliver Dyer, *Great Senators of the United States Forty Years Ago.*

... a temporary people's man, remarkable chiefly for his pomposity — swelling amidst his piles of papers and books, [looked] like a being designed by nature to be a good-humored barber (!) but forced by fate to make himself into a mock-heroic senator.

Harriet Martineau, in William Nisbet Chambers, *Old Bullion Benton: Senator from the New West.*

... as a popular orator, he was 'a rough-rider', and moved his audiences by the fervency and power of argument, illustration, and invective. He wielded the force of a cyclone; was a 'steam-engine in breeches'; never indulged in poetical quotations, anecdotes, or flights of fancy.

Colonel William T. Switzler, in William M. Meigs, *The Life of Thomas Hart Benton.*

BENTON, THOMAS HART
1889—1975 Artist

I wallowed in every cockeyed ism that came along, and it took me ten years to get all that modernist dirt out of my system. And my genius notions were dispelled in a hurry. The Quarter was overrun with geniuses — one supergenius and two embryoes with money from home to print a manifesto, and a new school was born. I was no good anywhere. In the company of such hardened internationalists as George Grosz, Wyndham Lewis, Epstein, Rivera, and that Stein woman, I was merely a roughneck with a talent for fighting, perhaps, but not for painting — as it was cultivated in Paris.

On himself, in Thomas Craven, *Thomas Hart Benton.*

In late years I have gained a kind of freedom. I don't stew around any more. I just go to work and do my stuff. I don't know, of course, the ultimate value of what I do. I don't care much about it. But I have a sort of inner conviction that for all the possible limitations of my mind and the distorting effects of my processes, for the contradicting struggles and failures I have gone through with, I have come to something that is in the image of America and the American people of my time. This conviction is in me pretty deeply.

I do not pretend to represent what could be called typical of America. I have never experienced anything that I could really say was typical of this country. The typical is a generality which does not interest me. My American image is made up of what I have come across, of what was 'there' in the time of my experience — no more, no less. My historical murals, because of this, are full of anachronisms. I paint the past through my own life experiences. I

feel that an anachronism with life is better than any academically correct historical rehash. . . .

Expressing the release of soul that I have come to feel, I often hum to myself when I work. I nearly always hum the same tune. It's one of these hill-billy tunes called 'Prisoner for Life.'

Ibid.

I do not characterize my art by any 'ism'. I have been called an advocate of regionalism. This is a word, however, without much meaning, a typical art critic's refuge which saves him (or her) the bother of thinking. The subject matter of my art has dealt with the whole of American culture, historical as well as actual. In representing the actual culture it has run from coast to coast, a pretty big region. Technically and psychologically its roots reach into all the aesthetic conceptions of the historical world, from ancient Egypt and India through Greece, Renaissance Italy and French Impressionism to those present environmental experiences which now do most to stimulate it. I would like to think of my art as representing Americanism. Maybe it does. Those psychophantic lovers of only that which is imported dislike it enough to make me hopeful.

On himself, *Thomas Benton Answers Questions.*

During the 1930s Thomas Hart Benton held a commanding and conspicuous position in American art. Controversial in the extreme, both as an artist and as a social commentator, he generated the degree of publicity associated with such other artists as Picasso, Dali, and Rivera in that highly polemic decade. To some he was one of the best contemporary painters, savior (and instigator) of a truly American stream of art. To others he was a 'bully' and a 'loudmouth,' vehement and highly vocal in his opinions, prolific and notably successful in his art, but limited or even of negative value from an aesthetic point of view. In either case the intensity of feeling he aroused was consistent. Few observers of the fortunes of American art were neutral toward him.

Matthew Baigell, *Thomas Hart Benton.*

A little, swarthy and cocky man. Benton resembles a well-nourished Sicilian bootblack rather than a midwest oldstock American. When I first got acquainted with him, I called upon him frequently, apparently always in time to help him carry about the studio his 400 lb. murals which he was painting for the New School of Social Research. (I posed for the negro with the drill and learned egg-tempera as a reward.) The time was summer and it was amusing to watch Benton, muscular in his underwear, sit low in an armchair, survey the mural, suddenly load his brush with a lot of tempera goo, crouch like a cat, spring across the room in a flying tackle, scrub the brush around in great circles, catch his breath, and then resume his place in the chair.

Benton is a colorful, scrappy, uncouth person, with a demonic energy and a strong tendency to publicize himself. All this is to his credit. If he were to hibernate or vegetate or dress like Fred Astaire, he would be hamstrung undoubtedly. Let him have his flash-bulbs, his harmonicas, his windmills, his mules, his little Pickaninnies and Persephones, it's all part of his constitution.

Reginald Marsh, 'Thomas Benton', *Demcourier*.

BERENSON, BERNARD

1865–1959 Art Historian

Life has taught me that it is not for our faults that we are disliked and even hated but for our qualities.

On himself, *The Passionate Sightseer*, from the diaries, 1957.

He was supposed to have invented a trick by which one could tell infallibly the authorship of any Italian painting, and he made an enemy of every owner of a picture he would not ascribe to Raphael, Giorgione, Tintoretto or Titian. He ranked with astrologers, palmists and fortune-tellers, while he was a pet of rich collectors. . . .

Van Wyck Brooks, *The Confident Years: 1885–1915*.

If we take Mr Berenson seriously we are committing the sin of the too logical German.

Howard Hannay, 'Mr Berenson's Theory of Art', in *London Mercury*, April 1921.

. . . a little tiny man, more of a genial fox than roaring lion, spruce and grey, so formally and neatly dressed that he looked like a miniature banker in Wall Street, though his voice was gentler.

Eric Linklater, *The Art of Adventure*.

So the aesthetic fox goes to work as an adventurer. His nose is well taught, he has the true critic's sense of quality. His observation is acute, his deduction logical. He has scholarship, perception, a good memory, and the indispensable training in method.

Ibid.

Little wonder that the last years of his life had become so precious to him that, as he said, he would willingly stand at 'street corners hat in hand begging passers-by to drop their unused minutes into it.'

John Walker, Introduction to Hanna Kiel ed., *The Bernard Berenson Treasury*.

BERESFORD, WILLIAM CARR

1768–1854 General

Wellington paid the greatest tribute to him when he declared that if he were removed by death or illness he would recommend Beresford to succeed him, not because he was a great general, but because he alone could 'feed an army'.

Henry Morse Stephens, in the *Dictionary of National Biography*.

BERKELEY, GEORGE, BISHOP

1685–1753 Philosopher

I observed that though we are satisfied his doctrine is not true, it is impossible to refute it. I never shall forget the alacrity with which Johnson answered, striking his foot with mighty force against a large stone, till he rebounded from it, 'I refute it *thus*.'

James Boswell, *Life of Johnson*.

When Bishop Berkeley said 'there was no matter',
    And proved it — 'twas no matter what he said:
They say his system 'tis in vain to batter,
    Too subtle for the airiest human head;
And yet who can believe it? I would shatter
    Gladly all matters down to stone or lead,
Or adamant, to find the world a spirit,
And wear my head, denying that I wear it.

What a sublime discovery 'twas to make the
    Universe universal egotism,
That's all ideal — *all ourselves*!. . . .
    Lord Byron, *Don Juan*, canto xi.

There was a young man who said, 'God
Must think it exceedingly odd
    If he finds that this tree
    Continues to be
When there's no one about in the Quad.'
    Ronald Knox, *Limerick*.

Dear Sir:
    Your astonishment's odd:
I am always about in the quad.
    And that's why the tree
    Will continue to be,
Since observed by,
    Yours faithfully,
      GOD.
    Anon., Rejoinder.

Manners with Candour are to *Benson* giv'n,
To Berkeley, ev'ry Virtue under Heav'n.
    Alexander Pope, *Epilogue to the Satires*, Dialogue II.

And God-appointed Berkely that proved all things a
                                          dream,
That this pragmatical, preposterous pig of a world,
                                          its farrow
     that so solid seem,
Must vanish on the instant if the mind but change
                                          its theme.
     William Butler Yeats, *Blood and the Moon.*

BESSBOROUGH, LADY (HENRIETTA FRANCES PONSONBY)

1761–1821 Society Woman

. . . good-natured tumultuous Lady Bessborough.
     Lady Granville, Letter to Lady Morpeth,
     17 August 1820.

BETHUNE, MARY MCLEOD

1875–1955 Educator, Civil Rights Advocate

I believe, first of all, in God, and next to all, in
Mary McLeod Bethune.
     On herself, in Emma Gelders Steine, *Mary
     McLeod Bethune.*

I don't mind being different. I don't want to be
Jim-Crowed to a back seat because I'm black and
I don't want to be ushered to a front seat because
I'm not white so they can 'palaver' over me.
     Ibid.

She had been as relentless as a frail plant pushing
aside a heavy stone. And she had impressed upon
the lives of countless young the stamp of her
own indomitable character. She was a mighty
mother to the youth of the world.
     Rackham Holt, *Mary McLeod Bethune.*

. . . this remarkable woman who stayed in the
South to create a school on whose campus no
Jim Crow was permitted. . . . It took gall and guts
to defy law and custom, and she had plenty of
both.
     Milton Meltzer, *Langston Hughes.*

She had the kind of eloquence that flowed from
strength of conviction. Her earnestness was like a
magnet that picked up the hearts as well as the
minds of her listeners. Her language was plain with a
Biblical plainness. In her deep contralto voice, it
sounded like poetry.
     Emma Gelders Steine, *Mary McLeod Bethune.*

Through the intonations of her speech, she could
build a simple statement into a dramatic charge
that brought forth in the minds of her listeners all
the calls ever uttered in the tradition of leadership
from Moses to modern times.
     Henry Winslow, in *ibid.*

BETTERTON, THOMAS

1635–1710 Actor, Dramatist

For who can hold to see the Foppish Town
Admire so bad a Wretch as Betterton?
Is't for his Legs, his Shoulders or his Face,
His formal Stiffness, or his awkward Grace,
A Shop for Him had been the fittest place?
But Brawn Tom the Playhouse needs must chuse
The Villians Refuge, and Whores Rendezvouse:
Where being Chief, each playing Drab to swive,
He takes it as his chief prerogative.
     Anon., *Satyr on the Players, circa* 1684.

I have lately been told by a gentleman who has
frequently seen Mr *Betterton* perform this part of
Hamlet, that he has observ'd his Countenance
(which was naturally ruddy and sanguine) in this
scene of the fourth act where his Father's Ghost
appears, thro' the violent and sudden Emotions of
Amazement and Horror, turn instantly on the
Sight of his Father's Spirit, as pale as his Neckcloth,
when every Article of his Body seem'd to be
affected with a tremor inexpressible; so that, had
his Father's Ghost actually risen before him, he
could not have been seized with more real agonies;
and this was felt so strongly by the audience, that
the blood seem'd to shudder in their veins likewise,
and they in some Measure partook of the Astonishment and Horror, with which they saw this excellent
Actor affected.
     Anon., in *Laureat,* 1740.

When I acted the Ghost with Betterton, instead of
my awing him, he terrified me. But divinity hung
round that man.
     Barton Booth, in Thomas Davies, *Dramatic
     Miscellanies.*

Betterton had so just a sense of what was true or
false Applause, that I have heard him say, he never
thought any kind of it equal to an attentive Silence;
that there were many ways of deceiving the Audience
into a loud one; but to keep them husht and quiet
was an Applause which only Truth and Merit could
arrive at: of which Art there never was an equal
Master to himself. From these various Excellencies,
he had so full a possession of the Esteem and
Regard of his Auditors, that upon his Entrance into

every Scene, he seem'd to seize upon the Eyes and Ears of the giddy and inadvertent! To have talk'd or look'd another way would then have been thought Insensibility or Ignorance. In all his Soliloquies of Moment, the strong Intelligence of his Attitude and Aspect drew you into such an impatient Gaze, and eager Expectation, that you almost imbib'd the Sentiment with your Eye before the Ear could reach it.

Colley Cibber, *Apology for the Life of Colley Cibber.*

Archbishop Tillotson was very well acquainted with Betterton, and continued that acquaintance, even after he was in that high station. One day, when Betterton came to see him at Lambeth, that prelate asked him how it came about that after he had made the most moving discourse that he could, was touched deeply with it himself, and spoke it as feelingly as he was able, yet he could never move people in the Church near so much as the other did on stage? 'That,' says Betterton, 'I think is easy to be accounted for: 'tis because you are only *telling* them a story, and I am *showing* them facts.'

Joseph Spence, *Anecdotes.*

Had you been to Night at the Playhouse, you had seen the force of action in Perfection: Your admired Mr *Betterton* behaved himself so well, that, tho' now about Seventy, he acted Youth; and by the prevalent Power of proper Manner, Gesture, and Voice, appear'd through the whole *Drama* a young Man of great Expectation, Vivacity, and Enterprize. The Soliloquy where he began the celebrated Sentence of, *To be, or not to Be*! The Expostulation where he explains with his Mother in her closet, the noble Ardour, after seeing his Father's Ghost, and his generous Distress for the Death of *Ophelia*, are each of them Circumstances which dwell strongly on the Minds of the Audience, and would certainly affect their Behaviour on any parallel Occasions in their own Lives.

Tatler, 22 September 1709.

BETTY, WILLIAM HENRY WEST

1791—1874 Actor

Betty is performing here, I fear, very ill, his figure is that of a hippopotamus, his face like the bull and *mouth* on the pannels of a heavy coach, his arms are fins fattened out of shape, his voice the gargling of an alderman with the quinsy, and his acting altogether ought to be natural, for it certainly is like nothing that *Art* has ever yet exhibited on the stage.

Lord Byron, Letter to Lady Melbourne, September 1812.

BEVAN, ANEURIN

1897—1960 Politician

Bevan Done and lost his friends — one-quarter Bloody Revolution one-quarter Pacifist one-half Same policy as Tories but with jobs.

Lord Beaverbrook, April 1958, in A. J. P. Taylor, *Beaverbrook.*

He was like a fire in a room on a cold winter's day.

Constance Cummings, in Michael Foot, *Aneurin Bevan.*

The outrageous ranter started so softly; his wit was delicate; he dealt in paradox and satire. His sentences were uttered with the perfect, if unconscious, timing of an actor. He seemed to wrestle with the problem of his audience, and, as the argument mounted in intensity, the language became direct and simple. As he spoke, a glowing clarity pierced the clouds and the story ended in a blaze of sunshine. ... He was always primarily a debater; his perorations might rise to a tremendous emotional climax, but the argument always came from the intellect.

Michael Foot, *Aneurin Bevan.*

Nye was born old and died young.

Jennie Lee, in *ibid.*

He enjoys prophesying the imminent fall of the capitalist system, and is prepared to play a part, any part, in its burial, except that of mute.

Harold Macmillan, Addressing the House of Commons, 1934.

Goebbels, though not religious, must thank Heaven
For dropping in his lap Aneurin Bevan;
And, doubtless, this pious mood invokes
An equal blessing on the trusty Stokes.
How well each does his work as a belittler
Of Germany's arch-enemy! Heil Hitler.

A. A. Milne, on Bevan's opposition to Churchill, in the *News Chronicle,* Autumn 1942.

Nye Bevan had a precise and concrete response to precise and concrete stimuli. But he joined this to a comprehensive, abstract and ideological political sensibility. . . . There seemed deep in him the feeling that any society founded on private ownership, no matter how diversified and agreeable in its outward manifestations, was essentially wicked, and that any society founded on public ownership, no matter how cruel and arbitrary its outward manifestations, was potentially good. In practice, this feeling was always being challenged and defeated by hard facts, which as a realistic and creative politician, he was prepared to recognize. But in the late evening ideology would control his conversation and colour his attitude.

Arthur Schlesinger, Jr, *Attitudes Towards America*, 1964.

BEVIN, ERNEST

1881–1951 Statesman

... When I took this job on I knew it wouldn't be a daisy. In fact, no Foreign Secretary has had to keep so many plates in the air at the same time. But what I said to my colleagues at the time was this: 'I'll take on the job. But don't expect results before three years.' Now it's patience you want in this sort of thing. I'm not going to throw my weight about 'ere in Paris. I'm just going to sit sturdy 'ere and 'elp.

On himself, at the Paris Peace Conference, 1946, in Harold Nicolson, Diary.

A turn-up in a million.

On himself, in *Dictionary of National Biography*.

A speech from Ernest Bevin on a major occasion had all the horrific fascination of a public execution. If the mind was left immune, eyes and ears and emotions were riveted.

Michael Foot, *Aneurin Bevan*.

... His public character had a curious duality. Capable of great suppleness in negotiation and sensitive to the mutual interests which made industrial co-operation desirable, he presented in public an image which was dogmatic, over-bearing, uncompromising, and egotistical. In negotiation he was a realist who understood the need for compromise. On the public platform he permitted himself every licence of venom, innuendo, and the grossest partiality.

Lord Francis-Williams, in the *Dictionary of National Biography*.

The familiar saying that Bevin always treated the Soviet Union as if it were a breakaway faction of the Transport and General Workers' Union. ...

Kingsley Martin, *Harold Laski*.

He objected to ideas only when others had them.

A. J. P. Taylor, *English History 1914–1945*.

Bevin thought he was Palmerston wearing Keir Hardie's cloth cap, whereas he was really the Foreign Office's Charlie McCarthy.

Konni Zilliacus, in Kingsley Martin, *Harold Laski*.

BEWICK, THOMAS

1753–1828 Wood Engraver, Author, Naturalist

Peace to Bewick; not a great man at all; but a very true of his sort, a well completed and a very *enviable* — living there in communion with the skies and woods and brooks, not here in ditto with the London Fogs, the roaring witchmongeries, and rail-way yellings and howlings.

Thomas Carlyle, Letter to John Ruskin, 20 December 1865.

The nobles of his day left him to draw the frogs, and pigs, and sparrows — of his day, which seemed to him, in his solitude, the best types of its Nobility. No sight or thought of beautiful things was ever granted him; — no heroic creature, goddess-born — how much less any native Deity — ever shone upon him. To his utterly English mind, the straw of the sty, and its tenantry, were abiding truth; — the cloud of Olympus, and its tenantry, a child's dream. He could draw a pig, but not an Aphrodite.

John Ruskin, *Ariadne Florentina*.

Pre-eminently a vulgar or boorish person, though of splendid honour and genius; his vulgarity shows in nothing so much as in the poverty of the details he has collected, with the best intentions, and the shrewdest sense, for English ornithology. His imagination is not cultivated enough to enable him to choose, or arrange.

John Ruskin, *Love's Meinie*.

See also J. M. W. Turner

BIERCE, AMBROSE GWINETT

1842–1914? Journalist, Author

I have the supremest contempt for my books — as books. As a journalist I believe I am unapproachable in my line; as an author, a slouch!

On himself, in Richard O'Connor, *Ambrose Bierce*.

I know how to write a story for magazine readers for whom literature is too good, but I will not do so, so long as stealing is more honorable.

Ibid.

Never obliged to match his wits with first-rate minds, he rode his hobbies freely and indulged his whims, dogmatizing at his ease with a too facile cynicism that overexpressed his somewhat acrid spirit.

Van Wyck Brooks, *The Confident Years: 1885–1915*.

Born in a log cabin, he defied [Horatio] Alger's law and did not become President.

Clifton Fadiman, *The Selected Writings of Clifton Fadiman: Portrait of a Misanthrope.*

He made a business of cracking skulls and ideas. Product of three disillusioning experiences, pioneer life, war, and journalistic uproars, he ended up with almost nothing that he could regard as sacred. He was an all-inclusive cynic.

C. Hartley Grattan, *Bitter Bierce.*

He was close on to six feet tall, of military bearing, and of such extraordinary vitality that young ladies asserted they could feel him ten feet away.

Ibid.

'God Almighty' Bierce they called him; what he did not find to his liking, he sought to change with regard for no one or no institution. While he lacked the satirical genius of a Pope or a Dryden, he was one American satirist who did not sell out to the Gilded Age.

Carlin T. Kindilien, *American Poetry in the Eighteen Nineties.*

He was a survivor of the Enlightenment sickened with the hopelessness which infected many writers as the nineteenth century moved toward its close. He saw life as patternless, spun by a tragic irony, woven by a mocking satisfaction.

Grant C. Knight, *The Critical Period in American Literature.*

He repeated himself endlessly, for his harp had a single string; but in the history of his *genre* Ambrose Bierce must undoubtedly have a small but secure place.

Stanley J. Kunitz and Howard Haycraft eds, *American Authors 1600–1900.*

Bierce would bury his best friend with a sigh of relief, and express satisfaction that he was done with him.

Jack London, in Paul Fatout, *Ambrose Bierce, The Devil's Lexicographer.*

He was a fierce and stern moralist living in what he believed to be an age of moral looseness. For three decades he exposed, with apparently perverse relish, the rottenness of American life, its political corruption, its moral debasement, its economic chicanery.

Jay Martin, *Harvest of Change, American Literature 1865–1914.*

For all our professed delight in and capacity for jocosity, we have produced so far but one genuine wit — Ambrose Bierce — and, save to a small circle, he remains unknown today.

H. L. Mencken, in Richard O'Connor, *Ambrose Bierce.*

But there was no more discretion in Bierce than you will find in a runaway locomotive.

H. L. Mencken, 'Ambrose Bierce', in *The American Scene*, selected and edited by Huntington Cairns.

More than war wounds, more than asthma contracted in graveyards, more than bitterness engendered by domestic strife, more than disillusionment with an imperfect world, frontier journalism, through its unusual freedom, created the satirist who was later to be hailed as its anathema.

Franklin Walker, *San Francisco's Literary Frontier.*

BILLINGTON, ELIZABETH

1768–1818 Singer

Her face was beautiful and expressive, her figure graceful; her voice possessed a peculiar sweetness of tone, and was of great extent, but wanted what Dr Burney would call *calibre.* The most scientific songs she executed with bewitching taste and affecting pathos; and though her voice was not overpowerful, it possessed great variety, and a most perfect shake.

Anon., *The Manager's Note-Book*, 1837–8.

When Haydn, the composer, called on Sir J. Reynolds, as he was engaged in painting the portrait of Mrs Billington, 'I like the portrait,' said Haydn, 'much; but you have painted Billington listening to the angels; you should rather have made the angels listening to her.'

George Raymond, *Memoirs of R. W. Elliston.*

Her voice was powerful, and resembled the tone of a clarionet.

W. Clark Russell, *Representative Actors.*

BILLY THE KID (WILLIAM H. BONNEY)

1859–81 Desperado

Billy the Kid took sides with the people of the country to fight for our property and our lives. He stood with us to the end, brave and reliable. He never pushed in his advice or opinions, but he had a wonderful presence of mind; the tighter the place the more he showed his cool nerve and quick brain.

... That he ever killed as many men as he is given credit for, or ever killed for money is absurd.

> Frank Coe, in Frazier Hunt, *The Tragic Days of Billy the Kid.*

All who ever knew Billy will testify that his polite, cordial and gentlemanly bearing invited confidence and promised protection — the first of which he never betrayed and the latter he was never known to withhold. Those who knew him best will tell you that in his most savage and dangerous moods his face always wore a smile. He eat [sic] and laughed, drank and laughed, rode and laughed, talked and laughed, fought and laughed, and killed and laughed.

> Pat F. Garrett, *The Authentic Life of Billy the Kid.*

BINGHAM, GEORGE CALEB

1811–79 Painter

I have frequently been told, in conversation with persons who have obtained their ideas of Art from books, that an artist should give to his productions something more than nature presents to the eye. That in painting a portrait for instance, he should not be satisfied with giving a true delineation of the form and features of his subject, with all the lines of his face which mark his individuality, but in addition to these should impart to his work the *soul* of his sitter. I cannot but think that this is exacting from an artist that which rather transcends the limits of his powers, great as they may be.

> On himself, Lecture, 1879, *Art, the Ideal of Art, and the Utility of Art.*

By becoming to some extent an itinerant, and painting upon moderate terms, he found himself full of business, and though in total darkness in regard to color, his drawing generally gave so strong a likeness that many of his unsophisticated patrons looked upon his productions as the perfection of the 'divine art.' He astonished them, too, by his facility of execution, frequently commencing and finishing a portrait in the same day. It is said that he painted, in this manner, twenty-five in the course of thirty days.

> Anon., in *Columbia Statesman*, 31 August 1849.

Bingham lived in a day when it was the picture rather than the way it was made which occupied the amateur's attention. No elaborate pseudo-technical verbiage was erected between his pictures and his audience. If he painted a tree, it was a tree and not a sign pointing to some obscure world of special values with which this cult or that was trying to prove its superior sensibility. Painting was plainer and more matter of fact in Bingham's days. There were no painters' painters nor was one supposed to need some special training or some occult capacity to determine whether or not one liked an artist's work. A picture was not directed to coteries of previous experts but to ordinary people who might buy it and put it in their homes. This was healthy and as it should be and, though Bingham lived in a world which was still close to the wilderness and faced hard times now and then, he had a public and was a successful artist. He painted for a living world and painted what that world could understand — its own life.

> Thomas Hart Benton, Preface to Albert Christ-Janer, *George Caleb Bingham of Missouri.*

To Bingham's way of thinking, it always became necessary to leave the secluded life. He was an Aristotelian: he believed that there are a thousand ways to be wrong, but only one way to be right.

> Albert Christ-Janer, *ibid.*

Inevitable in the early maturing strength of Bingham were traits of impatient bluntness which asserted themselves when he became provoked by differences of opinion. As a dogma lies at the basis of all action, so action is virile in exact proportion to the deep-seatedness of the dogma; as action is the result of belief, so the belief is revealed in the intensity of the act. With Bingham there was no half truth; he believed only in truth. His acts, then, were sometimes violent, his pen frequently vitriolic and his painting, at least once, polemic.

> *Ibid.*

In his personal appearance, Bingham was not a striking figure. Small of stature, five feet eight inches in height, and weighing never more than one hundred and fifty pounds, of delicate constitution always, there was yet a dynamic quality in the man that distinguished him in any crowd. I think this quality sprang from the fact that he was the very embodiment of moral and physical courage, *le chevalier sans peur et sans reproche.*

> C. B. Rollins, 'Some Recollections of George Caleb Bingham', *Missouri Historical Review*, July 1926.

BIRD, ROBERT MONTGOMERY

1806–54 Playwright, Author

I am entirely of too discursive and diffuse a turn to shine in a nutshell ... I have always been more disposed to count by *Acts* and *Chapters*, than by lines and paragraphs.

> On himself, in Curtis Dahl, *Robert Montgomery Bird.*

He had so many irons in the fire that he was never able to forge any single one into a weapon with which to conquer his world.
　Curtis Dahl, *ibid.*

BIRKENHEAD, EARL OF (FREDERICK EDWIN SMITH)

1872–1930 Statesman

The trouble with Lord Birkenhead is that he is so un-Christlike.
　Margot Asquith, in C. M. Bowra, *Memories.*

Your father fought hard and clean. He never concealed that he wanted the prizes of life. When they came to him he took them with dignity and without any illusions about their value. When hard knocks came he met them with great high spirits. He bore no man a grudge, and he never struck a foul blow.
　Lord Beaverbrook, Letter to the second Lord Birkenhead, 21 September 1934.

This dark Hermes.
　Henry Channon, Diary, 1 May 1934.

... a man with the vision of an eagle but with a blind spot in his eye.
　Andrew Bonar Law, 1917, in A. J. P. Taylor, *Beaverbrook.*

BLACK HAWK

1767–1838 War Chief of the Sauk Nation

I am now an obscure member of a nation, that formerly honored and respected my opinions. The path to glory is rough, and many gloomy hours obscure it. May the Great Spirit shed light on yours — and that you may never experience the humility that the power of the American government has reduced me to, is the wish of him, who, in his native forests, was once as proud and bold as yourself.
　On himself (in 1833 to General H. Atkinson, who defeated him), in T. C. McLuhan, *Touch The Earth.*

I fought hard. But your guns were well aimed. The bullets flew like birds in the air, and whizzed by our ears like the wind through the trees. My warriors fell around me; it began to look dismal. I saw my evil day at hand. The sun rose dim on us in the morning, and at night it sank in a dark cloud, and looked like a ball of fire. That was the last sun that shone on Black Hawk. His heart is dead, and no longer beats quick in his bosom. He is now a prisoner to the white men; they will do with him as they wish. But he can stand torture and is not afraid of death. He is no coward. Black Hawk is an Indian.
　On himself (upon his surrender in 1832), in *ibid.*

I —— am —— a man —— and you —— are —— another.
　On himself (after his surrender upon meeting President Andrew Jackson), in Carl Sandburg, *Abraham Lincoln, The Prairie Years.*

BLACK, HUGO LA FAYETTE

1886--1971 Jurist

When I was forty my doctor advised me that a man in his forties shouldn't play tennis. I heeded his advice carefully and could hardly wait until I reached 50 to start again.
　On himself, in *Think*, February 1963.

BLACK, JOSEPH

1728–79 Scientist

In one department of his lecture he exceeded any I have ever known, the neatness and unvarying success with which all the manipulations of his experiments were performed. His correct eye and steady hand contributed to the one; his admirable precautions, foreseeing and providing for every emergency, secured the other. I have seen him pour boiling water or boiling acid from a vessel that had no spout into a tube, holding it at such a distance as made the stream's diameter small, and so vertical that not a drop was spilt. ... The long table on which the different processes had been carried out was as clean at the end of the lecture as it had been before the apparatus was planted upon it. Not a drop of liquid, not a grain of dust remained.
　Henry, Lord Brougham, *Lives of Men of Letters and Science who flourished in the Time of George III.*

He has less nonsense in his head than any man living.
　Adam Smith, in Henry, Lord Brougham, *Lives of Men of Letters and Science who flourished in the Time of George III.*

BLACKETT, PATRICK MAYNARD STUART, BARON

1897–1975 Scientist

The year 1932 was the most spectacular year in the history of science. Living in Cambridge, one could not help picking up the human, as well as the intellectual, excitement in the air. James Chadwick, grey-faced after a fortnight of work with three hours' sleep a night, telling the Kapitsa Club (to which any young man was so proud to belong) how he had discovered the neutron; P. M. S. Blackett, the most handsome of men, not quite so authoritative as usual, because it seemed too good to be true, showing plates which demonstrated the existence of the positive electron; John Cockcroft, normally about as much given to emotional display as the Duke of Wellington, skimming down King's Parade and saying to anyone whose face he recognized: 'We've split the atom! We've split the atom!'
> C. P. Snow, *Variety of Men.*

BLACKMORE, SIR RICHARD

1653–1729 Poet

See who ne'er was nor will be half-read!
Who first sung Arthur, then sung Alfred;
Praised great Eliza in God's anger,
Till all true Englishmen cried, 'Hang her!' . . .
Maul'd human wit in one thick satire;
Next in three books sunk human nature:
Undid Creation at a jerk,
And of Redemption made damn'd work.
Then took his Muse at once, and dipt her
Full in the middle of the Scripture.
> John Gay, *Verses to be Placed Under the Picture of England's Arch-Poet.*

He said, the criticks had done too much honour to Sir Richard Blackmore, by writing so much against him.
> Samuel Johnson, in James Boswell, *Life of Johnson.*

Remains a difficulty still,
To purchase fame by writing ill.
From Flecknoe down to Howard's time
How few have reached the low sublime!
For when our high-born Howard died,
Blackmore alone his place supplied.
> Jonathan Swift, *Poetry: A Rhapsody.*

BLACKSTONE, SIR WILLIAM

1723–80 Jurist

Any lawyer who writes so clearly as to be intelligible

. . . is an enemy to his profession.
> Francis Hargrave, in Croake James, *Curiosities of Law and Lawyers.*

This legal classic is the poetry of the law, just as Pope is logic in poetry.
> Judge John Marshall, in Albert J. Beveridge, *Life of John Marshall.*

BLAINE, JAMES GILLESPIE

1830–93 Statesman

Blaine! Blaine! J. G. Blaine
Continental Liar from the State of Maine.
> Anon., Campaign slogan, 1884 election, in D. H. Elletson, *Roosevelt and Wilson: A Comparative Study.*

Blaine! Blaine The Man from Maine
We've had him once, we'll have him again.
> *Ibid.*

Thanks for heart and voice and vote,
> Blaine for Maine!

Thanks for Freedom's flag afloat,
> Once again!

Thanks for treason quick to threaten,
Boldly met, and balked and beaten;
Thanks for heart and voice and brain,
> Blaine of Maine!
> Anon., in D. S. Muzzey, *James G. Blaine.*

Blaine was the only man ever nominated to the Presidency in spite of the fact that the public knew perfectly well he was dishonest. Garfield was thought to have been dishonest, but only in the mildest sort of way; Blaine was known to have been dishonest, and on a big scale.
> Herbert Agar, *The People's Choice, from Washington to Harding: A Study in Democracy.*

For ways that are dark
And tricks that are vain,
I name Speaker Blaine,
And that I dare maintain.
> Benjamin F. Butler, in A. K. Adams, *The Home Book of Humorous Quotations.*

On the whole he is the completest gladiator in debate I know of.
> James Abram Garfield, in T. C. Smith, *The Life and Letters of J. A. Garfield*, vol. 2.

Wallowing in corruption like a rhinoceros in an African pool.
> E. L. Godkin, in Allen Churchill, *The Roosevelts.*

Like an armed warrior, like a plumed knight, James G. Blaine marched down the halls of the American Congress and threw his shining lance full and fair against the brazen foreheads of the defamers of his country and the maligners of his honor.

Robert Ingersoll, 1876, in David Barr Chidsey, *The Gentleman from New York — A Life of Roscoe Conkling.*

His talents were oratorical and his tastes political in a personal and party sense.

Ellis P. Oberholtzer, *History of the U.S. Since the Civil War.*

No man in our annals has filled so large a space and left it so empty.

Charles Edward Russell, in D. S. Muzzey, *James G. Blaine.*

See also Theodore Roosevelt

BLAIR, ERIC, see under ORWELL, GEORGE

BLAKE, ROBERT

1599—1657 Admiral

His life can show no private irregularities, no scandals to excite the curiosity of the prurient or the avaricious; nor has it any lessons in intrigue or finesse. It thus lacks the stimulus of sex, wealth, and power. . . . And how typically were his qualities those which Englishmen like to claim as their own — reticence, aversion to publicity, abhorrence of the theatrical, and the sense that, in the great moments of life, it should be thought only to do faithfully, leaving glory to follow good deeds.

Roger Beadon, *Robert Blake.*

R est here in peace the sacred dust
O f valiant Blake, the good, the just,
B elov'd of all on every side;
E ngland's honour, once her pride,
R ome's terror, Dutch annoyer,
T ruth's defender, Spain's destroyer.

B ring no dry eyes unto this place;
L et not be seen in any case,
A smiling or an unsad face.
K indle desires in every breast
E ternally with him to rest.

George Harrison, *Epitaph Acrostic, . . . on board the Dunbar in the Downs,* 11 August 1657.

I do not reckon myself equal to Blake.

Horatio Nelson, Letter to Earl of St Vincent, 1797.

Mr Coventry . . . discoursed largely and bravely to me concerning the different sorts of valours, the active and passive valour. For the latter he brought as an instance Generall Blacke, who in the defending of Taunton and Lime for the Parliament did through his stubborn sort of valour defend it the most *opiniastrement* that ever any man did anything — and yet never was the man that ever made any attaque by land or sea, but rather avoyded it on all, even fair occasions.

Samuel Pepys, Diary, 4 June 1664.

BLAKE, WILLIAM

1757—1827 Poet, Artist

Having spent the Vigour of my Youth & Genius under the Opression of Sr Joshua [Reynolds] & his Gang of Cunning Hired Knaves Without Employment & as much as could possibly be Without Bread, The Reader must expect to Read in all my Remarks on these Books Nothing but Indignation & Resentment. While S^r· Joshua was rolling in Riches, Barry was Poor & Unemploy'd except by his own Energy; Mortimer was call'd a Madman, & only Portrait Painting applauded & rewarded by the Rich & Great. Reynolds & Gainsborough Blotted & Blurred one against the other & Divided all the English World between them. Fuseli, indignant, almost hid himself. I am hid.

On himself, *Annotations to Reynolds's Discourses.*

I do not pretend to Paint better than Rafael or Mich. Angelo or Julio Romano or Alb. Durer, but I do Pretend to Paint finer than Rubens or Remb^t· or Correggio or Titian.

On himself, 'Public Address', from *Note Book,* 1810.

Self-educated *William Blake*
Who threw his spectre in the lake,
Broke off relations in a curse
With the Newtonian Universe,
But even as a child could pet
The tigers Voltaire never met,
Took walks with them through Lambeth, and
Spoke to Isaiah in the Strand,
And heard inside each mortal thing
Its holy emanation sing.

W. H. Auden, *New Year Letter.*

Blake saw a treeful of angels at Peckham Rye,
And his hands could lay hold on the tiger's terrible
heart,
Blake knew how deep is Hell, and Heaven how high,
And could build the universe from one tiny part.

William Rose Benét, *Mad Blake.*

Be a god, your spirit cried;
Tread with feet that burn the dew;
Dress with clouds your locks of pride;
Be a child, God said to you.
     Olive Dargan, *To William Blake.*

I lived; I toiled — day in, day out,
Endless labour, shafts of bliss,
For three score years and ten,
     And then;
I watched, with speechless joy and grief,
My last and loveliest spring
     Take wing.

Think you, I grudged the travailing?
I, who am come to this.
     Walter de la Mare, *A Lifetime: Epitaph for
     William Blake.*

Blake ... knew what interested him, and he therefore presents only the essential, only, in fact, what
can be presented, and need not be explained. And
because he was not distracted, or frightened, or
occupied in anything but exact statements, he
understood. He was naked, and saw man naked,
and from the centre of his own crystal. To him
there was no more reason why Swedenborg should
be absurd than Locke. He accepted Swedenborg,
and eventually rejected him, for reasons of his own.
He approached everything with a mind unclouded
by current opinions. There was nothing of the
superior person about him. This makes him terrifying.
     T. S. Eliot, *The Sacred Wood.*

Blake is damned good to steal from!
     Henry Fuseli, in Alexander Gilchrist, *Life of
     Blake.*

I was having these Blake visions. So. The thing I
understood from Blake was that it was possible
to transmit a message through time which could
reach the enlightened, that poetry had a definite
effect, it wasn't just pretty, or just beautiful, as I
had understood pretty beauty before ... But
anyway the impression I got was that it was like
a kind of time machine through which he could
transmit, Blake could transmit, his basic consciousness and communicate it to somebody else after he
was dead — in other words, build a time machine.
     Allen Ginsberg, in *Paris Review.*

This seer's ambition soared too far;
     He sank, on pinions backward blown;
But, tho' he touched nor sun nor star,
     He made a world his own.
     Edmund Gosse, *William Blake.*

He has no sense of the ludicrous, and, as to God, a
worm crawling in a privy is as worthy an object as
any other, all being to him indifferent. So to Blake
the Chimney Sweeper etc. He is ruined by vain
struggles to get rid of what presses on his brain — he
attempts impossibles.
     William Hazlitt, in Henry Crabb Robinson, Diary,
     1811.

For me the most poetical of all poets is Blake. I find
his lyrical note as beautiful as Shakespeare's and
more beautiful than anyone else's; and I call him
more poetical than Shakespeare, even though
Shakespeare has so much more poetry, because
poetry in him preponderates more than in
Shakespeare over everything else, and instead of
being confounded in a great river can be drunk
pure from a slender channel of its own.
     A. E. Housman, *The Name and Nature of Poetry.*

Blake is the only painter of imaginative pictures,
apart from landscape, that England has produced.
And unfortunately there is so little Blake, and even
in that little the symbolism is often artificially
imposed. Nevertheless, Blake paints with real
intuitional awareness and solid instinctive feeling.
He dares handle the human body, even if he sometimes makes it a mere ideograph. And no other
Englishman has even dared handle it with alive
imagination.
     D. H. Lawrence, *Introduction to his Paintings.*

William Blake was our arch-Policeman. Had Blake,
instead of passing his time with Renaissance bogeys
and athletes, painted his wife and himself naked in
their conservatory (as, in a more realistic tradition,
he quite conceivably might have done), the result
would have been very similar to Renaissance
portraits.
     Percy Wyndham Lewis, 'Policeman and Artist',
     in *Vortices and Notes.*

His eye was the finest I ever saw: brilliant, not
roving, clear and intent; yet susceptible; it flashed
with genius or melted with tenderness. It could also
be terrible. Cunning and falsehood quailed under it,
but it was never busy with them. It pierced them
and turned away. Nor was the mouth less expressive;
the lips flexible and quivering with feeling. I yet
recall it when, on one occasion, dwelling upon the
exquisite parable of the Prodigal, he began to repeat
a part of it; but at the words: 'When he was yet a
great way off, his father saw him', could go no
further; his voice faltered and he was in tears.
     Samuel Palmer, Letter to Alexander Gilchrist,
     1855.

He died on Sunday Night at 6 Oclock in a most
glorious manner. He said He was going to that

Country he had all His life wished to see & expressed Himself Happy hoping for Salvation through Jesus Christ. Just before he died his Countenance became fair. His eyes Brighten'd and he burst out singing of the things he saw in Heaven.

George Richmond, Letter to Samuel Palmer, 15 August 1827.

He is not so much a disciple of Jacob Böhmen and Swedenborg as a fellow Visionary. He lives, as they did, in a world of his own, enjoying constant intercourse with the world of spirits. He receives visits from Shakespeare, Milton, Dante, Voltaire, etc. etc. etc., and has given me repeatedly their very words in their conversations. His paintings are copies of what he saw in his Visions. His books (and his MSS. are immense in quantity) are dictations from the spirits. He told me yesterday that when he writes it is for the spirits only; he sees the words fly about the room the moment he has put them on paper, and his book is then published. A man so favoured, of course, has sources of wisdom peculiar to himself.

Henry Crabb Robinson, Letter to Dorothy Wordsworth, 1826.

The impression that his drawings once made is fast, and justly, fading away, though they are not without noble merit. But his poems have much more than merit; they are written with absolute sincerity, with infinite tenderness, and, though in the manner of them diseased and wild, are in verity the words of a great and wise mind, disturbed, but not deceived by its sickness; nay, partly exalted by it, and sometimes giving forth in fiery aphorism some of the most precious words of existing literature.

John Ruskin, *The Eagle's Nest.*

Blake, in the hierarchy of the inspired, stands very high indeed. If one could strike an average among poets, it would probably be true to say that, as far as inspiration is concerned, Blake is to the average poet, as the average poet is to the man in the street. All poetry, to be poetry at all, must have the power of making one, now and then, involuntarily ejaculate: 'What made him think of that?' With Blake, one is asking the question all the time.

Lytton Strachey, *Books and Characters.*

Blake is the only poet who sees all temporal things under a form of eternity. To him reality is merely a symbol, and he catches at its terms, hastily and faultily, as he catches at the lines of the drawing-master, to represent, as in a faint image, the clear and shining outlines of what he sees with the imagination; through the eye, not with it, as he says. Where other poets use reality as a spring-board into space, he uses it as a foothold on his return from flight.

Arthur Symons, *William Blake.*

There is no doubt that this poor man was mad, but there is something in the madness of this man which interests me more than the sanity of Lord Byron and Walter Scott.

William Wordsworth, in Henry Crabb Robinson, *Reminiscences.*

That William Blake
Who beat upon the wall
Till Truth obeyed his call.
William Butler Yeats, *An Acre of Grass.*

See also Thomas Gainsborough, William Butler Yeats

BLAKELOCK, RALPH ALBERT

1847—1919 Painter

Harriet Monroe and other critics misinterpreted Blakelock's paintings when they used such terms as '... wild, sweet strangeness — a fantastic delicacy and grace' in describing Blakelock's painting. There is a forbidding, even at times, sinister quality which emerges in almost all of his work. The small human figures, which often inhabit his canvases may indeed be charming and delicate — even sweet — but it is their very sweetness and innocence which contrasts with the pressing, ominous, forbidding quality of the landscape that finally creates the subtle atmosphere of terror.

David Gebhard, *The Enigma of Ralph A. Blakelock.*

Throughout his entire career Blakelock was a very uneven painter. His best canvases come very near to being masterpieces, and his poorest are scarcely worthy of the most trivial painter.... In short, in his duller moods, he was a mere imitator of himself. He plagiarized his own pictures and several critics have expressed the opinion that it would not be at all strange if some of his inferior work should in the future come to be condemned as forgeries.

Frederick W. Morton, in *ibid.*

His forms became more simplified over the years as ideas were borrowed from nature and reinvented, and many of his pictures seem, in their remote stillness, to be dreamed rather than seen. The best of Blakelock appeals to a deep, poetic apprehension for he was a visionary who, with a sensuous feeling for texture, revealed a universal experience rather than described a particular subject. Against skies that gleam or glow with light, trees are silhouetted — sometimes massive — sometimes outlined as delicately as lacework. These luminous skies never depict weather but are lighted by the golden tones of dawn and sunset or the silver of twilight and moonlight. Generally, a magical yet ominously melancholy atmosphere exists.

Phyllis Stuurman, in *ibid*.

BLESSINGTON, MARGUERITE, COUNTESS

1789—1849 Hostess, Author

Miladi seems highly literary. . . . She is also very pretty even in a morning, — a species of beauty on which the sun of Italy does not shine so frequently as the chandelier. Certainly, English women wear better than their continental neighbours of the same sex.

Lord Byron, *Letters and Journals*, 2 April 1823.

> Hospitable heart
> Whom twenty summers more and more endear'd;
> Part on the Arno, part where every clime
> Sent its most grateful sons, to kiss thy hand,
> To make the humble proud, the proud submiss,
> Wiser the wisest, and the brave more brave.

Walter Savage Landor, *In Memoriam Lady Blessington*.

Lady Blessington was naturally lively, good-humoured, mirthful, full of drollery, and easily amused. Her perception of the ridiculous was quick and keen. If there was anything absurd in a subject or object presented to her, she was sure to seize on it, and to represent the idea to others in the most ridiculous aspect possible. This turn of mind was not exhibited in society alone; in private it was equally manifested.

Dr Madden, *The Literary Life and Correspondence of the Countess of Blessington*.

Unlike all other beautiful faces that I have seen, hers was at the time of which I speak [sc. 1822], neither a history nor a prophecy . . . but rather a star to kneel before and worship . . . an end and a consummation in itself, not a promise of anything else.

P. G. Patmore (on seeing her standing before her portrait by Sir Thomas Lawrence at the Royal Academy Exhibition), in R. H. Stoddard, *Personal Recollections of Lamb, Hazlitt, and Others*.

BLOOMER, AMELIA JENKS

1818—94 Social Reformer

We all felt that the dress was drawing attention from what we thought to be of far greater importance — the question of woman's right to better education, to a wider field of employment, to better remuneration for her labour, and to the ballot for the protection of her rights. In the minds of some people the short dress and woman's rights were inseparably connected. With us, the dress was but an incident, and we were not willing to sacrifice greater questions to it.

On herself, in Charles N. Gattey, *The Bloomer Girls*.

> Heigh ho,
> Thro' sleet and snow,
> Mrs Bloomer's all the go.
> Twenty tailors take the stitches,
> Plenty of women wear the breeches,
> Heigh ho,
> Carrion crow!

Anon., in Ida Harper, *Life and Work of Susan B. Anthony*.

> Listen, females all
> No matter what your trade is,
> Old Nick is in the girls,
> The Devil's in the ladies!
> Married men may weep,
> And tumble in the ditches,
> Since women are resolved
> To wear the shirts and breeches.

Anon., 1851 broadsheet, *I'll be a Bloomer*.

. . . you must take Mrs Bloomer's suggestions with great caution, for she has not the spirit of the true reformer. At the first Woman's Rights Convention, but four years ago, she stood aloof and laughed at us. It was only with great effort and patience that she has been brought up to her present position. In her paper she will not speak against the Fugitive Slave Law, nor in her work to put down intemperance will she criticize the equivocal position of the church. She trusts to numbers to build up a cause rather than to principles, to the truth and right. Fatal Error! . . .

Susan B. Anthony, Letter to Elizabeth Cady Stanton, in Alma Lutz, *Created Equal: a Biography of Elizabeth Cady Stanton*.

BLOW, JOHN

1648—1708 Composer

It does not appear that Purcell, whom he did himself the honour to call his scholar, . . . ever threw notes about at random, in his manner, or insulted the ear with lawless discords, which no concords can render tolerable.

Dr Charles Burney, *A General History of Music*.

BOADICEA, QUEEN

— d. 62 Warrior

The Greek historian Dio Cassius, who lived about a century after Boadicea, when her fame and figure were already legendary, describes her as fierce and lofty, with a harsh voice and huge masses of fair hair. Those who remember Florence Austral as Brünhilde will be immediately struck by the resemblance.

Nicolas Bentley, *Golden Sovereigns.*

The citizens of London implored Suetonius to protect them, but when he heard that Boadicea, having chased Cerialis towards Lincoln, had turned and was marching south, he took the hard but right decision to leave them to their fate.

Winston Churchill, *History of the English-Speaking Peoples.*

Although, as a Stoic, Seneca officially despised riches, he amassed a huge fortune . . . Much of this he acquired by lending money in Britain; according to Dio, the excessive rates of interest that he exacted were among the causes of revolt in that country. The heroic Queen Boadicea, if this is true, was heading a rebellion against capitalism as represented by the philosophic apostle of austerity.

Bertrand Russell, *History of Western Philosophy.*

Julius Caesar advanced very energetically, throwing his cavalry several thousands of paces over the River Flumen; but the Ancient Britons, though all well over military age, painted themselves true blue or *woad*, and fought as heroically under their dashing queen, Woadicea, as they did later in thin red lines under their good queen Victoria.

W. C. Sellar and R. J. Yeatman, *1066 and All That.*

Boadicea, with her daughters before her in a chariot, went up to tribe after tribe, protesting that it was indeed unusual for Britons to fight under the leadership of a woman. 'But now,' she said, 'it is not as a woman descending from noble ancestry, but as one of the people that I am avenging lost freedom, my scourged body, the outraged chastity of my daughters. Roman lust has gone so far that not our very persons, not even age or virginity, are left unpolluted. . . . This is a woman's resolve; as for men, they may live and be slaves.' . . . Great glory, equal to that of our old victories, was won on that day. Some indeed say that there fell little less than eighty thousand of the Britons, with a loss to our soldiers of about four hundred, and only as many wounded. Boadicea put an end to her life by poison.

Tacitus, *Annals,* translated by A. J. Church and W. J. Brodribb.

The rising of Boadicea is the exception that proves the rule of the easy submission of East and South to Roman influence.

G. M. Trevelyan, *History of England.*

See also Hengist and Horsa

BODLEY, SIR THOMAS

1545—1613 Scholar, Diplomat

Thy treasure was not spent on *Horse* and *Hound*,
Nor that new *Mode*, which doth old States
                        confound. . . .
Th'hast made us all thine *Heirs*: whatever we
Hereafter write, 'tis thy *Posterity.*
This is thy *Monument!* here thou shalt stand
Till the times fail in their last grain of Sand.
And whereso'er thy silent *Reliques* keep,
This Tomb will never let thine honour sleep.
Still we shall think upon thee; all our fame
Meets here to speak one *Letter* of thy name.
Thou cans't not dye! Here thou art more than safe
When every *Book* is thy large *Epitaph.*

Henry Vaughan, *On Sir Thomas Bodley's Library.*

BOGART, HUMPHREY DE FOREST

1899—1957 Actor

Bogie was a curious mixture. He wasn't cynical. He didn't expect too much, he never realized he would leave the kind of mark he has left. He never tried to impress anyone. I've never known anyone who was so completely his own man. He could not be led in any direction unless it was the direction he chose to go. . . . He didn't think he owed anybody anything except good work.

Lauren Bacall, in Earl Wilson, *The Show Business Nobody Knows.*

He had tremendous respect for the acting profession — for real actors, not for flukes. He always felt one should work at one's trade and not just sit back and wait for that wonderful part because if you do, chances are nothing will come along. Even if things are not as good as you'd like them to be, you can still learn. You're functioning. Perhaps you're not using all of yourself but some of yourself.

Ibid.

Bogart anticipated the later day of the faintly or heavily neurotic sophisticate who was likely to be anti-heroic if not actively villainous. Bogie was heroic, but he tended to be the abashed or reluctant hero.

Charles Champlin, in Gabe Esso, *The Films of Clark Gable.*

Bogart is so much better than any other tough-guy actor. [He] can be tough *without* a gun. Also he has a sense of humor that contains that grating undertone of contempt.
　Raymond Chandler, *Raymond Chandler Speaking.*

Humphrey Bogart is probably the most subtle bad man (genus American) the films have produced.
　Otis Ferguson, *The Films of Otis Ferguson.*

His yes meant yes, his no meant no; . . . there was no bunkum about Bogart.
　Katharine Hepburn, in Joe Hyams, *Bogie.*

Bogie and I were good friends, and he gave me some good advice. He said 'Whatever it is, be against it'. I told him 'I've got a lot of scars already from being an againster'. He said 'You've got a lot of scars, but you're still alive'.
　Robert Mitchum, in Earl Wilson, *The Show Business Nobody Knows.*

Bogie had a manner, a personality — yes, an immense talent — that has made him almost immortal. Working with him, I think I understood it better than his fans. For all his outward toughness, insolence, braggadocio, and contempt (and those were always part of the characters he played, though they were not entirely within Bogie), there came through a kind of sadness, loneliness, and heartbreak (all of which *were* very part of Bogie the man). I always felt sorry for him — sorry that he imposed upon himself the façade of the character with which he had become identified.
　Edward G. Robinson, *All My Yesterdays.*

Bogart became a mythic figure, with his harrowed face, sharp, expressionless eyes, twisted mouth, weary walk; a figure mingling cynicism and duty as the moral man in an immoral society and soon finding, in the films and in life, a perfect companion in Lauren Bacall, raucous and lovely, one of the best of the satiric women.
　Arthur Schlesinger Jr, 'When the Movies Really Counted', in *Show*, April 1963.

Probably no other actor of his era has fit a detective part so perfectly. Humphrey Bogart. Wry, detached, anti-Establishment, a man with the sure masculinity of whiskey straight . . . Bogart was unflinching, outspoken, cynical and a realist; a tough guy in a trenchcoat, a man's man.
　David Zinman, *Fifty Classic Motion Pictures.*

BOLEYN, ANNE

1507–36 Queen Consort to Henry VIII

Neither did I at any time so far forget myself in my exaltation, or received queenship, but that I always looked for such an alteration as now I find; for the ground of my preferment being on no surer foundation than your grace's fancy, the least alteration was fit and sufficient (I know) to draw that fancy to some other subject. You have chosen me from a low estate to be your queen and companion, far beyond my desert or desire.
　On herself, Last Letter to Henry VIII (attributed by Bishop Burnet, in his *History of the Reformation*).

At the opening of the year 1536 Anne Boleyn's position rested on two supports: the life of Catherine of Aragon and the prospect of a prince. Never was fortune more cruel. On January 7th Catherine died, and on the twenty-ninth, the day of the funeral, Anne gave premature birth to a male child. She had miscarried of her saviour. The tragedy must obviously move to a close; and it moved swiftly. On May 2nd she was arrested and sent to the tower, accused of adultery with five men, one of whom was her brother. In the subsequent trials all were found guilty, and the law took its course. Anne herself was executed on May 18th. Whether she was guilty or not, no human judgement can now determine, and contemporaries differed. In all probability she had been indiscreet. If she had gone further, if she had really committed adultery — and that possibility cannot be lightly dismissed — then it is likely that a desperate woman had taken a desperate course to give England its prince and save herself from ruin. Whatever the truth, she had played her game and lost.
　J. E. Neale, *Queen Elizabeth.*

For something like five years she succeeded in holding him [Henry VIII] at arms' length, a remarkable performance, all things considered, and probably indicative that there was considerably more of cold calculation than of passion in Anne's attitude.
　Conyers Read, *The Tudors.*

BOLINGBROKE, VISCOUNT (HENRY ST JOHN)

1678–1751 Statesman

Whilst I loved much, I never loved long, but was inconstant to them all for the sake of all.
　On himself, Letter to Charles Wyndham, 26 December 1735.

He has been a most mortifying instance of the violence of human passions, and of the weakness of the most improved and exalted human reason. His virtues and his vices, his reason and his passions, did not blend themselves by a gradation of tints, but formed a shining and a sudden contrast. Here the darkest, there the most splendid colours; and both rendered more striking from their proximity.

Lord Chesterfield, *Letters*, vol. 4, 12 December 1749.

The brilliant metal attracts the lightning bolt – the splendour of Bolingbroke's talents drew upon him his ruin. Self-interest is a marvellous antidote to pity; and the minister could never begin to commiserate the man he could not cease to fear.

George Wingrove Cooke, *Memoirs of Lord Bolingbroke.*

It was his inspiring pen that . . . eradicated from Toryism all those absurd and odious doctrines which Toryism had adventitiously adopted, clearly developed its essential and permanent character . . . and in the complete reorganization of the public mind laid the foundation for the future accession of the Tory party to power.

Benjamin Disraeli, *Vindication of the British Constitution.*

When he was appointed Minister, a woman of the streets was said to have cried. . . . 'Seven thousand guineas a year, my girls, and all for us!'

Michael Foot, *The Pen and the Sword.*

Those who were most partial to him could not but allow that he was ambitious without fortitude, and enterprising without resolution; that he was fawning without insinuation, and insincere without art; that he had admirers without friendship, and followers without attachment; parts without probity, knowledge without conduct, and experience without judgment.

Lord Hervey, *Memoirs*, vol. 1.

He was passionate, partisan, and an opportunist, but in his endeavours to maintain the continuity of tory ideas of government while easing toryism out of its adherence to older formulations of its beliefs that were no longer applicable to changing circumstances, Bolingbroke prefigures the essential characteristics of the great tory leaders who came after him.

Sydney Wayne Jackman, *Man of Mercury.*

Sir, he was a scoundrel and a coward; a scoundrel for charging a blunderbuss against religion and morality; a coward because he had not resolution to fire it off himself, but left half a crown to a beggarly Scotchman to draw the trigger after his death.

Samuel Johnson, in James Boswell, *Life of Johnson.*

. . . it is to be noted that it was not until he had most signally failed as a statesman that he began to acquire a reputation as a political philosopher, and had he been able to make up his mind during the last few weeks of Anne's reign, he could have presented the country with a Patriot King in the person of James III instead of merely a volume on the need for one.

Sir Charles Petrie, *The Four Georges.*

Lord Bolingbroke is something superior to anything I have seen in human nature. You know I don't deal much in hyperboles: I quite think him what I say.

Alexander Pope, in Joseph Spence, *Anecdotes.*

Lord Bolingbroke quitted the Pretender, because he found him incapable of making a good prince. He himself, if in power, would have been the best of ministers. – These things will be proved one of these days. The proofs are ready, and the world *will* see them.

Ibid.

Lord Bolingbroke's father said to him on his being made a lord, 'Ah, Harry, I ever said you would be hanged, but now I find you will be beheaded.'

Joseph Spence, *ibid.*

His Conceptions are very superficial; but he expresses those Conceptions with much grace and address. Tho' he has not judgment to choose the right part, he can either speak, write, or debate upon what he does pursue, or take into his thoughts, with a most specious force and energy. Thus, though it was the most painful thing imaginable to a wise man to hear him harangue, there was little help against him, for he charmed all who had not deep discerning.

Richard Steele, *The Englishman.*

. . . he was fond of mixing pleasure and business, and of being esteemed excellent at both; upon which account he had a great respect for the characters of Alcibiades and Petronius, especially the latter, whom he would gladly be thought to resemble.

Jonathan Swift, *An Enquiry into The Behaviour of the Queen's Last Ministry.*

See also Jonathan Swift

BOONE, DANIEL

1734—1820 Pioneer

I had not been two years at the licks before a
d——d Yankee came, and settled down *within an
hundred miles of me*!!
  On himself, in Henry Nash Smith, *Virgin Land*.

We have been honored by a visit from col. BOONE,
the first settler of Kentucky; he lately spent two
weeks with us ... The colonel cannot live without
being in the woods. He goes a hunting twice a year
to the remotest wilderness he can reach; and hires a
man to go with him, whom he binds in written
articles to take care of him, and bring him home,
dead or alive.
  Anon., Fort Osage Army officer commenting on
  Boone at age 82, in *Western Spy*, 5 January 1816.

As Daniel Boone himself used to say, all you needed
for happiness was 'a good gun, a good horse, and a
good wife. . . .'
  John E. Bakeless, *Daniel Boone*.

When Daniel Boone goes by, at night,
The phantom deer arise
And all lost, wild America
Is burning in their eyes.
  Stephen Vincent Benét, *Daniel Boone*.

'Tis true he shrank from men even of his nation
  When they built up unto his darling trees, —
He moved some hundred miles off, for a station
  Where there were fewer houses and more ease.
  Lord Byron, *Don Juan*, canto vii.

[A] companion for owls, separated from the chearful
society of men, scorched by the Summer's sun, and
pinched by the Winter's cold, an instrument ordained
to settle the wilderness.
  John Filson, *The Discovery, Settlement, and
  Present State of Kentucke*.

A Nimrod by instinct and physical character, his
home was in the range of woods, his beau ideal the
chase, and forests full of buffaloes, bear and deer.
More expert at their own arts, than the Indians
themselves, to fight them, and foil them, gave scope
to the exulting consciousness of the exercise of his
own appropriate and peculiar powers.
  Timothy Flint, *Indian Wars of the West*.

He wanted a frontier, and the perils and pleasures of
a frontier life, not wealth; and he was happier in his
log-cabin, with a loin of venison and his ramrod for
a spit, than he would have been amid the great profusion of modern luxuries.
  James H. Perkins, in *North American Review*,
  January 1846.

See also Gary Cooper

BOOTH, EDWIN THOMAS

1833—93 Actor

[I could not] paint with big brushes — the fine
touches come in spite of me, and it's all folly to say:
'Don't elaborate, don't refine it' — I can't help it.
I'm too damned genteel and exquisite, I s'pose, and
some buster with a big voice and a broadaxe
gesticulation will oust me one of these fine days.
  On himself, in Toby Cole and Helen Krich
  Chinoy, *Actors on Acting*.

There's but one Hamlet to my mind: that's my
brother Edwin. You see, between ourselves, he *is*
Hamlet — melancholy and all.
  John Wilkes Booth, in Eleanor Ruggles, *Prince
  of Players: Edwin Booth*.

When Edwin Booth played Hamlet, then
The camp drab's tears could not but flow.
Then Romance lived and breathed and burned.
She felt the frail queen-mother's woe,
Thrilled for Ophelia, fond and blind,
And Hamlet, cruel, yet so kind,
And m'oaned, his proud words hurt her so.
  Vachel Lindsay, *Edwin Booth in California*.

Edwin had everything but guts: if he had had a little
more that was absolutely gross in his composition
he would have been altogether first class instead of
just a little short of it.
  Walt Whitman, in Horace Traubel, *With Walt
  Whitman in Camden*, vol. 1.

Edwin Booth's Hamlet was the simple, absolute
realization of Shakespeare's haunted prince, and
raised no question and left no room for inquiry
whether the Danes in the Middle Ages wore velvet
robes or had long flaxen hair. It was dark,
mysterious, afflicted, melancholy.
  Willian Winter, in Eleanor Ruggles, *Prince of
  Players: Edwin Booth*.

See also John Booth

BOOTH, JOHN WILKES

1838—65 Actor, Assassin

I have too great a soul to die like a criminal.
  On himself, in A. K. Adams, *The Home Book of
  Humorous Quotations*.

He is full of the true grit. I am delighted with him and feel the name of Booth to be more of a hydra than snakes and things ever was.

Edwin Booth, in Eleanor Ruggles, *Prince of Players: Edwin Booth.*

John was much too melodramatic. ... Although some of his tones were remarkably like Edwin's, his face onstage was wooden, and the performance had reminded Cary of nothing so much as 'a blood-and-thunder melodrama full of sheet iron and burnt rosin and ghosts and other horrors', he had once seen in the old Federal Street Theatre in Boston.

Richard Cary, as paraphrased in *ibid.*

He was mad with his own ego, possessed of a theatrical vanity that gnawed incessantly for fame. As an actor, John Wilkes Booth already owned national recognition, but he lusted after a kind of immortality completely unrelated to his profession. He desperately wanted to be remembered as a political and military hero, a savior of his romanticised version of the Old South.

Jay Robert Nash, *Bloodletters and Badmen.*

John had his share of their father in him: the very hairs of his head acted. The Harvard-educated Dick Cary might find him bombastic, yet there were critics who already rated him higher than his more polished brother — 'the best of living Romeos', one of them considered him. The passion of his embrace lifted Juliet out of her shoes. Desdemona winced at the bang of his scimitar when as Othello he flung himself on her body. His Hamlet was mustachioed, hot-blooded, definitely insane. After *Richard III* he slept smothered in oysters to heal the bruises got during a stage battle fought in deadly earnest.

Eleanor Ruggles, *Prince of Players: Edwin Booth.*

What he was after was to be '*the* Booth', to shoulder his way ahead of his brothers, to approach the level of his father's fame, and it was this ambition that kept him in the North even after war broke out and the South he loved was fighting gloriously. When Edwin sailed for England John saw his chance. He starred in St. Louis, in Chicago, then in Baltimore; and here in the city most intimately associated with all the Booths his posters proclaimed defiantly: I AM MYSELF ALONE!

Ibid.

See also Carl Sandburg

BOOTH, JUNIUS BRUTUS

1796—1852 Actor

What, Booth dead? Then there are no more actors!

Rufus Choate, in Eleanor Ruggles, *Prince of Players: Edwin Booth.*

He was a magnetic little man. Although very short, with stumpy legs, he carried himself imperiously; his blue-gray eyes looked black by gaslight; his commanding, delicately formed nose was faintly Oriental; his ears, pierced for earrings, were curiously pointed — 'I'm a real satyr!' he liked to boast.

Eleanor Ruggles, in *ibid.*

Booth illustrated Plato's rule that to the forming of an artist of the very highest rank a dash of insanity (or what the world calls insanity) is indispensable. Without question Booth was royal heir and legitimate representative of the Garrick-Kemble-Siddons dramatic traditions but he vitalized and gave an unnameable *race* to those traditions with his own electric personal idiosyncracy. (As in all art-utterance it was the subtle and powerful something *special to the individual* that really conquered).

Walt Whitman, in Toby Cole and Helen Krich Chinoy, *Actors on Acting.*

BOOTH, 'GENERAL' WILLIAM

1829—1912 Founder of the Salvation Army

... This vehement person who ... unroofed the slum to Victorian respectability, and spoke of himself as a moral scavenger netting the very sewers, was of a singularly delicate constitution. ... It was this extreme sensitiveness to squalor and suffering which made him so effective in unveiling the dark places of civilization. He saw sharply what others scarcely saw at all, and he felt as an outrage what others considered to be natural.

Harold Begbie, in the *Dictionary of National Biography.*

Booth led boldly with his big brass drum —
(Are you washed in the blood of the Lamb?)
The Saints smiled gravely and they said: 'He's come.'
(Are you washed in the blood of the Lamb?)
Walking Lepers followed, rank on rank,
Lurching bravos from the ditches dank,
Drabs from the alleyways and drug fiends pale —
Minds still passion-ridden, soul-power frail: —
Vermin-eaten saints with moldy breath,
Unwashed Legions with the ways of Death —
(Are you washed in the blood of the Lamb?)

Vachel Lindsay, *General William Booth Enters Into Heaven.*

It was William Booth who explained the authoritarian framework of his Salvation Army by remarking that if Moses had operated through committees, the Israelites never would have got across the Red Sea.

Edward Morello, in *New York World-Telegram and Sun,* 28 July 1965.

BORAH, WILLIAM EDGAR

1865—1940 Politician

... he was always winding himself up but never struck twelve.
    Anon., in John Chalmers Vinson, *William E. Borah and the Outlawry of War.*

He gives the impression of vigilant mental watchfulness manifested in physical tension ... his chin suggests will power and obstinacy — the force of immovability. His mouth is hard, lips thin, twisting at the corners when he talks, catching at the words he forces past them, squeezing them so that they come forth a torrent of hard, wounding projectiles. ... When he works to a climax in debate or speech, he leans slightly forward, his voice acquires almost a shrill tone, cuts like a knife, twists like a rapier, and then suddenly thunders like a 16 inch gun.
    Anon., in *Boston Herald,* 21 May 1923.

... that prince of blatherskites, Senator Borah, whose big mouth and tiny mentality have made his name a by-word of reproach wherever decent Americans gather.
    Anon., in *Fort Wayne News,* March 1922.

His career is notable in a hundred ways and celebrated in none.
    Anon., in *Detroit News,* 24 December 1921.

Here is the case of an honest politician, almost intellectually honest, whose restless vanity raises controversial points at a time when the world was approaching a merciful surcease. If Mr. Borah cannot be persuaded to give himself a rest, surely his undoubted patriotism might well induce him to give the country a rest.
    Anon., in *Wall Street Journal,* 12 May 1925.

... a host unto himself.
    Walter Lippmann, in R. J. Maddox, *William E. Borah and American Foreign Policy.*

When he reascends Olympus it might be appropriate to canonize him as the patron saint of political mischief makers, for Washington will be a far duller place without him.
    William C. Murphy, in Marian C. McKenna, *Borah.*

He is the only American whose brains seem properly baked; the others are all either crumbs or gruel. Perhaps that is because he is the only genuine one hundred per center.
    George Bernard Shaw to George S. Vierck, in *ibid.*

He was a war-party leader with a peace-party's instincts: a [Henry Cabot] Lodge turned pacifist, and a [Robert] La Follette for the War.
    John Chalmers Vinson, *William E. Borah and the Outlawry of War.*

The Titan, Borah, in his only avocation, rides regularly in Rock Creek Park, his only regret that he must proceed in the same direction as the horse.
    Robert M. Washburn, *Springfield Union,* 1925.

BORDEN, LIZZIE ANDREW

1860—1927 Alleged Murderesss

Lizzie Borden took an ax
And gave her mother forty whacks;
And when she saw what she had done
She gave her father forty-one.
    Anon., *Lizzie Borden.*

There's no evidence of guilt
    Lizzie Borden
That should make your spirit wilt,
    Lizzie Borden
Many do not think that you
Chopped your father's head in two,
It's so hard a thing to do
Lizzie Borden.
    A. L. Bixby, *To Lizzie.*

Lizzie is queer, but as for her being guilty I say 'no', decidedly 'no'.
    Emma Borden, in *New York Times,* 3 June 1927.

BOSWELL, JAMES

1740—95 Author

I am a being very much consisting of feelings. I have some fixed principles. But my existence is chiefly conducted by the powers of fancy and sensation. It is my business to navigate my soul amidst the gales as steadily and smoothly as I can.
    On himself, *Journal,* 26 March 1775.

An honest self-portrait is extremely rare because a man who has reached the degree of self-consciousness presupposed by the desire to paint his own portrait has almost always developed an ego-consciousness which paints himself painting himself, and introduces artificial highlights and dramatic shadows. As an autobiographer, Boswell is almost alone in his honesty.

I determined, if the Cyprian Fury should seize

me, to participate my amorous flame with a
genteel girl.
Stendhal would never have dared write such a
sentence. He would have said to himself: 'Phrases
like *Cyprian Fury* and *amorous flame* are clichés; I
must put down in plain words exactly what I mean.'
But he would have been wrong, for the Self thinks
in clichés and euphemisms, not in the style of the
Code Napoléon.
W. H. Auden, *The Dyer's Hand.*

I felt a strong sensation of that displeasure which his
loquacious communications of every weakness and
infirmity of the first and greatest good man of these
times has awakened in me, at his first sight; and,
though his address to me was courteous in the
extreme, and he made a point of sitting next me, I
felt an indignant disposition to a nearly forbidding
reserve and silence. How many starts of passion
and prejudice has he blackened into record, that else
might have sunk, for ever forgotten, under the pre-
ponderance of weightier virtues and excellences!
Angry, however, as I have long been with him, he
soon insensibly conquered, though he did not
soften me: there is so little of ill-design or ill-nature
in him, he is so open and forgiving for all that is
said in return, that he soon forced me to consider
him in a less serious light, and change my resentment against his treachery into something like
commiseration of his levity; and before we parted
we became good friends.
Fanny Burney, Letter to Mrs Phillips, June 1792.

Silly, snobbish, lecherous, tipsy, given to high-flown
sentiments and more than a little of a humbug,
Boswell is redeemed by a generosity of mind, a concentration on topics that will always appeal . . .
and a naivety that endeared him to the great minds
he cultivated. He needed Johnson as ivy needs an
oak.
Cyril Connolly, *The Evening Colonnade.*

Jamie, you have a light head, but a damned heavy
a———; and, to be sure, such a man will run easily
down hill, but it would be severe work to get him
up.
Lord Eglinton, in Boswell, *London Journal,*
9 May 1763.

You have but two topics, yourself and me, and I'm
sick of both.
Samuel Johnson, in *ibid.*, May 1776.

Boswell is a very *clubable* man.
Samuel Johnson (proposing Boswell as a member
of his evening Club), in James Boswell, *Life of
Johnson.*

If general approbation will add anything to your
enjoyment, I can tell you that I have heard you
mentioned as *a man whom everybody likes.* I think
life has little more to give.
Samuel Johnson, Letter to Boswell, 3 July 1778.

Lues Boswelliana, or disease of admiration.
T. B. Macaulay, *Essays:* 'Earl of Chatham'.

Homer is not more decidedly the first of Heroic
poets, Shakespeare is not more decidedly the first
of dramatists, Demosthenes is not more decidedly
the first of orators, than Boswell is the first of biographers. He has no second.
T. B. Macaulay, 'Samuel Johnson', in *Edinburgh
Review,* November 1831.

He longed passionately to pull himself together.
Men who had nobly succeeded had an irresistible
attraction for him. With them for a while his better
self was uppermost.
Desmond MacCarthy, *Criticism.*

See Boswell (but who for such drudg'ry more fit?)
Collect the vile refuse of poor Johnson's wit;
And fir'd with zeal for the scavenger's warm on't,
Indite what Same did, when his wisdom lay dormant.
Anthony Pasquin (John Williams), *The Children
of Thespis.*

It would be difficult to find a more shattering
refutation of the lessons of cheap morality than
the life of James Boswell. One of the most extraordinary successes in the history of civilization was
achieved by an idler, a lecher, a drunkard, and a
snob. Nor was this success of that sudden explosive
kind . . .; it was the supreme expression of an entire
life. Boswell triumphed by dint of abandoning himself, through fifty years, to his instincts. The
example, no doubt, is not one to be followed rashly.
Self-indulgence is common, and Boswells are rare.
Lytton Strachey, *Portraits in Miniature.*

His collected journals make up the most extraordinary biography, the most determined effort of a
human being to put himself totally on record, to be
found anywhere. Compared with Boswell, Rousseau
is evasive, Henry Miller reticent.
John Wain, *Samuel Johnson.*

Jemmy had a sycophantish, but a sincere admiration
of the genius, erudition and virtue of Ursa-Major,
and in recording the noble growlings of the Great
Bear, thought not of his own Scotch snivel.
John Wilson, *Noctes Ambrosianae.*

See also Henry Adams, Samuel Johnson, Damon
Runyon

BOTTOMLEY, HORATIO WILLIAM

1860—1933 Journalist, Financier

I'm Bottomley . . . I hold the unique distinction of having gone through every court in the country — except one . . . the Divorce Court . . . Although I'm nominally a bankrupt, I *never* had a better time in my *life*.
> On himself, Speaking to the Business League, Summer 1912.

I have not had your advantages, gentlemen. What poor education I have received has been gained in the University of Life.
> On himself, Speaking at the Oxford Union, 1921.

A wire I'll send to a gentleman friend
I'll call him Horatio B.
He's noted today for seeing fair play,
In a country that claims to be free.
If you feel in a plight, to his journal you write
And get reparation in full.
So you'll all say with me, Good luck to H.B.
And continued success to *John Bull*.
> Anon., Pantomime jingle, 1915

At the end of the war Bottomley had the public by the ears, the Government by the hand and his past by the throat.
> 'Tenax' [Edward Bell], *The Gentle Art of Exploiting Gullibility*.

England's Greatest Living Humbug.
> Reuben Bigland, Telegram to Bottomley, November 1920.

He had two brains, that man. One linked up with his tongue and the other thought while he talked.
> Sir Harry Preston, *Leaves from my Unwritten Diary*.

An acquaintance finding him stitching mail bags in prison, said: 'Ah, Bottomley, sewing?' Bottomley replied: 'No, reaping.'
> A. J. P. Taylor, *English History 1914—1945*.

BOURNE, RANDOLPH SILLIMAN

1886—1918 Author, Journalist

Never being competent to direct and manage any of the affairs of the world myself, I will be forced to set off by myself in the wilderness, howling like a coyote that everything is being run wrong.
> On himself, in Charles A. Madison, *Critics & Crusaders*.

Owing to a fall in infancy, he was deformed, hunchbacked, with a stunted body, large head, and heavy features; only those who recognized the keenness of his mind and the beauty of his spirit could forget his physical appearance. . . .
> Ernest Sutherland Bates, 'Randolph Silliman Bourne', in Allen Johnson ed., *Dictionary of American Biography*.

In his early death America lost a writer of great promise, a critic at home in philosophy, education, politics, and literature but homeless in his contemporary world.
> *Ibid.*

He was the conductor of innumerable diverse inspirations, a sort of clearing-house of the best living ideas of the time; through him the young writer and the young thinker came into contact with whatever in the modern world he most needed.
> Van Wyck Brooks, *Emerson and Others*.

What attracted him was the common struggle and aspiration of youth and poverty and the creative spirit everywhere, the sense of a new socialized world groping its way upward. It was this rich ground-note in all his work that made him, not the critic merely, but the leader.
> Van Wyck Brooks, in Charles A. Madison, *Critics & Crusaders*.

Above all Bourne was the perfect child of the prewar Enlightenment; when its light went out in 1918, he died with it.
> Alfred Kazin, *On Native Grounds*.

It is not, therefore, as a reformer in action that Bourne looms largest. It is as a writer who brought to political discussion the sensitiveness of a poet, the polemical skill of a journalist, the magic of a mastercraftsman in words, the analytical power and sweep of a social thinker.
> Max Lerner, in Louis Filler, *Randolph Bourne*.

Yet his premises have dignity and his philosophy has strength. And even an opponent will find that his own convictions taste sweeter if they have survived the chastening ordeal of being tested against Randolph Bourne's thought.
> Max Lerner, 'Randolph Bourne and Two Generations', in *Twice a Year*.

Few Americans possessed his enthusiasm for the deepening and enrichment of our indigenous culture. He early sought to remove the layer of rust and rot which crusted the minds of many Americans.
> Charles A. Madison, *Critics & Crusaders*.

BOW, CLARA

1905—65 Actress

In Miss Bow, the emergent flapper found her pre-destined model, pointing to such novelties as a boyish figure, short shirts, step-ins, chain smoking, a vanity case of precious metal with flask to match, necking, petting parties and the single standard.

Lloyd Morris, *Not So Long Ago.*

In a series of highly successful films after *It* in 1927, Bow summed up the spirit of the decade, but she fell foul of her own life style. ... She once said 'Being a sex symbol is a heavy load to carry, especially when one is tired, hurt and bewildered'. Possibly the most poignant epitaph for a breed of star she helped to create.

Clyde Jeavons and Jeremy Pascal, *A Pictorial History of Sex in the Movies.*

Elinor Glyn ... discovered in Clara Bow the epitome of 'It'. 'It was this: a strange magnetism which attracts both sexes ... there must be a physical attraction but beauty is unnecessary.' Probably Bow as the 'It' Girl was a studio scheme with which Elinor Glyn was happy to comply, but in the founding of the whole silly syndrome, Bow was an entirely worthy centrepiece. Even if the whole thing, including what she did on the screen, was evolved from the sort of girl she was, her life and career still seem to have been dreamed up by one of her script-writers.

David Shipman, *The Great Movie Stars.*

The 20's would have been quite different without Clara Bow: she was totally representative of the era, but to what extent she created the flapper and how much derived from her could probably never be calculated. With her bob, her cupid's-bow lips, her saucer eyes, her beads and bangles and her jiggles, she shook up cinema audiences everywhere: she was the bee's knees, she was the cat's pyjamas. She was gay and vivacious, as befitted the new emancipated woman; ... To the extent that the age was vulgar, she was vulgar, and was dismissed as such by Anita Loos, who considered that she succeeded in being at one and the same time innocuous and flashy.

Ibid.

BOWIE, JAMES

1796—1838 Adventurer

Colonel [William] Travis died like a hero, gun in hand, stretched across the carriage of a cannon, but the boastful Bowie died like a woman, almost concealed beneath a mattress.

Edward S. Sears, 'The Low Down on Jim Bowie', in Moody C. Boatright and Donald Day eds, *From Hell to Breakfast.*

BOYCE, WILLIAM

1710—79 Composer

Dr. Boyce, with all due reverence for the abilities of Handel, was one of the few of our Church composers who neither pillaged nor servilely imitated him. There is an original and sterling merit in his productions, founded as much on the study of our own masters, as on the best models of other countries, that gives to all his works a peculiar stamp and character of his own, for strength, clearness, and facility, without any mixture of styles, or extraneous and heterogeneous ornaments.

Dr Charles Burney, *A General History of Music.*

BOYLE, RICHARD, see under BURLINGTON, EARL OF

BOYLE, HON. ROBERT

1627—91 Natural Philosopher

He is very tall (about six foot high) and streight, very temperate, and vertuouse, and frugall: a Batcheler; keepes a Coach; sojournes with his sister, the Lady Ranulagh. His greatest delight is Chymistrey. He haz at his sister's a noble Laboratory, and severall servants (Prentices to him) to looke to it. He is charitable to ingeniose men that are in want, and foreigne Chymists have had large proofe of his bountie, for he will not spare for cost to gett any rare Secret.

John Aubrey, *Brief Lives.*

Many physicians, and other ingenious men, went into the society for natural philosophy [the Royal Society]. But he who laboured most, at the greatest charge, and with the most success at experiments, was Robert Boyle, the earl of Cork's youngest son. He was looked on by all who knew him as a very perfect pattern. He was a very devout Christian, humble and modest, almost to a fault, of a most spotless and exemplary life in all respects. He was highly charitable; and was a mortified and self-denied man that delighted in nothing so much as in the doing good. He neglected his person, despised the world, and lived abstracted from all pleasures, designs, and interests.

Gilbert Burnet, *History of His Own Time.*

I went to the Society where were divers Experiments in Mr. Boyls Pneumatique Engine. We put in a snake but could not kill it, by exhausting the aire, onely make it extreamly sick, but the chick died of Convulsions out right, in a short space.

John Evelyn, Diary, 25 April 1661.

I went to Lon: din'd at my Lord Falklands, made visits, & return'd: Mr Boile had now produced his Invention of dulcifying Sea-Water, like to be of mighty consequence.

Ibid.

It has plainly astonish'd me to have seen him so often recover when he has not been able to move, or bring his hand to his mouth; and indeed the contexture of his body, during the best of his health, appeared to me so delicate, that I have frequently compar'd him to a crystal or Venice glass; which tho' wrought never so thin and fine, being carefully set up, would outlast the hardier metals of daily use.

John Evelyn, Letter to Henry Wotton, March 1696.

I took boat at the Old Swan, and there up the river all alone as high as Putney almost, and then back again, all the way reading, and finishing Mr. Boyle's book of Colours, which is so chymical, that I can understand but little of it, but understand enough to see that he is a most excellent man.

Samuel Pepys, Diary, 2 June 1667.

A late distinguished professor, indeed, guiltless of any purpose of jesting or playing upon words, once gravely summed up the memorabilia of Boyle's history in the singular epitome, that he was 'the son of the Earl of Cork and the father of modern chemistry'.

George Wilson, in *British Quarterly Review*, 1849.

See also Robert Hooke

BRACEGIRDLE, ANNE

1663?—1748 Actress

Mrs *Bracegirdle* was now but just blooming to her Maturity; her Reputation as an Actress gradually rising with that of her Person; never any Woman was in such general Favour of her Spectators, which, to the last Scene of her Dramatick Life, she maintain'd by not being unguarded in her private Character. This Discretion contributed not a little to make her the *Cara*, the Darling of the Theatre: for it will be no extravagant thing to say,

Scarce an Audience saw her that were less than half of them Lovers, without a suspected Favourite among them.

Colley Cibber, *Apology for the Life of Colley Cibber.*

PIOUS Celinda goes to Pray'rs,
　　Whene'r I ask the Favour;
Yet, the tender Fool's in Tears,
　　When she believes I'll leave her.
Wou'd I were free from this Restraint,
　　Or else had Power to win her!
Wou'd she could make of me a Saint,
　　Or I of her a Sinner!
　　William Congreve, in Anthony Aston, *A Brief Supplement to Colley Cibber's Lives.*

She seems to have been a cold, vain, and interested coquette, who perfectly understood how much the influence of her charms was increased by the fame of a severity which cost her nothing, and who could venture to flirt with a succession of admirers in the just confidence that no flame which she might kindle in them would thaw her own ice.

T. B. Macaulay, *History of England.*

BRADFORD, JOHN

1510?—55 Gentleman

There, but for the grace of God, goes John Bradford.
　　On himself, attributed, watching criminals on their way to execution.

BRADFORD, WILLIAM

1589/90—1657 Pilgrim Leader

Though I am grown aged, yet I have had a longing desire to see with my own eyes something of that most ancient language and holy tongue in which the Law and Oracles of God were writ, and in which God and Angels spake to the holy patriarchs of old time; and what names were given to things from the Creation. And though I cannot attain to much herein, yet I am refreshed to have seen some glimpse hereof, as Moses saw the land of Canaan afar off. My aim and desire is to see how the words and phrases lie in the holy text, and to discern somewhat of the same, for my own content.
　　On himself, *Of Plymouth Plantation.*

From my years young in dayes of Youth,
God did make known to me his Truth,
And call'd me from my Native place
For to enjoy the Means of Grace.

In Wilderness he did me guide,
And in strange lands for me provide.
In Fears and Want, through Weal and Woe,
As Pilgrim pass'd I to and fro. . . .
  On himself, *Certain Verses left by Governor Bradford.*

BRADLEY, FRANCIS HERBERT

1846—1924 Philosopher

. . . It seems the greatest sign of friendship that he can give anyone is to take them to see his dog's grave. There are those who would not sit down among the angels, he says in his book, if their dogs were not admitted with them.
  Bertrand Russell, Letter to Alys Russell, December 1895.

See also J. E. McTaggart

BRADSHAW, JOHN

1602—59 Judge, Regicide

My brother Henry must heir the land
My brother Frank must be at his command
Whilst I, poor Jack, shall do that
Which all the world will wonder at.
  On himself, scribbled on a tombstone in Macclesfield Churchyard, when a boy, according to legend.

Bold and resolute, with a small organ of veneration, and a great lack of modesty, and not encumbered with any nice delicacy of feeling.
  Edward Foss, *Judges of England.*

A stout man, and learned in his profession. No friend to Monarchy.
  Bulstrode Whitelocke, *Memorials of the English Affairs,* 31 October 1659.

BRADSTREET, ANNE

Circa 1612—72 Poet

To be wrenched from the libraries and the courtesies of the Old World to the bleakness of peril of the new was not entirely to the girl's liking, and a pardonable homesickness for England shows now and then through the verses she wrote as a solace for her duties as a homemaker and mother of eight children.
  Grant C. Knight, *American Literature and Culture.*

Her breast was a brave Pallace, a Broad-street,
Where all heroick ample thoughts did meet,
Where nature such a Tenement had tane,
That other Souls, to hers, dwelt in a lane.
  John Norton, in Helen Campbell, *Anne Bradstreet and Her Time.*

BRANDEIS, LOUIS DEMBITZ

1856—1941 Jurist

. . . a lawyer who has not studied economics and sociology is very apt to become a public enemy.
  On himself, in Samuel J. Konefsky, *The Legacy of Holmes and Brandeis.*

As is so often true of one's image of the ideal, so Brandeis' conception of the social function of the able lawyer was no doubt a reflection of his own experience and motivations. He believed that lawyers of large affairs owed the community the benefit of their superior talents; they were lawyer-statesmen.
  Samuel J. Konefsky, *The Legacy of Holmes and Brandeis.*

Fifty-nine when Wilson nominated him to the Supreme Court, Brandeis in physical appearance was a lean man slightly above average height, whose vigorous pace and gestures marked him as one who had in no wise slowed down. There was just a touch of gray around the edges of his hair, which was generally cut short and somewhat tousled. The prominent dark eyes of his student days had receded into sockets shadowed by dark eyebrows, and the lines of his narrow, clean-shaven face had since his mid-forties given him somewhat the look of Abraham Lincoln. There was a quick keenness about him, however, that was quite different from the . . . brooding quality of the Emancipator President. . . . His speaking voice was soft when low volume was called for and his consonants were clear without the harsh exaggeration of the declaimer.
  A. L. Todd, *Justice on Trial: The Case of Louis D. Brandeis.*

For Brandeis was a liberal by affirmation and championed his causes not out of disinterest, but out of strong beliefs. A Jeffersonian democrat who passionately feared the 'curse of bigness,' he fought for the rights of states to use their police powers effectively and experimentally in order to preserve a federal system he considered essential for a democratic society.
  Melvin F. Urofsky, *A Mind of One Piece: Brandeis and American Reform.*

See also Felix Frankfurter

BRANGWYN, SIR FRANK (FRANÇOIS GUILLAUME)

1867—1956 Painter

Whistler had led us almost to believe that etching could be only a dainty thing — he set up the axiom to conceal his own limitations. Mr. Brangwyn flings Whistler's laws to the winds, and using large or small plates just as they suit his mood and are fit to express his intentions, he makes etching yield up majestic qualities which were utterly beyond Whistler's range.
> Haldane MacFall, in W. Shaw-Sparrow, *Frank Brangwyn and his Art.*

It is felt abroad that Brangwyn alone in his work symbolises the daring manliness of the British temperament; that he alone represents his time and race, showing courage, indomitable energy, and blending knowledge of the East with an intense sympathy for the grim stress and strain of Western industrialism.
> W. Shaw-Sparrow, *ibid.*

If you are sensitive to the throbbing tide of energy in creative work, you will find it a fatigue to follow with dramatic pleasure the constructional workmanship of two or three Brangwyns in a single sitting. I have felt the same fatigue when watching a strong athlete run in a great race, and there is, in fact, a certain resemblance between the nervous energy of the trained athlete and the constructive energy shown by Brangwyn.
> *Ibid.*

BREAKSPEAR, NICHOLAS, see ADRIAN IV

BRIGHT, JOHN

1811—89 Orator, Statesman

It is not my duty to make this country the knight-errant of the human race.
> On himself, speaking in 1855, in A. J. P. Taylor, *Beaverbrook.*

I have seen so much intrigue and ambition, so much selfishness and inconsistency in the character of many so-called statesmen, that I have always been anxious to disclaim the title. I have been content to describe myself as a simple citizen, who honestly examines such questions as affect the public weal and honestly offers his counsels to his countrymen.
> On himself, receiving the Freedom of the City of Edinburgh, 1868.

The only man in public life who has risen to eminence without being corrupted by London Society.
> H. H. Asquith, in R. B. Haldane, *Autobiography.*

. . . always ready for a chat and a fulmination, and filling up the intervals of business with 'Paradise Regained' . . . his opinion on men and things . . . is strong, clear, and honest, however one-sided. But he flies off provokingly into pounds, shillings, and pence when one wants him to abide for a little among deeper and less tangible motives, powers and arguments.
> Caroline Fox, Letter to Lucy Hodgkin, May 1861.

In Bright there was an unlimited self-confidence which amounted to corruption of the soul.
> Lord John Morley, in J. H. Morgan, *John Viscount Morley.*

It is not personalities that are complained of. A public man is right in attacking persons. But it is his attacks on *classes* that have given offence. . . .
> Lord Palmerston, in conversation with Richard Cobden, June 1859.

BRONTË, ANNE

1820—49 Novelist

She had, in the course of her life, been called on to contemplate near at hand and for a long time, the terrible effects of talents misused and faculties abused; hers was naturally a sensitive, reserved, and dejected nature; what she saw sank very deeply into her mind; it did her harm. She brooded over it till she believed it to be a duty to reproduce every detail . . . as a warning to others. . . . This well-meant resolution brought on her misconstruction and some abuse, which she bore, as it was her custom to bear whatever was unpleasant, with mild, steady patience. She was a very sincere and practical Christian, but the tinge of religious melancholy communicated a sad shade to her brief, blameless life.
> Charlotte Brontë, *Biographical Notice.*

A sort of literary Cinderella.
> George Moore, *Conversation in Ebury Street.*

Anne Brontë serves a twofold purpose in the study of what the Brontës wrote and were. In the first place, her gentle and delicate presence, her sad, short story, her hard life and early death, enter deeply into the poetry and tragedy that have always been entwined with the memory of the Brontës, as women and as writers; in the second, the books and poems that she wrote serve as matter of comparison by which to test the greatness of her two sisters. She is the measure of their genius — like them, but not with them.

Mrs Humphry Ward, Preface to the Haworth edition of the Brontës' Works.

BRONTË, (PATRICK) BRANWELL

1817—48 Artist

My aim, sir, is to push out into the open world, and for this I trust not poetry alone; that might launch the vessel, but could not bear her on. Sensible and scientific prose, bold and vigorous efforts in my walk in life, would give a further title to the notice of the world; and then again poetry ought to brighten and crown that name with glory. . . . Surely, in this day, when there is not a *writing* poet worth a sixpence, the field must be 'open, if a better man can step forward.

On himself, Letter to William Wordsworth, 19 January 1837.

I shall never be able to realise the too sanguine hopes of my friends, for at twenty-eight I am a thoroughly *old man* — mentally and bodily. Far more so, indeed, than I am willing to express. . . . My rude rough acquaintances here ascribe my unhappiness solely to causes produced by my sometimes irregular life because they have no other pains than those resulting from excess or want of ready cash. They do not know that I would rather want a shirt than want a springy mind, and that my total want of happiness, were I to step into York Minster now, would be far, far worse than their want of a hundred pounds when they might happen to need it, and that if a dozen glasses or a bottle of wine drives off their cares, such cures only make me outwardly passable in company but *never* drive off mine.

On himself, Letter to Joseph Leyland, 24 January 1847.

A Brother — sleeps he here? —
Of all his gifted race
Not the least-gifted; young,
Unhappy, beautiful; the cause
Of many hopes, of many tears.
O Boy, if here thou sleep'st, sleep well!
On thee too did the Muse
Bright in thy cradle smile:
But some dark Shadow came
(I know not what) and interpos'd.

Matthew Arnold, *Haworth Churchyard*.

The Brontë son did not fulfil his early promise; his great misfortune was that he was a man. If he had been constrained, as were his sisters, by the spirit of the times; if he had been compelled, for want of other

outlet, to take up his pen or else burst, he might have been known to-day, as rather more than the profligate brother of the Brontës.

Muriel Spark, *The Brontë Letters*.

BRONTË, CHARLOTTE

1816—55 Novelist

She showed that abysses may exist inside a governess and eternities inside a manufacturer.

G. K. Chesterton, *Twelve Types*.

I have read *Jane Eyre*, mon ami, and shall be glad to know what you admire in it. All self-sacrifice is good — but one would like it to be in a somewhat nobler cause than that of a diabolical law which chains a man body and soul to a putrefying carcase. However, the book *is* interesting — only I wish the characters would talk a little less like the heroes and heroines of police reports.

George Eliot, Letter to Charles Bray, 11 June 1848.

Charlotte Brontë, one cannot but feel after comparing her early work with modern bestsellers, was only unlike them in being fortunate in her circumstances, which gave her a cultured background, and in the age in which she lived, which did not get between her and her spontaneities.

Q. D. Leavis, *Fiction and the Reading Public*.

We shall not attempt to resolve the much agitated question of the sex of the author of these remarkable works. All that we shall say on the subject is, that if they are the productions of a woman, she must be a woman pretty nearly unsexed; and Jane Eyre strikes us as a personage much more likely to have sprung ready armed from the head of a man, and that head a pretty hard one, than to have experienced, in any shape, the softening influence of female creation.

James Lorimer, in *North British Review*, August 1849.

Had Brontë herself not grown up in a house of half-mad sisters with a domestic tyrant for father, no 'prospects', as marital security was referred to, and with only the confines of governessing and celibacy staring at her from the future, her chief release the group fantasy of 'Angria', that collective dream these strange siblings played all their lives, composing stories about a never-never land where women could rule, exercise power, govern the state, declare night and day, death and life — then we would never have heard from Charlotte. . . . Had that been the case, we might never have known what a resurrected soul wished to tell upon emerging from several millennia of subordination.

Kate Millett, *Sexual Politics.*

I believe she would have given all her genius and all her fame to be beautiful. Perhaps few women ever existed more anxious to be pretty than she, and more angrily conscious of the circumstance that she was *not* pretty.

George Smith, in *Critic*, January 1901.

I wish you had not sent me Jane Eyre. It interested me so much that I have lost (or won if you like) a whole day in reading it at the busiest period, with the printers I know waiting for copy. Who the author can be I can't guess — if a woman she knows her language better than most ladies do, or has had a 'classical' education. It is a fine book though — the man & woman capital — the style very generous and upright so to speak. I thought it was Kinglake for some time.

W. M. Thackeray, Letter to W. S. Williams, 23 October 1847.

It amuses me to read the author's naïve confession [in *Villette*] of being in love with 2 men at the same time; and her readiness to fall in love at any time. The poor little woman of genius! the fiery little eager brave tremulous homely-faced creature! I can read a great deal of her life as I fancy in her book, and see that rather than have fame, rather than any other earthly good or mayhap heavenly she wants some Tomkins or another to love her and be in love with. But you see she is a little bit of a creature without a penny worth of good looks, thirty years old I should think, buried in the country, and eating up her own heart there, and no Tomkins will come.

W. M. Thackeray, Letter to Lucy Baxter, 11 March 1853.

Charlotte Brontë was surely a marvellous woman. If it could be right to judge the work of a novelist from one small portion of one novel, and to say of an author that he is to be accounted as strong as he shows himself to be in his strongest morsel of work, I should be inclined to put Miss Brontë very high indeed. . . . Therefore, though the end of the book is weak, and the beginning not very good, I venture to predict that *Jane Eyre* will be read among English novels when many whose names are now better known shall have been forgotten.

Anthony Trollope, *Autobiography.*

March 21. Read to Albert out of that melancholy, interesting book, *Jane Eyre* . . . May 13. We dined alone and talked and read, going on reading till past 11 in that intensely interesting novel *Jane Eyre* . . . May 21. We remained up reading in *Jane Eyre* till ½ p. 11 — quite creepy . . . August 4. At near 10 we went below and nearly finished reading that most interesting book *Jane Eyre*. A peaceful, happy evening.

Queen Victoria, Diary, 1858.

Has it ever been sufficiently recognized that Charlotte Brontë is first and foremost *an Irishwoman*, that her genius is at bottom a Celtic genius? The main characteristics indeed of the Celt are all hers — disinterestedness, melancholy, wildness, a wayward force and passion, for ever wooed by sounds and sights to which other natures are insensible — by murmurs from the earth, by colours in the sky, by tones and accents of the soul, that speak to the Celtic sense as to no other . . . . Then, as to the Celtic pride, the Celtic shyness, the Celtic endurance, — Charlotte Brontë was rich in them all.

Mrs Humphry Ward, Preface to the Haworth edition of the Brontës' Works.

BRONTË, EMILY JANE

1818—48 Novelist

She —
(How shall I sing her?) — whose soul
Knew no fellow for might,
Passion, vehemence, grief,
Daring, since Byron died.
Matthew Arnold, *Haworth Churchyard.*

In Emily's nature the extremes of vigour and simplicity seemed to meet. Under an unsophisticated culture, inartificial tastes, and an unpretending outside lay a secret power and fire that might have informed the brains and kindled the veins of a hero; but she had no worldly wisdom; her powers were unadapted to the practical business of life: she would fail to defend her most manifest rights, to consult her most legitimate advantage. An interpreter ought always to have stood between her and the world.

Charlotte Brontë, Preface to *Wuthering Heights.*

Posterity has paid its debt to her too generously, and with too little understanding.

Ivy Compton-Burnett, Letter to Anthony Powell.

I've been greatly interested in *Wuthering Heights*, the first novel I've read for an age, and the best (as regards power and sound style) for two ages. . . : But it is a fiend of a book, an incredible monster, combining all the stronger female tendencies from Mrs Browning to Mrs Brownrigg. The action is laid in Hell, — only it

seems places and people have English names there.
D. G. Rossetti, Letter to William Allingham,
19 September 1854.

BRONTËS (COLLECTIVELY)

Literary criticism of the Brontës has been a long
game of masculine prejudice wherein the player either
proves they can't write and are hopeless primitives,
whereupon the critic sets himself up like a schoolmaster to edit their stuff and point out where they
went wrong, or converts them into case histories from
the wilds, occasionally prefacing his moves with a few
pseudo-sympathetic remarks about the windy house
on the moors, or old maidhood, following with an
attack on every truth the novels contain, waged by
anxious pedants who fear Charlotte might 'castrate'
them or Emily 'unman' them with her passion.
Kate Millett, *Sexual Politics*.

BROOKE, RUPERT CHAWNER

1887—1915 Poet

If I should die, think only this of me:
That there's some corner of a foreign field
That is forever England.
On himself, *The Soldier*.

The thoughts to which he gave expression in the very
few incomparable war sonnets which he has left behind will be shared by many thousands of young men
moving resolutely and blithely forward into this, the
hardest, the cruellest, and the least-rewarded of all the
wars that men have fought. They are a whole history
and revelation of Rupert Brooke himself. Joyous,
fearless, versatile, deeply instructed, with classic
symmetry of mind and body, he was all that one
would wish England's noblest sons to be in days when
no sacrifice but the most precious is acceptable, and
the most precious is that which is most freely proffered.
Winston Churchill, Obituary in *The Times*,
26 April 1915.

The death of Rupert Brooke fills me more and more
with the sense of the fatuity of it all. He was slain by
bright Phoebus' shaft — it was in keeping with his
general sunniness — it was the real climax of his pose.
I first heard of him as a Greek god under a Japanese
sunshade, reading poetry in his pyjamas, at Grantchester, — at Grantchester upon the lawns where the
river goes. Bright Phoebus smote him down. It is all
in the saga.
D. H. Lawrence, Letter to Lady Ottoline Morrell,
30 April 1915.

He energized the Garden-Suburb ethos with a certain
original talent and the vigour of a prolonged adolescence. His verse exhibits a genuine sensuousness
rather like Keats's (though more energetic) and something that is rather like Keats's vulgarity with a Public
School accent.
F. R. Leavis, *New Bearings in English Poetry*.

He was, in a sense, very neurotic. I think he was very
highly-strung. Supposing he had been alive today, his
early experiences wouldn't have made him so. But in
that day and age, in his class, men knew as little about
sex really as women did. He fell in love and induced
a woman to live with him and then grew out of love
with her. He thought she was with child by him, and
then she had a miscarriage, and the whole thing put
a terrible guilt complex in him. But once he'd got
over that, he seemed extraordinarily sane and
balanced.
Cathleen Nesbitt, in *Listener*, 20 January 1972.

I suppose by the time you get this you will have seen
about Rupert's death. . . . It was impossible not to
like him, impossible not to hope that he might like
one again; and now. . . . The meaninglessness of Fate
is intolerable; it's all muddle and futility. After all
the pother of those years of living, to effect — simply
nothing. It is like a confused tale, just beginning and
then broken off for no reason, and for ever. One
hardly knows whether to be sorry even. One is just
left with a few odd memories — until they too vanish.
Lytton Strachey, Letter to Duncan Grant,
25 April 1915.

Rupert had immense charm when he wanted to be
charming, and he was inclined to exploit his charm so
that he seemed to be sometimes too much the professional charmer. He had a very pronounced streak
of hardness, even cruelty, in his character, and his
attitude to all other males within a short radius of
any attractive female was ridiculously jealous — the
attitude of a farmyard cock among the hens.
Leonard Woolf, *Beginning Again*.

Yeats talked about you the other night. He thinks
you are likely to be a considerable person if you can
get rid of what he calls 'languid sensuality' and get in
its place 'robust sensuality'. I suppose you will understand this.
William Butler Yeats, reported in St John Ervine,
Letter to Brooke, January 1913.

He is the handsomest man in England, and he wears
the most beautiful shirts.
William Butler Yeats, in conversation, January
1913.

BROOKS, VAN WYCK

1886—1963 Author

He was a Ruskin come alive in New York in 1915, a sensitive, dynamic, brilliant young American who had found his standards in the great Victorian critics of materialism.
Alfred Kazin, *On Native Grounds.*

As a biographer his half-hearted Freudian analyses and self-indulgent lyricism directly encouraged less gifted 'interpreters' in biography to mistake their prejudices for facts and to write bad poetry when they meant to write biography.
Ibid.

He wrestled with the whole of American culture, with its literature and philosophy and their relation to the society they came from, and he did so in the very language of his subject. *His* conclusions, ironical, subtly contemptuous, but ultimately inspiring, could not be repudiated on the ground that he was incapable of understanding the things he dealt with.
Bernard Smith, 'Van Wyck Brooks', in Malcolm Cowley ed., *After the Genteel Tradition.*

As a practising critic, he wanted more than anything else a great literature made 'out of American life' — a literature that would constitute the soul of his people, at once born of the race's spiritual experiences and upholding those experiences for the race to live by.
Ibid.

His career was one long sustained attempt to realize a community of art and letters working and located at the very heart of American civilization. During his lifetime American literature came of age, and it did so to the accompaniment of his voice exhorting writers to meet their responsibility with courage and dignity — and with pride in their membership in a great community.
James R. Vitelli, *Van Wyck Brooks.*

However, it was not his ideas, which were few and broad, so much as a tone and a style, and an ability to invoke usable images and myths — his establishment, in short, of a distinct attitude toward literature as a guiding force in civilization — which he contributed to the making of modern American literature.
Ibid.

Although he turned out to be a critic of divided mind, a man whose life was broken in half, in one respect his career was all of a piece: from first to last he sought to transform America from an industrial

jungle into a place fit for the realization of Emerson's Romantic dream.
William Wasserstrom, *Van Wyck Brooks.*

BROUGHAM, HENRY PETER, LORD BROUGHAM AND VAUX

1778—1868 Statesman, Author

Never was there a subject that Grey did not say the Government was gone if I did not speak, and generally if I did not undertake it. All this necessarily led to my *interfering* . . . as to *domineering* it is possibly true. I am of a hasty and violent, at least vehement, nature, and not bred in courts or offices, and never was a subaltern, therefore I am a bad courtier. However I meant no harm and never grudged work; and always, both in and out of Parliament, was working as hard as a horse for the party, and never once for myself or to thwart them.
On himself, Letter to Lord Spencer, January 1835.

If the Lord Chancellor only knew a little law he would know something of everything. . . .
Anon., in G. W. E. Russell, *Collections and Recollections.*

He was a kind of prophet of knowledge. His voice was heard in the streets. He preached the gospel of the alphabet; he sang the praises of the primer all day long.
Walter Bagehot, *Biographical Studies*: 'Lord Brougham'.

If he were a horse, nobody would buy him; with that eye, no one could answer for his temper.
Ibid.

Mr. Brougham's mountain is delivered, and behold! — the mouse. The wisdom of the reformer could not overcome the craft of the lawyer. Mr. Brougham, after all, is not the man to set up a simple, natural, and rational administration of justice against the entanglements and technicalities of our English law proceedings.
Jeremy Bentham, Memorandum: 'On Brougham's Law Reform', after Brougham's speech of 7 February 1828.

Beware lest blundering Brougham destroy the sale,
Turn beef to bannocks, cauliflower to kail.
Lord Byron, *English Bards and Scotch Reviewers.*

The honourable and learned gentleman having in the course of his parliamentary life supported or proposed *almost every species of innovation* which could be practised on the constitution it was not very easy for ministers to do anything without seeming to borrow from him. Break away in what direction they would, whether to the right or to the left, it was all alike. 'Oh,' said the honourable gentleman, 'I was there before you: you would not have thought of that if I had not given you a hint.' . . . There was no noise astir for the good of mankind in any part of the world, but he instantly claimed it for his thunder.

> George Canning, in the House of Commons,
> in Walter Bagehot, *Biographical Studies*:
> Lord Brougham.

The fault of Mr. Brougham is, that he holds no intellect at present in great dread, and, consequently, allows himself on all occasions to run wild. Few men hazard more unphilosophical speculations; but he is safe, because there is no one to notice them. On all great occasions, Mr. Brougham has come up to the mark; an infallible test of a man of genius.

> Benjamin Disraeli, *The Young Duke*.

This curious and versatile creature . . . after acting Jupiter one day in the House of Lords, is ready to act Scapin anywhere else the next. . . .

> Charles Greville, Diary, 9 August 1839.

His eye is as fine an eye I ever saw. It is like a lion's, watching for prey. It is a clear grey, the light vibrating at the bottom of the iris, and the cornea shining, silvery and tense. I never before had the opportunity of examining Brougham's face with the scrutiny of a painter, and I am astonished at that extraordinary eye.

> Benjamin Haydon, *Autobiography*.

He is at home in the crooked mazes of rotten boroughs, is not baffled by Scotch law, and can follow the meaning of one of Mr Canning's speeches.

> William Hazlitt, *The Spirit of the Age*.

. . . As author, lawyer and politician, he is *triformis*, like Hecate: and in every one of his three forms he is *bifrons*, like Janus; the true Mr Facing-both-ways of Vanity Fair.

> Thomas Love Peacock, *Crotchet Castle*: The
> Reverend Dr. Folliott.

Lo! in Corruption's lumber-room,
The remnants of a wondrous broom;
That walking, talking, oft was seen,
Making stout promise to sweep clean;
But evermore, at every push,
Proved but a stump without a brush.
Upon its handle-top, a sconce,
Like Brahma's, looked four ways at once,
Pouring on king, lords, church and rabble

Long floods of favour-currying gabble;
From four-fold mouth-piece always spinning
Projects of plausible beginning,
Whereof said sconce did ne'er intend
Than any one should have an end;
Yet still by shifts and quaint inventions,
Got credit for its good intentions,
Adding no trifle to the store,
Wherewith the devil paves his floor.
Worn out at last, found bare and scrubbish,
And thrown aside with other rubbish,
We'll e'en hand o'er the enchanted stick,
As a choice present for Old Nick,
To sweep, beyond the Stygian lake,
The pavement it has helped to make.

> Thomas Love Peacock, in *Examiner*,
> August 1831.

Bias of honour, place, wealth, worldly good,
Drew all away; he would not so be drawn.
Truth's and Right's soldier from the first he stood,
And in the thickest darkness looked for dawn.

> Tom Taylor, in *Punch*, 30 May 1868.

. . . he might have been any *one* of ten first-rate kinds of men, but . . . he tried to be *all* ten, and has failed.

> *The Times*, in Walter Bagehot, *Biographical Studies*: 'Sir George Cornewall Lewis'.

He was one of those characters in real life who would appear incredible in fiction. He was so marvellously ill-favoured as to possess some of the attractiveness of a gargoyle. He had neither dignity, nor what a Roman would have called gravity. As Lord Chancellor, he distinguished himself by belching from the Woolsack.

> Esmé Wingfield-Stratford, in L. Levinson ed.,
> *Bartlett's Unfamiliar Quotations*.

See also John Cavanagh, Harriet Martineau

BROUN, HEYWOOD CAMPBELL
1888—1939 Journalist

The trouble with me is that I inherited an insufficient amount of vengeful feeling. Kings, princes, dukes and even local squires rode their horses so that they stepped upon the toes of my ancestors, who did nothing about it except to apologize. I would then have joined more eagerly in pulling down the Bastille, but if anybody had caught me at it and given me a sharp look I'm afraid I would have put it back again.

> On himself, in Robert E. Drennan ed., *Wit's End*.

His speech was slow and steady like the movement of the walking beam on an old-fashioned Mississippi steamboat, and like the walking beam it conveyed an impression of great power gently and only partially used.

Bruce Bliven, *Heywood Broun.*

Heywood Broun and I had one thing in common: he was fired from as many newspapers as I have been fired out of political parties.

Fiorello La Guardia, in *Heywood Broun as He Seemed to Us.*

Beneath that partly guileful naivete there was great wisdom and shrewdness in Heywood, and humor of most endearing ricochet.

Christopher Morley, *Heywood*, in *In Memoriam.*

With his great bulk, there was a spirit that was solid and delicate, giant-like and gentle. He was a gallant knight who smiled at his own gallantries and his own generosities.

Edward G. Robinson, in *Heywood Broun as He Seemed to Us.*

. . . no matter for whom he worked he wore no man's collar.

Franklin D. Roosevelt, in *Heywood Broun.*

A gin-drinking, poker-playing, wicked old reprobate.

Herbert B. Swope, in *Heywood Broun as He Seemed to Us.*

No one is so impotent that, meeting Broun face to face, he cannot frighten him into any lie. Any mouse can make this elephant squeal. Yet, I know no more honest being, for, when not threatened, his speech is an innocent emptying of his mind as a woman empties her purse, himself genuinely curious about its contents.

Alexander Woollcott, in Edwin P. Hoyt, *Alexander Woollcott: The Man Who Came to Dinner.*

BROUNCKER, WILLIAM, VISCOUNT

1620?—84 First President of the Royal Society

What should be our final judgement of Brouncker as a mathematician? I am afraid that I cannot be as enthusiastic as I should like to be. One must be more exacting in judging a man who had every scientific advantage that his age offered, and was in touch with all the ablest mathematicians of his time, than in the case of a man less favourably placed. He was certainly an able man, and his continued fraction approximation to $4/\pi$ was admirable. But in all the other papers I have mentioned he was pretty close to what others

had done, and sometimes done better; a sad verdict.

J. L. Coolidge, *The Mathematics of Great Amateurs.*

I perceive he is a rotten-hearted, false man as any else I know, even as Sir W. Pen himself, and, therefore, I must beware of him accordingly, and I hope I shall.

Samuel Pepys, Diary, 29 January 1666—7.

BROWN, FORD MADOX

1821—93 Painter

There were in Brown two incongruous spirits, one, desire for combination with a power in favour with the world, the other in open defiance of sedate taste; with all his variableness it was certainly not then notable that he had become a seeker after new truths.

William Holman-Hunt, *Pre-Raphaelitism and the Pre-Raphaelite Brotherhood.*

He would make no concessions and play no tricks, he was obstinate and rancorous, and he is so rare an example of popularity forfeited that by every rule of the game, he should have appeared today in force only to confound the generations that misjudged him. He is, however, not quite up to his part. The sincerity that shines out in him lights up not only the vulgarity of his age, but too many of his own perversities and pedantries.

Henry James, 'Lord Leighton and Ford Madox Brown', in *Harper's Weekly*, 1897.

Do you not see that his name never occurs in my books — do you think that would be so if I *could* praise him, seeing that he is an entirely worthy fellow? But pictures are pictures, and things that ar'n't ar'n't.

John Ruskin, Letter to Ellen Heaton, March 1862,

BROWN, JOHN

1800—59 Abolitionist

I am fully persuaded that I am worth inconceivably more to hang than for any other purpose.

On himself, 2 November 1859, in Burton Stevenson, *The Home Book of Quotations.*

Nature obviously was deeply intent in the making of him. He is of imposing appearance, personally, — tall, with square shoulders and standing; eyes of deep gray, and couchant, as if ready to spring at the least rustling, dauntless yet kindly; his hair shooting

backward from low down on his forehead; nose trenchant and Romanesque; set lips, his voice suppressed yet metallic, suggesting deep reserves; decided mouth; the countenance and frame charged with power throughout. ... I think him about the manliest man I have ever seen, — the type and synonym of the Just.
    Amos Bronson Alcott, in *ibid.*

Let no man pray that Brown be spared. Let Virginia make him a martyr. Now, he has only blundered. His soul was noble: his work miserable. But a cord and a gibbet would redeem all that, and round up Brown's failure with a heroic success.
    Henry Ward Beecher, in Oswald Garrison Villard, *John Brown.*

... A stone eroded to a cutting edge
By obstinacy failure and cold prayers ...
And with a certain minor prophet air
That fooled the world to thinking him half-great
When all he did consistently was fail.
    Stephen Vincent Benét, *John Brown's Body.*

John Brown is dead, he will not come again,
A stray ghost-walker with a ghostly gun.
    Ibid.

... when John Brown stretched forth his arm the sky was cleared — the armed hosts of freedom stood face to face over the chasm of a broken union, and the clash of arms was at hand.
    Frederick Douglass, speech at Storer College at Harper's Ferry, May 1882.

... the most ideal of men, for he wanted to put all his ideals into action.
    Ralph Waldo Emerson, in W. E. B. Du Bois, *John Brown.*

Was John Brown justified in his attempt; Yes, if Washington was in his, if Warren and Hancock were in theirs. If men are justified in striking a blow for freedom, when the question is one of a three penny tax on tea, then, I say, they are a thousand times more justified, when it is to save fathers, mothers, wives and children from the slave-coffle and the auction block, and to restore them their God-given rights.
    William Lloyd Garrison, in *Liberator,* 16 December 1859.

John Brown's body lies a-mouldering in the grave
But his soul goes marching on.
    C. S. Hall, *John Brown's Body.*

The death of Brown is more than Cain killing Abel: it is Washington slaying Spartacus.
    Victor Hugo, *A Word Concerning John Brown to Virginia,* 2 December 1859.

The Portent
Hanging from the beam,
    Slowly swaying (such the law),
Gaunt the shadow on your green,
    Shenandoah!
The cut is on the crown
(Lo John Brown),
And the stabs shall heal no more.

Hidden in the cap
    Is the anguish none can draw;
So your future veils its face,
    Shenandoah!
But the streaming beard is shown
(Weird John Brown),
The meteor of the War.
    Herman Melville, in F. O. Matthiessen ed., *The Oxford Book of American Verse.*

John Brown has loosened the roots of the slave system; it only breathes, — it does not live — hereafter.
    Wendell Phillips at the funeral of John Brown, in Oswald Garrison Villard, *John Brown.*

I speak for the slave when I say that I prefer the philanthropy of Captain Brown to that philanthropy which neither shoots me nor liberates me.
    Henry David Thoreau, in John Bartlett, *Familiar Quotations.*

... Some eighteen hundred years ago Christ was crucified; this morning, perchance, Captain Brown was hung. These are the two ends of a chain which is not without its links. He is not Old Brown any longer; he is an angel of light.
    Henry David Thoreau, *A Plea for Captain John Brown.*

I would now sing how an old man, tall with white
          hair,
    mounted the scaffold in Virginia.
(I was at hand, silent I stood with teeth shut close, I
          watched
I stood very near you old man when cool and
          indifferent,
but trembling with age and your inheal'd wounds
you mounted the scaffold.)
    Walt Whitman, *Leaves of Grass.*

See also John Peter Altgeld

BROWN, JOHN MASON

1900—69 Critic

. . . minister of fine arts to the people at large.
Brooks Atkinson, in Serrell Hillman, 'One Man
Chautauqua', in *Esquire*, April 1960.

John would rather be caught in a loincloth on Times
Square than with a sloppy phrase.
Norman Cousins, in *ibid.*

. . . the remarkable thing about John is that he has
made his living entirely out of talent. He isn't like
most of us, who sell insurance or bonds and use our
gifts on the side.
Henry Cabot Lodge, in *ibid.*

He treads the most extraordinary delicate line
between principle and popularity, and he never
seems to injure either. He doesn't respond to vulgar
drives, whether ambition, sex or money.
Marya Mannes, in *ibid.*

The Confederate Aristotle.
Charles Poore, in *New York Times.*

BROWN, ROBERT

1773—1858 Naturalist

I saw a good deal of Robert Brown, 'facile Princeps
Botanicorum', as he was called by Humboldt. He
seemed to me to be chiefly remarkable for the
minuteness of his observations and their perfect
accuracy. His knowledge was extraordinarily great,
and much died with him, owing to his excessive
fear of ever making a mistake. He poured out his
knowledge to me in the most unreserved manner,
yet was strangely jealous on some points. I called on
him two or three times before the voyage of the
Beagle, and on one occasion he asked me to look
through a microscope and describe what I saw.
This I did, and believe now that it was the marvellous
currents of protoplasm in some vegetable cell. I
then asked him what I had seen; but he answered
me, 'That is my little secret'.
Charles Darwin, *Autobiography.*

Perhaps no naturalist ever recorded the results of his
investigations in fewer words and with greater precision than Robert Brown: certainly no one ever
took more pains to state nothing beyond the precise
point in question. Indeed we have sometimes fancied
that he preferred to enwrap rather than to explain
his meaning; to put it into such a form that, unless
you follow Solomon's injunction and dig for the

wisdom as for hid treasure, you may hardly
apprehend it until you have found it all out for
yourself, when you will have the satisfaction of
perceiving that Mr. Brown not only knew all about
it, but put it upon record long before.
Asa Gray, in *Nature*, 4 June 1874.

BROWNE, SIR THOMAS

1605—82 Physician, Author

I dare, without usurpation, assume the honourable
style of Christian.
On himself, *Religio Medici*, part 1.

Lord, deliver me from myself.
On himself, *Religio Medici*, part 2.

It would be difficult to describe Browne adequately;
exuberant in conception and conceit, dignified,
hyper-latinistic, a quiet and sublime enthusiast; yet
a fantast, a humourist, a brain with a twist; egotistic
like Montaigne, yet with a feeling heart and an active
curiosity, which, however, too often degenerates
into a hunting after oddities.
Samuel Taylor Coleridge, *Literary Remains.*

Next morning, I went to see Sir Thomas Browne . . .;
his whole house and garden being a paradise and
cabinet of rareties, and that of the best collection,
especially medals, books, plants, and natural things.
Amongst other curiosities, Sir Thomas had a
collection of the eggs of all the fowl and birds he
could procure, that country (especially the promontory of Norfolk) being frequented, as he said,
by several kinds which seldom or never go farther
into the land, as cranes, storks, eagles, and variety
of water-fowl.
John Evelyn, Diary, 17 October 1671.

Browne . . . is a pre-eminent example of the class of
writer with whom it is form, not substance, that is
of the first importance. He is interesting almost
exclusively to the student and lover of style.
Edmund Gosse, *Sir Thomas Browne.*

Sir Thomas Browne seemed to be of opinion that
the only business of life was to think, and that the
proper object of speculation was, by darkening
knowledge, to breed more speculation, and 'find no
end in wandering mazes lost'. He chose the incomprehensible and impracticable as almost the only
subjects fit for a lofty and lasting contemplation, or
for the exercise of a solid faith. . . . He pushes a
question to the utmost verge of conjecture, that he
may repose on the certainty of doubt . . . he

delighted in the preternatural and visionary, and he only existed at the circumference of his nature.

William Hazlitt, *Character of Sir T. Browne as a Writer.*

His style is, indeed, a tissue of many languages; a mixture of heterogeneous words, brought together from distant regions, with terms originally appropriated to one art, and drawn by violence into the service of another. He must, however, be confessed to have augmented our philosophical diction; and in defence of uncommon words and expressions, we must consider, that he had uncommon sentiments.

Samuel Johnson, *Life of Browne.*

Who would not be curious to see the lineaments of a man who, having himself been twice married, wished that mankind were propagated like trees!

Charles Lamb, as reported by William Hazlitt, 'On Persons One would wish to have Seen', in *New Monthly Magazine,* January 1826.

It is interesting — or at least amusing — to consider what are the most appropriate places in which different authors should be read. Pope is doubtless at his best in the midst of a formal garden, Herrick in an orchard, and Shelley in a boat at sea. Sir Thomas Browne demands, perhaps, a more exotic atmosphere. One could read him floating down the Euphrates, or past the shores of Arabia; and it would be pleasant to open the *Vulgar Errors* in Constantinople, or to get by heart a chapter of the *Christian Morals* between the paws of a Sphinx.

Lytton Strachey, *Books and Characters.*

His immense egotism has paved the way for all psychological novelists, autobiographers, confession-mongers, and dealers in the curious shades of our private life. He it was who first turned from the contacts of man with man, to their lonely life within.

Virginia Woolf, *The Common Reader.*

See also Samuel Taylor Coleridge, Robert Louis Stevenson

BROWNING, ELIZABETH BARRETT
1806–61 Poet

The Greatest Novel Reader in the World.
On herself, Proposed epitaph.

The simple truth is that *she* was the poet, and I the clever person by comparison.

Robert Browning, Letter to Isa Blagden, 19 August 1871.

Mrs Browning's death is rather a relief to me, I must say. No more Aurora Leighs, thank God! A woman of real genius, I know; but what is the upshot of it all? She and her sex had better mind the kitchen and the children; and perhaps the poor. Except in such things as little novels, they only devote themselves to what men do much better, leaving that which men do worse or not at all.

Edward Fitzgerald, in W. A. Wright, *Letters and Literary Remains of Edward Fitzgerald.*

The poetess was everything I did not like. She had great cavernous eyes, glowering out under two big bushes of black ringlets, a fashion I had not beheld before. She never laughed, or even smiled, once, during the whole conversation, and through all the gloom of the shuttered room I could see that her face was hollow and ghastly pale. *Mamma mia*! but I was glad when I got out into the sunshine again.

Mrs Hugh Fraser, *A Diplomatist's Wife in Many Lands.*

We had some tea and some strawberries. . . . There was no very noteworthy conversation; the most interesting topic being that disagreeable and now wearisome one of spiritual communications, as regards which Mrs Browning is a believer, and her husband an infidel. . . . Browning and his wife had both been present at a spiritual session held by Mr Home, and had seen and felt the unearthly hands, one of which had placed a laurel wreath on Mrs Browning's head. Browning, however, avowed his belief that these hands were affixed to the feet of Mr Home, who lay extended in his chair, with his legs stretched far under the table. The marvellousness of the fact . . . melted strangely away in his hearty gripe, and at the sharp touch of his logic; while his wife, ever and anon, put in a little gentle word of expostulation.

Nathaniel Hawthorne, *French and Italian Notebooks.*

Her physique was peculiar: curls like the pendant ears of a water spaniel and poor little hands — so thin that when she welcomed you she gave you something like the foot of a young bird.

Frederick Locker, *My Confidences.*

She was just like a King Charles Spaniel, the same large soft brown eyes, the full silky curls falling round her face like a spaniel's ears, the same pathetic wistfulness of expression. Her mouth was too large for beauty, but full of eloquent curves and movements. Her voice was very expressive, her manner gentle but full of energy. At times she became intense in tone and gesture, but it was so spontaneous, that nobody could ever have thought it assumed as is the fashion with later poets and poetesses.

Mrs David Ogilvy, *Recollections of Mrs Browning.*

Fate has not been kind to Mrs Browning as a writer. Nobody reads her, nobody discusses her, nobody troubles to put her in her place. One has only to compare her reputation with Christina Rossetti's to trace her decline. Christina Rossetti mounts irresistibly to the first place among English women poets. Elizabeth, so much more loudly applauded during her lifetime, falls farther and farther behind.

Virginia Woolf, *The Second Common Reader.*

See also Robert Browning, Charlotte Cushman

BROWNING, ROBERT

1812—89 Poet

That bard's a Browning; he neglects the form:
But ah, the sense, ye gods, the weighty sense!
On himself, *The Inn Album.*

As to my own Poems — they must be left to Providence and that fine sense of discrimination which I never cease to meditate upon and admire in the public: they cry out for new things and when you furnish them with what they cried for, 'it's *so* new', they grunt.

On himself, Letter to John Ruskin, 10 December 1855.

I can have but little doubt that my writing has been, in the main, too hard for many I should have been pleased to communicate with; but I never designedly tried to puzzle people, as some of my critics have supposed. On the other hand, I never pretended to offer such literature as should be a substitute for a cigar, or a game of dominoes, to an idle man. So perhaps, on the whole, I get my deserts and something over — not a crowd, but a few I value more.

On himself, Letter to W. G. Kingsland, 1868.

Browning is a man with a moderate gift passionately desiring movement and fulness, and obtaining but a confused multitudinousness.

Matthew Arnold, Letter to A. H. Clough, 1848—9.

Robert Browning
Immediately stopped frowning
And started to blush
When fawned on by Flush.

W. H. Auden, *Academic Graffiti.*

He is at once a student of mysticism and a citizen of the world. He brings to the club-sofa distinct visions of old creeds, intense images of strange thoughts: he takes to the bookish student tidings of wild Bohemia, and little traces of the *demi-monde.* He puts down what is good for the naughty, and what is naughty for the good. Over women his easier writings exercise that imperious power which belongs to the writings of a great man of the world upon such matters. He knows women, and therefore they wish to know him.

Walter Bagehot, *Wordsworth, Tennyson, and Browning.*

It became a favourite pastime for ingenious brains to construe the craggiest passages in Browning, and to read him was for long in England the mark of a taste for nimble intellectual exercise rather than for a love of poetry. . . . His ideas were new, for poetry — and for that reason people thought them at first obscure — but they were quite clear. Only he had as it were a stutter in his utterance.

Rupert Brooke, *Browning.*

God knows I too understand very well what it is to be 'unintelligible' so-called. It is the effort of a man with very much to say, endeavouring to get it said in a not sordid or unworthy way, to men who are at home chiefly in the sordid, the prosaic, inane and unworthy. I see you pitching big crags into the dirty bottomless morass, trying to found your marble work, — Oh, it is a tragic condition withal! — But yet you must mend it, and alter. A writing man is there to be understood: let him lay that entirely to heart, and conform to it patiently; the sooner the better!

Thomas Carlyle, Letter to Browning, 25 April 1856.

Browning used words with the violence of a horse-breaker, giving out the scent of a he-goat. But he got them to do their work.

Ford Madox Ford, *The March of Literature.*

He introduced jazz into English verse, on account of his mixed blood no doubt. There is black blood in him somewhere, that is why he was called Browning — it comes out in the tom-tom of his verse. . . . He anticipated cross-words. He kept so many people guessing that he got a reputation for depth and for poetry out of all proportion to the beauty he evoked in words. Instead of 'fundamental brainwork', there is only something foundered beneath the surface. . . . The nearest he got to poetry was . . . Mrs Browning. . . . His muse is as much invalid as his wife was invalide.

Oliver St J. Gogarty, *As I Was Going Down Sackville Street.*

Other poets say anything — say everything that is in them. Browning lived to realize the myth of the Inexhaustible Bottle.
W. E. Henley, in *Athenaeum*, 22 August 1885.

Indeed I hold with the old fashioned criticism that Browning is not really a poet, that he has all the gifts but the one needful and the pearls without the string; rather one should say nuggets and rough diamonds. I suppose him to resemble Ben Johnson, only that Ben Johnson had more real poetry.
Gerard Manley Hopkins, Letter to R. W. Dixon, 12 October 1881.

The idea, with Mr Browning, always tumbles out into the world in some grotesque hind-foremost manner; it is like an unruly horse backing out of his stall, and stamping and plunging as he comes. His thought knows no simple stage — at the very moment of its birth it is a terribly complicated affair.
Henry James, in *Nation*, 20 January 1876.

Shelley . . . is a light, and Swinburne is a sound — Browning alone is a temperature.
Henry James, 'The Novel in "The Ring and the Book".'

How can Mr Browning help England? By leaving henceforth 'the dead to bury the dead', in effete and enervating Italy, and casting all his rugged genial force into the questions and the struggles of that mother-country to whom, and not to Italy at all, he owes all his most valuable characteristics.
Charles Kingsley, in *Fraser's Magazine*, February 1851.

Browning! Since Chaucer was alive and hale,
No man hath walk'd along our roads with step
So active, so inquiring eye, or tongue
So varied in discourse.
Walter Savage Landor, *To Robert Browning*.

Behold him shambling go,
At once himself the showman and the show,
Street preacher of Parnassus, roll on high
His blinking orbs, and rant tautology,
While gaping multitudes around the monk
Much wonder if inspired, or simply drunk.
William Leech, *The Obliviad*.

Old Hippety-Hop o' the accents.
Ezra Pound, *Mesmerism*.

Robert Browning is unerring in every sentence he writes of the Middle Ages; always vital, right and profound; so that in the matter of art, with which we have been specially concerned, there is hardly a principle connected with the mediaeval temper, that he has not struck upon in those seemingly careless and too rugged lines of his.
John Ruskin, *Modern Painters*.

Mr Browning intends apparently to finish a laborious life in an access or paroxysm of indiscriminate production. He floods acres of paper with brackets and inverted commas. He showers octavos on the public with a facility and grace like that of a conjuror scattering shoulder-knots and comfits out of a confederate's hat. What! we exclaim, all this monstrous quantity of verse out of no more of a poet than can be buttoned into one single-breasted waistcoat!
Robert Louis Stevenson, in *Vanity Fair*, 11 December 1875.

Mr Browning has in the supreme degree the qualities of a great debater or an eminent leading counsel; his finest reasoning has in its expression and development something of the ardour of personal energy and active interest which inflames the argument of a public speaker; we feel . . . how many a first rate barrister or parliamentary tactician has been lost in this poet.
A. C. Swinburne, *George Chapman*.

To charge him with obscurity is as accurate as to call Lynceus purblind, or complain of the sluggish action of the telegraph wire. He is something too much the reverse of obscure; he is too brilliant and subtle for the ready reader to follow with any certainty the track of an intelligence which moves with such incessant rapidity.
Ibid.

This bard's a Browning! — there's no doubt of that:
But, ah, ye gods, *the sense!* Are we so sure
If sense be sense unto our common-sense,
Low sense to higher, high to low, no sense,
All sense to those, all sense no sense to these?
That's where your poet tells! — and you've no right
(Insensate sense with sensuous thought being mixed)
To ask analysis!
Bayard Taylor, in *New York Daily Tribune*, 4 December 1875.

He has plenty of music in him, but he cannot get it out.
Alfred, Lord Tennyson, in Hallam Tennyson, *Tennyson: A Memoir by his Son*.

Mr Browning asks too much of his readers. He has no right to expect that for the sake of the good things which he has to bestow he will find readers to encounter the difficulties of his style which he deliberately sets in their way. It is sometimes as difficult to follow out the line of his thought as to keep up with an argument conducted by Kant, or Schelling, or Hegel.

The Times, 11 January 1865.

Meredith is a prose Browning, and so is Browning. He used poetry as a medium for writing in prose.

Oscar Wilde, *The Critic as Artist*.

In art, only Browning can make action and psychology one.

Oscar Wilde, Letter to H. C. Marillier, *circa* November 1885.

See also Matthew Arnold, John Donne, John Keats

BRUCE, JAMES

1730—94 African Traveller

JOHNSON: Why, Sir, he is not a distinct relater; and I should say, he is neither abounding nor deficient in sense. I did not perceive any superiority of understanding. BOSWELL: But will you not allow him a nobleness of resolution in penetrating into distant regions? JOHNSON: That, Sir, is not to the present purpose. We are talking of his sense. A fighting cock has a nobleness of resolution.

James Boswell, *Life of Johnson*.

He made me feel so very short as I sat next to him, that had not Mr Burney [a cousin], who is still less than myself been on the other side, I should have felt quite pitiful. But what very much diverted me was, that whenever I turned to see Mr Burney, I found his head leaning behind my chair, to peer at Mr Bruce, as he would have done at any outlandish animal. Indeed, no eye was off him; though I believe he did not perceive it, as he hardly ever himself looks at anybody. He seems quite satisfied with thinking of his own consequence.

Fanny Burney, Diary.

Bruce, drooping, bending in despondency over the fountains of the Nile must ever form a most striking picture, exemplifying the real practical difference which exists between moral and religious exertions; for although, among men, he had gained his prize, it may justly be asked, what was it worth? The course of a river is like the history of a man's life. All of it that is useful to us is worth knowing: but the source of the one is the birth of the other, and the 'hillock of green sod' is 'the infant mewling and puking in the nurse's arms.'

Major F. B. Head, *Life of Bruce*.

Conscious of his own integrity, and not suspecting that in a civilized country the statements of a man of honour would be disbelieved, he did not think it necessary gradually and cautiously to prepare his hearers for a climate and scenery altogether different from their own, but, as if from a balloon, he at once landed them in Abyssinia, and suddenly showed them a vivid picture to which he had been long accustomed. ... In short he told them the truth, the whole truth, and nothing but the truth, but the mind of man, like his stomach, can only contain a certain quantity, and the dose which Bruce gave to his hearers was more than they had power to retain.

Ibid.

For several hours every effort was made to restore him to the world; all that is usual, customary, and useless in such cases was performed. There was the bustle, the hurry, the confusion, the grief unspeakable, the village leech, his lancet, his phial, and his little pill; but the lamp was out, — the book was closed, — the lease was up — the game was won — the daring, restless, injured spirit had burst from the covert, and was — away!

Ibid.

Someone asked him what musical instruments were used in Abyssinia. Bruce hesitated, not being prepared for the question; and at last said, 'I think I only saw one *lyre* there.' George Selwyn whispered his next man, 'Yes; and there is one less since he left the country.'

John Pinkerton, *Walpoliana*.

BRUCE, LENNY (LEONARD ALFRED SCHNEIDER)

1926—66 Comedian

I'm Super-Jew!

On himself, shouted as he leapt from a window in an apparent, though unsuccessful, suicide attempt.

Though he leaves a red-faced litter of bluenoses and blow-hard columnists in his wake, Bruce remains the most powerful after-dinner monologist since Teddy Roosevelt.

Anon., in *Show Business Illustrated*, April 1962.

Usually he worked on the rim of danger. He let the weird notions run. When one clicked, it'd lock in in Bruce's mind, and he'd get the rush all comics do who move off the moment. Bruce did it more than other comics did. He took the chances.. He was not afraid to fall flat on his arse with new material. There were those that saw him go gurgling down the drain one night and make thunder the next.

Philip Berger, *The Last Laugh*.

Bruce's words and gestures said too clearly just what people are saying now in words not so beautiful or piercing and in gestures much more meaningful: that America proposes Christian Love and Democratic Goodness, and dispenses death and hate and corruption and lies.

John Cohen, *The Essential Lenny Bruce.*

Instead of working out of phony show-biz 'charm' and cuteness and carefully rehearsed topicality, Lenny Bruce was hitting the late fifties' mainline — the sense of smothered rage.

Albert Goldman, *Ladies and Gentlemen, Lenny Bruce!!*

He always suffered from verbal disabilities: a tendency to singsong, a habit of mumbling, a coy and uncomfortable relation with the mike. Only late at night, when he was working to a very hip crowd and the Methedrine was scalding through his veins could he ever attain the energy level of the parent style. When he did, though, he produced the most dazzling poetry of his entire career.

Ibid.

Never had he achieved more perfectly his ideal of coming on like an oral jazzman. He didn't want laughter anymore, he hated applause — 'Please don't applaud!' he would beg. 'It breaks my rhythm!' — he just wanted to get so far down into his own head that he felt that he was totally alone. He needed three thousand people so he could be alone! — self-absorbed, brooding and contemplative, like he was sitting with lizard eyes blinking on his own toilet bowl!

Ibid.

His gospel was freedom, sexual freedom, racial freedom, religious freedom, cliché freedom, hate freedom — in short, happiness through truth. Bruce enraged many people, including some arresting officers and psychiatrists and judges and prosecutors and critics who by the record of their lives and deeds were at least as sick as he was. But wasn't that what his whole *shtick* was about?

Jerry Tallmer, in John Cohen, *The Essential Lenny Bruce.*

BRUDENELL, JAMES THOMAS, see under CARDIGAN, EARL OF

BRYAN, WILLIAM JENNINGS

1860–1925 Politician

You ask me why 'tis thus

That I make this outward show,
Because my millionaire employer
Says 'Bryan men must go.'
And I have got a wife at home
With little ones to feed,
And must appear to think and vote
To suit the gold bugs' greed.

Anon., in *New York Times*, 1 November 1896.

. . . money-grabbing, selfish, office seeking, favour hunting, publicity-loving, marplot from Nebraska.

Anon., in D. H. Elletson, *Roosevelt and Wilson: A Comparative Study.*

W. J. Bryan not only suffers for his principles and mortifies his flesh, as he has every right to do, but he insists that others should suffer and be mortified.

Anon., in *Daily Express*, in John A. Garraty, 'Bryan: The Progressives, Part 1', *American Heritage*, December 1961.

There with an audience of some few hundreds of bronzed farmers who believed in him as their deliverer, the man who could lead them out of the bondage of debt, who could stay the drought and strike water from the rock, I heard him make the greatest speech of his life. Surely that was eloquence of the old stamp that was accounted divine, eloquence that reached through the callus of ignorance and toil and found and awoke the stunted souls of men.

Willa Cather, *Round Up: A Nebraska Reader.*

We put him to school and he wound up by stealing the schoolbooks.

Ignatius Donnelly (on the connection between Bryan and Populism), in Louis W. Koenig, *Bryan: A Political Biography of William Jennings Bryan.*

. . . a halfbaked glib little briefless jack-leg lawyer . . . grasping with anxiety to collar that $50,000 salary, promising the millennium to everybody with a hole in his pants and destruction to everybody with a clean shirt.

John Hay, in Paolo E. Coletta, 'The Bryan Campaign of 1896', in P. W. Glad, *William Jennings Bryan: A Profile.*

One could drive a prairie schooner through any part of his argument and never scrape against a fact.

David Houston, in John A. Garraty, 'A Leader of the People', in *ibid.*

He is too good a Christian to run a naughty world and he doesn't hate hard enough. . . .

Franklin K. Lane, in Patrick Devlin, *Too Proud to Fight: Woodrow Wilson's Neutrality.*

I brag and chant of Bryan, Bryan, Bryan, Bryan,
Candidate for president who sketched a silver zion.
  Vachel Lindsay, *Bryan, Bryan, Bryan, Bryan.*

Prairie avenger, mountain lion,
Bryan, Bryan, Bryan, Bryan.
Gigantic troubadour, speaking like a siege gun,
Smashing Plymouth Rock with his boulders from the
  West.
  '*Ibid.*

With him, words take the place of actions. He thinks
that to say something is to do something, which is an
imperfect view of administration.
  Henry Cabot Lodge, Letter to Sturgis Bigelow,
  23 May 1913.

Unlike Douglas who took to drink when Lincoln defeated him, Bryan took to smiles and religion . . . if
he woke in another life, he surely found no Methodist
heaven, no pitching of golden crowns around the
glassy sea, and no lamb; but he found great powers
and forces and strange wonderful processes moving
to worlds not realized; and perhaps smiled that he
had been such a fool and made so much trouble for
the countrymen.
  Edgar Lee Masters, 27 July 1925, in P. W. Glad,
  William Jennings Bryan: A Profile.

Tnere were many . . . who believed that Bryan was
no longer merely human, but had lifted himself up to
some level or other of the celestial angels. . . . It
would have surprised no one if he had suddenly begun to perform miracles . . . I saw plenty of his customers approach him stealthily to touch his garments.
. . . Those with whom he shook hands were made
men.
  H. L. Mencken, in L. W. Levine, *Defender of the
  Faith, William Jennings Bryan, The Last Decade,
  1915–1925.*

The President of the United States may be an ass,
but he at least doesn't believe that the earth is square,
and that witches should be put to death, and that
Jonah swallowed the whale.
  H. L. Mencken, in John A. Garraty, 'Bryan: The
  Progressives, Part 1', *American Heritage,*
  December 1961.

Again and again I am reminded of the danger of having to do with cranks. A certain orderliness of mind
and conduct seems essential for safety in this short
life. Spiritualists, bone-rubbers, anti-vivisectionists,
all sort of anti's in fact, those who have fads about
education or fads against it. Perfectionists, Daughters
of the Dove of Peace, sons of the Roaring Torrent,
Itinerant peace-mongers — all these may have a real
genius among them once in forty years, but look for

an exception to the common run of yellow dogs and
damnfools among them, is like opening oysters with
the hope of finding pearls. It's the common man we
want and the uncommon common man when we can
find him — never the crank. This is the lesson of
Bryan.
  Walter Hines Page, in Burton J. Hendrick, *The
  Life and Letters of Walter H. Page.*

[Bryan] Had rather be wrong than president.
  Thomas B. Reed, in Thomas A. Bailey, 'The
  Election of 1900', in P. W. Glad, *William
  Jennings Bryan: A Profile.*

A kindly man and well meaning in a weak kind of
way.
  Theodore Roosevelt, in D. H. Elletson, *Roosevelt
  and Wilson: A Comparative Study.*

What a disgusting, dishonest fakir Bryan is! When I
see so many Americans running after him, I feel very
much as I do when a really lovely woman falls in love
with a cad.
  Elihu Root, Letter to William M. Laffa, 31
  October 1900.

His mind was like a soup dish, wide and shallow; it
could hold a small amount of nearly anything, but
the slightest jarring spilled the soup into somebody's
lap.
  Irving Stone, *The Also Ran.*

The Great Inevitable.
  Woodrow Wilson, in Walter Lord, *The Good Years.*

He is *absolutely* sincere. That is what makes him
dangerous.
  Woodrow Wilson, in L. W. Levine, *Defender of
  the Faith, William Jennings Bryan, The Last
  Decade, 1915–1925.*

See also Franklin D. Roosevelt, Theodore Roosevelt

BRYANT, WILLIAM CULLEN
1794–1878 Poet, Editor

I do not like politics any better than you do; but they
get only my mornings, and you know politics and a
belly-ful are better than poetry and starvation.
  On himself, Undated letter to Charles Dana, in
  Charles H. Brown, *William Cullen Bryant.*

Poetry often seems for Bryant something hallowed
and set apart, like a best parlor filled with marmoreal
statuary that is only opened up on Sundays. It is a

little difficult to speak naturally or breathe very deeply in it.

> Marius Bewley, in *William Cullen Bryant*, in Perry Miller ed., *Major Writers of America*, vol. I.

He was the first American poet who was wholly sympathetic with the atmosphere and feeling of the country and who expressed its inner moods and reflected the landscape, the woods and the fields as if America itself was speaking through him.

> Van Wyck Brooks, *The World of Washington Irving*.

. . . a very pleasant man to associate with, but rather cold, I should imagine, if one should seek to touch his heart with one's own.

> Nathaniel Hawthorne, upon first meeting Bryant, in John Bigelow, *William Cullen Bryant*.

He did not have the audacity, the frenzy of the great poet. His themes were homely, his ideas those of his generation. Instead of burning with the spark of nature's fire he warmed his hands by a comfortable hearthside or sat close to the smoky lamp of the scholar.

> Grant C. Knight, *American Literature and Culture*.

He was my master in verse. . . .

> Henry Wadsworth Longfellow, in Charles H. Brown, *William Cullen Bryant*.

He is very nice reading in summer, but *inter Nos*, we don't want *extra* freezing in winter; Take him up in the depth of July, my advice is, When you feel an Egyptian devotion to ices.

> James Russell Lowell, *A Fable for Critics*.

There is Bryant, as quiet, as cool, and as dignified, As a smooth, silent iceberg, that never is ignified, Save when by reflection 'tis kindled o'nights With a semblance of flame by the chill Northern Lights

> *Ibid.*

His was essentially a self-pollenizing nature that needed few contacts with other minds. He lived within himself, little swayed by modes of thought, slowly maturing the native fruit of his speculation.

> Vernon Louis Parrington, *Main Currents in American Thought*, vol. 2.

It has always seemed to me Bryant, more than any other American, had the power to suck in the air of spring, to put it into his song, to breathe it forth again . . . never a wasted word — the last superfluity struck off a clear nameless beauty pervading and overarching all the work of his pen.

> Walt Whitman, in Edgar Lee Masters, *Whitman*.

BUCHANAN, GEORGE
1506—82 Scholar, Author

In a conversation concerning the literary merits of the two countries, a Scotchman, imagining that on this ground he should have an undoubted triumph over him, exclaimed, 'Ah, Dr Johnson, what would you have said of Buchanan, had he been an Englishman?' — 'Why, Sir, (said Johnson, after a little pause), I should *not* have said of Buchanan, had he been an *Englishman*, what I will now say of him as a *Scotchman*, — that he was the only man of genius his country ever produced.'

> James Boswell, *Life of Johnson*.

BUCHANAN, JAMES
1791—1868 Fifteenth United States President

If you are as happy, my dear sir, on entering this house as I am in leaving it and returning home, you are the happiest man in the country.

> On himself, to Abraham Lincoln at the White House the day of his retirement, 4 March 1861.

President James Buchanan is known as The Only President Who Never Married, and thus has become extremely useful in quizzes and crossword puzzles.

> Richard Armour, *It All Began With Columbus*.

The Constitution provides for every accidental contingency in the Executive — except a vacancy in the mind of the President.

> Senator Sherman of Ohio, in A. K. Adams, *The Home Book of Humorous Quotations*.

There is no such person running as James Buchanan. *He is dead of lockjaw*. Nothing remains but a platform and a bloated mass of political putridity.

> Thaddeus Stevens, in Fawn M. Brodie, *Thaddeus Stevens, Scourge of the South*.

BUCK, PEARL SYDENSTRICKER
1892—1973 Author

My whole life presents a unity. Everything I have done, even my writing, grows out of a fascinated interest in human beings, in the wonders of their minds and hearts, their sensitivities, their needs, and the essential loneliness of their position in the universe.

> On herself, in Theodore F. Harris, *Pearl Buck*.

. . . a capable, bustling novelist of the journalist school.

> V. S. Pritchett, in Paul A. Doyle, *Pearl S. Buck*.

East versus West, Victorian versus twentieth-century values: her life and work turn on their interplay.

Dody Weston Thompson, 'Pearl Buck', in Warren G. French and Walter E. Kidd eds, *American Winners of the Nobel Literary Prize.*

BUCKINGHAM, FIRST DUKE OF (GEORGE VILLIERS)

1592—1628 Statesman, Royal Favourite

Who rules the Kingdom? The King!
Who rules the King? The Duke!
Who rules the Duke? The Devil!
Anon., Contemporary graffiti.

But it is generally given to him who is the little god at court, to be the great devil in the country. The commonalty hated him with a perfect hatred; and all miscarriages in Church and state, at home, abroad, at sea and land, were charged on his want of wisdom, valour, or loyalty.

John Felton, a melancholy, mal-contented gentleman, and a sullen soldier, apprehending himself injured, could find no other way to revenge his conceived wrongs, than by writing them with a point of a knife in the heart of the Duke, whom he stabbed at Portsmouth, Anno Domini, 1629. It is hard to say how many of this nation were guilty of this murder, either by public praising, or private approving thereof.

His person, from head to foot could not be charged with any blemish, save that some hypercritics conceived his brows somewhat overpendulous, a cloud which in the judgement of others was by the beams of his eyes sufficiently dispelled.

Thomas Fuller, *The History of the Worthies of England.*

On tuesday his Grace was present at ye acting of K. Hen. 8 at ye Globe, a play bespoken of purpose by himself; whereat he stayd till ye Duke of Buckingham was beheaded, & then departed. Some say, he should rather have seen ye fall of Cardinall Woolsey, who was a more lively type of himself, having governed this kingdom 18 yeares, as he hath done 14.

Robert Gell, Letter, 9 August 1628.

. . . His ascent was so quick, that it seemed rather a flight than a growth, and he was such a darling of fortune, that he was at the topp, before he was seen at the bottome. . . . If he had an immediate ambition, with which hee was charged, and is a weede (if it bee a weede) apt to grow in the best soyles, it does not appear that it was in his nature, or that he brought it with him to the Courte, but rather found it there, and was a garment necessary for that ayre: nor was

it more in his power to be without promotion and titles, and wealth, then for a healthy man to sit in the sunn, in the brightest dogge days, and remayne without any warmth: he needed no ambition who was so seated in the hertes of two such masters.

Edward Hyde, Earl of Clarendon, *History of the Rebellion.*

Christ has his John, and I have my George.
James I, Attributed.

The King cast a glancing eye towards him, which was easily observed by such as observed their Prince's humour . . . then one gave him his place of Cupbearer, that he might be in the King's eye; another sent to his Mercer and Taylor to put good cloathes on him; a third to his Sempster for curious linnen, and all as in-comes to obtain offices upon his future rise; then others took upon themselves to be his Braccoes, to undertake his quarrels upon affronts, put upon him by *Somerset's* Faction. So all hands helped to the piecing up this new Favourite.

Anthony Weldon, *Court and Character of James I.*

No one dances better, no man runs or jumps better. Indeed he jumped higher than ever Englishman did in so short a time, from a private gentleman to a dukedom.

Arthur Wilson, *The History of Great Britain.*

See also James I

BUCKINGHAM, SECOND DUKE OF (GEORGE VILLIERS)

1628—87 Statesman

He had no principles of religion, vertue, or friendship. Pleasure, frolick, or extravagant diversion was all that he laid to heart. He was true to nothing, for he was not true to himself. He had no steadiness or conduct: He could keep no secret, nor execute any design without spoiling it. He could never fix his thoughts, nor govern his estate, tho' then the greatest in *England.* He was bred about the King: and for many years he had a great ascendent over him: But he spake of him to all persons with that contempt, that at last he drew a lasting disgrace upon himself.

Gilbert Burnet, *History of My Own Time.*

A Duke of Bucks, Is one that has studied the whole Body of Vice. His parts are disproportionate to the whole, and like a Monster he has more of some, and less of others than he should have. He has pulled down all that Fabrick that Nature raised in him, and built himself up again after a model of his own. He

has dam'd up all those Lights, that Nature made into
the noblest Prospects of the World, and opened other
little blind Loopholes backward, by turning Day into
Night, and Night into Day. His appetite to his
Pleasures is diseased and crazy, like the Pica in a
Woman, that longs to eat that, which was never made
for food, or a Girl in the Green-sickness that eats
Chalk and Mortar. . . . He endures Pleasures with less
Patience, than other Men do their Pains.

Samuel Butler, *The Character of A Duke of
Bucks.*

A Man so various, that he seem'd to be,
Not one, but all Mankind's Epitome.
Stiff in Opinions, always in the wrong;
Was Everything by starts and Nothing long:
But, in the course of one revolving Moon,
Was Chymist, Fidler, Statesman, and Buffoon;
Then all for Women, Painting, Rhyming, Drinking,
Besides ten thousand Freaks that died in thinking.
Blest Madman who could every Hour employ
With something New to wish or to enjoy!
Railing and praising were his usual Theams;
And both (to shew his Judgement) in Extreams:
So over Violent or over Civil,
That every Man with him was God or Devil.
In squandring Wealth was his peculiar Art:
Nothing went unrewarded, but Desert.
Begger'd by Fools, whom still he found too late:
He had his Jest, and they had his Estate.

John Dryden, *Absalom and Achitophel.*

The King had constant Intelligence of all his Behaviour . . . but . . . his Majesty had no Apprehension,
believing it impossible for the Duke to keep his Mind
long bent upon any particular Design, or to keep and
observe those Hours and Orders of sleeping and eating, as Men who pretend to Business are obliged to;
and that it was more impossible, for him to make
and preserve a Friendship with any serious Persons,
whom he could never restrain himself from abusing
and making ridiculous, as soon as he was out of their
Company. Yet with all these Infirmities and Vices
He found a Respect and Concurrence from Men of
different Tempers and Talents, and had an incredible
Opinion with the People.

Edward Hyde, Earl of Clarendon, *The Life of
Edward Earl of Clarendon, written by himself.*

Buckingham was a sated man of pleasure who had
turned to ambition as a pastime.

T. B. Macaulay, *History of England.*

They do tell me here that the Duke of Buckingham
hath surrendered himself to Secretary Morrice and is
going to the Tower. Mr Fenn at the table says that he
hath been taken by the Wach two or three times of
late at unseasonable hours, but so disguised that they

could not know him (and when I came home, by and
by, Mr Lowther tells me that the Duke of Buckingham doth dine publicly this day at Wadlows, at the
Sun Tavern and is mighty merry, and sent word to
the Lieutenant of the Tower that he would come to
him as soon as he had dined): Now, how sad a
thing it is when we come to make sport of proclaiming men traitors and banishing them, and putting
them out of their offices and Privy Council, and of
sending to and going to the Tower. God have mercy
on us.

Samuel Pepys, Diary, 28 June 1667.

In the worst inn's worst room with mat half-hung,
The floors of plaister and the walls of dung,
On once a flock-bed, but repair'd with straw,
With tape-ty'd curtains, never meant to draw,
The George and Garter dangling from the bed
Where tawdry yellow strove with dirty red,
Great Villiers lies — alas! how chang'd from him,
That life of pleasure, and that soul of whim!
Gallant and gay, in Cliveden's proud alcove,
The bow'r of wanton Shrewsbury and love;
Or just as gay, at Council, in a ring
Of mimick'd Statesmen, and their merry King.
No Wit to flatter left of all his store!
No Fool to laugh at, which he valu'd more.
There, Victor of his health, of fortune, friends,
And fame, this lord of useless thousands ends.

Alexander Pope, *Epistle iii, to Allen Lord
Bathurst.*

The witty Duke of Buckingham was an extreme bad
man. His duel with Lord Shrewsbury was concerted
between him and Lady Shrewsbury. All that morning
she was trembling for her gallant, and wishing the
death of her husband; and, after his fall, 'tis said
the Duke slept with her in his bloody shirt.

Alexander Pope, in Joseph Spence, *Anecdotes.*

But when degrees of Villany we name,
How can we choose but think of B(uckingham)?
He who through all of them has boldly ran,
Left ne're a Law unbroke by God or Man.
His treasur'd sins of Supererrogation,
Swell to a summ enough to damn a Nation:
But he must here, perforce, be left alone,
His acts require a Volumn of their own.

John Wilmot, Earl of Rochester, *Rochester's
Farewell.*

BUCKLE, HENRY THOMAS

1821—62 Historian

I suppose you think [history] is an account of human
life in general; Buckle you see abstracts life, and

makes it an account for the improvement of our tools.

Richard Simpson, Letter to Lord Acton,
9 June 1858.

BULL, JOHN

1563?—1628 Composer

The Bull by force
In Field doth Raigne,
But Bull by Skill
Good will doth gayne.

Anon., from the portrait of Bull in the Oxford
Music School, 1589.

I have been frequently astonished, in persuing Dr. Bull's lessons, at the few new and pleasing passages which his hand suggested to his pen. It has been said, that the late Dr. Pepusch preferred Bull's compositions to those of Couperin and Scarlatti, not only for harmony and contrivance, but air and modulation: an assertion which rather proves that the Doctor's taste was *bad*, than Bull's Music *good*. Though I should greatly admire the hand, as well as the patience, of any one capable of playing his compositions; yet, *as Music*, they would afford me no kind of pleasure: *Ce sont des notes, & rien que des notes;* there is nothing in them which excites rapture. They may be heard by a lover of Music with as little emotion as the clapper of a mill, or the rumbling of a post-chaise.

Dr Charles Burney, *A General History of Music.*

He made the invention of new difficulties of every kind which could impede or dismay a performer his sole study.

Ibid.

Of all the bulls that live, this hath the greatest asses ears.

Elizabeth I, Attributed.

The queens will being to know the said music, her Grace was at that time at the virginals: whereupon, he, being in attendance, Master Bull did come by stealth to hear without, and by mischance did sprawl into the queens Majesties Presence, to the queens great disturbance. She demanding incontinent the wherefore of such presumption, Master Bull with great skill said that wheresoever Majesty and Music so well combined, no man might abase himself too deeply; whereupon the queen's Majesty was mollified and said that so rare a Bull hath sung as sweet as Byrd.

Peter Philips, *A Briefe Chronicle.*

Dr. Bull hearing of a famous musician belonging to a certain cathedral at St. Omer's, he applied himself as a novice to him, to learn something of his faculty, and to see and admire his works. This musician, after some discourse had passed between them, conducted Bull to a vestry or music-school joining to the cathedral, and shewed to him a lesson or song of forty parts, and then made a vaunting challenge to any person in the world to add one more part to them, supposing it to be so complete and full that it was impossible for any mortal man to correct or add to it; Bull thereupon desiring the use of pen, ink and ruled paper, such as we call musical paper; prayed the musician to lock him up in the said school for two or three hours; which being done, not without great disdain by the musician, Bull in that time or less, added forty more parts to the said lesson or song. The musician thereupon being called in, he viewed it, tried it, and retried it; at length he burst out into a great ecstasy, and swore by the great God that he that added those forty parts must either be the Devil or Dr. Bull, etc. Whereupon Bull making himself known, the musician fell down and adored him.

Anthony à Wood, *Fasti Oxonienses*

This is the same Person who was admitted Bach: of Musick of this University, in 1586, as I have told you under that year, and would have proceeded in the same place, had he not met with clowns and rigid Puritans there that could not endure Church Musick . . . he became chief Organist to K. *James* I, was so much admired for his dexterous hand on the Organ, that many thought that there was more than Man in him. At length being possess'd with crotchets, as many Musicians are, he went beyond the Seas and died.

Ibid.

BUNYAN, JOHN

1628—88 Religious Writer

I have not for these things fished in other men's waters; my Bible and Concordance are my only library in my writing.

On himself, *To the Christian Reader, Prefaratory to Solomon's Temple Spiritualized.*

. . . but yet I did not think
To shew to all the world my pen and ink
In such a mode; I only thought to make
I knew not what; nor did I undertake
Thereby to please my neighbour; no, not I,
I did it mine own self to gratify.

On himself, 'The Author's Apology for His Book', prefaced to the *Pilgrim's Progress.*

Bunyan was a man of abnormal imagination. His imagination was vivid, active, flaming Dantean. It gave light → often lurid light — and heat, and form, and colour, to all he saw. It made his thoughts stand out in blazing sun-bright relief, or sink into seas of gloomy shadow: it gave glory and sweetness, and celestial tone to all his joys, and put cruel edge, and piercing point, on all his sorrows. He was a nervous man, too, one whose soul-harp was high-strung, answerable in quivers of pain, and shrieking harps of repulsion to every jar or discord; and his conscience was a lynx-eyed tyrant, unsleeping and remorseless . . . Bunyan's English is tinker's and soldier's and preacher's English. It is the English of the Bible, of the Ironsides, and of the village green.

Robert Blatchford, *My Favourite Books.*

Nowhere perhaps, except in Homer, is there such perfect description by the use of merely plain words. . . . The Elstow tinker produced an original thing, if an original thing was ever produced.

G. K. Chesterton, Introduction of *Pilgrim's Progress.*

Bunyan was never, in our received sense of the word, wicked. He was chaste, sober, honest; but he was a bitter blackguard; that is, damned his own, or his neighbour's eyes on slight, or no occasion, and was fond of a row. . . . The transmutation of actual reprobates into saints is doubtless possible; but like many recorded facts of corporeal alchemy, it is not supported by modern experiments.

Samuel Taylor Coleridge, *The Literary Remains of Samuel Taylor Coleridge,* 1836—9.

His piety was baffled by his genius, and the Bunyan of Parnassus had the better of the Bunyan of the Conventicle.

Samuel Taylor Coleridge, The Egerton MSS, British Museum.

Mr Bunyan . . . preached so New-Testament-like, that he made me admire and weep for joy, and give him my affections. And he was the first man that ever I heard preach to my unenlightened understanding and experience, for methought all his sermons were adapted to my condition, and had apt similitudes, being full of the love of God, and the manner of its secret working upon the soul, and of the soul under the sense of it, that I could weep for joy, most part of his sermons.

Charles Doe, *Experiences of Charles Doe.*

Bunyan was not merely the first of English Allegorists; he is one of the founders of the English novel, and the forerunner of Defoe.

Sir Charles Firth, Introduction to *Pilgrim's Progress.*

Put your Shakespearian hero and coward, Henry V and Pistol, or Parolles, beside Mr Valiant, and Mr Fearing, and you have a sudden revelation of the abyss that lies between the fashionable author who could see nothing in the world but personal aims and the tragedy of their disappointment, or the comedy of their incongruity, and the field preacher who achieved virtue and courage by identifying himself with the purpose of the world as he understood it. The contrast is enormous: Bunyan's coward stirs your blood more than Shakespeare's hero, who actually leaves you cold and secretly hostile. You suddenly see that Shakespeare, with all his flashes and divinations, never understood virtue and courage, never conceived how any man who was not a fool, could, like Bunyan's hero, look back from the brink of the river of death, over the strife and labour of his pilgrimage, and say, 'yet do I not repent me'; or, with the panache of a millionaire, bequeath 'my sword to him that shall succeed me in my pilgrimage, and my courage and skill to him that can get it.'

George Bernard Shaw, 'Epistle Dedicatory to A. B. Walkley', Preface to *Man and Superman.*

He was greatly served . . . by a certain rustic privilege of his style, which like the talk of strong, uneducated men, when it does not impress by its force, still charms by its simplicity. . . . We have to remark in him, not the parts where inspiration fails and is supplied by cold and merely decorated invention, but the parts where faith has grown to incredulity, and his characters become so real to him that he forgets the end of their creation. We can follow him step by step, into the trap which he lays for himself by his own entire good faith and triumphant liberality of vision, till the trap closes and shuts him in an inconsistency.

Robert Louis Stevenson, Introduction to *Pilgrim's Progress.*

Pilgrim's Progress, about a man that left his family, it didn't say why. I read considerable in it now and then. The statements was interesting but tough.

Mark Twain, *The Adventures of Huckleberry Finn.*

He merely told his own story, and said it may be yours also.

Ola Elizabeth Winslow, *John Bunyan.*

John Bunyan came into English literature and history by a side door.

Ibid.

Why do you call Bunyan a mystic? It is not possible to make a definition of mysticism to include him.

William Butler Yeats, Letter to his Father, 24 June 1918.

See also Daniel Defoe, Henry James

BURBAGE, RICHARD

1567?—1619 Actor

He's gone, & with him what a world are dead,
Which he revivd to be revived soe.
No more young Hamlett, ould Heironymoe.
King Leer, the greved Moore, and more beside,
That lived in him, have now for ever dy'de.
Oft have I seene him leape into the grave,
Suiting the person which he seem'd to have
Of a sad lover with so true an eye,
That theer I would have sworne, he meant to dye.
Oft Have I seene him play this part in ieast,
Soe lively, that spectators and the rest
Of his sad crew, whilst he but seem'd to bleed,
Amazed, thought even then hee dyed in deed.
> John Fletcher (?), *An elegie on the death of
> the famous actor Rich: Burbage who died 13
> Martij Ao. 1618.*

Astronomers and Star-gazers this year,
Write but of four eclipses — five appear;
Death interposing Burbage, and their staying,
Hath made a visible eclipse of playing.
> Thomas Middleton, *On the death of that great
> master in his art and quality painting and playing,
> R. Burbage.*

I am convinced that if Burbage were to rise from the dead and accept an invitation from Sir Henry Irving to appear at the Lyceum he would recoil beaten the moment he realized that he was to be looked at as part of an optical illlusion through a huge hole in the wall, instead of being practically in the middle of the theatre.
> George Bernard Shaw, in *Saturday Review*,
> 20 July 1895.

He is a man famous as our English Roscius; one who fitteth the action to the word, the word to the action most admirably.
> Earl of Southampton, in W. Clark Russell,
> *Representative Actors.*

Whatsoever is commendable in the grave Orator, is most exquisitely perfect in him; for by a full and significant action of body, he charmes our attention: sit in a full Theater, and you will think you see so many lines drawne from the circumference of so many eares, whiles the *Actor* is the *Centre*. He doth not strive to make nature monstrous, she is often seen in the same scaene with him, but neither on Stilts nor Crutches; and for his voice 'tis not lowei than the prompter, nor lowder than the Foile and

Target. By his action he fortifies morall precepts with example; for what we see him personate we thinke truely done before us; a man of a deepe thought might apprehend the Ghosts of our ancient *Heroes* walk't againe, and take him (at severall times) for many of them. Hee is much affected to painting, and 'tis a question whether that make him an excellent Plaier, or his playing an exquisite painter. Hee adds grace to the Poets labours: for what in the Poet is but ditty, in him is both ditty and musicke. . . . All men have beene of his occupation: and indeed, what he doth fainedly, that doe others essentially. . . .
> John Webster (ascribed), *Character of an Excellent Actor*, 1615.

See also Shakespeare

BURBANK, LUTHER

1849—1926 Horticulturalist

Old man Burbank is gone. Perhaps you remember him. He was a great man in a garden. His wife often said Luther had ten green thumbs. What a witty woman she must have been! Burbank was the wizard who crossed all those fruits and vegetables until he had the poor plants in such a confused and jittery condition that they could never decide whether to enter the dining room on the meat platter or the dessert dish.
> Groucho Marx, in an undated letter to Warner
> Brothers Studio.

See also Thomas Alva Edison

BURDETT, SIR FRANCIS

1770—1844 Radical

. . . all were agreed that our debts should increase
Excepting the Demagogue Francis.
That rogue! how could Westminster chuse him again
To leaven the virtue of these honest men!
> Lord Byron, *The Devil's Drive.*

. . . The general *football* Sir F. Burdett, kicked at by all, and owned by none.
> Lord Byron, Letter to John Hanson, 15 January
> 1809.

He saw, that a blaze of talent had burst forth. He saw that, if a Reform really took place, he would be *nothing* in that line of talent. He could not endure the idea of standing amidst a crowd of second or third rates; therefore he began to halt; to consider; to hesitate; to damp. We were going *too fast*; we exceeded *his bounds*, who, before, had *no bounds*. Till now he had been undisputed chief; that pleased him well, and he zealously and sincerely strove for the victory. But, when he found that the victory, if won, would leave him a disputed truncheon, he stopt short, and left us to the mercy of our foes, choosing rather to eke out his life as the *chief* of an unsuccessful, than to live an *associate* in a successful cause.

William Cobbett, *A History of the Last Hundred Days of English Freedom.*

Sir Francis Burdett, whose name once filled all mouths in England, no longer attracts much political attention. He probably struck his first notes on too high a key, not to fall into an octave below, before the air was finished.

James Fenimore Cooper, Letter to William Jay, 1828.

It so happened that the French Revolution was co-incident with Burdett's appearance in public life, & so in the confusion of circumstances it turned out, that he was looked upon as a Jacobin, when in reality he was a Jacobite.

Benjamin Disraeli, *Reminiscences.*

In one of his last speeches in Parliament, (then re-formed, & full of quiet middle class people) on the expenses of elections, he greatly denounced them, & observed that he had a right to give an opinion on this subject, as there was a period in his life, when parliamentary contests had reduced him to a state of absolute beggary. There was a murmur of admiring incredulity. 'I assure you, Sir,' he continued, 'I am indulging in no exaggeration. Honourable gentlemen may not believe it, but I can assure them there was a time, when Lady Burdett had only one pair of horses to her carriage!'

The effect of this remark in one of the early re-formed Parliaments full of retired tradesmen, many of whom had amassed wealth, but had never plucked up courage to keep a carriage, may be conceived. It was the most patrician definition of poverty ever made.

Ibid.

Sir Francis Burdett has often been left in a minority in the House of Commons, with only one or two on his side. We suspect, unfortunately for his country, that History will be found to enter its protest on the same side of the question!

William Hazlitt, *The Spirit of the Age*

He appeared in the extremest glory of bad taste, on the day of the opening of the new parliament, in a triumphal car — his face pale, his air languid, his . . . foot so placed on a footstool as to appear to be

trampling on a figure inscribed 'Venality and Corruption'.

Harriet Martineau, *History of England 1800–1815.*

. . . if I were base enough to seek the destruction of those institutions which we both profess to revere, I will tell [the honourable baronet] what instrument I should choose. I would take a man of great wealth, of patrician family, of personal popularity, aye, and of respectable talents. I am satisfied that such a one, while he scattered abroad the firebrands of sedition, under pretence that he went all lengths for the people, would be the best agent for destroying their liberties and happiness.

William Wilberforce, Speech in the House of Commons, 1817.

See also Horne Tooke

BURGHLEY, LORD (WILLIAM CECIL)

1520—98 Statesman

The only faithful Watchman for the realme,
That in all tempests never quit the helme,
But stood unshaken in his Deeds and Name,
And labour'd in the worke; not with the fame:
That still was good for goodness' sake, nor thought
Upon reward, till the reward him sought.
Whose Offices and honours did surprize,
Rather than meet him: And, before his eyes
Clos'd to their peace, he saw his branches shoot,
And in the noblest Families tooke root.
Of all the Land, who now, at such a Rate
Of divine blessing, would not serve a State?

Ben Jonson, *Epigram on William Lord Burghley.*

When the treasurer, in the latter part of his life, was much afflicted with gout, the queen always made him sit down in her presence with some obliging expression. 'My Lord,' she would say, 'we make use of you, not for your bad legs, but for your good head.'

John Macdiarmid, *Lives of British Statesmen.*

See also Edmund Spenser

BURKE, EDMUND

1729—97 Author, Statesman

You observe very rightly that no fair man can believe me to be Authour of Junius. Such a supposition might tend indeed to raise the estimation of my powers of writing above their just value. Not one of my friends does, upon that flattering principle, give me for the writer; and when my Enemies endeavour to fix Junius upon me, it is not for the sake of giving me the Credit of an able performance. My friends I have satisfied; my Enemies shall never have any direct satisfaction from me. The Ministry, I am told are convinced of my having written Junius, on the authority of a miserable Booksellers preface.

On himself, Letter to Charles Townshend, 17 October 1771.

I possessed not one of the qualities, nor cultivated one of the arts, that recommend men to the favour and protection of the great. I was not made for a minion or a fool. As little did I follow the trade of winning the hearts, by imposing on the understandings of the people.

On himself, *Letter to A Noble Lord*, 1796.

Burke loved to evade the arbitration of principle. He was prolific of arguments that were admirable but not decisive. He dreaded two-edged weapons and maxims that faced both ways. Through his inconsistencies we can perceive that his mind stood in a brighter light than his language. . . . Half of his genius was spent in making the secret that hampered it.

Lord Acton, in the Rev. Robert Murray, *Edmund Burke*.

His speeches on behalf of the colonies were so long and loud that they were called oratorios. In one of these, he pleaded with the King to lift the tax burden from the colonists and put it back on the English, who were accustomed to it. But by the time Burke had finished speaking the King was an old man and had become hard of hearing. Thus Burke's pleas fell on deaf ears.

Richard Armour, *It All Started With Columbus*.

When Johnson was ill and unable to exert himself as much as usual without fatigue, Mr Burke having been mentioned, he said: 'That fellow calls forth all my powers. Were I to see Burke now, it would kill me.'

James Boswell, *Life of Johnson*.

Such Spirit — such Intelligence — so much energy when serious, so much pleasantry when sportive, — so manly in his address, so animated in his conversation, so eloquent in Argument, so exhilarating in trifling — ! O, I shall rave about him till I tire you.

Fanny Burney, Diary.

Yet never, Burke, thou drankst Corruption's bowl!
Thee stormy Pity and the cherished lure
Of Pomp and proud Precipitance of soul
Wildered with meteor fires. Ah, Spirit pure!
The error's mist had left thy purged eye:

So might I clasp thee with a Mother's joy.

Samuel Taylor Coleridge, *Monody on the Death of Chatterton*.

Here lies our good Edmund, whose genius was such
We scarcely can praise it, or blame it too much;
Who, born for the Universe, narrowed his mind,
And to party gave up what was meant for mankind.

Oliver Goldsmith, *Retaliation*.

Is he like Burke, who winds into a subject like a serpent?

Oliver Goldsmith, in James Boswell, *Life of Johnson*.

He was so fond of arbitrary power that he could not sleep on his pillow unless he thought the king had a right to take it from under him.

Henry Grattan, in R. J. McHugh, *Henry Grattan*.

Burke understands everything but gaming and music. In the House of Commons I sometimes think him only the second man in England; out of it he is always the first.

Gerard Hamilton, in James Prior, *Memoir of the Life and Character of the Right Honourable Edmund Burke*.

Oft have I wondered that on Irish Ground
No poisonous reptiles ever yet were found;
Reveal'd the secret strands of nature's work,
She sav'd her venom to create a Burke.

Warren Hastings, in A. M. Davies, *Warren Hastings*.

The only specimen of Burke is, *all that he wrote*.

William Hazlitt, *English Literature*, 9, *The Character of Mr. Burke*.

You could not stand five minutes with that man beneath a shed, while it rained, but you must be convinced you had been standing with the greatest man you had ever seen.

Samuel Johnson, Attributed to Mrs Piozzi.

As he rose like a rocket, he fell like a stick.

Thomas Paine, *Letter to His Addressors*.

See also Lord Howe, James Mackintosh, Thomas Paine

BURLINGTON, EARL OF (RICHARD BOYLE)

1694—1753 Patron

Never were protection and great wealth more generously and more judiciously diffused than by this great person, who had every quality of a genius and artist, except envy.

Horace Walpole, *Anecdotes of Painters in England.*

Under the auspices of Lord Burlington and Lord Pembroke, architecture . . . recovered its genuine lustre. The former, the Apollo of arts, found a proper priest in the person of Mr. Kent.

Ibid.

BURNE-JONES, SIR EDWARD COLEY

1833—98 Painter

The Golden Age was with us while he stayed:
  For the Seven Ages knew him, and their wings
  Were stilled for him to paint; the Wizard Kings
Showed him the Orient treasures which they laid
At the Infant's feet, the Courts of Love obeyed
  His incantations; every Myth which brings
  Light out of darkness seemed imaginings
Of God, or things that God himself had made.

Wyke Bayliss, *Five Great Painters of the Victorian Era.*

The magician who held in his hand the crystal of romance.

Ibid.

It is the art of culture, of reflection, of intellectual luxury, of aesthetic refinement, of people who look at the world and at life not directly, as it were, and in all its accidental reality, but in the reflection and ornamental portrait of it furnished by art itself in other manifestations; furnished by literature, by poetry, by history, by erudition.

Henry James, 'The Picture Season in London', in *Galaxy*, August 1877.

Mr. Burne-Jones's figures have a way of looking rather sick; but if illness is capable of being amiable — and most of us have had some happy intimation that it is — Mr. Burne-Jones accentuates this side of the case.

Henry James, 'London Pictures', in *Atlantic Monthly*, August 1882.

His design was a child of the imagination, which had led him into an enchanted land, hidden behind high, rocky mountains, where Knights and Princesses rode through dark forests and wandered dreaming by moated granges, or looked out from towers of brass, and about whose shores mermaids swam and centaurs stamped their hairy hoofs.

William Rothenstein, *Men and Memories.*

I generally go and see Burne-Jones when there's a fog. He looks so angelic, painting away there by candlelight.

Ellen Terry, Letter to George Bernard Shaw, 29 October 1896.

BURNET, GILBERT, BISHOP

1643—1715 Historian

A portly prince, and goodly to the sight,
He seem'd a son of Anak for his height:
Like those whom stature did to crowns prefer;
Black-brow'd, and bluff, like Homer's Jupiter;
Broad-back'd, and brawny-built for love's delight,
A prophet form'd to make a female proselyte.
A theologue more by need than genial bent;
By breeding sharp, by nature confident.

John Dryden, *The Hind and the Panther.*

There prevailed in those days an indecent custom; when the preacher touched any favourite topick in a manner that delighted his audience [of MPs], their approbation was expressed by a loud *hum*, continued in proportion to their zeal and pleasure. When Burnet preached, part of his congregation *hummed* so loudly and so long, that he sat down to enjoy it, and rubbed his face with his handkerchief.

Samuel Johnson, *Lifes of Poets: Sprat.*

Burnet's *History of his own Times* is very entertaining. The style, indeed, is mere chit-chat. I do not believe that Burnet intentionally lied; but he was so much prejudiced that he took no pains to find out the truth. He was like a man who resolves to regulate his time by a certain watch, but will not inquire whether the watch is right or not.

Samuel Johnson, in James Boswell, *Life of Johnson.*

See also George I, John Wilmot

BURNEY, FRANCES (FANNY), (MADAME D'ARBLAY)

1752—1840 Novelist, Diarist

Miss Burney is a real wonder. What she is, she is intuitively. Dr. Burney told me she had had the fewest advantages of any of his daughters, from some peculiar circumstances. And such has been her timidity, that he himself had not any suspicion of her powers.

Samuel Johnson (in conversation with Mrs Thrale), in Fanny Burney, Diary, 20 June 1779.

We are, therefore, forced to refuse to Madame d'Arblay a place in the highest rank of art; but we cannot deny that, in the rank to which she belonged, she had few equals, and scarcely any superior. The variety of humours which is to be found in her novels is immense; and though the talk of each person separately is monotonous, the general effect is not monotony, but a very lively and agreeable diversity. Her plots are rudely constructed and improbable, if we consider them in themselves. But they are admirably framed for the purpose of exhibiting striking groups of eccentric characters.

T. B. Macaulay, in *Edinburgh Review*, January 1843.

Was introduced by Rogers to Made. D'Arblay . . . an elderly lady with no remains of personal beauty but a gentle manner and a pleasing expression of countenance. She told me she had wished to see two persons — myself of course being one, the other Geo. Canning. This was really a compliment to be pleased with, a nice little handsome [pat] of butter made up by a neat-handed Phillis of a dairy maid instead of the grease fit only for cart-wheels which one is dozed with by the pound.

Sir Walter Scott, *Journal*, 18 November 1826.

The jealousy of accomplished weepers came to a head in Fanny Burney, who became positively cattish about an unfortunate girl called Sophy Streatfield, because the latter was able to cry at will. It was because Fanny herself was probably the second-best weeper in the kingdom, and could not endure to be beaten.

T. H. White, *The Age of Scandal.*

See also Elizabeth Montagu

BURNS, JOHN ELLIOT

1858—1943 Labour Leader, Politician

Mr John Burns is the only gaol-bird in the Ministry.

W. T. Stead, in *Review of Reviews*, January 1906.

BURNS, ROBERT

1759--96 Poet

I don't well know what is the reason oɪ ıt, but somehow or other, though I am, when I have a mind, pretty generally beloved, yet I never could get the art of commanding respect: I imagine it is owing to my being deficient in what Sterne calls 'that understrapping virtue of discretion.' I am so apt to a *lapsus linguae*, that I sometimes think the character of a certain great man I have read of somewhere is very much *à-propos* to myself — that he was a compound of great talents and great folly.

On himself, *Journal*, May 1784.

Read Burns to-day. What would he have been, if a patrician? We should have had more polish — less force — just as much verse, but no immortality — a divorce and a duel or two, the which had he survived, as his potations must have been less spirituous, he might have lived as long as Sheridan, and outlived as much as poor Brinsley.

Lord Byron, *Journal*, 16 November 1813.

What an antithetical mind! — tenderness, roughness — delicacy, coarseness — sentiment, sensuality — soaring and grovelling, dirt and deity — all mixed up in that one compound of inspired clay!

Lord Byron, *Journal*, 13 December 1813.

And rustic life and poverty
Grew beautiful beneath his touch. . . .
Whose lines are mottoes of the heart,
Whose truths electrify the sage.

Thomas Campbell, *Ode to the Memory of Burns.*

A Burns is infinitely better educated than a Byron.

Thomas Carlyle, *Note Books*, November 1831.

It was a curious phenomenon, in the withered, unbelieving, secondhand Eighteenth Century, that of a Hero starting up, among the artificial pasteboard figures and productions, in the guise of Robert Burns. Like a little well in the rocky desert places, — like a sudden splendour of Heaven in the artificial Vauxhall! People knew not what to make of it. They took it for a piece of the Vauxhall fire-work; alas, it *let* itself be so taken, though struggling half-blindly, as in bitterness of death, against that! Perhaps no man had such a false reception from his fellow-men. . . . You would think it strange if I called Burns the most gifted British soul we had in all that century of his: and yet I believe the day is coming when there will be little danger in saying so.

Thomas Carlyle, *On Heroes and Hero Worship.*

His face was deeply marked by thought, and the habitual expression intensely melancholy. His frame was very muscular and well proportioned, though he had a short neck, and something of a ploughman's stoop: he was strong, and proud of his strength. I saw him one evening match himself with a number of masons; and out of five-and-twenty practised hands, the most vigorous young men in the parish, there was only one that could lift the same weight as Burns.

Allan Cunningham, in J. G. Lockhart, *Life of Burns.*

His muse and teaching was common sense, joyful, aggressive, irresistible. Not Latimer, nor Luther struck more telling blows against false theology than did this brave singer. The Confession of Augsburg, the Declaration of Independence, the French Rights of Man, and the 'Marseillaise', are not more weighty documents in the history of freedom than the songs of Burns.

Ralph Waldo Emerson, Speech given at a Centenary Burns dinner in Boston, 25 January 1859.

He had a strong mind, and a strong body, the fellow to it. He had a real heart of flesh and blood beating in his bosom — you can almost hear it throb. Some one said, that if you had shaken hands with him, his hand would have burnt yours. The Gods, indeed, 'made him poetical'; but nature had a hand in him first ... He held the plough or the pen with the same firm, manly grasp; nor did he cut out poetry as we cut out watch-papers, with finical dexterity, nor from the same flimsy materials.

William Hazlitt, Lectures on the English Poets.

Poor unfortunate fellow — his disposition was southern — how sad it is when a luxurious imagination is obliged in self defence to deaden its delicacy in vulgarity, and riot in things attainable that it may not have leisure to go mad after things which are not.

John Keats, Letter to Tom Keats, 7 July 1818.

My word, you can't know Burns unless you can hate the Lockharts and all the estimable bourgeois and upper classes as he really did — the narrow-gutted pigeons. ... Oh, why doesn't Burns come to life again, and really salt them!

D. H. Lawrence, Letter to Donald Carswell, 5 December 1927.

Burns wrote not so much from memory as from perception; not after slow deliberation, but from instantaneous impulse; the fire that burns through his compositions was not elaborated spark by spark, from mechanical friction, in the closet; — no, it was in the open field, under the cope of heaven, this poetical Franklin caught his lightnings from the cloud while it passed over his head, and he communicated them, too, by a touch, with electrical swiftness and effect.

James Montgomery, in Eclectic Review, May 1809.

Burns of all poets is the most a man.
D. G. Rossetti, On Burns.

His person was strong and robust; his manners rustic, not clownish; a sort of dignified plainness and simplicity, which received part of its effect, perhaps, from one's' knowledge of his extraordinary talents ... I would have taken the poet, had I not known what he was, for a very sagacious country farmer of the old Scotch school, i.e. none of your modern agriculturists, who keep labourers for their drudgery, but the douce gudeman who held his own plough. There was a strong expression of sense and shrewdness in all his lineaments; the eye alone, I think, indicated the poetical character and temperament.

Sir Walter Scott, in J. G. Lockhart, Life of Burns.

Notwithstanding the spirit of many of his lyrics, and the exquisite sweetness and simplicity of others, we cannot but deeply regret that so much of his time and talents were frittered away in compiling and composing for musical collections. ... This constant waste of his power and fancy in small and insignificant compositions, must necessarily have had no little effect in deterring him from undertaking any grave or important task.

Sir Walter Scott, in Quarterly Review, no. 1.

A dreamer of the common dreams,
A fisher in familiar streams,
He chased the transitory gleams
    That all pursue;
But on his lips the eternal themes
    Again were new.
William Watson, The Tomb of Burns.

I mourned with thousands, but as one
More deeply grieved, for he was gone
Whose light I hailed when first it shone,
    And showed my youth
How verse may build a princely throne
    On humble truth.
William Wordsworth, At the Grave of Burns.

Burns has been cruelly used, both dead and alive. The treatment which Butler and others have experienced has been renewed in him. He asked for bread — no, he did not ask it, he endured the want of it with silent fortitude — and ye gave him a stone. It is worse than ridiculous to see the people of Dumfries coming forward with their pompous mausoleum, they who persecuted and reviled him with such low-minded malignity.

William Wordsworth, Letter to John Scott, 11 June 1816.

See also John Knox, J. M. Synge, William Wordsworth

BURNSIDE, AMBROSE EVERETT

1824–81 Soldier

There was no ... intention to sacrifice but, if stupidity be culpability, few generals of ancient or modern times rank with Burnside in the guilt of manslaughter.
    Carl Russell Fish, *The American Civil War*.

He could easily fall asleep while signing papers, and even when standing. In short, he had something of a 'brigandish air' about him which appealed to people.
    Warren W. Hassler Jr, *Commanders of the Army of the Potomac*.

Few men, probably, have risen so high upon so slight a foundation as he. . . . Nobody could encounter his smile and receive the grasp of his hand without being for some time under a potent influence. It is probably true that that man's manners made his fortune.
    General Francis Winthrop Palfrey, *The Antietam and Fredericksburg*.

BURR, AARON

1756–1836 Politician

The rule of my life is to make business a pleasure and pleasure my business.
    On himself, in A. K. Adams, *The Home Book of Humorous Quotations*.

. . . a grave, silent, strange sort of animal . . .
    On himself, in Frank Monaghan, *John Jay*.

Oh, Aaron Burr, what hast thou done?
Thou hast shooted dead that great Hamilton.
You got behind a bunch of thistle
And shot him dead with a big hoss-pistol.
    Anon., in Bernard Mayo, *Henry Clay, Spokesman of the New West*.

Aaron Burr — may his treachery to his country exalt him to the scaffold, and hemp be his escort to the republic of dust and ashes.
    Anon., toast at the time of the trial of Aaron Burr, in F. F. Beirne, *Shout Treason: The Trial of Aaron Burr*.

For what wise purpose did the Almighty stay
His avenging rod on that eventful day?
Why struck he not the m——r to the ground,
Who could with coolness aim so deep a wound?
Who could with sullen disappointment's gloom

Plot for his country so reverse a doom,
And with malignant envy's direful hand
Deluge in tears Columbia's happy land,
Tear from a much-lov'd wife her bosom friend,
Cause her, alas! with sorrow to descend,
Into that grave where all her joys now lie!
Ah! little reptile, knows't thou too must die?
    Anon., in *New York Commercial Advertiser*, 18 July 1804.

. . . the Mephistopheles of politics.
    Henry Adams, *History of the United States*, vol. 2.

Burr's life, take it altogether, was such as in any country of sound morals his friends would be desirous of burying in profound oblivion. The son and grandson of two able and eminent Calvinistic divinities, he had no religious principles, and little, if any sense of reverence to a moral Governor of the Universe. . . . He lived and died as a man of the world — brave, generous, hospitable and courteous, but ambitious, rapacious, faithless and intriguing. This character raised him within a hair's breadth of a gibbett and a halter for treason, and left him, for the last thirty years of his life a blasted monument of Shakespeare's vaulting ambition.
    John Quincy Adams, in Samuel H. Wandell, *Aaron Burr in Literature*.

Just before the end of his life [Alexander] Hamilton engaged in a duel with Aaron Burr, a disappointed presidential candidate who never got beyond the vice-presidency. It is not known whether Burr shot (1) straighter or (2) sooner, but (3) he was declared the winner, and Hamilton, his time being up, (4) expired. One of the unanswered questions of history is why the ambitious Burr shot Hamilton instead of Jefferson, which would have given him the presidency. It would, however, have established a bad precedent for vice-presidents.
    Richard Armour, *It All Started With Columbus*.

He is in every sense a profligate; a voluptuary in the extreme, with uncommon habits of expense. . . . He is artful and intriguing to an inconceivable degree . . . bankrupt beyond redemption except by the blunder of his country . . . he will certainly attempt to reform the government a la Bonaparte . . . as unprincipled and dangerous a man as any country can boast — as true a Catiline as ever met in midnight conclave.
    Alexander Hamilton, Letter to James A. Bayard, 6 August 1800.

Secretly turning liberty into ridicule, he knows as well as most men how to make use of that name. In a word, if we have an embryo Caesar in the United States, 'tis Burr.

> Alexander Hamilton, in Herbert E. Parmet and Marie B. Hecht, *Aaron Burr, Portrait of an Ambitious Man.*

Fallen, proscribed, prejudged, the cup of bitterness has been administered to him with an unsparing hand. It has almost been considered as culpable to evince toward him the least sympathy or support, and many a hollow-hearted catiff have I seen, who basked in the sunshine of his bounty when in favor, who now skulked from his side, and even mingled among the most clamorous of his enemies. The ladies alone have felt or at least have had candour and independence enough to express their feelings which do honor to humanity.

> Washington Irving, 7 July 1807, in Samuel H. Wandell, *Aaron Burr in Literature.*

I never thought him an honest, frank-dealing man, but considered him as a crooked gun or other perverted machine, whose aim or shot you could never be sure of.

> Thomas Jefferson, Letter to William B. Giles, April 1807.

Burr's conspiracy had been one of the most flagitious of which history will ever furnish an example ... but he who could expect to effect such objects by the aid of American citizens, must be perfectly ripe for Bedlam.

> Thomas Jefferson, Letter to E. Du Pont de Nemours, 14 July 1807.

He was always at market, if they had wanted him.

> Thomas Jefferson, in Fawn M. Brodie, *Thomas Jefferson, An Intimate History.*

Burr was practiced in every art of gallantry; he had made womankind a study. He never saw a beautiful face and form without a sort of restless desire to experiment upon it and try his power over the inferior inhabitant. ... He was one of those persons who systematically managed and played upon himself and others, as a skilled musician on an instrument.

> Harriet Beecher Stowe, *The Minister's Wooing.*

How misunderstood — how maligned.

> Woodrow Wilson to Walter Flavius McCaleb at the grave of Aaron Burr, in F. F. Beirne, *Shout Treason: The Trial of Aaron Burr.*

BURROUGHS, EDGAR RICE

1875—1950 Author

I am sorry that I have not led a more exciting existence, so that I might offer a more interesting biographical sketch; but I am one of those fellows who has few adventures and always gets to the fire after it is out.

> On himself, in Richard A. Lupoff, *Edgar Rice Burroughs: Master of Adventure.*

BURTON, SIR RICHARD FRANCIS

1821—90 Explorer

... the impaired health, the depression of spirits, and worse still, the annoyance of official correspondence, which to me have been the sole results of African Exploration.

> On himself, *The Lake Regions of Central Africa.*

... It is a *real* advantage to belong to some parish. It is a great thing, when you have won a battle, or explored central Africa, to be welcomed home by some little corner of the Great World, which takes a pride in your exploits, because they reflect honour upon itself. In the contrary conditions you are a waif, a stray; you are a blaze of light, without a focus. Nobody outside your own fireside cares.

> On himself, in Lady Isabel Burton, *The Life of Captain Sir Richard Francis Burton.*

I struggled for forty-seven years, I distinguished myself in every way I possibly could. I never had a compliment nor a 'Thank you', nor a single farthing. I translated a doubtful book in my old age, and I immediately made sixteen thousand guineas. Now that I know the tastes of England, we need never be without money.

> On himself, in A. Symons, *Dramatis Personae: A neglected genius.*

Elizabeth, not Victoria, should have been his queen.

> Desmond MacCarthy, *Portraits.*

The attraction that Burton exercised throughout life was the spell that audacity exercises upon others. He was violent, explosive, and romantic, but his emotional explosions were not empty detonations; they drove him onwards with the directness of a projectile.

> *Ibid.*

BURTON, ROBERT

1577—1640 Author

All my joys to this are folly,
Naught so sweet as Melancholy.

> On himself, *Anatomy of Melancholy.*

Like a roving spaniel, that barks at every bird he sees, leaving his game, I have followed all, saving that which I should, and may justly complain, and truly, *qui ubique est, nusquam est* [he who is everywhere is nowhere], which Gesner did in modesty, that I have read many books, but to little purpose, for want of good method; I have confusedly tumbled over divers authors in our libraries, with small profit for want of art, order, memory, judgement.

Ibid.

He added, that 'Burton's Anatomy of Melancholy' was also excellent, from the quantity of desultory information it contained, and was a mine of knowledge that, though much worked, was inexhaustible.

Lord Byron, in Lady Blessington, *Conversations of Lord Byron.*

Burton's *Anatomy of Melancholy*, he said, was the only book that ever took him out of bed two hours sooner than he wished to be.

Samuel Johnson in James Boswell, *Life of Johnson.*

He lived like a king, a despot in the realm of words.
Desmond MacCarthy, *Portraits.*

He was an exact Mathematician, a curious Calculator of Nativities, a general read Scholar, a thro'-pac'd Philologist, and one that understood the surveying of Lands well. As he was by many accounted a severe student, a devourer of Authors, a melancholy and humerous Person; so by others, who knew him well, a Person of great honesty, plain dealing and Charity. I have heard some of the Antients of *Ch. Ch.* often say that his company was very merry, facete and juvenile, and no Man in his time did surpass him for his ready and dextrous interlarding his common discourses among them with Verses from the Poets or Sentences from classical Authors.

Anthony à Wood, *Athenae Oxonienses.*

He . . . paid his last debt to Nature, in his Chamber at *Ch. Ch.* at, or very near that time, which he had some years before foretold from the calculation of his own nativity, which being exact, several of the *Students* did not forebeare to whisper among themselves, that rather than there should be a mistake in the calculation, he sent up his soul to heaven through a slip about his neck.

Ibid.

BUTE, EARL OF (JOHN STUART)

1713—92 Statesman

O Bute, if instead of contempt and of odium,

You wish to obtain universal eulogium,
From your breast to your gullet transfer the blue
                                        string,
Our hearts are all yours at the very first swing.
Anon., in Alan Lloyd, *The Wickedest Age.*

Enough of Scotland — let her rest in peace;
The cause removed, effects of course should cease;
Why should I tell how Tweed, too mighty grown,
And proudly swelled with waters not his own,
Burst o'er his banks, and, by Destruction led,
O'er our fair England desolation spread,
Whilst, riding on his waves, Ambition, plumed
In tenfold pride, the port of BUTE assumed,
Now that the river god, convinced, though late,
And yielding, though reluctantly, to Fate,
Holds his fair course, and with more humble tides,
In tribute to the sea, as usual, glides?
Charles Churchill, *The Candidate.*

On the whole the Earl of Bute might fairly be called a man of cultivated mind. He was also a man of undoubted honour. But his understanding was narrow, and his manners cold and haughty. His qualifications for the part of statesman were best described by Prince Frederick . . . 'Bute,' said his Royal Highness, 'you are the very man to be envoy at some small proud German court where there is nothing to do.'

T. B. Macaulay, *Essays: 'Chatham'.*

. . . his bottom was that of any Scotch nobleman, proud, aristocratical, pompous, imposing, with a great deal of superficial knowledge, such as is commonly to be met in France and Scotland, chiefly upon matters of natural philosophy, mines, fossils, a smattering of mechanics, a little metaphysics, and a very false taste in everything.

Lord Shelburne, in Alan Lloyd, *The Wickedest Age.*

He has a good person, fine legs, and a theatrical air of the greatest importance. There is an extraordinary appearance of wisdom, both in his look and manner of speaking; for whether the subject be serious or trifling, he is equally pompous, slow and sententious. Not content with being wise, he would be thought a polite scholar, but he has the misfortune never to succeed, except with those who are exceedingly ignorant.

James, Earl Waldegrave, in A. F. Scott, *Every One A Witness.*

The fondness he retained for power, his intrigues to preserve it, the confusion he helped to throw into almost every succeeding system, and his impotent and dark attempt to hang on the wheels of Government, which he only clogged, and to which he dreaded even being suspected of recommending drivers, all proved that neither virtue nor philosophy had the honour of dictating his retreat, but that fear, and fear only, was the immediate, inconsiderate and precipitate cause of his resignation.

Horace Walpole, *Memoirs.*

Lord Bute, when young, possessed a very handsome person, of which advantage he was not insensible; and he used to pass many hours, every day as his enemies asserted, occupied in contemplating the symmetry of his own legs, during his solitary walks by the side of the Thames.

Sir Nathaniel Wraxall, *History Memoirs Of His Own Time.*

BUTLER, BENJAMIN FRANKLIN

1818—93 Soldier

As to the powers and duties of the government of the United States, I am a Hamiltonian Federalist. As to the rights and privileges of a citizen, I am a Jeffersonian Democrat. I hold that the full and only end of government is to care for the people in their rights and liberties, and that they have the right and privilege to call on either the State or the United States, or both, to protect them in equality of powers, equality of rights, equality of privileges, and equality of burdens under the law. . . .

On himself, *Butler's Book.*

He appreciates . . . the exact frame of mind of a captured rebel city, and the various ingenious modes of escaping the just inflictions of penalty for treason. No veteran pedagogue ever understood the tricks of truant school boys better.

Anon., in *New York Times,* in *ibid.*

After outraging the sensibilities of civilized humanity . . . he returns, reeking with crime, to his own people, and they receive him with joy . . . the beastliest, bloodiest poltroon and pickpocket the world ever saw.

Anon., in *Richmond Examiner,* in *ibid.*

This notorious demagogue and political scoundrel, having swilled three or four extra glasses of liquor, spread himself at whole length in City Hall last night . . . The only wonder is that a character so foolish, so grovelling and obscene, can for a moment be admitted into decent society anywhere out of the pale of prostitutes and débauchees.

Anon., in *ibid.*

In this section of the country Butler was the most

cordially despised and hated man who ever lived.

Anon., *New Orleans Times-Democrat,* 1893, in Frederick E. Hayes, *Third Party Movements Since The Civil War.*

The rebel tamer.

Anon., in Richard S. West Jr, *Lincoln's Scapegoat General: A Life of Benjamin F. Butler 1818—1893.*

A man whom all the waters of Massachusetts Bay cannot wash back into decency.

Anon., in *New York World,* 15 January 1863.

Now, there, I, Jefferson Davis, President of the Confederate States of America, and in their name do pronounce and declare the said Benjamin Butler to be a felon deserving of capital punishment. I do order that he shall no longer be considered or treated simply as a public enemy of the Confederate States of America, but as an outlaw and common enemy of mankind, and that, in the event of his capture, the officer of the capturing force do cause him to be immediately executed by hanging.

Jefferson Davis, in *Correspondence of Benjamin Butler,* vol. 2.

If there comes a time when there is an absolute dearth of news, when you can't think of anything to make an interesting letter, there is always one thing you can do, and that is to pitch into Ben Butler.

Murat Halstead to a group of fellow journalists, in the Washington *Evening Star,* 23 January 1899.

BUTLER, JOSEPH, BISHOP OF DURHAM

1692—1752 Author

Butler, Aristotle, Dante, Saint Augustine — my four doctors.

W. E. Gladstone, *Life of Cardinal Manning.*

Others had established the historical and prophetical ground of the Christian religion, and that sure testimony of its truth, which is found in its perfect adaptation to the heart of man. It was reserved for him to develop its analogy to the constitution and course of nature; and laying his strong foundations in the depth of that great argument, there to construct another and irrefragable proof, thus rendering Philosophy subservient to Faith, and finding in outward and visible things the type of those within the veil.

Robert Southey, *Epitaph on Bishop Butler.*

BUTLER, NICHOLAS MURRAY

BUTLER, NICHOLAS MURRAY

1862—1947 Educator, Scholar

... against everything new, everything untried, everything untested.
  Randolph Bourne, in Sherman Paul, *Randolph Bourne*.

As the self-appointed intellectual leader of the American plutocracy, he now calms the fears of the wealthy, now chides them gently when he wishes to do a little discreet begging for Columbia University.
  Dorothy Dunbar Bromley, 'Nicholas Murray Butler', in *American Mercury*, March 1935.

His conceit is consummate.... He has the bearing of a Roman emperor and he honestly believes that he was born to lead if not to rule.
  Ibid.

His discovery of the mass production of education in everything from scenario writing to Sanskrit has made his name something to conjure with in reverential collegiate circles.
  McAlister Coleman, 'Nicholas Murray Butler', in *Modern Monthly*, May 1933.

With his ideal of service and gospel of success, his Anglo-Saxon prejudices, absolute idealism in philosophy, and Republican political rectitude, he was the representative public man of the older generation, an intellectual Horatio Alger, the Captain of Learning who, in the *Columbia Monthly*, had told the undergraduates, 'don't Knock, Boost!'.
  Sherman Paul, *Randolph Bourne*.

BUTLER, SAMUEL

1612—80 Satirist, Poet

Satyricall Witts disoblige whom they converse with; and consequently make to themselves many Enemies and few Friends; and this was his manner and case. He was of leonine-coloured haire, sanguino-cholerique, middle sized, strong; a severe and sound judgement, high coloured; a good fellowe.
  John Aubrey, *Brief Lives*.

Who can read with pleasure more than a hundred lines or so of *Hudibras* at one time? Each couplet or quatrain is so whole in itself, that you can't connect them. There is no fusion.
  Samuel Taylor Coleridge, *Table Talk*, 3 July 1833.

His good sense is perpetually shining through all he writes; it affords us not the time of finding faults. We

pass through the levity of his rhyme, and are immediately carried into some admirable useful thought.
  John Dryden, *A Discourse Concerning the Original and Progress of Satire*.

Butler's Hudibras is a poem of more wit than any other in the language. The rhymes have as much genius in them as the thoughts; but there is no story in it, and but little humour ... The fault of Butler's poem is not that it has too much wit, but that it has not an equal quantity of other things. One would suppose that the starched manners and sanctified grimace of the times in which he lived, would of themselves have been sufficiently rich in ludicrous incidents and characters; but they seem rather to have irritated his spleen, than to have drawn forth his powers of picturesque imitation.
  William Hazlitt, *Lectures on the English Poets*.

There is in Hudibras a great deal of bullion which will always last. But to be sure the brightest strokes of his wit owed their force to the impression of the characters, which was upon men's mind at the time.
  Samuel Johnson, in James Boswell, *Life of Johnson.*

Those who had felt the mischiefs of discord, and the tyranny of usurpation, read *Hudibras* with rapture, for every line brought back to memory something known, and gratified resentment, by the just censure of something hated. But the book which was once quoted by Princes, and which supplied conversation to all the assemblies of the gay and witty, is now seldom mentioned, and even by those that affect to mention it, is seldom read.
  Samuel Johnson, in *Idler*, no. 59.

If exhaustible wit could give perpetual pleasure, no eye would ever leave half-read the work of Butler; for what poet has ever brought so many remote images so happily together? It is scarcely possible to peruse a page without finding some association of images that was never found before. By the first paragraph the reader is amused, by the next he is delighted, and by a few more strained to astonishment; but astonishment is a toilsome pleasure; he is soon weary of wondering, and longs to be diverted.
  Samuel Johnson, *Lives of Poets*.

This kind of stuff — the boisterous and obscure topical satire, the dismally comic mock-heroic poem, the social allusion sustained through hundreds of rhymed couplets, the academic tour de force, and the coy fugitive verses — is something intrinsically inartistic and anti-poetical, since its enjoyment pre-

126

supposes that Reason is somehow, in the long run, superior to Imagination, and that both are less important than a man's religious or political beliefs.
Vladimir Nabokov, *Commentary to Eugene Onegin.*

While Butler, needy wretch, was yet
Alive, No generous patron would a dinner give:
See him, when starv'd to death, and turn'd to dust,
Presented with a monumental bust.
The poet's fate is here in emblem shown,
He ask'd for bread, and he receiv'd a stone.
Samuel Wesley, Lines written on the erection of a monument to Butler in Westminster Abbey, 1681.

BUTLER, SAMUEL

1835—1902 Author

I am the *enfant terrible* of literature and science. If I cannot, and I know I cannot, get the literary and scientific big-wigs to give me a shilling, I can, and I know I can, heave bricks into the middle of them.
On himself, *Notebooks.*

The phrase 'unconscious humour' is the one contribution I have made to the current literature of the day.
Ibid.

Butler's books have worn well, far better than those of more earnest contemporaries like Meredith and Carlyle, partly because he never lost the power to use his eyes and to be pleased by small things, partly because in the narrow technical sense he wrote so well. When one compares Butler's prose with the contortions of Meredith and the affectations of Stevenson, one sees what a tremendous advantage is gained simply by not trying to be clever.
George Orwell, in *Tribune*, 21 July 1944.

When I admit neglect of Gissing,
They say I don't know what I'm missing.
Until their arguments are subtler,
I think I'll stick to Samuel Butler.
Dorothy Parker, *Sunset Gun.*

Butler obviously had a need to revolt against authority (as we see not only from his attitude to his own stern clerical father but from his attitude to all father-figures). He also had a need for security (witness his attitude to money, for him the stated root of all *good* — as it was in practice for his less honest contemporaries). He is therefore the most conservative and bourgeois of rebels, next to Dr Johnson. And most of his rebellion seems to be the product of

fear and thwarted rage, which resulted in destructiveness and possessiveness — somewhat incompatible qualities.
Allan Rodway, *English Comedy.*

Ardent Butlerite as I am, I cannot deny that Butler brought a great deal of his unpopularity on himself by his country parsonage unsociability and evangelical bigotry . . . Still, when all is said that can be said against Butler, the fact remains that when he was important he was so vitally important, and when he was witty he was so pregnantly witty, that we are forced to extend an unlimited indulgence to his weaknesses, and finally to embrace them as attractions.
George Bernard Shaw, *Pen Portraits and Reviews.*

Yet Butler, though he could be most amusing about people's mercenary motives, was too much a middle-class man himself to analyze the social system, in which, for all his financial difficulties, he occupied a privileged position. . . . For all his satiric insight, he had basically the psychology of the rentier.
Edmund Wilson, *The Shores of Light.*

See also George Gissing

BYNG, JOHN

1704—57 Admiral

The manner and cause of raising and keeping up the popular clamour and prejudice against me will be seen through   I shall be considered (as now I consider myself) a victim destroyed to divert the indignation and resentment of an injured and deluded people from the proper objects.
On himself, in Dudley Pope, *At Twelve Mr Byng Was Shot.*

For behaving so well in the ocean,
At least he deserves well a string,
And if he would sue for promotion,
I hope they will give him his swing.
Swing, swing, O rare Admiral Byng.
Anon., in Brian Tunstall, *Admiral Byng.*

Dans ce-pays-ci il est bon de tuer de temps en temps un amiral pour encourager les autres.
(In this country it's thought proper to kill an admiral from time to time, to encourage the others.)
Voltaire, *Candide.*

I never knew poor Byng enough to bow to.
Horace Walpole, Letter to Sir Horace Mann, 3 March 1757.

Some of the more humane officers represented to him, that his face being uncovered might throw reluctance into the executioners, and besought him to suffer a handkerchief. He replied with the same unconcern: 'If it will frighten *them*, let it be done; they would not frighten me.'

Horace Walpole, *Memoirs*.

BYRD, WILLIAM

1543–1623 Composer

Indeed, the best memorials of a professional man's existence are his surviving works; which, from their having been thought worthy of preservation by posterity, entitle him to a niche in the Temple of Fame, among the benefactors of mankind. The physician who heals the diseases, and alleviates the anguish of the body, certainly merits a more conspicuous and honourable place there; but the musician, who eminently sooths our sorrows, and innocently diverts the mind from its cares during health, renders his memory dear to the grateful and refined part of mankind, in every civilized nation.

Dr Charles Burney, *A General History of Music*.

Byrd's misfortune is that when he is not first-rate he is so rarely second-rate. . . .

Gustav Holst, 'My Favourite Tudor Composer', in *Midland Musician*, January 1926.

There be two whose benefits to us can never be requited: God, and our parents; the one for that He gave us a reasonable soul, the other for that of them we have our being. To these the prince and (as Cicero termeth him) the God of the Philosophers added our masters, as those by whose directions the faculties of the reasonable soul be stirred up to enter into contemplation and searching of more than earthly things, whereby we obtain a second being, more to be wished and much more durable than that which any man since the world's creation hath received of his parents, causing us to live in the minds of the virtuous, as it were, deified to the posterity. The consideration of this hath moved me to publish these labours of mine under your name, both to signify unto the world my thankful mind, and also to notify unto yourself in some sort the entire love and unfeigned affection which I bear unto you.

Thomas Morley, Dedication to *A Plain and Easy Introduction to Practical Music*.

BYRON, GEORGE GORDON NOEL, LORD

1788–1824 Poet

And be the Spartan's epitaph on me —

'Sparta hath many a worthier son than he.'
On himself, *Childe Harold*, canto iv.

I awoke one morning and found myself famous.
On himself, after the publication of the first cantos of *Childe Harold*, in Thomas Moore, *Life of Byron*.

Even I, — albeit I'm sure I did not know it,
Nor sought of foolscap subjects to be king, —
Was reckon'd, a considerable time,
The grand Napoleon of the realms of rhyme.
On himself, *Don Juan*, canto xi.

I perch upon a humbler promontory,
Amidst life's infinite variety:
With no great care for what is nicknamed glory,
But speculating as I cast mine eye
On what may suit or may not suit my story,
And never straining hard to versify,
I rattle on exactly as I'd talk
With anybody in a ride or walk.
Ibid., canto xv.

This morning I *swam* from *Sestos* to *Abydos*, the immediate distance is not above a mile but the current renders it hazardous, so much so, that I doubt whether Leander's conjugal powers must not have been exhausted in his passage to Paradise.
On himself, Letter to Henry Drury, 3 May 1810.

I am no Bigot to Infidelity — & did not expect that because I doubted the immortality of Man — I should be charged with denying ye. existence of God. — It was the comparative insignificance of ourselves & *our world* when placed in competition with the mighty whole of which it is an atom that first led me to imagine that our pretensions to eternity might be overrated. — This — & being early cudgelled to Church for the first ten years of my life — afflicted me with this malady — for after all it is I believe a disease of the mind as much as other kinds of Hypochondria.
On himself, Letter to William Gifford, 18 June 1813.

Well, — I have had my share of what are called the pleasures of this life, and have seen more of the European and Asiatic world than I have made a good use of . . . At five-and-twenty, when the better part of life is over, one should be *something*; and what am I? nothing but five-and-twenty — and the odd months. What have I seen? the same man all over the world, — ay, and woman too. Give *me* a Mussulman who never asks questions, and a she of the same race who saves one the trouble of putting them.
On himself, *Journal*, 14 November 1813.

I am sure my bones would not rest in an English grave, or my clay mix with the earth of that country. I believe the thought would drive me mad on my deathbed, could I suppose that any of my friends would be base enough to convey my carcass back to your soil.
On himself, Letter to John Murray, 7 June 1819.

I am like the tyger (in poesy), if I miss my first Spring, I go growling back to my Jungle. There is no second. I can't correct; I can't, and I won't.
Ibid., 18 November 1820.

There is something to me very softening in the presence of a woman, — some strange influence, even if one is not in love with them, — which I cannot at all account for, having no very high opinion of the sex. But yet, — I always feel in better humour with myself and every thing else, if there is a woman within ken. Even Mrs Mule, my firelighter, — the most ancient and withered of her kind, — and (except to myself) not the best-tempered — always makes me laugh.
On himself, *Journal,* 27 February 1814.

Now, if I know myself, I should say, that I have no character at all. . . . But, joking apart, what I think of myself is, that I am so changeable, being everything by turns and nothing long, — I am such a strange *melange* of good and evil, that it would be difficult to describe me. There are but two sentiments to which I am constant, — a strong love of liberty, and a detestation of cant, and neither is calculated to gain me friends.
On himself, in Lady Blessington, *Conversations with Lord Byron.*

I remember reading somewhere . . . a *concetto* of designating different living poets, by the cups Apollo gives them to drink out of. Wordsworth is made to drink from a wooden bowl, and my melancholy self from a skull, chased with gold. Now, I would add the following cups:- To Moore, I would give a cup formed like a lotus flower, and set in brilliants; to Crabbe, a scooped pumpkin; to Rogers, an antique vase, formed of agate; and to Colman, a champagne glass.
Ibid.

When Byron's eyes were shut in death,
We bow'd our head and held our breath.
He taught us little: but our soul
Had *felt* him like the thunder's roll.
Matthew Arnold, *Memorial Verses.*

What helps it now, that Byron bore,
With haughty scorn which mock'd the smart,
Through Europe to the Aetolian shore

The pageant of his bleeding heart?
That thousands counted every groan,
And Europe made his woe her own?
Matthew Arnold, *The Grande Chartreuse.*

. . . He had not the intellectual equipment of a supreme modern poet; except for his genius he was an ordinary nineteenth-century English gentleman, with little culture and no ideas.
Matthew Arnold, *Essays in Criticism:* 'Heinrich Heine'.

So long as Byron tried to write Poetry with a capital P, to express deep emotions and profound thoughts, his work deserved that epithet he most dreaded, *una seccatura.* As a thinker he was, as Goethe perceived, childish, and he possessed neither the imaginative vision — he could never invent anything, only remember — nor the verbal sensibility such poetry demands . . . His attempts to write satirical heroic couplets were less unsuccessful, but aside from the impossibility of equaling Dryden and Pope in their medium, Byron was really a comedian, not a satirist.
W. H. Auden, *The Dyer's Hand.*

I told him that he had rendered the most essential service to the cause of morality by his confessions, as a dread of similar disclosures would operate [more] in putting people on their guard in reposing dangerous confidence in men, than all the homilies that ever were written; and that people would in future be warned by the phrase of 'beware of being *Byroned*', instead of the old cautions used in past times.
Lady Blessington, *Conversations with Lord Byron.*

And poor, proud Byron, sad as grave
And salt as life; forlornly brave,
And quivering with the dart he gave.
Elizabeth Barrett Browning, *A Vision of Poets.*

He is the absolute monarch of words, and uses them, as Bonaparte did lives, for conquest, without more regard to their intrinsic value.
Lady Byron, Letter to Lady Anne Barnard, 2 December 1816.

If they had said the sun or the moon had gone out of the heavens, it could not have struck me with the idea of a more awful and dreary blank in the creation than the words: Byron is dead.
Jane Welsh Carlyle (on Byron's death), Letter to Thomas Carlyle.

A gifted Byron rises in his wrath; and feeling too surely that he for his part is not 'happy', declares the same in very violent language, as a piece of news that may be interesting. It evidently has surprised him much. One dislikes to see a man and poet reduced to proclaim on the streets such tidings.

Thomas Carlyle, *Past and Present*.

Close thy Byron, open thy Goethe.
Ibid.

The truth is that Byron was one of class who may be called the unconscious optimists, who are very often, indeed, the most uncompromising conscious pessimists, because the exuberance of their nature demands for an adversary a dragon as big as the world. But the whole of his essential and unconscious being was spirited and confident, and that unconscious being, long disguised and buried under emotional artifices, suddenly sprang into prominence in the face of a cold, hard, political necessity. In Greece he heard the cry of reality, and at the time that he was dying, he began to live.

G. K. Chesterton, *Twelve Types*.

It seems, to my ear, that there is a sad want of harmony in Lord Byron's verses. Is it not unnatural to be always connecting very great intellectual power with utter depravity? Does such a combination often really exist *in rerum natura*?

Samuel Taylor Coleridge, *Table Talk*, 1822.

W. Wordsworth calls Lord Byron the mocking bird of our Parnassian ornithology, but the mocking bird, they say, has a very sweet song of its own, in true notes proper to himself. Now I cannot say I have ever heard any such in his Lordship's volumes of warbles: and spite of Sir W. Scott, I dare predict that in less than a century, the Baronet's and the Baron's Poems will lie on the same shelf of oblivion, Scott be read and remembered as a novelist and the founder of a new race of novels, and Byron not remembered at all, except as a wicked lord who, from morbid and restless vanity, pretended to be ten times more wicked than he was.

Samuel Taylor Coleridge, marginalia in his copy of Pepys's *Memoirs*.

The world is rid of Lord Byron, but the deadly slime of his touch still remains.

John Constable, Letter to John Fisher, three weeks after Byron's death.

He seems to me the most *vulgar-minded* genius that ever produced a great effect in literature.

George Eliot, Letter, 21 September 1869.

Of Byron one can say, as of no other English poet of his eminence, that he added nothing to the language, that he discovered nothing in the sounds, and developed nothing in the meaning, of individual words. I cannot think of any other poet of his dis-

tinction who might so easily have been an accomplished foreigner writing English. . . . Just as an artisan who can talk English beautifully while about his work or in a public bar, may compose a letter painfully written in a dead language bearing some resemblance to a newspaper leader, and decorated with words like 'maelstrom' and 'pandemonium': so does Byron write a dead or dying language.

T. S. Eliot, *Byron*.

A coxcomb who would have gone into hysterics if a tailor had laughed at him.

Ebenezer Elliott, *The Village Patriarch*.

It is the workers who are most familiar with the poetry of Shelley and Byron. Shelley's prophetic genius has caught their imagination, while Byron attracts their sympathy by his sensuous fire and by the virulence of his satire against the existing social order. The middle classes, on the other hand, have on their shelves only ruthlessly expurgated 'family editions' of these writers. These editions have been prepared to suit the hypocritical moral standards of the bourgeoisie.

Friedrich Engels, *The Condition of the Working Class in England*, translated by W. C. Henderson and W. H. Chaloner.

He writes the thoughts of a city clerk in metropolitan clerical vernacular.

Ford Madox Ford, *The March of Literature*.

Lord Byron ist nur gross, wenn er dichtet, sobald er reflektiert ist er ein Kind.
(Byron is great in his talk, but a child in his reflections.)

J. W. von Goethe, *Conversations with Eckermann*.

Lord Byron is the spoiled child of fame as well as fortune. He has taken a surfeit of popularity, and is not contented to delight, unless he can shock the public. He would force them to admire in spite of decency and common sense . . . He is to be 'a chartered libertine' from whom insults are favours, whose contempt is to be a new incentive to admiration. His Lordship is hard to please: he is equally averse to notice or neglect, enraged at censure and scorning praise. He tries the patience of the town to the very utmost, and when they show signs of weariness or disgust, threatens to *discard* them. He says he will write on, whether he is read or not. He would never write another page, if it were not to court popular applause, or to affect a superiority over it.

William Hazlitt, *The Spirit of the Age*.

His poetry stands like a Martello tower by the side of his subject.
Ibid.

The charge we bring against Lord Byron is, that his writings have a tendency to destroy all belief in the reality of virtue — and to make all enthusiasm and constancy of affection ridiculous; and that this is effected, not merely by direct maxims and examples, of an imposing and seducing kind, but by the constant exhibition of the most profligate heartlessness, in the persons of those who had been transiently represented as actuated by the purest and most exalted emotions — and in the lessons of that very teacher who had been, but a moment before, so beautifully pathetic in the expression of the loftiest conceptions.

Francis Jeffrey, in *Edinburgh Review*, no. 72.

Byron! how sweetly sad thy melody!
    Attuning still the soul to tenderness
    As if soft Pity, with unusual Stress,
Had touch'd her plaintive lute, and thou, being by,
Hadst caught the tones, nor suffer'd them to die.

John Keats, *To Lord Byron*.

You speak of Lord Byron and me. There is this great difference between us. He describes what he sees, I describe what I imagine. Mine is the hardest task.

John Keats, Letter to George Keats, 1819.

The truth is, that what has put Byron out of favour with the public of late has not been his faults but his excellences. His artistic good ·taste, his classical polish, his sound shrewd sense, his hatred of cant, his insight into humbug above all, his shallow pitiable habit of being intelligible — these are the sins which condemn him in the eyes of a mesmerising, table-turning, spirit-rapping, spiritualising, Romanising generation, who read Shelley in secret, and delight in his bad taste, mysticism, extravagance, and vague and pompous sentimentalism. The age is an effeminate one, and it can well afford to pardon the lewdness of the gentle and sensitive vegetarian, while it has no mercy for the sturdy peer proud of his bull neck and his boxing, who kept bears and bulldogs, drilled Greek ruffians at Missolonghi, and 'had no objection to a pot of beer'; and who might, if he had reformed, have made a gallant English gentleman; while Shelley, if once his intense self-opinion had deserted him, would probably have ended in Rome as an Oratorian or a Passionist.

Charles Kingsley, *Thoughts on Shelley and Byron*.

Mad — bad — and dangerous to know.

Lady Caroline Lamb, *Journal*, 25 March 1812.

So we have lost another poet. I never much relished his ·Lordship's mind, and shall be sorry if the Greeks have cause to miss him. He was to me offensive, and I can never make out his great *power*, which his admirers talk of. Why a line of Wordsworth's is a lever to lift the immortal spirit! Byron can only

move the Spleen. He was at best a Satyrist, — in any other way· he was mean enough. I dare say I do him injustice; but I cannot love him, nor squeeze a tear to his memory.

Charles Lamb, Letter to Bernard Barton, 1824.

Byron dealt chiefly in felt and furbelow, wavy Damascus daggers, and pocket pistols studded with paste. He threw out frequent and brilliant sparks; but his fire burnt to no purpose; it blazed furiously when it caught muslin, and it hurried many a pretty wearer into an untimely blanket.

Walter Savage Landor, *Imaginary Conversations*.

He had a head which statuaries loved to copy, and a foot the deformity of which the beggars in the street mimicked.

T. B. Macaulay, *Essays*: 'Moore's Life of Byron'.

From the poetry of Lord Byron they drew a system of ethics, compounded of misanthropy and voluptuousness, in which the two great commandments were, to hate your neighbour, and to love your neighbour's wife.

Ibid.

To the Right Honourable Lord Byron . . . with that admiration of his poetic talents which must be universally and inevitably felt for versification undecorated with the meretricious fascinations of harmony, for sentiments unsophisticated by the delusive ardor of philanthropy, for narrative enveloped in all the cimmerian sublimity of the impenetrable obscure.

Thomas Love Peacock, Dedication of *Sir Proteus*.

A very interesting day. Rose late; at half-past ten joined Wordsworth in Oxford Road, and we then got into the fields and walked to Hampstead. We talked of Lord Byron. Wordsworth allowed him power, but denied his style to be English. Of his moral qualities we think the same. He adds there is insanity in Lord Byron's family, and that he believes Lord Byron to be somewhat cracked.

Henry Crabb Robinson, Diary, 24 May 1812.

Byron wrote, as easily as a hawk flies, and as clearly as a lake reflects, the exact truth in the precisely narrowest terms.

John Ruskin, *Praeterita*.

The aristocratic rebel, since he has enough to eat, must have other causes of discontent.

Bertrand Russell, *History of Western Philosophy*.

I remember saying to him [in 1815], that I really thought, that if he lived a few years longer, he would alter his sentiments. He answered rather sharply, 'I suppose you are one of those who prophesy that I will turn Methodist.' I replied — 'No. I don't expect your conversion to be of such an ordinary kind. I would rather look to see you retreat upon the Catholic faith, and distinguish yourself by the austerity of your penances.'

Sir Walter Scott, in Thomas Moore, *Notices of the Life of Lord Byron*.

Our Lord Byron — the fascinating — faulty — childish — philosophical being — daring the world — docile to a private circle — impetuous and indolent — gloomy and yet more gay than any other.

Mary Shelley, Letter to John Murray, 19 January 1830.

O mighty mind, in whose deep streams this age
Shakes like a reed in the unheeding storm,
Why dost thou curb not thine own sacred rage?

Percy Bysshe Shelley, *Fragment: Addressed to Byron*.

The fact is, that first, the Italian women with whom he associates are perhaps the most contemptible of all who exist under the moon — the most ignorant, the most disgusting, the most bigoted; countesses smell so strongly of garlic, that an ordinary Englishman cannot approach them. Well, L.B. is familiar with the lowest sort of these women, the people his gondolieri pick up in the streets. He associates with wretches who seem almost to have lost the gait and physiognomy of man, and who do not scruple to avow practices, which are not only not named, but I believe seldom even conceived in England. He says he disapproves, but he endures.

Percy Bysshe Shelley, Letter to Thomas Love Peacock, 1818.

The Coryphaeus of the Satanic School.

Robert Southey, in *London Courier*, replying to an attack by Byron, 1822.

Today Byron's dramas are hardly ever performed, and they are dismissed by most critics as ambitious failures. Yet they are of the first interest to anyone concerned with the idea of tragedy in modern literature. . . . The range of technical audacity is extreme. . . . Often Byron sought deliberately to surmount the limitations of the traditional stage in order to attain freer, larger forms of symbolic action. Like Aeschylus and Goethe, Byron was prepared to take grave risks, introducing to the theatre religious and philo-

sophic themes. He was the first major English poet since Milton to conceive of Biblical drama. And if Byron's plays are failures, they nevertheless contain within them preliminaries to some of the most radical aspects of modern drama.

George Steiner, *The Death of Tragedy*.

Of all remembered poets the most wanting in distinction of any kind, the most dependent for his effects on the most violent and vulgar resources of rant and cant and glare and splash and splutter.

Algernon C. Swinburne, *Wordsworth and Byron*.

As a boy I was an enormous admirer of Byron, so much so that I got a surfeit of him, and now I cannot read him as I should like to do. I was fourteen when I heard of his death. It seemed an awful calamity; I remember I rushed out of doors, sat down by myself, shouted aloud, and wrote on the sandstone: 'Byron is dead!'

Alfred, Lord Tennyson, in conversation with Frederick Locker-Lampson, 1869.

Ah, what a poet Byron would have been had he taken his meals properly, and allowed himself to grow fat — and not have physicked his intellect with wretched opium pills and acrid vinegar, that sent his principles to sleep, and turned his feelings sour! If that man had respected his dinner, he never would have written *Don Juan*.

W. M. Thackeray, *Memorials of Gormandizing*.

There lay the embalmed body of the Pilgrim — more beautiful in death than in life. The contraction of the muscles and skin had effaced every line that time or passion had ever traced on it; few marble busts could have matched its stainless white, the harmony of its proportions, and perfect finish. . . . To confirm or remove my doubts as to the cause of his lameness, I uncovered the Pilgrim's feet, and was answered — the great mystery was solved. Both his feet were clubbed, and his legs withered to the knee — the form and features of an Apollo, with the feet and legs of a sylvan satyr.

E. J. Trelawny, *Recollections of the Last Days of Shelley and Byron*.

My friend the apothecary o'er the way
Doth in his window Byron's bust display.
Once, at Childe Harold's voice, did Europe bow:
He wears a patent lung-protector now.

William Watson, *The Fall of Heroes*.

I hate the whole race of them, there never existed a more worthless set than Byron and his friends.

Duke of Wellington in conversation with Lady Salisbury, in Lord David Cecil, *The Cecils of Hatfield House.*

Lord Byron has spoken severely of my compositions. However faulty they may be, I do not think that I ever could have prevailed upon myself to print such lines as he has done.

William Wordsworth, *Opinions Expressed.*

See also Robert Burns, Isadora Duncan, Edmund Kean, Lady ·Caroline Lamb, John Masefield, William Wordsworth

C

CAEDMON

fl. 670 Poet

It sometimes happened at a feast that all the guests in turn would be invited to sing and entertain the company; then, when he saw the harp coming his way, he would get up from the table and go home. On one such occasion he had left the house in which the entertainment was being held and went out to the stable, where it was his duty that night to look after the beasts. There when the time came he settled down to sleep. Suddenly in a dream he saw a man standing beside him who called him by name. 'Caedmon,' he said, 'sing me a song.' 'I don't know how to sing,' he replied. 'It is because I cannot sing that I left the feast and came here.' The man who addressed him then said: 'But you shall sing to me.' . . . And Caedmon immediately began to sing verses in praise of God the Creator that he had never heard before. . . . When Caedmon awoke, he remembered everything that he had sung in his dream, and soon added more verses in the same style to a song truly worthy of God. Early in the morning he went to his superior the reeve, and told him about this gift that he had received. The reeve took him before the abbess, who ordered him to give an account of his dream and repeat the verses in the presence of many learned men, so that a decision might be reached by common consent as to their quality and origin. All of them agreed that Caedmon's gift had been given him by the Lord.
> Bede, *Ecclesiastical History of the English Nation*, translated by Leo Sherley-Price.

CALHOUN, JOHN CALDWELL

1782–1850 Statesman

When Calhoun took snuff, all South Carolina sneezed.
> Anon., in Hudson Strode, *Jefferson Davis, American Patriot, 1808–61*.

The sabled genius of the South who opposed northern property.
> John Quincy Adams, in Alfred Steinberg, *The First Ten*.

. . . tall, careworn, with furrowed brow, haggard and intensely gazing, looking as if he were dissecting the last abstraction which sprung from metaphysician's brain, and muttering to himself, in half-uttered tones, 'This is indeed a real crisis.'
> Henry Clay, in Richard Hofstadter, *The American Political Tradition*.

. . . young Hercules who carried the war on his shoulders.
> Alexander J. Dallas, *Dictionary of American Biography*.

. . . As a Senator he was the model of courtesy; he listened attentively to each one who spoke, neither reading nor writing when in his seat. . . . Wide as his knowledge, great as was his wisdom reaching toward prophetic limits, his opinions were but little derived from books or conversation. Dates he gathered on every hand, but his ideas were the elaboration of his brain, as much as his own, as is the honey not of the leaf, but of the bag of the bee.
> Jefferson Davis, in Hudson Strode, *Jefferson Davis: American Patriot*.

. . . a smart fellow, one of the first among second-rate men, but of lax political principles and a disordinate ambition not over-delicate in the means of satisfying itself.
> Albert Gallatin, in Gerald M. Capers, *John C. Calhoun – Opportunist. A Reappraisal*.

He marches and countermarches all who follow him until after having broken from the bulk of his followers he breaks from his friends one by one and expends them in breaking down his late associates — so all ends in ruins.
> John H. Hammond, in Richard Hofstadter, *The American Political Tradition*.

. . . the Marx of the masterclass.
> Richard Hofstadter, in *ibid*.

The green logs give forth more mysterious fires,
The hickory logs hum a more sinister tune,
While he thinks of Secessionist
JOHN C. CALHOUN;
And thinks he will soon
Be hanging Calhoun —

The new-made aristocrat, John C. Calhoun,
Who would wreck the Union —
John C. Calhoun.
    Vachel Lindsay, *Old Old Old Old
    Andrew Jackson.*

. . . the cast-iron man, who looks as if he had never
been born, and never could be extinguished.
    Harriet Martineau, *Retrospect of Western Travel.*

Mr. Speaker! I mean Mr. President of the Senate and
would-be President of the United States, which God
in His infinite mercy avert.
    John Randolph of Roanoke, in L. A. Harris,
    The Fine Art of Political Wit.

He could have demolished Newton, Calvin or even
John Locke as a logician.
    Daniel Webster, in *ibid.*

. . . he stood out as the great defender of federal as
opposed to centralized government, of cooperation
as against coercion; and in the process he made himself the supreme champion of minority rights and
interests everywhere.
    Charles M. Wiltse, *John C. Calhoun, Nationalist,
    1782–1828.*

. . . a giant of intellect, who was a child in party tactics.
    Henry A. Wise of Virginia, in Gerald M. Capers,
    John C. Calhoun – Opportunist. A Reappraisal.

CAMDEN, WILLIAM

1551–1623 Antiquary

He is the chaste model of all succeeding antiquaries.
    Anon., in *Biographical Magazine,* 1794.

Camden, most reverend head, to whom I owe
    All that I am in arts, all that I know.
(How nothing's that?) to whom my countrey owes
    The great renowne, and name wherewith shee
                                                    goes.
    Ben Jonson, *Epigrammes.*

What name, what skill, what faith hast thou in
                                                    things!
    What sight in searching the most antique springs!
What weight, and what authority in thy speech!
    Men scarce can make that doubt, but thou canst
                                                    teach.
    Ibid.

CAMPBELL, JOHN, BARON

1779–1861 Jurist

Edinburgh is now celebrated for having given us the
two greatest bores that have ever yet been known in
London, for Jack Campbell in the House of Lords is
just what Tom Macaulay is in private society.
    Lord Brougham, *circa* 1846, in *Dictionary of
    National Biography.*

If Campbell had engaged as an opera-dancer, I do not
say he would have danced as well as Deshayes, but I
feel confident he would have got a higher salary.
    J. Perry, in *Dictionary of National Biography.*

[His biographies] added another sting to death.
    Sir Charles Wetherell, on Campbell's *Lives of
    the Lord Chancellors,* in *Dictionary of
    National Biography.*

CAMPBELL, MRS PATRICK (BEATRICE STELLA)

1865–1940 Actress

On one occasion after a particularly wild 'tantrum'
she walked to the footlights and peered out at Yeats,
who was pacing up and down the stalls of the Abbey
Theatre. 'I'd give anything to know what you're
thinking,' shouted Mrs. Pat. 'I'm thinking,' replied
Yeats, 'of the master of a wayside Indian railway-
station who sent a message to his Company's
headquarters saying: "Tigress on the line: wire
instructions." '
    Gabriel Fallon, *Sean O'Casey: The Man I Knew.*

Even her diction is technically defective. In order to
secure refinement of tone, she articulates with the tip
of her tongue against her front teeth as much as possible. This enters for what it is worth into the method
of every fine speaker; but it should not suggest the
snobbish Irishman who uses it as a cheap recipe for
speaking genteel English; and once or twice Mrs
Campbell came dangerously near to producing this
mincing effect. For instance, 'One absorbing thought
which makes a sleeve of me,' is clearly not the excess of a genuine refinement of diction.
    George Bernard Shaw, in *Saturday Review,*
    1 June 1895.

I am convinced that Mrs Patrick Campbell could
thread a needle with her toes at the first attempt as
rapidly, as smoothly, as prettily, and with as much
attention to spare for doing anything else at the same
time as she can play an arpeggio.
    Ibid., 28 September 1895.

You will tell me no doubt that Mrs Patrick Campbell

cannot act. Who said she could? — who wants her to act? — who cares twopence whether she possesses that or any other second-rate accomplishment? On the highest plane one does not act, one *is*. Go and see her move, stand, speak, look, kneel — go and breathe the magic atmosphere that is created by the grace of all those deeds; and then talk to me about acting, forsooth!

> *Ibid.*, 7 March 1896.

Bah! You have no nerve; you have no brain: you are the caricature of an eighteenth century male sentimentalist, a Hedda Gabler titivated with odds and ends from Burne-Jones's ragbag. . . . You are an owl sickened by two days of my sunshine.

> George Bernard Shaw, Letter to Mrs Campbell,
> 11 August 1913.

If only you could write a true book entitled WHY, THOUGH I WAS A WONDERFUL ACTRESS, NO MANAGER OR AUTHOR WOULD EVER ENGAGE ME TWICE IF HE COULD POSSIBLY HELP IT, it would be a best seller. But you couldn't. Besides, you don't know. I do.

> *Ibid.*, 19 December 1938.

An ego like a raging tooth.

> William Butler Yeats, in Gabriel Fallon,
> *Sean O'Casey: The Man I Knew.*

CAMPBELL, THOMAS

1777–1844 Poet

C*** looks well, — seems pleased, and dressed to *sprucery*. A blue coat becomes him, — so does his new wig. He really looked as if Apollo has sent him a birthday suit, or a wedding-garment, and was witty and lively. . . . He abused Corinne's book, which I regret; because, firstly, he understands German, and is consequently a fair judge; and, secondly, he is *first-rate*, and, consequently, the best of judges. I reverence and admire him.

> Lord Byron, *Journal*, 5 December 1813.

Mr Campbell always seems to me to be thinking how his poetry will look when it comes to be hot-pressed on superfine wove paper, to have a disproportionate eye to points and commas, and dread of errors of the press. He is so afraid of doing wrong, of making the smallest mistake, that he does little or nothing. Lest he should wander irretrievably from the right path, he stands still. He writes according to established etiquette. He offers the Muses no violence. If he lights upon a good thought, he immediately drops it for fear of spoiling a good thing.

> William Hazlitt, *Lectures on the English Poets.*

I often wonder how Tom Campbell with so much real genius has not maintained a greater figure in the public eye than he has done of late. . . . Somehow he wants audacity — fears the public and, what is worse, fears the shadow of his own reputation. He is a great corrector too which succeeds as ill in composition as in education. Many a clever boy is flogged into a dunce and many an original composition corrected into mediocrity.

> Sir Walter Scott, *Journal*, 29 June 1826.

See also Walter Scott

CAMPBELL-BANNERMAN, SIR HENRY

1836–1908 Prime Minister

Personally I am a great believer in bed, in constantly keeping horizontal . . . the heart and everything else go slower, and the whole system is refreshed.

> On himself, Letter to Mrs Whiteley,
> 11 September 1906.

You'll do, you're cantie and you're couthy.

> W. E. Gladstone, on C-B's taking his seat in the
> Cabinet, February 1886, in John Wilson, *C.B.*
> *A life of Sir Henry Campbell-Bannerman.*

Mildly nefarious
Wildly barbarious
Beggar that kept the cordite down.

> Rudyard Kipling, recalling 'C-B' at the War
> Office, June 1901, in John Wilson, *ibid.*

. . . With no other leading Liberal of our time did diplomacy, transitory tactics, expediency of the hour, weigh lighter in the scale against principle.

> Lord Morley, *Recollections*

A jolly, lazy sort of man with a good dose of sense.

> Sir Alfred Pease, Diary, 13 May 1886.

CAMPION, EDMUND, SAINT

1540–81 Jesuit

It was not our death that ever we feared. But we knew that we were not lords of our own lives, and therefore for want of answer would not be guilty of our deaths. The only thing that we have now to say is, that if our religion do make us traitors, we are worthy to be condemned; but otherwise are, and have been, as good subjects as ever the Queen had.

> On himself, Speech at his Trial.

And indeed few who were reputed Scholars had more of Latine, or less of Greek, than he had.
Thomas Fuller, *The History of the Worthies of England.*

CANNING, GEORGE

1770–1827 Prime Minister

I know and have always known that I am — I would be either yours or nothing.
On himself, Letter to William Pitt, 1803.

. . . a heavier charge . . . that I am an adventurer. To this charge, as I understand it, I am willing to plead guilty. A representative of the people, I am one of the people, and I present myself to those who choose me only with the claims of character. . . . If to depend directly upon the people, as their representative in parliament; if, as a servant of the crown, to lean on no other support than that of public confidence — if that be to be an adventurer, I plead guilty . . . and I would not exchange that situation, to whatever taunts it may expose me, for all the advantages which might be derived from an ancestry of a hundred generations.
On himself, addressing his Liverpool constituents, 1816.

The turning of coats so common is grown,
That no one would think to attack it;
But no case until now was so flagrantly known
Of a schoolboy's turning his jacket.
Anon., verse by a Brooks's Club wit on Canning entering Parliament as a Tory, 1794.

Yet something may remain perchance to chime
With reason, and what's stranger still, with rhyme.
Even thy genius, Canning, may permit,
Who, bred a statesman, still was born a wit,
And never, even in that dull House, couldst tame
To unleaven'd prose thine own poetic flame;
Our last, our best, our only orator. . . .
Lord Byron, *The Age of Bronze.*

That is a name never to be mentioned . . . in the House of Commons without emotion. We all admire his genius; we all, at least most of us, deplore his untimely end; and we all sympathize with him in his fierce struggle with supreme prejudice and sublime mediocrity — with inveterate foes, and with — 'candid friends'.
Benjamin Disraeli, in the House of Commons, 28 February 1845.

Very well, gentlemen, since you are determined to have him, take him in God's name, but remember I tell you he will throw you all overboard.
George IV, to his Tory ministers, September 1822, in *Diary and Correspondence of Henry Wellesley 1st Lord Cowley 1790–1846.*

I hope he will be a degree less flat than he usually is, for, agreeable as he can be, he is much the most difficult person to get on with when he is not at his very best.
Lady Granville, Letter to Lady Morpeth, 21 January 1820.

Mr Canning has the luckless ambition to play off the tricks of a political rope-dancer, and he chooses to do it on the nerves of humanity!
William Hazlitt, *The Spirit of the Age,* 1824.

. . . the first logician of Europe.
Lord Holland, in Harriet Martineau, *History of the Thirty Years Peace.*

Canning was the strong man of [Perceval's] government — so strong that the others did not know what to make of him; and he did not know how to get on with them. He was the eagle in the dovecote, or rather among the owls. He fluttered the Volces in their Coriolo so tremendously that we find them heartily wishing that their gates had never shut him in among them . . . It seems as if his exuberant activity and boyish petulance and fun made him forget how old and wise he really was.
Harriet Martineau, *History of England 1800–1815.*

His absorbing idea was to be the political Atlas of England, to raise her on his shoulders.
Lady Morgan, Diary, August 1827.

It was Canning's temper that killed him.
Duke of Wellington, Letter to Lord Bathurst, 10 August 1827.

See also Lord Brougham, John Cavanagh

CANNING, STRATFORD, VISCOUNT STRATFORD DE REDCLIFFE

1786–1880 Diplomat

Thou third great Canning, stand among our best
And noblest, now thy long day's work hath ceased,
Here silent in our Minister of the West
Who wert the voice of England in the East.
Alfred Lord Tennyson, *Epitaph on Lord Stratford de Redcliffe,* in Westminster Abbey.

CANUTE (CNUT)

994?—1035 King of England

A noble figure he was, that great and wise Canute . . . trying to expiate by justice and mercy the dark deeds of his bloodstained youth; trying (and not in vain) to blend the two races over which he ruled; rebuilding the churches and monasteries which his father had destroyed . . .; rebuking, as every child has learned, his housecarles' flattery by setting his chair on the brink of the rising tide; and then laying his golden crown, in token of humility, on the high altar of Winchester, never to wear it more.
 Charles Kingsley, *Hereward the Wake.*

Canute began by being a Bad King on the advice of his Courtiers, who informed him (owing to a misunderstanding of the Rule Britannia) that the King of England was entitled to sit on the sea without getting wet. But finding that they were wrong he gave up this policy and decided to take his own advice in future — thus originating the memorable proverb, 'Paddle your own Canute' — and became a Good King and C. of E., and ceased to be memorable.
 W. C. Sellar and R. J. Yeatman, *1066 and All That.*

CAPONE, 'SCARFACE' AL(PHONSE)

1899—1944 Bootlegger

My rackets are run on strictly American lines and they're going to stay that way.
 On himself, in Claud Cockburn, *In Time of Trouble.*

Don't get the idea that I'm one of these goddam radicals. Don't get the idea that I'm knocking the American system.
 Ibid.

They talk about me not being on the legitimate. Why, lady, nobody's on the legit., when it comes down to cases; you know that.
 On himself, in Fred D. Pasley, *Al Capone, The Biography of A Self-Made Man.*

They call Al Capone a bootlegger. Yes, it's bootleg while it's on the trucks, but when your host at the club, in the locker room, or on the Gold Coast hands it to you on a silver tray, it's hospitality. What's Al Capone done, then? He's supplied a legitimate demand. Some call it bootlegging. Some call it racketeering. I call it a business. They say I violate the prohibition law. Who doesn't?
 Ibid.

A pleasant enough fellow to meet — socially — in a speakeasy — if the proprietor were buying Capone beer: a fervent handshaker, with an agreeable, ingratiating smile, baring a gleaming expanse of dental ivory: a facile conversationalist; fluent as to topics of the turf, the ring, the stage, the gridiron, and the baseball field; what the police reporters call 'a right guy'; generous — lavishly so, if the heart that beat beneath the automatic harnessed athwart the left armpit were touched.
 Fred D. Pasley in *ibid.*

He is Neapolitan by birth and Neanderthal by instinct.
 Ibid.

Capone bestrode Chicago like the Loop.
 Andrew Sinclair in *ibid.*

Al Capone's brief career was the interval between the last of the robber barons of crime and the age of the business man of crime. He used both the tommy-gun and the accountant to gut society; but he was too crude with the first tool and too naive with the second. His successors are harder fish to net.
 Ibid.

Al Capone was to crime what J. P. Morgan was to Wall Street, the first man to exert national influence over his trade.
 Ibid.

CAREW, THOMAS

1594/5—1640 Poet

An elegant court trifler.
 William Hazlitt, *Lectures on the Literature of the Age of Elizabeth.*

Carew, it seems to me, has claims to more distinction than he is commonly accorded; more than he is accorded by the bracket that, in common acceptance, links him with Lovelace and Suckling. He should be, for more readers than he is, more than an anthology poet. . . . To say this is not to stress any remarkable originality in his talent; his strength is representative, and he has individual force enough to be representative with unusual vitality.
 F. R. Leavis, *Revaluation.*

Tom Carew was next, but he had a fault,
That would not well stand with a Laureat;
His Muse was hard bound, and th'issue of's brain
Was seldom brought forth but with trouble and pain.
 John Suckling, *A Sessions of the Poets.*

CARLYLE, JANE BAILLIE WELSH

1801–66 Letter Writer

Jenny kissed me when we met,
    Jumping from the chair she sat in;
Time, you thief, who love to get
    Sweets into your list, put that in:
Say I'm weary, say I'm sad,
    Say that health and wealth have missed me,
Say I'm growing old, but add,
    Jenny kissed me.
    Leigh Hunt, in *Monthly Chronicle*.

CARLYLE, THOMAS

1795–1881 Historian, Essayist

Let me have my own way exactly in everything, and a sunnier and pleasanter creature does not exist.
    On himself, in A. K. Adams, *The Home Book of Humorous Quotations*.

That anyone who dressed so very badly as did Thomas Carlyle should have tried to construct a philosophy of clothes has always seemed to me one of the most pathetic things in literature.
    Max Beerbohm, *Works*.

I heard him growl a little about the [Crystal Palace] Exposition . . . 'a dreadful sight,' he called it: 'There was confusion enough in the universe, without building a crystal palace to represent it.' How like Carlyle!
    Elizabeth Barrett Browning, Letter to Mrs David Ogilvy, 25 July 1851.

It is so dreadful for him to try to unite the characters of the prophet and the mountebank; he has keenly felt it; and also he has been haunted by the wonder whether the people were not considering if they had had enough for their guinea.
    Jane Welsh Carlyle, of her husband as lecturer, 1840, in *The Journals of Caroline Fox*.

Carlyle has led us all out into the desert, and he has left us there.
    A. H. Clough, in conversation with R. W. Emerson, in E. E. Hale, *J. R. Lowell and his Friends*.

It is an idle question to ask whether his books will be read a century hence: if they were all burnt as the grandest of Suttees on his funeral pile, it would be only like cutting down an oak after its acorns have sown a forest. For there is hardly a superior or active mind of this generation that has not been modified by Carlyle's writings; there has hardly been an English book written for the last ten or twelve years that

would not have been different if Carlyle had not lived.
    George Eliot, in *Leader*, 27 October 1855.

He is like a lover or an outlaw who wraps up his message in a serenade, which is nonsense to the sentinel, but salvation to the ear for which it is meant.
    Ralph Waldo Emerson, *Papers from the Dial: 'Past and Present'*

We have never had anything in literature so like earthquakes as the laughter of Thomas Carlyle.
    Ralph Waldo Emerson, *ibid*.

Carlyle has been at issue with all the tendencies of his age. Like a John the Baptist, he has stood alone preaching repentance in a world which is to him a wilderness.
    J. A. Froude, *The Oxford Counter Reformation*.

The philosophy of Carlyle is simple, and it hardly changes all through his life. It is a revolt; or rather, a counter-revolution. In a word, it is *anti-mechanism*. Its main tenets are: (1) the universe is fundamentally not an inert automatism, but the expression or indeed incarnation of a cosmic spiritual life; (2) every single thing in the universe manifests this life, or at least could do so; (3) between the things that do and those that do not there is no intermediate position, but a gap that is infinite; (4) the principle of cosmic life is progressively eliminating from the universe everything alien to it; and man's duty is to further this process, even at the cost of his own happiness.
    John Holloway, *The Victorian Sage*.

The dynasty of British dogmatists, after lasting a hundred years and more, is on its last legs. Thomas Carlyle, third in the line of descent finds an audience very different from those which listened to the silver speech of Samuel Taylor Coleridge and the sonorous phrases of Samuel Johnson. . . . We smile at his clotted English.
    Oliver Wendell Holmes Sr, *Scholastic and Bedside Teaching*.

In the whole tone and temper of his teaching Carlyle is fundamentally the Puritan. The dogma of Puritanism he had indeed outgrown; but he never outgrew its ethics. His thought was dominated and pervaded to the end, as Froude rightly says, by the spirit of the creed he had dismissed. . . . It is, perhaps, the secret of Carlyle's imperishable greatness as a stimulating and uplifting power that, beyond any other modern writer, he makes us feel with him the supreme claims of the moral life, the meaning of our responsibilities, the essential spirituality of things, the indestructible reality of religion.

W. H. Hudson, Introduction to the Everyman edition of *Sartor Resartus* and *On Heroes and Hero Worship*.

That old Hebrew prophet, who goes to prince and beggar and says, 'If you do this or that, you shall go to Hell' — not the hell that priests talk of, but a hell on this earth.

Charles Kingsley, in F. E. Kingsley, *Charles Kingsley: Letters and Memories*.

Carlyle is abundantly contemptuous of all who make their intellects bow to their moral timidity by endeavouring to believe in Christianity. But his own creed — that everything is right and good which accords with the laws of the universe — is either the same or a worse perversion. If it is not a resignation of the intellect into the hands of fear, it is the subordination of it by a bribe — the bribe of being on the side of Power — irresistible and eternal Power.

John Stuart Mill, Diary, 22 February 1854.

I felt that he was a poet, and that I was not; that he was a man of intuition, which I was not; and that as such, he not only saw many things long before me, which I could only when they were pointed out to me, hobble after and prove, but that it was highly probable he could see many things which were not visible to me even after they were pointed out.

John Stuart Mill, *Autobiography*.

But the good his writings did me, was not as philosophy to instruct but as poetry to animate.

Ibid.

The old Ram Dass with the fire in his belly.

Lord Morley, *Recollections*.

There is, indeed, a considerable mystification about Carlyle's ideological stance, which may be one reason why contemporary readers, who like to be able to categorise their gurus, find him unappealing. On the one hand, he was authentically radical, in the sense of being outraged by the villanies and injustices of developing industrialism; on the other, he poured contempt on the notion of salvation through the franchise, supported Governor Eyre when he shot down rebel Jamaicans, and even ventured to disparage the abolition of slavery. His 'The Nigger Question' would undoubtedly nowadays get him into trouble with the Race Relations Board.

Malcolm Muggeridge, in *Observer*, 29 December 1974.

At bottom Carlyle is simply an English atheist who makes it a point of honor not to be one.

Friedrich Nietzsche, *The Twilight of the Idols*.

Art is not the same thing as cerebration. I imagine that by any test that could be devised, Carlyle would be found to be a more intelligent man than Trollope. Yet Trollope has remained readable and Carlyle has not: with all his cleverness he had not even the wit to write in plain straightforward English.

George Orwell, in *Tribune*, 2 November 1945.

Naturally, with his constitutional tendency to antagonism, his delight in strong words, and his unmeasured assumption of superiority, he was ever finding occasion to scorn and condemn and denounce. By use, a morbid desire had been fostered in him to find badness everywhere, unqualified by any goodness. He had a daily secretion of curses which he had to vent on somebody or something.

Herbert Spencer, *An Autobiography*.

The words in Carlyle seem electrified into an energy of lineament, like the faces of men furiously moved.

Robert Louis Stevenson, *On Some Technical Elements of Style in Literature*.

To be a prophet is to be a moralist, and it was the moral preoccupation in Carlyle's mind that was particularly injurious to his artistic instincts ... In his history, especially, it is impossible to escape from the devastating effects of his reckless moral sense.

Lytton Strachey, *Portraits in Miniature*.

Carlyle is a poet to whom nature has denied the faculty of verse.

Alfred, Lord Tennyson, Letter to W. E. Gladstone, *circa* 1870

Dr Pessimist Anticant was a Scotchman, who had passed a great portion of his early days in Germany. ... He had astonished the reading public by the vigour of his thoughts, put forth in the quaintest language. He cannot write English, said the critics. No matter, said the public; we can read what he does write, and that without yawning. And so Dr Pessimist Anticant became popular. Popularity spoilt him for all further real use, as it has done many another. While, with some diffidence, he confined his objurgations to the occasional follies or shortcomings of mankind ... it was all well; we were glad to be told our faults and to look forward to the coming millennium, when all men, having sufficiently studied the works of Dr Anticant, would become truthful and energetic. But the doctor mistook the signs of the times and the minds of men, instituted himself censor of things in general, and began the great task of reprobating everything and everybody, without further promise of any millennium at all. This was not so well; and, to tell the truth, our author did not succeed in his undertaking. His theories were all beautiful, and the code of morals that he taught us certainly an improvement on the practices of the age. We all of us could, and many of us did, learn much from the doctor while he chose to remain vague, mysterious, and cloudy: but when he became practical, the charm was gone.

Anthony Trollope, *The Warden.*

As a representative author, a literary figure, no man else will bequeath to the future more significant hints of our stormy era, its fierce paradoxes, its din, and its struggling parturition periods, than Carlyle. He belongs to our own branch of the stock too; neither Latin nor Greek, but altogether Gothic. Rugged, mountainous, volcanic, he was himself more a French Revolution than any of his volumes.

Walt Whitman, 'Death of Thomas Carlyle', in *Critic*, 12 February 1881.

See also Samuel Butler, Samuel Taylor Coleridge, Charles Dickens, J. A. Froude, Margaret Fuller, W. E. Gladstone, Gerard Manley Hopkins, D. H. Lawrence, George Bernard Shaw, Jonathan Swift, Algernon Swinburne, Anthony Trollope, H. G. Wells

CARNEGIE, ANDREW

1835–1919 Industrialist, Philanthropist

Man must have an idol — the amassing of wealth is one of the worst species of idolatry — no idol more debasing than the worship of money. Whatever I engage in I must push inordinately; therefore should I be careful to choose that life which will be the most elevating in its character. To continue much longer overwhelmed by business cares and with most of my thoughts wholly upon the way to make money in the shortest time, must degrade me beyond hope of permanent recovery.

On himself, in Matthew Josephson, *The Robber Barons.*

The man who dies thus rich dies disgraced.

On himself, 'Wealth', in *North American Review*, June 1889.

Pity the poor millionaire, for the way of the philanthropist is hard.

On himself, Letter to *Independent*, 26 July 1913.

Carnegie became so well known for his philanthropy that he became an Institution.

Richard Armour, *It All Started With Columbus.*

Never before in the history of plutocratic America had any one man purchased by mere money so much social advertising and flattery. No wonder that he

felt himself infallible, when Lords temporal and spiritual courted him and hung upon his words. They wanted his money, and flattery alone could wring it from him. . . . He had no ears for any charity unless labelled with his name. . . . He would have given millions to Greece had she labelled the Parthenon Carnegopolis.

Poultney Bigelow, *Seventy Summers*, vol. 2.

. . . until the moment of this death, he had remained to millions of his countrymen their prize showpiece of what they liked to think was the real essence of the American experience — the Americanized immigrant, the rugged individual, the self-made man, the Horatio Alger hero, the beneficent philanthropist, the missionary of secular causes, the democrat who could not only walk with but argue with kings.

Joseph Frazier Wall, *Andrew Carnegie.*

The public library was his temple and the 'Letters to the Editor' column his confessional.

Ibid.

CAROLINE AMELIA ELIZABETH OF BRUNSWICK

1768–1821 Queen Consort to George IV

No one in fact care for me; and this business has been more cared for as a political affair dan as de cause of a poor forlorn woman.

On herself, in Reginald Coupland, *Wilberforce.*

Most Gracious Queen, we thee implore
To go away and sin no more,
But if that effort be too great,
To go away at any rate.

Anon., in Lord Colchester, Diary, 15 November 1826.

If I must give up the Princess, I am resolved at least always to think that she would have been respectable, if the Prince had behaved only tolerably by her at first.

Jane Austen, Letter to Martha Lloyd, February 1813.

Fate wrote her a most tremendous tragedy, and she played it in tights.

Max Beerbohm, *King George the Fourth.*

If she was fit to be introduced as Queen to God she was fit to introduce to men.

Sir Benjamin Bloomfield, on the form of public prayer, in John Wilson Croker, Diary, 6 February 1820.

She would not have become as bad . . . if my father [George IV] had not been infinitely worse.
> Charlotte, Princess of Wales, in Geoffrey Wakeford, *Three Consort Queens*.

Damn the North! and damn the South! and damn Wellington! the question is, how am I going to get rid of this damned Princess of Wales?
> George IV, when Prince of Wales, October 1811, in W. H. Wilkins, *Mrs Fitzherbert and George IV*.

'Sir, your bitterest enemy is dead.'
'Is she, by God!' said the tender husband.
> George IV's response to Sir E. Nagle's attempt to tell him of Napoleon's death, in *The Journal of Hon. Henry Edward Fox*, 25 August 1821.

No proof of her guilt her conduct affords,
She sleeps not with couriers, she sleeps with the
> Lords.
> Lord Holland, *Epigram*, 17 August 1819, after Caroline had been observed to sleep during the first day of her trial.

Oh! deep was the sorrow and sad was the day,
When death took our gracious old Monarch away,
And gave us a Queen, lost to honour and fame,
Whose manners are folly, whose conduct is shame;
Who with aliens and vagabonds long having stroll'd,
Soon caught up their morals, loose, brazen, and bold.
> Theodore Hook, *Imitation of Bunbury's 'Little Grey Man'*.

Well, gentlemen, since you will have it so — 'God save the Queen', and may all your wives be like her!
> Duke of Wellington, to the men barring his way to champion the Queen's cause, in G. W. E. Russell, *Collections and Recollections*.

CAROLINE WILHELMINA OF ANSBACH

1683—1737 Queen Consort to George II

She was with regard to power as some men are to their amours, the vanity of being thought to possess what she desired was equal to the pleasure of the possession itself.
> Lord Hervey, *Memoirs*.

Here lies, wrapt up in forty thousand towels,
The only proof that Caroline had bowels.
> Alexander Pope, *Epigram on Queen Caroline*.

The qualities of Caroline of Ansbach were not moral qualities . . . but they were of a piece with the physical fortitude that had always upheld her. . . . Through force of circumstances, her proceedings were often devious; but in a certain robust integrity she never failed and, though she dissimulated she remained obstinately and grandly herself.
> Peter Quennell, *Caroline of England*.

What tho' the royal carcase must,
Squeez'd in a coffin, turn to dust?
Those elements her name compose,
Like atoms are exempt from blows.
> Jonathan Swift, *Directions for Making a Birthday Song*.

Oh! my Lord . . . if this woman should die, what a scene of confusion will here be! Who can tell into what hands the King will fall? Or who will have the management of him? I defy the ablest person in this Kingdom to foresee what will be the consequence of this great event.
> Sir Robert Walpole, in Lord Hervey, *Memoirs*.

CARPENTER, MARY

1807—77 Philanthropist

Shall I tell you that when she came to America I was a little disappointed that she seemed so much more the missionary than the guest, but doubtless I was expecting her to be *not Mary Carpenter*, and her errand-earnestness showed that we really had *her* with us.
> The Rev. W. C. Gannett, Letter to Rev. R. L. Carpenter, September 1877.

CARR, ROBERT, EARL OF SOMERSET

— d. 1645 Politician, Courtier

Thou was a man but of compounded part;
Nothing thy own, but thy aspiring heart;
Thy house Raleigh's, Westmoreland's thy land,
Overbury's thy wit, Essex thy wife. So stand,
By Aesop's Law, each bird may pluck his feather,
And thou stript naked art to wind and weather.
Yet care of friends, to shelter thee from cold,
Have mewed thee up in London's strongest hold.
Summer is set, and winter is come on,
Yet Robin Redbreast's chirping voice is gone.
> Anon., *Manuscript in Belvoir Castle*.

Blest pair of swans, O may you interbring
Daily new joys, and never sing:
Live till all grounds of wishes fail,
Till honour, yes, till wisdom grow so stale
That new great heights to try,
It must serve your ambition to die.
> John Donne, referring also to Lady Carr, *The Benediction*.

CARROLL, JOHN
1735–1815 Archbishop

Every one without exception, retraced and revived in his person the image of the Chief of the Apostles.
> Anon., Sulpitian, in John Shea, *Life of Archbishop Carroll.*

The Father of the American Church, and under God the author of its prosperity.
> Bishop Cheverus, 'Sermon Preached in the Catholic Church of St. Peter', 1810, in *ibid.*

The Irish suspected him of English sympathies, the French and German of being pro-Irish; the Jesuits were never altogether sure of him, yet other communities thought of him as being pro-Jesuit; ardent Republicans regarded him as an aristocrat and a Federalist. Yet he was unperturbed. . . .
> Richard J. Purcell, in *Dictionary of American Biography.*

CARROLL, LEWIS
(CHARLES LUTWIDGE DODGSON)
1832–98 Children's Writer

In answer to your question, 'What did you mean the Snark was?' will you tell your friend that I meant the Snark was a *Boojum.*
> On himself, Letter to May Barber, January 1897.

In writing it out, I added many fresh ideas, which seemed to grow of themselves upon the original stock; and many more added themselves when, years afterwards, I wrote it all over again for publication: but (this may interest some readers of 'Alice' to know) every such idea and nearly every word of the dialogue, *came of itself.* Sometimes an idea comes at night, when I have to get up and strike a light to note it down — sometimes when out on a lonely winter walk, when I have had to stop, and with half-frozen fingers jot down a few words which should keep the new-born idea from perishing — but whenever or however it comes, *it comes of itself.*
> On himself and the composition of *Alice, in Theatre,* April 1887.

Carroll's ego, a Humpty Dumpty (egg), was in perpetual peril of falling, never to be put together again. Indeed, Humpty Dumpty is the archetypal image of a Platonic man — seen as the union of white and yolk, yang and yin, enclosed within a thin shell of brittle skin. His defensive hypersensitivity to a little girl's curiosity is a reflection of a boy too long exposed to feminine eyes. It is the anguished cry of a little boy forced to spend the first years of his life in the almost exclusive company of sisters (of which Carroll ultimately had seven).
> Judith Bloomingdale, 'Alice as *Anima*: The Image of Woman in Carroll's Classic', in Robert Phillips, *Aspects of Alice.*

As Jung has also stated, the man possessed by the *anima* sees all of life as a game or puzzle. This perception seems to be the missing link between the two personalities of Charles Dodgson and Lewis Carroll. The pedantic mathematician, poor lecturer to boys at Oxford, is at the same time the fascinating teller of enchanted tales to little girls.
> *Ibid.*

To make the dream-story from which *Wonderland* was elaborated seem Freudian one has only to tell it.
> William Empson, *Some Versions of Pastoral.*

The symbolic completeness of Alice's experience is, I think, important. She runs the whole gamut; she is a father in getting down the hole, a fetus at the bottom, and can only be born by becoming a mother and producing her own amniotic fluid. Whether Carroll's mind played the trick of putting this into the story or not, he has the feelings that would correspond to it. A desire to include all sexuality in the girl-child, the least obviously sexed of human creatures, the one that keeps its sex in the safest place, was an important part of their fascination for him.
> *Ibid.*

. . . Carroll was not selfish, but a liberal-minded, liberal-handed egotist, but his egotism was all but second childhood.
> Harry Furniss, *Confessions of a Caricaturist.*

Although the first book has all the trappings of romance, including a quest for identity, a magic garden, magical transformations, and the luxuriance of perpetual springtime and a perpetual beginning, it ends with a trial, and there are no trials in utopias. It is strangely reminiscent of Carroll's experience upon seeing a sign that he thought read 'Romancement', only to discover, upon getting closer, that it actually said 'Roman cement'.
> Jan B. Gordon, 'The Alice Books and Metaphors of Victorian Childhood', in Robert Phillips, *Aspects of Alice.*

Carroll's superiority over Barrie is that his mawkish writings are his dull ones — he never succeeds in making sentimentality seductive.
> Florence Becker Lennon, *Lewis Carroll.*

Does the regimentation of Charles's own life suggest a repressed desire to be temperamental and unpunctual? He just missed the complete absurdity of Kant, whose neighbours in Königsberg set their watches by his regular afternoon walk; but he succumbed to the tyranny of time in fact, while trying to escape it in theory. A true Carrollian situation.

Florence Becker Lennon, *Victoria Through the Looking-Glass*.

Under the guise of nonsense he shows the ephemerality and unimportance of our most cherished categories, including time and space, and his social criticism is present by implication. The pacifists of 1914 might have described the soldiers fraternizing in the trenches in terms of the wood where things have no names. The stern categories called them back to the logical-nonsensical business of murdering one another as the fawn that trustfully allowed Alice to put her arms around its neck inside the wood emerged suddenly, exclaiming, 'Why — I'm a fawn — and you're a human child!'

Ibid.

In Lewis Carroll's writings the oral trauma (or the oral situation, to express the same thing more cautiously) is always breaking through the polite superficialities. For example, we attend a 'Mad Tea-Party' with Alice, the March Hare, the Mad Hatter, and the Dormouse. It is a *mad* tea-party. The March Hare *is* as mad as a March Hare, and so is the Mad Hatter; while Dormouse (*dormeuse*), with his continual tendency to fall asleep, represents withdrawal. In view of all this we expect to find a duplication of schizophrenic mechanisms in this part of the narrative, and we are not disappointed.

Géza Róheim, 'Magic and Schizophrenia', in Robert Phillips, *Aspects of Alice*.

He never found a role for himself in the world, either, and remained a portmanteau personality, now open as Lewis Carroll, now closed behind the armour of Charles L. Dodgson. He could not grasp the essential role of an adult, masculine person and he fumbled for his identity only to find it was usually expressed in a soft, feminine, plastic identification with young girl-children. He was a pedantic, forbidding adult as Charles L. Dodgson and in this role openly presented himself to the world, but as Lewis Carroll he became an adult, unmarried, secluded male spinster.

John Skinner, 'Lewis Carroll's Adventures in Wonderland', *American Imago*, vol. 4, 1947.

Carroll's special genius, perhaps, lies in his ability to disguise charmingly the seriousness of his own concern, to make the most playful quality of his work

at the same time its didactic crux.

Patricia Spacks, *Logic and Language in Through the Looking-Glass*.

His great delight was to teach me his Game of Logic. Dare I say this made the evening rather long, when the band was playing outside on the parade, and the moon was shining on the sea?

Irene Vanbrugh, in Robert Phillips, *Aspects of Alice*.

CARSON, CHRISTOPHER ('KIT')
1809–68 Frontiersman

He was not dressed in the outlandish habiliments with which fancy, since the time of Boone, instinctively invests the hunter and the trapper, but in genteel American costume ... Carson is rather under the medium height, but his frame exceedingly well knit, muscular, symmetrically proportioned. His hair, a light auburn, and worn long, falls back from a forehead high, broad and indicating more than a common share of intellect. The general contour of his face is not handsome, and yet not unpleasing. But that which at once arrests and almost monopolizes your attention is the eye — such an eye! gray, searching, piercing, as if with every glance he would reach the well-springs of thought, and read your very silent imaginings.

Arkansas Gazette & Democrat, 13 June 1851.

Kit Carson was one of the famous frontiersmen of his day. He was also a back-woodsman. For this reason he is said to have known the West backwoods and forewoods. As a young man he was a scout; as a boy, he was a boy scout. The daring deeds of Kit Carson are in no way minimized in a book about them which was written by Kit Carson.

Richard Armour, *It All Started With Columbus*.

See also Gary Cooper

CARTERET, JOHN, EARL GRANVILLE
1690–1763 Statesman

A careless, lolling, laughing love of self; a sort of Epicurean ease, roused to action by starts and bounds — such was his real character. For such a man to be esteemed really great, he must die early! He must dazzle as he passes, but he cannot bear a close and continued gaze.

Lord Mahon, *History of England, 1713–1783*.

He might have lectured upon public law. He might have taken his seat in a synod and taught the Canonists. Yet in public life no rust of pedantry ever dimmed his keen and brilliant intellect.

Ibid.

He was precipitate in his manner and rash in his projects; but though there was nothing he would not attempt, he scarce ever took any measures necessary to the accomplishment. He would profess amply, provoke indiscriminately, oblige seldom. It is difficult to say whether he was oftener intoxicated by wine or ambition: in fits of the former, he showed contempt for everybody; in rants of the latter, for truth. His genius was magnificent and lofty; his heart without gall or friendship, for he never tried to be revenged on his enemies, or to serve his friends.

Horace Walpole, *Memoirs.*

Commanding beauty, smooth'd by cheerful grace,
Sat on the open features of his face.
Bold was his language, rapid, glowing, strong,
And science flow'd spontaneous from his tongue.
A genius, seizing systems, slighting rules,
And void of gall, with boundless scorn of fools,
Ambition dealt her flambeau to his hand,
And Bacchus sprinkled fuel on the brand . . .
Unhurt, undaunted, undisturb'd he fell,
Could laugh the same, and the same stories tell:
And more a sage than he who bade await
His revels till his conquests were complete,
Our jovial statesman either sail unfurl'd,
And drank his bottle, tho' he miss'd the world.

Horace Walpole, in Basil Williams, *Carteret and Newcastle.*

Like a true Cornishman, indifferent, as is said, to what the rest of England was doing or thinking, he scorned the necessary condescensions of statesmen to secure the co-operation of fellow ministers, parliament, or people.

Basil Williams, *The Whig Supremacy.*

CARUSO, ENRICO

1873—1921 Singer

The Man With the Orchid-Lined Voice.
Edward L. Bernays, Caruso's publicist, in numerous press releases.

He lived his own life so noiselessly, with such concentration, such intensity, such inner stillness, that he had no need to draw on the lives of others to replenish it. He held his life in his hands, and he was never surprised by it because he gave to it all his attention. Being so full, so rich in himself, he could not absorb the kaleidoscopic life of other people. This is the reason why, when I am asked what Caruso thought of his contemporaries, I cannot answer. He didn't think of them — he greeted them.

Dorothy Caruso, *Enrico Caruso, His Life and Death.*

His records had made him known to millions, including a significant majority of non-opera-goers, but the Caruso cult owed as much to his almost magnetic rapport with the public, both on and off stage. . . . The beaming smile, lit by flashing white teeth, radiated an urchin exuberance and *joie de vivre.* Only Caruso would dare to go before the Metropolitan curtain, pat his stomach and implore the audience to go home 'because I'm so hungry and want my supper'.

Stanley Johnson, *Caruso.*

Recordings had won him the affection of millions, who sat by their phonographs and thrilled to the impassioned arias. His countrymen wept in exile over nostalgic folk songs winewarm with sunlight. . . . To New York's Little Italy he was far more than a voice; he had become a symbol of hope and laughter in adversity. They identified fiercely, patriotically, with the chubby little man who had escaped from a Neapolitan slum to win storybook success on alien soil but still spoke broken English and remained as Italian as macaroni.

Ibid.

I had a great veneration for that big boy, because he was such a baby, and God had given him so much that the gift was too colossal for his comprehension. Such a sentimentalist! Such a rich nature wasted upon superficial whims and ambition! What a child he was, that man with his broad shoulders and enormous chest. . . .

Lou Tellegen, *Women Have Been Kind.*

CARVER, GEORGE WASHINGTON

1864—1943 Agricultural Chemist, Educator

Isn't it fantastic that George Washington Carver found over 300 uses for the lowly peanut — but the South never had any use for George Washington Carver?

Dick Gregory, *From the Back of the Bus*

CASTLE, VERNON BLYTHE

1887—1918 Dancer

Catalysts and popularizers rather than reformers or

CASTLEMAINE

innovators, the Castles were perhaps the first large expression of modern mass society and its cult of good taste, its How To Lessons, its obsession with The Correct Thing. Old social barriers that had defended 'taste' and confined it to the wealthy were crumbling. Now, on all levels of society but the lowest, The Correct Thing was simply what the Castles did, two fine dancers with a sense of the moment and a flair for self-promotion. Their mixture of common sense and frivolity, of youthful exuberance and refinement, were what the early teens of the century demanded. They fused the decorum of the mansion ballroom and the vitality of the streets ... Their reign was short ... Vernon was killed in 1918. But through them masses of Americans discovered their dances and their dance music, their democratic right to elegance and the pursuit of fun.
>Arlene Croce, *The Fred Astaire and Ginger Rogers Book*.

CASTLEMAINE, COUNTESS OF, see under VILLIERS, BARBARA

CASTLEREAGH, VISCOUNT
(ROBERT STEWART, MARQUESS OF LONDONDERRY)

1739–1821 Statesman

A wretch never named but with curses and jeers!
>Lord Byron, *The Irish Avatar*.

The intellectual eunuch Castlereagh.
>Lord Byron, *Don Juan*, canto i (fragment).

That sad inexplicable beast of prey —
That Sphinx, whose words would ever be a doubt,
Did not his deeds unriddle them each day —
Than monstrous hieroglyphic — that long spout
Of blood and water, leaden Castlereagh!
>Lord Byron, *Don Juan*, canto ix.

Last night I toss'd and turned in bed,
But could not sleep — at length I said,
I'll think of Viscount C — stl — r — gh,
And of speeches — that's the way.
>Thomas Moore, *Insurrection of the Papers*.

Q. Why is a Pump like V-sc--nt C-stl-r--gh?
A. Because it is a slender thing of wood,
That up and down its awkward arm doth sway,
And coolly spout and spout and spout away,
In one weak, washy, everlasting flood!
>Thomas Moore, *A Riddle*.

I met Murder on the way —
He had a mask like Castlereagh —
Very smooth he looked, yet grim;
Seven blood-hounds followed him:
All were fat; and well they might
Be in admirable plight,
For one by one, and two by two,
He tossed them human hearts to chew
Which from his wide cloak he drew.
>Percy Bysshe Shelley, *The Mask of Anarchy*.

See also Henry Addington

CATHER, WILLA SIBERT

1873–1947 Author

I have never faced the typewriter with the thought that one more chore had to be done.
>On herself, in Mildred R. Bennett, *The World of Willa Cather*.

As she burned herself away in her writing, she had less and less to give; and she did not have that saving sense of humour which has from the beginning of time enabled others to laugh at themselves. Her religion of Art she took very seriously.
>*Ibid.*

Willa Cather never wrangled with abstractions or creeds, never struggled with politics or the pressing history of the front pages. She was concerned with the concrete process of observing life.
>E. K. Brown, *Willa Cather*.

She manipulated European and American values with as much subtlety as Henry James, but with an intent wholly different from James's. Like James, however, and to an even greater degree, she remained an American novelist: she saw life in terms of the possibilities provided by the New World, and her vision darkened only when those possibilities seemed to fail.
>David Daiches, *Willa Cather*.

For the whole range of Cather's values, standards, tastes, and prejudices, her tone is that of an inherent aristocrat in an equalitarian order, of an agrarian writer in an industrial order, of a defender of the spiritual graces in the midst of an increasingly materialistic culture.
>Maxwell Geismar, *The Last of the Provincials*.

Those who admire writing which selects with a quick ear, which eliminates all but the one unique word, which frowns upon anything suggestive of superfluity, will approve of Willa Cather's watchfulness,

146

her conscientious efforts to become a master. Those who hope rather to find in a novel life itself, prodigal, sweet, painful, disordered and bemused, will regret the loss of the story-teller in the development of the stylist.
    Grant C. Knight, *American Literature and Culture.*

Her style is so deftly a part of her theme that to the uncomprehending, to the seeker after verbal glass jewels, she is not perceivable as a 'stylist' at all.
    Sinclair Lewis, 'A Hamlet of the Plains', in James Schroeter ed., *Willa Cather and Her Critics.*

And she has got such a grip upon her materials — upon the people she sets before them — that both take on an extraordinary reality. I know of no novel that makes the remote folk of the western prairies more real than *My Antonia* makeš them, and I know of none that makes them seem better worth knowing.
    H. L. Mencken, 'My Antonia', in *ibid.*

When Willa talked of what she hated, her whole personality changed. Her chin hardened, her shoulders pushed forward, and one felt that the rigors of her life had made her tough or touchy. Her emotional nature was disciplined on the surface; but not far below burned a fiery surface.
    Elizabeth Shepley Sergeant, *Willa Cather.*

As in an iceberg, the greater part of her load was submerged. That of course made her masterful, and somewhat alarming.
    Ibid.

The disappearance of the old frontier left Miss Cather with a heritage of the virtues in which she had been bred but with the necessity of finding a new object for them. Looking for the new frontier she found it in the mind.
    Lionel Trilling, 'Willa Cather', in Malcolm Cowley ed., *After the Genteel Tradition.*

Having freed herself from the bondage of 'plot' as she has freed herself from an inheritance of the softer sentiments, Miss Cather has learned that ultimate interest of fiction inheres in character.
    Carl Van Doren, 'Willa Cather', in James Schroeter ed., *Willa Cather and Her Critics.*

Hers is to move on the sunlit face of the earth, with the gracious amplitude of Ceres, bidding the soil yield richly, that the other kind of artist, who is like Persephone and must spend half of his days in the world under the world, may be refreshed on emergence.
    Rebecca West, 'The Classic Artist', in *ibid.*

The most sensuous of writers, Willa Cather builds her imagined world almost as solidly as our five senses build the universe around us.
    Ibid.

CATHERINE OF ARAGON

1485—1536 Queen Consort to Henry VIII

I have done England little good, but I should be sorry to do it any harm.
    On herself, Attributed.

A pious woman toward God, (according to her devotion), frequent in prayer, which she always performed on her bare knees, nothing else between her and the earth interposed; little curious in her clothes, being wont to say, she accounted no time lost but what was laid out in dressing of her though art might be more excusable in her, to whom nature had not been over-bountiful. She was rather staid, than stately; reserved, than proud; grave from her cradle, insomuch that she was a matron before she was a mother. This her natural gravity increased with her apprehended injuries, settled in her reduced age into a habit of melancholy, and that terminated into a consumption of the spirits.
    Thomas Fuller, *Church History of Britain.*

CATHERINE OF BRAGANZA

1638—1705 Queen Consort to Charles II

The *Queene* arived, with a traine of Portugueze Ladys in their monstrous fardingals or *Guard-Infantas*: their complexions *olivaster*, & sufficiently unagreeable: *Her majestie* in the same habit, her foretop long & turned aside very strangely: She was yet of the handsomest Countenance of all the rest, & tho low of stature pretily shaped, languishing and excellent Eyes, her teeth wronging her mouth by stiking a little too far out: for the rest sweete & lovely enough.
    John Evelyn, Diary, 30 May 1662.

Mr Coventry tells me today that the Queene hath a very good night last night; but yet it is strange that she still raves and talks of little more than of her having of children, and fancies now that she hath three children and that the girle is very like the King. And this morning about 5 a-clock, waked (the Physician feeling her pulse, thinking to be better able to judge, she being still and asleep, waked her) and the first word she said was, 'How do the children?'
    Samuel Pepys, Diary, 27 October 1663.

... the Queene is very well again, and the King lay with her on Saturday night last. And that she speaks now very pretty English and makes her sense out now and then with pretty phrases   as, among others, this is mightily cried up — that meaning to say she did not like such a horse so well as the rest, he being too prancing and full of tricks, she said he did 'make too much vanity'.

Samuel Pepys, Diary, 4 January 1664.

A little woman, no breeder.
Anthony à Wood, *Life and Times*, 20 May 1662.

CATLIN, GEORGE
1796–1872 Artist

... my mind was continually reaching for some branch or enterprise of the art, on which to devote a whole life-time of enthusiasm; then a delegation of some ten or fifteen noble and dignified-looking Indians, from the wilds of the 'Far West', suddenly arrived in the city, arrayed and equipped in all their classic beauty, — with shield and helmet, — with tunic and manteau, — tinted and tasselled off, exactly for the painter's palette! In silent and stoic dignity, these lords of the forest strutted about the city for a few days, wrapped in their pictured robes, with their brows plumed with quills of the war-eagle, attracting the gaze and admiration of all who beheld them. . . . And the history and customs of such a people, preserved by pictorial illustrations, are themes worthy of the lifetime of one man, and nothing short of the loss of my life, shall prevent me from visiting their country, and of becoming their historian. . . .

On himself, in Vivian Varney Guyler, *George Catlin*.

It is but to paint the splendid panorama of a world entirely different from anything seen or painted before; a vast country of green fields, where men are all red; where meat is the staff of life; where no laws but those of honor are known; where buffaloes range, and the elk, mountain sheep, and fleet-bounding antelope . . . where the wolves are white and bears grizzly . . . where the rivers are yellow and white men are turned savages . . . the dogs are all wolves, women are slaves, men are lords. . . . For all those . . . yet uncorrupted by the vices of civilized acquaintance . . . for the character and preservation of these noble fellows I am an enthusiast, and it is for these uncontaminated people that I would be willing to devote the energies of my life.

On himself, in Harold McCracken, *George Catlin and the Old Frontier*.

CAVANAGH, JOHN
Early nineteenth-century Fives player

He was a fine, sensible, manly player, who did what he could, but that was more than any one else could even affect to do. His blows were not undecided and ineffectual — lumbering like Mr. Wordsworth's epic poetry, nor wavering like Mr. Coleridge's lyric prose, nor short of the mark like Mr. Brougham's speeches, nor wide of it like Mr. Canning's wit, nor foul like the *Quarterly*, nor *let* balls like the *Edinburgh Review*. Cobbett and Junius together would have made a Cavanagh.

William Hazlitt, *Table Talk: The Indian Jugglers*.

CAVENDISH, HON. HENRY
1731–1810 Natural Philosopher

A greater contrast between two men of science, both eminent benefactors to the same branch of knowledge, can hardly be imagined than Cavendish offers to Priestley. He was thoroughly educated in all branches of the Mathematics and Natural Philosophy; he studied each systematically; he lived retired from the world among his books and his instruments, never meddling with the affairs of active life; he passed his whole time in storing his mind with the knowledge imparted by former inquirers and in extending its bounds. Cultivating science for its own sake, he was slow to appear before the world as an author; had reached the middle age of life before he gave any work to the press; and though he reached the term of four-score, never published a hundred pages. His methods of investigation were nearly as opposite as this diversity might lead us to expect; and in all the accidental circumstances of rank and wealth the same contrast is to be remarked. He was a duke's grandson; he possessed a princely fortune; his whole expenditure was on philosophical pursuits; his whole existence was in his laboratory or his library.

Henry, Lord Brougham, *Lives of Men of Letters and Science*.

Mr. Cavendish received no one at his residence; he ordered his dinner daily by a note which he left at a certain hour on the hall table, where the housekeeper was to take it, for he held no communication with his female domestics, from his morbid shyness. It followed, as a matter of course, that his servants thought him strange, and his neighbours deemed him out of his mind. He hardly ever went into society. The only exceptions I am aware of are an occasional christening at Devonshire or Burlington House, the meetings of the Royal Society, and Sir Joseph Banks' weekly conversaziones. At both the latter places I have met him, and recollect the shrill cry he uttered as he shuffled quickly from room to room, seeming to be annoyed if looked at, but sometimes approaching to hear what was passing among others. His face was intelligent and mild, though, from the nervous irritation which he seemed to feel, the expression could hardly be called calm. It is not likely that he ever should have been induced to sit for his picture; the result therefore of any such experiment is wanting. His dress was of the oldest fashion, a greyish green coat and waistcoat, with flaps, a small cocked hat, and his hair dressed like a wig (which possibly it was) with a thick clubbed tail. His walk was quick and uneasy; of course he never appeared in London unless lying back in the corner of his carriage. He probably uttered fewer words in the course of his life than any man who ever lived to fourscore years, not at all excepting the monks of La Trappe.

Ibid.

He seems in his application of mathematics to physics to have disregarded elegance, and even simplicity, and to have chosen always the shortest and most certain path to his object.

Ibid.

Two striking figures at these meetings were Cavendish and Wollaston — the former the shyest and most taciturn of men; listening intently when discussion was going on, but never taking part in it; and shrinking out of sight if reference were made to himself or his own researches.

Sir Henry Holland, *Recollections of Past Life.*

CAVENDISH, MARGARET, DUCHESS OF NEWCASTLE

1624?--74 Author

On the subject of a literary wife, I must introduce to the acquaintance of the reader Margaret Duchess of Newcastle. . . . Her labours have been ridiculed by some wits; but had her studies been regulated, she would have displayed no ordinary genius. The *Connoisseur* has quoted her poems, and her verses have been imitated by Milton.

Isaac D'Israeli, *Curiosities of Literature.*

A dear favourite of mine, of the last century but one -- the thrice noble, chaste, and virtuous, — but again somewhat fantastical, and original-brain'd, generous Margaret Newcastle.

Charles Lamb, *Elia.*

The whole story of this lady is a romance, and all she doth is romantic. Her footmen in velvet coats, and

herself in an antique dress as they say, and was the other day at her own play, *The Humorous Lovers*; the most ridiculous thing that ever was wrote, but yet she and her Lord mightily pleased with it, and she at the end made her respect to the players from her box, and did give them thanks.

Samuel Pepys, Diary, 11 April 1667.

Her works at length amounting to thirteen folios, ten of them in print. This enormous mass of her writings is now so completely consigned to oblivion, that probably scarcely any English scholar living has read more of them than a few lines descriptive of melancholy quoted in the 'Connoisseur' . . . and praised beyond their desert.

Robert Southey, *Commonplace Book* (4th Series).

She succeeded during her lifetime in drawing upon herself the ridicule of the great and the applause of the learned. But the last echoes of that clamour have now all died away; she lives only in the few splendid phrases that Lamb scattered upon her tomb; her poems, her plays, her philosophies, her orations, her discourses — all those folios and quartos in which, she protested, her real life was shrined — moulder in the gloom of public libraries, or are decanted into tiny thimbles which hold six drops of their profusion. Even the curious student, inspired by the words of Lamb, quails before the mass of her mausoleum, peers in, looks about him, and hurries out again, shutting the door.

Virginia Woolf, *The Common Reader.*

She could write when she was young. But her fairies, if they survived at all, grew up into hippopotami. . . . She became capable of involutions, and contortions and conceits. . . . She similized, energetically, incongruously, eternally; the sea became a meadow, the sailors shepherds, the mast a maypole. The fly was the bird of summer, trees were senators, houses ships. . . . Truly, 'my Lady Sanspareille hath a strange spreading wit'. Worse still, without an atom of dramatic power, she turned to play-writing.

Ibid.

CAVENDISH, RICHARD

Eighteenth-century Gentleman

Mr Sheridan told us of Mr Richard Cavendish, who had a trick of swinging his arm round when talking, that, walking up Bond Street with a friend, he found, on stopping, that he had drawn seven hackney coaches to him.

Lord Broughton, *Recollections of a Long Life, 4 June 1810.*

CAVENDISH, THOMAS

1560—92 Circumnavigator

Thus having circumnavigated the whole Earth, let his Ship no longer be termed the *Desire*, but the *Performance*; He was the *third* man, and *second* Englishman, of such universal undertakings.
> Thomas Fuller, *The History of the Worthies of England*.

CAVENDISH, WILLIAM, DUKE OF DEVONSHIRE

1592—1676 Statesman

Newcastle on's horse for entrance next strives
  Well stuffd was his cloak-bag, and so were his
                                breeches.
And unbutt'ning the place where Nature's posset-
                                maker lives,
  Pulls out his wife's poems plays essays and
                                speeches.

'Whoop' quoth Apollo, 'What the de'il have we here?
  Put up thy wife's trumpery good noble Marquis,
And home again, home again, take thy career
  To provide her fresh straw and a chamber that
                                dark is.'
> Anon., *The Session of the Poets*, 1668.

CAXTON, WILLIAM

1422—91 Printer

It was in the year 1474 that our first press was established in Westminster Abbey, by William Caxton: but in the choice of his authors, that liberal and industrious artist was reduced to comply with the vicious taste of his readers; to gratify the nobles with treatises on heraldry, hawking and the game of chess, and to amuse the popular credulity with romances of fabulous knights, and legends of more fabulous saints.
> Edward Gibbon, *An Address*.

CECIL, EDGAR ALGERNON ROBERT GASCOYNE, VISCOUNT OF CHELWOOD

1864—1958 Statesman, Co-Founder of the League of Nations

Lord Robert ... with a permanent stoop ... gave one the impression when he was denouncing the [Welsh·Disestablishment] Bill of a benevolent hawk, if there be such a bird, anxious to swoop upon the Liberal Party to remove it from its evil environment of Radicalism and Nonconformity and secure it body and soul for the Church.
> Lord Winterton, *Orders for the Day*.

CECIL, ROBERT, EARL OF SALISBURY

1563—1612 Statesman

Here lieth Robin Crookback, unjustly reckoned
A Richard the Third, he was Judas the Second ...
> Anon., from a manuscript collection of verses on Robert Cecil's death.

Here lies, thrown down for worms to eat,
Little bossive that was so great.
Not Robin Goodfellow, or Robin Hood
But Robin th'encloser of Hatfield Wood,
Who seemed as sent from Ugly Fate
To spoil the Prince, and rot the State,
Owning a mind of dismal ends
As trap for foes and tricks for friends.
But now in Hatfield lies the Fox
Who stank while he lived and died of the Pox.
> Anon., popular celebration of Salisbury's death.

He was no fit counsellor to make affairs better, yet he was fit to stop them from getting worse.
> Francis Bacon, in David Cecil, *The Cecils of Hatfield House*.

Though there are many indications of his having possessed a kindly and affectionate nature, he seems never to have had a friendship. Life was to him a game which he would play for high stakes, and men and women were only pieces upon the board, set there to be swept off by one side or the other or allowed to stand so long only as the risk of letting them remain there was not too great.
> Augustus Jessop, in the *Dictionary of National Biography*.

It is an unwholesome thing to meet a man in the morning which hath a wry neck, a crooked back and a splay foot.
> John Mylles, servant of the Earl of Essex, in David Cecil, *The Cecils of Hatfield House*.

He had a full mind in an imperfect body. ... In a chair he had both a sweet and a grave presence, as if nature understanding how good a counsellor he would make, gave him no more beauty of person anywhere else, of purpose because it should not move him into action.
> Sir Henry Wotton, *The Character of Sir Robert Cecil*.

... Sometimes the less did he seem to be eloquent, the more he was; for he did not confine speaking well to one law of phrase or style, but varied his method in it, according to the bringing up of the person he conferred with, and the nature of the argument, whereby he cleared it a passage to the hearer's apprehension, were he of a quality either learned or unlearned. The capacity of the learned he gave satisfaction unto, the unlearned did give both a satisfaction, and a capacity to be satisfied.

Ibid.

His making ready to die was the greatest blessing of his life to him; for he never went to bed without cares till then, but had alarums everywhere to wake him, save in his conscience: when death came to be his business, he was in peace, and so died.

Ibid.

The Queen was wont to call Sir Robert Cecil her register of remembrances.

Sir Henry Wotton, *Table Talk*.

See also Mary Herbert

CECIL, WILLIAM, see under BURGHLEY, LORD

CERF, BENNETT

1898–1971 Publisher

Everyone has a streak of pure unadulterated ham. Many won't admit it. I revel in it.

On himself, in *New York Times*, 29 August 1971.

He was King of the Eclectics, and there is no successor to the throne.

Anon., in *Saturday Review*, 11 September 1971.

He had style, splendor, and swoosh. But all the joyousness, excitement, and fireworks associated with his name should not be allowed to obscure his main aim and achievement in life. He set out to be a book publisher, and he became one of the very best.

Ibid.

CHADWICK, SIR EDWIN

1800–90 Reformer, Philanthropist

He exhibits a curious example of the strictly legal as opposed to the scientific and practical order of mind. ... The legal mind, like Mr Chadwick's, first jumps to a conclusion or theory, in fact makes a case, and then devotes all its powers to support that case, rejects ... every circumstance, ... every practical and scientific fact, that contradicts its settled theory. ... Hence it is that reports drawn up by Mr Chadwick's Board of Health ignore the daily instance of choking-up of the pipe sewers, which he declared to be 'self-cleansing'. ... Hence, tables of the cost of sewerage works in various towns are published in the 1854 report, with one-half of the cost omitted, and instances of total failure are cited as triumphant successes. Mr Chadwick settled his system in 1848, and he would rather believe all the world wrong, rather see London made impassable, than permit himself to doubt that his theories, his dry water-works, and choked-up pipes are not perfection. ...

Anon., *Engineers and Officials*, 1856.

... he babbled too much, not of green fields, but of sewage. I remember Lord Farrar when president [of the Political Economy Club] calling Mr Chadwick to order and in tones of thunder saying, 'The subject is taxation not drainage.'

Sir J. MacDonnell, Political Economy Club, *Journal*, 5 July 1905.

I may say in brief that he is one of the contriving and organizing minds of the age; a class of mind of which there are very few, and still fewer who apply those qualities to the practical business of government. He is, however, one of the few men I have known who has a passion for the public good; and nearly the whole of his time is devoted to it in one form or another.

John Stuart Mill, Letter to James Henderson, August 1868.

CHAMBERLAIN, (ARTHUR) NEVILLE

1869–1940 Prime Minister

While war was still averted, I felt I was indispensable, for no one else could carry out my policy. Today the position has changed. Half a dozen people could take my place while war is in progress. ... It was of course a grievous disappointment that peace could not be saved, but I know that my persistent efforts have convinced the world that no part of the blame can lie here. That consciousness of moral right, which it is impossible for the Germans to feel, must be a tremendous force on our side.

On himself, Letter to his Sister, 10 September 1939.

... You, like the late Bonar Law, always understate your case. That is part of your character. But you do not make headway on this understatement. You

make it on character. So do not be deceived.
    Lord Beaverbrook, Letter to Chamberlain,
    7 June 1934.

The worst thing I can say about democracy is that it
has tolerated the right hon. Gentleman for four and
a half years.
    Aneurin Bevan, speaking in Parliament of
    Chamberlain as Minister of Health, 23 July 1929.

Listening to a speech by Chamberlain is like paying
a visit to Woolworths; everything in its place and
nothing above sixpence.
    Aneurin Bevan, in *Tribune*, 1937.

Neville Chamberlain is no better than a Mayor of
Birmingham, and in a lean year at that. Furthermore
he is too old. He thinks he understands the modern
world. What should an old hunks like him know of
the modern world?
    Lord Hugh Cecil, in Lord David Cecil, *The Cecils
    of Hatfield House*.

Without policy or direction, without philosophy or
morality, being pushed from pillar to post by the
dictators of Europe ... The puny son of one who
could at least be called courageous, however mistaken ..., has disgraced not only his native city ...
but his country and the whole civilised world as
well. ... The people of Birmingham have a specially
heavy responsibility, for they have given the world
the curse of the present British Prime Minister.
    Sir Stafford Cripps, speaking in Birmingham,
    18 March 1938.

No man that I know is less tempted than Mr
Chamberlain to cherish unreal illusions.
    Lord Halifax, February 1939, in Keith Feiling,
    Life of Neville Chamberlain.

Chamberlain's great fault was that he sneered at
people; he sneered at the Labour Members and they
never forgave him ...
    Lord Halifax, in Harold Nicolson, Diary,
    June 1954.

Well, he seemed such a nice old gentleman, I thought
I would give him my autograph as a souvenir.
    Adolph Hitler, attributed, in *The Penguin
    Dictionary of Modern Quotations*.

Look at his head. The worst thing Neville
Chamberlain ever did was to meet Hitler and let
Hitler see him.
    David Lloyd George, in conversation in
    Parliament, 3 September 1939.

He has appealed for sacrifice. The nation is prepared
for every sacrifice so long as it has leadership. I say
solemnly that the Prime Minister should give an
example of sacrifice, because there is nothing which
can contribute more to victory in this war than that
he should sacrifice the seals of office.
    David Lloyd George, to the House of Commons,
    May 1940.

He saw foreign policy through the wrong end of a
municipal drainpipe.
    David Lloyd George, attributed.

As Priam to Achilles for his son,
So you, into the night, divinely led,
To ask that young men's bodies, not yet dead,
Be given from the battle not begun.
    John Masefield, in Keith Feiling, *Life of Neville
    Chamberlain*.

I think it is the combination of real religious fanaticism with spiritual trickiness which makes one dislike
Mr Chamberlain so much. He has all the hardness of
a self-righteous man, with none of the generosity of
those who are guided by durable moral standards.
    Harold Nicolson, Diary, 26 April 1939.

He was a meticulous housemaid, great at tidying up.
    A. J. P. Taylor, *English History 1914–1945*.

See also Robert A. Taft

CHAMBERLAIN SIR (JOSEPH) AUSTEN

1863–1937 Statesman

Austen has at last gone home.
    Stanley Baldwin, tribute in the House of
    Commons, 17 March 1937.

Sir Austen Chamberlain said, when he was Foreign
Secretary, that he loved France like a mistress. Poor
Sir Austen doesn't know anything about mistresses.
    Lord Beaverbrook, Letter to Roy Howard,
    8 December 1931.

Austen always played the game and always lost it.
    Lord Birkenhead, comment (undated), in
    A. J. P. Taylor, *English History 1914–1945*.

Austen — alas! is a son of a Father and when the
Father is dead, the son's stock will drop heavily.
    Rudyard Kipling, 1911, in A. J. P. Taylor,
    Beaverbrook.

... the mind and manners of a clothes-brush ...
    Harold Nicolson, Diary, 6 June 1936.

He was very independent ... when the post of Chancellor [of the Exchequer] was offered to him — complained that he had not been sent for by the P.M., but that the office had just been thrown at him — like a bone at a dog. 'Stop a minute, Austen,' said the P.M. to him, 'there is a good deal of meat on that bone.'
> Frances Stevenson, Diary, 5 March 1919.

CHAMBERLAIN, JOSEPH

1836–1914 Statesman

I have been called the apostle of the Anglo-Saxon race, and I am proud of the title. I think the Anglo-Saxon race is as fine as any on earth.
> On himself, 1900, in H. Wickham Steed, *Through Thirty Years.*

They see me sitting on the Terrace with a big cigar, and they think me lazy, but when I go back to the Office, I make things hum ...
> On himself, in J. L. Garvin, *Life of Joseph Chamberlain.*

Mr. Chamberlain is no ephemeron, no mere man of the hour. He is the man of tomorrow, and the day after tomorrow.
> *African Review*, 15 March 1902.

'Moatlhodi': The Man who Rights Things.
> Title conferred on Chamberlain by the Bechuana chiefs, 1895, in J. L. Garvin, *Life of Joseph Chamberlain.*

... the master of the feast has the manners of a cad and the tongue of a bargee.
> H. H. Asquith, Letter to Herbert Gladstone, October 1900.

The difference between Joe and me is the difference between youth and age: I am age.
> Arthur Balfour, in Denis Judd, *Balfour and the British Empire.*

Mr. Chamberlain was incomparably the most live, sparkling, insurgent, compulsive figure in British affairs ... 'Joe' was the one who made the weather. He was the man the masses knew. He it was who had solutions for social problems; who was ready to advance, sword in hand if need be, upon the foes of Britain; and whose accents rang in the ears of all the young peoples of the Empire and of lots of young people at its heart.
> Winston Churchill, *Great Contemporaries.*

Mr. Chamberlain who looked and spoke like a cheesemonger.
> Benjamin Disraeli, Letter to Lady Bradford, August 1880.

He is a man worth watching and studying: of strong self-consciousness under most pleasing manners and I should think of great tenacity of purpose: expecting to play an historical part, and probably destined to it.
> W. E. Gladstone, Letter to Lord Granville, June 1877.

I do not see how a dissolution can have any terrors for him. He has trimmed his vessel, and he has touched his rudder in such a masterly way, that in whichever direction the winds of heaven may blow they must fill his sails.
> W. E. Gladstone, in a Home Rule speech, House of Commons, 8 June 1886.

... He was not born, bred or educated in the ways which alone secure the necessary tact and behaviour of a real gentleman.
> Sir Edward Hamilton, Diary, 3 December 1899.

The peace of shocked Foundations flew
> Before his ribald questionings.
He broke the Oracles in two,
> And bared the paltry wires and strings.
He headed desert wanderings;
> He led his soul, his cause, his clan
A little from the ruck of Things.
> *Once on a time there was a Man.*
> Rudyard Kipling, *Things and the Man.*

Oh, Joe was a great man. He woke the Colonial Office up and it has been going to sleep ever since.
> Sir Henry Lambert, *circa* 1918, in Sir Ralph Furse, *Aucuparius.*

... Dangerous as an enemy, untrustworthy as a friend, but fatal as a colleague.
> Sir Hercules Robinson, Letter to Sir Graham Bower, in Lady Longford, *Jameson's Raid.*

The Chamberlain family govern the country as if they were following hounds — where according to hunting conventions it is mean-spirited to look before you leap.
> Lord Salisbury, Letter to A. J. Balfour, 21 September 1904.

Well, I could live for Balfour, but I could die for Chamberlain. He says what he means to do — and why — and then he does it.
> Sir Henry Morton Stanley, Letter to his wife, *circa* 1900.

He was a man full of ambition, bringing the instincts of a commercial traveller to the affairs of the Empire. Pushfulness was to be the watchword of his Colonial administration.
William T. Stead, in *Review of Reviews*, 1899.

By temperament he is an enthusiast and a despot. A deep sympathy with the misery and incompleteness of most men's lives, and an earnest desire to transform this, transforms political action into a religious crusade; but running alongside this genuine enthusiasm is a passionate desire to crush opposition to his will.
Beatrice Webb, Diary, 12 January 1884.

See also A. J. Balfour, Theodore Roosevelt

CHAMBERS, SIR WILLIAM

1723—96 Architect

WILL CHAMBERS screw'd from Britain's purse,
   Five hundred thousand pound,
To raise a pile, when part was rais'd,
   It tumbled to the ground.
But let not Scorn annoy the Knight,
   Or make his worth her prey;
He sure deserves a nation's thanks,
   Who makes the *base* give way.
Anthony Pasquin (John Williams), *Epigrammatic Apology for Sir William Chambers.*

SIR WILLIAM! cover'd with Chinese renown,
Whose houses are no sooner *up* than *down*,
Don't heed the discontented Nation's cry:
   Thine are *religious* houses! very *humble*;
   Upon their *faces* much inclin'd to tumble;
So *meek*, they cannot keep their heads on *high.*
Peter Pindar (John Wolcot), *Lyric Odes for 1785*, Ode 7.

CHANDLER, RAYMOND THORNTON

1888—1959 Author

Having just read the admirable profile of Hemingway in the *New Yorker* I realize that I am much too clean to be a genius, much too sober to be a champ, and far, far, too clumsy with a shotgun to live the good life.
On himself, in Philip Durham, *Down These Mean Streets a Man Must Go.*

He can write a scene with an almost suffocating vividness and sense of danger — if he does not add three words too many to make it funny.
John Dickson Carr, in *New York Times Book Review*, 24 September 1950.

Chandler brought together in one personification a representative folk hero; a combination of the American frontier hero, war hero, political hero, athletic hero, and chivalric hero. Although he was only a symbol — albeit a symbol of honor in all things — Raymond Chandler's knight went among the people in the language of the people.
Philip Durham, *Down These Mean Streets a Man Must Go.*

The obvious accomplishment of his thrillers is to generate a sort of nervous tension which is the literary analogue to the tension generated by being an American.
George P. Elliott, *A Piece of Lettuce.*

What holds his books together and makes them so compulsively readable, even to alpha minds who would not normally think of reading a thriller, is the dialogue. There is a throw-away, down-beat quality about Chandler's dialogue, whether wisecracking or not, that takes one happily . . . .
Ian Fleming, in *London Magazine*, December 1959.

CHANEY, ALONZO ('LON')

1883—1930 Actor

When you hear a person talk you begin to know him better. My whole career has been devoted to keeping people from knowing me. It has taken me years to build up a sort of mystery surrounding myself, which is my stock in trade. And I wouldn't sacrifice it by talking.
On himself, in *New York Times*, 6 July 1930.

The Fates . . . dealt with Alonzo Chaney much as they would the hero of a Greek tragedy. The length of the thread when cut was far too short, but it was a golden thread, bright with accomplishment and success, twisted with heartache and hardship, and interwoven with irony. No dramatist could have created a more extraordinary story: that of a man born on April Fools' Day of deaf mute parents, who learned to communicate with his hands and body, and died of throat cancer on the threshold of a new career in which he would have been able to use his expressive voice.
Robert G. Anderson, *Faces, Forms, Films: The Artistry of Lon Chaney.*

How odd that it is most often Lon Chaney who walks beside me [in memory]. That rugged, cantankerous, stay-away-from-me guy who invented screen make-up — and behind him I see as background the crowds that gathered for miles when they heard he

was dead. The telephone company going mad as their lines jammed for hours for people to cry *it mustn't be true.*
  Adela Rogers St Johns, *The Honeycomb.*

See also Boris Karloff, Bela Lugosi

CHANNING, WILLIAM ELLERY

1780—1842 Clergyman

He had neither insight, courage, nor firmness. . . . He had been selected by a set of money-making men as their representative for piety.
  Maria Weston Chapman, in Jack Mendelsohn, *Channing the Reluctant Radical.*

Our bishop.
  Ralph Waldo Emerson, in Perry Miller, *The Transcendentalists.*

Dr. Channing, whilst he lived, was the star of the American Church. . . . He was made for the public; his cold temperament made him the most unprofitable private companion; but all America would have been impoverished in wanting him.
  Ralph Waldo Emerson, *Historic Notes of Life and Letters in New England.*

A remarkable man, his instinct of progress grew stronger the more he travelled, and the further he went, for he surrounded himself with young life.
  Theodore Parker, *Theodore Parker's Experience as a Minister.*

If persons were of a timid disposition, or of an anxious temperament, he did not think their opinion about religious doctrine of any importance; because he thought these weaknesses inclined them to dependence on the prevalent common creed, which he thought was driven into people by a system of intimidation.
  Elizabeth Palmer Peabody, Letter to William Sprague, 18 August 1858.

. . . not so much a conscientious intellect as an intellectual conscience.
  The Rev. Ephraim Peabody, Letter to William Sprague, 15 June 1852.

CHAPLIN, SIR CHARLES

1889—1977 Actor

Of all the comedians he worked most deeply and most shrewdly within a realization of what a human being is, and is up against. The Tramp is as centrally representative of humanity, as many-sided and as mysterious as Hamlet, and it seems unlikely that any dancer or actor can ever have excelled him in eloquence, variety or poignancy of motion . . . the finest pantomime, the deepest emotion, the richest and most poignant poetry are in Chaplin's work.
  James Agee in Theodore Huff, *Charles Chaplin.*

The world was his oyster, and he, after his first faltering two-reelers, was its pearl.
  John Mason Brown, *Book of the Month Club News*, 1964.

Chaplin does not wish to give himself to any emotion, to any situation, to any life. Life draws him too terribly for that. Whatever he feels must immediately arouse its opposite; so that Chaplin may remain untouched — immaculate and impervious in himself.
  Waldo Frank, *Scribners Magazine* September 1929.

There were two sides to Charlie, as there are to most clowns. The first was the fantastic cock of the walk who kidded our sacred institutions and solemn paraphernalia with merciless acumen. He kept a slop bucket in a safe and investigated a clock with a can opener. He slapped bankers on the back, and pinched a pretty cheek when he saw one. He had nothing but wit, grace, and agility with which to oppose the awful strength of custom and authority, but his weapons were a good deal more than sufficient.
  The other Charlie was a beggar for sympathy and an apostle of pity. He pitied everything that stumbled or whimpered or wagged a tail, particularly he pitied himself. There has never been a portrait of self-pity so vivid or so shocking as Charlie with a rose in his hand.
  Robert Hatch, *Reporter* 25 November, 1952.

The Zulus know Chaplin better than Arkansas knows Garbo.
  Will Rogers, *Atlantic Monthly* August, 1939.

CHAPMAN, GEORGE

1559—1634 Poet, Dramatist

Cloud-grapling *Chapman*, whose Aerial minde Soares at Philosophy, and strikes it blinde.
  Anon., 'On the Time-Poets', in *Choyce Drollery.*

The learned Shepherd of faire Hitching hill.
  William Browne, *Britannia's Pastorals.*

The Earl of Mulgrave and Mr Waller, two of the best judges of our age, have assured me they could never read over the translation of Chapman without incredible transport.

John Dryden, Dedication of *Miscellanies*, vol. 3.

I have sometimes wondered, in the reading, what was become of those glaring colours which amazed me in *Bussy D'Amboys* upon the theatre; but when I had taken up what I supposed a fallen star, I found I had been cozened with a jelly; nothing but a cold dull mass, which glittered no longer than it was shooting; a dwarfish thought dressed up in gigantic words.

John Dryden, Dedication of *The Spanish Friar*.

He is, like Marston, a philosophic observer, a didactic reasoner; but he has both more gravity in his tragic style, and more levity in his comic vein. His *Bussy d'Ambois*, though not without interest or some fancy, is rather a collection of apothegms or pointed sayings in the form of a dialogue, than a poem or a tragedy. In his verses the oracles have not ceased. Every other line is an axiom in morals — a libel on mankind, if truth is a libel. He is too stately for a wit in his serious writings, too formal for a poet. . . . Our author aims at the highest things in poetry, and tries in vain wanting imagination and passion, to fill up the epic moulds of tragedy with sense and reason alone, so that he often runs into bombast and turgidity — is extravagant and pedantic at one and the same time.

William Hazlitt, *Lectures on the Age of Elizabeth*.

Oft of one wide expanse had I been told
That deep-brow'd Homer ruled as his demesne;
Yet never did I breathe its pure serene
Till I heard Chapman speak out loud and bold:
Then felt I like some watcher of the skies
When a new planet swims into his ken;
Or like stout Cortez when with eagle eyes
He star'd at the Pacific — and all his men
Look'd at each other with a wild surmise —
Silent, upon a peak in Darien.

John Keats, *On First Looking into Chapman's Homer*.

When one thinks of the donnish insolence and perpetual thick-skinned swagger of Chapman over his unique achievements in sublime balderdash, and the opacity that prevented Webster, the Tussaud Laureate, from appreciating his own stupidity . . . it is hard to keep one's critical blood cold long enough to discriminate in favor of any Elizabethan whatever.

George Bernard Shaw, in *Saturday Review*, 19 February 1898.

Of all the Elizabethans, Chapman is nearest to Seneca. His vision of human affairs was stoic, and his style had a natural darkness and complication. . . .

In Chapman's conviction that violence breeds violence and that evil will not be mocked, there is something of the lucid grief of Tacitus. Yet simultaneously, Chapman was striving for success on the popular stage. Hence he gave to the audience its due ration of physical brutality, witchcraft, and amorous intrigue. His ghosts are as bloody as any in the Elizabethan theatre, his murders as frequent. But the stress of conflicting ideals proved too great. There is no unity of design in Chapman's plays. Amid the thickets of rhetoric there are sudden clearings where the grimness of his political vision carries all before it. But no proportion is sustained, as if a severe Palladian threshold gave sudden access to a baroque interior.

George Steiner, *The Death of Tragedy*.

CHARLES I

1600—49

As I was going by Charing Cross,
I saw a black man upon a black horse;
They told me it was King Charles the First —
Oh dear, my heart was ready to burst.
Nursery rhyme, traditional.

When I was a Freshman at Oxford 1642, I was wont to go to *Christ Church* to see King *Charles* I at supper: where I once heard him say, 'That as he was hawking in *Scotland,* he rode into the Quarry, and found the covey of Partridges falling upon the Hawk'; and I do remember this expression further, *viz*, and I will swear upon the Book 'tis true. When I came to my Chamber, I told this story to my Tutor; said he, *That Covey was London.*

John Aubrey, *Miscellanies*.

There was a Seam in the middle of his Fore-head, (downwards) which is a very ill sign in Metoposcopie.
Ibid.

King Charles the First, after he was condemned, did tell Colonel *Tomlinson*, that he believed, *That the English Monarchy was now at an end*: About half an Hour after, he told the Colonel, *That now he had Assurance by a strong impulse on his Spirit, that his Son should reign after him*. This information I had from *Fabian Phillips* Esq of the Inner-Temple, who had good Authority for the truth of it.
Ibid.

Never have I beheld features more unfortunate.
Gianlorenzo Bernini, attributed, on seeing Van Dyck's Charles I in three positions.

With Queen Bess for a husband, how happy had it been! There is a real selectness, if little nobleness of nature in him; his demeanor everywhere is that of a man who at least has no doubt that he is able to command. Small thanks to him perhaps; — had not all persons from his very birth been inculcating this lesson on him? He has, if not the real faculty to command, at least the authentic pretension to do it, which latter of itself will go far in this world.

Thomas Carlyle, *Historical Sketches.*

Charles knew his power; & Cromwell and Ireton knew it likewise, and knew, that it was the power of a Man who was within a yard's Length of a Talisman, only not within an arm's length, but which in that state of the public mind could he but have once grasped, would have enabled him to blow up Presbeyterian and Independent. If ever a lawless act was defensible on the principle of self-preservation, the murther of Charles might be defended.

Samuel Taylor Coleridge, *Notes on the English Divines*, 'Richard Baxter'.

His mind was an open book where all who chose might read, and he committed to paper more indiscretions than any ruler in history.

Wilbur Cortez, in W. C. Abbott, *Writings and Speeches of Oliver Cromwell.*

Upon some discourses with him, the King uttering these words to him, 'I shall play my game as well as I can,' Ireton replied, 'If your Majesty have a *game* to play, you must give us also the liberty to play ours.' Colonel Hutchinson privately discoursing with his cousin about the communications he had had with the king, Ireton's expressions were these: 'He gave us words, and we paid him in his own coin, when we found he had no real intention of the people's good, but to prevail by our factions, to regain by art what he had lost in fight.'

Lucy Hutchinson, *Memoirs of Colonel Hutchinson.*

He was the worthyest gentleman, the best husbande, the best father, and the best Christian, that the age in which he lyved had produced, and if he was not the best kinge, if he was without some parts and qualityes which have made some kings greate and happy, no other Prince was ever unhappy, who was possessed of half his virtues and indowments, and so much without any kinde of vice.

Edward Hyde, Earl of Clarendon, *History of The Rebellion.*

'T is not enough (thy pietie is such)
To cure the call'd *Kings Evill* with thy touch;
But thou wilt yet a Kinglier maistrie trie,
To cure the *Poets Evill*, Povertie:

And, in these cures, do'st so thy selfe enlarge,
As thou dost cure our *Evill*, at thy charge.
. . .
What can the *Poet* wish his *King* may doe,
But, that he cure the Peoples Evill too?
Ben Jonson, *An Epigram to K Charles for a 100 pounds he sent me in my Sicknesse.*

He said, that if he were necessitated to take any particular profession of life, he could not be a lawyer, adding his reasons: 'I cannot (saith he) defend a bad, nor yield in a good cause'.

Archbishop Laud, *Diary*, 1 February 1623.

He died in the beginning of his climacterical year, fatal many times where killing directions in the nativity threaten.

William Lilly, *Life and Death of Charles The First.*

He did not greatly court the ladies, nor had he a lavish affection unto many; he was manly and well fitted for venerial sports, yet rarely frequented illicit beds: I do not hear of above one or two natural children he had or left behind him. He had exquisite judgement by the eye, and *physionomy*, to discover the virtuous from the wanton; he honoured the virtuous; and was very shy and choice in wandering those ways; and when he did it, it was with much cautiousness and secrecy: nor did he prostitute his affection, but unto those of exquisite persons or parts; and this the queen well knew, nor did she wink at it.

William Lilly, *True History of King James I and King Charles I.*

We charge him with having broken his coronation oath; and we are told that he kept his marriage vow! We accuse him of having given up his people to the merciless inflictions of the most hot-headed and hardhearted of prelates; and the defence is, that he took his little son on his knee and kissed him! We censure him for having violated the articles of the Petition of Right, after having, for good and valuable consideration, promised to observe them; and we are informed that he was accustomed to hear prayers at six o'clock in the morning! It is to such considerations as these, together with his Vandyke dress, his handsome face, and his peaked beard, that he owes, we verily believe, most of his popularity with the present generation.

T. B. Macaulay, *Essays*: 'Milton'.

He seems to have learned from the theologians whom he most esteemed that between him and his subjects there could be nothing of the nature of mutual contract; that he could not, even if he would, divest himself of his despotic authority; and that in every promise which he made, there was an implied reserva-

tion that such promise might be broken in case of necessity, and that of the necessity he was the sole judge.
T. B. Macaulay, *History of England.*

He nothing common did nor mean
Upon that memorable scene,
But with his keener eye
The axe's edge did try;

Nor call'd the Gods, with vulgar spite,
To vindicate his helpless right;
But bow'd his comely head
Down, as upon a bed.
Andrew Marvell, *An Horatian Ode upon Cromwell's Return from Ireland.*

A Glorious Prince this Parliament
The King should be, did swear,
But now we understand they meant
In heaven and not here.

King and no King was once a play
Or fable on the stage.
But see! It is become this day
The moral of our age.
Marchamont Nedham, *A Short History of the English Rebellion compiled in verse.*

King Charles the First walked and talked
Half an hour after his head was cut off.
'Peter Puzzlewell', *A Choice Collection of Riddles, Charades and Rebuses.*

We wish we had rather endured thee (O Charles) than have been condemned to this mean tyrant [Cromwell]: not that we desire any kind of slavery, but that the Quality of the Master something graces the condition of the slave.
Edward Sexby, *Killing No Murder.*

His way of arguing was very civil and patient; for he seldom contradicted another by his authority, but by his reason: nor did he by any petulant dislike quash another's arguments; and he offered his exception by this civil introduction, *By your favour Sir, I think otherwise on this or that ground*: yet he would discountenance any bold or forward addresse unto him ... He had a great plainnes in his own nature, and yet he was thought even by his Friends to love too much a versatile man; but his experience had thorowly weaned him from this at last. ... And tho' he was of as slow a pen, as of speech; yet both were very significant: and he had that modest esteem of his own parts, that he would usually say, *He would willingly make his own dispatches, but that he found it better to be a cobler than a Shoomaker.* I have bin in company with very learned men, when I have

brought them their own papers back from him, with his alterations, who ever confest his amendments to have bin very material.
Sir Philip Warwick, *Memories of the Reigne of King Charles I.*

Had his active courage equall'd his passive, the rebellious and tumultuous humor of those, who were disloyall to him, probably had been quashed in their first rise: for thro' out the English story it may be observ'd, that the souldier-like spirit in the Prince hath been ever much more fortunate and esteemed, than the pious.
Ibid.

How prophetically he spake, when the first reformers began to take the government asunder, which he resembled to a watch, telling the tamperers with it, that it was easy to disjoin the pieces, but hard to set them together again in good order, and so it proved.
Ibid.

See also Oliver Cromwell, George II, William Juxon, William Laud, Lord Strafford

CHARLES II

1630—85

As Nero once with harp in hand survey'd
His flaming Rome, and as that burn'd he play'd
So our great Prince, when the Dutch fleet arriv'd
Saw his ships burn'd, and, as they burn'd, he swiv'd.
So kind he was in our extremest need
He would those flames extinguish with his seed.
But against Fate all human aid is vain
His pr--- then proved as useless as his chain.
Anon., *Fourth Advice to a Painter.*

King Charles II was crowned at the very conjunction of the Sun and Mercury. ... As the King was at Dinner in Westminster Hall, it Thundered and Lightened extremely: the Canons and the Thunder played together.
John Aubrey, *Brief Lives.*

Arise Evans had a fungous Nose, and said it was revealed to him, that the King's Hand would Cure him: And at the first coming of King Charles II into St. James's Park, he kiss'd the King's Hand, and rubbed his Nose with it; which disturbed the King, but Cured him.
John Aubrey, *Miscellanies.*

He said once to my self, he was no atheist, but he could not think God would make a man miserable only for taking a little pleasure out of the way. He disguised his popery to the last. . . . He was affable and easy and loved to be made so by all about him. The great art of keeping him long was, the being easy, and the making every thing easy to him. He had made such observations on the *French* government, that he thought a King who might be checkt, or have his Ministers called to an account by a Parliament, was but a King in name. He had a great compass of knowledge, tho' he was never capable of much application or study. He understood the Mechanicks and Physick; and was a good Chymist, and much set on several preparations of Mercury, chiefly the fixing it. He understood navigation well: But above all he knew the architecture of ships so perfectly, that in that respect he was exact rather more than became a Prince. His apprehension was quick, and his memory good. He was an everlasting talker. He told his stories with a good grace: But they came in his way too often. He had a very ill opinion both of men and women; and did not think that there was either sincerity or chastity in the world out of principle, but that some had either the one or the other out of humour or vanity. He thought that no body did serve him out of love: And so he was quits with all the world, and loved others as little as he thought they loved him. He hated business, and could not be easily brought to mind any: but when it was necessary, and he was set to it he would stay as long as Ministers had work for him. The ruine of his reign and of all his affairs was occasioned chiefly by his delivering himself up at his first coming over to a mad range of pleasure.

Gilbert Burnet, *History of My Own Time*.

His recommending only his mistresses and their children to his brother's care would have been a strange conclusion to any other's life, but was well enough suited to all the other parts of his.

Ibid.

. . . He had so ill an opinion of mankind, that he thought the great art of living and governing was, to manage all things, and all persons, with a depth of craft and dissimulation. And in that few men in the world could put on the appearance of sincerity better than he could: Under which so much artifice was usually hid. He had great vices, but scarce any virtues to correct them: He had in him some vices that were less hurtful, which corrected his more hurtful ones. He was during the active part of his life given up to sloth and lewdness to such a degree, that he hated business, and could not bear the engaging in any thing that gave him much trouble, or put him under any constraint.

Ibid.

He loved to talk over all the stories of his life to every new man that came about him . . . He went

over these in a very graceful manner; but so often, and so copiously, that all those who had been long accustomed to them grew weary of them: And when he entered on those stories they usually withdrew: So that he often began them in a full audience, and before he had done there were not above four or five left about him. Which drew a severe jest from *Wilmot*, Earl of *Rochester*. He said, he wondered to see a man have so good a memory as to repeat the same story without losing the least circumstance, and yet not remember that he had told it to the same persons the very day before. This made him fond of strangers; for they hearkened to all his often repeated stories, and went away in a rapture at such an uncommon condescension in a King.

Ibid.

There were some moral and social values in his perfection in little things. He could not keep the Ten Commandments, but he kept the ten thousand commandments. His name is unconnected with any great acts of duty or sacrifice, but it is connected with a great many of those acts of magnanimous politeness, of a kind of dramatic delicacy which lie on the dim borderland between morality and art.

G. K. Chesterton, *Essays*: 'Charles II'.

He would fain be a Despot, even at the cost of being another's Underling . . . I look on him as one of the moral Monsters of History.

Samuel Taylor Coleridge, *Annotation to Lord Braybrooke's Edition of S. Pepys's Diary*.

A prince of many Virtues, & many great Imperfections, Debonaire, Easy of Accesse, not bloudy or Cruel: his Countenance fierce, his voice greate, proper of person, every motion became him, a lover of the sea, & skillfull in shipping, not affecting other studys, yet he had a laboratory and knew of many Empyrical Medicines, & the easier Mechanical Mathematics: Loved Planting, building, & brought in a politer way of living, which passed to Luxurie and intollerable expense: He had a particular Talent in telling stories & facetious passages of which he had innumerable, which made some bouffounes and vitious wretches too presumptuous, & familiar, not worthy the favours they abused: He tooke delight to have a number of little spaniels follow him, & lie in his bed-Chamber, where often times he suffered the bitches to puppy & give suck, which rendered it very offensive, & indeede made the whole Court nasty and stinking.

John Evelyn, Diary, 6 February 1685.

In some of the State Poems, Charles II is ridiculed under the nick-name of Old Rowley, which was an ill-favoured stallion kept in the Meuse, that was remarkable for getting fine colts. — Mrs Holford, a young lady much admired by Charles, was sitting in her apartment and singing a satirical ballad upon 'Old Rowley the King', when he knocked at the door. Upon her asking who was there? he, with his usual good humour replied, 'Old Rowley himself, Madam'.

James Granger, *Biographical History of England.*

JOHNSON: (taking fire at any attack on that Prince, for whom he had an extraordinary partiality): 'Charles the Second was licentious in his practice; but he always had a reverence for what was good. Charles the second knew his people and rewarded merit. The Church was at no time better filled than in his reign. He was the best King we have had from his time till the reign of his present Majesty, except James the second, who was a very good King, but unhappily believed that it was necessary for the salvation of his subjects that they should be Roman Catholics. *He* had the merit of endeavouring to do what he thought was for the salvation of the souls of his subjects, till he lost a great empire. *We* who thought that we should *not* be saved if we were Roman Catholics, had the merit of maintaining our religion at the expense of submitting ourselves to the government of King William, for it could not be done otherwise, — to the government of one of the most worthless scoundrels that ever existed. No; Charles the second was not such a man as (naming another King). He did not destroy his father's will. He took money, indeed from France; but he did not destroy those over whom he ruled: he did not let the French fleet pass ours.'

Samuel Johnson, in James Boswell, *Life of Johnson.*

And art thou borne, brave Babe?

Ben Jonson, *An Epigram on the Princes Birth.*

C--t is the mansion house where thou dost swell,
There thou art fix'd as tortoise is to shell,
Whose head peeps out a little now and then
To take the air, and then peeps in again.
Strong are thy lusts, in c--t th'art always diving
And I dare swear thou pray'st to die a-swiving.
How poorly squander'st thou thy seed away
Which should get kings for nations to obey!

John Lacy, *Satire.*

According to him every person was to be bought: but some people haggled more about the price than others; and when this haggling was very obstinate and very skilful, it was called by some fine name. The chief trick by which clever men kept up the price of their abilities, was called integrity. The chief trick by which handsome women kept up the price of their beauty was called modesty. The love of God, the love of country, the love of family, the love of friends, were phrases of the same sort, delicate and convenient synonymes for the love of self. Thinking thus of mankind, Charles naturally cared very little what they thought of him. Honor and shame were scarcely more to him than light and darkness to the blind.

T. B. Macaulay, *History of England.*

See in what Glory Charles now sits
    With Truth to conquer Treason
And prove he is the King of wits
    The world, himself, and Reason . . . .

The King the four great Bills must pass
    And none but Saints are free
The Irish and Cavaliers, alas!
    Must th'only rebels be . . . .

Thus Royal Charles lets to lease
    Lays sword and sceptre down
To shew he values us and Peace
    Above a glorious Crown.

Marchamont Nedham, *A Short History of the English Rebellion compiled in verse.*

Upon the Quarter-deck he fell in discourse of his escape from Worcester. Where it made me ready to weep to hear the stories that he told of his difficulties that he had passed through. As his travelling four days and three nights on foot, every step up to the knees in dirt, with nothing but a green coat and a pair of country breeches on and a pair of country shoes, that made him so sore all over his feet that he could scarce stir.

Yet he was forced to run away from a miller and other company that took them for rogues.

His sitting at table at one place, where the master of the house, that had not seen him in eight years, did know him but kept it private; when at the same table there was one that had been of his own Regiment at Worcester, could not know him, but made him drink the King's health and said that the King was at least four inches higher than he.

Another place, he was by some servants of the house made to drink, that they might know him not to be a Roundhead, which they swore he was.

In another place, at his Inn, the master of the house, as the King was standing with his hands on the back of a chair by the fire-side, he kneeled down and kissed his hand privately, saying that he would not ask him who he was, but bid God bless him whither that he was going. Then the difficulty of getting a boat to get into France, where he was fain to plot with the master thereof to keep his design from the four men and a boy (which was all his ship's company), and so got to Feckham in France.

At Roane, he looked so poorly that the people went into the rooms before he went away, to see

whether he had not stole something or other.
Samuel Pepys, referring back to Charles' escape from Worcester, Diary, 23 May 1660.

The King doth mind nothing but pleasures and hates the very sight or thoughts of business. That my Lady Castlemayne rules him; who he says have all the tricks of Aretin that are to be practised to give pleasure — in which he is too able, having a large ----. . . . If any of the sober counsellors give him sober advice and move him in anything that is to his good and honour, the other part, which are his counsellors of pleasure, take him when he is with my Lady Castlemayne and in a humour of delight and then persuade him that he ought not to hear or listen the advice of those old dotards or counsellors that were heretofore his enemies, when God knows it is they that nowadays do most study his honour.
Ibid., 15 May 1663.

In our way discoursing of the wantonness of the Court and how it minds nothing else. And I saying that that would leave the King shortly, if he did not leave it, he told me 'No', for the King doth spend most of his time in feeling and kissing them naked all over their bodies in bed — and contents himself, without doing all the other but as he finds himself inclined; but this lechery will never leave him.
Ibid., 16 October 1665.

Mr Pierce did also tell me as a great truth, as being told it by Mr Cowly who was by and heard it, — that Tom Killigrew should publicly tell the King that his matters were coming into a very ill state, but that yet there was a way to help all — which is, says he, 'There is a good honest able man that I could name, that if your Majesty would imploy and command to see all things well executed, all things would soon be mended; and this is one Charles Stuart, — who now spends his time in imploying his lips and his prick about the Court, and hath no other imployment. But if you would give him this imployment, he were the fittest man in the world to perform it.' This he says is most true.
Ibid., 8 December 1666.

It is strange how everybody do nowadays reflect upon Oliver [Cromwell], and commend him, what brave things he did, and made all the neighbors fear him, while here a Prince, come in with all the love and prayers and good liking of his people . . . hath lost all so soon.
Ibid., July 1677.

Mr Cooling, my Lord Chamberlain's secretary . . . says . . . that for a good while the King's greatest pleasure hath been with his fingers, being able to do no more. But it is a pretty thing he told us: how the King, once speaking of the Duke of Yorke's being maistered by his wife, said to some of the company by, that he would go no more abroad with this Tom Otter (meaning the Duke of York) and his wife. Tom Killigrew, being by, answered, 'Sir,' says he, 'pray, which is the best for a man to be, a Tom Otter to his wife or his mistress?' — meaning the King's being so to my Lady Castlemayne.
Ibid., 30 July 1667.

But Sir H Cholmly tells me that the King hath this good luck: that the next day he hates to have anybody mention what he had done the day before, nor will suffer anybody to gain upon him that way — which is a good quality.
Ibid., 23 September 1667.

If love prevailed with him more than any other passion, he had this for excuse, besides that his complexion was of an amorous sort, the women seemed to be the aggressors; and I have since heard the king say that they would sometimes offer themselves to his embrace. . . .
Sir John Reresby, *Memoirs.*

He was not an active, busy, or ambitious prince, but perfectly a friend to ease, and fond of pleasure; he seemed to be chiefly desirous of peace and quiet for his own time.
Ibid.

So have I seen a King at chess
(His rooks and knights withdrawn
His queen and bishops in distress
Shifting about grow less and less)
      With here and there a pawn.
      Charles Sackville, Earl of Dorset, *On the Young Statesmen.*

Those who knew his Face, fixed their Eyes there; and thought it of more importance to See than to Hear what he said. His face was as little a blab as most Mens, yet though it could not be called a prattling Face, it would sometimes tell tales to a good Observer. When he thought fit to be angry, he had a very peevish Memory; there was hardly a Blot that escaped him.
George Savile, Marquis of Halifax, *A Character of King Charles the Second.*

A Mistress either Dexterous in herself, or well instructed by those that are so, may be very useful to her Friends, not only in the immediate Hours of her Ministry, but by her Influences and Insinuations at other times. It was resolved generally by others, whom he should have in his Arms, as well as whom he should have in his Councils. Of a Man who was so capable of choosing, he chose as seldom as any Man that ever lived.

Ibid.

He lived with his Ministers as he did with his Mistresses; he used them, but he was not in love with them.

Ibid.

His Wit was not acquired by *Reading*; that which he had above his original Stock by Nature, was from Company, in which he was very capable to observe. He could not so properly be said to have a wit very much raised, as a plain, gaining, well-bred, recommending kind of Wit.

Ibid.

Kings are not born: they are made by artificial hallucination. When the process is interrupted by adversity at a critical age, as in the case of Charles II, the subject becomes sane and never completely recovers his kingliness.

George Bernard Shaw, 'Maxims for Revolutionists', in *Man and Superman.*

If in his early travels, and late administration, he seem'd a little biased to one sort of Religion; the first is only to be imputed to a certain easiness of temper, and a complaisance for that company he was then forced to keep: and the last was no more than his being tired (which he soon was in any difficulty) with those bold oppositions in Parliament; which made him almost throw himself into the arms of the *Roman Catholick* party, so remarkable in England for their loyalty, who embrac'd him gladly, and lull'd him asleep with those enchanting songs of absolute sovereignty, which the best and wisest of Princes are often unable to resist.

John Sheffield, Earl of Mulgrave, *A Character of Charles II.*

He had so natural an aversion to formality ... he could not on premeditation act the part of a King for a moment, either at Parliament or Council ... which carried him into the other extreme ... of letting all distinction and ceremony fall to the ground, as useless and foppish.

Ibid.

He loved ease and quiet, to which his unnecessary wars are so far from being a contradiction, that they are rather a proof of it; since they were made chiefly to comply with those persons, whose dissatisfaction would have proved more uneasy to one of his humour, than all that distant noise of cannon, which he would often listen to with a great deal of tranquillity.

Ibid.

In the Isle of Great *Britain* long since famous known,
For breeding the best C( ) in *Christendom*;
There reigns, and long may he reign and thrive,
The easiest Prince and best bred Man alive:
Him no ambition moves to seek Renown,
Like the *French* Fool to wander up and down,
Starving his subjects, hazarding his Crown.
Nor are his high desires above his strength:
His Scepter and his P---- are of a length,
And she that plays with one may sway the other,
And make him little wiser than his Brother ...
Poor Prince, thy P---- like the Buffoons at Court,
It governs thee because it makes thee sport;
Tho' Safety, Law, Religion, Life, lay on't,
'Twill break through all to its way to C---.
Restless he rolls about from Whore to Whore,
A merry Monarch, scandalous and poor.

John Wilmot, Earl of Rochester, *On King Charles by the Earl of Rochester, for Which he Was Banished the Court and Turned Mountebank.*

Here lies our Sovereign Lord the King,
Whose word no man relies on,
Who never said a foolish thing,
Nor ever did a wise one.

John Wilmot, Earl of Rochester, *Epitaph on Charles II.*

Chast, pious, prudent, C(harles) the Second
The miracle of thy Restauration,
May like to that of *Quails* be reckoned
Rain'd on the Israelitick Nation;
The wisht for blessing from Heav'n sent,
Became their curse and Punishment.

John Wilmot, Earl of Rochester, *The History of Insipids, a Lampoon.*

See also Second Duke of Buckingham, John Dryden, John Flamsteed, George III, Nell Gwyn, Thomas Hobbes, Edward Hyde, Louise de Kerouaille, George Monck, Samuel Pepys, William Petty, Duke of Monmouth, Frances Stuart, Barbara Villiers

CHARLOTTE SOPHIA

1744—1818 Queen Consort to George III

Yes, I do think that the *bloom* of her ugliness is going off.

Colonel Disbrowe (her chamberlain), in William Timbs, *A Century of Anecdote.*

CHARTRES, FRANCIS

1675—1732 Gambler, Brothel-Keeper, Money-Lender

HERE continueth to rot
The Body of FRANCIS CHARTRES,
Who with *inflexible constancy*,
and *Inimitable Uniformity* of Life
Persisted
In spite of *Age* and *Infirmities*
In the Practice of *Every Human Vice*;
Excepting *Prodigality* and *Hypocrisy*:
His insatiable *Avarice* exempted him from the first,
His matchless *Impudence* from the second.
Nor was he more singular
in the undeviating *Pravity* of his *Manners*
Than successful
In *Accumulating* WEALTH
For without *Trade* or *Profession*,
Without *Trust of Public Money*,
And without *Bribe-worthy* service
He acquired, or more properly created
A *Ministerial Estate*.
He was the only Person of his Time
Who cou'd cheat without the Mask of *Honesty*
Retain his Primeval *Meanness*
When possess'd of *Ten Thousand* a *Year*
And having daily deserved the *Gibbet* for what he
did,
Was at last condemn'd to it for what he *could
not do*.
Oh Indignant Reader!
Think not his Life useless to Mankind!
Providence conniv'd at his execrable Designs,
To give to After-ages
A conspicuous Proof and Example,
Of how small Estimation is *Exorbitant Wealth*
in the sight of GOD,
By his bestowing it on the most *Unworthy* of
ALL MORTALS.
Dr John Arbuthnot, *Epitaph*.

CHASE, SALMON PORTLAND

1808—73 Politician

I would rather that the people should wonder why
I wasn't President than why I am.
On himself, in Samuel H. Dodson, *Diary and
Correspondence of Salmon P. Chase*.

Chase is a good man, but his theology is unsound.
He thinks there is a fourth person in the Trinity.
Anon., Senatorial critic from Ohio, in T. G.
Belden and M. R. Belden, *So Fell the Angels,
Salmon Portland Chase*.

... like all strong-willed and self-asserting men, Mr.
Chase had the faults of his qualities. He was never
easy to drive in harness, or light in hand. He saw

vividly what was wrong, and did not always allow
for what was relatively right.
Henry Adams, *The Education of Henry Adams*.

Probably the most striking-looking of the ministers
is Mr. Chase, the Secretary of the Treasury. His head
would be a treasure to any sculptor as a model of
benevolence. His lofty, spacious forehead, his fresh,
smooth countenance, his portly figure, and his
pleasant, kindly smile, all seem to mark the stock
old philanthropist of the stage, created to be the
victim and providence of street beggars. One wonders
how so kind-looking a man can find it in his heart to
tax anybody.
Edward Dicey, *Six Months in the Federal States*.

... like the bluebottle fly, [will] lay his eggs in every
rotten spot he can find. I have shut my eyes, as far
as possible, to everything of the sort. Mr. Chase
makes a good secretary and I shall keep him where
he is. If he becomes President, all right, I hope we
may never have a worse man.
Abraham Lincoln, in T. G. Belden and M. R.
Belden, *So Fell the Angels, Salmon Portland
Chase*.

Seward comforts him. Chase he deems a necessity.
Gideon Welles, on Lincoln's relations with two
leading cabinet members, in *ibid*.

CHATHAM, FIRST EARL OF
(WILLIAM PITT THE ELDER)

1708—78 Statesman

The atrocious crime of being a young man . . . I shall
attempt neither to palliate nor to deny.
On himself, Speech in the Commons, replying to
Robert Walpole, January 1741.

Whilst Balaam was poor, he was full of renown,
But now that he's rich, he's the jest of the town:
Then let all men learn by his present disgrace
That honesty's better by far than a place.
Anon. lampoon, in J. H. Plumb, *Chatham*.

England has been a long time in labour, but she has
at last brought forth a man.
Frederick of Prussia, Attributed.

He loved England with an intense and personal love.
He believed in her power, her glory, her public virtue,
till England learnt to believe in herself.
John Richard Green, *A Short History of the
English People*.

Lord Chatham is a greater paradox than ever: — is
seen at home by no human creature; — absolutely by

none! rides twenty miles every day, — is seen on the road, and appears in perfect good health; but will now speak to no creature he meets. I am much persuaded all is quackery; — he is not mad; that is, no madder than usual.

David Hume, Letter to Sir Gilbert Elliot, July 1768.

He was the first Englishman of his time, and he had made England the first country in the world.

T. B. Macaulay, *Essays*: 'The Earl of Chatham'.

Pitt, as his sister often said, knew nothing accurately except Spenser's Fairy Queen.

Ibid.

It was Chatham, ignorant of men, ignorant of politics, who knew with utter certainty England's destiny and showed her the way to it.

J. H. Plumb, *England in the 18th Century*.

. . . he could create the sense in all who listened to him that he was the mouthpiece of destiny. The controlled wildness of his temperament gave a passion to his oratory which hypnotized criticism and stirred profoundly not only Parliament but the nation. He was the first politician England had known whose power rested on the magic symbolism of his own personality and beliefs.

Ibid.

Walpole acted decisively. He threw Pitt out of his army commission. 'We must muzzle,' he said, 'this terrible cornet of the horse.' As well might he attempt to stop a hurricane with a hairnet.

J. H. Plumb, *Chatham*.

You will ask, what could be beyond this? Nothing, but what was beyond what ever was, and that was Pitt! He spoke at past one, for an hour and thirty-five minutes: there was more humour, wit, vivacity, finer language, more boldness, in short, more astonishing perfections than even you, who are used to him, can conceive. . . .

Horace Walpole, Letter to the Hon. Henry Seymour Conway, 15 November 1755.

. . . this immaculate man has accepted the Barony of Chatham for his wife, with a pension of three thousand pounds a year for three lives. . . . The pension he has left *us* is a war for three thousand lives! perhaps for twenty times three thousand lives! . . . What! to sneak out of the scrape, prevent peace, and avoid the war! blast one's character, and all for the comfort of a paltry annuity, a long-necked peeress, and a couple of Grenvilles!

Horace Walpole, Letter to the Countess of Ailesbury, 10 October 1761.

See also Adam Smith

CHATTERTON, THOMAS

1752—70 Poet

An addiction to poetry is very generally the result of 'an uneasy mind in an uneasy body' . . . Chatterton, *I* think, mad.

Lord Byron, Letter to Leigh Hunt, November 1815.

O Chatterton! that thou wert yet alive!
Sure thou would'st spread the canvass to the gale,
And love with us the tinkling team to drive
O'er peaceful freedom's undivided dale;
And we, at sober eve, would round thee throng
Hanging, enraptured, on thy stately song!
And greet with smiles the young-eyed Poesy
All deftly masked as hoar Antiquity.

Samuel Taylor Coleridge, *Monody on the Death of Chatterton*.

Here comes one whose claims cannot be so easily set aside; they have been sanctioned by learning, hailed by genius, and hallowed by misfortune — I mean Chatterton. Yet I must say what I think of him, and that is not what is generally thought . . . I cannot find in Chatterton's works any thing so extraordinary as the age at which they were written. They have a facility, vigour, and knowledge, which were prodigious in a boy of sixteen, but which would not have been so in a man of twenty. He did not shew extraordinary powers of genius, but extraordinary precocity. Nor do I believe he would have written better, had he lived. He knew this himself, or he would have lived. Great geniuses, like great kings, have too much to think of to kill themselves.

William Hazlitt, *Lectures on the English Poets*.

C omfort and joy's forever fled
H e ne'er will warble more!
A h me! the sweetest youth is dead
T hat e'er tun'd reed before.
T he Hand of Mis'ry bowed him low,
E 'en Hope forsook his brain;
R elentless man contemn'd his woe:
T o you he sigh'd in vain.
O ppressed with want, in wild despair he cried
'N o more I'll live', swallowed the draught and died.

(Samuel) William Henry Ireland, *Acrostic on Chatterton*.

This is the most extraordinary young man that has

encountered my knowledge. It is wonderful how the whelp has written such things.

Samuel Johnson, in James Boswell, *Life of Johnson*.

O Chatterton! How very sad thy fate!
Dear child of sorrow — son of misery!
How soon the film of death obscur'd that eye,
Whence Genius mildly flash'd, and high debate.
How soon that voice, majestic and elate,
Melted in dying numbers! Oh! how nigh
Was night to thy fair morning. Thou didst die
A half blown flow'ret which cold blasts amate.

John Keats, *Sonnet to Chatterton*.

Gentlemen of the jury, the prisoner at the bar, Thomas Chatterton, is indicted for the uttering of certain poems composed by himself, purporting them to be the poems of one Thomas Rowley, a priest of the XVth century, against the so frequently disturbed peace of Parnassus, to the great disturbance and confusion of the antiquary society and likewise notoriously to the prejudice of the literary fame of the said Thomas Chatterton. The fact is stated to have been committed by the prisoner between the ages of fifteen and seventeen and the poems are admitted to be excellent.

'Trial of Thomas Chatterton', *New Review*, 1782.

The finest of the Rowley poems . . . rank absolutely with the finest poetry in the language . . . He was an absolute and untarnished hero.

Dante Gabriel Rossetti, Letter to Hall Caine.

He was an instance that a complete genius and a complete rogue can be formed before a man is of age.

Horace Walpole, Letter to William Mason, 24 July 1778.

I thought of Chatterton, the marvellous Boy,
The sleepless Soul that perished in his pride.

William Wordsworth, *Resolution and Independence*.

CHAUCER, GEOFFREY

c. 1340—1400 Poet

Bifil that in that seson on a day,
In Southwerk, at the Tabard as I lay
Redy to wenden on my pilgrimage
To Caunterbury with ful devout corage,
At nyght was come into that hostelrye
Wel nyne and twenty in a compaignye,
Of sondry folk, by aventure yfalle
In felaweshipe, and pilgrimes were they alle,
That toward Caunterbury wolden ryde.

The chambres and the stables weren wyde,
And wel we weren esed atte beste.

On himself, General Prologue to *The Canterbury Tales*.

Long had our dull forefathers slept supine,
Nor felt the raptures of the tuneful nine;
Till Chaucer first, a merry bard, arose,
And many story told in rhyme and prose.

Joseph Addison, *Account of the Greatest English Poets*.

He lacks the high seriousness of the great classics, and therewith an important part of their virtue.

Matthew Arnold, *Essays in Criticism*: 'The Study of Poetry'.

And Chaucer, with his infantine
Familiar clasp of things divine;
That mark upon his lip is wine.

Elizabeth Barrett Browning, *A Vision of Poets*.

Grete thankes, laude and honour ought to be gyven unto the clerkes, poetes and historiographs that have wreton many noble bokes of wisdom; . . . emong whom and in especial tofore alle other we ought to gyve a syngular laud unto that noble and grete philosopher Gefferey Chaucer, the whiche for his ornate wrytyng in our tongue may wel have the name of a laureate poete.

William Caxton, Proem to *The Canterbury Tales*.

Sunk in a Sea of Ignorance we lay,
Till *Chaucer* rose, and pointed out the Day,
A Joking Bard, whose Antiquated Muse,
In mouldy Words could solid Sense produce.

Samuel Cobb, *Poetae Britannici*.

It may be thought he was unusually likeable, especially to men, because of his wide conversational interests and lively fund of unexpected knowledge. As to women, it is less safe to conjecture. He has the whim in his poetry to represent himself as most unlikely to attract them. This may well be true. He knew too much about them.

Neville Coghill, *The Poet Chaucer*.

I take unceasing delight in Chaucer. His manly cheerfulness is especially delicious to me in my old age. How exquisitely tender he is, and yet how perfectly free from the least touch of sickly melancholy or morbid drooping! The sympathy of the poet with the subjects of his poetry is particularly remarkable in Shakespeare and Chaucer; but what the first effects by a strong act of imagination and mental metamorphosis, the last does without any effort, merely by the inborn kindly joyousness of his nature. How

well we seem to know Chaucer! How absolutely nothing do we know of Shakespeare!
    Samuel Taylor Coleridge, *Table Talk*, 15 March 1834.

As he is the Father of *English* Poetry, so I hold him in the same Degree of Veneration as the *Grecians* held *Homer*, or the *Romans Virgil*: He is a perpetual Fountain of good Sense; learned in all Sciences; and therefore speaks properly on all Subjects: As he knew what to say, so he knows also when to leave off; a Continence which is practis'd by few Writers.
    John Dryden, *Preface to the Fables*.

Chaucer, I confess, is a rough diamond; and must be polished e'er he shines.
    Ibid.

Chaucer followed Nature everywhere, but was never so bold to go beyond her.
    Ibid.

Chaucer is glad and erect.
    Ralph Waldo Emerson, *Representative Men*: 'Shakespeare'.

And gret wel Chaucer whan ye mete,
As mi disciple and mi poete,
For in the floures of his youthe,
In sondri wise, as he wel couthe,
Of Ditees and of songes glade,
The whiche he for mi sake made,
The lond fulfild is overal:
Whereof to him in special
Above all othre I am most holde.
    John Gower, *Confessio Amantis*.

It is not possible for any two writers to be more opposite in this respect. Spenser delighted in luxurious enjoyment; Chaucer in severe activity of mind. As Spenser was the most romantic and visionary, Chaucer was the most practical of all the great poets, and the most a man of business and the world.
    William Hazlitt, *Lectures on the English Poets*.

O maister deere and fadir reverent!
Mi maister Chaucer, flour of eloquence,
Mirour of fructuous entendement,
O universal fadir in science!
Allas! that thou thyn excellent prudence
In thi bed mortel mightist naght byqwethe;
What eiled Deth? allas! whi wolde he sle the?
    T. Hoccleve, *Regement of Princes*.

The history of our language is now brought to the point at which the history of our poetry is generally supposed to commence, the time of the illustrious Geoffrey Chaucer, who may perhaps, with great justice, be styled the first of our versifiers who wrote poetically. He does not, however, appear to have deserved all the praise which he has received, or all the censure he has suffered.
    Samuel Johnson, *Dictionary of the English Language*.

For many historians of literature, and for all general readers, the great mass of Chaucer's work is simply a background to the *Canterbury Tales*, and the whole output of the fourteenth century is simply a background to Chaucer.
    C. S. Lewis, *Allegory of Love*.

Sithe of our language he was the lode-sterre.
    John Lydgate, Prologue to *The Falls of Princes*.

[Chaucer] owre englishe gilt with his sawes,
Rude and boistous firste be olde dawes,
That was ful fer from al perfeccioun,
And but of litel reputacioun,
Til that he cam, and, thorugh his poetrie,
Gan oure tonge first to magnifie,
And adorne it with his elloquence, –
To whom honour, laude, and reuerence.
    John Lydgate, *Troy Book*.

I read Chaucer still with as much pleasure as almost any of our poets. He is a master of manners, of description, and the first tale-teller in the true enlivened natural way.
    Alexander Pope, in Joseph Spence, *Anecdotes*.

Dan Chaucer, well of English undefiled,
On Fame's eternal beadroll worthy to be filed.
    Edmund Spenser, *The Faerie Queene*, book 4.

Chawcer, undoubtedly, did excellently in his *Troilus and Cressid*: of whome, trulie, I knowe not whether to marvaile more, either that hee in that mistie time could see so clearly, or that wee in this cleare age, goe so stumblingly after him.
    Sir Philip Sydney, *Defence of Poesie*.

Mr. C. had talent, but he couldn't spel. No man has a right to be a lit'rary man onless he knows how to spel. It is a pity that Chawcer, who had geneyus, was so unedicated. He's the wus speller I know of.
    Artemus Ward, *Chaucer's Poems*.

He was a staunch churchman, but he laughed at priests. He was an able public servant and courtier, but his views upon sexual morality were extremely lax. He sympathized with poverty, but did nothing to improve the lot of the poor ... And yet, as we read him, we are absorbing morality at every pore.
    Virginia Woolf, *The Common Reader*.

See also Robert Browning, William Dunbar, John Gower, Shakespeare, Edmund Spenser

CHESTERFIELD, EARL OF (PHILIP DORMER STANHOPE)

1694—1773 Politician, Correspondent

Tyrawley and I have been dead these two years; but we don't choose to have it known.
On himself, in old age, in James Boswell, *Life of Johnson.*

He was never a prig, nor a snob: the aristocracy he admired was one of taste, feeling, behaviour, not that of birth, for which he had an honest contempt. His ideal of a gentleman is almost that of Newman: there is nothing silly nor ungenerous about it.
Bonamy Dobrée, *Anne to Victoria.*

This man I thought had been a Lord among wits; but, I find, he is only a wit among Lords!
Samuel Johnson, in James Boswell, *Life of Johnson.*

They teach the morals of a whore, and the manners of a dancing-master.
Ibid., referring to Chesterfield's Letters.

Chesterfield admired, and often quoted, Cardinal de Retz: 'I can truly call him a man of great parts, but I cannot call him a great man. He never was so much as in his retirement'. Was there not a touch of self-identification in that description?
Sir Lewis Namier, *Crossroads of Power.*

He had neither creative passion nor unity of purpose, and therefore lacked single-mindedness; and while ready to pursue an interesting line of enquiry or argument, he easily tired of drudgery — 'a half-lazy man'.
Ibid.

The only Englishman who ever argued for the art of pleasing as the first duty of life.
Voltaire, Letter to Frederick the Great, 16 August 1774.

The more curious part of all is that one perceives by what infinite assiduity and attention his lordship's own great character was raised and supported; and yet in all that great character what was there worth remembering but his bon mots? His few fugitive pieces that remain show his genteel turn for songs

and his wit: from politics he rather escaped well, than succeeded by them. In short, the diamond owed more to being brillianted and polished, and well set, than to any intrinsic worth or solidity.
Horace Walpole, Letter to the Countess of Upper Ossory, 9 April 1774.

I was too late for the post on Thursday, and have since got Lord Chesterfield's Letters, which, without being well entertained, I sat up reading last night till between one and two, and devoured above 140. To my great surprise they seem really written from the heart, not for the honour of his head, and in truth do no great honour to the last, nor show much feeling in the first, except in wishing for his son's fine gentlemanhood.
Ibid.

Here is a disillusioned politician, who is prematurely aged, who has lost his office, who is losing his teeth, who, worst fate of all, is growing deafer day by day. Yet he never allows a groan to escape him. He is never dull; he is never boring; he is never slovenly. His mind is as well-groomed as his body. Never for a second does he 'welter in an easy-chair.'
Virginia Woolf, Essays: 'Lord Chesterfield's Letters'.

CHESTERTON, GILBERT KEITH

1874—1936 Novelist, Poet, Critic

I believe the biographers or bibliographers of the future, if they find any trace of me at all, will say something like this: 'Chesterton, Gilbert Keith. From the fragments left by this now forgotten writer it is difficult to understand the cause even of such publicity as he obtained in his own day; nevertheless there is reason to believe that he was not without certain fugitive mental gifts. As Budger truly says, "The man who invented the two most exquisitely apt titles of *All Things Considered* and *A Shilling For My Thoughts* can have had no contemptible intelligence." ' And the grave (I hope) will for ever conceal the secret that they were both invented by you.
On himself, Letter to E. V. Lucas.

Apart from vanity or mock modesty (which healthy people always use as jokes) my real judgement of my own work is that I have spoilt a number of jolly good ideas in my time.
On himself, *Autobiography.*

I can, if you will let me, lay claim to one little modest negative virtue. I have always been free from envy.

In the year 1900 I had been considered a rather clever and amusing young man, but I felt no pang whatsoever at finding myself cut out at my own game by a sudden new-comer, named G. K. Chesterton, who was obviously far more amusing than I, and obviously a man of genius into the bargain.
    Max Beerbohm, *Lytton Strachey.*

Like all platform performers, he runs a constant risk of being trapped by his own style. Opinions get fed into the machine, and what emerges is not so much inaccurate as inappropriate. Everything takes on the same slightly hectic tone. But this is as much a basic characteristic of Chesterton's imagination as the result of journalistic habit, and aesthetic rather than an intellectual defect. He sees the world in terms of loud contrasts and garish colours: the picture has the boldness of a cartoon, but it lacks light and shade.
    John Gross, *The Rise and Fall of the Man of Letters.*

This liberal colleague of Mr Shaw's . . . is a sort of caricature of 'a Liberal' as seen by Rowlandson.
    Percy Wyndham Lewis, *The Art of Being Ruled.*

Poor G.K.C., his day is past —
Now God will know the truth at last.
    E. V. Lucas, mock epitaph, in Dudley Barker, *G. K. Chesterton.*

Chesterton is like a vile scum on a pond. . . . All his slop — it is really modern catholicism to a great extent, the *never* taking a hedge straight, the mumbo-jumbo of superstition dodging behind clumsy fun and paradox . . . I believe he creates a milieu in which art is impossible. He and his kind.
    Ezra Pound, Letter to John Quinn, 21 August 1917.

Wells and I, contemplating the Chesterbelloc, recognize at once a very amusing pantomime elephant, the front legs being that very exceptional and unEnglish individual Hilaire Belloc, and the hind legs that extravagant freak of French nature, G. K. Chesterton.
    George Bernard Shaw, 'The Chesterbelloc', in *New Age,* 15 February 1908.

Chesterton's resolute conviviality is about as genial as an *auto de fé* of teetotallers.
    George Bernard Shaw, *Pen Portraits and Reviews.*

Here lies Mr Chesterton,
Who to heaven might have gone,
But didn't when he heard the news
That the place was run by Jews.
    Humbert Wolfe, *Lampoons.*

See also Hilaire Belloc

CHOATE, JOSEPH HODGES
1832–1917 Lawyer, Diplomat

. . . a virulent enemy of the Irish race, hating the Irish as the devil hates holy water; his malevolence not confined to any class or section of Irish, abhorring them all, and whenever occasion offered to spit his venom at the Irish he has done it, and when no occasion offered he made it.
    Anon. newspaper editorial, in Beckles Willson, *American Ambassadors to England.*

Joe Choate drops into the northeast corner of the first car and hurls himself up as if he were to settle there for life and cared for no creature in the world, not thinking of himself or of his appearance. He sees no one in the car. His mind is elsewhere.
    Anon., New York Press, 1895, in *American Heritage,* April 1975.

See also Chauncey Depew

CHRISTIE, DAME AGATHA
1890–1976 Thriller Writer

. . . though I have given in to people on every subject under the sun, *I have never given in to anyone over what I write.*
    On herself, *Autobiography*

A sausage machine, a perfect sausage machine.
    On herself, in G. C. Ramsey, *Agatha Christie, Mistress of Mystery*

In a Christie, you know, for example, that the corpse is not a real corpse, but merely the pretext for a puzzle. You know that the policeman is not a real policeman, but a good-natured dullard introduced on to the scene to emphasize the much greater intelligence of Poirot or Miss Marple. You know that there will be no loving description of the details of physical violence. You know (or up to a few years ago, used to know) that, although the murderer is going to be hanged, you will be kept well at a distance from this displeasing event. You know that although people may fall in love you will not be regaled with the physical details of what they do in bed. You know, relaxing with a Christie, that for an hour or two you can forget the authentic nastiness of life and submerge yourself in a world where, no matter how many murders take place, you are essentially in never-never land.
    Edmund Crispin, in H. R. F. Keating, ed., *Agatha Christie, First Lady of Crime.*

As a person she had a quality of elusiveness which stemmed from her earliest days — a defensive resistance to inquisitive probing, an inbuilt armour off which any questionnaire was liable to glance like a spent arrow.

Sir Max Mallowan (Christie's husband), *Mallowan's Memoirs*.

Her skill was not in the tight construction of plot, nor in the locked-room mystery, nor did she often make assumptions about the scientific and medical knowledge of readers. The deception in these Christie stories is much more like the conjurer's sleight-of-hand. She shows us the ace of spades face up. Then she turns it over, but we still know where it is, so how has it been transformed into the five of diamonds?

Julian Symons, *Bloody Murder, From the Detective Story to the Crime Novel: a History*.

CHURCHILL, CHARLES

1731—64 Poet

Churchill was a poor, low, unprincipled, vicious, coarse creature, with smartness that was sometimes almost strength; and what to us must in such a person always be a mystery, he had a command over the English language, as far as his mind enabled him to get in it, which made everything he said tell, far beyond its native worth or power, and has secured him no contemptible place among English satirists.

Blackwood's Magazine, June 1828.

Lord Eglinton came to me this fore-noon. We talked of Churchill. My Lord owned he was a very clever fellow, but must in some degree be either a fool or a knave to abuse the Scotch so grossly.

James Boswell, *London Journal*, 25 January 1763.

The comet of a season.

Lord Byron, *Churchill's Grave*.

Blotting and correction was so much his abhorrence, that I have heard from his publisher he once energetically expressed himself, 'it was like cutting away one's own flesh'.

Isaac D'Israeli, *Curiosities of Literature*.

Nay, Sir, I am a very fair judge. He did not attack me violently till he found I did not like his poetry; and his attack on me shall not prevent me from continuing to say what I think of him, from an apprehension that it may be ascribed to resentment.

No, Sir, I called the fellow a blockhead at first, and I will call him a blockhead still.

Samuel Johnson, in James Boswell, *Life of Johnson*.

To be sure, he is a tree that cannot produce true fruit. He only bears crabs. But, Sir, a tree that produces a great many crabs is better than one which produces only a few crabs.

Samuel Johnson, in James Boswell, *London Journal*, 1 July 1763.

CHURCHILL, JENNIE JEROME (LADY RANDOLPH SPENCER-)

1854—1921 Society Lady

I shall never get used to not being the most beautiful woman in the room. It was an intoxication to sweep in and know every man had turned his head. It kept me in form.

On herself, in conversation with her sister Leonie, 1914, in Anita Leslie, *Jennie*.

Had Lady Randolph Churchill been like her face, she could have governed the world.

Margot Asquith, *Autobiography*.

CHURCHILL, JOHN, see under MARLBOROUGH, DUKE OF

CHURCHILL, LORD RANDOLPH HENRY SPENCER-

1849—95 Statesman

All great men make mistakes. Napoleon forgot Blücher, I forgot Goschen.

On himself, in Lady Dorothy Nevill, *Leaves from the Notebooks*.

He has thrown himself from the top of the ladder, and will never reach it again!

Mr George Moore (civil servant), on hearing of Lord Randolph's resignation as Chancellor of the Exchequer, 1886, in Mrs Cornwallis West, *Reminiscences of Lady Randolph Churchill*.

I have four departments — the Prime Minister's, the Foreign Office, the Queen, and Randolph Churchill; the burden of them increases in that order.

Lord Salisbury, 1886, in David Cecil, *The Cecils of Hatfield House*.

Did you ever know a man who, having had a boil on his neck, wanted another?

> Lord Salisbury, on being pressed to give Lord Randolph office after 1886, in *ibid.*

CHURCHILL, SIR WINSTON LEONARD SPENCER-

1874—1965 Prime Minister

It's no use sitting upon me, for I am india-rubber — and I bounce!

> On himself, to suppressive fellow-subalterns, Meerut 1898, in Lord Baden-Powell, *Indian Memories.*

Like a good many other Generals at this time, French disapproved of me. I was that hybrid combination of subaltern and widely-followed war-correspondent which was not unnaturally obnoxious to the military mind.

> On himself, recalling the Boer War, *Great Contemporaries.*

I would say to the House, as I said to those who have joined the Government: 'I have nothing to offer but blood, toil, tears and sweat.'

> On himself, Speech in the Commons, 13 May 1940.

Let me, however, make this clear, in case there should be any mistake about it in any quarter. We mean to hold our own. I have not become the King's First Minister in order to preside over the liquidation of the British Empire.

> On himself, Speech at the Mansion House, 10 November 1942.

I did not suffer from any desire to be relieved of my responsibilities. All I wanted was compliance with my wishes after reasonable discussion.

> On himself, in *The Second World War: The Hinge of Fate.*

I am ready to meet my Maker. Whether my Maker is prepared for the ordeal of meeting me is another matter.

> On himself, on his seventy-fifth birthday, 1949.

I have never accepted what many people have kindly said, namely that I inspired the nation. It was the nation and the races dwelling all round the globe that had the lion heart. I had the luck to be called upon to give the roar.

> On himself, Eightieth Birthday Speech, November 1954.

Always remember, that I have taken more out of alcohol than alcohol has taken out of me.

> On himself, in Quentin Reynolds, *By Quentin Reynolds.*

Winston's back.

> Radio message sent out to the Royal Navy by the Board of Admiralty in September 1939, when Churchill was re-appointed First Sea Lord.

I have always said that the key to Winston is to realize that he is mid-Victorian, steeped in the politics of his father's period, and unable ever to get the modern point of view. It is only his verbal exuberance and abounding vitality that conceal this elementary fact about him.

> L. S. Amery, *My Political Life.*

I don't deny that Winston has his sentimental side. ... And what is more, he cannot really tell lies. That is what makes him so bad a conspirator.

> Stanley Baldwin, 8 December 1937, in Harold Nicolson, Diary.

Then comes Winston with his hundred-horse-power mind and what can I do?

> Stanley Baldwin, in G. M. Young, *Stanley Baldwin.*

Churchill is a good judge in every matter which does not concern himself. There, his judgement is hopeless, and he is sure to come to a big crash in time. ... He is born to trouble, for like Jehovah in the hymn — 'He plants his footsteps on the deep and rides upon the storm'.

> Lord Beaverbrook, Letter to Sir Robert Borden, 10 June 1925.

The weakness in this Indian issue is, that Winston Churchill is making it his ladder for the moment. Churchill has the habit of breaking the rungs of any ladder he puts his foot on.

> Lord Beaverbrook, Letter to Arthur Brisbane, 20 October 1932.

Churchill on the top of the wave has in him the stuff of which tyrants are made.

> Lord Beaverbrook, *Politicians and the War.*

Churchill is essentially a man without rancour. He has been accused of being bad-tempered. It isn't true. He could get very emotional, but after bitterly criticizing you he had a habit of touching you, of putting his hand on your hand ... as if to say that his real feelings for you were not changed. A wonderful display of humanity.

> Lord Beaverbrook, in conversation, 1963, in A. J. P. Taylor, *Beaverbrook.*

I arrived at the conclusion that his chameleon-like character is founded upon a temperamental disability. He fills all the roles with such exceeding facility that his lack of political stability is at once explained.
    Aneurin Bevan, Speech in the House of
    Commons, July 1929.

The seven-league-boot tempo of his imagination hastens him on to the 'sunny uplands' of the future, but he is apt to forget that the slow steps of humanity must travel every inch of the weary road that leads there.
    Aneurin Bevan, in *Tribune*, 1940.

The man who may be the wrecker of the Tory Party, but was certainly saviour of the civilised world.
    Henry Channon, Diary, 9 April 1952.

Winston may in your eyes and in those with whom he has to work have faults, but he has the supreme quality which I venture to say very few of your present future Cabinet possess — the power, the imagination, the deadliness, to fight Germany.
    Clementine Churchill, Letter to H. H. Asquith,
    May 1915.

. . . In private conversation he tries on speeches like a man trying on ties in his bedroom to see how he would look in them.
    Lionel Curtis, Letter to Nancy Astor, 1912.

Since the beginning of this war two men, whom we had thought of as slowly and unwillingly retiring from public life, have emerged into a glare of prominence. I mean Mr Churchill and Mr Wells. They must be nearly contemporary; they were both men of celebrity, I remember, when I was a freshman. Both have spoken and written a great deal in the last thirty-odd years; neither possesses what one could call a *style*, though each has a distinct idiom: that of Mr Wells being more like a durable boiler suit, and that of Mr Churchill more like a court dress of rather tarnished grandeur from a theatrical costumier's.
    T. S. Eliot, in *New English Weekly*, 8 February
    1940.

. . . full of go, no doubt full of foolishness, but he will like his father make the fur fly.
    Mary Kingsley, Letter to John Holt, 10 May
    1899.

He is using our [Labour] people as a necessary lever for morale, but he is not surrendering a single position or privilege, and he does not think that they ought to be surrendered. . . . He has set his face backwards not forwards.
    Harold Laski, Letter to Felix Frankfurter,
    March 1942.

He has spoilt himself by reading about Napoleon.
    David Lloyd George, in Frances Stevenson,
    Diary, 19 May 1917.

Winston is an able man, but he is not a leader. He does not want men around him with understanding minds. He would rather not have them. He is intolerant of them. That is bad leadership.
    David Lloyd George, in A. J. Sylvester, Diary,
    25 June 1940.

Winston was nervous before a speech, but he was not shy . . . Winston would go up to his Creator and say that he would very much like to meet His Son, about Whom he had heard a great deal and, if possible, would like to call on the Holy Ghost. Winston *loved* meeting people.
    Ibid., 2 January 1937.

The first time you meet Winston you see all his faults and the rest of your life you spend in discovering his virtues.
    Lady Lytton, in Christopher Hassall, *Edward
    Marsh*.

His passion for the combative renders him insensitive to the gentle gradations of the human mind.
    Harold Nicolson, Diary, 19 December 1945.

He is a young man who will go far if he doesn't overbalance!
    Cecil John Rhodes, 1901, in J. G. McDonald,
    Rhodes: A Life.

As history it is beneath contempt, the special pleading of a defence lawyer. As literature it is worthless. It is written in a sham Augustan prose which could only have been achieved by a man who thought always in terms of public speech, and the antitheses clang like hammers in an arsenal.
    Evelyn Waugh, on Churchill's *Life of
    Marlborough*, in David Pryce-Jones, *Evelyn
    Waugh and His World*.

Winston is always expecting rabbits to come out of empty hats.
    Field-Marshall Lord Wavell, in Henry Channon,
    Diary, 30 May 1943.

When Mr Attlee is presiding in the absence of the Prime Minister the Cabinet meets on time, goes systematically through its agenda, makes the necessary decisions, and goes home after three or four hours' work. When Mr Churchill presides we never reach the agenda and we decide nothing. But we go home to bed at midnight, conscious of having been present at an historic occasion.
    Ellen Wilkinson, during the Second World War,
    in Kingsley Martin, *Harold Laski*.

See also Huey Long

CIBBER, COLLEY
1671–1757 Actor, Dramatist

It may be observable, too, that my Muse and my Spouse were equally prolifick; that the one was seldom the Mother of a Child, but in the same Year, the other made me the Father of a Play; I think we had a Dozen of each Sort between us; of both which kinds, some died in their Infancy, and near an equal number of each were alive when I quitted the Theatre — But it is no wonder, when a Muse is only call'd upon by Family Duty, she should not always rejoice in the Fruit of her Labour.

> On himself, *Apology for the Life of Mr. Colley Cibber,* 1740.

He was in Stature of the middle Size, his Complexion fair, inclinable to the Sandy, his Legs somewhat of the thickest, his Shape a little clumsy, not irregular, and his Voice rather shrill than loud or articulate, and crack'd extremely when he endeavour'd to raise it. He was in his younger Days so lean, as to be known by the Name of *Hatchet Face.*

> Anon., *The Laureat, or the Right Side of Colley Cibber Esq.*

In merry old England it once was a rule
The King had his Poet, and also his Fool.
But now we're so frugal, I'd have you to know it,
That Cibber can serve both for Fool and for Poet.

> Anon., attributed by Cibber to Alexander Pope, before 1742.

Dr Johnson as usual spoke contemptuously of Colley Cibber. 'It is wonderful that a man, who for forty years had lived with the great and witty, should have acquired so ill the talents of conversation; and he had but half to furnish: for one half of what he said, was oaths.' He, however allowed considerable merit to some of his comedies, and said there was no reason to believe the *Careless Husband* was not written by himself.

> James Boswell, *Life of Johnson.*

Colley Cibber was extremely haughty as a theatrical manager, and very insolent to dramatists. When he had rejected a play, if the author desired him to point out the particular parts of it which displeased him, he took a pinch of snuff, and answered in general terms, 'Sir, there is nothing in it to coerce my passions.'

> George Colman, *Random Records.*

He was known only for some years, by the name of Master Colley. After waiting impatiently for some time for the Prompter's Notice, by good fortune he obtained the honour of carrying a message on the stage, in some play, to Betterton. Whatever was the cause, Master Colley was so terrified, that the scene was disconcerted by him. Betterton asked, in some anger, who the young fellow was that had committed the blunder. Downes replied, 'Master Colley!' — 'Master Colley! then forfeit him!' — 'Why, Sir,' said the prompter, 'he has no salary.' — 'No!' said the old man; 'why then put him down 10s. a week, and forfeit him 5s.'

> Thomas Davies, *Dramatic Miscellanies.*

I have seen him at fault where it was least expected; in parts which he had acted a hundred times, and particularly in Sir Courtly Nice; but Colley dexterously supplied the deficiency of his Memory, by prolonging his ceremonious bow to the lady, and drawling out 'Your humble servant, Madam.' to an extraordinary length; then taking a pinch of snuff, and strutting deliberately across the stage, he has gravely asked the prompter, 'what is next?'

> *Ibid.*

This actor, though his vivacity was mixed with too much pertness, never offended by flatness and insipidity.

> *Ibid.*

So well did Cibber, though a professed libertine through life, understand the dignity of virtue, that no comic author has drawn more dignified and striking pictures of it. Mrs Porter, upon reading a part, in which Cibber had painted virtue in the strongest and most lively colours, asked him how it came to pass, that a man, who could draw such admirable portraits of goodness, should yet live as if he were a stranger to it? — 'Madam,' said Colley, 'the one is absolutely necessary, the other is not.'

> *Ibid.*

. . . for that you, not having the Fear of Grammar before your Eyes, on the   of   at a certain Place, called the *Bath* in the County of Somerset, in *Knightsbridge* in the County of *Middlesex,* in and upon the *English* Language an Assault did make, and then and there, with a certain Weapon, called a Goose-quill, value one Farthing, which you in your left Hand then held, several very broad Wounds, but of no Depth at all, on the said *English* Language did make, and so you the said Col. *Apol.* the said *English* Language did murder.

> Henry Fielding, in *Champion,* 17 May 1740.

Cibber! write all thy Verses upon Glasses,
The only way to save 'em from our A———s.

> Alexander Pope, *Epigram Occasioned by Cibber's Verses in Praise of Nash.*

Swearing and supperless the Hero sate,
Blasphemed his Gods, the Dice, and damn'd his Fate.
Then gnaw'd his pen, then dash'd it on the ground,
Sinking from thought to thought, a vast profound!
Plunged for his sense, but found no bottom there,
Yet wrote and flounder'd on, in mere despair.
Round him much Embryo, much Abortion lay,
Much future Ode, and abdicated Play;
Nonsense precipitate, like running Lead
That slip'd through cracks and Zig-zags of the Head;
All that on Folly Frenzy could beget,
Fruits of dull Heat, and Sooterkins of Wit.
Next o'er his Books his eyes began to roll,
In pleasing Memory of all he stole,
How here he sipp'd, now there he plundered snug,
And suck'd all o'er like an industrious Bug.
    Alexander Pope, *The Dunciad*, 1742.

Me Emptiness and Dulness could inspire,
And were my Elasticity and Fire.
Some Daemon stole my pen (forgive th'offence)
And once betray'd me into common sense:
Else all my prose and verse were much the same;
This, prose on stilts; that, poetry fall'n lame.
Did on the Stage my Fops appear confin'd?
My Life gave ampler lessons to mankind.
Did the dead Letter unsuccessful prove?
The brisk Example never fail'd to move.
    Ibid.

    The proud Parnassian sneer,
The conscious simper, and the jealous leer,
Mix on his look.
    Ibid.

Quoth *Cibber* to *Pope*, tho' in Verse you foreclose,
I'll have the last Word, for by G—d I'll write Prose.
Poor *Colley*, thy Reas'ning is none of the strongest,
For know, the last Word is the Word that lasts longest.
    Alexander Pope, *Epigram, On Cibber's
    Declaration that he will have the last word with
    Mr Pope.*

See also Samuel Foote, James Thomson

CLARE, JOHN
1793—1864 Poet

Still, I have been no one's enemy but my own. My easy nature, either in drinking or anything else, was always ready to submit to persuasions of profligate companions, who often led me into snares, and laughed at me in the bargain when they had done so; such things as at fairs, coaxed about to bad houses, those painted pills of poison, by whom many unguarded youths are hurried to destruction like the ox to the slaughter house, without knowing the danger that awaits them at the end.
    On himself, *Sketches from the Life of John
    Clare written by Himself.*

I have seen the original document authorizing the admission of poor Clare into the Asylum. . . . There is a string of printed questions which the examining Physician answers. To the query whether the malady was preceded by any serious or long continued mental emotion or exertion the answer is — 'After years addicted to *poetical prosing.*'
    G. J. de Wilde, Letter to F. Martin, 28 February 1865.

How good was Clare? At his best he was very good indeed, with a natural simplicity supported by a remarkable sense of language; meant what he said, considered it well before he wrote it down, and wrote with love. When he was not good, he was no worse, than any other not-good poet of his time.
    Robert Graves, in *Hudson Review*, Spring 1955.

One cannot help feeling some qualms concerning the late enormous puffing of the Northamptonshire peasant, John Clare. . . . There can be no doubt Clare is a man of talents and a man of virtue; but as to poetical genius, in the higher and the only proper sense of that word, I fear it would be very difficult to shew that he deserves half the fuss that has been made. Smoothness of versification and simplicity of thought seem to be his chief merits; but alas! in these days these are not enough to command or to justify such a sounding of the trumpet.
    J. G. Lockhart, in *Blackwood's Edinburgh
    Magazine*, June 1820.

The principal token of his mental eccentricity was the introduction of prize-fighting, in which he seemed to imagine he was to engage; but the allusion to it was made in the way of interpolation in the middle of the subject on which he was discoursing, brought in abruptly, and abandoned with equal suddenness, and an utter want of connexion with any association of ideas which it could be thought might lead to the subject at any time; as if the machinery of thought were dislocated, so that one part of it got off its pivot. . . . This was the only symptom of aberration of mind we observed about Clare.
    Cyrus Redding, in *English Journal*, 15 May 1841.

He was a peasant writing poetry, yet cannot be called a peasant poet, because he had behind him no tradition of peasant literature, but had to do what he could with the current forms of polite literature. The mastering of these forms absorbed much of his energy, so that for so singular a man he added little

of his own, and the result was only thinly tinged with his personality, hardly at all with the general characteristics of his class.
   Edward Thomas, *John Clare.*

CLARENDON, see under HYDE, EDWARD

CLARK, GEORGE ROGERS

1752—1818 Explorer, Soldier

I am a man and a warrior — not a counselor. I carry war in my right hand, and in my left, peace.
   On himself, in William English, *Conquest of the Country Northwest of the River Ohio.*

CLAY, HENRY

1777—1852 Statesman

I am the most unfortunate man in the history of parties; always run by my friends when sure to be defeated, and now betrayed when I, or any one, would be sure of election.
   On himself, in Marquis James, *Andrew Jackson: Portrait of a President.*

If there were two Henry Clays, one of them would make the other President of the United States.
   On himself, in James Ford Rhodes, *The McKinley and Roosevelt Administrations, 1897—1909.*

The moon was shining silver bright,
The stars with glory crowned the night,
   High on a limb 'the same old coon'
   Was singing to himself this tune: —
      Get out of the way, you're all unlucky
      Clear the track for Old Kentucky!
   Anon., Campaign song, 1844, in Glyndon G. van Deusen, *The Life of Henry Clay.*

He wires in and wires out,
And leaves the people still in doubt,
Whether the snake that made the track,
Was going South or coming back.
   Anon., 1844, in Charles Sellars, *James K. Polk — Continentalist, 1843—46.*

Adams, Clay and Company. Would to God they were like Jonah in the Whale's belly; and the door locked, key lost, and not a son of Vulcan within a million miles to make another.
   Anon., in *National Intelligencer*, 6 October 1828.

He comes, he comes, the gallant Clay,
And millions cheer him on his way;
The little fox [Van Buren] just snuffs the breeze,
And sneaks away without the cheese
Oh yes, the manly tread of Harry
Does such fear and terror carry
Renard to his burrow flees.
   Anon., 1844 election jingle, in Meade Minnigerode, *Presidential Years, 1787—1860.*

. . . [The] standard of Henry Clay should consist of his armorial bearings, which ought to be a pistol, a pack of cards, and a brandy bottle.
   Anon., in *ibid.*

. . . [had an] undigested system of ethics.
   John Quincy Adams, in Marie B. Hecht, *John Quincy Adams, A Personal History of an Independent Man.*

He prefers the specious to the solid, and the plausible to the true. . . .
   John C. Calhoun, in L. A. Harris, *The Fine Art of Political Wit.*

I don't like Henry Clay. He is a bad man, an impostor, a creator of wicked schemes. I wouldn't speak to him, but by God, I love him.
   John Calhoun, in John F. Kennedy, *Profiles in Courage.*

He is in fact the spoiled child of society; everybody loves him, subscribes to his opinions, and finds excuses for his foibles.
   Philip Hone, Diary.

If he is like anybody, he does not know it. He has never studied models, and if he had, his pride would have rescued him from the fault of imitation.
   Thomas F. Marshall, in Bernard Mayo, *Henry Clay: Spokesman of the New West.*

With joy, we welcome back the Spring.
Its sunny days and hours,
When '*Violets and Cedars*' white,
Speak, HOPE AND FAITH, in flowers.
But yet, *by far more* dear than all
It ushers in the day,
That gave *to us* — and to the world,
The LOVED ONE — HENRY CLAY.
Oh, Henry Clay, this is thy Natal day,
   To us more dear,
Each passing year
   Tho' thou art far away.
   William G. Mickell, *The Natal Day*, 12 April 1852.

. . . [The] ineffable meanness of the lion turned

spaniel in his fawnings on the masters whose hands he was licking for the sake of the dirty puddings they might have to toss to him.
Edmund Quincy, in John F. Kennedy, *Profiles in Courage.*

. . . like a mackerel in the moonlight; he shines and he stinks.
John Randolph of Roanoke, in Ray Gingers, *Joke book about American History.*

I was defeated, horse, foot and dragoons — cut up — and clean broke down — by the coalition of Blifil and Black George — by the combination, unheard of till then, of the Puritan with the black-leg.
John Randolph of Roanoke (reference to the alliance between John Quincy Adams and Clay in 1825), in Glyndon G. van Deusen, *The Life of Henry Clay.*

Clay could get more men to run after him to hear him speak, and fewer to vote for him, than any man in America.
Mr Shepperd of North Carolina, as reported by Alexander H. Stephens in a letter to his brother, January 1845.

No one knew better than the Cock of Kentucky which side his bread was buttered on: and he liked butter. A considerable portion of his public life was spent in trying to find butter for both sides of the slice.
Irving Stone, *They Also Ran.*

He was a chameleon; he could turn any color that might be useful to him. To read of his career one must have cork-screw eyes.
Ibid.

Henry Clay said 'I would rather be right than be president.' This was the sourest grape since Aesop originated his fable.
Ibid.

See also Thomas Hart Benton

CLEVELAND, DUCHESS OF, see under VILLIERS, BARBARA

CLEVELAND, JOHN

1613—58 Poet

Heliconean Dew.
On himself, Anagram of his name.

The delight and ornament of St John's [Cambridge] society. What service as well as reputation he did it, let his orations and epistles speak; to which the library oweth much of its learning, the chapel much of its pious decency, and the college much of its renown.
Anon., *Clievelandi Vindiciae,* 1677.

A general artist, pure latinist, exquisite orator, and eminent poet. His epithets were pregnant with meta-physics, carrying in them a difficult plainness, difficult at the hearing, plain at the considering thereof. Never so eminent a poet was interred with fewer (if any remarkable) elegies upon him.
Thomas Fuller, *The History of the Worthies of England.*

But to speak something of our friend Cleveland, that grand malignant of Cambridge, we hear that now he is at Newark, where he hath the title of advocate put upon him. His office and employment is to gather all college rents within the power of the king's forces in those parts, which he distributes to such as are turned out of their fellowships at Cambridge for their malignancy.
Kingdom's Weekly Intelligencer, 27 May 1645.

CLEVELAND, (STEPHEN) GROVER

1837—1908 Twenty-Second and Twenty-Fourth United States President

I am not concerning myself about what history will think, but contenting myself with the approval of a fellow named Cleveland whom I have generally found to be a pretty good sort of a fellow.
On himself, in D. H. Elletson, *Roosevelt and Wilson: A Comparative Study.*

It seemed to me that I am as much consecrated to a service as the religionist who secludes himself from all that is joyous in life and devotes himself to a sacred mission.
On himself, 1885, in Richard Hofstadter, *The American Political Tradition.*

Hurrah for Maria
Hurrah for the kid
I voted for Grover
And am damn glad I did.
Anon., Cleveland campaign slogan, 1884, referring to the rumour that Cleveland, a bachelor, had fathered the child of Maria Halpin of Buffalo, New York.

Ma! Ma! Where's my pa?
Gone to the White House,

Ha! Ha! Ha!
> Anon., 1884, campaign slogan, in Allan Nevins, *Grover Cleveland, A Study in Courage.*

'Tis better to vote for some billy goat,
That butts for his corn and his hay,
Than to vote for a man that has not the sand
To stand by his party a day.
> Anon., in Marcus Cunliffe, *American Presidents and the Presidency.*

Grover, Grover,
Four more years of Grover;
Out they go; in we go,
Then we'll be in clover.
> Anon., Campaign chant, in A. W. Dunn, *From Harrison to Harding: A Personal Narrative.*

You ask us to endorse Cleveland's fidelity. In reply, I say, he has been faithful unto death, the death of the Democratic party.
> Anon., at the Chicago Convention in 1896, in D. H. Elletson, *Roosevelt and Wilson: A Comparative Study.*

In ordering Old Glory pulled down at Honolulu, President Cleveland turned back the hands on the dial of civilization. Native rule, ignorant, naked, heathen, is reestablished; and the dream of an American republic at the cross roads of the Pacific . . . has been shattered by Grover Cleveland, the Buffalo lilliputian.
> Anon., New York *Commercial Advertiser*, 14 April 1893, in Allan Nevins, *Grover Cleveland.*

We have been told that the mantle of Tilden has fallen upon Cleveland. The mantle of a giant upon the shoulders of a dwarf!
> Bourke Cochran, in *ibid.*

The thing to me most attractive about the President is the moral atmosphere of the man, his lofty and devoted views and aims. Circumstances have made me well acquainted with not a few other men since the war, but without intending derogation of them, I must say that the President strikes me as remarkable and well nigh unique for a certain moral fervor in his views of public affairs. The fact is that the 'preacher blood' of the President has told in him more and more as his public and private responsibilities have increased.
> Richard Watson Gilder, letter in *New York Times*, 12 December 1888.

He was the flower of American political culture in the Gilded Age.
> Richard Hofstadter, *The American Political Tradition.*

He was not a cruel man, but he was dogmatic, obtuse, and insensitive.
> *Ibid.*

The contrast with [Chester] Arthur, who was a fine handsome figure, was very striking. Cleveland's coarse face, his heavy inert body, his great shapeless hands, confirmed in my mind the attacks made upon him during the campaign.
> Robert M. La Follette, *Autobiography.*

A man of force & stubbornness with no breadth of view, no training in our history & traditions & essentially coarse fibred & self sufficient.
> Henry Cabot Lodge, Letter to Anna Lodge, 31 May 1896.

. . . his whole huge carcass seemed to be made of iron. There was no give in him, no bounce, no softness. He sailed through American history like a steel ship loaded with monoliths of granite.
> H. L. Mencken, 'From a Good Man in a Bad Trade', in *American Mercury*, January 1933.

He came into office his own man, and he went out without yielding anything of that character for an instant.
> *Ibid.*

He restored honesty and impartiality to government at a time when the service had become indispensable to the health of the public. . . . To have bequeathed a nation such an example of iron fortitude is better than to have swayed parliaments or to have won battles or to have annexed provinces.
> Allen Nevins, *Grover Cleveland.*

Too conservative to be a great constructive statesman.
> Allen Nevins, in Richard Hofstadter, *The American Political Tradition.*

His Accidency.
> Theodore Roosevelt, in D. H. Elletson, *Roosevelt and Wilson: A Comparative Study.*

To nominate Grover Cleveland would be to march through a slaughter house into an open grave.
> Henry Watterson, *Louisville Courier-Journal*, referring to the nomination of 1892, in Burton Stevenson, *The Home Book of Quotations: Classical and Modern.*

I am prepared to believe that Grover Cleveland was a better President of the United States than he was a trustee of Princeton University.
> Woodrow Wilson, in D. H. Elletson, *Roosevelt and Wilson: A Comparative Study.*

See also Martin van Buren

CLIVE, ROBERT, LORD

1725–74 Imperial Administrator

Consider my position. A great prince was dependent on my pleasure; an opulent city lay at my mercy; its richest bankers bid against each other for my smiles; I walked through vaults which were thrown open to me alone, piled on either hand with gold and jewels! By God, Mr Chairman, at this moment I stand astonished at my own moderation.

On himself, address to Parliament, 1772.

Clive, like most men who are born with strong passions and tried by strong temptations committed great faults. But every person who takes a fair and enlightened view of his whole career must admit that our island, so fertile in heroes and statesmen, has scarcely ever produced a man more truly great either in arms or in council.

T. B. Macaulay, *Essays*: 'Lord Clive'.

A savage old Nabob, with an immense fortune, a tawny complexion, a bad liver and a worse heart.

Ibid.

Clive was a great soldier, a great administrator, a born leader of his fellows. The bluntness of his moral perceptions prevented him from being a great man!

Colonel Malleson, *Lord Clive*.

CLOUGH, ARTHUR HUGH

1819–61 Poet

His landscape painting is noteworthy for its truth and solidity. It is often too truthful to be good as art, resembling rather a coloured photograph than a picture. Something of the land-surveyor, one might say, mingles with the poet.

William Allingham, Diary.

He was one of [Thomas] Arnold's favourite pupils, because he gave heed so much to Arnold's teaching; and exactly because he gave heed to it was it bad for him. He required quite another sort of teaching: to be told to take things easily; not to try to be wise overmuch; to be 'something beside critical'; to go on living quietly and obviously, and see what truth would come to him.

Walter Bagehot, in *National Review*, October 1862.

I never met with anyone who was more thoroughly high-minded. I believe he acted all through life simply from the feeling of what was right. He certainly had great genius, but some want of will or some want of

harmony with things around him prevented his creating anything worthy of himself.

Benjamin Jowett, Letter to Florence Nightingale (shortly after Clough's death).

We have a foreboding that Clough, imperfect as he was in many respects, and dying before he had subdued his sensitive temperament to the sterner requirements of his art, will be thought a hundred years hence to have been the truest expression in verse of the moral and intellectual tendencies, the doubt and struggle towards settled convictions, of the period in which he lived. To make beautiful conceptions immortal by exquisiteness of phrase, is to be a poet no doubt; but to be a new poet is to feel and to utter that immanent life of things without which the utmost perfection of mere form is at best only wax or marble.

James Russell Lowell, *My Study Windows*.

. . . A grave gentlemanly man, handsome, greyhaired, with an air of fastidious languor about him.

Alfred Munby, Diary, 9 March 1859.

Those who knew him well know that in him a genius and character of no common order has passed away, but they will scarcely be able to justify their knowledge to a doubting world.

Dean Stanley, Obituary notice in *Daily News*, 9 January 1862.

At the age of sixteen, he was in the Sixth Form, and not merely a Praepostor, but head of the School House. Never did Dr Arnold have an apter pupil. This earnest adolescent, with the weak ankles and the solemn face, lived entirely with the highest ends in view. He thought of nothing but moral good, moral evil, moral influence, and moral responsibility. . . . Perhaps it is not surprising that a young man brought up in such an atmosphere should have fallen a prey, at Oxford, to the frenzies of religious controversy; that he should have been driven almost out of his wits by the ratiocinations of W. G. Ward; that he should have lost his faith; that he should have spent the rest of his existence lamenting that loss, both in prose and verse; and that he should have eventually succumbed, conscientiously doing up brown paper parcels for Florence Nightingale.

Lytton Strachey, *Eminent Victorians*.

There was a poor poet named Clough,
Whom his friends all united to puff,
    But the public, though dull,
    Had not such a skull
As belonged to believers in Clough.

Algernon C. Swinburne, *Essays and Studies*, *Matthew Arnold*.

COBB, IRVIN SHREWSBURY

1876—1944 Newspaperman, Author

You may praise, you may flatter I. Cobb as you will
But the band of his derby will fit him round still.
  Julian Street, in A. K. Adams, *The Home Book of Humorous Quotations.*

COBBETT, WILLIAM

1763—1835 Polemicist, Author, Agriculturist

I was born under a King and Constitution; but I was not born under the Six Acts.
  On himself, *The Last Hundred Days of English Freedom.*

Cobbett, through all his life a cheat,
Yet as a rogue was incomplete,
For now to prove a finished knave
To dupe and trick, he robs a grave.

The radicals seem quite elated,
And soon will be intoxicated
For Cobbett means to turn their brain
With his American Sham Paine.
  Anon., *circa* 1819, in Robert Huish, *Memoirs of the Late Mr. Cobbett Esq.*

Mr. C-B-T ask'd leave to bring in very soon
A Bill to abolish the Sun and the Moon.
The Honourable Member proceeded to state
Some arguments us'd in a former debate,
On the subject of Sinecures, Taxes, Vexations,
The Army and Navy, and Old Corporations; —
The Heavenly Bodies, like those upon Earth,
Had, he said, been corrupt from the day of their birth,
With reckless profusion expending their light,
One after another, by day and by night.
And what classes enjoy'd it? The Upper alone —
Upon such they had always exclusively shone;
But when had they ever emitted a spark,
For the people who toil under ground in the dark?
  Anon., *Speech of the Member for Odium.*

. . . a Philistine with six fingers on every hand and on every foot six toes, four-and-twenty in number: a Philistine the shaft of whose spear is like a weaver's beam.
  Matthew Arnold, *Essays in Criticism.*

Had I met him anywhere save in that room and on that occasion, I should have taken him for a gentleman farming his own broad estate. He seemed to have that kind of self-possession and ease about him, together with a certain bantering jollity, which are

so natural to fast-handed and well-housed lords of the soil.
  Samuel Bamford, *Passages in the Life of a Radical.*

The pattern John Bull of his century, strong as the rhinoceros, and with singular humanities and genialities shining through his thick skin.
  Thomas Carlyle, *Essay on Scott.*

It is especially his bad language that is always good. It is precisely the passages that have always been recognized as good style that would now be regarded as bad form. And it is precisely these violent passages that especially bring out not only the best capacities of Cobbett but also the best capacities of English.
  G. K. Chesterton, *William Cobbett.*

It is not true that he belonged successively to two parties: it is much truer to say that he never belonged to any. But in so far as there were elements of the Radical in him at the end, there had been traces of them from the beginning. And in so far as he was in one sense a Tory at the beginning, he remained a Tory to the end. The truth is that the confusion was not in Cobbett but in the terms Tory and Radical. They are not exact terms; they are nothing like so exact as Cobbett was.
  Ibid.

The fools who put Cobbett in prison probably did believe they were crushing a Jacobin, when they were really creating one. And they were creating a Jacobin out of the best Anti-Jacobin of the age.
  Ibid.

He was the imperfect martyr. The modern and popular way of putting it is to say that a man can really be a martyr without being by any means a saint. The more subtle truth is that he can even be a saint and still have that sort of imperfection.
  Ibid.

There was something cool about Cobbett, for all his fire; and that was his educational instinct, his love of alphabetical and objective teaching. He was a furious debater; but he was a mild and patient schoolmaster. His dogmatism left off where most dogmatism begins. He would always bully an equal; but he would never have bullied a pupil.
  Ibid.

A reviewer likened him to a porcupine. Nothing could have pleased him better. The name had obvious qualities. A porcupine was just what he meant and needed to be, in the hostile environment of Philadelphia. 'Peter Porcupine' he became, eagerly thanking the Democratic reviewer for teaching him that word.
  G. D. H. Cole, *Life of William Cobbett.*

As Walt Whitman represents and symbolises a phase of the expansion of young America, Cobbett represents and symbolises a phase of the dissolution of Old England.

Ibid.

He was one of the most striking refutations of Lavater I ever witnessed. Never were the looks of any man more completely at variance with his character. There was something so dull and heavy about his whole appearance, that any one, who did not know him, would at once set him down for some country clodpole, to use a favourite expression of his own, who not only never read a book, or had a single idea in his head, but who was a mere man of mortality, without a particle of sensibility of any kind in his composition.

James Grant, *Random Recollections of the House of Commons.*

Why will Mr. Cobbett persist in getting into Parliament? He will find himself no longer the same man. What member of Parliament, I should like to know, could write his Register? As a popular partisan, he may (for aught I can say) be a match for the whole Honourable House; but, by obtaining a seat in St. Stephen's Chapel, he would only be equal to a 576th part of it.

William Hazlitt, *Fugitive Writings*: 'On Personal Identity'.

He persuades himself that he is the fittest person to represent Westminster in Parliament, and he considers this point (once proved) tantamount to his return. He knows no more of the disposition or sentiments of the people of Westminster than of the inhabitants of the moon (except from what he himself chooses to say or write of them), and it is this want of sympathy which, as much as anything, prevents his being chosen. The exclusive force and bigotry of his opinions deprives them of half their influence and effect, by allowing no toleration to others, and consequently setting them against him.

William Hazlitt, *Fugitive Writings*: 'On Knowledge of the World'.

He has no comfort in fixed principles: as soon as anything is settled in his own mind, he quarrels with it. He has no satisfaction but in the chase after truth, runs a question down, worries and kills it, then quits it like vermin, and starts some new game, to lead him a new dance, and give him a fresh breathing through bog and brake, with the rabble yelping at his heels and the leaders perpetually at fault. This he calls sport-royal.

William Hazlitt, *The Spirit of the Age.*

He is not pledged to repeat himself. Every new Register is a kind of new Prospectus. He blesses himself from all ties and shackles on his understanding; he has no mortgage on his brain; his notions are free and unencumbered.

Ibid.

He is a kind of fourth estate in the politics of the country.

Ibid.

If his blows were straight forward and steadily directed to the same object, no unpopular Minister could live before him; instead of which he lays about right and left, impartially and remorselessly, makes a clear stage, has all the ring to himself, and then runs out of it, just when he should stand his ground. He throws his head into his adversary's stomach, and takes away from him all inclination for the fight, hits fair or foul, strikes at every thing, and as you come up to his aid or stand ready to pursue his advantage, trips up your heels or lays you sprawling.

William Hazlitt, *The Character of W. Cobbett M.P.*

Gnawed by the worm that never dies, his own wretchedness would ever prevent him from making any attempt in favour of human happiness. His usual occupation at home was that of a garrett scribbler, excepting a little *night business* occasionally, to supply unavoidable exigencies. Grub Street did not answer his purpose, and being scented by certain tipstaffs for something more than scribbling, he took *French leave* for France. His evil genius pursued him here [America], and *as his fingers were as long as ever,* he was obliged as suddenly to leave the Republic, which has now drawn forth all his venom, for her attempt to do him *justice.* On his arrival in this country, he figured some time as a pedagogue, but as this employment scarcely furnished him salt to his porridge, he having been literally without bread to eat, and not a second shirt to his back, he resumed his old occupation of scribbling, having little chance of success in the other employments, which drove him to this country. His talent at lies and Billingsgate rhetoric, introduced him to the notice of a certain foreign agent, who was known during the Revolution by the name of *Traitor.*

'Paul Hedgehog', *History of Peter Porcupine.*

The pride of purse persecuted him in America, and persecuted him no less in England, as it persecutes us all, and will continue to persecute, until in the fulness of its cup, it shall be laid low. The purseproud Americans were a democracy, and therefore in America, Mr. Cobbett was a royalist; the purseproud

English were an aristocracy, and therefore in England, Mr. Cobbett was a democrat.

Robert Huish, *Memoirs of the Late Mr. Cobbett Esq.*

All security in his constancy or consistency was out of the question. He would write for one side just as long as he thought he was looked up as the greatest man among his party, but no sooner did he find out that others were preferred to himself, that any other notions were entertained than his own, that all would not join in attacking what he attacked, and admiring what he admired, than he turned fiercely around, flew off to the other side, and called all those who had the presumption to his cast off opinions fools and knaves.

Ibid.

Somebody said of Cobbett, very truly, that there were two sorts of people he could not endure, those who differed from him and those who agreed with him. These last had always stolen his ideas.

John Stuart Mill, Letter to Robert Harrison, December 1864.

He was honest: he never saw more than one side of a subject at a time, and he honestly stated his impression of the side he saw.

Daniel O'Connell, in W. J. O'N. Daunt, *Personal Recollections of the Late Daniel O'Connell M.P.*

Though there is much in his notions which I abhor, there is something in his character which I respect . . . he has, by his own unassisted efforts, raised himself from a very humble condition to a situation of respect . . . and he has the manliness and good sense not to be ashamed to avow the fact.

Richard Brinsley Sheridan, Speech during Westminster Election, 15 November 1806.

See also John Cavanagh, Thomas Paine

COBDEN, RICHARD

1804–65 Statesman

I have a horror of losing my own individuality, which is to me as existence itself.

On himself, refusing Palmerston's offer of cabinet rank, June 1859.

Mr Cobden was very anomalous in two respects. He was a sensitive agitator . . . He never spoke ill of anyone. He arraigned principles, but not persons. We fearlessly say that after a career of agitation of thirty years, not one single individual has — we do not say a valid charge, but a producible charge — a charge

which he would wish to bring forward against Mr Cobden. You cannot find the man who says, 'Mr Cobden said this of me, and it was not true.'

Walter Bagehot, Obituary notice, 1865, in *Biographical Studies.*

The greatest political character the pure middle class of this country has yet produced.

Benjamin Disraeli, Speech in the Commons, 3 April 1865.

He is a good Fellow, but extremely sensitive to attentions, being like all Middle Class men who have raised themselves either by money making or by Talent very vain, under the semblance of not being so.

Lord Palmerston, Letter to Lord Cowley, 16 October 1859.

. . . having sadly mismanaged his own affairs just as he would, if he could, the affairs of the nation. . . .

Lord Palmerston, Letter to Lord John Russell, 4 December 1863.

COCHISE

— d. 1874 Paramount Chief of the Chiricahua Apache

When I was young I walked all over this country, east and west, and saw no other people than the Apaches. After many summers I walked again and found another race of people had come to take it. How is it? Why is it that the Apaches wait to die — that they carry their lives on their fingernails. They roam over the hills and plains and want the heavens to fall on them. The Apaches were once a great nation; they are now but few, and because of this they so carry their lives on their fingernails. . . .

On himself, in Dee Brown, *Bury My Heart at Wounded Knee.*

COCHRAN, SIR CHARLES BLAKE

1872–1951 Showman

It is, I am sure, through his failures that he has made his friends. No other theatrical manager that I have ever known can rally adherents so swiftly in catastrophe. Temperamental stars demand to be allowed to pawn their jewellery for him. Chorus girls, stage managers, members of his office staff eagerly offer him their services indefinitely for nothing. Even hardboiled backers rush through the flames with their cheque-books over their mouths to aid him, regard-

less of the fact that the flames are probably consuming many of their own investments.
Noël Coward, *Present Indicative*.

When things were good, he resembled a rooster; when bad, a benign bishop.
Vivian Ellis, in the *Dictionary of National Biography*.

He was an authority on art, and all things beautiful, including the feminine.
Ibid.

CODY, WILLIAM FREDERICK, 'BUFFALO BILL'

1846—1917 Showman

. . . a sharpshooter who had poison ivy on his hands and thus was bothered by an itching trigger finger.
Richard Armour, *It All Started With Columbus*.

Buffalo Bill's
defunct
            who used to
            ride a watersmooth-silver
                                stallion
and break onetwothreefourfive pidgeons justlike that
                                Jesus
he was a handsome man
                and what i want to know is
how do you like your blueeyed boy
Mister Death.
e.e. cummings, 'Portraits' in *Poems 1923—1954*.

See also Theodore Roosevelt

COHAN, GEORGE MICHAEL

1878—1942 Actor, Playwright, Composer, Producer

As a dancer, I could never do over three steps. As a composer, I could never find use for over four or five notes in my musical numbers. As a violinist, I could never learn to play above the first position. I'm a one-key piano player, and as a playwright, most of my plays have been presented in two acts for the simple reason that I could seldom think of an idea for a third act.
On himself, Letter to George Buck, 1940, in Ward Morehouse, *George M. Cohan, Prince of the American Theatre*.

I don't care what you say about me, as long as you say *something* about me, and as long as you spell my name right.
On himself, in John McCabe, *George M. Cohan, The Man Who Owned Broadway*.

From my earliest days I was profoundly impressed with the fact that I had been born under the Stars and Stripes, and that has had a great deal to do with everything I have written. If it had not been for the glorious symbol of Independence, I might have fallen into the habit of writing problem plays, or romantic drama, or questionable farce. Yes, the American flag is in my heart, and it has done everything for me.
Ibid.

I can write better plays than any living dancer and dance better than any living playwright.
On himself, in *Show*, March 1962.

Mr. Cohan gives a splendid performance. Although that adjective is exact, it seems hardly enthusiastic enough for the ripeness and kindliness and wisdom of his playing. He is quizzical in the style to which we are all accustomed from him, but the jaunty mannerisms and the mugging have disappeared. For the fact is that *Ah, Wilderness* has dipped deeper into Mr. Cohan's gifts and personal character than any of the antics he has written for himself. Ironic as it may sound, it has taken Eugene O'Neill to show us how fine an actor George M. Cohan is.
Brooks Atkinson, Review of *Ah, Wilderness*, in *New York Times*, 3 October 1933.

Mr. Cohan is an actor to whom one takes out an oath of allegiance as gladly as to the flag. His caperings, his head-tossings, his winks, his jauntiness, his winning personality, his authoritative friendliness and his jovial habit of laying a finger aside his nose like a smooth-shaven Santa Claus free to choose a better exit than a chimney — all these have long since turned us all into devoted Cohanians. We have not really minded when he has gone Broadway Pirandello in a big way. We have rallied round his high-flying flag. For we are devoted Cohan fans, make no mistake about it. . . .
John Mason Brown, reviewing *The Return of the Vagabond*, in *New York Post*, 18 May 1940.

One of the last things he said when the end was near came in response to an impulsive comment by Gene Buck. 'By God, George,' Buck said, 'no man ever did what you did in the theatre. No man. Doesn't that make you proud as hell?' Cohan aroused himself from his sedation and said with a warm grin lighting his still youthful features, 'No complaints, kid. No complaints.'
John McCabe, *George M. Cohan, The Man Who Owned Broadway*.

I care nothing for the famous nasalities of George M. Cohan. . . . But I know that with only a fraction of [Irving] Berlin's gifts as a composer, he had something which even Berlin lacks: the complete sense of the boards. His revues would have been desirable additions to each theatrical season if they had done no more than produce himself. His hard sense, his unimaginative but not unsympathetic response to everything that took place on the street and at the bar and on the stage made him a prince of reviewers — he was not without malice and he was wholly without philosophy. Perhaps that is why his revues were wonderfully gay.

Gilbert Seldes, *The Seven Lively Arts.*

George M. Cohan always dances interestingly; he has sardonic legs. . . .

Ibid.

COKE, SIR EDWARD

1552—1634 Jurist

He left an estate of eleven thousand pounds per annum. Sir John Danvers, who knew him, told me he had heard one say to him, reflecting on his great scraping of wealth, that his sonnes would spend his estate faster than he gott it; he replyed, They cannot take more delight in the spending of it than I did in the getting of it.

John Aubrey, *Brief Lives.*

His second wife, Elizabeth, the relickt of Sir William Hatton, was with Child when he married her: laying his hand on her belly (when he came to bed) and finding a Child to stirre, What, sayd he, Flesh in the Pott. Yes, quoth she, or els I would not have maried a Coke.

Ibid.

You converse with books, not men, and books especially human; and have no excellent choice with men who are the best books: for a man of action and employment you seldom converse with, and then but with your underlings; not freely, but as a schoolmaster with his scholars, ever to teach, never to learn. . . . You will jest at any man in public, without respect of the person's dignity or your own: this disgraceth your gravity more than it can advance the opinion of your wit. You make the law to lean too much to your opinion, whereby you show yourself to be a legal tyrant, striking with that weapon where you please, since you are able to turn the edge any way. . . . Having the living of a thousand you relieve few or none.

Francis Bacon, *An Expostulation to The Lord Chief Justice Coke.*

The cause of Liberty, I have heard, is much indebted to Coke. If that be synonymous with the cause of Parliament, as for the moment it doubtless was, the debt is probable. In the stretching of precedents, which he has of all sorts and ages, dug up from beyond Pluto and the deepest charnel-houses, and extinct lumber-rooms of Nature, which he produces and can apply and cause to fit by shrinking, or expanding, and on the whole, to suit any foot, — he never had a rival.

Thomas Carlyle, *Historical Sketches.*

Such, *Coke*, were thy beginnings, when thy good
    In others evill best was understood:
When, being the strangers helpe, the poor mans aide,
    Thy just defences made th'oppressor afraid.
Such was thy Processe, when Integritie,
    And skill in thee, now, grew Authoritie;
That clients strove, in Question of the Lawes
    More for thy Patronage, then for their Cause,
And that thy strong and manly Eloquence
    Stood up thy Nations fame, her Crownes defence,
And now such is thy stand; while thou dost deale
    Desired Justice to the publique Weale
Like Solon's selfe; explat'st the knottie Lawes
    With endlesse labours, whilst thy learning drawes
No lesse of praise, then readers in all kinds
    Of worthiest knowledge, that can take men's
                                        minds.
Such is thy All; that (as I sung before)
    None Fortune aided lesse, or Vertue more. . . .
    Ben Jonson, *An Epigram on Sir Edward Coke,
    When he was Lord Chief Justice of England.*

COLERIDGE, SAMUEL TAYLOR

1772—1834 Poet, Critic

My instincts are so far dog-like that I love being superior to myself better than my equals.

On himself, *Notebooks,* 1805.

Stop, Christian passer-by! — Stop, child of God,
And read with gentle breast. Beneath this sod
A poet lies, or that which once seem'd he. —
O, lift one thought in prayer for S.T.C.;
That he who many a year with toil of breath
Found death in life, may here find life in death!
Mercy for praise — to be forgiven for fame
He ask'd, and hoped, through Christ.
        Do thou the same!
    On himself, *Epitaph.*

Shall gentle Coleridge pass unnoticed here,
To turgid ode and tumid stanza dear? . . .
Yet none in lofty numbers can surpass
The bard who soars to elegize an ass;
So well the subject suits his noble mind
He brays, the laureat of the long-ear'd kind.
    Lord Byron, *English Bards and Scotch Reviewers.*

And Coleridge, too, has lately taken wing,
    But like a hawk encumber'd with his hood, —
Explaining metaphysics to the nation —
I wish he would explain his Explanation.
    Lord Byron, *Don Juan*, canto i (fragment).

How great a possibility; how small a realized result.
    Thomas Carlyle, Letter to Ralph Waldo Emerson,
    12 August 1834.

I should very much like to have heard Carlyle's complaint against Coleridge. I keep wavering between admiration of his exceedingly great perceptive and analytical power and other wonderful points, and inclination to turn away altogether from a man who had so great a lack of all reality and actuality.
    A. H. Clough, Letter to J. N. Simpkinson,
    February 1841.

. . . Coleridge reminded me of a barrel to which every other man's tongue acted as a spigot, for no sooner did the latter move, than it set his own contents in a flow.
    James Fenimore Cooper, *Gleanings in Europe: England.*

This illustrious man, the largest and most spacious intellect, the subtlest and the most comprehensive, in my judgement, that has yet existed amongst men.
    Thomas de Quincey, *Recollections of the Lake Poets.*

To take a more common illustration, did he [the reader] ever amuse himself by searching the pockets of a child — three years old, suppose, when buried in slumber . . .? I have done this. . . . Philosophy is puzzled, conjecture and hypothesis are confounded, in the attempt to explain the law of selection which *can* have presided in the child's labours: stones remarkable only for weight, old rusty hinges, nails, crooked skewers, stolen when the cook has turned her back, rags, broken glass, tea-cups having the bottom knocked out, and loads of similar jewels, were the prevailing articles in the *procès verbal.* Yet doubtless, much labour had been incurred, some sense of danger, perhaps, had been faced, and anxieties of a conscious robber endured, in order to amass this splendid treasure. Such in value were the robberies of Coleridge; such their usefulness to himself or anybody else: and such the circumstances of uneasiness under which he had committed them.
    Thomas de Quincey (on Coleridge's plagiarisms), *Samuel Taylor Coleridge.*

Coleridge was one of those unhappy persons . . . of whom one might say, that if they had not been poets, they might have made something of their lives, might even have had a career; or conversely, that if they had not been interested in so many things, crossed by such diverse passions, they might have been great poets. . . . For a few years he had been visited by the Muse (I know of no poet to whom this hackneyed metaphor is better applicable) and thenceforth was a haunted man. . . . He was condemned to know that the little poetry he had written was worth more than all he could do with the rest of his life. The author of *Biographia Literaria* was already a ruined man. Sometimes, however, to be a 'ruined man' is itself a vocation.
    T. S. Eliot, *The Use of Poetry and the Use of Criticism.*

Coleridge's metaphysical interest was quite genuine, and was, like most metaphysical interest, an affair of his emotions. But a literary critic should have no emotions except those immediately provoked by a work of art . . . Coleridge is apt to take leave of the data of criticism, and arouse the suspicion that he has been diverted into a metaphysical hare-and-hounds. His end does not always appear to be the return to the work of art with improved perception and intensified, because more conscious, enjoyment; his centre of interest changes, his feelings are impure.
    T. S. Eliot, *The Sacred Wood.*

He seemed to breathe in words.
    Thomas Colley Grattan, *Beaten Paths and Those Who Trod Them.*

He was the first poet I ever knew. His genius at that time had angelic wings, and fed on manna. He talked on for ever; and you wished him to talk on for ever. His thoughts did not seem to come with labour and effort; but as if borne on the gusts of genius, and as if the wings of his imagination lifted him from off his feet. His voice rolled on the ear like the pealing organ, and its sound alone was the music of thought. His mind was clothed with wings; and raised on them, he lifted philosophy to heaven.
    William Hazlitt, *Lectures on the English Poets.*

He is the man of all others to swim on empty bladders in a sea without shore or soundings: to drive an empty stage-coach without passengers or lading, and arrive behind his time; to write marginal notes without a text; to look into a millstone to foster the rising genius of the age; to 'see merit in the chaos of its elements, and discern perfection in the great obscurity of nothing,' as his most favourite author Sir Thomas Browne has it on another occasion.
    William Hazlitt, 'Explanations — Conversation on the Drama with Coleridge', in *London Magazine*, December 1820.

The round-faced man in black entered, and dissipated all doubts on the subject, by beginning to talk. He did not cease while he stayed; nor has he since, that I know of.

William Hazlitt, *My First Acquaintances with Poets.*

Mr Coleridge was reckoned handsome when young. He is now 'more fat than bard beseems', and his face does not strike at first sight; but the expression is kind, the forehead remarkably fine, and the eye, as you approach it, extremely keen and searching. It has been compared to Bacon's, who was said to have 'an eye like a viper'. At first, it seems reposing under the bland weight of his forehead.

Leigh Hunt, in *Examiner*, 21 October 1821.

Negative Capability, that is, when a man is capable of being in uncertainties, mysteries, doubts, without any irritable reaching after fact and reason — Coleridge, for instance, would let go by a fine isolated verisimilitude caught from the Penetralium of mystery, from being incapable of remaining content with half-knowledge.

John Keats, Letter to G. and T. Keats, 21 December 1817.

He was a mighty poet and
A subtle-souled psychologist;
All things he seemed to understand,
Of old or new, on sea or land,
Save his own soul, which was a mist.
Charles Lamb, *Coleridge.*

When I heard of the death of Coleridge, it was without grief. It seemed to me that he long had been on the confines of the next world, — that he had a hunger for eternity. I grieved then that I could not grieve. But since, I feel how great a part he was of me. His great and dear spirit haunts me. I cannot think a thought, I cannot make a criticism on men and books, without an ineffectual turning and reference to him. He was the proof and touchstone of all my cogitations.

Charles Lamb, *The Death of Coleridge.*

An archangel a little damaged.
Charles Lamb, Letter to William Wordsworth, 1816.

Coleridge was a muddle-headed metaphysician who by some strange streak of fortune turned out a few real poems amongst the dreary flood of inanity which was his wont.

William Morris, Letter to F. S. Ellis, 1894 or 1895.

Mr Coleridge, to the valuable information acquired from similar sources [old women and sextons],

superadds the dreams of crazy theologians, and the mysticism of German Metaphysics, and favours the world with visions in verse, in which the quadruple elements of sexton, old women, Jeremy Taylor, and Emanuel Kant are harmonized into a delicious poetical compound.

Thomas Love Peacock, *The Four Ages of Poetry.*

The mystic sentimentality of Coleridge, however, adorned by original imagery, can never interest the gay or frivolous, who are to be attracted by the quick succession of commonplace and amusing objects; and for the same reason the deep glances into the innermost nature of man and the original views of the relation of things which Coleridge's works are fraught with are a stumbling-block and an offence to the million, not a charm.

Henry Crabb Robinson, Diary, 9 October 1811.

Coleridge's great fault is that he indulges before the public in those metaphysical and philosophical speculations which are becoming only in solitude and with select minds. His two great characters are philosophers of Coleridge's own school. The one a sentimental moralist, the other a sophisticated villain; both are dreamers.

Ibid., 23 January 1813.

You will see Coleridge — he who sits obscure
In the exceeding lustre and the pure
Intense irradiation of a mind,
Which, through its own internal lightning blind,
Flags wearily through darkness and despair —
A cloud-encircled meteor of the air,
A hooded eagle among blinking owls.
Percy Bysshe Shelley, *Letter to Maria Gisbourne.*

To tell the story of Coleridge without the opium is to tell the story of Hamlet without mentioning the ghost.

Leslie Stephen, *Hours in a Library.*

His misfortune was to appear at a time when there was a man's work to do — and he did it not. He had not sufficient strength of character, but professed doctrines which he had ceased to believe, in order to avoid the trouble of controversy.

John Sterling, in Caroline Fox, *Journals*, January 1842.

Coleridge the innumerable, the mutable, the atmospheric; Coleridge who is part of Wordsworth, Keats, and Shelley; of his age and of our own; Coleridge whose written words fill hundreds of pages and overflow innumerable margins; whose spoken words still reverberate, so that as we enter his radius he seems not a man, but a swarm, a cloud, a buzz of words, darting this way and that, clustering, quivering, and hanging suspended. So little of this can be caught in any reader's net.

    Virginia Woolf, *The Death of the Moth.*

A noticeable man with large grey eyes,
And a pale face that seemed undoubtedly
As if a blooming face it ought to be,
Heavy his low-hung lip did oft appear,
Deprest by weight of musing Phantasy;
Profound his forehead was, though not severe.

    William Wordsworth, *Stanzas, Written in My Pocket Copy of Thomson's 'Castle of Indolence'.*

See also John Cavanagh, Edmund Kean, Thomas Paine, Sir Walter Scott, Shakespeare, William Wordsworth

COLET, JOHN

1466?—1519 Humanist

After the conflagration, his monument being broken, his coffin, which was lead, was full of a liquour which conserved the body. Mr. Wyld and Ralph Greatorex tasted it, and 'twas of a kind of insipid taste, something of an ironish tast. The body felt, to the probe of a stick which they thrust into a chinke, like brawne.

    John Aubrey, *Brief Lives* (on the examination of Colet's coffin in old St Paul's after the Great Fire).

COLLINS, WILLIAM

1721—59 Poet

I have finished lately eight volumes of Johnson's *Lives of the Poets.* In all that number I observe but one man ... whose mind seems to have had the slightest tincture of religion. His name was Collins. ... Of him there are some hopes. But from the lives of all the rest there is but one inference to be drawn — that poets are a very worthless wicked set of people.

    William Cowper, Letter to John Newton, 19 March 1784.

Still alive — happy if insensible of our neglect, not raging at our ingratitude.

    Oliver Goldsmith (after visiting him at Chichester), *Polite Literature of Europe.*

He is the only one of the minor poets of whom, if he had lived, it cannot be said that he might not have done the greatest things. The germ is there. He is sometimes affected, unmeaning, and obscure; but he also catches rich glimpses of the bowers of Paradise,

and has lofty aspirations after the highest seats of the Muses. With a great deal of tinsel and splendid patchwork, he has not been able to hide the solid sterling ore of genius.

    William Hazlitt, *Lectures on the English Poets.*

He had employed his mind chiefly upon works of fiction and subjects of fancy, and by indulging some peculiar habits of thought was eminently delighted with those flights of imagination which pass the bounds of nature, and to which the mind is reconciled only by a passive acquiescence in popular traditions. He loved fairies, genii, giants and monsters; he delighted to rove through the meanders of inchantment, gaze on the magnificence of golden palaces, to repose by the waterfalls of Elysian gardens.

    Samuel Johnson, *Lives of the Poets.*

See also William Cowper

COLLINS, (WILLIAM) WILKIE

1824—89 Novelist

I have been writing novels for the last five and thirty years, and I have been regularly in the habit of relieving the weariness which follows on the work of the brain ... by champagne at one time and old brandy (cognac) at another. If I live until January next, I shall be sixty-six years old, and I am writing another work of fiction. There is my experience.

    On himself, Letter to a correspondent enquiring about his use of stimulants, 20 May 1889.

I cannot tell you with what a strange dash of pride as well as pleasure I read the great results of your hard work. Because, as you know, I was certain from the *Basil* days that you were the Writer who would come ahead of all the Field — being the only one who combined invention and power, both humorous and pathetic, with that invincible determination to work, and that profound conviction that nothing of worth is to be done without work, of which triflers and feigners have no conception.

    Charles Dickens, Letter to Wilkie Collins, 20 September 1862.

The greatest novels have something in them which will ensure their being read, at least by a small number of people, even if the novel, as a literary form, ceases to be written. It is not pretended that the novels of Wilkie Collins have this permanence. They are interesting only if we enjoy 'reading novels'. But novels are still being written; and there is no contemporary novelist who could not learn something from Collins in the art of interesting and exciting the reader. So long as novels are written, the possibilities of melodrama must from time to time be re-explored. The contemporary 'thriller' is in danger of becoming stereotyped. . . . The resources of Wilkie Collins are, in comparison, inexhaustible.

T. S. Eliot, *Wilkie Collins and Dickens.*

He was soft, plump, and pale, suffered from various ailments, his liver was wrong, his heart weak, his lungs faint, his stomach incompetent, he ate too much and the wrong things. He had a big head, a dingy complexion, was somewhat bald, and his full beard was of a light brown colour. His air was of mild discomfort and fractiousness; he had a queer way of holding his hand, which was small, plump, and unclean, hanging up by the wrist, like a rabbit on its hind legs. He had strong opinions and prejudices, but his nature was obviously kind and lovable, and a humorous vein would occasionally be manifest. One felt he was unfortunate and needed succour.

Julian Hawthorne, *Shapes that Pass.*

To Mr Collins belongs the credit of having introduced into fiction those most mysterious of mysteries, the mysteries which are at our own doors. This innovation gave a new impetus to the literature of horrors. It was fatal to the authority of Mrs Radcliffe and her everlasting castle in the Apennines. What are the Apennines to us, or we to the Apennines? . . . Mrs Radcliffe's mysteries were romances pure and simple; while those of Mr Wilkie Collins were stern reality.

Henry James, in *Nation*, 9 November 1865.

What brought good Wilkie's genius nigh perdition?
Some demon whispered – 'Wilkie! have a mission.'
Algernon C. Swinburne, *Essay on Collins.*

Wilkie Collins seems so to construct his [novels] that he not only, before writing, plans everything on, down to the minutest detail, from the beginning to the end; but then plots it all back again, to see that there is no piece of necessary dove-tailing which does not dove-tail with absolute accuracy. The construction is most minute and most wonderful. But I can never lose the taste of the construction. . . . One is constrained by mysteries and hemmed in by difficulties, knowing, however, that the mysteries will be made clear, and the difficulties overcome at the end of the third volume. Such work gives me no pleasure.

Anthony Trollope, *Autobiography.*

COLTRANE, JOHN WILLIAM
1926–67 Musician

I think with John Coltrane's . . . albums . . . with the

general projection of Coltrane's charisma, many Black people who had previously been only marginally interested in Black music, in their own personal life style, and conditions in general, changed their life styles immensely. The reason for this rests in the tremendous spiritual reservoir which is found in Coltrane's music and that of his various disciples . . . Coltrane's music made us reevaluate ourselves, see ourselves more objectively, more clearly, and place ourselves in a position within society.

Charles Ellison, in Dominique-René De Lerma ed., *Reflections on Afro-American Music.*

COMPTON-BURNETT, DAME IVY
1884–1969 Novelist

I do not see why exposition and description are a necessary part of a novel. They are not of a play, and both deal with imaginary human beings and their lives. I have been told that I ought to write plays, but cannot see myself making the transition. I read plays with especial pleasure, and in reading novels I am disappointed if a scene is carried through in the voice of the author rather than the voices of the characters. I think that I simply follow my natural bent.

On herself, *Orion*, 1945.

There's not much to say. I haven't been at all deedy.
On herself (when asked about her life), in *The Times*, 30 August 1969.

To read almost any piece of Compton-Burnett's 'communal dialectics' is to experience a pleasure as intense as most available literary pleasures, and yet page after page . . . is marked by the triviality inseparable from fantasy. There are two things which decisively rescue Miss Compton-Burnett's work from this danger. One is her comic sense; the other a dyad composed of her hatred and her pity.

Kingsley Amis, *What Became of Jane Austen?*

[She] is almost entirely an auditory writer – the visible world is indicated, in her book, in the most perfunctory manner, the story is welded together entirely by means of dialogue, one has a sense of perpetually eavesdropping on her characters.

Jocelyn Brooke, *Elizabeth Bowen.*

To my sense, Miss Compton-Burnett is not exactly an artist. She is something less valuable but rarer – the inventor of a wholly original species of puzzle. It is probably the first invention of the kind since the crossword, which it far outdoes in imaginative depth. . . . Though her novels are not in themselves works of art, the rules of the puzzle are allusions to literary forms and conventions. Reading them is like playing some Monopoly for Intellectuals, in which you can buy, as well as houses and hotels, plaques to set up on them recording that a great writer once lived there.

Brigid Brophy, *Don't Never Forget*.

One of the mischievous originalities of Compton-Burnett is to have pursued this insular tendency to the extreme, making it her trademark. She produces Compton-Burnetts, as someone might produce ball-bearings . . . Hence the uniformity of labelling in her titles and the open-stock patterns of her incidents and dialogue. The author, like all reliable old firms, is stressing the *sameness* of the formula; senior service. She has no imitators. The formula is a trade secret.

Mary McCarthy, *The Writing on the Wall*.

She was looking formidably severe. I think she was severe. She saw life in the relentless terms of Greek tragedy, its cruelties, ironies — above all its passions — played out against a background of triviality and ennui.

Anthony Powell, in *Spectator*, 6 September 1969.

CONGREVE, WILLIAM

1670—1729 Dramatist

For my part I keep the Commandments, I love my neighbour as my selfe, and to avoid Coveting my neighbour's wife I desire to be coveted by her; which you know is quite another thing.

On himself, Letter to Mrs Edward Porter, Rotterdam, 27 September 1700.

When *Congreve* brim full of his Mistresses Charms,
    Who had likewise made bold with *Molier*
Came in piping hot from his *Bracegirdle*'s arms
    And would have it his title was clear,

Said *Apollo,* You did most discreetly to take
    A part that was easiest and best
Though the rules of Behaviour Distinction should
                                                    make
    And you'd not done amiss to chuse last.

But never pretend to be modest or Chast
    Th'*Old Batchelor* speaks you Obscene,
And *Love for Love* shews, notwithstanding your
                                                    hast,
    That your Thoughts are Impure and Unclean.

That meaning's lascivious your Dialogues bear
    Fit to grace the foul Language of *Stews*,
And tho' you are said to make a Wife of a Play'r

You in those make a Whore of your Muse.
    Anon., *The Tryal of Skill*, 1704.

The days of Comedy are gone, alas!
    When Congreve's fool could vie with Molière's
                                                    bête:
Society is smooth'd to that excess,
That manners hardly differ more than dress.
    Lord Byron, *Don Juan*, canto xiii.

The happy boldness in his finished toil
Smells more than Sh—r's Wit, or J—n's Oil.
    Samuel Cobb, *Poetae Britannici*, comparing
    Congreve with Shakespeare and Ben Jonson.

Wickedness is no subject for comedy. This was Congreve's great error, and almost peculiar to him. The Dramatis Personae, of Dryden, Wycherley, etc., are often *vicious*, obscene, etc., but not, like Congreve's wicked.

Samuel Taylor Coleridge, Note to Hartley Coleridge, *Northern Worthies: William Congreve*.

The charms of his conversation must have been very powerful, since nothing could console Henrietta Dutchess of Marlborough, for the loss of his company, so much as an automaton, or small statue of ivory, made exactly to resemble him, which every day was brought to table. A glass was put in the hand of the statue, which was supposed to bow to her grace and to nod in approbation of what she spoke to it.

Thomas Davies, *Dramatic Miscellanies*, 1784.

O that your Brows my Lawrel had sustain'd,
Well had I been Depos'd if You had Reign'd!
The Father had descended for the Son;
For only You are lineal to the Throne.
    John Dryden, Prologue, to Congreve's *Double Dealer*.

His Double Dealer is much censured by the greater part of the Town: and is defended only by the best Judges, who as you know, are commonly the fewest. Yet it gets ground daily, and has already been acted Eight times. The women thinke he has exposed their Bitchery too much; and the Gentlemen, are offended with him; for the discovery of their follyes: and the way of their Intrigues, under the notion of Friendship to their Ladyes Husbands.

John Dryden, Letter to William Walsh, December 1693.

Every page presents a shower of brilliant conceits, is a tissue of epigrams in prose, is a new triumph of wit, a new conquest over dullness. The fire of artificial raillery is nowhere else so well kept up. This style, which he was almost the first to introduce, and which he carried to the utmost pitch of classical refinement, reminds one exactly of Collins' description of wit as opposed to humour,

Whose jewels in his crisped hair
Are placed each other's light to share.
William Hazlitt, *Lectures on English Comic Writers.*

It is acknowledged with universal conviction, that the perusal of his works will make no man better; and that their ultimate effect is to represent pleasure in alliance with vice, and to relax those obligations by which life ought to be regulated.
Samuel Johnson, *Lives of the Poets.*

Congreve has merit of the highest kind; he is an original writer who borrowed neither the materials of his plot, nor the manner of his dialogue. Of his plays I cannot speak distinctly; for since I inspected them many years have passed; but what remains upon my memory is, that his characters are commonly fictitious and artificial, with very little of nature, and not much of life. He formed a peculiar idea of comick excellence, which he supposed to consist in gay remarks and unexpected answers; but that which he endeavoured, he seldom failed of performing. His scenes exhibit not much of humour, imagery, or passion, his personages are a kind of intellectual gladiators; every sentence is to ward or strike; the contest of smartness is never intermitted; his wit is a meteor playing to and fro with alternate coruscations. His comedies have therefore, in some degree, the operation of tragedies; they surprise rather than divert, and raise admiration oftener than merriment. But they are the works of a mind replete with images, and quick in combination.
Ibid.

No writers have injured the Comedy of England so deeply as Congreve and Sheridan. Both were men of splendid wit and polished taste. Unhappily they made all their characters in their own likeness. Their works bear the same relation to the legitimate drama which a transparency bears to a painting. There are no delicate touches, no hues imperceptibly fading into each other: the whole is lighted up with an universal glare. Outlines and tints are forgotten in the common blaze which illuminates all. The flowers and fruits of the intellect abound, but it is the abundance of a jungle, not of a garden, unwholesome, bewildering, unprofitable from its very plenty, rank from its very fragrance. Every fop, every boor, every valet, is a man of wit.
T. B. Macaulay, *Essays:* 'Machiavelli'.

Two kinds of ambition early took possession of his mind, and often pulled it in opposite directions. He was conscious of great fertility of thought and powers of ingenious combination. His lively conversation, his polished manners and his highly respectable connections, had obtained for him ready access to the best company. He longed to be a great writer. He longed to be a man of fashion. Either object was within his reach. But could he secure both? Was there not something vulgar in letters, something inconsistent with the easy apathetic graces of a man of the mode? . . . Could he forgo the renown of being the first wit of his age? Could he attain that renown without sullying what he valued quite as much, his character for gentility? The history of his life is the history of the conflict between these two impulses. In his youth, the desire of literary fame had the mastery; but soon the meaner ambition overpowered the higher, and obtained supreme dominion over his mind.
T. B. Macaulay, *ibid,* 'On the Comic Dramatists of the Restoration'.

Aye, Mr Tonson, he was Ultimus Romanorum!
Alexander Pope, in conversation with Jacob Tonson, November 1730.

The comedies of Congreve must be ranked among the most wonderful and glorious creations of the human mind, although it is quite conceivable that, in certain circumstances, and at a given moment, a whole bench of Bishops might be demoralised by their perusal.
Lytton Strachey, *Portraits in Miniature.*

For never did poetick mine before
Produce a richer vein or cleaner ore;
The bullion stamp'd in your refining mind
Serves by retail to furnish half mankind.
Jonathan Swift, *To Mr Congreve.*

Reading in these plays now, is like shutting your ears, and looking at people dancing. What does it mean? The measures, the grimaces, the bowing, shuffling and retreating, the cavaliers seuls advancing upon those ladies — those ladies and men twirling round at the end in a mad galop after which everybody bows, and the quaint rite is celebrated.
W. M. Thackeray, *The English Humourists.*

All this pretty morality you have in the comedies of William Congreve, Esquire, they are full of wit, such manners as he observes, he observes with great humour; but ah! it's a weary feast, that banquet of wit where no love is. It palls very soon; sad indigestions follow it, and lonely blank headaches in the mornings.
Ibid.

He writes as if he was so accustomed to conquer, that he has a poor opinion of his victims.
  Ibid.

The language is every where that of Men of Honour, but their Actions are those of Knaves; a proof that he was perfectly well acquainted with human Nature, and frequented what we call polite company.
  Voltaire, *Letters Concerning the English Nation,* no. 19, 1733.

See also Henry Fielding, John Kemble, Alexander Pope

CONKLING, ROSCOE

1829—88 Politician

He had not only the courage of his convictions, but, that rarer quality among public men, the courage of his contempt.
  Anon., in *New York World,* April 1888.

The contempt of that large-minded gentleman is so wilting, his haughty disdain, his grandiloquent swell, his majestic, super-eminent, over-powering turkey-gobbler strut has been so crushing to myself and all the men of this House, that I know it was an act of the greatest temerity for me to venture upon a controversy with him.
  James G. Blaine, in David Barr Chidsey, *The Gentleman from New York — A Life of Roscoe Conkling.*

Vain as a peacock, and a czar in arrogance.
  Matthew P. Breen, *Thirty Years of New York Politics.*

. . . a cold, selfish man, who had no right to live except to prey upon his fellow men.
  Clarence Darrow, in D. M. Jordan, *Roscoe Conkling of New York: A Voice in the Senate.*

Roscoe Conkling was created by nature for a great career, [that he missed it] was entirely his own fault. Physically he was the handsomest man of his time. His mental equipment nearly approached genius. He was industrious to a degree. His oratorical gifts were of the highest order, and he was a debater of rare power and resources. But his intolerable egotism deprived him of vision for supreme leadership . . . he made no lasting impression on the country. The reason was that his wonderful gifts were wholly devoted to partisan discussions and local issues.
  Chauncey Depew, in *ibid.*

Conkling is very strong, a great fighter, inspired more by his hates than his loves; desires and has followers rather than friends. He will be of more service in a minority than in a majority. In his long service he has done little constructive work.
  James A. Garfield, in David Barr Chidsey, *The Gentleman from New York — A Life of Roscoe Conkling.*

Conkling, after ten years of absolute despotism in New York . . . got the elephantiasis of conceit . . . a plain, old-fashioned case of sore-head.
  Ibid.

His ability is that of an ardent, indefatigable stump speaker and party manager. Indeed, the stump has in our time produced no such fustian as he pours from it.
  To politics, in any good sense of the word, Mr. Conkling has not contributed a single or fruitful idea; he is not the author of a single measure of value or importance; he has made no speech which any sensible man can bear to read — so that his political claims to the chief place on the bench of the greatest tribunal in the world are as paltry as his political ones.
  E. L. Godkin, on Roscoe Conkling as a candidate for the Supreme Court, 1873, in D. M. Jordan, *Roscoe Conkling of New York; A Voice in the Senate.*

I regard him as the greatest mind in public life or that has been in public life since the beginning of government.
  Ulysses S. Grant, in *Nation,* 7 October 1880.

. . . could look hyacinthine in just thirty seconds after the appearance of a woman.
  Horace Greeley, in *New York Tribune,* May 1871, in David Barr Chidsey, *The Gentleman from New York — A Life of Roscoe Conkling.*

. . . the pet of the Petticoats . . . the darling of the ladies gallery.
  Ibid.

No one can approach him. If anybody can approach him, without being conscious that there is something great about Conkling, Conkling himself is conscious of it. He walks in a nimbus of it. If Moses' name had been Conkling when he descended from the Mount, and the Jews had asked him what he saw there, he would have promptly replied, 'Conkling.'
  Ibid.

Conkling was then one of the handsomest men I ever met. He was over six feet tall, of slender build

CONNOLLY, CYRIL

and stood straight as an arrow. His hair was just
turning gray. A curl, described as Hyperion, rolled
over his forehead. An imperial added much to the
beauty of his Apollo-like appearance. His noble
figure, flashing eye and majestic voice made one
forget that he was somewhat foppish in his dress.
> T. C. Platt, *Autobiography.*

For I do not remember how many years, Mr.
Conkling was the supreme ruler of this State; the
Governor did not count, the legislatures did not
count; comptrollers and secretaries of State, and
what-not did not count. It was what Mr. Conkling
said.
> Elihu Root, in D. M. Jordan, *Roscoe Conkling
> of New York: A Voice in the Senate.*

. . . [like] one of those genii in the Arabian Nights,
who when the cork was taken out of the bottle rose
out, away to the clouds, to the utter amazement
and astonishment of all beholders.
> Allen Thurman, 6 June 1879, *Congressional
> Record, 46th Congress, 1st Session.*

Too proud to be corrupt.
> Senator Vest, in David Barr Chidsey, *The
> Gentleman from New York — A Life of Roscoe
> Conkling.*

. . . vigorous and vain, an egotistical coxcomb . . .
who would, at any time, sacrifice the right to benefit
his party.
> Gideon Welles, Diary.

See also Rutherford B. Hayes

CONNOLLY, CYRIL VERNON

1903—75 Author, Critic

I came to America tourist Third with a cheque for
ten pounds and I leave plus five hundred, a wife, a
mandarin coat, a set of diamond studs, a state room
and bath, and a decent box for the ferret. That's
what everybody comes to America to do and I
don't think I've managed badly for a beginner.
> On himself, Letter to Noel Blakiston, 2 April
> 1930.

I have just finished reading *Enemies of Promise.* . . .
More than [T.S.] Eliot or [Edmund] Wilson you
really write about writing in the only way which is
interesting to anyone except academics, as a real
occupation like banking or fucking with all its
attendant egotism, boredom, excitement and terror.
> W. H. Auden, Letter to Cyril Connolly,
> 15 November 1938.

190

He was easily moved to tears, sometimes for deep
and genuine reasons, sometimes for trivial ones —
the tears of a spoiled child of civilisation. At a
restaurant dinner given on some fairly grim PEN
Club Conference occasion, he was sitting opposite
me and I noticed the tears start in his eyes and then
trickle down each cheek. Suddenly he got up from
the table, came over to me, and insisted on our
changing places. Intense boredom with the conversation of the lady journalist on his left had
driven him to this extreme course of action.
> Stephen Spender, in *Times Literary Supplement,*
> 6 December 1974.

Horizon has been a fine magazine and Mr Connolly
an exceptional editor. It seemed to me a proof of his
merit, when I was in London at the end of the war,
that, in the literary and Left political worlds, almost
everybody complained about him and it, but that
everybody, at the same time, seemed in some degree
dependent on them.
> Edmund Wilson, *Classics and Commercials.*

CONRAD, JOSEPH (JÒZEF KORZENIOWSKI)

1857—1924 Novelist

My style may be atrocious — but it produces its
effect — is as unalterable as . . . the size of my feet
— and I will never disguise it in the boots of Wells's
(or anybody else's) making . . . I shall make my own
boots or perish.
> On himself, Letter to Fisher Unwin, 28 May
> 1896.

Let me ask, is my earnestness of no account? Is that
a Slavonic trait? And I am earnest, terribly earnest.
Carlyle bending over the history of Frederick called
the Great was a mere trifle, a volatile butterfly, in
comparison. For that good man had only to translate himself out of bad German into the English we
know, whereas I had to work like a coal miner in his
pit quarrying all my English sentences out of a black
night.
> On himself, Letter to Edward Garnett, 28 August
> 1908.

We could pardon his cheerless themes were it not for
the imperturbable solemnity with which he piles the
unnecessary on the commonplace.
> Anon., in *Literature*, 30 April 1898.

In appearance Mr Conrad suggests the seaman. His
figure is stalwart and short, his dark beard well
trimmed, and his walk nautical. Meet him near the
docks and one would write him down 'ship's captain'
without hesitation. But his eyes, curiously distinctive
and striking, mark him out from his kind. Ship

captain he may be, but his eyes proclaim him an artist.

Anon., in *Academy*, 20 February 1904.

I have just read his new book *The Nigger of the 'Narcissus'*, which has moved me to enthusiasm. Where did the man pick up that style, & that *synthetic* way of gathering up a general impression & flinging it at you? Not only his style, but his attitude, affected me deeply. He is so consciously an artist.

Arnold Bennett, Letter to H. G. Wells, 8 December 1897.

He was the most consummate, the most engrossed, the most practical, the most common-sensible and the most absolutely passionate man-of-action become conscious man-of-letters that this writer has ever known, read of or conceived of.

Ford Madox Ford, *The March of Literature*.

The politeness of Conrad to [Henry] James and of James to Conrad were of the most impressive kind. Even if they had been addressing each other from the tribunal of the Académie Française their phrases could not have been more elaborate or delivered more *ore rotundo*. James always addressed Conrad as '*Mon cher confrère*', Conrad almost bleated with the peculiar tone that the Marseillais get into their compliments '*Mon cher maître*' . . . every thirty seconds. When James spoke of me to Conrad he always said: '*Votre ami, le jeune homme modeste.*' They always spoke French together, James using an admirably pronounced, correct, and rather stilted idiom such as prevailed in Paris in the seventies. Conrad spoke with extraordinary speed, fluency, and incomprehensibility, a meridional French with as strong a Southern accent as that of garlic in *aioli*. . . . Speaking English he had so strong a French accent that few who did not know him well could understand him at first.

Ford Madox Ford, *Return to Yesterday*.

Conrad spent a day finding the *mot juste*; then killed it.

Ford Madox Ford, in Robert Lowell, *Notebook*.

What is so elusive about him is that he is always promising to make some general philosophic statement about the universe, and then refraining with a gruff disclaimer. . . . He is misty in the middle as well as at the edges . . . the secret casket of his genius contains a vapour rather than a jewel . . . we need not try to write him down philosophically, because there is, in this particular direction, nothing to write. No creed, in fact. Only opinions, and the right to throw them overboard when facts make them look absurd.

E. M. Forster, *Abinger Harvest*.

Read Conrad's new book. He is the strongest writer — in every sense of the word — at present publishing in English. Marvellous writing! The other men are mere scribblers in comparison. That a foreigner should write like this, is one of the miracles of literature.

George Gissing, Letter to Miss Collet, 24 December 1902.

It is agreed by most of the people I know that Conrad is a bad writer, just as it is agreed that T. S. Eliot is a good writer. If I knew that by grinding Mr Eliot into a fine dry powder and sprinkling that powder on Mr Conrad's grave, Mr Conrad would shortly appear, looking very annoyed at the forced return and commence writing, I would leave for London early tomorrow morning with a sausage grinder.

Ernest Hemingway, *Transatlantic Review*, 1924.

I read you as I listen to rare music — with deepest depths of surrender, and out of those depths I emerge slowly and reluctantly again to acknowledge that I return to life.

Henry James, Letter to Conrad, 1 November 1906.

Why this giving in before you start, that pervades all Conrad and such folks — the Writers among the Ruins. I can't forgive Conrad for being so sad and giving in.

D. H. Lawrence, Letter to Edward Garnett, 30 October 1912.

At present Conrad is out of fashion, ostensibly because of his florid style and redundant adjectives (for my part I like a florid style: if your motto is 'Cut out the adjectives', why not go a bit further and revert to a system of grunts and squeals, like the animals?), but actually, I suspect, because he was a gentleman, a type hated by the modern intelligentsia. He is pretty certain to come back into favour. One of the surest signs of his genius is that women dislike his books.

George Orwell, in *New English Weekly*, 23 July 1936.

He was very conscious of the various forms of passionate madness to which men are prone, and it was this that gave him such a profound belief in the importance of discipline. His point of view, one might perhaps say, was the antithesis of Rousseau's: 'Man is born in chains, but he can become free.' He becomes free, so I believe Conrad would have said, not by letting loose his impulses, not by being casual and uncontrolled, but by subduing wayward impulse to a dominant purpose.

Bertrand Russell, *Autobiography*.

I felt ... that he thought of civilized and morally tolerable human life as a dangerous walk on a thin crust of barely cooled lava which at any moment might break and let the unwary sink into fiery depths.
  Bertrand Russell, in Norman Sherry, *Conrad and his World.*

Mr Conrad is wordy; his story is not so much told as seen intermittently through a haze of sentences. His style is like river-mist; for a space things are seen clearly, and then comes a great grey bank of printed matter, page on page, creeping round the reader, swallowing him up. You stumble, you protest, you blunder on, for the drama you saw so cursorily has hold of you; you cannot escape until you have seen it out. You read fast, you run and jump, only to bring yourself to the knees in such mud as will presently be quoted. Then suddenly things loom up again, and in a moment become real, intense, swift.
  H. G. Wells, review of *An Outcast of the Islands,* in *Saturday Review,* 16 May 1896.

One could always baffle Conrad by saying 'humour'. It was one of our damned English tricks he had never learned to tackle.
  H. G. Wells, in Arthur Mizener, *Ford Madox Ford.*

See also Ford Madox Ford, D. H. Lawrence, James Thurber

CONSTABLE, JOHN

1776—1837 Painter

I never saw an ugly thing in my life; for let the form of an object be what it may — light, shade, and perspective will always make it beautiful.
  On himself, in Charles R. Leslie, *The Life of John Constable.*

I should paint my own places best; painting is with me but another word for feeling, and I associate 'my careless boyhood' with all that lies on the banks of the Stour. Those scenes made me a painter, and I am grateful.
  On himself, Letter to John Fisher, 23 October 1821.

We have found out Mr. Constable's secret, he is a Cornelius Ketel; see Hardung's excellent catalogue of portraits, No. 153: 'Ketel took it into his head to lay aside his brushes and to paint with his fingers only; and at length, finding these tools too easy, undertook to paint with his toes.' We rather suspect that Turner is sometimes a little inclined to this fail-

ing, but never so perfectly *in toto* as Mr. Constable this year.
  Anon., in *Morning Chronicle,* 1831.

Where real business is to be done, you are the most energetic and punctual of men. In smaller matters, such as putting on your breeches, you are apt to lose time in deciding which leg shall go in first.
  John Fisher, Letter to Constable, 3 July 1823.

I like de landscapes of Constable; he is always picturesque, of a fine colour, and de lights always in de right places; but he makes me call for my great coat and umbrella.
  Henry Fuseli, in Charles R. Leslie, *The Life of John Constable.*

He possessed that innate, and only real gentility, of which the test is conduct towards inferiors and strangers; he was a gentleman to the poorest of his species, a gentleman in a stage-coach, nay, more, a gentleman at a stage-coach Inn dinner.
  Charles R. Leslie, *ibid.*

Whether he portray the solemn burst of the approaching tempest — the breezy freshness of morning — or the still deepness of a summer noon — every object represented, from the grandest masses to the smallest plant or spray, seems instinct with, as it were, and breathing the very spirit of the scene. His figures, too, seem naturally called forth by, and form part of, the landscape; we never ask whether they are well placed — there they are, and unless they choose to move on, there they must remain. His quiet lanes and covert nooks serve to introduce a romantic or sentimental episode to divide, not heighten, the interest; all is made subservient to the one object in view, the embodying of a pure apprehension of natural effect.
  W. Purton, in Charles R. Leslie, *The Life of John Constable.*

Unteachableness seems to have been a main feature of his character, and there is corresponding want of veneration in the way he approaches nature herself. His early education and associations were also against him: they induced in him a morbid preference of subjects of a lower order.
  John Ruskin, *Modern Painters.*

COOK, JAMES

1728—79 Navigator, Explorer

... a plain, sensible man with an uncommon attention to veracity. Sir John gave me an instance. It was supposed that Cook had said he had seen a nation of men like monkeys and Lord Monboddo had been very happy with this. Sir John happened to tell Cook of this. 'No,' he said, 'I did not say they were like monkeys, I said their faces put me in mind of monkeys.' There was a distinction very fine, but sufficiently perceptible . . . . He seemed to have no desire to make people stare, and being a man of steady moral principles, as I thought, did not try to make theories out of what he had seen to confound virtue and vice.

    James Boswell, in Alan Moorehead, *The Fatal Impact*.

When Cook — lamented, and with tears as just
As ever mingled with heroic dust —
Steer'd Britain's oak into a world unknown,
And in his country's glory sought his own,
Wherever he found man, to nature true,
The rights of man were sacred in his view.
He sooth'd with gifts, and greeted with a smile,
The simple native of the new-found isle;
He spurn'd the wretch that slighted or withstood
The tender argument of kindred blood,
Nor would endure that any should controul
His free-born brethren of the southern pole.

    William Cowper, *Charity*.

He takes people as he finds them, and he is deeply interested in them. He possesses that fundamental curiosity of the real explorer who does not necessarily want to arrive at some goal but who is driven on and on, always eager to see the other side of the next hill, and only infinity is the end.

    Alan Moorehead, *The Fatal Impact*.

Had those advent'rous spirits, who explore
Through ocean's trackless wastes, the far-sought
                         shore,
Whether of wealth insatiate, or of power
Conquerors who waste, or ruffians who devour:
Had these possess'd, O Cook! thy gentle mind,
Thy love of arts, thy love of humankind;
Had these pursued thy mild and liberal plan,
Discoveries had not been a curse to man!
Then, bless'd Philanthropy! thy social hands
Had link'd dissever'd worlds in brothers' bands;
Careless, if colour, or if clime divide;
Then lov'd, and loving, man had liv'd, and died.

    Hannah More, in Andrew Kippis, *Cook's Voyages*.

The story of his life does not lend itself to exploitation by cheap biographers. He was not a 'great lover', he was a great worker; there was nothing scandalous or equivocal or cheaply sensational in his career; and nobody ever made fewer mistakes.

    William Plomer, in Bonamy Dobree ed., *Anne to Victoria*.

COOK, THOMAS

1808—92 Travel Agent

It seems that some enterprising and unscrupulous man has devised the project of conducting some forty or fifty persons, irrespective of age and sex, from London to Naples and back for a fixed sum.

    Charles Lever, article *circa* 1886, in Edmund Swinglehurst, *The Romantic Journey*.

. . . The excursion monger.

    Alfred Munby, Diary, July 1861.

COOLIDGE, (JOHN) CALVIN

1872—1933 Thirtieth United States President

Perhaps one of the most important accomplishments of my administration has been minding my own business.

    On himself, at a news conference, 1 March 1929.

I think the American people wants a solemn ass as a President. And I think I'll go along with them.

    On himself, to Ethel Barrymore, reported in *Time*, 16 May 1955.

I have noticed that nothing I never said ever did me any harm.

    On himself, *Congressional Record*.

[He had] not an international hair on his head.

    Anon., in Marcus Cunliffe, *American Presidents and the Presidency*.

[He had] the mentality of a small town Rotarian.

    Anon., *The Socialist Call*, 1923.

He's not brilliant but he's safe.

    Anon., common saying when Coolidge was Governor of Massachusetts, in C. M. Fuess, *Calvin Coolidge*.

He is not impatient with mediocrity and is understood by mediocrity.

    Alfred Pearce Dennis, *The Man Who Became President*, in Edward C. Lathem ed., *Meet Mr. Coolidge*.

It is said of Von Moltke that he could be silent in seven languages. Calvin Coolidge, as I knew him, could at least be silent in one. Fundamentally, his quality of silence was only another phase of his instinct for frugality. The logic is clear enough; a man who is naturally frugal in expenditure, whether for dress, food or amusement, will be frugal in the expenditure of speech.

    Ibid.

COOLING, RICHARD

His name was Calvin
What could you expect
From one whose namesake
Was of God's elect
    Kensal Green (Colin Hurry), *Premature Epitaphs.*

When an excited man rushed up to Wilson Mizner
and said, 'Coolidge is dead,' Mizner asked, 'How do
they know?'
    Alva Johnston, *The Legendary Mizners*; also
    attributed to Dorothy Parker.

He laughed until you could hear a pin drop.
    Ring Lardner, in Robert E. Drennan ed., *Wit's
    End.*

Surely no one will write of these years since August,
1923, that an aggressive President altered the destiny
of the Republic. Yet it is an important fact that no
one will write of these same years that the Republic
wished its destiny to be altered.
    Walter Lippmann, in Edward C. Lathem ed.,
    Meet Calvin Coolidge.

Mr. Coolidge's genius for inactivity is developed to a
very high point. It is far from being an indolent
activity. It is a grim, determined alert inactivity
which keeps Mr. Coolidge occupied constantly . . . .
Inactivity is a political philosophy and a party program with Mr. Coolidge.
    Walter Lippmann, *Men of Destiny.*

Though I yield to no one in my admiration for Mr.
Coolidge, I do wish he did not look as if he had been
weaned on a pickle.
    Alice Roosevelt Longworth, Attributed, in
    *Crowded Hours — Reminiscences of Alice
    Roosevelt Longworth.*

He slept more than any other President, whether by
day or night. Nero fiddled, but Coolidge only snored.
When the crash came at last and Hoover began to
smoke and bubble, good Cal was safe in Northampton, and still in the hay.
    H. L. Mencken, in *American Mercury*, April 1933.

There were no thrills while he reigned, but neither
were there any headaches. He had no ideas but he
was not a nuisance.
    H. L. Mencken, in Ishbel Ross, *Grace Coolidge
    and her Era.*

'You must talk to me, Mr. Coolidge, I made a bet
today that I could get more than two words out of
you.'
    'You lose,' said the Vice-President with a poker
face, and let it go at that.
    Ishbel Ross, in *ibid.*

He has lived and will die, no matter where fate sends
him, Cal Coolidge, of Northampton, of Ludlow and
of Plymouth, the small-town American who is more
typical of America than our cosmopolitan boulevardier. No boulevardier — Calvin Coolidge. One flag,
one country, one conscience, one wife, and never
more than three words will do him all his life.
    William Allen White, in *ibid.*

. . . this runty, aloof, little man, who quacks through
his nose when he speaks.
    William Allen White, in C. M. Fuess, *Calvin
    Coolidge.*

. . . the slit-mouthed Puritan.
    Art Young, in William Allen White, *A Puritan in
    Babylon.*

COOLING, RICHARD

— d. 1697 Civil Servant

Mr Cooling, my Lord Chamberlain's secretary . . .
proved very drunk, and did talk, and would have
talked all night with us, I not being able to break
loose from him, he holding me by the hand. . . . Thus
he went on, and speaking then of my Lord Sandwich,
whom he professed to love exceedingly, says Cooling, 'I know not what, but he is a man methinks that
I could love for himself, without other regards; and
by your favour,' says he, 'by God there is nothing to
be beloved *propter se* but a cunt.' And so he talked
very lewdly. And then took notice of my kindness
to him on shipboard seven years ago, when the King
was coming over, and how much he was obliged to
me; but says, 'Pray look upon this acknowledgement
of a kindness in me to be a miracle; for,' says he, 'it
is against the law at Court for a man that borrows
money of me, even to but his place with, to own it
the next Sunday.' And then told us his horse was a
Bribe, and his boots a bribe; and told us he was made
up of bribes, as an Oxford scholar is set out with
men's goods when he goes out of town, and that he
makes every sort of tradesman to bribe him; and invited me home to his house, to taste of his bribe-wine.
I never heard so much vanity from a man in my life.
    Samuel Pepys, Diary, 30 July 1667.

COOPER, ANTHONY ASHLEY, see under
SHAFTESBURY, FIRST AND SEVENTH EARLS

COOPER, GARY (FRANK JAMES)

1901–61 Actor

That fellow is the world's greatest actor. He can do

194

with no effort what the rest of us spent years trying to learn; to be perfectly natural.

John Barrymore, in Jane Mercer, *Great Lovers of the Movies*.

Every line in his face spelled honesty. So innate was his integrity he could be cast in phony parts, but never look phony himself.

Tall, gaunt as Lincoln, cast in the frontier mold of Daniel Boone, Sam Houston, Kit Carson, this silent Montana cowpuncher embodied the true-blue virtues that won the West; durability, honesty, and native intelligence.

Frank Capra, *The Name Above the Title*.

Gary is an embodiment of the old saying that art consists in concealing its own artfulness. After seeing him on the screen, any young man might say, 'Shucks, I could do that.' The young man would be wrong.

Cecil B. De Mille, *Autobiography*.

More people can be found with a knowledge of the likes and dislikes of Mr. Gary Cooper than with the simplest idea of the main precepts of, say, Jesus Christ.

Otis Ferguson, *The Film Criticism of Otis Ferguson*.

For film producer Arthur Jacobs, and many others, Gary Cooper 'was the greatest film star there has ever been'. He personified the quiet American. This tall, handsome, soft-spoken hero, slow to anger but lethal when roused, driven by an unshakeable honesty and determination to do the right thing, seemed to grow directly from Cooper's own personality . . . .

Cooper was totally a creation of the movies. A film-star long before he became a true actor, he never appeared on the legitimate stage. . . . He deliberately set narrow limits on the exercise of his art and had an intuitive sense of what was right for him. He knew that his tremendous popularity sprang from his simple, natural screen personality and saw himself as the prototype 'Mr. Average Joe American. Just an average guy from the middle of America'.

Jane Mercer, *Great Lovers of the Movies*.

The silent stars move silently, especially Gary Cooper, who came from the Great Open Spaces where men *were* silent.

Adela Rogers St Johns, *The Honeycomb*.

Gable made them squirm in the movies next to their wives or their Saturday night dates. With his handsome face, confident manner and lightning wit, he made every little man feel inferior. But Cooper. Coop was one of them. He was taciturn and gangly. He was dusty and rumpled. And he said 'Yup'. But he

was not one to be messed with. He was one of the fastest draws in the great outdoors. He was an expert horseman and knew how to use his dukes, too. He gave the ineloquent little guy comfort and assurance as he left that dark world of make-believe. Cooper, himself, was not unaware of his image. He knew that 'identification' was his touchstone. Once asked to give his reason for success, Cooper replied 'Mostly, I think it's because I look like the guy down the street'. He told many interviewers 'I'm just an ordinary Joe who became a movie star'.

David Zinman, *Fifty Classic Motion Pictures*.

See also Cecil B. De Mille, Alan Ladd

COOPER, JAMES FENIMORE
1789—1851 Author

Cooper is the fighting Quaker of American literature.
Henry Seidel Canby, *Classic Americans*.

His Americanism was a raging lifelong combat which engendered such heat that his books are hot with the fire and clogged with the ashes of the conflagration.
Ibid.

At the bar of heaven Cooper would have answered: first, I am gentleman, next, I was a sailor, third, I am a patriot, and fourth, and with some derogation, I am a maker of light literature.
Ibid.

Fenimore Cooper has probably done more than any writer to present the Red Man to the White Man.
D. H. Lawrence, *Studies in Classic American Literature*.

. . . Cooper is responsible for the fathering of those aboriginal heroes, lovers, and sages, who have long formed a petty nuisance in our literature.
Francis Parkman, in George P. Winston, *John Fiske*.

Fenimore Cooper was the barometer of a gusty generation, sensitive to every storm on the far horizon. No other observer of that changing generation suffered so keenly in mind and conscience from the loosening of ancient ties, and none labored so hard to keep his countrymen to the strait path of an old-fashioned rectitude.
Vernon Louis Parrington, *Main Currents in American Thought*, vol. 2.

Testy, opinionated, tactless, forever lugging in disagreeable truths by the ears, he said many wise things so blunderingly as to make truth doubly offensive,

COPLEY, JOHN SINGLETON

and he hewed at his art so awkwardly as well-nigh to destroy the beauty of his romance.
Ibid.

A Yankee American to the verge of phobia, and yet he is not a democrat — he abominates the mob. An aristocrat to his fingertips, and yet he is a republican — he will knock you down if you tread not softly about the constitution.
Fred Lewis Pattee, in *American Mercury*, March 1925.

Like all badly educated people he confounded flowery and inflated circumlocution with beauty of style. His taste to the last was sophomoric.
Ibid.

In one place in *Deerslayer*, and in the restricted space of two thirds of a page, Cooper has scored 114 offenses against literary art out of a possible 115. It breaks the record.
Mark Twain, *Fenimore Cooper's Literary Offenses*, in Edmund Wilson ed., *The Shock of Recognition.*

If Cooper had any real knowledge of Nature's ways of doing things, he had a most delicate art in concealing the fact.
Ibid.

In his little box of stage properties he kept six or eight cunning devices, tricks and artifices for his savages and woodsmen to deceive and circumvent each other with, and he was never so happy as when he was working these innocent things and seeing them go.
Ibid.

Everytime a Cooper person is in peril, and absolute silence is worth four dollars a minute, he is sure to step on a dry twig. There may be a hundred handier things to step on, but that wouldn't satisfy Cooper. Cooper requires him to turn out and find a dry twig; and if he can't do it, go and borrow one. In fact, the Leatherstocking series ought to have been called the Broken Twig Series.
Ibid.

See also John Pope

COPLEY, JOHN SINGLETON

1738—1815 Artist

. . . poor America! I hope the best but I fear the worst. Yet certain I am She will finally Imerge from her present Callamity and become a Mighty Empire, and it is a pleasing reflection that I shall stand amongst the first of the Artists that shall have led the Country to the knowledge and cultivation of the fine Arts, happy in the pleasing reflection that they will one Day shine with a luster not inferior to what they have done in Greece or Rome in my Native Country.
On himself, Letter to Henry Pelham, in Jules David Prown, *John Singleton Copley.*

Copley remains a trifle hard and rigid; here and there his surfaces are more like carving than painting. As for suggestiveness, he rendered perfectly and exhaustively all that he saw, and he saw nothing that he could not render. He was definite, as we say; but that adventurous vision of the indefinite which has brushed with its wings all the very greatest works of art is never reflected here.
Henry James, 'Duveneck and Copley', in *Nation*, September 1875.

I visited Mr. Copley a few days since. He is very old and infirm. I think his age is upward of seventy, nearly the age of Mr. [Benjamin] West. His powers of mind have almost entirely left him; his late paintings are miserable; it is really a lamentable thing that a man should outlive his faculties.
Samuel F. B. Morse, Letter of 17 September 1811, in *Nation*.

COPLEY, JOHN SINGLETON, THE YOUNGER, see under LORD LYNDHURST

COPPE, ABIEZER

1619—72 Ranter

First all my strength my forces were utterly routed, my house I dwelt in fired, my father and mother forsook me, the wife of my bosome loathed me, mine old name was rotted perished; and I was utterly plagued consumed, dammed rammed and sunk into nothing, into the bowels of the still eternity (my mother's wombe) out of which I came naked and whereto I returned again naked. And lying a while there, rapt up in silence, at length (the body's outward forme being awake all this while) I heard with my outward ear, (to my apprehension) a most terrible thunderclap, and after that a second. And upon the second thunderclap, which was exceeding terrible, I saw a great body of light, like the light of the sun, and red as fire, in the forme of a drum (as it were) whereupon with exceeding trembling and amazement on the flesh, and with joy unspeakable in the spirit, I clapt my hands and cryed out, Amen halelujah, halelujah amen. And so lay trembling sweating and smoking (for the space of half an howre) at length with a loud voice I (inwardly) cried out, Lord what wilt thou do with me: my most excellent majesty and eternall glory (in me) answered and said, Fear not, I will take thee up into my everlasting kingdom. But thou shalt (first) drink a bitter cup, a bitter cup, a bitter cup; whereupon (being filled with exceeding amazement) I was thrown into the belly of hell (and take what you can of it in these expressions, though the matter is beyond expression), I was among all the devils in hell, even in their most hideous crew. And under all this terror and amazement there was a little spark of transcendent, unspeakable glory, which survived, and sustained itself, triumphing, exulting and exalting itself above the fiends.

On himself, Preface to *The Fiery Flying Roll*.

... The arrogant and wild deportment of Mr Copp the great Ranter, who made the Fiery Roll, who being brought before the Committee of Examinations, refused to be uncovered, and disguised himself into a madness, flinging apples and pears about the room, whereupon the Committee returned him to Newgate whence he came.

Weekly Intelligencer, 1–8 October 1649.

CORNELL, KATHARINE

1893–1974 Actress

The great ones have a little something extra. To love of the theatre, to intelligence and willingness to work, they bring a personal incandescence that cannot be acquired or imitated. Katharine Cornell was one of these. Something psychological happened when she made an entrance. Audiences could not be indifferent to her presence. Although she was not pretty, she was beautiful — dark eyes, dark hair, a somber, patient voice, and a slightly withdrawn personality. It was as if she could not quite let go. There was about her, some strange foreboding that was not deliberate but was inherent in her personality and suggested inner resources of understanding and passion that could not be entirely liberated on the stage. She was not spectacular, she was electric.

Brooks Atkinson, *Broadway*.

The last lady of the American theatre (as I sometimes think of her). . . .

Kenneth Tynan, 'Genius Without Portfolio: Orson Welles', in *Show*, November 1961.

CORNWALLIS, CHARLES, MARQUIS

1738–1805 Soldier

Hail, great destroyer (equall'd yet by none)
Of countries not thy master's, nor thine own;
Hatch'd by some demon on a stormy day,
Satan's best substitute to burn and slay . . .
Unnumber'd ghosts, from earth untimely sped,
Can take no rest till you, like them, are dead —
Then die, my Lord; that only chance remains
To wash away dishonourable stains,
For small advantage would your capture bring,
The plundering servant of a bankrupt king.

Philip Freneau, *To Lord Cornwallis*.

Tir'd with long acting on this bloody stage,
Sick of the follies of a wrangling age,
Come with your fleet and help me to retire
To Britain's coast, the land of my desire —
For me the foe their certain captive deem,
And every schoolboy takes me for his theme —
Long, much too long in this hard service try'd,
Bespatter'd still, be-devil'd and bely'd;
With the first chance that favouring fortune sends
I'll fly, converted, from this land of fiends:
Convinc'd, for me, she has no gems in store,
Nor leaves one triumph even to hope for more.

Philip Freneau, *Epistle from Lord Cornwallis to Sir Henry Clinton*.

His mind was of a character not uncommon. It was entirely passive; the impressions it received from without remained undisturbed by any process from within. . . . The mental constitution of the Marquess Cornwallis might be described in few words as being of the highest order of the commonplace.

Edward Thornton, *History of the British Empire in India*, vol. 4.

CORVO, BARON (FREDERICK ROLFE)

1860–1913 Novelist

Rolfe's vice was spiritual more than it was carnal: it might be said that he was a pander and a swindler, because he cared for nothing but his faith. He would be a priest or nothing, so nothing it had to be and he was not ashamed to live on his friends; if he could not have Heaven, he would have Hell, and the last footprints seem to point unmistakably towards the Inferno.

Graham Greene, *The Lost Childhood*.

Frederick Rolfe was a fantastic figure of the nineties. . . . The whole decade is now a little ridiculous, ridiculous decadence as well as ridiculous pietism.

They said of Rolfe that he was certainly possessed of a devil. At least his devil is still alive, it hasn't turned into a sort of golliwog, like the bulk of the nineties' devils. . . . He seems to have been a serpent of serpents in the bosom of all the nineties. That in itself endears him to one. The way everyone dropped him with a shudder is almost fascinating.

D. H. Lawrence, in *Adelphi*, December 1925.

Rolfe deserves a kinder epitaph than the belated *amende* of the *Aberdeen Free Press*. Who could improve on his own: 'Pray for the repose of his soul. He was so tired.'? Or, as he once wrote to a friend who accused him of selfishness: 'Selfish? Yes, selfish. The selfishness of a square peg in a round hole.'

A. J. A. Symons, *The Quest for Corvo*.

The books by which readers know him are but an earnest of what he might have done, and less than half of what he did. And yet, frustrated though he was, only the unimaginative will regard him as a failure, for he realized himself, brought the medieval atmosphere into modern days, and lived in the time of telephones as if in an age of rapiers.

A. J. A. Symons, *Essays and Biographies*.

Frederick William Rolfe . . . remains one of those writers more read about than read. . . . He wrote with great care, and with a sharpness, vivacity, and variety of epithet that give immediate and continuing pleasure, but he was not in any serious sense a novelist or even a writer of fiction. His emotionally injured self is the sole character of his fictions, with everybody else seen through the haze of his paranoia, like figures in a fun-fair mirror. . . . The long air-raid siren wail of self-justification precludes sympathy. To read much of Rolfe is to become powerfully aware that we are in the presence of a classic bore. This is not to say that the life is boring, only the work.

Julian Symons, in *Times Literary Supplement*, 3 January 1975.

CORYATE, THOMAS

1577?—1617 Traveller

In Surat being over-kindly used by some of the English, who gave him Sack, which they had brought from *England*, he calling for, as soon as he first heard of, it, and crying, *Sack, Sack, is there such a thing as Sack? I pray give me some Sack*, and drinking of it moderately, (for he was very temperate) it increased his flux which he had then upon him: and this caused him within a few days after his very tedious and troublesome travels, (for he went most

on foot), at that place to come to his journeys end. . . . For if one should go to the extremest part of the world East, another West, another North, and another South, they must all meet at last together in the Field of Bones, wherein our traveller hath now taken up his lodging.

Anthony à Wood, *Athenae Oxonienses*.

COTMAN, JOHN SELL

1782—1842 Painter, Engraver

I think Cotman's a very overrated reputation. Unlike [John] Crome, he was, I think, the slave of his water-colour technique, instead of its master.

Roger Fry, *Reflections on British Painting*.

[Roger] Fry could perceive only technical skill and inevitable correctness in Cotman's work. For myself, a Cotman drawing here and there shows the exquisite and final flawlessness of a Sung vase or a Yuan painting, yielding an instant of emotion before its dissolution into purest thought.

Martin Hardie, *Water-Colour Painting in Britain*.

With Crome a line was only part of a framework to suggest where light and dark and colour should be placed. With Cotman lines were the very bones on which the life of the work was supported. Even in his watercolours, they are essential to the whole design, used like the leading in a glass window, though not so obtrusively, to enclose the coloured shapes.

Ibid.

COTTON, JOHN

1584—1652 Clergyman

Whatever he delivered in the pulpit was soon put into an order of court, if of a civil, or set up as a practice in the church, if of an ecclesiastical concernment.

Anon., in William Cullen Bryant, *A Popular History of the United States*.

Mr. Cotton had such an insinuating and melting way in his preaching, that he would usually carry his very adversary captive after the triumphant chariot of his rhetoric.

The Rev. William Hubbard, in William Sprague, *Annals of the American Pulpit*.

The Cato of his age for his gravity, but having a glory with it which Cato had not.

Cotton Mather, in *ibid.*

He was the unmitred pope of a pope-hating common-wealth.

Moses Coit Tyler, *A History of American Literature.*

See also Cotton Mather

COURTAULD, SAMUEL

1876–1947 Industrialist, Art Collector

Art was to him, in his own phrase, 'religion's next-of-kin'.

T. S. R. Boase, in the *Dictionary of National Biography 1941–50.*

COWARD, SIR NOËL PIERCE

1899–73 Actor, Dramatist

It was ... a pleasant game to be discovered sobbing wretchedly in the corners of railway carriages or buses in the hope that someone would take pity on me and perhaps give me tea at Fuller's. This was only rarely successful, the only two responses I can recall being both clergymen. One talked to me for a long time, and told me to trust in God and every-thing would come right, and the other pinched my knee and gave me sixpence. Of the two, I preferred the latter.

On himself, *Present Indicative.*

With *Fallen Angels, On with the Dance,* and *The Vortex* all running at once, I was in an enviable position. Everyone but Somerset Maugham said that I was a second Somerset Maugham, with the exception of a few who preferred to describe me as a second Sacha Guitry.

Ibid.

My body has certainly wandered a good deal, but I have an uneasy suspicion that my mind has not wandered nearly enough.

Ibid.

I've sometimes thought of marrying — and then I've thought again.

On himself, in Ward Morehouse, in *Theatre Arts,* November 1956.

There is evidence in his work of sincerity, but one feels that it is in him rather than in his plays.

St John Irvine, *Good Housekeeping,* 1927.

Mr Coward's gift as a dramatist ... is that his dialogue has the rhythm of modern life, which is more broken and much quicker than that of twenty years ago. He understands, too, that it is more important that a joke on the stage should be spontaneous than witty. If it is also a brilliant piece of wit, so much the better, but the important thing is that it should seem spontaneous.

Desmond MacCarthy, *Humanities.*

It is a proof of Mr Coward's adroitness that he has managed to disguise the grimness of his comedy, and to conceal from the audience that his con-ception of love is desolating and false.

Ibid., on *Private Lives.*

See also Edna Ferber

COWLEY, ABRAHAM

1618–67 Poet

Nature wrought wonders then; when *Shakespear*
                 dy'd
Her dearest *Cowley* rose, drest in her gaudy Pride.
So from great Ruines a new Life she calls,
And builds an *Ovid* when a *Tully* falls.

Samuel Cobb, *Poetae Britannici.*

To him no author was known,
Yet what he wrote was all his own;
Horace's wit, and Virgil's state,
He did not steal, but emulate.
And when he would like them appear,
Their garb, but not their clothes, did wear.

John Denham, *Elegy on Cowley.*

He could never forgive any conceit which came in his way; but swept like a drag-net, great and small.

John Dryden, Preface to *Fables Ancient and Modern.*

I received the sad news of Abraham Cowley's death, that incomparable poet and virtuous man, my very dear friend, and was greatly deplored.

John Evelyn, Diary, 1 August 1667.

In Cowley there is an inexhaustible fund of sense and ingenuity, buried in inextricable conceits, and entangled in the cobwebs of the schools. He was a great man, not a great poet.

William Hazlitt, *Lectures on the English Poets.*

Cowley, like other poets who have written with narrow views, and, instead of tracing intellectual pleasures in the mind of man, paid their court to

temporary prejudices, has been at one time too much praised, and too much neglected at another.
Samuel Johnson, *Lives of the Poets.*

Who now reads Cowley? if he pleases yet,
His moral pleases, not his pointed wit;
Forgot his Epic, nay Pindaric Art,
But still I love the language of his Heart.
Alexander Pope, *Imitations of Horace*, book 2,
epistle 1.

Cowley, I think, would have had grace, for his mind was graceful, if he had had any ear, or if his taste had not been vitiated by the pursuit of wit; for false wit always deviates into tinsel or pertness.
Horace Walpole, Letter to Mr Pinkerton,
June 1785.

See also William D'Avenant, Andrew Marvell

COWPER, WILLIAM

1731—1800 Poet

I sing the sofa.
On himself, *The Task.*

I have no more right to the name of a poet than a maker of mousetraps has to that of an engineer.
On himself, Letter to William Unwin, *circa* 1785.

It is evident that this species of composition [the letter] exactly harmonized with the temperament and genius of Cowper. Detail was his forte and quietness his element. Accordingly, his delicate humour plays over perhaps a million letters, mostly descriptive of events which no one else would have thought worth narrating, and yet which, when narrated, show to us, and will show to persons to whom it will be yet more strange, the familiar, placid, easy ruminating provincial existence of our great grandfathers.
Walter Bagehot, *William Cowper.*

His taste lay in a smiling, colloquial, good-natured humour; his melancholy was a black and diseased melancholy, not a grave and rich contemplativeness.
Sir E. Brydges, *Recollections of Foreign Travel.*

They say poets never or rarely go *mad.* Cowper and Collins are instances to the contrary (but Cowper was no poet).
Lord Byron, Letter to Annabella Millbanke,
29 November 1813.

With all his boasted simplicity and love of the country, he seldom launches out into general descriptions of nature: he looks at her over his clipped hedges, and from his well-swept garden-walks; or if he makes a bolder experiment now and then, it is with an air of precaution, as if he were afraid of being caught in a shower of rain, or of not being able, in case of any untoward accident, to make good his retreat home. He shakes hands with nature with a pair of fashionable gloves on.
William Hazlitt, *Lectures on the English Poets.*

The fairest critic, and the sweetest bard.
James Hurdis, *Address to Criticism.*

I could forgive a man for not enjoying Milton; but I would not call that man my friend who should be offended by 'the divine chit-chat of Cowper'.
Charles Lamb, quoting Coleridge's phrase,
Letter to Coleridge, 5 December 1796.

I say, what a nice clear hand Cowper has got! and how neatly the poor old sod turns a compliment and all the while being able to write the most tragic lines ever writ, about his own damnation and one of the worst — for horrid suffering — of these in the Sapphic metre too. Think of that.
John Cowper Powys, Letter to Nicholas Ross,
27 May 1943.

COZENS, JOHN ROBERT

1752—79 Watercolourist

Cozens was all poetry.
John Constable, Letter to John Fisher,
4 August 1821.

With Cozens comes a new element: the personal subjective emotion that was to find a like expression in the poetry of Wordsworth and his contemporaries.
Martin Hardie, *Water-Colour Painting in Britain.*

CRABBE, GEORGE

1754—1832 Poet

His mildness in literary argument struck me with surprise in so stern a poet of nature, and I could not but contrast the unassumingness of his manners with the originality of his powers. In what may be called the ready-money small-talk of conversation, his facility might not perhaps seem equal to the known calibre of his talents; but in the progress of conversation I recollect remarking that there was a vigilant shrewdness that almost eluded you by keeping its watch so quietly. Though an oldish man when I saw him, he was not a *laudator temporis acti*, but a decided lover of later times.

Thomas Campbell, Letter in *Life of George Crabbe by his Son*.

He exhibits the smallest circumstances of the smallest things. He gives the very costume of meanness; the nonessentials of every trifling incident. . . . He describes the interior of a cottage like a person sent there to distrain for rent. He has an eye to the number of arms in an old worm-eaten chair, and takes care to inform himself and the reader whether a joint-stool stands upon three legs or four. . . . He takes an inventory of the human heart exactly in the same manner as of the furniture of a sick room: his sentiments have very much the air of fixtures; he gives you the petrifaction of a sigh, and carves a tear, to the life, in stone. . . . Crabbe's poetry is like a museum, or curiosity-shop.

William Hazlitt, *Lectures on the English Poets*.

Mr Crabbe, it must be confessed, is a repulsive writer. He contrives to 'turn diseases into commodities', and makes a virtue of necessity. He puts us out of conceit with this world, which perhaps a severe divine should do; yet does not, as a charitable divine ought, point to another. His morbid feelings droop and cling to the earth, grovel where they should soar; and throw a dead weight on every aspiration of the soul after the good or beautiful.

William Hazlitt, *The Spirit of the Age*.

Crabbe is a writer of great power, but of a perverse and morbid taste. He gives the very objects and feelings he treats of, whether in morals, or rural scenery, but he gives none but the most uninteresting, or the most painful. His poems are a sort of funeral dirge over human life, but without pity, without hope. He has neither smiles, nor tears, for his readers.

William Hazlitt, 'A Critical List of Authors', in *Select British Poets*.

Comparing the smartnesses of Crabbe with Young's. . . . Young moralised at a distance on some external appearances of the human heart; Crabbe entered it *on all fours*, and told the people what an ugly thing it is inside.

Walter Savage Landor, *Imaginary Conversations*.

Wordsworth . . . told Anne and I a story the object of which was to show that Crabbe had not imagination. He, Sir George Beaumont and Wordsworth were sitting together in Murray the bookseller's back-room. Sir George after sealing a letter blew out the candle which had enabled him to do so and

exchanging a look with Wordsworth began to admire in silence the undulating thread of smoke which slowly arose from the expiring wick when Crabbe put on the extinguisher.

Sir Walter Scott, Journal, 3 January 1827.

He had formed an attachment in early life to a young woman who, like himself, was absolutely without fortune; he wrote his poems to obtain patronage and preferment. . . . He *pushed* (as the world says) for patronage with these poems, and succeeded; got preferment sufficient, and married. It was not long before his wife became deranged, and when all this was told me by one who knew him well, five years ago, he was still almost confined in his own house, anxiously waiting upon this wife in her long and hopeless malady. A sad history! It is no wonder that he gives so melancholy a picture of human life.

Robert Southey, Letter to J. N. White, 30 September 1808.

He has a world of his own. There is a 'tramp, tramp, tramp,' a merciless sledgehammer thud about his lines which suits his subjects.

Alfred, Lord Tennyson (in conversation), in Hallam Tennyson, *Alfred Tennyson, A Memoir*.

The sum of all is, that nineteen out of twenty of Crabbe's Pictures are mere matters of fact; with which the Muses have just about as much to do as they have with a Collection of medical reports, or of Law Cases.

William Wordsworth, Letter to Samuel Rogers, 29 September 1805.

See also Lord Byron, Daniel Defoe, Samuel Johnson

CRAIG, EDWARD GORDON

1872—1966 Designer

Consider Craig's very odd profession. He has presented himself to the world, and to some extent conquered it, in the capacity of a Thwarted Genius.

George Bernard Shaw, in *Observer*, 8 November 1931.

CRANE, (HAROLD) HART

1899—1932 Poet, Writer

One must be drenched in words, literally soaked in them, to have the right ones form themselves into the proper pattern at the right moment.

On himself, in Malcolm Cowley, *A Second Flowering*.

Hart, Hart. . . . He did so much that was outrageous, but so much that was unaffectedly kind or exuberant and so much that kept us entertained. Nobody yawned when Hart was there.

Malcolm Cowley, in *ibid.*

There were many reasons for his suicide, including his frenzied drinking, his sexual quandary, his lack of money — or prospects of earning it and his feeling that poets had no place in American life, at least during those early years of the Depression. He used to fling up his arms and shout 'What good are poets today! The world needs men of action.'

Ibid.

In spite of a robust constitution he suffered from a number of recurring ailments, including acidosis, urethritis, urticaria (or plain hives), constipation, crabs, and rose fever. These he treated with home remedies, chiefly canned tomatoes, larkspur lotion, and an enema bag. He tried to stay away from doctors, possibly because he was afraid of being given the obvious advice: stop drinking.

Ibid.

In the same way Hart tried to charm his inspiration out of its hiding place with a Cuban rumba and a pitcher of hard cider.

Malcolm Cowley, *Exile's Return.*

Essentially Crane was a poet of ecstasy or frenzy or intoxication . . . . Essentially he was using rhyme and meter and fantastic images to convey the emotional states that were induced in him by alcohol, jazz, machinery, laughter, intellectual stimulation, the shape and sound of words and the madness of New York in the late Coolidge era.

Ibid.

Someone told me that when poor Hart finally met his end by jumping overboard from the Havana boat the last his friends on deck saw of him was a cheerful wave of the hand before he sank and drowned. That last friendly wave was very like Hart Crane.

John Dos Passos, *The Best Times.*

Crane finds in America a principle of unity and absolute faith, through the integration of such symbols as Columbus, Pocahontas, Rip Van Winkle, Poe, Whitman, the subway, and, above all, Brooklyn Bridge, an image of man's anonymous creative power unifying past and present.

James D. Hart, *The Oxford Companion to American Literature.*

The numberless friendships he made during his life with people of all sorts — from bar-flies and taxi-drivers to eccentric spinsters — witnessed the abundant, almost promiscuous, affection for humanity, collectively and individually which he shared with Whitman.

Philip Horton, *Hart Crane.*

He resented the encroachments of rationalism on any part of the poet's province, and, like the natural Platonist he was, consistently maintained that poetry, to remain true to its own nature, must transcend the dictates of scientific logic, and function only according to the laws of its own making.

Ibid.

Crane was the archetype of the modern American poet whose fundamental mistake lay in thinking that an irrational surrender of the intellect to the will would be the basis of a new mentality.

Allen Tate, in Louis Untermeyer ed., *Modern American Poetry, A Critical Anthology.*

See also James Joyce

CRANE, STEPHEN
1871–1900 Author

I was a Socialist for two weeks but when a couple of Socialists assured me I had no right to think differently from any other Socialist and then quarrelled with each other about what Socialism meant, I ran away.

On himself, in Jay Martin, *Harvests of Change, American Literature, 1865–1914.*

I had thought that there could be only two worse writers than Stephen Crane, namely two Stephen Cranes.

Ambrose Bierce, in Richard O'Connor, *Ambrose Bierce.*

This young man has the power to feel. He knows nothing of war, yet he is drenched in blood. Most beginners who deal with this subject splatter themselves merely with ink.

Ambrose Bierce, referring to Crane's *The Red Badge of Courage*, in John Berryman, *Stephen Crane.*

Crane was a preternaturally sensitive man; he saw everything, he heard, tasted, felt everything with the exquisite aptitude of a convalescent. The tremor of a butterfly's wing was not too slight to escape him. . . .

Van Wyck Brooks, in Richard M. Weatherford ed., *Stephen Crane, The Critical Heritage.*

He drank life to the lees, but at the banquet table where other men took their ease and jested over their wine, he stood a dark and silent figure, sombre as Poe himself, not wishing to be understood; and he took his portion in haste, with his loins girded, and his shoes on his feet, and his staff in his hand, like one who must depart quickly.

Willa Cather, 'When I Knew Stephen Crane', in Maurice Bassan ed., *Stephen Crane, A Collection of Critical Essays.*

He was thin to emaciation, his face was gaunt and un-shaven, a thin dark moustache straggled on his upper lip, his black hair grew low on his forehead and was shaggy and unkempt. His grey clothes were much the worse for wear and fitted him so badly it seemed un-likely he had ever been measured for them.

Ibid.

But Crane's work detonated on the mild din of that attack on our literary sensibilities with the impact and force of a twelve-inch shell charged with a very high explosive. Unexpected it fell amongst us; and its fall was followed by a great outcry.

Joseph Conrad, Preface to Crane's *The Red Badge of Courage.*

. . . the coolest man, whether army officer or civilian, that I saw under fire at any time during the war.

Richard Harding Davis, referring to Crane during the Spanish-American war, in R. W. Stallman, *Stephen Crane.*

With all his endowments he was not an admirable character. He gave out the effect of being an alley cat so far as habit went. And during the days when I first knew him in New York City he was living like an outcast. Although not a drinking man, he smoked incessantly and sometimes was thought to have used a drug of some kind.

Hamlin Garland, in *ibid.*

Tolstoy made the writing of Stephen Crane on the Civil War seem like the brilliant imagining of a sick boy who had never seen war but had only read the battle chronicles and seen the Brady photographs that I had read and seen at my grandparents' house.

Ernest Hemingway, *A Moveable Feast.*

Crane's virtues as a writer come from the honesty and the clarity with which he recorded what he saw; his weaknesses are the result of his failure to discover why he saw as he did.

Granville Hicks, *The Great Tradition.*

. . . he is the first expression of the opening mind of a new period, or, at least, the early emphatic phase of a new initiative — beginning, as a growing mind must needs begin, with the record of impressions, a record of a vigor and intensity beyond all precedent.

H. G. Wells, in Richard M. Weatherford ed., *Stephen Crane, The Critical Heritage.*

Stephen Crane was a vortex of intensity in a generally stagnant sea. He was an artist not as the age under-stood that word but as the world at large understands it. I do not say that he was a great artist or that he was even of the first rank, but what he had was the real thing and he adulterated it with nothing else.

Edmund Wilson, *The Shores of Light.*

CRANFIELD, LIONEL, EARL OF MIDDLESEX

1575—1645 Court Financier

By nature a planner and executant, not a politician, he was the victim, in the first place, of an illusion which may be called, perhaps, the administrator's fallacy — the belief, that is to say, that efficient management, combined with public spirit and a logically unanswerable case, can hold its own against interests and ambitions wielding personal and politi-cal power. Enjoying almost to the end the confidence of James, Middlesex both exaggerated, in the second place, the value of the King's support and under-estimated the capacity for mischief of the royal en-tourage. His proposals for abolishing superfluous offices, for further departmental economies, for pruning grants and pensions, and for transferring patronage from King to Treasurer were obviously sound sense; but, not less obviously, they were odious to influential individuals and groups who had the royal ear. It is not surprising, therefore, that they should have fallen on stony ground, and that the few of them which were partially adopted should not have long survived their detested author's fall.

R. H. Tawney, *Business and Politics under James I.*

CRANMER, THOMAS

1489—1556 Archbishop of Canterbury, Reformer

I protest before you all, there was never man came more unwillingly to a bishopric than I did to that: insomuch that when King Henry did send for me in post, that I should come over, I prolonged my journey by seven weeks at the least, thinking that he would be forgetful of me in the mean time.

On himself, Statement at His Examination, in John Foxe, *Acts and Monuments.*

CRASHAW, RICHARD

... a name which deserves to be held in everlasting
execration; a name which he could not pronounce
without almost doubting of the justice of God, were
it not for our knowledge of the fact, that the cold-
blooded, most perfidious, most impious, most blasphemous caitiff expired at last, amidst those flames
which he himself had been the chief cause of kindling.
   William Cobbett, *A History of the Protestant
   Reformation.*

And when the wood was kindled, and the fire began
to burn near him, stretching out his Arm, he put his
right hand into the flame, which he held so stedfast
and unmoveable (save that once with the same hand
he wiped his face) that all men might see his hand
burned before his Body was touched.
   John Foxe, *Acts and Monuments.*

Cranmer has got the right sow by the ear.
   Henry VIII, referring to Cranmer's part in his
   divorce from Katherine of Aragon.

See also Hugh Latimer, Mary I

CRASHAW, RICHARD

1613?–49 Poet

What he might eate or weare he took no thought;
His needfull foode he rather found than sought.
He seekes no downes, no sheetes, his bed's still made.
If he can find a chaire or stoole, he's lay'd;
When day peepes in, he quitts his restless rest,
And still, poore soule, before he's up he's dres't.
   Thomas Carre, *Anagram on the Name of Crashaw.*

Crashaw seems in his poems to have given the first
ebullience of his imagination, unshapen into form,
or much of, what we now term, sweetness.
   Samuel Taylor Coleridge, *Table Talk.*

Poet and Saint! to thee alone are giv'n
The two most Sacred Names of Earth and Heav'n.
   Abraham Cowley, *On the Death of Mr Crashaw.*

At times ... his passion for heavenly objects is imperfect because it is partly a substitute for human
passion.
   T. S. Eliot, *For Lancelot Andrewes.*

CRAZY HORSE (TASHUNCA-UITCO)

circa 1849–77 Chief of the Oglala Sioux

We did not ask you white men to come here. The

Great Spirit gave us this country as a home. You had
yours. We did not interfere with you. The Great
Spirit gave us plenty of land to live on, and buffalo,
deer, antelope and other game. But you have come
here; you are taking my land from me; you are killing
off our game, so it is hard for us to live. Now, you
tell us to work for a living, but the Great Spirit did
not make us to work, but to live by hunting. You
white men can work if you want to. We do not interfere with you, and again you say, why do you not
become civilized? We do not want your civilization!
We would live as our fathers did, and their fathers
before them.
   On himself, in T. C. McLuhan, *Touch The Earth.*

We do not hunt the troops, and never have, they
have always hunted us on our own ground. They tell
us they want to civilize us. They lie; they want to kill
us, and they sneak upon us when we are asleep to do
it. I only wish we had the power to civilize them.
We would certainly do so; but we would do it fairly,
we would not kill their women and children in their
own country and in their beds. And if we gave them
a home to live in and told them as long as they stayed
there they would be safe, they would be safe there.
We would not go there the next day and kill them
all, as they do us.
   On himself (immediately before his surrender in
   1877), in Fred M. Haas, *The Great Sioux Nation.*

Since the time of his youth Crazy Horse had known
that the world men lived in was only a shadow of
the real world. To get into the real world, he had to
dream, and when he was in the real world everything
seemed to float or dance. In this real world his horse
danced as if it were wild or crazy, and this was why
he called himself Crazy Horse.
   Dee Brown, *Bury My Heart at Wounded Knee.*

CRICHTON, JAMES (THE ADMIRABLE)

1560?–82 Prodigy

He is distinguished by a birth-mark or mole, beneath
his right eye. He is master of ten languages. These are
Latin and Italian in which he is excellently skilled;
Greek, in which he has composed epigrams; Hebrew,
Chaldaic, Spanish, French, Flemish, English and
Scotch; and he is also acquainted with the German.
He is deeply skilled in philosophy, in theology, and
in astrology; in which science he holds all the calculations of the present day to be erroneous. On philosophical and theological questions he has frequently
disputed with very able men, to the astonishment of
all who have heard him. He possesses a thorough
knowledge of the Cabbala. His memory is so astonish-

ing, that he knows not what it is to forget; and whenever he has once heard an oration he is ready to repeat it again, word for word, as it was delivered. He composes Latin verses upon any subject which is proposed to him, and in every different kind of metre. Such is his Memory, that although these verses have been extempore, he will repeat them backwards, beginning from the last word in the verse. His orations are unpremeditated and beautiful. He is also able to discourse on political questions with much solidity. In his person he is extremely beautiful. His address is that of a finished gentleman, even to a wonder; and his manner, in conversation, the most gracious that can be imagined. He is, in addition to all this, a soldier at all points, and has for two years sustained an honourable command in the wars of France. He has attained to great excellence in the accomplishments of leaping and dancing, and to a remarkable skill in the use of every sort of arms; of which he has already given proofs. He is a remarkable horseman, and breaker of horses, and an admirable jouster.

Anon., *Broadsheet*, 1580, found in a copy of Castiglione's *Courtier*, translated from the Italian by P. F. Tytler, 1834.

. . . When Urquhart plunged this charmed figure into the ferment of his fantastic imagination, there emerged a Crichton more admirable than ever, a transcendent Crichton, a unicorn of alchemist's gold. Scot had answered unto Scot: an eccentric had elaborated a prodigy: and there resulted a rhapsody which glorified and fixed the legend in an unrivalled erection of baroque English prose.

Hamish Miles, Introduction to Thomas Urquhart, *The Life and Death of the Admirable Crichtoun.*

. . . Matchless Crichtoun, seeing it now high time to put a gallant catastrophe to that so-long-dubious combat, animated with a divinely-inspired fervencie, to fulfil the expectation of the ladyes and crown the Duke's illustrious hopes, changeth his garb, falls to act another part, and, from defender, turns assailant: never did art so grace nature, nor nature second the precepts of art with so much liveliness, and such observancie of time, as when, after he had struck fire out of the steel of his enemie's sword, and gained the feeble thereof, with the fort of his own, by angles of the strongest position, he did, by geometrical flourishes of straight and oblique lines, so practically execute the speculative part, that, as if there had been Remora's and secret charms in the variety of his motion, the fierceness of his foe was in a trice transqualified into the numbness of a pageant. Then it was that, to vindicate the reputation of the Duke's family, and expiate the blood of the three vanquished gentlemen, he alonged a stoccade de pied ferme; then recoyling, he advanced another thrust, and lodged it home; after which, retiring again, his right foot did

beat the cadence of the blow that pierced the belly of this Italian; whose heart and throat being hit with the two former stroaks, these three franch bouts given in upon the back of the other; besides that, if lines were imagined drawn from the hand that livered them to the places which were marked by them, they would represent a perfect Isosceles Triangle, with a perpendicular from the top-angle, cutting the basis in the middle; they likewise give us to understand, that by them he was to be made a sacrifice of atonement for the slaughter of the three aforesaid gentlemen, who were wounded in the very same parts of their bodies by other such three venees as these, each whereof being mortal: and his vital spark exhaling as his blood gushed out, all he spoke was this. That seeing he could not live, his comfort in dying was, that he could not dye by the hand of a braver man, after the uttering of which words he expiring, with the shril clareens of trumpets, bouncing thunder of artillery, bethwacked beating of drums, universal clapping of hands, and loud acclamations of joy for so glorious a victory, the air above them was so rarified by the extremity of the noise and vehement sound, dispelling the thickest and most condensed parts thereof, that . . . the very sparrows and other flying fowls were said to fall to the ground, for want of aire enough to uphold them in their flight.

Sir Thomas Urquhart, *The Life and Death of the Admirable Crichtoun.*

All this while, the admirable Scot, (for so from thence forth he was called) minding more his hawking, hunting, tilting, vaulting, riding of well managed horses, tossing of the pike, handling of the musket, flourishing of colours, dancing, fencing, swimming, jumping, throwing of the barr, playing at the tennis, baloon, or long-catch; and sometimes at the house of games of dice, cards, playing at the chess, Billiards, troumadam and other such-like chamber-sports, singing, playing on the lute, and other musical instruments, masking, balling, revelling, and which did most of all divert, (or rather distract him from his speculations and serious employments) being more addicted to, and playing closer the courtship of handsome ladyes, and a jovial cup in the company of Bacchanalian blades, than the forseeing how to avoid, shun and escape, the snares, grins, and nets of the hard, obscure, and hidden arguments, riddles, and demands to be made, framed and woven by the professors, doctors, and others of that thrice-renown'd university. . . .

Ibid.

He made pedantry romantic. Out of the dry bones of dead philosophies he produced a wonderful effect. We can well believe that neither his mind nor his tongue weighed heavily on abstruse subjects. They touched them and were off. I have likened him to a butterfly, brilliant in colour and light on wing, but he was a butterfly who fed on Cabbages.

Charles Whibley, *The Admirable Crichton*.

I remembered, when I was in Italy, there was a Scottish Gentleman of most rare and singular parts who was a retainer to the Duke of that country; hee was a singular good Scholler, and as good a souldier; it chanced one night, the young prince, either upon some spleen, or false suggestion, or to trie the scots valour, met him in a place where he was wont to haunt, resolving either to kill, wound, or beat him; and for this effect conducted with him two of the best fencers he could find; the Scot had but one friend with him; in fine, a quarrel was pickt — they all drew; the Scot presently ran one of the fencers throw, and killed him in a trice; with that he bended his forces to the Prince, who, fearing lest that which was befallen the fencer, might happen upon himselfe, he exclaimed out instantly that he was the Prince, and therefore willed him to look about him what he did. The Scot, perceiving well that he was, fell down upon his knees, demanding pardon at his hands, and gave the Prince his naked rapier; who no sooner had received it, but with the same sword he ran him thorow to death; the which barabrous fact, as it was condemned of all men, so it sheweth the precipitation of his passionate ireful heart.

Thomas Wright, *The Passions of the Mind in General*.

CRIPPS, SIR (RICHARD) STAFFORD

1889–1952 Statesman

. . . He is, at the moment, the pivotal point of Labour policy. Also he is . . . one of the leaders of the future. This tall, buoyant scientist with the dark, piercing eyes, has about him the candour of a boy. That is the secret of his present stand. Comparatively new to political leadership, his interest is to discover, with a scientist's logic and lack of sentimentality, the exact implications of the present position and, having discovered them, to take the people . . . into his confidence. . . . Far from having disrupted the Labour Party . . . he has given a lead which has rallied the whole of the younger generation of Socialists to his side.

British Weekly, 5 October 1933.

Our white Gandhi . . . .

Brendan Bracken, Letter to Lord Beaverbrook, 11 November 1947.

. . . the modern Savonarola.

Henry Channon, on Cripps's Budget, Diary, 6 August 1948.

There but for the grace of God, goes God.

Sir Winston Churchill, on Cripps as Chancellor of the Exchequer, in Louis Kronenberger, *The Cutting Edge*.

The trouble is, his chest is a cage in which two squirrels are at war, his conscience and his career.

Winston Churchill, in Lord Moran, *Diary*.

The perfect Octavius.

Michael Foot, *Aneurin Bevan*.

It was his supreme and rare merit that he knew the difference between a good argument and a bad one.

Douglas Jay, in W. T. Rodgers ed., *Hugh Gaitskell 1906–63*.

I still fear his Messianic complex; and I am not sure that his optimism has not a touch of dangerous hubris in it. But . . . he is a tonic to the public, and his influence is as good as it is great.

Harold Laski, Letter to Felix Frankfurter, March 1942.

Cripps is superb at things but no good, as always, at persons. . . .

Ibid, May 1947.

. . . a rich man, with rich pals around him, and they are the biggest danger to the Labour party in this country. You will find those chaps where Mosley is before much longer.

J. McGurk of the Mineworkers' Federation, to the Labour Party Conference, October 1937.

. . . the cold ruthlessness of a hanging judge. . . .

Michael Postan, in W. T. Rodgers ed., *Hugh Gaitskell 1906–63*.

CROCKETT, DAVID

1786–1836 Frontiersman

I am at liberty to vote as my conscience and judgment dictate to be right, without the yoke of any party on me, or the driver at my heels, with the whip in his hands, commanding me to 'gee-whoa-haw' just at his pleasure.

On himself, in the *National Cyclopedia of American Biography*, vol. 4.

. . . fame is like a shaved pig with a greased tail, and it is only after it has slipped through the hands of some thousands, that some fellow, by mere chance, holds on to it!

On himself, in Richard M. Dorson ed., *Davy Crockett, American Comic Legend*.

I always had the praise o' raisin the tallest and fattest and sassyest gals in all America. They can out-run, out-jump, out-fight, and outscream any crittur in creation; and for scratchin', thar's not a hungry painter, or a patent horse-rake can hold a claw to 'em.
Ibid.

'Gentlemen,' says I, 'I'm Davy Crockett, the darling branch o' old Kentuck that can eat up a painter, hold a buffalo out to drink, and put a rifle ball through the moon.'
Ibid.

That's no human flesh in all creation that's so partial to home and the family circle, square, kitchen, barn, log-hut, pig-pen or fire-place as a Kentuckian. For my own part, I war in the habit, every mornin', of lightin' my pipe, and givin' all my domestic circle — wimmin, colts, wild cats, and kittens — an all-squeezin' hug all round; and the way the brute portion of 'em showed thar sharp ivories, and grinned back double extra satisfaction, war indeed upwards of gratifying to my mortal and sympathetic natur.
Ibid.

His favourite costume was a coonskin cap and a buckskin jacket. It is assumed that he wore trousers of some sort, although they are not mentioned.
Richard Armour, *It All Started With Columbus.*

CROKER, JOHN WILSON

1780–1857 Essayist, Politician

For two-and-twenty years I never quitted that room without a kind of uneasiness like a truant boy.
On himself and his work in the Admiralty, Letter to John Murray, 1838.

I filled an important office in glorious times, and with illustrious colleagues and friends, of whom I am more proud than I ever could be of any successes of my own.
On himself, Letter to Lord Hatherton, 1 February 1857.

He was, in short, a man who possessed, in very remarkable degree, a restless instinct for adroit baseness.
Benjamin Disraeli, caricaturing Croker as 'Rigby', in *Coningsby.*

. . . that impudent leering Croker . . . I detest him more than cold boiled veal.
T. B. Macaulay, Letter to Hannah M. Macaulay, 1831.

Mr Killthedead . . . a great compounder of narcotics, under the denomination of BATTLES, for he never heard of a deadly field, especially if dotage and superstition, to which he was very partial, gained the advantage over generosity and talent, both of which he abhorred, but immediately seizing his goosequill and foolscap,
He fought the Battle o'er again,
And thrice he slew the slain.
Thomas Love Peacock, *Melincourt.*

CROME, JOHN

1768–1821 Painter

The little stout man whose face is very dark, and whose eye is vivacious; that man has attained excellence, destined some day to be acknowledged, though not till he is cold and his mortal part returned to its kindred clay. He has painted, not pictures of the world, but English pictures, such as Gainsborough himself might have done; beautiful rural pieces, with trees which might well tempt the wild birds to perch upon them: thou needest not run to Rome, brother, where lives the old Mariolater, after pictures of the world, whilst at home there are pictures of England; nor needest thou even to go to London, the big city, in search of a master, for thou hast one at home in the old East Anglian town who canst instruct thee whilst thou needest instruction.
George Borrow, *Lavengro.*

I remember meeting my old friend Mr. John Crome, of Norwich (some of whose landscapes are not surpassed even by those of Gainsborough) with several of his pupils, on the banks of the Yare. 'This is our Academy,' he cried out triumphantly, holding up his brush.
John Burnet, *Landscape Painting.*

Crome is the quiet man at the party whom chatterers fail to notice. His true subject was not the Norfolk countryside but the stillness at the heart of it.
D. and T. Clifford, *John Crome.*

His trees made no concession to what the academic artist . . . expected of them; they are, if one could say so, plebeian trees, unversed in the elegant and well-bred airs that Gainsborough's assume. Thus it is apparent that so far from deriving an essential and guiding principle from Gainsborough, Crome really ranged himself in the opposite camp, the camp of the Realists set over against the Classicists.
H. Collins-Baker, *Crome.*

CROMPTON, SAMUEL
1753—1827 Inventor

Another estimable and modest man, a working weaver, named Samuel Crompton, carried the mechanism of spinning a stage further, by his admirable invention of the mule, which combined the principles of Arkwright's water-frame and Hargreaves's jenny. He knew nothing of the principles of mechanics save what he had patiently taught himself; but he was very persevering, and by working assiduously in his leisure hours during a period of about four years, he was at length enabled to perfect his invention. Being of a retiring and unambitious disposition, however, he protected it by no patent; and the principal regret expressed by him was, that public curiosity would not allow him 'to enjoy his little invention to himself in his garret', and to earn by his manual labour the fruits of his ingenuity and perseverance.

Samuel Smiles, *Self-help*.

In the summer of 1811 he visited the manufacturing districts, and collected information connected with the progress and extent of the cotton manufacture. Encouraged by what he had seen everywhere on his journey, he was assisted, on his return, to present a petition to Parliament for a recompense from the country. The committee, to whom the memorial was referred for examination, reported that Mr. Crompton was *entitled* to a *material reward*. Crompton thought his gift should bring him 50,000*l*.; the mechanical public thought he would obtain 25,000*l*.; great, therefore, was the astonishment of every one when Parliament granted him only 5,000*l*. No member engaged in manufacture, or connected with Lancashire, had generosity enough, or respect for justice, to protest against such a mockery of a reward being conferred. At the moment the sorry sum was granted, 360 factories, containing 4,600,000 spindles, were at work, spinning annually 40,000,000 pounds weight of cotton into yarn, and employing 70,000 persons directly in spinning, and 150,000 persons weaving the yarn into cloth, making 660,000 persons depending for their daily bread on the use of the *mule*. Yet Mr. Crompton, the ingenious author of all this extraordinary prosperity and wealth, had not, after thirty years toil and bodily labour, been able to raise himself or his family above the condition of common labourers, employing only their own hands in working three of his small muslin-wheels.

Bennet Woodcroft, *Brief Biographies of Inventors of Machines for the Manufacture of Textile Fabrics*.

CROMWELL, OLIVER
1599—1658 Lord Protector

I need pity. I know what I feel. Great place and business in the world is not worth the looking after.
On himself, Letter to Richard Mayor, 17 July 1650.

I am neither heir nor executor to Charles Stuart.
On himself, repudiating a royal debt, August 1651.

When I went there, I did not think to have done this. But perceiving the spirit of God so strong upon me, I would not consult flesh and blood.

On himself, on his forcible dissolution of Parliament in April 1653, in James Heath, *Flagellum, or the Life and Death, Birth and Burial of Oliver Cromwell*.

I was by birth a gentleman, living neither in any considerable height, nor yet in obscurity. I have been called to several employments in the nation, — to serve in parliaments, — and (because I would not be over tedious) I did endeavour to discharge the duty of an honest man in those services, to God, and His people's interest, and of the Commonwealth; having, when time was, a competent acceptation in the hearts of men, and some evidences thereof.
On himself, Speech to the First Parliament of the Protectorate, 12 September 1654.

Mr Lely, I desire you would use all your skill to paint my picture truly like me, and not flatter me at all; but remark all these roughnesses, pimples, warts and everything as you see me, otherwise I never will pay a farthing for it.
On himself, in Horace Walpole, *Anecdotes of Painting*.

This great man is risen from a very low and afflicted condition; one that hath suffered very great troubles of soul, lying a long time under sore terrors and temptations, and at the same time in a very low condition for outward things; in this school of afflictions he was kept, till he had learned the lesson of the Cross, till his will was broken into submission to the will of God. . . . Religion was laid into his soul with the hammer and the fire . . . .
Anon., Contemporary, in C. Firth, *Oliver Cromwell*.

You shall scarce speak to Cromwell about anything, but he will lay his hand on his breast, elevate his eyes, and call God to record; he will weep, howl and repent, even while he doth smite you under the first

rib . . . Oh Cromwell! Wither art thou aspiring? . . .
He that runs may read and foresee the intent, a new
regality.

Anon. Leveller Tract, *The Hunting of the Foxes.*

During a great part of the eighteenth century most
Tories hated him because he overthrew the
monarchy, most Whigs because he overthrew Parliament. Since Carlyle wrote, all liberals have seen in
him their champion, and all revolutionists have
apotheosized the first great representatives of their
school; while, on the other side, their opponents
have hailed the dictator who put down anarchy. Unless the socialists or the anarchists finally prevail —
and perhaps even then — his fame seems as secure as
human reputation is likely to be in a changing world.

W. C. Abbott, *Writings and Speeches of Oliver Cromwell.*

The commonest charge against Cromwell is hypocrisy — and the commonest basis for that is defective chronology.

Ibid.

Oliver Cromwell had certainly this afflatus. One that
I knew that was at the Battle of *Dunbar*, told me
that Oliver was carried on with a Divine impulse; he
did Laugh so excessively as if he had been Drunk; his
Eyes sparkled with Spirits. He obtain'd a great
Victory; but the action was said to be contrary to
Human Prudence. The same Fit of Laughter seized
Oliver Cromwell just before the Battle of *Naseby*; as
a Kinsman of mine, and a great favourite of his,
Colonel J.P. then present, testified. Cardinal *Mazerine*
said, That he was a Lucky Fool.

John Aubrey, *Miscellanies.*

. . . he thought Secrecy a Vertue, and Dissimulation
no Vice, and Simulation, that is, in plain English, a
Lie, or Perfidiousnesse to be a tollerable Fault in case
of Necessity.

Richard Baxter, *Reliquiae Baxterianae.*

He was of a sanguine complexion, naturally of such
a vivacity, hilarity and alacrity as another man is
when he hath drunken a cup too much.

Ibid.

And as he went on, though he yet resolved not what
form the New Commonwealth should be moulded
into, yet he thought it but reasonable, that he should
be the Chief Person who had been the chief in the
Deliverance.

Ibid.

When he quitted the Parliament, his chief dependence was on the Army, which he endeavoured by

all means to keep in unity, and if he could not bring
it to his sense, he, rather than suffer any division in
it, went-over himself and carried his friends with him
into that way which the army did choose, and that
faster than any other person in it.

Sir John Berkley, *Memoirs of Sir John Berkley.*

He gart kings ken they had a lith in their neck.

Alexander Boswell, Lord Auchinleck, in James
Boswell, *Tour of the Hebrides.*

. . . A devotee of law, he was forced to be often
lawless; a civilian to the core, he had to maintain
himself by the sword; with a passion to construct,
his task was chiefly to destroy; the most scrupulous
of men, he had to ride roughshod over his own
scruples and those of others; the tenderest, he had
continually to harden his heart; the most English of
our greater figures, he spent his life in opposition to
the majority of Englishmen; a realist, he was condemned to build that which could not last.

John Buchan, *Oliver Cromwell.*

Cromwell was a man in whom ambition had not
wholly suppressed, but only suspended, the sentiments of religion.

Edmund Burke, *Letters,* 1791.

As close as a Goose
Sat the *Parliament-House*
    To hatch the royal Gull;
    After much fiddle-faddle,
The Egg proved addle
And *Oliver* came forth *Nol.*

Samuel Butler, *A Ballad.*

Sylla was the first of victors; but our own
The sagest of usurpers, Cromwell; he
Too swept off senates while he hewed the throne
Down to a block — immortal rebel! See
What crimes it costs to be a moment free
And famous through all ages.

Lord Byron, *Childe Harold,* canto iv.

I confess I have an interest in this Mr Cromwell; and
indeed, if truth must be said, in him alone. The rest
are historical, dead to me; but he is epic, still living.
Hail to thee, thou strong one; hail across the longdrawn funeral-aisle and night of Time! . . .

Thomas Carlyle, *Historical Sketches.*

In spite of the stupor of Histories, it is beautiful . . .
to see how the memory of Cromwell, in its huge inarticulate significance, not able to *speak* a wise word
for itself to any one, has nevertheless been growing
steadily clearer and clearer in the popular English
mind; how from the day when high dignitaries and

pamphleteers of the Carrion species did their ever-memorable feat at Tyburn, onwards to this day the progress does not stop.

> Thomas Carlyle, *Letters and Speeches of Oliver Cromwell.*

His Grandeur he deriv'd from Heaven alone,
    For he was great e'er fortune made him so
And Wars like Mists that rise against the Sun
    Made him but greater seem, not greater grow.

No borrow'd Bays his Temples did adorn,
    But to our Crown he did fresh Jewels bring;
Nor was his Vertue poison'd soon as born,
    With the too early Thoughts of being King.

> John Dryden, *Heroick Stanzas consecrated to the Memory of His Highness Oliver.*

The Protector, *Oliver*, now affecting *King-ship*, is petition'd to take the Title on him, by all his new made sycophant Lords &c: but dares not for feare of the *Phanatics*, not thoroughly purged out of his rebell army. (29 March 1657)

Saw the superb Funerall of the *Protectors*: ... but it was the joyfullest funerall that ever I saw, for there was none that cried, but dogs, which the souldiers hooted away with a barbarous noise; drinking and taking *tabacco* in the streets as they went. (22 November 1658)

This day (o the stupendious, & inscrutable Judgements of God) were the Carkasses of that arch-rebell *Cromwell*, *Bradshaw* the Judge who condemned his Majestie & *Ireton*, son in law to the Usurper, draged out of their superbe Tombs (in Westminster among the Kings), to *Tyburne* & hanged on the Gallows there from 9 in the morning til 6 at night, & then buried under that fatal and ignominious Monument, in a deepe pitt: Thousands of people (who has seene them in all their pride and pompous insults) being spectators: looke back at November 22, 1658, & be astonish'd — And fear God & honor the King, but meddle not with them who are given to change. (30 January 1661)

> John Evelyn, *Diary.*

That slovenly fellow which you see before us, who hath no ornament in his speech; I say that sloven, if we should ever come to have a breach with the King (which God forbid) in such case will be one of the greatest men of England.

> John Hampden, speaking to Lord Digby in the House of Commons, overheard by Sir Richard Bulstrode.

If you prove not an honest man, I will never trust a fellow with a great nose for your sake.

> Sir Arthur Haslerig, *A Word to Generall Cromwell*, 1647.

During his short residence there [Cambridge University] ... he was more famous for his exercises in the Fields than in the Schools (in which he never had the honour of, because no worth and merit to, a degree) being one of the chief match-makers and players at Foot-ball, Cudgels, or any other boysterous sport or game.

> James Heath, *Flagellum, or the Life and Death, Birth and Burial of Oliver Cromwell.*

The domestic administration of Cromwell, though it discovers great abilities, was conducted without any plan either of liberty or arbitrary power: perhaps his difficult situation admitted of neither. His foreign enterprises though full of intrepidity were pernicious to national interest and seem more the result of impetuous fury or narrow prejudices, than of cool foresight and deliberation. An eminent personage he was however in many respects, and even a superior genius, but unequal and irregular in his operations. And though not defective in any talent, except that of elocution, the abilities which in him were most admirable and which most contributed to his marvellous success, were the magnanimous resolution of his enterprises, and his peculiar dexterity in discovering the character, and practising on the weaknesses of, mankind ... his subsequent usurpation was the effect of necessity as well as ambition. ... And upon the whole, his character does not appear more extraordinary and unusual by the mixture of so much absurdity with so much penetration, than by his tempering such violent ambition, and such enraged fanaticism with so much regard to justice and humanity.

> David Hume, *History of England.*

... In a word, as he was guilty of many Crimes against which Damnation is denounced, and for which Hell-fire is prepared, so he had some good qualities which have caused the Memory of some Men in all Ages to be celebrated; and he will be look'd upon by Posterity as a brave badd man.

> Edward Hyde, Earl of Clarendon, *History of the Rebellion.*

A complex character such as that of Cromwell, is incapable of creation, except in times of great civil and religious excitement, and one cannot judge of the man without at the same time considering the contending elements by which he was surrounded. It is possible to take his character to pieces, and, selecting one or other of his qualities as a corner-stone, to build around it a monument which will show him as a patriot or a plotter, a Christian man or a hypocrite, a demon or a demi-god as the sculptor may choose.

> F. A. Inderwick, *The Interregnum, 1648–60.*

God hath honoured you . . . not only in giving you extraordinary large room in the affections of thousands and tens of thousands of his chosen ones, but in hanging upon your back the glory of all their achievements, by means of which you have been made mighty and great, formidable and dreadful in the eyes of the great ones of the world, and truly myself and all others of my mind that I could speak with, have looked upon you as the most absolute single-hearted great man in England, untainted or unbiased with ends of your own. . . .

John Lilburne, *Jonah's Cry.*

'I am,' said he, 'as much for a government by consent as any man; but where shall we find that consent? Amongst the Prelatical, Presbeyterian, Independent, Anabaptist, or Leveling Parties?' . . . Then he fell into the commendation of his own government, boasting of the protection and quiet which the people enjoyed under it, saying, that he was resolved to keep the nation from being imbrued in blood. I said that I was of the opinion too much blood had been already shed, unless there were a better account of it. 'You do well,' said he, 'to charge us with the guilt of blood; but we think there is a good return for what hath been shed.'

Edmund Ludlow, Interview with Cromwell, August 1656.

His body was wel compact and strong, his stature under 6 foote (I beleeve about two inches) his head so shaped, as you might see it a storehouse and shop both of a vast treasury of natural parts. His temper exceeding fyery as I have known, but the flame of it kept downe, for the most part, or soon allayed with those moral endowments he had. He was naturally compassionate towards objects in distresse, even to an effeminate measure; though God had made him a heart, wherein was left little roume for any feare, but what was due to himselfe, of which there was a large proportion, yet did he exceed in tenderness towards sufferers. A larger soule, I thinke, hath seldom dwelt in a house of clay than his was.

John Maidston, Letter to John Winthrop, 24 March 1659.

So restless *Cromwel* could not cease
In the inglorious Arts of Peace,
    But through adventrous War,
    Urged his active Star. . . .

    And, if we would speak true,
    Much to the Man is due.
Who, from his private Gardens, where
He liv'd reserved and austere,
    As if his highest plot
    To plant the Bergamot,
Could by industrious Valour climbe

To ruine the great Work of Time,
    And cast the Kingdome old
    Into another Mold. . . .

A *Ceasar* he ere long to *Gaul,*
To Italy an *Hannibal,*
    An to all States not free
    Shall *Clymacterick* be.
Andrew Marvell, *An Horation Ode upon Cromwel's Return from Ireland.*

Cromwell, our chief of men, who through a cloud,
    Not of war only, but detractions rude,
    Guided by faith and matchless fortitude,
    To peace and truth thy glorious way has
            ploughed
And on the neck of crowned Fortune proud
    Has reared God's trophies, and his work pursued,
    While Darwen stream with blood of Scots
            imbrued,
    And Dunbar field resounds thy praises loud,
And Worcester's laureate wreath. Yet much remains
    To conquer still; peace hath her victories
    No less renowned than war: new foes arise,
Threatening to bind our souls with secular chains:
    Help us to save free conscience from the paw
    Of hireling wolves whose gospel is their maw.
John Milton, *Sonnet XVI, To the Lord General Cromwell.*

At dinner we talked much of Cromwell, all saying he was a brave fellow and did owe his crown he got to himself, as much as any man that ever got one.

Samuel Pepys, Diary, 8 February 1667.

He was a practical mystic, the most formidable and terrible of all combinations, uniting an inspiration derived from the celestial and supernatural with the energy of a mighty man of action; a great captain, but off the field seeming, like a thunderbolt, the agent of greater forces than himself; no hypocrite, but a defender of the faith; the raiser and maintainer of the Empire of England.

Lord Rosebery, in W. C. Abbott, *The Writings and Speeches of Oliver Cromwell.*

To your Highness justly belongs the honour of dying for the people: and it cannot choose but be an unspeakable consolation to you in the last moments of your life, to consider with how much benefit to the world you are like to leave it. Tis then only (my lord) the titles you now usurp will be truly yours, you will then indeed be the deliverer of your country . . .

All this we hope from your Highness' happy expiration, who are the true Father of your country — for while you live we can call nothing ours, and

CROMWELL, RICHARD

it is from your death that we hope for our inheritances. . . .

There is indeed that necessity which we think there is of saving the vineyard of the Commonwealth if possible by destroying the wild boar that is broke into it.
Edward Sexby, *Killing No Murder.*

Whilst he was cautious of his own words, (not putting forth too many lest they should betray his thoughts) he made others talk until he had, as it were, sifted them, and known their most intimate designs.
Sir William Waller, *Recollections.*

I . . . had occasion to converse with Mr Cromwell's physician, Dr Simcott, who assured me that for many years his patient was a most splenetick man and had phansies about the cross in that town; and that he had been called up to him at midnight, and such unseasonable hours very many times, upon a strong phansy, which made him believe he was then dying; and there went a story of him, that in the day-time, lying melancholy in his bed, be believed the spirit appeared to him, and told him that he should be the greatest man, (not mentioning the word king) in this Kingdom. Which his uncle, Sir Thomas Steward, who left him all the little estate Cromwell had, told him was traiterous to relate.
Sir Philip Warwick, on Cromwell's early manhood, in *Memoirs of Sir Philip Warwick.*

Cromwell: 'What if a man should take upon him to be king?'
Whitelocke: 'I think that Remedy would be worse than the Disease.'
Cromwell: 'Why do you think so?'
Whitelocke: 'As to your own Person the Title of King would be of no Advantage, because you have the full Kingly Power in you already . . . I apprehend indeed, less Envy and Danger, and Pomp, but not less Power, and real Opportunities of doing Good in your being General than would be if you had assumed the Title of King.'
Bulstrode Whitelocke, *Memorialls of English Affairs.*

He would sometimes be very cheerful with us, and laying aside his greatness he would be exceeding familiar with us, and by way of diversion would make verses with us, and everyone must try his fancy. He commonly called for tobacco, pipes, and a candle, and would now and then take tobacco himself; then he would fall again to his serious and great business.
Ibid.

In short, every Beast hath some evil Properties; but Cromwel hath the Properties of all evil Beasts.
Archbishop John Williams to King Charles at Oxford, in Hackett, *Life of Archbishop Williams.*

. . . the English Monster, the Center of Mischief, a shame to the British Chronicle, a pattern for Tyranny, Murther and Hypocrisie, whose bloody *Caligula, Domitian,* having at last attained the height of his *Ambition,* for Five years space, he wallowed in the blood of many Gallant and *Heroick* Persons. . . .
Gerard Winstanley, *Loyal Martyrology.*

See also Charles II, Thomas Fairfax, Thomas Hobbes, Henry Ireton, Thomas Jefferson, Theodore Roosevelt

CROMWELL, RICHARD

1626–1712 Lord Protector

Next him his Son and *Heir apparent*
Succeeded, though a lame *Vicegerent*;
Who first laid by the *Parliament,*
The only *Crutch* on which *he leant*;
And then sunk underneath the *State,*
That rode him above *Horseman's Weight.*
Samuel Butler, *Hudibras,* part III, canto ii.

His humanity, ingenuousness, and modesty, the mediocrity of his abilities, and the docility with which he submitted to the guidance of persons wiser than himself, admirably qualified him to be the head of a limited monarchy.
T. B. Macaulay, *History of England.*

Richard the fourth just peeping out of squire
(No fault so much as the old one was his sire
For men believed though all went in his name
He'd but be tenant till the landlord came.)
When on a sudden all amazed we found
The seven years Babel tumbled to the ground,
And he, poor heart, thanks to his cunning kin,
Was soon in cuerpo honest Dick again.
(*in cuerpo* = naked)
Robert Wild, *Iter Boreale.*

CROMWELL, THOMAS, EARL OF ESSEX

1485?–1540 Statesman, Administrator

Of what generacyon thou were no tonge can tell,
Whether of Chayme, or Syschemell,
Or else sent to us frome the deuyll of hell.
Synge trolle on away.
Ballad on his death, in Percy's *Reliques of Ancient English Poetry,* vol. 2. (Chayme and Syschemell are Cain and Abel.)

He was the first chief minister that England had ever had, who was baseborn and yet not a cleric. He stood completely outside the great religious movement of his time, and only made use of it to further his own political ends. He came at a time when things were in an unsettled state and ready for a change: his personality, emotionless, practical, stern, impressed itself on every phase of the national life.

R. B. Merriman, *Life and Letters of Thomas Cromwell.*

For Thomas Cromwell was a freak in English history, and that, perhaps, is why he has been so disliked: an iron-fisted bureaucrat who crammed into his brief reign the kind of process which in England, we like to maintain, is carried out insensibly, over centuries. He overhauled the machinery of government as it had never been overhauled since the reign of Henry II; and he overhauled it so drastically that much of it was not radically altered till the reign of Victoria. In six hundred years of history he stands out as the most radical of modernisers. Modern history, if it begins anywhere, begins, in England, with him.

H. R. Trevor-Roper, *England's Moderniser.*

See also Stephen Gardiner

CROSBY, (HARRY LILLIS) 'BING'

1901?–1977 Actor, Singer

If I've achieved any success as a warbler it's because I've managed to keep the kind of naturalness in my style, my phrasing, and my mannerisms which any Joe Doakes possesses.

They feel no kinship for a singer with a wonderful register and an elaborate range. They realize that he's achieved something they can never hope to achieve. But it's my hunch that most men feel that if they had gotten the opportunities I've had they could have done just as well. I don't doubt that there's a lot of truth in that. I'm certainly not a handsome figure, being on the short, dumpy side, and with hair that is thinning or has thinned. I have no glamour, no continental suavity, no bedroom eyes. So they figure I'm just one of the guys they run into every day at the pool room, or at the ball game, or at the office, or out hunting, or on the golf course.

On himself, *Call Me Lucky*

If I hadn't found something as easy as singing to earn me a living, I'm afraid the name of Crosby would be adding to the clutter of the stalls that peddle learning to the American public at two fifty a volume. In short, ever since Mother Crosby lent me a hand with my first grammar school composition on why a fly

can walk a ceiling, a phenomenon that's always fascinated me, I've cherished a yen to hunt and peck my way into the charmed circle of literati. However the lure of the open road, a topless flivver and a set of second hand drums were my undoing. The gypsy got the best of the bard and the Shakespeare in me has been groaning with frustration ever since.

On himself in a telegram to the radio editor of the Lincoln, Nebraska, *Star*, in Barry Ulanov, *The Incredible Crosby.*

I tell you . . . there's just no other gate like that Bing gate; he's the toppest . . . the peerest.

Louis Armstrong in J. T. H. Mize, *Bing Crosby and the Bing Crosby Style.*

I've used an expression — I've been criticised for using it — yet I say it very lovingly: . . . once Bing hit success, he placed himself in a little Cellophane bag and he zipped it up and he just will not allow anyone to get inside that bag. He doesn't want to be told that he's good.

Bob Hope, in Charles Thompson, *Bing.*

There was once a famous thing that he did while on a television show; he was asked by the interviewer why it was he had this calm about him and a sort of unruffled air? He reached into his pocket and pulled out an enormous wad of dollar bills, and he said 'that helps!'

Stefanie Powers in *ibid.*

Bing sings like all people think they sing in the shower.

Dinah Shore in J. T. H. Mize, *Bing Crosby and the Bing Crosby Style.*

CROSSMAN, RICHARD HOWARD STAFFORD

1907–74 Labour Politician, Journalist

I am an old-fashioned Zionist who believes that anti-Semitism and racialism are endemic.

On himself, Diary, 29 September 1964.

Minister, you have a very peculiar taste — the kind of peculiar taste which will enable you to enjoy the things that are said about you when your health is proposed.

Dame Evelyn Sharp, in Richard Crossman, Diary, 27 October 1964.

CRUIKSHANK, GEORGE

1792–1878 Cartoonist

The genius of Cruikshank has been cast away in an utterly ghastly and lamentable manner: his superb line-work, worthy of any class of subject, and his powers of conception and composition, of which I cannot venture to estimate the range in their degraded application, having been condemned, by his fate, to be spent either in rude jesting, or in vain war with conditions of vice too low alike for record or rebuke, among the dregs of the British populace.
    John Ruskin, *The Cestus of Aglaia.*

A fine rough English diamond.
    W. M. Thackeray, *An Essay on the Genius of George Cruikshank.*

There must be no smiling with Cruikshank. A man who does not laugh outright is a dullard, and has no heart. Even the old 'Dandy of Sixty' [George IV] must have laughed at his own wondrous grotesque image, as they say Louis Philippe did, who saw all the caricatures that were made of himself. And there are some of Cruikshank's designs which have the blessed faculty of creating laughter as often as you see them.
    Ibid.

CUMBERLAND, DUKE OF, ERNEST AUGUSTUS, KING OF HANOVER

1771–1851

Satan next took the army list in hand
  Where he found a new 'Field Marshal';
And when he saw this high command
  Conferred on his Highness of Cumberland,
'Oh were I prone to cavil – or were I not the Devil,
I should say this was somewhat partial;
  Since the only wounds that this Warrior gat
Were from God knows whom – and the Devil
               knows what!'
    Lord Byron, *The Devil's Drive.*

... what the country cares about is to have a life more, whether male or female, interposed between the succession and the King of Hanover.
    Lord Clarendon, Letter to Lord Granville on the birth of Princess Victoria, November 1840.

No government can last that has him either for a friend or an enemy.
    Lord Grey, in Earl of Stanhope, *Notes of Conversations with the Duke of Wellington 1831–51.*

The then Duke of Cumberland (the *foolish* Duke, as he was called), came one night into Foote's green-room at the Haymarket Theatre. 'Well, Foote,' said he, 'Here I am, ready as usual, to swallow all your good things.' – 'Upon my soul,' replied Foote, 'Your Royal Highness must have an excellent digestion, for you never bring any up again.'
    Samuel Rogers, *Table Talk.*

Go instantly, and take care that *you don't get pelted*!
    The Duke of Wellington, advice to Cumberland on William IV's death, June 1837.

CUMMINGS, EDWARD ESTLIN

1894–1962 Poet

I did not decide to become a poet – I was always writing poetry.
    On himself, in Bethany K. Dumas, *E. E. Cummings: A Remembrance of Miracles.*

Cummings' inventions, too, are sometimes gimcrack and wasted, but the best of them have enriched the common language.
    Malcolm Cowley, *A Second Flowering.*

He was the most brilliant monologuist I have known. What he poured forth was a mixture of cynical remarks, puns, hyperboles, outrageous metaphors, inconsequence, and tough-guy talk spoken from the corner of his wide expressive mouth: pure Cummings, as if he were rehearsing something that would afterwards appear in print.
    Ibid.

Of course he was a lyric poet in the bad-boy tradition, broadly speaking, of Catullus and Villon and Verlaine.
    Ibid.

His mind was essentially extemporaneous. His fits of poetic fury were like the maenadic seizures described in Greek lyrics.
    John Dos Passos, *The Best Times.*

Cummings's delight in certain things were contagious as a child's. Christmas tree balls, stars, snowflakes. Elephants were his totem. I would never have enjoyed snow so much if I hadn't walked around Washington Square with Cummings in a snowstorm. He loved mice. He had a great eye for sparrows and all pert timid brighteyed creatures.
    Ibid.

He made an attempt to break down certain barriers between himself and his reader. He did this by treating his reader with a greater degree of intimacy than his reader was always prepared for. Many of his poems have the external features of highly intimate letters.

> Bethany K. Dumas, *E. E. Cummings: A Remembrance of Miracles.*

His endeavor is to represent direct experience by the very form of his work as well as by its meaning; it is a sort of super-verbalism that drives some readers to frenzy and others to disgust, but conceals in its depths, if one have sufficient patience and tolerance, much brilliant irony and much poignant beauty.

> Stanley J. Kunitz and Howard Haycraft eds, *Twentieth Century Authors.*

Cummings was one of a continuous line of American artists who have challenged the nation to reassess fundamental aims and values ... Cummings' poetry is one long letter, pregnant with joy, addressed to most people from an immigrant in nowhere.

> Barry A. Marks, *E. E. Cummings.*

He has not so much tried to give life to words but to their grammatical-syntactical context: to give life not to the substance of a sentence but to its structure.

> Roy Harvey Pearce, *The Continuity of American Poetry.*

... he replaces the old poetic conventions with equally limited conventions of his own.

> Allen Tate, in Stanley J. Kunitz and Howard Haycraft eds, *Twentieth Century Authors.*

Cummings, responding to French art, always admiring the French civilization, nonetheless spent most of his life in the United States. He was a goldfinch needing a native tree to sing from.

> Eve Triem, *E. E. Cummings.*

I think of Cummings as Robinson Crusoe at the moment when he first saw the print of a naked human foot in the sand. That ... implied a new language — and a readjustment of conscience.

> William Carlos Williams, in Roy Harvey Pearce, *The Continuity of American Poetry.*

Cummings's style is an eternal adolescent, as fresh and often as winning but as half-baked as boyhood. ... He has apparently no faculty for self-criticism. One imagines him giving off poems as spontaneously as perspiration and with as little application of the intellect.

> Edmund Wilson, in S. V. Baum ed., *E. E. Cummings and the Critics.*

See also W. H. Auden

CURLL, EDMUND
1675—1747 Bookseller

There is indeed but one bookseller eminent among us for this abomination [sc. printing indecent books], and from him the crime takes the just denomination of *Curlicism.* The fellow is a contemptible wretch in a thousand ways: he is odious in his person, scandalous in his fame; he is marked by nature.

> Anon., in *Weekly Journal, or Saturday Post,* 5 April 1718.

Curll was in person very tall and thin, an ungainly, awkward, white-faced man. His eyes were a light grey, large, projecting, gogle, and purblind. He was splayfooted and baker-kneed. He had a good natural understanding, and was well acquainted with more than the title-pages of books. He talked well on some subjects, and was not an infidel.... He was a debauchee.

> Thomas Amory, *The Life of John Buncle.*

The caitiff Vaticide.

> Alexander Pope, *The Dunciad,* Book II.

CURZON, GEORGE NATHANIEL, MARQUESS CURZON OF KEDLESTON
1859—1925 Statesman

I met Curzon in Downing Street, from whom I got the sort of greeting a corpse would give to an undertaker.

> Stanley Baldwin, attributed, 1933, after Baldwin became Prime Minister — a job that Curzon always wanted.

Kipling once said to me of Curzon, that his activity was the product of bad health. Ordinary existence was barred to him. So his iron corset may have been responsible for his ill-directed drive and energy which enabled him to destroy the independence of the House of Lords.

> Lord Beaverbrook, *Don't Trust to Luck.*

Britannia's butler.

> Max Beerbohm, in Cecil Beaton, *The Strenuous Years.*

.... He told me once that the secret of life was ASSUMPTION. Few people will challenge what appears to be a fait accompli.

> Henry Channon, Diary, 23 March 1925.

215

... above all a *savant* and an historian and not a man of action ... he would bore the Cabinet by endless discourses and when asked for his policy would look disconcerted and astonished.

H. A. L. Fisher, in conversation with Harold Nicolson, 11 October 1933.

Curzon was not perhaps a great man, but he was a supreme Civil Servant.

David Lloyd George, in conversation with Harold Nicolson, 6 July 1936.

In parliamentary life, he was to be one who stayed to get his feet wet before deciding that a ship was sinking.

Leonard Mosley, *The Glorious Fault.*

Ah, those Curzonian dissertations! ... As if some stately procession proceeding orderly through Arcs de Triomphe along a straight wide avenue: outriders, escorts, bands; the perfection of accoutrements, the precise marshalling of detail, the sense of conscious continuity, the sense of absolute control. The voice rising at moments in almost histrionic scorn, or dropping at moments into a hush of sudden emotion; and then a flash of March sunshine, a sudden dart of eighteenth-century humour, a pause while his wide shoulders rose and fell in rich amusement. And all this under a cloud of exhaustion, under a cloud of persistent pain.

Harold Nicolson, *Some People.*

... He achieved successes rather than success. Had his will been as forceful as his intellect, his determination as constant as his industry, he might have triumphed over his own anachronisms. But the tense self-preoccupation of the chronic invalid robbed him of all elasticity and he failed to adapt himself to the needs of a transitional age which did not like him and which he did not like. He will live less by his achievements than by his endeavours: he will live as a man of great ambition and some egoism, who was inspired by a mystic faith in the imperial destiny of his country and devoted to that faith unexampled industry, great talents and an abiding energy of soul.

Harold Nicolson, in the *Dictionary of National Biography.*

My name is George Nathaniel Curzon,
I am a most superior person,
My cheek is pink, my hair is sleek,
I dine at Blenheim once a week.

After lines by Cecil Spring-Rice, in *The Masque of Balliol.*

See also Lord Kitchener

216

CUSHING, CALEB
1800—79 Politician

Yes, yes, I know where he is, You will find him up in the Athenaeum Library. He thinks there's a book up there which has got something in it he doesn't know, but I guess he'll find himself mistaken.

Colonel Barnes, in Claude M. Fuess, *The Life of Caleb Cushing.*

In the 'gentle art of making enemies' he was altogether too adept. Unfortunately too, he seemed temperamentally unable to make conciliatory advances; like the proud Duke in Browning's poem, he chose 'never to stoop'.

Claude M. Fuess, *The Life of Caleb Cushing.*

Lay aside, all yet dead,
For in the next bed
Reposes the body of Cushing;
He has crowded his way
Through the world, as they say,
And even though dead will keep pushing.

Hannah F. Gould, proposed epitaph, in Claude M. Fuess, *The Life of Caleb Cushing.*

Speaking of Cushing, he [Franklin Pierce] told me that the unreliability, the fickleness, which is usually attributed to him is an actual characteristic, but that it is intellectual, not moral. He has such comprehensiveness, such mental variety and activity, that, if left to himself, he cannot keep fast hold of one view of things, and so cannot, without external help, be a consistent man. He needs the influence of a more single and stable judgment to keep him from divergency, and on this condition, he is a most inestimable coadjutor. As regards learning and ability, he has no superior.

Nathaniel Hawthorne, from *The French and Italian Notebooks of Nathaniel Hawthorne.*

General C. is a dreffle smart man:
He's ben on all sides that give places or pelf;
But consistency still wuz a part of his plan, —
He's ben true to *one* party, an' that is himself.
James Russell Lowell, 1847, in M. M. C. Hodgson, *Caleb Cushing.*

Few men more versatile have played their part
On the world's shifting stage; not even he
Whom glorious Dryden, with consummate art,
Portrayed as 'all mankind's epitome!'
Jurist profound, and in affairs of State
Of counsel apt; a tried diplomatist,
Spain, China, England, felt his power insist
Upon his country's cause; in strong debate
His fervid spirit led the fiery van;

This scholar versed in tongues, this earnest man
By studious toil who won the title 'Great',
A stormy course for Fame's proud guerdon ran;
Through years not oft vouchsafed to human kind
 Still grandly towered the strength of Cushing's
 mind.
 George Lunt, in Claude M. Fuess, *The Life of Caleb Cushing.*

... one of the most brilliant special pleaders of his time. He was especially adept at finding precedents and arguments for whatever course of action the Executive desired.
 Roy Meredith, *Lincoln's Contemporaries.*

... his utterances smacked of the study, for he quoted from the *Iliad* with the same facility as did other members from the Bible.
 James Ford Rhodes, *History of the United States from the Compromise of 1850.*

CUSHING, HARVEY WILLIAMS

1869–1939 Neurological Surgeon

I remember the time when Mrs. Cushing took me to see [J.S.] Sargent's portrait of my master. I was speechless, stuttered something about its being a remarkable work of art and ducked out. Sargent had caught the mean look in the eyes and the disdainful sneer on the lips which his pupils had seen so often when, they had fallen short of his fastidious expectations. When he first saw it he is said to have remarked, 'Looks like I'd been weaned on a pickle'.
 Percival Bailey, in *The Founders of Neurology.*

See also Calvin Coolidge

CUSHMAN, CHARLOTTE SAUNDERS

1816–76 Actress

Bigotry itself must stand abashed before the life of our dead Queen, whose every thought and act were given for years to an art which ignorance and envy have battled in vain for centuries.
 Lawrence Barrett, in *New York Herald,* February 1876.

[George Eliot, George Sand and Elizabeth Barrett Browning] do not stand as high in their respective professions as she stands on the stage. They tasted but gingerly of the world's applause; she drained the brimming goblet.
 James McVicker, in Joseph Leach, *Bright Particular Star.*

... [James] Murdoch thought her not unlike a 'female Richelieu' and was convinced that 'wealth had no more devoted worshipper.' Men, on the whole, were put off by a streak of hardness in her character and were apt to say, disparagingly, that she not only thought like a man but looked like one. But Miss Cushman was the first actress on the American stage to evoke perpetual feminine adulation, and actors may also have been exasperated by her capacity, whether on the stage or off, for infatuating women.
 Lloyd Morris, *Curtain Time.*

The rare pleasure taken by this brawny, deep-voiced woman in playing men's parts was indulgently interpreted as the whim of a great actress, and she was very great, and in 1860 was at her peak. But as Hamlet or as Romeo, Cardinal Wolsey or Claude Melnotte, her peculiar, hollow tones, which seemed to belong to neither sex, hit on the ear perplexingly. Her large bosom, which couldn't be concealed, contrasted strangely with her masculine features, she looked neither man nor woman. Mary Devlin had once been her Juliet and during those performances, Miss Cushman confessed, she did indeed wish 'that she had been a *man*!'
 Eleanor Ruggles, *Prince of Players: Edwin Booth.*

[The role of Meg Merrilies] was her sure moneymaker. Actors playing with her these days whispered that as she gave her final death shriek in the part, she pounded her breast, which was known to be on fire with cancer, so as to make her famous cry one of real agony.
 Ibid.

She was the source and mainspring of the whole tragedy. She was inhuman, terrible, incredible, and horribly fascinating.
 John Rankin Towse, on Cushman as Lady Macbeth, in Toby Cole and Helen Krich Chinoy, *Actors On Acting.*

CUSTER, GEORGE ARMSTRONG

1839–76 Soldier

Cut off from aid, abandoned in the midst of incredible odds; waving aloft the sabre which had won him victory so often; the pride and glory of his comrades, the noble Custer fell: bequeathing to the nation his sword, to his comrades an example, to his friends a memory; and to his beloved one a hero's name.
 Lawrence Barrett, in Frederick Whittaker, *A Complete Life of Gen. George A. Custer.*

The North was given new hope when Custer's cavalry victories made the headlines, for up to that time

Union cavalry victories were a rarity. It was natural that he became the *beau ideal* of cavalry. Generals who *led* men were rare; generals who *won* battles were rarer. It is no wonder that he was idolized from President Lincoln down. All the world loves a winner.

Lawrence A. Frost, *The Custer Album.*

CUTHBERT

circa 635—87 Saint

In order to make more widely known the height of glory attained after death by God's servant Cuthbert. . . . Divine Providence guided the brethren to exhume his bones. After eleven years, they expected to find his flesh reduced to dust and the remains withered, as is usual in dead bodies; and they proposed to place them in a new coffin on the same site but above ground level, so that he might receive the honours due to him. When they informed Bishop Eadbert of their wish, he gave approval and directed that it should be carried out on the anniversary of his burial. This was done, and when they opened the grave, they found the body whole and incorrupt as though still living and the limbs flexible, so that he looked as if he were asleep rather than dead. Furthermore all the vestments in which he was clothed appeared not only spotless but wonderfully fresh and fair.

Bede, *Ecclesiastical History of the English People,* translated by Leo Sherley-Price.

CUTLER, SIR JOHN

1608?—93 Merchant

Sir John Cutler had a pair of black worsted stockings which his maid darned so often with silk that they became at last a pair of silk stockings.

Dr Arbuthnot, in the *Dictionary of National Biography.*

Resolve me, Reason, which of these is worse,
Want with a full, or with an empty purse?
Thy life, more wretched, Cutler, was confess'd,
Arise and tell me, was thy death more bless'd?
Cutler saw tenants break, and houses fall,
For very want; he could not build a wall.
His only daughter in a stranger's pow'r,
For very want; he could not pay a dow'r.
A few grey hairs his rev'rend temples crown'd
'Twas very want that sold them for two pound.
What ev'n deny'd a cordial at his end,
Banish'd the doctor, and expell'd the friend?
What but a want, which you perhaps think mad,
Yet numbers feel the want of what he had.
Cutler and Brutus, dying both exclaim,
'Virtue! and Wealth! what are ye but a name!'

Alexander Pope, *Epistle iii, to Allen Lord Bathurst, Of the Use of Riches.*

D

DALTON, JOHN
1766—1844 Chemist

Mr. Dalton's aspect and manner were repulsive. There was no gracefulness belonging to him. His voice was harsh and brawling, his gait stiff and awkward; his style of writing and conversation dry and almost crabbed. In person he was tall, bony, and slender. He never could learn to swim: on investigating this circumstance he found that his specific gravity as a mass was greater than that of water; and he mentioned this in his lectures on natural philosophy in illustration of the capability of different persons for attaining the art of swimming. Independence and simplicity of manner and originality were his best qualities. Though in comparatively humble circumstances he maintained the dignity of the philosophical character. As the first distinct promulgator of the doctrine that the elements of bodies unite in definite proportions to form chemical compounds, he has acquired an undying fame.

Humphry Davy, in W. C. Henry, *Memoirs of the Life and Scientific Researches of John Dalton.*

In his lectures he used to quote the *Optics* of Newton, saying that Newton had expressed his views almost as well as he could express them himself. Whatever came into his mind, from any source, he seemed always to consider his own property. He was a very disinterested man, and had no ambition beyond that of being thought a great philosopher. He was a very coarse experimenter, and almost always found the results he required, trusting to his head rather than to his hands. Memory and observation were subordinate qualities in his mind; he followed with ardour analogies and inductions, and however his claims to originality may admit of question, I have no doubt that he was one of the most original philosophers of his time, and one of the most ingenious.

Ibid.

For several years of his life he was in the habit every Thursday afternoon, when the weather permitted, of taking exercise in the open air, and of spending a few hours in company with a few intimate friends, in the enjoyment of his favourite diversion of bowling. . . . On these occasions his spirits were buoyant and cheerful, and he entered into the sport with all the keen relish of boyhood. Sometimes, when a fall of snow had taken place, he has been known to request that the snow might be swept from the bowling green that he might not be disappointed of his game. When it came to his turn to bowl, he threw his whole soul into his game, and after he had delivered the bowl from his hand, it was not a little amusing to spectators to see him running after it across the green, stooping down as if talking to the ball, and waving his hands from one side to the other exactly as he wished the bias of the ball to be, and manifesting the most intense interest in its coming near to the point at which he aimed. A small sum, a few pence, was played for each game, in order to pay for the use of the green, and Dalton set down in his pocket-book with the minutest accuracy, the amount of his losses or gains.

Samuel Giles, in *ibid.*

Dalton's habits of association and reasoning were slow and somewhat laborious, even when he was merely perusing the deductions of other mathematicians. In reading the Principia with him, I observed that he would rarely combine ratios by a mental process, but insisted upon my writing them down on a slate, under one another, and then deliberately effecting their combination. There was nothing fitful or impulsive in his nature; no sudden gleams of inspiration. He was ever calm, thoughtful, passionless. Imagination had absolutely no part in his discoveries: except, perhaps, as enabling him to gaze, in mental vision, upon the ultimate atoms of matter, and as shaping forth those pictorial representations of unseen things, by which his earliest as well as his latest philosophical speculations were illustrated.

W. C. Henry, in *ibid.*

What chemists took from Dalton was not new experimental laws but a new way of practicing chemistry (he himself called it the 'new system of chemical philosophy'), and this proved so rapidly fruitful that only a few of the older chemists in France and Britain were able to resist it.

Thomas S. Kuhn, *The Structure of Scientific Revolutions.*

He was not a fluent speaker, and when, as President, he had to make a few remarks when the reader of a paper stopped, he is reported to have sometimes contented himself by saying, 'This paper will no doubt be found interesting by those who take an interest in it'.

J. J. Thomson, *Recollections and Reflections*.

DANA, CHARLES ANDERSON

1819–97 Journalist

I have always felt that whatever the Divine Providence permitted to occur I was not too proud to report.

On himself, in L. Ziff, *The American 1890's*.

. . . one of the most eclectic of American scholars, one of the most executive of American minds.

Samuel Bowles, in Candace Stone, *Dana and the Sun*.

But bless ye, Mr Dana! May you live a thousan' years
To sorta keep things lively in this vale of human
tears. . . .

Eugene Field, in Frank Luther Mott, *American Journalism, A History: 1690–1960*.

. . . poor, despised, disgraced, Old Ananias!
Joseph Pulitzer, in W. A. Swanberg, *Pulitzer*.

. . . a poltroon in an hour of danger.
Ibid.

A master of the half-hidden barb, the deadly understatement, the parody, the pointed doggerel, Dana could skewer a victim in the most gentlemanly language . . .

W. A. Swanberg, *Pulitzer*.

DANBY, EARL OF (THOMAS OSBORNE)

1631–1712 Statesman

The Cabal had bequeathed to him the art of bribing Parliaments, an art still rude, and giving little promise of the rare perfection to which it was brought in the following century. He improved greatly on the plan of the first inventors. They had merely purchased orators: but every man who had a vote might sell himself to Danby.

T. B. Macaulay, *History of England*.

. . . his short neck, his legs uneven, the vulgar said, as those of a badger, his forehead low as that of a baboon, his purple cheeks, and his monstrous length of chin. . . .

Ibid.

The Earl of Danby thought he could serve himself of this plot of Oates, and accordingly endeavoured at it; but it is plain that he had no command of the engine; and instead of his sharing the popularity of nursing it, he found himself so intrigued that it was like a wolf by the ears; he could neither hold it nor let it go; and, for certain, it bit him at last: just as when a barbarous mastiff attacks a man, he cries poor cur! and is pulled down at last. So the Earl's favour did but give strength to the creature to worry him. Herein he failed, 1. In joining to aid a design of which he did not know the bottom. 2. In thinking a lord Treasurer that had enriched himself and his family could ever be popular.

Roger North, *Life of the Right Hon. Francis North, Lord Baron Guildford*.

By conserving the national finances he hoped to establish royal independence; by bribing the lesser members of the Commons he obtained the votes of the obscure, even though they cost him the diatribes of the eminent; for he rejoiced more in the votes of ninety-nine silent legislators than the conversion of one notable opponent. He was not the first English statesman to use bribery or influence, but he was the first to realise the value of organised system and personal mediocrity in the methods and material of politics, with which aids he contrived to establish Charles's absolutism on a basis, if not of consent, at least of negotiation and influence.

David Ogg, *England in the Reign of Charles II*

See also Lord Shaftesbury

DANIELS, JOSEPHUS

1862–1948 Journalist, Diplomat

When I was a lad I pondered some
On the horrible effects of the Demon Rum
I scorned to dally with the dread highball
And I never saw a bottle of champagne at all.
I kept away from guzzling men
And now I am the ruler of U.S.N.

J. C. Furnass, *The Life and Times of the Late Demon Rum*.

D'ARBLAY, MADAME, see under
BURNEY, FANNY

DARROW, CLARENCE SEWARD

1857–1938 Lawyer, Social Reformer

I don't believe in God because I don't believe in Mother Goose.

On himself, A. K. Adams, *The Home Book of Humorous Quotations*.

We know life is futile. A man who considers that his life is of very wonderful importance is awfully close to a padded cell.
On himself, in a lecture at the University of Chicago, 1929, on 'Facing Life Fearlessly: Omar Khayyam and A. E. Housman'.

I do not believe in the law of hate. I may not be true to my ideals always, but I believe in the law of love, and I believe you can do nothing with hatred. I would like to see a time when man loves his fellow-man and forgets his color or his creed. We will never be civilized until that time comes.
On himself, in A. and L. Wemberg eds, *Verdicts out of Court*.

He advised that Methodists be accepted as jurymen because their religious emotions can be transmuted into love and charity; but warned against taking Presbyterians because they knew right from wrong.
Harry Golden, *For 2¢ Plain*.

I had a visit not long ago from Clarence Darrow, the great American barrister for defending murderers. He had only a few days in England, but could not return home without seeing me, because he had so often used my poems to rescue his clients from the electric chair. Loeb and Leopold owe their life sentence partly to me; and he gave me a copy of his speech, in which, sure enough, two of my pieces are misquoted.
A. E. Housman, *Letters*.

Darrow's journey among the barbarians of the universe encompassed the stammering years of America's young adulthood. His presence along the way added much to the tumultuous years into which the lawyer was, as he liked to think, haphazardly thrown. In spite of his feeling that reality is grim, that futility and dread of annihilation are requisites for straight thinking and that poverty and relentless fate haunt mankind constantly, the infinite paradox on which he built all of his work and art predicted the hope 'that tomorrow will be less irksome than today.'
Abe C. Ravitz, *Clarence Darrow and the American Literary Tradition*.

DARWIN, CHARLES ROBERT

1809—82 Naturalist

Early in 1856 Lyell advised me to write out my views pretty fully, and I began at once to do so on a scale three or four times as extensive as that which was afterwards followed in my *Origin of Species*; yet it was only an abstract of the materials which I had collected and I got through about half the work on this scale. But my plans were overthrown, for early in the summer of 1858 Mr. Wallace, who was then in the Malay archipelago, sent me an essay *On the Tendency of Varieties to depart indefinitely from the Original Type*; and this essay contained exactly the same theory as mine. Mr. Wallace expressed the wish that if I thought well of his essay, I should send it to Lyell for perusal. The circumstances under which I consented at the request of Lyell and Hooker to allow of an abstract from my MS., together with a letter to Asa Gray, dated September 5, 1857, to be published at the same time with Wallace's Essay, are given in the *Journal of the Proceedings of the Linnean Society*, 1858, p. 45. I was at first very unwilling to consent, as I thought Mr. Wallace might consider my doing so unjustifiable, for I did not then know how generous and noble was his disposition. The extract from my MS. and the letter to Asa Gray had neither been intended for publication, and were badly written. Mr. Wallace's essay, on the other hand, was admirably expressed and quite clear. Nevertheless, our joint productions excited very little attention, and the only published notice of them which I can remember was by Professor Haughton of Dublin, whose verdict was that all that was new in them was false, and what was true was old. This shows how necessary it is that any new view should be explained at considerable length in order to arouse public attention.
On himself, *Autobiography*.

I have no patience whatever with these gorilla damnifications of humanity.
Thomas Carlyle, in Edward Latham, *Famous Sayings*.

In his personal character and relations, Darwin stands out in later nineteenth-century England, not as the vanguard of twentieth-century biology, but as one of his own 'living fossils', an eighteenth-century savant living in the railway age. He still preserved the conception of the integrity and supremacy of the intellect . . . and could never have imagined that his beloved natural history would be less altered by the acceptance of his revolutionary ideas that it was destined to be by the social changes which as a good liberal he supported.
R. A. Crowson, in S. A. Barnett, *A Century of Darwin*.

If the pursuit of truth be worthy of reverence, there could be no other earthly resting-place for a man who by his proof of the fact of evolution was the Copernicus, and by his establishment of the principle of natural selection was the Newton of the realm of living things: Charles Darwin.

Sir Gavin de Beer, *Reflections of a Darwinian.*

Darwin's thesis that species evolve was not a new one. A. R. Wallace reached a similar conclusion simultaneously with Darwin, and Lamarck and Erasmus Darwin were evolutionists two generations before him. There are reasons to think that Descartes and Buffon made the same discovery more than a century earlier. . . . Darwin obviously had predecessors who anticipated some of his discoveries. But Darwin did what none of his predecessors had done; he adduced in favour of his evolutionary views a store of facts which biologists could interpret in no way other than that in which Darwin interpreted them.

Theodosius Dobzhansky, in S. A. Barnett, *A Century of Darwin.*

It is no secret that . . . there are many to whom Mr. Darwin's death is a wholly irreparable loss. And this not merely because of his wonderfully genial, simple, and generous nature; his cheerful and animated conversation, and the infinite variety and accuracy of his information; but because the more one knew of him, the more he seemed the incorporated ideal of a man of science.

T. H. Huxley, in *Nature*, 1882.

Though he cannot be said to have proved the truth of his doctrine, he does seem to have proved that it *may* be true, which I take to be as great a triumph as knowledge and ingenuity could possibly achieve on such a question. Certainly nothing can be at first sight more entirely implausible than his theory, and yet after beginning by thinking it impossible, one arrives at something like an actual belief in it, and one certainly does not relapse into complete disbelief.

John Stuart Mill, Letter to Alexander Bain, April 1860.

I do not see that Darwin's supreme service to his fellow men was his demonstration of evolution — man could have lived on quite as happily and perhaps more morally under the old notion that he was specially made in the image of his Maker. Darwin's supreme service was that he won for man absolute freedom in the study of the laws of nature.

H. F. Osborn, *Impressions of Great Naturalists.*

What Galileo and Newton were to the seventeenth century, Darwin was to the nineteenth.

Bertrand Russell, *History of Western Philosophy.*

I never know whether to be more surprised at Darwin himself for making so much of natural selection, or at his opponents for making so little of it.

Robert Louis Stevenson, *'From his Note Book'.*

These two [Darwin and T. H. Huxley] were very great men. They thought boldly, carefully and simply, they spoke and wrote fearlessly and plainly, they lived modestly and decently; they were mighty intellectual liberators.

H. G. Wells, *Experiment in Autobiography.*

See also Erasmus Darwin, Benjamin Disraeli, T. H. Huxley, Charles Lyell, John Stuart Mill

DARWIN, ERASMUS

1731–1802 Poet, Physician

No envy mingles with our praise,
    Though could our hearts repine
At any poet's happier lays,
    They would, they must, at thine.

But we, in mutual bondage knit
    Of friendship's closest tie,
Can gaze on even Darwin's wit
    With an unjaundic'd eye;

And deem the bard, whoe'er he be,
    And howsoever known,
Who would not twine a wreath for thee,
    Unworthy of his own.

William Cowper, *Lines addressed to Dr. Darwin, Author of The Botanic Garden.*

A young man once asked him in, as he thought, an offensive manner, whether he did not find stammering very inconvenient. He answered, 'No Sir, it gives me time for reflection, and saves me from asking impertinent questions.'

Ernst Krause, *Erasmus Darwin.*

. . . that eager mind, whom fools deride
For laced and periwigged verses on his flowers;
Forgetting how he strode before his age,
And how his grandson caught from his right hand
A fire that lit the world . . . .

Alfred Noyes, *The Torchbearers.*

See also Charles Darwin

D'AVENANT, SIR WILLIAM

1606–68 Dramatist

The King knights *Will* for fighting on his side,
    Yet when *Will* comes for fighting to be tried,
There is not one in all the Armies can
    Say they ere felt, or saw this fighting man.

Strange that the Knight should not be known i'th
                                                Field,
  A Face well charg'd, tho nothing in his Shield.
Sure fighting *Will* like *Basilisk* did ride
  Among the Troops, and all that saw *Will* dy'd,
Else how could *Will* for fighting be a Knight,
  And none alive that ever saw *Will* fight.
    Anon., *Upon Fighting Will, circa* 1644.

Such were his virtues that they could command
A general applause from every hand:
His *Exit* then, this on record shall have
A *Clap* did usher *D'Avenant* to his grave.
    Anon., *Epitaph*, in Anthony à Wood, *Athenae
    Oxonienses.*

He gott a terrible clap of a black handsome wench
that lay in Axe-yard, Westminster, whom he thought
on when he speakes of Dalga in *Gondibert*, which
cost him his Nose, with which unlucky mischance
many witts were too cruelly bold.
    John Aubrey, *Brief Lives.*

Sir *William* walking by *Temple* Bar, a Fish-mongers
Boy, in watering his Fish upon the Stall, sprinkled
the *Laureat*: who snuffling loudly, complained of
the abuse. The Master Begged the Knight's Pardon,
and was for Chastising his Servant with some Expos-
tulations, as well as a Cudgel. *Zounds, Sir,* cry'd the
Boy, *its very hard I must be corrected for my
Cleanliness, the Gentleman blew his Nose upon my
Fish, and I was washing it off, that's all.* The Jest
pleas'd Sir *William* so well, that he gave him a piece
of Money. Since I have given you one old Jest upon
the Nose of Sir *William*, I'll venture to throw in
another. As he was walking along the *Mews*, an importunate Beggar-woman teiz'd him for Charity, with
often repeating, *Heaven bless your Eye-sight! God
preserve your Worship's Eye-sight* — Why, what's the
Matter with my Eye-sight, Woman? reply'd Sir
William, *I find no Defect there. Ah! good Sir! I wish
you never may,* return'd the Beggar, *for should your
sight ever fail you, you must borrow a Nose of your
Neighbour to hang your Spectacles on.*
    W. R. Chetwood, *A General History of the
    Stage.*

I am Old *Davenant* with my Fustian Quill;
  Tho' skill I have not,
  I must be writing still
    On *Gondibert*,
  That is not worth a Fart.
Waller, & Cowley, 'tis true have prais'd my Book,
  But how untruly
  All that read may look;
    Nor can *old Hobbs*
Defend me from dry Bobbs.

Then no more I'll dabble, nor pump Fancy dry,
  To compose a Fable
Shall make *Will. Crofts* to cry
  O gentle Knight,
Thou writ'st to them that shite.
    Sir John Denham and Friends, *The Author upon
    Himself.*

Mr Shakespear was his God-father & gave him his
name. (In all probability he got him). 'Tis further
said that one day going from school a grave Doctor
in Divinity met him, and ask'd him, *Child wither art
thou going in such hast?* to wch the child reply'd *O
Sir my Godfather is come to Town, & I am going to
ask his blessing.* To wch the Dr. said, *Hold Child,
you must not take the name of God in vaine.*
    Thomas Hearne, Diary, 1709.

He is a scholar of Donne's and took his sententious-
ness and metaphysics from him.
    Alexander Pope, *Conversation.*

The sort of verse Davenant makes choice of in his
Gondibert might contribute much to the vitiating
his style; for thereby he obliges himself to stretch
every period to the end of four lines: Thus the sense
is broken perpetually with parentheses, the words
jumbled in confusion, and darkness spread over all;
but it must be acknowledged, that Davenant had a
particular talent for the manners; his thoughts are
great, and there appears something roughly noble
through the whole.
    Thomas Rymer, in Theophilus Cibber, *Lives of
    the Poets.*

DAVIDSON, JO

1883–1952 Sculptor

I had brought some photos of my sculpture. Gandhi
looked at them intently and said:
'I see you make heroes out of mud.'
And I retorted: 'And sometimes vice-versa.'
    On himself, in *Between Sittings.*

Portrait making began to occupy the major part of
my time. My approach to my subjects was very
simple. I never had them pose but we just talked
about everything in the world. Sculpture, I felt, was
another language altogether that had nothing to do
with words. As soon as I got to work, I felt this other
language growing between myself and the person I
was 'busting.' I felt it in my hands. Sometimes the
people talked as if I was their confessor. As they
talked, I got an immediate insight into the sitters.
    Ibid.

This young man, who has studied in Paris, one is tempted to say, at the feet of Rodin, is a sculptor born, one who has not allowed his enormous facility to decline into dilettante methods. His touch is personal, crisply nervous, virile and not too impressionistic; the feeling for line, for structural foundation, never deserts him. That slight perpetual novelty which should season any art production, is seldom absent. There is an imaginative element, too, in his slightest effort. A torso for him is a cosmos, and he shows several that are as beautiful in their way as the Greek; indeed, when they are most beautiful they are Greek. . . .

James Gibbons Hunneker, in the New York *Sun*, 13 April 1911.

Jo believes it inevitable that a miracle will be wrought to crown his own effort with success, yet he is a shade respectful and astonished when he meets with the same success in others. He did not choose his sitters because they had prospered, though he believes in success and is himself the hero of the success story, one of Horatio Alger's.

Alice B. Toklas, in *New York Times Sunday Review*, 1951.

DAVIES, JOHN

1565?—1618 Poet

JOHN DAVIES of Hereford (for so he constantly styled himself) was the greatest Master of the Pen that England in his age beheld, for 1. Fast-writing, so incredible his expedition. 2. Fair-writing, some minutes consultation being required to decide, whether his lines were written or printed. 3. Close-writing, A Mysterie indeed, and too Dark for my Dimme Eyes to discover. 4. Various-writing, Secretary, Roman, Court and Text. . . . Our Davies had also some pretty excursions into Poetry and could flourish matter as well as Letters, with his Fancy as well as his Pen.

Thomas Fuller, *The History of the Worthies of England.*

His work . . . is voluminous, . . . the production of a man who had little better to offer than journalism, but for whom the times did not provide the opening of a journalist.

George Saintsbury, *Elizabethan Literature.*

DAVIES, SIR JOHN

1569—1626 Poet, Attorney-General

Jo. Davys goes waddling with his arse out behind as though he were about to make everyone that he meets a wall to pisse against.

John Manningham, Diary.

At length he died suddenly in his House in the *Strand.* . . . It was then commonly rumour'd that his Prophetical Lady had foretold his death in some manner, on the *Sunday* going before. For while she sate at Dinner by him, she suddenly burst out with Tears: Whereupon he asking her what the matter was, she answered, Husband, these are your Funeral Tears; to which he made reply, Pray therefore spare your Tears now, and I will be content that you shall laugh when I am dead.

Anthony à Wood, *Athenae Oxonienses.*

DAVIS, JEFFERSON

1808—89 President of the Confederacy

Jeff Davis rides a snow-white horse;
Abe Lincoln rides a mule.
Jeff Davis is a gentleman;
Abe Lincoln is a fool.

Anon. children's song, in Richard B. Harwell, 'Lincoln and the South', in R. G. Newman ed., *Lincoln for the Ages.*

We'll hang Jeff Davis to a sour apple tree,
As we go marching on.

Anon. soldiers' marching song, in W. E. Woodward, *Meet General Grant.*

Oh, the muskets they may rattle
And the cannon they may roar,
But we'll fight for you, Jeff Davis,
Along the Southern shore.

Anon., in Hudson Strode, *Jefferson Davis: Tragic Hero.*

There is no doubt that Jefferson Davis and other leaders of the South have made an army; they are making it appears, a navy; and they have made what is more than either, they have made a nation.

William Ewart Gladstone, speech at Newcastle-upon-Tyne, 7 October 1862.

. . . ambitious as Lucifer and cold as a lizard.

Sam Houston, in Carl Sandburg, *Abraham Lincoln: The Prairie Years and the War Years.*

The fact is, he is the kind of person I should expect to rescue one from a mad dog at any risk, but to insist upon a stoical indifference to the fright afterward.

Varina Howell, in Allen Tate, *Jefferson Davis: His Rise and Fall.*

224

... a man who thought in terms of principles rather than of possibilities and who cared more about proving he was right than about gaining success.

David M. Potter, in 'Jefferson Davis and the Political Factors in Confederate Defeat', in D. E. Fehrenbacher ed., *The Leadership of Abraham Lincoln.*

I am amazed that any man of judgment should hope for the success of any cause in which Jefferson Davis is a leader. There is contamination in his touch. If secession was 'the holiest cause that tongue or sword of mortal ever lost or gained,' he would ruin it! He will bear a great amount of watching. . . . He is not a cheap Judas. I do not think he would have sold the Saviour for thirty shillings; but for the successorship to Pontius Pilate he would have betrayed Christ and the apostles and the whole Christian Church.

Winfield Scott, in Charles W. Elliott, *Winfield Scott: The Soldier and the Man.*

See also Theodore Roosevelt, Thaddeus Stevens

DAVIS, RICHARD HARDING

1864—1916 Journalist, Author

Fresh, boyish, daring, manly, he suggested the well-groomed adventurer who lunched at Delmonico's or Sherry's and was off at three for some new revolution in Hayti or some war in Greece and who returned a few months later leaner and more bronzed than ever to be greeted with nods from all the club-windows that he passed.

Van Wyck Brooks, *The Confident Years: 1885—1915.*

He was one of those magnetic types, often otherwise second-rate, who establish patterns of living for others of their kind, and the notion of the novelist as war-correspondent which prevailed so long in American writing began in the early nineties undoubtedly with him.

Ibid.

He had the rare faculty of stirring by a phrase the imaginations of men, of including in a phrase a picture, an event — a cataclysm.

Winston Churchill, in *R.H.D., Appreciations of Richard Harding Davis.*

... those who knew him were less interested in the books than in the man himself — the generous, romantic, sensitive individual whose character and characteristics made him a conspicuous figure everywhere he went — and he went everywhere.

Finley Peter Dunne, in *ibid.*

The way to attend a war, for any right-thinking American correspondent, was to watch Richard Harding Davis and try to approximate his distinguished style. You needed almost as many wardrobe changes as a touring matinee idol, since it was necessary to be properly dressed for a legation garden party or scrambling up hills to catch a panoramic view of battle, which you then described in Olympian prose.

Richard O'Connor, *Jack London.*

... the glamour boy of turn-of-the-century America. . . .

Richard O'Connor, *The Scandalous Mr. Bennett.*

I knew nothing of his writing but he was clearly a robust flower of American muscular Christianity — healthy and wealthy, and, in America, wise.

William Rothenstein, *Richard Harding Davis: His Day.*

He was of that college boy's own age, but already an editor — already publishing books! His stalwart good looks were as familiar to us as were those of our own football captain; we knew his face as we know the face of the President of the United States, but we infinitely preferred Davis's.

Booth Tarkington, in Larzer Ziff, *The American 1890's.*

DAVY, SIR HUMPRHY

1778—1829 Natural Philosopher

Sir H. Davy's greatest discovery was Michael Faraday.

Anon., in the *Oxford Companion to English Literature.*

Sir Humphrey Davy
Abominated gravy.
He lived in the odium
Of having discovered Sodium.

E. C. Bentley, *Biography for Beginners.*

I was introduced to Mr. Davy, who has rooms adjoining mine in the Royal Institution: he is a very agreeable and intelligent young man, and we have interesting conversations in an evening: the principal failing in his character is, that he does not smoke.

John Dalton, Letter to John Rothwell, 10 January 1804

Davy possessed the capability, as Faraday does, of devoting all the powers of his mind to the practical and experimental investigation of a subject in all its bearings, and such a mind will rarely fail, by dint of mere industry and patient thinking, in producing results of the highest order.

Samuel Smiles, *Self-help*.

Most persons have probably heard of the letter sent to him from Italy, which reached him safely, though it only bore the mysterious superscription:-

SIROMFREDEVI
LONDRA.

C. R. Weld, *A History of the Royal Society*.

There is an entertaining anecdote illustrative of his popularity, even among the more humble classes. He was passing through the streets one fine night, when he observed a man showing the moon through a telescope. He stopped to look at the earth's satellite, and tendered a penny to the exhibitor. But the latter, on learning that his customer was no less a person than the great Davy, exclaimed with an important air, that 'he could not think of taking money from a brother philosopher'.

Ibid.

See also Michael Faraday

DAY LEWIS, CECIL

1904—72 Poet

My later work, as far as I may judge, presents a good deal more variety both in subject matter and in verse forms, a more sensuous appeal, and a greater flexibility of line, than my earlier.... What happens, as far as I can make out, is that I have some deep violent experience which, like an earthquake, throws up layers of my past that were inaccessible to me poetically till then. During the last war, for instance, I found myself able to use in verse for the first time images out of my own childhood. The new material thrown up, the new contours which life presents as a result of the seismic experience, may demand a new kind of poem. It is here that change of technique appears.

On himself, Introduction to *Selected Poems*.

DAY LEWIS JOINS UP. Cecil Day Lewis, the poet (a member of the International Association of Writers for the Defence of Culture) has joined the selection Committee of the BOOK SOCIETY.... On this Committee, Mr Day Lewis no doubt will be Change, Revolution, Youth, the Rising Generation. But this ends his stance as the Poet writing thrillers ... and establishes him as the Thriller Writer, the Underworld Man, the yesterday's newspaper, the grease in the sink-pipe of letters who has been posed for ten years as spring water.... Mr Day Lewis and his Legend are now liquidated: the liquid has flowed to

its oily shape and low level in the old sardine tin of Respectability. Mr Lewis has drained himself off, a Noyes, a Binyon, a Squire, a dullard. We can get along without him.

Geoffrey Grigson, in *New Verse*, May 1937.

Day-Lewis was a handsome man, in dress something of a dandy (in the best sense) and with a similar taste in such things as motor cars. In first coming into a room he might give the impression of austerity, but quite soon the mask would relax into its attractive lines of humour. He was, in fact, no mean anecdotalist, often against himself, at one time he had an hilarious story of catching his own dental plate before it could fly into the stalls after an impassioned end to a poetry reading.

Obituary in *The Times*, 23 May 1972.

DEBS, EUGENE VICTOR

1855—1926 Socialist

While there is a lower class I am in it, while there is a criminal element I am of it, and while there is a soul in prison I am not free.

On himself, during his trial at Canton Ohio, 16 June 1913.

I am not a ... leader. I don't want you to follow me or anything else. If you are looking for a Moses to lead you out of the ... wilderness, you will stay right where you are. I would not lead you into this promised land if I could, because if I could lead you in, someone else could lead you out.

On himself, in Emmet John Hughes, *The Ordeal of Power: A Political Memoir of the Eisenhower Years*.

Our engineer is E. V. Debs,
On him there are no spider webs;
And no one, now, the fact denies,
That on our union are no flies.

Anon., in McAlister Coleman, *Eugene V. Debs: A Man Afraid*.

Debs has a face that looks like a death's head ... as the arch 'Red' talked he was bent at the hips like an old old man, his eerie face peering up and out at the crowd like an necromancer leading a charm.

Anon., in *Los Angeles Times*, 11 September 1908.

Away with him! He utters the word 'Love'.
Dark-souled incendiary, madman forlorn,
He dares put humanity above
Discretion. Better never have been born

Than this to have offended! Learn, good brother,
   That Love and Pity are forgotten fables
Told by the drowsy years to one another
   With nothing in them to supply our tables.
These are the days of hungry common sense
   Millions of men have died to bring these days;
And more must die ere these good days go hence;
   For God moves still in most mysterious ways.
And Debs, Debs, Debs, you are out-weighed, out-
                                   priced,
These are the days of Caesar, not of Christ —
And yet — suppose — when all was done and said
There *were* a Resurrection from the Dead!
   John Cowper Powys, *To Eugene Debs.*

Under Debs' fighting leadership American Socialism
... entered its period of national popularity. Debs
himself remained curiously apart from the top direction of the Socialist movement. He could rival neither
Hillquit as an organizer nor DeLeon as a theoretician;
he neither dominated party conventions nor contributed important new doctrines. But he had
achieved a passionate sense of urgency of the class
struggle and a passionate vision of future society
liberated from capitalism.
   Arthur M. Schlesinger Jr, Introduction to
   Writings and Speeches of Eugene Debs.

... clearly the White House is the only safe place for
an honest man like Debs.
   George Bernard Shaw, in Ruth Le Prade ed.,
   Debs and the Poets.

[To hear him] was to listen to a hammer riveting a
chamber in Hell for the oppressors of the poor.
   Art Young, *On My Way.*

DEE, JOHN

1527–1608 Mathematician, Astrologer

He used to distill Egge-shells, and 'twas from hence
that Ben Johnson had his hint of the *Alkimist,* whom
he meant.
   John Aubrey, *Brief Lives.*

DEFOE, DANIEL

1661?–1731 Author, Polemicist

A true Malignant, Arrogant and Sour,
And ever Snarling at Establish'd Power.
   Anon., *The True-Born Hugonot, &c. A Satyr,
   1703.*

As in the case of Goethe, one hesitates to write
down that in ninety per cent of his writings outside
Moll Flanders Defoe is an insufferable bore. Nothing
is more dreary than the continual repetition of his
accounts of piratical adventures and sneak-thieving
in the lives of dull villains. ... With the one exception of his Moll all Defoe's characters are completely
invisible and utterly, not so much dead, as unalive in
the sense that tailors' dummies are unalive.
   Ford Madox Ford, *The March of Literature.*

Daniel Defoe, who spent his whole life, and wasted
his strength in asserting the right of Dissenters to a
toleration (and got no thanks for it but the pillory),
was scandalized at the proposal of the general principle, and was equally strenuous in excluding
Quakers, Anabaptists, Socinians, Sceptics, and all
who did not agree in the *essentials* of Christianity,
that is, who did not agree with him, from the benefit
of such an indulgence to tender consciences.
   William Hazlitt, *Fugitive Writings: On Party
   Spirit.*

The narrative manner of De Foe has a naturalness
about it beyond that of any other novel or romance
writer. His fictions have all the air of true stories. It
is impossible to believe, while you are reading them,
that a real person is not narrating to you every where
nothing but what really happened to himself. To
this, the extreme *homeliness* of their style mainly
contributes. We use the word in its best and heartiest
sense — that which comes *home* to the reader.
   Charles Lamb, *On the Secondary Novels of De
   Foe.*

Few will acknowledge all they owe
To persecuted, brave Defoe.
Achilles, in Homeric song,
May, or he may not, live so long
As Crusoe; few their strength had tried
Without so staunch and safe a guide.
What boy is there who never laid
Under his pillow, half afraid,
That precious volume, lest the morrow
For unlearnt lesson might bring sorrow?
But nobler lessons he has taught
Wide-awake scholars who fear'd naught:
A Rodney and a Nelson may
Without him not have won the day.
   Walter Savage Landor, *Daniel Defoe.*

Earless on high, stood unabash'd De Foe.
   Alexander Pope, *The Dunciad,* book ii.

That glorious old Non-con, De Foe, sharing with
Bunyan the literary honours of the sect, and
acknowledging no other chief than Milton.
   Henry Crabb Robinson, Letter to Thomas Robinson, 6 May 1848.

His great forte is his power of Vraisemblance.
  Sir Walter Scott, *Journal*, 8 May 1827.

So grave, sententious, dogmatical a Rogue, that
there is no enduring him.
  Jonathan Swift, *A Letter Concerning the
  Sacramental Test.*

He belongs, indeed, to the school of the great plain
writers, whose work is founded upon a knowledge
of what is most persistent, though not most seductive, in human nature. . . . He is of the school of
Crabbe and of Gissing, and not merely a fellow-pupil
in the same stern place of learning, but its founder
and master.
  Virginia Woolf, *The Common Reader.*

See also Robert Louis Stevenson

DEKKER, THOMAS

1570?—1641? Dramatist

Deckar excels in giving expression to certain habitual,
deeply rooted feelings, which remain pretty much
the same in all circumstances, the simple uncom-
pounded elements of nature and passion.
  William Hazlitt, *Lectures on the Age of
  Elizabeth.*

He clubbed with *Webster* in writing three Plays; and
with *Rowley* and *Ford* in another: and I think I
may venture to say, that these Plays as far exceed
those of his own Brain, as a platted Whip-cord
exceeds a single Thread in Strength.
  Gerard Langbaine, *Account of the English
  Dramatic Poets.*

Thomas Decker, a great pains taker in the dramatick
strain, and as highly conceited of those pains he
took; a high-flyer in wit, even against *Ben Johnson*
himself.
  William Winstanley, *Lives of the Most Famous
  English Poets.*

DE LA MARE, WALTER JOHN

1873—1956 Poet

One might say that, in every poet, there dwells an
Ariel, who sings, and a Prospero, who comprehends.
. . . Though the role of Prospero in de la Mare's
poetry is much greater than one may realize on a
first reading, it would not be unfair, I think, to call
him an Ariel-dominated poet. . . . His most obvious
virtues, those which no reader can fail to see

immediately, are verbal and formal, the delicacy of
his metrical fingering and the graceful architecture
of his stanzas.
  W. H. Auden, *Forewords and Afterwords.*

De la Mare offers nothing optimistic or comforting.
Human consciousness and human destiny remain
for him inexplicable puzzles. Life is transient and
death is final. His fantasy is rooted in no shared convictions or religious traditions, not even in the
superstitions of folklore. It derives its authority
solely from its appeal to the hinterland of the mind.
  W. W. Robson, *Modern English Literature.*

The delight of knowing the poet de la Mare needs
no translating into logic. But I must testify to one
gift wherein he outshines anyone I have been
lucky enough to meet. He has wisely warned us to
'look thy last on all things lovely every hour'. To this
I can add that I have never been in his company
without a sense of heightened and deepened perception. After talking to him, one goes away seeing
the world, for a while, with rechristened eyes.
  Siegfried Sassoon, *Siegfried's Journey.*

Walter de la Mare, perhaps because he had already
so much the air of being an inhabitant of the shades,
seemed confident in his modesty and modest in his
confidence. In his charming way, de la Mare can
make admissions about himself far more damaging
than those of other writers. 'It's strange, isn't it,' he
said, 'that I have a kind of sixth sense by which if
my name is printed in a newspaper I know at once
and turn immediately to it.' De la Mare has the
childlike profound innocence which accepts and
wonders at every phenomenon and is not shocked.
  Stephen Spender, *World Within World.*

Walter de la Mare owes much to Christina [Rossetti],
and, if there is any labelling to be done, I would
put you and de la Mare, that questioning poet, in
the same compartment & mark it 'Subtlety and
Sensitivity. Perishable. With Care.'
  Dylan Thomas, Letter to Pamela Hansford
  Johnson, 1933.

DE LEON, DANIEL

1852—1914 Socialist

. . . ardent student of history though he was, could
never apply its lessons to his immediate situations.
He had no fear of factionalism. In truth, he seemed
to welcome the opportunity to expel those whom
he called heretics. It gave him a feeling of power.
Like many intellectuals he sought compensation in
emotional outbursts, for a sedentary life at an

editorial desk. This he found by acting the part of an American Robespierre guillotining his victims. He became increasingly arbitrary. Every manifesto which issued from his pen was to be accepted as Holy Writ. Not until the coming of the American Communists in 1920 was there such strutting insistence on rigid adherence to doctrine as De Leon exhibited.

    McAlister Coleman, *Eugene V. Debs: A Man Unafraid.*

De Leon would have been politically sound if he had not been economically hollow.

    William D. Haywood, *Bill Haywood's Book.*

De Leon's tragedy lay in the fact that he was more Marxian than his master.

    Lillian Symes and Travers Clement, *Rebel America.*

DELIUS, FREDERICK

1862–1934 Composer

The ugliness of some of his music is really masterly.

    Anon., in *Sun*, criticism of Delius's concert on 30 May 1899.

While Beecham was rehearsing a new work by Frederick Delius in Queen's Hall, the composer was sitting up in the circle.

'Was that all right, Fred?' Beecham called out into space.

'Yes, except for the horns, perhaps,' came back the voice of Delius.

'Gentlemen, we'll try from bar X again.' . . .

'Yes, that was all right,' called out Delius.

'Oh good,' said Sir Thomas. 'You know there are no horns in that passage.'

    Leslie Ayre, *The Wit of Music.*

His features had that mingled cast of asceticism and shrewdness one mentally associates with high-ranking ecclesiastics. I was also struck by a general air of fastidiousness and sober elegance rarely to be observed in artists of any kind. Unexpectedly contrasting, but not unpleasing, was his style of speech, of which the underlying basis was recognizably provincial. Not for him was the blameless diction so laboriously inculcated and standardized in our leading public schools and ancient universities. He loyally preserved his preference for the Doric dialect of that great northern county of broad acres, which looks down and with compassion upon the miminy-piminy refinements of the softer south. Upon this had been grafted a polyglot mish-mash, acquired during his twenty-four years self-imposed exile from England. Both French and German words interlarded his sentences, and he always spoke of the 'orchester'.

    Sir Thomas Beecham, *Frederick Delius.*

Delius contrived whenever possible to spend his holidays in Norway. . . . Such was his tireless energy that before he took a cottage overlooking the hills he usually walked and climbed above; occasionally Jelka went with him and once the 'then' Mr. Beecham also, whom he never forgave for forgetting the sandwiches the day they lunched on a glacier.

    Eric Fenby, *Delius.*

Delius is . . . a pantheistic mystic whose vision has been attained by an all-embracing acceptation, a 'yea-saying' to life.

    Philip Heseltine, *Delius.*

One feels that all Delius' music is evolved out of the emotions of a past that was never fully realized when it was present, emotions which only became real after they had ceased to be experienced.

    Ibid.

Harmony with Delius has always been more of an instinct than an accomplishment.

    Ibid.

His greatest admirer could hardly describe Delius as a master of form, and even Mr. Cecil Gray, in the course of a highly laudatory essay, has admitted that many passages in Delius's music would retain the major element of their charm if all trace of melodic line were removed.

    Constant Lambert, *Music Ho!*

It is dangerous to hear Delius's music too often, for its sensuous autumnal beauty induces a profound nostalgia, a passionate and fruitless desire to stop the clocks, to recapture the past. I was once told of a man who on hearing Delius's more sensuous music was seized by an almost uncontrollable urge to remove all his clothing and engage in Pan-like diversions quite unsuited to his profession — which was that of a solicitor's clerk. He was, fortunately, sufficiently controlled to limit his response to the urge to the privacy of his chamber.

    Alec Robertson, *More Than Music.*

A provincial Debussy.

    A. J. P. Taylor, *English History 1914–1945.*

Delius, in spite of his bewitching harmonic experiments (or is it because of them?) belongs mentally to the eighties.

    Ralph Vaughan Williams, 'Gustav Holst', in *Music and Letters*, 1920.

DELMONICO, LORENZO

1813—81 Restaurateur

There never was a sight so fair
As at Delmonico's last night;
When feathers, flowers, gems, and lace
Adorned each lovely form and face;
A garden of all thorns bereft,
The outside world behind them left.
> Anon., contemporary newspaper verse, in
> Lately Thomas, *Delmonico's.*

As Delmonico goes, so goes the dining.
> Anon., in Lately Thomas, *Delmonico's.*

A practical apostle of health and decent living . . .
who deserves canonization in the American calendar.
> James Ford Rhodes, *History of the United States
> 1850—1877.*

Men might break or disappear or die — but . . . his
cisterns were always open to every falling drop of
prosperity.
> Sam Ward, *Lyrical Recreations.*

DE MILLE, CECIL BLOUNT

1881—1959 Motion Picture Director

It was soon obvious that CB lacked a sense of
humour. He was nearly as bad as Flo Ziegfeld. In
the hundred ceremonials of his life — all artificial
and all right out of the corniest movie imaginable —
he saw nothing funny.
> Norman bel Geddes, *Miracle in the Evening.*

Cecil B. de Mille,
Rather against his will,
Was persuaded to leave Moses
Out of 'The Wars of the Roses'.
> Nicolas Bentley, *Clerihew.*

A sturdily built, sun-bronzed man came toward me
with his hand extended in greeting and although I
had never met DeMille, nor seen a picture of him, I
knew that this must be he. The pongee sports shirt,
well-tailored riding breeches, leather puttees and
Napoleonic stride seemed to proclaim the fact that
here was the director to end all directors. 'My God,'
I thought. 'It's an American Benito Mussolini'.
> Charles Bickford, *Bulls, Balls, Bicycles and
> Actors.*

As far as directors were concerned, Cecil B. DeMille
mounted the greatest show on earth. Commanding
absolute loyalty from his staff, he directed as

though chosen by God for this one task. To suit his
role, he wore breeches and high boots, and carried a
revolver. The boots supported his legs, he explained,
and protected him from the snakes so often found
at his California ranch; the snakes inspired the
revolver as well. Cynics wondered whether the
serpents in the picture business caused him to wear
such garb at the studio.
> Kevin Brownlow, *The Parade's Gone By.*

Never have I seen a man with so pre-eminent a
position splash so fondly about in mediocrity, and,
like a child building a sand castle, so serenely convinced that he was producing works of art. . . .
Inspirationally and imaginatively, CB was sterile.
His stories, situations, and characters were, almost
without exception, unintelligent, unintuitive, and
psychologically adolescent. CB was the foreman in
a movie factory; he fitted the parts together and
demanded that they move as he thought they
should. It was an early form of automation.
> Norman bel Geddes, *Miracles in the Evening.*

He held the belief that he got the best work from
people when he had stripped their nerves raw, when
they could no longer think, when they acted through
an instinct of rage and desperation. If they turned in
a fair piece of work and he struck them across the
mouth, they'd turn in a better one the next day. He
regularly set his entire staff by the ears by demanding publicly their individual opinions on one another's work while he sat aloof in Olympian calm
until matters had reached a broth of discussion. He
then stepped in and resolved the trouble by Jovian
fiat.
> Agnes de Mille, *Dance to the Piper.*

He rode the fluctuating business deeps as on a surf-
board, with gaiety and bravado. If he had any
doubts as to his own ability or scope, he never
expressed them. He had doubts about his colleagues';
he expected the worst in business dealings and was
always ready. He was himself a phenomenally
shrewd man who augmented an instinct for popular
taste with bold and astonishing business coups. His
success was a world success, and he enjoyed every
minute of it, and it lasted. He kept sex, sadism,
patriotism, real estate, religion and public relations
dancing in midair like jugglers' balls for fifty years.
> Agnes de Mille, *Speak To Me, Dance With Me.*

Cecil de Mille moved in legends. The first, and one
that he struggled very hard to promote, was that
he was the world's greatest moving-picture director.
He was certainly the best known, more widely
hailed than even Griffith or Eisenstein! I heard
his name in Russia, years after his death. Albert

Speer uses it again and again in his autobiography as a synonym for grandiose, overblown opulence.
Ibid.

The first motion picture which I remember seeing was *The Sign of the Cross*. Another early film which made an impact on me was Cecil B. DeMille's *King of Kings*. This probably taught me more about the life of Christ than did a great deal of the Sunday school training I had as a boy.
Billy Graham, in *Show,* April 1963.

Cecil DeMille's evangelical films are the nearest equivalent today to the glossy German colour prints which sometimes decorated mid-Victorian Bibles. There is the same complete lack of period sense, the same stuffy horsehair atmosphere of beards and whiskers, and, their best quality, a child-like eye for details which enabled one to spend so many happy minutes spying a new lamb among the rocks, and unobtrusive dove or a mislaid shepherd.
Graham Greene, reviewing *The Crusades* in *Spectator,* 30 August 1935.

I had great admiration for him, but I never saw anything that I thought was good. If I tried to tell people to do some of the things he did, I would burst into laughter. Yet he made it work. I learned an awful lot from him by doing exactly the opposite. I once asked Gary Cooper how on earth he could read those goddam lines. 'Well,' he said 'when DeMille finishes talking to you, they don't seem so bad. But when you see the picture, then you kind of hang your head.'
Howard Hawks, in Kevin Brownlow, *The Parade's Gone By.*

Like most great film makers, he began as an artist, and was gradually overwhelmed by the need to prove himself as a businessman. He was not only harassed by the need to marry God and Moloch in his work; he was harassed by the need to marry them in himself. His life struggle until he gave up as a personal artist was not only against the men who held the purse strings of the industry in New York; it was between his body and his soul.
Charles Higham, *Cecil B. De Mille.*

I prefer to call DeMille a great actor and a great showman rather than a hypocrite. He had the capacity to absolutely believe what he was doing and saying while he was doing and saying it. If he happened to be talking about the virtue of the American home, he'd believe it at the moment, though he was violating it in his personal life. If he happened to be making a film like *The Ten Commandments* in which one of the Command-

ments was 'Thou shalt not commit adultery', he saw no conflict in that he himself was committing adultery. There was a dichotomy in his moral code, a comfortable, yet somehow sincere dichotomy.
Jesse Lasky Jr, in Walter Wagner, *You Must Remember This.*

For his great films he had devised what proved to be an infallible formula. He packed the screen with impressive pageantry, supported by complex plots and subplots, and into each scene he measured out a careful soupçon of pure suspense. He drew his sense of scenic composition and balance from such carefully studied illustrators as the great Frenchmen Gustave Doré and Job. It did not concern him in the least that in the opinion of 'serious' film makers his works were considered as artistically significant as Barnum and Bailey's Circus. He feared only one thing — that an audience might be bored.
Jesse Lasky Jr, *Whatever Happened to Hollywood?*

Unabashed by criticism from the erudite, DeMille interlaced fact and fancy into what he publicized as 'historical drama.' Short on fact but long on fancy, his artificially inseminated pictures appealed to the uncritical, who came away from the theatres wagging their heads with satisfaction: they had enjoyed themselves and had had a refresher course in history.
Frances Marion, *Off With Their Heads.*

DeMille's films were, indeed, all the wish-dreams of the Twenties. They depicted lives of luxury and leisure, of moral freedom. More practically, they offered people examples of 'how to go on', instructed audiences in contemporary manners and etiquette. DeMille shaped, as much as he reflected the life of the Twenties, from the bath tub to the dinner table.
David Robinson, *Hollywood in the Twenties.*

Nothing in his distinguished career persuades me that the movies are any the better for it and I am quite willing to uphold the contrary.
Gilbert Seldes, *The Seven Lively Arts.*

When I saw one of his pictures, I wanted to quit the business.
King Vidor, in Kevin Brownlow, *The Parade's Gone By.*

DEMUTH, CHARLES

1883–1935 Artist

John Marin and I drew our inspiration from the same source, French modernism. He brought his up in

buckets and spilt much along the way. I dipped mine out with a teaspoon, but I never spilled a drop.
    On himself, in Andrew Carnduff Ritchie, *Charles Demuth*.

'What would you most like to do, to know, to be? (In case you are not satisfied.)' Demuth: 'Lay bricks. What it's all about. A brick layer.' 'What do you look forward to?' Demuth: 'The past.'
    On himself, 1929, in David Gebhard, *Charles Demuth*.

DENHAM, SIR JOHN

1615—69 Poet

His eie was a kind of light goose-grey, not big, but it had a strange piercingness, not as to shining and glory, but (like a Momus) when he conversed with you he look't into your very thoughts.
    John Aubrey, *Brief Lives*.

I went to London to visit my Lord of Bristol, having been with Sir John Denham (his Majesty's surveyor) to consult with him about the placing of his palace at Greenwich, which I would have had built between the river and the Queen's house, so as a large square cut should have let in the Thames like a bay, but Sir John was for setting it on piles at the very brink of the water, which I did not assent to, and so came away, knowing Sir John to be a better poet than architect.
    John Evelyn, Diary, 19 October 1661.

He appears to have had, in common with almost all mankind, the ambition of being upon proper occasions *a merry fellow*, and, in common with most of them, to have been by nature, or by early habits, debarred from it. Nothing is less exhilarating than the ludicrousness of Denham: he does not fail for want of efforts; he is familiar, he is gross, but he is never merry.
    Samuel Johnson, *Lives of the Poets*.

If Sir John Denham had not the name of being mad, I believe in most companies he would be thought wittier than ever he was.
    Lord Lisle, Letter to Sir William Temple, 26 September 1667.

DEPEW, CHAUNCEY MITCHELL

1834—1928 Lawyer, Politician

On the 23rd of April Shakespeare, St George and myself were born, and I am the only survivor.
    On himself, in John W. Leonard ed., *Best Things By Chauncey M. Depew*.

Mr. Depew says that if you open my mouth and drop in a dinner, up will come a speech. But I warn you that if you open your mouths and drop in one of Mr. Depew's speeches, up will come your dinners.
    Joseph H. Choate, in Leon A. Harris, *The Fine Art of Political Wit*.

I am reminded of Chauncey Depew, who said to the equally obese William Howard Taft at a dinner before the latter became President, 'I hope, if it is a girl, Mr. Taft will name it for his charming wife.' To which Taft responded 'If it is a girl, I shall, of course name it for my lovely helpmate of many years. And if it is a boy, I shall claim the father's prerogative and name it Junior. But, if as I suspect it is only a bag of wind, I shall name it Chauncey Depew.'
    Senator Robert Kerr, in *ibid*.

. . . made corruption respectable in the eyes of the people.
    Carl Schurz, in George C. Eggleston, *Recollections of a Varied Life*.

DE QUINCEY, THOMAS

1785—1859 Author

I was necessarily ignorant of the whole art and mystery of opium-taking: and what I took, I took under every disadvantage. But I took it: — and in an hour, oh! heavens! what a revelation! what an upheaving, from its lowest depths, of the inner spirit! what an apocalypse of the world within me! That my pains had vanished, was now a trifle in my eyes: this negative effect was swallowed up in the immensity of those positive effects which had opened before me — in the abyss of divine enjoyment thus suddenly revealed.
    On himself, *Confessions of an English Opium-Eater*.

A little, artless, simple-seeming body, in a blue coat and black neckerchief (for his dress is singular), with his hat in his hand, steals gently among the company with a smile, turning timidly round the room — it is De Quincey, the Opium Eater and that abstruse thinker in logic and metaphysics XYZ.
    John Clare, *Fragment on the Londoners*.

He walked with considerable rapidity . . . and with an odd one-sided, and yet straightforward motion, moving his legs only, and neither his arms, head, nor any other part of his body. . . . His hat, which had the antediluvian aspect characteristic of the rest of his clothes, was generally stuck on the back of his head, and no one who ever met that antiquated figure, with that strangely dreamy and intellectual face, making its way rapidly, and with an oddly deferential air, through any of the streets of Edinburgh ... could ever forget it.

J. R. Findley, *Personal Recollections of Thomas De Quincey.*

He is a *very* nice man — I can go on reading and reading him. I laughed over *Goethe* yesterday. I like him, De Quincey, because he also dislikes such people as Plato and Goethe, whom I dislike.

D. H. Lawrence, Letter to Catherine Carswell, 1919.

He is a remarkable and very interesting young man; very diminutive in person, which, to strangers, makes him appear insignificant; and so modest, and so very shy that even now I wonder how he ever had the courage to address himself to my Brother by letter. I think of this young man with extraordinary pleasure, as he is a remarkable instance of the power of my Brother's poems, over a lonely and contemplative mind, unwarped by any established laws of taste ... a pure and innocent mind!

Dorothy Wordsworth, Letter to Lady Beaumont, 6 December 1807.

DERBY, FOURTEENTH EARL OF (EDWARD GEORGE GEOFFREY SMITH STANLEY)

1799–1869 Prime Minister

No generosity, never, to friend or foe; never acknowledged help, a great aristocrat, proud of family and wealth. He only agreed to [the Reform Bill] as he would of old have backed a horse at Newmarket, hated Disraeli, only believed in him as he would have done in an unprincipled trainer. He wins, that is all. He knows the garlic given, etc. He says to those without: 'All fair, gentlemen?'

Lord Clarendon, 1867, in G. W. E. Russell, *Sixty Years of Empire.*

Is there a real Stanley? I believe it is a mere myth sung to lull Newdegate [the Whip].

Benjamin Disraeli, 1848, in Robert Blake, *Disraeli.*

It is a strange thing to see Stanley [at Knowsley]; he is certainly the most natural character I ever saw; never seems to think of throwing a veil over any part of himself: it is the straightforward energy which is the cause of this, that makes him so comfortable as he is. In London he is one of the great political Leaders, and the second orator in the House of Commons, and here he is a lively rattling Sportsman, apparently devoted to racing and rabbit-shooting,

gay, boisterous, almost clownish in his manners, without a particle of refinement, and if one did not know what his powers are and what his position is, it would be next to impossible to believe that the Stanley of Knowsley could be the Stanley of the House of Commons.

Charles Greville, Diary, 18 July 1837.

One after one the Lords of Time advance;
Here Stanley meets — how Stanley scorns! — the
                       glance;
The brilliant chief, irregularly great,
Frank, haughty, rash, the Rupert of Debate;
Nor gout nor toil his freshness can destroy,
And time still leaves all Eton in the boy.
First in the class, and keenest in the ring,
He saps like Gladstone, and he fights like spring!
Yet who not listens, with delighted smile,
To the pure Saxon of that silver style?
In the clear style a heart as clear is seen,
Prompt to the rash, revolting to the mean.

Lord Lytton, in G. W. E. Russell, *The Queen's Prime Ministers.*

... never pays compliments, you know, that's not his way.

Lord John Manners, in Benjamin Disraeli, Letter to his sister, 11 March 1849.

To threaten and not to act upon it was too often tried formerly, and was also a maxim of Lord Derby, who was the most difficult and unsatisfactory minister she or indeed anyone had to deal with.

Queen Victoria, Letter to Lord Granville, 30 August 1880.

DERBY, SEVENTEENTH EARL OF (EDWARD STANLEY)

1865–1948 Politician

D. is a very weak-minded fellow I am afraid, and, like the feather pillow, bears the marks of the last person who has sat on him! I hear he is called in London 'genial Judas'!

Douglas Haig, Diary, January 1914.

DEVEREUX, ROBERT, EARL OF ESSEX

1567–1601 Court Figure

The strange air engulfed him. The strange land — charming, savage, mythical — lured him on with indulgent ease. He moved, triumphant, through a new peculiar universe of the unimagined and the unreal. ... All was vague, contradictory, and unaccountable;

DEWEY, GEORGE

and the Lord Deputy, advancing further and further into the green wilderness, began — like so many others before and after him — to catch the surrounding infection, to lose the solid sense of things, and to grow confused over what was fancy and what was fact.
> Lytton Strachey, on Essex in Ireland, *Elizabeth and Essex.*

DEWEY, GEORGE

1837—1917 Sailor

Oh dewy was the morning
Upon the first of May,
And Dewey was the admiral
Down in Manila Bay.
And dewy were the Regent's eyes,
The orbs of royal blue,
And dew we feel discouraged;
I dew not think we dew.
> Eugene Ware, in Topeka *Capital,* 10 May 1853.

DEWEY, JOHN

1859—1952 Philosopher, Pedagogue

In the bedlam of tragedy, melodrama and light opera in which we live, Dewey is still the master of the commonplace.
> C. E. Ayres, 'Dewey and His "Studies in Logical Theory" ', in Malcolm Cowley and Bernard Smith eds, *Books That Changed Our Minds.*

Not only is his own style dull, but his dullness infects everybody who has anything to write about his theories of education.
> Max Eastman, *Heroes I Have Known..*

He imparted a new freshness, a sturdy and mature optimism, to the best spirits in contemporary society. As a psychologist he opened the mind to new vistas; as a student of ethics, he projected a radiant vision of modern conduct.
> Alfred Kazin, *On Native Grounds.*

His name is used as a charm within the profession and an exorcism without. This is an interesting fate for the century's most consistent foe of dogmatism.
> Albert Lynd, 'Who Wants Progressive Education?', in Reginald D. Archambault ed., *Dewey on Education, Appraisals.*

DEWEY, THOMAS EDMUND

1902—71 Lawyer, Politician

The Boy Orator of the Platitude.
> Anon., in James T. Patterson, *Mr. Republican, a biography of Robert A. Taft.*

. . . snatched defeat from the jaws of victory.
> Anon., in R. D. Challener and John Fenton, 'Which Way America? Dulles Always Knew', in *American Heritage,* June 1971.

Dues to Dewey
Let Dewey do it! And Dewey did.
Dewey's 'magic' was simply that
He did the job he was working at!
But do we duly do honour to
The work of Dewey? We do! We do!
> Berton Braley, in Robert Hughes, *Thomas E. Dewey, Attorney for the People.*

He is just about the nastiest little man I've ever known. He struts sitting down.
> Mrs Dykstra, 8 July 1952, in James T. Patterson, *Mr. Republican, a biography of Robert A. Taft.*

Dewey, cool, cold, low-voiced, was like a softly growling bull terrier willing to take on all comers if he could get in one good bite.
> Edwin C. Hill, on Dewey's courtroom manner, in Rupert Hughes, *Thomas E. Dewey, Attorney for the People.*

. . . who, when he had nothing to do, went home and cleared his bureau drawers.
> Harold Ickes, in Robert Shogan, '1948 Election', in *American Heritage,* June 1968.

Dewey has thrown his diaper in the ring.
> Harold Ickes, in Leon A. Harris, *The Fine Art of Political Wit.*

. . . (resembled) the little man on the wedding cake.
> Alice Roosevelt Longworth, in Booth Mooney, *Roosevelt and Rayburn, A Political Partnership.*

You can't make soufflé rise twice.
> Attributed to Alice Roosevelt Longworth, on the 1948 nomination, in James T. Patterson, *Mr. Republican, a biography of Robert A. Taft.*

. . . Dewey did not possess many of the outward attributes of the successful politician. He was lacking in warmth, spontaneity . . . moved as if he had been wound up by a spring but not too tightly, and spoke with earnestness but without passion.
> Booth Mooney, *Roosevelt and Rayburn, A Political Partnership.*

You really have to get to know Dewey to dislike him.
  James T. Patterson, *Mr. Republican, a biography of Robert A. Taft.*

You ought to hear him. He plays the part of the heroic racket-buster in one of those gangster movies. He talks to the people as if they were the jury and I were the villain on trial for my life.
  Franklin D. Roosevelt, in Robert E. Sherwood, *Roosevelt and Hopkins, An Intimate History.*

Clad each day in a pair of platitudes.
  Norman Thomas, in Murray B. Seidler, *Norman Thomas, Respectable Rebel.*

Dewey is a ruthless man who considers shooting at sunrise as a cure for inefficiency ... when a few men get control of the economy of a nation, they find a front man to run the country for them.
  Harry S. Truman, in Victor Lasky, *J.F.K. The Man and the Myth.*

The trouble was he'd forgot what it was like to have to work for a living and it showed on him, which is why he lost the election.
  Harry S. Truman, on the 1948 campaign, in M. Miller, *Plain Speaking – An Oral Biography of Harry S. Truman.*

... there was something about that other fellow (Thomas E. Dewey, the Republican candidate for President, then governor of New York) that people just never did trust. He had a mustache, for one thing, and since those days, during the war, people were aware of Hitler, that mustache didn't do him any good.
  Ibid.

DIBDIN, CHARLES

1745–1814 Actor

Charles Dibdin comes forward with bronze-burnish'd
face;
Unletter'd, ill-manner'd, presuming and loud,
To push his bold front in the rhyme-weaving croud;
His career has been mark'd like a mere April day,
Where storms, rain and sunshine, by turns hold the
sway:
How he groans with despair at the scourges of Heav'n;
Now he laughs o'er the wages his follies have giv'n;
Blaspheming this month, amid filth in a garret,
In the next, gorging high, on his carp, cod and claret,
Like the bird of the east, by his weakness misled,
He'll with pride shew his breech – so the fool hides
his head.

The thing mounts to *alt'* in his passionate fires,
His brains are *piano*, and *bass* his desires ....
  Anthony Pasquin (John Williams), *The Children of Thespis.*

DICKENS, CHARLES

1812–70 Novelist

I have great faith in the poor; to the best of my ability I always endeavour to present them in a favourable light to the rich; and I shall never cease, I hope, until I die, to advocate their being made as happy and as wise as the circumstances of their condition, in its utmost improvement, will admit of their becoming.
  On himself, Letter to J. V. Staples, 3 April 1844.

Nothing can be more indefinite than his religion, nor more human. He loves his neighbour for his neighbour's sake, and knows nothing of sin, when it is not crime. Of course this shuts out half of psychology from his sight, and partly explains that he has so few characters and so many caricatures. His humour ... is only the second cause of his caricaturing and has found its grave in it.
  Lord Acton, Letter to Richard Simpson, December 1861.

My own experience in reading Dickens, and I doubt whether it is an uncommon one, is to be bounced between violent admiration and violent distaste almost every couple of paragraphs, and this is too uncomfortable a condition to be much alleviated by an inward recital of one's duty not to be fastidious, to gulp down the stuff in gobbets like a man.
  Kingsley Amis, *What Became of Jane Austen?*

Charles Dickens
Could find nothing to say to chickens,
But gossiping with rabbits
Became one of his habits.
  W. H. Auden, *Academic Graffiti.*

How true to Nature, even to their most trivial details, almost every character and every incident in the works of the great novelist ... really were.... But none, except medical men, can judge of the rare fidelity with which he followed the great Mother through the devious paths of disease and death. In reading *Oliver Twist* and *Dombey and Son*, or *The Chimes*, or even *No Thoroughfare*, the physician often felt tempted to say, 'What a gain it would have been to physic if one so keen to observe and so facile to describe had devoted his powers to the medical art.'
  British Medical Journal, 18 June 1870.

Dickens's achievement was to create serious literary art out of pop material . . . He also worked in a climate of Christian evangelism that allowed big unqualified moral gestures. Language and morality add dimensions to his cartoons and turn them into literature. We lack enthusiasm and are embarrassed by moral fervour and grandiloquence alike. That is why our attitude to Dickens is ambivalent — nostalgia mixed with distaste, *nausée* in the presence of the spreading chestnut tree.

    Anthony Burgess, *Urgent Copy.*

Poor Dickens's latter years were a melancholy aspect, do they not? — in the feverish pursuit of loud effects and money.

    George Eliot, Letter to John Blackwood, 20 February 1874.

At twenty-three Charles Dickens had already made a name for himself as a transcriber of the words of others, being probably the fastest and most accurate reporter ever to take down the inanities of the House of Commons. Politicians have their uses: their dullness may have driven Dickens to original composition.

    Clifton Fadiman, *The Selected Writings of Clifton Fadiman: Pickwick & Dickens.*

Dickens' people are nearly all flat . . . Nearly every one can be summed up in a sentence, and yet there is this wonderful feeling of human depth. . . . It is a conjuring trick; at any moment we may look at Mr Pickwick edgeways and find him no thicker than a gramophone record. But we never get the sideways view. . . . Those who dislike Dickens have an excellent case. He ought to be bad. He is actually one of our big writers, and his immense success with types suggests that there may be more in flatness than the severer critics admit.

    E. M. Forster, *Aspects of the Novel.*

While reading him I have the impression that I am contemplating one of Fra Angelico's *Last Judgement* where you have the redeemed, the damned and the indeterminate (not too numerous!) over whom angel and demon struggle. The balance that weighs them all, as in an Egyptian bas-relief, reckons only the positive or negative quality of their virtue. Heaven for the just: for the wicked, Hell. Herein Dickens is true to the opinion of his countrymen and of his time.

    André Gide, *Dostoyevsky* (Dent's translation).

And on that grave where English oak and holly
    And laurel wreaths entwine,
Deem it not all a too presumptuous folly —
    This spray of Western pine!
    Bret Harte, *Dickens in Camp.*

One of Dickens's most striking peculiarities is that, whenever in his writing he becomes emotional, he ceases instantly to use his intelligence. The overflowing of his heart drowns his head and even dims his eyes; for, whenever he is in the melting mood, Dickens ceases to be able and probably ceases even to wish to see reality. His one and only desire on these occasions is just to overflow, nothing else. Which he does, with a vengeance and in an atrocious blank verse that is meant to be poetical prose and succeeds only in being the worst kind of fustian.

    Aldous Huxley, *Vulgarity in Literature.*

Such at least was to be the force of the Dickens imprint, however applied in the soft clay of our generation; it was to resist so serenely the wash of the waves of time. To be brought up thus against the author of it, or to speak at all of one's early consciousness of it and of his presence and power, is to begin to tread ground at once sacred and boundless, the associations of which, looming large, warn us off even while they hold. He did too much for us surely ever to leave us free — free of judgement, free of reaction, even should we care to be, which heaven forbid: he laid his hand on us in a way to undermine as in no other case the power of detached appraisement.

    Henry James, *A Small Boy and Others.*

An old lady told me once that she had lunched with the Dickens family when she was a child (you must imagine a table full of children) and that Dickens had sat down without a word, leaning his head on his hand in an attitude of profound despondency. One of the Dickens children whispered to her, in commiseration, and explanation, 'Poor Papa is in love again!'

    Desmond MacCarthy, *Criticism.*

Called on Dickens. . . . Asked Dickens to spare the life of Nell in his story, and observed that he was cruel. He blushed.

    W. C. Macready, Diary, 21 January 1841.

He violated every rule of art
Except the feeling mind and thinking heart.
    John Macy, *Couplets in Criticism.*

It may be that it is because this high seriousness is lacking in Dickens's novels that, for all their great merits, they leave us faintly dissatisfied. When we read them now with great French and Russian novels in mind, and not only theirs, but George Eliot's, we are taken aback by their naïveté. In comparison with them, Dickens's are scarcely adult.

    W. Somerset Maugham, *Ten Novels and Their Authors.*

No one thinks first of Mr Dickens as a writer. He is at once, through his books, a friend. He belongs among the intimates of every pleasant-tempered and large-hearted person. He is not so much the guest as the inmate of our homes. He keeps holidays with us, he helps us to celebrate Christmas with heartier cheer, he shares at every New Year in our good wishes: for, indeed, it is not in his purely literary character that he has done most for us, it is as a man of the largest humanity, who has simply used literature as the means by which to bring himself into relation with his fellow-men.

Charles Eliot Norton, in *North American Review*, April 1868.

In its attitude towards Dickens the English public has always been a little like the elephant which feels a blow with a walking-stick as a delightful tickling . . . Dickens seems to have succeeded in attacking everybody and antagonising nobody.

George Orwell, *Charles Dickens*.

Who call him spurious and shoddy
Shall do it o'er my lifeless body.
I heartily invite such birds
To come outside and say those words!

Dorothy Parker, *Sunset Gun*.

Dickens was not the first or the last novelist to find virtue more difficult to portray than the wish for it.

V. S. Pritchett, *Books in General*.

The fact is, Mr Dickens writes too often and too fast; on the principle, we presume, of making hay whilst the sun shines, he seems to have accepted at once all engagements that were offered to him. . . . If he persists much longer in this course, it requires no gift of prophecy to foretell his fate — he has risen like a rocket, and he will come down like the stick.

Quarterly Review, October 1837.

The literary loss is infinite — the political one I care less for than you do. Dickens was a pure modernist — a leader of the steam-and-whistle party *par excellence* — and he had no understanding of any power of antiquity except a sort of jackdaw sentiment for cathedral towers. He knew nothing of nobler power of superstition — was essentially a stage manager, and used everything for effect on the pit. His Christmas meant mistletoe and pudding — neither resurrection from dead, nor rising of new stars, nor teaching of wise men, nor shepherds. His hero is essentially the ironmaster.

John Ruskin (on Dickens's death), Letter to Charles Eliot Norton, 19 June 1870.

Charles Dickens, whose books, though classed as novels and duly hampered with absurd plots which nobody ever remembers, are really extraordinarily vivid parables. All the political futility which has forced men of the calibre of Mussolini, Kemal, and Hitler to assume dictatorship might have been saved if people had only believed what Dickens told them in *Little Dorrit*.

George Bernard Shaw, Introduction to *Collected Prefaces*.

He seems, as a general rule, to get his first notions of an abuse from the discussions which accompany its removal, and begins to open his trenches and mount his batteries as soon as the place to be attacked has surrendered.

James Fitzjames Stephen, in *Edinburgh Review*, July 1857.

A list of the killed, wounded and missing amongst Mr Dickens's novels would read like an *Extraordinary Gazette*. An interesting child runs as much risk there as any of the troops who stormed the Redan.

James Fitzjames Stephen, *Cambridge Essays*.

He was successful beyond any English novelist, probably beyond any novelist that has ever lived, in exactly hitting off the precise tone of thought and feeling that would find favour with the grocers. As Burke said of George Grenville and the House of Commons, Dickens hit the average Englishman of the middle-classes between wind and water.

Leslie Stephen, *The Writings of W. M. Thackeray*.

All children ought to love him. I know two that do, and read his books ten times for once that they peruse the dismal preachments of their father. I know one who when she is happy reads *Nicholas Nickleby*; when she is unhappy reads *Nicholas Nickleby*; when she is tired reads *Nicholas Nickleby*; when she is in bed reads *Nicholas Nickleby*; when she has nothing to do reads *Nicholas Nickleby*; and when she has finished the book reads *Nicholas Nickleby* over again. This candid young critic, at ten years of age, said, 'I like Mr Dickens's books much better than your books, Papa;' and frequently expressed her desire that the latter author should write a book like one of Mr Dickens's books. Who can?

W. M. Thackeray, *Charity and Humour* (lecture).

Of Dickens's style it is impossible to speak in praise. It is jerky, ungrammatical, and created by himself in defiance of rules — almost as completely as that created by Carlyle. To readers who have taught themselves to regard language, it must therefore be unpleasant. . . . No young novelist should ever dare to imitate the style of Dickens. If such a one wants a model for his language, let him take Thackeray.

Anthony Trollope, *Autobiography*.

No man ever kept himself more aloof than Dickens from the ordinary honours of life. No titles were written after his name. He was not CB, or DCL, or FRS, nor did he ever attempt to become MP. What titles of honour may ever have been offered to him, I cannot say; but that titles were offered I do not doubt. . . . He . . . had a noble confidence in himself, which made him feel that nothing Queen, Parliament or Minister, could do for him would make him greater than he was. No title to his ear could have been higher than that name which he made familiar to the ears of all reading men and women.

Anthony Trollope, in *St. Paul's Magazine*, July 1870.

Of all such reformers Mr Sentiment is the most powerful. It is incredible the number of evil practices he has put down: it is to be feared he will soon lack subjects, and that when he has made the working classes comfortable, and got bitter beer put into proper-sized pint bottles, there will be nothing further for him left to do. Mr Sentiment is certainly a very powerful man, and perhaps not the less so that his good poor people are so very good; his hard rich people so very hard; and the genuinely honest so very honest. Namby-pamby in these days is not thrown away if it be introduced in the proper quarters. Divine peeresses are no longer interesting, though possessed of every virtue, but a pattern peasant or an immaculate manufacturing hero may talk as much twaddle as one of Mrs Ratcliffe's heroines, and still be listened to.

Anthony Trollope, *The Warden*.

We warn Wellington and Peel, we warn Toryism in general, against this young writer. If they had at their disposal the Bastilles and *lettres-de-cachet* of another day, we would advise their prompt application, as soon as he shall set foot in England again. . . . There is nothing in any of the books he has yet produced of a manifest political character, or of any probable political design. Yet there is that in them all which is calculated to hasten on the great crisis of the English Revolution (speed the hour!) far more effectively than any of the open assaults of Radicalism or Chartism.

United States Magazine and Democratic Review, April 1842.

He is a very great loss. He had a large loving mind and the strongest sympathy with the poorer classes. He felt sure a better feeling, and much greater union of classes, would take place in time. And I pray earnestly it may.

Queen Victoria, Diary, 11 June 1870.

See also Rudyard Kipling, D. H. Lawrence, Lord Lytton, W. Somerset Maugham, Gilbert Murray, Charles Reade, Tobias Smollett, H. G. Wells

DICKINSON, EMILY ELIZABETH

1830—86 Poet

Some keep the Sabbath going to church;
I keep it staying at home,
With a bobolink for a chorister,
And an orchard for a dome.

On herself, *Poems*, part II, no. 54.

I find ecstasy in living — the mere sense of living is joy enough.

On herself, referring to her seclusion, in Theodora Ward, *The Capsule of the Mind*.

I had no portrait, now, but am small, like the Wren, and my Hair is bold, like the chestnut Bur, and my eyes, like the Sherry in the Glass, that the guest leaves.

On herself, undated letter to Thomas Wentworth Higginson.

I had no monarch in my life, and cannot rule myself; and when I try to organize, my little force explodes and leaves me bare and charred.

On herself, undated letter to Thomas Wentworth Higginson.

And ultimately one simply sighs at Miss Dickinson's singular perversity, her lapses and tyrannies, and accepts them as an inevitable part of the strange and original genius that she was. The lapses and tyrannies become a positive charm — one even suspects they were deliberate.

Conrad Aiken, 'Emily Dickinson', in *Bookman*, October 1924.

. . . an eccentric, dreamy, half-educated recluse in an out-of-the-way New England village (or anywhere else) cannot with impunity set at defiance the laws of gravitation and grammar.

Thomas Bailey Aldrich, 'Re Emily Dickinson', in Caesar R. Blake and Carlton F. Wells eds, *The Recognition of Emily Dickinson*.

Miss Dickinson's versicles have a queerness and a quaintness that have stirred a momentary curiosity in emotional bosoms. Oblivion lingers in the immediate neighborhood.

Ibid.

Emily Dickinson is the perfect flowering of a rare but recognizable variety of the New England Gentlewoman of the past — the lily-of-the-valley variety, virginal, sequestered, to the passing eye most delicate and demure, but ringing all the while spicy bells of derision and delight.

Katharine Bates, in Klaus Lubbers, *Emily Dickinson.*

Emily Dickinson went to the one source open to such a solitary as she was; she dipped into her heart for her poetry, writing her verse simply as an easement to surcharged feelings.

Russell Blankenship, *American Literature As An Expression of the National Mind.*

Emily Dickinson had discovered that in the America of the nineteenth century one of the few ways to have a set of manners which was not open to anomaly and subversion was to become a recluse. The idea that one might become an expatriate would hardly have occurred to her.

Richard Chase, *Emily Dickinson.*

In a life so retired it was inevitable that the main events should be the death of friends, and Emily Dickinson became a prolific writer of notes of condolence.

Northrop Frye, 'Emily Dickinson', in Perry Miller ed., *Major Writers of America*, vol. 2.

... Emily Dickinson sought to speak the uniqueness of her experience in a personal tongue by reconstituting and revitalizing — at the risk of eccentricity — the basic verbal unit.

Albert Gelpi, *Emily as Appollonian*, in Richard H. Rupp ed., *Critics on Emily Dickinson.*

I saw her but twice, face to face, and brought away the impression of something as unique and remote as Undine or Mignon or Thekla.

Thomas Wentworth Higginson, in Conrad Aiken, 'Emily Dickinson', in *Bookman*, October 1924.

Emily, the quintessence and distillation of the Puritan spirit, poured out her pure nectar in rare and precious drops.

Stanley J. Kunitz and Howard Haycraft eds, *American Authors, 1600–1900.*

She was small, she was obstinate, she was not as wise as she ended by thinking herself; but her voice was unique, and she flung out the short cry of her gay or pain or mockery with a note that cannot be forgotten.

Percy Lubbock, 'Determined Little Anchoress', in Caesar R. Blake and Carlton F. Wells eds, *The Recognition of Emily Dickinson.*

To this determined little anchoress, so carefully shut up in her provincial cell, nothing was sacred and nothing daunting; she made as free with heaven and hell, life and death, as with the daisies and butterflies outside her window.

Ibid.

Her poetic strategy depended upon the 'language of surprise', wit, paradox, and irony, to reveal the naked soul in dramatic conflict with established conventions.

John B. Pickard, *Emily Dickinson.*

and in your halfcracked way you chose
silence for entertainment,
chose to have it out at last
on your own premises.

Adrienne Rich, in Albert J. Gelpi, *Emily Dickinson.*

Her poetry is a magnificent personal confession, blasphemous and, in its self-revelation, its honesty, almost obscene. It comes out of an intellectual life towards which it feels no moral responsibility. Cotton Mather would have burnt her for a witch.

Allen Tate, 'New England Culture and Emily Dickinson', in Caesar R. Blake and Carlton F. Wells eds, *The Recognition of Emily Dickinson.*

She was the antithesis of the hurried pushing America which forced itself onward to unique material prosperity and had no time to stabilize its mind and soul.

A. C. Ward, 'A Major American Poet', in Caesar R. Blake and Carlton F. Wells eds, *The Recognition of Emily Dickinson.*

Fascinating as the meaning or ideas in her poetry may be, and important as are her metaphors, verse, architecture, rhythm, and euphony, it is her study of the individual word and her masterly discovery of the right word that chiefly defines her distinction.

Henry W. Wells, *Introduction to Emily Dickinson.*

Hers was an essentially modern spirit, learning, as we have not yet fully learned, to make the best of a world that has undergone an intellectual fragmentation bombing.

George F. Whicher, 'Emily Dickinson among the Victorians', in Caesar R. Blake and Carlton F. Wells eds, *The Recognition of Emily Dickinson.*

She was inattentive to superficial polish, but at a time when poetry was like furniture put together with putty, gilded, and heavily upholstered, she preserved in her writing the same instinct of sound workmanship that made the Yankee Clipper, the

Connecticut clock, and the New England doorway objects of beauty.

George F. Whicher, 'A Centennial Appraisal', in *ibid.*

... of all great poets, she is the most lacking in taste; there are innumerable beautiful lines and passages wasted in the desert of her crudities; her defects, more than those of any other great poet that I have read, are constantly at the brink, or pushing beyond the brink, of her best poems.

Yvor Winters, *Maule's Curse.*

DIGBY, SIR KENELM

1603—65 Author, Diplomat, Virtuoso

Sir *Kenelm Digby* was a person very eminent and notorious throughout the whole course of his life from his Cradle to his Grave; ... He was a Man of very extraordinary Person and Presence, which drew the Eyes of all Men upon him, which were more fixed by a wonderful graceful Behaviour, a flowing Courtesy and Civility, and such Volubility of Language, as surprized and delighted; and though in another Man it might have appeared to have somewhat of Affectation, it was marvellous graceful in him, and seemed natural to his Size, and Mould of his Person, to the Gravity of his Motion, and the Tune of his Voice and Delivery. He had a fair Reputation in Arms. ... In a Word, he had all the Advantages that Nature, and Art, and an excellent Education could give him; which with great Confidence and Presentness of Mind, buoyed him up against all those Prejudices and Disadvantages ... which would have suppressed and sunk any other Man, but never clouded or eclipsed him from appearing in the best Places, and the best Company, and with the best Estimation and Satisfaction.

Edward Hyde, Earl of Clarendon, *The Life ... written by Himself.*

The very Pliny of our age for lying.

Henry Stubbes, *Animadversions on Glanville.*

DILLINGER, JOHN

1902—34 Gangster

A jail is just like a nut with a worm in it. The worm can always get out.

On himself, in Robert Cromie, *Dillinger, A Short and Violent Life.*

Stranger, stop and wish me well,
Just say a prayer for my soul in Hell.
I was a good fellow, most people said,
Betrayed by a woman all dressed in red.

Anon., chalked on an alley wall outside the Biograph Theater just after Dillinger was shot dead, in *ibid.*

Dillinger is not just one bad man against the United States. He is, unfortunately, a symbol of crime in its latter day aspects in America. He is crime on rubber tires, crime armed with the finest killing devices known to science.

Anon., Indiana newspaper editorial in 1934, in *ibid.*

A certain Mr Hoover called Dillinger a rat. What does he mean by that? At least Mr Dillinger is a gentleman. Could we say the same about you? We would like to see you serve some time. Perhaps your attitude on life would be different.

Anon., Letter to the editor of an Indiana newspaper shortly after Dillinger's escape from Crown Point Jail in March 1934, in *ibid.*

Johnnie's just an ordinary fellow. Of course he goes out and holds up banks and things, but he's really just like any other fellow, aside from that.

Mary Kinder (a mistress of Dillinger's), in *ibid.*

He liked people and people liked him — until he was crossed, and then he became dangerous. He wanted what he wanted when he wanted it — and he wanted to come by it easily. He was not driven to crime by his environment or by his associations but sought it out and let it lead him.

Ralph de Toledano, *J. Edgar Hoover.*

DISNEY, WALTER E.

1901—66 Film Producer

I love Mickey Mouse more than any woman I've ever known.

On himself, in Walter Wagner, *You Must Remember This.*

[His is] an imagination that can perceive all sorts of fantastic attitudes and action in things so common, so near to anyone's hand, that the sudden contrast of what they might be with what they certainly are not is universally droll, and not to be resisted. Add an uncanny eye for characteristic detail. Add a limitless invention, a happy choice of what seems the best medium for Mr. Disney's peculiar talents, its perfection and the combination of it with sound. But his gifts, like a speaker I heard of once, need no introduction, having already endeared themselves to children and associate professors. They are restricted gifts, I suppose; what is astonishing about the man is that he can make an endlessly amusing operetta out of some old razor blades, a needle and a thread, and perhaps a few soft-shell crabs.

Otis Ferguson, *The Film Criticism of Otis Ferguson.*

Because Walt Disney has always had his eye on his business and no time for fooling around, the wind raised by those responsible for the dither about him as a Significant Subject has passed over in an interesting way. The air clears and he becomes what he was in the first place: common and everyday, not inaccessible, not in a foreign language, not suppressed or sponsored or anything. Just Disney, making another to go into all the big gaudy houses and tank-town houses all over the country, under Extra Added Attractions.

Ibid.

Walt was a rugged individualist. He admired Henry Ford. He thought Ford was the cat's ass. Maybe Ford and Walt were the last of the great ones, the last of great rugged individualists. Maybe that was why they were impatient with people of lesser talent and impatient with themselves, when they made mistakes.

Ward Kimball, in Walter Wagner, *You Must Remember This.*

Walt's virtue is all they want to perpetuate. The great doer of good, the manufacturer of children's entertainment. Sure, he was that. But he said 'shit' and the rest of the words, and as I've said, he'd talk about turds for thirty minutes without pausing for breath.

At the bottom line Walt was a down-to-earth farmer's son who just happened to be a genius.

Ibid.

Disney's animal world was one in which violence, conflict, ruthless physical force and utter desperation were normal, accepted elements of experience. It was a world in which kind-heartedness was associated with brutality, in which contempt for the weak prevailed; in which conscience had become a kind of stupidity.... This was a society in which aggression paid out, inhumanity was practical, and power, being right, was always admirable.

Lloyd Morris, *Not So Long Ago.*

Disney made audiences roar with laughter by endowing such inanimate objects as steam-shovels and rocking chairs with human emotions. Was he not

depicting a world in which scientists would speculate about the analogies between electronic 'thinking machines' and the human brain? His pictures were pure fantasy, and almost pure fable, but what they reported about twentieth century existence afforded little warrant for optimism or complacence. That they seemed so funny to so many Americans was, in itself, socially significant. It indicated the extent to which a mood of disillusion had overtaken the nation. It testified that an old faith was in temporary eclipse, and that a traditional dream had, for the time, ceased to be potent.

Ibid.

There was always something obsessive about Walt Disney's personality. His single-minded concentration on his career, his possessiveness about his business, his unwillingness to share its management with any outsiders, his singular identification with The Mouse (Mickey), the paternalism and the parsimony that marked his dealings with employees.... In later years he even patroled the vast reaches of Disneyland, leaving instructions on sheets of blue note paper that he alone in the organization used. In short, he carried the search for perfection to absurd lengths.

Richard Schickel, *The Disney Version.*

See also W. H. Auden

DISRAELI, BENJAMIN, EARL OF BEACONSFIELD
1804—81 Prime Minister, Author

Though I sit down now, the time will come when you will hear me.

On himself, Maiden speech, 7 December 1837.

This is the third time that, in the course of six years, during which I have had the lead of the Opposition in the House of Commons, I have stormed the Treasury Benches: twice, fruitlessly, the third time with a tin kettle to my tail which rendered the race hopeless. You cannot, therefore, be surprised, that I am a little wearied of these barren victories, which like Alma, Inkerman, and Balaclava, may be glorious but are certainly nothing more.

On himself, Letter to Lady Londonderry, 2 February 1854.

I am myself a gentleman of the Press, and I bear no other scutcheon.

On himself, Speech in the House of Commons, 18 February 1863.

My lord, I am on the side of the angels.
On himself, rejecting Darwinianism at the Oxford Diocesan Society, November 1864.

Yes, I have climbed to the top of the greasy pole.
On himself, reminiscence on his being elected Prime Minister.

I am dead: dead, but in the Elysian fields.
On himself, on being welcomed to the House of Lords.

You have accused me of being a flatterer. It is true. I am a flatterer. I have found it useful. Everyone likes flattery; and when you come to Royalty you should lay it on with a trowel.
On himself, *circa* 1880, in G. W. E. Russell, *Collections and Recollections.*

I will not go down to posterity talking bad grammar.
On himself, correcting his last speech for *Hansard*, 31 March 1881.

I had rather live but I am not afraid to die.
On himself, last authentically recorded words, April 1881.

When I want to read a novel I write one.
On himself, attributed.

He was quite remarkable enough to fill a volume of Éloge. Someone wrote to me yesterday that no Jew for 1800 years has played so great a part in the world. That would be no Jew since St Paul; and it is very startling.
Lord Acton, Letter to Mrs Drew, 24 April 1881.

Gladstone: Mr. Disraeli, you will probably die by the hangman's noose or a vile disease.
Disraeli: Sir, that depends upon whether I embrace your principles or your mistress.
George E. Allen, *Presidents I have Known.*

[By Bentinck's death] Disraeli was soon left absolutely alone, the only piece upon the board on that side of politics that was above the level of a pawn . . . He was like a subaltern in a great battle where every superior officer was killed or wounded.
Duke of Argyll, *Autobiography and Memoirs.*

He is a self-made man, and worships his creator.
John Bright, in A. K. Adams, *The Home Book of Humorous Quotations.*

I wish D[israeli] had a touch even of the slightest sentiment.
Lord Cairns, Letter to Richard Cross, 1877.

. . . a man who is *never beaten*. Every reverse, every defeat is to him only an admonition to wait and catch his opportunity of retrieving his positon.
William Ewart Gladstone, Letter to Malcolm MacColl, 11 August 1877.

The downfall of Beaconfieldism is like the vanishing of some vast magnificent castle in an Italian romance.
William Ewart Gladstone, writing of the Liberal victory of 1880.

I think your being the Leader of the Tory party is the greatest triumph that Liberalism has ever achieved.
François Guizot, 1848, in Benjamin Disraeli, *Reminiscences.*

What strikes me most singular in you is, that you are fonder of Power than of Fame.
Edward Bulwer Lytton, in *ibid.*

As for D'Israeli and his Sybil, I cannot imagine its being received as testimony, or supposed to be anything but a commonplace story.
John Stuart Mill, Letter to Dr W. G. Ward, Spring 1849.

The Great Panjandrum.
Alfred Munby, Diary, 16 July 1874.

Here's to the man who rode the race, who took the time, who kept the time, and who did the trick.
Sir Mathew Ridley, toast to Disraeli at the Carlton Club, 13 April 1867.

The conversion of the Cabinet and the party to household suffrage was a feat which showed that there was nothing strong enough in either to resist his will. For all practical purposes Mr. Disraeli . . . is the Conservative Party. . . . The worst alternative that can happen is his continuance in power. He is under a temptation to Radical measures to which no other Minister is subject: because he can only remain in power by bringing stragglers from his adversary's army — and the stragglers are the men of extreme opinions. He can forward Radical changes in a way that no other Minister could do — because he alone can silence and paralyze the forces of Conservatism. And in an age of singularly reckless statesmen he is I think beyond question the one who is least restrained by fear or scruple.
Lord Salisbury, Letter to a Mr Gaussen, 11 May 1868.

. . . the potent wizard himself, with his olive complexion and coal black eyes, and the mighty dome of his forehead (no Christian temple, be sure), is un-

like any living creature one has met . . . The face is more like a mask than ever and the division between him and mere mortals more marked. I would as soon have thought of sitting down at table with Hamlet, or Lear, or the Wandering Jew . . . England is the Israel of his imagination, and he will be the Imperial Minister before he dies — if he gets the chance.
Sir John Skelton, *Table Talk of Shirley*.

In whatever he has written he has affected something which has been intended to strike his readers as uncommon and therefore grand. Because he has been bright and a man of genius he has carried his object as regards the young. He has struck them with astonishment and aroused in their imagination ideas of a world more glorious, more rich, more witty, more enterprising than their own. But the glory has been the glory of pasteboard and the wealth has been the wealth of tinsel. The wit has been the wit of hairdressers, and the enterprise the enterprise of mountebanks.
Anthony Trollope, *An Autobiography*.

The present man will do well, and will be particularly loyal and anxious to please me in every way. He is vy. peculiar, but vy. clever and sensible and vy. conciliatory.
Queen Victoria, Letter to the Crown Princess of Prussia, 29 February 1868.

See also Earl of Derby, William Ewart Gladstone, Rudyard Kipling, Theodore Roosevelt

DISRAELI, MRS MARY ANN

1792—1874

She is an excellent creature, but she never can remember which came first, the Greeks or the Romans.
Benjamin Disraeli, attributed.

DIX, DOROTHEA LYNDE

1802—87 Humanitarian

I am naturally timid and diffident, like all my sex.
On herself, in *Dictionary of American Biography*.

She studied language as the soldier guards his sword, to make it cut.
Mary S. Robinson, 'Dorothea Dix', *The Century Illustrated Monthly Magazine*, January 1893.

DODGSON, CHARLES LUTWIDGE, see under CARROLL, LEWIS

DODWELL, HENRY

1641—1711 Jacobite

He has set his heart on being a martyr, and I have set mine on disappointing him.
William III, attributed.

DONNE, JOHN

1573—1631 Poet, Dean of St Paul's

John Donne, Anne Donne, Un-done.
On himself, Letter to his Wife (announcing his dismissal from the service of Sir Thomas Egerton).

Reader! I am to let thee know,
Donne's Body only, lyes below:
For, could the grave his Soul comprize,
Earth would be richer than the skies.
Anon. epitaph, written on the wall above Donne's grave the day after his burial.

He was the one English love poet who was not afraid to acknowledge that he was composed of body, soul, and mind; and who faithfully recorded all the pitched battles, alarms, treaties, sieges, and fanfares of that extraordinary triangular warfare.
Rupert Brooke, *John Donne*.

With Donne, whose muse on dromedary trots,
Wreathe iron pokers into true-love knots;
Rhyme's sturdy cripple, fancy's maze and clue,
Wit's forge and fire-blast, meaning's press and screw.
Samuel Taylor Coleridge, *On Donne's Poetry*.

See lewdness and theology combined, —
A cynic and a sycophantic mind;
A fancy shared party per pale between
Death's heads and skeletons and Aretine! —
Not his peculiar defect or crime,
But the true current mintage of the time.
Such were the establish'd signs and tokens given
To mark a loyal churchman, sound and even,
Free from papistic and fanatic leaven.
Samuel Taylor Coleridge, from the *Literary Remains*.

To read Dryden, Pope, &c., you need only count syllables; but to read Donne you must measure

Time, and discover the *Time* of each word by the sense of Passion.

Samuel Taylor Coleridge, *Notes, Theological, Political and Miscellaneous*.

Few writers have shown a more extraordinary compass of powers than Donne; for he combined what no other man has ever done — the last sublimation of subtlety with the most impassioned majesty.

Thomas De Quincey, in *Blackwood's Magazine*, December 1828.

Would not Donne's *Satires*, which abound with so much wit, appear more charming, if he had taken care of his words, and of his numbers? But he followed Horace so very close, that of necessity he must fall with him; and I may safely say it of this present age, that if we are not so great wits as Donne, yet certainly we are better poets.

John Dryden, *A Discourse Concerning the Origine and Progress of Satire*.

Were he translated into numbers, and English, he would yet be wanting in the dignity of expression. ... He affects the metaphysics, not only in his satires, but in his amorous verses, where nature only should reign; and perplexes the minds of the fair sex with nice speculations of philosophy, when he should engage their hearts and entertain them with the softnesses of love.

Ibid.

About Donne there hangs the shadow of the impure motive; and impure motives lend their aid to a facile success. He is a little of the religious spellbinder, the Reverend Billy Sunday of his time, the flesh-creeper, the sorcerer of emotional orgy. We emphasize this aspect to the point of grotesque. Donne had a trained mind; but without belittling the intensity or the profundity of his experience, we can suggest that this experience was not perfectly controlled, and that he lacked spiritual discipline.

T. S. Eliot, *Lancelot Andrewes*.

Tennyson and Browning are poets, and they think; but they do not feel their thought as immediately as the odour of a rose. A thought to Donne was an experience; it modified his sensibility. When a poet's mind is perfectly equipped for its work, it is constantly amalgamating disparate experience; the ordinary man's experience is chaotic, irregular, fragmentary. The latter falls in love, or reads Spinoza, and these two experiences have nothing to do with each other, or with the noise of the typewriter or the smell of cooking; in the mind of the poet these experiences are always forming new wholes.

T. S. Eliot, *The Metaphysical Poets*.

Donne, I suppose, was such another
Who found no substitute for sense,
To seize and clutch and penetrate;
Expert beyond experience,

He knew the anguish of the marrow
The ague of the skeleton;
No contact possible to flesh
Allayed the fever of the bone.

T. S. Eliot, *Whispers of Immortality*.

Donne's vocabulary can be very pure and plain; it is close to the natural prose, which is *staccato* and monosyllabic, of love and anger.

Oliver Elton, *The English Muse*.

Of Donne I know nothing but some beautiful verses to his wife, dissuading her from accompanying him on his travels abroad, and some quaint riddles in verse, which the Sphinx could not unravel.

William Hazlitt, *Lectures on the English Poets*.

Dr Donne's verses are like the peace of God; they pass all understanding.

King James I, saying recorded by Archbishop Plume.

He esteemeth John Done the first poet in the World, in some things: his verses of the Lost Chaine he heth by heart. ... Affirmeth Done to have written all his best pieces ere he was 25 years old.

Ben Jonson, in *Conversations with William Drummond*.

That Done, for not keeping of accent, deserved hanging.

Ibid.

That Done himself, for not being understood, would perish.

Ibid.

The extraordinary force of originality that made Donne so potent an influence in the seventeenth century makes him now at once for us, without his being the less felt as of his period, contemporary — obviously a living poet in the most important sense. And it is not any eccentricity or defiant audacity that makes the effect here so immediate, but rather an irresistible rightness.

F. R. Leavis, *Revaluation*.

A. N. Whitehead once defined religion as 'What the individual does with his own solitariness';· nearly all Donne's serious poetry, his love-poetry no less than his religious poetry ... is in this sense essentially, not merely nominally, religious, is a record of what the poet has been doing with his solitariness. This solitariness, this privateness, this self-containedness, this, together with the often dialectical and dramatic expression of it, is, it seems to me, the most important difference between the serious poetry of Donne and the so-called Metaphysical School and that of Jonson and the Classical or Horatian School.

J. B. Leishmann, *The Monarch of Wit.*

Donne had no imagination, but as much wit, I think, as any writer can possibly have.

Alexander Pope, in Joseph Spence, *Anecdotes.*

Language lyes speechlesse; and Divinity,
Lost such a Trump as even to Extasie
Could charme the Soule, and had an Influence
To teach best judgements, and please dullest Sense.
The Court, the Church, the Universitie,
Lost Chaplaine, Deane, and Doctor, All these, Three.
It was his Merit, that his Funerall
Could cause a losse so great and generall.

Henry Valentine, *Elegie Upon the Incomparable Dr Donne.*

The Recreations of his youth were *Poetry*, in which he was so happy, as if nature and all her varieties had been made only to exercise his sharp wit, and high fancy; and in those pieces which were facetiously Composed and carelessly scattered (most of them being written before the twentieth year of his age) it may appear by his choice Metaphors, that both *Nature* and all the *Arts* joyned to assist him with their utmost skill. It is a truth, that in his penitential years, viewing some of those pieces that had been loosely (God knows too loosely) scattered in his youth, he wish't they had been abortive, or so short liv'd that his own eyes had witnessed their funerals: But though he was no friend to them, he was not so fallen out with heavenly Poetry as to forsake that: no not in his declining age; witnessed then by many Divine Sonnets, and other high, holy, and harmonious Composures.

Izaac Walton, *Life of Dr John Donne.*

Verses have Feet given 'em, either to walk graceful and smooth, and sometimes with Majesty and State, like Virgil's, or to run light and easie, like Ovid's, not to stand stock-still, like Dr. Donne's, or to hobble like indigested Prose.

Robert Wolseley, Preface to *Valentinian.*

His verse has the deliberate bareness of those who refused to avail themselves of the current usage. It has the extravagance of those who do not feel the pressure of opinion, so that sometimes judgement fails them, and they heap up strangeness for strangeness sake. He is one of those nonconformists, like Browning and Meredith, who cannot resist glorifying

their nonconformity by a dash of wilful and gratuitous eccentricity.

Virginia Woolf, *The Second Common Reader.*

I notice that the more precise and learned the thought the greater the beauty, the passion; the intricacy and subtleties of his imagination are the length and depth of the furrow made by his passion. His pedantry and his obscenity — the rock and loam of his Eden — but make me the more certain that one who is but a man like us all has seen God.

W. B. Yeats, Letter to H. J. C. Grierson, 14 November 1912.

See also William D'Avenant, T. S. Eliot, Hugh Latimer, Andrew Marvell

DOS PASSOS, JOHN RODRIGO

1896—1970 Novelist, Historian

John Dos Passos is a better biographer than a poet, a better poet than historian, a better historian than a novelist. He chose to write novels; therefore his best novels are those which make most use of his other talents, which are considerable.

John D. Brantley, *The Fiction of John Dos Passos.*

As a result of the family situation he had spent a lonely childhood in luxury hotels, always moving from city to city, always feeling himself the alien, always speaking the language with a foreign accent whether he was in France or Italy or Belgium — or in England, where he first went to school, or later among rich Americans at the Choate School in Connecticut — and never feeling at home except on trains or ocean steamers, where he could spend most of his time with a book held close to his gollywog glasses.

Malcolm Cowley, *A Second Flowering.*

Sometimes in reading Dos Passos you feel that he is two novelists at war with each other. One of them is a late-Romantic, a tender individualist, an esthete traveling about the world in an ivory tower that is mounted on wheels and coupled to the last car of the Orient Express. The other is a hard-minded realist, a collectivist, a radical historian of the class struggle.

Malcolm Cowley ed., *After the Genteel Tradition.*

Over a period of forty years, in some thirty published volumes, John Dos Passos has carried on a romantic, constantly disappointed love affair with the United States. His books, crowded with personal experiences

---

DOUGLAS, STEPHEN

and historic events, are at once celebrations, indictments, and pleas for reform.
Robert Gorham Davis, *John Dos Passos.*

For what is so significant about Dos Passos is that though he is a direct link between the post-war decade and the crisis novel of the depression period, the defeatism of the lost generation has been slowly and subtly transferred by him from persons to society itself.
Alfred Kazin, *On Native Grounds.*

Dos Passos certainly came closer to Socialism than most artists in his generation; yet it is significant that no novelist in America has written more somberly of the dangers to individual integrity in a centrally controlled society.
Ibid.

The picture of the United States which he painted was no trivial or enchanting landscape in pastels of a sweet land of liberty and hope; it was a grim and lugubrious representation, Hogarthian in its cynically penetrating detail of the squalor and misery of a machine-dominated, monopoly-ridden civilization.
John H. Wrenn, *John Dos Passos.*

DOUGLAS, STEPHEN ARNOLD
1813–61 Politician

I could travel from Boston to Chicago by the light of my own effigies.
On himself, in 1854, commenting on the numbers of figures in effigy burned of Douglas across the country in response to his stance on slavery, in James Ford Rhodes, *History of the United States.*

... between the negro and the crocodile, he took the side of the negro. But between the negro and the white man, he would go for the white man.
On himself, as reported by the *New York Tribune,* 6 December 1858.

... [a] steam engine in britches.
Anon., in George F. Milton, *The Eve of Conflict.*
Daniel Webster was described in similar fashion.

His face was convulsed, his gesticulations frantic, and he lashed himself into such a heat that if his body had been made out of combustible matter, it would have burnt out. In the midst of his roaring, to save himself from choking, he stripped off and cast away his cravat, and unbuttoned his waistcoat, and had the air and aspect of a half-naked pugilist.
And this man comes from the judicial bench, and passes for an eloquent orator.
John Quincy Adams, in Gerald M. Capers, *Stephen A. Douglas.*

Douglas never can be president, Sir. No, Sir; Douglas never can be president, Sir. His legs are too short, Sir. His coat, like a cow's tail, hangs too near the ground, Sir.
Thomas Hart Benton, in William Nisbet Chambers, *Old Bullion Benton: Senator from the New West.*

The Kansas-Nebraska bill was not the product of one of the South's best minds. Stephen Arnold Douglas, its author, was what was known in that day as a Northern man with Southern principles — that is to say, a practical politician.
Paxton Hibben, *Henry Ward Beecher: An American Portrait.*

Douglas will cling to the Democratic banner as long as a *shred* is *left*; his party may kick him, beat him, but as long as he has a hope of being taken up as a candidate for the Presidency he will humble himself too *low* to be respected by his party.
R. P. Letcher, in Robert W. Johannsen, *Stephen A. Douglas.*

... I did keep a grocery, and I did sell cotton, candles and cigars, and sometimes whiskey; but I remember in those days Mr. Douglas was one of my best customers. Many a time have I stood on one side of the counter and sold whiskey to Mr. Douglas on the other side, but the difference between us now is this: I have left my side of the counter, but Mr. Douglas still sticks to his tenaciously as ever.
Abraham Lincoln, in Leon A. Harris, *The Fine Art of Political Wit.*

When he invites any people willing to have slavery, to establish it, he is blowing out the moral lights around us. When he says he 'cares not whether slavery is voted down or voted up,' — that it is a sacred right of self government — he is in my judgment penetrating the human soul and eradicating the light of reason and the love of liberty in this American people.
Abraham Lincoln, Ottawa, 1850, in Damon Wells, *Stephen Douglas: The Last Years, 1857–61.*

As thin as the homoeopathic soup that was made by boiling the shadow of a pigeon that had been starved to death.
Abraham Lincoln, on Douglas's powers of reasoning, in Keith W. Jennison, *The Humorous Mr. Lincoln.*

246

He had improvised as States's Attorney and Judge when he knew little law and no jurisprudence. He had improvised as a young Congressman supporting Polk and the Mexican War. He had improvised policies and bills; above all the reckless measure, the worst Pandora's box in our history, for organizing Kansas Territory. As he improvised he battled implacably, for he loved nothing more than political combat. The great weakness of the born improviser is that he over simplifies the problem he faces and forgets that remote results were far more important than the immediate effect.

    Allan Nevins, *The Emergence of Lincoln*, vol. 1.

The great volcano of American politics was in a state of eruption. When the flow subsided, old landmarks were found to be either greatly altered or obliterated. Two new masses were prominent on the political landscape, the Republican Party and the Solid South. Douglas had disappeared.

    Roy Nicholas, in Gerald M. Capers, *Stephen A. Douglas.*

[A] legislative dictator, intolerant yet irresistible.

    William H. Seward, in Damon Wells, *Stephen Douglas: The Last Years, 1857–61.*

He appears to have been called *The Little Giant* more because he was little than because he was a giant.

    Irving Stone, *They Also Ran.*

... the squire of slavery, its very Sancho Panza — ready to do all its humiliating offices.

    Charles Sumner, in Gerald M. Capers, *Stephen A. Douglas.*

... a brutal vulgar man without delicacy or scholarship [who] looks as if he needed clean linen and should be put under a shower bath.

    Charles Sumner, in D. H. Donald, *Charles Sumner and the Coming of the Civil War.*

His basic error was one of timing. He continued to preach the virtues of compromise to an age which had largely become disillusioned with the concept.

    Damon Wells, *Stephen Douglas: The Last Years, 1857–61.*

DOUGLASS, FREDERICK

1817?–95 Abolitionist

It was not what you describe as oratory, or eloquence. It was sterner, darker, deeper than these. It was a volcanic outbreak of human nature, long pent-up in slavery and now at last bursting its imprisonment. It was the storm of insurrection; and I could not but think as he stalked to and fro upon the platform, roused up like the Numidian Lion, how that terrible voice of his would ring through the pine glades of the South, in the day of her visitation, calling the insurgents to battle, and striking terror to the hearts of the dismayed and despairing mastery.

    Anon., in *Liberator*, 9 July 1841.

Frederick Douglass used to tell me that when he was a Maryland slave, and a good Methodist, he would go into the farthest corner of the tobacco fields and pray to God to bring him liberty; but God never answered his prayers until he prayed with his heels.

    Susan B. Anthony, in R. C. Dorr, *Susan B. Anthony.*

And he was no soft-tongued apologist;
    He spoke straightforward, fearlessly uncowed;
The sunlight of his truth dispelled the mist,
    And set in bold relief each dark-hued cloud;
To sin and crime he gave their proper hue,
And hurled at evil what was evil's due.

    Paul Laurence Dunbar, *Frederick Douglass.*

When it is finally ours, this freedom, this liberty, this
beautiful and terrible thing, needful to man as air,
usable as the earth; When it belongs at last to our
        children,
when it is truly instinct, brain-matter, diastole,
        systole,
reflect action; When it is finally won; When it is more
than the gaudy mumbo-jumbo of politicians:
this man, this Douglass, this former slave, this Negro
beaten to his knees, exiled, visioning a world
where none is lonely, none hunted, alien,
this man, superb in love and logic, this man
shall be remembered — oh, not with statues'
        rhetoric,
not with legends and poems and wreaths of bronze
        alone,
but with the lives grown out of his life, the lives
fleshing his dream of the needful, beautiful thing.

    Robert E. Hayden, *Frederick Douglass.*

He stood there like an African prince, conscious of his dignity and power, grand in his proportions, majestic in his wrath, as with keen wit, satire, and indignation he portrayed the bitterness of slavery.

    Elizabeth Cady Stanton, in Alma Lutz, *Created Equal: A Biography of Elizabeth Cady Stanton.*

The life of Frederick Douglass is the history of American slavery epitomized in a single human experience. He saw it all, lived it all, and overcame it all.

    Booker T. Washington, *Frederick Douglass.*

DOWLAND, JOHN

1563?–1626? Musician, Composer

He complains much of public neglect, but these complaints were never known to operate much in favour of the complainants, any more than those made to a mistress or lover whose affection is diminishing, which seldom has any other effect than to accelerate aversion. As a composer, the public seem to have been right in withdrawing that favour from Downland, which had been granted on a *bad basis*; but with regard to his performance, we have nothing to say.
   Dr Charles Burney, *A General History of Music.*

He was the *rarest Musician* that his *Age* did behold: Having travailed beyond the Seas, and compounded *English* with *Foreign Skill* in their *faculty.* . . . A cheerful *Person* he was passing his days in lawful merriment, truly answering the *anagram* made of him,
   Johannes Doulandus
   Annos Ludendo Hausi.
   [I passed the years in playing.]
   Thomas Fuller, *The History of the Worthies of England.*

That Dowland missed many opportunities of advancing his fortunes may perhaps be justly attributed to a rambling disposition, which led him to travel abroad and neglect his duty in the chapel.
   Sir John Hawkins, *A General History of the Science and Practice of Music.*

Here Philomel in silence sits alone,
In depth of winter, on the bared brier,
Whereas the rose had once her beautie shown,
Which lords and ladies did so much desire:
But fruitless now; in winter's frost and snow
It doth despis'd and unregarded grow.

So since (old friend) thy yeares have made thee
                                    white,
And thou for others, hast consum'd thy spring,
How few regard thee, whome thou didst delight,
And farre, and neare came once to heare thee sing:
Ingratefull times, and worthles age of ours,
That lets us pine, when in hath cropt our flowers.
   Henry Peacham, *Minerva Brittanna.*

He seems to have suffered from too much artistic temperament.
   A. L. Rowse, *The Elizabethan Renaissance.*

DOYLE, SIR ARTHUR CONAN

1859–1930 Author

My contention is that Sherlock Holmes *is* literature on a humble but not ignoble level, whereas the mystery writers most in vogue now are not. The old stories are literature, not because of the conjuring tricks and the puzzles, not because of the lively melodrama, which they have in common with many other detective stories, but by virtue of imagination and style. These are fairy-tales, as Conan Doyle intimated in his preface to his last collection, and they are among the most amusing of fairy-tales and not among the least distinguished.
   Edmund Wilson, *Classics and Commercials.*

Conan Doyle, a few words on the subject of. Don't you find as you age in the wood, as we are both doing, that the tragedy of life is that your early heroes lose their glamour?. . . . Now, with Doyle I don't have this feeling. I still revere his work as much as ever. I used to think it swell, and I still think it swell.
   P. G. Wodehouse, *Performing Flea.*

DRAKE, SIR FRANCIS

1540?–96 Circumnavigator, Admiral

As for the Expedition of Sir *Francis Drake* in the Year 1587, for the Destroying of the *Spanish* Shipping and Provision upon their own Coast, as I cannot say that there intervened in that Enterprise any sharp Fight or Encounter, so nevertheless it did straightly discover, either that *Spain* is very weak at Home, or very slow to move, when they suffered a small fleet of *English* to make an hostile Invasion or Incursion upon their Havens and Roads from *Cadiz* to Cape *Sacre*, and thence to *Cascous*, and to fire, sink, and carry away at the least ten thousand Ton of their greater Shipping, besides fifty or sixty of their smaller Vessels, and that in the sight and under the favour of their Forts, and almost under the Eye of their great Admiral, the best Commander of *Spain* by Sea, the Marquis de *Santa Cruce*, without ever being disputed with in any Fight of Importance: I remember *Drake*, in the vaunting Stile of a Soldier, would call the Enterprise the Singeing of the King of *Spain*'s Beard.
   Francis Bacon, *Considerations Touching a War with Spain.*

DRAKE he's in his hammock an' a thousand mile
                                    away
   (Capten, art tha' sleepin' there below?)
Slung away between the round shot in Nombre Dios
                                    Bay
   An' dreamin' arl the time o' Plymouth Hoe.
   Henry Newbolt, *Drake's Drum.*

The Spanish Armada was a convoy of transports rather than a fleet of battleships, and when Drake singed the Spanish King's beard at Cadiz, he was not hurling an impudent insult at imposing dignity but demonstrating the effectiveness of naval guns which were almost as good as Nelson's at Trafalgar.
    A. F. Pollard, *The Elizabethans and the Empire.*

He was more skilful in all poyntes of Nauigation, then any that euer was before his time, in his time, or since his death, he was also of a perfect memory, great Observation, Eloquent by Nature, Skilfull in Artillery, Expert and apt to let blood, and giue Physicke unto his people according to the Climate, hee was low of stature, of strong limbs, broad breasted, round headed, browne hayre, full Bearded, his eyes round, large and cleare, well fauoured, fayre, and of a cheerefull countenance.
    John Stow, *Annales.*

DREISER, THEODORE

1871–1945 Author

To sit up and criticize me for saying 'vest' instead of 'waistcoat', to talk about my splitting the infinitive and using vulgar commonplaces here and there, when the tragedy of a man's life is being displayed, is silly. More, it is ridiculous. It makes me feel that American Criticism is the joke that English authorities maintain it to be.
    On himself, in Philip L. Gerber, *Theodore Dreiser.*

It was the ponderous battering ram of his novels that opened the way through the genteel reticences of American nineteenth-century fiction for what seemed to me to be a truthful description of people's lives. Without Dreiser's treading out a path for naturalism none of us would have had a chance to publish even.
    John Dos Passos, *The Best Times.*

Dreiser may be as great as Michelangelo, or Tolstoi or Wagner, or less great or more. When you are beside a mountain you can't see its relative importance.
    Ford Madox Ford, 'Portrait of Dreiser', in Alfred Kazin and Charles Shapiro eds, *The Stature of Theodore Dreiser.*

He was still in his intellectual menopause, just as his society was in the transitional state between Christian endeavor and civilization.
    Maxwell Geismar, *The Last of the Provincials.*

Dreiser was the first American to portray with truth and power our modern world of commerce and mechanization, the first to portray the dismal depersonalization of the individual which results from urbanization and intensifying societal pressure to conform, the first to draw us frankly and grimly as a nation of status-seekers.
    Philip L. Gerber, *Theodore Dreiser.*

He cannot die — though here's an end to strife —
Who hacked his way through literature to life.
    Kensal Green (Colin Hurry), *Premature Epitaphs.*

With his proverbial slovenliness, the barbarisms and incongruities whose notoriety has preceded him into history, the bad grammar, the breathless and painful clutching at words, the vocabulary dotted with 'trig' and 'artistic' that may sound like a sales-man's effort to impress, the outrageous solecisms that give his novels the flavor of sand, he has seemed the unique example of a writer who remains great despite himself.
    Alfred Kazin, *On Native Grounds.*

He stumbled into the naturalist novel as he has stumbled through life. It is doubtful that he would have become a novelist of the fight for realism in American letters had it not been won before he arrived on the scene . . . .
    Ibid.

Like Whitman, Dreiser, in compensating for a lack of education and culture, strove painfully for an elaborate vocabulary, and like Whitman, is at his worst when his style is least natural.
    Alexander Kern, 'Dreiser's Difficult Beauty', in Alfred Kazin and Charles Shapiro eds, *The Stature of Theodore Dreiser.*

. . . Dreiser more than any other man, marching alone, usually unappreciated, often hated, has cleared the trail from Victorian and Howellsian timidity and gentility in American fiction to honesty and boldness and passion of life. Without his pioneering, I doubt if any of us could, unless we liked to be sent to jail, seek to express life and beauty and terror.
    Sinclair Lewis, in an address on receiving the Nobel Prize in Literature, in Erik Karlfeldt, *Why Sinclair Lewis Won the Nobel Prize.*

Soul enwrapped demi-urge
Walking the earth,
Stalking Life!
    Edgar Lee Masters, 'Theodore Dreiser', in Alfred Kazin and Charles Shapiro eds, *The Stature of Theodore Dreiser.*

I spent the better part of forty years trying to induce him to reform and electrify his manner of writing, but so far as I am aware with no more effect than if I had sought to persuade him to take up golf or abandon his belief in non-Euclidian arcana.

H. L. Mencken, in Philip L. Gerber, *Theodore Dreiser*.

If we can imagine an old-fashioned ladies' sewing-circle, decorously exchanging local gossip over cakes and tea, suddenly invaded by an iceman in his working clothes, who enters without embarrassment, plants himself massively in the middle of the sofa, and begins to regale the company with anecdotes of the gas-house district, we may form some notion of the effect produced by Dreiser's first novels.

George F. Whicher, 'The Twentieth Century', in Arthur Hobson Quinn ed., *The Literature of the American People*.

His style is atrocious, his sentences are chaotic, his grammar and syntax faulty; he has no feeling for words, no sense of diction. His wordiness and his repetitions are unbearable, his cacophonies incredible.

T. K. Whipple, *Spokesmen*.

But it is unlikely that future readers will care to acquaint themselves at first hand with the work of the trail-breaker. The labor of reading Dreiser is too arduous and not sufficiently profitable. Too often, while engaged with one of his novels, one has that sense of grinding despair that comes in nightmares when one is being pursued over endless wastes of soft sand. The experience, however instructive, is too painful to be sought out by normal humanity.

Ibid.

DRESSLER, MARIE (LEILA KORBER)

1869—1934 Actress

I was born homely. And for fifty years it has been my lot to make my living on the stage, where the first requisite for a woman's success is supposed to be a face that's easy on the eyes. I was born serious and I have earned my bread by making other people laugh.

Sometimes I think I have had more trouble and more joy and more fun than any woman alive.

All my life I've been a trouper. My earliest memories are of packing and moving, catching trains, settling down briefly, packing again. Home was simply where my mother was. Physically, the word had no meaning for me until I was twenty-five years old and a Broadway success.

On herself, *My Own Story*.

She was the biggest star of her time ... a sort of low comedian and hokey-pokey, too. She ruled in musical comedy and in low comedy. As time went on she acquired a kind of peculiar distortion, a magnificence. She was a law unto herself. She'd mug and carry on ... but she knew how to make an entrance with great aplomb, great effect.

George Cukor, in Gavin Lambert, *On Cukor*.

Every cinemagoer knew that Dressler had triumphed over adversity: thus she had a very special meaning during the years of the Depression. It was once said that she was the Heart of America, just as Douglas Fairbanks Sr. was the son of America and Mary Pickford its girl next door. ... The public wanted to see the pessimistic and worldly wise Dressler. Her normal expression was one of extreme scepticism — she of course being the only sane person around.

David Shipman, *The Great Movie Stars*.

DREW, JOHN

1853—1927 Actor

John Drew's acting was so perfectly effortless that it didn't seem to be acting. Some people used to say, without realizing what a tribute they were paying him, that he only played himself, that 'he didn't act but just behaved'.

Ethel Barrymore, *Memories*.

Drew not only was a humorist of repute but became noted as an unfailing gentleman, meticulous of dress and elegant of conduct. He did not enjoy off-color stories or smutty remarks. When an acquaintance one day dealt him a salty tale at the bar, Drew said, 'I do not think you know me well enough to tell that kind of story.'

Gene Fowler, *Good Night Sweet Prince*.

... the Beau Brummel of the American stage.

Margaret Case Harriman, *Blessed Are the Debonair*.

The great public seldom complained about the monotony of Drew's roles. It was Drew that they came to see, and not the play in which he was appearing and the more he seemed to be acting himself the better they were pleased. Very early in Drew's starring career his supreme elegance furnished American women with a criterion which they applied to American men. As a result, by the turn of the century he had considerable influence on masculine deportment, attire and social attitude. The 'Drew reformation' made the male residents of Fifth Avenue and Newport seem almost as distinguished as their butlers, and from these exalted precincts a cult of well-bred worldliness spread over the country.

Lloyd Morris, *Curtain Time.*

What he has played most congenially, and with the manliest humor of his time, have been the roles of gentlemen.... The reason is a simple one; he was born with a taste for the better side of things and the cleaner surfaces of life. He has found them more interesting and more congenial than mire, and if he should ever deal with mire he would deal with it cleanly. Here was the nature of the man always present in his acting; and I think it has been because of that and because of his humor — his own distinctive humor — that he has charmed the best American public throughout so many fortunate years.

Booth Tarkington, Introduction to John Drew, *My Years on the Stage.*

DRYDEN, LADY ELIZABETH

circa 1638—1714 The poet's wife

Here lies my wife.
Here let her lie!
Now she's at rest
And so am I.

John Dryden, [proposed] *Epitaph for his Wife.*

See also John Dryden

DRYDEN, JOHN

1631—1700 Poet

He the black Paths of Sin had travell'd o'er
And found out Vices all unknown before,
To sins once hid in shades of gloomy Night,
He gave new Lustre and reduc'd to Light.
His *Muse* was prostitute upon the Stage,
And's *Wife* was Prostitute to all the age.

Anon., *The Tory-Poets, A Satyr.*

Though many may write in verse, though they may in a certain sense be masters of the art of versification, Dryden and Pope are not classics of our poetry, they are classics of our prose.

Matthew Arnold, *Essays in Criticism*, Second Series.

There *Dryden* sits with modest smile,
The master of the middle style.

W. H. Auden, *New Year Letter.*

If Dryden's plays had been as good as their prefaces he would have been a dramatist indeed.

Harley Granville Barker, *On Dramatic Method.*

Even John Dryden penned none but mawky plays.

John Bee, *Works of Samuel Foote.*

I told him that Voltaire, in a conversation with me, had distinguished Pope and Dryden thus: — 'Pope drives a handsome chariot with a couple of neat trim nags, Dryden a coach, and six stately horses!' JOHNSON: 'Why Sir, the truth is, they both drive coaches and six, but Dryden's horses are either galloping or stumbling; Pope's go at a steady, even trot.'

James Boswell, *Life of Johnson.*

Dryden's genius was of that sort which catches fire by its own motion: his chariot-wheels got hot by driving fast.

Samuel Taylor Coleridge, *Table Talk.*

Take his Verses, and divest them of their Rhimes, disjoint them in their Numbers, transpose their Expressions, make what Arrangement and Disposition you please of his Words, yet shall there Eternally be Poetry, and something which will be found incapable of being resolv'd into absolute Prose: An incontestable Characteristick of a truly Poetical Genius.

William Congreve, *Epistle Dedicatory to Dryden's Works.*

He was certainly a mechanical maker of verses, and in every line he ever wrote, we see indubitable marks of the most indefatigable industry and labour.... With the unwearied application of a plodding Flemish painter, who draws a shrimp with the most minute exactness, he had all the genius of one of the first masters. Never, I believe, were such talents and such drudgery united.

William Cowper, Letter to Unwin, 5 January 1782.

The depreciation or neglect of Dryden is not due to the fact that his work is not poetry, but to a prejudice that the material, the feelings, out of which he built is not poetic. Thus Matthew Arnold observes, in mentioning Dryden and Pope together, that 'their poetry is conceived and composed in their wits, genuine poetry is conceived in the soul'. Arnold was, perhaps, not altogether the detached critic when he wrote this line; he may have been stirred to a defence of his own poetry, conceived and composed in the soul of a mid-century Oxford graduate.

T. S. Eliot, *Essays*: 'John Dryden'.

They tell me my old Acquaintance Mr Dryden has left off the Theatre and wholly applies himself to the Controversies between the two Churches. Pray Heaven! this strange alteration in him portends nothing disastrous to the State; but I have all along observed, That Poets do Religion as little service by

drawing their Pens for it, as the Divines do Poetry by pretending to Versification.
Sir George Etherege, Letter to the Duke of Buckingham, March 1687.

You have a war in England between the Hind and the Panther. Generall Dryden in an expert Captain, but I always thought him fitter for execution than for Counsill.
Sir George Etherege, Letter tó Henry Guy, 14 August 1687.

Remember Dryden, & be blind to all his faults.
Thomas Gray, Letter to James Beattie, 2 October 1765.

Dryden was a better prose-writer, and a bolder and more varied versifier than Pope. He was a more vigorous thinker, a more correct and logical declaimer, and had more of what may be called strength of mind than Pope, but he had not the same refinement and delicacy of feeling.
William Hazlitt, *Lectures on the English Poets*.

Dryden's comedies have all the point that there is in ribaldry, and all the humour that there is in extravagance. I am sorry I can say nothing better of them. He was not at home in this kind of writing, of which he was himself conscious. His play was *horseplay*. His wit (what there is of it) is ingenious and scholar-like, rather than natural and dramatic.
William Hazlitt, *Lectures on the English Comic Writers*.

He is the most masculine of our poets; his style and his rhythms lay the strongest stress of all our literature on the naked thew and sinew of the English language.
Gerard Manley Hopkins, Letter to Robert Bridges, 6 November 1887.

The power that predominated in his intellectual operations was rather strong reason than quick sensibility. Upon all occasions that were presented, he studied rather than felt, and produced sentiments not such as nature enforces, but meditation supplied. With the simple and elemental passions, as they spring separate in the mind, he seems not much acquainted; and seldom describes them but as they are complicated by the various relations of society, and confused in the tumults and agitations of life.
Samuel Johnson, *Lives of the Poets*.

The father of English criticism.
Ibid.

We feel that he never heartily and sincerely praised any human being, or felt any real enthusiasm for any subject he took up.
John Keble, *Lectures on Poetry*.

His mind was of a slovenly character, — fond of splendor, but indifferent to neatness. Hence most of his writings exhibit the sluttish magnificence of a Russian noble, all vermin diamonds, dirty linen and inestimable sables.
T. B. Macaulay, 'John Dryden', in *Edinburgh Review*, January 1828.

Mr *Dryden* is a mere Renegado from *Monarchy*, *Poetry*, and good *Sense*.
Luke Milbourne, *Dryden's Virgil*, 1698.

Ev'n copious Dryden, wanted, or forgot,
The last and greatest Art, the Art to blot.
Alexander Pope, *Imitations of Horace*, Epistle II, i.

I learned versification wholly from Dryden's works; who had improved it much beyond any of our former poets, and would, probably, have brought it to its perfection, had not he been unhappily obliged to write so often in haste.
Alexander Pope, in Joseph Spence, *Anecdotes*.

He does not seem to have lived on very amicable terms with his wife, Lady Elizabeth, whom, if we may believe the lampoons of the time, he was compelled by one of her brothers to marry. Thinking herself neglected by the bard, and that he spent too much time in his study, she one day exclaimed, 'Lord, Mr. Dryden, how can you be always poring over those musty books? I wish I were a book, and then I should have more of your company.' 'Pray, my dear,' replied old John, 'if you do become a book let it be an almanack, for then I shall change you every year.'
Sir James Prior, *Life of Edmond Malone*.

An old gelt mastiff has more mirth than thou,
When thou a kind of paltry mirth would'st show.
Good humour thou so awkwardly putt'st on
It sits like modish clothes upon a clown . . .
Pied thing! Half wit! half fool! and for a knave,
Few men than this, a better mixture have:
But thou canst add to that, coward and slave.
Thomas Shadwell, ascribed, *The Medal of John Bayes*.

It was King Charles the Second who gave Dryden the hint for writing his poem called 'The Medal'. One day, as the king was walking in the Mall, and talking with Dryden, he said, 'If I was a poet, and I think I am poor enough to be one, I would write a poem on such a subject, in the following manner:' and then gave him the plan for it. — Dryden took the hint, carried the poem as soon as it was finished to the king, and had a present of a hundred broad pieces for it.

Joseph Spence, *Anecdotes.*

If Dryden failed to produce plays to match his talent, it is because he was working at a time when the very possibility of serious drama was in doubt. The Athenian and the Elizabethan past threw a lengthening shadow over the future of the dramatic imagination. Dryden was the first of numerous playwrights who found between themselves and the act of theatric invention a psychological barrier. The greatness of past achievement seemed insurmountable.

George Steiner, *The Death of Tragedy.*

Read all the prefaces of Dryden,
For these our critics much confide in,
(Tho' merely writ at first for filling
To raise the volume's price, a shilling.)
Jonathan Swift, *On Poetry.*

Our great Dryden has carried it as far as it would go, and with incredible success. He has often said to me in confidence, that the world would have never suspect him to be so great a poet, if he had not assured them so frequently in his prefaces that it was impossible they could either doubt or forget it.

Jonathan Swift, *A Tale of a Tub.*

See also Ambrose Bierce, John Donne, Henry Fielding, Samuel Johnson, Edmund Kean, Andrew Marvell, Philip Massinger, Thomas Otway, Alexander Pope

DU BOIS, WILLIAM EDWARD BURGHARDT

1868—1963 Historian

Doubtless Du Bois is the only alleged leader of an oppressed group of people in the world today who condemns revolution. In other words, he would continue to defend and maintain the status quo . . . .

Anon. editorial, in Francis L. Broderick and August Meier eds, *Negro Protest Thought in the Twentieth Century.*

He just got it into his head that he should be an aristocrat and ever since that time has been keeping his very beard as an aristocrat; he has been trying to be everything else but a Negro.

Marcus Garvey, in Elliott M. Rudwick, *W. E. B. Du Bois, A Study in Minority Group Leadership.*

Du Bois was the race prophet with gigantic ideas which were never implemented. He was the man in a big center chair at an international conclave — playing a role he seemed to like best of all.

Elliott M. Rudwick, in *ibid.*

Du Bois is more of the artist, less of the statesman; he conceals his passionate resentment all too thinly. He batters himself into rhetoric against these walls.

H. G. Wells, in Emma Louis Thronbrough ed., *Booker T. Washington.*

DULLES, JOHN FOSTER

1888—1959 Lawyer, Government Official

. . . who spent most of his time on aeroplanes and invented Brinkmanship, the most popular game since monopoly.

Richard Armour, *It All Started With Columbus.*

J.F.D. the wooliest type of useless pontificating American. . . . Heaven help us!

Sir Alexander Cadogan, Diary, 13 July 1942.

I know you're right to this extent — people just don't like that personality of Foster's, while they do like me. The fact remains that he just knows more about foreign affairs than anybody I know. In fact, I'll be immodest and say that there's only one man I know who has seen *more* of the world and talked with more people and *knows* more than he does — and that's me. And I can't take his job and move over there . . . .

Dwight Eisenhower, to Emmet John Hughes, 1960, in Hughes's *The Ordeal of Power: A Political Memoir of the Eisenhower Years.*

Dulles was indisputably the conceptual fount, as well as the prime mover of United States foreign policy. . . . He was the informing mind, indeed almost the sole keeper of the keys to the ramified web of understandings and relationships that constituted America's posture of categorical anti-Communism and limitless strategic concern.

Townsend Hoopes, *The Devil and John Foster Dulles.*

. . . his real gift lay in adversary proceedings, in tactics, in handling (if not really solving) the urgent problem at hand, a problem not infrequently exacerbated by his own previous tactics. He lacked in large measure the statement's dispassionate vision and the courage to peer across the perilous divide to the bristling trenches of alien ideology, to identify there, and then to build upon, the hidden elements of possible reconciliation.

Ibid.

DUNBAR, WILLIAM

As Secretary, he lived, acted, spoke, reacted, advanced, retreated, threatened, courted, summarized, analysed, briefed, cross-examined, responded, appealed, objected, thrust, parried — like a lawyer.
  Emmet John Hughes, *The Ordeal of Power: A Political Memoir of the Eisenhower Years.*

Mr. Dulles' moral universe makes everything quite clear, too clear . . . self-righteousness is the inevitable fruit of simple moral judgments.
  Reinhold Niebuhr, 'The Moral World of John Foster Dulles', in *New Republic*, 1 December 1958.

. . . to cross him was to cross the deity.
  Jamison Parker, in Townsend Hoopes, *The Devil and John Foster Dulles.*

The world's longest range misguided missile.
  Walter Reuther, attributed.

Smooth is an inadequate word for Dulles. His prevarications are so highly polished as to be aesthetically pleasurable.
  I. F. Stone, 24 January 1953, in *John Foster Dulles: Portrait of a Liberator.*

Dulles is a man of wily and subtle mind. It is difficult to believe that behind his unctuous manner he does not take a cynical amusement in his own monstrous pomposities.
  Ibid.

No one pretends that in his six years at the State Department Mr. Dulles has won affection. The Department knows the Secretary as a cold, arrogant and ruthless man who has been exhausting himself running around the world because he really trusts no one. . . . A life long servant of the most materialistic forces in our society, a Big Lawyer for the Big Money, a pre-war apologist for Japanese aggression and Nazi expansion, an exponent of Machiavellianism so long as the Axis was winning, an advocate of a Christian peace as soon as its defeat was foreseen, Mr. Dulles by his constant invocation of Christianity and freedom has succeeded in making these ideals suspect in the minds of uncommitted millions who hear in them only the tom-toms beating for a new war.
  Ibid.

See also Adlai Stevenson

DUNBAR, WILLIAM
1465?—1530 Poet

Dunbar writes so scathingly of women that, when

he treats of them in a complimentary vein, doubts have been cast upon his authorship.
  J. W. Baxter, *Dunbar.*

His work lacks Chaucer's comic poise, its smiling abstention (or apparent abstention) from personal involvement. What is worse is that his personal involvement seems at times merely professional. He carries to excess medieval insouciance about inconsistency, so that in his work as a whole the only unity is that of literary zeal. His Muse turns to any subject with whorish readiness; the energy and enthusiasm, the verbal virtuosity, therefore, come at last to seem factitious.
  Allan Rodway, *English Comedy.*

This darling of the Scottish Muses has been justly raised to a level with Chaucer by every judge of poetry, to whom his obsolete language has not rendered him unintelligible. In brilliancy of fancy, in force of description, in the power of conveying moral precepts with terseness, and marking lessons of life with conciseness and energy, in quickness of satire, and in poignancy of humour, the Northern Maker may boldly aspire to rival the Bard of Woodstock.
  Sir Walter Scott, *Memoir of George Ballantyne.*

DUNCAN, ISADORA
1878—1927 Dancer

Wasn't it Nietzsche who said that he wouldn't believe in a God who could not dance? Neither could I.
  On herself, in Lou Tellegen, *Women Have Been Kind.*

My Art is just an effort to express the truth of my Being in gesture and movement. It has taken me long years to find even one absolutely true movement. Words have a different meaning. Before the public which has thronged my representations I have had no hesitation. I have given them the most secret impulses of my soul. From the first I have only danced my life. As a child I danced the spontaneous joy of growing things. As an adolescent, I danced with joy turning to apprehension of the first realisation of tragic undercurrents; apprehension of the pitiless brutality and crushing progress of life. . . . Later on I danced my struggle with this same life, which the audience had called death, and my wrestling from it is ephemeral joys.
  On herself, *My Life.*

254

Isadora, Isadora, when the greatest writers and artists of the world have vied with one another to describe or portray you, how can I with my poor stumbling pen dare to give even the faintest outline of your grace and unearthly beauty! You, an antique goddess reborn that man might again catch a glimpse of pure beauty, and for this daring act the gods have sent you heartaches and sorrows beyond the scope of human comprehension, and which you bore like a martyr.

Mary Desti, *The Untold Story: The Life of Isadora Duncan.*

From far antiquity came Isadora bringing to moderns all the grace of movement, suppleness of body, charm and lightness of raiment, long sealed in the secret archives of sculptural Greece. Once in many cycles such a being is bórn and no matter in what earthly guise or in what form the message is delivered, it is always religious. No religious ceremony has ever moved its believers to a higher ecstasy than did Isadora's dance. . . . This goddess in a poor frail human body, what glimpses of heaven she gave us through her pure inspiration and marvellous interpretations of art.

Ibid.

Isadora, who had an un-American genius for art, for organizing love, maternity, politics and pedagogy on a great personal scale, had also an un-American genius for grandeur.

Janet Flanner, *Paris Was Yesterday.*

Great artists are tragic. Genius is too large, and it may have been grandeur that proved Isadora's undoing — the grándeur of temporary luxury, the grandeur of permanent ideals.

She was too expansive for personal salvation. She had thousands of friends. What she needed was an organized government. She had had checkbooks. Her scope called for a national treasury. It was not for nothing that she was hailed by her first name only, as queens have been, were they great Catharines or Marie Antoinettes.

As she stepped into the machine that was to be her final enemy, Isadora's last spoken words were, by chance, 'Je vois la gloire!'

Ibid.

A Paris *couturier* once said woman's modern freedom in dress is largely due to Isadora. She was the first artist to appear uncinctured, barefooted, and free. She arrived like a glorious bounding Minerva in the midst of a cautious corseted decade. The clergy, hearing of (though supposedly without ever seeing) her bare calf, denounced it as violently as if it had been golden. Despite its longings, for a moment America hesitated, Puritanism rather than poetry coupling lewd and nude in rhyme. But Isadora, originally from California but by then from Berlin, Paris and other points, arrived bearing her gifts as a Greek. She came like a figure from the Elgin marbles. The world over, and in America particularly, Greek sculpture was recognised to be almost notorious for its purity. The overpowering sentiment for Hellenic culture, even in the unschooled United States, silenced the outcries. Isadora had come as antique art and with such backing she became a cult.

Ibid.

As an artist, Isadora made her appearance in our plain and tasteless republic before the era of the half-nude revue, before the discovery of what is now called our Native Literary School, even before the era of the celluloid sophistication of the cinema. . . . What America now has, and gorges on in the way of sophistication, it then hungered for. Repressed by generations of Puritanism, it longed for bright, visible, and blatant beauty presented in a public form the simple citizenry could understand. Isadora appeared as a half-clothed Greek . . . .

Ibid.

Isadora not only danced but was demanded all over America and Europe. On the Continent she was more widely known than any other American of that decade, including Woodrow Wilson and excepting only Chaplin and Fairbanks, both of whom, via a strip of celluloid, could penetrate to remote hamlets without ever leaving Hollywood. But Isadora went everwhere in the flesh. She danced before kings and peasants. She danced from the Pacific to London, from Petrograd to the Black Sea, from Athens to Paris and Berlin. . . . For thirty years her life was more exciting and fantastic than anything Zola or Defoe ever fabricated for their heroines. Her companies were the great public talent of our generation — Duse, D'Annunzio, Bakst, Bernhardt, Picabia, Brancusi, Anatole France, Comtesse Anna de Noailles, Sardou, Ellen Terry.

Ibid.

All her life Isadora had been a practical idealist. She had put into practice certain ideals of art, maternity, and political liberty which people prefer to read as theories on paper. Her ideals of human liberty were not unsimilar to those of Plato, to those of Shelley, to those of Lord Byron, which led him to die dramatically in Greece. All they gained for Isadora were the loss of her passport and the presence of the constabulary on the stage of the Indianapolis Opera House, where the chief of police watched for sedition in the movement of Isadora's knees.

Ibid.

Isadora seemed to embody the best and worst of an artist. She had genuine talent, some mystical insight, but she was a bit bogus as well. She had that touch of vulgarity which I think art and people connected with it could well profit by. Although she put it there as much as anyone by her work and life, she negated the esoteric idea of Art because she couldn't help but give it her own humanity. And though she was usually drunk or broke or shacked up with some ne'er-do-well, she always survived. She was just a great person and *that* was her art.

Ken Russell, in John Baxter, *An Appalling Talent.*

... a woman whose face looked as if it had been made of sugar and someone had licked it ....

George Bernard Shaw, in Hesketh Pearson, *Bernard Shaw, a Postscript.*

I beheld the dance I had always dreamed of, a flowing of movement into movement, an endless interweaving of motion and music, satisfying every sense as a flower does, or a phrase of Mozart's.

Edith Wharton, in Edward Wagenknecht, *Seven Daughters of the Theatre.*

DUNDAS, HENRY, see under
MELVILLE, LORD

DUNSTAN, SAINT

924—88 Archbishop of Canterbury

St. Dunstan, as the story goes,
Once pulled the devil by his nose,
With red hot tongs, which made him roar,
That could be heard ten miles or more.

Nursery Rhyme, traditional.

See also Ethelred

DURAND, ASHER BROWN

1796—1886 Artist

It is better to make shoes, or dig potatoes, or follow any other honest calling to secure a livelihood, than seek the pursuit of Art for the sake of gain ... I would sooner look for figs on thistles than for the higher attributes of art from one whose ruling motive in its pursuit is money ... it is only through the religious integrity of motive by which all real Artists have been actuated, that it still preserves its original purity, impressing the mind through the visible forms of material beauty, with a deep sense of the invisible and immaterial, for which end all this world's beauty and significance, beyond the few requirements of our animal nature, seems to be expressly given.

On himself, in John K. Howat, *The Hudson River and its Painters.*

DUVEEN, JOSEPH, BARON

1869—1939 Art dealer

Early in life, Duveen ... noticed that Europe had plenty of art and America had plenty of money, and his entire astonishing career was the product of that simple observation.

S. N. Behrman, *Duveen.*

DWIGHT, TIMOTHY

1752—1817 Clergyman

A man of extraordinary qualities, but one on whom almost every mental gift had been conferred in fuller measure than poetical genius.

Henry Adams, *The United States in 1800.*

His voice divine revives the promised land,
The Heaven-taught leader and the chosen band.

Joel Barlow, *The Vision of Columbus.*

His mind resembled a well-arranged volume, in which each subject forms a separate section, and each view of that subject forms a separate page. He perfectly well knew the order of the subjects; could turn to any page at will; and always found each impression as distinct and perfect as when first formed.

William T. Dwight and Sereno E. Dwight, *Memoir of the Life of President Dwight.*

On account of his noble person — the perfection of the visible man — he exercised a power in his day and generation somewhat beyond the natural scope of his mental endowments.

S. G. Goodrich, in Moses Coit Typer, *Three Men of Letters.*

I never knew the man who took so deep an interest in everything — the best mode of cultivating a cabbage, as well as the phenomena of the heavens, or the employments of the angels.

N. W. Taylor, in William Sprague, *Annals of the American Pulpit.*

DYER, GEORGE

1755—1841 Author

At length George Dyer's phrenesis has come to a crisis; he is raging and furiously mad. I waited upon the heathen, Thursday was a se'nnight; the first symptom which struck my eye and gave me incontrovertible proof of the fatal truth was a pair of nankeen pantaloons four times too big for him, which the said Heathen did pertinaciously affirm to be new. They were absolutely ingrained with the accumulated dirt of ages; but he affirmed them to be clean.

Charles Lamb, Letter to Thomas Manning, 27 December 1800.

I found him busy as a moth over some rotten archive, rummaged out of some seldom-explored press, in a nook at Oriel. With long poring, he is grown almost into a book. He stood as passive as one by the side of the old shelves. I longed to new-coat him in russia, and assign him his place.

Charles Lamb, *Oxford in the Vacation.*

E

EAGELS, JEANNE

1894–1929 Actress

After five years of imprisonment in the success of *Rain*, the madness of the caged came upon poor Jeanne Eagels, and in a sense she died of that madness. Hers was the desperation and the death of the trapped.

> Alexander Woollcott, *The Portable Woollcott*.

EAKINS, THOMAS

1844–1916 Artist

My honors are misunderstanding, persecution, & neglect, enhanced because unsought.

> On himself, Letter to Harrison Morris, 1894.

The big artist does not sit down monkey-like and copy a coal-scuttle or an ugly old woman like some Dutch painters have done, nor a dung pile, but he keeps a sharp eye on Nature and steals her tools. He learns what she does with light, the big tool, and then color, then form, and appropriates them to his own use. Then he's got a canoe of his own, smaller than Nature's, but big enough for every purpose. ... With this canoe he can sail parallel to Nature's sailing. He will soon be sailing only where he wants to, ... but if ever he thinks he can sail another fashion from Nature or make a better-shaped boat, he'll capsize or stick in the mud, and nobody will buy his pictures or sail with him in his old tub. If a big painter wants to draw a coal-scuttle, he can do it better than the man that has been doing nothing but coal-scuttles all his life ... The big painter sees the marks that Nature's big boat made in the mud and he understands them and profits by them.

> On himself, in Gordon Hendricks, *The Life and Work of Thomas Eakins*.

Tom Eakins was somewhat hipped on nudes.

> Mrs Whiteman, in Gordon Hendricks, *The Life and Work of Thomas Eakins*.

I never knew of but one artist and that's Tom Eakins who could resist the temptation to see what they thought ought to be rather than what is.

> Walt Whitman, in *American Self-Portraits, 1670–1973*, an exhibition catalogue.

EARP, WYATT BERRY STAPP

1848–1929 Lawman

Wyatt's reputation and attainment, such as they were, may have been acclaimed by the Dodge City gang, but elsewhere he was merely another of the flotsam of the frontier.

> E. Bartholomew, *Wyatt Earp*.

EDDINGTON, SIR ARTHUR STANLEY

1882–1944 Astrophysicist

On one occasion when Smart found him engrossed with his fundamental theory, he asked Eddington how many people he thought would understand what he was writing — after a pause came the reply, 'Perhaps seven'.

> A. V. Douglas, *The Life of Arthur Stanley Eddington*.

His intellectual environment was that of many of the keenest minds of his age. He lived through a period rich in new ideas to which his powerful mind contributed its own quota. Stellar movements, radiation pressure, the physics of the stars and nebulae and galaxies, relativity, quantum theory, the significance of the constants of nature — to harmonise all these, to formulate a fundamental theory was his vision, and towards its realisation he pressed forward with superb confidence.

> *Ibid.*

EDDY, MARY MORSE BAKER

1821–1910 Founder of the Church of Christ Scientist

Jesus was called Christ only in the sense that you

say, a Godlike man. I am only a Godlike woman, God-anointed and I have done a work that none others could do.

On herself, Letter to Augusta Stevenson, 1900.

You can no more separate Mrs. Eddy from Science and Health than you can Moses from the Commandments, or Jesus from the Sermon on the Mount.

Anon., in Calvin C. Hill, 'Some Precious Memories of Mary Baker Eddy', in *We Knew Mary Baker Eddy*.

I hail with joy your voice speaking an assured word for God and Immortality, and my joy is heightened that these words are of woman's devisings.

Amos Bronson Alcott, address to Mary Baker Eddy, 1876.

. . . a brass god with clay legs.

Mark Twain (Samuel Clemens), *Christian Science*.

What she has really 'discovered' are ways and means of perverting and prostituting the science of healing to her own ecclesiastical aggrandizement, and to the moral and physical depravity of her dupes.

Mrs Josephine Curtis Woodbury, 'Quimbyism, or the Paternity of Christian Science', in *Arena*, 1899.

EDGAR (EADGAR)

944–75

It is a sign of Edgar's competence as a ruler that his reign is singularly devoid of recorded incident.

F. M. Stenton, *Anglo-Saxon History*.

EDGEWORTH, MARIA

1767–1849 Novelist

I have made up my mind to like no Novels really, but Miss Edgeworth's, Yours & my own.

Jane Austen, Letter to her niece Anna Lefroy, 1814.

She was a nice little unassuming 'Jeanie Deans-looking body' as we Scotch say — and, if not handsome, certainly not ill-looking. Her conversation was as quiet as herself. One would never have guessed she could write *her name*.

Lord Byron, *Letters and Journals*, 19 January 1821.

That is the great clue to bourgeois psychology: the reward business. It is screamingly obvious in Maria Edgeworth's tales, which must have done unspeakable damage to ordinary people. Be good, and you'll have money. Be wicked, and you'll be penniless at last.

D. H. Lawrence, *Introduction to his Paintings*.

I have not the pen of our friend Maria Edgeworth, who writes all the while she laughs, talks, eats, and drinks — and I believe, though I do not pretend to be so far in the secret, all the time she sleeps too. She has good luck in having a pen which walks at once so unweariedly and so well.

Sir Walter Scott, Letter to Joanna Baillie, 1825.

EDISON, THOMAS ALVA

1847–1931 Inventor

Since Edison suffered from insomnia, he invented the electric light, so that he could read at night. He had to sweat it out, and this led him to make his famous remark: 'Genius is about 2 per cent inspiration and 98 per cent perspiration.'

Richard Armour, *It All Started With Columbus*.

Edison was a giant. He had gigantic successes and gigantic failures. He had a giant's zest, a giant's power of recuperation and, until his last years, a giant's vision. If he had invented only the electric light bulb, he would have been noteworthy. That he also gave us the microphone, the kinetoscope, the phonograph and scores of other devices makes him one of the greatest inventors the world has ever known. Most important, he pioneered the industrial research laboratory, thus making possible the technological progress which enabled us to put a man on the moon. Whether he would have thought such a project worthwhile is doubtful. But once it was achieved, he would have been ready with a dozen ideas for turning it to good advantage. Making invention profitable was his main aim in life.

Keith Ellis, *Thomas Edison: Genius of Electricity*.

One day while Mr. Edison and I were calling on Luther Burbank in California, he asked us to register in his guest book. The book had a column for signature, another for home address, another for occupation and a final one entitled 'Interested in'. Mr. Edison signed in a few quick but unhurried motions. . . . In the final column he wrote without an instant's hesitation: 'Everything'.

Henry Ford, *Mr Friend Mr. Edison*.

Was it true, as legend had it, that Mr. Edison, like Napoleon, slept but four hours? Yes, said Mr. Ford, but Mr. Edison slept twice and sometimes *three times* a day.

Gene Fowler, *Skyline.*

He thwarted time and space . . .
. . . But what a bore
It is to hear
The Gramophone next door.

Kensal Green (Colin Hurry), *Premature Epitaphs.*

At the age of ten, young Thomas Alva's mind was an electric·thunderstorm rushing through the fields of truth.

J. Lewis Young, *Edison and His Phonograph.*

EDWARD I

1239—1307

I should not be a better king, however splendidly I was dressed.

On himself, attributed.

In a word: As the arm of King Edward I was accounted the measure of a yard, generally in England: so his actions are an excellent model and a praiseworthy platform for succeeding princes to imitate.

Thomas Fuller, *Church History of Britain.*

. . . Edward, however exceptionable his character may appear on the head of justice, is the model of a politic and warlike king: he possessed industry, penetration, courage, vigilance, and enterprise: he was frugal in all expenses that were not necessary: he knew how to open the public treasures on a proper occasion: he punished criminals with severity: he was gracious and affable to his servants and courtiers; and being of a majestic figure, expert in all military exercises, and in the main well proportioned in his limbs, notwithstanding the great length and the smallness of his legs, he was as well qualified to captivate the populace by his exterior appearance, as to gain the approbation of men of sense by his more solid virtues.

But the chief advantage which the people of England reaped, and still continue to reap, from the reign of this great prince, was the correction, extension, amendment, and establishment of the laws, which Edward maintained in great vigour, and left much improved to posterity; for the acts of a wise legislator commonly remain, while the acquisitions of a conqueror often perish with him. This merit has justly gained to Edward the appellation of the English Justinian.

David Hume, *History of England.*

Edward I preferred masterfulness to the arts of political management. In that sense he belonged less to the future than to the past.

K. B. McFarlane, *Edward I.*

. . . Edward's posthumous career among scholars has not been as spectacular as that of the Conqueror, but it is not entirely unremarkable. During the last two centuries he has been turned from a strong ruler into a national king; from a national king into an aspiring tyrant; and now from an aspiring tyrant into a conventional, if competent, lord.

G. Templeman, *Edward I and the Historians.*

EDWARD II

1284—1327

For it was commonly reported that he had devoted himself privately from his youth to the arts of rowing and driving chariots, digging pits and roofing houses; also that he wrought as a craftsman with his boon companions by night, and at other mechanical arts, besides other vanities and frivolities wherein it doth not become a king's son to busy himself.

The Chronicle of Lanercost, translated by Sir Herbert Maxwell.

No *Prince* ever ascended the *English Throne* with *greater,* or used it with *less* advantage to himself.

Thomas Fuller, *The History of the Worthies of England.*

Edward somme tyme kyng was brought from Kenelworthe to the castell of Berkeley, where he was sleyne with a hoote broche putte thro the secrete place posterialle. Wherefore mony peple say that he diede a martir and did mony miracles; nevertheless kepynge in prison, vilenes and obprobrious dethe cause not a martir, but if the holynesse of lyfe afore be correspondent. . . . But women luffynge to goe in pilgremage encrease moche the rumour of suche veneracion, untille that a feble edifienge falle down.

Ranulf Higden, *Polychronicon* (from an old translation).

He knew himself to be the Divine Victim, the incarnate God, and that sooner or later his life might be demanded of him. Piers Gaveston, the earl of Lancaster, the younger Despenser, might all die in his stead, but the call for sacrifice came to him in the end. Nothing else will account for his behaviour.

Margaret Murray, *The Divine King in England.*

He is still, as Stubbs truly said, the first king after the Norman Conquest who was not a man of business. Tall, well-built, strong and handsome, he had no serious purpose in life, no better policy than to amuse himself and to save himself worry and trouble. He is one of the best mediaeval examples of the brutal and brainless athlete, established on a throne. He was not, I suspect, exceptionally vicious or depraved. He was just incompetent, idle, frivolous, and incurious. Most of his distractions, for which his nobles severely blamed him, seem to us harmless enough; but contemporary opinion saw something ignoble and unkingly in a monarch who forsook the society of the magnates, his natural associates, and lived with courtiers, favourites, officials on the make, and even men of meaner estate, grooms, watermen, actors, buffoons, ditchers and delvers and other craftsmen.

T. F. Tout, *The Captivity and Death of Edward of Carnarvon.*

EDWARD III

1312—77

In this season the king of Englande toke pleasure to newe reedefy the castell of Wyndsore, the whiche was begonne by kynge Arthure. And there first beganne the table rounde, whereby sprange the fame of so many noble knightes throughout all the worlde. Then Kyng Edwarde determyned to make an order and a brotherhood of a certayne nombre of knyghtes, and to be called knyghtes of the blewe garter: and a feest to be kept yerely at Wynsore on saynt Georges day.

Jean Froissart, *Chronicles*, translated from the French by John Bourchier, Lord Berners.

See also John Gower

EDWARD IV

1442—83

This Monarch was famous only for his Beauty and his Courage, of which the Picture we have here given of him, and his undaunted Behaviour in marrying one Woman while engaged to another, are sufficient proofs.

Jane Austen, *The History of England.*

He was of visage louelye, of bodye myghtye, stronge, and cleane made: howe bee it in his latter dayes, wyth ouer liberall dyet, sommewhat corpulente and boorelye, and nathelesse not vncomelye; he was of

youthe greatlye geuen to fleshlye wantonnesse, from whiche healthe of bodye, in great prosperitye and fortune, wythoute a specyall grace hardelye refraineth.

Sir Thomas More, *The Historie of Kyng Rycharde the Thirde.*

See also Henry VI

EDWARD V

1470—83

He is commonly called King Edward the fifth, though his head was ask'd, but never *married* to the English *Crown*; and therefore, in all the Pictures made of him, a distance interposed, *forbiddeth* the *banes* betwixt them.

Thomas Fuller, *The History of the Worthies of England*, Westminster.

EDWARD VI

1537—53

And here, to use the example of Plutarch, in comparing kings and rulers, the Latins and the Greeks together, if I should seek with whom to match this noble Edward, I find not with whom to make my match more aptly, than with good Josias: for, as the one began his reign at eight years of age, so the other began at nine. Neither were their acts and zealous proceedings in God's cause much discrepant: for as mild Josias plucked down the hill altars, cut down the groves, and destroyed all monuments of idolatry in the temple, the like corruptions, dross, and deformities of popish idolatry (crept into the church of Christ of long time) this evangelical Josias, King Edward, removed and purged out of the true temple of the Lord. Josias restored the true worship and service of God in Jerusalem, and destroyed the idolatrous priests! King Edward likewise, in England abolishing idolatrous masses and false invocation, reduced again religion to a right sincerity; and more would have brought to perfection, if life and time had answered to his godly purpose. And though he killed not, as Josias did, the idolatrous sacrificers, yet he put them to silence, and removed them out of their places.

John Foxe, *Acts and Monuments.*

EDWARD VII

1841—1910

Bertie has remarkable social talent. He is lively, quick and sharp when his mind is set on anything, which is seldom. ... But usually his intellect is of no more use than a pistol packed in the bottom of a trunk if one were attacked in the robber-infested Apennines.
> Prince Albert, Letter to Princess Frederick William, 1 December 1858.

Across the wires the electric message came:
'He is no better, he is much the same.'
> Alfred Austin, attributed.

He wasn't clever, but he always did the right thing, which is better than brains.
> Lord Fisher, Letter to Reginald McKenna, 14 May 1910.

The greatest monarch we've ever had — on a race-course.
> Lord Northcliffe, attributed.

Poor Bertie — his is not a nature made to bear sorrow, or a life without amusement and excitement -- he gets bitter and irritable.
> Queen Victoria, Letter to the Empress Frederick, 12 June 1892.

See also Lord Fisher

EDWARD VIII (subs. THE DUKE OF WINDSOR)

1894—1972

What does it matter if I am shot? — I have four brothers.
> On himself, Letter to Kitchener, on accompanying his regiment to France, 1914.

I have found it impossible to carry the heavy burden of responsibility and to discharge my duties as King as I would wish to do without the help of the woman I love.
> On himself, Broadcast, 11 December 1936.

Hark! The herald angels sing —
Mrs Simpson pinched our king.
> Anon., in Cleveland Amory, *Who Killed Society?*

The King told [the Duke of Kent] that over two years ago while he knew he was an excellent Prince of Wales and liked the job, he nevertheless felt that he could never 'stick' being King as he puts it, he

was afraid of being a bad one. He could never tolerate the restrictions, the etiquette, the loneliness; so perhaps if this issue had not arisen something else would have.
> Henry Channon, Diary, 8 December 1936.

The Bill was read. The King was still King Edward. The Clerk bowed 'Le Rois le veult' and Edward, the beautiful boy King with his gaiety and honesty, his American accent and nervous twitching, his flair and glamour was part of history.
> *Ibid.*, 11 December 1936.

Think what you like of him, it was very largely due to him that his going was not cataclysmic. His determination that what he did should not be politically upsetting was as strong as his resolve to do it.
> Sir Colin Coote, in *Daily Telegraph*, 29 May 1972.

From his childhood onward this boy will be surrounded by sycophants and flatterers by the score and will be taught to believe himself as of a superior creation. A line will be drawn between him and the people he is to be called upon some day to reign over. In due course, following the precedent which has already been set he will be sent on a tour round the world, and probably rumours of a morganatic alliance will follow and the end of it all will be the country will be called upon to foot the bill.
> James Keir Hardie, to the House of Commons, 28 June 1894, on the motion to congratulate Queen Victoria on the prince's birth.

... He was born to be a salesman. He would be an admirable representative of Rolls Royce. But an ex-King cannot start selling motor-cars.
> Duchess of Windsor, in Harold Nicolson, Diary, 28 May 1947.

See also Harpo Marx

EDWARD THE CONFESSOR

— d. 1066

Throughout the whole of his reign people were rushing about all over the country attacking each other. ... And throughout the whole thing, there was Edward, as cool as a cucumber, down on his knees praying from morning till night; what for, no one knows, unless it was that he should be kept out of trouble. If so, it just shows the power of prayer.
> Nicolas Bentley, *Golden Sovereigns*.

And so, with the Kingdom made safe on all sides . . . the most kindly King Edward passed his life in security and peace, and spent much of his time in the glades and woods in the pleasures of hunting. After divine service, which he gladly and devoutly attended every day, he took much pleasure in hawks and birds of that kind which were brought before him, and was really delighted by the baying and scrambling of the hounds.
    Vita Aedwardi Regis, translated by F. Barlow.

A certain young woman . . . had an infection of the throat and of those parts under the jaw which, from their likeness to an acorn, are called glands. These had so disfigured her face with an evil smelling disease that she could scarcely speak to anyone without great embarrassment. She was informed in a dream that if she were washed in water by King Edward she would be cured of this most troublesome pox. . . . And when the king heard of it, he did not disdain to help the weaker sex, for he had the sweetest nature, and was always charming to all suitors. A dish of water was brought; the king dipped in his hands; and with the tips of his fingers he anointed the face of the young woman and the places infected with the disease. . . . Those diseased parts that had been treated by the smearing of the king softened and separated from the skin; and, with the pressure of the hand, worms together with pus and blood came out of various holes. . . . And hardly had she been at court a week, when all foulness washed away, the grace of God moulded her with beauty.
    Ibid.

And not to omit his attitude and appearance, he was a very proper figure of a man — of outstanding height, and distinguished by his milky white hair and beard, full face and rosy cheeks, thin white hands, and long translucent fingers; in all the rest of his body he was an unblemished royal person. Pleasant, but always dignified, he walked with eyes downcast, most graciously affable to one and all.
    Ibid.

EDWARD PRINCE OF WALES (THE BLACK PRINCE)

1330—76

Let the boy win his spurs.
    Edward III, attributed, at the Battle of Creçy, 1345.

See also George III

EDWARDS, JONATHAN

1703—58 Clergyman

I have a constitution in many respects peculiarly unhappy, attended with flaccid solids, vapid, sizy, and scarce fluids, and a low tide of spirits; often occasioning a kind of childish weakness and contemptibleness of speech, presence and demeanor, with a disagreeable dullness and stiffness.
    On himself, Letter to the trustees of New Jersey College, 1757.

The quintessence of Puritanism.
    Anon., popular encomium, in Sydney Ahlstrom, *A Religious History of the American People.*

The greatest of theologians; combining in a degree that is quite unexampled, the profoundly intellectual with the devotedly spiritual and sacred, and realizing in his own person a most rare, yet most beautiful, harmony between the simplicity of the Christian pastor on the one hand, and on the other, all the strength and prowess of a giant in philosophy; so as at once to minister . . . to the hearers of his plain congregation, and yet in the high field of authorship to have traversed in a way, that none have ever done before him, the most inaccessible places, and achieved such a mastery as had never till his time been realized, over the most arduous difficulties of our science.
    Thomas Chalmers, in William Sprague, *Annals of the American Pulpit.*

The ablest metaphysician of the period between Leibniz and Kant.
    Franklin Bowditch Dexter, *Biographical Sketches of the Graduates of Yale College.*

He was the last medieval American — at least among the intellectuals.
    Peter Gay 'A Loss of Mastery; Puritan Historians in Colonial America', in D. Levin, *Jonathan Edwards.*

The meeting house remembered!
You stood on stilts in the air,
but you fell from your parish.
'All rising is by a winding stair.'
    Robert Lowell, *Jonathan Edwards in Western Massachusetts.*

He believed in the worst God, preached the worst sermons, and had the worst religion of any human being who ever lived on this continent.
    M. M. Richter, *Jonathan Edwards.*

See also William Fox

EDWARDS, OLIVER

1711—91? Gentleman

I have tried too in my time to be a philosopher; but, I don't know how, cheerfulness was always breaking in.
  On himself, in James Boswell, *Life of Johnson*.

EDWIN (EADWINE), KING OF NORTHUMBRIA

585?—633

So peaceful was it in those parts of Britain under King Edwin's jurisdiction that the proverb still runs that a woman could carry her newborn babe across the island from sea to sea without any fear of harm. Such was the king's concern for the welfare of his people that in a number of places where he had noticed clear springs adjacent to the highway he ordered posts to be erected with brass bowls hanging from them, so that travellers could drink and refresh themselves. And so great was the people's affection for him, and so great was the awe in which he was held, that no one wished or ventured to use these bowls for any other purpose.
  Bede, *Ecclesiastical History of the English People*, translated by Leo Sherley-Price.

Within his own dominions, Eadwine displayed a genius for civil government which shows how completely the mere age of conquest had passed away. With him began the English proverb so often applied to after kings: 'A woman with her babe might walk scatheless from sea to sea in Eadwine's day.'
  J. R. Green, *A Short History of the English People*.

EGREMONT, EARL OF, see under WYNDHAM, SIR CHARLES

EINSTEIN, ALBERT

1879—1955 Scientist

Three wonderful people called Stein;
There's Gert and there's Ep and there's Ein.
Gert writes in blank verse,
Ep's sculptures are worse
And nobody understands Ein.
  Anon., in Ronald W. Clark, *Einstein: The Life and Times*.

Here Einstein lies;
  At least, they laid his bier
Just hereabouts —
  Or relatively near.
    Kensal Green (Colin Hurry), *Premature Epitaphs*.

Even today Einstein's general theory attracts men principally on aesthetic grounds, an appeal that few people outside of mathematics have been able to feel.
  Thomas S. Kuhn, *The Structure of Scientific Revolutions*.

One day at Fenner's just before the last war, G. H. Hardy and I were talking about Einstein. Hardy had met him several times, and I had recently returned from visiting him. Hardy was saying that in his lifetime there had only been two men in the world, in all the fields of human achievement, science, literature, politics, anything you like, who qualified for the Bradman class. One was Lenin and the other Einstein.
  C. P. Snow, *Variety of Men*.

His public life, as soon as the general theory was published (his fame had already mounted *before* the confirmation), was unlike that which any other scientist is likely to experience again. No one knows quite why, but he sprang into the public consciousness, all over the world, as the symbol of science, the master of the twentieth-century intellect, to a large extent the spokesman for human hope. It seemed that, perhaps as a release from the war, people wanted a human being to revere. It is true that they did not understand what they were revering. Never mind, they believed that here was someone of supreme, if mysterious, excellence.
  Ibid.

It did not last: the Devil howling *Ho,*
Let Einstein be, restored the status quo.
  J. C. Squire, in *The Faber Book of Comic Verse* (cf. Alexander Pope's couplet on Isaac Newton).

Entering Tom Quad one day, [Gilbert] Murray caught sight of Einstein sitting there with a far-away look on his face. The far-away thought behind that far-away look was evidently a happy one, for, at that moment, the exile's countenance was serene and smiling. 'Dr. Einstein, do tell me what you are thinking', Murray said. 'I am thinking,' Einstein answered, 'that after all, this is a very small star'.
  Arnold J. Toynbee, *Acquaintances*.

When Einstein came to England and was lionized after the war, he was entertained by Haldane. Einstein I know and can converse with very interestingly, in a sort of Ollendorfian French about politics, philosophy and what not, and it is one of the lost good things of my life, that I was never able to participate in the mutual exploration of these two stupendously incongruous minds. Einstein must have been like a gentle bright kitten trying to make friends with a child's balloon, very large and un-accountably unpuncturable.

H. G. Wells, *Experiment in Autobiography.*

See also Aldous Huxley

EISENHOWER, DWIGHT DAVID

1890—1969 Thirty-Fourth United States President

Each of us has his portion of ego. At least one night I dreamed that the 22nd amendment [limiting a President to two terms] had been repealed — and it wasn't wholly a nightmare.
On himself, in *New York Times,* 13 May 1962, when asked if he would like to be back in the White House.

I feel like bawling on my own shoulder.
On himself, in *New York World-Telegram and Sun,* 5 November 1953, on the anniversary of his election.

There is one thing about being President: nobody can tell you when to sit down.
On himself, attributed.

Ike is running like a dry creek.
Anon., in Peter F. Drucker, 'The Effective Executive', in *American Heritage Pictorial History of the Presidents.*

Golf had long symbolized the Eisenhower years — played by soft, boring men with ample waistlines who went around rich men's country-club courses in the company of wealthy businessmen and were tended by white-haired, dutiful Negroes.
David Halberstam, *The Best and the Brightest.*

Eisenhower was a subtle man, and no fool, though in pursuit of his objectives he did not like to be thought of as brilliant; people of brilliance, he thought, were distrusted.
Ibid.

As an intellectual, he bestowed upon the games of golf and bridge all the enthusiasm and perseverance that he withheld from books and ideas.
Emmet John Hughes, *The Ordeal of Power: A Political Memoir of the Eisenhower Years.*

He was the great tortoise upon whose back the world sat for eight years. We laughed at him; we talked wistfully about moving; and all the while we never knew the cunning beneath the shell.
Murray Kempton, 'The Underestimation of Dwight D. Eisenhower', in *Esquire,* September 1967.

What he would have liked said of him is that he achieved the highest objective of his or any other modern Presidency: in a nuclear world, teeming with violence on all sides, he successfully 'waged peace' for the eight years of his incumbency.
Arthur Larson, *Eisenhower: The President Nobody Knew.*

I read a very interesting quote by Senator Kerr of Oklahoma. In summing up Ike, he said 'Eisenhower is the only living unknown soldier.' Even this is giving him all the best of it.
Groucho Marx, Letter to Goodman Ace, in *The Groucho Letters.*

. . . President Eisenhower's whole life is proof of the stark but simple truth — that no one hates war more than one who has seen a lot of it.
Richard M. Nixon, Radio-Television Address, Moscow, August 1959.

He has done as much as any man of his limited gifts could do in this era of bad feeling to maintain before the world an image of the United States as being still a nation of free men and free institutions engaged in an experiment of some splendor and one that derives its justification from the hope that it will be useful to all humanity.
Richard H. Rovere, *The Eisenhower Years.*

Mr. Roosevelt liked to associate with the ruling families of Europe. He delighted in calling kings and princes by their first names. Mr. Eisenhower has some measure of the same attitude toward giants of American industry and finance. There are few peasants among his social companions.
Merriman Smith, *Meet Mister Eisenhower.*

Not long ago it was proved that Dwight D. Eisenhower was descended from the royal line of Britain, a proof if one were needed that everyone is descended from everyone.
John Steinbeck, *Travels with Charley.*

The General has dedicated himself so many times, he must feel like the cornerstone of a public building.
Adlai Stevenson, in Leon A. Harris, *The Fine Art of Political Wit.*

If I talk over the people's head, Ike must be talking under their feet.
Ibid.

Golf is a fine release from the tensions of office, but we are a little tired of holding the bag.
Ibid.

Senator Taft is the greatest living authority on what General Eisenhower thinks. ... The Republicans have a 'me too' candidate running on a 'yes but' platform, advised by a 'has been' staff ... General Eisenhower employs the three monkeys standard of campaign morality: see no evil — if it's Republican; hear no evil — unless it is Democratic; and speak no evil — unless Senator Taft says it's all right.
Ibid.

... complex human societies depend for the final decisions of war and peace on a group of elderly men any sensible plant personnel manager ... would hesitate to hire.
Here we have at the top a cardiac case whose chief interest is in getting away from his job as often as possible for golf and bridge.
I. F. Stone, 'What the Berlin Crisis Really Shows', 9 March 1959, in *The Best of I. P. Stone's Weekly.*

See also Henry Luce, Adlai Stevenson, Harry S. Truman

ELDON, LORD (JOHN SCOTT)

1751—1838 Statesman

If I were to begin life again, d——n my eyes, but I would begin as an agitator.
On himself, in Walter Bagehot, *Biographical Studies: Lord Brougham.*

I daresay I have myself been twenty times within an hour or a day of being out of office. The partiality of two Sovereigns has kept me in when nothing else could.
On himself, in Frances Hawes, *Henry Brougham.*

Found dead, a rat — no case could sure be harder;
Verdict — Confined a week in Eldon's larder.
Anon., contemporary.

He is a thorough-bred Tory ... but [has] never flinched, never gone back, never missed his way; he is an *out-and-outer* in this respect. His allegiance has been without flaw ... his implicit understanding is a kind of taffeta-lining to the Crown. ...
William Hazlitt, *The Spirit of the Age.*

By heartiness with which Lord Eldon is always found rejoicing in his own conscientiousness, as in a special gift of Providence, it seems as if he could not suppose that other men could ordinarily desire and endeavour to do their duty.
Harriet Martineau, on Eldon's retirement as Lord Chancellor, 1827, in *History of the Thirty Years Peace.*

A few more drops of Eldonine, and we should have had the People's Charter.
Quarterly Review, late 1850s.

Next came Fraud, and he had on,
Like Eldon, an ermined gown;
His big tears, for he wept well,
Turned to mill-stones as they fell.

And the little children, who
Round his feet played to and fro,
Thinking every tear a gem,
Had their brains knocked out by them.
Percy Bysshe Shelley, *The Mask of Anarchy.*

Lord Eldon and the Court of Chancery sat heavy on mankind.
Sydney Smith, in Walter Bagehot, *Biographical Studies: Lord Brougham.*

ELEANOR OF AQUITAINE

1122?—1204 Queen Consort to Henry II

She was the wife of that most pious King Louis, but she managed to secure an unlawful divorce and married Henry, and this in spite of the charge secretly made against her that she had shared Louis's bed with Henry's father, Geoffrey.
Walter Map, *De Nugis Curialium,* translated from the Latin by F. Tupper and M. B. Ogle.

See also Henry II

ELGAR, SIR EDWARD WILLIAM

1857—1934 Composer

If I write a tune you all say it's commonplace — if I don't, you all say it's rot.
On himself, Letter to A. J. Jaeger, 20 October 1898.

Lovely day: sun — zephyr — view — window open — liver — pills — proofs — bills — weed-killer — yah!
Ibid., 20 May 1900.

I have worked hard for forty years & at last, Providence denies me a decent hearing of my work: so I submit — I always said God was against art and I still believe it. Anything obscene or trivial is blessed in this world and has a reward — I ask for no reward — only to live & to hear my work.
Ibid., 9 October 1900.

Oh! Elgar's work's a d———able work,
The warmest work o' the year,
A work to tweak a teetotaller's beak
And make a methody swear.
Ibid., 14 November 1900.

I feel Gibbonsy, Croftish, Byrdlich & foolish all over.
Ibid.

Edward Elgar, BICYCLE & ORATORIO MONGER.
On himself, sending his bicycle to A. J. Jaeger, 6 February 1903.

I love Elgar's music. It makes me go away feeling I'm a very *bad* man.
Anon. concert-goer, in Atez Orga, *The Proms.*

During a long telephone conversation with Neville Cardus, [Sir Thomas] Beecham was discoursing upon British composers from Purcell onwards.
'But what about Elgar?' asked Cardus.
'What about him?' said Sir Thomas. 'Isn't he well?'
Leslie Ayre, *The Wit of Music.*

He is furious with me for drastically cutting his A flat symphony — it's a very long work, the musical equivalent of the Towers of St. Pancras Station — neo-Gothic you know.
Thomas Beecham, in Neville Cardus, *Sir Thomas Beecham.*

It is all so original, so individual & subjective that it will take the British public 10 years to let it soak into its pachydermal mind. . . .
A. J. Jaeger, on *The Apostles*, Letter to Elgar, 18 August 1903.

Elgar's music is as national in its way as the music of Vaughan Williams but, by using material that in type can be related back to the nineteenth-century German composers, Elgar avoids any suspicion of provincial dialect, even though his national flavour is sufficiently strong to repel certain countries — France in particular.
Constant Lambert, *Music Ho!*

Elgar was the last serious composer to be in touch with the great public.
Ibid.

. . . the aggressive Edwardian prosperity that lends so comfortable a background to Elgar's finales is now as strange to us as the England that produced *Greensleeves* and *The Woodes so wilde*. Stranger, in fact, and less sympathetic. In consequence much of Elgar's music, through no fault of its own, has for the present generation an almost intolerable air of smugness, self-assurance and autocratic benevolence.
Ibid.

The English public is curious. It can only recognise one composer at a time. Once it was Sullivan. Now it is Elgar.
C. H. H. Parry, attributed, 1918, in Michael Kennedy, *Portrait of Elgar.*

He used to bring in hedgehogs from the woods and feed them in the house; he sat in the strawberry bed and wished that someone would bring him champagne in a bedroom jug.
Dora M. Powell, *Edward Elgar: Memories of a Variation.*

In the matter of friendship we are, and I thank God for it, on terms of equality, but try as I may I can never forget that *you* have written a *Gerontius* and I have only listened to it! — the gap *awes* me!
Leo Francis Schuster, Letter to Elgar, 1903.

Edward Elgar, the figurehead of music in England, is a composer whose rank it is neither prudent nor indeed possible to determine. Either it is one so high that only time and posterity can confer it, or else he is one of the Seven Humbugs of Christendom.
George Bernard Shaw, 'Sir Edward Elgar', *Music and Letters.*

If I were a king, or a Minister of Fine Arts, I would give Elgar an annuity of a thousand a year on condition that he produced a symphony every eighteen months.
Ibid.

The landlady in Pickwick whose complaint of her husband was that 'Raddle aint like a man' would have said, if destiny had led her to the altar with the composer of the great symphony in A flat, 'Elgar aint like a musician'.
Ibid.

The Apostles . . . places British music once more definitely in the first place European rank, after two centuries of leather and prunella.
George Bernard Shaw, Letter to *Daily News*, 9 June 1922.

He has given us a Land of Hope and Glory; and we have handed him back the glory and kept all the hope for ourselves.

George Bernard Shaw, Letter to *The Times*, 20 December 1932.

. . . Popular and official recognition had the sense to recognize in Elgar a master, in spite of our inveterate prejudice against everybody who does not profess and call himself an amateur.

Donald Tovey, in *Music and Letters*, January 1935.

To the careful observer there is nothing to occasion astonishment or require explanation in the fact that the same Elgar who produced the mystical exaltation of *Gerontius* was an enthusiastic follower of horse-racing.

Sir Jack Westrup, *Sharps and Flats*.

ELIOT, CHARLES WILLIAM

1834—1926 Educator

But it was not in his character to participate in anything as a mere equal. He participated as a benevolent St. Bernard would enter into the play of puppies. Wherever he chanced to be, he towered above his associates.

Rollo Walter Brown, *Lonely Americans*.

He was not a political figure, nor an artist, nor a thinker: he was the embodiment of a mood of the American people, a sincere, important, and yet passing mood: and he belongs to a class of men who fill a great place in the public eye and are suddenly and ungratefully forgotten; — the class of worthies.

John Jay Chapman, *Memories and Milestones*.

Eliot's zeal was for the promotion of human welfare. Knowledge for the sake of knowledge or art for art's sake made him impatient; knowledge applicable to life excited his enthusiasm

Henry James, *Charles W. Eliot*.

ELIOT, GEORGE (MARY ANN EVANS)

1819—80 Novelist

Whatever may be the success of my stories, I shall be resolute in preserving my incognito, having observed that a *nom de plume* secures all the advantages without the disagreeables of reputation. Perhaps, therefore, it will be well to give you my prospective name, as a tub to throw to the whale in case of curious in-

quiries, and accordingly I subscribe myself, best and most sympathizing of editors, Yours very truly, George Eliot.

On herself, Letter to John Blackwood, 4 February 1857.

My artistic bent is not at all to the presentation of eminently irreproachable characters, but to the presentation of mixed human beings in such a way as to call forth tolerant judgment, pity, and sympathy. And I cannot stir a step aside from what I *feel* to be *true* in character. If anything strikes you as untrue to human nature in my delineations, I shall be very glad if you will point it out to me, that I may reconsider the matter. But alas! inconsistencies and weaknesses are not untrue.

On herself, Letter to John Blackwood, 18 February 1857.

It seems as if the sun had gone out. You cannot think how much I owed her. Of eighteen or twenty writers by whom I am conscious that my mind has been formed, she was one. Of course I mean ways, not conclusions. In problems of life and thought, which baffled Shakespeare disgracefully, her touch was unfailing. No writer ever lived who had anything like her power of manifold, but disinterested and impartially observant sympathy.

Lord Acton, Letter to Mary Gladstone, 27 December 1880.

Mrs Lewes sat on the sofa by me and talking to me only in a low sweet voice; her face is repulsively ugly from the immense size of the chin, but when she smiles it lights up amazingly and she looks both good and loving and gentle.

Lady Amberley, *Amberley Papers*.

In her brain-development the Intellect greatly predominates; it is very large, more in length than in its peripheral surface. In the Feelings, the Animal and Moral regions are about equal; the moral being quite sufficient to keep the animal in order and in due subservience, but would not be spontaneously active. The social feelings were very active, particularly the adhesiveness. She was of a most affectionate disposition, always requiring some one to lean upon, preferring what has hitherto been considered the stronger sex, to the other and more impressible. She was not fitted to stand alone.

Charles Bray, phrenological report, *Autobiography*.

I found out in the first two pages that it was a woman's writing — she supposed that in making a door, you last of all put in the *panels*!

Thomas Carlyle (after reading *Adam Bede*), in G. H. Haight, *George Eliot*.

I never saw such a woman. There is nothing a bit masculine about her; she is thoroughly feminine and looks and acts as if she were made for nothing but to mother babies. But she has a power of *stating* an argument equal to any man; equal to any man do I say? I have never seen any man, except Herbert Spencer, who could state a case equal to her. ... She didn't talk like a blue-stocking — as if she were aware she had got hold of a big topic — but like a plain woman, who talked of Homer as simply as she would of flat-irons.

John Fiske, Letter to his Wife, 1873.

I have seldom seen a grander face! I have read somewhere that she looked like a horse — a great mistake, as, although her face is long and narrow, it is only as Dante's was. It expresses elevation of thought, kindness, power and *humour* ... She reminds you continually of a man — a bright, gentle, lovable, philosophical man — without being a bit *masculine*.

Bret Harte, Letter, 1880.

The overdone reputation of the Evans-Eliot-Lewes-Cross woman (poor creature! one ought not to speak slightingly, I know), half real power, half imposition.

Gerard Manley Hopkins, Letter to Robert Bridges, October 1886.

A person whose life and opinions were in notorious antagonism to Christian practice in regard to marriage and Christian theory in regard to dogma. How am I to tell the Dean [Stanley] to do that which, if I were in his place, I should most emphatically refuse to do? ... One cannot eat one's cake and have it too.

T. H. Huxley, refusing to support a plan to bury her in Poets' Corner in Westminster Abbey.

In this vast ugliness resides a most powerful beauty which, in a very few moments steals forth and charms the mind, so that you end as I ended, in falling in love with her. Yes, behold me literally in love with this great horse-faced blue-stocking. I don't know in what the charm lies, but it is thoroughly potent. An admirable physiognomy — a delightful expression, a voice soft and rich as that of a counselling angel — a mingled sagacity and sweetness — a broad hint of a great underlying world of reserve, knowledge, pride and power — a great feminine dignity and character in these massively plain features — a hundred conflicting shades of consciousness and simpleness — shyness and frankness — graciousness and remote indifference — these are some of the more definite elements of her personality. ... Altogether, she has a larger circumference than any woman I have ever seen.

Henry James, Letter to his Father, 10 May 1869.

George Eliot seems to us among English romancers to stand alone. Fielding approaches her, but to our mind she surpasses Fielding. Fielding was didactic — the author of *Middlemarch* is really philosophic.

Henry James, in *Galaxy*, March 1873.

You see, it was really George Eliot who started it all. ... And how wild they all were with her for doing it. It was she who started putting all the action inside. Before, you know, with Fielding and the others, it had been outside. Now I wonder which is right?. ... You know I can't help thinking there ought to be a bit of both.

D. H. Lawrence, in Jessie Chambers, *D. H. Lawrence: A Personal Record.*

George Eliot had the heart of Sappho; but the face, with the long proboscis, the protruding teeth of the Apocalyptic horse, betrayed animality.

George Meredith, in *Fortnightly Review,* July 1909.

She ... taking as her text the three words which have been used so often as the inspiring trumpet-calls of men, — the words, *God, Immortality, Duty* — pronounced, with terrible earnestness, how inconceivable was the *first*, how unbelievable the *second*, and yet how peremptory and absolute the *third*. Never, perhaps, have sterner accents affirmed the sovereignty of impersonal and unrecompensing Law. I listened, and night fell; her grave, majestic countenance turned toward me like a sibyll's in the gloom; it was as though she withdrew from my grasp, one by one, the two scrolls of promise, and left me the third scroll only, awful with inevitable fates. And when we stood at length and parted, amid that columnar circuit of the forest-trees, beneath the last twilight of starless skies, I seemed to be gazing, like Titus at Jerusalem, on vacant seats and empty halls, — on a sanctuary with no Presence to hallow it, and heaven left lonely of a God.

F. W. H. Myers, in *Century Magazine*, November 1881.

George Sand is often immoral; but she is always beautiful. ... But in the English Cockney school, which consummates itself in George Eliot, the personages are picked up from behind the counter and out of the gutter; and the landscape, by excursion train to Gravesend, with return ticket for the City-road.

John Ruskin, *Fiction, Fair and Foul.*

George Eliot's reputation was ... enormous, in spite of the protests of Ruskin, and of the alliterative vituperations of Swinburne. ... The late Lord

ELIOT, T. S.

Bryce, in a public eulogy of Tolstoy, could think of nothing more complimentary to say of him than that as a novelist he was second only to George Eliot.
George Bernard Shaw, *Pen Portraits and Reviews.*

She was not, she used to say, either an optimist or a pessimist, but a 'meliorist' — a believer that the world could be improved, and was perhaps slowly improving, though with a very strong conviction that the obstacles were enormous and the immediate outlook not especially bright.
Leslie Stephen, *George Eliot.*

It is, I think, the defect of George Eliot that she struggles too hard to do work that shall be excellent. She lacks ease. Latterly the signs of this have been conspicuous in her style, which has always been and is singularly correct, but which has become occasionally obscure from her too great desire to be pungent. It is impossible not to feel the struggle, and that feeling begets a flavour of affectation. In *Daniel Deronda*, of which at this moment only a portion has been published, there are sentences which I have found myself compelled to read three times before I have been able to take home to myself all that the writer has intended.
Anthony Trollope, *Autobiography.*

It has made a deep impression on me. Albert likes and is much interested.
Queen Victoria (after reading *Adam Bede*), Journal, 29—30 October 1859.

See also Charlotte Cushman, Thomas Hardy, Henry James, George Meredith

ELIOT, THOMAS STEARNS

1888—1965 Poet

How unpleasant to meet Mr Eliot!
With his features of clerical cut,
And his brow so grim
And his mouth so prim
And his conversation, so nicely
Restricted to What Precisely
And If and Perhaps and But.
On himself, *Five Finger Exercises.*

Whether one writes a piece of work well or not seems to me a matter of crystallisation — the good sentence, the good word, is only the final stage in the process. ... The words come easily enough, in comparison to the core of it — the *tone* — and nobody can help one in the least with that. Any-

thing *I* have picked up about writing is due to having spent (as I once thought, wasted) a year absorbing the style of F. H. Bradley — the finest philosopher in English.
On himself, Letter to Lytton Strachey, 1 June 1919.

The years between fifty and seventy are the hardest. You are always being asked to do things and yet you are not decrepit enough to turn them down.
On himself, in *Time*, 23 October 1950.

One can only say that if Mr Eliot had been pleased to write in demotic English *The Waste Land* might not have been, as it just is to all but anthropologists, and literati, so much waste-paper.
Anon., in *Manchester Guardian*, 1922.

Mr Eliot does not convince us that his weariness is anything but a habit, an anti-romantic reaction, a new Byronism which he must throw off if he is not to become a recurring decimal in his fear of being a mere vulgar fraction.
Anon., in *Times Literary Supplement* (review of *Ara vus Prec*), 18 March 1920.

Mr Eliot, always evasive in the grand manner, has reached a stage at which he can no longer refuse to recognize the limitations of his medium; he is sometimes walking very near the limits of coherency. But it is the finest horses which have the most tender mouths, and some unsympathetic tug has sent Mr Eliot's gift awry. When he recovers control we shall expect his poetry to have gained in variety and strength from this ambitious experiment.
Anon., in *Times Literary Supplement* (review of *The Waste Land*), 20 September 1923.

Eliot started in the enormous confusion of war and post-war England, handicapped in every way. Yet by merit, tact, produce and pertinacity he succeeded in doing what no other American has done — imposing his personality, taste, and even many of his opinions on literary England.
Richard Aldington, in Charles Norman, *Ezra Pound.*

When things began to happen to our favourite spot,
A key missing, a library bust defaced,
    Then on the tennis-court one morning
    Outrageous, the bloody corpse and always,

Day after day, the unheard-of drought, it was you
Who, not speechless with shock but finding the right
    Language for thirst and fear, did most to
    Prevent a panic.
W. H. Auden, *For T. S. Eliot.*

As to the influence of this Lloyds Bank clerk
Upon the state of English poetry, I think
It was imperious. By this I mean
He restored to us what had almost gone,
The moral and intellectual porphyrogenitive.
And what had been, before his hegemony,
Expedience and a chaffering of poetic riff raff
Underwent, during his magistracy, the
Imposition of rigorous definitions
And that sense of spiritual onus
Inherent in all Pascalian interpretations.
Also he loved bad jokes.

    George Barker, 'Elegaics for T. S. Eliot', from
Dreams of a Summer Night.

I don't know why Eliot should feel so badly about
things. There is no reason why he should have to
write in that 'I-cannot-be-gay' manner. He did not
have to go through the war.

    Edmund Blunden, in *New Verse*, June 1945.

When the news of Eliot's death came through,
commercial television had just presented an abridgement of Middleton's *The Changeling*. Watching it,
I thought that this could never have happened if
Eliot hadn't opened our eyes to the greatness of
the Jacobeans. Spike Milligan, on a comic TV show,
could say, 'Not with a banger but a wimpy', and
most of the audience caught the reference. Weather
forecasters would joke about April being the
cruellest month. Demagogues would quote John
Donne and novelists make titles out of Donne's
poems or religious meditations. The metaphysical
poets, still quaint and unreadable in my schooldays,
became A-level set-books. And, though not everybody could follow Eliot to the final austerities of
Anglicanism, Royalism and Classicism, his affirmation of the importance of tradition was accepted
even by the *avant-garde*. For, with Eliot, the past
was not a dull and venerable ancestor but a living
force which modified the present and was in turn
modified by it. Time was not an army of unalterable law; time was a kind of ectoplasm.

    Anthony Burgess, *Urgent Copy*.

Of course, when you think of it, 'The Waste Land'
was the first great cutup collage.

    William Burroughs, *Paris Review*.

As the years went by, the astringent, sparkling,
quality deserted Eliot's prose, which was apt to
become arid and sometimes pontifical, bowed
down by the honours and ex-cathedra authority
which society had bestowed on him. During the
war he suddenly found himself accepted as something we were fighting for, like the Four Freedoms
or Big Ben. In the Thirties the image had been
formed of the cat-addict and cheese-taster, the
writer of pawky blurbs, the church-warden, the
polite deflater.

    Cyril Connolly, *The Evening Colonnade*.

Eliot is a great poet because he purified the words
of the tribe in novel, beautiful and many-meaninged
ways, not because he extended the field of subject-
matter available to poetic treatment: he didn't.

    Aldous Huxley, *Literature and Science*.

That awful boresome man? You can't be serious!
Why he's so *stoopid*! He's such a *bore*, don't you
know? I have to tell him all the clues!

    Henry Bradshaw Isherwood (on doing cross-
words with TSE in their Club), in Christopher
Isherwood, *Kathleen and Frank*.

Mr Eliot's best criticism, directed for the most part
on the poetry of the past, is immediately related to
his own problems as a poet — a poet confronted
with the task of inventing the new ways of using
words that were necessary if there was to be a contemporary poetry. The interest it shows Mr Eliot
taking in his subjects is correspondingly restricted.
But the restriction can be seen to be a condition of
the extraordinary cogency of the criticism — the
clean finality with which it does what was necessary
for his essential purposes. Never was there a finer
economy.

    F. R. Leavis, *The Common Pursuit*.

Mr T. S. Eliot has even made a virtue of developing
himself into an incarnate Echo, as it were (though
an *original* Echo, if one can say that). This imitation method, of the *creator-as-scholar* . . . does not
appeal to me extremely, I confess.

    Percy Wyndham Lewis, Letter to *Spectator*,
2 November 1934.

He is very yellow and glum. Perfect manners. He
looks like a sacerdotal lawyer — dyspeptic, ascetic,
eclectic. Inhibitions. Yet obviously a nice man and a
great poet. My admiration for him does not flag.
He is without pose and full of poise. He makes one
feel that all cleverness is an excuse for thinking hard.

    Harold Nicolson, Diary, 2 March 1932.

Eliot has remained aloof, but if forced at the pistol's
point to choose between Fascism and some more
democratic form of Socialism, would probably
choose Fascism.

    George Orwell, *Inside the Whale*.

The fearful despair that is almost normal in modern
times. You get the same kind of thing, though only
just touched upon, in Eliot's poems. With E, how-

ever, there is also a certain sniffish 'I told you so' implication, because as the spoilt darling of the *Church Times* he is bound to point out that all this wouldn't have happened if we had not shut our eyes to the Light.

George Orwell, Letter to Brenda Salkeld,
June 1933.

Sage Homme

These are the poems of Eliot
By the Uranian Muse begot;
A Man their Mother was,
A Muse their Sire.

How did the printed Infancies result
From Nuptials thus doubly difficult?

If you must needs enquire
Know diligent Reader
That on each Occasion
Ezra performed the Caesarean Operation. . . .

Ezra Pound, Letter to T. S. Eliot, 24 December 1921.

Mr Eliot . . . is at times an excellent poet and . . . has arrived at the supreme Eminence among English critics largely through disguising himself as a corpse.

Ezra Pound, in *Front*, November 1930.

Our venbl. friend Possum.

Ezra Pound, Letter to Wyndham Lewis,
3 August 1939.

His was the true Dantescan voice — not honoured enough, and deserving more than I gave him. . . . Recollections? let some thesis writer have the satisfaction of 'discovering' whether it was in 1920 or '21 that I went from Excideuil to meet a ruck-sacked Eliot. Days of walking — conversation? literary? *le papier Fayard* was then the burning topic. Who is there now for me to share a joke with? Am I to write 'about' the poet Thomas Stearns Eliot? or my friend 'the Possum'? Let him rest in peace. I can only repeat, but with the urgency of 50 years ago: READ HIM.

Ezra Pound (on Eliot's death), in *Sewanee Review*, Winter 1966.

He was a smash of a poet.

Ezra Pound, attributed, in Robert Lowell,
Notebook.

I would sometimes spend the night at Chester Terrace. I remember how on one such occasion I woke early and presently became conscious that the door of my room, which was on the ground floor, was slowly and silently being opened. I lay still and saw first a hand and then an arm reach round the door and lift from a hook the bowler hat that was hanging there. It was a little before seven o'clock and Mr Eliot was on his way to an early communion service. It was the first intimation I had had of his conversion to the Christian faith. This reticence was maintained in all his private affairs.

Herbert Read, *T. S. Eliot — A Memoir*.

This morning two of my pupils came together to ask me a question about work. One, named Eliot, is very well-dressed & polished, with manners of the finest Etonian type, the other is an unshaven Greek, appropriately named Demos, . . . The two were obviously friends, and had on neither side the slightest consciousness of social difference. I found they were not nearly so well grounded as I had thought; they were absolutely candid, & quite intelligent, but obviously had not been taught with the minute thoroughness that we practise in England. Window-dressing seems irresistible to Americans.

Bertrand Russell, Letter to Lady Ottoline Morrell, March 1914.

The secret of Eliot's influence over the young lay in the paradox of his personality. With a gesture of reversing current theories about the self-expressing poet, he dramatized a necessary shift in sensibility, from a subjective concern with the poet's self to an objective one with the values of a civilization end-lessly created in men's minds. He wrote a new, a really new poetry, which set up connections with the old, the really old.

Stephen Spender, in Allen Tate, *T. S. Eliot, the Man and his Work*.

Poet Eliot had dinner with me on Monday — rather ill and rather American: altogether not quite gay enough for my taste. But by no means to be sniffed at.

Lytton Strachey, Letter to Dora Charrington, 14 May 1919.

[Some poets], like Eliot, have become so aware of the huge mechanism of the past that their poems read like scholarly conglomerations of a century's wisdom, and are difficult to follow unless we have an intimate knowledge of Dante, the Golden Bough, and the weather-reports in Sanskrit.

Dylan Thomas, Letter to Pamela Hansford Johnson, 1933.

Pope Eliot.

Dylan Thomas, Letter to Geoffrey Grigson, 1934.

I am made a little tired at hearing Eliot, only in his

early forties, present himself as an 'agèd eagle' who asks why he should make the effort to stretch his wings.

Edmund Wilson, *Axel's Castle*.

I think that Mr Eliot has written some of the loveliest single lines in modern poetry. But how intolerant he is of the old usages and politenesses of society — respect for the weak, consideration for the dull! As I sun myself upon the intense and ravishing beauty of one of his lines, and reflect that I must make a dizzy and dangerous leap to the next, and so on from line to line, like an acrobat flying precariously from bar to bar, I cry out, I confess, for the old decorums, and envy the indolence of my ancestors who, instead of spinning madly through mid-air, dreamt quietly in the shade with a book.

Virginia Woolf, *The Captain's Death Bed*.

Pale, marmoreal Eliot was there last week, like a chapped office boy on a high stool, with a cold in his head, until he warms a little, which he did. 'The critics say I am learned and cold,' he said. 'The truth is I am neither.'

Virginia Woolf, Diary, 1921.

See also Ford Madox Ford, A. E. Housman, James Joyce, Wyndham Lewis, Logan Pearsall Smith, Edith Sitwell, Lytton Strachey, William Carlos Williams

ELIZABETH I

1533–1603

But if I continue in the kind of life I have begun, I doubt not but God will so direct mine owne and youre counsaile, that ye shall not need to doubt of a successor, which may be more beneficial to the Commonwealth, then he which may be borne of me, considering that the sisse of the best Princes many time degenerateth. And to me it shall be a full satisfaction both for the memoriall of my name, and for my glory also, if when I shall let my last breath, it be ingraven upon my Marble Tombe, *Here lyeth ELIZABETH, which raigned a Virgin, and dyed a Virgin*.

On herself, Speech to her first Parliament, 1559.

I am more afraid of making a fault in my Latin than of the Kings of Spain, France, Scotland, the whole house of Guise, and all of their confederates.

On herself, in F. Chamberlin, *The Sayings of Queen Elizabeth*.

I would rather be a beggar and single than a queen and married.

Ibid.

I grieve, yet dare not shew my discontent;
I love, and yet am forced to seem to hate;
I dote, but dare not what I ever meant;
I seem stark mute, yet inwardly doe prate;
I am, and am not — freeze, and yet I burn;
Since from myself my other self I turn.

Ibid., written when her suitor, the Duke of Alençon, left her for the last time in 1582.

I am your anointed Queen. I will never be by violence constrained to do anything. I thank God I am endued with such qualities that if I were turned out of the Realm in my petticoat I were able to live in any place in Christome.

Ibid.

I know I have the body of a weak and feeble woman; but I have the heart and stomach of a king, and of a King of England too, and think foul scorn that Parma, or Spain, or any prince of Europe should dare to invade the borders of my realm; to which, rather than any dishonour shall grow by me, I myself will take up arms, I myself will be your general, judge, and rewarder of every one of your virtues in the field.

Ibid., speaking at Tilbury in 1588.

The Queen of Scots is lighter of a fair son, and I am but a barren stock.

Ibid., at the time of the birth of the future James I.

Though God hath raised me high, yet this I count the glory of my crown: that I have reigned with your loves.

On herself, in 'Golden' Speech, 1601.

Oh dearest Bess
I like your dress;
Oh sweet Liz
I like your phiz;
Oh dearest Queen
I've never seen
A face more like
A soup-tureen.

Anon., in Arnold Silcock, *Verse and Worse*.

The Protestants Religion being now by authority of Parliament established, Queene ELIZABETHs first and chiefest care was, for the most constant defence thereof, against all the practises of all men amidst the enemies in that behalfe; neither indeed did she ever suffer the least innovation therein. Her second care was, to hold an even course in her whole life, and all her actions. Whereupon she tooke for her motto, Semper eadem, that is, Alwayes the same.

William Camden, *Annales*, translated by 'R.N.'.

For, which of the kings of this land before her Majesty, had theyr banners ever seene in the Caspian sea? which of them hath ever dealt with the Emperor of Persia, as her Majesty hath done, and obteined for her merchants large & loving privileges? who ever saw before this regiment, an English Ligier in the stately porch of the Grand Signor at Constantinople? who ever found English Consuls & Agents at Tripolis in Syria, at Aleppo, at Babylon, at Balsara, and which is more, who ever heard of Englishmen at Goa before now? what English shippes did heertofore ever anker in the mighty river of Plate? passe and repasse the unpassable (in former opinion) straight of Magellan, range along the coast of Chili, Peru, and all the backside of Nova Hispania, further then any Christian ever passed, travers the mighty bredth of the South sea, land upon the Luzones in despight of the enemy, enter into alliance, amity, and traffike with the princes of the Moluccaes, & the Isle of Java, double the famous Cape of Bona Speranza, arrive at the Isle of Santa Helena, & last of al returne home richly laden with the commodities of China, as the subjects of this now flourishing monarchy have done?

Richard Hakluyt, *The Principall Navigations, Voiages and Discoveries of the English Nation . . ., The Epistle Dedicatorie.*

When she smiled it was pure sunshine, that everyone did choose to bask in, if they could: but anon came a storm from a sudden gathering of clouds, and the thunder fell in wondrous manner on all alike.

Sir John Harrington, *Nugae Antiquae.*

Twenty years later, when England and the courts of Europe were agog with the idea that Queen Elizabeth might marry the Earl of Leicester, Lord Leicester told the French Ambassador that he had known Elizabeth since she was a child of eight, and from that very time she had always said: 'I will never marry'. Little notice was paid to the words. It did not occur to anyone, it seems, to look back and recall that when Elizabeth was eight years and five months old, Catherine Howard was beheaded.

Elizabeth Jenkins, *Elizabeth the Great.*

Queen Elizabeth never saw her self after she became old in a true glass. They painted her and somytymes would vermilion her nose, she had always about Christmas evens set dice, that threw sixes or five, & she knew not they were other, to make her win &

esteame herself fortunate. That she had a membrana on her which made her uncapable of man, though for her delight she tried many, att the coming of Monsieur, ther was a French Chirurgion who took in hand to cut it, yett fear stayed her & his death.

Ben Jonson, in *Conversations with William Drummond of Hawthornden.*

But Elizabeth's genius was opportunist. She was well content to win a practical victory without inflicting a constitutional defeat. She left unused powers which her unique personality rendered unnecessary. She overlooked offences the commission of which immediately served as a precedent for committing them anew.

J. E. Neale, *The Commons Privilege of Free Speech in Parliament.*

An element of lovemaking in diplomacy was always very much to her taste.

Conyers Read, *Mr. Secretary Walsingham and the Policy of Queen Elizabeth.*

It is hard to get at the truth about Queen Elizabeth. She has become one of the articles of the English national faith, and good Englishmen from John Hayward to John Neale have conspired together to glorify her.

Conyers Read, *The Tudors.*

She brought England through a very perilous passage into smooth waters. Unfortunately for her successors the chart by which she steered her erratic course was destroyed with her death.

Ibid.

Queen Elizabeth is the greatest of English, perhaps of all modern sovereigns. In a period remarkable for long and sanguinary wars, she made her name respected abroad without a waste of blood or treasure; and, in a time of great political ferment, she maintained the most absolute authority at home, without any loss of the affections of her people. She obtained glory without conquest, and unlimited power without odium.

Lord John Russell, *The English Government and Constitution.*

It was happy for the country that Queen Elizabeth found it in her interest to embrace the Protestant religion, and that, by the foolish as well as atrocious plots of the Roman Catholics, she was forced to cultivate still more strongly the affections of the Protestant party. Boast as we may of our Constitution, had Queen Elizabeth been a Roman Catholic, or James II. a Protestant, there would have been no liberty in England.

Ibid.

It may be said of Elizabeth, that if ever there was a monarch whose conduct seemed, according to the speech of the old heathen, to be governed alternately by two souls of a very different disposition and character, the supposition might be applied to her. Possessing more than masculine wisdom, magnanimity, and fortitude on most occasions, she betrayed, at some unhappy moments, even more than female weakness and malignity.

Sir Walter Scott, *History of Scotland*.

Of fayre *Eliza* be your siluer song,
    That blessed wight:
The flowre of Virgins, may shee florish long,
    In princely plight.
For shee is *Syrinx* daughter without spotte,
Which Pan the shepheards God of her begot:
    So sprong her grace
    Of heauenly race,
No mortall blemishe may her blotte.

Edmund Spenser, *The Shepheardes Calendar*, *April*.

A deep instinct made it almost impossible for her to come to a fixed determination upon any subject whatever. Or, if she did, she immediately proceeded to contradict her resolution with the utmost violence, and, after that, to contradict her contradiction more violently still.

Lytton Strachey, *Elizabeth and Essex*.

See also Richard Burton, Sir Martin Frobisher, J. A. Froude, Fulke Greville, Richard Grenville, Lady Jane Grey, Henry VII, Charles Kingsley, Sir Walter Raleigh, Franklin D. Roosevelt, Edmund Spenser, Christopher Tye, Queen Victoria, Francis Walsingham, John Whitgift

ELLISTON, ROBERT WILLIAM

1774–1831 Actor

He cannot retire into himself with that complacent studiousness which feels easy in the absence of bustle and in the solitary enjoyment of its own powers; in soliloquy therefore, which is nothing but thinking loudly, he is too apt to declaim; and in this respect he is like those common actors, who think of nothing but their profession and forget that declamation is of all styles of speaking the most unfit for soliloquies, because they ought never to have the air of being made for effect.

Leigh Hunt, *Critical Essays on the Performers of the London Theatres*.

He appropriates almost exclusively to himself the hero of genteel comedy, that character which attracts the regard of the fair and the fashionable, and that in its happiest point of view unites the most natural attractiveness of social pleasure, with the nicest repellents of gross familiarity.

Ibid.

He had three distinguished excellencies — dry humour, gentlemanly mirth, and fervid gallantry. His features were a little too round, and his person latterly became a great deal too much so. But we speak of him in his best days. His face, in one respect, was of that rare order which is peculiarly fitted for the expression of enjoyment: it laughed with the eyes as well as mouth. His eyes, which were not large, grew smaller when he was merry, and twinkled with glee and archness; his smile was full of enjoyment, and yet the moment he shook his head with a satirical deprecation, or dropped the expression of his face into an inuendo, nothing could be drier or more angular than his mouth. . . . And then his voice was remarkable for its union of the manly with the melodious; and as a lover, nobody approached him. Certainly nobody approached a woman as he did.

Leigh Hunt, 'The Death of Elliston', in *Tatler*, 10 July 1831.

His feelings follow each other like the buckets on a water-wheel, full one instant and empty the next.

Leigh Hunt, in Christopher Murray, *Robert William Elliston, Manager*.

'I like Wrench,' a friend was saying to him one day, 'because he is the same natural, easy creature, *on* the stage, that he is *off*.' 'My case exactly,' retorted Elliston — with a charming forgetfulness, that the converse of a proposition does not always lead to the same conclusion — 'I am the same person *off* the stage that I am *on*.' The inference, at first sight; seems identical; but examine it a little, and it confesses only, that the one performer was never, and the other always, *acting* . . . .

Charles Lamb, 'Ellistoniana' in *Englishman's Magazine*, August 1831.

One proud day to me he took his roast mutton with us in the Temple, to which I had superadded a preliminary haddock. After a rather plentiful partaking of the meagre banquet, not unrefreshed with the humbler sort of liquors, I made a sort of apology for the humility of the fare, observing that for my own part I never ate but of one dish at dinner. 'I too never eat but one thing at dinner' — was his reply — then after a pause — 'reckoning fish as nothing.'

Ibid.

Kenny told me that Charles Lamb, sitting down once to play whist with Elliston, whose hands were very dirty, said, after looking at them for some time, 'Well, Elliston, if *dirt* was trumps, what a hand you would have!'
Thomas Moore, *Memoirs, Journal and Correspondence.*

When Elliston was in a dying state at his house in Black-friar's road, his friend, Mr Durrant was near him, and being anxious his patient should take some medicine prescribed for him, said, 'Come, come, Elliston, you must indeed swallow this. Take it, and you shall have a wine glass of weak brandy and water!' Elliston raised his eyes, and, with still a comic smile, replied, 'Ah, you rogue — bribery and — corruption.'
George Raymond, *Memoirs of R. W. Elliston.*

Elliston was never in repose — his lamp perpetually exhausting, though no illumination was necessary — the fire of his imagination constantly under the blow-pipe, though no immediate work was passing through the furnace.
Ibid.

Elliston, who was one of those who consider no behaviour towards the other sex worthy the term civility which falls short of a positive declaration of love — like our forefathers, who fancied their hospitality poor, unless they made their guests dead drunk — used to relate a smart rebuke he once received in one of these moments of stage-coach *innamoramenti.* Addressing himself to a fair fellow-passenger in language somewhat savouring of *Young Wilding,* and perceiving the lady less favourable to his suit than he had expected, concluded by hoping he had not exceeded the bounds of decorum. 'Perhaps not sir', replied she; 'but your limits of decorum are so extremely liberal that you may possibly lose your way in the excursion.'
Ibid.

Such, alas, was poor Elliston! — one of those who appeared to regard righteousness as a liberal host does his best wine, using but little of it himself, and reserving his stock for the benefit of his friends.
Ibid.

A wretched Tragedian. — his attempts at dignity are ludicrous. He is a fine bustling comedian but he bustles in tragedy also.
Henry Crabb Robinson, Diary, 4 April 1811.

If thrown overboard in rags from one side of a ship, he would appear before his tormentors could turn round, upon the other side of the deck, dressed as a gentleman, ready to begin the world again.
Francis Wemyss, *Twenty-six Years of the Life of an Actor and Manager.*

EMERSON, RALPH WALDO

1803—82 Essayist, Poet

There was something bleached and dry, in the best of this verse, like that of an age-old wisdom, exposed for thousands of years to sun and wind, and a strong, clear, bracing mountain air seemed to have blown upon it.
Van Wyck Brooks, *The Flowering of New England, 1815—1865.*

He is the vital spirit of intellectual joy breaking out in a New England become numb and dead except to industrial development and dry moralizing.
Henry Seidel Canby, *Classic Americans.*

Like most poets, preachers, and metaphysicians, he burst into conclusions at a spark of evidence.
Ibid.

Emerson was a poet by bent, a philosopher by training, but in the synthesis of all his faculties and most of all his will, a preacher — and preaching, good preaching, is literature.... His merits are the qualities of controlled and eloquent persuasion; his faults the faults of a pulpiteer.
Ibid.

He was a philosopher not only of the over-soul but of the pragmatic experience; he was prophet not only of the American dream of democracy but of the universal religion of human brotherhood and individual integrity.
Frederic Ives Carpenter, *Emerson Handbook.*

There is throughout Emerson's poetry, as throughout all of the New England poetry, too much thought, too much argument. Some of his verse gives the reader a very curious and subtle impression that the lines are a translation.
John Jay Chapman, 'Emerson', in Edmund Wilson ed., *The Shock of Recognition.*

His works are all one single attack on the vice of the age, moral cowardice. He assails it not by railings and scorn, but by positive and stimulating suggestion. The imagination of the reader is touched by every device which can awake the admiration for heroism, the consciousness of moral courage.
Ibid.

Emerson was of course the prophet who gave no importance to groups or institutions and refused to think of history as a process. When he discussed Montaigne or Shakespeare, it was not against the background of their times, but rather as 'representative men' whom he might meet at any dinner of the Saturday Club.
Malcolm Cowley, *A Second Flowering*.

Thinking of Emerson as the one citizen of the New World fit to have his name uttered in the same breath with that of Plato, one may without presumption believe that even if Emerson has no system, none the less he is the prophet and herald of any system which democracy may henceforth construct and hold by.
John Dewey, in Frederic Ives Carpenter, *Emerson Handbook*.

... that everlasting rejecter of all that is, and seeker for he knows not what. ...
Nathaniel Hawthorne, in Edward Wagenknecht, *Nathaniel Hawthorne: Man and Writer*.

His mission was the liberation of men from chains that were self-forged and self-imposed. He challenged the individual to achieve his own salvation, and his optimism blinded him to the obstacles placed in the individual's path, to the handicaps imposed by accidents of nature and injustices of society.
Granville Hicks, *The Great Tradition*.

He seemed like an exotic transplanted from some angelic nursery.
Oliver Wendell Holmes, in W. L. Schroeder, *Oliver Wendell Holmes, An Appreciation*.

... the Buddha of the West.
Oliver Wendell Holmes, in Edward Everett Hale, *James Russell Lowell and His Friends*.

Rarely has a man so accurately known the limits of his genius or so unfailingly kept within them.
William James, Address at the Emerson Centenary in Concord, in Milton R. Konvitz and Stephen E. Whicher eds, *Emerson, A Collection of Critical Essays*.

There comes Emerson first, whose rich words, every
one,
Are like gold nails in temples to hang trophies on;
Whose prose is grand verse, while his verse, the Lord
knows,
Is some of it pr — No 'tis not even prose.
James Russell Lowell, *A Fable for Critics*.

I could readily see in Emerson, notwithstanding his merit, a gaping flaw. It was, the insinuation, that had

he lived in those days when the world was made, he might have offered some valuable suggestions.
Herman Melville, in William Ellery Sedgwick, *Herman Melville, The Tragedy of Mind*.

Yet I think Emerson is more than a brilliant fellow. Be his stuff begged, borrowed, or stolen, or of his own domestic manufacture he is an uncommon man. Swear he is a humbug — then he is no common humbug.
Herman Melville, Letter to Evert Duychinck, 3 March 1849.

One of the seven humbugs of Xtiandom.
William Morris, attributed, in Logan Pearsall Smith, Letter to R. C. Trevelyan, 16 July 1927.

... was like a young god making experiments in creation: he botched the work and always began on a new and better plan.
George Santayana, in Richard Chase, *Walt Whitman*.

His constant refrain is the omnipotence of imaginative thought; its power first to make the world, then to understand it, and finally to rise above it.
George Santayana, 'Emerson', in Milton R. Konvitz and Stephen E. Whicher eds, *Emerson, A Collection of Critical Essays*.

Emerson's writing has a cold, cheerless glitter, like the new furniture in a warehouse, which will come of use by and by.
Alexander Smith, *Dreamthorp*.

... a gap-toothed and hoary-headed ape, carried at first into notice on the shoulder of Carlyle, and who now in his dotage spits and chatters from a dirtier perch of his own finding and fouling: corphaeus or choragus of his Bulgarian tribe of autocophagous baboons, who make the filth they feed on.
Algernon C. Swinburne, Letter, 30 January 1874.

He has what none else has; he does what none else does. He pierces the crust the envelope the secrets of life. He joins on equal terms the few great sages and original seers. He represents the freeman, America, the individual.
Walt Whitman, in Edgar Lee Masters, *Whitman*.

EPSTEIN, SIR JACOB

1880–1959 Sculptor

From life's grim nightmare he is now released
Who saw in every face the lurking beast.

'A loss to Art', say friends both proud and loyal,
'A loss', say others, 'to the Café Royal.'
   Anon., in Arnold Silcock, *Verse and Worse.*

Epstein is a great sculptor. I wish he would wash, but
I believe Michel Angelo *never* did, so I suppose it is
part of the tradition.
   Ezra Pound, in Charles Norman, *Ezra Pound.*

See also Albert Einstein

ERNEST AUGUSTUS, see under
CUMBERLAND, DUKE OF

ERSKINE, THOMAS, LORD

1750—1823 Lord Chancellor

Crazy Lord Erskine is an Ass-
  -ortment of all follies:
He was the first to slur the Queen;
But since his trip to Gretna Green,
  He's wondrous kind to dollies.
   Theodore Hook, *Ass-Ass-Ination.*

The tongue of Cicero and the soul of Hampden.
   Lord John Russell, in *Dictionary of National
   Biography.*

ESSEX, EARL OF, see under
DEVEREUX, ROBERT

ETHELRED THE UNREADY

968?—1016

Ethelread the Unready ... was called the Unready
because he was never ready when the Danes were.
Rather than wait for him the Danes used to fine him
large sums called Danegeld, for not being ready. But
though they were always ready, the Danes had very
bad memories and often used to forget that they had
been paid the Danegeld and come back for it almost
before they had sailed away. By that time Ethelread
was always unready again.
   W. C. Sellar and R. J. Yeatman, *1066 and All
   That.*

The evils which give a sinister complexion to the age
were the results of conditions which from their very
nature were temporary. They were the effects of a
state of war under a king of singular incompetence.
Their ultimate cause was realized clearly enough by

the unknown man or woman who first described
him as 'Aethelred unraed' — 'Aethelred No-Counsel'.
In the last resort they all arose from the fact that in
a series of crises, each of which demanded a concentration of the national energy, the king could neither
give direction to his people nor hold his greater subjects firmly to their allegiance.
   F. M. Stenton, *Anglo-Saxon History.*

The career of his life is said to have been cruel in the
beginning, wretched in the middle, and disgraceful in
the end.
   William of Malmesbury, *History of the Kings of
   England,* translated by J. Sharpe.

Dunstan, indeed, had foretold his worthlessness,
having discovered it by a filthy token: for, when
quite an infant, the bishops standing round, as he
was immersing in the baptismal font, he defiled the
sacrament by a natural evacuation: at which Dunstan, being extremely angered, exclaimed, 'By God,
and his mother, this will be a sorry fellow.' I have
read, that when he was ten years of age, hearing it
noised abroad that his brother was killed, he so irritated his furious mother by his weeping, that, not
having a whip at hand, she beat the little innocent
with some candles she had snatched up. ... On this
account he dreaded candles, during the rest of his
life, to such a degree, that he would never suffer the
light of them to be brought into his presence.
   Ibid.

ETHEREGE, SIR GEORGE

1635?—91 Dramatist

How happy should I be cou'd I love the rustling of
papers so well as I have done the rustling of Petty
coats, cou'd I with as much pleasure harken to the
Ministers, when they talk of alliances and changes
in affaires of State, as I used to do the women when
they tattled of who is well with who, and who is
false to such a one.
   On himself, Letter to William Jephson, 24 May
   1688.

You know I am a well-wisher to Laziness.
   On himself, Letter to the Earl of Middleton, 13
   December 1688.

Yet there's Sr George, that honest Man ne'er fails;
Always of Women writes, and always rails;
For which, the Gods have plagued him to the height,
And for his Comfort sent him such a Wife:
A wife that represents all Forms; a Bitch,
A Wizard, wrinkled Woman, & a Witch.
   Anon., *An Answer to the Satyr on the Court
   Ladies.*

I allow it to be nature, but it is nature in its utmost corruption and degeneracy.

Richard Steele, on *The Man of Mode*, in *Spectator*, May 1711.

Etherege writes *Airy Songs*, and soft *Lampoons*,
The best of any Man; as for your *Nouns*,
Grammar, and *Rules of Art*, he knows 'em not,
Yet writ two Talking *Plays* without one Plot.

John Wilmot, Earl of Rochester, with the Duke of Buckingham, *Timon*.

EVELYN, JOHN

1620—1706 Diarist, Virtuoso

In fine, a most excellent person he is, and must be allowed a little for a little conceitedness; but he may well be so, being a man so much above others. He read me, though with too much gusto, some little poems of his own, that were not transcendent, yet one or two very pretty epigrams: among others, of a lady looking in at a grate and being pecked at by an eagle that was there.

Samuel Pepys, Diary, 5 November 1665.

His writing is opaque rather than transparent; we see no depths through it, nor any very secret movements of his mind or heart. He can neither make us hate a regicide, nor love Mrs Godolphin beyond reason. But he writes a diary, and he writes it supremely well. Even as we drowse, somehow or other the bygone gentleman sets up, through three centuries, a perceptible tingle of communication, so that without laying stress on anything in particular, stopping to dream, stopping to laugh, stopping merely to look, we are yet taking notice all the time.

Virginia Woolf, *The Common Reader*, 1925.

See also Samuel Pepys

F

FAIRBANKS, DOUGLAS

1883–1939 Actor

His energy was reserved for the massive action spectaculars with which he enchanted America through the twenties, and when sound ended the fashion he declined to a slightly pathetic ex-idol pursuing beautiful women around Europe. He died at fifty-six in 1939, his tanned body apparently untouched by age but actually so muscle-bound that the blood could barely circulate. He had not so much died, some friends thought, as run down.

John Baxter, *Stunt*.

The career and phenomenal popularity of Douglas Fairbanks followed naturally from the fashion for outdoor adventures [Tom] Mix and the serial stars created. Fairbanks refurbished it for the twenties, identifying his films with the expansive policies of his hero, Teddy Roosevelt, whose wary pacifism and doctrine of 'preparedness' he lived by. His personal philosophy was an almost childish optimism, and an adulation of physical fitness expressed in simplistic slogans, mostly expansions of *mens sana in corpore sano*. 'One of the best things in this little old world is enthusiasm' he said in one of the inspirational books ghosted by his secretary Kenneth Davenport. 'To be successful you must be happy; to be happy you must be enthusiastic; to be enthusiastic you must be healthy; and to be healthy you must keep mind and body healthy.'

Ibid.

He was by nature very athletic, and enjoyed doing stunts just for the fun of it, off stage. If he saw a gate, rather than go through the gate he'd hop over it. If he saw a desk, he'd rather vault over the desk than walk round it.

Douglas Fairbanks Jr, in John Baxter, *Stunt*.

Douglas Fairbanks was a man who never read *anything*. Even his method of deciding on scripts was to glance over them rapidly and then hand them to someone more fond of reading than he ... Douglas would do *anything* to get out of reading the printed word. It was not lack of intelligence or intellectual curiosity that prevented him — simply the fact that he couldn't bear to sit still long enough. Father [hotelier Frank Case, manager of The Algonquin] once said to me, in a bewildered kind of way, 'I don't know how I can be so fond of a man who has never read a book.'

Margaret Case Harriman, *The Vicious Circle*.

Behind those acrobatic stunts and that schoolboy exuberance, there was real genius. His leaps, and fights, and swift, violent trajectories were thrilling to watch, but they were inventive, too; they had about them the quality of beauty and surprise. He was an unconscious harlequin. Everything he did had poise and rhythm. . . . We may have forgotten the names of the pictures, but that tough, stocky little figure, that friendly grin, and the sense of almost illimitable mastery of space and time stays with us.

C. A. Lejeune, in David Shipman, *The Great Movie Stars*.

Doug was so energetic, so frenetic, so able to run extremely fast in the wrong direction that he was the perfect figure to embody a human trait gone frenziedly wrong. But often he played the opposite role, the healthy embodiment of a positive trait that overcomes the erring ways of those misguided folks who crept unknowingly in the wrong direction . . . Doug's physical energy was the perfect center for fast-moving, breezy films that took the business of making films rather lightly and showed how easily human error can be corrected with a little zest, a little effort, and a lot of jumping around.

Gerald Mast, *The Comic Mind*.

In his early films, made at the time of the First World War, Douglas Fairbanks represented all young democratic Americans, quick-thinking, fast-acting, self reliant and self-made. Ridiculing all fashionable affectations, Fairbanks preached the gospel of pep, the merits of clean living, the obligation to take everything with a smile, the claims of traditional decencies. . . . Again and again, in his pictures, Fairbanks demonstrated how ambition, alertness, daring and perpetual hustle would inevitably bring a young American to success, rewarding him both with the fortune he hoped for and the girl of his choice.

Lloyd Morris, *Not So Long Ago*.

Douglas had always faced a situation the only way he knew how, by running away from it.

Mary Pickford, *Sunshine and Shadow*.

Thomas Edison devoted his life to machines intended to make thinking unnecessary for the masses. Fairbanks is devoting his to pictures calculated to keep their minds off the fact that they do not think.

Terry Ramsaye, in Lloyd Morris, *Not So Long Ago*.

Doug did want to explore the Gobi Desert and climb the Matterhorn and Mary [Pickford] never in her life wanted to do anything but make movies. Doug had the innocent snobbery that dearly loved a lord, so when he went to London, poor Doug was ensnared by the daughter of a stable hand who had married the not-quite-bright heir to a title and could thus be called My Lady. When Mary found out about the Anglophobia flirtation she went quite mad. Unfaithful to HER? *Off with his head.*

Adela Rogers St Johns, *The Honeycomb*.

See also Marie Dressler

FAIRFAX, THOMAS, LORD

1612–71 Soldier, Statesman

But as for myself, and what I have done, I may say with Solomon, *I looked on all the works that my hands had wrought, and on the labour that I had laboured to do, and behold, all was vanity, and vexation of spirit.*

On himself, *A Short Memorial*.

For General they chose Sir Thomas Fairfax. . . . This man was chosen because they supposed to find him a man of no quickness of Parts, of no Elocution, of no suspicious plotting Wit, and therefore one that *Cromwell* could make use of at his pleasure. And he was acceptable to sober Men, because he was Religious, Faithful, Valiant, and of a grave, sober, resolved Disposition; very fit for Execution, and neither too Great, nor too Cunning to be Commanded by the Parliament.

Richard Baxter, *Reliquiae Baxterianae*.

Fairfax, whose name in armes through Europe rings
   Filling each mouth with envy, or with praise,
   And all her jealous monarchs with amaze,
   And rumours loud, that daunt remotest kings,
Thy firm unshak'n vertue ever brings
   Victory home, though new rebellions raise
   Thir Hydra heads, and the fals North displaies
   Her brok'n league, to impe their serpent wings,
O yet a nobler task awaites thy hand;
   For what can Warr, but endless warr still breed,
   Till Truth, and Right from Violence be freed,
And Public Faith cleard from the shamefull brand
   Of Public Fraud. In vain doth Valour bleed
   While Avarice, and Rapine share the land.

John Milton, *On the Lord Gen. Fairfax at the siege of Colchester*.

Taller as some say when he is in the field than at home.

Joshua Sprigge, *Anglia Rediviva*.

I have observed him at councils of war that he hath said little but hath ordered things expressly contrary to the judgement of all his council; and in action in the field I have seen him so highly transported that scarce anyone durst speak a word to him and he would seem more like a man distracted and furious than of his ordinary mildness and so far different temper.

Bulstrode Whitelocke, *Memorials of English Affairs*.

FARADAY, MICHAEL

1791–1867 Scientist

I cannot suppress the remark that the pair Faraday-Maxwell has a most remarkable inner similarity with the pair Galileo-Newton — the former of each pair grasping the relations intuitively, and the second one formulating those relations exactly and applying them quantitatively.

Albert Einstein, *Autobiographical Notes*, translated by P. A. Schlipp.

The truth is that Faraday in spite of his many contributions to chemistry was by nature a physicist.

Sir Harold Hartley, *Studies in the History of Chemistry*.

The prince of scientific expositors, Faraday, was once asked, 'How much may a popular lecturer suppose his audience knows?' He replied emphatically, 'Nothing.' Mine was not exactly a popular audience, but I ought not to have forgotten Faraday's rule.

T. H. Huxley, in L. Huxley, *Life and Letters of Thomas Henry Huxley*.

Faraday, on the other hand, shews up his unsuccessful as well as his successful experiments, and his crude ideas as well as his developed ones, and the reader, however inferior to him in inductive power, feels sympathy even more than admiration, and is tempted to believe that, if he had the opportunity, he too would be a discoverer.

J. C. Maxwell, *A Treatise on Electricity and Magnetism*.

281

My kind friend, Professor Faraday, was most attentive, and insisted on superintending the hanging-up of the drawings, and when the lecture was over, would help pack up the specimens, and worked until eleven o'clock, and saw me into my carriage, — this was genuine kindness; and it is this great man's natural character.

Benjamin Silliman, Letter to Dr Mantell, 17 May 1850.

In like manner, Professor Faraday, Sir Humphry Davy's scientific successor, made his first experiments in electricity by means of an old bottle, while he was still a working bookbinder. And it is a curious fact that Faraday was first attracted to the study of chemistry by hearing one of Sir Humphry Davy's lectures on the subject at the Royal Institution. A gentleman, who was a member, calling one day at the shop where Faraday was employed in binding books, found him poring over the article 'Electricity' in an Encyclopaedia placed in his hands to bind. The gentleman, having made inquiries, found he was curious about such subjects, and gave him an order of admission to the Royal Institution, where he attended a course of four lectures delivered by Sir Humphry. He took notes of the lectures, which he showed to the lecturer, who acknowledged their scientific accuracy, and was surprised when informed of the humble position of the reporter. Faraday then expressed his desire to devote himself to the prosecution of chemical studies, from which Sir Humphry at first endeavored to dissuade him; but the young man persisting, he was at length taken into the Royal Institution as an assistant; and eventually the mantle of the brilliant apothecary's boy fell upon the worthy shoulders of the equally brilliant bookbinder's apprentice.

Samuel Smiles, *Self-help*.

Faraday said of his discovery of the phenomenon of electromagnetic induction that it was a babe, and no one could say what it might do when it grew to manhood.

J. J. Thomson, *Recollections and Reflections*.

See also Sir Humphry Davy

FARQUHAR, GEORGE

1678–1707 Dramatist

My outside is neither better nor worse than my Creator made it, and the Piece being drawn by so great an Artist, twere Presumption to say there were many Strokes amiss. I have a Body qualified to answer all the Ends of its Creation, and that's sufficient.

As to the Mind, which in most men wears as many changes as their Body, so in me, 'tis generally drest like my Person in black. Melancholy is its every Day Apparel; and it has hitherto found few Holidays to make it change its Clothes. In short, my Constitution is very Splenetick, and yet very amorous; both which I endeavour to hide, lest the former should offend others, and the latter might incommode myself. And my Reason is so vigilant in restraining these two Failings, that I am taken for an easy-natur'd Man with my own Sex, and an ill-natur'd Clown by yours.

I have very little Estate, but what lies under the Circumference of my Hat; and should I, by mischance, come to lose my Head, I should not be worth a Groat, but I ought to thank Providence that I can by three Hours Study live one and twenty with Satisfaction to myself, and contribute to the Maintenance of more Families than some who have Thousands a Year.

On himself, *The Picture*.

He seems to have been a Man of Genius, rather sprightly than great, rather flowery than solid. His Comedies are diverting, because his Characters are natural, and such as we frequently meet with; but he has used no art in drawing them, nor does there appear any Force of Thinking, or deep Penetration into Nature, in any of his Performances; but rather a superficial View, pleasant enough to the Eye, tho' capable of leaving no great impression on the Mind. He had, it must be allowed, a lively imagination; but then it was not capable of any great Compass. He had wit, too; but it was of such a Kind, that it rather lost than gained by being dwelt upon; and it is certainly true, that his Comedies in general owe their success as much to the Player as to any thing intrinsically excellent in themselves.

Anon., 'Some Memoirs of George Farquhar', in Farquhar, *Works*, 1772.

Our author having received a college exercise from his tutor, upon the miracle of our Saviour's walking upon the water, and coming into the hall for examination the next day, it was found that he had not brought his exercise written as the rest had done; at which the lecturer being displeased, Farquhar offered to make one extempore; and after considering some time, he observed, that he thought it no great miracle, since the man that is born to be hanged, &c. The impiety of this reply quite extinguished all the approbation he expected from its wit.

Baker, Jones and Reed eds, *Biographia Dramatica*.

While Mr *Farquhar* was in *Trinity* College *Dublin*, he sent to a Gentleman to borrow Burnet's History of the *Reformation*, but the Gentleman sent him word

he never lent any Book out of his Chamber, but if he would come there he should make use of it as long as he pleas'd. A little while later, the Owner of the Book sent to borrow Mr *Farquhar*'s Bellows, he return'd him the Complement, — *I never lend my Bellows out of my own Chamber, but if he be pleas'd to come there, he should make use of them as long as he would.*
W. R. Chetwood, *A General History of the Stage.*

He makes us laugh from pleasure, oftener than from malice. He somewhere prides himself in having introduced on the stage the class of comic heroes here spoken of, which has since become a standard character, and which represents the warm-hearted, rattle-brained, thoughtless, high-spirited young fellow, who floats on the back of his misfortunes without repining, who forfeits appearances, but saves his honour, — and he gives us to understand that it was his own.
William Hazlitt, *Lectures on the English Comic Writers.*

FARRAGUT, DAVID GLASGOW

1801—70 Sailor

The sea upon the bar is smooth
Yet perilous the path
Where Gaines' and Morgan's bristling guns
Belch forth their rebel wrath.
And, close behind, their ironclads
Loom in the breaking day;
But Farragut is leading us
And we will clear the way.
Anon., in *Army and Navy Journal,* 3 September 1864, in reference to the battle of Mobile Bay.

Oh, never through all time shall be forgot
His last brave deed, now told by every lip,
When on he sailed, amid a storm of shot
Lashed in the rigging of his staunched old ship.
Anon., in *Harper's Weekly,* 10 September 1864.

Nothing was left to chance that could be anticipated. When the time for action came, his composure, quickness of perception, resolution, and command of his fleet proved invincible. . . . The lesson of his life is that his success was no accident.
Anon., in *Nation,* 1 January 1880.

Now then, your broadsides, shipmates all,
With grape well loaded down!
May garlands filled with sunshine fall
To gild his silvered crown!
I give the name that fits him best, —

Ay, better than his own, —
The Sea King of the Sovereign West
Who made his mast a throne!
Oliver Wendell Holmes, *A Toast to the Vice-Admiral.*

Oh! while Atlantic's breast
Bears a white rail,
While the Gulf's towering crest
Tops a green vale,
Men thy bold deeds shall tell
Old Heart of Oak,
Daring Dave Farragut
Thunderbolt stroke.
William T. Meredith, 'Farragut', in Burton E. Stevenson, *The Home Book of Verse.*

FASTOLFE, SIR JOHN

1378?—1459 Knight

Nor is our Comedian [Shakespeare] excusable, by some alteration of his name, writing him *Sir John Falstafe*, (and making him the *property of pleasure* for King *Henry* the fifth to abuse) seeing the *vicinity* of sounds intrench on the memory of *that worthy Knight*, and few do heed the *inconsiderable difference* in spelling of their names.
Thomas Fuller, *The History of the Worthies of England.*

FAULKNER, WILLIAM CUTHBERT

1897—1962 Author

Art is simpler than people think because there is so little to write about. All the moving things are eternal in man's history and have been written before, and if a man writes hard enough, sincerely enough, humbly enough, and with the unalterable determination never never to be quite satisfied with it he will repeat them, because art like poverty takes care of its own, shares its bread.
On himself, in Michael Millgate, 'Faulkner: The Problem of Point of View', in L. W. Wagner ed., *William Faulkner, Four Decades of Criticism.*

I think I have written a lot and sent it off to print before I actually realized strangers might read it.
On himself, in Malcolm Cowley, *A Second Flowering.*

I like to think of the world I created as being a kind of keystone in the universe; that, small as the keystone is, if it were ever taken away the universe itself would collapse.
Ibid.

There is no such thing as bad whiskey. Some whiskeys just happen to be better than others. But a man shouldn't fool with booze until he's fifty; then he's a damnfool if he doesn't.

> On himself, in J. R. Cofield, 'Many Faces, Many Moods', in James W. Webb and A. Wigfall Green, *William Faulkner of Oxford*.

It is as if Mr Faulkner, in a sort of hurried despair, had decided to try to tell us everything, absolutely everything, every last origin or source or quality or qualification, and every possible future or permutation as well, in one terrifically concentrated effort: each sentence to be, as it were, a microcosm. And it must be admitted that the practice is annoying and distracting.

> Conrad Aiken, 'William Faulkner: The Novel as Form', in L. W. Wagner ed., *William Faulkner, Four Decades of Criticism*.

Small wonder if even the most passionate of Mr Faulkner's admirers ... must find, with each new novel, that the first fifty pages are always the hardest, that each time one must learn all over again *how* to read this strangely fluid and slippery and heavily mannered prose, and that one is even, like a kind of Laocoon, sometimes tempted to give it up.

> *Ibid.*

Finally Faulkner's noblest characters are willing to face the fact that most men can learn the deepest truths about themselves and about reality only through suffering. Hurt and pain and loss are not mere accidents to which the human being is subject; nor are they mere punishments incurred by human error; they can be the means to the deeper knowledge and to the more abundant life.

> Cleanth Brooks, 'William Faulkner, Vision of Good and Evil', in L. W. Wagner ed., *William Faulkner, Four Decades of Criticism*.

The truth is that Faulkner unites in his work two of the dominant trends in American literature from the beginning: that of the psychological horror story as developed by Hawthorne, Poe, and Stephen Crane, among others; and that of realistic frontier humor, with Mark Twain as its best example. If you imagine Huckleberry Finn living in the House of Usher and telling uproarious stories while the walls crumble about him, that will give you the double quality of Faulkner's work at its best.

> Malcolm Cowley, in Otis E. Wheeler, 'Some Uses of Folk Humor by Faulkner', in F. W. Wagner ed., *William Faulkner, Four Decades of Criticism*.

There in Oxford (Mississippi), Faulkner performed a labor of imagination that has not been equaled in our time, and a double labor: first, to invent a Mississippi county that was like a mythical kingdom, but was complete and living in all its details; second, to make his story of Yoknapatampha County stand as a parable or legend of all the Deep South.

> Malcolm Cowley, *A Second Flowering*.

Another salient facet of Faulkner's style is his vocabulary. He apparently loved words and never forgot a word that he had read or heard. When the language did not offer the exact term for his purpose he did not hesitate to telescope, to forge, or to coin the necessary implement of his trade; ...

> Walter K. Everett, *Faulkner's Art and Characters*.

Even those who call Mr. Faulkner our greatest literary sadist do not fully appreciate him, for it is not merely his characters who have to run the gauntlet but also his readers.

> Clifton Fadiman, in *New Yorker*, 21 April 1934.

Mr. Faulkner, of course, is interested in making your mind, rather than your flesh creep.

> *Ibid.*

Old Corndrinking Mellifluous.

> Ernest Hemingway, in Carlos Baker, *Ernest Hemingway, A Life Story*.

Poor Faulkner. Does he really think big emotions come from big words?

> Ernest Hemingway, in A. E. Hotchner, *Papa Hemingway*.

Faulkner's work can be difficult: it abounds in humbled time sequences, involuted narrative structures, mangled syntax, and torturous diction. It demands from the reader that he take psychic and intellectual risks. One must bring to his novels a capacity for concentration, a readiness to abandon set notions about life and literature, and above all, a willingness to expose oneself to a gamut of feelings.

> Irving Howe, 'William Faulkner', in Perry Miller ed., *Major Writers of America*, vol. 2.

Faulkner's 'special world,' his great subject, is the South: the Southern memory, the Southern reality, the Southern myth.

> *Ibid.*

The problem that faces every student of Faulkner's writing is its lack of a center, the gap between his power and its source, that curious abstract magnificence (not only a magnificence of verbal resources alone) which holds his books together, yet seems to arise from debasement or perplexity or a calculating terror.

Alfred Kazin, *On Native Grounds.*

If respect for the human is the central fact of Faulkner's work, what makes that fact significant is that he realizes and dramatizes the difficulty of respecting the human.

Robert Penn Warren, 'William Faulkner', in L. W. Wagner ed., *William Faulkner, Four Decades of Criticism.*

Faulkner was shy. Faulkner was arrogant. Faulkner went barefoot on the streets of Oxford [Mississippi]. Faulkner tore up his driveway to discourage visitors.

James W. Webb and A. Wigfall Green, *William Faulkner of Oxford.*

See also Huey Long

FAWCETT, DAME MILLICENT (MRS HENRY FAWCETT)

1849–1929 Suffragette

In common with the great majority of suffrage workers, I wish to continue the agitation on constitutional lines, yet I feel that the action of the prisoners has touched the imagination of the country in a manner which quieter methods did not succeed in doing.

On herself, Letter to *The Times,* 29 October 1906.

It was obvious that to work for political freedom represented only one phase of a many sided movement. The most important departments dealt with 1) education 2) an equal moral standard between men and women 3) professional and industrial liberty and 4) political status. My special experience and training fitted me for work on behalf of the fourth of these; but I recognised that this was only one side of the whole question and I was likewise convinced that whoever worked on any of these branches was, whether he knew it or not, really helping on the other three.

On herself, *What I Remember.*

I can never feel that setting fire to houses and churches and letter-boxes and destroying valuable pictures really helps to convince people that women ought to be enfranchised.

On herself, in R. Fulford, *Votes for Women.*

A trim, prim little figure with a clear pleasant voice.

Sylvia Pankhurst, *The Suffragette Movement.*

The tales of her early struggles belong to Elizabeth [Garrett Anderson]'s life and not to her sister's. But it is important to remember that all through Millicent's school days, and through the young lady period that follows, this adventure was going on. It lit and kept burning Millicent's enthusiasm for the Cause.

R. Strachey, *Millicent Garrett Fawcett.*

FELL, DR JOHN

1625–86 Dean of Christ Church, Bishop of Oxford

I do not love thee, Doctor Fell,
The reason why I cannot tell,
But this one thing I know full well:
I do not love thee, Doctor Fell.

Thomas Brown, *Epigrams,* after Martial.

Stickt in holding up the college discipline; 4 times in a day at public service in the cathedral, twice at home; loved to have tales brought to him, and be flatterd, and therefore the most obnoxious in his house would choose to please him that way to save themselves. These persons he favoured more; allowed them the chambers that they desired, allowed them pupills, his countenance — while the sober partie that could not or would not tell tales were browbeaten. The college was so much at his beck that he flew further and endeavored to govern the University.

Anthony à Wood, *Life and Times,* 30 November 1660.

A waggish scholar of Ch. Ch. did thus characterize Dr Fell, ... Dr Fell, who is a long leane man, he called the *Jack.*

Ibid.

FENTON, ELIJAH

1683–1730 Poet, Translator

Fenton was tall and bulky, inclined to corpulence, which he did not lessen by much exercise, for he was very sluggish and sedentary, rose late, and when he had risen sat down to his book or papers. A woman, that once waited on him in a lodging, told him, as she said, that he would 'lie-a-bed, and be fed with a spoon'.

Samuel Johnson, *Lives of the Poets.*

This modest Stone what few vain Marbles can
May truly say, here lies an honest Man.
A Poet, blest beyond the Poet's fate,
Whom Heav'n kept sacred from the Proud and Great.
Foe to loud Praise, and Friend to learned Ease,

FERBER, EDNA

Content with Science in the Vale of Peace.
Calmly he look'd on either Life, and here
Saw nothing to regret, or there to fear;
From Nature's temp'rate feast rose satisfied,
Thank'd Heav'n that he had liv'd, and that he dy'd.
    Alexander Pope, *Epitaph on Mr Elijah Fenton.*

Poor Fenton! He died of indolence and inactivity; let it not be your fate, but use exercise.
    Alexander Pope, Letter to John Gay,
    21 July 1730.

Fenton's productions are more characterised by indecency than wit. He is said to have been a moral man. What must have been the morality of an age when a moral man could write such poems.
    Robert Southey, *Specimens.*

FERBER, EDNA

1887–1968 Author

Being an old maid is like death by drowning, a really delightful sensation after you cease to struggle.
    On herself, in Robert E. Drennan ed., *Wit's End.*

To this day I regard myself as a blighted Bernhardt.
    Ibid.

Miss Ferber, who was fond of wearing tailored suits, showed up at the Round Table one afternoon sporting a new suit similar to one Noël Coward was wearing. 'You look almost like a man,' Coward said as he greeted her. 'So,' Miss Ferber replied, 'do you.'
    Robert E. Drennan, *Wit's End.*

She writes a novel as a modern athletic girl might wear a crinoline and a bustle. She manages the trick, but she is self-conscious and filled with secret amusement over the masquerade.
    William McFee, in *New Republic*, 15 September 1926.

She squares off at her job in workmanlike fashion and turns out a nationally advertised product that looks as sound as this year's model always does, until next year's model comes along.
    T. S. Matthews, in *New Republic*, 6 March 1935.

FIELD, EUGENE

1850–95 Author

I am a Yankee by pedigree and education, but I was born in that ineffably uninteresting city, St. Louis.
    On himself, in Slason Thompson, *Eugene Field.*

Reform away, reform away, but as for me, the world is good enough for me as it is. I am a thorough optimist. In temperament I'm a little like old Horace — I want to get all the happiness out of the world that's possible.
    On himself, in *ibid.*

. . . he became in his later years the children's poet; and the simplicity and imaginative power of the child mind had for him the strongest appeal of all.
    Charles H. Dennis, *Eugene Field's Creative Years.*

. . . a tall, thin-haired man with a New England face of the Scotch type, rugged, smoothly shaven, and generally very solemn — suspiciously solemn in expression.
    Hamlin Garland, in Jean Holloway, *Hamlin Garland.*

See also James Whitcomb Riley

FIELDING, HENRY

1707–54 Novelist

Charg'd with writing of bawdy, this was F————'s
                reply:
Tis what DRYDEN and CONGREVE have done as
                well as I.
Tis true — but they did it with this good pretence,
With an ounce of rank bawdy went a pound of good
                sense:
But thou hast proportion'd, in thy judgement
                profound,
Of good sense scarce an ounce, and of bawdy a
                pound.
    Anon., *The Grub Street Journal*, 3 August 1732.

Fielding's essence . . . was a bold spirit of bounding happiness . . . Fielding was a reckless enjoyer. He saw the world — wealth and glory, the best dinner and the worst dinner, the gilded *salon* and the low sponging-house — and he saw that they were good. Down every line of his characteristic writings there runs this elemental energy of keen delight.
    Walter Bagehot, in *National Review,* April 1864.

Fielding, hearing that a friend of his was dejected because he was so deeply in debt, said to his informant, 'Is that all? How happy I should be if I could only get £500 deeper in debt than I am already.'
    E. H. Barker, *Literary Anecdotes and Contemporary Reminiscences.*

286

A novel, which, like a beggar, should always be kept 'moving on'. Nobody knew this better than Fielding, whose novels, like most good ones, are full of inns.
Augustine Birrell, *Obiter Dicta*.

The most singular genius which their island ever produced, whose works it has long been the fashion to abuse in public and to read in secret.
George Borrow, *The Bible in Spain*.

Fielding being mentioned, Johnson exclaimed, 'he was a blockhead'; and upon my expressing my astonishment at so strange an assertion, he said, 'What I mean by his being a blockhead is, that he was a barren rascal.'
James Boswell, *Life of Johnson*.

There are very different kinds of laughter: you make me laugh with pleasure; but I often laugh, and am angry at the same time with the facetious Mr Fielding.
Lady Dorothy Bradshaigh, Letter to Samuel Richardson, 27 March 1750.

The prose Homer of human nature.
Lord Byron, quoted in notes to Anderson's edition of Byron, *Don Juan*.

... how charming, how wholesome, Fielding always is! To take him up after Richardson is like emerging from a sick room heated by stoves into an open lawn, on a breezy day in May.
Samuel Taylor Coleridge, *Table-Talk*, 5 July 1834.

There were no plays, no operas, no masquerades, no balls, no public shews, except at the little theatre in the Hay-market, then known by the name of F———g's scandal-shop; because he frequently exhibited there certain drolls, or, more properly, invectives against the ministry; in doing which it appears extremely probable, that he had two views; the one to get money, which he very much wanted, from such as delighted in low humour, and could not distinguish true satire from scurrility; and the other in the hope of having some post given him by those whom he had abused, in order to silence his dramatic talent.
Eliza Haywood, *The History of Miss Betsy Thoughtless*.

All these books have the same fault, which I cannot easily pardon, being very mischievous. They place a merit in extravagant passions, and encourage young people to hope for impossible events to draw them out of the misery they choose to plunge themselves into, expecting legacies from unknown relations, and generous benefactors to distressed virtue, as much out of nature as fairy treasures. Fielding has really a fund of true humour, and was to be pitied at his first entrance into the world, having no choice (as he said himself) but to be a hackney writer or a hackney coachman. His genius deserved a better fate, but I cannot help blaming that continued indiscretion (to give it the softest name) that has run through his life, and I am afraid still remains.
Lady Mary Wortley Montagu, Letter to Lady Bute, 23 July 1754.

I am sorry for Henry Fielding's death, not only as I shall read no more of his writings, but I believe he lost more than others, as no man enjoyed life more than he did ... His happy constitution (even when he had, with great pains, half demolished it) made him forget everything when he was before a venison pasty or over a flask of champagne, and I am persuaded he has known more happy moments than any prince upon earth. His natural spirits gave him rapture with a cookmaid, and cheerfulness when he was fluxing in a garret.
Ibid., 22 September 1755.

I have not been able to read any more than the first volume of Amelia. Poor Fielding! I could not help telling his sister, that I was equally surprised at and concerned for his continued lowness. Had your brother, said I, been born in a stable, or been a runner at a sponging-house, we should have thought him a genius, and wished he had had the advantage of a liberal education, and of being admitted into good company; but it is beyond my conception, that a man of family, and who had some learning, and who really is a writer, should descend so excessively low, in all his pieces.
Samuel Richardson, Letter to Lady Dorothy Bradshaigh, 23 February 1752.

The genius of Cervantes was transfused into the novels of Fielding, who painted the characters, and ridiculed the follies of life with equal strength, humour and propriety.
Tobias Smollett, *Continuation of the Complete History of England*.

Fielding had as much humour perhaps as Addison, but, having no idea of grace, is perpetually disgusting.
Horace Walpole, Letter to Mr Pinkerton, June 1785.

See also George Eliot, Henry James, Ring Lardner, Samuel Richardson, Sir Walter Scott, W. M. Thackeray

FIELDS, W. C. (WILLIAM CLAUDE DUKENFIELD)

1880—1946 Comedian, Actor

I am free of all prejudice. I hate everyone equally.
    On himself, in an article by Jerome Beatty Jr,
    in *Saturday Review*, 28 January 1967.

I always keep a supply of stimulant handy in case I
see a snake — which I also keep handy.
    On himself, in Carey Ford, *The Time of
    Laughter.*

By God, I was born lonely!
    On himself, in Will Fowler, 'Why W. C. Fields
    Hated Christmas', in *Show Business Illustrated*,
    2 January 1962.

Fields is not only a funny man with a fair bag of
tricks; he creates a type. Nature's nobleman, let us
say, considerably beery and with a strong touch of
the sideshow barker. A blend of Jiggs the impenitent
household man, and a promoter of itinerant shell
games. But his manner of getting these things into
stage terms is not so easily reducible to words. He
is not a star playing a buffoon, but is completely
within the role; he is his own hero and his own
dupe and must accept this, to make the best of it.
And when there is no best to make, why, you must
be sad for him — because he is so earnest, because
he moves with such absurd gravity and concentration.
    Otis Ferguson, *The Film Criticism of Otis
    Ferguson.*

He is usually down but he is never right out, and yet
there is in him a kind of humor so deeply seated
that familiarity becomes somehow a further extension of our delight in this figure that is already
American legend, having built itself up by giving
itself away. If there was ever a great clown in this
time of changeover from the beer and music-hall to
the universal distribution of radio and films, I would
say it was in the person and the character and the
undying if corny gusto of Bill Fields, who moved
mountains until they fell on him, and then brushed
himself off and looked around for more.
    Ibid.

Bill Fields was never happy. He was always troubled
about something, and always complaining. He
trusted no one, not even his manager. His face,
speech, and manner never lost the cynical bitterness
of his hard early life. He had plenty of friends, but
few close ones. . . . Fields was much more than just
a comedian. He was one of the great creators of
theatre humour, as Mark Twain was of literary
humour. His use of his voice was masterful. The
wheezy twang he developed is unforgettable, as is
the mixture of back alley and drawing room in his
whole approach to acting.
    Norman bel Geddes, *Miracles In the Evening.*

To watch Mr. Fields, as Dickensian as anything
Dickens ever wrote, is a form of escape for poor
human creatures: we who are haunted by pity, by
fear, by our sense of right and wrong, who are
tongue-tied by conscience, watch with envious love
this free spirit robbing the gardener of ten dollars,
cheating the country yokels by his own variant
of the three-card trick, faking a marriage certificate,
and keeping up all the time, in the least worthy and
the most embarrassing circumstances, his amazing
flow of inflated sentiments.
    Graham Greene, reviewing *Poppy* in *Spectator*,
    17 July 1936.

Nearly everything Bill tried to get into his movies
was something that lashed out at the world . . . The
peculiar thing is that although he thought he was
being pretty mean there wasn't any real sting in it.
It was only funny. Bill never really wanted to hurt
anybody. He just felt an obligation.
    Gregory La Cava, in Robert L. Taylor,
    W. C. Fields.

Like his colleagues of the 'twenties, he bore with
fortitude the persecution of wives, children, bill
collectors, bank investigators and the law. But what
created the delicious tensions in the Fields films
was the sense of violence lurking underneath — the
anticipated joy of the moment when he would
kick Baby LeRoy or, as in 'If I Had a Million', use
his new-found fortune to bash in the automobiles
of the reckless drivers who had dented his own
cherished jalopy. In time the full-fledged Fields
arose — a cunning, swaggering figure, capable of
exploiting every opening and mastering every crisis.
'Never Give a Sucker An Even Break' was the title
of one of his films; it crystallised the new mood in
movie comedy. Fields's pictures were scratchy and
patchy, but I do not think that anyone has been so
funny since.
    Arthur Schlesinger Jr, 'When the Movies Really
    Counted', in *Show*, April 1963.

The great man is recognized as one of the original
antiheroes so currently in vogue with today's 'let it
all hang out' generation. Despite the possible reper-
cussions Fields uses his humor to kick society in the
groin and with a fervor gratifying to all mankind.
When he snarls at little brats, punches obnoxious in-
laws or outfoxes sly con men, he is rebelling against
the impositions of an unreasonable society. . . .
Modern day audiences . . . tend to identify with and

idolize this rasping misfit, aggressively at odds with society, who not only refuses to knuckle under, but brandishing his caustic wit, mounts an assault of his own.

Michael M. Taylor, *Fields For President.*

He had read of the keen critical rejection of failures such as Wagner's operas, Lincoln's Gettysburg Address, Walt Whitman's poems and Christ's Sermon on the Mount, and he was sensibly impressed.

Robert Lewis Taylor, *W. C. Fields.*

See also Florenz Ziegfeld

FIENNES, WILLIAM, VISCOUNT SAY AND SELE ('THE GODFATHER')

1582—1662 Puritan Politician

He being ill natur'd, cholerick, severe and rigid, and withal highly conceited of his own worth, did expect great matters at Court; but they failing he sided therefore with the discontented party the Puritan, and took all occasions cunningly to promote a Rebellion. For so it was, that several years before the Civil War began, he being looked upon at that time the *Godfather* of that party, had meetings of them in his house at *Broughton*, where was a room and passage thereunto, which his Servants were prohibited to come near: and when they were of a compleat number, there would be great noises and talkings heard among them, to the admiration of those that lived in the house, yet could they never discern their Lords companions.

Anthony à Wood, *Athenae Oxonienses.*

FILLMORE, MILLARD

1800—74 Thirteenth United States President

Millard Fillmore inherited the presidency from Zachary Taylor. This was discovered when Taylor's will was read. . . . The possessor of a keen historical sense, Fillmore was saving the Civil War for Lincoln who could handle it.

Richard Armour, *It All Started With Columbus.*

I'll tell you, at a time when we needed a strong man, what we got was a man that swayed with the slightest breeze. About all he ever accomplished as President, he sent Commodore Perry to open up Japan to the West, but that didn't help much as far as preventing the Civil War was concerned.

Harry S. Truman, in M. Miller, *Plain Speaking — An Oral Biography of Harry S. Truman.*

A Vain and Handsome Mediocrity.

Glyndon G. Van Deusen, *Thurlow Weed, Wizard of the Lobby.*

FIRBANK, (ARTHUR ANNESLEY) RONALD

1886—1926 Novelist

Firbank, whose appearance was as orchidaceous as his fictional fantasies, behaved so strangely that all attempts at ordinary conversation became farcical. His murmured remarks were almost inaudible, and he was too nervous to sit still for more than half a minute at a time. The only coherent information he gave me was when I heavily inquired where his wonderful fruit came from. 'Blenheim', he exclaimed with an hysterical giggle, and then darted away to put a picture-frame straight. . . . Watching him through the jungle of orchids, I found it hard to believe that this strange being could have any relationship with the outside world. He was as unreal and anomalous as his writings.

Siegfried Sassoon, *Siegfried's Journey.*

His most rational response to my attempts at drawing him out about literature and art was 'I adore italics, don't you?'

Ibid.

See also Evelyn Waugh

FISHER, JOHN

1459—1535 Humanist, Bishop of Rochester

Henry the Seventh gave him the bishopric of Rochester; which he, following the rule of the primitive church, would never change for a better: he used to say, his church was his wife, and he would never part with her because she was poor.

Gilbert Burnet, *History of the Reformation.*

See also St Thomas More

FISHER, JOHN ARBUTHNOT, LORD FISHER OF KILVERSTONE

1841—1920 Admiral of the Fleet

Fear God and Dread Nought.

Fisher's motto, inscribed on his coat of arms when he was elevated to the peerage.

I was Jekyll and Hyde! *Jekyll* in being successful in my work at the Admiralty — but *Hyde* as a failure in Society! that I talked too freely and was reported to say (which of course is a lie) that the King would see me through anything! That it was bad for me and bad for him as being a Constitutional Monarch.

> On himself, Letter to Lord Esher,
> 19 August 1908.

[He] spoke, wrote, and thought in large type and italics, when writing he underlined his argument with two, three, or even four strokes with a broad-nibbed pen, and when talking, with blows of his fist on the palm of the other hand. 'I wish you would stop shaking your fist in my face,' said King Edward [VII] when being subjected to some of Fisher's forcible arguments.

> Sir Reginald H. S. Bacon, *The Life of Lord Fisher of Kilverstone.*

. . . be Machiavellian, and play upon the delicate instrument of public opinion with your fingers and not with your feet, however tempting the latter may be.

> Lord Esher, Letter to Fisher, 21 October 1906.

The lurid imagery and ferocious invective of much of his correspondence (his enemies were all 'skunks', 'pimps', 'sneaks', or worse, often with a harsh modifying adjective like 'pestilent' or 'damnable') give the impression of a man writing at breakneck speed with a pen dipped in molten lava; The expressions with which he closed his letters to intimates, such as 'Yours till Hell freezes' and 'Yours till charcoal sprouts', were characteristic.

> Professor A. J. Marder, *From the Dreadnought to Scapa Flow.*

He was a mixture of Machiavelli and a child, which must have been extraordinarily baffling to politicians and men of the world.

> Esther Meynell, *A Woman Talking.*

FISK, JAMES, JR

1834—72 Financier

. . . the glaring meteor, abominable in his lusts, and flagrant in his violation of public decency . . . .

> Henry Ward Beecher, in Matthew Josephson,
> *The Robber Barons.*

He loved the crush of crowds, loved to move among the admiring glances drawn to him, dressed in a scarlet-lined cape, a frilled shirt over his expansive bosom, in the center of which sat the immense flashing diamond sparkler of wide fame. . . . There was an aura about him, compounded of his gaudy costumes (as a colonel of a militia regiment), his sensational frauds, his scandalous private life, and his charities to poor old women or newsboys who approached him. In song and story, 'Fisk never went back on the poor.'

> Matthew Josephson, *The Robber Barons.*

FISKE, JOHN

1842—1901 Historian, Philosopher

He has after all done no more than to tell better what other men painfully toiled to tell as best they could.

> Albert B. Hart, in Milton Berman, *John Fiske.*

FISKE, MINNIE MADDERN (MARIE AUGUSTA DAVEY)

1865—1932 Actress

As soon as I suspect a fine effect is being achieved by accident, I lose interest. I am not interested in unskilled labor. An accident — that is it. The scientific worker is an even worker. Any one may achieve on some rare occasion an outburst of genuine feeling, a gesture of imperishable beauty, a ringing accent of truth, but your scientific actor knows how he did it. He can repeat it again and again and again.

> On herself, in *Minnie Maddern Fiske. Her Views On Actors, Acting and the Problems of Production, as told to Alexander Woollcott.*

More than anybody I've ever known, Mrs. Fiske had at her finger tips all the hard-won tricks of the actor's trade. With a flutter of her white eyelids she could suggest the tremulous pride of youth; with a single shrug she could evoke the resignation of age. Every gesture, every inflection was informed with understanding and truth. She was sincerity's self.

> Marie Dressler, *My Own Story.*

It was some time after she came upon the stage that I asked myself if she were beautiful, but when I once thought of it, I was very sure she was — at least some of the time. Managers demanded beauty. She was a cloud through which the sun was ever trying to shine.

> Katherine Goodale, *Behind the Scenes With Edwin Booth.*

In the theatre of his mind, as [St John Ervine] wrote, it is improbable that he saw anyone so nervous, so darting, so brittle, so gleaming as Minnie Maddern Fiske.

> Alexander Woollcott, *The Portable Woollcott.*

FITZGERALD, EDWARD

1809—83 Poet, Translator

No man's life makes the mumbo-jumbo of psychologists and Freudians more trivial or absurd. Fitzgerald loved men, particularly two men, and knew no sexual attraction to women. Whether or not he could be called homosexual in medico-legal parlance, whether or not anything he did could have laid him open ... to a charge of gross indecency, is of little consequence. He loved Posh, his big Viking-like fisherman. . . . Who cares whether or not they went to bed together?
Rupert Croft-Cooke, *Feasting with Panthers*.

These pearls of thought in Persian gulfs were bred,
Each softly lucent as a rounded moon;
The diver Omar plucked them from their bed,
Fitzgerald strung them on an English thread.
James Russell Lowell, *In a Copy of Omar Khayyam*.

Fitzgerald's 'Omar' is worth all the Persian scholarship of a century.
Ezra Pound, *The New Age*, 1917.

FITZGERALD, FRANCIS SCOTT KEY

1896—1940 Author

We're too poor to economize. Economy is a luxury ... our only salvation is in extravagance.
On himself, in Paul Sann, *The Lawless Decade*.

Drink heightens feeling. When I drink, it heightens my emotions and I put it in a story. But then it becomes hard to keep reason and emotion balanced. My stories written when sober are stupid — like the fortune-telling one. It was all reasoned out, not felt.
On himself, in Andrew Turnbull, *Scott Fitzgerald*.

Do you know what my own story is? Well, I was always the poorest boy at a rich man's school. Yes, it was that way at prep schools, and at Princeton, too.
On himself, in Morley Callaghan, *That Summer in Paris*.

I who knew less of New York than any reporter of six months' standing and less of its society than any hall-room boy in a Ritz stag line, was pushed into the position not only of spokesman for the time but of the typical product of that same moment.
On himself, in Nancy Milford, *Zelda Fitzgerald*.

Sometimes I don't know whether Zelda and I are real or whether we are characters in one of my novels.
On himself, in Malcolm Cowley, *A Second Flowering*.

A writer like me must have an utter confidence, an utter faith in his star ... I once had it. But through a series of blows, many of them my own fault, something happened to that sense of immunity and I lost my grip.
On himself, in Arthur Mizener, *The Far Side of Paradise, A Biography of F. Scott Fitzgerald*.

Fitzgerald never got rid of anything; the ghosts of his adolescence, the failures of his youth, the doubts of his maturity plagued him to the end. He was supremely a part of the world he described, so much a part that he made himself its king and then, when he saw it begin to crumble, he crumbled with it and led it to death.
John Aldridge, 'Fitzgerald: The Horror and the Vision of Paradise', in Arthur Mizener, *F. Scott Fitzgerald: A Collection of Critical Essays*.

All the channels of Fitzgerald's sensibility seem to have anticipated their end in Gatsby; and all the dissident shapes that obstructed the progress of his search seem to find their apotheosis in Gatsby's romantic dream.
Ibid.

One of Scott's troubles was that he had never been able to think clearly. The thing to do with such a 'marvelous talent' as his was to use it. Instead he had made the mistake of loving youth so much that he had jumped straight from there to senility without passing through manhood in between.
Carlos Baker, *Ernest Hemingway, A Life Story*.

I often feel about Fitzgerald that he couldn't distinguish between innocence and social climbing.
Saul Bellow, *Paris Review*.

The self-consciousness of Fitzgerald is a barrier which we are never able to pierce. He sees himself constantly not as a human being, but as a man in a novel or in a play. Every move is a picture and there is a camera man behind each tree.
Heywood Broun, in Arthur Mizener, *The Far Side of Paradise, A Biography of F. Scott Fitzgerald*.

It was as if all his novels described a big dance to which he had taken ... the prettiest girl ... and as if at the same time he stood outside the ballroom, a little Midwestern boy with his nose to the glass, wondering how much the tickets cost and who paid for the music.
Malcolm Cowley, in Arthur Mizener, *ibid.*

I always feel that Daddy was the key-note and prophet of his generation and deserves remembrance as such since he dramatized the last post-war era and gave the real significance to those gala and so-tragically fated days. He tabulated and greatly envied football players and famous athletes and liked girls from popular songs, he loved gorging on canned voluptés at curious hours and, . . . was the longest and most exhaustive conversationalist I *ever* met.

> Zelda Fitzgerald, speaking about F. Scott Fitzgerald, in Nancy Milford, *Zelda Fitzgerald*.

In fact, Mr Fitzgerald — I believe that is how he spells his name — seems to believe that plagiarism begins at home.

> Zelda Fitzgerald, in her review of *The Beautiful and Damned*, in Nancy Milford, *Zelda Fitzgerald*.

His talent was as natural as the pattern that was made by the dust on a butterfly's wings. At one time he understood it not more than the butterfly did and he did not know when it was brushed or marred. Later he became conscious of his damaged wings and of their construction and he learned to think and could not fly any more because the love of flight was gone and he could only remember it when it had been effortless.

> Ernest Hemingway, *A Moveable Feast*.

Fitzgerald had the ability to seize hold of a fleeting moment and to convey its impact without waiting for the intervention of reason to remove the rawness of reality.

> Milton Hindus, *F. Scott Fitzgerald, An Introduction and Interpretation*.

Fitzgerald's life has, apart from its close connection with his work, a considerable interest of its own; it was a life at once representative and dramatic, at moments a charmed and beautiful success to which he and his wife, Zelda, were brilliantly equal, and at moments disastrous beyond the invention of the most macabre imagination.

> Arthur Mizener, *The Far Side of Paradise, A Biography of F. Scott Fitzgerald*.

It is fitting that Fitzgerald, the aesthete of nostalgia of the escape clause without question, should be the first American to formulate his own philosophy of the absurd.

> Wright Morris, 'The Function of Nostalgia: F. Scott Fitzgerald', in Arthur Mizener, *F. Scott Fitzgerald: A Collection of Critical Essays*.

Still, Scott Fitzgerald's life had indeed a legendary quality — for which he himself was in part responsible. It was characteristic that, as a small boy,

he should decide he was not the son of his parents. Instead, as he went around earnestly telling the neighbors, he had been wrapped up in a blanket, to which was pinned a piece of paper emblazoned with the name of the royal House of Stuart!

> Henry Dan Piper, *F. Scott Fitzgerald, A Critical Portrait*.

It is a mistake to say . . . that Fitzgerald was a spokesman for the very rich. He was interested in the rich only in their relationship to the middle class, and he wrote about them invariably from a middle-class point of view. If his writings are preoccupied with money, this is because money is the preoccupation of the middle class. People with inherited wealth usually interest themselves in other things.

> *Ibid.*

Possibly some personal insecurity on the author's part helped to accentuate this compensatory dream of endless revelry and glitter, this hollow ritual of delights partaken without emotion by suave young men and lacquered maidens.

> Arthur Hobson Quinn ed., *The Literature of the American People*.

In his brief career Fitzgerald tested in imaginative terms the occupations of gilded youth, of the impressively rich, of the socially elite, and found them sterile . . . . He had done his best to find security and satisfaction in the dream-world of riches and exclusiveness. With entire honesty he was proclaiming the failure of his attempt when his career closed.

> *Ibid.*

Fitzgerald was indeed a romantic who wished time to stand still forever at the hour of youth so that an aesthetic paradise might be super-imposed upon life's harsh actuality. This could only be done, it seemed, by the power of money, and accordingly Fitzgerald wrote for money.

> D. S. Savage, 'The Significance of F. Scott Fitzgerald', in Arthur Mizener, *F. Scott Fitzgerald: A Collection of Critical Essays*.

The first of the last generation.

> Gertrude Stein, in John Malcolm Brinnin, *The Third Rose*.

Fitzgerald was perhaps the last notable writer to affirm the Romantic fantasy, descended from the Renaissance, of personal ambition and heroism, of life committed to, or thrown away for, some ideal of self.

> Lionel Trilling, 'F. Scott Fitzgerald', in Arthur Mizener, *F. Scott Fitzgerald: A Collection of Critical Essays*.

A faun, with waving blond hair parted in the middle and an expression half-serious, half-humorous, he radiated a perceptiveness, a sense of discovery that made you tingle when you were with him. He was living the American dream — youth, beauty, money, early success — and he believed in these things so passionately that he endowed them with a certain grandeur.

Andrew Turnbull, *Scott Fitzgerald*.

Into *Tender Is the Night* he put his hard-earned beliefs: that work was the only dignity; that it didn't help a serious man to be too much flattered and loved; that money and beauty were treacherous aides; that honor, courtesy, courage — the old-fashioned virtues — were the best guides after all.

Ibid.

It is true that Fitzgerald has been left with a jewel which he doesn't know quite what to do with. For he has been given imagination without intellectual control of it; he has been given the desire for beauty without an aesthetic ideal; and he has been given a gift for expression without very many ideas to express.

Edmund Wilson, *The Shores of Light*.

See also John O'Hara

FLAMSTEED, JOHN

1646—1719 First Astronomer Royal

My letters being shown King Charles, he startled at the assertion of the fixed stars' place being false in the catalogue; said, with some vehemence, 'He must have them anew observed, examined and corrected, for the use of his seamen;' and further, (when it was urged to him how necessary it was to have a good stock of observations taken for correcting the motions of the moon and planets), with the same earnestness 'he must have it done'. And when he was asked Who could, or who should, do it? 'The person (says he) that informs you of them'. Whereupon I was appointed to it, with the incompetent allowance aforementioned.

On himself, *History of His Own Life*.

He realized better than any of his contemporaries what was needed most in his day for the promotion of astronomy. His work was marked by no brilliant discoveries; but, by unflagging industry and scrupulous care, by systematic observations and insistence upon accuracy, he bequeathed to his successors an immense treasure of observations. His name will always be honoured as that of the first great British

observer who established precise astronomy upon secure foundations, and is enrolled among those who have made permanent contributions to the advancement of astronomy.

Sir Harold Spencer Jones, in *Nature*, 31 August 1946.

FLAXMAN, JOHN

1755—1826 Sculptor

You, O Dear Flaxman, are a Sublime Archangel, My Friend and Companion from Eternity; in the Divine bosom is our Dwelling place.

William Blake, Letter to Flaxman, 21 September 1800.

I mock thee not, tho' I by thee am Mocked.
Thou call'st me Madman, but I call thee Blockhead.

William Blake, *MS Note-Book 1808—11*.

Very feeble & slow, his lamp is expiring, little fruit can be expected from so old a stock however golden its former productions — his religious, learned & contemplative mind is too little of this world to feel powerfully the attractions of art & this will still diminish as he draws closer to the objects of his thoughts.

C. R. Cockerell, Diary, March 1825.

In these designs of Flaxman [on Dante], you have gentlemanly feeling, and fair knowledge of anatomy, and firm setting down of lines, all applied, in the foolishest and worst possible way; you cannot have a more finished example of learned error, amiable want of meaning, and bad drawing with a steady hand.

John Ruskin, *The Elements of Drawing*.

FLECKER, (HERMAN) JAMES ELROY

1884—1915 Poet, Dramatist

Judging from my latest efforts I shall go down to fame (if I go) as a sort of Near East Kipling.

On himself, Letter to Frank Savery, 10 January 1912.

His conversation was variegated, amusing, and enriched with booty from the by-ways of knowledge. He was always and restlessly driven by his mind down such paths. He sought beauty everywhere, but preferred, for the most of his life, to find her decoratively clad.

Rupert Brooke, Obituary in *The Times*, 6 January 1915.

The great debt of gratitude which contemporary English poetry owes to James Flecker lies in the fact that in an age of anarchy in verse he took the trouble to master the technique of his art, in an age of formlessness he upheld the finest traditions of form.

Douglas Goldring, *Academy*, 1915.

A Gadarene Greek, and kinsman of Meleager, whose poems he came too near worshipping to hope to translate — spendthrift of emotion, loving men and sometimes women, showy, joyous, (sinking when ill soon to despair).

T. E. Lawrence, *An Essay on Flecker*.

See also W. H. Auden

FLECKNOE, RICHARD

— d. 1678? Poet

I write chiefly to avoid idleness, and print to avoid the imputation (of idleness), and as others do it to live after they are dead, I do it only not to be thought dead whilst I am alive.

On himself, in Augustine Birrell, *Andrew Marvell*.

That I use some broad words sometimes, 'tis but to conform to the pattern I imitate: *Brughel* representing, without any dishonesty, here a *Boor* shitting, there a *Boorinne* pissing, to render the vulgar more ridiculous (are properly the subjects of ridiculousness) and whose follies, abuses, and vices, are properly the subject of Satyre: for the rest never was *Indian* contriving feathers into picture, more careful of their shadows, than I not to give *umbrage* unto any, who reverence Authority, honour all noble Persons, and especially am a devoted servant unto Ladies.

On himself, Preface to *The Diarium or Journall*.

All human things are subject to decay,
And when fate summons, monarchs must obey.
This Flecknoe found, who, like Augustus, young
Was call'd to empire, and had govern'd long;
In prose and verse, was own'd, without dispute,
Thro' all the realms of *Nonsense*, absolute.

John Dryden, *MacFlecknoe*.

So thin
He stands, as if he only fed had been
With consecrated Wafers: and the *Host*
Hath sure more flesh and blood then he can boast.
This *Basso Relievo* of a Man,
Who as a Camel tall, yet easly can
The Needles Eye thread without any stich,
(His only impossible is to be rich).

Andrew Marvell, *Fleckno*.

See also Richard Blackmore

FLEMING, SIR ALEXANDER

1881—1955 Bacteriologist

'Pain in the mind' was not the spur that drove him to do research, as it was with Wright, but rather an urge to do a job better than the next man. Competition was the breath of life to him. Wright and he made a fine team. Wright supplied the ideas, which Fleming usually received in silence, and then went away and devised some neat trick for working them out. It was a joy to see him at work at his bench — the slick, apparently casual, but always efficient technique. If anything went wrong he was quite unperturbed and proceeded to do the job better.

L. Colebrook, in *Biographical Memoirs of Fellows of the Royal Society*.

Wright, chaffing him, used to say that medical research was just a game to him — and there was some truth in that. On one occasion, when King George and Queen Mary were due to visit the laboratories at St. Mary's, Wright wanted Fleming to display some of his bench technique. He did, but suspecting that it might not interest them very much, he also prepared one of his famous bacterial 'rock gardens' from all the available microbes which produced growths of vivid colouring. The story goes that when the Queen saw this she whispered to King George 'What is the use of this?' It was no use — but it amused Fleming.

Ibid.

The catalogue of Fleming's published work leaves little room for doubt that he had to an unusual degree the almost intuitive faculty for original observation coupled with a high degree of technical inventiveness and skill. He had in fact most of the qualities that make a great scientist: an innate curiosity and perceptiveness regarding natural phenomena, insight into the heart of a problem, technical ingenuity, persistence in seeing the job through and that physical and mental toughness that is essential to the top-class investigator.

R. Cruickshank, in the *Journal of Pathology and Bacteriology*, 1956.

FLEMING, IAN LANCASTER

1908—64 Novelist

Probably the fault about my books is that I don't take them seriously enough and meekly accept having my head ragged off about them in the family circle.... You, after all, write 'novels of suspense' — if not sociological studies — whereas my books are straight pillow fantasies of the bang-bang, kiss-kiss variety.

On himself, Letter to Raymond Chandler.

His work combined a passionate interest in the externals of the modern world — its machinery and furniture, in the widest sense of both words — with a strong, simple feeling for the romantic and the strange: the gipsy encampment, the coral grove, the villain's castle, the deadly garden, the mysterious island. Fleming technologized the fairy-tale for us, making marvellous things seem familiar, and familiar things marvellous. He was a great popular writer.

Kingsley Amis, *What Became of Jane Austen?*

Your descriptive passages, as usual, are very good indeed ... I am willing to accept the centipede, the tarantulas, the land crabs, the giant squid ... I am even willing to forgive your reckless use of invented verbs — 'I inch, Thou inches, He snakes, I snake, We Palp, They palp', etc, but what I will neither accept nor forgive is the highly inaccurate statement that when it is eleven a.m. in Jamaica, it is six a.m. in dear old England. This, dear boy, to put not too fine a point on it, is a f------ lie. When it is eleven a.m. in Jamaica, it is *four p.m.* in dear old England, and it is carelessness of this kind that makes my eyes steel slits of blue.

Noël Coward, Letter to Fleming on the publication of *Dr No*.

As you know I am a confirmed Fleming fan — or should it be addict. The combination of sex, violence, alcohol and — at intervals — good food and nice clothes is, to one who lives such a circumscribed life as I do, irresistible.

Hugh Gaitskell, Letter to Fleming on the publication of *Dr No*.

The trouble with Ian is that he gets off with women because he can't get on with them.

Rosamond Lehmann, in John Pearson, *Life of Ian Fleming*.

I gave myself a treat, or what I expected to be a treat, by reading Ian Fleming's adventure story about James Bond, called *Goldfinger*. I had been told that it was as good as Simenon. This is nonsense ... Fleming is so fantastic as to arouse disbelief. This story is too improbable to arouse interest, nor do I like the underlying atmosphere of violence, luxury and lust. I regard it as an obscene book, 'liable to corrupt'.

Harold Nicolson, Diary, 22 November 1959.

FLETCHER, JOHN
1579—1625 Dramatist

The admirable zeal of the Department of Inland Revenue, which a few years earlier had sought to obtain income tax returns from the authors of *The Beggar's Opera*, written over two hundred years before, was now directed to the case of Fletcher, who died in 1625. One day I received a request for his address, which they had been unable to trace, and on the principle of being helpful whenever possible, I replied that to the best of my knowledge it was on the south side of Southwark Cathedral, that he had been there for quite a time and in all probability was not intending an early removal.

Sir Thomas Beecham, *A Mingled Chime*.

Twixt *Johnsons* grave, and *Shakespeare's* lighter
                        sound,
His muse so steer'd that something still was found,
Nor this, nor that, nor both, but so his owne,
That 'twas his marke, and he was by it knowne.

William Cartwright, *Upon the Dramatick Poems of Mr John Fletcher*.

Thou, as if struck with the same generous darts,
Which burne, and raigne in noble lovers hearts,
Hath cloth'd affections in such native tires,
And so describ'd them in their owne true fires,
Such moving sighs, such undissembled teares,
Such charms of language, such hopes mixed with
                        fears,
Such grants after denials, such pursuits
After despaire, such amorous recruits,
That some who sate spectators have confest
Themselves transformed to what they saw exprest,
And felt such shafts steale through their captiv'd
                        sence,
As made them rise Parts, and goe Lovers thence.

William Cartwright, *Another*, prefixed to the 1647 Folio of Beaumont and Fletcher.

As we in Humane Bodies see, that lose
An Eye or Limb, the Vertue and the Use
Retreat into the other Eye or Limb,
And make it double. So I say of him:
Fletcher was *Beaumont's* Heir, and did inherit
His searching Judgement, and unbounded Spirit.
His Plays were printed therefore, as they were
Of *Beaumont* too, because his Spirit's there.

Sir Aston Cockain, *Verse Epistle to his Cosen Charles Cotton*.

There is a kind of Comedy, which, whoever produces must be capable of Tragedy (Cervantes, Shakspere) — but there is another kind, and that too highly amusing, which is quite heterogeneous. Of this latter

Fletcher was a great master. The surface and all it's flowers and open pleasures, serious or light, were his Property — all his eye can see, ear hear, — nothing more.

> Samuel Taylor Coleridge, Annotation to Beaumont and Fletcher, *Fifty Comedies and Tragedies.*

He does not well always; and when he does, he is a true Englishman; he knows not when to give over. If he wakes in one scene, he commonly slumbers in another.

> John Dryden, 'Defence of the Epilogue', appended to *The Conquest of Granada.*

Though he treated love in perfection, yet Honour, Ambition, Revenge, and generally all the stronger Passions, he either touch'd not, or not masterly. To conclude all; he was a Limb of Shakespeare.

> John Dryden, *Preface to Troilus and Cressida, or Truth found too late.*

Fletcher was above all an opportunist, in his verse, in his momentary effects, never quite a pastiche; in his structure ready to sacrifice everything to the single scene . . . Fletcher had a cunning guess at feelings, and betrayed them.

> T. S. Eliot, *Essays:* 'Philip Massinger'

The wit of Fletcher is excellent, like his serious scenes, but there is something strained and far-fetched in both. He is too mistrustful of Nature; he always goes a little on one side of her.

> Charles Lamb, *On the Elizabethan Dramatists.*

Oldwit: I knew Fletcher, my friend Fletcher, and his maid Joan. Well, I shall never forget him; I have supped with him at his house on the Bankside: he loved a fat loin of pork of all things in the world. And Joan his maid had her beer-glass of sack; and we all kissed her, i'faith, and were as merry as passed.

> Thomas Shadwell, *Bury Fair.*

Mr. Fletcher surviving Mr. Beaumont, wrote good Comedies of himself . . . . Though some think them inferior to the former, and no wonder if a single thread was not so strong as a twisted one.

> William Winstanley, *Lives of the Most Famous English Poets.*

See also Francis Beaumont, Philip Massinger, Thomas Middleton, Shakespeare

FLYNN, ERROL LESLIE

1909—59 Actor

My problem lies in reconciling my gross habits with my net income.

> On himself, in Jane Mercer, *Great Lovers of the Movies.*

Screen loving is such a self-conscious thing for me that I find myself drawing back, growing cold. In fact, I can think of only two, John Barrymore and John Gilbert — not Flynn — who could actually give a literal sexual feeling to a scene with a woman without being self-conscious about it. As for me, there is something in such a private scene that I cannot get myself to do even with the most delightful leading ladies.

> On himself, in *My Wicked Wicked Ways.*

Handsome, arrogant and utterly enchanting, Errol was something to watch. His arrivals on the set always reminded me of Alfred Lunt's vaudeville turn as an M.C. in Robert Sherwood's *Idiot's Delight.* Flanked by four to six blondes, arms linked, Errol would strut in at about eleven. One expected them to go into a routine, which no doubt they did. He was already the stud of the Warner stable and had or would co-star with everyone on the lot. . . . Infinitely charming Errol was possessed of his own demon. His drive was in an entirely different direction and probably enhanced by his hushed but recurrent tuberculosis which was soon to keep him out of military service. At the time, he was unquestionably the most wholesomely beautiful satyr.

> Bette Davis, *The Lonely Life.*

A magnificent specimen of the rampant male.

> David Niven, *The Moon's A Balloon.*

More recent actors in tights just aren't in the running; and, in the Talkie period, no actor swashed so blithe a buckle.

> David Shipman, *The Great Movie Stars.*

He had a mediocre talent, but to all the Walter Mittys of the world he was all the heroes in one magnificent, sexy, animal package.

> Jack L. Warner, *My Hundred Years in Hollywood.*

FOLIOT, GILBERT

— d. 1187? Bishop of London and Thomas à Becket's antagonist

Disappointed ambition, perhaps all the more painful because unacknowledged, the unwillingness to admit virtue in the recently converted publican, an inborn dislike of anything noisy or violent, of any trace of *panache*; the strong personal bias, the unfortunate series of accidents which made him an almost *ex officio* leader of the opposition and advocate of the king — all these contributed to make of Gilbert Foliot the adversary of the archbishop and, once adversary, his talents and reputation made him inevitably the one to whom all who opposed the archbishop looked for leadership and counsel.

David Knowles, *The Episcopal Colleagues of Archbishop Thomas Becket.*

FOOTE, ANDREW HULL

1806—63 Sailor

He prays like a saint and fights like the devil.
Rear Admiral Francis H. Gregory, in Robert Debs Heinl Jr, *The Dictionary of Military and Naval Quotations.*

FOOTE, SAMUEL

1720—77 Actor, Dramatist

Comedy, on the other hand, I define to be an exact representation of the peculiar manners of that people among whom it happens to be performed; a faithful imitation of singular absurdities, particular follies, which are openly produced as criminals are publicly punished, for the correction of individuals, and as an example to the whole community. This is, sir, one of the happy points which every comic author should have in view, and is distinguished by the Roman critic as the *utile*; the other point, the *dulce,* I conceive to be the fable, construction, machinery, conduct, plot, and incidents of the piece: in short, sir, the vehicle, which is to render the wholesome physic of reproof palateable to the squeamish patient.
On himself, *Letter to the Reverend Author of Remarks Critical and Christian on 'The Minor'.*

If we do not take liberties with our friends, with whom can we take liberties?
On himself, in J. Cradock, *Literary and Miscellaneous Memoirs.*

Thou Mimic of *Cibber* — of *Garrick,* thou Ape!
Thou Fop in *Othello*! thou Cypher in Shape!
Thou Trifle in Person! thou Puppet in Voice!
Thou Farce of a Player! thou Rattle for Boys!
Thou Mongrell! thou dirty face Harlequin Thing!
Thou Puff of bad Paste! thou Ginger-bread King!
Anon., 'On a Pseudo Player', in W. R. Chetwood, *A General History of the Stage.*

Equally improbable is the supposition that he either entertained personal likes or dislikes for any of the characters from whom he drew, or that his motives were really of a public nature, and propelled him onward to further the general weal. If he really admired a deformity of the mind, and ascribed it to the heart, while he assumed the face and dress of the offender, this genial feeling must have been created by reflecting on the plaudits which would accompany a successful hit-off of the subject under treatment. His public feeling we may safely ascribe to the prospect of private emolument, and consider that his philanthropy was solely swayed by the probable receipts of his theatrical treasury.
John Bee, *Works of Samuel Foote.*

Often our Foote was under the dire necessity of drawing upon his genius to support this body.
Ibid.

Boswell: Pray, Sir, is not Foote an infidel? *Johnson*: I do not know, Sir, that the fellow is an infidel; but if he be an infidel, he is an infidel as a dog is an infidel; that is to say, he has never thought upon the subject. *Boswell*: I suppose, Sir, he has thought superficially, and seized the first notions which occurred to his mind. *Johnson*: Why, then, Sir, still he is like a dog, that snatches the piece next him. Did you never observe that dogs have not the power of comparing? A dog will take a small bit of meat as readily as a large when both are before him.
James Boswell, *Life of Johnson.*

On the 26th of October we dined together at the Mitre tavern. I found fault with Foote for indulging his talent of ridicule at the expense of his visitors, which I colloquially termed making fools of his company. *Johnson*: Why, Sir, when you go to see Foote you do not go to see a saint: you go to see a man who will be entertained at your house, and then bring you on a public stage; who will entertain you at his house, for the very purpose of bringing you on a public stage. Sir, he does not make fools of his company; they whom he exposes are fools already; he only brings them into action.
Ibid.

By turns transform'd into all kinds of shapes,
Constant to none, Foote laughs, cries, struts, and
scrapes:
Now in the centre, now in van or rear,
The Proteus shifts, bawd, parson, auctioneer.
His strokes of humour, and his bursts of sport
Are all contain'd in this one word, *distort.*
Charles Churchill, *The Rosciad.*

. . . there is no Shakespeare or Roscius upon record who, like Foote, supported a theatre for a series of years by his own acting, in his own writings, and for ten years of the time upon a *wooden leg*! This prop to his person I once saw standing by his bedside, ready dressed in a handsome silk stocking, with a polished shoe and gold buckle, awaiting the owner's getting up. It had a kind of tragi-comical appearance; and I leave to inveterate wags the ingenuity of punning upon a Foote in bed, and a leg out of it.

George Colman, *Random Records.*

He had little regard for the feelings of others: if he thought of a witty thing that would create laughter, he said it ... and of this I can give one notable example. If Foote ever had a serious regard for any one, it was for Holland, yet at his death, or rather indeed, after his funeral, he violated all decency concerning him. Holland was the son of a baker at Hampton, and ... died rather young, and Foote attended as one of the mourners. He was really grieved; and the friend from whom I had the account, declared that his eyes were swollen with tears; yet when the gentleman said to him afterwards, 'So, Foote, you have just attended the funeral of our dear friend Holland;' Foote instantly replied, 'Yes, we have just shoved the little baker into his oven.'

J. Cradock, *Literary and Miscellaneous Memoirs.*

'My scenes,' he said on one occasion, 'have been collected from general nature and are applicable to none but those who through consciousness are compelled to a self-application. To that mark, if comedy directs not her aim, her arrows are shot in the air; for by what touches no man, no man will be amended.' This plea has not been admitted, however. Whenever Foote is now named it is as a satirist of peculiarities, not as an observer of character: it is as a writer whose reputation has perished with the personalities that alone gave it zest, it is as a comedian who so exclusively addressed himself to the audience of his theatre that posterity has been obliged to decline having any business or concern with him.

John Forster, *Biographical Essays.*

Foote is quite impartial, for he tells lies of everybody.

Samuel Johnson, in James Boswell, *Life of Johnson.*

There is a witty satirical story of Foote. He had a small bust of Garrick placed upon his bureau. 'You may be surprised (said he), that I allow him to be so near my gold; — but you will observe, he has no hands.'

Ibid.

Bygrove: He has wit to ridicule you, invention to frame a story of you, humour to help it about; and when he has set the town a laughing, he puts on a familiar air and shakes you by the hand.

Arthur Murphy, *Know Your Own Mind.*

Foote gives a dinner — large company — characters come one by one: — sketches them as they come: — each enters — he glad to see each — At Dinner, his wit, affectation, pride: his expense, his plate, his jokes, his stories; — all laugh; — all go, one by one — all abused, one by one; his toadeaters stay; — he praises himself — in a passion against all the world.

Arthur Murphy, Scheme for projected play, among his papers.

See also Duke of Cumberland, Oliver Goldsmith

FORBES-ROBERTSON, SIR JOHNSTON

1853—1937 Actor

He can present a dramatic hero as a man whose passions are those which have produced the philosophy, the poetry, the art, and the statecraft of the world, and not merely those which have produced its weddings, coroners' inquests, and executions.

George Bernard Shaw, in *Saturday Review*, 2 October 1897.

FORD, FORD MADOX (FORD HERMANN HUEFFER)

1873—1939 Author

I am not, you understand, a pessimist: I don't want our civilization to pull through. I want a civilization of small men each labouring two small plots — his own ground and his own soul. Nothing else will serve my turn.

On himself, *Provence.*

I happened to be in a company where a fervent young admirer exclaimed: 'By Jove, the *Good Soldier* is the finest novel in the English language!' whereupon my friend Mr John Rodker, who has always had a properly tempered admiration for my work, remarked in his clear, slow drawl: 'Ah yes. It is, but you have left out a word. It is the finest French novel in the English language!'

On himself, Dedicatory Letter to Stella Ford, 1927, *The Good Soldier.*

I learned all I know of Literature from Conrad — and England has learned all it knows of Literature from me.

On himself, in conversation with Herbert Read.

He understood what a man undertakes in becoming a writer. He understood the obligation taken on.

There was a real aristocracy in Ford. He was a professional writer who didn't soil his tools. He was unashamed, firm, a real workman, a man who understood what it is that gives a man's own life some significance.

Sherwood Anderson, *Coronet*, August 1940.

... He presented a wonderful appearance of a bland, successful gentleman, whose shabbiness was mere eccentricity and who regarded a preoccupation with the relative merits of Foyot and Larve, Vionnet and Poiret, the Ritz and the Hotel George V, as very natural and necessary.

Stella Bowen, in Douglas Goldring, *The Last Pre-Raphaelite*.

... His mind was like a Roquefort cheese, so ripe that it was palpably falling to pieces.

Van Wyck Brooks, in *ibid*.

As to Ford he is a sort of lifelong habit.

Joseph Conrad, Letter to H. G. Wells, 1905.

You must not mind Hueffer; that is his way. He patronizes me; he patronizes Mr Conrad; he patronizes Mr James. When he goes to Heaven he will patronize God Almighty. But God Almighty will get used to it, for Hueffer is all right!

Stephen Crane, in Ford Madox Ford, *Return to Yesterday*.

His forlorn attempts to throw a smoke-screen round himself produced through the distorted haze, the apparition of a monster, like a pink elephant, absurd, bizarre, immense.

Edward Crankshaw, in *National Review*, 1948.

So fat and Buddhistic and nasal that a dear friend described him as an animated adenoid.

Norman Douglas, in R. A. Cassell, *Ford Madox Ford*.

I don't suppose failure disturbed him much: he had never really believed in human happiness, his middle life had been made miserable by passion, and he had come through — with his humour intact, his stock of unreliable anecdotes, the kind of enemies a man ought to have, and a half-belief in a posterity which would care for good writing.

Graham Greene, *The Lost Childhood*.

It is not that Ford is difficult to read — in the sense that James is sometimes difficult, or Meredith. But you have to follow him in a mood of alert relaxation; you must not mind being mystified, detained, dragged backward, pulled forward, cheated, hoaxed. You must suspend curiosity and wait patiently until he is ready to explain ... Ford's approach to his audience is extraordinarily disingenuous, playful and sly. He would have made an ideal Ancient Mariner — accosting you with the air of one who asks only a minute of your time ... and then enweaving and enwinding you in his great, dazzlingly complicated web.

Christopher Isherwood, *Exhumations*.

O Father O'Ford, you've a masterful way with you,
Maid, wife and widow are wild to make hay with
                      you,
Blonde and brunette turn-about run away with you,
You've such a way with you, Father O'Ford.

James Joyce, Letter to Harriet Weaver, 1931.

[Ford] daubs his dove-grey kindliness with a villainous selfish tar, and hops forth a very rook among rooks, but his eyes, after all, remain like the Shulamite's, dove's eyes.

D. H. Lawrence, Letter to Violet Hunt.

Hueffer was a flabby lemon and pink giant, who hung his mouth open as though he were an animal at the Zoo inviting buns — especially when ladies were present. ... This ex-collaborator with Joseph Conrad was himself, it always occurred to me, a typical figure out of a Conrad book — a caterer, or corn-factor, coming on board — blowing like a porpoise with the exertion — at some Eastern port.

Percy Wyndham Lewis, *Rude Assignment*.

Master, mammoth mumbler.

Robert Lowell, *Life Studies*.

I knew him for twelve years, in a great many places and situations, and I can testify that he led an existence of marvellous discomfort, of insecurity, of deep and pressing anxiety as to his daily bread; but no matter where he was, whatever his sufferings were, he sat down daily and wrote, in his fine crabbed hand, with pen, the book he was working on at the moment; and I never knew him when he was not working on a book.

Katherine Anne Porter, in *New Directions*, no. 7, 1942.

He had all his faults, like his moustache, out in front where everyone cd see Yum. au fond a serious character as J.J. the Reverend Eliot and even ole Unc Wim the yeaT were NOT.

Ezra Pound, Letter to Brigit Patmore, 1952.

I once told Fordie that if he were placed naked and alone in a room without furniture, I would come back in an hour and find total confusion.

Ezra Pound, in V. S. Pritchett, *The Working Novelist*.

Freud Madox Fraud.
    Osbert Sitwell, in R. Phelps and P. Deane,
    The Literary Life, 1968.

Ford is a long blond with a drawling manner. . . .
What he is really or if he is really, nobody knows
now and he least of all; he has become a great
system of assumed personas and dramatized selves.
    H. G. Wells, *Experiment in Autobiography*.

Mr Ford Madox Ford is the Scholar Gipsy of
English letters: he is the author who is recognised
only as he disappears round the corner. It is impossible for anybody with any kind of sense about
writing to miss some sort of distant apprehension of
the magnificence of his work: but unfortunately
this apprehension usually takes the form of enthusiastic but belated discoveries of work that he
left on the doorstep ten years ago.
    Rebecca West, in *Daily News*, 2 April 1915.

            . . . Thank God you
    were not delicate, you let the world in
and lied! damn it you lied grossly
        sometimes. But it was all, I
see now, a carelessness, the part of a man
        that is homeless here on earth. . . .
    William Carlos Williams, *To Ford Madox Ford
    in Heaven*.

Traditionalist, *révolté*; Catholic, skeptic; agrarian
and internationalist; 'small producer' and restless
migrant; democratic, ritual-lover, and iconoclast;
fond father, erring husband, harassed lover; loyal to
England, to Germany, and to France -- he was all
these by turns and never fully succeeded in stabiliz-
ing or centering his personal or artistic loyalties.
    Morton Danwen Zabel, *Craft and Character in
    Modern Fiction*.

FORD, HENRY

1863—1947 Industrialist

History is more or less bunk. It's tradition. We don't
want tradition. We want to live in the present and
the only history that is worth a tinker's dam is the
history we make today.
    On himself, in *Chicago Tribune*, 25 May 1916.

Ford is a 'natural businessman' just as he is a 'natural
mechanic', and he is the rarest of all types, in that
he is a combination of the two.
    Thomas Alva Edison, in John Kenneth Galbraith,
    The Liberal Hour.

Machines, he said, were made to free mankind

To live the life of sport and of mind.
Let's hope the end will justify the means
That turned mankind from men into machines.
    Kensal Green (Colin Hurry), *Premature Epitaphs*.

He was acquisitive without limit and egotistic without deviation. His mind was astonishingly simple.
He could concentrate on a single idea almost as
perfectly as the inmate of a State Asylum who can
remember the number of every car which passes the
gate.
    Jonathan Norton Leonard, *The Tragedy of
    Henry Ford*.

I think he would rather be the maker of public
opinion than the manufacturer of a million automobiles a year, which only goes to show that in
spite of the fact that he sticks out his tongue at
history, he would nevertheless not object to making
a little of it himself.
    Samuel S. Marquess, *Henry Ford*.

The ordinary mortal is content to hitch his wagon
to a star. This is a sport too tame for Henry Ford.
He prefers to hang on to the tail of a comet. It is
less conventional, more spectacular and furnishes
more thrills.
    Ibid.

This demigod of the machine age had somehow
stitched together the incompatibles of the struggle
for existence. He was the idol of an American middle
class which wants to eat its cake and have it too, the
venerated symbol of a system under which people
aspire to be neither so self-seeking that they lose
caste nor so good that they must spend their days in
poverty.
    Keith Sward, *The Legend of Henry Ford*.

See also Walt Disney, Herbert Hoover

FORD, JOHN

1586?—1639? Dramatist

Deep in a dump John Ford alone was got
With folded arms and melancholy hat.
    Anon., 'On the Time-Poets', in *Choyce
    Drollery etc*.

He was a well-wisher to the muses, . . . and may be
known by an anagram instead of his name, generally
printed on the title page, viz: FIDE HONOR.
    Theophilus Cibber, *Lives of the Poets*.

He is a master of the brief mysterious words, so

calm in seeming, which well up from the depths of despair. He concentrates the revelation of a soul's agony into a sob or a sigh. The surface seems calm; we scarcely suspect that there is anything beneath; one gasp bubbles up from the drowning heart below, and all is silence.

Havelock Ellis, Introduction to Ford's Plays.

It has been lamented that the play of his which has been most admired, ('Tis Pity She's a Whore) had not a less exceptionable subject. I do not know, but I suspect that the exceptionableness of the subject is that which constitutes the chief merit of the play . . . but I do not find much other power in the author, (generally speaking) than that of playing with edged tools, and knowing the use of poisoned weapons. And what confirms me in this opinion is the comparative inefficiency of his other plays.

William Hazlitt, *Lectures on the Age of Elizabeth.*

He sought for sublimity, not by parcels in metaphors or visible images, but directly where she has her full residence in the heart of man; in the actions and sufferings of the greatest minds. There is a grandeur of the soul above mountains, seas, and the elements. Even in the poor perverted reason of Giovanni and Isabella, we discover traces of that fiery particle, which in the irregular starting from out of the road of beaten action, discovers something of a right line even in obliquity, and shows hints of an improvable greatness in the lowest descents and degradations of our nature.

Charles Lamb, *Specimens of Dramatic Poets.*

The Poetry of Ford . . . might . . . be likened to a mountain lake shut in by solitary highlands, without visible outlet or inlet, seen fitlier by starlight than by sunlight. . . . For nothing is more noticeable in this poet, than the passionless reason, and equable tone of style with which in his greatest works he treats of the deepest and most fiery passions, the quiet eye with which he searches out the darkest issues of emotion, the quiet hand with which he notes them down.

Algernon C. Swinburne, *Essays and Studies.*

Ford is rather a sculptor of character than a painter.
Ibid.

Ford's dominion was limited to one simple form of power, the knowledge and mastery of passion, properly so called, the science of that spiritual state in which the soul suffers from some dominant thought or feeling.
Ibid.

See also Thomas Dekker

FORD, JOHN (SEAN O'FEENEY)

1895–1973 Motion Picture Director

You say someone's called me the greatest poet of the Western saga. I am not a poet, and I don't know what a Western saga is. I would say that is horseshit. I'm just a hard-nosed, hardworking, run-of-the-mill director.

On himself, in Walter Wagner, *You Must Remember This.*

To be quite blunt, I make pictures for money, to pay the rent. There are some great artists in the business. I am not one of them.
Ibid.

John Ford is the Compleat Director . . . the dean of directors, — undoubtedly the greatest and most versatile in films. A megaphone has been to John Ford what the chisel was to Michelangelo: his life, his passion, his cross.

Ford cannot be pinned down or analyzed. He is pure Ford -- which means pure great. John is half-tyrant, half-revolutionary; half-saint, half-satan; half-possible, half-impossible; half-genius, half-Irish — but *all* director and *all* American.

Frank Capra, *The Name Above the Title.*

Just as [D.W.] Griffith portrayed the South in false colors in *The Birth of a Nation*, so Ford distorted the history of the West for generations of young people, failing to convey its Spartan crudity, its dryness, its competitiveness under the shadows of the mesas. In his world, as in Griffith's, men were staunch and powerful, women were bony pioneers or melting frails; his Irishness suffused his portraits of the figures of the past, giving his work at best the feel of an O'Casey, at worst a boisterous militancy. His range was wide — all the way from expressionist melodrama (*The Informer*) to historical pageantry (*Mary of Scotland*) and even the *roman policier* (*Gideon's Day*). But it is for his Westerns that Ford chiefly deserves to be remembered.

Charles Higham, *The Art of the American Film.*

Whatever John Ford wants, John Ford gets.
Edward G. Robinson, *All My Yesterdays.*

I like the old masters, by which I mean John Ford, John Ford . . . and John Ford.
Orson Welles, in Walter Wagner, *You Must Remember This.*

FORDYCE, GEORGE

1736–1802 Physician

Dr Fordyce sometimes drank a good deal at dinner.

He was summoned one evening to see a lady patient, when he was more than half-seas-over, and conscious that he was so. Feeling her pulse, and finding himself unable to count its beats, he muttered, 'Drunk by God!' Next morning, recollecting the circumstance, he was greatly vexed: and just as he was thinking what explanation of his behaviour he should offer to the lady, a letter from her was put into his hand. 'She too well knew,' said the letter, 'that he had discovered the unfortunate condition in which she was when he last visited her; and she entreated him to keep the matter secret in consideration of the enclosed (a hundred-pound banknote).'
Samuel Rogers, *Table-Talk*.

FORRESTER, CECIL SCOTT

1899—1966 Author

My distaste for my own work lingers on surprisingly. A father looking down at his first-born for the first time may experience a sense of shock, but he generally recovers from it rapidly enough; after a day or two he thinks it is a very wonderful baby indeed. My life would be happier if I reacted in the same way towards my books — the odd thing being that even as it is there are very few people who lead a happier life than mine, despite all the feelings that I have just been describing. I must be like the princess who felt the pea through seven mattresses; each book is a pea.
On himself, *The Hornblower Companion*.

FORSTER, EDWARD MORGAN

1879—1970 Novelist

'Only connect ...', the motto of *Howards End*, might be the lesson of all his work. His heroes and heroines ... are the precursors of the left-wing young people of today; he can be used by them as a take-off in whatever direction they would develop. Thus the parable form of Forster's novels may survive the pamphlet form of Shaw's plays, despite their vigorous thinking, because Forster is an artist and Shaw is not. Much of his art consists in the plainness of his writing for he is certain of the truth of his convictions and the force of his emotions.
Cyril Connolly, *Enemies of Promise*.

There is more in him than ever comes out. But he is not dead yet. I hope to see him pregnant with his own soul. ... He sucks his dummy — you know, those child's comforters — long after his age. But

there is something very real in him, if he will not cause it to die. He is *much* more than his dummy-sucking, clever little habits allow him to be.
D. H. Lawrence, Letter to Bertrand Russell, 12 February 1915.

Forster's world seemed a comedy, neatly layered and staged in a garden whose trim privet hedges were delicate with gossamer conventions. About its lawns he rolled thunderstorms in teacups, most lightly, beautifully.
T. E. Lawrence, in *Spectator*, 6 August 1927.

Interviewer: What writers have you learned the most from, technically?
Mailer: E. M. Forster, I suppose. I wouldn't say he is necessarily one of the novelists I admire most. But I have learned a lot from him ... Forster gave my notion of personality a sufficient shock that I could not manage to write in the third person. Forster, after all, had a developed view of the world; I did not.
Norman Mailer, in *Paris Review*.

E. M. Forster never gets any further than warming the teapot. He's a rare fine hand at that. Feel this teapot. Is it not beautifully warm? Yes, but there ain't going to be no tea.
Katherine Mansfield, Journal, May 1917.

He's a mediocre man — and knows it, or suspects it, which is worse; he will come to no good, and in the meantime he's treated rudely by waiters and is not really admired even by middle-class dowagers.
Lytton Strachey, Letter to James Strachey, 3 February 1914.

See also D. H. Lawrence

FOSTER, STEPHEN COLLINS

1826--64 Composer

His finest songs are warp and woof of the life of the nation, and they will endure. This is really folk music, despite the known authorship of Foster's melody and verse — folk art, which the American people have taken to themselves as their own.
Olin Downes, in Irene Downes ed., *Olin Downes on Music*.

That was the great tragedy of his life: his utter incapacity to exploit his genius as it deserved. Ingenuous, impractical, maladjusted to his environment, given to dreams and fancies that carried him away from reality, he was incapable of looking after himself. He wasted his life as well as his genius; and his closing days saw him an impoverished drunkard in the gutters of New York's Bowery.

David Ewen, *Songs of America.*

Stephen Foster was a child of his place and time. The problem of Southern slavery was pressing ever more strongly on Northern consciousness. The growing propaganda for abolition inspired anger in some, dedicated fervor in others, but sentimentality in most — sentimentality toward an oppressed people and toward the environment in which they lived and suffered. This Northern reaction to the subject of the Negro and his slavery, one of the most vital issues of the period, finds a voice in Stephen Foster's songs.

David Ewen, *Great Men of America's Popular Song.*

Foster is the first pop composer but he lived in prehistoric times. . . .

Ian Whitcomb, *After the Ball: Pop Music from Rag to Rock.*

FOX, CHARLES JAMES

1749--1806 Statesman

I certainly am ambitious by nature, but I really have, or think I have totally subdued the passion. I have still as much vanity as ever, which is a happier passion by far: because great reputation I think I may acquire and keep, great situation I never can acquire, nor if acquired, keep without making sacrifices I never will make.

On himself, Letter to Richard Fitzpatrick, 3 February 1778.

At Almacks' of pigeons I am told there are flocks,
But it's thought the completest is one Mr Fox.
If he touches a card, if he rattles a box,
Away fly the guineas of this Mr Fox.
He has met, I'm afraid, with so many bad knocks,
The cash is not plenty with this Mr Fox,
In gaming 'tis said he's the stoutest of cocks,
No man can play deeper than this Mr Fox,
And he always must lose, for the strongest of locks
Cannot keep any money for this Mr Fox.
No doubt such behaviour exceedingly shocks
The friends and relations of this Mr Fox.

Anon., in John W. Derry, *Charles James Fox.*

Sheridan told us that when Mr Fox went to see the *Gamester*, there appeared, in the next morning's newspapers, paragraphs stating how much the great profligate orator had been affected, and how bitterly he had wept. 'Whereas,' said Mr Sheridan, 'the truth was, Fox listened, as was his custom, attentively; and when Beverley, in the play, said that he would borrow money upon the reversion of his uncle's estate, Fox turned to me and whispered, "Rather odd, hey, that he had not thought of that before." '

Lord Broughton, *Recollections of a Long Life.*

His spirit is not owing to his ignorance of the state of men and things; he well knows what snares are spread about his path, from personal animosity, from court intrigues, and possibly from popular delusion. But he has put to hazard his ease, his security, his interest, his power, even his darling popularity, for the benefit of a people whom he has never seen. This is the road that all heroes have trod before him.

Edmund Burke, Speech on 1 December 1783.

He seems to have the particular talent of knowing more about what he is saying and with less pains than anybody else — his conversation is like a brilliant player of billiards, the strokes follow one another, piff paff.

Georgiana, Duchess of Devonshire, in E. Lascelles, *Charles James Fox.*

What is that fat gentleman in such a passion about?

Lord Eversley, as a child in the gallery of the House of Commons, in G. W. E. Russell, *Collections and Recollections.*

About sunset on the 13th September he said: 'I die happy, but I pity you.' Then, as if that were a little sententious, he looked up at his wife, and said: 'It don't signify, my dearest, dearest Liz.'

Christopher Hobhouse, *Fox.*

A namesake of Charles James Fox having been hung at Tyburn, the latter enquired of Selwyn whether he had attended the execution? 'No,' was Selwyn's reply, 'I make a point of never frequenting rehearsals.'

G. H. Jesse, *George Selwyn and his Contemporaries.*

Fox (in his earlier days I mean), Sheridan, Fitzpatrick, &c led *such* a life! Lord Tankerville assured me that he has played cards at Brookes's from ten o'clock at night till near six o'clock the next afternoon, a waiter standing by to tell them 'whose deal it was,' they being too sleepy to know.

Samuel Rogers, *Table-Talk.*

With his passion, his power, his courage, his openness, his flashes of imagination, his sympathetic errors, above all his supreme humanity, Fox was a sort of lax Luther, with the splendid faults and

qualities of the great reformer.
Lord Rosebery, *Pitt*.

If ever from an English heart
O here let prejudice depart,
O partial feeling cast aside,
Record that Fox a Briton died!
When Europe crouched to France's yoke,
When Austria bent and Prussia broke,
And the firm Russian's purpose brave
Was bartered by a timorous slave,
E'en then dishonour's peace he spurned,
The sullen olive-branch returned,
Stood for his country's glory fast,
And nailed her colours to the mast.
Sir Walter Scott, *Marmion*.

He was not a political adventurer, but a knight-errant roaming about in search of a tilt, or, still better, of a mêlée; and not much caring whether his foes were robbers or true men, if only there were enough of them.
Sir George Otto Trevelyan, *The Early History of Charles James Fox*.

'There are but forty of them,' said Thurlow of the Opposition of 1793, 'but there is not one of them who would not willingly be hanged for Fox.'
Henry Offley Wakeman, *Life of Charles James Fox*.

Charles James Fox was one of those vigorous exuberancies of genius, which this country, where nothing restrains or contracts the mind, pushes forth from time to time. . . . He was as agreeable as strong sense divested of graces and wit could make him; and as little disagreeable as such overbearing presumption could allow.
Horace Walpole, *Memoirs*.

See also Lord North

FOX, WILLIAM

1879–1952 Motion Picture Producer

What do I need friends for when I am sitting on my money bags?
On himself, in Glendon Allvine, *The Greatest Fox Of Them All*.

I always bragged of the fact that no second of those contained in the twenty-four hours ever passed but that the name of William Fox was on the screen, being exhibited in some theatre in some part of the world.
Ibid.

In his inexorable scaling of the heights any man who reaches the top can look back at ambitions crushed and egos wounded. Whether he be Sammy Glick or William Fox, he has magnificently earned his hatred. With more compulsive drive than furriers [Marcus] Loew or [Adolph] Zukor, or glove salesman Goldfish, Fox slashed ahead with that shrewd ruthlessness which they practiced and called *chutzpah*.
Glendon Allvine, in *ibid*.

Fox . . . probably unwittingly adapted to the screen a technique of moral teaching that had been brought to its eloquent efficacy in the sermons of Jonathan Edwards. Sin is a universal malady, the world is full of snares and temptations, yet mankind must aspire to virtue; and the more alluring the temptations resisted, the greater the merit of man's moral victory. . . . Could Fox justly be blamed because the American people were more impressed by the delights of sin than by its inevitable punishment?
Lloyd Morris, *Not So Long Ago*.

William Fox was dour and pugnacious, and many think he was the most greedily ambitious of all the moguls. And yet Adolph Zukor, the Warners, Nicholas Schenck and others all played the power game with equal savagery. Perhaps it was because Fox was a loner that he drew so little sympathy in his time of distress and was forgotten so soon after. He was poor at public relations, hating to be interviewed or have his picture printed. . . . Few knew of his lavish bequests to artistic and charitable organizations, or of the fact that he dearly loved many of his employees and readily gave expensive watches as gifts. Forgotten were his pioneering contributions to the film industry. There were no sons, as in the case of Lewis Selznick, to carry on his name and fight to vindicate it.
Norman Zierold, *The Moguls*.

FOXE, JOHN

1516?–87 Martyrologist

At length, having farther endeared himself, he then told her, That she would not only grow well of that Consumption, but also live to an exceeding great age. At which words the sick Gentlewoman a little moved, and earnestly beholding Master Fox: As well might you have said (quoth she) that if I should throw this Glass against the Wall, I might believe it would not break to pieces; and holding a Glass in her hand, out of which she had newly drunk, she threw it forth; neither did the Glass, first by chance lighting on a little Chest standing by the Bedside, and afterwards falling upon the ground, either break nor crack in any place about it: And the event fell out accordingly. For the Gentlewoman, being then threescore years of age, lived afterwards for all example of felicity, seldom seen in the off-spring of any Family, being able, before the 90 years of her age (for she lived longer) to reckon three hundred and three score of her Childrens Children and Grandchildren.

> Anon. Memoir of his life, in a Preface to John Foxe, *Acts and Monuments*.

John Foxe, in his so-called *Book of Martyrs*, told the story in detail a few years afterwards, with a venomous bias to be sure but with a respect for facts which entitles him to a high place among honest historians.

> Conyers Read, in his account of the Marian persecutions, in *The Tudors*.

FRANCIS, SIR PHILIP (JUNIUS)

1740–1818 Man of Letters, Editor

Junius has sometimes made his satire felt, but let not injudicious admiration mistake the venom of the shaft for the vigour of the bow. He has sometimes sported with lucky malice; but to him that knows his company, it is not hard to be sarcastick in a mask. While he walks like Jack the Giant-killer in a coat of darkness, he may do much mischief with little strength. Novelty captivates the superficial and thoughtless; vehemence delights the discontented and turbulent. He that contradicts acknowledged truth will always have an audience, he that vilifies established authority will always find abettors.

> Samuel Johnson, *Thoughts on the Late Transactions respecting Falkland's Islands*.

Junius was clearly a man not destitute of real patriotism and magnanimity, a man whose vices were not of the sordid kind. But he must also have been a man in the highest degree arrogant and insolent, a man prone to malevolence, and prone to the error of mistaking his malevolence for public virtue.

> T. B. Macaulay, *Warren Hastings*.

When I was at Balliol in the early 1890s ... I was called upon to read an essay on the Letters of Junius to the Master, it was in the last years of Jowett. In my essay I gave reasons for concluding that it was not Francis who was the hidden author. Jowett listened to me with attention, when I had finished ... the Master said that he was inclined to agree with me, and gave to me the astonishing reasons that 'when he was a young man he knew a very intimate friend of Sir Philip Francis, who, he thought, was much too vain a man to have kept it to himself if he really had been the author.'

> Viscount Samuel, Letter to *The Times*, 18 September 1962.

You know as much of [John] Wilkes and [Charles] Townshend as I do .... The famous *Junius* seems at last to issue from the shop of the former, though the composition is certainly above Wilkes himself. The styles are often blended, and very distinguishable, but nobody knows who it is that deigns to fight in disguise under Wilkes's banner.

> Horace Walpole, Letter to Horace Mann, 22 October 1771.

FRANKFURTER, FELIX

1882–1965 Jurist

... [while] Brandeis and Holmes impressed their philosophy upon a generation of lawyers through their opinions from the Supreme Bench Frankfurter, on the other hand, is exerting his influence upon the men just before they cross the threshold into the profession.

> Anon., 'Declines Position on Supreme Court of Massachusetts', in *Nation*, July 1932.

Small, quick, articulate, jaunty, Frankfurter was inexhaustible in his energy, and his curiosity, giving off sparks like an overcharged electric battery. He loved people, loved conversation, loved influence, loved life. Beyond his sparkling personal qualities, he had an erudite and incisive legal intelligence, a resourceful approach to questions of public policy, and a passion for raising the standards of public service. And ... what Mr. Justice Holmes had not unkindly described in 1920 as 'an unimaginable gift of wiggling in wherever he wants to!'

> Max Freedman ed., *Roosevelt and Frankfurter: Their Correspondence, 1928–1945*.

FRANKLIN, BENJAMIN

1706–90 Statesman, Scientist

> The body of
> Benjamin Franklin, printer,
> (Like the cover of an old book,
> Its contents worn out,
> And stript of its lettering and gilding)
> Lies here, food for worms!
> Yet the work itself shall not be lost,
> For it will, as he believed, appear once more,
> In a new
> And more beautiful edition,
> Corrected and amended
> By its Author!
> On himself, suggested epitaph, in L. A. Harris, *The Fine Art of Political Wit*.

Oh! had he been wise to pursue
The Track for his Talent designed,
What a tribute of praise had been due
To the teacher and friend of mankind.

But to covet political fame
Was in him a degrading ambition,
For a spark which from Lucifer came
Had kindled the blaze of sedition.
  Anon., 1764 Pennsylvania election jingle.

The best talents in France were blind disciples of
Franklin and Turgot, and led the blind to destruc-
tion.
  John Adams, in Esmond Wright, 'Benjamin
  Franklin, A Tradesman in the Age of Reason', in
  Wilbur R. Jacobs ed., *Benjamin Franklin, States-*
  man, Philosopher or Materialist?

The history of our Revolution will be one continued
lie from one end to the other. The essence of the
whole will be that Dr. Franklin's electrical rod smote
the earth and out sprang General Washington. That
Franklin electrified him with his rod — and thence
forward these two conducted all the policy, negotiations, legislatures, and war.
  John Adams, Letter to Dr Benjamin Rush,
  4 April 1790.

Franklin's reputation was more universal than that
of Leibnitz or Newton, Frederick or Voltaire, and
his character more beloved and esteemed than any
or all of them . . . His name was familiar to government and people, to kings, courtiers, nobility, clergy,
and philosophers, as well as plebians. . . . When they
spoke of him they seemed to think he was to restore
the golden age . . . .
  John Adams, *Works*, vol. 1.

Thrift, industry, and determination were essential
virtues in the building of a nation, but they were not,
then or at any other time in history, of sufficient
human dignity to build a philosophy on. . . . The
vulgarity he spread is still with us.
  Charles Angoff, *A Literary History of the*
  American People.

When Franklin was seventy, he was sent to Paris to
see what he could do to improve relations with the
French, and he is said to have done extremely well
despite his age. He died full of honors, *escargots*,
pâté, and *vin rouge*.
  Richard Armour, *It All Started With Columbus.*

. . . a crafty and lecherous old hypocrite . . . whose
very statue seems to gloat on the wenches as they
walk the States House yard.
  William Cobbett, in Esmond Wright, 'Benjamin

Franklin, A Tradesman in the Age of Reason',
in Wilbur R. Jacobs ed., *Benjamin Franklin,*
Statesman, Philosopher or Materialist?

Benjamin Franklin, incarnation of the peddling,
tuppenny Yankee.
  Jefferson Davis, in Burton Stevenson, *The Home*
  Book of Quotations.

A philosophical Quaker full of mean and thrifty
maxims.
  John Keats, Letter to George and Georgiana
  Keats, 14—31 October 1818.

And now, I, at least, know why I can't stand Benjamin. He tries to take away my wholeness and my
dark forest, my freedom. For how can any man be
free, without an illimitable background? And Benjamin tries to shove me into a barbed-wire paddock and
make me grow potatoes or Chicagoes.
  D. H. Lawrence, *Studies in Classic American*
  Literature.

Prudence is a wooden Juggernaut, before whom
Benjamin Franklin walks with the portly air of a
high priest.
  Robert Louis Stevenson, *Crabbed Age and Youth.*

What an adroit old adventurer the subject of this
memoir was! In order to get a chance to fly his kite
on Sunday he used to hang a key on the string and
let on to be fishing for lightning.
  Mark Twain, *The Late Benjamin Franklin.*

His mind was a federation of purposes, working harmoniously together. . . . His mind grew as his world
grew.
  Carl Van Doren, *Benjamin Franklin.*

. . . in spite of his personal tang, he seems to have
been more than any single man: a harmonious human
multitude.
  Ibid.

The natural philosophers in power believe that Dr.
Franklin has invented a machine of the size of a
toothpick case and materials that would reduce St.
Paul's to a handful of ashes.
  Horace Walpole, 1778, in Carl Van Doren,
  Benjamin Franklin.

We admire, I think, the lusty good sense of the man
who triumphs in the world that he accepts, yet at
the same time we are uneasy with the man who wears
so many masks that we are never sure who is behind
them.
  John William Ward, 'Who was Benjamin

Franklin?', in Wilbur R. Jacobs ed., *Benjamin Franklin, Statesman, Philosopher or Materialist?*

He is our wise prophet of chicanery, the great buffoon, the face on the penny stamp.
    William Carlos Williams, *In the American Grain.*

He was father of all the Yankees.... His worldly wisdom was suited to the philosophers in Paris and in Edinburgh; it was suited, too, to the old wives in the chimney corner, summing up a lifetime of neighbourly experience.
    Esmond Wright, 'Benjamin Franklin, A Tradesman in the Age of Reason', in Wilbur R. Jacobs ed., *Benjamin Franklin, Statesman, Philosopher or Materialist?*

See also Benjamin Thompson, Noah Webster

FRAZER, SIR JAMES GEORGE

1854—1941 Anthropologist

Often he showed himself capable of brilliant and far-reaching hypotheses in his use of the comparative method. His knowledge was purely theoretical; in all probability he had never seen a savage in the flesh. Despite his strong prejudices and fixed ideas, he attached singularly little importance to his theories, and was ever ready to change his opinions in the light of new evidence. He failed, however, really to understand the cultural, sociological, and psychological implications of his data. Just as he refused to read adverse criticisms and reviews of his books, so he was content completely to ignore ... the findings of the psycho-analytical school, and was out of touch with current sociological theory. For him it sufficed to describe in vivid and graceful language exotic ideas and practices, without attempting to discover their deeper meaning ... or the function they fulfil in an organized society.... So ... he was mainly impressed by what seemed to him the utter futility of the world he surveyed.
    E. O. James, in *Dictionary of National Biography 1941—50.*

FREDERICK AUGUSTUS, see under
YORK AND ALBANY, DUKE OF

FREDERICK LOUIS

1707—51 Prince of Wales

I did not think ingrafting my half-witted coxcomb

upon a madwoman would mend the breed.
    George II, attributed.

Here lies Fred,
Who was alive and is dead:
Had it been his father,
I had much rather;
Had it been his brother,
Better than another;
Had it been his sister,
No one would have missed her;
Had it been the whole generation,
Better for the nation:
But since 'tis only Fred,
Who was alive and is dead —
There's no more to be said.
    Horace Walpole, *Memoirs of George II.*

FRÉMONT, JOHN CHARLES

1813—90 Explorer, Politician, Soldier

Free soil, free labor, and Frémont.
    Anon. 1856 Republican anti-slavery platform slogan, in Henry Nash Smith, *Virgin Land.*

He endured terrible hardships, including the failure of many persons to put the accent in his name, even though he reminded them repeatedly
    Richard Armour, *It All Started With Columbus.*

California was discovered by John C. Frémont. This was thought unnecessary by the Mexicans and the Indians who were living there at the time, but they could not speak English and so did not count.
    Ibid.

Frémont, if anyone ever did, fitted perfectly the requirements of the romantic hero-symbol of an age of expansionism. Handsome, intelligent, mercurial, born of an uncertain liaison and therefore with something of a Byronic legacy, he was a self-made cavalier. Famous as a lover, eager as a student, admired and befriended by his elders, he could command the allegiance of an astonishing range of people from congressmen and savants to mountain men and Indians.
    William H. Goetzmann, *Exploration and Empire.*

I fancied I could see Frémont's men, hauling the cannon up the savage battlements of the Rocky Mountains, flags in the air, Frémont at the head, waving his sword, his horse neighing wildly in the mountain wind, with unknown and unnamed empires at every hand.
    Joaquin Miller, *Overland in A Covered Wagon.*

FRENCH, DANIEL

FRENCH, DANIEL CHESTER

1850—1931 Sculptor

I'd like to live to be two thousand years old and just sculp all the time.
> On himself, in Margaret French Cresson, *Daniel Chester French*.

FRENCH, JOHN DENTON PINKSTONE, EARL OF YPRES

1852—1925 Soldier

He is not an intriguer, but just a passionate little man with, as you say, hot temper and uncontrolled feelings. Anyone can work him up into a sort of mad suspicion, so that he falls an easy prey to the people around him.
> Lord Fisher, Letter to Lord Stamfordham, December 1915.

His normal apoplectic expression, combined with the tight cavalryman's stock which he affected in place of collar and tie, gave him an appearance of being perpetually on the verge of choking, as indeed he often was, emotionally if not physically.
> Barbara Tuchman, *The Guns of August*.

FRERE, SIR HENRY BARTLE EDWARD

1815—84 Statesman, Governor of India

I want to shake hands with the man who has done his duty.
> Man in a British railway station crowd, October 1880.

See also Winston Churchill, Lord Haig

FRICK, HENRY CLAY

1849—1919 Industrialist, Art Collector

... in his palace, seated on a Renaissance throne under a Baldachino and holding in his little hand a copy of the *Saturday Evening Post*.
> Anon., in Matthew Josephson, *The Robber Barons*.

FROBISHER, SIR MARTIN

1535?—94 Navigator

Martin, admiral of fifty tons, anchored solemnly in front of the Queen's palace where she was holding her court, and fired a salute, We can imagine Her Majesty, interrupted in a conversation with Walsyngham, discussing, of course, the extraordinary news that the Spanish army in Flanders was not only without a general and without wages, but that the soldiers were going off in companies to loot the villages of Catholic Brabant. The ladies in waiting called Her Majesty's attention to the scene across the river — the diminutive flotilla of — what was the name — Captain Martin Fyrbussher. Bound wither? Ah yes, for Cathay.
> William McFee, *Sir Martin Frobisher* (on his salute of the Queen at Greenwich).

FROST, ROBERT LEE

1874—1963 Poet

I never dared be radical when young
For fear it would make me conservative
    when old.
> On himself, *Precaution*.

I guess I don't take life very seriously. It's hard to get into this world and hard to get out of it. And what's in between doesn't make much sense. If that sounds pessimistic, let it stand. There's been too much vaporous optimism voiced about life and age.
> On himself, in an interview with Robert Peterson in November 1962, in Edward Connery Latham ed., *Interviews with Robert Frost.*

You can see the deliberateness with which the scholar seeks his material after he gets going, but a poet never lives in that way at all. All the best things he ever uses are things he didn't know he was getting when he was getting them. A poet never takes notes. You never take notes in a love affair.
> On himself, in an interview with C. Day Lewis in 1957, in Edward Connery Latham ed., *Interviews with Robert Frost*.

I'd just as soon play tennis with the net down.
> On himself, commenting on the writing of free verse, in *Newsweek*, 30 January 1956.

When Robert Frost was asked to explain one of his poems he replied 'What do you want me to do — say it over again in worser English?'
> H. E. F. Donohue, in *New York Herald Tribune Book Weekly*.

Although his blank verse is colloquial, it is never loose, for it possesses the pithy, surcharged economy indigenous to the New Englander.
> James D. Hart, *The Oxford Companion to American Literature*.

For Frost there must always be in poetry the reconciliation between the cadence, the rhythm, of the spoken sentence and the cadence, the rhythm, of the meter. Lacking this reconciliation of these two elements in sound, the intended poem, as such, has failed. Achieving it, the poem combines manner and matter with its own subtle music which is as natural as it is unmistakable.

Lawrence Thompson, *Fire and Ice, The Art and Thought of Robert Frost*.

He is a poet of the minor theme, the casual approach, and the discreetly eccentric attitude.

Yvor Winters, 'Robert Frost: or, the Spiritual Drifter as Poet', in James M. Cox ed., *Robert Frost, A Collection of Critical Essays*.

FROUDE, JAMES ANTHONY

1818—94 Historian

I am going to stick to the History ... and I believe I shall make something of it. At any rate one has substantial stuff between one's fingers to be moulding at, and not those slime and sea sand ladders to the moon 'opinion'.

On himself, Letter to A. H. Clough, 22 November 1853.

Well, when the Liberals are in, Mr Froude is sometimes a Conservative. When the Conservatives are in, Mr Froude is always a Liberal.

His butler's response to a canvassing agent, in Herbert Paul, *Life of Froude*.

[Carlyle's] doctrine of heroes ... comes next in atrocity to the doctrine that the flag covers the goods, that the cause justifies its agents, which is what Froude lives for.

Lord Acton, Letter to Mrs Drew, 10 February 1881.

He himself used to say that the interest of life to a thinking man was exhausted at thirty, or thirty-five. After that there remained nothing but the disappointment of earlier visions and hopes. Sometimes there was something almost fearful in the gloom, and utter disbelief, and defiance of his mind.

Sir George Colley, in Herbert Paul, *Life of Froude*.

... in Froude's case the loss of his faith turned out to be rather like the loss of a heavy port manteau, which one afterwards discovers to have been full of old rags and brickbats.

Lytton Strachey, *Eminent Victorians*.

Froude informs the Scottish youth
That parsons do not care for truth.
The Reverend Canon Kingsley cries
History is a pack of lies.
What cause for judgments so malign?
A brief reflection solves the mystery —
Froude believes Kingsley a divine,
And Kingsley goes to Froude for history.

William Stubbs, Letter to J. R. Green, 17 December 1871.

... a desultory and theoretical littérateur who wrote more rot on the reign of Elizabeth than Gibbon required for all the Decline and Fall ....

Algernon Turnor, Letter to Sir Henry Ponsonby, 13 May 1878.

See also Charles Kingsley

FRY, ROGER ELIOT

1866—1934 Art Critic, Painter

His scholarship was impressive, he had studied painting with the thoroughness he brought to all his undertakings, he was at home in galleries all over Europe, he was a formidable art historian; but when he began to paint, he was Mr. Facing Both-Ways; a thousand theories assailed him, paralysing every stroke of the brush.

M. Lilly, *Sickert The Painter and His Circle*.

See also J. S. Cotman

FULLER, (SARAH) MARGARET (MARCHIONESS OSSOLI)

1810—50 Transcendentalist, Social Reformer, Critic

'Tis an evil lot to have a man's
ambition and woman's heart.

On herself, in Faith Chipperfield, *In Quest of Love, The Life and Death of Margaret Fuller*.

I now know all the people worth knowing in America, and I find no intellect comparable to my own.

On herself, in Arthur W. Brown, *Margaret Fuller*.

No person has appeared among us whose conversation and morals have done more to corrupt the minds and hearts of our Boston community. For religion she substitutes art; for the Divinity ... she would give us merely the Beautiful.

Orestes Brownson, in Arthur W. Brown, *Margaret Fuller*.

All the art, the thought and nobleness in New England . . . seemed related to her, and she to it.
    Ralph Waldo Emerson, in William Harlan Hale, *Horace Greeley, Voice of the People.*

We are taught by her how lifeless and outward we were, what poor Laplanders burrowing under the snows of prudence and pedantry.
    Ralph Waldo Emerson, in Arthur W. Brown, *Margaret Fuller.*

. . . the loftiest soul that has yet irradiated the form of an American woman.
    Horace Greeley, in Faith Chipperfield, *In Quest of Love, The Life and Death of Margaret Fuller.*

Not only had she mastered Oriental scripture, German epic poetry, Icelandic saga, Greek, Italian, Middle English, and the obscurities of Immanuel Kant, but she hurled all this cultural heritage at you with intent to inspire you with it if you were sympathetic or stagger you with it if you were not.
    William Harlan Hale, *Horace Greeley, Voice of the People.*

She was a great humbug; of course with much talent, and much moral ideality, or else she could not have been so great a humbug. But she had stuck herself full of borrowed qualities, which she chose to provide herself with, but which had no root in her.
    Nathaniel Hawthorne, in Randall Stewart, *Nathaniel Hawthorne.*

'I accept the universe' is reported to have been a favourite utterance of our New England transcendentalist Margaret Fuller; and when someone repeated this phrase to Thomas Carlyle, his sardonic comment is said to have been, 'Gad! she'd better.'
    William James, *The Varieties of Religious Experience.*

She always keeps asking if I don't observe a Particular likeness 'twixt her and Minerva.
    James Russell Lowell, in James D. Hart, *The Oxford Companion to American Literature.*

In no sense an artist, scarcely a competent craftsman, she wrote nothing that bears the mark of high distinction either in thought or style. Impatient of organization and inadequately disciplined, she threw off her work impulsively, not pausing to shape it to enduring form.
    Vernon Louis Parrington, *Main Currents in American Thought.*

She wrote so gracelessly and effusively, and sometimes with such lack of simple clarity, that reading her was anything but a pleasure even to her friends and neighbors.
    Bernard Smith, *Forces in American Criticism.*

Wheresoever her eye rests our indolence and indulgence, our way of life and want of heroic action are shamed.
    Henry David Thoreau, in Faith Chipperfield, *In Quest of Love, The Life and Death of Margaret Fuller.*

. . . to whom Venus gave everything except beauty, and Pallas everything except wisdom.
    Oscar Wilde, in Arthur W. Brown, *Margaret Fuller.*

FULTON, ROBERT

1765—1815 Engineer, Inventor, Artist

He was a prophet, inasmuch as he foresaw the outcome of this grand revolution [the introduction and operation of steam-vessels], in which he was so active a participant and agent; and he was a statesman, in that he weighed justly and fully the enormous consequences of the introduction of steam navigation as an element of national greatness; but he has been recognized neither as prophet nor as statesman, both of which he was, but as the inventor of the steamboat — which he was not.
    Robert H. Thurston, *Robert Fulton.*

G

GABLE, (WILLIAM) CLARK

1901—60 Actor

I'm not much of an actor but I'm not bad unless it's one of those things outside my comprehension. I work hard. I'm no Adonis and I'm as American as the telephone poles I used to climb to make a living. So men don't get sore if their womenfolk like me on the screen. I'm one of them, they know it, so it's a compliment to them.

They see me broke, in trouble, scared of things that go bump in the night but coming out fighting, they see me making love to Jean Harlow or Claudette Colbert and they say, If he can do it I can do it, and figure it'll be fun to go home and make love to their wives.

They see life with a high price tag on it, but they get an idea that no price is too high if it's *life*.

I'm not going to make any motion pictures that don't keep right on telling them that about a man. Let's get that understood. The things a man has to have are hope and confidence in himself against odds, and sometimes he needs somebody, his pal or his mother or his wife or God, to give him that confidence. He's got to have some inner standards worth fighting for or there won't be any way to bring him into conflict. And he must be ready to choose death before dishonour without making too much song and dance about it. That's all there is to it.

On himself, in Adela Rogers St Johns, *The Honeycomb*.

He was unabashed virility, but the world moves towards unisex. He was an outdoorsman, but the outdoors is being macadamized in our day. He portrayed men of action and instinct, and we survivors feel paralyzed by numbers, rules, costs and awareness. . . . To think about Gable now is to experience an almost unutterable nostalgia, not only for the gruff and dashing figure he was but for the unsubtle and straightforward period in which he moved.

Charles Champlin, Foreword to Gabe Essoe, *The Films of Clark Gable*.

Gable the Kind — impudent, free, rascally, courageous, resourceful, direct, uncomplicated, charming, all-male but without need to overassert it, sane and self-reliant, gallant and natural — remains what we would wish to be, but what we sense we can now fully be only in spirit. We make do with lesser and more brittle gods.

Ibid.

Gable's ruthless realism made him the first great antihero of American movies, a Don Quixote in reverse, who saw the windmill in every giant and the whore in every lady. Before a generation coined the term, he invented *cool*. He was able to wade through the worst of MGM's syrupy sentimentality and shake it off, without a single ruffle to his feathers. . . .

René Jordan, *Clark Gable*.

Gable belonged to a time when there was still a taint of effeminacy to the acting profession. In real life, his father was a laborer who pleaded with him to come back to the oil fields where real men should be, instead of making faces on stage and screen. . . . Gable never forgot this and became the epitome of the star who is slightly ashamed of his trade and lets everyone notice it. . . .

Ibid.

The movies desperately needed someone like Gable and he was in the right place at the right time with the right face. Ears too big, manners too rough, he emerged as the popular thirties Everyman. Men could identify with him as he went about dispensing vicarious thrills such as telling the boss where to get off or bringing the haughty heiress down a peg. For women, he was a promise of powerful earthy sexuality that could hopefully be found at the Woolworth counter.

Ibid.

Allowing for all possible distortions, this is still a paradoxical life. A man who professed not to be an actor, just a lucky guy, nonetheless spent years of hard work learning a trade he was diffident about. On screen, he was supremely confident, but underneath he was frightened. Never forgetting his initial poverty, he feared his past and had a tendency to hide it like a half-gnawed bone. His stinginess was legendary. He lived in mortal dread of losing his financial status. The brash adventurer of the movies was really a man who would risk nothing. Grudgingly

he accepted almost every role they threw his way, never wanting to antagonise the studio powers. He married MGM and was a true organization man. When he left the studio in which he had reigned as king, it was a shattering blow on a par with an abdication.
    Ibid.

Gable. The King. An exaggeration of A Man.
    Adela Rogers St Johns, *The Honeycomb*.

What is a star? Who the hell knows? I know a lot of good actors who are not stars, and maybe some stars who are not good actors. Gable was a star, all right, and he put it on the line that he was *not* an actor ... but he made an impression with what he *did*.
    Spencer Tracy, in Larry Swindell, *Spencer Tracy*.

See also Carole Lombard

GAINSBOROUGH, THOMAS

1727—88 Painter

He was sure the perplexities of rendering art like a human resemblance, from human blocks, was a trial of patience that would have tempted holy St. Anthony to cut his own throat with his palette-knife.
    H. Angelo, *Reminiscences*.

That ingenious Proteus, Gainsborough, who is so becoming and so excellent in every shape he assumes.
    James Barry, *An Account of a Series of Pictures in the Great Room of the Society of Art, Manufactures, and Commerce, at the Adelphi*.

His subjects are softened and sentimentalised too much, it is not simple unaffected nature that we see, but nature sitting for her picture.
    William Hazlitt, 'On Gainsborough's Pictures', in *Champion*, 31 July 1814.

The charm of Gainsborough is indefinable: there is always something amateurish about him, and one feels like calling him the first (beyond all comparison) of the amateurs. It is not the charm of vigour, but the charm of facility, and of a correctness and softness of style so perfect that they never had occasion to dream of mannerism.
    Henry James, 'The Old Masters at Burlington House', in *Nation*, 1 February 1877.

Gainsborough was a fashionable portrait-painter. He never painted anything or anybody that any Englishman of the day could not have seen and in his turn observed 'from the life'. And yet he was as much a

fantastic as William Blake in his way. He did not see his sitters, or only saw them in a trance: a very mild, superficial trance, but nevertheless a palpable one. The fancies that hung around them, the flavour of their lives, their illusions about themselves, or about each other, all went to his head as they floated into his studio to be painted, like some enervating bergamot. He was doped with the graceful existence of all these pretty people, and that is how he worked. He saw nothing but pale blue clichés, and never a man or woman. Blake's Jehovah is a far realler person, or at least you can imagine him in the Tottenham Court Road more readily. You would take him for a Hampstead Nature crank, with his long hair, bare feet, and night-shirt.
    P. Wyndham Lewis, 'Painting of the Soul', in *Athenaeum*, December 1919.

Nothing can be more strongly expressive of Gainsborough's acknowledged goodness of heart, and of his ardent love for the profession, than the exclamation uttered whilst expiring — 'We are all going to Heaven, and Vandyke is of the party.'
    James Northcote, *The Life of Sir Joshua Reynolds*.

It is certain, that all those odd scratches and marks, which, on a close examination, are so observable in Gainsborough's pictures, and which even to experienced painters appear rather the effect of accident than design: this chaos, this uncouth and shapeless appearance, by a kind of magic, at a certain distance assumes form, and all the parts seem to drop into their proper places.
    Joshua Reynolds, *Fourteenth Discourse*, 10 December 1788.

The landscape of Gainsborough is soothing, tender, and affecting. The stillness of noon, the depths of twilight, and the dews and pearls of the morning, are all to be found on the canvases of this most benevolent and kind-hearted man. On looking at them we find tears in our eyes, and know not what brings them.
    John Ruskin, Lecture at the Royal Institution, 16 June 1836.

The greatest colourist since Rubens, and the last, I think, of legitimate colourists; that is to say, of those who were fully acquainted with the power of their material; pure in his English feeling, profound in his seriousness, graceful in his gaiety.
    John Ruskin, *Modern Painters*.

Nature was his master, for he had no other.
    Philip Thicknesse, *A Sketch of the Life and Paintings of Thomas Gainsborough, Esq.*

See also John Crome, Sir Thomas Lawrence, Henry Raeburn

GAITSKELL, HUGH TODD NAYLOR

1906—63 Statesman

I became a Socialist . . . not so much because I was a passionate advocate of public ownership but because I came to hate and loathe social injustice, because I disliked the class structure of our society, because I could not tolerate the indefensible difference of status and income which disfigures our society. I hated the insecurity that affected such a large part of our community while others led lives of security and comfort. I became a Socialist because I hated poverty and squalor.

On himself, at the Labour Party Conference, 1955.

A desiccated calculating machine.

Aneurin Bevan, in W. T. Rodgers ed., *Hugh Gaitskell 1906—63*.

Hugh Gaitskell developed naturally from boyhood to maturity in a singularly straight line.

Maurice Bowra, in W. T. Rodgers ed., *ibid*.

Gaitskell has a Wykehamistical voice and manner and a 13th century face.

Henry Channon, Diary, 10 April 1951.

. . . Morally, he was in the bravest of all categories: he flinched, but he always went on.

Roy Jenkins, in W. T. Rodgers ed., *Hugh Gaitskell 1906—63*.

He had reasoned himself into international socialism, but his vision of the future was one of England's Jerusalem.

Michael Postan, in *ibid*.

GALLATIN, ABRAHAM ALFONSE ALBERT

1761—1849 Diplomat, Statesman

Gallatin is a man of first-rate talents, conscious and vain of them, tortuous in his paths, born in Europe, disguising and yet betraying a supercilious prejudice of European superiority of intellect, and holding principles pliable to circumstances, occasionally mistaking the left for the right-handed wisdom.

John Quincy Adams, Diary, November 1821.

. . . is the only man in the United States who understands, through all the laberinths that [Alexander] Hamilton involv'd it, the precise state of the Treasury, and the resources of the country.

Pierce Butler, Letter to James Monroe, 27 September 1816.

The Gentleman from Geneva has an accent not unlike that of a wandering Israelite . . . admirably adapted . . . for augmenting the discordant howlings of a synagogue.

William Cobbett, *Porcupine's Works*, vol. 3.

. . . a man of most singular sagacity and penetration; he could read the very thoughts of men in their faces and develop their designs; a man of few words, made no promises but to real favorites [who] ever sought to enhance his own interest, power, and aggrandisement by the most insatiate avarice on the very vitals of the unsuspecting nation.

William Duane, *Aurora*, 3 September 1811.

Commas and points he sets exactly right,
And 'twere a sin to rob him of his mite.

Alexander Hamilton, in Alexander Balinsky, *Albert Gallatin, Fiscal Theories and Policies*.

GALSWORTHY, JOHN

1867—1933 Author

For that is, my dear Jack, what you are — a humanitarian moralist.

Joseph Conrad, Letter to Galsworthy.

We had dinner with Galsworthy the night before we left and I was rather disappointed in him. I can't stand pessimism with neither irony nor bitterness.

F. Scott Fitzgerald, Letter to Shane Leslie, 24 May 1921.

Galsworthy had not quite enough of the superb courage of his satire. He faltered, and gave in to the Forsytes. It is a thousand pities. He might have been the surgeon the modern soul needs so badly, to cut away the proud flesh of our Forsytes from the living body of men who are fully alive. Instead, he put down the knife and laid on a soft sentimental poultice, and helped to make the corruption worse.

D. H. Lawrence, *Phoenix*.

The thing that strikes one about Galsworthy is that though he's trying to be iconoclastic, he has been utterly unable to move his mind outside the wealthy bourgeois society he is attacking. . . . All he conceives to be wrong is that human beings are a little too inhumane, a little too fond of money, and aesthetically not quite sensitive enough. When he sets out to depict what he conceives as the desirable type of human being, it turns out to be simply a cultivated, humanitarian version of the upper-middle-class *rentier*, the sort of person who in those days used to haunt picture galleries in Italy and subscribe heavily to the Society for the Prevention of Cruelty to Animals.

George Orwell, *The Rediscovery of Europe*.

Galsworthy was a bad writer, and some inner trouble, sharpening his sensitiveness, nearly made him into a good one; his discontent healed itself, and he reverted to type. It is worth pausing to wonder in just what form the thing is happening to oneself.

George Orwell, in *New Statesman and Nation*, 12 March 1938.

The fact is that neither Mr Galsworthy nor Mr Kipling has a spark of the woman in him. Thus all their qualities seem to a woman, if one may generalise, crude and immature. They lack suggestive power. And when a book lacks suggestive power, however hard it hits the surface of the mind it cannot penetrate within.

Virginia Woolf, *A Room of One's Own*.

GAMBART, ERNEST

1814—1902 Art Dealer

There is an old he-wolf called Gambart,
Beware of him thou a lamb art,
   Else thy tail and thy toes
   And thine innocent nose
Will be ground by the grinders of Gambart.

Dante Gabriel Rossetti, in *The Times*, January 1976.

GARDINER, STEPHEN

1483?—1555 Bishop of Winchester

I will not here speak of that which hath been constantly reported to me touching the monstrous making and mishaped fashion of his feet and toes, the nails whereof were said not to be like to other mens, but to crook downwards, and to be sharp like the Claws of ravening Beasts.

John Foxe, *Acts and Monuments*.

It does not appear that he ever believed the Papal supremacy to be of the essence of the Church, although he came to look upon it as the bulwark of

episcopal power and of orthodoxy. Had he lived to see the impotence and utter subordination of the episcopate effected by the Council of Trent he might have judged otherwise.

J. A. Miller, *Stephen Gardiner and the Tudor Reaction*.

He was a man of marked reserve, of circumspection, caution, prudence — 'a man of great forecast', as Thirlby said of him in the days of [Thomas] Cromwell's ascendancy; one who had often said to Thirlby that 'he would not be compassed to enter into dangerous things by any man, before the King, but . . . he would go with and follow'.

Ibid.

GARFIELD, JAMES ABRAM

1831—81 Twentieth United States President

[The President] is the last person in the world to know what the people really want and think.

On himself, in *John M. Taylor, Garfield of Ohio: The Available Man*.

. . . though I am receiving what I suppose to be the usual number of threatening letters on that subject. Assassination can be no more guarded against than death by lightning; and it is best not to worry about either.

Ibid.

While I am not indifferent to the good opinion of men who think me fit for the presidency, I am still wholly disinclined to believe that any result will come out of it other than some general talk. I have so long and so often seen the evil effects of the presidential fever upon my associates and friends that I am determined it shall not seize upon me.

On himself, Diary, 5 February 1878.

When I was a lad I scarce went to school
But bossed the career of a towpath mule;
I urged him from Spring until late in the fall
To pull a big boat on the raging canal.
My urging of that mule was so ef-fi-ci-ent,
That now I am a candidate for President.
I rolled up my trousers as high as could be,
And relied upon that mule to educate me;
I soon learned so many of his tricks and ways
Which helped me very much at the counting in of
                    Hayes
At the counting in I was such an in-stru-ment,
That now I am a candidate for President.

Anon., Campaign Song 1880.

He lacked the quickness of perception, the promptness of decision, the fertility of resource which are so valuable in wrestling advantages from the majority or in opposing legitimate obstacles to their advance.

Anon., in *New York Times*, 11 December 1880.

Every President who dies in office, whether from bacteria or bullets, is regarded as a martyr to the public weal, at least to some degree. James A. Garfield, whose troubled six months were marred by office mongering, was probably helped, as far as reputation was concerned by his assassination.

Thomas A. Bailey, *Presidential Greatness*.

He rushes into a fight with the horns of a bull and the skin of a rabbit.

Jeremiah Black, in John M. Taylor, *Garfield of Ohio: The Available Man*.

Garfield has an interest everywhere . . . but in the Kingdom of Heaven.

Oliver P. Brown, in *ibid*.

Garfield has shown that he is not possessed of the backbone of an angle-worm.

Ulysses S. Grant, in *ibid*.

. . . He is the ideal candidate because he is the ideal self made man.

Rutherford B. Hayes, 1880, in Marcus Cunliffe, *American Presidents and the Presidency*.

Who of us, having heard him here or elsewhere, speaking upon a question of great national concern, can forget the might and majesty, the force and directness, the grace and beauty of his utterances.

William McKinley, in Theodore Clarke Smith, *The Life and Letters of James Abram Garfield*, vol. 2.

One of the noblest sentences ever uttered was uttered by Mr. Garfield before he became President. He was a member of Congress, as I remember it, at the time of Lincoln's assassination. He was at the old Fifth Avenue Hotel and they begged him to go out and say something to the people. He went out and after he had attracted their attention, he said this beautiful thing: 'My fellow citizens, the President is dead, but the Government lives and God Omnipotent reigns.'

Woodrow Wilson, Address, Helena, Montana, 11 September 1919.

GARFIELD, JOHN

1913–52 Actor

His climb from bare poverty to stardom illustrated

for him one of the most cherished folkways of our people. His feeling never changed that he had been mandated by the American people to go in there and 'keep punching' for them. His success, as he felt it, was the common property of millions, not peculiarly his own.

Clifford Odets, in *New York Times*, 25 May 1952.

John Garfield may have been the representative hero of the films in the thirties. Tough, aggressive, cynical he was society's victim, the wronged man pushed too far, or society's gadfly, the guy with a chip on his shoulder. He either tangled with the law and lost, or simply held to his personal code and survived.

Ted Sennett, *Warner Brothers Presents*.

Projected on the screens of the world, he was the Eternal Outsider, obliged to glimpse paradise but not to dwell there. John Garfield was the vagabond hood, the urban ne'er do well, the diamond-in-the-rough prodigy, the nervously embattled G.I. In every guise he conveyed an inner turbulence. As a primitive but idealistic sinner, he was as formidable as steel but vulnerably naive, volatile but plaintive. He was a game competitor but a born loser — urgently forceful and forcefully attractive, but never the master of his fate. Because the cards were stacked against him in the script, he was finally pathetic.

Larry Swindell, *Body and Soul: The Story of John Garfield*.

GARLAND, HAMLIN

1860–1940 Author

As a writer I have always been among the minority. I believe in dignity, decorum and grace, and I decline the honor of those who pander to the appetite of millions. . . .

On himself, in Jean Holloway, *Hamlin Garland*.

Garland was for the utter annihilation of the audacious brood that stood in the path of realism. . . .

Eugene Field, in *ibid*.

He has a certain harshness and bluntness, an indifference to the more delicate charms of style, and he has still to learn that though the thistle is full of an unrecognized poetry, the rose has a poetry, too, even overpraise cannot spoil.

William Dean Howells, in *ibid*.

One follows the progress of the man with the constant sense that he is steering by faulty compasses, that fate is leading him into paths too steep and rocky — nay, too dark and lonely — for him.

H. L. Mencken, in *ibid.*

Neither an outstanding artist nor an original mind, he had rather the capacity to reflect the most cogent intellectual, social, and aesthetic ideas of his own day while concomitantly representing the continuity of American radical individualism.

Donald Pizer, *Hamlin Garland's Early Work and Career.*

. . . Garland remains of importance as the historian of the Middle Border, recording in artistic prose one of the great eras of American development; and as the young rebel of the early nineties, breaking with crude, powerful assault the hold of the genteel tradition over our realism.

Walter Fuller Taylor, *The Story of American Letters.*

GARLAND, JUDY (FRANCES GUMM)

1922—69 Singer, Actress

If I'm such a legend, then why am I so lonely? If I'm such a legend, then why do I sit at home for hours staring at the damned telephone, hoping it's out of order, even calling the operator asking her if she's *sure* it's not out of order? Let me tell you, legends are all very well if you've got somebody around who loves you, some man who's not afraid to be in love with Judy Garland.

On herself, in John Gruen, *Close-Up.*

. . . To watch her pouring out her devotion to 'Dear Mr. Gable' and the great, big, wonderful world of the movies was a pleasure almost voyeuristic. One was seeing not the simulated emotions of an accomplished actress, but the real emotions of a real, vulnerable girl passing across her face and coloring her urgent, husky, . . . voice with an extraordinary absence of self-consciousness, self-censorship. She gave everything, without reserve — which was to be her triumph and finally, perhaps her tragedy.

John Russell Taylor and Arthur Jackson, *The Hollywood Musical.*

Even with her personal problems, her well-known addiction to 'Wake-me-up-put-me-to-sleep-now-calm-me-down' pills, her unpredictable behavior with concert promoters, showing up hours late and, reportedly, not at all on a few occasions, she was undisputedly a one-of-a-kind human being and artist. No one could deny this. She had played the

enfant terrible over and over throughout her stormy career. Yet prominent, talented people from virtually every walk of life idolized her, swore by her, defended and protected her, a combined show of fealty unrivaled in the business.

Mel Tormé, *The Other Side of the Rainbow with Judy Garland on the Dawn Patrol.*

GARNER, JOHN NANCE

1868—1967 Politician

Worst damfool mistake I ever made was letting myself be elected Vice-President of the United States. Should have stuck with my old chores as Speaker of the House. I gave up the second most important job in the Government for one that didn't amount to a hill of beans. I spent eight long years as Mr. Roosevelt's spare tire. I might still be Speaker if I hadn't let them elect me Vice-President.

On himself, in Frank X. Tolbert, 'What is Cactus Jack Up to Now', in *Saturday Evening Post*, 2 November 1963.

GARRICK, DAVID

1717—79 Actor

The painter dead, yet still he charms the eye,
While England lives his fame can never die.
But he who struts his hour upon the stage
Can scarce extend his fame for half an age.
No pen nor pencil can the actor save;
The art and artist share one common grave.

On himself, in Edgar Pemberton, 'The Marvel of Mary Anderson', *Munsey's Magazine*, vol. 32, 1904—5.

The voice of this performer is clear, impressive, and affecting; agreeable though not harmonious; sharp, though not dissonant; strong, though not extensive. In declamation it is uncommonly forcible; in narrative, unaffectedly simple. Wanting power at the top, it sometimes sinks where the passions meet with any violent agitation; yet, in general, Mr Garrick has so peculiar a method of adapting it, that we scarcely perceive it should rise where it is unhappily limited: and we are almost induced to believe, that it ought to rise no farther than the particular key to which he has the power of extending it.

Anon., *A Critical Examen of Mr Garrick's Abilities as an Actor.*

That Garrick *ranted* a little, and 'died hard', too *hard*, is upon record.

John Bee, *Works of Samuel Foote.*

Dr Burney having remarked that Mr Garrick was beginning to look old, he [Johnson] said, 'Why, Sir, you are not to wonder at that; no man's face has more wear and tear.'

James Boswell, *Life of Johnson*.

Sir Joshua Reynolds observed, with great truth, that Johnson considered Garrick to be as it were his *property*. He would allow no man either to blame or to praise Garrick in his presence, without contradicting him.

Ibid.

I presume to animadvert on his eulogy on Garrick, in his *Lives of the Poets* 'You say, Sir, his death eclipsed the gaiety of nations.' *Johnson*: 'I could not have said more or less. It is the truth; *eclipsed*, not *extinguished*; and his death *did* eclipse; it was like a storm.' *Boswell*: But why nations? Did his gaiety extend farther than his own nation? *Johnson*: 'Why, Sir, some exaggeration must be allowed . . .'

Ibid.

Johnson, indeed, had thought more upon the subject of acting than might be generally supposed. Talking of it one day to Mr Kemble, he said, 'Are you, Sir, one of those enthusiasts who believe yourself transformed into the very character you represent?' Upon Mr Kemble's answering that he had never felt so strong a persuasion himself; 'To be sure not, Sir, (said Johnson); the thing is impossible. And if Garrick really believed himself to be that monster, Richard the Third, he deserved to be hanged every time he performed it.'

Ibid.

I never saw in my life such brilliant piercing eyes as Mr. Garrick's are. In looking at him, when I have chanced to meet them, I have really not been able to bear their lustre.

Fanny Burney, Diary, 1771.

He took off Dr Johnson most admirably. Indeed I enjoyed it doubly from being in his company; his *see-saw*, his *pawing*, his very *look, and* his voice! My *cot*! what an astonishing thing it is that he [Garrick] has not a good ear for music! He took him off in a speech (that has *stuck in his gizzard* ever since some friendly person was so obliging as to repeat it to him). Indeed, I should much wonder if it did not, for it would have been a severe speech if it had been said upon who it would, much more upon Garrick, indeed, I think it must have been exaggerated, or if not, that it was a very severe, ill-natured, unjust thing. 'Yes, yes, Davy has some convivial pleasantries in him, but 'tis a futile Fellow.' A little while after, he took him off in one of his *own convivial pleasantries*, 'No Sir; I'm for the musick of the ancients, it has been corrupted so.'

Fanny Burney, *Journal*, 1777.

If manly sense, if Nature link'd with art;
If thorough knowledge of the human heart;
If powers of acting, vast and unconfin'd;
If fewest faults with greatest beauties joined;
If strong expression, and strange powers which lie
Within the magic circle of the eye;
If feelings, which few hearts, like his, can know,
And which no face so well as his, can show
Deserve the preference; — Garrick! take the chair,
Nor quit it — till thou place an equal there.

Charles Churchill, *The Rosciad*.

I have seen you with your magic hammer in your hand, endeavouring to beat your ideas into the heads of creatures who had none of their own. I have seen you, with lamb-like patience, endeavouring to make them comprehend you, and I have seen you when that could not be done — I have seen your lamb turned into a lion; by this your great labour and pains the public was entertained; *they* thought they all acted very fine; they did not see you pull the wires.

Kitty Clive, in W. Clark Russell, *Representative Actors*.

Damn him, he could act a gridiron!

Kitty Clive, in William Archer, *Introduction to the Dramatic Essays of Leigh Hunt*.

Our Garrick's a salad, for in him we see
Oil, vinegar, sugar, and saltness agree.

Oliver Goldsmith, in James Boswell, *Life of Johnson*.

Here lies David Garrick, describe me who can,
An abridgement of all that was pleasant in man;
As an actor, confest without rival to shine,
As a wit, if not first, in the very first line,
Yet with talents like these, and an excellent heart,
The man had his failings, a dupe to his art;
Like an ill-judging beauty, his colours he spread,
And beplaistered with rouge his own natural red.
On the stage he was natural, simple, affecting,
'Twas only that, when he was off, he was acting:
With no reason on earth to go out of his way,
He turn'd and he varied full ten times a day
Tho' secure of our hearts, yet confoundedly sick
If they were not his own by finessing and trick,
He cast off his friends, as a huntsman his pack,
For he knew when he pleas'd he could whistle them
back.

Oliver Goldsmith, *Retaliation*.

Did I tell you about Mr Garrick, that the Town are

horn-mad after; there are a dozen Dukes of a night at Goodmans Fields sometimes, & yet I am stiff in the opposition.
Thomas Gray, Letter to Chute, 24 May 1742.

We have heard it mentioned that once . . . while he was kneeling to repeat the curse, the first row in the pit stood up to see him better; the second row, not willing to lose the precious moments by remonstrating, stood up too; and so, by a tacit movement, the entire pit rose to hear the withering imprecation, while the whole passed in such cautious silence that you might have heard a pin drop.
William Hazlitt, in *London Magazine*, June 1820.

But what are the hopes of man! I am disappointed by that stroke of death, which has eclipsed the gaiety of nations and impoverished the public stock of harmless pleasure.
Samuel Johnson, *Lives of the Poets*: 'Edward Smith'.

'Garrick,' said Dr Johnson, 'begins to complain of the fatigue of the stage. Sir, a man that bawls turnips all day for his bread does twice as much.'
Samuel Johnson, in J. Cradock, *Literary and Miscellaneous Memoirs*.

Garrick's conversation is gay and grotesque. It is a dish of all sorts, but all good things. There is no solid meat in it: there is a want of sentiment in it. Not but that he has sentiment sometimes, and sentiment too, very powerful, and very pleasing; but it has not its full proportion in his conversation.
Samuel Johnson, in James Boswell, *Life of Johnson*.

Like Charles the imperial, enfeebled and hoary,
Great Garrick retir'd, o'er laden with glory:
He had run round the circle of Honour's career,
And knew ev'ry blessing which feeling makes dear;
But his vanity sated, his wishes were o'er;
For his hope grey diseas'd, and his joys were no more,
Like the young Macedonian, he wept when he knew,
That no graces of art were now left to subdue;
And that spirit which long was subservient to Fame,
Retreated within, and corroded his frame;
Where Nature's base particles entering in strife,
It subjected his wisdom, and fed on his life.
Anthony Pasquin (John Williams), *The Children of Thespis*.

Garrick . . . made himself a slave to his reputation. Amongst the variety of arts observed by his friends to preserve that reputation, one of them was to make himself rare. It was difficult to get him, and when you had him, as difficult to keep him. He

never came into company but with a plot how to get out of it. He was for ever receiving messages of his being wanted in another place. It was a rule with him never to leave any company saturated. Being used to exhibit himself at a theatre or a large table, he did not consider an individual as worth powder and shot.
Sir Joshua Reynolds, *Notes on Garrick*.

The grace of action, the adapted mien —
Faithful as nature to the varied scene;
Th'expressive glance — whose subtle comment draws
Entranc'd attention and a mute applause;
Gesture that marks, with force and feeling fraught,
A sense in silence, and a will in thought;
Harmonious speech, whose pure and liquid tone
Gives verse a music scarce confess'd its own.
Richard Brinsley Sheridan, *Verses to the Memory of Garrick, Spoken as a Monody at the Theatre Royal in Drury Lane*, March 1779.

See also Thomas Arne, Samuel Foote, Edmund Kean

GARRISON, WILLIAM LLOYD
1805—79 Abolitionist, Editor

Confine me as a prisoner — but bind me not as a slave
Punish me as a criminal — but hold me not as a chattel.
Torture me as a man — but drive me not like a beast.
Doubt my sanity — but acknowledge my immortality.
On himself, on the wall of the jail in Boston where he was confined for the night, 1835.

He is the Atlas of abolition. Had not God made *his* forehead strong against the foreheads of the people, the bark of abolition would have been wrecked on the rocks and quicksands of human expediency. So he says, I believe in my soul, we have all overvalued Garrison. And as to himself, pride has driven him mad. I cannot bear to see this ignoble idolatry among abolitionists.
Gamaliel Bailey of New York, 14 October 1837, in G. M. Frederickson ed., *William Lloyd Garrison*.

He was equipped by taste and temperament for free-lance journalism and for nothing else. As a journalist he was brilliant and provocative; as a leader for the anti-slavery host he was a name, an embodied motto, a figurehead of fanaticism.
Gilbert H. Barnes, *The Anti-Slavery Impulse*.

God never raised up such men as Garrison, and

others like him, as the ministers of his mercy for purposes of peaceful reform, but only as the fit and fearful ministers of his vengeance upon a people incorrigibly wicked.

Lyman Beecher, *Autobiography.*

Would find nothing to do in a lonely world, or a world with half-a-dozen inhabitants.

Ralph Waldo Emerson, in Russel B. Nye, *William Lloyd Garrison and the Humanitarian Reformers.*

There's Garrison, his features very
Benign for an incendiary;
Beaming forth sunshine through his glasses
On the surrounding lads and lasses.

James Russell Lowell, in C. M. Fuess, *Daniel Webster*, vol. 2.

. . . he will shake our nation to its center, but he will shake slavery out of it.

Samuel May, in Howard Zinn, *Abolitionists, Freedom-Riders, and the Tactics of Agitation.*

This martyrdom theme is central to Garrison's personality. It recurs again and again in his editorials, his speeches, his personal letters and his verse. It would seem that he felt the closer he approached martyrdom the greater would be the success of his agitation on behalf of the slave.

Walter M. Merrill, *Against Wind and Tide.*

[His] overgrown self-conceit had wrought him into the belief that his mighty self was abolition incarnate.

Amos A. Phelps, in Russel B. Nye, *William Lloyd Garrison and the Humanitarian Reformers.*

Champion of those who groan beneath
   Oppression's iron hand:
In view of penury, hate and death,
   I see thee fearless stand.
Still bearing up thy lofty brow,
   In the steadfast strength of truth,
In manhood stealing well the vow
   And promise of thy youth.

John Greenleaf Whittier, *To William Lloyd Garrison.*

GARRY, SPOKANE

1811—92 Indian missionary

I was born by these waters. The earth here is my mother. If the Great Father will not give me land at this place, I will not go to another reservation, but

will stay here until the whites push me out, and out, and out until there is no more out.

On himself, speaking in 1878 in response to a US Government proposal to move his people away from the Spokane River.

GARVEY, MARCUS MOZIAH

1887—1940 Political Organizer

It's a pity the cannibals do not get hold this man.

Anon., 1924, in Robert G. Weisbord, 'Marcus Garvey, Pan-Negroist', in *Race*, April 1970.

When the curtain dropped on the Garvey theatricals, the black man of America was exactly where Garvey had found him, though a little bit sadder, perhaps a bit poorer — if not wiser.

Ralph Bunch, in Gunnar Myrdal, *An American Dilemma: The Negro Problem and Modern Democracy.*

American Negro leaders are not jealous of Garvey. They are not envious of his success, they are simply afraid of his failure, for his failure would be theirs. He can have all the power and money that he can efficiently and honestly use, and if in addition he wants to prance down Broadway in a green shirt, let him — but do not let him foolishly overwhelm with bankruptcy and disaster one of the most interesting spiritual movements of the modern Negro world.

W.E.B. Du Bois, 'Marcus Garvey', in *Crisis*, December 1920—January 1921.

. . . without arms, money, effective organization of base of operations, Mr. Garvey openly and wildly talks of 'conquest' and of telling white Europeans in Africa to 'get out!' of becoming himself a black Napoleon!

Ibid.

A Jamaican Negro of unmixed stock, squat, stocky, fat and sleek, with protruding jaws, and heavy jowls, small bright pig-like eyes and rather bull-dog-like face. Boastful, egotistic, tyrannical, intolerant, cunning, shifty, smooth and suave, avaricious; as adroit as a fencer in changing front, as adept as a cuttlefish in beclouding an issue he cannot meet, prolix to the nth degree in devising new schemes to gain the money of poor ignorant Negroes; gifted at self-advertisement, without shame in self laudation, promising ever, but never fulfilling, without regard for veracity, a lover of pomp and tawdry finery and garish display, a bully with his own folk but servile in the presence of the Man, a sheer opportunist and a demagogic charlatan.

Robert W. Gagnall of the National Association

for the Advancement of Colored People, *Messenger*, March 1923.

. . . commentary on Marcus Garvey has usually taken the form of a Black and White Minstrel Show built around the general theme of a crazy egotistic and noisy Black who thought up a scatterbrained scheme to remove the Black people from their American paradise to the African jungle.
    Marcus Garvey Jr., 'Garveyism: Some Reflections on its Significance for Today', in John H. Clarke and Amy J. Garvey, *Marcus Garvey and the Vision of Africa*.

He had energy and daring and the Napoleonic personality. The personality that draws masses of followers . . . he had great power and possibilities within his grasp, but his deficiencies as a leader outweighed his abilities. To this man came an opportunity such as comes to few men, and he clutched greedily at the glitter and let the substance slip from his fingers.
    James Weldon Johnson, in *ibid*.

. . . it was in short racial fascism. He seemed to believe honestly that the best way to right the wrong of his people was to retort by adopting the modus operandi of the racial imperialists he was fighting. . . . He himself declared that his movement was fascistic. He said 'We were the first fascists . . . Mussolini copied fascism from me. . . .'
    J. A. Rogers, *World's Great Men of Color*.

If the assumption some of us possess that the exponent of an ideal should be pale, hungry-eyed, worn thin by vigils, is a general one, then Marcus Garvey is a disappointing figure. He is black, apparently too well-fed, exceedingly well groomed. In short, he does not look like himself. It is when he speaks, whether in the privacy of his office or in the glare of the lights of Liberty Hall, that one recognizes the man for what he is and for what he wants to be, a black leader of black people.
    Worth Tuttle, 'The New Nation in Harlem', in *The World Tomorrow*, 4 September 1925.

GASKELL, ELIZABETH CLEGHORN

1810—65 Novelist

She lives in a large, cheerful, airy house, quite out of Manchester smoke; a garden surrounds it, and, as in this hot weather the windows were kept open, a whispering of leaves and perfume of flowers always pervades the rooms. Mrs Gaskell herself is a woman of whose conversation and company I should not

tire. She seems to me kind, clever, animated, and unaffected.
    Charlotte Brontë, Letter to George Smith, 1 July 1851.

A natural unassuming woman whom they have been doing their best to spoil by making a lioness of her.
    Jane Welsh Carlyle, Letter, 17 May 1849.

The outstanding fact about Mrs Gaskell is her femininity. . . . We have only to look at the portrait of Mrs Gaskell, soft-eyed, beneath her charming veil, to see that she was a dove. In an age whose ideal of woman emphasized the feminine qualities at the expense of all others, she was all a woman was expected to be; gentle, domestic, tactful, unintellectual, prone to tears, easily shocked. So far from chafing at the limits imposed on her activities, she accepted them with serene satisfaction.
    David Cecil, *Early Victorian Novelists*.

Last night I met Mary Barton, otherwise called Mrs Gaskell. She is neither young (past 30) nor beautiful; very retiring, but quite capable of talking when she likes — a good deal of the clergyman's wife about her. Rather hard-featured, in the Scotch style.
    A. H. Clough, Letter to Anne Clough, 9 February 1849.

Paraclete of the Bartons!
    Walter Savage Landor, *To the Author of Mary Barton*.

GAVESTON, PIERS, EARL OF CORNWALL

— d. 1312 Royal Favourite

He himself, confident that he had been confirmed for life in his earldom, albeit he was an alien and had been preferred to so great dignity solely by the king's favour, had now grown so insolent as to despise all the nobles of the land; among whom he called the Earl of Warwick (a man of equal wisdom and integrity) 'the Black Dog of Arden.' When this was reported to the earl, he is said to have replied with calmness: 'If he call me a dog, be sure that I will bite him, so soon as I shall perceive my opportunity.'
    The Chronicle of Lanercost, translated by Sir Herbert Maxwell.

GAVESTON: I must have wanton Poets, pleasant
                                                    wits,
Musitians, that with touching of a string
May draw the pliant king which way I please:
Therefore ile have Italian maskes by night,

Sweete speeches, comedies, and pleasing showes,
And in the day when he shall walk abroad,
Like *Sylvian* Nimphes my pages shall be clad,
My men like Satyres grazing on the lawnes,
Shall with their Goate feete daunce an antick hay.
Sometimes a lovelie boy in *Dians* shape,
With haire that gilds the water as it glides,
Crownets of pearl about his naked armes,
And in his sportfull hands an Olive tree,
To hide those parts which men delight to see,
Shall bathe him in a spring. . . .

Christopher Marlowe, *Edward II*, Act I, Scene I.

See also Edward II

GAY, JOHN

1685–1732 Dramatist

The contempt of the world grows upon me, and I now begin to be richer and richer, for I find I could every morning I wake, be content with less than I aimed at the day before. I fancy in time, I shall bring myself into that state which No man ever knew before me, in thinking I have enough. I really am afraid to be content with so little, lest my good friends should censure me for indolence, and the want of laudable ambition, so that it will be absolutely necessary for me to improve my fortune to content them. How solicitous is mankind to please others.

On himself, Letter to Jonathan Swift, 18 February 1727.

Life is a Jest, and all Things show it;
I thought so once, but now I know it.

On himself, *Proposed Epitaph*, in Letter to Alexander Pope, October 1727.

For writing in the cause of Virtue, and against the fashionable vices, I am lookt upon at present as the most obnoxious person almost in England. . . . Mr. Pope tells me that I am dead and that this obnoxiousness is the reward of my inoffensiveness in my former life.

On himself, Letter to Jonathan Swift, 18 March 1728.

Cou'd any man but you think of trusting John Gay with his money; none of his friends wou'd ever trust him with his own whenever they cou'd avoid it. . . .

Lord Bathurst, Letter to Jonathan Swift, 19 April 1731.

I have been told of an ingenious observation of Mr Gibbon, that, 'The Beggar's Opera may, perhaps, have sometimes increased the number of highwaymen: but that it has had a beneficial effect in refining that class of men, making them less ferocious, more polite, — in short, more like gentlemen.' Upon this, Mr Courtenay said, that 'Gay was the Orpheus of Highwaymen.'

James Boswell, Note to *Life of Johnson*.

Gay is a great eater. 'As the French Philosopher used to prove his existence by *Cogito ergo sum*, the greatest proof of Gay's existence is *Edit, ergo est*.'

William Congreve, as reported by Joseph Spence, *Anecdotes*.

He was a satirist without gall. He had a delightful placid vein of invention, fancy, wit, humour, description, ease, and elegance, a happy style, and a versification which seemed to cost him nothing. His *Beggar's Opera* indeed has stings in it, but it appears to have left the writer's mind without any.

William Hazlitt, *A Critical List of Authors*.

Much however must be allowed to the author of a new species of composition, though it be not of the highest kind. We owe to Gay the ballad Opera; a mode of comedy which at first was supposed to delight only by its novelty, but has now by the experience of half a century been found so well accommodated to the disposition of a popular audience, that it is likely to keep long possession of the stage. Whether this new drama was the product of judgement or luck, the praise of it must be given to the inventor; and there are many writers read with more reverence, to whom such merit of originality cannot be attributed.

Samuel Johnson, *Lives of the Poets*.

Of manners gentle, of Affections mild;
In Wit, a Man; Simplicity, a Child;
With native Humour temp'ring virtuous Rage,
Form'd to delight at once and lash the age;
Above Temptation, in a low Estate,
And uncorrupted ev'n among the Great;
A safe Companion, and an easy Friend,
Unblam'd thro' Life, lamented in thy End.
These are Thy Humours! not that here thy Bust
Is mix'd with Heroes, or with Kings thy dust;
But that the worthy and the Good shall say,
Striking their pensive bosoms — *Here* lies *Gay*.

Alexander Pope, *Epitaph on Mr Gay*, in *Westminster Abbey*.

He has Merit, Good nature, and Integrity, three qualities that I fear are too often lost upon great men; or at least are not all three a match for that one which is opposed to them, Flattery. I wish it may not soon or late displace him from the Favour

he now possesses, and seems to like.
    Alexander Pope, Letter to Martha Blount, 1715.

We have liv'd little together of late, and we want to be physicians for one another. It is a remedy that agreed very well with us both for many years . . . I believe we both of us want whetting.
    Alexander Pope, Letter to Gay, 23 October 1730.

Good God, how often are we to die before we go quite off this stage? In every friend we lose a part of ourselves, and the best part. . . . Would to God the man we have lost had not been so amiable, nor so good!
    Alexander Pope, Letter to Jonathan Swift,
    5 December 1732.

Gay was quite a natural man, wholly without art or design, and spoke just what he thought and as he thought it.
    Alexander Pope, in Joseph Spence, *Anecdotes.*

Upon the whole I deliver my judgement; that nothing but servile attachment to a party, affectation of singularity, lamentable dullness, mistaken zeal, or studied hypocrisy, can have any objection against this excellent moral performance of Mr Gay.
    Jonathan Swift, on the Beggar's Opera, *Intelligencer*, no. 3.

A coach and six horses is the utmost exercise you can bear, and this onely when you can fill it with Such company as is best Suited to your tast, and how glad would you be if it could waft you in the air to avoyd jolting. . . . You mortally hate writing onely because it is the thing you chiefly ought to do as well to keep up the vogue you have in the world, as to make you easy in your fortune; you are mercifull to every thing but money, your best friend, whom you treat with inhumanity.
    Jonathan Swift, Letter to Gay, May 1732.

With . . . kind lordly folks, a real Duke and Duchess, as delightful as those who harboured Don Quixote, and loved that dear old Sancho, Gay lived, and was lapped in cotton, and had his plate of chicken, and his saucer of cream, and frisked, and barked, and wheezed, and grew fat, and so ended.
    W. M. Thackeray, *The English Humourists.*

See also John Fletcher, Jonathan Swift

GEORGE I

1660–1727

I hate all Boets and Bainters.
    On himself, in Lord Campbell, *Life of Mansfield.*

When Henry the Eighth left the Pope in the lurch,
The Protestants made him the head of the Church;
But George's good subjects, the Bloomsbury people,
Instead of the Church, made him head of the steeple.
    Anon., in Sir H. M. Imbert Terry, *A Constitutional King.*

God in His wrath sent Saul to trouble Jewry,
And George to England in a greater fury;
For George in sin as far exceedeth Saul
As ever Bishop Burnet did Saint Paul.
    Anon., in *ibid.*

The man had his big burden, big honours so called, absurd enough, some of them, in this world; but he bore them with a certain gravity and discretion: a man of more probity, insight, and general human faculty than he now gets credit for. His word was sacred to him. He had the courage of a Wolf, or Lion-Man; quietly royal in that respect at least. His sense of equity, of what was true and honourable in men and things, remained uneffaced to a respectable degree; and surely it has resisted much.
    Thomas Carlyle, in Lewis Melville, *The First George.*

No woman came amiss of him, if they were very willing and very fat . . . the standard of His Majesty's taste made all those ladies who aspired to his favour, and who were near the statutable size, strain and swell themselves like the frogs in the fable to rival the bulk and dignity of the ox. Some succeeded, and others burst.
    Lord Chesterfield, in A. F. Scott, *Every One A Witness.*

George I was lazy and inactive even in his pleasures, which therefore were lowly sensual. He was coolly intrepid and indolently benevolent. . . . Importunity alone could make him act, and then only to get rid of it.
    Lord Chesterfield, in *ibid.*

George I kept his wife in prison because he believed that she was no better than he was.
    Will Cuppy, *The Decline and Fall of Practically Everybody.*

George the First knew nothing and desired to know nothing; did nothing and desired to do nothing; and the only good thing that is told of him is that he wished to restore the crown to its hereditary successor.
    Samuel Johnson, in James Boswell, *Life of Johnson.*

A dull, stupid and profligate King, full of drink and

low conversation, without dignity of appearance or manner, without sympathy of any kind with the English people and English ways, and without the slightest knowledge of the English language.

Justin McCarthy, in Lewis Melville, *The First George.*

The natural honesty of his temper, joined with the narrow notions of a low education, made him look upon his acceptance of the crown as an act of usurpation, which was always uneasy to him.

Lady Mary Wortley Montagu, in *ibid.*

He was passively good-natured, and wished all mankind enjoyed quiet, if they would let him do so.
Ibid.

In private life he would have been called an honest blockhead; and Fortune, that made him a king, added nothing to his happiness, only prejudiced his honesty, and shortened his days. No man was ever more free from ambition; he loved money, but loved to keep his own, without being rapacious of other men's.
Ibid.

The king was heard to say in the drawing-room, upon the falling of the South Sea stock: 'We had very good luck; for we sold out last week.'

Joseph Spence, *Anecdotes.*

The King, observing with judicious eyes,
The state of both his universities,
To Oxford sent a troop of horse, and why?
That learned body wanted loyalty;
To Cambridge books, as very well discerning
How much that loyal body wanted learning.

Joseph Trapp, *On George I's Donation to Cambridge.*

The King to Oxford sent a troop of horse
For Tories own no argument but force.
With equal skill to Cambridge books he sent,
For Whigs admit no force but argument.

Sir William Browne, *Riposte to Trapp.*

See also William III

GEORGE II

1683—1760

The best, perhaps, that can be said of him is that on the whole, all things considered, he might have been worse.

Justin McCarthy, *A History of the Four Georges.*

O strutting Turkey-cock of Herrenhausen! O naughty little Mahomet! In what Turkish paradise are you now, and where be your painted houris? . . . Friends, he was your fathers' King as well as mine — let us drop a respectful tear over his grave.

W. M. Thackeray, *The Four Georges.*

He had no favourites and indeed no friends, having none of that expansion of heart, none of those amiable connecting talents, which are necessary for both. This, together with the sterility of his conversation, made him prefer the company of women, with whom he rather sauntered away than enjoyed his leisure hours. He was addicted to women, but chiefly to such as require little attention and less pay.

Lord Chesterfield, in A. F. Scott, *Every One A Witness.*

He had the haughtiness of Henry VIII without his spirit; the avarice of Henry VII, without his exactions; the indignities of Charles I, without his bigotry for his prerogative; the vexation of King William, with as little skill in the management of parties; and the gross gallantry of his father, without his goodnature or his honesty: — he might perhaps have been honest, if he had never hated his father, or had ever loved his son.

Horace Walpole, *Memoirs.*

Content to bargain for the gratification of his two predominant passions, Hanover and money, he was almost indifferent to the rest of his royal authority, provided exterior observance was not wanting; for he comforted himself if he did not perceive the diminution of Majesty, though it was notorious to all the rest of the world.
Ibid.

GEORGE III

1738—1820

I desire what is good; therefore, everyone who does not agree with me is a traitor.

On himself, in Sir John Fortescue ed., *The Correspondence of George III.*

Men of less principle and honesty than I pretend to may look on public measures and opinions as a game; I always act from conviction.

On himself, in Richard Pares, *George III and the Politicians.*

I will rather risk my Crown than do what I think personally disgraceful, and whilst I have no wish

but for the good and prosperity of my country, it
is impossible that the nation shall not stand by me;
if they will not, they shall have another King.
Ibid.

Throughout the greater part of his life George III
was a kind of consecrated obstruction.
Walter Bagehot, *The English Constitution.*

George the Third
Ought never to have occurred.
One can only wonder
At so grotesque a blunder.
Edmund Clerihew Bentley, *Biography for
Beginners.*

[Dr Johnson] said to Mr Barnard, 'Sir, they may
talk of the king as they will; but he is the finest
gentleman I have ever seen.' And he afterwards
observed to Mr Langton, 'Sir, his manners are those
of as fine a gentleman as we may suppose Louis the
Fourteenth or Charles the Second.'
James Boswell, *Life of Johnson.*

There was no doubt to which type King George
belonged. Without any attempt to make himself
cheap or popular in a common way, he appealed to
the most vital of his subjects. In character and convictions he was the average Briton of his day, or
what the average Briton aspired to be. He was John
Bull.
John Brooke, *George III.*

In the first year of freedom's second dawn
    Died George the Third; although no tyrant, one
Who shielded tyrants, till each sense withdrawn
    Left him nor mental nor external sun:
A better farmer ne'er brushed dew from lawn,
    A worse king never left a realm undone!
He died — but left his subjects still behind,
One half as mad — and 'tother no less blind.
Lord Byron, *The Vision of Judgement.*

He ever warr'd with freedom and the free:
    Nations as men, home subjects, foreign foes,
So they utter'd the word 'Liberty!'
    Found George the Third their first opponent.
                                                    Whose
History was ever stain'd as his will be
    With national and individual woes?
I grant his household abstinence; I grant
His neutral virtues, which most monarchs want;

I know he was a constant consort; own
    He was a decent sire, and middling lord.
All this is much and most upon a throne;
    And temperance, if at Apicius' board,

Is more than at an anchorite's supper shown.
    I grant him all the kindest can accord;
And this was well for him, but not for those
Millions who found him what oppression chose.
Ibid.

He came to his sceptre young; he leaves it old:
    Look to the state in which he found his realm,
And left it; and his annals too behold,
    How to a minion first he gave the helm;
How grew upon his heart a thirst for gold,
    The beggar's vice, which can but overwhelm
The meanest hearts; and for the rest, but glance
Thine eye along America and France.

'Tis true, he was a tool from first to last
    (I have the workmen safe); but as a tool
So let him be consumed. From out the past
    Of ages, since mankind have known the rule
Of monarchs — from the bloody rolls amass'd
    Of sin and slaughter — from the Caesar's school,
Take the worst pupil; and produce a reign
More drench'd with gore, more cumber'd with the
                                                    slain
Ibid.

O Sov'reign of an isle renown'd
    For undisputed sway
Wherever o'er yon gulph profound
    Her navies wing their way,
With juster claim she builds at length
    Her empire on the sea,
And well may boast the waves her strength,
    Which strength restor'd to Thee.
William Cowper, *On the Benefit Received By
His Majesty from Sea Bathing.*

Covetous only of a virtuous praise,
His life a lesson to the land he sways:
To touch the sword with conscientious awe,
Nor draw it but when duty bids him draw;
To sheathe it in the peace-restoring close
With joy beyond what victory bestows;
Blest country, where these kingly glories shine;
Blest England, if this happiness be thine!
William Cowper, *Table Talk.*

So much unaffected good nature and propriety
appears in all he says and does that it cannot but
endear him to all; but whether anything can long
endear a King, or an angel in this strange factious
country I cannot tell. I have the best opinion
imaginable of him; not from anything he does or
says just now, but because I have a moral certainty
that he was in his nursery the honestest, most true
and good-natured child that ever lived. . . . What the
child was, the man most certainly is, in spite of temporary appearances.
Lady Hervey, in Alan Lloyd, *The Wickedest Age.*

There is a certain continuity in his prejudices, but hardly any in his policy.

F. S. Oliver, *The Endless Adventure.*

His madness can best be explained as the breakdown of too costly a struggle to maintain this artificial character — the reserve and equanimity imposed upon a hot temper and anxious nerves, to say nothing of his resolute fidelity to a hideous queen, and a regimen of violent and exaggerated abstinence designed to counteract strong passions and a tendency to fat.

Richard Pares, *George III and the Politicians.*

His maxims, in mid-career, were those of a conscientious bull in a china shop.

Ibid.

FROM Grief's afflictive bed uprose,
Great GEORGE resumes his septr'd sway;
    As Fate, in pity to our woes,
Restor'd his intellectual day.

Anthony Pasquin (John Williams), *An Ode, on His Majesty's Recovery.*

It is true that George III could only think of one thing at a time, but as that is also one of the most prominent characteristics of the English people, what might have proved a source of weakness served as an additional bond of union between him and them.

Sir Charles Petrie, *The Four Georges.*

How canst thou seriously declare
    That George the Third
With Cressy's Edward can compare,
    Or Harry? — 'Tis too bad, upon my word:
George is a clever King, I needs must own,
And cuts a jolly figure on the throne.

Peter Pindar (John Wolcot), *Instructions to A Celebrated Laureate.*

If he is to be blamed, it must not be for what he did, but for what he was — an unbalanced man of low intelligence. And if he is to be praised, it is because he attempted to discharge honourably tasks that were beyond his powers.

J. H. Plumb, *Men and Places.*

When an old lady asked him [John Wolcot, 'Peter Pindar'] if he did not think he was a very bad subject of our most pious King George, he replied, 'I do not know anything about that, Madam, but I *do* know the king has been a devilish good subject for me.'

Cyrus Redding, *Fifty Years Recollections.*

By a certain persistent astuteness; by the dexterous utilising of political rivalries; by cajoling some men and betraying others; by a resolute adroitness that turned disaster and even disease into instruments of his aim, the King realised his darling object, of converting the dogeship to which he had succeeded, into a real and to some extent a personal monarchy.

Lord Rosebery, *Pitt.*

For the King himself, he seems all good-nature and wishing to satisfy everybody; all his speeches are obliging. I saw him again yesterday, and was surprised to find the levee room had lost so entirely the air of the lion's den. This Sovereign don't stand in one spot, with his eyes fixed royally on the ground, and dropping bits of German news; he walks about and speaks to everybody. I saw him afterwards on the throne, where he is graceful and genteel, sits with dignity, and reads his answers to addresses well. . . .

Horace Walpole, Letter of 1760, in A. F. Scott, *Every One A Witness.*

Early one morning he met a boy in the stables at Windsor and said: 'Well, boy! what do you do? What do they pay you?' 'I help in the stable,' said the boy, 'But they only give me victuals and clothes.' 'Be content,' said George, 'I have no more.'

Beckles Willson, *George III.*

Ward of the Law! — dread Shadow of a King!
Whose realm had dwindled to one stately room;
Whose universe was gloom immersed in gloom,
Darkness as thick as life o'er life could fling,
Save haply for some feeble glimmering
Of Faith and Hope — if thou, by nature's doom,
Gently hast sunk into the quiet tomb,
Why should we bend in grief, to sorrow cling,
When thankfulness were best? — Fresh-flowing tears,
Or, where tears flow not, sigh succeeding sigh,
Yield to such after-thought the sole reply
Which justly it can claim. The Nation hears
In this deep knell, silent for threescore years
An unexampled voice of awful memory!

William Wordsworth, *On the Death of His Majesty.*

See also George Cruikshank, Lord Liverpool

GEORGE IV

1762–1830

Arthur [Wellington] is king of England, [Daniel]

O'Connell is king of Ireland, and I suppose I am Dean of Windsor.
> On himself, on the issue of Catholic Emancipation, February 1829, in Lord Colchester, *Diary*.

He was certainly a Sybarite, but his faults were exaggerated. He was to the full as true a man as his father. He would embrace you, kiss you — seized on the Duke of Wellington and kissed him. He certainly could be the most polished of gentlemen, or the exact opposite.
> Lord Aberdeen, in G. W. E. Russell, *Collections and Recollections*.

Alvanley, — who's your fat friend?
> Beau Brummel, at the Cyprian's Ball, 1813.

But still there is unto a patriot nation,
  Which loves so well its country and its king,
A subject of sublimest exultation —
  Bear it, ye Muses, on your brightest wing!
Howe'er the mighty locust, Desolation
  Strip your green fields, and to your harvest cling,
Gaunt famine never shall approach the throne —
Though Ireland starve, great George weighs twenty stone.
> Lord Byron, *Don Juan*, canto viii.

And where is 'Fum' the Fourth, our 'royal bird'?
Gone down, it seems, to Scotland to be fiddled
  Unto by Sawney's violin, we have heard:
'Caw me, caw thee' — for six months hath been hatching
This scene of royal itch and loyal scratching.
> *Ibid.*, canto ix.

As a son, as a husband, as a father, and especially as an *adviser of young men*, I deem it my duty to say that, on a review of his whole life, I can find no one good thing to speak of, in either the conduct or the character of this King; and, as an Englishman, I should be ashamed to show my head, if I were not to declare that I deem his reign (including his regency) to have been the most unhappy for the people that England has ever known.
> William Cobbett, in *Political Register*, 3 July 1830.

King George IV believed that he was at the Battle of Waterloo, and indeed commanded there, and his friends were a little alarmed; but Knighton [his Physician], who was a sensible man, said: 'His Majesty has only to leave off curaçao and rest assured he will gain no more victories.'
> Benjamin Disraeli, *Lothair*.

The dandy of sixty, who bows with a grace,

And has taste in wigs, collars, cuirasses, and lace;
Who to tricksters and fools leaves the State and its treasure,
And, while Britain's in tears, sails about at his pleasure.
> William Hone, *The Political House that Jack Built*.

How Monarchs die is easily explain'd
  And thus it might upon the Tomb be chisell'd,
As long as George the Fourth could *reign* he reign'd,
  And then he mizzled.
> Thomas Hood, *On a Royal Demise*.

A corpulent Adonis of fifty.
> Leigh Hunt, in *London Examiner*, 1813.

Ye politicians, tell me, pray,
  Why thus with woe and care rent?
This is the worst you can say, —
Some wind has blown the Whig away,
  And left the *Heir Apparent*.
> Charles Lamb, *Epigram*.

A noble, hasty race he ran,
  Superbly filthy and fastidious;
He was the world's first gentleman,
  And made the appellation hideous.
> W. M. Praed, Proposed *Epitaph*, 1825.

An oak tree cannot rise out of macaroons and madeira on the green baize of a card table.
> J. B. Priestley, *Prince of Pleasure*.

. . . the worst anchoring ground in Europe.
> Lord Thurlow, in Christopher Hobhouse, *Fox*.

GEORGES I, II, III AND IV

George the First was always reckoned
Vile, but viler George the Second;
And what mortal ever heard
Any good of George the Third?
When from earth the Fourth descended
God be praised, the Georges ended.
> Walter Savage Landor, *Epigram*.

GEORGE V
1865—1936

Thank God, I am an optimist, and I believe in the commonsense of the people of this country.
> On himself, Letter to a friend, in the *Dictionary of National Biography*.

. . . give yourself more . . . rest from the everlasting functions & speeches which get on one's nerves. I warned you what it would be like, these people think one is made of stone & that one can go on for ever. . . .
> On himself, Letter to the Prince of Wales, 12 October 1919.

The life of the King is moving slowly to its close.
> B.B.C. radio news bulletin, in Henry Channon, Diary, 20 January 1936.

. . . The prestige of the monarchy, and the influence of the monarchy, in the prudent and conscientious hands of King George have waxed rather than waned. . . . No Cabinet, however strong, could afford to disregard the difficulties and doubts put forward by a sovereign who has no interest in party politics, and whose experience is reinforced by continuity and immutability.
> Earl of Birkenhead, *America Revisited.*

The Prince of Wales gives one the feeling of being feeble and hating his position, none of the tact of his Father and, they say, obstinate.
> Kathleen Isherwood, Diary, 7 May 1910.

He is all right as a gay young midshipman. He may be all right as a wise old King. But the intervening period when he was Duke of York just shooting at Sandringham, is hard to manage or swallow. For seventeen years he did nothing at all but kill animals and stick in stamps.
> Harold Nicolson, Diary, 17 August 1949.

See also Alexander Fleming

GEORGE VI

1895—1952

Everything is going nowadays. Before long, I shall also have to go.
> On himself, in conversation with Vita Sackville-West, February 1948, in Harold Nicolson, Diary.

. . . looked lonely and wistful as all the males of this family do on State occasions.
> Henry Channon, observing the King's first levée, Diary, 6 February 1937.

The children can't go without me. I can't leave the King, and of course the King won't go.
> Queen Elizabeth's comment on leaving war-time London, 1941.

GEORGE, HENRY

1839—97 Economic Theorist

He was a tribune of the people, poor for their sake when he might have been rich by mere compromising; without official position for their sake when he might have had high offices by merely yielding a part of his convictions to expediency.
> Anon. obituary, in Henry George Jr, *The Life of Henry George.*

It is the thorough fusion of insight into actual facts and forces, with the recognition of their bearing upon what makes human life worth living, that constitutes Henry George one of the world's great social philosophers.
> John Dewey, in Charles A. Madison, *Critics and Crusaders.*

No 'mere theorist' was Henry George, as some of the tongues and pens of his time glibly dubbed him. He was not the inventor even of the theory which they were pleased to label his 'hobby', nor did he ever claim to be. He was the human mouthpiece of a primary truth.
> Louis F. Post, *The Prophet of San Francisco.*

His capacity for wrath, righteous wrath, was comprehensive. Show him a wrong, whether social or individual, whether it affected him or his or not, and he could say 'damn' — feel it, too — with more religious fervor than some pious people put in their prayers.
> *Ibid.*

GERMAIN, LORD GEORGE, see under SACK-VILLE, VISCOUNT

GERONIMO

1829—1909 Warrior of the Chiricahua Apache

I don't fight Mexicans with cartridges. I fight them with rocks and keep my cartridges to fight the white soldiers.
> On himself, in Britton Davis, *The Truth About Geronimo.*

Once I moved about like the wind. Now I surrender to you and that is all.
> On himself, upon surrender to General Crook in 1886, in Alexander B. Adams, *Geronimo.*

Forty five years old, erect as a lodge-pole, every outline of his symmetrical form indicating strength, endurance, arrogance. Abundant black hair draping his shoulders, stern, paint-smeared features, those vindictive eyes, the livid scar, Geronimo, the renegade, strategist, trickster, killer of palefaces — now under arrest, but still defiant.

> Joseph Clum (an Indian Agent, recollecting Geronimo upon moment of his capture in 1887), in Woodworth Clum, *Apache Agent.*

GERSHWIN, GEORGE

1898–1937 Composer

Gershwin had charisma — there was no doubt about that — since even in his late adolescence, world-famous popular-song composers and performers were impressed by him and sensed that he was quite special. There was something about his open sincerity (which some have confused with ingenuousness), his overbrimming enthusiasms, his electrifying excitement, the high sense of purpose which revealed themselves not only in what he said but in the way his face glowed as he spoke, that instantly made George Gershwin a dynamic, magnetizing presence.

> David Ewen, *George Gershwin: His Journey to Greatness.*

From Gershwin emanated a new American music not written with the ruthlessness of one who strives to demolish established rules, but based on a new native gusto and wit and awareness. His was a modernity that reflected the civilization we live in as excitingly as the headline in today's newspaper.

> Ira Gershwin, in Edward Jablonski and Lawrence D. Stewart, *The Gershwin Years.*

We remember a young man
Who remained naive in a sophisticated world
We remember a smile
That was nearly always on his face
A cigar
That was nearly always in his mouth
He was a lucky young man
Lucky to be so in love with the world
And lucky because the world was so in love with him.

> Oscar Hammerstein in Merle Armitage, ed., *George Gershwin.*

During his start in analysis I said to him 'Does it help your constipation George?' (I used to make fun of analysis).

He answered, 'No, but now I understand why I have constipation.'

> Oscar Levant, *Memoirs of an Amnesiac.*

Once when George was speaking about a girl he'd

been in love with who'd just married someone else, he said, 'If I wasn't so busy, I'd be upset.'

> *Ibid.*

. . . A creature of the glitter and tinsel of Tin Pan Alley, Broadway, Hollywood, and the news media, he also hobnobbed with some of the most important names in serious music and was often the object of their admiration. Gershwin was a living, breathing, striving, plotting mass of contradictions — always on the run, always out to conquer the world, always seeking the adulation of the vast, unknown public (possibly this was the love affair he was eternally seeking). . . . He was a child of his age who never became old enough to outlive his usefulness.

> Charles Schwartz, *George Gershwin: His Life and Music.*

Many musicians do not consider George Gershwin a serious composer. But they should understand that, serious or not, he is a composer — that is, a man who lives in music and expresses everything, serious or not, sound or superficial, by means of music, because it is his native language . . . he expressed musical ideas; and they were new. . . .

> Arnold Schoenberg, in Robert Kimball and Alfred Simon, *The Gershwins.*

See also Oscar Levant, Cole Porter

GIBBON, EDWARD

1737–94 Historian

To the University of Oxford I acknowledge no obligation; and she will as willingly renounce me for a son, as I am willing to disclaim her for a mother. I spent fourteen months at Magdalen College; they proved the fourteen months the most idle and unprofitable of my whole life.

> On himself, *Autobiography.*

A matrimonial alliance has ever been the object of my terror rather than of my wishes. I was not very strongly pressed by my family or my passions to propagate the name and race of the Gibbons, and if some reasonable temptations occurred in the neighbourhood, the vague idea never proceeded to the length of a serious negotiation.

> *Ibid.*

When I contemplate the common lot of mortality, I must acknowledge that I have drawn a high prize in the lottery of life.

> *Ibid.*

The time is not far distant, Mr Gibbon, when your most ludicrous self-complacency, . . . your affected moral purity perking up every now and then from the corrupt mass like artificial roses shaken off in the dark by some Prostitute on a heap of manure, your heartless scepticism, . . . your tumid diction, your monotonous jingle of periods, will be still more exposed and scouted than they·have been. Once fairly knocked off from your lofty bedizened stilts, you will be reduced to your just level and true standards.

William Beckford, note in a copy of *The Decline and Fall of the Roman Empire.*

Gibbon's style is detestable; but it is not the worst thing about him.

Samuel Taylor Coleridge, *Table Talk*, 15 August 1833.

When I read a chapter in Gibbon, I seem to be looking through a luminous haze or fog; figures come and go, I know not how or why, all larger than life, or distorted and discoloured; nothing is real, vivid, true; all is scenical, and, as it were, exhibited by candlelight.

Ibid.

Johnson's style was grand and Gibbon's elegant; the stateliness of the former was sometimes pedantic, and the polish of the latter was occasionally finial. Johnson marched to kettle-drums and trumpets; Gibbon moved to flutes and hautboys: Johnson hewed passages through the Alps, while Gibbon levelled walks through parks and gardens.

George Colman, *Random Records.*

His person looked as funnily obese
As if a pagod, growing large as man,
Had rashly waddled off its chimney piece,
To visit a Chinese upon a fan.
Such his exterior; curious 'twas to scan!
And oft he rapped his snuffbox, cocked his snout,
And ere his polished periods he began,
Bent forwards, stretching his forefinger out,
And talked in phrases round as he was round about.

George Colman, *The Luminous Historian.*

Another damned, thick, square book! Always scribble, scribble, scribble! Eh! Mr. Gibbon?

William Henry, Duke of Gloucester, attributed.

There is no Gibbon but Gibbon and Gibbon is his prophet. The solemn march of his cadences, the majestic impropriety of his innuendo are without rivals in the respective annals of British eloquence and British indelicacy.

Philip Guedella, *Supers and Supermen.*

Gibbon pulled together in his mind a mass of facts such as erudition never before, and seldom since, accumulated; and — here is the miracle — his attitude towards all those facts is consistent. If his account is remote from actuality, all its incidents are equidistant from the serene centre of his judgement. . . .

Desmond MacCarthy, *Criticism.*

Heard of the death of Mr. Gibbon, the calumniator of the despised Nazarene, the derider of Christianity. Awful dispensation! He too was my acquaintence. Lord, I bless thee, considering how much infidel acquaintence I have had, that my soul never came into their secret! How many souls have his writings polluted! Lord preserve others from their contagion.

Hannah More, Diary, 19 January 1774.

Those other mysteries of the past, love and religion . . . eluded him among the shades as they also escaped him in the bright daylight of his own life. But he saw enough to raise some statues from the dead, and it is glory enough for any writer that he can turn a living sun to light the mortal darkness of the past.

E. J. Oliver, *Gibbon and Rome.*

In some passages he drew the thread of his verbosity finer than the staple of his argument.

Richard Porson, in William Cooke, *Memoirs of Samuel Foote.*

Porson thought Gibbon's *Decline and Fall* beyond all comparison the greatest literary production of the eighteenth century, and was in the habit of repeating long passages from it. Yet I have heard him say that 'there could not be a better exercise for a schoolboy than to turn a page of it into English.'

Samuel Rogers, *Table Talk.*

Happiness is the word that immediately rises to the mind at the thought of Edward Gibbon. . . . His father died at exactly the right moment, and left him exactly the right amount of money.

Lytton Strachey, *Portraits in Miniature.*

Gibbon's style is probably the most exclusive in literature. By its very nature it bars out a great multitude of human energies. It makes sympathy impossible, it takes no cognisance of passion, it turns its back upon religion with a withering smile. But that was just what was wanted. Classic beauty came instead. By the penetrating influence of style — automatically, inevitably — lucidity, balance, and precision were everywhere introduced; and the

miracle of order was established over the chaos of a thousand years.
Ibid.

See also J.A. Froude, John Gay, Samuel Johnson

GIBBONS, GRINLING

1648–1721 Statuary

I asked if he were unwilling to be made known to some Great men; for that I believed it might turne to his profit; he answerd, he was yet but a beginner; but would yet not be sorry to sell off that piece; I asked him the price, he told me 100 pounds, In good earnest the very frame was worth the mony, there being nothing even in nature so tender, & delicate as the flowers & festoones about it, & yet the workε was very stronge; but in the Piece above 100 figures of men &c; I found he was likewise Musical, & very Civil, sober & discreete in his discourse: There was onely an old Woman in the house; so desiring leave to visit him sometimes, I tooke my leave.
John Evelyn, Diary, 18 January 1671.

GIBBONS, JAMES, CARDINAL

1834–1921 Clergyman

Our Cardinal stands with the same devotion to his country as Richelieu had for France, cultivating a citizenship as unstained as Newman, and while reaching out to even a broader audience than Cardinal Manning, he still remains preeminent in his unquestioned devotion to the Holy Church.
Archbishop Glennon, 1911, in James J. Walsh, *Our American Cardinals.*

The Cardinal is a trump.
Theodore Roosevelt, in Arline Boucher and John Tehan, *Prince of Democracy.*

GIBBONS, ORLANDO

1583–1625 Composer

It is proportion that beautifies every thing, this whole Universe consists of it, and Musicke is measured by it.
On himself, *First Set of Madrigals and Motets.*

The purists . . . on account of the confusion arising from all parts singing different words at the same

time, pronounce the style, in which his full anthems are composed, to be vicious.
Dr Charles Burney, *A General History of Music.*

The subjects of Orlando Gibbons's madrigals are so simple and unmarked, that if they were now to be executed by instruments alone, they would afford very little pleasure to the greatest friends of his productions, and those of the same period. At the time they were published, however, there was nothing better with which to compare them, and the best Music which good ears can obtain, is always delightful, till better is produced.
Ibid.

The best hand in England.
John Chamberlain, Letter to Sir Dudley Carleton, 12 June 1625.

The best Finger of the Age.
John Hacket, *Scrinia Reservata.*

GIFFORD, WILLIAM

1756–1826 Journalist, Editor of *Quarterly Review*

'Why slumbers Gifford?' once was ask'd in vain;
Why slumbers Gifford? let us ask again.
Are there no follies for his pen to purge?
Are there no fools whose backs demand the
                                    scourge . . .
Arouse thee, Gifford! be thy promise claim'd,
Make bad men better, or at least ashamed.
Lord Byron, *English Bards and Scotch Reviewers.*

Mr Gifford, in short, is possessed of that sort of learning which is likely to result from an overanxious desire to supply the want of the first rudiments of education; that sort of wit, which is the offspring of ill-humour or bodily pain; that sort of sense, which arises from a spirit of contradiction and a disposition to cavil at and dispute the opinions of others; and that sort of reputation, which is the consequence of bowing to established authority and ministerial influence.
William Hazlitt, *The Spirit of the Age.*

He was a man of rare attainments and many excellent qualities. . . . As a commentator he was capital could he have but suppressed his rancour against those who had preceded him in the task but a misconstruction or misinterpretation, nay the misplacing of a comma, was in Gifford's eyes a crime worthy of the most severe animadversions. The same fault of extreme severity went through his critical labours and in general he flagellated with so little pity that people lost their sense for the criminal's guilt in dislike of the savage pleasure which the executioner seemed to take in inflicting the punishment.

Sir Walter Scott, *Journal*, 17 January 1827.

GILBERT, JOHN

1897—1936 Actor

He was . . . a Latin Lover with a difference. He smiled a good deal rather than smouldering, and, instead of a smooth shining cap of hair close to his head, he sported an unruly, appealing mop of dark curls. His love-making lacked Valentino's menace but more than compensated for this by its impetuosity and sincerity. For, as Alexander Walker says, while Valentino was a romantic by adoption, John Gilbert was 'a romantic by conviction'. His was an impulsive passionate temperament off-screen as well as on, and this conveyed itself to audiences, who were captivated by the powerful display of sensibilities allied to his obvious physical charms. If he had any menace, it was perhaps in the rakish-mess of his moustache (grown to counterbalance a rather bulbous nose). The quality contrasted appealingly with his youthful impatience and sincerity in love-making. It was an intriguing combination.

Jane Mercer, *Great Lovers of the Movies*.

See also Errol Flynn

GILBERT, WILLIAM

1540—1603 Natural Philosopher

Gilbert shall live, till loadstones cease to draw,
Or British fleets the boundless oceans awe . . .
John Dryden, *To My Honor'd Friend, Dr. Charleton*.

Gilbert is often thought of solely as an experimenter, and it is true that he was one of the first to design experiments specifically to test theories, but, as has often happened in the history of science, his theoretical ideas have been forgotten, because of a mistaken view that a theory which is later superseded is not interesting, whereas carefully performed experiments are part of the permanent structure of science.

Mary B. Hesse, *Forces and Fields*.

In an age of empiricism and ignorance he rescued the study of the magnet from the atmosphere of occult mysticism with which it was surrounded, and placed it for ever on a scientific basis.

Silvanus P. Thompson, *Gilbert, of Colchester*.

Among the honourable Assertors of this Liberty, I must reckon *Gilbert*, who having found an admirable Correspondence between his *Terella*, and the great *Magnet* of the Earth, thought, this Way, to determine this great Question, and spent his Studies and Estate upon this Enquiry; by which *obiter*, he found out many admirable magnetical Experiments: this Man would I have adored, not only as the sole Inventor of Magneticks, a new Science to be added to the Bulk of Learning, but as the Father of the new Philosophy; *Cartesius [Descartes]* being but a Builder-upon his Experiments.

Sir Christopher Wren, Inaugural Address, Gresham College, 1657.

GILBERT, SIR WILLIAM SCHWENK

1836—1911 Dramatist, Lyricist

I feel like a lion in a den of Daniels.
On himself, in Hesketh Pearson, *Lives of the Wits*.

I am a crumbling man — a magnificent ruin, no doubt, but still a ruin — and like all ruins I look best by moonlight. Give me a sprig of ivy and an owl under my arm and Tintern Abbey would not be in it with me.

On himself, in Leslie Ayre, *The Gilbert and Sullivan Companion*.

I know how good I am, but I do not know how bad I am.
On himself, in *ibid*.

I found myself politely described in the official list as Mr. William Gilbert, *playwright*, suggesting that my work was analogical to that of a wheelwright, or a shipwright, as regards the mechanical character of the process by which our respective results are achieved. There is an excellent word, 'dramatist', which seems to fit the situation, but it is not applied until we are dead, and then we become dramatists, as oxen, sheep and pigs are transfigured into beef, mutton and pork on their demise. You never hear of a novel-wright or a picture-wright or a poem-wright, and why a playwright?
On himself, in *ibid*.

His foe was folly and his weapon wit.
Anthony Hope (Sir Anthony Hope Hawkins), *Inscription* on the memorial tablet to Gilbert on London's Victoria Embankment, 1915.

You say that in serious opera, you must more or less sacrifice yourself. I say that this is just what I have been doing in all our joint pieces.
Sir Arthur Sullivan, Letter to Gilbert, 12 March 1889.

Another week's rehearsal with WSG & I should have gone raving mad. I had already ordered some straw for my hair.

Sir Arthur Sullivan, Letter to Frank Burnard, 12 March 1896, about *The Chieftain*.

See also Henry Irving, Arthur Sullivan

GILBERT (W.S.) AND SULLIVAN (ARTHUR)

1836–1911 and 1842–1900

Gilbert and Sullivan did not like each other as men; nor did either want to write operettas.

Lord Robert Cecil, Introduction to *The Savoy Operas*.

With Gilbert and Sullivan I am sure one will have something better than the dull farce of the Colonel. I am looking forward to being greatly amused.

Oscar Wilde, Letter to George Grossmith, 1881, anticipating the first night of *Patience*.

That pair of sparkling guys.

Stephen Williams, in Leslie Ayre, *The Gilbert and Sullivan Companion*.

GILLRAY, JAMES

1757–1815 Caricaturist

The inventive faculties of such a mind as his — its aptitude to seize upon the most prominent features of passing events; the exhaustless fecundity of thought that occupied the remotest corner of his crowded compositions; his comprehensive knowledge of the human visage, its passions and expression; his original perceptions of physiognomy, as exhibited in a never-ending variety of masks, easily likened to all, and copied individually from none; his characters, like Shakespeare's, though creations of his own brain, yet fitting and consistent in form, action, and attributes.

H. Angelo, *Reminiscences*.

Gillray was one of those unaffected wights who accomplish what he undertook without scientific parade, and even without the appearance of rule, or preconcerted plan.

Ibid.

Poor Gillray was always hipped, and at last sank into that deplorable state of mental aberration, which verifies the couplet, so often quoted, wherein the consanguinity of wit to madness is so eminently proved.

Ibid.

Gillray is the man — for the man of the People.

George III, in *ibid.*

Gillray ridicules excess in terms of excess, but his ridicule is fired by a profound distrust, and by fear that sometimes seems to try to control a hostile, superhuman force by giving it a known human face. His hero, often John Bull in one form or another, is usually being imposed upon: a sucker. At other times, his caricatures seem to be statements of pure revulsion against the mendacious uplift of fashionable high art.

David Piper, *The English Face*.

GIRTIN, THOMAS

1775–1802 Watercolourist

Where his predecessors had been calm and dispassionate, Girtin was hot and impulsive. Where their brain had directed and controlled the hand, Girtin's brain, eye and hand were working in unison. Girtin knew that chance must play its part in a successful engagement with watercolour. One has the feeling that whereas the artists before him achieved their results by recognised principles and built up their work to a steady foreseen finish, Girtin never quite knew what had happened, or how the result was achieved, till he saw his drawing as an accomplished thing.

Martin Hardie, *Water-Colour Painting in Britain*.

If poor Tom had lived, I should have starved.

J. M. W. Turner, attributed.

GISSING, GEORGE ROBERT

1857–1903 Novelist

Strange how . . . I am possessed with the idea I shall not live much longer. Not a personal thought but is coloured by this conviction. I never look forward more than a year or two at the utmost, it is the habit of my mind, in utter sincerity, to expect no longer tenure of life than that. I don't know how this has come about; perhaps my absolute loneliness has something to do with it. Then I am haunted by the idea that I am consumptive; I never cough without putting a finger to my tongue, to see if there is a sign of blood.

On himself, Diary, June 1888.

Strange thing that I, all of whose joys and sorrows come from excess of individuality, should be remarkable among men for my yieldingness to everyone and anyone in daily affairs. No man I ever met *habitually* sacrifices his own pleasures, habits, intentions to those of a companion, purely out of fear to annoy the latter. It must be a sign of extreme weakness, and it makes me the slave of men unspeakably inferior.

Ibid., October 1888.

Some of his conclusions were conservative, but at heart he was a late-Victorian rebel against the power of convention. His rebellion was muted because he was preoccupied with failure. He had collected as great a store of specialized information about people who failed as Samuel Smiles had collected of people who succeeded.

Asa Briggs, *Victorian Cities*.

He seems to me above all a case of saturation, and it is mainly his saturation that makes him interesting — I mean especially in the sense of making him singular. The interest would be greater were his art more complete; but we must take what we can get, and Mr Gissing has a way of his own. The great thing is that his saturation is with elements that, presented to us in contemporary English fiction, affect us as a product of extraordinary oddity and rarity: he reeks with the savour, he is bowed beneath the fruits, of contact with the lower, with the lowest middle-class, and that is sufficient to make him an authority — *the* authority in fact — on a region vast and unexplored.

Henry James, in *Harper's Weekly*, 31 July 1897.

Gissing's novels are a protest against the form of self-torture that goes by the name of respectability. Gissing was a bookish, over-civilised man, in love with classical antiquity, who found himself trapped in a cold, smoky, Protestant country where it was impossible to be comfortable without a thick padding of money between yourself and the outer world. Behind his rage and querulousness there lay a perception that the horrors of life in late-Victorian England were largely unnecessary. The grime, the stupidity, the ugliness, the sex-starvation, the furtive debauchery, the vulgarity, the bad manners, the censoriousness — these things were unnecessary, since the puritanism of which they were a relic no longer upheld the structure of society.

George Orwell, *George Gissing*.

When I admit neglect of Gissing,
They say I don't know what I'm missing.
Until their arguments are subtler,
I think I'll stick to Samuel Butler.

Dorothy Parker, *Sunset Gun*.

See also Samuel Butler, Daniel Defoe

GLADSTONE, WILLIAM EWART

1809—98 Prime Minister

All the world over, I will back the masses against the classes.

On himself, Speech at Liverpool, June 1886.

He talked shop like a tenth muse.

Anon. comment on Gladstone's Budget speeches, in G. W. E. Russell, *Collections and Recollections*.

Ah, Oxford on the surface, *but* Liverpool below.

An old Whig's comment in the House of Commons on Gladstone's Budget, February 1860, in Walter Bagehot, *Biographical Studies: Mr Gladstone*.

His other pre-eminent characteristic is the union of theory and policy . . . in Mr Gladstone there is all the resource and policy of the heroes of Carlyle's worship, and yet he moves scrupulously along the lines of the science of statesmanship.

Lord Acton, Letter to Mrs Drew, 14 December 1880.

If there were no Tories, I am afraid he would invent them.

Lord Acton, Letter to Mrs Drew, 24 April 1881.

Who equals him in earnestness? Who equals him in eloquence? Who equals him in courage and fidelity to his convictions? If these gentlemen who say they will not follow him have anyone who is equal, let them show him. If they can point out any statesman who can add dignity and grandeur to the stature of Mr Gladstone, let them produce him!

John Bright, Speech at Birmingham, 22 April 1867.

An almost spectral kind of phantasm of a man — nothing in him but forms and ceremonies and outside wrappings.

Thomas Carlyle, *Letters*, March 1873.

An old man in a hurry.

Lord Randolph Churchill, Speech to the Electors of South Paddington, June 1886.

. . . they told me how Mr. Gladstone read Homer for fun, which I thought served him right.

Winston Churchill, *My Early Life*.

He was generally thought to be very pusillanimous in dealing with foreign affairs. That is not at all the impression I derived. He was wholly ignorant.

Lord Cromer, Letter to Lord Newton, 29 November 1913.

A sophisticated rhetorician, inebriated with the exuberance of his own verbosity, and gifted with an egotistical imagination, that can at all times command an interminable and inconsistent series of arguments to malign his opponents, and glorify himself.
    Benjamin Disraeli, Speech at Knightsbridge, July 1878.

Posterity will do justice to that unprincipled maniac Gladstone — extraordinary mixture of envy, vindictiveness, hypocrisy, and superstition; and with one commanding characteristic — whether Prime Minister, or Leader of Opposition, whether preaching, praying, speechifying or scribbling — never a gentleman!
    Benjamin Disraeli, Letter to Lord Derby, 1878.

What you say about Gladstone is most just. What restlessness! What vanity! And what unhappiness must be his! Easy to say he is mad. It looks like it. My theory about him is unchanged: a ceaseless Tartuffe from the beginning. That sort of man does not get mad at 70.
    Benjamin Disraeli, Letter to Lady Bradford, 3 October 1879.

. . . when you have to deal with an earnest man, severely religious and enthusiastic, every attempted arrangement ends in unintelligible correspondence and violated confidence.
    Benjamin Disraeli, on being in Opposition, Letter to Montague Corry, 29 January 1881.

He has not a single redeeming defect.
    Benjamin Disraeli, in A. K. Adams, *The Home Book of Humorous Quotations*.

What's the matter with Gladstone? He's all right.
    George and Weedon Grossmith, *Diary of a Nobody*.

If you were to put that man on a moor with nothing on but his shirt, he would become whatever he pleased.
    T. H. Huxley, in Ernest Scott, *Lord Robert Cecil's Goldfield Diary*.

I don't object to Gladstone always having the ace of trumps up his sleeve, but merely to his belief that the Almighty put it there.
    Henry Labouchere, in Hesketh Pearson, *Lives of the Wits*.

He has one gift most dangerous to a spectator, a vast command of a kind of language, grave and majestic, but of vague and uncertain import.
    T. B. Macaulay, *Essays*, 'Gladstone on Church and Sate'.

In Committee . . . Gladstone, thin haired, with gaunt penetrating face, is restless; talks to this one & that; wipes his spectacles; unfolds clean pocket handkerchief suggestive of Womankind.
    Alfred Munby, Diary, 4 July 1870.

'Well,' said Dizzy [being asked to define the distinction between 'misfortune' and 'calamity'], 'if Mr. Gladstone fell into the Thames, it would be a misfortune; but, if someone pulled him out, it would be a calamity.'
    Hesketh Pearson, *Lives of the Wits*.

The faculty of concealing his thoughts in words, of separating conviction from argument, was not the least striking of the great statesman's talents.
    Agnes Repplier, *Life of Gladstone*.

The defects of his strength grow on him. All black is very black, all white very white.
    Lord Rosebery, Diary, 4 August 1887.

Oddly enough, about half his compatriots, including a great many of the well-to-do, regarded him as either mad or wicked or both. When I was a child, most of the children I knew were conservatives, and they solemnly assured me, as a well-known fact, that Mr. Gladstone ordered twenty top-hats from various hatters every morning, and that Mrs. Gladstone had to go round after him and disorder them.
    Bertrand Russell, *Unpopular Essays*: 'Eminent Men I Have Known'.

Lord Palmerston was quite right when he said to me 'Mr. Gladstone is a very dangerous man'. And so vy. arrogant, tyrannical & obstinate with no knowledge of the World or human nature. Papa felt this strongly. Then he was a fanatic in religion — All this & much want of égard towards my feelings (tho' since I was so ill that was better) led him to make him a vy dangerous & unsatisfactory Premier.
    Queen Victoria, Letter to her eldest daughter, 24 February 1874.

She must say . . . that *she* has felt that Mr Gladstone would have liked to *govern* HER as Bismarck governs the Emperor.
    Queen Victoria, Memorandum to her Private Secretary, Gen. Sir Henry Ponsonby, 18 November 1874.

He speaks to Me as if I was a public meeting.
    Queen Victoria, in George W. E. Russell, *Collections and Recollections*.

See also Lord Derby, Benjamin Disraeli, Henry Irving, Lord Palmerston, Queen Victoria

GLASGOW, ELLEN ANDERSON GHOLSON

1874–1945 Author

But the inner substance of my work has been universal human nature — or as I have always believed — and if the great Balzac had not been ahead of me, I should have called [my] books the Human Comedy.
> On herself, Letter to James Branch Cabell, 28 October 1943.

I suppose I am a born novelist, for the things I imagine are more vital and vivid to me than the things I remember.
> On herself, undated Letter to J. Donald Adams, in Blair Rouse, *Ellen Glasgow*.

I dread to finish a novel for you know when one is writing the world of the book seems almost more real than the other. When you are done, life is a blind alley for a while. I don't mean I'm happy when I'm working, but I'm less happy when I'm not.
> On herself, in E. Stanly Godbold Jr, *Ellen Glasgow and the Woman Within*.

Highly individual in American letters is her ability to pass with equal authority from country to city, from rusticity to sophistication, from tobacco field to the drawing room, from irony to tragedy.
> Louis Auchincloss, *Ellen Glasgow*.

Thus Ellen Glasgow, the first novelist to picture the true Southern life, was also the first to take the South out of the South. She gave it in fiction a touch of the universal.
> Van Wyck Brooks, *The Confident Years: 1885–1915*.

Southern romance is dead. Ellen Glasgow has murdered it.
> Carl Van Doren, in E. Stanly Godbold Jr, *Ellen Glasgow and the Woman Within*.

She was capable of searching for a word or a phrase for hours, and then of getting up from her bed to write it down when it came to her unexpectedly in her sleep.
> Edward Wagenknecht, *Cavalcade of the American Novel*.

GLENDOWER, OWEN (OWAIN AB GRUFFYDD OF GLYNDWR)

1359?–1416? Welsh Prince

HOTSPUR: . . . sometimes he angers me

With telling me of the mouldwarp and the ant,
Of the dreamer Merlin and his prophecies,
And of a dragon and a finless fish,
A clip-wing'd griffin and a moulten raven,
A couching lion and a ramping cat,
And such a deal of skimble-skamble stuff
As puts me from my faith. I tell you what, —
He held me last night at least ten hours
In reckoning up the several devils' names
That were his lackeys: I cried hum, and well, go to,
But mask'd him not a word. O, he's as tedious
As a tired horse, a railing wife;
Worse than a smoky house: I had rather live
With cheese and garlic in a windmill, far,
Than feed on cates and have him talk to me
In any summer-house in Christendom.
> William Shakespeare, *Henry IV, Part I*, Act III, Scene i.

GLYN, ELINOR

1864–1943 Novelist

Would you like to sin
With Elinor Glyn
On a tiger skin?
Or would you prefer
To err
With her
On some other fur?
> Anon. rhyme.

Mrs. Glynn achieved the paradox of bringing not only 'good taste' to the colony [Hollywood], but also 'sex appeal'. She coined the word 'It', and taught Rudolph Valentino to kiss the palm of a lady's hand rather than its back.
> Cecil Beaton, Introduction to *Three Weeks*.

I didn't know. Truly, I didn't know. Mine is a life sheltered to the point of stuffiness. I attend no movies, for any motion-picture theater is as an enlarged and a magnificently decorated lethal chamber to me. I have read but little of Madame Glyn. I did not know that things like *It* were going on. I have misspent my days. When I think of all those hours I flung away in reading Henry James and Santayana, when I might have been reading of life, throbbing, beating, perfumed life, I practically break down. Where, I ask you, have I been, that no true word of Madame Glyn's literary feats has come to me?
> Dorothy Parker, in *New Yorker*, 26 November 1927.

Copyright cannot exist in a work of a tendency so grossly immoral as this.
> Justice Younger, in an action for infringement of

copyright brought by Elinor Glyn in 1915, over *Three Weeks*.

See also Clara Bow

GLYNN, JOHN

1722–79 Radical

Sir, he was a Wilkite, which I never was.
John Wilkes, attributed, in conversation with George II.

GODDARD, ROBERT HUTCHINGS

1882–1945 Scientist

It has been said that one cannot today design a rocket, construct a rocket, or launch a rocket without infringing one or more of the 214 Goddard patents.
G. Edward Pendray, in Eugene M. Emme, *The History of Rocket Technology*.

GODKIN, EDWIN LAWRENCE

1831–1902 Journalist

I have always told you that your fatal defect was the incapacity to make a popular blunder. Not that you can't blunder just as others; we are all quick enough at that; but all your blunders are on the wrong side; they don't even make friends. What I want to see is some good, idiotic, gushing, *popular* blundering.
Henry Adams, undated Letter to Godkin.

A superficial reader and thinker, Godkin's strength as a publicist and critic lay in his ability to use words persuasively — to clothe the ideas he embraced in seductively attractive garb and to make all others appear odious and ridiculous by comparison.
William M. Armstrong, *E. L. Godkin and American Foreign Policy 1865–1900*.

Impulsive, hypercritical, and intolerant though he sometimes was, his volatile pen may have had a distinct sobering effect on an age that needed forcefully to be reminded of its shortcomings. . . .
Ibid.

Godkin and *The Nation* fought against all the American shibboleths, the love of display, the love of conquest, the defence of war, the contempt for peace, the flouting of national creeds once held sacred, high tariffs, grafts and greed, machine government, boss government, ostentatious wealth and shoddy thinking.
Van Wyck Brooks, *New England: Indian Summer 1865–1915*.

To my generation, his was certainly the towering influence in all thought concerning public affairs, and indirectly his influence has certainly been more pervasive than that of any other writer of the generation, for he influenced other writers who never quoted him, and determined the whole current of discussion.
William James, in Rollo Ogden ed., *Life and Letters of Edwin Lawrence Godkin*.

Godkin the righteous, known of old,
Priest of the nation's moral health,
Within whose *Post* we daily read
The Gospel of the Rights of Wealth.
McCready Sykes, in William M. Armstrong, *E. L. Godkin and American Foreign Policy 1865–1900*.

In all the field of American daily journalism there is not one today to measure up to him as critic, writer, or scientific student of politics — nor one pen so brilliant, so brave, so free and so unrestricted.
Oswald Garrison Villard, *Some Newspapers and Newspaper-Men.*

GODOLPHIN, SIDNEY, EARL

1645–1712 Statesman

He affected being useful without popularity; and the inconsiderable sum of money, above his paternal estate, which he left at his death, showed that he had indeed been the nation's treasurer, and not his own, and effectually confuted the vile calumnies of his enemies and successors.
Sarah Churchill, Duchess of Marlborough, *Correspondence, Sketches and Opinions.*

Godolphin had been bred a page at Whitehall, and had early acquired all the flexibility and the self-possession of a veteran courtier. . . . 'Sidney Godolphin,' said Charles, 'is never in the way, and never out of the way'. This pointed remark goes far to explain Godolphin's extraordinary success.
T. B. Macaulay, *History of England.*

GODWIN, MARY, see under WOLLSTONECRAFT, MARY

GOLDSMITH, OLIVER

1728—74 Poet, Dramatist

Of our friend Goldsmith he said, 'Sir, he is so much afraid of being unnoticed that he often talks merely lest you should forget that he is in the company.' *Boswell*: 'Yes, he stands forward.' *Johnson*: 'True, Sir, but if a man is to stand forward he should wish to do it, not in an awkward posture, not in rags, not so as that he shall only be exposed to ridicule.' *Boswell*: 'For my part I like very well to hear honest Goldsmith talk away carelessly.' *Johnson*: 'Why, yes, Sir; but he should not like to hear himself.'
James Boswell, *Life of Johnson.*

I told him what Goldsmith had said to me a few days before, 'As I take my shoes from the shoemaker, and my coat from the tailor, so I take my religion from the priest.' I regretted this loose way of talking. *Johnson:* 'Sir, he knows nothing; he has made up his mind about nothing.'
Ibid.

One of the performers of the Haymarket Theatre, was observing to Foote, 'What a *hum-drum* kind of man Dr Goldsmith appeared to be in the Green-room, compared with the figure he made in his poetry.' — 'The reason of that,' said he, 'Is, the *Muses* are better companions than the *Players.*'
William Cooke, *Memoirs of Samuel Foote.*

Poor fellow! he hardly knew an ass from a mule, nor a turkey from a goose, but when he saw it on the table.
Richard Cumberland, *Memoirs.*

Here, Hermes, says Jove, who with nectar was mellow,
Go fetch me some clay — I will make an odd fellow:
Right and wrong shall be jumbled — much gold and some dross;
Without cause be he pleased, without cause be he cross;
Be sure as I work to throw in contradictions,
A great love of truth; yet a mind turn'd to fictions;
Now mix these ingredients, which warmed in the baking,
Turn to learning, and gaming, religion, and raking.
With the love of a wench, let his writings be chaste;
Tip his tongue with strange matter, his pen with fine taste;
That the rake and the poet o'er all shall prevail,
Set fire to the head, and set fire to the tail:
For the joy of each sex, on the world I'll bestow it:
This Scholar, Rake, Christian, Dupe, Gamester, and Poet,
Thro' a mixture so odd, he shall merit great fame,

And among brother mortals, be *Goldsmith* his name!
When on earth this strange meteor no more shall appear,
You Hermes, shall fetch him, — to make us sport here!
David Garrick, *Jupiter and Mercury, a Fable.*

Here lies Nolly Goldsmith, for shortness called Noll,
Who wrote like an angel, and talk'd like poor Poll.
David Garrick, *Impromptu Epitaph.*

At the breaking up of an evening at a tavern, he entreated the company to sit down, and told them if they would call for another bottle they should hear one of his *bon mots*: — they agreed, and he began thus: — 'I was once told that Sheridan the player, in order to improve himself in stage gestures, had looking glasses, to the number of ten, hung about his room, and that he practised before them; upon which I said, then there were ten ugly fellows together.' — The company were all silent: he asked why they did not laugh, which they not doing, he, without tasting the wine, left the room in anger.
Sir John Hawkins, *Life of Samuel Johnson, LL.D.*

Dr Goldsmith is one of the first men we have as an author at present, and a very worthy man too. He has been loose in his principles, but he is coming right.
Samuel Johnson, in James Boswell, *London Journal.*

I received one morning a message from poor Goldsmith that he was in great distress, and as it was not in his power to come to me, begging that I would come to him as soon as possible. I sent him a guinea and promised to come to him directly. I accordingly went as soon as I was drest, and found that his landlady had arrested him for his rent, at which he was in a violent passion. I perceived that he had already changed my guinea, and had got a bottle of Madeira and a glass before him. I put the cork into the bottle, desired he would be calm, and began to talk to him of the means by which he might be extricated. He then told me that he had a novel ready for the press, which he produced to me. I looked into it, and saw its merit; told the landlady I should soon return, and, having gone to a bookseller, sold it for sixty pounds. I brought Goldsmith the money, and he discharged his rent, not without rating his landlady in a high tone for having used him so ill.
Samuel Johnson, in James Boswell, *Life of Johnson.*

Goldsmith should not be forever attempting to shine in conversation: he has not the temper for it,

he is so much mortified when he fails. Sir, a game of jokes is composed partly of skill, partly of chance; a man may be beat at times by one who has not the tenth part of his wit. Now Goldsmith's putting himself against another, is like a man laying a hundred to one who cannot spare the hundred. It is not worth the man's while. A man should not lay a hundred to one, unless he can easily spare it, though he has a hundred chances for him, he can get but a guinea: and he may lose a hundred. Goldsmith is in this state. When he contends, if he gets the better, it is a very little addition to a man of his literary reputation: if he does not get the better, he is miserably vexed.
Ibid.

It is amazing how little Goldsmith knows. He seldom comes where he is not more ignorant than anyone else.
Ibid.

No man was more foolish when he had not a pen in his hand, or more wise when he had.
Ibid.

'Ah, Madam' cried he, 'Goldsmith was not scrupulous; but he would have been a great man if he had known the real value of his own internal resources.'
Samuel Johnson, in Fanny Burney, Diary, 1778.

He was of a sociable disposition. He had a very strong desire, which I believe nobody will think very peculiar or culpable, to be liked, to have his company sought after by his friends. To this end, for it was a system, he abandoned his respectable character as a writer or a man of observation to that of a character which nobody was afraid of being humiliated in his presence. This was his general principle, but at times, observing the attention paid to the conversation of others who spoke with more premeditation, and the neglect of himself, though greedy and impatient to speak, he then resolved to be more formal and to carry his character about with him. But as he found he could not unite both, he naturally relaxed into his old manner, and which manner, it must be acknowledged, met with all success for the purposes he intended it.
Sir Joshua Reynolds, *Notes on Goldsmith.*

Goldsmith's mind was entirely unfurnished. When he was engaged in a work, he had all his knowledge to find, which when he found, he knew how to use, but forgot it immediately after he had used it.
Ibid.

His nature is truant; in repose it longs for change: as on a journey it looks back for friends and quiet. He passes today in building an air-castle for tomor-

row, or in writing yesterday's elegy; and he would fly away this hour, but that a cage and necessity keep him.
W. M. Thackeray, *The English Humourists.*

It is this detached attitude and width of view that give Goldsmith his peculiar flavour as an essayist. Other writers pack their pages fuller and bring us into closer touch with themselves. Goldsmith, on the other hand, keeps just on the edge of the crowd so that we can hear what the common people are saying and note their humours.
Virginia Woolf, *Essays*: 'The Captain's Death Bed'.

See also Washington Irving

GOLDWYN, SAMUEL (SAMUEL GOLDFISH)
1882—1974 Motion Picture Producer

For years I have been known for saying 'Include me out.'
On himself, in an address at Balliol College, Oxford, 1 March 1945.

I am a rebel. I defy every convention. I make a picture to please me — if it pleases me there is a good chance that it will please other people. But it has to please me first.
On himself, in Lloyd Morris, *Not So Long Ago.*

A self-made man may prefer a self-made name.
Judge Learned Hand, on granting permission for Samuel Goldfish to change his name to Samuel Goldwyn, in Bosley Crowther, *The Lion's Share.*

I think of Samuel Goldwyn as an American Primitive, possessed of a superior instinct for the profession in which he finally found himself. This is not to say that he was not often duped or snowed or conned. Those who retain a part of their innocence are easy prey for those who have lost all theirs.
Garson Kanin, *Hollywood.*

'I was always an independent, even when I had partners,' said Goldwyn near the end of his career, when his pictures had won more than a score of Academy Awards. After falling out with two sets of partners, he never took on any more. For the next three decades he made films, close to 80 of them, by himself, always putting up his own money. 'It's not that I wanted all the profits,' he explains, 'But because I never wanted others to lose.'
Norman Zierold, *The Moguls.*

See also William Fox

GOMPERS, SAMUEL

1850–1924 Labor Leader

I am a working man and in every nerve, in every fiber, in every aspiration, I am on the side which will advance the interests of my fellow workingmen. I represent my side, the side of the toiling wage-earning masses in every act and in every utterance.

On himself, in Thomas R. Brooks, *Toil and Trouble, a History of American Labor.*

He strode full fronted throughout Europe, so sure of himself and his entire equipment of ideas, so conscious of the immense power of American labor behind him, that he scattered to the right and left all peoples of all nations. He told British, French, and Italian labor leaders, quite positively, what they must do to be saved.

Ray Stannard Baker, in B. Mandel, *Samuel Gompers.*

He sought to win recognition for labor in all civic aspects of American life: an entry and a hearing at the White House; an official voice in the government, i.e. the Department of Labor; respectful relations with employers; representation in community agencies, etc. To become respectable — this was Gompers', and Labor's aim.

Daniel Bell, *The Great Totem*, in Gerald Emanuel Stearn ed., *Gompers, Great Lives Observed.*

Samuel Gompers is the greatest totem of the American labor movement, and the rules of endogamy and other taboos he set down have become the prescribed rules of American labor.

Ibid.

He knew enough to advocate radical principles when these would advance his own position in the labor movement, and he was fully prepared to abandon them the moment he felt that they were proving to be an obstacle to his career.

Philip S. Foner, *History of the Labor Movement in the United States*, vol. 2.

Had Mr. Gompers been able to add six inches to his height, he would have been one of our great tragedians.

John Frey, in *Washington Herald*, 5 September 1938.

. . . a myriad-sided nature; a creature of poetry and practical action; a dreamer, yet a doer of the world's work; a soul of storm while diffusing sunshine — a combination of wholly opposing characteristics . . . I love him next to my mother.

Rose Lee Guard, in B. Mandel, *Samuel Gompers.*

Sam was very short and chunky with a big head that was bald in patches, resembling a child suffering with ringworm. He had small snapping eyes, a hard cruel mouth, wide with thin drooping lips, heavy jaws, a personality vain, conceited, petulant and vindictive.

'Big Bill' Haywood, *The Autobiography of William D. Haywood.*

He believed the government should do nothing for labor that labor could do for itself through its trade unions.

B. Mandel, *Samuel Gompers.*

. . . wholly un-American in appearance: short; with large eyes, dark complexion, heavy-lined face, and hair slightly curly but looking motheaten — he was impressive. As I sat in the audience . . . I wrote the name 'Marat' on a slip of paper and handed it to my companion. He nodded.

Walter G. Merrit, *Destination Unknown.*

The A.F. of L. voted down the socialism that aims for peace through means of the ballot, but it did not vote down the socialism that President Gompers stands for — mob force socialism. It is this mob force socialism that we have to combat as much as the other.

David M. Parry, in Max Hayes, 'The World of Labor', in *International Socialist Review*, January 1904.

[The advent of Gompers] signified a labour movement reduced to an opportunistic basis, accepting the existence of capitalism and having for its objective the enlargement of the bargaining power of the wage-earner in the sale of his labour.

Selig Perlman, in Stuart Bruce Kaufman, *Samuel Gompers and the Origins of the American Federation of Labor, 1848–1896.*

All his vital expressions rose and fell together as though controlled by some inner mechanism. One moment, the mobile mask would be cunningly furtive and quizzical, then intimately and wistfully kind; then again it would glow with a self-righteous passion that in retrospect seemed grotesque. It was a congenitally histrionic face, and its outlay in spiritual energy bespoke an enormous vitality.

Benjamin Stolberg, in B. Mandel, *Samuel Gompers.*

Like a piece of worn-out buffalo robe which has lain in the garret and been chewed by the moths since 1890, and then been thrown out in the rain and laid in the gutter for a year or two, and then been dragged by a puppy dog to cut his teeth on.

Mark Sullivan, description of Gompers' hair,

'Labour in the New World', in *Colliers'*, 21 December 1918.

See also John L. Lewis

GORDON, CHARLES GEORGE (GORDON OF KHARTOUM)

1833–86 Soldier

I am not the *rescued lamb*, and I will not be.
On himself, Diary, September 1884.

It is quite painful to see men tremble so when they come to see me, that they cannot hold the match to their cigarette.
On himself, Diary, September 1884.

In ten or twelve years' time . . . some of us will be quite passé; no one will come and court us. . . . Better a ball in the brain than to flicker out unheeded.
On himself, Diary, November 1884.

I like my religious views, they were and are a greatcoat to me.
On himself, in Anthony Nutting, *Gordon: Martyr and Misfit*.

Too late! Too late to save him.
In vain, in vain, they tried.
His life was England's glory,
His death was England's pride.
Anon. song after Gordon's death.

A man who habitually consults the Prophet Isaiah when he is in a difficulty is not apt to obey the orders of any one.
Lord Cromer, Letter to Lord Granville, 1884.

He has an immense name in Egypt – he is popular at home. He is a strong but sensible opponent of slavery. He has a small bee in his bonnet.
Lord Granville, Letter to W. E. Gladstone, November 1883.

Horrible as it is to us I imagine that the manner of his death was not unwelcome to himself. Better wear out than rust out, and better break than wear out.
T. H. Huxley, Letter to S. J. Donnelly, February 1885.

The man of England, circled by the sands.
George Meredith, *Epigram*.

. . . One of the very few friends I ever had who came

up to my estimate of the Christian hero.
Lord Wolseley, in Julian Symons, *England's Pride*.

GORDON, GEORGE HAMILTON, see under ABERDEEN, EARL OF

GOULD, (JASON) 'JAY'

1836–92 Financier

I needed the good will of the legislature of four states. I formed the legislative bodies with my own money. I found that it was cheaper that way.
On himself, in André Siegfried, *America at Mid-Century*.

In a Republican district, I was a Republican; in a Democratic district I was a Democrat; in a doubtful district I was doubtful; but I was always for Erie!
On himself, in Matthew Josephson, *The Robber Barons*.

. . . one of the most sinister figures that have ever flitted bat-like across the vision of the American people. . . .
Anon., in *ibid.*

Gould, who had only *agents* rather than confidants or allies, seemed to enjoy most the role of 'the one against all'; self-contained, impassive to all pleas or reproaches, he seemed content with his loneliness. For most of his days he lived . . . 'in the necessary isolation of a ship's commander when on sea duty.' At times he seemed to soar above the others like a destroying angel.
Matthew Josephson, *ibid.*

GOWER, JOHN

1325?–1408 Poet

O moral Gower, this book I directe
To thee.
Geoffrey Chaucer, *Troilus and Criseyde*, Book V.

He that reads the works of Gower will find smooth numbers and easy rhymes, of which Chaucer is supposed to have been the inventor, and the French words, whether good or bad, of which Chaucer is charged as the inventor.
Samuel Johnson, *Dictionary of the English Language*

If there had been no Chaucer, Gower would have

had a respectable place in history as the one 'correct' English poet of the Middle Ages, as the English culmination of that courtly medieval poetry which had its rise in France and Provence two or three hundred years before. The prize for style would have been awarded to Gower; as it is, he deserves rather more consideration than he has generally received in modern times. It is easy to pass him over and to say that his correctness is flat, his poetical art monotonous. But at the very lowest valuation he did what no one else except Chaucer was able to do; he wrote a large amount of verse in perfect accordance with his own critical principles, in such a way as to stand minute examination; and in this he thoroughly expressed the good manners of his time.

W. P. Ker, *Medieval English Literature.*

In order to feel fully how much he [Chaucer] achieved, let any one subject himself to a penitential course of reading in his contemporary Gower. . . . Gower has positively raised tediousness to the precision of science, he has made dullness an heirloom for the students of our literary history. . . . He is the undertaker of the fair mediaeval legend, and his style has the hateful gloss, that seemingly unnatural length, of a coffin.

James Russell Lowell, *My Study Windows.*

If Chaucer had not existed, the compositions of John Gower, the next poet in succession, would alone have been sufficient to rescue the reigns of Edward III and Richard II from the imputation of barbarism.

Thomas Warton, *History of English Poetry.*

GRABLE, (ELIZABETH RUTH) BETTY

1916—73 Actress

[I'm] strictly an enlisted man's girl.
On herself, in Richard Schickel, *The Stars.*

One of the most famous pin-ups of all time. . . . The classic pose — the one-piece swimming suit, high heels, and delicate ankle bracelet — seemed to say, 'Follow me home, boys, I'm what you're fighting for'.

Mark Gabor, *The Pin Up: A Modest History.*

The greatest of all the pin-ups was undoubtedly Betty Grable. She was the 'Gam Girl', on account of her fabulous legs — insured by Twentieth Century Fox for $1,000,000 (more even than Astaire's). Grable's appeal is difficult to understand today. She wasn't a siren; she wasn't even particularly erotic.

. . . She was a warm-hearted hoyden with an ever-ready shoulder to cry on, a brash, slightly vulgar attraction, and a homeliness, a feeling of being real, that the other pin-ups never had. The guy in his bunk at sea, on watch in some jungle outpost, or waiting on stand-by through long nights to fly the next mission, could look at Grable and those legs and feel that, given the chance, he could find solace with this brand of sympathetic, almost maternal woman. He didn't have a hope in hell of making it with [Ann] Sheridan or the others, but Grable, he felt, could be had.

Clyde Jeavons and Jeremy Pascall, *A Pictorial History of Sex in the Movies.*

Her special forte was the backstage musical in which her famous legs were put on display on the most absurd of pretexts. Miss Grable's beauty — if that is the word for it — was of the common sort. Nor did she offer much in the way of character maturity. She was, at best, a sort of great American floozie, and her appeal to lonely GIs was surely that of every hash-house waitress with whom they ever flirted.

Richard Schickel, *The Stars.*

GRACE, WILLIAM GILBERT

1848—1915 Cricketer

I puts the ball where I likes, and that beggar, he puts it where he likes.

J. C. Shaw (Nottinghamshire bowler), in Lord Hawke, *Memorial Biography of W. G. Grace.*

W. G. Grace was by no conceivable standard a good man. He was in theory a country doctor, took ten years to get qualified, and must have been a much worse one than Doyle, particularly since Grace played cricket six days a week all the summer. At that time cricket was the national game. Grace was the star cricketer and one of the greatest of all Victorian heroes. He played as an amateur, and amateurs were not supposed to be paid. That did not prevent Grace making large sums of money out of the game. He was a cheat, on and off the cricket field. He exhibited almost the exact opposite of Doyle's virtues, including extreme meanness, trickery, and, perhaps oddest of all, physical cowardice.

C. P. Snow, Introduction to A. C. Doyle, *The Case-book of Sherlock Holmes.*

GRANT, ULYSSES SIMPSON

1822—85 Eighteenth United States President

The truth is I am more of a farmer than a soldier. I take little or no interest in military affairs, and, although I entered the army thirty-five years ago and have been in two wars, in Mexico as a young lieutenant, and later, I never went into the army without regret and never retired without pleasure.

On himself, to Otto von Bismarck, in W. E. Woodward, *Meet General Grant.*

I know only two tunes; one of them is 'Yankee Doodle' and the other isn't.

On himself, in *ibid.*

I had been a light smoker previous to the attack on Donelson. . . . In the accounts published in the papers I was represented as smoking a cigar in the midst of the conflict; and many persons, thinking, no doubt, that tobacco was my chief solace, sent me boxes of the choicest brands. . . . As many as ten thousand were soon received. I gave away all I could get rid of, but having such a quantity on hand I naturally smoked more than I would have done under ordinary circumstances. I have continued the habit ever since.

On himself, to General Porter, in *ibid.*

Since the beginning of the government, we have had no elected President who has raised up such hosts of bitter enemies in his own political party as Grant. . . . The bitter enmities incurred are all personal, and they show that his temper incapacitates him for success in a political position. His intellect is so narrow that nobody can respect him and his jealous temper causes him to regard every Republican statesman who can possibly become a rival as his personal enemy.

Anon., in *New York World,* 14 March 1871.

To the politicians it seemed that Grant regarded the presidency 'as a candy cornucopia from which he is to extract a sugar plum for the good little boys who have given him some of their plum cake.'

Ibid., 9 March 1869.

With the conventional air of assumed confidence, everyone publicly assured everyone else that the President himself was the saviour of the situation, and in private assured each other that if the President had not been caught this time, he was sure to be trapped the next, for the ways of Wall Street were dark and double.

Henry Adams, *The Education of Henry Adams.*

Grant was five feet eight inches and slightly stooped. He had cold blue eyes and a big jaw hidden behind a scrubby, messy light brown beard which went well with his scrubby, messy uniform.

Herbert Agar, in Lord Longford, *Abraham Lincoln.*

The greatest general of the North was U. S. Grant, who is not to be confused with U.S. Mail or U.S. Steel. In a picture of the Northern generals, all of whom have identical untidy black whiskers, he is usually the one in the center with his coat unbuttoned.

Richard Armour, *It All Started With Columbus.*

All his military greatness came of the plainest possible qualities, developed to an astonishing degree.

Adam Badeau, in W. E. Woodward, *Meet General Grant.*

. . . The people are tired of a man who has not an idea above a horse or a cigar. . . .

Joseph Brown, 12 December 1871, in William B. Hesseltine, *Ulysses S. Grant.*

He is an incurable borrower and when he wants to borrow he knows of only one limit — he wants all you've got. When I was poor he borrowed fifty dollars of me; when I was rich he borrowed fifteen thousand men.

General Bruckner, to Mark Twain, in Bernard DeVoto ed., *Mark Twain in Eruption.*

Early in 1869 the cry was for 'no politicians' but the country did not mean 'no brains'.

William Clafin, Letter to W.E. Chandler, 22 August 1870.

He does not march, nor quite walk, but pitches along as if the next step would bring him on his nose.

Richard Henry Dana, in William B. Hesseltine, *Ulysses S. Grant.*

[Grant could] afford to be a deaf-and-dumb candidate, but this country can't afford to elect a deaf-and-dumb President.

Horace Greeley, in *New York Tribune,* 1867.

How is it that Grant, who was behind at Fort Henry, drunk at Donelson, surprised at Shiloh, and driven back from Oxford, Miss., is still in command? . . .

Murat Halstead, Letter to Salmon P. Chase, 19 February 1863.

We all thought Richmond, protected as it was by our splendid fortifications and defended by our army of veterans, could not be taken. Yet Grant turned his face to our Capital, and never turned it away until we had surrendered. Now, I have carefully searched the military records of both ancient and modern history, and have never found Grant's superior as a general. I doubt if his superior can be found in all history.

Robert E. Lee, in James Grant Wilson, *General Grant*.

When Grant once gets possession of a place, he holds on to it as if he had inherited it.
    Abraham Lincoln, Letter to General Benjamin Butler, 22 June 1864.

I can't spare this man; he fights.
    Abraham Lincoln, in J. F. C. Fuller, *The Generalship of Ulysses S. Grant*.

For 'twas there to our Ulysses
    That Lee gave up the fight
Now boys, 'To Grant for President
    And God defend the right!'
    Miles O'Reilly, in *New York Tribune*, 2 September 1868.

Grant stood by me when I was crazy, and I stood by him when he was drunk, and now we stand by each other.
    General William Tecumseh Sherman, attributed, circa 1870, in Robert Debs Heinl Jr, *The Dictionary of Military and Naval Quotations*.

I knew him as a cadet at West Point, as a lieutenant of the Fourth Infantry, as a citizen of St Louis, and as a growing general all through the bloody Civil War. Yet to me he is a mystery and I believe he is a mystery to himself.
    General William Tecumseh Sherman, in Warren W. Hassler Jr, *Commanders of the Army of the Potomac*.

I always liked the way Grant said that he knew what the other generals would do because after all they had been to school at West Point together and the Mexican war together and the others acted like generals but he acted like one who knew just what the generals opposite him would do because that one had always been like that at West Point and after all what can anybody change to, they have to be what they are and they are so Grant always knew what to do.
    Gertrude Stein, *Everybody's Autobiography*.

He is a scientific Goth, resembling Alaric, destroying the country as he goes and delivering the people over to starvation. Nor does he bury his dead, but leaves them to rot on the battlefield.
    John Tyler, Letter to Sterling Price, 7 June 1864.

GRANVILLE, EARL, see under CARTERET, JOHN

GRANVILLE, AUGUSTUS BOZZI

1783—1872 Physician

You know Mrs. Carlyle said that Owen's sweetness reminded her of sugar of lead. Granville's was that plus butter of antimony!
    Jane Welsh Carlyle, as reported in Leonard Huxley, *Life and Letters of Thomas Henry Huxley*.

GRATTAN, HENRY

1746—1820 Irish Politician

Grattan, after all, was no great thing — full of wit and fire and folly — more failure than success in his antithesis, and his piety and religious cant was offensive, as, after all, whatever may be its merit in an individual, it is only used in a speech for the worst of purposes.
    H. G. Bennett, in *The Creevey Papers*.

Ever glorious Grattan! the best of the good!
    So simple in heart, so sublime in the rest!
With all which Demosthenes wanted endued,
    And his rival or victor in all he possess'd.

Ere Tully arose in the zenith of Rome,
    Though unequall'd, preceded, the task was
                                    begun —
But Grattan sprung up like a god from the tomb
    Of ages, the first, last, the saviour, the *one*!

With the skill of an Orpheus to soften the brute;
    With the fire of Prometheus to kindle mankind;
Even Tyranny listening sate melted or mute,
    And Corruption shrunk scorch'd from the glance
                                    of his mind.
    Lord Byron, *The Irish Avatar*.

I was much struck with the simplicity of Grattan's manners in private life. They were odd, but they were natural. Curran used to take him off, bowing to the very ground, and 'thanking God' he had no peculiarities of gesture or appearance. Rogers used to call him 'a sentimental harlequin,' but Rogers backbites everybody, and Curran, who used to quiz his great friend Godwin to his very face, could hardly respect a fair mark of mimicry in another.
    Lord Byron, in Stephen Gwynn, *Henry Grattan and his times*.

On a cool and critical contemplation of his original mind and character, it may be fearlessly asserted that he was more a poet than an orator or statesman. It is confessedly admitted on all sides that he is the most poetical of orators, ancient or modern.

Nor does his failure in the poems he wrote contradict in any degree the theory now put forward, namely, that Grattan is to be considered rather as the poet of Irish political passion and national ambition, than as the statesman expounding her wants and providing for her necessities.
D. O. Madden, *Speeches of the Rt. Hon. Henry Grattan.*

To all Irishmen he gave the wing-beat of his words and the example of his integrity; so that both Parnell and Pearse looked back across the bleak stretch of the nineteenth century and knew him for a man whose ways might not be theirs, whose name might be forgotten, but whose work had become part of the structure of Ireland.
R. J. McHugh, *Henry Grattan.*

GRAY, ASA

1810—88 Scientist

At Dubuque I first met a number of men of whom I had often heard but with whom I had not previously come into direct contact. Most prominent among them was Gray. Someone, I remember, looked out of the window and said: 'There goes Asa Gray. If he should say that black was white, I should see it already turning whitish.'
David Starr Jordan, *The Days of a Man.*

GRAY, THOMAS

1716—71 Poet

I shall be but a shrimp of an author.
On himself, Letter to Horace Walpole, 25 February 1768.

Gray, a born poet, fell upon an age of reason.
Matthew Arnold, *Essays in Criticism*, 'Gray'.

Mr Johnson attacked Mr Gray, and said he was a dull fellow. I said he was reserved and might appear dull in company. But surely he was not dull in his poetry, though he might be extravagant. 'No, Sir,' said Mr Johnson. 'He was dull in company, dull in his closet, dull everywhere. He was dull in a new way; and this made many people think him great. He was a mechanical poet.'
James Boswell, *London Journal*, 28 March 1775.

Shut away in the ivory tower of his intense shyness, Gray's conception of Gothic was gradually transformed. He inherited the view that Gothic buildings

were a haphazard jumble of ornaments which might, at best, be individually attractive. He grew to have a serious love of Gothic architecture and an historical attitude towards it not very different from our own. . . . Despite his retired life Gray had some influence on the taste of his time; but he was too lazy, too sensitive, perhaps, to be a very effective champion of the Gothic Revival.
Kenneth Clark, *The Gothic Revival.*

His Letters are inimitably fine. If his poems are sometimes finical and pedantic, his prose is quite free from affectation. He pours his thoughts out upon paper as they arise in his mind; and they arise in his mind without pretence, or constraint, from the pure impulse of learned leisure and contemplative indolence. He is not here on stilts or in buckram; but smiles in his easy chair, as he moralises through the loopholes of retreat, on the bustle and raree-show of the world. . . . He had nothing to do but to read and to think, and to tell his friends what he read and thought. His life was a luxurious, thoughtful dream.
William Hazlitt, *Lectures on the English Poets.*

Awful, pleasing, persecuted Gray.
James Hurdis, *Tears of Affection.*

Sir, I do not think Mr Gray a superior sort of poet. He has not a bold imagination, nor much command of words. The obscurity in which he has involved himself will not make us think him sublime.
Samuel Johnson, in James Boswell, *London Journal*, 25 June 1763.

Mr Gray's love of and knowledge of Gothic architecture are all known; he contended particularly for the superiority of its effect in churches; and, besides, admired the elegance and good taste of many of its ornaments. I remember him saying, though I have forgotten the building to which the observation was applied, 'Call this what you will, but you must allow that it is beautiful.'
Norton Nichols, *Reminiscences.*

I would rather have written that poem [The Elegy], gentlemen, than take Quebec.
James Wolfe, the night before he was killed at Quebec, attributed.

He failed as a poet, not because he took too much pains, and so extinguished his animation, but because he had very little of that fiery quality to begin with, and all his pains were of the wrong sort. . . . I do not profess to be a person of very various reading; nevertheless, if I were to pluck out of Gray's tail all the feathers which I know belong to other birds, he

would be left very bare indeed.
William Wordsworth, in R. P. Gillies, *Memoirs.*

See also A. E. Housman, Sir Walter Scott

GREELEY, HORACE

1811–72 Editor, Political Leader

. . . tow-headed, and half-bald at that . . . slouching in dress; goes bent like a hoop, and so rocking in his gait that he walks down both sides of the street at once.
On himself, in William Harlan Hale, *Horace Greeley, Voice of the People.*

. . . the repentant male Magdalen of New York journalism.
James Gordon Bennett Sr, in Glyndon G. Van Deusen, *Horace Greeley, Nineteenth-Century Crusader.*

. . . poor Greeley . . . nincompoop without genius.
Ibid.

With such a head as is on his shoulders the affairs of the nation could not, under his direction, be wisely administered; with such manners as his, they could not be administered with common decorum; with such associates as he has taken to his bosom, they could not be administered with common integrity.
William Cullen Bryant, referring to Greeley as a presidential candidate, in Charles H. Brown, *William Cullen Bryant.*

To each fanatical delusion prone,
He damns all creeds and parties but his own;
And faction's fiercest rabble always find
A kindred nature in the Tribune's mind;
Ready each furious impulse to obey,
He raves and ravens like a beast of prey.
William J. Grayson, in William Harlan Hale, *Horace Greeley, Voice of the People.*

He was experimental, self-contradictory, explosive, irascible, and often downright wrongheaded. He preached thrift and could not practice it himself. He promoted conservative Whiggism and became a socialist immediately thereafter. He talked pacifism, but turned into one of the foremost fomentors of the Civil War.
William Harlan Hale, in *ibid.*

His very look and bearing were cast in part: his moon-faced stare, his flapping trousers, his squeaky slang, his sputtering profanities, his unpredictable

oddities, and his general air of an owlish, rustic sage all helped make a popular legend of him in his lifetime.
Ibid.

An incorrigible idealist, clearly, was this Yankee plebian . . . a strange, child-like figure, with his round moon-face, eyes blinking through spectacles, and a fringe of whiskers that invited the pencil of the cartoonist — yet carrying the sorrows of the world in his heart and vexing his soul with all the problems of society. . . .
Vernon Parrington, in Frank Luther Mott, *American Journalism, A History: 1690–1960.*

GREENAWAY, (CATHERINE) KATE

1846–1901 Artist, Illustrator

She ruled in a small realm of her own, like the island-valley of Avalon, 'deep-meadowed, happy, fair with orchard lawns', a land of flowers and gardens, of red brick houses with dormer windows, peopled by toddling boys and little girls clad in long, high-waisted gowns, muffs, pelisses and mob-caps. In all her work there is an atmosphere of an earlier peace and simple piety that recalls Izaak Walton and 'fresh sheets that smell of lavender'. The curtains and frocks of dimity and chintz, the houses with the reddest and pinkest of bright bricks, the 'marigolds all in a row' in gardens green as can be, . . . the lads and lasses with rosy cheeks and flaxen curls, all make for what is best in the best of all possible worlds.
Martin Hardie, *Water-Colour Painting in Britain.*

GREENE, ROBERT

1560?–92 Dramatist, Pamphleteer

Greene, is the pleasing Object of an eie;
Greene, pleasde the eies of all that lookt uppon him.
Greene, is the ground of everie Painters die:
Greene, gave the ground, to all that wrote upon him.
Nay more the men, that so Eclipst his fame:
Purloynde his Plumes, can they deny the same?
'R.B., Gent', *Greene's Funeralle*

A rakehell: a makeshift: A scribling foole:
A famous Bayrd in Citty, and Schoole.
Now sicke as a dog: and ever Brainesick:
Where such a raving, and desperate Dick?
Gabriel Harvey, *Four Letters and Certain Sonnets.*

See also Thomas Nashe

GREENOUGH, HORATIO

1805—52 Sculptor

The men who have reduced locomotion to its simplest elements, in the trotting wagon and the yacht 'America', are nearer to Athens at this moment than they who would bend the Greek temple to every use. I contend for Greek principles, not Greek things.

On himself, in Sylvia E. Crane, *White Silence*.

Greenough had thus essayed a resolution of the central problem inherent in evolving an American aesthetic. From the wellsprings of antiquity through his neoclassical experience in Italy, he discovered 'the germ of future architecture.' Aided by the evolutionists, he found confirmation of his theories in nature through the fundamental law of adaptation. It was his unique contribution to fuse the strands of evolution and neo-classicism into one organic principle of functionalism in architecture. He thus evolved the rockbound law that form should follow function and be subservient to it, nothing more.

Sylvia E. Crane, *ibid*.

[Greenough's] tongue was far cunninger in talk than his chisel [was] to carve.

Ralph Waldo Emerson, Letter to Thomas Carlyle, in Sylvia E. Crane, *ibid*.

GREGORY, ISABELLA AUGUSTA, LADY

1852—1932 Author

Now that the Abbey Players are world-renowned, I begin to realize that with such an audience and such actors an author is hardly needed. Good acting covers a multitude of defects. It explains the success of Lady Gregory's plays.

Oliver St J. Gogarty, *As I Was Going Down Sackville Street*.

She has been to me mother, friend, sister and brother. I cannot realize the world without her — she brought to my wavering thoughts steadfast nobility. All day the thought of losing her is like a conflagration in the rafters. Friendship is all the house I have.

William Butler Yeats (written during an illness of Lady Gregory's), *Journal*, 4 February 1909.

Sound of a stick upon the floor, a sound
From somebody that toils from chair to chair;
Beloved books that famous hands have bound,
Old marble heads, old pictures everywhere;
Great rooms where travelled men and children found

Content or joy; a last inheritor
Where none has reigned that lacked a name and fame
Or out of folly into folly came.

William Butler Yeats, *Coole Park and Ballylee*.

GRENVILLE, GEORGE

1712—70 Prime Minister

Grenville's character was stern, melancholy and pertinacious. Nothing was more remarkable in him than his inclination always to look on the dark side of things. He was the raven of the House of Commons, always croaking defeat in the midst of triumphs, and bankruptcy with an overflowing exchequer.

T. B. Macaulay, *Essays*: 'Chatham'.

We are inclined to think, on the whole, that the worst administration which has governed England since the Revolution was that of George Grenville. His public acts may be classed under two heads, outrages on the liberty of the people, and outrages on the dignity of the crown.

Ibid.

. . . a fatiguing orator and indefatigable drudge; more likely to disgust than to offend. . . . As all his passions were expressed by one livid smile, he never blushed at the variations in his behaviour . . . scarce any man ever wore in his face such outward and visible marks of the hollow, cruel, and rotten heart within.

Horace Walpole, *Memoirs*.

His ambition was equal to Pitt's; and his plodding, methodic genius made him take the spirit of detail for ability. Avarice, which he possessed in no less proportion than his other passions, concurred to lead him from a master who browbeat and treated him superciliously to worship the rising sun.

Ibid.

GRENVILLE, SIR RICHARD

1541—91 Naval Commander

Here die I, Richard Grenville, with a joy full and quiet mind, for that I have ended my life as a true soldier ought to do, that hath fought for his countrey, Queene, religion, and honour, whereby my soule most joyfully departeth out of this bodie, and shall alwaies leave behind it an everlasting fame as a valiant and true soldier that hath done his dutie, as he was bound to do.

On himself, dying words, attributed.

GRESHAM, SIR THOMAS

1519?—79 Merchant, Benefactor

... the Wealthiest Citizen in *England* of his age, and the founder of *two* stately Fabricks, the *Old Exchange*, a kind of Colledge for merchants, and *Gresham Colledge*, a kind of Exchange for Scholars.
> Thomas Fuller, *The History of the Worthies of England*.

... the greatest English financier of the century, the government's constant adviser and Royal agent in Antwerp, Sir Thomas Gresham. He was a remarkable man: a sort of combination of a Pierpoint Morgan and Keynes of his day.
> A. L. Rowse, *The England of Elizabeth*.

GREVILLE, CHARLES CAVENDISH FULKS

1794—1865 Diarist

I try to find out the truth, and the best conclusions at which my mind can arrive are really *truth* to me. . . .
> On himself, Diary, 2 April 1847.

No. I do not feel attracted to them [the *Memoirs*]. I remember the author, and he was the most conceited person with whom I have ever been brought in contact, although I have read Cicero and known Bulwer Lytton.
> Benjamin Disraeli, 1875, in G. W. E. Russell, *Collections and Recollections*.

For fifty years he listened at the door,
He heard some secrets and invented more.
These he wrote down, and women, statesmen, kings
Became degraded into common things.
> Lord Winchilsea, on the publication of Greville's *Memoirs*.

GREVILLE, FULKE, FIRST BARON BROOKE

1554—1628 Poet

Servant to Queen Elizabeth
Councillor to King James and
Friend to Sir Philip Sidney.
> On himself, *Epitaph*.

GREY, CHARLES, EARL

1764—1845 Prime Minister

Mark my words, within two years you will find that we have become unpopular, for having brought forward the most aristocratic measure that ever was proposed in parliament.
> On himself, in conversation with Lord Sidmouth, *a propos* the Reform Bill, April 1832.

I have been in the company of no distinguished man in Europe, so much my senior, with whom I have felt myself more at ease, or who has appeared to me better to understand the rights of all in a drawing room.
> James Fenimore Cooper, *Gleanings in Europe: England*.

Grey with his dam'd cocked-up nose. . . .
> George IV, in Roger Fulford, *The Trial of Queen Caroline*.

I hope God will forgive you on account of this Bill; I don't think I can.
> Lord Sidmouth, remark about the Reform Bill, April 1832.

GREY, EDWARD, VISCOUNT GREY OF FALLODON

1862—1933 Statesman

I think he is a man rather to see difficulties than to help people over them.
> Arthur Acland, Letter to H. H. Asquith, 1900.

... he always created difficulties. . . . He never came down into the arena and therefore got a false reputation. He was absolutely worthless. By the second year of the war Grey had completely crumpled up. He was pure funk.
> David Lloyd George, in conversation with A. J. Sylvester, 5 May 1933.

He was a mean man, . . . I am glad I trampled upon his carcase. He would have pursued me even from his grave.
> David Lloyd George, justifying his criticism of Grey in his *War Memoirs*, in Frances Stevenson, Diary, 29 October 1934.

GREY, LADY JANE (DUDLEY)

1537—54 Pretender to the English Throne

I founde her, in her Chamber, reading Phaedon Platonis in Greeke, and that with as much delite, as some ientlemen would read a merie tale in Bocase. After salutation, and dewtie done, with some other

taulke, I asked hir, whie she would leese soch pastime in the Parke? smiling she answered me: I wisse, all their sporte in the Parke is but a shadoe to that pleasure, that I find in Plato. . . .
    Roger Ascham, *The Scholemaster.*

Whatever might be the cause, she preserved the same appearance of knowledge, and the contempt of what was generally esteemed pleasure, during the whole of her life, for she declared herself displeased with being appointed Queen, and while conducting to the scaffold, she wrote a sentence in Latin and another in Greek on seeing the dead body of her husband accidentally passing that way.
    Jane Austen, *The History of England.*

Her contribution to English history was the revelation of a beautiful, devoted, unselfish, Christian spirit under circumstances in which the main springs of human action are almost certain to be revealed.
    Conyers Read, *The Tudors.*

See also Mary I

GREY, ZANE

1872—1939 Author

If Zane went out with a mosquito net to catch minnows, he could make it sound like a Roman Gladiator setting forth to slay whales in the Tiber.
    Robert H. Davis, in Jean Karr, *Zane Grey, Man of the West.*

. . . the 20th Century heir of the dime novel. . . .
    James D. Hart, *The Oxford Companion to American Literature.*

GRIFFITH, DAVID (LEWELYN) WARK

1875—1948 Film Director

I made them *see*, didn't I? . . . I changed everything. Remember how small the world was before I came along. I made them see it both ways in time as well as in space. . . .
    I brought it all to life. I moved the whole world onto a twenty-foot screen. I was a greater discoverer than Columbus. I condensed history into three hours and made them live it. They still remember Mae Marsh trimming her dress with cotton and putting coal dust on it to look like Ermine when the Colonel, her brother came home. *Griffith touches,* eh? They still talk about Griffith touches.
    On himself, in Adela Rogers St Johns, *The Honeycomb.*

I never saw [Griffith] dressed in anything but a high, stiff collar, a grey felt hat, high shoes with brass hooks and pulling-loops at the back, and one of a succession of suits none of which could have been less than fifteen years old, and all of which were woefully out of style. He looked like a hard-up, itinerant high-school teacher. His face was grave. When he smiled it was with the benign rigidity of a stone buddha. His nose, like his face, was long and thin, and he had a pronounced under-lip, upon which rested an endless succession of cigarettes.
    Norman bel Geddes, *Miracle In the Evening.*

Brought up in poverty and without adequate education, Griffith had aspirations to be a great writer, in particular a great playwright. Now he was hailed as the Shakespeare of the screen and he walked with the great of his time, the wealthy and the socially prominent. Although he knew that he had poured his heart into *The Birth of a Nation*, and *Intolerance*, he must have been a bit bewildered to have achieved such success in the medium he had originally despised. His was an intuitive genius, and fame made him self-conscious. His deliberate striving for artistic excellence or for popularity in his later films led him at times to descend into mannerism. The financial failure of *Intolerance* made him painfully aware of the need to cater more to popular taste, yet he was never sure of what popular taste was.
    Eileen Bowser, *D. W. Griffith.*

It was the fate of David Wark Griffith to have a success unknown in the entertainment world until his day, and to suffer the agonies which only a success of that magnitude can engender when it is past. Even the [Motion Picture Academy of Arts and Sciences] presentation of an Oscar in 1936 did little to ease Griffith's heartache. There was no solution for Griffith but a kind of frenzied beating on the barred doors of one day after another. Unfortunately, when he is dead, a man's career has but one tense. The laurels are fresh on the triumphant brow. He lies here, the embittered years forgotten — David Wark Griffith — the Great.
    Charles Brackett, at Griffith's funeral, 1948, in Lillian Gish, *The Movies, Mr. Griffith and Me.*

Many people who drink heavily — and I think Griffith was one of them — are not reeling drunk, but their senses are dulled. They're too soaked to respond properly. I don't know exactly why Griffith began drinking, whether out of some personal unhappiness or because his world was beginning to float away. He loved the grand world and was very proud of having met people like Winston Churchill. The last years of his life were terribly sad, anyway.

I'm afraid that drinkers end by alienating people, and they get terribly lonely. Imagine, dwindling away like that for almost twenty years after having practically invented silent pictures.

George Cukor, in Gavin Lambert, *On Cukor.*

. . . Griffith had no rivals. He was the teacher of us all. Not a picture has been made since his time that does not bear some trace of his influence. He did not invent the close-up or some of the other devices with which he has sometimes been credited, but he discovered and he taught everyone how to use them for more beautiful effect and better storytelling on the screen. Above all, he taught us how to photograph thought, not only by bringing the camera close to a player's eyes, but by such devices, novel and daring in their time, as focusing it on a pair of hands clasped in anguish or on some symbolic object that mirrored what was in the player's mind. He did much to teach the motion picture camera its own special language; and for that I, like every other worker in motion pictures, am his debtor.

Cecil B. De Mille, *The Autobiography of Cecil B. De Mille.*

With him, we never felt we were working for a salary. He inspired in us his belief that we were involved in a medium that was powerful enough to influence the whole world.

Lillian Gish, *The Movies, Mr. Griffith and Me.*

His footprints were never asked for, yet no one ever filled his shoes.

Hedda Hopper, *From Under My Hat.*

He believed that he was a genius, or wanted to believe it. He was proud of the social superiority that his forebears had taken for granted. Yet he saw himself trapped by poverty in an occupation unworthy of an artist, and inadmissible by a gentleman. He was working only for money enough to buy his freedom from detested drudgery. But the more money he made, the more he seemed to need; he squandered it recklessly, perhaps because he could never take it seriously as an end in itself. Since money was the public measure of success, his vanity was nourished by setting a low value on it. . . . He never completely overcame his contempt for his profession, or the feeling that, for him, success in it was a kind of failure. But the restlessness induced by his conflicting emotions found an outlet in continuous experiment. To shatter the stereotyped formulas that every other maker of pictures accepted as binding; to undertake fearlessly what nobody had ever attempted before; this gave Griffith a perverse satisfaction.

Lloyd Morris, *Not So Long Ago.*

Everywhere, Mr. Griffith now gives us excesses — everything is big; the crowds, the effects, the rainstorms, the ice floes, and everything is informed with an overwhelming dignity. He has long ago ceased to create beauty — only beautiful effects, like set pieces in fireworks. And he was the man destined by his curiosity, his honesty, his intelligence, to reach the heights of the moving picture.

Gilbert Seldes, *The Seven Lively Arts.*

GUTHRIE, (WOODROW WILSON) 'WOODY'

1912—67 Folk Singer

They called me everything from a rambling honkytonk hitter to a waterlogged harmonica player. One paper down in Kentucky said what us Okies needed next to three good square meals a day was some good music lessons.

On himself, in Howard Taubman, *Music on My Beat: An Intimate Volume of Shop Talk.*

When Oklahoma talks to New York, New York hadn't ought to get restless and nervous, and when Chicago says something to Arizona, that ought not to cause trouble. I ain't mad at nobody that don't get mad at me. Looks like whatever you try to do, somebody jumps up and hollers and raises cain — then the feller next to him jumps up and hollers how much he likes it.

On himself, in *ibid.*

Woody always claimed that he could not theorize, that he couldn't keep up with us and our book learning. He'd bow out of an argument rather than get tangled up in four-syllable words. But he had a number of sound theories about songwriting. I only wish we had been able to learn them better.

Pete Seeger, in J. M. Schwartz ed., *The Incompleat Folksinger.*

GWYN, NELL (ELEANOUR)

1650—87 Actress, Mistress to Charles II

Hard by the Mall lives a wench call'd Nell,
  King Charles the Second he kept her.
She hath got a trick to handle his pr———,
  But never lays hands on his sceptre.
All matters of state from her soul she does haste,
  And leave to the politic bitches.
The whore's in the right, for 'tis her delight
  To be scratching just where it itches.

Anon., *Nell Gwynne.*

Our good King Charles the Second

Too flippant of treasure and moisture
  Stoop'd from the Queen infecund
To a wench of orange and oyster.
Consulting his cazzo he found it expedient
To engender Don Johns on Nell the Comedian.
    Anon., *A Ballad called The Haymarket Hectors.*

She was low in stature, and what the French call
mignonne and *piquante*, well-formed, handsome,
but red-haired, and rather *embonpoint*; of the
enjoué she was a complete mistress. Airy, fantastic,
and sprightly, she sang, danced, and was exactly
made for acting light, showy characters, filling them
up, as far as they went, most effectually. On the
front of Bagnigge Wells, one of her country houses,
where she entertained the King with concerts, there
was a bust of her, and though it was wretchedly
executed, it confirmed the correctness of Lely's
pencil. She had remarkably lively eyes, but so small
they were almost invisible when she laughed; and a
foot, the least of any woman in England.
    Anon., *The Manager's Note-Book.*

Let not poor Nelly starve!
    Charles II, attributed last words.

She continued to hang on her cloaths with her usual
negligence when she was the King's mistress, but
whatever she did became her.
    James Granger, *Biographical History of England.*

She was, or affected to be very orthodox, and a
friend to the clergy and the Church. The story of
her paying the debt of a worthy clergyman, whom,
as she was going through the city, she saw some
bailiffs hurrying to prison, is a known fact; as is also
that of her being insulted in her coach at Oxford, by
the mob, who mistook her for the Duchess of Portsmouth. Upon which, she looked out of the window,
and said, with her usual good humour, *Pray, good
people, be civil; I am the protestant whore.* This
laconic speech drew on her the blessings of the
populace.
    Ibid.

The King and Duke of York was at the play; but so
great performance of a comical part was never, I
believe, in the world before as Nell hath done this,
both as mad girle, and then, most and best of all,
when she comes in like a young gallant; and hath
the motions and carriage of a spark, the most that
ever I saw any man have. It makes me, I confess,
admire her.
    Samuel Pepys, on seeing her play Florimel in
    Dryden's *Mayden Queene*, Diary, 2 March 1667.

This you'd believe, had I but time to tell you,
The pain it costs to poor laborious *Nelly*
While she employs Hands, Fingers, Lips and Thighs,
E're she can raise the Member she enjoys.
    John Wilmot, Earl of Rochester, *On King
    Charles.*

H

HAGGARD, SIR HENRY RIDER

1856—1925 Novelist

Only little people are vain. How anybody can be
vain, amazes me. I know that in my own small way
I grow humbler year by year.
    On himself, Journal, 23 March 1915.

Sir Rider Haggard
Was completely staggered
When his bride-to-be
Announced 'I AM SHE!'
    W. H. Auden, *Academic Graffiti*.

Even your imagination is out of the fifth form.
    Andrew Lang, Letter to Rider Haggard.

Will there never come a season
Which shall rid us from the curse
Of a prose which knows no reason
And an unmelodious verse:
When the world shall cease to wonder
At the genius of an Ass,
And a boy's eccentric blunder
Shall not bring success to pass:
When mankind shall be delivered
From the clash of magazines,
And the inkstand shall be shivered
Into countless smithereens:
When there stands a muzzled stripling,
Mute, beside a muzzled bore:
When the Rudyards cease from kipling
And the Haggards Ride no more.
    J. K. Stephen, *A Protest in Verse*.

HAIG, DOUGLAS, EARL

1861—1928 Soldier

With the publication of his Private Papers in 1952,
he committed suicide 25 years after his death.
    Lord Beaverbrook, *Men and Power*.

What a rascal Haig was. One of the biggest rascals in
a long time. Twisting turning conspiring against
French, pushing him out, conniving with the King.
Oh he is a disgraceful story.
    Lord Beaverbrook, message to Frank Owen,
    1959.

Haig had a first-rate General Staff mind.
    Lord Haldane, *An Autobiography*.

He was a remote, almost God-like figure, in whom
we had complete trust. His personality and his inflexible belief in victory inspired every single man.
His was the only army of the great nations at war
which did not break.
    Sir John Kennedy, in *Scotsman*, 15 August 1959.

Haig was devoid of the gift of intelligible and coherent expression.
    David Lloyd George, *War Memoirs*.

We may not like the psychological basis of Haig's
imperturbability. We may condemn the system that
moulded him. But it could not have been a 'small'
man who bore that massive responsibility, and
worked out his behaviour by the creed of a world in
whose destruction he himself was taking, unwittingly, a major part.
    John Terraine, in *New Statesman and Nation*,
    1952.

He's quite all right, but he's too — cautious: he will
be so fixed on not giving the Boers a chance, he'll
never give himself one.
    Colonel Wolls-Sampson, in B. H. Liddel Hart,
    History of the First World War.

HAKLUYT, RICHARD

1552?—1616 Geographer, Chronicler

In a word, many of such useful tracts of sea adventures, which before were scattered as several ships,
Mr. Hakluyt hath embodied into a fleet, divided
into three squadrons, so many several volumes; a
work of great honour to England, it being possible
that many ports and islands in America, which being
base and barren, bear only a bare name for the
present, may prove rich places for the future.
    Thomas Fuller, *The History of the Worthies of
    England*.

351

HALE, EDWARD EVERETT

1822–1909 Author

The rough-and-ready Hale . . . had kept the faith and gusts of the early republic. With his air of an untidy Pilgrim father, he seemed to say that Gilead still had its balm.

Van Wyck Brooks, *New England: Indian Summer 1865–1915.*

His religion was his life, and he knew no other. It would never have occurred to him to think of himself as anything other than a child of God, intent upon his Father's business.

Charles Reynolds Brown, *They Were Giants.*

In the vast range of his work he was always an artist in his ethics and a moralist in his art.

William Dean Howells, in Jean Holloway, *Edward Everett Hale.*

Dr Hale's gift was for inspiration, rather than for organization; it was for him to initiate, rather than to demonstrate.

Francis Greenwood Peabody, *Reminiscences of Present-Day Saints.*

HALE, SIR MATTHEW

1609–76 Judge

I remember about 1646 (or 1647) that Mr John Maynard (now Sir John, and serjeant) came into Middle Temple Hall, from Westminster Hall, weary with business, and hungry, when we had newly dined. He sate-down by Mr Bennet Hoskyns (the only son of Serjeant Hoskyns the Poet) since Baronet, and some others; who having made an end of their Commons, fell unto various Discourse, and what was the meaning of the text (Rom. v. 7). 'For a just man one would dare to die; but for a good man one would willingly die.' They askt Mr Maynard what was the difference between a just man and a good man. He was beginning to eate, and cryed: — Hoh! you have eaten your dinners, and now have leasure to discourse; I have not. He had eate but a Bitt or two when he reply'd: — I'le tell you the difference presently: serjeant Rolle is a just man, and Mathew Hal is a good man; and so fell to make an end of his dinner. And there could not be a better interpretation of this text. For serjeant Rolle was just but by nature penurious; and his wife made him worse: Mathew Hale was not only just, but wonderfully Charitable and open handed, and did not sound a trumpet neither, as the Hypocrites doe.

John Aubrey, *Brief Lives.*

One of his [fencing] masters told him he could teach him no more, for he was now better at his own trade than himself was. This Mr Hale looked on as flattery; so, to make the master discover himself, he promised him the house he lived in, for he was his tenant, if he could hit him a blow on the head; and bade him do his best for he would be as good as his word: so after a little engagement, his master, being really superior to him, hit him on the head, and he performed his promise, for he gave him the house freely; and was not unwilling at that rate to learn to distinguish flattery from plain and simple truth.

Gilbert Burnet, *Life of Sir Mathew Hale.*

When he was a practitioner, differences were often referred to him, which he settled, but would accept of no reward for his pains, though offered by both parties together, after the agreement was made; for he said in those cases he was made a judge, and a judge ought to take no money. If they told him, he lost much of his own time in considering their business, and so ought to be acknowledged for it; his answer was, as one that heard it told me, 'Can I spend my time better than to make people friends? Must I have no time allowed me to do good in?'

Ibid.

It is said he was once caught. A courtier who had a cause to be tried before him, got one to go to him as from the King, to speak for favour to his adversary, and so carried his point; for the chief justice could not think any person to be in the right that came so unduly recommended.

Roger North, *The Life of Right Hon. Francis North, Baron Guildford.*

He became the cushion exceedingly well: his manner of hearing patient, his directions pertinent, and his discourses copious and, although he hesitated often, fluent. His stop for a word, by the produce always paid for the delay; and on some occasions he would utter sentences heroic.

Ibid.

This great man was most unfortunate in his family; for he married his own servant maid, and then for excuse said there was no wisdom below the girdle.

Ibid.

HALE, NATHAN

1755–76 Spy

I only regret that I have but one life to lose for my country.

On himself, at his execution, 22 September 1776.

. . . Nathan Hale, who was on the American side and thus a good spy, went to his death bravely when he was caught by the British. He cheerfully remarked that he wished he could be hanged more often for his country. Benedict Arnold, as we have seen, refused to be hanged even once, which was niggardly and disloyal.

Richard Armour, *It All Started With Columbus.*

HALIFAX, MARQUIS OF, see under SAVILE, GEORGE

HALLÉ, SIR CHARLES

1819—95 Musician

I created for myself a singular test by which to know if a piece of music was beautiful or not. There was a spot, a bench under a tree by the side of a very small water-fall, where I loved to sit and 'think music'. Then, going in my mind through a piece of music such as Beethoven's 'Adelaide', or the Cavatina from 'Der Freischutz', I could imagine that I heard it in the air surrounding me, that the whole of nature sang it, and then I knew that it was beautiful. Many pieces would not stand that test, however hard I tried, and these I rejected as indifferent.

On himself, *Autobiography.*

I felt that the whole musical education of the public had to be undertaken.

Ibid.

The noise of the brass had, I am ashamed to say, brought the unwilling tears to my eyes, and caused them to overflow enough to attract attention. Hallé, who was waiting for his term of martyrdom, caught sight of this little tragedy, and began the first of a series of kindnesses to me in which he never failed to his dying day, by cheering me up with little jokes, and soothing my small nerves most effectually. He told me that if I cried at the brass, I should have a much worse time in later life. I reminded him of this episode in later years, and he said it was no wonder that the Dublin brass had moved me to tears, for it had nearly had the same effect upon himself.

C. V. Stanford, *Pages from an Unwritten Diary.*

I saw one sight in Venice which alone repaid the journey: Charles Hallé in a frock-coat and a white top hat reading the *Daily Telegraph* while seated in a gondola and floating under the Bridge of Sighs.

Ibid.

HALLECK, HENRY WAGER

1815—72 Soldier, Administrator

Originates nothing, anticipates nothing, takes no responsibility, plans nothing, suggests nothing, is good for nothing.

Gideon Welles, Diary, 1862.

HALLEY, EDMUND

1656—1742 Astronomer

At 9 years old, his father's apprentice taught him to write, and arithmetique. He went to Paule's schoole to Dr. Gale: while he was there he was very perfect in the caelestiall Globes in so much that I heard Mr. Moxton (the Globe-maker) say that if a star were misplaced in the Globe, he would presently find it. He studied Geometry, and at 16 could make a dyall, and then, he said, thought himselfe a brave fellow. At 16 went to Queen's Colledge in Oxon, well versed in Latin, Greeke, and Hebrew: where, at the age of nineteen, he solved this useful Probleme in Astronomie, never donne before, viz. *from 3 distances given from the Sun, and Angles between, to find the Orbe,* for which his name will be ever famous.

John Aubrey, *Brief Lives.*

I have no esteem of a man who has lost his reputation both for skill candor & Ingenuity by silly tricks ingratitude & foolish prate. & yt I value not all or any of the shams of him and his Infidel companions being very well satisfied that if Xt and his Appostles were to walk againe upon earth, they should not scape free from ye calumnies of their venomous tongues, but I hate his ill manners not the man, were he either honest or but civil there is none in whose company I could rather desire to be.

John Flamsteed, Letter to Isaac Newton, 24 February 1692.

Halley, the astronomer, of whom it was remarked, that 'he could believe any thing but the Scriptures', talking against Christianity as wanting mathematical demonstration, was stopped by Newton, who said, 'Man, you had better hold your tongue; you have never sufficiently considered the matter'.

M. Noble, *A Biographical History of England.*

HAMILTON, ALEXANDER

1757—1804 Statesman

In this dark and insidious manner did this intriguer lay schemes in secret against me, and, like the worm

at the root of the peach, did he labor for twelve years, underground and in darkness, to girdle the root, while all the axes of the Anti-Federalists, Democrats, Jacobins, Virginia debtors to English merchants, and French hirelings, chopping as they were for the whole time at the trunk, could not fell the tree.
> John Adams, 20 July 1807, in Zoltan Haraszti, *John Adams and the Prophets of Progress.*

. . . bastard brat of a Scottish peddlar.
> John Adams, in James B. Peabody ed., *John Adams, A Biography in his own Words.*

Born on a speck more obscure than Corsica, from an original not only contemptible but infamous, with infinitely less courage and capacity than Bonaparte, he would in my Opinion, if I had not controuled the Fury of his Vanity, instead of relieving this country from Confusion as Bonaparte did France, he would have involved it in all the Bloodshed and distractions of foreign and civil War at once.
> John Adams, on the death of Hamilton, in *ibid.*

Hamilton is really a colossus to the anti-republican party. Without numbers, he is a host within himself.
> Thomas Jefferson, Letter to James Madison, 21 September 1795.

. . . not only a monarchist, but for a monarchy bottomed on corruption.
> Thomas Jefferson, in Richard B. Morris, 'Alexander Hamilton After Two Centuries', in J. E. Cooke ed., *Alexander Hamilton, a Profile.*

To the cause of American Union he gave unstintingly of his energy and devotion, and yet he had little love for the people whose power and material well-being he sought to advance. . . . The supreme irony of Hamilton's achievement is that the methods by which he sought to lay the economic foundations of the American union actually aggravated political sectionalism in the United States — the very eventuality he most dreaded.
> John C. Miller, *Alexander Hamilton: Portrait in Paradox.*

He worked for the peace, prosperity, and freedom of the entire community. His client was not a class but the country.
> Broadus Mitchell, *Heritage from Hamilton.*

Hamilton was an administrative genius, perhaps the greatest America has yet produced. He believed in a strong executive, guarded the Presidency from encroachments upon its power by the legislative branch of the government, and assumed an influence in Washington's cabinet system which is un-matched in the annals of the American cabinet system. Concerning himself with every phase of public policy, he was more than merely Secretary of the Treasury. He was in fact Washington's prime minister.
> Richard B. Morris, 'Alexander Hamilton After Two Centuries', in J. E. Cooke ed., *Alexander Hamilton, a Profile.*

As the creative organizer of a political state answering the needs of a capitalistic order — a state destined to grow stronger as imperialistic ambitions mount — he seems the most modern of our eighteenth-century leaders, one to whom our industrialism owes a very great debt, but from whom our democratic liberalism has received nothing.
> Vernon L. Parrington, *Hamilton and the Leviathan State*, in *ibid.*

[Hamilton's] touch of the heroic, the touch of the purple, the touch of the gallant, the dashing, the picturesque.
> Theodore Roosevelt, Letter to Governor Morris, 28 November 1910.

He smote the rock of the natural resources, and abundant streams of revenue gushed forth. He touched the dead corpse of public credit, and it sprang open upon its feet.
> Daniel Webster, Speech in the Senate, 10 March 1831.

See also Aaron Burr, Albert Gallatin, Robert F. Kennedy

HAMILTON, EMMA, LADY

1761?—1815 Society Lady

Brave Emma! — Good Emma! — If there were more Emmas, there would be more Nelsons.
> Lord Nelson, on leaving for his last voyage, in Robert Southey, *Life of Nelson.*

See also Horatio Nelson

HAMPDEN, JOHN

1594—1643 Statesman

He was rather of reputation in his own Country, then of publique discourse or fame in the Kingdom, before the businesse of Shippmony, but then he grew the argument of all tounges, evry man enquyringe who and what he was, that durst, at his owne charge supporte the liberty and property of the

kingdome, and reskue his Country from being made a prey to the Courte.
> Edward Hyde, Earl of Clarendon, *History of the Rebellion.*

He had a head to contrive, a tongue to persuade, and a hand to execute, any mischief.
> *Ibid.*

Without question, when he first drew the sword, he threw away the scabbard.
> *Ibid.*

Hampden was very well read in History; and I remember the first time I ever saw that of Davila of the Civil Wars of France, it was lent me under the title of 'Mr Hampden's *Vade Mecum*'.
> Sir Philip Warwick, *Memoirs.*

HANCOCK, JOHN

1736/7—93 Merchant, Politician

There! John Bull can read my name without spectacles.
> On himself, on signing the Declaration of Independence, in Herbert S. Allan, *John Hancock, Patriot in Purple.*

Yes, there is the place where the great John Hancock was born . . . John Hancock! A man without head and without heart — the mere shadow of a man! — and yet a Governor of Old Massachusetts.
> John Adams, 1791, in L. Sears, *John Hancock, the Picturesque Patriot.*

See also John Brown

HAND, (BILLINGS) LEARNED

1872—1961 Jurist

I think of Cervantes' advice: 'Try to win the second prize. For the first is always by favor. The second goes for pure merit.' The praises of Judge Hand have been earned, not by occupying the highest bench, but by pure merit.
> Jerome Frank, commenting on Hand's failure to be appointed to the Supreme Court, in Marvin Schick, *Learned Hand's Court.*

HANDEL, GEORGE FREDERICK

1685—1759 Composer

He was perhaps as great a genius in music as Mr Pope was in poetry; the musical composition of the one being as expressive of the passions, as the happy versification of the other excelled in harmony.
> Anon., in *Scots Magazine*, April 1759.

Of his peers Beethoven was perhaps the most generous in his appraisal of Handel. 'He was the greatest composer that ever lived. I would uncover my head, and kneel before his tomb.' And again, when forty volumes of Arnold's edition, the gift of A. A. Stumpff . . . came to him in 1826: 'There is the truth.'
> Ludwig van Beethoven, in Percy M. Young, *Handel.*

To many he remains the greatest dreamer in music the world has ever known. His whole life was a dream; and his every effort was a votive offering to his temple of dreams — that temple which he sought to make beautiful.
> Newman Flower, *George Frideric Handel.*

Of Handel it is however remarkable that his vocal fugues are not yet antiquated, whereas but few of his airs probably would be found still to please the ear.
> Johann Nicolaus Forkel, 1802, in H. T. David and A. Mendel, *The Bach Reader.*

If Income Tax collectors ever indulge in community singing, I have no doubt that they sing the choruses from the *Messiah*, for the *Messiah* is the first great anthem of man's enslavement by materialism.
> Compton Mackenzie, in G. Hughes and H. van Thal, *The Music Lover's Companion.*

Ah, a German and a genius! a prodigy, admit him!
> Jonathan Swift, attributed last words.

We have heard what Gluck, Mozart, Haydn and Beethoven said about Handel. What they did in the Potteries may be remembered as a greater tribute. In 1892 the Hanley Glee and Madrigal Society received an invitation to sing Gaul's *Israel in the Wilderness* at the Crystal Palace. The Invitation was declined because the choir preferred to stay at home to practise *Israel in Egypt*.
> Percy M. Young, *Handel.*

See also R. B. Sheridan

HANNA, MARCUS ALONZO

1837—1904 Politician, Capitalist

Where is Hanna, bulldog Hanna,
Low-browed Hanna, who said: 'Stand pat'?

Gone to his place with old Pierpont Morgan
Gone somewhere . . . with lean rat Platt.
    Vachel Lindsay, *Bryan, Bryan, Bryan, Bryan.*

See also William McKinley

HARCOURT, LEWIS, FIRST VISCOUNT

1863—1922 Statesman

I have myself a constitutional dislike to limelight,
which often disfigures that which it is intended to
adorn.
    On himself, Speech to the Corona Club, 18 June
    1912.

Few men have appealed less to the gallery than Mr
Harcourt. He does not scan far horizons. He does
not declare any vision of a promised land. He has no
passionate fervour for humanity and is too honest
to pretend any. He is a practical politician, with no
dithyrambs. He loves the intricacies of the campaign more than the visionary gleam, the actual
more than the potential, present facts more than
future fancies. He is the man without a dream.
    A. G. Gardiner, *Prophets, Priests and Kings.*

HARCOURT, SIR WILLIAM GEORGE GRAN-
VILLE VENABLES VERNON

1827—1904 Statesman

Harcourt was full to the brim of old Whig traditions
and stories, many of the latter scandalous in the
highest degree. He was an admirable and ready Constitutional lawyer; a good old-fashioned parliamentary bruiser.
    Augustine Birrell, *Things Past Redress.*

. . . The big salmon will always be sulking under his
stone, and ready for occasional plunges which will
not always be free from a sinister intention.
    Sir Henry Campbell-Bannerman, Letter to H. H.
    Asquith, December 1898.

HARDIE, JAMES KEIR

1856—1915 Socialist, Labour Leader

I understand what Christ suffered in Gethsemane
as well as any man living.
    On himself, speaking to friends after hostility in
    Aberdare, 6 August 1914.

I am of that unfortunate class who never knew what
it was to be a child in spirit. Even the memories of
boyhood and young manhood are gloomy.
    On himself, in Kenneth O. Morgan, *Keir Hardie.*

[He] deliberately chooses this policy as the only
one he can boss. His only chance of leadership lies
in the creation of an organisation 'agin the Government'; he knows little and cares less for any constructive thought or action.
    Beatrice Webb, in Kitty Muggeridge and Ruth
    Adam, *Beatrice Webb: A Life.*

HARDING, WARREN GAMALIEL

1865—1923 Twenty-Ninth United States President

I have no trouble with my enemies but my goddam
friends, White, they are the ones who keep me walking the floor nights.
    On himself, to William Allen White, 1923, in
    David Lewis Cohn, *The Fabulous Democrats.*

Everybody's second choice.
    Anon., in Francis Russell, *President Harding: His
    Life and Times 1865—1923.*

When you get hearts on fire for Harding, you have
generated enough heat to set Lake Michigan boiling
and turn the Chicago River into a pot roast.
    Anon., in *ibid.*

He was an excellent 'mixer', he had the inestimable
gift of never forgetting a man's face or his name,
and there was always a genuine warmth in his handshake, a real geniality in his smile. He was a regular
he-man according to the sign manual of the old days
— a great poker player, and not at all averse to putting a foot on the brass rail.
    Anon., in *ibid.*

Few deaths are unmingled tragedies. Harding's was
not, he died in time.
    Samuel Hopkins Adams, in *The American
    Heritage Pictorial History of the Presidents,*
    vol. 2.

Harding became president as a result of mistaken
identity. The Republican presidential convention
was held in a smoke-filled room, and visibility was
so poor that Harding was mistaken for Hoover.
    Richard Armour, *It All Started With Columbus.*

I am more and more under the opinion that for
President we need not so much a brilliant man as
solid, mediocre men, providing they have good

sense, sound and careful judgment and good manners. All these Harding has.

Richard Washburn Child, in Francis Russell, *President Harding: His Life and Times 1865–1923.*

Harding, You're the Man for us.
We think the country's ready
For another man like Teddy.
We need another Lincoln
To do the country's thinkin'
      Mist-er Hard-ding
        You're the man for us.
Al Jolson, campaign song, 1919.

Absolute knowledge have I none.
But my aunt's washerwoman's sister's son
Heard a policeman on his beat
Say to a laborer on the street
That he had a letter just last week —
A letter which he did not seek —
From a Chinese merchant in Timbuctoo,
Who said that his brother in Cuba knew
Of an Indian chief in a Texas town,
Who got the dope from a circus clown,
That a man in Klondike had it straight
From a guy in a South American state,
That a wild man over in Borneo
Was told by a woman who claimed to know,
Of a well-known society rake,
Whose mother-in-law will undertake
To prove that her husband's sister's niece
Has stated plain in a printed piece
That she has a son who never comes home
Who knows all about the Teapot Dome.

Henry Cabot Lodge, in *The American Heritage Pictorial History of the Presidents*, vol. 2.

You speak of Harding's English. He has an affectation for odd words which I do not share, words like 'normalcy' . . . but I should not have said that his writing was at all what you seem to think it. Perhaps I am less sensitive about it because I have been through eight years with a man who wrote English very well without saying anything.

Henry Cabot Lodge to John Morse, in John A. Garraty, *Henry Cabot Lodge.*

Harding was not a bad man. He was just a slob.

Alice Roosevelt Longworth, in Ishbel Ross, *Grace Coolidge and her Era.*

His speeches leave the impression of an army of pompous phrases moving over the landscape in search of an idea. Sometimes these meandering words would actually capture a struggling thought and bear it in triumphantly a prisoner in their midst until it died of servitude and overwork.

Senator William McAdoo, in Leon A. Harris, *The Fine Art of Political Wit.*

. . . a tin horn politician with the manner of a rural corn doctor and the mien of a ham actor.

H. L. Mencken, in *Baltimore Evening Sun,* 15 June 1920.

Keep Warren at home. Don't let him make any speeches. If he goes out on a tour somebody's sure to ask him questions, and Warren's just the sort of damned fool that will try to answer them.

B. Penrose, in *The American Heritage Pictorial History of the Presidents,* vol. 2.

If ever there was a he-harlot, it was this same Warren G. Harding.

William Allen White, in Francis Russell, *President Harding: His Life and Times 1865–1923.*

. . . Harding stood there on the rostrum, the well-schooled senatorial orator, with his actor's sharply chiseled face, with his greying hair and massive black eyebrows, with his matinee-idol manner, tiptoeing eagerly into the national limelight; which — alas — he was to catch and keep from that day until he fell in tragedy.

Ibid.

He has a bungalow mind.

Woodrow Wilson, in Thomas A. Bailey, *Woodrow Wilson and the Great Betrayal.*

HARDY, THOMAS

1840–1928 Author

People call me a pessimist; and if it is pessimism to think, with Sophocles, that 'not to have been born is best', then I do not reject the designation. . . . I do not see that we are likely to improve the world by asseverating, however loudly, that black is white, or at least that black is but a necessary contrast and foil, without which white would be white no longer. That is mere juggling with a metaphor. But my pessimism, if pessimism it be, does not involve the assumption that the world is going to the dogs, and that Ahriman is winning all along the line. On the contrary, my practical philosophy is distinctly meliorist.

On himself, in William Archer, *Real Conversations.*

I never cared for life, life cared for me.
And hence I owe it some fidelity. . . .

On himself, *Epitaph.*

Thomas Hardy
Was never tardy
When summoned to fulfill
The Immanent Will.

W. H. Auden, *Academic Graffiti.*

My first Master was Thomas Hardy, and I think I was very lucky in my choice. He was a good poet, perhaps a great one, but not *too* good. Much as I loved him, even I could see that his diction was often clumsy and forced and that a lot of his poems were plain bad. This gave me hope where a flawless poet might have made me despair. He was modern without being too modern. His world and sensibility were close enough to mine . . . so that, in imitating him, I was being led towards not away from myself, but they were not so close as to obliterate my identity. If I looked through his spectacles, at least I was conscious of a certain eyestrain. Lastly, his metrical variety, his fondness for complicated stanza forms, were an invaluable training in the craft of making.

    W. H. Auden, *The Dyer's Hand.*

Hardy went down to botanize in the swamps, while Meredith climbed toward the sun. Meredith became, at his best, a sort of daintily dressed Walt Whitman; Hardy became a sort of village atheist brooding and blaspheming over the village idiot.

    G. K. Chesterton, *The Victorian Age in Literature.*

The work of Thomas Hardy represents an interesting example of a powerful personality uncurbed by any institutional attachment or by submission to any objective beliefs: unhampered by any ideas, or even by what sometimes acts as a partial restraint upon inferior writers, the desire to please a large public. He seems to me to have written as nearly for the sake of 'self-expression' as a man well can; and the self which he had to express does not strike me as a particularly wholesome or edifying matter of communication. He was indifferent even to the prescripts of good writing: he wrote sometimes overpoweringly well, but always very carelessly; at times his style touches sublimity without ever having passed through the stage of being good.

    T. S. Eliot, *After Strange Gods.*

Hardy seems to me essentially a poet, who conceives of his novels from an enormous height. They are to be tragedies or tragi-comedies, they are to give out the sound of hammer-strokes as they proceed; in other words Hardy arranges events with emphasis on causality, the ground plan is a plot, and the characters are ordered to acquiesce in its requirements. . . . This, as far as I can make out, is the flaw running through Hardy's novels: he has emphasized causality more strongly than his medium permits.

    E. M. Forster, *Aspects of the Novel.*

The unpopularity of Mr Hardy's novels among women is a curious phenomenon. If he had no male admirers, he could almost cease to exist. It is not merely that the mass of girls who let down their back-hair to have a long cry over Edna Lyall or Miss Florence Warden do not appreciate his books, but even educated women approach him with hesitation and prejudice. This is owing to no obvious error on the novelist's part; he has never attacked the sex, or offended its proprieties. But there is something in his conception of feminine character which is not well received. The modern English novelist has created, and has faithfully repeated, a demure, ingenuous, and practically inhuman type of heroine. . . . But Mr Hardy's women are moulded of the same flesh as his men; they are liable to flutterings and tremblings; they are not always constant even when they are 'quite nice'; and some of them are actually 'of a coming-on disposition'.

    Edmund Gosse, in *Speaker*, 13 September 1890.

A fact about the infancy of Mr Hardy has escaped the interviewers and may be recorded here. On the day of his birth, during a brief absence of his nurse, there slipped into the room an ethereal creature, known as the Spirit of Plastic Beauty. Bending over the cradle she scattered roses on it, and as she strewed them she blessed the babe. 'He shall have an eye to see moral and material loveliness, he shall speak of richly-coloured pastoral places in the accent of Theocritus, he shall write in such a way as to cajole busy men into a sympathy with old, unhappy, far-off things.' She turned and went, but while the nurse still delayed, a withered termagant glided into the room. From her apron she dropped toads among the rose-leaves, and she whispered: 'I am the genius of False Rhetoric, and led by me he shall say things ugly and coarse, not recognizing them to be so, and shall get into a rage about matters that call for philosophic calm, and shall spoil some of his best passages with pedantry and incoherency. He shall not know what things belong to his peace, and he shall plague his most loyal admirers with the barbaric contortions of his dialogue.

    Edmund Gosse, in *Cosmopolis*, January 1896.

He complained that they [the critics] accused him of pessimism. One critic singled out as an example of gloom his poem on the woman whose house burned down on her wedding night. 'Of course it's a humorous piece,' said Hardy, 'and the man must have been thick-witted not to see that. On reading his criticism, I went through my last collection of poems with a pencil, marking them S, N, and C according as they were sad, neutral, or cheerful. I found them in pretty equal proportions; which nobody could call pessimism.'

    Robert Graves, *Goodbye to All That.*

What a commonplace genius he has; or a genius for the commonplace, I don't know which. He doesn't rank so terribly high, really. But better than Bernard Shaw, even then.

D. H. Lawrence, Letter to Martin Secker, 24 July 1928.

By the side of George Eliot . . . Meredith appears as a shallow exhibitionist . . . and Hardy, decent as he is, as a provincial manufacturer of gauche and heavy fictions that sometimes have corresponding virtues.

F. R. Leavis, *The Great Tradition*.

The gloom is not even relieved by a little elegance of diction.

Lytton Strachey, review of Hardy's poems, *Satires of Circumstance, New Statesman*, 19 December 1914.

There is one thing which not the dullest reader can fail to recognize — the persistency with which there alternately smoulders and flames through the book Mr Hardy's passionate protest against the unequal justice meted by society to the man and woman associated in an identical breach of the moral law. In his wrath, Mr Hardy seems at times almost to forget that society is scarcely more unjust than nature. He himself proposes no remedy, suggests no escape — his business not being to deal in nostrums of social therapeutics. He is content to make his readers pause, and consider, and pity; and very likely he despairs of any satisfactory solution of the problem which he presents with such disturbing power and clothes with a vesture of such breathing and throbbing life.

William Watson, in *Academy*, 6 February 1892.

No one has written worse English than Mr Hardy in some of his novels — cumbrous, stilted, ugly, and inexpressive — yes, but at the same time so strangely expressive of something attractive to us in Mr Hardy himself that we would not change it for the perfection of Sterne at his best. It becomes coloured by its surroundings; it becomes literature.

Virginia Woolf, *The Moment*.

See also John Cowper Powys

HARIOT, THOMAS

1560—1621 Mathematician, Astronomer

He did not like (or valued not) the old storie of the Creation of the World. He could not beleeve the old position; he would say *ex nihilo nihil fit* nothing comes of nothing. But a *nihilum* killed him at last: for in the top of his Nose came a little red speck (exceeding small) which grew bigger and bigger, and at last killed him. I suppose it was that which the Chirurgians call a *noli me tangere*.

John Aubrey, *Brief Lives*.

HARLEY, ROBERT, EARL OF OXFORD

1661—1724 Statesman

This mischievous darkness of his soul was written on his countenance and plainly legible in a very odd look, disagreeable to everybody at first sight, which being joined with a constant, awkward motion or agitation of his head and body, betrayed a turbulent dishonesty within, even in the midst of all those familiar airs, jocular bowing and smiling, which he always affected to cover what could be covered.

Anon., in Michael Foot, *The Pen and The Sword*.

. . . the man himself was of all men the least interesting. There is indeed a whimsical contrast between the very ordinary qualities of his mind and the very extraordinary vicissitudes of his fortune.

T. B. Macaulay, *History of England*.

He constantly had, even with his best friends, an air of mystery and reserve which seemed to indicate that he knew some momentous secret, and that his mind was labouring with some vast design. In this way he got and long kept a high reputation for wisdom. It was not till that reputation had made him an Earl, a Knight of the Garter, Lord High Treasurer of England, and master of the fate of Europe, that his admirers began to find out that he was really a dull puzzleheaded man.

Ibid.

The Earl of Oxford is a person of as much virtue, as can possibly consist with the love of power; and his love of power is no greater than what is common to men of his superior capacities; neither did any man ever appear to value it less, after he had obtained it, or exert it with more moderation. He is the only instance that ever fell within my memory, or observation, of a person passing from a private life, through the several stages of greatness, without any perceivable impression upon his temper and behaviour.

Jonathan Swift, *An Enquiry Into the Behaviour of the Queen's Last Ministry*.

HARLOW, JEAN (HARLEAN CARPENTER)

1911—37 Actress

Jean Harlow was very soft about her toughness.

George Cukor, in Gavin Lambert, *On Cukor*.

There is no sign that her acting would ever have progressed beyond the scope of the restless shoulders and the protuberant breasts; her technique was the gangster's technique — she toted a breast like a man totes a gun.

Graham Greene, reviewing *Saratoga*, in *Night and Day*, 26 August 1937.

The 'platinum blonde' hair and pleasing curves of Miss Jean Harlow broke all of Hollywood's glamor records during the nineteen-thirties. . . . Essentially, the girl portrayed by Miss Harlow expressed the American male's boredom with the traditional concept of 'romance', with the doctrine that fulfillment in love is a primary objective in life; and perhaps also with the restless discontent and implied superiority of the American woman. For this girl was earthy, humorous, hard-boiled. She made no pretensions to culture or refinement. For her, sex and love were by no means inseparable, and she mocked at prudery and puritanism, at fastidiousness and pretentiousness. Brought up in a fiercely competitive world, without advantages or protection, she had learned to defend herself adequately and to value, at their specific practical worth, the goods she might hope to secure. Warm-hearted, gay, gaudy, her lack of subtlety and deviousness amounted to a kind of honesty — and to anxious businessmen, during the Great Depression, she seemed entirely desirable.

Lloyd Morris, *Not So Long Ago*.

Harlow's hip-swinging, gum-chewing, slangy, wisecracking characterisations were a delight. She perfectly understood the roles she invariably played (even to the point of asking her agent, when he phoned with a new part, 'What kinda whore am I this time?') and she brightened every picture she was in. She knew what she was, the audience knew what she was (and revelled in her), even the censor knew what she was, but she got away with it all because she had immense humour, treated sex as fun and could tell the public all they wanted to know about the character she played without ever needing to resort to heavy-handed verbal explanations.

Clyde Jeavons and Jeremy Pascall, *A Pictorial History of Sex in the Movies*.

A square-shooter if there ever was one.

Spencer Tracy, in Larry Swindell, *Spencer Tracy*.

See also Marilyn Monroe

HARMSWORTH, ALFRED, see under NORTHCLIFFE, LORD

HARRINGTON, JAMES

1611—77 Political Theorist

He grew to have a phancy that his Perspiration turned to Flies, and sometimes to Bees; and he had a versatile timber house built in Mr Hart's garden (opposite to St James's parke) to try the experiment. He would turne it to the sun, and sitt towards it; then he had his fox-tayles there to chase away and massacre all the Flies and Bees that were to be found there, and then shut his *Chassees*. Now this Experiment was only to be tried in Warme weather, and some flies would lie so close in the cranies and cloath (with which it was hung) that they would not presently shew themselves. A quarter of an hower after perhaps, a fly or two, or more, might be drawen out of the lurking holes by the warmth; and then he would crye out, Doe you not see it apparently that these come from me? 'Twas the strangest sort of madness that ever I found in any one: talke of any thing els, his discourse would be very ingeniose and pleasant. . . .

John Aubrey, *Brief Lives*.

HARRIS, FRANK

1856—1931 Author, Journalist

In fact Frank Harris has no feelings. It is the secret of his success. Just as the fact that he thinks that other people have none either is the secret of the failure that lies in wait for him somewhere on the way of Life.

Oscar Wilde, Letter to More Adey, 12 May 1897.

To survive you one must have a strong brain, an assertive ego, a dynamic character. In your luncheon-parties, in old days, the remains of the guests were taken away with the *débris* of the feast. I have often lunched with you in Park Lane and found myself the only survivor.

Oscar Wilde, Letter to Frank Harris, 13 June 1897.

Frank Harris is invited to all the great houses in England — once.

Oscar Wilde, in A. K. Adams, *The Home Book of Humorous Quotations*.

See also A. E. Housman

HARRIS, JOEL CHANDLER

1848—1908 Author, Journalist

As for myself — though you could hardly call me

a real, sure enough author — I never have anything but the vaguest ideas of what I am going to write; but when I take my pen in hand, the dust clears away and the 'other fellow' takes charge.

On himself, Letter to his daughters, 1898.

You know, of course, that so far as literary art is concerned, I am poverty-stricken; and you know too, that my style and methods will cause you to pull your hair.

On himself, Letter to William Dean Howells, 1 June 1900.

If merit be aptly appraised, to Joel Chandler Harris will always go the credit for making a section famous with legends — legends which were engrafted on Southern soil. If he had done no more than give a delineation of the plantation, his place in literature would be secure. However, he did more than this — he preserved from oblivion the lore significant for an insight not only into a people but into a past.

Stella Brewer Brookes, *Joel Chandler Harris — Folklorist.*

Harris, who read Grimm and the *Arabian Nights*, knew every by-path in the woods, hunted foxes with the hounds, treed 'coons with the Negroes, and, lingering in the quarters, spent hours and hours watching the dances and listening to the songs and the stories that had come from Africa more often than not.

Van Wyck Brooks, *The Times of Melville and Whitman.*

Masked as a cornfield journalist, a harmless darky, and a jovial farmer, Harris satirized the South emerging in his time by questioning all of the values it was developing. Fearing the results of writing direct satire, he adopted personae who could transmute and suppress the satirical into the allegorical impulse.

Jay Martin, *Harvest of Change, American Literature, 1865—1914.*

In reality the stories are only alligator pears — one eats them merely for the sake of the dressing.

Mark Twain, Letter to J. C. Harris, 1881.

HARRISON, BENJAMIN

1833—1901 Twenty-Third United States President

The President is a good deal like the old camp horse that Dickens described; he is strapped up so he can't fall down.

On himself, Letter to William McKinley, 4 February 1892.

. . . he sweated ice water.

Anon., in Jules Ables, *The Rockefeller Millions.*

The Boys in Blue and soldiers true
    Are shouting loud for General Ben.
While from the river to the lakes
    He draws a host of loyal men.
But nowhere in the Hoosier state
    A single voice or vote he gains
From Copperheads or ex-Confeds
    For they all march with Uncle James.

Anon. campaign song when Harrison ran unsuccessfully for Governor of Indiana, 1876.

We're going to work tonight
    We're going to work all day;
If you've any money to bet on the race
    Don't bet on the free trade bay.

Ben Harrison is a thoroughbred
There are no flies upon his head
No clogs or heavy weights he wears,
Protection is the flag he bears.

Anon. campaign slogan, 1888.

The grandson of the old Harrison speaks as if he were picking his flint. In the meantime the hour is one of the quietest in the history of the land.

George Alfred Townsend, in *Cincinnati Inquirer.*

You may be interested in knowing that we have one of the smallest Presidents the U.S. has ever known. He is narrow, unresponsive and, oh, so cold. The town is full of grumblers. Nobody appears to like H., though, of course, many tolerate him for what he can give out; there is no administration element in town. . . .

. . . Senators call and say their say to him, and he stands silent. . . . As one Senator says: 'It's like talking to a hitching post.'

Walter Wellman, Letter to Walter Q. Gresham, 20 March 1889.

The people trusted Harrison. They had never been told things by Harrison which they discovered after the campaign was over to be vote-catching tom-foolery. He never deceived them with promises he did not expect to keep. He did not try to flatter them by pretending to believe their judgment infallible.

William Allen White, in Henry J. Sievers, *Benjamin Harrison: Hoosier Statesman.*

See also Robert A. Taft

HARRISON, WILLIAM HENRY

1773—1841 Ninth United States President

Some folks are silly enough as to have formed a plan to make a President of the United States out of this Clerk and Clodhopper.
    On himself, Letter to Stephen Van Rensselaer, 1836.

When Martin was housed like a chattel,
    Opposed to the war as you know,
Our hero was foremost in battle,
    And conquered at Tippecanoe.
    Anon., *Washington Globe*, 11 June 1840.

Tippecanoe And Tyler Too!
    Anon. campaign slogan.

His name is *Harrison*; upon the banks
Of conscious Thames he played his warlike pranks,
And then a Gov'ner of North Western land
He held o'er wolves and Indians wide command.
Upon the Senate floor, besides, he stood, and
Talked of Rome, much to his country's good.
'Tis even said, to market he doth send
His corn and pigs, 'The Farmer of North Bend.'
With such a grand ballon [*sic*] he cannot fail
Direct into the *Mansion White* to sail
You may depend sir, Martin will feel blue
When e'er we shout 'hurrah for Tippecanoe.'
    Anon., in *Albany Argus*, 5 January 1836.

Make way for old Tip, turn out, turn out,
Make way for old Tip, turn out!
'Tis the people's decree,
Their choice he shall be,
So Martin Van Buren turn out, turn out,
So Martin Van Buren turn out!
    Anon., 1840 campaign song.

Let Van from his coolers of silver drink wine,
And lounge on his cushioned settee,
Our man on his buckeye bench can recline,
Content with hard cider is he.
Then a shout for each freeman, a shout for each state,
To the plain, honest husbandman true,
And this be our motto, the motto of fate,
Hurrah for old Tippecanoe!
    Ibid.

Harrison comes in upon a hurricane; God grant he may not go out upon a wreck!
    John Quincy Adams, Diary, vol. 10.

[An] active but shallow mind, a political adventurer not without talents but self-sufficient, vain and indiscreet.
    John Quincy Adams, in A. Steinberg, *The First Ten.*

Harrison was the first president to die in office. He had been in his office for thirty days, working on new tariff laws, and probably over-taxed himself.
    Richard Armour, *It All Started With Columbus.*

The American eagle has taken his flight which is supplied by the cider barrell. . . . Hurrah for Tippecanoe is heard more frequently than Hurrah for the Constitution, and whatever may be the result of the election, the Hurrah is heard and felt in every part of the United States.
    Philip Hone, Diary.

General Harrison was sung into the Presidency.
    Ibid.

The President is the most extraordinary man I ever saw. He does not seem to realize the vast importance of his elevation. . . . He is as tickled with the Presidency as is a young woman with a new bonnet.
    Martin Van Buren, in A. Steinberg, *The First Ten.*

See also John Tyler, Martin Van Buren

HART, WILLIAM S.

1872—1946 Actor

My friends, I love the art of making motion pictures. It is as the breath of life to me. The rush of the wind that cuts your face, the pounding hoofs of the pursuing posse; out there in front, a fallen tree trunk that spans a yawning chasm. The noble animal under you that takes it in the same old ground-eating gallop. The shots of the baffled ones that remain behind. And then . . . the clouds of dust through which comes the faint voice of the director. 'OK, Bill. OK. Glad you made it. Great stuff, Bill. Great stuff, and say, Bill, give old Fritz a pat on the nose for me, will you?' Oh, the thrill of it all!
    On himself, Introduction, filmed for the sound re-issue of *Tumbleweeds*, 1938.

William S. Hart was the strong silent man of the movies for ten years after 1914. His steely gaze, adamant honesty, determination, daring and hearty goodness were passionately enjoyed week in and week out by old and young. . . . Always he was 'a one-woman man, nature's nobleman who fights a mob to victory single-handed.' 'Quick on the guns as William S. Hart' became an American proverb.
    Lewis Jacobs, *The Rise of the American Film.*

Hart's West was refreshingly new, tough and dirty, sometimes brutal and bawdy. If the character he portrayed was the familiar good-bad man, his mixture of nobility and baseness was never completely predictable. He might bow to the heroine's innocence . . . or he might simply seduce her.

Donald W. La Badie, 'The Last Round-Up', in *Show*, September 1962.

He is a strange figure now, with his stiff walk, his mirthless face, his mid-Victorian morality. . . . And yet there is still an oddly noble, even poetic quality about the man — perhaps because of his very strangeness, perhaps because of the sentimental romanticism with which he invests the land and the horses and the heroines with whom he comes into contact; perhaps more because of the character which was to become a commonplace, but which he first created: the 'good-bad man', the hero with a past for whom his present mobility is a kind of atonement, and who will always ride off into the sunset rather than commit another person to the burden of a lasting attachment.

David Robinson, *Hollywood in the Twenties*.

I saw my first movie in Atlanta, Georgia, during World War I. It was a William S. Hart western and was shown in a small neighbourhood theatre with player piano and a ten-cent admission. . . . As for lasting influence of the William S. Hart Westerns and the serialized thrillers of those early days, I am not especially aware of one, unless it be that the 'Good-uns' somehow managed to overcome the 'Bad-uns'.

Dean Rusk, in *Show*, April 1963.

Bill Hart was a second-rate Shakespearean actor. He had played Messala in *Ben Hur* on the stage and had never been farther west than Jersey City. He had a mean rugged countenance, and so that fine showman Tom Ince, second only to Griffith, made him come to Hollywood and do some Western into which that face fitted.

He was scared to death of horses.

Adela Rogers St Johns, *The Honeycomb*.

See also Tom Mix.

HARTE, (FRANCIS) BRET

1836–1902 Author

You cannot possibly hate pen and ink as I do who live in it and by it perpetually.

On himself, Undated letter to his wife.

. . . Bret Harte illuminated everything he touched. Now in shilling-shockers contracted for, years in advance at so many pounds a hundred words, he slaughters cowboys to make cockneys 'sit up', or

hashes up a short story to serve as jam between commercial sandwiches in sloppy popular magazines.

Ambrose Bierce, in George R. Stewart Jr, *Bret Harte, Argonaut and Exile*.

What he had written, out of a real desire to express the spirit of the region he knew, was, he discovered, merely entertainment for his readers. He accepted — harassed, one must admit, by personal difficulties and financial troubles — the role of entertainer, and as an entertainer survived for thirty years his death as an artist.

Granville Hicks, *The Great Tradition*.

. . . our Theocritus at last, and from California, whence we least expected him.

James Russell Lowell, in Edward Wagenknecht, *James Russell Lowell, Portrait of a Many-Sided Man*.

He was showy, meretricious, insincere; and he constantly advertised these qualities in his dress. He was distinctly pretty, in spite of the fact that his face was badly pitted with smallpox. In the days when he could afford it — and in the days when he couldn't — his clothes always exceeded the fashion by a shade or two.

Mark Twain, in Maxwell Geismar, *Mark Twain, An American Prophet*.

He hadn't a sincere fiber in him. I think he was incapable of emotion for I think he had nothing to feel with.

Mark Twain, in E. Hudson Lond, *Mark Twain, Handbook*.

Harte's dainty self-complacencies extended to his carriage and gait. His carriage was graceful and easy, his gait was of the mincing sort, but was the right gait for him, for an unaffected one would not have harmonized with the rest of the man and the clothes.

Mark Twain, in Bernard De Voto ed., *Mark Twain in Eruption*.

Harte, in a mild and colorless way, was that kind of man — that is to say, he was a man without a country; no, not a man — man is too strong a term; he was an invertebrate without a country.

Ibid.

He was an incorrigible borrower of money; he borrowed from all his friends; if he ever repaid a loan the incident failed to pass into history.

Mark Twain, *Autobiography*.

See also Mark Twain

HARVEY, WILLIAM

1578—1657 Physician

Ah! my old Friend Dr. Harvey — I knew him right well. He made me sitt by him 2 or 3 hours together in his meditating apartment discoursing. Why, had he been stiffe, starcht, and retired, as other formall Doctors are, he had known no more than they. From the meanest person, in some way, or other, the learnedst man may learn something. Pride has been one of the greatest stoppers of the Advancement of Learning.

John Aubrey, *Brief Lives.*

I have heard him say, that after his Booke of the *Circulation of the Blood* came-out, that he fell mightily in his Practize, and that 'twas beleeved by the vulgar that he was crack-brained; and all the Physitians were against his Opinion, and envyed him; many wrote against him.

Ibid.

He was very Cholerique; and in his young days wore a dagger (as the fashion then was) but this Dr. would be apt to draw-out his dagger upon every slight occasion.

Ibid.

He was not tall; but of the lowest stature, round faced, olivaster complexion; little Eie, round, very black, full of spirit; his haire was black as a Raven, but quite white 20 yeares before he dyed.

Ibid.

I remember he kept a pretty young wench to wayte on him, which I guesse he made use of for warmeth-sake as King David did, and tooke care of her in his Will, as also of his man servant.

Ibid.

And I remember that when I asked our famous *Harvey*, in the only Discourse I had with him, (which was but a while before he dyed) What were the things that induc'd him to think of a *Circulation of the Blood?* He answer'd me, that when he took notice that the Valves in the Veins of so many several Parts of the Body, were so Plac'd that they gave free passage to the Blood Towards the Heart, but oppos'd the passage of the Venal Blood the Contrary way: He was invited to imagine, that so Provident a Cause as Nature had not so Plac'd so many Valves without Design: and no Design seem'd more probable, than That, since the Blood could not well, because of the interposing Valves, be sent by the Veins to the Limbs; it should be Sent through the Arteries, and Return through the Veins, whose Valves did not oppose its course that way.

Robert Boyle, *A Disquisition about the Final Causes of Natural Things.*

Coy Nature, (which remain'd, though Aged grown,
A Beauteous virgin still, injoyd by none,
Nor seen unveil'd by any one)
When Harvey's violent passion she did see,
Began to tremble and to flee,
Took Santuary like *Daphne* in a tree:
There Daphne's lover stop't, and thought it much
The very Leaves of her to touch,
But *Harvey* our *Apollo*, stopt not so,
Into the Bark, and root he after her did goe.
Abraham Cowley, *Ode upon Dr. Harvey.*

And truly when ever He hath been pleased to give any of his own Inventions leave to see the light, He hath not deported Himself with Ostentation, or superciliousness, after the custome of many, as if an Oak had spoken, or he had deserved a draught of Hens Milk: but, His Dictates were Oraculous, and Merits above the reach of Elogie, or Reward: but, with exceeding Modesty, as if onely casually, or without any difficultie of inquest, he had fallen upon the Discovery of those Mysteries, which, indeed, he long searched into with profest diligence, and study indefatigable.

George Ent, *Epistle Dedicatory* to Harvey's *Anatomical Exercitations.*

Dr. Harvey was ever afraid of becoming blind: early one morning, for he always rose early, his housekeeper coming into his chamber to call him, opened the window shutters, told him the hour, and asked him if he would not rise. Upon which he asked if she had opened the shutters; she replied yes — then shut them again — she did so — then open them again. But still the effect was the same to him, for he had awakened stone blind. Upon which he told her to fetch him a bottle, (which she herself had observed to stand on a shelf in his chamber for a long time), out of which he drank a large draught, and it being a strong poison, which it is supposed he had long before prepared and set there for this purpose, he expired within three hours after.

Edward Hasted, *The History and Topographical Survey of the County of Kent.*

He is the first Englishman of whom we know enough to say that he was definitely what we now mean by 'a scientific man'. He viewed the problems of life as we view them, he observed the facts as we observe them, he experimented as we experiment, and he reasoned as we reason.

Sir Wilmot Herringham, 'William Harvey at St. Bartholomew's', in *St. Bartholomew's Hospital Journal,* 1928.

In merit, Harvey's rank must be comparatively low indeed. So much had been discovered by others, that little more was left for him to do than to dress it up into a system; and *that*, every judge in such matters will allow, required no extraordinary talents. Yet, easy as it was, it made him *immortal*. But none of his writings shew him to have been a man of uncommon abilities. It were easy to quote many passages, which bring him nearly to a level with the rest of mankind. He lived almost thirty years after Asellius published the Lacteals, yet, to the last, seemed most inclined to think, that no such vessels existed. Thirty hours at any time, should have been sufficient to remove all his doubts.

William Hunter, *Two Introductory Lectures to his Last Course of Anatomical Lectures.*

HASSAM, (FREDERICK) CHILDE

1859—1935 Artist

A seeker of sunlight and bright skies, a watcher of the myriad atmospheric changes in our common day, an avid observer of all forms of human endeavor with hands and brains, he came to look upon New York as the most fascinating city on earth. It held all sorts of people. It had all kinds of weather, especially the good. He knew its nobility and its squalor. He called its skyline incomparable. He painted The Hovel and the Skyscraper, The Flatiron Flower Shop, Flower Girls, The Old Bottle Man, Hodcarriers, Bricklayers. Himself a worker, he liked to picture workers. He painted downtown and uptown.

Adeline Adams, *Childe Hassam.*

These are the reasons why I like your work, built up 'on the knowledge of a lifetime,' and not upon expressionism, cubism, incompetence and conceit, the backbone of the rot and rubbish foisted by strange sharpers and incompetents — there are lots of blatant Americans, as they call themselves, among them, — fooling the most gullible and ignorant public in the world, crying they know not why, save as an investment, for art and getting artlessness, but cocksure in the valor of their ignorance.

Joseph Pennell, Letter to Hassam, 23 February 1923.

HASTINGS, LADY ELIZABETH

1682—1739 Philanthropist

Though her mien carries much more invitation than command, to behold her is an immediate check to loose behaviour; to love her was a liberal education.

Sir Richard Steele, in *Tatler*, no. 49.

HASTINGS, WARREN

1732—1818 Colonial Administrator

What age is it permitted me to look back upon, with my bodily and mental faculties, though impaired, not destroyed; and as my memory presents to me the record of times past, to be able to say 'quorum pars non parva fuit', and like a grain of sand in the way of the ball of a billiard table, to have given its excentrick direction to the rolling events of the world, which they would have obtained, if I had never existed.

On himself, Letter to Edward Baber, 6 October 1815.

I gave you all, and you have rewarded me with confiscation, disgrace, and a life of impeachment.

On himself, to the House of Commons, in A. M. Davies, *Warren Hastings*, 1935.

A mouth extending fierce from ear to ear,
With fangs like those which wolves and tigers wear;
Eyes, whose dark orbs announce, and sullen mood,
A lust of rapine, and a thirst of blood;
Such Hastings was, as by the Commons painted,
(Men shuddered as they look'd, and women
                    fainted —). . . .
Yet he has friends! And they, — nay (strange to tell!)
His very wife, who ought to know him well,
Whose daily sufferings from the worst of men
Should make her wish the wretch impeach'd again, —
Believe him gentle, meek, and true of heart —
O Hastings, what a hypocrite thou art!

On himself, on his portrait painted by Lemuel Abbott, in A. M. Davies, *ibid.*

He tried to see India with the eyes of an Indian, his successors saw it with the eyes of Englishmen. He sought to give India the things he knew it needed: they sought to give it the things they thought would benefit it.

A. M. Davies, in *ibid.*

We can hardly wonder that his popularity with the Bengalees was such as no later ruler has ever attained, or that after a century of great events Indian mothers still hush their infants with the name of Warren Hastings.

John Richard Green, *A Short History of the English People.*

His principles were somewhat lax. His heart was somewhat hard. But though we cannot with truth describe him either as a righteous or as a merciful ruler, we cannot regard without admiration the amplitude and fertility of his intellect, his rare talents for command, for administration, and for controversy, his dauntless courage, his honourable poverty, his fervent zeal for the interests of state, his noble equanimity, tried by both extremes of fortune and never disturbed by either.

T. B. Macaulay, *Essays*: 'Warren Hastings'.

The just fame of Hastings rises still higher, when we reflect that he was not bred a statesman; that he was sent from school to a counting house; and that he was employed during the prime of his manhood as a commercial agent, far from all intellectual society.

Ibid.

His capacity for decision, his grasp of essentials, and his combination of daring and dogged determination were of incalculable value in the dangerous last years of his reign. Had a strange combination of circumstances not kept him in power long after he would have been recalled under modern conditions of communication, it is difficult to think of any other man then concerned in Indian affairs who would have averted disaster.

Lucy S. Sutherland, *The East India Company in 18th Century Politics*.

HATHAWAY, ANNE

1556—1623 Shakespeare's Wife

She hath a way so to control
To rapture the imprisoned soul
And sweetest Heaven on earth display,
That to be Heaven Ann hath a way;
     She hath a way
     Ann Hathaway —
To be Heaven's self Ann hath a way.
     Charles Dibdin, *A Love Ditty*.

HAWKSMOOR, NICHOLAS

1661—1736 Architect

[Vanbrugh's] approach to architecture was basically simple whereas Hawksmoor's may fairly be called basically complex.

K. Downes, *Hawksmoor*.

In terms of architecture, the Mausoleum remote on its lonely hill is his greatest achievement. It is one of the last Baroque buildings in the freedom of its sources and the intensity of its direct assault on the emotions. But its geometrical simplicity and its sombre severity look forward to the age of neo-classicism. And the strangeness — even when sources have been analysed — of many of Hawksmoor's formal devices, has found recognition only in the present century's exploration of the subconscious. Ultimately the quality and character of his work cannot be put into prose. Its language is the one he knew best and knew as few other English architects have known: the eloquence of stone.

Ibid.

He was always inclined by his temperament toward that which is sombre and awe-inspiring. Like Michael Angelo's, his architecture was great tragedy.

H. S. Goodhart-Rendel, *Nicholas Hawksmoor*.

Poor Hawksmoor, What a Barbarous Age, have his fine, ingenious Parts fallen into. What wou'd Mons[r]: Colbert in France have given for Such a Man?

Sir John Vanbrugh, Letter, August 1721.

See also Christopher Wren

HAWTHORNE, NATHANIEL

1804—64 Author

I have another great difficulty in the lack of materials; for I have seen so little of the world that I have nothing but thin air to concoct my stories of, and it is not easy to give a life-like semblance to such shadowy stuff.

On himself, Letter to Henry Wadsworth Longfellow, 1838.

I sat down by the wayside of life like a man under enchantment, and a shrubbery sprung up around me, and the bushes grew to be saplings, and the saplings became trees, until no exit appeared possible, through the tangling depths of my obscurity.

On himself, in Malcolm Cowley ed., Introduction to *Nathaniel Hawthorne, The Selected Works*.

I am slow to feel — slow, I suppose, to comprehend and, like the anaconda, I need to lubricate any object a great deal before I can swallow it and actually make it my own.

On himself, in Mark Van Doren, *Nathaniel Hawthorne*.

I doubt whether I have ever really talked with half a dozen persons in my life, men or women.

Ibid.

I don't want to be a doctor, and live by men's diseases; nor a minister to live by their sins; nor a lawyer to live by their quarrels. So I don't see there's anything left for me but to be an author.

Ibid.

Hawthorne was against sin. Without it, though, he would never have become a great author.
Richard Armour, *American Lit Relit*.

In the life history of Nathaniel Hawthorne are no high surges of drama and excitement, no flaming and sulfurous sins over which biographers can exercise their rhetoric and pseudo-psychologists ponder the inhibition, the trauma, the concealed loathing which might, if one looks far enough, color the writings. The Story is quite otherwise: Hawthorne's life was commonplace, even dull.
Edward H. Davidson, 'Nathaniel Hawthorne', in Perry Miller ed., *Major Writers of America*, vol. 1.

Nathaniel Hawthorne's reputation as a writer is a very pleasing fact, because his writing is not good for anything, and this is a tribute to the man.
Ralph Waldo Emerson, in Jay B. Hubbell, *Who Are The Major American Writers?*

My father was two men, one sympathetic and intuitional, the other critical and logical; altogether they formed a combination that could not be thrown off its feet.
Julian Hawthorne, in Edward Wagenknecht, *Nathaniel Hawthorne: Man and Writer*.

He has the look all the time, to one who doesn't know him, of a rogue who suddenly finds himself in a company of detectives. But in spite of his rusticity, I felt a sympathy for him amounting to anguish. . . .
Henry James Sr, Letter to Ralph Waldo Emerson, 1861.

He combined in a singular degree the spontaneity of the imagination with a haunting care for moral problems. Man's conscience was his theme but he saw it in the light of a creative fancy which added, out of its own substance, an interest, and, I may almost say, an importance.
Henry James Jr, *Hawthorne*.

Had he been born without the poetic imagination, he would have written treatises on the Origin of Evil.
James Russell Lowell, in J. Donald Crowley ed., *Hawthorne, The Critical Heritage*.

There is Hawthorne, with genius so shrinking and
rare
That you hardly at first see the strength that is there;
A frame so robust, with a nature so sweet,
So earnest, so graceful, so lithe and so fleet,
Is worth a descent from Olympus to meet.
James Russell Lowell, *A Fable for Critics*.

Where Hawthorne is known, he seems to be deemed a pleasant writer, with a pleasant style — a sequestered, harmless man, from whom any deep or weighty thing would hardly be anticipated — a man who means no meanings.
Herman Melville, 'Hawthorne and His Mosses', in Edmund Wilson ed., *The Shock of Recognition*.

He has the purest style, the finest taste, the most available scholarship, the most delicate humor, the most touching pathos, the most radiant imagination, the most consummate ingenuity; and with these varied good qualities he has done *well* as a mystic.
Edgar Allen Poe, in *ibid*.

Although a Yankee, he partakes of none of the characteristics of a Yankee. His thinking and his style have an antique air. His roots strike down through the visible mold of the present, and draw sustenance from the generations under ground.
Alexander Smith, *Dreamthorp*.

Hawthorne — the half man of genius who never could carry out an idea or work it through to the full result. . . .
Algernon Charles Swinburne, Letter to John H. Ingram, 9 January 1875.

There never surely was a powerful, active, continually effective mind less round, more lop-sided, than that of NATHANIEL HAWTHORNE.
Anthony Trollope, *The Genius of Nathaniel Hawthorne*, in B. Bernard Cohen, *The Recognition of Nathaniel Hawthorne*.

But Hawthorne, when you have studied him, will be very precious to you. He will have plunged you into melancholy, he will have overshadowed you with black forebodings, he will almost have crushed you with imaginary sorrows; but he will have enabled you to feel yourself an inch taller during the process.
Ibid.

Hawthorne can be casual, desultory, even pedagogic in his method; he can be pale and dull. At his worst, he has much feeble and conventional allegory and much that is fanciful rather than truly imaginative, and he had a tiresome weakness for dioramas, processions, and exhibits.
Edward Wagenknecht, *Cavalcade of the American Novel*.

Nathaniel Hawthorne had his limitations as an artist and as a man. His range as a writer was more deep than wide; there were aspects of experience that did not interest him very much; he often said no where most men say yes.
    Edward Wagenknecht, *Nathaniel Hawthorne: Man and Writer.*

. . . he never seemed to be doing anything, and yet he did not like to be disturbed at it.
    John Greenleaf Whittier, in Mark Van Doren, *Nathaniel Hawthorne.*

See also Henry James, Edgar Allen Poe, Robert Louis Stevenson

HAY, JOHN MILTON

1838—1905 Politician

I would not do for a Methodist preacher for I am a poor horseman. I would not suit the Baptists for I dislike water. I would fail as an Episcopalian, for I am no ladies' man.
    On himself, in A. K. Adams, *The Home Book of Humorous Quotations.*

HAYDON, BENJAMIN ROBERT

1786—1846 Historical Painter

The basis of my character was earnestness of feeling. I took up everything as if my life depended on it, and not feeling sufficient gratification in simply doing all that I could, my imagination was never satisfied if I did not call on the aid and blessing of God to correct and fortify my resolve.
    On himself, *Autobiography.*

Haydon hardly contemplated a teaspoon without a desire to shout and hurl himself at it.
    Edmund Blunden, Introduction to Haydon, *Autobiography.*

Painters with poets for the laurels vie:
But should the laureat bands thy claims deny,
Wear thou thy own green palm, Haydon, trium-
                                        phantly.
    Charles Lamb, *Poem to Haydon.*

Haydon believed himself Phidias in the morning, and retired as Michael Angelo at night.
    John Ruskin, *Sir Joshua and Holbein* (first draft, 1860).

Haydon! let worthier judges praise the skill
Here by thy pencil shown in truth of lines
And charm of colours; I applaud those signs
Of thought, that give the true poetic skill.
    William Wordsworth, *To B. R. Haydon, On Seeing His Picture of Napoleon Buonaparte on the Island of St. Helena.*

HAYES, RUTHERFORD BIRCHARD

1822—93 Nineteenth United States President

Mr. Hayes came in by a majority of one, and goes out by unanimous consent.
    Anon., in John M. Taylor, *Garfield of Ohio: The Available Man.*

Rutherford, the Rover.
    Anon., in *Chicago Times*, 6 September 1878.

His Fraudulency.
    Anon. contemporary newspaper headline, in Harry Barnard, *Rutherford B. Hayes and his America.*

Conkling and Hayes
Is the ticket that pays.
    Anon., Vaudeville song.

The tide is in, the tide is in,
    I hear its deaf'ning roar,
Its mighty waves, with thundering din,
    Are bursting on the shore.
Fling wide, fling wide our flag afar.
    And strike for happier days;
Count every stripe and every star
    A People's pledge for Hayes.
    Anon., *The Popular Tide for Hayes.*

He recognized nothing, and neither authorized nor repudiated anybody. According to the newspaper accounts he would hardly go further in political discussion than to accede to the proposition that there was a republican form of government and that this was the hundredth year of the national government.
    Anon., in *Nation*, February 1877.

[He had] good sense, like a horse.
    Sardis Birchard, in Harry Barnard, *Rutherford B. Hayes and his America.*

No painful, care-worn wrinkles, indicative of infirmities or misfortunes, to provoke a grudge against nature, or engender sourness toward mankind. Nor does he wear a smirking face, as if he were a candidate for admiration; but a fine sunny countenance.
    Thomas C. Donaldson, *Memoirs.*

The policy of the President has turned out to be a give-away from the beginning. He has nulled suits, discontinued prosecutions, offered conciliation everywhere in the South, while they have spent their time in whetting their knives for any Republican they could find.

James Abram Garfield, in Harry Barnard, *Rutherford B. Hayes and his America*.

It may be asked whether this man of destiny has any marked peculiarities. I answer none whatever. Neither his body nor his mind runs into rickety proportions.

Judge William Johnston, in H. J. Eckenrode, *Rutherford B. Hayes: Statesman of Reunion*.

See also Chester A. Arthur

HAYLEY, WILLIAM

1745—1820 Poet, Biographer

Thy friendship oft has made my heart to ache:
Do be my Enemy for Friendship's sake.

William Blake, *Epigram*.

William Hayley, Esq. of Earthem, in Sussex, one of the humerous *genteel poets* of the present age, who have judgment without genius, and harmony without thought.

Anthony Pasquin (John Williams), *The Children of Thespis*.

HAZLITT, WILLIAM

1778—1830 Essayist

Without the aid of prejudice and custom, I should not be able to find my way across the room.

On himself, *Sketches and Essays*: 'On Prejudice'.

Well, I've had a happy life.

On himself (last words), in W. C. Hazlitt, *Memoirs of William Hazlitt*.

Hazlitt, the pit-trumpet of Mr Kean at Drury Lane.

Anon., in Philadelphia *National Gazette*, 7 February 1821.

If Hazlitt was a godsend to Kean, Kean was scarcely less of a godsend to Hazlitt. The critic made the actor's reputation, but the actor made the critic's immortality *as* a theatrical critic. If Hazlitt had not had Kean to write about, he would certainly have written much less with far inferior life and gusto,

and would probably never have collected his articles.

William Archer, Introduction to *Hazlitt on Theatre*, 1895.

Hazlitt . . . sits a silent picture of severity. If you were to watch his face for a month you would not catch a smile there. His eyes are always turned towards the ground, except when one is turned up now and then with a sneer that cuts a bad pun and a young author's maiden table-talk to atoms.

John Clare, *Fragment on the Londoners*.

His manners are 99 in a 100 singularly repulsive.

Samuel Taylor Coleridge, Letter to Thomas Wedgwood, 16 September 1803.

Hazlitt possesses considerable Talent; but it is diseased by a morbid hatred of the Beautiful, and killed by the absence of the Imagination, & alas! by a wicked Heart of embruted Appetites. Poor wretch! he is a melancholy instance of the awful Truth — that man cannot be on a Level with the Beasts — he must be above them or below them.

Samuel Taylor Coleridge, Letter to Hugh J. Rose, 25 September 1816.

Under this stone does William Hazlitt lie
Thankless of all that God or man could give.
He lived like one who never thought to die,
He died like one who dared not hope to live.

Samuel Taylor Coleridge, *Epitaph*.

Hazlitt . . . had perhaps the most uninteresting mind of all our distinguished critics.

T. S. Eliot, *Essays*: 'John Dryden'.

William Hazlitt . . . owned that he could not bear young girls; they drove him mad. So I took him home to my old nurse, where he recovered perfect tranquility.

Charles Lamb, Letter to William Wordsworth, 26 June 1806.

To the play itself . . . he paid scarcely any attention, even when he went there in his capacity as a writer for the critical journals; for, notwithstanding the masterly truth and force of most of his decisions on plays and actors, I will venture to say, that in almost every case, except those of his two favourites, Kean and Liston, they might be described as the result of a few hasty glances and a few half-heard phrases. From these he drew instant deductions which took others hours of observation to reach, and as many more of labour to work out.

P. G. Patmore, *My Friends and Acquaintances*.

Though we are mighty fine fellows nowadays, we cannot write like Hazlitt.
Robert Louis Stevenson, *Virginibus Puerisque*.

See also Edmund Kean, Robert Louis Stevenson

HEARST, WILLIAM RANDOLPH

1863—1951 Newspaper Proprietor

Please remain. You furnish the pictures and I'll furnish the war.
On himself, Telegram to artist Frederic Remington who desired to return to America from Cuba where he said there was no war in progress, March 1908.

He wrote so much about the Yellow Peril that his journalism took its distinctive coloration from the subject.
Richard Armour, *It All Started With Columbus*.

See also Louella Parsons

HEMINGWAY, ERNEST MILLER

1899—1961 Author

I'm Ernie Hemorrhoid, the poor man's Pyle.
On himself, when putting on a war correspondent's uniform, in Robert Macerving, *Hemingway in Cuba*.

All good books have one thing in common — they are truer than if they had really happened, and after you've read one of them you will feel that all that happened, happened to you and then it belongs to you forever: the happiness and unhappiness, good and evil, ecstasy and sorrow, the food, wine, beds, people and the weather. If you can give that to readers, then you're a writer. That's what I was trying to give them in *For Whom The Bell Tolls*.
On himself, in A. E. Hotchner, *Papa Hemingway*.

Wearing underwear is as formal as I ever hope to get.
Ibid.

But my writing is nothing. My boxing is everything.
On himself, in Morley Callaghan, *That Summer in Paris*.

Always remember this. If you have a success, you have it for the wrong reasons. If you become popular it is always because of the worst aspects of your work. They always praise you for the worst aspects. It never fails.
Ibid.

When I have an idea, I turn down the flame, as if it were a little alcohol stove, as low as it will go. Then it explodes and that is my idea.
On himself, in James R. Mellow, *Charmed Circle: Gertrude Stein & Co.*

If a writer of prose knows enough about what he is writing about, he may omit things that he knows, and the reader, if the writer is writing truly enough, will have a feeling of those things as strongly as though the writer had stated them. The dignity of movement of an iceberg is due to only one-eighth of it being above water.
On himself, in Malcolm Cowley, *A Second Flowering*.

A great writer seems to be born with knowledge. But he really is not; he has only been born with the ability to learn in a quicker ratio to the passage of time than other men and without conscious application, and with an intelligence to accept or reject what is already presented as knowledge.
Ibid.

I had learned already never to empty the well of my writing, but always to stop when there was still something there in the deep part of the well, and let it refill at night from the springs that fed it.
On himself, in *A Moveable Feast*.

The tragic view of life comes out in his perennial contrast of the permanence of nature and the evanescence of man. But he does not repine. Here is nature and here is man. Here also is something about the nature of manhood.
Carlos Baker, *Hemingway: Writer as Artist*.

And as for Hemingway himself, why was he always hardening himself up? The answer was obvious. Anyone close to him knew he was really soft and sentimental. It was amusing to remember the Hemingway who had first come to Montparnasse. Ask anybody. Why had he been wearing those three heavy sweaters to make himself look husky and powerful?
Morley Callaghan, *That Summer in Paris*.

Hemingway wanted to make his readers feel the emotion directly — not as if they were being told about it, but as if they were taking part in it. The best way to produce this effect, he decided as a first theorem, was to set down exactly, in their proper sequence, the sights, sounds, touches, tastes, and smells that had evoked an emotion he remembered feeling. Then, without auctorial comments and without ever saying that he or his hero had been frightened, sad, or angry, he could make the reader feel the emotion for himself.
Malcolm Cowley, *A Second Flowering*.

A literary style . . . of wearing false hair on the chest.
> Max Eastman, review of *Death in the Afternoon*, in Carlos Baker, *Ernest Hemingway, A Life Story*.

He is a great writer. If I didn't think so I wouldn't have tried to kill him. . . . I was the champ and when I read his stuff I knew he had something. So I dropped a heavy glass skylight on his head at a drinking party. But you can't kill the guy. He's not human.
> F. Scott Fitzgerald, in Jed Kiley, *Hemingway, A Title Fight in Ten Rounds*.

His inclination is toward megalomania and mine toward melancholy.
> F. Scott Fitzgerald, in Carlos Baker, *Ernest Hemingway, A Life Story*.

There are pieces and paragraphs of your work that I read over and over — in fact I stopped myself doing it for a year and a half because I was afraid that your particular rhythms were going to creep in on mine by a process of filtration.
> F. Scott Fitzgerald, Letter to Hemingway, 1 June 1934.

Hemingway's words strike you, each one, as if they were pebbles fetched fresh from a brook. They live and shine, each in its place. So one of his pages has the effect of a brook-bottom into which you look down through the flowing water. The words form a tessellation, each in order beside the other.
> Ford Madox Ford, in Edmund Wilson, *The Wound and the Bow*.

He comes and sits at my feet and praises me. It makes me nervous.
> Ford Madox Ford, in Arthur Mizener, *The Saddest Story, A Biography of Ford Madox Ford*.

For Hemingway courage is a permanent element in a tragic formula: life is a trap in which a man is bound to be beaten and at last destroyed, but he emerges triumphant, in his full stature, if he manages to keep his chin up.
> W. M. Frohock, *The Novel of Violence in America*.

He's the original Limelight Kid, just you watch him for a few months. Wherever the limelight is, you'll find Ernest with his big lovable boyish grin, making hay.
> Robert McAlmon, in Malcolm Cowley, *A Second Flowering*.

Famous at twenty-five; thirty a master.
> Archibald MacLeish, in Carlos Baker, *Hemingway: Writer as Artist*.

When I first met Hemingway he had a truly sensitive capacity for emotion, and that was the stuff of the first stories; but he was shy of himself and he began to develop, as a shield, a big Kansas City-boy brutality about it, and so he was 'touchy' because he was really sensitive and ashamed that he was. Then it happened. I saw it happening and tried to save what was fine there, but it was too late. He went the way so many other Americans have gone before, the way they are still going. He became obsessed with sex and violent death. . . .
> Gertrude Stein, in John Malcolm Brinnin, *The Third Rose*.

Despite Hemingway's preoccupation with physical contests, his heroes are almost always defeated physically, nervously, practically: their victories are moral ones.
> Edmund Wilson, *The Wound and the Bow*.

HENDERSON, ARTHUR

1863—1935 Labour Leader, Statesman

We will support Henderson as a rope supports a man who is hanged.
> V. I. Lenin, in a message from the Russian Communist Party to the British Labour Party, 1920, in A. J. P. Taylor, *English History 1914—1945*.

HENDRIX, JIMI (JAMES MARSHALL)

1942—70 Musician

A psychedelic hootchie-kootchie man, swathed in red and orange, he was magnificent, at the very edge of the believable and totally real.
> Michael Lydon, *Rock Folk*.

HENGIST (d. 488) AND HORSA (d. 455)

Jutish Warlords

What went on between the death of Boadicea and the emergence on the scene of Alfred, nobody seems to have the faintest idea. . . . For a time, the land was ruled by squabbling gangs of Nordic nonentities, among whom the names of Hengist and Horsa ring a dim sort of bell. These were the Vikings, who lumbered about in the twilight of the Dark Ages wearing hats tastefully trimmed with cows' horns.
> Nicholas Bentley, *Golden Sovereigns*.

HENRI, ROBERT

1865–1929 Painter

I dashed into action with my pen and rattled off two or three pages which were to convince you that first of all there is a God, proven beyond doubt of all reasoning beings by Nature itself, and secondly that what I objected to was not the belief in and worship of a God, but the fact that the worship is not simple and direct enough — that I would have God proven by nature — Nature is the book — there is no other — nature has proven the existence of a supreme power to all the world — to those who have never been reached by printed books.

On himself, in William Innes Homer, *Robert Henri and His Circle*.

I don't ever expect to paint Academic architectural historical subjects. I hope I may never have any more use for a T-square than a fiddler has — pure go easy unplumbed nature's enough for me.

Ibid.

Many critics as well as many artists mistake my leavings out and my accentuations and suppressions for lack of completion, they being so set in their belief that art is the business supply of reproducing *things* — they have not learned yet that the *idea* is what is intended to be presented and the thing is but the material *used* for its expression. What they mistake for my undevelopment is the very sign of development and instead of being short of the point they seem to think is attainment, I am really beyond that point, having shed the unnecessary, and passed on into the freer field of expression.

Ibid.

In Philadelphia in the nineties, there was a group of newspaper artists, plain and rather normal young men making their livings as craftsmen — and we became painters because Robert Henri had that magic ability as a teacher which inspires and provokes his followers into action. He was a catalyst; he was an emancipator, liberating American art from its youthful academic conformity, and liberating the individual artist from repressions that held back his natural creative ability.

William Innes Homer, *Robert Henri and His Circle*.

In a portrait by Henri, the human subject usually appears in the center of an otherwise unoccupied space. His sitters do not exist so much in a given environment, but by a *fait accompli*, a fiat of event. Though they are complete beings, and the face of each is a psychological costume (so to speak), their world is incomplete — they often exist in a space as unfinished as the vacant lots and excavations in a Henri scene of the Manhattan shore of the East River.

Leslie Katz, *Robert Henri*.

HENRY I

1068–1135

The king praises no one whom he has not resolved to ruin.

Bishop Bloet, in Henry of Huntingdon, *History of England*, translated by T. Forester.

For, he was very wanton, as appeareth by his numerous natural issue, no fewer than *fourteen*, all by him publicly owned; the males highly advanced, the females richly married, which is justly reported to his praise, it being *lust* to *beget*, but *love* to *bestow* them. His sobriety otherwise was admirable, whose temperance was of proof against any meat objected to his appetite, *Lampreys* alone excepted, on a surfeit whereof he died, *Anno Domini* 1135.

Thomas Fuller, *The History of the Worthies of England*.

Henry I was not a creator of institutions; he contributed nothing to the theory of kingship or to the philosophy of government. He created men. It was his contribution to English government and society to insert into the social fabric men with a direct interest in royal government; men who depended on royal government for their rise, and on its continuance for their survival.

R. W. Southern, *The Place of Henry I in English History*.

After his death, a monk of Bec saw him in a vision thrust into hell each morning and rescued by the prayers of monks each evening.

Ibid.

HENRY II

1133–89

This King Henry was wise, valiant, and generally fortunate. His faults were such as speak him man, rather than a vicious one. Wisdom enough he had for his work, and work enough for his wisdom, being troubled in all his relations. His wife, Queen Eleanor, brought a great portion, (fair provinces in France), and a great stomach with her; so that it is questionable, whether her froward spirit more drove her husband away from her chaste, or Rosamond's fair face more drew him to her wanton, embraces. His sons (having much of the mother in them) grew up, as in age, in obstinacy against him.

Thomas Fuller, *Church History of Britain*.

Henry II, king of England, had a reddish complexion, rather dark, and a large round head. His eyes were grey, bloodshot, and flashed in anger. He had a fiery countenance, his voice was tremulous, and his neck a little bent forward; but his chest was broad, and his arms were muscular. His body was fleshy, and he had an enormous paunch, rather by the fault of nature than from gross feeding. For his diet was temperate, and indeed in all things, considering he was a prince, he was moderate and even parsimonious. In order to reduce and cure, as far as possible, this natural tendency and defect, he waged a continual war, so to speak, with his own belly by taking immoderate exercise. . . . At the first dawn of day he would mount a fleet horse, and indefatigably spend the day in riding through the woods, penetrating the depths of forests, and crossing the ridges of hills. On his return home in the evening he was seldom seen to sit down, either before he took his supper or after; for, notwithstanding his own great fatigue, he would weary all his court by being constantly on his legs.

Giraldus Cambrensis, *The Conquest of Ireland*, translated from the Latin by T. Forester.

He travelled incessantly, and in stages intolerable, like a public carrier, and, in this matter, he showed scant consideration for his retinue. In dogs and birds he was most expert, and exceeding fond of hunting. He passed nights without sleep and was untiring in his activities. Whenever in his dreams passion mocked him with vain shapes, he used to curse his body, because neither toil nor fasting was able to break or weaken it. I, however, ascribe his activities not to his incontinence but to his fear of becoming too fat.

Walter Map, *De Nugis Curialium*, translated from the Latin by F. Tupper and M. B. Ogle.

See also Eleanour of Aquitaine

HENRY IV

1367—1413

At last, as he was praying before the shrine of St. Edward at Westminster Abbey, he was seized with a terrible fit, and was carried into the Abbot's chamber, where he presently died. It had been foretold that he would die at Jerusalem, which certainly is not, and never was, Westminster. But, as the Abbot's room had long been called the Jerusalem chamber, people said it was all the same thing, and were quite satisfied with the prediction.

Charles Dickens, *A Child's History of England*.

HENRY V

1387—1422

Owre kyng went forth to Normandy,
With grace and myyt of chivalry;
The God for hym wrouyt marvelously. . . .
    Anon., Ballad in Percy, *Reliques of Ancient English Poetry*.

The Kinge daylie and nightlie in his owne person visited and searched the watches, orders and stacions of euerie part of his hoast, and whom he founde dilligent he praised and thanked, and the negligent he corrected and chastised.

Anon., *The First English Life of King Henry the Fifth* (on his conduct during a siege).

But after the sermon was ended, the Kinge commaunded the Fryer to be brought before him; to whome in open audience he saide these wordes: 'Ye asked me this day in your sermon what I was that thus oppressed the people of Christ's profession, to wch at that time it was not convenient to make aunswere, and therefore nowe I aunswere you thus: I am the scourge of God, sent to punish the people of God for there synns.' And that aunswere made he commaunded euerie man to avoide the chamber, except the Fryer, wch they two only were together in secret communicacion by the space of two or three howers.

Ibid. (on his encounter with St Vincent Ferrier while on campaign in France).

And before he was Kyng, what tyme regnyd he Prince of Walyes, he fyll & yntendyd gretly to riot, and drew to wylde company. . . . And thanne he beganne to reigne for Kyng, & he rememberyd the gret charge & warrship that he shulde take upon hym; And anon he commaundyd al his peple that were attendaunt to his mysgovernaunce afore tyme, & all his housolde, to come before hym. And when they herde that, they were ful glad, for they subposyd that he wolde a promotyd them into gret offices. . . . But for all that, the Prynce kept his countynance ful sadly unto them, And sayde to them: 'Syrys, ye are the peple that I haue cherysyd and mayntyngd in Ryot & wylde governance; and here I geve you all in commaundment, & charge you, that from this day forward that ye forsake all misgovernaunce, lyve aftyr the lawys of Almyghty God, & aftyr the lawys of oure lande. And who that doyth the contrarye, I make feythfull promyse to God, that he shal be trewly ponisyd accordyng to the law, withoute eny favour or grace.'

The Brut Chronicle.

HENRY VI

In the year of our lord 1415, Henry V King of England called together the prelates and lords of his kingdom, and asked their advice, on peril of their souls, whether he had a better grievance against the kingdom of Scotland or against the kingdom of France, to go to war about.

> *The Book of Pluscarden*, translated by F. J. H. Skene.

Henry V was not the bluff patriot king of Shakespeare's plays; he was a dour and martial fanatic, obsessed by religion and his legal rights.

> John Bowle, *England, A Portrait*.

HOTSPUR: He made me mad
To see him shine so brisk, and smell so sweet,
And talk so like a waiting gentlewoman
Of guns, and drums, and wounds — God save the
                                       mark! —
And telling me the sovereignest thing on earth
Was parmeceti for an inward bruise.

> William Shakespeare, *Henry IV, Part I*.

For these Frenchmen, puffed up with pride and lacking in foresight, hurling mocking words at the ambassadors of the King of England, said foolishly to them that as Henry was but a young man, they would send him little balls to play with and soft cushions to rest on until he should have grown to a man's strength. When the king heard these words he was much moved and troubled in spirit; yet he addressed these short, wise and honest words to those standing around him: 'If God wills, and if my life shall be prolonged with health, in a few months I shall play with such balls in the Frenchmen's court-yards that they will lose the game eventually and for their game win but grief. And if they shall sleep too long on their cushions in their chambers, I will awake them, before they wish it, from their slumbers at dawn by beating on their doors.'

> John Strecche (on the King's reaction to insults from the ambassadors of the Dauphin), *The Chronicle for the Reign of Henry V*, translated by A. R. Myers.

See also George III, Sir John Falstolfe

HENRY VI

1421–71

And the same nyghte that Kynge Edwarde came to Londone, Kynge Herry, beyinge inwarde in presone in the Toure of Londone, was put to dethe, the xxj day of Maij, on a Tywesday nyght, betwyx xj and xij of the cloke, beyinge thenne at the Toure the Duke of Gloucestre, brother to Kynge Edwarde, and

many other; And on the morwe he was chestyd and brought to Paulys, and his face was opyne that every manne myghte see hyme; and in hys lyinge he bledde one the pament there; and afterward at the Blake Fryres was broughte and there he blede new and fresche; and from thens he was caryed to Chyrchesey in a bote, and buryed there in our Lady chapelle.

> John Warkworth, *Chronicle* (on Henry's death and burial at Chertsey).

HENRY VII

1457–1509

He was a Prince, sad, serious, and full of thoughts, and secret observations, and full of notes and memorials of his own hand, especially touching persons. As, who to employ, whom to reward, whom to inquire of, to whom to beware of, what were the dependencies, what were the factions, and the like; keeping, as it were, a journal of his thoughts.

> Francis Bacon, *History of the Reign of Henry VII*.

What the man lacked apparently was any personal charm. They called his son later Bluff King Hal and his granddaughter Good Queen Bess, but none ever gave Henry VII a nickname. He never seems to have caught the popular imagination. What contemporaries chiefly remarked in him was his wisdom, by which they meant his sound common sense. Men feared him, admired him, depended on him, but they did not love him.

> Conyers Read, *The Tudors*.

. . . Henry Tydder, son of Edmund Tydder, son of Owen Tydder, whiche of his ambitiousness and insociable covetise, encroacheth and usurpid upon hym the name and title of royall estate of this Realme of Englond, where unto he hath no maner interest, right, title, or colour, as every man wel knowoth; for he is discended of bastard blood bothe of ffather side and of mother side, For the said Owen the graunfader was bastard borne, and his moder was daughter un to John, Duke of Somerset, sone unto John, Erle of Somerset, sonne unto Dame Katryne Swynford, and of ther indouble avoutry gotyn, wherby evidently apperith that no title can nor may in him, which fully entendeth to entre this Realme, purposyng a conquest.

> Richard III, *The Proclamation against Henry Tudor*, 1485.

See also John Fisher, George II, Richard III

HENRY VIII
1491–1547

  Passetyme with good cumpanye
I love, and shall unto I dye,
  Gruche so wylle, but none deny,
So God plecyd, so lyf woll I.
    For my pastaunce'
    Hunte, syng, & daunce,
    My hert is sett:
      All godely sport
      To my comfort,
    Who shall me lett?
  On himself, in Horace Walpole, *Catalogue of Royal and Noble Authors.*

Bluff Henry the Eighth to six spouses was wedded:
One died, one survived, two divorced, two beheaded.
  Anon., nursery rhyme, *circa* 1750.

. . . Nothing can be said in his vindication, but that his abolishing Religious Houses and leaving them to the ruinous depredations of time has been of infinite use to the landscape of England in general, which probably was a principal motive for his doing it, since otherwise why should a Man who was of no Religion himself be at so much trouble to abolish one which had for ages been established in the Kingdom?
  Jane Austen, *The History of England.*

Henry the Eighth
Took a thuctheththion of mateth.
He inthithted that the monkth
Were a lathy lot of thkunkth.
  E. C. Bentley, *More Biography.*

After all thes Solempnytes and Costly tryumphes fynesshed And that our naturall yong, lusty, And Coragious prynce And souerayn lord kyng herre the viiith entreng in to the flower of pleasaunt youthe had taken vppon hyme the Regall Septour and themperyall Dyademe of this fertill and plentifull Realme of Englond wche at that tyme florysshed in all aboundance of welthe & Riches whereof he was inestymably garnysshid & furnyshed called than the golden world such grace of plenty Raygned than wt in this Realme.
  George Cavendish, *The Life and Death of Cardinal Wolsey.*

I repayring to your Majesty into your prevey Chambre Fynding your grace not as pleasaunte as I trustyd to have done I was so bolde as to aske your grace how ye lykyd the quene Whereunto your grace Sobyrly answeryd saying That I was not all men Surelye my lorde as ye know. I lykyd her beffor not well but now I lyke her moche woorse For quoth your highness I haue Felte her belye and her brestes and therby, as I can Judge She Sholde be noe Mayde which strake me so to the harte when I Felt them that I hadde nother will nor Corage to procede any ferther in other matyrs, saying I have left her as good a mayde as I founde her. . . .
  Thomas Cromwell, Letter to Henry VIII, June 1540 (reminding Henry of his words to Cromwell, after his wedding night with Anne of Cleves).

Then, there is a great story belonging to this Field of the Cloth of Gold, showing how the English were distrustful of the French, and the French of the English, until Francis rode alone one morning to Henry's tent; and, going in before he was out of bed, told him in joke that he was his prisoner; and how Henry jumped out of bed and embraced Francis; and how Francis helped Henry to dress, and warmed his linen for him; and how Henry gave Francis a splendid jewelled collar, and how Francis gave Henry, in return, a costly bracelet. All this and a great deal more was so written about, and sung about, and talked about at that time (and indeed since that time too), that the world has had good cause to be sick of it, for ever.
  Charles Dickens, *A Child's History of England.*

The plain truth is, that he was a most intolerable ruffian, a disgrace to human nature, and a blot of blood and grease upon the History of England.
  Ibid.

Henry VIII perhaps approached as nearly to the ideal standard of perfect wickedness as the infirmities of human nature will allow.
  Sir James Mackintosh, *History of England*, vol. 2.

If a lion knew his own strength, hard were it for any man to rule him.
  Sir Thomas More, attributed.

Could you but see how nobly he is bearing himself, how wise he is, his love for all that is good and right, and specially his love of learning, you would need no wings to fly into the light of this new risen and salutary star. Oh, Erasmus, could you but witness the universal joy, could you but see how proud our people are of their new sovereign, you would weep for pleasure. Heaven smiles, earth triumphs, and flows with milk and honey and nectar. This king of ours is no seeker after gold, or gems, or mines of silver. He desires only the fame of virtue and eternal life.
  Lord Mountjoy, Letter to Erasmus, translated by J. A. Froude (on the accession of Henry).

. . . If all the pictures & patterns of a merciless Prince were lost in the World, they might all again be painted to the life, out of the story of this King.
   Sir Walter Raleigh, *The Historie of the World*.

Possibly he had an Oedipus complex: and possibly from this derived a desire for, yet horror of, incest, which may have shaped some of his sexual life.
   Richard Scarisbrick, *Henry VIII*.

The Rose both White and Red
In one Rose now doth grow:
Thus thorough every sted
Thereof the fame doth blow.
Grace the seed did sow:
England, now gather floures,
Exclude now all doloures.
   John Skelton, *A Laud and Praise Made for Our Sovereign Lord the King*.

The king no sooner heard she [Anne of Cleves] had landed at Rochester, than he went thither incognito, to see his future comfort, and found her so different from her picture, which had been drawn by Hans Holbein, that in the impatience of his disappointment he swore they had brought him a Flanders mare.
   Tobias Smollett, *The History of England*.

The imperial Stature, the colossal stride,
Are yet before me; yet do I behold
The broad full visage, chest of amplest mould,
The vestments 'broidered with barbaric pride:
And lo! a poniard, at the monarch's side,
Hangs ready to be grasped in sympathy
With the keen threatenings of that fulgent eye,
Below the white-rimmed bonnet, far descried.
   William Wordsworth, *Recollection of the Portrait of King Henry Eighth, Trinity Lodge, Cambridge*.

See also Anne Boleyn, John Fisher, George I, George II, Henry VII, Catherine Howard, Jane Seymour, Thomas Wolsey

HENRY, PATRICK

1736—99 Statesman, Orator

Is life so dear or peace so sweet, as to be purchased at the price of chains and slavery? Forbid it, Almighty God! I know not what course others may take, but as for me, give me liberty or give me death!
   On himself, Speech, Virginia Convention, 23 March 1775.

. . . [Henry] is a real half-Quaker-moderate and mild, and in religious matters a saint; but the very devil in politics; a son of thunder.
   Roger Atkinson, in Moses Coit Tyler, *Patrick Henry*.

. . . the forest-born Demosthenes.
   Lord Byron, in Robert Meade, *Patrick Henry, Practical Revolutionary*.

It was of little importance whether a country was ruled by a despot with a tiara on his head, or by a demagogue in a red cloak, a caul-bare wig, . . . although *he should profess on all occasions to* bow to the *majesty of the people*.
   Francis Corbin, 1788, in *ibid*.

. . . all tongue, without either head or heart.
   Thomas Jefferson, in Bernard Mayo, *Myths and Men*.

. . . drew all natural rights from a purer source — the feelings of his own heart.
   Thomas Jefferson, *Works*, vol. 12.

The Belgian hare could nothing to you show,
   Profile Patrick — what a family man!
   Henry Aylett Sampson, *Sonnets and Other Poems*.

It is said that the edicts of Mr. H. are unregistered with less opposition in the Virginia Assembly than those of the grand monarch by his parliaments. He has only to say, Let this be law, and it is law.
   George Washington, Letter to James Madison, 1788.

HEPWORTH, DAME BARBARA

1903—75 Sculptor

It's so natural to work large — it fits one's body. This doesn't mean that I don't like working small because I do. It's refreshing, like painting or drawing, but I've always wanted to go to my arm's length and walk round things, or climb up them. I kept on thinking of large works in a landscape: this has always been a dream in my mind.
   On herself, in A. Bowness, *The Complete Sculpture of Barbara Hepworth*.

What she does she does admirably. It is rather like the work of a maker of musical instruments. If anyone would know how to make a beautiful belly to a mandolin or a lute it is she. If she were a potter, she would be a potter of distinction and resource.

But she comes at a time — as does Mr. Moore — when artists are working in a vacuum.

Percy Wyndham Lewis, in *Listener*, October 1946.

HERBERT, EDWARD, LORD HERBERT OF CHERBURY

1583—1648 Courtier, Philosopher

James Ussher, Lord Primate of Ireland, was sent for by him, when in his death-bed, and he would have received the sacrament. He sayd indifferently of it that *if there was good in any-thing 'twas in that*, or *if it did no good 'twould doe no hurt*. The Primate refused it, for which many blamed him. He then turned his head to the other side and expired very serenely.

John Aubrey, *Brief Lives*.

HERBERT, GEORGE

1593—1633 Poet

Another exquisite master of this species of style, when the scholar and the poet supplies the material, but the perfect well-bred gentleman, the expression and the arrangement, is George Herbert.

Samuel Taylor Coleridge, *Biographia Literaria*.

In the sincerity and brightness of his imagination, I saw that George Herbert represented the theology of the Protestant Church in a perfectly central and deeply spiritual manner. . . . The code of feeling and law written in these verses may be always assigned as a standard of the purest unsectarian Christianity; and whatever has been wisest in thought or happiest in the course of my following life was founded at this time on the teaching of Herbert.

John Ruskin, *Praeterita*.

Thus he liv'd, and thus dy'd like a Saint, unspotted of the World, full of Alms-deeds, full of Humility, and all the examples of a vertuous life; which I cannot conclude better, than with this borrowed observation:
— All must to their cold Graves;
But the religious actions of the just,
Sweet smell in death, and blossom in the dust.
Mr *George Herberts* have done so to this, and will doubtless do so to succeeding Generations . . . I wish (if God shall be so pleased) that I may be so happy as to dye like him.

Izaac Walton, *Life of George Herbert*.

And HERBERT: he, whose education,
Manners, and parts, by high applauses blown,
Was deeply tainted with Ambition;

And fitted for a Court, made that his aim:
At last, without regard to Birth or Name,
For a poor Country-Cure, does all disclaim.

Where, with a soul compos'd of Harmonies,
Like a sweet Swan, he warbles, as he dies
His makers praise, and, his own obsequies.
Charles Wotton, *To My Old, and Most Worthy Friend, Mr IZAAC WALTON*.

HERBERT, MARY, COUNTESS OF PEMBROKE

1561—1621 Patroness

She was very salacious, and she had a Contrivance that in the Spring of the yeare, when the Stallions were to leape the Mares, they were to be brought before such a part of the house, where she had a *vidette* (a hole to peep out at) to looke on them and please herselfe with their Sport; and then she would act the like sport herselfe with *her* stallions. One of her great Gallants was Crooke-back't Cecill, Earl of Salisbury.

John Aubrey, *Brief Lives*.

Underneath this sable hearse
Lies the subject of all verse:
Sidney's sister, Pembroke's mother.
Death, ere thou hast slain another
Fair and learn'd and good as she,
Time shall throw a dart at thee.
William Browne, *On the Countess Dowager of Pembroke*, 1621 (formerly ascribed to Ben Jonson).

HEREWARD 'THE WAKE'

fl. 1070—1 Saxon Warrior

The next moment the door of the bower was thrown violently open, and in swaggered a noble lad eighteen years old. His face was of extraordinary beauty, save that the lower jaw was too long and heavy, and that his eyes wore a strange and almost sinister expression, from the fact that the one of them was grey and the other blue. He was short, but of immense breadth of chest and strength of limb; while his delicate hands and feet and long locks of golden hair marked him of most noble, and even, as he really was, of ancient royal race.

Charles Kingsley, *Hereward the Wake*.

The military drama of the conquest closed with the vast siege operations conducted by William against the Isle of Ely defended by Hereward. Hereward was a man of the Fenland district, with a genius for amphibious guerilla warfare in that difficult country. But his resistance only began after the rest of England had been conquered, and the event was therefore never in doubt. It was but the last and noblest of a series of regional revolts undertaken too late.

    G. M. Trevelyan, *History of England*.

HERRICK, ROBERT

1591—1674 Poet

As wearied *Pilgrims*, once possest
Of long'd-for lodging, go to reast:
So I, now having rid my way;
Fix here my Button'd Staffe and stay.
Youth (I confess) hath me mis-led;
But Age hath brought me right to Bed.
    On himself, *His own Epitaph*.

The Ariel of poets, sucking 'where the bee sucks' from the rose-heart of nature, and reproducing the fragrance idealized.

    Elizabeth Barrett Browning, *The Greek Christian Poets and the English Poets*.

That which is chiefly pleasant in these Poems is now and then a pretty Floury and Pastoral gale of Fancy, a vernal prospect of some Hill, Cave, Rock, or Fountain; which but for the interruption of other trivial passages might have made up none of the worst Poetic Landskips.

    Edward Phillips, *Theatrum Poetarum*.

Of all our poets this man appears to have had the coarsest mind. Without being intentionally obscene, he is thoroughly filthy, and has not the slightest sense of decency. In an old writer, and especially one of that age, I never saw so large a proportion of what may truly be called either trash or ordure.

    Robert Southey, *Commonplace Book* (4th Series).

The greatest song-writer — as surely as Shakespeare is the greatest dramatist — ever born of English race.

    Algernon C. Swinburne, *Studies in Prose and Poetry*.

HERSCHEL, SIR WILLIAM

1738—1822 Astronomer

In the evening Mr. Herschel came to tea. I had once seen that very extraordinary man at Mrs. de Luc's, but was happy to see him again, for he has not more fame to awaken curiosity, than sense and modesty to gratify it. He is perfectly unassuming, yet openly happy; and happy in the success of those studies which would render a mind less excellently formed presumptuous and arrogant. The King has not a happier subject than this man, who owes wholly to His Majesty that he is not wretched: for such was his eagerness to quit all other pursuits to follow astronomy solely, that he was in danger of ruin, when his talents, and great and uncommon genius, attracted the King's patronage. He has now not only his pension, which gives him the felicity of devoting all his time to his darling study, but he is indulged in license from the King to make a telescope according to his new ideas and discoveries, that is to have no cost spared in its construction, and is wholly to be paid for by His Majesty.

    Fanny Burney, Diary, 1786.

In constructing the seven-foot reflector, he finished no fewer than two hundred specula before he produced one that would bear any power that was applied to it, — a striking instance of the persevering laboriousness of the man. While sublimely gauging the heavens with his instruments, he continued patiently to earn his bread by piping to the fashionable frequenters of the Bath Pump-room. So eager was he in his astronomical observations, that he would steal away from the room during an interval of the performance, give a little turn to his telescope, and contentedly return to his oboe.

    Samuel Smiles, *Self-help*.

Oh, but I have better news for you, Madam, if you have any patriotism as a citizen of this world and wish its longevity. Mr. Herschel has found out that our globe is a comely middle-aged personage, and has not so many wrinkles as seven stars, who are evidently our seniors. Nay, he has discovered that the Milky Way is not only a mob of stars, but that there is another dairy of them still farther off, whence I conclude comets are nothing but pails returning from milking, instead of balloons filled with inflammable air.

    Horace Walpole, Letter to the Countess of Upper Ossory, 4 July 1785.

Oh, I must stop: I shall turn my own brain, which, while it is launching into an ocean of universes, is still admiring pismire Herschel. That he should not have a *wise* look does not surprise me — he may be stupified by his own discoveries.

    Horace Walpole, Letter to the Countess of Upper Ossory, 6 September 1787.

HERVEY, JOHN, LORD

1696—1743 Author

P. Let *Sporus* tremble — *A.* What? that thing of silk,
Sporus, that mere white curd of Ass's milk?
Satire or sense, alas! can *Sporus* feel?
Who breaks a butterfly upon a wheel?
P. Yet let me flap this bug with gilded wings,
This painted child of dirt, that stinks and stings;
Whose buzz the witty and the fair annoys,
Yet wit ne'er tastes, and beauty ne'er enjoys:
So well-bred spaniels civilly delight
In mumbling of the game they dare not bite.
Eternal smiles his emptiness betray,
As shallow streams run dimpling all the way.
Whether in florid impotence he speaks,
And, as the prompter breathes, the puppet squeaks;
Or, at the ear of *Eve*, familiar Toad,
Half froth, half venom, spits himself abroad,
In puns, or politics, or tales, or lies,
Or spite, or smut, or rhymes, or blasphemies.
    Alexander Pope, *Epistle to Dr. Arbuthnot.*

HEYWOOD, THOMAS

— d. 1650? Dramatist

    ...and *Heywood* Sage,
Th' Apologetic Atlas of the Stage;
Well of the Golden Age he could entreat,
But little of the Mettal, he could get;
Threescore sweet Babes he fashion'd at a Lump,
For he was Christen'd in *Parnassus* Pump;
The Muses Gossip to *Aurora*'s Bed,
And ever since that time his Face was Red.
    Anon., in Gerald Langbaine, *Account of the English Dramatic Poets.*

He was attempting to reach his audience's tears by new means; for no domestic tragedy so far as we know had made the erring wife lovable and the deceived husband dignified. Shakespeare himself is more conservative in tragedy and, infinitely subtler though his treatment of motives may be, he does not essay new problems of conduct or paradoxical situations. Except that it is unformed by any message, is not illustrative of any sociological criticism, and is more humane, *A Woman Killed with Kindness* — a tragedy of a middle class household — anticipates the bloodless tragedies of Ibsen. In another way Heywood may be regarded as the forerunner of Richardson, the school of sensibility, and the *comédie larmoyante* of the eighteenth century.
    A. M. Clark, *Thomas Heywood, Playwright and Miscellanist.*

In the work of nearly all of his contemporaries who are as well known as he there is at least some inchoate pattern; there is, as it would often be called, personality. Of those of Heywood's plays which are worth reading, each is worth reading for itself, but none throws any illumination upon any other. . . . Heywood's is a drama of common life, not, in the highest sense, tragedy at all; there is no supernatural music from behind the wings. He would in any age have been a successful playwright.
    T. S. Eliot, *Essays*: 'Thomas Heywood'.

His manner is simplicity itself. There is nothing supernatural, nothing startling or terrific. He makes use of the commonest circumstances of everyday life, and of the easiest tempers, to shew the workings, or rather the inefficacy of the passions, the *vis inertiae* of tragedy. His incidents strike from their very familiarity, and the distresses he paints invite our sympathy, from the calmness and resignation with which they are borne.
    William Hazlitt, *On Lyly, Marlowe, Heywood, etc.*

Generosity, courtesy, temperance in the depths of passion; sweetness, in a word, and gentleness; Christianism; and true hearty Anglicism of feelings shaping that Christianism; shine through his beautiful writings in a manner more conspicuous than those of Shakespeare, but only more conspicuous, inasmuch as, in Heywood, these qualities are primary, in the other subordinate to poetry. I love them both equally, but Shakespeare has most of my wonder. Heywood should be known to his countrymen as he deserves. His plots are almost invariably English.
    Charles Lamb, *On the Elizabethan Dramatists.*

Heywood is no great hand at a villain.
    Algernon C. Swinburne, *The Age of Shakespeare.*

'Tis said, that he not only acted himself almost every day, but also wrote each day a Sheet: and that he might loose no time, many of his Plays were composed in the Tavern, on the back-side of Tavern Bills, which may be the Occasion that so many of them be lost.
    William Winstanley, *Lives of the Most Famous English Poets.*

HICKOK, JAMES BUTLER 'WILD BILL'

1837—76 Soldier, Frontiersman

He is said never to have killed a man except in self-defense, but he was defending himself almost constantly.
    Richard Armour, *It All Started With Columbus.*

HILDRETH, RICHARD

The Prince of Pistoleers.
  Joseph G. Rosa, *They Called Him Wild Bill: The Life and Adventures of James Butler Hickok.*

HILDRETH, RICHARD

1807–65 Historian, Editor, Lawyer

As venomous and deaf as an adder. . . .
  Richard Henry Dana, in Arthur M. Schlesinger Jr, 'The Problem of Richard Hildreth', in *New England Quarterly*, June 1940.

He was a tall, thin man, absent, silent: already a phantom of himself. . . .
  William Dean Howells, in Donald E. Emerson, *Richard Hildreth.*

HILL, JOE (JOEL HÄGGLUND)

1879–1915 Labor Leader

I dreamed I saw Joe Hill last night,
Alive as you and me.
Says I: 'But Joe, you're ten years dead.'
'I never died,' says he . . .

And standing there as big as life
And smiling with his eyes,
Joe says, 'What they forgot to kill
Went on to organize.'
  Two verses of five of 'The Ballad of Joe Hill'.

Singer of manly song, laughter and tears,
Singer of Labor's wrongs, joys, hopes and fears.

Though you were one of us, what could we do?
Joe, there were none of us needed like you.

Utah has drained your blood, white hands are wet,
We of the 'surging flood,' NEVER FORGET!

High lead and black unbending — 'rebel true blue.'
Into the night unending, Why was it you?
  Ralph Chaplin, in William D. Haywood, *Bill Haywood's Book.*

HILL, 'SIR' JOHN

1716?–75 Physician, Playwright

With sleek appearance, and with ambling pace,
And type of vacant head with vacant face,
The Proteus Hill put in his modest plea, —
'Let favour speak for others, Worth for me.' —

For who, like him, his various powers could call
Into so many shapes, and shine in all?
Who could so nobly grace the motley list,
Actor, Inspector, Doctor, Botanist?
Knows any one so well, — sure no one knows —
At once to play, prescribe, compound, compose?
  Charles Churchill, *The Rosciad.*

For Physick & Farces, his equal there scarce is
His Farces are Physick, his Physick a Farce is.
  David Garrick, Letter to Dr John Hawkesworth, *circa* January 1759.

HILLIARD, NICHOLAS

1537–1619 Miniaturist, Goldsmith

              A hand, or eye,
By Hilliard drawne, is worth an history,
By a worse painter made.
  John Donne, *The Storme.*

In his younger days, the want of an eminent master to direct him, was supply'd in a great measure by his strong affection to the study of nature therefore in his workes, tho his lines are just and true, yet they are generally pale and livid without that force & strength of Coloring more conspicuous in other masters of later date.
  George Vertue, *Notebooks.*

Though Hilliard copied the neatness of his model (Holbein), he was far from attaining that nature and force which that great master impressed on his most minute works. Hilliard arrived at no great strength of colouring, his faces are pale, and void of any variety of tints, the features, jewels and ornaments expressed by lines as slender as a hair.
  Horace Walpole, *Anecdotes of Painting in England.*

Hilliard is the central artistic figure of the Elizabethan age, the only English painter whose work reflects, in its delicate microcosm, the world of Shakespeare's earlier plays.
  Ellis Waterhouse, *Painting in Britain 1530–1790.*

HOARE, SAMUEL JOHN GURNEY, VISCOUNT TEMPLEWOOD

1880–1959 Statesman

He has all the materials that go to the making of a leader of the Conservative party. He is not stupid, but he is very dull. He is not eloquent, but he talks well. He is not honest (politically), but he is most evangelical, a great leader in the Church of England.

He has a little money, but not too much. He always conforms to the party policy. He knows not Ishmael, but he is well acquainted with the life-story of Jacob.

Lord Beaverbrook, Letter to Arthur Brisbane, 20 October 1932.

He was a Cato defending himself; for forty minutes he held the House [of Commons] breathless, and at last sat down . . . and burst into tears. . . . It may have been only a Mea Culpa; but to me . . . it was the voice of a large section of sensible England; perhaps the swan-song of a certain Conservative spirit. . . .

Henry Channon, recording Hoare's resignation speech, Diary, 19 December 1935.

HOBBES, THOMAS

1588—1679 Philosopher

I am about to take my last voyage, a great leap in the dark.

On himself, attributed last words.

Here lies *Tom Hobbes*, the Bug-bear of the Nation, Whose *Death* hath frighted *Atheism* out of *Fashion*.

Anon., *An Elegie upon Mr. Thomas Hobbes of Malmesbury, Lately Deceased.*

In fine, after a thousand shams and fobs
Ninety years eating and immortal jobs,
Here matter lies, and that's an end of Hobbes.

Anon. in a London broadsheet, 1679.

O that he had spent all the time
In hard translations and in rhyme
Which he spent in opposing truths by
which to Heaven we climb.

Anon., *The True Effigies of the Monster of Malmesbury*, 1680.

His extraordinary Timorousness Mr. Hobs doth very ingeniosely confess and atributes it to the influence of his Mother's Dread of the Spanish Invasion in 88, she being then with child of him.

John Aubrey, *Brief Lives.*

When he was a Boy he was playsome enough, but withall he had even then a contemplative Melancholinesse; he would gett him into a corner, and learn his Lesson by heart presently. His haire was black, and his schoolfellows were wont to call him *Crowe*.

Ibid.

'Twas pitty that Mr. Hobbs had not began the study of the Mathematics sooner, els he would not have layn so open. But one may say of him, as one sayes of Jos. Scaliger, that where he erres, he erres so ingeniosly, that one had rather erre with him then hitt the marke with Clavius.

Ibid.

The witts at Court were wont to bayte him. But he feared none of them, and would make his part good. The King would call him *the Beare*: Here comes the Beare to be bayted: (this is too low witt to be published).

Ibid.

He alwayes avoided, as much as he could, to conclude hastily.

Ibid.

He desired not the reputation of his wisdome to be taken from the cutt of his beard, but from his reason.

Ibid.

He had read much, if one considers his long life; but his contemplation was much more than his reading. He was wont to say that if he had read as much as other men, he should have knowne no more then other men.

Ibid.

When Mr. T. Hobbes was sick in France, the Divines came to him, and tormented him (both Roman Catholic, Church of England, and Geneva). Sayd he to them, Let me alone, or els I will detect all your Cheates from Aaron to yourselves.

Ibid.

Ah! poor Hobbes, he possessed fine talents: in forming his theories, however, he fancied the first link of his chain was fastened to a rock of *adamant*, but it proved to be a rock of *ice*.

Samuel Taylor Coleridge, 'Retrospect of Friendly Communications with the Poet Coleridge', in *Christian Observer*, May 1845.

Mr. *Hobbs*, in the Preface to his own bald Translation of the *Ilias*, (studying Poetry as he did Mathematicks, when it was too late) Mr. *Hobbs*, I say, begins the praise of *Homer* where he should have ended it.

John Dryden, Preface to *Fables Ancient and Modern.*

His strong mind and body appear to have resisted all impressions but those which were derived from the downright blows of matter: all his ideas seemed to lie like substances in his brain: what was not a solid, tangible, distinct, palpable object was to him nothing.

William Hazlitt, *On the Writings of Hobbes.*

The contradiction is apparent. Hobbes, the small bourgeois, the clever boy making good at Oxford, is taken into the service of one of the most conservative of the great feudal families, which still ruled large tracts of the economically backward north of England. When Hobbes takes his noble pupils on the grand tour of Europe he meets the most advanced intellects of his time — Galileo, Descartes, Gassendi. He comes home to discuss their ideas with the Duke of Newcastle.

Christopher Hill, *Puritanism and Revolution.*

Finally, Hobbes abandoned the old games of text swapping and precedent hunting for logical argument. That is to say, he made reason, not authority, the arbiter of politics. Paradoxically, it is the absolutist Hobbes who demonstrated that the state exists for man, that it is the product of human reason, and therefore that political theory is a rational science.

Ibid.

But now here was Hobbes making contract the basis of morality! Justice is the keeping of covenants: no contract, no injustice. Nowhere is the fundamentally 'bourgeois' nature of Hobbes's approach to the state and to morality more apparent than in this, the foundation of both.

Ibid.

Hobbes's politics are fitted only to promote tyranny, and his ethics to encourage licentiousness. Though an enemy to religion, he partakes nothing of the spirit of scepticism; but is as positive and dogmatical as if human reason, and his reason in particular, could attain a thorough conviction in these subjects.

David Hume, *History of England.*

When God vouchsafed to make man after his own Image, and in his own Likeness, and took so much delight in him, as to give him the command and dominion over all the Inhabitants of the Earth, the Air, and the Sea, it cannot be imagin'd but that at the same time he endued him with Reason, and all the other noble Faculties which were necessary for the administration of that Empire, and the preservation of the several Species which were to succeed the Creation; and therefore to uncreate him to such baseness and villany in his nature, as to make man such a Rascal, and more a Beast in his frame and constitution than those he is appointed to govern, is a power that God never gave to the Devil; nor

hath any body assum'd it, till Mr. Hobbes took it upon him.

Edward Hyde, Earl of Clarendon, *A Brief View and Survey of the Leviathan.*

There are two conclusions which reasonably result from Mr. Hobbes his Axioms, and which may prove beneficial to him; the first is, that we may believe that he doth not himself believe one word in his Book that we find fault with: for writing is at least an external thing as speaking, and therefore keeping his heart right, he might have the same liberty the Prophet gave *Naaman*, and write what his Sovereign *Cromwell* commanded him, or what he discern'd would be acceptable to him, that it would procure him his protection, which ought to have the same force with him as his command. The other is, that when ever he shall be commanded by the King, to retract, and recant whatever is condemned in this Book, he will cheerfully, and with a better conscience renounce them all, and write an other Book more reasonably in the confutation of his errors in this. But then he is upon an other disadvantage, which is very grievous to an honest man, that when he makes that recantation, no man will believe that it is the thoughts of his heart, but only his profession with his tongue, which being but an extended thing, he doth signify his obedience to that authority to which he is subject, without any remorse for the wickedness of his former writing.

Ibid.

. . . It hath bin always a lamentation amongst Mr. Hobbes his Friends, that he spent too much time in thinking, and too little in exercising those thoughts in the company of other Men of the same, or of as good faculties; for want whereof his natural constitution, with age, contracted such a morosity, that doubting and contradicting Men were never grateful to him.

Ibid.

There are several passages in Hobbes's translation of Homer, which, if they had been writ on purpose to ridicule that poet, would have done very well.

Alexander Pope, in Joseph Spence, *Anecdotes.*

Where he is wrong, he is wrong from over-simplification, not because the basis of his thought is unreal or fantastic. For this reason, he is still worth refuting.

Bertrand Russell, *History of Western Philosophy.*

Hobbes clearly proves that ev'ry Creature
Lives in a State of War by Nature.

Jonathan Swift, *On Poetry: A Rhapsody.*

What other things go under his name, I know not as yet: sure it is, if several persons of credit may be believed, that a certain Scholar, who was made a Bishop sometime after the restauration of K. *Ch.* 2, did say it openly in the time of *Oliver*, . . . that *he had rather be the author of one of Mr. Hobbes his books, than to be King of England.*

Anthony à Wood, *Athenae Oxoniensis.*

Confirmed also that Thomas Hobs died at Hardwick within 12 miles of Chatsworth, that on his death bed he should say that he was 91 yeares finding out a hole to go out of this world, and at length found it. He died on 4 Dec. Thursday. . . . An ill-natured man they say, proud, scornful. . . . Hobs his Leviathan hath corrupted the gentry of the nation, hath infused ill principles into them, atheisme. . . . Mr Hobs a person of verie acute parts, quick apprehension to the last, ready to answer whatsoever is proposed, and would understand what you meane before you are at the end of half your discourse.

Anthony à Wood, *Life and Times*, 10 December 1679.

See also William D'Avenport, John Locke

HOGARTH, WILLIAM

1697—1764 Painter, Engraver

With the death of Hogarth, almost all the old school of humorous designers disappeared. He was the great luminary of this species of art, and when his light went out, all the lesser lights were extinguished.

H. Angelo, *Reminiscences.*

Oft have I known Thee, HOGARTH, weak and vain,
Thyself the idol of thy awkward strain,
Thro' the dull measure of a summer's day,
In phrase most vile, prate long long hours away,
Whilst Friends with Friends all gaping sit, and gaze
To hear a HOGARTH babble HOGARTH's praise.

Charles Churchill, *An Epistle to William Hogarth.*

He who should call the Ingenious Hogarth a Burlesque Painter, would, in my Opinion, do him very little Honour: for sure it is much easier, much less the Subject of Admiration, to paint a Man with a Nose, or any other Feature of a preposterous Size, or to expose him in some absurd or monstrous Attitude, than to express the Affections of Men on Canvas. It hath been thought a vast Commendation of a Painter, to say his Figures *Seem to breathe*; but surely, it is a much greater and nobler Applause, *that they appear to think.*

Henry Fielding, Preface to *Joseph Andrews.*

He was essentially what the French so conveniently call *primaire*, i.e. a man whose limited and reach-me-down culture gives him a ready answer to any problem, who becomes dogmatic, narrow-minded, positive and self-satisfied.

Roger Fry, *Reflections on British Painting.*

He does not represent folly or vice in its incipient, or dormant, or *grub* state, but fully grown, with wings, pampered into all sorts of affectation, airy, ostentatious, and extravagant. Folly is there seen at its height — the moon is at the full — at 'the very error of the time.' There is a perpetual collision of eccentricities — a tilt and tournament of absurdities — the prejudices and caprices of mankind are let loose, and set together by the ears, as in a bear-garden.

William Hazlitt, 'On Mr. Wilkie's Pictures', in *Champion*, 5 March 1815.

Other pictures we look at — his prints we read.

Charles Lamb, *On the Genius and Character of Hogarth in Essays and Sketches.*

He has seldom drawn a mean or insignificant countenance. Hogarth's mind was eminently reflective; and, as it has been well observed of Shakespeare, that he has transfused his own poetical character into the persons of his drama (they are all more or less *poets*), Hogarth has impressed a *thinking character* upon the persons of his canvas.

Ibid.

Hogarth has never been admitted to rank high as a painter, but certainly so as a moralist; yet it has, of late, been discovered that his small pictures possess considerable dexterity of execution: as to his larger pieces, they appear to be the efforts of imbecility; he was totally without the practice required for such works.

James Northcote, *The Life of Sir Joshua Reynolds.*

See also Evelyn Waugh

HOGG, JAMES

1770—1835 Author

The said Hogg is a strange being, but of great, though uncouth, powers. I think very highly of him, as a poet; but he, and half of these Scotch and Lake troubadours, are spoilt by living in little circles and petty societies.

Lord Byron, Letter to Tom Moore, 3 August 1814.

The honest grunter.
Sir Walter Scott, *Journal*, 12 December 1825.

When supper was half over, James Hogg, the Ettrick Shepherd, appeared. A chair had been designedly left vacant for him between the two aristocrats. His approach was discernible before his person was visible; for he came straight from a cattle fair, and was reeking with the unsavory odours of the sheep and pigs and oxen, in whose company he had been for hours. Nevertheless he soon made himself at home with the fair ladies on each side of him: somewhat too much so, for, supper over, the cloth withdrawn, and the toddy introduced, the song going round, and his next door neighbours being too languid in their manner of joining in the chorus to please him, he turned first to the right hand, then to the left, and slapped both of them on their backs with such good will as to make their blade bones ring again; then, with a yell of an Ojibbaway Indian, he shouted forth 'Noo then, leddies, follow me! Heigh tutti, tutti! Heigh tutti, tutti!'
Julian Charles Young, *Journal*.

HOLMES, OLIVER WENDELL

1809—94 Essayist, Poet, Teacher

I have, in common with yourself, a desire to leave the world a little more human than if I had not lived; for a true humanity is, I believe, our nearest approach to Divinity, while we work out our atmospheric apprenticeships on the surface of this second-class planet.
On himself, Letter to Harriet Beecher Stowe, 1860.

To be 70 years young is sometimes far more cheerful than to be forty years old.
On himself, Letter to Julia Ward Howe, 27 May 1879.

I was always patient with those who thought well of me, and accepted all their tributes with something more than resignation.
On himself, in Vernon Louis Parrington, *Main Currents in American Thought*, vol. 2.

He was a poet laureate by avocation, always prepared to present his bouquet at a banquet or an ode at a country fair.
Van Wyck Brooks, *The Flowering of New England 1815—1865*.

Holmes was an aristocrat even to the extent of having a slight repugnance to people who smelled too much of mere literary pursuits.
Alexander Cowie, *The Rise of the American Novel*.

Holmes came out late in life, with a strong sustained growth for two or three years, like old pear trees which have done nothing for ten years, and at last begin and grow great.
Ralph Waldo Emerson, in George Arms, *The Fields Were Green*.

There was nothing Miltonic about him. There were few stops to his organ.
Grant C. Knight, *American Literature and Culture*.

Read with sprightly vivacity to a group of sympathetic listeners at the mellowest hour of the dinner, his occasional verse must have sparkled brightly and have gone off with such a crackle of laughter as to convince the Back Bay that the asthmatic little gentleman with bubbling spirits was a veritable poet. . . .
Vernon Louis Parrington, *Main Currents in American Thought*, vol. 2.

Not since Robert Treat Paine had there been such a master of Yankee small talk. . . . But like every talker his discursiveness is inveterate; he wanders far in pursuit of his point and sometimes returns empty-handed. He was always an amateur; life was too agreeable for him to take the trouble to become an artist.'
Ibid.

He kept the windows of his mind open to the winds of scientific inquiry that were blowing briskly to the concern of orthodox souls. Many a barnacled craft was floundering in those gales, and Holmes watched them going-down with visible satisfaction.
Vernon Louis Parrington, in Robert Allen Skotheim, *American Intellectual Histories and Historians*.

Holmes' influence lay rather in his contribution to the spread of ideas, to the unabashed scrutiny of the physician who healed the human body and tried through his sympathy and understanding to help the souls of the disheartened and the unhappy by the magic medicine of laughter.
Arthur Hobson Quinn, 'The Establishment of National Literature', in Arthur Hobson Quinn ed., *The Literature of the American People*.

. . . fat as a baloon — he weighed as much as three hundred, and had double chins all the way down to his stomach.
Mark Twain, in Kenneth S. Lynn, *William Dean Howells, An American Life*.

HOLMES, OLIVER WENDELL JR

1841—1935 Jurist

One of my old formulas is to be an enthusiast in the front part of your heart and ironical at the back.
On himself, in James B. Peabody ed., *The Holmes—Einstein Letters.*

Judges are apt to be naif, simple-minded men, and they need something of Mephistopheles. We too need education in the obvious — to learn to transcend our own convictions and to leave room for much that we hold dear to be done away with short of revolution by the orderly change of law.
On himself, 'Law and the Court', 1913, in *Collected Legal Papers.*

He was an aristocrat and a conservative. He did not prefer, he said, a world with a hundred million bores in it to one with ten. The fewer the people who do not contribute beauty or thought, the better. He had little sympathy with the sufferings and failure of mankind, and no urgent desire to change their lot. He thought that in the last analysis man rightly preferred his own interest to that of his neighbor, and did not believe in the Christian precept to love thy neighbor as thyself, which was the test of the meddling missionary: if men thought more about their jobs and less about themselves and their neighbors, they would accomplish more in the world.
Francis Biddle, *Justice Holmes, Natural Law, and the Supreme Court.*

Men called the doctor's son the Great Dissenter. The title was misleading. *To want something fiercely and want it all the time* — this is not dissent but affirmation. The things Holmes wanted were great things, never to be realized. How can man realize the infinite? *Have faith and pursue the unknown.*
Catherine Drinker Bowen, *Yankee From Olympus: Justice Holmes and His Family.*

Within his breast he carries the secret of eternal youth, and he carries it with an incomparable grace.
Charles Evans Hughes, in Merlo J. Pusey, *Charles Evans Hughes.*

See also Felix Frankfurter

HOLST, GUSTAV THEODORE

1874—1934 Composer

My idea of composition is to spoil as much MS paper as possible.
On himself, Letter to Ralph Vaughan Williams, 15 April 1932.

I couldn't bear to think that I was going to 'drift apart' from you musically speaking. (If I do, who shall I have to crib from?)
Ralph Vaughan Williams, Letter to Holst, 1925.

He has a mind which is heir to all the centuries and has found out the language in which to express that mind.
Ralph Vaughan Williams, 'Gustav Holst', in *Music and Letters*, 1920.

If to have 'lived' it is necessary to have eloped with a *prima donna*, to have played mean tricks on one's friends, to be dirty and drunken — if life means no more than that, then indeed the word has little meaning for a man like Holst. But if to live may be summed up in the words 'Whatsoever thy hand findeth to do, do it with thy might,' then Holst has lived to the full; he has learnt his lesson in the hard school of necessity; he has not run away from the battle but has fought and won.
Ralph Vaughan Williams, *ibid.*

HOMER, WINSLOW

1836—1910 Artist

The life that I have chosen gives me my full hours of enjoyment for the balance of my life. The Sun will not rise, or set, without my notice, and thanks.
On himself, in Lloyd Goodrich, *Winslow Homer.*

Some years later when a dealer was having trouble selling another of his compositions because it was too stark, Homer wrote sardonically, 'If you want more sentiment put into this picture I can with one or two touches, in five minutes' time, give it the stomach ache that will suit any customer.'
James Thomas Flexner, *The World of Winslow Homer.*

His style was highly selective. He saw things in a big way: he simplified, he eliminated, he concentrated on the large forms and movements. This bigness of style had been instinctive from the first; as he matured it became a deliberate process. 'Never put more than two waves in a picture; it's fussy,' he once said.
Lloyd Goodrich, *Winslow Homer.*

Before Mr. Homer's little barefoot urchins and little girls in calico sun-bonnets, straddling beneath a cloudless sky upon the natural rail fence, the whole effect of the critic is instinctively to contract himself, to double himself up, as it were, so that he can creep into the problem. . . . [Homer] is almost barbarously simple, and, to our eye, he is horribly ugly; but there is nevertheless something I like about him. What is it? For ourselves, it is not his subjects. We frankly confess that we detest his subjects — his barren plank fences . . . his flat-breasted maidens, suggestive of a dish of rural doughnuts and pie. . . . He has chosen the least pictorial features of the least pictorial range of scenery and civilization; he has resolutely treated them as if they *were* pictorial, as if they were every inch as good as Capri or Tangiers; and, to reward his audacity, he has incontestably succeeded.

Henry James, in James Thomas Flexner, *The World of Winslow Holmes.*

HONE, WILLIAM

1780—1842 Radical Pamphleteer, Publisher

Hone the publisher's trial you must find very amusing; and as an Englishman very encouraging.

John Keats, Letter to his Brother, 1817.

The acquittal of Hone is enough to make one out of love with English Juries.

William Wordsworth, Letter to T. Monkhouse, 1818.

HOOD, THOMAS

1835—74 Poet

Urn a lively Hood.

On himself, shortly before dying.

HOOKE, ROBERT

1635—1703 Physicist

He is but of middling stature, something crooked, pale faced, and his face but little belowe, but his head is lardge; his eie full and popping, and not quick; a grey eie. He haz a delicate head of haire, browne, and of an excellent moist curle. He is and ever was very temperate, and moderate in dyet, etc. As he is of prodigious inventive head, so is a person of great vertue and goodness. Now when I have sayd his Inventive faculty is so great, you cannot imagine his Memory to be excellent, for they are like two Bucketts, as one goes up, the other goes downe. He is certainly the greatest Mechanick this day in the World.

John Aubrey, *Brief Lives.*

Hooke was the most important scientific figure of the period following the Restoration. Possibly Boyle had more prestige, but this was partly compounded of respect for his high rank and for his high conception of the duties of that rank. He was not in fact so well equipped for science as Hooke. He was unmathematical; the prolixity of his writing reflects a certain want of mental incisiveness, and his range was comparatively limited. The striking characteristic of Hooke's scientific work is the mastery he displayed over an enormous field.

Margaret 'Espinasse, *Robert Hooke.*

I returned home, calling at Woo[d]cot, & Durdens by the way: where I [found] Dr. Wilkins, Sir William Pettit, & Mr. Hooke contriving Charriots, new rigges for ships, a Wheele for one to run races in, & other mechanical inventions, & perhaps three such persons together were not to be found else where in Europ, for parts and ingenuity.

John Evelyn, Diary, 7 September 1665.

Above all, Mr. Boyle to-day was at the meeting [of the Royal Society], and above him Mr. Hooke, who is the most, and promises the least, of any man in the world that ever I saw.

Samuel Pepys, Diary, 15 February 1664.

As to his person, he made but a mean appearance, being short of stature, very crooked, pale, lean, and of a megre aspect, with lank brown hair, which he wore till within three years of his death, and his features were not the most regular; but in his younger days he had a sharp, ingenious look, and was very active. And he used to say, he was strait till about sixteen years of age, when being of a thin and weak habit, he first grew awry by frequently using a turner's lathe, and other inclining exercises. His inventive faculty was surprisingly great, which he imployed with indefatigable industry, always contenting himself with little sleep, and that very irregular; for he seldom went to bed till two or three a clock in the morning, and frequently not at all, but pursued his studies the whole night, and took a short nap in the day. This continual expense of spirits, accompanied with a recluse life, may be supposed to have easily produced a melancholy, accompanied with a mistrust and jealousy, which increased with his years. For at first he was communicative with his discoveries and inventions, till, as he was wont to say, some persons improving upon his hints published them for their own, which at last rendered him close and reserved even to a fault; by which means many things are lost, which he affirmed he knew.

J. Ward, *The Lives of the Professors of Gresham College.*

Being from his childhood ingeniously given, [he] was sent to the college school at Westminster, where, in one week's time, he made himself master of the first six books of Euclid, to the admiration of Mr. Busby his master, in whose house he lodged and dieted. He also did there, of his own accord, learn to play 20 lessons on the organ, and invented thirty several ways of flying, as he and Dr. Wilkins of Wadham coll. have reported.

Anthony à Wood, *Athenae Oxonienses.*

HOOKER, JOSEPH, 'FIGHTING JOE'

1814—79 Soldier

In the 'Fifties', when out in California at the Gold Rush, he became famous for his 'glad eye' for ladies of easy virtue, whence the Californians invented the name 'Hookers' for the type of ladies the debonaire lieutenant liked ·so well. Likewise he communed with John Barleycorn and was said to be a three bottle man.

George Fort Milton, *Conflict: The American Civil War.*

HOOKER, RICHARD

1554?—1600 Theologian

. . . indeed, my lord, I have received more satisfaction in reading a leaf, or paragraph, in Mr. Hooker, though it were but about the fashion of churches, or church-music, or the like, but especially of the Sacraments, than I have had in the reading particular large treatises written but of one of these subjects by others, though very learned men: and I observe there is in Mr. Hooker no affected language; but a grave, comprehensive, clear manifestation of reason, and that backed with the authority of the Scripture, the Fathers and Schoolmen.

James I (hearing of Hooker's death), in Izaak Walton, *Life of Hooker.*

. . . he designed to write a deliberate, sober treatise of the Church's power to make canons for the use of ceremonies, and by law to impose an obedience to them, as upon her children; and this he proposed to do in eight books of the Laws of Ecclesiastical Polity; intending therein to shew such arguments as should force an assent from all men, if reason, delivered in sweet language, and void of provocation, were able to do it: and, that he might prevent all prejudice, he wrote before it a large preface or epistle to the Dissenting Brethren, wherein there were such bowels of love, and such a commixture of that love with reason, as was never exceeded but in holy writ. . . .

Izaak Walton, *Life of Hooker.*

HOOKER, THOMAS

1586?—1647 Clergyman

. . . a clergyman who, in a dim church, interpreted the Gospel according to his own lights. He would also accept no money for his preaching, which set a low wage standard for others; he was therefore scorned as a free thinker. Many of his parishioners believed his stern words about hell and followed him to Hartford, where he guaranteed their protection in the hereafter and sold them the first fire-insurance policies.

Richard Armour, *It All Started With Columbus.*

And Hooker of vast endowment, a strong will, and an energetic mind; ingenuous in his temper, and open in his professions; trained to benevolence by the discipline of affliction; versed in tolerance by his refuge in Holland; choleric, yet gentle in his affections; firm in his faith, yet readily yielding to the power of reason; the peer of the reformers without their harshness; the devoted apostle to the humble and the poor; severe towards the proud; mild in his soothings of a wounded spirit; glowing with the raptures of devotion, and kindling with the messages of redeeming love; his eye, voice, gesture, and whole frame animate with the living vigor of heartfelt religion. . . .

George Bancroft, in William Sprague, *Annals of the American Pulpit.*

To see three things was holy Austin's wish:
Rome in her Flower, Christ Jesus in the Flesh,
And Paul i'th Pulpit; Lately men might see
Two first, and more, in Hooker's Ministry.

John Cotton, in Perry Miller, *Errand into the Wilderness.*

His natural temper was cheerful and courteous; but it was accompanied with such a sensible grandeur of mind, as caused his friends, without the help of astrology, to prognosticate that he was born to be considerable.

Cotton Mather, in William Prague, *Annals of the American Pulpit.*

. . . the one rich pearl with which Europe more than repaid America for the treasures from her coast.

Ezekiel Rogers, in *ibid.*

HOOVER, HERBERT CLARK

1874—1964 Thirty-First United States President

I was in favor of giving former Presidents a seat in the Senate until I passed 75 years. Since then I have

less taste for sitting on hardbottomed chairs during long addresses.
> On himself, Interview given in retirement.

Mellon pulled the whistle,
Hoover rang the bell,
Wall Street gave the signal
And the country went to hell.
> Anon., song of the Bonus Marchers, 1932.

Hoover isn't a stuffed shirt. But at times he can give the most convincing impersonation of a stuffed shirt you ever saw.
> Anon., in E. Lyons, *Herbert Hoover.*

Facts to Hoover's brain are as water to a sponge; they are absorbed into every tiny interstice.
> Bernard M. Baruch, in D. Hinshaw, *Herbert Hoover: American Quaker.*

If you put a rose in Hoover's hand it would melt.
> Gutzon Borghum, in William E. Leuchtenburg, *Franklin D. Roosevelt and the New Deal.*

. . . He is not a complicated personality, but rather a personality of monolithic simplicity. With no reflection on anyone, it might be said that whenever and wherever Herbert Hoover has mystified people or has been misunderstood by them, nearly always it has been because he is an extremely plain man living in an extremely fancy age.
> James M. Cox, in Springfield, in Ohio, *Sun*, 10 August 1949.

It would be difficult to imagine a less political and popularly ingratiating personality than that of this round, sedentary, factual-minded man who seems incapable of pretending to be anything that he does not know himself to be.
> Herbert Croly, 'How is Hoover?', in *New Republic*, 27 June 1928.

If Wall Street grabbed your final cent,
That's right, impeach the President.
If Europe seethes with discontent,
Denounce the cause — our President.
> Arthur Guiterman, in E. Lyons, *Herbert Hoover.*

He is, in short, a very plain man; a bit stodgy, somewhat too conservative for his times; given to fundamental principles and abstract expression rather than to quick-witted extemporization and easy affability. But put him in an appointive rather than an elective job, give him work to do of the sort that can benefit everybody, and Herbert Hoover shows up at his best.
> David Hinshaw, *Herbert Hoover: American Quaker.*

Hard on H. to go out of office to the sound of crashing banks. Like the tragic end of a tragic story. . . . The history of H's administration is Greek in its fatality.
> Agnes Meyer, Diary, 25 February 1933.

It was like sitting in a bath of ink to sit in his room.
> Henry Stimson, Diary, 18 June 1931.

One may say that Hoover has regarded our entire business structure as a single factory, conceiving himself as it were, consulting engineer for the whole enterprise. Having this conception, Hoover set about applying to the whole business structure of the United States principles similar to those which Henry Ford applied to the manufacture of automobiles.
> Mark Sullivan, in E. Lyons, *Herbert Hoover.*

Such a little man could not have made so big a depression.
> Norman Thomas, Letter to Murray B. Seidler, 3 August 1960.

See also Warren G. Harding

HOOVER, J(OHN) EDGAR

1895—1972 First Director of the Federal Bureau of Investigation.

In foreign countries people are forced by their governments to submit to their gestapos. In this country, Hoover has the voluntary support of all those who delight in gangster movies and ten-cent detective magazines.
> Anon., in *New Republic*, 19 February 1940.

Hoover and the FBI were one — creator and creation. He served eight Presidents as the world's most powerful policeman. With a genius for administration and popular myth, he fashioned his career as an improbable bureaucratic morality play peopled by bad guys and G-men.
> Anon., in *Time*, 15 May 1972.

As an administrator, he was an erratic, unchallengeable czar, banishing agents to Siberian posts on whimsy, terrorizing them with torrents of implausible rules, insisting on conformity of thought as well as dress.
> *Ibid.*, 22 December 1975.

A shrewd bureaucratic genius who cared less about crime than about perpetuating his crime-busting image. With his acute public relations sense, he

managed to observe his bureau's failings while magnifying its sometime successes. Even his fervent anti-communism has been cast into doubt; some former aides insist that he knew the party was never a genuine internal threat to the nation but a useful popular target to ensure financial and public support for the F.B.I.
Ibid.

The Federal Bureau of Investigation, the G-Men and Mr. J. Edgar Hoover form one of the most important elements of the American myth — symbols of perfection in detective methods, wholesome anti-communism, ruthless pursuit of gangsters and spies, and of a dedicated puritanical but unself-seeking chief above and outside politics; the nation's watchdog and the President's counsellor.
Cyril Connolly, in Arthur M. Schlesinger Jr, *A Thousand Days: John Kennedy in the White House.*

The truth is that the FBI of our collective memory never really existed outside of the very fertile and imaginative mind of its eternal Director, Citizen John Edgar Hoover. To him, all high adventure was possible in the cause of Right, all moral victories over obvious evil inevitable, so long as faith in the all-encompassing power of his good office was absolute.
J. Robert Nash, *Citizen Hoover.*

He was a charmer. He was a brilliant chameleon. But he was also a master con man. That takes intelligence of a certain kind, an astuteness, a shrewdness. He never read anything that would broaden his mind or give depth to his thinking. I never knew him to have an intellectual or educated friend.
William Sullivan, in *Time*, 22 December 1975.

[Of] medium height, inclined to be chubby, and of dark complexion. His full lips forbid a stern mouth, but he has a piercing glance, which those who have left his service say is the result of practice before a mirror. Hoover walks with a rather mincing step, almost feminine. This gait may be a relic of his valedictorian days, for at all times he appears to be making his way as though the caution of a teacher not to race to the rostrum was ringing in his ears.
Walter Trohan, in *Chicago Tribune*, 21 June 1936.

No women are among his intimates, for Hoover — and he would have every G-Man be likewise — is a woman hater. This may be due to his cardinal creed as a crimefighter, the traditional French directive: *Cherchez la Femme* ('Look for the woman').
Ibid.

HOPKINS, GERARD MANLEY
1844—89 Poet

Sprung Rhythm, as he calls it in his sober and sensible preface, is just as easy to write as other forms of verse; and many a humble scribbler of words for music-hall songs has written it well. But he does not: he does not make it audible. . . . Also the English language is a thing which I respect very much, and I resent even the violence Keats did to it; and here is a lesser than Keats doing much more. . . . His manner strikes me as deliberately adopted to compensate by strangeness for the lack of pure merit, like the manner which Carlyle took up after he was thirty.
A. E. Housman, Letter to Robert Bridges, 30 December 1918.

He is likely to prove, for our time and the future, the only influential poet of the Victorian age, and he seems to me the greatest.
F. R. Leavis, *New Bearings in English Poetry.*

Hopkins is what people call a writer's writer. He writes in a very strange, twisted style — perhaps it is a bad style, really: at any rate, it would be a bad one to imitate — which is not at all easy to understand but which appeals to people who are professionally interested in points of technique.
George Orwell, *The Meaning of a Poem.*

The useful, but monotonous, in their day unduly neglected, as more recently unduly touted, metrical labours of G. Manley Hopkins.
Ezra Pound, *The Nineteenth Century and After.*

We must remember that Hopkins died prematurely. If he had lived longer, and continued his development towards a more austere and 'smoother' style, the technical elaborations of his middle years would have fallen into perspective. It would then have been beyond doubt that Hopkins was not an English eccentric but an English classic.
W. W. Robson, *Modern English Literature.*

See also A. E. Housman

HOPKINS, HARRY LLOYD
1890—1946 Politician

Mr. Hopkins is a bull-headed man whose high place in the New Deal was won by his ability to waste more money in quicker time on more absurd undertakings than any other mischievous wit in Washington could think of.

> Anon., in *Chicago Tribune* (enlarged and framed by Hopkins), in Robert E. Sherwood, *Roosevelt and Hopkins, An Intimate History*.

If Roosevelt ever becomes Jesus Christ, he should have Harry Hopkins as his prophet.

> Anon., in *Time*, February 1934.

Lord Root of the Matter.

> Winston Churchill (suggested title should Hopkins ever be awarded a peerage), in Robert E. Sherwood, *Roosevelt and Hopkins, An Intimate History*.

The fire-eating administrator of Federal Emergency Relief, Harry L. Hopkins, may safely be credited with spoiling the Thanksgiving Day dinners of many conservatives who had been led to believe that President Roosevelt's recent zig to the right would not be followed by a zag to the left.

> Delbert Clark, in *New York Times*, 2 December 1934.

He had the purity of St. Francis of Assisi combined with the sharp shrewdness of a race track tout.

> Joseph E. Davis, in S. F. Charles, *Minister of Relief, Harry L. Hopkins and the Depression*.

Harry is the perfect ambassador for my purposes. He doesn't even know the meaning of the word 'protocol'. When he sees a piece of red tape, he just pulls out those old garden shears of his and snips it. And when he's talking to some foreign dignitary, he knows how to slump back in his chair and put his feet up on the conference table and say, 'Oh, *yeah?*'

> Franklin Roosevelt, in Robert E. Sherwood, *Roosevelt and Hopkins, An Intimate History*.

The rise of Franklin Roosevelt to power was due more to the extraordinary circumstances of the times than to any clever conspiracy; but Harry Hopkins, in the promotion of his own slender chances, was impelled to connive, plot and even to misrepresent, and this was undoubtedly the least creditable phase of his public career.

> Robert E. Sherwood, in *ibid*.

. . . he was generally regarded as a sinister figure, a backstairs intriguer, an Iowan combination of Machiavelli, Svengali and Rasputin.

> *Ibid*.

HOPPER, EDWARD

1882–1967 Artist

My aim in painting has always been the most exact transcription possible of my most intimate impressions of nature. If this end is unattainable, so, it can be said, is perfection in any other ideal of painting or in any other of man's activities.

> On himself, in *Edward Hopper*.

Edward Hopper is an American — nowhere but in America could such an art have come into being. But its underlying classical nature prevents its being merely local or national in its appeal. It is my conviction, anyhow, that the bridge to international appreciation is the national bias, providing, of course, it is subconscious. An artist to gain a world audience must belong to his own peculiar time and place; the self-conscious internationalists, no less than the self-conscious nationalist, generally achieve nothing but sterility. But more than being American, Hopper is — just Hopper, thoroughly and completely himself.

> Charles Burchfield, in Alfred H. Barr Jr, *Edward Hopper*.

Hopper's chief subject matter was the physical face of America. His attitude toward the native scene was not simple. He once said to me, speaking of his early years, that after France this country seemed 'a chaos of ugliness'. No artist was more aware of the architectural disorder and monotony of our cities, the dreariness of our suburbs, the rawness of our countryside, ravaged by industry and high-speed transportation. But beneath this awareness lay a deep emotional attachment.

> Lloyd Goodrich, *Edward Hopper*.

In exactly conveying the mood of these particular places and hours, Hopper's art transcended realism and became highly personal poetry. His poetry was never sentimental; it had too direct a relation to actualities. Where a sentimentalist would have made such themes banal, with him they were completely fresh and genuine. Banality, indeed, was inherent in much of his subject matter, but the strength of his feeling for familiar reality transformed banality into authentic poetry.

> *Ibid*.

The pervading sense of loneliness in Hopper's art is linked to his reserved emotional attitude towards human beings, and to its corollary, the strong emotion he concentrates on the non-human elements of the world in which he lives. There is a transference of emotion from humanity to its setting analogous to the landscapist's transference to nature.

> *Ibid*.

HOPPER, HEDDA

1890—1966 Journalist

Being a Hollywood reporter as well as an actress I'm more or less on both sides of the fence.
On herself, in George Eells, *Hedda and Louella.*

Timid? As timid as a buzzsaw.
Casey Shawhan, in *ibid.*

HORSA, see under HENGIST

HOUDINI, HARRY (EHRICH WEISS)

1874—1926 Magician, Escapologist

The man who walked through walls.
Anon., in William Lindsay Gresham, *Houdini.*

Ehrich Weiss never doubted his destiny. Crushing defeats, snubs, family pleading for other ambitions did not stop him. Although tireless practice never gave him the polished ease of the star sleight-of-hand performer, he hacked and carved his place on the heights by inventing a whole new form of magic. He hurled at the universe a challenge to bind, fetter, or confine him so that he, in turn, could break free. He triumphed over manacles and prison cells, the wet-sheet packs of insane asylums, webs of fish net, iron boxes bolted shut — anything and everything human ingenuity could provide in an attempt to hold him prisoner. His skill and daring finally fused deeply with the unconscious wish of Everyman; to escape from chains and leg irons, gibbets and coffins . . . by magic.
William Lindsay Gresham, in *ibid.*

He was no master-manipulator of cards and coins, in spite of his ambition to be remembered as a wizard of dexterity. But he did manipulate life and circumstance and the imagination of men.
Ibid.

HOUGHTON, BARON (RICHARD MONCKTON MILNES)

1809—85 Politician, Author

There is only one post fit for you, and that is the office of perpetual president of the Heaven and Hell Amalgamation Society.
Thomas Carlyle, in T. E. Wemyss Reid, *Life of Lord Houghton.*

HOUSMAN, ALFRED EDWARD

1859—1936 Poet

If a line of poetry strays into my memory, my skin bristles so that the razor ceases to act.
On himself, *The Name and Nature of Poetry.*

As to your enquiry, I have not published any poem, since the last that you have seen. The other day I had the curiosity to reckon up the complete pieces, printed and unprinted, which I have written since 1896, and they only come to 300 lines. . . . In barrenness, at any rate, I hold a high place among English poets, excelling even Gray.
On himself, Letter to Witter Eynner, 28 February 1910.

Tell him that the wish to include a glimpse of my personality in a literary article is low, unworthy, and American. Tell him that some men are more interesting than their books but my book is more interesting than its man. Tell him that Frank Harris found me rude and Wilfrid Blunt found me dull. Tell him anything else that you think will put him off.
On himself, Letter to Grant Richards (his publisher, about a prospective interview), 27 September 1927.

Down to Cambridge with old Gaselee. . . . We dress for dinner. Black tie. We assemble. A. E. Housman and a don disguised as a Shropshire Lad. We have 1789 Madeira and Haut Brion and tripe and oysters and grouse-pie and mushrooms. The firelight flits on the silver of the smaller combination room and there are red shades, highly inflammable, to each candle. Housman is dry, soft, shy, prickly, smooth, conventional, silent, feminine, fussy, pernickety, sensitive, tidy, greedy, and a touch of a toper. 'What is this, my dear Gaselee?' 'This is Estrella 1789.' 'A perfect wine.' Yet not eighteenth-century and still less 1890. A *bon bourgeois* who has seen more sensitive days. He does not talk much except about food. And at 10.30 he rises to take his leave. All his movements are best described in such Trollope expressions.
Harold Nicolson, Diary, 26 September 1931.

Housman was Masefield with a dash of Theocritus.
George Orwell, *Inside the Whale.*

Though now and again a young admirer paid him the tribute of imitation, he cannot truthfully be said to have exercised any influence on the poetry of his day. As a poet he lived in a vacuum, shut off from the developments of his time; one need only consider Gerard Manley Hopkins and Mr Eliot to appreciate, by contrast, the completeness of his isolation.
John Sparrow, *Independent Essays.*

HOUSTON, SAMUEL

1793–1863 Soldier, Politician

. . . I wish no prouder epitaph to mark the board or slab that may lie on my tomb than this: 'He loved his country, he was a patriot; he was devoted to the Union.' If it is for this that I have suffered martyrdom, it is sufficient that I stand at quits with those who have wielded the sacrificial knife.

On himself, in Llerena Friend, *Sam Houston, The Great Designer.*

An honest man no party platform needs,
He follows right, and goes where justice leads.
Anon. election slogan, New York, 29 May 1860.

He was in a class by himself, having gone to a small school. When Texas became a republic, he was its first president, and when Texas joined the Union he became a senator. In Washington, he was feared and respected by his fellow senators, possibly because he always carried a knife. They addressed him as 'the distinguished Senator from Texas.' He referred to them as 'You-all'.

Richard Armour, *It All Started With Columbus.*

. . . It was easy to believe in his heroism. He was fifty five years old . . . a magnificent barbarian, somewhat tempered by civilization. He was of large frame, of stately carriage and dignified demeanor and had a lion-like countenance capable of expressing fiercest passions. His dress was peculiar, but it was becoming to his style. The conspicuous features of it were a military cap, and a short military cloak of fine blue broadcloth, with a blood-red lining. Afterward, I occasionally met him when he wore a vast and picturesque sombrero and a Mexican blanket.

Oliver Dyer, *Great Senators of the United States.*

The President is General Houston of your acquaintance. His career . . . has been strange and wild. . . . A domestic tempest of desperate violence, and calamitous consequences; habitual drunkenness; a residence of several years amongst the Cherokee Indians; residing amongst them as a chieftain, and begetting sons and daughters; a sudden reappearance on this stage with better hopes and purposes, and commensurate success, — but still with unreclaimed habits. Finally, however, a new connexion with a young and gentle woman brought up in fear of God, conquered no doubt as women have been from the beginning and will be to the end by a glowing tongue, but in good revenge making conquest of his habits of tremendous cursing and passionate love of drink.

Captain Elliot, Letter to Henry Unwin Addington, 15 November 1842.

. . . looked like a prophet inspired by a vision unfolding the events of a thousand years to come.
John Salmon Ford, *Memoirs.*

For all the mauling that he had received at the hands of the world, Sam Houston retained the sensitive nature of his boyhood. He was not a happy warrior, but a brooding man in the stormy quest of repose.

Marquis James, *The Raven: A Biography of Sam Houston.*

His republic! That is true; for the country literally belongs to him and the people [are] his slaves. I can regard Texas as very little more than *Big Drunk's* big ranch.

Mirabeau B. Lamar, *Lamar Papers.*

Wires in and wires out
And leave the people all in doubt
Whether the snake that made the track
Was going South or coming back.
Marshall Mendian, 1854, in Llerena Friend, *Sam Houston, The Great Designer.*

. . . I find the President extremely courteous. When he out for general inspection, this seldom oftener than once in sunshine, between eleven & two, he . . . dresses himself gaudily in self peculiar taste viz., black silk velvet gold lace crimson vest and silver spurs takes a graduating glass, stops a moment before the mirror . . . and adjusts his shappo . . . and lastly the requisite inibriating sip·that makes himself again *Hector* up on his feet and no longe(r) the wounded Achilise of San Jacinto . . . and with a tread of dominion in his aroganic step strides . . . across his own nominated metropolis . . . to the bar keeper.

William D. Redd, Letter to Mirabeau Lamar, 23 May 1837.

He exhibited a propensity which to his friends seemed unaccountable and injudicious: it was to make enemies of persons who were desirous of friendly relations with him. He acted on one of Talleyrand's strange maxims, 'Would you rise, make enemies.'

Ashbell Smith, Ashbell Smith Papers.

See also Gary Cooper

HOWARD, CATHERINE

– d. 1542 Queen Consort to Henry VIII

Within eighteen months the intrigues in which Catherine had indulged since the age of twelve were uncovered, and she was charged with having committed adultery since her marriage with her cousin Culpepper. During the investigations she escaped from her apartment in Hampton Court and rushed down the gallery towards the chapel where she knew the King was at mass. The guards caught her before she could reach him, and she was dragged back, shrieking: a scene that impressed itself so vividly on the public mind, that the gallery is said to be haunted still.

Elizabeth Jenkins, *Elizabeth the Great.*

See also Elizabeth I

HOWARD, HENRIETTA, COUNTESS OF SUFFOLK

1681–1767 Mistress to George II

. . . A wise, discreet, honest and sincere courtier, who will promise no farther than she can perform, and will always perform what she does promise.

Lady Betty Germaine, Letter to Jonathan Swift, 8 February 1733.

If it was not for you we would forswear all Courts; and really it is the most mortifying thing in nature, that we can neither get into the Court to live with you, nor you get into the country to live with us; so we will take up with what we can get that belongs to you, and make ourselves as happy as we can in your house.

Alexander Pope, Letter to Mrs Howard, 20 June 1726.

Nor warp'd by passion, aw'd by rumour,
Not grave thro' pride, or gay through folly,
An equal mixture of good humour,
And sensible soft melancholy.

Alexander Pope, *To A Certain Lady at Court.*

HOWARD, HENRY, see under SURREY, EARL OF

HOWARTH, HUMPHREY

fl. 1800 Physician

Humphrey Howarth, the surgeon, was called out, and made his appearance in the field stark naked, to the astonishment of the challenger, who asked him what he meant. 'I know,' said H., 'that if any part of the clothing is carried into the body by a gunshot wound, festering ensues; and therefore I have met

you thus.' His antagonist declared that, fighting with a man in *puris naturalibus* would be quite ridiculous; and accordingly they parted without further discussion.

Samuel Rogers, *Table Talk.*

HOWE, JULIA WARD

1819–1910 Author, Reformer

. . . a personality serenely throned as queen among her American sisters, yet apparently unconscious of her sovereignty.

Ellen M. Mitchell, *Julia Ward Howe.*

She could always discover sunlight behind the shadows and the clouds; evil to her was but the promise of good, and good the promise of something better.

Ibid.

HOWE, RICHARD, EARL

1726–99 Admiral of the Fleet

His rigid brow seemed to give to every lineament of his countenance the harshness of an Article of War, yet under that unfavourable physiognomy a more humane mind never did honour to nature.

Anon., in Oliver Warner, *A Portrait of Lord Nelson.*

'Give us Black Dick and we fear nothing,' echoed from the line at Spithead to the floor of the House of Commons.

Ira D. Grubber, *The Howe Brothers and the American Revolution.*

Lord Howe's ideas were commonly either so ill conceived by himself, or so darkly and ambiguously expressed, that it was by no means easy to comprehend his precise meaning. This oracular and confused mode of delivery, rendered still more obscure by the part of the house where he usually sat, which was on a back row at a distance from the Speaker's chair, increased however the effect of his oratory; and seemed to exemplify Burke's assertion, that 'Obscurity is a Source of the Sublime.'

Sir Nathaniel Wraxall, *Historical Memoirs of His Own Time.*

HOWELLS, WILLIAM DEAN

1837–1920 Author

. . . the lousy cat of our letters.

Ambrose Bierce, in Paul Fatout, *Ambrose Bierce, The Devil's Lexicographer.*

For all his timidity and quaint propriety, his almost feminine domesticity, no one better understood or presented the transition from the old America to the new than this dean of American letters who at the height of his fame and influence cast his lot in with the protestants and rebels of his generation.

Henry Steele Commager, *The American Mind.*

You have such a rare faculty of not liking things in a likable manner. Anyone can be charmingly enthusiastic, but so few can be even tolerably sceptical. . . .

Bret Harte, Undated letter to Howells.

Limited by his way of living and his views on morality, confused in his thinking and condemned by that confusion to work with superficial phenomena, Howells was grievously handicapped in his attempt to make an enduring record of the life of his country and his time.

Granville Hicks, *The Great Tradition.*

Mr Howells was one of the gentlest, sweetest, and most honest of men, but he had the code of a pious old maid whose great delight was to have tea at the vicarage.

Sinclair Lewis, in Jay B. Hubbell, *Who Are the Major American Writers?*

. . . the sweetest socialist that ever was. . . .

James Russell Lowell, in Edward Wagenknecht, *James Russell Lowell, Portrait of a Many-Sided Man.*

. . . for years Howells was the Dean of American letters, and there was no one else on the faculty.

John Macy, in Alfred Kazin, *On Native Grounds.*

The writer who could thus understand the varieties of American life, and portray them both lovingly and shrewdly, was himself, as his audience came to believe, the man who best symbolized America. By 1900, when the New England Sages and Whitman were all dead, it was Howells who, combining their traditions, stood alone as the American Sage, preserving the idea of culture and transmitting a sense of its relevance.

Jay Martin, *Harvests of Change, American Literature 1865–1914.*

The truth about Howells is that he really has nothing to say, for all the charm he gets into saying it. His psychology is superficial, amateurish, often nonsensical; his irony is scarcely more than a polite facetiousness; his characters simply refuse to live.

H. L. Mencken, *Prejudices: First Series.*

Henry James went to France and read Turgenev. W. D. Howells stayed at home and read Henry James.

George Moore, *Confessions of a Young Man.*

And so Howells, perforce, became a specialist in women's nerves, an analyst of the tenuous New England conscience, a master of Boston small-talk. It was such materials that shaped his leisurely technique until it falls about his theme with the amplitude of crinoline.

Vernon Louis Parrington, *Main Currents in American Thought*, vol. 3.

He remained a 'nice' person, neurotically fastidious, acquiescent to the power wielded by the middle-class Victorian woman in determining moral and cultural standards. He became, indeed, the chief spokesman for the 'genteel female', aiding and abetting her efforts to keep this country's literature emasculated and cheerful.

Bernard Smith, *Forces in American Criticism.*

If he had been as thorough-going as his program demanded, he would have been the American Zola; he became instead our masculine Jane Austen.

George Snell, *The Shapers of American Fiction 1789–1947.*

. . . an author so prolific during the sixty years between his earliest book and his latest that he amounts almost to a library in himself, as editor and critic so influential that he amounts almost to a literary movement.

Carl Van Doren, in Edward Wagenknecht, *Cavalcade of the American Novel.*

HUBERT DE BURGH

— d. 1243 Statesman

Hubert had served King John as Chamberlain, as castellan of Chinon, as sheriff of Norfolk, as justiciar. He was an ambitious man, who had had to win a place for himself. He was self-seeking and tended to take the colour of the baronial society which he desired to enter. His determination to maintain the interests of the Crown and the well-being of England on the basis of a strong centralized administration was not, and could not be divorced from his desire to maintain himself. His marriage in 1221 to Margaret, the sister of the king of the Scots, and his creation as earl of Kent raised him to the level but did not give him the stability of, the earl of Chester or the earl of Pembroke. He had always to think of his position, and to secure it by the possession of land and castles, by the choice of friends, the care-

ful selection of his clerks and agents, the cultivation of the good-will of the king. The violence of the storm which broke upon him in 1232 shows how hard his efforts to hold his own must have been. He was not liked, had never been accepted, and nothing was too bad to say about him.
Sir Maurice Powicke, *The Thirteenth Century*.

HUGHES, CHARLES EVANS

1862—1948 Jurist

How I dislike writing opinions! I prefer arguments — and let some one else have the responsibility of decision.
On himself, after being appointed to the World Court, in Merlo Pusey, *Charles Evans Hughes*.

You have sent me forth to the doubtful combats of public life. Sometimes I have returned with my shield, and at least once I returned upon it, but I have always come back. While it is a privilege to hold public office, it is the life beyond the political grave that is the best. In one respect the servant of the people is like the Apostle — he 'dies daily.'
On himself, in *ibid*.

. . . a shining illustration of that peculiar type of citizen developed in this country during the present generation — the citizen who personally opposes vice and is a punisher of small crimes, but who shows no indignation at the larger forms of legalized robbery.
William Jennings Bryan, in Samuel Hendel, *Charles Evans Hughes and the Supreme Court*.

Hughes took over the reins [as Chief Justice of the Supreme Court] with the easy grace of one long familiar with his task, although he had never presided over a court before. His piercing eyes and finely chiseled nose, his broad forehead, his white beard and bushy brows, standing out in contrast to his black robe, gave him the appearance of Mr. Justice himself.
Merlo Pusey, *Charles Evans Hughes*.

. . . it is not merely what Mr. Hughes has done that has shed honor upon all. . . . It is what he has stood for. He never sought an office; he never administered an office with a view to keeping it longer, or with a view to getting another. He never attempted to build up a personal political machine for his own aggrandizement. He never abandoned or suppressed an opinion which he thought ought to be expressed, in order to please anybody. . . . He subdued his idealism to the uses of mankind.
Elihu Root, in *ibid*.

HUGHES, HOWARD ROBARD

1905—76 Film Maker, Industrialist, Inventor

I want to be unobtrusive.
On himself, in an interview with United Press International's Aline Mosby.

In a nation which increasingly appears to prize social virtues, Howard Hughes remains not merely anti-social but grandly, brilliantly, surpassingly asocial. He is the last private man, the dream we no longer admit.
Joan Didion, *Slouching Towards Bethlehem*.

The spook of American Capitalism . . . suspicious and withdrawn, elusive to the point of being almost invisible, he is loath to give anything up, loath to admit error. . . . There is one aspect of his character about which his former associates are agreed: he abhors making a decision.
Fortune Magazine; cited in Elaine Davenport and Paul Eddy with Mark Hurwitz, *The Hughes Papers*.

In a sense, Howard Hughes, America's bashful billionaire, epitomizes the dilemma of twentieth century America: inventive, brilliant, fantastic, overwhelming in technical precocity and accomplishment — suspicious, complex, contradictory, and sometimes downright antediluvian in social outlook.
Albert B. Gerber, *Bashful Billionaire*.

Hughes was the only man I ever knew who had to die to prove he had been alive.
Walter Kane in James Phelan, *Howard Hughes, The Hidden Years*.

A man whose life, more than that of any other man, resembles the most improbable Grade B Spectacular in glorious Vistavision.
John Keats, *Howard Hughes*.

An earlier generation mistook him for a blend of Charles Lindbergh, Tom Swift and his electric locomotive, and Jimmy Stewart, in *Mr. Smith Goes to Washington*, and made him an American folk hero. . . . Today's feverish cult of the conspiracy pictures him as an American folk demon. They see him as a giant puppet master, a one-man Illuminati manipulating this nation and others. If he was not the master of the CIA, they cry, he was at least its premier agent.
James Phelan, *Howard Hughes, The Hidden Years*.

HUGHES, (JAMES) LANGSTON

1902—67 Author

And one must bear in mind that with Langston Hughes Harlem is both place and symbol. When he depicts the hopes, the aspirations, the frustrations, and the deep-seated discontent of the New York ghetto, he is expressing the feelings of Negroes in black ghettos throughout America.

Arthur P. Davis, 'The Harlem of Langston Hughes' Poetry', in Seymour L. Gross and John Edward Hardy eds, *Images of the Negro in American Literature.*

Behind the warm smile of his dark eyes there was a grave dignity, and a polite reserve which communicated itself at once. He was very likeable and easy to get on with, but at the same time one felt an impenetrable, elusive remoteness which warded off all undue familiarity.

Arthur Koestler, in Milton Meltzer, *Langston Hughes.*

Do not let any lionizers stampede you. Hide and write and study and think. . . .

Vachel Lindsay, Undated letter to Hughes.

HUME, DAVID

1711—76 Philosopher, Historian

I assure you, that without running any of the heights of scepticism, I am apt in a cool hour to suspect, in general, that most of my reasonings will be more useful by furnishing hints and exciting people's curiosity, than as containing any principles that will augment the stock of knowledge, that must pass to future ages.

On himself, Letter to Francis Hutcheson, March 1740.

My views of *things* are more conformable to Whig principles; my representation of *persons* to Tory prejudices. Nothing can so much prove that men commonly regard more persons than things, as to find that I am commonly numbered among the Tories.

On himself, Letter to Dr Clephane, 1756.

A room in a sober discreet family, who would not be averse to admit a sober, discreet, virtuous, regular, quiet, goodnatured man of a bad character — such a room, I say, would suit me extremely.

On himself, Letter to Dr Clephane, September 1757.

Never literary attempt was more unfortunate than my Treatise of Human Nature. It fell *dead-born from the press.*

On himself, *My Own Life.*

. . . I was, a man of mild disposition, of command of temper, of an open, social, and cheerful humour, capable of attachment, but little susceptible of enmity, and of great moderation in all my passions. Even my love of literary fame, my ruling passion, never soured my temper, notwithstanding my frequent disappointments. My company was not unacceptable to the young and careless, as well as to the studious and literary; and as I took a particular pleasure in the company of modest women, I had not reason to be displeased with the reception I met from them. In a word, though most men, anywise eminent, have found reason to complain of calumny, I never was touched, or even attacked, by her baleful tooth; and though I wantonly exposed myself to the rage of both civil and religious factions, they seemed to be disarmed in my behalf of their wonted fury. My friends never had occasion to vindicate any one circumstance of my character and conduct: not but that the zealots, we may well suppose, would have been glad to invent and propagate any story to my disadvantage, but they could never find any which they thought would wear the face of probability. I cannot say there is no vanity in making this funeral oration of myself; but I hope it is not a misplaced one; and this is a matter of fact which is easily cleared and ascertained.

On himself, in *ibid.*

Is it right in you, Sir, to hold up to our view, as 'perfectly wise and virtuous', the *character* and *conduct* of one, who seems to have been possessed with an incurable antipathy to all that is called RELIGION; and who strained every nerve to explode, suppress, and extirpate the spirit of it among men, that its very name, if he could effect it, might no more be had in remembrance?

Anon., *A Letter to Adam Smith*, 1777.

Hume is always idiomatic, but his idioms are constantly wrong; many of his best passages are on that account curiously grating and puzzling; you feel they are very like what an Englishman would say, but yet that, after all, somehow or other they are what he never would say; — there is a minute seasoning of imperceptible difference which distracts your attention, and which you are for ever stopping to analyse.

Walter Bagehot, in Alexander Bain, *James Mill.*

David Hume ate a swinging great dinner,
    And grew every day fatter and fatter;
And yet the huge bulk of a sinner
    Said there was neither spirit or matter.

J. H. Beattie, in *The Faber Book of Comic Verse.*

Hume owned that he had never read the New Testament with attention. Here then was a man who had been at no pains to inquire into the truth of religion, and had continually turned his mind the other way. It was not to be expected that the prospect of death would alter his way of thinking, unless GOD should send an angel to set him right.

James Boswell, *Life of Johnson.*

A few weeks before his death, when there were dining with him two or three of his intimate companions, one of them, Dr. Smith, happening to complain of the world as spiteful and ill-natured, 'No, no', said Mr. Hume, 'here am I, who have written on all sorts of subjects calculated to excite hostility, moral, political and religious, and yet I have no enemies, except indeed, all the Whigs, all the Tories, and all the Christians'.

Henry Lord Brougham, *Men of Letters and Science in the Time of George III.*

But he was always careless about the offensive application of his principles; forgetting that if there be anything in a set of opinions calculated deeply and permanently to outrage the feelings of mankind, the probability at least is, that they have something about them unsound, — that the mass of the public are right, and the solitary philosopher wrong.

J. H. Burton, *Life and Correspondence of David Hume.*

Nature, I believe, never formed any man more unlike his real character than David Hume. The powers of phisiognomy were baffled by his countenance; neither could the most skilful, in that science, pretend to discover the smallest traces of the faculties of his mind, in the unmeaning features of his visage. His face was broad and flat, his mouth wide, and without any other expression than that of imbecility. His eyes vacant and spiritless, and the corpusculence of his whole person was far better fitted to communicate the idea of a turtle-eating Alderman, than of a refined philosopher.

James Caulfield, Earl of Charlemont, in Francis Hardy, *Memoirs of The Political and Private Life of James Caulfield Earl of Charlemont*, 1812.

A letter from Hume overpaid the labour of ten years.
Edward Gibbon, *Autobiography.*

Our Davie's a fine good-natured crater, but uncommon wake-minded.
Catherine Hume (Hume's mother), attributed, in J. H. Burton, *Life of Hume.*

For the sake of this beloved object, DELIBERATE DOUBT, there is no mischief he is not ready to commit, even to the unhinging the national Religion, and unloosing all the hold it has on the minds of the people. And all this for the selfish and unnatural lust of *escaping* from right reason and common sense, *into the calm, though obscure regions of philosophy.* But here we have earthed him; rolled up in the Scoria of a *dogmatist* and *Sceptic*, run down together. He has been long taken for a Philosopher: and so perhaps he may be found — like Aristotle's statue in the block.

Richard Hurd, *Remarks on Mr. David Hume's Essay on the Natural History of Religion.*

Why, Sir, his style is not English, the structure of his sentences is French. Now the French structure and the English structure may, in the nature of things, be equally good. But if you allow the English language is established, he is wrong. My name might originally have been Nicholson, as well as Johnson; but were you to call me Nicholson now, you would call me very absurdly.

Samuel Johnson, in James Boswell, *Life of Johnson.*

. . . He had a vanity of being thought easy. It is more probable that he should assume an appearance of ease, than so very improbable thing should be, as a man not afraid of going (as, in spite of his delusive theory, he cannot be sure but he may go) into an unknown state, and not being uneasy at leaving all he knew. And you are going to consider that upon his own principle of annihilation he had no motive to speak the truth.

Ibid.

The philosophy of Hume was nothing more than the analysis of the word 'cause' into uniform sequence.
Benjamin Jowett, Introduction to Plato, *Parmenides.*

Hume, from whose fascinating narrative [i.e. Hume's *History*] the great mass of the reading public are still contented to take their opinions, hated religion so much that he hated liberty for having been allied with religion, and has pleaded the cause of tyranny with the dexterity of an advocate, while affecting the impartiality of a judge.

T. B. Macaulay, *Essays*: 'Milton'.

Hume is an accomplished advocate: Without positively asserting much more than he can prove, he gives prominence to all the circumstances which support his case; he glides lightly over those which are unfavourable to it; his own witnesses are applauded and encouraged; the statements which seem to throw discredit on them are controverted; the contradictions into which they fall are explained away; a clear and connected abstract of their evidence is given. Everything that is offered on the other side is scrutinized with the utmost severity; — every suspicious circumstance is a ground for comment and invective; what cannot be denied is extenuated, or passed by without notice; concessions even are sometimes made — but their insidious candour only increases the effect of the vast mass of sophistry.

T. B. Macaulay, in *Edinburgh Quarterly*, vol. 47.

David, who there supinely designs to lie,
The fattest hog in Epicurus' sty,
Though drunk with Gallic wine and Gallic praise,
David shall bless Old England's halcyon days.

William Mason, *An Heroic Epistle to Sir William Chambers*.

Accordingly, France had Voltaire, and his school of negative thinkers, and England (or rather Scotland) had the profoundest negative thinker on record, David Hume: a man, the peculiarities of whose mind qualified him to detect failures of proof, and want of logical consistency, at a depth which the French Sceptics, with their comparatively feeble powers of analysis and abstraction, stopt far short of, and which German subtlety alone could thoroughly appreciate, or hope to rival.

J. S. Mill, *Dissertations*: 'Bentham'.

Hume possessed powers of a very high order; but regard for truth formed no part of his character. He reasoned with surprising acuteness; but the object of his reasonings was not to attain truth, but to show that it was unattainable. His mind, too, was completely enslaved by a taste for literature; not those kinds of literature which teach mankind to know the causes of their happiness and misery, that they may seek the one and avoid the other; but that literature which without regard for truth or utility, seeks only to excite emotion.

J. S. Mill, in *Westminster Review*, October 1824.

No man is without his failings; and his great views of being singular, and a vanity to show himself superior to most people, led him to advance many axioms that were dissonant to the opinion of others, and led him into sceptical doctrines only to show how minute and puzzling they were to other folk; in so far, that I have often seen him (in various companies, according as he saw some enthusiastic person there) combat either their religious or political principles; nay, after he had struck them dumb, take up the argument on their side with equal good humour, wit and jocoseness, all to show his pre-eminency.

George Nicholl, in *Edinburgh Magazine*, 1802.

Hume, for example, suffered from the illusion about sensations that I have described. His system was a sort of psychology without bodies, and he treated sensations as if they had a criterion of identity rather like, indeed too like, the criterion of identity of material objects. And many other philosophers have made the same kind of mistake.

David Pears, in Bryan Magee, *Modern British Philosophy*.

Hume's philosophy, whether true or false, represents the bankruptcy of eighteenth-century reasonableness. He starts out, like Locke, with the intention of being sensible and empirical, taking nothing on trust, but seeking whatever instruction is to be obtained from experience and observation. But having a better intellect than Locke's, a greater acuteness in analysis, and a smaller capacity for accepting comfortable inconsistencies, he arrives at the disastrous conclusion that from experience and observation nothing is to be learnt.

Bertrand Russell, *History of Western Philosophy*.

The growth of unreason throughout the nineteenth century and what has passed of the twentieth is a natural sequel to Hume's destruction of empiricism. It is therefore important to discover whether there is any answer to Hume within the framework of a philosophy that is wholly or mainly empirical. If not, there is no intellectual difference between sanity and insanity. The lunatic who believes that he is a poached egg is to be condemned solely on the ground that he is in a minority, or rather — since we must not assume democracy — on the ground that the government does not agree with him.

Ibid.

Upon the whole, I have always considered him, both in his lifetime and since his death, as approaching as nearly to the idea of a perfectly wise and virtuous man, as perhaps the nature of human frailty will permit.

Adam Smith, Letter to William Strachan, November 1776.

No mortal being was ever more completely divested of the trammels of the personal and the particular, none ever practised with a more consummate success the divine art of impartiality.

Lytton Strachey, *Portraits in Miniature*, 1931.

See also Francis Bacon, John Knox

HUMPHREY, DUKE OF GLOUCESTER

1391–1447 Statesman

To dine with Duke *Humphrey*. . . . For *Humphrey Duke* of Gloucester (commonly called the *good*

Duke) was so hospitable, that every man of *Fashion*, otherwise *unprovided*, was welcome to *Dine* with him. . . . But after the Death of good Duke Humphrey (when many of his former Almsmen were at a losse for a meals meat) this proverb did *alter its copy*, to Dine with *Duke Humphrey*, importing, to be *Dinnerlesse*.

Thomas Fuller, *The History of the Worthies of England.*

HUNT, HENRY ('ORATOR HUNT')

1773—1835 Radical Politician

. . . the incarnation of an empty, blustering, restless, ignorant, and selfish demagogue. . . .

Harriet Martineau, *History of the Thirty Years Peace.*

HUNT, (JAMES HENRY) LEIGH

1784—1859 Essayist, Poet

He is perhaps, a little opinionated, as all men who are the *centre* of circles, wide or narrow — the Sir Oracles, in whose name two or three are gathered together — must be, and as even Johnson was; but, withal, a valuable man, and less vain than success, and even the consciousness of preferring 'the right to the expedient' might excuse.

Lord Byron, Journal, 1 December 1813.

He is a good man, with some poetical elements in his chaos; but spoilt by the Christ-Church Hospital and a Sunday newspaper, — to say nothing of the Surrey gaol, which conceited him into a martyr. But he is a good man. When I saw *Rimini* in MS., I told him that I deemed it good poetry at bottom, disfigured only by a strange style. His answer was, that his style was a system, or *upon system*, or some such cant; and, when a man talks of system, his case is hopeless.

Lord Byron, Letter to Thomas Moore, 1 June 1818.

He improves upon acquaintance. The author translates admirably into the man. Indeed the very faults of his style are virtues in the individual. His natural gaiety and sprightliness of manner, his high animal spirits, and the *vinous* quality of his mind, produce an immediate fascination and intoxication in those who come in contact with him, and carry, off in society whatever in his writings may to some seem flat and impertinent. From great sanguineness of temper, from great quickness and unsuspecting simplicity, he runs on to the public as he does at his own fireside, and talks about himself, forgetting that he is not always among friends.

William Hazlitt, *The Spirit of the Age.*

What though, for showing truth to flatter'd state,
Kind Hunt was shut in prison, yet has he
In his immortal spirit, been as free
As the sky-searching lark, and as elate.
Minion of grandeur! think you he did wait?
Think you he nought but prison walls did see,
Till, so unwilling, thou unturn'dst the key?
Ah, no! far happier, nobler was his fate!
In Spenser's halls he strayed, and bowers fair,
Culling enchanted flowers; and he flew
With daring Milton through the fields of air:
To regions of his own his genius true
Took happy flights. Who shall his fame impair
When thou art dead, and all thy wretched crew?

John Keats, *Sonnet written on the day that Mr Leigh Hunt left Prison.*

One of those happy souls
Which are the salt of the earth, and without whom
The world would smell like what it is — a tomb.

P. B. Shelley, Letter to Maria Gladstone, 1 July 1820.

L.H. was our spiritual grandfather, a free man. . . . A light man, I daresay, but civilised, much more so than my grandfather in the flesh. These free, vigorous spirits advance the world, and when one lights on them in the strange waste of the past one says 'Ah, you're my sort' — a great compliment.

Virginia Woolf, *A Writer's Diary*, 13 August 1921.

See also John Keats

HUNTER, JOHN

1728—93 Surgeon

He had, now, indeed arrived at the highest rank in his profession; was consulted by all those surgeons who were attached to Mr. Pott during that gentleman's lifetime; he was almost adored by the rising generation of medical men, who seemed to quote him as the Schools, at one time, did Aristotle.

Joseph Adams, *Memoirs of the Life and Doctrines of the late John Hunter, Esq.*

John Hunter once saying to Lord Holland, 'If you wish to see a great man you have one before you. I consider myself a greater man than Sir Isaac Newton.' Explained then why; that discoveries which lengthen life and alleviate sufferings are of infinitely more importance to mankind than any thing relating to the stars, &c. &c.

Thomas Moore, Diary, 4 October 1829.

The limitations of John Hunter are obvious. He was hampered by a defective education. He had an almost medieval respect for words as words. He could not express himself clearly, either in writing or by word of mouth, when he dealt with the more difficult problems of surgery, which he knew existed but was unable to solve for want of the ancillary sciences. He was a gross teleologist. His metaphors were often strained and sometimes wholly false. He was confessedly ignorant of the work of his surgical colleagues and foreign contemporaries, and . . . he suffered from frequent and severe attacks of illness which would have incapacitated any one possessed of a less dauntless spirit. But when we have said this we have said all there is to say against him as a man.
    Sir D'Arcy Power, *The Hunterian Oration*, 14 February 1925.

I have been ill of the gout in four or five parts, and produced from one of my fingers a chalkstone, that I believe is worthy of a place in Mr. Hunter's collection of human miseries — he best knows whether it is qualified to be a candidate there — I do know that on *delivery* I had it weighed, and its weight was four grains and [a] half.
    Horace Walpole, Letter to the Rev. Robert Nares, 5 October 1793.

HUNTINGTON, HENRY EDWARDS

1850—1927 Financier, Art Collector

Huntington, with his large, deeply lined face, his long nose and black beard, might have sat for Holbein as a great vassal of the Renaissance period, or some militant prince of the Church.
    Matthew Josephson, *The Robber Barons*.

HUSKISSON, WILLIAM

1770—1830 Statesman

It's all over with me; bring me my wife, and let me die.
    On himself, after being run over by 'The Rocket' at Parkside Station, 15 September 1830.

He is not a good debater, and is still worse at those great speeches. . . . He is *au fait* in all official and financial details, and has a great deal of what the French call *administrative* experience but the defects of his manner and voice prevent him being a useful speaker, for no one is useful whom the House [of Commons] merely tolerates — who, on the contrary, does not force them to attend to him. . . .
    John Wilson Croker, Letter to Sir Robert Peel, 25 August 1822.

He goes [to the King] . . . with as much latitude as the Whigs can consistently give him, with his conciliatory prudence, his unpretending sagacity, his easy small talk, and above all with a perfect knowledge of the ground he treads on, and a conviction that the King must be managed, and with the skill and ability to do it.
    Lady Granville, Letter to Lady Carlisle, 31 August 1827.

Oh! he is a very good bridge for rats to run over.
    Duke of Wellington, on making Huskisson a Cabinet Minister, in Lord Holland, Diary, 8 March 1828.

HUTCHINSON, ANNE

1591—1643 Religious Reformer

A woman that preaches better Gospell than any of your black-coats that have been at the Ninnyversity, a woman of an other kind of spirit, who hath had many revelations of things to come.
    Anon., in William Cullen Bryant, *A Popular History of the United States*.

A dear saint and servant of God.
    William Hutchinson, in Winifred Rugg, *Unafraid*.

You have not only to deal with a woman this day . . . that never had any true Grace in her heart. . . . Yea, this day she hath shewed herselfe to be a Notorious Imposter.
    The Rev. Thomas Shepard, speaking at Hutchinson's heresy trial, in Emery Battis, *Saints and Sectaries*.

A dangerous instrument of the Devil raised up by Satan amongst us.
    The Rev. John Wilson, at Hutchinson's excommunication trial, 1638, in Winifred Rugg, *Unafraid*.

A woman not fit for our society.
    John Winthrop, in *ibid*.

HUXLEY, ALDOUS LEONARD

1894—1963 Novelist

He is at once the truly clever person and the stupid person's idea of the clever person; he is expected to be relentless, to administer intellectual shocks.
    Elizabeth Bowen, in *Spectator*, 11 December 1936.

The great Mahatma of all misanthropy . . . this pedant who leeringly gloated over how crayfish copulated (through their third pair of legs) but could never have caught or cooked one; let alone broken in a horse, thrown and branded a steer, flensed a whale, or slaughtered, cut, cured, and cooked anything at all.

Roy Campbell, *Light on a Dark Horse.*

People will call Mr Aldous Huxley a pessimist; in the sense of one who makes the worst of it. To me he is that far more gloomy character; the man who makes the best of it.

G. K. Chesterton, *The Common Man.*

Mr Aldous Huxley, who is perhaps one of those people who have to perpetrate thirty bad novels before producing a good one, has a certain natural — but little developed — aptitude for seriousness. Unfortunately, this aptitude is hampered by a talent for the rapid assimilation of all that isn't essential and by a gift for chic. Now, the gift for chic, combined with the desire for seriousness, produces a frightful monster: a chic religiosity.

T. S. Eliot, *La Nouvelle Revue Française*, 1 May 1927, translated by Thomas M. Donnan.

To begin with, Huxley, though he is more like Max Beerbohm than any other living writer (an ambiguity which I shall let stand, as it works either way), belongs as distinctly to the present day as does Beerbohm to the '90's. He has an utterly ruthless habit of building up an elaborate and sometimes almost romantic structure and then blowing it down with something too ironic to be called satire and too scornful to be called irony.

F. Scott Fitzgerald (reviewing *Crome Yellow*), in *St Paul Daily News*, 26 February 1922.

Aldous Huxley sits there and without looking at you, or at anyone else in particular, emits streams of impersonal sound, like a sort of loudspeaker, about the habits of bees and ants, the excretions of elephants, and sexual intercourse among whales. By a kind of studied fastidiousness avoiding reticent language: For aren't we the unashamed Intelligentsia? And as he speaks a look of anxiety comes on the faces of the women present as though they would be unspeakably shocked if anyone thought they could possibly be shocked by anything.

William Gerhardie, *Memoirs of a Polyglot.*

I don't like his books; even if I admire a sort of desperate courage of repulsion and repudiation in them. But again, I feel only half a man writes the books — a sort of precocious adolescent.

D. H. Lawrence, Letter to Lady Ottoline Morrell, 5 February 1929.

The novelist must be able to get into the skin of the creatures of his invention, see with their eyes and feel with their fingers; but Aldous Huxley sees them like an anatomist. He dissects out their nerves, uncovers their arteries with precision, and peers into the ventricles of their hearts. The process gives rise in the reader to a certain discomfort.

W. Somerset Maugham, Introduction to *Modern English and American Literature.*

You were right about Huxley's book [*Ape and Essence*] — it is awful. And do you notice that the more holy he gets, the more his books stink with sex. He cannot get off the subject of flagellating women.

George Orwell, Letter to Richard Rees, 3 March 1949.

You could always tell by his conversation which volume of the *Encyclopedia Britannica* he'd been reading. One day it would be Alps, Andes and Apennines, and the next it would be the Himalayas and the Hippocratic Oath.

Bertrand Russell, Letter to R. W. Clark, July 1965.

As a young man, though he was always friendly, his silences seemed to stretch for miles, extinguishing life, when they occurred, as a snuffer extinguishes a candle. On the other hand, he was (when uninterrupted) one of the most accomplished talkers I have ever known, and his monologues on every conceivable subject were astonishing floriated variations of an amazing brilliance.

Edith Sitwell, *Taken Care Of.*

He was the tallest English author known to me. He was so tall (and thin, so that he seemed to stretch to infinity) that when, long ago, he lived in Hampstead, ribald little boys in that neighbourhood used to call out to him: 'Cole up there, guv'nor?'

Frank Swinnerton, *The Georgian Literary Scene.*

Aldous Huxley, as [D. H. Lawrence's] direct protagonist, preaches the sermon of the intellect; his god is cellular, and his heaven a socialist Towards. He would, as someone brighter than myself has said, condense the generative principle into a test-tube; Lawrence, on the other hand, would condense the world into the generative principle, and make his apostles decline not cogitare but copulare.

Dylan Thomas, Letter to Pamela Hansford Johnson, 1933.

It used to be fashionable to call him 'intelligent', but he was never particularly intelligent. His habit of reading the *Encyclopaedia Britannica* gives the quality of his appetite for facts and ideas; his

interest in the great intellectual movements that were bringing most light in his own time was on exactly the same level as his interest in a twelfth-century heresy, a queer species of carnivorous plant, a special variety of Romanesque architecture or a Greek poet surviving in fragments. Freud, Lenin, Einstein, Joyce — he sometimes expressed about them, in his casual essays, opinions as obtuse and philistine as those of the ordinary Fleet Street journalist.
Edmund Wilson, *Classics and Commercials.*

All raw, uncooked, protesting. A descendant, oddly enough, of Mrs H[umphrey] Ward: interest in ideas; makes people into ideas.
Virginia Woolf (on reading *Point Counter Point*), *A Writer's Diary*, 23 January 1935.

See also D. H. Lawrence, Harpo Marx

HUXLEY, THOMAS HENRY

1825—95 Man of Science

Men differ greatly in their manner of meeting criticism and reacting to it. Huxley found controversy the spice of life. He once testified that a polemic was as little abhorrent to him 'as gin to a reclaimed drunkard'. And a published reply from an opponent evoked the testimony that it 'caused such a flow of bile that I have been the better for it ever since'.
W. B. Cannon, *The Way of an Investigator.*

In the sharpest contrast to Darwin stands the figure of T. H. Huxley, inventor and popularizer of the very word biology (Darwin would have called himself a naturalist to the end of his days), and prototype of the non-museum professional biologist. Huxley's efforts were devoted at least as much to establishing the professional status and training of biologists as to purely intellectual propaganda for Darwinism. It was not until students trained in the schools of biology fathered by Huxley began to erupt into systematic work that the influence of Darwin's teachings about species began to make itself felt.
R. A. Crowson, in S. A. Barnett, *A Century of Darwin.*

Huxley is a very genial, comfortable being — yet with none of the noise and windy geniality of some folks here.
Henry James, Letter to William James, 29 March 1877.

Huxley's solicitude for Darwin's strength was characteristic of him. He often alluded to himself as 'Darwin's bull dog'.
H. F. Osborn, *Impressions of Great Naturalists.*

I have sometimes described him as one who is continually taking two irons out of the fire and putting three in; and necessarily, along with the external congestion entailed, there is apt to come internal congestion.
Herbert Spencer, *An Autobiography.*

As I knew Huxley he was a yellow-faced, square-faced old man, with bright little brown eyes, lurking as it were in caves under his heavy grey eyebrows, and a mane of grey hair brushed back from his wall of forehead. He lectured in a clear firm voice without hurry and without delay, turning to the blackboard behind him to sketch some diagram, and always dusting the chalk from his fingers rather fastidiously before he resumed.
H. G. Wells, *Experiment in Autobiography.*

See also Charles Darwin, George Lewes, Charles Lyell

HYDE, ANNE, DUCHESS OF YORK

1637—71 Court Figure

Paint her with oyster lip and breath of fame
Wide mouth that 'sparagus may well proclaim
With Chanc'llors belly and so large a rump,
There (not behind the coach) her pages jump . . .
Andrew Marvell, *Last Instructions to a Painter.*

The Duke of York in all things but his amours was led by the nose by his wife.
Samuel Pepys, Diary, 30 October 1668.

March 31, f, died Ann, Duchess of York. . . . She died with eating and drinking; died fast and fustie; salacious; lecherous.
Anthony à Wood, *Life and Times*, 31 March 1671.

HYDE, EDWARD, EARL OF CLARENDON

1609—74 Historian, Statesman

He knew well upon how slippery Ground he stood, and how naturally averse the Nation was from approving an exorbitant Power in any Subject.
On himself, on his own position as Chancellor to Charles II, *The Life . . . of Edward Earl of Clarendon, . . . by himself.*

He was always pressing the King to mind his affairs, but in vain. He was a good Chancellor, only a little too rough, but very impartial in the administration of justice. He never seemed to understand foreign affairs well: and yet he meddled too much in them.

He had too much levity in his wit, and did not always observe the decorum of his post. He was high, and was apt to reject those who addressed themselves to him with too much contempt. He had such a regard to the King, that when places were disposed of, even otherwise than as he advised, yet he would justify what the King did, and disparage the pretensions of others, not without much scorn; which created him many enemies. He was indefatigable in business, tho' the gout did often disable him from waiting on the King: yet, during his Credit, the King came constantly to him when he was laid up by it.

Gilbert Burnet, *History of My Own Time.*

I found him in his bed Chamber very Sad: The Parliament had accused him, & he had enemies at Court, especialy the boufoones & Ladys of Pleasure, because he thwarted some of them and stood in their way, I could name some of the chiefe, The truth is he made few friends during his grandure among the royal Suffrers; but advanced the old rebells, that had mony enough to buy places: he was however (though no considerable Lawyer), one who kept up the forme & substance of things in the nation with more solemnity than some would have, & was my particular kind friend on all occasions.

John Evelyn, Diary, 27 August 1667.

No man wrote abler state papers. No man spoke with more weight and dignity in council and in parliament. No man was better acquainted with general maxims of statecraft. No man observed the varieties of character with a more discriminating eye. It must be added that he had a strong sense of moral and religious obligation, a sincere reverence for the laws of his country, and a conscientious regard for the honour and interest of the Crown. But his temper was sour, arrogant and impatient of opposition. Above all, he had been long an exile; and this circumstance alone would have completely disqualified him for the supreme direction of affairs.

T. B. Macaulay, *History of England.*

When *Clarindon* had discern'd beforehand,
   (As the cause can eas'ly foretell the Effect)
At once three Deluges threat'ning our Land;
   'Twas the season he thought to turn Architect.

Us, *Mars*, and *Apollo*, and *Vulcan* consume;
   While he the Betrayer of *England* and *Flander*,
Like the King-fisher chuseth to build in the Broom,
   And nestles in flames like the Salamander.
   Andrew Marvell, *Clarendon's House-Warming.*

He did plainly say he would not direct me in anything, for he would not put himself into the power of any man to say that he did so and so; but plainly told me as if he would be glad I did something.

Lord, to see how we poor wretches dare not do the King good service for fear of the greatness of these men.

Samuel Pepys, Diary, 14 July 1664.

And endeed, I am mad in love with my Lord Chancellor, for he doth comprehend and speak as well, and with the greatest easiness and authority, that ever I saw man in my life. I did never observe how much easier a man doth speak, when he knows all the company to be below him, then in him; for though he spoke endeed excellent well, yet his manner and freedom of doing it, as if he played with it and was informing only the rest of the company, was mighty pretty.

Ibid., 13 October 1666.

Mr Hater tells me at noon, that some rude people have been, as he hears, at my Lord Chancellor's, where they have cut down the trees before his house and broke his windows; and a gibbet either set up before, or painted on his gate, and these words writ — 'Three sights to be seen; Dunkirke, Tanger, and a barren Queen.'

Ibid., 14 June 1667.

He did say the other day at his table — 'Treachery?' says he, 'I could wish we could prove there was anything of that in it, for that would imply some wit and thoughtfulness; but we are ruined merely by folly and neglect'.

Ibid., 12 July 1667.

With what a gorgeous sinuosity, with what a grandiose delicacy, [Clarendon] elaborates through his enormous sentences, the lineaments of a soul.

Lytton Strachey, *Portraits in Miniature:* 'Macaulay'.

Those who look on History as a mere means of strengthening the Whig position, will doubtless convict Clarendon of monstrous partiality, and it may be confessed that he thought it no part of his duty to look back upon events with the eyes of a Roundhead.

Charles Whibley, *Edward Hyde.*

It has been pointed out that he had little sense of natural scenery or of history's dramatic elements. He'did not see the persons of his drama against any background, natural or artificial. His world has not houses, nor courts, nor fields. The personages of his drama seem to move hither and thither, in vast, vacant spaces. He was interested supremely in men, not things, in the conflict of wills and the passions of the mind. History for him was 'Character in Action'.

Ibid.

I

INCHBALD, ELIZABETH

1753—1821 Novelist, Dramatist

The impediment in her speech was of that peculiar nature, that it rather imparted an entertaining characteristic to her conversation, than diminished its force. . . . One morning waiting on a manager who shall be nameless, with a new play, the gentleman *suddenly* became so violently enamoured, that, dispensing with all preparatory courtesies, he commenced a personal attack, *sans ceremonie*; on which, the lady seizing him by his tail with one hand, with the other rang the bell, till assistance appeared. Ever afterwards, when speaking of this love *rencontre*, she used whimsically to stammer out,

'How f—ortunate for me he did NOT W—EAR a W—IG.'

Frederick Reynolds, *Life and Times of Frederick Reynolds.*

INNESS, GEORGE

1825—94 Artist

I once met him in the White Mountains and we spent several hours talking together, or rather he talked and I listened, about a theory he had of color intertwined in a most ingenious way with Swedenborgianism, in which he was a devout believer. Toward the latter part of the evening I became quite dizzy, and which was color and which religion I could hardly tell!

D. Maitland Armstrong, in Nicolai Cikovsky Jr, *George Inness.*

George Inness is here and thinks it attractive for the artist — As his theory is 'Subject is nothing, treatment makes the picture' I can believe he is satisfied.

Frederic E. Church, writing from Thomasville, Georgia, 18 March 1890.

He can be as sensitive as he is powerful in his rendering of nature's phenomena. The aerial distances and perspective of his best moods are subtle and delicate, like nature herself. We can breathe in his atmosphere, and travel far and wide in his landscape. . . . Unlike the generality of our landscape art, his does not hint a picture so much as a living realization of the affluence of nature. Inness gives with equal facility the drowsy heat, hot shimmer, and languid quiet of a summer's noon, or the storm-weighed atmosphere, its dark masses of vapor, and the wild gathering of thunder-clouds, with their solemn hush before the tempest breaks. He uses sunlight sparingly, but it glows on his canvas, and turns darkness into hope and joy. . . . The spirit of his landscapes alone is American.

James Jackson Jarves, *The Art-Idea.*

IRETON, HENRY

1611—51 Regicide

A tall black thief, with bushy curled hair, a meagre envious face, sunk hollow eyes, a complection between choler and melancholy, a four square Machiavellian head, and a nose of the fifteens.

Anon., *The Man in the Moon*, 1, 1649.

One brave heart, and subtle-working brain . . . a man able with his pen and his sword: 'very stiff in his ways.'

Thomas Carlyle, *Letters and Speeches of Oliver Cromwell.*

One line of mine begets many of his, which I doubt makes him sit up too late.

Oliver Cromwell, Letter to his Daughter, Bridget Ireton, 25 October 1646.

No man could prevail so much, nor order Cromwell so far, as Ireton could.

Bulstrode Whitelocke, *Memorials of English Affairs.*

IRVING, SIR HENRY

1838—1905 Actor

It is the fate of actors to be judged by echoes which are altogether delusive — when they have passed out of immediate ken, and some fifty years hence some old fool with be saying — there never was an actor like Irving.

On himself, Letter, 1891.

If our young playgoers saw Irving, they would burst like electric lightbulbs. If you saw Irving, you don't need to be told what he was like. If you did not, what's the good? This age has its Robert Taylors, and Jessie Mathewses. Why tamper with fragrance? Why cloud the dewy present with immortal dust? It lives, we remember, and the young generation doesn't care.

James Agate, in *ibid.*

Suppose, for instance, Gladstone, who possesses the quality to a wonderful extent, was dramatised. I mean the character. Irving could not play it. Ungoverned rage, sorrow, dread, he can depict, but not pure mental force. He well expresses the emotion of a mind acted on but not of a mind acting on others. He lacks what one may call the muscle and sinew of the brain.

James Albery, Letter to Frank Archer, 1873.

Somebody asked Gilbert if he had been to see Irving in *Faust*. 'I go to the pantomime,' said Gilbert, 'only at Christmas.'

Leslie Ayre, *The Gilbert and Sullivan Companion.*

He had, in acting, a keen sense of humour — of sardonic, grotesque, fantastic humour. He had an incomparable power for eeriness, for stirring a dim sense of mystery; and not less masterly was he in invoking a dim sense of horror. His dignity was magnificent in purely philosophic or priestly gentleness, or in the gaunt aloofness of philosopher or king. He could be benign with a tinge of malevolence, and arrogant with an undercurrent of sweetness.

Max Beerbohm, in *Saturday Review*, 21 October 1905.

He danced, he did not merely walk — he sang, he by no means merely spoke. He was essentially artificial, in distinction to being merely natural.

Edward Gordon Craig, *Henry Irving.*

One of his stage-tricks is very effective, but quite unworthy of a great artist. He is fond, whenever the scene permits, of shutting down every light — leaving the stage in utter darkness, lit only by the solitary lamp or dull fire which may be in the room; while he has directed from the prompt place or the flies, a closely focussed calcium — which shines only and solely upon *his* face and head; so that you can only see a lot of spectral figures without expression moving about the scene — and one ghostly lighted

face shining out of the darkness; an expressive face to be sure — but after all the entirety of the drama disappears, and a conjuror-like exhibition of a sphinx-like wonder takes its place.

Augustin Daly, Letter to his Brother, 18 September 1878.

He never 'suffered fools gladly'. I remember an occasion at the Garrick Club, when a new member, anxious to claim familiar acquaintance with him, came up to him, and said: 'Hello, Irving, an extraordinary thing has just happened to me. A total stranger stopped me in the street and said: "God bless me, is that you?" ' And Irving replied, in his characteristic staccato: 'And — er — was it?'

Edward Heron-Allen, in Saintsbury and Palmer eds, *We Saw Him Act.*

I wish they wouldn't make such a white-winged angel of father. He was never that.

Laurence Irving, in Edward Gordon Craig, *Henry Irving.*

Speaking to my mother one day about various dignitaries of the Church, I said: 'They're always faintly disappointing in real life, aren't they?' 'Yes,' she replied. 'You see, you saw Irving as Beckett —'

Naomi Jacob, in Saintsbury and Palmer eds, *We Saw Him Act.*

His voice is apparently wholly unavailable for purposes of declamation. To say that he speaks badly is to go too far; to my sense he simply does not speak at all — in any way that, in an actor, can be called speaking. He does not pretend to declaim, or dream of declaiming. . . . It is of course by his picturesqueness that Mr Irving has made his place; by small ingenuities of 'business' and subtleties of action; by doing as a painter does who 'goes in' for colour when he cannot depend on his drawing.

Henry James, 'The London Theatres', in *Galaxy*, 1877.

How little Mr Irving is Romeo it is not worth while even to attempt to declare; he must know it of course, better than anyone else, and there is something very touching in so extreme a sacrifice of one's ideal.

Henry James, in *Atlantic Monthly*, August 1882.

His Hamlet was not Shakespeare's Hamlet, nor his Lear Shakespeare's Lear: they were both avatars of the imaginary Irving in whom he was so absorbingly interested. His huge and enduring success as Shylock was due to his absolutely refusing to allow Shylock to be the discomfited villain of the piece. The Merchant of Venice became the Martyrdom of Irving, which was, it must be confessed, far finer than the tricking of Shylock. His Iachimo, a very fine performance, was better than Shakespeare's Iachimo, and not a bit like him. On the other hand his Lear was an impertinent intrusion of a quite silly conceit of his own into a great play. His Romeo, though a very clever piece of acting, wonderfully stage-managed in the scene where Romeo dragged the body of Paris down a horrible staircase into the tomb of the Capulets, was an absurdity, because it was impossible to accept Irving as Romeo, and he had no power of adapting himself to an author's conception: his creations were his own and they were all Irving.

George Bernard Shaw, *Pen Portraits and Reviews*.

He does not merely cut plays, he disembowels them.
George Bernard Shaw, in *Saturday Review*, 26 September 1896.

Of the theatre at large he knew almost nothing; for he never left his own stage. I am exaggerating when I say that he regarded an author as a person whose business it was to provide plays at five shillings an act, and, in emergencies, to write the fifth act whilst the fourth was being performed; and yet in spite of his intercourse with Tennyson, Traill, Wills, and Comyns Carr, I believe that this caricature of his attitude gives a juster impression of it than any statement of the sober facts.

George Bernard Shaw, Introduction to *Ellen Terry and Bernard Shaw, a Correspondence*.

I grant his intellectuality dominates his other powers and gifts, but I have never seen in living man or picture, such distinction of bearing. A splendid figure, and his face very noble. A superb brow; rather small dark eyes which can at moments become immense, and hang like a bowl of dark liquid with light shining through; a most refined curving Roman nose, strong and delicate in line, and *cut clean* (as all his features); a smallish mouth, and full of the most wonderful teeth, even at 55; lips most delicate and refined — firm, firm, firm — and with a rare smile of the most exquisite beauty, and quite-not-to-be-described kind. (He seems always ashamed of his smile, even in very private life, and will withdraw it at once in public.) His chin, and the line from ear to chin, is firm, extremely delicate, and very strong and clean defined. He has an ugly ear! Large, flabby, ill-cut, and pasty looking, pale and lumpy. His hair is superb; beautiful in 1867, when I first met him, when it was blue-black like a raven's wing, it is even more splendid now when it is liberally streaked with white. It is rather long and hangs in lumps on his neck, which is now like the neck of a youth of 20! His skin is

very pale, delicate, refined, and stretched tightly over his features. Under the influence of strong emotion, it contracts more, and turning somewhat paler, a grey look comes into his face, and the hollows of his cheeks and eyes show up clearly.
Ellen Terry, *Notes on Irving*.

I was at Tewkesbury yesterday, and felt how like he *really* is to the great Abbey there, but his admiration is for something of quite another sort. He tries to be like Milan Cathedral. He never admires the right thing.
Ibid.

His *self* was to him on a first night what the shell is to a lobster on dry land.
Ellen Terry, *The Story of My Life*.

See also Edmund Kean

IRVING, WASHINGTON

1783—1859 Author, Diplomat

I have no command of my talents, such as they are, and have to watch the varyings of my mind as I would those of a weathercock.
On himself, Undated letter to Sir Walter Scott.

I have never found, in anything outside of the four walls of my study, an enjoyment equal to sitting at my writing-desk with a clean page, a new theme, and a mind awake.
On himself, in Theodore Tilton, *Half an Hour at Sunnyside*.

It has been a matter of marvel to my European readers, that a man from the wilds of America should express himself in tolerable English. I was looked upon as something new and strange, in literature.
On himself, in his Introduction to *Bracebridge Hall*.

Not a great man, not even a great author, though a good chronicler, an excellent story-teller, a skilful essayist, and adept in romantic coloring; not in accord with progress in America but the most winning spokesman for the Federalist hope; a musician with a few themes, and the minor ones the best, and many played perfectly — that is Washington Irving.
Henry Seidel Canby, *Classic Americans*.

He proved that the barbarous American could write as the captains of 1812 had proved that Americans

could fight at sea, he tickled John Bull's romantic rib. . . .
>   *Ibid.*

Indeed Irving's reputation is the remarkable achievement of a style that sometimes rests upon little else than its own suavity.
>   *Ibid.*

A smooth polished clever amiable man — excellent for an acquaintance but for a bosom friend — *no*!
>   Thomas Carlyle, in Stanley T. Williams, *The Life of Washington Irving*.

. . . I don't go upstairs to bed two nights out of seven . . . without taking Washington Irving under my arm; and, when I don't take him, I take his brother Oliver Goldsmith.
>   Charles Dickens, in Ernest Boll, 'Dickens and Irving', in *Modern Language Quarterly*, December 1944.

Irving's literary significance begins with his instinctive realization, important in his day in a nation as puritanical in background as the United States, that literature's first function is to engage and entertain the reader. He had a healthy respect for the priority of style, the way a thing is said, to message or moral.
>   William L. Hedges, 'Washington Irving', in Perry Miller ed., *Major Writers of America*, vol. 1.

Here lies the gentle humorist, who died
>   In the bright Indian Summer of his fame!
>   Marks his secluded resting-place beside
The river that he loved and glorified.
>   Here in the autumn of his days he came,
>   But the dry leaves of life were all aflame
With tints that brightened and were multiplied.
How sweet a life was his; how sweet a death!
>   Living, to wing with mirth the weary hours,
>   Or with romantic tales the heart to cheer;
Dying, to leave a memory like the breath
>   Of summers full of sunshine and of showers,
>   A grief and gladness in the atmosphere.
>   Henry Wadsworth Longfellow, *In The Churchyard at Tarrytown*.

. . . Irving in the end was immolated on the altar of romanticism. The pursuit of the picturesque lured him away into sterile wastes, and when the will-o'-the-wisp was gone he was left empty.
>   Vernon Louis Parrington, *Main Currents in American Thought*, vol. 2.

Irving's style is essentially a fusion of the witty and the poetic: wit enlivens poetry, and poetry tempers wit.

Carl Van Doren, Introduction to *Tales by Washington Irving*.

I never enthused over him: Irving was suckled on the Addisonian-Oxford-Cambridge milk.
>   Walt Whitman, in Edgar Lee Masters, *Whitman*.

See also Thomas Wolfe

ISAACS, RUFUS DANIEL, MARQUESS OF READING

1860–1935 Judge, Civil Servant

He has no trace of hardness, and though intensely ambitious is never selfish. By race a Jew, he is British to the core, neither touchy, restless nor suspicious, but combines wisdom with caution and has the laugh of an English schoolboy. What attracts me in him is his untirable capacity for simple enjoyment, his gravity and insight, and a critical faculty that never cuts.
>   Margot, Lady Asquith, *Autobiography*.

. . . a man who 'thinks to scale'. . . .
>   Lord Moulton, in *ibid.*

IVES, CHARLES E.

1874–1954 Composer, Insurance Executive

How far can the composer be held accountable? . . . after all is said and sung. . . .
>   On himself, in Ned Rorem, *Music and People*.

And in America, today, we find one of the deepest-rooted of these [indigenous] growths — the one which is the most sturdy, luxurious, savorous, and thorny, too — in the music of Charles Ives.
>   Olin Downes, in Irene Downes ed., *Olin Downes on Music*.

Now Ives is nothing if not a nationalistic American composer. The forces conveyed by his music are deeply, typically American. They are the essences of a practical people, abrupt and nervous and ecstatic in their movements and manifestations — brought into play with a certain reluctance and difficulty, but when finally loosed, jaggedly, abruptly, almost painfully released, with something of an hysteric urgency; manifested sometimes in a religious and mystical elevation, but almost invariably in patterns that have a paroxysmal suddenness and abruptness and violence.
>   Paul Rosenfeld, in Herbert A. Leibowitz ed., *Musical Impressions: Selections from Paul Rosenfeld's Criticism*.

J

JACK, 'CAPTAIN'

1837?—73 Modoc War Chief

I am but one man. I am the voice of my people. Whatever their hearts are, that I talk. I want no more war. I want to be a man. You deny me the right of a white man. My skin is red; my heart is a white man's heart; but I am a Modoc. I am not afraid to die. I will not fall on the rocks. When I die, my enemies will be under me. Your soldiers began on me when I was asleep on Lost River. They drove us to these rocks, like a wounded deer. . . .
> On himself, in Dee Brown, *Bury My Heart at Wounded Knee.*

JACKSON, ANDREW

1767—1845 Seventh United States President

Not only was Jackson not a consistent politician, he was not even a real leader of democracy . . . he always believed in making the public serve the ends of the politicians. Democracy was good talk with which to win the favor of the people and thereby accomplish ulterior motives. Jackson never really championed the cause of the people.
> T. P. Abernethy, in Arthur M. Schlesinger Jr, *The Age of Jackson.*

Incompetent both by his ignorance and by the fury of his passions. He will be surrounded and governed by incompetent men, whose ascendency over him will be secured by their servility and who will bring to the Government of the nation nothing by their talent for intrigue.
> John Quincy Adams, in Meade Minnigerode, *Presidential Years, 1787—1860.*

Andrew Jackson was a popular president. He swore he would shake hands with everyone in town and kept his promise. This delayed the business of his administration for several weeks, until they could take off the bandages. One of the first things President Jackson did, after flexing his fingers, was to reward those who had cast more than one ballot for him by appointing them postmasters, judges, generals, and garbage collectors. It was in this last

connection that one of his friends made the famous remark, 'To the victors belong the spoils.'
> Richard Armour, *It All Started With Columbus.*

Except an enormous fabric of Executive power, the President has built up nothing. . . . He goes for destruction, universal destruction.
> Henry Clay, in Glyndon G. Van Deusen, *The Life of Henry Clay.*

The *sagacity* of General Jackson was the admiration of the sophist and the wonder of the savage; it unravelled the meshes of both, without the slightest seeming effort.
> George M. Dallas, Eulogy delivered at Philadelphia, 26 June 1845.

His stern, inflexible adherence to Democratic principles, his unwavering devotion to his country, and his intrepid opposition to her enemies, have so long thwarted their unhallowed schemes of ambition and power, that they fear the potency of his name on earth, even after his spirit shall have ascended to heaven.
> Stephen Douglas, 6 January 1844, in Robert W. Johannsen, *Stephen A. Douglas.*

He was a simple, emotional, and unreflective man with a strong sense of loyalty to personal friends and political supporters; he swung to the democratic camp when the democratic camp swung to him.
> Richard Hofstadter, *The American Political Tradition.*

[He] has slain the Indians & flogged the British & . . . therefore is the wisest & greatest man in the nation.
> P. H. Magnum of Orange County, North Carolina, 15 April 1824, in Marquis James, *Andrew Jackson — Portrait of a President.*

Andrew Jackson was eight feet tall
His arm was a hickory limb and a maul.
His sword is so long he dragged it on the ground.
Every friend was an equal. Every foe was a hound.
> Vachel Lindsay, *The Statue of Old Andrew Jackson.*

Little advanced in civilization over the Indians with

whom he made war.

Elijah Hunt Mills, in Marquis James, *Andrew Jackson — Portrait of a President.*

An overwhelming proportion of the material power of the Nation was against him. The great media for the dissemination of information and the molding of public opinion fought him. Haughty and sterile intellectualism opposed him. Musty reaction disapproved him. Hollow and outworn traditionalism shook a trembling finger at him — all but the people of the United States.

Franklin D. Roosevelt, Jackson Day Address, 8 January 1936.

. . . that the chief who violated the Constitution, proscribed public virtue and patriotism and introduced high handed corruption into public affairs and debauchery into private circles was the first President who received insult to his person and was an object of assassination.

William Henry Seward, 1835, in G. G. Van Deusen, *William Henry Seward.*

Nobody knows what he will do when he does
                                          come . . .
My opinion is
That when he comes he will bring a breeze with
                                          him.
Which way it will blow I cannot tell. . . .
My FEAR is stronger than my HOPE.

Daniel Webster, in William Nisbet Chambers, *Old Bullion Benton, Senator from the New West.*

See also James K. Polk

JACKSON, THOMAS JONATHAN 'STONEWALL'

1824—63 Soldier

I don't profess any romantic indifference to life; and, certainly, in my own private relations, I have as much that is dear to any to wish to live for as any man. But I do not desire to survive the independence of my country.

On himself, in Elihu S. Riley, *Stonewall Jackson.*

There is Jackson, standing like a stone wall. Let us determine to die here, and we will conquer.

Brigadier General Barnard E. Bee to his brigade at the first battle of Bull Run, 21 July 1862.

Stonewall Jackson, wrapped in his beard and his silence.

Stephen Vincent Benét, *John Brown's Body.*

You are better off than I am, for while you have lost your *left*, I have lost my *right* arm.

General Robert E. Lee, in a note to Jackson when the latter was mortally wounded at Chancellorsville, 4 May 1863.

Such an executive officer the sun never shone on. I have but to show him my design, and I know that if it can be done it will be done. No need for me to send or watch him. Straight as the needle to the pole he advances to the execution of my purpose.

Robert E. Lee, in G. F. R. Henderson, *Stonewall Jackson and the American Civil War.*

The sun's bright lances rout the mists
    Of morning and, by George,
Here's Longstreet struggling in the lists,
    Hemmed in an ugly gorge.
Pope and his Yankees! — whipped before —
'Bayonet and grape!' hear Stonewall roar.
'Charge Stuart! Pay off Ashby's score!'
    In 'Stonewall Jackson's Way.'

John Williamson Palmer, *Stonewall Jackson's Way.*

Outwardly Jackson was not a stonewall for it was not his nature to be stable and defensive, but vigorously active. He was an avalanche from an unexpected quarter. He was a thunderbolt from a clear sky. And yet he was in character and will more like a stonewall than any man I have known.

James Power Smith, in Elihu S. Riley, *Stonewall Jackson.*

He became one of the Great Captains, famed not only in his own embattled Confederacy, but also in the land of his enemies and beyond foreign seas. He came to epitomize the good and the virtue of what was finally a lost cause, and people would say that had he lived the cause might have fared differently. But death struck him down at the height of a military fame enjoyed by no other Civil War figure, struck him down at the high point of Confederate success.

Frank E. Vandiver, *Mighty Stonewall.*

JAMES I (VI OF SCOTLAND)

1566—1625

I will govern according to the common weal, but not according to the common will.

On himself, in a Reply to a demand of the House of Commons, 1621.

I am sure ye would not have me renounce my religion for all the world. I am not a Monsieur who can shift his religion as easily as he can shift his shirt

when he comes in from tennis.
On himself, attributed.

Sound as also his head, which was very full of brains; but his blood was wonderfully tainted with melancholy.
Anon., Post-mortem on the King.

Death's Iron Hand hath clos'd those eyes
   Which were at once three kingdoms' spies;
Both to foresee and to prevent
   Daungers as soon as they were ment:
That head whose working braine alone
   Wrought all men's quiet but its owne
Now lyes at rest; o let him have
   The peace he lent us, in the grave.
Anon., in Edmund Howe, *Continuation of Stow's Annales, or Generall Chronicle.*

It was one of King James' Maxims, to take no favourite but what was recommended to him by his Queen, that if she afterwards complained of this Dear One, he might answer, It is long of yourself: for you were the party that commended him unto me. Our old master took delight strangely in things of this nature.
Archbishop George Abbot, in *Biographia Britannica.*

King James was Bacon's Primum Mobile.
William Blake, *Annotations to Bacon.*

This King James, with his large hysterical heart, with his large goggle-eyes, glaring timorously-inquisitive on all persons and objects, as if he would either look through them, or else be fascinated by them, and, so to speak, start forth *into* them, and spend his very soul and eyesight in the frustrate attempt to look through them, — remains to me always a noticeable, not unloveable, man. For every why he has his wherefore ready; prompt as touch-wood blazes up, with prismatic radiance, that stonishing lynx-faculty.
Thomas Carlyle, *Historical Sketches.*

The King was excessively addicted to hunting and drinking, not ordinary French and Spanish wines, but strong Greek wines, and though he would divide his hunting from drinking these wines, yet he would compound his hunting with drinking these wines, and to that purpose he was attended by a special officer, who was as much as could be always at hand, to fill the King's cup in his hunting when he called for it. . . . Whether it was from drinking these wines or from some other cause, the King became so lazy and unwieldy, that he was *trust* on horseback, and as he was set, so he would ride,

without otherwise poising himself on his saddle; nay, when his hat was set on his head, he would not take the pains to alter it, but it sat as it was upon him.
Roger Coke, *Detection of the Court and State of England.*

The loathsome Lackwit, James I.
Samuel Taylor Coleridge, Notebook.

Who would not be thy subject, James, t'obey
   A Prince, that rules by'example, more than sway?
Whose manners draw, more then they powers con-
                straine.
Ben Jonson, *Epigrammes.*

Of James the First, as of John, it may be said that, if his administration had been able and splendid, it would probably have been fatal to our country, and that we owe more to his weakness and mean-ness than to the wisdom and courage of much better sovereigns. He came to the throne at a critical moment. The time was fast approaching when either the king must become absolute, or the parliament must control the whole executive administration. Had James been like Henry the Fourth, like Maurice of Nassau, or like Gustavus Adolphus, a valiant, active, and politic ruler, had he put himself at the head of the protestants of Europe, . . . had he found himself, after great achievements, at the head of fifty thousand troops, brave, well-disciplined, and devotedly attached to his person, the English par-liament would soon have been nothing more than a name. . . .
T. B. Macaulay, *History of England.*

As no other reason appeared in favour of their choice but handsomeness, so the love the King showed was as amorously conveyed as if he had mis-taken their sex, and thought them ladies; which I have seen *Somerset* and *Buckingham* labour to resemble in the effeminateness of their dressings; though in w----- looks, and wanton gestures, they exceeded any part of womankind my conversation did ever cope withal. Nor was his love, or whatever else posterity will please to call it . . . carried on with a discretion sufficient to cover a less scanda-lous behaviour; for the King's kissing them after so lascivious a mode in public, and upon the theatre, as it were of the world, prompted many to imagine some things done in the tyring-house, that exceed my expressions no less than they do my experience; and therefore left floating on the waves of conjec-ture, which hath in my hearing tossed them from one side to another.
Francis Osborn, *Works.*

Old friends are best. King James used to call for his

old shoes; they were easiest for his feet.
John Selden, *Table Talk.*

An omniscient umpire whom no one consulted.
Hugh Trevor-Roper, *Archbishop Laud.*

Hee was naturally of a timourous disposition, which
was the reason of his quilted Doublets: His eyes
large, ever rowling after any stranger came in his
prescence, insomuch, as many for shame have left
the roome, as being out of countenance: His beard
was very thin: His tongue too large for his mouth,
which ever made him speak full in the mouth, and
made him drink very uncomely, as if eating his
drink, which came out into the cup of each side of
his mouth: His skin was as soft as Taffeta Sarsnet,
which felt so, because hee never washt his hands,
onely rubb'd his fingers ends slightly with the wet
end of a napkin: His legs were very weake, having
had (as was thought) some foul play in his youth,
or rather before he was born, that he was not able
to stand at seven years of age, that weaknesse made
him ever leaning on other mens shoulders, his walke
was ever circular.
Sir Anthony Weldon, *The Court and Character
of King James.*

Nor must I forget to let you know how perfect the
King was in the art of dissimulation, or to give it
his own phrase (*King-craft*); The Earle of Somerset
never parted from him with more seeming affection
than at this time, when he knew *Somerset* would
never see him more; and had you seen that seeming
affection (as the author himself did) you would
rather have believed he was in his rising than setting.
The Earl, when he kissed his hand, the King hung
about his neck, slabbering his cheeks, saying: for
God's sake, when shall I see thee again; On my Soul,
I shall neither eat nor sleep until you come again;
the Earl told him on Monday (this being on the
Friday) for God's sake let me, said the King, shall I,
shall I? Then lolled about his neck: then for God's
sake give thy lady this kiss for me; in the same manner at the stayres head, at the middle of the stayres,
and at the stayres foot; the Earl was not in his
coach when the King used these very words (in the
hearing of four servants, one of whom was *Somerset*'s great creature, and of the Bed-Chamber, who
reported it instantly to the Author of this History)
I shall never see his face more.
Ibid.

Hee was so crafty and cunning in petty things, as
the circumventing any great man, the change of a
Favourite, &c. insomuch as a very wise man was
wont to say, hee beleeved him the wisest foole in
Christendome, meaning him wise in small things,
but a foole in weighty affaires.
Ibid.

James's humour was a tumbling wit that turned
things upside down and heaped together incongruous thoughts and images in a hurly-burly jumble,
as when he prayed the Pope to permit him the
hawking of the stream in purgatory. His mind
passed easily from topic to topic, and he applied
the vocabulary of one set of ideas to things entirely
different, throwing discordant images into grotesque
juxtaposition. His wit was the rollicking foolery of
the court jester, enriched by his extensive knowledge.
D. Harris Willson, *King James VI and I.*

He was born a King, and from that height, the less
fitted to look into inferior things; yet few escaped
his knowledge, being, as it were, a *Magazine* to
retain them. His stature was of the *Middle Size*;
rather tall than low, well set and somewhat plump,
of a ruddy complexion, his hair of a light brown, in
his full perfection, had at last a tincture of white. If
he had any predominant *Humor* to Ballance his
Choler, it was sanguine, which made his *Mirth Witty.*
His beard was scattering on the Chin, and very thin;
and though his clothes were seldom fashioned to
the *Vulgar* garb, yet in the whole man he was not
uncomely. He was a King in understanding, and was
content to have his subjects ignorant in many things.
Arthur Wilson, *The History of Great Britain.*

My Lord Montjoy, reprehended by the King for
taking tobacco, answered, 'By that your Majesty
shall have a little more practice in England, you will
find greater faults to pardon amongst us.'
Sir Henry Wotton, *Table Talk.*

See also John Bull, Duke of Buckingham, Fulke
Greville, Walter Raleigh

JAMES II

1633—1701

He is every way a perfect Stuart, and hath the advantage of his brother only that he hath ambition and
thoughts of something he hath not, which gives him
industry and address even beyond his natural parts.
Yet his conduct, courage, judgement and honour are
not much to be confided in. . . . His religion suits
well with his temper; heady, violent, and bloody,
who easily believes the rashest and worst of counsels to be most sincere and hearty. . . . His interest
and design are to introduce a military and arbitrary

government in his brother's time.
    Anon., *Report Drawn up for the Earl of Shaftesbury, circa* 1680.

When James II was crowned (according to the Ancient Custom, the Peers go to the Throne, and kiss the King). The Crown was almost kissed off his Head. An Earl did sett it right: and as he came from the Abbey to Westminster-Hall, the Crown tottered extreamly.
    The Canopy carried over King James II's Head by the Wardens of the Cinque Ports, was torn by a Puff of Wind, as he came to Westminster-Hall: it hung down very lamentably. I saw it. 'Twas Cloath of gold, and my strength (I am confident) could not have rent it, and it was not a windy day.
    The top of his Scepter (Flower de Lis) did then fall, which the Earl of Peterborough took up.
    John Aubrey, *Brief Lives.*

. . . He has even been called dull. He was not dull; but he was cut off. His mind was isolated, and to a whole group of appreciations, impervious. . . . Complexity did not bewilder him, rather he missed it altogether. . . . He could scheme with things, but not against schemers. . . . He thought in straight lines.
    Hilaire Belloc, *James II.*

That Prince had taken a fancy to Sir Charles' Daughter (though it seems she was not very handsome) and, in consequence of his intrigues with her, he created Miss Sedley Countess of Dorchester. This honour, so far from pleasing, greatly shocked Sir Charles. However libertine himself had been, yet he could not bear the thoughts of his daughter's dishonour; and with regard to this her exaltation, he only considered it as rendering her more conspicuously infamous. He therefore conceived a hatred for the King; and from this, as well as other motives, readily joined to dispossess him of the throne.
    A witty saying of Sedley's on this occasion, is recorded. 'I hate ingratitude (said Sir Charles); and therefore, as the King has made my daughter a countess, I will endeavour to make his daughter a queen:' meaning the Princess Mary, married to the Prince of Orange, who dispossessed James of the throne at the ever-glorious Revolution.
    David Erskine Baker, Isaac Reed and Stephen Jones eds, *Biographia Dramatica*, 1812.

I do affirm that he was the most honest and sincere man I ever knew: a great and good Englishman, and a high protector of trade, and had nothing so much at heart as the glory and strength of the fleet and navy.
    Thomas Bruce, Earl of Ailesbury, *Memoirs.*

It makes one's flesh creep to think that such a man should have been the ruler of millions. . . . A Prince whose malignant cruelties made him loathed by his contemporaries, and whose revolting predilections unless we ascribe them to a diseased brain, are not only a slur on the age which tolerated them, but a disgrace to the higher instincts of our common nature.
    H. Buckle, *History of Civilization.*

He was bred with high notions of the kingly authority, and laid it down for a maxim, that all who opposed the King were rebels in their hearts. He was perpetually in one amour or another, without being very nice in his choice: Upon which the King said once, he believed his Brother had his mistresses given him by his Priests for penance. . . . He was naturally eager and revengeful: And was against the taking off any that set up in an opposition to the measures of the Court, and who by that means grew popular in the House of Commons. He was for rougher methods. He continued for many years dissembling his religion, and seemed zealous for the Church of *England*: But it was chiefly on design to hinder all propositions that tended to unite us among our selves.
    Gilbert Burnet, *History of My Own Time.*

James was naturally candid and sincere and a firm friend, till his affairs and his religion wore out all his first principles and inclinations.
    Ibid.

I am weary of travelling and am resolved to go abroad no more. But when I am dead and gone, I know not what my brother will do: I am much afraid that when he comes to wear the Crown he will be obliged to travel again. And yet I will take care to leave my kingdoms to him in peace, wishing he may long keep them so. But this hath all of my fears, little of my hopes, and less of my reason.
    Charles II, in Christopher Falkus, *Charles II.*

It were almost incredible to tell you, at the latter end of King *James's* Time (though the Rod of Arbitrary Power was always shaking over us) with what Freedom and Contempt the Common People in the open Streets talk'd of his wild Measures to make a whole Protestant Nation Papists; and yet, in the height of our secure and wanton Defiance of him, we of the Vulgar had no farther Notion of any Remedy for this Evil than a satisfy'd Presumption that our Numbers were too great to be mastered by his mere Will and Pleasure; and that though he might be too hard for our Laws, he would never be able to get the better of our Nature; and that to drive all *England* into Popery and Slavery he would find would be teaching an old Lion to dance.

Colley Cibber, *Apology for the Life of Colley Cibber.*

It is only too probable that James's bigotry alone baffled his despotism — and that he might have succeeded in suppressing the liberties of his country, if he would, — for a time at least — have kept aloof from its Religion. It should be remembered in excuse for the supporters of James II, that, the practicability of conducting the affairs of the state with and by Parliament, had not yet been demonstrated.

Samuel Taylor Coleridge, Annotation to Lord Braybrooke's Edition of Pepys's Diary.

If he had a point of religion, it was the religion of Mary Tudor's kind, which stirred him to cruelty and revenge and drove him to a career of treason against the religion and freedom of his people.

H. M. Gwatkin, *Church and State in England.*

King James was not the first prince who loved justice, hated iniquity and died in exile; yet there never was, perhaps, any ruler of any country, who in his lifetime suffered so much from the disloyalty of his own family, and the ingratitude of his friends, and, after his death, from the injustice of posterity.

Malcolm V. Hay, *Enigma of James II.*

Had James ruled in Spain, or even in seventeenth century France, history might now be resounding with his praises, voiced not only by Spaniards or Frenchmen, but by Englishmen. But as he ruled in England, he still waits his apologist.

David Ogg, *England in the Reigns of James II and William III.*

My Lord [Sandwich] . . . telling me the story of how the Duke of Yorke hath got my Lord Chancellor's daughter with child, and that she doth lay it to him, and that for certain he did promise her marriage, and had signed it with his blood, but that he by stealth had got the paper out of her Cabinett. And that the King would have him marry her, but that he would not. So that the thing is very bad for the Duke and for them all. But my Lord doth make light of it, as a thing that he believes is not a new thing to the Duke to do abroad. Discoursing concerning what if the Duke should marry her, my Lord told me that among his father's many old sayings that he had writ in a book of his, this is one: that he that doth get a wench with child, and marries her afterward it is as if a man should shit in his hat and then clap it upon his head.

Samuel Pepys, Diary, 7 October 1660.

The Duke of York hath not got Mrs Middleton, as I was told the other day, but says that he wants not her, for he hath others and hath always had, and that he hath known them brought through the Matted Gallery at White-hall into his closet. Nay, he hath come out of his wife's bed, and gone to others laid in bed for him.

Ibid., 24 June 1667.

Except he became a protestant, his friends would be obliged to leave him, like a garrison one could no longer defend.

George Savile, Marquis of Halifax, in *Memoirs of Sir John Reresby.*

Under the morose face there seemed to be a heart of stone.

Alexander Smellie, *Men of the Covenant.*

He would have been an excellent King of Spain.

Charles Whibley, *George Jeffreys.*

See also Charles II, Elizabeth I, Anne Hyde, Barbara Villiers

JAMES, HENRY

1843—1916 Novelist

I suspect the age of letters is waning, for our time. It is the age of Panama Canals, of Sarah Bernhardt, of Western wheat-raising, of merely material expansion. Art, form, may return, but I doubt that I shall live to see them — I don't believe they are eternal, as the poets say. All the same, I shall try to make them live a little longer!

On himself, Letter to Thomas Perry, February 1881.

I have not the least hesitation in saying that I aspire to write in such a way that it would be impossible to an outsider to say whether I am at a given moment an American writing about England or an Englishman writing about America . . . and so far from being ashamed of such an ambiguity I should be exceedingly proud of it, for it would be highly civilised.

On himself, in Pelham Edgar, *Henry James, Man and Author.*

Nothing is my *last word* about anything — I am interminably supersubtle and analytic — and with the blessing of heaven, I shall live to make all sorts of representations of all sorts of things. It will take a lot cleverer person than myself to discover my last impression — amongst all these things — of anything.

On himself, Letter to Mrs F. H. Hill, 21 March 1879.

We are Americans born — *il faut en prendre son parti*. I look upon it as a great blessing; and I think that to be an American is an excellent preparation for culture. We have exquisite qualities as a race, and it seems to me that we are ahead of the European races in the fact that more than either of them we can deal freely with forms of civilization not our own, can pick and choose and assimilate and in short (aesthetically &c) claim our property wherever we find it.

On himself, Letter to Thomas Perry, 20 September 1867.

I desire to offer myself for Naturalization in this country, that is, to change my status from that of American citizen to that of British subject. I have assiduously and happily spent here all but 40 years, the best years of my life, and I find my wish to testify at this crisis to the force of my attachment and devotion to England, and to the cause for which she is fighting, finally and completely irresistible. It brooks at least no inward denial whatever. I can only testify by laying at her feet my explicit, my material and spiritual allegiance, and throwing into the scale of her fortune my all but imponderable moral weight — 'a poor thing but mine own'.

On himself, Letter to H. H. Asquith, 28 June 1915.

In Heaven there'll be no algebra,
No learning dates or names,
But only playing golden harps
And reading Henry James.

Anon., in Edward Stone, *The Battle and the Books: Some Aspects of Henry James.*

It's not that he 'bites off more than he can chaw', as T. G. Appleton said of Nathan, but he chaws more than he bites off.

Mrs Henry Adams, Letter to her Father, December 1881.

Henry James
Abhorred the word *Dames*,
And always wrote 'Mommas'
With inverted commas.

W. H. Auden, *Academic Graffiti*.

Few writers have had less journalistic talent than James, and this is his defect, for the supreme masters have one trait in common with the childish scribbling mass, the vulgar curiosity of a police-court reporter. One can easily imagine Stendhal or Tolstoi or Dostoievski becoming involved in a barroom fight, but James, never. I have read somewhere a story that once, when James was visiting a French friend, the latter's mistress, unobserved,

filled his top hat with champagne, but I do not believe it because, try as I will, I simply cannot conceive what James did and said when he put his hat on.

W. H. Auden, *The Dyer's Hand.*

Despite his resolute self-suppression for his 'form's' sake, Mr Henry James, through his books, stands out as clearly to me as any preacher I have ever seen perched up in a pulpit. And I do not happen to have heard any preacher in whom was a moral fervour so great as (with all its restraint) is Mr James' fervour, or one whose outlook on the world seemed to me so fine and touching and inspiring, so full of reverence for noble things and horror of things ignoble.

Max Beerbohm, *Around Theatres.*

On the credit side: He is a truly marvellous craftsman. By which I mean that he constructs with exquisite never-failing skill, and that he writes like an angel. Even at his most mannered and his most exasperating, he conveys his meaning with more precision and clarity than perhaps any other living writer. He is never, never clumsy, nor dubious, even in the minutest details. . . . But on the debit side: — He is tremendously lacking in emotional power. Also his sense of beauty is over-sophisticated and wants originality. Also his attitude towards the spectacle of life is at bottom conventional, timid and undecided. Also he seldom chooses themes of first-class importance, and when he does choose such a theme he never fairly bites it and makes it bleed. Also his curiosity is limited. It seems to me to have been specially created to be admired by super-dilettanti.

Arnold Bennett, in *New Age*, October 1910.

I can find no better example of the Superfine Young Man than Mr Henry James . . . highly finished, perfectly machined, icily regular, thoroughly representative. . . . For the first quarter of an hour of our conversation with him we are largely impressed with his variety, his catholicity; after that comes a certain indescribable sense of vagueness, of superficiality, of indifferentism; finally, if we must give the thing a name, a forlorn feeling of vacuity, of silliness.

Robert Buchanan, in *Universal Review*, March 1889.

He is never in deep gloom or in violent sunshine. But he feels deeply and vividly every delicate shade. We cannot ask for more.

Joseph Conrad, Letter to John Galsworthy, February 1899.

Civilisation at its highest pitch was the master pas-

sion of his mind and his preoccupation with the international aspects of character and custom issued from the conviction that the rawness and rudeness of a young country were not incapable of cure by contact with more developed forms, and that the process of assimilation was already under way.
Pelham Edgar, *Henry James, Man and Author.*

The current of English literature was not appreciably altered by his work during his lifetime; and James will probably continue to be regarded as the extraordinarily clever but negligible curiosity.
T. S. Eliot, 'Henry James, In Memory', in Edmund Wilson ed., *The Shock of Recognition.*

Henry James is an author who is difficult for English readers, because he is an American; and who is difficult for Americans, because he is European; and I do not know whether he is possible to other readers at all.
T. S. Eliot, 'A Prediction', in Leon Edel ed., *Henry James, A Collection of Critical Essays.*

. . . the nicest old lady I ever met.
William Faulkner, in Edward Stone, *The Battle and the Books: Some Aspects of Henry James.*

Mr James, to put the matter shortly, has preferred to enquire into the habits of the comfortable classes and of their dependants, and no other human being has made the serious attempt to enquire with an unbiased mind into the habits and necessities of any other class or race of the habitable globe as it is.
Ford Madox Ford, *Henry James.*

Many readers cannot get interested in James, although they can follow what he says (his difficulty has been much exaggerated), and can appreciate his effects. They cannot grant his premise, which is that most of human life has to disappear before he can do us a novel.
E. M. Forster, *Aspects of the Novel.*

We sat in a detached room — glimpse of fine study as we passed. H.J. very kind. Laid his hand on my shoulder and said: 'Your name's Moore.'
E. M. Forster, Diary, 1908.

James's so-called obscurity was never an offence to me; indeed, this charge against an author is invariably a spur. After forcing myself once to read and understand Kant, I profess to be able to find a meaning in any book where there is a meaning to be found, and so I set myself to unravel several of James's obscurities. The knots were soon loosed, but alas! I had nothing for my pains. 'Much ado about nothing,' I said to myself, and tossed the

book aside, never again to be reopened. The admirers of James, I soon discovered, were all people of no importance as judges of literature; would-be geniuses, for the most part, or society women.
Frank Harris, *My Life and Loves.*

The truth is that Mr James's cosmopolitanism is, after all, limited; to be really cosmopolitan, a man must be at home even in his own country.
Thomas Wentworth Higginson, *Short Studies of American Authors.*

One of the reasons James found the American scene difficult to deal with was that its brief past had been embodied in so few visible forms.
Harold T. McCarthy, *Henry James, The Creative Process.*

Henry James's fictions are like the cobwebs which a spider may spin in the attic of some old house, intricate, delicate and even beautiful, but which at any moment the housemaid's broom with brutal common sense may sweep away.
W. Somerset Maugham, *The Vagrant Mood.*

Much of Henry James is what the French, whom he so extravagantly admired, dismiss with a shrug of the shoulders as *littérature.* He did not live, he observed life from a window, and too often was inclined to content himself with no more than what his friends told him they saw when *they* looked out of a window. But what can you know of life unless you have lived it? . . . In the end the point of Henry James is neither his artistry nor his seriousness, but his personality, and this was curious and charming and a trifle absurd.
W. Somerset Maugham, *A Writer's Notebook.*

. . . we have Henry James a deserter made by despair; one so depressed by the tacky company at the American first table that he preferred to sit at the second table of the English.
H. L. Mencken, in Edward Stone, *The Battle and the Books: Some Aspects of Henry James.*

The interviewer in us would like to ask Henry James why he never married; but it would be in vain to ask, so much does he write like a man to whom all action is repugnant. He confesses himself on every page, as we all do. On every page James is a prude.
George Moore, *Confessions of a Young Man.*

PROVINCIALISM . . . Galdos, Turgenev, Flaubert, Henry James, the whole fight of modern enlightenment is against this. . . . Henry James in his unending endeavour to provide a common language, an

idiom of manners and meanings for the three nations, England, America, France. Henry James was, despite any literary detachments, the crusader, both in his internationalism, and in his constant propaganda against personal tyranny, against the hundred subtle forms of personal oppressions and coercions. Idiots said he was untouched by emotion.
    Ezra Pound, *The New Age*, 1917.

When he isn't being a great and magnificent author, he certainly can be a very fussy and tiresome one.
    Ezra Pound, Letter to John Quinn, 4 June 1918.

When he died one felt there was no one to ask about anything. Up to then one felt someone knew.
    Ezra Pound, in *Paris Review*.

James felt buried in America; but he came here [England] to be embalmed.
    George Bernard Shaw, Letter to Molly Tompkins.

As always with great aestheticians there is a certain vulgarity in his work, and this vulgarity found its expression in violence. It is vulgarity of a kind that we never find in the work of coarser writers like Fielding, Smollett and Lawrence, but which we always are conscious of in writers like Flaubert, or Jane Austen, or Wilde.
    Stephen Spender, in Cyril Connolly, *Enemies of Promise*.

It was once irreverently remarked, by a non-Jacobean too-ready with historical analogy, that there were three Henry Jameses — James the First, James the Second, and the Old Pretender.
    Frank Swinnerton, *The Georgian Literary Scene*.

There has probably been no other major novelist whose work has been so often criticized not so much for what it is but for what certain critics think it should have been. One critic, whose name I do not know, becoming impatient of the carpers, once said that they criticized Henry James as they might criticize a cat for not being a dog.
    James Thurber, *The Wings of Henry James*.

I can't stand George Eliot, & Hawthorne & those people; I see what they are at, a hundred years before they get to it, & they just tire me to death. And as for the *Bostonians*, I would rather be damned to John Bunyan's heaven than read that.
    Mark Twain, Letter to William Dean Howells, July 1885.

Leviathan retrieving pebbles . . . a magnificent but painful hippopotamus resolved at any cost, even at the cost of its dignity, upon picking up a pea.
    H. G. Wells, *Boon*.

James never scuffled with Fact; he treated her as a perfect and unchallenkeable lady; he never questioned a single stitch or flounce of the conventions and interpretations in which she presented herself. He thought that for every social occasion a correct costume could be prescribed and a correct behaviour defined. On the table (an excellent piece) in his hall at Rye lay a number of caps and hats, each with its appropriate gloves and sticks, a tweed cap and a stout stick for the Marsh, a soft comfortable deerstalker if he were to turn aside to the Golf Club, a light-brown felt hat and a cane for a morning walk down to the Harbour, a grey felt with a black band and a gold-headed cane of greater importance, if afternoon calling in the town was afoot.
    H. G. Wells, *Experiment in Autobiography*.

To you literature like painting is an end, to me literature like architecture is a means, it has a use.
    H. G. Wells, Letter to James, 8 July 1915.

James is developing, but he will never arrive at passion, I fear.
    Oscar Wilde, Letter to Robert Ross, 12 January 1899.

Can you possibly imagine Henry James without an accompaniment of corsets and Prince Alberts with striped trousers.
    William Carlos Williams, in Edward Stone, *The Battle and the Books: Some Aspects of Henry James*.

We must admit that Henry James has conquered. That courtly, worldly, sentimental old gentleman can still make us afraid of the dark.
    Virginia Woolf, 'The Ghost Stories', in Leon Edel ed., *Henry James, A Collection of Critical Essays*.

See also Willa Cather, Ford Madox Ford, Elinor Glyn, William Dean Howells, John Singer Sargent, Logan Pearsall Smith, Hugh Walpole, Edith Wharton

JAMES, JESSE WOODSON

1847—82 Desperado

Jesse had a wife to mourn all her life.
Two children they were brave.
'Twas a dirty little coward that shot Mr. Howard
And laid Jesse James in his grave.

It was Bob Ford, the dirty little coward,
I wonder how does he feel,
For he ate of Jesse's bread and slept in Jesse's bed,
Then he laid Jesse James in his grave.

Jesse was a man, a friend to the poor,
He never would see a man suffer pain;
And with his brother Frank he robbed the Gallatin
                                        bank
And stopped the Glendale train.
  The Ballad of Jesse James, in Homer Croy, *Jesse
  James Was My Neighbor.*

He never shot a light out in his life, never took a
drink at a bar as he watched in the mirror some
other man with a view of disposing of him, never
rode down a street shooting right and left for the
fun of it. He was in the business of train and bank
robbery. And he made a success of it as no other
man in America has ever done.
  Homer Croy, *Jesse James Was My Neighbor.*

Not one among all the hired cowards, hard on the
hunt for blood money, dared face this wonderful
outlaw, even one against twenty, until he had disarmed himself and turned his back to his assassin,
the first and only time in a career which has passed
from the realms of an almost fabulous romance into
that of history.
  Major John Edwards, in Carl W. Breihan, *The
  Complete and Authentic Life of Jesse James.*

Jesse James shot children, but only in fact not in
folklore.
  John Greenway, *The Inevitable Americans.*

JAMES, WILLIAM

1842—1910 Philosopher, Psychologist

James confronted all dogma with skepticism and
made skepticism itself a dogma.
  Henry Steele Commager, in Robert Allen
  Skotheim, *American Intellectual Histories and
  Historians.*

He was almost a Columbus as an explorer of the
inner world. . . .
  John Dewey, *Characters and Events.*

He was not a philosopher who by taking pains
acquired a literary gift; he was an artist who gave
philosophic expression to the artist's sense of the
unique, and to his love of the individual.
  Ibid.

. . . James tossed on the rubbish heap all the absolutisms of the nineteenth century: Deism, Transcen-
dentalism, orthodox Christianity, and classical
physics.
  Ralph Gabriel, in Robert Allen Skotheim, *American Intellectual Histories and Historians.*

James took philosophy as he took life — seriously.
He felt that, like tragic poetry, it was distinguished
by its noble theme.
  Ralph Barton Perry, *The Thought and Character
  of William James.*

It would be incongruous . . . to expect of him that
he should build a philosophy like an edifice to go
and live in for good. Philosophy to him was rather
like a maze in which he happened to find himself
wandering, and what he was looking for was the
way out.
  George Santayana, in Bernard P. Brennan,
  William James.

JARRELL, RANDALL

1914—65 Educator, Author

He gives you, as all great or good writers do, a foothold in a realm where literature itself is inessential,
where your own world is more yours than you
could ever have thought, or even felt, but is one you
have always known.
  James Dickey, 'Randall Jarrell', in Robert Lowell,
  Peter Taylor and Robert Penn Warren eds,
  Randall Jarrell.

He was bearded, formidable, bristling, with a high-
pitched nervous voice and the wariness of a porcupine.
  Stanley Kunitz, 'Out of the Cage', in *ibid.*

His gifts, both by nature and by a lifetime of hard
dedication and growth, were wit, pathos, and brilliance of intelligence. These qualities, dazzling in
themselves, were often so well employed that he
became, I think, the most heartbreaking English
poet of his generation.
  Robert Lowell, 'Randall Jarrell', in *ibid.*

He died, you might say, because his heart was in the
right place and his heart was even stronger than his
intellect. Jarrell was split between his heart and
mind.
  Karl Shapiro, *Randall Jarrell.*

If God were a writer and wrote a book that Randall
did not think was good, Randall would not have
hesitated to give it a bad review. And if God complained, I think Randall would then set about showing God what was wrong with his sentences.
  Robert Watson, 'Randall Jarrell: The Last Years',
  in Robert Lowell, Peter Taylor and Robert Penn
  Warren eds, *Randall Jarrell.*

JAY, JOHN

1745—1829 Jurist, Statesman, Diplomat

One John, surnamed Jay, journeyed into a far country, even unto Great Britain. 2. And the word of Satan came unto him saying, make thou a covenant with this people whereby they may be enabled to bring the *Americans* into bondage, as heretofore. 3. And John answered unto Satan, of a truth. . . . Let me find grace in thy sight, that I may secretly betray my country and the place of my nativity. . . .

> Anon., parody on the Jay Treaty, in Frank Monaghan, *John Jay*.

Damn John Jay! Damn every one that won't damn John Jay! Damn every one that won't put lights in his windows and sit up all night damning John Jay!!!

> Anon., 1794, in Herbert Alan Johnson, *John Jay*.

He argues closely but is long-winded and self-opinioned. He can beat opposition to what he advocates provided regard is shown to his ability. He may be attached by good treatment but will be unforgiving if he thinks himself neglected. . . . Almost every man has a weak spot, and Mr. Jay's weak spot is Mr. Jay.

> Mr Elliott, in Samuel Flagg Bemis, *John Jay*, in *American Secretaries of State and their diplomacy*, vol. 1.

At length on rapid wings of fate,
Ardent to save the sinking State . . .
No party rage disturb'd his rest,
No vile detraction shook his breast . . .
Peace on his path her sun-beams spread,
And glory arch'd around his head.
  Swift starting from their darksome *den*,
The nightly haunt of thieves and *men*,
Our democrats, broke forth in fury
And sentenced Jay *sans* Judge or Jury. . . .

> Lemuel Hopkins, *Guillotina or a Democratic Dirge*.

I suspect that Jay has been betrayed by his anxiety to couple us with England, and to avoid returning with his finger in his mouth. . . . It is apparent that those most likely to be in the secret of the affair do not assume an air of triumph.

> James Madison, Letter to Thomas Jefferson, 15 February 1795, commenting on the Jay Treaty.

JEFFERS, (JOHN) ROBINSON

1887—1962 Poet

I made three dozen negatives of Jeffers [Robinson] — used all my negatives; and developed the moment I got home. It was another grey day, but now I realize, knowing him better, that Jeffers is more himself on grey days. He belongs to stormy skies and heavy seas. Without knowing his work one would feel in his presence greatness.

I did not find him silent — rather a man of few words. Jeffers' eyes are notable: blue, shifting — but in no sense furtive — as though they would keep their own secrets — penetrating all-seeing eyes. Despite his writing I cannot call him misanthropic; his is the bitterness of despair over humanity he really loves.

> Edward Weston, 1929, in Nancy Newhall, *Edward Weston*.

JEFFERSON, THOMAS

1743—1826 Third United States President

Cease, cease old man, for soon you must,
  Your faithless cunning, pride, and lust,
    Which Death shall quickly level:
Thy cobweb'd Bible ope again;
  Quit thy blaspheming crony, Paine,
    And think upon the Devil.

Resume thy shells and butterflies,
  Thy beetles' heads, and lizards' thighs,
    The state no more controul:
Thy tricks, with sooty *Sal* give o'er;
  Indulge thy body, Tom, no more;
    But try to save thy *soul*.

> Anon., Philadelphia *Port Folio*, 22 January 1803.

The gloomy night before us flies,
The Reign of Terror now is o'er;
Its gags, inquisitors and spies,
Its herds of harpies are no more.
Rejoice, Columbia's sons, rejoice,
To tyrants never bend the knee,
But join with heart and soul and voice,
For Jefferson and Liberty!

> Anon., Election poem, 1800.

Our ships all in motion,
Once whitened the ocean,
  They sail'd and return'd with a cargo.
Now, doom'd to decay
They have fallen a prey
  To Jefferson, worms, and Embargo.

> Anon., in *Repertory*, Boston, 15 July 1808.

. . . could be painted only touch by touch, with a fine pencil, and the perfection of the likeness depended upon the shifting and uncertain flicker of its

semi-transparent shadows.
Henry Adams, in Adrienne Koch ed., *Thomas Jefferson, Great Lives Observed.*

Ambition is the subtlest Beast of the Intellectual and Moral Field. It is wonderfully adroit in concealing itself from its owner. . . . Jefferson thinks he shall by this step get a Reputation of a humble, modest, meek man, wholly without ambition or vanity. He may even have deceived himself into this Belief. But if a Prospect opens, the World will see and he will feel, that he is as ambitious as Oliver Cromwell though no soldier.
John Adams, Letter to John Quincy Adams, 3 January 1794.

You should remember that Jefferson was but a boy to me. I was at least ten years older than him in age and more than twenty years older than him in politics.
John Adams, Letter to Benjamin Rush, 25 October 1809.

I held levees once a week, that all my time might not be wasted by idle visits. Jefferson's whole eight years was a levee. . . .
Jefferson and Rush were for liberty and straight hair. I thought curled hair was as republican as straight.
John Adams, Letter to Benjamin Rush, 25 December 1811.

Thomas Jefferson still survives.
John Adams, last words. Jefferson in fact was already deceased.

His genius is of the old French school. It conceives better than it combines.
John Quincy Adams, Diary, 23 November 1804.

He saw the gross inconsistency between the principles of the Declaration of Independence and the fact of negro slavery, and he could not, or would not, prostitute the faculties of his mind to the vindication of that slavery which from his soul he abhorred. Mr. Jefferson had not the spirit of martyrdom. He would have introduced a flaming denunciation of slavery into the Declaration of Independence, but the discretion of his colleagues struck it out.
Ibid., 27 January 1831.

Jefferson was not only a statesman but an inventor. His many inventions include the dumb waiter, the decimal system of coinage, . . . the swivel chair, the University of Virginia and the Democratic Party. An extremely versatile person, he was also an architect, thus saving a fee when he built his home. Deeply

religious, Jefferson was for a time minister to France. In his spare time, he was a farmer and an aristocrat.
Richard Armour, *It All Started With Columbus.*

Jeffersonian Democracy simply meant the possession of the federal government by the agrarian masses led by an aristocracy of slave-owning planters.
Charles A. Beard, *The Economic Origins of Jeffersonian Democracy.*

For life was freakish
But life was fervent,
And I was always
Life's willing servant.
Stephen Vincent Benét, *Thomas Jefferson.*

. . . the first modern to state in human terms the principles of democracy.
John Dewey, in Adrienne Koch ed., *Thomas Jefferson, Great Lives Observed.*

I think this is the most extraordinary collection of human talent, of human knowledge, that has ever been gathered at the White House — with the possible exception of when Thomas Jefferson dined alone.
John F. Kennedy, Speech at the White House to honor forty-nine Nobel Prize Winners, 1962, in *New York Times*, 30 April 1962.

. . . was saturated with democracy in the worst form, and he remained to the last day of his life a sterile worshipper of the people.
John B. McMaster, *The History of the United States*, vol. 2.

It may be said of him as has been said of others that he was a 'walking library', and what can be said of but few such prodigies, that Genius of Philosophy ever walked hand in hand with him.
James Madison, Letter to Samuel Harrison Smith, November 1826.

The patriot, fresh from freedom's councils come,
Now pleased retires to lash his slaves at home;
Or woo, perhaps, some black Aspasia's charms,
And dream of Freedom in his bondsmaid's arms.
Thomas Moore, in Fawn M. Brodie, *Thomas Jefferson, An Intimate History.*

A gentleman of thirty two who could calculate an eclipse, survey an estate, tie an artery, plan an edifice, try a cause, break a horse, dance a minuet and play the violin.
James Parton, *Life of Thomas Jefferson.*

. . . the moonshine philosopher of Monticello.

Timothy Pickering, in Adrienne Koch ed., *Thomas Jefferson, Great Lives Observed.*

I cannot live in this miserable, undone country, where, as the Turks follow their sacred standard, which is a pair of Mahomet's breeches, we are governed by the old red breeches of that prince of projectors, St Thomas of Cantingbury; and surely, Becket himself never had more pilgrims at his shrine than the Saint of Monticello.
John Randolph of Roanoke, in L. A. Harris, *The Fine Art of Political Wit.*

. . . the old Sachem of our tribe.
John Taylor, in George Dangerfield, *The Era of Good Feelings.*

See also John Adams, Aaron Burr, Cecil B. De Mille, John Marshall, Martin Van Buren, Frank Lloyd Wright

JEFFREY, FRANCIS, LORD

1773—1850 Critic

Never mind his damning the North Pole. *I* have heard him speak disrespectfully of the equator.
Sydney Smith, in Harriet Martineau, *Autobiography.*

JEFFREYS, GEORGE, BARON JEFFREYS OF WEM

1645—89 Judge

He hath in great perfection the three chief qualifications of a lawyer: boldness, boldness, boldness.
Anon., in the *Hatton Correspondence.*

He has been so much chased, that I began my critical examination of his history in the hope and belief that I should find that his misdeeds had been exaggerated, and that I might be able to rescue his memory from some portion of the obloquy under which it labours; but I am sorry to say that in my matured opinion, although he appears to have been a man of high talents, of singularly agreeable manners, and entirely free from hypocrisy, his cruelty and his political profligacy have not been sufficiently exposed or reprobated.
Lord Campbell, *Lives of the Chancellors.*

The many Hundreds that he hanged in the West, shews he was a stout Man, his Entrails Brass, and his Heart Steel; and this was necessary in the Post where the King had placed him. — Hang, draw and quarter was part of his Loyalty; and yet we may call him a merciful Judge. For he had such Respect for the Souls of Men, that he scarce hanged any but those who were innocent, and of those he sentenced 200 in a forenoon. If he excelled in one thing more than another, 'twas in his haste to send Whiggs to Heaven: for Hang Men first, and try 'em afterwards . . . was his peculiar Talent.
John Dunton, *The Merciful Assizes.*

There was a fiendish exultation in the way he pronounced sentence on offenders. Their weeping and imploring seemed to titillate him voluptuously; and he loved to scare them into fits by dilating with luxuriant amplification on all the details of what they were to suffer. Thus when he had an opportunity of ordering an unlucky adventuress to be whipped at the cart's tail, 'Hangman,' he would exclaim, 'I charge you to pay particular attention to this lady! Scourge her soundly, man! It is Christmas; a cold time for Madam to strip in! See that you warm her shoulders thoroughly. . . .'
T. B. Macaulay, *History of England.*

He took a pleasure in mortifying fraudulent attorneys, and would deal forth his severities with a sort of majesty. He had extraordinary natural abilities, but little acquired beyond what practice in affairs had supplied. He talked fluently, and with spirit; and his weakness was he could not reprehend without scolding; and in such Billingsgate language as should not come out of the mouth of any man. He called it 'giving a lick with the rough side of his tongue'.
Roger North, *Life of Francis North.*

JELLICOE, JOHN RUSHWORTH, EARL

1859—1935 Admiral

Sailor with a flawed cutlass.
Correlli Barnett, *The Swordbearers.*

Jellicoe was the only man on either side who could lose the war in an afternoon.
Winston Churchill, *The World Crisis.*

He fought to make a German victory impossible rather than a British victory certain.
Cyril Falls, *The First World War.*

JENKINSON, ROBERT BANKS, see under LIVERPOOL, LORD

JENYNS, SOAME

1704–89 Writer, Wit

Here lies a little ugly nauseous elf,
Who judging only from its wretched self,
Feeby attempted, petulant and vain,
The 'Origin of Evil' to explain.
> Anon., *Epitaph on Soame Jenyns* (a reply to
> Jenyns's attack on Johnson after Johnson's
> death), in James Boswell, *Life of Johnson.*

Though metaphysicks spread the gloom of night,
By reason's star he* guides our aching sight;
The bounds of knowledge marks, and points the way
To pathless wastes, where wilder'd sages stray;
Where, like a farthing link-boy, Jennings stands,
And the dim torch drops from his feeble hands.
(*Johnson)
> John Courtenay, *Literary and Moral Character of
> Dr Johnson.*

Soame Jenyns was an old woman and his vocabulary was as trite as could be; and yet, because he
wrote in the eighteenth century, he put his poor
words and thoughts into shipshape sentences.
> A. E. Housman, Review of vols 13–14 of the
> *Cambridge History of English Literature.*

JEROME, JEROME KLAPKA

1859–1927 Author

I think I may claim to have been, for the first
twenty years of my career, the best abused author
in England. *Punch* invariably referred to me as
' 'Arry K'Arry', and would then proceed to solemnly
lecture me on the sin of mistaking vulgarity for humour and impertinence for wit. . . . Max Beerbohm
was always very angry with me. The *Standard*
spoke of me as a menace to English letters. . . . At
the opening dinner of the Krasnapolski restaurant
in Oxford Street (now the Frascati), I was placed
next to Harold Frederick, just arrived from America.
I noticed that he had been looking at me with
curiosity. 'Where's your flint hammer?' he asked me
suddenly. 'Left it in the cloakroom?' He explained
that he had visualized me from reading the English
literary journals, and had imagined something prehistoric.
> On himself, *My Life and Times.*

I did not intend to write a funny book, at first. I did
not know I was a humorist. I have never been sure
about it. In the middle ages, I should probably have
gone about preaching and got myself burned or
hanged.
> *Ibid.*

Costume, dandaical or not, is in the highest degree
expressive. . . . The bowler of Mr Jerome K. Jerome
is a perfect preface to all his works.
> Max Beerbohm, *Dandies and Dandies.*

JERVIS, JOHN, EARL ST VINCENT

1735–1823 Admiral

My old oak.
> George IV, attributed.

JEWETT, SARAH ORNE

1849–1909 Author

Cute little spider down in Maine
(All the time we need her)
Spin some silvery webs again
To catch the flying reader.
> Thomas Bailey Aldrich, urging Miss Jewett to
> write.

She was neither philosopher nor sociologist, but she
was an observer and interpreter who did the type of
observing that precedes speculation and the kind of
interpreting that resists collectivization.
> Richard Cary, *Sarah Orne Jewett.*

Your voice is like a thrush's in the din of all the
literary noises that stun us so.
> William Dean Howells, in *ibid.*

JOHN, KING

1167?–1216

Five years did King John lie under this sentence of
excommunication; in which time we find him more
fortunate in his martial affairs than either before or
after. For he made a successful voyage into Ireland,
(as greedy a grave for English corpses, as a bottomless bag for their coin), and was very triumphant in
a Welsh expedition, and stood on honourable terms
in all foreign relations.
> Thomas Fuller, *Church History of Britain.*

'Foul as it is, hell itself is defiled by the fouler
presence of John.' The terrible view of his contemporaries has passed into the sober judgement of
history. . . . John was the worst outcome of the
Plantaganets. He united into one mass of wickedness
their insolence, their selfishness, their unbridled
lust, their cruelty and tyranny, their shamelessness,

JOHN OF GAUNT

their superstition, their cynical indifference to
honor or truth.
  J. R. Green, *The History of the English People.*

King John was not a good man —
  He had his little ways,
And sometimes no one spoke to him
  For days and days and days.
  A. A. Milne, *Now We Are Six.*

If Bouvines had been won, John would have been
the dominant power in Western Europe. With Philip
Augustus humbled there would have been little
chance that Otto's enemies could destroy his imperial power. The papacy would have had to bow to
the victorious cousins. And the English baronage,
appeased by the recovery of their continental lands
would hardly have considered revolt against so
powerful a monarch.
  Sidney Painter, *King John.*

He was the very worst of all our kings: a man whom
no oaths could bind, no pressure of conscience, no
consideration of policy, restrain from evil; a faithless son, a treacherous brother, an ungrateful
master; to his people a hated tyrant. Polluted with
every crime that could disgrace a man, false to every
obligation that should bind a king, he had lost half
his inheritance by sloth, and ruined and desolated
the rest. Not devoid of natural ability, craft or
energy, with his full share of the personal valour
and accomplishments of his house, he yet failed in
every design he undertook, and had to bear humilia-
tions which, although not without parallel, never
fell on one who deserved them more thoroughly or
received less sympathy under them. In the whole
view there is no redeeming trait; John seems as
incapable of receiving a good impression as of carrying into effect a wise resolution.
  Bishop William Stubbs, *The Constitutional History of England.*

His death saved the kingdom for his descendants.
  Ibid.

Unfortunately for his reputation, John was not a
great benefactor to monasteries which kept
chronicles.
  W. C. Warren, *King John.*

John handled the situation [Magna Carta] with a
sensitivity to the delicate balance and a resourceful
ingenuity which, whatever one thinks of him as a
man, can only enhance his reputation as a ruler of
consummate ability.
  Ibid.

It is impossible, the evidence being what it is, to

pronounce finally upon his character as a man, but
it seems clear that he was inadequate for the tasks
confronting him as king. Even in his achievements
there was always something missing. He subdued
nations to his will, but brought only the peace of
fear; he was an ingenious administrator, but expedients came before policy; he was a notable judge,
but chicanery went along with justice; he was an
able ruler, but he did not know when he was squeezing too hard; he was a clever strategist, but his military operations lacked that vital ingredient of
success — boldness. He had the mental abilities of
a great king, but the inclinations of a petty tyrant.
  Ibid.

Lo! John self-stripped of his insignia: — crown
Sceptre and mantle, sword and ring laid down
At a proud Legate's feet! The spears that line
Baronial halls, the opprobrious insult feel;
And angry Ocean roars a vain appeal.
  William Wordsworth, *Papal Abuses.*

See also Herbert de Burgh, James I

JOHN OF GAUNT, DUKE OF LANCASTER

1340—99 Statesman

King Richard: Old John of Gaunt, time-honour'd
Lancaster. . . .
  William Shakespeare, *Richard II*, Act I, Scene i.

JOHN OF SALISBURY

— d. 1180 Jurist

The style of John of Salisbury, far from being equal
to that of Augustin, Eutropius, and a few more of
those early ages, does not appear to me by any
means elegant; sometimes he falls upon a good expression, but the general effect is not very classical.
  Henry Hallam, *Introduction to the Literature of
Europe.*

JOHN, AUGUSTUS EDWIN

1878—1961 Artist

John! John!
How he's got on!
  He owes it, he knows it, to me!
Brass earrings I wear,
And I don't do my hair,
  And my feet are as bare as can be;
When I walk down the street,

All the people I meet
    They stare at the things I have on!
When Battersea-Parking
You'll hear folks remarking:
    'There goes an Augustus John!'
    Song in Revue, in *Monster Matinee*, March 1917.

You who revel in the quick
And are Beauty's Bolshevik;
For you know how to undress
And expose her loveliness.
    Oliver St John Gogarty, *Ode 'To Augustus John'*.

Admiring women gaze upon
This gay memorial to John
Whose bold, discerning eye would scan
Things missed by another man.
    Kensal Green (Colin Hurry), *Premature Epitaphs*.

He had become one of the most popular men in the country. In Soho restaurants 'Entrecôte à la John' was eaten; in theatres any actor impersonating an artist was indistinguishable from him; in several novels he was instantly recognizable as 'the painter'.
    Michael Holroyd, *Augustus John*.

That standard celebrity.
    Percy Wyndham Lewis, *Blasting and Bombardiering*.

It was his Rembrandtesque drawings of stumpy brown people, followed by his tribes after tribes of archaic and romantic Gitanos and Gitanas that made him the legitimate successor to Beardsley and Wilde and in exploiting the inveterate exoticism of the educated Englishman and Englishwoman, stamped himself, barbaric chevelure and all, on what might be termed the Augustan decade.
    Percy Wyndham Lewis, *History of the Largest Independent Society in England*.

John, indeed, is the last of the great improvisers; he was made to throw off his fancies at white heat; and he alone is able to draw nudes in any position, at any angle, as Tiepolo could.
    William Rothenstein, *Men and Memories, 1900–22*.

He is a spiritual gypsy, and scorns the arm-chair thoughts of sluggish minds; he takes his subject by assault, never by cunning.
    Ibid.

When I think of him, I often feel that the only thing to do is to chuck up everything and make a dash for some such safe secluded office-stool as is pressed by dear Maynard [Keynes]'s bottom. The dangers of freedom are appalling! In the meantime it seems to me that one had better buy up every drawing by him that's on the market. For surely he's bound to fizzle out; and then the prices!
    Lytton Strachey, Letter to Duncan Grant, 12 April 1907.

He exaggerates every little hill and hollow of the face till one looks like a gypsy, grown old in wickedness and hardship. If one looked like any of his pictures the country women would take the clean clothes off the hedges when one passed, as they do at the sight of a tinker.
    William Butler Yeats, Letter to John Quinn, 4 October, 1907.

JOHNSON, ANDREW

1808–75 Seventeenth United States President

What will the aristocrats do, with a railsplitter for President, and a tailor for Vice President.
    On himself, in Fawn M. Brodie, *Thaddeus Stevens: Scourge of the South*.

. . . an insolent drunken brute, in comparison with whom Caligula's horse was respectable.
    Anon., in *New York World*, 1865.

Like a boy whistling down ghosts, the vehemence with which he boasts of his plebian origin shows that it is a sore spot with him, and the pains which he takes to remind us that he was a tailor prove that he is constantly haunted by that unwelcome fact.
    Anon., in *Nation*, 6 September 1866.

He came to office metaphorically speaking, foaming at the mouth. He was so tremendous in his denunciation of treason and smiled so savagely that 'rebels must take back seats' in the work of reconstruction that sensible men were afraid that wisdom was to be swallowed up in wrath and revenge defy reason.
    Anon., in *Harper's Weekly*, 6 May 1867.

His mind had one compartment for right and one for wrong, but no middle chamber where the two could commingle.
    Howard K. Beale, in Michael L. Benedict, *The Impeachment and Trial of Andrew Johnson*.

This angry man, dizzy with the elevation to which assassination has raised him, frenzied with power and ambition, does not seem to know that not he but the men who made the Constitution placed it in the people's hands. They placed Andrew Johnson in the people's hands also; and when those hands shall drop their votes into the ballot box, Andrew Johnson and his policy of arrogance and usurpation will be snapped like a willow wand.

Roscoe Conkling, in David Barr Chidsey, *The Gentleman from New York — A Life of Roscoe Conkling.*

One of the people by birth, he remained so by conviction.

Jefferson Davis, in George F. Milton, *The Age of Hate.*

. . . a poor white, steeped in the limitations, prejudices, and ambitions of his social class.

W. E. B. Du Bois, in Eric L. McKitrick, *Andrew Johnson: A Profile.*

If Andy Johnson was a snake, he would hide in the grass and bite the heels of rich men's children.

Isham G. Harris, in Michael L. Benedict, *The Impeachment and Trial of Andrew Johnson.*

Like an aching tooth, everyone (sic) is impatient to have the old villain out.

Joseph Medill to John Logan, in Eric L. McKitrick, *Andrew Johnson: A Profile.*

[He] reduced the Presidency to the level of a grog house.

John Sherman, in William B. Hesseltine, *Ulysses S. Grant.*

Andrew Johnson practised the politics of nostalgia; and he discovered in his own career, in which he took infinite pride, full vindication of his old-fashioned social philosophy. He was a self-made man, the embodiment of the American success story, though hardly one of its more attractive products.

Kenneth M. Stampp, *Andrew Johnson: The Last Jacksonian.*

You will remember that in Egypt He sent frogs, locusts, murrain, lice, and finally demanded the first-born of everyone of the oppressors. Almost all of these have been taken from us. We have been oppressed with taxes and debts, and He has sent us worse than lice, and has afflicted us with Andrew Johnson.

Thaddeus Stevens, August 1866, in Fawn M. Brodie, *Thaddeus Stevens.*

JOHNSON, (JONATHAN) EASTMAN

1824—1906 Artist

Johnson depicted the myth — and myth is the col-

lective fantasy of a nation — that hard work was not only virtuous but joyful. To a young nation struggling to become a major power this idealization of the working farmer and pioneer was, we can see now, a national necessity.

Patricia Hills, *Eastman Johnson.*

He . . . preaches no ugly gospel of discontent, as does so much of the contemporary French and Flemish art of this genre; his Nantucket neighbors know nothing of the *protestation douloureuse de la race asservie à la glebe*; there is no *cri de la terre* arising from his cranberry marshes or his hay-stuffed barns.

William Walton, in *ibid.*

JOHNSON, LIONEL PIGOT

1867—1902 Poet

I looked with wonder at the young scholar, who, it proved, was but a year younger than myself, being twenty-three. Not an advanced age, indeed, but not even the knowledge that he was Lionel Johnson could make him look more than fifteen, and he never seemed to look older as long as he lived. . . . His little, almost tiny, figure, was so frail that it reminded one of that old Greek philosopher who was so light of weight that he filled his pockets with stones for fear the wind might blow him away.

Richard Le Gallienne, *The Romantic '90s.*

Johnson stands out with an austere light behind him like the aureoled head of a little saint.

Katherine Tynan, *Memories.*

Lionel Johnson comes the first to mind,
That loved his learning better than mankind,
Though courteous to the worst; much falling he
Brooded upon sanctity
Till all his Greek and Latin learning seemed
A long blast upon the horn that brought
A little nearer to his thought
A measureless consummation that he dreamed.

William Butler Yeats, *In Memory of Major Robert Gregory.*

JOHNSON, LYNDON BAINES

1908—73 Thirty-Sixth United States President

I have said that I believe in the tight fist and the open mind — a tight fist with money and an open mind to the needs of America.

On himself, Speech at Washington D.C., 4 December 1964.

I am going to build the kind of nation that President Roosevelt hoped for, President Truman worked for and President Kennedy died for.
On himself, in *Sunday Times*, December 1964.

I seldom think of politics more than eighteen hours a day.
On himself, in Henry A. Zeiger, *Lyndon B. Johnson: Man and President*.

Hey, hey, LBJ! How many kids did you kill today?
Anon. anti-Vietnam war chant.

At last after more than two years in the hot glare of public and private scrutiny, it still is necessary to approach Lyndon Johnson as one approaches an artichoke — layer by layer, with each leaf yielding no more than a hint of what lies at the heart.
Philip L. Geyelin, *Lyndon B. Johnson and the World*.

Face-saving, the President observed, was not his major purpose in life. 'While you're trying to save your face,' he declared, 'you're losing your ass.'
Ibid.

. . . we have many people that have thin skins, Lyndon Johnson is one. His skin is a millionth of an inch thick.
Senator Barry M. Goldwater, in Leon A. Harris, *The Fine Art of Political Wit*.

We now have a President who tries to save money by turning off lights in the White House, even as he heads toward a staggering addition to the national debt. 'L.B.J.' should stand for Light Bulb Johnson.
Barry M. Goldwater, Speech in Chicago, 10 April 1964.

He was trying to get everyone on board in an office where the best decisions are often the loneliest ones.
David Halberstam, *The Best and the Brightest*.

His social vision did not go beyond the classic prescriptions for dealing with injustice: give everybody an equal start, above all education, and meanwhile keep the niggers off your porch.
Christopher Lasch, 'The Presidential Mystique', in H. W. Quint and M. Cantor eds, *Men, Women and Issues in American History*, vol. 2.

We've got a wild man in the White House, and we are going to have to treat him as such.
Senator Eugene McCarthy, in Alfred Steinberg, *Sam Johnson's Boy*.

. . . a damn independent boy; independent as a hog on ice.

Sam Rayburn, in Alfred Steinberg, *Sam Johnson's Boy*.

Everybody is in doubt about whether President Johnson is a conservative progressive or a progressive conservative, and he is in clover.
James Reston, in *New York Times*, 9 September 1964.

He is an incorrigible believer. He believes in everything that works.
James Reston in *New York Times Magazine*, 17 January 1965.

He doesn't have the best mind on the Democratic side of the Senate; he isn't the best orator; he isn't the best parliamentarian. But he is the best combination of all those qualities.
Senator Richard Russell, in *Time*, 22 June 1953.

. . . he was the great legislative prestidigitator of his time. Not since James F. Bynes had Congress seen a man so skilled in modifying a measure to enlist the widest possible support, so adept at the arts of wheedling, trading and arm-twisting, so persistent and so persuasive.
Arthur M. Schlesinger Jr, *A Thousand Days, John F. Kennedy in the White House*.

A great, raw man of immense girth, wandering as a stranger in the Pepsi generation. Coarse, earthy — a brutal intrusion into the misty Kennedy renaissance that still clung to the land.
Hugh Sidey, *A Very Personal Presidency*.

He learned how to seize authority from the lazy or slow, threaten and storm the weak, flatter the vain, promise the greedy, buy off the stubborn, and isolate the strong.
Alfred Steinberg, *Sam Johnson's Boy*.

. . . Johnson's strategy is too slick to talk about and so subtle that only a few fellow con-men appreciate it.
I. F. Stone, *In a Time of Torment*.

He is one of the most long-winded men in Washington; a Rabbit, with a remarkably small stock of basic ideas; these consist of a few cliches about freedom, which he translates largely into the freedom of the entrepreneur to make a buck.
Ibid.

I sleep each night a little better, a little more confidently because Lyndon Johnson is my President. For I know he lives and thinks and works to make sure that for all America and indeed, the growing

body of the free world, the morning shall always come.
    Jack Valenti, in Hugh Sidey, *A Very Personal Presidency*.

Johnson's instinct for power is as primordial as a salmon's going upstream to spawn.
    Theodore H. White, *The Making of the President – 1964*.

JOHNSON, SAMUEL (DOCTOR)

1709–84 Critic, Poet, Lexicographer

I have protracted my work till most of those whom I wished to please have sunk into the grave, and success and miscarriage are empty sounds; I therefore dismiss it with frigid tranquility, having little to fear or hope from censure or from praise.
    On himself, Preface to his *Dictionary of the English Language*.

If I had no duties, and no reference to futurity, I would spend my life in driving briskly in a post-chaise with a pretty woman.
    On himself, in James Boswell, *Life of Johnson*.

You must not mind me, madam; I say strange things, but I mean no harm.
    On himself, in Fanny Burney, Diary, 23 August 1778.

The groans of Learning tell that Johnson dies.
Adieu, rough critic, of Colossal size!
Grateful, ye virtues, round his grave attend,
And boldly guard your energetic friend!
Ye vices keep aloof – a foe to you!
Yet one, the subtlest of your tribe, he knew;
In silence, Envy, to his fame be just,
And, tho' you stain'd his spirit, spare his dust.
    Anon. *Epitaph*, published in several newspapers in February 1796 under the name of Anna Seward (who disavowed it).

Our knowledge of Johnson comes to us solely and exclusively through Boswell's spectacles. . . . Not one man in a thousand . . . has ever dipped into any single thing that Johnson wrote.
    Anon., in *Temple Bar*, June 1892.

The Hercules of literature.
    Mrs Anna Laetitia Barbauld, Preface to *Rasselas*, 1810.

That pompous preacher of melancholy moralities.
    Jeremy Bentham, *The Book of Fallacies*.

'Oho', said Dr Johnson
To Scipio Africanus,
'If you don't own me a Philosopher,
I'll kick your Roman Anus.'
    William Blake, *An Island in the Moon*.

When I put down Mr Johnson's sayings, I do not keep strictly to chronology. I am glad to collect the gold dust, as I get by degrees as much as will be an ingot.
    James Boswell, Journal, 14 April 1775.

He turned to me and said, 'I look upon *myself* as a good-humoured fellow.' The epithet *fellow* applied to the great lexicographer, the stately moralist, the masterly critic, as if he had been *Sam* Johnson, a mere pleasant companion, was highly diverting; and this light notion of himself struck me with wonder. I answered, also smiling, 'No, no, Sir; that will *not* do. You are good-natured, but not good-humoured. You are irascible. You have not patience with folly and absurdity. I believe you would pardon them if there were time to deprecate your vengeance; but punishment follows so quick after sentence that they cannot escape.'
    Ibid.

Johnson: Well, we had a good talk.
Boswell: Yes, Sir, you tossed and gored several persons.
    James Boswell, *Life of Johnson*.

I compared him . . . to a warm West-Indian climate, where you have a bright sun, quick vegetation, luxuriant foliage, luscious fruits; but where the same heat sometimes produces thunder, lightning, and earthquakes in a terrible degree.
    Ibid.

Sastres told me that Dr Brocklesby, who attended Johnson in his last illness, although an infidel was forced by Johnson to kneel when the latter prayed. Brocklesby would not always finish the prayer, and Johnson kept turning round in a violent rage, exclaiming: 'Why will you not say, Amen?'
    Lord Broughton, *Recollections of a Long Life*.

Indeed, the freedom with which Dr Johnson condemns whatever he disapproves is astonishing.
    Fanny Burney, Diary, 23 August 1778.

That Johnson's stile is obscure, the testimony of all unlearned readers abundantly confirms; and from the same authority the cause may be stated to be his perpetual affectation of expressing his thoughts by the use of polysyllables of Latin derivation: a fault, which confines to men of erudition the most animating enforcements of virtue and the most salutary rules of conduct, by disqualifying all those who have not been made acquainted by a liberal education with the Latin appellations for things, or those, from whose memories the common use of the English names has in the course of time effaced them.

Robert Burrowes, *Essay on the Stile of Doctor Samuel Johnson.*

Rough Johnson, the great moralist.
Lord Byron, *Don Juan*, canto xiii.

Our English Lexiphanes.
Archibald Campbell, *Lexiphanes, a Dialogue.*

Shall we not say, of this great mournful Johnson too, that he guided his difficult confused existence wisely; led it *well*, like a right-valiant man? That waste chaos of Authorship by trade; that waste chaos of Scepticism in religion and politics, in life-theory and life-practice; in his poverty, in his dust and dimness, with the sick body and the rusty coat: he made it do for him, like a brave man. Not wholly without a loadstar in the Eternal; he had still a loadstar, as the brave all need to have: with his eye set on that, he would change his course for nothing in these confused vortices of the lower sea of Time. 'To the Spirit of Lies, bearing death and hunger, he would in no wise strike his flag.' Brave old Samuel: *ultimus Romanorum!*

Thomas Carlyle, *On Heroes and Hero Worship.*

POMPOSO (insolent and loud,
Vain idol of a *scribbling* crowd,
Whose very name inspires an awe,
For what his Greatness hath decreed,
Like Laws of PERSIA and of MEDE,
Sacred thro' all the realm of *Wit*,
Must never of Repeal admit. . . .)
Charles Churchill, *The Ghost.*

Who wit with jealous eye surveys,
And sickens at another's praise.
Ibid.

He for subscribers baits his hook,
And takes your cash, but where's the book?
No matter where; wise fear, you know,
Forbids the robbing of a foe;
But what, to serve our private ends,
Forbids the cheating of our friends?
Ibid., referring to Johnson's Dictionary.

. . . Old dread-death and dread-devil Johnson, that teacher of moping and melancholy. . . . If the writings of this time-serving, mean, dastardly old pensioner had got a firm hold of the minds of the people at large, the people would have been bereft of their very souls. These writings, aided by the charm of pompous sound, were fast making their way, till light, reason, and the French revolution came to drive them into oblivion; or, at least, to confine them to the shelves of repentant, married old rakes, and those old stock-jobbers with young wives standing in need of something to keep down the unruly ebullitions which are apt to take place while the 'dearies' are gone hobbling to 'Change.

William Cobbett, *Journal*, November 1821.

Dr Dread-Devil . . . said, that there were *no trees* in Scotland. I wonder how they managed to take him round without letting him see trees. I suppose that lick-spittle Boswell, or Mrs Piozzi, tied a bandage over his eyes, when he went over the country which I have been over. I shall sweep away all this bundle of lies.

William Cobbett, *Tour of Scotland.*

Dr Johnson seems to have been really more powerful in discoursing *viva voce* in conversation than with his pen in hand. It seems as if the excitement of company called something like reality and consecutiveness into his reasonings, which in his writings I cannot see. His antitheses are almost always verbal only; and sentence after sentence in the *Rambler* may be pointed out to which you cannot attach any definite meaning whatever.

Samuel Taylor Coleridge, *Table-Talk*, 1 November 1833.

Nor was his energy confin'd alone
To friends around his philosophick throne;
Its influence wide improv'd our letter'd isle,
And lucid vigour mark'd the general style:
As Nile's proud waves, swol'n from their oozy bed,
First o'er the neighbouring meads majestick spread;
Till gathering force, they more and more expand,
And with new virtue fertilise the land.

John Courtenay, *Moral and Literary Character of Dr. Johnson.*

The Caliban of literature.
Gilbert Cowper, in James Boswell, *Life of Johnson.*

Those who demand of poetry a day-dream, or a metamorphosis of their own feeble desires and lusts, or what they believe to be 'intensity' of passion, will not find much in Johnson. He is like Pope and Dryden, Crabbe and Landor, a poet for those who want poetry and not something else, some stay for their own vanity.

T. S. Eliot, *Eighteenth-Century Poetry.*

A dangerous person to disagree with.
T. S. Eliot, *The Metaphysical Poets.*

We arrive, then, at Johnson, the most tragic of all our major literary figures, a great writer whose still living writings are always ignored, a great honest man who will remain forever a figure of half fun because of the leechlike adoration of the greatest and most ridiculous of all biographers. For it is impossible not to believe that, without Boswell, Johnson for us today would shine like a sun in the heavens whilst Addison sat forgotten in coffee houses.

Ford Madox Ford, *The March of Literature.*

Rabelais and all other wits are nothing compared with him. You may be diverted by them; but Johnson gives you a forcible hug, and shakes laughter out of you whether you will or no.

David Garrick, in James Boswell, *Life of Johnson.*

There is no arguing with Johnson; for if his pistol misses fire, he knocks you down with the butt end of it.

Oliver Goldsmith, in *ibid.*

Johnson to be sure has a roughness in his manner; but no man alive has a more tender heart. *He has nothing of the bear but his skin.*

Ibid.

If you were to make little fishes talk, they would talk like whales.

Ibid.

Dr Johnson's morality was as English an article as a beefsteak.

Nathaniel Hawthorne, *Our Old Home. Lichfield and Uttoxeter.*

Johnson wrote a kind of rhyming prose, in which he was as much compelled to finish the different clauses of his sentences, and to balance one period against another, as the writer of heroic verse is to keep to lines of ten syllables with similar terminations. He no sooner acknowledges the merits of his author in one line than the periodical revolution of his style carries the weight of his opinion completely over to the side of objection, thus keeping up a perpetual alternation of perfections and absurdities.

William Hazlitt, *Characters of Shakespeare's Plays.*

I am not . . . saying that Dr Johnson was a man without originality, compared with the ordinary run of men's minds, but he was not a man of original thought or genius, in the sense in which Montaigne or Lord Bacon was. He opened no new vein of precious ore, nor did he light upon any single pebbles of uncommon size and unrivalled lustre. We seldom meet with any thing to 'give us pause'; he does not set us thinking for the first time.

William Hazlitt, *Lectures on the English Comic Writers.*

Here lies poor Johnson; reader have a care;
Tread lightly, lest you rouse a sleeping bear.
Religious, moral, generous, and humane
He was; but self-sufficient, rude, and vain;
Ill-bred, and overbearing in dispute,
A scholar and a Christian and a brute.

Soame Jenyns, *Epitaph on Samuel Johnson.*

In this country, to those seriously interested in literature, the cult of Johnson is an exasperation and a challenge. . . . Johnson, one finds oneself having again and again to insist, was not only the Great Clubman; he was a great writer and a great highbrow — or would have been, if the word, and the conditions that have produced it, had existed; that is, he assumed a serious interest in things of the mind, and, for all his appeal to 'the common reader', was constantly engaged in the business of bringing home to his public and his associates, whose cult of him was a tribute to the force with which he did it, that there were standards in these things above the ordinary level of the ordinary man.

F. R. Leavis, *The Common Pursuit.*

In the foreground is that strange figure which is as familiar to us as the figures of those among whom we have been brought up, the gigantic body, the huge massy face, seamed with the scars of disease, the brown coat, the black worsted stockings, the grey wig with the scorched foretop, the dirty hands, the nails bitten and pared to the quick.

T. B. Macaulay, *Essays:* 'Boswell's Life of Johnson'.

What a singular destiny has been that of this remarkable man! To be regarded in his own age as a classic, and in ours as a companion! To receive from his contemporaries that full homage which men of genius have in general received only from posterity! To be more intimately known to posterity than other men are known to their contemporaries! . . . The reputation of those writings, which he probably expected to be immortal, is every day fading; while those peculiarities of manner and that careless table-talk the memory of which, he probably thought, would die with him, are likely to be remembered as long as the English language is spoken in any quarter of the globe.

T. B. Macaulay, *ibid.*

We cannot be in Johnson's company long, without becoming aware that what draws us to him so closely is that he combined a disillusioned estimate of human nature sufficient to launch twenty little cynics, with a craving for love and sympathy urgent enough to turn a weaker nature into a benign sentimentalist.

Desmond MacCarthy, *Criticism*.

Gibbon and Dr Johnson . . . were the victims of bad theories. I can read every word that Dr Johnson wrote with delight, for he had good sense, charm and wit. . . . He knew good English when he saw it. . . . But when he himself sat down to write . . . he mistook the orotund for the dignified. He had not the good breeding to see that simplicity and naturalness are the truest mark of distinction.

W. Somerset Maugham, *The Summing Up*.

The *Rambler* is certainly a strong misnomer. He always plods in the beaten road of his predecessors, following the *Spectator* (with the same pace a pack-horse would do a hunter) in the style that is proper to lengthen a paper. . . . I should be glad to know the name of this laborious author.

Lady Mary Wortley Montagu, Letter to Lady Bute, 23 July 1754.

O rough, pure, stubborn, troubled soul: for whom
    A smile of special tenderness men keep —
Who prayed for strength 'to regulate my room',
    And 'preservation from immoderate sleep'.

Christopher Morley, *On a Portrait of Dr Samuel Johnson, LL.D.*

Now that the old lion is dead, every ass thinks he may kick at him.

Samuel Parr, in James Boswell, *Life of Johnson*.

Dr Johnson's sayings would not appear so extraordinary, were it not for his *bow-wow way*.

Lord Pembroke, in *ibid*.

The conversation of Johnson is strong and clear, and may be compared to an antique statue, where every vein and muscle is distinct and bold. Ordinary conversation resembles an inferior cast.

Bishop Thomas Percy, in *ibid*.

I own I like not Johnson's turgid style,
That gives an inch th'importance of a mile;
Casts of manure a waggon-load around
To raise a simple daisy from the ground;
Uplifts the club of Hercules — for what? —
To crush a butterfly or brain a gnat;
Creatures a whirlwind from the earth to draw
A goose's feather or exalt a straw;
Sets wheels on wheels in motion — such a clatter:
To force up one poor nipperkin of water;

Bids ocean labour with tremendous roar,
To heave a cockle-shell upon the shore.
Alike in every theme his pompous art,
Heaven's awful thunder, or a rumbling cart!

Peter Pindar (John Wolcot), *On Dr. Samuel Johnson*.

Mr Johnson did not like anyone who said they were happy, or who said anyone else was so. 'It is all *cant* (he would cry), the dog knows he is miserable all the time.'

Mrs Piozzi (Hester Lynch Thrale), *Anecdotes of Johnson*.

Mrs Thrale justly and wittily . . . said that Johnson's conversation was by much too strong for a person accustomed to obsequiousness and flattery; it was *mustard in a young child's mouth*.

Mrs Piozzi, in James Boswell, *Life of Johnson*.

Terribly afraid of free-thinking, though not hostile to free-eating. . . . A great author, notwithstanding his *Dictionary* is imperfect, his *Rambler* pompous, his *Idler* inane, his *Lives* unjust, his poetry inconsiderable, his learning common, his ideas vulgar, his *Irene* a child of mediocrity, his genius and wit moderate, his precepts worldly, his politics narrow, and his religion bigoted.

Robert Potter, *The Art of Criticism as Exemplified by Dr Johnson's Lives of the Most Eminent English Poets*.

I at once and for ever recognized in him a man entirely sincere, and infallibly wise in the view and estimate he gave of the common questions, business, and ways of the world. I valued his sentences not primarily because they were symmetrical, but because they were just, and clear. . . . No other writer could have secured me, as he did, against all chance of being misled by my own sanguine and metaphysical temperament. He taught me carefully to measure life, and distrust fortune; and he secured me, by his adamantine common-sense, from being caught in the cobwebs of German metaphysics, or sloughed in the English drainage of them.

John Ruskin, *Praeterita*.

When we consider the rank which Dr Johnson held, not only in literature, but in society, we cannot help figuring him to ourselves as the benevolent giant of some fairy tale, whose kindnesses and courtesies are still mingled with a part of the rugged ferocity imputed to the fabulous sons of Anak, or rather, perhaps, like a Roman dictator, fetched from his farm, whose wisdom and heroism still relished of his rustic occupation.

Sir Walter Scott, *Lives of the Novelists*.

Dr Johnson, whose sophistry in criticism has been fatal to the general poetic taste of this period, elevated the style of prose composition much above the water-gruel mark. His splendid example demonstrates, that efflorescence and strength of language united, are necessary to form the perfection of writing in prose as well as in verse.

Anna Seward, Letter to William Seward, 1795.

I have not wasted my life trifling with literary fools in taverns as Johnson did when he should have been shaking England with the thunder of his spirit.

George Bernard Shaw, Preface to *Misalliance*.

Garrick, had he called Dr Johnson Punch, would have spoken profoundly and wittily, whereas Dr Johnson, in hurling that epithet at him, was but picking up the cheapest sneer an actor is subject to.

George Bernard Shaw, Preface to *Plays Pleasant and Unpleasant*.

A writer of gigantick fame in these days of little men.

Thomas Sheridan, *Life of Swift*.

That great Cham of literature.

Tobias Smollett, Letter to John Wilkes, 16 March 1759.

Of those who have thus survived themselves most completely, left a sort of personal seduction behind them in the world, and retained, after death, the art of making friends, Montaigne and Samuel Johnson certainly stand first.

Robert Louis Stevenson, *Familiar Studies of Men and Books*.

Great is thy prose; great thy poetic strain;
Yet to dull coxcombs are they great in vain.
When weak opponents would thy strength defeat,
Thy words, like babbling parrots, they repeat;
But mixed with theirs, the vigour all is fled,
The letter living, but the spirit dead:
Their want of powers these insects will not see;
Bombast in them, is the sublime in thee.

Percival Stockdale, *The Remonstrance*.

Johnson's aesthetic judgements are almost invariably subtle, or solid, or bold; they have always some good quality to recommend them — except one: they are never right.

Lytton Strachey, *Books and Characters*.

He is a man of a very clear head, great power of words, and a very gay imagination; but there is no disputing with him. He will not hear you, and having a louder voice than you, must roar you down.

Dr John Taylor, in James Boswell, *Life of Johnson*.

Of the POLITICAL WRITINGS of Dr Johnson, it would be injurious to the interests of truth, and to the common rights of human nature, to speak in terms of much commendation. . . . Many positions are laid down, in admirable language, and in highly polished periods, which are inconsistent with the principles of the English constitution, and repugnant to the common rights of mankind. As a political writer, he makes much more use of his rhetoric than of his logic, and often gives his readers high sounding declamation instead of fair argument.

Joseph Towers, *An Essay on the Life, Character, and Writings of Dr Samuel Johnson*.

His works are the Antipodes of Taste, & he is a Schoolmaster of truth, but never its parent; for his doctrines have no novelty, and are never inculcated with indulgence either to the froward child, or to the Dull one. He has set nothing in a new light, yet is as diffuse as if we had every thing to learn. Modern Writers have improved on the Ancients only by conciseness: Dr Johnstone, like the Chymists of Laputa, endeavours to carry back what has been digested to its pristine & crude principles.

Horace Walpole, *General Criticism of Dr Johnson's Writings*.

As an author, Johnson's fame was, to tell the truth, scarcely more than contemporary; for it depended upon *novelty of style*, in an age which loved personal novelties like the clothes of the later Brummell. To them, the not-ungraceful antithetical balancing feats with which he wrote of 'amorous propensities' rather than 'love' were new and strange. As a lexicographer, he was of importance. As a conversationalist, the equivalent of our modern 'brains trust' — who would have been lost without the microphone of Boswell — he was of the first rank.

T. H. White, *The Age of Scandal*.

See also Henry Adams, James Boswell, David Garrick, Edward Gibbon, Leigh Hunt, Soame Jenyns, Elizabeth Montagu, William Warburton

JOLSON, AL (ASA YOELSON)

1888—1950 Singer, Actor

It was easy enough to make Jolson happy at home. You just had to cheer him for breakfast, applaud wildly for lunch, and give him a standing ovation for dinner.

George Burns, in Michael Freedland, *Jolson*.

Show Business dubbed him 'The King' and for 40 years he reigned supreme. He was the only entertainer who could dismiss the cast at eleven o'clock — hold the audience for an hour and have them shouting for more. On such occasions, he had to pay the stage hands overtime. When asked about this, he said 'It was worth it — they loved me out there.'
Eddie Cantor, *The Way I See It.*

There was something electric about him that sent a thrill up your spine. He sang and talked; but he was more than just a singer or an actor — he was an *experience.*
Eddie Cantor, *Take My Life.*

Born in Russia, he sang of Dixie and a Sewanee River he never saw until he was forty. He once said 'I've got so much dough that fourteen guys couldn't spend it in their lifetimes. But I'd rather die than quit this business'.
Michael Freedland, *Jolson.*

The spectacle of Jolson's vitality had the same quality as the impression I got from the New York sky line — one had forgotten that there still existed in the world a force so boundless, an exaltation so high, and that anyone could still storm Heaven with laughter and cheers.
Gilbert Seldes, *The Seven Lively Arts.*

JONES, INIGO

1573—1652 Architect, Designer

Our only learned architect.
George Chapman, Dedication of *Musaeus* to Jones, 1616.

He was more of an artist, by education than Wren, had a finer taste in art, had seen more of the best works of the great Italian and ancient Roman masters, had associated more with wits and men of the world than his eminent successor; but he was less of a mathematician, had a less expanded mind, and was less of a philosopher.
J. Elmes, *Sir Christopher Wren.*

Dominus Do-all.
Ben Jonson, attributed.

He had the painstaking, syntactical temperament of the artist, a gift he shared with Milton. For Milton in returning to the correct traditions of antiquity, tidied up the loose ends of the English language left by the Elizabethan poets and set exacting standards of versification. Inigo Jones did a similar service for architecture and in his own we have a forewarning of the severely grand, minatory and organ note of Milton's poetry.
James Lees-Milne, *The Age of Inigo Jones.*

To place him intelligibly one must think of him not in an English but a European context; one must see him, let us say, as an architectural Rubens — an individual of altogether exceptional genius whose vision and energy transferred a Mediterranean phenomenon to the still half Gothic north. His architecture challenges not merely the English but the European achievements of his time.
J. Summerson, *Architecture in Britain 1530—1830.*

Not to be equalled by whatsoever great masters in his time for boldness, softness, sweetness, and sureness of touch.
Anthony Van Dyck, in John Webb, *A Vindication of Stone-Heng, Restored.*

It was Vox Europae that named Inigo Jones Vitruvius Britannicus, being much more, than at home, famous in remote parts, where he lived many years.
John Webb, Preface to *A Vindication of Stone-Heng, Restored.*

JONES, JOHN PAUL

1747—92 Sailor

I have not yet begun to fight!
On himself, to the British Captain Pearson of HMS *Serapis* when asked if he was prepared to surrender at the battle off Flamborough Head, Yorkshire, 25 September 1779.

I hope you will be convinced that in the British prints I have been censured unjustly. I was, indeed, born in Britain, but I do not inherit the degenerate spirit of that fallen nation, which I at once lament and despise. It is far beneath one to reply to their hirely invectives. They are strangers to the inward approbation that greatly . . . rewards the man who draws his sword only in support of the dignity of freedom.
On himself, in Lincoln Lorenz, *John Paul Jones: Fighter for Freedom and Glory.*

I have not drawn my sword in our glorious cause for hire, but in support of the dignity of human nature and the divine feelings of philanthropy. I hoisted with my own hands the flag of freedom the first time it was displayed on board the *Alfred* in the Delaware; and I have attended it ever since with

veneration on the ocean.
> On himself, in a comment to Samuel Huntington, in *ibid.*

Pray, tell us good neighbors, whence all this affray?
(Quoth Trim) all this packing and posting away,
With cart-loads of luggage, aunts, sisters, and wives,
All driving as if 'twas a race for their lives?
Has d'Orvilliers' vast navy invaded our coast?
Is Amherst cut off at Coxheath with his host? . . .
Cox-coxcomb! yield the road, or I'll break all your
> bones,
The pi-pirate, trai-traitor comes, d--m him, Paul
> Jones! . . .
> Anon., *Paul Jones or the Fife Coast Garland.*

'Out booms! Out booms!' our skipper cried
> 'Out booms and giver her sheet!'
And the swiftest keel that was ever launched
> Shot ahead of the British fleet.
And amidst a thundering shower of shot
> With stunsails hoisting away,
Down the North Channel Paul Jones did steer
> Just at the break of day.
> Anon., in Samuel Eliot Morison, *John Paul Jones: A Sailor's Biography.*

Chief among our naval heroes was John Paul Jones, who is well remembered. At least he is better remembered than if his name had been merely John Jones. He commanded a stout vessel named the *Bonjour Richard.* It was he, who after his ship was sunk, declared, 'I have just begun to fight.' He was a brave man, but slow to anger.
> Richard Armour, *It All Started With Columbus.*

In faded naval uniform, Paul Jones lingers visible here; like a wineskin from which the wine is drawn. Like a ghost of himself. Low in his once loud bruit; scarcely audible, save with extreme tedium, in ministerial ante-chambers; in this or the other charitable dining rooms, mindful of the past. What changes, culminatings and declinings! . . . Poor Paul! hunger and dispiritment track thy sinking footsteps; once, or at most twice, in this Revolution-tumult the figure of thee emerges; mute, ghost-like, as 'with stars twinkling through'.
> Thomas Carlyle, in Samuel Eliot Morison, *John Paul Jones: A Sailor's Biography.*

JONSON, BENJAMIN

1573—1637 Dramatist, Poet

O rare Ben Jonson.
> *Epitaph in Westminster Abbey.*

Tudicio: The wittiest fellow of a bricklayer in England.
Ingenioso: A meere Empyrick, one that getts what he hath by observation, and makes onely nature privy to what he endites, so slow an Inventor, that he were better betake himself to his old trade of Bricklaying, a bould whorson, as confident now in making of a booke, as he was in times past in laying of a brick.
> Anon., *Second Part of The Return from Parnassus, circa* 1601—2.

Ben: Johnson was at a taverne and in comes Bishoppe Corbett (but not so then) into the next roome; Ben: Johnson calls for a quart of *raw* wine, gives it to the tapster: 'Sirrha' sayes he, 'carry this to the gentleman in the next chamber, and tell him I *sacrifice* my service to him'; the fellow did so, and in those words: 'Friend,' sayes Dr Corbett, 'I thanke him for his love, but pr'y thee tell hym from mee he's mistaken for *sacrifices* are allwayes *burn't.*'
> Anon., in *Merry Passages and Jests*, by Sir Nicholas L'Estrange.

Shakespear seeing Ben Johnson in a necessary-house, with a book in his hand reading it very attentively, said he was sorry his memory was so *bad*, that he could not *sh-te without a book.*
> Anon., *Shakespeare's Jests, or the Jubilee Jester, circa* 1769.

He was, (or rather had been) of a cleare & faire skin his habit was very plaine. I have heard Mr Lacy the Player say, that he was wont to weare a coat like a coach-mans coate, with slitts under the armepitts. he would many times exceed in drinke: Canarie was his beloved liquour: then he would tumble home to bed; and when he had thoroughly perspired, then to studie.
> John Aubrey, *Brief Lives.*

Aristotle and the others haunted him . . . and stiffened a talent and a method already by nature sufficiently stiff.
> Harley Granville Barker, *On Dramatic Method.*

Seldom or never could he consummate the business — it is the final creative act — by setting a character free.
> *Ibid.*

'Tis said that Benjamin was no such Rabbi neither, for I am informed his learning was but Grammar high.
> Mrs Aphra Behn, *An Epistle to the Reader, of The Dutch Lover.*

Whoe hath his flock of caqueling Geese compard

To thy tun'd quire of Swans? . . .
Thomas Carew, *To Ben Johnson uppon Occasion of his Ode to Himself.*

O Ben, my rare friend, is this in very deed thou? There in the body with thy rugged sagacities and genialities; with thy rugged Annandale face and unquenchable laughing eyes —; like a rock hiding in it perennial limpid wells! My rare friend there is in thee something of the lion I observe: — thou art the rugged stonemason, the harsh, learned Hodman; yet hast strains too of a noble softness, melodious as the voice of wood doves, fitfully thrilling as the note of nightingales now and then! Rarer I have not met with. A sterling man, a true singer-heart, — born of my native valley too; to whom and to which be all honour!
Thomas Carlyle, *Historical Sketches of Notable Persons and Events in the Reigns of James I and Charles I.*

Doctor: The last remedy, like Pigeons to the soles of the feet, must be to apply my dear Friend Mr *Johnson's* Works, but they must be apply'd to his head.
Codshead: Oh, have a care Doctor, he hates *Ben. Johnson*, he has an Antipathy to him.
Crambo: Oh, I hate *Johnson*, oh, oh, dull, dull, oh oh no Wit.
Doctor: 'Tis you are dull . . . dull! he was the Honour of his Nation, and the Poet of Poets. . . .
William Cavendish, Duke of Newcastle, *The Triumphant Widow, or The Medley of Humours.*

Next Jonson sat; in ancient learning train'd
His rigid judgement Fancy's flights restrain'd
Correctly pruned each wild luxurious thought,
Mark'd out her course, nor spared a glorious fault;
The book of man he read with nicest art,
And ransack'd all the secrets of the heart;
Exerted penetration's utmost force,
And traced each passion to its proper source;
And strongly mark'd in liveliest colours drew,
And brought each foible forth to public view:
The coxcomb felt a lash in every word,
And fools, hung out, their brother fools deterred.
His comic humour kept the world in awe,
And laughter frightened folly more than law.
Charles Churchill, *The Rosciad.*

Whilst Shakespeare gave us wit as salt to our meat, Ben Jonson gave wit as salt instead of meat.
Samuel Taylor Coleridge, *Bristol Lectures.*

I ought very particularly to call your attention to the extraordinary skill shown by Ben Jonson in contriving situations for the display of his characters. In fact his care and anxiety in this matter led him to do what scarcely any of the dramatists of that age did — that is, invent his plots.
Samuel Taylor Coleridge, *Literary Remains.*

He could not but be a Species of himself: tho' like the Mammoth and Megatherion fitted & destined to live only during a given period, and then to exist a Skeleton, hard, dry, uncouth perhaps, yet massive, and not to be contemplated without that mixture of Wonder and Admiration, or more accurately that middle somewhat between both for which we want a term — not quite even with the latter, but far above the mere former.
Samuel Taylor Coleridge, Annotation to Copy of Anderson's *British Poets*, vol. 4.

It was a constant complaint of the old actors who lived in Queen Anne's time, that if Jonson's plays were intermitted for a few years, they could not know how to personate his characters, they were so difficult, and their manners so distant, from those of all other authors. To preserve them required a kind of stage learning, which was traditionally hoarded up.
Thomas Davies, *Dramatic Miscellanies.*

After he was reconciled with the Church & left of to be a recusant at his first communion in token of true Reconciliation, he drank out all the full cup of wyne.
William Drummond, in *Conversations with William Drummond of Hawthornden.*

in his youth given to Venerie. he thought the use of a maide, nothing in comparison to ye wantoness of a wife & would never have ane other Mistress. he said two accidents strange befell him, one that a man made his owne wyfe to Court him, whom he enjoyed two yeares ere he knew of it, & one day finding them by chance Was passingly delighted with it, one other lay diverse tymes with a woman, who shew him all that he wished except the last act, which she would never agree unto.
Ibid.

He heth consumed a whole night in lying looking to his great toe, about which he hath seen tarters and turks Romans and Carthaginions feight in his imagination.
Ibid.

He is a great lover and praiser of himself, a contemner and Scorner of others, given rather to losse a friend, than a Jest, jealous of every word and action of those about him (especially after drink which is one of the Elements in which he liveth), a dissembler of ill parts which raigne in him, a bragger of some good that he wanteth, thinketh nothing well but what either he himself, or some of his friends

and Countrymen hath said or done. he is passionately kynde and angry, carelesse either to gaine or keep, Vindictive, but if he be well answered, at himself . . . for any religion as being versed in both, interpreteth best sayings and deeds often to the worst: oppressed with fantasie, which hath ever mastered his reason, a generall disease in many poets. his inventions are smooth and easie but above all he excelleth in a translation.
Ibid.

He was not only a professed imitator of Horace, but a learned plagiary of all the others; you track him everywhere in their snow.
John Dryden, *An Essay of Dramatic Poesy.*

As he did not want imagination, so none ever said he had much to spare.
Ibid.

Wise *Johnson*'s talent in observing lay,
But others' follies still made up his play.
John Dryden, ascribed, *Covent Garden Drolery*, 1672.

Johnson with skill dissected human kind,
And show'd their faults that they their faults might find;
But then, as all anatomists must do,
He to the meanest of mankind did go,
And took from Gibbets such as he would show.
Ibid.

The reputation of Jonson has been of the most deadly kind that can be compelled upon the memory of a great poet. To be universally accepted; to be damned by the praise that quenches all desire to read the book; to be afflicted by the imputation of the virtues which excite the least pleasure; and to be read only by historians and antiquaries — this is the most perfect conspiracy of approval. For some generations the name of Jonson has been carried rather as a liability than as an asset in the balance-sheet of English literature. . . . Poetry of the surface cannot be understood without study . . . the immediate appeal of Jonson is to the mind; his emotional tone is not in the single verse, but in the design of the whole.
T. S. Eliot, *Essays*: 'Ben Jonson'.

His type of personality found its relief in something falling under the category of burlesque or farce — though when you are dealing with a *unique* world, like his, these terms fail to appease the desire for definition. . . . Jonson poses as a satirist. But satire like Jonson's is great in the end not by hitting off its object, but by creating it; the satire is merely the

means which leads to the aesthetic result, the impulse which projects a new world into a new orbit.
Ibid.

Thy labours shall outlive thee; and, like gold,
Stampt for continuance, shall be current where
There is a sun, a people, or a year.
John Fletcher, *To My Worthy Friend Ben Jonson, on his Catiline*, 1611.

His parts were not so *ready* to *run of themselves* as *able to answer the* spur, so that it may be truly said of him, that he had an *Elaborate wit* wrought out by his own industry. He would sit silent in learned company, and suck in (besides wine) their several humours into his observation. What was *ore* in others, he was able to refine to himself.
Thomas Fuller, *The History of the Worthies of England.*

He may be said to mine his way into a subject, like a mole, and throws up a prodigious quantity of matter on the surface, so that the richer the soil in which he labours, the less dross and rubbish we have.
William Hazlitt, *On Beaumont and Fletcher.*

There are people who cannot taste olives — and I cannot much relish Ben Jonson, though I have taken some pains to do it, and went to the task with every sort of good will. I do not deny his power or his merit; far from it: but it is to me of a repulsive and unamiable kind.
William Hazlitt, *On Shakespeare and Ben Jonson*

When I a verse shall make,
Know I have praid thee,
For old *Religions* sake,
Saint *Ben* to aide me.

Make the way smooth for me,
When I, thy *Herrick*,
Honouring thee, on my knee
Offer my *lyrick*.

Candles Ile give to thee,
And a new Altar;
And thou Saint Ben, shalt be
Writ in my Psalter.
Robert Herrick, *His Prayer to Ben Johnson.*

You were mad when you writ your *Fox*, and madder when you writ your *Alchymist*; you were mad when you writ *Catilin*, and stark mad when you writ *Sejanus*; but when you writt your *Epigrams* and the *Magnetick Lady* you were not so mad. Excuse me that I am so free with you. The madness I mean is that divine Fury, that heating

and heightening Spirit, which *Ovid* speaks of.
  James Howell, *Epistolae Ho-Elianae, To My Father Ben Jonson.*

I was invited yesternight to a solemne supper by B J . . . there was good company, excellent cheer, choice wines, and joviall welcome; one thing intervened which almost spoyld the relish of the rest, that B began to engrosse all the discourse, to vapour extreamly of himselfe, and by vilifying others to magnifye his owne *muse: T. Ca.* busd me in the eare, that though Ben had barreld up a great deal of knowledge, yet it seemes he had not read the *ethiques*, which among other precepts of morality forbid self commendation, declaring it to be an ill favoured solecism in good manners.
  James Howell, *A New Volume of Letters.*

His naturall advantages were judgement to order and governe fancy, rather than excesse of fancy, his productions being slow and upon deliberation, yett then aboundinge with great witte and fancy and will lyve accordingly, and surely as he did exceedingly exalte the English language, in eloquence, propriety, and masculyne expressions, so he was the best judge of, and fittest to prescribe rules to poetry and poetts, of any man who had lyved with or before him. . . . His conversation was very good and with the men of most note, and he had for many yeares an extraordinary kindnesse for Mr Hyde, till he founde he betook himself to businesse, which he believed ought never to be preaferred before his company: He lyved to be very old, and till the Palsy made a deepe impression upon his body and his minde.
  Edward Hyde, Earl of Clarendon, *The Life of Edward Earl of Clarendon, written by Himself.*

Then Jonson came, instructed from the school,
To please in method, and invent by rule.
His studious patience and laborious art,
By regular approach, assail'd the heart.
Cold approbation gave the lingering bayes,
For those who durst not censure, scarce could praise.
A mortal born, he met the general doom,
But left, like Egypt's Kings, a lasting tomb.
  Samuel Johnson, *Prologue at the Opening of the Drury Lane Theatre.*

I wonder how you ever durst invay
In Satire, Epigram, or Libell-play
against the manners of the tyme, or men
in full examples of all mischiefs, when
no ill thou could so taske dwells not in thee,
and there the store house of your plotte wee see.
For thou, that hast in thee so many waies
of practizd mischief, hast begott thy bayes

in reading of they selfe, tickling the age,
stealing all equal glory from the stage,
that I confesse with like forme thou hast writt
of good and badd things, not with equall witt.
The reason is, or may be quickly showne,
the good's translation, butt the ill's thyne owne.
  Inigo Jones, *To His false friend Mr Ben Johnson*, after 1619.

What he has is immense gusto, and an intellectual, fundamentally hostile and contemptuous sense of human folly; he boasted himself a good hater, a good fighter, and a master of his craft, and he was all three.
  Desmond MacCarthy, *Humanities.*

In the rest of his Poetry, for he is not wholly Dramatic, as his Underwoods, Epigrams, etc, he is sometimes bold and strenuous, sometimes Magisterial, sometimes Lepid and full enough of conceit, and sometimes a Man, as other Men are.
  Edward Phillips, *Theatrum Poetarum.*

His lines did relish mirth, but so severe,
That as they tickled, they did wound the ear.
Well then, such virtue cannot die, though stones
Loaded with epitaphs do press his bones:
He lived to me; spite of this martyrdom,
Ben, is the self-same poet in the tomb.
    You that can aldermen new wits create,
    Know, Jonson's skeleton is laureat.
    H. Ramsay, *Upon the Death of Benjamin Jonson.*

    And everie Comedie
      He did intend
    An Errata page should be,
To show men faults and teach 'em how to mend.
    Edward Ravenscroft, *Commendatory Verses*, prefixed to Edward Howard, *The Six Days Adventure, or the New Utopia.*

The State and mens affaires are the best playes
Next yours.
  Sir John Roe, *Verse Letter To Ben Jonson*, 6 January 1604.

I can't read Ben Jonson, especially his comedies. To me he appears to move in a wide sea of glue.
  Alfred, Lord Tennyson, in *Alfred Lord Tennyson, A Memoir by His Son.*

To know Ben Jonson was in Jonson's eyes a liberal profession.
  Charles Whibley, *Edward Hyde.*

Every half quarter of an Hour a glass of Sack must be sent of an errand into his Guts, to tell his Brains

they must come up quickly, and help out with a line.
Robert Wilde, *The Benefice.*

See also Beaumont and Fletcher, Robert Browning, John Dee, Thomas Dekker, John Donne, Thomas Middleton, Shakespeare

JONSON, BENJAMIN

1597—1603 Ben Jonson's son

Rest in soft peace, and, asked, say here doth lie
Ben Jonson his best piece of poetry:
For whose sake, henceforth, all his vows be such
As what he loves may never like too much.
Ben Jonson, *On My First Son.*

JOPLIN, JANIS

1943—70 Singer

I'd rather not sing than sing quiet.
On herself, in Lillian Roxon, *Rock Encyclopedia.*

. . . Janis's dramas gave the impression of a very self-centered girl, still possessed by a need for constant reassurance — that she could sing, that she was liked, that she was, above all noticed. She worried constantly about reactions to her performances, though certain that she was destined in this world to attain some special place. 'She was a lot looser in the beginning,' Nancy Getz said, 'but still she was harsh. It was "fuck off, and if you don't like it, split".'
Myra Friedman, *Buried Alive.*

Janis became renowned — and by far too many people, loved — for her wildness, her drinking, her loveless sexual abandon and all of that gobbling frenzy that fulfilled the fantasy of the age. Everyone was sucking on it like a gargantuan leech. Her NOW was theirs. In no time, she was her raw and royal majesty, up on Mount Olympus, wrapped in her imperial lynx coat, with a bottle of Southern Comfort for a scepter and for a throne of glory, a deadly cage.
Ibid.

Perhaps, too, along with her infantilism, it was the temper of the times that increased Janis's tendency to act out in the first place and use sex as the prime arena in which she dramatized all her difficulties. In the same way that loneliness, joy, craving, and despair were highly eroticized in performance, so were the troubles that pulled at her heart acutely sexualized from day to day. The difference was that, onstage, that eroticism provided a magnificent release — for her and for her audiences. Offstage, it did little more than drag her further into the darkness of confusion.
Ibid.

Cameras played over those rugged features of hers as if she were an incredible beauty and, in her very own way, she is. Men's eyes go glassy as they think about her. Writers rape her with words as if there weren't any other way to deal with her. No one had gotten as excited about anyone for years as people did about Janis Joplin. She was a whole new experience for everyone. People had to readjust their thinking because of her. Her voice, for instance. Chicks are not supposed to sing that way, all hoarse and insistent and footstamping. They're not supposed to sound as if they're shrieking for delivery from some terrible, urgent, but not entirely unpleasant, physical pain.
Lillian Roxon, *Rock Encyclopedia.*

Janis Joplin said the forty or fifty minutes she performed on stage was like going to bed with her favorite lover. 'It's like a hundred orgasms with the man you love.'
Earl Wilson, *The Show Business Nobody Knows.*

JOSEPH (CHIEF)

circa 1840—1904 Chief of the Nez Percé

I see the whites all over the country gaining wealth, and see their desire to give us lands which are worthless. . . . The earth and myself are of one mind. The measure of the land and the measure of our bodies are the same. Say to us, if you can say it, that you were sent by the Creative Power to talk to us. Perhaps you think the Creator sent you here to dispose of us as you see fit. If I thought you were sent by the Creator I might be induced to think you had a right to dispose of me. . . . I never said the land was mine to do with as I chose. The one who has the right to dispose of it is the one who has created it. I claim a right to live on my land, and accord you the privilege to live on yours.
On himself, in T. C. McLuhan, *Touch The Earth.*

I have carried a heavy load on my back ever since I was a boy. I learned then that we were but few, while the white men were many, and that we could not hold our own with them. We were like deer. They were like grizzly bears. We had a small country. Their country was large. We were contented to let things remain as the Great Spirit Chief made them. They were not; and would change the rivers and mountains if they did not suit them.

On himself, 'An Indian's Views of Indian Affairs', in *North American Review*, 1879.

I am tired of fighting. Our chiefs are killed. Looking Glass is dead. The old men are all killed. It is the young men who say yes or no. He who led the young men is dead. The little children are freezing to death. My people, some of them, have run away to the hills and have no blankets, no food; no one knows where they are, perhaps freezing to death. I want time to look for my children and see how many of them I can find. Hear me, my chiefs, I am tired; my heart is sick and sad. From where the sun now stands, I will fight no more forever.

On himself (upon his surrender in 1877), in Merrill D. Beal, *'I Will Fight No More Forever'*.

JOWETT, BENJAMIN

1817–93 Scholar

Did you ever hear the story of a man who asked his physician whether he was not dangerously ill? 'No sir, but you are dangerously old.' So I too have come to the creaky places of life.

On himself in old age, Letter to Lady Wemyss.

Jowett, in his day, did probably more than any other single man to let some fresh air into the exhausted atmosphere of the [Oxford] common rooms, and to widen the intellectual horizons of the place. . . . He never at any time (I should think) had anything definite to teach.

H. H. Asquith, Letter to Lady Horner, 26 October 1891.

First come I; my name is Jowett.
There's no knowledge but I know it.
I am Master of this College:
What I don't know isn't knowledge.

H. C. Beeching, *The Masque of Balliol*.

See also Sir Philip Francis

JOYCE, JAMES AUGUSTINE

1882–1941 Author

My mind rejects the whole social order and Christianity — home, the recognized virtues, classes of life, and religious doctrines. . . . I cannot enter the social order except as a vagabond.

On himself, Letter to Nora Barnacle, 1904.

It is not my fault that the odor of ashpits and old weeds and offal hangs round my stories. I seriously believe that you will retard the course of civilization in Ireland by preventing the Irish people from having a good look at themselves in my nicely polished looking glass.

On himself. Letter to Grant Richards, who had abandoned plans to publish *Dubliners*, 1906.

Mr. Joyce has desophisticated language. And it is worth while remarking that no language is so sophisticated as English. It is abstracted to death. Take the word 'doubt': it gives us hardly any sensuous suggestion of hesitancy, of the necessity for choice, of static irresolution. Whereas the German 'Zweifel' does, and, in a lesser degree, the Italian 'dubitare'. Mr. Joyce recognizes how inadequate 'doubt' is to express a state of extreme uncertainty, and replaces it by 'in twosome twiminds'.

Samuel Beckett, in Sylvia Beach ed., *Our Exagmination . . . of Work in Progress*.

Shakespeare said pretty well everything, and what he left out, James Joyce, with a nudge from meself, put in.

Brendan Behan, in Sean McCann, *The Wit of Brendan Behan*.

The key to reading *Ulysses* is to treat it like a comedian would — as a sort of gag book.
Ibid.

You must not stink I am attempting to ridicul (de sac!) you or to be smart, but I am so disturb by my inhumility to onthorstand most of the impslocations constrained in your work that (although I am by nominals dump and in fact I consider myself not brilliantly ejewcatered but still of above Averroege men's tality and having maid the most of the oporto unities I kismet) I am writing you, dear mysterre Shame's Voice, to let you no how bed I feeloxerab out it all.

'Vladimir Dixon' (probably Joyce himself), Letter to 'Mister Germ's Choice', in Sylvia Beach ed., *Our Exagmination . . . of Work in Progress*.

I am inclined to think that Mr Joyce is riding his method to death.
Ford Madox Ford, *Thus to Revisit*.

Joyce is horrified and fascinated by the human body; it seems to him ritually unclean and in direct contact with all the evil in the universe, and though to some of us this seems awful tosh, it certainly helps him to get some remarkable literary effects.
E. M. Forster, review of *Ulysses*, 1926.

Ulysses is a dogged attempt to cover the universe

with mud, an inverted Victorianism, an attempt to make crossness and dirt succeed where sweetness and light failed, a simplification of the human character in the interests of Hell.

E. M. Forster, *Aspects of the Novel.*

I never got very much out of *Ulysses.* I think it's an extraordinary book, but so much of it consists of rather lengthy demonstrations of how a novel ought *not* to be written, doesn't it? He does show nearly every conceivable way it should not be written, and then goes on to show how it might be written.

Aldous Huxley, in *Paris Review.*

It is a fact of crucial significance in the history of the novel this century that James Joyce opened the first cinema in Dublin in 1909. Joyce saw very early on that film must usurp some of the prerogatives which until then had belonged almost exclusively to the novelist. . . . Film is an excellent medium for showing things, but it is very poor at taking an audience inside characters' minds, at telling it what people are thinking. Joyce saw this at once, and developed the technique of interior monologue within a few years of the appearance of the cinema.

B. S. Johnson, *Aren't You Rather Young to be Writing Your Memoirs?*

My God, what a clumsy olla putrida James Joyce is! Nothing but old fags and cabbage-stumps of quotations from the Bible and the rest, stewed in the juice of deliberate, journalistic dirty-mindedness.

D. H. Lawrence, Letter to Aldous Huxley, 15 August 1928.

The champion Penman.

Percy Wyndham Lewis, *Blasting and Bombardiering.*

In retailing the thoughts, half-thoughts, perceptions or inattentions of Bloom and Mrs Bloom, he has sunk a shaft down into the welter of nonsense which lies at the bottom of the mind, and pumping up this stuff (it is an astounding hydraulic feat) presented it as a criticism of life.

Desmond MacCarthy, *Criticism.*

Considered as a book . . . *Finnegans Wake* must be pronounced a complete fiasco.

Malcolm Muggeridge, in *Time and Tide,* 20 May 1939.

He was very spruce and nervous and chatty. Great rings upon little twitching fingers. Huge concave spectacles which flicked reflections of the lights as he moved his head like a bird, turning it with that definite insistence to the speaker as blind people do who turn to the sound of a voice. . . . He told me that a man had taken Oolissays to the Vatican and had hidden it in a prayer-book, and that it had been blessed by the Pope. He was half-amused by this and half-impressed. He saw that I would think it funny, and at the same time he did not think it wholly funny himself. My impression . . . was . . . of a very nervous and refined animal — a gazelle in a drawing-room. His blindness increases that impression. I suppose he is a real person somewhere, but I feel that I have never spent half-an-hour with anyone and been left with an impression of such brittle and vulnerable strangeness.

Harold Nicolson, Letter to Vita Sackville-West, 4 February 1934.

Ulysses . . . I rather wish I had never read it. It gives me an inferiority complex. When I read a book like that and then come back to my own work, I feel like a eunuch who has taken a course in voice production and can pass himself off fairly well as a bass or a baritone, but if you listen closely you can hear the good old squeak just the same as ever.

George Orwell, Letter to Brenda Salkeld, September 1934.

Joyce's influence in so far as I consider it sanitary, is almost exclusively Flaubert's influence, extended. That is to say Flaubert invented a sort of specific for literary diabetes. Injections of this specific into Maupassant and weaker injections into Kipling, Steve Crane, etc., prevented a good deal of diabetes (sugar in the wrong place) . . . Joyce got some of the real stuff, full strength, or in words already used: Wrote English as clean and hard as Flaubert's French.

Ezra Pound, in *English Journal* (Chicago), May 1933.

In Ireland they try to make a cat cleanly by rubbing its nose in its own filth. Mr Joyce has tried the same treatment on the human subject. I hope it may prove successful.

George Bernard Shaw, Letter to Sylvia Beach, 11 June 1921.

He was not only the greatest literary stylist of his time. He was also the only living representative of the European tradition of the artist who carries on with his creative work unaffected by the storm which breaks around him in the world outside his study.

Stephen Spender, in *Listener,* 23 January 1941.

He is a *good* writer. People like him because he is incomprehensible and anybody can understand him. But who came first, Gertrude Stein or James Joyce?

Do not forget that my first great book, *Three Lives*, was published in 1908. That was long before *Ulysses*. But Joyce *has* done *something*. His influence, however, is local.

Gertrude Stein (in conversation), in Samuel Putnam, *Paris was our Mistress*.

As for Ulysses, I *will not* look at it, *no*, NO.

Lytton Strachey, Letter to James Strachey, 7 May 1922.

If mimicry and impersonation made great literature, 'Ulysses' would be a great book. It is, I think, a great Irish performance, which in a hundred years' time will have for connoisseurs of literature an interest comparable to that of 'Euphues'.

Frank Swinnerton, *The Georgian Literary Scene*.

Experiment? God forbid! Look at the results of experiment in the case of a writer like Joyce. He started off writing very well, then you can watch his going mad with vanity. He ends up a lunatic.

Evelyn Waugh, in *Paris Review*, 1962.

Your work is an extraordinary experiment and I will go out of my way to save it from destruction or restrictive interruption. It has its believers and its following. Let them rejoice in it. To me it is a dead end.

H. G. Wells, Letter to Joyce, 23 November 1928.

Mr Joyce's indecency in *Ulysses* seems to me the conscious and calculated indecency of a desperate man who feels that in order to breathe he must break the windows. At moments, when the window is broken, he is magnificent. But what a waste of energy!

Virginia Woolf, *The Captain's Death Bed*.

My own contribution, five and sixpence, is given on condition he [T. S. Eliot] puts publicly to their proper use the first 200 pages of Ulysses. Never have I read such tosh. As for the first 2 Chapters we will let them pass, but the 3rd 4th 5th 6th — merely the scratching of pimples on the body of the bootboy at Claridges. Of course, genius *may* blaze out on page 652 but I have my doubts. And this is what Eliot worships.

Virginia Woolf, Letter to Lytton Strachey (who had written to offer his support for the Eliot Fellowship Fund), 24 August 1922.

My considered opinion, after long reflection, is that whilst in many places the effect of *Ulysses* on the reader undoubtedly is somewhat emetic, nowhere does it tend to be an aphrodisiac. *Ulysses* may, therefore, be admitted to the United States.

John M. Woolsey, US District Judge, in his judgment after the prosecution of *Ulysses* for obscenity.

I saw Joyce in Dublin; he said his mother was still alive, and it was uncertain whether she would die or not. He added 'but these things really don't matter.'

William Butler Yeats, Letter to Lady Gregory, April 1903.

A cruel playful mind like a great soft tiger cat.

William Butler Yeats, Letter to Olivia Shakespear, 8 March 1922.

See also W. H. Auden, Jane Austen, Ford Madox Ford, Aldous Huxley, D. H. Lawrence, Gertrude Stein, Lytton Strachey, Leonard Woolf

'JUNIUS', see under SIR PHILIP FRANCIS; also, EDMUND BURKE

JUXON, WILLIAM
1582–1663 Archbishop of Canterbury

One in whom nature had not omitted, but grace hath ordered, the tetrarch humour of choler, being admirably master of his pen and his passion. For his abilities, he was successively preferred by King Charles the First, Lord Bishop of Hereford and London, and for some years Lord Treasurer of England; a troublesome place in those times, it being expected that he should make *much brick* (though not altogether without yet) with very little *straw* allowed unto him.

Thomas Fuller, *The History of the Worthies of England*.

He had a perfect command of his passion, (an happines not granted to all clergymen in that age, though Privy Councillors), slow, not of speech as a defect, but to speak, out of discretion, because when speaking he plentifully paid the principal and interest of his auditors' expectation. No hands having so much money passing through them had their fingers less soiled therewith. . . . In this particular, he was happy above others of his order, that whereas many may be said in some sort to have left their Bishopricks (flying into the King's quarters for safety) he staid at home till his bishoprick left him, roused from his swan's nest at Fulham for a bird of another feather to build therein.

This reverend Prelate, Dr Juxon, then Bishop of

JUXON, WILLIAM

London, was of a meek spirit and of a solid and steddy judgment; and having addicted his first studies to the Civil Law, (from which he took his title of Doctor, tho' he afterwards took on him the Ministry) this fitted him the more for secular and state affairs. His temper and prudence wrought so upon all men, that tho' he had the two most invidious characters, both in the Ecclesiastical and Civil State; one of a Bishop, the other of a Lord Treasurer: yet neither drew envy on him; tho' the humour of the times tended to brand all great men in Employment.

Sir Philip Warwick, *Memoirs of the Reign of Charles I.*

In 1648 he had the honour and happiness, if it may

be so called, to attend K Charles I of blessed memory in his most disconsolate condition, and to administer comfort, ghostly counsel and the Sacrament to him, and to be also present with him on the Scaffold, when he was beheaded before his own door by his most rebellious subjects, to the great horrour and amazement of all the world. Afterwards this holy Bishop retired to his Mannour of *Little Compton* in *Glocestershire*, near to *Chipping Norton* in *Oxfordshire*, where he spent several years in a retired and devout condition, and now and then, for health's sake, rode a hunting with some of the neighbouring and loyal gentry.

Anthony à Wood, *Athenae Oxonienses.*

See also Seth Ward

K

KARLOFF, BORIS (WILLIAM HENRY PRATT)

1887—1969 Actor

Like the late Lon Chaney, he reached stardom with the sole assistance of the make-up man. Any face would have done as well on a big body, and any actor could have produced the short barks and guttural rumbles, the stiff, stuffed sawdust gestures, which was all his parts required of him.
  Graham Greene, reviewing *The Black Room* in *Spectator*, 20 September 1935.

See also Bela Lugosi

KAUFMAN, GEORGE S.

1889—1961 Playwright, Journalist

Over my dead body.
  On himself, a proposed epitaph, in Robert E. Drennan ed., *Wit's End*.

When I was born I owed twelve dollars.
  Ibid.

It's nice to have company when you come face to face with a blank page.
  On himself, referring to his frequent collaborations with playwrights, in Howard Teichmann, *George S. Kaufman, An Intimate Portrait*.

One day at the Round Table, Aleck Woollcott made a remark which·George Kaufman felt derided his Jewish ancestry. After defining his position to Woollcott, G.S.K. got up from his seat and said, 'I am now walking away from this table, out of the dining room, and out of this hotel.' Then surveying the group, he spotted Dorothy Parker — who was of both Jewish and Gentile parentage — and added, 'And I hope that Mrs. Parker will walk out with me — half way.'
  Robert E. Drennan, *Wit's End*.

He was like a dry cracker. Brittle.
  Edna Ferber, in Howard Teichmann, *George S. Kaufman, An Intimate Portrait*.

He would die of shame if anyone were to call him 'cultured' and he would be as unlikely to quote Shakespeare as Walter Pater would have been to talk cockney.
  Joseph Wood Krutch, *The American Drama Since 1918*.

Kaufman molded me. Kaufman gave me the walk and the talk.
  Groucho Marx, in Howard Teichmann, *George S. Kaufman, An Intimate Portrait*.

He had great integrity, George did. You never had to watch him when he was dealing.
  Harpo Marx, in *ibid*.

Kaufman has shown Americans how ridiculous some of their most cherished institutions are: their rotary clubs, their hypocritical adoration of women, their thirst for the dollar, their worship of material success. To have become successful by condemning the pet notions of his audience is an unusual accomplishment.
  Joseph Mersand, *The American Drama Since 1930*.

He was responsible for marrying very high farce with very high comedy, and with his wit, it came out satire.
  George Oppenheimer, in Howard Teichmann, *George S. Kaufman, An Intimate Portrait*.

KEAN, CHARLES JOHN

1811—68 Actor

Charles is getting on tonight, he's acting very well. I suppose that is because he is acting with me.
  Edmund Kean, attributed, in H. N. Hillebrand, *Edmund Kean*.

His tone somewhat dogmatic but I prefer him in the dining room to him on the stage.
  Henry Crabb Robinson, Diary, 17 July 1856.

KEAN, EDMUND

1787–1833 Actor

Fight for me, I have no resources in myself; mind is gone, and body is hopeless. God knows my heart. I would do, but cannot. Memory, the first of goddesses has forsaken me, and I am left without a hope but from those old resources that the public and myself are tired of. Damn, God damn ambition. The soul leaps, the body falls.

> On himself, Letter to the editor of *Star*, March 1830.

Mr Kean would seem to apply literally to his art, the lesson of Demosthenes with regard to Oratory — action, action, action. His limbs have no repose or steadiness in scenes of agitated feeling; his hands are kept in unremitting and the most rapid, convulsive, movement; seeking, as it were, a resting place in some part of his upper dress, and occasionally pressed together on the crown of his head. I have marked the process to be the same in his personation of different characters, and I think I may assert that there is no eye which a habit of this kind would not strike as untoward and incongruous. The wild groping of the fingers about the neck and breast reminded me of Dryden's conceit in one of his tragedies, of the fumbling of the tenants of the cemeteries, at the day of resurrection, for their dispersed limbs.

> 'Betterton', in Philadelphia *National Gazette*, 7 February 1821.

With . . . Byron to a private pit box to see Mr Kean in Richard. He was extremely happy; and is a very short man with a piercing black eye. 'Off with his head; so much for Buckingham,' was given thus: The instant he received the news of Buckingham being prisoner he said quickly, 'Off with his head,' and then, advancing to the front of the stage, added with a savage smile, 'So much for Buckingham'. He gave a sportive ferocity to the character, which I think it requires. His scene with Lady Anne was highly finished. His expostulation with Stanley in the North, 'What do they do in the north?' with a loud, shrill taunting interrogatory, had an extraordinary effect; and lastly, his combat with Richmond was surprising. He continued pushing with his hand after he had received his wound, and dropped his sword as if he had not lost his weapon, and showed by his vacant stare that he was struggling with the effect of the fatal blow. It was only in a sudden that death could seize, then he fell flat backwards at once.

> Lord Broughton, *Recollections of a Long Life*.

He said he always felt his part when acting with a pretty woman, and then only.

> *Ibid.*

Just returned from seeing Kean in Richard. By jove, he is a soul! Life — nature — truth — without exaggeration or diminution. Kemble's Hamlet is perfect; — but Hamlet is not Nature. Richard is a man; and Kean is Richard. Now to my own concerns.

> Lord Byron, *Journal*, 19 February 1814.

Was not Iago perfection? particularly the last look. I was *close* to him (in the orchestra), and never saw an English countenance half so expressive. I am acquainted with no *im*material sensuality so delightful as good acting.

> Lord Byron, Letter to Thomas Moore, May 1814.

Kean is original; but he copies from himself. His rapid descents from the hyper-tragic to the infra-colloquial though sometimes productive of great effect are often unreasonable. To see him act is like reading Shakespeare by flashes of lightning. I do not think him thorough-bred gentleman enough to play Othello.

> Samuel Taylor Coleridge, *Table Talk*.

Kean did not simply say the lines but physically performed them, losing himself in a part, and so rediscovering himself; and like the musical virtuosi of the period with their interpolated cadenzas, he opened up spaces between the lines for the silent play of temperament.

> Peter Conrad, in *Times Literary Supplement*, 29 August 1975.

He should not be set above Garrick, whose wide range he lacked; nor should Kemble, exponent of virtue, suffer by false comparison with the exponent of villainy. Kean's was the fierce flame of crime exultant, and the true contrast is with Irving's baleful glow of crime repentant.

> M. Willson Disher, in *Oxford Companion to the Theatre*.

Novelty will always command notice in London, and Kean's acting, happily, was a novelty on the English stage. His croaking tones — his one-two-three-hop step to the right, and his equally brusque motions to the left — his retching at the back of the stage whenever he wanted to express passion — his dead stops in the middle of sentences — his hirre hurre, hop hop hop! over all passages where sense was to be expressed, took amazingly.

> *Edinburgh Magazine*, vol. 16, 1824.

The only 'lord' he could tolerate was Lord Byron, — a fatal fancy on his part, if, as I have reason to think, the example of the poet influenced most banefully the conduct of the actor.

Thomas Colley Grattan, *Beaten Paths and Those Who Trod Them.*

We found him, as was usual after the performance of any of his principal parts, stretched on a sofa, retching violently, and throwing up blood. His face was half-washed — one side deadly pale, the other deep copper colour.

Ibid.

He presented a mixture of subdued fierceness, unsatisfied triumph, and suppressed dissipation.

Ibid.

Our highest conception of an actor is, that he shall assume the character once for all and be it throughout, and trust to this conscious sympathy for the effect produced. Mr Kean's manner of acting is, on the contrary, rather a perpetual assumption of his part, always brilliant and successful, almost always true and natural, but yet always a distinct effort in every new situation, so that the actor does not seem entirely to forget himself, or to be identified with the character. The extreme elaboration of the parts injures the broad and massy effect; the general impulse of the machine is retarded by the variety and intricacy of the movements. But why do we try this actor by an ideal theory? Who is there that will stand the same test?

William Hazlitt, 'Mr Kean's Richard', in *Morning Chronicle*, 15 and 21 February 1814.

There is in Mr Kean, an infinite variety of talent, with a certain monotony of genius.

William Hazlitt, 'Mr Kean's Duke Aranza', in *Examiner*, 10 December 1815.

Mr Kean's acting is not of the patrician order; he is one of the people, and what might be termed a *radical* performer.

William Hazlitt, 'Mr Kean as Coriolanus', in *London Magazine*, no. 11, February 1820.

One simply cannot see a man like that as the clear-eyed guider of his destiny. Beside Byron, Shelley, Coleridge, Wordsworth and Hazlitt he is a baby. Yet Fate, or the Time-spirit, or environment, or whatever you may choose to call the impulsive drift of the age in which he lived put him up beside them, so that he gave preeminent expression in his own art to ideas harmonious with theirs, and filled his niche. . . . He flashed upon the world on the twenty-sixth

of January 1814, completely formed and astonishingly new, like a bomb thrown out of the mortar of destiny.

H. N. Hillebrand, *Edmund Kean.*

It is not by his faults but by his excellencies that we measure a great man. The strength of a beam is measured by its weakest part, that of a man by his strongest. Thus estimated, Edmund Kean was incomparably the greatest actor I have seen, although even warm admirers must admit that he had many and serious defects.

George Henry Lewes, *On Actors and the Art of Acting.*

Kean was not only remarkable for the intensity of passionate expression, but for a peculiarity I have never seen so thoroughly realised by another although it is one which belongs to the truth of passion, namely, the expression of *subsiding emotion*. Although fond, far too fond, of abrupt transitions — passing from vehemence to familiarity, and mingling strong lights and shadows with Caravaggio force of unreality — nevertheless his instinct taught him what few actors are taught — that a strong emotion, after discharging itself in one massive current, continues for a time expressing itself in feebler currents.

Ibid.

One of his means of effect — sometimes one of his tricks — was to make long pauses between certain phrases. For instance, on quitting the scene, Sir Edward Mortimer has to say warningly, 'Wilford, remember!' Kean used to pause after 'Wilford,' and during the pause his face underwent a rapid succession of expressions fluently melting into each other, and all tending to one climax or threat; and then the deep tones of 'remember!' came like muttered thunder. Those spectators who were unable to catch these expressions considered the pause a mere trick; and sometimes the pauses were only tricks, but often they were subtle truths.

Ibid.

He was a real innovator. But the parts he could play were few. He had no gaiety; he could not laugh; he had no playfulness that was not as the playfulness of a panther showing her claws every moment.

Ibid.

He preys upon it as a victim, instead of hugging it to his bosom, and wearing it in his heart.

The New England Palladium, March 1821, on Kean's deficiency in 'keeping up' a character.

A rotatory movement of the hand, as if describing the revolution of a spinning jenny; multiplied slaps upon his forehead, and manual elevation of his fall of hair; repeated knocking upon his own breast, and occasional rapping at the chests of others; the opening of his ruffles, like a schoolboy run riot from the playground, and a strange indistinct groping inside of his shirt, as if in search of something uncommonly minute, filled up the round of his action, while a voice most unmusical, exerted to a harsh and painful screech, afforded the finishing touch to a Romeo decidedly the worst we ever witnessed on the London boards.
Sun, January 1815.

Mrs. Dimond offers me a place in her box tonight, whence will be seen Massinger's horrible *Sir Giles Overreach*, played by Mr Kean. If he can stretch that hideous character as he does others, quite beyond all the authors meant or wished, it will shock us too much for endurance, though in these days people do require mustard to everything.
Mrs Piozzi (Hester Lynch Thrale), Letter to Sir James Fellowes, 27 December 1816.

March 16 . . . Kean about three o'clock in the morning, ordered a hackney coach to his door, took a lighted candle, got in, and rode off. He was not heard of till the Thursday noon when they found him in his room at the theatre fast asleep wrapt up in a large white greatcoat. He then sent for a potence, some ginger etc., and said, 'Send me Lewis or the other woman. I must have a fuck, and then I shall do.' He had it. They let him sleep until about six when they awoke him, dressed him, and he acted but was not very sober. After the play we got him to supper at Sigel's lodgings and got him to a bedroom and locked him up till the morning.
James Winston, Diary, 1825.

See also William Hazlitt, W. C. Macready, Sarah Siddons

KEATON, (JOSEPH FRANK) 'BUSTER'

1895–1966 Actor

Keaton's face ranked almost with Lincoln's as an early American archetype; it was haunting, handsome, almost beautiful, yet it was irreducibly funny; he improved matters by topping it off with a deadly horizontal hat, as flat and thin as a phonograph record. One can never forget Keaton wearing it, standing erect at the prow as his little boat is being launched. The boat goes grandly down the skids and, just as grandly, straight on to the bottom.

Keaton never budges. The last you see of him, the water lifts the hat off the stoic head and it floats away.
James Agee, *Agee on Film*, vol. 1.

Keaton worked strictly for laughs, but his work came from so far inside a curious and original spirit that he achieved a great deal besides, especially in his feature-length comedies. . . . He was the only major comedian who kept sentiment almost entirely out of his work, and he brought pure physical comedy to its greatest heights. Beneath his lack of emotion he was also uninsistently sardonic; deep below that, giving a disturbing tension and grandeur to the foolishness, for those who sensed it, there was in his comedy a freezing whisper not of pathos but of melancholia. With the humor, the craftsmanship and the action there was often, besides, a fine, still and sometimes dreamlike beauty.
Ibid.

No other comedian could do as much with the deadpan. He used this great, sad, motionless face to suggest various related things: a one-track mind near the track's end of pure insanity: mulish imperturbability under the wildest of circumstances: how dead a human being can get and still be alive: an awe-inspiring sort of patience and power to endure, proper to granite but uncanny in flesh and blood. Everything that he was and did bore out this rigid face and played laughs against it. When he moved his eyes, it was like seeing them move in a statue. His short-legged body was all sudden, machine like angles, governed by a daft aplomb. When he swept a semaphorelike arm to point, you could almost hear the electrical impulse in the signal block. When he ran from a cop his transitions from accelerating walk to easy jog trot to brisk canter to headlong gallop to flogged-piston spring — always floating above this frenzy, the untroubled, untouchable face — were as distinct and as soberly in order as an automatic gearshift.
Ibid.

This was my dead-pan boy, hero of a hundred movies, Frustration's Mime, pursued, put-upon, persecuted by humans as well as objects suddenly possessed of a malevolent life and will of their own.
Paul Gallico, in Rudi Blesh, *Keaton*.

. . . A practical man, driven by this horror of the ridiculous, he is the great realist among the comedians. Yet he is a surrealist, too (perhaps surrealism has to exist beside realism). His imagination envisaged surreal happenings, and his phenomenal skills enabled him to realise his visions. Being, consciously, a realist, he justifies his visions by framing them into dreams. It is dreams in *CONVICT 13* and *SHER-*

LOCK JUNIOR which liberate the images of fantasy: the little convict bounding up and down on the hangman's elastic rope; the cinema projectionist who emerges from sleep into a dream, then enters that other dream which is the cinema screen.
David Robinson, *Buster Keaton*.

Keaton's greatest creation, of course, was himself. He appeared in many different roles, father and son, millionaire and bum, halfwit and scholar, cowhand and stockbroker, fugitive and man-about-town, ardent lover and oppressed husband. He was a fine and conscientious actor, and gave all these characters their own validity. Yet ultimately they all fuse into one figure, a small, solitary animal with a face of other-worldly beauty and great melancholy unsmiling eyes that gaze unflinchingly outwards upon a world which must always dwarf him, but cannot diminish him; because behind those eyes there is a soul.
Ibid.

KEATS, JOHN

1795—1821 Poet

When I have fears that I may cease to be
  Before my pen has glean'd my teeming brain,
Before high-piled books, in charactery,
  Hold like rich garners the full ripen'd grain;
When I behold, upon the night's starr'd face,
  Huge cloudy symbols of a high romance,
And think that I may never live to trace
  Their shadows, with the magic hand of chance;
And when I feel, fair creature of an hour,
  That I shall never look upon thee more,
Never have relish in the faery power
  Of unreflecting love; — then on the shore
Of the wide world I stand alone, and think
Till love and fame to nothingness do sink.
  On himself, *Sonnet*.

I never wrote one single Line of Poetry with the least Shadow of public thought.
  On himself, Letter to J. H. Reynolds, 9 April 1818.

I think I shall be among the English Poets after my death.
  On himself, Letter to George and Georgiana Keats, October 1818.

I would sooner fail than not be among the greatest.
  On himself, Letter to James Hessey, 9 October 1818.

I have two luxuries to brood over in my walks, your Loveliness and the hour of my death. O that I could have possession of them both in the same minute.
  On himself, Letter to Fanny Brawne, July 1819.

Give me books, fruit, french wine and fine weather and a little music out of doors, played by somebody I do not know.
  On himself, Letter to Fanny Brawne, 29 August 1819.

This grave contains all that was mortal of a young English poet, who, on his death bed, in the bitterness of his heart at the malicious power of his enemies, desired these words to be graven on his tombstone, 'Here lies one whose name was writ in water.'
  Epitaph, on his tombstone in Rome.

To exalt into greatness one whose achievement was actually that of an often delightful, if often awkward, decorative poet may have . . . harmful consequences. Any presumption that Keats might in time have become a major artist is cast in doubt by the fact that it is unpromising theories about poetry that derive from defects of character, quite as much as bad influences and the results of illness, which vitiate his existing work.
  Kingsley Amis, *What Became of Jane Austen?*

What harm he has done in English Poetry. As Browning is a man with a moderate gift passionately desiring movement and fulness, and obtaining but a confused multitudinousness, so Keats with a very high gift, is yet also consumed with this desire: and cannot produce the truly living and moving, as his conscience keeps telling him. They will not be patient neither understand that they must begin with an Idea of the world in order not to be prevailed over by the world's multitudinousness: or if they cannot get that, at least with isolated ideas: and all other things shall (perhaps) be added unto them.
  Matthew Arnold, Letter to A. H. Clough, 1848—9.

  And Keats the real
Adonis with the hymeneal
Fresh vernal buds half sunk between
His youthful curls, kissed straight and sheen
In his Rome-grave, by Venus queen.
  Elizabeth Barrett Browning, *A Vision of Poets*.

John Keats, who was kill'd off by one critique,
  Just as he really promised something great,
If not intelligible, without Greek
  Contrived to talk about the Gods of late,
Much as they might have been supposed to speak.
  Poor fellow! His was an untoward fate;

'Tis strange the mind, that very fiery particle,
Should let itself be snuff'd out by an article.
   Lord Byron, *Don Juan*, canto xi.

A tadpole of the Lakes.
   Lord Byron, Journal, 15 March 1820.

Johnny Keats's *piss-a-bed* poetry.
   Lord Byron, Letter to John Murray, 12 October 1820.

Such writing is a sort of mental masturbation — he is always f--gg--g his *Imagination*. I don't mean he is *indecent*, but viciously soliciting his own ideas into a state, which is neither poetry nor any thing else but a Bedlam vision produced by raw pork and opium.
   Ibid., 9 November 1820.

'Who killed John Keats?'
   'I', says the Quarterly,
   So savage and Tartarly;
''Twas one of my feats.'

'Who shot the arrow?'
   'The poet-priest Milman
   (So ready to kill man),
Or Southey or Barrow.'
   Ibid., 30 July 1821.

Almost any young gentleman with a sweet tooth might be expected to write such things. *Isabella* might have been written by a seamstress who had eaten something too rich for supper and slept upon her back.
   Jane Welsh Carlyle, to Robert Browning, in William Allingham, Diary.

Keats is a miserable creature, hungering after sweets which he can't get; going about saying, 'I am so hungry; I should so like something pleasant!'
   Thomas Carlyle, in Wemyss Reid, *Life, Letters, and Friendships of R. M. Milnes.*

I began on our friend Keats new Vol — find the same fine flowers spread if I can express myself in the wilderness of poetry — for he launches on the sea without compass — & mounts pegasus without saddle or bridle as usual & if those cursd critics coud be shood out of fashion with their rule & compass & cease from making readers believe a Sonnet cannot be a Sonnet unless it be precisely 14 lines & a long poem as such unless one first sits down to wiredraw out regular argument & then plod after it in a regular manner the same as Taylor cuts out a coat for the carcase — I say then he may push off first rate — but he is a child of nature warm and wild.
   John Clare, Letter to James Hessey, 4 July 1820.

It is not, we say, that the author has not powers of language, rays of fancy, and gleams of genius — he has all these; but he is unhappily a disciple of the new school of what has been somewhere called Cockney poetry; which may be defined to consist of the most incongruous ideas in the most uncouth language. . . . This author is a copyist of Mr [Leigh] Hunt, but he is more unintelligible, almost as rugged, twice as diffuse, and ten times more tiresome and absurd than his prototype.
   J. W. Croker, in *Quarterly Review*, April 1818.

Keats has written many beautiful passages, but the general character of his poetry cannot be too much condemned — beyond all other injurious to a taste not yet formed. It is 'sicklied o'er with the very palest cast of thought', & at best resembles one of those beauties who fed upon rose-leaves instead of wholesome flesh, fish, & fowl.
   George Darley, Letter to Miss Darley, 9 January 1842.

Mr KEATS is also dead. He gave the greatest promise of genius of any poet of his day. He displayed extreme tenderness, beauty, originality, and delicacy of fancy; all he wanted was manly strength and fortitude to reject the temptations of singularity in sentiment and expression. Some of his shorter and later pieces are, however, as free from faults as they are full of beauties.
   William Hazlitt, *Select British Poets.*

In what other English poet (however superior to him in other respects) are you so *certain* of never opening a page without lighting upon the loveliest imagery and the most eloquent expressions? Name one. Compare any succession of their pages at random, and see if the young poet is not sure to present his stock of beauty; crude it may be, in many instances; too indiscriminate in general; never, perhaps, thoroughly perfect in cultivation; but there it is, exquisite of its kind, and filling envy with despair.
   Leigh Hunt, *Imagination and Fancy.*

Keats, at a time when the phrase had not yet been invented, practised the theory of art for art's sake. He is the type, not of the poet, but of the artist. He was not a great personality, his work comes to us as a greater thing than his personality. When we read his verse, we think of the verse, not of John Keats.
   F. R. Leavis, *Revaluation.*

Keats caught cold in training for a genius, and, after a lingering illness, died. . . . But death, even the death of the radically presumptuous profligate, is a serious thing; and as we believe that Keats was made presumptuous chiefly by the treacherous puffing of his cockney fellow gossips, and profligate in his poems merely to make them saleable, we regret that he did not live long enough to acquire common sense, and abjure the pestilent and perfidious gang who betrayed his weakness to the grave, and are now panegyrising his memory into contempt.

Literary Gazette and Journal of Belles Lettres,
Review of Shelley's *Adonais,* 8 December 1821.

We venture to make one small prophecy, that his bookseller will not a second time venture £50 upon any thing he can write. It is a better and a wiser thing to be a starved apothecary than a starved poet; so back to the shop Mr John, back to 'plasters, pills, and ointment boxes', &c. But, for Heaven's sake, young Sangrado, be a little more sparing of extenuatives and soporifics in your practice than you have been in your poetry.

J. G. Lockhart, in *Blackwood's Magazine,* August 1818.

The genius of the lamented person to whose memory I have dedicated these unworthy verses, was not less delicate and fragile than it was beautiful; and where canker-worms abound, what wonder, if it's young flower was blighted in the bud? The savage criticism on his *Endymion,* which appeared in the *Quarterly Review,* produced the most violent effect on his susceptible mind; the agitation thus originated ended in the rupture of a blood-vessel in the lungs; a rapid consumption ensued, and the succeeding acknowledgements from more candid critics, of the true greatness of his powers, were ineffectual to heal the wound thus wantonly inflicted.

Percy Bysshe Shelley, Preface to *Adonais.*

I weep for Adonais — he is dead!
O, weep for Adonais! though our tears
Thaw not the frost which binds so dear a head!
And thou, sad Hour, selected from all years
To mourn our loss, rouse thy obscure compeers,
And teach them thine own sorrow, say: 'With me
Died Adonais; till the Future dares
Forget the Past, his fate and fame shall be
An echo and a light unto eternity!'

P. B. Shelley, *Adonais.*

Yet thou hast won the gift Tithonus missed:
Never to feel the pain of growing old,
  Nor lose the blissful sight of beauty's truth,
But with the ardent lips Urania kissed
  To breathe thy song, and, ere thy heart grew cold,
    Become the Poet of Immortal Youth.

Henry Van Dyke, *Keats.*

It is in Keats that one observes the beginning of the artistic renaissance of England. Byron was a rebel, and Shelley a dreamer; but in the calmness and clearness of his vision, his self-control, his unerring sense of beauty, and his recognition of a separate realm for the imagination, Keats was the pure and serene artist, the forerunner of the Pre-Raphaelite school.

Oscar Wilde, reported in *New York World,* 1882.

His art is happy, but who knows his mind?
I see a schoolboy when I think of him,
With face and nose pressed to a sweet-shop window,
For certainly he sank into his grave
His senses and his heart unsatisfied,
And made — being poor, ailing and ignorant,
Shut out from all the luxury of the world,
The coarse-bred son of a livery-stable keeper —
Luxuriant song.

William Butler Yeats, *Ego Dominus Tuus.*

See also Rupert Brooke, Samuel Taylor Coleridge, Gerard Manley Hopkins, Rudyard Kipling, James Wolfe, William Butler Yeats

KELVIN, LORD, see under THOMSON, WILLIAM

KEMBLE, JOHN PHILIP

1757—1823 Actor

Lo, Kemble comes, the Euclid of the stage;
Who moves in given angles, squares a start,
And blows his Roman beak by rules of art;
Writhes with a grace to agony unknown,
And gallops half an octave in a groan.

Anon., *The Thespiad,* 1809.

Hamlet, whose sensibility is so keenly alive, that every trifle administers fresh pangs to his distress, was converted by Mr Kemble into a dry scolastic personage, uttering wise saws with a sneer, and delivering his ironies with a spruce air and a smart tone, such as is used by forward boys and girls on their introduction into the world, when they wish to excite attention to their abortive bon-mots and unfledged sarcasms.

Anon., in *Examiner,* 1814.

The Garrick school was all *rapidity* and *Passion,* while the Kemble school was so full of *paw* and *pause,* that, at first, the performers, thinking their new competitors had either lost their cues, or forgotten their parts, used frequently to prompt them.

Ann Crawford, *circa* 1785, in Frederick Reynolds, *Life and Times of Frederick Reynolds.*

Mr Kemble's pauses are I believe, very judicious, though to many they appeared long. The actor must take into the account the tone of the audience; for the rule of acting, in conformity to the rule of speaking, must not contradict the general sense. A player cannot, with safety to himself, affect to appear wiser than his judges.

Thomas Davies, *Dramatic Miscellanies.*

The very tone of Mr Kemble's voice has something retrospective in it — it is an echo of the past.

William Hazlitt, 'Mr Kean's Macbeth', in *Champion*, 13 November 1814.

He is . . . as shy of committing himself with nature, as a maid is of committing herself with a lover. All the proper forms and ceremonies must be complied with, before 'they two can be made one flesh'. Mr Kemble sacrifices too much to decorum. He is chiefly afraid of being contaminated by too close an identity with the characters he represents. This is the greatest vice in an actor, who ought never to *bilk* his part. He endeavours to raise Nature to the dignity of his own person and demeanour, and declines with a graceful smile and a wave of the hand, the ordinary services she might do him.

William Hazlitt, 'Mr Kemble's Sir Giles Over-reach', in *Examiner*, 5 May 1816.

He is the very still-life and statuary of the stage; a perfect figure of a man; a petrification of sentiment, that heaves no sigh and sheds no tear; an icicle upon the bust of Tragedy.

Ibid.

In that prodigious prosing paper, the *Times*, which seems to be written as well as printed by a steam engine, Mr Kemble is compared to the ruin of a magnificent temple, in which the divinity still resides. This is not the case. The temple is unimpaired; but the divinity is sometimes from home.

William Hazlitt, on Kemble as Macbeth, 'Mrs Siddons', in *Examiner*, 16 June 1816.

We feel more respect for John Kemble in a plain coat than for Lord Chancellor on the woolsack. He is surrounded to our eyes with a greater number of imposing recollections: he is a more reverend piece of formality; a more complicated tissue of costume. We do not know whether to look upon this accomplished actor as Pierre, or King John, or Coriolanus, or Cato, or Leontes, or the Stranger. But we see in him a stately hieroglyphic of humanity; a living monument of departed greatness; a sombre comment on the rise and fall of kings.

William Hazlitt, 'On Actors and Acting', in *Examiner*, 5 January 1817.

I have known him make an eternal groan upon the interjection *Oh!* as if he were determined to show that his misery had not affected his lungs; and to represent an energetical address he has kept so continual a jerking and nodding of the head, that at last, if he represented anything at all, it could be nothing but St Vitus' Dance. By this study of nonentities it would appear that he never pulls out his handkerchief without a design upon the audience, that he has as much thought in making a step as making a speech, in short that his very finger is eloquent and that nothing means something. . . . He does not present one the idea of a man who grasps with the force of genius, but of one who overcomes by the toil of attention.

Leigh Hunt, *Critical Essays on the Performers of the London Theatres*, 1807.

Mr Kemble insists that the word *rode* should be *rod*, *beard* is metamorphosed into *bird*, he never *pierces* the heart, but *purses* it, and *virtue* and *merchant* become in the dialogue of the kitchen *varchue* and *marchant*. The strong syllable *er* appears to be an abomination, and is never allowed utterance; Pope says

To err is human, to forgive divine

but Mr Kemble will not consent to this, he says

To air is human —

making the moralist say that it is the nature of man to dry his clean shirt or to take a walk. . . .

Ibid.

Kemble was missed by those who had been used to him; but he was missed rather as a picture than a man.

Leigh Hunt, 'The Death of Elliston,' in *Tatler*, 10 July 1831.

He was no more to be compared to his sister than stone is to flesh and blood.

Leigh Hunt, *Autobiography.*

Mr Kemble must be struck to the heart's core, or not at all: he must be wounded to the soul with grief despair or madness.

Mrs Inchbald, in *New British Theatre with Critical Remarks by Mrs Inchbald.*

No man could deliver brilliant dialogue — the dialogue of Congreve or Wycherley — because none understood it half so well as John Kemble. His *Valentine*, in 'Love for Love', was to my recollection, faultless. He flagged sometimes in the intervals of tragic passion; he would slumber over the level parts of an heroic character; his *Macbeth* has been known to nod. But he always seemed to me to be particularly alive to pointed and witty dialogue. The relaxing levities of tragedy have not been touched by any since him. The playful court-bred spirit in which he condescended to the players in *Hamlet*, the sportive relief which he threw into the darker shades of *Richard*, disappeared with him. He had his sluggish moods, his torpors, but they were the halting-stones and resting-places of his tragedy, politic savings and restings of the breath, husbandry of the lungs, whose nature pointed him to be an economist, rather, I think, than errors of Judgement.

    Charles Lamb, *On the Artificial Comedy of the Last Century.*

One night, when John Kemble was performing at some country theatre one of his most favourite parts, he was much interrupted from time to time, by the squalling of a young child in one of the galleries. At length, angered by this rival performance, Kemble walked with solemn step to the front of the stage, and addressing the audience in his most tragic tones, said, 'Ladies and Gentlemen, unless the play is stopped, the child cannot possibly go on.'

    Tom Moore, *Memoirs, Journal and Correspondence.*

In KEMBLE, behold all the shadows of learning,
An eye that's expressive, a mind half discerning;
Tho' the sense of the scene in its quickness must
                       center,
Yet pause must ensue, ere the hero will enter:
Well skill'd in the family secrets of mumming,
'Tis a trick that implies a great actor is coming:
But the time that's prescrib'd for the art being out,
Then on rushes John in an outrageous rout,
With a nice painted face, and a complacent grin,
Like an excellent sign to an ill-manag'd inn;
With the lineal brow, heavy, dismal, and murky,
And shoulders compress'd, like an over-trus'd
                       turkey.
    Yet he has his merits, tho' crude and confin'd,
The faint sickly rays of — a half letter'd mind.

    Anthony Pasquin (John Williams), *The Children of Thespis.*

When Kemble was living at Lausanne, he used to feel rather jealous of Mont Blanc; he disliked to hear people always asking, 'How does Mont Blanc look this morning?'

    Samuel Rogers, *Table Talk.*

See also David Garrick, Edmund Kean, W. C. Macready

KEMPENFELT, RICHARD

1718–82 Naval Commander

Toll for the brave!

Brave Kempenfelt is gone;
His last sea-fight is fought,
His work of glory done.

    William Cowper, *Loss of the Royal George.*

His sword was in its sheath,
His fingers held the pen,
When Kempenfelt went down
With twice four hundred men.

    Ibid.

KENNEDY, JOHN FITZGERALD

1917–63 Thirty-Fifth United States President

I guess he [Harry S. Truman] will apologize for calling me an S.O.B. and I will apologize for being one.

    On himself, in Victor Lasky, *J.F.K.: The Man and the Myth.*

It has recently been observed that whether I serve one or two terms in the Presidency, I will find myself at the end of that period at what might be called an awkward age — too old to begin a new career and too young to write my memoirs.

    On himself, in Leon A. Harris, *The Fine Art of Political Wit.*

An idealist without illusions.

    On himself, in Arthur M. Schlesinger Jr, *A Thousand Days, John F. Kennedy in the White House.*

It's really quite a Roman administration — great dinners, great tours, great redecoration. Kennedy is undoubtedly talented, but ever since he was a tiny boy he's had one idea — succeeding. His speaking style is pseudo-Roman: 'Ask not what your country can do for you. . . .' Why not say, 'Don't ask . . .'? 'Ask not . . .' is the style of a man playing the role of being President, not of a man being President.

    Herb Gold, in *New York Post*, 1 June 1962.

He was the most perceptive of critics, he could pick out a sentence or a paragraph and see its weakness. Even though he might not have understood the analytic basis for its weakness, he had a feel for it, and this was uncanny.

    Walter Heller, in Arthur M. Schlesinger Jr, *A Thousand Days, John F. Kennedy in the White House.*

Under Kennedy, nothing of major consequence bearing his stamp made much headway in the early years of the New Frontier. Seldom before in United States history has any President been so consistently rebuffed by the legislators — not of the Opposition

party, but of both parties. The hostility to Kennedy's 'must' proposals was not partisan. It was bipartisan.
Victor Lasky, *J.F.K.: The Man and the Myth.*

There is something very eighteenth century about this young man. He is always on his toes during our discussion. But in the evening there will be music and wine and pretty women.
Harold Macmillan, in *New York Journal-American*, 21 January 1962.

[Kennedy had] the wisdom of a man who senses death within him and gambles that he can cure it by risking his life.
Norman Mailer, in Arthur M. Schlesinger Jr, *A Thousand Days, John F. Kennedy in the White House.*

Kennedy, in the supercilious arrogance which Harvard inculcates in lace-curtain Irish, doggedly mispronounced ordinary words. . . . This was the true Rooseveltian contempt for the common man. He seems afraid to be taken for a valid American.
Westbrook Pegler, *New York Journal-American*, 7 October 1960.

There is a lot of he-coon ingrained in the hide of the new President. He strikes me as practically cold all the way, with a hard blue eye on Valhalla.
Robert Ruark, *New York World Telegram and Sun*, 21 December 1960.

It is said the President is willing to laugh at himself. That is fine. But when is he going to extend that privilege to us?
Mort Sahl, in Victor Lasky, *J.F.K.: The Man and the Myth.*

. . . an historian manqué. The historical mind can be analytical, or it can be romantic. The best historians are both, Kennedy among them.
Arthur M. Schlesinger Jr, *A Thousand Days, John F. Kennedy in the White House.*

. . . a skeptical mind, a laconic tongue, enormous personal charm, an agreeable disdain for the rituals of Massachusetts politics and a detachment from the niceties of American liberalism.
Ibid.

He felt neither uplifted nor weighed down by power. He enjoyed the Presidency, thinking not of its power but its opportunities, and he was sobered by the Presidency, thinking not of its power but its obligations. He was a strong President primarily because he was a strong person.
Theodore Sorenson, *Kennedy.*

. . . perhaps the truth is that in some ways John Fitzgerald Kennedy died just in time. He died in time to be remembered as he would like to be remembered, as ever-young, still victorious, struck down undefeated, with almost all the potentates and rulers of mankind, friend and foe, come to mourn at his bier. For somehow one has the feeling that in the tangled dramaturgy of events, this sudden assassination was for the author the only satisfactory way out. The Kennedy Administration was approaching an impasse, certainly at home, quite possibly abroad, from which there seemed no escape.
I. F. Stone, 'We All Had A Finger On That Trigger', in Neil Middleton ed., *The Best of I. F. Stone.*

The liberals like his rhetoric and the conservatives like his inaction.
Norman Thomas, in Murray B. Seidler, *Norman Thomas, Respectable Rebel.*

. . . a great believer in the doctrine that politics is the science of the possible . . . his low estimate of the possible has left him pretty much a captive to the conservatives.
Norman Thomas, in *New America*, 6 October 1961.

The intellectual playboy was not, after all, another F.D.R. It was not necessary to fear him and might be risky to follow him. Since a leader requires, above all, the respect of his followers, in losing at the outset the essential respect of the Eighty-seventh Congress, John Kennedy had lost whatever chance he had had to remake his country.
Tom Wicker, *J.F.K. and L.B.J. The Influence of Personality Upon Politics.*

See also Robert F. Kennedy, Adlai Stevenson

KENNEDY, ROBERT FRANCIS
1925–68 Politician

I was the seventh of nine children. And when you come from that far down, you have to struggle to survive.
On himself, in B. G. Clinch, *The Kennedy Neurosis.*

He was that kind of a terrier of a man.
McGeorge Bundy, in George Plimpton ed., *Interviews by Jean Stein, American Journey: The Life and Times of Robert Kennedy.*

It was impossible to watch Robert Kennedy among the mobs in the streets in 1968, without realising that most of the people who surged around him would not have been in the least surprised if he had walked upon the waters.
Henry Fairlie, *The Kennedy Promise, The Politics of Expectation.*

That was the Kennedy way. You bit off more than you could chew, and then you chewed it.
Gerald Gardner, *Robert Kennedy in New York.*

There were several qualities which set him apart from others in office. The first was total confidence in his relationship with the President. The second was an almost absolute insistence on being well and honestly briefed. The third was a capacity, indeed an instinct, to see world events not so much in terms of a great global chess game, but in human terms. As such he retained his commonsense, it was at least as strong as his ideology, (when others were talking about a surgical air strike against Cuba during the missile crisis, he said very simply he did not want his brother to be Tojo of the 1960's). Out of all of this came the final characteristic, the capacity to grow, change and to admit error.
David Halberstam, *The Best and the Brightest.*

. . . the highest-ranking withdrawn adolescent since Alexander Hamilton in 1794.
Murray Kempton, in 'Bobby: To Be or Not to Be', in *Newsweek*, 29 January 1968.

I see Jack in older years as the nice rosy-faced old Irishman with the clay pipe in his mouth, a rather nice broth of a boy. Not Bobby. Bobby could have been a revolutionary priest.
Alice Roosevelt Longworth, in George Plimpton ed., *Interviews by Jean Stein, American Journey: The Life and Times of Robert Kennedy.*

His death seemed like the death of one's own adolescence. It's partly his character and something athletic about him, which is typical of school boys; he's very much sort of Massachusetts Eastern shore, he's almost the Eastern Seaboard boy.
Robert Lowell, in *ibid.*

He is an active principle. . . . Something compassionate, something witty, has come into the face. Something of sinew.
Norman Mailer, in Arthur M. Schlesinger Jr, *A Thousand Days, John F. Kennedy in the White House.*

It is the conjunction of moral certainty about right and wrong with calculated opportunism which accounts for Kennedy's reputation for ruthlessness. He gives the impression that personal success and the triumph of right are interchangeable.
Hans J. Morgenthau, in N. G. Clinch, *The Kennedy Neurosis.*

He had an existential dimension. He defined and created himself in action, and learned about everything from experience. His end was always unknown. He dared death repeatedly. He was preoccupied with suffering and despair. When his brother died, he passed through a night of dread, and learned about the absurd.
Jack Newfield, in Henry Fairlie, *The Kennedy Promise, The Politics of Expectation.*

. . . he was fundamentally a hack, but he could be awed by the radicals.
Robert Scheer, in George Plimpton ed., *Interviews by Jean Stein, American Journey: The Life and Times of Robert Kennedy.*

His obvious characteristics are energy, vindictiveness, and simple mindedness about human motives which may yet bring him down. To Bobby the world is black or white. Them and Us. He has none of his brother's human ease or charity.
Gore Vidal, March 1963, in Margaret Laing, *Robert Kennedy.*

KENT, ROCKWELL

1882—1971 Artist

Of my own drawings, prints and paintings there is little I would say. They must stand on their own feet, pretending to be nothing but just what in fact they are: my own attempts to show in line, or paint on canvas how beautiful I've found the world to be. If to the viewer's eyes *my* world appears less beautiful than his, I'm to be pitied and the viewer praised.
On himself, in *Rockwell Kent: The Early Years.*

So beautiful to me is the 'Almighty's' world and all the beings He has made to live in it that despite 'His' stern injunction against the making of 'graven images' I have become so inveterate a maker of them as to be termed an Artist.
Ibid.

Kent has looked about him with a spirit of youth and fighting strength. He wastes no despair over the debacle of civilization. He ignores this parasitic disease that has hecked and stunted so many lives and turns with gusto toward the earth which still remains and those men who still inhabit the earth itself. His view of stripped and simple forms of earth, rock, sea and air shows the enthusiasm of the anatomist for bone and muscle and the passion of the lover for beloved flesh. He regards earth as an organic thing of strong living body, whose limbs are mountains and hillslopes, whose natural habitation is clear air and moving water. He draws earth as another might draw the exciting and desirable strong body of a man or woman. His earth is essentially a naked savage earth living out of doors, not so much a cruel and terrifying savage as a wild and free one.

Grant H. Code, in *Demcourier*, 1937.

Rockwell Kent is probably the most versatile man alive. Now that I have written this and have remembered Kent's activities, the sentence looks like an understatement. He is so multiple a person as to be multifarious; sometimes (in spite of the physical evidence) I suspect he is not a person at all, but an Organization — possibly The Rockwell Kent Joint and Associated Enterprises, Inc. I have known him as a painter, pamphleteer, poet (in private), politician (a poor one), propagandist, lecturer, explorer, architect (he redesigned my home in the Adirondacks), grave-digger, farmer, illustrator, Great Dane-breeder, type-designer, xylographer ('wood-engraver' to the uninitiated), friend, and general stimulator. In all these capacities he has been publicized; he has even attained legendary proportions.

Louis Untermeyer, 'Kent — the Writer', in *Demcourier*, 1937.

. . . Rockwell Kent, the painter, is essentially a contemplative observer and interpreter of Nature's grand design, in which Man, if he appears at all, is a tiny symbol subsumed to the rhythm and muted drama of the landscape.

Richard V. West, in *Rockwell Kent: The Early Years*.

KENT, WILLIAM

1686–1748 Architect

William Kent was one of those generally accomplished persons who can do everything up to a certain point, and nothing well.

Sir Reginald Blomfield, *A History of Renaissance Architecture in England 1500–1800*.

Burlington unbyass'd knows thy worth;
His judgement in thy master-strokes can trace
Titian's strong fire and Guido's softer grace;
But, oh consider, e'er thy works appear,
Canst thou unhurt the tongue of envy hear?
John Gay, *Epistle to Paul Methuen*.

A certain pedestrianism, as of one who moves slowly with a heavy tread, may debar Kent from the name of genius, but his were among the most varied and solemn talents of our race.

Sacheverell Sitwell, *British Architects and Craftsmen*.

He was not a thinker; he was only a second-rate artist with a well-developed sense of decoration.

J. Summerson, *Architecture in Britain 1530–1830*.

Mahomet imagined an Elysium, but Kent created many.

Horace Walpole, *Anecdotes of Painters in England*.

Kent leaped the fence, and saw that all Nature was a garden.

Horace Walpole, *On Modern Gardening*.

Mr. Kent's passion, clumps — that is, sticking a dozen trees here and there till a lawn looks like a ten of spades.

Horace Walpole, Letter to Sir Horace Mann, 20 June 1743.

See also Robert Adam, John Vanbrugh.

KERN, JEROME DAVID

1885–1945 Composer

I am trying to do something for the future of American music, which today has no class whatsoever and is mere barbaric mouthing.

On himself, Letter to *New York Times*, 1920.

Who is this Jerome Kern whose music towers in an Eiffel way above the average primitive hurdy-gurdy accompaniment of the present-day musical comedy?

Alan Dale, in David Ewen, *Great Men of America's Popular Song*.

A small, amicable, quiet man, with tremendous stores of nervous energy, Kern wore horn-rimmed glasses, smoked constantly, poured forth hundreds of facile tunes with a radio blaring in his ears, and modestly called himself a dull fellow with little talent and lots of luck.

Wesley Towner, in Max Wilk, *They're Playing Our Song*.

KEROUAC, (JEAN LOUIS) JACK

1922—69 Author

My work comprises one vast book like Proust's *Remembrance of Things Past*, except that my remembrances are written on the run instead of afterwards in a sickbed.
    On himself, in Bernard Duffey, 'Jack Kerouac', in Joseph J. Waldemeir ed., *Recent American Fiction*.

He was a man whose life was directed by what he felt under his skin, not inside his head.
    Ann Charters, *Kerouac*.

Kerouac couldn't join forces with the anarchist radicals or the Liberal Left, and he couldn't attend the conservatives' fund-raising dinner or contribute beyond his taxes to the bureaucracy of the paper-shufflers, so he felt himself caught in the middle. There was only one solution, to drop out in the great American tradition of Thoreau, Mark Twain and Daniel Boone.
    Ibid.

As the man who'd thought up the term 'beat generation', Kerouac insisted that he alone understood it. It meant 'beatific', trying to be in a state of beatitude, like St. Francis, trying to love all life, being utterly sincere and kind and cultivating 'joy of heart'.
    Ibid.

Kerouac . . . tried LSD only once. This was with Timothy Leary at Harvard in January 1961. After this experience with LSD Kerouac was sure it had been introduced into America by the Russians as part of a plot to weaken the country.
    Ibid.

. . . American lonely Prose Trumpeter of drunken
                    Buddha Sacred Heart.
    Allen Ginsberg, in Ann Charters, *Kerouac*.

A candid kid, Kerouac at times stumbles on some good details about hitch-hiking and turns of phrase about his discontents, though much sinks under sophomoric 'real straight talk about souls' and the indiscriminate reportage about the gang.
    Kingsley Widmer, *The Literary Rebel*.

Yet, of course, there appears some charm in childishness, and intermittently Kerouac's kidworld opens into some direct and suggestive responsiveness of a rebel on the road, Junior division.
    Ibid.

See also Joseph McCarthy

KEROUAILLE, LOUISE RENÉE DE, DUCHESS OF PORTSMOUTH AND AUBIGNY

1649—1734 Mistress to Charles II

Portsmouth, that pocky bitch
    A damn'd Papistical drab
An ugly deform'd witch
    Eaten up with the mange and scab

This French hag's pocky bum
    So powerful is of late
Although its both blind and dumb
    It rules both Church and State.
    Anon., *A Satire*, 1680.

Lowly born and meanly bred,
Yet of this nation is the head;
For half Whitehall make her their court,
Though the other half make her their sport.
Monmouth's tower, Jeffrey's advance,
Foe to England, spy to France,
False and Foolish, proud and bold,
Ugly, as you see, and old;
In a word, her mighty Grace
Is whore in all things but her face.
    Anon., 1682.

Following his Majestie this morning through the Gallerie, I went (with the few who attended him) into the Dutchesse of Portsmouth's dressing roome, within her bed-chamber, where she was in her morning loose garment, her maides combing her, newly out of her bed: His Majestie and the Gallants standing about her: but that which ingag'd my curiositie, was the rich and splendid furniture of this woman's Appartment, now twice or thrice, puld down and rebuilt, to satisfie her prodigal & expensive pleasures, whilst her Majestie dos not exceede, some gentlemens ladies furniture and accomodation. . . . Lord what contentment can there be in the riches and splendor of this world, purchas'd with vice and dishonor.
    John Evelyn, Diary, 4 October 1683.

. . . a very fine woman she was, but most think she was sent on purpose to ensnare the king, who most readily ran into toils of that sort.
    Sir John Reresby, *Memoirs*.

The last especially was quite out of the Definition of an ordinary Mistress: the Causes and the Manner of her first being introduced were very different. A very peculiar Distinction was spoken of, some extraordinary Solemnities that might Dignify, though not sanctify, her function. Her Chamber was the true Cabinet Council. The King did always by his Councils, as he did sometimes by his Meals; he sat down out of form, with the *Queen*, but he supped *below stairs*.

    George Savile, Marquis of Halifax, *A Character of King Charles the Second*.

See also Nell Gwyn, Barbara Villiers

KEYNES, JOHN MAYNARD, BARON

1883—1946 Economist

I work for a Government I despise for ends I think criminal.

    On himself at the Treasury, Letter to Duncan Grant, December 1917.

I was a voice crying in the wilderness and had, therefore, to cry loudly. . . .

    On himself, on Reparations, Letter to Professor Calvin Hoover, 6 December 1945.

. . . in conversation when Keynes was present there was never any point in saying anything because he always thought of a better remark than yours before you had time to think of it. His wit was shattering and his capacity for rudeness was unequalled. But he was completely disinterested, bore no malice however fierce the controversy, and was so charming that even those wounded could not bear a grudge.

    Anon., Obituary article in *New Statesman*, 27 April 1946.

In the highest degree he possessed that ingenuity which turns commonplace into paradoxes and paradoxes into truisms, which discovers — or invents — similarities and differences, and associates disparate ideas — that gift of amusing and surprising with which very clever people, and only very clever, can by conversation give a peculiar relish to life.

    Clive Bell, *Old Friends*.

Keynes is the Treasury man in Paris — clear headed, self confident, with an unerring memory and unsurpassable digestion. But while he is one of the most influential men behind the scenes . . . he looks at large political problems too much from the aspect of currency and exchange; . . . in large affairs his advice is often based upon premises which may be correct in technique, but utterly misleading in practice. . . . He is a wonderful fellow, but has passed his life in cloister and has had no experience in handling men or in assessing their temperaments.

    Lord Crawford and Balcarres, Diary, 9 April 1919.

He went about the world carrying with him everywhere a feeling of the bishop *in partibus*. True salvation was elsewhere, among the faithful at Cambridge. When he concerned himself with politics and economics he left his soul at home. This is the reason for a certain hard, glittering, inhuman quality in most of his writing.

    Bertrand Russell, *Autobiography*.

Keynes's intellect was the sharpest and clearest that I have ever known. When I argued with him, I felt that I took my life in my hands, and I seldom emerged without feeling something of a fool. I was sometimes inclined to feel that so much cleverness must be incompatible with depth, but I do not think this feeling was justified.

    Ibid.

. . . it is one of his queer characteristics that one often wants, one cannot tell why, to make a malicious attack on him, and that, when the time comes, one refrains, one cannot tell why. His sense of values, and indeed all his feelings, offer the spectacle of a complete paradox. He is a hedonist and a follower of [G. E.] Moore; he is lascivious without lust; he is an Apostle without tears.

    Lytton Strachey, in Milo Keynes ed., *Essays on John Maynard Keynes*.

See also Sir Thomas Gresham, Augustus John

KIDD, WILLIAM

circa 1645—1701 Pirate

This person in the gaudy clothes
Is worthy Captain Kidd
They say he never buried gold
I think, perhaps, he did.
They say it's all a story that
His favorite little song
Was 'Make these lubbers walk the plank!'
I think, perhaps, they're wrong.
    Stephen Vincent Benét, *Captain Kidd*.

KING, EDWARD

1612—37 Poet

For Lycidas is dead, dead ere his prime,
Young Lycidas, and hath not left his peer:
Who would not sing for Lycidas? he well knew
Himself to sing, and build the lofty rhyme.
He must not flote upon his wat'ry bier
Unwept, and welter to the parching wind,
Without the meed of some melodious tear.
    John Milton, *Lycidas*.

Although Milton endows Lycidas with the power of song, the extant specimens of King's verse — Latin contributions to various volumes chiefly celebrating events in the Royal family — are wholly undistinguished.

> A. S. P. Woodhouse and Douglas Bush, *Variorum Commentary on the Poems of Milton.*

KING, MARTIN LUTHER, JR

1929–68 Civil Rights Advocate, Clergyman

I want to be the white man's brother, not his brother-in-law.

> On himself, in *New York Journal-American,* 10 September 1962.

Yes, if you want to say that I was a drum major, say that I was a drum major for justice; say that I was a drum major for peace; I was a drum major for righteousness. And all of the other shallow things will not matter. . . .

> On himself, suggesting his own eulogy in a sermon delivered 4 February 1968, in Coretta Scott King, *My Life with Martin Luther King, Jr.*

The irony . . . is that King's name retains its huge symbolic strength even while his principles, his strategies, and many of his apparent accomplishments slide into deepening eclipse.

> Anon., in *Newsweek,* 26 January 1970.

The kindest statement which can be made about the role of Reverend Martin Luther King in Birmingham is that it is unusual behavior for a commander in a winning battle to urge his troops not to fight as hard and to negotiate a surrender when victory is in sight.

> Anon., in *Liberator,* June 1963.

Conventional commentators these days like to speak of King's nobility, and the purity of his humanism, and they sigh that the world is not ready for him. But it is more accurate to say that King is not ready for the world.

> Andrew Kopkind, in David L. Lewis, *Martin Luther King.*

Martin Luther King was a dreamer. His assumption that black clergymen could take power in the ghettos was, by far, the most ethereal dream he ever entertained.

> Louis Lomax, 'When "Non Violence" Meets "Black Power" ', in C. Eric Lincoln ed., *Martin Luther King, Jr. A Profile.*

He got the peace prize, we got the problem. I don't want the white man giving me medals. If I'm following a general, and he's leading me into battle, and the enemy tends to give him rewards, or awards, I get suspicious of him. Especially if he gets a peace award before the war is over.

> Malcolm X, in Peter Goldman, *The Death and Life of Malcolm X.*

Martin Luther King's primary concern is in defending the white man, and if he can elevate the black man's condition at the same time, then the black man will be elevated. But if it takes a condemnation of the white man in order to elevate the black man, you'll find that Martin Luther King will get out of the struggle. Martin Luther King isn't preaching love — he's preaching love the white man.

> *Ibid.*

In a movement in which respect is accorded in direct proportion to the number of times one has been arrested, King appears to keep the number of times he goes to jail to a minimum. In a movement in which successful leaders are those who share in the hardships of their followers, in the risks they take, in the beatings they receive, in the length of time they spend in jail, King tends to leave prison for other important engagements.

> August Meier, 'The Conservative Militant', in C. Eric Lincoln ed., *Martin Luther King, Jr. A Profile.*

He had charisma — a down-to-earth sincerity, an ability to wear the mantle of the church in such a way as to suggest a special closeness to God. He won the grudging admiration of white Americans and the support of millions of foreigners through his dignity, his willingness to take verbal abuse, to go to jail quietly — and to turn the other cheek in the process — in order to achieve his goals.

> Carl T. Rowan, *The Consequences of Decision.*

He stood in that line of saints which goes back from Gandhi to Jesus; his violent end, like theirs, reflects the hostility of mankind to those who annoy it by trying hard to pull it one more painful step farther up the ladder from ape to angel.

> I. F. Stone, 'The Fire Has Only Just Begun', in Neil Middleton ed., *The Best of I. F. Stone.*

He was a Negro, but with
a soul as pure as the white snow.
He was killed by whites
with black souls.
When I received this news
that same bullet entered me.
That bullet killed him,
but by that bullet I was reborn,
and I was reborn a Negro.

> Yevgeny Yevtushenko, upon hearing of King's assassination, translated in William Robert Miller, *Martin Luther King, Jr.*

KINGSLEY, CHARLES
1819—75 Author

I have seen Mr Kingsley, 'Christian socialist' & author of 'Alton Locke' &c — & was much struck by his originality & intenseness. Few men have pleased me more. With every tendency to wildness & exaggerated colouring, he never can speak or write otherwise than according to a noble nature, I am sure.

> Elizabeth Barrett Browning, Letter to Mrs David Ogilvy, 3 September 1852.

Hast thou read Kingsley's 'Westward-ho!'? . . . a fine foe-exterminating book of Elizabeth's time, done and written in the religious spirit of Joshua and David. For Spaniards read Russians, and it is truly a tract for the times, *selon toi.*

> Caroline Fox, Letter to Elizabeth Carne, June 1855.

We sat out the service in the Cathedral [at Chester] — nestling, so to speak, in the old brown stalls of the choir — and heard Canon Kingsley preach. The service and the *mise en scène* were almost agreeable but poor Kingsley is in the pulpit a decidedly weak brother. His discourse (on the Athanasian Creed) was, intellectually, flat and, sentimentally, boyish.

> Henry James, Letter to his Father, 29 May 1872.

He has attempted (as I may call it) to *poison the wells.*

> Cardinal Newman, *Apologia Pro Vita Sua.*

Froude informs the Scottish youth
That parsons do not care for truth.
The Reverend Canon Kingsley cries
History is a pack of lies.
What cause for judgements so malign?
A brief reflection solves the mystery —
Froude believes Kingsley a divine,
And Kingsley goes to Froude for history.

> Bishop William Stubbs, Letter to J. R. Green, 17 December 1871.

The name of Kingsley, naturalist, health reformer, poet and preacher, on the one hand silenced as an advocate of socialism, on the other denounced as a propagator of impurity, may stand for the meeting-place of all the forces at work on the younger imagination of the years when, as it seemed to those who recalled the sordid and sullen past, England was renewing itself.

> G. M. Young, *Victorian England.*

See also J. A. Froude, Shakespeare

KIPLING, (JOSEPH) RUDYARD
1865—1936 Author

K is for Kipling
    A builder of rhymes,
Who 'lest we forget'
    All our national crimes
Sets them forth at great length
    In large type in *The Times.*

> Anon., Alphabet of Authors, *circa* 1902.

There are some poets, Kipling for example, whose relation to language reminds one of a drill sergeant: the words are taught to wash behind their ears, stand properly at attention and execute complicated maneuvers, but at the cost of never being allowed to think for themselves. There are others, Swinburne for example, who remind one more of Svengali: under their hypnotic suggestion, an extraordinary performance is put on, not by raw recruits, but by feeble-minded schoolchildren.

> W. H. Auden, *The Dyer's Hand.*

What is it then, that makes Kipling so extraordinary? Is it not that while virtually every other European writer since the fall of the Roman Empire has felt that the dangers threatening civilization came from *inside* that civilization (or from inside the individual consciousness), Kipling is obsessed by a sense of dangers threatening from *outside*?

> W. H. Auden, *Forewords and Afterwords.*

His poems in their quantity, their limitation to one feeling at a time, have the air of brilliant tactical improvisations to overcome sudden unforeseen obstacles, as if, for Kipling, experience were not a seed to cultivate patiently and lovingly, but an unending stream of dangerous feelings to be immediately mastered as they appear.

> *Ibid.*

The fact is that Mr Kipling appears not perfectly to understand the pandemonium and nerve-strain of war; it seldom surges up in his pages of that appalling misery which brought seasoned men down in the shell holes . . . crying, and 'whacked to the wide'. He makes constant stern attempts at actuality; he constantly falls short, in expression merely strained, in sheer want of comprehension. To those who were in the line, his technical phraseology will seem incongruous. . . . As to the multitudinous enigma of war atmosphere, Mr Kipling has not written much that convinces us.

> Edmund Blunden, on Kipling's *The Irish Guards in the Great War, Nation and Athenaeum,* 28 April 1923.

Wot! haven't you heard of Kiplingson? whose name
  and fame have spread
As far as the Flag of England waves, and the Tory
  prints are read?

I was raised in the lap of Jingo, sir, till I grew to the
  height of a man,
And a wonderful Literary Gent, I emerged upon
  Hindostan!

I sounded the praise of the Empire, sir, I pitch'd out
  piping hot
The new old stories of British bounce (see Lever and
  Michael Scott);

And rapid as light my glory spread, till thro'
  Cockaigne it flew,
And I grew the joy of the Cockney cliques, and the
  pet of the Jingo Jew!
  Robert Buchanan, *The Ballad of Kiplingson.*

Mr Rudyard Kipling has asked in a celebrated epigram what they can know of England who only
England know. It is a far deeper and sharper question to ask: 'What can they know of England who
know only the world?' . . . Mr Kipling does certainly know the world; he is a man of the world,
with all the narrowness that belongs to those imprisoned in that planet. He knows England as an
intelligent English gentleman knows Venice. He has
been to England a great many times; he has stopped
there for long visits. But he does not belong to it,
or to any place. . . . Mr Kipling, with all his merits,
is the globe-trotter; he has not the patience to become part of anything. So great and genuine a man
is not to be accused of a merely cynical cosmopolitanism; his cosmopolitanism is his weakness.
  G. K. Chesterton, *Heretics.*

Some of his work is of impeccable form and because
of that little thing he shall sojourn in Hell only a
very short while.
  Joseph Conrad, Letter to R. B. Cunningham
  Graham, 1897.

His candour has deceived many into thinking him
too near a simpleton to yield much that can be of
use to them in exploring life. They are inclined to
take too literally Mr Max Beerbohm's vision of him
dancing a jig with Britannia upon Hampstead Heath,
and have thought her as much belittled by his hat,
as he is made ridiculous by her helmet. Really it is
only the high finish of his art which has made him
seem to lack subtlety, for he does not display the
workings of his mind, his doubts, and his gropings.
He drives his thought to a conclusion, and only

when it has reached the force of an intuition . . .
does he clothe it in symbols.
  Bonamy Dobrée, in *Monthly Criterion,* December 1927.

Mr Kipling is a laureate without laurels. He is a
neglected celebrity. The arrival of a new book of his
verse is not likely to stir the slightest ripple on the
surface of our conversational intelligentsia.
  T. S. Eliot, in *Athenaeum,* May 1919.

In him we have a writer of gifts almost as great as
gifts could be. To read merely, let us say *Stalky &
Co.* is to be almost overwhelmed by the cleverness
in handling incident and in suggesting atmosphere.
But at a certain stage of his career Mr Kipling
became instinct with the desire to be of importance,
with the result that, using his monumental and semi-
biblical language, alternating it with his matchless
use of colloquialisms, Mr Kipling set out to attack
world problems from the point of view of the
journalists' club smoking-room and with the ambitions of a sort of cross between the German Emperor and a fifth-form public-schoolboy.
  Ford Madox Ford, *The Critical Attitude.*

We, the mere novelists of nowadays, are nearly all
of us woman-ridden. . . . But Kipling's women are
— just women. . . . Kipling puts women in their
place, whether the kitchen or the drawing-room.
And because he does so, the woman who appreciates any but his stories of children is a rarity, to be
either married or made a pal of, according to your
temperament, as soon as found.
  Gilbert Frankau, in *London Magazine,* August
  1928.

KIPLING, RUDYARD, Poet Laureate and Recruit-
ing Sergeant, was born all over the world, some
eighteen years ago. After a lurid infancy at Westward Ho! in the company of Stalky & Co., he emigrated to India at the age of six and swallowed it
whole. In the following year the British Empire was
placed in his charge, and it is still there. A misgiving
that England may have gone too far struck him in
1897, he wrote 'The Recessional', but there are
signs that he has since forgotten it.
  C. L. Graves and E. V. Lucas, *Lives of the
  'Lustrious.*

Sir, we welcome in you one who has used the great
gifts given to you for no small or mean or unworthy
purpose, but rather to advance the interests of your
country, and to stir your fellows to a truer and
loftier patriotism. We welcome in you a poet, a
patriot, an Englishman of whom we are proud —
(cheers) — and what, perhaps, is best of all, one of
whom we may say in every relation of private and

public life, Here is a man whose heart is in the right place. (Loud cheers.)

Rider Haggard, introducing Kipling in a speech at the Anglo-African Writers' Club, 20 May 1898.

I commented on the fact that he had wide fame and was known as 'the great Mr Kipling', which should be a consolation to him. He thrust the idea aside with a gesture of disgust. 'What is it worth — what *is* it all worth?' he answered. Moreover he went on to show that anything which any of us did *well* was no credit to us: that it came from somewhere else: 'We are only telephone wires.'

Rider Haggard, Journal, 22 May 1918.

He has drawn masters as they have never been drawn before: the portraits may be cruel, biased, not sufficiently representative; but how they live! He has put the case for the unathletic boy with convincing truth. He depicts, too, very faithfully, the curious camaraderie which prevails nowadays between boys and masters. . . . And above all, Mr Kipling knows the heart of a boy. He understands, above all men, a boy's intense reserve upon matters that lie deepest within him, and his shrinking from and repugnance to unrestrained and blatant discussion of these things.

Ian Hay, *The Lighter Side of School Life.*

In his earliest time I thought he perhaps contained the seeds of an English Balzac; but I have given that up in proportion as he has come down steadily from the simple in subject to the more simple — from the Anglo-Indians to the natives, from the natives to the Tommies, from the Tommies to the quadrupeds, from the quadrupeds to the fish, and from the fish to the engines and screws.

Henry James, Letter to Grace Norton, 25 December 1897.

The one great fault in Mr Kipling's work is, not its 'brutality', nor its fondness for strong effects, but a certain taint of bad manners, from the literary point of view. He insists upon spicing his stories with an ill-flavoured kind of gossip, wholly irrelevant, and very offensive. . . . Too often, when reading Mr Kipling, we are forced to say, 'That would make a good special report', or 'That's a telling bit of war correspondence.'

Lionel Johnson, in *Academy*, 17 October 1891.

In fact, Mr Kipling is, both by temperament and by conviction, a Tory. But it is not necessary to agree with the whole of a writer to be glad of him, and this is especially true of Mr Kipling. . . . Perhaps as one grows older and better acquainted with the works and ways of his God of Things as They Are, one is inclined to agree with him more rather than

less; nor need the doing so imply our senectitude, for we must recall that Mr Kipling thought the same at twenty as he does now, that his young shoulders were born with a strangely old Tory head upon them. He saw the Thing as It Is from a very early age.

Richard Le Gallienne, in *Munsey's Magazine*, November 1919.

To put the thing in its shortest possible way, Kipling is first and foremost the poet of work. It is really remarkable how poetry and fiction before his time had avoided this subject. They had dealt almost exclusively with men in their 'private hours' — with love-affairs, crimes, sport, illness and changes of fortune. . . . A whole range of strong sentiments and emotions — for many men, the strongest of all — went with them. For, as Pepys once noted with surprise, there is a great pleasure in talking of business. It was Kipling who first reclaimed for literature this enormous territory.

C. S. Lewis, *Literature and Life.*

This pickle has a peculiar mordant quality which distinguishes it from all others. The chief ingredient is unwashed English, chopped, broken, and bruised with a brazen instrument. Then work in chips and fragments of cynicism, 'B.V.' [James Thomson]'s poems, the seven cardinal sins, the *Soldier's Pocket Book*, the *Civil Service Regulations*, Simla manners, profanity, an Ekka pony, the Southern Cross, and genius. Spice with a Tipperary brogue.

E. V. Lucas, 'Literary Recipe for Kipling Chutnee', in *Privateer*, 1892.

Mr Kipling's world is a barrack full of oaths and clatter of sabres; but his language is copious, rich, sonorous. One is tempted to say that none since the Elizabethans has written so copiously. Others have written more beautifully, but no one that I can call to mind at this moment has written so copiously. Shelley and Wordsworth, Landor and Pater, wrote with part of the language; but who else, except Whitman, has written with the whole language since the Elizabethans?

George Moore, *Avowals.*

It became, as years passed, almost a game to invent new dresses for his work — uniform editions, pocket editions, the Edition de Luxe in red and gold, the Bombay Edition, the Service Edition intended for the pack or pocket of soldiers in the 1914 War. There were, also, school editions, and gigantic volumes in which all the dog stories or all the Mowgli stories or all the humorous stories were assembled, and year by year the wise men held their breath and wondered whether by now the public demand for old wine in new bottles was exhausted.

The cautious feared it might be, but they were always wrong.

Charles Morgan, *The House of Macmillan*.

The huge paradox of Kipling is never more apparent than when you read the reviews of a new book of his. This extraordinary writer, whom we are accustomed to see billed as speaking to the world's hugest fiction audience, is really the subtlest of highbrows. His finest things would bore the slackwit reader just as Shakespeare does. . . . He writes a story ostensibly about big howitzers, and it is really a lover's tribute to Jane Austen. He writes a story apparently about wireless, and it means nothing save to a student of Keats.

Christopher Morley, in *Saturday Review of Literature*, 2 October 1926.

For my own part I worshipped Kipling at thirteen, loathed him at seventeen, enjoyed him at twenty, despised him at twenty-five, and now again rather admire him. The one thing that was never possible, if one had read him at all, was to forget him. . . . If he had never come under imperialist influences, and if he had developed, as he might well have done, into a writer of music-hall songs, he would have been a better and more lovable writer. In the rôle he actually chose, one was bound to think of him, after one had grown up, as a kind of enemy, a man of alien and perverted genius.

George Orwell, in *New English Weekly*, 23 January 1936.

Rudyard the dud yard,
Rudyard the false measure,
Told 'em that glory
Ain't always a pleasure,
But said it wuz glorious nevertheless
To lick the boots of the bloke
That makes the worst mess.

Ezra Pound, *Poems of Alfred Venison (Alf's Fourth Bit)*.

Kipling has done more than any other since Disraeli to show the world that the British race is sound at core and that rust or dry-rot are strangers to it.

Cecil Rhodes, in J. G. McDonald, *Rhodes: A Life*.

Kipling is too clever to live.

Robert Louis Stevenson, Letter to Henry James, August 1890.

Mr Kipling . . . stands for everything in this cankered world which I would wish were otherwise.

Dylan Thomas, Letter to Pamela Hansford Johnson, 1933.

He is a stranger to me but he is a most remarkable man — and I am the other one. Between us we cover all knowledge; he knows all that can be known and I know the rest.

Mark Twain, *Autobiography*.

. . . You're *our* partic'lar author, you're our patron an' our friend,
You're the poet of the cuss-word and the swear,
You're the poet of the people where the red-mapped lands extend.

Edgar Wallace, welcoming Kipling to Cape Town, January 1898.

As one turns over the pages of his *Plain Tales from the Hills*, one feels as if one were seated under a palm-tree reading life by superb flashes of vulgarity. The bright colours of the bazaars dazzle one's eyes. The jaded commonplace Anglo-Indians are in exquisite incongruity with their surroundings. The mere lack of style in the storyteller gives an odd journalistic realism to what he tells us. From the point of view of literature Mr Kipling is a man of talent who drops his aspirates. From the point of view of life he is a reporter who knows vulgarity better than anyone has ever known it. Dickens knew its clothes. Mr Kipling knows its essence. He is our best authority on the second-rate. He terrifies us by his truth, and makes his sordid subject matter marvellous by the brilliancy of its setting.

Oscar Wilde, 'The Critic as Artist', in *Nineteenth Century*, 1890.

It's odd, this hostility to Kipling. How the intelligentsia do seem to loathe the poor blighter, and how we of the *canaille* revel in his stuff. One thing I do think is pretty unjust — when they tick him off for not having spotted the future of the India Movement and all that sort of thing. I mean, considering he left India for ever at the age of about twenty-two.

P. G. Wodehouse, *Performing Flea*.

I myself had served for many years with soldiers, but had never heard the words or expressions that Rudyard Kipling's soldiers used. Many a time did I ask my brother Officers whether they had heard them. No, never. But sure enough, a few years later, the soldiers thought, and talked, and expressed themselves exactly like Rudyard Kipling had taught them in his stories. . . . Rudyard Kipling made the modern soldier.

Sir George Younghusband, *A Soldier's Memories in Peace and War*.

See also John Galsworthy, Rider Haggard, James Joyce, Christopher Marlowe, H. G. Wells

KITCHENER, HORATIO HERBERT, EARL OF KHARTOUM AND BROOME

1850—1916 Soldier

He is to Lord Curzon what the broadsword is to the rapier.
    Anon. comment in a Simla newspaper, 1908.

The great armies that he called into being are his living monument, and no nobler monument has been raised to man.
    Obituary in *The Times*, 1916.

The great poster.
    Margot, Lady Asquith, in A. J. P. Taylor, *English History 1914—1945*.

I don't think Ld. Kitchener is a model of good taste.
    Alice Balfour, Diary, 6 June 1899.

He is . . . terribly bureaucratic, and does not see with sufficient clearness the difference between forming a country and commanding a regiment.
    Lord Cromer, Letter to Lord Salisbury, April 1899.

Lord K. is playing hell with its lid off at the War Office — What the papers call 'standing no nonsense' but which often means 'listening to no sense'.
    Lady Jean Hamilton, Diary, 12 August 1914.

He is fearfully wrong-headed sometimes, but he is always *homme sérieux* practising himself, and enforcing upon others, the highest standard of *workmanlike* strenuousness, indefatigable industry and iron perseverance. Great qualities these in a wishy-washy world.
    Lord Milner, Letter to Lady Edward Cecil, January 1902.

On 5 June the *Hampshire*, with Kitchener on board, struck a mine within two hours of leaving Scapa Flow. Kitchener and most of the crew were drowned. So perished the only British military idol of the first World war. The next morning [Lord] Northcliffe burst into his sister's drawing-room with the words: 'Providence is on the side of the British Empire after all.'
    A. J. P. Taylor, *English History 1914—1945*.

See also Theodore Roosevelt

KNELLER, SIR GODFREY (GOTTFRIED KNILLER)

1646—1723 Painter

                     . . . where true Design,
Postures unforc'd, and lively Colours joyn,
Likeness is ever there; but still the best,
Like proper Thoughts in lofty Language drest,
Where Light, to shades descending, plays, not strives,
Dyes by degrees, and by degrees revives.
Of various Parts a perfect whole is wrought;
Thy Pictures think, and we Divine their Thought.
    John Dryden, *To Sir Godfrey Kneller*.

That man of wigs and drapery.
    John Fisher, Letter to John Constable, 9 May 1823.

The portraits of Kneller, for example, seem all to have been turned in a machine; the eye-brows are arched as if by a compass; the mouth curled, and the chin dimpled, the head turned on one side, and the hands placed in the same affected position. He thought that beauty and perfection were *one* and he very consistently reduced this principle to practice.
    William Hazlitt, 'Character of Sir Joshua Reynolds', in *Champion*, 30 October 1814.

Kneller, by Heav'n and not a Master taught,
Whose Art was Nature, and whose Pictures thought;
Now for two ages having snatch'd from fate
Whate'er was Beauteous, or Whate'er was Great,
Lies crown'd with Princes Honours, Poets Lays,
Due to his Merit, and brave Thirst of Praise.
Living, great Nature fear'd he might outvie
Her works; and dying, fears herself may die.
    Alexander Pope, *Epitaph on Sir Godfrey Kneller*, in Westminster Abbey.

As I was sitting by Sir Godfrey Kneller one day, whilst he was drawing a picture, he stopped and said, 'I can't do so well as I should do, unless you flatter me a little, pray flatter me, Mr. Pope! you know I love to be flattered.'
    Alexander Pope, in Joseph Spence, *Anecdotes*.

The fool has got a country house near Hampton Court, and is so busy about fitting it up (to receive nobody), that there is no getting him to work.
    Sir John Vanbrugh, Letter to J. Tonson, 15 June 1703.

There can be no doubt that Kneller was the dominant artistic figure of his age in England. His mature portrait style reflects with relentless objectivity the fashionable world under the reign of three Sovereigns with no leanings towards the arts. The downright shoddiness of much of his enormous output is a mirror of the cynicism of his age, but he had a wonderfully sharp eye for character, could draw and paint a face with admirable economy, and maintains, even in his inferior work, a certain virility and down-to-earth quality which is refreshing after the languishments of the age of Lely. He was one of the first to concentrate on the portrait as a document concerned with the likeness of a historical personality rather than as a work of art.

Ellis Waterhouse, *Painting in Britain 1530–1790.*

When Kneller in his last hours was dreading the approach of death Pope tried to comfort him by saying that as he had been a good man in this world the Almighty would be sure to look after him in the next, but the painter was too much attached to his country house and its material comforts to be interested in the possible joys of Heaven. 'Ah, my good friend, Mr. Pope,' he cried, 'I wish God would allow me to stay at Whitton.'

William T. Whitley, *Artists and their Friends in England.*

See also Alexander Pope

KNOX, HENRY

1750–1806 Soldier, Politician

The resources of his genius supplied the deficit of means.

George Washington, Report to the Continental Congress after the siege and battle of Yorktown, 1781.

KNOX, JOHN

1505–72 Scottish Reformer

One is tempted almost to say that there was more of Jesus in St Theresa's little finger than in John Knox's whole body.

Matthew Arnold, *Literature and Dogma.*

This that Knox did for his Nation, I say, we may really call a resurrection as from death. It was not a smooth business; but it was welcome surely, and cheap at that price, had it been far rougher. On the whole, cheap at any price; — as life is. The people began to *live*: they needed first of all to do that, at what cost and costs soever. Scotch Literature and Thought, Scotch Industry; James Watt, David Hume, Walter Scott, Robert Burns: I find Knox and the Reformation acting in the heart's core of every one of these persons and phenomena; I find that without the Reformation, they would not have been.

Thomas Carlyle, *On Heroes and Hero-Worship.*

I saw him everie day of his doctrine go hulie and fear, with a furring of martriks about his neck, a staff in an hand, and guid godlie Robert Ballanden, his servand, halding upe the uther oxtar, from the Abbay to the paroche kirk; and be the said Richart and another servant, lifted upe to the pulpit, whar he behivit to lean at his first entrie; bot or he haid done with his sermont, he was sa active and vigorous that he was lyk to ding that pulpit in blads, and fly out of it.

James Melvill, *The Lyff of John Knox.*

Whose love is given over-well
Shall look on Helen's face in hell,
Whilst they whose love is thin and wise
May view John Knox in Paradise.

Dorothy Parker, in *The Faber Book of Comic Verse.*

A man of a fearless heart and a fluent eloquence; violent, indeed, and sometimes coarse, but the better fitted to obtain influence in a coarse and turbulent age, — capable at once of reasoning with the wiser nobility, and inspiring with his own spirit and zeal the fierce populace. Toleration, and that species of candour which makes allowance for the prejudices of birth or situation, were unknown to his uncompromising mind; and this deficiency made him the more fit to play the distinguished part to which he was called.

Sir Walter Scott, *History of Scotland.*

Knox was always very conscious of his own position, heroic or otherwise, and spoke about it without concealment. This is not the greatest sort of man perhaps, but a very serviceable penetrating sort of man for all that, who makes everything serve.

Robert Louis Stevenson, *Selections from his Notebook.*

The lantern of his analysis did not always shine with a very serviceable light; but he had the virtue, at least, to carry it into many places of fictitious holiness, and was not abashed by the tinsel divinity that hedged kings and queens from his contemporaries.

Robert Louis Stevenson, *John Knox.*

KOUSSEVITZKY, SERGEI ALEXANDROVITCH

1874–1951 Musician

The only ground for our authority is the love for us and for our work; and if this were absent, all else would be futility and emptiness — however well we might be 'armed' with knowledge and skill. . . . But for such love to be able to arise it is necessary first

of all that we ourselves do not smoulder like dying
embers, but are aflame with sacred love for that
which we serve . . . for living art and living men.

On himself, in Hugo Leichtentritt, *Serge Koussevitsky: The Boston Symphony Orchestra and
the New American Music.*

Some time ago I heard the Boston Orchestra in New
York, under Koussevitsky. It was like meeting a
beautiful woman of the year 1900 — now middle-
aged, simpering, and hideously frescoed.

H. L. Mencken, Letter to Isaac Goldberg, 6 May
1925.

No matter how wrong one may think him about any
given musical rendition, there always seems to be

room for his conception and for one's own in the
same concert hall.

Virgil Thomson, *The Musical Scene.*

KYD, THOMAS

1558—94 Dramatist

Sporting Kyd, or Marlowe's mighty line.

Ben Jonson, *To The Memory of Shakespeare.*

Murderous topics were always congenial to the
dramatist.

Sir Sidney Lee, in *Dictionary of
National Biography.*

L

LADD, ALAN WALBRIDGE

1913–64 Actor

Hard, bitter and occasionally charming, he is after all a small boy's idea of a tough.
> Raymond Chandler, *Raymond Chandler Speaking*.

In the hierarchy of tough-guy stars, Alan Ladd holds an honoured name: through 50 or so formula pictures he strolled, stone-faced, in roles which fitted him as snugly as the iron strapped to his side. No one ever pretended that he could act. He got to the top, therefore, by a combination of determination and luck.
> David Shipman, *The Great Movie Stars*.

Actors like Gary Cooper or Gregory Peck are in themselves, as material objects, 'realistic', seeming to bear in their bodies and their faces mortality, limitation, the knowledge of good and evil. Ladd is a more 'aesthetic' object, with some of the 'universality' of a piece of sculpture: his special quality is in his physical smoothness and serenity, unworldly and yet not innocent, but suggesting that no experience can really touch him.
> Robert Warshow, *The Immediate Experience*.

LAEMMLE, CARL

1867–1939 Motion Picture Producer

Uncle Carl Laemmle
Has a very large family.
> Anon., coined after the revelation in 1936 that Laemmle had more than seventy relatives working in sinecures at the Universal Studios.

A Bavarian Jew of immense cunning.
> Bob Thomas, *Selznick*.

. . . Carl Laemmle was the prototype of the more than slightly mad movie mogul, impulsive, quixotic, intrepid, unorthodox, and unpredictable. Only the gossip columnists could consider him otherwise, for to them he was always dependably good copy. . . .
> Norman Zierold, *The Moguls*.

LA FARGE, JOHN

1835–1910 Artist

No one has struggled more against his destiny than I; nor did I for many years fully acquiesce in being a painter, though I learned the methods and studied the problems of my art. I had hoped to find some other mode of life, some other way of satisfying the desire for a contemplation of truth, unbiassed, free, and detached.
> On himself, in Cecilia Waern, *John La Farge*.

La Farge's mind was opaline with infinite shades and refractions of light, and with color toned down to the finest gradations.
> Henry Adams, in Royal Cortissoz, *John La Farge*.

The task of painting him is so difficult as to scare any literary artist out of his wits. The thing cannot be done. It is like the attempt of the nineteenth-century writers to describe a sunset in colors. Complexity cannot be handled in print to that degree. . . .
> Henry Adams, in Alfred Frankenstein, *American Self-Portraits 1670–1973*.

. . . he flung out a myriad invisible tentacles of understanding, electric filaments which in an instant identified him with the subject of his thought and made him free of its innermost secrets. And what he gathered through these magical processes he brought back and put before you, slowly with an almost oracular deliberation, but in such living words and with such artistic balancing of his periods, that you saw what he saw, felt what he felt, and waited in positive tense enjoyment for the unfolding of the next mental picture. You watched and waited in absolute security but sometimes a little breathlessly, for La Farge was a past master of the parenthesis and he hated to let go of his collateral lines of thought.
> Royal Cortissoz, *John La Farge*.

An innovator in art represents not so much the distillation of a given epoch or culture as the emergence of a particular artistic personality capable of articulating a still inchoate vision in his milieu. John La Farge, although heir to the climate of nineteenth-century Romanticism, was nevertheless the precursor of a more pragmatic generation, more audaciously analytical, more in tune with the spirit of scientific inquiry. With wide-ranging interests and insatiable curiosity, he became the spokesman of an outlook that was prophetic of America in the twentieth century.

Henry A. La Farge, *John La Farge.*

LA FOLLETTE, ROBERT MARION

1855–1925 Statesman

It is hard to say the right thing about Bob La Follette. You know, he lived 150 years.

Senator William Edgar Borah, 1925, in Frederic A. Ogg, *Robert M. La Follette in Retrospect.*

That famous phrase, 'I do not choose',
Is once more headlined in the news;
La Follette thinks it's much more fun
To make it read 'You shall not run.'

George Rothwell Brown, in H. G. Warren, *Herbert Hoover and the Great Depression.*

Robert M. La Follette, Sr. of Wisconsin, a ceaseless battler for the underprivileged in an age of special privilege, a courageous independent in an era of conformity, who fought memorably against tremendous odds and stifling inertia for the social and economic reforms which ultimately proved essential to American progress in the 20th. century.

John F. Kennedy, in Robert S. Maxwell ed., *La Follette: Great Lives Observed Series.*

But if there was any expression or any suggestion of a lack of faith in the common man, in 'the plain people', a fighting look came into his eyes and a vibrant ring into his voice, and a stream of arguments, which he seemed almost unable to restrain, overwhelmed the unhappy critic.

Max Otto, in *ibid.*

. . . if the Senator from Wisconsin had his will, if the Kaiser had his will, liberty would become a memory, honor a tradition, and tyranny the ruling power throughout this world.

Senator Joseph T. Robinson, 6 October 1917, in *ibid.*

See also Franklin D. Roosevelt

LA GUARDIA, FIORELLO HENRY

1822–1947 Politician

I invented the low blow.

On himself, in Arthur Mann, *La Guardia Comes to Power.*

I can out demagogue the best of demagogues.

On himself, during the 1919 campaign, in *ibid.*

I never thought I had enough Jewish blood in my veins to justify boasting of it.

On himself, in *ibid.*

Seven times he's won elections,
Seven times he's reached the top.
He is proud he's an American
And he's proud he is a wop!
Just remember Chris Columbus . . .
Now join in the chorus all . . .
We are following La Guardia
To his chair in City Hall.

Anon. campaign song.

It goes against the grain of real Americans to have anybody by the name of La Guardia telling the American people how to run their government. If he doesn't like our laws, he ought to go back to the country whence his ancestors came. . . . No state but New York would disgrace itself by sending such a man as La Guardia to Congress and keeping him there. New York has been a cesspool into which immigrant trash has been dumped for so long that it can scarcely be considered American any more.

Anon., in *Denver Post*, 9 June 1930.

La Guardia, with his social progressivism, could make out of New York a gigantic laboratory for civil reconstruction.

Paul Blanshard, 'La Guardia Versus McKee', in *Nation*, 25 October 1933.

They have counted nine over Fiorello upon occasion but never ten.

Heywood Broun, in Arthur Mann, *La Guardia: A Fighter Against His Times.*

That in exploiting racial and religious prejudices La Guardia would run circles around the bosses he despised and derided. When it came to raking ashes of Old World hates, warming ancient grudges, waving the bloody shirt, turning the ear to ancestral voices, he could easily out demagogue the demagogues. And for what purpose? To redress old wrongs abroad? To combat foreign levy or malice domestic? To produce peace on the Danube, the Nile, the Jordan? Not on your tintype. Fiorello La Guardia knew better. He knew that the aim of the rabble rouser is simply to shoo into office for entirely extraneous, illogical and even silly reasons the muni-

cipal officials who clean city streets, teach in schools, protect, house and keep healthy, strong and happy millions of people crowded together here.
Robert Moses, *La Guardia, A Salute and a Memoir.*

If it's La Guardia or bust, I prefer bust!
Joseph M. Price, in Arthur Mann, *La Guardia Comes to Power.*

He was half Italian, half Jewish, and wholly American. He was born in New York but spent his childhood and youth in Arizona. From the Southwest he brought more than a fondness for sombrero-brimmed hats so broad they made the stout little fellow look like a perambulating mushroom; he brought something of the breezy independence of the frontier. No figure in American politics ever thumbed his nose so brashly at party regularity and got away with it.
I. F. Stone, in *The Truman Era.*

He is remembered as New York's best mayor when what he longed to be was America's First Progressive President.
Rexford Guy Tugwell, *The Art of Politics as Practiced by Three Great Americans.*

. . . come up and see me sometime, and bring La Guardia.
Mae West, after La Guardia had described a show of hers as indecent, in Arthur Mann, *La Guardia: A Fighter Against His Times.*

LAHR, BERT (IRVING LAHRHEIM)

1895–1967 Actor

God must have laughed when Bert Lahr was born.
Brooks Atkinson, in John Lahr, *Notes on a Cowardly Lion.*

Mr. Lahr is an actor in the pantomime tradition who has a thousand ways to move and a hundred ways to make the story interesting and theatrical, and touching, too. His long experience as a bawling mountebank has equipped Mr. Lahr to represent eloquently the tragic comedy of one of the lost souls of the earth.
Brooks Atkinson, Review of *Waiting for Godot,* in *New York Times,* 20 April 1966.

The Beauty Part showed him in the golden twilight of his preposterous maturity, the last and most marvellous of the American clowns cradled by burlesque.
Alistair Cooke, reviewing S. J. Perelman's play *The Beauty Part, Guardian,* 13 June 1963.

LAMB, LADY CAROLINE

1785–1828 Novelist

. . . Lady Caroline Lamb defined truth to be what one thinks at the moment.
Lord Broughton, *Recollections of a Long Life,* December 1815.

But — the *little French lady!* — here I hardly know how to write! — To the tales told about *her, scandal* is nothing — INFAMY enwraps them! — I could only be glad no certainty hung upon them — at least, that no conviction had indisputably marked them in my belief, — though *that way,* all concurred to make my suspicions incline to give credit to what previously had been told me. — What these tales are, perhaps you may both know: that Lady Elizabeth Forster, a Daughter of Lord Bristol, & by birth *an Hervey,* — who is parted from her Husband, by consent, though not by divorce, is Mother to this Child — & that the Duke of Devonshire is its Father! — The Child, whom they call *La petite Caroline,* is about 4 years old: fat, & full of mincing little affectations & airs, but not handsome, though she has a sort of Face that may grow up to more advantage.
Fanny Burney, Diary, August 1791.

I have much to do & little time to do it in — certainly not an instant to spare to a person for whom the iron (to use her metaphor) retains all the *heat* but none of the flexibility . . . I know not whom I may love but to the latest hour of my life I shall hate that woman. — *Now* you know my sentiments — they will be the same on my deathbed. —— To her I do not express this because I have no desire to make her uncomfortable — but such is the state of my mind towards her for reasons I shall not refer to & I beg to be spared from meeting her until we may be chained together in Dante's Inferno.
Lord Byron, Letter to Lady Melbourne, 5 April 1813.

A word to you of Lady Caroline Lamb — I speak from experience — *keep clear of her* — (I do not mean as a woman — that is all fair) she is a villainous *intrigante* — in every sense of the word — mad & malignant — capable of all & every mischief — above all — guard your *connections* from her society — with all her apparent absurdity there is an indefatigable & active spirit of meanness & destruction about her — which delights & often succeeds in inflicting misery.
Lord Byron, Letter to James Wedderburn Webster, 4 September 1815.

I was more sinned against than sinning.
Lord Byron, in Lady Blessington, *Conversations of Lord Byron.*

She was the most dynamic personality that had appeared in London society for a generation. . . . Slight, agile, and ethereal, with a wide-eyed wilful little face, and curly short hair, she still looked a child; like something less substantial even, — 'the Sprite', people called her, 'the Fairy Queen, Ariel'. Her fresh lisping voice, too, trained though it was to linger cooingly on the syllables in the approved Devonshire House manner, was a child's voice; 'Lady Caroline', said an irritated rival, 'baas like a sheep.'

Lord David Cecil, *Melbourne.*

I did not make what is called 'love' to her till I saw how acceptable it would be. In short, she appeared to feel for me even more than I felt for her. It is but justice to her to say that we had every opportunity of acting ill; though I was young and almost in love, though everything conspired to tempt her, I believe she resisted what few women would have done.

Edward Bulwer Lytton, Letter to his Mother, 14 January 1825.

Several women were in love with Byron, but none so violently as Lady Caroline Lamb. She absolutely besieged him. He showed me the first letter he received from her; in which she assured him that, if he was in any want of money, 'all her jewels were at his service.' They frequently had quarrels; and more than once, on coming home, I have found Lady C. walking in the garden, and waiting for me, to beg that I would reconcile them.

Samuel Rogers, *Table-Talk.*

LAMB, CHARLES

1775—1834 Essayist

I am, in plainer words, a bundle of prejudices — made up of likings and dislikings.

On himself, *Essays of Elia*, 'Imperfect Sympathies.'

I love to lose myself in other men's minds. When I am not walking, I am reading; I cannot sit and think. Books think for me.

On himself, *Last Essays of Elia, Detached Thoughts on Books and Reading.*

My attachments are all local, purely local. I have no passion . . . to groves and vallies. The rooms where I was born, the furniture which has been before my eyes all my life, a book case which has followed me about . . . wherever I have moved — old chairs, old tables, streets, squares, where I have sunned myself, my old school, — these are my mistresses. Have I

not enough, without your mountains?

On himself, Letter to William Wordsworth, 30 January 1801.

Anything awful makes me laugh. I misbehaved once at a funeral.

On himself, Letter to Robert Southey, 1815.

How I like to be liked, and what I do to be liked!

On himself, Letter to Dorothy Wordsworth, 8 January 1821.

Charles Lamb . . . now a Gentleman at large, can remember few specialities in his life worth noting except that he once caught a swallow flying (*teste sua manu*); below the middle stature, cast of face slightly Jewish, with no Judaic tinge in his complexional religion; stammers abominably and is therefore more apt to discharge his occasional conversation in a quaint aphorism or a poor quibble than in set and edifying speeches; has consequently been libelled as a person always aiming at wit, which, as he told a dull fellow that charged him with it, is at least as good as aiming at dulness; a small eater but not drinker; confesses a partiality for the production of the juniper berry, was a fierce smoker of Tobacco, but may be resembled to a volcano burnt out, emitting only now and then a casual puff.

On himself, *Autobiographical sketch*, 10 April 1827.

May my last breath be drawn through a pipe and exhaled in a pun.

On himself, in A. K. Adams, *The Home Book of Humorous Quotations.*

In everything that relates to science, I am a whole encyclopedia behind the rest of the world.

On himself, in *ibid.*

He is very fond of snuff, which seems to sharpen up his wit every time he dips his plentiful finger into his large bronze-coloured box: and then he sharpens up his head, throws himself backward in his chair, and stammers at a joke or pun with an inward sort of utterance ere he can give it speech, till his tongue becomes a sort of packman's strop turning it over and over till at last it comes out whetted as keen as a razor: and expectation, when she knows him, wakens into a sort of danger as bad as cutting your throat.

John Clare, *Fragment on the Londoners.*

His sayings are generally like women's letters; all the pith is in the postscript.

William Hazlitt, *Boswell Redivivus.*

There is a spirit in Mr Lamb's productions, which is in itself *anti-critical*, and tends so much to reconcile us to all that is in the world, that the effect is almost neutralizing to everything but complacency and a queer admiration — his very criticisms chiefly tend to overthrow the critical spirit.

Leigh Hunt, in *Examiner*, March 1819.

And Lamb, the frolic and the gentle,
Has vanished from his lonely hearth.

William Wordsworth, *Extempore Effusion upon the Death of James Hogg.*

See also R. W. Elliston, Robert Louis Stevenson

LAMB, WILLIAM, see under MELBOURNE, VISCOUNT

LAMBERT, JOHN

1619—83 Soldier

My Lord did seem to wonder much why Lambert was so willing to be put into the Toure, and thinks he hath some design in it; but I think that he is so poor that he cannot use his liberty for debts if he were at liberty — and so it is as good and better for him to be there then anywhere else.

Samuel Pepys, Diary, 7 March 1660.

LANDOR, WALTER SAVAGE

1775—1864 Poet

What is it that Mr Landor wants, to make him a poet? His powers are certainly very considerable, but he seems to be totally deficient in that modifying faculty, which compresses several units into one whole. . . . Hence his poems, taken as wholes, are unintelligible; you have eminences excessively bright, and all the ground around and in between them in darkness. Besides which, he has never learned, with all his energy, how to write simple and lucid English.

Samuel Taylor Coleridge, *Table Talk*, 1 January 1834.

Consider . . . one of the very finest poets of the first part of the nineteenth century: Landor. He is an undoubted master of verse and prose; he is the author of at least one long poem which deserves to be much more read than it is; but his reputation has never been such as to bring him into comparison with Wordsworth. . . . Wordsworth was an essential part of history; Landor only a magnificent by-product.

T. S. Eliot, *The Use of Poetry and the Use of Criticism.*

Landor . . . is very eighteenth century. He differs from Wordsworth in having no new life to offer. What he offers, in prose as well as in verse, is literature. If his phrasing is 'clean-cut', it is not because it defines and conveys sharply any strongly felt significance; to say 'clean-cut' is merely to intimate that he affects a 'lapidary' manner. He cultivates this for its own sake, choosing his themes as occasions for exercising it.

F. R. Leavis, *Revaluation.*

Landor has not been a popular author. His collected works are nevertheless the best substitute for a University education that can be offered to any young man in a hurry.

Ezra Pound, in *Future*, November 1917.

See also Samuel Johnson, Rudyard Kipling

LANIER, SIDNEY

1842—81 Poet, Musician, Critic

My flute is my faucet; it lets out just what I have put in. If I can become beautiful, the soul running through my flute will be beautiful also.

On himself, in Aubrey Harrison Starke, *Sidney Lanier.*

His language, too often over-wrought, was sometimes silly or namby-pamby, with too much of the mawkish adolescent in the quality of the feeling, and there were elements in his writing too of the high-flown Southern oratorical style and the feverish exaltation of tuberculosis.

Van Wyck Brooks, *The Times of Melville and Whitman.*

Thinking of himself as a knight and minstrel, he imagined that the new Confederate nation would embody all that was finest in the chivalric life, and later his prose and verse abounded in figures of paladin and paynim, the tournament and the battle-axe and cross-bow.

Ibid.

. . . the Sir Galahad of American Literature.

Thomas Wentworth Higginson, in Aubrey Harrison Starke, *Sidney Lanier.*

Never simple, never easy, never in one single lyric

natural and spontaneous for more than one stanza, always concealing his barrenness and tameness by grotesque violence to language and preposterous storm of sound, Lanier appears to me to be as conclusively not a poet of genius as any ambitious man who ever lived, labored, and failed.

Walt Whitman, in *ibid.*

In Lanier the chivalric romance of the South was to merge with German romanticism and to become inflated and irised, made to drip with the dews of idealism. . . .

Edmund Wilson, *Patriotic Gore.*

If one reads very much of Lanier, one is tempted in the long run to lose patience with him. He is at once insipid and florid. He is noble, to be sure, but his nobility is boring; his eloquence comes to seem empty.

Ibid.

LANSBURY, GEORGE

1859—1940 Newspaperman, Labour Politician

. . . not a very clear head, but with a heart that reaches beyond the stars.

Harold Laski, Letter to Maurice Firuski, August 1920.

The most lovable figure in modern politics.

A. J. P. Taylor, *English History 1914—1945.*

LANSDOWNE, MARQUIS OF, see under SHEL-BURNE, LORD

LARDNER, RINGGOLD WILMER

1885—1933 Author, Journalist

He [William Howard Taft] looked at me as if I was a side dish he hadn't ordered.

On himself, in A. K. Adams, *The Home Book of Humorous Quotations.*

Where do they get that stuff about me being a satirist? I ain't no satirist. I just listen.

On himself, in Walton R. Patrick, *Ring Lardner.*

Lardner simply did not see life in terms of politics and economics and sociology but in terms of games. Even after he stopped writing about organized sports, his characters kept using the language of sports and they played games like bridge and horse-

shoes, mainly to kill time and to kill their endless boredom.

Otto Friedrich, *Ring Lardner.*

Jupiter on tiptoes.

Ernest Hemingway, in Carlos Baker, *Ernest Hemingway, A Life Story.*

His specialty lay in his ability to report with seeming unconsciousness the appalling mediocrity and varity of the middle-class soul.

George F. Whicher, 'The Twentieth Century', in Arthur Hobson Quinn ed., *The Literature of the American People.*

Mr Lardner does not waste a moment when he writes in thinking whether he is using American slang or Shakespeare's English; whether he is remembering Fielding or forgetting Fielding; whether he is proud of being American or ashamed of not being Japanese; all his mind is on his story. Hence, incidentally, he writes the best prose that has come our way.

Virginia Woolf, in Walton R. Patrick, *Ring Lardner.*

LASKI, HAROLD JOSEPH

1893—1950 Political Author

Yes, my friend, we are both Marxists, you in your way, I in Marx's.

On himself, reply to an interrupter at a public meeting, in Kingsley Martin, *Harold Laski.*

I have the feeling that I am already a ghost in a play that is over.

On himself, Letter to Felix Frankfurter, September 1947.

Your chairman today is an example of that dangerous species who, so far as my knowledge goes, is in our movement rarely trusted and never praised — the species whose professional work is criticism and thought. . . . I represent something a little different from the past, British by birth, middle class by origin, Jewish by inheritance — symbolic of the vital fact that the Labour party knows no boundaries save those which are defined by faith in its principles and policies.

On himself, as acting chairman of the 1944 Labour Party Conference, in Kingsley Martin, *Harold Laski.*

[Laski has] had a backdoor key to the White House. A surprising number of us, Professor, have begun to think it is time to change the lock.

Mr Woodruff of Michigan, on Roosevelt's friendship with Laski, in *Congressional Record*, 6 February 1946.

LASKY, JESSE L.

1880–1956 Motion Picture Producer

. . . Vaudeville was at its height; and the height of vaudeville was in the Lasky productions of musical plays, short but always well constructed, well cast, well mounted, well directed. There was a Lasky touch, a Lasky finish and polish about his productions that made them unique . . . if the bill included a Lasky musical, you left the vaudeville theater well satisfied and with a lilt. Lasky was a showman's showman.

Cecil B. De Mille, *Autobiography*.

Aside from a nefarious indulgence of overblown romanticism, his wholesome, if not always harmless, pleasure was arranging outdoor adventures up mountains and down unknown rivers. . . . He was lowered on lassos by cowboys to become the only man ever to have managed a descent down the arch of the towering Rainbow Natural Bridge in Utah. He completed three expeditions down the Colorado River, in the days when it was still an uncharted wilderness. He landed among hostile natives, reported to be cannibals, on the island of Tiburon off the coast of Mexico, and got his Bell and Howell smashed with a rock. . . . Perhaps this man, who spent his life fabricating thrills and adventures for the masses imprisoned in humdrum pursuits, needed something beyond the sheer reward of wealth itself. It was difficult to reconcile the daredevil of the Rio de las Balsas, the Colorado, Tiburon Island, with the suave, cool, mild-mannered executive on the other end of a cigar, but in many ways the adventurer was the more real figure.

Jesse Lasky Jr, *Whatever Happened to Hollywood?*

LATIMER, HUGH, BISHOP OF WORCESTER

1485–1555 Martyr

Then they brought a Faggot, kindled with fire, and laid the same down at D. *Ridleys* feet. To whom Mr. *Latimer* spake in this manner; Be of good comfort, Mr. *Ridley*, and play the man, we shall this day light such a candle by Gods grace in *England*, as I trust shall never be put out.

John Foxe, *Acts and Monuments*.

He was no great scholar: he knew no Greek: he took his doctrinal position from Cranmer and left disputation to Ridley. He was a preacher, and a court preacher, too. Not a fashionable court preacher, like John Donne or the great Jesuit preachers of the next century, exploring and illuminating the intimate spiritual recesses of rich patrons and great ladies, but a tribune of the people who preached his message menacingly, like Hosea or Amos, to the face of Kings.

H. R. Trevor-Roper, *Hugh Latimer and the English Commonwealth*.

See also Mary I

LATROBE, BENJAMIN HENRY

1764–1820 Architect, Engineer

My principles of good taste are rigid in Grecian architecture. I am a bigoted Greek in the condemnation of the Roman architecture of Baalbec, Palmyra, and Spalatro. . . . Wherever, therefore, the Grecian style can be copied without impropriety I love to be a mere, I would say a slavish copyist, but the forms & the distribution of the Roman & Greek buildings which remain, are in general, inapplicable to the objects & uses of our public buildings. Our religion requires a church wholly different from the temples, our legislative assemblies and our courts of justice, buildings of entirely different principles from their basilicas; and our amusements could not possibly be performed in their theatres & amphitheatres. . . .

On himself, in Talbot Hamlin, *Benjamin Henry Latrobe*.

I believe I am the first who, in our own country, has endeavored & partly succeeded, to place the profession of architect and civil engineer on that footing of responsibility which it occupies in Europe. But I have not so far succeeded as to make it an eligible profession for one who has the education & the feelings of a gentleman. . . . The best in all our great cities is in the hands of mechanics who disgrace the art but possess the public confidence, and under the false appearance of economy have infinitely the advantage in this degrading competition. With them the struggle will be long & harrassing. . . . Fascinating and honorable as is the profession, it is not lucrative.

On himself, in *ibid*.

LAUD, WILLIAM

1573–1645 Archbishop of Canterbury

He is half a precisian in the outward man; he loveth

little bands, short hair, grave looks; but had rather
be slain at Tyburn than preach in a cloak.
  Anon., *The Character of an Untrue Bishop.*

Although he came with confidence to the scaffold,
and the blood wrought lively in his cheeks, yet
when he did lye down upon the block he trembled
every joint of him; the sense of something after
death, and the undiscovered country unto which
his soul was wandering startling his resolution, and
possessing every joint of him with an universal
palsey of fear.
  Anon., in *Post* (London), January 1644.

William Lawd (Arch-bishop of Canterbury) in a
Sermon Preached before the Parliament, about the
beginning of the Reign of King Charles I affirms
the Power of Prayer to be so great, that though
there be a Conjunction or Opposition of Saturn or
Mars (as there was one of them then) it will overcome the malignity of it.
  John Aubrey, *Brief Lives.*

This little man with his horseshoe brows, and prim
mouth, and sharp restless eyes is too subtle a figure
for an easy verdict. It is clear that he had great
natural gifts of head and heart. . . . [But] . . . there
was a cold donnish insensitiveness about him . . .
he applied the brain of a college pedant to the
spacious life of England.
  John Buchan, *Oliver Cromwell.*

He had no inconsiderable faith to preach, but no
gifts to make it acceptable. He was a devoted priest,
and a great ecclesiastic, but what the world sought
was a prophet.
  Ibid.

A busy logical faculty, operating entirely on
chimerical element of obsolete delusions, a vehement shrill-voiced character, confident in its own
rectitude, as the narrowest character may the
soonest be. A man not without affections, though
bred as a College Monk, with little room to develop
them; of shrill, tremulous, partly feminine nature
capable of spasms, of most hysterical obstinacy, as
female natures are. Prone to attach itself, if not
from love, at least from the need of help. A most
attaching creeper-plant, something of the bramble
species in it. The bramble will prick you to the
bone, while the oak to your handling is sleek; the
bramble by its very prickers and climbing, will train
itself aloft, and be found at the tops of the highest
trees; you shall judge thereby if it was not a strong
shrub, that bramble! Dr William Laud has pricked
a man or two that handled him. . . .
  Thomas Carlyle, *Historical Sketches.*

Poor old Laud, and his surplices.
  Thomas Carlyle, *Letters and Speeches of Oliver
  Cromwell.*

He pluckt down Puritans and Property, to build up
Paul's and Prerogative.
  Lord Falkland, as paraphrased by Sir Philip
  Warwick, *Memoirs of the Reign of Charles I.*

The one second-rate Englishman who had exercised
a wide influence upon the history of the world.
  H. A. L. Fisher, *History of Europe.*

But Courtiers most complained, that he persecuted
them, not in their proper places, but what in an
ordinary way he should have taken from the *hands*
of inferior officers, that He with a *long* and *strong
Arm* reached to himself over all their heads. Yet
others plead for him, that he abridg'd their *bribes*
not *fees*, and it vexed them that He struck their
fingers with the *dead-palsie*, so that they could not
(as formerly) have a *feeling* for Church preferments.
  Thomas Fuller, *Church History of Britain.*

He was very plain in apparel, and sharply checkt
such Clergymen whom he saw goe in rich or gaudy
cloaths, commonly calling them the *Church-
Triumphant.* Thus as *Cardinal Woolsey* is reported
the first Prelate, who made *Silks* and *Sattens*
fashionable amongst clergy-men; so this Arch-bishop
first retrenched the usual wearing there-of. Once at
a Visitation in *Essex* one in *Orders* (of good estate
and extraction) appeared before him very gallant in
habit, whom Dr *Laud* (then Bishop of London)
publickly reproved, shewing him the plainness of
his own apparel. My *Lord* (said the Minister) *you
have better cloaths at home, and I have worse,*
whereat the Bishop rested very well contented.
  Ibid.

He wore his hair very close, and though in the beginning of his greatness, many measured the length of
men's stricktness by the shortness of their hair, yet
some will say, that since, out of antipathy to conform to his example, his opposites have therein indulged more liberty to themselves.
  Ibid.

One of low stature, but high parts; piercing eyes,
cheerful countenance, wherein gravity and pleasantness were well compounded; admirable in his
naturals, unblameable in his morals, being very strict
in his conversation. Of him I have written in my
Ecclesiastical History: though I confess it was somewhat too soon for one with safety and truth to treat
of such a subject. Indeed I could instance some kind
of coarse venison, not fit for food when first killed;

and therefore cunning cooks bury it for some hours in the earth, till the rankness thereof being mortified thereby, it makes most palateable meat. So the memory of some persons newly deceased are neither fit for the writers or readers repast until some competent time after their interment.

Thomas Fuller, *The History of the Worthies of England.*

The Stye of all pestilential filth that hath infested the state and government of this commonwealth.

Sir Harbottle Grimston, Supporting Motion for the Impeachment of Archbishop Laud.

He was a man of great parts and very exemplar virtues, allyed and discredited by some unpopular naturall infirmityes, the greatest of which was, (besydes a hasty sharpe way of expressinge himselfe) that he believed innocence of hearts, and integrity of manners, was a guarde strong enough to secure any man, in his voyage through this worlde, in what company soever he travelled, and through what wayes soever he was to passe, and sure never any man was better supplyed with that provisyon.

Edward Hyde, Earl of Clarendon, *History of the Rebellion.*

The greatest Want the Archbishop had, was of a true Friend, who would seasonably have told him of his Infirmities, and what People spake of him; and . . . such a Friend would have been very acceptable to him.

Edward Hyde, Earl of Clarendon, *The Life . . . written by Himself.*

Laud hath a restless spirit, and cannot see when things are well, but loves to bring matters to a pitch of reformation floating in his own brain.

James I, attributed.

Nor deem, when Learning her last prize bestows
The glitt'ring eminence exempt from foes;
See, when the vulgar 'scapes, despis'd or aw'd,
Rebellions vengeful talons seize on Laud.
From meaner minds though smaller fines content
The plunder'd palace, or sequester'd rent,
Mark'd out by dangerous parts, he meets the shock,
And fatal Learning leads him to the block.

Samuel Johnson, *The Vanity of Human Wishes.*

You would be ruled by nobody, nor communicate yourself to any that I know, nor make yourself any party at Court, but stood upon yourself: it may be that was your fault.

Sir John Lamb, Letter to Laud, 1641.

Being a man of the Church, his ascendant is Capricornus, the cusp of the ninth house: Saturn is Lord of the sign, now in Aries his fall; a long time retrograde, and now positied in the twelfth of the figure, or fourth from his ascendant; so that the heavens represent him in condition of mind, of a violent spirit, turbulent and envious, a man involved in troubles, imprison'd, &c. Jupiter, a general significator of Churchmen, doth somewhat also represent his condition, being of that eminency he was of in our commonwealth. Jupiter, as you see, is retrograde, and with many fixed stars of the nature of Mars and Luna: an argument he was deep laden with misfortunes, and vulgar clamours at this present.

William Lilly, *Horoscope of William Laud,* 30 December 1644.

His understanding was narrow; and his commerce with the world had been small. He was by nature rash, irritable, quick to feel for his own dignity, slow to sympathise with the sufferings of others, and prone to the error, common in superstitious men, of mistaking his own peevish and malignant moods for emotions of pious zeal.

T. B. Macaulay, *History of England.*

Many writers have been tempted to digress from their immediate topic in order to dismiss Laud in an epigram: but between his grandiose design and its calamitous event the gulf is too vast for so delicate a bridge. What single definition can embrace his comprehensive social ideal, and his narrow-minded application of it: his tolerant theology and his intolerant methods: his huge efforts and their tenuous results: the social justice which he advocated, and the savage punishments which he inflicted? Yet the ideal, and the practical, in Laud's policy cannot be treated apart, for his ideal was only expressed in his practice — 'Thorough' is not the motto of a doctrinaire — and his practice, though shaped by an ideal, was plainly inspired by his acute appreciation of actual conditions.

Hugh Trevor-Roper, *Archbishop Laud.*

He who looks upon him thro' those canons, which in Synod passed in his time, will find him a true Assertor of Religion, Royalty, and Property; and that his grand designe was no other, than that of our first Reformation. . . . And untill this Nation is blest with such a spirit, it will lye in that darknes and confusion the Sects at this time have flung it into.

Sir Philip Warwick, *Memoirs of the Reign of King Charles I.*

LAUDERDALE, DUKE OF (JOHN MAITLAND)

1616—82 Statesman

This haughty monster with his ugly claws,

First temper'd poison to destroy our laws;
Declares the Council edicts are beyond
The most authentic statutes of the land;
Sets up in Scotland, *a la mode de France*,
Taxes, excise, and army does advance.
This saracen his country's freedom broke
To bring upon our necks the heavier yoke.
This is the savage pimp without dispute
First brought his mother for a prostitute;
Of all the miscreants ever went to hell
This villain rampant bears away the bell.

    Anon., *An Historical Poem*, 1680.

He made a very ill appearance: He was very big: His
hair red, hanging odly about him: His tongue was
too big for his mouth, which made him bedew all
that he talked to: And his whole manner was rough
and boisterous, and very unfit for a Court. He was
very learned, not only in *Latin*, in which he was a
master, but in *Greek* and *Hebrew*. He had read a
great deal of divinity, and almost all the historians
ancient and modern: So that he had great materials.
He had with these an extraordinary memory, and
copious but unpolished expression. He was a man,
as the Duke of *Buckingham* called him to me, of a
blundering understanding. He was haughty beyond
expression, abject to those he saw he must stoop to,
but imperious to all others. He had a violence of
passion that carried him often to fits like madness,
in which he had no temper. If he took a thing
wrong, it was a vain thing to study to convince him:
That would rather provoke him to swear, he would
never be of another mind: He was to be let alone:
And perhaps he would have forgot what he had said,
and come about of his own accord. He was the
coldest friend and the violentest enemy I ever
knew: I felt it too much not to know it.

    Gilbert Burnet, *History of My Own Time*.

LAUGHTON, CHARLES

1899—1962 Actor

We got on very well — in spite of his strange habits,
such as a terrific prejudice concerning Jews and
needing strange off-stage noises to get himself in the
mood for acting. He was the first actor I encountered who prepared to make a laughing entrance by
going around doing *ha-ha!* sounds for hours.

    George Cukor, in Gavin Lambert, *On Cukor*.

I always admired his courage in revealing the sensual
side of his nature with such honesty and power. In
the part of Angelo he trod the stage like an evil bat,
with the billowing silk sleeves of his black gown
flapping round him as he prowled up and down the
stage, and he had immense drive, with a strong vein
of poetic imagination which gave his performance
colour and excitement. One might say, perhaps, that
whereas [Leslie] Faber and [Cedric] Hardwicke
were highly skilled dyed-in-the-wool professionals,
Laughton was an inspired amateur. The first two
men were perfectionists, calculating their acting to
a nicety, and both struck me as being basically
modest men, dry, witty, cynical. Laughton was
more of an exhibitionist. His monsters were vicious
with a kind of childlike naiveté fascinating in its
contradictions. In *Macbeth* he made a sensation only
in the Banquet Scene when confronted with the
Ghost of Banquo, while in *King Lear* his scene on
Dover Cliff made the greatest impression. He could
not find and sustain the progression necessary to
achieve either of these great parts to the full. How
often stage and screen, dividing the loyalties of
talented actors, have played havoc with their sense
of direction and crippled their potentialities in consequence.

    Sir John Gielgud, *Distinguished Company*.

Charles Laughton was a total actor. His range was
wide — no screen actor has come anywhere near so
large a compass of characterizations, each one vivid
and individual. He was a big, brazen, show-off actor.
He went overboard sometimes and, in some of the
poor films he made, he got near to chewing the
scenery; but as well as the bold, daring gesture — the
hallmark of the great actor — he could perform with
infinite delicacy. . . . He was one of the few film-
stars able to overcome an unprepossessing personal
appearance and go on to receive wide audience
acceptance.

    David Shipman, *The Great Movie Stars*.

LAUREL, STAN (ARTHUR STANLEY JEFFERSON) AND HARDY, OLIVER

1890—1965 and 1892—1957 Comedians

That kind of junk [elaborate film criticism] annoys
the hell out of me. What people like that don't
understand and never will understand is that what
we were trying to do was to make people laugh in as
many ways as we could, without trying to prove a
point or show the world its troubles or get into
some deep meaning. Why the hell do you have to
explain why a thing is funny? We were trying to do
a very simple thing, give some people some laughs,
and that's all we were trying to do.

    Stan Laurel on himself, in John McCabe, *The
Comedy World of Stan Laurel*.

As a team, they complemented each other perfectly,
not only physically, but also in terms of personality.

Laurel was the eternal innocent — trusting, babyish, so stupid that when a good idea comes to him it is gone before he can grasp it and make use of it, and with a streak of childish maliciousness in him which comes to the surface when pressed a little too far. Hardy on the other hand, was completely adult — the bon vivant and gallant of the old school, with flowery gestures and eloquent speech, pompous and opinionated, and only temporarily deflated when his ego is punctured — as it always was, without fail!

> Joe Franklin, *Classics of the Silent Screen.*

Of all the silent comedians, Laurel and Hardy are perhaps the most threatening to women, as they combine the physical ruination with misogyny. One epicene and gross, the other emaciated, they are an aesthetic offense. With their disaster-prone bodies and their exclusive relationship that not only shuts out women but questions their very necessity, they constitute a two-man wrecking team of female — that is, civilized and bourgeois — society.

> Molly Haskell, *From Reverence to Rape.*

LAW, ANDREW BONAR

1858–1923 Prime Minister

I am afraid I shall have to show myself very vicious, Mr Asquith, this session. I hope you will understand.

> On himself, speaking to Herbert Asquith in February 1912, in Roy Jenkins, *Asquith.*

Has not the brains of a Glasgow baillie.

> H. H. Asquith, speaking to David Lloyd George, in Frances Stevenson, Diary, 27 November 1916.

It is fitting that we should have buried the Unknown Prime Minister by the side of the Unknown Soldier.

> H. H. Asquith, on the interment of Law's ashes in Westminster Abbey, 1923.

Of course the most characteristic thing to those who knew him would be a ginger cake and a glass of milk, to which I brought him home pretty nearly every night for about four years!

> Stanley Baldwin, Letter to Lord Beaverbrook, 18 December 1928.

He was almost devoid of Conservative principles. This Presbyterian from Canada had no imaginative reverence for the traditions and symbols of the past, no special care for vested interests, no attachment whatever to the Upper Classes, the City, the Army, or the Church. . . . [His] Conservatism . . . proceeded from caution, scepticism, lack of faith, a

distrust of any intellectual process which proceeded more than one or two steps ahead or any emotional enthusiasm which grasped at an intangible object, and an extreme respect for all kinds of *Success.*

> John Maynard Keynes, *Essays in Biography.*

Bonar would never make up his mind on anything. Once a question had been decided, Bonar would stick to it and fight for it to a finish, but he would never help in the taking of a decision.

> David Lloyd George, in A. J. Sylvester, *Life with Lloyd George.*

I told Bonar that . . . I had been to a Mozart concert and the music was wonderful. Bonar casually and languidly remarked: 'I don't care for music.' As we motored along, there was the Mediterranean blue sea on one side and the rolling snow-capped Alpes Maritimes on the other. This inspired me to exclaim: 'Look, Bonar, what a wonderful scene that is.' 'I don't care for scenery,' remarked Bonar. Presently we came to a bridge . . . I said to Bonar: 'Look, Bonar, aren't those handsome women?' 'I don't care for women,' remarked Bonar very drily. 'Then what the hell do you care for?' I asked. Then in his very soft voice, and quieter still, Bonar replied: 'I like bridge.'

> *Ibid.*

. . . the public have never realised the creative common-sense of Bonar Law — he was the most constructive objector that I have ever known. . . .

> David Lloyd George, in Harold Nicolson, Diary, 6 July 1936.

Bonar always jibs a good deal before taking a long jump. . . .

> Frances Stevenson, Diary, 16 March 1920.

See also Lord Beaverbrook

LAWRENCE, DAVID HERBERT

1885–1930 Novelist, Poet, Painter, Playwright

I always say, my motto is 'Art for my sake'.

> On himself, Letter to Ernest Collings, 24 December 1912.

I'll do my life work, sticking up for the love between man and woman.

> On himself, Letter to Sally Hopkin, 25 December 1912.

I'm like Carlyle, who, they say, wrote 50 volumes on the value of silence.

> On himself, Letter to Ernest Collings, 17 January 1913.

I *know* I can write bigger stuff ·than any man in England.

On himself, Letter to Edward Garnett, April 1913.

A book should either be a bandit or a rebel or a man in a crowd. People should either run for their lives, or come under the colours, or say *how do you do?* I hate the actor-and-the-audience business. An author should be in among the crowd, kicking their shins or cheering on to some mischief or merriment. That rather cheap seat in the gods where one sits with fellows like Anatole France and benignly looks down on the foibles, follies and frenzies of so-called fellow-men just annoys me. After all the world is not a stage — not to me: nor a theatre: nor a show-house of any sort. . . . Whoever reads me will be in the thick of the scrimmage, and if he doesn't like it — if he wants a safe seat in the audience — let him read somebody else.

On himself, Letter to Carlo Linati, 22 January 1925.

I don't know how much you sympathise with my work — perhaps not much. But, anyhow, you know it is quite sincere, and that I sincerely believe in restoring the other, the phallic consciousness, into our lives: because it is the source of all real beauty, and all real gentleness. And those are the two things, tenderness and beauty, which will save us from horrors.

On himself, Letter to Harriet Monroe, 15 March 1928.

About *Lady C.* — you mustn't think I advocate perpetual sex. Far from it. Nothing nauseates me more than promiscuous sex in and out of season. But I want, with *Lady C.*, to make an *adjustment in consciousness* to the basic physical realities. I realize that one of the reasons why the common people often keep — or kept — the good *natural glow* of life, just warm life, longer than educated people, was because it was still possible for them to say fuck! or shit without either a shudder or a sensation. If a man had been able to say to you when you were young and in love: an' if tha shits, an' if tha pisses, I'm glad, I shouldna want a woman who couldna shit nor piss — surely it would have been a liberation to you, and it would have helped to keep your heart warm.

On himself, Letter to Lady Ottoline Morrell, 28 December 1928.

One of the great denouncers, the great missionaries the English send to themselves to tell them they are crass, gross, lost, dead, mad and addicted to un-natural vice. I suppose it is a good thing that these chaps continue to roll up, though in this case I wonder whether as much silly conduct has not been encouraged as heartless conduct deterred. However that may be, it is a chilling disappointment to take an actual look at the denunciations and be confronted not only by egomania, fatuity and gimcrack theorizing, but bitterness and censoriousness as well. It might even be more intelligent to leave Lawrence on his pinnacle, inspiring, unapproachable and unread.

Kingsley Amis, *What Became of Jane Austen?*

One might . . . say that, in their attitude towards art, the formal verse writer is a catholic, the free verse writer a protestant. And Lawrence was, in every respect, very protestant indeed. As he himself acknowledged, it was through [Walt] Whitman that he found himself as a poet, found the right idiom of poetic speech for his demon. On no other poet, so far as I know, has Whitman had a beneficial influence; he could on Lawrence because, despite certain superficial resemblances, their sensibilities were utterly different.

W. H. Auden, *The Dyer's Hand.*

I am a tremendous admirer of Lawrence. I should hesitate to go as far in admiration as that very distinguished critic E. M. Forster, who believes that he was 'the greatest imaginative novelist of our time'. In my opinion, Lawrence lacked one quality — the power to discipline and control his faculties. . . . Lawrence seemed to me sometimes to suffer from a delusion similar to the delusion of the sick man who thinks that if a given quantity of medicine will do him good, twice the quantity will do him twice the good. . . . Still, I would say that no finer work has been done in our time than Lawrence's finest. . . . In the future no first editions of present-day writers will be more passionately and expensively sought for than Lawrence's, unless perhaps Joyce's. I regard this as certain.

Arnold Bennett, in *Evening Standard*, 12 April 1930.

'Character' for Lawrence belonged to the dead past — to a way of life that he strove to transcend. Character, of course, was amusing and interesting, and would, of course, persist. But the interest in it was a literary interest and, so far as life goes, was static. Character — which Lawrence savoured as well as anybody — had been *used* as a demonstration of life until it had become stereotyped — a *made* instead of a spontaneous thing.

Catherine Carswell, *The Savage Pilgrimage.*

The picture of D. H. Lawrence suggested by the obituary notices of 'competent critics' is of a man morose, frustrated, tortured. . . . Lawrence was as little morose as any open clematis flower, as little tortured or sinister or hysterical as a humming-bird. Gay, skilful, clever at everything, furious when he felt like it but never grieved or upset, intensely amusing, without sentimentality or affectation, almost always right in his touch for the *content* of things or persons, he was at once the most harmonious and the most vital person I ever saw.

Catherine Carswell, Letter to *Time and Tide*, 14 March 1930.

Lawrence, as the early lyricism of his pre-war books evaporated, became a master of the colloquial style. Though his work is marred by carelessness, repetition, and want of ear and a tendency to preach and rant which ill-health accentuated, it is always vigorous, thoughtful and alive, the enemy of elaboration and artifice, of moral hypocrisy and verbal falseness.

Cyril Connolly, *Enemies of Promise*.

Since he had dismissed the brain for the belly-worship of his creed, the vision of a peaceful and rational society could have no attractions for him. He was an enemy of the mind; and though somehow he might have repudiated this as shrilly as he repudiated all accepted standards, he remained a mouthpiece of reaction in contemporary letters. The 'mindless, eyeless, hysterical mass-consciousness' with which his work is identified has become the bane of modern Europe.

Roger Dataller, *The Plain Man and the Novel*.

The Rainbow, a novel by Mr D. H. Lawrence, . . . is . . . more hideous than any imaginable reality. The thing is done so coldly, so pompously, so gravely that it is like a savage rite. There is not a gleam of humour in the fog of eloquent lubricity. The thud, thud, thud of hectic phrases is intolerably wearisome. They pound away like engines, grinding out a dull monotonous tune of spiritless sensuality. . . . The deadliest enemies of literature are the foes in its own household. . . . The injury done to letters by men of genius who violate the ancient sanctities is profound and far-reaching. If Mr Lawrence were not greater than his offence, his offence would not be so rank. But he possesses the heavenly gift of glamour. He can weave veils of shimmering meretriciousness round unnameable and unthinkable ugliness. He can lift the rainbow out of the sunlight and set its arch over the pit from whose murky brink every healthy foot ought to shrink in fear and abhorrence.

James Douglas, Review of *The Rainbow*, in *Star*, 22 October 1915.

In the work of D. H. Lawrence . . . is found the profoundest research into human nature, as well as the most erratic and uneven writing, by any writer of our generation.

T. S. Eliot, in *Vanity Fair*, July 1923.

He kept his trivialities for poetry in the way most writers of both keep them for prose.

D. J. Enright, in *New Statesman*, 30 October 1964.

This pictorial account of the day-to-day life of an English gamekeeper is full of considerable interest to outdoor minded readers, as it contains many passages on pheasant-raising, the apprehending of poachers, ways to control vermin, and other chores and duties of the professional gamekeeper. Unfortunately, one is obliged to wade through many pages of extraneous material in order to discover and savour those sidelights on the management of a midland shooting estate, and in this reviewer's opinion the book cannot take the place of J. R. Miller's *Practical Gamekeeping*.

Field and Stream review of *Lady Chatterley's Lover*.

The Press can make a great to-do about the innocuous, blameless and essentially minor poetry of Edward Thomas (to take but one example); they politely refuse to discuss the questionable, but essentially major effort of a D. H. Lawrence. Is it any wonder that such an attitude drives a man to sheer fanaticism?

John Gould Fletcher, in *Poetry* (Chicago), August 1918.

I cannot say that I liked Lawrence much. He remained too disturbing even when I got to know him well. He had so much need of moral support to take the place of his mother's influence that he kept one — everyone who at all came into contact with him — in a constant state of solicitude. He claimed moral support imperiously — and physical care too.

Ford Madox Ford, *Mightier than the Sword*.

Lawrence himself is, as far as I know, the only prophetic novelist writing to-day — all the rest are fantasists or preachers: the only living novelist in whom the song predominates, who has the rapt bardic quality, and whom it is idle to criticize. He invites criticism because he is a preacher also — it is this minor aspect of him which makes him so difficult and misleading — an excessively clever preacher who knows how to play on the nerves of his congregation. Nothing is more disconcerting than to sit down, so to speak, before your prophet, and then suddenly to receive his boot in the pit of your stomach.

E. M. Forster, *Aspects of the Novel*.

I'll tell you a poet with a method that is a method: Lawrence. I came across a poem of his in a new *Imagiste* Anthology just published here, and it was such a poem that I wanted to go right to the man that wrote it and say something.

Robert Frost, Letter to Edward Garnett, 12 June 1915.

Lawrence thought every woman should
Be shown that her desires are good,
That *amor naturale*'s error
Lies in obeying Ego's terror.
Lawrence, too, contrived to train us
In the importance of the anus,
Not *Sade*-like as a matter of course,
But to return us to a Source
Which, with some conscientious plumbing
Could liberate the Second Coming.

John Fuller, *The Art of Love.*

It's not good enough to spend time and ink in describing the penultimate sensations and physical movements of people getting into a state of rut. . . . The body's never worthwhile, and the sooner Lawrence recognizes that, the better — the men we swear by — Tolstoy, Turgenev, Chekov, Maupassant, Flaubert, France — knew that great truth, they only use the body, and that sparingly, to reveal the soul.

John Galsworthy, Letter to Edward Garnett, 13 April 1914.

At one time . . . a certain inner circle of the leaders of literary fashion . . . pretended to consider Mr Lawrence the white hope of English letters; and they succeeded in making his books the vogue among a section of the London intelligentsia. It became the correct thing to admire Mr Lawrence — until he suddenly applied the acid test of the value of these protestations and of this admiration by publishing *The Rainbow*. Then what a change of front! The deafening silence, broken only by the sound of the white rabbits of criticism scuttling for cover, which formed the sequel to *The Rainbow* prosecution, will not soon be forgotten by those who were in London at the time. Not one of Mr Lawrence's fervent boosters ventured into print to defend him; not one of his brother authors (save only Mr Arnold Bennett, to whom all honour is due) took up the cudgels on his behalf. English novelists are proverbially lacking in *esprit de corps*, but surely they were never so badly shown up as when they tolerated the persecution of a distinguished *confrère* without making a collective protest.

Douglas Goldring, *Reputations.*

Lawrence's special and characteristic gift was an extraordinary sensitiveness to what Wordsworth called 'unknown modes of being'. He was always intensely aware of the mystery of the world, and the mystery was always for him a *numen*, divine. Lawrence could never forget, as most of us almost continuously forget, the dark presence of the otherness that lies beyond the boundaries of man's conscious mind. This special sensibility was accompanied by a prodigious power of rendering the immediately experienced otherness in terms of literary art.

Aldous Huxley, Introduction to *The Letters of D. H. Lawrence.*

To be with Lawrence was a kind of adventure, a voyage of discovery into newness and otherness. For, being himself of a different order, he inhabited a different universe from that of common men — a brighter and intenser world, of which, while he spoke, he would make you free. . . . For Lawrence, existence was one continuous convalescence; it was as though he were newly re-born from a mortal illness every day of his life.

Ibid.

Though without any of Nietzsche's nobility of character and capacity to endure neglect and solitude, Lawrence in his slight way, often recalls Nietzsche, another poet enmeshed in the will, and solacing his impotence with dreams of new forms of life in which he would be the master.

Hugh Kingsmill, *D. H. Lawrence.*

It makes me laugh when I think of that American doctor who 'looked at literature' who wrote about Lawrence and saw only a diseased prurient mind in him. I think all he wanted to see was disease. Because Ursula and Birkin, in *Women in Love*, have a good meal with beetroot and ham and venison pastry, he reads some horror into beetroot and ham and pastry. I think the horror was in the good doctor's mind, for what horror is there in beetroot or ham or venison pastry? Good to eat they are, that's all. Lawrence was so direct, such a real puritan! He hated any *haut-goût* or lewdness. Fine underclothing and all the apparatus of the seducing sort were just stupid to him. All tricks; why tricks? Passionate people don't need tricks.

Frieda Lawrence, *Not I, But the Wind. . . .*

I have heard so much about 'form' . . . why are you English so keen on it? Their own form wants smashing in almost any direction, but they can't come out of their snail house. I know it is so much safer. That's what I love Lawrence for, that he is so plucky and honest in his work, he dares to come out in the open and plants his stuff down bald and naked; really he is the only revolutionary worthy of the name, that I know; any new thing must find a new shape, then afterwards one can call it 'art'.

Frieda Lawrence, Letter to Edward Garnett, 1912.

Then there is his sanity, his poise. There is a tendency among certain critics, especially in Germany, to regard D. H. Lawrence as a neurotic. That foolish legend will, we trust, be killed by this publication. The whole correspondence of D. H. Lawrence pulsates with sanity, even in little things. 'Don't you,' he writes, 'think it's nonsense when M. says that my world is not the ordinary man's world, and that I am a sort of animal with a sixth sense? . . . They all seem determined to make a freak of me — to save their own short-failings, and make them "normal".' Lawrence was obviously exceptional, even eccentric, but he was not a neurotic.

F. R. Leavis, Review of Lawrence's *Letters*, in *New Statesman*, 1 October 1932.

Is there no name later than Conrad's to be included in the great tradition? There is, I am convinced, one: D. H. Lawrence. Lawrence, in the English language, was the great genius of our time (I mean the age, or climatic phase, following Conrad's).

F. R. Leavis, *The Great Tradition*.

Lawrence had excuses for his prophetic passion. Civilized life is certainly threatened with impoverishment by education based on crude and defective psychology, by standardization at a low level, and by the inculcation of a cheap and shallow emotional code. Lawrence's genius has done much to make this more widely and keenly realized than before. It is a great service.

F. R. Leavis, *For Continuity*.

What Lawrence offers is not a philosophy or an *oeuvre* — a body of literary art — but an experience, or, to fall back on the French again, an *expérience*, for the sense of 'experiment' is needed too. In him the human spirit explored, with unsurpassed courage, resource and endurance, the representative, the radical and central problems of our time. Of course he went into dangerous places, and laid himself open to reprehension as setting dangerous examples and inciting to dangerous experiments. But if he earned reprehension, we owe him gratitude for earning it.

Ibid.

Lawrence is placed — is, in fact, distinctly *passé*; we are no longer (if we ever were) very much impressed by him. He had, of course, a kind of genius, but to take him seriously as an intellectual and spiritual force, a force that could affect our attitude to-

wards life and the problems of our time — it's amusing to think that there were once earnest souls who did so. To-day, while recognizing the queerly limited gifts he dissipated, we hardly bother to smile at his humourless fanaticisms. At least, that's the impression one gets from the literary world to-day (I mean the milieu in which fashions are set and worn and the higher reviewing provided for).

F. R. Leavis, *The Common Pursuit*.

He sees more than a human being ought to see. Perhaps that's why he hates humanity so much.

Vernon Lee, in Aldous Huxley, Introduction to *Letters of D. H. Lawrence*.

We know what sort of picture D. H. Lawrence would paint if he took to the brush instead of the pen. For he did so, luckily, and even held exhibitions. As one might have expected, it turned out to be incompetent Gauguin.

Percy Wyndham Lewis, *Men Without Art*.

Lawrence's animal natures, just because of their irreducible obscenity, are the purest bodies in our current literature. Animated by a metaphysical conception they act through obedience to fundamental laws of nature. Of these laws Lawrence admits his complete ignorance. He created his metaphysical world by faith; he proceeds only by intuition. He may have been utterly wrong, but he is absolutely consistent.

Henry Miller, *The Cosmological Eye*.

Lawrentian sexuality seems to be guided by somewhat the same principle one finds expressed in Rainwater's study of the working class (also the doctrine of the nineteenth-century middle classes) — 'sex is for the man'. Lawrence's knowledge of Freud was sketchy and secondhand, but he appears to be well acquainted with the theories of female passivity and male activity and doubtless found them very convenient. Ladies — even when they are 'cunt' — don't move.

Kate Millett, *Sexual Politics*.

It is a book that piques one's curiosity in many ways. To begin with, what is the sex of 'D. H. Lawrence'? The clever analysis of the wayward Lettie, surely a woman's woman, and the particular way in which physical charm is praised almost convince us that it is the work of a woman; while, if so, we must wonder greatly at the sympathetic understanding of the male point of view as interpreted in the reflections of the supposed narrator of the book.

Morning Post, Review of *The White Peacock*, 9 February 1911.

All his life long Lawrence laboured to convince himself and other people that sexual desire carried its own validity: that the spiritual and the sexual were distinct. In fact, he never could believe it. What he did believe was something quite different, and quite true, namely that, in a man and woman who are whole, as he was never whole, the spiritual and the sexual might be one. . . . He believed in a harmony which was impossible for him personally to achieve without a physical resurrection.

John Middleton Murry, *Son of Woman.*

In *St Mawr* Lawrence the critic sets out with the Freudian interpretation in his mind to make up a story about a horse. But the symbol has not really caught fire in the mind of Lawrence the creator. As a result, the horse never takes on real symbolic significance, but becomes a sort of grotesque caricature of Lawrence himself. In his identification of himself with the horse Lawrence even goes so far as to make the wretched animal have no foals *because it doesn't want to.* Lawrence, it should be remembered, had no children, nor did many of his characters.

Norman Nicholson, *Man and Literature.*

Lawrence at first sight does not seem to be a pessimistic writer, because, like Dickens, he is a 'change-of-heart' man and constantly insisting that life here and now would be all right if only you looked at it a little differently. But what he is demanding is a movement away from our mechanised civilisation, which is not going to happen, and which he knows is not going to happen. . . . The kind of life that he is always pointing to, a life centring round the simple mysteries — sex, earth, fire, water, blood — is merely a lost cause.

George Orwell, *Inside the Whale.*

Like other civilized communities we have laws against obscenity which must be rigorously enforced. It is not enough to keep a sharp eye upon picture-postcard shops and to terrorize small boys who chalk ribald nonsense on blank walls. When a publisher like Mr Martin Secker sends out a novel by Mr D. H. Lawrence which flouts the most elementary canons of decency, the police should be equally alert. It should be remembered, moreover, that Mr Lawrence is an old offender, and that the edition of his former book, *The Rainbow*, was unceremoniously seized by the police. Undeterred by this experience, Mr Lawrence has penned another novel, *Women in Love*, which justly merits the fate of its predecessor. I do not claim to be a literary critic, but I know dirt when I smell it and here it is in heaps — festering, putrid heaps which smell to high Heaven.

W. Charles Pilley, Review of *Women in Love*, in *John Bull*, 17 September 1921.

Detestable person but needs watching. I think he learned the proper treatment of modern subjects before I did.

Ezra Pound, Letter to Harriet Monroe, March 1913.

Lawrence's teachings are interesting because they are a compendium of what a whole generation wanted to feel, until Hitler arose, just after Lawrence's death, and they saw where the dark unconsciousness was leading them. Seen in this light, Lawrence represented the last phase of the Romantic movement: random, irresponsible egotism, power for power's sake, the blood cult of Rosenberg. And Lawrence was representative, because tens of thousands of people in England and Europe were uprooted people, like himself.

V. S. Pritchett, *The Living Novel.*

He stands towards our day much as Richard Wagner stood towards his own. . . . He holds the mirror up to men in their most secret trouble. There must be folk in thousands who have been made to live more truly through his work. Each book has been a tearing new experience. It is characteristic that the angriest of the opposition to him has broken from the archaic ranks of the romantic males and the cast-iron feminists. And it is with Wagner and the other artists who have beaten out the rhythm for their ages that D. H. Lawrence must come permanently to rest: one of those stars which, seen or lost to sight, help hold the planet on its course.

Paul Rosenfeld, *Men Seen.*

Lawrence is very like Shelley — just as fine, but with a similar impatience of fact. The revolution he hopes for is just like Shelley's prophecy of banded anarchs fleeing while the people celebrate a feast of love. His psychology of people is amazingly good up to a point, but at a certain point he gets misled by love of violent colouring.

Bertrand Russell, Letter to Lady Ottoline Morrell, July 1915.

Lawrence is a long line of people, beginning with Heraclitus & ending with Hitler, whose ruling motive is hatred derived from megalomania, & I am sorry to see that I was once so far out in estimating him.

Ibid, February 1937.

What at first attracted me to Lawrence was a certain dynamic quality and a habit of challenging assumptions that one is apt to take for granted. . . . But this is not to say that there was anything good in his ideas. They were the ideas of a sensitive would-be despot who got angry with the world because it would not obey. When he realized that other people existed, he hated them. But most of the time he lived in a solitary world of his own imaginings, peopled by phantoms as fierce as he wished them to be.

Bertrand Russell, *Autobiography*.

Lawrence, though most people did not realize it, was his wife's mouthpiece. He had the eloquence, but she had the ideas. She used to spend part of every summer in a colony of Austrian Freudians at a time when psychoanalysis was little known in England. Somehow, she imbibed prematurely the ideas afterwards developed by Mussolini and Hitler, and these ideas she transmitted to Lawrence, shall we say, by blood-consciousness.

Ibid.

Mr Lawrence looked like a plaster gnome on a stone toadstool in some suburban garden. At the same time he bore some resemblance to a bad self-portrait by Van Gogh. He had a rather matted, dank appearance. He looked as if he had just returned from spending an uncomfortable night in a very dark cave, hiding, perhaps, in the darkness, from something which, at the same time, he on his side was hunting.

Edith Sitwell, *Taken Care Of*.

In many ways I liked it — the ordinary Lawrenceisms were less in evidence — and it was excellent to attack that subject frontally. But I complain of a sad lack of artistic intention — of creative powers thrown away — of an obsession with moralising. To say nothing of a barbaric, anti-civilization outlook, which I disapprove of.

Lytton Strachey, on reading *Lady Chatterley's Lover*, Letter to Roger Senhouse, 23 October 1928.

[Aldous Huxley] would, as someone brighter than myself has said, condense the generative principle into a test-tube; Lawrence, on the other hand, would condense the world into the generative principle, and make his apostles decline not cogitare but copulare.

Dylan Thomas, Letter to Pamela Hansford Johnson, 1933.

It is typical of the physically weak to emphasize the strength of life (Nietzsche); of the apprehensive and complex-ridden to emphasize its naivete and dark wholesomeness.

Ibid.

Like Hitler, Lawrence gives an impression of proceeding somnambulistically — arms outstretched, vision confident but unseeing, footfall certain because unconscious. Many of his ideas, indeed, par-

ticularly in his last years, were decidedly Hitlerian; much in *Apocalypse* could have gone straight into *Mein Kampf*.

Times Literary Supplement, Review of Richard Aldington's *Portrait of a Genius, But . . .* , 1950.

It seems to us now that his system, for all its fervour, was largely negative, a mere assertion of his denial of the system of his upbringing. His God, for instance, must be the exact opposite of the 'gentle Jesus' of his childhood. . . . Fascism finally succeeded, at least temporarily, in making the synthesis that eluded Lawrence.

Rex Warner, *The Cult of Power*.

See also W. H. Auden, Aldous Huxley, Wilfred Owen, Henry James, Bertrand Russell, Dylan Thomas, Virginia Woolf

LAWRENCE, GERTRUDE

1898–1952 Singer, Actress

Gertie has an astounding sense of the complete reality of the moment, and her moments, dictated by the extreme variability of her moods, change so swiftly that it is frequently difficult to discover what, apart from eating, sleeping, and acting, is true of her at all.

Noël Coward, *Present Indicative*.

LAWRENCE, SIR THOMAS

1769–1830 Painter

He was sensible that his own pictures 'had too much of a metallic appearance, — too many shining lights.'

Joseph Farington, Diary, 22 July 1798.

Lawrence is one of our greatest masters. I use the word master in rather a narrow sense. I do not mean by it quite the same as one of our greatest artists. I mean that he showed a consummate mastery over the means of artistic expression — that he had an unerring eye and hand. That is to say, that when he looked at anything, say a man's head, he seized at once the relations and proportions of its parts, and could draw this with unwavering precision. In this respect a man like Reynolds was a bungler in comparison, and even Gainsborough was hardly his equal. But whereas in Gainsborough's case the vision was, as it were, polarized by a peculiar melodious rhythm which was inherent in him, the vision that Lawrence grasped so surely was relatively commonplace and undistinguished.

Roger Fry, *Reflections on British Painting*.

Lawrence . . . made his art into a trade.
  Lord Gower, *Romney and Lawrence.*

His manner was elegant, but not high bred. He had too much that air of always submitting. He had smiled so often & so long, that at last his smile wore the appearance of being set in enamel.
  Benjamin R. Haydon, Diary, 9 January 1830.

Lawrence's characterisations tend in fact to have a double aim: to portray the public, superficial creature of fashion and society in poise and dress, and, primarily in the face, to indicate the more private sensibilities of the heart, in the parted lips, the dilated brilliant eyes, the sable curls in profusion on the forehead high and pale.
  David Piper, *The English Face.*

He is, from habit of coaxing his subjects I suppose, a little too fairspoken, otherwise very pleasant.
  Sir Walter Scott, Diary, 3 October 1827.

LAWRENCE, THOMAS EDWARD (OF ARABIA)

1888—1935 Author, Soldier

All the subject provinces of the Empire, to me were not worth one English boy.
  On himself, Introduction to *Seven Pillars of Wisdom.*

I drew these tides of men into my hands
And wrote my will across the sky in stars.
  Ibid.

I was an Irish nobody. I did something. It was a failure. And I became an Irish nobody again.
  On himself, as reported by William Butler Yeats, in Percy Wyndham Lewis, *Blasting and Bombadiering.*

Arabian Lawrence, who, whatever his claims as a man, was surely a sonorous fake as a writer.
  Kingsley Amis, *What Became of Jane Austen?*

As I walked with him down Piccadilly, my mind went back to an interrogation in Nazareth. What, the German Intelligence officer had asked, did I think about the secret letter which Djemal Pasha had received from the Emir Faisal, suggesting to the Turks terms for Arab neutrality, after the British reverse at Es Salt? I had said it sounded a very tall tale indeed; whereat the German produced a photograph of a letter bearing what he declared to be Faisal's signature. The same photostat was shown to some Australian prisoners in Nazareth. What did all this mean? — I now asked Lawrence as we stood at a

corner. He looked oddly at me beneath the streetlamp, and said: 'I wrote it myself. Or rather, I caused it to be written — I don't write good Arabic you know. We were in a hole east of Amman, waiting on Allenby, and I wanted to gain a few days' grace'. I watched him depart along Down Street. His small, spare frame disappeared suddenly in the shadows: he was expert at giving the illusion of a vanishing trick.
  Alan Bott, *Eastern Flights.*

. . . a bore and a bounder and a prig. He was intoxicated with his own youth, and loathed any milieu which he couldn't dominate. Certainly he had none of a gentleman's instincts, strutting about Peace Conferences in Arab dress.
  Henry Channon, Diary, 25 May 1935.

He frankly envied poets. He felt that they had some sort of secret which he might be able to grasp and profit from. He made Charles Doughty his chief hero. . . . Lawrence told me: 'When I asked Doughty why he had made that Arabian journey, his answer was that he had gone there "to redeem the English language from the slough into which it has fallen since the' time of Spenser".' These words of Doughty's seem to have made a great impression on Lawrence, and largely account, I think, for his furious keying-up of style in *The Seven Pillars.*
  Robert Graves, *Goodbye to All That.*

Even in his writing, Lawrence was a man of the conscious will. He *wanted* to write well, and he wrote about as well as a conscious will can make one write. But the consciously willed style always . . . stops short of the best, the genuinely good. . . . As a character, I find Lawrence extremely interesting. . . . He had . . . a self-will of heroic, even of Titanic, proportions; and one has the impression that he lived for the most part in one of the more painful corners of the inferno. He is one of those great men for whom one feels intensely sorry, because he was nothing but a great man.
  Aldous Huxley, Letter to Victoria Ocampo, 1946.

There are those who have tried to dismiss his story with a flourish of the Union Jack, a psychoanalytical catchword or a sneer; it should move our deepest admiration and pity. Like Shelley and like Baudelaire, it may be said of him that he suffered, in his own person, the neurotic ills of an entire generation.
  Christopher Isherwood, *Exhumations.*

He was retiring and yet craved to be seen, he was sincerely shy and naively exhibitionist. He had to rise above others and then humble himself, and in his self-inflicted humiliation demonstrate his superi-

ority. A deep cleavage in his own life lay at the root of it.
    Lewis B. Namier, in A. W. Lawrence, *T. E. Lawrence by His Friends.*

It should be noted that there is now no intelligentsia that is not in some sense 'left'. Perhaps the last right-wing intellectual was T. E. Lawrence.
    George Orwell, *The Lion and the Unicorn.*

A callow and terrified Marbot, placed in command of a sardonic Napoleon at Austerlitz and Jena, would have felt much as your superiors must in command of Lawrence the great.
    George Bernard Shaw, Letter to Lawrence, 17 December 1922.

Lawrence was a pure undiluted actor. A few weeks before his death I asked my wife, who was an intimate friend of his, why we had not seen him for some time. 'Oh,' she said, 'he's such an infernal liar!'
    George Bernard Shaw, in Hesketh Pearson, *Bernard Shaw, a Postscript.*

Lawrence licentiate to dream and to dare.
    Sir Ronald Storrs, *Orientations.*

LAZARUS, EMMA

1849—87 Poet, Essayist.

The poems have important merits, and I observe that my poet gains in skill as the poems multiply, and she may at last confidently say, I have mastered the obstructions, I have learned the rules. . . .
    Ralph Waldo Emerson, Undated letter to Emma Lazarus.

You should not write songs for *your* people, but for *the* people.
    Henry George, Undated letter to Emma Lazarus.

She never attached any great value to poetical fame; a purely literary career seemed to her too unreal, too detached from the world of the living, to offer any genuine reward. But once she enlisted in the army of Jewish nationalism, she lived like a woman possessed, her eyes not upon her own career, but upon the fulfillment of the promise of Israel. It was in that cause that her character had its fullest flowering.
    Allen Lesser, *Weave a Wreath of Laurel.*

I liked your sonnet about the Statue much better than I like the Statue itself. But your sonnet gives its subject a *raison d'être* which it wanted before

quite as much as it wanted a pedestal.
    James Russell Lowell, referring to the Statue of Liberty, Undated letter to Emma Lazarus.

Since Miriam sang of deliverance and triumph by the Red Sea, the Semitic race has had no braver singer.
    John Greenleaf Whittier, in H. E. Jacob, *The World of Emma Lazarus.*

LEACOCK, STEPHEN BUTLER

1869—1944 Author

Presently I shall be introduced as 'this venerable old gentleman' and the axe will fall when they raise me to the degree of 'grand old man'. That means on our continent any one with snow-white hair who has kept out of jail till eighty.
    On himself, *Three Score and Ten.*

LEAR, EDWARD

1812—88 Author, Artist

'How pleasant to know Mr. Lear!'
Who has written such volumes of stuff!
Some think him ill-tempered and queer,
But a few think him pleasant enough.
    On himself, Preface to *Nonsense Songs.*

I am almost thanking God that I was never educated, for it seems to me that 999 of those who are so, expensively and laboriously, have lost all before they arrive at my age — and remain like Swift's Strulbruggs — cut and dry for life, making no use of their earlier-gained treasures: whereas, I seem to be on the threshold of knowledge.
    On himself, Letter to Chichester Fortescue, 2 September 1859.

I went to the city today, to put the £125 I got for the 'Book of Nonsense' into the funds. It is doubtless a very unusual thing for an artist to put by money, for the whole way from Temple Bar to the Bank was *crowded* with carriages and people — so immense a sensation did this occurrence make. And all the way back it was the same, which was very gratifying.
    On himself, Letter to Lady Waldegrave, 4 November 1862.

Archbishop Tait . . . was always most kind to me, and once said in a big party, when I had been singing 'Home she brought her warrior' and people were crying — 'Sir! You ought to have half the Laureate-ship!'

On himself, Letter to Lord Carlingford, 9 December 1882.

Considering that I myself in 1833 had every sort of syphilitic disease, who am I to blame others, who have had less education and more temptation.

On himself, Diary, 20 February 1885.

His non-sense is not vacuity of sense: it is a parody of sense, and that is the sense of it. 'The Jumblies' is a poem of adventure, and of nostalgia for the romance of foreign voyage and exploration; 'The Yongy-Bongy-Bo' and 'The Dong with a Luminous Nose' are poems of unrequited passion — 'blues' in fact.

T. S. Eliot, *The Music of Poetry.*

Never was there a man who could so live into the feelings of a child.

Mrs Hugh Fraser, *A Diplomat's Wife in Many Lands.*

Some inner conflict, aggravated by indifferent health and insufficient wealth drove him to cut capers with words and images and ideas. And so, by accident, he becomes the laureate of nonsense, objectivising for his own relief and, as it happens, for our delight, that wilfulness which ever kept him a child in a world that was already in its second childhood.

Holbrook Jackson, Introduction to *The Complete Nonsense of Edward Lear.*

He really *lived* upon the letters of his distant friends more than any man I have ever known.

Franklin Lushington, Letter to Hallam Tennyson, March 1888.

Even today, epilepsy is a lonely disease, and although the idea of 'demoniac possession' can now be laughed at, there are still irrational lingerings of shame. In the early nineteenth century it was obscured by ignorance and old wives tales, and one of these was that attacks could be brought on by masturbation. Lear certainly believed that there could be a connection between the two, and as an adult he constantly blamed the attacks on his lack of will power. The usual threat offered to a little boy was that his penis would drop off and, like the Pobble whose toes disappeared when the scarlet flannel wrapper was taken away, Edward must sometimes have thought that he would be happier without it; the Pobble was given a feminine concoction of 'Lavender water tinged with pink', and perhaps this was the best solution.

Vivien Noakes, *Edward Lear, the Life of a Wanderer.*

The illustration to the written Nonsenses are often clichés of a skilled draughtsman, not much interested in human figures as such, but with considerable experience in drawing birds and animals — birds especially. When his hand was left to itself it seems to have sought the lines of least resistance in the form of amiable harpies, sometimes with birds' legs, and usually with vestigial wings functioning as arms.

Brian Reade, *Edward Lear's Parrots.*

Illyrian woodlands, echoing falls
    Of water, sheets of summer glass,
    The long divine Peneian pass,
The vast Akrokeraunian walls,

Tomohrit, Athos, all things fair,
    With such a pencil, such a pen,
    You shadow forth to distant men,
I read, and felt that I was there.

Alfred, Lord Tennyson, *To E.L. on his Travels in Greece.*

LEE, ANN

1736—84 Founder of the Shakers in America

Let names and sects and parties
Accost my ears no more,
My ever blessed Mother,
Forever I'll adore.
Appointed by kind-heaven
My Saviour to reveal
Her doctrine is confirmed
With an external seal.

Anon., from Shaker hymn 'Mother'.

Me have some love from Mother Ann
Me love it love it dearly
She called me her little son
And made me feel cheerly.

Anon. Shaker song.

The woman clothed with the sun.

Anon., popular description, in Edward T. Jones ed., *Notable American Women*, vol. 2.

A common prostitute.

Isaac Backus, in William G. McLoughlin, *Isaac Backus and the American Pietistic Tradition.*

The graceful motion of her hands, the beautiful appearance of her countenance, and the heavenly melody of her voice, made her seem like a glorious inhabitant of the heavenly world, singing praises to God.

Thankful Barce, in Edmund Andrews, *The People Called Shakers.*

LEE, GYPSY ROSE (ROSE LOUISE HOVICK)

1914–70 Ecdysiast

I am not a stripper. A stripper is a woman who puts on a sex spectacle. My act is straight comedy.
On herself, in Art Cohn, *The Nine Lives Of Michael Todd.*

The Best Undressed Woman In America.
Mike Todd, Slogan for *Streets of Paris* presentation at New York 1939 World's Fair.

LEE, NATHANIEL

1653?–92 Dramatist

There in a Den remov'd from human Eyes,
Possest with Muse, the Brain-sick Poet lyes,
Too miserably wretched to be nam'd;
For Plays, for Heroes, and for Passion fam'd
Thoughtless he raves his sleepless Hours away,
In Chains all nights, in Darkness al the Day.
And if he gets some Intervals from Pain,
The Fit returns; he foams, and bites his Chain,
His Eye-balls rowl, and he grows mad again.
Anon., *A Satyr on the Poets.*

The truth is, the poet's imagination ran away with his reason. While in Bedlam, he made that famous witty reply to a coxcomb scribbler who had the cruelty to jeer him with his misfortune, by observing that it was an easy thing to write like a madman: *'No* (said Lee) *it is* not *an easy thing to write like a madman; but it is very easy to write like a fool.'*
Baker, Reed and Jones eds, *Biographica Dramatica.*

Lee was a mad poet it is said, who described, in frantic verse, the actions of a mad hero.
Thomas Davies, *Dramatic Miscellanies.*

He was so esteemed and beloved that before his misfortune we always called him *Honest Nat* and afterwards *poor Nat.*
'W.G.', in *Gentleman's Magazine*, 1745.

LEE, ROBERT EDWARD

1807–70 Soldier

Posterity will rank Lee above Wellington or Napoleon, before Saxe or Turenne, above Marlborough or Frederick, before Alexander or Caesar. . . . In fact, the greatest general of this or any other age. He has made his own name, and the Confederacy he served,

immortal.
Anon. editorial, *Montreal Telegraph*, written as a eulogy on Lee's death.

Here was a man who remains great, although he failed. . . . Here was a man who failed grandly, a man who said that 'human virtue should be equal to human calamity,' and showed that it could be equal to it, and so, without pretense, without display, without self-consciousness, left an example that future Americans may study with profit as long as there is an America.
Gamaliel Bradford, in Margaret Sanborn, *Robert E. Lee: The Complete Man 1861–1870.*

What General Lee's feelings were I do not know, as he was a man of much dignity, with an impassable face, it was impossible to say whether he felt inwardly glad that the end had finally come, or felt sad over the result, and was too manly to show it. Whatever his feelings, they were entirely concealed from my observation; but my own feelings . . . were sad and depressed. I felt like anything rather than rejoicing at the downfall of a foe who had fought so long and valiantly, and had suffered so much for a cause.
Ulysses S. Grant, in *ibid.*

He was a foe without hate, a friend without treachery, a soldier without cruelty, and a victim without murmuring. He was a public officer without vices, a private citizen without wrong, a neighbor without hypocrisy, and a man without guilt. He was Caesar without his ambition, Frederick without his tyranny, Napoleon without his selfishness and Washington without his reward.
Benjamin H. Hill, in Robert Debs Heinl Jr, *The Dictionary of Military and Naval Quotations.*

Lee is the only man I know whom I would follow blindfold.
Stonewall Jackson, Letter of May 1862.

If I were on my death bed, and the President should tell me that a great battle was to be fought for the liberty or slavery of the country, and asked my judgment as to the ability of a commander, I would say with my dying breath, let it be Robert E. Lee.
General Winfield Scott, in Burke Davis, *They Called Him Stonewall.*

An angel's heart, an angel's mouth,
Not Homer's could alone for me
Hymn well the great Confederate South,
Virginia first and *Lee!*
Philip Stanhope Worsley, inscribed in a presentation copy of his translation of the *Iliad* to General Lee, January 1866.

LE FANU, JOSEPH SHERIDAN

1814—73 Novelist

It was his curious habit to write most of his stories in bed on scraps of paper and in pencil.
C. Litton Falkiner, in *Dictionary of National Biography*.

Those who possessed the rare privilege of Le Fanu's friendship, and only they, can form any idea of the true character of the man, for after the death of his wife, to whom he was most deeply devoted, he quite forsook general society, in which his fine features, distinguished bearing, and charm of conversation marked him out as the *beau-idéal* of an Irish wit and scholar of the old school. From this society he vanished so entirely that Dublin, always ready with a nickname, dubbed him 'The Invisible Prince.'
Temple Bar, vol. 50, 1877.

LEIGH, VIVIEN (VIVIAN MARY HARTLEY)

1913—67 Actress

She was often underrated because she was so beautiful.
George Cukor, in Gavin Lambert, *On Cukor*.

Why is Vivien Leigh beautiful? Well, to be outrageously romantic about it, she seems part flower. Tiny and fragile, she has skin like a white anemone petal, eyes as green and gracefully slanted as an Aeschynanthus leaf. The mouth suggests a cool, subtly defined wildflower; the entire head, an exquisite shape painted by some English master.
John Gruen, *Close-Up*.

LELY, SIR PETER (PIETER VAN DER FAES)

1618—80 Portrait Painter

Sir Peter, in his faces, preserves a languishing air, and a drowsy sweetness peculiar to himself.
The Biographical Magazine, 1794.

Th'amazed world shall henceforth find
None but my *Lilly* ever drew a *Mind*.
Richard Lovelace, *To my Worthy Friend Mr. Peter Lilly*.

Cheat *hocus-pocus*-Nature an Essay
O' th' Spring affords us, *Presto* and away;
You all the year do chain her, and her fruits,
Roots to their Beds, and flowers to their Roots.

Have not mine eyes feasted i' th' frozen *Zone*,
Upon a fresh new-grown Collation
Of Apples, unknown sweets, that seem'd to me
Hanging to tempt as on the fatal Tree;
So delicately limn'd I vow'd to try
My appetite impos'd upon my Eye.
You Sir alone, Fame and all conqu'ring Rime,
Files the set teeth of all devouring time.
Richard Lovelace, *Peinture*.

He had a very peculiar expression in the eyes of his female figures; a tender languishment, a look of blended sweetness and drowsiness, unattempted before his time by any master, which he certainly conceived to be graceful. But although, in some poetic forms, it might happen to have a desirable and poetic effect, yet, as his expression is the same in all, he is accounted a mannerist.
M. Pilkington, *The Gentleman's and Connoisseur's Dictionary of Painters*, 1798.

Lely supplied the want of taste with *clinquant*; his nymphs trail fringes and embroidery through purling streams. Add, that Vandyck's habits are those of the times; Lely's a sort of fantastic nightgowns, fastened with a single pin. The latter was in truth the ladies'-painter.
Horace Walpole, *Anecdotes of Painters in England*.

See also Oliver Cromwell, Nell Gwyn, Godfrey Kneller

L'ENFANT, PIERRE CHARLES

1754—1825 Town Planner, Engineer, Soldier

A man of many accomplishments, with an overflow of ideas and few competitors, he was the factotum of the new nation.
J. J. Jusserand, *L'Enfant and Washington*.

LENNOX, CHARLOTTE RAMSAY

1720—1804 Novelist

But gaily chearful may thy tuneful art
Enliven, soften, and enlarge the heart;
While bless'd with ease and happiness refin'd,
At once you ravish and instruct mankind.
Anon., Poem from *Gentleman's Magazine*.

L'ESTRANGE, SIR ROGER

1616—1704 Tory Journalist

He was one of the great corrupters of our language

by excluding vowels and other letters not commonly pronounced, and introducing part and affected phrases.
James Granger, *Biographical History of England.*

The pattern of bad writing.
Henry Hallam, *Literature of Europe.*

LETTSOM, JOHN COAKLEY

1744—1815 Physician

When people's ill, they comes to I,
  I physics, bleeds, and sweats 'em;
Sometimes they live, sometimes they die.
  What's that to I? I let's 'em.
  On himself, *Epigram.*

LEVANT, OSCAR

1906—72 Author, Actor, Musician

My behavior has been impeccable; I've been unconscious for the past six months.
  On himself, *The Memoirs of an Amnesiac.*

Underneath this flabby exterior is an enormous lack of character.
  Ibid.

I don't drink. I don't like it. It makes me feel good.
  On himself, in *Time*, 5 May 1950.

A character who, if he did not exist, could not be imagined.
  S. N. Behrman, Introduction to *A Smattering of Ignorance. Oscar Levant.*

For one year and one month he declared my house his house. For one year and one month he ate my food, played my piano, ran up my phone bill, burned cigarette holes in my landlady's furniture, monopolized my record player and my coffeepot, gave his guests the run of the joint, insulted my guests, and never stopped complaining. He was an insomniac. He was an egomaniac. He was a leech and a lunatic. . . . But I loved the guy.
  He honestly believed he was taking what was coming to him and nothing more. This was not to be confused with generosity, which Oscar didn't know how to accept. If anybody offered to help him out, his favorite reply was, 'Do me a favor — don't do me a favor'. But if it was he who asked the favor it was all right. Oscar was utterly unable to enjoy an equal relationship with anybody. It had to be one-sided, on his side, with the single exception of George Gershwin. Once I understood this and accepted it, I found Oscar to be one of the most rewarding men I had ever known. I lost a house, but I gained a friend.
  Harpo Marx, *Harpo Speaks.*

There is absolutely nothing wrong with Oscar Levant that a miracle cannot fix.
  Alexander Woollcott, in Margaret Case Harriman, *The Vicious Circle.*

See also Harpo Marx

LEVET(T), ROBERT

1701?—82 Physician

Officious, innocent, sincere,
  Of every friendless name the friend.
  Samuel Johnson, *On the Death of Mr. Levet.*

LEWES, GEORGE HENRY

1817—78 Author, Journalist

He was the son of a clown. He had the legs of his father in his brain.
  George Meredith, in *Fortnightly Review*, July 1909.

George Lewes, who was present, looked surprised and then cried out —
  'Oh, I'm not like that, I commence to write at once, directly the pen is in my hand! In fact, I boil at a low temperature!'
  'Indeed,' cut in Mr. Huxley, 'That is very interesting, for, as you know, to boil at a low temperature implies a vacuum in the upper region.'
  'Two', *Home Life with Herbert Spencer.*

LEWIS, JOHN LLEWELLYN

1880—1969 Labor Leader

Think of me as a coal miner, and you won't make any mistakes.
  On himself, in James A. Wechsler, *Labor Baron.*

Lewis is many things on many different occasions, but he is always 'regular', with himself as the chief arbiter of regularity. He is the grand walking delegate, the glorified organizer, the perfect boss in American labor.
  He has physical courage but no creative daring.

His morale is a matter of magnificent brow-beating rather than political subtlety. He moves slowly, with a wealth of objective detail, shrewdly enough, — but above all — callously.

    Anon., 'The Independent', 1925, in Cecil Carnes, *John L. Lewis, Leader of Labor*.

It takes courage to fight injustice,
    To champion decency,
To replace gloom with light and cheer
    In the hearts of the needy.

John L. Lewis, may God bless you,
    You have put up a noble fight.
The aged miners and the widows
    Send their blessings day and night.
    Anon., in *United Mine Workers Journal*, 1 July 1949.

. . . John L. Lewis, who has often been called the Jack Dempsey of Labor, could not be called either evolutionist or revolutionist very accurately. He did not begin his leadership with any particular set of ideas, any certain integrated list of ideals. Dempsey once said that he struck from where his hand was. That was the science he knew. John L. Lewis moved, in his strategy, like Dempsey punched. He was always primarily interested in the immediate step, but that step he took ruthlessly.

    Cecil Carnes, *John L. Lewis, Leader of Labor*.

. . . It is my opinion that Roosevelt had not really been able to put his heart into the contest against Willkie, who presented so indistinct a target; but a battle to discredit John L. Lewis loomed as a real pleasure.

    Harry L. Hopkins, in Saul D. Alinsky, *John L. Lewis*.

. . . They tell me he fights moving locomotives in the early morning just to warm up. He's the Huey Long of labor. That's what he is, the Huey Long of Labor.

    Huey Long, in Cecil Carnes, *John L. Lewis, Leader of Labor*.

Of those that kept their eyes open, and with the 'will to organize,' John L. Lewis was the only one who possessed the indispensable capacity to dramatize [in] his own person that the 'hour of labor's redemption has arrived.' By the early months of 1937 when the auto workers 'sat down,' Lewis was the 'George Washington of American labor.' Not many of the contemporaries will forget how the press and the radio issued bulletins on his journey to Detroit to meet the top men of General Motors. It is hard to conceive of the rise of American mass

production unionism without the confidence of victory radiating from his personality and self-assurance.

    [Samuel] Gompers and Lewis both faced the realities in their land — the one excelling in the art of persuasion within his own camp and of advocacy to the public at large, the other believing in power, the appearance no less than the substance. It looks as though the latter has missed becoming the acknowledged ancestor of the 'new nation' because of too much concern with being a 'crowned personage'!

    Professor Selig Perlman, Interview, 8 July 1949, in Saul D. Alinsky, *John L. Lewis*.

LEWIS, MERIWETHER

1774—1809 Explorer

I am no coward; but I am *so* strong, *so hard to die*. . . . If I had not done it, someone else would.
    On himself, dying words, having committed suicide, in John Bakeless, *Lewis and Clark*.

Lewis N. Clark was a trail blazer and a path breaker and a very good man in the bush because he never got poison ivy. He carried beads to give to the Indians, who sewed them on bookmarks, handbags, and watch fobs to sell to tourists at Albuquerque.
    Richard Armour, *It All Started With Columbus*.

Except for his height and his bow legs, he looked a little like Napoleon, or so a friend thought.
    John Bakeless, *Lewis and Clark*.

The importance of the Lewis and Clark expedition lay on the level of imagination: it was drama, it was the enactment of a myth that embodied the future. It gave tangible substance to what had been merely an idea, and established the image of a highway across the continent so firmly in the minds of Americans that repeated failures could not shake it.
    Henry Nash Smith, *Virgin Land*.

LEWIS, PERCY WYNDHAM

1884—1957 Novelist, Painter

I am a portmanteau-man.
    On himself, *Blasting and Bombardiering*.

I have been called a Rogue Elephant, a Cannibal Shark, and a crocodile. I am none the worse. I remain a caged, and rather sardonic, Lion in a particularly contemptible and ill-run Zoo.
    Ibid.

That lonely old volcano of the Right.
    W. H. Auden, in Roy Campbell, in *Time and Tide*, 7 July 1951.

We leave the Martyr's Stake at Abergwilly
To Wyndham Lewis with a box of soldiers (blonde)
Regretting one so bright should be so silly.
    W. H. Auden and Louis MacNeice, *Letters from Iceland*.

Let us admire, for instance, the admirable though somewhat negative qualities in the work of Mr. Lewis; the absence of vulgarity and false sentiment, the sobriety of colour, the painstaking search for design — without forgetting that in the Salon d'Automne or the Salon des Independants a picture by him would neither merit nor obtain from the most generous critic more than a passing word of perfunctory encouragement.
    Clive Bell, in *Athenaeum*, 5 March 1920.

One of his minor purposes is to disembowel his enemies, who are numerous, for the simple reason that he wants them to be numerous. He would be less tiresome if he were more urbane.
    Arnold Bennett, in *Evening Standard*, 28 April 1927.

What Lewis believes in most is himself and the measure he applies to his contemporaries is how far they differ from that yardstick and how far they stand in his way. His criticism also suffers from a lack of proportion. He will attack a writer on philosophical or moral grounds and then as violently for the most superficial and frivolous of errors; or he will turn from rending an important writer to maul an obscure and inconsiderable hack. He is like a maddened elephant which, careering through a village, sometimes leans against a house and carelessly demolishes the most compact masonry, trumpeting defiance to the inhabitants within, sometimes pursues a dog or a chicken or stops to uproot a shrub or bang a piece of corrugated iron.
    Cyril Connolly, *Enemies of Promise*.

In the work of Mr Lewis we recognize the thought of the modern and the energy of the cave-man.
    T. S. Eliot, reviewing Lewis's *Tarr*.

Lewis' drawing has the qualities of sculpture.
    Jacob Epstein, in Ezra Pound, Letter to John Quinn, 10 March 1916.

I do not think I have ever seen a nastier-looking man. . . . Under the black hat, when I had first seen them, the eyes had been those of an unsuccessful rapist.
    Ernest Hemingway, *A Moveable Feast*.

Wyndham Lewis gives a display of the utterly repulsive effect people have on him, but he retreats into the intellect to make this display. It is a question of manner and manners. The effect is the same. It is the same exclamation: They stink! My God, they stink!
    D. H. Lawrence, *Phoenix*.

Anyone who has read him will know that hard slap in the face that his sentences administer to the reader, the brief, challenging laugh that follows the slap and the sudden note of deadly and of often pessimistic seriousness that follows the laugh.
    E. Newton, in C. Handley-Read, *The Art of Wyndham Lewis*.

Enough talent to set up dozens of ordinary writers has been poured into Wyndham Lewis's so-called novels, such as *Tarr* or *Snooty Baronet*. Yet it would be a very heavy labour to read one of these books right through. Some indefinable quality, a sort of literary vitamin . . . is absent from them.
    George Orwell, in *Tribune*, 2 November 1945.

The whole public and even those of us who then knew him best, have been so befuddled with the concept of Lewis as EXPLOSIVE that scarcely anyone has had the sense or the patience to look calmly at his perfectly suave and equipoised observations of letters. The difference between a gun and a tree is a difference of tempo. The tree explodes every spring.
    Ezra Pound, in *Criterion*, July 1937.

A buffalo in wolf's clothing.
    Robert Ross, in Percy Wyndham Lewis, *Blasting and Bombadiering*.

He liked to shroud himself in mystery. After hiding for weeks he would suddenly reappear, having been, he would declare, in Sweden, or in some remote country; and he would hint at a conquest. His 'conquests' seemed for the most part to be Swedes, Germans, Poles, or Russians, shadowy figures whom one heard of, but never met. I was never sure whether, indeed, he ever had left England.
    William Rothenstein, *Men and Memories 1900–22*.

Mr Lewis's pictures appeared, as a very great painter said to me, to have been painted by a mailed fist in a cotton glove.
    Edith Sitwell, *Taken Care Of*.

When one sat to him, in his enormous studio, mice emerged from their holes, and lolled against the furniture, staring in the most insolent manner at the sitter. At last, when Tom Eliot was sitting to him, their behaviour became intolerable. They climbed on to his knee, and would sit staring up at his face. So Lewis bought a large gong which he placed near the mouse-hole, and, when matters reached a certain limit, he would strike this loudly, and the mice would retreat.

> Edith Sitwell, Letter to Lady Snow, 8 January 1959.

Wyndham Lewis, tall and thin, looked rather like a young frenchman on the rise, perhaps because his feet were very french, or at least his shoes. He used to come and sit and measure pictures. I cannot say that he actually measured with a measuring-rod but he gave all the effect of being in the act of taking very careful measurement of the canvas, the lines within the canvas and everything that might be of use. Gertrude Stein rather liked him.

> Gertrude Stein, *The Autobiography of Alice B. Toklas.*

LEWIS, SINCLAIR

1885–1951 Author

A dull fellow whose virtue — if there is any — is to be found only in his books.

> On himself, *Self-Portrait* (Berlin, August 1927).

He has written the sharpest parodies of the lush, rococo, euphemistic salestalk of American business life that we have, but he has also weighed down his novels with a heavy burden of unreal and exaggerated jargon, palmed off as common speech, with unfunny topical jokes, passed on as native humor, and the weight of that dated mockery grows heavier every year.

> Robert Cantwell, 'Sinclair Lewis', in Malcolm Cowley ed., *After the Genteel Tradition.*

For Lewis is the historian of America's catastrophic going-to-pieces — or at least of the going-to-pieces of her middle class — with no remedy to offer for the decline that he records.

> *Ibid.*

He was the first American to be measured and weighed and certified as an international giant of letters.

> Malcolm Cowley, *After the Genteel Tradition.*

Marked by a thin past and a narrow future, Lewis is indeed the Last Provincial of our letters: a provincial who wanders, homeless, between a barren and deteriorating hinterland and an increasingly appalling industrial order — a hinterland with which he feels no ties, an industrial order with which he cannot come to grips.

> Maxwell Geismar, *The Last of the Provincials.*

Sinclair Lewis has been called the Bad Boy of the national letters. In a way the celebrated critic of the national manners who established the new realism of the nineteen-twenties in the American mind and established the American mind in contemporary literature, whose literary career, lasting over a quarter of a century, has been marked by controversy, dispute, and perpetual ferment, deserves his title.

> *Ibid.*

He was a writer who drank, not, as so many have believed, a drunk who wrote.

> James Lundquist, *Sinclair Lewis.*

He was one of the worst writers in modern American literature, but without his writing one cannot imagine modern American literature. That is because, without his writing, we can hardly imagine ourselves.

> Mark Schorer, *Sinclair Lewis, An American Life.*

In him we have the doubly pathetic sight of a youth who is driven into an inner world even more bleak and barren than the exterior world that expelled him, who would gladly have chosen that world. And this difference from the novelistic pattern was to make for the real enigma of his novels, a persistent conflict of values that clashed no less within him.

> *Ibid.*

In any imaginable society he would be as noticeable as a bashful cyclone. He enters a room with a diffident insolence, bracing himself against what lies in wait for him. After all his harsh campaigns, he has still an eager, shy desire to please.

> Carl Van Doren, *Sinclair Lewis.*

He is a master of that species of art to which belong glass flowers, imitation fruit, Mme Tussaud's waxworks, and barnyard symphonies, which aims at deceiving the spectator into thinking that the work in question is not an artificial product but the real thing.

> T. K. Whipple, *Spokesmen.*

Lewis is the most successful critic of American society because he is himself the best proof that his charges are just.

> *Ibid.*

LILBURNE, JOHN

1614?—57 Leveller

Is *John* departed, and is *Lilburn* gone?
Farewell to both, to *Lilburn* and to *John*.
Yet, being dead, take this Advice from me,
Let them not both in one Grave buried be:
Lay *John* here, and *Lilburn* thereabout,
For, if they both should meet, they would fall out.
    Anon. near contemporary.

An Haberdasher of Small Wares,
In Politicks and State-Affairs.
    Samuel Butler, *Hudibras*, part III.

So suddenly addicted still
To's only Principle, his *will*,
That whatso'er it chanc'd to prove,
Nor force of Argument could move:
Nor *Law*, nor *Cavalcade* of *Ho'burn*
Could render half a Grain less stubborn,
For he at any Time would hang
For th'opportunity t'*harangue*:
And rather on a Gibbet dangle,
Than miss his dear Delight, to wrangle.
    Ibid.

John keeps a weekly rendezvous in the way of edification over Capen and Cock broth, at close meetings with the venerable agents and ambassadors from the most high and mighty adjutators, who if they could be once weaned from that learned opinion that monarchical government is anti-christian, are resolved to have no king but John; and then we shall have a John à London as famous as John à Leyden.
    Mercurius Pragmaticus, 9 November 1647.

LILLY, WILLIAM

1602—81 Astrologer

But this I well remember, the whole Nation was affrited by Lilly the Almanack [writer], who foretold what a dreadfull Eclipse (that which was called Black monday) it would be.
    John Evelyn, Diary.

I home by coach, taking Mr. Booker [the astrologer] with me, who did tell me a great many fooleries, which may be done by nativities, and blaming Mr. Lilly for writing to please his friends and to keep in with the times (as he did formerly to his own dishonour), and not according to the rules of art, by which he could not well err, as he had done.
    Samuel Pepys, Diary, 24 October 1660.

LINACRE, THOMAS

1460?—1524 Physician, Scholar

He was one of the first English Men that brought polite learning into our Nation, and it hath been justly questioned by some of the Goliaths of learning, whether he was a better Latinist or Grecian, or a better Grammarian or Physician.
    Anthony à Wood, *Athenae Oxonienses*.

LINCOLN, ABRAHAM

1809—65 Sixteenth United States President

Abraham Lincoln his hand and pen
He will be good but god knows when.
    On himself, childhood couplet.

As President, I have no eyes but constitutional eyes; I cannot see you.
    On himself, in a reply to South Carolina commissioners on the secession question.

I have now come to the conclusion never again to think of marrying, and for this reason: I can never be satisfied with anyone who would be blockhead enough to have me.
    On himself, 1 April 1838, after he was rejected by Mary Owen.

A new kind of historian [would be required] to comprehend the genius of a character so externally uncouth, so pathetically simple, so unfathomably penetrating, so irresolute and yet so irresistible, so bizarre, grotesque, droll, wise and perfectly beneficent as the great original thinker and statesman for whose death the whole land, even in the midst of victories unparalleled, is today draped in mourning.
    Anon., in *New York Herald*, 1865.

Fox populi.
    Anon., in *Vanity Fair*, 1863.

Lincoln is now popularly known for being 'heads' when one is matching pennies.
    Richard Armour, *It All Started With Columbus*.

His mind works in the right directions but seldom works clearly and cleanly. His bread is of unbolted flour, and much straw, too, mixes in the bran, and sometimes gravel stones.
    Henry Ward Beecher, Letter to Salmon Chase.

A tempering of will in these trotting months
Whose strong hoofs striking have scarred him again
        and again.

He still rules more by the rein than by whip or spur
But the reins are fast in his hands and the horses
know it.
He no longer says 'I think,' but 'I have decided.'
    Stephen Vincent Benét, in A. H. Jones, *Roosevelt's Image Brokers.*

. . . This man's appearance, his pedigree, his coarse low jokes and anecdotes, his vulgar similes and his frivolity, are a disgrace to the seat he holds. . . .
    John Wilkes Booth, in Lord Longford, *Abraham Lincoln.*

Mr. Lincoln is like a waiter in a large eating house where all the bells are ringing at once; he cannot serve them all at once and so some grumblers are to be expected.
    John Bright, *Cincinnati Gazette*, 1864.

Bankrupt of generals and fired by the genius of battle, King Abraham himself will don the nodding plume and buckle on the panoply of war. . . . From the awful picture thus evoked from the realms of the imagination, the mind recoils with horror. King Abraham charging at the head of his victorious legions, and joking even in the heat of battle, is a thought too terrific to dwell upon. Let us hope that this is only imagination . . . that if the great Abraham is to join the headless procession his ugly visage will be removed by his own betrayed countrymen — by the men whose rights he has denied, whose persons he has immured in his loathesome bastilles, whose sons and brothers he has murdered upon Southern battlefields — by that nation which the whole world despises now, because they regard this Buffoon as its type.
    John Esten Cooke, in Richard B. Harwell, 'Lincoln and the South', in R. G. Newman ed., *Lincoln for the Ages.*

We must be ready for, and let the clown appear, and hug ourselves that we are well off, if we have got good nature, honest meaning, and fidelity to public interest, with bad manners, — instead of an elegant roué and malignant self seeker.
    Ralph Waldo Emerson, in Denis Tilden Lynch, *'Boss Tweed' — The Story of a Grim Generation.*

His heart was as great as the world, but there was no room in it to hold a memory of a wrong.
    Ralph Waldo Emerson, *Letters and Social Aims: Greatness.*

Of one thing I feel sure, either he has become a Garrisonian Abolitionist or I have become a Lincoln Emancipationist, for I know that we blend, like kindred drops, into one.

William Lloyd Garrison, in Russel B. Nye, *William Lloyd Garrison and the Humanitarian Reformers.*

Lincoln had faith in time, and time has justified his faith.
    Benjamin Harrison, *Lincoln Day Address*, Chicago, 1898.

To become President, Lincoln had had to talk more radically on occasion than he actually felt; to be an effective President, he was compelled to act more conservatively than he wanted.
    Richard Hofstadter, in D. E. Fehrenbacher ed., *The Leadership of Abraham Lincoln.*

Hundreds of people are now engaged in smoothing out the lines on Lincoln's face — forcing all features to the common mold — so that he may be known, not as he really was, but, according to their poor standard, as he should have been.
    Robert G. Ingersoll, *Lincoln.*

Strange mingling of mirth and tears, of tragic and grotesque, of cap and crown, of Socrates and Rabelais, of Aesop and Marcus Aurelius — Lincoln, the greatest memory of the world.
    Ibid.

A bronzed lank man! His suit of ancient black
    A famous high-top hat and plain worn shawl
Make him the quaint great figure that men love,
    The prairie lawyer, master of us all.
    Vachel Lindsay, *Abraham Lincoln Walks at Midnight.*

Mr. Lincoln's perilous task has been to cast a rather shackly raft through the rapids, making fast the unrulier logs as he could snatch opportunity, and the country is to be congratulated that he did not think it his duty to run straight at all hazards, but cautiously to assure himself with his setting pole where the main current was, and keep steadily to that.
    James Russell Lowell, 1864, in D. E. Fehrenbacher ed., *The Leadership of Abraham Lincoln.*

The catastrophe of Lincoln, though it was a great shock, does not cloud the prospect. How could one have wished him a happier death? He died almost unconciously in the fulness of success, and martyrdom in so great a cause consecrates his name through all history. Such a death is the crown of a noble life.
    John Stuart Mill, Letter to Max Kyllman, May 1865.

His cadences sang the ancient song that where there

is freedom men have fought and sacrificed for it, and that freedom is worth men's dying for. For the first time since he became President he had on a dramatic occasion declaimed, howsoever it might be read, Jefferson's proposition which had been a slogan of the Revolutionary war — 'All men are created equal' — leaving no other inference than that he regarded the Negro slave as a man. His outwardly smooth sentences were inside of them gnarled and tough with the enigmas of the American experiment.
    Carl Sandburg, *Abraham Lincoln, the War Years.*

Out of the smoke and stench, out of the music and violent dreams of the war, Lincoln stood perhaps taller than any other of the many great heroes. This was in the mind of many. None threw a longer shadow than he. And to him the great hero was The People. He could not say too often that he was merely their instrument.
    Ibid.

Lincoln?
He was a mystery in smoke and flags
Saying yes to the smoke, yes to the flags,.
    Yes to the paradoxes of democracy,
    Yes to the hopes of government
Of the people by the people for the people,
    No to debauchery of the public mind,
    No to personal malice nursed and fed,
    Yes to the Constitution when a help.
No to the Constitution when a hindrance,
    Yes to man as a struggler amid illusions,
    Each man fated to answer for himself:
Which of the faiths and illusions of mankind
    Must I choose for my own sustaining light
To bring me beyond the present wilderness?
    Carl Sandburg, *The People, Yes.*

Indeed it may be said that if it was Lincoln's destiny to go down in history as the Great Emancipator, rarely has a man embraced his destiny with greater reluctance than he.
    Kenneth Stampp, in Lerone Bennett Jr, 'Was Abe Lincoln a White Supremacist?', in D. E. Fehrenbacher ed., *The Leadership of Abraham Lincoln.*

The Union with him in sentiment rose to the sublimity of religious mysticism; while his ideas of its structure and formation in logic rested upon nothing but the subtleties of sophism.
    Alexander H. Stephens, 1870, in *ibid.*

He is a barbarian, Scythian, Yahoo, a gorilla in respect of outward polish, but a most sensible, straightforward old codger.
    George Templeton Strong, in Allen Nevins ed., *The Diary of George Templeton Strong.*

Beside this corpse, that bears for winding-sheet
    The stars and stripes he lived to rear anew
Between the mourners at his head and feet
    Say, scurril-jester, is there room for YOU?

Yes, he had lived to shame me from my sneer,
    To lame my pencil, and confute my pen —
To make me own this kind of princes' peer,
    This rail-splitter a true-born king of men.
    Tom Taylor, in Lord Longford, *Abraham Lincoln.*

O Captain! My Captain! our fearful trip is done,
The ship has weather'd every rock, the prize we
                    sought is won.
The port is near, the bells I hear, the people all
                    exulting,
While follow eyes the steady keel, the vessel grim
                    and daring;
    But o heart! heart! heart!
        O the bleeding drops of red,
            Where on the deck my captain lies,
                Fallen cold and dead.
    Walt Whitman, *O Captain! My Captain!*

. . . the grandest figure on the crowded canvas of the drama of the nineteenth century.
    Walt Whitman, in Carl Sandburg, *Abraham Lincoln: The Prairie Years and the War Years.*

The only thing like passion or infatuation in the man was the passion for the Union of These States.
    Walt Whitman, 1886, in D. E. Fehrenbacher ed., *The Leadership of Abraham Lincoln.*

This dust was once a man,
Gentle, plain, just and resolute, under whose cau-
                    tious hand,
Against the foulest crime in history known in any
                    land or age,
Was saved the Union of these States.
    Walt Whitman, *This Dust was Once the Man.*

See also Matthew Arnold, Gary Cooper, Warren G. Harding, Charles A. Lindbergh, Dolly Madison, James K. Polk, Theodore Roosevelt, Carl Sandburg, William Henry Seward, Adlai Stevenson, Booth Tarkington, Martin Van Buren

LINDBERGH, CHARLES AUGUSTUS

1902—74 Aviator

How Lincoln would have held him
As gently as a babe —
And, come to think, by Jonathan!

The youngster looks like Abe.
    Anon., from popular American song of the late
    1920s.

We measure heroes as we do ships, by their displace-
ment. Colonel Lindbergh has displaced everything.
. . . He has displaced everything that is petty, that
is sordid, that is vulgar.
    Charles Evans Hughes, New York speech, June
    1927.

Alone, yet never lonely,
    Serene, beyond mischance,
The world was his, his only,
    When Lindbergh flew to France!
    Aline Michaelis, *Lindbergh*.

This boy is not our usual type of hero. He is all the
others rolled into one and multiplied by ten. . . .
    Will Rogers, syndicated column, 25 May 1927.

LINDSAY, (NICHOLAS) VACHEL

1879—1931 Poet

I think that the poet should believe in art for its
own sake, but the draughtsman inevitably moralizes.
Artists always preach, if it is nothing more than
their school of art. Art is pre-eminently didactic.
    On himself, in Edgar Lee Masters, *Vachel Lind-
    say, A Poet in America*.

I am not only sophisticated, but all my ancestors
were sophisticated.
    On himself, in T. K. Whipple, *Spokesmen*.

Fundamentally, Mr Lindsay was a remarkable poet;
altogether he never comes to as much as he should.
Probably he never had much of a chance. He grew
up in the Babbitt country. He was, when young, a
Babbitt himself, and to this day he has not ceased
trying to transmute the activities of Babbitry into
the stuff of dreams and fantasy.
    Heywood Broun, in *ibid*.

Still preaching the gospel of beauty, he tried to
stimulate a popular taste for poetry through a
method that he called 'the higher vaudeville', in
which his recitations were marked by a dramatic use
of gesture and chant, emphasizing his strong rhythms
and syncopations.
    James D. Hart, *The Oxford Companion to
    American Literature*.

He was, primarily, a rhyming John the Baptist singing to convert the heathen, to stimulate and en-

courage the half-hearted dreams that hide and are
smothered in sordid villages and townships.
    Louis Untermeyer ed., *Modern American Poetry,
    A Critical Anthology*.

Much of Lindsay will die; he will not live as either a
prophet or a politician. But the vitality which
impels the best of his galloping meters will persist;
his innocent wildness of imagination, outlasting his
naive programs, will charm even those to whom his
declamations are no longer a novelty. His gospel is
no less original for being preached through a saxo-
phone.
    Ibid.

After entangling himself in a snarl of childish and
delusive notions about the psychology of the creative process, he broke down in bewilderment and
exhaustion and took the shortest means of extri-
cating himself by suicide.
    George F. Whicher, 'The Twentieth Century',
    in Arthur Hobson Quinn ed., *The Literature of
    the American People*.

LIPPMANN, WALTER

1889—1974 Editor, Author

It was not Lippman's style to scare people: his
approach to world affairs was sober, reasoned,
judicious and restrained. But he came closer to
being a 'thunderer' than any other American journalist.
    Henry Brandon, in *Sunday Times* (London),
    15 December 1974.

The name that opened every door.
    Alastair Buchan, in *Observer*, 15 December 1974.

Walter Lippmann belonged, like his fellow countryman, Reinhold Niebuhr, to the great tradition of
Christian pessimism, the premise that man is inherently sinful and society inherently corrupt,
though both may redeem themselves. Certainly,
little happened in the long bridge of time that Lippmann traversed to undermine this premise while his
realism and historical knowledge formed a counter-
weight to the buoyancy and optimism of his
countrymen.
    Ibid.

He is a great man because he agrees with me.
    Lyndon B. Johnson, in Philip Geyelin, *Lyndon
    B. Johnson and the World*.

Walter. Look, don't think.
    Helen Lippmann, shouting to her husband at
    Seal Harbor, Maine, while he was climbing on
    some rocks.

LISTER, JOSEPH, BARON

1827—1912 Surgeon

His brow spreads large and placid, and his eye
Is deep and bright, with steady looks that still.
Soft lines of tranquil thought his face fulfill —
His face at once benign and proud and shy.
If envy scout, if ignorance deny,
His faultless patience, his unyielding will,
Beautiful gentleness and splendid skill,
Innumerable gratitudes reply.
His wise, rare smile is sweet with certainties,
And seems in all his patients to compel
Such love and faith as failure cannot quell.
We hold him for another Herakles,
Battling with custom, prejudice, disease,
As once the son of Zeus with Death and Hell.
    W. E. Henley, *The Chief.*

On only one occasion in the two years I worked
under him was there anything approaching the
nature of a boast, and that in an unassuming and
jocose manner. He was speaking of the importance
of the drainage of abscesses and referred to the time
when he was called to Balmoral to operate upon
Queen Victoria for an axillary abscess, and play-
fully said: 'Gentlemen, I am the only man who has
ever stuck a knife into the Queen!'
    J. R. Leeson, *Lister as I knew him.*

The methodical life of Lord Lister offers a strong
contrast to this. It is a life on which a neat pattern
is carefully imprinted, everything he did conforming to the one overriding motif of his work.
Subtract his professional and scientific activities
from his life and literally there is nothing of any
moment to record.
    Kenneth Walker, *Joseph Lister.*

We speak of the Homeric and Shakespearian ages, of
the pre-Hippocratic and post-Hippocratic epochs of
medicine, and of the pre-Newtonian and Newtonian
eras of physics. So also do medical historians talk of
pre-Listerian and post-Listerian surgery, and the difference between surgery as Lister found it and surgery as he left it is immense, far greater than most
of us realize.
    Ibid.

LIVERPOOL, EARL OF (ROBERT BANKS JENKINSON)

1770—1828 Prime Minister

. . . the Lord Liverpool seemingly-wise . . .
    Lord Byron, *The Devil's Drive.*

. . . the Arch-Mediocrity
    Benjamin Disraeli, *Coningsby.*

His test of priestly celebrity was the decent editor-
ship of a Greek play. He sought for the successors
of the apostles, for the stewards of the mysteries of
Sinai and Calvary, among third rate hunters after
syllables.
    Benjamin Disraeli, of Lord Liverpool's selection
    of bishops, in *Tancred.*

. . . always approached [George III] with a vacant
kind of grin, and had hardly anything businesslike
to say. . . .
    George III's complaint, in George Rose, Diary,
    30 September 1804.

The Earl of Liverpool, whom Madame de Stael is
said to have described as having 'a talent for silence'.
    Leigh Hunt, *Autobiography.*

Liverpool has acted as he always does to a friend in
personal questions — shabbily, timidly and ill.
    Lord Palmerston, Letter to William Temple, June
    1826.

LIVINGSTONE, DAVID

1813—73 Missionary

I never met a man who fulfilled more completely
my idea of a perfect Christian gentleman.
    Sir Bartle Frere, *Proceedings of the Royal Geo-
graphical Society,* 1874.

There is a group of respectable Arabs, and as I come
nearer I see the white face of an old man among
them. He has a cap with a gold band round it; his
dress is a short jacket of red blanket cloth; and his
pants — well, I didn't observe. I am shaking hands
with him. We raise our hats, and I say, 'Doctor
Livingstone, I presume?' and he says, 'Yes'.
    H. M. Stanley, *How I Found Livingstone.*

LLOYD GEORGE, DAVID, EARL LLOYD GEORGE OF DWYFOR

1863—1945 Prime Minister

I hate fences, I always feel like knocking down
every fence I come across!
    On himself, in Frances Stevenson, Diary,
    30 November 1915.

I never believed in costly frontal attacks either in

war or politics if there was a way round.
On himself, *War Memoirs*.

Lloyd George knew my father.
My father knew Lloyd George.
Anon., popular catch of the First World War.

Lloyd George has a bigger sound in American than
'Prime Minister'. . . . For Lloyd George is the man
who does things, and that means everything to
America.
Member of the American Luncheon Club speak-
ing to Lloyd George, in Frances Stevenson,
Diary, 9 April 1917.

He couldn't see a belt without hitting below it.
Margot, Lady Asquith, *Autobiography*.

He did not seem to care which way he travelled
providing he was in the driver's seat.
Lord Beaverbrook, *Decline and Fall of Lloyd
George*.

You know you are an acquired flavour, but, once
acquired, people like you very much.
John Burns, in conversation with Lloyd George,
in A. J. Sylvester, Diary, 5 January 1937.

With so much dishonour, you might have bought us
a little peace.
Lord Hugh Cecil, on his Irish policy, 1916, in
Lord David Cecil, *The Cecils of Hatfield House*.

Count not his broken pledges as a crime.
He *meant* them, HOW he meant them — at the time.
Kensal Green (Colin Hurry), *Premature Epitaphs*.

The trouble with Lloyd George is that he thinks in
images, not in concepts.
Lord Haldane, 1919, in Dudley Sommer, *Haldane of Cloan*.

. . . He could charm a bird off a branch but was himself always unmoved.
Tom Jones, in *Observer*, 25 January 1976.

. . . this extraordinary figure of our time, this siren,
this goat-footed bard, this half-human visitor to our
age from the hag-ridden magic and enchanted woods
of Celtic antiquity. One catches in his company that
flavour of final purposelessness, inner irresponsibi-
lity, existence outside or away from our Saxon good
and evil, mixed with cunning, remorselessness, love
of power, that lend fascination, enthralment, and
terror to the fair-seeming magicians of North-
European folklore. . . . Lloyd George is rooted in
nothing; he is void and without content; he lives and

feeds in his immediate surroundings; he is an instrument and a player at the same time which plays on
the company and is played on by them too; he is a
prism, as I have heard him described, which collects
light and distorts it and is most brilliant if the light
comes from many quarters at once; a vampire and a
medium in one.
John Maynard Keynes, *Essays in Biography*.

The little Welshman is peppery, but he means to
win — which is what matters!
Lord Kitchener, in Sir George Arthur, *Life of
Lord Kitchener*.

D[avid] is incapable of *achieving* anything, without
reducing all round him to nervous wrecks. In this
way he *distributes* his own nerves in a crisis, and, I
believe, saves himself in the process. I always used
to think it was an unnecessary bother . . . , but now
I perceive the more subtle psychology of it, and
realise that it is necessary for him to produce this
state of enervation in everyone else, in order that
he himself may derive some sort of nervous energy
which fortifies him.
Frances Stevenson, Diary, 29 March 1934.

L.G. said to me that once one had assured oneself
of food and shelter, which meant security, the next
thing that mattered was advertisement.
A. J. Sylvester, Diary, 27 April 1933.

A master of improvised speech and improvised policies.
A. J. P. Taylor, *English History, 1914-1945*.

See also Nancy Astor, Megan Lloyd George, Woodrow Wilson

LLOYD GEORGE, LADY MEGAN

1902—66 Politician

Megan Lloyd George, who hates the Tories more
than she loves England!
Henry Channon, Diary, 7 November 1950.

She is an amusing little person, but is getting rather
artificial. D[avid Lloyd George] thinks she is growing selfish, but that is not her fault, for she has not
been taught to be unselfish.
Frances Stevenson, Diary, 29 April 1917.

LOCKE, JOHN

1632—1704 Philosopher

. . . Locke, we feel, is not so much cleverer than ourselves as to be capable of playing tricks with us even if he wanted to do so. He is the Mr. Baldwin of philosophy, and he derives from his literary style some of the advantages which that statesman owed to his pipe and his pigs.

C. D. Broad, *Ethics and the History of Philosophy.*

Against Locke's philosophy I think it an unanswerable objection that, although he carried his throat about with him in this world for seventy-two years, no man ever condescended to cut it.

Thomas de Quincey, *On Murder Considered As One of the Fine Arts.*

Moderation, caution, a wish to examine every side of a question, and an unwillingness to decide till after the most mature and circumspect investigation, and then only according to the clearness of the evidence, seem to have been the characteristics of his mind, none of which denote the daring innovator, or maker of a system. What there is of system in his works is Hobbes's, . . . the deviation from its common sense and general observation are his own.

William Hazlitt, *On Locke's Essay on the Human Understanding.*

So religion and science were reconciled by limiting the sphere of each. Locke's synthesis performed a social function invaluable for his class. But it was woefully incomplete, for it left out the dialectical element of thought which the Puritan revolutionaries and the early scientists had grasped. It was the dogma of a static civilization.

Christopher Hill, *Puritanism and Revolution.*

Perhaps I rather restore the word, idea, to its original sense, from which Mr. *Locke* had perverted it, in making it stand for all our perceptions.

David Hume, *A Treatise on Human Nature,* part one, footnote.

Locke is the most fortunate of all philosophers. He completed his work in theoretical philosophy just at the moment when the government of his country fell into the hands of men who shared his political opinions. Both in practice and in theory, the views which he advocated were held, for many years to come, by the most vigorous and influential politicians and philosophers. His political doctrines, with the developments due to Montesquieu, are embedded in the American Constitution, and are seen to be at work whenever there is a dispute between President and Congress. The British Constitution was based upon his doctrines until about fifty years ago, and so was that which the French adopted in 1871.

Bertrand Russell, *History of Western Philosophy.*

No one has yet succeeded in inventing a philosophy at once credible and self-consistent. Locke aimed at credibility, and achieved it at the expense of consistency. Most of the great philosophers have done the opposite. A philosophy which is not self-consistent cannot be wholly true, but a philosophy which is self-consistent can very well be wholly false.

Ibid.

Some of Locke's opinions are so odd that I cannot see how to make them sound sensible. He says that a man must not have so many plums that they are bound to go bad before he and his family can eat them; but he may have as much gold and as many diamonds as he can lawfully get, because gold and diamonds do not go bad. It does not occur to him that the man who has the plums might sell them before they go bad.

Ibid.

What I have now done, I thought it my Duty to do, not with respect to my self, but to some of the Mysteries of our Faith; which I do not charge you with *opposing*, but with laying such Foundations as do tend to the Overthrow of them; and may have more, if your Way of *Certainty by Ideas* should obtain.

Edward Stillingfleet, Bishop of Worcester, *Answer to Mr. Locke's Second Letter.*

. . . Mr. Locke never loved the trade of disputing in public in the schools but was always wont to declaim against it as being rather invented for wrangling or ostentation than to discover truth.

James Tyrrell, according to Lady Masham, in Maurice Cranston, *John Locke.*

This great Man could never subject himself to the tedious Fatigue of Calculations, nor to the Dry Pursuit of Mathematical Truths, which do not at first present any sensible Objects to the Mind; and no one has given better Proofs than he, that 'tis possible for a Man to have a Geometrical Head, without the Assistance of Geometry.

Voltaire, *Letters Concerning the English Nation.*

This John Locke was a man of turbulent spirit, clamorous and never contented. The club wrote and took notes from the mouth of their master [Peter Stahl], who sat at the upper end of the table, but the said John Locke scorned to do it, so that while every man besides of the club were writing, he would be prating and troublesome.

Anthony à Wood, *Athenae Oxonienses.*

See also John C. Calhoun, David Hume, George Washington

LODGE, HENRY CABOT

1850—1924 Politician, Author

If Lodge says a thing he will do it, but if he will not do a thing he will say so, and usually in a manner that will make the person who made the request an enemy for life. . . . He considers himself so far superior to the ordinary run of people that the mere addition of another enemy to his long string means nothing to him one way or the other.
    Anon., in *Saturday Evening Post*, 7 May 1910.

. . . He is the gentleman and scholar in politics without the guilelessness and squeamishness of the said gentleman and scholar.
    Anon., in Samuel E. Morison, 'Memoir of Edward H. Clement', Massachusetts Historical Society, *Proceedings*, vol. 57.

Some men can engage in the fiercest political controversies without arousing personal animosity. Lodge was not one of them. . . . [He] could enrage his antagonists by making them feel their own impotence to enrage him.
    Anon., in *Outlook*, 19 November 1924.

[Lodge had] a hard enough time keeping his temper without stopping to consult his conscience.
    Thomas A. Bailey, *Woodrow Wilson and the Great Betrayal*.

In discussion he was one of those who care more for drowning his adversary than for discovering some common ground for possible agreement.
    Margaret Chanler, in John A. Garraty, *Henry Cabot Lodge*.

. . . [his mind was like the soil of New England] naturally barren, but highly cultivated.
    Chauncey M. Depew, in Thomas A. Bailey, *Woodrow Wilson and the Lost Peace*.

A degenerate son of Harvard.
    A. Lawrence Lowell, in Francis Russell, *President Harding: His Life and Times 1865-1923*.

He was as cool as an undertaker at a hanging.
    H. L. Mencken, in *Baltimore Evening Sun*, 15 June 1920.

Lodge's keynote speech was bosh, but it was bosh delivered with an air. . . . But Lodge got away with it because he was Lodge — because there was behind it his unescapable confidence in himself, his disarming disdain of discontent below, his unapologetic superiority.
    Ibid.

. . . the Oscar Wilde type [of statesman] who moves with an air of lugubrious pedantry and a solemn sense of weighty responsibility about the aisles of the chamber.
    William J. Stone, 1891, in John A. Garraty, *Henry Cabot Lodge*.

LODGE, THOMAS

1558—1625 Author

In witt, simple; in learning, ignorant; in attempt, rash; in name, Lodge.
    Stephen Gosson, *Playes Confuted in Five Actions*.

LOEB, JACQUES

1859—1924 Physiologist

As a person he always remained the tense and excitable figure of his youth, short, lean, and spikey in appearance, with pointed nose and chin and dark glinting eyes that could stab an opponent but also break up in laughter. He was an indefatigable, almost frenzied, worker, hungry for recognition and never satisfied with what he got, assailed by a perpetual sense of isolation from his peers, biting and dogmatic in his pronouncements but prepared to seek an opponent out with an ungrudging, 'You are right, I was wrong!'
    Donald Fleming, in Jacques Loeb, *The Mechanistic Conception of Life*.

Few scientists of Loeb's generation were as well known to the American public. As a materialist in philosophy, a mechanist in science, and a socialist in politics, he offended against the prevalent American orthodoxies. But he was correspondingly idolized by the dissenters and the debunkers — including Veblen, Mencken, and Sinclair Lewis — who increasingly set the intellectual tone.
    Donald Fleming, in *Dictionary of Scientific Biography*.

LOMBARD, CAROLE (JANE PETERS)

1909—42 Actress

All her life, Carole Lombard had been running a race with a swift, invisible opponent. I think she always knew that she would never live to be old. In all the time I knew her, I never heard her make any plans for her own future. She did not expect to follow the long trail. Perhaps that is why she tried to cram so much into her life, why she seemed to savor life — and particularly her life after she met Clark Gable — as few people ever did.

Anon., in Warren G. Harris, *Gable and Lombard.*

It is always a pleasure to watch those hollow Garbo features, those neurotic elbows and bewildered hands, and her voice has the same odd beauty a street musician discovers in old iron, scraping out heartbreaking and nostalgic street melodies.

Graham Greene, reviewing *Fools For Scandal*, in *Spectator*, 26 August 1938.

Miss Lombard was beautiful, deft, alert, ready for love but with her capacity for romance always tripped up by her unquenchable thirst for reality.

Arthur Schlesinger Jr, 'When The Movies Really Counted', in *Show*, April 1963.

LONDON, JACK

1876—1916 Writer

I tramped all through the United States, from California to Boston, and up and down, returning to the Pacific Coast by way of Canada, where I got into jail and served a term for vagrancy, and the whole tramping experience made me become a Socialist.

On himself, *Star Rover.*

I dream of beautiful horses and fine soil. I dream of the beautiful things I own. . . . And I write for no other purpose than to add to the beauty that now belongs to me. I write a book for no other reason than to add three or four hundred acres to my magnificent estate.

On himself, in Charles Child Walcutt, *Jack London.*

. . . small, dark, full of movement, with eyes that could glow like topazes when something exciting was happening. . . . I shall always think of him as the most lovable child I ever met. . . . Like Peter Pan, he never grew up, and he lived his own stories with such intensity that he ended by believing them himself.

Ford Madox Ford, in Richard O'Connor, *Jack London.*

Like his country, London was corporally mature, innerly a child. He mastered the outward circumstance of life, and then played with toys. The world was his by physical and intellectual possession: but he preferred to live in a nursery and blamed his excess drinking on the fact that no nurse was there to keep the liquor from his lips.

Waldo Frank, in Joan London, *Jack London.*

Grandiloquent without being a fraud, he was the period's greatest crusader and the period's most unashamed hack.

Alfred Kazin, *On Native Grounds.*

All his life he grasped whatever straw of salvation lay nearest at hand, and if he joined Karl Marx to the Superman with a boyish glee that has shocked American Marxists ever since, it is interesting to remember that he joined Herbert Spencer to Shelley, and astrology to philosophy, with as carefree a will.

Ibid.

. . . easy to criticize him, easy to deplore him, impossible to avoid him.

Fred Lewis Pattee, in Joan London, *Jack London.*

He was the true king of our story tellers, the brightest star that flashed upon our skies. He brought us the greatest endowment of genius and of brain, and the story of what America did to him is a painful one.

Upton Sinclair, in Richard O'Connor, *Jack London.*

He had made many mistakes and committed innumerable follies, but at least he had the satisfaction of knowing that they had been big ones. He had never played life 'the little way'.

Irving Stone, *Sailor on Horseback, The Biography of Jack London.*

LONG, HUEY PIERCE

1893—1935 Politician

Oh, hell, say that I'm *sui generis* and let it go at that.

On himself, in T. Harry Williams, 'The Gentle man from Louisiana: Demagogue or Democrat', *The Journal of Southern History*, vol. 26, February 1960.

The Prince of Piffle.

Anon., New Orleans newspaper item, 1923.

[A] sartorial aurora borealis.

Anon., in *New York Times*, in G. Wolfskill and J. A. Hudson, *All but the People: Franklin D. Roosevelt and his Critics, 1933—39.*

[His strength lay in] the terrible South that Stark Young and his sort ignore . . . the beaten, ignorant, Bible-ridden, White South. Faulkner occasionally really touches it. It has yet to be paid for.

Sherwood Anderson, in Arthur M. Schlesinger Jr, *The Politics of Upheaval.*

He would light on one part of you, sting you, and then, when you slapped at him, fly away to land elsewhere and sting again.
    Alben Barkley, in *ibid.*

The trouble with Senator Long is that he is suffering from halitosis of the intellect. That's presuming Emperor Long has an intellect.
    Harold Ickes, in G. Wolfskill and J. A. Hudson, *All but the People: Franklin D. Roosevelt and his Critics, 1933–39.*

He brought to his career a streak of genius, yet in his program and tactics he was as indigenous to Louisiana as pine trees and petroleum.
    V. O. Key Jr, *Southern Politics in State and Nation.*

He did not permit himself, in an oft-repeated pattern, to be hamstrung by a legislature dominated by old hands experienced in legislation and frequently under corporate retainer. He elected his own legislatures and erected a structure of political power both totalitarian and terrifying.
    Ibid.

He misused his fine mind, battered it, as a child might treat a toy the value and purpose of which he could not understand. He used his skills for the enrichment of his shoddy friends and for petty revenge upon his enemies. He used his mind to destroy the very foundations upon which his real reforms in Louisiana could permanently rest. He destroyed many things with his mind. And among them was himself.
    Raymond Moley, *The First New Deal.*

When it comes to arousing prejudice and passion, when it comes to ranting and raving, when it comes to vituperation and vilification, when it comes to denunciation and demagoguery, there is one who stands out by himself alone. He has many imitators but no equals.
    Jared Y. Sanders, *Tangpahoa Parish News,* 2 December 1926.

At bottom, Huey Long resembled . . . a Latin American dictator . . . like Vargas and Peron, Long was in revolt against economic colonialism, against the oligarchy, against the smug and antiquated past; like them, he stood in a muddled way for economic modernization and social justice; like them, he was most threatened by his own arrogance and cupidity, his weakness for soft living and his rage for personal power.
    Arthur M. Schlesinger Jr, *The Politics of Upheaval.*

He was a liar, and he was nothing but a damn demagogue.
    It didn't surprise me when they shot him. These demagogues, the ones that live by demagoguery. They all end up the same way.
    Harry S. Truman, in Merle Miller, *Plain Speaking – An Oral Biography of Harry S. Truman.*

. . . a Winston Churchill who has never been at Harrow.
    H. G. Wells, in Arthur M. Schlesinger Jr, *The Politics of Upheaval.*

He is the most formidable kind of brer fox, the self-abnegating kind that will profess ignorance, who will check his dignity with his hat if he can serve his plans by buffoonery.
    Rebecca West, in *ibid.*

See also John L. Lewis

LONGCHAMP, WILLIAM, BISHOP OF ELY

— d. 1197 Statesman

The Chancellor in name only, disturbed by the thought of his lost power and his present condition, tried in every way to get round the prohibition against his crossing the Channel, and in a variety of ways and more than once he made a laughing stock of himself. I shall not mention that he was caught and held both in a monk's habit and in woman's clothing, but it is well remembered what vast stores of goods and what enormous treasures the Flemings took from him when he landed at last in Flanders.
    Richard of Devizes, *Chronicle*, translated from the Latin by J. T. Appleby.

LONGFELLOW, HENRY WADSWORTH

1807—82 Poet

I am never indifferent, and never pretend to be, to what people say or think of my books. They are my children, and I like to have them liked.
    On himself, Letter to Richard Henry Stoddard, 19 May 1878.

Most of the time am alone; smoke a great deal; wear a broad-brimmed black hat, black frock-coat, a black cane. Molest no one. Dine out frequently. In winter go much into Boston society.
    On himself, in Thomas Wentworth Higginson, *Old Cambridge.*

Longfellow is to poetry what the barrel-organ is to music.
Van Wyck Brooks, in Newton Arvin, *Longfellow, His Life and Work.*

Longfellow's soul was not an ocean. It was a lake, clear, calm and cool. The great storms of the sea never reached it. And yet this lake had its depths. Buried cities lay under its surface.
Van Wyck Brooks, *The Flowering of New England 1815–1865.*

. . . a dandy Pindar. . . .
Margaret Fuller, in Thomas Wentworth Higginson, *Old Cambridge.*

Indeed it is as a Victorian that I see him; not, perhaps, an American Tennyson, but, in some ways, an American Victoria. It would be decidedly frivolous to dub him 'our late dear Queen' and yet his didactic obsessions, his insistence upon the purities of living . . . offer ample opportunity for so considering him.
Herbert S. Gorman, *A Victorian American, Henry Wadsworth Longfellow.*

He outreaches his grasp time and again, and his successes are to be found in those lesser moments when he plucks some brief and fragrant flower of fancy springing from his doorstep or from the calf-bound tomes upon his library table. It is humble enough but it serves.
Ibid.

. . . you reach and touch me always with the simple directness of a summer landscape, an evening sky, or a skylark's song. You rest me as Nature rests me always — on a lighter plane than my ordinary level. . . .
Bret Harte, Letter to Longfellow, 9 November 1875.

Longfellow appears . . . to be no more conscious of any earthly or spiritual trouble than a sunflower is — of which lovely blossom he, I know not why, reminded me.
Nathaniel Hawthorne, in Edward Wagenknecht, *Longfellow: A Full-Length Portrait.*

Here sits our Poet Laureate if you will,
Long has he worn the wreath and wears it still,
Kind, soft voiced, gentle, in his eyes there shines
The ray serene that filled Evangeline,
What tranquil joy his friendly presence gives!
Oliver Wendell Holmes, in Herbert G. Jones, *The Amazing Mr. Longfellow.*

Decorum, excessive moderation, and a bold didacticism that sometimes descends into downright foolish bathos; a lack of imaginative passion or the instinct of rebellion: all these have reduced him, in much of his writing, from a true poet to a cultural influence.
Stanley J. Kunitz and Howard Haycraft eds, *American Authors, 1600–1900.*

He educated America when America was in utter crudeness artistically. For years he was a kind of literary pastor leading his flocks, for the most part women, beside the still waters of Old World culture.
Fred Louis Pattee, *The First Century of American Literature, 1770–1870.*

His didactics are all out of place. He has written brilliant poems, by accident; that is to say, when permitting his genius to get the better of his conventional habit of thinking, a habit deduced from German study.
Edgar Allen Poe, *Longfellow's Ballads.*

Longfellow, reminiscent, polished, elegant, with the air of finest conventional library, picture-gallery or parlor, with ladies and gentlemen in them, and plush and rosewood, and ground-glass lamps, and mahogany and ebony furniture, and a silver inkstand and scented satin paper to write on.
Walt Whitman, in Edgar Lee Masters, *Whitman.*

. . . counteractant most needed for our materialistic, self-assertive, money-worshipping, Anglo-Saxon races, and especially for the present age in America.
Walt Whitman, in Gay Wilson Allen, *The Solitary Singer, A Critical Biography of Walt Whitman.*

See also Edgar Allen Poe, Ezra Pound

LORRE, PETER

1904–64 Actor

As satyr, humorist, and lethal snake, he shows, here as always, a complete feeling for the real juice of situations and the best way of distilling this through voice, carriage, motion. He is one of the true characters of the theatre, having mastered loose oddities and disfigurements until the total is a style, childlike, beautiful, unfathomably wicked, always hinting at things it would not be good to know.

His style is most happily luminous in the intense focus and supple motion of movie cameras, for the keynote of any scene can be made visual through him. In close-ups, it is through the subtle shifts of eyes, scalp, mouth lines, the intricate relations of head to shoulders and shoulders to body. In medium-shots of groups, it is through his entire motion as a sort of supreme punctuation mark and underlineation. A harmless statement is thrown off in a low voice, and it is felt like the cut of a razor in Lorre, immediately in motion — the eyes in his head and the head on his shoulders and that breathless caged walk raising a period to double exclamation points. Or the wrong question is asked, and the whole figure freezes, dead stop, and then the eventual flowering of false warmth, the ice within it.

Otis Ferguson, *The Film Criticism of Otis Ferguson.*

Lorre, with every physical handicap, can convince you of the goodness, the starved tenderness of his vice-entangled soul. Those marbly pupils in the pasty spherical face are like the eye pieces of a microscope through which you can see laid flat on the slide the entangled mind of a man: love and lust, nobility and perversity, hatred of itself and despair jumping out at you from the jelly.

Graham Greene, *Graham Greene On Film.*

LOVELACE, RICHARD

1618—58 Cavalier Poet

One of the handsomest men in England. He was an extraordinary handsome Man, but prowd. He wrote a poem called *Lucasta.*

John Aubrey, *Brief Lives.*

But when the beauteous Ladies came to know
That their deare *Lovelace* was endanger'd so:
Lovelace that thaw'd the most congealed brest,
He who lov'd best and them defended best.
Whose hand so rudely grasps the steely brand,
Whose hand so gently melts the Ladies hand
They all in mutiny though yet undrest
Sally'd and would in his defence contest.

Andrew Marvell, *To his Noble Friend Mr Richard Lovelace Upon His Poems.*

Richard Lovelace, an approv'd both Souldier, Gentleman & Lover, and a fair pretender to the Title of Poet. . . . As to the last of his Qualifications, a Man may discern therein sometimes those sparks of a Poetic fire, which had they been the main design, and not Parergon, in some work of Heroic argument, might happily have blaz'd out into the perfection of sublime Poesy.

Edward Phillips, *Theatrum Poetarum.*

Richard Lovelace . . . became a Gent. Commoner of *Glocester Hall* in the beginning of the Year 1634, and in that of his age 16, being then accounted the most amiable and beautiful Person that every Eye beheld, a Person also of innate modesty, virtue and courtly deportment, which made him then, but especially after, when he retired to the great City, much admired and adored by the Female Sex. In 1636, when the King and Queen were for some days entertained at *Oxon.*, he was, at the request of a great Lady belonging to the Queen, made to the Archb. of *Cant.* then Chancellor of the University, actually created, among other Persons of Quality, Master of Arts, tho' but of two Years standing; at which time his Conversation being made public, and consequently his ingenuity and generous Soul discovered, he became as much admired by the Male, as before by the Female, Sex.

Anthony à Wood, *Athenae Oxonienses.*

LOWELL, AMY

1874—1925 Poet, Critic

The future's her goose and I dare say she'll wing it,
Though the triumph will need her own power to
　　　　　　　　　　　　　　　sing it.
Although I'm no prophet, I'll hazard a guess
She'll be rated by time as more rather than less.

On herself, *A Critical Fable.*

. . . her self-imposed discipline of producing rapidly written, monumental quantities of prose and verse, distracted her mind from recurrent cycles of pain. The habit of writing had its reward as self-imposed therapy, but it could not remove the cause of illness. If Amy Lowell was not ideally well-balanced, she was eminently sane.

Horace Gregory, *Amy Lowell.*

. . . Amy Lowell's nineteenth-century heritage seems greater than of any public literary figure who appeared on lecture platforms in the cause of the 'new poetry' which flowered so rapidly between 1912 and 1920. It no longer seems so extraordinary that her ethical and moral principles were so very New England-Victorian, that she dressed in a mode that was at least ten years 'behind the times'.

Ibid.

. . . how much nicer, finer, bigger you are intrinsically, than your poetry is.

D. H. Lawrence, Letter to Amy Lowell, November 1914.

When I get through with that girl she'll think she was born in free verse.

Ezra Pound, in Horace Gregory, *Amy Lowell.*

. . . our only hippo-poetess.

Ezra Pound, in Charles Norman, *Ezra Pound.*

Amy Lowell was a dynasty in herself.
 Elsie Sergeant, in S. Foster Damon, *Amy Lowell.*

The colors with which her works are studded seem like bits of bright enamel; every leaf and flower has a lacquered brilliance. To compensate for the lack of the spirit's warmth, Miss Lowell feverishly agitates all she touches; nothing remains quiescent.
 Louis Untermeyer, *Modern American Poetry, A Critical Anthology.*

When she reached her accustomed suite at the Belmont Hotel, in New York City, where she stopped several times a year, every large mirror had to be swathed in black, every clock stopped, and the sixteen pillows produced.
 Clement Wood, *Amy Lowell.*

Amy Lowell, neither distinguished poet nor great critic, was still Amy Lowell and played her part well. The rest may ultimately be largely silence.
 Ibid.

Her bodily frame was excessively stout and ungainly; her face held something childish, self-consciously prim, and almost mediocre, with a sleek urbanity of self-assurance grown from her long cultural background.
 Ibid.

LOWELL, JAMES RUSSELL

1819—91 Author, Diplomat, Teacher

There is Lowell, who's striving Parnassus to climb
With a whole bale of isms tied together with rhyme,
He might get on alone, spite of brambles and boulders,
 But he can't with the bundle he has on his shoulders.
 On himself, *A Fable for Critics.*

I am the first poet who has endeavored to express the American Ideas and I shall be popular by and by.
 On himself, in George Arms, *The Fields Were Green.*

As an artist, our poet did not walk steady; and though he did not spill all from his cup, he spilled much.
 George Arms, *ibid.*

Lowell was a bookman, pure and simple, born and bred in an alcove; and he basked and ripened in the sun of books till he grew as mellow as a meerschaum.
 Van Wyck Brooks, *The Flowering of New England 1815—1865.*

Once more the health of Nature's favored son,
The poet, critic, patriot, all in one;
Health, honor, friendship ever round him wait
In life's fair field beyond the seven-barred gate!
 Oliver Wendell Holmes, in Martin Duberman, *James Russell Lowell.*

At the first encounter with people he was always apt to have a certain frosty shyness, a smiling cold, as from the long, high-sunned winters of his Puritan race; he was not quite himself till he had made you aware of his quality: then no one could be sweeter, tenderer than he; then he made you free of his whole heart; but you must be his captive before he could do that.
 William Dean Howells, in Edward Wagenknecht, *James Russell Lowell, Portrait of a Many-Sided Man.*

He was strong without narrowness, he was wide without bitterness and glad without fatuity.
 Henry James, in Arthur Hobson Quinn, 'The Establishment of National Literature', in Quinn ed., *The Literature of the American People.*

He had no standards other than ethical, only likes and dislikes; no interesting ideas, only a pottering concern for the text; no historical backgrounds, only isolated figures dwelling in a vacuum. He was puzzled over new schools and unfamiliar technic, and was at ease only in praising established reputations and confirming approved judgments.
 Vernon Louis Parrington, *Main Currents in American Thought*, vol. 2.

Lowell was not a grower — he was a builder. He *built* poems: he didn't put in the seed, and water the seed, and send down his sun — letting the rest take care of itself: he measured his poems — kept them within the formula.
 Walt Whitman, in Edgar Lee Masters, *Whitman.*

He was a man of great talent — I do not deny it: and skill, yes, skill — I do not deny that. But inspiration? I doubt it.
 Ibid.

A poet, statesman, and an American in one! A sort of three-headed Cerberus of Civilisation, who barks when he is baited, and is often mistaken for a lion, at a distance.
 Oscar Wilde, Letter to Mrs Alfred Hunt, 17 February 1881.

LUCE, HENRY ROBINSON

1898—1967 Publisher

I am a Protestant, a Republican and a free-enterpriser,

which means I am biased in favor of God, Eisenhower and the stockholders of Time Inc. — and if anybody who objects doesn't know this by now, why the hell are they still spending 35 cents for the magazine?

On himself, in W. A. Swanberg, *Luce and His Empire*.

I'm a Jesuit of journalism — a persuader.
On himself, in John Kobler, *Luce, His Time, Life, and Fortune*.

I think it is Mr Luce's unique contribution to American journalism that he placed into the hands of the people yesterday's newspaper and today's garbage homogenized into one neat package.
Herbert Lawrence Block (Herblock), in W. A. Swanberg, *Luce and His Empire*.

He was, as he saw it, God's classmate, and any slanting or twisting of journalism was for God and Yale. . . . His publications have little merit, or much contact with reality. He wanted it that way, for he himself was remote and felt little comfort with the ordinary citizens he bamboozled.
Stephen Longstreet, in *ibid*.

He really thought there was nothing he could not do, so he often did it.
Archibald MacLeish, in *ibid*.

But this exterior conceals the most arrogant conceit and the most ruthlessly hard-boiled self-assurance it has ever been my privilege to come up against.
Cyrus Sulzberger, in *ibid*.

Everybody who encountered him felt his enormous energy and noticed his nervous pacing and his chain-smoking, and the tension that made him repeat phrases as if the words were under pressure, shot out of a gun.
W. A. Swanberg, in *ibid*.

LUDLOW, EDMUND

1617—92 Regicide

A common, handfast, honest, dull, and indeed partly wooden man.
Thomas Carlyle, *Letters and Speeches of Oliver Cromwell*.

LUGOSI, BELA

1882—1956 Actor

It is useless to debate whether he was a good actor or not; Lugosi *was* Dracula: the actor's identification with the part is complete. He may not conform to the Stoker description (as does John Carradine, for example) but he left an indelible mark on the role and, consequently, on the horror film as, well. Where [Lon] Chaney remained human and pathetic, Lugosi appeared totally evil. As Count Dracula, he neither asked for nor needed the audience's sympathy. Even Lugosi's nonvillain roles he imbued with malevolence, as in *The Black Cat* and *The Invisible Ray*. To his other roles — mad scientist, necromancer, monster, or mere red herring — he brought a kind of corn-ball, demented poetry and total conviction.
Carlos Clarens, *An Illustrated History of the Horror Film*.

Poor old Bela. It was a strange thing. He really was a shy, sensitive and talented man. But he made a fatal mistake. He never took the trouble to learn our language and consequently he was very suspicious of tricks, fearful of what he regarded as scene-stealing. Later, when he realized I didn't go in for such nonsense we became friends. But we never really socialised. Our lives, our tastes, were quite different. Ours was simply a professional relationship.
Boris Karloff, in John Brosnan, *The Horror People*.

For some people, he was the embodiment of dark, mysterious forces, a harbinger of evil from the world of shadow. For others he was merely a ham actor appearing in a type of film unsuitable for children and often unfit for adults.
Arthur Lennig, *The Count*.

If Lugosi chews the scenery at times, he chews with grandiose vigor, and often that chewing provides our only nourishment. This much can be said; he is never dull. When he is on the screen, the film moves, and when he is not, the film is generally a species of the 'undead'.
Ibid.

An extraordinary man, the screen Lugosi does not worry about the welfare of his victims, nor does he ever have qualms of conscience. 'Freedom and power, but above all, power! Power over all trembling creatures, over the whole ant-heap!' says Raskolnikov. The screen Lugosi lived life on a cosmic stage, not in the middle-class closet. He does not care what his neighbours think. In fact, if he had his way, he'd kill them all off because they annoy him. What Lugosi appealed to, then, is the unsocial side of ourselves, a *reductio ad absurdum* of our supposed 'territorial imperative'. He was also, in a peculiar sense, a revolutionary. Like the Marx Brothers, the screen Lugosi disliked the establishment. The

Marx Brothers, however, tore down the establishment, after making a mockery of it, and substituted sheer anarchy. The Lugosi character also tore it down, but was eager to replace it with his own rule. He was not, then, opposed to authority, but only to someone else's employment — and enjoyment — of it. He did not want power for some utopia, but basically for the sheer joy of running the whole show his own way.

    Ibid.

LUHAN, MABEL DODGE

1879—1962 Author

She's American, plebian,
Sexed all over in a way you laugh and like,
Unintellectual, unsensitive,
Unkind, if kindness is quick sympathy,
Though kind as summer when she thinks of it.
    Max Eastman, in Albert Parry, *Garrets and Pretenders.*

Sit silently and secrete intensity;
Go passionately nowhere and go fast;
Have thoughts, but never to their peril, think;
Be meaningful and moonish and bizarre,
A personage of art and ecstasy.
    Ibid.

Mrs. Luhan treated her husbands and lovers like possessions of the same order as the beautiful objects with which she filled her houses. She collected people and arranged them like flowers. Her New York *salon* was only one of many; wherever she went, she loved to combine people in startling new juxtapositions.
    Christopher Lasch, *The New Radicalism in America.*

Except for her vast memoir, an extraordinary effort of introspection, the life of Mable Dodge Luhan was that of another rich and restless woman, a footnote in the cultural history of Bohemia.
    Ibid.

She was a stoutish woman with a very sturdy fringe of heavy hair over her forehead, heavy long lashes and very pretty eyes and a very old fashioned coquetry.
    Gertrude Stein, in *ibid.*

LUTYENS, SIR EDWIN LANDSEER

1869—1944 Architect

The nature of Lutyens's aesthetic honesty can per-

haps be crystallised by saying that he aimed at the utmost truth in *architecture's* reflection of life. Architecture's reflection of *life*, be it observed; not of abstract values, nor of structural means, nor of a building's functional purpose, but of the humanity that men of the renaissance age were accustomed to transfer to the forms and proportions of architecture.
    C. Hussey, *The Life of Sir Edwin Lutyens.*

I had proposed that we should lunch together at the Garrick Club, because I had obviously to ask father if he had any serious objection to the writing or the writer of this essay. But, when I broached the matter, he merely mumbled in obvious embarrassment: 'Oh, my!' — just as his father used to do. Then, as the fish was served, he looked at me seriously over the rims of his two pairs of spectacles and remarked: 'The piece of cod passeth all understanding.'
    Robert Lutyens, *Sir Edwin Lutyens.*

That most delightful, good-natured, irresponsible, imaginative jester of genius.
    Vita Sackville-West, *Pepita.*

LYELL, SIR CHARLES

1797—1875 Geologist

There were two men to whom Darwin's debt was great: Malthus, to whom reference has already been made, and Lyell, the propounder of the principle of uniformitarianism in natural processes. Darwin was steeped in this principle, and Thomas Henry Huxley showed that its application to the realm of living beings inevitably led to evolution.
    Sir Gavin de Beer, *Reflections of a Darwinian.*

Lyell's function was mainly that of a critic and exponent of the researches of his contemporaries, and of a philosophical writer thereon, with a rare faculty of perceiving the connection of scattered facts with each other, and with the general principles of science. As Ramsay once remarked to me, 'We collect the data, and Lyell teaches us to comprehend the meaning of them'.
    Sir Archibald Geikie, *The Founders of Geology.*

See also Charles Babbage, Charles Darwin

LYLY, JOHN

1554—1606 Dramatist, Author

The only Rare Poet of that Time, the Witty, Comi-

cal, Facetiously-Quick, and unparalell'd *John Lilly*.
> Edward Blount, Address to the Reader, in Lyly's
> *Comedies*, 1632.

The noble Sydney . . .
>   . . . did first reduce
Our tongue from Lillies writing then in use;
Talking of stones, stars, plants, of fishes, flyes,
Playing with words, and idle similies,
As th'English, apes and very zanies be
Of every thing, that they doe heare and see,
So imitating his ridiculous tricks,
They spake and writ, all like meere lunatiques.
> Michael Drayton, *To My Most Dearely Loved*
> *Friend Henery Reynolds Esquire*.

Himself a mad lad, as ever twanged, never troubled
with any substance of wit or circumstance of
honesty, sometime the fiddlestick of Oxford, now
the very babble of London.
> Gabriel Harvey, *Advertisement for Papp-hatchett*
> *and Martin Marprelate*, 1590.

LYNDHURST, LORD (JOHN SINGLETON COPLEY THE YOUNGER)

1772—1863 Jurist

He wanted to serve a temporary purpose, and he did
so always. He regarded politics as a game; to be
played first for himself, and then for his party. He
did not act contrary to his opinion, but he did not
care to form a true opinion.
> Walter Bagehot, *Biographical Studies*: 'What
> Lord Lyndhurst really was'.

I tell you what, Lyndhurst, I wish I could make an
exchange with you. I would give you some of my
walking power and you should give me some of
your brains.
> Lord Brougham, comment in old age, attributed.

Lady Tankerville asked Lord Lyndhurst, whether he
believed in Platonic Friendship?
> 'After but not before,' was the reply.
> Benjamin Disraeli, *Reminiscences*.

LYTTELTON, GEORGE, BARON

1709—73 Politician

The friend who told you that I was nothing in faction gave a true character of me, and he may add, if
he pleases, that I am nothing in a Court. What,
therefore, have I to do in the political world? Certainly nothing, but like the chorus in the ancient
tragedies, give sober precepts of morality which
none of the actors regard.
> On himself, in Reginald Blunt, *Thomas, Lord*
> *Lyttelton*.

He trusted too much to the representations of
others and was always ready to leave the labour of
discriminating characters to those who found an
interest in deceiving him.
> Anon., in *St James's Chronicle*, September 1776.

Wrapped up like a Laputan in intense thought . . .
he leaves his hat in one room, his sword in another,
and would leave his shoes in a third if his buckles,
though awry, did not save them; his legs and arms
. . . seem to have undergone the *question extraordi-
naire*; and his head, always hanging upon one or
other of his shoulders, seems to have received the
first stroke of the block.
> Philip Dormer Stanhope, Earl of Chesterfield,
> *Letters*.

That man sat down to write a book, to tell the
world what the world had all his life been telling
him.
> Samuel Johnson, in James Boswell, *Life of John-
> son*.

>   From these abstracted of,
You wander through the philosophic world;
Where in bright train continual wonders rise
Or to the curious or the pious eye.
And oft, conducted by historic truth,
You tread the long extent of backward time,
Planning with warm benevolence of mind
And honest zeal, unwarped by party rage,
Britannia's weal — how from the venal gulf
To raise her virtue and her arts revive.
> James Thomson, *The Seasons: Spring*.

Absurdity was predominant in Lyttelton's composition: it entered equally into his politics, his apolo-
gies, his public pretences, his private conversations.
With the figure of a spectre, and the gesticulations
of a puppet, he talked heroics through his nose,
made declamations at a visit, and played cards with
scraps of history or sentences of Pindar.
> Horace Walpole, *Memoirs*.

LYTTON (BULWER-LYTTON), EDWARD GEORGE EARLE, LORD

1803—73 Author, Statesman

'Ada' used to shock Lytton by her barefaced atheism. He maintained a correspondence with her on
the Immortality of the Soul, which will probably
some day be published for he never wrote an invitation to dinner without an eye to posterity.
> At one time, he flattered himself, that he had a
little shaken her; she had hinted at some sort of

Pantheistic compromise. 'Never' said Lytton, 'I *must* have *identity*.'

He exceeded Cicero.

Benjamin Disraeli, *Reminiscences*.

Lytton's inflated language means an inflation of sentiment, and his pseudo-philosophic nonsense and preposterous rhetoric carry with them inevitably a debasing of the novelist's currency. But they were taken seriously by the general public.

Q. D. Leavis, *Fiction and the Reading Public*.

Lytton cashed his cheque on fame for ready money.

Desmond MacCarthy, *Experience*.

You talk of tinsel! why, we see
The old mark of rouge upon your cheeks.
You prate of Nature! you are he
That spilt his life among the cliques.

Alfred, Lord Tennyson, 'The New Timon and the Poets', in *Punch*, 28 February 1846 (a rejoinder to Bulwer-Lytton's attack on him in 'The New Timon').

If he would but leave off scents for his handkerchief, and oil for his hair: if he would but confine himself to three clean shirts in a week, a couple of coats in a year, a beef-steak and onions for dinner, his beaker a pewter pot, his carpet a sanded floor, how much might be made of him even yet.

W. M. Thackeray, Review of Lytton's *Ernest Maltravers*.

He thoroughly understood the political status of his own country, a subject on which Dickens, I think, was marvellously ignorant, and which Thackeray had never studied. He had read extensively, and was always apt to give his readers the benefit of what he knew. The result has been that very much more than amusement may be obtained from Bulwer's novels.

Anthony Trollope, *Autobiography*.

See also Thomas Beecham, Charles Greville, W. Somerset Maugham, Lord Palmerston, H. G. Wells

M

MACARTHUR, DOUGLAS

1880—1964 Soldier

Old soldiers never die; they just fade away.
> On himself, in an address to a joint session of the United States Congress, 19 April 1951.

I came through and I shall return.
> On himself, in a statement to reporters in Australia in 1943 having been evacuated from the Philippines during the Second World War.

The shadows are lengthening for me. The twilight is here. My days of old have vanished tone and tint; they have gone glimmering through the dreams of things that were. Their memory is one of wondrous beauty, watered by tears and coaxed and caressed by the smiles of yesterday. I listen vainly, but with thirsty ear, for the witching melody of faint bugles blowing reveille, of far drums beating the long roll. In my dreams I hear again the crash of guns, the rattle of musketry, the strange mournful mutter of the battlefield. But in the evening of my memory, always I come back to West Point. Always there echoes and re-echoes in my ears — Duty — Honor — Country.
> On himself, in a farewell address to the cadets of West Point, 12 May 1962.

Oh yes, I studied dramatics under him for twelve years.
> Dwight D. Eisenhower, in Quentin Reynolds, *By Quentin Reynolds.*

Let him go, let him go, we are the braver,
  Stain his hands with our blood, dye them forever.
Recall, oh ye kinsmen, how he left us to die,
  Starved and insulted by his infamous lie;
How he seduced us with boasts of defense;
  How he traduced us with plans of offense.
When his publicity chairman presides,
  Vaunts his fame as high as the Bay of Fundy
                                        tides —
Recollects bonus boys gassed out by him
  Remember Bataan boys sacrificed for him.
Try him, Tribunal of Public Opinion
  Brothers, condemn him through our dominion

Then when he stands before Judges Olympian,
  Quakes at his final court-martial: oblivion.
> Aquill Penn (pseud.), *The Lost Leader*, written in a Japanese prisoner of war camp in June 1943.

I fired him because he wouldn't respect the authority of the President. That's the answer to that. I didn't fire him because he was a dumb son of a bitch, although he was, but that's not against the law for generals. If it was half to three quarters of them would be in jail.
> Harry S. Truman, commenting on his removal of MacArthur from command of U.S. and U.N. Troops in Korea, in Merle Miller, *Plain Speaking: An Oral Biography of Harry S. Truman.*

MACAULAY, THOMAS BABINGTON, LORD

1800—59 Historian, Essayist, Politician

I am far from insensible to the pleasure of having fame, rank, and this opulence which has come so late.
> On himself, Journal, 1 January 1858.

He never starts except for the end in view. His hook and bait will only catch a particular fish, — there is no vague cast of the net.
> Lord Acton, Letter to William Ewart Gladstone, 21 June 1876.

The great apostle of the Philistines.
> Matthew Arnold, *Essays in Criticism:* 'Joubert'.

Macaulay is well for a while, but one wouldn't *live* under Niagara.
> Thomas Carlyle, in R. A. Milnes, *Notebook.*

. . . vague generalities handled with that brilliant imagination which tickles the ear and amuses the fancy without satisfying the reason.
> John Wilson Croker, to the House of Commons, 22 September 1831.

. . . His speeches are harangues and never replies.
> Charles Greville, Diary, 24 July 1831.

The worst of it is that Macaulay, like Rousseau, talked his nonsense so well that it still passes for gospel with all those who have advanced as far as reading, but have not as yet attained to thinking.
George Birkbeck Hill, *Footsteps of Dr Johnson.*

I wish that I was as cocksure of anything as Tom Macaulay is of everything.
William Lamb, Viscount Melbourne, attributed.

He has written some very brilliant essays — very transparent in artifice, and I suspect not over honest in scope and management, but he has written *no history.*
John G. Lockhart, Letter to John Wilson Croker, 12 January 1849.

His object is to strike, and he attains it; but it is by scene-painting — he aims at stronger effects than truth warrants, and so caricatures many of his personages as to leave it unaccountable how they have done what they did.
John Stuart Mill, commenting on Macaulay's *Essays*, Letter to Arthur Hardy, September 1856.

Macaulay is like the military kind who never suffered himself to be seen, even by the attendants of his bed-chamber, until he had had time to put on his uniform and jackboots.
John Morley, *Critical Miscellanies.*

Then the favourite comes with his trumpets and drums,
And his arms and his metaphors crossed.
W. M. Praed, undergraduate squib, 1820.

A sentence of Macaulay's . . . may have no more sense in it than a blot pinched between doubled paper.
John Ruskin, *Praeterita.*

He has occasional flashes of silence, that make his conversation perfectly delightful.
Sydney Smith, in Lady Holland, *Memoirs of Sydney Smith.*

To take Macaulay out of literature and society and put him in the House of Commons is like taking the chief physician out of London during a pestilence.
Ibid.

Macaulay is like a book in breeches.
Ibid.

I recognise our friend in almost every sentence — haunted by no doubts, exempt from every tinge of ill-nature, keeping out of all obscure depths, running

after every amusing incident or image, and making most captivating music as he crows and flaps his wings in the consciousness of strength and courage . . .
Sir James Stephen, Letter to the Rev. H. Melvill, December 1855.

. . . that style which, with its metallic exactness and its fatal efficiency, was certainly one of the most remarkable products of the industrial revolution.
Lytton Strachey, *Portraits in Miniature.*

He seems to have been created *en bloc.* His manner never changed; as soon as he could write at all — at the age of eight — he wrote in the style of his History. The three main factors in his intellectual growth, — the Clapham sect, Cambridge, Holland House — were not so much influences as suitable environments for the development of a predetermined personality. Whatever had happened to him he would always have been a middle class intellectual with whig views. . . . And there he is — squat, square and perpetually talking — on Parnassus.
Ibid.

See also Lytton Strachey

MCCARTHY, JOSEPH
1908—57 Politician

McCarthyism is Americanism with its sleeves rolled.
On himself, in a 1952 speech, in Richard Rovere, *Senator Joe McCarthy.*

McCarthy is the only major politician in the country who can be labelled 'liar' without fear of libel.
Joseph and Stewart Alsop, syndicated column, 3 December 1953.

Even more terrifying was Senator Joseph R. McCarthy, who thought there was a Communist under every bed, and often awoke people in the middle of the night with his poking around. During the day McCarthy looked for Communists in the State Department — under desks. A 'Joe Should Go' movement was started, and though its backers did not say where they thought Joe should go, everyone had a pretty good idea. Finally McCarthy was censored for something 'unbecoming a Senator.' No doubt it was his rumpled suit.
Richard Armour, *It All Started With Columbus.*

The late Joseph R. McCarthy, a United States Senator from Wisconsin, was in many ways the most gifted demagogue ever bred on these shores. No

bolder seditionist ever moved among us — nor any politician with a surer, swifter access to the dark places of the American mind.
Richard Rovere, *Senator Joe McCarthy.*

This sovereign of the assemblies was 'foul mouthed' all right, and 'a low mean fellow', and he wanted no one to think otherwise of him. He was a master of the scabrous and the scatological; his talk was laced with obscenity. He was a vulgarian by method as well as, probably, by instinct. He belched and burped in public. If he did not dissemble much, if he did little to hide from the world the sort of human being he was, it was because he had the shrewdness to see that this was not in his case necessary. He seemed to understand, as no other politician of this stature ever has, the perverse appeal of the bum, the mucker, the Dead End kid, the James Jones-Nelson Algren-Jack Kerouac hero of a nation uneasy in its growing order and stability. . . .
Ibid.

. . . this Typhoid Mary of conformity. . . .
Ibid.

MCCLELLAN, GEORGE BRINTON

1826—85 Soldier

For McClellan had always been the great symbol. He was the trumpets these soldiers had heard and the flags they had carried and the faraway, echoing cheers they had raised: the leader of an unreal army which had come marching out of the horn gates with golden light on its banners, an impossible sunrise staining the sky above its path, and now it had gone into the land of remembered dreams.
Bruce Caton, *The Army of the Potomac: A Stillness at Appomattox.*

[McClellan] is an admirable Engineer, but he seems to have a special talent for the stationary engine.
Abraham Lincoln, in Robert Debs Heinl Jr, *The Dictionary of Military and Naval Quotations.*

If I gave McClellan all the men he asks for they could not find room to lie down. They'd have to sleep standing up.
Abraham Lincoln, in Carl Sandburg, *Abraham Lincoln, The Prairie Years and the War Years.*

My dear McClellan:
If you don't want to use the army, I should like to borrow it for a while.
Yours respectfully,
A. Lincoln.

Abraham Lincoln, Letter to McClellan, complaining that the general was failing in his duties as commander in chief of the Army of the Potomac, in *ibid.*

So McClellan sent a telegram to Lincoln one day: 'Have captured two cows. What disposition should I make of them?' And Lincoln: 'Milk 'em, George.'
Carl Sandburg, *ibid.*

The General believed that he was the chosen instrument of the Almighty to save the Union, and acted accordingly.
John Russell Young, *Around the World with General Grant.* . . .

MCCORMICK, CYRUS HALL

1809—84 Industrialist, Inventor

In the early days, grain was cut with a scythe or sickle by a sickley old man who carried around an hourglass so that he would know when it was quitting time. He was called the Grim Reaper. This slow procedure was speeded up by Cyrus McCormick, familiarly known as Jack the Reaper, who developed a machine with a belt conveyor, which conveyed belts through the Middle West and was responsible for establishing the Corn Belt and the Bible Belt.
Richard Armour, *It All Started With Columbus.*

MCCULLERS, CARSON SMITH

1917—67 Author

I suppose my central theme is the theme of spiritual isolation. Certainly I have always felt alone.
On herself, in Mark Schorer, *The World We Imagine.*

. . . the machinery of love is the eternal flaw in Mrs McCullers' impersonal universe which alone has the power to liberate man from his fate of spiritual isolation.
Louis Auchincloss, *Pioneers and Caretakers.*

Mrs McCullers has always been concerned with exploring what Hawthorne called the 'labyrinth of the human heart' and what she has found therein has not always proved cause for rejoicing.
Oliver Evans, *The Ballad of Carson McCullers.*

. . . her dependence on the more decadently baroque elements in what is taken to be a Faulkner-

ian outlook has served her, as the saying goes, only
too well.

> Vivienne Koch, 'The Conservation of Caroline
> Gordon', in Louis D. Rubin Jr and Robert D.
> Jacobs eds, *Southern Renascence.*

Unlike too many other 'legends', her talent was as
real as her face. . . .

> Gore Vidal, in Melvin J. Friedman, 'Flannery
> O'Connor: Another Legend in Southern Fiction',
> in Robert E. Reiter ed., *Flannery O'Connor.*

Mrs McCullers, sometimes depicted as a sensational-
ist revelling in the grotesque, is more than that
because she is first of all the poetic symbolist, a
seeker after those luminous meanings which always
do transcend the boundaries of the stereotyped,
the conventional, and the so-called normal.

> Marguerite Young, in Oliver Evans, *The Ballad
> of Carson McCullers.*

MACDONALD, (JAMES) RAMSAY

1866–1937 Prime Minister

If God were to come to me and say, 'Ramsay,
would you rather be a country gentleman than a
Prime Minister?', I should reply, 'Please God, a
country gentleman.'

> On himself, in Harold Nicolson, Diary, 5 October
> 1930.

Ramsay MacDonald is trying to ride two horses. He
is trying to appear a strong, virile fellow, who is
justified in the eyes of the public, in running after
the great ladies in society. In short, a reincarnation
of Palmerston.

The other horse is the ailing, sick, weary Titan,
carrying the world on his shoulders. A brave, courageous creature, indomitable in his will-power in
the face of all the afflictions God has visited on
him — somewhat in spite of God.

The truth is, he is an old humbug.

> Lord Beaverbrook, Letter to Sir Robert Borden,
> 14 August 1932.

. . . the boneless wonder . . .

> Winston Churchill, comment on MacDonald's
> conciliation of his Roman Catholic supporters,
> 1931.

We know that he has, more than any other man,
the gift of compressing the largest amount of words
into the smallest amount of thought.

> Winston Churchill, Speech in the Commons,
> March 1933.

Ramsay was like the fellow who said: 'I'ze eating
very well indeed. I'ze drinking very well indeed.
But it's when I'ze asked to do anything in the way
of work that I feels all wrong.'

> Winston Churchill, 1933, in A. J. Sylvester,
> *Life with Lloyd George.*

. . . MacDonald was conscientious almost to a fault,
and he never acquired the art of delegating responsibility; it was said of him that he had been known,
when prime minister, to look up trains for one of
his secretaries.

> Lord Elton, in the *Dictionary of National Bio-
> graphy 1931–40.*

He will not risk things. He will not see people. He
gets restive immediately a hint of criticism appears.
. . . He can't bear a big man near him.

> Harold Laski, Letter to Felix Frankfurter,
> February 1930.

He is leading the gentlemen of England, and there is
no price he would not pay for that. . . .

> *Ibid.,* 1931.

He had sufficient conscience to bother him, but not
sufficient to keep him straight.

> David Lloyd George, in A. J. Sylvester, Diary,
> 29 August 1938.

. . . he dramatizes his position as always. The defeated statesman surrounded by his devoted flock;
the devoted father having harmed his brilliant son;
Cincinnatus longing to return to his plough but
restrained by public duty . . . always there is something histrionic and therefore fraudulent about him.
I respect and admire him in many ways. But I do
see why many people regard him as a complete
humbug.

> Harold Nicolson, Diary, 20 November 1935.

I am haunted by mental decay such as I saw creeping over Ramsay MacDonald. A gradual dimming of
the lights.

> *Ibid.,* 28 April 1947.

There are no professions he ever made, no pledges
he ever gave to the country, and no humiliation to
which he would not submit if they would only
allow him still to be called the Prime Minister.

> Viscount Snowden, Speech in the House of
> Lords, 3 July 1934.

MacDonald owes his pre-eminence largely to the
fact that he is the only artist, the only aristocrat by
temperament and talent in a Party of plebeians and
plain men.

> Beatrice Webb, Diary, May 1930.

MCKIM, CHARLES FOLLEN
1847–1909 Architect

McKim saw in his dreams a civilization of law and order, cities rich, spacious, and necessarily conventional. He quickly grasped the adaptability of the architecture of Rome, Florence, and Tuscany, as well as the Louis XIV period of France, to the needs of America and devoted himself to the study of these styles, and what I have called the 'Renaissance of McKim, Mead, and White' is a wonderful adaptation of the styles of these periods to the needs of twentieth-century America.
> Alfred Hoyt Granger, *Charles Follen McKim.*

He stood for a national architecture, inspired by beauty and built upon the solid foundations of law, order, and tradition.
> *Ibid.*

Plunged into a world that did not know these masters, even by name, and that looked on Victorian Gothic as romantic archeology, but in no possible sense as architecture, McKim's inflexible nature had some hard rebuffs and conflicts. It required time and other influences to bring him to a sense of the great worth of the underlying principles of the Parisian training, but his sympathies were always more with the earlier than the later French masters. He never really liked modern French taste and he was, in fact, more close to Rome than to Paris.
> Robert Peabody, in *ibid.*

MCKINLEY, WILLIAM
1843–1901 Twenty-Fifth United States President

I would rather have my political economy founded upon the everyday experience of the puddler or the potter than the learning of the professor.
> On himself, in Paul W. Glad, *McKinley, Bryan and the People.*

The truth is, I didn't want the Philippines and when they came to us as a gift from the gods, I did not know what to do with them . . . I sought counsel from all sides — Democrats as well as Republicans — but got little help.
> On himself, in James Ford Rhodes, *The McKinley and Roosevelt Administration 1897–1909.*

Looking for all the world like a benign undertaker, he embalmed himself for posterity. Never permitting himself to be photographed in disarray, he would change his white vests, when wrinkled, several times a day.
> Thomas A. Bailey, *Presidential Greatness.*

President McKinley, the conservative's conservative, stepped gingerly into the lukewarm water of tropical imperialism when he reluctantly scooped up the Spanish Philippines, Guam, and Puerto Rico.
> *Ibid.*

The bullet that pierced Goebel's breast
Can not be found in all the West;
Good reason, it is speeding here
To stretch McKinley on his bier.
> Ambrose Bierce, in A. W. Johns, *The Man Who Shot McKinley.*

McKinley keeps his ear to the ground so close that he gets it full of grasshoppers much of the time.
> 'Uncle' Jo Cannon, in H. J. Sievers, *Benjamin Harrison: Hoosier President.*

I didn't believe one man should have so much service and another man should have none.
> Leon Czolgosz, after he had assassinated McKinley, in Margaret Leech, *In the Days of McKinley.*

It may be hard for Mack, bein' new at the business, to select the right man for the wrong place. But I'm sure he'll be advised by his friends, and from the list of candidates I've seen he'll have no trouble in findin' timber.
> 'Mr Dooley' (Finley Peter Dunne), on McKinley's problems as a new president, in Marcus Cunliffe, *American Presidents and the Presidency.*

I was more surprised to learn from the autopsy of the President that he was dying of old age at 58, if he had not been shot.
> John Hay, Letter to Henry Adams, 21 October 1901.

Where is McKinley, Mark Hanna's McKinley,
His slave, his echo, his suit of clothes?
Gone to join the shadows, with the pomps of that
time,
And the flame of that summer's prairie rose.
> Vachel Lindsay, *Bryan, Bryan, Bryan, Bryan.*

. . . had about as much backbone as a chocolate éclair.
> Theodore Roosevelt, as reported by Secretary Long, in D. H. Elletson, *Roosevelt and Wilson: A Comparative Study.*

. . . a mediaeval knight in the dusty arena of Ohio politics.
> Bellamy Storer, in Margaret Leech, *In the Days of McKinley.*

Not long ago we had two men running for the President. There was Mr. McKinley on the one hand and Mr. Bryan on the other. If we'd have had an 'Anti-Doughnut Party' neither would have been elected. I don't know much about finance, but some friends told me that Bryan was all wrong on the money question, so I didn't vote for him. I knew enough about the Philippines to have a strong aversion to sending our bright boys out there to fight with a disgraced musket under a polluted flag, so I didn't vote for the other fellow.

Mark Twain, in Philip S. Foner, *Mark Twain Social Critic.*

He weighed out his saccharine on apothecary scales, just enough and no more for the dose that cheers but does not inebriate.

William Allen White, in Paul W. Glad, *McKinley, Bryan and the People.*

. . . used too many hackneyed phrases, too many stereotyped forms. He shook hands with exactly the amount of cordiality and with precisely the lack of intimacy that deceived men into thinking well of him, too well of him.

Ibid.

He walked among men a bronze statue, for thirty years determinedly looking for his pedestal.

William Allen White, in Ralph G. Martin, *Ballots and Bandwagons.*

MACKINTOSH, SIR JAMES

1765—1832 Philosopher

Sir Jammy (the humane *code-softener*).
William Cobbett, *Journal*, 31 October 1825.

Mr. Mackintosh's Lectures were after all but a kind of philosophical centos. They were profound, brilliant, new to his hearers; but the profundity, the brilliancy, the novelty were not his own. He was like Dr. Pangloss (not Voltaire's, but Coleman's) who speaks only in quotations; and the pith, the marrow of Sir James's reasoning and rhetoric at that memorable period might be put within inverted commas.

William Hazlitt, *The Spirit of the Age.*

[S. T. Coleridge] thought him no match for Burke, either in style or manner. Burke was a metaphysician, Mackintosh a mere logician. Burke was an orator (almost a poet) who reasoned in figures, because he had an eye for nature: Mackintosh, on the other hand, was a rhetorician, who had only an eye for common-places.

William Hazlitt, *Fugitive Writings: My Acquaintance with Poets.*

Though thou'rt like Judas, an apostate black,
In the resemblance thou dost one thing lack;
When he had gotten his ill-purchas'd pelf,
He went away, and wisely hang'd himself:
This thou may do at last, yet much I doubt
If thou hast any bowels to gush out!

Charles Lamb, *Epigram.*

MCPHERSON, AIMEE SEMPLE

1890—1944 Evangelist

Your sister in the King's glad service.
On herself, in William G. McLoughlin, 'Aimee Semple McPherson', *Journal of Popular Culture*, Winter 1967.

The Barnum of religion.
Anon., in *Notable American Women*, vol. 2.

The bringing of the spirit of Christ into a community after the fashion of one of his real disciples like Mrs McPherson is doing more to destroy the powers of Satan, sin, and lawlessness in that community than all the police departments, sheriffs, and courts combined.

Judge Ben B. Lindsay, in Aimee Semple McPherson, *This Is That.*

She is a frank and simple fraud, somewhat like Texas Guinan, but more comical and not quite so cheap.

Morrow Mayo, 'Aimee Rises from the Sea', in *New Republic*, 25 December 1929.

Mrs. McPherson has the nerve of a brass monkey and the philosophy of the Midway — 'Never give a sucker an even break' — is grounded in her.

Ibid.

MACREADY, WILLIAM CHARLES

1793—1873 Actor

America!! Give me a crust in England. God speed me in my labours for my blessed family's sake. Amen! No *America.*
On himself, Diary.

Mr. Macready sometimes, to express uneasiness and agitation, composes his cravat as he would in a drawing-room.

William Hazlitt, in *Examiner*, 6 October 1816.

On the whole, we think Mr Macready's powers are better adapted to the declamation than to the acting of passion — that is, that he is a better orator than actor.

William Hazlitt, 'Mr Macready's Othello', in *Examiner*, 13 October 1816.

We do not always see the reason for his *fortes* and *pianos*: his grace looks more the effect of study than habit: his personal character does not seem so concerned in what he does. You are not sure what sort of person he will be when he leaves the stage.

Leigh Hunt, 'Macready as Virginius', in *Tatler*, 19 October 1830.

Consciousness of his imperfect declamation of blank verse . . . induced him to adopt what his admirers called his natural style of speaking it; which was simply chopping it up into prose.

Fanny Kemble, *Records of a Later Life*.

His declamation was mannered and unmusical; yet his intelligence always made him follow the winding meanings through the involutions of the verse, and never allowed you to feel, as you feel in the declamation of Charles Kean, and many other actors, that he was speaking words which he did not thoroughly understand. The trick of a broken and spasmodic rhythm might destroy the music proper to the verse, but it did not perplex you with false emphasis or intonations wandering at hazard.

George Henry Lewes, *On Actors and the Art of Acting*.

Macready it is said, used to spend some minutes behind the scenes, lashing himself into an imaginative rage by cursing *sotto voce*, and shaking violently a ladder fixed against the wall.

Ibid.

Macready a most horribly ugly fellow acted the part of a detected villain exquisitely.

Henry Crabb Robinson, Diary, 23 April 1817.

Macready's style was an amalgam of John Kemble and Edmund Kean. He tried to blend the classic art of the one with the impulsive intensity of the other; and he overlaid both with an outerplating of his own, highly artificial, and elaborately formal. He had, too, a mania, for inoculating everyone from his own system: he was a Narcissus in love with his own formalities; and he compelled, as far as he could, all within his influence to pay him the worship of imitation. It was I believe Mrs W. Clifford, mother-in-law of Harrison the singer who well rebuked his tyrannic egoism. He had been remorselessly hammering a speech into her ears at rehearsal, in his *staccato*, extra-syllabic manner, when she very

coolly, but very decidedly, told him that she much preferred her own style, and declined to change it for his; adding, as she opened her eyes and expanded her hands and mouth, with a strong *crescendo* emphasis on the word *all*:—

'If this goes on, we shall be ALL Macreadys!'
George Vandenhoff, *Dramatic Reminiscences*.

The fact is, beauty and grace in art were not Macready's study so much as exactitude; he had less a view to symmetry of form, than to proportion in measurement; the formal justness of a right angle would be more palpably satisfying to his eye, than the elegance of a curve; and his ear found more pleasure in accent than in melody. Thus he seized salient points of character, and gave them strong emphasis, and relief; he was less competent to make harmonious combinations of parts into a consistent whole. His power lay in passionate outbursts, not in philosophical analysis; hence his soliloquies were generally faulty, strained, violent, not toned down by the softening influence of thought.

Ibid.

MCTAGGART, JOHN MCTAGGART ELLIS

1866—1925 Philosopher

If Hegel be the inspired, and too often incoherent, prophet of the Absolute; and if Bradley be its chivalrous knight, ready to challenge anyone who dares to question its pre-eminence; McTaggart is its devoted and extremely astute family solicitor.

C. D. Broad, *Ethics and the History of Philosophy*.

MADISON, DOLLY PAYNE

1768—1849 Hostess

A dastardly act of the British was their landing soldiers on the shores of Chesapeake Bay without warning, and then proceeding to burn Washington. Fortunately Dolly Madison, the mistress of the White House, was a woman of great strength and presence of mind. She carried off everything of value, including the Declaration of Independence, the Mint, and the Washington Monument. After the British had gone, she returned everything to its place, thus establishing herself as the most honest public servant until Lincoln.

Richard Armour, *It All Started With Columbus*.

Affectation and her are farther asunder than the poles.

Anne Royall, *Southern Tour*.

MADISON, JAMES

1750/1—1836 Fourth United States President

Poor Madison the tremors has got,
'Bout this same arming the nation,
Too far to retract, he cannot
Go on — and he loses his station. . . .
As to powder and bullets and swords,
For as they were never intended,
They're a parcel of high sounding words
But never to *action* extended. . . .
  O! this is *great* Terrapin War!
  Anon., in *New York Evening Post*, 4 February
  1812.

Pardon me if I add that I think him a little too
much of a book politician, and too timid in his politics, for prudence and caution are opposites of
timidity.
  Fisher Ames, in Irving Brant, *The Fourth
  President, A Life of James Madison.*

Mr. Madison is wholly unfit for the storms of War.
Nature has cast him in too benevolent a mould.
Admirably adapted to the tranquil scenes of
peace — blending all the mild amiable virtues, he is
not fit for the rough and rude blasts which the conflicts of nations generate.
  Henry Clay, Letter to Caesar Rodney,
  29 December 1812.

Mr. Madison is, as I always knew him, slow in taking
his ground, but firm when the storm rises.
  Albert Gallatin, in Irving Brant, *The Fourth
  President, A Life of James Madison.*

Jemmy Madison — Oh, poor Jemmy, he is but a
withered little applejohn.
  Washington Irving, 1812, in George Dangerfield,
  The Era of Good Feelings.

. . . stimulating everything in the manner worthy of
a little commander-in-chief, with his little round hat
and huge cockade.
  Richard Rush, Letter to Benjamin Rush, 20 June
  1812.

I did not like his looks any better than I like his
Administration.
  Daniel Webster, in R. N. Current, *Daniel Webster
  and the Rise of National Conservatism.*

He had as much to do as any man in framing the
constitution, and as much to do as any man in ad-
ministering it.
  Daniel Webster, in Harold S. Schultz, *James
  Madison.*

See also Martin Van Buren

MAHAN, ALFRED THAYER

1840—1914 Sailor, Historian

It was inevitable that the English-German imperialistic rivalry should have ended in struggle: it was
this American's unenviable distinction however to
have armed both foes, ideologically and physically,
for the contest.
  Louis M. Hacker, 'The Incendiary Mahan', in
  Scribner's Magazine, April 1934.

. . . Mahan, the maritime Clausewitz, the Schlieffen
of the sea.
  Barbara W. Tuchman, *The Guns of August.*

There had been naval histories before, but Mahan's
power of generalization, his ability to subordinate
details to the central theme, and to trace the logic
of events and their significance for later times, made
him truly the first 'philosopher of sea power'.
  Allan Westcott, 'Alfred Thayer Mahan', in Dumas
  Malone ed., *Dictionary of American Biography.*

MAITLAND, JOHN, see under LAUDERDALE, DUKE OF

MALCOLM X (MALCOLM LITTLE)

1925—65 Civil Rights Activist, Religious Leader

The slaying of Malcolm X has shown again that
hatred, whatever its apparent justification, however
it may be rationalized, turns on itself in the end. . . .
Now the hatred and violence he preached has over-
whelmed him and he has fallen at the hands of
Negroes.
  Anon., in *New York Herald Tribune*, in J. H.
  Clarke, *Malcolm X: the man and his times.*

Black history began with Malcolm X.
  Eldridge Cleaver, in Peter Goldman, *The Death
  and Life of Malcolm X.*

If you knew him you would know why we must
honor him: Malcolm was our manhood, our living,
black manhood! This was his meaning to his people.
And, in honoring him, we honor the best in ourselves. . . . However much we may have differed
with him or with each other about him and his value
as a man, let his going from us serve only to bring
us together, now. . . . And we will know him then
for what he was and is — a Prince — our own black
shining Prince! -- who didn't hesitate to die, because
he loved us so.
  Ossie Davis, eulogy, in Eldridge Cleaver, *Soul
  On Ice.*

He meant to haunt us — to play on our fears and quicken our guilts and deflate our dreams that everything was getting better — and he did.
    Peter Goldman, *The Death and Life of Malcolm X.*

He spoke like a poor man and walked like a king.
    Dick Gregory, in *ibid.*

He was always challenging the white man, always debunking the white man. I don't think he was ever under any illusion that a powerless black minority could mount a physical challenge to a powerful white majority and survive. But they could mount a psychological challenge, and if they were persistent, they might at least produce some erosion in the attitudes and the strategies by which the white man has always protected himself and his interests. His challenge was to prove that you are as great as you say you are, that you are as loving as you say you are, that you are as altruistic as you say you are, that you are as *superior* as you say you are.
    C. Eric Lincoln, in *ibid.*

He was a kind of alter ego for people who were too vulnerable and too insecure to say what they really felt regarding our situation in America. He wanted them to understand the inconsistencies between what the white man said and what the white man did, and to prove by these inconsistencies that there was no magic in being white. He was trying to strip the white man of his mystique, and that made him a demagogue for most white people.
    Ibid.

Malcolm was a destroyer of myths and the webs of mystification. . . . He was a black son and brother who had audaciously returned to us from a very long trip through lands ruled by god-kings and magician-tricksters. He brought back the truth about the racket of racism, oppression and imperialism. . . .
    Patricia Robinson, 'Malcolm X, Our Revolutionary Son and Brother', in John Henry Clarke ed., *Malcolm X: The man and his time.*

Malcolm's failures were a failure of leadership style and a failure to evolve a sound organizational base for his activities. Thus Malcolm is a domestic victim of the protest style. Malcolm tried to employ the protest style with all the dramatizing rhetoric and verbal pyrotechnics at his command in order to mobilize an effective organization. The protest style is just not suited to the task of mobilization.
    Charles E. Wilson, in *ibid.*

MALORY, SIR THOMAS
1400?–70? Author

In our forefathers tyme, when papistrie, as a standyng pool, covered and overflowed all England, fewe bookes were read in our tong, savyng certaine bookes Chevalrie, as they sayd, for pastime and pleasure, which, as some say, were made in Monasteries, by idle Monkes, or wanton Chanons: as for example, *Morte Arthure*: the whole pleasure of which booke standeth in two speciall poyntes, in open mans slaughter, and bold bawdrie: In which book those be counted the noblest Knightes, that do kill most men without any quarrell, and commit fowlest aduoulteries by subtlest shifts. . . . This is good stuffe, for wise men to laughe at, or honest men to take pleasure at.
    Roger Ascham, *The Schoolmaster.*

Malory's description of himself as 'the servant of Jesu both day and night' has been assumed to imply that he was a priest, but his description of himself as a 'knight' confutes the suggestion. Pious ejaculation at the conclusion of their labours is characteristic of medieval authors.
    Sidney Lee, in *Dictionary of National Biography.*

His fundamental merit is not so much his Latin fluency and facility as his art of combining pathos and simplicity, romance and epic straightforwardness. His language has all the strength of an oration, all the ease of a popular tale.
    Eugène Vinaver, *Malory.*

MALTHUS, THOMAS ROBERT
1766–1834 Political Economist, Clergyman

Had Adeline read Malthus? I can't tell;
  I wish she had: his book's the eleventh commandment,
Which says, 'Thou shalt not marry,' unless *well*:
  This he (as far as I can understand) meant:
'Tis not my purpose on his views to dwell,
  Nor canvass what 'so eminent a hand' meant;
But certes it conducts to lives ascetic,
Or turning marriage into arithmetic.
    Lord Byron, *Don Juan*, canto xv.

They hunted together in search of Truth, and huzzaed when they found her, without caring who found her first; and indeed I have seen them both put their able hands to the windlass to drag her up from the bottom of that well in which she so strangely loves to dwell.
    Maria Edgeworth, on the friendship between Malthus and David Ricardo, in John Maynard Keynes, *Essays in Biography.*

Mr. Malthus's system is one, 'in which the wicked cease from troubling, and in which the weary are at rest.' To persons of an irritable and nervous disposition, who are fond of kicking against the pricks, who have tasted of the bitterness of the knowledge of good and evil, and to whom whatever is amiss in others sticks not merely like a burr, but like a pitch-plaister, the advantage of such a system is incalculable.

William Hazlitt, *Reply to the Essay on Population by the Rev. T. R. Malthus.*

Malthus is a real moral philosopher, and I would almost consent to speak as inarticulately, if I could think and act as wisely.

Sydney Smith, Letter to a friend, July 1821.

Philosopher Malthus came here last week. I got an agreeable party for him of unmarried people. There was only one lady who had had a child; but he is a good-natured man, and, if there are no appearances of approaching fertility, is civil to every lady.

Ibid., 1831.

MANNING, HENRY EDWARD, CARDINAL

1808—92 Theologian

I am conscious of a desire to be in such a position (1) as I had in times past, (2) as my present circumstances imply, (3) as my friends think me fit for, (4) as I feel my own faculties tend to. But, God being my helper, I will not seek it by the lifting of a finger or the speaking of a word.

On himself, Diary, *circa* 1851.

I am a Mosaic Radical.

On himself, in old age, in Lytton Strachey, *Eminent Victorians.*

I do not know whether I am on my head or my heels when I have active relations with you. In spite of my friendly feelings, this is the judgment of my intellect.

Cardinal Newman, Letter to Manning, 1866.

. . . As he entered the ante-room where one awaited his approach, the most Protestant knee instinctively bent. •

G. W. E. Russell, *Collections and Recollections.*

If God gives me strength to undertake a great wrestling-match with infidelity, I shall owe it to [Manning].

Cardinal Wiseman, in Lytton Strachey, *Eminent Victorians.*

See also James Gibbons

MANSFIELD, KATHERINE (KATHERINE MANSFIELD BEAUCHAMP)

1888—1923 Author

Trying to read her after Chekhov was like hearing the carefully artificial tales of a young old-maid compared to those of an articulate and knowing physician who was a good and simple writer.

Ernest Hemingway, *A Moveable Feast.*

Katherine Mansfield's life is so fascinating because — despite its surface tangle of moods, impetuous reactions and rash decisions — it presents a very simple symbolic pattern. This is a variant of the Garden of Eden theme. An apple of knowledge is eaten, with bitter consequences, And then, under the curse and blessing of that knowledge, comes the attempt to regain the paradise. It is a deeply moving story but not really a tragic one, for it ends in sight of success.

Christopher Isherwood, *Exhumations.*

I do not know whether my impression of her was just, but it was quite different from other people's. Her talk was marvellous, much better than her writing, especially when she was telling of things that she was going to write, but when she spoke about people she was envious, dark, and full of alarming penetration in discovering what they least wished known and whatever was bad in their characteristics.

Bertrand Russell, *Autobiography.*

I think that in some abstruse way [John Middleton] Murry corrupted and perverted and destroyed Katherine both as a person and a writer. She was a very serious writer, but her gifts were those of an intense realist, with a superb sense of ironic humour and fundamental cynicism. She got enmeshed in the sticky sentimentality of Murry and wrote against the grain of her own nature. At the bottom of her mind she knew this, I think, and it enraged her.

Leonard Woolf, *Beginning Again.*

We could both wish that our first impression of K.M. was not that she stinks like a — well, civet cat that had taken to street walking. In truth, I'm a little shocked by her commonness at first sight; lines so hard and cheap. However, when this diminishes, she is so intelligent and inscrutable that she repays friendship.

Virginia Woolf, *A Writer's Diary*, 11 October 1917.

See also A. E. Housman

MANSFIELD, EARL OF (WILLIAM MURRAY)

1705—93 Judge

My desire to disturb no man for conscience sake is pretty well known and, I hope, will be had in remembrance.
> On himself, in Bonamy Dobrée ed., *Anne to Victoria.*

I will not do that which my conscience tells me is wrong upon this occasion, to gain the huzzas of thousands, or the daily praise of all the papers which come from the press: I will not avoid doing what I think is right, though it should draw on me the whole artillery of libels; all that falsehood and malice can invent, or the credulity of a deluded populace can swallow.
> On himself, in *ibid.*

He [Johnson] would not allow Scotland to derive any credit from Lord Mansfield; for he was educated in England. 'Much,' said he, 'may be made of a Scotchman, if he be *caught* young.'
> James Boswell, *Life of Johnson.*

Sir, you may as well maintain that a carrier, who has driven a pack-horse between Edinburgh and Berwick for thirty years, does not know the road, as that Lord Mansfield does not know the law of England.
> James Boswell, *Journal of A Tour of the Hebrides.*

Loyalty, Liberty, and Law,
Impatient of the galling chain,
And yoke of pow'r, resum'd their reign;
And burning with the glorious flame
Of public virtue, Mansfield came.
> Charles Churchill, *The Ghost.*

So then — the Vandals of our isle,
　Sworn foes to sense and law,
Have burnt to dust a nobler pile
　Than ever Roman saw!

And MURRAY sighs o'er Pope and Swift,
　And many a treasure more,
The well-judg'd purchase and the gift
　That grac'd his letter'd store.

Their pages mangled, burnt, and torn,
　The loss was *his alone*;
But ages yet to come shall mourn
　The burning of *his own*.
> William Cowper, *On the Burning of Lord Mansfield's Library Together with his MSS by the Mob in the Month of June 1780.*

The vigour of Lord Mansfield's eloquence was weakened by the craft of his profession, which begot subtlety, and by the timid disingenuousness of his heart, which did not permit him to throw out his mind with honesty; a specious — a false — a pleasing — an accomplished, and a mischievous citizen.
> Henry Grattan Jr, *Memoirs of Henry Grattan.*

　　Mansfield, the just and intrepid;
Wise Judge, by the craft of the Law ne'er seduced
　　　　　　　　　from its purpose;
And when the misled multitude raged like the winds
　　　　　　　　　in their madness,
Not to be moved from his rightful resolves.
> Robert Southey, *A Vision of Judgment X.*

MANSFIELD, RICHARD

1854—1907 Actor

The excitement of a first night is actual suffering; the nervousness actual torture. Yet as I walk . . . to the theatre . . . and note the impassive, imperturbable faces of the passers-by, I must confess to myself that I would not change places with them — no, not for worlds. I have something that is filling my life brimful of interest. . . . It's like a battle. I shall win or die.
> On himself, in *Harper's Weekly*, 24 May 1890.

I have more inward quaverings and doubtings and more horrible fears and misgivings and nervous spasms than occur to most men after fourteen years of campaigning, and I even now never face the footlights . . . without suffering an agony of fright.
> On himself, in *Chicago Herald-Examiner*, April 1893.

For each role he built a definite, different, distinct character. Of course one could discern the style of the master as one can of Whistler whether it be a portrait of a great lady or a misty vision of the Thames. So, too, this actor's canvases were signed Richard Mansfield.

One can understand that he had little time for trivia or indeed for the smaller amenities. He was abrupt, he rarely encouraged conversation, for he was husbanding the hours and even the minutes. There was so much that he wished to accomplish and maybe he had long sensed that he had not too many years ahead.
> Douglas Wood, 'The Last of the Giants', in *Show*, September 1963.

MARCY, WILLIAM LEARNED

1786—1857 Lawyer, Politician

I know of no man who possesses greater facility than the Secretary of State of turning an unwelcome visitor into an icicle.
>   Anon., *New York Times*, December 1855.

He has enough of the witchery of mischievous fun and tact to make him racy as a politician and delightful as an acquaintance. He is as piquantly [sic] mischievous as Mephistopheles himself. . . .
>   Fitzwilliam Byrdsall, Letter to James Buchanan, 1 December 1851.

. . . the celebrated William L. Marcy, author of the political maxim, 'To the victor belong the spoils'.
>   H. L. Mencken, *The American Language: An Inquiry into the Development of English in the United States.*

. . . gifted with a dry sense of humor, he had a way of laughing silently, while he shook like a bowlful of jelly. He was never averse to playing his own game while gently smiling on (and at) others.
>   Allan Nevins, *Ordeal of the Union*, vol. 2.

MARLBOROUGH, DUKE OF (JOHN CHURCHILL)

1650—1722 Soldier

Unbounded courage and compassion join'd,
Tempering each other in the victor's mind,
Alternately proclaim him good and great,
And make the hero and the man complete.
>   Joseph Addison, *The Campaign.*

'Twas then great Marlbro's mighty soul was prov'd,
That in the shock of charging hosts unmov'd,
Amidst confusion, horror and despair,
Examin'd all the dreadful scenes of war;
In peaceful thought the field of death survey'd,
To fainting squadrons sent the timely aid,
Inspir'd repuls'd battalions to engage,
And taught the doubtful battle where to rage.
>   *Ibid.*

And glory long has made the sages smile;
   'Tis something, nothing, words, illusion, wind —
Depending more upon the historian's style
   Than on the name a person leaves behind:
Troy owes to Homer what whist owes to Hoyle:
   The present century was growing blind
To the great Marlborough's skill in giving knocks,
Until his late Life by Archdeacon Coxe.
>   Lord Byron, *Don Juan*, canto iii.

A note of what is to bee got to the Duke of Marl.'s History. Vigilance, Sobriety, Regularity, Humility, Presence of Mind, Voyd of Capriciousness, execution of orders well given, Health proceeding from temperance, Early up, Never taken at a Why Not.
>   Sarah Churchill, Duchess of Marlborough, in Iris Butler, *Rule of Three.*

He never rode off any field except as a victor. He quitted war invincible; and no sooner was his guiding hand withdrawn than disaster overtook the armies he had led.
>   Winston Churchill, *Marlborough*, vol. 1.

By his invincible genius in war and his scarcely less admirable qualities of wisdom and management he had completed that glorious process that carried England from her dependency upon France . . . to ten years' leadership of Europe. Although this proud task was for a space cast aside by faction . . . the greatness of Britain and her claims to empire were established upon foundations that have lasted to this day. He had proved himself the 'good Englishman' he aspired to be, and History may declare that if he had had more power his country would have had more strength and happiness, and Europe a surer progress.
>   *Ibid.*

Dost thou recall to mind with joy, or grief,
Great Marlborough's actions, that immortal chief,
Whose slightest trophy rais'd in each campaign,
More than suffic'd to signalize a reign?
>   William Congreve, *A Letter to Lord Viscount Cobham.*

Of honour or the finer sentiments of mankind he knew nothing; and he turned without a shock from guiding Europe and winning great victories to heap up a matchless fortune by peculation and greed. He is perhaps the only instance of a man of real greatness who loved money for money's sake.
>   John Richard Green, *A Short History of the English People.*

In life's last scene what prodigies surprise,
Fears of the brave, and follies of the wise!
From Marlborough's eyes the streams of dotage
                                                   flow,
And Swift expires a driv'ller and a show.
>   Samuel Johnson, *The Vanity of Human Wishes.*

Threescore, I think, is pretty high;
'Twas time in conscience he should die.
This world he cumber'd long enough;
He burnt his candle to the snuff;
And that's the reason, some folks think,
He left behind so great a stink.

Behold his funeral appears,
Nor widow's sighs, nor orphan's tears,
Wont at such times each heart to pierce,
Attend the progress of his hearse.
But what of that, his friends may say,
He had those honours in his day.
True to his profit and his pride,
He made them weep before he dy'd.
    Nathaniel Mist (also attributed to Jonathan
    Swift), in Michael Foot, *The Pen and the Sword*.

That impenetrable reserve under graceful and courteous manners; those unceasing contacts and cor-
respondences with opponents; that iron parsimony
and personal frugality, never relaxed in the blaze
of fortune and abundance; that hatred of waste
and improvidence in all their forms. . . .
    A. L. Rowse, *The Early Churchills*.

In Marlborough's fashion of war-making there was
emphatically no nonsense. He never wasted a man
or a movement; he never executed a single manoeuvre for show; he never, either in words or deeds,
indulged in gasconading. Probably no man ever had
such a superhuman business as he had put on his
shoulders in the business of at once fighting half
Europe and keeping the other half in fighting
order. . . .
    George Saintsbury, *Life of Marlborough*.

'Great praise the Duke of Marlbro' won,
    And our good Prince Eugene.'
'Why 't was a very wicked thing!'
    Said little Wilhelmine.
'Nay . . nay . . my little girl', quoth he,
    'It was a famous victory.

'And everybody praised the Duke
    Who this great fight did win.'
'But what good came of it at last?'
    Quoth little Peterkin.
'Why that I cannot tell,' said he,
'But 't was a famous victory.'
    Robert Southey, *The Battle of Blenheim*.

. . . the Victor of Blenheim, alike in all virtues
                                    accomplish'd,
Public or private, he; the perfect soldier and
                                    statesman,
England's reproach and her pride; her pride for his
                                    noble achievements,
Her reproach for the wrongs he endur'd.
    Robert Southey, *A Vision of Judgment*.

It was Marlborough who first taught us to be proud
of our standing army as a national institution, and
the spirit of confidence which pervaded Wellington's
army in the Peninsula, and to a still more remark-

able degree shows itself now in Queen Victoria's
army, may be said to have been born at Blenheim,
baptized at Ramillies, and confirmed at Oudenarde.
    Lord Wolseley, *Life of Marlborough*.

See also Robert E. Lee, Lord Peterborough,
Jonathan Swift

MARLOWE, CHRISTOPHER

1564—93 Dramatist

Marlowe was happy in his buskin Muse —
Alas, unhappy in his life and end;
Pity it is that wit so ill should dwell,
Wit lent from heaven, but vices sent from hell.
Our theatre hath lost, Pluto hath got,
A tragic penman for a dreary plot.
    Anon., in *The Return From Parnassus*.

Hee saieth & verely beleveth that one Marlowe is
able to shewe more sounde reasons for Atheisme
than any devine in Englande is able to geve to prove
devinitie that Marloe tolde him that hee hath read
the Atheist lecture to Sr Walter Raliegh & others.
    Anon., in *Remembraunces of Words and Matter
    againste Ric Cholmeley*.

Next Marlowe, bathed in the Thespian Springs,
Had in him those brave translunary things
That your first poets had: his raptures were
All air and fire, which made his verses clear,
For that fine madness still he did retain,
Which rightly should possess a poet's brain.
    Michael Drayton, *Of Poets and Poetry*.

It is pertinent, at least, to remark that Marlowe's
'rhetoric' is not, or not characteristically, Shakespeare's rhetoric; that Marlowe's rhetoric consists
in a pretty simple huffe-snuffe bombast, while
Shakespeare's is more exactly a vice of style, a tortured perverse ingenuity of images which dissipates
instead of concentrating the imagination, and which
may be due in part to influences by which Marlowe
was untouched. Next, we find that Marlowe's vice
is one which he was gradually attenuating, and even,
what is more miraculous, turning into a virtue. And
we find that this poet of torrential imagination
recognized many of his best bits (and those of one
or two others), saved them, and reproduced them
more than once, almost invariably improving them
in the process.
    T. S. Eliot, *Essays*: 'Christopher Marlowe'.

But the direction in which Marlowe's verse might
have moved, had he not 'dyed swearing', is quite
un-Shakespearian, is toward . . . intense and serious

and indubitably great poetry, which, like some great painting and sculpture, attains its effects by something not unlike caricature.

Ibid.

With Shakespeare, with Webster, death is a sudden severing of life; their men die, conscious to the last of some part at least of their surroundings, influenced, even upheld, by that consciousness, and preserving the personality and characteristics they have possessed through life. . . . In Marlowe's Faustus alone, all this is set aside. He penetrates deeply into the experience of a mind isolated from the past, absorbed in the realisation of its own destruction.

Una Ellis-Fermor, *Christopher Marlowe.*

Wonder not (for with thee wil I first begin) thou famous gracer of Tragedians, that *Greene* who hath said with thee like the foole in his heart, there is no God, should nowe give glory unto his greatnesse: for penetrating is his power, his hand lies heavy upon me, he hath spoken unto me with a voice of thunder, and I have felt he is a God that can punish enemies. Why should thy excellent wit, his gift be so blinded that thou should give no glory to the giver? . . . Is it pestilent Machivilian pollicie that thou hast studied?

Robert Greene, *Greenes Groatsworth of Wit bought with a million of Repentance.*

There is a lust of power in his writings, a hunger and thirst after unrighteousness, a glow of the imagination unhallowed by any thing except its own energies. His thoughts burn within him like a furnace with bickering flames; or throwing out black smoke and mists, that hide the dawn of genius, or like a poisonous mineral, corrode the heart.

William Hazlitt, *Lectures on the Dramatic Literature of the Age of Elizabeth.*

It was Marlowe who first wedded the harmonies of the great organ of blank verse which peals through the centuries in the music of Shakespeare. It was Marlowe who first captured the majestic rhythms of our tongue, and whose 'mighty line' is the most resounding note in England's literature. . . . He stands foremost and apart as the poet who gave us, with a rare measure of richness, the literary form which is the highest achievement of expression.

Henry Irving, Speech unveiling a statue, Canterbury, 1891.

. . . That things esteemed to be doon by the devine power might have aswell been don by observation of men all which he wold so sodenlie take slight occasion to slyp out as I and many others in regard of his other rashness in attempting soden pryvie iniuries to men did overslypp thogh often reprehend

him for it & for which God is my witnes aswell by my lordes commaundment as in hatred of his life and thoughts I left & did refraine his companie.

Thomas Kyd, Letter to Sir John Puckering, May 1593.

Marlowe's dramatic heroes stand alone in their singularity and singlemindedness. Conscious at every moment of their identity, they are supremely self-conscious at the moment of death. From what we know of Marlowe's own character, we may fairly suppose that he threw a good deal of himself into these monomaniac exponents of the first person; egoists, exhibitionists, infidels, outsiders.

Harry Levin, *Christopher Marlowe, the Overreacher.*

Marlowe enjoyed his strategic position because his background was still sustained by the mythical and the universal, even while he was engaged in bringing the factual and the personal in the foreground.

Ibid.

Marlowe . . . was perhaps good enough to make it possible to believe that if he had been born thirty years ago, he might now be a tolerable imitator of Mr Rudyard Kipling.

George Bernard Shaw, in *Saturday Review*, 25 May 1895.

Marlowe, the moment the exhaustion of the imaginative fit deprives him of the power of raving, becomes childish in thought, vulgar and wooden in humour, and stupid in his attempts at invention. He is the true Elizabethan blank-verse beast, itching to frighten other people with the superstitious terrors and cruelties in which he does not himself believe, and wallowing in blood, violence, muscularity of expression and strenuous animal passion as only literary men do when they are thoroughly depraved by solitary work, sedentary cowardice, and starvation of the sympathetic centres. It is not surprising to learn that Marlowe was stabbed in a tavern brawl; what would be utterly unbelievable would be his having succeeded in stabbing anyone else.

Ibid., 11 July 1896.

The infernal tradition that Marlowe was a great dramatic poet instead of a xvi century Henley throws all the blame for his wretched half-achievement on the actor. Marlowe had words and a turn for their music, but nothing to say — a barren amateur with a great air.

George Bernard Shaw, Letter to Harley Granville Barker, 2 September 1903.

The first English poet whose powers can be called sublime was Christopher Marlowe.

Algernon C. Swinburne, *The Age of Shakespeare.*

Nor was any great writer's influence on his fellows more utterly and unmixedly an influence for good. He first, and he alone, guided Shakespeare into the right way of work; his music, in which there is no echo of any man's before him, found its own echo in the more prolonged but hardly more exalted harmony of Milton's. He is the greatest discoverer, the most daring and intrepid pioneer, in all our poetic literature. Before him was neither genuine blank verse nor genuine tragedy in our language. After his arrival the way was prepared, the paths were made straight, for Shakespeare.

> *Ibid.*

It so hapned that at Detford, a little village about three miles distant from London, as he went to stab with his ponyard one named Ingram, that had invited him thither to a feast, and was then playing at tables, he quickly perceyving it, so avoyded the thrust, that withal drawing out his dagger for his defence hee stabd this Marlowe into the eye, in such sort, that his braines comming out at the daggers point, hee shortly after dyed.

> William Vaughan, *Golden Grove*, 1600.

See also Thomas Kyd, Thomas Nashe, Sir Walter Raleigh

MARSHAL, WILLIAM, EARL OF PEMBROKE AND STRIGUIL

— d. 1219 Regent

'Have you enough money to live on?' he asked the monk. When the latter produced forty-eight pounds, William pointed out that so small a sum would not keep them. The monk hastened to explain that he did not intend to live on the principal but to invest the money and use only the interest. William was profoundly shocked. 'At usury! By the spear of God that will not do. Seize the money Eustace. Since you do not wish to return to a virtuous life, go, and may the devil guide you.'

> Sidney Painter (describing his encounter with an eloping monk and lady), *William Marshal*.

The sagacious and honest policy of the earl of Pembroke drew to him all save those who were hopelessly committed to the invader. He placed the country under a government which included all elements, and which, whilst it could not suppress all jealousies, found room for all energies.

> William Stubbs, *Constitutional History* (on his conduct at the beginning of the reign of Henry III).

MARSHALL, GEORGE CATLETT JR

1880–1959 Soldier, Politician

I thought that the continual harping on the name of [Chief Justice] John Marshall was rather poor business. It was about time for someone else to swim for the family.

> On himself, in Forrest C. Pogue, *George Catlett Marshall, Education of a General 1880–1939*.

. . . it [the Marshall Plan] was the most unsordid act in history.

> Winston Churchill, in Merle Miller, *Plain Speaking: An Oral Biography of Harry S. Truman.*

General Marshall is not only willing, he is eager to play the role of a front man, for traitors.

The truth is this is no new role for him, for Gen. George C. Marshall is a living lie . . . unless he himself was desperate, he could not possibly agree to continue as an errand boy, a front man, a stooge, or a co-conspirator for this administration's crazy assortment of collectivist, cutthroat crackpots and Communist fellow-traveling appeasers. . . .

> Senator William Jenner, opposing Marshall's nomination as Secretary of Defense, *Congressional Record.*

At times the ice-cold military mind asserted itself, and this was dangerous when it came to dealing with people who wore no uniform and were not obedient to military commands. There was a streak of the dictator in him, something forbidding and proud; he could not hide it.

> Robert Payne, *The Marshall Story.*

In a war unparalleled in magnitude and horror, millions of Americans gave their country outstanding service. General of the Army George C. Marshall gave it victory.

> Harry S. Truman, Speech on 26 November 1945.

MARSHALL, JOHN

1755–1835 Jurist

. . . he formulated, more tellingly than any one else and for a people whose thought was permeated with legalism, the principles on which the integrity and ordered growth of their Nation have depended. Springing from the twin rootage of Magna Charta and the Declaration of Independence, his judicial statesmanship finds no parallel in the salient features of its achievement outside our own annals.

> Edward S. Corwin, *John Marshall and the Constitution.*

Marshall's intrinsic achievements are too solid and his personal quality too homespun to tolerate mythical treatment. It is important not to make untouchable dogmas of the fallible reasoning of even our greatest judge. . . .

Felix Frankfurter, in John Marshall, Bicentennial Celebration 1955, *Final Report.*

Marshall was not a bookish lawyer though he was no stranger to books. He could, as wise judges do, make them his servants. He eschewed precedents such as were then available in his opinions for the Court. But he showed mastery in the treatment of precedents where they have been relied on for an undesirable result.

Ibid.

To a great degree, the measure of Marshall's influence . . . was in his qualities of character and personal leadership. The eminence acquired by the Supreme Court during that period and the strength imparted to the Constitution are less the work of Marshall the convinced Federalist than of Marshall the man. Here was a statesman, not a zealot; an empiricist, not a dogmatist; a leader, not a tyrant.

Donald G. Morgan, 'Marshall, the Marshall Court, and the Constitution', in W. Melville Jones ed., *Chief Justice John Marshall: A Reappraisal.*

See also George C. Marshall

MARSTON, JOHN

1575?—1634 Dramatist

Marston is a writer of great merit, who rose to tragedy from the ground of comedy, and whose *forte* was not sympathy, either with the stronger or softer emotions, but an impatient scorn and bitter indignation against the vices and follies of men, which vented itself either in comic irony or in lofty invective. He was properly a satirist.

William Hazlitt, *Lectures on the Age of Elizabeth.*

Jo. MARSTONE the last Christmas, when he daunced with Alderman Mores wives daughter, a Spaniard borne, fell into a strange commendation of her wit and beauty. When he had done, she thought to pay him home, and told him she *thought* he was a poet. ''Tis true,' said he, 'for poets feigne and lye, and soe did I, when I commended your beauty, for you are exceedingly foule.'

John Manningham, Diary, 21 November 1602.

He abhors such writers, and their works; and hath professed himself an enemy to all such as stuff their scenes with ribaldry, and lard their lines with scur-

rilous taunts and jests; so that whatsoever, even in the spring of his years, he hath presented upon the private and public theatre, now in his autumn and declining age he need not be ashamed of.

William Sheares, *Epistle Dedicatory . . . to The Workes of John Marston.*

No sooner has he said anything especially beautiful, pathetic, or sublime, than the evil genius must needs take his turn, exact, as it were, the forfeit of his bond, impel the poet into some sheer perversity, defame the form and flow of the verse with some preposterous crudity or flatulence of phrase which would discredit the most incapable or the most fantastic novice. And the worst of it all is, that he limps or stumbles with either foot alternately. At one moment, he exaggerates the licence of artificial rhetoric, the strain and swell of the most hyperbolical poetic diction: at the next, he falls flat upon the naked level of insignificant or offensive realism.

Algernon C. Swinburne, *The Age of Shakespeare.*

The Muse of this poet is . . . no giddy girl, but a strong woman with fine irregular features, large and luminous eyes, broad intelligent forehead, eyebrows so thick and close together that detraction might call her beetle-browed, powerful mouth and chin, fine contralto voice (with an occasional stammer), expression alternately repellent and attractive, but always striking and sincere. No one has ever found her lovely; but there are times when she has a fascination of her own which fairer and more famous singers might envy her; and the friends she makes are as sure to be constant as she, for all her occasional roughness and coarseness, is sure to be loyal in the main to the nobler instincts of her kind and the loftier traditions of her sisterhood.

Ibid.

MARTINEAU, HARRIET

1802—76 Author

I cannot think of any future as at all probable, except the 'annihilation' from which some people recoil with so much horror. I find myself here in the universe, — I know not how, whence, or why. I see everything in the universe go out and disappear, and I see no reason for supposing that it is not an actual and entire death. And for *my* part, I have no objection to such an extinction. I well remember the passion with which W. E. Forster said to me, 'I had rather be damned than annihilated.' If he once felt five minutes' damnation, he would be thankful for extinction in preference. The truth is, I care little about it any way.

On herself, Letter to Henry G. Atkinson, 19 May 1876.

I see no reason why the existence of Harriet Martineau should be perpetuated.

On herself, attributed last words.

Know that a great new light has arisen among English women. In the words of Lord Brougham, 'There is a deaf girl at Norwich doing more good than any man in the country'. . . . She has a vast store of knowledge on many deep and difficult subjects; a wonderful store for a person scarcely thirty, and her observation of common things must have been extraordinary correct as well as rapid.

Lucy Aikin, Letter to Dr Channing, 15 October 1832.

I cannot but praise a person whose one effort seems to have been to deal perfectly honestly and sincerely with herself, although for the speculations into which this effort has led her I have not the slightest sympathy.

Matthew Arnold, Letter to his Mother, May 1855.

I fancied you would be struck by Miss Martineau's lucid and able style. She is a very admirable woman — and the most logical intellect of the age, for a woman. On this account it is that the men throw stones at her, and that many of her own sex throw dirt; but if I begin of this subject I shall end by gnashing my teeth.

Elizabeth Barrett Browning, Letter to H. S. Boyd, 24 December 1844.

Miss Martineau makes herself an object of envy by the success of her domestic arrangements. She has built a cottage near her house, placed in it a Norfolk dairymaid, and has her poultry-yard, and her piggery, and her cowshed; and Mrs Wordsworth declares she is a model in her household economy, making her servants happy, and setting an example of activity to her neighbours.

Henry Crabb Robinson, Letter to Miss Fenwick, 15 January 1849.

My scholars are welcome to read as much Voltaire as they like. His voice is mighty among the ages. Whereas they are entirely forbidden Miss Martineau, — not because she is an infidel, but because she is a vulgar and foolish one.

John Ruskin, Fors Clavigera, Letter 87.

See also Mary Wollstonecraft

MARVELL, ANDREW

1621–78 Poet

He was a great master of the Latin tongue; an excellent poet in Latin or English: for Latin verses there was no man could come into competition with him. . . . He kept bottles of wine at his lodgeing, and many times he would drinke liberally by himselfe to refresh his spirits, and exalt his Muse.

John Aubrey, Brief Lives.

Politically he was a Parliamentarian, intellectually he was a rationalist, temperamentally he was a satirist. . . . He retained the mystical individualism of the Renaissance while recognizing its inadequacy, and as a consequence a tension is generated in his poetry comparable to that in the later poems of Yeats, who also had a foot in two cultural camps.

F. W. Bateson, English Poetry: A Critical Introduction.

The poems of Marvell . . . have much of that overactivity of fancy, that remoteness of allusion, which distinguishes the school of Cowley; but they have also a heartfelt tenderness, a childish simplicity of feeling, among all their complication of thought, which would atone for all their conceits, if conceit were indeed . . . an offence against poetic nature.

Hartley Coleridge, Biographia Borealis.

By way of flourishing my eyes, I have been looking into Andrew Marvell, an old favourite of mine, who led the way for Dryden in verse, and Swift in prose, and was a much better fellow than the last, at any rate.

Edward Fitzgerald, Letter to W. A. Wright, 20 January 1872.

Most facetious in his discourse, yet grave in his carriage, a most excellent preacher who like a good husband never broached what he had new brewed, but preached what he had pre-studied some competent time before.

Thomas Fuller, The History of the Worthies of England.

This is one of the great differences between Donne and Marvell: while Donne, one might almost say, devised entirely new ways of saying entirely new things, Marvell assimilated, recombined, and perfected from his contemporaries various new ways of saying old ones.

J. B. Leishman, Proceedings of the British Academy, 1961.

Among these saucy detractors, the most notorious was that vile fellow Marvell: whose life, from his youth upwards, was one scene of wickedness. He was naturally so pert and impudent, that he took upon him to write satires for the faction, in which there was more defamation than wit. His talent was in railing; in everything else he had a grovelling genius.

Samuel Parker, History of his Own Time.

MARX, (JULIUS HENRY) 'GROUCHO'

1890—1977 Comedian

They say a man is as old as the woman he feels. In that case I'm eighty-five. . . . I want it known here and now that this is what I want on my tombstone. Here lies Groucho Marx, and Lies and Lies and Lies. P.S. He never kissed an ugly girl.

On himself, *The Secret Word is Groucho.*

Please accept my resignation. I don't want to belong to any club that will accept me as a member.

On himself in a telegram to the Friar's Club, Hollywood. (There are various versions of this famous one-liner, all ostensibly authentic.)

My sex life is now reduced to fan letters from an elderly lesbian who would like to borrow $800; phone calls from a flagrant fairy with chronic low blood pressure (he'd like to get in pictures); and Pincus' dog who howls mournfully under my window every night.

On himself in a letter to Harry Kurnitz, 3 October 1950.

What put him in a better mood was being mistaken for someone else — like the day a Beverly Hills dowager, obviously on the lookout for a non-Japanese gardener to work her own place, drove by in a Cadillac and stopped in front of father's house. Father was dressed in old pants and a sweatshirt, and he was down on his hands and knees in a flower bed, working with a trowel.

'Oh gardener,' the dowager called out the window to the crouched figure in the garden, 'how much does the lady of the house pay you a month?'

'Oh I don't get paid in dollars,' answered Father. 'The lady of the house just lets me sleep with her.'

Arthur Marx, *Son of Groucho.*

On his climb up the ladder he has enjoyed life to the utmost. He has shaken hands with Presidents, danced cheek to cheek with Marlene Dietrich, played baseball with Lou Gehrig, traded backhands with Jack Kramer, strummed guitar duets with the great Segovia, and he's insulted nearly everyone worth insulting.

Arthur Marx, *Life With Groucho.*

MARX, (ADOLPH) 'HARPO'

1893—1964 Comedian, Musician

I was the same kind of father as I was a harpist — I played by ear.

On himself, in Harpo Marx, *Harpo Speaks.*

I've played piano in a whorehouse. I've smuggled secret papers out of Russia. I've spent an evening on the divan with Peggy Hopkins Joyce. I've taught a gangster mob how to play Pinchie Winchie. I've played croquet with Herbert Bayard Swope while he kept Governor Al Smith waiting on the phone. I've gambled with Nick the Greek, sat on the floor with Greta Garbo, sparred with Benny Leonard, horsed around with the Prince of Wales, played Ping-pong with George Gershwin. George Bernard Shaw has asked me for advice. Oscar Levant has played private concerts for me at a buck a throw. I have golfed with Ben Hogan and Sam Snead. I've basked on the Riviera with Somerset Maugham and Elsa Maxwell. I've been thrown out of the casino at Monte Carlo. Flush with triumph at the poker table, I've challenged Alexander Woollcott to anagrams and Alice Duer Miller to a spelling match. I've given lessons to some of the world's greatest musicians. I've been a member of the two most famous Round Tables since the days of King Arthur — sitting with the finest creative minds of the 1920's at the Algonquin in New York, and with Hollywood's sharpest professional wits at the Hillcrest. . . .

The truth is, I had no business doing any of these things. I couldn't read a note of music. I never finished the second grade. But I was having too much fun to recognize myself as an ignorant upstart.

On himself, in *ibid.*

One of Harpo's more disconcerting penchants was for running around in the nude. He would invite a group of friends to his house and greet them in the drawing room stark naked and smiling.

Norman bel Geddes, *Miracle In the Evening.*

Harpo's worldly activities had embraced pimps, thieves, whores, dowagers, royalty and statesmen. He had come out of the early vaudeville circuits which were the slums of entertainment. His cruise upward from these lowest of stage alleys to a place among the theatre's elite had been full of bawdy adventure. Yet there had come out of it a man mysteriously innocent. . . .

This same innocence that endeared him to his audiences, Harpo brought off the stage and offered to his friends. It was an innocence that rose out of Harpo's good will toward people. No envy or worry was to be noted in him. He enjoyed all he met, even fools. There were no bad meals, bad ball games, bad shows or bad people in his world. There were a few outside of it, like Nazis and bigots. Harpo went after them with a ferocity that marked his chase of villains on the stage.

But in his private world all was pleasant. If he felt displeased by anything going on in front of him, he smiled, closed his eyes and fell asleep. He was

able to fall asleep in a dentist's chair and remain asleep while having a tooth filled.
Ben Hecht, *A Child of the Century*.

One could never be sure in accepting a dinner invitation to Harpo's whether one's companions would be H. G. Wells and Don Budge, or Somerset Maugham and Salvador Dali. Frequently the combinations were even more remarkable — Aldous Huxley and Maxie Rosenbloom.
Oscar Levant, *A Smattering of Ignorance*.

M-G-M emasculated Harpo, turning him into a cute, childlike imp who honks rather than a lecherous, asocial man of nature who grabs and unmasks. M-G-M kept the angelic pixy and deleted the brash vulgarity and blatant sexuality. He became a child-man rather than a natural man. Harpo had always been more at home with children than with adults in the Paramounts. ... At M-G-M his relationship to animals became a conventional one rather than a bizarre and irrational kinship between natural man and other creatures.
Gerald Mast, *The Comic Mind*.

MARY I

1516—58

'When I am dead and my body is opened,' she said to those around her, 'ye shall find CALAIS written on my heart'. I should have thought, if anything were written on it, they would have found the words —JANE GREY, HOOPER, ROGERS, RIDLEY, LATIMER, CRANMER, AND THREE HUNDRED PEOPLE BURNT ALIVE WITHIN FOUR YEARS OF MY WICKED REIGN, INCLUDING SIXTY WOMEN AND FORTY LITTLE CHILDREN. But it is enough that their deaths were written in Heaven.
Charles Dickens, *A Child's History of England*.

The lady Mary my sister came to me to Whestminster, wheare after salutacions she was called with my counsel into a chambre, where was declared how long I had suffered her masse against my will in hope of her reconciliation, and how no, being no hope, which I perceived by her lettres, except I saw some short amendment, I could not beare it. She answerid that her soul was God's, and by her faith she wold not chaung, nor dissemble her opinion with contrary doinges. It was said I constrained not her faith, but willed her not as a king to rule but as a subject to obey. And that her exaumple might breed to much inconvenience.
Edward VI, *Chronicle*.

It was her particular misfortune that the two things in the world to which she was devoted, her husband and her religion, were the two things which most estranged her from her people.
Conyers Read, *The Tudors*.

MARY II

1662—94 Queen Consort to William III

Oft have we heard of impious sons before
Rebelled for crowns their royal parents wore;
But of unnatural daughters rarely hear
'Till those of hapless James and old king Lear
But worse than cruel lustful Goneril thou!
She took but what her father did allow;
But thou, more impious, robb'st thy father's brow.
Him both of power and glory you disarm,
Make him by lies the people's hate and scorn,
Then turn him forth to perish in a storm.
Anon., *The Female Parricide*, 1689.

Her understanding, though very imperfectly cultivated, was quick. There was no want of feminine wit and shrewdness in her conversation; and her letters were so well expressed that they deserved to be well spelt.
T. B. Macaulay, *History of England*.

See also Henry Purcell, William III

MARY STUART, QUEEN OF SCOTS

1542—87

Mary, Mary, quite contrary,
    How does your garden grow?
With silver bells, and cockle shells,
    And pretty maids all in a row.
    Nursery Rhyme, traditionally taken to refer
    to Mary.

The meanest hind in fair Scotland
    May rove their sweets amang;
But I, the Queen of a' Scotland,
    Maun lie in prison strang.
I was the Queen o' bonie France,
    Where happy I hae been;
Fu' lightly rase I in the morn,
    As blythe lay down at e'en;
And I'm the Sovereign of Scotland,
    And mony a traitor there;
Yet here I lie in foreign hands
    And never-ending care.
    Robert Burns, *Lament of Mary Queen of Scots*.

Let men patiently abide, and turn unto their God, and then shall he either destroy that whore in her whoredom, or else he shall put it in the hearts of a multitude to take the same vengeance upon her that has been taken of Jezebel and Athaliah, yea, and of others of whom profane histories make mention; for greater abomination was never in the nature of any woman than is in her, whereof we have but seen only the buds. . . .

John Knox, *History of the Reformation in Scotland.*

There was one more ceremony to accomplish. The executioner must exhibit the head and speak the customary words. The masked black figure stooped and rose, crying in a loud voice: 'Long live the Queen!' But all he held in his hand that had belonged to the rival queen of hearts was a kerchief, and pinned to it an elaborate auburn wig. Rolled nearer the edge of the platform, shrunken and withered and grey, with a spare silver stubble on the small shiny skull was the head of the martyr. Mary Stuart had always known how to embarrass her enemies.

Garrett Mattingly, *The Defeat of the Spanish Armada.*

Fresch, fulgent, flurist, fragrant flour, formois
Lantern to lufe, of ladeis lamp and lot,
Cherie maist chaist, cheif charbucle and chois;
Smaill sweit smaragde, smelling but smit of smot. . . .

Alexander Scot, *Ane New Zeir Gift To the Quene Mary Quhen scho come first hame.*

This may be truly said, that if a life of exile and misery, endured with almost saintly patience, from the 15th of June, 1567, until the day of her death, upon the 8th of February, 1587, could atone for crimes and errors of the class attributed to her, no such penalty was ever more fully discharged than by Mary Stuart.

Sir Walter Scott, *History of Scotland.*

It would be idle to dwell on the story of this princess, too well known for having the misfortune to be born in the same age, in the same island with, and to be handsomer than Elizabeth. Mary had the weakness to set up a claim to a greater kingdom than her own, without any army; and was at last reduced by her crimes to be a saint in a religion which was opposite to what her rival professed out of policy.

Horace Walpole, *Catalogue of the Royal and Noble Authors.*

. . . the most notorious whore in all the world.

Peter Wentworth, in J. E. Neale, *Peter Wentworth.*

See also Elizabeth I

MARY, VICTORIA MARY AUGUSTA LOUISE OLGA PAULINE CLAUDINE AGNES

1867—1953 Queen Consort to George V

Queen Mary looking like the Jungfrau, white and sparkling in the sun.

Henry Channon, Diary, 22 June 1937.

MASEFIELD, JOHN

1878—1967 Poet

Masefield gloomyish, and very precise in diction. Fine voice. Diction of a public speaker.

Arnold Bennett, Journal, 14 December 1918.

A nervous, generous, correct man, very sensitive to criticism. . . . He wrote in a hut in his garden, surrounded by tall gorse-bushes, and only appeared at meal-times. In the evening he used to read his day's work over to Mrs Masefield, and they corrected it together.

Robert Graves, *Goodbye to All That.*

He's a horrible sentimentalist — the cheap Byron of the day — his stuff is Lara 1913.

D. H. Lawrence, Letter to Edward Garnett, 3 March 1913.

Masefield was the first Georgian poet to arouse excitement in more than a clique. Since that time, which was in 1911, he has been subjected to so much condemnation on the part of successive schools of poets that he is rather in the position of Nanki Poo in 'The Mikado', when Ko-Ko explains that he is 'as good as dead — practically he *is* dead.' Nanki Poo, of course, is not at all dead, and in fact is upon the stage at the time.

Frank Swinnerton, *The Georgian Literary Scene.*

MASON, GEORGE

1725—92 Statesman

By refusing to support the unamended Constitution, by doggedly defending local, state, and regional interests against the trading of too much liberty for too much authority, by steering shy of open political hassles except in line of duty to his beloved state of Virginia, Mason forfeited acclaim that history laid generously upon both his friends and his adversaries. His achievements as an intellectual leader, and as a consultant to other intellectual leaders, were obscured by the tumult of those final years.

Robert Allen Rutland, *George Mason, Reluctant Statesman.*

MASSINGER, PHILIP

1583–1640 Dramatist

Massinger that knowes
The strength of Plot to write in verse and prose:
Whose easie Pegassus will amble ore
Some threescore miles of Fancy in an houre.
   Anon., *On the Time-Poets*, in *Choyce Drollery*.

Massinger's verse . . . is the nearest approach to the language of real life at all compatible with a fixed metre. In Massinger, as in all our poets before Dryden, in order to make harmonious verse in the reading, it is absolutely necessary that the meaning should be understood; when the meaning is once seen, then the harmony is perfect.
   Samuel Taylor Coleridge, *Notes for a Lecture*.

The comic Scenes in Massinger not only do not harmonize with the tragic, not only interrupt the feeling, but degrade the characters that are to form any Part in the action of the Piece so as to render them unfit for any *tragic interest* — as when a gentleman is insulted by a mere Blackguard — it is the same as if any other action of nature had occurred, as if a Pig had run under his legs, or his horse threw him.
   Ibid.

Massinger, in his grasp of stagecraft, his flexible metre, his desire in the sphere of ethics to exploit both vice and virtue, is typical of an age which had much culture, but which, without being exactly corrupt, lacked moral fibre.
   A. H. Cruickshank, *Philip Massinger*.

His ways of thinking and feeling isolated him from both the Elizabethan and the later Caroline mind. He might almost have been a great realist; he is killed by conventions which were suitable for the preceding literary generation, but not for his. Had Massinger been a greater man, a man of more intellectual courage, the current of English literature immediately after him might have taken a different course. The defect is precisely a defect of personality. He is not, however, the only man of letters who, at the moment when a new view of life is wanted, has looked at life through the eyes of his predecessors, and only at manners through his own.
   T. S. Eliot, *Essays*: 'Philip Massinger'.

Massinger makes an impression by hardness and repulsiveness of manner. In the intellectual processes which he delights to describe, 'reason panders will': he fixes arbitrarily on some object which there is no motive to pursue, or every motive combined against it, and then by screwing up his heroes or heroines to the deliberate and blind accomplishment of this, thinks to arrive at 'the true pathos and sublime of human life'. This is not the way. He seldom touches the heart or kindles the fancy. . . . For the most part his villains are a sort of *lusus naturae*; his impassioned characters are like drunkards or madmen. Their conduct is extreme and outrageous, their motives unaccountable and weak; their misfortunes are without necessity, and their crimes without temptation, to ordinary apprehensions.
   William Hazlitt, *Lectures on the Age of Elizabeth*.

See also Thomas Middleton

MATHER, COTTON

1662/3–1727/8 Clergyman, Author, Politician

Grim Cotton Mather
Was always seeing witches
Daylight, moonlight,
They buzzed about his head,
Pinching him and plaguing him
With aches and pains and stitches,
Witches in his pulpit,
Witches by his bed.
   Stephen Vincent Benét, *Cotton Mather*.

His printed works . . . will not convey to Posterity, nor give to strangers, a just Idea of the real Worth and great Learning of the Man. It was conversation and Acquaintance with him, in his familiar and occasional Discourses and private Communications that discovered the vast compass of his Knowledge and the Projections of his Piety; more . . . than all his Pulpit exercises.
   Benjamin Colman, in John Sibley, *Biographical Sketches of Graduates of Harvard University*.

He was pious, but not affected; serious without moroseness; grave, but not austere; affable without meanness; and facetious, without levity.
   The Rev. Joshua Gee, Funeral sermon, 1727/8.

'What good shall I do?' was the Subject of his daily Tho'ts.
   Samuel Mather, *Life of Cotton Mather*.

Mather is named Cotton Mather. What a name! . . . should he resemble and represent his venerable grandfathers, John Cotton and Richard Mather, in piety, learning, elegance of mind, solid judgement, prudence and wisdom, he will bear away the palm; and I trust that, in this youth, Cotton and Mather will be united and flourish again.
   Urian Oakes, *Harvard College Commencement Address*, 1678.

It is ... evident that his judgement was not equal to his other faculties; that his passions, which were naturally strong and violent, were not always under proper regulation; that he was weak, credulous, enthusiastic, and superstitious.

B. Pierce, *History of Harvard University.*

The prominent infirmity of his nature was a childish incredulity. It extended to almost everything; and in nothing was it more manifest than in constantly recognising extraordinary interpositions in answer to his prayers.

William B. Sprague, *Annals of the American Pulpit.*

MATHER, INCREASE

1639—1723 Clergyman, Author, Politican

He was one of a very *Gentlemanly Behaviour*; full of Gravity, with all the Handsome *Carriage*, as well as *Neatness*, of a *Gentleman*. . . . His *Words* were *few* as *Wise Mens* used to be; and much on the *Guard*. . . . Pertinent, and Ponderous, and Forcible.

Anon., in John Sibley, *Biographical Sketches of Graduates of Harvard University.*

He spoke with a Grave and Wise *Deliberation*: But on some Subjects, his Voice would rise for the more *Emphatical Clauses*, as the Discourse went on; and anon come on with such a Tonitraous Cogency, that the Hearers would be struck with an Awe, like what would be Produced on the Fall of thunderbolts.

Anon. contemporary, in *ibid.*

A most excellent preacher he was, using great plainness of speech, with much light and heat, force and power; for he taught as one having authority, commanding reverence from all that heard him; whilst he spake . . . with the most awful reverence himself.

The Rev. Benjamin Colman, funeral sermon, 1723.

He appears to have been affected quite enough by *ungrateful* returns for his services; and had no very moderate sense of his own importance.

B. Pierce, in John Sibley, *Biographical Sketches of Graduates of Harvard University.*

The name Increase was given him 'because of the never to be forgotten *Increase*, of every sort, wherewith GOD favoured the Country, about the time of his nativity.'

John L. Sibley, in *ibid.*

MAUGHAM, (WILLIAM) SOMERSET

1874—1965 Novelist

My first book, published in 1897, was something of a success. Edmund Gosse admired and praised it. After that I published other books and became a popular dramatist . . . I used to meet Gosse once or twice a year and continued to do so for twenty years, but I never met him without his saying to me in his unctuous way: 'Oh, my dear Maugham, I liked your *Liza of Lambeth* so much. How wise you are never to have written anything else.'

On himself, *A Writer's Notebook.*

I discovered my limitations and it seemed to me that the only sensible thing was to aim at what excellence I could within them. I knew that I had no lyrical quality, I had a small vocabulary and no efforts that I could make to enlarge it much availed me. I had little gift of metaphors; the original and striking simile seldom occurred to me. Poetic flights and the great imaginative sweep were beyond my powers . . . I knew that I should never write as well as I could wish, but I thought with pains I could arrive at writing as well as my natural defects allowed. On taking thought it seemed to me that I must aim at lucidity, simplicity and euphony. I have put these three qualities in the order of the importance I assigned to them.

On himself, *The Summing Up.*

I always reserve to myself the privilege of changing my mind. It's the only one elderly gentlemen share with pretty women.

On himself, *The Aide.*

Most writers discipline themselves to working certain hours, then knock off for relaxation until the morrow. Charles Morgan writes for a limited time each day, after which he goes out to cut wood; Willie Maugham has a stopwatch by his side and, on completion of the day's quota, goes to the terrace and prepares for the elaborate ritual of the dry martini.

Cecil Beaton, *The Strenuous Years.*

Willie can be extremely capricious. He can turn violently against an old friend for some quite small reason: a guest who has upheld unpopular views, who has been argumentative or shown bad manners at the card table, has been told to pack his bags and leave forthwith. Willie admitted that his temper was so violent that he could quite well imagine, in a moment of rage, killing someone. . . . One day recently Willie was walking in the garden with his companion, Alan Searle, when they stopped in their tracks to watch the progress of a snail. Alan picked up a small bit of gravel and tossed it at the snail. Willie shouted: 'Don't do that!' Alan threw another little pebble. The next thing Alan knew he was lying with an unrecognizable face in a nearby hospital.

Ibid.

W. Somerset Maugham prefers small parties,
'Four is a wonderful number,' he decrees.
'Six is all right, and eight will do in a pinch.
After that, it's not a party: it's a rabble.'

Bennett Cerf, *The Laugh's On Me.*

Maugham thinks with pleasure of the civilized and wealthy society of the eighteenth century, he has made his own life wealthy and civilized and therefore would like to believe that the prose of the eighteenth century is the best. But supposing a new age of 'great tragic issues' is now in being, then a prose of humour, tolerance, and horsesense will seem frivolous and archaic! And what writer could have been more lucid and simple, more admired by Maugham than Swift who, living in the heart of that courteous and cultivated age, contrived to go mad in it?

Cyril Connolly, *Enemies of Promise.*

Somerset Maugham I met only once, on the steps of the Opera. He looked exceedingly wicked. . . . Two fundamental failings rob him of greatness. His works do not suggests those 'mysteries' which, as Proust puts it, 'have their explanation probably only in other worlds and a presentiment of which is precisely what moves us most in life and in art'. His other fault is the fear of appearing old-fashioned.

William Gerhardie, *Memoirs of a Polyglot.*

He is for our day, I suppose, what Bulwer-Lytton was for Dickens's: a half-trashy novelist, who writes badly, but is patronized by half-serious readers, who do not care much about writing.

Edmund Wilson, *Classics and Commercials.*

See also Harpo Marx

MAXWELL, JAMES CLERK

1831—79 Physicist

Before Maxwell, Physical Reality, in so far as it was to represent the processes of nature, was thought of as consisting in material particles, whose variations consist only in movements governed by partial differential equations. Since Maxwell's time, Physical Reality has been thought of as represented by continuous fields, governed by partial differential equations, and not capable of any mechanical

interpretation. This change in the conception of Reality is the most profound and the most fruitful that physics has experienced since the time of Newton.

Albert Einstein, in J. J. Thomson et al., *James Clerk Maxwell. A Commemoration Volume.*

It was this power of profound physical intuition, coupled with adequate, although not outstanding, mathematical technique, that lay at the basis of Maxwell's greatness. Yet he was perhaps less remarkable in the possession of a vivid physical imagination than in the strict control he kept over it. He never allowed it to run away with him. No matter how clearly he saw physical concepts in his mind's eye, he never made the mistake of identifying them with ultimate physical reality. He saw too deeply into things ever to imagine that what he saw was the ultimate stratum of all — final and absolute truth.

J. Jeans, in *ibid.*

There are however in every science certain exceptional individuals, who appear divinely blest, and radiate an influence far beyond the borders of their land and thus directly inspire and expedite the researches of the whole world. Among these is to be counted James Clerk Maxwell.

Max Planck, in *ibid.*

See also Michael Faraday

MAYER, LOUIS BURT

1885—1957 Motion Picture Producer

I remembered him as a hard-faced, badly-spoken and crass little man. . . . [He] wore a two-hundred-and-fifty-dollar suit, had the glibness of a self-taught evangelist and was mantled in the arrogance of success.

Charles Bickford, *Bulls, Balls, Bicycles and Actors.*

The reason so many people showed up at his funeral was because they wanted to make sure he was dead.

Samuel Goldwyn, in Bosley Crowther, *Hollywood Rajah.*

Throughout his life — even in later years when he tossed aside the moral principles so deeply ingrained in him in childhood — Mayer looked on himself as the saintliest of humans. He strove to prove it by devotion to wholesome films picturing men and women in heroic terms, and even those characters tarnished by sin reached ultimate perfection through love. He wanted all his movies to fade out with bells peeling, rose petals softening the path of

lovers until the camera gazed mistily on a handsome and triumphant groom embracing a beautiful blushing bride in the inevitable happy ending.
Arthur Marx, *Mayer and Thalberg.*

I will say that it was clear that behind his gutta-percha face and roly-poly figure (contained in some of the best tailoring I've ever seen) it was evident there was a man of steel — but well-mannered steel, the very best quality steel, which meant the hardest and most impenetrable steel.
Edward G. Robinson, *All My Yesterdays.*

He had a Judaic sense of his position. He saw his stars as members of a family in which love, honour and obedience were venerated and rewarded, while the neglect of them earned self-righteous retribution. His relations with his stars were well summed up by what he himself innocently said to the director of his beloved Andy Hardy series: 'A boy may hate his father, but he always *respects* him.'
Alexander Walker, *Stardom.*

MEADE, GEORGE GORDON
1815—72 Soldier

. . . who, in a word, holds his place by virtue of no personal qualification but in deference to a presumed, fictitious, perverted, political necessity, and who hangs upon the neck of Gen. Grant like an Old Man of the Sea whom he longs to be got rid of, and whom he retains solely in deference to the weak complaisance of this constitutional Commander-in-Chief.
Henry Ward Beecher, in *Independent*, 13 October 1864.

What is most of all attractive about Meade's intellectual make-up is his absolute candor. There is no bluff, no swagger, no pretension, no attempt to throw dirt into the eyes of posterity.
Gamaliel Bradford, *Union Portraits.*

MELBOURNE, VISCOUNT (WILLIAM LAMB)
1779—1848 Statesman, Prime Minister

I hate to be considered ill-used; I have always thought complaints of ill-usage contemptible, whether from a seduced disappointed girl, or a turned-out Prime Minister.
On himself, in Emily Eden, Letter to Mrs Lister, 23 November 1834.

Lord Melbourne sees [the Queen] every day for a couple of hours, and his situation is certainly the most dictatorial, the most despotic, that the world has ever seen. Wolsey and Walpole were in strait waistcoats compared to him.
John Wilson Croker, Letter to Sir Robert Peel, 15 August 1837.

I have no doubt [Melbourne] is passionately fond of [the Queen], as he might be of his daughter if he had one; and the more because he is a man with a capacity for loving without anything to love. It is become his province to educate, instruct and form the most interesting mind and character in the world.
Charles Greville, *The Greville Memoirs.*

. . . the person who makes me feel safe and comfortable.
Queen Victoria, Diary, 4 July 1838.

MELVILLE, HERMAN
1819—91 Author

Though I wrote the Gospels in this century, I should die in the gutter.
On himself, Letter to Nathaniel Hawthorne, 29 June 1851.

What I feel most moved to write, that is banned, — it will not pay. Yet, altogether, write the *other* way I cannot.
Ibid.

Until I was twenty-five I had no development at all. From my twenty-fifth year I date my life. Three weeks have scarcely passed, at any time between then and now, that I have unfolded within myself.
On himself, Undated letter to Nathaniel Hawthorne.

A rover, whose imagination had been disciplined neither by Puritanism nor by a formal education, he lashed, like his own whales, into bloody foam when the lance of doubt finally struck him through.
Henry Seidel Canby, *Classic Americans.*

Melville's idea of art is much more Promethean; he thought of a work of art as something never finished, something that remained living, organic, and emergent.
Richard Chase, 'Herman Melville', in Perry Miller ed., *Major Writers of America*, vol. 1.

Normally he was not a man of noticeable appearance; but when the narrative inspiration was on him, he looked like all the things he was describing — savages, sea-captains, the lovely Fayaway in her canoe, or the terrible Moby Dick himself.
Julian Hawthorne, in Eleanor Melville Metcalf, *Herman Melville.*

But Melville's imagination has a tendency to wildness and metaphysical extravagance; and when he trusted to it alone, he becomes difficult and sometimes repulsive . . . and now and then his speculations and rhapsodies have a tinge almost of insanity.
Julian Hawthorne and Leonard Lemmon, 'Herman Melville, An Early Sea Novelist', in Watson G. Branch ed., *Melville, The Critical Heritage.*

He can neither believe, nor be comfortable in his unbelief; and he is too honest and courageous not to try to do one or the other.
Nathaniel Hawthorne, in Carl Van Doren, *The American Novel 1789–1939.*

We have had writers of rhetoric who had the good fortune to find a little in a chronicle of another man and from voyaging, of how things, actual things can be, whales for instance, and this knowledge is wrapped in the rhetoric like plums in a pudding. Occasionally it is there, alone, unwrapped in pudding, and it is good. This is Melville.
Ernest Hemingway, in Carlos Baker, *Hemingway: Writer as Artist.*

Melville has the strange, uncanny magic of sea-creatures, and some of their repulsiveness. He isn't quite a land animal. There is something slithery about him. Something always half-seas-over. In his life they said he was mad — or crazy. But he was over the border.
D. H. Lawrence, *Studies in Classical American Literature.*

His vocabulary was large, fluent, eloquent, but it was excessive, inaccurate and unliterary. He wrote too easily, and at too great length, his pen sometimes running away from him, and from his readers.
Richard Henry Stoddard, 'Herman Melville', in Watson G. Branch ed., *Melville, The Critical Heritage.*

See also Frank Lloyd Wright

MELVILLE, VISCOUNT (HENRY DUNDAS)
1742–1811 Statesman

The mind of Mr Dundas was active and meddling,

and he was careful to exhibit the appearance of a great share in the government of India: but what was it, as President of the Board of Control, that he ever did? He presented, as anybody might have presented, the Company's annual budget, and he engrossed an extraordinary share of their patronage. But I know not any advice which he ever gave, for the government of India, that was not either very obvious or very wrong.
James Mill, *The History of British India.*

Now thou art off, I long to see,
In thine own language, 'Who wants me?'
It will not be at all surprising
To catch thee, HARRY, advertising.
If mad to face a second storm,
Take an Advertisement in form.
'A steady Man, near sixty years of age,
Would very willingly engage
As Butler to a Minister of State,
And overlook the Plate.
But should the Plate by chance be carried off,
And not a hogshead or a bottle left;
He begs to say, he won't be fool enough
To answer for the leakage or the theft.
If wanted he can have, by God's good grace,
An excellent character from his last place.
Please to direct to Mr H. Dundas,
At the old sign — the Bottle and the Glass.'
'Peter Pindar' (John Wolcot), *Odes to the Ins and Outs.*

The Right Honourable Gentleman is indebted to his memory for his jests, and to his imagination for his facts.
Richard Brinsley Sheridan, Reply to Dundas in the House of Commons.

Never did any man conceal deeper views of every kind under the appearance of careless inattention to self-interest. In him was exemplified the remark that 'Ars est celare Artem', and the seeming want of caution or artifice in his ordinary intercourse, capacitated him for contending successfully with men of more habitual self-command.
Nathaniel Wraxall, *Memoirs.*

MENCKEN, HENRY LOUIS
1880–1956 Author, Editor

The older I grow the more I distrust the familiar doctrine that age brings wisdom.
On himself, in *Prejudices*, series 3.

If after I depart this vale, you remember me and

have thought to please my ghost, forgive some sinner and wink your eye at a homely girl.
On himself, December 1921, in H. L. Mencken ed., *The Smart Set.*

I've made it a rule never to drink by daylight and never to refuse a drink after dark.
On himself, in A. K. Adams, *The Home Book of Humorous Quotations.*

I get little enjoyment out of women, more out of alcohol, most out of ideas.
On himself, in Edgar Kemler, *The Irreverent Mr. Mencken.*

I never listen to debates. They are dreadful things indeed. The plain truth is that I am not a fair man, and don't want to hear both sides. On all known subjects, ranging from aviation to xylophone-playing, I have fixed and invariable ideas. They have not changed since I was four or five.
On himself, Letter to Jim Tully, 1940.

He is vigorous, boisterous and Rabelaisian, good-humored and intolerant as a humbug; a libertarian and an immoralist; a hedonist, but of the simplest tastes; he is a naturally irreligious, irreverent, easy-going, individualist, wholly without sentiment where his interests are involved, and convinced that self-help and self-reliance are all that one requires to succeed.
Ernest Boyd, *H. L. Mencken.*

To him Pegasus was just a runaway horse.
Benjamin de Casseres, *Mencken and Shaw.*

My regret is that Mencken does not contradict himself more. Logic is his sin.
Ibid.

This precocious Baltimore journalist, formerly cub reporter, ghost writer, and literary handy man, drama critic, columnist, and editorializer: this hard-bitten and professional purveyor of public opinion emerges, in his late twenties, as a full-blown Mencken out of Nietzsche's brow, and for almost another decade there was to be little change in his basic point of view.
Maxwell Geismar, *The Last of the Provincials.*

He edited a magazine called 'The Smart Set' which is like calling Cape Kennedy 'Lovers' Lane'.
Ben Hecht, *Letters from Bohemia.*

What he believed in and what his readers wanted to be told were soon indistinguishable; his work became a series of circus tricks, a perpetual search for some new object of middle-class culture to be-

labor and some new habit or caprice of *Homo Americanus* to ridicule.
Alfred Kazin, *On Native Grounds.*

But if Mencken had never lived, it would have taken a whole army of assorted philosophers, monologists, editors, and patrons of the new writing to make up for him. As it was, he not only rallied all the young writers together and imposed his skepticism upon the new generation, but also brought a new and uproarious gift for high comedy into a literature that had never been too quick to laugh.
Ibid.

On all grounds he despised the average American. But as one wordmaster to another, he admired him with an unblushing patriotism.
Edgar Kemler, *The Irreverent Mr. Mencken.*

The more he reflected upon the Fascist experiment, the more he believed that Fascism, for better or for worse, had a promising future in the Western world, and that an 'intelligent Fascism' operated by incorruptible naval officers might be just the thing for America.
Ibid.

Mencken's most valuable single contribution to American criticism was his fight to purge our literature of its puritanism and gentility. By jumping on the bodies of timid critics and timid novelists alike, by discrediting their flabby values and bloodless evasions, he more than any other man opened up pioneer spaces, and enabled us, at least technically, to come of age.
Louis Kronenberger, 'H. L. Mencken', in Malcolm Cowley ed., *After the Genteel Tradition.*

He launched a massive attack on everything this country held inviolate, on most of what it held self evident. He showed how our politics was dominated by time-servers and demagogues, our religion by bigots, our culture by puritans. He showed how the average citizen, both in himself and in the way he let himself be pulled round by the nose, was a boob.
Ibid.

He simply hid a conservative's tastes under a fire-brand's vocabulary.
Ibid.

Mencken came in like a lion. Like a revolutionary, overthrowing half the props that supported America's conception of itself — and not merely its beliefs and moralities, but its peace of mind.
Ibid.

He upset all the applecarts and charged through all the china shops, bellowing his impatience of all restraint and exulting in the triumph of the ego.
    George F. Whicher, 'The Twentieth Century', in Arthur Hobson Quinn ed., *The Literature of the American People*.

MEREDITH, GEORGE

1828—1909 Novelist, Poet

Mr Meredith, the only living novelist in England who rivals Ouida in sheer vitality, packs tight all his pages with wit, philosophy, poetry, and psychological analysis. His obscurity, like that of Carlyle and Browning, is due less to extreme subtlety than to the plethoric abundance of his ideas. He cannot stop to express himself. If he could, he might be more popular.
    Max Beerbohm, *Ouida*.

At his best, a sort of daintily dressed Walt Whitman.
    G. K. Chesterton, *The Victorian Age in Literature*.

Though fashion may turn and raise him a bit, he will never be the spiritual power he was about the year 1900. His philosophy has not worn well. His heavy attacks on sentimentality — they bore the present generation, which pursues the same quarry but with neater instruments, and is apt to suspect any one carrying a blunderbuss of being a sentimentalist himself . . . What with the faking, what with the preaching, which was never agreeable and is now said to be hollow, and what with the home counties posing as the universe, it is no wonder Meredith now lies in the trough.
    E. M. Forster, *Aspects of the Novel*.

He spoke as one afoot will wind
A morning horn ere men awake;
His note was trenchant, turning kind.
He was of those whose wit can shake
And riddle to the very core
The counterfeits that Time will break.
    Thomas Hardy, *George Meredith*.

By the side of George Eliot . . . Meredith appears as a shallow exhibitionist (his famous 'intelligence' a laboured and vulgar brilliance).
    F. R. Leavis, *The Great Tradition*.

In George Meredith there is nothing but crackjaw sentences, empty and unpleasant in the mouth as sterile nuts. I could select hundreds of phrases which Mr Meredith would probably call epigrams, and I would defy anyone to say they were wise, graceful or witty.
    George Moore, *Confessions of a Young Man*.

Meredith is, to me, chiefly a stink. I should never write on him as I detest him too much ever to trust myself as critic of him.
    Ezra Pound, Letter to John Quinn, 4 June 1918.

Ah! Meredith! Who can define him? His style is chaos illumined by flashes of lightning. As a writer he has mastered everything except language: As a novelist he can do everything except tell a story: as an artist he is everything except articulate.
    Oscar Wilde, *The Decay of Lying*.

Meredith deserves our gratitude and excites our interest as a great innovator. Many of our doubts about him and much of our inability to frame any definite opinion of his work comes from the fact that it is experimental and thus contains elements that do not fuse harmoniously — the qualities are at odds: the one quality that binds and concentrates has been omitted. To read Meredith, then, to our greatest advantage we must make certain allowances and relax certain standards. We must not expect the perfect quietude of a traditional style nor the triumphs of a patient and pedestrian psychology.
    Virginia Woolf, *The Second Common Reader*.

See also Robert Browning, Samuel Butler, John Donne, Ford Madox Ford, Thomas Hardy

MIDDLETON, THOMAS

1570?—1627 Dramatist

Facetious Middleton, thy witty Muse
Hath pleased all that books or men peruse.
If any thee despise, he doth but show,
Antipathy to wit in doing so:
Thy fame's above his malice, and 'twill be
Dispraise enough for him to censure thee.
    Anon., *Wit's Recreations*.

Squibbling Middleton.
    Anon., from a poem in Gerard Langbaine, *Account of the English Dramatic Poets*.

He remains merely a name, a voice, the author of certain plays, which are all of them great plays. He has no point of view, is neither sentimental nor cynical; he is neither resigned, nor disillusioned, nor romantic; he has no message. He is merely the name which associates six or seven great plays. . . . [The] mixture of tedious discourse and sudden reality is everywhere in the work of Middleton, in his comedy also. In *The Roaring Girl* we read with toil through a mass of conventional intrigue, and suddenly realise that we are, and have been for some time without knowing it, observing a real and unique human being. In reading the *Changeling*, we may think, till almost the end of the play, that we have been concerned merely with a fantastic Elizabethan morality, and then discover that we are looking on at a dispassionate exposure of fundamental passions of any time and any place.

    T. S. Eliot, *Essays*: 'Thomas Middleton'.

He is lamentably deficient in the plot and dénouement of the story. It is like the rough draught of a tragedy, with a number of fine things thrown in, and the best made use of first; but it tends to no fixed goal, and the interest decreases, instead of increasing, as we read on, for want of previous arrangement and an eye to the whole . . . . The author's power is *in* the subject, not *over* it; or he is in possession of excellent materials which he husbands very ill. This character, though it applies more particularly to Middleton, might be applied generally to the age.

    William Hazlitt, *Lectures on the Age of Elizabeth*.

He was contemporary with those famous Poets, *Johnson*, *Fletcher*, *Massinger*, and *Rowley*, in whose Friendship he had a large Share; and tho' he came short of the two former in Parts, yet like the *Ivy* by the Assistance of the *Oak*, (being joyn'd with them in several Plays), he climbed up to some considerable height of Reputation.

    Gerard Langbaine, *Account of the English Dramatic Poets*.

See also T. S. Eliot

MILBANKE, ANNABELLA, LADY BYRON

1792—1860

The Princess of Parallelograms.
    Lord Byron, in conversation with Lady Melbourne.

MILL, JAMES

1773—1836 Philosopher

He argues against oppression less because he loves the oppressed many, than because he hates the oppressing few.
    Jeremy Bentham, according to John Bowring, *Memoirs of Bentham*.

He is an Aristotelian of the fifteenth century, born out of due season.
    T. B. Macaulay, 'Mill's Essay on Government', in *Edinburgh Review*, March 1829.

Our objection to the essay of Mr. Mill is fundamental. We believe that it is utterly impossible to deduce the science of government from the principles of human nature.
    Ibid.

My father exercised a far greater personal ascendency than Bentham. He was sought for the vigour and instructiveness of his conversation, and used it largely as an instrument for the diffusion of his opinions. I have never known any man who could do such ample justice to his best thoughts in colloquial discussion. His perfect command over his great mental resources, the terseness and expressiveness of his language, and the moral earnestness, as well as intellectual force of his delivery, made him one of the most striking of all argumentative conversers.
    John Stuart Mill, *Autobiography*.

In his views of life he partook of the character of the Stoic, the Epicurean, and the Cynic, not in the modern but the ancient sense of the word. In his personal qualities the Stoic predominated. His standard of morals was Epicurean, inasmuch as it was utilitarian, taking as the exclusive test of right and wrong the tendency of actions to produce pleasure or pain. But he had (and this was the Cynic element) scarcely any belief in pleasure; at least in his later years, of which alone, on this point, I can speak confidently. He was not insensible to pleasures; but he deemed very few of them worth the price which, at least in the present state of society, must be paid for them.
    Ibid.

All his work as a thinker was devoted to the service of mankind, either by the direct improvement of their beliefs and sentiments, or by warring against the various influences which he regarded as obstacles to their progress; and while he put as much conscientious thought and labour into everything he did, as if he had never done anything else, the subjects on which he wrote took as wide a range as if he had written without any labour at all.
    John Stuart Mill, Preface to James Mill, *Analysis of the Human Mind*.

MILL, JOHN STUART

1806—73 Philosopher

I have not any great notion of the advantage of

what the 'free discussion' men call the 'collision of opinions', it being my creed that Truth is *sown* and germinates in the mind itself, and is not to be struck *out* suddenly like fire from a flint by knocking another hard body against it; so I accustomed myself to *learn* by inducing others to deliver their thoughts, and to teach by scattering my own, and I eschewed occasions of controversy (except occasionally with some of my old Utilitarian associates).

On himself, Letter to Thomas Carlyle, May 1833.

I have never, at least since I had any convictions of my own, belonged to the benevolentiary, soup-kitchen school. Though I hold the good of the species (or rather of its separate units) to be the ultimate end (which is the alpha and omega of my utilitarianism), I believe with the fullest belief that this end can in no other way be forwarded but by the means you speak of, namely, by each taking for his exclusive aim the development of what is best in *himself*.

Ibid., January 1834.

You may think it presumptuous in a man to be finishing a treatise on logic and not to have made up his mind finally on these great matters. But mine professes to be a logic of experience only, and to throw no further light upon the existence of truths not experimental, than is thrown by showing to what extent reasoning from experience will carry us. Above all mine is a logic of the indicative mood alone — the logic of the imperative, in which the major premiss says not *is* but *ought*, I do not meddle with.

On himself, Letter to John Sterling, November 1839.

I know that compromises are often inevitable in practice, but I think they should be left to the enemy to propose — reformers should assert principles and only *accept* compromises.

On himself, Letter to W. J. Fox, end of 1849.

I did not invent the word, but found it in one of [John] Galt's novels, the *Annals of the Parish*, in which the Scotch clergyman, of whom the book is a supposed autobiography, is represented as warning his parishioners not to leave the Gospel and become utilitarians. With a boy's fondness for a name and a banner I seized on the word, and for some years called myself and others by it as a sectarian appellation, and it came to be occasionally used by some others holding the opinions which it was intended to designate.

On himself and the origin of the term Utilitarianism, in *Autobiography of John Stuart Mill*.

Ask yourself whether you are happy, and you cease to be so. The only chance is to treat, not happiness, but some end external to it, as the purpose of life. Let your self-consciousness, your scrutiny, your self interrogation, exhaust themselves on that; and if otherwise fortunately circumstanced, you will inhale happiness with the air you breathe, without dwelling on it or thinking about it, without either forestalling it in imagination, or putting it to flight by fatal questioning. This theory now became the basis of my philosophy of life. [1826]

Ibid.

I am thus one of the very few examples, in this country, of one who has not thrown off religious belief, but never had it: I grew up in a negative state with regard to it. I looked upon the modern exactly as I did upon the ancient religion, as something which in no way concerned me.

Ibid.

In his mind, philosophy seemed to mean chiefly advanced views in politics and in ethics; which, of course, came into collision with religious orthodoxy and the received commonplaces of society. Such a view of the functions of a University would not be put forth by any man that had ever resided in a University; and this is not the only occasion when Mill dogmatized on Universities in total ignorance of their working.

Alexander Bain, commenting on Mill's critique of Sedgwick, in *John Stuart Mill*.

He was all his life possessed of the idea that differences of character, individual and national, were due to accidents and circumstances that might possibly be, in part, controlled; on this doctrine rested his chief hope in the future. He would not allow that human beings at birth are so very different as they afterwards turn out.

Ibid.

He grants that women are physically inferior, but seems to think that this does not affect their mental powers. He never takes account of the fact, that the large diversion of force for the procreative function must give some general inferiority in all things where that does not come in, unless women are made on the whole much stronger than men. In an allusion to his experience of the Independent States of India, he tells us that in three cases out of four, if a superior instance of good government occurs, it is in a woman's reign; which looks like the fallacy of proving too much.

Ibid.

He would not, however, I think, ever have been a working-men's champion on their own lines. He would not have held out any tempting bribe of immediate amelioration such as to inspire the highest efforts of the existing generation. His most sanguine hopes were of a very slow progress in all things; with the sole exception, perhaps, of the equality-of-women question, on which his feelings went farther than on any other.

Ibid.

Mill laid up in his capacious mind a variety of things; but, with all his getting, he got this special understanding — the understanding of principles. If you wanted, at any time, to commend yourself to his favourable regards, you had but to start a doctrinal discussion — to bring a new *logos* to his view.

Ibid.

Ah poor fellow! he had to get himself out of Benthamism; and all the emotions and sufferings he has endured have helped him to thoughts that never entered Bentham's head. However, he is still too fond of demonstrating everything. If John Mill were to get up to heaven, he would be hardly content till he had made out how it all was. For my part, I don't much trouble myself about the machinery of the place; whether there is an operative of angels, or an industrial class, I'm willing to leave all that.

Thomas Carlyle, in Caroline Fox, *Journal.*

This method of early, intense application he would not recommend to others; in most cases it would not answer, and where it does, the buoyancy of youth is entirely superseded by the maturity of manhood, and action is very likely to be merged in reflection. 'I never was a boy,' he said, 'never played at cricket; it is better to let Nature have her own way.'

Caroline Fox, *ibid.*

I am reading that terrible book of John Mill's on Liberty, so clear and calm and cold; he lays it on one as a tremendous duty to get oneself well contradicted, and admit always a devil's advocate into the presence of your dearest, most sacred truths, as they are apt to grow windy and worthless without such tests; if indeed they can stand the shock of arguments at all. He looks through you like a basilisk, relentless as Fate . . . Mill makes me shiver, his blade is so keen and unhesitating.

Caroline Fox, Letter to E. C. Carne, *circa* 1860.

We well knew Mr. Mill's intellectual eminence before he entered Parliament. What his conduct there principally disclosed, at least to me, was his singular moral elevation. I remember now that at the time, more than twenty years back, I used familiarly to call him the Saint of Rationalism, a phrase roughly and partially what I now mean. Of all the motives, stings and stimulants that reach men through their egoism in Parliament, no part could move or even touch him. His conduct and his language were, in this respect, a sermon. Again, though he was a philosopher, he was not, I think, a man of crotchets.

William Ewart Gladstone, in W. L. Courtney, *Life of John Stuart Mill.*

One who has produced by his books a strong impersonal impression rarely produces a personal impression to correspond. The faculties which have caused his superiority as a writer are not, in all cases, accompanied by the faculties which give superiority in personal discourse or in debate; and this is especially the case when he has to address those with whom he is so little in sympathy as Mill was with the humdrum rank and file of our legislators.

Herbert Spencer, *An Autobiography.*

As for Mill as a thinker — a man who knew nothing of Plato and Darwin gives me very little. His reputation is curious to me. I gain nothing, I have gained nothing from him — an arid, dry man with moods of sentiment — a type that is poor, and, I fancy, common. But Darwinism has of course shattered many reputations besides his, and I hope that individual liberty has had its day, for a time. His later religious views show an outstanding silliness and sentimentality.

Oscar Wilde, Letter to W. L. Courtney, 1889.

MILLAIS, SIR JOHN EVERETT

1829—96 Artist

Given an object to be rendered as we see it — beautiful or ugly, exalted or commonplace, animate or inanimate — then Millais, with palette and brush and a little colour, putting the right touch and the right colour in the right place, with the minimum of effort and the maximum of result, will paint it as neither Leighton nor Angelo nor Raphael could have painted it, as it has never been painted, except perhaps by Velasquez.

Wyke Bayliss, *Five Great Painters of the Victorian Era.*

This strangely unequal painter — a painter whose imperfectly great powers always suggest to me the legend of the spiteful fairy at the christening feast. The name of Mr. Millais's spiteful fairy is vulgarity.

Henry James, 'The Grosvenor Gallery', in *Nation,* 23 May 1878.

He at last the champion great Millais
Attaining Academic opulence,
   Wind up his signature with A.R.A.
So rivers merge in the perpetual sea;
   So luscious fruit must fall when over-ripe
And so the consummated P.R.B.
   Christina Rossetti, in William Rossetti, *Dante
   Gabriel Rossetti.*

I am not sure whether he may not be destined to
surpass all that has yet been done in figure-painting,
as Turner did all past landscape.
   John Ruskin, *Academy Notes,* 1856.

He was an angelic and blustering personification of
John Bull, what the Germans call *der Stock-
Engländer.* He answered to the *stage* idea of the
superior officer, although the superior officer is
characterised rather by the gentleness, the tact and
the scrupulous sympathy which command by persuasion. Millais was a man who . . . *ne se doutait
de rien.*
   Walter Richard Sickert, in *Fortnightly Review,*
   June 1929.

When Millais said 'Art', he meant British Art. And
when he said 'British Art', he meant the painting
of John Everett Millais.
   Ibid.

Millais' was a complex and multiple career. He had
a keen sense of the touching mystery of childish
facial expression. His *Blind Girl* is a miracle by
which he will survive. That was his proper scale.
Running through all his work, from his book illustrations to the later pictures, is a certain wooden-
ness in the figures. His interest was in faces.
   Walter Richard Sickert, in *Manchester Guardian,*
   2 March 1926.

MILLAY, EDNA ST VINCENT

1892—1950 Author

. . . the reason I am a poet is entirely because you
wanted me to be and intended I should be, even
from the very first. You brought me up in the tradition of poetry, and everything I did you encouraged. I can not remember once in my life when you
were not interested in what I was working on, or
even suggested that I should put it aside for something else.
   On herself, Undated letter to her mother.

Edna St. Vincent Millay became, in effect, the unrivaled embodiment of sex appeal, of the It-girl of
the hour, the Miss America of 1920.
   Elizabeth Atkins, *Edna St. Vincent Millay and
   Her Times.*

The crystallization of the myriad curiosities of sensation, of agonies and joys, of hates and loves into
a deeply satisfying poetic empathy within a man's
heart during his little span of life — this is for Millay
the kernel of pure good in the universe.
   Ibid.

She gave voice to a new freedom, a new equality,
the right of the woman to be as inconstant in love
as the man and as demanding of variety.
   Hildegarde Flanner, 'Two Poets: Jeffers and
   Millay', in Malcolm Cowley ed., *After the
   Genteel Tradition.*

. . . the career of Edna Millay presented the still
sadder spectacle of a poet who withered on the
stalk before attaining fruition.
   George F. Whicher, 'The Twentieth Century',
   in Arthur Hobson Quinn ed., *The Literature
   of the American People.*

See also Dorothy Parker

MILLER, (ALTON) GLENN

1901—44 Musician

His world of all blacks and all whites, but few grays,
was encased in an exasperatingly brittle and hard
shell. Though always deeply dedicated to the
public's understanding and appreciation of his
music, he allowed only a few privileged friends the
opportunity to understand and appreciate the man
who had created it.
   George T. Simon, *Glenn Miller and His Orchestra.*

But Glenn Miller was different. He made jazz. He
was musicianly. He represented the climax of forty
years of popular music — from the crudities of rag-
time through the Mickey-Mouseness of early dance
music and the undisciplined jazz bands to the sleek
but win swingy all-purpose music of Glenn Miller.
Who could ask for anything more?
   Ian Whitcomb, *After the Ball: Pop Music from
   Rag to Rock.*

MILLS, C. WRIGHT

1916—62 Author, Educator

C. Wright Mills was a man of passionate commitment to the values he cherished most: truth, reason,
and freedom. He was concerned with these values
in their totality, as living realities which manifest
themselves in the realm of existence as well as in
the realm of ideas.
   Fred H. Blum, 'C. Wright Mills: Social Conscience and Social Values', in Irving L. Horowitz
   ed., *The New Sociology.*

He was, rather, an empiricist who could not wait for the science to catch up with him.

Rose K. Goldsen, 'Mills and the Profession of Sociology', in *ibid.*

Mills was a strenuous defender of virile liberty and a screamer. He hit hard at the injustices of the social order. He chose to be a sociologist because he saw it as the profession that had the concepts and skills — and thus the responsibility — to expose and correct such injustices.

Ibid.

Mills was an angry man, with the disciplined, directed anger of the humanist in an irrational society — for what is humanism if not anger with unreason?

Ralph Miliband, 'C. Wright Mills', in G. William Domhoff and Hoyt B. Ballard eds, *C. Wright Mills and the Power Elite.*

The trouble with Mills was that he never managed to emancipate himself from a view of the intellectual as the free man, in duty bound to help make others free. Such a romantic, naive belief is inconvenient; it poses a threat. No wonder he made enemies in the academic fraternity.

Ibid.

He was a man on his own, with both the strength and also the weakness which go with that solitude. He was on the Left, but not of the Left, a deliberately lone guerilla, not a regular soldier. He was highly organized, but unwilling to *be* organized, with self-discipline the only discipline he could tolerate.

Ibid.

MILLS, ROBERT

1781—1855 Architect, Engineer

Who would have believed that the designer of the Washington Monument and the Bunker Hill Monument could keep his name from becoming a household word? To have planned *either* of these monoliths ought to be enough to insure the planner's fame; to have planned *both of them* would be to take a bond of fate. Yet . . . probably very few readers could remember having heard his name. We are interested in him . . . not because he is famous, but *because he ought to be famous.*

Anon., *New York Evening Post*, 7 June 1920.

MILTON, JOHN

1608—74 Poet, Polemicist

. . . Sad task, yet argument

Not less but more Heroic than the wrath
Of stern *Achilles* on his Foe pursu'd
Thrice Fugitive about Troy Wall; or Rage
Of *Turnus* for Lavinia disespous'd,
Or *Neptune's* ire or *Juno's*, that so long
Perplex'd the *Greek* and *Cytherea's* Son;
If answerable style I can obtain
Of my Celestial Patroness, who deigns
Her nightly visitation unimplor'd,
And dictates to me slumb'ring, or inspires
Easy my unpremeditated Verse;
Since first this Subject for Heroic Song
Pleas'd me long choosing, and beginning late;
Not sedulous by Nature to indite
Wars, hitherto the only Argument
Heroic deem'd, chief maistry to dissect
With long and tedious havoc fabl'd Knights
In Battles feign'd; the better fortitude
Of Patience and Heroic Martyrdom
Unsung; or to describe Races and Games,
Or tilting Furniture, emblazon'd Shields,
Impresses quaint, Caparisons and Steeds;
Bases and tinsel Trappings, gorgeous Knights
At Joust and Tournament; then marshall'd Feast
Serv'd up in Hall with Sewers, and Seneschals;
The skill of Artifice or Office mean,
Not that which justly gives Heroic name
To Person or to Poem. Mee of these
Nor skill'd nor studious, higher Argument
Remains, sufficient of itself to raise
That name, unless an age too late, or cold
Climate, or Years damp my intended wing
Deprest; and much they may, if all be mine,
Not Hers who brings it nightly to my Ear.

On himself, *Paradise Lost*, Book IX.

I must confess, that I think his Stile, tho' admirable in general, is in some Places too much stiffened and obscured by the frequent Use of those Methods, which *Aristotle* has prescribed for the raising of it.

Joseph Addison, in *Spectator*, no. 285.

Our Language sunk under him, and was unequal to that greatness of soul which furnished him with such glorious conceptions.

Ibid., no. 297.

He is our great artist in style, our one first-rate master in the grand style.

Matthew Arnold, *Mixed Essays:* 'A French Critic on Milton'.

He had abroun hayre. His complexion exceeding faire — he was so faire that they called him *the Lady of Christ's College.*

John Aubrey, *Brief Lives.*

But in Milton, the Father is Destiny, the Son a Ratio of the five senses, & the Holy-ghost a Vacuum!

Note: the reason Milton wrote in fetters when he wrote of Angels & God, and at liberty when of Devils & Hell, is because he was a true Poet and of the Devil's party without knowing it.

William Blake, *The Marriage of Heaven and Hell.*

As for his syntax, it never troubles those who leave it alone.

Douglas Bush, *English Literature in the Earlier 17th Century.*

If fallen in evil days on evil tongues,
   Milton appealed to the Avenger, Time,
If Time, the Avenger, execrates his wrongs,
   And makes the word 'Miltonic' mean *'sublime'*,
He deign'd not to belie his soul in songs,
   Nor turn his very talent to a crime;
He did not loathe the Sire to laud the Son,
But closed the tyrant-hater he begun.

Lord Byron, *Don Juan*, canto i (fragment).

Milton's the prince of poets — so we say;
   A little heavy, but no less divine.

Ibid., canto iii.

The words of Milton are true in all things, and were never truer than in this: 'He who would write heroic poems must make his whole life a heroic poem.'

Thomas Carlyle, *Essays: 'Burns'.*

Indeed, the whole of Milton's poem [*Paradise Lost*] is such barbarous trash, so outrageously offensive to reason and to common sense that one is naturally led to wonder how it can have been tolerated by a people, amongst whom astronomy, navigation, and chemistry are understood.

William Cobbett, *Year's Residence in the United States.*

Shakespeare is the Spinozistic deity — an omnipresent creativeness. Milton is the deity of prescience; he stands *ab extra*, and drives a fiery chariot and four, making the horses feel the iron curb which holds them in.

Samuel Taylor Coleridge, *Table Talk.*

High poetry is the translation of reality into the ideal under the predicament of succession of time only. The poet is an historian, under condition of moral power being the only force in the universe. The very grandeur of his subject ministered a difficulty to Milton. The statement of a being of high intellect, warring against the Supreme Being, seems to contradict the idea of a Supreme Being. Milton precludes our feeling this, as much as possible, by keeping the peculiar attributes of divinity less in sight, making them to a certain extent allegorical only. Again poetry implies the language of excitement; yet how to reconcile such language with God? Hence Milton confines the poetic passion in God's speeches to the language of Scripture.

Samuel Taylor Coleridge, *Lecture on Milton*, March 1819.

Milton has carefully marked in his Satan the intense selfishness, the alcohol of egotism, which would rather reign in hell than serve in heaven. To place this lust of self in opposition to denial of self or duty, and to show what exertions it would make, and what pains endure to accomplish its ends, is Milton's particular object in the character of Satan. But around this character he throws a singularity of daring, a grandeur of sufferance and a ruined splendour, which constitute the very height of poetic sublimity.

Ibid.

Greece, sound thy Homer's, Rome thy Virgil's
          name,
But England's Milton equals both in fame.

William Cowper, *To John Milton.*

Ages elaps'd ere Homer's lamp appear'd,
And ages ere the Mantuan swan was heard:
To carry nature lengths unknown before,
To give a Milton birth, ask'd ages more.
Thus genius rose and set at order'd times,
And shot a day-spring into distant climes,
Ennobling ev'ry region that he chose;
He sunk in Greece, in Italy he rose;
And, tedious years of Gothic darkness pass'd,
Emerg'd all splendour in our isle at last.

William Cowper, *Table Talk.*

So far as I perceive anything [in *Paradise Lost*], it is a glimpse of a theology that I find in large part repellent, expressed through a mythology which would better have been left in the Book of Genesis, upon which Milton has not improved.

J. S. Diekhoff, *Milton's Paradise Lost.*

Many people will agree that a man may be a great artist, and yet have a bad influence. There is more of Milton's influence in the badness of the bad verse of the eighteenth century than of anybody else's: he certainly did more harm than Dryden and Pope. . . . But . . . there is a good deal more to the charge against Milton than this; and it appears a good deal more serious if we affirm that Milton's poetry could *only* be an influence for the worse, upon any poet whatever. It is more serious, also, if we affirm that Milton's bad influence may be traced much farther than the eighteenth century, and much farther than upon bad poets: if we say that it was an influence against which we still have to struggle.

T. S. Eliot, *Essays and Studies.*

To say that the work of a poet is at the farthest possible remove from prose would once have struck me as condemnatory: it now seems to me simply, when we have to do with Milton, the precision of its peculiar greatness. As a poet, Milton seems to me probably the greatest of all eccentrics. His work illustrates no general principles of good writing; the only principles of writing that it illustrates are such as are valid only for Milton himself to observe.
T. S. Eliot, *Essays: 'Milton II'.*

It is only in the period that the wave-length of Milton's verse is to be found: it is his ability to give a perfect and unique pattern to every paragraph, such that the full beauty of the line is found in its context, and his ability to work in larger musical units than any other poet — that is to me the most conclusive evidence of Milton's supreme mastery. The peculiar feeling, almost a physical sensation of a breathless leap, communicated by Milton's long periods, and by his alone, is impossible to procure from rhymed verse.
Ibid.

I suppose that in Satan determining to destroy the innocent happiness of Eden, for the highest political motives, without hatred, not without tears, we may find some echo of the Elizabethan fulness of life that Milton as a poet abandoned, and as a Puritan helped to destroy.
William Empson, *Some Versions of Pastoral.*

I should say that Milton's experience of propaganda is what makes his later poetry so very dramatic; that is, though he is a furious partisan, he can always imagine with all its force exactly what the reply of the opponent would be. As to his integrity, he was such an inconvenient propagandist that the Government deserve credit for having the nerve to appoint and retain him.
William Empson, *Milton's God.*

Yet shall he mount, and keep his distant way
Beyond the limits of a vulgar fate,
Beneath the Good how far — but far above the
Great.
Thomas Gray, *The Progress of Poesy.*

Milton, therefore, did not write from casual impulse, but after a severe examination of his own strength, and with a resolution to leave nothing undone which it was in his power to do. He always labours, and almost always succeeds. He strives hard to say the finest things in the world, and he does say them. He adorns and dignifies his subject to the utmost: he surrounds it with every possible association of beauty or grandeur, whether moral, intellec-

tual, or physical. He refines on his descriptions of beauty; loading sweets on sweets, till the sense aches at them. . . . In Milton, there is always an appearance of effort.
William Hazlitt, *Lectures on the English Poets.*

Malt does more than Milton can,
To justify God's ways to man.
A. E. Housman, *A Shropshire Lad*, lxii.

It is not strange that Milton received no encouragement after the restoration: it is more to be admired that he escaped with his life. Many of the cavaliers blamed extremely that lenity towards him, which was so honourable in the king, and advantageous to posterity.
David Hume, *The History of England.*

Milton's republicanism was, I am afraid, founded in an envious hatred of greatness, and a sullen desire of independence; in petulance impatient of controul, and pride disdainful of superiority. . . . It is to be suspected, that his predominant desire was to destroy rather than to establish, and that he felt not so much the love of liberty as repugnance to authority.
Samuel Johnson, *Lives of the Poets.*

He thought woman made only for obedience, and man only for rebellion.
Ibid.

Milton never learned the art of doing little things with grace; he overlooked the milder excellence of suavity and softness; he was a *Lion* that had no skill in *dandling the Kid.*
Ibid.

The characteristick quality of his poem is sublimity. He sometimes descends to the elegant, but his element is the great. He can occasionally invest himself with grace; but his natural port is gigantick loftiness. He can please when pleasure is required; but it is his peculiar power to astonish.
Ibid.

The plan of *Paradise Lost* has this inconvenience, that it comprises neither human actions nor human manners. The man and woman who act and suffer, are in a state which no other man or woman can ever know. The reader finds no transaction in which he can be engaged; beholds no condition in which he can by any effort of imagination place himself; he has, therefore, little natural curiosity or sympathy.
Ibid.

We read Milton for instruction, retire harassed and overburdened, and look elsewhere for recreation; we desert our master, and seek for companions.
Ibid.

Milton would not have excelled in dramatick writing; he knew human nature only in the gross, and had never studied the shades of character, nor the combinations of concurring, or the perplexity of contending passions.
Ibid.

The truth is, that both in prose and verse, he had formed his style by a perverse and pedantick principle. He was desirous to use English words with a foreign idiom. This in all his prose is discovered and condemned, for there judgement operates freely, neither softened by the beauty nor awed by the dignity of his thoughts; but such is the power of his poetry that his call is obeyed without resistance, the reader feels himself in captivity to a higher and nobler mind, and criticism sinks in admiration.
Ibid.

Milton, Madam, was a genius that could cut a Colossus from a rock; but could not carve heads upon cherry-stones.
Samuel Johnson, in James Boswell, *Life of Johnson.*

I have but lately been on my guard against Milton. Life to him would be death to me. Miltonic verse cannot be written but in the vein of art — I wish to devote myself to another sensation.
John Keats, Letter to George and Georgiana Keats, 17 September 1819.

Milton almost requires a solemn service of music to be played before you enter upon him:
Charles Lamb, *Last Essays of Elia:* 'Detached Thoughts on Books and Reading'.

Milton seems to the colleges profound because he wrote of hell, a great place, and is dead.
Stephen Leacock, *Charles Dickens.*

Even in the first two books of *Paradise Lost* . . . we feel, after a few hundred lines, our sense of dissatisfaction growing into something stronger. In the end we find ourselves protesting — protesting against the routine gesture, the heavy fall, of the verse, flinching from the foreseen thud that comes so inevitably, and, at last, irresistibly: for reading *Paradise Lost* is a matter of resisting, of standing up against, the verse-movement, of subduing it into something tolerably like sensitiveness, and in the end our resistance is worn down; we surrender at last to the monotony of ritual.
F. R. Leavis, *Revaluation.*

Nearly every sentence in Milton has that power which physicists sometimes think we shall have to attribute to matter — the power of action at a distance.
C. S. Lewis, *A Preface to Paradise Lost.*

The most striking characteristic of the poetry of Milton is the extreme remoteness of the associations by means of which it acts upon the reader. Its effect is produced, not so much by what it expresses, as by what it suggests; not so much by the ideas which it directly conveys, as by other ideas which are connected with them. He electrifies the mind through conductors.
T. B. Macaulay, *Essays:* 'Milton'.

The spirits of Milton are unlike those of almost all other writers. His fiends, in particular, are wonderful creations. They are not metaphysical abstractions. They are not wicked men. They are not ugly beasts. They have no horns, no tails, none of the fee-faw-fum of Tasso and Klopstock. They have just enough in common with human nature to be intelligible to human beings. Their characters are, like their forms, marked by a certain dim resemblance to those of men, but exaggerated to gigantic dimensions, and veiled in mysterious gloom.
Ibid.

If ever despondency and asperity could be excused in any man, they might have been excused in Milton. But the strength of his mind overcame every calamity. Neither blindness, nor gout, nor age, nor penury, nor domestic afflictions, nor political disappointments, nor abuse, nor proscription, nor neglect, had power to disturb his sedate and majestic patience. His spirits do not seem to have been high, but they were singularly equable.
Ibid.

Poetry is what Milton saw when he went blind.
Don Marquis, in Edward Anthony, *O Rare Don Marquis.*

When I beheld the Poet blind, yet bold,
In slender Book his vast Design unfold,
Messiah Crown'd, *God's* reconciled Decree,
Rebelling *Angels*, the Forbidden Tree,
Heav'n, Hell, Earth, Chaos, All; the Argument
Held me a while misdoubting his Intent,
That he would ruine (for I saw him strong)
The sacred Truths to Fable and old Song,
(So *Sampson* groap'd the Temples Posts in spight)
The World o'rewhelming to revenge his Sight.
Andrew Marvell, *On Mr. Milton's Paradise Lost.*

Where couldst thou Words of such a compass find?
Whence furnish such a vast expense of Mind?

Just Heav'n Thee, like *Tiresias*, to requite,
Rewards with *Prophesie* thy loss of Sight.
Ibid.

To pass under the spell of Milton is to be con-
demned to imitate him. It is quite different with
Shakespeare. Shakespeare baffles and liberates;
Milton is perspicuous and constricts.
John Middleton Murry, *Heaven and Earth.*

Milton's style, in his Paradise Lost, is not natural;
'tis an exotic style. — As his subject lies a good deal
out of our world, it has a particular propriety in
those parts of the poem: and, when he is on earth,
wherever he is describing our parents in Paradise,
you see he uses a more easy and natural way of writing. — Though his formal style may fit the higher
parts of his own poem, it does very ill for others
who write on natural and pastoral subjects.
Alexander Pope, in Joseph Spence, *Anecdotes.*

Milton's Devil as a moral being is far superior to his
God, as one who perseveres in some purpose which
he has conceived to be excellent, in spite of adversity and torture, is to one who in the cold security
of undoubted triumph inflicts the most horrible
revenge upon his enemy, not from mistaken notions
of inducing him to repent of a perseverance in
enmity, but with the alleged design of exasperating
him to new torments. Milton has so far violated
the popular creed (if this shall be judged a violation), as to have alleged no superiority of moral
virtue to his God over his Devil. And this bold
neglect of direct moral purpose is the most decisive
proof of Milton's genius.
Percy Bysshe Shelley, *Defence of Poetry.*

The greater proportion of Milton's art is employed
in finding violent coesmas. His favourite trick of
leaving one word, especially a verb, isolated at the
beginning of a new line, is a case in point: at the
end of that wonderful passage on the fall of Mulci-
ber, he seems to have felt the necessity for some
exceptionally strong coesma — as it were, a dam
after such a stream of sweetness — and he attained
what he wanted by simply breaking off the metre
with the unassimilable word 'Again'.
Robert Louis Stevenson, *Selections from his
Note Book.*

O mighty-mouth'd inventor of harmonies,
O skill'd to sing of Time or Eternity,
God-gifted organ-voice of England,
Milton, a name to resound for ages.
Alfred, Lord Tennyson, *Milton.*

The New World honors him whose lofty plea
For England's freedom made her own more sure,

Whose song, immortal as its theme, shall be
Their common freehold while both worlds
endure.
John Greenleaf Whittier, *On the Milton Window.*

It requires more than a willing suspension of disbelief to read Milton; it requires a willing suspension
of intelligence. A good many years ago I found
Milton's procedure more nearly defensible than I
find it now; I find that I grow extremely tired of the
meaningless inflation, the tedious falsification of the
materials by way of excessive emotion.
Yvor Winters, *The Function of Criticism.*

That mighty orb of song, The divine Milton.
William Wordsworth, *The Excursion.*

Milton! thou shouldst be living at this hour:
England hath need of thee: she is a fen
Of stagnant waters.
William Wordsworth, *National Independence and
Liberty.*

Thy soul was like a Star, and dwelt apart;
Thou hadst a voice whose sound was like the sea:
Pure as the naked heavens, majestic, free,
So didst thou travel on life's common way,
In cheerful godliness; and yet thy heart
The lowliest duties on herself did lay.
Ibid.

See also Joel Barlow, William Cowper, Daniel Defoe,
Oliver Wendell Holmes Sr, Leigh Hunt, Inigo Jones,
Isaac Newton, Bertrand Russell, Carl Sandburg,
Edmund Spenser, Alfred, Lord Tennyson, Roger
Williams, Richard Wilson, William Wordsworth

MITCHELL, (WILLIAM) 'BILLY'

1879–1936 Soldier, Aviator

As a patriotic American citizen, I can stand by no
longer and see these disgusting performances by
the navy and war departments, at the expense of
the lives of our people, and the delusion of the
American public . . . I considered it my duty to tell
what I knew, although it meant sure disciplinary
action and probably court-martial.
On himself, in Isaac Don Levine, *Mitchell's
Pioneer of Air Power.*

The army is about to take the only course open to
it in the case of Colonel William Mitchell . . . he will
be arrested. In the natural course of events he will
be court-martialed. In all probability he will be
found guilty as charged. . . . . Getting rid of Col.
Mitchell will not, however, get rid of the issues he

has raised nor will it greatly better the conditions in American aviation . . . 'Mitchellism' will remain after Col. Mitchell is gone. It is easy to riddle some of his charges and debate others, but they have made a powerful impression upon the country. . . . It loves his dashing, slashing tactics, for it admires the fighter . . .

Anon., in *New York Evening Post*, in *ibid*.

He would rather be truthful for his country's sake than be silent for the sake of his job in Washington. . . . We may wait a hundred years for another such display of courage.

Anon, in *Cleveland Press*, in *ibid*.

He is a firebrand, a stormy petrel, an eagle, and vulture; vain, contemptuous, courageous, a martyr to the truth —

Roger Burlingame, *General Billy Mitchell: Champion of Air Defense*.

MITFORD, NANCY

1905—73 Novelist

Evelyn Waugh liked the company of young women and took them to nightclubs, though he never danced. His terms of praise were unusual. Very high was 'Nice short girl' — Evelyn was very conscious of being himself on the short side — or of Nancy Mitford, 'Nice cheap girl to take out for the evening. Costs you only eighteen and six for an orangeade in a night-club.'

Maurice Bowra, *Memories*.

Nancy had been named after the Nancies of seafaring ballads, and her thick, dark, curly hair, worn (after the ill-fated shingling) in a very short upsweep, her tall, fashionably boyish figure and her penchant for the exotic did give her something of the aspect of an elegant pirate's moll.

Jessica Mitford, *Hons and Rebels*.

I have long revered you as an agitator — agitatrix, *agitateuse*? — of genius. You have only to publish a few cool reflections on 18th-century furniture to set gangs on the prowl through the Faubourg St. Germain splashing the walls with 'Nancy, go home'.

Evelyn Waugh, *Open Letter to the Hon Mrs Peter Rodd (Nancy Mitford) on a Very Serious Subject*.

MIX, (THOMAS HEZEKIAH) TOM

1880—1940 Actor

As gaudy in dress as [William S.] Hart had been simple, he was prone to wear white evening suits, purple tuxedos, cowboy outfits decorated with diamonds. Over the gate of his Beverly Hills mansion, his monogram shone in electric lights. When he supplanted Hart in the nation's affections, he brought with him an idealized conception of the cowboy as a clean-living, sportsmanlike fellow that was to linger on the screen for years.

Donald W. La Badie, 'The Last Round-up', in *Show*, September 1962.

He was a helluva engineer. He rode superbly. He figured out stunts scientifically, and broke every bone in his body doing them.

Cliff Lyons, in John Baxter, *Stunt*.

As I look back now, Tom was as elegant on a horse as Fred Astaire on a dance floor, and that's the elegantest there is.

Adela Rogers St Johns, *The Honeycomb*.

They say he rides like part of the horse, but they don't say what part.

Robert E. Sherwood, in Robert E. Drennan ed., *Wit's End*.

MONCK, GEORGE, DUKE OF ALBEMARLE

1608—70 Soldier, Statesman

Little General Monk
Sat upon a trunk,
Eating a crust of bread;
There fell a hot coal
And burnt in his clothes a hole,
Now little General Monk is dead.

Nursery rhyme, traditional.

His nature was cautious and somewhat sluggish; nor was he at all disposed to hazard sure and moderate advantages for the chance of obtaining even the most splendid success. He seems to have been impelled to attack the new rulers of the commonwealth less by the hope that, if he overthrew them, he should become great, than by the fear that, if he submitted to them, he should not even be secure.

T. B. Macaulay, *History of England*.

My Lord Albemarle, I hear, doth bear through and bustle among them and will not be removed from the King's good opinion and favour, though none of the Cabinett; but yet he is envied enough.

Samuel Pepys, Diary, 15 May 1663.

But who shall find a pen fit for thy glory
Or make posterity believe thy story.

Robert Wild, *Iter Boreale*.

'Twas at his rising that our day begun;
But he the morning star to Charles our sun.
He took Rebellion rampant by the throat,
And made the canting Quaker change his note.
His hand it was that wrote, (we saw no more)
Exit Tyrannus over Lambert's Door.
Like to some subtle lightning so his words
Dissolved in their scabbards rebels' swords.
He with success the sov'reign skill hath found
To dress the weapon and so heal the wound.
George and his boys, as spirits do they say
Only by walking scare our foes away.
    Ibid.

MONMOUTH, DUKE OF (JAMES FITZROY SCOTT)

1649—85 Soldier

This Perkins a Prince whose excellency lies
In cutting of capers and storming dirt pies;
He aims at a crown for his noddle unfit
As Howe for a Duchess or he for a wit.
    He danceth, he skippeth,
    He frisketh, he leapeth
To trumpet and drums he manfully trippeth —
But his Highness, God bless him has come safely
                                            back,
To the shame and confusion of Perkin Warbeck.
    Anon., *A Ballad Called Perkins Figary.*

Disgrac'd, undone, forlorn, made Fortune's sport
Banish'd the Kingdom first, and then the Court;
Out of my places turn'd, and out of doors
And made the meanest of your sons of whores,
The scene of laughter, and the common chats
Of your salt bitches and your other brats;
Forc'd to a private life, to whore and drink
On my past grandeur and my folly think.
Would I had been the brat of some mean drab
Whom fear or shame had caus'd to choke or stab
Rather than be the issue of a King
And by him made so wretched scorn'd a thing.
    Anon., *Letter of the Duke of Monmouth to the
    King.*

Have I done all that royal dad could do
And do you threaten now to be untrue?
Oh! that my pr--- when I thy dam did f---
Had in some turkey's a---, or cow's been stuck!
Then I had been when the base deed was done
Sure to have got no rebel to my son.
    Anon., *The King's Answer.*

To lure, like Monmouth, associates, and humble
followers on fools' errands to their doom can find
no defenders.
    Winston Churchill, *Marlborough, His Life and
    Times.*

Of all this Numerous Progeny was none
So Beautiful so Brave as *Absalom*:
Whether inspir'd by some diviner Lust
His father got him with a greater Gust,
Or that his Conscious Destiny made way
By manly Beauty to Imperial Sway.
    John Dryden, *Absalom and Achitophel.*

What faults he had (for who from faults is free?)
His father could not or he would not see.
Some warm excesses which the law forbore
Were constru'd Youth that purg'd by boiling o'r:
And *Ammon*'s Murder, by a specious Name
Was call'd a Just Revenge for injur'd Fame.
    Ibid.

Within a few years he was to become a serious element in politics, because of two things, his Protestantism, and his illegitimacy. The events of the Popish Plot placed a substantial premium on the first, while the second commended him to those who thought that a weak claim to the throne was the best guarantee of constitutional rule.
    David Ogg, *England in the Reign of Charles II.*

See also Louise de Keroualle

MONROE, JAMES

1758—1831 Fifth United States President

Monroe was there, and Armstrong bold,
No bolder man might be,
And Rush, the Attorney-Gen-e-ral,
All on their horses three.
    Anon., satirical comment on the sacking of
    Washington by the British during the War of
    1812, in Arthur Styron, *The Last of the Cocked
    Hats.*

There behold him for a term of eight years, strengthening his country for defence by a system of combined fortifications, military and naval, sustaining her rights, her dignity and honor abroad; soothing her dissensions, and conciliating her acerbities at home; controlling by a firm although peaceful policy the hostile spirit of the European Alliance against Republican South America, exhorting by the mild compulsion of reason, the shores of the Pacific from the stipulated acknowledgement of Spain; and leading back the imperial autocrat of the North, to his lawful boundaries, from his hastily asserted dominion over the Southern Ocean. This strengthening and consolidating the federative edifice of his country's Union, till he was entitled to say, like Augustus Caesar of his imperial city, that he had

found her built of brick and left her constructed of marble.
John Quincy Adams, in Harry Ammon, *James Monroe, The Quest for National Identity*.

[Tranquility was] the pole-star of his policy. . . . There is a slowness, want of decision and a spirit of procrastination in the President, which perhaps arises from his situation than his personal character.
John Quincy Adams, in A. Steinberg, *The First Ten*.

. . . a mind, anxious and unwearied in the pursuit of truth and right, patient of inquiry, patient of contradiction, courteous even in the collision of sentiment, sound in its ultimate judgments, and firm in its final conclusions.
John Quincy Adams, Eulogy, in Daniel C. Gilman, *James Monroe*.

James Monroe came from Virginia, the mother of presidents. Little is known of his father, except that he was devoted to Virginia.
Richard Armour, *It All Started With Columbus*.

. . . is one of the most improper and incompetent that could be selected. Naturally dull and stupid; extremely illiterate; indecisive to a degree that would be incredible to one who did not know him; pusillanimous, and of course hypocritical; has no opinion on any subject and will always be under the government of the worst men.
Aaron Burr, Letter to his son-in-law, Governor of South Carolina, 1816, commenting on James Monroe as a presidential candidate.

I have known many much more rapid in reaching a conclusion, but few with a certainty so unerring.
John C. Calhoun, Letter to S. L. Gouverneur, 8 August 1818.

His services as President might be summed up in four words — he personified an interim. The War of 1812 . . . was merely the symptom of a profound change in domestic and international relations. After the shock of such a change, an interim was necessary; and if the interim was necessary, the personification was honorable.
George Dangerfield, *The Era of Good Feelings*.

He was a man whose soul might be turned wrong side outwards without discovering a blemish to the world.
Thomas Jefferson, in Daniel C. Gilman, *James Monroe*.

. . . one of those respectable mediocrities in high public station, with whom people are apt to sym-

pathize in their troubles, especially when unnecessarily attacked and humiliated by persons of greatly superior ability.
Carl Schurz, *Life of Henry Clay*, vol. 1.

MONROE, MARILYN (NORMA JEANE BAKER)
1926–62 Actress

When I just wrote 'this is the end of Norma Jean' I blushed as if I had been caught in a lie. Because this sad, bitter child who grew up too fast is hardly ever out of my heart. With success all around me, I can still feel her frightened eyes looking out of mine. She keeps saying 'I never lived, I was never loved', and often I get confused and think it's I who am saying it.
On herself, in *My Story*.

A sex symbol becomes a thing. I hate being a thing.
On herself, in Jeremy Pascall and Clive Jeavons, *A Pictorial History of Sex in the Movies*.

She had this absolute, unerring touch with comedy. In real life she didn't seem funny, but she had this touch. She acted as if she didn't quite understand why it was funny, which is what made it so funny. She could also do low comedy — pratfalls and things like that — but I think her friends told her it wasn't worthy of her. As a director, I really had very little influence on her. All I could do was make a climate that was agreeable to her. Every day was an agony of struggle for her, just to get there. It wasn't just willfulness, it was . . . like the comedy, something she didn't seem to understand.
George Cukor, in Gavin Lambert, *On Cukor*.

There's been an awful lot of crap written about Marilyn Monroe, and there may be an exact psychiatric term for what was wrong with her. I don't know — but truth to tell, I think she was quite mad. The mother was mad, and poor Marilyn was mad. I know people who say 'Hollywood broke her heart' and all that, but I don't believe it. She was very observant and tough-minded and appealing, but she had this bad judgment about things. She adored and trusted the wrong people. She was very courageous — you know that book *Twelve Against the Gods*? Marilyn was like that, she had to challenge the gods at every turn, and eventually she lost.
Ibid.

If she was a victim of any kind, she was a victim of friends.
Ibid.

Marilyn was not just another love goddess; she was one of the first love children, crossing over from America's conscience-ridden past into today's more open society. That she didn't quite make it to the other side had more to do with the harsh fundamentalism foisted upon her as Norma Jean than with her later intent as Marilyn.

Fred Lawrence Guiles, *Norma Jean*.

She catered to these fantasies and played these roles because she was afraid that if she stopped — which she did once and for all with sleeping pills — there would turn out to be nothing there, and therefore nothing to love. She was never permitted to mature into a warm, vibrant woman, or fully use her gifts for comedy, despite the signals and flares she kept sending up. Instead, she was turned into a figure of mockery in the parts she played and to the men she played with.

Molly Haskell, *From Reverence to Rape*.

The times being what they were, if she hadn't existed we would have had to invent her, and we did, in a way. She was the fifties' fiction, the lie that a woman has no sexual needs, that she is there to cater to, or enhance, a man's needs. She was the living embodiment of half of one of the more grotesque and familiar pseudo-couples — the old man and the 'showgirl', immortalized in *Esquire* and *Playboy* cartoons.

Ibid.

A phenomenon of nature, like Niagara Falls and the Grand Canyon.

Nunnally Johnson, in William Manchester, *The Glory and the Dream*.

As a classic comedienne of grace, delicacy and a happy wonder, she certainly has had no peer since Billie Burke or Ina Claire. The lightness, justness and rhythm of her clowning often held hints of something more penetrating. Her comic tone was sometimes disturbingly ironic; her personal style was more lyric than naturalistic.

Lincoln Kirstein, in Edward Wagenknecht, *Seven Daughters of the Theatre*.

So we think of Marilyn who was every man's love affair with America. Marilyn Monroe who was blonde and beautiful and had a sweet little rinky-dink of a voice and all the cleanliness of all the clean American backyards. She was our angel, the sweet angel of sex, and the sugar of sex came up from her like a resonance of sound in the clearest grain of a violin. Across five continents the men who knew the most about love would covet her, and the classical pimples of the adolescent working his first gas pump would also pump for her, since Marilyn was

deliverance, a very Stradivarius of sex, so gorgeous, forgiving, humorous, compliant and tender that even the most mediocre musician would relax his lack of art in the dissolving magic of her violin.

Norman Mailer, *Marilyn*.

At various times her immense appeal was attributed to her breathless voice, her incandescence, her ash-blonde hair, her moist-lipped mouth, her dreamy blue eyes, and that tremulous gait. It was more elusive than that — and more earthy. Marilyn's need to be desired was so great that she could make love to a camera. Because of this, her lust aroused lust in audiences, sometimes even among women. There was nothing subtle about it. She was no tease. She was prepared, and even eager, to give what she offered. By the time she was fourteen the fathers of her friends had pawed her, and one summer an off-duty policeman had cut through a screen door to get to her. She never pretended to be shocked or even resentful. . . . She exulted in her carnality. As a rising star she posed naked for a calendar. She didn't need the fifty dollars; she just liked the idea.

William Manchester, *The Glory and the Dream*.

After *Yank* ran a picture of her in an article on women in war work she was given a screen test. . . . The first man to see the rushes said: 'I got a cold chill. This girl had something I hadn't seen since silent pictures. This is the first girl who looked like one of those lush stars of the silent era. Every frame of the test radiated sex.' Billy Wilder, who later directed her in *Some Like It Hot*, called it 'flesh impact' and said the only other stars who had it were Clara Bow, Jean Harlow, and Rita Hayworth.

Ibid.

She was the bastard daughter of a paranoid schizophrenic . . . a girl with a desperate, insatiable yearning to be wanted. . . . Her first husband taught her sexual ecstasy on a Murphy bed. She gloried in it and would pursue it for the rest of her life, but it wasn't enough; she craved the adoration of millions.

Ibid.

It's Mae West, Theda Bara, and Bo Peep all rolled into one.

Groucho Marx, in Marilyn Monroe, *My Story*.

She played the game, and she paid the price. What it costs to swing such a career as she had can never be known except by the person who experiences it, but surely the editors of *Vogue* did not exaggerate when they said, 'That she withstood the incredible, unknowable pressures of her public legend as long as she did is evidence of the stamina of the human spirit.'

Edward Wagenknecht, *Seven Daughters of the Theatre*.

Hollywood didn't kill Marilyn Monroe. It's the Marilyn Monroes who are killing Hollywood. Marilyn was mean. Terribly mean. The meanest woman I have ever met around this town. I have never met anybody as mean as Marilyn Monroe nor as utterly fabulous on the screen, and that includes Garbo.

But I miss her. It was like going to the dentist, making a picture with her. It was hell at the time, but after it was all over, it was wonderful.

Billy Wilder, in Earl Wilson, *The Show Business Nobody Knows.*

Marilyn Monroe was the meteor of show business. There were many small, dim stars floating in the sky when the meteor streaked across the heavens. Its flash and fire blotted them into oblivion. Then suddenly the meteor was spent, plunged into darkness, and the small, dim stars could be seen floating in the sky again.

Earl Wilson, *ibid.*

MONTAGU, ELIZABETH

1720—1800 Author, Hostess

Mrs Montagu, a lady distinguished for having written an Essay on Shakespeare, being mentioned — [Joshua] *Reynolds*: 'I think that essay does her honour.' [Samuel] *Johnson*: 'Yes, Sir, it does *her* honour, but it would do nobody else honour. I have, indeed, not read it all. But when I take up the end of a web, and find it packthread, I do not expect, by looking further, to find embroidery. Sir, I will venture to say, there is not one sentence of true criticism in her book. . . . No, Sir, there is no real criticism in it: none showing the beauty of thought, as formed on the workings of the human heart.'

James Boswell, *Life of Johnson.*

He told us, 'I dined yesterday at Mrs Garrick's with Mrs Carter, Miss Hannah More, and Miss Fanny Burney. Three such women are not to be found. . . .' *Boswell*: 'Might not Mrs Montagu have been a fourth?' *Johnson*: 'Sir, Mrs Montagu does not make a trade of her wit; but Mrs Montagu is a very extraordinary woman; she has a constant stream of conversation, and it is always impregnated; it has always meaning.'

Ibid.

To the same Patroness resort,
(Secure of favour at her court)
Strong Genius, from whose forge of thought

Forms rise, to quick perfection wrought,
Which, though new-born, with vigour move,
Like Pallas springing arm'd from Jove —
Imagination, scatt'ring round
Wild roses over furrow'd ground,
Which Labour of his frowns beguile,
And teach Philosophy a smile —
All these to MONTAGU'S repair,
Ambitious of a shelter there.

William Cowper, *On Mrs Montagu's Feather Hangings.*

She is not only the finest genius, but the finest lady I ever saw; she lives in the highest style of magnificence; her apartments are in the most splendid taste; but what baubles are these when speaking of a Montagu!

Hannah More, in Rebecca West, *Elizabeth Montagu.*

It is a life that knew only once the touch of defeat, yet it radiates a low degree of light and heat. It dispenses through the ages hardly more warmth than chandeliers blazing away behind the closed windows of a great house; and even in its own day it could not relieve Mrs Montagu herself from a sensation of debilitating chill. For what saves her record from being intolerable is that she was the first to think it so.

Rebecca West, *ibid.*

. . . she was a romantic by temperament. The ardour with which she proclaims her own coldness, the passion with which she professes moderation, betray her type. For this reason she is uneasy as she is distinguished; and though her gifts were clear cut, the fuzzy outlines of a pretentious thinker and pedant blur the image of a woman of action which she should have stamped on the page of history, profoundly respectable in power and generosity.

Ibid.

She deserved the respect of contemporary society because she was as fine a justification for its capitalist system as the time provided, and not to remember her as that today is to withhold justice.

Ibid.

MONTAGU, LADY MARY WORTLEY

1689—1762 Belle Lettriste

Lady Mary lived before the age in which people waste half their lives in washing the whole of their persons.

Walter Bagehot, *Estimations in Criticism.*

. . . Bye the bye, her Ladyship, as far as I can judge, has lied, but not half so much as any other woman would have done in the same situation.

Lord Byron, Letter to Mrs Catherine Gordon Byron, 28 June 1810.

Rufa, whose eye quick-glancing o'er the Park
Attracts each light gay meteor of a Spark,
Agrees as ill with Rufa studying Locke,
As Sappho's diamonds with her dirty smock,
Or Sappho at her toilet's greasy task,
With Sappho fragrant at an evening Mask:
So morning Insects that in Muck begun,
Shine, buzz, and fly-blow in the setting sun.

Alexander Pope, *Moral Essays*, Epistle II.

She was, like her age, cold and hard; she was infinitely unromantic; she was often cynical, and sometimes gross. . . . She was, in fact, almost devoid of those sympathetic feelings which appear to us to be the essence of all goodness; so that she is read now, when she is read at all, simply for her wit. But, in reality, she was something more than a brilliant letter-writer; she was a moralist.

Lytton Strachey, *Biographical Essays*.

Alas! in her bedraggled Italian adventures, what kind of *jouissance* was it that she found? That she refused to palliate her situation, that she faced her wretched failure without flinching and without pretence — there lay the intellectual eminence which lifts her melancholy history out of the sordid into the sublime. There is something great, something not to be forgotten, about the honesty with which she looked into the worthlessness of things, and the bravery with which she accepted it.

Ibid.

Lady Mary is arrived; I have seen her; I think her avarice, her art, and her vivacity are all increased. Her dress, like her language, is a *galimatias* of several countries; the groundwork rags and the embroidery nastiness. She needs no cap, no handkerchief, no gown, no petticoat, and no shoes.

Horace Walpole, Letter to Sir Horace Mann, 2 February 1762.

MONTAGU, JOHN, see under SANDWICH, EARL OF

MONTEFIORE, SIR MOSES HAIM

1784—1885 Philanthropist

The tree under whose shadows thousands of his brethren found shelter.

Dr Louis Loewe, *An Address Delivered at the Memorial Service*.

MONTGOMERY, ROBERT

1807—55 Poet

Montgomery has likewise given us a new volume. . . . How is his strain marred by his devotedness to a monstrous system of religion! I cannot easily understand how a mind so benevolent as his should have found the peace he says he has under his tremendous belief.

Lucy Aikin, Letter to Dr Channing, 13 May 1835.

Satan Montgomery.

Caroline Bowles, Letter to Robert Southey, 20 August 1832.

His writings bear the same relation to poetry as a Turkey-carpet bears to a picture. There are colours in the Turkey-carpet out of which a picture might be made. There are words in Mr Montgomery's verses which, when disposed in certain orders and combinations, have made, and will again make good poetry. But, as they now stand, they seem to be put together on principle, in such a manner as to give no image of anything in the 'heavens above, or in the earth beneath, or in the waters under the earth.'

T. B. Macaulay, *Essays*: 'Robert Montgomery's Poems'.

He is a fine young man, who has been wickedly puffed and wickedly abused, and who is in no little danger of being spoiled by forcing. . . . He has rushed in where angels fear to tread. He has attempted subjects which ought never to be attempted, and in which it is impossible not to fail; yet these very subjects have obtained for him popularity, and the profit without which he could not have obtained the education of which he was worthy, as well as ambitious. When he lowers his flight, I wish he may not find that he has weakened his wings by straining them.

Robert Southey, Letter to Caroline Bowles, 26 August 1832.

MOODY, DWIGHT LYMAN

1837—99 Evangelist

A terrier-like aspect — a sort of look which, if he had been given to fighting wild beasts at Ephesus or anywhere else, would have boded ill for the wild beasts.

Anon., in *Advance*, 4 March 1875.

For denominations he cared nothing; for Christianity he would give up his life.

Anon., in *Independent*, 28 December 1899.

And we shall not soon forget his incomparable frankness, his broad undenominationalism, his sledge-hammer gestures, his profuse diction, which stops neither for colons nor commas; his trueness, which never becomes conventional; his naturalness which never whines; his abhorrence of Phariseeism . . . his mastery of his subject, his glorious self-confidence, his blameless life, and his unswerving fealty to his conscience and to his work.

Anon., in Bernard Weisberger, *They Gathered at the River*.

Having heard Moody I am satisfied
But I shall not come to him to be saved.
He is not my idea of a Saviour.
I do not believe in him
Nor his God
Nor his method of swaying sinners nor his stories
                which sound like lies.
I Walt tell him he is an ignorant charlatan, a mis-
                taken enthusiast,
   and that Boston will ere long desire him to *git*.
Walt Whitman, from a parody of his *Passage to India*.

MOORE, GEORGE AUGUSTUS

1852–1933 Author

I came into the world apparently with a nature like a smooth sheet of wax, bearing no impress, but capable of receiving any; of being moulded into all shapes. Nor am I exaggerating when I say I think that I might equally have been a Pharaoh, an ostler, a pimp, an archbishop, and that in the fulfilment of the duties of each a certain measure of success would have been mine.

On himself, *Confessions of a Young Man*.

Whatever was in his mind, no matter where he was nor what his audience, he said. And when he had nothing to say, he said nothing. Which of these courses in an average drawing-room needs the greater courage — to say anything, or to say simply nothing? I think I used to rate Moore's silences his finer triumph. They were so unutterably blank. And yet, in some remote way, they so dominated the current chatter. It was impossible not to watch him during them. He sat rather on the edge of his chair, his knees together, his hands hanging limp on either side of him. Limply there hung over his brow a copious wisp of blonde hair, which wavered as he turned the long white oval of his face from one speaker to another. He sat wide-eyed, gaping, listening — no, one would not have said 'listening' but hearing: it did not seem that his ears were sending in any reports to his brain. It would be an understatement to say that his face was as a mask which revealed nothing. His face was as a mask of gauze through which Nothing was quite clearly visible. And then, all of a sudden, there would appear — Something. There came a gleam from within the pale-blue eyes, and a sort of ripple passed up over the modelling of the flaccid cheeks, the chin suddenly receded a little further, — and *Voilà Moore qui parle! Silence, la compagnie! Moore parle*.

Max Beerbohm, *George Moore*.

. . . that old pink petulant walrus.

Henry Channon, Diary, 20 May 1941.

We should really be much more interested in Mr Moore if he were not quite so interested in himself. We feel as if we were being shown through a gallery of really fine pictures, into each of which, by some useless and discordant convention, the artist had represented the same figure in the same attitude. 'The Grand Canal with a distant view of Mr Moore', 'Effect of Mr Moore through a Scotch Mist', 'Mr Moore by Firelight', 'Ruins of Mr Moore by Moonlight'.

G. K. Chesterton, *Heretics*.

Susan Mitchell sensed something lacking. Women are like that. She wrote, 'Some men kiss and do not tell, some kiss and tell; but George Moore told and did not kiss.'

Oliver St John Gogarty, *As I Was Walking down Sackville Street*.

The technical perfection of the novels of Mr George Moore does not prevent them from being faultlessly dead.

Q. D. Leavis, *Fiction and the Reading Public*.

Well, he's a bhit of a bhank-holiday fellow, ye know, Moore is.

Edward Martyn, in Max Beerbohm, *George Moore*.

'Do you know George Moore?' I asked him [Oscar Wilde] one day when he had been rolling the British Zola's novels round the ring. 'Know him? I know him so well that I haven't spoken to him in ten years.'

Vincent O'Sullivan, *Aspects of Wilde*.

An inveterate romancer, whose crimson inventions . . . suggested that he had been brought into the world by a union of Victor Hugo and Ouida.

George Bernard Shaw, *Pen Portraits and Reviews*.

George Moore . . . looked like a very prosperous Mellon's Food baby.
> Gertrude Stein, *The Autobiography of Alice B. Toklas.*

George Moore is always conducting his education in public.
> Oscar Wilde, in conversation with Max Beerbohm.

That vague formless obscene face.
> Oscar Wilde, Letter to Reginald Turner, February 1899.

He leads his readers to the latrine and locks them in.
> Oscar Wilde, in Hesketh Pearson, *The Life of Oscar Wilde.*

Moore once had visits from the Muse
But fearing that she would refuse
An ancient lecher took to geese
He now gets novels at his ease.
> William Butler Yeats, Journal, 9 March 1909.

Moore dismissed his sixth cook the day I left — six in three weeks. One brought in a policeman, Moore made so much noise. Moore brought the policeman into the dining room and said 'Is there a law in this country to compel me to eat that abominable omelette?'
> William Butler Yeats, Letter to Lady Gregory, May 1901.

See also Lytton Strachey, William Wordsworth

MOORE, GEORGE EDWARD

1873—1958 Philosopher

Moore's my man.
> J. L. Austin, attributed, in Bryan Magee, *Modern British Philosophy.*

I have never but once succeeded in making him tell a lie, and that was by a subterfuge. 'Moore,' I said, do you *always* speak the truth?' 'No,' he replied. I believe this to be the only lie he ever told.
> Bertrand Russell, *Autobiography*, vol. 1.

One of the pet amusements of all Moore's friends was to watch him trying to light a pipe. He would light a match, and then begin to argue, and continue until the match burnt his fingers. Then he would light another, and so on, until the box was finished. This was no doubt fortunate for his health, as it provided moments during which he was not smoking.
> *Ibid.*

. . . G. E. Moore was a perfect March Hare. His gown was always covered with chalk, his cap was in rags or missing, and his hair was a tangle which had never known the brush within man's memory. Its order and repose were not improved by an irascible habit of running his hand through it. He would go across town to his class, with no more formal footwear than his bedroom slippers, and the space between these and his trousers (which were several inches too short) was filled with wrinkled white socks.
> Norbert Wiener, *Ex-Prodigy.*

See also Lord Keynes, Ludwig Wittgenstein

MOORE, SIR JOHN

1761—1809 Soldier

I should not be pardonable if I omitted mentioning, in the fullest manner, the abilities and heroism of General Moore. I have seen so much of his conduct that I can speak confidently. To him you may safely look as a most promising officer; he goes to England covered with honourable scars, and were I king of England I would administer a salve.
> Sir Ralph Abercrombie, Letter to William Huskisson.

Not a drum was heard, not a funeral note,
    As his corpse to the rampart we hurried;
Not a soldier discharged his farewell shot
    O'er the grave where our hero we buried.

We buried him darkly at dead of night,
    The sods with our bayonets turning;
By the struggling moonbeam's misty light
    And the lantern dimly burning.

No useless coffin enclosed his breast,
    Not in sheet or in shroud we wound him;
But he lay like a warrior taking his rest,
    With his martial cloak around him.

Few and short were the prayers we said,
    And we spoke not a word of sorrow;
But we steadfastly gazed on the face that was dead,
    And we bitterly thought of the morrow.

We thought, as we hollow'd his narrow bed
    And smoothed down his lonely pillow,
That the foe and the stranger would tread o'er his
                  head,
    And we far away on the billow!

Lightly they'll talk of the spirit that's gone
    And o'er his cold ashes upbraid him, —

But little he'll rock, if they let him sleep on
   In the grave where a Briton has laid him.

But half of our heavy task was done
   When the clock struck the hour for retiring:
And we heard the distant and random gun
   That the foe was sullenly firing.

Slowly and sadly we laid him down,
   From the field of his fame fresh and gory;
We carved not a line, and we raised not a stone —
   But we left him alone with his glory.
   William Cowper, *The Burial of Sir John Moore
   at Corunna*.

It is considered as fortunate for his Reputation
that he fell. The mildest disapprobation is of his
Talents, which NOW it is said have always been
overrated. His power consisted in laborious application to details, but prov'd to be greatly deficient
when task'd by the command of a large Army. His
Indecision and Ruinous Retreat (in which they say
Thousands were sacrific'd from absolute Fatigue)
produc'd everything short of a Mutiny, so that when
the Men were congratulated after the Victory by
their Officers, they loudly exclaimed, 'No thanks to
others! Why didn't we do this before?'
   Sir Thomas Lawrence, Letter to Joseph Farring-
ton, 1809.

I have made up my mind to my three eldest boys
going with General Sir John Moore, because — what
is their object in life? — *fame*, and where can they
learn to deserve it better than in such a moment?
   Lady Sarah Napier, in Carola Oman, *Sir John
Moore*.

When you are a man, come to me, and I will give
you a real sword, for your dear Uncle's sake.
   Lady Hester Stanhope, in a note accompanying
a gift of toys to Moore's nephew John, 1809.

MOORE, MARIANNE CRAIG

1887—1972 Poet

Anything that is a stumbling block to my reader is
a matter of regret to me and punctuation ought to
be exact. Under ordinary circumstances, it is as
great a hardship to me to be obliged to alter punctuation as to alter words, though I will admit that
at times I am heady and irresponsible.
   On herself, Letter to Ezra Pound, 19 January
1919.

Did laboratory studies affect my poetry? I am sure
they did. I found the biology courses — minor,
major and histology — exhilarating. I thought, in
fact, of studying medicine. Precision, economy of
statement, logic employed to ends that are disinterested, drawing and identifying, liberate — at
least have some bearing on — the imagination, it
seems to me.
   On herself, in an interview with Donald Hall, in
Donald Hall ed., *Marianne Moore, A Collection
of Critical Essays*.

She takes the museum piece out of its glass case,
and sets it against the living flower. She produces
living plants out of the herbarium and living animals
from the bestiary.
   Louise Boyan, 'American Timeless', in *Quarterly
Review of Literature*, vol. 4, no. 2.

With a concern to narrow limits, to reduce the
means of expression to what is indispensable, she
understands, like certain painters, the necessity of
not going beyond the line. Thus the firmness of the
contours, the self-containment of the poem, which
often goes by a crooked mile to its usually ringing,
often epigrammatic close.
   Jean Carriague, *Marianne Moore*.

And there is one final, and 'magnificent' compliment: Miss Moore's poetry is as 'feminine' as
Christina Rossetti's, one never forgets that it is
written by a woman; but with both one never
thinks of this as anything but a positive virtue.
   T. S. Eliot, *Essays*: 'Marianne Moore'.

Miss Moore's relation to the soil is not a simple one,
or rather it is to various soils — to that of Latium
and to that of Attica I believe (or at least to that of
the Aegean littoral) as well as most positively to soil
(well top-dressed) of America.
   Ibid.

Miss Moore's work has been an interweaving of perception and creation, the two reinforcing and
extending each other: her interest has been in
exploring the details of her 'object' in order to give
both an accurate delineation of it and a suggestive
presentation of the values she believes it to exemplify. In so doing, she had pleased nearly all the
prominent members of her poetic generation.
   Bernard F. Engel, *Marianne Moore*.

If there is a theme that runs from first to last in
Marianne Moore's poems, it is the theme of self-
defense. The very style of the early poems is defensive, wit and irony and extreme precision being a
kind of armor to hide feeling. Never quite to
commit oneself is a defense.
   Donald Hall, *Marianne Moore*.

Miss Moore leaves the stones she picks up carefully uncut, but places them in an unimaginably complicated and difficult setting, to sparkle under the Northern Light of her continual irony.
  Randall Jarrell, 'Her Shield', in Donald Hall ed., *Marianne Moore, A Collection of Critical Essays*.

Although her early verses present no difficulties, her more characteristic lines seem to erect a barrier of jagged clauses, barbed quotations and suspicious structures between herself and her audience.
  Louis Untermeyer, *Modern American Poetry, A Critical Anthology*.

It is a talent which diminishes the tom-toming on the hollow men of a wasteland to an irrelevant pitter-patter. Nothing is hollow or waste to the imagination of Marianne Moore.
  William Carlos Williams, 'Marianne Moore', in Donald Hall ed., *Marianne Moore, A Collection of Critical Essays*.

MOORE, THOMAS

1779—1852 Poet, Author

Lalla Rookh
Is a naughty book
By Tommy Moore,
Who has written four;
Each warmer
Than the former,
So the most recent
Is the least decent.
  Anon., *On T. Moore's Poems*.

Moore always smiles whenever he recites;
He smiles, you think, approving what he writes?
And yet in this no vanity is shown:
A modest man may like what's not his own.
  Anon., in *Elegant Extracts*.

Mr. Moore *is* a *poet*, and therefore is *not* a reasoner.
  Peregrine Bingham, in *Westminster Review*, January 1824.

Young Catullus of his day
As sweet, but as immoral, in his lay!
  Lord Byron, *English Bards and Scotch Reviewers*.

The poet of all circles, and the idol of his own.
  Lord Byron, Dedication to *The Corsair*.

In society, he is gentlemanly, gentle, and altogether more pleasing than any individual with whom I am acquainted. . . . He has but one fault — and that one I daily regret — he is not *here*.
  Lord Byron, Journal, 22 November 1813.

He was an actor all through his existence, the mask has fallen from his hand in death, and Lord John Russell has picked it up.
  T. Crofton Croker, Letter to T. C. Grattan, 5 July 1853.

Highly gifted, yet meanly endowed; he had too much genius for so little independence of spirit. He rose above the depressing influences of low birth to sink under the caresses of the high-born.
  Thomas Colley Grattan, *Beaten Paths and Those Who Trod Them*.

Mr Moore's Muse is another Ariel, as light, as tricksy, as indefatigable, and as humane a spirit. His fancy is for ever on the wing, flutters in the gale, glitters in the sun. Every thing lives, moves, and sparkles in his poetry, while over all love waves his purple light. His thoughts are as restless, as many, and as bright as the insects that people the sun's beam.
  William Hazlitt, *Lectures on the English Poets*.

He looked as if begotten between a toad and cupid.
  Theodore Hook, in Thomas Colley Grattan, *Beaten Paths and Those Who Trod Them*.

When Moore is merry he ceases to be a poet so utterly that we are tempted to ask when did he begin.
  George Bernard Shaw, *Pen Portraits and Reviews*.

See also Lord Byron, Alexander Pope, William Butler Yeats

MORDAUNT, CHARLES, see under PETERBOROUGH, EARL OF

MORE, HANNAH

1745—1833 Writer

This lady, excellent as she was, and incapable of practising any studied deceit, had, however, an instinct of worldly wisdom, which taught her to refrain from shocking ears polite with too harsh or too broad an exposure of all which she believed. This, at least, if it were any duty of hers, she considered, perhaps, as already fulfilled by her writings; and, moreover, the very tone of good breeding which she had derived from the good company she had kept made her feel the impropriety of lecturing her visitors even when she must have thought them in error.
  Thomas de Quincey, *Autobiography*.

Mrs Hannah More is another celebrated modern poetess, and I believe still living. She has written a great deal which I have never read.

William Hazlitt, *Lectures on the English Poets*.

If, instead of belonging to a trumpery gospel faction, she had only watched over those great points of religion in which the hearts of every sect of Christians are interested, she would have been one of the most useful and valuable writers of her day.

Sydney Smith, in *Edinburgh Review*, April 1809.

Much as I love your writings, I respect yet more your heart and your goodness. You are so good, that I believe you would go to heaven, even though there were no Sunday, and only six *working* days in the week.

Horace Walpole, Letter to Mrs H. More, 1788.

See also Elizabeth Montagu, Mary Wollstonecraft

MORE, SIR THOMAS

1478–1535 Statesman, Author, Saint

I pray Sir give me aid in my going up; as for my coming down I can make shift for myself.
    On himself, attributed, as he ascended the scaffold for his execution.

You will never get credit for beheading me, my neck is so short.
    On himself, attributed, remark made to his executioners.

Memorandum that in his Utopia his lawe is that the young people are to see each other stark naked before marriage. Sir [William] Roper, of Eltham in Kent, came one morning, pretty early, to my lord, with a proposall to marry one of his daughters. My lord's daughters were then both together a bed in a truckle-bed in their father's chamber asleep. He carries Sir [William] into the chamber and takes the sheet by the corner and suddenly whippes it off. They lay on their Backs, and their smocks up as high as their armpitts. This awakened them, and immediately they turned on their Bellies. Quoth Roper, I have seen both sides, and so gave a patt on her Buttock he made choice of, sayeing, Thou art mine. Here was all the trouble of the wooing.

John Aubrey, *Brief Lives*.

He is of middle height, well shaped, complexion pale, without a touch of colour in it save when the skin flushes. The hair is black, shot with yellow, or yellow shot with black; beard scanty, eyes grey, with dark spots — an eye supposed in England to indicate genius, and to be never found except in remarkable men. The expression is pleasant and cordial, easily passing into a smile, for he has the quickest sense of the ridiculous of any man I ever met.

Desiderius Erasmus, Letter to Ulrich von Hutten, translated by J. A. Froude.

When *More* some time had Chancellor been
    No more suits did remain,
The same shall never more be seen
    Till *More* be there again.
    Thomas Fuller, *The History of the Worthies of England*.

Sir Thomas More's Life of Edward V., written about 1500, appears to me the first example of good English language; pure and perspicuous, well-chosen, without vulgarisms or pedantry.

Henry Hallam, Introduction to *The Literature of Europe*.

None who read the *Utopia* can deny that its author drank deep of the finest spirit of his age. None can question that he foresaw the main lines along which the political and social ideals of the Renaissance were to develop in the future. There is hardly a scheme of social or political reform that has been enunciated in later epochs of which there is no definite adumbration in More's pages. But he who passes hastily from the speculations of More's *Utopia* to the record of More's subsequent life and writings will experience a strange shock. Nowhere is he likely to be faced by so sharp a contrast between precept and practice, between enlightened and vivifying theory in the study, and adherence in the workaday world to the unintelligent routine of bigotry and obscurantism.

Sir Sidney Lee, *Great Englishmen of the Sixteenth Century*.

When we reflect that Sir Thomas More was ready to die for the doctrine of transubstantiation, we cannot but feel some doubt whether the doctrine of transubstantiation may not triumph over all opposition. More was a man of eminent talents. He had all the information on the subject that we have, or that, while the world lasts, any human being will have.

T. B. Macaulay, *Essays*: 'Ranke's History of the Popes'.

. . . No such culprit stood at any European bar for a thousand years. It is rather from caution than from necessity that the ages of Roman domination are excluded from the comparison. It does not seem that in any moral respect Socrates himself could claim a superiority.

Sir James Mackintosh, *Life of Sir Thomas More*.

Catholics ought to see in More, that mildness and candour are the true ornaments of all modes of faith. Protestants ought to be taught humility and charity from this instance of the wisest and best of men falling into what they deem the most fatal errors. All men in the fierce contests of contending factions should, from such an example, learn the wisdom to fear lest in their most hated antagonists they may strike down a Sir Thomas More.
Ibid.

This Sir Thomas More, after he had bine brought upp in the Latine tongue at Saint Anthonies in London, was by his father's procurement receaved into the house of the right reuerend, wise, and learned prelate Cardinall Morton; where, thoghe he was younge of yeares, yet wold he at Christmas tyde sodenly sometimes steppe in among the players, and neuer studyeng for the matter, make a parte of his owne there presently among them, which made the lookers-on more sporte than all the plaiers beside. In whose witt and towardnes the Cardinall much delightinge, wold often say of him vnto the nobles that divers tymed dined with him: 'This child here wayting at the table, whosoever shall live to see it, will prove a mervailous man.'
William Roper, *The Lyfe of Sir Thomas Moore.*

So on a tyme, walking with me alonge the teames side at Chelsey, in talking of other things he said vnto me: 'Nowe wold to our Lord, sonne Roper, vppon condicion that three things were well established in Christendome, I were put in a sack, and here presently caste into the Thames.'
'What greate things be those, Sir,' quoth I, 'that should moue you so to wish?'
'In faith, sonne, they be these,' said he. 'The first is, that where the moste part of Christen princes be at mortall warre, they were all at an uniuersall peace. The second, that wheare the Church of Christe is at this presente sore afflicted with many errors and heresees, it were setled in a perfect vniformity of religion. The third, that where the kings matter of his mariage is nowe come question, it were to the glory of god and quietnes of all partes brought to a good conclusion.'
Ibid.

And albeit his mynde served him to the second daughter, for that he thought her the fairest and best favoured, yeat when he considered that it wold be both greate greif and some shame also to the eldest to see your yonger sister in mariage preferred before her, he then of a certayne pity framed his fancy towardes her, and soon after maryed her.
Ibid., on More's choice of a wife among the three daughters of Master Colte.

Who, with a generous, tho mistaken Zeal,
Withstood a brutal tyrant's useful rage,
Like CATO firm, like ARISTIDES just,
Like rigid CINCINNATUS nobly poor,
A dauntless Soul erect, who smil'd on Death.
James Thomson, *The Seasons, Summer.*

. . . More and his fellow-martyr Fisher were not canonised for four centuries; and some explanation is required of this surprising delay. Partly, no doubt, it was due to the view held of More in Rome. Like Newman long afterwards, More was suspect as a Liberal Catholic, a Catholic who appealed (as he still appeals) to Protestants, who was indeed himself half-Protestant. Belonging to the age and sharing the views of his friend Erasmus, he had doubted the value of monasticism, wished to reduce the externals of worship, to admit lay reason into dogmatic studies, to meet reform half-way and salvage thereby a purified religion. But in fact, when Rome was saved it was not by such measures: the Counter-Reformation was not a compliance with Reform but a defiance of it. . . .
H. R. Trevor-Roper, *Sir Thomas More and the English Lay Recusants.*

See also George Orwell

MORGAN, JOHN PIERPONT

1837—1913 Banker, Financier, Art Collector

I owe the public nothing.
On himself, in Matthew Josephson, *The Robber Barons.*

It's Morgan's, it's Morgan's,
The great financial Gorgon's. . . .
Anon. song.

Mr. Morgan buys his partners; I grow my own.
Andrew Carnegie, attributed.

Morgan's ruby nose added to his personal fame and with some humor he once said it 'would be impossible for me to appear on the streets without it.' His nose, he remarked on another occasion, 'was part of the American business structure.'
Stewart Holbrook, *The Age of the Moguls.*

See also Al Capone, Thomas Gresham, Mark Hanna

MORLAND, GEORGE

1763—1804 Painter

The father, proud of having produced such a son,

naturally boasted the precocity of his abilities; but this adulation too soon laid the foundation of that insolence and self-will which the young painter cherished and indulged as he approached manhood, and was the main cause of his profligacy, premature mental and bodily decay, and ultimate ruin.

H. Angelo, *Reminiscences*.

He valued his pencil as the means of acquiring not distinction, but the gold wherewith to charm away creditors and liquidate tavern bills. The pictures which he dashed off according to the craving of the hour, are numerous and excellent. They are all facsimiles of low nature — graphic copies of common life — their truth is their beauty, and if they have anything poetical about them, it lies in the singular ease and ruminating repose which is the reigning character of many.

Allan Cunningham, *The Lives of the Most Eminent British Painters*.

He is the rustic painter for the people; his scenes are familiar to every eye, and his name is on every lip. Painting seemed as natural to him as language is to others, and by it he expressed his sentiments and his feelings and opened his heart to the multitude.

Ibid.

MORLEY, THOMAS

1557—1604? Musician

MORLEY! would any try whither MORe LYeth
  In our ENGLISH, to merit
  Or in th'ITALIAN spirit
Who in regard of his each wit defieth?
  Anon., *To the Author, First Book of Madrigals to Four Voices*.

Master Morley supposing, perhaps, that the harmony which was to be heard through the clattering of knives, forks, spoons, and plates, with the gingling of glasses, and clamorous conversation of a city-feast, need not be very accurate or refined, was not very nice in setting parts to these tunes, which are so far from correct, that almost any one of the city waits would, in musical cant, have *vamped* as good an accompaniment.

Dr Charles Burney, *A General History of Music*.

Such was old Orpheus cunning
That senseless things drew near him
And herds of beasts to hear him
The stock, the stone, the Ox, the Ass came running.
MORLEY! but this enchanting
To thee, to be the Musick-God is wanting.
And yet thou needst not fear him;

Draw thou the Shepherd still and Bonny-lasses,
And envy him not stocks, stones, Oxen, Asses.
  Michael Drayton, attributed, *Mr. M.D. to the Author*, in *The First Book of Balletts to Five Voyces*.

Death hath deprived me of my dearest friend,
My dearest friend is dead and laid in grave,
In grave he rests until the world shall end,
The world shall end, as end must all things have.
All things must have an end that nature wrought,
That nature wrought, must unto dust be brought.
  Thomas Weelkes, *A Remembrance of My Friend Mr. Thomas Morley, Airs or Fantastic Spirits*.

MORRELL, LADY OTTOLINE VIOLET ANNE

1873—1938 Hostess

I did not know I loved you till I heard myself telling you so — for one instant I thought 'Good God, what have I said?' and then I knew it was the truth.
  Bertrand Russell, Letter to Ottoline Morrell, March 1911.

. . . Loving you is like loving a red-hot poker, which is a worse bedfellow than even Lytton's umbrella: every caress brings on agony.
  Bertrand Russell, Letter to Ottoline Morrell, June 1912.

MORRIS, WILLIAM

1834—96 Poet, Painter, Designer

His method, his mingling of the couplet measure and the old stanza in his tales . . . looks somehow like writing in ruins.
  R. W. Dixon, Letter to Gerard Manley Hopkins, 4 November 1881.

Morris . . . had just been talking to some members of a ship's crew whom he had met in Fenchurch Street. They had remained for some time under the impression that he was a ship's captain. This had pleased him very much, for it was his ambition to be taken for such a man. . . . With a grey beard like the foam of the sea, with grey hair through which he continually ran his hands, erect and curly on his forehead, with a hooked nose, a florid complexion and clean, clear eyes, dressed in a blue serge coat, and carrying, as a rule, a satchel, to meet him was always, as it were, to meet a sailor ashore.
  Ford Madox Ford, *Ancient Lights*.

He's an extraordinary example, in short of a delicate sensitive genius and taste, served by a perfectly healthy body and temper.

Henry James, Letter to Alice James, 12 March 1869.

Morris is our only improvisatore, perhaps the only great improvisatore that ever lived. He could go to his study and write five hundred lines of *The Earthly Paradise* and return quite cheerful and happy, as if nothing extraordinary had happened; and these five hundred lines were never casual — every one was perfect.

George Moore, Letter to Nancy Cunard, 1921.

Rossetti did not much like Morris, and one of Morris's characteristics he despised. Rossetti, who was the soul of generosity himself, thought that the penuriousness of Morris, who was rich, corresponded ill with his fine humanitarian sentiments. 'Did anyone ever hear of Topsy giving a penny to anybody?' Rossetti would ask.

Vincent O'Sullivan, *Aspects of Wilde.*

I can't understand how a man who, on the whole, enjoys dinner — and breakfast — and supper — to that extent of fat — can write such lovely poems about Misery.

John Ruskin, Letter to Joan Agnew, 21 January 1870.

I feel nothing but elation when I think of Morris. My intercourse with him was so satisfying that I should be the most ungrateful of men if I asked for more. You can lose a man like that by your own death, but not by his. And so, until then, let us rejoice in him.

George Bernard Shaw (on Morris's death), in *Saturday Review*, 10 October 1896.

The dream-world of Morris was as much the antithesis of daily life as with other men of genius, but he was never conscious of the antithesis and so knew nothing of intellectual suffering.

William Butler Yeats, *Autobiographies.*

The one perfectly happy and fortunate poet of modern times.

William Butler Yeats, *Ideas of Good and Evil.*

See also Alfred, Lord Tennyson, Virginia Woolf, William Butler Yeats

MORSE, SAMUEL FINLEY BREESE

1791—1872 Artist, Inventor

I do not speak of *portrait-painters*; had I no higher thoughts than being a first-rate portrait-painter, I would have chosen a far different profession. My ambition is to be among those who shall revive the splendor of the fifteenth century; to rival the genius of a Raphael, a Michael Angelo, or a Titian; my ambition is to be enlisted in the constellation of genius now rising in this country; I wish to shine, not by a light borrowed from them, but to strive to shine the brightest.

On himself, Letter to his Mother, 3 May 1815.

Alas the very name of pictures produces a sadness of heart I cannot describe. Painting has been a smiling mistress to many, but she has been a cruel jilt to me. I did not abandon her; she abandoned me.

On himself, Letter to James Fenimore Cooper, 1849.

I have many yearnings towards painting and sculpture, but that rigid faculty called reason, so opposed often to imagination, reads me a lecture to which I am compelled to bow. . . . No, I have made the sacrifice of my profession to establish an invention which is doing mankind a great service. I pursued it long enough to found an institution (the Academy of Design) which, I trust, is to flourish long after I am gone. . . .

On himself, Letter to Nathaniel Jocelyn, 20 January 1864.

Communication was improved by S. O. S. Morse, who invented the telegraph and organized the first union of telegraph operators in the West, known as the Western Union. He also developed the secret code that bears his name. Morse's first message on the telegraph was the reverent question, 'What hath God wrought?' which is Morse code for 'don't write, telegraph.'

Richard Armour, *It All Started With Columbus.*

He makes good portraits, strong likenesses; . . . but he cannot design. There is no poetry about his paintings, and his prose consists of straight lines, which look as if they had been stretched to their utmost tension to form clothes-lines.

Philip Hone, Diary, 15 May 1833.

Even the telegraph was seen as an extraneous enterprise which Morse expected would free him to paint all the harder. Although his soaring imagination informed him at once that his invention was to be of vast importance to mankind, although his religious idealism assured him that he was divinely and wondrously appointed to this task, he nevertheless continued to think of himself as a painter. He could not know the decades of labor and contention in which his telegraph was to involve him, nor could he foresee what a cruel and ungrateful mistress art was to prove.

Harry B. Wehle, *Samuel F. B. Morse.*

MORTON, JOHN, CARDINAL

1420?–1500 Statesman

He was a great instrument in advancing a voluntary contribution to the king through the land; persuading prodigals to part with their money, because they did spend it most, and the covetous, because they might spare it best; so making both extremes to meet in one medium, to supply the king's necessities.

Thomas Fuller, on 'Morton's Fork', *The History of the Worthies of England.*

See also Sir Thomas More

MORTON, SARAH WENTWORTH APTHORP

1759–1846 Poet

[The] American Sappho.

Robert Treat Paine Jr, in *The National Cyclopaedia of American Biography.*

MOSES, ANNA MARY ROBERTSON, 'GRANDMA'

1860–1961 Artist

In such a world the paintings of Grandma Moses provide a sense of peace and adjustment to the natural laws by which we must live or be destroyed. In Grandma Moses' world there is the same zest and understanding of the eternal importance of small things which one finds in the peasant pictures of Pieter Breughel. His pictures have the robustness and earthiness of a Flemish male. Those of Grandma Moses are infused with the quality of a New England woman who had divided her life between two of the most beautiful parts of the world — the Shenandoah Valley and the hills of Vermont. But both Breughel and Grandma Moses tell you essentially the same thing — that every day life is good and amusing and filled with richness and variety and beauty, if you choose to find it.

Louis Bromfield, *Grandma Moses, American Primitive.*

MOTT, LUCRETIA COFFIN

1793–1880 Suffragette, Reformer

The Roman Lucretia, by the wrongs she endured, and the tragical and suicidal death she suffered, kindled the flames of rebellion, changed the form of government in her day, and founded a republic. Our Yankee Lucretia is no doubt, ambitious to follow the example of her great prototype; . . . Lucretia the first raised a republic, Lucretia the second is bent on ruining one.

Anon., in *New York Weekly Herald,* 28 December 1848.

Lucretia Mott
Like the serpent and the dove,
Thou hast wisdom and love;
Thy faith by thy deeds is shown forth
Thy liberal mind
Chains of sect cannot bind;
Thy sect is the righteousness of earth.

Anon., in *Liberator,* 15 January 1841.

. . . not quite enough an abstractionist for me and her will is more illuminated than her mind.

Ralph Waldo Emerson, in Otelia Cromwell, *Lucretia Mott.*

Her courage is no merit, one almost says, where triumph is so sure.

Ralph Waldo Emerson, in Lloyd C. M. Hare, *The Greatest American Woman.*

. . . she rules like a queen on the platform, and when she looked as if she desired anything we all sprang to see what it might be.

Thomas Wentworth Higginson, in *ibid.*

She spoke gratefully of intellectual light as a guide to the spiritual truth, and anticipated and prayed for an ultimate universal diffusing of both.

Harriet Martineau, *Retrospect of Western Travel.*

Having known Lucretia Mott, not only in the flush of life, when all her faculties were at their zenith, but in the repose of advanced age, her withdrawal from our midst seems as natural and as beautiful as the changing foliage of some grand oak from the spring-time to the autumn.

Elizabeth Cady Stanton, in Lloyd C. M. Hare, *The Greatest American Woman.*

MUIR, JOHN

1838–1914 Naturalist, Explorer

Do behold the King in his glory, King Sequoia!

Behold! Behold! seems all I can say. Some time ago I left all for Sequoia and have been and am at his feet; fasting and praying for light, for is he not the greatest light in the woods, in the world? Where are such columns of sunshine, tangible, accessible, terrestrialized? . . . I'm in the woods, woods, woods, and they are in *me-ee-ee*.

On himself, Letter to Mrs Ezra S. Carr.

I am very, very blessed. The Valley is full of people, but they do not annoy me. I revolved in pathless places and in higher rocks than *the world* and his ribbony wife can reach.

On himself, Letter to Mrs Ezra S. Carr, 29 July 1870.

I am hopelessly a mountaineer. . . . Civilization and fever and all the morbidness that has been hooted at me have not dimmed my glacial eye, and I care to live only to entice people to look at Nature's loveliness. My own special self is nothing.

On himself, Letter to Mrs Ezra S. Carr, 7 October 1874.

I have not yet in all my wanderings found a single person so free as myself. Yet I am bound to my studies, and the laws of my own life. At times I feel as if driven with whips, and ridden upon. When in the woods I sit at times for hours watching birds or squirrels. . . . Yet I am swept onward in a general current that bears on irresistibly.

On himself, Letter to Sarah Muir Galloway, 26 February 1875.

I was once free as any pine-playing wind, and feel that I have still a good length of line, but alack! there seems to be a hook or two of civilization in me that I would fain pull out, yet *would not pull out* — O, O, O!!!

On himself, in William Bade ed., *The Life and Letters of John Muir*, vol. 2.

. . . I feel like a flake of glass through which light passes, but which, conscious of the inexhaustibleness of its sun fountain, cares not whether its passing light coins itself into other forms or goes unchanged — neither charcoaled nor diamonded! Moreover, I find that though I have a few thoughts entangled in the fibres of my mind, I possess no words into which I can shape them. You tell me that I must be patient and reach out and grope in lexicon granaries for the words I want. But if some loquacious angel were to touch my lips with literary fire, bestowing every word of Webster, I would scarce thank him for the gift, because most of the words of the English language are made of mud, for muddy purposes, while those invented to contain

spiritual matter are doubtful and unfixed in capacity and form, as wind-ridden mist-rags.

Ibid.

. . . I have everywhere testified to my friends, who should also be yours, my happiness in finding you — the right man in the right place — in your mountain tabernacle, and have expected when your guardian angel would pronounce that your probation and sequestration in the solitudes and snows had reached their term, and you were to bring your ripe fruits so rare and precious into waiting society.

Ralph Waldo Emerson, Letter to John Muir, 5 February 1872.

MUNI, PAUL (MUNI WEISENFREUND)

1895–1967 Actor

Paul was a most attractive man, I thought. Evidently he did not think so and usually retreated behind a beard. Transference is one thing, but I sincerely believe the audience wants to become familiar with certain physical attributes that are ever present in each performance. Mr. Muni seemed intent on submerging himself so completely that he disappeared. His wife used to say 'I've lived with more men than any other woman'. There is no question that his technique as an actor was superb. But for me, beneath the exquisite petit point of details, the loss of his own sovereignty worked conversely to rob some of his characterisations of blood. It is a criticism that I aim at the naturalist actors. Paul's intellect was always at work. He fought the good fight and added greatly to the dignity and respectability of Hollywood.

Bette Davis, *The Lonely Life.*

He never wanted a paying customer to say, 'I know exactly what to expect of him!' He was continually, restlessly searching for a change. He didn't want to be stuck in a rut. Having been typed as a bearded child, he sought barefacedly to surprise audiences, to give them what they didn't anticipate, even what they didn't want. This was the reason for his successes and perhaps equally the reason for his failures. His test for a role: did the man have substance? When you touched him, was he flesh? Was the character larger, deeper, broader, more intelligent than the man he downgraded and despised — the nothing Muni?

Jerome Lawrence, *Actor.*

To Paul Muni, acting was not just a career, but an obsession. Despite enormous success on Broadway and in Hollywood, he threw himself into each role with a sense of dedication that can only be ex-

plained one way; he was pursued by a fear of failure.
Arthur Miller, in *ibid.*

Muni Weisenfreund . . . became Paul Muni and my most potent competition. He played *Pasteur* and *Zola*; *I* could have. I played *Ehrlich* and *Reuter*; *he* could have. The Brothers Warner regarded us as two sides of a coin and did not hesitate to exploit the situation. I disliked Muni and Muni detested me.
Edward G. Robinson, *All My Yesterdays.*

Something of the Yiddish stage's patriarchal traditions determined his predilection for playing characters considerably older than himself. Such a flair was also a kind of defiant anti-stardom, since it involved sinking his identity into a character and projecting his own personality only when it was a means of clarifying a dramatic point. He never gave himself wholeheartedly to a film career, and consequently escaped many of the degradations that lay in wait for those who did.
Alexander Walker, *Stardom.*

He was the master character actor. Others achieved stardom by projecting their strong personalities onto the screen. Muni turned the procedure around. He erased his identity. He transformed the character into the actor.
David Zinman, *Fifty Famous Motion Pictures.*

MURRAY, GEORGE GILBERT AIMÉ

1866—1957 Classical Scholar, Translator

The really great event of the last few weeks has been Gilbert Murray. I fear I should fall into schoolgirlishness if I ventured to tell you how much I liked him. You will judge when I say that no woman in my earlier years made me talk more about myself than he has now . . . I found him so gentle, so sweetly reasonable — almost the ideal companion. Even could I forgive his liking Dickens, and Tennyson.
Bernard Berenson, Letter to Bertrand Russell, 22 March 1903.

We need a number of educated poets who shall at least have opinions about Greek drama, and whether it is or is not of any use to us. And it must be said that Professor Gilbert Murray is not the man for this. Greek poetry will never have the slightest vitalizing effect upon English poetry if it can only appear masquerading as a vulgar debasement of the eminently personal idiom of Swinburne. These are strong words to use against the most popular

Hellenist of his time; but we must witness of Professor Murray ere we die that these things are not otherwise but thus.
T. S. Eliot, *The Sacred Wood.*

Gentle-voiced and with the spiritual look of the strict vegetarian, [he was] doing preliminary propaganda work for the League of Nations. Once, as I sat talking to him in his study about Aristotle's *Poetics*, while he walked up and down, I suddenly asked: 'Exactly what is the principle of that walk of yours? Are you trying to avoid the flowers on the rug, or are you trying to keep to the squares?' My own compulsion-neuroses made it easy for me to notice them in others. He wheeled around sharply: 'You're the first person who has caught me out,' he said. 'No, it's not the flowers or the squares; it's a habit that I have got into of doing things in sevens. I take seven steps, you see, then I change direction and go another seven steps, then I turn around. I consulted Browne, the Professor of Psychology, about it the other day, but he assured me it isn't a dangerous habit. He said: "When you find yourself getting into multiples of seven, come to me again." '
Robert Graves, *Goodbye to All That.*

MURRAY, JOHN

1778—1843 Publisher

He is a rogue of course, but a civil one.
Jane Austen, Letter to Cassandra Austen, 17 October 1815.

I believe M. to be a good man, with a personal regard for me. But a bargain is in its very essence a *hostile* transaction . . . even between brethren, [it] is a declaration of war.
Lord Byron, Letter to Douglas Kinnaird, 14 July 1821.

The most timid of God's booksellers.
Lord Byron, in Thomas Medwin, *Conversations of Lord Byron.*

Southey says, in alteration of Byron's phrase, that M. is the most timorous not of God's but of the Devil's booksellers.
Sir Walter Scott, Journal, 7 December 1825.

See also Sir Walter Scott

MURRAY, WILLIAM, see under MANSFIELD, LORD

MURROW, EDWARD R.

1908—65 Broadcaster

Murrow. The right man in the right place in the right era. An innately elegant man in an innately inelegant profession. A rare figure, as good as his legend. His presence was so strong that it still lives.

. . . His voice was steeped in civility, intelligence, and compassion. He was a man who, much as Lindbergh did, spanned the oceans and shortened distance and heightened time.

David Halberstam, in *Washington Post*,
28 December 1975.

N

NAPIER, SIR CHARLES JAMES

1782–1853 Soldier, Administrator

The hundred-gun ship has taken the little cock-boat in tow, and it will follow for ever over the ocean of time.
> On himself, when praised by the Duke of Wellington, 1843.

Peccavi — I have Scinde.
> On himself, attributed, in *Punch*, 1843.

A fiery lynx-eyed man with the spirit of an old knight in him more than in any modern I have ever met.
> Thomas Carlyle, in Rosamond Lawrence, *Charles Napier: Friend and Fighter.*

When he went into a campaign he took with him but a piece of soap and a pair of towels; he dined off a hunch of bread and a cup of water. 'A warrior', said he, 'should not care for wine or luxury, for fine turbans or embroidered shulwars; his talwar should be bright, and never mind whether his papooshes are shiny.' Napeer Singh was a lion indeed. . . . But this lion, though the bravest of animals, was the most quarrelsome that ever lashed a tail and roared in a jungle.
> W. M. Thackeray, *The Tale of Koompanee Jehan.*

NASH, JOHN

1752–1835 Architect

My thick, squat, dwarf figure with round head, snub nose, and little eyes.
> On himself, Letter to Sir John Soane, 1822.

Augustus at Rome was for building renown'd,
And of marble he left what of brick he had found;
But is not our Nash, too, a very great master?—
He finds us all brick and leaves us all plaster.
> Anon., in *Quarterly Review*, vol. 34, 1826.

Nash embodied everything which the nineteenth century hated about the eighteenth.
> John Summerson, *Architecture in Britain 1530–1830.*

NASH, OGDEN

1902–71 Poet

Being both viable and friable I wish to prolong my existence.
> On himself, in *Saturday Evening Post.*

He has a Democritean streak which entitled him to the respect due to a philosopher, albeit a laughing one.
> Anon., in Clifton Fadiman, *Party of One.*

As a poet Nash works under two disadvantages: he is a humorist, and he is easy to understand.
> Clifton Fadiman, *ibid.*

He writes about what we share — the common cold rather than the uncommon Highland lass.
> *Ibid.*

Nash is a true household poet in that he really understands the joys and sorrows of domestic life. He does not, like the folksy household poet, sentimentalize them. He is always the understanding host, never the unwelcome guest.
> *Ibid.*

Hurrah, Mr Nash, for your writings laughable!
We liked you surly, we love you affable,
And think your poems designed for the nursery
Almost the best in your bulging versery.
> Phyllis McGinley, in *Saturday Review of Literature*, 10 October 1936.

Nash is the laureate of a generation which had to develop its own wry, none-too-joyful humor as the alternative to simply lying down on the floor and screaming.
> Russell Maloney, in *New York Times Book Review*, 14 October 1945.

He has become, in a strictly Shakespearean sense, America's number one fool, though in any other sense he is nobody's fool.
> George F. Whicher, in *Atlantic Monthly*, December 1942.

NASHE, THOMAS

1567–1601 Author

He can raile (what mad Bedlam cannot raile?) but the favour of his railing, is grosely fell, and smelleth noysomly of the pumps, or a nastier thing. His gayest floorishes, are but Gascoignes weedes, or Tarletons trickes, or Greenes crankes, or Marlowes bravados: his jestes, but the dregges of common scurrilitie, the shreds of the theater, or the of-scouring of new Pamflets: his freshest nippitatie, but the froth of stale inventions, long since lothsome to quick tastes: his shroving ware, but lenten stuffe, like the old pickle herring: his lustiest verdure, but rank ordure, not to be named in Civilitie, or Rhetorique.
  Gabriel Harvey, *Pierces Supererogation*.

NATION, CARRY AMELIA MOORE

1846–1911 Temperance Agitator

. . . a bulldog running along at the feet of Jesus, barking at what He doesn't like.
  On herself, in Herbert Asbury, *Carry Nation*.

Sing a song of six joints,
  With bottles full of rye;
Four and twenty beer kegs,
  Stacked up on the sly.
When the kegs were opened,
  The beer began to sing,
'Hurrah for Carry Nation,
Her work beats anything.'
  Anon., satire in *ibid*.

. . . Carrie Nation was responsible for legislation that required printing the alcoholic content on the label so that sick people would know whether they were getting enough alcohol to do them any good.
  Richard Armour, *It All Started With Columbus*.

There came to our town an old pelican
Whose manner was scarcely angelican:
  To a man who sold beer
  She said, 'Say, look here!
If you want me to save you from helican.'
  Ironquill (pseud.), in *The Capital* (Topeka).

Mrs. Nation thoroughly believes in her mission. She is a harmless paranoiac animated by a compelling obsession. She does not impress me as a fanatic. The word 'zealot' best describes her. Dumpy in figure, plain but neat in dress, the possessor of a soft, melodious voice, she seems to be the incarnation of motherly benevolence.
  Shannon Mountjoy, in *Muskogee Times-Democrat*, 10 November 1907.

She keeps telling me that she smashes saloons because her first husband died of drink, and that she is afraid I will do the same. She says she has visions from the Lord, and I have often found her beside the bed at night talking to an unseen being who she claimed was Jesus Christ.
  David Nation, in Herbert Asbury, *Carry Nation*.

NEDHAM, MARCHAMONT

1620–78 Journalist

Here lies *Britannicus*, Hell's barking cur,
That son of Belial who kept damned stir:
And every Munday spent his stock of spleen
In venomous railing on the King and Queen
Who, though they both in goodness may forgive him
Yet, (for his safety) we'll in hell receive him.
  Anon., *Mercurius Britannicus His Welcome to Hell*.

[He] had very great influence upon numbers of inconsiderable persons, such who have a strange presumption that all must needs be true that is in print. He was then the *Goliath* of the *Philistines*, the great Champion of the late Usurper, whose pen in comparison to others was like a weavers beam. . . . He was a person endowed with quick natural parts, was a good humantian Poet and boon Droll: and had he been constant to his Cavaleering principles he would have been loved by, and admired, of all; but being mercenary, and valuing money and sordid interest, rather than conscience, friendship, or love to his Prince, was much hated by the Royal Party to his last, and many cannot yet endure to hear him spoken of.
  Anthony à Wood, *Athenae Oxonienses*.

See also William Prynne

NELSON, HORATIO, VISCOUNT

1758–1805 Admiral

Before this time tomorrow I shall have gained a peerage, or Westminster Abbey.
  On himself, shortly before the Battle of the Nile, August 1798, in Robert Southey, *Life of Nelson*.

Nelson for ever — any time
Am I his to command in prose or rhyme!

Give me of Nelson only a touch,
And I save it, be it little or much:
Here's one our Captain gives, and so
Down at the word, by George, shall it go!
They say that at Greenwich they point the beholder
To Nelson's coat, 'still with tar on the shoulder:
'For he used to lean with one shoulder digging,
'Jigging, as it were, and zig-zag-zigging
'Up against the mizzen-rigging!'
    Robert Browning, *Nationality in Drinks.*

He brought heroism into the line of duty.
    Joseph Conrad, in Robert Debs Heinl Jr, *The Dictionary of Military and Naval Quotations.*

Rarely has a man been more favored in the hour of his appearing, never one so fortunate in the moment of his death.
    Alfred Thayer Mahan, *The Life of Nelson.*

He leads: we hear our Seaman's call
    In the roll of battles won;
For he is Britain's Admiral
    Till the setting of her sun.
    George Meredith, *Trafalgar Day.*

The love she [Lady Hamilton] makes to Nelson is not only ridiculous, but disgusting: not only the rooms, but the whole house, staircase and all, are covered with nothing but pictures of her and him, of all sizes and sorts, and representations of his naval actions, coats-of-arms, pieces of plate in his honour, the flag-staff of L'Orient, &c. — an excess of vanity which counteracts its purpose. If it was Lady Hamilton's house there might be a pretence for it; to make his own house a meer looking-glass to view himself all day is bad taste.
    Lord Minto, Letter to Lady Minto, March 1802.

'Do you know,' said he to Mr. Ferguson, 'what is shown on board the commander-in-chief? No. 39!' Mr. Ferguson asked what that meant? — 'Why, to leave off action! Now damn me if I do! You know, Foley', turning to the captain, 'I have only one eye, — I have a right to be blind sometimes,' — and then putting the glass to his blind eye, in that mood of mind which sports with bitterness, he exclaimed, 'I really do not see the signal!' Presently he exclaimed, 'Damn the signal! Keep mine for closer battle flying! That's the way I answer such signals. Nail mine to the mast!'
    Robert Southey, on the Battle of Copenhagen, *Life of Nelson.*

It was Nelson's maxim, that, to negotiate with effect, force should be at hand, and in a situation to act.
    Ibid.

Presently, calling [Captain] Hardy back, he said to him, in a low voice, 'Don't throw me overboard'; and he desired that he might be buried by his parents, unless it should please the king to order otherwise. Then, reverting to his private feelings: 'Take care of my dear Lady Hamilton, Hardy; take care of poor Lady Hamilton. — Kiss me, Hardy,' said he. Hardy knelt down and kissed his cheek: and Nelson said, 'Now I am satisfied. Thank God, I have done my duty.'
    Ibid., describing Nelson's death at Trafalgar.

In his own country the king granted these honourable augmentations to his armourial ensign: a chief undulated, *argent*; thereon waves of the sea; from which a palm-tree issuant, between a disabled ship on the dexter, and a ruinous battery on the sinister, all proper; and for his crest, on a naval crown, *or*, the chelengk, or plume, presented to him by the Turk, with the motto *Palman qui meruit ferat.*
    Ibid., describing Nelson's acclaim after the Battle of the Nile.

Always in his element and always on his element.
    G. M. Trevelyan, *History of England.*

See also Daniel Defoe, Sir Francis Drake

NEVILLE, RICHARD, EARL OF WARWICK (THE KINGMAKER)

1428—71 Statesman

He should be thought of as the forerunner of Wolsey rather than as the successor of Robert of Belesme, or the Bohuns and Bigods. That the world remembers him as a turbulent noble is a misfortune. Such a view is only drawn from a hasty survey of the last three or four years of his life, when under desperate provocation he was driven to use for personal ends the vast feudal power that lay ready to his hand. If he had died in 1468, he would be remembered in history as an able soldier and statesman, who with singular perseverance and consistency devoted his life to consolidating England under the house of York.
    C. W. Oman, *Warwick the Kingmaker.*

NEWCASTLE, DUKE OF (THOMAS PELHAM-HOLLES)

1693—1768 Statesman

. . . the Duke of Newcastle . . . made his entry with as much alacrity and noise as usual, mightily out of breath though mightily in words, and in his hand a bundle of papers as big as his head and with little more in them.

Lord Hervey, in Lewis Namier, *Crossroads of Power*.

No man was so unmercifully satirised. But in truth he was himself a satire ready made. All that the art of a satirist does for other men, nature had done for him.

T. B. Macaulay, *Essays:* 'Horace Walpole's Letters'.

He was a living, moving, talking caricature. His gait was a shuffling trot, his utterance a rapid stutter; he was always in a hurry; he was never in time; he abounded in fulsome caresses and hysterical tears. His oratory resembled that of Justice Shallow. It was nonsense, effervescent in animal spirits and impertinence.

Ibid.

On Friday this august remnant of the Pelhams went to court for the first time. At the foot of the stairs he cried and sunk down: the yeomen of the guard were forced to drag him up under the arms. When the closet-door opened, he flung himself at his length at the King's feet, sobbed, and cried, 'God bless your Majesty! God preserve your Majesty!' and lay there howling and embracing the King's knees, with one foot extended, that my Lord Coventry . . . endeavouring to shut the door, caught his grace's foot, and made him roar out with pain.

Horace Walpole, Letter to Richard Bentley, 17 March 1754.

. . . Newcastle had nobody to attend him but Sir Edward Montagu, who kept pushing him all up the gallery. From thence he went into the hazard-room, and wriggled, and shuffled, and lisped, and winked, and spied. . . . You would have died to see Newcastle's pitiful and distressed figure — nobody went near him: he tried to flatter people, that were too busy to mind him; in short, he was quite disconcerted; his treachery used to be so sheathed in folly, that he was never out of countenance; but it is plain he grows old.

Horace Walpole, Letter to George Montagu, 26 April 1759.

Newcastle had two ruling passions, devotion to the Hanoverian succession and its instrument the Whig party, and a love of power, which to satisfy him, must be amply recognized, for it was not enough for him to pull the strings, if the puppets were not consciously dancing to his tune.

Basil Williams. *Carteret and Newcastle*.

NEWMAN, JOHN HENRY, CARDINAL

1801–90 Theologian

Point 4. I shall come back from Rome with a prestige, as if I had a blunderbuss in my pocket.

On himself, Personal memorandum, 15 January 1854.

From the age of fifteen, dogma has been the fundamental principle of my religion: I know no other religion; I cannot enter into the idea of any other sort of religion; religion, as a mere sentiment, is to me a dream and a mockery.

On himself, *History of my Religious Opinions*.

It's true these have been years of strife, but after all there's the Cardinal's Hat.

On himself, dying words, August 1890.

To me he seems to have been the most artificial man of our generation, full of ecclesiastical loves and hatred. Considering what he really was, it is wonderful what a space he has filled in the eyes of mankind. In speculation he was habitually untruthful and not much better in practice. His conscience had been taken out and the Church put in its place. Yet he was a man of genius, and a good man in the sense of being disinterested.

Benjamin Jowett, Letter to Margot Tennant, 22 May 1891.

It is remarkably interesting, it is like listening to the voice of one from the dead.

Cardinal Manning, comment on Newman's *Apologia pro Vita Sua*, 1864.

Poor Newman! He was a great hater!

Cardinal Manning, *circa* 1891, in Lytton Strachey, *Eminent Victorians*.

When Newman was a child he 'wished that he could believe the Arabian Nights were true.' When he came to be a man, his wish seems to have been granted.

Lytton Strachey, in *ibid*.

See also James Gibbons, Sir Thomas More

NEWTON, SIR ISAAC

1642–1727 Natural Philosopher, Mathematician

I don't know what I may seem to the world, but, as to myself, I seem to have been only like a boy playing on the sea shore, and diverting myself in now and then finding a smoother pebble or prettier shell

than ordinary, whilst the great ocean of truth lay all undiscovered before me.
    On himself, in Joseph Spence, *Anecdotes*.

Reason and Newton, they are quite two things:
For so the swallow and the sparrow sings,
Reason says Miracle, Newton says Doubt.
    William Blake, *You Don't Believe*.

That God is colouring Newton does show.
    William Blake, *To Venetian Artists*.

When Newton saw an apple fall, he found
    In that slight startle from his contemplation —
'Tis *said* (for I'll not answer above ground
    For any sage's creed or calculation) —
A mode of proving that the earth turned round
    In a most natural whirl, called 'gravitation';
And this is the soul mortal who could grapple,
Since Adam, with a fall, or with an apple.
    Lord Byron, *Don Juan*, canto x.

Newton *was* a great man, but you must excuse me if I think that it would take many Newtons to make one Milton.
    Samuel Taylor Coleridge, *Table Talk*.

        Newton, childlike sage!
Sagacious reader of the works of God.
    William Cowper, *The Task*.

Enough of this. Newton forgive me. You found the only way that, in your day, was at all possible for a man of the highest powers of intellect and creativity. The concepts that you created still dominate the way we think in physics, although we now know that they must be replaced by others farther removed from the sphere of immediate experience if we want to try for a more profound understanding of the way things are interrelated.
    Albert Einstein, *Autobiographical Notes*.

I also saw Sir Isaac Newtons (now made knight at the Queenes entertaining at Oxon) the burning Glasse which dos such wonders as that of the K. of France which cost so much, dos not come-neere, it penetrating Cast Iron of all Thicknesse, vitrifies Brick, mealts all sorts of mettals in a moment.
    John Evelyn, Diary, 22 April 1705.

Mr. Newton's approbation is more to me than the cry of all the ignorant in the world.
    John Flamsteed, attributed.

The most interesting part of the Life of Newton is his prefigurative boyhood; his unceasing fabrication of mills and traps; the speed, swift as light, with which he recovered lost ground; and the Herculean

grasp of mind by which he only once perused an abstruse volume and held its contents firm as a vice.
    T. D. Fosbroke, *Biographical Anecdotes of Dr. Jenner*.

One trait of his early disposition is told of him: he had then a rude method of measuring the force of the wind blowing against him, by observing how much further he could leap in the direction of the wind, or blowing on his back, than he could leap the contrary way, or opposed to the wind; an early mark of his original infantine genius.
    William Hutton, *Philosophical and Mathematical Dictionary*.

Must a theory of motion explain the cause of the attractive forces between particles of matter or may it simply note the existence of such forces? Newton's dynamics was widely rejected because, unlike both Aristotle's and Descartes's theories, it implied the latter answer to the question. When Newton's theory had been accepted, a question was therefore banished from science. That question, however, was one that general relativity may proudly claim to have solved.
    Thomas Kuhn, *The Structure of Scientific Revolutions*.

Anecdote of Newton, showing his extreme absence; inviting a friend to dinner and forgetting it: the friend arriving, and finding the philosopher in a fit of abstraction. Dinner brought up for *one*: the friend (without disturbing Newton) sitting down and dispatching it, and Newton, after recovering from his reverie, looking at the empty dishes and saying, 'Well really, if it wasn't for the proof before my eyes, I could have sworn that I had not yet dined'.
    Thomas Moore, Diary, 18 January 1828.

At some seldom times when he designed to dine in hall, would turn to the left hand and go out into the street, when making a stop he found his mistake, would hastily turn back, and then sometimes instead of going into hall, return to his chamber again.
    Humphrey Newton, Letter to John Conduit, 1728.

Sir Isaac had a favourite little dog, named Diamond: this animal ranged uncontrolled through his study; and once, during his master's absence, overturned a lighted candle, which fell upon a manuscript that he had laboured many years to complete — it was reduced to ashes! the immortal Newton merely exclaimed, 'Oh, Diamond! Diamond! thou little knowest the mischief thou hast done'.
    M. Noble, *A Biographical History of England*.

Nature and Nature's laws lay hid in Night:
God said, Let Newton be! and all was light.
   Alexander Pope, *Epitaph for Sir Isaac Newton.*

Sir Isaac Newton, though so deep in Algebra and
Fluxions, could not readily make up a common
account: and, when he was Master of the Mint, used
to get somebody to make up his accounts for him.
   Alexander Pope, in Joseph Spence, *Anecdotes.*

What I have known with respect to myself, has
tended much to lessen both my admiration, and my
contempt, of others. Could we have entered into the
mind of Sir Isaac Newton, and have traced all the
steps by which he produced his great works, we
might see nothing very extraordinary in the process.
   Joseph Priestley, *Memoirs written by Himself.*

The second occupant of the Lucasian chair was
Newton. There is hardly a branch of modern mathematics, which cannot be traced back to him, and of
which he did not revolutionize the treatment; and
in the opinion of the greatest mathematicians of
subsequent times — Lagrange, Laplace, and Gauss —
his genius stands out without an equal in the whole
history of mathematics.
   W. W. Rouse Ball, *A History of the Study of
   Mathematics at Cambridge.*

He was thus able to ennunciate his law of universal
gravitation: 'Every body attracts every other with a
force directly proportional to the product of their
masses and inversely proportional to the square of
the distance between them'. From this formula he
was able to deduce everything in planetary theory:
the motions of the planets and their satellites, the
orbits of comets, the tides. It appeared later that
even the minute departures from elliptical orbits on
the part of the planets were deducible from Newton's law. The triumph was so complete that Newton was in danger of becoming another Aristotle,
and imposing an insuperable barrier to progress. In
England, it was not till a century after his death that
men freed themselves from his authority sufficiently
to do important original work in the subjects of
which he had treated.
   Bertrand Russell, *History of Western Philosophy.*

Newton, when at school, stood at the bottom of the
lowermost form but one. The boy above Newton
having kicked him, the dunce showed his pluck by
challenging him to a fight, and beat him. Then he
set to work with a will, and determined also to van-
quish his antagonist as a scholar, which he did, rising
to the top of his class.
   Samuel Smiles, *Self-help.*

Pray, Sir Isaac, may I ask you what is your opinion

of the immortality of the soul? — [asked Signora
Antonio Cocchi].
   — Madam, I'm an experimental Philosopher.
   Joseph Spence, *Anecdotes.*

Newton and Cuvier lowered themselves when the
one accepted an idle knighthood, and the other became a baron of the empire.
   Herbert Spencer, in L. Huxley, *Life and Letters
   Of Thomas Henry Huxley.*

Have ye not listened while he bound the Suns
And planets to their spheres? th'unequal task
Of human-kind till then. Oft had they roll'd
O'er erring man the year, and oft disgraced
The pride of Schools, before their course was
                                    known
Full in its causes and effects to him,
All piercing sage! who sat not down and dream'd
Romantic schemes, defended by the din
Of specious words, and tyranny of names;
But, bidding his amazing mind attend,
And with heroic patience years on years
Deep-searching, saw at last the System dawn,
And shine, of all his race, on him alone.
   James Thomson, *To The Memory of Sir Isaac
   Newton.*

Sir Isaac Newton, they say, was so absorbed in his
pursuits, as to be something of a changeling in
worldly matters; and when he descended to earth
and conjecture he was no phenomenon.
   Horace Walpole, Letter to the Countess of
   Upper Ossory, 6 September 1787.

I do not dislike the French from the vulgar antipathy between neighbouring nations, but for their
insolent and unfounded airs of superiority. In arms
we have almost always outshone them: and till they
have excelled Newton, and come near to Shakespeare, pre-eminence in genius must remain with us.
   Horace Walpole, Letter to Hannah More, 14
   October 1787.

One of Sir I. Newton's philosophical friends abroad
had sent him a curious prism, which was taken to
the Custom-house, and was at that time a scarce
commodity in this kingdom. Sir Isaac, laying claim
to it, was asked by the officers what the value of
the glass was, that they might accordingly regulate
the duty. The great Newton, whose business was
more with the universe than with duties and draw-
backs, and who rated the prism according to his
own idea of its use and excellence, answered, 'That
the value was so great that he could not ascertain it'.
Being again pressed to set some fixed estimate upon
it, he persisted in his reply, 'That he could not say
what it was worth, for that the value was in-

estimable'. The honest Custom-house officers accordingly took him at his word, and made him pay a most exorbitant duty for the prism, which he might have taken away upon only paying a rate according to the weight of the glass!

C. R. Weld, *A History of the Royal Society.*

The pathetic desire of mankind to find themselves starting from an intellectual basis which is clear, distinct, and certain, is illustrated by Newton's boast, *hypotheses non fingo* [I do not frame hypotheses], at the same time when he enunciated his law of universal gravitation. This law states that every particle of matter attracts every other particle of matter; though at the moment of enunciation only planets and heavenly bodies had been observed to attract 'particles of matter'.

Alfred North Whitehead, *The Function of Reason.*

The antechapel where the statue stood
Of Newton with his prism and silent face,
The marble index of a mind forever
Voyaging through strange seas of thought alone.
William Wordsworth, *The Prelude*, book 30.

See also John C. Calhoun, Charles Darwin, Michael Faraday, Benjamin Franklin, Edmund Halley, John Hunter, Lord Rutherford, J. M. W. Turner, George Washington

NIEBUHR, REINHOLD

1892–1971 Theologian

Hawk-nosed and saturnine, Reinhold Niebuhr is, nevertheless, a cheerful and gracious (though conversationally explosive) man. An intellectual's intellectual, he nevertheless lectures and preaches with the angular arm-swinging of a revivalist.

Anon., in *Time*, 8 March 1948.

A scholar whose writing often taxes the understanding.

Anon., in *ibid.*, 19 February 1951.

The leading liberal opponent of pacificism.

James Loeb, in *ibid.*, 8 March 1948.

The troubler of my peace.

Dr William Temple, in *ibid.*, 8 March 1948.

NIGHTINGALE, FLORENCE

1820–1910 Hospital Reformer

What a comfort it was to see her pass. She would speak to one, and nod and smile to as many more; but she could not do it to all you know. We lay there by the hundreds; but we could kiss her shadow as it fell and lay our heads on the pillow again content.

A patient in the Crimean War, in Cecil Woodham-Smith, *Florence Nightingale.*

There was a great deal of romantic feeling about you 23 years ago when you came home from the Crimea (I really believe that you might have been a Duchess if you had played your cards better!). And now you work on in silence, and nobody knows how many lives are saved by your nurses in hospitals (you have introduced a new era in nursing): how many thousand soldiers who would have fallen victims to bad air, bad drainage and ventilation, are now alive owing to your forethought and diligence; how many natives of India (they might be counted probably by hundreds of thousands) in this generation and in generations to come have been preserved from famine, oppression and the load of debt by the energy of a sick lady who can scarcely rise from her bed. . . . Like Dr. Pusey you are a Myth in your own lifetime. Do you know that there are thousands of girls about the age of 18 to 23 named after you? Everyone has heard of you and has a sweet association with your name.

Benjamin Jowett, Letter to Florence Nightingale, December 1879.

If you prefer to do your work rather by moving the hidden springs than by allowing yourself to be known to the world as doing what you really do, it is not for me to make any observations on this preference (inasmuch as I am bound to presume you have good reasons for it) other than to say that I much regret that this preference is so very general among women.

John Stuart Mill, Letter to Florence Nightingale, December 1867.

Miss Nightingale did inspire awe, not because one felt afraid of her *per se*, but because the very essence of *Truth* seemed to emanate from her, and because of her perfect fearlessness in telling it.

William Richmond, in *The Richmond Papers.*

Yet her conception of God was certainly not orthodox. She felt towards Him as she might have felt towards a glorified sanitary engineer; and in some of her speculations she seems hardly to distinguish between the Deity and the Drains.

Lytton Strachey, *Eminent Victorians.*

You are, I know, well aware of the high sense I entertain of the Christian devotion which you have displayed during this great and bloody war, and I need hardly repeat to you how warm my admiration is for your services, which are fully equal to those of my dear and brave soldiers, whose sufferings·you have had the *privilege* of alleviating in so merciful a manner. I am, however, anxious of marking my feelings in a manner which I trust will be agreeable to you, and therefore send you with this letter a brooch, the form and emblems of which commemorate your great and blessed work, and which, I hope, you will wear as a mark of the high approbation of your Sovereign!

Queen Victoria, Letter to Florence Nightingale, January 1856.

NOLLEKENS, JOSEPH

1737—1823 Sculptor

Nollekens was much superior to any other, in knowledge of the figure & in execution. He had not much mind, but great experience.

N. Marchant, in Joseph Farington, Diary, April 1806.

To the beauties of the immortal Shakespeare he was absolutely insensible, nor did he ever visit the theatre when his plays were performed; though he was actively alive to a pantomime, and frequently spoke of the capital and curious tricks in Harlequin Sorcerer. He also recollected with pleasure Mr. Rich's wonderful and singular power of scratching his ear with his foot like a dog; and the street-exhibition of Punch and his wife delighted him beyond expression.

J. T. Smith, *Nollekens and His Times*

NORTH, FREDERICK, EARL OF GUILFORD

1732—92 Prime Minister

I was the creature of Parliament in my rise; when I fell I was its victim. I came among you without connexion. It was here I was first known; you raised me up; you pulled me down. I have been the creature of your opinion and your power, and the history of my political life is one proof which will stand against and overturn a thousand wild assertions, that there is a corrupt influence in the Crown which destroys the independence of this House.

On himself, in W. Baring Pemberton, *Lord North*.

Heber told me a capital jest of Frederick North at Algiers. North asked the Dey permission to see his women. After some parley the Dey said, 'He is so ugly, let him see them all'.

Lord Broughton, *Recollections of a Long Life*.

He was a man of admirable parts, of general knowledge, of versatile understanding, fitted for every sort of business, of infinite wit and pleasantry, of a delightful temper, and with a mind most perfectly disinterested; but it would be ·only to degrade myself by a weak adulation, and not to honour the memory of a great man, to deny that he wanted something of the vigilance and spirit of command that the time required.

Edmund Burke, in Alan Lloyd, *The Wickedest Age*.

When Barré stern, with accents deep,
Calls up Lord North and murders sleep,
And if his Lordship rise to speak,
Then wit and argument awake.

David Garrick, in Alan Valentine, *Lord North*.

Were I ambitious of any other Patron than the Public, I would inscribe this work to a statesman, who, in a long, a stirring, and at length an unfortunate administration, had many political opponents, almost without a personal enemy; who has retained, in his fall from power, many faithful and disinterested friends; and who, under the pressure of severe infirmity, enjoys the lively vigour of his mind and the felicity of his incomparable temper. Lord North will permit me to express the feelings of friendship in the language of truth.

Edward Gibbon, Dedication prefixed to *The Decline and Fall of the Roman Empire*.

The noble lord in the blue ribbon is actuated in all his measures by the most disinterested zeal for his country. He wants only one quality to make him a great and distinguished statesman; I mean a more despotic and commanding temper.

Lord Melville, in Nathaniel Wraxall, *Memoirs*.

LORD NORTH told Charles Fox, as they both
                sipp'd their broth,
  I know by Britannia's queer looks,
That the wench is offended such foes should unite,
  And will scratch us both *out of her books*.
Thús Fox, in reply, damn it, North, never mind,
  Should she curse our new creed of belief,
She may black that page where our names have long
                stood,
  For we both must *turn o'er a new leaf*.

Anthony Pasquin (John Williams), *An Epigram Written at the time of the Coalition between Lord North and Charles Fox.*

Lord North was a coarse and heavy man, with a wide mouth, thick lips, and puffy cheeks, which seemed typical of his policy.

J. H. Rose, in Sir Charles Petrie, *The Four Georges.*

Two large prominent eyes that rolled about to no purpose (for he was utterly short-sighted), a wide mouth, thick lips and inflated visage, gave him the air of a blind trumpeter. A deep untuneable voice, which, instead of modulating, he enforced with unnecessary pomp, a total neglect of his person, and ignorance of every civil attention, disgusted all who judge by appearance, or without their approbation till it is courted. But within that rude casket were enclosed many useful talents. . . . What he did, he did without a mask, and was not delicate in choosing his means.

Horace Walpole, *Memoirs*.

He had neither system nor principles nor shame; sought neither the favour of the Crown or of the people, but enjoyed the good luck of fortune with a gluttonous Epicurism that was equally careless of glory or disgrace.

Ibid.

He possessed a classic mind, full of information, and always enlivened by wit, as well as sweetened by good humour.

Nathaniel Wraxall, *Memoirs*.

NORTHCLIFFE, VISCOUNT (ALFRED CHARLES WILLIAM HARMSWORTH)

1865–1922 Journalist, Newspaper Proprietor

Have you heard? The Prime Minister has resigned and Northcliffe has sent for the King.

Anon., popular saying, 1919, in Hamilton Fyfe, *Northcliffe*.

. . . the greatest figure who ever strode down Fleet St.

Lord Beaverbrook, *Politicians and the War*.

The late Lord Northcliffe would not print anything in criticism of himself. He would always print the words of praise. Even from the publicity point of view, he was wrong.

Lord Beaverbrook, Letter to Tom Driberg, 3 December 1952.

The democracy knows you as the poisoner of the streams of human intercourse, the fermenter of war, the preacher of hate, the unscrupulous enemy of human society.

A. G. Gardner, *Open Letter to Northcliffe*, December 1914.

Northcliffe: the trouble with you, Shaw, is that you look as if there were a famine in the land. *Shaw*: The trouble with you, Northcliffe, is that you look as if you were the cause of it.

George Bernard Shaw, attributed, in *The Penguin Modern Dictionary of Quotations*.

He is an extraordinarily commonplace man, with a very good brain for business. He is rather dull to talk to, very vain, but kind-hearted I should say. Nothing original. Those are the men that get on.

Frances Stevenson, Diary, 19 May 1917.

He aspired to power instead of influence, and as a result forfeited both.

A. J. P. Taylor, *English History, 1914–1945*.

See also Lord Kitchener

NORTON, CHARLES ELIOT

1827–1908 Editor, Teacher, Author

Charles Eliot Norton had the moral and spiritual qualities, of a stoic kind, which are possible without the benefits of revealed religion. And living as he did in a non-Christian society, and in a world which, as he saw it on both sides of the Atlantic, showed signs of decay, he maintained the standards of the humanism that he knew.

T. S. Eliot, in Kermit Vanderbilt, *Charles Eliot Norton*.

He was an idealist whom his strong common sense bound to daily duty. With the dialectic of despair which many mistakenly imagined was his working hypothesis, he had a practical wisdom which was radiant with welcome for any good thing done or said.

William Dean Howells, 'Charles Eliot Norton', in *North American Review*, December 1912.

The great thing, whatever turn we take, is to find before us perspectives and to have a weight to them; in accordance with which wisdom the world he lived in received for long no firmer nor more gallant and generous impress than that of Charles Eliot Norton.

Henry James, *Notes on Novelists*.

He was a man of the highest natural gifts, in their kind; observant and critical rather than imaginative, but with an all-persuading sympathy and sensibility, absolutely free from envy, ambition, or covetousness: a scholar from his cradle, not only now a *man* of the world, but a *gentleman* of the world.

John Ruskin, in Kermit Vanderbilt, *Charles Eliot Norton*.

And to that height illumined of the mind
He calls us still by the familiar way,

Leaving the sodden tracks of life behind,
Befogged in failure, chilled with love's decay —
Showing us, as the night-mists upward wind,
How on the heights is day and still more day.
    Edith Wharton, *For Professor Norton's Eightieth Birthday.*

NOVELLO, IVOR (DAVID IVOR DAVIES)

1893—1951 Actor, Composer

It is time that some official recognition were shown of his achievement in keeping the British flag flying over Ruritania.
    Anon., in *Evening Standard*, 1951.

It was a shock to discover that Ivor Novello was addicted to Nescafé.
    Gabriele Annan, Review of Sandy Wilson's *Ivor in Times Literary Supplement*, 19 December 1975.

I lift my hat to Mr Novello. He can wade through tosh with the straightest face: the tongue never visibly approaches the cheek. Both as actor and as author he can pursue adventures too preposterous even for the films and do it with that solemn fixity of purpose which romantic melodrama inexorably demands.
    Ivor Brown, in *Observer*, 1935.

My image of this romantic handsome youth who had composed 'Keep the home fires burning' drooped and died and lay in the gutter between the tramlines and the kerb. The reason for this was that I had caught him in a completely 'off' moment. He was not sitting at a grand piano. He was not in naval uniform. The eager Galahad expression which distinguished every photograph of him was lacking. His face was yellow, and he had omitted to shave owing to a morning rehearsal. He was wearing an odd overcoat with an Astrakhan collar, and a degraded brown hat, and if he had suddenly produced a violin from somewhere and played the 'Barcarole' from *The Tales of Hoffmann*, I should have given him threepence from sheer pity.
    Noël Coward, *Present Indicative.*

He could make that poker funny, but I really can't tell you how.
    Zena Dare, in Sandy Wilson, *Ivor.*

The funeral was like a Coronation — the streets were lined with crowds all the way. I looked out of the car window and said, 'Look who's standing there!' It was Lady Churchill.
    Phyllis Monkman, in *ibid.*

Mr Novello plays the King with all the assurance of a man who has gauged public taste down to the last emotional millimetre.
    Milton Shulman, in *Evening Standard*, reviewing *King's Rhapsody*, 1949.

NOVELLO, VINCENT

1781—1861 Editor, Composer, Organist

Vincent, you, who with like mastery
Can chase the notes with fluttering finger-tips
Like fairies down a hill hurrying their trips,
Or sway the organ with firm royalty;
Why stop ye on the road?
    Leigh Hunt, *Sonnet to Henry Robertson, John Gattie and Vincent Novello, Not Keeping their Appointed Hour.*

But when this master of the spell, not content to have laid a soul prostrate, goes on, in his power, to inflict more bliss than lies in her capacity to receive, — impatient to overcome her 'earthly' with his 'heavenly,' — still pouring in, for protracted hours, fresh waves and fresh from the sea of sound, or from that inexhausted *German* ocean, above which, in triumphant progress, dolphin-seated, ride those Arions *Haydn* and *Mozart*, with their attendant Tritons, *Bach*, *Beethoven*, and a countless tribe, whom to attempt to reckon up would but plunge me again in the deeps, — I stagger under the weight of harmony, reeling to and fro at my wits' end; — clouds, as of frankincense, oppress me — priests, altars, censers, dazzle before me — the genius of *his* religion hath me in her toils — a shadowy triple tiara invests the brow of my friend, late so naked, so ingenuous — he is Pope, — and by him sits, like as in the anomaly of dreams, a she-Pope too, — tri-coroneted like himself! — I am converted, and yet a Protestant; — at once *malleus hereticorum*, and myself grand heresiarch: or three heresies centre in my person: — I am Marcion, Elbion, and Cerinthus — Gog and Magog — what not? — till the coming in of the friendly supper-tray dissipates the figment, and a draught of true Lutheran beer (in which chiefly my friend shows himself no bigot) at once reconciles me to the rationalities of a purer faith; and restores to me the genuine unterrifying aspects of my pleasant-countenanced host and hostess.
    Charles Lamb, *Essays of Elia*, 'A Chapter on Ears'.

O

OAKLEY, ANNIE (PHOEBE MOZEE)

1860–1926 Sharp shooter

Little Sure-Shot.
  Sitting Bull's nickname for Oakley.

OATES, LAWRENCE EDWARD GRACE

1880–1912 Antarctic Explorer

I am just going outside, and may be some time.
  On himself, Last Message, in R. F. Scott,
  Antarctic Diary, 16 March 1912.

OATES, TITUS

1649–1705 Perjurer

As I'm informed on Monday last you sat
As dismal as a melancholy cat,
Folding your arms, and pulling down your hat
Over your eyes and groaning in a chair,
As if you did for God knows what despair.
Fye, Doctor, fye! You know it is a folly,
Thus to submit and yield to melancholy.
  Thomas Brown, *Advice to Dr. Oates. . . . When
  a Prisoner in the King's Bench.*

What need you care whose dunghill, Sir, you shit
                                            on!
Those who take up the sword for G--- must fight
                                            on.
But if your sadness does proceed from fear
Of being mounted on a *three-legged mare*
And (in a *line*) to preach a sermon there;
Well may you melancholy be and vex,
Because the jade does always break the necks
Of those that ride upon her. . . .
  Ibid.

A comical passage happen'd at the *Commons*, which
I think very well worth sending you: the Doctor
going thither for a licence, two scurvy questions
were asked him: The first was, Whether he would
have a licence to marry a boy or a girl? The second,

whether he would have a licence for *behind*, or
before?
  Thomas Brown, *The Widow's Wedding, or a True
  Account of Doctor Oates's Marriage.*

The Articles of Marriage were as follows: Imprimis,
the Doctor promises, *in verba Sacerdotis*, never to
keep a male-servant in his house under sixty, and to
hang up a picture of the destruction of *Sodom* in
his bedchamber; . . . *Item* The Doctor promises that
he will never offer to attack, either in bed or couch,
joint-stool or table, the body of the aforesaid *Mrs.
Margaret Wells, a parte post*, but to comfort,
refresh, and relieve her *a parte ante*, giving the aforesaid *Mrs. Margaret Wells*, in case he offend after that
manner, full leave to make herself amends *before*, as
she pleases. As also on a second trespass, to burn his
peace-maker: However with this proviso, that whenever the aforesaid *Mrs. Margaret Wells* happens to be
under the dominion of the moon, that is to say,
whenever it is term-time with the aforesaid *Mrs.
Margaret Wells*, then the above-mentioned Doctor
shall have full power, liberty and authority, to enter
the *Westminster-Hall* of her body at which door he
pleases.
  Ibid.

Malchus, a puny Levite, void of sense
And grace, but stuff'd with noise and impudence,
Was his prime tool — so venomous a brute
That every place he liv'd in spew'd him out.
Lies in his mouth, and malice in his heart
By nature grew, and were improv'd by art.
Mischief his pleasure was, and all his joy
To see his thriving calumny destroy
Those whom his double heart and forked tongue
Surer than viper's teeth to death had stung.
  John Caryll, *Naboth's Vineyard.*

Sunk were his Eyes, his Voice was harsh and loud,
Sure signe he neither Cholerick was, nor Proud:
His long Chin prov'd his Wit; his Saint-like Grace
A Church Vermilion, and a *Moses*'s Face.
His Memory miraculously great,
Could Plots, exceeding mans belief, repeat;
Which therefore cannot be accounted Lies,
For humane Wit could never such devise.
Some future Truths are mingled in his Book;
But where the Witness fail'd, the Prophet spoke.
  John Dryden, *Absalom and Achitophel.*

'Tis Oates, bare Oates, which is become
The health of England, bane of Rome
And wonder of all Christendom.
And therefore Oates has well deserved
From musty barn to be preferr'd
And now in Royal Court preserv'd;
That like Hesperian fruit Oates may
Be watched and guarded night and day;
Which is but just retaliation
For having guarded a whole nation.
    Richard Duke, *A Paneygeric upon Oates*.

For my part, I do looke on *Oates* as a vaine, insolent man, puff'd up, with the favour of the Commons, for having discovered something realy true; as more especialy detecting the dangerous intrigue of Coleman, proved out of his owne letters; & of a general designe, which the Jesuiticall party of the Papists ever had, & still have to ruine the Church of England; but that he was trusted with those great secrets he pretended, or had any solid ground for what he accused divers noble men of, I have many reasons to induce my contrary beliefs.
    John Evelyn, Diary, 18 July 1679.

Oates, who had but two days before ben pilloried at severall places, & whip't at the Carts tails from Newgate to Algate; was this day placed in a sledge (being not able to go by reason of his so late scourging) & dragd from Prison to Tyburn, & whip'd againe all the way, which some thought to be very severe and extraordinary; but in case he were gilty of the perjuries, & so of the death of many innocents, as I feare he was; his punishment was but what he well deserv'd: I chanc'd to pass in my Coach just as Execution was doing on him: *A strange revolution*.
    Ibid., 22 May 1685.

Such a mans Testimonie should not be taken against the life of a Dog.
    At the trial of Lord Stafford, in *ibid.*,
    6 December 1680.

The fact that Oates was an active and practising homosexual has always been known, but historians have evaded one obvious conclusion; that this explains the astonishing ease with which he was admitted to certain Catholic circles which one would have supposed barred to a disreputable Anglican clergyman with heterodox leanings.
    J. P. Kenyon, *The Popish Plot*.

Whene'er it swore, to prove the oaths were true
Out of its mouth at random halters flew.
Round some unwary neck, by magic thrown
Though still the cunning Devil sav'd its own.
    Thomas Otway, Prologue to Aphra Behn, *City Heiress*.

By birth he was an Anabaptist, by prudence a clergyman, by profession a perjurer.
    John Pollock, *The Popish Plot*.

See also Lord Danby

OCKHAM, WILLIAM
—d. 1349? Philosopher

Occam is best known for a maxim which is not to be found in his works, but has acquired the name of 'Occam's razor'. This maxim says: 'Entities are not to be multiplied without necessity.' Although he did not say this, he said something which has much the same effect, namely: 'It is vain to do with more what can be done with fewer.' That is to say, if everything in some science can be interpreted without assuming this or that hypothetical entity, there is no ground for assuming it. I have myself found this is a most fruitful principle in logical analysis.
    Bertrand Russell, *History of Western Philosophy*.

O'CONNELL, DANIEL
1775—1847 Politician

I can drive a coach and six through any act of Parliament.
    On himself, in Edward Latham, *Famous Sayings*.

We do not reckon Mr O'Connell among the sincere Repealers. He knows too much to believe that repeal can be obtained except by force, and he has too much to lose, to desire a sanguinary contest in which power would accompany not the qualities which he possesses, popular eloquence and legal knowledge, but those which he wants, military skill and indifference to danger.
    Anon., in *Edinburgh Review*, January 1844.

Generally, an agitator is a rough man of the O'Connell type, who says anything himself, and lets others say anything. You 'peg into me and I will peg into you, and let us see which will win,' is his motto.
    Walter Bagehot, 1865, *Biographical Studies*.

His fame blazed like a straw bonfire, and has left behind it scarce a shovelful of ashes. Never any public man had it in his power to do so much good for his country, nor was there ever one who accomplished so little.
    J. A. Froude, *Short Studies*.

He possessed to the highest degree the eloquence of a demagogue, but he possessed also the sagacity

of a statesman and the independence of a patriot . . . the noblest instance of his moderation is furnished by his constant denunciations of rebellion . . . he exhausted all his eloquence in contrasting the advantages of constitutional agitation with the horrors of war; he exhibited at all times . . . an almost Quaker detestation of force.
W. E. H. Lecky, *The Leaders of Public Opinion in Ireland.*

Once to my sight the giant thus was given:
Walled by wide air, and roofed by boundless heaven,
Beneath his feet the human ocean lay,
And wave on wave flowed into space away.
Methought no clarion could have sent its sound
Even to the centre of the hosts around;
But, as I thought, rose the sonorous swell
As from some church tower swings the silvery bell.
Aloft and clear, from airy tide to tide
It glided, easy as a bird may glide;
To the last verge of that vast audience sent,
It played with each wild passion as it went;
Now stirred the uproar, now the murmur stilled,
With sobs or laughter answered as it willed.
Then did I know what spells of infinite choice,
To rouse or lull hath the sweet human voice;
Then did I seem to seize the sudden clue
To that grand troublous Life Antique — to view,
Under the rockstand of Demosthenes,
Mutable Athens heave her noisy seas.
Lord Lytton, on O'Connell's oratory in the House of Commons, in G. W. E. Russell, *Collections and Recollections.*

He was a lawyer; and never could come to the point of denying and defying all British law. He was a Catholic . . . and would not see that the Church had ever been the enemy of Irish Freedom. He was an aristocrat . . . and the name of a Republic was odious to him . . . his success as a Catholic Agitator ruined both him and his country . . . by eternally half-unsheathing a visionary sword, which friends and foes alike knew to be a phantom. . . .
John Mitchel, *Jail Journal.*

The only way to deal with such a man as O'Connell is to hang him up and erect a statue to him under the gallows.
Sydney Smith, *Table-talk.*

See also George III, George IV

O'CONNOR, (MARY) FLANNERY

1925—64 Author

Flannery O'Connor's characters are almost all fana-

tic, suffering from what we might diagnose as an acute sense of dislocation of place.
Melvin J. Friedman, 'Flannery O'Connor: Another Legend in Southern Fiction', in Robert E. Reiter ed., *Flannery O'Connor.*

What we can know for sure is that Flannery O'Connor created a remarkable art, unique in its time. Unlike any Southern writer before her, she wrote in praise of ice in the blood.
Josephine Hendin, *The World of Flannery O'Connor.*

O'Connor became more and more the pure poet of the Misfit, the oppressed, the psychic cripple, the freak — of all of those who are martyred by silent fury and redeemed through violence.
Ibid.

O'Connor wrote about what she knew best: what it means to be a living contradiction. For her it meant an eternal cheeriness and loathing for life; graciousness and fear of human contact, acquiescence and enduring fury.
Ibid.

ODETS, CLIFFORD

1906—63 Playwright

If you have acquired by now the distressing sense that I am situating myself historically, correct! Talent should be respected.
On himself, in the preface of *Six Plays by Clifford Odets.*

My only interest in the theatre is to write plays for a collection like the Group Theatre, a collective of writers, directors, actors and other theatre craftsmen who form and work out a collective technique to express a collective ideology.
On himself, in Fred B. Millet, *Contemporary American Authors.*

I believe in the vast potentialities of mankind . . . I want to find out how mankind can be helped out of the animal kingdom into the clear sweet air.
On himself, Letter to John Mason Brown, 1935.

Honestly, Clifford, unless you turn out to be a genius, no one will ever speak to you.
Stella Adler, in Gerald Weales, *Clifford Odets, Playwright.*

He hits hard, and below the belt if need be. But at least he hits.
John Mason Brown, *Dramatis Personae.*

. . . the leading proletarian playwright, although he has been less concerned with the problems of the worker than with the 'fraud' of middle-class civilization, deprived by economic insecurity of its former status and becoming aware that its cherished ideals no longer correspond to realities.

James D. Hart, *The Oxford Companion to American Literature.*

Both in his personal life and in his plays, Odets grappled with the true American tragedy, the widespread, highly contagious worship of a tawdry success measured in terms of money and status. Odets' dramas constituted an open wrestling match with something seldom displayed on our stages, conscience.

Emony Lewis, *Stages.*

Now the point I am trying to make is not that Clifford Odets is a good playwright nor that his work is better than anything else in New York. The first fact is pretty widely known and the second is obvious.

Archibald MacLeish, in Gerald Weales, *Clifford Odets, Playwright.*

In the drama the shrillest horn-blower of them all is Clifford Odets. Mr Odets is certainly determined not to let die the legend that he is the White Hope of the American theatre. Not even by living in Hollywood and receiving the shekels of the mammon of movies, has daunted his faith in himself. And by blowing his horn hard enough he has convinced a few otherwise sensible critics that the Hope has become a reality.

Grenville Vernon, in *ibid.*

ODO OF BAYEUX, EARL OF KENT

—d. 1097 Statesman

. . . he was governor of all England, under the king, after the death of William Fitz-Osborn. He had wonderful skill in accumulating treasure; possessed extreme craft in dissembling; so that, though absent, yet, stuffing the scrips of the pilgrims with letters and money, he had nearly purchased the Roman papacy from the citizens. But when, through the rumour of his intended journey, soldiers eagerly flocked to him from all parts of the kingdom, the king, taking offence, threw him into confinement; saying, that he did not seize the bishop of Bayeux, but the Earl of Kent. His partisans being intimidated by threats, discovered such quantities of gold, that the heap of precious metal would surpass the belief of the present age; and at last, many sackfuls of wrought gold were also taken out of the rivers,

which he had secretly buried in certain places.

William of Malmesbury, *Chronicles of the Kings of England*, translated by J. A. Giles.

OGLETHORPE, JAMES EDWARD

1696—1785 Founder of Georgia

Founded Georgia, gave it laws and trade,
He saw it flourish, and he saw it fade.

Anon., in *Gentleman's Magazine*, 4 June 1785.

The gentleness of Oglethorpe's nature appeared in all his actions. He was merciful to the prisoner; a father to the emigrant; the unwavering friend of Wesley; the constant benefactor of the Moravians; honestly zealous for the conversion of the Indians; invoking for the Negro the panoply of the Gospel. He was, for a commercial age, the representative of that chivalry which neither fear nor reproach, and felt a stain on honor like a wound.

George Bancroft, *History of the United States.*

The Last Leaf on the Tree
My grandmamma has said —
Poor old lady, she is dead
    Long ago —
That he had a Roman nose,
And his cheek was like a rose
    In the snow.
But now his nose is thin
And it rests upon his chin
    Like a staff.
And a crook is in his back
And a melancholy crack
    In his laugh.
I know it is a sin
For me to sit and grin
    At him here;
But the old three-cornered hat,
And the breeches, and all that
    Are so queer.

Oliver Wendell Holmes, in *The Oxford Book of American Verse.*

The finest figure you ever saw. He perfectly realizes all my ideas of Nestor. His literature is great, his knowledge of the world extensive, and his faculties as bright as ever; he is one of the three persons still living who were mentioned by Pope. . . . He was the intimate friend of Southern, the tragic poet, and of all the wits of that time. He is perhaps the oldest man of a *gentleman* living. . . . He is quite a . . . chevalier, heroic, romantic, and full of the old gallantry.

Hannah More, in Robert William, *Memoirs of the Life of Mrs Hannah More.*

Can I forget the Generous Bard
Who, touched with human woe, redressive searched
Into the horror of the gloomy jail?
Unpitied and unheard where misery moans;
Where sickness pines; where thirst and hunger burn,
And poor misfortunate feels the lash of vice.
> James Thomson, *Winter*, from *The Seasons*
> (Varient edition), inspired by the philanthropic
> work of Oglethorpe.

I am a Methusalem from the scenes I have seen;
yet, t'other day, I made an acquaintance with one a
little my senior; yet we are to be very intimate for
a long time for my new friend is but ninety-four.
It is General Oglethorpe; I had not seen him these
twenty years, yet knew him instantly. As he did not
recollect me, I told him it was a proof how little
he was altered and I how much. I said I would visit
him; he replied 'No, no; I can walk better than you;
I will come to you.' He is alert, upright, has his eyes,
ears, and memory fresh. If you want any particulars
of the last century, I can procure them.
> Horace Walpole, Letter to the Countess of Upper
> Ossory, 18 February 1783.

. . . his very long life was the great curiosity and the
moment he is dead the rarity is over; and as he was
but ninety-seven, he will not be a prodigy compared
with those who reached to a century and a half.
He is like many who make a noise in their own time
from some singularity, which is forgotten, when it
comes to be registered with others of the same
genius, but more extraordinary in their kind.
> *Ibid.*, 7 July 1785.

                    . . . the Prisons Open'd
Yet Britain cease thy captives' woes to mourn.
To break the chains, see Oglethorpe was born.
> Samuel Wesley Jr, *Poems*.

O'HARA, JOHN HENRY

1905—70 Author

To put the matter in the simplest possible terms, the
middle brows like O'Hara because his books remind
them of the life they imagine themselves to be leading.
> John W. Aldridge, *Time to Murder and Create*.

O'Hara's men and women dance around the Victorian traditions of class distinction and sexual restraint like savages around a cross left by murdered
missionaries and now adorned with shrunken heads.
> Louis Auchincloss, *Reflections of a Jacobite*.

Mr O'Hara can write like a streak, but he just won't

think, or at any rate he won't think in his novels.
> Clifton Fadiman, *Party of One*.

I had to admit that in his old-fashioned way O'Hara
was still romantic about sex, like Scott Fitzgerald
he thought of it as an upper-class prerogative.
> Alfred Kazin, *Contemporaries*: 'Lady Chatterley
> in America'.

Mr. O'Hara's world is populated by the cheap, vulgar, debased and self-destroyed. His reaction to it
is a mixture of sardonic scorn, savage contempt
and romantic wonder.
> Orville Prescott, *In My Opinion*.

O. HENRY (WILLIAM SYDNEY PORTER)

1862—1910 Author

This is that dubious hero of the press
Whose slangy tongue and insolent address
Were spiced to rouge on Sunday afternoon
The man with yellow journals round him strewn.
We laughed and dozed, then roused and read again,
And vowed O. Henry funniest of men.
He always worked a triple-hinged surprise
To end the scene and make one rub his eyes.
> Vachel Lindsay, *The Knight in Disguise*.

OLDCASTLE, SIR JOHN, LORD COBHAM

—d. 1417 Soldier

Stage-poets have themselves been very bold with,
and others very merry at, the memory of Sir John
Oldcastle; whom they have fancied a boon companion, a jovial roister, and yet a coward to boot,
contrary to the credit of all chronicles, owning him
a martial man of merit. The best is, Sir John Falstaff
hath relieved the memory of Sir John Oldcastle,
and of late is substituted buffoon in his place; but
it matters as little what petulant poets, as what
malicious papists, have written against him.
> Thomas Fuller, *Church History of Britain*.

Sir John Oldcastle, Lord Cobham, was the most
conspicuous of the first heretics, or, in other words,
of the first who preferred death to insincerity,
under the new law for burning heretics.
> Sir James Mackintosh, *History of England*,
> vol. 10.

OLDENBURG, HENRY

1615—77 Natural Philosopher

It was mainly by his immense correspondence that

Oldenburg forwarded the cause of science, or, as it was then called, of the 'new experimentall learning', by that and by his assiduous discharge of secretarial and editorial work. Without being a man of brilliant genius, he was just such an intelligent, reliable, energetic, and conscientious worker as was needed at that time to form a centre for the new movement.

H. Rix, in *Nature*, 2 November 1893.

OLDFIELD, ANNE

1683—1730 Actress

I was too young to view her first Dawn on the Stage, but yet had the infinite Satisfaction of her Meridian Lustre, a Glow of Charms not to be beheld but with a trembling Eye, which held her Influence till set in Night.

W. R. Chetwood, *A General History of the Stage.*

The Part of *Sophonisba* . . . was reputed the Cause of her Death; for in her Execution she went beyond Wonder, to Astonishment! From that Time, her Decay came slowly on, and never left her till it conducted her to eternal Rest . . .

Ibid.

I have observ'd several with promising Dispositions, very desirous of Instruction at their first setting out; but no sooner had they found their least Account in it, than they were as desirous of being left to their own Capacity, which they then thought would be disgrac'd by their seeming to want any farther Assistance. But this was not Mrs *Oldfield's* way of thinking; for to the last Year of her Life, she never undertook any Part she liked, without being importunately desirous of having all the Helps in it that another could possibly give her. By knowing so much herself, she found out how much more there was of Nature needful to be known.

Colley Cibber, *Apology fror the Life of Colley Cibber.*

She was in Stature just rising to that height, where the graceful can only begin to show itself; of a lively aspect, and a command in her mien, that like the principal figure in the finest painting, first seizes and longest delights, the eye of the spectators. Her voice was sweet, strong, piercing, and melodious; her pronunciation voluble, distinct, and musical; and her emphasis always placed where the spirit of the sense, in her periods, only demanded it. If she delighted more in the higher comic than in the tragic strain, 'twas because the last is too often written in lofty disregard of nature. But in characters of modern life, she found occasion to add the

particular air and manner which distinguished the different humours she presented; whereas in tragedy the manner of speaking varies as little as the blank verse it is written in. . . . The ornaments she herself provided . . . seemed in all respects the *paraphernalia* of a woman of quality.

Colley Cibber, Preface to *The Careless Husband.*

Mrs. Oldfield happened to be in some danger in a Gravesend Boat, and when the rest of the passengers lamented their imagined approaching fate, she, with a conscious dignity, told them their deaths would be only a private loss; — 'But I am a public concern'.

Thomas Davies, *Dramatic Miscellanies.*

Odious! in woollen! 'twould a saint provoke! —
Were the last words which poor Narcissus spoke. —
No! Let a charming chintz and brussels lace
Wrap my cold limbs and shade my lifeless face.
One would not, sure, be frightful when one's dead;
And Betty, give this cheek a little red.

Alexander Pope, characterizing Mrs Oldfield as a coquette, in *Epistle to Richard Temple, Viscount Cobham.*

OLMSTED, FREDERICK LAW

1822—1903 Landscape Architect

In effect, Olmsted's was not a retreat from the growth of industrial America; it was a necessary corollary to that growth. Particularly in an age of rapid social and physical change, man needed to remind himself of a natural order that was permanent and of a beauty more subtle than that of bricks and mortar. It was this quality of life which Olmsted sought to create through his many parks and communities. Like Olmsted's writing, publishing, and Civil War hospital activities, landscape architecture provided a means for him to render a social service to help solve the problems of a changing nation.

Julius Fabos, Gordon T. Milde and V. Michael Weinmayr, *Frederick Law Olmsted, Sr.*

As he stood, in 1857, on the threshold of his career as a planner and channeler of the growth of the bustling, changing American nation, Olmsted could be fairly described as a romantic, a trained engineer, an experienced farmer, a cosmopolitan man, a sharp observer and social critic, an accomplished writer, a proven manager, and a man of understanding and compassion. This extraordinary combination of traits and abilities in conjunction with that quality that makes a man an artist was to enable Olmsted to design some of the most outstanding, construc-

tive achievements of nineteenth-century America.
Ibid.

Two factors exacerbated this tension between goals and forms. The first was the subordination of the humanitarian and scientific aspirations of Olmsted and Vaux to the demands of the new industrial expansion. In an age that accepted social Darwinism as a rationale for social action, the survival of the fittest seemed more important than the alleviation of human distress through ecological engineering. The second was the growth in power and prestige of men of industrial wealth, for whom Olmsted worked with increasing frequency. While they generally appreciated his technical and administrative ability, and the impressive scale of his work, they usually neither shared nor fully comprehended his social and scientific goals.

Albert Fein, *Frederick Law Olmsted and the American Environmental Tradition.*

Of all American artists, Frederick Law Olmsted, who gave the design for the laying out of the grounds of the World's Fair, stands first in the production of great works which answer the needs and give expression to the life of our immense and miscellaneous democracy. The buildings which surround the Court of Honor, so-called, at Chicago, make a splendid display of monumental architecture. They show how our ablest architects have studied the work of the past, and the arrangement of the buildings according to the general plan produces such a superb effect in the successful grouping in harmonious relations of vast and magnificent structures.

Charles Eliot Norton, in Albert Fein, *ibid.*

O'NEILL, EUGENE GLADSTONE

1888—1953 Playwright

In 1920 I had honestly never heard of the Pulitzer Prize, or if I had, hadn't listened. So when a wire reached me . . . saying I had won it my reaction was a disdainful raspberry — 'Oh, a damned medal! And one of those presentation ceremonies! I won't accept it!'

On himself, in Arthur and Barbara Gelb, *O'Neill.*

Most modern plays are concerned with the relation between man and man, but that does not interest me at all. I am interested only in the relation between man and God.

On himself, in Jordan Y. Miller, *Eugene O'Neill,* in Warren G. French and Walter E. Kidd eds,. *American Winners of the Nobel Literary Prize.*

I intend to use whatever I can make my own, to write about anything under the sun in any manner that fits the subject. And I shall never be influenced by any consideration but one: Is it the truth as I know it — or, better still, feel it?

On himself, in an interview in the *Philadelphia Public Ledger,* 1923.

If one does not like O'Neill, it is not really him that one dislikes: it is our age — of which like the rest of us he is more the victim than the master.

Eric Bentley, 'Trying to Like O'Neill', in John Gassner ed., *O'Neill. A Collection of Critical Essays.*

Though he possesses the tragic vision, he cannot claim the tragic tongue.

John Mason Brown, in Frederic I. Carpenter, *Eugene O'Neill.*

Eugene O'Neill died as he (largely) had lived in frustration and anguish, mental and physical anguish. For all his delving, he had not solved the mystery of man's eternal struggle with himself and an overwhelming universe. The closest he came to a solution was his belief, stated so forcibly in *The Iceman Cometh,* that man must cling to his illusions or perish.

Jean Gould, *Modern American Playwrights.*

. . . Mr Eugene O'Neill, who has done nothing much in American drama save to transform it utterly, in ten or twelve years, from a false world of neat and competent trickery to a world of splendor and fear and greatness . . . he has seen life as not to be neatly arranged in the study of a scholar but as a terrifying, magnificent, and often quite horrible thing akin to the tornado, the earthquake, the devastating fire.

Sinclair Lewis, address as the recipient of the Nobel Prize for Literature, in John Mason Brown, *Dramatis Personae.*

. . . O'Neill is a fairly tall young man, dark, wiry, nervous, of interesting rather than handsome countenance, serious, and shy to the point of being easily embarrassed. . . . He hates the idea of publicity and the searching impertinences of interviewers with the same enthusiasm as the devil hates baptismal fonts.

Burns Mantle, *American Playwrights of Today.*

At twenty, almost on a dare, he had married a girl he hardly knew, fathered a child he never saw until nearly twelve years later, went gold prospecting in Honduras, contracted malaria, and was divorced before he was twenty-two. He failed as a newspaper reporter, became intimate with all the more famous New York and Connecticut bordellos, to which he was guided by his brother, James; evidence all of

fast becoming a hopeless alcoholic; and, after attempting suicide, contracted a severe enough lung infection to place him in a Connecticut tuberculosis sanitarium for six months at the age of twenty-four.
> Jordan Y. Miller, 'Eugene O'Neill', in Warren G. French and Walter E. Kidd eds, *American Winners of the Nobel Literary Prize*.

The truth about O'Neill is that he is the only American playwright who has what might be called 'size'. There is something relatively distinguished about even his failures; they sink not trivially but with a certain air of majesty, like a great ship, its flags flying, full of holes.
> George Jean Nathan, 'Eugene O'Neill', in Alan S. Downer ed., *American Drama and Its Critics*.

Strindberg is in his grave, and the German expressionists are already on their way to the cemetery. O'Neill should give up buying tin wreaths and following funeral processions. His path lies in the other direction.
> *Ibid.*

He'll probably never write a good play again.
> George Bernard Shaw, upon hearing that O'Neill had sworn off drinking, in Arthur and Barbara Gelb, *O'Neill*.

The plays of Eugene O'Neill have never seemed to be solely of the theatre. They have, as it were, followed one out into the noisy streets and into the privacy of one's room, into the greater privacy, even of one's inner thoughts and feelings, and not for a few hours or days, but with a certain timeless insistency.
> Richard Dana Skinner, *Eugene O'Neill*.

Life and death, good and evil, spirit and flesh, male and female, the all and the one, Anthony and Dionysius — O'Neill's is a world of these antithetical absolutes such as religion rather than philosophy conceives, a world of pluses and minuses; and his literary effort is an algebraic attempt to solve these equations.
> Lionel Trilling, 'Eugene O'Neill', in Malcolm Cowley ed., *After the Genteel Tradition*.

His interest is not the minutiae of life, not its nuances and humor, but its 'great inscrutable forces'.
> *Ibid.*

O'Neill gave birth to the American theatre and died for it.
> Tennessee Williams, in Arthur and Barbara Gelb, *O'Neill*.

See also George M. Cohan

OPIE, JOHN
1761—1807 Painter

I mix them with my brains, sir.
> On himself, being asked how he mixed his colours.

ORWELL, GEORGE (ERIC ARTHUR BLAIR)
1903—50 Author

Every line of serious work that I have written since 1936 has been written, directly or indirectly, *against* totalitarianism and *for* democratic Socialism, as I understand it. It seems to me nonsense, in a period like our own, to think that one can avoid writing of such subjects. Everyone writes of them in one guise or another. It is simply a question of which side one takes and what approach one follows.
> On himself, *Why I Write*.

I often feel that I will never pick up a book by Orwell again until I have read a frank discussion of the dishonesty and hysteria that mar some of his best work.
> Kingsley Amis, *What Became of Jane Austen?*

Some of your American readers may not realise Mr Orwell's status in this country and take his commentary seriously. We all like him here, though the standard of his pamphleteering is going down of late, and we know him as the preacher of a doctrine of Physical Courage as an Asset to the left-wing intellectual, and so forth. I think we all agree that he is pretty thoroughly out of touch with any writing under thirty years of age.
> Alex Comfort, in *Partisan Review*, 1942.

He would not blow his nose without moralising on conditions in the handkerchief industry.
> Cyril Connolly, *The Evening Colonnade*.

Good prose, he once wrote, should be 'like a window pane'. Of course his critical style is not quite as transparent as this suggests, nor would it be as powerful if it were. Orwell the critic is as imaginative as Orwell the novelist. He puts across his points with a cartoonist's pictorial shorthand. . . . There are blunt generalizations which need to be argued out . . . and obsessions which have to be discounted. But how few flaws there were in that window pane, if you compare him with any of his contemporaries who wrote about politics with the same degree of anger and intensity.
> John Gross, *The Rise and Fall of the Man of Letters*.

Mr Orwell . . . is a silly billy. He's full of political

tittletattle — but he gets it all wrong. He thinks people are always falling in love with political Stars. I am so glad that emotional public schoolboy has transferred his excitable loyalties to the Partisans.

Percy Wyndham Lewis, Letter to Dwight Macdonald, 26 January 1947.

Orwell's mania to identify himself with the poor and outcast in England. . . . They had been wronged by his class, and he must somehow make it up. So he stayed in workhouses, consorted with down-and-outs, and in *The Road to Wigan Pier* gave what he considered to be an authentic picture of working-class life. Actually, as I occasionally ventured to remark to him, I think his data was derived much more from the *News of the World* and seaside picture postcards — two of his ruling passions — and even from Dickens, than from direct observation.

Malcolm Muggeridge, in M. Gross, *The World of George Orwell*.

Orwell . . . could recognize the putrescence seeping out of the pores of the time, and was unable to lift his nostrils clear . . . Orwell's strength and significance is that . . . he never looked for the familiar deodorant of self-deception or sought out the sweetened balms of elegant literary evasion. He sniffed and wrote on the same quivering reflex.

Denis Potter, in *The Times*, 5 October 1968.

There was something about him, the proud man apart, the Don Quixote on a bicycle (and if Saint Thomas More was the first Englishman, as one historian called him, then Orwell was perhaps the last) that caught one's imagination right away. That made one think of a knight errant and of social justice as the Holy Grail. One felt safe with him; he was so intellectually honest. His mind was a court where the judge was the lawyer for the defence.

Paul Potts, in *London Magazine*, March 1957.

George Orwell was the wintry conscience of a generation which in the thirties had heard the call of the rasher assumptions of political faith. He was a kind of saint and, in that character, more likely in politics to chastise his own side than the enemy.

V. S. Pritchett (on Orwell's death), in *New Statesman*, 1950.

Thoroughgoing, Orwell changed his identity with his name. Curiously though, the change is not *so* radical: he exchanged ordinarinesses. On to the terrifying *tabula rasa* that was Eric Blair he etched the familiar features — the spiv's moustache, the centre parting, the short back and sides — the persona of the ordinary bloke, someone whose name

might have been George Hair-oil. . . . [In] Miss Buddicom's account of their first meeting . . . Orwell was standing on his head. Asked why, he replied, 'You are noticed more if you stand on your head than if you are the right way up.' It is irresistibly symbolic. He continued to get the same effect by turning the world upside down.

Craig Raine, in *New Statesman*, 17 May 1974.

If we are to expose antecedents, Orwell himself does not come off very well. Comrade Orwell, the former police official of British imperialism . . . Comrade Orwell, former fellow-traveller of the pacifists . . . Comrade Orwell, former extreme left-winger, ILP partisan and defender of Anarchists. . . . And now Comrade Orwell who returns to his old imperialist allegiances and works at the BBC conducting British propaganda to fox the Indian masses! It would seem that Orwell himself shows to a surprising degree the over-lapping of left-wing, pacifist and reactionary tendencies of which he accuses others!

George Woodcock, in *Partisan Review*, 1942.

OSBORNE, THOMAS, see under DANBY, EARL OF

OTIS, JAMES

1725—83 Politician, Publicist

He talks so much and takes up so much of our time, and fills it with trash, obsceness, profaneness, nonsense and distraction, that we have no[ne] left for rational amusements or inquiries . . . I never saw such an object of admiration, reverence, contempt, and compassion, all at once . . . I fear, I tremble, I mourn for the man and for his country; many others mourn over him, with tears in their eyes.

John Adams, *Papers*, 1.

OTWAY, THOMAS

1652—85 Dramatist

I must confess, I had often a titillation to poetry, but never durst venture on my muse, till I got her into a corner in the country; and then, like a bashful young lover, when I had her in private, I had courage to fumble, but never thought she would have produced anything; till at last, I know not how, ere I was aware, I found myself father of a dramatic birth.

On himself, Preface to *Don Carlos*.

I am a wretch of honest race
My parents not obscure, nor high in titles were;
They left me Heir to no Disgrace.
My Father was (a thing now rare)
Loyall and brave, my Mother chast and fair.
Their pledge of Marriage-vows was only I;
Alone I liv'd their much lov'd fondled boy.
On himself, *The Poet's Complaint of His Muse.*

But Wine does now the Poet's breast inspire,
Wine, that doth kindle all our youthful fire,
Wine that makes *Ot—y* write and fools admire;
His verse of wine stinks worse than bawdy Punk
For he never writes a verse but when he is drunk.
Anon., *The Tory Poets.*

Life up your Heads, ye Tories of the Age
Lett Otway tumble Shadwell from the stage,
Otway who long, (leane loyalty preserving)
Has shown a wonder and grown fat with starving.
Anon., *A Supplement to the late Heroic Poem.*

Otway has followed nature in the language of his tragedy, and therefore shines in the passionate part of it, more than any of our English poets. As there is something familiar and domestic in the fable of his Tragedy, more than in those of any other poet, he has little pomp, but great force in his expression. For which reason, though he has admirably succeeded in the tender and melting part of his tragedies, he sometimes falls into too great a familiarity of phrase in those parts, which, by Aristotle's rule, ought to have been raised and supported by the dignity of expression.
Anon., in *Spectator*, 14 April 1711.

His person was of the middle size, inclinable to fatness. He had a thoughtful, speaking eye, and that was all.
Anon., in *Gentleman's Magazine*, 1745.

But everyone knows Mr Otway's good Nature, which will not permit him to shock any one of our Sex to their Faces.
Aphra Behn, *Familiar Letters of Love, Gallantry and Several Occasions.*

To Thomas Otway was reserved the honour of giving tragedy its true and genuine tone of language, divested of unnatural flight and unnecessary pomp.
Thomas Davies, *Dramatic Miscellanies.*

There is . . . extant a joke which Otway is said to have played off on Dryden, when their relations were strained. . . . It is said that they lived in houses facing each other, and Otway wrote sarcastically on Dryden's door one night
Here Dryden lives, a poet and a wit.

to which Dryden replied the next night by writing on Otway's door:
Here Otway lives — exactly opposite.
J. C. Ghosh, *Works of Thomas Otway.*

He had susceptibility of feeling, and warmth of genius; but he had not equal depth of thought or loftiness of imagination, and indulged his mere sensibility too much, yielding to the immediate impression or emotion excited in his own mind, and not placing himself enough in the minds and situations of others, or following the workings of nature sufficiently with keenness of eye and strength of will into its heights and depths, its strongholds as well as its weak sides.
William Hazlitt, *On Ancient and Modern Literature.*

Otway's comedies do no sort of credit to him: on the contrary, they are as desperate as his fortunes.
William Hazlitt, *Lectures on English Comic Writers.*

Otway is a turbid winter torrent, with the sob and moan of anguished, stifled human love in it, whirling us to a catastrophe without hope. . . . The comic scenes in Otway therefore, though unfortunately gross and repulsive, are absolutely needed for relaxation of the tense strain. For he makes the impression of being almost all supreme crisis and desperate situation, like terrific peaks where the earth-cloud hangs in gloom, only soothed by the low warble of water, among mosses, or casual song of little bird, only broken by flashes of livid lightning — and all the rest barren steep.
Roden Noel, Introduction to Otway's *Works.*

'Tis a talent of nature rather than an effect of judgement to write so movingly.
Alexander Pope, in Joseph Spence, *Anecdotes.*

Tom O(tway) came next, Tom S(hadwell's) dear
Zany;
And swear for *Heroicks*, he writes best of any;
Don Carlos his Pockets so amply had fill'd,
That his *Mange* was quite cur'd, and his *Lice*, were
all kill'd.
But *Apollo*, had seen his Face on the *Stage*,
And prudently did not think fit to engage,
The scum of a *Play-house*, for the Prop of an *Age*.
John Wilmot, Earl of Rochester, *A Session of the Poets.*

OWEN, SIR RICHARD

1804—92 Naturalist

Owen believes that no animal has sensation unless

furnished with a brain, therefore the cuttlefish is
the lowest creature which can effectively be treated
with cruelty. Examined a long series of skulls: those
of babies so much phrenologically better than
grown persons — which Owen thinks quite natural,
as they came uncontaminated from the Author of
all Goodness, and degenerate after contact with the
world.

Caroline Fox, *Journals*, May 1842.

See also Augustus Granville

OWEN, ROBERT

1771—1858 Socialist

The mission of my life appears to be, to prepare the
population of the world to understand the vast importance of the second creation of Humanity, from
the birth of each individual, through the agency of
man, by creating entirely new surroundings in which
to place all through life, and by which a new human
nature would appear to arise from the new surrounding.

On himself, *The Life of Robert Owen by Himself.*

During my childhood, and for many years afterward, it never occurred to me that there was anything in my habits, thoughts, and actions different
from those of others of my age; but when looking
back and comparing my life with many others, I
have been induced to attribute my favourable
difference to the effects produced at an early period
when my life was endangered by the spoonful of
scalding flummery. Because from that time I was
compelled to notice the effects produced by different kinds of food on my constitution, which had
also been deeply injured in its powers of digestion.
Ibid.

This gentleman is for establishing innumerable
communities of paupers! Each is to be resident in
an *inclosure*, somewhat resembling a barrack establishment, only more extensive. I do not clearly
understand whether the sisterhoods and brother-
hoods are to form distinct communities, or whether
they are to mix promiscuously; but I perceive they
are to be under a very *regular discipline*; and that
wonderful peace, happiness and national benefit
are to be the result!

William Cobbett, *Political Register*, 2 August
1817.

You came among us a rich man among the poor and
did not call us a rabble. There was no sneer upon

your lips, no covert scorn in your tone.

Ebenezer Elliott, in an address sent to Owen by
the Sheffield Trade Unionists, 1834.

English Socialism arose with Owen, a manufacturer,
and proceeds therefore with great consideration
towards the bourgeoisie and great injustice toward
the proletariat in its methods, although it culmin-
ates in demanding the abolition of the class antagonism between bourgeoisie and proletariat.

Friedrich Engels, *Condition of the Working
Class.*

The doctrine of Universal Benevolence, the belief
in the Omnipotence of Truth, and in the Perfect-
ibility of Human Nature, are not new, but 'Old,
old' Master Robert Owen; — why then do you say
that they are new? They are not only old, but super-
annuated, they are dead and buried, they are reduced to mummy, they are put in the catacombs at
Paris, they are sealed up in patent coffins, they have
been dug up again and anatomised, they have been
drawn quartered and gibbeted, they have become
black, dry, parched in the sun, loose, and rotten,
and are dispersed to all the winds of Heaven!

William Hazlitt, *Political Essays.*

He was the first publicist among us who looked with
royal eyes upon children. He regarded grown
persons as being proprietors of the world — bound
to extend the rites of hospitality to all arrivals in it.

George Holyoake, *History of Co-operation.*

I must confess, also, that I was one of those who, at
one time, was favourably impressed with many of
Mr. Owen's views, and, more especially, with those
of a community of property. This notion has a
peculiar attraction for the plodding, toiling, ill-
remunerated sons and daughters of labour.

William Lovett, *Life and Struggles.*

Robert Owen brought to the task the necessary
skill, but the demoralising effects of our institutions left him no materials to work upon.

Bronterre O'Brien, footnote to his translation of
Buonarroti's *History of Babeuf's Conspiracy.*

My father made another still greater mistake. A
believer in the force of circumstances and of the instinct of self interest to reform all men, however
ignorant or vicious, he admitted into his village
all comers, without recommendatory introduction
or any examination whatever. This error was the
more fatal, because it is in the nature of any novel
experiment, or any putting forth of new views
which may tend to revolutionize the opinions or
habits of society, to attract to itself . . . waifs and
strays from the surrounding society; men and

women of crude, ill-considered, extravagant notions; nay, worse, vagrants who regard the latest heresy but as a stalking horse for pecuniary gain, or a convenient cloak for immoral demeanour.

Robert Dale Owen, on the failure of New Harmony, *Threading My Way*.

His mind never fairly met any other mind, — though towards the close of his life he had a strange idea that it did, and that, too, by means of spirit-mediums. Yet, in the very same breath in which he insisted upon the reality of his communications with departed spirits, he maintained that the new-found power was 'all electricity'.

F. A. Packard, *Life of Robert Owen*.

Mr. Owen then was, and is still, persuaded that he was the first who ever observed that man was the creature of his circumstances. On this supposed discovery he founded his system. Never having read a metaphysical book, nor held a metaphysical conversation, nor having even heard of the disputes concerning free-will and necessity, he had no clear conception of his subject, and his views were obscure. Yet he had all along been preaching and publishing and projecting and predicting in the fullest conviction that he could command circumstances or create them, and place men above their control when necessary.

Francis Place, in Graham Wallace, *Life of Francis Place*.

Owen may be described as one of those intolerable bores who are the salt of the earth. To the Whigs and political economists he appeared chiefly as a bore.

Leslie Stephen, in *Dictionary of National Biography*.

OWEN, WILFRED

1893—1918 Poet

My subject is War, and the pity of War. The poetry is in the pity.

On himself, Preface to *Poems*.

I am held peer by the Georgians; I am a poet's poet.

On himself, Letter to his Mother, January 1918.

It is now quite clear that the fundamental biographic fact about Owen is that he was his mother's boy: his family situation was sufficiently like that of D. H. Lawrence for the comparison to be made. . . . What the *Letters* cry out on nearly every page is that it was she Owen's mother who magnetised his love, his intimacy, his tenderness. . . . Of the 673 Owen letters that survive, 631 are to her. . . . It is their frequency, their atmosphere of being written to someone who understands and appreciates everything, and above all their explicit declarations that drive the point home.

Philip Larkin, in *Encounter*, March 1975.

When I excluded Wilfred Owen [from *The Oxford Book of Modern Verse*], whom I consider unworthy of the poets' corner of a country newspaper, I did not know I was excluding a revered sandwich-board Man of the revolution & that some body has put his worst & most famous poem in a glass-case in the British Museum — however if I had known it I would have excluded him just the same. He is all blood, dirt & sucked sugar stick.

William Butler Yeats, Letter to Dorothy Wellesley, 21 December 1936.

P

PAGE, WALTER HINES

1855—1918 Journalist, Diplomat

Page could reject a story with a letter that was so complimentary and make everybody feel so happy that you could take it to a bank and borrow money on it.

    O. Henry, in Burton J. Hendrick, *The Life and Letters of Walter H. Page.*

His taste was for the roast beef of literature, not for the side dishes and the trimmings, and his appreciation of the substantial work of others was no surer than this instinct for his own performance.

    Ellery Sedgwick, in Burton J. Hendrick, *ibid.*

PAINE, THOMAS

1737—1809 Revolutionary, Author

My country is the world, and my religion is to do good.

    On himself, *The Rights of Man.*

I am proud to say that with a perseverance undismayed by difficulties, a disinterestedness that compelled respect, I have not only contributed to raise a new empire in the world, founded on a new system of government, but I arrived at an eminence in political literature, the most difficult of all lines to succeed and excel in, which aristocracy, with all its aids, has not been able to reach or to rival.

    On himself, in David Freeman Hawke, *Paine.*

I know not whether any man in the world has had more influence on its inhabitants or affairs for the last thirty years than Tom Paine. There can be no severer satyr on the age. For such a mongrel between pig and puppy, begotten by a wild boar on a bitch wolf, never before in any age of the world was suffered by the poltroonery of mankind, to run through such a career of mischief. Call it then the Age of Paine.

    John Adams, Letter to Benjamin Waterhouse, 29 October 1805.

What a poor ignorant, malicious, short-sighted, crapulous mass, is Tom Paine's *Common Sense.*

    John Adams, Letter to Thomas Jefferson, 22 June 1819.

. . . has no country, no affections that constitute the pillars of patriotism.

    John Quincy Adams, Letter to John Adams, 3 April 1797.

There never was a man less beloved in a place than Paine in this, having at different times disputed with everybody. The most rational thing he could have done would have been to have died the instant he had finished his *Common Sense*, for he never again will have it in his power to leave the world with so much credit.

    Sarah Franklin Bache, Letter to Benjamin Franklin, 14 January 1781.

His private life disgraced his public character, certain immoralities, and low and vulgar habits, which are apt to follow in the train of almost habitual drunkeness, rendered him a disgusting object for many of the latter years of his life, though his mental faculties retained much of their former luster.

    Joel Barlow, in an open letter to *Raleigh Register*, 18 October 1809.

In digging up your bones, Tom Paine,
    Will. Cobbett has done well:
You visit him on earth again,
    He'll visit you in hell.
    Lord Byron, *Epigram*.

Nor is our England without her missionaries. . . . Her Paine: rebellious Staymaker; unkempt; who feels that he, a single Needleman, did, by his *Common Sense* Pamphlet, free America; — that he can will free all this World, perhaps even the other.

    Thomas Carlyle, *The French Revolution.*

Thomas Paine invented the name of the Age of Reason; and he was one of those sincere but curiously simple men who really did think that the age of reason was beginning, at about the time when it was really ending.

    G. K. Chesterton, *William Cobbett.*

At his expiring flambeau I lighted my taper.
William Cobbett, in Audrey Williamson, *Thomas Paine: His Life, Work and Times.*

An illiterate mechanic, who mistaking some disturbance of his nerves for a miraculous call proceeds alone to convert a tribe of savages, whose language he can have no natural means of acquiring, may have been misled by impulses very different from those of high self-opinion; but the illiterate perpetrator of the 'Age of Reason', must have had *his* conscience stupefied by the habitual intoxication of presumptuous arrogance, and his common-sense over-clouded by the vapours of his heard.
Samuel Taylor Coleridge, *The Friends:* 'Essay IV'.

Sturdy Tom Paine, biographers relate,
Once with his friends engaged in warm debate.
Said they, 'Minorities are always right';
Said he, 'The truth is just the opposite'.
Finding them stubborn, 'Frankly now,' asked he,
'In this opinion do ye all agree;
All, every one, without exception?' When
They thus affirmed unanimously, — 'Then
Correct,' said he, 'My sentiment must be,
For I myself am the minority.'
Richard Garnett, *Tom Paine.*

A mouse nibbling at the wing of an archangel.
Robert Hall, in Gregory's *Life of Paine.*

Regardless of why he did it, Paine introduced into American journalism the personal report, whose authority stemmed as much from an awareness of who wrote it as from the strength of thought and style. While leading a revolution on the political front, he had also initiated one in polemic literature.
David Freeman Hawke, *Paine.*

Tom mounted on his sordid load,
And bawled d––n ye, clear the road;
His shovel grasp'd firm in his hands,
Which far and near the street commands,
No hardy mortal dares approach,
Whether on horseback, foot or coach;
None in his wits the risk would choose,
Who either wears a coat or hose,
So — in pomp, on Billingsgate,
His arms display'd in burlesque state;
Scurrility and imprudence,
Bombast and Bedlam eloquence,
Defiance bids — to COMMON SENCE.
Frances Hopkinson, in *Pennsylvania Evening Post,* 6 February 1776.

Paine was a Quaker by birth and a friend by nature.

The world was his home, mankind were his friends, to do good was his religion.
Alice Hubbard, *An American Bible.*

Paine thought more than he read.
Thomas Jefferson, Letter to J. Cartwright, 1824.

Janius is our own,
Who props a bank, altho' he scorn'd a throne;
And, should his heart with just resentments burn,
Would scorn a bank and prop a throne in turn;
But should both bank and throne reject the job,
Would damn them both and idolize the mob;
And if all three should scorn the honest fellow,
For *Daniel Shays* and *Liberty* would bellow.
Peter Markoe, in David Freeman Hawke, *Paine.*

[That] mere adventurer *from England*, without fortune, without family or connections, ignorant even of grammar.
Gouverneur Morris, in David Freeman Hawke, *Paine.*

In the best of times, he had a larger share of every other sense than of common sense, and lately the intemperate use of ardent spirits has I am told, considerably impaired the small stock, which he originally possessed.
Gouverneur Morris, Letter to Thomas Jefferson, 6 March 1794.

He seems cocksure of bringing about a revolution in Great Britain and I think it quite as likely he will be promoted to the pillory.
Gouverneur Morris, Diary, 16 February 1792.

Tom Paine has triumphed over Edmund Burke and the swine are now courted electors.
George Bernard Shaw, Preface to *Man and Superman.*

Paine's brandy is less to the purpose than Pitt's port, and much less to the purpose than Coleridge's opium . . . his writings were the product of brains certainly not sodden by brandy, but clear, vigorous, and in some ways curiously free from passion.
Leslie Stephen, in Audrey Williamson, *Thomas Paine: His Life, Work and Times.*

What he gave to English people was a new rhetoric of radical egalitarianism, which touched the deepest responses of the 'free-born Englishman' and then penetrated the sub-political attitudes of the urban working people.
E. P. Thompson, *The Making of the English Working Class.*

It would be difficult to name any human composition [*Common Sense*] which has had an effect at once so instant, so extended and so lasting. . . . It was pirated, parodied and imitated; and translated into the language of every country where the new republic had well-wishers. It worked nothing short of miracles and turned Tories into Whigs.

George Trevelyan, *History of the American Revolution.*

Can nothing be done in our Assembly for poor Paine? Must the merits of *Common Sense* continue to glide down the stream of time unrewarded by this country? His writings certainly have had a powerful effect upon the public mind. Ought they not, then, to meet an adequate reward?

George Washington, Letter to James Madison, 12 June 1784.

It was pre-eminently from him that the working classes and working class movements of the nineteenth century first learnt to think, and what they learnt was common sense, toleration, reason, humanity, a hatred of privilege and the abuse of power, a love of liberty in life, speech, and thought. It was in fact from Tom Paine that they learnt to lisp the language of democracy.

Leonard Woolf, *Tom Paine.*

If Mr. Paine should be able to rouse up the lower classes, their interference will probably be marked by wild work, and all we now possess, whether in private property or public liberty, will be at the mercy of a lawless and furious rabble.

Christopher Wyvill, in David Freeman Hawke, *Paine.*

See also Charles Willson Peale, Ida Tarbell

PALMER, SAMUEL

1805—81 Painter

I have beheld as in the spirit, such nooks, caught such glimpses of the perfumed and enchanted twilight — of natural midsummer, as well as, at other times of day, other scenes, as passed thro' the intense purifying separating transmuting heat of the soul's infabulous alchymy, would divinely consist with the severe and stately port of the human, as with the moon thron'd among constellations, and varieties of lesser glories, the regal pomp and glistening brilliance and solemn attendance of her starry train.

On himself, Letter to George Richmond, November 1827.

If you've a mangy cat to draw, christen it Palmer.

On himself, Letter to George Richmond, 19 August 1836.

There are two pictures by a Mr. Palmer so amazing that we felt the most intense curiosity to see what manner of man it was who produced such performances. We think if he would show himself with a label round his neck, *The Painter of A View in Kent,* he would make something of it at a shilling a head. What the Hanging Committee means by hanging these pictures without the painter to explain them is past conjecture.

Anon., in *European Magazine,* 1825.

You feel . . . that Palmer is telling you not what he has seen but of his thoughts — his thoughts of the glory of the sun, the magic of moonlight, the mystery of the stars, thatched cottages couched under immemorial trees; the enigmatic beauty of lanterns swinging in the night; lamp-light giving gold to a window-blind; the goodness of harvest and ripe fruitage; men that drive the plough and scatter the grain; all the bounty and beauty that make the history and happiness of rural England.

M. Hardie, *Water-Colour Painting in Britain.*

PALMERSTON, VISCOUNT (HENRY JOHN TEMPLE)

1784—1865 Prime Minister

I have . . . been acting the part of a very distinguished tightrope dancer and much astonishing the public by my individual performances and feats. . . . . So far, so well; but even Madame Sacqui, when she had mounted her rope and flourished among her rockets, never thought of making the rope her perch, but providently came down to avoid a dangerous fall.

On himself, Letter to Stephen Sulivan, December 1852.

Die, my dear doctor! That's the *last* thing I shall do.

On himself, attributed last words.

If the Devil has a son
It is surely Palmerston.

Anon., popular catch.

[He] is tolerated because he is cheerful and wounds no pride, and because he is old and excites no envy. . . .

Lord Acton, Letter to Richard Simpson, 1862.

A man of the world is not an imaginative animal, and Lord Palmerston was by incurable nature a man of the world: keenly detective in what he could realise by experience — utterly blind, dark, and impervious to what he could not so realise.

Walter Bagehot, *Biographical Studies:* 'Lord Palmerston'.

Do the exact opposite of what [Palmerston] did. His administration at the Foreign Office was one long crime.

John Bright, advice to Lord Rosebery, in latter's Diary, 17 March 1886.

He was plucky and Palmerston to the last moment.

Lord Clarendon, Letter to Lord Granville, October 1865.

. . . a Conservative Minister working with Radical tools and keeping up a show of Liberalism in his foreign policy.

Lord Derby, 1856, in Robert Blake, *Disraeli.*

Palmerston . . . seems now the inevitable man, and tho' he is really an imposter, utterly exhausted, and at best only ginger beer and not champaign, and now an old painted Pantaloon, very deaf, very blind, and with false teeth, which would fall out of his mouth when speaking, if he did not hesitate and halt so in his talk — he is a name which the country resolves to associate with energy, wisdom, and eloquence, and will until he has tried and failed. . . .

Benjamin Disraeli, Letter to Lady Londonderry, 2 February 1854.

Lytton who was always mourning over his lost youth, & was ridiculously made up, delighted in Palmerston, leading the House of Commons at 76! He sat opposite him with an expression of contemplative admiration. It was not however his wit, or his eloquence, or his dexterity that excited this sentiment. It was his age. 'That man,' he said to me one day 'is a future.'

Benjamin Disraeli, *Reminiscences.*

'The Prime Minister . . . was upwards of 80 years of age. He ate for dinner two plates of turtle-soup; he was then served very amply to a plate of cod and oyster sauce, he then took a paté, afterwards he was helped to two very greasy-looking entrees; he then despatched a plate of roast mutton; there then appeared before him the largest, & to my mind the hardest, slice of ham that ever figured on the table of a nobleman, yet it disappeared, just in time for him to answer the enquiry of his butler "Snipe, my lord, or pheasant?" He instantly replied pheasant: thus completing the ninth dish of meat at that meal. I need not now tell you what is the state of his health.' This is a literal report of an anecdote told by the Speaker with much grave humor.

Ibid.

Your dexterity seems a happy compound of the smartness of an attorney's clerk and the intrigue of a Greek of the lower empire.

Benjamin Disraeli, attributed.

It was easy to settle affairs with Palmerston because he was a man of the world, and was therefore governed by the principle of honor.

Benjamin Disraeli, Letter to Montague Corry, 29 January 1881.

In the march of his epoch he was behind the eager but before the slow.

Sir Henry Bulwer Lytton, *The Life of Henry John Temple, Viscount Palmerston.*

Of all kinds of ability, ingenuity is perhaps the least likely to expand into genius, or to exhaust itself with years.

Harriet Martineau, *History of England 1800–1815.*

A strong hand, firm will, are necessary to compel the Greek Government to perform a duty of equity and of justice. That strong hand can only be yours, my Lord; that firm will my just rights lead me to hope will be yours likewise.

David (Don) Pacifico, Letter to Lord Palmerston, 8 October 1847.

His style was not only devoid of ornament and rhetorical device, but it was slipshod and untidy. . . . He eked out his sentences with 'hum' and 'hah'; cleared his throat, and flourished his pocket-handkerchief, and sucked his orange; he rounded his periods with 'You know what I mean,' and 'all that sort of thing'; and seemed actually to revel in an anticlimax. It taxed the skill of the reporters' gallery to trim his speeches into decent form; and yet no one was listened to with keener interest, no one was so much dreaded as an opponent, and no one ever approached him in the art of putting a plausible face upon a doubtful policy, and making the worse appear the better cause. Palmerston's Parliamentary success is a perfect illustration of the doctrine laid down by Demosthenes. If what really matters is that the speaker should have the same predilections as the majority, and should entertain the same likes and dislikes as his country, Palmerston was unsurpassed.

G. W. E. Russell, *Sixty Years of Empire.*

That wretched Pam seems to me to get worse and worse. There is not a particle of veracity or noble feeling that I have ever been able to trace in him.

He manages the House of Commons by debauching it, making all parties laugh at one another, . . . by substituting low ribaldry for argument, bad jokes for principle, and an openly-avowed vainglorious imbecile vanity as a panoply to guard himself from the attacks of all thoughtful men. I think, if his life lasts long, it must cost us the slight remains of Constitutional Government which exist among us.
> Bishop Wilberforce, in *ibid.*

See also W. E. Gladstone, Ramsay MacDonald, Theodore Roosevelt

PANKHURST, DAME CHRISTABEL HENRIETTE

1858—1928 Suffragette

She knows everything and can see through everything.
> Mrs Drummond, Speech, as reported in *Suffragette*, 12 December 1913.

Christabel cared less for the political vote itself than for the dignity of her sex, and she denounced the false dignity earned by submission and extolled the true dignity accorded by revolt. She never made any secret of the fact that to her the means were even more important than the end. Militancy to her meant the putting off of the slave *spirit*.
> Emmeline Pethwick-Lawrence, *My Part in a Changing World.*

Christabel, who possessed in a high degree a flair for the intricacies of a complex political situation, had conceived the militant campaign as a whole. She never doubted that the tactics she had evolved would succeed in winning the cause. She dreaded all the old plausible evasions and she feared the old ingrained inferiority complex in the majority of women. Thus she could not trust her mental offspring to the mercies of untrained political minds.
> *Ibid.*

Christabel may well have been a lesbian, but the evidence is circumstantial rather than explicit: she never married and the copious documents relating to her life do not allude to any heterosexual involvements. All the available evidence indicates that she had stronger emotional attachments to women than to men. As far as the history of the WSPU is concerned the exact nature of Christabel's sex-life is less significant than the fact that by 1913 she had grown into a state of mind in which she was completely adverse to any form of co-operation with men.
> Andrew Rosen, *Rise up Women.*

PANKHURST, EMMELINE

1858—1928 Suffragette

The argument of the broken pane of glass is the most valuable argument in modern politics.
> On herself, in *Votes for Women*, 23 February 1912.

When I began this Militant Campaign I was a Poor Law Guardian, and it was my duty to go through a workhouse infirmary, and I shall never forget seeing a little girl of thirteen lying on a bed playing with a doll. I was told she was on the eve of becoming a mother, and she was infected with a loathsome disease, and on the point of bringing, no doubt, a diseased child into the world. Was that not enough to make me a militant Suffragette? We women suffragists have a great mission — the greatest mission the world has ever known. It is to free half the human race, and through that freedom to save the rest.
> On herself, Speech, in *Votes for Women*, 25 October 1912.

What an extraordinary mixtue of idealism and lunacy! Hasn't she the sense to see that the very worst method of campaigning for the franchise is to try and intimidate or blackmail a man into giving her what he would gladly give her otherwise.
> David Lloyd George, in Richard Lloyd George, *Lloyd George.*

She was as she instinctively knew, cast for a great role. She had a temperament akin to genius. She could have been a queen on the Stage or in the Salon. Circumstances had baulked her in the fulfilment of her destiny. But the smouldering spark leapt into flame when her daughter Christabel initiated militancy. It was fed by a passion for her first born. She dwelt on the name of her daughter 'Christabel the Annointed One', the young deliverer who was to emancipate the new generation of women. Mrs. Pankhurst was driven on by her 'daemon' to fulfil her destiny and to provide herself, as she said, with a 'niche in history'.
> Emmeline Pethwick-Lawrence, *My Part in a Changing World.*

PARKER, DOROTHY ROTHSCHILD

1893—1967 Writer, Essayist

Four be the things I'd been better without:
Love, curiosity, freckles and doubt.
> On herself, *Inventory.*

I require only three things of a man. He must be handsome, ruthless, and stupid.

On herself, in John Keats, *You Might As Well Live.*

But I, despite expert advice
Keep doing things I think are nice,
And though to good I never come —
Inseparable my nose and thumb.

On herself, in Robert E. Drennan ed., *Wit's End.*

I was following in the exquisite footsteps of Miss Edna St. Vincent Millay, unhappily in my own horrible sneakers.

Ibid.

Mrs Parker remarked, at the reception following her remarriage to Alan Campbell: 'People who haven't talked to each other in years are on speaking terms again today — including the bride and groom.'

Ibid.

Discussing a job with a prospective employer, Mrs Parker explained, 'Salary is no object; I want only enough to keep body and soul apart.'

Ibid.

If I had any decency, I'd be dead. Most of my friends are.

Ibid. (on her seventieth birthday).

This is on me.

Ibid. (proposed epitaph).

Excuse my dust.

On herself, *Her Own Epitaph.*

This belle dame sans merci has the ruthlessness of the great tragic lyricists whose work was allegorized in the fable of the nightingale singing with her breast against a thorn. It is disillusion recollected in tranquility where the imagination has at last controlled the emotions. It comes out clear, and with the authentic sparkle of a great vintage.

Henry Seidel Canby, in John Keats, *You Might As Well Live.*

Mrs Parker once collided with Clare Boothe Luce in a doorway. 'Age before beauty,' cracked Mrs Luce. 'Pearls before swine,' said Mrs Parker, gliding through the door.

Robert E. Drennan ed., *Wit's End.*

She was an elfin woman who had two kinds of magic about her. Her first magical quality was that no one could ever consider her dispassionately, and the other was that no one could precisely define her.

John Keats, *You Might As Well Live.*

Petite, pretty, and deadly as an asp. . . .

Howard Teichmann, *George S. Kaufman, An Intimate Portrait.*

. . . a combination of Little Nell and Lady Macbeth.

Alexander Woollcott, in Robert E. Drennan ed., *Wit's End.*

I found her in hospital typing away lugubriously. She had given her address as Bedpan Alley and represented herself as writing her way out. There was a hospital bill to pay before she dared to get well. . .

Alexander Woollcott, *While Rome Burns.*

See also Calvin Coolidge, George S. Kaufman

PARKMAN, FRANCIS

1823—93 Historian

If the weakness of Parkman's prose lies in his most self-consciously heroic diction and his trite imagery, its great strength comes from his acute sense of specific place and specific fact, and from his brilliant control of the pace of his narrative.

David Levin, *History As Romantic Art.*

. . . he hobbled on, through those streets already submerged by the tide of alien immigrants, a patrician, a Puritan of the Puritans, remote, inscrutable, indomitable.

Bliss Perry, 'Some Personal Qualities of Francis Parkman', in *Yale Review*, April 1924.

Intense of purpose, impetuous in pursuit, intolerant of idleness, effeminacy, and indifference, emphatic in belief, dependent on himself alone, pleasant to his acquaintance, beloved by his friends, he fought his way through fifty years of achievement, a worthy comrade to those great figures in his histories whom he has lifted to fame and honor.

Henry Dwight Sedgwick, *Francis Parkman.*

Silent in pain, patient in accomplishment, modest in victory, gentle in bearing, and yet determined to grimness, he proved himself lawful heir of the best Puritan traits.

Ibid.

Parkman seemed to think of himself as living in a time when all heroes were dead or about to pass forever from the scene. In this sense, for all his

obsession with concreteness and veracity, he appears to have undertaken a task no less amorphous than depicting the decline and fall of the human will.
William R. Taylor, 'Francis Parkman', in Marcus Cunliffe and Robin W. Winks eds, *Pastmasters*.

And his greatness lies in his ability to make these creatures of his mind come alive on the pages which he laboriously compiled, so that the reader is translated into an enthralling new world, whose history is a great drama played out by a heroic company.
Mason Wade, *Francis Parkman, Heroic Historian*.

And the hardships of his private life, his engrossing and exhausting struggle with blindness, insanity, rheumatism, arthritis, and perhaps other disorders, although one cannot but admire him for his strength of character in dealing with them, unquestionably limited both his scholarship and his understanding to the point where he is relatively a minor figure.
Yvor Winters, *The Anatomy of Nonsense*.

PARNELL, CHARLES STEWART
1846—91 Irish Leader

The impression made by one of his more elaborate speeches might be compared to that which one receives from a grey sunless day with an east wind, a day in which everything shows clear, but also hard and cold.
James Bryce, *Studies in Contemporary Biography*.

It is a very dangerous thing to approach an expiring cat.
Sir William Harcourt, Letter to William Ewart Gladstone, 22 November 1890.

That man suspected his own shadow. He was unhappy and saw little good in the world, but I do think he meant well by Ireland.
Cecil J. Rhodes, in J. G. McDonald, *Rhodes: A Life*.

The Bishops and the Party
That tragic story made,
A husband that had sold his wife
And after that betrayed;
But stories that live longest
Are sung above the glass,
And Parnell loved his country,
And Parnell loved his lass.
William Butler Yeats, *Come Gather Round Me, Parnellites*.

The fall of Parnell left Ireland with a dead god instead of a leader.
G. M. Young, *Victorian England: Portrait of an Age*.

PARRINGTON, VERNON LOUIS
1871—1929 Historian, Philologist

The past five years I have spent in study and writing, up to my ears in the economic interpretation of American history and literature, getting the last lingering Harvard prejudices out of my system.
On himself, Letter to former Harvard classmates, 1913.

Officially I am a teacher of English literature, but in reality my business in life is to wage war on the crude and selfish materialism that is biting so deeply into our national life and character.
On himself, Letter to the Rev. L. N. Linebaugh, 16 June 1908.

He has yanked Miss Beautiful Letters out of the sphere of the higher verbal hokum and fairly set her in the way that leads to contact with pulsating reality — that source and inspiration of all magnificent literature.
Charles Beard, in Richard Hofstadter, *The Progressive Historians*.

He had warmth of feeling, a most unacademic contempt for convention, and a healthy distrust of all buncombe.
Granville Hicks, 'The Critical Principles of V. L. Parrington', in *Science and Society*, Fall 1939.

It was the grass-roots radical, the Populist, the Jeffersonian liberal, even the quasi-Marxist in him, that combined to make him so outstanding a Progressive intellectual.
Alfred Kazin, *On Native Grounds*.

. . . Parrington came to be essentially Jeffersonian in his outlook: a natural aristocrat, a religious skeptic, a man of learning yet rooted to the soil and ever hopeful that the plasticity of life allowed the potential fulfillment of democratic dreams.
Robert A. Skotheim and Kermit Vanderbilt, 'Vernon Louis Parrington', in *Pacific Northwest Quarterly*, July 1962.

What Whitman accomplished for American poetry, Parrington achieved for intellectual history. He felled the timber for later historians to come into finer proportions.
Ibid.

And whenever the liberal historian of America finds occasion to take account of the national literature, . . . it is Parrington who is his standard and guide.
Lionel Trilling, in Richard Hofstadter, *The Progressive Historian*.

PARRY, SIR CHARLES HUBERT HASTINGS

1848–1918 Composer

It is a good thing Parry died when he did; otherwise he might have set the whole Bible to music.
Frederick Delius, in Philip Heseltine, *Delius*.

I cannot stand Parry's orchestra: it's dead and never more than an *organ part arranged*.
Edward Elgar, Letter to A. J. Jaeger, March 1898.

That healthy vigorous beefsteak optimism of Parry.
Gustav Holst, Letter to Ralph Vaughan Williams, 1903.

With many composers you gradually become aware that they have the defects of their qualities. With Parry the process is reversed; it is only by degrees that you discover him to possess the qualities of his defects.
R. O. Morris, *Music and Letters*, March 1920.

As a composer he has ceased to be for the simple reason that as a composer he never was.
Parry's music is not an artist's picture of the emotions with which it deals; it is only a guide book to the emotions, a conscientiously constructed chart of them, done by a plodding cartographer without the visionary inner eye.
Ernest Newman, in *Musical Courier*, 1919.

I respect Mr. Parry; I enjoy his musical essays; I appreciate his liberal views; I know the kindly feelings his pupils at the Royal College have for him. If he would only be content with an overture, I should praise it to the skies sincerely; for I like to hear just one specimen of shipshape professional composition in sonata form occasionally. But I really cannot stand four large doses of it in succession — *Allegro con spirito*, in C; *Andante sostenuto*, in A minor; *Allegro scherzoso* (*scherzoso* indeed!) in F; and *Moderato*, with variations (two repeats in each) — twelve variations, as I am a living man!
George Bernard Shaw, in *Star*, 24 May 1889.

Parry never tried to divorce art from life: he once said to me 'Write choral music, as befits an Englishman and a democrat.'
Ralph Vaughan Williams, talking at the Composer's Concourse, 1957.

PARSONS, LOUELLA

1881?–1972 Journalist

The first person I ever cared deeply and sincerely about was — myself.
On herself, in George Eells, *Hedda and Louella*.

. . . she never avoids phrases like 'the reason is because' unless it is impossible not to do so, and she likes her infinitives split.
Anon., in *ibid*.

Hearst's Hollywood Stooge.
Joel Faith, in *ibid*.

You turn the whole nation into a swerving circle without too much needle.
Bob Hope, in *ibid*.

PASSFIELD, LORD, see under WEBB, SIDNEY

PATER, WALTER HORATIO

1839–94 Critic, Essayist

Even then [in my childhood] I was angry that he should treat English as a dead language, bored by that sedulous ritual wherewith he laid out every sentence as in a shroud — hanging, like a widower, long over its marmoreal beauty or ever he could lay it in his book, its sepulchre.
Max Beerbohm, *Works*: 'Diminuendo'.

Mr Walter Pater's style is, to me, like the face of some old woman who has been to Madame Rachel and had herself enamelled. The bloom is nothing but powder and paint and the odour is cherryblossom.
Samuel Butler, *Notebooks*.

Faint, pale, embarrassed, exquisite Pater! He reminds me, in the disturbed midnight of our actual literature, of one of those lucent match boxes which you place, on going to bed, near the candle, to show you, in the darkness, where you can strike a light: he shines in the uneasy gloom — vaguely, and has a phosphorescence, not a flame.
Henry James, Letter to Edmund Gosse, 13 December 1894.

Alma Pater.
Osbert Lancaster, written on a photograph of Pater when Lancaster was at Oxford, in John Betjeman, *Summoned by Bells*.

So you are going to see Pater! That will be delightful. But I must tell you one thing about him, to save you from disappointment. You must not expect him to talk like his prose. Of course, no true artist ever does that. But, besides that, he never talks about anything that interests him. He will not breathe one golden word about the Renaissance. No! he will probably say something like this: 'So you wear cork soles in your shoes? Is that really true? And do you find them comfortable? . . . How extremely interesting!'
> Oscar Wilde, in Richard Le Gallienne, *The Romantic '90s.*

See also George Kaufman, Rudyard Kipling, William Wordsworth

PATTON, GEORGE SMITH

1885—1945 Soldier

I know that my ambition is selfish and cold yet it is not a selfish selfishness for instead of sparing me, it makes me exert myself to the uttermost to attain an end which will do neither me nor anyone else any good. . . . I will do my best to attain what I consider — wrongly perhaps — my destiny.
> On himself, in Martin Blumenson, *The Patton Papers.*

Old Blood and Guts.
> Anon., in *ibid.*

Patton was an acolyte to Mars.
> Colonel J. J. Farley, 17 November 1964, in Robert Hebs Heinl Jr, *The Dictionary of Military and Naval Quotations.*

PAXTON, SIR JOSEPH

1801—65 Architect, Landscape Designer

His life was simple, his ingenuity unfailing, his energy unbounded, his health robust, his taste dubious.
> R. Furneaux-Jordan, *Sir Joseph Paxton.*

From his earliest days at Chatsworth, Paxton displayed, as fully as any man of his time, that thoroughly Victorian blend of romanticism and realism. If the Chatsworth cascades and fountains were conceived as a faerie fantasy, the pumps and pipes and jets, designed in the Estate Office, were efficient and durable. It was the marriage of these two opposed ways of thought which lifted Paxton's talents to the level of genius.
> *Ibid.*

The quantity of bodily industry which that Crystal Palace expresses is very great. So far it is good.

The quantity of thought it expresses is, I suppose, a single and very admirable thought of Sir Joseph Paxton's, probably not a bit brighter than thousands of thoughts which pass through his active and intelligent brain every hour — that it might be possible to build a greenhouse larger than ever greenhouse was built before. This thought, and some very ordinary algebra, are as much as all that glass can represent of human intellect.
> John Ruskin, *The Stones of Venice,* Appendix 7.

PEABODY, GEORGE

1795—1869 Financier, Philanthropist

Let all the rich, who mean, when they shall die
To do great things by legacy,
How to make sure a worthy end, and see
And taste the pleasure, learn of Peabody.
> George T. Dole, poem delivered before the Phi Beta Kappa Society of Yale University, 1868.

. . . Like Jesus Christ, he had a wound in the side, this wound was the misery of others. It was not blood that flowed from this wound: it was gold which now came from a heart. . . . It was on the face of [such] men that we can see the smile of God.
> Victor Hugo, *Elegy on George Peabody.*

PEACOCK, THOMAS LOVE

1785—1866 Novelist

A minor master . . . far more energetically original than the chorus of drowsy Victorian and Edwardian eulogy would imply. That enchanting urbanity, which gave him command of a whole range between witty seriousness and demented knockabout, was something which disappeared from the English novel almost before it had properly arrived.
> Kingsley Amis, *What Became of Jane Austen?*

The art of satire, in his hands, resolved itself into a kind of cookery; almost, indeed, into the concoction of a simple dish, with much the same ingredients, which the *chef* spends fifteen years in garnishing and making perfect; which is named after him, and copied by others, but of which the open secret dies with him.
> Oliver Elton, *A Survey of English Literature.*

When one reads Peacock aloud one soon notices that the style is tuned to the cadence of the human voice rather than to the sweep of the eye, which accounts for so much of its balance and variations of rhythm and tone. Wilson thought of flute music in connection with the qualities of clarity and purity of tone in Peacock's style, but the roundness and fullness of the style evoke the sound of the French horn as well.

George Bernard Shaw, Preface to *Man and Superman*.

His fine wit
Makes such a wound, the knife is lost in it;
A strain too learned for a shallow age,
Too wise for selfish bigots; let his page
Which charms the chosen spirits of the time,
Fold itself up for the serener clime
Of years to come, and find its recompense
In that just expectation.

Percy Bysshe Shelley, *Letter to Maria Gisborne*.

Mr Peacock is on a visit with us this winter. He is a very mild, agreeable man, and a good scholar. His enthusiasm is not very ardent, nor his views very comprehensive, but he is neither superstitious, ill-tempered, dogmatical, nor proud.

Percy Bysshe Shelley, Letter to T. J. Hogg, 21 November 1811.

PEAKE, MERVYN LAURENCE

1911—68 Novelist

To canalize my chaos. To pour it out through the gutters of Gormenghast. To make not only tremendous stories in paint that approximate to the visual images in Gormenghast, but to create arabesques, abstracts, of thrilling colour, worlds on their own, landscapes and roofscapes and skyscapes peopled with hierophants and lords — the fantastic and the grotesque, and to use paint as though it were meat and drink.

On himself, Letter to Maeve Gilmore.

His inglorious war was spent first as a gunner on the Isle of Sheppey, then as a sapper in Blackpool, where — his mechanical incompetence being exposed — he employed his artistic gifts printing beautiful cards saying 'Only officers may use this lavatory.'

Anon., in *Times Literary Supplement*, 25 June 1970.

Peake has been praised, but he has also been mistrusted. His prose works are not easily classifiable: they are unique as, say, the books of Peacock or Lovecraft are unique. . . . It is difficult, in post-war English writing, to get away with big rhetorical

gestures. Peake manages it because, with him, grandiloquence never means diffuseness; there is no musical emptiness in the most romantic of his descriptions; he is always exact.

Anthony Burgess, Introduction to *Titus Groan*.

For Mervyn, going down into the underground was not a straightforward, upright, and still journey down an escalator, but a sliding descent down the rail. I could never summon up courage to follow, so that sometimes he would reach the bottom, go up the other escalator, and pass me by once more at, it seemed, even greater speed, in time to take my hand as I staidly tripped off the bottom step. We often went to Lyons for meals, and I suppose we were neither of us the most regular looking customers . . . Mervyn sometimes ordered stewed camel. It probably wasn't very funny, and the waitresses obviously thought not.

Maeve Gilmore, *A World Away*.

To whom it may concern, I wish to recommend Mr Mervyn Peake as a draughtsman of great distinction, who might be most suitably employed in war records.

Augustus John, Letter, 28 December 1939.

PEALE, CHARLES WILLSON

1741—1827 Painter

I must say something on painting which has employed some of my thoughts, as essential to us painters — which I hope you will take no offense at. Truth is better than a high finish. The Italians say give me a true outline & you may fill it up with Turd.

On himself, in Charles Coleman Sellers, *Charles Willson Peale*.

What [Tom] Paine was with the pen, Peale would now seek to be with the brush — a propagandist of revolution and the Age of Reason.

Charles Coleman Sellers, *ibid.*

In a portrait artist's face one often finds the artist also, and this is true of Peale. There are exceptions, but the Peale face is almost always recognizable at once in an expression of gentle, intelligent affability. The eyes are warm, the mouth approves. These are faces of the Enlightenment, the Age of Reason. When you see them in the mass, as in the great Independence Hall collection, the impression is that of an audience as a favorite lecturer raises his eyes to address them.

Ibid.

PEARSON, DREW (ANDREW RUSSELL)

1897—1969 Journalist

I operate by sense of smell. If something smells wrong, I go to work.
> On himself, in Oliver Pilat, *Drew Pearson*.

. . . adapted the untiring and often merciless skill of investigative political reporting to the modern idiom of the insider's gossip.
> Anon., Obituary, in *New York Times*.

Pearson is America's No 1 keyhole peeper, muck-raker, propaganda peddling prostitute of the nation's press and radio.
> Senator William Jenner of Indiana, in Morris A. Bealle, *All American Louse*.

He is not a sunnavabitch. He is only a filthy brain child, conceived in ruthlessness and dedicated to the proposition that Judas Iscariot was a piker.
> *Ibid.*

. . . an unprincipled, degenerate liar — but with a tremendous audience both in the newspapers and on the airwaves — a man who has been able to sugar-coat his wares so well that he has been able to fool vast numbers of people with his fake piety and false loyalty.
> Senator Joseph McCarthy, in Herman Klurfeld, *Behind the Lines*.

Years ago, when he first came to Washington, he was nearly all one color, having only about the normal number of spots on his escutcheon. Today, by rolling in the muck virtually all of his working hours, he has more spots than you can shake a leopard at.
> Eleanor Patterson, in *ibid*.

. . . a miscalled newscaster specializing in falsehoods and smearing people with personal and political motivation.
> Westbrook Pegler, in Oliver Pilat, *Drew Pearson*.

. . . a large man with the learned look of a Midwest college professor of Latin; socially aloof but responsive in conversation; phyically strong, able to sling a heavy bag of manure across his shoulder at the farm; and mentally tough, not merely hard, from the constant necessity of making painful decisions.
> Oliver Pilat, *Drew Pearson*.

. . . this S.O.B. makes a racket, a business, a mint of money writing fiction in the guise of news reporting.
> Walter Winchell, in *ibid*.

PEARY, ROBERT EDWIN

1856—1920 Explorer

. . . As I look about on the scenery that a few years ago would have filled me with enthusiasm, as I think of my high hopes then, and contrast them with my present lack of energy, of interest, of elation; as I think of the last four years and what I have been through . . . it all seems so small, so little worth the while that I could cry out in anguish of spirit.
> On himself, in J. E. Weems, *Peary, The Explorer and the Man*.

. . . My feelings are not of the brightest. I think of four years ago when in spite of the setback of not getting my ship farther north, I looked full of life and hope and anticipation at this . . . shore mellow in the August sunlight, and dreamed of what I should accomplish. Now a maimed old man, unsuccessful after the most arduous work. . . . Has the game been worth the candle?
> *Ibid.*

I don't want to live and die without accomplishing anything or without being known beyond a narrow circle of friends. I would like to acquire a name which would be an 'open sesame' to circles of culture and refinement anywhere, a name which would make my mother proud and which would make me feel that I was the peer of anyone I might meet.
> *Ibid.*

I can hear the yelping of the dogs, the shouting of the drivers, and the forward rush of every man and sledge, as after days of weary travel across the ragged sea ice, every man and dog spurts for the shore of that untrodden land lying a few yards ahead in the brilliant Arctic sunlight.
> *Ibid.*, on arriving at the North Pole.

Despite his many feats . . . Peary generally regarded the opening fifty-two years of his life as being comprised of one failure after another, and considering the goal he had set for himself one must agree with his stern assessment. Paradoxically, however, his final success, when it did come, actually seemed to be more of a climactic tragedy; for his most notable achievement, the one that won him the enduring fame he had yearned for when young, became muddled by a ridiculous controversy that caused him and his family boundless grief and that probably shortened his life.
> J. E. Weems, *ibid*.

The curious peered intently at the man who had endured so many bitter years in such a remote place, wondering what he was really like.
They saw a hard, erect, slender man whose fifty

years did not show from a distance. The broadest part of him was at his chest, and his hair and his drooping moustache were still auburn . . . Peary's ruddy face had been drawn by brutally cold weather, and the deep lines there were indicative of many bitter years.

Ibid.

See also Millard Fillmore

PEEL, JOHN

1776—1857 Huntsman

D'ye ken John Peel with his coat so gay?
D'ye ken John Peel at the break of the day?
D'ye ken John Peel when he's far far away
With his hounds and his horn in the morning?

'Twas the sound of his horn called me from my bed,
And the cry of his hounds has me oft-times led;
For Peel's view halloo would waken the dead,
Or a fox from his lair in the morning.
John Woodcock Graves, *John Peel.*

PEEL, SIR ROBERT

1788—1850 Prime Minister

I shall leave a name execrated by every monopolist, but it may be . . . sometimes remembered with expressions of goodwill in the abodes of those whose lot it is to labour and to earn their daily bread in the sweat of their brow, when they shall recruit their exhausted strength with abundant and untaxed food, the sweeter because it is no longer unleavened with a sense of injustice.
On himself, repealing the Corn Laws in the Commons.

His offence is not merely an offence against party, but against morals.
Anon., in *Morning Herald*, 30 June 1846, after the fall of the Tory government.

[Disraeli] attributed Peel's great power and effect in the House to having always had Blue Books by heart, and having thereby the appearance of a fund of greater knowledge than he really possessed.
William Beresford, Letter to Lord Stanley, September 1849.

Did he ever see a truth before it was forced on him by circumstances rather than reasonings? Never, perhaps. It is however a noble enough commendation

that he did not sacrifice the good of his country (when once seen clearly) even to the preservation of his personal consistency, and for this thing, if not for another, we should all bless his memory.
Elizabeth Barrett Browning, Letter to Mrs David Ogilvy, 28 August 1850.

Sir Robert Peel was a man who had stupidity in the soul. It went, as it often does, along with all the talents of a man of business and a man of the world. He was the kind of man who only knows things by their labels, and has not only no comprehension but no curiosity touching their substance or what they are made of.
G. K. Chesterton, *William Cobbett.*

If there is a word between persuasive and coaxing, I should select it as the one that best describes the manner of Mr Peel. The latter would do him great injustice, as it wants his dignity, and argument, and force; and the former would . . . do injustice to the truth.
James Fenimore Cooper, *Gleanings in Europe: England.*

The right honourable gentleman caught the Whigs bathing, and walked away with their clothes.
Benjamin Disraeli, Speech, February 1845, referring to the opening of letters by governments.

His life has been a great appropriation clause. He is a burglar of other's intellect . . . there is no statesman who has committed political petty larceny on so great a scale.
Benjamin Disraeli, to the House of Commons, 15 May 1847.

. . . he, like some smaller men, is . . . very sensible of the sweetness of the cheers of opponents.
William Ewart Gladstone, Diary, 30 June 1846.

Peel died at peace with all mankind; even with Disraeli. The last thing he did was to cheer Disraeli. It was not a very loud cheer, but it *was* a cheer; it was distinct. I sat next to him.
William Ewart Gladstone, in Benjamin Disraeli, *Reminiscences.*

Peel! what is Peel to me? Damn Peel?
Lord Lyndhurst, speaking to his fellow peers about amending the Municipal Reform Bill, 1835.

In the administration of public affairs, as surely as a great act or measure is impracticable, you forthwith achieve it.
Harriet Martineau, Letter to Peel, 22 February 1846.

His smile was like the silver plate on a coffin.
   Daniel O'Connell, in G. M. Trevelyan, *British History in the Nineteenth Century*.

He has abundance of human honesty and not much of Divine faith; he will never do a dishonourable thing, he will be ashamed of doing a religious one.
   Lord Shaftesbury, Diary, 24 July 1841.

The truth is that Peel is afraid of the Opposition, his colleagues and his supporters, He is afraid to place himself on high ground. He never fixes his mind on any good principle to be held in discussion; nor on any principle at all till he gets into the House of Commons; and then he seeks for one which he thinks will be safe.
   Duke of Wellington, Letter to Mrs Arbuthnot, April 1828.

I have no small talk and Peel has no manners.
   Duke of Wellington, in G. W. E. Russell, *Collections and Recollections*.

That is a gentleman, who never sees the end of a campaign.
   Duke of Wellington, in Benjamin Disraeli, *Reminiscences*.

See also Charles Dickens

PEELE, GEORGE

1556–96 Poet

This person was living, in his middle age, in the latter end of Q. *Elizabeth*, but when, or where he dyed, I cannot tell; for so it is, and always hath been, that most Poets dye poor, and consequently obscurely, and a hard matter it is to trace them to their graves.
   Anthony à Wood, *Athenae Oxonienses*.

PEIRCE, CHARLES SANDERS

1839–1914 Philosopher

Just as there are many fogies — old and young — who with idle conservatism dispute the value of my work, so, unless the whole congregation of logicians experiences a regeneration, I expect the day will come when another generation of old and young fogies will be equally indisposed to admit that there is any corner of the whole field that I have not turned up, and put into the right condition.
   On himself, in Ernest Nagel, 'Charles S. Peirce, Pioneer of Modern Empiricism', in *Philosophy of Science*.

He readily gave the impression of being unsocial, possibly cold, more truly retiring. At bottom the trait was in the nature of a refined shyness, an embarrassment in the presence of the small talk and introductory salutations intruded by convention to start one's mind.
   Joseph Jastrow, 'Charles S. Peirce as a Teacher', in *Journal of Philosophy, Psychology and Scientific Methods*, 21 December 1916.

Deeply mathematical, his thinking had not the trace of a scholastic quality; there was no love of the tool for its own sake, but an admiration of its cutting edge as the issue of human care and skill.
   Ibid.

But he was always somewhat proud of his ancestry and connections, overbearing towards those who stood in his way, indifferent to the consequences of his acts, quick to take affront, highly emotional, easily duped, and with, as he puts it, 'a reputation for not finding things'.
   Paul Weiss, Charles Sanders Peirce, in *Dictionary of American Biography*.

. . . Peirce's career with ideas is most absorbing, for his life story is primarily the record of an intellect; an intellect masculine in its boldness and sweep, vast in its learning, austere in its self-discipline and comparable to that of Leibniz in its combination of mathematical, logical, scientific, and metaphysical power.
   Frederic Harold Young, 'Charles Sanders Peirce', in Philip P. Wiener and Frederic H. Young eds, *Studies in The Philosophy of Charles Sanders Peirce*.

PELHAM-HOLLES, THOMAS, see under NEWCASTLE, DUKE OF

PENN, WILLIAM

1644–1718 Founder of Pennsylvania

Quoth Martyr Charles to William Penn,
   'Tis best to let things be:
They're used to looking up at you,
   And they can see through me.
   Anon., *Notes and Queries*, Tenth series, vol. 10: 227.

Quoth Martyr Charles to William Penn,
   Nay, broadbrim, no such curse;
Whitehall was surely bad enough,
   Your City Hall were worse.
   Anon., in *ibid.*, vol. 11: 55.

. . . an intemperate meal for a boundless liberty of conscience.

Anon., in Bonamy Dobrée, *William Penn*.

William Penn . . . came to America to collect some land the King owed his father. He belonged to a frightened religious Sect known as the Quakers. So that he would not be forgotten, he gave his name to the Pennsylvania Railroad, the Pennsylvania Station, and the state prison, which is known as the Penn.

Richard Armour, *It All Started With Columbus*.

The first Sense he had of God was when he was 11 years old at Chigwell, being retired into a chamber alone; he was so suddenly surprized with an inward comfort and (as he thought) an externall glory in the roome that he has many times sayd that from thence he had the Seale of Divinity, and Immortality, that there was a God and that the Soule of man was capable of enjoying his divine communications. His schoolmaster was not of his Perswasion. . . .

John Aubrey, *Brief Lives*.

. . . in a century when theological argument was regarded as the chief end of man, Penn yielded to the prevalent fashion of striving to unscrew the inscrutable and indulged in the futile custom of dogmatizing about the unknowable.

William Bull, *William Penn: A Topical Biography*.

He had such an opinion of his own faculty of persuading, that he thought none could stand before it: 'Tho he was singular in that opinion: For he had a tedious luscious way, that was not apt to overcome a man's reason, tho' it might tire his patience.

Gilbert Burnet, *History of His Own Time*.

Penn's primary goal in life was to defend and spread the message of spiritual Christianity and to make its power operative in societies beset by sin. Despite his strenuous efforts God's kingdom did not come to Europe, England or Pennsylvania, and his will was not done 'on earth as it is in heaven.' By the last years of his life Penn had come to realize that he would pass from the kingdom of 'this world' to the Kingdom of God only when he passed through the portals of death.

Melvin B. Endy Jr, *William Penn and Early Quakerism*.

He will always be mentioned with honour as a founder of a colony, who did not in his dealings with a savage people, abuse the strength derived from civilization, and as a lawgiver who, in the age of persecution, made religious liberty the corner

stone of a polity. But his writings and his life furnish abundant proofs that he was not a man of strong sense. He had no skill in reading the characters of others. His confidence in persons less virtuous than himself led him into great errors and misfortunes. His enthusiasm for one great principle sometimes impelled him to violate other great principles which he ought to have held sacred.

T. B. Macaulay, *History of England*.

Mrs Turner tells me that Mr Will Pen, who is lately come over from Ireland, is a Quaker again, or some very melancholy thing; that he cares for no company, nor comes into any — which is a pleasant thing, after his being abroad so long — and his father such a hypocritical rogue, and at this time an atheist.

Samuel Pepys, Diary, 29 December 1667.

He was learned without vanity, apt without forwardness, facetious in conversation yet weighty and serious, of an extraordinary greatness of mind, yet void of the strain of ambition, as free from rigid gravity as he was clear of unseemly levity. A man, a scholar, a Friend, a minister surpassing in superlative endowments whose memorial will be valued by the wise and blessed with the just.

Testimony of Reading Quarterly Meeting, in C. O. Peare, *William Penn, A Biography*.

PEPYS, SAMUEL

1633–1703 Diarist, Naval Administrator

. . . among the rest Mr Christmas my old schoolfellow, with whom I had much talk. He did remember that I was a great roundhead when I was a boy, and I was much afeard that he would have remembered the words that I said the day that the King was beheaded (that were I to preach upon him my text should be: 'The memory of the wicked shall rot'); but that I found afterward that he did go away from schoole before that time.

On himself, Diary, 1 November 1660.

. . . So by coach with my wife and Mercer to the park; but the King being there, and I nowadays being doubtful of being seen in any pleasure, did part from the Tour, and away out of the Park to Knightsbridge and there eat and drank in the coach, and so home, and I, after a while at my office, home to supper and to bed — having got a great Cold, I think by pulling off my periwigg so often.

Ibid., 24 April 1665.

Lay very long in bed, discoursing with Mr Hill of most things of a man's life, and how little merit doth prevail in the world, but only favour — and that for myself, chance without merit brought me in, and that diligence only keeps me so, and will, living as I do among so many lazy people, that the diligent man becomes necessary, that they cannot do anything without him. And so told him of my late business of the victualling and what cares I am in to keep myself, having to do with people of so different factions at Court, and yet must be fair with them all — which was very pleasant discourse for me to tell.

Ibid., 1 November 1665.

Music and women I cannot but give way to, whatever my business is.

Ibid., 9 March 1666.

And so to Mrs Martin and there did what je voudrais avec her, both devante and backward, which is also muy bon plazer.

Ibid., 3 June 1666.

The truth is, I do indulge myself a little more the pleasure, knowing that this is the proper age of my life to do it, and out of my observation that most men do thrive in the world do forget to take pleasure during the time that they are getting their estate but reserve that till they have got one, and then it is too late for them to enjoy it with any pleasure.

Ibid., 10 March 1666.

To church; and with my mourning, very handsome, and new periweg, make a great show.

Ibid., 31 March 1667.

And so I betake myself to that course, which is almost as much as to see myself go into the grave; for which, and all the discomforts that will accompany me being blind, the good God prepare me!

Ibid., last entry, 31 May 1669.

In S. Pepys, the *Understanding* is *hypertrophied* to the necrosis or marasmus of the Reason and Imagination, while far-sighted (yet Oh! how short-sighted) Self-interest fills the place of Conscience.

Samuel Taylor Coleridge, Annotation to copy of Pepys's Diary, ed. Lord Braybrooke, 1825.

Pepys's only ground of morality was Prudence — a shrewd Understanding in the service of Self-love, his conscience. He was a *Pollard* man without the *Top* (i.e., the Reason as the source — of *Ideas*, or immediate yet not sensuous truths, having their evidence in themselves; and the Imagination, or idealising Power, of symbols mediating between the Reason and the Understanding); but on this account more broadly and luxuriantly branching out from the upper Trunk. For the sobriety and steadfastness of a worldly self-interest substitute inventive Fancy, Will-wantonness (*stat pro ratione voluntas*), and a humourous sense of the emptiness and dream-likeness of human pursuits — and Pepys would have been the *Panurge* of the incomparable Rabelais.

Ibid.

The Paul Pry of his day.

David Masson, in *Quarterly Review*, July and October 1856.

Matter-of-factly, like the screech of a sash-window being thrown open, begins one of the greatest texts in our history and in our literature. The subject of this biography turns his head to us across the centuries and addresses us as though we were across the room. Not to be moved is to be deficient in humanity.

Richard Ollard, *Pepys*.

Conviviality . . . was not second but first nature to Pepys.

Ibid.

Pepys's animating principle bureaucratised his surroundings just as culture put into a glass of milk transforms it into yoghurt.

Ibid.

Among the famous characters of the period were Samuel Pepys, who is memorable for keeping a Diary and going to bed a great deal, and his wife Evelyn, who kept another memorable Diary, but did not go to bed in it.

W. C. Sellar and R. J. Yeatman, *1066 and All That*.

The man, you will perceive, was making reminiscences — a sort of pleasure by ricochet, which comforts many in distress, and turns some others into sentimental libertines; and the whole book, if you will but look at it in that way, is seen to be a work of art to Pepys's own address.

Robert Louis Stevenson, *Samuel Pepys*.

Here we have a mouth pouting, moist with desires; eyes greedy, protuberant, and yet apt for weeping too, a nose great alike in character and dimensions; and altogether a most fleshly, melting countenance. The face is attractive by its promise of reciprocity. I have used the word *greedy*, but the reader must not suppose that he can change it for that closely kindred one of *hungry*, for there is here no aspiration, no waiting for better things, but an animal joy in all that comes. It could never be the face of an artist; it is the face of a *viveur* — kindly, pleased and pleasing, protected from excess and upheld in

contentment by the shifting versatility of his de-sires.
Ibid., on Pepys's portrait.

He had a kind of idealism in pleasure; like the princess in the fairy story, he was conscious of a rose-leaf out of place.
Ibid.

He has no idea of truth except for the diary. He has no care that a thing shall be, if it but appear.
Ibid.

'Tis never any drudgery to wait on Mr Pepys, whose conversation, I think, is more nearly akin to what we are taught to hope for in Heaven, than that of anybody else I know.
Humphrey Wanley, in Richard Ollard, *Pepys*.

See also Rudyard Kipling.

PERCEVAL, SPENCER

1762—1812 Prime Minister

It is a great misfortune to Mr. Perceval to write in a style that would disgrace a washerwoman.
George IV, *Letters*, 1812.

. . . the principle of Perceval's Administration was *peculating bigotry — bigotted peculation!* In the name of the Lord he plundered the people — pious and enlightened Statesman! he would take their money only for the good of their souls!
Daniel O'Connell, speaking at the Limerick Aggregate Catholic meeting, 24 July 1812.

Mr Perceval is a *very* little man.
Lord Sidmouth, Letter to Hiley Addington, 8 October 1809.

PERRY, OLIVER HAZARD

1785—1819 Sailor

We have met the enemy and they are ours. . . .
On himself, in announcing American victory over the British at the naval battle of Lake Erie, 10 September 1813.

Another victory occurred when Commodore Perry, on his way back from discovering the North Pole, swept the British from Lake Erie. The place has been kept tidy ever since.
Richard Armour, *It All Started With Columbus*.

PERSHING, JOHN JOSEPH

1860—1948 Soldier

When the last bugle is sounded, I want to stand up with my soldiers.
On himself, in *The Yanks are Coming* by the eds. of *Army Times*.

Oh to be in Paris now that Pershing's there!
To hear the waves of welcome that greet him
everywhere;
To see the children and the girls a-pelting him with
flowers,
And feel that every petal is meant for us and
ours. . . .
Anon., on Pershing's arrival in France as the head of the United States Expeditionary Force in World War I.

Pershing inspired confidence but not affection. Personal magnetism seemed lacking; he won followers and admirers but not personal worshippers. Plain in word, sane and direct in action, he applied himself to all duty and all work with a manifest purpose, not only of succeeding in what he attempted, but of surpassing, guiding and directing his followers in what was before them.
Roger L. Bullard, in Donald Smythe, *Guerrilla Warrior: The Early Life of John J. Pershing*.

Everybody thanked him and nobody gave him anything. I guess they figure that at his age he only needs half a salary as he will only eat half as much and only need half as good a place to sleep.
Will Rogers, on Pershing's retirement as Chief of Staff of the United States Army, in *The Yanks Are Coming* by the eds of *Army Times*.

He was no tin soldier and certainly no figurine saint.
Donald Smythe, *Guerrilla Warrior: The Early Life of John J. Pershing*.

PETERBOROUGH, EARL OF (CHARLES MORDAUNT)

1658—1735 Soldier, Admiral, Diplomat

Peterborough may be described as a polite, learned and amorous Charles the Twelfth. . . . What Peterborough was to Bolingbroke as a writer, he was to Marlborough as a general. . . . He was in truth the last of the knights errant. . . . His virtues and vices were those of the Round Table.
T. B. Macaulay, *The War of the Succession in Spain*.

A bitter woman summed him up as a man who to vileness of soul had joined a sort of knight errantry. An enthusiastic admirer fondly pictured him as a hangdog he dearly loved, and the ramblingest lying rogue on earth.

William Stebbing, *Peterborough.*

The standard of stature in the gallery of the War of the Spanish Succession is not so heroic that it could afford without a struggle to part with the one type not drearily commonplace.

Ibid.

Everybody has read how a London mob, mistaking, which must have been difficult for the blindest mob, the restless wiry earl for the stately and serene Duke of Marlborough, was threatening violence, when Peterborough disabused it. . . . 'In the first place, I have only five guineas in my pocket, and secondly, here they are entirely at your service.'

Ibid.

. . . a player at the game of life, for whom thrones, armies, senates, hearts, honour, were pawns to be moved hither and thither for sport; a streak of phosphoric light, trailing, full of illusions and full of charm, across fifty years of English annals; one of the most fantastically bright spirits that ever gaily dug holes for history to fill up.

Ibid.

I never knew or heard of anybody so volatile and so fixed as your Lordship. You, while your imagination is carrying you through every corner of the world . . . can at the same time remember to do offices of favour and kindness to the meanest of your friends; and in all your scenes you have passed, have not been able to attain that one quality peculiar to a great man, of forgetting everything but injuries.

Jonathan Swift, in E. B. G. Warburton, *Life of Peterborough.*

His career was a series of unconnected actions. His motives were mere impulses. He sailed with all canvas spread, but without a rudder; he admitted of no rule of duty, and his sole, but unacknowledged end, was the gratification of his inordinate self-esteem.

E. B. G. Warburton, *ibid.*

See also Alexander Pope

PETTY, SIR WILLIAM

1623—87 Political Economist

I remember about 1660 there was a great difference between him and Sir Hierome Sanchy, one of Oliver's knights. They printed one against the other:

This knight was wont to preach at Dublin. The Knight had been a soldier, and challenged Sir William to fight with him. Sir William is extremely short-sighted, and being the challengee it belonged to him to nominate place and weapon. He nominated for the place, a darke Cellar, and the weapon to be a great Carpenter's Axe. This turned the Knight's challenge into ridicule, and so it came to nought.

John Aubrey, *Brief Lives.*

Thence to White-hall, where in the Duke's chamber the King came and stayed an hour or two, laughing at Sir W Petty, who was there about his boat, and at Gresham College in general. At which poor Petty was I perceive at some loss, but did argue discreetly and bear the unreasonable follies of the King's objections and other bystanders with great discretion — and offered to take odds against the King's best boats; but the King would not lay, but cried him down with words only. Gresham College he mightily laughed at for spending time only in weighing of ayre, and doing nothing else since they sat.

Samuel Pepys, Diary, 1 February 1664.

In *Dec.* 1650 his name was wonderfully cried up for being the chief person in the recovery to life of one *Ann Green*, who was hang'd in *Oxford Castle* on the 14 of the same month, for making away her bastard child; at which time, instead of recovering her, he intended to have her made an anatomy.

Anthony à Wood, *Athenae Oxonienses.*

PETTY, WILLIAM, MARQUIS OF LANSDOWNE, see under SHELBURNE, LORD

PHILIP, 'KING' (METACOMET)

—d. 1676 Sachem of the Wampanoag Nation

The writers of his time and for one hundred fifty years afterward considered him at once a skilled and devious plotter and a spoiled child who revolted against a benign and paternalistic master race for 'fancied slights' urged on by the devil. Above all, he was a fiend incarnate, who waged barbarous warfare against a population which fought with Christian chivalry, or at most responded to extreme provocation with 'Cromwellian thoroughness.'

Charles T. Burke, *Puritans At Bay.*

PHILIPS, AMBROSE

1674—1749 Poet

Namby Pamby.

Henry Carey, *Namby Pamby: or a Panegyric on the New Versification.*

Men sometimes suffer by injudicious kindness; Philips became ridiculous, without his own fault, by the absurd admiration of his friends, who decorated him with honorary garlands which the first breath of contradiction blasted.
Samuel Johnson, *Lives of the Poets.*

. . . a good Whig and a middling poet.
T. B. Macaulay, *Essays:* 'Addison'.

If Justice Philips' costive head
Some frigid rhymes disburses;
They shall like Persian tales be read
And glad both babes and nurses.
Jonathan Swift, *Sandys's Ghost.*

PHILLIPS, WENDELL

1811—84 Abolitionist

He was about the only Bostonian of his time who wore no middle name and he was therefore considered half naked.
Frank Sullivan, *A Garland of Ibids.*

PICKETT, GEORGE EDWARD

1825—75 Soldier

'Tis Pickett's charge at Gettysburg:
How terrible it is to see
Great armies making history:
Long lines of muskets belching flame!
No need of gunners taking aim
When from that thunder cloud of smoke
The lightning kills at every stroke!
If there's a place resembling hell,
'Tis where, 'mid shot and bursting shell,
Stalks Carnage arm in arm with Death,
A furnace-blast in every breath,
On Pickett's charge at Gettysburg.
Fred Emerson Brooks, *Pickett's Charge.*

PIERCE, FRANKLIN

1804—69 Fourteenth United States President

Come rally all, the bugle call
Above the field is heard;
With Pierce and King the breezes ring,
And all the land is stirred;
The hill tops and the valleys pour
Their legions to the fight,
From sea to sea, from shore to shore,

The council fires burn bright!
So boys fling out the standard sheet,
And let the welkin ring;
We're bound to give the Whigs defeat
With gallant Pierce and King.
Anon. campaign song, 1848.

We Polked you in 1844 and we shall Pierce you in 1852.
Anon. Democratic Party election slogan referring to the comparative anonymity of two presidential candidates who were elected.

Two generals are in the field,
Frank Pierce and Winfield Scott;
Some think that Frank's a fightin man,
And some think he is not.
'Tis said that when in Mexico
While leading on his force,
He took a sudden fainting fit
And tumbled off his horse!
Anon. campaign song, 1848.

Many persons have difficulty remembering what President Franklin Pierce is best remembered for, and he is therefore probably best forgotten.
Richard Armour, *It All Started With Columbus.*

The country 'gone with a rush' [for Pierce]. A New Hampshire Democratic, doughface, militia colonel, a kind of third-rate county, or at most, state politician, President of the United States!
Richard Henry Dana, in Charles Francis Adams, *Richard Henry Dana.*

. . . a man who cannot be befriended; whose miserable administration admits but of one excuse, imbecility. Pierce was either the worst, or he was the weakest, of all our Presidents.
Ralph Waldo Emerson, in Mark Van Doren, *Nathaniel Hawthorne.*

There are scores of men in the country that seem brighter than he is, but [he] has the directing mind, and will move them about like pawns on a cheeseboard, and turn all their abilities to better purpose than they themselves could do. . . . He is deep, deep, deep. But what luck withal! Nothing can ruin him.
Nathaniel Hawthorne to Horatio Bridge, in Ray F. Nichols, *Franklin Pierce, Young Hickory of the Granite Hills.*

It was said that the delicate matter of his excessive conviviality was talked over with him and he promised to walk circumspectly should he become President.
James Ford Rhodes, in Meade Minnigerode, *Presidential Years 1787—1860.*

. . . a small politician, of low capacity and mean surroundings, proud to act as the servile tool of men worse than himself but also stronger and abler. He was ever ready to do any work the slavery leaders set him, and to act as their attorney in arguing in its favor, — to quote [Thomas Hart] Benton's phrase, with 'undaunted mendacity, moral callosity [and] mental obliquity.'
>Theodore Roosevelt, *Life of Thomas Hart Benton.*

He's got the best picture in the White House, Franklin Pierce, but being President involves a little bit more than just winning a beauty contest, and he was another one that was a complete fizzle . . . Pierce didn't know what was going on, and even if he had, he wouldn't of known what to do about it.
>Harry S. Truman, in Merle Miller, *Plain Speaking: An Oral Biography of Harry S. Truman.*

Every man of solid understanding both in congress and elsewhere, who had aided this ill-starred scion of the Granite State in his efforts to reach the Presidency, became satisfied of his utter incompetency for the performance of the duties devolved upon him.
>D. L. Yulee, Letter to Stephen A. Douglas, 28 January 1853.

PIKE, ZEBULON MONTGOMERY

1779—1813 Soldier, Explorer

Pike's name remains perpetuated in a great natural monument more than 14,000 feet in height, an honour totally unjustified and totally undeserved.
>John Terrell, *Zebulon Pike.*

PINKERTON, ALLAN

1819—84 Detective

From cooper to copper.
>Anon., popular expression referring to Pinkerton's early career as a barrel maker.

PITT, WILLIAM, THE ELDER, see under CHATHAM, FIRST EARL OF

PITT, WILLIAM (THE YOUNGER)

1759—1806 Prime Minister

He was the parent of more practical reforms in administration and political economy than almost any other English statesman. . . . But he approached them with his eye, not on the horizon like a man of the study, but always on the treacherous and broken ground at his feet.
>Arthur Bryant, *The Years of Endurance.*

He was not merely a chip of the old block, but the old block itself.
>Edmund Burke, commenting upon Pitt's maiden speech, February 1781.

With death doom'd to grapple,
>Beneath this cold slab, he
Who lied in the Chapel
>Now lies in the Abbey.
>Lord Byron, *Epitaph for William Pitt.*

>Pitt too had his pride,
And as a high-soul'd minister of state is
Renown'd for ruining Great Britain gratis.
>Lord Byron, *Don Juan,* canto ix.

And oh! if again the rude whirlwind should rise,
>The dawnings of peace should fresh darkness
>>deform,
The regrets of the good and the fears of the wise
>Shall turn to the Pilot that weathered the Storm.
>George Canning, *Song,* 1802.

Pitt is to Addington
As London is to Paddington.
>George Canning, *The Oracle.*

If I should smoke . . . William would instantly call for a pipe.
>William Pitt the Elder (Earl of Chatham), in John Ehrmann, *The Younger Pitt.*

That he may be regretted by those who were looking up to his power for emoluments, or for *shelter*; by the numerous swarm of 'blood-suckers and muck-worms'; that his loss may be regretted, and deeply regretted, by these, I am far from meaning to deny; but that he is regretted by the *people of England* is a falsehood which, come whence it will, never shall pass uncontradicted by me.
>William Cobbett, *Political Register,* 1 February 1896.

The great snorting bawler.
>William Cobbett, *Rural Rides*

Mr Pitt's fault as an Englishman and statesman was that he came into place against the constitution and supported himself in place by exercising the power of the throne . . . his eloquence was so great he could explain even ev'ry disaster into almost the contrary. His choice of words was perfect, his voice beautiful, and his way of putting aside the question when he chose, and fascinating the minds of men, extraordinary. He died calm and resign'd and took the sacrament before his death.

> Georgiana, Duchess of Devonshire. Letter to the Marquis of Hartington, 23 January 1806.

Sick of thy taxes, while the wearied nation
Drags her last penny forth, and fears starvation;
Whose voice is loud, and daily waxing louder;
List to the serious sound, and damn the Powder.
To thee, responsible for every blunder,
Her mildest murmurs should be claps of thunder.

No ringlets now around her neck to wave,
Phyllis must hide the reddening shame, or shave!
At thee she flings her curses, Pitt, and cries —
At thee she darts the lightnings of her eyes;
And thinks that Love ne'er warm'd Him who could
vex
With wanton strokes of cruelty the Sex.

> 'Peter Pindar' (John Wolcot), *Hair Powder — A Plaintive Epistle.*

Pitt deem'd himself an Eagle — what a flat!
  What was he? A poor wheeling, fluttering Bat —
An Imp of Darkness — busy catching flies!
  Here, there, up, down, off, on — shriek, shriek —
          snap, snap —
His gaping mouth a very lucky trap,
  Quick seizing for his hungry maw — Supplies.

> 'Peter Pindar' (John Wolcot), *Odes to the Ins and Outs,* II.

Thou thoughtest we should all wear mourning,
  Black, weeping all for thy returning —
All with white handkerchiefs to catch wet sorrow:
  Ah! know there are not ten who care
  Five farthings were they now to hear
That thou wert in a jail tomorrow.

> *Ibid.*

Pitt was endowed with mental powers of the first order; his readiness, his apprehension, his resource were extraordinary; the daily parliamentary demand on his brain and nerve power he met with serene and inexhaustible affluence; his industry, administrative activity, and public spirit were unrivalled; it was perhaps impossible to carry the force of sheer ability further; he was a portent.

> Earl of Rosebery, *Pitt.*

From the dead eighteenth century his figure still faces us with a majesty of loneliness and courage. There may have been men both abler and greater than he, though it is not easy to cite them; but in all history there is no more patriotic spirit, none more intrepid, and none more pure.

> *Ibid.*

See also Thomas Paine, James Wolfe

POCAHANTAS

circa 1595—1617 Princess of the Tidewater Confederacy

In the obscurely tragic life of Pocahantas there is possibly no more fitting scene than her release. In a busy hostelry near the waterside, where London ends and the encircling sea begins, Pocahantas sank to her death in ever-strange arms. No-one, perhaps least of all her husband, saw life or death as she saw it, and no-one could offer her comprehensible solace.

> Philip Barbour, *Pocahantas And Her World.*

Were there two sides to Pocahantas?
Did she have a fourth dimension?

> Ernest Hemingway, in Philip Young, 'The Mother of Us All', *Kenyon Review*, 1962.

Our Mother, Pocahontas
Her skin was rosy copper-red.
And high she held her beauteous head.
Her step was like a rustling leaf:
Her heart a nest, untouched of grief.
She dreamed of sons like Powhatan,
And through her blood the lightning ran.
Love-cries with the birds she sung,
Bird like
In the grape-vine swung.
The Forest, arching low and wide
Gloried in its Indian bride.

> Vachel Lindsay, *Our Mother Pocahontas.*

. . . when inconstant Fortune turned our peace to war, this tender Virgin would still not spare to dare to visit us, and by her our jars have been oft appeased, and our wants still supplied; were it the policy of her father thus to employ her, or the ordinance of God thus to make her his instrument, or her extraordinary affection to our Nation, I know not: but of this I am sure; when her father with the utmost of his policy and power, sought to surprise me, having but eighteen with me, the dark night could not affright her from coming through the irksome woods, and with watered eyes gave me intelligence, with her best advice to escape his fury; which had he known, he had surely slain her. Jamestown with her wild train she as freely frequented, as her father's habitation, and during the time of two or three years, she next under God, was still

POE, EDGAR ALLEN

the instrument to preserve this Colony from death,
famine, and utter confusion which if in those times,
had once been dissolved, Virginia might have lain
as it was at our first arrival to this day.
  John Smith, *The General Historie of Virginia,
  The Fourthe Book.*

Shopworn by sentimentality, Pocahantas endures
and stands with the most appealing of our saints.
She has passed subtly into our folklore, where she
lives as a popular fable — a parable taught children
who carry some vague memory of her through their
lives. She is an American legend, a woman whose
actual story has blended with imaginary elements
in time become traditional.
  Philip Young, 'The Mother of Us All', in *Kenyon
  Review*, 1962.

POE, EDGAR ALLEN

1809—49 Poet, Critic, Author

I never was in the *habit* of intoxication.... But, for
a brief period, while I resided in Richmond, and
edited the *Messenger* I certainly did give way, at
long intervals, to the temptation held out on all
sides by the spirit of Southern conviviality.
  On himself, Letter to Dr J. E. Snodgrass, 1 April
  1841.

I've got an idea that if Poe had been an exemplary,
conventional, tax-oppressed citizen like Longfellow,
his few poems, as striking as they are, would not
have made so great a stir.
  Thomas Bailey Aldrich, Letter to William
  Stedman, 1900.

. . . an unmanly sort of man whose love-life seems
to have been largely confined to crying in laps and
playing house.
  W. H. Auden, in Richard Wilbur, 'Edgar Allen
  Poe', in Perry Miller ed., *Major Writers of
  America*, vol. 1.

Edgar Allen Poe
Was passionately fond of roe.
He always liked to chew some
When writing anything gruesome.
  Edmund Clerihew Bentley, *More Biography.*

It is high irony that Poe should have invented the
detective story, that stand-by for breadwinning
of the hack writer, and yet half starved himself.
  Henry Seidel Canby, *Classic Americans.*

Poe's poetry began as a presumably passionate ex-

pression of the mind and imagination of Edgar Poe;
it ended as a commentary on and a 'philosophy'
of the whole Romantic concept of the creative
imagination.
  Edward H. Davidson, *Poe, A Critical Study.*

That Poe had a powerful intellect is undeniable: but
it seems to me the intellect of a highly gifted young
person before puberty. The forms which his lively
curiosity takes are those in which a pre-adolescent
mentality delights: wonders of nature and of
mechanics and of the supernatural, cryptograms and
cyphers, puzzles and labyrinths, mechanical chess-
players and wild flights of speculation.
  T. S. Eliot, *Essays.*

The jingle man,
  Ralph Waldo Emerson, in *ibid.*

He had, to a morbid excess, that desire to rise which
is vulgarly called ambition, but no wish for the
esteem or the love of his species; only the hard wish
to succeed — not shine, not serve — succeed, that he
might have the right to despise a world which galled
his self-conceit.
  Rufus Griswold, in Arthur Hobson Quinn, *Edgar
  Allen Poe.*

The substance of Poe is refined; it is his form that
is vulgar. He is, as it were, one of Nature's gentle-
men, unhappily cursed with incorrigible bad taste.
  Aldous Huxley, 'Vulgarity in Literature', in
  Robert Regan ed., *Poe, A Collection of Critical
  Essays.*

With all due respects to the very original genius of
the author of the 'Tales of Mystery', it seems to us
that to take him with more than a certain degree
of seriousness is to lack seriousness one's self.
  Henry James, *Comments.*

He was an adventurer into the vaults and cellars
and horrible underground passages of the human
soul. He sounded the horror and the warning of his
own doom.
  D. H. Lawrence, *Studies in Classic American
  Literature.*

Poe had a pretty bitter doom. Doomed to seethe
down his soul in a great continuous convulsion of
disintegration, and doomed to register the process.
And then doomed to be abused for it, when he had
performed some of the bitterest tasks of human
experience that can be asked of a man. Necessary
tasks too. For the human soul must suffer its own
disintegration, consciously, if ever it is to survive.
  Ibid.

602

I love him in this blatant, well-fed place.
Of all the faces, his the only face
Beautiful, tho' painted for the stage,
Lit up with song, then torn with cold, small rage,
Shames that are living, loves and hopes long dead,
Consuming pride, and hunger, real, for bread.
Vachel Lindsay, *The Wizard in the Street.*

The hurrying great ones scorn his Raven's croak,
And well may mock his mystifying cloak
Inscribed with runes from tongues he has not read,
To make the ignoramus turn his head.
The artificial glitter of his eyes
Has captured half-grown boys. They think him wise
Some shallow player-folk esteem him deep,
Soothed by his stead wan's mesmeric sweep.
Ibid.

. . . three-fifths of him genius and two-fifths sheer
fudge. . . .
James Russell Lowell, *A Fable for Critics.*

The emphasis in Poe is almost always on the psychological aspect, on the inner response rather than the external stimulus.
David M. Rein, 'The Appeal of Poe Today', in Richard P. Benton ed., *New Approaches to Poe.*

Above all, Poe is great because he is independent of cheap attractions, independent of sex, of patriotism, of fighting, of sentimentality, snobbery, gluttony, and all the rest of the vulgar stock-in trade of his profession. This is what gives him his superb distinction.
George Bernard Shaw, 'Edgar Allen Poe', in Eric W. Carlson ed., *The Recognition of Edgar Allen Poe.*

Poe is a kind of Hawthorne with delirium tremens.
Leslie Stephen, *Hours in a Library.*

. . . Poe's verses illustrate an intense faculty for technical and abstract beauty, with the rhyming art to excess, an incorrigible propensity toward nocturnal themes, a demoniac undertone behind every page — and, by final judgment, probably belong among the electric lights of imaginative literature, brilliant and dazzling, but with no heat.
Walt Whitman, *Edgar Poe's Significance.*

See also J. C. Powys, Alfred, Lord Tennyson, Thomas Wolfe

POLK, JAMES KNOX

1795–1849 Eleventh United States President

. . . a more ridiculous, contemptible and forlorn

candidate was never put forth by any party. Mr. Polk is a sort of fourth or rather fortieth rate lawyer and small politician in Tennessee, who by accident was once Speaker of the House. . . . He was rejected even by his own State as Governor — and now he comes forward as candidate of the great democracy.
Anon., in *New York Herald.*

. . . he is sold soul and body to that grim idiot, half albino, half negro, the compound of democracy and of slavery, which, by the slave representation in Congress, rules and ruins the Union.
John Quincy Adams, in *ibid.*

James K. Polk and his Mexican war, the man inhumane and void of integrity, the measure an injustice practised upon a weaker neighbour.
Hubert Howe Bancroft, *Retrospection.*

Polk's mind was rigid, narrow, obstinate, far from first-rate. . . . But if his mind was narrow it was powerful and he had guts. If he was orthodox, his integrity was absolute and he could not be scared, manipulated, or brought to heel. No one bluffed him, no one moved him with direct or oblique pressure. Furthermore, he knew how to get things done, which is the first necessity of government, and he knew what he wanted done, which is the second. . . . He was to be the only 'strong' President between Jackson and Lincoln. He was to fix the mold of the future in America down to 1860, and therefore for a long time afterward. That is who James Polk was.
Bernard De Voto, in Saul Braun, in *The American Heritage History of the Presidents of the United States.*

. . . a victim of the use of water as a beverage.
Samuel Houston, in Llerena Friend, *Sam Houston, The Great Designer.*

Polk's appointments all in all are the most damnable set that was ever made by any President since the government was organized. . . . He has a set of interested *parasites* about him, who flatter him until he does not know himself. He seems to be acting upon the principle of hanging an old friend for the purpose of making two new ones. . . . There is one thing I will say . . . I *never betrayed a friend or [was] guilty of the black sin of ingratitude.* I fear Mr. Polk cannot say as much.
Andrew Johnson, in Eric L. McKitrick, *Andrew Johnson: A Profile.*

Had it not been for the press, James K. Polk might as well have retired to a monastery instead of occupying the White House as far as his Presidential

contacts with the public were concerned.
    James E. Pollard, *The Presidents and the Press*.

By carrying the flag to the Pacific he gave America
her continental breadth and ensured her future significance in the world . . . Polk's aggressive course
toward Mexico outraged moralists at the time and
since, but no responsible person has yet proposed
that his work be undone.
    Arthur M. Schlesinger, *A Yardstick for
    Presidents, Paths to the Present*.

. . . He was not fastidious; he was not thoughtful
of the rights of other peoples, other races, other
political parties than his own. . . . His motto for
Americans and white men was to keep what they
had and catch what they could.
    James Schouler, *History of the United States*.

See also Franklin Pierce

POLLOCK, JACKSON

1912—56 Artist

We're all of us influenced by Freud, I guess. I've
been a Jungian for a long time . . . painting is a
state of being. . . . Painting is self-discovery. Every
good artist paints what he is.
    On himself, in Francis V. O'Connor, *Jackson
    Pollock*.

Abstract painting is abstract. It confronts you.
There was a reviewer a while back who wrote that
my pictures didn't have any beginning or any end.
He didn't mean it as a compliment, but it was. It
was a fine compliment.
    Ibid.

The idea of an isolated American painting, so popular in this country during the 'thirties, seems absurd
to me, just as the idea of creating a purely American
mathematics or physics would seem absurd. . . . And
in another sense, the problem doesn't exist at all; or,
if it did, would solve itself: An American is an
American and his painting would naturally be qualified by that fact, whether he wills it or not. But the
basic problems of contemporary painting are independent of any one country.
    Ibid.

My painting does not come from the easel. I hardly
ever stretch my canvas before painting. I prefer to
tack the unstretched canvas to the hard wall or the
floor. I need the resistance of a hard surface. On the
floor I am more at ease. I feel nearer, more a part of
the painting, since this way I can walk around it,

work from the four sides and literally be *in* the
painting. This is akin to the method of the Indian
sand painters of the West. I continue to get further
away from the usual painter's tools such as easel,
palette, brushes, etc. I prefer sticks, trowels, knives
and dripping fluid paint or a heavy impasto with
sand, broken glass and other foreign matter added.
When I am *in* my painting, I'm not aware of what I
am doing. It is only after a sort of 'get acquainted'
period that I see what I have been about. I have no
fears about making changes, destroying the image,
etc., because the painting has a life of its own. I
try to let it come through. It is only when I lose
contact with the painting that the result is a mess.
Otherwise there is pure harmony, an easy give and
take, and the painting comes out well.
    On himself, *Possibilities*.

Before I get started on my own stuff and forget
everything else I want to tell you I think the little
sketches you left around here are magnificent.
Your color is rich and beautiful. You've the stuff
old kid — all you have to do is keep it up. You
ought to give some time to drawing — but I do not
somehow or other feel the lack of drawing in the
stuff left here. It seems to *go* without it.
    Thomas Hart Benton, Letter to Pollock, 1935.

What is thought to be Pollock's bad taste is in
reality simply his willingness to be ugly in terms of
contemporary taste. In the course of time this
ugliness will become a new standard of beauty.
Besides, Pollock submits to a habit of discipline
derived from cubism; and even as he goes away from
cubism he carries with him the unity of style with
which it endowed him when in the beginning he
put himself under its influence. Thus Pollock's
superiority to his contemporaries in his country
lies in his ability to create a genuinely violent and
extravagant art without losing stylistic control.
His emotion starts out pictorially; it does not have
to be castrated and translated in order to be put
into a picture. . . .
    Clement Greenberg, in *Nation*, 13 April 1946.

Lee Krasner also introduced Pollock to Hans
Hofmann. When Hofmann first saw his paintings he
recognized that Pollock 'worked from the heart,'
but suggested that he could profit from enrolling in
his school and working from nature. Pollock replied: 'I am nature.'
    Francis V. O'Connor, *Jackson Pollock*.

'Talent, will, genius,' as George Sand wrote Flaubert,
'are natural phenomena like the lake, the volcano,
the mountain, the wind, the star, the cloud.'
Pollock's talent is volçanic. It has fire. It is unpredictable. It is undisciplined. It spills itself out in a

mineral prodigality not yet crystalized. It is lavish, explosive, untidy.

But young painters, particularly Americans, tend to be too careful of opinion. Too often the dish is allowed to chill in the serving. What we need is more young men who paint from inner impulse without an ear to what the critic or spectator may feel — painters who will risk spoiling a canvas to say something in their own way. Pollock is one.

James Johnson Sweeney, in Francis V. O'Connor, *Jackson Pollock*.

The nervous, if rough, calligraphy of Pollock's work may hide a protest against the cool architectural objectivity of the abstractionist mode as it makes its subjective statement. Pollock does not seem to be especially talented, there being too much of an air of baked-macaroni about some of his patterns, as though they were scrambled baroque designs.

Parker Tyler, in *View*, May 1945.

PONSONBY, HENRIETTA, see under BESSBOROUGH, LADY

PONTIAC

—d. 1769 Chief of the Ottowa Nation

I mean to destroy the English and leave not one upon our lands.

On himself, in Allan W. Eckert, *The Conquerors*.

. . . there is reason to judge of Pontiac, not only as a savage possessed of the most refined cunning and treachery natural to the Indians, but as a person of extraordinary abilities . . . he keeps two secretaries, one to write for him, and the other to read the letters he receives, and he manages them so as to keep each of them ignorant of what is transacted by the other.

General Thomas Gage, Letter to Lord Halifax, 1764.

Among all the wild tribes of the continent, personal merit is indispensable to gaining or preserving dignity. Courage, resolution, address, and eloquence are sure passports to distinction. With all these Pontiac was pre-eminently endowed, and it was chiefly to them, urged to their highest activity by a vehement ambition, that he owed his greatness. He possessed a commanding energy and force of mind, and in subtlety and craft could match the best of his wily race. But though capable of acts of magnanimity, he was a thorough savage, with a wider range of intellect than those around him, but

showing all their passions and prejudices, their fierceness and treachery. His faults were the faults of his race; and they cannot eclipse his nobler qualities.

Francis Parkman, *The Conspiracy of Pontiac*.

POPE, ALEXANDER

1688—1744 Poet

I left no calling for this idle trade,
No duty broke, no father disobey'd.
The Muse but serv'd to ease some friend, not Wife,
To help me thro' this long disease, my Life.

On himself, *Epistle to Dr. Arbuthnot*.

Yes I am proud; I must be proud to see
Men, not afraid of God, afraid of me.

On himself, *Epilogue to the Satires*.

Heroes and Kings! your distance keep;
In peace let one poor Poet sleep,
Who never flatter'd folks like you:
Let Horace blush, and Virgil too.

On himself, *For One Who Would Not be Buried in Westminster Abbey*.

Wordsworth says somewhere that wherever Virgil seems to have composed 'with his eye on the object', Dryden fails to render him. Homer invariably composes 'with his eye on the object', whether the object be a moral or a material one: Pope composes with his eye on his style, into which he translates his object, whatever it is.

Matthew Arnold, *On Translating Homer*.

If Wordsworth had Pope in mind when he advised Poets to write 'in the language really used by men' he was singularly in error. Should one compare Pope at his best with any of the Romantics, including Wordsworth, at their best, it is Pope who writes as men normally speak to each other and the latter who go in for 'poetic' language.

W. H. Auden, *Forewords and Afterwords*.

As I get older, and the times get gloomier and more difficult, it is to poets like Horace and Pope that I find myself more and more turning for the kind of refreshment I require.

W. H. Auden, in *New Yorker*, 22 February 1969.

It is a pretty poem, Mr. Pope, but you must not call it Homer.

Richard Bentley, on Pope's translation, in Samuel Johnson, *Lives of the Poets*.

I spoke against his Homer, and the portentuous cub never forgives.

    Richard Bentley, in Francis Wrangham, *British Plutarch*.

One whom it was easy to hate, but still easier to quote.

    Augustine Birrell, *Obiter Dicta*.

I told him that Voltaire, in a conversation with me, had distinguished Pope and Dryden thus:– 'Pope drives a handsome chariot, with a couple of neat trim nags; Dryden, a coach and six stately horses.' *Johnson*: 'Why, Sir, the truth is, they both drive coaches and six; but Dryden's horses are either galloping or stumbling: Pope's go at a steady even trot.'

    James Boswell, *Life of Johnson*.

I wonder he is not thrashed; but his littleness is his protection; no man shoots a wren.

    William Broome, Letter to Elijah Fenton, 3 May 1728.

Better to err with Pope, than shine with Pye.

    Lord Byron, *English Bards and Scotch Reviewers*.

I took Moore's poems and my own and some others, and went over them side by side with Pope's, and I was really astonished (I ought not to have been so) and mortified at the ineffable distance in point of sense, harmony, effect, and even *imagination*, passion, and *invention*, between the little Queen Anne's man, and us of the Lower Empire.

    Lord Byron, Letter to John Murray, 1817.

Those miserable mountebanks of the day, the poets, disgrace themselves and deny God, in running down Pope, the most *faultless* of Poets, and almost of men.

    Lord Byron, Letter to John Murray, 4 November 1820.

I have a dark suspicion that a modern poet might manufacture an admirable lyric out of almost every line of Pope.

    G. K. Chesterton, *Twelve Types*.

O for another Dunciad — a POPE
    To purge this dump with his gigantic boot —
Drive fools to water, aspirin or rope —
    Make idle lamp-posts bear their fitting fruit:
Private invective's far too long been mute.

    Alex Comfort, 'Letter to an American Visitor', in *Tribune*, 4 June 1943.

Then Pope, as harmony itself exact,
In verse well disciplin'd, complete, compact,
Gave virtue and morality a grace,
That, quite eclipsing Pleasure's painted face,
Levied a tax of wonder and applause,
Ev'n on the fools that trampled on their laws.
But he (his musical finesse was such,
So nice his ear, so delicate his touch)
Made poetry a mere mechanic art;
And ev'ry warbler has his tune by heart.

    William Cowper, *Table-Talk*.

Let us take the initial and final letters of his Surname, *viz.*, *A. P--E*, and they give you the Idea of an *Ape*. — *Pope* comes from the Latin word *Popa*, which signifies a little Wart; or from *Poppysma*, because he was continually *popping* out squibs of wit, or rather *Po-pysmata*, or *Po-piams*.

    John Dennis, *Daily-Journal*, 11 June 1728.

. . . Pope's translation [of Homer] is a portrait endowed with every merit except that of likeness to the original.

    Edward Gibbon, *Autobiography*.

Europe has not as yet recovered from the Renaissance, nor has English poetry recovered from Alexander Pope.

    Oliver St J. Gogarty, *As I Was Going Down Sackville Street*.

It is natural to wish the finest writer, one of them, we ever had should be an honest man. It is for the interest even of that virtue whose friend he professed himself, and whose beauties he sung, that he should not be found a dirty animal. . . . It is not from what he told me about himself, that I thought well of him, but from a humanity and goodness of heart, ay, and greatness of mind, that runs through his private correspondence, not less apparent than are a thousand little vanities and weaknesses mixed with those good qualities, for nobody ever took him for a philosopher.

    Thomas Gray, Letter to Horace Walpole, 3 February 1746.

It cannot be denied, that his chief excellence lay more in diminishing, than in aggrandizing objects; in checking, not in encouraging our enthusiasm; in sneering at the extravagances of fancy or passion, instead of giving a loose to them; in describing a row of pins and needles, rather than the embattled spears of Greeks and Trojans; in penning a lampoon or a compliment, and in praising Martha Blount.

    William Hazlitt, *Lectures on the English Poets*.

When I hear anyone say, with definite emphasis, that Pope was a poet, I suspect him of calling in

ambiguity of language to promote confusion of thought. That Pope was a poet is true; but it is one of those truths which are beloved of liars, because they serve so well the cause of falsehood. That Pope was not a poet is false; but a righteous man, standing in awe of the last judgement and the lake which burneth with fire and brimstone, might well prefer to say it.
A. E. Housman, *The Name and Nature of Poetry*.

It is surely superfluous to answer the question that has once been asked, Whether Pope was a poet? otherwise than by asking in return, If Pope be not a poet, where is poetry to be found?
Samuel Johnson, *Lives of the Poets*.

His more ambitious works may be defined as careless thinking carefully versified.
James Russell Lowell, *My Study Windows*.

No poet? Calculated commonplace?
Ten razor blades in one neat couplet case!
John Macy, *Couplets in Criticism*.

Pope courted with the utmost assiduity all the old men from whom he could hope a legacy: the Duke of Buckingham, Lord Peterborough, Sir Godfrey Kneller, Mr Wycherley, Mr Congreve, Lord Harcourt etc., and I do not doubt projected to sweep the Dean's [Jonathan Swift's] whole inheritance if he could have persuaded him to throw up his Deanery and come die in his house; and his general preaching against money was meant to induce people to throw it away that he might pick it up.
Lady Mary Wortley Montagu, Letter to Lady Bute.

Mr. Addison wrote a letter to Mr. Pope, when young, in which he desired him not to list himself under either party: 'You,' says he, 'who will deserve the praise of the whole nation, should not content yourself with the half of it.'
Joseph Spence, *Anecdotes*.

He was, in modern parlance, a nérvosé. Abnormally sensitive to stimuli, his frail organization responded frantically to the slightest outward touch. If you looked at him he would spit poison, and he would wind himself into an endless mesh-work of intrigues and suspicions if you did not. But it was not only in malignity and contortions that Pope's sensitiveness showed itself; throughout his life he gave proof of a tenderness which was something more than a merely selfish susceptibility, and of a power of affection as unmistakeable as his power of hate.
Lytton Strachey, in *Spectator*, 20 November 1909.

In POPE, I cannot read a Line,
But with a Sigh, I wish it mine;

When he can in one Couplet fix
More Sense than I can do in Six:
It gives me such a jealous Fit,
I cry, Pox take him, and his Wit.
Jonathan Swift, *On the Death of Dr Swift*.

You . . . are a kind of Hermit, how great a noise you make soever by your Ill nature in not letting the honest Villains of the Times enjoy themselves in this world, which is their only happiness, and terrifying them with another. I should have added in my libel that of all men living you are most happy in your Enemies and your Friends: and I will swear you have fifty times more Charity for mankind than I could ever pretend to.
Jonathan Swift, Letter to Alexander Pope, 1 May 1733.

His Libels have been thrown out with so much Inveteracy, that, not to dispute whether they *should* come from a *Christian*, they leave it a question whether they *could* come from a *Man*.
Lewis Theobald, Preface to *The Works of Shakespeare*, 1733.

The sublime and the pathetic are the two chief nerves of all genuine poetry. What is there transcendently sublime or pathetic in Pope?
Joseph Warton, *Essay on the Writings and Genius of Pope*.

See also Ambrose Bierce, William Blackstone, John Donne, John Dryden, John Gay, G. F. Handel, Samuel Johnson, Godfrey Kneller, Lord Mansfield, Walter Raleigh, Richard Savage, Jonathan Swift, William Wordsworth

POPE, JOHN

1822—92 Soldier

[Pope] was utterly outgeneralled; he never knew where his enemy was; he fought to no purpose. But when he did fight, it was with a will beyond his discretion.
Theodore A. Dodge, *A Bird's Eye View of Our Civil War*.

Pope is an imaginative chieftain and ranks next to [James Fenimore] Cooper as a writer of fiction.
George Templeton Strong, in Allan Nevins and M. H. Thomas eds, *The Diary of George Templeton Strong*, vol. 3.

It cannot be denied that the estimate of his character held by the officers under his command was not of a kind to elicit that hearty and zealous cooperation needed for the effective conduct of great military operations. [Pope] had the misfortune to be of all men the most *disbelieved*.

William Swinton, *Campaigns of the Army of the Potomac.*

PORSON, RICHARD

1759—1808 Greek Scholar

I went to Frankfurt, and got drunk
With that most learned professor, Brunck;
I went to Worts, and got more drunken
With that more 'learn'd professor, Ruhnken.

On himself, *Facetiae Cantabrigiensis.*

I doubt if I could produce any original work which would command the attention of posterity. I can be known only by my notes: and I am quite satisfied if, three hundred years hence, it shall be said that 'one Porson lived towards the close of the eighteenth century, who did a great deal for the text of Euripedes.'

On himself, in William Maltby, *Porsoniana.*

Porson was walking with a Trinitarian friend; they had been speaking of the Trinity. A buggy came by with three men in it: 'There,' says he, 'is an illustration of the Trinity.' 'No,' said his friend Porson, 'you must show me one man in *three* buggies, if you can.'

E. H. Barker, *Literary Recollections and Contemporary Reminiscences.*

Sometimes, at a later period, when he was able enough to pay for a dinner, he chose, in a fit of abstinence, to go without one. I have asked him to stay and dine with me; and he has replied, 'Thank you, no; I dined yesterday.'

William Maltby, *Porsoniana.*

Tooke used to say that 'Porson would drink ink rather than not drink at all.' Indeed, he would drink anything. He was sitting with a gentleman, after dinner, in the chambers of a mutual friend, a Templar, who was then ill, confined to bed. A servant came into the room, sent thither by his master for a bottle of embrocation which was on the chimney-piece. 'I drank it an hour ago,' said Porson.

Ibid.

See also Robert Southey

608

PORTER, COLE

1893—1964 Composer, Lyricist

. . . the Adlai Stevenson of songwriters. . . . He was an aristocrat in everything he did and everything he wrote. Everything had class — even a little pop song like 'Don't Fence Me In.' There are not other writers like him . . . Cole wrote exquisite melodies. . . . He had that commercial instinct. He was also lucky to have lived and died at the right time, because he lived in an era of flourish.

Richard Adler, in George Eells, *The Life that Late He Led; A biography of Cole Porter.*

Cole Porter's songs, like the man who wrote them, were always exquisitely groomed, possessed culture, breeding, and social background, and were smart and urbane, often with a touch of cynicism as spice. Porter's songs reflected the attitudes, experiences, and the *Weltanschauung* of one who had been everywhere and had seen everything. . . .

David Ewen, *Great Men of America's Popular Song.*

Porter deliberately chose to be a snob, at least to all appearances. He inherited money and loved it; but he made much more by himself and loved it as well. He spent freely and gained it freely; he even complained about taxes in a lighthearted vein. 'My ninety-two percent, I suppose, supports some unknown government bureau,' he said. He was determined to be a gay divorcé from life and never abandoned the pose.

Richard G. Hubler, *The Cole Porter Story.*

Of all the theatre men only Cole Porter truly seemed to have been born into café society, to be the perfect smart cracker gentleman. He had a million dollars and a beautiful wife (so sophisticated that she didn't know how to open a door). . . . He wore gold garters and had visited India, China, Japan, Cambodia but he liked the music of Bali best. As he floated down the Rhine in a boat he composed 'You're the Top'. . . .

Ian Whitcomb, *After the Ball: Pop Music from Rag to Rock.*

Overall, I find Rodgers warmer, Arlen more hip, Gershwin more direct, Vernon Duke more touchable, Berlin more practical. But no one can deny that Porter added a certain theatrical elegance, as well as interest and sophistication, wit, and musical complexity to the popular song form.

Alec Wilder, *American Popular Song: The Great Innovators, 1900—50.*

PORTLAND, EARL OF, see under BENTINCK, WILLIAM

PORTSMOUTH, DUCHESS OF, see under KEROUAILLE, LOUISE DE

POUND, EZRA WESTON LOOMIS

1885–1972 Poet

O Helpless few in my country
O remnant enslaved! . . .

Take thought:
I have weathered the storm
I have beaten out my exile.
    On himself, *The Rest*.

I am also at work on a cryselephantine poem of immeasurable length which will occupy me for the next four decades unless it becomes a bore.
    On himself, referring to initial work on the
    Cantos, in a letter to Milton Bronner,
    21 September 1915.

How did it go in the madhouse? Rather badly. But what other place could one live in America?
    On himself, on his imprisonment in St Eliza-
    beth's Hospital, Washington, D.C., in Charles
    Norman, *Ezra Pound*.

I see they call me Mussolini's boy. I only saw the bastard once. No German or Italian was ever in position to give me an order. So I took none. But a German near my home at Rapallo told me they were paying good money for broadcasts. That was a fatal mistake.
    On himself, referring to the start of his Italian
    broadcasts, in Charles Norman, *Ezra Pound*.

The bays that formerly old Dante crowned
Are worn today by Ezra Loomis Pound.
    Anon., in *Punch*, 22 January 1913.

His costume — the velvet jacket and the open-road shirt — was that of the English aesthete of the period. There was a touch of Whistler about him; his language, on the other hand, was Huckleberry Finn's.
    Sylvia Beach, *Shakespeare and Company*.

Mr Pound is humane, but not human.
    e.e. cummings, in Michael Reck, Ezra Pound.

Pound did not create the poets: but he created a

situation in which for the first time, there was a 'modern movement in poetry' in which English and American poets collaborated, knew each other's works and influenced each other. . . . If it had not been for the work that Pound did in the years of which I have been talking, the isolation of American poets might have continued for a long time.
    T. S. Eliot, 'Ezra Pound', in *Poetry: A Magazine
    of Verse*, 1946.

I have never known a man, of any nationality, to live so long out of his native country without seeming to settle anywhere else.
    T. S. Eliot, 'Ezra Pound', in Walter Sutton ed.,
    Ezra Pound, A Collection of Critical Essays.

A minister of the arts without portfolio.
    Horace Gregory, *Ezra Pound*.

In fact my complaint against Ezra is that, having attracted one time and again with the promise of delightful cerebral embraces, he is forever bidding me adieu with no more than a languid handshake — a suave, a fastidious, an irreproachable, but still a handshake . . . he has always about him the air of a mimic. . . . He does not present to me a style — but a series of portrayals. . . . To me Pound remains the exquisite showman minus the show.
    Ben Hecht, *Pounding Ezra*.

. . . the man who taught me to distrust adjectives.
    Ernest Hemingway, in K. L. Goodwin, *The
    Influence of Ezra Pound*.

Any poet born in this century or in the last ten years of the preceding century who can honestly say that he has not been influenced by or learned greatly from the work of Ezra Pound deserves to be pitied rather than rebuked . . . the best of Pound's writing — and it is in the Cantos — will last as long as there is any literature.
    Ernest Hemingway, in Carlos Baker, *Ernest
    Hemingway, A Life Story*.

Pound has spent his life trying to live down a family scandal:— he's Longfellow's grand-nephew.
    D. H. Lawrence, Letter to Robert Graves.

He has no real creative theme. His versification and his *Procédés* are servants to wilful ideas and platform vehemences. His moral attitudes and absolutisms are bullying assertions, and have the uncreative blatancy of one whose Social Credit consorts naturally with Fascism and anti-Semitism.
    F. R. Leavis, 'Ezra Pound', in Walter Sutton ed.,
    Ezra Pound, A Collection of Critical Essays.

Ezra Pound, I feel, is probably a poet of a higher

and rarer order than it is easy at times to realize, because of much irrelevant dust kicked up by his personality as it rushes, strides or charges across the temporal scene.

Percy Wyndham Lewis, in William Van O'Connor, *Ezra Pound.*

The United States, for all that it lay over the ocean, presented a broad target, and he fired away. His preoccupation with it, which never left him, was that of a lover who abuses his mistress through the mails and then wonders why she doesn't love him.

Charles Norman, *Ezra Pound.*

A village explainer, excellent if you were a village, but if you were not, not.

Gertrude Stein, in Malcolm Cowley, *Exile's Return.*

But the world will know him mainly as that rare thing, a poet. And when the broadcasts and the manias, the economics and the sense of justice are but footnotes in some learned history, men will remember him because he was one of the few to whom is granted the gift of giving words to that which is beyond words.

Noel Stock, *The Life of Ezra Pound.*

To talk over a poem with him is like getting you to put a sentence into dialect. All becomes clear and natural. Yet in his own work he is very uncertain, often very bad though very interesting sometimes. He spoils himself by too many experiments and has more sound principles than taste.

William Butler Yeats, Letter to Lady Gregory.

Ezra Pound has made flux his theme; plot, characterization, logical discourse, seem to him abstractions unsuitable to a man of his generation.

William Butler Yeats, 'Ezra Pound', in Walter Sutton ed., *Ezra Pound, A Collection of Critical Essays.*

See also William Carlos Williams

POWER, TYRONE EDMUND

1914—58 Actor

I've done an awful lot of stuff that's a monument to public patience.

On himself, in David Shipman, *The Great Movie Stars.*

POWERS, HIRAM

1805—73 Sculptor

Sculptor! Thy hand has moulded into form

The haggard features of a toil-worn face,
And whosoever views thy work shall trace
An age of sorrows, and a life of storm.
And canst thou mould the heart? for that is warm,
Glowing with tenderness for all its race,
Instinct with all the sympathies that grace
The pure and artless bosoms where they swarm.
Artist! may fortune smile upon thy hand!
Go forth and rival Greece's art sublime.
Return, and bid the statesmen of thy Land
Live in thy marble through all after time.
Oh, catch the fire from heaven Prometheus stole
And give the lifeless block a breathing soul.

John Quincy Adams, *To Hiram Powers.*

For one, there was Hiram Powers, who was also in Florence and whose reputation for a while was all-European, — 'the first sculptor of his age,' as a Florentine authority called him, 'without a rival,' said Thorwaldsen, 'in the making of busts.' 'The entrance of Powers upon the field,' this patriarch of sculptors said, 'constituted an era in art'; and replicas of 'The Greek Slave', about which Mrs. Browning wrote a poem, were bought for great houses in England and Russia. Powers even represented in his busts the 'porosities of the skin,' a perfection that seemed incredible to good critics of the time, and Queen Victoria admired this 'fair stone' that shamed the 'strong' by its 'thunder of white silence,' in Mrs. Browning's poem.

Van Wyck Brooks, *The Dream of Arcadia.*

It was rather Powers's character than his statues and his busts that many, like the Brownings, found delightful, for his talk was fresh, original and full of bone and muscle and his ideas were square, tangible and solid. Hawthorne, who said all this, was always glad to listen to the mill-stream of Hiram Powers's talk, whether about the buckeyes of Ohio, the hunters of the West or the dangers of blood-transfusion and the effects of draughts.

Ibid.

A very instructive man [who] sweeps one's empty and dead notions out of the way with exceeding vigor, but when you have his ultimate thought and perception you feel inclined to think and see a little further for yourself. He sees too clearly what is within his range to be aware of any region of mystery beyond.

Nathaniel Hawthorne, in Sylvia Crane, *White Silence.*

He is a man of great mechanical talent and natural strength of perception, but with no poetry in his composition, and I think no creative power. . . .

William Wetmore Story, Letter to James Russell Lowell, in Henry James, *William Wetmore Story.*

POWYS, JOHN COWPER

1872–1963 Novelist

Yes, I am a born Clown and therefore just suited to write fairy stories as I have done since I was ten years old when at Dorchester, Dorset, Thomas Hardy taught me to like Edgar Allen Poe, and Poe taught me about those 'Mimes in the form of God on high, blind puppets that come and go at bidding of vast formless things that move the scenery to and fro and flap from out their condor wings invisible woe.'
On himself, Letter to Nicholas Ross, 9 February 1960.

My 'lecturing' really was . . . a sort of focussing, through one single twisting, leaping, shuffling, skipping, bowing and scraping human figure, of some special comic-tragic vein in the planetary consciousness . . . I often found it *impossible to stop*. That was my worst fault as a lecturer. I used to *try* to stop; and even begin my peroration; but something, some delicate nuance, some metaphysical nicety, would come sliding into my brain, and I would go whirling on again in my spiral dance, like that mad storm god in Hiawatha. There were even times when I would lecture without a pause and in a constant mounting crescendo for no less than two hours!
On himself, *Autobiography*.

He seemed like one of the Gods returned to earth from Olympus or Valhalla, or a flaming Montezuma, not in spangled loin cloths and beaten discs of thin gold, but in modern dress.
Nicholas Ross, *J.C.P. and J.R.N.R.* (an introduction to Powys's letters to Ross).

PRESCOTT, WILLIAM HINCKLING

1796–1859 Historian

He narrates events in their order of time with considerable skill, but the causes of the events, their place in the general history of the race, or their influence in special on the welfare of the nation, he does not appreciate. He tells the fact for the fact's sake.
Theodore Parker, *The American Scholar*.

PRESLEY, ELVIS ARON

1935–77 Singer

I was on the show (at Overton Park, Memphis) as an extra added single . . . and I came out on stage and uh, uh, I was scared stiff. My first big appearance, in front of an audience. And I came out and I was doin' a fast-type tune, uh, one of my first records, and ever'body was hollerin' and I didn't know what they were hollerin' at. Ever'body was screamin' and ever'thing, and, uh I came off stage and my manager told me they were hollerin' because I was wigglin'. Well, I went back out for an encore and, I, I, I kind-a did a little more and the more I did, the wilder they went.
On himself in an interview with *TV Guide*, 1956.

Elvis Presley, the Hillbilly Cat, Swivel-Hips, the King of Rock and Roll, the King of Bebop, the King of Country Music, simply, the King.
Michael Bane, *Country Music*, December 1977.

So Elvis Presley came, strumming a wierd guitar and wagging his tail across the continent, ripping off fame and fortune as he scrunched his way, and, like a latter-day Johnny Appleseed, sowing seeds of a new rhythm and style in the white souls of the new white youth of America, whose inner hunger and need was no longer satisfied with the antiseptic white shoes and whiter songs of Pat Boone. 'You can do anything,' sang Elvis to Pat Boone's white shoes, 'but don't you step on my Blue Suede Shoes!'
Eldridge Cleaver, *Soul On Ice*.

The hair was a Vaseline cathedral, the mouth a touchingly uncertain sneer of allure. One, two-wham! Like a berserk blender the lusty young pelvis whirred and the notorious git-tar slammed forward with a jolt that symbolically deflowered a generation of teenagers and knocked chips off 90 million older shoulders. Then out of the half-melted vanilla face came a wild black baritone came bawling in orgasmic lurches. *Whu-huh-huh-huh f'the money! Two f'the show! Three t'git riddy naa GO CAAT GO!*
Brad Darrach, *Life*, Winter 1977.

Mr Presley made another television appearance last night on the Milton Berle show over Channel 4 . . . he might possibly be classified as an entertainer. Or, perhaps quite as easily as an assignment for a sociologist.
Jack Gould, *New York Times*, 7 June 1956.

Mr Presley has no discernible singing ability. His specialty is rhythm songs which he renders in an undistinguished whine; his phrasing, if it can be called that, consists of the stereotyped variations that go with a beginner's aria in a bathtub. For the ear he is an unutterable bore. . . .
Ibid.

From watching Mr Presley it is wholly evident that his skill lies in another direction. He is a rock-and-roll variation of one of the most standard acts in show business: the 'virtuoso of the hootchy-kootchy. His one specialty is an accented movement of the body that heretofore has been primarily indentified with the repertoire of the blonde bomb-shells of the burlesque runway. The gyration never had anything to do with the world of popular music and still doesn't.
Ibid.

For Elvis there was no escape in art, since his original triumph was his very artlessness. He didn't write songs, nor did he aspire to anything more than success. Even his films were no more than a magnification of his image, a further reinforcement of the impossible perfection which transformed him, like all our public figures, from a living presence into an all-purpose, economy-rate icon.
Peter Gurnalnick, *Country Music*, December 1977.

The key phrases are pressure from other people, investments mushrooming and dying strangely.
Antonia Lamb. Horoscope forecast prepared for Elvis in 1970.

He really wants to idolize womanhood, but there is a Victorian fascination with wicked women. He dislikes mature or older women, prefers the young girls and the mother images. He has very strong sex drives, but a lot of his sexual energy is sublimated in his work. Sex is important mainly as a physical need. He is also hung up on ritual and fetishes.
Antonia Lamb in Jerry Hopkins, *Elvis a Biography*.

PRIESTLEY, JOSEPH

1733–1804 Theologian, Man of Science

Of Dr. Priestley's theological works, he [Samuel Johnson] remarked, that they tended to unsettle every thing, and yet settled nothing.
James Boswell, *Life of Johnson*.

He is one of the most voluminous writers of any age or country, and probably he is of all voluminous writers the one who has the fewest readers.
Henry, Lord Brougham, *Lives of Men of Letters and Science who flourished in the Time of George III.*

The attention of Dr. Priestley, the founder of a new

department of science, and the discoverer of many gases, was accidentally drawn to the subject by the circumstance of his residing in the neighbourhood of a large brewery. Being an attentive observer, he noted, in visiting the brewery, the peculiar appearances attending the extinction of lighted chips in the gas floating over the fermented liquor. He was forty years old at the time, and knew nothing of chemistry; he obtained access, however, to books, which taught him little, for as yet nothing was known on the subject. Then he commenced experimenting, devising his own apparatus, which was of the rudest description. The curious results of his first experiments led to others, which in his hands shortly became the science of pneumatic chemistry.
Samuel Smiles, *Self-help*.

The most seditious hand-bills were . stuck up in London and Birmingham, and Dr. Priestley is said to have boasted that at the latter he could raise 20,000 men; and so indeed he has, but against himself.
Horace Walpole, Letter to Mary Berry, 20 July 1791.

See also Henry Cavendish

PRIMROSE, ARCHIBALD PHILIP, see under ROSEBERY, EARL OF

PRIOR, MATTHEW

1664–1721 Poet

Nobles and heralds, by your leave,
　Here lies what once was Matthew Prior;
The son of Adam and of Eve,
　Can Bourbon or Nassau go higher?
　On himself, *Epitaph*.

Mrs Thrale disputed with him (*sc.* Johnson) on the merit of Prior. He attacked him powerfully; said, he wrote of love like a man who had never felt it: his love verses were college verses . . . Mrs Thrale stood to her gun with great courage . . . till he at last silenced her by saying, 'My dear Lady, talk no more of this. Nonsense can be defended but by nonsense.'
James Boswell, *Life of Johnson*.

No one has exceeded him in the laughing grace with which he glances at a subject that will not bear examining, with which he gently hints at what cannot be directly insisted on, with which he half conceals, and half draws aside the veil from some of the Muses' nicest mysteries. His Muse is, in fact, a giddy

wanton flirt, who spends her time in playing at snap-dragon and blind-man's buff, who tells what she should not, and knows more than she tells.
William Hazlitt, *Lectures on the English Poets.*

Tradition represents him as willing to descend from the dignity of the poet and statesman to the low delights of mean company. His Chloe probably was sometimes ideal; but the woman with whom he co-habited was a despicable drab of the lowest species.
Samuel Johnson, *Lives of the Poets.*

Most of his faults brought their excuse with them.
Ibid.

Is not Prior the most indecent of tale-tellers, not even excepting La Fontaine; and how often do we see his works in female hands!
Sir Walter Scott, in J. G. Lockhart, *Life of Scott.*

PRITCHARD, HANNAH

1711—68 Actress

This lady was so very natural an actress, and was so powerfully affected by her feelings, that she seldom retired from any great tragic part without being in some degree affected by a stomachic complaint.
William Cooke, *Memoirs of Samuel Foot.*

PRYNNE, WILLIAM

1600—69 Pamphleteer, Politician

The more I am beat down, the more I am lift up.
On himself, in William M. Lamont, *Marginal Prynne.*

Here earless William Pryn doth lye
And so will eternally
For when the last trump sounds to appeare
He that hath eares then let him heare.
Anon., in Anthony à Wood, *Life and Times.*

[He] . . . arrived at such an Athletick Habit in the career of writing, that if he may not scribble, and print too, he cannot live, and if he live, he must write, and if he write, it must be against governments.
Anon., *To the Supreme Authority of England, Scotland, and Ireland,* 1659.

His manner of studie was thus: he wore a long quilt cap, which came 2 or 3, at lest, inches over his eies, which served him as an Umbrella to defend his

Eies from the light. About every three houres his man was to bring him a roll and a pot of Ale to refocillate his wasted spirits; so he studied and dranke, and munched some bread; and this main-tained him till night, and then, he made a good Supper: now he did well not to dine, which breaks off one's fancy, which will not presently be re-gained: and 'tis with Invention as a flux, when once it is flowing, it runs amaine: if it is checked, flows but *guttim:* and the like for perspiration, check it and 'tis spoyled.
John Aubrey, *Brief Lives.*

He delivers the words as a Parrat, that pronounceth the Syllables, but not as a man that understands the meaning.
Sir Richard Baker, *Theatrum Triumphans.*

The negative aim of his pamphlets was to check the growth of Popery. Their positive aim was to raise the moral standards of the country. He wanted England to be a community where men were ab-stemious, serious-minded, short-haired, and shunned plays.
William M. Lamont, *Marginal Prynne.*

. . . one of your freinds not long since told me, *there was as great disproportion betwixt you and me, to write upon controverting the things of God, as there is betwixt a tall cedar and a little shrub:* unto which I replyed, *goe you, and tell the tall Cedar, the little shrub will have a bout with him.*
John Lilburne, *A Copie of a Letter to Mr William Prynne Esq.*

Mr Prinn . . . did discourse with me a good while alone in the garden about the laws of England, tell-ing me the many faults in them; and among others, their obscurity through multitude of long statutes, which he is about to abstract out of all of a sort, and as he lives, and parliaments come, get them put into laws and the other statutes repealed; and then it will be a short work to know the law — which appears a very noble good thing.
Samuel Pepys, Diary, 25 April 1666.

[Francis Finch] told me Mr Prin's character; that he is a man of mighty labour and reading and memory, but the worst judge of matters, or layer-together of what he hath read, in the world — (which I do not however believe him in); that he believes him very true to the King in his heart, but can never be re-conciled to Episcopacy. That the House doth not lay much weight upon him or anything he says.
Ibid., 3 July 1666.

Looke here Thou *that hast* malice *to the Stage,*
And Impudence *enough for the whole Age;*
Voluminously-Ignorant! *be vext*
To read this Tragedy, and thy owne be next.
James Shirley, 'Commendatory Verses' to John
    Ford's *Love's Sacrifice.*

M. Nedham the Weather-cock tells us, that *he was*
one of the greatest paper worms that ever crept
into a closet of a library, &c. and others that *he*
never intended an end in writing books, and that
his study or reading *was not only a wearisomeness*
to the flesh, but to the ears.
    Anthony à Wood, *Athenae Oxonienses.*

PUGIN, AUGUSTUS WELBY NORTHMORE

1812–52 Architect

I am such a locomotive being always flying about.
    On himself, Letter, January 1841.

I have passed my life in thinking of fine things,
studying fine things, designing fine things and realising very poor ones.
    On himself, *Remarks on Articles in The Rambler.*

Pugin is the Janus of the Gothic Revival; his buildings look back to the picturesque past, his writings
look forward to the ethical future.
    Kenneth Clark, *The Gothic Revival.*

The true bent of Pugin's mind was towards the
theatre, and his earliest successes achieved in reforming the scenery and decorations of the stage;
and throughout his life the theatrical was the only
branch of his art which he perfectly understood.
    J. Fergusson, *History of Modern Architecture.*

He was in the habit of wearing a sailor's jacket,
loose pilot trousers, jack-boots, and a wide-awake
hat. In such a costume landing on one occasion
from the Calais Boat, he entered, as was his custom,
a first-class railway carriage, and was accosted with
a 'Halloa, my man, you have mistaken, I think, your
carriage.' 'By Jove,' was his reply, 'I think you are
right; I thought I was in the company of gentlemen.'
    B. Ferrey, *Recollections of A. W. N. Pugin.*

Always before his eyes and before those of the more
enlightened of his followers was a vision of a time
near at hand when natural building should have
been relearnt by Christian workers — all workers
of that time having become Christian — in a service
that was perfect freedom.
    H. S. Goodhart-Rendel, *Victorian Conservanda.*

He had a most sincere love for his profession, a
hearty honest enthusiasm for pixes and piscinas; and
though he will never design so much as a pix or a
piscina thoroughly well, yet better than most of
the experimental architects of the day. Employ
him by all means, but on small work. Expect no
cathedrals of him: but no one at present, can design
a better finial.
    John Ruskin, *The Stones of Venice*, Appendix
    XII.

See also Sir Gilbert Scott

PULITZER, JOSEPH

1847–1911 Journalist

J. P. did not build an original situation, but he was
wonderfully effective in seizing upon an old situation and breathing new life into what looked like
a corpse.
    James Wyman Barrett, *Joseph Pulitzer and His*
    World.

As a writer of editorials, his ideas were strong, definite, challenging, but his style was not brilliant: he
was too fond of reiteration, even alliteration; his
effects were labored. In reading a J. P. editorial,
you can feel the man suffer while he works.
    Ibid.

Poor, misguided, selfish vulgarian. . . .
    James Gordon Bennett, in W. A. Swanberg,
    Pulitzer.

He was the damnedest best man in the world to
have in a newspaper office for one hour in the
morning. For the remainder of the day he was a
damned nuisance.
    John A. Cockerill, in *ibid.*

. . . this Dick Turpin of journalism. . . .
    Charles Anderson Dana, in James Wyman Barrett,
    Joseph Pulitzer and His World.

The insuperable obstacle in the way of his social
progress is not the fact that he is a Jew, but in certain offensive personal qualities . . . his face is
repulsive, not because the physiognomy is Hebraic,
but because it is Pulitzeresque . . . cunning, malice,
falseness, treachery, dishonesty, greed, and venal
self-abasement have stamped their unmistakable
traits . . . no art can eradicate them.
    Ibid.

He came to this country, not to promote the cause

of his race or his native land, but to push the fortunes of that part of Jewry which is situated over the soles of his boots and under the hat that covers his head.

Charles Anderson Dana, in W. A. Swanberg, *Pulitzer*.

. . . undoubtedly semi-neurasthenic, a disease-demonized soul, who could scarcely control himself in anything, a man who was fighting an almost insane battle with life itself, trying to be omnipotent and what not else, and never to die.

Theodore Dreiser, in George Juergens, *Joseph Pulitzer and The New York World*.

A towering figure in National and International journalism has passed away; a mighty democratic force in the life of the Nation and in the activity of the world has ceased; a great power uniformly exerted in behalf of popular rights and human progress is ended. Joseph Pulitzer is dead.

William Randolph Hearst, in W. A. Swanberg, *Pulitzer*.

He used to be a socialist when he was poor but now that he has acquired wealth he is just like the rest of the capitalists.

Ibid.

The only consideration which guides this fellow in the control of his precious paper is to keep out of the reach of criminal prosecution.

Leander Richardson, in George Juergens, *Joseph Pulitzer and The New York World*.

It was by this appeal to the basest passions of the crowd that Mr Pulitzer succeeded; like many another he deliberately stooped for success, and then, having achieved it, slowly put on garments of righteousness.

Oswald Garrison Villard, *Some Newspapers and Newspaper-Men*.

PURCELL, HENRY

1658?—95 Composer

Musick is yet but in its Nonage, a forward Child, which gives hope of what it may be hereafter in *England*, when the Masters of it shall find more Encouragement. 'Tis now learning *Italian*, which is its best Master, and studying a little of the *French* Air, to give it somewhat more of Gayety and Fashion. Thus being farther from the Sun, we are of later Growth than our Neighbor Countries, and must be content to shake off our Barbarity by degrees.

On himself, Preface to *Dioclesian*.

He was so superior to all his predecessors, that his compositions seemed to speak a new language; yet, however, different from that to which the public had been long accustomed, it was universally understood. His songs seem to contain whatever the ear could then wish, or heart could feel.

Dr Charles Burney, *A General History of Music*.

So changeable is taste in Music, and so transient the favour of any particular style, that its history is like that of a ploughed field: such a year it produced wheat, such a year barley, peas or clover; and such a year lay fallow. But none of the productions remain, except, perhaps, a small part of last year's crop, and the corn or weeds that now cover its surface. Purcell, however, was such an excellent cultivator of his farm on Parnassus, that its crops will be long remembered, even after time has devoured them.

Ibid.

Purcell . . . had always an inferior band to the Italian opera composers, as well as inferior fingers, and an inferior audience, to write for.

Ibid.

Mark how the lark and linnet sing,
    With rival notes
    They strain their warbling throats,
To welcome in the spring.
    But in the close of night
When Philomel begins her heav'nly lay,
    They cease their mutual spight,
Drink in her Music with delight,
And list'ning and silent, and silent and list'ning,
    And list'ning and silent obey.

So ceas'd the rival crew when Purcell came,
They sung no more, or only sung his fame.
Struck dumb they all admir'd the godlike man:
    The godlike man
    Alas! too soon retir'd
    As he too late began.
We beg not hell our Orpheus to restore:
    Had he been there,
    Their sovereign's fear
    Had sent him back before.
The pow'r of harmony too well they know
Would long ere this have tun'd their jarring sphere,
    And left no hell below.

The heav'nly choir, who heard his notes from high,
Let down the scale of Music from the sky:
    They handed him along,
    And all the way he taught, and all the way they
                                                          sung.
Ye brethren of the lyre, and tuneful voice,

Lament his lot, but at your own rejoice.
Now live secure and linger out your days,
The gods are pleas'd alone with Purcell's lays,
   Nor know to mend their choice.
   John Dryden, *Ode on the Death of Mr. Henry Purcell.*

Nor were his beauties to his art confin'd,
His form appear'd the product of his mind.
A conquering sweetness in his visage dwelt,
His eyes would warm, his wit like light'ning melt.
Pride was the sole aversion of his eye,
Himself as humble as his art was high.
   'R. G.', *On the death of the late famous Mr. Henry Purcell, circa* 1695.

The queen [Mary II] having a mind one afternoon to be entertained with music, sent to Mr Gostling, then one of the chapel, and afterwards subdean of St Paul's, to Henry Purcell and Mrs. Arabella Hunt, who had a very fine voice, and an admirable hand on the lute, with a request to attend her; they obeyed her commands; Mr Gostling and Mrs. Hunt sang several compositions of Purcell, who accompanied them on the harpsichord; at length the queen beginning to grow tired, asked Mrs. Hunt if she could not sing the old Scots ballad 'Cold and raw', Mrs. Hunt answered yes, and sang it to her lute. Purcell was all the while sitting at the harpsichord unemployed, and not a little nettled at the queen's preference of a vulgar ballad to his music; but seeing her majesty delighted with this tune, he determined that she should hear it upon another occasion: and accordingly in the next birthday song . . . he composed an air to the words 'May her bright example chace Vice in troops out of the land,' the bass whereof is the tune to Cold and Raw. . . .
   Sir John Hawkins, *A General History of the Science and Practice of Music.*

The Orfeus Brittanicus, Mr. H. Purcell, who unhappily began to shew his great skill before the reform of musick *al'Italliana*, and while he was warm in the persuit of it, dyed; but a greater musicall genius England never had.
   Roger North, *The Musicall Grammarian.*

A mate to a cock, and corn tall as wheat,
Is his Christian name who in musick's compleat:
His surname begins with the grace of a cat,
And concludes with the house of a hermit; note that.
His skill and performance each auditor wins,
But the poet deserves a good kick on the shins.
   Mr Tomlinson, *The Pleasant Musical Companion*, 1701, translated from the original Latin by Sir John Hawkins.

I know no other case where musical genius has come into the world so manifestly at the wrong time and place. . . .
   Donald F. Tovey, *Essays and Lectures on Music.*

Judgments of Purcell's art have differed according to individual reactions. Some have found it feminine and yielding, others have been struck by its boisterous energy. In art as in religion we are apt to discover what we hope to find, to judge the source by the extent to which it supplies our own thirst. What no one will fail to find in Purcell at his best is a spring of life, a vitality that glows with the effort of the whole man. To listen is to share an experience, to catch some of his glancing fire and to have a part in his aching regret. He was a man of changing moods and sympathies, ready to boast, to worship, to sigh and to lament. He could bid the trumpets to sound for majesty, or seeking flight from love's sickness find the fever in himself.
   Sir Jack Westrup, *Purcell.*

See also John Blow

PYM, JOHN

1584–1643 Parliamentarian

The most popular man, and the most able to do hurte, that hath lived in any tyme.
   Edward Hyde, Earl of Clarendon, *History of the Rebellion.*

Q

QUANTRILL, WILLIAM CLARKE

1837—65 Bandit

He raged against Kansas day and night. He thought of nothing but the humiliation and destruction of her people. That is why he sought authority in Richmond to raise a regiment of outlaws. For then he could shed blood like water in Kansas. Then would the sky be blackened with the smoke rising from the scourging of Kansas, and the land filled with the lamentations of the orphans and the homeless widows — a sacrifice required, demanded, cried for by the hideous, monstrous, misshapen thing Quantrill called his soul. 'Kansas should be laid waste at once.' That was his cry, his thought day and night — his life.
>   William E. Connelley, *Quantrill and the Border Wars.*

Because of Quantrill, widows wailed, orphans cried, maidens wept.
>   *Ibid.*

. . . he was not entirely a demon — But history will record him a desperately bad man — a highway robber of the darkest shade & a desperate leader of a set of the most desperate Demons that ever disgraced the name of man — infinitely worse than he was. None of them with bravery enough to meet an enemy — But they took every advantage of the surroundings — by treachery to drench the earth with blood & carnage.
>   Abraham Ellis (a robbery victim of Quantrill), in Charles Boer, *Varmit Q.*

QUARLES, FRANCIS

1592—1644 Poet

My mouth's no dictionary; it only serves as the needful interpreter of my heart.
>   On himself, 'To the Reader', *Feast for Worms.*

Or where the pictures for the page atone,
And Quarles is sav'd by beauties not his own.
>   Alexander Pope, *The Dunciad*, Book i.

QUILLER COUCH, SIR ARTHUR THOMAS

1863—1944 Author, Academic

Judged by subsequent Cambridge standards, he often seems impossibly florid, and on the whole his critical methods are what can only be described as under-ingenious. But in 1912 the world was younger, and professors could still talk about criticism in terms of an adventure.
>   John Gross, on Quiller-Couch's tenure as King Edward VII Professor at Cambridge, *The Rise and Fall of the Man of Letters.*

In Cambridge memories, there must linger many and varied pictures of Q: there was the professorial figure clad, literally, in a wedding-garment in preparation for the lecture-room; there was the figure of the countryman, in tweeds, strolling into the Pitt Club for lunch; there was the Commodore's figure, ready to spend an afternoon with the Cruising Club; there was the post-prandial figure in his rooms in Jesus, dispensing good talk, good liquor and good fellowship to his guests. And at the back of it all was the sense of style, a sense which governed his dress and his manners as surely as his writing.
>   S. C. Roberts, Introduction to Quiller-Couch's *Memories and Opinions.*

R

RADCLIFFE, ANN

1764—1823 Novelist

Charming as were all Mrs Radcliffe's works, charming even as were the works of all her imitators, it was not in them, perhaps, that human nature, at least in the midland counties of England, was to be looked for.

    Jane Austen, *Northanger Abbey*.

The great enchantress of that generation.

    Thomas de Quincey, *Confessions of an English Opium-Eater*.

Her descriptions of scenery, indeed, are vague and wordy to the last degree . . . her characters are insipid, the shadows of a shade, continued on, under different names, through all her novels: her story comes to nothing. But in harrowing up the soul with imaginary horrors, and making the flesh creep, and the nerves thrill, she is unrivalled among her fair country-women. . . . She makes her readers twice children.

    William Hazlitt, *Lectures on the English Comic Writers*.

I am going into scenery whence I intend to tip you a Damosel Radcliffe — I'll cavern you, and grotto you, and waterfall you, and wood you, and immense-rock you, and tremendous sound you, and solitude you.

    John Keats, Letter to J. H. Reynolds, 14 March 1818.

Mrs Radcliffe makes an appeal less to the nerves than to the imagination, using as we have seen the desiccated idiom of the age, like Scott, and she does achieve a total effect.

    Q. D. Leavis, *Fiction and the Reading Public*.

RAEBURN, SIR HENRY

1756—1823 Painter

When Sir Henry Raeburn has to render a hand, an arm, a leg, he usually draws it far better than Gainsborough, or even than Sir Joshua; but his manly and respectable work lacks a certain charm which one always finds in theirs. The touch of fancy is absent; it is plain, nutritive prose. . . . It is Presbyterian art.

    Henry James, in *Nation*, 1 February 1877.

RAGLAN, LORD (FITZROY JAMES HENRY SOMERSET)

1788—1855 Soldier

Hallo! don't carry away that arm till I have taken off my ring.

    On himself, during his operation after Waterloo, 1815.

Not since we landed has Raglan shown one particle of military knowledge . . . I wish they would reinforce us with a new Commander-in-Chief, and put this one in petticoats and send him home.

    Robert Portal, Letter to his Mother from the Crimea, October 1854.

RAINEY, GERTRUDE MALISSA NIX PRIDGETT, 'MA'

1886—1939 Singer

[Ma Rainey was] a short, dark woman with a warm, impish expression who tried to compensate for her basic physical shapelessness by glittering with artificial brilliance. Ma's wild, stringy hair, flaring up in uncombed disarray, was held in some semblance of order by a tiara that was sometimes studded with diamonds. When she could get them, diamonds gleamed in her ears and covered her fingers. A necklace of $20 gold pieces brightened her pudgy neck. For more than 30 years she toured the South, usually playing in tents lit by kerosene lanterns that cast eerie shadows around her as she rolled out the blues in a deep, earthy, majestically pulsant voice, her only movement a slow, rhythmic, almost hypnotic swaying.

    John S. Wilson, 'The Blues', in *Show Business Illustrated*, 17 October 1961.

RALEIGH, SIR WALTER

1552?—1618 Adventurer, Author, Statesman

If any man accuseth me to my face, I will answer him with my mouth; but my tail is good enough to return an answer to such who traduceth me behind my back.

> On himself, in Thomas Fuller, *The History of the Worthies of England.*

Old Sir Thomas Malette, one of the Judges of the Kings Bench, knew Sir Walter Ralegh and sayd that notwithstanding his great Travells, Conversation, Learning, etc., yet he spake broad Devonshire to his dyeing day.

> John Aubrey, *Brief Lives.*

He loved a wench well; and one time getting up one of the Mayds of Honour up against a tree in a Wood ('twas his first Lady) who seemed at first boarding to be somewhat fearfull of her Honour, and modest, she cryed, sweet Sir Walter, what doe you me ask? Will you undoe me? Nay, sweet Sir Walter! Sweet Sir Walter! Sir Walter! At last, as the danger and the pleasure at the same time grew higher, she cryed in the extasey, Swisser Swatter Swisser Swatter.

> *Ibid.*

Mr Walt humbled himselfe to his Father, and promised he would behave himself mightily mannerly. So away they went. . . . He sate nexte to his Father and was very demure at least half dinner time. Then sayd he, I this morning, not having the feare of God before my eies, but by the instigation of the devill, went to a Whore. I was very eager of her, kissed and embraced her, and went to enjoy her, but she thrust me from her, and vowed I should not *For your father lay with me but an hower ago.* Sir Walt, being so strangely supprized and putt out of his countenance at so great a Table, gives his son a damned blow over the face; his son, as rude as he was, would not strike his father, but strikes over the face of the Gentleman that sate next to him, and sayed *Box about, 'twill come to my Father anon.* 'Tis now a common used Proverb.

> *Ibid.*

He tooke a pipe of Tobacco a little before he went to the scaffold, which some formall persons were scandalised at, but I thinke twas well and properly donne, to settle his spirits.

> *Ibid.*

I will prove you the notoriousest traitor that ever came to the bar. . . . Nay, I will prove all; thou art a monster; thou has an English face but a Spanish heart.

> Edward Coke, at Raleigh's trial, 17 November 1603.

I have known many persons who turned their gold into smoke, but you are the first to turn smoke into gold.

> Queen Elizabeth I (on his introduction of tobacco into England), in F. Chamberlin, *The Sayings of Queen Elizabeth.*

This Captain Raleigh coming out of Ireland to the English Court in good habit (his clothes being then a considerable part of his estate) found the Queen walking, till, meeting with a plashy place, she seemed to scruple going thereon. Presently Raleigh cast and spread his new plush cloak on the ground; whereon the Queen trod gently, rewarding him afterwards with many suits, for his free and seasonable tender of so fair a foot-cloth. Thus an advantageous admission into the first notice of a Prince is more than half a degree to preferment.

> Thomas Fuller, *The History of the Worthies of England.*

Only my father would keep such a bird in a cage.

> Prince Henry, attributed, son to James I, on Raleigh's continuing imprisonment in the Tower.

Ralegh . . . might almost have served as a living model for Marlowe's theatrical heroes.

> Harry Levin, *Christopher Marlowe, the Overreacher.*

In talking over the design for a dictionary that might be authoritative for our English writers, Mr Pope rejected Sir Walter Ralegh twice, as too affected.

> Joseph Spence, *Anecdotes.*

He was one that fortune had pickt up out of purpose, of whom to make an example, or to use as her Tennis-Ball, thereby to show what she could do; for she tost him up of nothing, and to and fro to greatness, and from thence down to little more than to that wherein she found him (a bare Gentleman).

> Anthony à Wood, *Athenae Oxonienses.*

See also Christopher Marlowe, Lord Shaftesbury

RAMSAY, ALLAN

1713—84 Portrait Painter

Benevolence of various kinds; man who would not give half a crown, wd. get up in the middle of night & ride to serve you ten miles in heavy rain.

> James Boswell, Journal, 17 May 1778.

His marriage to his art implied no fervent devotion: it was fundamentally a *mariage de convenance,* promising serenity and harmony rather than the ful-filment of a grand passion; and one feels that he achieved these qualities in his paintings out of the clear knowledge that they represented the limits beyond which his genius could not carry him.

A. Smart, *The Life and Art of Allan Ramsay.*

His pictures are much superior in merrit than other portrait painters — his mens pictures strong likeness firm in drawing — and true flesh colouring natural tinctures. his Lady delicate and Genteel — easy free likeness. their habits and dresses well disposed and airy. his flesh tender his silks & satins &c shineing beautiful & clean — with great Variety.

George Vertue, *Notebooks.*

RANDOLPH (OF ROANOKE), JOHN

1773—1833 Politician

His face is livid, gaunt his white body, his breath is green with gall; his tongue drips poison.

John Quincy Adams, in Edward Boykin, *The Wit and Wisdom of Congress.*

RANK, JOSEPH ARTHUR, LORD

1888—1972 Industrialist, Film Magnate

A deeply and sincerely religious man, he was strongly motivated by the belief that he was selec-ted by Divine Providence to provide the people of this country with the best quality flour and bread, the stuff of life as he liked to call it, at the cheapest price.

Sir Ernest Chain, in *The Times*, 5 April 1972.

RANSOM, JOHN CROWE

1882—1974 Author

Ransom seems in his poems, as most modern poets do not, sympathetic and charming, full of tender-ness and affection, wanting the light and sorry for the dark — moral and condemning only when he has to be, not because he wants to be; loving neither the sterner vices nor the sterner virtues.

Randall Jarrell, 'John Ransom's Poetry', in Thomas Daniel Young ed., *John Crowe Ransom.*

He is an academic poet, always seeking his most potent effect from the built-in paradox of his poetics: the intensification of feeling that comes from ascetic techniques.

Thornton H. Parsons, *John Crowe Ransom.*

Reading him we are at once delighted and made pro-foundly aware of what it is to be men with all the burden and glory of our contradictions. This, I believe, is how Ransom, that genial pluralist, would like to have it.

John C. Stewart, *John Crowe Ransom.*

A Water-Colorist.

Edmund Wilson, in Thornton H. Parsons, *John Crowe Ransom.*

RATHBONE, (PHILIP ST JOHN) BASIL

1892—1967 Actor

. . . a neat and tidy actor with an immaculate ex-terior.

Brooks Atkinson, Review of *Romeo and Juliet*, in *New York Times*, 21 December 1934.

READE, CHARLES

1814—84 Novelist

Reade was a much better informed man than Dickens, and in some ways more public-spirited. He really hated the abuses he could understand . . . and he probably helped to alter public opinion on a few minor but important points. But it was quite beyond him to grasp that, given the existing form of society, certain evils *cannot* be remedied. Fasten upon this or that minor abuse, expose it, drag it into the open, bring it before a British jury, and all will be well — that is how he sees it. Dickens at any rate never imagined that you can cure pimples by cutting them off.

George Orwell, *Essays*: 'Charles Dickens'.

If you have the sort of mind that takes pleasure in dates, lists, catalogues, concrete details, descriptions of processes, junk-shop windows and back numbers of *Exchange and Mart*, the sort of mind that likes knowing exactly how a mediaeval catapult worked or just what objects a prison-cell of the eighteen-forties contained, then you can hardly help enjoying Reade. He himself, of course, did not see his work in quite this light.

George Orwell, in *New Statesman and Nation*, 17 August 1940.

It has generally been his object to write down some abuse with which he has been particularly struck, — the harshness, for instance, with which paupers or lunatics are treated, or the wickedness of certain classes, — and he always, I think, leaves upon his readers an idea of great earnestness of purpose. But he has always left at the same time on my mind so strong a conviction that he has not really understood his subject, that I have found myself ever taking the part of those whom he has accused. So good a heart, and so wrong a head, surely no novelist ever before had combined!

Anthony Trollope, *Autobiography.*

REITH, JOHN CHARLES WALSHAM, LORD

1889—1971 Communications Pioneer

A figure of Ariel sculpted by Eric Gill in the late 1920's for the façade of the British Broadcasting Corporation building, has had a peculiar and almost embarrassing history. Lord Reith, then head of the BBC, complained that the sculptor had emphasized Ariel's reproductive organ beyond necessity. Gill refused to make any changes. It was decided to submit the matter to arbitration; Sir Israel Gollancz, the noted Shakespearian scholar and editor, and Isreal Zangwill the novelist were among the Shakespearians deputized to investigate. After concluding that Ariel's approximate age should be thirteen, they called in a Doctor, who agreed with Lord Reith that for such a boy the genitals were overemphasized. The necessary surgery was performed and the statue of Ariel put into the place it still occupies on the building.

Louis Marder, *His Exits and His Entrances.*

REMINGTON, FREDERIC

1861—1909 Artist, Author

Evening overtook me one night in Montana and by good luck I made the camp-fire of an old wagon freighter who shared his coffee and bacon with me. I was nineteen years of age and he was a very old man . . . During his long life he had followed the receding frontiers . . . . 'And now' he said, 'there is no more West. In a few years the railroad will come along the Yellowstone. . . .' He had his point of view and he made a new one for me . . . I saw men all ready swarming into the land. I knew the derby hat, the smoking chimneys, the cord-binders, and the thirty-day notes were upon us in a restless surge. I knew the wild riders and the vacant land were about to vanish forever . . . and the more I considered the subject, the bigger the forever loomed. Without knowing exactly how to do it, I began to try to record some facts around me, and the more I looked the more the panorama unfolded.

On himself, in *Collier's*, 18 May 1905.

I remember this subject of the Santiago campaign

with awe . . . I remember my own emotions, which were numerous, interesting, and, on the whole, not pleasant. I am yet unable to decide whether sleeping in a mud-puddle, the confinement of a troopship, or being shot at is the worst. They are irritating and when done on an empty stomach, with the object of improving one's mind, they are extravagantly expensive. However, they satisfy a life of longing to see men do the greatest thing which men are called on to do.

The creation of things by men in time of peace is of every consequence, but it does not bring forth the tumultuous energy which accompanies the destruction of things by men in war. He who has not seen war only half comprehends the possibilities of his race.

On himself, in Peter H. Hassrick, *Frederic Remington.*

What success I have had has been because I have a horseman's knowledge of a horse. No one can draw equestrian subjects unless he is an equestrian himself.

Ibid.

Though somewhat heavy-set and prone to suffer in the heat, Remington prided himself in facing such tests against nature. The ambiance of military life with its air of self-reliance, masculine bravura and adventure was his chosen stage. With camera, sketch pad and notebook he recorded the cavalry's manoeuvers in every phase. . . . Probably most impressive to his eastern eye however was the landscape itself. 'In Arizona', he noted in his diary, 'nature allures with her gorgeous color and then repels with the cruelty of her formations [,] waterless barren and desolate — cactus sharp thorns — vast tiresome expanses and serrated peaks.'

Peter H. Hassrick, *Ibid.*

His whole life as a documentary artist was dedicated to the singular thesis of being the pictorial historian of our Old West. His horizon was broad both historically and geographically. Most of what he recorded was from firsthand intimate association, at time when the Western frontier was in its most exciting full bloom . . . Remington's artistic credo was truthful realism and the 'little people' who are always the human grist for the mill of history, rather than the organized campaigns, spectacular events, and the big names that are the meat of most historians.

Harold McCracken, *The Frederic Remington Book.*

REUTHER, WALTER PHILIP

1907—70 Labor Leader

It's hard to guess where Walter's ideas come from. If you have an idea that is worth anything, you might as well give it to him because if you don't, he'll steal it from you.
Anon., in Jack Stieber, *Governing the UAW*.

Walter Reuther has attempted to dictate to the black community ever since the UAW came to power. He has been a Jekyll and Hyde — a liberal around the country, and in Detroit, where he tried to control political power he is a ruthless despot.
Anon. Detroit black power leader, in *Washington Post*, 9 January 1969.

[There were] four generals in Detroit: Ford, Chrysler, General Motors and General Reuther.
Anon., common saying, in Jean Gould and Lorena Hickok, *Walter Reuther, Labor's Rugged Individualist*.

. . . a labor leader turned radical political . . . I can think of nothing more detrimental to this nation than for any President to owe his election to, and thereby be a captive of, a political boss like Walter Reuther.
Richard M. Nixon, in P. Cormier and W. J. Eaton, *Reuther*.

Walter Reuther is the most dangerous man in Detroit because no one is more skillful at bringing about revolution without seeming to disturb the existing forms of society.
George Romney, in Thomas R. Brooks, *Toil and Trouble*.

REVERE, PAUL

1735—1818 Silversmith, Revolutionary

Although hardly a man is now alive who remembers the entire poem that was written about his exploits, Paul Revere got up at midnight and awakened everyone with his cries. He had seen a light in the steeple of Old North Church, and knew at once that the British were coming by land or sea. Accompanied by William Dawes, he carried the news from Boston to Concord and from Ghent to Aix. When dawn broke, the countryside swarmed with countrymen.
Richard Armour, *It All Started With Columbus*.

Paul Revere was more than a figure on horseback, more than a great silversmith, bell-caster, powder-maker and shrewd leader of Boston's artisans. He was the handyman of the Revolution. He helped to plant the Tree of Liberty, and lived to enjoy its fruits.
G. Donald Dallas, *The Spirit of Paul Revere*.

For, borne on the night-wind of the Past,
Through all our history, to the last,
In the hour of darkness and peril and need,
The people will wake and listen to hear
The hurrying hoof-beats of that steed,
And the midnight message of Paul Revere.
Henry Wadsworth Longfellow, *Paul Revere's Ride*.

REYNOLDS, SIR JOSHUA

1723—92 Painter

When S^r J---- R---- died
All Nature was degraded;
The King drop'd a tear into the Queen's Ear,
And all his Pictures faded.
William Blake, *Annotations to Reynolds's Discourses*.

I consider Reynolds's Discourses to the Royal Academy as the Simulations of the Hypocrite who smiles particularly where he means to Betray. His Praises of Rafael is like the Hysteric Smile of Revenge. His Softness & Candour, the hidden trap & the poisoned feast. He praises Michel Angelo for Qualities which Michel Angelo abhorr'd, & he blames Rafael for the only Qualities which Rafael valued. Whether Reynolds knew what he was doing is nothing to me: the Mischief is just the same whether a Man does it Ignorantly or Knowingly. I always consider's True Art & True Artists to be particularly Insulted & Degraded by the Reputation of these Discourses, As much as they were Degraded by the Reputation of Reynolds's Paintings, & that such Artists as Reynolds are at all times Hired by the Satans for the Depression of Art — A Pretence of Art, to destroy Art.
Ibid.

O reader behold the philosopher's grave!
He was born quite a fool but he died quite a knave.
William Blake, *Epitaph*.

It is . . . to Reynolds that the honour of establishing the English school belongs.
John Constable, Lecture at the Royal Institution, June 1836.

Damn him, how various he is!
  Thomas Gainsborough, in E. Waterhouse, *Painting in Britain 1530–1790*.

Here Reynolds is laid, and to tell you my mind,
He has not left a better or wiser behind;
His pencil was striking, resistless and grand,
His manners were gentle, complying and bland;
Still born to improve us in every part,
His pencil our faces, his manners our heart:
To coxcombs averse, yet most civilly staring,
When they judged without skill he was still hard of
                                                hearing:
When they talk'd of their Raphaels, Correggios and
                                                stuff,
He shifted his trumpet, and only took snuff.
  Oliver Goldsmith, *Retaliation*.

Never had mortal a purer eye for Color.
  Benjamin Robert Haydon, Diary, 21 April 1840.

He became rich by the accumulation of borrowed wealth, and his genius was the offspring of taste. He combined and applied the materials of others to his own purposes, with admirable success; he was an industrious compiler, or skilful translator, not an original inventor in art.
  William Hazlitt, 'Character of Sir Joshua Reynolds', in *Champion*, 30 October 1814.

They [the *Discourses*] are subdued, mild, unaffected, thoughtful, — containing sensible observations on which he laid too little stress, and vague theories which he was not able to master. There is the same character of mind in what he wrote, as of eye in what he painted. His style is gentle, flowing, and bland: there is an inefficient outline, with a mellow, felicitous, and delightful filling-up. In both, the taste predominates over the genius — the manner over the matter!
  William Hazlitt, in *Edinburgh Review*, August 1820.

I know of no man who has passed through life with more observation than Reynolds.
  Samuel Johnson, in James Boswell, *The Life of Samuel Johnson*.

The link that united him to Michel Angelo was the sense of ideal greatness; the noblest of all perceptions. It is this sublimity of thought that marks the first-rate genius; this impelling fancy which has nowhere its defined form, yet every-where its image; and while pursuing excellence too perfect to be attained, creates new beauty that cannot be surpassed!
  Sir Thomas Lawrence, Address to the Students of the Royal Academy, 1823.

He assumed, that invention was little more than a new combination of such images as have been already treasured up in the memory, so that he whose mind was best stored with images would most certainly be the most capable of invention; and thus, that he who was best acquainted with the compositions of others, would be the most capable of originality.
  James Northcote, *The Life of Sir Joshua Reynolds*.

His pictures in general possess a degree of merit to mere portraits; they assume the rank of history.
  Ibid.

His theory and his practice are evidently at variance; he speaks of the cold painters of portraits, and ranks them on a level with the epigrammatist and the sonnetteer, yet devoted his life to portraits. How to account for this dereliction of his theory may be difficult; the reason given by himself was, that he adapted his style to the taste of the age in which he lived; and again, that a man does not always do what he would, but what he can.
  Ibid.

Compar'd, to other painting-men,
Thou art an eagle to a wren!
  'Peter Pindar' (John Wolcot), *Lyric Odes to the Royal Academicians* 1782, Ode I.

He rejoices in showing you his skill; and those of you who succeed in learning what painter's work really is, will one day rejoice also, even to laughter — the highest laughter which springs of pure delight, in watching the fortitude and fire of a hand which strikes forth its will upon the canvas as easily as the wind strikes it on the sea. He rejoices in all abstract beauty and rhythm and melody of design; he will never give you a colour that is not lovely, nor a shade that is unnecessary, nor a line that is ungraceful. But all his power and all his invention are held by him subordinate — and the more obediently because of their nobleness, — to his true leading purpose of setting before you such likeness of the living presence of an English gentleman or an English lady, as shall be worthy of being looked upon for ever.
  John Ruskin, *Lectures on Art*, IV.

Nearly every word that Reynolds wrote was contrary to his own practice; he seems to have been born to teach all error by his precept, and all excellence by his example; he enforced with his lips generalization and idealism, while with his pencil he was tracing the patterns of the dresses of the belles of his day; he exhorted his pupils to attend

only to the invariable, while he himself was occupied in distinguishing every variation of womanly temper; and he denied the existence of the beautiful, at the same instant that he arrested it as it passed, and perpetuated it for ever.
John Ruskin, *Modern Painters*.

Sir Joshua is the ablest man I know on a canvas.
George Selwyn, attributed, on hearing that Reynolds intended standing for Parliament.

Sir Joshua Reynolds used great quantities of snuff, and he would take it so freely when he was painting, that it frequently inconvenienced those sitters who were not addicted to it: so that by sneezing they much deranged their positions, and often totally destroyed expressions which might never return.
J. T. Smith, *Nollekens and His Times*.

All his own geese are swans, as the swans of others are geese.
Horace Walpole, Letter to the Countess of Upper Ossory, December 1786.

See also David Garrick, Sir Thomas Lawrence, Elizabeth Montagu, Henry Raeburn, George Romney

RHODES, CECIL JOHN

1853—1902 Imperialist

Some people like to have cows in their parks. I like to have people.
On himself, opening Groote Schuur to the public, in Cecil Headlam, *Milner Papers*.

So little done, so much to do. . . .
On himself, dying words, in J. G. McDonald, *Rhodes: A Life*.

Africa possessed my bones.
On himself, in *ibid*.

He has grey curly hair and a face like a jubilee bonfire.
Lionel Curtis, *With Milner in South Africa*.

Dreamer devout, by vision led
Beyond our guess or reach,
The travail of his spirit bred
Cities in place of speech.
So huge the all-mastering thought that drove —
So brief the term allowed —

Nations, not words he linked to prove
His faith before the crowd.
Rudyard Kipling, *The Burial*.

A new Elizabethan.
Lord Rosebery, in Elizabeth Pakenham, *Jameson's Raid*.

Too big to get through the gates of hell.
Olive Schreiner, in *ibid*.

I admire him, I frankly confess it; and when his time comes I shall buy a piece of the rope for a keepsake.
Mark Twain, *Following the Equator*.

RHODES, JAMES FORD

1848—1927 Historian

Mr Rhodes has seen America a part of the time through the windows of a country house and the remainder of the time through the windows of the Centennial Club.
Charles A. Beard, in Robert Cruden, *James Ford Rhodes*.

With little command of the varied resources of his native tongue, he had no knack for the well-turned sentence, the apt phrase; he lacked that sense of the comic, the tragic or the ironic which can transform history into literature.
Robert Cruden, *ibid*.

He watches the wheels go round and describes a portion of the machinery; too often, however, the reader is left to guess at the motive forces which supply the power.
Lester B. Shippee, in *ibid*.

. . . the last great workman of the school that did not distinguish between nationalism and Northernism.
Nathaniel W. Stephenson, in Robert Auden, *James Ford Rhodes*.

RICE, SIR STEPHEN

1637—1715 Politician

'I will drive', he used to say, 'a coach and six through the Act of Settlement.'
T. B. Macaulay, *History of England*.

RICHARD I, COEUR DE LION

1157—99

Richard's neglect was England's good fortune. Left almost to their own devices, with the king first at the other end of the world and then immersed in his preoccupations with his continental lands, the barons of England developed a sense of collective responsibility for the good governance of their country that would never have come into being if their king had been constantly among them, directing the affairs of the country with a strong hand.

J. J. Appleby, *England Without Richard.*

Coeur-de-Lion was not a theatrical popinjay with greaves and steel-cap on it but a man living upon victuals.

Thomas Carlyle, *Past and Present.*

The inadequacy of our insular method in popular history is perfectly shown in the treatment of Richard Coeur de Lion. His tale is told with the implication that his departure for the crusade was something like the escapade of a schoolboy running away to sea. It was, in this view, a pardonable or lovable prank; whereas in truth it was more like a responsible Englishman now going to the Front. Christendom was nearly one nation, and the Front was the Holy Land.

G. K. Chesterton, *A Short History of England.*

Richard I was rather a knight-errant than a king. His history is more that of a Crusade than of a reign.

Sir James Mackintosh, *History of England.*

He was the least English of all the kings of England; and the fact that he was and continued to be almost a stranger to the country which he was called upon to govern accounts for his initial mistakes. He came to England on 13 August 1189, and left it, after four months, on 12 December. He revisited it, when he was released from captivity, on 13 March 1194, and after a stay of two months returned to France where he spent the remainder of his life. These six months were all that he devoted to his kingdom in his ten years' reign. He used England as a bank on which to draw and overdraw in order to finance his ambitious exploits abroad. . . . Twice in the course of four years England was called upon to furnish money on a wholly unprecedented scale: first for the crusade, and secondly for the king's ransom when he fell into the hands of the emperor on his return.

A. L. Poole, *From Domesday Book to Magna Carta.*

But this king, amongst all the princes of the Christ-ian name that the round circle of the world embraces, alone is worthy of the honour of a leader and the name of a king, for he began his work well, he continued it even better, and, if he remains with you a while longer, he will finish it perfectly.

Safadin, the brother of Saladin, Sultan of Egypt, in Richard of Devizes, *Chronicle*, translated by J. T. Appleby.

RICHARD II

1367—1400

On Saint Matthew's day [21 September], just two years after the beheading of the earl of Arundel, I, the writer of this history, was in the Tower, wherein King Richard was a prisoner, and I was present while he dined, and I marked his mood and bearing, having been taken thither for that very purpose by Sir William Beauchamp. And there and then the king discoursed sorrowfully in these words: 'My God! a wonderful land is this, and a fickle; which has exiled, slain, destroyed, or ruined so many kings, rulers, and great men, and is ever tainted and toileth with strife and variance and envy'; and then he recounted the histories and names of sufferers from the earliest habitation of the kingdom.

Adam of Usk, *Chronicle*, translated by A. R. Myers.

The gallant boy of Smithfield became an early modern tyrant; neurotic, introspective and revengeful — so 'treacherous' said his enemies, that he was 'a disgrace to the whole realm.' Nor was he interested in campaigns in France. Artistic and extravagant — 'he kept the greatest port and maintained the most plentiful house that ever any King of England did'. He was also far too sensitive: brought back the body of his favourite, Robert de Vere, Earl of Oxford, who had been exiled in the Low Countries; opened his coffin, contemplated his friend's face, stroked the fingers and adorned them with jewels before a splendid reburial.

John Bowle, *England, A Portrait.*

. . . his reign is the first attempt of an English king to rule as an autocrat *on principle*, and as such it is a tragedy complete in itself. It has an artistic unity independent alike of earlier and later events, just because Richard II suddenly and violently tried to break with the *modus vivendi* of centuries. The modern notion of Divine Right can be traced back to Richard II and no further.

V. H. Galbraith, *A New Life of Richard II.*

Gaunt: His rash fierce blaze of riot cannot last,

For violent fires soon burn out themselves. . . .
Shakespeare, *Richard II*, Act II, Scene i.

A weak, vain, frivolous, and inconstant prince; without weight to balance the scales of government; without discernement to chuse a good ministry; without virtue to oppose the measures and advice of evil counsellors, even when they happened to clash with his own principles and opinion. He was a dupe to flattery, a slave to ostentation, and not more apt to give up his reason to the suggestion of sycophants and vitious ministers, than to sacrifice those ministers to his safety. He was idle, profuse, and profligate, and, though brave by starts, naturally pusillanimous and irresolute. His pride and resentment prompted him to cruelty and breach of faith: while his necessities obliged him to fleece his people, and degrade the dignity of his character and station.
Tobias Smollett, *The History of England from the Descent of Julius Caesar to the Treaty of Aix-la-Chapelle.*

See also John Gower

RICHARD III

1452–85

He contents the people wherever he goys best that ever did prince; for many a poor man that hath suffred wrong many days have be relevyd and helpyd by hym and his commands in his progresse. And in many grete citeis and townis were grete summis of mony gif hym, which he hath refusyd. On my trouth, I lykyd never the condicion of any prince so well as his; God hathe sent hym to us for the welfare of us al. . . .
Thomas Langton, Bishop of St David's, Letter to the Prior of Christ Church Monastery, Oxford, 1483.

Robespierre vindicating, in the midst of massacre, the existence of a God of mercy, is like our own Richard III issuing his Proclamation against Vice after the murder of his nephews. The sentiments professed by either may be admirable in themselves, but they only serve to deepen the general abhorrence of the character they contrast.
Edward Bulwer Lytton, *The Reign of Terror.*

Richarde the thirde sonne, of whom we nowe entreate, was in witte and courage egall with either of them, in bodye and prowesse farre vnder them bothe, little of stature, ill fetured of limmes, croke backed, his left shoulder much higher then his right,
hard fauored of visage, and suche as in states called warlye, in other menne otherwise, he was malicious, wrathfull, enuious and, from afore his birth, euer frowarde. . . . None euill captaine was hee in the warre, as to whiche his disposicion was more metely then for peace. . . . He was close and secrete, a deepe dissimuler, lowlye of countenaunce, arrogant of heart, outwardly coumpinable where he inwardely hated, not letting to kisse whom he thoughte to kyll; dispitious and cruell, not for evill will alway, but ofter for ambicion, and either for the suretie or encrease of his estate. Frende and foo was muche what indifferent, where his aduantage grew, he spared no man's deathe, wose life withstode his purpose.
Sir Thomas More, *The Historie of Kyng Rycharde the Thirde.*

The truth I take to have been this. Richard, who was slender and not tall, had one shoulder a little higher than the other: a defect, by the magnifying glasses of party, by distance of time, and by the amplification of tradition, easily swelled to shocking deformity; for falsehood itself generally pays so much respect to truth as to make it the basis of its superstructure.
Horace Walpole, *Historic Doubts on the Life and Reign of King Richard the Third.*

In 1485 the only difference between Richard III and Henry VII was that Henry proved successful.
C. H. Williams, *Henry VII.*

RICHARD, EARL OF CORNWALL

1209–72 King of the Romans

Richard of Alemaigne, whil that he was kyng,
He spende al is tresour opon swyvyng. . . .
Ballad, in Percy's *Reliques of Ancient English Poetry.*

The archbishop of Cologne advised his brethren to choose some one rich enough to support the dignity, not strong enough to be feared by the electors: both requisites met in the Plantagenet Richard, earl of Cornwall, brother of the English Henry III. He received three, eventually four votes, came to Germany and was crowned at Aachen. But three of the electors, finding that the sums he had paid to them were smaller than those received by others, seceded in disgust, and chose Alfonso X of Castile, who, shrewder than his competitor, continued to watch the stars at Toledo, enjoying the splendours of his title while troubling himself about it no further than to issue now and then a proclamation.
James Bryce, *The Holy Roman Empire.*

RICHARDSON, HENRY HOBSON

1838—86 Architect

The significance of Richardson can now be made clearer. He was not the first modern architect: he was the last great traditional architect: a reformer and not an initiator. Dying when he did, his architecture remained entirely within the historic past of traditional masonry architecture, cut off almost entirely from the new cycle which extends from the mid-eighties into the twenties of the present century.
>   Henry-Russell Hitchcock Jr, *The Architecture of H. H. Richardson and His Times*.

Richardson's tragedy was not his early death: it was his excessive popularity, which led to overproduction. The tragedy of the great individual genius is often enough due to too general an acceptance of that genius. A universal demand for the product of one man cannot be supplied except with counterfeits.
>   *Ibid.*

RICHARDSON, SAMUEL

1689—1761 Novelist

I confess that it has cost, and still costs, my philosophy some exertion not to be vexed that I must admire, aye, greatly admire, Richardson. His mind is so very vile a mind, so cozy, hypocritical, praisemad, canting, envious, concupiscent.
>   Samuel Taylor Coleridge, *Animae Poetae*.

Erskine: 'Surely, Sir, Richardson is very tedious.'
Johnson: 'Why, Sir, if you were to read Richardson for the story, your impatience would be so much fretted, that you would hang yourself. But you must read him for the sentiment, and consider the story as only giving occasion to the sentiment.'
>   James Boswell, *Life of Johnson*.

The most extraordinary contrast that ever was presented between an author and his works.
>   William Hazlitt, 'On Persons One Would wish to have Seen', in *New Monthly Magazine*, January 1826.

There is more knowledge of the heart in one letter of Richardson's than in all *Tom Jones*.
>   Samuel Johnson, in *ibid*.

You think I love flattery, and so I do; but a little too much always disgusts me. That fellow Richardson, on the contrary, could not be contented to sail quietly down the stream of his reputation, without longing to taste the froth from every stroke of the oar.
>   Samuel Johnson, *Miscellanies*.

I was such an old fool as to weep over *Clarissa Harlowe* like any milkmaid of sixteen over the *Ballad of the Ladies Fall*. To say truth, the first volume softened me by a near resemblance of my maiden days, but on the whole 'tis most miserable stuff. . . . Yet the circumstances are so laid as to inspire tenderness, and I look upon this and *Pamela* to be two books that will do more general mischief than the works of Lord Rochester.
>   Lady Mary Wortley Montagu, Letter to Lady Bute, 1 March 1752.

The follies of modern novel writing render it impossible for young people to understand the perfection of the human nature in his conception, and delicacy of finish in his dialogue, rendering all his greater scenes unsurpassable in their own manner of art. They belong to a time of the English language in which it could express with precision the most delicate phases of sentiment, necessarily now lost under American, Cockney, or scholastic slang.
>   John Ruskin, *Praeterita*.

The works of Richardson . . . are pictures of high life as conceived by a bookseller, and romances as they would be spiritualized by a Methodist preacher.
>   Horace Walpole, Letter to Sir Horace Mann, 20 December 1764.

See also Thomas Heywood

RIDLEY, NICHOLAS

1500?—55 Bishop of London, Martyr

But Master Ridley by reason of the evil making of the fire unto him, because the wooden faggits were laid about the goss, and over high built, the fire burned first beneath, being kept down by the wood. Which when he felt, he desired them for Christs sake to let the fire come unto him, Which when his Brother in law heard, but he had not understood, intending to rid him out of his pain (for the which cause he gave attendance) as one in such sorrow, not well advised what he did, heaped faggots upon him, so that he clean covered him, which made the fire more vehement beneath, that it burned clean all his nether parts, before it once touched the upper, and that made him leap up and down under the faggots and often desire them to let the fire come unto him, saying: I cannot burn. Which indeed appeared well: for after his legs were consumed by reason of his struggling through the pain (whereof he had no release, but only his contentation in God) he showed that side toward us clean, shirt and all untouched with flame. Yet in all this torment he forgot not to call unto God still, having in his mouth, Lord have mercy upon me, intermingling his cry, let the fire come unto me, I cannot burn. In which pains he laboured till one of the standers by with his bill pulled off the Faggots above, and where he saw the fire flame up, he wrested himself unto that side. And when the flame touched the Gun-powder, he was seen stirr no more, but burned on the other side, falling down at Master *Latimers* feet.

John Foxe, *Acts and Monuments.*

See also Hugh Latimer, Mary I

RILEY, JAMES WHITCOMB

1849–1916 Poet

My work did itself. I'm only the willer bark through which the whistle comes.
On himself, in Stanley J. Kunitz and Howard Haycraft eds, *American Authors, 1600–1900.*

He is troubled, worried, fretted, vexed and haunted; and hopes wiser minds will have the opportunity of making his literary foundlings the subject of investigation.
On himself, in Marcus Dickey, *The Maturity of James Whitcomb Riley.*

I never know whether I can write another good thing or not — but what am I saying? I never *wrote* anything, I *found* it.
On himself, in *ibid.*

The fine, noble things that Riley wrote of would have been far finer, far nobler, had they touched life and reality rather than conventional tear-ducts.
Anon., Obituary in *New York Tribune.*

His muse was a truant, and he was a runaway schoolboy who kept the heart of a boy into manhood and old age, which is one definition of genius.
Henry A. Beers, 'The Singer of the Old Swimmin' Hole', in *Yale Review*, October 1919.

His pathos is bathos, his sentiment sediment, his 'homely philosophy' brute platitudes — beasts of the field of thought.
Ambrose Bierce, in Paul Fatout, *Ambrose Bierce, Bierce.*

. . . affects the sensibilities like the ripple of a rill of buttermilk falling into a pig-trough.
Ambrose Bierce, in Paul Fatout, *Ambrose Bierce, The Devil's Lexicographer.*

. . . a humble crop gathered from the corners of rail fences, from the vines which clamber upon the porches of small villages, and from the weedy sidewalks of quiet towns far from the great markets of the world.
Hamlin Garland, on Riley's poetry, in Stanley J. Kunitz and Howard Haycraft eds, *American Authors, 1600–1900.*

. . . the poet of our common life.
William Dean Howells, in Richard Crowder, *Those Innocent Years.*

. . . the unctuous, over-cheerful, word-mouthing, flabby-faced citizen who condescendingly tells Providence, in flowery and well-rounded periods, where to get off.
Hewitt Howland, in Richard Crowder, *ibid.*

Riley will always be the poet of the man who remembers that once he was a boy; of the city dweller who remembers that once his life was in the country; of the unfortunate who recall that once their lives were prosperous; of the prosperous who recollect that once they were unhappy.
John A. Howland, *James Whitcomb Riley In Prose and Pictures.*

Sentimentalism was the marketable commodity which 'Sunny Jim' Riley picked up at the beginning of his career and successfully peddled during the Nineties. In the fourteen volumes of this collected work, a reader of American poetry may see the last full expression of the sentimental tradition in American poetry — and the reasons for its disappearance.
Carlin T. Kindilien, *American Poetry in the Eighteen Nineties.*

He was not interested, as Eugene Field was, in expanding or exploring a child's imagination; he looked only for a situation that would bring tears to a reader's eyes. The poem was never written for the child; it was written to commercialize the child's feelings.
Ibid.

ROBERTS, FREDERICK SLEIGH, FIRST EARL OF KANDAHAR, PRETORIA AND WATERFORD

1832—1914 Soldier

He says his prayers every night, and leaves the rest to God.
Lady Roberts, in J. L. Garvin, *Life of Joseph Chamberlain.*

ROBERTSON, PATRICK, LORD

1794—1855 Author

Here lies that peerless paper peer Lord Peter,
Who broke the laws of God and man and metre.
Sir Walter Scott, *Epitaph.*

ROBESON, PAUL

1898—1976 Singer, Civil Rights Campaigner

. . . Paul Robeson strikes me as having been made out of the original stuff of the world. In this sense he is coeval with Adam and the redwood trees of California. He is a fresh act, a fresh gesture, a fresh effort of creation. I am proud of belonging to his race. For, of course, we are both members of the one sometimes fulsomely described as human.
Alexander Woollcott, in Marie Seton, *Paul Robeson.*

ROBINSON, EDWARD G. (EMMANUEL GOLDENBERG)

1893—1973 Actor

I was not exactly an ideal leading man. I was short, swarthy, and stocky, hardly significant competition for a theatre that worshipped tall and handsome actors like John Barrymore and Lou Tellegen. The few parts I would play — and they would be few indeed, it was subliminally predicted — would not be Anglo-Saxon. The predictions were wrong. I played an Anglo-Saxon — *once.*
On himself, in *All My Yesterdays.*

That one unfailing actor.
Alexander Woollcott, *The Portable Woollcott.*

See also Paul Muni

ROBINSON, EDWIN ARLINGTON

1869—1935 Poet

No poet ever understood loneliness or separateness better than Robinson or knew the self-consuming furnace that the brain can become in isolation, the suicidal hellishness of it, doomed as it is to feed on itself in answerless frustration, fated to this condition by the accident of birth, which carries with it the hunger for certainty and the intolerable load of personal recollection.
James Dickey, 'The Many Truths', in Ellsworth Barnard ed., *Edwin Arlington Robinson, Centenary Essays.*

Another odd thing about Robinson is that his best work and his worst are yet remarkably alike. The qualities that make the good poems good are the same qualities that make the bad poems bad; it is only a question of how Robinson's method works out in, 'takes to', the situation he is depicting, and often the difference between good, bad, and mediocre is thin indeed.
Ibid.

Man, individual man, is the moral center of Robinson's poetry. He begins with a nineteenth-century interest in character and carries over its corresponding ideal of the whole or complete person. We know all too well that the twentieth century is the age of alienation, and alienated man can be found with ease and in abundance in Robinson's poetry.
W. R. Robinson, 'The Alienated Self', in Ellsworth Barnard ed., *Edwin Arlington Robinson, Centenary Essays.*

Always defeat — always failure: surely the theme of human failure, with all its variations and nuances, has been treated so exhaustively by no other poet as by Robinson. One would not have believed there were so many ways to fail.
T. K. Whipple, *Spokesmen.*

I cannot call Robinson disillusioned; I cannot believe that he ever entertained an illusion about this world. One cannot imagine him as a child with a child's eager interest and trustfulness. One pictures him, judging from his poetry, as a gloomy little boy, on his guard against the world, hostile toward a hostile universe.
Ibid.

ROBINSON, SIR THOMAS

1700?—77 Civil Servant

Unlike my subject will I frame my song,

It shall be witty and it shan't be long.
Lord Chesterfield, *Epigram*.

ROCHE, SIR BOYLE

1743—1807 Irish Politician

Every time he opens his mouth he puts his foot in it.
Anon., *circa* 1770.

ROCHESTER, EARL OF, see under WILMOT, JOHN

ROCKEFELLER, JOHN DAVISON

1839—1937 Industrialist, Philanthropist

I believe the power to make money is a gift of God . . . to be developed and used to the best of our ability for the good of mankind. Having been endowed with the gift I possess, I believe it is my duty to make money and still more money, and to use the money I make for the good of my fellow man according to the dictates of my conscience.
On himself, in Matthew Josephson, *The Robber Barons*.

I'm bound to be rich! *Bound to be rich!*
Ibid.

I had no ambition to make a fortune. Mere money-making has never been my goal. I had an ambition to build.
On himself, in Allen Nevins, *Study in Power: John D. Rockefeller*, vol. 1.

I have ways of making money you know nothing of.
On himself, 1872, in Jules Abels, *The Rockefeller Millions*.

Rockefeller's voice may not be the voice of God, but nevertheless it speaks the final word, for whoever opposes Rockefeller has lost before the battle starts.
Anon., in William H. Allen, *Rockefeller*.

St. John of the Rocks.
Anon., popular nickname, in *Life*, 6 July 1911.

In a career that knew no calm but the unstable equilibrium of a colossus about to battle or the exhaustion of boa constrictor satiety, not the least dramatic is this triumphant John D. Rockefeller when ninety and his canonization as the apostle of

business by one hundred million fellow citizens.
William H. Allen, *Rockefeller*.

He is the father of trusts, the world's foremost pioneer centralizer of business machinery and power, the vaulting apostle and exemplar of business efficiency, the demonstrator-in-chief of cooperation's superiority over competition, — always for cooperators and frequently for consumers.
Ibid.

Rockefeller made his money in oil, which he discovered at the bottom of wells. Oil was crude in those days, but so was Rockefeller. Now both are considered quite refined.
Richard Armour, *It All Started With Columbus*.

. . . the paramount engineer of the world's notables, a sort of lone-wolf with whom aloofness has been second nature.
Richard Gilbert Collier, *Famous Living Americans*.

John D. Rockefeller can be fully described as a man made in the image of the ideal money maker. . . . An ideal money-maker is a machine the details of which are diagrammed on the asbestos blueprints which paper the walls of hell.
Thomas Lawson, in Jules Abels, *The Rockefeller Millions*.

While his subtle, ruminative, daring mind solved large problems by an acid process of thought, he presented to the world a front of silence which was like smooth steel.
Allen Nevins, *Study in Power: John D. Rockefeller*, vol. 1.

. . . another St. Francis of Assisi.
John Singer Sargent, in Evan Charteris, *Sargent*.

ROCKINGHAM, MARQUIS OF (CHARLES WATSON WENTWORTH)

1730—82 Prime Minister

His virtues were his arts. In opposition he respected the principles of government; in administration he provided for the liberties of the people. He employed his moment of power in realizing everything which he had proposed in a popular situation — the distinguishing mark of his public conduct. Reserved in profession, sure in performance, he laid the foundation of a solid confidence.
Edmund Burke, *Epitaph on Rockingham*, carved on a monument at Wentworth Woodhouse.

He could neither speak nor write with ease, and was handicapped by inexperience, boils, and a passion for Newmarket.

O. A. Sherard, *A Life of John Wilkes.*

Rockingham himself was a high-minded man with that type of negative virtue which wealth and position make easy. In the midst of a corrupt generation he was too rich to accept a bribe and too unimaginative to offer one. In the midst of a loose people he preserved an admirably starchy disposition.

Ibid.

ROCKNE, KNUTE KENNETH

1888–1931 American Football Coach

Rockne wanted nothing but 'bad losers'. Good losers get into the habit of losing.

George E. Allen, *Presidents Who Have Known Me.*

ROGERS, SAMUEL

1763–1855 Poet

'They tell me I say ill-natured things,' he observed in his slow, quiet, deliberate way; 'I have a weak voice; if I did not say ill-natured things, no one would hear what I said.'

Henry Taylor, *Autobiography.*

See also Lord Byron, Sir Walter Scott

ROGERS, WILL (WILLIAM PENN ADAIR ROGERS)

1879–1935 Comedian

I don't make jokes; I just watch the government and report the facts.

On himself, in a syndicated column.

My folks didn't come over on the *Mayflower*, but they were there to meet the boat.

Ibid.

Well, there was a move on foot for making fewer and worse pictures so they hired me.

On himself, in William Cahn, *A Pictorial History of the Great Comedians.*

I never met a man I didn't like.

On himself.

Well, all I know is just what I read in the papers.

On himself. This line, originally used to preface his Ziegfeld Follies performances, later opened his newspaper column.

He is practically the only public figure I know who has kept his hair, his wife, and his sense of humor twenty-five years.

Marie Dressler, *My Own Story.*

There was already a tendency to confuse Rogers with the national boobies to whom his frequent social pronouncements linked him. But he was in the first place a show figure, even in his worst things one could not help recognizing him as a very good one. And where his political views gained their weight with the populace of this country was from the character he had created of a typical American — a man in suspenders and stocking feet, unpretending, kind, bashful, not knowing about all these here newfangled customs and ideas, but (and here is where he became the ideal of the type rather than the type) disposing of them with native shrewdness, moving toward a final triumph over everything that was new or fancy or politically not right. Too homey and dependent on the old gags of faith in a simple world for comfort, there was still a certain common-man homeliness and goodness about him that everyone could see at once, a wholesome impatience with frippery and a running mumble of irony against it. In this created character he was a valuable property, just as he would be in real life, on a farm say, heckling the cows and squinting at the tarmal weather. He was one of the naturals of show business, and it is not pleasant to lose him.

Otis Ferguson, *The Film Criticism of Otis Ferguson.*

We remember Will Rogers with gratitude and affection because he knew how to revive the spirit of laughter in hearts that had known too much of the distractions and anxieties of a busy world. His mission in life was to cheer, to comfort and to console.

There was something infectious about his humor. His appeal went straight to the heart of the nation. Above all things, in a time grown too solemn and somber he brought his countrymen back to a sense of proportion.

Will Rogers knew out of the fullness of a blithe heart that few things in life are to be taken seriously and that our troubles multiply if we take them tragically. And so he showed us all how to laugh. From him we can learn anew the homely lesson that the way to make progress is to build on what we have,

to believe that today is better than yesterday and that tomorrow will be better than either.
> Franklin D. Roosevelt, Letter to Walter Harrison, 1938.

The bosom friend of senators and congressmen was about as daring as an early Shirley Temple movie.
> James Thurber, in Joe McCarthy ed., *Fred Allen's Letters*.

Hell, Will *has* to be a great actor; why, he's acting even when the camera's not there. He has to act just to be able to keep talking the way he does, with all that colloquial speech when he knows better, and after all the proper talking he's been exposed to. I can't do what Will does. I can play a thug, or a country boob or a flatfoot cop, but if somebody said, 'Now act like Spencer Tracy', I wouldn't know what to do.
> Spencer Tracy, in Larry Swindell, *Spencer Tracy*.

See also Florenz Ziegfeld

ROLFE, FREDERICK, see under CORVO, BARON

ROMNEY, GEORGE

1734–1802 Painter

Romney in the mean time shy, private, studious and contemplative; conscious of all the disadvantages and privations of a very stinted education; of a habit naturally hypochondriac, with aspen nerves, that every breath could ruffle, was at once in art the rival, and in nature the very contrast of Sir Joshua [Reynolds].
> Richard Cumberland, *Memoirs*.

Sir Joshua [Reynolds] disliked Romney so much that he would not even allude to him by name, but in after-years, when he had to refer to him, spoke of him as 'the man in Cavendish Square'.
> Lord Ronald Gower, *Romney and Lawrence*.

My more than father.
> Lady Hamilton, 1791, in H. Gambin, *George Romney and His Art*.

[He] painted many good heads, but in a mannered way. He had some taste & sensibility, and represented beautiful women in a captivating manner, but He never cd. make a picture altogether exquisite. He had no eye for the harmony of the whole,

& his colours were often coarse & discordant, not rendered with feeling.
> Ozias Humphrey, in Joseph Farington, Diary, 26 August 1803.

He is *par excellence*, a painter of handsome men and women, and the interpreter of a certain high-bred, aquiline sensibility of repression.
> David Piper, *The English Face*.

Romney, as a portrait painter, had the dispassionate eye of the camera in expert professional hands, who know that the instrument cannot lie but are not concerned in making it tell the truth.
> E. Waterhouse, *Painting in Britain 1530–1790*.

ROOSEVELT, (ANNA) ELEANOR

1884–1962 Humanitarian

She ain't stuck up, she ain't dressed up, and she ain't afeared to talk.
> Anon., 1933, in *Anna Eleanor Roosevelt: Memorial Addresses in the House of Representatives, Joint Committee on Printing*.

A symbol of compassion in a world of increasing righteousness.
> Henry Kissinger, in Joseph Lash, *Eleanor: the Years Alone*.

Eleanor is a Trojan mare.
> Alice Roosevelt Longworth, in James Brough, *Princess Alice*.

No woman has ever so comforted the distressed or so distressed the comfortable.
> Claire Booth Luce, in *Anna Eleanor Roosevelt: Memorial Addresses in the House of Representatives, Joint Committee on Printing*.

There have been famous women known the world over for their profiles on coins or their images in light but the world knows Eleanor Roosevelt by heart.
> Archibald MacLeish, in *ibid*.

She *lived* equality, freedom, and democracy . . . She put those ideals into flesh.
> Frances Perkins, in *ibid*.

Falsity withered in her presence. Hypocrisy left the room.
> Adlai Stevenson, address at the Democratic National Convention, 1962.

She would rather light a candle than curse the

darkness, and her glow has warmed the world.
    Adlai Stevenson, address to the United Nations
    General Assembly, 9 November 1962.

See also Franklin D. Roosevelt

ROOSEVELT, FRANKLIN DELANO

1882—1945 Thirty-Second United States President

God has led the President by the hand for a long
while, but even God gets tired sometimes.
    Anon. clergyman, in *Spectator*, 5 February 1943.

Roosevelt is my shepherd, I am in want
He maketh me to lie down on park benches;
He leadeth me beside the still factories.
He disturbeth my soul:
He leadeth me in the Paths of destruction for his
                                Party's sake.
Yea, though I walk through the valley of recession,
I anticipate no recovery
For he is with me;
His promises and pipe dreams they no longer fool
                                me.
He preparest a reduction in my salary in the pre-
                    sence of my creditors;
He anointeth my small income with taxes;
Surely unemployment and poverty shall follow me
                all the days of the New Deal,
And I will dwell in a mortgaged house forever.
    Anon., in G. Wolfskill and J. A. Hudson, *All But
    the People: Franklin D. Roosevelt and his Critics,
    1933—39.*

It is a mystery to me how each morning he selects
the few things he *can* do from the thousands he
should do.
    Anon., in W. E. Binkley, *The Man in the White
    House.*

And they say you don't know the people.
And they say you want to be a dictator. . . .

In fact, to tell you a secret, they say you are
                                terrible.
And, if I may speak from the record, we know
                                them, too.
And that's jake with us, because we know.
And we know you never were a Fuehrer and never
                                will be,
Not a Fuehrer, just a guy in pitching for the bunch
                                of us,
For all of us, the whole people.

A big guy pitching, with America in his heart.
A man who knows the tides and ways of the people
As Abe Lincoln knew the wind on the prairies,

And has never once stopped believing in them.
(The slow, tenacious memory of the people,
Somehow, holding on to the Lincolns, no matter
                                who yelled
against them. . . .)
A country squire from Hyde Park with a Harvard
                                accent.
Who never once failed the people
And whom the people won't fail.
    Stephen Vincent Benét, in *New York Post*,
    5 November 1940.

I'd rather be right than Roosevelt.
    Heywood Broun, in Robert E. Drennan ed.,
    Wit's End.

Roosevelt had exploded one of the most popular
myths in America. . . . He had dissociated the concept of wealth from the concept of virtue.
    James MacGregor Burns, *Roosevelt: The Lion
    and the Fox.*

Restless and mercurial in his thinking, a connoisseur
of theories but impatient with people who took
theories seriously, he trusted no system except the
system of endless experimentation.
    Eric Goldman, *Rendezvous With Destiny.*

No personality has ever expressed the American
popular temper so articulately or with such exclusiveness. In the Progressive era national reform
leadership was divided among Theodore Roosevelt,
Wilson, Bryan, and La Follette. In the age of the
New Deal it was monopolized by one man, whose
passing left American liberalism demoralized and all
but helpless.
    Richard Hofstadter, 'Franklin D. Roosevelt:
    The Patrician as Opportunist', in W. E. Leuchten-
    burg ed., *Franklin D. Roosevelt, A Profile.*

[A] chameleon on plaid.
    Herbert Hoover, in James MacGregor Burns,
    Roosevelt: The Lion and the Fox.

. . . would rather follow public opinion than lead it.
    Harry Hopkins, in G. Wolfskill and J. A. Hudson,
    *All But the People: Franklin D. Roosevelt and
    his Critics, 1933—39.*

. . . the man who started more creations than were
ever begun since Genesis — and finished none.
    Hugh Johnson, 1937, in *ibid.*

He was the only person I ever knew — anywhere —
who was never afraid. God, how he could take it
for us all.
    Lyndon Baines Johnson, in James MacGregor
    Burns, *Roosevelt: The Lion and the Fox.*

... make no mistake, he is a force — a man of superior but impenetrable mind, but perfectly ruthless, a highly versatile mind which you cannot foresee.
Carl G. Jung, 1936, in Arthur M. Schlesinger Jr, 'Behind the Mask', in W. E. Leuchtenburg ed., *Franklin D. Roosevelt, A Profile*.

I have always found Roosevelt an amusing fellow, but I would not employ him, except for reasons of personal friendship, as a geek in a common carnival.
Murray Kempton, in Victor Lasky, *J. F. K., The Man and the Myth*.

Roosevelt is a Jeffersonian democrat, projected into the industrial age. Deeply religious, profoundly American, an aristocrat with that magnanimity of spirit which loathes cruelty and special privileges, he is less concerned with inferences from a system than with adaptation of intuitions.
Harold J. Laski, in *New Statesman and Nation*, 14 March 1942.

... an amiable man with ... philanthropic impulses ... without any important qualifications.
Walter Lippmann, in G. Wolfskill and J. A. Hudson, *All But the People: Franklin D. Roosevelt and his Critics, 1933—39*.

He's so doggone smart that fust thing I know I'll be working fer him — and I ain't goin' to.
Huey Long, in Arthur Schlesinger, *The Politics of Upheaval*.

... two-thirds mush and one-third Eleanor.
Alice Roosevelt Longworth, in G. Wolfskill and J. A. Hudson, *All But the People: Franklin D. Roosevelt and his Critics, 1933—39*.

I am advocating making him a king in order that we may behead him in case he goes too far beyond the limits of the endurable. A president, it appears, cannot be beheaded, but kings have been subjected to the operation from ancient times.
H. L. Mencken, in *ibid*.

If he became convinced tomorrow that coming out for cannibalism would get him the votes he so sorely needs, he would begin fattening a missionary in the White House backyard come Wednesday.
H. L. Mencken, in W. E. Leuchtenburg ed., *Franklin D. Roosevelt, A Profile*.

To look on his policies as the result of a unified plan ... was to believe that the accumulation of stuffed snakes, baseball pictures, school flags, old tennis shoes, and the like in a boy's bedroom were the design of an interior decorator.
Raymond Morley, in James MacGregor Burns, *Roosevelt: The Lion and the Fox*.

[His] mentality was not intellectual in the sense in which that word is ordinarily used. . . . He had to have feeling as well as thought. His emotions, his intuitive understanding, his imagination, his moral and traditional bias, his sense of right and wrong — all entered into his thinking, and unless these flowed freely through his mind as he considered a subject, he was unlikely to come to any clear conclusions or even to a clear understanding.
Frances Perkins, in D. M. Potter, 'Sketches for the Roosevelt Portrait', in W. E. Leuchtenburg ed., *Franklin D. Roosevelt, A Profile*.

... the Great Uncertainty. No one knows what he thinks or what he will do tomorrow.
Amos Pinchot, Letter to Felix Frankfurter, 1935.

[If Roosevelt was] as busy as Rabbit and as bouncy as Tigger, he was too often, I fear, as big a bluffer as Owl.
Clinton Rossiter, in James MacGregor Burns, *John Kennedy, A Political Profile*.

Mr Roosevelt did not carry out the Socialist platform, unless he carried it out on a stretcher.
Norman Thomas, in G. Wolfskill and J. A. Hudson, *All But the People: Franklin D. Roosevelt and his Critics, 1933—39*.

Some personalities make their effect by masterfulness. . . . Others get their way by persuasion. Roosevelt played both roles. It was by masterfulness that he rallied the American people from the economic depression, it was by persuasiveness that he afterwards led them step by step, to oppose the aggressor powers in World War II.
Arnold J. Toynbee, in *New York Times Magazine*, 8 November 1959.

He was, I knew then, not made President, but a born one. . . . No monarch, I thought, unless it may have been Elizabeth or her magnificent Tudor father, or maybe Alexander or Augustus Caesar, can have given quite that sense of serene presiding, of gathering up into himself, or really representing, a whole people.
Rexford G. Tugwell, 'The Experimental Roosevelt', in W. E. Leuchtenburg ed., *Franklin D. Roosevelt, A Profile*.

The most effective transmitting instrument possible for the coming of the New World order. He is eminently 'reasonable' and fundamentally implacable.

He demonstrates that comprehensive new ideas can be taken up, tried out and made operative in general affairs without rigidity or dogma. He is continuously revolutionary in a new way without ever provoking a stark revolutionary crisis.

> H. G. Wells, in Arthur M. Schlesinger Jr, 'Behind the Mask', in *ibid*.

Poetry, religion, and Franklin D.
The three abominations be.
Why mince words? I do not feel
Kindly toward the Nouveau Deal
Hopkins peddles quack elixir
Tugwell is a phony fixer
  Another lapse
  For Homo saps
Yahweh!

> E. B. White, in 'H. L. Mencken meets a Poet in the West Side YMCA', from *The Fox of Peaback and other Poems*.

Roosevelt and I took office at the same time, only my company is running at a profit while his company is running at a loss.

> Wendel Willkie, in Irving Stone, *They Also Ran*, referring to Willkie's becoming head of Commonwealth and Southern at the time Roosevelt was elected President.

In the beginning, Franklin created the A A A and the NRA. And the NRA was without form, and void; and the Astor yacht was upon the face of the deep.

> Howard Wolf, 'Greener Pastures', in G. Wolfskill and J. A. Hudson, *All But the People: Franklin D. Roosevelt and his Critics, 1933–39*.

See also Heywood Broun, Harry Hopkins, John F. Kennedy, John L. Lewis, Norman Thomas, Harry S. Truman, Wendel Willkie.

ROOSEVELT, THEODORE

1858–1919 Twenty-Sixth United States President

The great virtue of my radicalism lies in the fact that I am perfectly ready, if necessary, to be radical on the conservative side.

> On himself, to William Howard Taft, 4 September 1906.

I am as strong as a bull moose and you can use me to the limit.

> On himself, in a speech, 14 October 1912.

I wish to preach, not the doctrine of ignoble ease, but the doctrine of the strenuous life.

> On himself, speech before the Hamilton Club of Chicago, 10 April 1899.

There is a homely adage which runs, 'Speak softly and carry a big stick; you will go far'. . . .

> On himself, speech at Minnesota State Fair, 2 September 1901.

You called me a megalomaniac — I called you a Serpent's tooth.

> On himself, to William Howard Taft, in Franklin P. Adams, *T.R. to W.H.T.*

How I wish I wasn't a reformer, Oh Senator! But I suppose I must live up to my part, like the Negro minstrel who blacked himself all over!

> On himself, Letter to Chauncey Depew, in Richard Hofstadter, *The American Political Tradition*.

The White House is a bully pulpit!

> On himself, in Hamilton Basso, *Mainstream*.

A smack of Lord Cromer, Jeff Davis a touch of him;
A little of Lincoln, but not very much of him;
Kitchener, Bismarck and Germany's Will,
Jupiter, Chamberlain, Buffalo Bill.

> Anon., *Roosevelt!*

Roosevelt was never a mere sounding board for the popular mind. He had rather, in his halcyon days, an absolute sense of political pitch. He struck the notes that the chorus awaited. This he did intuitively, for he contained within him the best and the worst of America, the whole spectrum from practical enlightenment and sound moral judgement to sentimentalism and braggadocio. He could touch greatness and he could skirt cheapness. . . .

> John M. Blum, *The Republican Roosevelt*.

Nobody likes him now but the people.

> Lord Bryce, in Lawrence F. Abbott ed., *The Letters of Archie Butt, Personal Aide to President Roosevelt*.

Now look, that damned cowboy is President of the United States.

> Mark Hanna, in a conversation with H. H. Kohlsaat, 16 September 1901.

. . . he raises intelligence to the quick flash of intuition.

> John Hay, in E. E. Morison, introduction, *The Letters of Theodore Roosevelt*, vol. 5.

Workingmen believed
He busted trusts,
And put his picture in their windows.
'What he'd have done in France!'
They said.
Perhaps he would —
He could have died
Perhaps,
Though generals rarely die except in bed,
As he did finally.
And all the legends that he started in his life
Live on and prosper
Unhampered now by his existence.
    Ernest Hemingway, *T. Roosevelt.*

. . . he was the master therapist of the middle classes.
    Richard Hofstadter, *The American Political
Tradition.*

The Constitution rides behind
    And Big Stick rides before,
Which is the rule of precedent
    In the reign of Theodore.
    Wallace Irwin, *The Ballad of Grizzly Gulch.*

Roosevelt is the keenest and ablest living interpreter of what I would call the superficial public sentiment of a given time and he is spontaneous in his
response to it; but he does not distinguish between
that which is a mere surface indication of a sentiment and the building up by a long process of
education of a public opinion which is as deep
rooted as life. . . .
    Robert La Follette, *La Follette's Autobiography:
A Personal Narrative of Political Experiences.*

When the stuffed prophets quarrel, when the saw-
                    dust
    comes out, I think of Roosevelt's genuine sins.
Once more my rash love for that cinnamon bear,
    Begins!
    Vachel Lindsay, *Roosevelt.*

Where is Roosevelt, the young dude cowboy,
Who hated Bryan, then aped his way?
Gone to join the shadows with mighty Cromwell
And tall King Saul, till the judgement day.
    Vachel Lindsay, *Bryan, Bryan, Bryan, Bryan.*

[He] understood the psychology of the mutt.
    Medill McCormick, in Richard Hofstadter, *The
American Political Tradition.*

                The talk begins.
He's dressed in canvas khaki, flannel shirt,
Laced boots for farming, chopping trees, perhaps;
A stocky frame, curtains of skin on cheeks
Drained slightly of their fat; gash in the neck
Where pus was emptied lately; one eye dim,

And growing dimmer; almost blind in that.
And when he walks he rolls a little like
A man whose youth is fading, like a cart
That rolls when springs are old. He is a moose,
Scarred, battered from the hunters, thickets, stones;
Some finest tips of antlers broken off,
And eyes where images of ancient things
Flit back and forth across them, keeping still
A certain slumberous indifference
Or wisdom, it may be.
    Edgar Lee Masters, *At Sagamore Hill.*

He hated all pretension save his own pretension.
    H. L. Mencken, *Prejudices, Second Series.*

But Roosevelt was never polite to an opponent;
perhaps a gentleman, by what pass as American
standards, he was surely never a gentle man. In a
political career of nearly forty years he was never
even fair to an opponent. All his gabble about the
square deal was merely so much protective coloration. No man, facing him in the heat of controversy,
ever actually got a square deal. He took extravagant
advantages; he played to the worst idiocies of the
mob; he hit below the belt almost habitually. One
never thinks of him as a duelist, say of the school
of Disraeli, Palmerston and, to drop a bit, Blaine.
One always thinks of him as a glorified bouncer
engaged eternally in cleaning out barrooms — and
not too proud to gouge when the inspiration came
to him, or to bite in the clinches, or to oppose the
relatively fragile brass knuckles of the code with chair
legs, bung-starters, cuspidors, demijohns and ice
picks.
    Ibid.

Tempted sufficiently, he would sacrifice anything
and everything to get applause. Thus the statesman
was debauched by the politician and the philosopher was elbowed out of sight by the popinjay.
    Ibid.

He was, in his dealings with concrete men as in his
dealings with men in the mass, a charlatan of the
very highest skill — and there was in him, it goes
without saying, the persuasive charm of the charlatan as well as the daring deviousness, the humanness of naïveté as well as the humanness of chicane.
He knew how to woo — and not only boobs.
    Ibid.

But most of all he was a skillful broker of the possible, a broker between the past and the present,
between the interest groups pushing the government
one way and the other, between his own conscience
and his opportunities. An able, ambitious nondoc-
trinaire, a moralist with a deep love for his country
and an abiding sense of responsibility, he was of

that *genus sui generis*, a democratic politician.
George E. Mowry, *The Era of Theodore Roosevelt 1900–1912*.

He had a talent for innocency. All things with which he associated himself fell in his mind easily into the category of goodness.
Amos R. E. Pinchot, *History of the Progressive Party 1912–1916*.

Theodore Roosevelt thought with his hips.
Lincoln Steffins, in James MacGregor Burns, *Roosevelt: The Lion and the Fox*.

Yet so strong was this young Roosevelt — hard-muscled, hard-voiced even when the voice cracked in falsetto. With hard, wriggling jaw muscles, and snapping teeth, even when he cackled in raucous glee, so completely did the personality of this man overcome me that I made no protest and accepted his dictum as my creed.
William Allen White, *Autobiography*.

Roosevelt bit me and I went mad.
William Allen White, in Richard Hofstadter, *The American Political Tradition*.

Teddy was reform in a derby, the gayest, cockiest, most fashionable derby you ever saw.
William Allen White, in Eric Goldman, *Rendezvous With Destiny*.

I was a young arrogant protagonist of the divine rule of the plutocracy . . . [Roosevelt] shattered the foundation of my political ideals. As they crumbled then and there, politically, I put his heel on my neck and I became his man.
William Allen White, in *ibid*.

Our hero is a man of peace,
    Preparedness he implores;
His sword within his scabbard sleeps,
    But mercy, how it snores.
McLandburgh Wilson, in A. K. Adams, *The Home Book of Humorous Quotations*.

See also Douglas Fairbanks, Warren G. Harding, Franklin D. Roosevelt, William Howard Taft, Woodrow Wilson

ROSEBERY, EARL OF (ARCHIBALD PHILIP PRIMROSE)
1847–1929 Prime Minister

I must plough my furrow alone. That is my fate, agreeable or the reverse; but before I get to the end of that furrow it is possible that I may find myself not alone.
On himself, Speech to the City Liberal Club, 19 July 1901.

He failed to separate the awkward incidents of the hour from the long swing of events, which he so clearly understood. Toughness when nothing particular was happening was not the form of fortitude in which he excelled. He was unduly attracted by the dramatic, and by the pleasure of making a fine gesture.
Winston Churchill, *Great Contemporaries*.

[He was] sometimes called 'Nature's Welfare State'. This is in reference to the fact that by marrying a Rothschild, being Prime Minister and winning the Derby, he demonstrated that it was possible to improve one's financial status and run the Empire without neglecting the study of form.
Claud Cockburn, *Aspects of English History*.

He is subjective, personal, a harp responsive to every breeze that blows. . . . He passes quickly through the whole gamut of emotion. . . . He is a creature of moods and moments, and spiritually he often dies young.
A. G. Gardiner, *Prophets, Priests and Kings*.

He is morbidly suspicious, which I do not attribute to politics, but to a point in his character, strengthened by Newmarket training.
Lord Granville, Letter to William Ewart Gladstone, 23 December 1882.

Without you the new Government would be ridiculous, with you it is only impossible.
Sir William Harcourt, Letter to Rosebery, August 1892.

I believe he funked the future which he saw before him — that he felt called upon to say something on politics in general and give a lead, and that he did not know what to say and so took up his hat and departed.
Sir William Harcourt, in A. G. Gardiner, *Life of Sir William Harcourt*.

He is a one-eyed fellow in blinkers.
David Lloyd George, September 1932, in A. J. Sylvester, *Life with Lloyd George*.

A dark horse in a loose box.
John Morley, in A. G. Gardiner, *Life of Sir William Harcourt*.

Rosebery who, though brilliant and attractive, is

not a serious person. Rosebery's enigmatic attitude creates a factitious interest in him, but it is a betrayal of his weakness.

Goldwin Smith, Letter to James Bryce, 1902.

[Gladstone's] successor is a poor creature who would be, if he could, like him & who, like him, would willingly sell England for power. But when he tries to roar like a lion, he only brays like an ass.

Sir Garnett Wolseley, Letter to the Duke of Cambridge, June 1896.

ROSSETTI, CHRISTINA GEORGINA

1830—94 Poet

Miss Christina was exactly the pure and docile-hearted damsel that her brother portrayed God's Virgin pre-elect to be.

William Holman-Hunt, *Pre-Raphaelitism and the Pre-Raphaelite Brotherhood.*

I think she is the best poet alive. . . . The worst of it is you cannot lecture on really pure poetry any more than you can talk about the ingredients of pure water — it is adulterated, methylated, sanded poetry that makes the best lectures. The only thing that Christina makes me want to do, is cry, not lecture.

Sir Walter Raleigh, in Virginia Woolf, *Second Common Reader.*

Christina Rossetti is too little known, except by some of her moralistic verses; she had a most delicate command of rhythm, . . . a delicate sense of the sound of words, and a highly competent technical ability which never appeared laboured because of its simplicity. . . . But it is her perspective of life that interests me most: sweet, small & narrow, delicate to the point of elusion.

Dylan Thomas, Letter to Pamela Hansford Johnson, 1933.

Christine [sic] has the great distinction of being a born poet, as she seems to have known very well herself. But if I were bringing a case against God she is one of the first witnesses I should call. It is melancholy reading. First she starved herself of love, which meant also life; then of poetry in deference to what she thought her religion demanded . . . Consequently, as I think, she starved into austere emaciation a very fine original gift.

Virginia Woolf, *A Writer's Diary*, 5 August 1918.

See also Walter De La Mare, Marianne Moore

ROSSETTI, DANTE GABRIEL

1828—82 Poet, Painter

The Rossetti Exhibition. I have been to see it and am pleased to find it more odious than I had even dared to hope.

Samuel Butler, *Notebooks.*

I should say that Rossetti was a man without any principles at all, who earnestly desired to find some means of salvation along the lines of least resistance.

Ford Madox Ford, *Ancient Lights.*

The writer's father once declared that D. G. Rossetti wrote the thoughts of Dante in the language of Shakespeare — to which this writer replied that Rossetti would have been better employed if he had written the thoughts of Rossetti in the language of Victoria.

Ford Madox Ford, *The March of Literature.*

I do not want to overrate Rossetti. I can see plainly enough that his technical power as a poet was far superior to his skill of hand as a painter; his draughtmanship sometimes leaves a good deal to be desired, and even his palette was not as rich as that of the great masters. But there was what one critic has well called the 're-birth of wonder' in all his work; to him the world was an enchanted place and his women were all heroines of the spirit.

Frank Harris, *My Life and Loves.*

Personally he struck me as an unattractive, poor man. I suppose he was horribly bored! — But his pictures, as I saw them in his room, I think decidedly strong. They were all large, fanciful portraits of women, of the type *que vous savez*, narrow, special, monotonous but with lots of beauty and power.

Henry James, Letter to John La Farge, 20 June 1869.

Rossetti, dear Rossetti
    I love your work,
but you were really
    a bit of a jerk.
George MacBeth, *Pictures from an Exhibition.*

He had some of the greatest qualities of genius, most of them indeed; what a great man he would have been but for the arrogant misanthropy that marred his work, and killed him before his time: the grain of humility which makes a great man one of the people and no lord over them, he lacked, and with it lost the enjoyment of life which would have kept him alive, and sweetened all his work for him and us.

William Morris (on Rossetti's death), Letter to William Bell Scott, 27 April 1882.

He was the only one of our modern painters who taught disciples for love of them. He was not really an Englishman, but a great Italian tormented in the Inferno of London; doing the best he could, and teaching the best he could; but the 'could' shortened by the strength of his animal passions, without any trained control, or guiding faith.

John Ruskin, *Praeterita.*

Mr. Rossetti threw more than half his strength into literature, and in that precise measure, left himself unequal to his appointed task in painting.

John Ruskin, *On the Old Road.*

A prince among parasites.

James McNeill Whistler, in Joseph and Elizabeth Robins Pennell, *The Whistler Journal.*

Rossetti is not a painter, Rossetti is a ladies' maid!

James McNeill Whistler, in R. Emmons, *The Life and Opinions of Walter Richard Sickert.*

See also William Morris

ROTHKO, MARK (MARCUS ROTHKOVICH)

1903—70 Artist

The unfriendliness of society to his activity is difficult for the artist to accept. Yet this very hostility can act as a lever for true liberation. Freed from a false sense of security and community, the artist can abandon his plastic bankbook, just as he has abandoned other forms of security. Both the sense of community and of security depend on the familiar. Free of them, transcendental experiences become possible.

On himself, in Peter Selz, *Mark Rothko.*

As I have grown older, Shakespeare has come closer to me than Aeschylus, who meant so much to me in my youth. Shakespeare's tragic concept embodies for me the full range of life from which the artist draws all his tragic materials, including irony; irony becomes a weapon against fate.

On himself, in *ibid.*

Holding tenaciously to humanist values, he paints pictures which are in fact related to man's scale and his measure. But whereas in Renaissance painting man was the measure of space, in Rothko's painting space, i.e. the picture, is the measure of the man.

Peter Selz, *ibid.*

An Apollonian intensity becomes evident in Rothko's work once we go beyond the immediate sensual appeal of the beautiful color relationships. In her interpretaions of Rothko's work, Dore Ashton has compared it with Greek drama, 'to the fatalism, the stately cadence and the desperately controlled shrieks.' Indeed, his work does not so much resolve agitation as contain it, in the sense of holding it within bounds. These apparently quiet, contemplative surfaces are only masks for underlying turmoil and passion.

Ibid.

ROTHSCHILD, LIONEL NATHANIEL DE, BARON

1808—79 Banker, Philanthropist

My opponents say that I cannot take my seat. That is rather my affair than theirs. I have taken the best advice. I feel assured that as your representative, as the representative of the most wealthy, the most important, the most intelligent constituency in the world, I shall not be refused admission to Parliament on account of any form of words whatsoever.

On himself, addressing voters in the City of London, August 1847.

For eleven years we've had the M.P. question screaming in every corner of the house.

Baroness de Rothschild, comment on her husband's eventual admission to the House of Commons, 1858.

ROTHSCHILD, SIR NATHAN MEYER, BARON ROTHSCHILD OF TRING

1840—1915 Banker, Philanthropist

I've got to keep breathing: it'll be my worst business mistake if I don't.

On himself, comment on the financial disruptions of war, 1915, in Frederic Morton, *The Rothschilds.*

I go to the bank every morning and when I say 'no' I return home at night without a worry. But when I say 'yes' it's like putting your finger into a machine — the whirring wheels may drag your whole body in after the finger.

On himself, in Virginia Cowles, *The Rothschilds: A Family of Fortune.*

Those who know him well appreciate him, but he requires to be very well known to be appreciated, for his manner is always uncertain and rarely caressing.

Anon., in *Vanity Fair*, 9 June 1888.

Is Lord Rothschild the dictator of this country? Are we really to have all the ways of reform, financial and social, blocked simply by a notice board: 'No thoroughfare. By order of Nathaniel Rothschild'.

David Lloyd George, defending his Budget taxation plans against opposition, 1909.

ROWE, NICHOLAS

1674–1718 Poet Laureate, Dramatist

A Gentleman, who lov'd to lie in Bed all Day for his Ease, and to sit up all Night for his Pleasure.

John Dennis, *Original Letters*.

The genius of Rowe was slow and timid, and loved the ground.

William Hazlitt, 'The Fair Penitent', in *Examiner*, 10 March 1816.

ROWLANDSON, THOMAS

1756–1827 Painter, Caricaturist

He burlesqued even the burlesque.

H. Angelo, *Reminiscences*.

The latter once gave offence, by carrying a pea-shooter into the life-academy, and, whilst old Moser was adjusting the female model, and had just directed her contour, Rowlandson let fly a pea, which making her start, she threw herself entirely out of position, and interrupted the gravity of the study for the whole evening. For this offence, Master Rowlandson went near to getting himself expelled.

Ibid.

To think of Regency England is to think in terms of Rowlandson.

M. Hardie, *Water-Colour Painting in Britain*.

Rowlandson was a more serious person than is often supposed . . . and he was tough; but he could be unemotional, detached, even bored, the last surely an odd characteristic for an artist. For all his preoccupation with the bawdy, he could be as close to Jane Austen as he was to Smollett.

John Hayes, *Rowlandson: Watercolours and Drawings*.

Rowlandson had more feeling for individual comic incident than for an artistic or intellectual whole; his larger compositions, complex and skilful though they often are, seem very often to be imposed upon the material rather than a truly organic growth from the nature of the subject-matter.

Ibid.

The essentials of the man are in his line, his exuberance, and the content and humour of his *reportage*; his world is the ordinary world and the ordinary man's response to it.

Ibid.

About the year 1780, Rowlandson emerges clearly as the master of an individual style in drawing and etching social subjects. Vigorous, ornate, emphatic and brilliant, the style was no slapdash corruption of commonplace excellence used for an unworthy and cheap object, but a careful and cultivated instrument admirably suited for reflecting, as had come into fashion in England from the Continent, the ideas and habits of a consciously picturesque and somewhat luxurious age.

A. P. Oppe, *Thomas Rowlandson*.

ROYCE, JOSIAH

1855–1916 Philosopher, Teacher

Josiah Royce is one of the most versatile minds in the history of American thought. He writes as a man of broad and humane culture. He should be read primarily because reading him is a liberal education.

Vincent Buranelli, *Josiah Royce*.

You are still the centre of my gaze, the pole of my mental magnet. When I write, 'tis with one eye on the page, and one on you!

William James, Letter to Royce, 26 September 1900.

That elfin figure with the unconventional dress and slouching step, that face which blended the infant and the sage, that total personality, as amused, amusing, and intent on righteousness as Socrates himself.

George Herbert Palmer, 'Josiah Royce', in Clifford Barrett ed., *Contemporary Idealism in America*.

Similarly, his thinking was marred by profusion and sheer power, rather than by refinement, pointedness, or focal illumination. He carried big guns but they were too big to hit the center of a small target.

Ralph Burton Perry, 'Josiah Royce', in Dumas Malone ed., *Dictionary of American Biography*.

There was a suggestion about him of the benevolent ogre or the old child, in whom a preternatural sharpness of insight lurked beneath a grotesque mask.

George Santayana, *Character and Opinion in the United States.*

His was a Gothic and scholastic spirit, intent on devising and solving puzzles, and honouring God in systematic works, like the coral insect or the spider; eventually creating a fabric that in its homely intricacy and fullness arrested and moved the heart, the web of it was so vast, and so full of mystery and yearning.

Ibid.

RUNYON, (ALFRED) DAMON

1884—1946 Author

... hired Hessian at the Typewriter.
On himself, in Edwin P. Hoyt, *A Gentleman of Broadway.*

He lived, by preference, amid the tinsel and the glaring lights of midnight, the sheen of asphalt in the rainy blackness, and the wistful crackling of discarded want-ads that curled around his legs in the biting winds of January.
Edwin P. Hoyt, *ibid.*

In truth, he stands at the center of the Broadway microcosm like its very demiurge, who had called his creature into existence for the essential purpose of gaining self-expression through them.
Jean Wagner, *Runyonese.*

... Broadway Boswell.
Ed Weiner, *The Damon Runyon Story.*

RUPERT, PRINCE, COUNT PALATINE OF THE RHINE

1619—82 Soldier

... the last Elizabethan, and the first Whig.
John Buchan, Lord Tweedsmuir, Preface to George Edinger, *Rupert of the Rhine.*

A man who hath had his hand very deep in the blood of many innocent men.
Oliver Cromwell, Letter to David Lesley, 14 August 1650.

He was the last knight errant; he was the first liberal politician.
George Edinger, *Rupert of the Rhine.*

The Prince was rough, and passionate, and loved not debate, liked what was proposed, as he liked the persons who proposed it.
Edward Hyde, Earl of Clarendon, *History of the Rebellion.*

Rupert that knew not fear, but health did want,
Kept state, suspended in a *chaise-volante*;
All save his head shut in that wooden case,
He show'd but like a broken weatherglass;
But arm'd in a whole lion cap-a-chin
Did represent the Hercules within.
Dear shall the Dutch his twinging anguish know
And feel what valour whet with pain can do.
Andrew Marvell, *Second Advice to a Painter.*

But above all I observed how he [Lord Fitzharding] observed from the Prince that Courage is not what men take it to be, a contempt of death; 'For', says he, 'how chagrin the Prince was the other day when he thought he should die — having no more mind to it than another man; but,' says he, 'some men are more apt to think they shall escape than another man in fight, while another is doubtful he shall be hit. But when the first man is sure he shall die, as now the Prince is, he is as much troubled and apprehensive of it as any man else. For,' says he, 'since we told him that we believe he would overcome his disease, he is as merry, and swears and laughs and curses, and doth all the things of a man in health, as ever he did in his life' — which methought was a most extraordinary saying, before a great many persons there of quality.
Samuel Pepys, Diary, 15 January 1665.

RUSH, BENJAMIN

1745—1813 Physician, Revolutionary

Bleeding Puff. — From the New—York Paper. — 'This day there is to be a meeting of the trustees of Columbia College. The object of their meeting is to invite Dr. Benjamin Rush to a professorship of the practice of physic in Columbia College. A correspondent is happy in remarking, that there are few obstacles in a choice which must result in so many advantages to Columbia College. *He is a man born to be useful to society'.*
And so is a *musquito*, a *horse-leech*, a *ferret*, a *pole cat*, a *weazel*: for these are all bleeders, and understand their business full as well as Doctor Rush does his.
William Cobbett, *Peter Porcupine's Works.*

Even today, Rush is still commonly known as a signer of the Declaration of Independence and as a bleeder, the deed of the pen alone saving him from the total disgrace of the lancet. And as if his heavy reliance upon bloodletting were not enough to assure his historical obloquy, Rush dared to commit the unforgivable sin of criticizing George Washington.

Donald J. D'Elia, in *Transactions of the American Philosophical Society*.

RUSH, RICHARD

1780—1859 Lawyer, Diplomat, Statesman

Never were abilities so much below mediocrity so well rewarded; no, not since Caligula's horse was made Consul.

John Randolph of Roanoke, on the appointment of Rush as Secretary of the Treasury, in Edward Boykin ed., *The Wit and Wisdom of Congress*.

See also James Monroe

RUSKIN, JOHN

1819—1900 Author

Yesterday, I came on a poor little child lying flat on the pavement in Bologna — sleeping like a corpse — possibly from too little food. I pulled up immediately — not in pity, but in *delight* at the folds of its poor little ragged chemise over the thin bosom — and gave the mother money — not in charity, but to keep the flies off it while I made a sketch. I don't see how this is to be avoided, but it is very hardening.

On himself, Letter to his parents, 1845.

For myself, I am never satisfied that I have handled a subject properly till I have contradicted myself at least three times.

On himself, Inaugural Address at the Cambridge School of Art, 1858.

I was still in the bonds of my old Evangelical faith; and, in 1858, it was with me, Protestantism or nothing: the crisis of the whole turn of my thoughts being one Sunday morning, at Turin, when, from before Paul Veronese's Queen of Sheba, and under quite overwhelmed sense of his God-given power, I went away to a Waldensian chapel, where a little squeaking idiot was preaching to an audience of seventeen year old women and three louts, that they were the only children of God in Turin; and that all the people in Turin outside the chapel, and all the

people in the world out of sight of Monte Viso, would be damned. I came out of the chapel, in sum of twenty years of thought, a conclusively unconverted man.

On himself, *Fors Clavigera*, Letter 76, April 1877.

You hear of me, among others, as a respectable architectural man-milliner; and you send for me that I may tell you the leading fashion.

On himself, *The Crown of Wild Olive*.

The Doctors say it was overwork and worry, which is partly true, and partly not. *Mere* overwork or worry might have soon ended me, but it would not have driven me crazy. I went crazy about St. Ursula and the other saints, — chiefly young-lady saints.

On himself, Letter to Charles Eliot Norton, July 1878.

I takes and paints,
Hears no complaints,
And sells before I'm dry;
Till savage Ruskin
He sticks his tusk in,
Then nobody will buy.

Anon., 'Poem by a Perfectly Furious Academician', in *Punch*.

A bottle of beautiful soda-water.

Thomas Carlyle, Letter to John Carlyle, 27 November 1855.

We should read Ruskin for the very quality of his mind which, when abused, makes him unreadable: his refusal to consider any human faculty in isolation. This characteristic, which produced the intellectual chaos of his later works, also allowed him to make his original and important discoveries.

Kenneth Clark, *Ruskin Today*.

It is through the visual imagination, and the images thrown up by it, that Ruskin becomes accessible . . . the visual dimension is not his weakness, but his strength. The images are the constructs of his argument, they do more than 'convey' what he is saying: they are what he is saying.

Robert Hewison, *John Ruskin: The Argument of the Eye*.

He is a chartered libertine — he has possessed himself by prescription of the function of a general scold.

Henry James, 'On Whistler and Ruskin', in *Nation*, 19 December 1878.

Leave to squeamish Ruskin
Popish Apennines,
Dirty stones of Venice

And his gas-lamps seven;
We've the stones of Snowdon
And the lamps of heaven.
  Charles Kingsley, *Letter to Thomas Hughes.*

It is long since there has been an age of which it could be said, as truly as of this, that nearly all the writers, even the good ones, were but commentators: expanders and appliers of ideas borrowed from others. Among those of the present time I can think only of two . . . who seem to draw what they say from a source within themselves: and to the practical doctrines and tendencies of both these, there are the gravest objections. Comté, on the Continent; in England (ourselves excepted) I can think only of Ruskin.
  John Stuart Mill, Diary, 21 January 1854.

. . . rising up & down on his toes, after his manner, with his hands in his tail-pockets, and finally jaunting downstairs in the same springy fashion, with the prim smile of Sir Oracle upon his dry lips.
  Alfred Munby, Diary, 8 November 1860.

The bulk of Ruskin's writing is not invalidated because of his attack on Whistler. A certain girlish petulance of style that distinguished Ruskin was not altogether a defect. It served to irritate and fix attention, where a more evenly judicial writer might have remained unread.
  W. R. Sickert, 'The Spirit of the Hive', in *New Age*, 26 May 1910.

. . . What greater sarcasm can Mr. Ruskin pass upon than that he preaches to young men what he cannot perform! Why, unsatisfied with his own conscious power, should he choose to become the type of incompetence by talking for forty years of what he has never done!
  James McNeill Whistler, *Whistler v Ruskin: Art and Art Critics.*

We are told that Mr. Ruskin has devoted his long life to art, and as a result is 'Slade Professor' at Oxford. In the same sentence we have thus his position and its worth. It suffices not, Messieurs! A life passed among pictures does not make a painter — else the policeman in the National Gallery might assert himself. As well allege that he who lives in a library must needs die a poet. Let not Mr. Ruskin flatter himself that more education makes the difference between himself and the policeman both standing gazing in the gallery.
  James McNeill Whistler, *The Gentle Art of Making Enemies.*

There is hardly a page of his writings which can be properly apprehended until it is collated with the condition of his mind and the circumstances of his life not only at the general period within which the book falls, but on the actual day on which that particular page was written.
  R. H. Wilenski, *John Ruskin.*

The mind of Ruskin, endowed with every gift except the gift to organize the others, was more tumultuous than the tumult in which it was involved. The deceptive lucidity of his intoxicating style displayed, or concealed, an intellect as profound, penetrating, and subtle as any that England has seen; and as fanciful, as glancing, and as wayward as the mind of a child.
  G. M. Young, *Victorian England.*

See also Van Wyck Brooks

RUSSELL, BERTRAND ARTHUR WILLIAM, THIRD EARL
1872—1970 Philosopher

I can only say that, while my own opinions as to ethics do not satisfy me, other people's satisfy me still less.
  On himself, *Reply to My Critics.*

I have a perfectly cold intellect, which insists upon & respects nothing. It will sometimes hurt you, sometimes seem cynical, sometimes heartless. It is very much more dominant at certain times than at others. You won't much like it. But it belongs with my work — I have deliberately cultivated it, & it is really the main thing I have put discipline into. In time I believe you will not mind it, but the sudden absolute cessation of feeling when I think must be trying at first. And nothing is sacred to it — it looks at everything quite impartially, as if it were someone else.
  On himself, Letter to Lady Ottoline Morrell, April 1911.

I like mathematics because it is *not* human & has nothing particular to do with this planet or with the whole accidental universe — because, like Spinoza's God, it won't love us in return.
  On himself, Letter to Lady Ottoline Morrell, March 1912.

I don't know how other people philosophise, but what happens with me is, first, a logical instinct that the truth must lie in a certain region, and then an attempt to find its exact whereabouts in that region. I trust the instinct absolutely, though it is blind and dumb; but I know no words vague enough to express it. If I do not hit the exact point in the region, contradictions and difficulties still beset me; but though I know I must be more or less wrong, I don't think I am in the wrong region.

On himself, Letter to F. H. Bradley, January 1914.

Here I have not a care in the world: the rest to nerves and will is heavenly. One is free from the torturing question: What more might I be doing? Is there any effective action that I haven't thought of? Have I a right to let the whole thing go and return to philosophy? Here I have to let the whole thing go, which is far more restful than choosing to let it go and doubting, if one's choice is justified. Prison has some of the advantages of the Catholic Church.

On himself, Letter from prison to Frank Russell, May 1918.

I have missed much by not dying here, as the Chinese were going to have given me a terrific funeral in Central Park, & then bury me on an island in the Western Lake, where the greatest poets & emperors lived, died, and were buried. Probably I should have become a God. What an opportunity missed.

On himself, Letter from China to Lady Ottoline Morrell after an announcement of his death, May 1921.

I'm as drunk as a Lord, but then I am one, so what does it matter?

On himself, in Ralph Schoenmann ed., Bertrand Russell, Philosopher of the Century.

I have a certain hesitation in starting my biography too soon for fear of something important having not yet happened. Suppose I should end my days as President of Mexico; the biography would seem incomplete if it did not mention this fact.

On himself, Letter to Stanley Unwin, November 1930.

At the age of eleven, I began Euclid, with my brother as my tutor. This was one of the great events of my life, as dazzling as first love. I had not imagined that there was anything so delicious in the world. After I had learned the fifth proposition, my brother told me that it was generally considered difficult, but I found no difficulty whatever. This was the first time it had dawned upon me that I might have some intelligence.

On himself, Autobiography.

I was told that the Chinese said they would bury me by the Western Lake and build a shrine to my memory. I have some slight regret that this did not happen, as I might have become a god, which would have been very *chic* for an atheist.

Ibid.

I have always thought respectable people scoundrels and I look anxiously at my face every morning for signs of my becoming a scoundrel.

On himself, in Alan Wood, *The Passionate Sceptic.*

Although we may oppose the plan
Of giving womenfolk a vote,
Still to the ordinary man
Few things are more engaging than
The Russell of the Petticoat.

Anon., *circa* 1907, during Russell's campaign for Women's Suffrage.

Said Lord Russell to Lady Cecilia,
I certainly wish I could feel ya,
    Your data excite me,
    It would surely delight me
To sense your unsensed sensibilia.

Anon., contemporary, in Ronald W. Clark, *Life of Bertrand Russell.*

[His] lack of spiritual depth became painfully evident during the first World War, when Russell, although (to do him justice) he never minimized the wrong done to Belgium, perversely maintained that, war being evil, the aim of statesmanship should be to bring the war to an end as soon as possible, which would have been achieved by British neutrality and a German victory. It must be supposed that mathematical studies had caused him to take a wrongly quantitative view which ignored the question or principle involved.

Anon., premature obituary, in *Listener*, 1937.

The Ass in the Lion's Skin and the Wolf in Sheep's Clothing represent familiar human types, but we have no image for the traitor who pretends to be a Mugwump.

An undated War Office article of Summer 1916.

I believe that it can be shown that all Russell's philosophy has been based on this quest for reassurance. It is sceptical in the sense that it questions all claims, but it also tries to find a solid base for them. The reason why Russell was always attempting to reduce things was to give fewer hostages to fortune.

A. J. Ayer, in Bryan Magee, *Modern British Philosophy.*

Hither flock all the crowd whom love has wrecked
Of intellectuals without intellect
And sexless folk whose sexes intersect:
All who in Russell's burly frame admire
The 'lineaments of gratified desire',
And of despair have baulked the yawning precipice
By swotting up his melancholy recipes
For 'happiness' — of which he is the cook

And knows the weight, the flavour, and the look,
Just how much self-control you have to spice it
                                    with:
How to 'rechauffe' the stock-pot of desire
Although the devil pisses on the fire:
How much long-suffering and how much bonhomie
You must stir up, with patience and economy,
To get it right: . . .
    Roy Campbell, *The Georgiad.*

Meeting [D. H.] Lawrence, I told him how enchanted I had been by the lucidity, the suppleness and
pliability of Bertrand Russell's mind. He sniffed.
'Have you seen him in a bathing-dress?' he asked.
'Poor Bertie Russell! He is all Disembodied Mind.'
    William Gerhardie, *Memoirs of a Polyglot.*

He is not a philosopher in the accepted meaning of
the word; not a lover of wisdom; not a searcher
after wisdom; not an explorer of that universal
science which aims at the explanation of all phenomena of the universe by ultimate causes; that in the
opinion of your deponent and multitudes of other
persons he is a sophist; practices sophism; that by
cunning contrivances, tricks and devices and by
mere quibbling, he puts forth fallacious arguments
and arguments that are not supported by sound
reasoning; and he draws inferences which are not
justly deduced from a sound premise; that all his
alleged doctrines which he calls philosophy are just
cheap, tawdry, worn out, patched up fetishes and
propositions, devised for the purpose of misleading
the people.
    Joseph Goldstein, prosecuting counsel, in the
    New York court case against Russell, 1940.

If I were the Prince of Peace, I would choose a less
provocative Ambassador.
    A. E. Housman, in Alan Wood, *Bertrand Russell,
    The Passionate Sceptic.*

The enemy of all mankind, you are, full of the lust
of enmity. It is *not* the hatred of falsehood which
inspires you. It is the hatred of people, of flesh
and blood. It is a perverted, mental blood-lust. Why
don't you own it.
    D. H. Lawrence, Letter to Bertrand Russell,
    September 1915.

What ails Russell is, in matters of life and emotion,
the inexperience of youth. He is, vitally, emotionally, much too inexperienced in personal contact
and conflict, for a man of his age and calibre. It
isn't that life has been too much for him, but too
little.
    D. H. Lawrence, Letter to Lady Ottoline Morrell,
    1915.

Lord Russell explained that he had two models for
his own style — Milton's prose and Baedeker's guide-
books. The Puritan never wrote without passion,
he said, and the cicerone used only a few words in
recommending sights, hotels, and restaurants.
Passion was the voice of reason, economy the signature of brilliance.
    Ved Mehta, *Fly and the Fly-Bottle.*

In one of his books he speaks very favourably of
adultery, but he does so in the scientific way in
which one might say a word for the method of
least squares, the hookworm, or a respectable volcano. Multitudes of other men, both lay and clerical, have thought along the same lines, and if they
have kept their ideas diligently to themselves, then
the crypto-Earl's frank-blabbing is only the more to
his credit.
    H. L. Mencken, in *Baltimore Sun*, May 1940.

He only feels life through his brain, or through sex,
and there is a gulf between these two separate
departments.
    Lady Ottoline Morrell, in Robert Gathorne-
    Hardy, *Ottoline at Garsington.*

It's not just a question of clarity, it's a question of
professional ethics.
    Karl Popper, commending Russell's style in
    Bryan Magee ed., *Modern British Philosophy.*

Russell thought one ought to know a lot about, say,
the rods and cones in the eye, and I don't pretend
to know anything about them, and, if I may speak a
bit rudely, I don't want to.
    Gilbert Ryle, in *ibid.*

Russell had many aristocratic attributes which infused his entire sensibility. It provided him with
strength when standing out against orthodoxy but
it sapped his confidence in the outcome of dramatic
change. He was influenced by bourgeois trepidations
which dissolved revolutionary transformation into
categories like 'mass society'. He felt that excellence
came from the special nurturing of individual talent
and that mediocrity or cultural decline would
follow the overthrow of privilege. He desired its
overthrow but he mourned in advance some of the
consequences as he saw them.
    Ralph Schoenmann, *Bertrand Russell and the
    Peace Movement.*

His writings were most pessimistic, but he himself
always appeared in the best of spirits — a feature
which I had also noticed in pessimists on frontier
expeditions. Apparently the way to really enjoy
oneself is to be full of dark forebodings and expect
the worst; then if the worst actually happens it is

only what one had expected, and if anything less than the worst occurs one can be in uproarious good-humour.

Sir Francis Younghusband, *The Light of Experience.*

See also Ludwig Wittgenstein

RUSSELL, JOHN, FIRST EARL

1792–1878 Prime Minister

Finality Jack.
Nick-name, derived from his view that the 1832 Reform Bill represented the fullest extent of the Franchise.

The foreign policy of the Noble Earl . . . may be summed up in two truly expressive words, 'meddle' and 'muddle'.

Lord Derby, Speech in the House of Lords, February 1864.

All great catastrophes which have occurred in our external affairs of late years have arisen from slight circumstances. The noble Lord could not find time to prevent the siege of a town, and so he invaded a country. So it was in all his policy. There was an alternation from fatal inertness to still more terrible energy. With him it was ever one step from collapse to convulsion. We commence by neglecting our duties, we terminate by violating their rights.

Benjamin Disraeli, Speech in the House of Commons, referring to Afghanistan, June 1842.

If a traveller were informed that such a man was leader of the House of Commons, he may well begin to comprehend how the Egyptians worshipped an insect.

Benjamin Disraeli, attributed.

He has risen with adversity. He seemed below par as a leader in 1835, when he had a clear majority, and the ball nearly at his feet: in each successive year the strength of his Government has fallen and his own has risen.

William Ewart Gladstone, 1841, in A. Wyatt Tilby, *Lord John Russell.*

How formed to lead, if not too proud to please!
His fame would fire you, but his manners freeze.
Like or dislike, he does not care a jot;
He wants your vote, but your affections not;
Yet human hearts need sun as well as oats —
So cold a climate plays the deuce with votes.

Lord Lytton, in G. W. E. Russell, *Collections and Recollections.*

So much for these statesmen of ours — they always remind me of what Southey said to me at Keswick; pointing in a little Bible-book for children, in size and shape an inch cube, to a woodcut of Samson with a gate on his back about twenty times his own size, he said, 'That is Lord John Russell carrying away the British Constitution'; and sure enough that is about the proportion between the men and the work they have in hand.

John Stuart Mill, Letter to John Sterling, July 1833.

To have begun with disapprobation, to have fought through many difficulties, to have announced and acted on principles new to the day in which he lived; to have filled many important offices, to have made many speeches, and written many books; and in his whole course to have done much with credit and nothing with dishonour, and so to have sustained and advanced his reputation to the very end, is a mighty commendation.

Lord Shaftesbury, Diary, Summer 1878.

If, instead of being the brightest ornament of the Senate, and the man to whom the country may point as that most rare of beings, a truly honest politician, he had been a member of the prize-ring, he could not have known better how and where to apply his knock-down blow.

Sir John Shelley, Letter to the Duke of Bedford, 30 November 1845.

The people along the [Devonshire] road were very much disappointed by his smallness. I told them he was much larger before the [Reform] bill was thrown out, but was reduced by excessive anxiety about the people. This brought tears into their eyes.

Sydney Smith, in Lady Holland, *Memoirs of Sydney Smith.*

Johnny has upset the coach.
Lord Stanley, note passed to Sir James Graham in the House of Commons on Russell's speech to the House on Irish Disestablishment, 1834.

A man of much talent, who leaves a name behind him, kind and good, with a great knowledge of the Constitution, who behaved very well on many trying occasions; but he was impulsive, very selfish (as shown on many occasions, especially during Lord Aberdeen's administration), vain, and often reckless and impulsive.

Queen Victoria, Diary, 29 May 1878.

See also Thomas Moore, Queen Victoria

RUSSELL, LILLIAN

1861–1922 Actress, Entertainer

Artistically Lillian Russell added little to theatrical history except an aptitude for commercializing sex appeal, a process on which Hollywood would infinitely elaborate, and of course her amazing ability to hit high C eight times in a performance. [But she and Diamond Jim Brady] together embellished the art of consumption, not the noblest endeavor in the world as we look back on it from the viewpoint of our diminished and soon-to-be-overtaxed resources. With their twelve-course dinners, their gold-plated bicycles, their encrustations of personal jewelry, their private railroad cars, they represented the ultimate vulgarization of the Horatio Alger legend.
  John Burke, *Duet in Diamonds*.

Her figure was on the hefty side. But around her lay an aura of beauty and calm assurance — she looked the way homely Jim [Brady] felt. He soon discovered that she liked to eat as much as he did. Lovely Lillian would retire to the ladies' room to remove her corset. Back at the table, she would almost match him, course for course.
  Allen Churchill, in 'Them As Has 'Em, Wears 'Em', in *Show*, April 1962.

La Russell was the great beauty of her day and the toast of the town. I can still recall the rush of pure awe that marked her entrance on the stage. And then the thunderous applause that swept from orchestra to gallery, to the very roof.
  Marie Dressler, *My Own Story*.

Whether she liked it or not, Lillian Russell was for a quarter of a century one of the most conspicuous figures on the English-speaking stage. Darling of the critics, idol of orchestra and gallery alike, she held public favor for an unprecedented period. She was a golden beauty who stampeded men's senses. Even if she had possessed no voice — and her voice was magnificent — she would have been a great success. The cold-blooded press went into ecstasies over her flawless features, her acting, her incomparable charm.
  Ibid.

Destiny and the cornfields of Iowa shaped her for the stage!
  Tony Pastor, in *ibid.*

RUTH, GEORGE HERMAN 'BABE'

1895–1948 Baseball Player

Here comes Jack with his newest babe.
  Anon. coach for the Baltimore Orioles, watching the young Ruth trot out to the playing field with head coach Jack Dunn at his first day of spring training, in Tom Meany, *Babe Ruth*.

God dressed in a camel's hair polo coat and flat camel's hair cap, God with a flat nose and little piggy eyes, a big grin, and a fat black cigar sticking out of the side of it.
  Paul Gallico, in *Dictionary of American Biography*.

Who is this Baby Ruth? And what does she do?
  George Bernard Shaw, to an American journalist, in Tom Meany, *Babe Ruth*.

I wonder where my Babe Ruth is tonight?
He grabbed his hat and coat and ducked from sight.
He may be at some cozy roadside inn,
Drinking tea — or maybe gin.
He may be at a dance, or may be in a fight.
I know he's with a dame,
I wonder what's her name,
I wonder where my Babe Ruth is tonight?
  William J. Slocum, parody sung at the New York Baseball Writers' Dinner, 1926.

RUTHERFORD, ERNEST, BARON RUTHERFORD OF NELSON AND CAMBRIDGE

1871–1937 Physicist

As I was standing in the drawing-room at Trinity, a *clergyman* came in. And I said to him: 'I'm Lord Rutherford'. And he said to me, 'I'm the Archbishop of York'. And I don't suppose either of us believed the other.
  On himself, in C. P. Snow, *Variety of Men*.

I went to no more lectures, except to Rutherford, whom I could not resist. He would boom on, talking about all kinds of interesting things, occasionally producing gems like 'integral $y. dx$; dx is small, we will neglect this'. He talked so easily and informally, he knew it all in an instinctive, relaxed way and the answer always somehow came out right. As someone said: 'The α particles were his friends, he knew what they would do' (there was a story, which I have not verified, that in one of his early papers the mass of an α particle came out as 3.3 on which he commented: 'we take four as the nearest integer').
  Sir Edward Bullard, in *Nature*, 30 August 1974.

An early breakthrough in spending money [at the Cavendish laboratory] was the purchase of the doughnut magnet, designed by Cockcroft, which was used to focus α particles. Rutherford, when showing it to a visitor, said: 'That cost as much as a research student for a year — but it does twice as much work'.

Ibid.

On the occasion of one of his discoveries, the writer said to him: 'You are a lucky man, Rutherford, always on the crest of the wave!' To which he laughingly replied, 'Well! I made the wave, didn't I?' and he added soberly, 'At least to some extent.'

A. S. Eve and J. Chadwick, in *Obituary Notices of Fellows of the Royal Society.*

Voltaire once said that Newton was more fortunate than any other scientist could ever be, since it could fall to only one man to discover the laws which govern the universe. Had he lived in a later age, he might have said something similar of Rutherford and the realm of the infinitely small; for Rutherford was the Newton of atomic physics. In some respects he was more fortunate than Newton; there was nothing in Rutherford's life to compare with the years which Newton spent in a vain search for the philosopher's stone, or with Newton's output of misleading optical theories, or with his bitter quarrels with his contemporaries. Rutherford was ever the happy warrior — happy in his work, happy in its outcome, and happy in its human contacts.

Sir James Jeans, in *ibid.*

The greater the achievements of a scientist the more exactly and briefly can they be described. Rutherford created the modern study of radioactivity; he was the first to understand that it is the spontaneous disintegration of the atom of radioactive elements. He was the first to produce the artificial disintegration of the nucleus and finally he was the first to discover that the atom has a planetary system. Each of these achievements is sufficient to make a man a great physicist.

P. L. Kapitza, in *Proceedings of the Royal Society of London.*

He was a big, rather clumsy man, with a substantial bay window that started in the middle of the chest. I should guess that he was less muscular than at first sight he looked. He had large staring blue eyes and a damp and pendulous lower lip. He didn't look in the least like an intellectual. Creative people of his abundant kind never do, of course, but all the talk of Rutherford looking like a farmer was unperceptive nonsense. His was really the kind of face and physique that often goes with great weight of character and gifts. It could easily have been the soma of a great writer.

C. P. Snow, *Variety of Men.*

The difficulty is to separate the inner man from the Rutherfordiana, much of which is quite genuine. From behind a screen in a Cambridge tailor's, a friend and I heard a reverberating voice; 'That shirt's too tight round the neck. Every day I grow in girth. *And* in mentality.'

Ibid.

His estimate of his own powers was realistic, but if it erred at all, it did not err on the modest side. 'There is no room for this particle in the atom as designed by *me*,' I once heard him assure a large audience. It was part of his nature that, stupendous as his work was, he should consider it ten per cent more so.

Ibid.

RYDER, ALBERT PINKHAM

1847–1917 Artist

Have you ever seen an inch worm crawl up a leaf or twig, and then clinging to the very end, revolve in the air, feeling for something to reach something? That's like me. I am trying to find something out there beyond the place on which I have a footing.

On himself, in James Thomas Flexner, *The World of Winslow Homer.*

I threw my brushes aside; they were too small for the work in my hand. I squeezed out big chunks of pure moist color and taking my palette knife, I laid on blue, green, white and brown in great sweeping strokes . . . I saw nature springing into life upon my dead canvas. It was better than nature, for it was vibrating with the thrill of a new creation. Exultantly I painted until the sun sank below the horizon, then I raced around the fields like a colt let loose, and literally bellowed for joy.

On himself, in *ibid.*

The artist should fear to become the slave of detail. He should strive to express his thought and not the surface of it. What avails a storm cloud accurate in form and color if the storm is not therein?

On himself, in Lloyd Goodrich, *Albert P. Ryder.*

The artist needs but a roof, a crust of bread and his easel, and all the rest God gives him in abundance. He must live to paint and not paint to live. He cannot be a good fellow; he is rarely a wealthy man, and upon the potboiler is inscribed the epitaph of his art. . . . The artist should not sacrifice his ideals to a landlord and a costly studio. A rain-tight roof, frugal living, a box of colors and God's sunlight through clear windows keep the soul attuned and the body vigorous for one's daily work.

On himself, in *ibid.*

S

SAARINEN, EERO
1910—61 Architect

Except for a rather brief excursion into sculpture, it never occurred to me to do anything but to follow in my father's footsteps and become an architect. As his partner, I often contributed technical solutions and plans, but only within the concept he created. A better name for architect is form-giver and until his death in 1950, when I started to create my own form, I worked within the form of my father.

On himself, in *Eero Saarinen, on His Work*.

I think of architecture as the total of man's manmade physical surroundings. The only thing I leave out is nature. You might say it is man-made nature. It is the total of everything we have around us, starting from the largest city plan, including the streets we drive on and its telephone poles and signs, down to the building and house we work and live in and does not end until we consider the chair we sit in and the ash tray we dump our pipe in. It is true that the architect practices on only a narrow segment of this wide keyboard, but that is just a matter of historical accident. The total scope is much wider than what he has staked his claim on. So, to the question, what is the scope of architecture? I would answer: It is man's total physical surroundings, outdoors and indoors.

On himself, in *ibid*.

I am a child of my period. I am enthusiastic about the three common principles of modern architecture: function, structure, and being part of our time. The principle of respecting function is deeply imbedded in me as it is in others of this period. But, like others, I do not look to it to solve my architectural problems. Sometimes, however, the problem and the time are ripe for an entirely new functional approach to a problem (as in the new jet airport for Washington), and at such moments function may become the overwhelming principle in directing the formula of design.

On himself, in *ibid*.

SACAGAWEA
circa 1787—1812 Squaw of the Mandan Nation

She was always busy, digging edible roots they were familiar with and finding strange ones, tailoring buckskins, making moccasins, explaining novelties, cool and swift in emergencies. . . . She is remarkable, this girl who may have been no more than seventeen in 1805, and of whom no word is directly reported since she could speak only Shoshone and Minnetaree. She is better known than any other Indian woman and she has unusual resourcefulness, staunchness, and loyalty, a warmth that can be felt through the rugged prose of men writing with their minds on a stern job, and a gaiety that is childlike and yet not the childishness we have associated with primitives.

Bernard De Voto, *Westward the Course of Empire*.

. . . she seems to possess the folly or the philosophy of not suffering her feelings to extend beyond the anxiety of having plenty to eat and a few trinkets to wear.

Captains Meriwether Lewis and William Clark, in Nicholas Biddle ed., *The Journals of the Expedition under the Command of Captains Lewis and Clark*.

SACCO, NICOLA, and VANZETTI, BARTOLOMEO
1891—1927 and 1888—1927 Alleged Anarchists

They long ago entered that great domain of human psychology in which time at last evaluates all things truly, making the calendar of intolerance and injustice complete from 399 B.C. to 1927 A.D.

Anon., in *St. Louis Post Dispatch*, in Michael Musmanno, *After Twelve Years*.

On this day, Nicola Sacco and Bartolomeo Vanzetti, dreamers of the brotherhood of man, who hoped it might be found in America, were done to a cruel death by the children of those who fled long ago to this land of hope and freedom.

Anon. note left in the reading room of the Boston Atheneum, 23 August 1927, in Howard Fast, *The Passion of Sacco and Vanzetti*.

These men were castaways upon our shore, and we, an ignorant and savage tribe, have put them to death because their speech and their manners were different from our own and because to the untutored mind that which is strange is in its infancy ludicrous, but in its prime, dangerous and to be done away with.
Edna St Vincent Millay, *Fear*.

Sacco is a heart, a faith, a character, a man; a lover of nature and of mankind. A man who gave all, who sacrificed all to the cause of Liberty and to his love for Mankind.
Bartolomeo Vanzetti, notes prepared for court statement, in Herbert Ehrmann, *The Untried Case*.

Never in our full life could we hope to do such work for tolerance, for justice, for man's understanding of men as now we do by accident. . . . The last moment belongs to us — that agony is our triumph.
Bartolomeo Vanzetti, statement to judge preparing to deliver death sentence, in Eugene Lyons, *The Life and Death of Sacco and Vanzetti*.

See also Ben Shahn

SACKVILLE, VISCOUNT (LORD GEORGE GERMAIN)

1716—85 Soldier, Statesman

Sackvilles alone anticipate defeat,
And ere they dare the battle, sound retreat.
Charles Churchill, *The Candidate*.

As those rare acts which Honour taught
Our daring sons where Granby fought,
Or those which, with superior skill,
SACKVILLE achiev'd by standing still.
Charles Churchill, *The Ghost*.

Fear and self-interest were the motives that led men to acquiesce to his political power. He had long since demonstrated that those who opposed him were likely to suffer for it; that he could be unforgiving to men who stood in his way, and revengeful to those who openly opposed him. If he could not break a man, he could damage his reputation by the subtle arts of organized insinuation.
Alan Valentine, *Lord George Germain*.

SACKVILLE-WEST, VICTORIA MARY (VITA)

1892—1962 Novelist, Poet

Viti is not a person one can take for granted. She is a dark river moving deeply in shadows. She really does not care for the domestic affections. She would wish life to be conducted on a series of *grandes passions*. Or she thinks she would. In practice, had I been a passionate man, I should have suffered tortures of jealousy on her behalf, have made endless scenes, and we should now have separated, I living in Montevideo as H.M. Minister and she breeding Samoyeds in the Gobi desert.
Harold Nicolson, Diary, 24 December 1933.

One unspoken friendship I always felt confident in, though little was said between us: this was with Vita Sackville-West. Working always in her garden, caring for her friends, her flowers and her poetry, modest and never interesting herself in literary disputes, her friendship had the freedom of silence and watchfulness about it.
Stephen Spender, *World Within World*.

One of these days, though, I shall sketch here, like a grand historical picture, the outlines of all my friends. . . . It might be a most amusing book. The question is how to do it. Vita should be Orlando, a young nobleman.
Virginia Woolf, *A Writer's Diary*, 18 September 1927.

SAINT-GAUDENS, AUGUSTUS

1848—1907 Sculptor

You can do anything you please. It's the way it's done that makes the difference. . . .
I thought that art seemed to be the concentration of the *experience* and *sensation* of life in painting, literature, sculpture, and particularly acting, which accounts for the desire in artists to have realism. However, there is still the feeling of the lack of something in the simple representation of some indifferent action. The imagination must be able to bring up the scenes, incidents, that impress us in life, condense them, and the truer they are to nature the better. The imagination may condemn that which has impressed us beautifully as well as the strong, or characteristic, or ugly. . . .
On himself, in Buckner Hollingsworth, *Augustus Saint-Gaudens*.

I suppose that every earnest effort toward great sincerity, or honesty, or beauty, in one's production is a drop added to the ocean of evolution to the something higher that I suppose we are rising slowly (damned slowly) to. . . . But whatever it is, the passage is terribly sad and tragic, and to bear up against what seems at times the great doom that is over us, love and courage are the great things. I try to express it without entering into any philosophy or definition of art. . . .

I once told Schiff that at times I thought beauty must mean — at least — some goodness.

On himself, in *ibid.*

St. Gaudens was a child of Benvenuto Cellini smothered in an American cradle.

Henry Adams, in Louis Hall Tharp, *Saint-Gaudens and the Gilded Era.*

He was a draughtsman, a designer, who expressed himself with equal feeling for the *ensemble* whether he worked in the round or in relief. He was a true impressionist who saw a work as a whole before he began, and who kept the impression before him until the end. Although he laboured at detail, he always strove to keep the detail subservient to the *ensemble.* In studying his work we feel that it is completely under control, impulse is chastened by consideration. He was an eclectic with, if the term be allowed, more individualism than eclecticism, yet he never allowed his individuality to master the temperament of his sitter. Facile cleverness he abhorred. He avoided mere realism, desiring to mould what he selected from life into a pattern framed by the artist's vision.

C. Lewis Hind, in Buckner Hollingsworth, *Augustus Saint-Gaudens.*

His was a negative period, disclaiming the pseudo-classicism of the previous generation, but not yet established on a positive basis. In the midst of aesthetic uncertainties that leaned heavily on European taste, Saint-Gaudens could and did affirm his belief in his own country and its future in art.

Buckner Hollingsworth, in *ibid.*

Augustus Saint-Gaudens who needs not mortal years in doing immortal work.

Charles Eliot, Dedication in Buckner Hollingsworth, *ibid.*

ST JOHN, HENRY, see under BOLINGBROKE, VISCOUNT

ST VINCENT, EARL, see under JERVIS, JOHN

SALISBURY, THIRD MARQUIS OF (ROBERT ARTHUR TALBOT GASCOYNE CECIL)

1830—1903 Prime Minister

. . . If the Conservatives abandoned the principles for which I joined them, I should walk for the last time down the steps of the Carlton Club without casting a glance of regret behind me.

On himself, in Lord David Cecil, *The Cecils of Hatfield House.*

I do not understand what people mean when they talk of the burden of responsibility. I could understand what they mean by the burden of decision — I feel it . . . trying to make up my mind whether or not to take a greatcoat with me. I feel it in exactly the same way and no more when I am writing a dispatch upon which peace or war may depend. Its degree depends on the materials for decision that are available and not in the least on the magnitude of results which may follow. With the results I have nothing to do.

Ibid.

. . . when he came . . . to explain in dulcet tones the entire fulfilment of the treaty of Berlin, he shone like the peaceful evening star. But sometimes he is like the red planet Mars, and occasionally he flames in the midnight sky, not only perplexing nations but perplexing his own nearest friends and followers.

The Duke of Argyll, speaking in the House of Lords, May 1879.

. . . that strange powerful inscrutable and brilliant obstructive deadweight at the top.

Lord Curzon, in Lord David Cecil, *The Cecils of Hatfield House.*

He is a great master of gibes and flouts and jeers.

Benjamin Disraeli, to the House of Commons, 5 August 1874.

Sal. seems most prejudiced and not to be aware that his principal object in being sent to Const[antinople] is to keep the Russians out of Turkey, not to create an ideal existance for Turkish Xtians. He is more Russian than Ignatyev: *plus Arabe que l'Arabie!*

Benjamin Disraeli, Letter to Lord Derby, 28 December 1876.

I am always very glad when Lord Salisbury makes a great speech. . . . It is sure to contain at least one blazing indiscretion which it is a delight to remember.

A. E. Parker, Earl of Morley, Speech at Hull, 25 November 1887.

I have a few glass cases in which I put those people who by their excellence deserve them. Now take Lord Salisbury. I have a fine glass case for him. As a statesman he stands alone. There is no-one who can fairly be compared with him. He is always reliable, always good; and therefore I have made a glass case for him. . . .

Cecil Rhodes, in Philip Jourdan, *Cecil Rhodes: His Private Life.*

. . . Of Lord Salisbury I can only observe that the combination of such genuine amiability in private life with such calculated brutality in public utterance is a psychological phenomenon which might profitably be made the subject of a Romanes Lecture at Oxford.

> G. W. E. Russell, *Sixty Years of Empire: The Queen's Prime Ministers*.

My greatest Prime Minister.

> Queen Victoria, in Lord David Cecil, *The Cecils of Hatfield House*.

SANDBURG, CARL

1878—1967 Author

Here is the difference between Dante, Milton, and me. They wrote about hell and never saw the place. I wrote about Chicago after looking the town over for years and years.

> On himself, in Harry Golden, *Carl Sandburg*.

He is submerged in adolescence. . . . Give Sandburg a mind, and you perhaps destroy him.

> Sherwood Anderson, Letter to Van Wyck Brooks, December 1919.

In a generation in which most poets set themselves more manageable and more opportune tasks, he undertook to be the poet of a people among whom the sources of poetry, though by no means exhausted, were untapped, grown over, and all but completely forgotten.

> Newton Arrin, 'Carl Sandburg', in Malcolm Cowley ed., *After the Genteel Tradition*.

This son of an immigrant Swede railroad worker, this ex-housepainter, ex-dishwasher, ex-newspaperman, has done more than all but two or three other writers of his time to keep somewhat open and unclogged the channels that ought to flow between the lives at the base of society and the literary consciousness.

> *Ibid.*

. . . a pacifist between wars.

> Robert Frost, in Harry Golden, *Carl Sandburg*.

On the day that God made Carl He didn't do anything else that day but sit around and feel good.

> Edward Steichen, in *ibid.*

The great mid-West, that vast region of steel mills and slaughterhouses, of cornfields and prairies, of crowded cities and empty skies, spoke through Carl Sandburg.

> Louis Untermeyer, *Modern American Poetry, A Critical Anthology*.

Under close scrutiny Sandburg's verse reminds us of the blobs of living jelly or plankton brought up by deep-sea dredging; it is a kind of protoplasmic poetry, lacking higher organization.

> George F. Whicher, 'The Twentieth Century', in Arthur Hobson Quinn ed., *The Literature of the American People*.

. . . there are moments when one is tempted to feel that the cruellest thing that has happened to Lincoln since he was shot by Booth has been to fall into the hands of Carl Sandburg.

> Edmund Wilson, in Gay Wilson Allen, *Carl Sandburg*.

SANDWICH, EARL OF (JOHN MONTAGU)

1718—92 Statesman

Consult his person, dress, and air,
He seems, which strangers well might swear,
The master, or, by courtesy,
The captain of a colliery.
Look at his visage, and agree
Half-hang'd he seems, just from the tree
Escaped; a rope may sometimes break,
Or men be cut down by mistake.

> Charles Churchill, *The Duellist*.

Too honest (for the worst of men
In forms are honest, now and then)
Not to have, in the usual way,
His bills sent in; too great to pay:
Too proud to speak to, if he meets
The honest tradesman whom he cheats:
Too infamous to have a friend;
Too bad for bad men to commend,
Or good to name; beneath whose weight
Earth groans; who hath been spared by Fate
Only to show, on Mercy's plan,
How far and long God bears with man.

> *Ibid.*

To run a horse, to make a match,
To revel deep, to roar a catch,
To knock a tottering watchman down,
To sweat a woman of the town;
By fits to keep the peace, or break it,
In turn to give a pox, or take it;
He is, in faith, most excellent,
And, in the world's most full intent,
A true choice spirit, we admit;
With wits a fool, with fools a wit.

> *Ibid.*

'Lord! sister,' says Physic to Law, 'I declare,
Such a sheep-biting look, such a pick-pocket air!

Not I for the Indies: — You know I'm no prude, —
But his nose is a shame, — and his eyes are so lewd!
Then he shambles and straddles so oddly — I fear —
No — at our time of life 'twould be silly, my dear.'
    'I don't know,' says Law, 'but methinks for his
                look,
'Tis just like the picture in Rochester's book;
Then his character, Phyzzy — his morals — his life —
When she died, I can't tell, but he once had a wife.
They say he's no Christian, loves drinking and
                whoring,
And all the town rings of his swearing and roaring!
His lying and filching and Newgate-bird tricks; —
Not I — for a coronet, chariot and six.'
    Thomas Gray, *The Candidate* or *The Cambridge Courtship.*

Only a fortnight before he laid the Essay on Woman before the House of Lords, he had been drinking and singing loose catches with [John] Wilkes at one of the most dissolute clubs in London. Shortly after the meeting of Parliament, the Beggar's Opera was acted at Covent Garden theatre. When Macheath uttered the words — 'That Jemmy Twitcher should peach me I own surprises me', — pit, boxes and galleries burst into a roar which seemed likely to bring the roof down. From that day Sandwich was universally known by the nickname of Jemmy Twitcher.
    T. B. Macaulay, *Essays*: 'Chatham'.

Sandwich had a predilection to guilt, if he could couple it with artifice and treachery.
    Horace Walpole, *Memoirs.*

SARGENT, JOHN SINGER

1856—1925 Artist

Every time I paint a portrait I lose a friend.
    On himself, attributed.

I can't paint *views*. I can paint objects; I can't paint *views*.
    On himself, in Donelson F. Hoopes, *Sargent Watercolors.*

I *hate* to paint portraits! I hope never to paint another portrait in my life. Landscape I like, but, most of all, decoration, where the really aesthetic side of art counts for so much more. Portraiture may be all right for a man in his youth, but after forty I believe that manual dexterity deserts one, and, besides, the colour-sense is less acute. Youth can better stand the exactions of a personal kind that are inseparable from portraiture. I have had

enough of it. I want now to experiment in more imaginary fields.
    On himself, in Richard Ormond, *John Singer Sargent.*

It is positively dangerous to sit to Sargent. It is taking your face in your hands.
    Anon., to W. Graham Robertson, in *ibid.*

His advice to a fellow-painter was: 'Begin with Frans Hals, copy and study Frans Hals, after that go to Madrid and copy Velasquez, leave Velasquez, till you have got all you can out of Frans Hals'.
    Harold Acton, *The Memoirs of an Aesthete.*

As Henry James had admirably said, perception with Sargent was already by itself a kind of execution. It is true that for the most part, he, like Velasquez, was occupied with facts, not ideas. He told Arthur Rubinstein that he treated his themes objectively, not subjectively and therefore when his sitters were uninteresting, Sargent's portraits were not great successes.
    Martin Birnbaum, *John Singer Sargent; A Conversation Piece.*

Sargent did not reject the moderns. He understood their creeds and restlessness. Like many of us, he recognized the value of their vision, without sympathizing with them, but he had not patience with rebels who profaned beauty like prostitutes, who enjoyed shocking you with their violence and refused to submit themselves to artistic routine and discipline.
    Ibid.

Sargent's portrait of Henry James is nearly finished, and I hear is a masterpiece. There is a plaid waistcoat in it, heaving like a sea in storm, which is said to be prodigious.
    Edmund Gosse, Letter to Thomas Hardy, 1913.

It is difficult to imagine a young painter less in the dark about his own ideal, more lucid and more responsible from the first about what he desires.
    Henry James, 'John S. Sargent', in *Harper's Weekly*, October 1887.

He is various and experimental; if I am not mistaken, he sees each work that he produces in a light of its own, not turning off successive portraits according to some well-tried receipt which has proved useful in the case of their predecessors; nevertheless there is one idea that pervades them all, in a different degree, and gives them a family resemblance — the idea that it would be inspiring to know just how Velasquez would have treated the theme.
    Ibid.

John is very stiff, a sort of completely accentless mongrel, not at all like Curtis or Newman; rather French, faubourg sort of manners. Ugly, not at all changed in feature, except for a beard. He was very shy, having I suppose a vague sense that there were poets about. . . .

Vernon Lee (Violet Paget), in Richard Ormond, *John Singer Sargent.*

Sargent used frequently to halt his painting to rest his sitters by playing to them. Dr. Playfair's maid once commented of his practice: 'Isn't it nice that Mr. Sargent feels like painting when he tires of playing the piano.'

David McKibbin, *Sargent's Boston.*

Sargent's conventional success inevitably alienated him from the *avant-garde.* He had become an establishment figure, and his fashionable portraits were interpreted as the products of mammon. There was a touch of malice and envy in the attitude of those artists who had known him in the days when he was still struggling to establish a reputation. Mary Cassatt called him a 'buffoon', while Whistler condescendingly told the Pennells: 'I wouldn't, for a moment, have anyone think I was saying anything about Sargent, who is a good fellow, but as for his work it is neither better nor worse than that of the usual Academician.' The attitude of the older Impressionists is summed up in the correspondence of Camille Pissarro and his son, Lucien. The latter wrote in 1891 that he had recently been invited to lunch with Sargent: 'He was very, very nice. I don't like his painting; he doesn't seem to me to be much of an artist.' His father replied: 'Monet had told me that he is very kind. As for his painting, that, of course, we can't approve of; he is not an enthusiast but rather an adroit performer, and it was not for his painting that Mirbeau wanted you to meet him. He is a man who can be very useful.'

Richard Ormond, *John Singer Sargent.*

While painting, he rushed bull-like at his canvas, spluttering and gasping, and muttering imprecations and incantations to himself in the throes of creation. 'Demons!', repeated several times, was his favourite expression.

Ibid.

What relation have Sargent's men and women to the drama of life and death? Sargent rarely succeeded in removing his figures from the model stand, from the Louis XV chair or settee dear to the new rich, from pearl necklaces and glittering medals, and Worth dresses of velvet and satin.

William Rothenstein, *Men and Memories 1872–1900.*

I have said that he has the supreme virtue in a portrait-painter of an eye for character. He has a great gift for placing his shapes where he wishes, safely and firmly. The colour is *quelconque*, and the quality of execution is slippery, and has no beauty or distinction of its own. The paintings might be described as able black-and-white sketches on a large scale, in adequate colours. The problem of turning out satisfactory likenesses with a certain brilliant allure, and the little touches of piquant provocation that respectable women are always so anxious to secure, has seldom been solved by an abler hand or a juster eye.

Walter Richard Sickert, in *New Age,* 9 May 1910.

An American, born in Italy, educated in France, who looks like a German, speaks like an Englishman, and paints like a Spaniard.

William Starkweather, 'The Art of John S. Sargent', in *Mentor,* October 1924.

A sepulchre of dulness and propriety.

James MacNeill Whistler, in Richard Ormond, *John Singer Sargent.*

See also Harvey Cushing, William Butler Yeats

SARGENT, SIR MALCOLM
1895–1967 Conductor

I spend up to six hours a day waving my arms about and if everyone else did the same they would stay much healthier.

On himself, in Leslie Ayre, *The Wit of Music.*

After one of my concerts, a critic wrote that I had given a 'perfunctory' performance of a certain work. . . . I was annoyed about it and pointed out that, whereas he was entitled to give an opinion about my performance, to say that it was 'perfunctory' was to suggest that I had not given proper attention to the job I was paid to do.

Some time later the same critic wrote a notice of another of my concerts. He began, 'If one did not know that Malcolm Sargent takes meticulous care over the preparation of his concerts, one might have thought that this was a perfunctory performance —'

There was nothing else for it. We became friends and remained so through the years.

On himself, in Leslie Ayre, *The Proms.*

'What do you have to know to play the cymbals?' someone asked Sir Malcolm Sargent. 'Nothing,' was the reply. 'Just when.'

Leslie Ayre, *The Wit of Music.*

I couldn't care less about *you*. *I'm* having the time of my life. It's the most wonderful feeling of neurotic power in the world. I think I would rather do this than anything I know. I would travel anywhere in the world to conduct a symphony orchestra. . . . Say, does Malcolm Sargent talk this much?

Danny Kaye, conducting the London Philharmonic Orchestra.

You have only to see the eyes of a choral society screwing into him like a thousand gimlets to know what he means to them. . . . He plays upon their imaginations and minds like a mesmerist.

Bernard Shore, *The Orchestra Speaks.*

SASSOON, SIEGFRIED LORRAINE

1886—1967 Author

A booby-trapped idealist.

On himself, *Siegfried's Journey.*

At first I only noticed his sticking-out ears and obvious embarrassment, but a closer scrutiny revealed great charm and a certain sweetness and grave strength in his countenance.

Lady Cynthia Asquith, Diary, 15 November 1917.

Siegfried Sassoon lunched with me at the Reform yesterday. He expected some decoration for admittedly fine bombing work. . . . Sassoon was uncertain about accepting a home billet if he got the offer of one. I advised him to accept it. He is evidently one of the reckless ones. He said his pals said he always gave the Germans every chance to pot him. He said he would like to go out once more and give them another chance to get him, and come home unscathed. He seemed jealous of the military reputation of poets.

Arnold Bennett, Journal, 9 June 1917.

He speaks slowly, enunciating the words as if they pained him, in a voice that has something of the troubled thickness apparent in the voices who emerge from a deep grief. . . . And all the while he will be breathing hard like a man who has swum a distance. One would think that he communed with himself, save that, at the pauses, he shoots a powerful glance at the listener.

Robert Nichols, Introduction to American edition of Sassoon's *Counterattack.*

SAVAGE, RICHARD

— d. 1743 Poet

Savage my name, unblest my native morn,

Who to the ills of poetry was born.
From Pope deputed, from my heart's ally,
To yonder camp I tend, a dauntless spy.
Through great and many dangers safe I go,
My only guard my falsehood to the foe.

Thomas Cooke, *The Battle of the Poets.*

Hack, spendthrift, starveling, duellist in turn;
Too cross to cherish yet too fierce to spurn;
Begrimed with ink or brave with wine and blood;
Spirit of fir and manikin of mud;
Now shining clear, now fain to starve and skulk;
Star of the cellar, pensioner of the bulk;
At once the child of passion and the slave;
Brawling his way to an unhonoured grave —
That was DICK SAVAGE.

W. E. Henley, *Hawthorn and Lavender.*

There are no proper judges of his conduct who have slumbered away their time on the down of plenty, nor will any wise man presume to say, 'Had I been in Savage's condition, I should have lived or written better than Savage.'

Samuel Johnson, *Lives of the Poets.*

SAVILE, GEORGE, MARQUIS OF HALIFAX

1633—95 Author, Politician

He confessed he could not swallow down every thing that divines imposed on the world: He was a Christian in submission: He believed as much as he could, and he hoped that God would not lay it to his charge, if he could not digest iron, as an ostrich did, nor take into his belief things that must burst him: If he had any scruples, they were not sought for, nor cherished by him: for he never read an atheistical book.

Gilbert Burnet, *History of My Own Times.*

When he talked to me as a philosopher of his contempt for the world, I asked him, what he meant by getting so many new titles, which I call'd the hanging himself about with bells and tinsel. He had no other excuse for it, but this, that, since the world were such fools as to value those matters, a man must be a fool for company: He considered them but as rattles: Yet rattles please children: So these might be of use to his family.

Ibid.

Jotham of pregnant wit and piercing thought,
Endowed by nature, and by learning taught
To move Assemblies, but who only tried
The worse awhile, then chose the better side;
Nor chose alone, but turned the balance too;
So much the weight of one brave man can do.

John Dryden, *Absalom and Achitophel.*

But is there any other beast that lives
Who his own harm so wittily contrives?
Will any dog that hath his teeth and stones
Refin'dly leave his bitches and his bones
To turn a wheel and bark to be employ'd
While Venus is by rival dogs enjoy'd?
Yet this fond man, to get a statesman's name
Forfeits his friends, his freedom, and his fame.
    John Dryden and John Sheffield, Earl of Mulgrave, *Essay Upon Satire*.

This man, who possessed the finest genius and most extensive capacity of all employed in public affairs during the present reign, affected a species of neutrality between the parties, and was esteemed the head of that small body known as Trimmers. This conduct, which is more natural to men of integrity than of ambition, could not, however procure him the former character, and he was always, with reason, regarded as an intriguer rather than a patriot.
    David Hume, *History of England*.

He passed from faction to faction. But instead of adopting and inflaming the passions of those whom he joined, he tried to diffuse amongst them something of the spirit of those whom he had just left.
    T. B. Macaulay, *Essays: 'Sir William Temple'*.

His understanding was keen, sceptical, inexhaustibly fertile in distinctions and objections; his taste refined, his sense of the ludicrous exquisite; his temper placid and forgiving, but fastidious, and by no means prone either to malevolence or to enthusiastic admiration. Such a man could not long be constant to any band of political allies. He must not, however be confounded with the vulgar crowd of renegades. For though, like them, he passed from side to side, his transition was always in the direction opposite to theirs. He had nothing in common with those who fly from extreme to extreme, and who regard the party which they have deserted with an animosity far exceeding that of consistent enemies. His place was between the hostile divisions of the community, and he never wandered far beyond the frontier of either. The party to which he at any moment belonged was the party which, at that moment, he liked least, because it was the party of which, at that moment he had the nearest view. He was therefore always severe upon his violent associates, and was always in friendly relations with his moderate opponents.
    T. B. Macaulay, *History of England*.

His writings were the fruit, not of failure and disgrace, but of a bold and dangerous political career. In consequence they are few; but they are untinged by the bitterness of disappointment. If he saw through the vulgar charms of power, it was not with

envy, as unattainable, nor with disgust, as sour; it was with the sane intellectual judgement of one who has known and valued it at its proper estimation.
    Hugh Trevor-Roper, *Historical Essays*.

SAYERS, DOROTHY LEIGH

1893—1957 Author

Her slickness in writing has blinded many readers to the fact that her stories, considered as detective stories, are very bad ones. They lack the minimum of probability that even a detective story ought to have, and the crime is always committed in a way that is incredibly tortuous and quite uninteresting.
    George Orwell, in *New English Review*, 23 January 1936

Of Dorothy (Leigh) Sayers . . . it is not easy to write fairly. For her whole-hearted admirers, a diminished but still considerable band, she is the finest detective story writer of the twentieth century, to those less enthusiastic her work is long-winded and ludicrously snobbish.
    Julian Symons, *Bloody Murder*.

I had often heard people say that Dorothy Sayers wrote well, and I felt that my correspondents had been playing her as their literary ace. But, really, she does not write very well: it is simply that she is more consciously literary than most of the other detective-story writers and that thus she attracts attention in a field which is mostly on a sub-literary level. In any serious department of fiction, her writing would not appear to have any distinction at all.
    Edmund Wilson, *Classics and Commercials*.

SCHLESINGER, ARTHUR MEIER

1888—1965 Historian

The slightly built, gray-haired professor with a whimsical smile was considered capable rather than colorful.
    Anon., Obituary notice in *New York Times*, 31 October 1965.

SCHURZ, CARL

1829—1906 Diplomat, Politician

[He] brought justice and the Indian together.
    Anon., in Joseph Schafer, *Carl Schurz — Militant Liberal*.

. . . a political career consistent only in the frequency and agility of its changes.
> James G. Blaine, *Twenty Years of Congress*, vol. 2.

He has not become rooted and grounded anywhere, has never established a home, is not identified with any community, is not interwoven with the interests of any locality or of any class, has no fixed relation to Church or State, to professional, political, or social life, has acquired none of that companionship and confidence which unite old neighbors in the closest ties, and give to friendship its fullest developments, its most gracious attributes.
> *Ibid.*

. . . an insatiate appetite for opposition.
> Louis A. Coolidge, in C. M. Fuess, *Carl Schurz, Reformer (1829–1906)*.

Few persons know that this red-beard Teuton has the eloquence of Demosthenes and the fire of Kossuth.
> Charles A. Dana, in C. M. Fuess, *ibid.*

. . . his trial of organization after organization, as if he were a political taster instead of a political teacher.
> George Hope, in C. M. Fuess, *ibid.*

For more than fifty years there was hardly a bad cause in our political life which did not have reason to fear this German-born master of English speech.
> Bliss Perry, in C. M. Fuess, *ibid.*

He must be undermining somebody to be entirely virtuous.
> 'Gath', George Alfred Townsend, in *Cincinnati Enquirer*, 18 November 1885.

SCOTT, CHARLES PRESTWICH

1846–1932 Editor of *Guardian*

He makes righteousness readable.
> James Bone, attributed.

SCOTT, SIR GEORGE GILBERT

1811–78 Architect

I was awakened from my slumbers by the thunder of [Augustus] Pugin's writings. I well remember the enthusiasm to which one of them excited me, one night when travelling by railway, in the first years of their existence. I was from that moment a new man.

Old things (in my practice) had passed away, and, behold, all things had become new, or every aspiration of my heart had become mediaeval. What had for fifteen years been a labour of love only, now became the one business, the one aim, the one overmastering object of my life. I cared for nothing as regarded my art, but the revival of gothic architecture. I did not know Pugin, but his image in my imagination was like my guardian angel, and I often dreamed that I knew him.
> On himself, *Personal and Private Recollections*.

We may be now too near to the Victorian age to be able to judge its heroes impartially; but will anyone ever admire the works of Scott? It is hard to believe that they will, for there is nothing particular in them to admire.
> Basil Clarke, *Church Builders of the Nineteenth Century*.

Gilbert Scott was the supreme model of a Samuel Smiles self-made man . . . with all the vigour and all the lack of subtlety that one would expect.
> R. Furneaux-Jordan, *Victorian Architecture*.

It must have seemed so easy in his day to be a Gothic architect, and he should have proved to us that it was impossible. In this way he was a teacher if we would learn.
> W. R. Lethaby, *Philip Webb and His Work*.

It is always tempting to choose an individual or two in order to epitomise a movement or an age, and in the case of Sir George Scott the temptation is irresistible. For not only was he the leading architect of the Gothic Revival in its respectable phase, but also he seems completely representative of what we have come to consider the Victorian character. His religion was not romantic in the Pugin manner; his self-assurance was, on the surface at least, colossal; his instinct for combining financial success with a rather smug morality seems to be the very essence of his time; and his enormous output of bad and indifferent architecture reflects that Victorian philistinism that sprang from the moralisation of art.
> R. Turnor, *Nineteenth Century Architecture in Britain*.

SCOTT, JAMES FITZROY, see under MONMOUTH, DUKE OF

SCOTT, JOHN, see under ELDON, EARL OF

SCOTT, ROBERT FALCON

1868—1912 Antarctic Explorer

. . . For my own sake I do not regret this journey, which has shewn that Englishmen can endure hardships, help one another, and meet death with as great a fortitude as ever in the past. We took risks, we knew we took them; things have come out against us, and therefore we have no cause for complaint, but bow to the will of Providence, determined still to do our best to the last.

> On himself, 'Message to the Public', written shortly before his death, March 1912.

. . . in such a heart as Scott's it was human endeavour that mattered, not mere ambition to achieve.

> Herbert G. Ponting, *The Great White South*.

SCOTT, SIR WALTER

1771—1832 Author

Scott became the historiographer-royal of feudalisms.

> Matthew Arnold, *Essays in Criticism*: 'Heinrich Heine'.

Walter Scott has no business to write novels, especially good ones. — It is not fair. — He has Fame and Profit enough as a Poet, and should not be taking the bread out of other people's mouths. — I do not like him, & do not mean to like *Waverley* if I can help it — but fear I must.

> Jane Austen, Letter to Anna Austen, 28 September 1814.

'I think,' continued Byron, after a pause, 'that Scott is the only very successful genius that could be cited as being as generally beloved as a man, as he is admired as an author; and, I must add, he deserves it, for he is so thoroughly good-natured, sincere, and honest, that he disarms the envy and jealousy his extraordinary genius must excite.'

> Lady Blessington, *Conversations with Lord Byron*.

And think'st thou, Scott! by vain conceit perchance,
On public taste to foist thy stale romance
Though Murray with his Miller may combine
To yield thy muse just half-a-crown per line?
No! when the sons of song descend to trade,
Their bays are sear, their former laurels fade.
Let such forgo the poet's sacred name
Who rack their brains for lucre, not for fame.

> Lord Byron, *English Bards and Scotch Reviewers*.

He is undoubtedly the Monarch of Parnassus, and the most *English* of bards. I should place Rogers next in the living list . . . Moore and Campbell both *third* — Southey and Wordsworth and Coleridge — the rest δἰπολλοι — thus: —

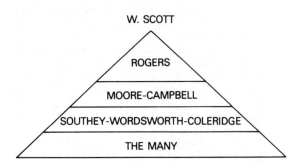

> Lord Byron, Journal, 24 November 1813.

. . . Grand work, Scotch Fielding, as well as great English Poet — wonderful man! I long to get drunk with him.

> *Ibid.*, 5 January 1821.

It can be said of him, When he departed, he took a man's life along with him. No sounder piece of British manhood was put together in that eighteenth century of Time.

> Thomas Carlyle, *Critical and Miscellaneous Essays*, vol. 4, Scott'.

The truth is, our best definition of Scott were perhaps even this, that he was, if no great man, then something much pleasanter to be, a robust, thoroughly healthy and withal very prosperous and victorious man. An eminently well-conditioned man, healthy in body, healthy in soul; we will call him one of the *healthiest* of men.

> Thomas Carlyle, in *London and Westminster Review*, January 1838.

The Waverley Novels . . . spread Gothic sentiment to every class of reader. . . . They described real historical events and associated them with clear description of Gothic architecture. . . . Scott was a more reliable guide to the Middle Ages than previous Gothic poets and novelists; for, like Gray and Warton, he combined literature with archaeology. It was the wealth of archaeological detail in Scott's novels which made his picture of the Middle Ages so satisfying, and so much more influential than the mere melancholy of the poets.

> Kenneth Clark, *The Gothic Revival*.

Walter Scott's poems and novels . . . both supply instance and solution of the *present* conditions and components of popularity, viz. to amuse without requiring any effort of thought, and without exciting any deep emotion. The age seems *sore* from excess of stimulation, just as, a day or two after a thorough debauch and long sustained drinking match, a man feels all over like a bruise.

Samuel Taylor Coleridge, Letter to Thomas Allsop, January 1821.

Scott's prodigious facility and the conventional unreality of his view of life ruined the English novel. By means of his enormous reputation he was enabled to debase the intellectual and moral currency in this department of literature to the lowest possible limit. It is a curious illustration of our attitude towards these things that Scott's method of paying off his debts by feverish literary production seems only to arouse our unqualified admiration. The commercial instinct in our British breasts is so highly developed that we glory in the sight of a great man prostituting his fame to make money, especially in a good cause. If he had paid off his debts at the gaming table, or even at the stock exchange, perhaps we should have been shocked. As he only flung his own genius and art on to the table to play against a credulous public his virtue remains immaculate.

Havelock Ellis, in *Savoy Magazine*, October 1896.

On Waterloo's ensanguined plain
Lie tens of thousands of the slain;
But none, by sabre or by shot,
Fell half so flat as Walter Scott.

Thomas, Lord Erskine, *On Scott's 'The Field of Waterloo'*.

The public has done for good with the slipshod methods of amateur literary hacks like Scott. That Scott will live as an historical figure we need neither doubt nor regret. He was, like Chateaubriand and like Goethe, a good man. . . . His very last words — spoken to his son-in-law — were: 'Be a good man, my dear, be a *good* man.' A good *man*, you observe, not a good biographer or a good writer to the signet. And the proudest boast of Scott was that he had never in all the immense array of his hack scrapbag written one word that the purest maiden seated in the privacy of her bedchamber could not read without a blush. That too is historic.

Ford Madox Ford, *The March of Literature*.

For my own part I do not care for him, and find it difficult to understand his continued reputation. . . . When we fish him out of the river of time . . . he is seen to have a trivial mind and a heavy style. He cannot construct. He has neither artistic detachment nor passion, and how can a writer who is devoid of both, create characters who will move us deeply? . . . He only has a temperate heart and gentlemanly feelings, and an intelligent affection for the countryside: and this is not basis enough for great novels.

E. M. Forster, *Aspects of the Novel*.

Sir Walter Scott is undoubtedly the most popular writer of the age — the 'lord of the ascendant' for the time being. He is just half what the human intellect is capable of being: if you take the universe, and divide it into two parts, he knows all that it *has been*; all that it *is to be* is nothing to him. . . . He is 'laudator temporis acti' — a '*prophesier* of things past'. The old world is to him a crowded map; the new one a dull, hateful blank. He dotes on all well-authenticated superstitions; he shudders at the shadow of innovation. . . . Sir Walter would make a bad hand of a description of the *Millenium*, unless he could lay the scene in Scotland five hundred years ago.

William Hazlitt, *The Spirit of the Age*.

His works (taken together) are almost like a new edition of human nature. This is indeed to be an author!

William Hazlitt, *English Literature*.

Walter Scott is the most popular of all the poets of the present day, and deservedly so. He describes that which is most easily and generally understood with more vivacity and effect than any body else. He has no excellences, either of a lofty or recondite kind, which lie beyond the reach of the most ordinary capacity to find out; but he has all the good qualities which all the world agree to understand.

William Hazlitt, *Lectures on the English Poets*.

Scott was a born story-teller: we can give him no higher praise. Surveying his works, his character, his method, as a whole, we can liken him to nothing better than to a strong and kindly elder brother, who gathers his juvenile public about him at eventide, and pours out a stream of wondrous improvisation. . . . And thoroughly to enjoy him, we must again become as credulous as children at twilight.

Henry James, in *North American Review*, October 1864.

Scott appears hemmed in, his prose is curiously fatigued — the clumsy, unrealised descriptions of thrilling actions, the rhetorical outbursts in 'the language of passion', the conscientious oil-paintings of historical scenes and characters, drag their slow lengths along often ridiculously.

Q. D. Leavis, *Fiction and the Reading Public*.

These, then, are the moral services, — many and great, — which Scott has rendered, positively and negatively, consciously and unconsciously, to society. He has softened national prejudices; he has encouraged innocent tastes in every region of the world; he has imparted to certain influential classes the conviction that human nature works alike in all; he has exposed priestcraft and fanaticism; he has effectively satirized eccentricities, unamiablenesses, and follies; he has irresistibly recommended benignity in the survey of life, and indicated the glory of a higher kind of benevolence; and finally, he has advocated the rights of women.

Harriet Martineau, in *Tait's Edinburgh Magazine*, January 1833.

During the first quarter of this century a great poet was raised in the North, who . . . has contributed by his works, in prose and verse, to prepare men for some closer and more practical approximation to Catholic truth. The general need of something deeper and more attractive than what had offered itself elsewhere, may be considered to have led to his popularity; and by means of his popularity he re-acted on his readers, stimulating their mental thirst, feeding their hopes, setting before them visions, which, when once seen, are not easily forgotten, and silently indoctrinating them with nobler ideas, which might afterwards be appealed to as first principles.

Cardinal Newman, in *British Critic*, April 1839.

He has the rare talent of pleasing all ranks and classes of men, from the peer to the peasant, and all orders and degrees of mind, from the philosopher to the man-milliner 'of whom nine make a taylor'. On the arrival of *Rob Roy*, as formerly on that of *Marmion*, the scholar lays aside his Plato, the statesman suspends his calculations, the young lady deserts her hoop, the critic smiles as he trims his lamp, thanking God for his good fortune, and the weary artisan resigns his sleep for the refreshment of the magic page.

Thomas Love Peacock, *An Essay on Fashionable Literature*.

It has been impossible, hitherto, to make the modern reader understand the vastness of Scott's historical knowledge, underneath its romantic colouring, nor the concentration of it in his eternally great poems and romances. . . . He must be read with the care which we give to Chaucer; but with the greater reward, that what is only a dream in Chaucer, becomes to us, understood from Scott, a consummate historical morality and truth. . . . The literally *Scotch* novels . . . *are*, whatever the modern world may think of them, as faultless, throughout, as human work can be: and eternal examples of the

ineffable art which is taught by the loveliest nature to her truest children.

John Ruskin, *Praeterita*.

As his books are play to the reader, so they were play to him. He conjured up the romantic with delight, but he hardly had the patience to describe it. He was a great day-dreamer, a seer of fit and beautiful and humorous visions, but hardly a great artist; hardly, in the manful sense, an artist at all. . . . A great romantic — an idle child.

Robert Louis Stevenson, *A Gossip on Romance*.

Either Scott the novelist is swallowed whole and becomes part of the body and brain, or he is rejected entirely. There is no middle party in existence — no busybodies run from camp to camp with offers of mediation. For there is no war.

Virginia Woolf, *The Moment*.

I don't like to say all this, or to take to pieces some of the best reputed passages of Scott's verse, especially in the presence of my wife, because she thinks me too fastidious; but as a poet Scott *cannot* live, for he has never in verse written anything addressed to the immortal part of man. In making amusing stories in verse, he will be superseded by some newer versifier; what he writes in the way of natural description is merely rhyming nonsense.

William Wordsworth, in conversation (reported by Mrs Davy), 11 July 1844.

See also Lord Byron, John Knox, Pontiac, Ann Radcliffe, Shakespeare, William Wordsworth

SCOTT, WINFIELD

1786—1866 Soldier

Sir, I am the greatest coward in America! I will prove it. I fought this battle sir, against my judgment, I think the President of the United States ought to remove me for doing it, I did all in my power to make the army efficient. I deserve removal because I did not stand up, when my army was sent in a condition for fighting, and resist it to the last.

On himself, in a conversation with Abraham Lincoln, in John G. Nicolay and John Hay, *Abraham Lincoln: A History*.

Old Fuss and Feathers.

Anon. popular nickname for Scott based on his preoccupation with the sartorial splendour of his uniforms.

His long life march is ended, His battles fought and won;

With solemn voices blended
Of drum and bell and gun
    Lay him down
    Whose renown
Is an unsetting sun.
    Anon., in *Harper's Weekly*, 16 June 1866.

That Scott was vain of many things there is no doubt. He took a special pride in his person — from all accounts, with full justification. Nor did he hesitate to invite attention to it, either verbally or by the surer method of enhancing its commanding appearance with the showiest trappings of his profession. Not even the gorgeously bedizened marshals of Napoleon wore their plumes, sashes, aiguillettes and glittering uniforms with more complacency than did this republican soldier whose imposing and symmetrical form was so well set off by such martial embellishments.
    Charles W. Elliott, *Winfield Scott: The Soldier and the Man.*

I don't know whether Scott is a *dotard* or a *traitor*! I can't tell which. He *cannot* or will not comprehend the condition in which we are placed and is entirely unequal to the emergency. . . . I am leaving nothing undone to increase our force — but that confounded old Gen'l always comes in the way — he is a fearful incubus. He understands nothing, appreciates nothing, and is ever in my way.
    General George B. McClellan, in William S. Myers, *A Study in Personality: George Brinton McClellan.*

See also Franklin Pierce

SCROGGS, SIR WILLIAM

1623?—83 Lord Chief Justice

The Chief was Arod, whose corrupted youth
Has made his soul an enemy to truth.
But nature furnished him with parts and wit
For bold attempts and deep intriguing fit;
Small was his learning and his eloquence
Did please the rabble, nauseate men of sense.
Bold was his spirit, nimble and loud his tongue,
Which more than law, or reason takes the throng.
Him, part by money, partly by her grace
The cov'tous Queen rais'd to a Judge's place,
And as he bought his place, he justice sold
Weighing his causes not by law but gold.
He made the Justice seat a common mart:
Well skill'd he was in the mysterious art
Of finding varnish for an unsound cause,
And for the sound, imaginary flaws.
    John Caryll, *Naboth's Vineyard.*

He was vulgar and profligate, a great winebibber, stained by coarse habits and the ignorant prejudices common to all of his day but the most temperate and learned, but a man of wit, shrewdness, strong character, and master of the talents which were necessary to secure success in the legal profession such as it then was.
    John Pollock, *The Popish Plot.*

SEDLEY, SIR CHARLES

1639—1701 Poet, Dramatist

I am apt to think you have 'bated something of your mettel since you and I were rivalls in other matters, tho' I hope you have not yet attained the perfection I have heard Sir Charles Sydlie brag of which is that when a short youth runs quick through every veine, and puts him in minde of his ancient prowesse, he thinks it not worth while to bestow motion on his *et cetera* muscle.
    Sir George Etherege, Letter to John Dryden, 20 March 1687.

Mr Batten telling us of a late triall of Sir Charles Sydly the other day before my Lord Chief Justice Foster and the whole Bench — for his debauchery a little while since at Oxford Kate's; coming in open day into the Balcone and showed his nakedness — acting all the postures of lust and buggery that could be imagined, and abusing of scripture, and as it were, from thence preaching a Mountebanke sermon from that pulpitt, saying that there he hath to sell such a pouder as should make all the cunts in town run after him — a thousand people standing underneath to see and hear him.
    And that being done, he took a glass of wine and washed his prick in it and then drank it off; and then took another and drank the King's health. . . . Upon this discourse, Sir J Mennes and Mr Batten both say that buggery is now almost grown as common among our gallants as in Italy, and that the very pages of the town begin to complain of their masters for it. But blessed be God, I do not to this day know what is the meaning of this sin, nor which is the agent nor which the patient.
    Samuel Pepys, Diary, 1 July 1663.

See also James II

SELWYN, GEORGE AUGUSTUS

1719—91 Wit, Politician

If I am alive I shall be glad to see him; if I am dead, he'll be glad to see me.
    Lord Holland, expecting Selwyn on his deathbed.

The beautiful Lady Coventry was one day exhibiting to him a splendid new dress, covered with large silver spangles the size of a shilling, and enquired of him whether he admired her taste. — 'Why,' he said, 'you will be change for a guinea.'

> G. H. Jesse, *George Selwyn and his Contemporaries.*

If, this gay fav'rite lost, they yet can live,
A tear to Selwyn let the Graces give!
With rapid kindness teach Oblivion's pall
O'er the sunk foibles of the man to fall;
And fondly dictate to a faithful Muse
The prime distinction of the friend they lose.
'Twas social wit, which, never kindling strife,
Blazed in the small sweet courtesies of life;
Those little sapphires round the diamond shone,
Lending soft radiance to the richer stone.

> Dr John Warner, *Epitaph on George Selwyn.*

See also Charles James Fox

SELZNICK, DAVID O.

1902—65 Motion Picture Producer

I have no middle name. I briefly used my mother's maiden name, Sachs. I had an uncle, whom I greatly disliked, who was also named David Selznick, so in order to avoid the growing confusion between the two of us, I decided to take a middle initial and went through the alphabet to find one that seemed to me to give the best punctuation, and decided on 'O'.

> On himself, in Rudy Behlmer, *Memo From David O. Selznick.*

Selznick has been described as overbearing, egocentric, aggressive, exhausting and impossible. Correspondent Lloyd Shearer once wrote that Selznick gave the impression that he stormed through life demanding to see the manager — and that, when the manager appeared, Selznick would hand him a twenty-page memo announcing his instant banishment to Elba.

> Rudy Behlmer, *ibid.*

He was a dynamic, flamboyant, spoiled, utterly egotistical man. Compared with Orson [Welles] he was semieducated and uninspired, but he had an infallible, instinctive sense of the motion picture business with its strange blend of blatant romanticism and commercial preoccupation. . . . For all his arrogance and exasperating self-indulgence, he was a man of intelligence and considerable charm — a typically Hollywood combination of oafishness and sophistication.

> John Houseman, *Runthrough.*

There was a kind of innocence that he had. Like all boys, he loved to play games, and there was a quality of game-playing in everything he did. He loved to dress up and to entertain, to play the host. He was kind of high and handsome; he couldn't do enough for his guests. He had a childish, young approach to picture making as well. Even the memos were a sign of his playfulness. He was *playing* at the game of being the producer.

> John Huston, in Bob Thomas, *Selznick.*

In truth, David was a bit of a snob. Despite his father's downfall, he believed that the Selznicks were among the elite of movie society, and he aimed to impress his contemporaries with that notion. He lived and acted accordingly. He chose his close acquaintances with care, and he nourished friendships with the rich and influential. He abhorred the common stereotype of the movie producer as an uncouth Jew, and he sought to divorce himself from such a view. More and more of his intimates were rich gentiles, and he declined to identify himself with the Jewish community of Hollywood.

> Bob Thomas, *ibid.*

SENNETT, MACK (MICHAEL SINNOTT)

1884—1960 Motion Picture Director

It wasn't me, the Old Man, who was so funny; it was the comical people I had around me. I called myself 'King of Comedy', a solemn and foolish title if there ever was one, but I was a harassed monarch. I worked most of the time. It was only in the evenings that I laughed.

> On himself, in *King of Comedy.*

Sennett wheedled his first financing out of a couple of ex-bookies to whom he was already in debt. He took his comics out of music halls, burlesque, vaudeville, circuses and limbo, and through them he tapped in on that great pipeline of horsing and miming which runs back unbroken through the fairs of the Middle Ages at least to ancient Greece. He added all that he himself had learned about the large and spurious gesture, the late decadence of the Grand Manner, as a stage-struck boy in East Berlin, Connecticut, and as a frustrated opera singer and actor. The only thing he claims to have invented is the pie in the face, and he insists 'Anyone who tells you he has discovered something new is a fool, or a liar or both'.

> James Agee, *Agee On Film*, vol. 1.

Mack knew how, but he didn't know why. He knew how to do slapstick but he never knew why he did. It was instinct with Mack.

> Hal Roach, *The Silent Picture*, Spring 1970.

A big, rough, tough plumber named Mack Sennett knew about gadgets such as movie cameras and klieg lights and about laughter from his mother, who, before he left Ireland, was buddies with the leprechauns. He put these together as Clowns and Keystone Cops, Chases, the original Sennett Comedies and Bathing Beauties, and made them a stone of the corner on which the Movies were built.
Adela Rogers St Johns, *The Honeycomb.*

I would like to recommend that his films be recirculated, particularly in countries that punish disrespect of too much law and too much order.
Josef von Sternberg, *Fun In a Chinese Laundry.*

SETTLE, ELKANAH
1648–1724 Poet

Doeg, though without knowing how or why
Made still a blund'ring kind of Melody;
Spurd boldly on, and Dash'd through Thick and
Thin,
Through Sense and Non-sense, never out nor in;
Free from all meaning, whether good or bad,
And in one Word, Heroically mad,
He was too warm on Picking-work to dwell,
But Faggoted his Notions as they Fell,
And, if they Rhim'd and Rattled, all was well.
Spightfull he is not, though he wrote a Satyr,
For still there goes some *Thinking* to ill-Nature:
He needs no more than Birds and Beasts to think,
All his Occasions are to eat and Drink.
If he call Rogue and Rascal from a Garrat
He means you no more mischief than a Parat.
John Dryden, *The Second Part of Absalom and Achitophel.*

There is something in *names* which one cannot help feeling. Now *Elkanah Settle* sounds so *queer*, who can expect much from that name?
John Wilkes, in James Boswell, *Life of Johnson.*

SEWARD, ANNA, 'THE SWAN OF LITCHFIELD'
1747–1809 Author

. . . here is Miss Seward with 6 tomes of the most disgusting trash, sailing over Styx with a Foolscap over her periwig as complacent as can be. — Of all Bitches dead or alive a scribbling woman is the most canine. — Scott is her Editor, I suppose because she lards him in every page.
Lord Byron, Letter to John Cam Hobhouse, 17 November 1811.

SEWARD, WILLIAM HENRY
1801–72 Politician

[A man] who has faith in everybody, and enjoys the confidence of nobody.
On himself, Letter to Thurlow Weed, 2 January 1862.

Nobody can apologize for insults but I, who never give any.
On himself, in Allan Nevins, *The Emergence of Lincoln*, vol. 1.

I did not regard Seward as exactly insincere, we generally knew at what hole he would go in, but we never felt quite sure as to where he would come out.
Anon., in Frederic Bancroft, *The Life of William Henry Seward.*

A subtle, quick man, rejoicing in power, given to perorate and to oracular utterances, fond of badinage, bursting with the importance of State mysteries.
Anon., in *The Times*, in *ibid.*

In '64 with peace secured
We will have our William Seward.
Anon. Glee Club song, New York Palace Garden, 1860.

A slouching slender figure; a head like a wise macaw; a beaked nose; shaggy eyebrows; unorderly hair and clothes; hoarse voice; off-hand manner; free talks, and perpetual cigar.
Henry Adams, *Education of Henry Adams.*

Undoubtedly Seward did too much thinking in ink; and a 'spend thrift verbosity' called 'the nightmare of foreign ministers' was sometimes the result.
Frederic Bancroft, *The Life of William Henry Seward.*

He was not the father of the Republican party; but he, more than any other man, was its master. He was not the first of antislavery champions; but of the great antislavery North, having a reasonable and worthy political purpose, he was, as Jefferson Davis said, 'the directing intellect.'
Ibid.

He stood up and talked as though he were engaged in conversation, and the effect was always great. It gave the impression of a man deliberating 'out loud' with himself.
Charles A. Dana, *Recollections.*

SEYMOUR, JANE

[His] natural tendencies were toward a government not merely paternal, but prodigal – on which . . .. [he endeavored] to make everyone prosperous, if not rich. . . . Few governors favored, few senators voted for more unwisely lavish expenditures than he.
Horace Greeley, *Recollections.*

. . . a dirty abolitionist sneak.
Mary Todd Lincoln, in Lord Longford, *Abraham Lincoln.*

Seward must be got out of the Cabinet. He is Lincoln's evil genius. He has been the President de Facto, and has kept a sponge saturated with chloroform to Uncle Abe's nose all the while.
Joseph Medill of the *Chicago Tribune* after the defeat at Fredericksburg, in Benjamin P. Thomas, *Abraham Lincoln.*

Seward with all his ability was in [Andrew] Johnson's hands only as clay in the hands of a potter.
Oliver P. Temple, in Eric L. McKitrick, *Andrew Johnson: A Profile.*

. . . it was well understood by those who knew him that he was an optimist, governed less by convictions and fixed laws than by expedients, and that he had more faith in his skill and management to govern and accomplish a purpose than in the constitution or any political principle.
Gideon Welles, *Lincoln's Administration.*

See also Salmon P. Chase

SEYMOUR, JANE

1509–37 Queen Consort to Henry VIII

Of all the wives of King *Henry* she only had the happiness to die in his full favour, the 14th of *Octob.* 1537. and is buried in the quire of *Windsor* Chappell, the King continuing in *real mourning* for her even all the *Festival* of *Christmas.*
Thomas Fuller, *The History of the Worthies of England.*

SHADWELL, THOMAS

1642–92 Dramatist

Tom writ, his readers still slept o'er his book;
For *Tom took opium*, and they opiates took.
Thomas Brown, *In Obitum T. Shadwell, pinguis memoriae 1693.*

Now stop your Noses, Readers all and some,
For here's a tun of Midnight work to come,
Og from a Treason Tavern rowling home.
Round as a Globe, and Liquored every chink,
Goodly and Great he Sayls behind his Link;
With all this Bulk there's nothing lost in *Og*
For ev'ry inch that is not Fool is Rogue:
A Monstrous Mass of foul corrupted matter,
As all the Devils had spew'd to make the Batter.
When wine has given him Courage to Blaspheme,
He curses God, but God before curst him;
And if Man could have reason, none has more,
That made his Paunch so rich, and him so Poor.
John Dryden, *The Second Part of Absalom and Achitophel.*

But though Heav'n made him poor (with rev'rence speaking)
He never was a Poet of God's making;
The Midwife laid her hand on his Thick Skull,
With this Prophetick blessing – *Be thou Dull;*
Drink, Swear and Roar, forbear no lewd Delight
Fit for thy Bulk, doe anything but write,
Thou art of lasting Make, like thoughtless men,
A strong Nativity – but for the Pen;
Eat Opium, mingle Arsenick in thy Drink
Still thou mayst live, avoiding Pen and Ink.
I see, I see, 'tis counsel giv'n in vain
For Treason, botcht in Rhime will be thy Bane,
Rhime is the Rock on which thou art to wreck,
'Tis fatal to thy Fame, and to thy Neck.
Ibid.

Shadwell alone my perfect image bears,
Mature in dulness from his tender years;
Shadwell alone of all my Sons is he
Who stands confirmed in full stupidity.
The rest to some faint meaning make pretence,
But Shadwell never deviates into sense.
John Dryden, *Mac Flecknoe.*

Thou last great Prophet of Tautology.
Ibid.

In thy fellonious heart, though venom lies,
It does but touch thy *Irish* pen, and dies.
Thy genius calls thee not to purchase fame
In keen Iambicke, but mild Anagram:
Leave writing Plays, and chuse for thy command
Some peaceful Province in Acrostick Land.
There thou maist wings display, and Altars raise,
And torture one poor word Ten thousand ways.
Ibid.

He has often call'd me an Atheist in print; I would believe more charitably of him, and that he only goes the *broad way,* because the other is too *narrow* for him. He may see, by this, that I do not delight to meddle with his course of life, and his immoralities, though I have a bead-roll of them. I have hitherto contented myself with the ridiculous part of him, which is enough, in all conscience, to employ one man; even without the story of his late fall at the Old Devil, where he broke no ribs, because the hardness of the stairs could reach no bones; and, for my part, I do not wonder how he came to fall, for I have always known him heavy; the miracle is, how he got up again.

John Dryden, *Vindication of 'The Duke of Guise'.*

They are to be pittied that fall under Mr Shadwell's lash. He lays on Heavily. His fools want mettle, and his witty men will scarce pass muster among the last recruits our General made for the Dog and Partridge.

Sir George Etherege, Letter to William Jephson, 24 May 1688.

The *Virtuoso* of Shadwell does not maintain his character with equal strength to the end, and this was that writer's general fault. Wycherley used to say of him that 'he knew how to start a fool very well, but that he was never able to run him down'.

Alexander Pope, in Joseph Spence, *Anecdotes.*

See also Thomas Otway

SHAFTESBURY, FIRST EARL OF (ANTHONY ASHLEY COOPER)

1621–83 Statesman

A little limping peer — though crazy yet in action nimble and as busy as a body-louse.

Anon., Letter to the Bishop of Meath, June 1680.

Greatest of men, yet man's least friend, farewell,
Wit's mightiest, but most useless miracle;
Where Nature all her richest treasures stor'd
To make one vast unprofitable hoard.
So high as thine no orb of fire could roll,
The brightest yet the most eccentric soul;
Whom 'midst wealth, honours, fame, yet want of ease,
No pow'r could e'er oblige, no state could please,
Be in thy grave with peaceful slumbers bless'd
And find thy whole life's only stranger, rest.

Anon., *Shaftesbury's Farewell*, February 1683.

Nature made him a perverse wight, whose nose
Extracts the essence of his gouty toes;
Double with head to tail he crawls apart:
His body's th'emblem of his double heart.

Anon., *The Cabal*, contemporary.

A little bobtail'd Lord, urchin of State,
A praisegod-Barebones-Peer whom all men hate,
Amphibious animal, half fool, half knave
... the rigling peer ...

John Ayloffe, *The Dream of the Cabal.*

His morals were of a piece with his religion, that is, he had very little of either morality or Christianity.

Gilbert Burnet, *History of My Own Time.*

'Mong these there was a *Politician*
With more heads than a *Beast in Vision*,
And more Intrigues in ev'ry one
Than all the Whores of Babylon:
So politic, as if one Eye
Upon the other were a Spy,
That, to trepan the one to think
The other blind, both strove to blink:
And in his dark pragmatic Way
As busy as a Child at Play.

Samuel Butler, *Hudibras*, part 3.

So little did he understand
The desp'rate Feats he took in Hand
For, when h'had got himself a Name
For Frauds and Tricks he spoil'd his Game;
Had forc'd his Neck into a Noose,
To shew his Play as *Fast* and *Loose*;
And when he chanc'd t'escape, mistook,
For Art and Subtlety, his Luck.

Ibid.

Dealing so long in sins of pomp and glory,
Who would have thought, (to make up Guzman's story)
Hypocrisy at last should enter in
And fix this floating mercury of sin.

John Caryll, *The Hypocrite.*

His body thus, and soul together vie
In vice's empire for the sov'reignty;
In ulcers that, this does abound in sin,
Lazar without, and Lucifer within.
The silver pipe is no sufficient drain
For the corruption of this little man,
Who, though he ulcers has in ev'ry part
Is nowhere so corrupt as in his heart.

Ibid.

Shaftesbury was fond of a simile from Sir Walter Raleigh's writings, that 'whosoever shall follow truth too near the heels it may haply strike out his teeth'. Raleigh had applied this to the writing of contemporary history; Shaftesbury transferred it to a politician seeking truth and pursuing it, in opposition to power, and amid the hypocrisies, self-seekings, meannesses and falsehoods of public men.

W. D. Christie, *Sir Anthony Ashley Cooper.*

A Name to all succeeding Ages curst,
For close Designs and crooked Counsels fit,
Sagacious, Bold and Turbulent of wit,
Restless, unfit in Principles and Place,
In Pow'r unpleased, impatient of Disgrace;
A fiery Soul, which working out its way,
Fretted the Pigmy Body to decay:
And o'r informed the Tenement of Clay.
A daring Pilot in extremity;
Pleas'd with the Danger, when the Waves went high
He sought the Storms; but, for a Calm unfit,
Would Steer too nigh the Sands to boast his Wit.
Great Wits are sure to Madness near alli'd
And thin Partitions do their Bounds divide;
Else, why should he, with Wealth and Honour blest,
Refuse his Age the needful Hours of Rest?
Punish a Body which he could not please,
Bankrupt of Life, yet prodigal of Ease?

And all to leave what with his Toil he won
To that unfeather'd two-legged thing, a Son;
Got, while his Soul did huddled notions trie;
And born a shapeless lump, like Anarchy.
In Friendship false, implacable in hate,
Resolved to Ruin or to Rule the State.
    John Dryden, *Absalom and Achitophel.*

Achitophel, grown weary to possess
A lawful Fame, and lazie Happiness,
Disdain'd the Golden Fruit to gather free
And lent the Crowd his Arm, to shake the Tree.
    Ibid.

A Martial Heroe first, with earl Care,
Blown, like a Pigmee by the Winds, to war.
A beardless Chief, a Rebel e'er a Man,
(So young his Hatred to his Prince began).
Next this, (how wildly will Ambition steer!)
A Vermin wriggling in th'usurper's ear,
Bartring his venal wit for sums of Gold,
He cast himself into the Saint-like mould,
Groan'd sigh'd and pray'd, while Godliness was Gain,
The lowdest bag-pipe of the Squeaking Train.
But as 'tis hard to cheat a juggler's eyes,
His open lewdness he cou'd ne'er disguise.
There split the Saint: for Hypocritique Zeal
Allows no Sins but those it can conceal. . . .
Pow'r was his aym; but, thrown from that pretence,
The Wretch turned loyal in his own defence,
And Malice reconcil'd him to his Prince.
    John Dryden, *The Medall.*

Behold him now exalted into Trust,
His Counsels oft convenient, seldom Just;
Ev'n in the most sincere advice he gave
He had a grudging still to be a Knave.
The Frauds he learnt in his Fanatique years

Made him uneasy in his lawful gears.
At best as little honest as he could:
And like white Witches, mischievously good.
To his first byass longingly he leans,
And *rather* would be great by wicked means.
    Ibid.

As by our little Machiavel we find
(That nimblest creature of the busy kind)
His limbs are crippled and his body shakes,
Yet his hard mind, which all this bustle makes,
No pity of his poor companion takes.
What gravity can hold from laughing out
To see that drag his feeble legs about
Like hounds ill coupled: Jowler lugs him still
Thro' hedges, ditches, and through all that's ill.
'Twere crime in any man but him alone
To use his body so, tho' 'tis his own;
Yet this false comfort never gives him o'er
That whilst he creeps, his vig'rous thought can soar.
    John Dryden and John Sheffield, Earl of Mul-
    grave, *Essay upon Satire.*

The King and the Duke of York used to call him
Little Sincerity, while with others at court, he went
under the title of *Lord Shiftesbury.*
    Augustus Jessop, *Note to Roger North's Life of
    . . . Lord Keeper Guildford.*

I have heard him also say that he desired no more of
any man but that he would talk; if he would but
talk said he, let him talk as he pleases. And, indeed,
I never knew anyone to penetrate so quick into
men's hearts, and from a small opening survey that
dark cabinet, as he would. He would understand
men's true errand as soon as they had opened their
mouths, and began their story in appearance to
another purpose.
    John Locke, *Fragment of Memoir of Shaftesbury.*

It is certain that, just before the Restoration, he
declared to the Regicides that he would be damned,
body and soul, rather than suffer a hair of their
heads to be hurt, and that, just after the Restoration, he was one of the judges who sentenced them
to death. It is certain that he was a principal
member of the most profligate Administration ever
known, and that he was afterwards a principal member of the most profligate Opposition ever known.

It is certain that, in power, he did not scruple to
violate the great fundamental principle of the
Constitution, in order to exalt the Catholics, and
that, out of power, he did not scruple to violate
every principle of justice, in order to destroy
them. . . . From the misguided friends of Toleration,
he borrowed their contempt for the Constitution,
and from the misguided friends of civil Liberty their

contempt for the rights of conscience . . . his life was such that every part of it, as if by a skilful contrivance reflects infamy on every other. We should never have known how abandoned a prostitute he was in place, if we had not known how desperate an incendiary he was out of it. . . . As often as he is charged with one treason, his advocates vindicate him by confessing two.

T. B. Macaulay, *Essay: 'Sir William Temple'*.

In place or out of place, he moved not the least from his purpose, or cast an eye towards returning into the interest of the Crown, upon any emergence that happened either of favour or displeasure. Therefore he was not a person so given to change as many thought when they nicknamed him my Lord Shiftsbury: his changes were, as Caesar's only *mutando rationem belli*.

Roger North, *Examen*.

The strands of idealism and scruple are closely woven into the texture of his career. He might have stepped out of one of Mr Gladstone's cabinets into the Cabal, and out of the Cabal into a Conclave of Whitechapel desperadoes; he was the Jekyll and Hyde of English politics, alike an apostle of enlightenment and progress, and an agent of force and falsehood, all the more formidable because his frame was small and his spirit unquenchable. He introduced into politics the new elements of advertisement and publicity, as Danby introduced those of organisation, and party management.

David Ogg, *England in the Reign of Charles II*.

SHAFTESBURY, SEVENTH EARL OF (ANTHONY ASHLEY COOPER)

1801–85 Philanthropist, Statesman

Silent, not offended, not puffed-up, not beguiled, *fully resolved never to do or accept anything*, however pressed by the strong claims of public necessity and public usefulness, which should, in the least degree, limit my opportunity or control my free action in respect of the Ten Hours Bill.

On himself, response to the Government Whip's offer of the Lord-Lieutenancy of Ireland, Diary, 17 April 1844.

The League hate me as an aristocrat; the landowners, as a Radical; the wealthy of all opinions, as a mover of inconvenient principles. The Tractarians loathe me as an ultra-Protestant; the Dissenters, as a Churchman; the High Church think me abominably low, the Low Church some degrees too high. I have no political party; the Whigs, I know, regard me as leaning very decidedly to the Conservatives;

the Conservatives declare that I have greatly injured the Government of Sir R. Peel. I have thus the approval and support of neither; the floating men of all sides, opinions, ranks, and professions, who dislike what they call a 'saint', join in the hatred, and rejoice in it. Every class is against me, and a host of partisans in every grade. The working people, catching the infection, will go next, and then, 'farewell, King'; farewell any hopes of further usefulness.

On himself, Diary, October 1845.

My habits are formed on metropolitan activity, and I must ever be groping where there is the most mischief.

On himself, Diary, 1847.

I cannot bear to leave the world with all the misery in it.

On himself, aged eighty-four, in G. W. E. Russell, *Collections and Recollections*.

You have given me the privilege of seeing one of the most impressive of all spectacles — a great English nobleman living in patriarchal state in his own hereditary halls.

Benjamin Disraeli, in *ibid*.

Lord Shaftesbury would have been in a lunatic asylum if he had not devoted himself to reforming lunatic asylums.

Florence Nightingale, quoted in *Times Literary Supplement*, 8 November 1974.

SHAHN, BEN

1898–1969 Artist

Then I got to thinking about the Sacco-Vanzetti case. . . . Ever since I could remember I'd wished that I'd been lucky enough to be alive at a great time — when something big was going on, like the Crucifixion. And suddenly I realized I was. Here I was living through another crucifixion. Here was something to paint!

On himself, in James Thrall Soby, *Ben Shahn*.

In Russia I went to a Jewish school, of course, where we *really read* the Old Testament. That story was about the ark being brought into the temple, hauled by six white oxen, and balanced on a single pole. The Lord knew that the people would worry about the ark's falling off the pole, so to test their faith He gave orders that no one was to touch it, no matter what happened. One man saw it beginning to totter, and he rushed up to help. He was struck dead. I refused to go to school for a week after we read that story. It seemed so damn unfair. And it still does.

On himself, in James Thrall Soby, *ibid*.

I'm sadly dulled to fame, too, now that it has come
at last, because during all those years of obscurity
I protected myself with the philosophy that a head-
ful of thoughts and roomful of paintings were the
important things in life even if the public never
found out about either. I still think so.
Ibid.

I was not the only artist who had been entranced by
the social dream, and who could no longer reconcile
that view with the private and inner objectives of
art. . . . The change in art, mine included, was
accomplished during World War II. For me, it had
begun during the late thirties when I worked in the
Resettlement Administration. I had then crossed
and recrossed many sections of the country, and
had come to know well so many people of all kinds
of belief and temperament, which they maintained
with a transcendent indifference to their lot in life.

Theories had melted before such experience. My
own painting then had turned from what is called
'social realism' into a sort of personal realism. I
found the qualities of people a constant pleasure. . . .
There were the poor who were rich in spirit, and the
rich who were also sometimes rich in spirit. . . .
Ibid.

Because of the 'hardening of his creative arteries'
and because, too, commerce came to him rather
than the other way around, Shahn has never seen
any conflict, nor indeed any distinction, between
his own art and his commercial art, if it can be so
called. 'I can make no distinction. The difference is
that you get paid pretty directly for commercial
art.'
Frank Getlein, *Ben Shahn.*

SHAKESPEARE, WILLIAM

1564–1616 Dramatist

How do you think, Reading could have assisted him
in such great Thoughts? It would only have lost
Time. When he found his Thoughts grow on him so
fast, he could have writ for ever, had he liv'd so
long.
Anon., *Essay Against Too Much Reading*, 1728.

There is something so wild, and yet so solemn in his
speeches of his ghosts, fairies, witches and the like
imaginary persons, that we cannot forbear thinking
them natural, though we have no rule by which to
judge of them, and must confess, if there are such
beings in the world, it looks highly probable as if
they should talk and act as he has represented them.
Joseph Addison, in *Spectator*, 1 July 1712.

Others abide our question. Thou art free.
We ask and ask — thou smilest and art still
Out-topping knowledge. For the loftiest hill,
Who to the stars uncrowns his majesty,

Planting his stedfast footsteps in the sea,
Making the heaven of heavens his dwelling-place,
Spares but the cloudy border of his base,
To the foil'd searching of mortality;

And thou, who didst the stars and sunbeams know,
Self-school'd, self-scann'd, self-honour'd, self-secure,
Didst tread on earth unguess'd at. — Better so!

All pains the immortal spirit must endure,
All weakness which impairs, all griefs which bow,
Find their sole speech in that victorious brow.
Matthew Arnold, *Shakespeare.*

I keep saying, Shakespeare, Shakespeare, you are as
obscure as life is.
Matthew Arnold, Letter to A. H. Clough,
December 1847.

Nothing could have been more fortunate for Shakespeare's development as a dramatist than his being
compelled for his livelihood — judging by his early
poems his youthful taste was something much less
coarse — to face the problems which the chronicle
play poses.
W. H. Auden, *The Dyer's Hand.*

Shakespeare is in the singularly fortunate position
of being, to all intents and purposes, anonymous.
W. H. Auden, *Forewords and Afterwords.*

The discovery which turned Shakespeare from a
good dramatist into a great one was that the outward clashing of character with character is poor
material beside the ferment in the spirit of a man,
confined by law or custom, or, inherited belief, or
netted round by alien circumstance or wills, but
quickening in their despite. It was a discovery due in
the England of Shakespeare's time, which the
Renaissance and the Reformation had set spiritually
free. It was due to be made in terms of drama; for
here was an art which, as no other could, showed
you the living, breathing man.
Harley Granville Barker, *On Dramatic Method.*

Shakespeare's form is apparent mainly in terms of
power. He works by means of contrast between
character and character, by tension and relaxation,
climax and anti-climax, by changes of tone and
pace, by every sort of variation between scene and
scene. We could illustrate the form of *King Lear*
by a chart, a sort of temperature chart, with plot,
and sub-plot and characters marked by ink lines of

different colours, zigzagging up and down and crossing and recrossing; the rise and fall to show volume of emotion, while a separate line could mark increase and decrease of pace. We can rightly call this form I think, for all that it is form in motion.
Ibid.

Whereas most romantic dramatists of his time made little attempt at relating story to character, Shakespeare seems to have asked himself, 'What conceivable kind of person would fit in with such a situation or perform such an action, however unlikely?' Much of his artistic skill was directed to making improbable actions plausible by inventing the right people to perform them.
Geoffrey Bullough, *Narrative and Dramatic Sources of Shakespeare.*

Shakespeare's name, you may depend on it, stands absurdly too high and will go down. He had no invention as to stories, none whatever. He took all his plots from old novels, and threw their stories into a dramatic shape, at as little expense of thought as you or I could turn his plays back again into prose tales. That he threw over whatever he did write some flashes of genius, nobody can deny: but this was all. Suppose anyone to have had the *dramatic* handling for the first time of such ready-made stories as Lear, Macbeth, &c. and he would be a sad fellow indeed, if he did not make something very grand of them.
Lord Byron, Letter to James Hogg, 24 March 1814.

Like a miraculous celestial Light-ship, woven all of sheet-lightning and sunbeams.
Thomas Carlyle, *Historical Sketches of Notable Persons and Events in the Reigns of James I and Charles I.*

Shakespeare to thee was dull, whose best jest lies
I' the Ladies questions, and the Fooles replyes;
Old fashion'd wit, which walkt from town to town
In turn'd Hose, which our fathers call'd the Clown;
Whose wit our nice times would obsceanness call,
And which made Bawdry pass for Comicall:
Nature was all his Art, thy veine was free
As his, but without his scurility; . . .
William Cartwright, *Upon the Dramatick Poems of Mr John Fletcher.*

Underwit: Item, *The Book of Cannons; Shakespeares* works. Why *Shakespeares* works?
Thomas: I had nothing for the Pike Men before.
Underwit: They are playes.
Thomas: Are not all your musteringes in the Country so, Sir; Pray read on.
William Cavendish, Duke of Newcastle, *The Country Captaine.*

Shakespere's intellectual action is wholly unlike that of Ben Jonson or Beaumont and Fletcher. The latter see the totality of a sentence or passage, and then project it entire. Shakespere goes on creating, and evolving B. out of A., and C. out of B., and so on, just as a serpent moves, which makes a fulcrum of its own body, and seems forever twisting and untwisting its own strength.
Samuel Taylor Coleridge, *Table Talk*, 5 March 1834.

Our myriad-minded Shakespeare.
Samuel Taylor Coleridge, *Biographia Literaria.*

Since he was resolved to drown the Lady [Ophelia] like a Kitten, he should have set her a swimming a little sooner. To keep her alive only to sully her Reputation, and discover the Rankness of her Breath, was very Cruel.
Jeremy Collier, *A Short View of the Immorality and Profaneness of the English Stage.*

As for *Shakespeare*, he is too guilty (of immodesty) to make an Evidence: but I think he gains not much by his Misbehaviour; he has commonly *Plautus's Fate*, where there is most smut there is least Sense.
Ibid.

His Volume is all up-hill and down; *Paradise* was never more pleasant than some part of it, nor *Ireland* and *Greenland* colder, and more uninhabitable than others. And I have undertaken to cultivate one of the most barren places in it. The trees are all Shrubs, and the Men Pigmies, nothing has any spirit or shape.
John Crowne, *Epistle Dedicatory to Henry the Sixth, the First Part, . . . Written by Mr Crown.*

Some say (good *Will*) which I, in sport do sing,
Hadst thou not plaid some Kingly parts in sport,
Thou hadst been a companion for a *King*;
And, beene a King among the meaner sort.
Some others raile; but, raile as they thinke fit,
Thou hast no rayling, but, a raigning Wit:
And honesty *thou sow'st, which they do reape,*
So, to increase their Stocke *which they do keepe.*
John Davies of Hereford, *The Scourge of Folly, circa* 1611.

But there is a wide difference in the management of their plots, between Shakespeare and Beaumont and Fletcher. Those of the former are altogether as improbable as the latter. But, under his direction, improbability lessens imperceptibly; the superstructure is so beautiful, that you forget the foundation. You survey the whole building with such delight, that you have not leisure to think of the enchanted ground on which it stands.
Thomas Davies, *Dramatic Miscellanies.*

He seems to have been the very Original of our *English* Tragical Harmony; that is the Harmony of Blank Verse, diversifyed often by Disyllable and Trisyllable Terminations. For that Diversity distinguishes it from Heroick Harmony, and, bringing it nearer to common Use, makes it more to gain Attention, and more firm for Action and Dialogue. Such verse we make when we are writing Prose; we make such verse in Common Conversation.

John Dennis, *On the Genius and Writings of Shakespeare.*

Shakespear having neither had Time to correct, nor friends to consult must necessarily have frequently left such faults in his Writings, for the Correction of which either a great deal of Time or a judicious and well-natur'd Friend is indispensably necessary.

Ibid.

But why doe I dead *Shakespeare's* praise recite,
Some second *Shakespeare* must of *Shakespeare*
                    write;
For mee tis needlesse, since an host of men,
Will pay to clap his praise, to free my pen.

Leonard Digges, *Commendatory verses to Shakespeares Poems.*

To begin with *Shakespeare*: he was the man who of all Modern, and perhaps Ancient Poets, had the largest and most comprehensive soul. All the Images of Nature were still present to him, and he drew them not laboriously but luckily: when he describes any thing, you more than see it, you feel it too. Those who accuse him to have wanted learning, give him the greater commendation: he was naturally learn'd; he needed not the spectacles of Books to read Nature; he look'd inwards, and found her there. I cannot say he is everywhere alike; were he so, I should do him injury to compare him with the greatest of Mankind. He is many times flat, insipid; his Comick wit degenerating into clenches, his serious swelling into Bombast. But he is alwayes great, when some great occasion is presented to him; no man can say he ever had a fit subject for his wit, and did not then raise himself as high above the rest of Poets.

John Dryden, *Essay on Dramatic Poesy.*

Shakspear (who with some errors not to be avoided in that age, had, undoubtedly a larger Soul of Poesie than ever any of our Nation) was the first, who to shun the pains of continuall rhyming, invented that kind of writing, which we call blanck verse, but the French, more properly, *Prose Mesuree,*: into which the *English* Tongue so naturally Slides, that in writing Prose 'tis hardly to be avoyded.

John Dryden, Dedication to *The Rival Ladies.*

Never did any author precipitate himself from such heights of thought to so low expressions, as he often does. He is the very *Janus* of poets; he wears, almost everywhere two faces: and you have scarce begun to admire the one, e're you despise the other.

John Dryden, *The Conquest of Granada: Defence of the Epilogue.*

Shakespear show'd the best of his skill in his *Mercutio* [*Romeo and Juliet*], and he said himself, that he was forc'd to kill him in the third Act, to prevent being kill'd by him. But, for my part, I cannot find he was so dangerous a person; I see nothing in him but what was so exceeding harmless, that he might have liv'd to the end of the play, and dy'd in his bed, without offence to any man.

Ibid.

His excellencies came and were not sought,
His words like casual Atoms made a thought:
Drew up themselves in rank and file, and writ,
He wondring how the devil it were such wit.
Thus like the drunken Tinker in his Play,
He grew a Prince and never knew which way.

John Dryden, *Covent Garden Drolery.*

If Shakespeare were stripped of all the bombasts in his passions, and dressed in the most vulgar words, we should still find the beauties of his thoughts remaining; if his embroideries were burnt down, there would still be silver at the bottom of the melting-pot.

John Dryden, Preface to *Troilus and Cressida.*

If the only way to prove that Shakespeare did not feel and think exactly as people felt and thought in 1815, or in 1860, or in 1880, is to show that he felt and thought as we felt and thought in 1927, then we must accept gratefully that alternative.

T. S. Eliot, *Shakespeare and the Stoicism of Seneca.*

I do not believe that any writer has ever exposed this *bovaryisme*, the human will to see things as they are not, more clearly than Shakespeare.

Ibid.

Shakespeare is the only biographer of Shakespeare.

Ralph Waldo Emerson, *Representative Men.*

'Shakespeare', says a Brother of the *Craft*, 'is a vast garden of criticism:' and certainly no one can be favoured with more weeders gratis.

Richard Farmer, *An Essay on The Learning of Shakespeare.*

Once when visiting Stratford-on-Avon with Toole, [Henry Irving] saw a rustic sitting on a fence, whom

they submitted to an interrogatory. 'That's Shakespeare's house, isn't it?' it was asked innocently. 'Yes.' 'Ever been there?' 'Noa.' 'How long has he been dead?' 'Dunno.' 'What did he do?' 'Dunno.' 'Did he not write?' 'Oh yes, he did summat.' 'What was it?' 'Well, I think he writ *Boible*.'
Percy Fitzgerald, *Henry Irving*.

A sycophant, a flatterer, a breaker of marriage vows, a whining and inconstant person.
Ebenezer Forsyth, *Shakespeare,: Some Notes on his Character and Writings*.

The name 'William Shakespeare' is very probably a pseudonym behind which a great unknown lies concealed. Edward de Vere, Earl of Oxford, a man who has been thought to be identifiable with the author of Shakespeare's works, lost a beloved and admired father while he was still a boy and completely repudiated his mother, who contracted a new marriage very soon after her husband's death.
Sigmund Freud, *An Outline of Psychoanalysis*, translated by James Strachey.

He was an eminent instance of the truth of that Rule, *Poeta non fit sed nascitur*, one is not made, but born a Poet. Indeed his learning was very little, so that as Cornish *diamonds* are not polished by any Lapidary, but are pointed and smoothed even as they are taken out of the Earth, so *nature* it self was all the *art* which was used upon him.
Thomas Fuller, *The History of the Worthies of England*.

Shake-spear . . . could turn with all tides, tack about and take advantage of all winds, by the quickness of his Wit and Invention.
Ibid.

I cannot read him, he is such a bombast fellow.
George II, attributed.

Far from the sun and summer-gale,
In thy green lap was Nature's Darling laid.
Thomas Gray, *The Progress of Poesy*.

As to the Soul, perhaps they may have none on the Continent; but I do think we have such things in England. Shakespear, for example, I believe had several to his own share.
Thomas Gray, Letter to Horace Walpole, March 1771.

There is an upstart Crow, beautified with our feathers, that with his *Tygers heart wrapped in a Players hide*, supposes he is as well able to bumbast out a blanke verse as the best of you: and being an absolute Johannes fac totum, is in his owne conceit the onely Shake-scene in a countrie.
Robert Greene, *Green's Groats-worth of Wit; bought with a Million of Repentaunce*.

The victim of spiritual emotions that involve criminatory reflections does not usually protrude them voluntarily on the consideration of society; and, if the personal theory be accepted, we must concede the possibility of our national dramatist gratuitously confessing his sins and revealing those of others, proclaiming his disgrace and avowing his repentance in poetical circulars distributed by the delinquent himself amongst his most intimate friends.
J. D. Halliwell-Phillips, on the Sonnets, *Outlines of the Life of Shakespeare*.

Homosexuality? No, I know nothing of the joys of homosexuality. My friend Oscar can no doubt tell you all about that. But I must say that if *Shakespeare* asked me, I would have to submit.
Frank Harris, attributed, remark over luncheon in the Café Royal.

The plays he purchased or obtained surreptitiously, which became his 'property', and which are now called his, were never set upon the stage in their original state. They were first spiced with obscenity, blackguardism and impurities, before they were produced; and this business he voluntarily assumed, and faithfully did he perform his share of the management in that respect. It brought *money* to the house.
Colonel Joseph C. Hart, *The Romance of Yachting*.

If *to invent according to Nature*, be the true definition of genius, Shakespeare had more of this quality than any other writer. He might be said to have been a joint-worker with Nature, and to have created an imaginary world of his own, which has all the appearance and truth of reality. His mind, while it exerted an absolute control over the stronger workings of the passions, was exquisitely alive to the slightest impulses, and most evanescent shades of character and feeling. The broad distinctions and governing principles of human nature are presented not in the abstract, but in their immediate and endless application to different persons and things. The local details, the particular accidents, have all the fidelity of history, without losing anything of their general effect.
William Hazlitt, 'Mr Kean's Macbeth', in *Champion*, 13 November 1814.

The striking feature of Shakespeare's mind was its generic quality, its power of communication with all other minds, — so that it contained a universe of thought and feeling within itself, and had no one particular bias, or exclusive excellence more than another. He was just like any other man, but that he was like all other men. He was the least of an egotist that it was possible to be. He was nothing in himself, but he was all that others were, or that they could become.

William Hazlitt, *On Shakespeare and Milton.*

His language is hieroglyphical. It translates thoughts into visible images. It abounds in sudden transitions and elliptical expressions. This is the source of his mixed metaphors, which are only abbreviated forms of speech. These, however give no pain from long custom. They have, in fact, become idioms in the language. They are the building and not the scaffolding, to thought.

Ibid.

Shakespeare was the least of a coxcomb of any one that ever lived, and much of a gentleman.

Ibid.

The fault, then, of Shakespeare's comic Muse is, in my opinion, that it is too good-natured and magnanimous. It mounts above its quarry. It is 'apprehensive, quick, forgetive, full of nimble, fiery, and delectable shapes': but it does not take the highest pleasure in making human nature look as mean, as ridiculous and contemptible as possible.

William Hazlitt, *On Shakespeare and Ben Jonson.*

Who shall say that he never proved a Tarquin to some unchronicled Lucrece?

W. Carew Hazlitt, *Shakespeare, Himself and His Work.*

His mind and hand went together: And what he thought, he uttered with that easinesse, that wee have scarce received from him a blot in his papers. But it is not our province, who onely gather his works and give them you, to praise him. It is yours that reade him.

John Heminge and Henry Condell, Address 'To the Great Variety of Readers', prefixed to the First Folio, 1623.

What is he? You might almost answer, He is the earth . . . the globe . . . existence. . . . In Shakespeare the birds sing, the rushes are clothed with green, hearts love, souls suffer, the cloud wanders, it is hot, it is cold, night falls, time passes, forests and multitudes speak, the vast eternal dream hovers over all. Sap and blood, all forms of the multiple reality, actions and ideas, man and humanity, the living and the life, solitudes, cities, religions, diamonds and pearls, dunghills and charnel houses, the ebb and flow of beings, the steps of comers and goers, all,

all are on Shakespeare and in Shakespeare; and, this genius being the earth, the dead emerge from it.

Victor Hugo, *William Shakespeare*, 1864, in L. Marder, *His Exits and Entrances.*

There was also *Shakespeere*, who (as *Cupid* informed me) creepes into the women's closets about bed time, and if it were not for some of the old out-of-date Grandames (who are set over the rest as their tutoresses) the young sparkish Girles would read in *Shakespeere* day and night, so that they would open the Booke or Tome, and the Men with a Fescue in their hands should point to the Verse.

John Johnson, *The Academy of Love, Describing ye folly of young men and ye fallacy of women.*

The dialogue of this author is often so evidently determined by the incident which produces it, and is pursued with so much ease and simplicity, that it seems scarcely to claim the merit of fiction, but to have been gleaned by diligent selection out of common conversation, and common occurrences.

Samuel Johnson, Preface to *The Plays of William Shakespeare.*

Shakespeare approximates the remote, and familiarises the wonderful; the event which he represents will not happen, but if it were possible, its effects would probably be such as he has assigned; and it may be said, that he has not only shown human nature as it acts in real exigencies, but as it would be found in trials, to which it cannot be exposed.

Ibid.

His tragedy seems to be skill, his comedy to be instinct.

Ibid.

The stream of Time, which is continually washing the dissoluble fabricks of other poets, passes without injury by the adamant of *Shakespeare*.

Ibid.

It is incident to him to be now and then entangled with an unwieldy sentiment, which he cannot well express, and will not reject; he struggles with it a while, and if it continues stubborn, comprises it in words such as occur, and leaves it to be disentangled and evolved by those who have more leisure to bestow upon it.

Ibid.

A quibble is to *Shakespeare*, what luminous vapours are to the traveller; he follows it at all adventures, it is sure to lead him out of his way, and sure to engulf him in the mire. It has some malignant power over his mind, and its fascinations are irresistible.

Whatever be the dignity or profundity of his disquisition, whether he be enlarging knowledge or exalting affection, whether he be amusing attention with incidents, or enchaining it in suspense, let but a quibble spring up before him, and he leaves his work unfinished. A quibble is the golden apple for which he will always turn aside from his career, or stoop from his elevation. A quibble, poor and barren as it is, gave him such delight, that he was content to purchase it, by the sacrifice of reason, propriety and truth. A quibble was to him the fatal *Cleopatra* for which he lost the world and was content to lose it.

    Ibid.

He found the *English* stage in a state of the utmost rudeness.

    Ibid.

The genius of *Shakespeare* was not to be depressed by the weight of poverty, nor limited by the narrow conversation to which men in want are inevitably condemned; the incumbrances of his fortune were shaken from his mind, *as dewdrops from a lion's mane.*

    Ibid.

    Soule of the Age!
The applause! delight! the wonder of our Stage!
My *Shakespeare*, rise; I will not lodge thee by
  Chaucer or *Spenser*, or bid *Beaumont* lye
A little further, to make thee a roome:
  Thou art a Moniment, without a Tombe,
And art alive still, while thy booke doth live,
  And we have wits to read, and praise to give.
    Ben Jonson, *To the Memory of my beloved, the Author Mr. William Shakespeare.*

He was not of an age, but for all time!
  And all the *Muses* still were in their prime,
When like *Apollo* he came forth to warme
  Our eares, or like a *Mercury* to charme!
    Ibid.

Yet must I not give Nature all; Thy Art,
  My gentle Shakespeare, must enjoy a part.
For though the Poets matter, Nature be,
  His Art doth give the fashion. And, that he,
Who casts to write a living line, must sweat,
  (Such as thine are) and strike the second heat
Upon the *Muses* anvile: turne the same,
  (And himselfe with it) that he thinks to frame;
Or for the lawrell, he may gaine a scorne,
  For a good *Poet's* made, as well as borne,
And such wert thou.

    Ibid.

Sweet swan of Avon!

    Ibid.

Shaksperr wanted Arte.
    Ben Jonson, in his *Conversations with William Drummond of Hawthornden.*

I remember, the Players have often mentioned it as an honour to *Shakespeare*, that in his writing, (whatsoever he penned) hee never blotted out a line. My answer hath been, would he had blotted a thousand.
    Ben Jonson, *Timber, or Discoverie made upon man and matter.*

His wit was in his owne power; would the rule of it had beene so too. Many times hee fell into those things, could not escape laughter: As when hee said in the person of Caesar, one speaking to him; *Caesar thou dost me wrong.* Hee replyed: *Caesar did never wrong, but with just cause*: and such like; which were ridiculous. But hee redeemed his vices, with his virtues. There was ever more in him to be praysed, than to be pardoned.
    Ibid.

Several things dove-tailed in my mind, and at once it struck me what quality went to form a man of achievement, especially in literature, and which Shakespeare possessed so enormously — I mean *Negative Capability*, that is, when a man is capable of being in uncertainties, mysteries, doubts, without any irritable reaching after fact and reason. Coleridge, for instance, would let go by a fine isolated verisimilitude caught from the Penetralium of mystery, from being incapable of remaining content with half-knowledge. This pursued through volumes would perhaps take us no further than this, that with a great poet the sense of Beauty overcomes every other consideration, or rather obliterates all consideration.
    John Keats, Letter to George and Thomas Keats, 28 December 1817.

A Man's life of any worth is a continual allegory, and very few eyes can see the Mystery of his life — a life, like the scriptures, figurative — which such people can no more make out than they can the Hebrew Bible. Lord Byron cuts a figure, but he is not figurative — Shakespeare led a life of Allegory: his works are the comments on it.
    John Keats, Letter to George and Georgiana Keats, 24 February 1819.

The direct controlling influence in his daily life, the special incentive to all his labours, was the desire to accumulate a fortune, and to secure those social advantages by which the possession of wealth is naturally accompanied. This was the counterpoise to the extravagant emotional and meditative tendencies of his nature. It was by this practical instinct that he held on to the realities of human existence, . . . that he resisted the ceaseless pressure of a restless imagination, — that he offered a determined front to the ever-rushing invasion of the wonder and mystery of this changeful world of time and place. It was the familiar landmark that fixed for him his own little home in the infinite ocean of life.

Thomas Kenny, *The Life and Genius of Shakespeare.*

To the critic of the poetry the word 'Shakespeare' stands alone for the dramatic life that persists in the plays, and any other 'Shakespeare' is a pure abstraction.

G. Wilson Knight, *Myth and Miracle.*

Not a single one is very admirable. . . . They are hot and pothery: there is much condensation, little delicacy; like raspberry jam without cream, without crust, without bread; to break its viscidity.

Walter Savage Landor, on Shakespeare's sonnets, *Imaginary Conversations — Southey and Landor.*

When I read Shakespeare I am struck with wonder
That such trivial people should muse and thunder
In such lovely language.

D. H. Lawrence, *When I read Shakespeare.*

Shake-speare was Godfather to one of Ben: Johnson's children, and after the christning being in a deepe study, Johnson came to cheere him up, and askt him why he was so Melancholy? no faith Ben: (sayes he) not I, but I have beene considering a great while what should be the fittest gift for me to bestow upon my God-child, and I have resolv'd at last; I pry'the what, sayes he? I' faith Ben: I'le e'en give him a douzen good Lattin Spoones, and thou shalt translate them.

Sir Nicholas L'estrange, *Merry Passages and Jeasts.*

Shakespeare is a good raft whereon to float securely down the stream of time; fasten yourself to that and your immortality is safe.

George Henry Lewes, *On Actors and the Art of Acting.*

Wee wondred (*Shake-speare*) that thou went'st so soone
From the Worlds-Stage, to the Graves-Tyring-roome.
Wee thought thee dead, but this thy printed worth,
Tels thy Spectators, that thou wentst but forth
To enter with applause. An Actors Art,
Can dye, and live, to acte a second part.
That's but an *Exit* of Mortalitie;
This, a Re-entrance to a Plaudite.

'I.M.', *To the Memorie of M. W. Shake-speare,* 1623.

Desmond McCarthy . . . said somewhere that trying to work out Shakespeare's personality was like looking at a very dark glazed picture in the National Portrait Gallery: at first you see nothing, then you begin to recognise features, and then you realise that they are your own.

Desmond MacCarthy, in Samuel Schoenbaum, *Shakespeare's Lives.*

Upon a tyme when Burbidge played Rich 3. there was a citizen greue soe farr in liking with him, that before shee went from the play shee appointed him to come that night unto her by the name of Ri: the 3. Shakespeare overhearing their conclusion went before, was intertained, and at his game ere Burbidge came. Then message being brought that Rich. the 3rd was at the dore, Shakespeare caused returne to be made that William the Conquerour was before Rich. the 3.

John Manningham, Diary, 13 March 1602.

On this planet, the reputation of Shakespeare is secure.

Louis Marder, *His Exits and His Entrances.*

The sweete witty soule of *Ovid* lives in mellifluous & hony-tongued *Shakespeare*, witnes his *Venus* and *Adonis*, his *Lucrece*, his sugred Sonnets among his private friends &c.

Francis Meres, *Palladia Tamia.*

The Muses would speak with Shakespeares fine filed phrase, if they would speak English.

Ibid.

What needs my Shakespeare for his honoured bones,
The labour of an age in piled stones?
Or that his hallowed reliques should be hid
Under a starry-pointing pyramid?
Dear Son of Memory, great heir of Fame,
What need'st thou such weak witness of thy name?
Thou in our wonder and astonishment
Hast built thyself a live-long monument.
For whilst to the shame of slow-endeavouring art
Thy easy numbers flow, and that each heart
Hath from the leaves of thy unvalued book
Those delphic lines with deep impression took,
Then thou our fancy of itself bereaving,
Dost make us marble with too much conceiving;
And so sepulchered in such pomp dost lie,
That kings for such a tomb would wish to die.

John Milton, *An Epitaph on the Admirable Dramatic Poet, W. Shakespeare.*

If Dr Gall the craniologist's assertion is to be believed, the organ of robbery (covetiveness) and the organ for forming good dramatic plots, are one and the same; he certainly proved himself a great adept

in the latter, and no doubt was so in the former.
> W. T. Moncrieff, *New Guide to the Spa of Leamington Priors*.

Him we may profess rather to feel than to understand; and it is safer to say, on many occasions, that we are possessed by him, than that we possess him.
> Maurice Morgann, *An Essay on the Dramatick Character of Sir John Falstaff*.

Shakespear, (whom you and ev'ry Play-house bill
Style the divine, the matchless, what you will)
For gain, not glory, wing'd his roving flight,
And grew immortal in his own despight.
> Alexander Pope, *Imitation of Horace*, Book II, epistle i.

The Poetry of *Shakespeare* was Inspiration indeed: he is not so much an Imitator as an Instrument, of Nature; and 'tis not so just to say that he speaks from her, as that she speaks thro' him.
> Alexander Pope, Preface to *The Works of Shakespeare*.

Players are just such judges of what is *right*, as Taylors are of what is *graceful*. And in this view it will be but fair to allow, that most of our Author's faults are less to be ascribed to his wrong judgement as a Poet, than to his right judgement as a Player.
> *Ibid.*

Shakespeare generally used to stiffen his style with high words and metaphors for the speeches of his Kings and great men. He mistook it for a mark of greatness. This is strongest in his early plays, but in his very last play, his *Othello*, what a forced language has he put into the mouth of the Duke of Venice!
> Alexander Pope, in Joseph Spence, *Anecdotes*.

His poetry has been cut into minute indigestible fragments, and used like wedding cake, not to eat, but to dream upon.
> Walter Raleigh, *Shakespeare*.

Shakespeare is like a picture full of anachronisms — geographical blunders, forgetfulness of his plot, and even sometimes of character — but he produces a high value picture because his mind is intent upon the general effect . . . he does not stoop to a cold explanation of his intention in the character, though perhaps a single line would be enough, but concluding that you are possessed with the character as much as he was himself.
> Sir Joshua Reynolds, *Notes on Shakespeare*.

In such an age, immortal Shakespeare wrote
By no quaint rules, nor hampering critics taught;

With rough majestic force he mov'd the heart,
And strength and nature made amends for art.
> Nicholas Rowe, Prologue to *Jane Shore*.

The top of his performance was the ghost in his own *Hamlet*.
> Nicholas Rowe, *Some Account of the Life, etc, of Mr William Shakespeare*, 1709.

From the quantitative data a portrait of the dramatist emerges. A bi-sexual personality, predominantly masculine, aggressive, prone to wide fluctuations of mood, this Shakespeare tried to suppress his feminine traits and justify his existence by vigorous, even ruthless action. The homosexual tendency helps to explain the poet's paranoic suspiciousness, his jealous imagining that other men have been coming between him and the woman or women he loves. Over the years sensuality and self-indulgence grew more and more repugnant to Shakespeare, but he did not easily accept spiritualised emotions — 'he could not admit the loving kindness of Christian charity without feeling threatened with overwhelming weakness.'
> Samuel Schoenbaum, *Shakespeare's Lives*, summarizing the conclusions of Harold Grier McCurdy, *The Personality of Shakespeare*.

The fact is, we are growing out of Shakespeare. Byron declined to put up with his reputation at the beginning of the nineteenth century; and now, at the beginning of the twentieth, he is nothing but a household pet. His characters still live; his word pictures of woodland and wayside still give us a Bank-holiday breath of country air; his verse still charms us; his sublimities still stir us; the commonplaces and trumperies of the wisdom which age and experience bring to all the rest of us are still expressed by him better than by anybody else; but we have nothing to hope from him, and nothing to learn from him — not even how to write plays, though he does that so much better than most modern dramatists.
> George Bernard Shaw, in *Saturday Review*, 11 July 1896.

In playing Shakespeare, play *to* the lines, *through* the lines, *on* the lines, but never *between* the lines. There simply isn't time for it. You would not stick five bars rest into a Beethoven symphony to pick up your drumsticks; and similarly you must not stop the Shakespeare orchestra for business. Nothing short of a procession or a fight should make anything so extraordinary as a silence during a Shakespearian performance.
> George Bernard Shaw, Letter to Ellen Terry, 23 September 1896.

With the single exception of Homer, there is no eminent writer, not even Sir Walter Scott, whom I can despise so entirely as I despise Shakespeare when I measure my mind against his.
George Bernard Shaw, in *Saturday Review*, 26 September 1896.

Even when Shakespeare, in his efforts to be a social philosopher, does rise for an instant to the level of a sixth-rate Kingsley, his solemn self-complacency infuriates me. And yet, so wonderful is his art, that it is not easy to disentangle what is unbearable from what is irresistible.
George Bernard Shaw, in *Saturday Review*, 5 December 1896.

My capers are part of a bigger design than you think: Shakespeare, for instance, is to me one of the Towers of the Bastille, and down he must come.
George Bernard Shaw, Letter to Ellen Terry, 27 January 1897.

Meanwhile
Immortal William dead, and turned to Clay
May stop a hole to keep the wind away.
Oh that the earth which kept the world in awe
Should patch a wall t'expel the winter's flaw!
George Bernard Shaw, *Shakes Versus Shav*.

Hope to mend Shakespear! or to match his Style!
'Tis such a Jest, would make a *Stoick* smile.
John Sheffield, Earl of Mulgrave, Prologue to his alteration of *Julius Caesar*, 1692.

Dr Young observed to me that Shakespeare's style where the hearts and manners of men was the subject, is always good. His bad lines generally [occur] where they are not concerned.
Joseph Spence, *Anecdotes*.

It is difficult to resist the conclusion that he was getting bored himself. Bored with people, bored with real life, bored with drama, bored, in fact, with everything except poetry and poetical dreams. He is no longer interested, one often feels, in what happens, or who says what, so long as he can find place for a faultless lyric, or a new unimagined rhythmical effect, or a grand and mystic speech. . . . Half enchanted by visions of loveliness, and half bored to death; on the one side inspired by a soaring fancy to the singing of ethereal songs, and on the other urged by a general disgust to burst occasionally through his torpor into bitter and violent speech. If we are to learn anything of his mind from his last works, it is surely this.
Lytton Strachey, *Books and Characters*: 'Shakespeare's Final Period'.

He was a most diligent spie upon Nature.
Nahum Tate, *The Loyal General, A Tragedy: Address to Edward Tayler*.

He is fair game, like the Bible, and may be made use of nowadays even for advertisements of soap and razors.
Ralph Vaughan Williams, Preface to *Sir John In Love*.

This enormous dunghill ['son énorme fumier'].
Voltaire, Letter to d'Argental, 19 July 1776.

Shakespeare, the poet of England, patriot and Tory has been pronounced a German by our foes. By what right do they claim a dramatist removed from them by a whole world of poetry and romance, a dramatist whose amplitude and generosity must be for ever unintelligible to them.
Charles Whibley, *Shakespeare, Patriot and Tory*.

We must be free or die, who speak the tongue
That Shakespeare spake; . . .
William Wordsworth, *National Independence and Liberty*.

Scorn not the Sonnet; Critic, you have frowned,
Mindless of its just honours; with this key
Shakespeare unlocked his heart.
William Wordsworth, *Miscellaneous Sonnets*.

Do you suppose for one moment that Shakespeare educated Hamlet and King Lear by telling them what he thought and believed? As I see it, Hamlet and Lear educated Shakespeare, and I have no doubt that in the process of that education he found out that he was an altogether different man to what he thought himself, and had altogether different beliefs.
William Butler Yeats, Letter to Sean O'Casey, 20 April 1928.

Shakespeare, — what *trash* are his works in the gross.
Edward Young, in Joseph Spence, *Anecdotes*.

See also Edward Alleyn, Francis, Beaumont, William Blake, John Bunyan, William D'Avenant, Chancery Depew, R. W. Emerson, George Eliot, Sir John Fastolfe, John Fletcher, Samuel Foote, James Gillray, Ann Hathaway, Robert Herrick, Thomas Heywood, Nicholas Hilliard, William Hogarth, Henry Irving, Ben Jonson, James Joyce, George Kaufman, Edmund Kean, Rudyard Kipling, Ring Lardner, Christopher Marlowe, John Milton, Elizabeth Montagu, Sir Isaac Newton, Joseph Nollekens, D. G. Rossetti, George Bernard Shaw, Herbert Beerbohm Tree, John Webster, William Wordsworth, William Butler Yeats

SHAW, GEORGE BERNARD

1856—1950 Dramatist

The first moral lesson I can remember as a tiny child was the lesson of teetotalism, instilled by my father, a futile person you would have thought him. One night, when I was about as tall as his boots, he took me out for a walk. In the course of it I conceived a monstrous, incredible suspicion. When I got home I stole to my mother and in an awestruck whisper said to her, 'Mamma, I think Papa's drunk.' She turned away with impatient disgust, and said 'When is he ever anything else?' I have never believed anything since: then the scoffer began. . . . Oh, a devil of a childhood, Ellen, rich only in dreams, frightful in realities.
On himself, Letter to Ellen Terry, 11 June 1897.

It is significant of the difference between my temperament and Mr Pinero's that when he, as a little boy, first heard Ever of Thee I'm Fondly Dreaming, he wept; whereas, at the same tender age, I simply noted with scorn the obvious plagiarism from Cheer Boys, Cheer.
On himself, in *Saturday Review*, 5 February 1898.

I have played my game with a conscience. I have never pretended that G.B.S. was real: I have over and over again taken him to pieces before the audience to show the trick of him. And even those who in spite of that cannot escape from the illusion, regard G.B.S. as a freak. The whole point of the creature is that he is unique, fantastic, unrepresentative, inimitable, impossible, undesirable on any large scale, utterly unlike anybody that ever existed before, hopelessly unnatural, and void of real passion. Clearly such a monster could do no harm, even were his example evil (which it never is).
On himself, 'Belloc and Chesterton', in *New Age*, 15 February 1908.

My plays must be acted, and acted hard. They need a sort of bustle and crepitation of life which requires extraordinary energy and vitality, and gives only glimpses and movements of the poetry beneath. The lascivious monotony of beauty which satisfies those who are slaves of art instead of masters of it is hideous in my plays.
On himself, Letter to Mrs Patrick Campbell, 3 July 1912.

He will fill his fountain pen with your heart's blood, and sell your most sacred emotions on the stage. He is a mass of imagination with no heart. He is a writing and talking machine that has worked for nearly forty years until its skill is devilish. . . . All his goods are in the shop window, and he'll steal *your* goods and put them there too.
On himself, Letter to Mrs Patrick Campbell, 8 November 1912.

I am like a dentist, there is so much that is wounding about my work.
On himself, Letter to Mrs Patrick Campbell, 8 December 1912.

My plays have the latest mechanical improvements; the action is not carried on by impossible soliloquys and asides; and my people get on and off the stage without requiring four doors to a room which in real life would only have one. But my stories are the old stories; my characters are the familiar harlequin and columbine, clown and pantaloon (note the harlequin's leap in the third act of Caesar and Cleopatra); my stage tricks and suspenses and thrills and jests are the ones in vogue when I was a boy, by which time my grandfather was tired of them.
On himself, 'Better than Shakespeare?', Preface to *Caesar and Cleopatra*.

I am of the true Shakespearian type: I understand everything and everyone and am nobody and nothing.
On himself, Letter to Frank Harris, 20 June 1930.

I am not a professional liar. I am even ashamed of the extent to which in my human infirmity I have been an amateur one.
On himself, *Love Among The Artists*.

I am as much a woman, as Lady So-and-So is a man: say ninety five per cent.
On himself, in Blanche Patch, *Thirty Years with GBS*.

You are talking to a man who is three-quarters of a ghost.
On himself, in his nineties, to a spiritualist, in *ibid*.

My only policy is to profess evil and do good.
On himself, in Stephen Winsten, *Bernard Shaw*.

His plays are a joy to watch, not because they purport to deal with social and political problems, but because they are such wonderful displays of conspicuous waste; the conversational energy displayed by his characters is so far in excess of what their situation requires, that, if it were to be devoted to practical action, it would wreck the world in five minutes. The Mozart of English letters he is not — the music of the Marble statue is beyond him — the Rossini, yes. He has all the brio, humour, cruel

clarity and virtuosity of that Master of *Opera Buffa*.
  W. H. Auden, Footnote to 'The Globe', in *The Dyer's Hand*.

It is all very well to believe, as Shaw did, that all criticism is prejudiced, but, with Shaw's dramatic criticism, the prejudice is more important than anything else.
  Eric Bentley, Introduction to *Shaw on Music*.

— Oh dear me — its too late to do anything but *accept* you and *love* you — but when you were quite a little boy somebody ought to have said 'hush' just once.
  Mrs Patrick Campbell, Letter to GBS, 1 November 1912.

I believe you have eaten your own heart.
  Ibid., 1 February 1939.

Yes: I am glad I invented you, and that it is the cleverest thing I ever did.
  Ibid.

God help us if he would ever eat a beef-steak.
  Mrs Patrick Campbell, in Bertrand Russell, *Autobiography*, vol. 2.

Some Nationalist Irishmen have referred to him contemptuously as a 'West Briton'. But this is really unfair; for whatever Mr. Shaw's mental faults may be, the easy adoption of an unmeaning phrase like 'Briton' is certainly not one of them. It would be much nearer the truth to put the thing in the bold and bald terms of an old Irish song, and to call him 'The anti-Irish Irishman'.
  G. K. Chesterton, *Essays*: 'Shaw the Puritan'.

He is a daring pilgrim who has set out from the grave to find the cradle. He started from points of view which no one else was clever enough to discover, and he is at last discovering points of view which no one else was ever stupid enough to ignore.
  Ibid.

There is at least one outstanding fact about the man we are studying: Bernard Shaw is never frivolous. He never gives his opinions a holiday; he is never irresponsible even for an instant. He has no nonsensical second self which he can get into as one gets into a dressing-gown; that ridiculous disguise which is yet more real than the real person.
  Ibid.

The simplest clues to life escape him, as he scales impossible pinnacles of unnecessary thought, only to slip down the other side.
  Edward Gordon Craig, *Ellen Terry and Her Secret Self*.

Has he not worked like a giant? — is he not the possessor of a gigantically card-indexed intellectual energy? Has he not made a mountain of money out of literature? Has he not risen to the highest position in the realms of pure journalism and been a steadying influence to those schools of thoughtlessness which are for ever proclaiming that beauty is truth, truth beauty, that aristocracy is uglier than it is painted, and that the Devil has all Stravinsky's best tunes. . . .
  Ibid.

His brain is a half-inch layer of champagne poured over a bucket of Methodist near-beer.
  Benjamin de Casseres, *Mencken and Shaw*.

Shaw is a Puritan who missed the Mayflower by five minutes.
  Ibid.

Shaw's relations with women have always been gallant, coy even. The number he has surrendered to physically have been few — perhaps not half a dozen in all — the first man to have cut a swathe through the theatre and left it strewn with virgins.
  Frank Harris, *Bernard Shaw*.

Shaw was . . . impatient with weakness and parasites — anything but a lover of the underdog. I grew to think of him as a little obstinate, English in mind, and not Celtic at all, and ·time has proved that theory to be correct.
  Ibid.

Mr Shaw, I don't know what we are going to talk about, because I agree with everything you have ever written or said.
  Leslie Henson, in Blanche Patch, *Thirty Years with GBS*.

Any sexual relationship which could not provide an alternative world, made largely out of words, tended to disgust him.
  Michael Holroyd, *GBS, Sex, and Second Childhood*.

He believed in art for action's sake.
  Ibid.

The eyes betray the passion and the pain
Of Jesus come again in cap and bells.
  Colin Hurry, *G.B.S.* (a sonnet).

I'm afraid *The Intelligent Woman's Guide* I shall have to leave to the intelligent woman: it is too boring for the intelligent man, if I'm any sample. Too much gas-bag.
  D. H. Lawrence, Letter to Martin Secker, 24 July 1928.

He has a curious blank in his make-up. To him all sex is infidelity and only infidelity is sex. Marriage is sexless, null. Sex is only manifested in infidelity, and the queen of sex is the chief prostitute. If sex crops up in marriage, it is because one party falls in love with somebody else, and wants to be unfaithful. Infidelity is sex and prostitutes know all about it. Wives know nothing and are nothing, in that respect.

> D. H. Lawrence, *A Propos of Lady Chatterley's Lover.*

I am just as genial a character as Mr. Bernard Shaw, to give you an idea. I am rather what Mr. Shaw would have been if he had been an artist — I here use 'artist' in the widest possible sense — if he had not been an Irishman, if he had been a young man when the Great War occurred, if he had studied painting and philosophy instead of economics and Ibsen, and if he had been more richly endowed with imagination, emotion, intellect and a few other things. (He said he was a finer fellow than Shakespeare. I merely preferred myself to Mr. Shaw.)

> Percy Wyndham Lewis, *Blasting and Bombardiering.*

That noisiest of all old cocks.
> *Ibid.*

Have you seen any more of your friends who worship Bernard Shaw? Tell them that Shaw is Carlyle & water, that he ought to have been a Quaker (cocoa and commercial dishonesty), that he has squandered what talents he may have had back in the '80's in inventing metaphysical reasons for behaving like a scoundrel, that he suffers from an inferiority complex towards Shakespeare, & that he is the critic, cultured critic (not very cultured but it is what B meant) that Samuel Butler prayed to be delivered from.

> George Orwell, Letter to Brenda Salkeld, March 1933.

He used blocks of water-lined paper of a green tint to rest the eyes, and on them he would turn out, between breakfast and lunch, an average of 1,500 words a day. The rate would depend on the intricacy of stage 'business', and with that he never had much patience. He once told me that he would rather write the whole dialogue of *Hamlet* than manage the entrance and the exit of the ghost. He would complete the dialogue of a long play inside two months.

> Blanche Patch, *Thirty Years with GBS.*

A strange lady giving an address in Zurich wrote him a proposal thus: 'You have the greatest brain in the world, and I have the most beautiful body; so we ought to produce the most perfect child.' Shaw asked: 'What if the child inherits my body and your brains?'

> Hesketh Pearson, *Bernard Shaw, His Life and Personality.*

Knowing he hated bloodsports and would agree with the sentiment, Lady Astor remarked, 'I hate killing for pleasure.' As he said nothing, one of her children probed: 'Do you hate killing for pleasure?' 'It depends upon whom you kill', he answered.

> Hesketh Pearson, *Lives of the Wits.*

He created a character adaptable to his parts because he was a born actor, not merely because he was nervous and timid; and he put forward his views with levity because he was a born clown, not solely because he wished to gain an audience. It is the combination of actor and critic, of clown and prophet, that makes him unique in literature. His was not simply the gaiety of the great artist, like Shakespeare, or Cervantes; it was as if a great teacher like Socrates or Christ, or Buddha could not resist the temptation to diversify his sermons with somersaults.

> Hesketh Pearson, *Bernard Shaw, a Postscript.*

1908 saw a stirring. By 1912 it was established, at least in Ormond St., that the cardboard Shaw and the suety Wells were NOT the voice.
> Ezra Pound, in *Criterion*, 1937.

He went through the fiery furnace, but never a hair
was missed
From the heels of our most Colossal Arch-Super-
Egotist.

> *Punch*, March 1917.

I think envy plays a part in his philosophy in this sense, that if he allowed himself to admit that goodness of things he lacks and others possess, he would feel such intolerable envy that he would find life unbearable. Also he hates self-control, and makes up theories with a view to proving that self-control is pernicious. I couldn't get on with *Man and Superman*: it disgusted me. I don't think he is a soul in Hell dancing on red-hot iron. I think his Hell is merely diseased vanity and a morbid fear of being laughed at.

> Bertrand Russell, Letter to Lowes Dickinson, July 1904.

George Too Shaw To Be Good.
> Dylan Thomas, Letter to Pamela Hansford Johnson, October 1933.

For one thing, it [*Heartbreak House*] is improvised work. Shaw admitted he made it up as he went along, not knowing from day to day what his characters would do or say or become. He always tended to work this way, regarding a play essentially as an organism with a life of its own; one need only nurture it and let it assume its own shape. He even used to keep a checkerboard at hand to remind himself who was onstage and who was off at any given moment in the writing. There is no doubt this method served him as well as any other; his night mind was not, to say the least, fantastic. I am sure deep in his unconscious there lurked not the usual nightmare monsters of the rest of us, but yards of thesis, antithesis, and synthesis, all neatly labelled and filed. Yet in *Heartbreak House* Shaw's improvisatory genius breaks down; he keeps marching into conversational culs-de-sac.

> Gore Vidal, *Essays:* 'Love love love'.

He hasn't an enemy in the world, and none of his friends like him.

> Oscar Wilde, in G. B. Shaw, *Sixteen Self Sketches*.

Mr Bernard Shaw has no enemies but is intensely disliked by all his friends.

> Oscar Wilde, in William Butler Yeats, *Autobiographies*.

This is the first generation in which the spirit of literature has been conquered by the spirit of the press, of hurry, of immediate interests, and Bernard Shaw is the Joseph whose prosperity has brought his brethren into captivity.

> William Butler Yeats, Letter to Edmund Gosse, 12 April 1910.

I agree about Shaw — he is haunted by the mystery he flouts. He is an atheist who trembles in the haunted corridor.

> William Butler Yeats, Letter to George Russell ('AE'), 1 July 1921.

Presently I had a nightmare that I was haunted by a sewing-machine that clicked and shone, but the incredible thing was that the machine smiled, smiled perpetually. Yet I delighted in Shaw, the formidable man. He could hit my enemies, and the enemies of those I loved, as I could never hit, as no living author that was dear to me could ever hit.

> William Butler Yeats, *Autobiographies*.

See also E. M. Forster, Thomas Hardy, Harpo Marx, Evelyn Waugh, Oscar Wilde

SHAW, RICHARD NORMAN

1831–1912 Architect

In designing, his favourite maxim . . . was 'keep it quiet.'

W. R. Lethaby, *Philip Webb and His Work*.

SHAW, T. E., see under LAWRENCE, T. E.

SHEELER, CHARLES

1883–1965 Artist

Perhaps the greatest value of art teaching is that the pupil may later have something to unlearn. The distance I traversed along the road from art school days to the present has been greater than the length of that sentence may imply.

From the casual portrayal of the momentary appearance of nature learned in art school, to the concept of a picture as having an underlying architectural structure to support the elements in nature which comprise the picture, was a long journey with many stop-overs along the way.

> On himself, in *Charles Sheeler*, a Museum of Modern Art Catalogue.

There is a strong contemporary sensibility in Sheeler's painting. It shares many of the qualities of present-day formalism, and emphasizes an aesthetic of austerity which most younger artists understand. Like many of them, Sheeler was a rigorous formalist who eliminated nonessentials. Irreducible man-made forms, anonymous surfaces, and, above all, cool imagery make him interesting to a new generation of geometrically oriented artists, even though his literalism is foreign to them. Sheeler — the inveterate classicist — synthesizes and corrects nature, eliminates imperfection, and subtly readjusts the world.

> Martin Friedman, *Charles Sheeler*.

To discover and separate these things from the amorphous, the conglomerate normality with which they are surrounded and of which before the act of 'creation' each is a part, calls for an eye to draw out that detail which is in itself the thing, to clinch our insight, that is, our understanding, of it. It is this eye for the thing that most distinguished Charles Sheeler — and along with it to know that every hair on every body, now or then, in its minute distinctiveness is the same hair, on every body anywhere, at any time, changed as it may be to feather, quill or scale.

The local is the universal. It was a banana to Cézanne.

> William Carlos Williams, Introduction to *Charles Sheeler*, Museum of Modern Art Catalogue.

SHEFFIELD, JOHN, EARL OF MULGRAVE AND NORMANBY

1648—1721 Poet

I am not so young now but that I can chew the cud of lechery with some satisfaction. You who are so amorous and vigorous may have your mind wholly taken up with the present, but we grave decay'd people, alas, are glad to steal a thought some times towards the past, and then are to ask God forgiveness for it too.

On himself, Letter to George Etherege, 7 March 1687.

SHELBURNE, EARL OF (WILLIAM PETTY, MARQUIS OF LANSDOWNE)

1737—1805 Politician

D--- it! I never could see through varnish, and there's an end.

Thomas Gainsborough, finding it impossible to paint Shelburne's portrait, in *The Autobiography of Mrs. Piozzi.*

The jesuit of Berkeley Square.

George III, in *The Correspondence of George III with Lord North.*

Do you know that I could never conceive the reason why they call you Malagrida, for Malagrida was a very good sort of man.

Oliver Goldsmith, in *Memoirs of the Earl of Charlemont.*

His falsehood was so constant and notorious, that it was rather his profession than his instrument. It was like a fictitious violin, which is hung out of a music shop to indicate in what goods the tradesman deals; not to be of service, nor to be depended on for playing a true note. He was so well known that he could only deceive by speaking truth. His plausability was less an artifice than a habit; and his smiles were so excited that, like the rattle of the snake, they warned before he had time to bite. Both his heart and his face were brave; he feared neither danger nor detection. He was as fond of insincerity as if he had been the inventor, and practised it with as little caution as if he thought nobody else had discovered the secret.

Horace Walpole, *Journal of the Reign of George III.*

SHELLEY, MARY WOLLSTONECRAFT

1797—1851 Authoress

As a child I scribbled; and my favourite pastime, during the hours given me for recreation, was to 'write stories'. Still I had a dearer pleasure than this, which was the formation of castles in the air — the indulging in waking dreams — the following up of trains of thought, which had for their subject the formation of a succession of imaginary incidents. My dreams were at once more fantastic and agreeable than my writings.

On herself, Introduction to *Frankenstein.*

Mrs Shelley is very clever, indeed it would be difficult for her not to be so; the daughter of Mary Wollstonecraft and Godwin, and the wife of Shelley, could be no common person.

Lord Byron, in Lady Blessington, *Conversations with Lord Byron.*

I believe that she has nothing of what is commonly called vices, and that she has considerable talent. . . . I am anxious that she should be brought up like a philosopher, even like a cynic. It will add greatly to the strength and worth of her character. I wish too that she should be *excited* to industry. She has occasionally great perseverance, but occasionally, too, she shows great need to be roused.

William Godwin, her father, Letter to William Baxter, June 1812.

The author seems to us to disclose uncommon powers of poetic imagination. The feeling with which we perused the unexpected and fearful, yet, allowing the possibility of the event, very natural conclusion of Frankenstein's experiment, shook a little even our firm nerves.

Sir Walter Scott, review of *Frankenstein,* in *Blackwood's Magazine,* March 1818.

SHELLEY, PERCY BYSSHE

1792—1822 Poet

Less oft is peace in Shelley's mind,
Than calm in waters, seen.

On himself, *To Jane: The Recollection.*

In this have I long believed, that my power consists in sympathy and that part of imagination which relates to sentiment and contemplation. I am formed, if for anything not in common with the herd of mankind, to apprehend the minute and remote distinctions of feeling, whether relative to external nature or the living things which surround us, and to communicate the conceptions which result from considering either the moral or the material universe as a whole.

On himself, Letter to William Godwin, 1817.

I have an unpurchasable mind.

On himself, in conversation with Henry Addington, 1802.

It always seems to me that the right sphere for Shelley's genius was the sphere of music, not of poetry.

Matthew Arnold, *Essays in Criticism*, 'Maurice de Guerin'.

A beautiful and ineffectual angel, beating in the void his luminous wings in vain.

Matthew Arnold, *Essays in Criticism*, 'Byron'.

Ah, did you once see Shelley plain,
    And did he stop and speak to you?
And did you speak to him again,
    How strange it seems, and new!

Robert Browning, *Memorabilia*.

Meantime, as I call Shelley a moral man, because he was true, simple-hearted, and brave, and because what he acted corresponded to what he knew, so I call him a man of religious mind, because every audacious negative cast up by him against the Divine was interpenetrated with a mood of reverence and adoration — and because I find him everywhere taking for granted some of the capital dogmas of Christianity, while most vehemently denying their historical basement.

Robert Browning, *Shelley*.

As to poor Shelley, who is another bugbear to you and the world, he is, to my knowledge, the *least* selfish and the mildest of men — a man who has made more sacrifice of his fortune and feelings for others than any I ever heard of. With his speculative opinions I have nothing in common, nor desire to have.

Lord Byron, Letter to Thomas Moore, 4 March 1822.

Shelley . . . was quietly, but necessarily expelled [from Oxford] . . . I say *quietly*, for, like most residents in Oxford, I never heard of it till long after; and *necessarily*, — for how could the society, which treated him and his sad case with tender consideration, keep such a rotten sheep in their fold?

C. V. Cox, *Recollections of Oxford*.

He is one of the many whom we cannot read without wonder, or without pain: when I consider his

powers of mind, I am proud that he was an Etonian: when I remember their perversion, I wish he had never been one. However, he has made his election; and where Justice cannot approve, Charity can at least be silent!

Etonian, 1821.

The splendours, the almost supernatural beauty of the active mind of Shelley will obviously forever gild his poems and blind one to the mediocrity of thousands of his inferior lines. But the gold is an exterior gold; we bring it ourselves to his shrine, and his shining soul only very seldom illuminates his poems from within. He is almost never natural; he is almost never not intent on showing himself the champion of freedom, the Satan of a Hanoverian Heaven.

Ford Madox Ford, *The March of Literature*.

As to Mr Shelley's virtues, if he belonged (as we understand he did), to a junta, whose writings tend to make our sons profligates, and our daughters strumpets, we ought justly to regret the decease of the Devil (if that were possible), as one of his co-adjutors. Seriously speaking, however, we feel no pleasure in the untimely death of this Tyro of the Juan school, that pre-eminent Academy of Infidels, Blasphemers, Seducers, and Wantons. We had much rather have heard, that he and the rest of the fraternity had been consigned to a Monastery of La Trappe, for correction of their dangerous principles, and expurgation of their corrupt minds.

Gentleman's Magazine, 1822.

Mr Shelley's style is to poetry what astrology is to natural science — a passionate dream, a straining after impossibilities, a record of fond conjectures, a confused embodying of vague abstractions — a fever of the soul, thirsting and craving after what it cannot have, indulging its love of power and novelty at the expense of truth and nature, associating ideas by contraries, and wasting great powers by their application to unattainable objects.

William Hazlitt, in *Edinburgh Review*.

He had a fire in his eye, a fever in his blood, a maggot in his brain, a hectic flutter in his speech, which mark out the philosophic fanatic.

William Hazlitt, *Table Talk*.

Shelley . . . might well call himself Ariel. All the most enjoying part of this poetry is Ariel — the 'delicate' yet powerful 'spirit', jealous of restraint, yet able to serve; living in the elements and the flowers; treading the 'ooze' of the salt deep, and running 'on the sharp wind of the north'; feeling for creatures unlike himself; 'flaming amazement' on them too, and singing exquisitest songs. Alas! and he suffered for years, as Ariel did in the cloven pine: but now he is out of it, and serving the purposes of Beneficence with a calmness befitting his knowledge and his love.

Leigh Hunt, *Imagination and Fancy.*

You, I am sure, will forgive me for sincerely remarking that you might curb your magnanimity, and be more of an artist, and load every rift of your subject with ore.

John Keats, Letter to Shelley, August 1820.

'Follow your instincts' is his one moral rule, confounding the very lowest animal instincts with those lofty ideas of right, which it was the will of Heaven that he should retain, ay, and love, to the very last, and so reducing them all to the level of sentiments. 'Follow your instincts' — But what if our instincts lead us to eat animal food? 'Then you must follow the instincts of me, Percy Bysshe Shelley. I think it horrible, cruel, it offends my taste.' What if our instincts lead us to tyrannise over our fellow-men? 'Then you must repress those instincts. I, Shelley, think that, too, horrible and cruel.' Whether it be vegetarianism or liberty, the rule is practically the same — sentiment: which, in his case, as in the case of all sentimentalists, turns out to mean at last, not the sentiments of mankind in general, but the private sentiments of the writer. This is Shelley; a sentimentalist pure and simple; incapable of anything like inductive reasoning.

Charles Kingsley, *Thoughts on Shelley and Byron.*

For Shelley's nature is utterly womanish. Not merely his weak points, but his strong ones, are those of a woman. Tender and pitiful as a woman; and yet, when angry, shrieking, railing, hysterical as a woman. The physical distaste for meat and fermented liquors, coupled with the hankering after physical horrors, are especially feminine. The nature of a woman looks out of that wild, beautiful, girlish face — the nature: but not the spirit.

Ibid.

That 'quivering intensity', offered in itself apart from any substance, offered instead of any object, is what, though it may make Shelley intoxicating at fifteen, makes him almost unreadable, except in very small quantities of his best, to the mature. Even when he is in his own way unmistakably a distinguished poet . . . it is impossible to go on reading him at any length with pleasure; the elusive imagery, the high-pitched emotions, the tone and movement, the ardours, ecstasies, and despairs, are too much the same all through. The effect is of vanity and emptiness (Arnold was right) as well as monotony.

F. R. Leavis, *Revaluation.*

But Shelley had a hyper-thyroid face.

Sir John Squire, *Ballade of the Glandular Hypothesis.*

Shelley, lyric lord of England's lordliest singers, here first heard
Ring from lips of poets crowned and dead the Promethean word
Whence his soul took fire, and power to out-soar the sunward-soaring bird.

Algernon C. Swinburne, *Eton: An Ode.*

Mr Shelley and his disciples — the followers (if I may so call them) of the PHANTASTIC SCHOOL, labour to effect a revolution. . . . They would transfer the domicile of poetry to regions where reason, far from having any supremacy or rule, is all but unknown, an alien and an outcast; to seats of anarchy and abstraction, where imagination exercises the shadow of an authority, over a people of phantoms, in a land of dreams.

Henry Taylor, Preface to *Philip van Artevelde.*

Shelley should not be read, but inhaled through a gas pipe.

Lionel Trilling, in Clifton Fadiman, *Enter Conversing.*

See also Robert Browning, Lord Byron, Samuel Taylor Coleridge, Isadora Duncan, John Keats, Rudyard Kipling, D. H. Lawrence, T. E. Lawrence, Jack London, William Wordsworth, William Butler Yeats.

SHERIDAN, PHILIP HENRY
1831—88 Soldier

The facile hand of politics, of material greed, never reached out and touched him. He had the variety of mind — fortunate for its possessor — that is convinced of the unchanging correctness, the universal inclusiveness, of its few and uncomplicated tenets. No imagination, none of that distracting sense of proportion alluded to as a sense of humor, existed to fill him with bothersome doubts.

Joseph Hergesheimer, *Sheridan: A Military Narrative.*

The terrible grumble, and rumble, and roar,
Telling the battle was on once more,
And Sheridan twenty miles away.

Thomas Buchanan Read, *Sheridan's Ride.*

The general is a stumpy, quadrangular little man, with a forehead of no promise and hair so short that it looks like a coat of black paint. But his eyes and mouth show force, and of all our chieftains he alone has displayed the capacity of handling men in actual shock of battle, turning defeat into victory, rallying a broken fugitive mob and hurling them back upon the enemy.

George Templeton Strong, in Allan Nevins and M. H. Thomas eds, *The Diary of George Templeton Strong.*

SHERIDAN, RICHARD BRINSLEY

1751–1816 Statesman, Dramatist

For my own Part when I read for Entertainment, I had much rather view the Characters of Life as I would wish they *were* than as they *are*: therefore I hate Novels, and love Romances. The Praise of the best of the former, their being *natural*, as it is called, is to me their greatest Demerit.

On himself, Letter to Thomas Grenville, 30 October 1772.

What I write in a Hurry I always feel to be not worth reading, and what I try to take Pains with, I am sure never to finish. . . .

On himself, Letter to David Garrick, 10 January 1778.

I have had to struggle with the disadvantages of uncertain income. These in all cases are known to be great, but they are particularly formidable to a man of sanguine temper, blessed with but a small share of resolution, who might expect much from the exertions of talent, who forms hopes which are never realised, and makes to himself promises he is unable to perform.

On himself, *In his own Defence, before the Lord Chancellor.*

How unceasingly do I meditate on Death, and how continually do I act as if the thought of it had never crossed my mind.

On himself, Letter to his Wife, November 1804.

Sure I am, that there is no Person who has been near to me and confidentially acquainted with my private affairs and personal difficulties and who has witness'd my conduct under them that has not been confirmed or improved in principle and integrity in his views and transactions in this Life. You will forgive my having said thus much of myself — it may be egotism, but it is Fact.

Ibid., 20 April 1810.

You told me lately in one of your Letters that I was too apt to eat the calf in the Cow's belly, apologizing for the homeliness of the Phraze, and dared me

to deny it. I do not wholly deny it, but I do assert that in most of the great cases in which I have suffered by eagerness of anticipation the cause has been more infinitely in the roguery and insincerity of others than even in my own credulity and indolence.

Ibid., November 1814.

Good at a fight, but better at a play;
Godlike in giving, but the devil to pay.

Lord Byron, *On a Cast of Sheridan's Hand.*

Not that I do not admire and prefer his unequalled conversation; but — that '*but*' must only be intelligible to thoughts I cannot write.

Lord Byron, Journal, 12 December 1813.

He, the watchman, found Sherry in the street, fuddled and bewildered, and almost insensible. 'Who are you, Sir?' — no answer. 'What's your name?' — a hiccup. 'What's your name?' — Answer, in a slow, deliberate, and impassive tone — 'Wilberforce!!!' Is not that Sherry all over? — and, to my mind, excellent. Poor fellow, *his* very dregs are better than the 'first sprightly runnings' of others.

Lord Byron, Letter to Thomas Moore, 31 October 1815.

Every man has his element: Sheridan's is hot water.

Lord Eldon, in Lord Broughton, *Recollections of a Long Life.*

O vat a *clevare* fellow dat Sheridan is! — shall I tell you? — *Oui*, — Yes I vill — *Biendonc* — I could no never see him at de theatre, so *je vais chez lui* — to his house in Hertford-street, muffled in great coat, and I say, '*Domestique!* — you hear?' — 'Yes'. — 'Well, den, tell your master dat M. ---- de Mayor of Stafford be below.' *Domestique* fly — and on de instant, I be shown into de drawing-room. In von more minute, Sheridan leave his dinner party, enter de room hastily, stop suddenly, stare, and say, — 'How dare you, Grim, play me such a trick?' Then putting himself into a passion, he go on, — 'Go, sare! — get out of my house.' 'Begar,' say I, placing my back against the door, 'not till you pay me my forty pounds,' — and then, I point to de pen, ink, and paper, on von small tables in de corner, and say — 'Dere! — write me the check, and de Mayor shall go *vitement — entendez vous?* If not, *morbleu*, I vill ----'

'Oh!' interrupted de *clevare* man, 'If I must, Grim, I must,' — and as if he were *très pressé* — very hurry — he write de draft, and pushing it into my hand, he squeeze it, and I do push it into my pocket. Vell den, I do make haste to de banker's, and giving it to de clerks, I say, 'Four Tens if you please, Sare.' — 'Four tens!' he say with much surprise — 'de draft be only for four pounds!' o! vat a *clevare* fellow dat Sheridan is! But I say — 'If you please, sare, *donnez-moi donc*, those four pounds.' And den he say, 'Call again to-morrow!' Next day I meet de manager in de street, and I say, 'Mistare Sheridan, have you forget?' and den he laugh, and say, 'Vy, Grim, I recollected afterwards — I left out the *O*?' — O! vat a *clevare* fellow dat Sheridan is!

Giuseppe Grimaldi, in Frederick Reynolds, *Life and Times of Frederick Reynolds.*

We cannot help thinking that there are marks of an uneasy turn of mind in all Sheridan's productions. There is almost always some real pain going on amongst his characters. They are always perplexing, mortifying, or distressing one another; snatching their jokes out of some misery, as if they were playing at snap-dragon. . . . Sheridan's comedy is all-stinging satire. His bees want honey.

Leigh Hunt, on *The School for Scandal*, in *Tatler*, 27 October 1830.

It is said that, as he sat at the Piazza Coffee-house, during the fire [in Drury Lane], taking some refreshment, a friend of his having remarked on the philosophic calmness with which he bore his misfortune, Sheridan answered, 'A man may surely be allowed to take a glass of wine *by his own fireside*.'

Thomas Moore, *Memoirs of the Life of R. B. Sheridan.*

To such minutiae of effect did he attend, that I have found in more than one instance, a memorandum made of the precise place in which the words 'Good God, Mr Speaker,' were to be introduced.

Ibid.

The only time he could have found for this pre-arrangement of his thoughts (of which few, from the apparent idleness of his life, suspected him,) must have been during the many hours of the day that he remained in bed, — when, frequently, while the world gave him credit for being asleep, he was employed in laying the framework of his wit and eloquence for the evening.

Ibid.

His hours of composition, as long as he continued to be an author, were at night, and . . . he required a profusion of lights around him, while he wrote. Wine too, was one of his favourite helps to inspiration; — 'If the thought (he would say) is slow to come, a glass of good wine encourages it, and when it *does* come, a glass of good wine rewards it.'

Ibid.

Never examining accounts, nor referring to receipts, he seemed as if . . . he wished to make *paying* as like as possible to *giving*.

Ibid.

Propose what you will, and 'tis Brinsley can do't;
So fit for all things, yet, alas! fit for none,
Continually doing, yet *always undone*;
So beckon'd by Hope, yet by Hope so oft cheated,
For *ever contending*, yet *ever defeated*;
By much too sincere for a good politician,
Too eccentric to make a sound mathematician;
Too proud for attendance, too vain to beseech,
Too poor to be happy, too candid to preach:
Thus he swims in a strange indeterminate mean,
Neither hallow'd nor damn'd, but betwixt and between.
When Genius essays to effect his conversion,
Attachments obtrude and defeat the exertion;
Tho' Satire has arm'd him to regulate men,
Young Gratitude draws all the ink from his pen.
If to lacerate Folly he wings the keen dart,
It wounds his *best friend* in the core of his heart. . . .

Anthony Pasquin (John Williams), *The Children of Thespis.*

Somebody told me, (but not your Father) that the Opera Singers would not be likely to get any money out of Sheridan this year. 'Why, that fellow grows fat,' says I, 'like Heliogabalus, upon the tongues of nightingales.'

Mrs Piozzi (Hester Lynch Thrale), Letter to Fanny Burney, 22 November 1781.

Sheridan was listened to with such attention that you might have heard a pin drop.

Samuel Rogers, *Table Talk.*

Sheridan had very fine eyes, and he was not a little vain of them. He said to me on his death-bed, 'Tell Lady Besborough that my eyes will look up on the coffin-lid as brightly as ever.'

Ibid.

Sheridan wrote for the actor as Handel wrote for the singer, setting him a combination of strokes, which, however difficult some of them may be to execute finely, are familiar to all practised actors as the strokes which experience has shewn to be proper to the nature and capacity of the stage-player as a dramatic instrument. With Sheridan you are never in the plight of the Gentleman who stamped on a sheet of Beethoven's music in a rage, declaring that what cannot be played should not be written.

George Bernard Shaw, in *Saturday Review*, 27 June 1896.

The work of Sheridan begins to be taken at its true value — as a clever but emasculated *rifacimento* [*re-moulding*] .
Lytton Strachey, *Portraits in Miniature.*

At this period of his life, when he was not more than thirty-three years of age, his countenance and features had in them something peculiarly pleasing, indicative at once of intellect, humour, and gaiety. All these characteristics played about his lips when speaking, and operated with inconceivable attraction; for they anticipated as it were, to the eye, the effect produced by his oratory, on the ear, thus opening for him a sure way to the heart or the understanding.
Sir Nathaniel Wraxall, *Historical and Posthumous Memoirs.*

Fox outlived his vices; those of Sheridan accompanied him to the tomb.
Ibid.

See also Robert Burns, Charles James Fox, Sarah Siddons

SHERIDAN, THOMAS

1719—88 Actor

Why, Sir, Sherry is dull, naturally dull; but it must have taken a great deal of pains to become what we now see him. Such an excess of stupidity, Sir, is not in Nature.
Samuel Johnson, in James Boswell, *Life of Johnson.*

Sir, it is burning a farthing candle at Dover, to shew a light at Calais.
Ibid., on Sheridan's style.

See also Oliver Goldsmith

SHERMAN, WILLIAM TECUMSEH

1820—91 Soldier

In revolutions men fall and rise. Long before this war is over, much as you hear me praised now, you may hear me cursed and insulted. . . . Read history, read Coriolanus and you will see the true measure of popular applause. Grant, Sheridan and I are now the popular favorites, but neither of us will survive this war. Some other must rise greater than either of us, and he has not yet manifest himself. . . .
On himself, Letter to his Wife.

I will not accept if nominated, and will not serve if elected.
On himself, telegram to John B. Henderson, Chairman of the Republican National Convention at Chicago, declining the presidential nomination, 5 June 1884.

Sherman, hurrah, we'll go with him
Wherever it may be
Through Carolina's cotton fields
Or Georgia to the sea.
Anon., soldiers' marching song.

It would seem as if in him, all the attributes of man were merged into the enormities of the demon, as if Heaven intended in him to manifest depths of depravity yet untouched by a fallen race . . . unsated still in his demoniac vengeance he sweeps over the country like a simoom of destruction.
Anon., editorial in *Macon Telegraph* (Georgia), 5 December 1864.

We drink to twenty years ago,
When Sherman led our banner;
His mistresses were fortresses,
His Christmas gift — Savannah!
George B. Corkhill, toast at a dinner given in Sherman's honour in Washington, 8 February 1833.

No living American was so loved and venerated as he. To look upon his face, to hear his name, was to have one's love of country intensified. He served his country, not for fame, not out of a sense of professional duty, but for love of the flag and of the beneficent civil institutions of which it was the emblem. He was an ideal soldier, and shared to the fullest the *esprit de corps* of the army; but he cherished the civil institutions organized under the constitution, and was a soldier only that these might be perpetuated in undiminished usefulness and honor. . . .
President Benjamin Harrison, in *Congressional Record.*

No man of action has more completely attained the point of view of the scientific historian, who observes the movements of mankind with the same detachment as a bacteriologist observes bacilli under a microscope and yet with a sympathy that springs from his own common manhood. In Sherman's attainment of that philosophic pinnacle, soaring above the clouds of ignorance and passion, lies the explanation of much that seems perplexing and contradictory in his character — the dispassionateness of an impulsive man, the restfulness of a restless man, the patience of an impatient man, the sympathy of a relentless man.

Basil H. Liddell Hart, *Sherman: Soldier-Realist-American.*

SHERRINGTON, SIR CHARLES SCOTT

1857—1952 Physiologist

In the summer of 1915 he disappeared on a bicycle, presumably for a holiday, leaving no address: a collar stud, which was lost and could not be replaced, disclosed his whereabouts. He was a bench-worker 'incognito' at a munitions plant in Birmingham. His shift time, 7 a.m.—6 p.m., did not permit any visit to a shop to obtain a collar stud. His great interest in industrial fatigue — he was Chairman of the Industrial Fatigue Board in 1918 — had determined him to study fatigue 'in situ'. . . . He was then nearly 60.

C. E. R. Sherrington, *Charles Scott Sherrington, 1857—1952.*

SHIRLEY, JAMES

1596—1666 Poet

James, thou and I did spend some precious yeares
At Katherine-Hall; since when, we sometimes feele
In our poetick braines, (as plaine appeares)
A whirling tricke, then caught from Katherine's
wheele.

Thomas Bancroft, *To James Shirley.*

SHORT, REV. THOMAS

1789—1879 Oxford Academic

Match me such marvel, save in college port,
That rose-red liquor, half as old as Short.

Anon. Epigram, after J. W. Burgon.

SICKERT, WALTER RICHARD

1860—1942 Painter

Sickert's whole development can be interpreted as a series of experiments designed not only to discover the ideal handling of his medium but also to find out how far the method of painting devised to express this handling, and its outcome — style — can and cannot be programmed and systematized. The value Sickert placed on handling and his intense emotional involvement with paint were constantly

at war with his desire to tame his medium so as to make the execution of a painting almost mechanical.

W. Baron, *Sickert.*

As Sickert wrote to Miss Sands, he could not 'conceive heaven' without

'1. painting in a sunny room an iron bedstead in the morning

2. painting in a North light studio from drawings till tea-time

3. giving a few lessons to eager students of both sexes at night.'

Ibid.

There is cruelty, disgust, and sadness in the scenes and characters of his *genre* paintings, a pathos which never degenerates into sentimentality; and principally a disdainful discretion, a sort of self-defence, in his attitude towards human contacts — *noli me tangere.* He needs but a commonplace object well set in an uninteresting interior in order to evoke a dramatic quality, to suggest situations guessed rather than seen. All relations with Sickert have an extraordinary, a mysterious character.

Jacques Blanche, in R. Emmons, *The Life and Opinions of Walter Richard Sickert.*

Although he left the footlights for the studio so early, Sickert has been an actor all his life, the world his theatre, the gallery his stage, and the whole picture-going public his audience.

R. Emmons, *ibid.*

Sickert shows us a world which is drab, dirty, disillusioned, a world whose pleasures are mirthless and whose devil is boredom. A world, in fact, such as we know.

John Rothenstein, *The Artists of the 1890s.*

Sickert's genius for discovering the dreariest house and most forbidding rooms in which to work was a source of wonder and amusement to me. He himself was so fastidious in his person, in his manners, in the choice of his clothes; was he affecting a kind of dandyism *à rebours*?

William Rothenstein, *Men and Memories.*

SIDDONS, SARAH

1755—1831 Actress

When Mrs Siddons came into the room, there happened to be no chair ready for her, which he [Dr Johnson] observing, said with a smile, 'Madam, you who so often occasion a want of seats to other people, will the more easily excuse the want of one yourself.'

James Boswell, *Life of Johnson.*

My friend Douglas Kinnaird told a story, rather too long, about Mrs Siddons and Kean acting together at some Irish Theatre. Kean got drunk and Mrs Siddons got all the applause. The next night Kean acted Jaffier, and Mrs Siddons Belvidera, and then 'he got all the applause', and, said Sheridan, 'she got drunk I suppose.'
  Lord Broughton, *Recollections of a Long Life.*

I had however seen, and been half killed by Mrs Siddons in 'Belvidera'.
  Fanny Burney, Diary, January 1783.

I found her the Heroine of a Tragedy, — sublime, elevated, and solemn. In Face and person, truly noble, and commanding; in manners, quiet and stiff; in voice, deep and dragging; and in conversation, formal, sententious, calm and dry. I expected her to have been all that is interesting; the delicacy and sweetness with which she seizes every opportunity to strike and to captivate upon the stage had persuaded me that her mind was formed with that peculiar susceptibility, which, in different modes, must give equal powers to attract and to delight, in common life. But I was very much mistaken.
  Ibid., 15 August 1787.

She was the stateliest ornament of the public mind.
  William Hazlitt, 'Mrs Siddons', in *Examiner*, 16 June 1816.

She is out of the pale of all theories and annihilates all rules. Wherever she sits there is grace and grandeur, there is tragedy personified. Her seat is the undivided throne of the Tragic Muse. She had no need of the robes, the sweeping train, the ornaments of the stage; in herself she is as great as any being she ever represented in the ripeness and plenitude of her power.
  William Hazlitt, *Table Talk: Whether Actors ought to Sit in the Boxes.*

She can overpower, astonish, afflict, but she cannot win: her majestic presence and commanding features seem to disregard love, as a trifle to which they cannot descend.
  Leigh Hunt, *Critical Essays on the Performers of the London Theatres.*

Her voice appeared to have lost its brilliancy (like a beautiful face through a veil).
  Henry Crabb Robinson, Diary, 21 April 1812.

When without motion her arms are not genteel.
  Horace Walpole, Letter to the Countess of Upper Ossory, 3 November 1782.

SIDMOUTH, LORD, see under ADDINGTON, HENRY

SIDNEY, SIR PHILIP
1554—1626 Statesman, Soldier, Poet

Sidney did not keep a decorum in making every one speak as well as himself.
  Ben Jonson, in *Conversations with William Drummond of Hawthornden.*

So that whereas (through the fame of his high deserts) he was then, or rather before, in election for the Crown of *Poland*, the Queen of England refused to further his advancement, not out of emulation, but out of fear to lose the jewel of her times.
  Anthony à Wood, *Athenae Oxonienses.*

See also Fulke Greville, John Lyly, Edmund Spenser

SILLIMAN, BENJAMIN
1779—1864 Chemist, Natural Historian

He exercised, at that time, a wide and commanding influence on the science of the country, — gave dignity to its pursuit, was the eloquent expounder of its principles, the able advocate of its importance, and its defender against the denunciation of zealous, though narrow-minded, theologians.
  Joseph Henry, Letter to G. P. Fisher, 13 November 1865.

SIMMS, WILLIAM GILMORE
1806—70 Author

Here lies one who, after a reasonably long life, distinguished chiefly by unceasing labors, has left all his better works undone.
  On himself, in E. Winfield Parks, *William Gilmore Simms As Literary Critic.*

He poured out his material copiously, lavishly, with overrunning measure. His stories flow as generously as his Jamaica rum. His is a veritable geyser of invention, an abundant sea of salty speech.
  Vernon Louis Parrington, *Main Currents in American Thought*, vol. 2.

It was more or less in spite of his conscious aims that he now and then wrote about striking characters and situations through vivid pages in simple, nervous, racy language.
  Carl Van Doren, *The American Novel 1789—1939.*

SIMON, JOHN ALLESBROOK, VISCOUNT

1873–1954 Politician

Simon has sat on the fence so long that the iron has entered his soul.
> David Lloyd George, in A. J. P. Taylor, *English History 1914–1945.*

SINCLAIR, UPTON BEALL

1878–1968 Author, Socialist

He was one of those hypercompassionate men who cannot sleep at night when they think of ten-year-old children working in mills and who, convinced that society is ruled by organized greed, feel that the burden of changing it rests upon them.
> Van Wyck Brooks, *The Confident Years: 1885–1915.*

Few American public figures, let alone American inspirational novelists, have written so many books, delivered so many lectures, covered as much territory, advocated so many causes or composed so many letters to the editor, got mixed up in so many scandals, been so insulted, ridiculed, spied on, tricked and left holding the bag — few, in short, have jumped so nimbly from so many frying pans into so many fires, and none has ever managed to keep so sunny and buoyant while the flames were leaping around him.
> Robert Cantwell, 'Upton Sinclair', in Malcolm Cowley ed., *After the Genteel Tradition.*

This pale and soft-voiced ascetic, with his near-sighted smile, his disarming candor and his strongly prim and dated pre-war air of good-fellowship and enthusiasm, has been involved, ever since he began to write, in knock-down and drag-out conflicts of such ferocity and ruthlessness they might well demoralize a dozen hardened captains of industry.
> *Ibid.*

He was intense, nervous, chaste, easily influenced, perplexed about religious problems and worried about sex; an amateur violinist who lectured his sweet-hearts about venereal diseases, went on fantastic bicycle rides of a hundred miles a day and suffered from blinding surges of unfocused emotion that he interpreted as symptoms of genius.
> *Ibid.*

His socialism has always been of the emotional sort, a direct response to his own environment, and, as a result of his failure to undergo an intense intellectual discipline, he has never eradicated the effects of his bourgeois upbringing.
> Granville Hicks, *The Great Tradition.*

Here at home, his writings have been too searching of our native ills, too savage in their indictment of our frailties and sins, too revolutionary in their pleas for and programs of advance, to win acceptance still egotistically provincial even in higher critical circles.
> John Haynes Holmes, in James Lambert Harte, *This is Upton Sinclair.*

As guileless as a child, as tender as a woman, compassionate, chivalric, heroic in self-sacrifice, dedicated to righteousness, Sinclair has walked in our wicked and troubled world as did the apostles of old with the gospel of the kingdom. One knows not whether most to admire the author or to love the man.
> *Ibid.*

. . . propaganda for the sake of political action can and does in Sinclair's fiction become tedious. One gets tired of watching Mr Sinclair spy a capitalist behind every woodpile.
> Grant C. Knight, *American Literature and Culture.*

It is alive and warm. It is brutal with life. It is written of sweat and blood, and groans with tears. It depicts not what man ought to be, but what man is compelled to be in our world, in the Twentieth Century.
> Jack London, referring to Sinclair's *The Jungle*, in Jay Martin, *Harvests of Change, American Literature, 1865–1914.*

No man in American history has denounced more different people than you have, or in more violent terms, and yet no man that I can recall complains more bitterly when he happens to be hit. Why not stop caterwauling for a while, and try to play the game according to the rules?
> H. L. Mencken, Letter to Sinclair, 2 May 1936.

It seems to me that you are a professional messiah like any other, and would perform precisely like the rest if you got the chance. Once in power, you would certainly not be too polite to the money-mad widows and orphans whose stocks and bonds now haunt your dreams.
> *Ibid.*

You are now in class with Masters and Frost, loafers, hiders. Which is a damn pity, as you have been some good at alternating intervals.
> Ezra Pound, Letter to Sinclair, 26 September 1936.

SITTING BULL

circa 1831—90 Sachem of the Hunkpapa Sioux
Nation

I wish all to know that I do not propose to sell any
part of my country, nor will I have the whites cutting our timber along the rivers, more especially the
oak. I am particularly fond of the little groves of
oak trees. I love to look at them, because they
endure the wintry storm and the summer's heat and
— not unlike ourselves — seem to flourish by them.
On himself, in T. C. McLuhan, *Touch The Earth.*

When I was a boy the Sioux owned the world; the
sun rose and set on their land; they sent ten thousand men to battle. Where are the warriors today?
Who slew them? Where are our lands? Who owns
them? What white man can say I ever stole his land
or a penny of his money? Yet, they say I am a thief.
What white woman, however lonely, was ever captive or insulted by me? Yet they say I am a bad
Indian. What white man has ever seen me drunk?
Who has ever come to me hungry and unfed? Who
has ever seen me beat my wives or abuse my children? What law have I broken? Is it wrong for me to
love my own? Is it wicked for me because my skin is
red? Because I am a Sioux; because I was born
where my father lived; because I would die for my
people and my country?
Ibid.

SITWELL, DAME EDITH

1887—1964 Authoress

The most trying attitude of all that the public has
adopted is that of accusing me of trying to '*épater
le bourgeois*' — (such bad manners. One assumes
intelligence in one's audience) and of doing this in
order to get publicity. . . . That is the reason why I
live here in France, now, instead of in London; for
it is no use people trying to get at me and behave as
the crowds behave to the wretched lions and tigers
at the Zoo.
On herself, Letter to R. G. Howarth,
24 February 1937.

It is a dangerous thing to say, but I can say it to
you. Sometimes, when I begin a poem, it is almost
like automatic writing. Then I use my mind on it
afterwards.
On herself, Letter to Maurice Bowra,
24 January 1944.

Nobody has ever been more alive than I! I am like
an unpopular electric eel in a pond full of flatfish.
On herself, in John Lehmann, *A Nest of Tigers.*

When we come to compare the collected poems of
Dame Edith Sitwell with those of Yeats, or Mr Eliot
or Professor Auden, it will be found that hers have
the purest poetical content of them all.
Cyril Connolly, in *Sunday Times*, 29 July 1957.

Writers who detach tragedy from the persons who
suffer it are generally to be seen soon after wearing
someone else's bleeding heart on their own safe
sleeves — an odious transaction, and an odious transaction is what Dame Edith Sitwell's atomic poetry
seems to me to be.
D. J. Enright, in *New Statesman.*

The Sitwells belong to the history of publicity
rather than of poetry.
F. R. Leavis, *New Bearings in English Poetry.*

Edith — she is a poetess by the way — is a bad loser.
When worsted in argument, she throws Queensberry
Rules to the winds. She once called me Percy.
Percy Wyndham Lewis, *Blasting and Bombardier-
ing.*

Then Edith Sitwell appeared, her nose longer than
an ant-eater's, and read some of her absurd stuff.
Lytton Strachey, recalling an evening at Arnold
Bennett's house, Letter to Dora Carrington, 28
June 1921.

So you've been reviewing Edith Sitwell's latest
piece of virgin dung, have you? Isn't she a poisonous
thing of a woman, lying, concealing, flipping, pla-
giarising, misquoting, and being as clever a crooked
literary publicist as ever.
Dylan Thomas, Letter to Glyn Jones, 1934.

With the Sitwells, at Renishaw . . . Sachie likes talking about sex. Osbert very shy. Edith wholly
ignorant. We talked of slums. She said the poor
streets of Scarborough were terrible but that she did
not think that the fishermen took drugs very much.
She also said that port was made with methylated
spirit: she knew this for a fact because her char-
woman told her.
Evelyn Waugh, Diary, 23 August 1930.

My wife . . . liked delicate fantasy after the manner
of Edith Sitwell, to whom I am as appreciatively
indifferent as I am to the quaint patterns of old
chintzes, the designs on dinner plates or the charm
of nursery rhymes.
H. G. Wells, *Experiment in Autobiography.*

SMART, CHRISTOPHER

1722—71 Poet

Johnson: 'It seems as if his mind has ceased to

struggle with the disease; for he grows fat upon it.'
Burney: 'Perhaps, Sir, that may be from want of
exercise.' Johnson: 'No, Sir; he has partly as much
exercise as he used to have, for he digs in the
garden. Indeed, before his confinement, he used for
exercise to walk to the ale-house; but he was *carried*
back again. I did not think he ought to be shut up.
His infirmities were not noxious to society..He insisted on people praying with him; and I'd as lief pray
with Kit Smart as any one else. Another charge was,
that he did not love clean linen; and I have no passion for it.'
James Boswell, *Life of Johnson*.

Mr Morgan argued with him . . . in vain. . . . 'Pray,
Sir, (said he) whether do you reckon Derrick or
Smart the best poet'; Johnson at once felt himself
roused; and answered, 'Sir, there is no settling the
point of precedency between a louse and a flea.'
Ibid.

Smart loved to hear me play upon my flute, and I
have often soothed the wanderings of his melancholy by some favourite air; he would shed tears
when I played, and generally write some lines afterwards.
John Kempe, 'Memoir', in *Gentleman's Magazine*,
1823.

Smart's melancholy shewed itself only in a preternatural excitement to prayer — taking *au pied de la
lettre* our blessed Saviour's injunction to *pray without ceasing.* — So that beginning by regular addresses
to the Almighty, he went on to call his friends from
their dinners, or beds, or places of recreation, whenever that impulse towards prayer pressed upon his
mind. In every other transaction of life no man's
wits could be more regular than those of Smart.
Mrs Piozzi (Hester Lynch Thrale), *The British
Synonymy*.

SMILES, SAMUEL

1812–1904 Author, Social Reformer

My object in writing out *Self-Help*, and delivering it
at first in the form of lectures, and afterwards rewrit-
ing and publishing it in the form of a book, was principally to illustrate and enforce the power of George
Stephenson's great word — PERSEVERANCE.
On himself, *Autobiography*.

He was 'fonder of frolic than of learning' when a
young man and was not even thrifty. 'I thought,'
he said, 'that the principal use of money was to be
spent.' He even forced open his money box with a
table knife in order to collect the few pennies he

had bothered to save. His later life was an exercise
in self-discipline; before he moulded others, he set
out to mould himself. This is perhaps the most important thing about him as a person.
Asa Briggs, *Victorian People*.

Remember only that you live in our terrific, untidy,
indifferent empirical age, where not one single problem is solved and not one single Accepted Idea from
the past has any more any magic. Our Lord and his
teachings are dead; and the late Smiles and his.
Ford Madox Ford, Letter to Lucy Masterman,
23 January 1913.

I remember Dr Smiles as the kindest old man, with a
white head and beard, full of sympathy for children
and love for animals. He even took an interest in my
doll, and was particularly keen about my money-box,
frequently asking how it was getting on. Sometimes
he dropped in a penny by way of encouragement. I
see it all now. He knew that if a child be taught to
save and take care of its pennies that child will
generally grow up thrifty, whereas money easily
gained is readily lost, while he who buys what he
does not want frequently ends up by wanting what
he cannot buy.
Mrs Alec Tweedie, in Thomas Bowen, *Life and
Works of Smiles*.

See also Gilbert Scott

SMITH, ADAM

1723–90 Political Economist

He was the most absent man in company that I ever
saw — moving his lips and talking to himself, and
smiling in the midst of large companies. If you
awakened him from his reverie, and made him
attend to the subject of the conversation, he immediately began a harangue, and never stopped till he
told you all he knew about it, and with the utmost
philosophical ingenuity.
Alexander Carlyle, in R. B. Haldane, *Adam
Smith*.

'Be seated, gentlemen,' said Smith on one occasion.
'No,' replied Pitt, 'we will stand till you are first
seated; for we are all your scholars.'
C. R. Fay, *Adam Smith and the Scotland of His
Day*.

His achievements are not accidents. If the architects'
plans are compared with history, they will be found
to have been executed in large part by the builders
of the nineteenth century.
Francis W. Hirst, *Adam Smith*.

Smith has issued from the seclusion of a professorship of morals, from the drudgery of a commis-
sionership of customs, to sit in the council-chamber
of princes. His word has rung through the study to
the platform. It has been proclaimed by the agitator,
conned by the statesman, and printed in a thousand
statutes.

Ibid.

A very noticeable figure he was as he went up and
down the High Street, and he used to tell himself
the observations of two market women about him
as he marched past them one day. 'Hegh sirs!' said
one, shaking her head significantly, 'And he's well
put on too!' rejoined the other, surprised that one
who appeared from his dress to be likely to have
friends should be left by them to walk abroad alone.

John Rae, *Life of Adam Smith.*

See also David Hume

SMITH, ALFRED EMANUEL

1873—1944 Politician

[He] could make statistics sit up, beg, roll over and
bark.

Anon., in Oscar Handlin, *Al Smith and His
America.*

. . . ruined by associating with rich men — a thing
far more dangerous to politicians than even booze
or the sound of their own voices.

H. L. Mencken, in Richard O'Connor, *The First
Hurrah.*

The plain fact is that Al, as a good New Yorker, is
as provincial as a Kansas farmer. He is not only not
interested in the great problems that heave and
lather the country: he has never heard of them.

H. L. Mencken, July 1927, in *A Carnival of
Buncombe.*

The man you ran against ain't a candidate, he is just
a victim.

Will Rogers, Letter to Smith, when the latter was
returned for a fourth term as governor of New
York, in Richard O'Connor, *The First Hurrah.*

The Happy Warrior of the political battlefield.

Franklin D. Roosevelt, at the Democratic National Convention, 1924.

He exchanged the old blue serge suit for a white tie
and tails, the brown derby for a top hat. He took
off the square-toe brogans with which he had
climbed from the sidewalks of New York to dizzy

heights and put on a pair of pumps. It takes a damn
good acrobat to do that while at the top of the
ladder.

Mayor Jimmy Walker of New York, in Richard
O'Connor, *The First Hurrah.*

SMITH, BESSIE

circa 1898—1937 Singer

'It's a long, old road' as Bessie Smith puts it, 'but
it's got to find an end.' And so, she wearily, doggedly informs us, 'I picked up my bag, baby, and I
tried it again'. Her song ends on a very bitter and
revealing note. 'You can't trust nobody, you might
as well be alone/Found my long-lost friend, and I
might as well stayed at home!' Still, she was driven
to find that long-lost friend, to grasp again, with
fearful hope, the unwilling, unloving, human hand.

James Baldwin, 'Four AM', in *Show*, October
1964.

This was no actress, no imitator of women's woes;
there was no pretense. It was the real thing.

Carl van Vechten, in John S. Wilson, 'The Blues',
in *Show Business Illustrated*, 17 October 1961.

SMITH, DAVID

1906—65 Sculptor

My sculpture grew from painting. My analogy and
reference is with color. Flash reference and after-
image vision is historied in painting. I chew the fat
with painters. My student days, WPA days, Romany
Marie and McSorley days were with painters —
Graham, Davis, Resnikoff, De Kooning, Xceron,
Edgar Levy, Gorky, Stella, etc. In these early days
it was Cubist talk. Theirs I suppose was the Cubist
canvas, and my reference image was the Cubist
construction. The lines then had not been drawn by
the pedants — in Cubist talk, Mondrian and Kandinsky were included.

On himself, 'Notes on My Work', in *Arts Magazine*, February 1960.

I believe in perception as being the highest order of
recognition. My faith in it comes as close to an ideal
as I have. When I work, there is no consciousness of
ideals — but intuition and impulse.

Ibid.

I believe in any revolutionary idea when it's necessary — in any push against what I believe is wrong.
You do it in defense of your own convictions, even

if you feel it won't work. Revolutionary action is never lost. Something comes out of it finally.

On himself, 'Interview by Katherine Kuh', in *Artist's Voice*, 1962.

[He] is one of these artists on the order of Balzac who not only can afford their mistakes, but even need them. . . . His inability or unwillingness, to exercise self-criticism may permit Smith to indulge in illustrative cuteness or decorative whimsicality, or to descend to petty effects, but it encourages him at the same time to accept the surprises of his temperament. We get the sense of a headlong, reckless, artist who is confident of his ability to redeem in another piece whatever may go wrong in the one at hand.

Clement Greenberg, in Jane Harrison Cone, *David Smith*.

SMITH, FREDERICK EDWIN, see under BIRKEN-HEAD, EARL OF

SMITH, JOSEPH

1805—44 Prophet of the Church of Jesus Christ of the Latter Day Saints

No man knows my history. . . . If I had not experienced what I have, I could not have believed it myself.

On himself, Funeral sermon, 4 April 1844, in Fawn Brodie, *No Man Knows My History*.

This Joe Smith is undoubtedly one of the greatest characters of the age. He indicates as much talent, originality, and moral courage as Mahomet, Odin, or any of the great spirits that have hitherto produced the revolutions of past ages.

Anon., in *New York Herald*, 7 November 1842.

Who is this modern Knight with his magic lamp? It is the Green Mountain boy of old Vermont — the ignorant farmer of western New York, the unlettered fool of sectarian tales; the scourge and terror of outlawed Missouri, the favorite Military Chieftain of Illinois . . . the admired of millions . . . the dread of politicians, the revered of savages; the stumbling block of nations, and the wonder of the world; and to cap the climax, he is 'Jo Smith the Mormon Prophet.'

Anon., in *Boston Correspondent*, 22 May 1844.

The source of his power lay not in his doctrine but in his person, and the rare quality of his genius was due not to his reason but to his imagination.

Fawn Brodie, *No Man Knows My History*.

. . . best endowed with that kingly facility which directs, as by intrinsic right, the feeble or confused souls who are looking for guidance.

Josiah Quincy, *Figures of the Past from the Leaves of Old Journals*.

The Saints, the Saints, his only pride,
For them he lived, for them he died.
Their joys were his, their sorrows too;
He loved the Saints, he loved Nauvoo.

John Taylor, *The Seer*.

Whenever he found his speech growing too modern — which was about every sentence or two — he ladled in a few such scriptural phrases as 'exceeding sore', 'and it came to pass', etc., and made things satisfactory again. 'And it came to pass' was his pet. If he had left that out, his Bible would have been only a pamphlet.

Mark Twain, in M. H. Werner, *Brigham Young*.

Once in the world's history we were to have a Yankee prophet, and we have had him in Joe Smith.

John Greenleaf Whittier, *A Mormon Conventicle*.

SMITH, (LLOYD) LOGAN PEARSALL

1865—1946 Author

I love money; just to be in the room with a millionaire makes me less forlorn.

On himself, *Trivia*.

People say that life is the thing, but I prefer reading.
Ibid.

How can you say that my life is not a success? Have I not for more than sixty years got enough to eat and escaped being eaten?
Ibid.

Mr. Smith, with his dear eccentric spinsters with whom he loves to take tea and about whom, after their deaths, he writes droll but unsympathetic memoirs, with his rummaging in old English country houses for hitherto unpublished documents of mild antiquarian interest, is the ghost of James's Passionate Pilgrim, himself a little spectral in his prime, the last and faintest incarnation of Eliot's Mr. Prufrock, who has forgotten even the eagles and the trumpets and the mermaids riding seaward on the waves.

Edmund Wilson, *The Bit Between My Teeth*.

SMITH, SYDNEY

1771—1845 Wit

The Smiths never had any arms, and have invariably

693

sealed their letters with their thumbs.
> On himself, in Earl of Ilchester ed., *The Journal of Elizabeth Lady Holland, 1791—1811.*

When I am in the pulpit, I have the pleasure of see-ing my audience nod approbation while they sleep.
> On himself, attributed.

The whole of my life has passed like a razor — in hot water or a scrape.
> *Ibid.*

My idea of heaven is eating *pâtés de fois gras* to the sound of trumpets.
> *Ibid.*

You and I are the exceptions to the laws of nature; you have risen by your gravity, and I have sunk by my levity.
> On himself, remark to his brother.

I cannot cure myself of punctuality.
> On himself, in Douglas Jerrold ed., *Bon-Mots of Sydney Smith.*

SMITHERS, LEONARD

1861—1909 Publisher

He loves first editions, especially of women.
> Oscar Wilde, Letter to Reginald Turner, 10 August 1897.

SMOLLETT, TOBIAS GEORGE

1721—71 Novelist

A beggar asking Dr Smollett for alms, he gave him, through mistake, a guinea. The poor fellow, on per-ceiving it, hobbled after him to return it; upon which, Smollett returned it to him, with another guinea as a reward for his honesty, exclaiming at the same time, 'What a lodging has honesty taken up with.'
> Anon., *Anecdotes of Books and Authors.*

Smollett's 'Travels in France and Italy' . . . gives the impression of a sound, sincere personality, not very cultured in the arts, but immensely well informed, and breathing a hard, comfortable common sense at every pore. A doctor's personality, and yet still more the personality of a police magistrate; slightly less *doux*, and more downright, than that of Fielding.
> Arnold Bennett, Journal, 25 September 1907.

It is extremely strange that both Mr Dickens and Mr Thackeray, two men whose writings were so singu-larly pure, should have quoted Smollett as such a witty writer, and have considered him, or affected to consider him, their master; it would puzzle any one to find a witty passage in Dickens or Thackeray with a *double entendre* in it; it would puzzle any man to find a funny passage in Smollett without one.
> Henry Kingsley, *Fireside Studies.*

For a short period during the interregnum between Pope and Johnson he was a kind of literary Protector.
> Thomas Seccombe, *The Age of Johnson.*

Next Sm–ll–t came. What author dare resist
Historian, critic, bard, and novellist?
'To reach thy temple, honour'd Fame,' he cry'd
'Where's, where's an avenue I have not try'd?'
> Cuthbert Shaw, *The Race.*

See also Henry James, Thomas Rowlandson

SOANE, SIR JOHN

1753—1837 Architect

We are anxious that Mr. Soane, as an Architect, may be now and for ever alone. 'Let him stand for a genius' at once 'the glory and the shame' of the Art. No exertions should be spared to check the adop-tion of his manner. It is the most pernicious and vitiated. Nature, common sense, propriety, simpli-city, are all immolated to his idol, Novelty.
> Anon., in *Guardian*, 27 May 1821.

I know your constitution somewhat; it is too eager for stormy weather and easily becomes feverish.
> Rowland Burdon, Letter to Soane, 2 April 1812.

Soane affected an originality of form and decora-tion, which, not being based on any well-understood constructive principle, or any recognised form of beauty, has led to no result, and to us now appears little less than ridiculous.
> J. Fergusson, *History of the Modern Styles of Architecture.*

His handling of exterior orders is posthumously Baroque. His delight in the syncopated silhouette is essentially Picturesque — so is his concern as an interior designer with the interplay of sunlight and shadow and reflected space. And his obsession with death and destruction . . . can only be understood in terms of the sublime.
> J. Mordaunt-Crook, *The Greek Revival.*

He never possessed any real strength, moral or intellectual. He had more sensitiveness than feeling, more perseverance than power, more fancy than genius, more petulance than ardour.

    George Wightwick, *Recollections*.

SOMERSET, FITZROY JAMES HENRY, see under LORD RAGLAN

SOUSA, JOHN PHILIP

1854—1932 Composer, Bandmaster

In certain of his strains he struck an incomparably popular and vital note. He said the national thing in a certain way that no one else ever achieved, and that could be said only of this nation. . . . There is national braggadocio of the imperialistic era: Uncle Sam in his striped hat, goatee, and trousers, out to lick the world, by gum.

    Olin Downes, in Irene Downes ed., *Olin Downes on Music*.

Sousa was no Beethoven. Nonetheless, he was Sousa.

    Deems Taylor, *Of Men and Music*.

He wrote marches for this [US Marine] band, including 'Stars and Stripes Forever', a neatly assembled flame of controlled fire, guaranteed to make the lame walk.

    Ian Whitcomb, *After the Ball: Popular Song from Rag to Rock*.

SOUTHEY, ROBERT

1774—1843 Poet

Robert the Rhymer who lived at the Lakes
Describes himself thus, to prevent mistakes;
Or rather, perhaps, be it said, to correct them,
There being plenty about for those who collect
                    them. . . .
A man he is by nature merry,
Somewhat Tom-foolish, and comical, very;
Who has gone through the world, not mindful of
                    pelf,
Upon easy terms, thank Heaven, with himself. . . .
Having some friends whom he loves dearly
And no lack of foes, whom he laughs at sincerely;
And never for great, nor for little things,
Has he fretted his guts to fiddle-strings.

    On himself, *Robert the Rhymer*.

Me judice, I am a good poet, but a better historian.

    On himself, Letter to William Taylor.

My ways are as broad as the king's high-road, and my means lie in an ink-stand.

    On himself, in Edward Latham, *Famous Sayings*.

He seems to have been without taint of worldliness; London, with its pomp and vanities, learned coteries with their dry pedantry rather scared than attracted him; he found his prime glory in his genius, and his chief felicity in home-affections. I like Southey.

    Charlotte Brontë, Letter to William Smith Williams, 12 April 1850.

He had written praises of a Regicide;
    He had written praises of all kings whatever;
He had written for republics far and wide,
    And then against them bitterer than ever;
For pantisocracy he once had cried
    Aloud, a scheme less moral than 'twas clever;
Then grew a hearty anti-jacobin —
    Had turned his coat — and would have turned his
                    skin.

    Lord Byron, *The Vision of Judgment*.

Bob Southey! You're a poet — Poet laureate,
    And representative of all the race,
Although 'tis true that you've turned out a Tory at
    Last — yours has lately been a common case.

    Lord Byron, Dedication to *Don Juan*.

Yesterday, at Holland-house, I was introduced to Southey — the best looking bard I have seen for some time. To have that poet's head and shoulders, I would almost have written his Sapphics. He is certainly a prepossessing person to look on, and a man of talent, and all that.

    Lord Byron, Letter to Thomas Moore, 27 September 1813.

Southey is lean as a harrow; *dun* as a tobacco-*spluchan*; no chin (I mean the smallest), *snubbed* Roman nose, vehement brown eyes, huge *white* head of hair; when he rises, — all legs together. . . . Well-informed, rational; a good man: but perhaps so striking for nothing as for his excitability and irritability.

    Thomas Carlyle, Letter to Alexander Carlyle, 27 February 1835.

The living undertaker of epics.

    William Hazlitt, *Lectures on the English Poets*.

He seems to me to be a man of gentle feelings & bitter opinions. His opinions make him think a great many things abominable which are not so; against which accordingly he thinks it would be right, & suitable to the fitness of things, to express great indignation: but if he really feels this indignation, it is only by a voluntary act of the imagination that he conjures it up, by representing the thing to his own mind in colours suited to that passion.

John Stuart Mill, Letter to John Sterling, 20–22 October 1831.

Beneath these poppies buried deep,
    The bones of Bob the bard lie hid;
Peace to his manes; and may he sleep
    As soundly as his readers did! ...

Death, weary of so dull a writer,
    Put to his books a *finis* thus.
Oh! may the earth on him lie lighter
    Than did his quartos upon us!
Thomas Moore, *Epitaph on Robert Southey.*

Mr Southey wades through ponderous volumes of travels and old chronicles, from which he carefully selects all that is false, useless and absurd, as being essentially poetical; and when he has a commonplace book full of monstrosities, strings them into an epic.

Thomas Love Peacock, *The Four Ages of Poetry.*

A celebrated poet, Mr Feathernest, to whom the Marquis had recently given a place in exchange for his conscience. It was thought by Mr Feathernest's friends, that he had made a very good bargain. The poet had, in consequence, burned his Odes to Truth and Liberty, and had published a volume of Panegyrical Addresses 'to all the crowned heads in Europe', with the motto, 'Whatever is at court, is right.'

Thomas Love Peacock, *Melincourt.*

... I told Porson that Southey had said to me, 'My *Madoc* has brought me in a mere trifle; but that poem will be a valuable possession to my family.' Porson answered, '*Madoc* will be read — when Homer and Virgil are forgotten.'

Samuel Rogers, *Table Talk.*

See also John Keats, John Murray, Lord Russell, Sir Walter Scott.

SPARKS, JARED

1789–1866 Editor, Historian

He was looked upon as the Nestor of American historians. ...

John Spencer Bassett, *The Middle Group of American Historians.*

He could not let the father of his country speak of 'Old Put', he changed the phrase to 'General Putman'. He could not allow Washington to speak of a

sum of money as a 'flea-bite'. The sum was 'totally inadequate to our demands'. In short, he bowdlerized the political fathers, in the spirit of a neoclassical age.

Van Wyck Brooks, *The Flowering of New England, 1815–1865.*

... a professional eulogist.

Theodore Roosevelt, in Harvey Wish, *The American Historian.*

SPENCER, HERBERT

1820–1903 Philosopher, Psychologist

My *Principles of Psychology* is not 'caviare to the public', but cod-liver oil, for although it is nasty to take at the time, it does good afterwards.

On himself, in 'Two', *Home Life with Herbert Spencer.*

You see, I am like an elephant's trunk, which roots up trees and picks up sixpences.

Ibid.

It has never been my way to set before myself a problem and puzzle out an answer. The conclusions at which I have from time to time arrived, have not been arrived at as solutions to questions raised; but have been arrived at unawares — each as the ultimate outcome of a body of thoughts which slowly grew from a germ.

On himself, in *An Autobiography.*

The expression often used by Mr. Herbert Spencer of the Survival of the Fittest is more accurate, and is sometimes equally convenient.

Charles Darwin, *The Origin of Species.*

I feel rather mean when I read him: I could bear, and rather enjoy feeling that he was twice as ingenious and clever as myself, but when I feel that he is about a dozen times my superior, even in the master art of wriggling, I feel aggrieved. If he had trained himself to observe more, even at the expense, by the law of balancement, of some loss of thinking power, he would have been a wonderful man.

Charles Darwin, Letter to J. D. Hooker, December 1866.

He was very thin skinned under criticism, and shrank from argument; it excited him overmuch, and was really bad for his health. His common practice when pressed in a difficult position, was to finger his pulse and saying: 'I must not talk any more', to abruptly leave the discussion unfinished.

Of course, wicked people put a more wicked interpretation on this habit than it should in fairness bear.

Sir Francis Galton, in David Duncan, *Life of Spencer*.

Mr. Spencer is a very considerable writer, and I set great store by his works. But we are very old friends, and he has endured me as a sort of 'devil's-advocate' for thirty-odd years. He thinks that if I can pick no holes in what he says he is safe. But I pick a great many holes, and we agree to differ.

T. H. Huxley, Letter to Lady Welby, April 1884.

Oh! you know, Spencer's idea of a tragedy is a deduction killed by a fact.

T. H. Huxley, in Herbert Spencer, *An Autobiography*.

He is so good that he ought to be better. His *a priori* system is more consistent than Hamilton's, but quite as fundamentally absurd; in fact there is the same erroneous assumption at the bottom of both. And most of his general principles strike me as being little more than verbal or at most empirical generalizations, with no warrant for their being considered laws.

John Stuart Mill, Letter to Alexander Bain, March 1864.

He is a considerable thinker, though anything but safe — and is on the whole an ally, in spite of his Universal Postulate. . . . His notion that we cannot think the annihilation or diminution of force I remember well — and I thought it out-Whewelled Whewell. The conservation of thought has hardly yet got to be believed, and already its negation is declared inconceivable. But this is Spencer all over; he throws himself with a certain deliberate impetuosity into the last new theory that chimes with his general way of thinking, and treats it as proved as soon as he is able to found a connected exposition of phenomena upon it.

Ibid.

See also George Eliot, Jack London

SPENSER, EDMUND

1552?—99 Poet

Old *Spencer* next, warm'd with Poetick Rage,
In Antick Tales amus'd a Barb'rous Age;
An Age that yet uncultivate and Rude,
Where-e're the Poet's Fancy led, pursu'd
Through pathless Fields, and unfrequented Floods,
To Dens of Dragons, and Enchanted Woods.

Joseph Addison, in *Annual Miscellany*, 1694.

At *Delphos* shrine, one did a doubt propound,
Which by th'Oracle must be released,
Whether of poets were the best renown'd:
Those that survive, or they that are deceased?
The Gods made answer by divine suggestion,
While *Spencer* is alive, it is no question.

Francis Beaumont, *On Mr Edm. Spencer, Famous Poet*.

Spencer . . .
. . . lost a *Noble* Muse in *Fairy-land*.

Knightly Chetwood, *Commendatory Verses prefixed to An Essay on Translated Verse, by the Earl of Roscommon*.

Our ancient verse, (as homely as the Times),
Was rude, unmeasur'd, only lagg'd with Rhymes:
Number and Cadence, that have since been Shown,
To those unpolish'd Writers were unknown.
Fairfax was He, who, in that Darker Age,
By his just Rules restrain'd Poetic Rage;
Spencer did next in Pastorals excel,
And taught the Noble Art of Writing well:
To stricter Rules the Stanza did restrain,
And found for Poetry a richer Veine.

John Dryden, *The Art of Poetry*.

Spencer more than once insinuates, that the Soul of *Chaucer* was transfus'd into his Body; and that he was begotten by him Two hundred years after his Decease. *Milton* has acknowledg'd to me, that *Spenser* was his Original.

John Dryden, Preface to *The Fables*.

Discouraged, scorn'd, his writings vilified,
Poorly — poor man — he liv'd; poorly — poor man — he died.

Phineas Fletcher, *The Purple Island*, canto 4.

There passeth a story commonly told and believed, that *Spencer* presenting his Poems to Queen *Elizabeth*: She highly affected therewith, commanded the Lord *Cecil* Her Treasurer, to give him an hundred pound; and when the Treasurer (a good Steward of the Queens money) alledged that sum was too much, then *give him* (quoth the Queen) *what is reason*; to which the Lord consented, but was so busied, belike, about matters of higher concernment, that *Spencer* received no reward; Whereupon he presented this petition in a small piece of paper to the Queen in her Progress,

I was promis'd on a time,
To have reason for my rhyme;
From that time unto this season,
I receiv'd nor rhyme nor reason.

Hereupon the Queen gave strict order (not without some check to her Treasurer) for the present payment of the hundred pounds, the first intended unto him.

Thomas Fuller, *The History of the Worthies of England*.

The poet of imaginative Protestantism.
S. R. Gardiner, *Cromwell's Place in History*, 1897.

The Nobility of the Spensers has been illustrated and enriched by the trophies of Marlborough, but I exhort them to consider the Faerie Queene as the most precious jewel of their coronet.
Edward Gibbon, *Memoirs*.

It is said he was a Stranger to Mr *Sidney* (afterwards Sir *Philip*) when he had begun to write his *Fairy Queen*, and that he took occasion to go to *Leicester*-House, and to introduce himself by sending in to Mr *Sidney* a Copy of the Ninth Canto of the First Book of that Poem. Mr *Sidney* was much surpriz'd with the Description of *Despair* in that Canto, and is said to have shewn an unusual kind of Transport on the Discovery of so new and uncommon a Genius. After he had read some Stanza's, he turn'd to his Steward, and bid him give the Person that brought those verse Fifty Pounds; but upon reading the next Stanza, he order'd the Sum to be doubled. The Steward was no less surpriz'd than his Master, and thought it his Duty to make some Delay in executing so sudden and lavish a Bounty; but upon reading one Stanza more, Mr *Sidney* rais'd his Gratuity to Two Hundred Pounds, and commanded the Steward to give it immediately, lest as he read further, he might be tempted to give away his whole Estate. From this time he admitted the Author to his Aquaintance and Conversation, and prepar'd the way of his being known and receiv'd at Court.
J. Hughes, *The Life of Mr Edmund Spenser*.

That virtue therefore which is but a youngling in the contemplation of evil, and knows not the utmost that vice promises to her followers, and rejects it, is but a blank virtue, not a pure; her whiteness is but an excremental whiteness; Which was the reason why our sage and serious Poet Spenser, whom I dare be known to think a better teacher than Scotus or Aquinas, describing true temperance under the person of Guion, brings him in with his palmer through the cave of Mammon, and the bower of earthly bliss that he might see and know, and yet abstain.
John Milton, *Areopagitica*.

See also Ben Jonson, Leigh Hunt, Shakespeare, William Butler Yeats

STANFORD, SIR CHARLES VILLIERS
1852–1924 Composer

I apologize for anything I have said, am saying, or may at any future time say.
On himself, *Pages from an Unwritten Diary*, 1914.

I shall always prefer beauty of tone to strength of music.
Ibid.

The stuff I hate and which I know is ruining any chance for good music in England is stuff like Stanford's which is neither fish, flesh, fowl nor good red-herring.
Edward Elgar, Letter to A. J. Jaeger, 11 December 1898.

Difficult to please, and most glad to be pleased.
Ivor Gurney, in *Music and Letters*, July 1924.

Stanford is all crotchets and fads and moods.
Gustav Holst, Letter to Ralph Vaughan Williams, 1903.

His very facility prevented him from knowing when he was genuinely inspired and when his work was routine stuff.
Ralph Vaughan Williams, at the Composers' Concourse, 1957.

See also Ralph Vaughan Williams

STANHOPE, LADY HESTER LUCY
1776–1839 Eccentric

Lady Hester's was a nose of wild ambitions, of pride grown fantastical, a nose that scorned the earth, shooting off, one fancies, towards some eternally eccentric heaven. It was a nose, in fact, altogether in the air.
Lytton Strachey, *Books and Characters*: 'Lady Hester Stanhope'.

STANHOPE, PHILIP DORMER, see under CHESTERFIELD, LORD

STANLEY, EDWARD GEORGE GEOFFREY SMITH, see under DERBY, EARL OF

STANLEY, SIR HENRY MORTON

1841–1904 Explorer

I am partial to adventures, but I never attempt the impossible.
> On himself, to King Leopold II, April 1890, in Frank Hird, *H. M. Stanley: The Authoritative Life.*

He went not forth to conquer but to pave;
And though from half a world he hath removed
The cloud of death and darkness, those he loved
Lie far in some unvisitable grave.
Wherefore our England now goes forth to meet him
With hands outstretched, and silent — eye to eye,
Because her heart is full and tears are by;
So does our England greet him
And brings the long lost, weary wanderer home.
> Anon., *Welcome to Stanley.*

Mr. Stanley's elocution is bad, though it improves as he gets into his discourse. . . . If he has half the courage before an average civilized audience that he showed in the wilds of Africa he can at once overcome his deficiencies. To do this he, of course, must forego his manuscript, and, forgetting the singsong and doleful monotone in which his voice is too often pitched, simply talk to his auditors of what he saw, heard and suffered while doing his duty so nobly to the Herald, to humanity, and to science.
> Anon. *Herald* reporter commenting on Stanley's first lecture in America, in Arthur Montefiore, *Life of Henry M. Stanley.*

He represented both the old romance of adventurous travel and the new romance of mechanical efficiency. It was his luck to do considerable things exactly at the time when exploration had become scientific, but had not ceased to be picturesque. A generation before, there was glamour, but little good business in the conquest of the wild; on the whole, the betting was decidedly on the wild. A generation later the glamour had largely departed, though the business was very good business indeed. But in the high and palmy days of Stanley, the explorer had the best of both worlds. He was admired as a disinterested knight errant, and rewarded handsomely for not being one.
> E. T. Raymond, *Portraits of the Nineties.*

The nineteenth century had a pathetic faith in its Press, and even in the American Press; and it revelled in the vision of one strong, silent man, by the power of a mighty banking account, hurling a second strong, silent man across a dark continent to the succour of a third strong, silent man.
> *Ibid.*, also referring to J. C. Bennett of the *New York Herald.*

In the mixture of the absurd and the serious . . . Mark Twain compared Stanley favorably with Columbus: Columbus started out to discover America, but all he had to do was to sit in his cabin and hold his grip and sail straight on, and America would discover itself. Here it was, barring his passage the whole length and breadth of the South American continent, and he couldn't get by it. He'd got to discover it. But Stanley started out to find Dr. Livingstone, who was scattered abroad, as you may say, length and breadth of a vast slab of Africa as big as the United States. It was a blind kind of search.
> Mark Twain, reported in Arthur Montefiore, *The Life of Henry M. Stanley.*

STANTON, EDWIN MCMASTERS

1814–69 Politician

I do not see how he survives, why he is not crushed and torn to pieces. Without him I should be destroyed.
> Abraham Lincoln, Letter to George Julian and Owen Lovejoy.

. . . the man's public character is a public mistake.
> Abraham Lincoln, Comment to T. S. Barnett.

[Stanton] is the most unmitigated scoundrel I ever knew, heard or read of; if Stanton had lived during Jesus' lifetime, Judas Iscariot would have remained a respected member of the fraternity of apostles.
> George Brinton McClellan, in Benjamin P. Thomas and Harold M. Hyman, *Stanton: The Life and Times of Lincoln's Secretary of War.*

All men die and death does not change faults into virtues.
> Manton Marble, in *New York World* (on the death of Stanton), 1869.

Stanton was a dangerous foe — a sleuth hound sort of a man who never lost his scent or slackened his purpose.
> Samuel Ward, in Benjamin P. Thomas and Harold M. Hyman, *Stanton: The Life and Times of Lincoln's Secretary of War.*

STANTON, ELIZABETH CADY

1815–1902 Suffragette

If Mrs Stanton would attend a little more to her domestic duties and a little less to those of the great public, perhaps she would exalt her sex quite as much as she does by quixotically fighting wind-mills in their gratuitous behalf, and might possibly set a notable example of domestic felicity. No married woman can convert herself into a feminine Knight of the Rueful Visage and ride about the country attempting to redress imaginary wrongs without leaving her own household in a neglected condition that must be an eloquent witness against her.

> Anon., in *New York Sunday Times*, January 1868.

Heigh! ho! the carrion crow
Mrs Stanton's all the go:
Twenty tailors take the stitches,
Mrs Stanton wears the breeches.

> Anon. song quoted by Elizabeth Stanton in a letter to Elizabeth Smith Miller (Mrs Stanton's bloomer costume made good election propaganda for her husband).

As usual when she had fired her gun she went home and left me to finish the battle.

> Susan B. Anthony, after Mrs Stanton had addressed a convention on the subject of divorce, June 1860.

... that such mental powers must be hampered with such a *clumsy body* — oh — if we could only give her elasticity of limbs — and locomotive powers.

> Susan B. Anthony, Letter to Elizabeth Smith Miller, 15 February 1892.

Mrs Stanton is my sentence maker, my pen artist.

> Susan B. Anthony, in Ida Husted Harper, *Life and Work of Susan B. Anthony*, vol. 1.

STEELE, SIR RICHARD

1672—1729 Essayist, Dramatist, Politician

As to the vilest of mankind it would be a glorious world if I were. For I would not conceal my thought in favour of an injured man, though all the powers on earth gainsaid it, to be made the first man in the nation.

> On himself, Letter to Jonathan Swift, 26 May 1713.

He maintained a perpetual struggle between reason and appetite.

> Theophilus Cibber, *Lives of the Poets*.

It is our belief that no man so much as Steele has suffered from *compassion*. It was out of his own bitter experience that he shrewdly called it, himself, the best disguise of malice, and said that the most apposite course to cry a man down was to lament him.

> John Forster, *Biographical Essays*.

Wit more piercing and keen, a reflective spirit of wider scope, a style more correct and pure, even humour more consummate than his own, will be found in the way of comment upon life, among his friends and fellow-labourers: but for that which vividly brings actual life before us, which touches the heart as with a present experience, which sympathises to the very core with all that moves the joy or sorrow of his fellows, and which still, even as then can make the follies of men ridiculous, and their vices hateful without branding ridicule or hate upon the men themselves — we must turn to Steele.

> *Ibid.*

The comedies of Steele were the first that were written expressly with a view not to imitate the manners, but to reform the morale of the age. The author seems to be all the time on his good behaviour, as if writing a comedy was no very creditable employment, and as if the ultimate object of his ambition was a dedication to the Queen. Nothing can be better meant, or more inefficient.

> William Hazlitt, *The Comic Writers of Last Century*.

A scholar among rakes, and a rake among scholars.

> T. B. Macaulay, *Essays*: 'The Life and Writings of Addison'.

I am recreating my mind with the brisk sallies and quick turns of wit, which Mr Steele in his liveliest and freest humours darts about him.

> Alexander Pope, Letter to Caryll, 14 August 1713.

Methinks I hear thee loud as trumpet,
As bagpipe shrill, or oyster-strumpet;
Methinks I see thee, spruce and fine,
With coat embroider'd richly shine
And dazzle all the idol faces
As through the hall thy worship paces. . . .

> Jonathan Swift, *Imitations of Horace*, ode 1, book 2.

But if I may with freedom talk,
All this is foreign to thy walk:
Thy genius has perhaps a knack
At trudging in a beaten track,
But is for state-affairs as fit
As mine for politicks or wit.
Then let us both in time grow wise,
Nor higher than our talents rise;
To some snug cellar we'll repair
From duns and debts, and drown our care.

> *Ibid.*

STEFFENS, (JOSEPH) LINCOLN

1866—1936 Journalist, Reformer

The thing for me to do, I decided, was to leave the universities, go into business or politics, and see, not what thinkers thought, but what practical men did and why.

On himself, in Charles A. Madison, *Critics and Crusaders*.

I have not lived in vain. The world which I tried so hard, so dumbly, to change has changed me. . . . My life was worth my living. And as for the world in general, all that was or is or ever will be wrong with that is my — our thinking about it.

On himself, in Russell M. Horton, *Lincoln Steffens*.

I always thought he was at his best, doing his greatest work — in the sense of complete self-fulfillment — in the days when he was still the eager, observant, thirsty reporter striving first of all to understand. When the conscious reformer stepped in and took him over the less effective he seemed — to me — to be.

Ray Stannard Baker, in Russell M. Horton, *ibid*.

What Steffens gives is a hard ground lit by a cool, clear light: the seeing of things as things in fact are.

Barrows Dunham, Introduction to Ella Winters and Herbert Shapiro eds, *The World of Lincoln Steffens*.

This little Machiavellian, itinerant preacher went up and down upon the earth shaking it in his own way. He said the same things over and over, gently, subtly, and unendingly.

Mabel Dodge Luhan, in Russell M. Horton, *ibid*.

. . . he never let up on these fishing expeditions into the deep sea currents, the sun spots and ice floes, of his swarming, alive mind.

Carl Sandburg, in Russell M. Horton, *Lincoln Steffens*.

He had ways kin to Socrates, the asker of questions, whims allying him to Diogenes, who with mockery and a lantern sought an honest man by daylight in the streets of Athens. . . .

Ibid.

STEIN, GERTRUDE

1874—1946 Poet, Author

Think of the Bible and Homer, think of Shakespeare and think of me.

On herself, in B. L. Reid, *Art by Subtraction*.

Now listen! I'm no fool. I know that in daily life we don't go around saying 'is a . . . is . . . is . . .' Yes, I'm no fool; but I think that in that line the rose is red for the first time in English poetry for a hundred years.

On herself, in John Malcolm Brinnin, *The Third Rose*.

I have been the creative literary mind of the century.

Ibid.

Reading Gertrude Stein at length is not unlike making one's way through an interminable and badly printed game book.

Richard Bridgeman, *Gertrude Stein in Pieces*.

While she believed that most writers failed to allow writing to express all that it could, in her own practice she scrupulously saw to it that writing expressed less than it would.

John Malcolm Brinnin, *The Third Rose*.

The supreme egocentric of the most perfect clique of egocentrics.

Oscar Cargill, in B. L. Reid, *Art by Subtraction*.

To produce pure proletarian art the artist must be at one with the worker; this is impossible, not for political reasons, but because the artist never is at one with any public. The grandest attempt to escape from this is provided by Gertrude Stein, who claims to be a direct expression of the Zeitgeist (the present stage of the dialectic process) and therefore to need no other relation to a public of any kind. She has in fact a very definite relation to her public, and I should call her work a version of child-cult. . . .

William Empson, *Some Versions of Pastoral*.

My notion is that Miss Stein has set herself to solve, and has succeeded in solving, the most difficult problem in prose composition — to write something that will not arrest the attention in any way, manner, shape, or form. If you think this is easy, try it. I know of no one except Miss Stein who can roll out this completely non-resistant prose, prose that puts you at once in a condition resembling the early stages of grippe — the eyes and legs heavy, the top of the skull wandering around in an uncertain and independent manner, the heart ponderously, tiredly beating.

Clifton Fadiman, in B. L. Reid, *Art by Subtraction*.

Miss Stein was a past master in making nothing happen very slowly.

Clifton Fadiman, *The Selected Writings of Clifton Fadiman*: 'Puzzlements'.

What an old covered-wagon she is!
  F. Scott Fitzgerald, in John Malcolm Brinnin,
  The Third Rose.

Gertrude Stein and me are just like brothers. . . .
  Ernest Hemingway, in John Malcolm Brinnin,
  ibid.

Eschewing Joyce's concern with myth and historical
cycles and Proust's obsession with memory, Miss
Stein is primarily concerned with the concept of the
continuous and ongoing present.
  Michael Hoffman, *The Development of Abstrac-*
  tionism in the Writings of Gertrude Stein.

Gertrude Stein's prose-song is a cold, black suet-
pudding. We can represent it as a cold suet-roll of
fabulously reptilian length. Cut it at any point, it is
the same thing; the same heavy, sticky, opaque mass
all through, and all along . . . it is mournful and
monstrous, composed of dead and inanimate
material. It is all fat, without nerve. . . .
  Percy Wyndham Lewis, in John Malcolm Brinnin,
  The Third Rose.

She was a golden brown presence, burned by the
Tuscan sun and with a golden glint in her warm
brown hair. She was dressed in a warm brown cor-
duroy suit. She wore a large round coral brooch and
when she talked, very little, or laughed, a good deal,
I thought her voice came from this brooch. It was
unlike anyone else's voice — deep, full, velvety like
a great contralto's, like two voices. She was large
and heavy with delicate small hands and a beautifully modelled and unique head. It was often compared to a Roman emperor's. . . .
  Alice B. Toklas, upon first meeting Miss Stein,
  What is Remembered.

She has outdistanced any of the symbolists in using
words for pure purposes of suggestion — she has
gone so far that she no longer even suggests.
  Edmund Wilson, in B. L. Reid, *Art by Subtrac-*
  tion.

See also Albert Einstein, Percy Wyndham Lewis,
Alice B. Toklas

STEINBECK, JOHN ERNST

1902—68 Author

Biology and myth provide the two poles of Steinbeck's world, tide pool and paradise.
  Joseph Fontenrose, *John Steinbeck, An Intro-*
  duction and Interpretation.

Exploring as broadly as possible the secret of the
species man, he presented himself simultaneously
as storyteller, fabulist, critic of social institutions,
innovative stylist, and appraiser of experience in
philosophical terms.
  James Gray, *John Steinbeck.*

His remarkable, almost uncanny ability to meet the
intellectual and emotional needs of a depression-
trained reading public contrasts vividly with the
work of those novelists who, with almost missionary
zeal, were trying to influence the public mind.
  Frederick J. Hoffman, *The Modern Novel in*
  America.

Nothing in his books is so dim, insignificantly
enough, as the human beings who live in them, and
few of them are intensely imagined as human beings
at all.
  Alfred Kazin, *On Native Grounds.*

After a dozen books Steinbeck still looks like a distinguished apprentice, and what is so striking in his
work is its inconclusiveness, his moving approach
to human life and yet his failure to be creative with
it.
  Ibid.

His career is something of a casualty, and a casualty
I think in this particular case of an unlucky wedding
between art and rebellion which developed into a
fatal marital hostility between the poetic and the
political impulse. His career to date has the shape of
a suggestive, a representative, and a completely
honourable failure.
  R. W. B. Lewis, 'John Steinbeck, The Fitful
  Daemon', in Carl Bode ed., *The Young Rebel in*
  American Literature.

The world of John Steinbeck's novels is a beautiful
warm valley with disaster hanging over it. This is the
essential feature story after story. Steinbeck may
change his outlook, as he has from the lyric to the
sociological, or he may change his technical
approach, as he has from romantic to dramatic narrative, but the valley microcosm remains as the
setting of his work, and his people continue to be
foredoomed with an almost calvinistic regularity.
  Harry Thornton Moore, *The Novels of John*
  Steinbeck.

STEPHEN, KING

circa 1097–1154

Stephen was no hero. Although he was an excellent
warrior and showed enterprise and speed in the

beginning of campaigns and sieges, he too often failed to complete them; and though he seemed cheerful and gay, beneath the surface he was mistrustful and sly. He was basically smallminded, and as a result he did not inspire the devotion which his grandfather or uncle had inspired; even his panegyrist, the author of the *Gesta Stephani*, found him colourless.

R. H. C. Davis, *King Stephen*.

He was a man of great renown in the practice of arms, but for the rest almost an incompetent, except that he was rather inclined to evil.

Walter Map, *De Nugis Curialium*, translated from the Latin by F. Tupper and M. B. Ogle.

STEPHEN, SIR LESLIE

1832–1904 Editor, Historian

His accomplishments as editor, biographer, historian of ideas, essay-writing alpinist are still fairly common knowledge, while his criticism has a tart flavour which recommends it to modern tastes, and marks him off from all but a tiny handful of his contemporaries. It is true that latter-day admirers have sometimes paid too much attention to his purely negative virtues as a critic, but it must be conceded that these are an essential part of his appeal. He knew how to make short work of mawkishness or affectation. He was expert at showing up impostors for what they were. In an age of histrionics he kept a cool head, and his lack of enthusiasm can be infectious.

John Gross, *The Rise and Fall of the Man of Letters*.

Leslie Stephen in old age was much given to groaning audibly, like many distinguished Victorians, particularly if they were widowers. . . . Mr Gibbs was an old friend of the Stephen family and at more or less regular intervals used to come and dine with them at Hyde Park Gate. He had been tutor for six or seven years to the Prince of Wales . . . and in spite or because of this was a bit of a bore. . . . On the nights when Mr Gibbs came to dinner, towards 10 o'clock, Leslie Stephen would start groaning and saying at intervals quite audibly: 'O why doesn't he go; O why doesn't he go!'

Leonard Woolf, *Beginning Again*.

STEPHENS, ALEXANDER HAMILTON

1812–83 Politician

My God, there is nothing about him but lungs and brains.

Anon., 1855, in R. R. Von Abele, *Alexander H. Stephens*.

A little way up the aisle sits a queer-looking bundle. An immense cloak, a high hat, and peering somewhere out of the middle a thin, pale, sad little face. This brain and eyes enrolled in countless thicknesses of flannel and broadcloth wrappings belong to Hon. Alexander H. Stephens, of Georgia. How anything so small and sick and sorrowful could get here all the way from Georgia is a wonder. If he were to draw his last breath at any instant you would not be surprised. If he were laid out in his coffin he need not look any different, only when the fires would have gone out in those burning eyes.

Ibid., 1876.

Mr. Stephens is slightly above medium height, and painfully thin in appearance. His head is small and flat; his forehead low, and partially covered with straight dark, lustre-lacking hair; and his cheek, thin, wrinkled, and of parchment texture. His walk, his features, his figure bespeak great physical emaciation. You look in vain for some outward manifestation of that towering, commanding intellect which has held the congregated talent of the country spellbound for hours . . . but you still feel convinced that the feeble, tottering being before you is all brain — brain in the head, brain in the arms, brain in the legs, brain in the body — that the whole man is charged and surcharged with electricity of intellect, that a touch would bring forth the divine spark.

Anon., in E. Ramsay Richardson, *Little Aleck*.

Alexander Stephens does not emulate the modesty of the rose. He positively refuses to 'pine upon the bush.' He is not only ready to be plucked, but means to oblige somebody to pluck him. He feels that his dear Georgia can not get along without him in Washington. . . . This little irrepressible human steam engine, with a big brain and scarcely any body, is one of the most accomplished parliamentarians the world has ever seen. . . . Let him come back.

Ibid., on Stephens' return to Congress after the Civil War.

I could swallow him whole and never know the difference.

Judge Walter T. Colquitt, in *ibid*.

Never have I seen so small a nubbin come out of so much husk.

Abraham Lincoln, on meeting Stephens, in R. R. Von Abele, *Alexander H. Stephens*.

STEPHENSON, GEORGE

1781—1848 Inventor

Stephenson, the great Engineer, told Lichfield that he had travelled on the Manchester and Liverpool railroad for many miles at the rate of a mile a minute, but his doubt was not how fast his Engines could be made to go, but at what pace it would be proper to stop, that he could make them travel with greater speed than any bird can cleave the air, and he had ascertained that 400 miles an hour was the extreme velocity which the human frame could endure.

Charles Greville, Diary, 28 January 1834.

The whole secret of Mr. Stephenson's success in life was his careful improvement of time, which is the rock out of which fortunes are carved and great characters formed. He believed in genius to the extent that Buffon did when he said that 'patience is genius'; or as some other thinker put it, when he defined genius to be the power of making efforts. But he never would have it that he was a genius, or that he had done anything which other men, equally laborious and persevering as himself, could not have accomplished. He repeatedly said to the young men about him: 'Do as I have done — persevere!'

Samuel Smiles, *Lives of the Engineers*.

See also Samuel Smiles

STERNE, LAURENCE

1713—68 Author

Ah, I am as bad as that dog Sterne, who preferred whining over 'a dead ass to relieving a living mother' — villain — hypocrite — slave — sycophant! but *I* am no better.

Lord Byron, Journal, 1 December 1813.

Much as has been said against him, we cannot help feeling his immense love for things around him; so that we may say of him, as of Magdalen, 'much is forgiven him, because he loved much.' A good simple being after all.

Thomas Carlyle, *Lectures on the History of Literature*.

Sterne's morals are bad, but I don't think they can do much harm to any one whom they would not find bad enough before. Besides, the oddity and erudite grimaces under which much of his dirt is hidden take away the effect for the most part; although, to be sure, the book [*Tristram Shandy*] is scarcely readable by women.

Samuel Taylor Coleridge, *Table Talk*, 18 August 1833.

Mr Sterne it may be supposed, was no great favourite with Dr Johnson, and a lady once ventured to ask the grave Doctor, 'how he liked Yorick's sermons'. — 'I know nothing about them, Madam,' was his reply. But sometime afterwards, forgetting himself, he severely censured them; and the lady very aptly retorted; 'I understood you to say, Sir, that you had never read them.' — 'No, Madam, I did read them, but it was in a stage coach; I should not have even deigned to have looked at them, had I been at large.'

J. Cradock, *Literary and Miscellaneous Memories*.

His works consist only of *morceaux* — of brilliant passages.

William Hazlitt, *Lectures on the English Comic Writers*.

Tristram Shandy may perhaps go on a little longer; but we will not follow him. With all his drollery there is a sameness of extravagance which tires us. We have just a succession of Surprise, surprise, surprise.

David Hume, in James Boswell, *Private Papers from Malahide Castle*.

That great spunky unflincher.

B. S. Johnson, *See the Old Lady Decently*.

Nothing odd will do long. *Tristram Shandy* did not last.

Samuel Johnson, in James Boswell, Journal, 26 March 1776.

The immense popularity of Sterne, which elicited one volume of *Tristram Shandy* after another, is astonishing to the twentieth century, in which its only readers are probably those specifically concerned with literature, for to the general reader it is interminably dull, without either plot or point. Sterne requires careful and persevering reading, but the reward is an extremely subtle kind of pleasure.

Q. D. Leavis, *Fiction and the Reading Public*.

Oh, bless'd Compassion! Angel Charity!
More dear one genuine deed perform'd for thee,
Than all the periods Feeling e'er can turn,
Than all thy soothing pages, polish'd STERNE!
Hannah More, *Sacred Dramas (Sensibility)*.

Soon after *Tristram* appeared, Sterne asked a Yorkshire lady of fortune and condition whether she had read his book. 'I have not, Mr Sterne,' was the answer; 'and, to be plain with you, I am informed it is not proper for female perusal.' — 'My dear good lady,' replied the author, 'do not be gulled by such stories; the book is like your young heir there,' (pointing to a child of three years old, who was roll-

ing on the carpet in his white tunic) 'he shows at times a good deal that is usually concealed, but it is all in perfect innocence!'
Sir Walter Scott, *Laurence Sterne*.

See also Thomas Hardy, W. M. Thackeray

STEVENS, THADDEUS

1792—1868 Politician, Lawyer

You have heard that I am one of the devil's children and that this club foot of mine is proof of my parentage.
On himself, in *Gettysburg Star and Sentinel*, 7 July 1874.

I wish I were the owner of every Southern slave, that I might cast off the shackles from their limbs, and witness the rapture which would excite them in the first dance of their freedom.
On himself, in Fawn M. Brodie, *Thaddeus Stevens, Scourge of the South*.

Whoever cracked Thaddeus Stevens' skull would let out the brains of the Republican Party.
Anon., saying in *ibid*.

. . . Your old friend, Thad. Stevens, as soon as he has fixed our currency, is going to regulate by law the rising of the sun, so that the days shall be of equal length all the year round.
Charles Francis Adams Jr, Letter to his Father.

[Stevens'] mind, so far as his sense of obligation to God was concerned, was a howling wilderness.
Jeremiah Black, in Alphonse B. Miller, *Thaddeus Stevens*.

This man in his den was as much a revolutionist as Marat in his tub. Had he lived in France in the days of the Terror, he would have pushed one of the triumvirate desperately for his place, have risen rapidly to the top through his genius and audacity and will, and probably have died by the guillotine with the sardonic smile upon his face.
Claude A. Bowers, *The Tragic Era*.

His reputation remains many-sided partly because his character and history were full of paradoxes and contradictions. He was a humanitarian lacking in humanity; a man of boundless charities and vindictive hates; a Calvinist convinced that all men are vile who nevertheless cherished a vision of the Promised Land where all men should be equal before the law; a revolutionary who would carve up the estates of the 'bloated aristocrats' of the South, but in the

same breath offer to defend Jefferson Davis in his trial for treason. . . .
Fawn M. Brodie, *Thaddeus Stevens, Scourge of the South*.

He was an abolitionist, before there was such a party name.
O. J. Dickey, in *Congressional Globe*, 17 December 1868.

> To the Memory of
> Thaddeus Stevens
> Ah, Alas, Alas,
> the
> Great unchained
> is
> Chained at last.

John H. McClellan, in Fawn M. Brodie, *Thaddeus Stevens, Scourge of the South*.

Scholar, wit, zealot of liberty, part fanatic, part gambler, at his worst a clubfooted wrangler possessed of endless javelins, at his best a majestic and isolated figure wandering in an ancient wilderness thick with thorns, seeking to bring justice between man and man — who could read the heart of limping, poker-faced old Thaddeus Stevens?
Carl Sandburg, *Abraham Lincoln, The War Years*.

Nobody said more in fewer words or gave to language a sharper bite. Speech was with him a cat-o'-nine-tails, and woe to the victim on whom the terrible lash descended.
Charles Sumner, in Alphonse B. Miller, *Thaddeus Stevens*.

STEVENS, WALLACE

1879—1955 Poet, Businessman

Life is an affair of people not of places. But for me life is an affair of places and that is the trouble.
On himself, in William Burney, *Wallace Stevens*.

Stevens' place is therefore clearly in the tradition of existentialist romanticism. The fertile fact or sensation is primary; everything including the existence or non-existence of God, follows from that. The only order worth looking for is the order of chaos itself.
William Burney, in *ibid*.

But until the end of his life his poetic style remained marked by a kind of intelligent dandyism, never soft or merely pretty, always hard as a diamond and regally controlled.
Max J. Herzberg, *The Reader's Encyclopedia of American Literature*.

At the bottom of Stevens' poetry there is wonder and delight, the child's or animal's or savage's — man's — joy in his own existence, and thankfulness for it.

> Randall Jarrell, 'The Collected Poems of Wallace Stevens', in Ashley Brown and Robert S. Haller eds, *The Achievement of Wallace Stevens.*

Wallace Stevens was really very much annoyed at being catalogued, categorized, and compelled to be scientific about what he was doing — to give satisfaction, to answer the teachers. He wouldn't do that. He was independent.

> Marianne Moore, in Charles Tomlinson ed., *Marianne Moore, A Collection of Critical Essays.*

The irony, the humor, the self-satire, are means by which Stevens' comic imagination keeps the proper distance from things, even if they are his own ideas, and protects the poet from defining the world by his own passions.

> Robert Pack, *Wallace Stevens.*

The merging of the abstract and the mental with the concrete and the sensual is perhaps the most characteristic quality of Stevens' style. If a poem begins with a generalization, he will proceed to illustrate it, or, if a poem commences with a series of illustrative particulars, it will end with a generalization.

> *Ibid.*

Taken generally, Stevens' perspective is that of the man of art, the museum — and concert-goer, the student of French poetry . . . the aesthete in the best sense of the word.

> Delmore Schwartz, in Stanley J. Kunitz and Howard Haycraft eds, *Twentieth Century Authors.*

Something of the talent of a Sherlock Holmes is needed to penetrate Stevens' oblique implications. His poetry is keyed to readers who delight in solving puzzles.

> George F. Whicher, 'The Twentieth Century', in Arthur Hobson Quinn ed., *The Literature of the American People.*

His gift for combining words is baffling and fantastic but sure: even when you do not know what he is saying, you know that he is saying it well.

> Edmund Wilson, 'Wallace Stevens and E. E. Cummings', in S. U. Baum ed., *e. e. cummings and the Critics.*

STEVENSON, ADLAI EWING

1900—65 Statesman, Diplomat, Lawyer

Someone asked . . . how I felt [on being defeated for the Presidency by Dwight Eisenhower] and I was reminded of a story that a fellow townsman of ours used to tell — Abraham Lincoln. They asked him how he felt once after an unsuccessful election. He said he felt like a little boy who has stubbed his toe in the dark. He said that he was too old to cry, but it hurt too much to laugh.

> On himself, Speech of 5 November 1952.

I regret that I have but one law firm to give to my country.

> On himself, referring to the Kennedy administration's use of lawyers from his Chicago office.

It's an odd thing to say, but everybody who has served at the United Nations has known me personally or by my writings or travel. And they were about 98 percent pro-Democratic during my campaigns. I've often said it was a damn shame I ran for President of the wrong country.

> On himself, in Alden Whitman, *Portrait, Adlai E. Stevenson, Politician, Diplomat, Friend.*

Through all the placid confidence of the Eisenhower era and the clumsy crusades of Dulles, he reminded the world that there was another America — sensitive, self critical, thoughtful and visionary. At home he kept the light of intellect burning through a period when it was not fashionable to think.

> Anon., in *The Times*, 14 July 1965.

. . . Adlai Stevenson, no matter how many holes his shoe soles bore, no matter how steeped he was in the lore of Lincoln, couldn't fool them [the voters] he wasn't folks.

> Anon., in *Newsweek*, 26 July 1965.

. . . unexceptional as a glass of decent Beaujolais.

> *Ibid.*

The verdict may be that it was not only his wit but his psyche that was out of phase with the times. He remained a gentleman in the face of a declining political market for civility.

> Henry S. Ashmore, in Edward P. Doyle ed., *As We Knew Adlai, The Stevenson Story by Twenty-Two Friends.*

He believed in us, perhaps more than we deserved. And so we came to believe in ourselves, more than we had.

> Lyndon Baines Johnson, in H. J. Muller, *Adlai Stevenson: A Study in Values.*

My God, in this job, he's got the nerve of a burglar.

> John F. Kennedy, commenting on Stevenson as United States Ambassador to the United Nations, in *Time*, 24 February 1961.

Stevenson himself hasn't even backbone training, for he is a graduate of Dean Acheson's spineless school of diplomacy which cost the free world 600,000,000 former allies in the past seven years of Trumanism.

> Richard M. Nixon, 10 October 1952, in S. G. Brown, *Conscience in Politics: Adlai E. Stevenson in the 1950s.*

You would be as likely, in fact, to find Adlai Stevenson in public without his pants as without the protective armor of his calm, urbane self-assurance.

> Cabell Phillips, in *New York Times Magazine*, September 1965.

... Stevenson had made Kennedy's rise possible. ... His lofty conception of politics, his conviction that affluence was not enough for the good life, his impatience with liberal clichés, his contempt for conservative complacency, his summons to the young, his demand for new ideas, his respect for people who had them, his belief that history afforded no easy answers, his call for strong public leadership — all this set the tone for a new era of Democratic politics.

> Arthur M. Schlesinger Jr, *A Thousand Days, John Kennedy in the White House.*

The real trouble with Stevenson is that he's no better than a regular sissy.

> Harry S. Truman, in Merle Miller, *Plain Speaking, An Oral Biography of Harry S. Truman.*

He was called an egg-head, and he tossed back a Latinism of his own devising: 'Via ovum cranium difficilis est' (The way of the egghead is hard').

> Alden Whitman, *Portrait, Adlai E. Stevenson, Politician, Diplomat, Friend.*

See also Dwight Eisenhower, Cole Porter

STEVENSON, ROBERT LOUIS (BALFOUR)

1850—94 Author

I am a rogue at egotism myself; and, to be plain, I have rarely or never liked a man who was not.

> On himself, Letter to an Australian admirer, *circa* 1877.

I have played the sedulous ape to Hazlitt, to Lamb, to Wordsworth, to Sir Thomas Browne, to Defoe, to Hawthorne, to Montaigne, to Baudelaire and to Obermann.

> On himself, *Memories and Portraits.*

I am an Epick writer with a k to it, but without the necessary genius.

> On himself, Letter to Henry James, December 1892.

There is always in his work a certain clean-cut angularity which makes us remember that he was fond of cutting wood with an axe.

> G. K. Chesterton, *Twelve Types.*

Stevenson seemed to pick the right word up on the point of his pen, like a man playing spillikins.

> G. K. Chesterton, *The Victorian Age in Literature.*

Valiant in velvet, light in ragged luck,
Most vain, most generous, sternly critical,
Buffoon and poet, lover and sensualist;
A deal of Ariel, just a streak of Puck,
Much Antony, of Hamlet most of all,
And something of the Shorter-Catechist.

> W. E. Henley, *In Hospital.*

Two legendary figures dominated the literary background of my generation in its youth; the Dying Wanderer and the Martyred Dandy, Stevenson and Oscar Wilde. ... Wilde's legend has persisted, almost undiminished ... Stevenson's legend — as distinct from the popularity of his work — seems quite extinguished. Why should this be so? It is no sufficient explanation to say that Stevenson was a poseur. All legendary figures have been poseurs of one sort or another. But Stevenson's poses now seem fatally lacking in style and conviction. He was half-hearted about them; and he changed them too often. The general effect is confused.

> Christopher Isherwood, *Exhumations.*

The question really is, however, for the critical spirit, whether Louis's work itself doesn't pay somewhat for the so complete exhibition of the man & the life ... the books are jealous and a certain supremacy and mystery (above all) has, as it were, gone from them. The achieved legend and history that has *him* for subject, has made, so to speak, light of *their* subjects, and their claim to represent him. ... He had of course only to be then himself less picturesque and none of us who knew him would have had him so by an inch. But the fact remains that the *exhibition* that has overtaken him has helped and that he is thus as an artist and creator in some degree the victim of himself.

> Henry James, Letter to Graham Balfour, Stevenson's official biographer.

I think of Mr. Stevenson as a consumptive youth weaving garlands of sad flowers with pale, weak hands, or leaning to a large plate-glass window and scratching thereon exquisite profiles with a diamond pencil.

George Moore, *Confessions of a Young Man.*

Stevenson's letters most disappointing also. I see that romantic surroundings are the worst surroundings possible for a romantic writer. In Gower Street, Stevenson could have written a new *Trois Mousquetaires*. In Samoa he wrote letters to the *Times* about Germans. I see also the traces of a terrible *strain* to lead a natural life. To chop wood with any advantage to oneself or profit to others, one should not be able to describe the process. In point of fact the natural life is the unconscious life. Stevenson merely extended the sphere of the artificial by taking to digging.

Oscar Wilde, Letter to Robert Ross, 6 April 1897.

See also Samuel Butler

STEWART, ROBERT, see under CASTLEREAGH, VISCOUNT

STIEGLITZ, ALFRED

1864—1946 Photographer

There is something in me which seeks a balance, a relationship which can be put in a formula. But there is also something in me which, as soon as I have found the formula, insists upon kicking the stuffing out of it.

On himself, in Herbert J. Seligmann, *Alfred Stieglitz Talking.*

I have seen some of his feelings, black and white as his photographs, with the same subtle meaning that perhaps even beautiful color could never answer. Stieglitz was trying to let people see that photography was an art, and at the same time showing Picasso who was trying to make his art 'more photographic.' When asked what Stieglitz means to me as an artist, I answer: everything. Because I value his opinion as one who has always known.

I do not think I could have existed as a painter without that super-encouragement and the battle he has fought day by day for twenty-five years. He is without a doubt the one who has done the most for art in America.

Arthur G. Dove, 'A Different One', in Waldo Frank et al., *America and Alfred Stieglitz.*

In America, Alfred Stieglitz has been the great outstanding pioneer among photographers who have a true devotion to a specifically camera expression.

He has not essayed imitation of the techniques of drawing, painting, or lithography, but, far from deprecating the literal accuracy of the machine, has exploited its peculiar possibilities without reservation. Thus, though we infer from his work a reason functioning to discriminate, he has deferred to the machine's testimony on content material with a passivity that parallels inevitable human passivity in experiencing fact.

Evelyn Scott, 'A Note on the Esthetic Significance of Photography', in *ibid.*

Stieglitz had said that the art business reminded him, though he had never been in one, of a house of prostitution, where women, even virgin girls, were at the command of men with money; money ruled. In an emergency, if all the girls were busy and a man came, with money, in haste, the proprietress of the house could step in and fill the place of one of the girls. But this a picture dealer could never do for an artist. At which, said Stieglitz, Montross was horrified.

Herbert J. Seligmann, *Alfred Stieglitz Talking.*

This is true of his feeling about America. Here he stayed to fight the unequal battle for the creative spirit against machine industrialism. He would not become an expatriate, and he unhesitatingly sacrificed to his self-appointed task what would have been easier and more pleasant living in Europe. The depth of his love is to be measured by the violence of his half-century-long effort to rouse and provoke a living response.

Ibid.

He was of his time, and ahead of his time, in that he understood intuitively the creative resources of the machine. He impressed the sensibility of the human spirit on processes which dominant industrialism could use only for the crude purposes of mass production. So he achieved through the refinements of photo-engraving and other reproductive processes results which are miracles of revelation and delicacy.

Ibid.

I remember him dark and I felt him having white hair. He can do both of these things or anything. Now that sounds as if it were the same thing or not a difficult thing but it is just is, it is a difficult thing to do two things as one, but he just can that is what Stieglitz is and he is important to every one oh yes he is whether they know it or not oh yes he is. There are some who are important to every one whether any one knows anything of that one or not and Stieglitz is such a one, he is that one, he is indeed, there is no question but that he is such a one, he is that one, he is indeed, there is no question but that he is such a one no question indeed, but that he is one, who is an important one for every one, no matter whether they do or whether they do not know anything about any such thing about any such one about him

That is what Stieglitz is.
Any one can recognize him.
Any one does know that there are such ones, all of us do know that
Stieglitz is such a one.
That he is one.
291
 Gertrude Stein, *Stieglitz*.

The life work of Alfred Stieglitz, covering a period of almost fifty years of creative experiment, projects a complete analysis and synthesis of a machine, the camera. Using the methods and materials which belong exclusively to photography, Stieglitz has demonstrated beyond doubt that when the camera machine is guided by a very sensitive and deeply perceptive artist, it can produce perfectly embodied equivalents of unified thought and feeling. This unity may be called vision of life — of forces taking form in life.
 Paul Strand, 'Alfred Stieglitz and a Machine', in Waldo Frank et al., *America and Alfred Stieglitz*.

So Stieglitz turned the 'mechanical eye' of the camera from the things which people do or build, directly to the things which people are. He has given portraiture, in any medium, the new significance of a deliberate attempt to register the forces whose sum constitutes an individual, whose sum therefore documents the world of that individual. These amazing portraits, whether they objectify faces or hands, the torso of a woman, or the torso of a tree, suggest the beginning of a penetration of the scientific spirit into the plastic arts. Through photographic line, form, and tonal values, Stieglitz has gone beyond mere picture making, beyond any empty gesture of his own personality made at the expense of the thing or the person in front of him. He has examined our world of impulse and inhibition, of reaching out and of withdrawal, in a spirit of disinterested inquiry oriented by a wistful love. Photographs of things and people — of sun and cloud shapes — become equivalents of a deeply critical yet affirmative inquiry into contemporary life. They are the objective and beautiful conclusions of that inquiry.
 Ibid.

STILES, EZRA

1727–95 Scholar

Ezra Stiles succeeded as a college president partly because the job brought out the worst in him. All his life he had fought against vanity and had it well in hand by the time Yale called him. In New Haven it revived and proved an asset.
 Edmund S. Morgan, *The Gentle Puritan, A Life of Ezra Stiles, 1727–1795*.

The great wig he wore whenever he stepped outside and the velvet cap with which he replaced it when sitting in his study both added to the appearance of antique decay.
 Ibid.

. . . both a living polyglot and a living encyclopedia.
 Benjamin Silliman, in Francis Parsons, 'Ezra Stiles of Yale', in *New England Quarterly*, June 1936.

STILLWELL, JOSEPH WARREN

1883–1946 Soldier

Lean to the point of gauntness, perpetually squinting through steel-rimmed glasses as a result of a near-blinded eye injured in a World War I explosion, profane, irascible, well disciplined in body, undisciplined in tongue Stillwell was totally lacking in the art of diplomatic finesse. A man with a compulsion to speak and damn the consequences, he sounded off against colleagues and superiors with a zest that caused momentary amusement but ultimate dislike. The nickname 'vinegar Joe', applied in affection, became a damaging trademark.
 Forrest C. Pogue, *George C. Marshall: Ordeal and Hope 1939–1942*.

STOPES, MARIE CHARLOTTE CARMICHAEL

1880–1958 Advocate of Birth Control

Dr. Marie Stopes
After reading the Lives of the Popes,
Remarked: 'What a difference it would have made
                          to these Pages
If I had been born in the Middle Ages.'
 Hon. Mrs Geoffrey Edwards, in Arnold Silcock, *Verse and Worse*.

I think you should insist on the separation in the public mind of your incidental work as a scientific critic of methods of contraception with your main profession as a teacher of matrimonial technique.
 George Bernard Shaw, Letter to Marie Stopes, October 1928.

STORY, WILLIAM WETMORE

1819—95 Sculptor

Story, as we have noted, was frankly and forcibly romantic, and with a highly cultivated quality in his romance; so that he penetrated the imagination of his public as nobody else just then could have done. He told his tale with admirable emphasis and straightness, with a strong sense both of character and of drama, so that he created a kind of interest for the statue which had been, without competition, up to that time, reserved for the picture. He gave the marble something of the colour of the canvas; he in any case offered the observer a spectacle and, as nearly as possible, a scene. It was a question if not always absolutely of an action perpetrated, at least of one meditated, prepared, remembered or prompted, and, with that, of a state of feeling, a state of expression, to which association could lend a glamour. He chose his subjects, for the most part, among figures already consecrated to the imagination — by history, poetry, legend — and so offered them with all their signs and tokens, their features and enhancements.

Henry James, *William Wetmore Story*.

He had served no apprenticeship to his craft and mystery, had not only not been through the mill, but had not even undergone preparation for that discipline. It is difficult, in truth, to see what mill, at that season, and in all the conditions, would have struck him as turning for him, what apprenticeship, to the deeper initiation, he could conveniently have served.

Ibid.

STOWE, HARRIET ELIZABETH BEECHER

1811—96 Author, Humanitarian

[I] no more thought of style or literary excellence than the mother who rushes into the street and cries for help to save her children from a burning house, thinks of the teachings of the rhetorician or the elocutionist.

On herself, referring to *Uncle Tom's Cabin*, in Forrest Wilson, *Crusader in Crinoline, The Life of Harriet Beecher Stowe*.

Today I have taken my pen from the last chapter of *Uncle Tom's Cabin* and I think you will understand me when I say that I feel as if I had written some of it almost with my heart's blood. I look upon it almost as a despairing appeal to a civilised humanity. . . .

On herself, Letter to Horace Mann, March 1852.

I am a little bit of a woman, — somewhat more than forty, about as thin and dry as a pinch of snuff; never very much to look at in my best of days, and looking like a used-up article now.

On herself, Letter to Mrs Fallen, 1853.

My vocation is simply that of painter, and my object will be to hold up in the most lifelike and graphic manner possible slavery, its reverses, changes, and the negro character, which I have had ample opportunities for studying. There is no arguing with *pictures*, and everybody is impressed by them, whether they mean to be or not.

On herself, in Edward Wagenknecht, *ibid.*

I make no mental effort of any sort; my brain is tired out. It was a woman's brain and not a man's, and finally from sheer fatigue and exhaustion in the march and strife of life it gave out before the end was reached. And now I rest me, like a moored boat, rising and falling on the water, with loosened cordage and flapping sail.

On herself, Letter to Oliver Wendell Holmes, 5 February 1893.

But the final proof of Mrs Stowe's power was that she created the Southern romance, — and that, three generations later, Southern writers still had to reckon with her picture.

Van Wyck Brooks, *The Flowering of New England 1815—1865*.

. . . Harriet Beecher Stowe, whose *Uncle Tom's Cabin* was the first evidence to America that no hurricane can be so disastrous to a country as a ruthlessly humanitarian woman.

Sinclair Lewis, Introduction to Paxton Hibben, *Henry Ward Beecher: An American Portrait*.

She lived in a world of confusion, fatigue, and cloudy abstraction, and she suffered at times from a Messianic complex.

Edward Wagenknecht, *Cavalcade of the American Novel*.

To her who in our evil time
Dragged into light the nation's crime
With strength beyond the strength of men
And, mightier than their sword, her pen. . . .

John Greenleaf Whittier, in Johanna Johnston, *Runaway to Heaven, The Story of Harriet Beecher Stowe*.

See also Ida Tarbell

STRACHEY, (GILES) LYTTON

1880—1932 Author, Historian

It seems to me that I live neither for happiness nor

for duty. I like being happy. I scheme to be happy; I want to do my duty, and I sometimes even do it. But such considerations seem to affect me only sporadically and vaguely; there is something else which underlies my actions more fundamentally, which guides, controls, and animates the whole. It is ambition. I want to excel, to triumph, to be powerful, and to glorify in myself. I do not want a vulgar triumph, a vulgar power; fame and riches attract me only as subsidiary ornaments of my desire. What I want is the attainment of a true excellence, the development of noble qualities, and the full expression of them — the splendour of a spiritual success. It is true that this is an egotistical conception of life; but I see no harm in such an egotism.

On himself, Address to the Apostles, 11 May 1912.

To preserve, for instance, a becoming brevity — a brevity which excludes everything that is redundant and nothing that is significant — that, surely is the first duty of the biographer. The second, no less surely, is to maintain his own freedom of spirit.

On himself, Preface to *Eminent Victorians*.

It is not his [the historian's] business to be complimentary; it is his business to lay bare the facts of the case, as he understands them. That is what I have aimed at in this book — to lay bare the facts of some cases, as I understand them, dispassionately, impartially, and without ulterior intentions. To quote the words of a Master — 'Je n'impose rien; je ne propose rien; j'expose.'

Ibid.

Incapable of creation in life or in literature, his writings were a substitute for both.

T. R. Barnes, *Scrutiny*.

Lytton Strachey peered at everyone through thick glasses, looking like an owl in daylight. He is immensely tall, and could be even twice his height if he were not as bent as sloppy asparagus.

Cecil Beaton, Diary, 1923.

An emaciated face of ivory whiteness above a long square-cut auburn beard, and below a head of very long sleek dark brown hair. The nose was nothing if not aquiline, and Nature had chiselled it with great delicacy. The eyes, behind a pair of gold-rimmed spectacles, eyes of an inquirer and cogitator, were large and brown and luminous. The man to whom they belonged must, I judged, though he sat stooping low down over his table, be extremely tall. He wore a jacket of brown velveteen, a soft shirt, and a dark red tie. I greatly wondered who he was. He looked rather like one of the Twelve Apostles, and I

decided that he resembled especially the doubting one, Thomas, who was also called Didymus.

Max Beerbohm, on seeing Strachey for the first time in the Savile Club, in May 1912, *Mainly on the Air*.

Dear Lytton Strachey said to me: first I write one sentence: then I write another. That's how I write. And so I go on. But I have a feeling writing ought to be like running through a field.

Max Beerbohm (in conversation), in Virginia Woolf, *A Writer's Diary*, 1 November 1938.

There was seldom anything tense in a conversation with Lytton; it drifted hither and thither in that pleasant atmosphere, gay, truthful (cynical if you will — the terms are interchangeable almost), amusingly and amusedly censorious. Lytton brought a literary and historical flavour into his talk so that, if the past were discussed sometimes as though it were the present, the perplexities and misfortunes of his contemporaries were treated often as though they came from the pages of Saint-Simon or Horace Walpole.

Clive Bell, *Old Friends*.

I prefer Joyce to you. He does not taunt me, but leads me on, points to very far horizons, and shows me a way that leads there. He promises new discoveries, new methods, new beauties — you don't promise anything. You just are.

Gerald Brenan, Letter to Strachey, 1921.

One observed a number of discordant features — a feminine sensibility, a delight in the absurd, a taste for exaggeration and melodrama, a very mature judgement, and then some lack of human substance, some hereditary thinness in the blood that at times gave people who met him an odd feeling in the spine. He seemed almost indecently lacking in ordinariness.

Gerald Brenan, *South from Granada*.

Eminent Victorians is the work of a great anarch, a revolutionary textbook on bourgeois society written in the language through which the bourgeois ear could be lulled and beguiled, the Mandarin style. And the bourgeois responded with fascination to the music, like seals to the Eriskay love-lilt.

Cyril Connolly, *Enemies of Promise*.

Lytton Strachey was unfit [for war service], but instead of allowing himself to be rejected by the doctors preferred to appear before a military tribunal as a conscientious objector. He told us of the extraordinary impression caused by an air-cushion which he inflated in court as a protest against the hardness of the benches. Asked by the chairman the usual question: 'I understand, Mr Strachey, that you have a conscientious objection to war?', he replied (in his curious falsetto voice): 'Oh, no, not at all, only to *this* war.' And to the chairman's other stock question, which had previously never failed to embarrass the claimant: 'Tell me, Mr Strachey, what would you do if you saw a German soldier trying to violate your sister?' he replied with an air of noble virtue: 'I would try to get between them.'

Robert Graves, *Goodbye to All That.*

At another party, the conversation turned to the question of which great historical character the people there would most have liked to go to bed with. The men voted for Cleopatra, Kitty Fisher and so on, but when it came to Lytton's turn he declared shrilly: 'Julius Caesar!'

Michael Holroyd, *Lytton Strachey.*

On one occasion, some friends were discussing George Moore's extensive revisions to his novels, and one of them asked Lytton about his own amendments. 'I write very slowly, and in faultless sentences,' he replied. And this was hardly an exaggeration.

Ibid.

Much of the present interest in the nineteenth century is often written and spoken of as a reaction against Strachey; but I do not at all feel it so. . . . The views of history with which I grew up were almost entirely created by Victorians; and Strachey did not necessarily contradict them; he directed attention to a rather different Victorian field, and he also woke me up to the possibility of treating the Victorians themselves as interesting, problematical, extremely relevant to my own life and the general life I was born into.

Humphry House, *All in Due Time.*

Strachey is never direct: and not, I think, in himself wholesome. But I don't know him, and my memory of his books tangles itself with my memory of Henry Lamb's marvellous portrait of an outraged wet mackerel of a man, dropped like an old cloak into a basket-chair. If the portrait meant anything it meant that Lytton Strachey was no good.

T. E. Lawrence, Letter to Robert Graves, 1 October 1927.

The steeds that draw the chariot of his life seem to be curiously ill-matched: one so dignified and serious, and so high-stepping, and of the old English breed, so well versed in the manners and traditions of the last four centuries; the other so feminine, nervous, hysterical, shying at imaginary obstacles, delighting in being patted and flattered and fed with sugar.

Lady Ottoline Morrell, *Early Memoirs.*

In Strachey, because there is no *Sturm und Drang*, because he dislikes *Sturm und Drang* too much even to overcome it, as the artist must, there is no joy.

Edwin Muir, Letter to Stephen Hudson, 8 May 1925.

Pass a person through your mind, with all the documents, and see what comes out. That seems to be your method. Also choose them, in the first place, because you dislike them.

Walter Raleigh, commenting on *Eminent Victorians,* Letter to Strachey, May 1918.

His style is unduly rhetorical, and sometimes, in malicious moments, I have thought it not unlike Macaulay's. He is indifferent to historical truth and will always touch up the picture to make the lights and shades more glaring and the folly or wickedness of famous people more obvious. These are grave charges, but I make them in all seriousness.

Bertrand Russell, *Autobiography.*

The man who brilliantly ruined the art of biography.

George Sherburn, Introduction to *Selections from Pope.*

Lytton Strachey was a major Bloomsbury idol of this time. I knew him but slightly, and don't like his work. Also his letters to Virginia Woolf, now published, make me blush from head to foot, with the exclamations of 'oh deary Mary me!' and the enumeration of Countesses known and dimly related to them. . . . He seemed to have been cut out of very thin cardboard.

Edith Sitwell, *Taken Care Of.*

Eliot . . . seemed less alarming than, for example, Lytton Strachey, who could soar far above one with his wit and then follow this up with the depth-charge of one of his famous prolonged silences.

Stephen Spender, in Allen Tate, *T. S. Eliot, the Man and his Work.*

He combined strikingly their [the Bloomsbury Group's] gaiety with their intermittent chilliness. Sometimes he would play childish games such as 'Up Jenkins', which we played one Christmas. Often he would gossip brilliantly and maliciously. At times there was something insidious about his giggling manner; at times he would sit in his chair without saying a word.

Stephen Spender, *World Within World.*

I have just finished Elizabeth [*Elizabeth and Essex*]. . . . It is much your greatest work. And its success bears out my theory as against your own — or what used to be your view. You used to tell me that your strength was satire and satire alone, so you must choose people whom you did not much like in order to satirize them. I thought the argument bad then, and now the time gives proof of it. Your best book has been written about people to whom you are spiritually akin — far more akin than to the Victorians. And it is not a piece of satire but a piece of life.

G. M. Trevelyan, Letter to Lytton Strachey, 25 November 1928.

His biographical method, though novel in England, was already an old story in France. Sainte-Beuve was the great master of it, and Strachey's ironic tone has something in common with his. The weaknesses as well as the virtues of Strachey's style are the result of his imitation of French models. He is lucid and cool and precise, but he is terribly given to clichés. The penalty of trying to reproduce in English the chaste and abstract vocabulary of French is finding one's language become pale and banal.

Edmund Wilson, *The Shores of Light*.

He has fabricated, chiefly from eighteenth-century material, a very discreet code of manners of his own, which allows him to sit at the table with the highest in the land and to say a great many things under cover of that exquisite apparel which, had they gone naked, would have been chased by the men-servants from the room.

Virginia Woolf, *The Captain's Death Bed*.

See also Ottoline Morrell

STRAFFORD, EARL OF (THOMAS WENTWORTH)

1593–1641 Statesman

And so, thorough let us go, and spare not.
On himself, Letter to William Laud, 15 May 1634.

He was a simple man of strong affections, and he wrote the most endearing letters to his children.
John Buchan, *Oliver Cromwell*.

It is on his eight years of Irish government that his chief title to fame must rest and it may fairly be said that no British pro-Consul ever undertook a severer labour, or in a short time produced more miraculous results.
Ibid.

Wentworth is a man of dark countenance, a stern down-looking man, full of thoughts, energies, — of tender affections gone mostly to the shape of pride and sorrow, of rage sleeping in stern composure, kept strictly under lock and key: cross him not abruptly, he is a choleric man, and from under his dark brows flashes a look not pleasant to me. Poor Wentworth, his very nerves are all shattered, he lives in perpetual pain of body, such a force of soul has he to exert. He must bear an Atlas burden of Irish and other unreasons: from a whole chaos of angry babble he has to extract the word or two of meaning, and compress the rest into silence. A withered figure, scathed and parched as by internal, and external fire. Noble enough; yes, and even beautiful and tragical; at all events, terrible enough. He reverences King Charles, which is extremely miraculous, yet partially to be comprehended; King Charles, and I think, no other creature under this sky. Nay, at bottom, King Charles is but his Talismanic Figure, his conjuration Formula, with which he will conjure the world; he must not break or scratch that figure, or where were he? At bottom does not even reverence King Charles; he looks into the grim sea of fate stretching dark into the Infinite and the Eternal, and himself alone there; and reverences in strange ways only that, and what holds of that. A proud, mournful, scathed and withered man, with a prouder magazine of rage lying in him.

Thomas Carlyle, *Historical Sketches*.

My Lord of Strafford's condition is happier than mine.
Charles I, attributed, on agreeing to Strafford's execution, May 1641.

Here lies wise and valiant dust
Huddled up 'twixt fit and just,
Strafford who was hurried hence
'Twixt treason and convenience.
He lived and died here in a mist,
A Papist and a Calvinist.
His Prince's nearest joy and grief,
He had, yet wanted all relief.
The prop and ruin of the State;
The People's violent love and hate;
One in extremes, loved and abhorr'd.
Riddles lie here, or in a word
Here lies blood, and let it lie
Speechless still, and never cry.
John Cleveland, ascribed, in a Broadsheet of 1641.

I . . . beheld on Tower-hill the fatal stroke, which sever'd the wisest head in England from the Shoulders of the Earle of Strafford, whose crime coming under the cognizance of no human-Law, a new one was made, not to be a precedent, but his destruction, to such exorbitancy were things arrived.
John Evelyn, Diary, 12 May 1641.

He was no doubte of great observation, and a piercing judgement both into things and persons, but his too good skill in persons made him judge the worse of things, for it was his misfortune to be of a tyme wherin very few wise men were aequally imployed with him . . . and decerning many defects in most men, he too much neglected what they sayd or did. Of all his passyons his pryde was most predominant, which a moderate exercise of ill fortune might have corrected and reformed, and which was by the hande of heaven strangely punished, by bringing his destruction upon him, by two thinges, that he most despised, the people, and Sr Harry Vane.

Edward Hyde, Earl of Clarendon, *History of the Rebellion*.

He is dead with more honour than any of them will gain which hunted after his life.

William Laud, attributed, 1644.

He was the first Englishman to whom a peerage was a sacrament of infamy, a baptism into the communion of corruption. As he was the earliest of that hateful list, so was he also by far the greatest; eloquent, sagacious, adventurous, intrepid, ready of invention, immutable of purpose, in every talent which exalts or destroys nations pre-eminent, the lost archangel, the Satan of the Apostacy.

T. B. Macaulay, *Essays*: 'Hallam's Constitutional History'.

Sure I am, that his station was like those turfs of earth or sea-banks, which by the storm swept away, left all the in-land to be drown'd by popular tumult.

Sir Philip Warwick, *Memoires of the Reigne of King Charles I*.

STUART, CHARLES EDWARD LOUIS PHILIP CASIMIR

1720–88 The Young Pretender

Over the water and over the lea,
   And over the water to Charley.
Charley loves good ale and wine,
   And Charley loves good brandy,
And Charley loves a pretty girl,
   As sweet as sugar candy.

Over the water and over the lea,
   And over the water to Charley.
I'll have none of your nasty beef,
   Nor I'll have none of your barley;
But I'll have some of your very best flour
   To make a white cake for my Charley.
Nursery Rhyme, traditional.

An' Charlie he's my darling, my darling, my darling,
Charlie he's my darling, the young Chevalier.
   Robert Burns, *Charlie he's my darling*, refrain.

God bless the King, I mean the Faith's Defender;
God bless — no harm in blessing — the Pretender;
But who Pretender is, or who is King,
God bless us all — that's quite another thing.
   John Byrom, *To an Officer in the Army*.

Only ladies in Highland industry shops speak of him with any affection, which seems appropriate since all Charles bequeathed to Scotland that was of any benefit was a tourist industry.

Margaret Forster, *The Rash Adventurer*.

STUART, FRANCES TERESA, DUCHESS OF RICHMOND AND LENNOX

1647–1702 Mistress to Charles II

But without doubt the King's Passion was stronger towards that other Lady than ever it was to any other Woman: and she carried it with that Discretion and Modesty, that she made no other Use of it than for the Convenience of her own Fortune and Subsistence, which was narrow enough; never seemd disposed to interpose in the least Degree in Business, nor to speak ill of any Body; which Kind of Nature and Temper, the more inflamed the King's Affection, who did not in his Nature love a Busy Woman, and had an Aversion from speaking with any Woman, or hearing them speak, of any Business, but to that Purpose he thought them all made for, however, they broke in afterwards upon him to all other Purposes.

Edward Hyde, Earl of Clarendon, *The Life of Edward Earl of Clarendon*.

At my Goldsmith's did observe the King's new Medall, where in little there is Mrs Stewards face, as well done as ever I saw anything in my whole life, I think — and a pretty thing it is that he should choose her face to represent Britannia by.

Samuel Pepys, Diary, 25 February 1667.

The King begins to be mightily reclaimed, and sups every night with great pleasure with the Queene: and yet, it seems, he is mighty hot upon the Duchess of Richmond; insomuch that, upon Sunday was se'ennight at night, after he had ordered his Guards and Coach to be ready to carry him to the park, he did on a sudden take a pair of oars or sculler, and all alone, or but one with him, go to Somerset House, and there, the garden door not being open, himself clamber over the wall to make a visit to her; which is a horrid shame.

Ibid., 19 May 1668.

STUART, GILBERT

1755—1828 Artist

No man ever painted history if he could obtain employment in portraits.
On himself, in E. P. Richardson, *Gilbert Stuart*.

When Stuart the painter died, a eulogium on his character appeared in one of the American papers, in which it was said that he left the brightest prospects in England, and returned to his own country, from his admiration of her new institutions, and a desire to paint the portrait of Washington. On hearing this, Sir Thomas Lawrence said: 'I knew Stuart well; and I believe the real cause of his leaving England was his having become tired of the inside of some of our prisons.' 'Well, then', said Lord Holland, 'after all, it was his love of freedom that took him to America.'
Charles Robert Leslie, *Autobiography*.

He was particularly eloquent on the subject of arts and artist; and when he wished he could wield the weapons of satire and ridicule with peculiar force, seize the strong point of character, placing it so dexterously in the light he wished, that the impression was irresistible and not easily effaced.
John Neagle, in E. P. Richardson, *Gilbert Stuart, a National Gallery Catalogue*.

The method of Stuart is given in these few words. It was his habit to throw his subject off his guard, and then, by his wonderful powers of conversation, he would call up different emotions in the face he was studying. He chose the best or that which he thought most characteristic, and with the skill of genius used it to animate the picture. And this portrait of John Adams is a remarkable work, for a faithful representation of the extreme age of the subject would have been painful in inferior hands. But Stuart caught a glimpse of the living spirit shining through the feeble and decrepit body. He saw the old man at one of those happy moments when the intelligence lights up the wasted envelope, and what he saw he fixed upon the canvas.
Josiah Quincy, in E. P. Richardson, *ibid.*

John Neal, who knew Stuart, saw his portraits in his own image: 'A man of noble type himself, robust and hearty, with a large frame, and the bearing of one who might stand before kings, all Stuart's men look as if they were predestined statesmen, or had sat in council, or commanded armies. ...' This untroubled calm was the essence of the neo-classic portrait. As [Washington] Allston was to observe, Stuart had 'the faculty of distinguishing between the accidental and the permanent.'
E. P. Richardson, in *ibid.*

He nails the face to the canvas.
Benjamin West, attributed, in William Temple Franklin, Letter to Benjamin Franklin, 9 November 1784.

See also George Washington

STUART, JAMES EWELL BROWN (JEB)

1833—64 Soldier

. . . the Confederate lion, the shaking of whose mane and angry roar kept the Jackal North in a perpetual terror.
Anon., Editorial, in *Richmond Examiner*, 17 May 1864.

His horse furniture and equipment were polished leather and bright metal, and he liked to wear a red rose in his jacket when the roses bloomed, and a love knot of red ribbon when flowers were out of season. His soft, fawn-coloured hat was looped up on the right with a gold star, and adorned with a curling ostrich feather. His boots sported little knightly spurs of gold — admiring ladies, even those who never saw him in their lives, sent him such things. He went conspicuous all gold and glitter, in the front of great battles and in a hundred little cavalry fights, which killed men just as dead as Gettysburg . . . for Jeb Stuart was the first cavalier of the South. . . .
John W. Thomason Jr, *Jeb Stuart*.

STUART, JAMES FRANCIS EDWARD

1688—1766 The Old Pretender

The spring of his whole conduct is fear, fear of the horns of the devil and of the flames of hell. . . . He has all the superstition of a Capuchin, but I found in him no tincture of the religion of a Prince.
Henry St John, Viscount Bolingbroke, Letter to the Earl of Mar, 27 March 1716

Modern psychologists would hint at traumas set up by the circumstances of his birth, his abrupt departure from England, the uncertainty of life at Saint Germain, his father's doctrine of the divine right of kings conflicting so obviously against the will of the people. And they would no doubt be correct. James Francis Edward was a born loser.
Christopher Sinclair-Stevenson, *Inglorious Rebellion*.

STUART, JOHN, see under BUTE, EARL OF

STUART, JOHN
715

STUART, MARY, see under MARY QUEEN OF
SCOTS

STUBBS, GEORGE

1724–1806 Painter, Anatomist

The wide Creation waits upon his call,
He paints each species and excels in all,
Whilst wondering Nature asks with jealous tone,
Which Stubbs's labours are and which her own?
  Anon., Pamphlet by 'An Impartial Hand', in
  Exhibition, 1766.

Stubbs is useful, but his Horses are not broad
enough in light & shadow for a Painter. They may
be just as correct without violating the principles of
effect. They are delicate, minute, & sweetly drawn,
with great character, but they want substance, for
they have hardly any light & shadow.
  Benjamin Robert Haydon, Diary, 25 April 1826.

'Tis said that nought so much the temper rubs
Of that ingenious artist, Mister Stubbs,
As calling him a horse-painter — how strange
That Stubbs the title should desire to change!
  Peter Pindar (John Wolcot), *Lyric Odes to the
  Royal Academicians*, 1782, Ode 7.

Well pleas'd thy horses, Stubbs, I view,
  And eke thy dogs, to *homely* nature true:
Let modern artist match thee, if they can —
  Such animals thy genius suit:
  Then stick, I beg thee, to the brute.
And meddle not with woman, nor with man.
  Ibid., Ode 15.

He certainly stands in that company of artists —
Dürer being one of its representatives — who, from
the centre of their nature, have enjoyed a wide-
ranging and unassailable capacity and whose works
have the characteristic named by Sir Henry Wotton
in his definition of good architecture, 'firmness', a
principle implying the most comprehensive definition of craftsmanship and requiring mental discipline as well as skill of hand. Unlike Hogarth, who
said that he had to get things wrong before he got
them right, Stubbs possessed a natural virtuosity,
which he never forfeited or lost but which was always unpretentious in its effect.
  Basil Taylor, *Stubbs*.

In the 1760s Stubbs was to be the most talented,
responsive and versatile interpreter of such an icono-
graphy of rural life: his work should be seen in this
context and not regarded — as it has been formerly
— as one unusually refined and distinguished manifestation of sporting art.
  Ibid.

SULLIVAN, SIR ARTHUR SEYMOUR

1842–1900 Composer

We all have the same eight notes to work with.
  On himself, attributed, when accused of plagiar-
  izing.

In all the pieces we have written together I have invariably subordinated my views to your own.
  W. S. Gilbert, Letter to Sullivan, 30 March 1884.

You are an adept in your profession & I am an
adept in mine. If we meet, it must be as master &
master — not as master & servant.
  Ibid., 19 March 1889.

He is like a man who sits on a stove and then com-
plains that his backside is burning.
  W. S. Gilbert, in Leslie Ayre, *The Gilbert and
  Sullivan Companion.*

A composer of the rarest genius, who, because he
was a composer of the rarest genius, was as modest
and unassuming as a neophyte should be but seldom is.
  Ibid.

It has been said that he was lucky in his chief colla-
borator: it should be added that no man ever more
thoroughly deserved his luck.
  Sir Henry Hadow, *English Music.*

They trained him to make Europe yawn; and he
took advantage of their teaching to make London
and New York laugh and whistle.
  George Bernard Shaw, in *Scots Observer*,
  6 September 1890.

Sullivan's genius was in making it impossible for
opera-goers subsequently to tell whether the words
or the tunes came first.
  Percy M. Young, *A Critical Dictionary of Composers and Their Music.*

See also W. S. Gilbert, Gilbert and Sullivan

SULLIVAN, JOHN LAWRENCE

1858–1918 Boxer

'*East side, west side, all around the town
The tots sang: "Ring a rosie--"
"London Bridge is falling down." '*
And . . .
John L. Sullivan
The strong boy
Of Boston

Broke every single rib of Jake Kilrain.
Vachel Lindsay, *John L. Sullivan, The Strong Boy of Boston.*

SULLIVAN, LOUIS HENRY

1856—1924 Architect

The true function of the architect is to initiate such buildings as shall correspond to the real needs of the people: . . . to vitalize building materials, to animate them with a subjective significance and value, to make them a visible part of the social fabric, to infuse into them the true life of the people, to impart to them the best that is in the people.
On himself, in Hugh Morrison, *Louis Sullivan.*

I value spiritual results only. I say spiritual results precede all other results, and indicate them. I can see no efficient way of handling this subject on any other than a spiritual or psychic basis.
It is for this reason that I say all mechanical theories of art are vanity, and that the best of rules are but as flowers planted over the graves of prodigious impulses which splendidly lived their lives, and passed away with the individual men who possessed these impulses. This is why I say that it is within the souls of individual men that art reaches its culminations. This is why I say that each man is a law unto himself.
On himself, in Hugh Morrison, *ibid.*

Sullivan's life-long search in architecture was for a 'rule so broad as to admit of no exceptions.' This rule, as he evolved it from his experience with Nature, is the simple one that *form follows function.* To Sullivan, this was simply natural law. It was a direct adaptation of a great biological principle to the sphere of architecture.
Hugh Morrison, in *ibid.*

In the field of architecture, I believe, it remained for Louis Sullivan to integrate romanticism and realism, to achieve a synthesis both in theory and in practice completely expressive of modern life, and to make possible the renewal of architecture as a creative art based on those fundamentals that have always existed in the great architecture of past. In this sense he was the first modern architect.
Ibid.

Sullivan was the first American architect to think consciously of his relations with civilization. Richardson and Root both had good intuitions, and they had made effective demonstrations; but Sullivan knew what he was about, and what is more important, he knew what he ought to be about.
Lewis Mumford, in Hugh Morrison, *ibid.*

SUMNER, CHARLES

1811—74 Politician, Abolitionist

A foul-mouthed poltroon, [who] when caned for cowardly vituperation falls to the floor in an inanimate lump of incarnate cowardice.
Anon., in *Richmond Examiner*, 1856.

Sumner's mind had reached the calm of water which receives and reflects images without absorbing them; it contained nothing but itself.
Henry Adams, *The Education of Henry Adams.*

. . . hates slavery more than he loves the Constitution, and . . . to reach and throttle the one he is willing to march over the prostrate form of the other.
Orville H. Browning, in David Donald, *Charles Sumner and the Rights of Man.*

. . . the most completely nothin' of a mon that ever crossed my threshold, — naught whatsoever in him or of him but wind and vanity.
Thomas Carlyle, in D. H. Donald, *Charles Sumner and the Coming of the Civil War.*

. . . the great orb of the State Department who rises periodically in his effulgence and sends his rays down the steep places here to cast a good many dollars into the sea.
Roscoe Conkling, in David Donald, *Charles Sumner and the Rights of Man.*

He identifies himself so completely with the universe that he is not at all certain whether he is a part of the universe or the universe is a part of him.
S. S. Cox, *Why We Laugh.*

It characterizes the man for me that he hates Charles Sumner, for it shows that he cannot discriminate between a foible and a vice.
Ralph Waldo Emerson, in David Donald, *Charles Sumner and the Rights of Man.*

A man of huge and distempered vanity.
William Ewart Gladstone, in *ibid.*

He works his adjectives so hard that if they ever catch him alone, they will murder him.
E. L. Godkin, in *ibid.*

He was essentially a free-lance, an independent in politics, the first great Mugwump of Massachusetts.
Archibald H. Grimke, *The Life of Charles Sumner: The Scholar in Politics.*

It sometimes seemed as if Sumner thought the Rebellion itself was put down by speeches in the Senate, and that the war was an unfortunate and most annoying, though trifling disturbance, as if a fire-engine passed by.
George F. Hoar, *Autobiography*, vol. 1.

Rero, rero, riddety rad;
This morning my baby caught sight of her Dad.
Quoth she, 'Oh Daddy, where have you been?'
'With Mann and Sumner, a-putting down sin!'
Julia Howes, in D. H. Donald, *Charles Sumner and the Coming of the Civil War*.

By degrees, Sumner had come to stand for something the South wanted exterminated from the Union; he was perhaps the most perfect impersonation of what the South wanted to secede from.
Carl Sandburg, *Abraham Lincoln: The War Years*.

Wherever wrong doth right deny,
Or suffering spirits urge their plea,
Here is a voice to smite the lie,
A hand to set the captive free.
John Greenleaf Whittier, in Ida Husted Harper, *Life and Work of Susan B. Anthony*, vol. 2.

SUNDAY, WILLIAM ASHLEY, 'BILLY'

1862—1935 Evangelist

A rube of the rubes.
On himself, in Sydney Ahlstrom, *A Religious History of the American People*.

Measured in terms of claimed converts and net profits . . . Billy Sunday was the greatest high-pressure and mass conversion Christian evangel that America, or the world, has known.
Anon., in *New York Times*, 7 November 1935.

The acrobat dervish of evangelism.
Ibid.

He outrages every rule of church decorum, and slaps in the face all our traditions of dignity and reverence in worship; but not for a moment is he a clown, much less a mountebank.
Anon., in *National Cyclopaedia of American Biography*.

SURREY, EARL OF (HENRY HOWARD)

1517?—47 Poet

Sir Thomas Wyatt

Never went on a diet,
Unlike the Earl of Surrey,
Who ate nothing but curry.
W. H. Auden, *Academic Graffiti*.

Surrey, the *Granville* of a former Age:
Matchless his Pen, victorious was his Lance;
Bold in the Lists, and graceful in the Dance.
Alexander Pope, *Windsor-Forest*.

The first English classical poet.
Thomas Warton, *History of English Poetry*.

SWIFT, JONATHAN

1667—1745 Author

Yet malice never was his aim;
He lash'd the vice, but spared the name;
No individual could resent,
Where thousands equally were meant.
On himself, *On the Death of Dr Swift*.

Poor Pope will grieve a month, and Gay
A week, and Arbuthnot a day.
St. John himself will scarce forbear
To bite his pen, and drop a tear.
The rest will give a shrug, and cry,
'I'm sorry — but we all must die!'
Ibid.

Good God! what a genius I had when I wrote that book.
On himself (of *The Tale of a Tub*), in Walter Scott, *Life of Swift*.

I shall be like that tree, I shall die at the top.
On himself, attributed.

When people ask me how I governed Ireland, I say that I pleased Dr. Swift.
Lord Carteret, Letter to Swift, March 1737.

Swift was *anima Rabelaisii habitans in sicco* — the soul of Rabelais dwelling in a dry place.
Samuel Taylor Coleridge, *Table Talk*.

Cousin Swift, you will never be a poet.
John Dryden, in Samuel Johnson, *Lives of the Poets*.

He possessed the Talents of a Lucian, a Rabelais, and a Cervantes, and in his Works exceeded them all. He employed his Wit to the noblest Purposes, in ridiculing as well Superstition in Religion as Infidelity, and several Errors and Immoralities which sprung up from time to time in his Age; and lastly, in the Defence of his Country, against several pernicious Schemes of wicked Politicians. Nor was he only a Genius and a Patriot: he was in private Life a good and charitable Man, and frequently lent Sums of Money without Interest to the Poor and Industrious; by which means many Families were preserved from Destruction.

Henry Fielding, Obituary notice in *True Patriot*, 5 November 1745.

Dr Tyrrell asked Carlyle whom he considered the greatest writer of English Prose. 'Swaft! for his parfaict lucidity.'

Oliver St J. Gogarty, *As I Was Going Down Sackville Street*.

Swift's reputation as a poet has been in a manner obscured by the greater splendour, by the natural force and inventive genius of his prose writings. . . . Swift shone as one of the most sensible of the poets; he is also distinguished as one of the most nonsensical of them. No man has written so many lack-adaisical, slip-shod, tedious, trifling, foolish, fantastical verses as he, which are so little an imputation on the wisdom of the writer; and which, in fact, only shew his readiness to oblige others, and forget himself.

William Hazlitt, *Lectures on the English Poets*.

In life's last scene what prodigies surprise,
Fears of the brave, and follies of the wise!
From Marlb'rough's eyes the streams of dotage flow,
And Swift expires a driv'ler and a show.

Samuel Johnson, *The Vanity of Human Wishes*.

Swift has a higher reputation than he deserves. His excellence is strong sense; for his humour, though very well, is not remarkably good. I doubt whether *A Tale of a Tub* be his; for he never owned it, and it is much above his usual manner.

Samuel Johnson, in James Boswell, *Life of Johnson*.

Nobody can deny but religion is a comfort to the distressed, a cordial to the sick, . . . therefore whoever would argue or laugh it out of the world without giving some equivalent for it ought to be treated as a common enemy. But when this language comes from a churchman who enjoys large benefices and dignities from that very church he openly despises it is an object of horror for which I want a name, and can only be excused by madness, which I think the Dean was always strongly touched with. His character seems to me a parallel with that of Caligula, and had he had the same power, would have made the same use of it.

Lady Mary Wortley Montagu, Letter to Lady Bute, 23 June 1754.

We are right to think of Swift as a rebel and iconoclast, but except in certain secondary matters, such as his insistence that women should receive the same education as men, he cannot be labelled 'left'. He is a Tory anarchist, despising authority while disbelieving in liberty, and preserving the aristocratic outlook while seeing clearly that the existing aristocracy is degenerate and contemptible.

George Orwell, *Politics vs Literature*.

Jonathan Swift
Had the gift,
By fatherige, motherige,
And by brotherige,
To come from Gutherige,
But now is spoil'd clean,
And an Irish Dean.

Alexander Pope, *Lines on Swift's Ancestors*.

I'll send you my bill of fare said Lord B[olingbroke] when trying to persuade Dr. Swift to dine with him. — 'Send me your bill of company,' was Swift's answer to him.

Joseph Spence, *Anecdotes*.

That brute, who hated everybody that he hoped would get him a mitre, and did not.

Horace Walpole, Letter to George Montagu, 20 June 1766.

Swift has sailed into his rest;
Savage indignation there
Cannot lacerate his breast.
Imitate him if you dare,
World-besotted traveller; he
Served human liberty.

William Butler Yeats, *Swift's Epitaph*.

See also Lord Mansfield, Duke of Marlborough, Andrew Marvell, Somerset Maugham, Alexander Pope

SWINBURNE, ALGERNON CHARLES

1837—1909 Poet

Having Mr. Swinburne's defence of his prurient poetics, *Punch* hereby gives him his royal license to change his name to what is evidently its true form — Swine-born.

Anon., Review of *Poems and Ballads*, in *Punch*, 1866.

As to Swinburne's verses . . . they are 'florid impotence', to my taste, the *minimum* of thought and idea in the *maximum* of words and phraseology.

Nothing said and nothing done with, left to stand alone and trust for its effect in its own worth.

Robert Browning, Letter to Isa Blagden, 22 March 1870.

I attempt to describe Mr. Swinburne; and lo! the Bacchanal screams, the sterile Dolores sweats, serpents dance, men and women wrench, wriggle, and form in an endless alliteration of heated and meaningless words, the veriest garbage of Baudelaire flowered over with the epithets of the Della Cruscans.

Robert Buchanan, in *Contemporary Review*, October 1871.

It is probable that there is not much to be gained by an absolute system of prosody; by the erudite complexities of Swinburnian metre. With Swinburne, once the trick is perceived and the scholarship appreciated, the effect is somewhat diminished. When the unexpectedness, due to the unfamiliarity of the metres to English ears, wears off and is understood, one ceases to look for what one does not find in Swinburne; the inexplicable line with the music that can never be recaptured in other words. Swinburne mastered his technique, which is a great deal, but he did not master it to the extent of being able to take liberties with it, which is everything.

T. S. Eliot, *Reflections on 'Vers Libre'*.

The words of condemnation are words which express his qualities. You may say 'diffuse'. But the diffuseness is essential; had Swinburne practised greater concentration his verse would be, not better in the same kind, but a different thing. His diffuseness is one of his glories.

T. S. Eliot, *The Sacred Wood*.

The poetry is not morbid, it is not erotic, it is not destructive. These are adjectives which can be applied to the material, the human feelings, which in Swinburne's case do not exist. The morbidity is not of human feeling but of language.

Ibid.

[Emerson] condemned Swinburne severely as a perfect leper and a mere sodomite, which criticism recalls Carlyle's scathing description of that poet — as a man standing up to his neck in a cesspool, and adding to its contents.

Interview with Ralph Waldo Emerson, in *Frank Leslie's Illustrated Newspaper*, 3 January 1874.

It was important, at meals, to keep the wine or beer or spirits out of Swinburne's reach. If this were not done, as often by host or hostesses not aware of his weakness, he would gradually fix his stare upon the bottle as if he wished to fascinate it, and then, in a moment, flash or pounce upon it, like a mongoose on a snake, drawing it towards him as though it resisted and had to be struggled with. Then, if no one had the presence of mind to interfere, a tumbler was filled in a moment, and Swinburne had drained it to the last drop, sucking-in the liquid with a sort of fiery gluttony, tilting the glass into his shaking lips, and violently opening and shutting his eyelids. It was an extraordinary sight, and one which never failed to fill me with alarm, for after that the Bacchic transition might come at any moment.

Edmund Gosse, Manuscript Notes on Swinburne.

It is curious that though Sade is the author who most influenced Swinburne, and though Swinburne's writings are full of sadism properly so called, his own propensities were those of Rousseau and Sacher-Masoch. It is true that these are cheaper to indulge, but that does not seem to have been the reason.

A. E. Housman, Letter to Edmund Gosse, 20 January 1919.

There was, indeed — I say it with unabated reverence — something absurd, as it were misbegotten, about Swinburne, which no truthful picture can omit; something that made people turn and laugh at him in the streets, as I once saw some carters do as he went by on Wimbledon Common, with his eccentric dancing, one might even say epileptic, gait, his palms spread open behind him in a tense nervous way. He was certainly an odd, scarcely human, figure.

Richard Le Gallienne, *The Romantic '90s*.

Take him at his best he is by far the best — finest poet; truest artist — of the young lot — when he refrains from pointing a hand at the genitals.

George Meredith, Letter to Frederick Greenwood, 1 January 1873.

A sea blown to storm by a sigh.

George Meredith, in Siegfried Sassoon, *George Meredith*.

A mind all aflame with the feverish carnality of a schoolboy over the dirtiest passages in Lemprière.

John Morley, reviewing *Poems and Ballads*, in *Saturday Review*, 1866.

Of Swinburne it is certainly true that, unless we know something of his life . . . we cannot grasp the true nature of his poetic talent. That talent was a rich, yet infertile, growth, like the desert aloe or cactus suddenly throwing out a splendid spire of blossoms, which rapidly declines and decays, as if exhausted by its riotous thrust. The poet's extravagances of conduct were an inseparable part of his creative evolution. He did cease to write memorable poems because his health and nerves were shattered, or because pale ale is less suited to the creation of works of literature than midnight draughts of fiery spirit. But, just as in writing he felt obliged to follow a course of furious self-expenditure and continued to drive his imagination so long as imagination lasted, in life, too, his *daimon* impelled him to squander health and energy, till he sank at length into complete collapse and Watts-Dunton . . . called at Great James Street to remove a helpless stretcher-case.

> Peter Quennell, *The Singular Preference*.

Swinburne . . . expresses in verse what he finds in books as passionately as a poet expresses what he finds in life.

> George Bernard Shaw, in *Saturday Review*, 11 July 1896.

He is a reed through which all things blow into music.

> Alfred, Lord Tennyson (in conversation), in Hallam Tennyson, *Alfred Tennyson, A Memoir*.

Isn't he the damnedest simulacrum!

> Walt Whitman, attributed.

Mr. Swinburne is already the Poet Laureate of England. The fact that his appointment to this high post has not been degraded by official confirmation renders his position all the more unassailable.

> Oscar Wilde, in *Idler*, April 1895.

You know, Watts is a solicitor and the business of a solicitor is to conceal crime. Swinburne's genius has been killed, and Watts is doing his best to conceal it.

> Oscar Wilde (of Swinburne's retirement to Putney with Theodore Watts-Dunton), in Vincent O'Sullivan, *Aspects of Wilde*.

See also Robert Browning, George Eliot, Rudyard Kipling

SYDENHAM, THOMAS

1624—89 Physician

Strange things have been said in jest, or in earnest, concerning the studies necessary to form a physician. Sydenham advised Sir Richard Blackmore to read Don Quixote. He probably spoke in jest. But it is impossible to read Sydenham and not perceive that his mind did in truth hardly admit any auxiliary to the exercise of its own observation.

> P. M. Latham, *Lectures on Subjects Connected with Clinical Medicine*.

He was famous for his cool regimen in the small-pox, which his greatest adversaries have been since forc'd to take up and follow. He was also famous for his method of giving the bark after the paroxysm in agues, and for his laudanum.

> Anthony à Wood, *Athenae Oxonienses*.

SYMONDS, JOHN ADDINGTON

1840—93 Author

Mr Soddington Symonds.

> Algernon C. Swinburne, Letter to Theodore Watts-Dunton, 1 September 1894.

SYNGE, JOHN MILLINGTON

1871—1909 Dramatist

When I was writing 'The Shadow of the Glen' I got more aid than any learning could have given me from a chink in the floor of the old Wicklow house where I was staying, that let me hear what was being said by the servant girls in the kitchen.

> On himself, Preface to *The Playboy of the Western World*.

He had, however, nothing to show but one or two poems and impressionistic essays, full of that kind of morbidity that has its root in too much brooding over methods of expression, and ways of looking upon life, which come, not out of life, but out of literature, images reflected from mirror to mirror.

> William Butler Yeats (describing first meeting Synge in Paris, 1899), Preface to First Edition of *The Well of the Saints*.

Synge has just had an operation on his throat and has come through it all right. . . . When he woke out of the ether sleep, his first words, to the great delight of the doctor, who knows his plays, were: 'May God damn the English, they can't even swear without vulgarity.' This tale delights the Company, who shudder at the bad language they have to speak in his plays.

> William Butler Yeats, Letter to John Quinn, 4 October 1907.

He was a solitary, undemonstrative man, never asking pity, nor complaining, nor seeking sympathy . . . all folded up in brooding intellect, knowing nothing of new books and newspapers, reading the great masters alone; and he was but the more hated because he gave his country what it needed, an unmoved mind where there is a perpetual Last Day, a trumpeting and coming up to judgement.

> William Butler Yeats, *The Cutting of An Agate*.

And that enquiring man John Synge comes next,
That dying chose the living world for text
And never could have rested in the tomb
But that, long travelling, he had come
Towards nightfall upon certain set apart
In a most desolate stony place,
Towards nightfall upon a race
Passionate and simple like his heart.
  William Butler Yeats, *In Memory of Major
  Robert Gregory.*

Whenever he tried to write drama without dialect, he wrote badly, and he made several attempts, because only through dialect could he escape self-expression, see all that he did from without, allow his intellect to judge the images of his mind as if they had been created by some other mind. His objectivity was, however, technical only, for in those images paraded all the desires of his heart.
  William Butler Yeats, *Autobiographies.*

He was the only man I have ever known incapable of a political thought or of a humanitarian purpose.
  Ibid.

In Paris, Synge once said to me, 'We should unite stoicism, asceticism, and ecstasy. Two of them have often come together, but the three, never.'
  Ibid.

Synge was the rushing up of the buried fire, an explosion of all that had been denied or refused, a furious impartiality, an indifferent turbulent sorrow. His work, like that of Burns, was to say all the people did not want to have said.
  Ibid.

T

TAFT, ROBERT ALPHONSO

1889—1953 Politician

[The] Dagwood Bumstead of American Politics.
> Anon., in *Time*, 1940.

Every time he stood up to speak, I wanted to fight him.
> Senator George Aiken of Vermont, in James T. Patterson, *Mr. Republican*.

It must be said that as far as his opinions on foreign policy were concerned, Senator Taft was more than Mr Republican. He was Mr American. It was he, perhaps better than anyone else, who voiced the doubts and prejudices, the hopes and fears, the frustrations, the hesitations, and the dissatisfactions that the American people felt as they slowly and ponderously went about the business of adjusting to their changed role in the world.
> John P. Armstrong, 'The Enigma of Senator Taft and American Foreign Policy', in *Review of Politics*, vol. 17, no. 2, April 1955.

. . . : the man who would lead the Congressional Republicans out of their inertia and defeatism, reshape their program, and make them an articulate opposition to the liberals and internationalists of the New Deal and the Fair Deal.
> James MacGregor Burns, *The Deadlock of Democracy*.

Throughout his Senate years, Taft would seek to lift his party above opportunism and to fix it to firm principles. He was a man of party because, like Burke, he understood that in modern society freedom and order cannot endure without the apparatus of responsible political party. In serving party, he meant to serve his country; there was no inconsistency in loyalty to both.
> Russell Clark and James McClellan, *The Political Principles of Robert A. Taft*.

We're looking over a four-leaf clover
That we overlooked before;
One leaf is courage, the second is fight,
Third is our party, that always is right;
No need explainin' the one remainin'
It's Bob Taft whom we adore.

Let's put Taft over — the four-leaf clover
That we'll overlook no more.
> Richard Guylay, Campaign Song, 1948.

. . . he has a positive genius for being wrong. He is an authentic living representative of the old Bourbons of whom it was said that they 'learned nothing and forgot nothing.'
> Marvin Harrison, *Robert A. Taft, Our Illustrious Dunderhead*.

. . . has all the limitations of Neville Chamberlain, the same complacency, the same incapacity to foresee, the same apathy in action . . . to nominate him now would be to invite for the nation a disaster of preparedness, for Mr. Taft a tragic ordeal.
> Walter Lippmann, in *New York Herald Tribune*, 25 June 1940.

. . . was the very opposite of the hollow men with their fabricated personalities. The inner man was the solidest part of Taft, and at the core he was so genuine and just, so rational and compassionate that he commanded the confidence of men when he could never convince them.
> Walter Lippmann, in Malcolm Moos, *The Republicans: A History of Their Party*.

. . . is industrious, prudent, monogamous, proper in speech and comportment, law-abiding, church-going and presumably God-fearing, a good provider, a believer in education, a tree-grower, a good caretaker of the temple of the soul.
> Richard Rovere, 'Taft: Is this the Best We've Got?', in *Harper's Magazine*, April 1948.

. . . whose slight build and undistinguished bearing give him the appearance of an elderly boy.
> I. F. Stone, 8 January 1948, 'The Imponderable of Leadership: It Just Wasn't There', in *The Truman Era*.

He was the son of a Republican president and was shrewdly able to use this fact to advantage in exploiting the Republican viewpoint. He had a sense of dynasty. Like Quincy Adams and Benjamin Harrison, he wanted to keep the presidency in the family.
> Harry S. Truman, *1945: Year of Decisions: Memoirs by Harry S. Truman*, vol. 1.

See also Dwight Eisenhower

TAFT, WILLIAM HOWARD

1857—1930 Twenty-Seventh United States
President

I have proven to be a burdensome leader and not
one that aroused the multitude . . . I am entirely
content to serve in the ranks.
> On himself, to Dr Wesley Hill, in *The American
> Heritage Pictorial History of the Presidents of
> the United States.*

. . . can be depended upon to stand for property
rights whenever they come into conflict with human
rights.
> Anon., in *Literary Digest*, 16 July 1921.

[The] very Progressivism which President Taft
provoked [should] uncompromisingly have resented
Chief Justice Taft.
> Anon., in *The New Republic*, 1921.

The amiable, goodnatured, subthyroid Taft had the
misfortune to follow the crusading, club-brandishing,
hyperthyroid Roosevelt, much as a dim star follows
a blazing comet. The Nation felt let down.
> Thomas A. Bailey, *Presidential Greatness.*

Taft had served so long under Theodore Roosevelt
as a trouble shooter and yes-man that he never recovered from the subordinate experience. . . . When
someone addressed him as 'Mr. President', he would
instinctively turn around to see where Roosevelt
was.
> *Ibid.*

The Great Postponer.
> William Jennings Bryan, in Oswald Garrison
> Villard, *The Fighting Years.*

. . . He loathed being President and being Chief
Justice was all happiness for him. He fought against
being President and yielded to the acceptance of
that heritage because of the insistence of Mrs Taft—
very ambitious in that direction. It had always been
the ambition of his life to be on the Supreme Court.
Taft once said that the Supreme Court was his
notion of what heaven must be like.
> Felix Frankfurter, *Reminiscences.*

He was a bad President, but a good sport.
> Felix Frankfurter, in *The New Republic.*

. . . the only man in American political history who
can, with complete accuracy, be described as a
creature of destiny.
> Henry Pringle, in Alpheus Thomas Mason,
> *William Howard Taft.*

[A president who] meant well but meant well
feebly.
> Theodore Roosevelt, 1912, in *The American
> Heritage Pictorial History of the Presidents
> of the United States.*

I am the seventh son of a seventh daughter and I
have clairvoyant powers. I see a man weighing three
hundred and fifty pounds. There is something hanging over his head. I cannot make out what it is. . . .
At one time it looks like the presidency, then again
it looks like the chief justiceship.
> Theodore Roosevelt (offering Taft a remarkable
> choice, 1908).

Taft stuck at a water-tank railroad station and learning that the train would only stop if a number of
passengers wished to come aboard, telegraphed to
the conductor. 'Stop at Hicksville. Large party
waiting to catch train.'
> Malcolm Ross, in F. C. Hicks, *William Howard
> Taft: Yale Professor of Law and New Haven
> Citizen.*

When I suggested to him that he occupy a Chair of
Law at the University he said that he was afraid that
a chair would not be adequate, but that if we would
provide a Sofa of Law, it might be all right.
> Anson Phelps Stokes, 1912, in *ibid.*

Will was then at his stoutest. He sat down in the
very small theater seat and seemed to overflow. He
looked at me smilingly and said: 'Horace, if this
theater burns, it has got to burn around me.'
> Horace Dutton Taft, *Memories and Opinions.*

See also Chauncey Depew

TALLIS, THOMAS

circa 1510—85 Composer

Ye sacred muses, race of Jove
Whom Musicks' love delighteth
Come down from Christ all heavens above
To Earth where sorrow dwelleth.
In mourning weeds, with tears in eyes,
Tallis is dead and Musick dies.
> Anon., set to music by William Byrd, 1585.

TANEY, ROGER BROOK

1777—1864 Jurist

. . . he is old, very old. The infirmities of age have
bowed his venerable form. Earth has no further

object of ambition for him; and when he shall sink into his grave after a long career of high office in our country, I trust . . . that he will leave behind him. . . the noblest evidence that he died, as he had lived, a being honorable to the earth from which he sprang, and worthy of the heaven to which he aspired.

Anon., in *New York Tribune*, 7 March 1857.

His name, proclaimed Charles Sumner in the United States Senate, was to be 'hooted down the pages of history.'

Carl Brent Swisher, 'Mr. Chief Justice Taney', in Allison Dunham ed., *Mr Justice*.

Judge Story thinks the Supreme Court is gone, and I think so too.

Daniel Webster, commenting on Taney's appointment, in Sidney H. Asch, *The Supreme Court and Its Great Justices*.

TARBELL, IDA MINERVA

1857–1944 Author, Journalist

The only reason I am glad that I am a woman is that I will not have to marry one.

On herself, in Mary E. Tomkins, *Ida M. Tarbell*.

. . . beautiful with virtue.

Ray Stannard Baker, in *ibid*.

Miss Tarbarrel.

John D. Rockefeller, in Jules Abels, *The Rockefeller Millions*.

Not a word. Not a word about that misguided woman.

John D. Rockefeller, asked to comment on Miss Tarbell's *The History of the Standard Oil Company*, in Ida Minerva Tarbell, *All in a Day's Work*.

. . . Tarbell joins the select company of propagandists like Thomas Paine and Harriet Beecher Stowe whose works were like bugle calls to battle.

Mary E. Tomkins, *Ida M. Tarbell*.

. . . Tarbell is remembered as the journalist who bested the robber barons in a fair fight and scotched the reptilian principle of special privilege that they had attempted to substitute for the historic American principle of equal opportunity.

Ibid.

Muckraking crusader for the middle class, liberated New Woman who yet remained womanly, promoter of the values of Old America, and a person of unquestioned integrity, she was a sort of national maiden aunt. . . .

Ibid.

TARKINGTON, (NEWTON) BOOTH

1869–1946 Author

I'm more afraid of using up my eyes and right hand than the supplies of the mystic workman under the outer layers. I don't force that chap . . . But when I *let* him be one, he's a Simon Legree driving *me*. . . . He *always* wants to go on: *wants* to use my strength to the last thimble of it.

On himself, Undated letter to Hamlin Garland, in James Woodress, *Booth Tarkington, Gentleman from Indiana*.

I wish I'd kept my old reputation . . . I'm so darn dignified now that the only alleviating thing . . . is that most of the school children under the 7A grade . . . think I'm the man that killed Abraham Lincoln.

On himself, after receiving many honorary degrees, in James Woodress, *ibid*.

. . . from first to last, under various disguises, he has always been as he is to-day, a successful exponent of glorified melodrama.

Frederick Taber Cooper, *Some American Story Tellers*.

You have achieved two things that I had believed almost impossible in American fiction — you have written of average people without becoming an average writer and you have treated that American girl without sentimentality.

Ellen Glasgow, Undated letter to Tarkington, in James Woodress, *Booth Tarkington, Gentleman from Indiana*.

There was a young feller called Booth
Whose habits at times were uncouth
    Once he sat a whole day
    Drinking absinthe frappé
Then tossed off six quarts of vermouth.

Oliver Herford, in James Woodress, *ibid*.

I tremble a little for you. Now you must go on and be of the greatest.

William Dean Howells, talking to the young Tarkington, in James Woodress, *ibid*.

He wrote with the confident touch of a man unconfused by speculations. His manner was light and allusive. He had a rapid, joyous, accurate eye, invention and good temper.

Carl Van Doren, *The American Novel 1789–1939*.

Having kept faith in his life with the best traditions of American experience, he remained in death a member of Wordsworth's one great society — 'the noble living and the noble dead'.

James Woodress, *Booth Tarkington, Gentleman from Indiana.*

Totally lacking in guile and pretense, he was a man of integrity, a generous humanist, an inveterate optimist, and an old-fashioned gentleman.

Ibid.

TARLTON, RICHARD

—d. 1588 Actor

The partie nowe is gone,
    and closlie clad in claye,
Of all the jesters in the lande,
    he bare the praise awaie.

John Scottowe, British Library MS Harley 3885, f. 19.

TAYLOR, JEREMY, BISHOP

1613—67 Religious Author

Jer. Taylor's discursive intellect dazzle-darkened his intuition. The principle of becoming all things to all men, if by *any* means he might save *any*, with him as with Burke, thickened the protecting epidermis of the tact-nerve of truth into something like a callus. But take him all in all, such a miraculous combination of erudition, broad, deep, and omnigenous; of logic subtle as well as acute, and as robust as agile; of psychological insight, so fine yet so secure! of public prudence and practical *sageness* that one ray of *creative Faith* would have lit up and transfigured into wisdom, and of genuine imagination, with its streaming face unifying all at one moment like that of the setting sun when through an interspace of blue sky no larger than itself, it emerges from the cloud to sink behind the mountain, but a face seen only at *starts*, when some breeze from the higher air scatters, for a moment, the cloud of butterfly fancies, which flutter round him like a morning-garment of ten thousand colours — (now how shall I get out of this sentence? the tail is too big to be taken up into the coilers mouth) — well, as I was saying, I believe such a complete man hardly shall we meet again.

Samuel Taylor Coleridge, Letter to John Kenyon, 3 November 1814.

TAYLOR, ZACHARY

1784—1850 Twelfth United States President

I think I hear his cheerful voice,
'On column! Steady! Steady!'
So handy and so prompt was he
We called him Rough and Ready.

Anon. soldier's ditty, composed during the Seminole Wars, *circa* 1837.

Nero fiddled while Rome was burning; and the President may laugh and grow fat in his easy chair while the republic is rocking with earthquakes. If it should chance to be swallowed up, or riven to atoms, it is nothing to him; he has washed his hands of the dirty business of governing, and you must look to the agents, not to the principal.

Anon., *The Democratic Review*, June 1850.

General Taylor is remembered as the only president who ever rode a horse up the steps of the Capitol. Eminent historians agree that he was probably the only president who ever wanted to. At any rate, it is fortunate for the custodians of the building that this bad precedent has not been followed.

Richard Armour, *It All Started With Columbus.*

Indifferent specimen of the Lord of Creation. He is a short, thick-set man looking neither like the President of a great nation nor a military hero tho' he bears both honors and the last not undeservedly. If he had rested at the climax, history would have accorded him an unmodified distinction.

Margaret Gardiner, in Robert Seager II, *and Tyler too — A Biography of John and Julia Gardiner Tyler.*

Jesus is the most respectable person in the United States. Jesus sits on the President's chair. Zachary Taylor sits there, which is the same thing, for he believes in war, and in the Jesus who gave the Mexicans hell.

William Lloyd Garrison, in Russel B. Nye, *William Lloyd Garrison and the Humanitarian Reformers.*

He really is a most simple-minded old man. He has the least show or pretension about him of any man I ever saw; talks as artlessly as a child about affairs of state, and does not seem to pretend to a knowledge of anything of which he is ignorant. He is a remarkable man in some respects; and it is remarkable that such a man should be President of the United States.

Horace Mann, *Life of Horace Mann.*

. . . quite ignorant for his rank, and quite bigoted in

his ignorance . . . few men have ever had a more comfortable, labor-saving contempt for learning of every kind.

Winfield Scott, *Memoirs*, vol. 2.

TECUMSEH

1768?—1813 Chief of the Shawnee Nation

My heart is a stone: heavy with sadness for my people; cold with the knowledge that no treaty will keep the whites out of our lands; hard with the determination to resist as long as I live and breathe. Now we are weak and many of our people are afraid. But hear me: a single twig breaks, but the bundle of twigs is strong. Someday I will embrace our brother tribes and draw them into a bundle and together we will win our country back from the whites.

On himself, in T. C. McLuhan, *Touch The Earth*.

I am a Shawnee. My forefathers were warriors. Their son is a warrior. From them I take only my existence, from my tribe I take nothing. I am the maker of my own fortune, and Oh! that I could make that of my Red People, and of my country, as great as the conceptions of my mind, when I think of the spirit that rules the universe. I would not then come to Governor Harrison to ask him to tear up the treaty [of 1807], and to obliterate the landmark, but I would say to him, 'Sir, you have liberty to return to your own country.'

On himself, in *ibid*.

Where today are the Pequot? Where are the Narragansett, the Mohican, the Pakanoket, and many other once powerful tribes of our people? They have vanished before the avarice and the oppression of the White Man, as snow before a summer sun.

Will we let ourselves be destroyed in our turn without a struggle, give up our homes, our country bequeathed to us by the Great Spirit, the graves of our dead and everything that is dear and sacred to us. I know you will cry with me 'Never! Never!'

On himself, in Dee Brown, *Bury My Heart at Wounded Knee*.

TELFORD, THOMAS

1757—1834 Engineer

He was laborious, pains-taking, and skilful; but, what was better, he was honest and upright. He was a most reliable man; and hence he came to be extensively trusted. Whatever he undertook, he endea-

voured to excel in. He would be a first-rate hewer, and he became so. He was himself accustomed to attribute much of his success to the thorough way in which he had mastered the humble beginnings of this trade. He was even of the opinion that the course of manual training he had undergone, and the drudgery, as some would call it, of daily labour — first as an apprentice, and afterwards as a journeyman mason — had been of greater service to him than if he had passed through the curriculum of a University.

Samuel Smiles, *Lives of the Engineers*.

Telford it was, by whose presiding mind
The whole great work was plann'd and perfected;
Telford, who o'er the vale of Cambrian Dee,
Aloft in air, at giddy height upborne,
Carried his navigable road, and hung
High o'er Menai's straits the bending bridge.

Robert Southey, *Inscriptions for the Caledonian Canal*.

TEMPLE, HENRY JOHN, see under PALMERSTON, VISCOUNT

TEMPLE, SIR WILLIAM

1628—99 Statesman, Author

It was his constitution to dread failure more than he desired success, to prefer security, comfort, repose, leisure, to the turmoil and anxiety which are inseparable from greatness; and this natural languor of mind, when contrasted with the malignant enemy of the keen and restless spirits among whom his lot was cast, sometimes appears to resemble the moderation of virtue. But we must own that he seems to us to sink into littleness and meanness when we compare him, we do not say with any high ideal standard of morality, but with many of those frail men, who, aiming at noble ends, but often drawn from the right path by strong passions and strong temptations, have left to posterity a doubtful and checkered fame.

T. B. Macaulay, *Essays: 'Sir William Temple'*.

TENNIEL, SIR JOHN

1820—1914 Artist, Illustrator

Tenniel used his pen to attack fraud and corruption and to ridicule folly. He seemed to inherit from his father, who was 'an instructor in arms', something of the equanimity of a fencer. Fair and good-natured in his work, he gave to political cartooning a dignity it did not possess before. His study of the Elgin Marbles and other pieces of sculpture as a lad imparted to his work something of the dignity of sculpture.

H. Hubbard, *Some Victorian Draughtsmen.*

Tenniel has much of the largeness and symbolic mystery of imagination which belong to the great leaders of classic art: in the shadowy masses and sweeping lines of his great compositions, there are tendencies, which might have won his adoption into the school of Tintoret; and his scorn of whatever seems to him dishonest or contemptible in religion, would have translated itself into awe in the presence of its vital power.

John Ruskin, *The Art of England.*

TENNYSON, ALFRED, LORD

1809—92 Poet

'Artist first, then Poet,' some writer said of me. I should answer, 'Poeta nascitur non fit'; indeed, 'Poeta nascitur et fit.' I suppose I was nearer thirty than twenty before I was anything of an artist.

On himself (note written in 1890), in Hallam Tennyson, *Tennyson, A Memoir.*

Baron Alfred T. de T.
   Are we at last in sweet acord?
I learn — excuse the girlish glee —
   That you've become a noble lord;
So now that time to think you've had
   Of what it makes charming girls,
Perhaps you find they're not so bad —
   Those daughters of a hundred earls.

Anon., *The Vere de Vere to Tennyson.*

As for Mr Halfred he was a 'dacious one. He used to be walking up and down the carriage drive hundreds of times a day, shouting and holloaing and preaching, with a book always in his hand and such a lad for making sad work of his clothes . . . down on his heels and his coat unlaced and his hair anyhow. He was a rough 'un was Mister Halfred and no mistake.

An old servant at Somersby Rectory, in H. D. Rawnsley, *Memories of the Tennysons.*

To drawing-room as usual, where Tennyson had his port. Barnes no wine. Tennyson said, 'Modern fame is nothing: I'd rather have an acre of land. I shall go down, down! I'm up now. Action and reaction.'

William Allingham, Diary, 4 October 1863.

The real truth is that Tennyson, with all his temperament and artistic skill, is deficient in intellectual power; and no modern poet can make very much of his business unless he is pre-eminently strong in this.

Matthew Arnold, Letter to his Sister, 1860.

He had a large, loose-limbed body, a swarthy complexion, a high, narrow forehead, and huge bricklayer's hands; in youth he looked like a gypsy; in age like a dirty old monk; he had the finest ear, perhaps, of any English poet; he was also undoubtedly the stupidest; there was little about melancholia that he didn't know; there was little else that he did.

W. H. Auden, Introduction to *A Selection from the Poems of Alfred Lord Tennyson.*

If Wordsworth is the great English poet of Nature, then Tennyson is the great English poet of the Nursery . . . i.e., his poems deal with human emotions in their most primitive states, uncomplicated by conscious sexuality or intellectual rationalization.

Ibid.

He is very natural & simple, & rather abrupt in his manner from a constitutional shyness; a man to revolt against any effort to make him 'shine'. He doesn't shine — but you do not feel it difficult to believe him to be a great man whether he speaks or is silent. I assure you he smoked his pipe (a real clay pipe) after tea, — with just a word of mere form to ascertain if it would throw me into fits or not.

Elizabeth Barrett Browning, Letter to Mrs David Ogilvy, 25 July 1851.

He seems . . . in truth but a *long*, lazy kind of man, at least just after dinner — Yet there is something naive about him — the genius you see too.

Robert Browning, 1846, after seeing Tennyson for the first time, at a public dinner.

Virgil was no good because Tennyson ran him, and as for Tennyson — well, Tennyson goes without saying.

Samuel Butler, *Notebooks.*

Alfred is one of the few British and foreign figures (a not increasing number I think) who are and remain beautiful to me, a true human soul, or some authentic approximation thereto, to whom your own soul can say, 'Brother!'

Thomas Carlyle, in Hallam Tennyson, *Tennyson, A Memoir.*

He could not think up to the height of his own towering style.

G. K. Chesterton, *The Victorian Age in Literature.*

Tennyson is a great poet, for reasons that are perfectly clear. He has three qualities which are seldom found together except in the greatest poets: abundance, variety, and complete competence. We therefore cannot appreciate his work unless we read a good deal of it. We may not admire his aims: but whatever he sets out to do, he succeeds in doing, with a mastery that gives us the sense of confidence that is one of the major pleasures of poetry. . . . He had the finest ear of any English poet since Milton.

T. S. Eliot, Introduction to Tennyson's *Poems.*

I remember him well, a sort of Hyperion.

Edward Fitzgerald (describing Tennyson at Cambridge), in Hallam Tennyson, *Tennyson, A Memoir.*

No, you cannot read the *Idylls of the King* except in minute doses because of the sub-nauseating sissiness — there is no other convenient word — of the points of view of both Lord Tennyson and the characters that he projects . . . and because of the insupportable want of skill in the construction of sentences, the choice of words and the perpetual ampliation of images.

Ford Madox Ford, *The March of Literature.*

Tennyson had the British Empire for God, and Queen Victoria for Virgin Mary.

Lady Gregory, in William Butler Yeats, Journal, 17 March 1909,

You call Tennyson 'a great outsider'; you mean, I think, to the soul of poetry. I feel what you mean, though it grieves me to hear him depreciated, as of late years has often been done. Come what may he will be one of our greatest poets. To me his poetry appears 'chryselephantine'; always of precious mental material and each verse a work of art, no botchy places, not only so but no half-wrought or low-toned ones, no drab, no brown-holland; but the form, though fine, not the perfect artist's form, not equal to the material.

Gerard Manley Hopkins, Letter to R. W. Dixon, 1879.

Tennyson was not Tennysonian.

Henry James, *The Middle Years.*

I would he were as his poems.

Edward Lear, Diary, 11 July 1865.

Tennyson, while affecting to dread observation, was none the less no little vain, a weakness of which Meredith gave me this amusing illustration. Tennyson and William Morris were once walking together on a road in the Isle of Wight. Suddenly in the distance appeared two cyclists wheeling towards them. Tennyson immediately took alarm, and, turning to Morris, growled out, 'Oh, Morris, what shall I do. Those fellows are sure to bother me!' Thereupon Morris drew him protectively to his side. 'Keep close to me,' he said, 'I'll see that they don't bother you.' The cyclists came on, sped by without a sign, and presently disappeared on the horizon. There was a moment or two of silence, and then Tennyson, evidently huffed that he had attracted no attention, once more growled out, 'They never even looked at me!'

Richard Le Gallienne, *The Romantic '90s.*

The great length of his mild fluency: the yards of linen-drapery for the delight of women.

George Meredith, in Frank Harris, *My Life and Loves.*

Brahms is just like Tennyson, an extraordinary musician, with the brains of a third rate village policeman.

George Bernard Shaw, Letter to Pakenham Beatty, 4 April 1893.

Tennyson, who was nothing if not a virtuoso, never produced a success that will bear reading after Poe's failures.

George Bernard Shaw, *Pen Portraits and Reviews.*

Tennyson's knowledge of nature — nature in every aspect — was simply astonishing. His passion for 'star-gazing' has often been commented upon by readers of his poetry. Since Dante no poet in any land has so loved the stars. He had an equal delight in watching the lightning; and I remember being at Aldworth once during a thunder-storm when I was alarmed at the temerity with which he persisted, in spite of all remonstrances, in gazing at the blinding lightning. For moonlight effects he had a passion equally strong, and it is especially pathetic to those who know this to remember that he passed away in the light he so much loved — in a room where there was no artificial light — nothing to quicken the darkness but the light of the full moon.

Theodore Watts-Dunton, *Impressions of Tennyson.*

See also Matthew Arnold, John Donne, Henry Wadsworth Longfellow, Gilbert Murray, William Wordsworth

TERRY, DAME (ALICE) ELLEN

1847—1928 Actress

Do you know, I have no weight on the stage; unless I have heavy robes I can't keep on the ground.
    On herself, Letter to George Bernard Shaw.

E. T. was persuadable — especially on Mondays — less so on Tuesdays. On Wednesday, people around her found it difficult to make her understand what it was they were trying to say — but by the time Thursday arrived she could be counted on to do the very thing they didn't expect. Friday she devoted to telling them that it didn't hurt, and that they must be brave and not cry — Saturday was always a half-holiday, spent in promising her advisers that she would be good next week — and on Sunday she generally drove away to Hampton Court with Irving, waving her lily white hand.
    Edward Gordon Craig, *Ellen Terry and Her Secret Self.*

Miss Ellen Terry is 'aesthetic'; not only her garments but her features themselves bear the stamp of the new enthusiasm. She has a charm, a great deal of a certain amateurish, angular grace, a total lack of what the French call *chic*, and a countenance very happily adapted to the expression of pathetic emotion. To this last effect her voice also contributes; it has a sort of monotonous, husky thickness which is extremely touching, though it gravely interferes with the modulation of many of her speeches.
    Henry James, in *Nation*, 12 June 1879.

To learn Imogen requires a Bishop's wife, not *you*.
    George Bernard Shaw, Letter to E. T., 28 August 1896.

Ellen's skin does not fit her body more closely than Lady Cicely Brassbound [a character in *Captain Brassbound's Conversion*, one of Shaw's plays] fits her; for I am a first class ladies tailor, and I love Ellen and Ellen loves me.
    George Bernard Shaw, Letter to Mrs Patrick Campbell, 3 July 1912.

One may say that her marriages were adventures and her friendships enduring.
    George Bernard Shaw, in C. St J. Constable ed., *Ellen Terry and Bernard Shaw, A Correspondence.*

The contrast between herself and [Henry] Irving could hardly have been stronger. She, all brains and sympathy, scattering them everywhere and on everybody: he, all self, concentrating that self on his stage as on a pedestal. She, able to express herself effortlessly with her pen, raining letters all over the place on the just and the unjust: he preferring to keep a staff of literary henchmen to write his letters and lectures, which sometimes did him only sorry justice. But the combination worked. Everything went from her, and everything came to him. They were extrovert and introvert, and thus to a sufficient extent complemented one another whilst the Lyceum sun was at its zenith.
    George Bernard Shaw, *Ellen Terry and Bernard Shaw, a Correspondence.*

She was an extremely beautiful girl and as innocent as a rose. When Watts kissed her, she took for granted she was going to have a baby.
    George Bernard Shaw, in Stephen Winston, *Days with Bernard Shaw.*

Judging from the banquet, Lady Macbeth seems an economical housekeeper and evidently patronises local industries for her husband's clothes and the servants' liveries, but she takes care to do all her own shopping in Byzantium.
    Oscar Wilde, on Ellen Terry in Irving's revival of *Macbeth*, 29 December 1888.

THACKERAY, WILLIAM MAKEPEACE

1811—63 Novelist

William Makepeace Thackeray
Wept into his daiquiri,
When he heard St. John's Wood
Thought he was no good.
    W. H. Auden, *Academic Graffiti.*

Thackeray, like Sterne, looked at everything — at nature, at life, at art — from a *sensitive* aspect. His mind was, to some considerable extent, like a woman's mind. It could comprehend abstractions when they were unrolled and explained before it, but it never naturally created them; never of itself, and without external obligation, devoted itself to them. The visible scene of life — the streets, the servants, the clubs, the gossip, the West End — fastened on his brain. These were to him reality. . . . The sick wife in the next room, the unpaid baker's bill, the lodging-house keeper who doubts your solvency; these, and such as these, — the usual accompaniments of an early literary life, — are constantly alluded to in his writings. Perhaps he could never take a grand enough view of literature, or accept the truth of 'high art', because of his natural tendency to this stern and humble realism.
    Walter Bagehot, in *National Review*, April 1864.

He dissects his victims with a smile; and performs

the cruellest of operations on their self-love with a pleasantry which looks provokingly very like good-nature.

Robert Bell, review of *Vanity Fair*, in *Fraser's Magazine*, 1848.

I approve Mr Thackeray. This may sound presumptuous perhaps, but I mean that I have long recognized in his writings genuine talent, such as I admired, such as I wondered at and delighted in. No author seems to distinguish so exquisitely as he does dross from ore, the real from the counterfeit.

Charlotte Brontë, Letter to W. S. Williams, 28 October 1847.

Thackeray is unique. I *can* say no more, I *will* say no less.

Charlotte Brontë, Letter to W. S. Williams, 29 March 1848.

George Smythe said, that, as they say, novelists always draw their own characters, he wished Thackeray would draw his own — that would be a character! The Cynic Parasite!

Benjamin Disraeli, *Reminiscences*.

If Mr Thackeray falls short of Fielding, much of whose peculiar power and more of whose manner he has inherited or studiously acquired, it is because an equal amount of large cordiality has not raised him entirely above the region of the sneering, into that of simple uncontaminated human affection. His satiric pencil is dipped in deeper colours than that of his prototype. Not Vanity Fair so properly as Rascality Fair is the scene he lays open to our view; and he never wholly escapes from his equivocal associations, scarcely ever lays aside for a whole page his accustomed sneer. His is a less comfortable, and on the whole therefore, let us add, a less true view of society than Fielding's.

John Forster, review of *Vanity Fair*, in *Examiner*, July 1848.

Finished that brilliant, bitter book, 'Vanity Fair'; it shows great insight into the intricate badness of human nature, and draws a cruel sort of line between moral and intellectual eminence, as if they were most commonly dissociated, which I trust is no true bill.

Caroline Fox, *Journals*, November 1849.

The great accusation against him has been cynicism and hardness. In that charge most of us from time to time have joined. But, going into the more solemn and careful account which we must make with the dead, we think that charge should be withdrawn. The charge has been made and sustained, because in his fierce campaign against falsehood, meanness and vulgarity, he did his work only too thoroughly, and hunted those vices high and low, into every hole and corner where they had taken refuge. If he found a mere soupçon of one of them in his own favourite characters . . . he dragged it to the light; and then the world, or part of it, said, 'The man cannot understand a perfect character.' It was because he understood what a perfect character should be so well that the charge was made against him.

Henry Kingsley, in *Macmillan's Magazine*, February 1864.

As a satirist, it is his business to tear away the mask from life, but as an artist and a teacher he grievously errs when he shows us *everywhere* corruption underneath the mask. His scepticism is pushed too far. While trampling on cant, while exposing what is base and mean, and despicable, he is not attentive enough to honour, and to paint what is high, and generous, and noble in human nature.

G. H. Lewes, in *Morning Chronicle*, March 1848.

Thackeray settled like a meat-fly on whatever one had got for dinner, and made one sick of it.

John Ruskin, *Fors Clavigera*.

It is a terrible thing to be taught by a master of his craft that in life there is little to excite admiration — nothing to inspire enthusiasm. It is fearful to have insight into the human heart, and to detect in that holy of holies not even one solitary spark of the once pure flame. . . . Guilt is among us — crime abounds — falsehood is around and about us; but, conscious as we are of these facts, we know that man may yet trust to his fellow man, and that evil is not permitted to outweigh good. A series of novels, based upon the principle which Mr Thackeray delights to illustrate would utterly destroy this knowledge and render us a race of unbelievers — animals less happy than the brutes who, dumb and unreasoning as they are, can still consort together and derive some consolation from their companionship.

The Times, 22 December 1852.

Among all our novelists his style is the purest, as to my ear it is also the most harmonious. Sometimes it is disfigured by a slight touch of affectation, by little conceits which smell of the oil; — but the language is always lucid. The reader, without labour, knows what he means, and knows all that he means.

Anthony Trollope, *Autobiography*.

See also Charles Dickens, Lord Lytton, Tobias Smollett.

THOMAS À BECKET

1118?–70 Archbishop of Canterbury, Statesman

. . . For three hundred years, he was accounted one of the greatest saints in heaven, as may appear from the accounts in the ledger-books of the offerings made to the three greatest altars in Christ's Church in Canterbury. The one was to Christ, the other to the Virgin, and the third to St. Thomas. In one year there was offered at Christ's altar, 31.2s.6d; to the Virgin's altar, 631.5s.6d; but to St. Thomas's altar, 8321.12s.3d.
    Gilbert Burnet, *History of the Reformation.*

. . . your Becket was a noisy egoist and hypocrite; getting his brains spilt on the floor of Canterbury Cathedral, to secure the main chance, — somewhat uncertain how!
    Thomas Carlyle, *Past and Present.*

You are the Archbishop in revolt against the King;
    in rebellion to the King and the law of the land;
You are the Archbishop who was made by the King;
    whom he met in your place to carry out his command.
You are his servant, his tool and his jack,
You wore his favours on your back,
You had your honours all from his hand; from him
    you had the power, the seal and the ring.
This is the man who was the tradesman's son: the
    backstairs brat who was born in Cheapside;
This is the creature that crawled upon the King;
    swollen with blood and swollen with pride.
Creeping out of the London dirt,
Crawling up like a louse on your shirt,
The man who cheated, swindled, lied; broke his
    oath and betrayed his King.
    T. S. Eliot, *Murder in the Cathedral* (the four knights accuse Becket).

During which his office, who braver than Becket? None in the court wore more costly clothes, mounted more stately steeds, made more sumptuous feasts, kept more jovial company, brake more merry jests, used more pleasant pastimes. In a word, he was so perfect a layman, that his parsonages of Bromfield, and St. Maryhill in London, with other ecclesiastical cures, whereof he was pastor, might even look all to themselves, he taking no care to discharge them.
    Thomas Fuller, *Church History of Britain.*

Will no one free me of this turbulent priest?
    Henry II, attributed.

A bearer of the iniquity of the clergy.
    Henry VIII, Royal Proclamation of November 1538.

Other saints had borne testimony by their sufferings to the general doctrine of Christianity; but Becket had sacrificed his life to the power of the clergy; and this peculiar merit challenged, and not in vain, a suitable acknowledgement of his memory.
    David Hume, *History of England.*

A minister of iniquity.
    John of Salisbury, *Entheticus II.*

There is probably no hour in medieval history of which the details are so well known, and so revealing of character, as is the last hour of the archbishop's life, from about half-past two to half-past three on that dark December afternoon.
    David Knowles, *Archbishop Thomas Becket: A Character Study.*

When they returned to the dead archbishop Robert of Merton, his confessor, showed those around him the hairshirt, which even his own clerks had never seen, beneath the monastic habit and the canon's rochet that he was wearing. The hairshirt and drawers were sewn tightly round the body and thighs, but could be opened at the back for the daily scourging. The whole garment was alive with vermin, and the monks remarked to each other that the martyrdom by sword was more tolerable than this other never-ceasing martyrdom.
    Ibid.

In the seven years (1155–62) in which he held that office, the Angevin chancery became the most perfect piece of administrative machinery that Europe had yet known.
    T. F. Tout, on Becket's service as Lord Chancellor, *The Place of St. Thomas of Canterbury in History: a Centenary Study.*

THOMAS, DYLAN MARLAIS

1914–53 Poet

It is typical of the physically weak to emphasize the strength of life (Nietzsche): of the apprehensive and complex-ridden to emphasize its naivete and dark wholesomeness (D. H. Lawrence); of the naked-nerved and blood-timid to emphasize its brutality and horror (Me!).
    On himself, Letter to Pamela Hansford Johnson, 1933.

I should say I wanted to write poetry in the beginning because I had fallen in love with words. The first poems I knew were nursery rhymes, and before I could read them for myself I had come to love just the words of them, the words alone. What the words stood for, symbolised, or meant, was of very secondary importance; what mattered was the *sound* of them as I heard them for the first time on the lips of the remote and incomprehensible grown-ups who seemed, for some reason, to be living in my world. And these words were, to me, as the notes of bells, the sounds of musical instruments, the noises of wind, sea, and rain, the rattle of milkcarts, the clopping of hooves on cobbles, the fingering of branches on a window pane, might be to someone, deaf from birth, who has miraculously found his hearing. I did not care what the words said, overmuch, nor what happened to Jack & Jill & the Mother Goose rest of them; I cared for the shapes of sound that their names, and the words describing their actions, made in my ears; I cared for the colours the words cast on my eyes.

On himself, in *Texas Quarterly*, Winter 1961.

Myself, I believe it possible that if one kept one's ear close to the dirt of Dylan Thomas's grave in Wales, one might overhear that fruity voice murmuring ironically to itself a variation on the last words of the dying Vespasian: 'I think I am becoming a near myth.'

George Barker, in *Listener*, 4 December 1965.

In America, visiting British writers are greeted at cocktail parties by faculty wives with 'Can you screw as good as Dylan?'

Anthony Burgess, *Urgent Copy*.

Dylan wore a green porkpie hat pulled down level with his slightly bulging eyes: like the agate marbles we used as Alley Taws when I was a boy in France, but a darker brown. His full lips were set low in a round full face, a fag-end stuck to the lower one. His nose was bulbous and shiny. He told me afterwards that he used to rub it up with his fist before the mirror every morning until it shone satisfactorily; as a housewife might polish her doorknob or I the silver-topped malacca cane that I affected in those days.

Julian Maclaren-Ross, *Memoirs of the Forties*.

       . . . Young and gay
A bulbous Taliessin, a spruce and small
Bow-tied Silenus roistering his way
Through lands of fruit and fable, well aware
That even Dionysus has his day.

Louis MacNeice, *Autumn Sequel*.

There is a story of the friend in the funeral parlour, who looked down at the poet's painted face, loud suit and carnation in his buttonhole, only to declare, 'He would never have been seen dead in it.'

Andrew Sinclair, *Dylan Thomas*.

I think it was Whitman who said that 'even in religious fervor there is always a touch of animal heat.' Both religious fervour and animal heat were in his poetry, to the highest degree. His poetry was the 'pure fire compressed into holy forms' of which one of Porphyry's Oracles spoke. The generation of those poems was attended by 'the great heat' that Aristotle said 'attended the generation of lions.' To him, blood was spirit.

Edith Sitwell, *Taken Care Of*.

The great thing to remember about Dylan was that he was a complete chameleon and could adapt himself to any company and play any role. He was, in fact, a natural born actor. . . . His favourite role was that of a Welsh country gentleman for which in later days he dressed in hairy tweeds and carried a knobbed walkingstick. Alternative he could be a B.B.C. actor and verse reader, for which he wore a light grey smooth tweed suit. The role of the drunken Welsh poet with 'fag in the corner of the mouth, and dirty raincoat, and polo sweater' sometimes lasted for a week or more, but not longer. He had an extremely flexible voice and could suit it to any of these roles.

Donald Taylor, in Constantine Fitzgibbon, *Life of Dylan Thomas*.

His passion for lies was congenital: more a practice in invention than a lie. He would tell quite unnecessary ones, which did not in any way improve his situation: such as, when he had been to one cinema, saying it was another, and making up the film that was on: and the obvious ones, that only his mother pretended not to see through, like being carted off the bus into his home, and saying he had been having coffee, in a café, with a friend.

Caitlin Thomas, *Leftover Life to Kill*.

THOMAS, MARTHA CAREY

1857—1935 Educator, Women's Rights Advocate

If I ever live and grow up my *one* aim and concentrated purpose *shall be* and *is* to show that women *can learn, can reason, can compete* with men in the grand fields of literature and science and conjecture that open before the nineteenth century, that a woman can be a woman and a *true* one without having all her time engrossed by dress and society.

On herself, in Edith Finch, *Carey Thomas of Bryn Mawr*.

She had no time and no use for casual chitchat. Compelled by courtesy to suffer it, the warmth of her manner chilled to bare civility, the heavy eyelids dropped slightly over the brilliant eyes, her face became a mask of controlled impatience and distaste.

Edith Finch, *ibid.*

THOMAS, NORMAN MATTOON

1884–1968 Socialist, Politician

However, uneasy as I am about being spoken of too well by too many men, I don't feel I'm obliged to go out and smash somebody's window to prove that I'm not respectable.

On himself, in *Playboy*, November 1966.

Roosevelt: Norman, I'm a damn sight better politician than you. *Thomas*: Certainly Mr. President, you're on that side of the desk and I'm on this.

On himself, *Autobiography*.

My actual transition to socialism was slow and gradual. There was no vision of any 'Road to Damascus.' There was no great moment of any kind.

On himself, *Reminiscences*, part 1.

I would rather be right than be president but I am perfectly willing to be both.

On himself, 'The Dissenter's Role in a Totalitarian Age', in *New York Times Magazine*, 20 November 1949.

I appreciate the flowers only I wish the funeral hadn't been so complete.

On himself, on being congratulated for running an unsuccessful but high calibre campaign, in *The Unofficial Observer, American Messiahs.*

. . . even as an inveterate loser, he has been one of the most influential individuals in 20th century American politics. His ideas have received from his rivals the supreme compliment of plagiarism and from the American people the accolade of acceptance.

Anon., in *Washington Post*, 20 November 1959.

. . . conveyed . . . [the] feeling that there is something glorious about being forever engaged. He seemed always just back from the side of the sharecroppers or being egged by the friends of Frank Hague. In that guise, he represented the only available piece of that buried tradition of the American radical about whom Dos Passos wrote. The old libertarian dream of spending one's life in lonely combat against every form of enslavement, to the extent that it was not a Communist confusion, appeared to us to have no vessel but Norman Thomas.

Murray Kempton, *Part of Our Time: Some Ruins and Monuments of the Thirties.*

Like a veteran Shakespeare player, he needs but to be thrown a cue to reply with the answering soliloquy and the rest of the play. He has a perfect sense of timing and an accurate feel for dramatic values. He can let an audience and an opponent relax, then suddenly, with a verbal shaft, skewer the opponent and jerk the audience to attention. He can explode and harangue when the necessity presents itself. His personality is imposing and his wit is quick.

Harry MacArthur, in Washington (Sunday) *Star*, 25 November 1948.

My objection to Norman Thomas can be put briefly: he is a liberal, not a socialist. A socialist, as I use the term anyway, is one who has taken the first simple step *at least* of breaking with present day bourgeoise society . . . [Thomas's] role has always been that of left opposition *within the present society*, the fighting crusader in small matters . . . and the timid conformist in big matters. . . .

Dwight MacDonald, *Politics*, October 1944.

. . . while they were giving him ear they would have at least enjoyed a rare and exhilarating pleasure, to wit, that of listening to a political speech by a really intelligent and civilized man. . . . It is not often in this great Republic that one hears a political hullabaloo that is also a work of art.

H. L. Mencken, in *Baltimore Sun*, 18 October 1948.

. . . the speaker poked gentle but devastating fun at all the clowns in the political circus, by no means forgetting himself. There was not a trace of rancor in his speech, and not a trace of Messianic bombast . . . his voice is loud, clear and a trifle metallic. He never starts a sentence that doesn't stop, and he never accents the wrong syllable in a word or the wrong word in a sentence.

Ibid.

His essential contribution indeed, was to keep moral issues alive at a moment when the central emphasis was on meeting economic emergencies. At his best, Thomas gave moving expression to an ethical urgency badly needed in politics, to a sense of the relation between means and ends and of the inestimable value of the individual human being. . . .

Arthur M. Schlesinger Jr, *The Age of Roosevelt*, vol. 2.

. . . called himself a Socialist as a result of misunderstanding.

Leon Trotsky, in Harry Fleischman, *Norman Thomas, a biography.*

THOMPSON, SIR BENJAMIN (COUNT RUMFORD)

1753—1814 Physicist, Social Reformer

These, Virtue, are thy triumphs, that adorn
Fitliest our nature, and bespeak us born
For loftiest action, not to gaze and run
From clime to clime, or batten in the sun,
Dragging a drony flight from flower to flower,
Like summer insects in a gaudy hour;
Nor yet, o'er love-sick tales with fancy range
And cry, 'Tis Pitiful, 'tis passing strange!'
But on life's varied views to look around
And raise expiring sorrow from the ground:
And he, who thus hath born his part assign'd
In the sad fellowship of human kind,
Or for a moment soothed the bitter pain
Of a poor brother — has not lived in vain!
    Samuel Taylor Coleridge, *Count Rumford.*

The Triumvirate of the memorable embarkation will consist of the grand Gibbon, Henry Laurens, Esquire, President of Congress, and Mr. Secretary, Colonel, Admiral, Philosopher Thompson.
    Edward Gibbon, Letter to Lord Sheffield, 17 September 1785.

Yet all shall read, and all that page approve
When public spirit meets with public love.
Thus late where poverty with rapine dwelt,
Rumford's kind genius the Bavarian felt,
Not by romantic charities beguiled,
But calm in project and in mercy mild,
Where'oer his wisdom guided, none withstood,
Content with peace and practicable good
Round him the labourers throng, the nobles wait,
Friend of the poor and guardian of the state.
    Thomas J. Mathias, *The Pursuits of Literature.*

An educated person's general knowledge would be unlikely to include even enough material for a thumbnail sketch of Rumford and his work, and yet in his lifetime few men were more widely known. He had given his name to a type of fire-grate. A French soldier grumbling about the *maigreur* of his soup would refer to it disdainfully as Rumford's soup. The poor in more than one capital city would see his name or his portrait on tickets entitling them to free dinners. He was the personal friend of more than one king and well known to many others. In science his name stood high: he had received the Copley Medal from the Royal Society and honours from many other learned bodies. All these distinctions and a host of others gave him a fame almost equal to that of his contemporary and fellow countryman Benjamin Franklin. None the less Count Rumford has receded into the background of history.
    W. J. Sparrow, *Knight of the White Eagle.*

The great characteristic of Rumford's whole career is that *all* his practical work was strictly philosophical, and most of his philosophical work was eminently and directly practical.
    W. Mattieu Williams, in *Notices of the Proceedings at the Meetings of the Members of the Royal Institution of Great Britain.*

THOMSON, JAMES

1700—48 Poet

Dr Johnson said that Thomson had a true poetical genius, the power of viewing everything in a poetical light. That his fault was such a cloud of words sometimes that the sense could hardly peep through. He said Shiels, who compiled Cibber's *Lives of the Poets*, was one day with him. He took down Thomson and read a good portion to Shiels, and then asked if this was not very fine. Shiels was high in admiration. 'Well,' said Dr Johnson, 'I have missed every other line.'
    James Boswell, *Journal*, 11 April 1776.

Remembrance oft shall haunt the shore
When Thames in summer wreaths is drest
And oft suspend the dashing oar
To bid his gentle spirit rest.
    William Collins, *Ode on the Death of Mr Thomson.*

Thomson, the kind-hearted Thomson, was the most indolent of mortals and of poets. But he was also one of the best both of mortals and of poets. Dr Johnson makes it his praise that he wrote 'no line which dying he would wish to blot.' Perhaps a better proof of his honest simplicity, and inoffensive goodness of disposition, would be that he wrote no line which any other person living would wish that he should blot. . . . As critics, however, not as moralists, we might say on the other hand — 'Would he had blotted a thousand!'
    William Hazlitt, *Lectures on the English Poets.*

Among his peculiarities was a very unskilful and inarticulate manner of pronouncing any lofty or solemn composition. He was once reading to Doddington, who, being himself a reader eminently elegant, was so much provoked by his odd utterance, that he snatched the paper from his hand, and told him that he did not understand his own verses.
    Samuel Johnson, *Lives of the Poets.*

THOMSON, SIR WILLIAM, BARON KELVIN

1824—1907 Scientist, Inventor

Thirty years later another undergraduate of Peterhouse, named William Thomson, better known to fame as Lord Kelvin, was so certain he would be top of the [examination] list that he sent his servant to find out who was second. (It was William Thomson.)

    B. V. Bowden, *Faster than Thought.*

Lord Kelvin appeared to have the unique power of carrying on two trains of thought, or attending to two things at a time. At meals or in company his eyes at times had an abstracted or far-away look as if his mind was 'voyaging o'er strange seas of thought alone,' but yet he could still attend apparently to what was going on around him. At lunch I remember one day when his mind had apparently been pondering some abstruse scientific question, and Lady Thomson had been discussing plans for an afternoon excursion, Sir William suddenly looked up and said, 'At what times does the dissipation of energy begin?'

    Sir Ambrose Fleming, *Memories of a Scientific Life.*

His mind was extraordinarily fertile in ideas. . . . Even in a lecture, if a new idea occurred to him, he would start off on a new tack. This made him very discursive and often very lengthy. . . . He has been known to have lectured for the hour before reaching the subject of the lecture.

    J. J. Thomson, *Recollections and Reflections.*

THOREAU, HENRY DAVID

1817—62 Essayist, Poet, Transcendentalist

I should not talk so much about myself if there were anybody else whom I knew as well.

    On himself, in *Walden.*

I would rather sit on a pumpkin and have it all to myself than be crowded on a velvet cushion.

    On himself, in *ibid.*

My life hath been the poem I would have writ,
But I could not both live and utter it.

    On himself, in Walter Harding, *The Days of Henry Thoreau.*

You may rely on it that you have the best of me in my books, and that I am not worth seeing personally.

    On himself, Letter to a friend, 1856.

Much do they wrong our Henry, wise and kind,
Morose who name thee, cynical to men,
Forsaking manners civil and refined
To build thyself in Walden woods a den, —
There flout society, flatter the rude kind:
We better knew thee, loyal citizen!
Thou, Friendship's all-adventuring pioneer,
Civility itself would civilize.

    Amos Bronson Alcott, in F. B. Sanborn, *The Life of Henry David Thoreau.*

When a pious visitor inquired sweetly, 'Henry, have you made your peace with God?' he replied 'We have never quarrelled.'

    Brooks Atkinson, *Henry Thoreau, the Cosmic Yankee.*

He liked to administer doses of moral quinine, and he never thought of sugaring his pills.

    Van Wyck Brooks, *The Flowering of New England 1815—1865.*

Thoreau's quality is very penetrating and contagious; reading him is like eating onions — one must look out or the flavor will reach his own page.

    John Burroughs, *Henry David Thoreau.*

Behind a mask of self-exaltation Thoreau performed as before a mirror — and first of all for his own edification. He was a fragile Narcissus embodied in a homely New Englander.

    Leon Edel, *Henry D. Thoreau.*

Henry does not feel himself except in opposition. He wants a fallacy to expose, a blunder to pillory, requires a little sense of victory, a roll of the drums, to call his powers into full exercise.

    Ralph Waldo Emerson, in Walter Harding, *The Days of Henry Thoreau.*

He was bred to no profession; he never married; he lived alone; he never went to church; he never voted; he refused to pay a tax to the state; he ate no flesh, he drank no wine, he never knew the use of tobacco; and, though a naturalist, he used neither trap nor gun.

    Ralph Waldo Emerson, in Mark Van Doren, *Henry David Thoreau, A Critical Study.*

Thoreau was sincerity itself, and might fortify the convictions of prophets in the ethical laws by his holy living. It was an affirmative experience which he refused to set aside.

    Ralph Waldo Emerson, 'Thoreau', in Edmund Wilson ed., *The Shock of Recognition.*

. . . the nullifier of civilization, who insisted on nibbling his asparagus at the wrong end.

    Oliver Wendell Holmes, in Jay B. Hubbell, *Who Are The Major American Writers?*

He had a noble face, with tossed hair, a distraught eye, and a fine aquilinity of profile . . . but his nose failed to add that foot to his stature which Lamb says a nose of that shape will always give a man.

    William D. Howells, in Henry Seidel Canby, *Thoreau.*

He was imperfect, unfinished, inartistic; he was worse than provincial — he was parochial.

    Henry James, *Life of Nathaniel Hawthorne.*

He seems to me to have been a man with so high a conceit of himself that he accepted without questioning, and insisted on our accepting, his defects and weaknesses of character as virtues and powers peculiar to himself.

    James Russell Lowell, 'Thoreau', in Edmund Wilson ed., *The Shock of Recognition.*

Viewed now from the heights of our decadence, he seems almost like an early Roman. The word virtue has meaning again, when connected with his name.

    Henry Miller, Preface to Henry David Thoreau, *Life Without Principle.*

By creating a classic image of the cynic hermit in ideal solitude Thoreau has demonstrated some of the meannesses of the demands of Time and Matter, and furnished the spirit and will for social criticism; he has made men acute critics, if not sensible shepherds, of their own sentiments.

    Mark Van Doren, *Henry David Thoreau, A Critical Study.*

THURBER, JAMES GROVER

1894–1961 Cartoonist, Writer, Playwright

With sixty staring me in the face, I have developed inflammation of the sentence structure and a definite hardening of the paragraphs.

    On himself, in *New York Post*, 30 June 1955.

I do not have a psychiatrist and I do not want one, for the simple reason that if he listened to me long enough, he might become disturbed.

    On himself, *Credos and Curios.*

The mistaken exits and entrances of my thirties have moved me several times to some thought of spending the rest of my days wandering aimlessly around the South Seas, like a character out of Conrad, silent and inscrutable. But the necessity for frequent visits to my oculist and dentist have prevented this.

    On himself, *My Life and Hard Times.*

My theories and views of literature vary with the lateness of the hour, the quality of my companions, and the quantity of liquor.

    On himself, in Fred B. Millet, *Contemporary American Authors.*

Freud discovered the Id, and Thurber named it Walter Mitty.

    Larry Adler, in *Sunday Times*, 5 October 1975.

While it is true that Thurber sees the human condition as bleak, this bleakness is nevertheless tempered by a margin of hope — that man may overcome the illusions which obstruct his view of reality, and may use comedy as a means of coming to terms with life.

    Stephen A. Black, *James Thurber: His Masquerade.*

Helen [Mrs Thurber] said some drunk dame told Jim at a party that she would like to have a baby by him. Jim said, 'Surely you don't mean by unartificial insemination!'

    Nunnally Johnson in a letter to Groucho Marx, 9 October 1961.

To Thurber and [E. B.] White it seemed that, the way things were going, sex as nature intended it was on the way out. After a while people would just sit around and read sex books. Boldly they undertook to save the human race from extinction. They also hoped to make some money.

    Dale Kramer, *Ross and the New Yorker.*

I cannot say that James Thurber's work has progressed. No more could I say that the new moon is more exquisite than the last one. I will not be so illiterate as to expand the perfect into the more perfect.

    Dorothy Parker, Preface to James Thurber, *Men, Women and Dogs.*

Above the still cool lake of marriage he saw rising the thin mist of Man's disparity with Woman. In his drawings one finds not only the simple themes of love and misunderstanding, but also the rarer and tenderer insupportabilities.

    E. B. White, in Charles S. Holmes, *The Clocks of Columbus, The Literary Career of James Thurber.*

TILDEN, SAMUEL JONES

1814—86 Politician

Mr. Tilden is incapable of doing the simplest thing without a mask.
    Anon., in *New York Herald*, 17 June 1880, urging Tilden to declare if he were a candidate.

Tweed and Tilden

'We was as brothers,' William said,
    'Till, siding with the foe,
You struck me, Sam, when I was down,
    A foul and trait'rous blow.'

'Forgive me, Bill,' said Oily Sam,
    'The Fates, not men, ordain;
When I have clutched the White House prize
    We'll brothers be again.'
    Anon., in *The Illustrated Hayes Song and Joke Book*.

My name is Sam Tilden;
I'm thoroughly skilled in
    All manner of slippery ways.
In New York I was brought up
And regularly taught up
    In the sharpest and trickiest 'lays'.

Chorus — O, I'm going to be a reformer,
    I am bound to be a reformer,
        I'll be a reformer or die.
    There's no use a-talking,
    Just dry up your squawking,
        For a red-hot reformer am I.
    Ibid.

His hour had come; he promptly grasped the leadership thus left open. Starting out for the Presidential nomination, his plan embraced three features: his stepping stone was the governorship, his shibboleth was administrative reform, his method was organization to a degree which has never been surpassed.
    James G. Blaine, *Twenty Years of Congress*, vol. 2.

He was admired, respected, and applauded but not loved — a human iceberg who fired his party and the American people to high action.
    A. C. Flick, *Samuel Jones Tilden*.

The combined power of rebellion, Catholicism and whiskey.
    James A. Garfield, 1876 (Garfield was under the impression that Tilden had won the election and this was his explanation).

In view of Mr. (Samuel J.) Tilden's Civil War record my advice is not to raise the flag.
    Mark Twain, in Philip S. Foner, *Mark Twain, Social Critic*.

Sam Tilden wants to overthrow Tammany Hall. He wants to drive me out of politics. He wants to stop the pickings, starve out the boys, and run the city as if 'twas a damned little country store in New Lebanon. He wants to bring the hayloft and cheesepress down to the city, and crush out the machine. He wants to get a crowd of reformers in the legislature ... who will cut down the tax levy below a living rate; and then, when he gets everything fixed to suit him, he wants to go the United States Senate.
    William Marcy 'Boss' Tweed, in A. C. Flick, *Samuel Jones Tilden*.

... It is like putting a 200 horse power engine in a ... craft built for only 100 horse power ... Tilden has too much mind for his body.
    Ibid.

See also Grover Cleveland

TOKLAS, ALICE BABETTE

1877—1967 Author, Literary Figure

I wish to God we had gone together as I always so fatuously thought we would — a bomb — shipwreck — just anything but this.
    On herself, referring to Gertrude Stein's death, in Margo Jefferson, 'Passionate Friends', in *Newsweek*, 7 January 1974.

Miss Toklas was incredibly ugly, uglier than almost anyone I had ever met. A thin, withered creature, she sat hunched in her chair, in her heavy tweed suit and her thick lisle stockings, impregnable and indifferent. She had a huge nose, a dark moustache, and her dark-dyed hair was combed into absurd bangs over her forehead.
    Otto Friedrich, 'The Grave of Alice B. Toklas', in *Esquire*, January 1968.

Tiny, nimble, and mustachioed....
    Arthur Gold and Robert Fizdale, 'How Famous People Look', in *Vogue*, February 1974.

I like a view but I like to sit with my back turned to it.
    Gertrude Stein, impersonating Miss Toklas.

Alice Toklas neither took life easy nor fraternized casually.
    Virgil Thomson, in Alden Whitman, *The Obituary Book*.

TOMKINS, THOMAS

—d. 1656 Composer

Yet thou wert mortal: now begin to live,
And end with only Time. Thy Muses give
What Nature hath deny'd, Eternity:
Gladly my younger Muse doth honour thee,
But mine's no praise. A large increase it has
That's multiply'd through strong affections glass.
Yet is thy worth the same, and were no other
Though as a Judge I spake, not as a Brother.
    This comfort have, this Art's so great, so free,
    None but the good can reach to censure thee.
    John Tomkins, *To my Brother the AUTHOR*.

And thou, great Master of melodius skill,
This holy harmony didst help to fill;
When in this dismal Cadence, no sound else
Was heard but Mournful groans, and mortal bells.
Thy hand an Organ was of ample good
To set in tune, and cheer the mourning mood.
According to thy Tenor, thou didst lend
Us Meanes, our low and base state to mend.
T'accomplish now this song of courtesy,
In triple time our thanks shall trebles be.
These lines are Brief, but know thy Restless song
Of fame, shall stand in notes both large and long.
    John Toy, *Worcester Elegy and Eulogy*.

TONE, THEOBALD WOLFE

1763—98 Irish Politician

He was a very slender, angular, rapid-moving man . . . nose rather long, I forget the shape, nothing remarkable; laughed and talked fast with enthusiasm about music and other innocent things, so that one could not possibly suspect him of plots and treasons.
    Miss Crampton, 1843, in Frank McDermot, *Theobald Wolfe Tone*.

In truth Tone was simply a brave, unassuming man, who was merry because he needed great reserves. . . . Tone, with his flute in his pocket, and a laugh always up his sleeve, was a hero with slippers — because the road, for him much longer and more arduous, brought him many a night to rest in his inn.
    Sean O'Faolain, *The Autobiography of Theobald Wolfe Tone*.

Wolfe Tone was a most extraordinary man and his history is the most curious history of those times. With a hundred guineas in his pocket, unknown and unrecommended, he went to Paris in order to overturn the British Government in Ireland. He asked for a large force; Lord Edward Fitzgerald for a small one. They listened to Tone. . . .
    Duke of Wellington, in *ibid*.

TONGE, ISRAEL

1621—80 Conspirator

[Titus] Oates's John the Baptist. . . .
    John Kenyon, *The Popish Plot*.

TOOKE, JOHN HORNE

1736—1812 Radical, Philologist

That he was crafty, however, as well as sagacious and reflecting, soon appeared manifest; and when he was found often to put others forward on the stage, while he himself prompted behind the scenes, or moved the wires of the puppet, a distrust of him grew up which enabled plain dealers, pursuing a more straightforward course, to defeat him when they happened to fall out, although their resources were in every respect incomparably less ample.
    Henry Brougham, *Statesman in the Time of George III*.

Sir Francis Burdett told us that Horne Tooke, when advised to take a wife said, 'With all my heart; whose wife shall it be?'
    Lord Broughton, *Recollections of a Long Life*.

The fellow who looks like a half-and-half person.
    James Fenimore Cooper, *Gleanings in Europe: England*.

He wanted effect and *momentum*. Each of his sentences told very well of itself, but they did not altogether make a speech. He left off where he began. His eloquence was a succession of drops, not a stream. His arguments, though subtle and new, did not affect the main body of the question. The coldness and pettiness of his manner did not warm the hearts or expand the understandings of his hearers. Instead of encouraging, he checked the ardour of his friends; and teazed, instead of overpowering his antagonists.
    William Hazlitt, considering Tooke as a Parliamentary speaker, in *The Spirit of the Age*.

Provided he could say a clever or a spiteful thing,

he did not care whether it served or injured the cause. Spleen or the exercise of intellectual power was the motive of his patriotism, rather than principle.
William Hazlitt, *ibid.*

See also Richard Porson

TOSCANINI, ARTURO

1867—1957 Conductor

After I die, I shall return to earth as a gatekeeper of a bordello and I won't let any of you — not a one of you [in the entire orchestra] — enter!
On himself, in Howard Taubman, *The Maestro: The Life of Arturo Toscanini.*

Any *asino* can conduct — but to make music . . . eh? Is *difficile*!
On himself, in Samuel Antek, *This Was Toscanini.*

Playing with Toscanini was a musical rebirth. The clarity, intensity, and honesty of his musical vision — his own torment — was like a cleansing baptismal pool. Caught up in his force, your own indifference was washed away. You were not just a player, another musician, but an artist once more searching for long-forgotten ideals and truths. You were curiously alive, and there was purpose and self-fulfillment in your work. It was not a job, it was a calling!
Samuel Antek, in *ibid.*

A glorified bandmaster!
Thomas Beecham, in Neville Cardus, *Sir Thomas Beecham.*

His assets are seldom found assembled together in one conductor: immense knowledge and experience, a natural way of absorbing tone, a keen ear, a prodigious memory, great force of personal will and conviction, and — greatest of all — a simple honesty equal to Verdi's. His interpretations were direct and unambiguous; he was incapable of that subtlety which depends on the oblique approach.
Neville Cardus, *Talking of Music.*

The man was supercharged; and it permeated the atmosphere, creating an aura of excitement that we didn't feel with other conductors. A concert can be a concert, or it can be a concert plus an event; and with Toscanini we had the double feature. But it was the dress rehearsals that were absolutely extraordinary: in that atmosphere of quiet and intense concentration we were hypnotized, and the ninety-five men functioned as one.
Bernard H. Haggin, *The Toscanini Musicians Knew.*

A reactionary in spirit, he has none the less revolutionized orchestral conducting by his radical simplification of its procedures. Almost wholly devoted to the playing of familiar classics, he has at the same time transformed these into an auditive image of twentieth-century America with such unconscious completeness that musicians and laymen all over the world have acclaimed his achievement without, I think, very much bothering to analyze it.
Virgil Thomson, *The Muscial Scene.*

See also Thomas Beecham

TOWNSHEND, CHARLES

1725—67 Politician

Protective poverty of heart was the contrived shield of his stricken, vulnerable self; gifted enough to be aware, however, dimly, of its ugliness and purpose, he consistently disguised or veiled it.
Sir Lewis Namier and John Brooke, *Charles Townshend.*

Charles Townshend is dead. All those parts and fire are extinguished; those volatile salts are evaporated; that first eloquence of the world is dumb; that duplicity is fixed; that cowardice terminated heroically.
Horace Walpole, Letter to Sir Horace Mann, 27 September 1767.

TRACY, SPENCER

1900—67 Actor

Spence is the best we have, because you don't see the mechanism at work. He covers up, never overacts, gives the impression he isn't acting at all. I try to do it, and I succeed, but not the way Spence does. He has direct contact with an audience he never sees.
Humphrey Bogart, in Larry Swindell, *Spencer Tracy.*

Spence was the kind of actor about whom you thought 'I've got a lot of things I could say to you, but I don't say them because you *know*', and next day everything I'd thought of telling him would be there in the rushes. Also, I was never sure whether

Spence was really listening when I talked to him. He was one of those naturally original actors who did it but never let you see him doing it.

George Cukor, in Gavin Lambert, *On Cukor*.

He has that poise and self-security that might pass as 'just being natural' until you try it on the stage for yourself. And . . . he blunts or turns aside any tin knife of the ludicrous that the situation may have pointed against him, simply by virtue of a steady intelligence, a cagey grasp of stage motion and effects, and something profound in the way of kindness and knowingness and cheer that needs no flurry of business for its projection, since it is received all around with the immediacy of air waves, and that, being profound, can never be made silly.

Otis Ferguson, *The Film Criticism of Otis Ferguson*.

The guy's good and there's nobody in this business who can touch him, so you're a fool to try. And don't fall for that humble stuff either; the bastard knows it!

Clark Gable, in Larry Swindell, *Spencer Tracy*.

Tracy, to my way of thinking, was the motion-picture actor incarnate.

Stanley Kramer, in Walter Wagner, *You Must Remember This*.

The face was unforgettable. It was craggy, freckled and roughhewn. It was tough and sturdy and sun-burned ' and later seamed with a network of wrinkles. Someone once said the lines would hold two days of rain. He himself said his face reminded him of a beat-up barn door.

David Zinman, *Fifty Classic Motion Pictures*.

TRAHERNE, THOMAS

1637—74 Poet

The naked Truth in many faces shewn,
Whose inward Beauties very few hav known,
A Simple Light, transparent Words, a Strain
That lowly creeps, yet maketh Mountains plain,
Brings down the highest Mysteries to sense
And keeps them there; that is our Excellence:
At that we aim.

On himself, *The Author to the Critical Peruser*.

When I came into the Country, and being seated among silent Trees, had all my Time in mine own Hands, I resolved to Spend it all, whatever it cost me, in Search of Happiness, and to Satiat that burning Thirst which Nature had Enkindled, in me from my Youth. In which I was so resolut, that I chose

rather to live upon 10 pounds a year, and to go in Lether Clothes, and feed upon Bread and Water, so that I might hav all my time clearly to my self: then to keep many thousands per annums in an Estate of Life where my Time would be Devoured in Care and Labour.

On himself, *Centuries*, iii.

He was a man of a cheerful and sprightly Temper, free from any thing of the sourness or formality, by which some great pretenders of Piety rather disparage and misrepresent true Religion, than recommend it; and therefore was very affable and pleasant in his Conversation, ready to do all good Offices to his Friends, and Charitable to the Poor almost beyond his ability.

Preface (possibly written by Susanna Hopton) to first edition of Traherne's *Thanksgivings*.

TREE, SIR HERBERT BEERBOHM

1853—1917 Actor-manager

It is difficult to live up to one's posters . . . When I pass my name in such large letters I blush, but at the same time instinctively raise my hat.

On himself, in Hesketh Pearson, *Beerbohm Tree*.

It was characteristic of his complexity that he was greatly amused at his own naivete. He once handed me a letter from a stranger who had seen him act on the previous night. 'That's very nice,' I said after reading it. 'Very,' said he, 'I can stand any amount of flattery so long as it's fulsome enough.'

Max Beerbohm, *From a Brother's Standpoint*.

I am afraid that as the years went by, and the gap between our ages was accordingly contracted, each of us found himself even more shy in the presence of the other than he was wont to be with people at large. An old friend of Herbert's once said to him, and me, in the course of a dinner in the 'Dome' of His Majesty's: 'You two, when you're together, always seem to be in an attitude of armed neutrality.' I suggested to Herbert that 'terrified love' would be a truer description.

Ibid.

He had not the animal vigour which is necessary to great excellence in violent tragedy or in robust comedy. He could make himself look like Falstaff; he understood and revelled in the character of Falstaff, but his performance lacked fundamental force. Hence the contradiction in his acting: his performance as a whole often fell short of high excellence, yet these same impersonations were lit by insight and masterly strokes of interpretation which made the spectator feel that he was watching the performance of the most imaginative of living actors. He had understood the character marvellously well. The same phenomenon would occur in parts in which the author himself had put next to nothing.

Desmond MacCarthy, *From the Stalls, circa* 1920.

With the amount of personal attention, Mr Tree, which you give to all your presentations, and the care you bestow on every detail, I really don't think you need an actual producer. Nor, with the constant supervision you so thoroughly exercise, have you any use for a stage-manager. What you really require are a couple of *tame, trained echoes*!

Hugh Moss, after an engagement, in Joe Graham, *An Old Stock-Actor's Memories.*

His fellow-manager went round to his dressing-room after a performance. Tree was sitting at his mirror removing his make-up. 'Well, what did you think of my Hamlet?' he asked. 'Quite frankly,' replied Hare, 'I didn't much care for it.' Tree absorbed this, and then tried again: 'No . . . but it's a good part, isn't it?'

Hesketh Pearson, *Beerbohm Tree.*

Confronted with a Shakespearian play, he stares into a ghastly vacuum, yet stares unterrified, undisturbed by any suspicion that his eyesight is failing, quite prepared to find the thing simply an ancient, dusty, mouldy, empty house which it is his business to furnish, decorate, and housewarm with an amusing entertainment.

George Bernard Shaw, in *Saturday Review*, 11 February 1905.

[He] turned to Shakespeare as to a forest out of which . . . scaffolding could be hewn without remonstrance from the landlord. . . . As far as I could discover, the notion that a play could succeed without any further help from the actor than a simple impersonation of his part, never occurred to Tree.

George Bernard Shaw, *From the Point of View of a Playwright.*

He had great admiration for the gypsies and their music, and told me that he had once resisted an impulse to visit them, lest he should become too fascinated by their life and unable to return home.

Iris Tree, *Memories.*

A charming fellow, and so clever: he models himself on me.

Oscar Wilde, in Hesketh Pearson, *Beerbohm Tree.*

TROLLOPE, ANTHONY
1815—82 Novelist

I find that, taking the books which have appeared under our names, I have published much more than twice as much as Carlyle. I have also published considerably more than Voltaire, even including his letters. . . . It will not, I am sure, be thought that, in making my boast as to quantity, I have endeavoured to lay claim to any literary excellence. . . . But I do lay claim to whatever merit should be accorded to me for persevering diligence in my profession. . . . More than nine tenths of my literary work has been done in the last twenty years, and during twelve of those years I followed also another profession. I have never been a slave to this work, giving due time, if not more than due time, to the amusements I have loved. But I have been constant, — and constancy in labour will conquer all difficulties.

On himself, *Autobiography.*

I was thinking today that nature intended me for an American rather than an Englishman. I think I should have made a better American yet I hold it higher to be a bad Englishman, than a good American, as I am not.

On himself, in C. P. Snow, *Trollope.*

Of all novelists in any country, Trollope best understands the role of money. Compared with him, even Balzac is too romantic.

W. H. Auden, *Forewords and Afterwords.*

What a pity it is that so powerful and idiomatic a writer should be so incorrect gramatically and scholastically speaking! Robert [Browning] insists on my putting down such phrases as these: 'The Cleeve was distant from Orley two miles, though it *could not be driven* under five.' 'One rises up the hill.' 'As good as *him.*' 'Possessing more *acquirements* than he would have *learned* at Harrow.' *Learning acquirements*! Yes, they are faults, and should be put away by a first-rate writer like Anthony Trollope. It's always worth while to be correct.

Elizabeth Barrett Browning (on reading *Orley Farm*), Letter to Isa Blagden, 1861.

Have you ever read the novels of Anthony Trollope? They precisely suit my taste, — solid and substantial, written on the strength of beef and through the inspiration of ale, and just as real as if some giant had hewn a great lump out of the earth, and put it under a glass case, with all its inhabitants going about their daily business, and not suspecting that they were being made a show of. And these books are just as English as a beef-steak.

Nathaniel Hawthorne, Letter to Joseph M. Field.

He has a gross and repulsive face and manner, but appears *bon enfant* when you talk with him. But he is the dullest Briton of them all.

Henry James, Letter to the James family, 1 November 1875.

His first, his inestimable merit was a complete appreciation of the usual. . . .

Henry James, *Partial Portraits*.

Trollope's fecundity was prodigious; there was no limit to the work he was ready to do. It is not unjust to say that he sacrificed quality to quantity. Abundance, certainly is in itself a great merit; almost all the greatest writers have been abundant. But Trollope's fertility was gross, importunate.

Ibid.

A big, red-faced, rather underbred Englishman of the bald-with-spectacles type. A good roaring positive fellow who deafened me till I thought of Dante's Cerberus.

James Russell Lowell, Letter, 20 September 1861.

Mr Trollope's success as a novelist for the time he was writing was almost wonderful, the more so because, as soon as death stopped his prolific pen, the author and the books died almost at the same time, for no one reads or thinks about Mr Trollope's novels now. And yet, in his time those who in society had not read his last novel were out of the fashion.

William Tinsley, *Random Recollections of an Old Publisher*, 1900.

See also A. E. Housman

TRUMAN, HARRY S.

1884–1972 Thirty-Third United States President

I don't know whether you fellows ever had a load of hay or a bull fall on you. But last night the moon, the stars and all the planets fell on me. If you fellows ever pray, pray for me.

On himself to newspapermen on becoming President, in Jonathan Daniels, *The Man of Independence*.

I never gave them hell, I just tell the truth and they think it's hell.

On himself, in *Look*, 3 April 1956.

If somebody throws a brick at me I can catch it and throw it back. But when somebody awards a decoration to me, I am out of words.

On himself, on receiving the Grand Cross of Merit of Austria, 7 May 1964.

I don't give a damn about *The Missouri Waltz* but I can't say it outloud because it's the song of Missouri. It's as bad as *The Star-Spangled Banner* so far as music is concerned.

On himself, in *Time*, 10 February 1958.

Among President Truman's many weaknesses was his utter inability to discriminate between history and histrionics.

Anon., in Douglas MacArthur, *Reminiscences*.

. . . a New Dealer who showed no desire to persecute business.

Anon., in *Harper's Magazine*, 1937.

Mr. Truman was unable to make the simple complex in the way so many men in public life tend to do. For very understandable reasons, of course. If one makes something complex out of something simple, then one is able to delay making up one's mind. And that was something that never troubled Mr. Truman.

Dean Acheson, in Merle Miller, *Plain Speaking, An Oral Biography of Harry S. Truman*.

Truman . . . seemed to stand for nothing more spectacular than honesty in war contracting, which was like standing for virtue in Hollywood or adequate rainfall in the Middle West.

George E. Allen, *Presidents Who Have Known Me*.

It has been said that Mr. Truman reversed the Roosevelt philosophy of tolerant accommodation toward the communist world, setting us a hard-line, anti-communist, counterrevolutionary course, resulting in hot and cold wars, a trillion dollars spent on armaments, and a reversal of priorities that has virtually plundered and wrecked our planet.

Bob Arthur, in Merle Miller, *Plain Speaking, An Oral Biography of Harry S. Truman*.

Truman was nominated by men speculating beyond the death of Roosevelt who knew what they wanted but did not know what they were getting.

Jonathan Daniels, *The Man of Independence*.

He is a man totally unfitted for the position. His principles are elastic, and he is careless with the truth. He has no special knowledge of any subject, and he is a malignant, scheming sort of an individual who is dangerous not only to the United Mine

Workers, but dangerous to the United States of America.
John L. Lewis, United Mine Workers Convention, 1948.

. . . was not able to make peace, because politically he was too weak at home. He was not able to make war because the risks were too great. President Eisenhower signed an armistice which accepted the partition of Korea and a peace victory because being himself the victorious commander in World War II and a Republican, he could not be attacked as an appeaser. President Truman and Secretary Acheson, on the other hand, never seemed able to afford to make peace on the only terms which the Chinese would agree to.
Walter Lippmann, in Bert Cochran, *Harry Truman and the Crisis Presidency*.

Truman had been sent to Washington by a man criticized throughout the country as a crook. I didn't see any future in an association like that. He was a guy — a punk — sent up by gangsters.
Victor Messall, when offered the post of Senator Truman's chief assistant, in Bert Cochran, *ibid*.

He was liked, he was admired, he evoked steadfast loyalty in many, but he could not inspire.
Cabell Phillips, *The Truman Presidency*.

. . . right on all the big things, wrong on most of the little ones.
Sam Rayburn, attributed.

He was distressingly petty in petty things; he was gallantly big in big things.
Clinton Rossiter, in Thomas A. Bailey, *Presidential Greatness*.

Mr. Truman believes other people should be 'free to govern themselves as they see fit' — so long as they see fit to see as we see fit.
I. F. Stone, 'With Malice Toward None — Except Half Mankind,' in *The Truman Era*.

Harry Truman proves the old adage that any man can become President of the United States.
Norman Thomas, in Murray B. Seidler, *Norman Thomas, Respectable Rebel*.

President Truman cannot prevent the tide from coming in or the sun from rising. But once America stands for opposition to change we are lost. America will become the most hated nation in the world.
Henry Wallace, in *New York Times*, 14 March 1947.

See also John F. Kennedy

744

TRUMBULL, JOHN
1756—1843 Artist

To preserve and diffuse the memory of the noblest actions; to impart to future generations the glorious lessons of human rights, and of the spirit with which these should be asserted and supported; and to transmit to posterity the personal resemblance of those who have been great actors in those illustrious scenes, are objects that give dignity to my profession, peculiar to my situation from having borne personally a humble part in the great events I am to describe. No other artist now living possesses this advantage, and no one can come after me to divide the honor of truth and authenticity, however easily I may hereafter be exceeded in elegance. I feel therefore some pride in accomplishing a work, such as has never been done before, and in which it is not easy that I should have a rival.
On himself, Letter to Thomas Jefferson.

TUCKER, SOPHIE (SOPHIE ABUZA)
1884—1966 Entertainer

The Last of the Red-Hot Mamas.
On herself, publicity introduction coined by her.

Keep breathing.
On herself, when asked the secret of her longevity on her eightieth birthday, 13 January 1964.

The approval and affection of the members of your own profession are a greater reward and more soul-satisfying than just popularity with the public and big money. . . . When it's about 5 or 6 am and the crowds have melted away and you're left alone to wipe off the make-up and take off your corsets and go to bed — and to bed *alone* — there's a lot of comfort in knowing that the men and women who work in show business have a respect for you and are fond of you. . . . Knowing, as you stretch your tired body out between the sheets with a sigh of relief, that you've done a good job, and the members of your own profession think you have, and say: 'Oh, Sophie's a good *schnuck*!' goes a hell of a long way.
On herself, in *Some of These Days*.

Sophie's entirely a night-club singer. Her style and material are hardly what you'd want at a Holy Name breakfast. But in the night clubs she's queen, she has no inhibitions and needs none, she sings the words we used to write on the sidewalks of New York. And you *hear* her.
Eddie Cantor, *Take My Life*.

TURNER, FREDERICK JACKSON

1861—1932 Historian

I am one of those who believes in breaking line fences, even at the risk of arrest for trespass, or disclosure of being an amateur, or something worse, breaking into the professional's game.

On himself, in Ray Allen Billington, *Frederick Jackson Turner*.

But this I know, that three qualities of the man's mind made upon me a profound and indelible impression. These qualities were: a lively and irrepressible intellectual curiosity; a refreshing freedom from personal preoccupations and didactic motives; a quite unusual ability to look out upon the wide world in a humane friendly way, in a fresh and strictly independent way, with a vision unobscured by academic inhibitions.

Carl Becker, 'Frederick Jackson Turner', in Howard W. Odum ed., *American Masters of Social Science*.

Turner was a down-to-earth, old-shoe type of mortal, not through affection, but because he cast himself in the role of the historical character he admired most: the Jackson Man.

Ray Allen Billington, *Frederick Jackson Turner*.

At times he seems a propagandist, at others a mere historicist, and on occasion, Whitmanesque. A man who touches the historian, the social scientist, the intellectual, the antiquarian, the mass subconscious mind, and the average citizen, man and boy, may not have been a great historian in the orthodox sense, but he was something of an intuitive genius.

Howard R. Lamar, 'Frederick Jackson Turner', in Marcus Cunliffe and Robin W. Winks eds, *Pastmasters*.

TURNER, JOSEPH MALLORD WILLIAM

1775—1851 Painter

Mr. Turner is a tubby little man and has every mark of feeding well, and 'sleeps o' nights'.

Anon., in *Morning Chronicle*, 1830.

Turner's one dream, the extraordinarily high aspiration of his life, was to gain a complete knowledge of light in all its phases.

E. Chesneau, *The English School of Painting*.

He seems to paint with tinted steam, so evanescent, and so airy. The public think he is laughing at them, and so they laugh at him in return.

John Constable, Letter to George Constable, 12 May 1836.

The Philosopher of Art and the Newton of Painting.

J. Elmes, *Sir Christopher Wren*.

[Benjamin] West has spoken in the highest manner of a picture in the Exhibition painted by Turner, that is what Rembrandt thought of but could not do.

Joseph Farington, Diary, 17 April 1801.

Sir George [Beaumont] said they [Turner's pictures] appeared to Him to be like the works of an old man who had ideas but had lost his power of execution.

Ibid., 5 April 1806.

Shortly before the end, Dr. Price, of Margate, who had attended Turner when he had been ill there, was summoned to London for a consultation with Mr. Bartlett. He is said to have told the patient that death was near. 'Go downstairs,' Turner said to the doctor, 'take a glass of sherry and then look at me again.' The doctor did so, but his opinion remained unchanged.

A. J. Finsberg, *The Life of J. M. W. Turner R.A.*

In the gallery was a gorgeous display of haunted dreams thrown on the canvas, rather in the way of hints and insinuations than real pictures, and yet the effect of some was most fascinating. The colouring almost Venetian, the imagination of some almost as grand as they were vague; but I think one great pleasure in them is the opportunity they give for trying to find out what he can possibly mean, and then you hug your own creative ingenuity, whilst you pretend to be astonished at Turner's. This especially refers to the Deluge and the Brazen Serpent.

Caroline Fox, Journals, May 1849.

At a dinner when I was present, a salad was offered to Turner, who called the attention of his neighbour at the table . . . to it in the following words: 'Nice cool green that lettuce, isn't it? and the beetroot pretty red — not quite strong enough; and the mixture, delicate tint of yellow that. Add some mustard, and then you have one of my pictures.'

William P. Frith, *My Autobiography and Reminiscences*.

I wonder whether Turner ever did have any distinctive personal experience before nature. He seems to me to have had so intense a desire to create, to do, to be so busy about picture-making that he never had the time for that.

Roger Fry, *Reflections on British Painting*.

All the taste and all the imagination being borrowed, his powers of eye, hand, and memory, are equal to any· thing. In general, his pictures are a waste of morbid strength. They give pleasure only by the excess of power triumphing over the barrenness of the subject.

William Hazlitt, in *Morning Chronicle*, 5 February 1814.

If you have ever in your life had one opportunity, with your eyes and heart open, of seeing the dew rise from a hill pasture, or the storm gather on a sea-cliff, and if you yet have no feeling for the glorious passages of mingled earth and heaven which Turner calls up before you into breathing tangible being, there is indeed no hope for your apathy, art will never touch you, nor nature inform.

John Ruskin, *Modern Painters*.

There is no test of our acquaintance with nature so absolute and unfailing, as the degree of admiration we feel for Turner's painting. Precisely as we are shallow in our knowledge, vulgar in our feeling, and contracted in our views of principles, will the works of this artist be stumbling-blocks to us: precisely in the degree to which we are familiar with nature, constant in our observation of her, and enlarged in our understanding of her, will they expand before our eyes into glory and beauty.

Ibid.

Like Bewick, he could draw *pigs* better than any other animal.

John Ruskin, *The Ruskin Collection*.

Turner made drawings of mountains and clouds which the public said were absurd. I said, on the contrary, they were the only true drawings of mountains and clouds ever made yet: and I proved this to be so, as only it could be proved, by steady test of physical science: but Turner had drawn his mountains rightly, long before their structure was known to any geologist in Europe; and has painted perfectly truths of anatomy in clouds which I challenge any meteorologist in Europe to explain to this day.

John Ruskin, *The Eagle's Nest*, vol. 3.

Views on the Thames, crude blotches, nothing could be more vicious.

Benjamin West, in Joseph Farington, Diary, 5 May 1807.

I have often heard my father describe the lectures. He declared you could hardly hear anything Turner said, he rambled on in such a very indistinct way which was most difficult to follow. My father said that at the General Assemblies he would make long speeches in an equally confused and rambling manner, and if interrupted or called to order for not confining himself to the subject in question, he would become angry and say, 'Nay, nay, if you make an abeyance of it I will sit down.' But though the subject matter of his lectures was neither listened to nor understood, they were well attended as he used to display beautiful drawings of imaginary buildings with fine effects of light and shade, on the wall behind his rostrum.

William T. Whitley, *Art in England 1800–20*.

See also John Constable, John Millais

TURNER, NAT

1800–31 Abolitionist

Having soon discovered [myself] to be great, I must appear so, and therefore studiously avoided mixing in society, and wrapped myself in mystery, devoting my time to fasting and praying.

On himself to Thomas Gray, *Confessions*.

Our insurrection, general, or not, was the work of fanaticism — General Nat was no preacher, but in his immediate neighborhood, he had acquired the character of a prophet; like a Roman Sybil, he traced his divination in characters of blood, one leaves alone in the woods; he would arrange them in some conspicuous place, have a dream telling him of the circumstance; and then send some ignorant black to bring them to him, to whom he would interpret their meaning. Thus, by means of this nature, he acquired an immense influence, over such persons as he took into his confidence. He, likewise, pretended to have conversations with the Holy Spirit; and was assured by it, that he was invulnerable. His escape, as he labored under that opinion is much to be regretted.

Anon., *Richmond Whig*, 17 September 1831.

Deep down inside, even when we didn't know his name, Nat Turner was always alive. Nat, by whatever we called him, or dreamed of him; Nat was our secret weapon, our ace in the hole, our private consciousness of manhood kept strictly between us.

Ossie Davis, 1968, 'Nat Turner Hero Reclaimed', in Eric Foner ed., *Nat Turner, Great Lives Observed*.

He stood erect, a man as proud
As ever to a tyrant bowed
Unwilling head or bent a knee
And longed, while bending, to be free:
And o'er his ebon features came
A shadow — 'twas of manly shame —
Aye, shame that he should wear a chain
And feel his manhood writhed with pain,

Doomed to a life of plodding toil,
Shamefully rooted to the soil!
He stood erect; his eyes flashed fire;
His robust form convulsed with ire;
'I will be free! I will be free!
Or, fighting, die a man!' cried he.
    T. Thomas Fortune, in *Cleveland Gazette*,
    22 November 1884.

TURPIN, (BERNARD) BEN

1869—1940 Motion Picture Comedian

Turpin, whose skinny, agile body, high forehead, and wildly crossed eyes made him one of the silliest looking clowns in film history, was the perfect embodiment of [Mack] Sennett's anti-romanticism and anti-heroism . . . Turpin's crossed eyes shot satiric deflating darts into the gaudy hot airfilled balloons that Hollywood passed off as art on its tinsel-blinded public.
    Gerald Mast, *The Comic Mind*.

Turpin came to us from the circus and the vaudeville stage. One of his demands on the studio as soon as his face became known all over the world was that we take out an insurance policy with Lloyds of London which would pay him one million dollars if his eyes ever came uncrossed. It took only the simplest examination by an honest oculist to assure Lloyds their money was safe. Ben's eyes were permanently fixed and so were his notions.
    This skinny, strutting little man with a Polish piano player's mane of hair and a neck like a string was obsessed by money and by the conviction that he couldn't be funny after 5 pm. He had a five o'clock quitting time in his contract. When the bell rang he left no matter what it cost the studio.
    Mack Sennett, *King of Comedy*.

We paid Turpin $1500 a week at the height of his powers. He invested all his money, bought apartment houses, and became a rich man. He always saved a few dollars a week by personally doing the janitor work at all his apartment houses.
    He seldom drove an automobile — a frantic thought at that; who knows how many directions he would have tried to drive at once? He preferred to save money by travelling by streetcar. As he would enter the trolley, he would draw his wren-like physique up to full strut and squeak, at the top of his voice, 'I'm Ben Turpin. Three thousand dollars a week!'
    Ibid.

TWACHTMAN, JOHN HENRY

1853—1902 Artist

In the work of John Twachtman we see his true character. Whatever may have been his outward action, his pictures reveal his inner spirit. Outwardly gruff, hedonistic, skeptical and insensitive; inwardly he was impressionable, sensitive and sincere. In manner bantering, didactic, inconsistent, careless; in spirit delicate, constant, naive and loving. An instinctive understanding of true aesthetic values gave poise and confidence; but a lack of patronage and a contempt for popular banalities created skepticism and incredulity. Thus we see in Twachtman, the man, a dual character. One instinctive, the other acquired; one real, the other affected. In judging the man we must make this distinction; in judging his art it is not necessary, for therein we find the man truly himself.
    Eliot Clark, *John Twachtman*.

Twachtman's attitude toward nature, his approach to his subject, was not that of a naturalist, a pantheist or a realist. It was more truly that of an artist. He was not curious about botanical structure or the absolute veracity of naturalistic form; he had not the religious feeling of the affinity of nature with its creator or its relation to man; nor was he a graphic reporter of realistic facts. He saw in nature the means for an arrangement for form and color; he sought not so much the beauty of a part as the relation of parts to an organized whole. He was not emotional in a romantic sense, that sense which is related more to the association of ideas or the symbolical suggestion of nature.
    Ibid.

TWAIN, MARK (SAMUEL LANGHORNE CLEMENS)

1835—1910 Writer

I am different from Washington. I have a higher and grander standard of principle. Washington could not lie. I *can* lie but I won't.
    On himself, in *Chicago Tribune*, 20 December 1871.

I have noticed my conscience for many years, and I know it is more trouble and bother to me than anything else I started with.
    On himself, in A. K. Adams, *The Home Book of Humorous Quotations*.

Twenty-four years ago, Madam, I was incredibly handsome. The remains of it are still visible through

the rift of time. I was so handsome that women became spellbound when I came in view. In San Francisco, in rainy seasons, I was frequently mistaken for a cloudless day.
  Ibid.

The reports of my death are greatly exaggerated.
  Ibid., when learning of his reported demise.

I don't mind what the opposition say of me, so long as they don't tell the truth about me; but when they descend to telling the truth about me, I consider that that is taking an unfair advantage.
  On himself, Speech delivered at Hartford, Connecticut, 26 October 1880.

I have never taken any exercise, except sleeping and resting, and I never intend to take any. Exercise is loathsome. And it cannot be any benefit when you are tired; and I am always tired.
  On himself, in Maxwell Geismar, *Mark Twain, An American Prophet.*

It's a long stretch between that first birthday speech and this one. That was my cradle song, and this is my swan song, I suppose. I am used to swan songs; I have sung them several times.
  On himself, *Essays:* 'Seventieth Birthday'.

My books are water; those of the great geniuses are wine. Everybody drinks water.
  On himself, May 1886 entry in his notebook, in Frederick Anderson ed., *Mark Twain, The Critical Heritage.*

Indeed I have been misjudged, from the very first. I have never tried in even one single little instance, to help cultivate the cultivated classes. I was not equipped for it, either by native gifts or training. And I never had any ambition in that direction, but always hunted for bigger game — the masses. I have seldom deliberately tried to instruct them, but have done my best to entertain them.
  On himself, Letter to Andrew Land, 1890.

[Bret Harte] trimmed and trained and schooled me patiently until he changed me from an awkward utterer of coarse grotesquenesses to a writer of paragraphs and chapters that have found a certain favor in the eyes of even some of the very decentest people in the land.
  On himself, in E. Hudson Long, *Mark Twain Handbook.*

Ah, well, I am a great and sublime fool. But then I am God's fool, and all His works must be contemplated with respect.
  On himself, in Edward Wagenknecht, *Mark Twain: The Man and His Work.*

Mark Twain was always a divine amateur. . . . He had no notion of construction, and very little power of self-criticism. He was great in the subordinate business of decoration, as distinguished from construction; but he would mingle together the very best and the very worst decorations.
  Arnold Bennett, in *Bookman*, June 1910.

His wife not only edited his works but edited him.
  Van Wyck Brooks, *The Ordeal of Mark Twain.*

. . . a hack writer who would not have been considered fourth rate in Europe, who tricked out a few of the old proven 'sure fire' literary skeletons with sufficient local color to intrigue the superficial and the lazy.
  William Faulkner, in Michael Millgate, *The Achievement of William Faulkner.*

His head was striking. He had the curly hair, the aquiline nose, and even the aquiline eye — an eye so eagle-like that a second lid would not have surprised me — of an unusual and dominant nature.
  Bret Harte, in E. Hudson Long, *Mark Twain Handbook.*

He glimmered at you from the narrow slits of fine blue-greenish eyes, under branching brows, which with age grew more and more like a sort of plumage, and he was apt to smile into your face with a subtle but amiable perception, and yet with a sort of remote absence; you were all there for him, but he was not all there for you.
  William Dean Howells, in Edward Wagenknecht, *Mark Twain: The Man and His Work.*

He was Southwestern, and born amid the oppression of a race that had no rights as against ours, but I never saw a man more regardful of negroes. He had a yellow butler when I first began to know him, because he said he could not bear to order a white man about, but the terms of his ordering George were those of the softest entreaty which command ever wore.
  William Dean Howells, 'My Mark Twain', in Edmund Wilson ed., *The Shock of Recognition.*

I love to think of the great and godlike Clemens. He is the biggest man you have on your side of the water by a damn sight, and don't you forget it. Cervantes was a relation of his.
  Rudyard Kipling, Undated letter to Frank Doubleday.

But who is this in sweeping Oxford gown
Who steers the raft, or ambles up and down,
Or throws his gown aside, and there in white
Stands gleaming like a pillar of the night?

The lion of high courts, with hoary mane,
Fierce jester that this boyish court will gain —
Mark Twain!
The bad world's idol:
Old Mark Twain.
  Vachel Lindsay, *The Raft.*

Mark Twain, our Chief with neither smile nor jest,
Leading to war our youngest and our best.

The Yankee to King Arthur's Court returns.
The sacred flag of Joan above him burns.

For she has called his soul from out of tomb.
And where she stands, there he will stand till doom.
  Vachel Lindsay, *Mark Twain and Joan of Arc.*

His capacity for truth was warped by his genius for burlesque, or it was diverted by respect for the crowd, and by his devotion to the god success. His imagination was fertile and vivid within its range, but in exercising it he chose situations and characters which lent themselves to exaggeration.
  Edgar Lee Masters, *Mark Twain, A Portrait.*

This genius from Missouri was sensitive and tremulous, he was griefstricken and remorseful, he was superstitious and overbelieving, yet skeptical. In some particulars he loved the beautiful, but he was vulgar. He had a certain affection for his fellows, yet he distrusted and even despised them.
  Ibid.

Mark Twain and I are in very much the same position. We have to put things in such a way as to make people, who would otherwise hang us, believe that we are joking.
  George Bernard Shaw, remark to Archibald Henderson.

See also Frank Lloyd Wright

TWEED, WILLIAM MARCY
1823—78 Politician

This is
  BOSS TWEED
  The Tammany Atlas who all sustains
  (A Tammany Samson perhaps for his pains),
  Who rules the city where Oakey reigns,
  The master of Woodward and Ingersoll
  And all of the gang on the City Roll,
  And formerly lord of 'Slippery Dick.'
  Who controll'd the plastering laid on so thick
  By the comptroller's plasterer, Garvey by name,
  The Garvey whose fame is the little game

Of laying on plaster and knowing the trick
Of charging as if he himself were a brick
      Of the well-plaster'd House
         That TWEED built.
  Anon., *The House that Tweed built.*

It is better to be one of Mr. Tweed's horses than a poor taxpayer of this city.
  Anon., in *New York Times*, 28 September 1870.

Mr. Tweed is inspired to all high and noble aims, by the contemplation of personal beauty and innocence as imbedded in a photograph of himself.
  Ibid., 26 January 1871.

No King, no Clown, to rule this town!
  William O. Bartlett, in *New York Sun, circa* 1870.

One of the most suave, sleek and oleaginous persons on earth is the New York professional politician, when things are going his way. . . . Had there been any doubt of his identity, it might have been easily determined by the size of his diamond and the conspicuous position it occupied upon his person. . . . The politician who had not got a diamond on his bosom was of little account among his fellows, and was looked upon as having neglected his opportunities. . . . But the days of the politicians' diamond glory are well nigh gone. . . . They went out with Boss Tweed, who set the political fashion, and who wore the most brilliant diamond of all.
  Matthew Breen, *Thirty Years of New York Politics.*

He had a benignant, paternal expression, as of a patriarch pleased to see his retainers happy. It was a magnificent rendering of Fagin and his pupils. You could imagine him trotting up and down in the character of an unsuspicious old gentleman with his handkerchief hanging out of his pocket, so that his scholars might show their skill in prigging a wipe. He knew which of that cheerful company was the Artful Dodger. . . . And he never doubted that he could buy every man in the room if he were willing to pay the price.
  George W. Curtis, in Alexander E. Callow Jr, *The Tweed Ring.*

His nose is half-Brougham, half-Roman, and a man with a nose of that sort is not a man to be trifled with.
  Francis G. Fairfield, *The Clubs of New York.*

Skilled to pull wires, he baffles Nature's hope
Who sure intended him to stretch a rope.
  James Russell Lowell, *The Boss.*

Inclosed you will find 9 cents, my contribution

toward the erection of a statue of Honorable W. M. Tweed. I send this for the purpose of showing my appreciation of the man who for the last ten years has defrauded the public, more especially the poor man, out of millions of dollars, so that his image may always remain to the public gaze for generations to come.

> Thomas McCue, in Denis Tilden Lynch, *'Boss' Tweed — The Story of a Grim Generation*.

Tweed's impudent serenity is sublime. Were he not a supreme scoundrel, he would be a great man.

> George Templeton Strong, in A. Nevins and M. H. Thomas eds, *The Diary of George Templeton Strong*.

Alas! alas! young men, look at the contrast — in an elegant compartment of a Wagner palace car, surrounded by wine, cards and obsequious attendants, going to his Senatorial place at Albany; then look again at the plain box . . . behold the low-studded room, looking out upon a mean little dingy court where, a prisoner, exhausted, forsaken, miserable, betrayed, sick, William M. Tweed lies a-dying. From how high up to how low down!

> Reverend De Witt Talmadge, in Alexander B. Callow Jr, *The Tweed Ring*.

See also Samuel J. Tilden

TWINING, RICHARD

1749—1824 Merchant

It seems as if Nature had curiously plann'd
    That men's names with their trades should agree;
There's Twining the Tea-Man, who lives in the
                        Strand,
    Would be *whining*, if robb'd of his T.

> Theodore Hook, *Epigram*.

TYE, CHRISTOPHER

circa 1497—1572 Musician

I oft have heard my father merrily speak
In your high praise; and thus his highness saith,
England one God, one truth, one doctor hath
For music's art, and that is Doctor Tye,
Admired for skill in music's harmony.

> William Shakespeare, *Henry VIII*.

Dr. Tye was a peevish and humoursome man, especially in his latter days, and sometimes playing on the organ in the chapel of Qu. Eliz. which contained much music, but little delight to the ear, she would send the verger to tell him that he played out of tune, whereupon he sent word that her ears were out of tune.

> Anthony à Wood, *Fasti Oxonienses*.

TYLER, JOHN

1790—1862 Tenth United States President

If the annexation of Texas shall crown off my public life, I shall neither retire ignominiously nor be soon forgotten.

> On himself, 1844, in Robert Seager II, *and Tyler too, A Biography of John and Julia Gardiner Tyler*.

Mr. Tyler is a graceful, easy speaker, with all that blandness of manner which belongs to the Virginia character. But there was nothing forceable or striking in his speech; no bright thoughts, no well-turned expressions; nothing that left an impression on the mind from its strength and beauty — *nothing that marked a great man*.

> Anon., in *Daily Pittsburgher*, 8 October 1840.

Tippicanoe and Tyler too!

> Anon., campaign slogan when Tyler ran for vice-president on the ticket headed by William Henry Harrison.

Mr. Tyler . . . styles himself President of the United States, and not Vice President acting as President, which would be the correct style. It is a construction in direct violation both of the grammar and context of the constitution, which confers upon the Vice President, on the decease of the President, not the office, but the duties of the said office.

> John Quincy Adams, in L. Falkner, *The President Who Wouldn't Retire*.

A political sectarian of the slave-drawing Virginian Jeffersonian school, principled against all improvement, with all the interests and passions and vices rooted in his moral and political constitution.

> John Quincy Adams, in Marie B. Hecht, *John Quincy Adams — A Personal History of an Independent Man*.

With all his court, in gaudy trappings of mock royalty, to receive the homage of hungry sycophants, under color of doing homage to the principles of Bunker Hill martyrdom.

> *Ibid.* (Tyler was a guest when Daniel Webster delivered an address on the completion of the Bunker Hill Monument.)

Although he was elected to office as a Wig, the Wigs later disowned him because he insisted on wearing his own hair. For a time he was a man without a party, which annoyed his wife who loved to entertain.

Richard Armour, *It All Started With Columbus*.

He was the first vice-president to become president through the death of a president, which was a good thing for him but a bad thing for Harrison.

Ibid.

But vanity in him, as in Mr. Adams, supplies all other wants and sustains a tottering statesman.

C. J. Ingersoll to Martin Van Buren, in Oliver P. Chitwood, *John Tyler, Champion of the Old South*.

Tip was Bank, Ty was anti-Bank; Tip was Tariff, Ty was anti-Tariff; Tip was Distribution, Ty was anti. In fact, Fellow citizens, Tip is Whig, Ty is Democrat.

John Winston, commenting that Tyler and Harrison, running mates in the 1840 election, disagreed on every political issue.

See also William Henry Harrison

V

VALENTINO, RUDOLPH (RUDOLPHO DI VALENTINA D'AUTONGUOLLA)

1895—1926 Actor

[He was] the symbol of everything wild and wonderful and illicit in nature.
  Anon., in *Life*, 15 January 1950.

Valentino had silently acted out the fantasies of women all over the world. Valentino and his world were a dream. A whole generation of females wanted to ride off into a sandy paradise with him. At thirteen I had been such a female.
  Bette Davis, *The Lonely Life*.

He had more sheer animal magnetism than any actor before or since. *The Sheik* and *Blood and Sand* placed Valentino on a pinnacle of adoration before he knew the *a b c*'s of screen acting. He became a far more accomplished actor later on, but women didn't attend his pictures to see him act. They went to swoon.
  Jesse Lasky, *I Blow My Own Horn*.

Here was a young man who was living daily the dream of millions of other young men. Here was one who was catnip to women. Here was one who had wealth and fame. And here was one who was very unhappy.
  H. L. Mencken, 'Appendix From Moronia', *Prejudices*, sixth series.

I began to observe Valentino more closely. A curiously naive and boyish young fellow, certainly not much beyond thirty, and with a disarming air of inexperience. To my eye, at least, not handsome, but nevertheless rather attractive. There was an obvious fineness in him; even his clothes were not precisely those of his horrible trade. He began talking of his home, his people, his early youth. His words were simple and yet somehow very eloquent. I could still see the mime before me, but now and then, briefly and darkly, there was a flash of something else. That something else, I concluded, was what is commonly called, for want of a better name, a gentleman.
  Ibid.

Valentino epitomised the continuing fascination of the public with exoticism. He was in direct descent from Theda Bara and indeed, has been described as 'quite simply a male vamp'. It's difficult to see today the magnetism that he evidently exerted; it has been said that he had the acting talents of the average wardrobe, and he certainly seemed to restrict his range to a great deal of eye rolling, eyebrow jerking and facial smouldering. This, however, was enough to ensure that during his lifetime and even fifty years after his death the name Valentino is synonymous with 'Great Lover'.
  Clyde Jeavons and Jeremy Pascall, *A Pictorial History of Sex in the Movies*.

Valentino was different and women knew it. His patent-leather hair, his smoky eyes, his habit of kissing women on the inside rather than the back of the hand, the way his chest heaved when consumed by passion, the manner in which he turned away, tight-lipped, when nearly overcome and, most of all, his cavalier, almost brutal treatment of women all conspired to make him the hottest, sexiest, most desirable male star of the 'twenties.
  Ibid.

For *lover* the thesaurus gives us Lothario, Romeo, Casanova, Don Juan; most people, I discover, give you *Valentino*. When they die young the wounds bleed, wounds that bleed leave scars to remember by.
  Adela Rogers St Johns, *The Honeycomb*.

See also John Gilbert, Elinor Glyn

VANBRUGH, SIR JOHN

1664—1726 Dramatist, Architect

We have always regarded his productions as rough jewels of inestimable worth.
  Robert and James Adam, *Works*.

His conceptions were far beyond his powers of execution, and his mind was possessed with a single idea, almost amounting to megalomania.
  Sir Reginald Blomfield, *A History of Renaissance Architecture in England 1500—1800*.

Under this stone, reader, survey
Dead Sir John Vanbrugh's house of clay.
Lie heavy on him earth! for he
Laid heavy loads on thee.
    Abel Evans, *Epitaph.*

He never faltered in his career; and from first to
last — at Blenheim and Castle Howard, as at Seaton
Delaval and Grimsthorpe — there is one principle
runs through all his designs, and it was a worthy one
— a lofty aspiration after grandeur and eternity.
    James Fergusson, *History of the Modern Styles
of Architecture.*

Others of our Comick Writers who have succeeded
most in that way, pick out Characters that are indeed diverting enough on the Stage, but which
scarce one sensible Man in a Thousand can read in
his Chamber, so much is left to the Action: but Mr
Van Brug's Characters are composed of that Part of
Nature, which is not so Monstrous to shock the
Reader, or Nauseate his Palate, but which yield a
pleasing Entertainment; he puts Folly into such a
Light, that it is as Diverting to the Reader as Spectator; and his Fools are so pleasing, that you are not
weary of their Company before they leave you.
    Charles Gildon, *Lives and Characters of the Eng-
lish Dramatic Poets . . . begun by Mr Langbain
. . . continued . . . by a Careful Hand,* 1699.

He discovers the utmost dramatic generalship in
bringing off his characters at a pinch, and by an
instantaneous *ruse de guerre*, when the case seems
hopeless in any other hands. The train of his associations, to express the same thing in metaphysical
language, lies in following the suggestions of his
fancy into every possible combination of cause and
effect, rather than into every possible combination
of likeness or difference.
    William Hazlitt, *Lectures on the English Comic
Writers.*

Vanbrugh used his weighty materials as a pigment,
and the sky his canvas, with a brush too wide to
allow any niceties of detail. Surely Mammon was his
Zeus.
    Edwin Lutyens, in C. Hussey, *The Life of Sir
Edwin Lutyens.*

To speak then of Vanbrugh in the language of a
painter, he had originality of invention, he understood light and shadow, and had great skill in
composition. To support his principal object, he
produced his second and third groups or masses; he
perfectly understood in his art what is the most
difficult in ours, the conduct of the back-ground; by
which the design and invention is set off to the
greatest advantage. What the back-ground is in

painting, in architecture is the real ground on which
the building is erected; and no architect took greater
care than he that his work should not appear crude
and hard; that is, it did not abruptly start out of the
ground without expectation or preparation.
    Sir Joshua Reynolds, *Discourse XIII*, December
1786.

Heaviness was the lightest of his faults. . . . The
Italian style . . . which he contrived to caricature
. . . is apparent in all his works; he helped himself
liberally to its vices, contributed many of his own,
and by an unfortunate misfortune adding impurity
to that which was already greatly impure, left it
disgusting and often odious.
    Sir Robert Smirke, *Manuscript Notes.*

In his bold flights of irregular fancy, his powerful
mind rises superior to common conceptions, and
entitles him to the high distinctive appellation of
the Shakespeare of Architects.
    Sir John Soane, *Lecture V to the Royal Aca-
demy.*

Van's Genius without Thought or Lecture
Is hugely turnd to Architecture.
    Jonathan Swift, *The History of Vanbrug's House.*

From such deep Rudiments as these,
Van is become by due Degrees,
For building fam'd; and justly reckon'd
At Court, *Vitruvius* the *Second.*
No Wonder; since wise *Authors* show,
That *best Foundations* must be *low.*
And now the *Duke* has wisely ta'en him
To be his *Architect* at *Blenheim.*
But Raillery for once apart,
If this Rule holds in ev'ry Art;
Or if his Grace were no more skill'd in
The Art of battering Walls than Building;
We might expect to see next Year
A *Mouse-trap* Man chief Engineer.
    Ibid.

Sir John was a man of Pleasure, and likewise a Poet,
and an Architect. The general Opinion is, that he is
as sprightly in his Writings as he is heavy in his
Buildings. 'Tis he who rais'd the famous Castle of
Blenheim, a ponderous and lasting Monument of
our unfortunate Battle of Hochstet. Were the Apartments but as spacious as the walls are thick, this
Castle would be commodious enough.
    Voltaire, *Letters Concerning the English Nation.*

He wanted eyes, he wanted all ideas of proportion,
convenience, propriety. He undertook vast designs,
and composed heaps of littleness. The style of no
age, no country, appears in his works; he broke

through all rule, and compensated for it by no imagination.

Horace Walpole, *Anecdotes of Painters in England.*

Vanbrugh dealt in quarries, and Kent in lumber.

Horace Walpole, Letter to Sir Horace Mann, 22 April 1775.

His humour was broad like his keystones, though not so heavy.

Lawrence Whistler, *Sir John Vanbrugh.*

Vanbrugh . . . was neither nursed nor tutored; he sprang into power like Athene, fully armed with imagination, and so great was the impression he made, that at once a new manner appeared in the chief works.

Ibid.

See also Nicholas Hawksmoor

VAN BUREN, MARTIN

1782–1862 Eighth United States President

Every paper almost that we open speaks contemptuously of Van Buren's prospects for the presidency; but they speak without knowledge of . . . the vast machine of intrigue and corruption that he has set in operation in every part of the Union — they do not see the fox prowling near the barn; the mole burrowing near the ground, the pilot fish who plunges deep in the ocean in one spot and comes up in another to breathe the air.

Anon., in *New York Courier and Enquirer,* 1835.

The Red Fox of Kinderhook.

Anon., common nickname for Van Buren.

Ole Tip he wears a homespun suit,
He has no ruffled shirt — wirt — wirt
But Mat he has the gold plate,
And he's a little squirt — wirt — wirt.

Anon., 1840 campaign song.

The masterspirit of his magic wand cast a spell over the heterogeneous mass, and the wolves and kids mingled together in peace and love.

Anon., commenting on Van Buren's ability to bring together disparate political groups, 1827.

Van, Van, Van, is a used-up man.

Anon., Whig Party chant, 1840.

[a] service dough-face . . . Madison had none of his obsequiousness, his sycophancy, his profound dis-

simulation and duplicity. In the last of these he much more resembles Jefferson though with very little of his genius. The most disgusting part of his character, his fawning servility, belonged neither to Jefferson nor to Madison.

John Quincy Adams, in L. Falkner, *The President Who Wouldn't Retire.*

It was he who conceived and constructed the gigantic patronage system which directly caused the death of two Presidents, nearly drove Lincoln insane and caused Cleveland to cry out, 'It makes me feel like resigning and hell is to pay.' It was he who mainly visualized and brought to pass the National Conventions where a people's choice can be conveniently nominated by a conclave of political jobholders. The adjective 'Vanburenish' . . . was coined as a synonym for vapid non-committalism, and Van Buren it was who set the style for candidates who agilely straddle the issues, who, no matter how much wire-pulling there has been back-stage, always declare themselves astonished and overcome at the honor of being 'called' by the People.

Holmes Alexander, *The American Talleyrand.*

Van Buren was not reelected, but his campaign was so hilarious that he was popularly acclaimed the Panic of 1837.

Richard Armour, *It All Started With Columbus.*

He stood on the dividing-line between the mere politician and the statesman — perfect in the arts of the one, possessing largely the comprehensive powers of the other.

James G. Blaine, *Twenty Years of Congress.*

He is not . . . of the race of the lion or the tiger; he belonged to a lower order — the fox.

John C. Calhoun, in Louis W. Koenig, *The Rise of the Little Magician.*

Good Lord? What is Van? For though simple he
                                                    looks,
'Tis a task to unravel his looks and his crooks,
With his depths and his shallows, his good and his
                                                    evil,
All in all he's a riddle must puzzle the Devil.

Davy Crockett, in Holmes Alexander, *The American Talleyrand.*

. . . his outward appearance like the unruffled surface of a majestic river, which covers rocks and whirlpools, but shows no mark of agitation beneath.

Philip Hone, in Holmes Alexander, *ibid.*

He rowed to his object with muffled oars.

John Randolph of Roanoke, in Edward Boykin ed., *The Wit and Wisdom of Congress.*

When he enters the Senate chamber in the morning, he struts and swaggers like a crow in the gutter. He is laced up in corsets, such as women in a town wear and, if possible, tighter than the best of them. It would be difficult to say from his personal appearance whether he was man or woman, but for his large red and gray whiskers. [He is] as opposite to General Jackson as dung is to a diamond . . . secret, sly, selfish, cold, calculating, distrustful, treacherous. . . . It is said that . . . he could laugh on one side of his face and cry on the other at one and the same time.

    Senator White, in A. Steinberg, *The First Ten.*

See also Henry Clay, William Henry Harrison

VANDERBILT, CORNELIUS

1794–1879 Financier, Capitalist

What do I care about the law? Hain't I got the power?

    On himself, in Matthew Josephson, *The Robber Barons.*

Vanderbilt made his money in ships thus, while others became captains of industry, he became a commodore. . . . One of his favorite expressions, which endeared him to everyone, was 'The public be damned.'

    Richard Armour, *It All Started With Columbus.*

VAN DOREN, MARK

1894–1972 Poet, Teacher

He is a poet of place, creating wonder from common things, finding miraculous the true apprehension of the ordinary experience.

    Grace Schulman, 'Mark Van Doren as an American', in *Nation*, 15 October 1973.

Too often Mr. Van Doren's poetry seems to be written for the easy reader, the person who thinks that by reading a narrative in verse he is achieving a greater stature than by reading a narrative in prose.

    James G. Southworth, *More Modern American Poets.*

VANE, SIR HENRY

1613–62 Statesman, Author

There never was such a prostitute sight,
That ere profaned this purer light

A hocus-pocus juggling Knight,
  Which nobody can deny.

His cunning state tricks and oracles,
His lying wonders and miracles,
Are turned at last into Parliament shackles
  Which nobody can deny.
    Anon., *Vanity of Vanities or Sir Henry Vane's Picture*, before 1662.

So much dissimulation and enthusiasm, such vast parts and such strong delusions, good sense and madness, can hardly be believed to meet in one man. He was successively a Presbyterian, Independent, Anabaptist, and Fifth Monarchy Man. In sum, he was the Proteus of his times, a mere hotch-potch of religion, chief ring-leader of all the frantic sectarians, of a turbulent spirit and working brain, of a strong composition of choler and melancholy, an inventor not only of whimseys in religion, but of crotchets in the state.

    Baker, Jones and Reed eds., *Biographia Britannica.*

A man, one rather finds, of light fibre this Sir Harry Vane. Grant all manner of purity and elevation; subtle, high discourse; much intellectual and practical dexterity: there is an amiable, devoutly zealous, very pretty man; but not a royal man; alas, no! On the whole rather a thin man. Whom it is even important to keep strictly subaltern. Whose tendency towards the Abstract, or Temporary-Theoretic, is irresistible: whose hold of the Concrete, in which lies always the Perennial, is by no means that of a giant, or born Practical King; — whose 'astonishing subtlety of intellect' conducts him not to new clearness, but to ever-new abstruseness, wheel within wheel, depth under depth; marvellous temporary empire of the air; — wholly vanished now and without meaning to any mortal. My erudite friend, the astonishing intellect that occupies itself in splitting hairs, and not in splitting some kind of cordage, and effectual draught-tackle to take the road with, is not to me the most astonishing of intellects!

    Thomas Carlyle, *Cromwell.*

Ther neede no more be sayd of his ability, then that he was chosen to cozen and deceave a whole nation, which excelled in craft and dissemblinge, which he did with notable pregnancy and dexterity, and preavayled with a people, which could not be otherwise preavayled upon, then by advancinge ther Idoll Presbitery, to sacrifice ther peace, ther interest, and ther fayth, to the erectinge a power and authority that resolved to persequte presbitery to an extirpation, and very neere brought ther purpose to passe.

    Edward Hyde, Earl of Clarendon, *History of the Rebellion.*

He was a perfect enthusiast, and without doubt did believe himself inspired, which so far clouded his reason and understanding (which in all matters without the verge of religion was inferior to that of few men) that he did at some time believe he was the person deputed to reign over the saints for a thousand years.

Ibid.

Vane, young in years but in sage counsel old
   Than whom a better senator ne'er held
   The helm of Rome, when gowns not arms repell'd
The fierce Epirot and the African bold, —
   Whether to settle peace or to unfold
   The drift of hollow states hard to be spell'd, —
   Then to advise how war may, best upheld,
Move by her two main nerves, iron and gold,
In all her equipage! — besides to know
   Both spiritual pow'r and civil what each means
   What severs each, thou hast learn'd, which few
                     have done.
The bounds of either sword to thee we owe:
   Therefore on thy firm hand Religion leans
   In peace, and reckons thee her eldest son.
   John Milton, *To Sir Henry Vane The Younger.*

See also Lord Strafford

VAUGHAN, HENRY

1622—95 Poet

There were two Vaughans (Twinnes) both very ingeniose, and writers. One writt a Poeme called *Olor Iscanus* (Henry Vaughan, the first-borne) and another booke of divine meditations. He is ingeniose, but prowd and humorous.
   John Aubrey, *Brief Lives.*

Above the voiceful windings of a river
An old green slab of simply graven stone
Shuns notice, overshadowed by a yew.
Here Vaughan lies dead, whose name flows on for
                     ever
Through pastures of the spirit washed with dew
And starlit with eternities unknown.
Here sleeps the Silurist; the loved physician;
The face that left no portraiture behind;
The skull that housed white angels and had vision
Of daybreak through the gateways of the mind.
   Siegfried Sassoon, *At the Grave of Henry Vaughan.*

Made his first entry into *Jesus* Coll. in *Mich.* Term 1638, aged 17 years: where spending two Years or more in Logicals under a noted Tutor, was taken thence and designed by his Father for the obtaining of some knowledge in the municipal Laws at *London.* But soon after the Civil War beginning, to the horror of all good Men, he was sent for home, followed the pleasant Paths of Poetry and Philology, became noted for his ingenuity, and published several Specimens thereof. . . . Afterwards applying his Mind to the study of Physic, became at length eminent in his own Country for the practice thereof, and was esteemed by Scholars *an ingenious Person, but proud and humorous.*
   Anthony à Wood, *Athenae Oxonienses.*

VAUGHAN WILLIAMS, SIR RALPH

1872—1958 Composer

[C.V.] Stanford would sometimes sigh deeply when I brought him my week's work and say he was hoping against hope.
   On himself, at the Composer's Concourse, 1957.

Reporter: Tell me, Dr. Vaughan Williams, what do you think about music?
RVW: It's a Rum Go!
   Leslie Ayre, *The Wit of Music.*

Hard, deep-seated Englishry, honest without gush, sensitive without lyrical rapture.
   A. H. Fox Strangways, in *Music and Letters*, March 1920.

In a work like Vaughan Williams's *Pastoral Symphony* it is no exaggeration to say that the creation of a particular type of grey, reflective, English-landscape mood has outweighed the exigencies of symphonic form. To those who find this mood sympathetic, their intense and personal emotional reaction will more than compensate for the monotony of texture and the lack of form, of which a well-disposed listener might perhaps be unduly conscious.
   Constant Lambert, *Music Ho!*

See also Edward Elgar

VEBLEN, THORSTEIN BUNDE

1857—1929 Economist, Social Theorist

We may now leave him in peace, remote and aloof in his Olympian privacy; whence may his stinging phrases continue to puncture our cherished illusions or to goad our lethargic minds.
   Paul T. Homan, 'Thorstein Veblen', in Howard W. Odum ed., *American Masters of Social Science.*

Veblen's style is characteristic of the man he was: precise yet ponderous, incisive yet indirect, witty yet long-winded.

Charles A. Madison, *Critics and Crusaders.*

Veblen was a strange creature, looked at through common sense eyes; and commentators have not known quite how to account for the distillation into so alien a vessel of an American Century's discontents.

Rexford Guy Tugwell, 'Veblen and Business Enterprise', in Malcolm Cowley and Bernard Smith eds, *Books That Changed Our Minds.*

The man who shook the world with his irony, and who opened the way to a new social system for the generation which should find the wit to resolve the conflicts he had pointed out, went slowly out of life, lonely, trivial, unappeased and disagreeable. But that was probably all in the character he had chosen out of those available to him.

Ibid.

. . . the philosophy of American business was riddled by the mordant ironies of Thorstein Veblen . . . who with the industry of a termite outbored the most boring of professional economists.

George F. Whicher, 'The Twentieth Century', in Arthur Hobson Quinn ed., *The Literature of the American People.*

He was likewise a master of devious implication, pungent epigram, and adhesive phrases that clung like leeches to the bloated form of capitalism.

Ibid.

VESEY, DENMARK

circa 1767–1822 Abolitionist

Vesey's example must be regarded as one of the most courageous ever to threaten the racist foundation of America. In him the anguish of Negro people welled up in nearly perfect measure. He stands today, as he stood yesterday . . . as an awesome projection of the possibilities for militant action on the part of a people who have — for centuries — been made to bow down in fear.

Sterling Stuckey, 'Remembering Denmark Vesey — Agitator or Insurrectionist?', *Negro Digest*, February 1966.

Among those of his color he was looked up to with awe and respect. His temper was impetuous and domineering in the extreme, qualifying him for the despotic rule of which he was ambitious. All his passions were ungovernable and savage; and to his numerous wives and children he displayed the haughty and capricious cruelty of an Eastern bashaw.

Official report on the insurrection, in Thomas Wentworth Higginson, 'Black Rebellion', in *Travellers and Outlaws.*

VICTORIA, QUEEN

1819–1901

. . . they wished to treat me like a girl, but I will show them that I am Queen of England.

On herself, Letter to Lord Melbourne on the Bedchamber Question, May 1839.

Lord John Russell may resign, and Lord Aberdeen may resign, but I *can't* resign.

On herself, speaking to Lord Clarendon on the formation of a government, January 1855.

The Queen herself, though it was tried in all ways, *never* could *before* her accession take the slightest interest in public affairs; but, the moment she felt the responsibility, she bent her neck to the yoke and worked hard, though she *hates* it *all* as much now as she did as a girl.

On herself, Memorandum to Sir Henry Ponsonby, 9 July 1872.

Oh if the Queen were a man, she would like to go and give those horrid Russians whose word one cannot trust such a beating.

On herself, Letter to Disraeli, January 1878.

Others but herself *may submit* to his [Gladstone's] democratic rule but *not the Queen.*

On herself, Memorandum to Sir Henry Ponsonby, 4 April 1880.

As I get older, I cannot understand the world. I cannot comprehend its littlenesses. When I look at the frivolities and littlenesses, it seems to me as if they were all a little mad.

On herself, Diary, *circa* 1885.

We are not amused.

On herself, attributed, remark probably made after she saw a horseguard attempting to imitate her, 1889.

How different, how very different, from the home life of our own dear Queen!

Anon., comment of a contemporary woman after a performance of *Antony and Cleopatra*, in Irvin S. Cobb, *A Laugh a Day.*

How shall we speak of an infinite loss . . . the un-imaginable touch of fate that extinguishes an epoch, that removes the central figure of all the world. . . . The golden reign is closed. The supreme woman of the world, best of the highest, greatest of the good, is gone. The Victorian age is over. Never, never was loss like this, so inward and profound that only the slow years can reveal its true reality. The Queen is dead.
    Anon., in *Daily Telegraph*, 23 January 1901.

It is indeed a pity that you find no consolation in the company of your children. The root of the trouble lies in the mistaken notion that, the func-tion of a mother is to be always correcting, scolding, ordering them about and organising their activities. It is not possible to be on happy friendly terms with people you have just been scolding.
    Prince Albert, Letter to Victoria,
    1 October 1856.

'I will have no melancholy in this house' is her formula — and not a bad one either in moments of anxiety.
    A. J. Balfour, Letter to Lord Salisbury,
    19 December 1899.

She was the greatest of Englishwomen — I had al-most said of Englishmen — for she added the highest of manly qualities to the personal delicacy of the woman.
    Joseph Chamberlain, Letter to Lord Milner,
    25 January 1901.

Your Majesty's life has been passed in constant com-munion with great men, and the knowledge and management of important transactions. Even if your Majesty were not gifted with those great abilities, which all must now acknowledge, this rare and choice experiment must give your Majesty an advan-tage in judgment, which few living persons, and probably no living Prince, can rival.
    Benjamin Disraeli, Letter to Queen Victoria,
    26 February 1868.

Murmurings of children in a dream. The royal project of gracious interposition with our rivals is a mere phantom. It pleases the vanity of a court deprived of substantial power. . . .
    Benjamin Disraeli, Letter to Lord Derby concern-ing the Queen's offer to mediate with the Liberals, 21 October 1866.

No it is better not. She would only ask me to take a message to Albert.
    Benjamin Disraeli, reply to the suggestion that the Queen visit him in his last illness, April 1881.

Her chief fault (in little things and great) seems to be impatience; in Sea phrase, She always wants to *go ahead*; she can't bear contradiction nor to be thwarted.
    Adolphus Fitzclarence, in Charles Greville, Diary, 24 September 1842.

To speak in rude and general terms, the Queen is in-visible, and the Prince of Wales is not respected. With the Queen, who abounds beyond all necessity in private and personal kindnesses to those having relations with her, it is a matter of great and ever increasing difficulty to arrange for any part of those formal ceremonial duties to the public, which in an ordinary state of things would go as matters of course. These parts of business are among the most difficult, and are the most painful, of the duties of my place; and it would be a relief to me if I could lay the blame upon the unhandy manner in which I perform them. The Queen's reluctance grows, and will grow, with age.
    William Ewart Gladstone, Letter to Earl Gran-ville, December 1870.

It was so awfully pathetic seeing Her drawn on a gun carriage by the eight cream coloured horses of Jubilee renown — but I never at any funeral felt so strongly before, that She Herself was not on the bier but watching it all from somewhere and rejoicing in Her people's loyalty.
    Kathleen Isherwood, Letter, 3 February 1901.

She's more of a man than I expected.
    Henry James (after reading the Queen's *Letters*), in E. M. Forster, Diary, 1908.

'Ave you 'eard o' the Widow at Windsor
  With a hairy gold crown on 'er 'ead?
She 'as ships on the foam — she 'as millions at 'ome,
  An' she pays us poor beggars in red.
    Rudyard Kipling, *The Widow at Windsor*.

Walk wide o' the Widow at Windsor,
  For 'alf o' Creation she owns:
We 'ave bought 'er the same with the sword an' the
                            flame,
  An' we've salted it down with our bones.
    Ibid.

The finest & most poetic thing that can be said about the Queen, is . . . that her virtues and powers are *not* those of a great woman, like Elizabeth or Catherine II . . . , but are the virtues and powers of an ordinary woman: things that any person, however humble, can appreciate and imitate . . . an example inestimably precious to the whole world.
    Alfred Munby, Letter to Austin Dobson, 4 July 1897.

You never saw anybody so entirely taken up with military affairs as she is.

    Lord Panmure, Letter to Lord Raglan, 1855.

Dear dead Victoria
    Rotted cosily;
In excelsis gloria,
    And R.I.P.
And her shroud was buttoned neat,
    And her bones were clean and round,
And her soul was at her feet
    Like a bishop's marble hound.
    Dorothy Parker, *Victoria.*

Her court was pure; her life serene;
    God gave her peace; her land reposed;
    A thousand claims to reverence closed
In her as Mother, Wife and Queen.
    Alfred, Lord Tennyson, *To The Queen.*

See also Prince Albert, Richard Burton, Duke of Cumberland, Duke of Marlborough, Lord Melbourne, Joseph Lister, Henry Wadsworth Longfellow, D. G. Rossetti, Alfred, Lord Tennyson, Oscar Wilde

VILLIERS, BARBARA, COUNTESS OF CASTLEMAINE, DUCHESS OF CLEVELAND

1641–1709 Mistress to Charles II, Court Figure

But ere I part, I Cleveland must behold —
The Amazon gamester with her keeper's gold,
Hedged in by rooks and sharpers to prove true
The proverb, 'lightly come and lightly go',
She for her soul cant give the dice-box o'er
'Till she's as poor and wretched as Jane Shore;
And she'll by sad experience find it worse
Than broke in visage to be broke in purse.
    Anon., *Tunbridge Satire.*

The Empress Massalina tir'd in lust at least,
But you could never satisfy this beast.
Cleveland I say, was much to be admir'd
For she was never satisfied or tired.
Full forty men a day have swived the whore,
Yet like a bitch she wags her tail for more.
    John Lacy, *Satire.*

This abandoned woman, not content with her complaisant husband, and her royal keeper, lavished her fondness on a crowd of paramours, of all ranks, from Dukes to rope-dancers. In the time of the Commonwealth she commenced her career of gallantry, and terminated it under Queen Anne, by

marrying, when a great-grandmother, that worthless fop, Beau Fielding.

    T. B. Macaulay, *Essays*: 'On the Comic Dramatists of the Restoration'.

Endeed I can never enough admire her beauty.

    Samuel Pepys, Diary, 7 September 1661.

Mr Povy and I in his coach to Hide-park, being the first day of the Tour there — where many brave ladies. Among others, Castlemayne lay impudently upon her back in her coach, asleep with her mouth open.

    Ibid., 19 March 1665.

Young Harry Killigrew is banished the Court lately for saying that my Lady Castlemayne was a little lecherous girl when she was young, and used to rub her thing with her fingers or against the end of forms, and that she must be rubbed with something else. This she complained to the King of — and he sent to the Duke of York, whose servant he is, to turn him away. The Duke of York hath done it, but takes it ill of my Lady that he was not complained to first. She attended him to excuse it, but ill blood was made by it.

    Ibid., 21 October 1666.

It seems she is with child, and the King says he did not get it; with that she made a slighting 'puh' with her mouth, and went out of the house, and never came in again till the King sent to Sir Dan. Harvey's to pray her. . . . But it seems she hath told the King that whoever did get it, he should own it; and the bottom of the quarrel is this; she is fallen in love with young Jermin, who hath of late lain with her oftener than the King and is now going to marry my Lady Falmouth. The King, he is mad at her entertaining Jermin, and she is mad at Jermin's going to marry from her, so they are all mad, and thus the Kingdom is governed.

    Ibid., 29 July 1667.

Thy strumpets Charles, have 'scaped no nation's ear;
Cleveland the van, and Portsmouth led the rear;
A brace of cherubs of as vile a breed
As ever was produced of human seed.
To all but thee the punks were ever kind,
Free as loose air, and gen'rous as the wind;
Both steer'd thy pego and the nations helm
And both betray'd thy pintle and thy realm.
    Thomas Sackville, Earl of Dorset (?), *A Faithful Catalogue of our Most Eminent Ninnies.*

If the Church of Rome has got by her no more than the Church of England has lost, the Matter is not much.

    Bishop Stillingfleet, on Castlemaine's conversion, 1663, in J. Oldmixon, *History of England.*

When she has jaded quite
Her almost Boundless appetite;
Cloy'd with the choicest Banquets of Delight,
She'll still drudge on in tastless Vice,
(As if she sinn'd for Exercise)
Disabling st(out)est Stallions every hour:
And when they can perförm no more,
She'll rail at 'em, and kick them out of Door.
    John Wilmot, Earl of Rochester, attributed,
    Pindarick.

Libell on the countess of Castlemayne's doore in
Merton Coll [January 1666]. . . . The reason why
she is not ducked 'Cause by Caesar she is - - -
    Anthony à Wood, *Life and Times.*

See also Charles II

VILLIERS, GEORGE, see under BUCKINGHAM,
DUKES OF

VON STERNBERG, JOSEF
1894—1969 Film Director

Instead of the Elinor Glyn plots of the day, I had in
mind a visual poem. Instead of flat lighting, shadows.
In the place of pasty masks, faces in relief, plastic
and deep-eyed. Instead of scenery which meant
nothing, an emotionalised background that would
transfer itself into my foreground. Instead of saccharine characters, sober figures moving in rhythm.
    On himself, of his first film *The Salvation Hun-
    ters.*

When they ask me what elements are necessary for a
director, I propose some absolutely horrible qualifications. I tell them he must know all the languages,
he must know the history of the theatre from its
beginnings, he must be an expert in psychoanalysis
and must have had some psychiatric training. He
must know every emotion. And they ask me 'Did
you know all this?' And I say 'No — but I never
asked anyone how to become a director.'
    On himself, Interview, December 1964, in Kevin
    Brownlow, *The Parade's Gone By.*

The only way to succeed is to make people hate
you. That way they remember you.
    On himself, to Clive Brook, in Kevin Brownlow,
    ibid.

Considered by some the greatest cameraman in the
world, von Sternberg's grasp of narrative was seldom
more than tenuous. The majority of his sound films
were carried by the visuals alone, for von Sternberg
had a richer sense of visuals than any director since
Maurice Tourneur. He not only understood the
subtle art of lighting — he knew that art direction
and set dressing could have an emotional effect as
well as fulfilling practical requirements. Von Sternberg could film the telephone directory and make it
exciting, mysterious and sensuous.
    Kevin Brownlow, in *ibid.*

Critical historians have evaluated Von Sternberg's
pictures as things of beauty but not a joy forever.
His artistry with a camera was rarely surpassed, but
he sometimes allowed pictorial effects to over-
shadow the story he was telling.
    Jesse Lasky, *I Blow My Own Horn.*

Sternberg's films are poetic without being symbolic. We need not search for slumbering allegories of
Man and God and Life, but rather for a continuous
stream of emotional autobiography. Sternberg's
exoticism is, then, less a pretense than a pretext for
objectifying personal fantasies. His equivalent
literary genre is not the novel or the short story of
the theatrical spectacle, but the closet drama un-
playable but for the meaningful grace of gesture and
movement.
    Andre Sarris, *The American Cinema.*

Jo has been his usual obnoxious, brilliant self; refusing to concede the merit of suggestions and then
acting upon them: making changes that would be
aggravating in any other director that turn out all
right. As with all his pictures, he makes silly things
look great. . . .
    David O. Selznick, Letter to Bud Schulberg, in
    Rudy Behlmer, *Memo From David O. Selznick.*

In a milieu with its easy contempt for aesthetic
values, the hieratic disdain of his style — which
ranks with the most patrician filmmaking in the
world — is a thrilling thing to see, as it always is
wherever work is touched, 'beyond the call of duty,'
with the vital grace of art.
    Herman G. Weinberg, *Josef von Sternberg.*

What I admire in him is not his cinematic genius
that reveals itself in his bird-of-prey eyes and his
lightning comprehension and control of any situation. That can be learned and may often be har-
bored in an individual. But what counts most and
makes him great is his endurance, his mind forcing
domination over his threadbare nerves, his stoicism
and monklike humility toward his work.
    Ibid.

VON STROHEIM, ERICH (OSWALD VAN NORDENWALL)

1885–1957 Film Director, Actor

This isn't the worst. The worst is that they stole twenty-five years of my life.

> On himself, on his death bed, while in great pain, in Thomas Quinn Curtis, *Von Stroheim*.

To measure fully the importance of this work, it is necessary to go back into history and put oneself in the period when it first appeared. It is among the most authentic work of our profession. The passage of time may have lessened its shock; the physical changes all around us may have disfigured it; the films that it influenced and the imitations it inspired have tended to blur its originality. But this work of Erich von Stroheim, even though mutilated by others, shines with a power and newness that a quarter of a century cannot diminish.

> René Clair, introducing a retrospective of von Stroheim's work at the Venice Film Festival, 1958.

Genius! In talking of films, what meaning can we give this word so devalued by hypocrisy and confused standards? An artist of genius is one who creates without imitating, and who draws out of the depths of his own being the least predictable part of his work. How many in the history of the cinema fit this definition? Whatever their number, Erich von Stroheim is at their head. He owed nothing to anyone. Yet it is to this man, who died in poverty, that every one of us is in debt.

> *Ibid.*

'This is a true honor' said [Billy] Wilder by way of introduction. 'In my opinion, you were twenty years ahead of your time.' 'Thirty' replied von Stroheim without smiling.

> Thomas Quinn Curtis, *Von Stroheim*.

He told me that if he should die tomorrow, there would be sorrow only in one group in Hollywood, the workmen, the laborers, the artisans. 'I had no trouble with them; never! I got on well with them for the plain reason that I was one of them. I have always stood with them better than I have with the wealthy and the powerful. I could *never* get on with vice-presidents.'

> Lloyd Lewis, in *ibid.*

Von Stroheim was the greatest director in the world. That's a fact, and no one who knows pictures would dispute it. But he was impossible, a crazy artist. If he had only been ten percent less himself and ten percent more reasonable, we would still be making pictures together.

> Louis B. Mayer, in *ibid.*

Some Hollywood flack, in a burst of inspiration, dubbed him the Man You Love to Hate. He was a short man, almost squat, with a vulpine smirk that told you, the moment his image flashed on the screen, that no wife or bank roll must be left unguarded. The clean-shaven bullet head, the glittering monocle, and the ram rod back (kept rigid by a corset it was whispered) were as familiar and as dear to the moviegoing public as the Pickford curls or Eugene O'Brien's pompadour. No matter what the background of the picture was — an English drawing room, a compartment on the Orient Express, the legation quarter of Peiping — he always wore tight-fitting military tunics, flaunted an ivory cigarette holder, and kissed ladies' hands profusely, betraying them in the next breath with utter impartiality. For sheer menace, he made even topnotch vipers like Lew Cody, Ivan Lebedeff, and Rockliffe Fellowes seem rank stumblebums by comparison. He was the ace of cads, a man without a single redeeming feature, the embodiment of Prussian Junkerism, and the greatest heavy of the silent film, and his name, of course, was Erich von Stroheim.

> S. J. Perelman, 'Cloudland Revisited: Vintage Swine', in *The Most of S. J. Perelman.*

Stroheim, who had brought to the silent film a sophistication and maturity the cinema was hardly to know again, and a unique, disturbing and horrific vision of an old world in decay but still destructively lingering, was a houseless giant in the era of sound pictures. Intermittently he acted, in America and France, his performances as striking as his films had been. He left behind a heart-breaking trail of unrealised projects. Hollywood's failure to contain this trying genius is one of the tragedies of the history of art.

> David Robinson, *Hollywood in the Twenties.*

W

WALLACE, HENRY AGARD

1888—1965 Politician

Much of what Mr. Wallace calls his global thinking is, no matter how you slice it, still Globaloney.
   Claire Booth Luce, Speech in the House of Representatives, 9 February 1943.

WALLER, EDMUND

1606—87 Poet

That admirable writer has the best and worst verses of any among our great English poets.
   Joseph Addison, in *Tatler*, no. 163.

One of the first refiners of our English language and poetrey. When he was a brisque young sparke, and first studyed Poetry; me thought, sayd he, I never sawe a good copie of English verses; they want smoothness; then I began to essay. I have severall times heard him say that he cannot versify when he will: but when the Fitt comes upon him, he does it easily, i.e. in plaine terms, when his Mercurius and Venus are well aspected.
   John Aubrey, *Brief Lives*.

He first made writing easily an art; first showed us to conclude the sense most commonly in distichs, which in the verse of those before him, runs on for so many lines together, that the reader is out of breath to overtake it.
   John Dryden, Dedication to *The Rival Ladies*.

Unless he had written, none of us could write.
   John Dryden, Preface to William Walsh, *A Dialogue Concerning Women*.

Waller belonged to the same class as Suckling — the sportive, the sparkling, the polished, with fancy, wit, elegance of style, and easiness of versification at his command. Poetry was the plaything of his idle hours — the mistress, to whom he addressed his verses, was his real Muse.
   William Hazlitt, 'A Critical List of Authors', in *Select British Poets*.

The general character of his poetry is elegance and gaiety. He is never pathetic, and very rarely sublime. He seems neither to have had a mind much elevated by nature nor amplified by learning. His thoughts are such as a liberal conversation and large acquaintance with life would easily supply. They had however then, perhaps, that grace of novelty which they are now often supposed to want by those who, having already found them in later books, do not know or inquire who produced them first. This treatment is unjust. Let not the original author lose by his imitators.
   Samuel Johnson, *Lives of the Poets*.

His importation of the French theory of the couplet as a kind of thought-coop did nothing but mischief.
   James Russell Lowell, 'Essay on Dryden', in *My Study Windows*.

See also George Chapman, William D'Avenant

WALPOLE, HORACE, FOURTH EARL OF ORFORD

1717—97 Author

It is charming to totter into vogue.
   On himself, Letter to G. A. Selwyn, December 1765.

He was a witty, sarcastic, ingenious, deeply-thinking, highly-cultivated, quaint, though evermore gallant and romantic, though very mundane, old bachelor of other days.
   Fanny Burney, *Memoirs of Dr Burney*.

Walpole! I thought not I should ever see
So mean a Heart as thine has proved to be;
Thou who in Luxury nursed, beholdst with Scorn
The boy who Friendless, Fatherless, Forlorn,
Asks thy high Favour . . .
                    . . . I shall live and stand
By Rowley's side when *Thou* are dead and damned.
   Thomas Chatterton, on Walpole's refusal to help him.

Walpole deserves his place as the central figure in every account of eighteenth-century medievalism.

He was not an originator. To give a new direction to taste, to furnish men's minds with a new Utopia, requires more imagination and independence than Walpole could command. But to catch and intensify new ideas as they float from mind to mind requires gifts too; and these gifts Walpole had. Wit, curiosity, a graceful style, and a good social position were more valuable assets than passionate conviction or massive learning.

Kenneth Clark, *The Gothic Revival.*

The conformation of his mind was such that whatever was little seemed to him great, and whatever was great seemed to him little.

T. B. Macaulay, 'Walpole', in *Edinburgh Review*, October 1833.

Walpole ought never to be confused with Walpole, who was quite different; it was Walpole who lived in a house called Strawberry Jam and spent his time writing letters to famous men (such as the Prime Minister, Walpole, etc.). Walpole is memorable for inventing the new policy of letting dogs go to sleep.

W. C. Sellar and R. J. Yeatman, *1066 and All That.*

He was mischievous and obscene; he gibbered and mocked and pelted the holy shrines with nutshells. And yet with what a grace he did it — with what ease and brilliancy and wit! . . . He is the best company in the world — the most amusing, the most intriguing — the strangest mixture of ape and Cupid that ever was.

Virginia Woolf, *Essays*, 'The Death of the Moth'.

A queer sort of imagination haunted the seemingly prosaic edifice of Walpole's mind. What but imagination gone astray and vagrant over pots and pans instead of firmly held in place was his love of knick-knacks and antiquities, Strawberry hills and decomposing royalties?

Ibid., 'Granite and Rainbow'.

See also Lytton Strachey

WALPOLE, SIR HUGH SEYMOUR

1884–1941 Author

I was a young man in a hurry, ambitious, greedy, excitable. I was not really vain. When he [Henry James] told me gently that I was an idiot and that my novels were worthless, I believed that, from his point of view, it must be so, and that if the world had been peopled with Henry Jameses I should certainly never publish a line. The world was not.

On himself, *The Apple Trees.*

Of Walpole it may truly be said that all there is in his books is his own: no divine spark has assisted him.

William Gerhardie, *Memoirs of a Polyglot.*

You bleat and jump like a white lambkin on the vast epistolary green which stretches before you co-extensive with life . . . I positively invite and applaud your gambols.

Henry James, Letter to Walpole, *circa* 1909.

I have little doubt that he would have given all his popularity to gain the esteem of the intelligentsia. He knocked humbly at their doors and besought them to let him in, and it was a bitterness to him that they only laughed.

Somerset Maugham, *A Writer's Notebook.*

How *cooooold* he be ainy goood? He knows naaaathing about saix!

Robertson Nicoll, in Frank Swinnerton, *The Georgian Literary Scene.*

WALPOLE, SIR ROBERT, FIRST EARL OF ORFORD

1676–1745 Prime Minister

Who killed Cock Robin?
I, said the Sparrow,
With my bow and arrow,
I killed Cock Robin.
    Nursery Rhyme, *circa* 1744, traditionally held to refer to Walpole's fall.

All the birds of the air
Fell a-sighing and a-sobbing
When they heard the bell toll
For poor Cock Robin.
    Ibid.

He would frequently ask young fellows at their first appearance in the world, while their honest hearts were yet untainted, 'Well, are you to be an old Roman? a patriot? You will soon come off of that and grow wiser.' And thus he was more dangerous to the morals than to the liberties of his country, to which I am persuaded he meant no ill in his heart.

Lord Chesterfield, *Letters and Characters*, vol. 2.

Profuse and appetent, his ambition was subservient to his desire of making a great fortune. He had more of the Mazarin than of the Richelieu. He would do mean things for profit, and never thought of doing great ones for glory.

Ibid.

I think 'tis thought a fault to wish anybody dead,
but I hope 'tis none to wish he might be hanged,
having brought to ruin so great a country as this
might have been.

    Sarah Churchill, *Opinions of Sarah, Duchess of
Marlborough.*

When Sir Robert Walpole was dismissed from all
his employments he retired to Houghton and
walked into the Library; when, pulling down a
book and holding it some minutes to his eyes, he
suddenly and seeming sullenly exchanged it for
another. He held that about half as long, and looking out a third returned it instantly to its shelf and
burst into tears. 'I have led a life of business so
long,' said he, 'that I have lost my taste for reading,
and now — what shall I do?'

    Mrs Piozzi (Hester Lynch Thrale), *Memoirs.*

He had a heightened awareness both of the world
and of men. From this sprang both his exquisite
taste and his finesse in human relations. He could
live outside his own character. He possessed
empathy, the quality to get, as it were, into the skin
of other human beings, to feel with them; an intuitive quality which, of course, could err, but more
often brilliantly clarified a common situation.

    J. H. Plumb, *Sir Robert Walpole.*

Seen him I have, but in his happier hour
Of Social Pleasure, ill-exchang'd for Pow'r;
Seen him, uncumber'd with the venal tribe,
Smile without Art, and win without a bribe.
Would he oblige me? Let me only find
He does not think me what he thinks mankind.
Come, come, at all I laugh he laughs, no doubt,
The only diff'rence is, I dare laugh out.

    Alexander Pope, *Epilogue to the Satires*,
    dialogue 1.

With favour and fortune fastidiously blest,
He's loud in his laugh, and he's coarse in his jest:
Of favour and fortune unmerited, vain,
A sharper in trifles, a dupe in the main.
Achieving of nothing — still promising wonders —
By dint of experience improving in blunders.
Oppressing true merit, exalting the base,
And selling his country to purchase his place.
A jobber of stocks by retailing false news —
A prater at court in the style of the stews:
Of virtue and worth by profession a giber,
Of juries and senates the bully and briber.
Though I name not the wretch, yet you know
                   whom I mean —
'Tis the cur-dog of Britain, and spaniel of Spain.

    Jonathan Swift, *A Character of Sir Robert
Walpole.*

He had some small smattering in books, but no manner of politeness; nor in his whole life, was ever
known to advance any one person, upon the score
of wit, learning or abilities for business. The whole
system of his ministry was corruption; and he never
gave bribe or pension, without frankly telling the
receivers what he expected from them, and
threatening them to put an end to his bounty, if
they failed to comply in every circumstance.

    Jonathan Swift, *An Account of the Court and
Empire of Japan.*

See also H. H. Asquith, Lord Chatham, Lord
Melbourne, Horace Walpole

WALSINGHAM, SIR FRANCIS

1530?–90 Statesman

Sir Francis Walsingham the Queenes Secretary,
Chancellour of the Dutchy of Lancaster, and order
of the Garter, dyed of a carnosity growing intra
testium tunicas, or rather through violence of
medecines. A man exceeding wise and industrious,
having discharged very honourable Embassies, a
most sharp maintainer of the purer Religion, a most
subtill searcher of hidden secrets, who knew excellently well how to winne mens minds unto him, and
to apply them to his own uses: insomuch, as in
subtilities and officious services he surpassed the
Queenes expectation, and the Papists accused him
as a cunning workman in complotting his businesses,
and alluring men into dangers, whilest he diligently
searched out their hidden practises against religion,
his Prince Countrey, and that to his so great charges,
that he weakened his private estate; and being surcharged with debt, he was buried by darke in Pauls
Church at London without any funerall solemnity.

    William Camden, *Annales*, translated by North.

Walsingham, who hath found himself taxed even
now by her words, took opportunity, and rising up,
protested that his mind was free of all malice: I
call God, said he, to record, that as a private person
I have done nothing unbeseeming an honest man;
nor as I hear the place of a public person, have I
done anything unworthy my place. I confess, that
being very careful for the safety of the Queen and
realm, I have curiously searched out the practices
against the same.

    William Cobbett, *State Trials* (his denial that he
    forged letters between Mary Queen of Scots and
    Babington).

He outdid the Jesuits in their own bowe and over-
reached them in their own equivocation, and mental

reservation; never setling a lye, but warily drawing out and discovering truth.

    D. Lloyd, *State Worthies*.

... the great Maecenas of this age,
As wel to al that civil artes professe,
As those that are inspired with martial rage. ...
    Edmund Spenser, *Sonnet to Walsingham Prefatory to the Faery Queen*.

See also Sir Martin Frobisher

WALTON, IZAAK

1593–1683 Author

And angling, too, that solitary vice,
    Whatever Izaak Walton sings or says:
The quaint, old, cruel coxcomb, in his gullet
Should have a hook, and a small trout to pull it.
    Lord Byron, *Don Juan*, canto xiii.

What Walton saw in angling was not that delight in the consciousness of accomplishment and intelligence which sends the true fisherman to the river and keeps him there, rejoicing in his strength, whether he kill or go away empty. It was rather the pretext — with a worm and perhaps a good supper at one end and a contemplative man at the other — of a day in the fields.
    W. E. Henley, *Walton*.

Did you ever light upon Walton's 'Complete Angler'? ... It breathes the very spirit of innocence, purity, and simplicity of heart; there are many choice old verses interspersed in it; it would sweeten a man's temper at any time to read it; it would Christianise every discordant angry passion.
    Charles Lamb, Letter to Coleridge, 28 October 1796.

WALWYN, WILLIAM

fl. 1649 Leveller

I never proposed any man for my enemy, but injustice, oppression, innovation, arbitrary power, and cruelty; where I found them, I ever opposed myself against them; but so, as to destroy the evil, but to preserve the person, and therefore all the war I have made ... hath been to get victory over the understandings of men, accounting it a more worthy and profitable a labour to beget friends to the cause I loved, rather than to molest men's persons, or confiscate men's estates.
    On himself, *The Fountain of Slander Discovered*.

... The complexion also of many of them being like the bellei of a toad, and to speak the truth, Worley was one of the properest gentlemen amongst them all, as he was the most remarkable and taken notice of, by reason of his habit and busie diligence; he went that day in a great white and brown basket-hilted beard, and with a set of teeth in his head much like a potfish, all staring and standing at some distance one from another, as if they had not been good friends. It may be conjectured he picks them twice a day with a bed-staffe, they looke so white and cleare; he was mighty diligent about the Commonwealthe that day, and the privileges of the subject, and all the fraternity came flocking about him on all occasions, as a company of turkeys do about a frogge, wondering at him as at a strange sight.
    John Bastwick, *A Just Defence of John Bastwick*.

WARBURTON, WILLIAM, BISHOP OF GLOUCESTER

1698–1779 Scholar

Orthodoxy is my doxy — heterodoxy is another man's doxy.
    On himself, in Joseph Priestley, *Memoirs*.

I am well informed, that Warburton said of Johnson, 'I admire him, but I cannot bear his style': and that Johnson being told of this, said, 'That is exactly my case as to him.'
    James Boswell, *Life of Johnson*.

The manner in which he [Dr Johnson] expressed his admiration of the fertility of Warburton's genius and of the variety of his materials, was, 'The table is always full, Sir. He brings things from the north, and the south, and from every quarter ... He carries you round and round, without carrying you forward to the point; but then you have no wish to be carried forward.'
    Ibid.

I am not really Learned enough to be a judge in Works of the nature & Depth of yours, but I travel thro your book [*The Divine Legation of Moses*], as thro an Amazing Scene of ancient Egypt or Greece, struck with Veneration & Wonder, but at every step wanting an instructor to tell me all I wish to know. Such you prove to me in the Walks of Antiquity & such you will prove to all Mankind.
    Alexander Pope, Letter to Warburton, 24 June 1740.

W. is a sneaking Parson, & I told him he flatterd.
  Alexander Pope, Letter to Martha Blount,
  August 1743.

WARD, ARTEMUS (CHARLES FARRAR BROWNE)

1834—67 Humorist

I am happiest when I am idle. I could live for months without performing any kind of labour, and at the expiration of that time I should feel fresh and vigorous enough to go right on in the same way for numerous more months.
  On himself, *Pyrotechny*.

WARD, JOHN WILLIAM, EARL DUDLEY OF CASTLE DUDLEY

1781—1833 Politician

Ward has no heart, they say; but I deny it:
He has a heart, and gets his speeches by it.
  Samuel Rogers, *Epigram*.

WARD, LESTER FRANK

1841—1913 Sociologist

. . . the diffusion of a great poet and a noble nature, scientifically gifted, treating his serious subject with simplicity and severity.
  Matthew Arnold, in Samuel Chugerman, *Lester F. Ward, the American Aristotle*.

The mind of a sage, the heart of a woman, the soul of a poet.
  Emily Palmer Cape, *Lester F. Ward, A Personal Sketch*.

As a whole, his works are easy but not light reading. There is no sugared pop for infant minds but solid food for adults; no lyrical paragraphs or sizzling propaganda but scientific ideas embedded firmly in a scientific base.
  Samuel Chugerman, *Lester F. Ward, The American Aristotle*.

Raised as he was under frontier conditions and in poverty, used to work with his hands as well as head, he was democratic through and through and hence preached the gospel of equal opportunity that

each might attain the best of which he was capable.
  James Quayle Dealey, 'Lester Frank Ward', in Howard W. Odum ed., *American Masters of Social Science*.

You are not only ahead of us [other American sociologists] in point of time, but we all know that you are head, shoulders, and hips above us in many respects scientifically. You are Gulliver among the Lilliputians.
  Albion W. Small, Letter to Ward, 7 December 1903.

WARD, SETH, BISHOP OF EXETER AND SALISBURY

1617—89 Mathematician, Clergyman

He is (without all manner of flattery) so prudent, learned, and good a man, that he honours his Preferment as much as the Preferment does him: and is such a one that cannot be advanced too high. My Lord Falkland was wont to say that he never knew any one that a paire of Lawne sleeves had not altered from himselfe, but only Bishop Juxon; had he knowne this excellent Prelate, he would have sayd he had knowne one more. As is the pattern of humility and courtesie, so he knowes to be trampled or worked upon. He is a Batchelour, and of a most magnificent and munificent mind.
  John Aubrey, *Brief Lives*.

Ward was a man of great reach, went deep in mathematical studies, and was a very dexterous man, if not too dexterous; for his sincerity was much questioned.
  Gilbert Burnet, *History of His Own Time*.

When he first went to the University, he was young and low of stature, and as he walked about the streets, the Doctors, and other grave Men, would frequently lay their Hands upon his white Head, for he had very fair Hair, and ask him of what College he was, and of what standing, and such like Questions, which was so great a vexation to him, that he was asham'd to go into the Town, and, as it were, forc'd to stay in the College and study.
  Walter Pope, *The Life of . . . Seth, Lord Bishop of Salisbury*.

WARD, WILLIAM GEORGE

1812—82 Theologian

Farewell, whose living like I shall not find,
  Whose Faith and Work were bells of full accord,

My friend, the most unworldly of mankind,
  Most generous of all Ultramontanes, Ward,
How subtle at tierce and quart of mind with mind,
  How loyal in the following of thy Lord.
  Alfred, Lord Tennyson, *In Memoriam, W. G. Ward.*

WARWICK, EARL OF, see under NEVILLE, RICHARD

WASHINGTON, BOOKER TALIAFERRO

1856—1915 Educationalist

Booker Washington is the combined Moses and Joshua of his people. Not only has he led them to the promised land, but still lives to teach them by example and precept how properly to enjoy it.
  Andrew Carnegie, in Emma Lou Thornbrough ed., *Booker T. Washington.*

Without money or armies or political power, he carried into the midst of the deep South, historical perspective, economic, social, and spiritual insights, and with all a great human understanding. Where others hated, he sympathized; where others argued, he understood; where others forced, he taught.
  Frank P. Graham, in Anson Phelps Stokes, *A Brief Biography of Booker Washington.*

He has lived heroic poetry, and he can, therefore, afford to talk simple prose.
  William Dean Howells, 'An Exemplary Citizen', in *North American Review*, July 1901.

As nearly as any man I have ever met, Booker T. Washington lived up to Micah's verse, 'What more doth the Lord require of thee than to do justice, and love Mercy and walk humbly with thy God.'
  Theodore Roosevelt, in Anson Phelps Stokes, *Booker Taliaferro Washington.*

. . . Washington avoided antagonism and concentrated on emphasizing harmony within the framework of the caste system. When he did complain, it was in terms of the effect which the inequity had, not upon the Negroes but upon the whites. He viewed everything from the whites' point of view.
  Elliot M. Rudwick, *W. E. B. Du Bois, A Study in Minority Group Leadership.*

WASHINGTON, GEORGE

1732—99 First United States President

I can't tell a lie, Pa; you know I can't tell a lie. I did cut it with my hatchet.
  On himself, when asked by his father how a cherry tree had come to be destroyed, in Mason Locke Weems, *Life of Washington.*

I am so hackneyed to the touches of the painter's pencils that I am now altogether at their beck . . . at first I was as impatient and as restive under the operation as a colt is of the saddle. The next time I submitted very reluctantly, but with less flouncing. Now no dray horse moves more readily to his thill than I do to the painter's chair.
  On himself, Letter to Francis Hopkinson, 1785.

My movements to the chair of Government will be accompanied by feelings not unlike those of a culprit who is going to the place of his execution.
  On himself, Letter to Henry Knox, 1 April 1789.

Perhaps the reason little folks
  Are sometimes great when they grow taller
is just because, like Washington,
  They do their best when they are smaller.
  Anon., in Dixon Wecter, *President Washington and Parson Weems.*

If there are spots in his character, they are like the spots in the sun, only discernible by the magnifying powers of a telescope. Had he lived in the days of idolatry, he had been worshipped like a god.
  Anon., in *Pennsylvania Journal*, 1777.

Instead of adoring a Washington, mankind should applaud the nation which educated him . . . I glory in the character of a Washington, because I know him to be only an exemplification of the American character.
  John Adams, 1785, in Marcus Cunliffe, *George Washington, Man and Monument.*

George Washington set many precedents, which, as the first President, he was in a good position to do.
  Richard Armour, *American Lit Relit.*

George Washington was therefore chosen to lead the brave but outnumbered colonists. He took command of his forces under a spreading chestnut tree in Cambridge, after which he returned home long enough to marry Martha Washington and make preparations to become the father of his country.
  Richard Armour, *It All Started With Columbus.*

767

. . . is a soldier, — a warrior; he is a modest man; sensible; speaks little; in action cool, like a bishop of his prayers.

> Roger Atkinson, in Moses Coit Tyler, *Patrick Henry*.

Where may the wearied eye repose
   When gazing on the Great,
Where neither guilty glory glows,
   Nor despicable state?
Yes-one-the first-the last-the best-
   The Cincinnatus of the West
      Whom Envy cannot hate,
Bequeathed the name of Washington,
To make men blush there was but one.

> Lord Byron, *Ode to Napoleon Buonaparte*.

He has become entombed in his own myth — a metaphorical Washington Monument that hides from us the lineaments of the real man.

> Marcus Cunliffe, *George Washington, Man and Monument*.

. . . every hero becomes a bore at last. . . . They cry up the virtues of George Washington — 'Damn George Washington!' is the poor Jacobin's whole speech and confutation.

> Ralph Waldo Emerson, *Representative Men*.

Washington was never truly a military man. He remained to the end of the war a civilian serving half-reluctantly in uniform.

> James Thomas Flexner, 'Cincinnatus Assayed: Washington in the Revolution', in James Morton Smith ed., *George Washington, A Profile*.

My fine crab-tree walking stick, with a gold head curiously wrought in the form of the cap of liberty, I give to my friend, and the friend of mankind, George Washington. If it were a sceptre, he has merited it and would become it.

> Benjamin Franklin, Will, 23 June 1789.

. . . Bold in the fight, whose actions might have aw'd
   A Roman Hero or a Grecian God.
   He, he, as first his gallant troops shall lead,
   Undaunted man, a second Diomede. . . .

> Philip Freneau, *American Liberty, a Poem*.

If, among all the pedestals supplied by history for public characters of extraordinary nobility and purity, I saw one higher than all the rest, and if I were required, at a moment's notice, to name the fittest occupant for it, I think my choice, at any time during the last forty-five years, would have lighted, and would now light upon Washington!

> William Ewart Gladstone, in Marcus Cunliffe, *George Washington, Man and Monument*.

Did anyone ever see Washington nude? It is inconceivable. He had no nakedness, but I imagine he was born with his clothes on, and his hair powdered, and made a stately bow on his first appearance in the world.

> Nathaniel Hawthorne, in Daniel Boorstin, 'The Mythologizing of George Washington', in James Morton Smith ed., *George Washington, A Profile*.

His mind was great and powerful, without being of the very first order; his penetration strong, though not so acute as that of a Newton, Bacon, or Locke; and as far as he saw, no judgment was ever sounder. It was slow in operation, being little aided by invention or imagination, but sure in conclusion.

> Thomas Jefferson, Letter to Dr Walter Jones, 2 January 1814.

. . . A Citizen, first in war, first in peace, first in the hearts of his countrymen.

> Henry (Light Horse Harry) Lee, Resolution proposed to Congress on the death of Washington, 26 December 1799.

Washington is the mightiest name of earth — long since the mightiest in the cause of civil liberty, still mightiest in moral reformation. . . . To add brightness to the sun or glory to the name of Washington is alike impossible. Let none attempt it. In solemn awe pronounce the name, and in its naked deathless splendor leave it shining on.

> Abraham Lincoln, 1842, in James Morton Smith ed., *George Washington, A Profile*.

Virginia gave us this imperial man
Cast in the massive mould
Of those high-statured ages old
Which into grander forms our mortal metal ran;
She gave us this unblemished gentleman:
What shall we give her back but love and praise
As in the dear old unestranged days
Before the inevitable wrong began?
Mother of states and undiminished men,
Thou gavest us a country, giving him. . . .

> James Russell Lowell, *Under the Old Elm*.

A simple gentleman of Virginia with no extraordinary talents had so disciplined himself that he could lead an insubordinate and divided people into ordered liberty and enduring union.

> Samuel Eliot Morison, 'The Young Man Washington', in James Morton Smith ed., *George Washington, A Profile*.

If George Washington should appear on earth, just as he sat to [Gilbert] Stuart, I am sure that he would be treated as an imposter, when compared with Stuart's likeness of him, unless he produced his credentials.

> John Neal, 1823, in E. P. Richardson, *Gilbert Stuart*.

Advice to a statuary who is to execute the statue of Washington.
Take from the mine the coldest, hardest stone,
It needs no fashion: it is Washington,
But if you chisel, let the stroke be rude,
And on his heart engrave — Ingratitude.

> Thomas Paine, in Dixon Wecter, *President Washington and Parson Weems*, in James Morton Smith ed., *George Washington, A Profile*.

Vain Britons, boast no longer, with proud indignity
By land your conquering legions, your matchless
                    strength at sea,
Since we, your braver sons incensed, our swords
                    have girded on,
Huzza, huzza, huzza, huzza, for war and Washington.

> Jonathan Mitchell Sewall, in William Alfred Bryan, *George Washington in American Literature, 1775–1865*.

. . . all his features were indicative of the most ungovernable passions, and had he been born in the forests, it was his opinion that he would have been the fiercest man among the savage tribes.

> Gilbert Stuart, in Samuel Eliot Morison, 'The Young Man Washington', in James Morton Smith ed., *George Washington, A Profile*.

G. Washington was abowt the best man this world sot eyes on. . . . He never slept over! . . . He luved his country dearly. He wasn't after the spiles. He was a human angil in a 3 kornered hat and knee britches.

> Artemus Ward (Charles Farrar Browne), in James Morton Smith ed., *ibid*.

The crude commercialism of America, its materialising spirit . . . are entirely due to the country having adopted for its national hero a man who was incapable of telling a lie.

> Oscar Wilde, *The Decay of Lying*.

Magic name! If none other under heaven can draw us to each other that talisman can touch the chords of unison, and clasp us hand to hand, and bind heart to heart, in the kindred heirship of one Patriot Father! — Before that august name Feud and Faction stand abashed: — Civil Discord hushes into awed silence: — schisms and sections are subdued and vanish, for, in the very naming of that name,

there is . . . the strength and beauty of National Union.

> Henry A. Wise, 22 February 1858, in William Alfred Bryan, *George Washington in American Literature, 1775–1865*.

See also John Adams, John Quincy Adams, John Brown, Alexander Hamilton, Robert E. Lee, John Marshall, Benjamin Rush, Mark Twain, 'Mad' Anthony Wayne, Noah Webster

WATSON-WENTWORTH, CHARLES, see under ROCKINGHAM, MARQUESS OF

WATT, JAMES
1736–1819 Engineer

He devoured every kind of learning. Not content with chemistry and natural philosophy, he studied anatomy, and was one day found carrying home for dissection the head of a child that had died of some hidden disorder.

> Henry, Lord Brougham, *Lives of Men of Letters and Science who flourished in the Time of George III*.

His peculiar achievement was to make use of science, for the first time in history, in conceiving a major invention, which has had the unique effect of giving mankind a dynamic outlook, in place of the ancient static belief that nothing very fundamentally changes.

> J. G. Crowther, *Scientists of the Industrial Revolution*.

I am sure that James Watt had no desire to establish a matriarchal family; yet by making it possible for men to sleep in places distant from those in which they work he has had this effect upon a great part of our urban populations.

> Bertrand Russell, *Why I am Not a Christian: The New Generation*.

Many distinguished inventors are found comparatively helpless in the conduct of business, which demands the exercise of different qualities, — the power of organizing the labor of large numbers of men, promptitude of action in emergencies, and sagacious dealing with the practical affairs of life. Thus Watt hated that jostling with the world, and contact with men of many classes, which are usually encountered in the conduct of any extensive industrial operation. He declared that he would rather face a loaded cannon than settle an account or make a bargain; and there is every probability that he would have derived no pecuniary advantage whatever from his great invention [i.e. the steam engine], or been able to defend it against the repeated attacks of the mechanical pirates who fell upon him in Cornwall, London, and Lancashire, had he not been so fortunate as to meet, at the great crisis of his career, with the illustrious Matthew Boulton, 'the father of Birmingham'.

Samuel Smiles, *Self-help.*

I look upon him, considering both the magnitude and the universality of his genius, as perhaps the most extraordinary man that this country ever produced.

William Wordsworth, in James P. Muirhead, Letter to his Mother, 1841.

See also John Knox

WAUGH, EVELYN ARTHUR ST JOHN

1903–66 Novelist

My 39th birthday. A good year. I have begotten a fine daughter; published a successful book; drunk over 300 bottles of wine and smoked 300 Havana cigars. I get steadily worse as a soldier with the passage of time but more humble and patient — as far as soldiering is concerned; I have about £900 in hand and no grave debts except to the government; health excellent except when impaired by wine; a wife I love; agreeable work in surroundings of great beauty. Well that is as much as one can hope for.

On himself, Diary, October 1942.

I regard writing not as investigation of character but as an exercise in the use of language, and with this I am obsessed. I have no technical psychological interest. It is drama, speech, and events that interest me.

On himself, in *Paris Review*, 1962.

No critic worth his salt would deny that Evelyn Waugh was one of the finest satirists in modern English literature, an artist of ruthless integrity whose savage indignation was distilled into consummately civilized prose. . . . He had the sharp eye of a Hogarth alternating with that of the Ancient Mariner.

Harold Acton, *Adam*, 1966.

Evelyn was attracted by the foibles of those who lived in large, aristocratic houses. He . . . fostered a fascination, though in many ways despising it, for the higher echelons of the Army and military etiquette. He drank port and put on weight, and attempted to behave in the manner of an Edwardian

aristocrat. He was very conscious of what a gentleman should or should not do: no gentleman looks out of a window, no gentleman wears a brown suit. In fact, Evelyn's abiding complex and the source of much of his misery was that he was not a six-foot tall, extremely handsome and rich duke.

Cecil Beaton, *The Strenuous Years.*

In literary calendars 1945 is marked as the year Waugh ended. It was the year of *Brideshead Revisited.* . . . After that it was clear he had been conclusively eaten by his successor, Mr Evelyn Waugh, English novelist, officer (ret.) and gentleman. Mr Waugh writes a prose as fluent, lovely and lacking in intellectual content as a weeping willow: Waugh had written — and, almost as much as written, *omitted* — in fragments and ellipses, like a fiercer Firbank.

Brigid Brophy, *Don't Never Forget.*

The satire of Evelyn Waugh in his early books was derived from his ignorance of life. He found cruel things funny because he did not understand them and he was able to communicate that fun.

Cyril Connolly, *Enemies of Promise.*

One phrase from 'Pinfold' is a true heartcry from Evelyn Waugh: 'Why does everybody except me find it so easy to be nice?' At times, when remonstrated with for not being 'nice', he would retort, 'You don't know how much nastier I would be if I hadn't become a Catholic.'

Tom Driberg, in *Observer Colour Magazine*, 20 May 1973.

Evelyn affected a grave demeanour of manner, he seldom laughed aloud, and a smile was very rewarding. He was a great comedian, and at times one was reminded of Charlie Chaplin, the little man, the figure of fun. It is difficult for me to understand why so many feared him — perhaps he could not resist attacking pretension and all forms of cowardice. And it must be admitted that sometimes he just liked to attack.

Anne Fleming, in David Pryce-Jones, *Evelyn Waugh and his World.*

If Mr Waugh would sternly root out the sentimentalities and adolescent values which have, so deplorably as it seems to many of us, coiled themselves about the enchanting comic spirit which is his supreme asset as a writer, and return to being the drily ironic narrator of the humours of his world and of his lavish inventive fancy, he would thereby increase his stature. . . . There is in nearly every writer . . . a soft-headed romantic, who will, if allowed, get out of hand. . . . In Mr Waugh's case, this romantic being, kept well under in earlier life, would seem to have temporarily seized the pen.

An unhappy and unsuitable partnership, overdue for dissolution.
    Rose Macaulay, in *Horizon*, December 1946.

Despite all Waugh's efforts to appear to be an irascible, deaf old curmudgeon, a sort of inner saintliness kept breaking through.
    Malcolm Muggeridge, in M. Gross, *The World of George Orwell.*

W's driving forces. Snobbery. Catholicism. . . . One cannot really be a Catholic & grown-up. Conclude. Waugh is *abt.* as good a novelist as one can be (i.e. as novelists go today) while holding untenable opinions.
    George Orwell, 'Manuscript Notebook', in *Collected Essays.*

My feeling is that these novels of Waugh's are the only things written in England that are comparable to Fitzgerald and Hemingway. They are not so poetic; they are perhaps less intense; they belong to a more classical tradition. But I think that they are likely to last and that Waugh, in fact, is likely to figure as the only first-rate comic genius that has appeared in England since Bernard Shaw.
    Edmund Wilson, *Classics and Commercials.*

See also Nancy Mitford

WAYNE, 'MAD' ANTHONY

1745–96 Soldier

Our streets, for many days, rang with nothing but the name of General Wayne. You are remembered constantly next to our good and great Washington, over our claret and Madeira. You have established the national character of our country; you have taught our enemies that bravery, humanity, and magnanimity, are the great national virtues of the Americans.
    General Nathaniel Greene, Letter to Anthony Wayne, after the battle of Stony Point.

General Wayne had a constitutional attachment to the sword, and this case of character had acquired strength from indulgence.
    Henry (Light Horse Harry) Lee, in Robert Debs Heinl Jr, *The Dictionary of Military and Naval Quotations.*

WEBB, MARTHA BEATRICE, LADY PASSFIELD

1858–1943 Economist, Socialist

To me hers is, *au fond*, a tiresome sort of mind, but she has lived, ever since she was eighteen, an independent and industrious and at times adventurous life. And it is to the credit both of her insight and character that, being lapped in bourgeois luxury, and really very good-looking, she finally at the age of thirty married Sidney Webb.
    H. H. Asquith, Letter to Mrs Harrisson, June 1927.

That she was a superior person is clear. But she was also insular because she was keenly aware of her own superiority. She is reported to have said once, when asked if she had ever felt shy, 'Oh, no. If I ever felt inclined to be scared going into a room full of people I would say to myself, "You're the cleverest member of one of the cleverest families in the cleverest class of the cleverest nation of the world, so what have you got to be frightened of?" ' Such assurance stunted her potential stature.
    David A. Shannon, Introduction to Beatrice Webb, *American Diary.*

There's no more mysticism in Beatrice than in a steam engine.
    H. G. Wells, in Desmond MacCarthy, 'The Webbs as I saw them' (essays).

. . . beneath the metallic façade and the surface of polished certainty, there was a neurotic turmoil of doubt and discontent, suppressed or controlled, an ego tortured in the old-fashioned religious way almost universal among the wise and good in the nineteenth-century. . . . She had, too, the temperament strongly suppressed, the passion and imagination, of an artist, though she would herself have denied this. Her defence against these psychological stresses was a highly personal form of mysticism. . . .
    Leonard Woolf, *Beginning Again.*

WEBB, SIDNEY JAMES, LORD PASSFIELD

1859–1947 Economist, Socialist

Lord Passfield, he says, is utterly useless, vacillating and weak. Lord Passover he calls him.
    Sir Donald Cameron, in Margery Perham, *East African Journey.*

Sidney is simply unconscious of all the little meanness which turns social intercourse sour; he is sometimes tired, occasionally bored, but never unkindly or anxious to shine, or be admired, and wholly unaware of the absence of, or presence of, social consideration. I verily believe that if he were thrown . . . into a company of persons all of whom wanted to snub him, he would take up the first book and become absorbed in it, with a sort of feeling that they were good-natured enough not to claim his attention, or that they did not perceive that he was reading on the sly. And the greater personages they happened to be, the more fully satisfied he would be at the arrangement; since it would relieve him of any haunting fear that he was neglecting his social duty and making others uncomfortable. On the other hand, whether in his own house or in another's, if some person is neglected or out of it, Sidney will quite unconsciously drift to them and be seen eagerly talking to them.

Beatrice Webb, *Our Partnership.*

. . . all the way through exactly what he appeared to be on the surface. He had no doubts or hesitations . . . for he knew accurately what could be known about important subjects or, if he did not actually know about it, he knew that he could obtain accurate knowledge about it with the aid of a secretary and an index card.

Leonard Woolf, *Beginning Again.*

WEBB, BEATRICE AND SIDNEY

(dates as above)

Old people are always absorbed in something, usually themselves; we prefer to be absorbed in the Soviet Union.

On themselves, in Kingsley Martin, 'The Webbs in retirement', in Margaret Cole (ed.), *The Webbs and their Work.*

Only once do I remember the Webbs going gay.

Blanche Patch, *Thirty Years with GBS.*

He did the work. She kept him at it.

J. H. Plumb, Lecture at Cambridge, *circa* 1965.

Sidney and Beatrice Webb . . . were the most completely married couple I have ever known. They were, however, very averse from any romantic view of love or marriage. Marriage was a social institution designed to fit instinct into a legal framework. During the first ten years of their marriage, Mrs. Webb would remark at intervals, 'as Sidney always says, marriage is the waste-paper basket of the emotions'.

Bertrand Russell, *Autobiography*, vol. 1.

How did the idea enter into your head that their relationship was frigid and inhuman? I used to live with them, and work with them a good deal, and you may take it from me that you couldn't be more wrong. Though Sidney, when they were working together could stick it out almost indefinitely, Beatrice would suddenly reach the end of her

tether, jump up, throw her pen away, fling herself on her husband, and half smother him with kisses. This might happen two or three times in a morning; and after each outbreak she would return to work with new vigour, and grind away like a slave until the need for a similar stimulant became imperative.

George Bernard Shaw, in Hesketh Pearson, *Bernard Shaw, a Postscript.*

Neither was puritanical; neither was capable of irony. And they were always helpful, which infuriated people who thought they did not need help.

Ibid.

WEBSTER, DANIEL

1782–1852 Statesman

I was born an American; I will live an American; I shall die an American.

On himself, Speech, July 1850.

A living lie, because no man on earth could be so great as he looked.

Anon., in John F. Kennedy, *Profiles in Courage.*

. . . the gigantic intellect, the envious temper, the ravenous ambition, and the rotten heart of Daniel Webster.

John Quincy Adams, in R. N. Current, *Daniel Webster and the Rise of National Conservatism.*

As a logic fencer, or parliamentary Hercules, one would incline to back him at first sight against all the extant world. The tanned complexion; that amorphous crag-like face; the dull black eyes under the precipice of brows, the dull anthracite furnaces needing only to be *blown*; the mastiff mouth accurately closed. . . .

Thomas Carlyle, Letter to Ralph Waldo Emerson, in Henry Cabot Lodge, *Daniel Webster.*

One of the great characteristics of Webster's eloquence is that he glows and burns and rises with the tide of hopeful passion of a great young nation.

Rufus Choate, in C. M. Fuess, *Daniel Webster*, vol. 1. 1782–1830.

Mr. Webster has two characters, which Proteus-like he can assume as his interests or necessities demand — the 'God-like' and the 'Hell-like' — the 'God-like Daniel' and 'Black Dan.!'

John J. Crittenden, in R. N. Current, *Daniel Webster and the Rise of National Conservatism.*

The word 'honor' in the mouth of Mr. Webster is

like the word 'love' in the mouth of a whore.
    Ralph Waldo Emerson, in Ray Gingers, *Joke Book about American History*.

Very expensive, and always in debt.
    Ralph Waldo Emerson, in C. M. Fuess, *Daniel Webster, vol. 2, 1832–52*.

A single look would be enough to wither up a whole volume of bad logic.
    Thomas Hamilton, in Bertha M. Rothe ed., *Daniel Webster Reader*.

. . . remembered best as the quasi-official rhapsodist of American nationalism.
    Richard Hofstadter, *The American Political Tradition*.

Unfortunately he sometimes paid in the wrong coin — not in legal tender — but in the confidence that people reposed in him.
    Gerald W. Johnson, in John F. Kennedy, *Profiles in Courage*.

Mr. Webster appeared like a great seventy-four gun ship, which required deeper water, larger space, and stronger wind to be set in motion.
    Benjamin Perry, in N. D. Brown, *Daniel Webster and the Politics of Availability*.

I would not attempt to vie with the honorable gentleman from Massachusetts in a field where every nigger is his peer and every billy-goat his master.
    John Randolph of Roanoke, believing that Webster had accused him of impotence.

Daniel Webster struck me much like a steam engine in trousers.
    Sidney Smith, in Lady Holland, *Memoirs*, vol. 1.

Good heavens, he is a small cathedral by himself.
    Sidney Smith, in Henry Cabot Lodge, *Daniel Webster*.

Webster looked like Coriolanus. He seemed to scorn, while he addressed the people.
    Charles Sumner, in R. N. Current, *Daniel Webster and the Rise of National Conservatism*.

God is only the president of the day, and Webster is his orator.
    Henry David Thoreau, *Walden*.

Thou,
Whom the rich heavens did so endow
With eyes of power and Jove's own brow . . .
New England's stateliest type of man,

In port and speech Olympia;
Whom no one met, at first, but took
A second awed and wondering look.
    John Greenleaf Whittier, *The Lost Occasion*.

So fallen! so lost! the light withdrawn
    Which once he wore!
The glory from his gray hairs gone
    Forevermore . . . .

Of all we loved and honored, naught
    Save power remains;
A fallen angel's pride of thought,
    Still strong in chains. . . .

Then pay the reverence of old days
    To his dead fame;
Walk backward, with averted gaze,
    And hide the shame!
    John Greenleaf Whittier, *Ichabod*.

See also Thomas Hart Benton, Noah Webster

WEBSTER, JOHN

1580?–1625? Dramatist

Webster was not, in the special sense of the word, a great dramatist, but was a great poet who wrote haphazard dramatic or melodramatic romances for an eagerly receptive but semi-barbarous public.
    William Archer, 'Webster, Lamb, and Swinburne', in *New Review*, 1893.

. . . The world called Webster is a peculiar one. It is inhabited by people driven like animals, and perhaps like men, only by their instincts, but more blindly and ruinously. Life there seems to flow into its forms and shapes with an irregular, abnormal, and horrible volume. That is ultimately the most distressing feature of Webster's characters, their foul and indestructible vitality. . . . A play of Webster's is full of the feverish and ghastly turmoil of a nest of maggots.
    Rupert Brooke, *John Webster and the Elizabethan Drama*.

I suppose you could define a pessimist as a man who thinks John Webster's *Duchess of Malfi* a great play; an optimist as one who believes it actable.
    Ronald Bryden, 'Blood Soaked Circus', in *Observer*, 18 July 1971.

Webster was much possessed by death
And saw the skull beneath the skin;
And breastless creatures under ground
Leaned backward with a lipless grin.

Daffodil bulbs instead of balls
Stared from the sockets of the eyes!
He knew that thought clings round dead limbs
Tightening its lusts and luxuries.
    T. S. Eliot, *Whispers of Immortality*.

Webster is a slow deliberate careful writer, very much the conscious artist. He was incapable of writing so badly or so tastelessly as Tourneur sometimes did, but he is never quite so surprising as Tourneur sometimes is. Moreover, Webster, in his greatest tragedies, has a kind of pity for *all* of his characters, an attitude towards good and bad alike which helps to unify the Webster pattern.
    T. S. Eliot, *Essays*: 'Cyril Tourneur'.

But hist! with him Crabbed (*Websterio*)
The *Play-wright, Cart-wright*: whether? either!
                    (ho —
No further). Looke as yee'd bee look't into:
Sit as ye woo'd be *Read*: *Lord*! who woo'd know
                    him?
Was ever man so mangled with a *Poem*?
See how he drawes his mouth awry of late,
How he scrubs: wrings his wrist: scatches his Pate.
A *Midwife*! helpe! By his *Braines Coitus*,
Some *Centaure* strange; some huge *Bucephalus*
Or *Pallas* (sure) ['s] ingendred in his *Braine*,
Strike, *Vulcan*, with thy hammer once againe.
This is the *crittick* that (of all the rest)
I'd not have view mee, yet I feare him least,
Heer's not a word *cursively* I have *Writ*,
But hee'l *Industriously* examine it.
And in some 12. monthes hence (or there *about*)
Set in a shamefull sheete, my errors *out*.
But what care I! It *will* be so obscure,
That none shall understand him (I am sure).
    Henry Fitzjeffrey, *Notes from Black-Fryers, in Certain Elegies done by Sundry Excellent Wits*.

To move a horror skilfully, to touch a soul to the quick, to lay upon fear as much as it can bear, to wean and weary a life till it is ready to drop and then step in with mortal instruments to take its last forfeit: this only a Webster can do.
    Charles Lamb, *Specimens of English Dramatic Poets*.

The vices and the crimes which he delights to paint, all partake of an extravagance which, nevertheless, makes them impressive and terrible, and in the retribution and the punishment, there is a character of corresponding wildness. But our sympathies, suddenly awakened, are allowed as suddenly to subside. There is nothing of what Wordsworth calls 'a mighty stream of tendency' in the events of his dramas. . . .
    'H. M.', in *Blackwood's Edinburgh Magazine*, 1818.

How lively are thy persons fitted, and
How pretty are thy lines! — thy Verses stand
Like unto pretious Jewels set in gold,
And grace thy fluent prose; I once was told
By one well skil'd in arts, he thought thy Play
Was onely worthy Fame to beare away
From all before it. . . .
    S. Sheppard, *On Mr Webster's Most Excellent Tragedy Called the White Devil, in Epigrams, Theological, Philosophical, and Romantic*, 1651.

Webster, it may be said, was as it were a limb of Shakespeare: but that limb, it might be replied, was the right arm.
    Algernon C. Swinburne, *The Age of Shakespeare*.

As to our Countryman *Webster*, tho' I am to confess obligations to him, I am not oblig'd to be blind to all his Faults. He is not without his incidents of *Horror*, almost as extravagant as those of the *Spaniard*. He had a strong and impetuous Genius, but withal a most wild and indigested one: He sometimes conceived nobly, but did not always express with clearness; and if he now and then soars handsomely, he as often rises into the Region of Bombast: his Conceptions were so eccentric, that we are not to wonder why we cannot ever trace him. As for Rules, he either knew them not, or thought them too servile a restraint. Hence it is, that he skips over *years* and *kingdoms* with an equal Liberty.
    Lewis Theobald, Preface to *The Fatal Secret*.

Webster is not concerned with humanity. He is the poet of bile and brainstorm, the sweet singer of apoplexy; ideally, one feels, he would have had all his characters drowned in a sea of cold sweat. His muse drew nourishment from Bedlam, and might, a few centuries later, have done the same from Belsen. I picture him plagued with hypochondria, probably homosexual, and consumed by feelings of persecution — an intensely neurotic mind, in short, at large in the richest, most teeming vocabulary that any age ever offered to a writer.
    Kenneth Tynan, 'A Sea of Cold Sweat', in *Observer*, 18 December 1960.

See also Thomas Dekker, Christopher Marlowe

WEBSTER, NOAH

1758–1843 Lexicographer

If my name's a terror to evil doers, mention it.
    On himself, in Harry R. Warfel, *Noah Webster, Schoolmaster to America*.

I have contributed in a small degree, to the instruction of at least four million of the rising generation; and it is not unreasonable to expect that a few seeds of improvement planted by my hand, may germinate and grow and ripen into valuable fruit, when my remains shall be mingled with the dust.

On himself, Letter to Timothy Pickering, 1817.

It is a melancholy proof of the amount of mischief one man of learning can do to society, that Webster's system of orthography is adopted and propagated.

William Cullen Bryant, in Harry R. Warfel, *Noah Webster, Schoolmaster to America.*

By the time he was a little over 30, this son of a New England farmer had hobnobbed with Washington and Franklin, pamphleteered for the adoption of the Constitution, gained renown as a lecturer on the English language and education, and hustled his books like an 18th-century Jacqueline Susann.

E. Jennifer Monaghan, 'Noah Webster', in *New York Times Book Review*, 21 September 1975.

The ease with which Webster walked about the Jericho of English lexicography, blowing his trumpet of destruction, was an American ease, born of a sense that America was a continent and not a province.

Horace E. Scudder, *Noah Webster.*

He had no conception of the enormous weight of the English language and literature, when he undertook to shovel it out of the path of American civilization.

Ibid.

Webster, the pioneer in many fields of endeavor on the American intellectual frontier, taught the masses to spell and read. He was truly the schoolmaster of the Republic.

Erwin C. Shoemaker, *Noah Webster, Pioneer of Learning.*

One of his greatest assets was his ability to appraise the past and present, to anticipate future needs, and to adopt the material at hand, be it books or ideas, to the requirements of the present and future.

Ibid.

In conversation he is even duller than in writing, if that is possible.

Juliana Smith, in E. Jennifer Monaghan, 'Noah Webster', in *New York Times Book Review*, 21 September 1975.

He became in effect a kind of intellectual frontiersman, as fertile of ideas as the frontiersman is fertile of mere material resources.

Edward Wagenknecht, in Erwin C. Shoemaker, *Noah Webster, Pioneer of Learning.*

WEDGWOOD, JOSIAH

1730—95 Potter, Designer, Manufacturer

Whether, O Friend of Art! your gems derive
Fine forms from Greece, and fabled Gods revive;
Or bid from modern life the portrait breathe,
And bind round Honour's brow the laurel wreath;
Buoyant shall sail, with Fame's historic page,
Each fair medallion o'er the wrecks of age;
Nor Time shall mar, nor Steel, nor Fire, nor Rust
Touch the hard polish of the immortal bust.

Erasmus Darwin, *The Loves of the Plants.*

WEED, THURLOW

1797—1882 Politician, Journalist

. . . . manipulation was an instinct of Mr. Weed; an object to be pursued for its own sake, as one plays cards; but he appeared to play with men as though they were only cards; he seemed incapable of feeling himself one of them. He took them and played them at their face value.

Henry Adams, *Education of Henry Adams.*

He is cool, calculating, a man of expedients, who boasts that for thirty years he has not in political affairs let his heart outweigh his judgment.

Samuel Bowles, 1860, in H. J. Hendrick, *Lincoln's War Cabinet.*

Writing slowly and with difficulty, he was for twenty years the most sententious and pungent writer of editorial paragraphs on the American press.

In pecuniary matters, he was generous to a fault while poor; he is said to be less so since he became rich; but I am no longer in a position to know. I cannot doubt, however, that if he had never seen Wall Street or Washington, had never heard of the Stock Board, and had lived in some yet undiscovered country, where legislation is never bought nor sold, his life would have been more blameless, useful, and happy.

Horace Greeley, *Recollections of a Busy Life.*

. . . Weed was as conservative as he was Republican. . . . To the end of his days he maintained his hostility to civil service reform and to free trade, his suspicions of trade unions and eight-hour days. But

775

the old spirit that had fought against slavery and on behalf of Catholics and antirenters, together with that shrewd political prescience so quick to sense the coming storm, was not wholly gone from the thinking of an ancient whose eightieth birthday came and went in the midst of the Gilded Age.
Glyndon G. Van Deusen, *Thurlow Weed, Wizard of the Lobby.*

There was an epic quality in the life of Thurlow Weed. His early years reflected the trials and struggles of young America, a frontier country filled with poverty and opportunity and hope. The growth of his political power coincided with and in a large measure reflected the growth of the power of industry and finance. Politician, journalist, millionaire, brimful of energy and action, more interested as he was in the end than in the means by which the end was achieved; his career came close to epitomising the strengths and weaknesses, the accomplishments and the failures of nineteenth century America.
Ibid.

WELLES, GIDEON

1802--78 Politician

[One] with feelings easily given to irritation and a man that is often lost in gloomy melancholy.
On himself, in H. J. Hendrick, *Lincoln's War Cabinet.*

I like to catch people in the suds, to fall upon them by surprise, when it is washing day, not only with their hands, but with their temper.
On himself, on his own writing, in R. S. West Jr, *Gideon Welles, Lincoln's Navy Department.*

Retire, O Gideon, to an onion farm
Ply any trade that's innocent and slow
Do anything, where you can do no harm
Go anywhere you fancy — only go.
Anon., in *Frank Leslie's Monthly*, 5 June 1862.

There was an old fogy named Welles
Quite worthy of cap and of bells,
For he th't that a pirate,
Who steamed at a great rate,
Would wait to be riddled with shells.
Anon., in *Punch*, in *New York World*, based on the Confederate raider *Florida*'s daylight run through the blockade into Mobile.

The country has never done him anything like justice. His patriarchal looks, his immense wig, his flowing beard, and his somewhat stolid manners,

and the names of 'Father Welles' and 'Noah' applied to him by the slang talkers and writers of the day, created an altogether false impression of him in the public mind. . . . His personal management of its [Navy Department's] affairs was intelligent, thorough, and efficient. More, perhaps, than any of his colleagues, he was given to minding his own business, and in the discharge of duty he was as inflexible as an old Roman.
Maunsell B. Field, *Memories of Many Men.*

As a sop to New England, Mr. Lincoln had made Gideon Welles of Connecticut, his Secretary of the Navy. He was tall and 'venerably insignificant', with a flowing beard and a huge gray wig. Welles had been a newspaperman in Hartford, and did not know the stem from the stern of a ship, but he was an industrious and capable administrator. He was also very irritable, and those who under valued him did not know that, with pen dipped in gall, he kept a diary. In one respect, Welles was unique among the Cabinet members — he did not think himself a better man than the President.
Margaret Leech, *Reveille in Washington.*

Welles is the most garrulous old woman you were ever annoyed by.
General George B. McClellan, Letter to his Wife, October 1861.

[Welles was] ironclad on this subject of Reconstruction and had not only fifteen inch guns leveled against Congress but was for running his prow into them.
Edwin M. Stanton, in R. S. West Jr, *Gideon Welles, Lincoln's Navy Department.*

WELLESLEY, ARTHUR, see under WELLINGTON, DUKE OF

WELLINGTON, DUKE OF (ARTHUR WELLESLEY)

1769—1852 Soldier, Prime Minister

I like to walk alone. . . .
On himself, Letter to Henry Wellesley, 7 July 1801.

It is a bad thing always to be fighting. While in the thick of it I am too much occupied to feel anything; but it is wretched just after. It is quite impossible to think of glory. Both mind and feelings are exhausted. I am wretched even at the moment of

victory, and I always say that next to a battle lost, the greatest misery is a battle gained.
> On himself, in Lady Frances Shelley, *Diary*.

. . . Nothing shall induce me to utter a word, either in public or in private, that I don't believe to be true. If it is God's will that this great country should be destroyed, and that mankind should be deprived of this last asylum of peace and happiness, let it be so; but as long as I can raise my voice, I will do so against the infatuated madness of the day.
> On himself, Letter to G. R. Gleig, 11 April 1831.

The only thing I am afraid of is fear.
> On himself, in Philip Henry Stanhope, *Conversations with the Duke of Wellington*.

To Stop The Duke Go For Gold.
> A slogan widely used in 1830, probably the inspiration of Francis Place.

The Duke of Wellington had exhausted nature and exhausted glory. His career was one unclouded longest day.
> Anon., Obituary in *The Times*, September 1852.

You are 'the best of cut-throats': — do not start;
The phrase is Shakespeare's, and not misapplied:
War's a brain-spattering, windpipe-slitting art,
  Unless her cause by Right be sanctified.
If you have acted *once* a generous part,
  The World, not the World's masters, will decide,
And I shall be delighted to learn who,
Save you and yours, have gained by Waterloo?
> Lord Byron, *Don Juan*, canto ix.

Never had mortal Man such opportunity,
  Except Napoleon, or abused it more:
You might have freed fall'n Europe from the Unity
  Of Tyrants, and been blest from shore to shore:
And *now* — What *is* your fame? Shall the muse tune
                                    it yet?
  Now that the rabble's first vain shouts are o'er?
Go — hear it in your famish'd Country's cries!
Behold the world! and curse your victories!
> *Ibid.*

He hated jobs and spoke the truth.
> Richard Cobden, in John Morley, *The Life of Richard Cobden*.

The Duke's government — a dictatorship of patriotism.
> Benjamin Disraeli, *Endymion*.

The Duke of Wellington brought to the post of first minister immortal fame; a quality of success which

would almost seem to include all others.
> Benjamin Disraeli, *Sybil*.

The Duke said '[Count] D'Orsay is the only painter who ever made me look like a gentleman.' Calling on D'Orsay one day in his studio, the Duke's portrait being on an easel, & that of the Marquess Wellesley, his brother, framed and suspended, D'Orsay said, looking from the easel to the framed picture 'Cock pheasant & Hen pheasant!'
> Benjamin Disraeli, *Reminiscences*.

The Duke of Wellington said, that going to the Opera in state (8 carriages & state liveries) he, as Master of the Horse, sitting in the same carriage as the Queen & the Prince Consort, the Duke said, 'How very ill men look when they smile.'
'Much worse when they frown' replied Albert.
> *Ibid.*

We would rather see his long nose in a fight than a reinforcement of 10,000 men a day.
> Captain John Kincaid, in Michael Glover, *Wellington as Military Commander*.

Great Chieftain, who takest such pains
  To prove — what is granted *nem con.*
With how mod'rate a portion of brains
  Some heroes contrive to get on.
> Thomas Moore, *Dog Day Reflections*.

After some further conversation . . . I observed to the Duke that his previous experience and trial of war in the Dutch campaign must have been very useful to him. 'Why — I learnt what one ought not to do, and that is always something.'
> Philip Henry Stanhope, *Conversations with the Duke of Wellington*.

Great in council and great in war,
Foremost captain of his time,
Rich in saving common-sense,
And, as the greatest only are,
In his simplicity sublime.
> Alfred, Lord Tennyson, *Ode on the Death of the Duke of Wellington*.

He was the pride and the *bon genie*, as it were of this country! He was the GREATEST man this country ever produced, and the most *devoted* and *loyal* subject, and the staunchest supporter the Crown ever had . . . Albert is much grieved.
> Queen Victoria, *Letters*.

If England should require her army again, and I should be with it, let me have 'Old Nosey' to command. Our interests would be sure to be looked into, we should never have occasion to fear an

enemy. There are two things we should be certain of. First, we should always be as well supplied with rations as the nature of the service would admit. The second is we should be sure to give the enemy a d——d good thrashing. What can a soldier desire more?
    Private Wheeler, *Letters*.

You are the only subject I shake hands with.
    William IV, Conversation with Wellington, in Lady Salisbury, *Diary*, 10 July 1835.

                Him the mighty deed
Elates not, brought far nearer the grave's rest,
As shows that time-worn face, for he such seed
Has sown as yields, we trust, the fruit of fame
In Heaven; hence no one blushes for thy name,
Conqueror, 'mid some sad thoughts, divinely blest!
    William Wordsworth, *On a Portrait of the Duke of Wellington*.

See also John Abernethy, Charles Dickens, George IV, Robert E. Lee, C. J. Napier

WELLS, HERBERT GEORGE

1866—1946 Author

I had rather be called a journalist than an artist, that is the essence of it.
    On himself, Letter to Henry James, 1915.

Every one of us who started writing in the nineties, was discovered to be 'a second' — somebody or other. In the course of two or three years I was welcomed as a second Dickens, a second Bulwer Lytton and a second Jules Verne. But also I was a second Barrie, though J. M. B. was hardly more than my contemporary, and, when I turned to short stories, I became a second Kipling. . . . Later on I figured as a second Diderot, a second Carlyle and a second Rousseau.
    On himself, *Experiment in Autobiography*.

I launched the phrase 'The war to end war' — and that was not the least of my crimes.
    On himself, in Geoffrey West, *H. G. Wells*.

The critics have been right. For as one looks back over Mr Wells's long and honorable record as a novelist one fails to recall a single vivid or credible character. They are all alike — and all alike in being rather colorless automata, mere puppets by which their manipulator has sought to demonstrate his successive attitudes toward a changing world.
    Conrad Aiken, in *Atlantic Monthly*, November 1926.

I suppose you'll have the common decency to believe me when I tell you I am always powerfully impressed by your work. Impressed is *the* word, O Realist of the Fantastic! whether you like it or not. And if you want to know what impresses me it is to see how you contrive to give over humanity into the clutches of the Impossible and yet manage to keep it down (or up) to its humanity, to its flesh, blood, sorrow, folly. *That* is the achievement!
    Joseph Conrad, Letter to Wells, 4 December 1898.

All Wells' characters are as flat as a photograph. But the photographs are agitated with such vigour that we forget their complexities lie on the surface and would disappear if it was scratched or curled up.
    E. M. Forster, *Aspects of the Novel*.

Wells impressed me as about the best mind that I had met in my many years in England: a handsome body and fine head. I had hoped extraordinary things from him, but the Great War seems to have shaken him, and his latest attempt to write a natural history of the earth chilled me. A history of humanity to the present time in which Shakespeare is not mentioned and Jesus is dismissed in a page carelessly, if not with contempt, shocks me.
    Frank Harris, *My Life and Loves*.

Your big feeling for life, your capacity for chewing up the thickness of the world in such enormous mouthfuls, while you fairly slobber, so to speak, with the multitudinous taste — this constitutes for me a rare and wonderful and admirable exhibition.
    Henry James, Letter to Wells, 3 March 1911.

Whatever Wells writes is not only alive, but kicking.
    Henry James, in G. K. Chesterton, *Autobiography*.

A whole generation of cocky, iconoclastic young men and women came into being . . . You were the most energetic and intimate of our fathers. You opened so many doors. You delighted and excited and angered us. You offered us all the world in tempting cans with lively labels: Socialism, Free Love, Marriage, Education, World Organization, and H. G. Wells's Patent Feminism — Very Perishable. Down they went. And gradually, on this varied if not always digestible diet, the children grew older.
    Freda Kirchwey, 'A Private Letter to H. G. Wells', in *Nation* (New York), 28 November 1928.

I like Wells, he is so warm, such a passionate declaimer or reasoner or whatever you like. But, ugh! — he hurts me. He always seems to be looking at life as a cold and hungry little boy in the street stares at a shop where there is hot pork.

D. H. Lawrence, Letter to A. D. McLeod, April 1913.

Perhaps in the end we should come back to his student ambitions for the secret of Wells's individuality as a short-story writer. The interest in biology has mated happily with his concern for the mass of human nature to make him a general practitioner in the disease of creation: his consciousness of life as an organism has made him the cosmic doctor.

T. E. Lawrence, in *Spectator*, 25 February 1928.

Mr Wells's directing idea — 'the re-orientation of loyalties through a realisation of the essential unity of our species' — is not trivial. To this he has devoted his life with a noble disinterestedness. . . . We may find it hard to like or respect him, but he is doing work that needs doing and that at the moment seems terribly urgent. Yet we must also remind ourselves that the more his kind of influence seems likely to prevail . . . the more urgent is drastic criticism. If he belongs to the past it is only in the sense that it has long been impossible to discuss him seriously except as a case, a type, a portent. As such, he matters.

F. R. Leavis, in *Scrutiny*, May 1932.

I have no hesitation whatever in saying that Wells, as he is, entertains me far more agreeably than Dickens. I know very well that the author of *David Copperfield* was a greater artist than the author of *Mr Polly*, just as I know that the Archbishop of Canterbury is a more virtuous man than my good friend, Fred the Bartender; but all the same, I prefer Wells and Fred to Dickens and the Archbishop.

H. L. Mencken, in *Smart Set*, July 1910.

His death on August 13, 1946, at the age of 79, came with a shock. England without H. G. Wells, to many of us, will hardly be England. 'Heavens, *what* a bourgeois!' Lenin exclaimed of him after a long and famous interview. Translated out of Marxian into English that reads: 'Heavens, *what* an Englishman!'

John Middleton Murry, in *Adelphi*, October–December 1946.

H. G. Wells is delighted with the failure of the League [of Nations], since it provides him with a perfect illustration of human muddle-headedness. He becomes more of a republican every day, and is in fact the only political thinker I know in England who seriously believes that it would be desirable or possible to abolish the monarchy in the country.

Harold Nicolson, Diary, 12 May 1936.

Dine with Sibyl [Lady Colefax]. H. G. Wells starts a long and well-expressed theory that *homo sapiens* has failed. Even as the dinosaur failed because he had concentrated upon size, so we have failed because we have not developed the right type of brain. So we will first destroy ourselves and then die out as a species. Just revert to mud and slime. 'And we shall deserve it', said Wells. Walter Elliot says that surely it won't be as bad as that. 'One thousand years more', says Wells; 'that's all that *homo sapiens* has before him.'

Ibid., 15 June 1939.

Back in the nineteen-hundreds it was a wonderful experience for a boy to discover H. G. Wells. There you were, in a world of pedants, clergymen and golfers, with your future employers exhorting you to 'get on or get out', your parents systematically warping your sexual life, and your dull-witted schoolmasters sniggering over their Latin tags; and here was this wonderful man who could tell you about the inhabitants of the planets and the bottom of the sea, and who *knew* that the future was not going to be what respectable people imagined.

George Orwell, in *Horizon*, August 1941.

The connecting link is Wells's belief in Science. He is saying all the time, if only the small shopkeeper could acquire a scientific outlook, his troubles would be ended. And of course he believes that this is going to happen, probably in the quite near future. A few more million pounds for scientific research, a few more generations scientifically educated, a few more superstitions shovelled into the dustbin, and the job is done.

George Orwell, *Essays*, 'The Rediscovery of Europe'.

He is a professor of the gruesome, a past master in the art of producing creepy sensations. . . . He spends his life imagining what would happen if one of the laws of nature were altered just a little — with terrifying results.

William T. Stead, in *Review of Reviews*, April 1898.

I stopped thinking about him when he became a thinker.

Lytton Strachey, in conversation with Hesketh Pearson, May 1921.

Wells never learnt how to write a novel which was a work of art. When advised of this, he bluffed after the manner of the defendant in an English Law Court charged with libel. This defendant answers the charge by saying that the words were never uttered, or alternatively that they do not bear the meaning put upon them, or again alternatively that they are in fact true, and legitimate comment. Wells, charged with being unaesthetic, replied that he never said he was, and alternatively that the aesthetes can't prove it, and anyway, Yah!

Frank Swinnerton, *The Georgian Literary Scene.*

The weak part of Wells' outfit is his lack of any detailed knowledge of social organisation — and this, I think, vitiates his capacity — for foreseeing the future machinery of government and the relation of classes. But his work is full of luminous hypotheses and worth careful study by those who are trying to look forward.

Beatrice Webb, Diary, December 1901.

The tragedy of H. G.'s life — his aptitude for 'fine thinking' and even 'good feeling' and yet his total incapacity for decent conduct. He says in so many words that directly you leave your study you inevitably become a cad and are indeed mean and dishonourable and probably cruel.

Ibid. (commenting on *The New Machiavelli*), 5 November 1910.

The Old Maid among novelists; even the sex-obsession that lay clotted on *Ann Veronica* and *The New Machiavelli* like cold white sauce was merely Old Maid's mania, the reaction towards the flesh of a mind too long absorbed in airships and colloids.

Rebecca West, review of Wells's novel *Marriage*, in *Freewoman*, 19 September 1912.

See also G. K. Chesterton, Winston Churchill, Harpo Marx, George Bernard Shaw

WENTWORTH, THOMAS, see under STRAFFORD, EARL OF

WESLEY, CHARLES

1707—88 Methodist

He was a Methodist in the truest sense, not only the first Methodist, but the complete Methodist, whose character and career crystallize perhaps more than any other the authentic spirit of the Revival. Rooted in catholic principle, fervent in evangelic appeal, second only to Whitefield as an evangelist, his recurring theme was 'O let me commend my Saviour to you!'

Frederick C. Gill, *Charles Wesley.*

Not unfrequently he has come to the house in the City Road, and having left the pony in the garden in front, he would enter, crying out, 'Pen and ink!

pen and ink!' These being supplied, he wrote the hymn he had been composing. When this was done, he would look round on those present and salute them with much kindness, ask after their health, give out a short hymn, and thus put all in mind of eternity.

Thomas Jackson, *Life of the Rev. Charles Wesley.*

WESLEY, JOHN

1703—91 Founder of Methodism

I look upon all the world as my parish.

On himself, Journal, June 1739.

Though I am always in haste, I am never in a hurry.

On himself, Letter, December 1777.

He seems to have been almost ubiquitous, and he moves with a rapidity reminding us of the flying angel who had the everlasting Gospel to preach, and he shines alike in his conflicts with nature and the still wilder tempests caused by the passions of men.

E. Paston Hood, *Vignettes of the Great Revival.*

It was 1791 . . . England was to pass unscathed through these troubled years, but the tumbrils might well have been seen in the streets of London, had not a little man in gown and hands taken the world for his parish, and changed the hearts of men.

Arnold Lunn, *John Wesley.*

To live for God while in this vale of tears,
He rose at four o'clock for threescore years;
Then spent the livelong day in something great and
good;
Nor loung'd one hour away, nor ever ling'ring stood.

That this is no romance, one instance hear,
And may it rend in twain each sluggard's ear!
His last day's work but one he plann'd, and thought
to ride
A HUNDRED MILES AND EIGHT, and preach and
write beside.

Thomas Olivers, in Maldwyn Edwards, *The Astonishing Youth.*

The Emperor Charles V, and his rival of France, appear at this day infinitely insignificant, if we compare them with Luther and Loyola; and there may come a time when the name of Wesley will be more generally known, and in remoter regions of the globe, than that of Frederick or of Catherine.

Robert Southey, *Life of John Wesley.*

WESLEY, SAMUEL SEBASTIAN

1810—76 Composer

His crabbedness and eccentricity, of which many stories are told, were chiefly due to an abnormal sensitiveness of ear. . . .
Sir Henry Hadow, *English Music.*

He has the gift, possessed by those alone who stand in the inner courts, of making music which first surprises us by its novelty and afterwards convinces us that it was inevitable; he leads us into paths hitherto untrodden and opens the way by which we can follow.
Ibid.

We walked on — it was a lovely summer's day in June — and soon reached that charming spot called 'The Nunneries'. We adjusted our rods and flies, and then the doctor took a general survey of the river, which at that spot was very low just then, and quite wadeable.
'Dear me, look! They are rising well on the other side of the river. Do you mind, Spark, as I'm not allowed to wade just now, taking off your shoes and stockings, tucking up your trousers, and carrying me across?'
'Doctor.' I said, 'I fear you'll be too heavy; but I'll do my best.'
'Oh!' he added quickly, *'that* will be all right, as I'll carry the things, rods and all!'
He got on my back; I noticed that he was getting his right arm free with the rod and flies in his hand; and just as I was suffering from the sharpness of the stones on my bare feet in the middle of the river, I said I feared I should fall with him. He exclaimed,—
'Now stand quite still; there's a fine trout rising just below there, and I can get at him nicely with a good throw.'
'Doctor! doctor!' I shouted, as well as my nearly exhausted state would allow, 'if I don't try to reach the bank at once, we *must* both tumble into the river.'
I managed just to get through, and fall on the bank breathless, and the doctor went clean over my head like a shuttlecock. He got up, and then stood for a moment regarding me with considerable contempt.
William Spark, *Musical Memories.*

As Wesley played the pedals much more than his predecessors, and was also much fuller in his harmonical combinations, the old [organ] blower felt that he would soon be unable to discharge the extra amount of work imposed upon him; and one evening, when Samuel Sebastian had been laying it on rather stronger than usual, the old man let out the wind, and turning to me with tears in his eyes, said — 'O Master William, I can't abide him; he'll be the death of me if he goes on like this long.'
And so it proved, for three weeks afterwards poor old Glen, the organ-blower, was carried to his last home, and died, if not of a broken heart, at least of insufficient wind.
Ibid.

[Sir Robert Prescott Stewart] had a great admiration for S. S. Wesley's work, and was anxious to hear him play. Knowing his peculiarities, he travelled down secretly to Winchester and sat himself down in a corner of the choir for service. But Wesley's quick eye detected him, and instead of the usual voluntary at the close, he played about eight commonplace bars and vanished.
C. V. Stanford, *Pages from an Unwritten Diary.*

WEST, BENJAMIN

1738—1820 Painter

The American Raphael.
Anon., in *Public Advertiser* (London).

West's pictures do not appear inviting.
Joseph Farington, Diary, February 1806.

One of the most accomplished skaters in America.
John Galt, *The Life, Studies, and Works of Benjamin West, Esq.*

Looked at West's picture, *Christ blessing the Sick.* . . . Hard, red, mean, well-composed; nothing can be more despicable than the forms. How the people have been duped! Yet, on the whole, it is one of his best pictures.
Benjamin R. Haydon, *Journal*, 3 April 1812.

Mr. West's name stands deservedly high in the annals of art in this country — too high for him to condescend to be his own puffer, even at second-hand. He comes forward, in the present instance, as the painter and the showman of the piece; as the candidate for public applause, and the judge who awards himself the prize; as the idol on the altar, and the priest who offers up the grateful incense of praise. He places himself, as it were, before his own performance, with a *Catalogue Raisonné* in his hand, and, before the spectator can form a judgement on the work itself, dazzles him with an account of the prodigies of art which are there conceived and executed.
William Hazlitt, on West's exhibiting of *Death on the Pale Horse*, in *Edinburgh Review*, December 1817.

WEST, let me whisper in thy ear
  Snug as a thief within a mill,
From me thou has no cause to fear;
  To panegyric will I turn my skill;
And if thy *picture* I am forc'd to blame,
I'll say most handsome things about the *frame*.
    Peter Pindar (John Wolcot), *Lyric Odes to the Royal Academicians*, 1783, ode 2.

The beauties of the art, his converse shows;
  His *canvass*, almost ev'ry thing that's bad!
Thus at th'Academy, we must suppose,
  A man more useful never could be had;
Who in himself, a host, so much can do;
Who is both precept and example too.
    Peter Pindar (John Wolcot), *Farewell Odes*, for 1786, ode 5.

That tame and wooden painter, West.
    A. W. N. Pugin, *Contrasts*.

We have an American, West, who deals in high history, and is vastly admired, but he is heavier than Guercino, and has still less grace, and is very inferior.
    Horace Walpole, Letter to Sir Horace Mann, 22 April 1775.

See also J. M. W. Turner

WESTON, EDWARD
1886–1958 Photographer

I do not wish to impose my personality upon nature (any of life's manifestations), but without prejudice or falsification to become *identified* with nature, to know things in their very essence, so that what I record is not an interpretation — *my* idea of what nature *should* be — but a *revelation*, — a piercing of the smoke screen artificially cast over life by irrelevant, humanly limited exigencies, into an absolute, impersonal recognition.
    On himself, in *The Daybooks*, vol. 2.

In trying to analyze my present work as compared to that of several years ago, I can best summarize that once my aim was interpretation; now it is presentation. Also, I could now, with opportunity produce one or more significant photographs a day 365 days a year. Any creative work should function as easily and naturally as breathing.
    On himself, 14 April 1926, in Nancy Newhall, *Edward Weston*.

So writing I do not place the artist on a pedestal, as a little god. He is only the interpreter of the inexpressible, for the layman, the link between the known and the unknown, the beyond. This is mysticism, — of course! How else can one explain why a combination of lines by Kandinsky, or a form by Brancusi, not obviously related to the cognized world, does bring such intense reponse.... Granted the eye becomes excited, Why?
    Ibid., 7 April 1930

Weston is, in the real sense, one of the few great creative artists of today. He has recreated the mother-forms and forces of nature; he has made these forms eloquent of the fundamental unity of the world. His work illuminates man's journey toward perfection of the spirit.
    Ansel Adams, in *ibid.*

... He was one of those who taught photography to be itself.
    Robinson Jeffers, in *ibid.*

WHARTON, EDITH NEWBOLD JONES
1862–1937 Author

Mrs Wharton at her best was an analyst of the paralysis that attends success. Hers was not a world where romance was apt to flourish.
    Louis Auchincloss, 'Edith Wharton and Her New York', in Irving Howe ed., *Edith Wharton, A Collection of Critical Essays.*

Mrs Wharton, do you know what's the matter with you? You don't know anything about life.
    F. Scott Fitzgerald, upon first meeting Mrs Wharton, in Grace Kellogg, *The Two Lives of Edith Wharton.*

The arena of her imagination is the forefront of social life, where manners reveal moral stress or bias, and accepted forms of conduct may break under the weight of personal desire.
    Irving Howe, 'The Achievement of Edith Wharton', in Irving Howe ed., *Edith Wharton, A Collection of Critical Essays.*

In the novels written during the last fifteen years of her life, Mrs Wharton's intellectual conservatism hardened into an embittered and querulous disdain for modern life; she no longer really knew what was happening in America; and she lost what had once been her main gift: the accurate location of the target she wished to destroy.
    Ibid.

... I take to her very kindly as regards her diabolical little cleverness, the quantity of intention and intelligence in her style and her sharp eye for an

interesting *kind* of subject . . . I want to get hold of the little lady and pump the pure essence of my wisdom and experience into her.
> Henry James, Letter to Mary Cadwalader Jones, 1902.

Your only drawback is not having the homeliness and the inevitability and the happy limitation and the affluent poverty of a country of your own.
> Henry James, Letter to Mrs Wharton, 1912.

Her great theme, like that of her friend Henry James, became the plight of the young and innocent in a world of greater intricacy than they were accustomed to.
> Alfred Kazin, 'Edith Wharton', in Irving Howe ed., *Edith Wharton, A Collection of Critical Essays.*

Edith Wharton knew well enough that one dynasty had succeeded another in American life; the consequences of that succession became the great subject of her best novels. But she was not so much interested in the accession of the new class as she was in the destruction of her own, in the eclipse of its finest spirits.
> *Ibid.*

Edith Wharton, who believed so passionately in the life of art that she staked her life upon it, remains not a great artist but an unusual American, one who brought the weight of her personal experience to bear upon a modern American literature to which she was spiritually alien.
> *Ibid.*

She was herself a novel of his, no doubt in his earlier manner.
> Percy Lubbock, referring to Edith Wharton and Henry James, in Millicent Bell, *Edith Wharton and Henry James, The Story of Their Friendship.*

With her ripe culture, her clear and clean intelligence, her classical spirit, her severe standards and austere ethics, Mrs Wharton is our outstanding literary aristocrat.
> Vernon L. Parrington, *Our Literary Aristocrat*, in Irving Howe ed., *Edith Wharton, A Collection of Critical Essays.*

She is as finished as a Sheraton sideboard, and with her poise, grace, high standards, and perfect breeding, she suggests as inevitably old wine and slender decanters.
> *Ibid.*

She brought to her novels a strong, if limited intelligence, notable powers of observation, and a genuine

desire to tell the truth — a desire which in some part she satisfied. But she was a woman in whom we cannot fail to see a limitation of heart, and this limitation makes itself manifest as a literary and moral deficiency in her work, and of *Ethan Frome* especially.
> Lionel Trilling, 'The Morality of Inertia', in Irving Howe ed., *Edith Wharton, A Collection of Critical Essays.*

WHARTON, THOMAS, MARQUIS OF WHARTON
1648—1715 Statesman

Unheard, came creeping out sly *Cataline*,
Father of *Faction*; who with Force unseen
Rowls on with steddy pace, the *Great Machine*.
Of antient Stock, in covert *Saw-pits* bold,
In Plots consummate and in tricks grown old,
Since among Knaves he holds the foremost place,
Old *Ferguson*'s footsteps, who so well can trace;
Tho' twice his marriage-bed has been betray'd
Good reasons still his Vengeance have allay'd.
The injury his former Spouse has done
The large Estate she left did well attone.
He is content his present Spouse should strole
To gain young Cully's to the Kit-Kat Bowl.
> Anon., *The Seven Wise Men.*

He was a man of great wit and versatile cleverness, and cynically ostentatious in his immorality, having the reputation of being the greatest rake and the truest Whig of his time.
> *Encyclopaedia Britannica*, 13th edition.

It is your lordship's particular distinction that you are master of the whole compass of business, and have signaliz'd yourself in all the different scenes of it. We admire some for the dignity, others for the popularity of their behaviour; some for their clearness of judgement, others for their happiness of expression; some for the laying of schemes, and others for the putting of them in execution: It is your lordship only who enjoys these several talents united, and that too in as great perfection as others possess them singly. Your enemies acknowledge this great extent in your lordship's character, at the same time that they use their utmost industry and invention to derogate from it. But it is for your honour that those who are now your enemies were always so.
> Joseph Addison, Dedication to fifth volume of *Spectator.*

In small things and great his devotion to his party constantly appeared. He had the finest stud in England; and his delight was to win plates from

Tories. Sometimes when, in a distant county, it was fully expected that the horse of a High Church squire would be first on the course, down came, on the very eve of the race, Wharton's Careless, who had ceased to run at Newmarket merely for want of competitors, or Wharton's Gelding, for whom Lewis the Fourteenth had in vain offered a thousand pistoles. A man whose mere sport was of this description was not likely to be easily beaten in any serious contest.

T. B. Macaulay, *History of England.*

The superiority of his genius consists in nothing else but an inexhaustible fund of political lies, which he plentifully speaks, and by an unparallel generosity forgets, and consequently contradicts, the next hour.

Jonathan Swift, in *Examiner*, no. 15, 1710.

The Ends he has gain'd by lying, appear to be more owing to the frequency than the Art of them; his lies being sometimes detected in an Hour, often in a Day, and always in a Week: . . . He is a Presbeyterian in Politicks and an Atheist in Religion; but he chuses at present to Whore with a *Papist* . . . With a good natural Understanding, a great fluency in Speaking, and no ill taste of Wit, he is generally the worst Companion in the World; his Thoughts being wholly taken up between Vice and Politicks, so that Bawdy Prophaneness, and Business fill up his whole Conversation. To gratify himself in the two· first, he makes choice of suitable Favourites, whose Talent reaches no higher than to entertain him with all the Lewdness that passes in Town.

Jonathan Swift, *A Short Character of His Ex. T. E. of Wharton.*

WHEATLEY, PHILLIS

circa 1753—84 Poet

. . . beneath the dignity of criticism.

Thomas Jefferson, in Edward D. Seeber, 'Phillis Wheatley', in *Journal of Negro History*, July 1939.

Here the fair volume shows the far-spread name
Of wondrous Wheatley, Afric's heir to fame.
Well is it known what flowing genius shines,
What force of numbers, in her polished lines;
With magic power the grand descriptions roll
Thick on the mind, and agitate the soul.

Joseph Ladd, in Edward D. Seeber, *ibid.*

. . . she sings like a canary in a cage, a bird that

forgets its native melody and imitates only what it hears.

William Long, in Chas Fred Heartman ed., *Phillis Wheatley.*

WHEWELL, WILLIAM

1794—1866 Academic

Someone having said of Whewell that his *forte* was science, 'Yes,' assented Sydney Smith, 'and his foible is omniscience.'

Sidney Smith, in Walter Jerrold, *A Book of Famous Wits.*

See also Herbert Spencer

WHISTLER, JAMES ABBOTT MCNEILL

1834—1903 Artist

I have hardly a warm personal enemy left.

On himself, in Joseph and Elizabeth Robins Pennell, *The Whistler Journal.*

I have also executed a good deal of distemper. . . .

On himself, *The Gentle Art of Making Enemies.*

To the question: 'Do you think genius is hereditary?' he replied: 'I can't tell you; heaven has granted me no offspring.'

On himself, in Hesketh Pearson, *Lives of the Wits.*

'What!' exclaimed the examiner: 'you do not know the date of the Battle of Buena Vista? Suppose you were to go out to dinner, and the company began to talk of the Mexican war, and you, a West Point man, were asked the date of the battle, what would you do?' 'Do? Why, I should refuse to associate with people who could talk of such things at dinner!'

On himself, in *ibid.*

A supposititious conversation in *Punch* brought about the following interchange of telegrams: —
From Oscar Wilde, Exeter, to J. McNeill Whistler, Tite St. — *Punch* too ridiculous — when you and I are together we never talk about anything except ourselves.
From Whistler, Tite St, to Oscar Wilde, Exeter. — No, no, Oscar, you forget — when you and I are together, we never talk about anything except me.

On himself, *The Gentle Art of Making Enemies.*

Art should be independent of all clap-trap — should

stand alone, and appeal to the artistic sense of eye or ear, without confounding this with emotions entirely foreign to it, as devotion, pity, love, patriotism, and the like. All these have no kind of concern with it; and that is why I insist on calling my works 'arrangements' and 'harmonies.'

Take the picture of my mother, exhibited at the Royal Academy as an 'Arrangement in Grey and Black.' Now that is what it is. To me it is interesting as a picture of my mother; but what can or ought the public to care about the identity of the portrait?

On himself, Letter to *World*, 22 May 1878.

Mr. Whistler's brave attempt to enlighten the Britishers is lost to us . . . But we can't despair, remembering as we do that the Whistlerian idea arose in the land of progress and Presidents, the land where Barnum blows and Whitman catalogues. . . .

Anon., Editorial in *London*, 18 August 1877.

Whistler once made London a half-way house between New York and Paris and wrote rude things in the visitors' book.

Max Beerbohm, in Katherine Lyon Mix, *Max and the Americans*.

Read any page of *The Gentle Art of Making Enemies*, and you will hear a voice in it, and see a face in it, and see gestures in it. And none of these is quite like any other known to you. It matters not that you never knew Whistler, never even set eyes on him. You see him and know him here. The voice drawls slowly, quickening to a kind of snap at the end of every sentence, and sometimes rising to a sudden screech of laughter; and, all the while, the fine fierce eyes of the talker are flashing out at you and his long nervous fingers are tracing extravagant arabesques in the air. No! you need never have seen Whistler to know what he was like. He projected through printed words the clear-cut image and clear-ringing echo of himself. He was a born writer, achieving perfection through pains which must have been infinite for that we see at first sight no trace of them at all. . . .

Max Beerbohm, in Stanley Weintraub, *Whistler: a biography*.

No man ever preached the impersonality of art so well; no man ever preached the impersonality of art so personally.

G K. Chesterton, reviewing *The Gentle Art of Making Enemies*.

Like the white lock of Whistler,
  That lit our aimless gloom,
Men showed their own white feather
  As proudly as a plume.

G. K. Chesterton, 'To Edmund Clerihew Bentley', *The Man Who Was Thursday*.

Mr. Whistler's experiments have no relation whatever to life; they have only a relation to painting.

Henry James, 'The Picture Season in London', in *Galaxy*, August 1877.

The effect of Whistler at his best is exactly to give to the place he hangs in — or perhaps I should say to the person he hangs for — something of the sense, of the illusion, of a great museum.

Henry James, 'The Grafton Galleries', in *Harper's Weekly*, 26 June 1897.

Lost in over-subtlety.

Augustus John, *Chiaroscuro*.

He was so isolated, so apart, in his work, that nothing has been more difficult for the historian of modern art than to place, to classify him . . . He turned his back on the history and archaeology in favour at the Academy, filling his canvas with no meaning whatever except whatever there may be in the beauty of rhythm and design.

Elizabeth and Joseph Pennell, *The Life of James McNeill Whistler*.

Respect for the great traditions of art always remained his standard: 'What is not worthy of the Louvre is not worthy of art,' he said again and again.

Ibid.

You had your searches, your uncertainties,
And this is good to know — for us, I mean,
Who bear the brunt of our America
And try to wrench her impulse into art.

Ezra Pound, *To Whistler, American.*

There's a combative Artist named Whistler
Who is, like his own hog-hairs, a bristler:
  A tube of white lead
  And a punch on the head
Offer varied attractions to Whistler.

Dante Gabriel Rossetti, in Elizabeth and Joseph Pennell, *The Life of James McNeill Whistler*.

I have seen, and heard much of Cockney impudence before now; but never expected to hear a coxcomb ask two hundred guineas for flinging a pot of paint in the public's face.

John Ruskin, *Fors Clavigera*.

'I only know of two painters in the world,' said a newly introduced feminine enthusiast to Whistler, 'yourself and Velasquez.' 'Why,' answered Whistler in dulcet tones, 'why drag in Velasquez?'

D. C. Seitz, *Whistler Stories*.

On the evening of February 20, 1885, Whistler in

faultless evening dress delivered at Prince's Hall, London, the 'Ten O'Clock,' his famous lecture summing up in beautifully polished prose his theories of aesthetics. He held his audience and made a profound impression, pointing out that people do not look *at* a picture, but *through* it, seeking for something to improve their mental or moral state. . . . Art can not be understood by everyone; only vulgarity is common to all. 'The Dilettante stalks abroad. The amateur is loosed. The voice of the aesthete is heard in the land, and catastrophe is upon us.' Art is not concerned with the scenic beauty of Switzerland but rather with a piece of Chinese blue porcelain or a painting by Velasquez. Art does not concern the multitude but only the few.
    Frederick A. Sweet, *Whistler*.

Fly away, butterfly, back to Japan
Tempt not a pinch at the hand of a man,
And strive not to sting ere you die away.
So pert and so painted, so proud and so pretty,
To brush the bright down from your wings were a
                                  pity —
Fly away, butterfly, fly away.
    Algernon C. Swinburne, in Stanley Weintraub, *Whistler: a biography*.

I never saw any one so feverishly alive as this little, old man, with his bright, withered cheeks, over which the skin was drawn tightly, his darting eyes, under their prickly bushes of eyebrow, his fantastically-creased black and white curls of hair, his bitter and subtle mouth, and, above all, his exquisite hands never at rest.
    Arthur Symons, *Studies in Seven Arts*.

A miniature Mephistopheles, mocking the majority.
    Oscar Wilde, in *Pall Mall Gazette*, 21 February 1885.

As for borrowing Mr. Whistler's ideas about art, the only thoroughly original ideas I have ever heard him express have had reference to his own superiority as a painter over painters greater than himself.
    Oscar Wilde, in *Truth*, January 1890.

With our James vulgarity begins at home, and should be allowed to stay there.
    Oscar Wilde, Letter to *World*.

Mr Whistler in pointing out that the power of the painter is to be found in his powers of vision, not in his cleverness of hand, has expressed a truth which needed expression, and which, coming from the lord of form and colour, cannot fail to have its influence. His lecture, the Apocrypha though it be for the people, yet remains from this time as the Bible for the painter, the masterpiece of masterpieces, the song of songs. It is true he has pronounced the panegyric of the Philistine, but I can fancy Ariel praising Caliban for a jest: and in that he has read the Commination Service over the critics, let all men thank him, the critics themselves indeed most of all, for he has now relieved them from the necessity of a tedious existence. . . .
    Oscar Wilde, in Stanley Weintraub, *Whistler: a biography*.

All his life Whistler committed the unpardonable offense of being himself; sprung of a nation where the *vox populi* is the *vox dei*, he hated the *vox populi*.
    John Butler Yeats, in *ibid*.

See also Sir Frank Brangwyn, Ezra Pound, Oscar Wilde

WHITE, WILLIAM ALLEN

1868—1944 Editor, Journalist, Author

His unpolished and unpretentious beliefs were so blended with cosmopolitan ideas that he was something of a composite American. Within the last twenty-odd years of his life, he became the folk hero of the middle class.
    Walter Johnson, *William Allen White's America*.

See also Theodore Roosevelt

WHITEFIELD, GEORGE

1714—70 Calvinist Methodist

I love those that thunder out the word! The Christian world is in a deep sleep. Nothing but a loud voice can waken them out of it!
    On himself, in Arnold A. Dallimore, *George Whitefield*.

I had rather wear out than rust out.
    On himself, attributed.

A second George Fox.
    Anon., contemporary denunciation of Whitefield, in Sydney Ahlstrom, *A Religious History of the American People*.

He looked as if he was cloathed with authority from ye great God and a sweet collome solemnity sat upon his brow and my hearing him preach gave me a heart wound by gods blessing.

  Anon., in William Warren Sweet, *Religion in Colonial America.*

How awfully, with what Thunder and Sound did he discharge the Artillery of Heaven upon us.

  Benjamin Colman, in Ola E. Winslow, *Jonathan Edwards.*

In the dreadfullest winter I ever saw, people wallowed in the snow day and night, for the benefit of his beastly brayings.

  Dr Timothy Cutler, in William Warren Sweet, *Religion in Colonial America.*

His eloquence had a wonderful Power over the Hearts and Purses of his Hearers.

  Benjamin Franklin, *The Autobiography of Benjamin Franklin.*

I never treated Whitefield's ministry with contempt; I believe he did good. He had devoted himself to the lower classes of mankind, and among them he was of use. But when familiarity and noise claim the praise due to knowledge, art and elegance, we must beat down such pretensions.

  Samuel Johnson, in James Boswell, *Life of Johnson.*

Whitefield's popularity is owing chiefly to his manner. He would be followed by crowds were he to wear a nightcap in the pulpit, or were he to preach from a tree.

  Samuel Johnson, in *ibid.*

I heard him once, and it was as low, confused, puerile, conceited, ill-natured, enthusiastic a performance as I ever heard.

  Jonathan Mayhew, 1740, in Ola E. Winslow, *Jonathan Edwards.*

Can anything but love beget love? This shone in his very countenance, and continually breathed in all his words, whether public or private. Was it not this which, quick and penetrating as lightning, flew from heart to heart? which gave life to his sermons, his conversation, his letters? Ye are witnesses.

  John Wesley, in J. B. Wakely, *Anecdotes of the Rev. George Whitefield.*

Now as an angel of blessing classed,
And now as a mad enthusiast.
Called in his youth to sound and gauge
The moral lapse of his race and age,
And sharp as truth, the contrast draw
Of human frailty and perfect law;
Possessed by the one dread thought that lent

Its goad to his fiery temperament,
Up and down the world he went,
A John the Baptist crying — Repent!

  John Greenleaf Whittier, *The Preacher.*

WHITEHEAD, ALFRED NORTH

1861—1947 Mathematician, Philosopher

He was a very modest man, and his most extreme boast was that he did try to have the qualities of his defects.

  Bertrand Russell, *Portraits From Memory.*

See also Charles Dickens

WHITGIFT, JOHN

1530—1604 Archbishop of Canterbury

Being made Archbishop of Canterbury, and of the pryvie Councell, he carried him selfe in that mylde and charitable course, that he was not only greatly approved by all the cleargie of England, but even by some of those, whom with his penn he might seem to have wounded: I mean the Puritans of whom he won divers to conformitye. In the Starre Chamber, he used to deliver his sentence in a good fashion, ever leaning to the mylder censure as best became his calling.

  Sir John Harington, *Nugae Antiquae.*

Of all the Bishops that ever were in that place, (I mean, in the see of Canterbury), none did ever so much hurt unto the Church of God, as he hath done, since his coming. No Bishop had ever such an aspiring and ambitious mind as he: no, not Stephen Gardiner of Winchester. None so tyrannous as he: no, not Bonner.

  'Martin Marprelate', *Dialogue of Tyrannical Dealing.*

Every year he entertained the queen [Elizabeth I] at one of his houses, so long as he was archbishop; and some years twice or thrice, where all things were performed in so seemly an order, that she went thence always exceedingly well pleased. And besides many public and gracious favours done unto him, she would salute him, and bid him farewell by the name of Black Husband; calling also his men her servants, as a token of her good contentment with their attendance and pains.

  Sir George Paule, *Life of Whitgift.*

. ... he was like the Ark, which left a blessing upon the place where it rested; and in all his employments

was like Jehoiada, that did good unto Israel. . . . His merits to the Queen, and her favours to him, were such that she called him *her little black husband*.
Izaak Walton, *Life of Hooker*.

WHITMAN, WALT

1819—92 Poet

I celebrate myself, and sing myself,
And what I assume you shall assume.
On himself, *Song of Myself*.

Do I contradict myself?
Very well then I contradict myself,
(I am large, I contain multitudes).
On himself, *ibid*.

There is something in my nature furtive like an old hen! You see a hen wandering up and down a hedge-row, looking apparently quite unconcerned, but presently she finds a concealed spot, and furtively lays an egg, and comes away as though nothing had happened! That is how I felt in writing *Leaves of Grass*.
On himself, in Edgar Lee Masters, *Whitman*.

I am as bad as the worst, but thank God I am as good as the best.
Ibid.

As America fully and fairly construed is the legitimate result and evolutionary outcome of the past, so I would dare claim for my verse.
On himself, in James Miller Jr, 'America's Epic', in Roy Harvey Pearce ed., *Whitman, A Collection of Critical Essays*.

In Whitman's works the elemental parts of a man's mind and the fragments of imperfect education may be seen merging together, floating and sinking in a sea of insensate egotism and rhapsody, repellent, divine, disgusting, extraordinary.
John Jay Chapman, 'Walt Whitman', in Francis Murphy ed., *Walt Whitman, A Critical Anthology*.

He had the bad taste bred in bone of all missionaries and palmists, the sign-manual of a true quack. This bad taste is nothing more than the offensive intrusion of himself and his mission into the matter in hand.
Ibid.

. . . we do not want to plant corn, to hoe it, to drive the crows away, to gather it, husk it, grind it, sift it, bake it, and butter it, before eating it, and then

take the risk of its being at last moldy in our mouths. And this is what you have to do in reading Mr Whitman's rhythm.
William Dean Howells, review of 'Drum-Taps', in Francis Murphy ed., *Walt Whitman, A Critical Anthology*.

It exhibits the effort of an essentially prosaic mind to life itself, by a prolonged muscular strain, into poetry.
Henry James, referring to *Leaves of Grass*, 'Mr Walt Whitman', in Edwin Haviland Miller ed., *A Century of Whitman Criticism*.

This awful Whitman. This post-mortem poet. This poet with the private soul leaking out of him all the time. All his privacy leaking out in a sort of dribble, oozing into the universe.
D. H. Lawrence, *Studies in Classic American Literature*.

He was the poet of the self's motion downwards into the abysses of darkness and guilt and pain and isolation, upwards to the creative act in which darkness was transmuted into beauty. When the self became lost to the world, Whitman was lost for poetry. But before that happened, Whitman had, in his own example, made poetry possible in America.
R. W. B. Lewis, 'Walt Whitman', in Perry Miller ed., *Major Writers of America*, vol. 1.

Whitman was like a prophet straying in a fog and shouting half-truths with a voice of great trumpets. He was seeking something, but he never knew quite what, and he never found it. He vanishes in the mist, and his words float back, dim, superb, to us behind him.
Amy Lowell, 'Walt Whitman and The New Poetry', in Francis Murphy ed., *Walt Whitman, A Critical Anthology*.

Whitman, despite his cosmic consciousness and mysticism, sang the seen — not the unseen. He sat at a loom throwing the shuttle and guiding the threads without any pattern other than that the fabric should be unmistakably American.
Edgar Lee Masters, *Whitman*.

He *is* America. His crudity is an exceeding great stench but it *is* America. He is a hollow place in the rock that echoes with his time. He *does* 'chant the crucial stage' and he is the 'voice triumphant.' He is disgusting. He is an exceedingly nauseating pill, but he accomplishes his mission. . . .
I honor him for he prophesied me while I can only recognize him as a forebear of whom I ought to be proud. . . . It is a great thing, reading a man to know not 'His tricks are as yet my tricks, but I can

easily make them mine' but 'His message is my message. We will see that men hear [it].'

Ezra Pound, *What I feel about Walt Whitman*, 1 February 1909.

The absence of any principle of selection or of a sustained style enables him to render aspects of things and of emotion which would have eluded a trained writer. He is, therefore, interesting even where he is grotesque or perverse.

George Santayana, *The Poetry of Barbarism*.

He is neither afraid of being slangy nor of being dull; nor, let me add, of being ridiculous. The result is a most surprising compound of plain grandeur, sentimental affectation, and downright nonsense.

Robert Louis Stevenson, 'The Gospel According to Walt Whitman', in Edwin Haviland Miller ed., *A Century of Whitman Criticism*.

. . . he is a writer of something occasionally like English, and a man of something occasionally like genius.

Algernon C. Swinburne, 'Whitmania', in *ibid*.

He occasionally suggests something a little more than human. You can't confound him with the other inhabitants of Brooklyn or New York. How they must shudder when they read him! He is awfully good.

Henry David Thoreau, Letter to Harrison Blake, 7 December 1856.

See also Theodore Dreiser, Thomas Hardy, William Dean Howells, Rudyard Kipling, D. H. Lawrence, George Meredith, Vernon Parrington, Dylan Thomas, Frank Lloyd Wright

WHITNEY, ELI

1765–1825 Inventor

. . . after having gratified every ambition and swung the country almost at his will . . . had thrown away the usual objects of political ambition like the ashes of smoked cigarettes; had turned to other amusements, satiated every taste, gorged every appetite, won every object that New York afforded, and not yet satisfied, had carried his field of activity abroad, until New York no longer knew what most to envy, his horses or his houses. . . .

Henry Adams, in Matthew Josephson, *The Robber Barons*.

WHITTIER, JOHN GREENLEAF

1807–92 Poet, Author

Phrenologically, I have too much self-esteem to be troubled by the opinions of others — and I love my friends too well to deny them the gratification (if it be one) of abusing me to their hearts' content.

On himself, in Edward Wagenknecht, *John Greenleaf Whittier, A Portrait in Paradox*.

His technical methods were stereotyped. The simplest and most conventional ballad metres, the sentiments, phrases and rhythms of other poets served him to the last. He had no pride of artistry. When editors revised his manuscripts, Whittier accepted their changes without remark.

Van Wyck Brooks, *The Flowering of New England, 1815–1865*.

Best loved and saintliest of our singing train.

Oliver Wendell Holmes, in Walter Fuller Taylor,. *The Story of American Letters*.

There is Whittier, whose swelling and vehement
                    heart
Strains the strait-breasted drab of the Quaker apart,
And reveals the live Man, still supreme and erect,
Underneath the bemummying wrappers of sect.

James Russell Lowell, 'A Fable for Critics', in Edmund Wilson ed., *The Shock of Recognition*.

It has been his chief glory not that he could speak inspired words, but that he spoke them for the despised, the helpless and the dumb; for those too ignorant to honor, too poor to reward him. Grace was given him to know his Lord in the lowest disguise, even in that of the poor hunted slave, and to follow him in heart into prison and unto death.

Harriet Beecher Stowe, in Edward Wagenknecht, *Harriet Beecher Stowe, The Known and the Unknown*.

Whittier's ambition, then, was to become a New England Burns, who, without glorifying lawless passion, would sing the worth of the common man, and transmute the daily routine of the farm into the fine metal of poetry.

Walter Fuller Taylor, *The Story of American Letters*.

. . . a sort of minor saint in outmoded Quaker dress.

Robert Penn Warren, *John Greenleaf Whittier's Poetry*.

WHITTINGTON, RICHARD (DICK)

—d. 1423 Lord Mayor of London

He travelled as far as Holloway, and there sat down on a stone to consider what course he should take; but while he was thus ruminating, Bow Bells, of which there were only six, began to ring; and he thought their sounds addressed him in this manner:

'Turn again, Whittington,
Thrice Lord Mayor of London.'

'Lord Mayor of London!' said he to himself; 'what would not one endure to be Lord Mayor of London, and ride in such a fine coach? Well, I'll go back again, and bear all the pummelling and ill-usage of Cicely rather than miss the opportunity of being Lord Mayor!'

Andrew Lang, 'The History of Whittington', in *The Blue Fairy Book*.

WILBERFORCE, WILLIAM

1759—1833 Philanthropist, Abolitionist

God Almighty has set before me two great objects, the suppression of the Slave Trade and the reformation of manners.

On himself, Diary, 1787.

They charge me with fanaticism. If to be feelingly alive to the sufferings of my fellow-creatures is to be a fanatic, I am one of the most incurable fanatics ever permitted to be at large.

On himself, in the House of Commons, 19 June 1816.

I saw what seemed a mere shrimp mount upon the table; but, as I listened, he grew, and grew, until the shrimp became a whale.

James Boswell, Letter to Dundas on Wilberforce at a public meeting in York on 25 March 1784.

Go, W---, with narrow skull,
Go home and preach away at Hull.
No longer to the Senate cackle
In strains that suit the tabernacle;
I hate your little wittling sneer,
Your pert and self-sufficient leer.
Mischief to trade sits on your lip,
Insects will gnaw the noblest ship.
Go, W---, begone, for shame,
Thou dwarf with big resounding name.

James Boswell, in J. Wesley Bready, *England: Before and After Wesley*.

O Wilberforce! thou man of black renown,
Whose merit none enough can sing or say,

Thou hast struck one immense Colossus down,
Thou moral Washington of Africa!
But there's another little thing, I own,
Which you should perpetrate some summer's day,
And set the other half of earth to rights;
You have freed the *blacks* — now pray shut up the whites.

Lord Byron, *Don Juan*, canto xiv.

Your friend, Mr Wilberforce, will be very happy any morning to hand your Ladyship to the guillotine.

Lord Grenville, comment to Lady Spencer on Wilberforce's pacificist amendment, January 1795.

He has two strings to his bow: — he by no means neglects his worldly interests, while he expects a bright reversion in the skies. Mr Wilberforce is far from being a hypocrite; but he is ... as fine a specimen of *moral equivocation* as can well be conceived.

William Hazlitt, *The Spirit of the Age*.

If I were called upon to describe [him] in one word, I should say he was the most 'amusable' man I ever met with in my life. Instead of having to think what subjects will interest him, it is perfectly impossible to hit one that does not. I never saw any one who touched life at so many points; and this the more remarkable in a man who is supposed to live absorbed in the contemplations of a future state.

Sir James Mackintosh, 1829, in R. I. and S. Wilberforce, *Life of Wilberforce*.

If this is madness, I hope that he will bite us all.

Mrs Sykes, comment to his mother on Wilberforce's 'conversion', Summer 1786.

See also Richard Brinsley Sheridan

WILDE, OSCAR FINGAL O'FLAHERTIE WILLS

1854—1900 Author, Dramatist, Wit

I rise sometimes after six, but don't do much but bathe, and although always feeling slightly immortal when in the sea, feel sometimes slightly heretical when good Roman Catholic boys enter the water with little amulets and crosses round their necks and arms that the good S. Christopher may hold them up.

I am now off to bed after reading a chapter of S. Thomas à Kempis. I think half-an-hour's warping of the inner man daily is greatly conducive to holiness.

On himself, Letter to William Ward, 26 July 1876.

I am so glad you like that strange coloured book of mine: it contains much of me in it. Basil Hallward is what I think I am; Lord Henry what the world thinks me; Dorian what I would like to be — in other ages, perhaps.

On himself, on *The Picture of Dorian Gray*, Letter to Ralph Payne, 12 February 1894.

What the paradox was to me in the sphere of thought, perversity became to me in the realm of passion.

On himself, *De Profundis*.

The two great turning points of my life were when my father sent me to Oxford, and when society sent me to prison.

Ibid.

The Gods had given me almost everything. I had genius, a distinguished name, high social position, brilliancy, intellectual daring: I made art a philosophy, and philosophy an art: I altered the minds of men and the colours of things: there was nothing I said or did that did not make people wonder: I took the drama, the most objective form known to art, and made it as personal a mode of expression as the lyric or the sonnet, at the same time I widened its range and enriched its characterisation: drama, novel, poem in rhyme, poem in prose, subtle or fantastic dialogue, whatever I touched I made beautiful in a new mode of beauty: to truth itself I gave what is false no less than what is true as its rightful province, and showed that the false and the true are merely forms of intellectual existence. I treated art as the supreme reality, and life as a mere mode of fiction: I awoke the imagination of my century so that it created myth and legend around me: I summed up all systems in a phrase, and all existence in an epigram.

On himself, Letter to Lord Alfred Douglas, *De Profundis*, January—March 1897.

Morality does not help me. I was a born antinomian. I am one of those who are made for exceptions, not for laws. But while I see that there is nothing wrong in what one does, I see that there is something wrong with what one becomes. It is well to have learned that.

Ibid.

The prisoner looks to liberty as an immediate return to all his ancient energy, quickened into more vital forces by long disuse. When he goes out he finds he still has to suffer. His punishment as far as its effects go, lasts intellectually and physically, just as it lasts socially. He has still to pay. One gets no receipt for the past when one walks out into the beautiful air.

On himself, Letter to Frank Harris, June 1897.

It is curious how vanity helps the successful man and wrecks the failure. In old days half of my strength was my vanity.

On himself, Letter to Robert Ross, 16 November 1897.

My writing has gone to bits — like my character. I am simply a self-conscious nerve in pain.

Ibid.

The three women I have most admired are Queen Victoria, Sarah Bernhardt, and Lily Langtry. I would have married any one of them with pleasure.

On himself in Vincent O'Sullivan, *Letters of Oscar Wilde*, footnote.

Mr Oscar Wilde is no poet, but a cleverish man who has an infinite contempt for his readers, and thinks he can take them in with a little mouthing verse.

Anon., Review in *Spectator*, 13 August 1881.

He has made of infamy a new Thermopylae.

Anon., in William Butler Yeats, *Autobiographies*.

From the beginning Wilde performed his life and continued to do so even after fate had taken the plot out of his hands.

W. H. Auden, *Forewords and Afterwords*.

Of his poems not one has survived, for he was totally lacking in a poetic voice of his own; what he wrote was an imitation of poetry-in-general.

Ibid.

The solution that, deliberately or accidentally, he found was to subordinate every other dramatic element to dialogue for its own sake and create a verbal universe in which the characters are determined by the kinds of things they say, and the plot is nothing but a succession of opportunities to say them.

Ibid., on Wilde's plays.

Mr Wilde was not, I think, what one calls a born writer. His writing seemed to be always rather an overflow of intellectual and temperamental energy than an inevitable, absorbing function.

Max Beerbohm, in *Saturday Review*, 8 December 1900.

He sipped at a weak hock and seltzer

As he gazed at the London skies
Through the Nottingham lace of the curtains
    Or was it his bees-winged eyes?
    John Betjeman, *The Arrest of Oscar Wilde at
    the Cadogan Hotel.*

That sovereign of insufferables.
    Ambrose Bierce, *Wasp* (San Francisco), 1882.

He . . . was really a charlatan. I mean by a charlatan
one sufficiently dignified to despise the tricks that
he employs . . . Wilde and his school professed to
stand as solitary artistic souls apart from the public.
They professed to scorn the middle class, and declared that the artist must not work for the bourgeois. The truth is that no artist so really great ever
worked so much for the bourgeois as Oscar Wilde.
No man, so capable of thinking about truth and
beauty ever thought so constantly about his effect
on the middle classes. He studied the Surbiton
school-mistress with exquisite attention, and knew
exactly how to shock, and how to please her. . . . He
descended below himself to be on top of others.
He became purposely stupider than Oscar Wilde
that he might seem cleverer than the nearest curate.
He lowered himself to superiority; he stooped to
conquer.
    G. K. Chesterton, in *Daily News*, 19 October
    1909.

Queerly enough, it was the very multitude of his
falsities that prevented him from being entirely
false. Like a many-coloured humming top, he was at
once a bewilderment and a balance. He was so fond
of being many-sided that among his sides he even
admitted the right side. He loved so much to multiply his souls that he had among them one soul at
least that was saved.
    Ibid.

His gaze was constantly fixed on himself; yet not
on himself, but on his reflection in the looking-
glass. . . . Introspection of the genuine kind he never
achieved . . . while Whistler was a prophet who liked
to play Pierrot, Wilde grew into a Pierrot who liked
to play the prophet.
    Harold Child, in *Times Literary Supplement*,
    18 June 1908.

Wilde's voice was of the brown velvet order — mellifluous — rounded — in a sense giving it a plummy
quality — rather on the adenotic side — but practically pure cello — and very pleasing.
    Franklin Dyall, in Hesketh Pearson, *Life of
    Oscar Wilde.*

Oscar Wilde did not dive very deeply below the surface of human nature, but found, to a certain extent

rightly, that there is more on the surface of life than
is seen by the eyes of most people.
    J. T. Grein, in *Sunday Special*, 9 December 1900.

Wilde: I wish I had said that.
Whistler: You will, Oscar, you will.
    L. C. Ingleby, *Oscar Wilde.*

He was, on his plane, as insufferable as a Methodist
is on his.
    H. L. Mencken, Introduction to Wilde's *A House
    of Pomegranates.*

Oscar Wilde's talent seems to me essentially rootless, something growing in a glass in a little water.
    George Moore, Letter to Frank Harris, in
    Pearson's Magazine, New York, March 1918.

It was Wilde's hard fate that he should have been
beaten in his own field by his own contemporaries.
We are told that as a talker he could not hold his
own with Whistler; we know for ourselves that he
was no match for him as a controversialist. We can
see, moreover, that in the comedy of manners he
has been equalled, if not surpassed by Mr Shaw,
with whom, as a writer of prose, he cannot even be
compared. . . . We, who are posterity for Wilde,
must confess that he is rather a pale ghost as an
artist. . . .
    John Middleton Murry, 'Oscar Wilde as a Tragic
    Hero', *Athenaeum*, 24 September 1920.

One has the impression that he never put out more
than half of his strength in his books.
    Vincent O'Sullivan, Letter to Frank Harris, in
    Pearson's Magazine, April 1918.

'Have you anything to declare?' asked the customs
official. 'No. I have nothing to declare'; he paused:
'except my genius.'
    Hesketh Pearson, on Wilde's arrival in New York,
    Life of Oscar Wilde.

The nineties, the early nineties when Wilde's talent
was in full fruition, seem now, at least in literature,
to be coloured by the personality of Wilde, and the
movement foolishly called decadent. But in the
nineties when Wilde was writing, he had a very few
silent friends, and a very great number of vociferous
enemies. His books were laughed at, his poetry parodied, his person not kindly caricatured, and even
when his plays won popular applause, this hostility
against him was only smothered, not choked. His
disaster ungagged it, and few men have been sent
to perdition with a louder cry of hounds behind
them.
    Arthur Ransome, *Oscar Wilde, A Critical Study.*

Men lived more vividly in his presence, and talked better than themselves.
  Ibid.

Too many of Wilde's paragraphs are perorations.
  Ibid.

His tasks were always too easy for him, he never strained for achievement, and nothing requires more generosity to forgive than success without effort. . . . He pawned much of himself to the moment, and was never able to redeem it.
  Ibid.

It was the very element of his tragedy that it could not be shared or alleviated; on the path he had henceforth to tread there could be no comrade; his offence was one at which charity itself stood embarrassed, and compassion felt the fear of compromise.
  E. T. Raymond, *Portraits of the Nineties.*

He says that *The Ballad of Reading Gaol* doesn't describe his prison life, but his life at Naples with Bosie [Lord Alfred Douglas], and that all the best stanzas were the immediate result of his existence there.
  Robert Ross, Letter to Leonard Smithers, 12 April 1898.

He was never quite sure himself where and when he was serious.
  Robert Ross, Letter to Adela Schuster, 23 December 1900.

There was also in Queen Victoria's reign a famous inventor and poet called Oscar Wilde who wrote very well but behaved rather beardsley; he made himself memorable by inventing Art, Asceticism, etc., and was the leader of a set of disgusting old gentlemen called 'the naughty nineties'.
  W. C. Sellar and R. J. Yeatman, *1066 and All That.*

He has the property of making his critics dull. They laugh angrily at his epigrams, like a child who is coaxed into being amused in the very act of setting up a yell of rage and agony . . . Mr Wilde, an arch-artist, is so colossally lazy that he trifles even with the work by which an artist escapes work.
  George Bernard Shaw, on *An Ideal Husband*, in *Saturday Review*, 12 January 1895.

Mr Wilde has written scenes in which there is hardly a speech which could conceivably be uttered by one real person at a real at-home; but the deflection from common sense is so subtle that it is evidently produced as a tuner tunes a piano: that is, he first tunes a fifth perfectly, and then flattens it a shade. If he could not tune the perfect fifth, he could not produce the practicable one.
  George Bernard Shaw, in *Saturday Review*, 4 May 1895.

When Oscar came to join his God,
Not earth to earth, but sod to sod,
It was for sinners such as this
Hell was created bottomless.
  Algernon C. Swinburne, *Oscar Wilde.*

What has Oscar in common with art, except that he dines at our tables and picks from our platters the plums for the pudding that he peddles in the provinces? Oscar — the amiable, irresponsible, esurient Oscar — with no more sense of a picture than he has of the fit of a coat — has the courage of the opinions . . . of others!
  James McNeill Whistler, Letter to *World*, 1885.

Bourgeois malgré lui.
  James McNeill Whistler, attributed.

I think his fate is rather like Humpty Dumpty's, quite as tragic and quite as impossible to put right.
  Constance Wilde, Letter to her brother, 26 March 1897.

His manner had hardened to meet opposition and at times he allowed one to see an unpardonable insolence. His charm was acquired and systematised, a mask which he wore only when it pleased him.
  William Butler Yeats, *Autobiographies.*

Wilde had arrived in Dieppe, and Dowson pressed upon him the necessity of acquiring 'a more wholesome taste.' They emptied their pockets onto the café table, and though there was not much, there was enough, if both heaps were put into one. Meanwhile the news had spread, and they set out accompanied by a cheering crowd. Arrived at their destination, Dowson and the crowd remained outside, and presently Wilde returned. He said in a low voice to Dowson. 'The first these ten years, and it will be the last. It was like cold mutton' . . . and then aloud, so that the crowd might hear him, 'But tell it in England, for it will entirely restore my character.'
  Ibid., describing Wilde's visit to a brothel after his release from prison.

See also Henry James, Henry Cabot Lodge, Shakespeare, Robert Louis Stevenson, James McNeill Whistler

WILDER, THORNTON NIVEN

1897—1975 Author, Playwright

I am interested in the drives that operate in society and in every man. Pride, avarice and envy are in every home. I am not interested in the ephemeral — such subjects as the adulteries of dentists. I am interested in those things that repeat and repeat and repeat in the lives of millions.
On himself, *New York Times*, 6 November 1961.

I constantly rewrite, discard and replace the cycle of plays. Some are on the stove, some are in the oven, some are in the waste-basket. There are no first drafts in my life. An incinerator is a writer's best friend.
Ibid.

I was an old man when I was 12; and now I *am* an old man, *and it's splendid.*
On himself, on his seventieth birthday.

Whenever I'm asked what college I attended, I'm tempted to reply Thornton Wilder!
Garson Kanin, *Washington Star*, 12 August 1975.

A wizard, a magus, a waver of wands who summons up shapes from chaos and conjures worlds out of clouds, all in an instant.
Michael Kernan, *Washington Post*, 18 November 1973.

Thornton Wilder . . . posed the same questions as Euripides, Sophocles and the other classic Greeks whose works fascinated and comforted him. And the reason that he couldn't answer the questions lay in the very face of literature; the writer, being mortal, doesn't know the answers any more than anyone else does. But he has the wit to keep on asking.
Rod MacLeish, *Washington Post*, 11 December 1975.

WILDMAN, SIR JOHN

1621?—93 Politician

And where's my old friend & fellow rebel Johnee Wildman? Mount Atlas stand on tiptoes where art thee? And behold a mighty stone fell from the skies into the bottom of the sea, and gave a mighty plump, and great was the fall of that stone, and so farewell, Johnee Wildman.
Richard Overton, July 1649, in Maurice Ashley, *John Wildman*.

WILKES, JOHN

1727—97 Radical

Give me a grain of truth . . . and I will mix it up with a great mass of falsehood, so that no chemist shall ever be able to separate them.
On himself, in Henry Crabb Robinson, Diary.

Nothing has been so obnoxious to me through life as a dead calm.
On himself, in Horace Bleackley, *Life of John Wilkes*.

I scarcely ever met with a better companion, he has inexhaustible spirits, infinite wit and humour, and a great deal of knowledge; but a thorough profligate in principle as in practice, hjs life is stained with every vice, and his conversation full of blasphemy and indecency. These morals he glories in; for shame is a weakness he has long since surmounted.
Edward Gibbon, in O. A. Sherard, *A Life of John Wilkes*.

Did we not hear so much of Jack Wilkes, we should think more highly of his conversation. Jack has great variety of talk, Jack is a scholar, Jack has the manners of a gentleman. But after hearing his name sounded from pole to pole as the phoenix of convivial felicity we are disappointed in his company.
Samuel Johnson, in James Boswell, *Life of Johnson*.

Wilkes had his revenge one night at Carlton House when the prince called for toasts. He gave 'The King — long life to him'. The prince, who detested his father and rejoiced in his illness, resented the words. 'Since when have you been so anxious over my parent's health?' he said. 'Since I had the pleasure of your royal highness's acquaintance,' answered Wilkes with a bow.
Raymond Postgate, *That Devil Wilkes*.

Wilkes telling stories against himself — as that of the old lady looking up at the signboard of one of the numerous Wilkes's Head Taverns, and muttering, 'Aye, he swings everywhere but where he ought.'
O. A. Sherard, *A Life of John Wilkes*.

Wantonness, rather than ambition or vengeance, guided his hand; and though he became the martyr of the best cause, there was nothing in his principles or morals that led him to care under what government he lived. To laugh and riot and scatter firebrands with him was liberty — Despotism will for ever reproach Freedom with the profligacy of such a saint.
Horace Walpole, *Memoirs*.

See also Sir Philip Francis, Lord Sandwich

WILKIE, SIR DAVID

1785—1841 Painter

When he has made a sketch for a picture & settled his design, He then walks about looking for a person proper to be a model for completing each character in his picture, & He then paints *everything from the life*. . . . He sometimes walks abt. for a *week* before He can meet with the character of head &c. that will suit him.

Joseph Farington, Diary, 12 December 1807.

January 2. Out on business. Called on Newton, who mentioned a saying of Wilkie's, which for his servility is a touch. 'To be acquainted with a Nobleman on pleasant terms is a good thing, but it is a great thing to be acquainted with one on any terms.' Up with your flap, David, and boo as you are kicked.

Benjamin R. Haydon, Diary, 1830.

Mr. Wilkie presents us with a sort of lenten fare, very good and wholesome, but rather insipid than overpowering.

William Hazlitt, 'On Mr. Wilkie's Pictures', in *Champion*, 5 March 1815.

WILKINS, TIMOTHY

—d. 1671 Epicurean

Timothy Wilkins died; lived and died an epicure; some men are soon chosen.

Anthony à Wood, *Life and Times*, October 1671.

WILKINSON, TATE

1739—1803 Actor-Manager

During his career as manager, if any member of his company had obstinately neglected to listen to his advice on any particular point of acting, or the like, he would mount, on some future night, into the gallery, and hiss most strenuously — an expedient which presently brought the trifler to his senses. On one occasion, being more than usually indignant at some very slovenly exhibition on the stage, his hiss was remarkably audible. The delinquent actor, however, seemed to have friends around him, for, on a cry of 'Turn him out!', poor Wilkinson was unceremoniously handed down from his own gallery, and ejected into the street. Notwithstanding, he still

maintained this useful and very disinterested experiment.

George Raymond, *Memoirs of R. W. Elliston.*

WILLIAM I ('THE CONQUEROR')

1027—87

When the famous William, 'the Conqueror' of England . . . had brought under his sway the farthest limits of the island, and had tamed the minds of the rebels by awful examples, to prevent error from having free course in fortune, he decided to bring the conquered people under the rule of written law. So, setting out before him the English Laws in their threefold versions, namely, Mercian law, Dane law and Wessex law, he repudiated some of them, approved others and added those Norman laws from overseas which seemed to him most effective in preserving the peace. Lastly, to give the finishing touch of all this forethought, after taking counsel he sent his most skilful councillors in circuit throughout the realm. By these a careful survey of the whole country was made, of its woods, its pastures and meadows, as well as of arable land, and was set down in common language and drawn up into a book; in order, that is, that every man may be content with his own rights, and not encroach unpunished on those of others.

Richard FitzNeal, attributed, *Dialogus Scaccario*, translated by Charles Johnson (on William's legislation and Domesday Book).

As far as mortal man can guide the course of things when he is gone, the course of our national history since William's day has been the result of William's character and of William's acts. Well may we restore to him the surname that men gave him in his own day. He may worthily take his place as William the Great alongside of Alexander, Constantine, and Charles.

E. A. Freeman, *William the Conqueror.*

William, indeed, seems to have been astute without wisdom, resolute without foresight, powerful without ultimate purpose, a man of very limited aims and very limited vision, narrow, ignorant and superstitious.

R. G. Richardson and G. O. Sayles, *The Governance of Mediaeval England.*

To receive the oath, he caused a parliament to be called. It is commonly said that it was in Bayeux that he had his great council assembled. He sent for all the holy bodies thither, and put so many of them together as to fill a whole chest, and then covered them with a pall; but Harold neither saw them, nor knew of their being there; for naught was shewn or told to him about it; and over all was a philactery, the best that he could select; OIL DE BOEF, as I have heard it called. When Harold placed his hand upon it, the hand trembled, and the flesh quivered; but he swore and promised upon his oath, to take Ele to wife, and to deliver up England to the duke: and thereunto to do all in his power, according to his might and wit, after the death of Edward, if he should live, so help him God and the holy relics there! Many cried 'God grant it!' and when Harold had kissed the saints, and had risen upon his feet, the duke led him to the chest, and made him stand near it; and took off the chest the pall that had covered it, and showed Harold upon what holy relics he had sworn: and he was sorely alarmed at the sight.

    Robert Wace, *Roman de Rou*, translated by
    Edgar Taylor (describing the ruse by which
    William tricked the future King Harold).

Seeing a large part of the hostile host pursuing his own troops, the prince thrust himself in front of those in flight, shouting at them and threatening them with his spear. Staying their retreat, he took off his helmet, and standing before them bareheaded, he cried: 'Look at me well. I am still alive and by the grace of God I shall yet prove victor. What is this madness which makes you fly, and what way is open for your retreat? You are allowing yourselves to be pursued and killed by men whom you could slaughter like cattle. You are throwing away victory and lasting glory, rushing into ruin and incurring lasting disgrace. And all for naught since by flight none of you can escape destruction.' With these words he restored their courage, and leaping to the front and wielding his death-dealing sword, he defied the enemy who merited death for their disloyalty to him their prince.

    William of Poitiers, *Life of William I*, translated
    by D. C. Douglas and G. W. Greenaway.

See also Edward I, Hereward the Wake, Odo of Bayeux

WILLIAM II

—d. 1100

There exists no proof as
To who shot William Rufus
But shooting him would seem
To have been quite a sound scheme.
    E. C. Bentley, *More Biography*.

Now when the King returned from across the sea, Anselm went to him, and humbly sought permission to go to Pope Urban at Rome for his archiepiscopal pallium. But the king flared up at the name of Urban, and said that he did not recognize him as pope, and that it was contrary to established usage to allow anyone in his kingdom to nominate a pope not of his choosing.

    Eadmer, *Life of St. Anselm*, translated by
    R. W. Southern.

Then was there flowing hair and extravagant dress; and then was invented the fashion of shoes with curved points; then the model for young men was to rival women in delicacy of person, to mince their gait, to walk with loose gesture, and half-naked. Enervated and effeminate, they unwillingly remained what nature had made them; the assailers of others' chastity, prodigal of their own. Troops of pathics and droves of harlots followed the court. . . .

    William of Malmesbury, describing William's
    court, in *Chronicle of the Kings of England*,
    translated by J. A. Giles.

A few countrymen conveyed the body, placed on a cart, to the cathedral at Winchester, the blood dripping from it all the way. Next year the tower fell; though I forebear to mention the different opinions on this subject, lest I should seem to assent too readily to unsupported trifles, more especially as the building might have fallen, through imperfect structure, even though he had never been buried there.

    Ibid.

See also Charles II, George II

WILLIAM III

1650—1702

There is one certain means by which I can be sure never to see my country's ruin: I will die in the last ditch.

    On himself, to the Duke of Buckingham,
    attributed.

What is the rhyme for porringer?
What is the rhyme for porringer?
The king he had a daughter fair
And gave the Prince of Orange her.
    Anon., Nursery Rhyme, traditional.

    For the case Sir is such
    The people think much
That your love is Italian, your government Dutch.
Ah! who could have thought that a low-country
                 stallion

And a Protestant Prince should prove an Italian.
    Anon., *circa* 1688.

King William thinks all
Queen Mary talks all
Prince George drinks all
And Princess Anne eats all.
    Anon., shortly after the Glorious Revolution of
    1688.

    He's ugly and crooked
    His nose it is hooked
The Devil to him is a beauty
    Nor father nor mother
    Nor sister nor brother
Can ever bring him to his duty.
    Anon., *circa* 1688.

A blockish damned Dutch mien, a hawkish beak,
With timorous eyes, who grunts when he should
                   speak.
Breathless and faint, he moves, or rather stumbles
Silent and dull he sits, and snorts or grumbles.
    Ibid.

He has gotten in part the shape of a man,
But more of a monkey, deny it who can;
He has the tread of a goose, and the legs of a swan,
    A dainty fine king indeed.
    Anon., *Coronation Ballad*, 1689.

Have you not seen on the stage come tell ho
A strutting thing called a Punchinello?
Of all things I know 'tis likest this fellow
    A dainty fine king indeed.
    Ibid.

He had a thin and weak Body, was brown haired, and of a clear and delicate Constitution: He had a *Roman* Eagle Nose, bright and sparkling Eyes, a large front, and a Countenance composed to gravity and authority: All his Senses were critical and exquisite. He was always asthmatical, and the dregs of the Small Pox falling on his Lungs, he had a constant deep Cough. His behaviour was solemn and serious, and commonly with a disgusting dryness, which was his Character at all times, except in a day of Battle: for then he was all fire, tho' without passion: He was then everywhere, and looked to every thing.
    Gilbert Burnet, *History of His Own Time.*

He had not a trace of that second sight of the battlefield which is the mark of military genius. He was no more than a resolute man of good common sense whom the accident of birth had carried to the conduct of war. It was in the sphere of politics that his inspiration lay. Perhaps he has never been surpassed in the sagacity, patience, and discretion of his statecraft. The combinations he made, the difficulties he surmounted, the adroitness with which he used the time factor, or played upon the weakness of others, the unerring sense of proportion and power of assigning to objectives their true priorities, all mark him for the highest fame.
    Winston Churchill, *Marlborough, His Life and Times.*

He would break a political opponent without pity, but he was never needlessly cruel, and was glad to treat foes no longer dangerous with contempt or indifference. He wasted no time on minor revenges. His sole vendetta was with Louis [XIV].
    Ibid.

Rejoice you sots, your idol's come again
To pick your pockets and kidnap your men.
Give him your moneys and his Dutch your lands
Ring not your bells ye fools, but wring your hands.
    Henry Hall, ascribed, *Upon the King's Return from Flanders.*

Hail happy William, thou art strangely great!
What is the cause, thy virtue, or thy fate?
For thee the child the parent's heart will sting;
For thee the Favorite will desert his King;
For thee the Patriot will subvert the laws;
For thee the Judge will still decide the cause;
For thee the Prelate will his church betray;
For thee the Soldier fights without his pay;
For thee the Freeman mortgages his hold;
For thee the Miser lavishes his gold;
For thee the Merchant loses all his store;
For thee the tradesman is content and poor;
For thee the sailor's pressed and starves on shore;
For thee the Senate our best laws suspend
And will make any new to serve thy end. . . .
And that this wonder may more wondrous seem
Thou never yet did'st one kind thing for them.
Rebels like witches, having signed the rolls
Must serve their Masters, though they damn their
                   souls.
    Henry Hall, or John Grubham Howe,
    A Panegyric.

His most illustrious antagonist, the great Condé, remarked, after the bloody day of Seneff, that the Prince of Orange had in all things borne himself like an old general, except in exposing himself like a young soldier.
    T. B. Macaulay, *History of England.*

He praised and reprimanded, rewarded and punished, with the stern tranquillity of a Mohawk chief.
    Ibid.

The feeling with which William regarded France explains the whole of his policy towards England. His public spirit was an European public spirit. The chief object of his care was not our island, not even his native Holland, but the great community of nations threatened with subjugation by one too powerful member.

Ibid.

He was in truth far better qualified to save a nation than to adorn a court. . . . He seldom came forth from his closet, and when he appeared in the public rooms, he stood among the crowd of courtiers and ladies, stern and abstracted, making no jest, and smiling at none. His freezing look, his silence, the dry and concise answers which he uttered when he could keep silence no longer, disgusted noblemen and gentlemen who had been accustomed to be slapped on the back by their royal masters. . . . He spoke our language, but not well. His accent was foreign: his diction was inelegant; and his vocabulary seems to have been no larger than was necessary for the transaction of business.

Ibid.

That character, almost devoid of the humanity and kindliness which we appreciate most of all in kings, seemed like a grim edifice or institution, divided into separate, independent compartments, connected by few corridors, and known to the world only from its cold, forbidding antechamber.

David Ogg, *England in the Reigns of James II and William III.*

He was the first English King who was a good European. The least forthcoming and the most inscrutable of monarchs, he nevertheless familiarized men with a new type of kingship, detached, dignified, and, in all impersonal matters, essentially just.

Ibid.

I do not doubt but King William came over with a view to the crown. Nor was he called upon by patriotism, for he was not an Englishman, to assert our liberties. No; his patriotism was of a higher rank. He aimed not at the crown of England for ambition, but to employ its forces and wealth against Louis XIV for the common cause of the liberties of Europe. The Whigs did not understand the extent of his views, and the Tories betrayed him. He has been thought not to have understood us; but the truth was he took either party as it was predominant, that he might sway the parliament to support his general plan.

Horace Walpole, Letter to William Mason, *circa* 1792.

See also George III

WILLIAM IV

1765–1837

Now, ladies and gentlemen, I wish you good-night. I will not detain you any longer from your amusements, and shall go to my own, which is to go to bed; so come along, my Queen.

On himself, to his guests at a party at St James's Palace, in Mary F. Sanders, *The Life and Times of Queen Adelaide.*

. . . he is an immense improvement on the last unforgiving animal [George IV]. This man at least *wishes* to make everybody happy. . . .

Emily Eden, Letter, August 1830.

Etiquette is a thing he cannot comprehend.

Charles Greville, Diary, 24 July 1830.

Of political dexterity and artifice he was altogether incapable, and although if he had been false, able, and artful, he might have caused more perplexity to his Whig Government and have played a better party game, it is perhaps fortunate for the Country, and certainly happy for his own reputation, that his virtues thus predominated over his talents.

Ibid., 25 June 1837.

They gave William IV a lovely funeral. It took six men to carry the beer.

Louis Untermeyer, *A Treasury of Laughter.*

See also Duke of Wellington.

WILLIAMS, JOHN

1582–1650 Archbishop of York

Most true it is, (as I am certainly informed from such as knew the privacies and casualties of his infancy), this Archbishop was but one degree removed from a misogynist, yet, to palliate his infirmity, to noble females he was most complete in his courtly addresses.

Thomas Fuller, *Church History of Britain.*

WILLIAMS, ROGER

circa 1603–83 Clergyman, Poet, Founder of Rhode Island

He was an eloquent preacher; stiff and self-confident in his opinions, ingenious, powerful and commanding in impressing them on others, inflexible in his adherence to them, and, by an inconsistency peculiar to religious enthusiasts, combining the most amiable and affectionate sympathies of the heart with the most repulsive and inexorable exclusion of conciliation, compliance, or intercourse with his adversaries in opinion.

John Quincy Adams, *Discourse on the New England Confederacy of 1643.*

Because of his unorthodox views, the Pilgrims branded him. They branded him as a heretic, and drove him from town to town, although he preferred to walk. This was why Roger Williams reluctantly left Plymouth and founded Rhode Island, which is not really an island and is so small that it is usually indicated on maps by the letters R.I. out in the Atlantic Ocean. It was once densely wooded. It is now densely populated.

Richard Armour, *It All Started With Columbus.*

He was the first person in modern Christianity to assert, in its plenitude, the doctrine of the liberty of conscience, the equality of opinions before the law; and in its defense he was the harbinger of Milton, the precursor and the superior of Jeremy Taylor.

George Bancroft, *History of the United States.*

Kind treatment could win him, but opposition could not conquer him.

William Bentley, *History of Salem.*

His teaching was well approved, for the benefit whereof I shall bless God, and am thankful to him even for his sharpest admonitions and reproofs, so far as they agreed with truth.

William Bradford, in William Sprague, *Annals of the American Pulpit.*

Differ and contend he must. For him a stagnant life was not worth living.

John G. Palfrey, *History of New England.*

A man of such discretion and inimitably sanctified parts, that an Archangel from heaven could not have shewn more goodness with less ostentation.

Sir Thomas Urquhart, 1653, in Samuel Brockunier, *The Irrepressible Democrat.*

WILLIAMS, WILLIAM CARLOS

1883—1963 Author, Physician

Whatever my life has been it has been single in purpose, single in design and constantly directed to the one end of discovery, if possible, of some purpose in being alive. . . . Poetry, an art, is what answer I have.

On himself, Letter to Norman Macleod, 1945.

I don't play golf, am not a joiner. I vote Democratic, read as much as my eyes will stand, and work at my trade day in and day out. When I can find nothing better to do, I write.

On himself, in Stanley J. Kunitz and Howard Haycraft eds., *Twentieth Century Authors.*

To the stuffy realism of the well-made novel Williams responds with the mockery and disarray of a kind of Dada novel. To a prefabricated form that he finds empty and rigid he answers with a comic flamboyance.

James E. Breslin, *William Carlos Williams.*

Poems, stories, letters show Williams worried about wasting his creative energies on the banal; and in such moods he imagined himself as a giant surrounded by smaller men, who were tearing at him savagely, drawing him down into the anonymous crowd.

Ibid.

The quest to which Williams addressed himself as early as 1912 is essentially the same as that to which his attention was turned five decades later: What is the measurable factor in language that will replace metrics as a basis for poetic composition?

John Malcolm Brinnin, 'William Carlos Williams', in Leonard Unger ed., *Seven Modern American Poets.*

Among the poets of his own illustrious generation, William Carlos Williams was the man on the margin, the incorrigible maverick, the embattled messiah.

Ibid.

I think he wouldn't make so much of the great American language if he were judicious about everything. And that is the beauty of it — he is willing to be reckless, and if you can't be that, what's the point of the whole thing?

Marianne Moore, in an interview with Donald Hall, in Charles Tomlinson ed., *Marianne Moore, A Collection of Critical Essays.*

. . . at any rate he has not in his ancestral endocrines the arid curse of our nation. None of his immediate forebears burnt witches in Salem, or attended assemblies for producing prohibitions.

Ezra Pound, in Noel Stock, *The Life of Ezra Pound.*

Williams' antagonism towards all things British, intensified by the expatriation of Pound and Eliot, was only a small part of his insistence on the use of America in American art. As a doctor, he was surrounded with the vernacular; sometimes crude, sometimes impassioned, but always real.

Linda Welshimer Wagner, *The Prose of William Carlos Williams*.

He avoids any suspicion of emotional heightening, and cultivates a flat, matter-of-fact, conversational tone, which might easily become intolerable if not combined with an extreme rapidity of pace and a startling succession of sensations.

George F. Whicher, 'The Twentieth Century', in Arthur Hobson Quinn ed., *The Literature of the American People*.

WILLKIE, WENDELL LEWIS

1892–1944 Lawyer, Politician

Trying to give Wilkie advice is just as effective as giving castor oil to the sphinx.

Anon., in Mary Earhart Dillon, *Wendell Willkie*.

. . . a master of timing releases, issuing denials before edition time, adding punch to a prepared speech, or making one on the spur of the moment letter-perfect enough to have been memorized, treating publishers, editors, and reporters with the skill needed to suggest to each that they were the sole beneficiaries of his gratitude and his confidence.

Anon. (1940), in James MacGregor Burns, *Roosevelt: The Lion and the Fox*.

. . . the barefoot boy of Wall Street had become the glamour boy of Hollywood.

Senator Rush D. Holt, in Mary Earhart Dillon, *Wendell Willkie*.

The rich man's Roosevelt; the simple, barefoot boy from Wall Street.

Harold L. Ickes, in Leon A. Harris, *The Fine Art of Political Wit*.

With him in the White House, the monied interests would be in full control and would expect the American brand of fascism as soon as he could set it up.

Harold L. Ickes, in Russell Clark and James McClellan, *The Political Principles of Robert A. Taft*.

He seemed to us like a man who had set out on a mule to defeat a German Panzer division, confident of his star, sure that he needed nothing more to rout the mechanized political forces against him. If it's an act, it's a good one.

Arthur Korck, *Memoirs*.

His part has been to save his country from an irreconcilable partisan division in the face of the most formidable enemies who were ever arrayed against all that America is and means. Historians will say . . . that second only to the Battle of Britain, the sudden rise and nomination of Willkie was the decisive event, perhaps providential, which made it possible to rally the free world when it was almost conquered. Under any other leadership but his the Republican party would in 1940 have turned its back upon Great Britain, causing all who still resisted Hitler to feel that they were abandoned.

Walter Lippmann, in Mary Earhart Dillon, *Wendell Willkie*.

A man wholly natural in manner, a man with no pose, no 'sweetness'; no condescension, no clever plausibleness . . . as American as the courtyard in the square of an Indiana county seat . . . a good, sturdy, plain, able Hoosier.

Booth Tarkington, in James MacGregor Burns, *Roosevelt: The Lion and the Fox*.

. . . a synthesis of Guffey's First Reader, the Genealogy of Indiana, the collected speeches of Tom Girdler and the New Republic. He agreed with Mr. Roosevelt's entire program of social reform and said it was leading to disaster.

Norman Thomas, in Joseph Barnes, *Willkie*.

He is simply a big, two-fisted, Middle Western American who happens to be at the same time a scholar and a gentleman. In any gathering he is about as anonymous and inconspicuous as a buffalo bull in a herd of range cattle.

Stanley Walker, *This is Wendell Willkie*.

See also John L. Lewis

WILMOT, JOHN, EARL OF ROCHESTER

1647–80 Poet, Libertine

Were I (who to my cost already am
One of those strange prodigious Creatures *Man*)
A Spirit free, to choose for my own share,
What Case of Flesh, and Blood, I pleas'd to weare,
I'd be a *Dog*, a *Monkey*, or a *Bear*.
Or any thing but that vain *Animal*,
Who is so proud of being rational.

On himself, *A Satyr Against Mankind*.

Talking of Rochester's Poems, he [Johnson] said, he had given them to Mr Steevens to castrate for the edition of the Poets for which he was to write Prefaces. Dr Taylor (the only time I ever heard him say any thing witty) observed, that 'if Rochester had

been castrated himself, his exceptionable poems would not have been written.' I asked if Burnet had not given a good Life of Rochester. *Johnson*: 'We have a good *Death*; there is not much *Life*.'
James Boswell, *Life of Johnson*.

I find it is not for me to contend any way with your Lordship, who can write better on the meanest subject than I can on the best.
John Dryden, Letter to Wilmot, 1673.

The sharpness of his satire, next to himself, falls most heavily on his friends, and they ought never to forgive him for commending them perpetually the wrong way, and sometimes by contraries,
John Dryden, Preface to *All for Love*.

The very name of Rochester is offensive to modest ears; yet does his poetry discover such energy of style and such poignancy of satire, as give ground to imagine what so fine a genius, had he fallen in a more happy age, and had followed better models, was capable of producing. The ancient satirists often used great liberty in their expressions; but their freedom no more resembles the licentiousness of Rochester than the nakedness of an Indian does that of a common prostitute.
David Hume, *History of England*.

As he cannot be supposed to have found leisure for any course of continued study, his pieces are commonly short, such as one fit of resolution would produce.
Samuel Johnson, *Lives of the Poets*.

His Sins were like his Parts, (for from them corrupted they sprang), all of them high and extraordinary. He seem'd to affect something singular and paradoxical in his Impieties, as well as in his Writings, above the reach and thought of other men. . . . For this was the heightening and amazing circumstance of his sins, that he was so diligent and industrious to recommend and propagate them. . . . Nay, so confirm'd was he in Sin, that he lived, and oftentimes almost died, a Martyr for it.
Robert Parsons, *A Sermon preached at the Earl of Rochester's Funeral*.

Here I saw my Lord Rochester and his lady, Mrs Mallet, who hath after all this ado, married him; and, as I hear some say in the pit, it is a great act of charity, for he hath no estate.
Samuel Pepys, Diary, 4 February 1667.

With no poetick ardors fir'd,
I press the bed where *Wilmot* lay;
That here he lov'd, or here expir'd,
Begets no numbers grave or gay.
Alexander Pope, *On Lying in the Earl of Rochester's Bed at Atterbury*.

Rail on, poor feeble scribbler, speak of me
In as ill terms as the world speaks of thee.
Sit swelling in thy hole like a vex'd toad,
And all thy pox and malice spit abroad
Thou canst blast no man's name by thy ill word;
Thy pen is full as harmless as thy sword.
Sir Car Scroope, *The Author's Reply*.

Mean in each action, lewd in every limb
Manners themselves are mischievous in him.
John Sheffield, Earl of Mulgrave, *An Essay on Satire*.

A Man whom the Muses were fond to inspire, and ashamed to avow.
Horace Walpole, *Catalogue of Royal and Noble Authors*.

Lord Rochester's poems have much more obscenity than wit, more wit than poetry, more poetry than politeness.
Ibid.

As Lord Rochester was immersed only in the vices of that reign, he was an innocent character compared to those who were plunged in its crimes.
Ibid.

The eager tendency and violent impulses of his natural temper, unhappily inclining him to the excesses of Pleasure and Mirth; which with the wonderful pleasantness of his unimitable humour, did so far engage the affections of the Dissolute towards him, that to make him delightfully ventrous and frollicksome to the utmost degree of riotous extravagancy, they for some years heightened his spirits (enflamed by wine) into one almost interrupted fit of wantonness and intemperance.
Anthony à Wood, *Athenae Oxonienses*.

See also Samuel Richardson

WILSON, EDMUND

1895—1972 Critic

. . . a vanishing type, the free man of letters.
Van Wyck Brooks, in Sherman Paul, *Edmund Wilson. A Study of Literary Vocation in Our Time*.

It is so damned easy for such as he, born into easy means, graduated from a fashionable university into a critical chair overlooking Washington Square, etc., to sit tight and hatch little squibs of advise to poets not to be so 'professional' as he claims they are, as though all the names he has just mentioned had been as suavely nourished as he. . . .

Hart Crane, Undated letter to Yvor Winters.

. . . the man in the iron necktie.

e. e. cummings, in Joseph Epstein, 'The Twenties', in *New York Times Book Review*, 15 June 1975.

Edmund Wilson embodied the idea of literature, not as some pastime or otherwise second-rate activity, but as a guide to life, a means of understanding the world, and a weapon for bringing order where chaos stood before.

Joseph Epstein, *ibid*.

The serious reader returns to Wilson for fresh air when the atmosphere of theoretical and academic critics either thins out or becomes stale.

Charles P. Frank, *Edmund Wilson*.

Wilson is not like other critics; some critics are boring even when they are original; he fascinates even when he is wrong.

Alfred Kazin, in Max J. Herzberg, *The Reader's Encyclopedia of American Literature*.

Above everything else, he was always the observing reader, the vibrant critical intelligence in whom everything joined toward dispassionate understanding.

Alfred Kazin, *On Native Grounds*.

By the catholicity of his interests, the freshness and directness of his performance, he seemed more than any other critic in America the experimentalist who worked with the whole tradition of literature in his bones.

Ibid.

A modernist and a scholar, he was the best example of the richness and exactitude that criticism in America had always missed in its modernist critics. In an age of fanaticisms and special skills, he stood out as the quiet arbiter, the private reader of patience and wisdom whose very skill gave him a public importance.

Ibid.

. . . quiet, reticent, and rather shy, his friends appropriately call him 'Bunny'!

Stanley J. Kunitz and Howard Haycroft eds, *Twentieth Century Authors*.

Literary critic, social reporter, travel writer, poet, playwright, short story writer, novelist, chronicler, and historian — he is our pre-eminent man of letters, perhaps the last of the great professionals, the genuine *littérateurs*.

Sherman Paul, *Edmund Wilson, A Study of Literary Vocation in Our Time*.

He was a master of the literary case or argument, marshalling his evidence with the cogency of a legal brief and pushing his point across in persuasive, common-sense prose.

Andrew Turnbull, *Scott Fitzgerald*.

WILSON, HARRIETTE

1789—1846 Courtesan

I shall not say why and how I became, at the age of fifteen, the mistress of the Earl of Craven. Whether it was love, or the severity of my father, or the winning arts of the noble lord, which induced me to leave my parental roof and place myself under his protection, does not now much signify; or, if it does, I am not in the humour to gratify curiosity in this matter.

On herself, *Memoirs*.

WILSON, RICHARD

1714—82 Painter

Poor Wilson! think of his fate, think of his magnificence. But the mind loses its dignity less in adversity than in prosperity. He is now walking arm in arm with Milton and Linnaeus. He was one of those appointed to show the world the hidden stores and beauties of nature.

John Constable, Letter to John Fisher, 9 May 1823.

His landscapes proclaim at once their classic calm, their mood of tranquil reverie; we are attracted at once by their wide spaces of sky, their distant sunlit clouds and the deep shade of their trees, but, alas! they do not hold up to their promise, and gradually as their emptiness of content, their merely scenic quality, make themselves felt the charm evaporates. They will not bear prolonged contemplation. One dreads to find out too clearly how the trick is done.

Roger Fry, *Reflections on British Painting*.

WILSON, (THOMAS) WOODROW

1856—1924 Twenty-Eighth United States President

He loved gay nonsense. He could play the fool enchantingly.
Anon., in S. B. McKinley, *Woodrow Wilson: A Biography.*

Here's to Woodrow, King Divine,
Who rules this place along with Fine
We hear he's soon to leave this town
To take on Teddy Roosevelt's crown.
Anon., Princeton students' song, *circa* 1908.

Mr. Wilson's name along the Allies is like that of the rich uncle, and they have accepted his manners out of respect for his means.
Anon., in *London Morning Post*, 1919, in Thomas A. Bailey, *Woodrow Wilson and the Lost Peace.*

An idealist, a philosopher, a moralist, a religionist, he was born; as someone has well said, halfway between the Bible and the dictionary, and he never lost his faith in the power of words.
Thomas A. Bailey, *Woodrow Wilson and the Peacemakers.*

He wore a sterilized, disinfected expression, yet he could suddenly confront a person or a camera with a momentary expression of almost lover-like understanding and affection.
William C. Bullitt, Introduction to William C. Bullitt and Sigmund Freud, *Thomas Woodrow Wilson: Twenty-eighth President of the United States — A Psychological Study.*

Mr. Wilson bores me with his Fourteen Points; why God Almighty has only ten.
Georges Clemenceau, in *The American Heritage Pictorial History of the Presidents.*

Lloyd George believes himself to be Napoleon but President Wilson believes himself to be Jesus Christ.
Georges Clemenceau, in Thomas A. Bailey, *Woodrow Wilson and the Lost Peace.*

How can I talk to a fellow who thinks himself the first man in two thousand years to know anything about peace on earth?
Ibid.

They say Wilson has blundered. Perhaps he has, but I notice he usually blunders forward.
Josephus Daniels, in S. B. McKinley, *Woodrow Wilson: A Biography.*

When he stepped from his lofty pedestal and wrangled with the representatives of other states upon equal terms, he became as common as clay.
Colonel Edward House, 29 June 1919, in Thomas A. Bailey, *Woodrow Wilson and the Lost Peace.*

Like Odysseus, he looked wiser when seated.
John Maynard Keynes, in Robert L. Heilbroner, *The Worldly Philosophers.*

A man can change one or two of his opinions for his own advantage and change them perfectly honestly, but when a man changes all the well considered opinions of a lifetime and changes them all at once for his own popular advantage it seems to me that he must lack in loyalty of conviction.
Henry Cabot Lodge, in John A. Garraty, *Henry Cabot Lodge.*

William Allen White had a Kansan's suspicion of anyone with a handshake 'like a ten-cent pickled mackerel in brown paper.'
Walter Lord, *The Good Years* (the reference is to Woodrow Wilson).

The University president who cashiered every professor unwilling to support Woodrow Wilson for the first vacancy in the Trinity.
H. L. Mencken, 'Star Spangled Men', in *New Republic*, 29 September 1920.

The air currents of the world never ventilated his mind.
Walter Hines Page, April 1917, in Patrick Devlin, *Too Proud to Fight: Woodrow Wilson's Neutrality.*

Byzantine logothete.
Theodore Roosevelt, in D. H. Elletson, *Roosevelt and Wilson: A Comparative Study.*

I feel certain that he would not recognize a generous impulse if he met it on the street.
William Howard Taft, in Alpheus Thomas Mason, *William Howard Taft.*

See also Franklin D. Roosevelt

WINCHELL, WALTER

1897—1972 Journalist

If only when my epitaph is readied, they will say, 'Here is Walter Winchell — with his ear to ground — as usual.'
On himself in Ed Weiner, *Let's Go To Press.*

At the start, I'm tense as a race horse at the barrier. I lose my breath, and then I'm off, selling the news as hard as a corner newsboy yelling, 'EXTRA'.
Ibid.

When you are in the brick-throwing racket, you must expect to get hit with one occasionally. My greatest thrill has been surviving my imitators.
Ibid.

I don't see why Walter Winchell is allowed to live.
Ethel Barrymore, in Bob Thomas, *Winchell.*

He is more like some freak of climate — a tornado, say, or an electric storm that is heard whistling and roaring far away, against which everybody braces himself; and then it strikes and does its whirling damage.
Alistair Cooke, 'Walter Winchell: "an American Myth" ', in *Listener*, 20 November 1947.

The three of us are all in the same business — libel — but Winchell seems to know where to stop.
H. L. Mencken, to George Jean Nathan, in Bob Thomas, *Winchell.*

Poor Walter. He's afraid he'll wake up some day and discover he's not Walter Winchell.
Dorothy Parker, in *ibid.*

Walter Winchell suffers from a chronic state of wild excitement, venom and perpetual motion of the jaw.
Eleanor Patterson, in Ed Weiner, *Let's Go To Press.*

Walter and I made the ideal companions, He loved to talk, and I couldn't do anything but listen.
Damon Runyon, in Bod Thomas, *Winchell.*

This is a dangerously ill-informed man who, in his tremendous egotism, who, with this great power, un-accompanied by greatness or nobility of thinking, is uttering sage opinions on what we should do....
Ed Sullivan, in *ibid.*

I suppose it would be easy to assemble evidence in support of the contention that Winchell is lacking in taste. He has a more valuable asset. For want of a better term, let us call it zest.
Alexander Woollcott, in *ibid.*

WINSTANLEY, GERRARD

fl. 1648—52 Leveller, Digger

Sometimes my heart hath been full of deadness and uncomfortableness, wading like a man in the dark and slabby weather; and within a little time I have been filled with such peace, light, life and fulness, that if I had two pairs of hands, I had matter enough revealed to have kept them writing a long time.
On himself, Preface to *Several Pieces Gathered into One Volume*

Being a friend to love wading through the bondage of the world.
On himself, Dedication to *Fire in the Bush.*

WINTHROP, JOHN

1588—1649 First Governor of Massachusetts Bay

The Father of New England.
Cotton Mather, in Henry J. Cowell, *John Winthrop, A Seventeenth Century Puritan Romance.*

WISE, STEPHEN SAMUEL

1874—1949 Rabbi

I am a Jew who is an American. I was a Jew before I was an American. I have been an American all my life, 64 years, but I've been a Jew for 4,000 years.
On himself, 'Jew in America', in *Time*, 20 June 1938.

The only rabbi born on St. Patrick's Day.
On himself, 'St. Patrick's Day Rabbi', in *Newsweek*, 25 March 1940.

I would rather think of my religion as a gamble than to think of it as an insurance policy.
On himself, attributed.

A man of vast and varied misinformation.
William Gaynor, in A. K. Adams, *The Home Book of Humorous Quotations.*

WISTER, OWEN

1860—1938 Author

To the fundamental doctrine of economy of means he shows blithe indifferences; in his long stories and his shorter ones alike, he refuses to trim his hedges or to prune back his vines, preferring to let them luxuriate, weed-like, in whatsoever direction they list.
Frederick Taber Cooper, *Some American Story Tellers.*

You have an air tight cinch on the West — others may monkey but you arrived with a horrible crash every pop.
Frederic Remington, in N. Orwin Rush, *Frederic Remington and Owen Wister, The Story of a Friendship, 1893—1909.*

WITHERS, GEORGE

1588—1667 Poet, Pamphleteer

To Him-selfe G. W. wisheth all happiness.
On himself, *Dedication of Abuses Stript and Whipt.*

Withers seems to have contemplated to a degree of idolatry his own possible virtue. He is for ever anticipating persecution and martyrdom; fingering, as it were, the flames, to try how he can bear them.
Charles Lamb, *On the Poetical Works of George Wither.*

Worthy Withers.
Alexander Pope, *Dunciad*, Book I.

Wither's motto. *Nec habeo, nec careo, nec curo.* Nor have I, nor want I, nor care I.
Anthony à Wood, *Athenae Oxonienses.*

This our Author . . . sided with the Presb. in the beginning of the Civil Wars rais'd by them, *an.* 1642, became an Enemy to the King and Regality, sold the Estate he had, and with the Moneys received for it rais'd a Troop of Horse for the Parliament, was made a Captain and soon after a Major, having this motto on his Colours, *Pro Rege, Lege, Grege*: but being taken Prisoner by the Cavaliers, Sir *Jo. Denham* the Poet (some of whose land at *Egham* in *Surry Wither* had got into his clutches) desired his Majesty not to hang him, *because that so long as* Wither *lived*, Denham *would not be accounted the worst Poet in* England.
Ibid.

WITTGENSTEIN, LUDWIG JOSEF JOHANN

1889—1951 Philosopher

. . . Wittgenstein, picking up a poker to emphasize a point, asked: 'Give me an example of a moral rule.' [Karl] Popper replied with: 'Not to threaten visiting lecturers with pokers.' Whereupon, Popper has written, 'Wittgenstein, in a rage, threw the poker down and stormed out of the room, banging the door behind him.' But not, according to some accounts, before Russell had pulled himself up in

his chair and roared out: 'Wittgenstein, it is you who is creating all the confusion.'
Ronald W. Clark, describing a philosophical meeting at Cambridge in 1946, in *The Life of Bertrand Russell.*

The fundamental thing about human languages is that they can and should be used to describe something; and this something is, somehow, the world. To be constantly and almost exclusively interested in the medium — in spectacle-cleaning — is a result of a philosophical mistake. This philosophical mistake can quite easily be traced in Wittgenstein.
Karl Popper, in Bryan Magee, *Modern British Philosophy.*

My German engineer, I think is a fool. He thinks nothing empirical is knowable — I asked him to admit that there was not a rhinoceros in the room, but he wouldn't.
Bertrand Russell, Letter to Lady Ottoline Morrell, November 1911.

You know the best remark [G. E.] Moore ever made? I asked him one time who his best pupil was, and he said, 'Wittgenstein'. I said, 'Why?' 'Because, Bertrand, he is my only pupil who always looks puzzled'.
Bertrand Russell, in Ved Mehta, *Fly and the Fly-Bottle.*

WODEHOUSE, SIR PELHAM GRENVILLE

1881—1975 Writer

One great advantage in being historian to a man like Jeeves is that his mere personality prevents one selling one's artistic soul for gold. In recent years I have had lucrative offers for his services from theatrical managers, motion-picture magnates, the proprietors of one or two widely advertised commodities, and even the editor of the comic supplement of an American newspaper, who wanted him for a 'comic strip'. But, tempting though the terms were, it only needed Jeeves' deprecating cough and his murmured 'I would scarcely advocate it, sir,' to put the jack under my better nature.
On himself, Introduction to *Jeeves Omnibus.*

With Sean O'Casey's statement that I am 'English literature's performing flea', I scarcely know how to deal. Thinking it over, I believe he meant to be complimentary, for all the performing fleas I have met have impressed me with their sterling artistry and that indefinable something which makes the good trouper.
On himself, *Performing Flea.*

The end of writing is the production in the reader's mind of a certain image and a certain emotion. And the means towards that end are the use of words in any particular language; and the complete use of that medium is the choosing of the right words and the putting of them in the right order. It is *this* which Mr Wodehouse does better, in the English language, than anyone else alive; or at any rate than anyone else whom I have read for many years past.

Hilaire Belloc, Introduction to *Week-end Wodehouse*.

He is, I believe, the only man living who speaks with equal fluency the American and English languages.

Max Eastman, *Enjoyment of Laughter*.

If my analysis of Wodehouse's mentality is accepted, the idea that in 1941 he consciously aided the Nazi propaganda machine becomes untenable and even ridiculous. . . . His moral outlook has remained that of a public-school boy, and according to the public-school code, treachery in time of war is the most unforgivable of all sins. But how could he fail to grasp that what he did would be a big propaganda score for the Germans and would bring a torrent of disapproval on his head? To answer this one must take . . . into consideration . . . Wodehouse's complete lack — so far as one can judge from his printed works — of political awareness. It is nonsense to talk of 'Fascist tendencies' in his books. There are no post-1918 tendencies at all.

George Orwell, *In Defence of P. G. Wodehouse*.

It was in the Edwardian epoch that he began to develop the style which has made him a national institution. But his stories use ancient devices of comedy. Some of his comic routines are as old as Aristophanes. Jeeves, like Sherlock Holmes, now belongs to folk-lore. He derives ultimately from the clever slaves of ancient literature.

W. W. Robson, *Modern English Literature*.

I confess I find myself slightly shocked when anybody admits to not liking Wodehouse, although I can see that this is an unreasonable reaction. But I think I can be dogmatic on a few points from my own observation; that Wodehouse has been more read than any other English novelist by his fellow novelists; that nobody with any genuine feeling for the English language has failed to recognise at least an element of truth in Belloc's judgment of 1934, that Wodehouse was 'the best writer of English now alive, the head of my profession'; that the failure of academic literary criticism to take any account of Wodehouse's supreme mastery of the English language or the profound influence he has had on every worth-while English novelist in the

past 50 years demonstrates in better and conciser form than anything else how the Eng. Lit. industry is divorced from the subject it claims to study.

Auberon Waugh, in *New Statesman*, 21 February 1975.

WOFFINGTON, MARGARET (PEG)

circa 1714—60 Actress

This agreable Actress in the Part of Sir *Harry* coming into the Greenroom said pleasantly, *In my Conscience, I believe half the Men in the House take me for one of their own Sex.* Another Actress reply'd, *It may be so, but in my Conscience! the other half can convince them to the Contrary.*

W. R. Chetwood, *A General History of the Stage*.

WOLFE, JAMES

1727—59 Soldier

> Wolfe, where'er he fought,
> Put so much of his heart into his act
> That his example had a magnet's force,
> And all were swift to follow whom all loved.
> William Cowper, *The Task*, book 2.

Mad, is he? then I hope he will *bite* some of my other generals.

George II, in Beckles Wilson, *Life and Letters of James Wolfe*.

> The sons of earth, the proud giants of old,
>   Have broke from their darksome abodes;
> And such is the news, that in heaven 'tis told,
>   They're marching to war with the gods.
> A council was held in the chamber of Jove,
>   And this was the final decree,
> That Wolfe should be call'd to the armies above,
>   And the charge was intrusted to me.

> To the plains of Quebec with the orders I flew,
>   He begg'd for a moment's delay;
> And cried, O forbear! Let me victory hear,
>   And then the command I'll obey.
> With a darkening film I encompass'd his eyes,
>   And convey'd him away in an urn,
> Lest the fondness he bore for his own native shore,
>   Should tempt him again to return.
> Thomas Paine, 'Death of General Wolfe', in *Pennsylvania Magazine*, March 1775.

What he accomplished was done in the years when the ordinary mortal is learning his business; he was to war what William Pitt, the son of the great commoner who sent him to Quebec, was later to politics, what Keats was to literature.

Edward Salmon, *General Wolfe.*

WOLFE, THOMAS CLAYTON

1900—38 Author

I will go everywhere and do everything. I will meet all the people I can. I will think all the thoughts, feel all the emotions I am able, and I will write, write, write.

On himself, in Malcolm Cowley, *A Second Flowering.*

His writing was a sort of chant, like the declamations of a Homeric bard.

Malcolm Cowley, *ibid.*

His persistent immaturity — still another fault that is often urged against him — was not so much a weakness of character as it was a feature of his literary policy. He had to play the part of an innocent in the great world. He had to have illusions, then lose them painfully, then replace them with others, because that repeated process was the story he wanted to tell.

Ibid.

Wolfe was never at home in those other languages that most persons employ in most of their intimate relations: the language of gestures, the language of hints and indirections. He was completely articulate only when he had a pencil in his long fingers, but then he was more at home than anyone else who has lived on this continent.

Ibid.

Tom's genius is gigantic, tremendous, immense in its prolific scope but he'll have to learn to cut down, choose, condense.

F. Scott Fitzgerald, in Andrew Turnbull, *Scott Fitzgerald.*

His end was so tragic that I am glad I knew him in carefree and fortunate times. He had that flair for the extravagant and fantastic which has been an American characteristic from Irving and Poe to Dashiell Hammett.

F. Scott Fitzgerald, 'My Generation', in Matthew J. Bruccoli ed., *Profile of F. Scott Fitzgerald.*

Naive, self-absorbed, full of homespun mysticism and adolescent grandeur, he cut his way blindly and noisily to achievement; by his passionate insistence on the importance of self, that self is the very center

of existence, he gave his fever and uncertainty a remarkable scope and something more than the dignity of the conventionally mature understanding.

Alfred Kazin, *On Native Grounds.*

He thought of himself as writing the last great epic of American nationality, certainly the last great American romance, as he perhaps did; but the epic was a personal quarrel, and the romance a vast inchoate yearning to the end.

Ibid.

He wrote one book all his life, as all the volumes he produced were chapters in it. . . .

Ibid.

He lived in a world in which man was forever haunted by his own promise and deflected from it.

Ibid.

His work and career, as they are now concluded, must stand as a classic example of creative activity motivated, shaped and limited by a singularly dramatic pattern of misevaluations.

Martin Maloney, 'A Study of Semantic States', in Leslie A. Field, Thomas Wolfe, *Three Decades of Criticism.*

The merits of Wolfe's work are probably more apparent at a first reading; its defects emerge with overpowering insistence on subsequent reflection and further acquaintance. It is hardly likely that the four unwieldy novels can long survive in a world which has proved itself too difficult for dinosaurs.

George F. Whicher, 'The Twentieth Century', in Arthur Hobson Quinn ed., *The Literature of the American People.*

WOLLSTONECRAFT, MARY (MARY GODWIN)

1759—97 Advocate of Women's Rights

I know what you are thinking of, but I have nothing to communicate on the subject of religion.

On herself, attributed last words, spoken to her husband.

In all probability had she been married well in early life, she had then been a happy woman and universally respected.

Anon., in *Monthly Visitor*, February 1798.

Her works will be read with disgust by every female who has any pretensions to delicacy; with detestation by everyone attached to the interests of religion and morality, and with indignation by anyone who might feel any regard for the unhappy

woman, whose frailties should have been buried in oblivion.
    Anon., in *Historical Magazine*, 1799.

Whilom this dame the Rights of Women writ,
    That is the title to the book she places,
Exhorting bashful womankind to quit
    All foolish modesty and coy grimaces,
And name their backsides as it were their faces;
    Such licence loose-tongued liberty adores,
Which adds to female speech exceeding graces;
    Lucky the maid that on her volume pores,
    A scripture archly fram'd for propagating whores.
    Anon., in the *Anti-Jacobin*, vol. 9, 1801.

For Mary verily would wear the breeches
God help poor silly men from such usurping b---s.
    Ibid.

Be happy. Resolve to be happy. You deserve to be so. Every thing that interferes with it, is weakness & wandering; & a woman, like you can, must, shall, shake it off. Afford, for instance, no food for the morbid madness, & no triumph to the misanthropical gloom, of your afternoon visitor. Call up, with firmness, the energies which I am sure you so eminently possess.
    William Godwin, Letter to Mary Wollstonecraft, 17 August 1796.

The strength of her mind lay in intuition. She was often right, by this means alone, in matters of mere speculation. Yet though perhaps in the strict sense of the term, she reasoned little, it is surprising what a degree of soundness is to be found in her determination. But if this quality was of use to her in topics that seem the proper province of reasoning, it was much more so in matters directly appealing to the intellectual taste. In a robust and unwavering judgement of this sort, there is a kind of witch-craft.
    William Godwin, *Memoirs of the author of a Vindication of the Rights of Women*.

Fierce passion's slave, she veer'd with every gust,
Love, Rights, and Wrongs, Philosophy, and Lust.
    T. J. Mathias, *The Shade of Alexander Pope on the Banks of the Thames*.

She devoted herself to the relief of her suffering fellow-beings with the ardour of a Saint Vincent de Paul, and in return she was considered by them a moral scourge of God. Because she had the courage to express opinions new to her generation, and the independence to live according to her own standard

of right and wrong, she was denounced as another Messalina.
    Elizabeth Robins Pennell, *Mary Wollstonecraft Godwin*.

See Wollstonecraft, whom no decorum checks,
Arise, the intrepid champion of her sex;
O'er humbled man assert the sovereign claim,
And slight the timid blush of virgin fame.
'Go, go, (she cries) ye tribes of melting maids,
Go, screen your softness in sequestered shades;
With plaintive whispers woo the unconscious grove,
And feebly perish, as despis'd ye love.
What tho' the fine Romances of Rousseau
Bid the frame flutter, and the bosom glow; ...
Soon shall the sex disdain the illusive sway,
And wield the sceptre in yon blaze of day; ...
Surpass their rivals in the powers of mind
And vindicate the *Rights of Womankind*.
    Richard Polwhele, *The Unsex'd Females*.

Hard was thy fate in all the scenes of life,
As daughter, sister, mother, friend, and wife;
But harder still thy fate in death we own,
Thus mourned by Godwin with a heart of stone.
    William Roscoe, in Elizabeth Robins Pennell, *Mary Wollstonecraft Godwin*.

A philosophizing serpent ... that hyena in petticoats.
    Horace Walpole, *Letters*.

Among the writers whose extravagant doctrines have not only been published in this country, but circulated with uncommon avidity, loaded with extravagant praise and insinuated into every recess, the name of Mary Wollstonecraft has obtained a lamentable distinction.
    Jane West, *Letters to a Young Man*.

Mary Wollstonecraft was a new sort of woman, the first of the moderns: she is still a modern woman: at moments I echo her impatient cry, 'Women are certainly great fools: but nature made them so,' and say that she is a woman of the future. Hannah More, Elizabeth Fry, Mrs Barbauld, Harriet Martineau all carry their dates and belong to their period; we admire and sometimes smile: Mary Wollstonecraft insists upon a more intimate reception.
    Mona Wilson, 'Mary Wollstonecraft', in Bonamy Dobrée ed., *Anne to Victoria*.

Many millions have died and been forgotten in the hundred and thirty years that have passed since she was buried; and yet as we read her letters and listen to her arguments and consider her experiments, above all, that most fruitful experiment, her relation with Godwin, and realize the high-handed and hot-blooded manner in which she cut her way to the quick of life, one form of immortality is hers undoubtedly: she is alive and active, she argues and experiments, we hear her voice and trace her influence even now among the living.

Virginia Woolf, *Essays:* 'Mary Wollstonecraft Godwin'.

See also Mary Shelley

WOLSEY, THOMAS, CARDINAL

1475?—1530 Archbishop, Statesman

Had I but served God as diligently as I have served the King, he would not have given me over in my gray hairs.

On himself, addressed to Sir William Kingston.

Little Boy Blue,
　Come blow your horn,
The sheep's in the meadow,
　The cow's in the corn;
But where is the boy
　Who looks after the sheep?
He's under a haycock,
　Fast asleep.
Will you wake him?
　No, not I,
For if I do,
　He's sure to cry.
Nursery Rhyme, traditionally taken to refer to Wolsey.

Item, that he, having the French pox, presumed to come and breathe on the king.
The Articles of Parliament Against Wolsey, 1529.

Thomas Wolsey, Cardinal, was a butcher's son, of Ipswych, in Suffolke. He was a fellowe of Magdalen Colledge in Oxford, where he was tutor to a young gentleman of Limmington, near Ilchester, *in com.* Somerset, in whose guift the presentation of that church is, worth the better part of 200 *li. per annum*, which he gave to his tutor, Wolsey. He had committed hereabout some debauchery (I thinke, drunke: no doubt he was of a high rough spirit), and spake derogatorily of Sir Amias Paulet (a Justice of Peace in the neighbourhood) who putt him into the stockes . . . which, when he came to be Cardinall, he did not forget; he layed a fine upon Sir Amias to build the gate of the Middle Temple. . . .

John Aubrey, *Brief Lives*.

The King was young and lusty, disposed all to mirth and pleasure and to follow his desire and appetite, nothing minding to travail in the busy affairs of this realm. The which the almosyner perceived very well; took upon him therefore to disburden the King of so weighty a charge and troublesome business, putting the King in comfort that he shall not need to spare any time of his pleasure for any business that should necessary happen in the council, as long as he, being there, having the King's authority and commandment, doubted not to see all things sufficiently furnished and perfected.

George Cavendish, *The Life and Death of Cardinal Wolsey*.

The once proud Cardinal was soon further disgraced, and wrote the most abject letters to his vile sovereign; who humbled him one day and encouraged him the next, according to his humour, until he was at last ordered to go and reside in his diocese of York. He said he was too poor; but I don't know how he made that out, for he took a hundred and sixty servants with him, and seventy-two cartloads of furniture, food, and wine.

Charles Dickens, *A Child's History of England*.

King Henry took just offence that the cardinal set his own arms above the king's on the gatehouse, at the entrance into the college. This was no verbal but a real *ego et rex meus*, excusable by no plea in manners or grammar; except only that, (which is rather fault than figure), a harsh down-right hysterosis. But, to humble the cardinal's pride, some afterwards set up, on a window, a painted mastiff-dog, gnawing the spadebone of a shoulder of mutton, to mind the cardinal of his extraction, being the son of a butcher; it being utterly improbable, (that some have fancied), that that picture was placed there by the cardinal's own appointment, to be to him a monitor of humility.

Thomas Fuller, *Church History of Britain*.

Their heads will catch cold who wait bare for a dead pope's triple crown. Wolsey may be an instance hereof, who, on every avoidance of St. Peter's chair, was sitting down therein, when suddenly someone or other clapt in before him!

Ibid.

In full-blown dignity, see Wolsey stand,
Law in his voice, and fortune in his hand:
To him the church, the realm, their pow'rs consign,
Thro' him the rays of regal bounty shine,
Turn'd by his nod the stream of honour flows,
His smile alone security bestows,
Still to new heights his restless wishes tow'r,
Claim leads to claim, and pow'r advances pow'r;
Till conquest unresisted ceas'd to please,

And rights submitted left him none to seize.
    Samuel Johnson, *Vanity of Human Wishes*.

Wolsey: I have ventur'd
Like little wanton boys that swim on bladders,
This many summers in a sea of glory,
But far beyond my depth; my high-blown pride
At length broke under me, and now has left me
Weary and old with service, to the mercy
Of a rude stream, that must for ever hide me.
    William Shakespeare, Henry VIII, Act III,
    Scene ii.

Katharine: he was a man
Of an unbounded stomach, ever ranking
Himself with princes; one that by suggestion
Tied all the kingdom; simony was fair play:
His own opinion was his law: i' the presence
He would say untruths, and be ever double
Both in his words and meaning. He was never,
(But where he meant to ruin) pitiful:
His promises were, as he then was, mighty,
But his performances, as he is now, nothing:
Of his own body he was ill, and gave
The clergy ill example.
    Ibid., Act IV, Scene ii.

Griffith:
He was a scholar, and a ripe and good one;
Exceeding wise, fair-spoken, and persuading;
Lofty and sour to them that lov'd him not,
But to those men that sought him sweet as summer.
    Ibid.

See also First Duke of Buckingham, William Laud,
Lord Melbourne, Richard Neville

WOOD, ANTHONY (À)

1632—95 Antiquary, Historian

He is so great an Admirer of a solitary and retired
Life, that he frequents no Assemblies of the said
University, hath no Companion in Bed or at Board,
in his Studies, Walks, or Journies, nor holds Communication with any, unless with some, and those
very few, of generous and noble spirits, that have in
some measure been Promoters and Encouragers of
the Work: and indeed all things considered he is but
a degree different from an Ascetick, as spending all
or most of his time, whether by Day or Night, in
Reading, Writing, and Divine Contemplation.
    On himself, in Oliver Lawson Dick ed., *Aubrey's
    Brief Lives*.

Merton Wood, with his Antiquitie,
Will live to all Eternitie.
    Anon., contemporary.

A little silly fellow who hath an ill designe to libell
honest men.
    Gilbert Burnet, remark reported to Wood, and
    noted in his *Life and Times*.

Just as naturally as a cuttle fish ejects poisonous
ink, so did Mr Wood eject spite.
    Llewellyn Powys ed., *Life and Times of Anthony
    à Wood*.

His indefatigable industry was so high, that through
earnestness he would burst out of bleeding suddenly, insomuch that he had a bason frequently
held under him that he might not spoil his papers.
    Richard Rawlinson, *Memoranda Relating to
    Wood*.

WOOD, EDWARD FREDERICK LINDLEY, EARL OF HALIFAX

1881—1959 Statesman

I have had enough obloquy for one life-time.
    On himself, 1938, on his vice-regal period, in
    A. J. P. Taylor, *English History 1914—1945*.

He is a typical example of a 'safeguarded' member
of the Conservative party. He was brought up with
a silver spoon in his mouth, and he has led a sheltered life. Bad speeches by him are praised as masterpieces of oratory; good speeches are looked upon as
unprecedented in history. . . . Honourable and trust-
worthy, his word can be relied upon, and his promises are always performed. He leads a splendid private
life . . . believing in a big God with long boots. . . .
Such a man, if he stumbles on the right course, will
do it through God's grace and not on account of
any worldly wisdom.
    Lord Beaverbrook, Letter to Arthur Brisbane,
    28 May 1930.

. . . he always appears a sort of Jesus in long boots.
The long boots are needed because he has had to
wade through the mud. But he was not responsible
for the mud, oh, dear no! Edward Wood could never
make anything so dirty as mud, and the last thing
he would think of, would be to throw it at others.
    Ibid.

He fascinates and bamboozles everyone. Is he saint
turning worldling, or worldling turned saint?
    Henry Channon, Diary, 16 February 1939.

It appears that during the Halifax reign in India
someone asked 'What is the Viceroy thinking?' and
the answer was 'Whom did he see last?'
    Ibid., 24 May 1939.

WOOD, GRANT

1892—1942 Artist

I suddenly realized that all the good ideas I ever had came to me while I was milking a cow.
On himself, in Darrell Garwood, *Artist in Iowa.*

Grant Wood is a quiet, friendly sort. When you meet him, you instinctively know that he belongs in that charmed category of persons who can't help being good natured. He is of medium height and plump — no signs of American Gothic here. He has a pug nose, sensitive and friendly like a rabbit's. Light russet would probably describe the color of his hair, although he himself insists that it is 'pink'. Smack in the middle of his square and essentially stubborn chin is an amazing cleft. In his feckless youth, he raised a spectacular patch of pink whiskers and a picture of him taken in this period reveals that the cleft parted the whiskers in the middle, giving somewhat the same effect as an open-face peanut butter sandwich. A very self-contained sort of person he is, with droll blue eyes behind unrimmed glasses, a low, soft voice, and a Buddha-like little smile.
Park Rinard and Arnold Pyle, *Grant Wood.*

Grant Wood came back to America, his new technique in hand, determined that American artists should paint not just America but that one locality in America that they knew best. This was the philosophy of Regionalism.
Margaret Thomas, *The Art of Grant Wood.*

WOOD, SIR HENRY JOSEPH

1869—1944 Conductor

A hundred seasons may elapse
Ere timber reach its prime.
Small wonder, then, we hope our Wood
Will go on beating time.
Anon., heard at the Savage Club, 1944.

It would not be true to say that Henry Wood . . . ever really walked on to a concert platform. His progress was more in the nature of an eager little trot, rather as though he were anxious that his reputation for punctuality should not be marred. . . .
Leslie Ayre, *The Proms.*

Wood was a great one for precise pitch and every player had to file past him and satisfy him that his instrument was in tune. For this purpose he first used an electric tuning-fork but, finding that it did not go on sounding long enough for his purpose, he devised another piece of apparatus, worked by a handle, on the principle of an organ-pipe. It had a small wind-chest containing three sets of bellows, each of which relieved the next as they successively ran out of breath. It remained absolutely in tune for years.
The players hated it.
Ibid.

No one could have called him a great conductor: but he carried 'usefulness' to the point of genius.
Victor Gollancz, *Journey Towards Music.*

He has been burning the candle at both ends & in the middle too & now he is a wreck.
A. J. Jaeger, Letter to Edward Elgar, 16 October 1902.

It was generous-minded Sir Henry Wood who first started mixed bathing in the sea of music.
Dame Ethel Smyth, *An Open Secret.*

I cannot imagine a situation in which he would fail to hit on the one kindly thing that can be said without verging on humbug. Once I remarked: 'What amazes me is the way you contrive to turn on the warm tap if it is humanly possible.'
'Well you don't want people to *catch cold*, do you?'
Dame Ethel Smyth, *A Final Burning of Boats.*

His self-confidence was wonderful — completely sure of himself, but in a humble rather than a cocksure way. Even in the war days, you would not hear him grumble about bad playing or indiscipline. It would just be, 'Poor darlings. They're all worried'.
Lady Jessie Wood, in Leslie Ayre, *The Proms.*

WOOLF, LEONARD SIDNEY

1880—1969 Author

I don't think he is an 'idiot', rather a perverse, partially-educated alien German, who has thrown in his lot violently with Bolshevism and Mr Joyce's 'Ulysses' and 'the great sexual emancipation' and all the rest of the nasty fads of the hour. It is no use for us to strive with such a man.
Edmund Gosse, Letter to Sidney Colvin, 1924.

There's a story that a week or two before the engagement he proposed in a train, and she accepted him, but owing to the rattling of the carriage he didn't hear, and took up a newspaper, saying 'What?' On which she had a violent revulsion and replied 'Oh, nothing!'
Lytton Strachey, Letter to Lady Ottoline Morrell, 12 June 1912.

WOOLF, (ADELINE) VIRGINIA

1882—1941 Novelist

People, like Arnold Bennett, say I can't create, or didn't in *Jacob's Room*, characters that survive. My answer is — but I leave that to the *Nation*: it's only the old argument that character is dissipated into shreds now; the old post-Dostoievsky arguments. I daresay it's true, however, that I haven't that 'reality' gift. I insubstantise, wilfully to some extent, distrusting reality - its cheapness.

On herself, *A Writer's Diary*, 19 June 1923.

I do not know how Virginia Woolf is thought of by the younger literary generation; I do know that by my own, even in the palmiest days of social consciousness, she was admired and loved much more than she realized. I do not know if she is going to exert an influence on the future development of the novel — I rather suspect that her style and her vision were so unique that influence would only result in tame imitation — but I cannot imagine a time, however bleak, or a writer, whatever his school, when and for whom her devotion to her art, her industry, her severity with herself — above all, her passionate love, not only or chiefly for the big moments of life but also for its daily humdrum 'sausage-and-haddock' details — will not remain an example that is at once an inspiration and a judge.

W. H. Auden, *Forewords and Afterwords*.

Great novels are devastatingly particular. Virginia Woolf's novels are too devastatingly vague. I lost patience when I discovered (from the luncheon in *Between the Acts* . . .) that she thought you need a corkscrew to open a bottle of champagne. For evocation, subtlety of mood, atmosphere — all the qualities the Lupians praise — the sensitive Mrs Woolf can be shamed by an old toughy like Simenon, who has the literary good sense to approach the intangible through the concrete.

Brigid Brophy, *Don't Never Forget*.

Virginia Woolf seemed to have the worst defect of the Mandarin style, the ability to spin cocoons of language out of nothing. The history of her literary style has been that of a form at first simple, growing more and more elaborate, the content lagging far behind, then catching up, till . . . she produced a masterpiece in *The Waves*.

Cyril Connolly, *Enemies of Promise*.

She is like a plant which is supposed to grow in a well-prepared garden bed — the bed of esoteric literature — and then pushes up suckers all over the place, through the gravel of the front drive, and even through the flagstones of the kitchen yard. She was full of interests, and their number increased as she grew older, she was curious about life, and she was tough, sensitive but tough.

E. M. Forster, *Virginia Woolf* (Reid Lecture).

Virginia had this reputation of being a rather malicious person — deservedly so, I think. Adrian — Virginia's brother, Vanessa and Clive and several others suddenly discovered they were no longer on speaking terms. So Adrian called on them and said 'Something's wrong between us — it must be the Goat' — that was Virginia's nickname. He got everyone to write down what Virginia had said about the others. We met a month later and read the notes aloud — and from that time, Virginia's power was broken for ever.

David Garnett, in *Observer Colour Supplement*, 5 March 1972.

Her works are very strange. They're very beautiful, aren't they? but one gets such a curious feeling from them. She sees with incredible clarity, but always as though through a sheet of plate glass. Her books are not immediate. They're very puzzling to me.

Aldous Huxley, in *Paris Review*.

Her genius was intensely feminine and personal — private, almost. To read one of her books was (if you liked it) to receive a letter from her, addressed specially to you. . . . Open *To the Lighthouse*, *The Common Reader*, or *The Waves*, read a couple of pages with appreciation, and you have become already a distant relative of the Bloomsbury Family. You can enter the inner sanctum, the Woolf drawing-room, and nobody will rise to greet you — for you are one of the party. 'Oh, come in,' says Virginia, with that gracious informality which is so inimitably aristocratic, 'you know everybody, don't you? We were just talking about Charles Tansley . . . poor Charles — such a prig. . . .' And so, scarcely aware, we float into our story.

Christopher Isherwood, *Exhumations*.

The reader not prepared to readjust himself to the technique of *Mrs Dalloway* or *To the Lighthouse* will get very little return for the energy he must lay out in wrestling with those involved periods. He is repaid by none of the obvious satisfactions he expects from a novel — no friendly characters, no reassuring conviction that life is as he wants it to be, no glow of companionship or stirring relation of action. . . . He is dimly aware of having missed the point and feels cheated, or at best impressed but irritated.

Q. D. Leavis, *Fiction and the Reading Public*.

After dinner . . . she would sit in her chair by the

fire, smoking the strong cigarette she rolled for herself in a long holder, and talk. She wanted to know about everybody and everything. What was young X writing? Was it true that So-and-so had broken his best friend's marriage? What did we think of the latest magazine? The latest production of *The Duchess of Malfi* or *Twelfth Night*? What on earth was she to answer to the old bore Z, who kept on writing her pompous fan-letters from America? She delighted in witty gossip, and would discuss the comic and tragic events of the day as keenly as the deepest problems of literature. There can never have been anyone on whom the mantle of acknowledged literary greatness lay less heavily.

John Lehmann, *Penguin New Writing*, no. 19.

She was extremely beautiful, with an austere intellectual beauty of bone and outline, with large melancholy eyes under carved lids, and the nose and lips, the long narrow cheek of a Gothic Madonna. Her voice, light, musical, with a throaty note in it, was one of her great charms. She was tall and thin, and her hands were astonishingly exquisite. She used to spread them out to the fire, and they were so transparent one fancied one saw the long fragile bones through the fine skin. There was something about her that made one think of William Morris and the New Age and the Emancipation of Women.

Rosamond Lehmann, *Penguin New Writing*, no. 7.

Mrs Woolf is charming, scholarly, intelligent, everything that you will: but here we *have* not a Jane Austen — a Felicia Hemans, rather, as it has been said.

Percy Wyndham Lewis, Letter to *Spectator*, 2 November 1934.

In Strachey, because there is no *Sturm und Drang* . . . there is no joy. And on this plane of judgement I may as well agree with you that Virginia Woolf is not a figure of sufficient importance to warrant a difference of opinion between us. She does not face the problem, and it may be that . . . I may have to put her down along with Strachey and Garnett among the forces which are imposing a premature and hardening limitation on contemporary literature — fencing it off into a small perfection which is a denial of further progress.

Edwin Muir, Letter to Stephen Hudson, 8 May 1925.

Virginia Woolf, I enjoyed talking to her, but thought *nothing* of her writing. I considered her 'a beautiful little knitter'.

Edith Sitwell, Letter to Geoffrey Singleton, 11 July 1955.

To be in her company was delightful. She enjoyed each butterfly aspect of the world and of the moment, and would chase the lovely creatures, but without damaging the coloured dust on their wings.

Edith Sitwell, *Taken Care Of.*

I think she has very grave faults. Absolutely self-absorbed and (no wonder), jealous of literary excellence; (couldn't see the point of D. H. Lawrence until he was dead). Ungenerous, indeed incapable of knowing what generosity means, I had almost said, but she recognizes it in others. . . . She is arrogant, intellectually, beyond words yet absolutely humble about her own great gift. Her integrity fascinates me. To save your life, or her own, she could not doctor what she thinks to be the truth.

Dame Ethel Smyth, Diary, 1933.

To have known Virginia Woolf is a great privilege, because it is to have known an extraordinary and poetic and beautiful human being. Some critics describe her as forbidding and austere. Her austerity was not that of a closed-in or a prudish mind. As with all genuinely intelligent people, one could discuss anything with her with the greatest frankness; she was far too interested in life to make narrow moral judgements. Perhaps she was a little too impatient towards stupidity and tactlessness; it is a gift to writers to suffer fools gladly. To be with her was a joy, because her delight and her awareness of everything around her communicated themselves easily and immediately to her friends. What was written on her beautiful unforgettable face was not severity at all, though there was some melancholy.

Stephen Spender, Obituary in *Listener*, 10 April 1941.

I am now in the middle of Virginia's [*To the Lighthouse*] — which I like, so far, much better than Mrs Dalloway. It really is most unfortunate that she rules out copulation — not the ghost of it visible — so that her presentation of things becomes little more, it seems to me, than an arabesque — an exquisite arabesque, of course.

Lytton Strachey, Letter to E. B. C. Lucas, 7 May 1927.

For me, this work seems very clever, very ingenious, but creatively unimportant. It was done — as so much modern un-creative writing is done — with the superficial wits; there was nothing in it for those who did not pride themselves upon intellectual superiority to the herd.

Frank Swinnerton, *The Georgian Literary Scene.*

See also Lytton Strachey, Leonard Woolf

WOOLLCOTT, ALEXANDER HUMPHREYS

1887—1943 Author, Critic

To all things clergic
I am allergic.
    On himself, in Samuel Hopkins Adams, *Alexander Woollcott, His Life and His World.*

You must have suspected more than once that I'm a pretty trivial, rootless person, a fellow of motley and diffused affections, permanently adrift.
    On himself, Letter to Robert Rudd.

. . . the smartest of Alecs.
    Heywood Broun, in Robert E. Drennan ed., *Wit's End.*

His life was what the marquees describe as a 'continuous performance.'
    John Mason Brown, Introduction to *The Portable Woollcott.*

He turned several books into bestsellers, single-handed. . . . Woollcott's enthusiasms could make a book a bestseller more surely than anything else.
    Bennett Cerf, in Samuel Hopkins Adams, *Alexander Woollcott, His Life and His World.*

I disliked Mr Woollcott intensely. In literary matters, he was a consistent champion of the second-rate and worse, and the charm that he turned on for the people he considered important was singularly lacking when he was dealing with people he considered his social inferiors. This is not my idea of the way a gentleman acts.
    Bennett Cerf, Letter to Edwin P. Hoyt, 1966.

. . . a New Jersey Nero who mistook his pinafore for a toga.
    Edna Ferber, in Edwin P. Hoyt, *Alexander Woollcott: The Man Who Came to Dinner.*

I want to be alone on this trip. I don't expect to talk to a man or woman — just Aleck Woollcott.
    Edna Ferber, in Robert E. Drennan ed., *Wit's End.*

. . . a persnickety fellow with more fizz than brain.
    Ben Hecht, in *ibid.*

He was a serious young man, a very active one, and a perfectly normal one until the end of his college years when he suffered a severe attack of the mumps and the complications that sometimes affect the male. After that attack the change in Aleck was apparent. He became, in effect, a eunuch, and he began to acquire eunuchoid characteristics. He grew pudgy and his hips broadened. . . . He grew mincing in his ways.
    Edwin P. Hoyt, *Alexander Woollcott: The Man Who Came to Dinner.*

He became Buddha-like in his fat. . . . The studied insult, the insulting term of endearment, even the dirty word at the dinner table — all these became Woollcottian hallmarks.
    Ibid.

Trivia was Aleck's declared business.
    Ibid.

Mr Woollcott was a perplexing man, given to many kindnesses and generosities, but at the same time he seemed to feel a need to find the minutest chinks in his friends' armor, wherein to insert a poisoned needle.
    John Keats, *You Might As Well Live.*

He looked like something that had gotten loose from Macy's Thanksgiving Day Parade.
    Harpo Marx, in Edwin P. Hoyt, *Alexander Woollcott: The Man Who Came to Dinner.*

Just a big dreamer with a sense of double entry.
    Harpo Marx, in Samuel Hopkins Adams, *Alexander Woollcott, His Life and His World.*

. . . a fat duchess with the emotions of a fish.
    Harold Ross, in Robert E. Drennan ed., *Wit's End.*

Old Vitriol and Violets.
    James Thurber, in *ibid.*

For in the Alexander Woollcott of today, retired at 42 after 20 years of journalism, are traces of a little boy — a little fat boy, impish, disagreeable, even obnoxious at times, but one who creates amusement and wins friends. Brought up in the Mauve Decade, he is irrevocably stamped with its tastes, its ideals in art and its sentimentalities.
    Danton Walker, in Edwin P. Hoyt, *Alexander Woollcott: The Man Who Came to Dinner.*

See also Robert Benchley, Edna Ferber

WOOLLEY, MONTY (EDGAR MONTILLION WOOLLEY)

1888—1963 Actor

These popping consonants, this practiced roar, this sarcasm without inner compulsion and ranting without the fire of rage — these are possibly necessary where there are people to be tickled in the back row, where motion needs overemphasis to keep the front rows awake, and where an actor has been so long in the same routine that he has felt it go stale and slipped into making it louder and busier, hence funnier. The camera eye picks this all up, shows relentlessly where it is false, and literally throws it at your head, back row or front.

Otis Ferguson, reviewing the film of *The Man Who Came to Dinner*, 1942, in *Film Criticism of Otis Ferguson*.

WORDSWORTH, WILLIAM

1770—1850 Poet

The principal object, then, proposed in these Poems was to choose incidents and situations from common life, and to relate or describe them, throughout, as far as was possible in a selection of language really used by men, and, at the same time, to throw over them a certain colouring of imagination, whereby ordinary things should be presented to the mind in an unusual aspect; and further, and above all, to make these incidents and situations interesting by tracing in them, truly though not ostentatiously, the primary laws of our nature: chiefly, as far as regards the manner in which we associate ideas in a state of excitement.

On himself, Preface to the *Lyrical Ballads*.

No poet, perhaps, is so evidently filled with a new and sacred energy when the inspiration is upon him; no poet, when it fails him, is so left 'weak as is a breaking wave'. . . . Wordsworth's poetry, when he is at his best, is inevitable, as inevitable as Nature herself. It might seem that Nature not only gave him the matter for his poem, but wrote his poem for him. He has no style. . . . When he seeks to have a style he falls into ponderosity and pomposity.

Matthew Arnold, *Wordsworth*.

But Wordsworth's eyes avert their ken
From half of human fate.

Matthew Arnold, *Stanzas in Memory of the Author of 'Obermann'*.

When Wordsworth tries to write according to his theories, the result is nearly always flat; to write well, he has to forget them.

W. H. Auden, *Forewords and Afterwords*.

Just for a handful of silver he left us,
    Just for a riband to stick in his coat —
Found the one gift of which fortune bereft us,
    Lost all the others she lets us devote;

They, with the gold to give, doled him out silver,
    So much was theirs who so little allowed:
How all our copper had gone for his service!
    Rags — were they purple, his heart had been
                                            proud!
We that had loved him so, followed him, honoured
                                            him,
    Lived in his mild and magnificent eye,
Learned his great language, caught his clear accents,
    Made him our pattern to live and to die!
Shakespeare was of us, Milton was for us,
    Burns, Shelley, were with us, — they watch from
                                            their graves!
He alone breaks from the van and the freemen,
    He alone sinks to the rear and the slaves!
    Robert Browning, *The Lost Leader*.

Next comes the dull disciple of thy school,
That mild apostate from poetic rule,
The simple Wordsworth, framer of a lay,
As soft as evening in his favourite May,
Who warns his friend 'to shake off toil and trouble,
And quit his books for fear of growing double',
Who, both by precept and example, shows
That prose is verse, and verse is merely prose;
Convincing all, by demonstration plain,
Poetic souls delight in prose insane
And Christmas stories tortured into rhyme
Contain the essence of the true sublime.

Lord Byron, *English Bards and Scotch Reviewers*.

And Wordsworth, in a rather long *Excursion*
    (I think the quarto holds five hundred pages),
Has given a sample from the vasty version
    Of his new system to perplex the sages;
'Tis poetry — at least by his assertion,
    And may appear so when the Dog Star rages —
And he who understands it would be able
To add a story to the Tower of Babel.

Lord Byron, Dedication to *Don Juan*.

Crazed beyond all hope.
    Ibid., canto i.

The great Metaquizzical poet.
    Lord Byron, Letter to John Murray, 19 January 1821.

I cannot help thinking that there is in Wordsworth's poems something of a spirit of withdrawal and seclusion from, and even evasion of, the actual world. . . . Retiring early from all conflict and even contact with the busy world, he shut himself from the elements which it was his business to encounter and master. This gives to his writings, compared with those of Scott or Byron, an appearance of sterility and unreality.

A. H. Clough, *Poems and Prose Remains*.

He is himself, and, I dare affirm, that he will hereafter be admitted as the first and greatest philosophical poet, the only man who has effected a complete and constant synthesis of thought and feeling and combined them with poetic forms, with the music of pleasurable passion, and with Imagination or the *modifying* power in that highest sense of the word. . . . Wordsworth is a poet, and I feel myself a better poet, in knowing how to honour *him* than in all my own poetic compositions, all I have done or hope to do.

> Samuel Taylor Coleridge, Letter to Richard
> Sharp, 1804.

He strides on so far before you, that he dwindles in the distance.

> Samuel Taylor Coleridge, quoted by William
> Hazlitt, in *Examiner*, 12 January 1817.

He was, upon the whole, not a well-made man. His legs were pointedly condemned by all female connoisseurs in legs; not that they were bad in any way which *would* force itself upon your notice — there was no absolute deformity about them; and undoubtedly they had been serviceable legs beyond the average standard of human requisition; for I calculate, upon good date, that with these identical legs Wordsworth must have traversed a distance of 175,000 to 180,000 English miles — a mode of exertion which, to him, stood in the stead of alcohol and all other stimulants whatsoever to the animal spirits; to which, indeed, he was indebted for a life of unclouded happiness, and we for much of what is most excellent in his writings.

> Thomas de Quincey, *Literary Reminiscences.*

Wordsworth is really the first, in the unsettled state of affairs in his time, to annex new authority for the poet, to meddle with social affairs, and to offer a new kind of religious sentiment which it seemed the peculiar prerogative of the poet to interpret.

> T. S. Eliot, *The Use of Poetry and the Use of
> Criticism.*

Is Wordsworth a bell with a wooden tongue?

> Ralph Waldo Emerson, *Journal*, 1863.

I have been poring over Wordsworth lately: which has had much effect in bettering my Blue Devils: for his philosophy does not abjure melancholy, but puts a pleasant countenance upon it, and connects it with humanity. It is very well, if the sensibility that makes us fearful of ourselves is diverted to become a cause of sympathy and interest with Nature and mankind: and this I think Wordsworth tends to do.

> Edward Fitzgerald, Letter to John Allen, 1832.

The difference between reading a long poem by Tennyson and a longer one by Wordsworth has always to the writer seemed to be this: with Tennyson you eat for a long time through a joint of fat, insipid meat to come now and then on the purple patch of a truffle; with Wordsworth you wander through the empty rooms of an immense grey castle hollowed out of primæval crags. From time to time, lying on a dusty stone floor, you will come upon a leaf from an illuminated Book of Hours, and once or twice upon a whole wall frescoed by Simone Martini.

> Ford Madox Ford, *The March of Literature.*

He evidently loves the monologue style of conversation, but shows great candour in giving due consideration to any remarks which others may make. His manner is simple, his general apperance that of the abstract thinker, whom his subject gradually warms into poetry.

> Caroline Fox, *Journals*, June 1842.

Wordsworth had quite the figure and air of a sturdy mountaineer in search of a stray sheep or goat. We had a scorching ramble of more than two hours in which Wordsworth *expanded* amazingly. . . . There were no bursts of information but a gradual development of it. He looked round, as we ascended, from time to time, at the prospect up and down and beyond the river; and he talked of painting, sketching, and many other subjects suggested by the scene. But he did not after all talk like a painter or a philosopher, and not one bit like a poet. There was an inflexible matter-of-fact manner and spirit in all he said, which came out in a rather hoarse and harsh *burr* that made it disagreeable as well as unimpressive. I could hardly believe in the man's identity, or be convinced that I walked beside the author so remarkable for his imaginative and vapoury abstractions.

> Thomas Colley Grattan, *Beaten Paths and Those
> Who Trod Them.*

Once as I was walking with Wordsworth in Pall Mall we ran into Christie's, where there was a very good copy of the Transfiguration, which he abused through thick and thin. In the corner stood the group of Cupid and Psyche kissing. After looking some time he turned round to me with an expression I shall never forget, and said, 'The Dev-ils!'

> Benjamin Robert Haydon, *Autobiography.*

He has produced a deeper impression, and on a smaller circle, than any other of his contemporaries. His powers have been mistaken by the age, nor does he exactly understand them himself. He cannot form a whole. He has not the constructive faculty. He can give only the fine tones of thought, drawn from his mind by accident or nature, like the sounds drawn from the Aeolian harp by the wandering gale. — He is totally deficient in all the machinery of poetry.

William Hazlitt, *Lectures on the English Poets.*

He has no fancy, no wit, no humour, little descriptive power, no dramatic power, great occasional elegance, with continual rusticity and boldness of allusion: but he is sublime without the Muse's aid, pathetic in the contemplation of his own and man's nature.

William Hazlitt, 'A Critical List of Authors', in *Select British Poets.*

The most original poet now living, and the one whose writings could the least be spared; for they have no substitutes elsewhere. The vulgar do not read them; the learned, who see all things through books, do not understand them; the great, despite the fashionable, may ridicule them; but the author has created himself an interest in the heart of the retired and lonely student of nature, which can never die.

William Hazlitt, *The Spirit of the Age.*

Coleridge has told me that he himself liked to compose in walking over uneven ground, or breaking through the straggling branches of a copsewood; whereas Wordsworth always wrote (if he could) walking up and down a straight gravel-walk, or in some spot where the continuity of his verse met with no collateral interruption.

William Hazlitt, in *Examiner*, 12 January 1817.

A modern Moses who sits on Pisgah with his back obstinately turned to that promised land, the Future; he is only fit for those old maid tabbies, the Muses.

Douglas Jerrold, Review of Wordsworth's Poems.

It may be said that we ought to read our contemporaries: that Wordsworth, etc., ought to have their due from us. But for the sake of a few fine imaginative or domestic passages, are we to be bullied into a certain Philosophy engendered in the whims of an Egotist? Every man has his speculations, but every man does not brood and peacock over them till he makes a false coinage and deceives himself.

John Keats, Letter to John H. Reynolds, 3 February 1818.

Separate from the pleasure of your company, I don't much care if I never see another mountain in my life.

Charles Lamb, Letter to Wordsworth, 30 January 1801.

Those who best know him seem to be most impressed with the catholic character of his ability. I have been told that Lockhart has said of him that he would have been an admirable country attorney. Now a man who could have been either Wordsworth or a country attorney could certainly have been anything else which circumstances had led him to desire to be.

John Stuart Mill, Letter to John Sterling, October 1831.

I needed to be made to feel that there was real, permanent happiness in tranquil contemplation. Wordsworth taught me this not only without turning away from, but with a greatly increased interest in the common feelings and common destiny of human beings.

John Stuart Mill, *Autobiography.*

Compared with the greatest poets, he may be said to be the poet of unpoetical natures, possessed of quiet and contemplative tastes. But unpoetical natures are precisely those which require poetic cultivation. This cultivation Wordsworth is much more fitted to give than poets who are intrinsically far more poets than he.

Ibid.

Is Wordsworth sleeping in peace on his bed of mud in the profundity of Pathos, or will he ever again wake to dole out a lyrical ballad?

Thomas Love Peacock, Letter, 1808.

Perhaps 'alive' is scarcely the word one would apply to the 'luminary' of the Lake District. Wordsworth drew his first orderly and deliberate breath in 1770; and continued the alternative processes of inhalation and exhalation until 1850.

Ezra Pound, in *Future*, September 1913.

Mr Wordsworth, a stupid man, with a decided gift for portraying nature in vignettes, never yet ruined anyone's morals, unless, perhaps, he has driven some susceptible persons to crime in a very fury of boredom.

Ibid., November 1917.

He had a mind which was somehow
    At once circumference and centre
Of all he might or feel or know;
Nothing went ever out, although
    Something did ever enter.

He had as much imagination
    As a pint-pot; — he never could
Fancy another situation,
From which to dart his contemplation
    Than that wherein he stood.

Percy Bysshe Shelley, *Peter Bell the Third.*

In honoured poverty thy voice did weave
Songs consecrate to truth and liberty, —
Deserting these, thou leavest me to grieve,
Thus having been, that thou shouldst cease to be.
    Percy Bysshe Shelley, *To Wordsworth.*

Wordsworth was a tea-time bore, the great Frost of literature, the verbose, the humourless, the platitudinary reporter of Nature in her dullest moods. Open him at any page: and there lies the English language not, as George Moore said of Pater, in a glass coffin, but in a large, sultry, and unhygienic box.
    Dylan Thomas, Letter to Pamela Hansford Johnson, 1933.

He found in stones the sermons he had already hidden there.
    Oscar Wilde, *The Decay of Lying.*

Wordsworth is so often flat and heavy partly because his moral sense has no theatrical elements, it is an obedience, a discipline which he has not created. This increases his popularity with the better sort of journalists, the *Spectator* writers, for instance, with all who are part of the machine and yet care for poetry.
    William Butler Yeats, *Memoirs.*

See also Lord Byron, John Cavanagh, Samuel Taylor Coleridge, Alexander Cozens, George Crabbe, Edmund Kean, Rudyard Kipling, W. S. Landor, D. H. Lawrence, Alexander Pope, Sir Walter Scott, Robert Louis Stevenson, Booth Tarkington, Alfred, Lord Tennyson, John Webster

WOTTON, SIR HENRY

1568—1639 Poet, Diplomat

His good old genially pious life.
    Thomas Carlyle, *Frederick the Great.*

What shall we say, since silent now is he,
Who when he spoke, all things would silent be!
Who had so many languages in store,
That only Fame shall speak of him in more.
Whom England now no more returned must see;
He's gone to heav'n, on his fourth embassy.
    Abraham Cowley, *An Elegy on Sir Henry Wotton.*

WREN, SIR CHRISTOPHER

1632—1723 Architect, Mathematician

As I am Dismiss'd, having worn out (by God's mercy) a long Life in the Royal service, and having made some Figure in the World, I hope it will be allowed me to Die in Peace.
    On himself, Letter to the Lords of the Treasury, 21 April 1719.

Sir Christopher Wren
Said, 'I am going to dine with some men.
If anybody calls
Say I am designing St. Paul's.'
    Edmund Clerihew Bentley, *Biography for Beginners.*

From the very first he was an inventor — keen, alert, and quick to make immediate use of actual observation and discovery; he had none of the dreamer's disease of inactivity; he seems indeed to have possessed a fertility of invention which sometimes tempted him to turn out work before it was mature, and to shirk the labour of fastidious finish inevitable to the scholar and the artist.
    Sir Reginald Blomfield, *A History of Renaissance Architecture in England 1500—1800.*

He thought of architecture basically, inside and outside, as solid geometry. . . . It is precisely the geometrical feeling in his architecture which makes it so seldom exciting — although Hawksmoor, building equally geometrically, contrived to excite. Wren is probably the most rational architect we have ever had, and the mind of the constructor of astronomical models and the solver of trigonometrical problems is expressed in his architecture.
    K. Downes, *Nicholas Hawksmoor.*

Wren's mind was finely balanced between cognition and inspiration. In science, he was capable of devising the theoretical formula to solve a problem but not bothering to proceed to the solution; on the other hand he found congenial the emphasis of post-Baconian science on experiment, because he needed visible results to maintain his interest. . . . This need may explain his involvement first with anatomy and then with architecture.
    Ibid.

That miracle of a youth.
    John Evelyn, Diary, 10 July 1654.

Wren's solutions are not adapted as the only possible ones; his architectural music is latitudinarian; his preferences are never exclusive to alternatives.
    V. Fürst, *The Architecture of Sir Christopher Wren.*

Wren's achievement is unique, it is wholly and completely of his soil and time. It is the epitome of an age which could confidently attempt to replace the

lost ideals of the past by the newly discovered criteria of its present; an age which could glory in the belief that the advance from the 'superstitions' of religion to the 'certainties' of science was not only a progression, but progress. In this light, Wren's achievement is supreme. That his successors for long deprecated his example, and that posterity for long scorned its heritage, was due to their incomprehension, not his genius.
    Ibid.

There scarce ever met in one man, in so great a perfection, such a Mechanical Hand, and so Philosophical a Mind.
    Robert Hooke, Preface to *Micrographia.*

Thro' several reigns we have patiently seen the noblest publick buildings perish (if I may say so) under the hand of one single court-architect; who, if he had been able to profit by experience, wou'd long since at our expense, have prov'd the greatest master in the world.
    The First Earl of Shaftesbury, *A Letter Concerning Design.*

He was not only in his profession the greatest man of that age, but had given more proofs of it than any other man ever did; yet for want of that natural freedom and audacity which is necessary in commerce with men, his personal modesty overthrew all his public actions.
    Richard Steele, in *Tatler*, 9 August 1709.

Generally, the City churches give a wonderful picture of Wren's mind during the central period of his career. It is an energetic, adventurous mind, proceeding by intellectual argument rather than by the intuitive conceptions of aesthetic entities to which all argument must be subordinated. Wren was, through and through, an empiricist. A design of his never *grows*: it is stated at once, then abruptly altered or wholly superseded.
    J. Summerson, *Architecture in Britain 1530–1830.*

As to his bodily Constitution, it was naturally rather delicate than strong, especially in his Youth, which seem'd consumptive; and yet, by a judicious Regularity and Temperance, (having acquir'd good Knowledge in Physick) he continued healthy, with little Intermission, even to this extreme old Age. Further 'tis observable, that he was happily endued with such an Evenness of Temper, a steady Tranquillity of Mind, and Christian Fortitude, that no injudicious Incidents, or Inquietude, of human Life,

Could ever ruffle or discompose; and was in Practice a *Stoick.*
    Christopher Wren Jr, *Parentalia.*

See also Inigo Jones

WRIGHT, FRANK LLOYD

1867–1959 Architect

Early in life I had to choose between honest arrogance and hypocritical humility. I chose honest arrogance and have seen no occasion to change.
    On himself, in Herbert Jacobs, *Frank Lloyd Wright.*

I have endeavored . . . to establish a harmonious relationship between ground plan and elevation of these buildings, considering the one as a solution and the other an expression of the conditions of a problem of which the whole is a project. I have tried to establish an organic integrity to begin with, forming the basis for the subsequent working out of a significant grammatical expression and making the whole, as nearly as I could, consistent.
    On himself, *An American Architecture.*

My grandfather, Frank Lloyd Wright, wore a red sash on his wedding night. That is glamour.
    Anne Baxter, in *Time*, 5 May 1952.

I agree that non-critical estimates of Frank Lloyd Wright are rather meaningless now. I would go further and say that critical estimates of Wright are also meaningless now. Sometime Frank Lloyd Wright will be re-evaluated — and his great concept of architecture where everything is all one organism, all one thing, will be appreciated.
    Eero Saarinen, *Eero Saarinen, on His Work.*

Wright's 'time, his day, his age' was that of late nineteenth-century America. He was the embodiment of its most tenacious attitudes: of its supreme confidence in the common future, and of its desperate, complimentary yearning for pre-industrial, sometimes pre-civilized, images and symbols to root itself upon. . . . As such, Wright was the heir, in architecture — and regarded himself as being so — of a tradition, in part Jeffersonian, which had previously found its best expression in the works of Melville, Whitman and Mark Twain. As they, in their writing, had celebrated at once the flux and flow which characterize modern times and the compulsion toward unity which is the democratic will, so he, in his architecture, sought to make the images of flow a fact, to celebrate continuous space, and to bring all together into shapes which were unified by his will.

Vincent Scully Jr, *Frank Lloyd Wright.*

WRIGHT, JOSEPH (OF DERBY)

1734—97 Painter

But see far off the modest Wright retire!
Alone he rules his Element of Fire:
Like Meteors darting through the gloom of Night,
His sparkles flash upon the dazzled sight;
Our eyes with momentary anguish smart,
And Nature trembles at the power of Art.
May the bold colours, claiming endless praise,
For ages shine with undiminish'd blaze,
And when the fierce VESUVIO burns no more,
May his red deluge down thy canvass pour.

William Hayley, *An Essay on Painting*, epistle 2.

In Wright's mind and in that of his Midlands contemporaries, modern science was no less of a miracle than the antique; the lecturer's equipment held the same beauty and purity of line and exacted the same devout contemplation.

Benedict Nicolson, *Joseph Wright of Derby.*

The Man Of Night!
O'er *woollen* hills, where gold and silver moons
Now mount like sixpences, and now balloons;
Where sea-reflections, nothing nat'ral tell ye,
So much like fiddle-strings, or vermicelli;
Where ev'ry thing exclaimeth, how severe!
'What *are* we?' and 'what business have we here?'

'Peter Pindar' (John Wolcot), *Lyric Odes for 1783*, ode 5.

WRIGHT, ORVILLE, and WRIGHT, WILBUR

1871—1948 and 1867—1912 Pioneer Aviators

This biplane is the shape of human flight.
Its name might better be First Motor Kite.
Its makers' name — Time cannot get that wrong,
For it was writ in heaven doubly Wright.

Robert Frost, *The Wrights' Biplane.*

WYATT, JAMES

1746—1813 Architect

Wyatt was an essentially romantic architect. His strength lay in scenic effect rather than in detail, and his imagination found freer play in towers and battlements than in garlands and cameos. Had Gothic been the natural language of his time, Wyatt would have been a greater architect: failing that he needed a tradition of Baroque.

Kenneth Clark, *The Gothic Revival.*

In his lifetime Wyatt enjoyed the reputation of having 'revived in this country the long forgotten beauties of Gothic architecture', but the real importance of his Gothic work lay in the manner in which it bridged the gap between the rococo Gothic in the mid-eighteenth century and the serious medievalism of the early nineteenth.

H. M. Colvin, in *Biographical Dictionary of English Architects.*

Everybody had employed him, and therefore everybody continued to do so. It would almost have been bad *ton* to seek for assistance elsewhere. Other practitioners might have his ability, but who had heard of them? In consulting a person of Mr. Wyatt's reputation, the world of fashion thought it was quite safe.

Sir Charles Eastlake, *The Gothic Revival.*

Beckford is much dissatisfied with Wyatt, who perpetually disappoints him. He said that if Wyatt can get near a large fire and have a bottle by him, he cares for nothing else.

Joseph Farington, Diary, 29 March 1804.

James Wyatt, of execrable memory.

A. W. N. Pugin, *Contrasts.*

WYCHERLEY, WILLIAM

1640?—1716 Dramatist

Mr Wycherley being indeed almost the only man alive, who has made Comedy instructive in its Fable; almost all the rest being contented to instruct by their characters.

John Dennis, *The Usefulness of the Stage.*

I must confess that I have no great Opinion of that which Men generally call Humility: in most Men, Humility is want of Heat; 'tis Phlegm, 'tis Impotence, 'tis a wretched Necessity, of which they who lie under it vainly endeavour to make a Virtue. But in a Man of Mr Wycherley's Make, 'tis Choice, 'tis Force of Mind, 'tis a Good, 'tis a generous Condescension, and what Force of Mind is there not requisite to bend back a Soul by perpetual Reflection, which would be always rising and eternally aspiring by virtue of its inborn Fire?

John Dennis, *The Select Works.*

In my Friend, every syllable, every Thought is masculine; his Muse is not led forth as to a Review, but as to a Battle; not adorn'd for Parade, but Execution; he would be tried by the Sharpness of his Blade, and not by the Finery; Like your Heroes of Antiquity he charges in Iron, and seems to despise all Ornament but intrinsick Merit. — Congreve is your familiar Acquaintance, you may judge of Wycherley by him: they have the same manly ways of Thinking and Writing, the same Candour, Modesty, Humanity and Integrity of Manners: It is impossible not to love them for their own sakes, abstracted from the merit of their Works.

George Granville, *A Letter with a Character of Mr Wycherley*.

He appears to have led, during a long course of years, that most wretched life, the life of a vicious old boy about town.

T. B. Macaulay, *Essays*: 'On the Comic Dramatists of the Restoration'.

In truth, Wycherley's indecency is protected against the critics as a skunk is protected against the hunters. It is safe because it is too filthy to handle, and too noisome even to approach.

Ibid.

Pope: His memory did not carry above a sentence at a time. These single sentences were good, but the whole was without connection and good for nothing but to be flung into maxims. *Spence*: In spite of his good sense, I could never read his plays with true pleasure, from the general stiffness of his style. *Pope*: Ay, that was occasioned by his being always studying for antitheses.

Joseph Spence, *Anecdotes*.

This Gentleman who pass'd his life among Persons of the highest Distinction, was perfectly well acquainted with their lives, and their Follies, and painted them with the strongest Pencil, and in the truest Colours. He has drawn a *Misanthrope*, or Man-hater, in Imitation of that of *Molière*. All *Wycherley*'s strokes are stronger and bolder than those of our *Misanthrope*, but then they are less delicate, and the Rules of Decorum are not so well observed in this Play. The English writer has corrected the only Defect that is in *Molière*'s Comedy, the Thinness of the Plot, which also is so dispos'd that the Characters in it do not enough raise our Concern. The English Comedy affects us, and the Contrivance of the Plot is very ingenious, but at the same time 'tis too bold for French manners.

Voltaire, *Letters Concerning the English Nation* (English edition).

See also John Kemble, Alexander Pope, Thomas Shadwell

WYCLIFFE, JOHN

— d. 1384 Religious and Social Reformer

John Wycleve was a grand dissembler, a man of little conscience, and what he did as to religion, was more out of vaine glory, and to obtaine unto him a name, than out of honestie.

Dr John Fell, in Anthony à Wood, *Life and Times*, June 1672.

To Lutterworth they come, — Sumner, Commissary, Official, Chancellor, Proctors, Doctors, and the servants (so that the remnant of the body would not hold out a bone, amongst so many hands) take what was left out of the grave, and burnt them to ashes, and cast them into Swift, a neighbouring brook running hard by. Thus this brook hath conveyed his ashes into Avon, Avon into Severn, Severn into the narrow seas, they, into the main ocean. And thus the ashes of Wickliffe are the emblem of his doctrine, which now, is dispersed all the world over.

Thomas Fuller, *Church History of Britain* (on the disinterment, burning and dispersal of Wycliffe's remains in accordance with a decree of the Council of Constance).

Wyclif had loved Oxford dearly — it is perhaps the only deep personal emotion he ever reveals — and in a passage, which must be the earliest of all the many tributes that have been paid to a city that has cast her spell over many minds, he writes of her fresh meadows and pleasant streams, her verdure 'branchy between towers', the soft airs that make of her a dwelling fit for angels, a very house of God and gate of heaven. Yet even this sweet Oxford had been deflowered by the friars; they had cast its prophet forth; he was an exile who would never see its spires again. Rue, not snapdragon, clung to the walls of Balliol, and the rector of Lutterworth swept his earliest home, along with Cain's castles, out of the new Jerusalem.

Dom David Knowles, *The Religious Orders in England*.

He was a master of irony, and no account of him is balanced which omits his elephantine playfulness.

Bernard L. Manning, in *The Cambridge Medieval History*, vol. 7, 1932.

Not least art thou, thou little Bethlehem
In Judah, for in thee the Lord was born;
Nor thou in Britain, little Lutterworth,
Least for in thee the word was born again.

Alfred, Lord Tennyson, *To Sir John Oldcastle*

The devil's instrument, church's enemy, people's confusion, heretics' idol, hypocrites' mirror, schism's broacher, hatred's sewer, lies' forger, flatteries' sink; who at his death despaired like Cain, and, stricken by the horrible judgment of God, breathed forth his wicked soul to the dark mansion of the black devil!

Thomas Walsingham, *Ypodigma Neustriae*, translated by Thomas Fuller.

WYLIE, ELINOR MORTON HOYT

1885–1928 Poet, Author

She makes imaginatively accessible to a broader range of sensibility whatever is most exquisite, dainty, fine, rare, fantastic, elegant, refined, delicate, and even ethereal in sensation and perception — things commonly accessible and acceptable only to the feminine, the effeminate or the epicene taste.

Thomas A. Gray, *Elinor Wylie*.

But in her novels she was obsessed by the need to make ornate pictures. Everywhere in them human beings are wrought into marble and ironwork, draped luxuriously like silk dolls, sculptured into a frieze and given a language so overwhelmingly rapturous as to become meaningless.

Alfred Kazin, *On Native Grounds*.

She possessed to the utmost degree the classic poetic temperament, and unlike most who possess it, it was in her only the outward expression of an inner power.

Stanley J. Kunitz and Howard Haycroft eds, *Twentieth Century Authors*.

. . . her beauty aroused more commotion than her fine poems or the delicate fantasies she called novels.

Lloyd Morris, in Max J. Herzberg, *The Readers' Encyclopedia of American Literature*.

Volatile as her temper was, she was actually as indestructible and resolute as water. She had a level of her own from which no circumstances could dam her long.

Carl Van Doren, Introduction to 'The Venetian Glass Nephew', in *Collected Prose of Elinor Wylie*.

WYNDHAM (WINDHAM), SIR CHARLES, EARL OF EGREMONT

1710–63 Statesman

Lord Egremont was a composition of pride, ill-nature, avarice, and strict good breeding; with such infirmity in his frame, that he could not speak truth on the most trivial occasion. He had humour, and did not want sense, but had neither knowledge of business, nor the smallest share of parliamentary abilities.

Horace Walpole, *Memoirs*.

Y

YATES, MARY ANN

1728—87 Actress

Mrs. Yates, to a very fine figure joins a very hand-some face, though not now in her *première jeunesse*: but the expression of her face is infinitely haughty and hard. With an *overdone* civility, as soon as our names were spoken, she rose from her seat hastily, and rather *rushed* towards, than meerly advanced to meet us; but I doubt not it was meant as the very *pink of politeness*.
> Fanny Burney, Diary, 1774.

Might figure give a title unto fame,
What rival should with Yates dispute her claim?
But justice may not partial trophies raise,
Nor sink the actress in the woman's praise,
Still hand in hand her words and actions go.
And the heart feels more than the features show;
For through the regions of that beauteous face,
We no variety of passions trace;
Dead to the soft emotions of the heart,
No kindred softness can those eyes impart:
The brow, still fix'd in sorrow's sullen frame
Void of distinction, marks all parts the same.
> Charles Churchill, *The Rosciad.*

Too much stumping about, and too much flumping about.
> Kitty Clive, in W. Clark Russell, *Representative Actors.*

On Mrs Yates rehearsing one morning at Drury-Lane Theatre a new part of a tragic princess, where at her death a *flourish of trumpets* was necessary, Hopkins the prompter, doubtful whether it was proper to go through the whole ceremony at that time, walked up softly to her as she lay seemingly dead upon the stage, and whispered, 'Madam! Madam!' — 'Well, what does the man want?' — 'Only, Madam, to know whether you would have the *flourish* now, or *wait for it till night.*'
> Samuel Foote, in William Cooke, *Memoirs of Samuel Foote.*

YEATS, WILLIAM BUTLER

1865—1939 Poet

No people hate as we [the Irish] do in whom that past is always alive, there are moments when hatred poisons my life and I accuse myself of effeminacy because I have not given it adequate expression. It is not enough to have put it into the mouth of a rambling peasant poet. Then I remind myself that though mine is the first English marriage I know of in the direct line, all my family names are English and that I owe my soul to Shakespeare, to Spenser and to Blake, perhaps to William Morris, and to the English language in which I think, speak and write, that everything I love has come to me through English, my hatred tortures me with love, my love with hate. I am like the Tibetan monk who dreams at his initiation that he is eaten by a wild beast and learns on waking that he himself is eater and eaten.
> On himself, *A General Introduction for my Work.*

We were the last romantics — chose for theme
Traditional sanctity and loveliness;
Whatever's written in what poets name
The book of the people; whatever most can bless
The mind of man or elevate to rhyme;
But all is changed, that high horse riderless,
Though mounted in that saddle Homer rode
Where the swan drifts upon a darkening flood.
> On himself, addressing Lady Gregory, *Coole Park and Ballylee.*

Under bare Ben Bulben's head
In Drumcliff churchyard Yeats is laid.
An ancestor was rector there
Long years ago, a church stands near,
By the road an ancient cross.
No marble, no conventional phrase;
On limestone quarried near the spot
By his command these words are cut:
> Cast a cold eye
> On life, on death.
> Horseman, pass by!
> On himself, *Under Ben Bulben.*

You were silly like us: your gift survived it all;
The parish of rich women, physical decay,
Yourself; mad Ireland hurt you into poetry.
> W. H. Auden, *In Memory of W. B. Yeats.*

To get the Last Poems of Yeats
You need not mug up on dates;
> All a reader requires
> Is some knowledge of gyres

And the sort of people he hates.
  W. H. Auden, *Academic Graffiti.*

'Yeats claimed,' said Sargent, 'that he could be a
chancellor or the ruler of a nation, if he chose! He
boasted that he could quell mobs! When he sat for
me he wore a velvet coat and a huge loose bow tie,
and a long lock of hair fell across his brow. He told
me that he did these things to remind himself of his
own importance as an artist!' 'Why,' quietly interrupted Fox, 'didn't he tie a string around his finger?'
  Martin Birnbaum, *John Singer Sargent; A Conversation Piece.*

Against this drab background of dreary modern
materialism, Willie Yeats was calmly walking about
as the Man Who Knew the Fairies. Yeats stood for
enchantment. . . . But I very specially rejoiced in the
fighting instinct which made the Irishman so firm
and positive about it. He was the real original
rationalist who said that the fairies stand to reason.
He staggered the materialists by attacking their abstract materialism with a completely concrete
mysticism.
  G. K. Chesterton, *Autobiography.*

Your omission of my work from the absurdly-named
Oxford Book of Modern Verse is exactly typical of
the attitude of the minor to the major poet. For
example Thomas Moore, the Yeats of the 19th century, would undoubtedly have excluded Keats and
Shelley from any anthology he had compiled.
  Lord Alfred Douglas, telegram to Yeats on the
  publication of *The Oxford Book of Modern
  Verse* (edited by Yeats).

Born into a world in which the doctrine of 'Art for
Art's sake' was generally accepted, and living on
into one in which art has been asked to be instrumental to social purposes, he held firmly to the
right view which is between these, though not in
any way a compromise between them, and showed
that an artist, by serving his art with entire integrity, is at the same time rendering the greatest
service he can to his own nation and to the whole
world.
  T. S. Eliot, *The Poetry of W. B. Yeats.*

He hammered on truth's anvil till he made
Such images as must endure,
Immortalised the house that has decayed,
The fallen lintel, rotted roof and floor;
Became what he created in his blood
Through years of thinking in the marrowbone —
Man and poet contracted into God
Beyond the certainties in book and stone.
  Brendan Kennelly, *Yeats.*

Yeats in spite of his paunch was elegant in a smooth
light suit and a just sufficiently crooked bow tie. His
manner was hierophantic, even when he said: 'This
afternoon I have been playing croquet with my
daughter.' . . . He confined the conversation to spiri-
tualism and the phases of the moon. . . . He talked a
great deal about the spirits to whom his wife, being
a medium, had introduced him. 'Have you ever seen
them?' Dodds asked. . . . Yeats was a little piqued.
No, he said grudgingly, he had never actually seen
them . . . but — with a flash of triumph - he had
often *smelt* them.
  Louis MacNeice, *The Strings are False.*

Comment on the question of Yeats's attitude to
Fascism has been bedevilled by the assumption that
a great poet must be, even in politics, 'a nice guy'.
If this be assumed then it follows that, as Yeats
obviously was a great poet, he cannot *really* have
favoured Fascism, which is obviously not a nice
cause. . . . If one drops the assumption, about poets
always having to be nice in politics, then the puzzle
disappears, and we see, I believe, that Yeats the man
was as near to being a Fascist as his situation and
the conditions of his own country permitted.
  Conor Cruise O'Brien, in A. Norman Jeffares
  and K. G. W. Cross, *In Excited Reverie.*

Translated into political terms, Yeats's tendency is
Fascist. Throughout most of his life, and long before Fascism was ever heard of, he had the outlook
of those who reach Fascism by its aristocratic route.
He is a great hater of democracy, of the modern
world, science, machinery, the concept of progress
— above all, of the idea of human equality. Much of
the imagery in his work is feudal, and it is clear that
he was not altogether free from ordinary snobbish-
ness. Later these tendencies took clearer shape and
led him to 'the exultant acceptance of authori-
tarianism as the only solution.'
  George Orwell, in *Horizon*, January 1943.

My stay at Stone Cottage [Yeats's home] will not be
in the least profitable. I detest the country. Yeats
will amuse me part of the time and bore me to
death with psychical research the rest. I regard the
visit as a duty to posterity.
  Ezra Pound, in Charles Norman, *Ezra Pound.*

An 'unbuttoned' Beethoven is often spoken of,
there was no unbuttoned Yeats either in his work or
in himself, and that is why I deny that he was guilty
of pose. He was fastidious in his person and his
choice of friends; he loathed pretentiousness in
others and so had none himself. The only art to
which he was almost wholly insensitive was music.
  Lennox Robinson, in A. Norman Jeffares and
  K. G. W. Cross, *In Excited Reverie.*

Yeats, in spite of his desire to be a public figure, was more apolitical than any fully responsible person alive.

Arland Ussher, *Three Great Irishmen.*

See also Mrs Patrick Campbell, Ford Madox Ford, Andrew Marvell, Edith Sitwell

YONGE, CHARLOTTE MARY

1823–1901 Novelist

You have become so *very dear* to me through your books, that I must beg the favour of addressing you in this term. I feel deep gratitude towards you for the pleasure and real moral benefit derived from your books. My royal pupil, Princess Margaret, too, owes very much to you.... With children, although gifted as my princess is, in a high degree there must be some *tempting inducements* to make them study more *willingly.*

Rose Arbesser (Governess of Princess Margaret of Italy), Letter to C. M. Yonge.

She practised definitely and on purpose many self-denials, of which she never spoke, and which only gradually became obvious to her friends. As for instance, until the necessities of the trade forced it on her, she never wrote stories in Lent.

Christabel Coleridge, *C. M. Yonge.*

She had a quiet, cheerful, healthy, well-balanced mind; she was wonderfully well read and well in-formed, and her memory was extraordinary. In conversation she was clever and humorous, and her laugh was quite infectious. . . . The only trait in her character which astounded me was that painful shyness which consumed and transfigured her in the presence of strangers.

Mrs M. E. Sumner, Letter to Christabel Coleridge.

YORK AND ALBANY, DUKE OF (FREDERICK AUGUSTUS)

1763–1827 Soldier

Oh, the brave old Duke of York,
    He had ten thousand men;
He marched them up to the top of the hill,
    And he marched them down again.
And when they were up, they were up,
    And when they were down, they were down,
And when they were only half-way up,
    They were neither up nor down.
Nursery Rhyme, traditional.

The Duke of York was spoken of, as a well meaning and an honest man, but as one scarcely on a level with the ordinary scale of human intellect. Neither he nor his brother [George IV], however, had any proper knowledge of *meum* and *tuum*, a fault that was probably as much owing to the flatterers that surrounded them, and to defective education, as to natural tendencies.

James Fenimore Cooper, *Gleanings in Europe: England.*

YOUNG, BRIGHAM

1801–77 Leader of the Mormons

Their leader in the early days in Utah was Bigamy Young. When he arrived in Salt Lake City he said to his followers, 'This is the place,' although he had never been there before. It was uncanny.

Richard Armour, *It All Started With Columbus.*

The Lion of the Lord.

W. W. Phelps, in Fawn Brodie, *No Man Knows My History.*

He is dreadfully married. He's the most married man I ever saw in my life.

Artemus Ward (Charles Farrar Browne), *Artemus Ward's Lecture.*

See also Cecil B. De Mille

YOUNG, EDWARD

1683–1765 Poet

When Young was writing a tragedy Grafton is said by Spence to have sent him a human skull, with a candle in it, as a lamp; and the poet is reported to have used it.

Herbert Croft, in Samuel Johnson, *Life of Young.*

A sort of cross between a sycophant and a psalmist.

George Eliot, in *Westminster Review*, January 1857.

Of Young's poems it is difficult to give any general character, for he has no uniformity of manner: one of his pieces has no great resemblance to another. He began to write early and continued long, and at different times had different modes of poetical excellence in view. His numbers are sometimes smooth and sometimes rugged; his style is sometimes concatenated and sometimes abrupt, sometimes dif-fusive and sometimes concise. His plan seems to have started in his mind at the present moment,

and his thoughts appear the effects of chance, sometimes adverse and sometimes lucky, with very little operation of judgement.
  Samuel Johnson, *Life of Young.*

Where Y---- must torture his invention
To flatter knaves, or lose his pension.
  Jonathan Swift (writing of the Court), *Rhapsody on Poetry.*

See also George Crabbe

YOUNG, THOMAS

1773—1829 Physician, Physicist, Egyptologist

When I was a boy, I thought myself a man; now I am a man, I find myself a boy.
  On himself, in George Peacock, *Life of Thomas Young.*

In like manner, the brilliantly-colored soap-bubbles blown from a common tobacco-pipe, — though 'trifles light as air' in most eyes, — suggested to Dr. Young his beautiful theory of 'interferences', and led to his discovery relating to the diffraction of light. Although great men are popularly supposed only to deal with great things, men such as Newton and Young were ready to detect the significance of the most familiar and simple facts; their greatness consisting mainly in their wise interpretation of them.
  Samuel Smiles, *Self-help.*

It is recorded of Young that, when requested by an acquaintance, who presumed somewhat upon his youthful appearance, to exhibit a specimen of his handwriting, he very delicately rebuked the inquiry by writing a sentence in his best style in fourteen different languages.
  John Tyndall, *New Fragments.*

Immediately after his return to England he became a fellow-commoner of Emanuel College, Cambridge. When the master of the college introduced him to those who were to be his tutors he jocularly said, 'I have brought you a pupil qualified to read lectures to his tutors'.
  Ibid.

Z

ZIEGFELD, FLORENZ
1869—1932 Impresario

As far as Ziegfeld was concerned, the only reason anyone came to any of his revues was to see his girls. Men came to see their bodies, and women came to see their clothes, if any. The comedians in his shows were there only to entertain the vulgarians who did not, or could not, sufficiently appreciate his girls . . . it does seem strange that the man who was responsible for bringing so much laughter to so many hated to laugh. He did not think Bert Williams was funny, nor Eddie Cantor, nor Ed Wynn, nor W. C. Fields, nor Will Rogers. Comedy annoyed him to such an extent that at the cue for comedian's entrance at a rehearsal or a performance, he would step into the lobby.
  Norman bel Geddes, *Miracle In the Evening.*

Others gave shows. He gave productions. He was everywhere. He hired actors, okayed songs, selected fabrics, created the ideas for costumes and scenery, found the top people to execute these designs, was an expert in lighting. I watched him but did not know him. His was a reserve that I, with all my audacity, dared not penetrate. . . . He was, in a way no other man ever achieved, a man whose daring and finesse changed the whole picture of Broadway. There was a time when his earnings were fifty thousand dollars a week. . . . There were times when he was broke. Money meant nothing to him; it was to spend, and with the taste to spend it, he introduced into the American theatre an era of lavishness and glamour that has never been surpassed.
  Eddie Cantor, *Take My Life.*

He was the kind of fellow who made people feel honored to have him owe them money.
  Buddy de Sylva, in *ibid.*

Florenz Ziegfeld was a man with an engaging smile and a hawklike nose and all the charm in the world when he wanted to have it, and show it. He had considerably more temperament than anybody he ever managed, all the way from Sandow the Strong Man and Anna Held to W. C. Fields and Marilyn Miller. He squandered money on his productions, his whims, his affectations. He wore imported lavender shirts, went in for 500-word conversations by long-distance telephone, sent to South Africa for baby elephants and often sent special messengers to Baltimore for terrapin.
  Ward Morehouse, in 'The Ziegfeld Follies: A Formula With Class', in *Theatre Arts*, May 1956.

Florenz Ziegfeld exerted a sorcery in the American theatre from the time of the starting of the Ziegfeld Follies in 1907 until his death in July of 1932. He took girls, lights, paint and canvas, silks and satins and lace and chiffon, billowy plumes and mountains of glittering beads and rhinestones, and fashioned it all into something of singular and stirring beauty.

He created a legend of perfection in show business which has lingered long after his passing. The Ziegfeld girl, bedecked and caparisoned with the best that money could buy, became the symbol of theatrical glamour. She still is, and to a great extent, for there are no show girls like her in the rather stark and grimly expense-conscious theatre of today.
  Ibid.

That was long ago, years before Ziegfeld's name became as recognizable as a trade-mark, a kind of universal guarantee that at any harlequinade presented by him you would behold more squanderous settings, lovelier pagentry, and damsels fairer to see than you would find on any other stage in the 'land.
  Alexander Woollcott, *The Portable Woollcott.*

Index of Persons Quoted

ABBOT, GEORGE James I
ABBOTT, W. C. Oliver Cromwell
ABERCROMBIE, SIR RALPH Sir
  John Moore
ABERDEEN, LORD (q.v.) George IV
ABERNETHY, T. P. Andrew Jackson
ACHESON, DEAN (q.v.) Harry S.
  Truman
ACLAND, ARTHUR Edward Grey
ACTON, LORD (q.v.) Edmund Burke,
  Charles Dickens, Benjamin Disraeli,
  George Eliot, J. A. Froude, W. E.
  Gladstone, T. B. Macaulay, Lord
  Palmerston
ACTON, HAROLD John Singer
  Sargent, Evelyn Waugh
ADAM OF USK Richard II
ADAM, ROBERT and JAMES Sir
  John Vanbrugh
ADAMS, ADELINE Childe Hassam
ADAMS, ANSEL Edward Weston
ADAMS, CHARLES FRANCIS Abigail
  Adams, John Quincy Adams
ADAMS JR, CHARLES FRANCIS
  Thaddeus Stevens
ADAMS, HENRY (q.v.) Chester A.
  Arthur, Joel Barlow, Aaron Burr,
  Salmon P. Chase, Timothy Dwight,
  E. L. Godkin, Ulysses S. Grant,
  Thomas Jefferson, John La Farge,
  Augustus Saint-Gaudens, William
  Henry Seward, Charles Sumner,
  Thurlow Weed, Eli Whitney
ADAMS, MRS HENRY Henry James
ADAMS, JOHN (q.v.) Samuel Adams,
  Benjamin Franklin, Alexander
  Hamilton, John Hancock, Thomas
  Jefferson, James Otis, Thomas
  Paine, George Washington
ADAMS, JOHN QUINCY (q.v.)
  Fisher Ames, Thomas Hart Benton,
  Aaron Burr, John C. Calhoun, Henry
  Clay, Stephen A. Douglas, Albert
  Gallatin, William Henry Harrison,
  Andrew Jackson, Thomas Jefferson,
  James Monroe, Thomas Paine, James
  K. Polk, Hiram Powers, John Ran-
  dolph, John Tyler, Martin Van Buren,
  Daniel Webster, Roger Williams
ADAMS, JOSEPH John Hunter
ADAMS, M. RAY Joel Barlow
ADAMS, SAMUEL HOPKINS Warren
  G. Harding
ADDINGTON, HENRY (LORD

SIDMOUTH) (q.v.) Lord Grey,
  Spencer Perceval
ADDISON, JOSEPH (q.v.) Geoffrey
  Chaucer, Duke of Marlborough, John
  Milton, Shakespeare, Edmund Spenser,
  Edmund Waller, Lord Wharton
ADLER, LARRY James Thurber
ADLER, RICHARD Cole Porter
ADLER, STELLA Clifford Odets
AGAR, HERBERT James G. Blaine,
  Ulysses S. Grant
AGATE, JAMES Sir Henry Irving
AGEE, JAMES Sir Charles Chaplin,
  Buster Keaton, Mack Sennett
AIKEN, CONRAD Emily Dickinson,
  William Faulkner, H. G. Wells
AIKEN, GEORGE Robert A. Taft
AIKIN, LUCY (q.v.) Harriet Martineau,
  Robert Montgomery
ALBERT, PRINCE (q.v.) Edward VII,
  Queen Victoria
ALBERY, JAMES Sir Henry Irving
ALCOTT, AMOS BRONSON (q.v.)
  Louisa May Alcott, John Brown,
  Mary Baker Eddy, Henry David
  Thoreau
ALCOTT, LOUISA MAY (q.v.) Amos
  Bronson Alcott
ALDINGTON, RICHARD T. S. Eliot
ALDRICH, THOMAS BAILEY (q.v.)
  Emily Dickinson, Sarah Orne Jewett,
  Edgar Allen Poe
ALDRIDGE, JOHN F. Scott Fitz-
  gerald, John O'Hara
ALEXANDER, HOLMES Martin Van
  Buren
ALLEN, FRED (q.v.) Jack Benny
ALLEN, GEORGE E. Benjamin
  Disraeli, Knute Rockne, Harry S.
  Truman
ALLEN, LEVI Ethan Allen
ALLEN, WILLIAM H. John D.
  Rockefeller
ALLINGHAM, WILLIAM A. H. Clough,
  Alfred, Lord Tennyson
ALLVINE, GLENDON William Fox
ALSOP, JOSEPH and STEWART
  Joseph McCarthy
AMBERLEY, LADY George Eliot
AMERY, L. S. H. H. Asquith, Sir
  Winston Churchill
AMES, FISHER (q.v.) James Madison
AMIS, KINGSLEY Jane Austen, Ivy
  Compton-Burnett, Charles Dickens,

Ian Fleming, John Keats, D. H.
  Lawrence, T. E. Lawrence, George
  Orwell, Thomas Love Peacock
AMORY, THOMAS Edmund Curll
ANDERSON, EDDIE 'ROCHESTER'
  Jack Benny
ANDERSON, ROBERT G. Lon Chaney
ANDERSON, SHERWOOD (q.v.)
  Ford Madox Ford, Huey Long, Carl
  Sandburg
ANGELO, HENRY James Barry, Thomas
  Gainsborough, James Gillray, William
  Hogarth, George Morland, Thomas
  Rowlandson
ANGLO-SAXON CHRONICLE Alfred
ANGOFF, CHARLES Benjamin
  Franklin
ANTEK, SAMUEL Arturo Toscanini
ANNAN, GABRIELE Noël Coward,
  Ivor Novello
ANTHONY, SUSAN B. (q.v.) Amelia
  Bloomer, Frederick Douglass,
  Elizabeth Cady Stanton
APPLEBY, J. J. Richard I
ARBESSER, ROSE Charlotte Yonge
ARBUCKLE, MINTA DURFEE
  Roscoe 'Fatty' Arbuckle
ARBUTHNOT, JOHN (q.v.) Queen
  Anne, Francis Chartres, Sir John
  Cutler
ARCHER, WILLIAM William Hazlitt,
  John Webster
ARGYLL, DUKE OF Benjamin
  Disraeli, Lord Salisbury
ARMOUR, RICHARD John Adams,
  John Quincy Adams, Samuel Adams,
  Chester A. Arthur, James Buchanan,
  Edmund Burke, Aaron Burr, Andrew
  Carnegie, Kit Carson, 'Buffalo Bill'
  Cody, Davy Crockett, John Foster
  Dulles, Thomas Alva Edison, Millard
  Fillmore, Benjamin Franklin, John C.
  Frémont, Ulysses S. Grant, Nathan
  Hale, Warren G. Harding, William
  Henry Harrison, Nathaniel Hawthorne,
  William Randolph Hearst, 'Wild Bill'
  Hickok, Thomas Hooker, Sam
  Houston, Andrew Jackson, Thomas
  Jefferson, John Paul Jones, Meri-
  wether Lewis, Abraham Lincoln,
  Joseph McCarthy, Cyrus McCormick,
  Dolly Madison, James Monroe,
  Samuel F. B. Morse, Carrie Nation,
  William Penn, Oliver Hazard Perry,

Franklin Pierce, Paul Revere, John D. Rockefeller, Zachary Taylor, John Tyler, Martin Van Buren, Cornelius Vanderbilt, George Washington, Roger Williams, Brigham Young
ARMS, GEORGE James Russell Lowell
ARMSTRONG, D. MAITLAND George Inness
ARMSTRONG, JOHN P. Robert A. Taft
ARMSTRONG, LOUIS (q.v.) Bing Crosby
ARMSTRONG, WILLIAM M. E. L. Godkin
ARNOLD, MATTHEW (q.v.) Branwell Brontë, Emily Brontë, Robert Browning, Lord Byron, Geoffrey Chaucer, William Cobbett, John Dryden, Thomas Gray, John Keats, John Knox, T. B. Macaulay, Harriet Martineau, John Milton, Alexander Pope, Sir Walter Scott, Shakespeare, Percy Bysshe Shelley, Alfred, Lord Tennyson, Lester Frank Ward, William Wordsworth
ARRIN, NEWTON Carl Sandburg
ARTHUR, BOB Harry S. Truman
ASCHAM, ROGER Lady Jane Grey, Thomas Malory
ASHMORE, HENRY S. Adlai E. Stevenson
ASQUITH, LADY CYNTHIA Siegfried Sassoon
ASQUITH, HERBERT HENRY, LORD (q.v.) Nancy, Lady Astor, John Bright, Joseph Chamberlain, Benjamin Jowett, Bonar Law, Beatrice Webb
ASQUITH, MARGOT, Lady (q.v.) Lord Birkenhead, Lady Randolph Churchill, Rufus Isaacs, Lord Kitchener, David Lloyd George
ASSER Alfred
ASTON, ANTHONY Elizabeth Barry
ASTOR, VISCOUNT Nancy, Lady Astor
ATKINS, ELIZABETH Edna St Vincent Millay
ATKINSON, BROOKS Fred Allen, John Barrymore, Lionel Barrymore, John Mason Brown, George M. Cohan, Katharine Cornell, Bert Lahr, Basil Rathbone, Henry David Thoreau
ATKINSON, ROGER Patrick Henry, George Washington
ATTLEE, CLEMENT (q.v.) Lord Beaverbrook
AUBREY, JOHN (q.v.) George Abbot, Thomas Allen, Edward Alleyn, Sir Francis Bacon, Francis Beaumont, Robert Boyle, Samuel Butler, Charles I, Charles II, Sir Edward Coke, John Colet, Oliver Cromwell, Sir William D'Avenant, John Dee, Sir John Denham, Sir Matthew Hale, Edmund

Halley, Thomas Hariot, James Harrington, William Harvey, Lord Herbert of Cherbury, Mary Herbert, Thomas Hobbes, Robert Hooke, James II, Ben Jonson, William Laud, Richard Lovelace, Andrew Marvell, John Milton, Sir Thomas Moore, William Penn, Sir William Petty, William Prynne, Sir Walter Raleigh, Henry Vaughan, Edmund Waller, Seth Ward, Thomas Wolsey
AUCHINCLOSS, LOUIS Ellen Glasgow, Carson McCullers, John O'Hara, Edith Wharton
AUDEN, W. H. (q.v.) Jane Austen, Sir Max Beerbohm, William Blake, James Boswell, Robert Browning, Lord Byron, Cyril Connolly, Walter De La Mare, Charles Dickens, John Dryden, T. S. Eliot, Sir H. Rider Haggard, Thomas Hardy, Henry James, Rudyard Kipling, D. H. Lawrence, Percy Wyndham Lewis, Edgar Allen Poe, Alexander Pope, Shakespeare, George Bernard Shaw, Earl of Surrey, Alfred, Lord Tennyson, W. M. Thackeray, Anthony Trollope, Oscar Wilde, Virginia Woolf, William Wordsworth, W. B. Yeats
AUSTEN, HENRY Jane Austen
AUSTEN, JANE (q.v.) Queen Caroline of Brunswick, Maria Edgeworth, Edward IV, Lady Jane Grey, Henry VIII, John Murray, Mrs Radcliffe, Sir Walter Scott
AUSTIN, ALFRED (q.v.) Edward VII
AUSTIN, J. L. (q.v.) G. E. Moore
AYER, A. J. J. L. Austin, Bertrand Russell
AYLOFFE, JOHN Lord Arlington, First Lord Shaftesbury
AYRE, LESLIE Frederick Delius, Sir Edward Elgar, Sir Henry Irving, Sir Malcolm Sargent, Sir Ralph Vaughan Williams, Henry Wood
AYRES, C. E. John Dewey

BACALL, LAUREN Humphrey Bogart
BACHE, SARAH FRANKLIN Thomas Paine
BACKUS, ISAAC (q.v.) Ann Lee
BACON, FRANCIS (q.v.) Robert Cecil, Sir Edward Coke, Francis Drake, Henry VII
BACON, SIR REGINALD H. S. Lord Fisher
BADEAU, ADAM Ulysses S. Grant
BAGEHOT, WALTER (q.v.) Queen Anne, Thomas Arnold, Lord Brougham, Robert Browning, A. H. Clough, Richard Cobden, William Cowper, Henry Fielding, George III, David Hume, Lord Lyndhurst, Lady Mary Wortley Montagu, Daniel

O'Connell, Lord Palmerston, W. M. Thackeray
BAIGELL, MATTHEW Thomas Hart Benton
BAILEY, GAMALIEL William Lloyd Garrison
BAILEY, PERCIVAL Harvey Cushing
BAILEY, THOMAS A. James A. Garfield, Henry Cabot Lodge, William McKinley, William Howard Taft, Woodrow Wilson
BAIN, ALEXANDER John Stuart Mill
BAINES, EDWARD Sir Richard Arkwright
BAKELESS, JOHN E. Daniel Boone, Meriwether Lewis
BAKER, CARLOS F. Scott Fitzgerald, Ernest Hemingway
BAKER, RAY STANNARD Samuel Gompers, Lincoln Steffens, Ida Tarbell
BAKER, SIR RICHARD William Prynne
BALDWIN, JAMES Bessie Smith
BALDWIN, STANLEY, LORD (q.v.) Austen Chamberlain, Sir Winston Churchill, Lord Curzon, Bonar Law
BALFOUR, ALICE Lord Kitchener
BALFOUR, ARTHUR (q.v.) Joseph Chamberlain, Queen Victoria
BAMFORD, SAMUEL William Cobbett
BANCROFT, FREDERIC William Henry Seward
BANCROFT, GEORGE (q.v.) Thomas Hooker, James Oglethorpe, Roger Williams
BANCROFT, HUBERT HOWE James K. Polk
BANCROFT, THOMAS James Shirley
BANE, MICHAEL Elvis Presley
BARBAULD, ANNA LAETITIA Samuel Johnson
BARBIROLLI, SIR JOHN (q.v.) Sir Thomas Beecham
BARBOUR, PHILIP Pocahontas
BARCE, THANKFUL Ann Lee
BARKER, E. H. Henry Fielding, Richard Porson
BARKER, GEORGE T. S. Eliot, Dylan Thomas
BARKER, HARLEY GRANVILLE (q.v.) John Dryden, Ben Jonson, Shakespeare
BARKLEY, ALBEN Huey Long
BARLOW, JOEL (q.v.) Benedict Arnold, Timothy Dwight, Thomas Paine
BARNES, COLONEL Caleb Cushing
BARNES, GILBERT H. William Lloyd Garrison
BARNES, T. R. Lytton Strachey
BARNETT, CORRELLI Lord Jellicoe
BARON, W. Walter Richard Sickert

BARRETT, JAMES WYMAN Joseph Pulitzer

BARRETT, LAWRENCE (q.v.) Charlotte Cushman, George Armstrong Custer

BARRINGTON, MRS RUSSELL Walter Bagehot

BARROW, SIR JOHN Lord Anson

BARRY, JAMES (q.v.) Thomas Gainsborough

BARRYMORE, ETHEL (q.v.) John Drew, Walter Winchell

BARRYMORE, JOHN (q.v.) Gary Cooper

BARTHOLOMEW, E. Wyatt Earp

BARTLETT, WILLIAM O. William Marcy Tweed

BARTON, MARGARET William Beckford

BARUCH, BERNARD M. (q.v.) Herbert Hoover

BASSETT, JOHN SPENCER George Bancroft, Jared Sparks

BASTWICK, JOHN William Walwyn

BATES, ERNEST SUTHERLAND Randolph Bourne

BATES, KATHARINE Emily Dickinson

BATESON, F. W. Andrew Marvell

BATHURST, LORD John Gay

BAXTER, ANNE Frank Lloyd Wright

BAXTER, BEVERLEY Lord Beaverbrook

BAXTER, JOHN Douglas Fairbanks

BAXTER, J. W. William Dunbar

BAXTER, RICHARD (q.v.) Oliver Cromwell, Lord Fairfax

BAY, W. V. N. Thomas Hart Benton

BAYLISS, WYKE Sir Edward Burne-Jones, Sir John Everett Millais

BEACH, SYLVIA Ezra Pound

BEADON, ROGER Robert Blake

BEALE, HOWARD K. Andrew Johnson

BEARD, CHARLES Carl Becker, Thomas Jefferson, Vernon Parrington, James Ford Rhodes

BEATON, CECIL Sir Max Beerbohm, Elinor Glyn, Somerset Maugham, Lytton Strachey, Evelyn Waugh

BEATTIE, J. H. David Hume

BEATTIE, LESTER M. John Arbuthnot

BEAUMONT, FRANCIS (q.v.) Edmund Spenser

BEAUMONT, SIR JOHN Francis Beaumont

BEAVERBROOK, LORD (q.v.) Stanley Baldwin, Aneurin Bevan, Lord Birkenhead, Austen Chamberlain, Neville Chamberlain, Sir Winston Churchill, Lord Curzon, Lord Haig, Samuel Hoare, David Lloyd George, Ramsay MacDonald, Lord Northcliffe, Edward Wood

BECKER, CARL (q.v.) George Bancroft, Frederick Jackson Turner

BECKETT, SAMUEL James Joyce

BECKFORD, WILLIAM (q.v.) Edward Gibbon

BEDE (q.v.) Aidan, Caedmon, Cuthbert, Edwin

BEE, BARNARD E. 'Stonewall' Jackson

BEE, JOHN John Dryden, Samuel Foote, David Garrick

BEECHAM, SIR THOMAS (q.v.) Frederick Delius, Sir Edward Elgar, John Fletcher, Arturo Toscanini

BEECHER, HENRY WARD (q.v.) John Brown, James Fisk Jr. Abraham Lincoln, George G. Meade

BEECHER, LYMAN William Lloyd Garrison

BEECHING, SIR H. C. Benjamin Jowett

BEERBOHM, MAX (q.v.) Thomas Carlyle, Queen Caroline of Brunswick, G. K. Chesterton, Lord Curzon, Sir Henry Irving, Henry James, Jerome K. Jerome, George Meredith, George Moore, Walter Pater, Lytton Strachey, Sir Herbert Beerbohm Tree, James McNeill Whistler, Oscar Wilde

BEERS, HENRY A. James Whitcomb Riley

BEETHOVEN, LUDWIG VAN G. F. Handel

BEGBIE, HAROLD William Booth

BEHAN, BRENDAN James Joyce

BEHLMER, RUDY David O. Selznick

BEHN, APHRA Ben Jonson, Thomas Otway

BEHRMAN, S. N. Lord Duveen, Oscar Levant

BEL GEDDES, NORMAN Cecil B. De Mille, W. C. Fields, D. W. Griffith, Harpo Marx, Florenz Ziegfeld

BELL, CLIVE Lord Keynes, Percy Wyndham Lewis, Lytton Strachey

BELL, DANIEL Samuel Gompers

BELL, EDWARD ('TENAX') Horatio Bottomley

BELL, ROBERT W. M. Thackeray

BELLOC, HILAIRE (q.v.) James II, P. G. Wodehouse

BELLOW, SAUL F. Scott Fitzgerald

BEMIS, SAMUEL FLAGG John Quincy Adams

BENÉT, STEPHEN VINCENT Maxwell Anderson, John James Audobon, Judah P. Benjamin, Daniel Boone, John Brown, 'Stonewall' Jackson, Thomas Jefferson, 'Captain' Kidd, Abraham Lincoln, Cotton Mather, Franklin D. Roosevelt

BENÉT, WILLIAM ROSE William Blake

BENNETT, ARNOLD (q.v.) Joseph Conrad, Henry James, D. H. Lawrence, Percy Wyndham Lewis, John Masefield, Siegfried Sassoon, Tobias Smollett, Mark Twain

BENNETT, H. G. Henry Grattan

BENNETT SR, JAMES GORDON (q.v.) Horace Greeley

BENNETT JR, JAMES GORDON (q.v.) Joseph Pulitzer

BENNETT, MILDRED R. Willa Cather

BENTHAM, JEREMY (q.v.) Lord Brougham, Lord Eldon, Samuel Johnson, James Mill

BENTLEY, EDMUND CLERIHEW Sir Francis Bacon, Hilaire Belloc, Sir Humphry Davy, George III, Henry VIII, Edgar Allen Poe, William II, Sir Christopher Wren

BENTLEY, ERIC Eugene O'Neill, George Bernard Shaw

BENTLEY, NICOLAS Alfred, Boadicea, Cecil B. De Mille, Edward the Confessor, Hengist and Horsa

BENTLEY, RICHARD (q.v.) Alexander Pope

BENTLEY, WILLIAM Samuel Adams, Roger Williams

BENTON, THOMAS HART (politician) (q.v.) John Quincy Adams, Stephen A. Douglas

BENTON, THOMAS HART (artist) (q.v.) George Caleb Bingham, Jackson Pollock

BERENSON, BERNARD (q.v.) Gilbert Murray

BERESFORD, WILLIAM (q.v.) Sir Robert Peel

BERGER, PHILIP Lenny Bruce

BERKLEY, SIR JOHN Oliver Cromwell

BERNARD, SIR FRANCIS Samuel Adams

BERNAYS, EDWARD L. Enrico Caruso

BERNINI, GIOVANNI Charles I

BESSBOROUGH, LADY (q.v.) Lord Aberdeen, Henry Addington,

BETJEMAN, SIR JOHN Oscar Wilde

BEVAN, ANEURIN (q.v.) Clement Attlee, Stanley Baldwin, Neville Chamberlain, Sir Winston Churchill, Hugh Gaitskell

BEWLEY, MARIUS William Cullen Bryant

BICKFORD, CHARLES Cecil B. De Mille, Louis B. Mayer

BIDDLE, FRANCIS Oliver Wendell Holmes Jr

BIERCE, AMBROSE (q.v.) Sir Francis Bacon, Stephen Crane, Bret Harte, William Dean Howells, William McKinley, James Whitcomb Riley, Oscar Wilde

BIGELOW, POULTNEY Andrew Carnegie

BIGLAND, REUBEN Horatio Bottomley

BILLINGS, JOHN S. S. F. Baird
BILLINGTON, MICHAEL Harley Granville Barker
BILLINGTON, RAY ALLEN Frederick Jackson Turner
BINGHAM, PEREGRINE Thomas Moore
BIRCH, MR Thomas Hart Benton
BIRCHARD, SARDIS Rutherford B. Hayes
BIRKENHEAD, LORD (F. E. SMITH) (q.v.) Stanley Baldwin, Austen Chamberlain, George V
BIRNBAUM, MARTIN John Singer Sargent, W. B. Yeats
BIRRELL, AUGUSTINE Matthew Arnold, Henry Fielding, Sir William Harcourt, Alexander Pope
BIXBY, A. L. Lizzie Borden
BLACK, JEREMIAH James A. Garfield, Thaddeus Stevens
BLACK, STEPHEN A. James Thurber
BLAINE, JAMES G. (q.v.) Judah P. Benjamin, Roscoe Conkling, Carl Schurz, Samuel J. Tilden, Martin Van Buren
BLAKE, WILLIAM (q.v.) Sir Francis Bacon, John Flaxman, William Hayley, James I, Samuel Johnson, John Milton, Sir Isaac Newton, Sir Joshua Reynolds
BLANCHE, JACQUES Walter Richard Sickert
BLANKENSHIP, RUSSELL Emily Dickinson
BLANSHARD, PAUL Fiorello La Guardia
BLATCHFORD, ROBERT John Bunyan
BLESSINGTON, LADY (q.v.) Lord Byron, Sir Walter Scott
BLIVEN, BRUCE Heywood Broun
BLOCK, HERBERT LAWRENCE Henry Luce
BLOET, BISHOP Henry I
BLOMFIELD, SIR REGINALD William Kent, Sir John Vanbrugh, Sir Christopher Wren
BLOOMFIELD, SIR BENJAMIN Queen Caroline of Brunswick
BLOOMINGDALE, JUDITH Lewis Carroll
BLOUNT, EDWARD John Lyly
BLUM, FRED H. C. Wright Mills
BLUM, JOHN M. Theodore Roosevelt
BLUNDEN, EDMUND T. S. Eliot, Benjamin R. Haydon, Rudyard Kipling
BOASE, T. S. R. Samuel Courtauld
BOGART, HUMPHREY (q.v.) Spencer Tracy
BOLINGBROKE, LORD (q.v.) James Francis Edward Stuart
BONE, JAMES C. P. Scott

BOOTH, BARTON Thomas Betterton
BOOTH, EDWIN (q.v.) John Wilkes Booth
BOOTH, JOHN WILKES (q.v.) Edwin Booth, Abraham Lincoln
BORAH, WILLIAM E. (q.v.) Robert La Follette
BORDEN, EMMA Lizzie Borden
BORGHUM, GUTZON Herbert Hoover
BORROW, GEORGE John Crome, Henry Fielding
BOSWELL, ALEXANDER Oliver Cromwell
BOSWELL, JAMES (q.v.) (see also Samuel Johnson) George Berkeley, James Bruce, George Buchanan, Edmund Burke, Charles Churchill, Colley Cibber, James Cook, John Dryden, Henry Fielding, Samuel Foote, David Garrick, John Gay, George III, Oliver Goldsmith, Thomas Gray, David Hume, Samuel Johnson, Lord Mansfield, Elizabeth Montagu, Alexander Pope, Joseph Priestley, Matthew Prior, Allan Ramsay, Samuel Richardson, Sarah Siddons, Christopher Smart, James Thomson, William Warburton, William Wilberforce, John Wilmot
BOTT, ALAN T. E. Lawrence
BOURNE, RANDOLPH (q.v.) Nicholas Murray Butler
BOWDEN, B. V. Charles Babbage, William Thomson
BOWEN, CATHERINE DRINKER Oliver Wendell Holmes Jr
BOWEN, ELIZABETH Aldous Huxley
BOWEN, STELLA Ford Madox Ford
BOWERS, CLAUDE A. Thaddeus Stevens
BOWERS, CLAUDE G. John Adams
BOWLE, JOHN Roger Bacon, Henry V, Richard II
BOWLES, CAROLINE Robert Montgomery
BOWLES, SAMUEL Charles A. Dana, Thurlow Weed
BOWRA, SIR MAURICE Hugh Gaitskell, Nancy Mitford
BOWSER, EILEEN D. W. Griffith
BOYAN, LOUISE Marianne Moore
BOYD, ERNEST H. L. Mencken
BOYLE, ROBERT (q.v.) William Harvey
BRACKEN, BRENDAN Sir Stafford Cripps
BRACKETT, CHARLES D. W. Griffith
BRADFORD, GAMALIEL Robert E. Lee, George B. Meade
BRADFORD, WILLIAM (q.v.) Roger Williams
BRADLEY, P. H. (q.v.) Matthew Arnold
BRADSHAIGH, LADY DOROTHY

Henry Fielding
BRALEY, BERTON Thomas Dewey
BRANDON, HENRY Walter Lippmann
BRANTLEY, JOHN D. John Dos Passos
BRAY, CHARLES George Eliot
BREEN, MATTHEW Roscoe Conkling, William Marcy Tweed
BRENAN, GERALD Lytton Strachey
BRESLIN, JAMES E. William Carlos Williams
BREWER, J. S. George Abbot
BRIDGEMAN, RICHARD Gertrude Stein
BRIDGES-ADAMS, W. Hilaire Belloc
BRIGGS, ASA George Gissing, Samuel Smiles
BRIGHT, JOHN (q.v.) Benjamin Disraeli, W. E. Gladstone, Abraham Lincoln, Lord Palmerston
BRINNIN, JOHN MALCOLM Gertrude Stein, William Carlos Williams
BROAD, C. D. Sir Francis Bacon, John Locke, J. E. McTaggart
BRODIE, FAWN Joseph Smith, Thaddeus Stevens
BROMFIELD, LOUIS Anna 'Grandma' Moses
BROMLEY, DOROTHY D. Nicholas Murray Butler
BRONTË, CHARLOTTE (q.v.) Jane Austen, Anne Brontë, Emily Brontë, Elizabeth Gaskell, Robert Southey, W. M. Thackeray
BROOKE, JOCELYN Ivy Compton-Burnett
BROOKE, JOHN George III
BROOKE, RUPERT (q.v.) Robert Browning, John Donne, J. E. Flecker, John Webster
BROOKES, STELLA BREWER Joel Chandler Harris
BROOKS, CLEANTH William Faulkner
BROOKS, FRED EMERSON George Pickett
BROOKS, VAN WYCK (q.v.) Thomas Bailey Aldrich, Bernard Berenson, Ambrose Bierce, Randolph Bourne, William Cullen Bryant, Stephen Crane, Richard Harding Davis, Ralph Waldo Emerson, Ford Madox Ford, Ellen Glasgow, E. L. Godkin, Edward Everett Hale, Joel Chandler Harris, Oliver Wendell Holmes, Sidney Lanier, Henry Wadsworth Longfellow, James Russell Lowell, Hiram Powers, Upton Sinclair, Jared Sparks, Harriet Beecher Stowe, Henry David Thoreau, Mark Twain, John Greenleaf Whittier, Edmund Wilson
BROOME, WILLIAM Alexander Pope
BROPHY, BRIGID Jane Austen, Ivy Compton-Burnett, Evelyn Waugh, Virginia Woolf

BROPHY, JAMES D. W. H. Auden
BROUGHAM, LORD (q.v.) Joseph Black, Lord Campbell, Henry Cavendish, David Hume, Lord Lyndhurst, Joseph Priestley, John Horne Tooke, James Watt
BROUGHTON, LORD Richard Cavendish, Charles James Fox, Samuel Johnson, Edmund Kean, Lady Caroline Lamb, Lord North, Sarah Siddons, John Horne Tooke
BROUN, HEYWOOD (q.v.) F. Scott Fitzgerald, Fiorello La Guardia, Vachel Lindsay, Franklin D. Roosevelt, Alexander Woollcott
BROWN, BEATRICE CURTIS Queen Anne
BROWN, CHARLES REYNOLDS Edward Everett Hale
BROWN, DEE Crazy Horse
BROWN, E. K. Willa Cather
BROWN, GEORGE ROTHWELL Robert La Follette
BROWN, IVOR Ivor Novello
BROWN, JOHN MASON (q.v.) Maxwell Anderson, Sir Charles Chaplin, George M. Cohan, Clifford Odets, Eugene O'Neill, Alexander Woollcott
BROWN, JOSEPH Ulysses S. Grant
BROWN, OLIVER P. James A. Garfield
BROWN, ROLLO WALTER Charles William Eliot
BROWN, THOMAS Dr John Fell, Titus Oates, Thomas Shadwell
BROWNE, CHARLES FARRAR see WARD, ARTEMUS
BROWNE, WILLIAM George Chapman, Mary Herbert
BROWNE, SIR WILLIAM George I
BROWNING, ELIZABETH BARRETT (q.v.) Matthew Arnold, Lord Byron, Thomas Carlyle, Geoffrey Chaucer, Robert Herrick, John Keats, Charles Kingsley, Harriet Martineau, Sir Robert Peel, Alfred, Lord Tennyson, Anthony Trollope
BROWNING, ORVILLE H. Charles Sumner
BROWNING, ROBERT (q.v.) Elizabeth Barrett Browning, Lord Nelson, Percy Bysshe Shelley, Algernon C. Swinburne, Alfred, Lord Tennyson, William Wordsworth
BROWNLOW, KEVIN Cecil B. De Mille, Josef von Sternberg
BROWNSON, ORESTES Margaret Fuller
BRUCE, THOMAS (EARL OF AYLESBURY) James II
BRUCKNER, GENERAL Ulysses S. Grant
BRUMMELL, BEAU George IV

BRYAN, WILLIAM JENNINGS (q.v.) Charles Evans Hughes, William Howard Taft
BRYANT, SIR ARTHUR William Pitt
BRYANT, WILLIAM CULLEN (q.v.) Horace Greeley, Noah Webster
BRYCE, JAMES Richard of Cornwall
BRYCE, LORD Charles Parnell, Theodore Roosevelt
BRYDEN, RONALD John Webster
BRYDGES, SIR E. William Cowper
BUCHAN, ALASTAIR Walter Lippmann
BUCHAN, JOHN Oliver Cromwell, William Laud, Prince Rupert, Lord Strafford
BUCHANAN, ROBERT John James Audubon, Henry James, Rudyard Kipling, Algernon C. Swinburne
BUCKLE, H. T. (q.v.) James II
BULL, MARY Susan B. Anthony
BULL, WILLIAM William Penn
BULLARD, SIR EDWARD Lord Rutherford
BULLARD, ROGER L. John J. Pershing
BULLITT, WILLIAM C. Woodrow Wilson
BULLOUGH, GEOFFREY Shakespeare
BUNCH, RALPH Marcus Garvey
BUNDY, MCGEORGE Robert F. Kennedy
BURANELLI, VINCENT Josiah Royce
BURCHFIELD, CHARLES Edward Hopper
BURDON, ROWLAND Sir John Soane
BURGESS, ANTHONY Charles Dickens, T. S. Eliot, Mervyn Peake, Dylan Thomas
BURGESS, GELETT Aubrey Beardsley
BURKE, CHARLES T. 'King' Philip
BURKE, EDMUND (q.v.) Oliver Cromwell, Charles James Fox, Lord North, William Pitt, Lord Rockingham
BURKE, JOHN Lillian Russell
BURLINGAME, ROGER William 'Billy' Mitchell
BURNET, GILBERT (q.v.) Richard Baxter, William Bentinck, Robert Boyle, Second Duke of Buckingham, Charles II, John Fisher, Sir Matthew Hale, Edward Hyde, James II, Duke of Lauderdale, William Penn, George Savile, First Lord Shaftesbury, Thomas à Becket, Seth Ward, William III, Anthony à Wood
BURNET, JOHN John Crome
BURNEY, DR CHARLES John Blow, William Boyce, John Bull, William Byrd, John Dowland, Orlando Gibbons, Thomas Morley, Henry Purcell
BURNEY, FANNY (q.v.) Thomas

Arne, Sir Joseph Banks, James Boswell, James Bruce, Edmund Burke, David Garrick, Sir William Herschel, Samuel Johnson, Lady Caroline Lamb, Sarah Siddons, Horace Walpole, Mary Ann Yates
BURNEY, WILLIAM Wallace Stevens
BURNS, GEORGE Al Jolson
BURNS, JAMES MACGREGOR Franklin D. Roosevelt, Robert A. Taft
BURNS, JOHN David Lloyd George
BURNS, ROBERT (q.v.) Mary Queen of Scots, Charles Edward Stuart
BURR, AARON (q.v.) James Monroe
BURROUGHS, JOHN Henry David Thoreau
BURROUGHS, WILLIAM T. S. Eliot
BURROWES, ROBERT Samuel Johnson
BURTON, J. H. David Hume
BUSH, DOUGLAS John Milton
BUTLER, BENJAMIN F. (q.v.) James G. Blaine
BUTLER, HUGH Dean Acheson
BUTLER, JOSEPHINE Elizabeth Garrett Anderson
BUTLER, PIERCE Albert Gallatin
BUTLER, SAMUEL (1612–80) (q.v.) Second Duke of Buckingham, Oliver Cromwell, Richard Cromwell, John Lilburne, First Lord Shaftesbury
BUTLER, SAMUEL (1835–1902) (q.v.) Walter Pater, Dante Gabriel Rossetti, Alfred, Lord Tennyson
BUTTERFIELD, L. H. Abigail Adams
BYRDSALL, FITZWILLIAM William L. Marcy
BYROM, JOHN Charles Edward Stuart
BYRON, LADY Lord Byron
BYRON, LORD (q.v.) William Beckford, George Berkeley, William Betty, Lady Blessington, Daniel Boone, Lord Brougham, Sir Francis Burdett, Robert Burns, Robert Burton, Thomas Campbell, George. Canning, Lord Castlereagh, Thomas Chatterton, Charles Churchill, Samuel Taylor Coleridge, William Congreve, William Cowper, Oliver Cromwell, Duke of Cumberland, Maria Edgeworth, Henry Fielding, George III, George IV, William Gifford, Henry Grattan, Patrick Henry, James Hogg, Leigh Hunt, Samuel Johnson, Edmund Kean, John Keats, Lady Caroline Lamb, Lord Liverpool, T. R. Malthus, Duke of Marlborough, Annabella Milbanke, John Milton, Lady Mary Wortley Montagu, Thomas Moore, John Murray, Sir Isaac Newton, Thomas Paine, William Pitt, Alexander Pope, Sir Walter Scott, Anna Seward,

Shakespeare, Mary Shelley, Percy Bysshe Shelley, Richard Brinsley Sheridan, Robert Southey, Laurence Sterne, Izaac Walton, George Washington, Duke of Wellington, William Wilberforce, William Wordsworth

CADOGAN, SIR ALEXANDER John Foster Dulles

CAIRNS, LORD Benjamin Disraeli

CALHOUN, JOHN CALDWELL (q.v.) Thomas Hart Benton, Henry Clay, James Monroe, Martin Van Buren

CALLAGHAN, MORLEY Ernest Hemingway

CAMBRENSIS, see GIRALDUS

CAMDEN, WILLIAM (q.v.) Elizabeth I, Sir Francis Walsingham

CAMERON, SIR DONALD Sidney Webb

CAMPBELL, ARCHIBALD Samuel Johnson

CAMPBELL, LORD Prince Albert, Judge Jeffreys

CAMPBELL, MRS PATRICK (q.v.) Tallulah Bankhead, Sir James Matthew Barrie, George Bernard Shaw

CAMPBELL, ROBERT E. William L. Marcy

CAMPBELL, ROY Aubrey Beardsley, Aldous Huxley, Bertrand Russell

CAMPBELL, THOMAS (q.v.) Robert Burns, George Crabbe

CAMPBELL-BANNERMAN, SIR HENRY (q.v.) Sir William Harcourt

CANBY, HENRY SEIDEL James Fenimore Cooper, Ralph Waldo Emerson, Washington Irving, Herman Melville, Dorothy Parker, Edgar Allen Poe

CANNING, GEORGE (q.v.) Lord Brougham, William Pitt

CANNON, 'UNCLE' JOE William McKinley

CANNON, W. B. T. H. Huxley

CANTOR, EDDIE Al Jolson, Sophie Tucker, Florenz Ziegfeld

CANTWELL, ROBERT Sinclair Lewis, Upton Sinclair

CAPE, EMILY PALMER Lester Frank Ward

CAPRA, FRANK Gary Cooper, John Ford

CARDUS, SIR NEVILLE Sir Thomas Beecham, Arturo Toscanini

CAREW, THOMAS (q.v.) Ben Jonson

CAREY, HENRY Ambrose Philips

CARGILL, OSCAR Gertrude Stein

CARLYLE, ALEXANDER Adam Smith

CARLYLE, JANE WELSH (q.v.) Jane Austen, Lord Byron, Thomas

Carlyle, Elizabeth Gaskell, Augustus Granville, John Keats

CARLYLE, THOMAS (q.v.) Amos Bronson Alcott, St Anselm, Sir Francis Bacon, George Bancroft, Jeremy Bentham, Thomas Bewick, Robert Browning, Robert Burns, Lord Byron, Charles I, William Cobbett, Sir Edward Coke, Samuel Taylor Coleridge, Oliver Cromwell, Richard Cromwell, Charles Darwin, George Eliot, George I, W. E. Gladstone, Lord Houghton, Henry Ireton, Washington Irving, James I, Samuel Johnson, John Paul Jones, Ben Jonson, John Keats, John Knox, William Laud, Edmund Ludlow, T. B. Macaulay, John Stuart Mill, John Milton, Sir Charles Napier, Thomas Paine, Richard I, John Ruskin, Sir Walter Scott, Shakespeare, Robert Southey, Laurence Sterne, Lord Strafford, Charles Sumner, Algernon C. Swinburne, Alfred, Lord Tennyson, Thomas à Becket, Sir Henry Vane, Daniel Webster, Sir Henry Wotton

CARNEGIE, ANDREW (q.v.) John Pierpont Morgan, Booker T. Washington

CARNES, CECIL John L. Lewis

CARPENTER, FREDERICK IVES Ralph Waldo Emerson

CARR, JOHN DICKSON Raymond Chandler

CARRE, THOMAS Richard Crashaw

CARRIAGUE, JEAN Marianne Moore

CARSWELL, CATHERINE D. H. Lawrence

CARTERET, LORD (q.v.) Jonathan Swift

CARTWRIGHT, WILLIAM John Fletcher, Shakespeare

CARTY, JOHN J. Alexander Graham Bell

CARUSO, DOROTHY Enrico Caruso

CARY, PHOEBE Susan B. Anthony

CARY, RICHARD John Wilkes Booth, Sarah Orne Jewett

CARYLL, JOHN Titus Oates, Sir William Scroggs, First Lord Shaftesbury

CATER, HAROLD DEAN Henry Adams

CATHER, WILLA (q.v.) William Jennings Bryan, Stephen Crane

CATON, BRUCE George B. McClellan

CAULFIELD, JAMES David Hume

CAUSLEY, CHARLES W. H. Auden

CAVENDISH, GEORGE Henry VIII, Thomas Wolsey

CAVENDISH, WILLIAM Ben Jonson, Shakespeare

CAXTON, WILLIAM (q.v.) Geoffrey Chaucer

CECIL, LORD DAVID Sir Max Beerbohm, Elizabeth Gaskell, Lady Caroline Lamb

CECIL, LORD HUGH Neville Chamberlain, David Lloyd George

CECIL, LORD ROBERT (q.v.) Gilbert and Sullivan

CERF, BENNETT (q.v.) Somerset Maugham, Alexander Woollcott

CHAIN, SIR ERNEST Lord Rank

CHALMERS, THOMAS Jonathan Edwards

CHAMBERLAIN, JOHN Orlando Gibbons

CHAMBERLAIN, JOSEPH (q.v.) Queen Victoria

CHAMPLIN, CHARLES Humphrey Bogart, Clark Gable

CHANDLER, RAYMOND (q.v.) Humphrey Bogart, Alan Ladd

CHANLER, MARGARET Henry Cabot Lodge

CHANNON, SIR HENRY Lord Birkenhead, Sir Winston Churchill, Sir Stafford Cripps, Lord Curzon, Edward VIII, Hugh Gaitskell, George VI, Samuel Hoare, T. E. Lawrence, Megan Lloyd George, Queen Mary, George Moore, Edward Wood

CHAPLIN, RALPH Joe Hill

CHAPMAN, GEORGE (q.v.) Inigo Jones

CHAPMAN, JOHN JAY Charles William Eliot, Ralph Waldo Emerson, Walt Whitman

CHAPMAN, MARIA WESTON William Ellery Channing

CHARLES I (q.v.) Lord Strafford

CHARLES II (q.v.) Nell Gwyn, James II

CHARLOTTE, PRINCESS OF WALES Queen Caroline of Brunswick

CHARTERS, ANN Jack Kerouac

CHASE, RICHARD Emily Dickinson, Herman Melville

CHATHAM, FIRST EARL OF (q.v.) William Pitt

CHATTERTON, THOMAS (q.v.) Horace Walpole

CHAUCER, GEOFFREY (q.v.) John Gower

CHENEY, EDNAH D. Louisa May Alcott

CHESNEAU, E. J. M. W. Turner

CHESTERFIELD, LORD (q.v.) John Arbuthnot, Lord Bolingbroke, George I, George II, Lord Lyttelton, Sir Thomas Robinson, Sir Robert Walpole

CHESTERTON, G. K. (q.v.) Alfred, St Anselm, Hilaire Belloc, Charlotte Brontë, John Bunyan, Lord Byron, Charles II, William Cobbett, Thomas Hardy, Aldous Huxley, Rudyard Kipling, George Meredith, George

Moore, Thomas Paine, Sir Robert Peel, Alexander Pope, Richard I, George Bernard Shaw, Robert Louis Stevenson, Alfred, Lord Tennyson, James McNeill Whistler, Oscar Wilde, W. B. Yeats

CHETWOOD, KNIGHTLY Edmund Spenser

CHETWOOD, W. R. Sir William D'Avenant, George Farquhar, Anne Oldfield, Margaret Woffington

CHEVERUS, BISHOP John Carroll

CHILD, HAROLD Oscar Wilde

CHILD, RICHARD WASHBURN Warren G. Harding

CHINARD, GILBERT John Adams

CHOATE, JOSEPH H. (q.v.) Chauncey Depew

CHOATE, RUFUS Junius Brutus Booth, Daniel Webster

CHRISTIE, W. D. First Lord Shaftesbury

CHRIST-JANER, ALBERT George Caleb Bingham

CHUGERMAN, SAMUEL Lester Frank Ward

CHURCH, FREDERIC E. George Inness

CHURCHILL, ALLEN Lillian Russell

CHURCHILL, CHARLES (q.v.) Thomas Arne, Lord Bute, Samuel Foote, David Garrick, 'Sir' John Hill, William Hogarth, Samuel Johnson, Ben Jonson, Lord Mansfield, Lord Sackville, Lord Sandwich, Mary Ann Yates

CHURCHILL, CLEMENTINE Sir Winston Churchill

CHURCHILL, LORD RANDOLPH (q.v.) W. E. Gladstone

CHURCHILL, SARAH, DUCHESS OF MARLBOROUGH (q.v.) Queen Anne, Lord Godolphin, Duke of Marlborough, Sir Robert Walpole

CHURCHILL, SIR WINSTON (q.v.) Queen Anne, Nancy, Lady Astor, Clement Attlee, Stanley Baldwin, Bede, Boadicea, Rupert Brooke, Joseph Chamberlain, Sir Stafford Cripps, Richard Harding Davis, W. E. Gladstone, Harry L. Hopkins, Lord Jellicoe, Ramsay MacDonald, Duke of Marlborough, George C. Marshall, Duke of Monmouth, Lord Rosebery, William III

CIBBER, COLLEY (q.v.) Elizabeth Barry, Thomas Betterton, Anne Bracegirdle, James II, Anne Oldfield

CIBBER, THEOPHILUS John Ford, Sir Richard Steele

CLAFIN, WILLIAM Ulysses S. Grant

CLAIR, RENÉ Erich von Stroheim

CLARE, JOHN (q.v.) Thomas De Quincey, William Hazlitt, John Keats, Charles Lamb

CLARENDON, see HYDE, EDWARD

CLARENDON, LORD Duke of Cumberland, Lord Derby, Lord Palmerston

CLARENS, CARLOS Bela Lugosi

CLARK, A. M. Thomas Heywood

CLARK, DELBERT Harry L. Hopkins

CLARK, ELIOT John Twachtman

CLARK, G. N. Richard Bentley

CLARK, KENNETH William Beckford, Thomas Gray, A. W. N. Pugin, John Ruskin, Sir Walter Scott, Horace Walpole, James Wyatt

CLARK, RONALD Ludwig Wittgenstein

CLARK, RUSSELL, and MCCLELLAN, JAMES Robert A. Taft

CLARKE, BASIL Sir George Gilbert Scott

CLARKE, J. F. John Abernethy

CLAY, HENRY (q.v.) John C. Calhoun, Andrew Jackson, James Madison

CLEAVER, ELDRIDGE Malcolm X, Elvis Presley

CLEMENCEAU, GEORGES Woodrow Wilson

CLEMENS, SAMUEL see TWAIN, MARK

CLEVELAND, JOHN (q.v.) Lord Strafford

CLIFFORD, D. and T. John Crome

CLINTON, DE WITT John Quincy Adams

CLIVE, KITTY David Garrick, Mary Ann Yates

CLOUGH, A. H. (q.v.) Thomas Arnold, Thomas Carlyle, Samuel Taylor Coleridge, Elizabeth Gaskell, William Wordsworth

CLUM, JOSEPH Geronimo

COBB, SAMUEL Geoffrey Chaucer, William Congreve, Abraham Cowley

COBBETT, WILLIAM (q.v.) Prince Arthur, Sir Francis Burdett, Thomas Cranmer, Benjamin Franklin, Albert Gallatin, George IV, Samuel Johnson, Sir James Mackintosh, John Milton, Robert Owen, Thomas Paine, William Pitt, Benjamin Rush, Sir Francis Walsingham

COBDEN, RICHARD (q.v.) Duke of Wellington

COCHRAN, BOURKE Grover Cleveland

COCKAIN, SIR ASTON John Fletcher

COCKBURN, CLAUD Lord Rosebery

COCKERELL, C. R. Robert Adam, John Flaxman

COCKERILL, JOHN A. Joseph Pulitzer

CODE, GRANT H. Rockwell Kent

COE, FRANK Billy the Kid

COGHILL, NEVILLE Geoffrey Chaucer

COHEN, JOHN Lenny Bruce

COKE, SIR EDWARD (q.v.) Sir Walter Raleigh

COKE, ROGER James I

COLE, G. D. H. William Cobbett

COLEBROOK, L. Sir Alexander Fleming

COLEMAN, MCALISTER Nicholas Murray Butler, Daniel De Leon

COLERIDGE, CHRISTABEL Charlotte Yonge

COLERIDGE, HARTLEY Andrew Marvell

COLERIDGE, SAMUEL TAYLOR (q.v.) Richard Baxter, Francis Beaumont, Sir Thomas Browne, John Bunyan, Edmund Burke, Samuel Butler, Lord Byron, Charles I, Charles II, Thomas Chatterton, Geoffrey Chaucer, William Congreve, Richard Crashaw, John Donne, John Dryden, Henry Fielding, John Fletcher, Edward Gibbon, William Hazlitt, George Herbert, Thomas Hobbes, James I, James II, Samuel Johnson, Ben Jonson, Edmund Kean, Walter Savage Landor, Philip Massinger, John Milton, Sir Isaac Newton, Thomas Paine, Samuel Pepys, Samuel Richardson, Sir Walter Scott, Shakespeare, Laurence Sterne, Jonathan Swift, Jeremy Taylor, Sir Benjamin Thompson, William Wordsworth

COLERIDGE, SARA Jane Austen

COLLEY, SIR GEORGE J. A. Froude

COLLIER, JEREMY Shakespeare

COLLIER, RICHARD GILBERT John D. Rockefeller

COLLINS, WILLIAM (q.v.) James Thomson

COLLINS-BAKER, H. John Crome

COLMAN, BENJAMIN Cotton Mather, Increase Mather, George Whitefield

COLMAN, GEORGE Colley Cibber, Samuel Foote, Edward Gibbon

COLQUITT, WALTER T. Alexander H. Stephens

COLVIN, H. M. James Wyatt

COMFORT, ALEX George Orwell, Alexander Pope

COMMAGER, HENRY STEELE William Dean Howells, William James

COMPTON-BURNETT, IVY (q.v.) Emily Brontë

CONDELL, HENRY Shakespeare

CONGREVE, WILLIAM (q.v.) Anne Bracegirdle, John Dryden, John Gay, Duke of Marlborough

CONKLING, ROSCOE (q.v.) Chester A. Arthur, Andrew Johnson, Charles Sumner

CONNELLEY, WILLIAM E. William Clarke Quantrill

CONNOLLY, CYRIL (q.v.) Joseph Addison, W. H. Auden, James Boswell, T. S. Eliot, E. M. Forster, J. Edgar Hoover, D. H. Lawrence, Percy Wyndham Lewis, Somerset Maugham, George Orwell, Dame Edith Sitwell, Lytton Strachey, Evelyn Waugh, Virginia Woolf

CONRAD, JOSEPH (q.v.) Stephen Crane, Ford Madox Ford, John Galsworthy, Henry James, Rudyard Kipling, Lord Nelson, H. G. Wells

CONRAD, PETER Edmund Kean

CONSTABLE, JOHN (q.v.) Lord Byron, Alexander Cozens, Sir Joshua Reynolds, J. M. W. Turner, Richard Wilson

COOKE, ALISTAIR Bert Lahr, Walter Winchell

COOKE, GEORGE WINGROVE Lord Bolingbroke

COOKE, JOHN ESTEN Abraham Lincoln

COOKE, THOMAS Richard Savage

COOKE, WILLIAM Oliver Goldsmith, Mrs Pritchard

COOLIDGE, J. L. Lord Brouncker

COOLIDGE, LOUIS A. Carl Schurz

COOPER, FREDERICK TABER Booth Tarkington, Owen Wister

COOPER, JAMES FENIMORE (q.v.) Joanna Baillie, Sir Francis Burdett, Samuel Taylor Coleridge, Lord Grey, Sir Robert Peel, John Horne Tooke, Duke of York

COOTE, SIR COLIN Edward VIII

CORBIN, FRANCIS Patrick Henry

CORKHILL, GEORGE B. William Tecumseh Sherman

CORTEZ, WILBUR Charles I

CORTISSOZ, ROYAL John La Farge

CORWIN, EDWARD S. John Marshall

COTTON, JOHN (q.v.) Thomas Hooker

COURTENAY, JOHN Soame Jenyns, Samuel Johnson

COUSINS, NORMAN John Mason Brown

COWARD, SIR NOËL (q.v.) C. B. Cochran, Ian Fleming, Gertrude Lawrence, Ivor Novello

COWIE, ALEXANDER Thomas Bailey Aldrich, Oliver Wendell Holmes

COWLEY, ABRAHAM (q.v.) Sir Francis Bacon, Richard Crashaw, William Harvey, Sir Henry Wotton

COWLEY, MALCOLM Hart Crane, e. e. cummings, John Dos Passos, Ralph Waldo Emerson, William Faulkner, F. Scott Fitzgerald, Ernest Hemingway, Sinclair Lewis, Thomas Wolfe

COWPER, GILBERT Samuel Johnson

COWPER, WILLIAM (q.v.) Joseph Addison, William Collins, James Cook, Erasmus Darwin, John Dryden, George III, Richard Kempenfelt, Lord Mansfield, John Milton, Elizabeth Montagu, Sir John Moore, Sir Isaac Newton, Alexander Pope, James Wolfe

COX, C. V. Percy Bysshe Shelley

COX, JAMES C. Herbert Hoover

COX, S. S. Charles Sumner

CRADOCK, J. Samuel Foote, Laurence Sterne

CRAIG, EDWARD GORDON (q.v.) Sir Henry Irving, George Bernard Shaw, Dame Ellen Terry

CRAMPTON, MISS Wolfe Tone

CRANE, HART (q.v.) Edmund Wilson

CRANE, STEPHEN (q.v.) Ford Madox Ford

CRANE, SYLVIA E. Horatio Greenough

CRANKSHAW, EDWARD Ford Madox Ford

CRAWFORD, ANN John Kemble

CRAWFORD, LORD Lord Keynes

CREEVEY, THOMAS Henry Addington

CRIPPS, SIR STAFFORD (q.v.) Neville Chamberlain

CRISPIN, EDMUND Agatha Christie

CRITTENDEN, JOHN J. Daniel Webster

CROCE, ARLENE Vernon Blythe Castle

CROCKETT, ALBERT STEVENS James Gordon Bennett Jr

CROCKETT, DAVY (q.v.) Martin Van Buren

CROFT, HERBERT Edward Young

CROFT-COOKE, RUPERT Edward Fitzgerald

CROKER, JOHN WILSON (q.v.) William Huskisson, John Keats, T. B. Macaulay, Lord Melbourne

CROKER, T. CROFTON Thomas Moore

CROLY, HERBERT Herbert Hoover

CROMER, LORD W. E. Gladstone, C. G. Gordon, Lord Kitchener

CROMWELL, OLIVER (q.v.) Henry Ireton, Prince Rupert

CROMWELL, THOMAS (q.v.) Henry VIII

CROWNE, JOHN Shakespeare

CROWNINSHIELD, FRANK George Bellows

CROWSON, R. A. Charles Darwin, T. H. Huxley

CROWTHER, J. G. James Watt

CROY, HOMER Jesse James

CRUDEN, ROBERT James Ford Rhodes

CRUICKSHANK, A. H. Philip Massinger

CRUICKSHANK, R. Sir Alexander Fleming

CUKOR, GEORGE Marie Dressler, D. W. Griffith, Jean Harlow, Charles Laughton, Vivien Leigh, Marilyn Monroe, Spencer Tracy

CUMBERLAND, RICHARD Richard Bentley, Oliver Goldsmith, George Romney

CUMMINGS, CONSTANCE Aneurin Bevan

CUMMINGS, E. E. (q.v.) 'Buffalo Bill' Cody, Ezra Pound, Edmund Wilson

CUMMINGS, W. H. Thomas Arne

CUNARD, EMERALD LADY H. H. Asquith

CUNLIFFE, MARCUS George Washington

CUNNINGHAM, ALLAN Robert Burns, George Morland

CUPPY, WILL George I

CURTIS, GEORGE W. William Marcy Tweed

CURTIS, LIONEL Sir Winston Churchill, Cecil Rhodes

CURTIS, THOMAS QUINN Erich von Stroheim

CURZON, LORD (q.v.) Stanley Baldwin, Lord Salisbury

CUTLER, TIMOTHY George Whitefield

CZOLGOSZ, LEON William McKinley

DAHL, CURTIS Robert Montgomery Bird

DAICHES, DAVID Willa Cather

DALE, ALAN Jerome Kern

DALLAS, ALEXANDER J. John C. Calhoun

DALLAS, G. DONALD Paul Revere

DALLAS, GEORGE MIFFLIN Andrew Jackson

DALTON, JOHN (q.v.) Sir Humphry Davy

DALY, AUGUSTIN Sir Henry Irving

DANA, CHARLES ANDERSON (q.v.) James Gordon Bennett Jr, Joseph Pulitzer, Carl Schurz, William Henry Seward

DANA, RICHARD HENRY Ulysses S. Grant, Richard Hildreth, Franklin Pierce

DANGERFIELD, GEORGE James Monroe

DANIEL, WALTER Ailred of Rievaulx

DANIELS, JONATHAN Harry S. Truman

DANIELS, JOSEPHUS (q.v.) Woodrow Wilson

DARE, ZENA Ivor Novello

DARGAN, OLIVE William Blake

DARLEY, GEORGE John Keats

DARRACH, BRAD Elvis Presley

DARROW, CLARENCE (q.v.) Roscoe Conkling

DARWIN, CHARLES (q.v.) Charles Babbage, Robert Brown, Herbert Spencer
DARWIN, ERASMUS (q.v.) Josiah Wedgwood
DATALLER, ROGER D. H. Lawrence
DAVIDSON, EDWARD H. Nathaniel Hawthorne, Edgar Allen Poe
DAVIES, A. M. Warren Hastings
DAVIES, JOHN (OF HEREFORD) (q.v.) Shakespeare
DAVIES, THOMAS Colley Cibber, William Congreve, Ben Jonson, John Kemble, Nathaniel Lee, Anne Oldfield, Thomas Otway, Shakespeare
DAVIS, ARTHUR P. Langston Hughes
DAVIS, BETTE George Arliss, Theda Bara, Errol Flynn, Paul Muni, Rudolph Valentino
DAVIS, JEFFERSON (q.v.) Benjamin Butler, John C. Calhoun, Benjamin Franklin, Andrew Johnson
DAVIS, JOSEPH E. Harry L. Hopkins
DAVIS, OSSIE Malcolm X. Nat Turner
DAVIS, R. H. C. King Stephen
DAVIS, RICHARD HARDING (q.v.) Stephen Crane
DAVIS, ROBERT GORHAM John Dos Passos
DAVIS, ROBERT H. Zane Grey
DAVY, SIR HUMPHRY (q.v.) John Dalton
DEALEY, JAMES QUAYLE Lester Frank Ward
DE BEER, SIR GAVIN Charles Darwin, Charles Lyell
DE CASSERES, BENJAMIN H. L. Mencken, George Bernard Shaw
DE LA MARE, WALTER (q.v.) William Blake
DE LEON, T. C. Judah P. Benjamin
D'ELIA, DONALD J. Benjamin Rush
DELIUS, FREDERICK (q.v.) Charles Parry
DE MILLE, AGNES Cecil B. De Mille
DE MILLE, CECIL B. (q.v.) Gary Cooper, D. W. Griffith, Jesse Lasky
DENHAM, SIR JOHN (q.v.) Abraham Cowley, Sir William D'Avenant
DENNIS, ALFRED PEARCE Calvin Coolidge
DENNIS, CHARLES H. Eugene Field
DENNIS, JOHN Alexander Pope, Nicholas Rowe, Shakespeare, William Wycherley
DEPEW, CHAUNCEY (q.v.) Roscoe Conkling, Henry Cabot Lodge
DE QUINCEY, THOMAS (q.v.) Samuel Taylor Coleridge, John Donne, John Locke, Hannah More, Mrs Radcliffe, William Wordsworth
DERBY, LORD (q.v.) Lord Palmerston, Lord Russell
DESTI, MARY Isadora Duncan

DE SYLVA, BUDDY Florenz Ziegfeld
DEVONSHIRE, DUCHESS OF (GEORGIANA) Charles James Fox, William Pitt
DE VOTO, BERNARD James K. Polk, Sacagawea
DEWEY, JOHN (q.v.) Ralph Waldo Emerson, Henry George, William James, Thomas Jefferson
DE WILDE, G. J. John Clare
DEXTER, FRANKLIN BOWDITCH Jonathan Edwards
DIBDIN, CHARLES (q.v.) Edward Alleyn, Anne Hathaway
DICEY, A. V. Henry Beaufort
DICEY, EDWARD Salmon P. Chase
DICKENS, CHARLES (q.v.) Wilkie Collins, Henry IV, Henry VIII, Washington Irving, Mary I, Thomas Wolsey
DICKEY, JAMES Randall Jarrell, Edwin Arlington Robinson
DICKEY, O. J. Thaddeus Stevens
DIDION, JOHN Howard R. Hughes
DIEKHOFF, J. S. John Milton
DIGGES, LEONARD Shakespeare
DISBROWE, COLONEL Queen Charlotte Sophia
DISHER, M. WILLSON Edmund Kean
DISRAELI, BENJAMIN (q.v.) Lord Aberdeen, Prince Albert, Lord Anson, Matthew Arnold, Lord Bolingbroke, Lord Brougham, Sir Francis Burdett, George Canning, Joseph Chamberlain, Richard Cobden, John Wilson Croker, Lord Derby, Mary Ann Disraeli, George IV, W. E. Gladstone, Charles Greville, Lord Liverpool, Lord Lyndhurst, Lord Lytton, Lord Palmerston, Sir Robert Peel, Lord Russell, Lord Salisbury, Seventh Lord Shaftesbury, W. M. Thackeray, Queen Victoria, Duke of Wellington
D'ISRAELI, ISAAC Margaret Cavendish, Charles Churchill
DIXON, R. W. William Morris
DOBRÉE, BONAMY Lord Chesterfield, Rudyard Kipling
DOBZHANSKY, THEODOSIUS Charles Darwin
DODGE, THEODORE A. John Pope
DOE, CHARLES John Bunyan
DOLE, GEORGE T. George Peabody
DONALDSON, THOMAS C. Rutherford B. Hayes
DONNE, JOHN (q.v.) Robert Carr, Nicholas Hilliard
DONNELLY, IGNATIUS William Jennings Bryan
DONOHUE, H. E. F. Robert Frost
DOS PASSOS, JOHN R. (q.v.) Hart Crane, e. e. cummings, Theodore Dreiser
DOUGLAS, LORD ALFRED William Butler Yeats

DOUGLAS, A. V. SIR Arthur Stanley Eddington
DOUGLAS, JAMES D. H. Lawrence
DOUGLAS, NORMAN Ford Madox Ford
DOUGLAS, STEPHEN A. (q.v.) Andrew Jackson
DOUGLASS, FREDERICK (q.v.) John Brown
DOVE, ARTHUR G. Alfred Stieglitz
DOWNES, K. Nicholas Hawksmoor, Sir Christopher Wren
DOWNES, OLIN Stephen C. Foster, Charles Ives, John Philip Sousa
DRABBLE, MARGARET Arnold Bennett
DRAYTON, MICHAEL John Lyly, Christopher Marlowe, Thomas Morley
DREISER, THEODORE (q.v.) Sherwood Anderson, Joseph Pulitzer
DRENNAN, ROBERT E. Tallulah Bankhead, Robert Benchley, Edna Ferber, George S. Kaufman, Dorothy Parker
DRESSLER, MARIE (q.v.) Lionel Barrymore, Minnie Fiske, Will Rogers, Lillian Russell
DRIBERG, TOM Evelyn Waugh
DRUMMOND, MRS Dame Christabel Pankhurst
DRUMMOND, WILLIAM ('DRUMMOND, OF HAWTHORNDEN') Ben Jonson
DRYDEN, JOHN (q.v.) Francis Beaumont, Second Duke of Buckingham, Gilbert Burnet, Samuel Butler, George Chapman, Geoffrey Chaucer, William Congreve, Abraham Cowley, Oliver Cromwell, John Donne, Elizabeth Dryden, Richard Flecknoe, John Fletcher, William Gilbert, Thomas Hobbes, Ben Jonson, Sir Godfrey Kneller, Duke of Monmouth, Titus Oates, Henry Purcell, George Savile, Elkanah Settle, Thomas Shadwell, First Lord Shaftesbury Shakespeare, Edmund Spenser, Jonathan Swift, Edmund Waller, John Wilmot
DUANE, WILLIAM Albert Gallatin
DU BOIS, W. E. B. (q.v.) Marcus Garvey, Andrew Johnson
DUKE, RICHARD William Bedloe, Titus Oates
DUMAS, BETHANY K. e. e. cummings
DUNBAR, PAUL LAURENCE Frederick Douglass
DUNDAS, HENRY see MELVILLE, LORD
DUNHAM, BARROWS Lincoln Steffens
DUNNE, FINLEY PETER Richard Harding Davis, William McKinley

DUNTON, JOHN Judge Jeffreys
DURHAM, PHILIP Raymond Chandler
DWIGHT, WILLIAM T. and SERENO E. Timothy Dwight
DYALL, FRANKLIN Oscar Wilde
DYER, OLIVER Thomas Hart Benton, Sam Houston
DYKSTRA, MRS Thomas Dewey

EADMER St Anselm, William II
EASTLAKE, SIR CHARLES James Wyatt
EASTMAN, MAX Robert Benchley, John Dewey, Ernest Hemingway, Mabel Dodge Luhan, P. G. Wodehouse
EDEL, LEON Henry David Thoreau
EDEN, EMILY Prince Albert, William IV
EDGAR, PELHAM Henry James
EDGEWORTH, MARIA (q.v.) Joanna Baillie, T. R. Malthus
EDINGER, GEORGE Prince Rupert
EDISON, THOMAS ALVA (q.v.) Henry Ford
EDWARD III (q.v.) Edward, the Black Prince
EDWARD VI (q.v.) Mary I
EDWARDS, MRS GEOFFREY Marie Stopes
EDWARDS, JOHN N. Jesse James
EGLINTON, LORD James Boswell, Charles Churchill
EINSTEIN, ALBERT (q.v.) Michael Faraday, J. C. Maxwell, Sir Isaac Newton
EISENHOWER, DWIGHT D. (q.v.) John Foster Dulles, Douglas MacArthur
ELDON, LORD (q.v.) Richard Brinsley Sheridan
ELGAR, SIR EDWARD (q.v.) Charles Parry, C. V. Stanford
ELIOT, CHARLES WILLIAM (q.v.) Augustus Saint-Gaudens
ELIOT, GEORGE (q.v.) Matthew Arnold, Charlotte Brontë, Lord Byron, Thomas Carlyle, Charles Dickens, Edward Young
ELIOT, THOMAS STEARNS (q.v.) Henry Adams, Lancelot Andrewes, Matthew Arnold, Francis Beaumont, William Blake, Lord Byron, Sir Winston Churchill, Samuel Taylor Coleridge, Wilkie Collins, Richard Crashaw, John Donne, John Dryden, John Fletcher, Thomas Hardy, William Hazlitt, Thomas Heywood, Aldous Huxley, Henry James, Samuel Johnson, Ben Jonson, Rudyard Kipling, Walter Savage Landor, D. H. Lawrence, Edward Lear, Percy Wyndham Lewis, Christopher Marlowe, Philip Massinger, Thomas

Middleton, John Milton, Marianne Moore, Gilbert Murray, Charles Eliot Norton, Edgar Allen Poe, Ezra Pound, Shakespeare, Algernon C. Swinburne, Alfred, Lord Tennyson, Thomas à Becket, John Webster, William Wordsworth, William Butler Yeats
ELIZABETH I (q.v.) John Bull, Sir Walter Raleigh
ELIZABETH, QUEEN MOTHER George VI
ELLIOT, CAPTAIN Sam Houston
ELLIOTT, CHARLES W. Winfield Scott
ELLIOTT, EBENEZER Lord Byron, Robert Owen
ELLIOTT, GEORGE P. Raymond Chandler
ELLIS, ABRAHAM William Clarke Quantrill
ELLIS, HAVELOCK John Ford, Sir Walter Scott
ELLIS, KEITH Thomas Alva Edison
ELLIS, VIVIAN C. B. Cochran
ELLIS-FERMOR, UNA Christopher Marlowe
ELLISON, CHARLES John Coltrane
ELMES, J. Inigo Jones, J. M. W. Turner
ELTON, OLIVER John Donne, Thomas Love Peacock
ELTON, LORD Ramsay MacDonald
EMERSON, RALPH WALDO (q.v.) John Quincy Adams, Amos Bronson Alcott, Washington Allston, Jane Austen, George Bancroft, John Brown, Robert Burns, Thomas Carlyle, William Ellery Channing, Geoffrey Chaucer, Margaret Fuller, William Lloyd Garrison, Horatio Greenough, Nathaniel Hawthorne, Oliver Wendell Holmes, Emma Lazarus, Abraham Lincoln, Lucretia Mott, John Muir, Franklin Pierce, Edgar Allen Poe, Shakespeare, Charles Sumner, Algernon C. Swinburne, Henry David Thoreau, George Washington, Daniel Webster, William Wordsworth
EMMONS, R. Walter Richard Sickert
EMPSON, WILLIAM Lewis Carroll, John Milton, Gertrude Stein
ENDY, MELVIN B. William Penn
ENGEL, BERNARD F. Marianne Moore
ENGELS, FRIEDRICH Lord Byron, Robert Owen
ENRIGHT, D. J. D. H. Lawrence, Dame Edith Sitwell
ENT, GEORGE William Harvey
EPSTEIN, SIR JACOB (q.v.) Percy Wyndham Lewis
EPSTEIN, JOSEPH Edmund Wilson
ERASMUS Sir Thomas More

ERSKINE, THOMAS, LORD, Sir Walter Scott
ESHER, LORD H. H. Asquith, Lord Fisher, Sir John French
'ESPINASSE, MARGARET Robert Hooke
ETHEREGE, SIR GEORGE (q.v.) John Dryden, Sir Charles Sedley, Thomas Shadwell
EVANS, ABEL Sir John Vanbrugh
EVANS, OLIVER Carson McCullers
EVE, A. S. and CHADWICK, J. Lord Rutherford
EVELYN, JOHN (q.v.) William Bedloe, Robert Boyle, Sir Thomas Browne, Catherine of Braganza, Charles II, Abraham Cowley, Oliver Cromwell, Sir John Denham, Grinling Gibbons, Robert Hooke, Edward Hyde, Louise de Keroualle, William Lilly, Sir Isaac Newton, Titus Oates, Lord Strafford, Sir Christopher Wren
EVERETT, WALTER K. William Faulkner
EVERSLEY, LORD Charles James Fox
EWEN, DAVID Stephen C. Foster, George Gershwin, Cole Porter

FABOS, JULIUS, MILDE, GORDON T., and WEINMAYR, V. MICHAEL Frederick Olmsted
FADIMAN, CLIFTON Ambrose Bierce, Charles Dickens, William Faulkner, Ogden Nash, John O'Hara, Gertrude Stein
FAIRBANKS, JR, DOUGLAS Douglas Fairbanks
FAIRFIELD, FRANCIS G. William Marcy Tweed
FAIRLIE, HENRY Robert F. Kennedy
FAITH, JOEL Louella Parsons
FALKINER, C. LITTON Sheridan Le Fanu
FALKLAND, LORD William Laud
FALLON, GABRIEL Mrs Patrick Campbell
FALLS, CYRIL Lord Jellicoe
FARINGTON, JOSEPH Sir Thomas Lawrence, J. M. W. Turner, Benjamin West, Sir David Wilkie, James Wyatt
FARLEY, J. J. George S. Patton Jr
FARMER, RICHARD Shakespeare
FAULKNER, WILLIAM (q.v.) Henry James, Mark Twain
FAY, C. R. Adam Smith
FEIN, ALBERT Frederick Olmsted
FELL, DR JOHN (q.v.) John Wycliffe
FENBY, ERIC Frederick Delius
FERBER, EDNA (q.v.) George S. Kaufman, Alexander Woollcott
FERGUSON, OTIS Humphrey Bogart, Gary Cooper, Walt Disney, W. C. Fields, Peter Lorre, Will Rogers, Spencer Tracy, Monty Woolley

FERGUSSON, JAMES A. W. N. Pugin, Sir John Soane, Sir John Vanbrugh

FERREY, B. A. W. N. Pugin

FIELD, EUGENE (q.v.) Charles A. Dana, Hamlin Garland

FIELD, MAUNSELL B. Gideon Welles

FIELDING, HENRY (q.v.) Colley Cibber, William Hogarth, Jonathan Swift

FILSON, JOHN Daniel Boone

FINCH, EDITH M. Carey Thomas

FINDLEY, J. R. Thomas De Quincey

FINK, RICHARD Horatio Alger

FINSBERG, A. J. J. M. W. Turner

FIRTH, SIR CHARLES John Bunyan

FISH, CARL RUSSELL Ambrose E. Burnside

FISHER, LORD (q.v.) Edward VII, Sir John French

FISHER, H. A. L. Lord Curzon, William Laud

FISHER, JOHN John Constable, Sir Godfrey Kneller

FISKE, JOHN (q.v.) George Eliot

FISKE, STEPHEN James Gordon Bennett Jr

FITZCLARENCE, LORD ADOLPHUS Queen Victoria

FITZGERALD, EDWARD (q.v.) Elizabeth Barrett Browning, Andrew Marvell, Alfred, Lord Tennyson, William Wordsworth

FITZGERALD, F. SCOTT (q.v.) Sherwood Anderson, John Galsworthy, Ernest Hemingway, Aldous Huxley, Gertrude Stein, Edith Wharton, Thomas Wolfe

FITZGERALD, PERCY Shakespeare

FITZGERALD, ZELDA F. Scott Fitzgerald

FITZJEFFREY, HENRY John Webster

FITZNEAL, RICHARD William I

FLAMSTEED, JOHN (q.v.) Edmund Halley, Sir Isaac Newton

FLANNER, HILDEGARDE Edna St Vincent Millay

FLANNER, JANET Isadora Duncan

FLEMING, SIR AMBROSE William Thomson

FLEMING, ANNE Evelyn Waugh

FLEMING, DONALD Jacques Loeb

FLEMING, IAN (q.v.) Raymond Chandler

FLETCHER, JOHN (q.v.) Richard Burbage, Ben Jonson

FLETCHER, JOHN GOULD D. H. Lawrence

FLETCHER, PHINEAS Edmund Spenser

FLEXNER, JAMES THOMAS Winslow Homer, George Washington

FLICK, A. C. Samuel J. Tilden

FLINT, TIMOTHY Daniel Boone

FLOWER, NEWMAN G. F. Handel

FONER, PHILIP S. Samuel Gompers

FONTENROSE, JOSEPH John Steinbeck

FOOT, MICHAEL Aneurin Bevan, Ernest Bevin, Lord Bolingbroke, Sir Stafford Cripps

FOOTE, SAMUEL (q.v.) Mary Ann Yates

FORD, FORD MADOX (q.v.) Robert Browning, Lord Byron, Joseph Conrad, Daniel Defoe, Theodore Dreiser, Ernest Hemingway, Henry James, Samuel Johnson, James Joyce, Rudyard Kipling, D. H. Lawrence, Jack London, William Morris, Dante Gabriel Rossetti, Sir Walter Scott, Percy Bysshe Shelley, Samuel Smiles, Alfred, Lord Tennyson, William Wordsworth

FORD, HENRY (q.v.) Thomas Alva Edison

FORD, JOHN SALMON Sam Houston

FORKEL, JOHANN N. G. F. Handel

FORSTER, E. M. (q.v.) Jane Austen, Joseph Conrad, Charles Dickens, Thomas Hardy, Henry James, James Joyce, D. H. Lawrence, George Meredith, Sir Walter Scott, H. G. Wells, Virginia Woolf

FORSTER, JOHN Samuel Foote, Sir Richard Steele, W. M. Thackeray

FORSTER, MARGARET Charles Edward Stuart

FORSYTH, EBENEZER Shakespeare

FORTUNE, T. THOMAS Nat Turner

FOSBROKE, T. D. Sir Isaac Newton

FOSS, EDWARD William Arden, John Bradshaw

FOWLER, GENE John Barrymore, John Drew, Thomas Alva Edison

FOX, CAROLINE John Bright, Charles Kingsley, John Stuart Mill, Richard Owen, W. M. Thackeray, J. M. W. Turner, William Wordsworth

FOXE, JOHN (q.v.) Thomas Cranmer, Edward VI, Stephen Gardiner, Hugh Latimer, Nicholas Ridley

FOX-STRANGWAYS, A. H. Sir Ralph Vaughan Williams

FRANCIS-WILLIAMS, LORD Ernest Bevin

FRANK, CHARLES P. Edmund Wilson

FRANK, JEROME Learned Hand

FRANK, WALDO Sir Charles Chaplin, Jack London

FRANKAU, GILBERT Rudyard Kipling

FRANKFURTER, FELIX (q.v.) John Marshall, William Howard Taft

FRANKLIN, BENJAMIN (q.v.) George Washington, George Whitefield

FRANKLIN, JOE Stan Laurel and Oliver Hardy

FRASER, MRS HUGH Elizabeth Barrett Browning, Edward Lear

FREEDLAND, MICHAEL Al Jolson

FREEDMAN, MAX Felix Frankfurter

FREEMAN, DOUGLAS SOUTHALL Dean Acheson

FREEMAN, E. A. William I

FREDERICK OF PRUSSIA Lord Chatham

FRENEAU, PHILIP Lord Cornwallis, George Washington

FRERE, SIR BARTLE (q.v.) David Livingstone

FREUD, SIGMUND Shakespeare

FREY, JOHN Samuel Gompers

FRIEDMAN, MELVIN J. Flannery O'Connor

FRIEDMAN, MYRA Janis Joplin

FRIEDRICH, OTTO Ring Lardner, Alice B. Toklas

FRIEND, JULIUS W. Sherwood Anderson

FRITH, WILLIAM P. J. M. W. Turner

FROHOCK, W. M. Ernest Hemingway

FROISSART, JEAN Edward III

FROST, LAWRENCE A. George Armstrong Custer

FROST, ROBERT (q.v.) D. H. Lawrence, Carl Sandburg, Orville and Wilbur Wright

FROUDE, J. A. (q.v.) Thomas Carlyle, Daniel O'Connell

FRY, ROGER (q.v.) Aubrey Beardsley, John Sell Cotman, William Hogarth, Sir Thomas Lawrence, J. M. W. Turner, Richard Wilson

FRYE, NORTHROP Emily Dickinson

FUESS, CLAUDE M. Caleb Cushing

FULLER, JOHN D. H. Lawrence

FULLER, MARGARET (q.v.) Amos Bronson Alcott, Washington Allston, Henry Wadsworth Longfellow

FULLER, THOMAS Adrian IV, Edward Alleyn, Lancelot Andrewes, Elias Ashmole, Elizabeth Barton, First Duke of Buckingham, Edmund Campion, Catherine of Aragon, Thomas Cavendish, John Cleveland, John Davies, John Dowland, Edward I, Edward II, Edward V, Sir John Fastolfe, Sir Thomas Gresham, Richard Hakluyt, Henry I, Henry II, Humphrey, Duke of Gloucester, King John, Ben Jonson, William Juxon, William Laud, Andrew Marvell, Sir Thomas More, Cardinal Morton, Sir John Oldcastle, Sir Walter Raleigh, Queen Jane Seymour, Shakespeare, Edmund Spenser, Thomas à Becket, Archbishop Williams, Thomas Wolsey, John Wycliffe

FURNASS, J. C. Josephus Daniels

FURNEAUX-JORDAN, R. Sir Joseph Paxton, Sir George Gilbert Scott

FURNISS, HARRY Lewis Carroll
FÜRST, V. Sir Christopher Wren
FUSELI, HENRY William Blake, John Constable

GABLE, CLARK (q.v.) Spencer Tracy
GABOR, MARK Betty Grable
GABRIEL, RALPH William James
GAGE, THOMAS Pontiac
GAGNALL, ROBERT W. Marcus Garvey
GAINSBOROUGH, THOMAS (q.v.) Sir Joshua Reynolds, Lord Shelburne
GAITSKELL, HUGH (q.v.) Ian Fleming
GALBRAITH, V. H. Richard II
GALLATIN, ALBERT (q.v.) Abigail Adams, John C. Calhoun, James Madison
GALLICO, PAUL Buster Keaton, 'Babe' Ruth
GALLOWAY, JOSEPH Samuel Adams
GALSWORTHY, JOHN (q.v.) D. H. Lawrence
GALT, JOHN Benjamin West
GALTON, SIR FRANCIS Herbert Spencer
GANNETT, REV. W. C. Mary Carpenter
GARDINER, A. G. Lord Harcourt, Lord Rosebery
GARDINER, MARGARET Zachary Taylor
GARDINER, S. R. Edmund Spenser
GARDNER, A. G. Lord Northcliffe
GARDNER, GERALD Robert F. Kennedy
GARFIELD, JAMES A. (q.v.) James G. Blaine, Roscoe Conkling, Rutherford B. Hayes, Samuel J. Tilden
GARLAND, HAMLIN (q.v.) Stephen Crane, Eugene Field, James Whitcomb Riley
GARNETT, DAVID Virginia Woolf
GARNETT, RICHARD Thomas Paine
GARRETT, PAT F. Billy The Kid
GARRICK, DAVID (q.v.) Thomas Arne, Oliver Goldsmith, 'Sir' John Hill, Samuel Johnson, Lord North
GARRISON, WILLIAM LLOYD (q.v.) John Brown, Abraham Lincoln, Zachary Taylor
GARVEY, MARCUS (q.v.) W. E. B. Du Bois
GARVEY, JR, MARCUS Marcus Garvey
GARVIN, J. L. Stanley Baldwin
GAUNT, WILLIAM Aubrey Beardsley
GAY, JOHN (q.v.) John Arbuthnot, Sir Richard Blackmore, William Kent
GAY, PETER Jonathan Edwards
GAYNOR, WILLIAM Stephen S. Wise
GEBHARD, DAVID Ralph A. Blakelock

GEE, JOSHUA Cotton Mather
GEIKIE, SIR ARCHIBALD Charles Lyell
GEISMAR, MAXWELL Willa Cather, Theodore Dreiser, Sinclair Lewis, H. L. Mencken
GELL, ROBERT First Duke of Buckingham
GELPI, ALBERT Emily Dickinson
GEM, S. H. Aelfric
GEORGE II (q.v.) Frederick Louis Prince of Wales, Shakespeare, James Wolfe
GEORGE III (q.v.) Henry Addington, James Gillray, Lord Liverpool, Lord Shelburne
GEORGE IV (q.v.) Henry Addington, George Canning, Queen Caroline of Brunswick, Lord Grey, Sir John Jervis, Spencer Perceval
GEORGE, HENRY (q.v.) Emma Lazarus
GERBER, ALBERT B. Howard R. Hughes
GERBER, PHILIP L. Theodore Dreiser
GERHARDIE, WILLIAM Arnold Bennett, Aldous Huxley, Somerset Maugham, Bertrand Russell, Sir Hugh Walpole
GERMAINE, LADY BETTY Henrietta Howard
GERSHWIN, IRA George Gershwin
GETLEIN, FRANK Ben Shahn
GEYELIN, PHILIP Lyndon B. Johnson
GHOSH, J. C. Thomas Otway
GIBBON, EDWARD (q.v.) William Caxton, David Hume, Lord North, Alexander Pope, Edmund Spenser, Sir Benjamin Thompson, John Wilkes
GIBBS, GEORGE John Adams
GIBBS, WOLCOTT John Barrymore
GIDDINGS, JOSHUA R. John Quincy Adams
GIDE, ANDRÉ Charles Dickens
GIELGUD, SIR JOHN Charles Laughton
GILBERT, W. S. (q.v.) Henry Irving, Sir Arthur Sullivan
GILDER, RICHARD WATSON Grover Cleveland
GILDON, CHARLES Sir John Vanbrugh
GILES, SAMUEL John Dalton
GILL, FREDERICK C. Charles Wesley
GILLRAY, JAMES (q.v.) Sir Joseph Banks
GILMORE, MAEVE Mervyn Peake
GINSBERG, ALLEN William Blake, Jack Kerouac
GIRALDUS CAMBRENSIS Henry II
GISH, LILLIAN D. W Griffith
GISSING, GEORGE (q.v.) Joseph Conrad

GLADSTONE, WILLIAM EWART (q.v.) Prince Albert, Joseph Butler, Sir Henry Campbell-Bannerman, Joseph Chamberlain, Jefferson Davis, Benjamin Disraeli, John Stuart Mill, Sir Robert Peel, Lord Russell, Charles Sumner, Queen Victoria, George Washington
GLASGOW, ELLEN (q.v.) Booth Tarkington
GLENNON, ARCHBISHOP James Gibbons
GLOUCESTER, DUKE OF Edward Gibbon
GODKIN, E. L. (q.v.) James G. Blaine, Roscoe Conkling, Charles Sumner
GODWIN, WILLIAM Mary Shelley, Mary Wollstonecraft
GOETHE, J. W. VON Lord Byron
GOETZMANN, WILLIAM H. John C. Frémont
GOFFIN, RICHARD Louis Armstrong
GOGARTY, OLIVER ST JOHN Robert Browning, Lady Gregory, Augustus John, George Moore, Alexander Pope, Jonathan Swift
GOLD, ARTHUR, and FIZDALE, ROBERT Alice B. Toklas
GOLD, HERB John F. Kennedy
GOLDEN, HARRY Clarence Darrow
GOLDMAN, ALBERT Lenny Bruce
GOLDMAN, ERIC Franklin D. Roosevelt
GOLDMAN, PETER Malcolm X
GOLDRING, DOUGLAS J. E. Flecker, D. H. Lawrence
GOLDSEN, ROSE K. C. Wright Mills
GOLDSMITH, OLIVER (q.v.) Edmund Burke, William Collins, David Garrick, Samuel Johnson, Sir Joshua Reynolds, Lord Shelburne
GOLDSTEIN, JOSEPH Bertrand Russell
GOLDWATER, BARRY Lyndon B. Johnson
GOLDWYN, SAMUEL (q.v.) Louis B. Mayer
GOLLANCZ, VICTOR Henry Wood
GOODALE, KATHERINE Minnie Fiske
GOODHART-RENDEL, H. S. Nicholas Hawksmoor, A. W. N. Pugin
GOODRICH, LLOYD Winslow Homer, Edward Hopper
GOODRICH, S. D. Timothy Dwight
GORDON, JAN B. Lewis Carroll
GORMAN, HERBERT S. Henry Wadsworth Longfellow
GOSSE, SIR EDMUND William Blake, Sir Thomas Browne, Thomas Hardy, John Singer Sargent, Algernon C. Swinburne, Leonard Woolf
GOSSON, STEPHEN Thomas Lodge
GOULD, HANNAH F. Caleb Cushing
GOULD, JACK Elvis Presley

GOULD, JEAN Eugene O'Neill
GOWER, JOHN (q.v.) Geoffrey Chaucer
GOWER, LORD RONALD Sir Thomas Lawrence, George Romney
GRAHAM, BILLY Cecil B. De Mille
GRAHAM, FRANK P. Booker T. Washington
GRANGER, ALFRED HOYT Charles F. McKim
GRANGER, JAMES Charles II, Nell Gwyn, Sir Roger L'Estrange
GRANT, JAMES William Cobbett
GRANT, ULYSSES S. (q.v.) Roscoe Conkling, James A. Garfield, Robert E. Lee
GRANVILLE, LADY Lady Bessborough, George Canning, William Huskisson
GRANVILLE, LORD C. G. Gordon, Lord Rosebery
GRANVILLE, GEORGE William Wycherley
GRATTAN, C. HARTLEY Ambrose Bierce
GRATTAN, HENRY (q.v.) Edmund Burke
GRATTAN, JR, HENRY (q.v.) Lord Mansfield
GRATTAN, THOMAS COLLEY Samuel Taylor Coleridge, Edmund Kean, Thomas Moore, William Wordsworth
GRAVES, C. L. and LUCAS, E. V. Rudyard Kipling
GRAVES, JOHN WOODCOCK Sir Robert Peel
GRAVES, ROBERT John Clare, Thomas Hardy, T. E. Lawrence, John Masefield, Gilbert Murray, Lytton Strachey
GRAY, ASA (q.v.) Robert Brown
GRAY, JAMES John Steinbeck
GRAY, THOMAS (q.v.) John Dryden, David Garrick, John Milton, Alexander Pope, Lord Sandwich, Shakespeare
GRAY, THOMAS A. Elinor Wylie
GRAYDON, ALEXANDER Ethan Allen
GRAYSON, WILLIAM J. Horace Greeley
GREELEY, HORACE (q.v.) James Gordon Bennett Jr, Roscoe Conkling, Margaret Fuller, Ulysses S. Grant, William Henry Seward, Thurlow Weed
GREEN, JOHN RICHARD Lord Chatham, Edwin, Warren Hastings, King John, Duke of Marlborough
GREEN, KENSAL (pseudonym of COLIN HURRY) Nancy, Lady Astor Stanley Baldwin, Arnold Bennett, Calvin Coolidge, Theodore Dreiser,

Thomas Alva Edison, Albert Einstein, Henry Ford, Augustus John, David Lloyd George
GREENBERG, CLEMENT Jackson Pollock, David Smith
GREENE, GRAHAM George Arliss, Baron Corvo, Cecil B. De Mille, W. C. Fields, Ford Madox Ford, Jean Harlow, Boris Karloff, Carole Lombard, Peter Lorre
GREENE, NATHANIEL 'Mad' Anthony Wayne
GREENE, ROBERT (q.v.) Christopher Marlowe, Shakespeare
GREENWAY, JOHN Jesse James
GREGORY, LADY AUGUSTA (q.v.) Alfred, Lord Tennyson
GREGORY, DICK George Washington Carver, Malcolm X
GREGORY, FRANCIS H. Andrew Foote
GREGORY, HORACE Amy Lowell, Ezra Pound
GREIN, J. T. Oscar Wilde
GRENVILLE, LORD (q.v.) William Wilberforce
GRESHAM, WILLIAM LINDSAY Harry Houdini
GREVILLE, CHARLES (q.v.) Prince Albert, Sir Joseph Banks, Lord Brougham, Lord Derby, T. B. Macaulay, Lord Melbourne, George Stephenson, William IV
GREY, LORD (q.v.) Duke of Cumberland
GRIGSON, GEOFFREY Cecil Day Lewis
GRIMALDI, GIUSEPPE Richard Brinsley Sheridan
GRIMKE, ARCHIBALD H. Charles Sumner
GRIMSTON, SIR HARBOTTLE William Laud
GRISWOLD, RUFUS Edgar Allen Poe
GROSART, ALEXANDER BALLOCH Sir William Alexander
GROSS, JOHN Walter Bagehot, Arnold Bennett, G. K. Chesterton, George Orwell, Sir Arthur Quiller-Couch, Sir Leslic Stephen
GROSSMITH, GEORGE and WEEDON W. E. Gladstone
GRUBBER, IRA D. Lord Howe
GRUEN, JOHN Vivien Leigh
GUARD, ROSE LEE Samuel Gompers
GUEDELLA, PHILIP Sir James Matthew Barrie, Edward Gibbon
GUILES, FRED LAWRENCE Marilyn Monroe
GUITERMAN, ARTHUR Herbert Hoover
GUIZOT, FRANÇOIS Benjamin Disraeli
GURNALNICK, PETER Elvis Presley

GURNEY, IVOR C. V. Stanford
GUYLAY, RICHARD Robert A. Taft
GUYOT, ARNOLD Louis Agassiz
GWATKIN, H. M. James II

HACKER, LOUIS Carl Becker, Alfred Thayer Mahan
HACKET, JOHN Orlando Gibbons
HADOW, SIR HENRY Thomas Arne, Sir Arthur Sullivan, S. S. Wesley
HAGGARD, SIR H. RIDER (q.v.) Rudyard Kipling
HAGGIN, BERNARD H. Arturo Toscanini
HAIG, DOUGLAS, LORD (q.v.) Edward Stanley
HAKLUYT, RICHARD (q.v.) Elizabeth I
HALBERSTAM, DAVID Dwight D. Eisenhower, Lyndon B. Johnson, Robert F. Kennedy, Edward R. Murrow
HALDANE, LORD Lord Haig, David Lloyd George
HALDIMAND, SIR FREDERICK Ethan Allen
HALE, WILLIAM HARLAN Margaret Fuller, Horace Greeley
HALIFAX, LORD Neville Chamberlain
HALIFAX, MARQUIS OF, see SAVILE
HALL, C. S. John Brown
HALL, DONALD Marianne Moore
HALL, HENRY William III
HALL, ROBERT Thomas Paine
HALLAM, HENRY John of Salisbury, Sir Roger L'Estrange, Sir Thomas More
HALLIWELL-PHILIPS, J. D. Shakespeare
HALSTEAD, MURAT Benjamin Butler, Ulysses S. Grant
HAMILTON, ALEXANDER (q.v.) John Adams, Aaron Burr, Albert Gallatin
HAMILTON, SIR EDWARD Joseph Chamberlain
HAMILTON, EMMA LADY (q.v.) George Romney
HAMILTON, GERARD Edmund Burke
HAMILTON, LADY JEAN Lord Kitchener
HAMILTON, THOMAS Daniel Webster
HAMMOND, JOHN H. John C. Calhoun
HAMMERSTEIN, OSCAR George Gershwin
HAMPDEN, JOHN (q.v.) Oliver Cromwell
HAND, LEARNED (q.v.) Samuel Goldwyn
HANNA, MARK (q.v.) Theodore Roosevelt

HANNAY, HOWARD Bernard
Berenson
HARCOURT, SIR WILLIAM (q.v.)
Charles Parnell, Lord Rosebery
HARDIE, JAMES KEIR (q.v.)
Edward VIII
HARDIE, MARTIN John Sell Cotman,
Alexander Cozens, Thomas Girtin,
Kate Greenaway, Samuel Palmer,
Thomas Rowlandson
HARDY, THOMAS (q.v.) George
Meredith
HARGRAVE, FRANCIS Sir William
Blackstone
HARINGTON, SIR JOHN John
Whitgift
HARRIMAN, MARGARET CASE
Tallulah Bankhead, John Drew,
Douglas Fairbanks
HARRINGTON, SIR JOHN Elizabeth I
HARRIS, FRANK (q.v.) Henry James,
Dante Gabriel Rossetti, Shakespeare,
George Bernard Shaw, H. G. Wells
HARRIS, ISHAM G. Andrew Johnson
HARRIS, NEIL Phineas T. Barnum
HARRISON, BENJAMIN (q.v.)
Abraham Lincoln, William Tecumseh
Sherman
HARRISON, GEORGE Robert Blake
HARRISON, MARVIN Robert A. Taft
HART, ALBERT B. John Fiske
HART, JAMES D. Sherwood Ander-
son, Hart Crane, Robert Frost, Zane
Grey, Vachel Lindsay, Clifford Odets
HART, JOSEPH Shakespeare
HARTE, BRET (q.v.) Charles Dickens,
George Eliot, William Dean Howells,
Henry Wadsworth Longfellow, Mark
Twain
HARTLEY, SIR HAROLD Michael
Faraday
HARVEY, GABRIEL Robert Greene,
John Lyly, Thomas Nashe
HASKELL, MOLLY Stan Laurel and
Oliver Hardy, Marilyn Monroe
HASLERIG, SIR ARTHUR Oliver
Cromwell
HASSLER, JR, WARREN W. Ambrose
E. Burnside
HASSRICK, PETER H. Frederic
Remington
HASTED, EDWARD William Harvey
HASTINGS, WARREN (q.v.) Edmund
Burke
HATCH, ROBERT Sir Charles Chaplin
HAVES, H. R. Henry Ward Beecher
HAWKE, DAVID FREEMAN Thomas
Paine
HAWKINS, SIR JOHN John Dowland,
Henry Purcell
HAWKINS, SIR JOHN Oliver
Goldsmith
HAWKS, HOWARD Cecil B. De Mille
HAWTHORNE, JULIAN Wilkie

Collins, Nathaniel Hawthorne,
Herman Melville
HAWTHORNE, NATHANIEL (q.v.)
Elizabeth Barrett Browning, William
Cullen Bryant, Caleb Cushing, Ralph
Waldo Emerson, Margaret Fuller,
Samuel Johnson, Henry Wadsworth
Longfellow, Herman Melville, Frank-
lin Pierce, Hiram Powers, Anthony
Trollope, George Washington
HAY, IAN Rudyard Kipling
HAY, JOHN (q.v.) William Jennings
Bryan, William McKinley, Theodore
Roosevelt,
HAY, MALCOLM V. James II
HAYDEN, ROBERT E. Frederick
Douglass
HAYDON, BENJAMIN R. (q.v.)
Jeremy Bentham, Lord Brougham,
Sir Thomas Lawrence, Sir Joshua
Reynolds, George Stubbs, Benjamin
West, Sir David Wilkie, William
Wordsworth
HAYES, JOHN Thomas Rowlandson
HAYES, RUTHERFORD B. (q.v.)
James A. Garfield
HAYLEY, WILLIAM (q.v.) Joseph
Wright
HAYWOOD, 'BIG BILL' Samuel
Gompers
HAYWOOD, ELIZA Henry Fielding
HAYWOOD, WILLIAM D. Daniel De
Leon
HAZARD, EBENEZER Ethan Allen
HAZLITT, WILLIAM (q.v.) Sir Francis
Bacon, James Barry, Francis
Beaumont, William Beckford, Jeremy
Bentham, William Blake, Lord
Brougham, Sir Thomas Browne, Sir
Francis Burdett, Edmund Burke,
Robert Burns, Samuel Butler, Lord
Byron, Thomas Campbell, George
Canning, Thomas Carew, John
Cavanagh, George Chapman, Thomas
Chatterton, Geoffrey Chaucer,
William Cobbett, Samuel Taylor
Coleridge, William Collins, William
Congreve, Abraham Cowley, William
Cowper, George Crabbe, Daniel
Defoe, Thomas Dekker, John Donne,
John Dryden, Lord Eldon, George
Farquhar, John Ford, Thomas
Gainsborough, David Garrick, John
Gay, William Gifford, Thomas Gray,
Thomas Heywood, Thomas Hobbes,
William Hogarth, Leigh Hunt, Samuel
Johnson, Ben Jonson, Edmund Kean,
John Keats, John Kemble, Sir
Godfrey Kneller, Charles Lamb, John
Locke, Sir James Mackintosh, W. C.
Macready, T. R. Malthus, Christopher
Marlowe, John Marston, Philip
Massinger, Thomas Middleton, John
Milton, Thomas Moore, Hannah More,

Thomas Otway, Robert Owen,
Alexander Pope, Matthew Prior, Mrs
Radcliffe, Sir Joshua Reynolds,
Samuel Richardson, Nicholas Rowe,
Sir Walter Scott, Shakespeare, Percy
Bysshe Shelley, Sarah Siddons,
Robert Southey, Sir Richard Steele,
Laurence Sterne, Jonathan Swift,
James Thomson, John Horne Tooke,
J. M. W. Turner, Sir John Vanbrugh,
Edmund Waller, Benjamin West,
William Wilberforce, Sir David Wilkie,
William Wordsworth
HAZLITT, W. CAREW Shakespeare
HEAD, F. B. James Bruce
HEARNE, THOMAS Sir William
D'Avenant
HEARST, WILLIAM RANDOLPH
(q.v.) Joseph Pulitzer
HEATH, JAMES Oliver Cromwell
HECHT, BEN Sherwood Anderson,
Harpo Marx, H. L. Mencken, Ezra
Pound, Alexander Woollcott
'HEDGEHOG, PAUL' William Cobbett
HEDGES, WILLIAM L. Washington
Irving
HELLER, WALTER John F. Kennedy
HEMINGE, JOHN and CONDELL,
HENRY Shakespeare
HEMINGWAY, ERNEST (q.v.) Joseph
Conrad, Stephen Crane, William
Faulkner, F. Scott Fitzgerald, Ring
Lardner, Percy Wyndham Lewis,
Katherine Mansfield, Herman
Melville, Pocahontas, Ezra Pound,
Theodore Roosevelt, Gertrude Stein
HENDIN, JOSEPHINE Flannery
O'Connor
HENLEY, W. E. Matthew Arnold,
Robert Browning, Joseph Lister,
Richard Savage, Robert Louis
Stevenson, Izaac Walton
HENRY II (q.v.) Thomas à Becket
HENRY VIII (q.v.) Thomas Cranmer,
Thomas à Becket
HENRY, PRINCE Sir Walter Raleigh
HENRY, JOSEPH Benjamin Silliman
HENRY, W. C. John Dalton
HENSON, LESLIE George Bernard
Shaw
HEPBURN, KATHARINE Humphrey
Bogart
HERBERT, A. P. Lord Baden-Powell
HERFORD, OLIVER Booth
Tarkington
HERGESHEIMER, JOSEPH Philip
Sheridan
HERON-ALLEN, EDWARD Sir Henry
Irving
HERRICK, ROBERT (q.v.) Ben
Jonson
HERRINGHAM, SIR WILMOT
William Harvey
HERSCHEL, SIR J. F. W. Francis
Baily

HERVEY, LORD (q.v.) Lord Bolingbroke, Queen Caroline Wilhelmina, Duke of Newcastle
HERVEY, LADY George III
HERZBERG, MAX J. Wallace Stevens
HESELTINE, PHILIP Frederick Delius
HESSE, MARY B. William Gilbert
HEWISON, ROBERT John Ruskin
HEYWOOD, THOMAS (q.v.) Edward Alleyn
HIBBEN, PAXTON Stephen A. Douglas
HICKS, GRANVILLE Stephen Crane, Nathaniel Hawthorne, Bret Harte, William Dean Howells, Vernon Parrington, Upton Sinclair
HIGDEN, RANULF Edward II
HIGGINSON, THOMAS WENTWORTH George Bancroft, Emily Dickinson, Henry James, Sidney Lanier, Lucretia Mott
HIGHAM, CHARLES Cecil B. De Mille, John Ford
HILL, BENJAMIN H. Robert E. Lee
HILL, CHRISTOPHER Sir Francis Bacon, Thomas Hobbes, John Locke
HILL, EDWIN C. Thomas Dewey
HILL, GEORGE BIRKBECK T. B. Macaulay
HILLEBRAND, H. N. Edmund Kean
HILLS, PATRICIA Eastman Johnson
HIND, C. LEWIS Augustus Saint-Gaudens
HINDUS, MILTON F. Scott Fitzgerald
HINSHAW, DAVID Herbert Hoover
HIRST, F. W. Adam Smith
HITCHCOCK JR, HENRY-RUSSELL Henry H. Richardson
HITLER, ADOLPH Neville Chamberlain
HOAR, GEORGE F. Charles Sumner
HOBHOUSE, CHRISTOPHER Charles James Fox
HOCCLEVE, T. Geoffrey Chaucer
HOELTJE, HUBERT H. Amos Bronson Alcott
HOFFMAN, FREDERICK J. John Steinbeck
HOFFMAN, MICHAEL Gertrude Stein
HOFSTADTER, RICHARD John C. Calhoun, Grover Cleveland, Andrew Jackson, Abraham Lincoln, Franklin D. Roosevelt, Theodore Roosevelt, Daniel Webster
HOGGART, RICHARD W. H. Auden
HOLBROOK, FLORENCE Jane Addams
HOLBROOK, STEWART John Pierpont Morgan
HOLLAND, LORD George Canning, Queen Caroline of Brunswick, George Selwyn
HOLLAND, SIR HENRY Sir Joseph Banks, Henry Cavendish

HOLLINGSWORTH, BUCKNER Augustus Saint-Gaudens
HOLLINS, C. B. George Caleb Bingham
HOLLOWAY, JOHN Thomas Carlyle
HOLMAN HUNT, WILLIAM Ford Madox Brown, Christina Rossetti
HOLMES, JOHN HAYNES Upton Sinclair
HOLMES SR, OLIVER WENDELL (q.v.) Henry Ward Beecher, Thomas Carlyle, Ralph Waldo Emerson, David G. Farragut, Henry Wadsworth Longfellow, James Russell Lowell, James Oglethorpe, Henry David Thoreau, John Greenleaf Whittier
HOLMES JR, OLIVER WENDELL (q.v.) Henry Adams, J. M. Harlan
HOLROYD, MICHAEL Thomas Arnold, Augustus John, George Bernard Shaw, Lytton Strachey
HOLST, GUSTAV (q.v.) William Byrd, Charles Parry, C. V. Stanford
HOLT, RACKHAM Mary McLeod Bethune
HOLT, RUSH D. Wendell Willkie
HOLYOAKE, GEORGE Robert Owen
HOMAN, PAUL T. Thornstein Veblen
HOME, SIR EVERARD Sir Joseph Banks
HOMER, WILLIAM INNES Robert Henri
HONE, PHILIP John Quincy Adams, Henry Clay, William Henry Harrison, Samuel F. B. Morse, Martin Van Buren
HONE, WILLIAM (q.v.) George IV
HOOD, E. PASTON John Wesley
HOOD, THOMAS (q.v.) George IV
HOOK, THEODORE Queen Caroline of Brunswick, Lord Erskine, Thomas Moore, Richard Twining
HOOKE, ROBERT (q.v.) Sir Christopher Wren
HOOPES, TOWNSEND John Foster Dulles
HOOVER, HERBERT (q.v.) Franklin D. Roosevelt
HOPE, ANTHONY W. S. Gilbert
HOPE, BOB Bing Crosby, Louella Parsons
HOPE, GEORGE Carl Schurz
HOPKINS, ARTHUR John Barrymore
HOPKINS, GERARD MANLEY (q.v.) Robert Browning, John Dryden, George Eliot, Alfred, Lord Tennyson
HOPKINS, HARRY L. (q.v.) John L. Lewis, Franklin D. Roosevelt
HOPKINS, LEMUEL John Jay
HOPKINSON, FRANCES Thomas Paine
HOPPER, HEDDA (q.v.) D. W. Griffith
HOPTON, SUSANNA Thomas Traherne
HORNER, FRANCIS Henry Addington

HORTON, PHILIP Hart Crane
HOUSE, EDWARD Woodrow Wilson
HOUSE, HUMPHRY Lytton Strachey
HOUSEMAN, JOHN David O. Selznick
HOUSMAN, A. E. (q.v.) William Blake, Clarence Darrow, Gerard Manley Hopkins, Soame Jenyns, John Milton, Alexander Pope, Bertrand Russell, Algernon C. Swinburne
HOUSTON, DAVID William Jennings Bryan
HOUSTON, SAMUEL (q.v.) Jefferson Davis, James K. Polk
HOWE, ED Henry Adams
HOWE, EDMUND Edward Alleyn
HOWE, IRVING Sherwood Anderson, William Faulkner, Edith Wharton
HOWE, JOHN GRUBHAM William III
HOWELL, JAMES Ben Jonson
HOWELL, VARINA Jefferson Davis
HOWELLS, WILLIAM DEAN (q.v.) Hamlin Garland, Edward Everett Hale, Richard Hildreth, Sarah Orne Jewett, James Russell Lowell, Charles Eliot Norton, James Whitcomb Riley, Booth Tarkington, Henry David Thoreau, Mark Twain, Booker T. Washington, Walt Whitman
HOWES, JULIA Charles Sumner
HOWLAND, HEWITT James Whitcomb Riley
HOWLAND, JOHN A. James Whitcomb Riley
HOYT, EDWIN P. Damon Runyon, Alexander Woollcott
HUBBARD, ALICE Thomas Paine
HUBBARD, H. Sir John Tenniel
HUBBARD, WILLIAM John Cotton
HUBLER, RICHARD G. Cole Porter
HUDSON, W. H. Thomas Carlyle
HUGHES, CHARLES EVANS (q.v.) Oliver Wendell Holmes Jr, Charles A. Lindbergh
HUGHES, EMMET JOHN John Foster Dulles, Dwight D. Eisenhower
HUGHES, J. Edmund Spenser
HUGHES, RUPERT John Adams
HUGO, VICTOR John Brown, George Peabody, Shakespeare
HUISH, ROBERT William Cobbett
HULL, WILLIAM William Penn
HUME, CATHERINE David Hume
HUME, DAVID (q.v.) Lord Chatham, Oliver Cromwell, Edward I, Thomas Hobbes, John Locke, John Milton, George Savile, Laurence Sterne, Thomas à Becket, John Wilmot
HUMPHREY, OZIAS George Romney
HUNNEKER, JAMES GIBBONS Jo Davidson
HUNT, LEIGH (q.v.) Jane Welsh Carlyle, Samuel Taylor Coleridge, R. W. Elliston, George IV, John

Keats, John Kemble, Charles Lamb, Lord Liverpool, W. C. Macready, Vincent Novello, Percy Bysshe Shelley, Richard Brinsley Sheridan, Sarah Siddons
HUNTER, WILLIAM William Harvey
HURD, RICHARD David Hume
HURDIS, JAMES William Cowper, Thomas Gray
HURRY, COLIN (see also Green, Kensal) George Bernard Shaw
HUSSEY, C. Sir Edwin Lutyens
HUSTON, JOHN David O. Selznick
HUTCHINSON, LUCY Charles I
HUTCHINSON, WILLIAM Anne Hutchinson
HUTTON, WILLIAM John Baskerville, Sir Isaac Newton
HUXLEY, ALDOUS (q.v.) Charles Dickens, T. S. Eliot, James Joyce, D. H. Lawrence, T. E. Lawrence, Edgar Allen Poe, Virginia Woolf
HUXLEY, T. H. (q.v.) Charles Babbage, Charles Darwin, George Eliot, Michael Faraday, W. E. Gladstone, C. G. Gordon, Herbert Spencer
HYDE, EDWARD, EARL OF CLARENDON (q.v.) Richard Bancroft, First Duke of Buckingham, Second Duke of Buckingham, Charles I, Oliver Cromwell, Sir Kenelm Digby, John Hampden, Thomas Hobbes, Ben Jonson, William Laud, John Pym, Prince Rupert, Lord Strafford, Frances Stuart, Sir Henry Vane

ICKES, HAROLD Thomas Dewey, Huey Long, Wendell Willkie
INCHBALD, ELIZABETH (q.v.) John Kemble
INDERWICK, F. A. Oliver Cromwell
INGERSOLL, C. J. John Tyler
INGERSOLL, ROBERT G. Henry Ward Beecher, James G. Blaine, Abraham Lincoln
INGLEBY, L. C. Oscar Wilde
IRELAND, WILLIAM HENRY Thomas Chatterton
IRVINE, ST JOHN Sir Noël Coward
IRVING, HENRY (q.v.) Christopher Marlowe
IRVING, LAURENCE Sir Henry Irving
IRVING, WASHINGTON (q.v.) Aaron Burr, James Madison
IRWIN, WALLACE Theodore Roosevelt
ISHERWOOD, CHRISTOPHER W. H. Auden, Ford Madox Ford, T. E. Lawrence, Katherine Mansfield, Robert Louis Stevenson, Virginia Woolf
ISHERWOOD, HENRY BRADSHAW T. S. Eliot

ISHERWOOD, KATHLEEN George V, Queen Victoria
ISRAEL, LEE Tallulah Bankhead

JACKMAN, SYDNEY WAYNE Lord Bolingbroke
JACKSON, GERALD Sir Thomas Beecham
JACKSON, HOLBROOK Edward Lear
JACKSON, THOMAS Charles Wesley
JACKSON, THOMAS 'STONEWALL' (q.v.) Robert E. Lee
JACOB, NAOMI Sir Henry Irving
JACOBS, LEWIS Theda Bara, William S. Hart
JAEGER, A. J. Sir Edward Elgar, Henry Wood
JAMES I. (q.v.) First Duke of Buckingham, John Donne, Richard Hooker, William Laud
JAMES, E. O. Sir James Frazer
JAMES SR, HENRY Nathaniel Hawthorne
JAMES JR, HENRY (q.v.) Henry Adams, Louisa May Alcott, Matthew Arnold, Ford Madox Brown, Robert Browning, Sir Edward Burne-Jones, Wilkie Collins, Joseph Conrad, John Singleton Copley Sr, Charles Dickens, Charles William Eliot, George Eliot, Gissing, Nathaniel Hawthorne, Winslow Homer, T. H. Huxley, Sir Henry Irving, Charles Kingsley, Rudyard Kipling, James Russell Lowell, Sir John Everett Millais, William Morris, Charles Eliot Norton, Walter Pater, Edgar Allen Poe, Sir Henry Raeburn, Dante Gabriel Rossetti, John Ruskin, John Singer Sargent, Sir Walter Scott, Robert Louis Stevenson, William Wetmore Story, Alfred, Lord Tennyson, Dame Ellen Terry, Henry David Thoreau, Anthony Trollope, Queen Victoria, Sir Hugh Walpole, H. G. Wells, Edith Wharton, James McNeill Whistler, Walt Whitman
JAMES, MARQUIS Sam Houston, Andrew Jackson
JAMES, WILLIAM (q.v.) Jane Addams Ralph Waldo Emerson, Margaret Fuller, E. L. Godkin, Joaiah Royce
JARRELL, RANDALL (q.v.) W. H. Auden, Marianne Moore, John Crowe Ransom, Wallace Stevens
JARVES, JAMES JACKSON George Inness
JASTROW, JOSEPH Charles S. Peirce
JAY, DOUGLAS Sir Stafford Cripps
JEANS, SIR JAMES J. C. Maxwell, Lord Rutherford

JEAVONS, CLYDE, and PASCALL, JEREMY Theda Bara, Clara Bow, Betty Grable, Jean Harlow, Rudolph Valentino
JEBB, R. C. Richard Bentley
JEFFERS, ROBINSON (q.v.) Edward Weston
JEFFERSON, THOMAS (q.v.) John Adams, Samuel Adams, Aaron Burr, Alexander Hamilton, Patrick Henry, James Monroe, Thomas Paine, George Washington, Phillis Wheatley
JEFFREY, FRANCIS, LORD (q.v.) Lord Byron
JEFFREYS, JUDGE (q.v.) Richard Baxter
JENKINS, ELIZABETH Elizabeth I, Catherine Howard
JENKINS, RALPH, and WARNER, GERTRUDE C. Henry Barnard
JENKINS, ROY Hugh Gaitskell
JENNER, WILLIAM George C. Marshall, Drew Pearson
JENYNS, SOAME (q.v.) Samuel Johnson
JERROLD, DOUGLAS William Wordsworth
JESSE, G. H. Charles James Fox, George Selwyn
JESSOPP, AUGUSTUS Robert Cecil, First Lord Shaftesbury
JOHN OF SALISBURY (q.v.) Adrian IV, Thomas à Becket
JOHN, AUGUSTUS (q.v.) Mervyn Peake, James McNeill Whistler
JOHNS, B. G. John Aubrey
JOHNSON, ANDREW (q.v.) James K. Polk
JOHNSON, B. S. James Joyce, Laurence Sterne
JOHNSON, GERALD Daniel Webster
JOHNSON, HUGH Franklin D. Roosevelt
JOHNSON, JAMES WELDON Marcus Garvey
JOHNSON, JOHN Shakespeare
JOHNSON, LIONEL (q.v.) Rudyard Kipling
JOHNSON, LYNDON BAINES (q.v.) Walter Lippmann, Franklin D. Roosevelt, Adlai E. Stevenson
JOHNSON, NUNNALLY Marilyn Monroe, James Thurber
JOHNSON, SAMUEL (q.v.) (see also JAMES BOSWELL) Joseph Addison, Mark Akenside, Queen Anne, Sir Richard Blackmore, Lord Bolingbroke, James Boswell, Sir Thomas Browne, Edmund Burke, Gilbert Burnet, Fanny Burney, Robert Burton, Samuel Butler, Charles II, Thomas Chatterton, Geoffrey Chaucer, Lord Chesterfield,

Charles Churchill, William Collins, William Congreve, Abraham Cowley, Sir John Denham, John Dryden, Elijah Fenton, Henry Fielding, Samuel Foote, Sir Philip Francis, David Garrick, John Gay, George I, Oliver Goldsmith, John Gower, Thomas Gray, David Hume, Ben Jonson, William Laud, Dr Robert Levett, Lord Lyttelton, Duke of Marlborough, John Milton, Ambrose Philips, Alexander Pope, Matthew Prior, Sir Joshua Reynolds, Samuel Richardson, Richard Savage, Shakespeare, Thomas Sheridan, Laurence Sterne, Jonathan Swift, James Thomson, Edmund Waller, George Whitefield, John Wilkes, John Wilmot, Thomas Wolsey, Edward Young

JOHNSON, STANLEY Enrico Caruso

JOHNSON, WALTER William Allen White

JOHNSTON, ALVA Calvin Coolidge

JOHNSTON, WILLIAM Rutherford B. Hayes

JOLSON, AL (q.v.) Warren G. Harding

JONES, SIR HAROLD SPENCER John Flamsteed

JONES, INIGO (q.v.) Ben Jonson

JONES, TOM David Lloyd George

JONSON, BEN (q.v.) Edward Alleyn, Sir Francis Bacon, Francis Beaumont, Lord Burghley, William Camden, Charles I, Charles II, Sir Edward Coke, John Donne, Elizabeth I, James I, Inigo Jones, Benjamin Jonson (his son), Thomas Kyd, Shakespeare, Sir Philip Sidney

JORDAN, DAVID STARR Asa Gray

JORDAN, RENÉ Clark Gable

JOSEPHSON, MATTHEW James Fisk Jr, Jay Gould, Henry E. Huntington

JOWETT, BENJAMIN (q.v.) A. H. Clough, David Hume, Cardinal Newman, Florence Nightingale

JOYCE, JAMES (q.v.) Ford Madox Ford

JUERGENS, GEORGE Horatio Alger

JUNG, CARL G. Franklin D. Roosevelt

JUSSERAND, J. J. Pierre Charles L'Enfant

KANE, WALTER Howard R. Hughes

KANIN, GARSON Samuel Goldwyn, Thornton Wilder

KAPITZA, P. L. Lord Rutherford

KARLOFF, BORIS (q.v.) Bela Lugosi

KATZ, LESLIE Robert Henri

KAYE, DANNY Sir Malcolm Sargent

KAZIN, ALFRED Henry Adams, Sherwood Anderson, Randolph Bourne, Van Wyck Brooks, John Dewey, John Dos Passos, Theodore Dreiser, William Faulkner, Jack London, H. L. Mencken, John O'Hara, Vernon Parrington, John Steinbeck, Edith Wharton, Edmund Wilson, Thomas Wolfe, Elinor Wylie

KEAN, EDMUND (q.v.) Charles Kean

KEATS, JOHN (q.v.) Francis Beaumont, Robert Burns, Lord Byron, George Chapman, Thomas Chatterton, Samuel Taylor Coleridge, Benjamin Franklin, William Hone, Leigh Hunt, John Milton, Mrs. Radcliffe, Shakespeare, Percy Bysshe Shelley, William Wordsworth

KEATS, JOHN Howard R. Hughes, Dorothy Parker, Alexander Woollcott

KEBLE, JOHN John Dryden

KELEN, EMERY Nancy, Lady Astor

KEMBLE, FANNY W. C. Macready

KEMLER, EDGAR H. L. Mencken

KEMPE, JOHN Christopher Smart

KEMPTON, MURRAY Dwight D. Eisenhower, Robert F. Kennedy, Franklin D. Roosevelt, Norman Thomas

KENNEDY, SIR JOHN Lord Haig

KENNEDY, JOHN F. (q.v.) Thomas Jefferson, Robert La Follette, Adlai E. Stevenson

KENNELLY, BRENDAN William Butler Yeats

KENNEY, CHARLES LAMB Michael Balfe

KENNY, THOMAS Shakespeare

KENYON, J. P. Titus Oates, Israel Tonge

KER, W. P. John Gower

KERN, ALEXANDER Theodore Dreiser

KERNAN, MICHAEL Thornton Wilder

KERR, ROBERT Chauncey Depew

KEY, V. O. Huey Long

KEYNES, LORD (q.v.) A Bonar Law, David Lloyd George, Woodrow Wilson

KIMBALL, WARD Walt Disney

KINCAID, JOHN Duke of Wellington

KINDER, MARY John Dillinger

KINDILIEN, CARLIN T. Ambrose Bierce, James Whitcomb Riley

KINGSLAKE, ALEXANDER WILLIAM Lord Cardigan

KINGSLEY, CHARLES (q.v.) Robert Browning, Lord Byron, Canute, Thomas Carlyle, Hereward, John Ruskin, Percy Bysshe Shelley

KINGSLEY, HENRY Tobias Smollett, W. M. Thackeray

KINGSLEY, MARY Sir Winston Churchill

KINGSMILL, HUGH D. H. Lawrence

KIPLING, RUDYARD (q.v.) Sir Henry Campbell-Bannerman, Austen Chamberlain, Joseph Chamberlain, Cecil Rhodes, Mark Twain, Queen Victoria

KIRCHWEY, FREDA H. G. Wells

KIRSTEIN, LINCOLN Marilyn Monroe

KISSINGER, HENRY Eleanor Roosevelt

KITCHENER, LORD (q.v.) H. H. Asquith, David Lloyd George

KNIGHT, GRANT C. Ambrose Bierce, Anne Bradstreet, William Cullen Bryant, Willa Cather, Oliver Wendell Holmes, Upton Sinclair

KNIGHT, G. WILSON Francis Beaumont, Shakespeare

KNOWLES, DAVID Gilbert Foliot, Thomas à Becket, John Wycliffe

KNOX, HENRY (q.v.) 'Mad' Anthony Wayne

KNOX, JOHN (q.v.) Mary Queen of Scots

KNOX, RONALD George Berkeley

KOCH, VIVIENNE Carson McCullers

KOESTLER, ARTHUR Langston Hughes

KONEFSKY, SAMUEL J. Louis Brandeis

KOPKIND, ANDREW Martin Luther King

KORCK, ARTHUR Wendell Willkie

KRAMER, DALE James Thurber

KRAMER, STANLEY Spencer Tracy

KRAUSE, ERNST Erasmus Darwin

KRONENBERGER, LOUIS H. L. Mencken

KRUTCH, JOSEPH WOOD Maxwell Anderson, George S. Kaufman

KUHN, THOMAS S. John Dalton, Albert Einstein, Sir Isaac Newton

KUNITZ, STANLEY Randall Jarrell

KUNITZ, STANLEY, and HAYCRAFT, HOWARD Ambrose Bierce, e. e. cummings, Emily Dickinson, Henry Wadsworth Longfellow, Edmund Wilson, Elinor Wylie

KYD, THOMAS (q.v.) Christopher Marlowe

LA BADIE, DONALD W. William S. Hart, Tom Mix

LABOUCHERE, HENRY W. E. Gladstone

LA CAVA, GREGORY W. C. Fields

LACY, JOHN Charles II, Barbara Villiers

LADD, JOSEPH Phillis Wheatley

LA FARGE, HENRY John La Farge

LA FOLLETTE, ROBERT M. (q.v.)

Grover Cleveland, Theodore Roosevelt

LA GUARDIA, FIORELLO (q.v.) Heywood Broun

LAMAR, HOWARD R. Frederick Jackson Turner

LAMAR, MIRABEAU B. Sam Houston

LAMB, ANTONIA Elvis Presley

LAMB, LADY CAROLINE (q.v.) Lord Byron

LAMB, CHARLES (q.v.) Jack Bannister, Sir Thomas Browne, Lord Byron, Margaret Cavendish, Samuel Taylor Coleridge, William Cowper, Daniel Defoe, Sir George Dyer, R. W. Elliston, John Fletcher, John Ford, George IV, Benjamin R. Haydon, William Hazlitt, Thomas Heywood, William Hogarth, John Kemble, Sir James Mackintosh, John Milton, Vincent Novello, Izaac Walton, John Webster, Goerge Withers, William Wordsworth

LAMB, SIR JOHN William Laud

LAMBERT, CONSTANT Frederick Delius, Sir Edward Elgar, Sir Ralph Vaughan Williams

LAMBERT, SIR HENRY Joseph Chamberlain

LAMBERT, RICHARD S. George Barrington

LAMONT, WILLIAM M. William Prynne

LANCASTER, OSBERT Walter Pater

LANDOR, WALTER SAVAGE (q.v.) Lady Blessington, Robert Browning, Lord Byron, George Crabbe, Daniel Defoe, Elizabeth Gaskell, The Four Georges, Shakespeare

LANE, FRANKLIN K. William Jennings Bryan

LANG, ANDREW Sir H. Rider Haggard, Dick Whittington

LANGBAINE, GERARD Thomas Dekker, Thomas Middleton

LANGHORNE, ELIZABETH Nancy, Lady Astor

LANGTON, THOMAS Richard III

LARDNER, RING (q.v.) Calvin Coolidge

LARKIN, PHILIP W. H. Auden, Wilfred Owen

LARRABEE, ERIC Sir Francis Bacon

LARSON, ARTHUR Dwight D. Eisenhower

LASCH, CHRISTOPHER Lyndon B. Johnson, Mabel Dodge Luhan

LASKI, HAROLD (q.v.) Sir Winston Churchill, Sir Stafford Cripps, George Lansbury, Ramsay MacDonald, Franklin D. Roosevelt

LASKY, JESSE (q.v.) Rudolph Valentino, Josef von Sternberg

LASKY JR, JESSE Cecil B. De Mille, Jesse Lasky

LASKY, VICTOR John F. Kennedy

LATHAM, P. M. John Abernethy, Thomas Sydenham

LAUD, WILLIAM (q.v.) Charles I, Lord Strafford

LAW, ANDREW BONAR (q.v.) H. H. Asquith, Lord Birkenhead

LAWRENCE, D. H. (q.v.) Arnold Bennett, William Blake, Rupert Brooke, Robert Burns, Joseph Conrad, James Fenimore Cooper, Baron Corvo, Thomas De Quincey, Maria Edgeworth, George Eliot, Ford Madox Ford, E. M. Forster, Benjamin Franklin, John Galsworthy, Thomas Hardy, Aldous Huxley, James Joyce, Percy Wyndham Lewis, Amy Lowell, John Masefield, Herman Melville, Edgar Allen Poe, Ezra Pound, Bertrand Russell, Shakespeare, George Bernard Shaw, H. G. Wells, Walt Whitman

LAWRENCE, FREDA D. H. Lawrence

LAWRENCE, JEROME Paul Muni

LAWRENCE, SIR THOMAS (q.v.) Sir John Moore, Sir Joshua Reynolds

LAWRENCE, T. E. (q.v.) J. E. Flecker, E. M. Forster, Lytton Strachey, H. G. Wells

LAWSON, THOMAS John D. Rockefeller

LEACOCK, STEPHEN (q.v.) Robert Benchley, John Milton

LEAR, EDWARD (q.v.) Alfred, Lord Tennyson

LEAVIS, F. R. Rupert Brooke, Thomas Carew, John Donne, T. S. Eliot, Thomas Hardy, Gerard Manley Hopkins, Samuel Johnson, John Keats, Walter Savage Landor, D. H. Lawrence, George Meredith, John Milton, Ezra Pound, Percy Bysshe Shelley, Dame Edith Sitwell, H. G. Wells

LEAVIS, Q. D. Charlotte Brontë, Edward Bulwer-Lytton, George Moore, Mrs Radcliffe, Sir Walter Scott, Laurence Sterne, Virginia Woolf

LECKY, W. E. H. Daniel O'Connell

LEE, HENRY (LIGHT HORSE HARRY) George Washington, 'Mad' Anthony Wayne

LEE, JENNIE Aneurin Bevan

LEE, ROBERT E. (q.v.) Ulysses S. Grant, 'Stonewall' Jackson

LEE, SIR SIDNEY Thomas Kyd, Sir Thomas Malory, Sir Thomas More

LEE, VERNON D. H. Lawrence,

John Singer Sargent

LEECH, HARPER, and CARROLL, JOHN CHARLES Philip D. Armour

LEECH, MARGARET Gideon Welles

LEECH, WILLIAM Robert Browning

LEES-MILNE, JAMES Inigo Jones

LEESON, J. R. Joseph Lister

LE GALLIENNE, RICHARD Lionel Johnson, Rudyard Kipling, Algernon C. Swinburne, Alfred, Lord Tennyson

LEHMANN, JOHN Virginia Wollf

LEHMANN, ROSAMOND Ian Fleming, Virginia Woolf

LEISHMAN, J. B. John Donne, Andrew Marvell

LEJEUNE, C. A. Douglas Fairbanks

LELAND, CHARLES GODFREY Phineas T. Barnum

LENIN, V. I. Arthur Henderson

LENNIG, ARTHUR Bela Lugosi

LENNON, FLORENCE BECKER Sir James Matthew Barrie, Lewis Carroll

LEONARD, JONATHAN NORTON Henry Ford

LERNER, MAX Randolph Bourne

LESLIE, CHARLES ROBERT John Constable, Gilbert Stuart

LESSER, ALLEN Emma Lazarus

L'ESTRANGE, SIR NICHOLAS Shakespeare

LETCHER, R. P. Stephen A. Douglas

LETHABY, W. R. Sir George Gilbert Scott, Richard Norman Shaw

LEVANT, OSCAR (q.v.) George Gershwin, Harpo Marx

LEVENSON, J. C. Henry Adams

LEVER, CHARLES Thomas Cook

LEVIN, DAVID Francis Parkman

LEVIN, HARRY Christopher Marlowe, Sir Walter Raleigh

LEWES, GEORGE HENRY (q.v.) Edmund Kean, W. C. Macready, Shakespeare, W. M. Thackeray

LEWIS, C. S. (q.v.) Geoffrey Chaucer, Rudyard Kipling, John Milton

LEWIS, EMONY Clifford Odets

LEWIS, JOHN L. (q.v.) Harry S. Truman

LEWIS, LLOYD Erich von Stroheim

LEWIS, MERIWETHER (q.v.) and CLARK, WILLIAM (q.v.) Sacagawea

LEWIS, PERCY WYNDHAM (q.v.) Thomas Arnold, W. H. Auden, Arnold Bennett, William Blake, G. K. Chesterton, T. S. Eliot, Ford Madox Ford, Thomas Gainsborough, Dame Barbara Hepworth, Augustus John, James Joyce, D. H. Lawrence, George Orwell, Ezra Pound, George Bernard Shaw, Dame Edith Sitwell, Gertrude Stein, Virginia Woolf

LEWIS, R. W. B. John Steinbeck,

Walt Whitman

LEWIS, SINCLAIR (q.v.) Henry Ward Beecher, Willa Cather, Theodore Dreiser, William Dean Howells, Eugene O'Neill, Harriet Beecher Stowe

LIDDELL HART, BASIL H. William Tecumseh Sherman

LILBURNE, JOHN (q.v.) Oliver Cromwell, William Prynne

LILLY, M. Roger Fry

LILLY, WILLIAM (q.v.) Charles I, William Laud

LINCOLN, ABRAHAM (q.v.) Salmon P. Chase, Stephen A. Douglas, Ulysses S. Grant, George B. Mc Clellan, Alexander H. Stephens, Edwin M. Stanton, George Washington

LINCOLN, C. ERIC Malcolm X

LINCOLN, MARY TODD William Henry Seward

LINDSAY, BEN B. Aimee Semple McPherson

LINDSAY, VACHEL (q.v.) John Peter Altgeld, Edwin Booth, William Booth, William Jennings Bryan, John C. Calhoun, Mark Hanna, Langston Hughes, Andrew Jackson, Abraham Lincoln, William McKinley, Pocahantas, Edgar Allen Poe, O. Henry, Theodore Roosevelt, John L. Sullivan, Mark Twain

LINKLATER, ERIC Bernard Berenson

LIPPMANN, HELEN Walter Lippman

LIPPMANN, WALTER (q.v.) Jane Addams, William Borah, Calvin Coolidge, Franklin D. Roosevelt, Robert A. Taft, Harry S. Truman, Wendell Willkie

LISLE, LORD Sir John Denham

LLOYD, D. Sir Francis Walsingham

LLOYD GEORGE, DAVID (q.v.) H. H. Asquith, Lord Beaverbrook, Neville Chamberlain, Sir Winston Churchill, Lord Curzon, Edward Grey, Lord Haig, A. Bonar Law, Ramsay MacDonald, Emmeline Pankhurst, Lord Rosebery, Baron N. M. Rothschild, John Simon

LOCKE, JOHN (q.v.) First Lord Shaftesbury

LOCKER, FREDERICK Elizabeth Barrett Browning

LOCKHART, J. G. William Beckford, John Clare, John Keats, T. B. Macaulay

LODGE, HENRY CABOT (q.v.) John Mason Brown, William Jennings Bryan, Grover Cleveland, Warren G. Harding, Woodrow Wilson

LOEB, JAMES Reinhold Niebuhr

LOEWE, DR LOUIS Sir M. H. Montefiore

LOMAX, LOUIS Martin Luther King

LONDON, JACK (q.v.) Ambrose Bierce, Upton Sinclair

LONG, HUEY (q.v.) John L. Lewis, Franklin D. Roosevelt

LONG, WILLIAM Phillis Wheatley

LONGFELLOW, HENRY WADSWORTH (q.v.) Washington Allston, Jane Austen, William Cullen Bryant, Washington Irving, Paul Revere

LONGSTREET, STEPHEN Henry Luce

LONGWORTH, ALICE ROOSEVELT Calvin Coolidge, Thomas Dewey, Warren G. Harding, Robert F. Kennedy, Eleanor Roosevelt, Franklin D. Roosevelt

LORD, WALTER William Allen White

LORIMER, JAMES Charlotte Brontë

LORING, A. K. Horatio Alger

LOTHIAN, LORD Nancy, Lady Astor

LOVELACE, RICHARD (q.v.) Sir Peter Lely

LOVETT, WILLIAM Robert Owen

LOWELL, A. LAWRENCE Henry Cabot Lodge

LOWELL, AMY (q.v.) Walt Whitman

LOWELL, JAMES RUSSELL (q.v.) William Cullen Bryant, A. H. Clough, Caleb Cushing, Ralph Waldo Emerson, Edward Fitzgerald, Margaret Fuller, William Lloyd Garrison, John Gower, Bret Harte, Nathaniel Hawthorne, William Dean Howells, Emma Lazarus, Abraham Lincoln, Edgar Allen Poe, Alexander Pope, Henry David Thoreau, Anthony Trollope, William Marcy Tweed, Edmund Waller, George Washington, John Greenleaf Whittier

LOWELL, ROBERT Jonathan Edwards, Ford Madox Ford, Robert F. Kennedy

LUBBOCK, PERCY Emily Dickinson, Edith Wharton

LUCAS, E. V. G. K. Chesterton, Rudyard Kipling

LUCE, CLAIRE BOOTH Eleanor Roosevelt, Henry Wallace

LUDLOW, EDMUND Oliver Cromwell

LUHAN, MABEL DODGE (q.v.) Lincoln Steffens

LUNDQUIST, JAMES Sinclair Lewis

LUNN, ARNOLD John Wesley

LUNT, GEORGE Caleb Cushing

LUSHINGTON, FRANKLIN Edward Lear

LUTYENS, SIR EDWARD (q.v.) Sir John Vanbrugh

LUTYENS, ROBERT Sir Edwin Lutyens

LYDGATE, JOHN Geoffrey Chaucer

LYDON, MICHAEL Jimi Hendrix

LYNDHURST, LORD (q.v.) Robert Peel

LYONS, CLIFF Tom Mix

LYND, ALBERT John Dewey

LYTTLETON, WILLIAM H. John Quincy Adams

LYTTON, EDWARD BULWER, LORD (q.v.) Lord Derby, Benjamin Disraeli, Lady Caroline Lamb, Daniel O'Connell, Richard III, Lord Russell

LYTTON, SIR HENRY Lord Palmerston

LYTTON, LADY Sir Winston Churchill

MACARTHUR, HARRY Norman Thomas

MACAULAY, THOMAS BABINGTON, LORD (q.v.) Lucy Aikin, Queen Anne, Lord Arlington, Francis Atterbury, Jane Austen, Sir Francis Bacon, Jeremy Bentham, James Boswell, Anne Bracegirdle, Second Duke of Buckingham, Fanny Burney, Lord Bute, Lord Byron, Robert Cecil, Charles I, Charles II, Lord Chatham, Lord Clive, William Congreve, John Wilson Croker, Richard Cromwell, Lord Danby, John Dryden, Sir Philip Francis, W. E. Gladstone, Lord Godolphin, George Grenville, Robert Harley, Warren Hastings, David Hume, Edward Hyde, James I, Judge Jeffreys, Samuel Johnson, William Laud, Mary II, James Mill, John Milton, George Monck, Robert Montgomery, Sir Thomas More, Duke of Newcastle, William Penn, Lord Peterborough, Ambrose Philips, Sir Stephen Rice, Lord Sandwich, George Savile, First Lord Shaftesbury, Sir Richard Steele, Lord Strafford, Sir William Temple, Barbara Villiers, Horace Walpole, Lord Wharton, William III, William Wycherley

MACAULAY, ROSE Evelyn Waugh

MACBETH, GEORGE Dante Gabriel Rossetti

MCADOO, WILLIAM Warren G. Harding

MCALMON, ROBERT Ernest Hemingway

MCCABE, JOHN George M. Cohan

MACCARTHY, DESMOND James Boswell, Sir Richard Burton, Robert Burton, Sir Noël Coward, Charles Dickens, Edward Gibbon, Samuel Johnson, Ben Jonson, James Joyce, Edward Bulwer Lytton, Shakespeare, Sir Herbert Beerbohm Tree

MCCARTHY, EUGENE Lyndon B. Johnson

MCCARTHY, HAROLD T. Henry James

MCCARTHY, JOSEPH (q.v.) Drew Pearson

MCCARTHY, JUSTIN George I, George II

MCCARTHY, MARY Ivy Compton-Burnett

MCCLELLAN, GEORGE B. (q.v.) Winfield Scott, Edwin M. Stanton, Gideon Welles

MCCLELLAN, JOHN H. Thaddeus Stevens

MCCORMICK, MEDILL Theodore Roosevelt

MCCRACKEN, HAROLD Frederic Remington

MCCUE, THOMAS William Marcy Tweed

MACDIARMID, JOHN Lord Burghley

MACDONALD, DWIGHT Norman Thomas

MACDONNELL, JAMES Sir Edwin Chadwick

MACFALL, HALDANE Sir Frank Brangwyn

MCFARLANE, K. B. Edward I

MCFEE, WILLIAM Sir Martin Frobisher

MCFEE, WILLIAM Edna Ferber

MCGINLEY, PHYLLIS Ogden Nash

MCGURK, J. Sir Stafford Cripps

MCHUGH, R. J. Henry Grattan

MACILWAIN, GEORGE John Abernethy

MACKENZIE, COMPTON G. F. Handel

MCKIBBIN, DAVID John Singer Sargent

MCKINLEY, WILLIAM (q.v.) James A. Garfield

MACKINTOSH, SIR JAMES (q.v.) Henry VIII, Sir Thomas More, John Oldcastle, Richard I, William Wilberforce

MACLAREN-ROSS, JULIAN Dylan Thomas

MACLAY, WILLIAM John Adams

MACLEISH, ARCHIBALD Ernest Hemingway, Henry Luce, Clifford Odets, Eleanor Roosevelt

MACLEISH, ROD Thornton Wilder

MCLOUGHLIN, WILLIAM G. Isaac Backus

MCMASTER, JOHN B. Thomas Jefferson

MACMILLAN, HAROLD Lord Alexander of Tunis, Aneurin Bevan, John F. Kennedy

MACNEICE, LOUIS W. H. Auden, Percy Wyndham Lewis, Dylan Thomas, William Butler Yeats

MACREADY, W. C. (q.v.) Charles Dickens

MACVICKER, JAMES Charlotte Cushman

MACY, JOHN Charles Dickens,

William Dean Howells, Alexander Pope

MADDEN, D. O. Henry Grattan

MADDEN, DR Lady Blessington

MADISON, CHARLES A. Sholem Asch, Randolph Bourne, Thornstein Veblen

MADISON, JAMES (q.v.) John Jay, Thomas Jefferson

MAGNUM, P. H. Andrew Jackson

MAHAN, ALFRED THAYER (q.v.) Lord Nelson

MAHON, LORD Francis Atterbury, John Carteret

MAIDSTON, JOHN Oliver Cromwell

MAILER, NORMAN E. M. Forster, John F. Kennedy, Robert F. Kennedy, Marilyn Monroe

MALCOLM X (q.v.) Martin Luther King

MALLESON, COLONEL Lord Clive

MALLET, DAVID Richard Bentley

MALLOWAN, SIR MAX Dame Agatha Christi

MALONEY, MARTIN Thomas Wolfe

MALONEY, RUSSELL Ogden Nash

MALTBY, WILLIAM Richard Porson

MANCHESTER, WILLIAM George Arliss, Marilyn Monroe

MANDEL, B. Samuel Gompers

MANN, HORACE Zachary Taylor

MANNERS, LORD JOHN Lord Derby

MANNES, MARYA John Mason Brown

MANNING, BERNARD L. John Wycliffe

MANNING, CARDINAL (q.v.) Lord Acton, Cardinal Newman

MANNINGHAM, JOHN Sir John Davies, John Marston, Shakespeare

MANSFIELD, KATHERINE (q.v.) E. M. Forster

MANTLE, BURNS Eugene O'Neill

MAP(PE), WALTER Queen Eleanour of Aquitaine, Henry II, King Stephen

MARBLE, MANTON Edwin M. Stanton

MARCHANT, N. Joseph Nollekens

MARDER, A. J. Lord Fisher

MARDER, LOUIS Lord Reith, Shakespeare

MARION, FRANCES Cecil B. De Mille

MARKOE, PETER Thomas Paine

MARKS, BARRY A. e. e. cummings

MARLOWE, CHRISTOPHER (q.v.) Piers Gaveston

MARQUESS, SAMUEL S. Henry Ford

MARQUIS, DON John Milton

MARSH, REGINALD Thomas Hart Benton

MARSHALL, JOHN (q.v.) Sir William Blackstone

MARSHALL, THOMAS F. Henry Clay

MARTIN, JAY Ambrose Bierce, Joel

Chandler Harris, William Dean Howells

MARTIN, KINGSLEY Ernest Bevin

MARTINEAU, HARRIET (q.v.) Matthew Arnold, Thomas Hart Benton, Sir Francis Burdett, John C. Calhoun, George Canning, Lord Eldon, Henry Hunt, Lucretia Mott, Lord Palmerston, Sir Robert Peel, Sir Walter Scott

MARTYN, EDWARD George Moore

MARVELL, ANDREW (q.v.) Charles I, Oliver Cromwell, Richard Flecknoe, Anne Hyde, Edward Hyde, Richard Lovelace, John Milton, Prince Rupert

MARX, ARTHUR Groucho Marx, Louis B. Mayer

MARX, GROUCHO Luther Burbank, Dwight D. Eisenhower, George S. Kaufman, Marilyn Monroe

MARX, HARPO (q.v.) George S. Kaufman, Oscar Levant, Alexander Woollcott

MARX, KARL Jeremy Bentham

MASEFIELD, JOHN (q.v.) Neville Chamberlain

MASON, WILLIAM David Hume

MASSON, DAVID Samuel Pepys

MAST, GERALD Douglas Fairbanks, Harpo Marx, Ben Turpin

MASTERS, EDGAR LEE William Jennings Bryan, Theodore Dreiser, Theodore Roosevelt, Mark Twain, Walt Whitman

MATHER, COTTON (q.v.) John Cotton, Thomas Hooker, John Winthrop

MATHER, SAMUEL Cotton Mather

MATHIAS, THOMAS J. Sir Benjamin Thompson, Mary Wollstonecraft

MATTHEWS, T. S. Edna Ferber

MATTINGLY, GARRETT Mary, Queen of Scots

MAUGHAM, W. SOMERSET (q.v.) Matthew Arnold, Jane Austen, Arnold Bennett, Charles Dickens, Aldous Huxley, Henry James, Samuel Johnson, Sir Hugh Walpole

MAXWELL, J. C. (q.v.) Michael Faraday

MAY, SAMUEL William Lloyd Garrison

MAYER, LOUIS B. (q.v.) Erich von Stroheim

MAYES, HERBERT Horatio Alger

MAYHEW, JONATHAN George Whitefield

MAYO, MORROW Aimee Semple McPherson

MEDILL, JOSEPH Andrew Johnson, William Henry Seward

MEHTA, VED Bertrand Russell

MEIER, AUGUST Martin Luther King

MELBOURNE, LORD (q.v.) T. B. Macaulay

MELTZER, MILTON Mary McLeod Bethune

MELVILL, JAMES John Knox

MELVILLE, LORD (HENRY DUNDAS) (q.v.) Lord North

MELVILLE, HERMAN (q.v.) John Brown, Ralph Waldo Emerson, Nathaniel Hawthorne

MENCKEN, H. L. (q.v.) Ambrose Bierce, William Jennings Bryan, Willa Cather, Grover Cleveland, Calvin Coolidge, Theodore Dreiser, Hamlin Garland, Warren G. Harding, William Dean Howells, Henry James, Serge Koussevitzky, Henry Cabot Lodge, William L. Marcy, Franklin D. Roosevelt, Theodore Roosevelt, Bertrand Russell, Upton Sinclair, Al Smith, Norman Thomas, Rudolph Valentino, H. G. Wells, Oscar Wilde, Woodrow Wilson, Walter Winchell

MENDIAN, MARSHALL Sam Houston

MERCER, JANE Gary Cooper, John Gilbert

MEREDITH, GEORGE (q.v.) Matthew Arnold, George Eliot, C. G. Gordon, G. H. Lewes, Lord Nelson, Algernon C. Swinburne, Alfred, Lord Tennyson

MEREDITH, ROY Calbe Cushing

MEREDITH, WILLIAM T. David G. Farragut

MERES, FRANCIS Shakespeare

MERRILL, WALTER M. William Lloyd Garrison

MERRIMAN, R. B. Thomas Cromwell

MERRIT, WALTER G. Samuel Gompers

MERSAND, JOSEPH George S. Kaufman

MESSALL, VICTOR Harry S. Truman

MEYER, AGNES Herbert Hoover

MEYNELL, ESTHER Lord Fisher

MICHAELIS, ALINE Charles Lindbergh

MICKELL, WILLIAM G. Henry Clay

MIDDLETON, THOMAS (q.v.) Richard Burbage

MILBOURNE, LUKE John Dryden

MILES, HAMISH James Crichton

MILIBAND, RALPH C. Wright Mills

MILL, JAMES (q.v.) Lord Melville

MILL, JOHN STUART (q.v.) Jeremy Bentham, Thomas Carlyle, Sir Edwin Chadwick, William Cobbett, Charles Darwin, Benjamin Disraeli, David Hume, Abraham Lincoln, T. B. Macaulay, James Mill, Florence Nightingale, Lord Russell, Robert Southey, Herbert Spencer, William Wordsworth

MILLAY, EDNA ST VINCENT (q.v.) Nicola Sacco and Bartolomeo Vanzetti

MILLER, ARTHUR Paul Muni

MILLER, HENRY Sherwood Anderson

D. H. Lawrence, Henry David Thoreau

MILLER, J. A. Stephen Gardiner

MILLER, JOAQUIN John C. Frémont

MILLER, JOHN C. Samuel Adams, Alexander Hamilton

MILLER, JORDAN Y. Eugene O'Neill

MILLETT, KATE Charlotte Brontë, D. H. Lawrence

MILLS, ELIJAH HUNT Andrew Jackson

MILNE, A. A. Aneurin Bevan, King John

MILNER, LORD Lord Kitchener

MILTON, GEORGE FORT Joseph Hooker

MILTON, JOHN (q.v.) Oliver Cromwell, Lord Fairfax, Edward King, Shakespeare, Edmund Spenser, Sir Henry Vane

MINTO, LORD Lord Nelson

MIST, NATHANIEL Duke of Marlborough

MITCHEL, JOHN Daniel O'Connell

MITCHELL, BROADUS Alexander Hamilton

MITCHELL, ELLEN M. Julia Ward Howe

MITCHELL, RUTH COMFORT Jane Addams

MITCHISON, NAOMI Elizabeth Garrett Anderson

MITCHUM, ROBERT Humphrey Bogart

MITFORD, JESSICA Nancy Mitford

MITFORD, MARY RUSSELL Jane Austen

MIZENER, ARTHUR F. Scott Fitzgerald

MOLEY, RAYMOND Huey Long

MONAGHAN, E. JENNIFER Noah Webster

MONCRIEFF, W. T. Shakespeare

MONKMAN, PHYLLIS Ivor Novello

MOONEY, BOOTH Thomas Dewey

MONTAGU, LADY MARY WORTLEY (q.v.) Henry Fielding, George I, Samuel Johnson, Alexander Pope, Samuel Richardson, Jonathan Swift

MONTGOMERY, JAMES Robert Burns

MOORE, GEORGE Lord Randolph Churchill

MOORE, GEORGE A. (q.v.) Arnold Bennett, Anne Brontë, William Dean Howells, Henry James, Rudyard Kipling, George Meredith, William Morris, Robert Louis Stevenson, Oscar Wilde

MOORE, HARRY THORNTON John Steinbeck

MOORE, MARIANNE (q.v.) Wallace Stevens, William Carlos Williams

MOORE, THOMAS (q.v.) Lord Castlereagh, R. W. Elliston, John Hunter,

Thomas Jefferson, John Kemble, Tom Moore, Sir Isaac Newton, Richard Brinsley Sheridan, Robert Southey, Duke of Wellington

MOOREHEAD, ALAN James Cook

MORDAUNT-CROOK, J. Sir John Soane

MORE, HANNAH (q.v.) James Cook, Edward Gibbon, Elizabeth Montagu, James Oglethorpe, Laurence Sterne

MORE, SIR THOMAS (q.v.) Edward IV, Henry VIII, Richard III

MOREHOUSE, WARD Florenz Ziegfeld

MORELLO, EDWARD William Booth

MORGAN, CHARLES Rudyard Kipling

MORGAN, CHARLES H. George Bellows

MORGAN, DONALD G. John Marshall

MORGAN, EDMUND S. Ezra Stiles

MORGAN, LADY George Canning

MORGANN, MAURICE Shakespeare

MORGENTHAU, HANS J. Robert F. Kennedy

MORISON, SAMUEL ELIOT George Washington

MORLEY, CHRISTOPHER Matthew Arnold, Heywood Broun, Samuel Johnson, Rudyard Kipling·

MORLEY, LORD JOHN Lord Acton, John Bright, Sir Henry Campbell-Bannerman, Thomas Carlyle, T. B. Macaulay, Lord Rosebery

MORLEY, JOHN Algernon C. Swinburne

MORLEY, RAYMOND Franklin D. Roosevelt

MORLEY, THOMAS (q.v.) William Byrd

MORRELL, LADY OTTOLINE (q.v.) Bertrand Russell, Lytton Strachey

MORRIS, GOUVERNEUR Thomas Paine

MORRIS, LLOYD Theda Bara, Clara Bow, Charlotte Cushman, Walt Disney, John Drew, Douglas Fairbanks, William Fox, D. W. Griffith, Jean Harlow, Elinor Wylie

MORRIS, RICHARD B. Alexander Hamilton

MORRIS, R. O. Charles Parry

MORRIS, WILLIAM (q.v.) Samuel Taylor Coleridge, Ralph Waldo Emerson, Dante Gabriel Rossetti

MORRIS, WRIGHT F. Scott Fitzgerald

MORRISON, HUGH Louis Sullivan

MORSE, SAMUEL FINLEY BREESE (q.v.) Washington Allston, John Singleton Copley

MORTON, FREDERICK W. Ralph A. Blakelock

MOSES, ROBERT Fiorello La Guardia
MOSELEY, LEONARD Stanley Baldwin, Lord Curzon
MOSS, HUGH Sir Hubert Beerbohm Tree
MOTLEY, JOHN LOTHROP George Bancroft
MOULTON, LORD Rufus Isaacs
MOUNTBATTEN, EARL Lord Alexander of Tunis
MOUNTJOY, LORD Henry VIII
MOUNTJOY, SHANNON Carrie Nation
MOWRY, GEORGE E. Theodore Roosevelt
MUGGERIDGE, MALCOLM Thomas Carlyle, James Joyce, George Orwell, Evelyn Waugh
MUIR, EDWIN Lytton Strachey, Virginia Woolf
MUMFORD, LEWIS Louis Sullivan
MUNBY, ALFRED A. H. Clough, Thomas Cook, Benjamin Disraeli, W. E. Gladstone, John Ruskin, Queen Victoria
MURPHY, ARTHUR Samuel Foote
MURPHY, WILLIAM C. William Borah
MURRAY, MARGARET Edward II
MURRAY, JOHN MIDDLETON D. H. Lawrence, John Milton, H. G. Wells, Oscar Wilde
MYERS, F. W. H. George Eliot
MYLLES, JOHN Robert Cecil

NABOKOV, VLADIMIR Samuel Butler
NAMIER, SIR LEWIS B. Lord Chesterfield, T. E. Lawrence, Charles Townshend
NAPIER, LADY SARAH Sir John Moore
NASH, JAY ROBERT John Wilkes Booth, J. Edgar Hoover
NATHAN, GEORGE JEAN Eugene O'Neill
NATION, DAVID Carrie Nation
NEAGLE, JOHN Gilbert Stuart
NEAL, JOHN George Washington
NEALE, J. E. Anne Boleyn, Elizabeth I
NEDHAM, MARCHAMONT (q.v.) Charles I, Charles II
NELSON, HORATIO, LORD (q.v.) Robert Blake, Emma Hamilton
NESBITT, CATHLEEN Rupert Brooke
NEVINS, ALLEN Grover Cleveland, Stephen A. Douglas, William L. Marcy, John D. Rockefeller
NEWBOLT, HENRY Sir Francis Drake
NEWFIELD, JACK Robert F. Kennedy
NEWMAN, ERNEST Charles Parry
NEWMAN, CARDINAL JOHN HENRY (q.v.) Jane Austen, Charles Kingsley, Cardinal Manning, Sir Walter Scott

NEWTON, E. Percy Wyndham Lewis
NEWTON, HUMPHREY Sir Isaac Newton
NICHOLAS, ROY Stephen A. Douglas
NICHOLL, GEORGE David Hume
NICHOLS, NORTON Thomas Gray
NICHOLS, ROBERT Siegfried Sassoon
NICHOLSON, NORMAN D. H. Lawrence
NICOLL, ROBERTSON Sir Hugh Walpole
NICOLSON, BENEDICT Joseph Wright
NICOLSON, HAROLD Clement Attlee, W. H. Auden, Lord Beaverbrook, Arthur Neville Chamberlain, Austen Chamberlain, Sir Winston Churchill, Lord Curzon, T. S. Eliot, Ian Fleming, George V, A. E. Housman, James Joyce, Ramsay MacDonald, Vita Sackville-West, H. G. Wells
NIEBUHR, REINHOLD (q.v.) John Foster Dulles
NIETZSCHE, FRIEDRICH Thomas Carlyle
NIGHTINGALE, FLORENCE (q.v.) Seventh Earl of Shaftesbury
NIVEN, DAVID Errol Flynn
NIXON, RICHARD M. Dwight D. Eisenhower, Walter Reuther, Adlai E. Stevenson
NIZER, LOUIS Sholem Asch
NOAKES, VIVIEN Edward Lear
NOBLE, M. Edmund Halley, Sir Isaac Newton
NOEL, RODEN Thomas Otway
NORMAN, CHARLES Ezra Pound
NORTH, ROGER Lord Danby, Sir Matthew Hale, Judge Jeffreys, Henry Purcell, First Lord Shaftesbury
NORTHCLIFFE, LORD (q.v.) Edward VII
NORTHCOTE, JAMES Thomas Gainsborough, William Hogarth, Sir Joshua Reynolds
NORTON, CHARLES ELIOT (q.v.) Charles Dickens, Frederick Olmsted
NORTON, JOHN Anne Bradstreet
NOYES, ALFRED Erasmus Darwin

OAKES, Urian Cotton Mather
OBERHOLTZER, ELLIS P. James G. Blaine
O'BRIEN, BRONTERRE Robert Owen
O'BRIEN, CONOR CRUISE William Butler Yeats
O'CONNELL, DANIEL (q.v.) William Cobbett, Sir Robert Peel, Spencer Perceval
O'CONNOR, FRANCIS V. Jackson Pollock
O'CONNOR, RICHARD James Gordon

Bennett Jr, Richard Harding Davis
ODETS, CLIFFORD (q.v.) John Garfield
O'FAOLAIN, SEAN Wolfe Tone
OGG, DAVID Lord Danby, James II, Duke of Monmouth, First Lord Shaftesbury, William III
OGILVY, MRS DAVID Elizabeth Barrett Browning
O. HENRY (q.v.) Walter Hines Page
OLIVER, E. J. Edward Gibbon
OLIVER, F. S. George III
OLIVER, PETER Samuel Adams
OLIVERS, THOMAS John Wesley
OLLARD, RICHARD Samuel Pepys
OMAN, C. W. Richard Neville
O'NEILL, WILLIAM Jane Addams
ONSLOW, ARTHUR William Bentinck
OPPE, A. P. Thomas Rowlandson
OPPENHEIMER, GEORGE George S. Kaufman
O'REILLY, MILES Ulysses S. Grant
ORMOND, RICHARD John Singer Sargent
ORRERY, LORD John Arbuthnot
ORWELL, GEORGE (q.v.) W. H. Auden, Samuel Butler, Thomas Carlyle, Joseph Conrad, Charles Dickens, T. S. Eliot, John Galsworthy, George Gissing, Gerard Manley Hopkins, A. E. Housman, Aldous Huxley, James Joyce, Rudyard Kipling, D. H. Lawrence, T. E. Lawrence, Percy Wyndham Lewis, Charles Reade, Dorothy Sayers, George Bernard Shaw, Jonathan Swift, Evelyn Waugh, H. G. Wells, P. G. Wodehouse, William Butler Yeats
OSBORN, FRANCIS James I
OSBORN, H. F. Charles Darwin, T. H. Huxley
O'SULLIVAN, VINCENT George Moore, William Morris, Oscar Wilde
OTTO, MAX Robert La Follette
OTWAY, THOMAS (q.v.) Titus Oates
OVERTON, JOHN HENRY Lancelot Andrewes
OVERTON, RICHARD Sir John Wildman
OWEN, ROBERT (q.v.) William Allen
OWEN, ROBERT DALE Robert Owen

PACIFICO, DAVID Lord Palmerston
PACK, ROBERT Wallace Stevens
PACKARD, F. A. Robert Owen
PAGE, WALTER HINES (q.v.) William Jennings Bryan, Woodrow Wilson
PAINE JR, ROBERT TREAT Sarah Morton
PAINE, THOMAS (q.v.) John Adams, Edmund Burke, George Washington, James Wolfe
PAINTER, SIDNEY King John,

William Marshal
PALFREY, FRANCIS W. Ambrose E.
  Burnside
PALFREY, JOHN G. Roger Williams
PALMER, GEORGE HERBERT Josiah
  Royce
PALMER, JOHN Williamson 'Stonewall'
  Jackson
PALMER, SAMUEL (q.v.) William
  Blake
PALMERSTON, LORD (q.v.) John
  Bright, Richard Cobden, Lord
  Liverpool
PANKHURST, SYLVIA Dame
  Millicent Fawcett
PANMURE, LORD Queen Victoria
PARES, RICHARD George III
PARKER, A. E. Lord Salisbury
PARKER, DOROTHY (q.v.) Margot,
  Lady Asquith, Samuel Butler, Charles
  Dickens, George Gissing, Elinor Glyn,
  John Knox, James Thurber, Queen
  Victoria, Walter Winchell
PARKER, JAMISON John Foster
  Dulles
PARKER, SAMUEL Andrew Marvell
PARKER, THEODORE John Adams,
  William Ellery Channing, William
  H. Prescott
PARKMAN, FRANCIS (q.v.) James
  Fenimore Cooper, Pontiac
PARR, SAMUEL Samuel Johnson
PARRINGTON, VERNON LOUIS (q.v.)
  Thomas Bailey Aldrich, Joel Barlow,
  William Cullen Bryant, James
  Fenimore Cooper, Margaret Fuller,
  Horace Greeley, Alexander Hamilton,
  Oliver Wendell Holmes, William
  Dean Howells, Washington Irving,
  James Russell Lowell, William
  Gilmore Simms, Edith Wharton
PARRY, C. H. H. (q.v.) Sir Edward
  Elgar
PARRY, DAVID M. Samuel Gompers
PARSONS, ROBERT John Wilmot
PARSONS, THORNTON H. John
  Crowe Ransom
PARTON, JAMES Thomas Jefferson
PASLEY, FRED D. Al Capone
PASQUIN, ANTHONY (pseudonym of
  John Williams) James Boswell, Sir
  William Chambers, Charles Dibdin,
  David Garrick, Geogre III, William
  Hayley, John Kemble, Lord North,
  Richard Brinsley Sheridan
PASTOR, TONY Lillian Russell
PATCH, BLANCHE George Bernard
  Shaw, Beatrice and Sidney Webb
PATMORE, P. G. Lady Blessington,
  William Hazlitt
PATTEE, FRED LEWIS Amos Bronson
  Alcott, Joel Barlow, James Fenimore
  Cooper, Jack London, Henry Wads-
  worth Longfellow

PATTERSON, ELEANOR Drew
  Pearson, Walter Winchell
PATTERSON, JAMES T. Thomas
  Dewey
PAUL, HERBERT Queen Anne
PAUL, SHERMAN Nicholas Murray
  Butler, Edmund Wilson
PAULE, SIR GEORGE John Whitgift
PAYNE, ROBERT George C. Marshall
PEABODY, ELIZABETH PALMER
  William Ellery Channing
PEABODY, EPHRAIM William Ellery
  Channing
PEABODY, FRANCIS GREENWOOD
  Edward Everett Hale
PEABODY, ROBERT Charles F.
  McKim
PEACHAM, HENRY John Dowland
PEACOCK, THOMAS LOVE (q.v.)
  Lord Brougham, Lord Byron, Samuel
  Taylor Coleridge, John Wilson
  Croker, Sir Walter Scott, Robert
  Southey, William Wordsworth
PEARCE, ROY HARVEY e. e.
  cummings
PEARS, DAVID David Hume
PEARSON, HESKETH W. E. Glad-
  stone, George Bernard Shaw, Sir
  Herbert Beerbohm Tree, Oscar Wilde
PEARSON, LESTER Dean Acheson
PEASE, SIR ALFRED Sir Henry
  Campbell-Bannerman
PEGLER, WESTBROOK John F.
  Kennedy, Drew Pearson
PEMBROKE, LORD Samuel Johnson
PENDRAY, G. EDWARD Robert H.
  Goddard
PENNELL, ELIZABETH ROBINS
  Mary Wollstonecraft
PENNELL, ELIZABETH and JOSEPH
  James McNeill
PENNELL, JOSEPH Childe Hassam
PENROSE, B. Warren G. Harding
PEPYS, SAMUEL (q.v.) Robert Blake,
  Robert Boyle, Lord Brouncker,
  Second Duke of Buckingham,
  Catherine of Braganza, Margaret
  Cavendish, Charles II, Richard Cool-
  ing, Oliver Cromwell, John Evelyn,
  Nell Gwyn, Robert Hooke, Anne
  Hyde, Edward Hyde, James II, John
  Lambert, William Lilly, George
  Monck, William Penn, Sir William
  Petty, William Prynne, Prince Rupert,
  Sir Charles Sedley, Frances Stuart,
  Barbara Villiers, John Wilmot
PERCIVAL, J. John Quincy Adams
PERCY, THOMAS Samuel Johnson
PERELMAN, S. J. Theda Bara, Erich
  von Stroheim
PERKINS, FRANCES Eleanor
  Roosevelt, Franklin D. Roosevelt
PERKINS, JAMES H. Daniel Boone
PERLMAN, SELIG Samuel Gompers,

John L. Lewis
PERRY, BENJAMIN Daniel Webster
PERRY, BLISS Francis Parkman,
  Carl Schurz
PERRY, J. Lord Campbell
PERRY, RALPH BARTON William
  James, Josiah Royce
PETHICK-LAWRENCE, LADY
  EMMELINE Dame Christabel Pank-
  hurst, Emmeline Pankhurst
PETRIE, SIR CHARLES Lord
  Bolingbroke, George III
PETTIGREW, THOMAS JOSEPH John
  Abernethy
PHELAN, JAMES Howard R. Hughes
PHELPS, AMOS A. William Lloyd
  Garrison
PHELPS, W. W. Brigham Young
PHILIPS, PETER John Bull
PHILLIPS, CABELL Adlai E. Steven-
  son, Harry S. Truman
PHILLIPS, EDWARD Robert Herrick,
  Ben Jonson, Richard Lovelace
PHILLIPS, WENDELL (q.v.) John
  Brown
PICKARD, JOHN B. Emily Dickinson
PICKERING, TIMOTHY Thomas
  Jefferson
PICKFORD, MARY Douglas Fairbanks
PIERCE, B. Cotton Mather, Increase
  Mather
PIGGOTT, MOSTYN Aubrey Beardsley
PILAT, OLIVER Drew Pearson
PILKINGTON, M. Sir Peter Lely
PILLEY, W. CHARLES D. H. Lawrence
PINCHOT, AMOS R. E. Franklin D.
  Roosevelt, Theodore Roosevelt
PINDAR, PETER (pseudonym of
  JOHN WOLCOT) Sir Joseph Banks,
  Sir William Chambers, George III,
  Samuel Johnson, Lord Melville,
  William Pitt, Sir Joshua Reynolds,
  George Stubbs, Benjamin West,
  Joseph Wright
PINKERTON, JOHN James Bruce
PIOZZI, MRS (HESTER LYNCH
  THRALE) Samuel Johnson, Edmund
  Kean, Richard Brinsley Sheridan,
  Christopher Smart, Sir Robert
  Walpole
PIPER, DAVID James Gillray, Sir
  Thomas Lawrence, George Romney
PIPER, HENRY DAN F. Scott
  Fitzgerald
PIZER, DONALD Hamlin Garland
PLACE, FRANCIS Robert Owen
PLANCK, MAX J. C. Maxwell
PLATT, T. C. Roscoe Conkling
PLOMER, WILLIAM James Cook
PLUMB, J. H. Lord Chatham, George
  III, Sir Robert Walpole, Beatrice and
  Sidney Webb
POE, EDGAR ALLEN (q.v.) Nathaniel
  Hawthorne, Henry Wadsworth
  Longfellow

POGUE, FORREST C. Joseph Stillwell

POLLARD, A. F. Sir Francis Drake

POLLARD, JAMES E. James K. Polk

POLLOCK, JOHN Titus Oates, William Scroggs

POLWHELE, RICHARD Mary Wollstonecraft

PONSONBY, M. Prince Albert

PONTING, HERBERT Robert Falcon Scott

POOLE, A. L. Richard I

POORE, CHARLES John Mason Brown

POPE, ALEXANDER (q.v.) Joseph Addison, Queen Anne, Sir Francis Bacon, Richard Bentley, George Berkeley, Lord Bolingbroke, Second Duke of Buckingham, Queen Caroline Wilhelmina, Geoffrey Chaucer, Colley Cibber, William Congreve, Abraham Cowley, Edmund Curll, Sir John Cutler, Sir William D'Avenant, Daniel Defoe, John Donne, John Dryden, Elijah Fenton, John Gay, Lord Hervey, Thomas Hobbes, Henrietta Howard, Sir Godfrey Kneller, John Milton, Lady Mary Wortley Montagu, Sir Isaac Newton, Anne Oldfield, Thomas Otway, Francis Quarles, Thomas Shadwell, Shakespeare, Sir Richard Steele, Earl of Surrey, Jonathan Swift, Sir Robert Walpole, William Warburton, John Wilmot, George Withers

POPE, WALTER Seth Ward

POPPER, SIR KARL Bertrand Russell, Ludwig Wittgenstein

PORSON, RICHARD (q.v.) Edward Gibbon

PORTAL, ROBERT Lord Raglan

PORTER, KATHERINE ANNE Ford Madox Ford

PORTER, KENNETH W. John Jacob Astor

POST, LOUIS F. Henry George

POSTAN, MICHAEL Sir Stafford Cripps, Hugh Gaitskell

POSTGATE, RAYMOND John Wilkes

POTTER, DAVID M. Jefferson Davis

POTTER, DENNIS George Orwell

POTTER, ROBERT Samuel Johnson

POTTS, PAUL George Orwell

POUND, EZRA (q.v.) W. H. Auden, Aubrey Beardsley, Hilaire Belloc, Arnold Bennett, Robert Browning, G. K. Chesterton, T. S. Eliot, Sir Jacob Epstein, Edward Fitzgerald, Ford Madox Ford, Gerard Manley Hopkins, Henry James, James Joyce, Rudyard Kipling, Walter Savage Landor, D. H. Lawrence, Percy Wyndham Lewis, Amy Lowell, George Meredith, George Bernard Shaw, Upton Sinclair, James McNeill Whistler, Walt Whitman, William Carlos Williams, William Wordsworth, William Butler Yeats

POWELL, ANTHONY Ivy Compton-Burnett

POWELL, DORA M. Sir Edward Elgar

POWER, SIR D'ARCY John Abernethy, John Hunter

POWERS, STEFANIE Bing Crosby

POWER-WATERS, ALMA John Barrymore

POWICKE, SIR MAURICE Hubert de Burgh

POWYS, JOHN COWPER (q.v.) William Cowper, Eugene V. Debs

POWYS, LLEWELYN Anthony à Wood

PRAED, W. M. George IV, T. B. Macaulay

PREECE, HAROLD Sam Bass

PRESCOTT, ORVILLE John O'Hara

PRESTON, SIR HARRY Horatio Bottomley

PRICE, JOSEPH M. Fiorello La Guardia

PRIESTLEY, J. B. George IV

PRIESTLEY, JOSEPH (q.v.) Sir Isaac Newton

PRINGLE, HENRY William Howard Taft

PRIOR, SIR JAMES John Dryden

PRITCHETT, V. S. Pearl S. Buck, Charles Dickens, D. H. Lawrence, George Orwell

PUGIN, A. W. N. (q.v.) Benjamin West, James Wyatt

PULITZER, JOSEPH (q.v.) Charles A. Dana

PURCELL, RICHARD J. John Carroll

PURTON, W. John Constable

PUSEY, MERLO Charles Evans Hughes

QUENNELL, PETER Matthew Arnold, Queen Caroline Wilhelmina, Algernon C. Swinburne

QUINCY, EDMUND Henry Clay

QUINCY, JOSIAH Joseph Smith, Gilbert Stuart

QUINN, ARTHUR HOBSON Sherwood Anderson, F. Scott Fitzgerald, Oliver Wendell Holmes

RAE, JOHN Adam Smith

RAINE, CRAIG W. H. Auden, George Orwell

RALEIGH, SIR WALTER (q.v.) Henry VIII

RALEIGH, SIR WALTER Christina Rossetti, Shakespeare, Lytton Strachey

RAMSAY, H. Ben Jonson

RAMSAYE, TERRY Theda Bara, Douglas Fairbanks

RANDOLPH, JOHN (q.v.) John Quincy Adams, John C. Calhoun, Henry Clay, Thomas Jefferson, Richard Rush, Martin Van Buren, Daniel Webster

RANSOME, ARTHUR Oscar Wilde

RASHDALL, H. Roger Bacon

RAVENSCROFT, EDWARD Ben Jonson

RAVITZ, ABE C. Clarence Darrow

RAWLINSON, RICHARD Anthony à Wood

RAYBURN, SAM Lyndon B. Johnson, Harry S. Truman

RAYMOND, E. T. Sir Henry Morton Stanley, Oscar Wilde

RAYMOND, GEORGE Elizabeth Billington, R. W. Elliston, Tate Wilkinson

READ, CONYERS Anne Boleyn, Elizabeth I, John Foxe, Lady Jane Grey, Henry VII, Mary I

READ, SIR HERBERT T. S. Eliot

READ, THOMAS BUCHANAN Philip Sheridan

READE, BRIAN Edward Lear

REDD, WILLIAM D. Sam Houston

REDDING, CYRUS John Clare, George III

REDDING, LEO L. James Gordon Bennett Jr

REED, THOMAS B. William Jennings Bryan

REIN, DAVID M. Edgar Allen Poe

REMINGTON, FREDERIC (q.v.) Owen Wister

PEPPLIER, AGNES W. E. Gladstone

RERESBY, SIR JOHN Charles II, Louise de Keroualle

RESTON, JAMES Lyndon B. Johnson

REUTHER, WALTER (q.v.) John Foster Dulles

REYNOLDS, FREDERICK Elizabeth Inchbald

REYNOLDS, SIR JOSHUA (q.v.) Thomas Gainsborough, David Garrick, Oliver Goldsmith, Shakespeare, Sir John Vanbrugh

REYNOLDS, R. A. Lord Cardigan

RHODES, CECIL JOHN (q.v.) Sir Winston Churchill, Rudyard Kipling, Charles Parnell, Lord Salisbury

RHODES, JAMES FORD (q.v.) Caleb Cushing, Lorenzo Delmonico, Franklin Pierce

RICH, ADRIENNE Emily Dickinson

RICHARD III (q.v.) Henry VII

RICHARD OF DEVIZES William Longchamp

RICHARDSON, SIR ALBERT Robert Adam

RICHARDSON, SIR B. W. John Arbuthnot

RICHARDSON, EDGAR P. Washington Allston, Gilbert Stuart

RICHARDSON, LEANDER Joseph Pulitzer

RICHARDSON, R. G. and SAYLES, G. O. William I

RICHARDSON, SAMUEL (q.v.) Henry Fielding

RICHMOND, GEORGE William Blake

RICHMOND, WILLIAM Florence Nightingale

RICHTER, M. M. Jonathan Edwards

RIDLEY, SIR MATTHEW Benjamin Disraeli

RINARD, PARK, and PYLE, ARNOLD Grant Wood

RIX, H. Henry Oldenburg

ROACH, HAL Mack Sennett

ROBERTS, LADY Lord Roberts

ROBERTS, S. C. Sir Arthur Quiller-Couch

ROBERTSON, ALEC Frederick Delius

ROBINSON, DAVID Cecil B. De Mille, William S. Hart, Buster Keaton, Erich von Stroheim

ROBINSON, EDWARD G. (q.v.) Ethel Barrymore, Humphrey Bogart, Heywood Broun, John Ford, Louis B. Mayer, Paul Muni

ROBINSON, HENRY CRABB William Blake, Lord Byron, Samuel Taylor Coleridge, Daniel Defoe, R. W. Elliston, Charles Kean, W. C. Macready, Harriet Martineau, Sarah Siddons

ROBINSON, SIR HERCULES Joseph Chamberlain

ROBINSON, JOSEPH T. Robert La Follette

ROBINSON, LENNOX William Butler Yeats

ROBINSON, MARY S. Dorothea Dix

ROBINSON, PATRICIA Malcolm X

ROBINSON, W. R. Edwin Arlington Robinson

ROBSON, W. W. Walter De La Mare, Gerard Manley Hopkins, P. G. Wodehouse

ROCHESTER, EARL OF, see WILMOT, JOHN

ROCKEFELLER, JOHN D. (q.v.) Ida Tarbell

RODWAY, ALLAN Samuel Butler, William Dunbar

ROE, SIR JOHN Ben Jonson

ROGERS, EZEKIEL Thomas Hooker

ROGERS, J. A. Marcus Garvey

ROGERS, SAMUEL (q.v.) Duke of Cumberland, Dr. George Fordyce, Charles James Fox, Edward Gibbon, Humphrey Howarth, John Kemble, Lady Caroline Lamb, Richard Brinsley Sheridan, Robert Southey, John William Ward

ROGERS, WILL (q.v.) Sir Charles Chaplin, Charles A. Lindbergh, John J. Pershing, Al Smith

RÓHEIM, GÉZA Lewis Carroll

ROLLINGS, C. B. George Caleb Bingham

ROMNEY, GEORGE Walter Reuther

ROOSEVELT, FRANKLIN DELANO (q.v.) Heywood Broun, Thomas Dewey, Harry L. Hopkins, Andrew Jackson, Will Rogers, Al Smith

ROOSEVELT, THEODORE (q.v.) William Jennings Bryan, Grover Cleveland, James Gibbons, Alexander Hamilton, William McKinley, Franklin Pierce, Jared Sparks, William Howard Taft, Booker T. Washington, Woodrow Wilson

ROOT, ELIHU William Jennings Bryan, Rosoe Conkling, Charles Evans Hughes

ROPER, WILLIAM Sir Thomas More

ROSA, JOSEPH G. 'Wild Bill' Hickok

ROSCOE, WILLIAM Mary Wollstonecraft

ROSE, J. H. Lord North

ROSEBERY, LORD (q.v.) Henry Addington, Oliver Cromwell, Charles James Fox, George III, W. E. Gladstone, William Pitt, Cecil Rhodes

ROSEN, ANDREW Dame Christabel Pankhurst

ROSENFELD, PAUL Charles Ives, D. H. Lawrence

ROSS, HAROLD Alexander Woollcott

ROSS, ISHABEL Calvin Coolidge

ROSS, MALCOLM William Howard Taft

ROSS, NICHOLAS J. C. Powys

ROSS, ROBERT Percy Wyndham Lewis, Oscar Wild

ROSSETTI, CHRISTINA (q.v.) Sir John Everett Millais

ROSSETTI, Daute Gabriel (q.v.) Emily Brontë, Robert Burns, Thomas Chatterton, Ernest Gambart, James McNeill Whistler

ROSSITER, CLINTON Franklin D. Roosevelt, Harry S. Truman

ROTHENSTEIN, SIR JOHN Walter Richard Sickert

ROTHENSTEIN, SIR WILLIAM Aubrey Beardsley, Sir Edward Burne-Jones, Richard Harding Davis, Augustus John, Percy Wyndham Lewis, John Singer Sargent, Walter Richard Sickert

ROTHSCHILD, BARONESS D. E. Rothschild

ROUSE BALL, W. W. Sir Isaac Newton

ROVERE, RICHARD H. Dwight D. Eisenhower, Joseph McCarthy, Robert A. Taft

ROWAN, CARL T. Martin Luther King Jr

ROWE, NICHOLAS (q.v.) Shakespeare

ROWSE, A. L. John Dowland, Sir

Thomas Gresham, Duke of Marlborough

ROXON, LILLIAN Janis Joplin

ROYALL, ANNE Dolly Madison

RUARK, ROBERT John F. Kennedy

RUDWICH, ELLIOTT W. E. B. Du Bois, Booker T. Washington

RUGGLES, ELEANOR Lawrence Barrett, John Wilkes Booth, Junius Brutus Booth, Charlotte Cushman

RUNYON, DAMON (q.v.) Walter Winchell

RUSH, RICHARD (q.v.) James Madison

RUSK, DEAN William S. Hart

RUSKIN, JOHN (q.v.) Thomas Bewick, William Blake, Ford Madox Brown, Robert Browning, Lord Byron, John Constable, George Cruikshank, Charles Dickens, George Eliot, John Flaxman, Thomas Gainsborough, Benjamin R. Haydon, George Herbert, Samuel Johnson, T. B. Macaulay, Harriet Martineau, Sir John Everett Millais, William Morris, Charles Eliot Norton, Sir Joseph Paxton, A. W. N. Pugin, Sir Joshua Reynolds, Samuel Richardson, Dante Gabriel Rossetti, Sir Walter Scott, Sir John Tenniel, W. M. Thackeray, J. M. W. Turner, James McNeill Whistler

RUSSELL, BERTRAND, LORD (q.v.) Sir Francis Bacon, Jeremy Bentham, Boadicea, Francis H. Bradley, Lord Byron, Joseph Conrad, Charles Darwin, T. S. Eliot, W. E. Gladstone, Thomas Hobbes, David Hume, Aldous Huxley, Lord Keynes, D. H. Lawrence, John Locke, Katherine Mansfield, G. E. Moore, Lady Ottoline Morrell, Sir Isaac Newton, William Ockham, George Bernard Shaw, Lytton Strachey, James Watt, Beatrice and Sidney Webb, Alfred North Whitehead, Ludwig Wittgenstein

RUSSELL, CHARLES E. James G. Blaine

RUSSELL, G. W. E. Lord Acton, Cardinal Manning, Lord Palmerston, Lord Salisbury

RUSSELL, JOHN LORD (q.v.) Elizabeth Garrett Anderson, Elizabeth I, Lord Erskine

RUSSELL, KEN Isadora Duncan

RUSSELL, RICHARD Lyndon B. Johnson

RUSSELL, W. CLARK Elizabeth Billington

RUTLAND, DUKE OF Henry Addington

RUTLAND, ROBERT ALLEN George Mason

RYLE, GILBERT Bertrand Russell

RYMER, THOMAS Sir William
D'Avenant

SAARINEN, EERO (q.v.) Frank Lloyd
Wright
SACKVILLE, CHARLES, EARL OF
DORSET Charles II
SACKVILLE, THOMAS Barbara
Villiers
SACKVILLE-WEST, VITA (q.v.) Sir
Max Beerbohm, Sir Edwin Lutyens
SAFADIN Richard I
SAHL, MORT John F. Kennedy
ST JOHN-STEVAS, NORMAN Walter
Bagehot
ST JOHNS, ADELA ROGERS Roscoe
'Fatty' Arbuckle, Lon Chaney, Gary
Cooper, Douglas Fairbanks, Clark
Gable, William S. Hart, Tom Mix,
Mack Sennett, Rudolph Valentino
SAINTSBURY, GEORGE John Davies,
Duke of Marlborough
SALISBURY, LORD (q.v.) Joseph
Chamberlain, Lord Randolph
Churchill, Benjamin Disraeli
SALMON, EDWARD James Wolfe
SAMPSON, HENRY AYLETT Patrick
Henry
SAMUEL, LORD Sir Philip Frances
SANDBURG, CARL (q.v.) Abraham
Lincoln, George B. McClellan,
Lincoln Steffens, Thaddeus Stevens,
Charles Sumner
SANDERS, JARED Y. Huey Long
SANTAYANA, GEORGE Ralph Waldo
Emerson, William James, Josiah
Royce, Walt Whitman
SARGENT, JOHN SINGER (q.v.)
John D. Rockefeller
SARRIS, ANDRE Josef von Sternberg
SASSOON, SIEGFRIED (q.v.) Walter
De La Mare, Ronald Firbank, Henry
Vaughan
SAVAGE, D. S. F. Scott Fitzgerald
SAVILE, GEORGE, MARQUIS OF
HALIFAX (q.v.) Charles II, James II,
Louise de Kerouaille
SAYLES, G. O. William I
SCARISBRICK, RICHARD
Henry VIII
SCHARLIEB, MARY Elizabeth
Garrett Anderson
SCHEER, ROBERT Robert F.
Kennedy
SCHICKEL, RICHARD Walt Disney,
Betty Grable
SCHLESINGER JR, ARTHUR M.
Aneurin Bevan, Humphrey
Bogart, Eugene V. Debs,
W. C. Fields, Lyndon B. Johnson,
John F. Kennedy, Carole Lombard,
Huey Long, James K. Polk, Adlai E.
Stevenson, Norman Thomas
SCHOENBAUM, SAMUEL
Shakespeare

SCHOENBERG, ARNOLD George
Gershwin
SCHOENMANN, RALPH Bertrand
Russell
SCHORER, MARK Sherwood
Anderson, Sinclair Lewis
SCHOULER, JAMES James K. Polk
SCHREINER, OLIVE Cecil Rhodes
SCHULMAN, GRACE Mark Van
Doren
SCHURZ, CARL (q.v.) Chauncey
Depew, James Monroe
SCHUSTER, LEO FRANCIS
Sir Edward Elgar
SCHWARTZ, CHARLES George
Gershwin
SCHWARTZ, DELMORE Wallace
Stevens
SCOT, ALEXANDER Mary Queen
of Scots
SCOTT, EVELYN Alfred Stieglitz
SCOTT, SIR WALTER (q.v.) Jane
Austen, Fanny Burney, Robert
Burns, Lord Byron, Thomas
Campbell, George Crabbe, Daniel
Defoe, William Dunbar, Maria
Edgeworth, Elizabeth I, Charles
James Fox, William Gifford, James
Hogg, Samuel Johnson, John Knox,
Sir Thomas Lawrence, Mary, Queen
of Scots, John Murray, Matthew Prior,
Lord Robertson, Mary Shelly,
Laurence Sterne
SCOTT, WINFIELD (q.v.) Jefferson
Davis, Robert E. Lee, Zachary
Taylor
SCOTTOWE, JOHN Richard
Tarlton
SCROOPE, SIR CAR John Wilmot
SCUDDER, HORACE E. Noah
Webster
SCULLY JR, VINCENT Frank Lloyd
Wright
SEARS, EDWARD S. James Bowie
SECCOMBE, THOMAS Tobias
Smollett
SEDGWICK, ELLERY Walter Hines
Page
SEDGWICK, HENRY DWIGHT
Francis Parkman
SEEGER, PETE Woody Guthrie
SEITZ, D. C. James McNeill Whistler
SELDEN, JOHN James I
SELDES, GILBERT George M. Cohan,
Cecil B. De Mille, D. W. Griffith, Al
Jolson
SELIGMANN, HERBERT J. Alfred
Stieglitz
SELLAR, W.C., and YEATMAN, R. J.
Alfred, Boadicea, Canute, Ethelred,
Samuel Pepys, Horace Walpole, Oscar
Wilde
SELLERS, CHARLES COLEMAN
Benedict Arnold, Charles Wilson
Peale

SELWYN, GEORGE (q.v.) Sir Joshua
Reynolds
SELZ, PETER Mark Rothko
SELZNICK, DAVID O. (q.v.) Josef von
Sternberg
SENNETT, MACK (q.v.) Roscoe
'Fatty' Arbuckle, Ben Turpin
SENNETT, TED John Garfield
SERGEANT, ELIZABETH SHEPLEY
Willa Cather
SERGEANT, ELSIE Amy Lowell
SEWALL, JONATHAN John Adams,
George Washington
SEWARD, ANNA (q.v.) Samuel
Johnson
SEWARD, WILLIAM H. (q.v.)
Stephen A. Douglas, Andrew Jackson
SEXBY, EDWARD Charles I, Oliver
Cromwell
SHADWELL, THOMAS (q.v.) John
Dryden, John Fletcher
SHAFTESBURY, FIRST EARL OF
(q.v.) Sir Christopher Wren
SHAFTESBURY, SEVENTH EARL
OF (q.v.) Sir Robert Peel, Lord
Russell
SHAKESPEARE, WILLIAM (q.v.)
Owen Glendower, Henry V, John of
Gaunt, Richard II, Christopher Tye,
Thomas Wolsey
SHANNON, DAVID Beatrice Webb
SHAPIRO, KARL Randall Jarrell
SHARP, DAME EVELYN Richard
Crossman
SHAW, CUTHBERT Tobias Smollett
SHAW, GEORGE BERNARD (q.v.)
Harley Granville Barker, Sir James
Matthew Barrie, Francis Beaumont,
Hilaire Belloc, William Borah, John
Bunyan, Richard Burbage, Samuel
Butler, Mrs Patrick Campbell,
George Chapman, Charles II,
G. K. Chesterton, Edward Gordon
Craig, Eugene V. Debs, Charles
Dickens, Isadora Duncan, Sir
Edward Elgar, George Eliot, Sir
Johnston Forbes-Robertson, Sir
Henry Irving, Henry James, Samuel
Johnson, James Joyce, T. E. Lawrence
Christopher Marlowe, George More,
Thomas Moore, William Morris,
Lord Northcliffe, Eugene O'Neill,
Thomas Paine, Charles Parry,
Thomas Love Peacock, 'Babe' Ruth,
Shakespeare, Richard Brinsley
Sheridan, Marie Stoes, Sir Arthur
Sullivan, Algernon C. Swinburne,
Alfred, Lord Tennyson, Dame Ellen
Terry, Sir Herbert Beerbohm Tree,
Mark Twain, Beatrice and Sidney
Webb, Oscar Wilde
SHAW, J. C. W. G. Grace
SHAWHAN, CASEY Hedda Hopper
SHAW-SPARROW, W. Sir Frank
Brangwyn

SHEARES, WILLIAM John Marston
SHEFFIELD, JOHN, EARL OF MULGRAVE (q.v.) Charles II, First Earl Shaftesbury, Shakespeare, John Wilmot
SHELBURNE, LORD (q.v.) Lord Bute
SHELLEY, SIR JOHN Lord Russell
SHELLEY, MARY (q.v.) Lord Byron
SHELLEY, PERCY BYSSHE (q.v.) Henry Addington, Sir Francis Bacon, Lord Byron, Lord Castlereagh, Samuel Taylor Coleridge, Lord Eldon, Leigh Hunt, John Keats, John Milton, Thomas Love Peacock, William Wordsworth
SHEPARD, ODELL Louisa May Alcott
SHEPARD, THOMAS Anne Hutchinson
SHEPPARD, S. John Webster
SHEPPERD, MR. Henry Clay
SHERARD, O. A. Lord Rockingham, John Wilkes
SHERBURN, GEORGE Lytton Strachey
SHERIDAN, RICHARD BRINSLEY (q.v.) William Cobbett, David Garrick, Lord Melville
SHERIDAN, THOMAS (q.v.) Samuel Johnson
SHERMAN, JOHN Andrew Johnson
SHERMAN, SENATOR James Buchanan
SHERMAN, WILLIAM T. (q.v.) Ulysses S. Grant
SHERRINGTON, C. E. R. Sir Charles Scott Sherrington
SHERWOOD, ROBERT E. Harry L. Hopkins, Tom Mix
SHIPMAN, DAVID Clara Bow, Marie Dressler, Errol Flyn, Alan Ladd, Charles Laughton
SHIPPEE, LESTER B. James Ford Rhodes
SHIRLEY, JAMES (q.v.) Francis Beaumont, William Prynne
SHOEMAKER, ERWIN C. Noah Webster
SHORE, BERNARD Sir Malcolm Sargent
SHORE DINAH Bing Crosby
SHULMAN, MILTON Ivor Novello
SIBLEY, JOHN Cotton Mather
SICKERT, WALTER RICHARD (q.v.) Sir John Everett Millais, John Ruskin, John Singer Sargent
SIDEY, HUGH Lyndon B. Johnson
SIDMOUTH, LORD see Henry Addington
SILLIMAN, BENJAMIN (q.v.) Michael Faraday, Ezra Stiles
SIMON, GEORGE T. Glenn Miller
SIMPSON, RICHARD Henry Thomas Buckle
SINCLAIR, ANDREW Al Capone,

Dylan Thomas
SINCLAIR, UPTON (q.v.) Jack London
SINCLAIR-STEVENSON, CHRISTOPHER James Francis Edward Stuart
SITTING BULL (q.v.) Annie Oakley
SITWELL, DAME EDITH (q.v.) Aldous Huxley, D. H. Lawrence, Percy Wyndham Lewis, Lytton Strachey, Dylan Thomas, Virginia Woolf
SITWELL, SIR OSBERT William Beckford, Ford Madox Ford
SITWELL, SIR SACHEVERELL William Kent
SKELTON, JOHN Henry VIII
SKELTON, SIR JOHN Benjamin Disraeli
SKINNER, JOHN Lewis Carroll
SKINNER, RICHARD DANA Eugene O'Neill
SKLAR, KATHRYN KISH Catherine Beecher
SKOTHEIM, ROBERT A. and VANDERBILT, KERMIT Vernon Parrington
SLOAN, JOHN Robert Henri
SLOCUM, WILLIAM J. 'Babe' Ruth
SMALL, ALBION W. Lester Frank Ward
SMALRIDGE, GEORGE Francis Atterbury
SMART, Alistair Allan Ramsay
SMELLIE, ALEXANDER James II
SMILES, SAMUEL (q.v.) John Abernethy, Sir Richard Arkwright, I. K. Brunel, Samuel Crompton, Sir Humphry Davy, Michael Faraday, Sir William Herschel, Sir Isaac Newton, Joseph Priestly, George Stephenson, Thomas Telford, James Watt, Thomas Young
SMIRKE, SIR ROBERT Sir John Vanbrugh
SMITH, ADAM (q.v.) Joseph Black, David Hume
SMITH, ALEXANDER Ralph Waldo Emerson, Nathaniel Hawthorne
SMITH, ASHBELL Sam Houston
SMITH, BERNARD Van Wyck Brooks, Margaret Fuller, William Dean Howells
SMITH, CHARLOTTE Jane Austen
SMITH, F.E., see BIRKENHEAD LORD
SMITH, GEORGE Charlotte Brontë
SMITH, GOLDWIN Lord Rosebery
SMITH, MRS GORDON Nancy, Lady Astor
SMITH, HARRY B. Lawrence Barrett
SMITH, HENRY NASH Meriwether Lewis
SMITH, JAMES POWER 'Stonewall' Jackson
SMITH, J. T. Joseph Nollekens, Sir Joshua Reynolds

SMITH, JOHN Pocahantas
SMITH, JULIANA Noah Webster
SMITH, LOGAN PEARSALL (q.v.) Matthew Arnold
SMITH, MERRIMAN Dwight D. Eisenhower
SMITH, OLIVER H. Henry Ward Beecher
SMITH, SIDNEY (q.v.) Lord Eldon, Francis Jeffrey, T. B. Macaulay, T. R. Malthus, Hannah More, Daniel O'Connell, Lord Russell, Daniel Webster, William Whewell
SMYTH, DAME ETHEL Henry Wood, Virginia Woolf
SMYTHE, DONALD John J. Pershing
SMOLLETT, TOBIAS (q.v.) Henry Fielding, Henry VIII, Samuel Johnson, Richard II
SMYTHE, JAMES MOORE John Arbuthnot
SNELL, GEORGE William Dean Howells
SNOW, C. P. P. M. S. Blackett, Albert Einstein, W. G. Grace, Lord Rutherford
SNOWDEN, VISCOUNT Ramsay MacDonald
SOANE, SIR JOHN (q.v.) Sir John Vanbrugh
SOMERVILLE, WILLIAM Joseph Addison
SORENSON, THEODORE John F. Kennedy
SOUTHAMPTON, EARL OF Richard Burbage
SOUTHERN, SIR R. W. Henry I
SOUTHEY, ROBERT (q.v.) Lucy Aikin, Joseph Butler, Lord Byron, Margaret Cavendish, George Crabbe, Elijah Fenton, Robert Herrick, Lord Mansfield, Duke of Marlborough, Robert Montgomery, Lord Nelson, Thomas Telford, John Wesley
SOUTHWORTH, JAMES G. Mark Van Doren
SPACKS, PATRICIA Lewis Carroll
SPARK, MURIEL Branwell Brontë
SPARK, WILLIAM S. S. Wesley
SPARROW, JOHN A. E. Housman
SPARROW, W. J. Sir Benjamin Thompson
SPEICHER, EUGENE George Bellows
SPENCE, JOSEPH Thomas Betterton, Lord Bolingbroke, John Dryden, George I, Sir Isaac Newton, Alexander Pope, Sir Walter Raleigh, Shakespeare, Jonathan Swift, William Wycherley
SPENCER, HERBERT (q.v.) Thomas Carlyle, T. H. Huxley, John Stuart Mill, Sir Isaac Newton
SPENDER, STEPHEN W. H. Auden, Cyril Connolly, Walter De La Mare,

T. S. Eliot, Henry James, James Joyce, Vita Sackville-West, Lytton Strachey, Virginia Woolf
SPENSER, EDMUND (q.v.) Geoffrey Chaucer, Elizabeth I, Sir Francis Walsingham
SPRAGUE, WILLIAM B. Cotton Mather
SPRIGGE, JOSHUA Lord Fairfax
SPRING-RICE, CECIL Lord Curzon
SQUIRE, SIR JOHN Albert Einstein, Percy Bysshe Shelley,
STALLMAN, R. W. James Gordon Bennett Jr
STAMPP, KENNETH Andrew Johnson, Abraham Lincoln
STANFORD, C. V. (q.v.) Sir Charles Hallé, S. S. Wesley
STANHOPE, LADY HESTER (q.v.) Sir John Moore
STANHOPE, PHILIP DORMER, see CHESTERFIELD, LORD
STANHOPE, PHILIP HENRY Duke of Wellington
STANLEY, A. P. Thomas Arnold
STANLEY, LORD Lord Russell
STANLEY, DEAN A. H. Clough
STANLEY, SIR HENRY MORTON (q.v.) Joseph Chamberlain, David Livingstone
STANTON, EDWIN M. (q.v.) Gideon Welles
STANTON, ELIZABETH CADY (q.v.) Susan B. Anthony, Frederick Douglass, Lucretia Mott
STARKWEATHER, WILLIAM John Singer Sargent
STEAD, William T. H. H. Asquith, John Burns, Joseph Chamberlain, H. G. Wells
STEBBING, WILLIAM Lord Peterborough
STEELE, SIR RICHARD (q.v.) Francis Atterbury, Lord Bolingbroke, Sir George Etherege, Elizabeth Hastings, Sir Christopher Wren
STEFFENS, LINCOLN (q.v.) Theodore Roosevelt
STEICHEN, EDWARD Carl Sandburg
STEIN, GERTRUDE (q.v.) F. Scott Fitzgerald, Ulysses S. Grant, Ernest Hemingway, James Joyce, Percy Wyndham Lewis, Mabel Dodge Luhan, George Moore, Ezra Pound, Alfred Stieglitz, Alice B. Toklas
STEINBECK, JOHN (q.v.) Dwight D. Eisenhower
STEINBERG, ALFRED John Quincy Adams, Lyndon B. Johnson
STEINE, EMMA G. Mary Mcleod Bethune
STEINER, GEORGE Lord Byron, George Chapman, John Dryden
STENTON, SIR F. M. Edgar, Ethelred

STEPHEN, SIR JAMES Richard Baxter, T. B. Macaulay
STEPHEN, JAMES FITZJAMES Charles Dickens
STEPHEN, J. K. Sir H. Rider Haggard
STEPHEN, SIR LESLIE (q.v.) Samuel Taylor Coleridge, Charles Dickens, George Eliot, Robert Owen, Thomas Paine, Edgar Allen Poe
STEPHENS, ALEXANDER H. (q.v.) Abraham Lincoln
STEPHENS, HENRY MORSE William Beresford
STEPHENSON, NATHANIEL W. James Ford Rhodes
STERLING, JOHN Samuel Taylor Coleridge
STEVENS, THADDEUS (q.v.) James Buchanan, Andrew Johnson
STEVENSON, ADLAI E. (q.v.) Dwight D. Eisenhower, Eleanor Roosevelt
STEVENSON, ELIZABETH Henry Adams
STEVENSON, FRANCES H. H. Asquith, Lord Beaverbrook, Austen Chamberlain, A. Bonar Law, David Lloyd George, Megan Lloyd George, Lord Northcliffe
STEVENSON, Robert Louis (q.v.) Matthew Arnold, Robert Browning, John Bunyan, Thomas Carlyle, Charles Darwin, Benjamin Franklin, William Hazlitt, Samuel Johnson, Rudyard Kipling, John Knox, John Milton, Samuel Pepys, Sir Walter Scott, Walt Whitman
STEWART, DONALD OGDEN Robert Benchley
STEWART, JOHN C. John Crowe Ransom
STILES, EZRA (q.v.) Ethan Allen
STILLINGFLEET, EDWARD John Locke, Barbara Villiers
STIMSON, HENRY Herbert Hoover
STOCK, NOEL Ezra Pound
STOCKDALE, PERCIVAL Samuel Johnson
STODDARD, RICHARD HENRY Herman Melville
STOKES, ANSON PHELPS William Howard Taft
STOLBERG, BENJAMIN Samuel Gompers
STONE, IRVING William Jennings Bryan, Henry Clay, Clarence Darrow, Stephen A. Douglas, Jack London
STONE, I. F. John Foster Dulles, Dwight D. Eisenhower, Lyndon B. Johnson, John F. Kennedy, Martin Luther King, Fiorello La Guardia, Robert A. Taft, Harry S. Truman
STONE, WILLIAM J. Henry Cabot Lodge

STORER, BELLAMY William McKinley
STORRS, SIR RONALD Lord Allenby, T. E. Lawrence
STORY, WILLIAM WETMORE (q.v.) Hiram Powers
STOW, JOHN Sir Francis Drake
STOWE, HARRIET BEECHER (q.v.) Catherine Beecher, Aaron Burr, John Greenleaf Wittier
STRACHEY, LYTTON (q.v.) Lord Acton, H. H. Asquith, John Aubrey, Sir Francis Bacon, Evelyn Baring, Sir Max Beerbohm, William Blake, James Boswell, Rupert Brooke, Sir Thomas Browne, Thomas Carlyle, A. H. Clough, William Congreve, Robert Devereux, T. S. Eliot, Elizabeth I, E. M. Forster, J. A. Froude, Edward Gibbon, Thomas Hardy, David Hume, Edward Hyde, Augustus John, Samuel Johnson, James Joyce, Lord Keynes, D. H. Lawrence, T. B. Macaulay, Lady Mary Wortley Montagu, Cardinal Newman, Florence Nightingale, Alexander Pope, Shakespeare, Richard Brinsley Sheridan, Dame Edith Sitwell, Hester Stanhope, H. G. Wells, Leonard Woolf, Virgina Woolf
STRACHEY, R. Dame Millicent Fawcett
STRAND, PAUL Alfred Stieglitz
STRECCHE, JOHN Henry V
STREET, JULIAN Irvin S. Cobb
STRONG, GEORGE TEMPLETON Abraham Lincoln, John Pope, Philip Sheridan, William Marcy Tweed
STUART, GILBERT (q.v.) George Washington
STUBBES, HENRY Sir Kenelm Digby
STUBBS, WILLIAM (BISHOP) J. A. Froude, King John, Charles Kingsley, William Marshal
STUCKEY, STERLING Denmark Vesey
STUURMAN, PHYLLIS Ralph A. Blakelock
SUCKLING, JOHN Thomas Carew
SULLIVAN, SIR ARTHUR (q.v.) W. S. Gilbert
SULLIVAN, ED Walter Winchell
SULLIVAN, FRANK Wendell Phillips
SULLIVAN, MARK Samuel Gompers, Herbert Hoover
SULLIVAN, WILLIAM J. Edgar Hoover
SULZBERGER, CYRUS Henry Luce
SUMMERSON, JOHN Inigo Jones, William Kent, John Nash, Sir Christopher Wren
SUMNER, CHARLES (q.v.) Stephen A. Douglas, Thaddeus Stevens, Daniel Webster

SUMNER, MRS M. E. Charlotte Yonge
SUTHERLAND, LUCY S. Warren Hastings
SWANBERG, WILLIAM A. Charles A. Dana, Henry Luce
SWARD, KEITH Henry Ford
SWEENEY, JAMES JOHNSON Jackson Pollock
SWEET, FREDERICK A. James McNeill Whistler
SWIFT, JONATHAN (q.v.) Queen Anne, John Arbuthnot, Mary Barber, Richard Bentley, Sir Richard Blackmore, Lord Bolingbroke, Queen Caroline Wilhelmina, William Congreve, Daniel Defoe, John Dryden, John Gay, G. F. Handel, Robert Harley, Thomas Hobbes, Lord Peterborough, Ambrose Philips, Alexander Pope, Sir Richard Steele, Sir John Vanbrugh, Sir Robert Walpole, Lord Wharton, Edward Young
SWINBURNE, ALGERNON CHARLES (q.v.) Robert Browning, Lord Byron, A. H. Clough, Wilkie Collins, Ralph Waldo Emerson, John Ford, Nathaniel Hawthorne, Robert Herrick, Thomas Heywood, Christopher Marlowe, John Marston, Percy Bysshe Shelley, John Addington Symonds, John Webster, James McNeill Whistler, Walt Whitman, Oscar Wilde
SWINDELL, LARRY John Garfield
SWINNERTON, FRANK Sir Max Beerbohm, Aldous Huxley, Henry James, James Joyce, John Masefield, H. G. Wells, Virginia Woolf
SWINTON, WILLIAM John Pope
SWISHER, CARL BRENT Roger B. Taney
SWITZLER, WILLIAM T. Thomas Hart Benton
SWOPE, HERBERT B. Heywood Broun
SYDNEY, SIR PHILIP Geoffrey Chaucer
SYKES, MCCREADY E. L. Godkin
SYKES, MRS William Wilberforce
SYLVESTER, A. J. David Lloyd George
SYMES, LILLIAN, and CLEMENT, TRAVERS Daniel De Leon
SYMONS, ARTHUR Aubrey Beardsley, William Blake, Sir Richard Burton, James McNeill Whistler
SYMONS, A. J. A. Baron Corvo
SYMONS, JULIAN Dame Agatha Christie, Baron Corvo, Dorothy Sayers

TACITUS Boadicea
TAFT, HORACE DUTTON William Howard Taft

TAFT, WILLIAM HOWARD (q.v.) Woodrow Wilson
TALLMER, JERRY Lenny Bruce
TALMADGE, DE WITT William Marcy Tweed
TARKINGTON, BOOTH (q.v.) Richard Harding Davis, John Drew, Wendell Willkie
TATE, ALLEN Hart Crane, e. e. cummings, Emily Dickinson
TATE, NATHUM Shakespeare
TAWNEY, R. H. Lionel Cranfield
TAYLOR, A. J. P. Ernest Bevin, Horatio Bottomley, Neville Chamberlain, Frederick Delius, Lord Kitchener, George Lansbury, David Lloyd George, Lord Northcliffe
TAYLOR, BASIL George Stubbs
TAYLOR, BAYARD Robert Browning
TAYLOR, DEEMS John Philip Sousa
TAYLOR, DONALD Dylan Thomas
TAYLOR, HENRY Samuel Rogers, Percy Bysshe Shelley
TAYLOR, JOHN Thomas Jefferson, Joseph Smith
TAYLOR, DR JOHN Samuel Johnson
TAYLOR, JOHN RUSSELL, and JACKSON, ARTHUR Judy Garland
TAYLOR, MICHAEL M. W. C. Fields
TAYLOR, N. W. Timothy Dwight
TAYLOR, ROBERT LEWIS W. C. Fields
TAYLOR, TOM Lord Brougham, Abraham Lincoln
TAYLOR, WALTER FULLER Hamlin Garland, John Greenleaf Whittier
TAYLOR, WILLIAM R. Francis Parkman
TEICHMANN, HOWARD Dorothy Parker
TELLEGEN, LOU Enrico Caruso, Isadora Duncan
TEMPLE, OLIVER P. William Henry Seward
TEMPLE, WILLIAM Reinhold Niebuhr
TEMPLEMAN, G. Edward I
TEMPLER, SIR GERALD Lord Alexander of Tunis
TENNYSON, ALFRED, LORD (q.v.) Alfred, Robert Browning, Lord Byron, Stratford Canning, Thomas Carlyle, George Crabbe, Ben Jonson, Edward Lear, Edward Bulwer Lytton, John Milton, Algernon C. Swinburne, Queen Victoria, W. G. Ward, Duke of Wellington, John Wycliffe
TERRAINE, JOHN Lord Haig
TERRELL, JOHN Zebulon Pike
TERRY, DAME ELLEN (q.v.) Sir Edward Burne-Jones, Sir Henry Irving

THACKERAY, W. M. (q.v.) Charlotte Brontë, Lord Byron, William Congreve, George Cruikshank, Charles Dickens, John Gay, George II, Oliver Goldsmith, Edward Bulwer Lytton, Sir Charles Napier
THICKNESSE, PHILIP Thomas Gainsborough
THEOBALD, LEWIS Alexander Pope, John Webster
THOMAS, BOB Carl Laemmle, David O. Selznick
THOMAS, CAITLIN Dylan Thomas
THOMAS, DYLAN (q.v.) Matthew Arnold, W. H. Auden, Walter De La Mare, T. S. Eliot, Aldous Huxley, Rudyard Kipling, D. H. Lawrence, Christina Rossetti, George Bernard Shaw, Dame Edith Sitwell, William Wordsworth
THOMAS, EDWARD John Clare
THOMAS, LATELY Lorenzo Delmonico
THOMAS, MARGARET Grant Wood
THOMAS, NORMAN (q.v.) Thomas Dewey, Herbert Hoover, John F. Kennedy, Franklin D. Roosevelt, Harry S. Truman, Wendell Willkie
THOMASON JR, JOHN W. Jeb Stuart
THOMPSON, DODY WESTON Pearl S. Buck
THOMPSON, E. P. Thomas Paine
THOMPSON, LAWRENCE Robert Frost
THOMPSON, SILVANUS P. William Gilbert
THOMPSON, DR W. H. A. J. Balfour
THOMSON, JAMES (q.v.) Alfred, Lord Lyttelton, Sir Thomas More, Sir Isaac Newton, James Oglethorpe
THOMSON, J. J. John Dalton, Michael Faraday, William Thomson
THOMSON, VIRGIL Serge Koussevitzky, Alice B. Toklas, Arturo Toscanini
THOREAU, HENRY DAVID (q.v.) Amos Bronson Alcott, John Brown, Margaret Fuller, Daniel Webster, Walt Whitman
THORNTON, EDWARD Lord Cornwallis
THRALE, HESTER LYNCH, see PIOZZI, MRS
THURBER, JAMES (q.v.) Fred Allen, Robert Benchley, Henry James, Will Rogers, Alexander Woollcott
THURLOW, LORD George IV
THURMAN, ALLEN Roscoe Conkling
THURSTON, ROBERT H. Robert Fulton
TICKELL, THOMAS Joseph Addison
TINSLEY, WILLIAM Anthony Trollope
TODD, A. L. Louis Brandeis

TODD, MIKE Gypsy Rose Lee
TOKLAS, ALICE B. (q.v.) Jo Davidson, Gertrude Stein
TOLEDANO, RALPH DE John Dillinger
TOMKINS, JOHN Thomas Tomkins
TOMKINS, MARY E. Ida Tarbell
TOMLINSON, MR Henry Purcell
TORMÉ, MEL Judy Garland
TOUT, T. F. Edward II, Thomas à Becket
TOVEY, DONALD Sir Edward Elgar, Henry Purcell
TOWNER, WESLEY Jerome Kern
TOWERS, JOSEPH Samuel Johnson
TOWNSEND, GEORGE ALFRED Benjamin Harrison, Carl Schurz
TOWSE, JOHN RANKIN Charlotte Cushman
TOY, JOHN Thomas Tomkins
TOYNBEE, ARNOLD J. Albert Einstein, Franklin D. Roosevelt
TRACY, SPENCER (q.v.) Clark Gable, Jean Harlow, Will Rogers
TRAPP, JOSEPH George I
TREE, IRIS Sir Herbert Beerbohm Tree
TRELAWNY, E. J. Lord Byron
TREVELYAN, G. M. Queen Anne, Boadicea, Hereward, Lord Nelson, Thomas Paine, Lytton Strachey
TREVELYAN, SIR GEORGE OTTO Charles James Fox
TREVOR-ROPER, HUGH R. Thomas Cromwell, James I, Hugh Latimer, William Laud, Sir Thomas More, George Savile
TRIEM, EVE e. e. cummings
TRILLING, LIONEL Willa Cather, F. Scott Fitzgerald, Eugene O'Neill, Vernon Parrington, Percy Bysshe Shelley, Edith Wharton
TROHAN, WALTER J. Edgar Hoover
TROLLOPE, ANTHONY (q.v.) Charlotte Brontë, Thomas Carlyle, Wilkie Collins, Charles Dickens, Benjamin Disraeli, George Eliot, Nathaniel Hawthorne, Edward Bulwer Lytton, Charles Reade, W. M. Thackeray
TROTSKY, LEON Norman Thomas
TRUMAN, HARRY S. (q.v.) Thomas Dewey, Millard Fillmore, Huey Long, Douglas MacArthur, George C. Marshall, Franklin Pierce, Adlai E. Stevenson, Robert A. Taft
TUCHMAN, BARBARA Sir John French, Alfred Thayer Mahan
TUGWELL, REXFORD GUY Fiorello La Guardia, Franklin D. Roosevelt, Thornstein Veblen
TURNBULL, ANDREW F. Scott Fitzgerald, Edmund Wilson
TURNER J. M. W. (q.v.) Thomas Girtin

TURNOR, ALGERNON J. A. Froude
TURNOR, R. Sir George Gilbert Scott
TUTTLE, WORTH Marcus Garvey
TWAIN, MARK (q.v.) (pseudonym of Samuel Clemens) Thomas Bailey Aldrich, Chester A. Arthur, Jane Austen, John Bunyan, James Fenimore Cooper, Mary Baker Eddy, Benjamin Franklin, Joel Chandler Harris, Bret Harte, Oliver Wendell Holmes, Henry James, Rudyard Kipling, William McKinley, Cecil Rhodes, Joseph Smith, Sir Henry Morton Stanley, Samuel J. Tilden
TWEED, WILLIAM M. (q.v.) Samuel J. Tilden
TWEEDIE, MRS ALEC Samuel Smiles
'TWO' G. H. Lewes
TYLER, JOHN Ulysses S. Grant
TYLER, MOSES COIT John Cotton
TYLER, PARKER Jackson Pollock
TYNAN, KATHERINE Lionel Johnson
TYNAN, KENNETH Katherine Cornell, John Webster
TYNDALL, JOHN Thomas Young
TYRRELL, JAMES John Locke

UNTERMAYER, LOUIS Rockwell Kent, Vachel Lindsay, Amy Lowell, Marianne Moore, Carl Sandburg, William IV
UROFSKY, MELVIN F. Louis Brandeis
URQUHART, SIR THOMAS James Crichton, Roger Williams
USSHER, ARLAND W. B. Yeats

VALENTI, JACK Lyndon B. Johnson
VALENTINE, ALAN Lord Sackville
VALENTINE, HENRY John Donne
VANBRUGH, IRENE Lewis Carroll
VANBRUGH, SIR JOHN (q.v.) Nicholas Hawksmoor, Sir Godfrey Kneller
VAN BUREN, MARTIN (q.v.) John Quincy Adams, William Henry Harrison
VANDENHOFF, GEORGE W. C. Macready
VAN DEUSEN, GLYNDON G. Millard Fillmore, Thurlow Weed
VANDIVER, FRANK E. 'Stonewall' Jackson
VAN DOREN, CARL Willa Cather, Benjamin Franklin, Ellen Glasgow, William Dean Howells, Washington Irving, Sinclair Lewis, William Gilmore Simms, Booth Tarkington, Elinor Wylie
VAN DOREN, MARK (q.v.) Henry David Thoreau
VAN DYCK, ANTHONY Inigo Jones
VAN DYKE, HENRY John Keats

VAN VECHTEN, CARL Bessie Smith
VAN WYCK, WILLIAM Emily Dickinson
VAUGHAN, HENRY (q.v.) Sir Thomas Bodley
VAUGHAN, WILLIAM Christopher Marlowe
VAUGHAN WILLIAMS, SIR RALPH (q.v.) Frederick Delius, Gustav Holst, Charles Parry, Shakespeare, C. V. Stanford
VERNON, GRENVILLE Clifford Odets
VERTUE, GEORGE Nicholas Hilliard, Allan Ramsay
VEST, SENATOR Roscoe Conkling
VICTORIA, QUEEN (q.v.) Prince Albert, Queen Alexandra, Charlotte Brontë, Lord Derby, Charles Dickens, Benjamin Disraeli, Edward VII, George Eliot, W. E. Gladstone, Lord Melbourne, Florence Nightingale, Lord Russell, Lord Salisbury, Duke of Wellington
VIDAL, GORE Jeremy Bentham, Robert F. Kennedy, Carson McCullers, George Bernard Shaw
VIDOR, KING Cecil B. De Mille
VILLARD, OSWALD GARRISON James Gordon Bennett Jr, E. L. Godkin, Joseph Pulitzer
VINAVER, EUGÈNE Thomas Malory
VINES, C. M. Lord Beaverbrook
VINSON, JOHN CHALMERS William Borah
VITELLI, JAMES R. Van Wyck Brooks
VOLTAIRE John Byng, Lord Chesterfield, William Congreve, John Locke, Shakespeare, Sir John Vanbrugh, William Wycherley
VON STERNBERG, JOSEF (q.v.) Mack Sennett

WACE, ROBERT William I
WADE, MASON Francis Parkman
WAGENKNECHT, EDWARD Ellen Glasgow, Nathaniel Hawthorne, Marilyn Monroe, Harriet Beecher Stowe, Noah Webster
WAGNER, JEAN Damon Runyon
WAGNER, LINDA W. William Carlos Williams
WAIN, JOHN James Boswell
WAKEMAN, HENRY O. Charles James Fox
WALDEGRAVE, LORD Lord Bute
WALKER, ALEXANDER Louis B. Mayer, Paul Muni
WALKER, DANTON Alexander Woollcott
WALKER, FRANKLIN Ambrose Bierce
WALKER, JIMMY Al Smith

WALKER, JOHN Bernard
Berenson
WALKER, KENNETH Joseph Lister
WALKER, STANLEY Wendell
Willkie
WALL, JOSEPH FRAZIER Andrew
Carnegie
WALLACE, EDGAR Rudyard Kipling
WALLACE, HENRY (q.v.) Harry S.
Truman
WALLACE, IRVING Phineas T.
Barnum
WALLER, SIR WILLIAM Oliver
Cromwell
WALPOLE, HORACE (q.v.) Robert
Adam, Mark Akenside, Queen Anne,
Lord Anson, Sir Joseph Banks, Lord
Burlington, Lord Bute, John Byng,
John Carteret, Lord Chatham,
Thomas Chatterton, Lord Chester-
field, Abraham Cowley, Henry Field-
ing, Charles James Fox, Sir Philip
Francis, Benjamin Franklin, Frederick
Louis, Prince of Wales, George II,
George III, George Grenville, Sir
William Herschel, Nicholas Hilliard,
John Hunter, Samuel Johnson,
William Kent, Sir Peter Lely, Lord
Lyttelton, Mary Queen of Scots,
Lady Mary Wortley Montagu, Hannah
More, Duke of Newcastle, Sir Isaac
Newton, Lord North, James Ogle-
thorpe, Joseph Priestley, Sir Joshua
Reynolds, Richard III, Samuel
Richardson, Lord Sandwich, Lord
Shelburne, Sarah Siddons, Jonathan
Swift, Charles Townshend, Sir John
Vanbrugh, Benjamin West, John
Wilkes, William III, John Wilmot,
Mary Wollstonecraft, Sir Charles
Wyndham
WALPOLE, SIR ROBERT (q.v.) Queen
Caroline Wilhelmina
WALSINGHAM, THOMAS John
Wycliffe
WALTON, IZAAC (q.v.) Sir Francis
Bacon, John Donne, George Herbert,
Richard Hooker, John Whitgift
WALTON, WILLIAM Eastman John-
son
WANLEY, HUMPHREY Samuel Pepys
WARBURTON, E. B. G. Lord Peter-
borough
WARD, ARTEMUS (pseudonym of
Charles Farrar Browne) (q.v.)
Geoffrey Chaucer, George Washing-
ton, Brigham Young
WARD, A. C. Emily Dickinson
WARD, MRS HUMPHRY Anne
Brontë, Charlotte Brontë
WARD, J. Robert Hooke
WARD, JOHN WILLIAM (q.v.)
Benjamin Franklin
WARD, SAM Lorenzo Delmonico

WARD, SAMUEL Edwin M. Stanton
WARD, SETH (q.v.) Sir Francis Bacon
WARE, EUGENE FITCH George
Dewey
WARKWORTH, JOHN Henry VI
WARNOCK, G. J. J. L. Austin
WARNER, JACK L. Errol Flynn
WARNER, DR JOHN George Selwyn
WARNER, REX D. H. Lawrence
WARREN, MERCY OTIS Samuel
Adams
WARREN, ROBERT PENN William
Faulkner, John Greenleaf Whittier
WARREN, W. C. King John
WARSHOW, ROBERT Alan Ladd
WARTON, JOSEPH Alexander Pope
WARTON, T. John Gower, Earl of
Surrey
WARWICK, SIR PHILIP Charles I,
Oliver Cromwell, John Hampden,
William Juxon, William Laud, Lord
Strafford
WASHBURN, ROBERT M. William
Borah
WASHINGTON, BOOKER T. (q.v.)
Frederick Douglass
WASHINGTON, GEORGE (q.v.)
Benedict Arnold, Patrick Henry,
Henry Knox, Thomas Paine
WASSERSTROM, WILLIAM Van
Wyck Brooks
WATERHOUSE, ELLIS Nicholas
Hilliard, Sir Godfrey Kneller,
George Romney
WATERTON, GEORGE John Quincy
Adams
WATSON, ROBERT Randall Jarrell
WATSON, WILLIAM Robert Burns,
Lord Byron, Thomas Hardy
WATTERSON, HENRY Grover Cleve-
land
WATTS-DUNTON, THEODORE
Alfred, Lord Tennyson
WAUGH, AUBERON P. G. Wodehouse
WAUGH, EVELYN (q.v.) Sir Max
Beerbohm, Hilaire Belloc, Sir Winston
Churchill, James Joyce, Nancy
Mitford, Dame Edith Sitwell
WAVELL, LORD Sir Winston Chur-
chill
WEBB, BEATRICE (q.v.) Joseph
Chamberlain, James Keir Hardie,
Ramsay MacDonald, Sidney Webb,
H. G. Wells
WEBB, JAMES W., and GREEN, A.
WIGFALL William Faulkner
WEBB, JOHN Inigo Jones
WEBSTER, DANIEL (q.v.) John C.
Calhoun, Alexander Hamilton
Andrew Jackson, James Madison,
Roger B. Taney
WEBSTER, JOHN (q.v.) Richard
Burbage
WEELKES, THOMAS Thomas Morley

WEEMS, J. E. Robert Peary
WEHLE, HARRY B. Samuel F. B.
Morse
WEINBERG, HERMAN G. Josef von
Sternberg
WEINER, ED Damon Runyon
WEISS, PAUL Charles S. Peirce
WELD, C. R. Sir Humphry Davy, Sir
Isaac Newton
WELDON, SIR ANTHONY First Duke
of Buckingham, James I
WELLES, GIDEON (q.v.) Salmon P.
Chase, Roscoe Conkling, Henry
Halleck, William Henry Seward
WELLES, ORSON John Ford
WELLINGTON, DUKE OF (q.v.) Lord
Byron, George Canning, Queen
Caroline of Brunswick, Duke of
Cumberland, William Huskisson, Sir
Robert Peel, Wolfe Tone
WELLMAN, WALTER Benjamin
Harrison
WELLS, DAMON Stephen A. Douglas
WELLS, H. G. (q.v.) Lord Beaver-
brook, Arnold Bennett, Joseph
Conrad, Stephen Crane, Charles
Darwin, W. E. B. Du Bois, Albert
Einstein, Ford Madox Ford, T. H.
Huxley, Henry James, James Joyce,
Huey Long, Franklin D. Roosevelt,
Dame Edith Sitwell, Beatrice Webb
WELLS, HENRY W. Emily Dickinson
WEMYSS, FRANCIS R. W. Elliston
WENTWORTH, PETER Mary, Queen
of Scots
WESLEY, JOHN (q.v.) George White-
field
WESLEY, SAMUEL (q.v.) Samuel
Butler, James Oglethorpe
WEST, BENJAMIN (q.v.) Gilbert
Stuart, J. M. W. Turner
WEST, JANE Mary Wollstonecraft
WEST, MAE Fiorello La Guardia
WEST, DAME REBECCA Willa Cather,
Ford Madox Ford, Huey Long, Eliza-
beth Montagu, H. G. Wells
WEST, RICHARD V. Rockwell Kent
WESTCOTT, ALLAN Alfred Thayer
Mahan
WESTON, EDWARD (q.v.) Robinson
Jeffers
WESTRUP, SIR JACK Sir Edward
Elgar, Henry Purcell
WETHERELL, SIR CHARLES Lord
Campbell
WHARTON, EDITH (q.v.) Isadora
Duncan, Charles Eliot Norton
WHARTON, THOMAS Earl of Surrey
WHEELER, PRIVATE Duke of
Wellington
WHIBLEY, CHARLES James Crichton,
Edward Hyde, James II, Ben Jonson,
Shakespeare
WHICHER, GEORGE F. Emily Dickin-
son, Theodore Dreiser, Ring Lardner,

Vachel Lindsay, H. L. Mencken, Edna St Vincent Millay, Ogden Nash, Carl Sandburg, Wallace Stevens, Thornstein Veblen, William Carlos Williams, Thomas Wolfe

WHIPPLE, T. K. Theodore Dreiser, Sinclair Lewis, Edwin Arlington Robinson

WHISTLER, JAMES MCNEILL (q.v.) Dante Gabriel Rossetti, John Ruskin, John Singer Sargent, Oscar Wilde

WHISTLER, LAWRENCE Sir John Vanbrugh

WHITCOMB, IAN Stephen C. Foster, Glenn Miller, Cole Porter, John Philip Sousa

WHITE, E. B. Robert Benchley, Franklin D. Roosevelt, James Thurber

WHITE, T. H. Fanny Burney, Samuel Johnson

WHITE, SENATOR Martin Van Buren

WHITE, THEODORE H. Lyndon B. Johnson

WHITE, WILLIAM ALLEN (q.v.) Calvin Coolidge, Warren G. Harding, Benjamin Harrison, William Mc-Kinley, Theodore Roosevelt

WHITEHEAD, Alfred North (q.v.) Sir Isaac Newton

WHITELOCKE, BULSTRODE John Bradshaw, Oliver Cromwell, Lord Fairfax, Henry Ireton

WHITEMAN, MRS Thomas Eakins

WHITLEY, WILLIAM T. Sir Godfrey Kneller, J. M. W. Turner

WHITMAN, ALDEN Adlai E. Stevenson

WHITMAN, WALT (q.v.) Edwin Booth, Junius Brutus Booth, John Brown, William Cullen Bryant, Thomas Carlyle, Ralph Waldo Emerson, Washington Irving, Sidney Lanier, Abraham Lincoln, Henry Wadsworth Longfellow, James Russell Lowell, Dwight Moody, Edgar Allen Poe, Algernon C. Swinburne

WHITTIER, JOHN GREENLEAF (q.v.) William Lloyd Garrison, Nathaniel Hawthorne, Emma Lazarus, John Milton, Joseph Smith, Harriet Beecher Stowe, Charles Sumner, Daniel Webster, George Whitefield

WICKER, TOM John F. Kennedy

WIDMER, KINGSLEY Jack Kerouac

WIENER, NORBERT G. E. Moore

WIGHTWICK, GEORGE Sir John Soane

WILBERFORCE, BISHOP Lord Palmerston

WILBERFORCE, WILLIAM (q.v.) Sir Francis Burdett

WILD(E), ROBERT Richard Cromwell, Ben Jonson, George Monck

WILDE, CONSTANCE Oscar Wilde

WILDE, OSCAR (q.v.) Matthew Arnold, Alfred Austin, Aubrey Beardsley, Sir Max Beerbohm, Robert Browning, Margaret Fuller, Gilbert and Sullivan, Frank Harris, Henry James, John Keats, Rudyard Kipling, James Russell Lowell, George Meredith, John Stuart Mill, George Moore, Walter Pater, Algernon C. Swinburne, George Bernard Shaw, Leonard Smithers, Robert Louis Stevenson, Dame Ellen Terry, Sir, Herbert Beerbohm Tree, George Washington, James McNeill Whistler, William Wordsworth

WILDER, ALEC Cole Porter

WILDER, BILLY Marilyn Monroe

WIDMER, KINGSLEY Jack Kerouac

WILENSKI, R. H. John Ruskin

WILKES, JOHN (q.v.) John Glyn, Elkanah Settle

WILKINSON, ELLEN Sir Winston Churchill

WILLEY, BASIL Sir Francis Bacon

WILLIAM III (q.v.) Henry Dodwell

WILLIAM IV (q.v.) Duke of Wellington

WILLIAM OF MALMESBURY Alfred, Ethelred, Odo of Bayeux, William II

WILLIAM OF POITIERS William I

WILLIAMS, BASIL John Carteret, Duke of Newcastle

WILLIAMS, C. H. Richard III

WILLIAMS, JOHN (q.v.) Oliver Cromwell

WILLIAMS, JOHN, see Pasquin, Anthony

WILLIAMS, STEPHEN Gilbert and Sullivan

WILLIAMS, TENNESSEE Eugene O'Neill

WILLIAMS, WILLIAM CARLOS (q.v.) e. e. cummings, Ford Madox Ford, Benjamin Franklin, Henry James, Marianne Moore, Charles Sheeler

WILLIAMS, W. MATTIEU Sir Benjamin Thompson

WILLKIE, WENDELL (q.v.) Franklin D. Roosevelt

WILLSON, BECKLES George III

WILLSON, D. HARRIS James I

WILMOT, JOHN, EARL OF ROCHESTER (q.v.) Second Duke of Buckingham, Charles II, Sir George Etherege, Nell Gwyn, Thomas Otway, Barbara Villiers

WILSON, ARTHUR First Duke of Buckingham, James I

WILSON, CHARLES E. Malcolm X

WILSON, DEMOND Jack Benny

WILSON, EARL Janis Joplin, Marilyn Monroe

WILSON, EDMUND (q.v.) Sherwood Anderson, W. H. Auden, Sir Max

Beerbohm, Robert Benchley, Samuel Butler, Cyril Connolly, Stephen Crane, e. e. cummings, Sir Arthur Conan Doyle, T. S. Eliot, F. Scott Fitzgerald, Ernest Hemingway, Aldous Huxley, Sidney Lanier, Somerset Maugham, John Crowe Ransom, Carl Sandburg, Dorothy Sayers, Logan Pearsall Smith, Gertrude Stein, Wallace Stevens, Lytton Strachey, Evelyn Waugh

WILSON, GEORGE Robert Boyle

WILSON, J. Joanna Baillie

WILSON, JOHN James Boswell

WILSON, JOHN Anne Hutchinson

WILSON, JOHN S. Gertrude 'Ma' Rainey

WILSON, MCLANDBURGH Theodore Roosevelt

WILSON, MONA Mary Wollstonecraft

WILSON, WOODROW (q.v.) Chester A. Arthur, William Jennings Bryan, Aaron Burr, Grover Cleveland, James A. Garfield, Warren G. Harding

WILTSE, CHARLES M. John C. Calhoun

WINCHELL, WALTER (q.v.) Drew Pearson

WINCHILSEA, LORD Charles Greville

WINDSOR, DUCHESS OF (MRS SIMPSON) Edward VIII

WINGFIELD-STRATFORD, ESMÉ Lord Brougham

WINSLOW, HENRY Mary McLeod Bethune

WINSLOW, OLA ELIZABETH John Bunyan

WINSTANLEY, GERARD (q.v.) Oliver Cromwell

WINSTANLEY, WILLIAM Francis Beaumont, Thomas Dekker, John Fletcher, Thomas Heywood

WINSTON, JAMES Edmund Kean

WINSTON, JOHN John Tyler

WINTER, WILLIAM Edwin Booth

WINTERS, YVOR Henry Adams, Emily Dickinson, Robert Frost, John Milton, Francis Parkman

WINTERTON, LORD Lord Cecil of Chelwood

WINTHROP, JOHN (q.v.) Thomas Hooker, Anne Hutchinson

WISE, HENRY A. John C. Calhoun, George Washington

WISEMAN, CARDINAL Cardinal Manning

WODEHOUSE, P. G. (q.v.) Arnold Bennett, Sir Arthur Conan Doyle, Rudyard Kipling

WOLF, HOWARD Franklin D. Roosevelt

WOLFE, HUMBERT Arnold Bennett,

G. K. Chesterton
WOLFE, JAMES (q.v.) Thomas Gray
WOLLS-SAMPSON, COLONEL Lord Haig
WOLSELEY, LORD C. G. Gordon, Duke of Marlborough
WOLSELEY, SIR GARNETT Lord Rosebery
WOLSELEY, ROBERT John Donne
WOOD, ANTHONY À (q.v.) Lord Arlington, Sir Arthur Aston, John Aubrey, John Bull, Robert Burton, Catherine of Braganza, Thomas Coryate, Sir John Davies, Dr John Fell, William Fiennes, Thomas Hobbes, Robert Hooke, Anne Hyde, William Juxon, Thomas Linacre, John Locke, Richard Lovelace, Marchamont Nedham, George Peele, Sir William Petty, William Prynne, Sir Walter Raleigh, Sir Philip Sidney, Thomas Sydenham, Christopher Tye, Henry Vaughan, Barbara Villiers, Timothy Wilkins, John Wilmot, George Withers
WOOD, CLEMENT Amy Lowell
WOOD, DOUGLAS Richard Mansfield
WOOD, LADY JESSIE Henry Wood
WOODBURY, JOSEPHINE CURTIS Mary Baker Eddy
WOODCOCK, GEORGE George Orwell
WOODCROFT, BENNET Samuel Crompton
WOODHOUSE, A. S. P. and BUSH, DOUGLAS Edward King
WOODRESS, JAMES Booth Tarkington
WOODRUFF, MR Harold Laski
WOLCOT, JOHN, see PINDAR, PETER
WOOLF, LEONARD (q.v.) Arnold Bennett, Rupert Brooke, Katherine Mansfield, Thomas Paine, Sir Leslie Stephen, Beatrice Webb, Sidney Webb
WOOLF, VIRGINIA (q.v.) Joseph Addison, Sir Max Beerbohm, Arnold Bennett, Sir Thomas Browne, Elizabeth Barrett Browning, Margaret Cavendish, Geoffrey Chaucer, Lord Chesterfield, Samuel Taylor Coleridge, Daniel Defoe, John Donne, T. S.

Eliot, John Evelyn, John Galsworthy, Oliver Goldsmith, Thomas Hardy, Leigh Hunt, Aldous Huxley, Henry James, James Joyce, Ring Lardner, Katherine Mansfield, George Meredith, Christina Rossetti, Vita Sackville-West, Sir Walter Scott, Lytton Strachey, Horace Walpole, Mary Wollstonecraft
WOOLCOTT, ALEXANDER (q.v.) Michael Arlen, George Arliss, Heywood Broun, Jeanne Eagels, Minnie Fiske, Oscar Levant, Dorothy Parker, Paul Robeson, Edward G. Robinson, Walter Winchell, Florenz Ziegfeld
WOOLSEY, JOHN M. James Joyce
WORDSWORTH, DOROTHY Thomas De Quincey
WORDSWORTH, WILLIAM (q.v.) Joanna Baillie, Bede, William Blake, Robert Burns, Lord Byron, Thomas Chatterton, Samuel Taylor Coleridge, George Crabbe, George III, Thomas Gray, Benjamin R. Haydon, Henry VIII, William Hone, King John, Charles Lamb, John Milton, Sir Isacc Newton, Sir Walter Scott, Shakespeare, James Watt, Duke of Wellington
WORSLEY, PHILIP STANHOPE Robert E. Lee
WOTTON, CHARLES George Herbert
WOTTON, SIR HENRY (q.v.) Sir Francis Bacon, Robert Cecil, James I
WRAXALL, NATHANIEL Lord Bute, Lord Howe, Lord Melville, Lord North, Richard Brinsley Sheridan
WREN, SIR CHRISTOPHER (q.v.) William Gilbert
WREN JR, CHRISTOPHER Sir Christopher Wren
WRENN, JOHN H. John Dos Passos
WRIGHT, ESMOND Benjamin Franklin
WRIGHT, THOMAS James Crichton
WYNTOUN, ANDREW Alexander II of Scotland
WYVILL, CHRISTOPHER Thomas Paine

YEATMAN, R. J., see SELLAR, W. C.

YEATS, JOHN BUTLER James McNeill Whistler
YEATS, WILLIAM BUTLER (q.v.) George Berkeley, William Blake, Rupert Brooke, John Bunyan, Mrs Patrick Campbell, John Donne, Lady Gregory, Augustus John, Lionel Johnson, James Joyce, John Keats, George Moore, William Morris, Wilfred Owen, Charles Parnell, Ezra Pound, Shakespeare, George Bernard Shaw, Jonathan Swift, J. M. Synge, Oscar Wilde, William Wordsworth
YEVTUSHENKO, YEVGENY Martin Luther King Jr
YOUNG, ART Calvin Coolidge, Eugene V. Debs
YOUNG, EDWARD (q.v.) Sir Francis Bacon, Shakespeare
YOUNG, FREDERIC HAROLD Charles S. Peirce
YOUNG, G. M. Charles Kingsley, Charles Parnell, John Ruskin
YOUNG, J. LEWIS Thomas Alva Edison
YOUNG, JOHN RUSSELL George B. McClellan
YOUNG, JULIAN CHARLES James Hogg
YOUNG, MARGUERITE Carson McCullers
YOUNG, PATRICIA Sir Thomas Beecham
YOUNG, PERCY G. F. Handel, Sir Arthur Sullivan
YOUNG, PHILIP Pocahontas
YOUNGER, JUSTICE Elinor Glyn
YOUNGHUSBAND, SIR GEORGE Rudyard Kipling
YOUNGHUSBAND, SIR FRANCIS Bertrand Russell
YULEE, D. L. Franklin Pierce

ZABEL, MORTON DANWEN Ford Modox Ford
ZIEROLD, NORMAN Theda Bara, William Fox, Samuel Goldwyn, Carl Laemmle
ZILLIACUS, KONNI Ernest Bevin
ZINMAN, DAVID Humphrey Bogart, Gary Cooper, Paul Muni, Spencer Tracy

GRAND PRIX
PRIX
CENTURY

GRAND PRIX
CENTURY

The first 100 years of the world's most
glamorous and dangerous sport

CHRISTOPHER HILTON

Haynes Publishing

First published in October 2005

A catalogue record for this book is
available from the British Library

ISBN 1 84425 120 9

Library of Congress control no. 2005926142

Published by Haynes Publishing, Sparkford,
Yeovil, Somerset, BA22 7JJ, UK
Tel: 01963 442030 Fax: 01963 440001
Int. tel: +44 1963 442030 Int. fax: +44 1963 440001
E-mail: sales@haynes.co.uk
Website: www.haynes.co.uk

Haynes North America, Inc.,
861 Lawrence Drive, Newbury Park,
California 91320, USA

Printed and bound in England by
J. H. Haynes & Co. Ltd, Sparkford

CONTENTS

Introduction   6

1   Dusty road   9
2   The Chaps   49

    Plate section   65–72

3   In Nuvolari's time   97
4   End of innocence   123
5   Shadowlands   150

    Plate section   169–176

6   In Fangio's time   192
7   In Clark's time   230
8   Safety first   263

    Plate section   273–280

9   Money men   313
10 In Senna's time   362

    Plate section   377–384

11 In Schumacher's time   416
12 The Centurions   457

    The major records   463
    Acknowledgements   465
    Bibliography   467
    Index   473

INTRODUCTION

The high brick walls of the factory beside the Seine formed a shield against preying eyes. Somewhere deep within, shrouded by absolute secrecy, three cars were being prepared: fast cars, racing cars.When they were ready, one of them had a trial run. It emerged from the factory gates – two brick pillars spanned by an arch of ornate, wrought iron bearing the words *Renault Fréres* – at a place called Boulogne-Billancourt on the rim of Paris.

The car turned on to the quayside, houses to its left, trees standing like sentries to the right in front of the river. This early spring day, sunlight fell on the trees creating a geometry of shadows. As the car moved it ran across these shadows.

The driver, a Hungarian, wore gloves, a stout leather jacket and cloth cap. He didn't have goggles because on this test run he wouldn't be stretching the car. He'd do a lot of that very soon, but not here and not now. His riding mechanic – who'd help change wheels, carry out running repairs and any other tasks – sat immobile beside him, similar jacket, similar cap. Both had moustaches and looked severe, the way people did in public in 1906.

The driver was Ferenc Szisz, known as François, and where he led many, many would follow, all the way to Michael Schumacher. The riding mechanic was known simply by the surname Marteau because riding mechanics were usually drawn from the working classes and that's how the working classes were known. Marteau translated means Hammer – in motor racing, it's as good a name as any.

At the end of the run the car went back through the gates and into the absolute secrecy again.

Some time after this, a small handpicked team in ordinary saloon cars drove to the provincial town of Le Mans 120 miles away and, methodically, explored the triangle of roads outside it. Once or twice Monsieur Renault himself came down and did that, too.

Very early in June he set up headquarters in a chateau near the village of Changé, outside Le Mans – sloping rooftops, verdant gardens – and the racing cars were brought. Day by day, the team prepared for the scrutineering in a tent in a field, and then made ready for 6:03 on the morning of 26 June and the first Grand Prix ever run.

The race started at 6am, with cars being sent off every 90 seconds, which is how a driver called Camille Jenatzy – Belgian, but by co-incidence of Hungarian origin – went at 6:07.30. The car he drove was a Mercedes.

When Szisz won the race, Louis Renault stood with tears flowing down his face. Some say it was for his brother Marcel – killed in a road race three years before – but the tears surely mingled with that profound intoxication of creating a machine and hiring a driver to beat the best that anybody could put against them. Louis Renault may have been the first man to cry in Grand Prix racing. He would not be the last.

Late winter, and three specially chartered Boeing 747 transport planes lifted off from England, Germany and Italy, bound for Melbourne, Australia. The little world born in 1906 had, a century later, become a global presence requiring jumbo jets to move it from continent to continent. There'd be the blood-red Ferraris from Italy, Williams with their BMW engines, Toyota from their base in Cologne, Sauber from Switzerland and – two arches across time – McLaren with Mercedes engines, and Renault moving 34 tonnes of freight and three cars. Renault's engines came from Viry-Châtillon, not far from Boulogne-Billancourt, the cars from their Enstone factory near Oxford.

Renault alone took 80 people, including 40 mechanics and technicians, 10 race engineers, 5 caterers, 10 people to handle media, marketing and hospitality. Each of the three cars had mechanics, an engine mechanic, a hydraulic specialist, an electronics specialist, a race engineer, a data engineer, a control systems engineer, an engine technician, an engine electronics technician…

The Renault of 1906, watched by a decorative crowd of great decorum in formal dress, averaged 62mph over almost 770 miles. Then everybody went away and didn't come back for a year. After the Australian Grand Prix in 2005 – watched by the world – Renault and all the other teams went to Malaysia, Bahrain, Imola, Spain, Monaco, the Nürburgring, Canada and the United States before they reached the circuit of Magny-Cours for the French Grand Prix in July and a century of racing.

That Grand Prix racing began in the pastureland of one French Department and ended in the pastureland of another, 180 miles away, is just one of those coincidences which make history so wonderfully unnerving. That, at Magny-Cours, a personable Spaniard called

Fernando Alonso put his Renault on pole and won crisply and cleanly one sun-blessed afternoon is another. Surely somewhere Up There a certain Ferenc Szisz nodded his approval. Alonso beat a Finn, Kimi Räikkönen, and his McLaren with its Mercedes engine...

Here is the story from that misty dawn to that sunny afternoon. It is one of the greatest human stories and it all happened just like this.

Chapter 1

DUSTY ROAD

In January 1886 a severe-looking man with a drooping moustache, Karl Benz, applied for and was granted a patent to manufacture a motor vehicle. It resembled a frail, skeletal rickshaw with a small wheel at the front and two big wheels at the back, steered by a handle.

Benz had a rival. A few months after patent's granting, another severe-looking man with a drooping moustache, Gottlieb Daimler, put one of his engines in a coach and created the horseless carriage.

The car had been born.[1]

Since recorded time, a horse had been the fastest means of transport over land. In the 19th century, and with a great suddenness, an era of innovation changed everything, and this new era moved to its own urgency, spread its own infinite possibilities. A Scot, James Watt,[2] coined the term 'horsepower', but British inventors developed steam for locomotion and by 1829 when Robert Stephenson built a locomotive driven by steam, the horse had become extinct as a serious means of transport.

Trains profoundly changed life in Britain, and then the world, but there was an inherent constriction to the freedom they brought because you could only go where the railway lines went. The car offered personal choice.

Steam needed big engines that weren't really practical, or even safe, for anything as small as a car. Daimler solved this with the internal combustion engine and soon a lot of companies started to make cars because enough rich people would buy them. The by-product was probably coincidental – as well as chugging around in them looking pleased with yourself, you could race them.

Competition seems to be a basic characteristic of man and originated with survival. Darwin's theory of evolution describes this. Even the simple acts of motion – walking, running, jumping, swimming – have become competitive events; and so have the simple acts of the hunt – throwing, sprinting, working as a team. The defensive mechanisms – punching, kicking, seizing an opponent to throw him down – have become boxing, kick-boxing, wrestling and judo. The spear has become the javelin, and the bow remains in archery. Rifle and pistol shooting are both Olympic events, and we still race horses just as we race bicycles. To do the same with cars was no more than extending man's basic characteristic to the technology which, in 1886, had appeared.

It didn't take long.

Soon enough, and there is something almost haunting about this, names familiar today would come in. Daimler and Benz were in already. In 1888, Michelin brothers Édouard and André set up a tyre company.[3] Peugeot had been making racing bikes but in 1889 produced a three-wheeler powered by steam. They soon understood Daimler's engine was the future and, in 1891, a Daimler-powered Peugeot went across France to Paris and on to Brest in Brittany. No petrol-driven vehicle had made such a journey before and it produced a sales surge, from five cars a year to 72.

In November 1892, an Italian champion cyclist who lived in Castel d'Ario – a sleepy little stone-clad town with a through road, a broad square and church spires near Mantua – had his fourth child, a son. He earned a good living by farming the fertile plain which encircles the town. The fourth-born was a lively little lad and, as was the way of it, would surely work the land as his father did and one day no doubt inherit some of it, toiling in anonymity. He was called Tazio Nuvolari. Far from tilling the soil he'd become, some insist to this day, the greatest driver who ever lived – but he was born before a race had been run. While Grand Prix racing was not yet in its birth pangs, here was its future.

The first race was in 1894, a trial of reliability and partly propaganda to *prove* that cars really could go faster than anything horse-drawn without exploding. Drivers had to cover the 78 miles from Paris to Rouen in eight and a half hours, and over a hundred entered. The internal combustion engine had not yet conquered all opposition and some of the vehicles were powered by steam, although they weren't really cars at all; some worked on electricity and, anyway, of the hundred entrants only 21 showed up.

A rich American newspaper owner based in Paris, Gordon Bennett, watched the start and was so captivated he even despatched a reporter to try to follow the event by bicycle, which is a lovely contradiction.

It is tempting to portray the era in terms of caricature, seeing them all as drooping moustaches under black hats perched on strange, pug-like vehicles bounce-bounce-bouncing along rough country lanes; and more tempting because having your photograph taken was an event to be treated very seriously – capturing your dignity for posterity – which is why they all look so severe. They were just being normal.

Then, of course, life was very different. No world war had yet been fought or imagined, no plane had ever flown, no man had ever travelled at the speed your saloon car will do effortlessly today. The west was a place of monarchies, rigid social strata and imperial certainties. Britain, made vastly wealthy by the Industrial Revolution, ruled the largest empire the world had ever seen and kept it in order with the largest navy. France had an extensive African empire and designs on being a global presence. And so it went. There was huge disparity between rich and poor, and by definition only the wealthy could buy cars. Racing would cost more again.

En route to Rouen the 21 race entrants halted at the small town of Mantes, just short of halfway, and reports suggest that the townspeople enjoyed seeing the cars as much as the drivers enjoyed having their lunch there. The diners could certainly afford the price if they could afford a car. The first of 19 who reached Rouen was a Count driving a steam tractor which could carry six people, and it received no award because of that. It took 6 hours 48 minutes, averaging 11mph and keeping Peugeots in second and third places.

All the vehicles had solid wheels. Michelin were the first to produce a practical rubber tyre for cars, in 1895, the year proper racing began, and a matrix was forged by necessity. Since there were no circuits, public roads had to be used with towns as markers. The first race ran from Paris to Bordeaux and back, 745 miles, and was won at an average speed of 14.9mph. That year, Italian and American racing began and the *Automobile Club de France* was formed.

The town-to-town matrix lasted until 1903. There would be twelve of these races, including Paris–Marseilles–Paris, in 1896. In October that year a certain Hon Charles Rolls journeyed to Paris to buy a Peugeot, which became Cambridge's first car. A Paris–Amsterdam–Paris race was staged in 1898. 'Manufacturers were already producing cars specifically for racing while drivers' names were becoming familiar and almost professional.'[4]

There was René de Knyff, a Belgian racing for France. He had a flowing beard and habitually wore a yachting cap.

There was another Belgian, red-bearded Camille Jenatzy, whose father had built the first factory making rubber in Belgium. Jenatzy won bicycle races but was also 'of a studious nature and when he obtained his degree as a civil engineer he abandoned sport (forever as he thought)'.[5] He wasn't happy in the family business and moved to Paris to get into motoring. He'd thought electric cars were the way to go and started making them...

In February 1898, a snowstorm paralysed the town of Modena on the plain outside Bologna. The snow was so deep that for two days a *petit bourgeois* merchant and landowner[6] could not reach the town hall to record the birth of his second son. The family surname was extremely common in the area, and when the boy was registered as Enzo Anselmo Ferrari, he took his place among the hundreds of other unremarkable, anonymous Ferraris. Yes, while Grand Prix racing was not yet into its birth pangs, here was its future.

That December, a Count with a name like a line of poetry – Gaston de Chasseloup-Laubat, younger brother of the man who founded the *Automobile Club de France* (the *ACF*) – took his chain-driven 40-horsepower electric car to a village road – Achères – outside Paris and did 39.2mph to claim the World Land Speed Record over a flying kilometre. This had a profound effect on Jenatzy who laid down a challenge for 1899. In January he and Chasseloup-Laubat met on the same road and Jenatzy pushed the record to 41mph. Chasseloup-Laubat responded with 43mph, and the possibilities which direct competition could, and did, create were being revealed moment by moment. It was more than that. It showed, seven decades before the rarefied, specialised craft – an aeroplane on land – pushed the record to 600mph that speeds could be increased in attainable increments. Each land speed record was also a way of saying to the motor racers: *You can go faster, too.*

Chasseloup-Laubat and Jenatzy agreed to do it again and went off to build bigger engines.[7] Jenatzy pushed it to 49mph and this was attracting so much attention the *ACF* drew up rules and sent officials along to supervise. Chasseloup-Laubat pushed it to 57mph, Jenatzy through the 100kmh barrier (62mph).

The increasing speed was reflected in the May 1899 Paris–Bordeaux race where the winner averaged 29mph.

A month later a company called Fabbrica Italiana Automobili Torino was founded, but you know it by its initials, FIAT, later styled Fiat.

That year, Daimler's agent in France, Emil Jellinek – who was also the dashing Austro-Hungarian consul in Nice – entered a Daimler in the 1899 Nice Speed Week. He understood the value of publicity. He raced the car under a pseudonym, using the Christian name of his nine-year-old daughter, Mercedes.

Newspaper tycoon Bennett thought the French were monopolising motor racing and decided to break that; and whatever Bennett wanted Bennett got. His father had founded the *New York Herald,* and that helped. Tall, handsome, he'd always got a lot of women. Once, for a bet, he drove a coach from Rhode Island to New York's Central Park, naked. He started, and won, the first trans-Atlantic yacht race. His engagement to a 'prominent Baltimore socialite' was terminated when he came to her New Year's party drunk and 'relieved himself in the grand piano.' Hence his exile in Paris.[8]

Now he'd get a motor race, an annual event of at least 550 kilometres (340 miles) between national teams chosen by their governing bodies; teams a maximum of three cars. The French were so strong that they held a ballot to pick theirs and it produced 'much bickering'.[9] The first of these races, known as the Gordon Bennett Trophy, was from Paris to Lyon in June 1900, with seven entries. De Knyff had a Panhard[10] and Jenatzy a Snoek-Bolide.[11] Karl Benz's son Eugen drove, naturally, a Benz while two American entries were elderly single-cylinder cars called Wintons. Jenatzy retired after hitting a lot of small animals – presumably dogs, cats, chickens and rabbits – along the route. One driver ran full into a St Bernard, jammed the steering, swerved across a ditch and went between two trees into a field.

Here was foreboding. Rising speed, the long and rough open roads, villages and towns – unpoliced and unpoliceable – were by definition potentially lethal and one must assume villagers had no experience of estimating speed, never having seen it before. In a race a month later, one car struck a cart and in another race a car struck a cow. In a race the year after, one car collided with a tram and another killed a boy standing in the middle of the road.

A rhythm of progress had been established. In 1902 the Land Speed Record was pushed to 75mph before another very rich American, William K. Vanderbilt, beat that and by year's end it stood at 77mph. In 1903, it would be beaten four times, once by Charles Rolls.

The foreboding deepened. Despite French Government reservations, the *ACF* organised a race from Paris to Madrid. It attracted 230 'very fast and sometimes dangerously flimsy cars'[12] which started from Versailles at intervals from 4am. As they thundered off into the dawn, they were about to kill road racing.

A tremendous duel developed between two Frenchmen, Fernand Gabriel and Marcel Renault, but Renault's car overturned, killing him; a riding mechanic died when a car hit a tree so hard that it broke up and parts were embedded in the tree itself; a mechanic died when a car hit a wall; a car veered into a crowd, killing the mechanic and a soldier.

The Spanish and French governments moved to stop the whole thing and did when it reached Bordeaux. The French Government was so nervous it ordered the cars to be hauled back to Paris by horses or on horse-drawn vehicles – a savage irony – but this proved unworkable and they were allowed to drive slowly. Even then one car struck a woman, injuring her. There would be no more town-to-town races.

The Bennett Trophy remained, and it assumed central importance.

In 1904, a third very rich American, Henry Ford, pushed the Land Speed Record to 91mph over the flying mile on frozen Lake St Clair, Michigan and others would push it through the 100. That same year the Hon Rolls was introduced to a Mr Royce in a London hotel.

The 1905 Bennett Trophy was run in the Auvergne region of France, the year the Land Speed Record reached 108mph. The Auvergne was preceded by an eliminating race and during it a Briton, Maurice Farman (sometimes referred to as Henry) missed a turn in his Panhard. He…

> found himself engaged in a short cut through the woods to the valley below. The two men [Farman and his riding mechanic] were thrown out, caught in the branches of the trees and held there while the car leapt along its wildly destructive path. Report has it that Farman, caught on a higher branch than his mechanic, pulled out his cigarette case and, looking down, quietly remarked: 'I wish you would pass me a match up, Tom.'[13]

As it seems, in this eliminator or the race itself, a US entry struck trouble and American manufacturers…

> were rather raw at the racing game in those days. [The car] broke its main oil feed pipe and had no facilities for repairing it. The men were of that rough Western type that never knows defeat. The mechanic sat on the frame of the machine, his legs dangling over, and with a can poured directly into the crankcase [but] more went on the outside than the in. They finished but as they stepped off the car oil was dripping from them in such quantities that [when] champagne was offered to them they could not hold the glass, they could not put it to their lips until some of the oil had been wiped away with a rag.[14]

Perhaps this is how a certain class of people saw themselves and their world, and how they wrote about it. Whatever, Rolls finished eighth in a Wolseley.

Two months later, Tazio Nuvolari's uncle Giuseppe took him to Brescia to watch a three-lap event with the leading manufacturers and drivers, including wild Victor Hémery, Vincenzo Lancia and Felice Nazzaro, clean shaven, a particularly studious-looking man. For anyone from solid, sleepy, virtually silent Castel d'Ario[15] it had to be intoxicating, 22 racing cars covering 500 kilometres and averaging a hundred kilometres an hour. Nuvolari had touched the passion which would ignite and rule the rest of his life.

The Bennett Trophy rules' limit of three cars per country irked the French because, compared to the strength of their automobile industry, they resented Switzerland with a sole manufacturer having the same and resented Mercedes entering three each from their German and Austrian factories.

The *ACF* found a solution. They'd organise their own race in 1906 under their own rules. They selected 64 miles of country roads outside the town of Le Mans as their circuit. To pacify the government they would make sure these roads were closed off and build extensive barriers to keep the spectators back from the cars.

They'd make it a monumental event spread over two days, six laps a day, giving a total distance of 769 miles – more than double the length of any race before. They'd find the perfect name for it, too, not the Championship of France, not the *Coupe*-this or the *Trophée*-that. No. It would be known as the Great Prize in motorsport.

Grand Prix racing was about to be born.

The year started with a flurry of World Land Speed Records, one of them set by Louis Chevrolet at Daytona, climaxing at 117mph over the flying mile but, beyond that, it was a time of solid beginnings.

On 5 May, three weeks before the French Grand Prix, a race called the Targa Florio, named for Vincenzo Florio who founded it, was run for the first time (and would continue until 1977). It represented a brutal test of man and machine: three laps totalling 277 miles of rugged Sicilian tracks and mountain roads which rose and fell, not to mention bandits and wolves. It attracted ten entries, including Lancia driving a Fiat and Alessandro Cagno who won it, in an Itala car. He'd make his mark, but doing something else.[16]

Maybe the Targa Florio was a staging post for Le Mans. Cagno took his Itala there while Florio himself (he hadn't competed in Sicily) took a Mercedes.

Le Mans is a typical French provincial town surrounded by verdant countryside, languid straight roads and strung out stone villages. The circuit did not touch on the town and that gave it a pastoral, almost rustic feel. The cars had a maximum weight of 1,000kg [2,204lb].

The Grand Prix attracted 34 entries, but only from France (25), Italy and Germany. The British were not tempted because they felt the French were using it to demonstrate their superiority and, even if the British did win, the French would claim they had lost it by accident.

The *ACF* was so determined to make the race a success it spent a considerable amount on the circuit although not nearly enough on its surface. (The expenditure was regained by grants from the town and hotel owners plus the entry fees.) Mindful of the Paris–Madrid fiasco...

> the towns are barricaded from end to end; villages are fenced, also there is not a single house, or cottage, or road, or lane, or footpath without its palisade. The total length of this palisading is 65,000 metres, or 40 miles. The tribunes – grandstands, the time-keeper's box, the telegraph boards etc – are situated at Montfort, about 20 kilometres from Le Mans [...] On the opposite side of the course a whole length of the frontage is given up to the firms competing in the race, so that they may be able to re-victual their cars.[17]

The circuit formed a triangle, another matrix, because every French Grand Prix to 1914 and on into the 1920s would follow that basic shape. This one began on the main road outside Montfort, a little town, and went towards Le Mans then turned sharp left 'at so short a radius that any car travelling at 30 miles an hour must run off.'[18]

That was on to the first full length of the triangle: it flowed in a straight line to a village and the other side of that in a straight line towards the town of St Calais, but the road was so bad there that the local council agreed to build a by-pass of roughly laid planking in a field.

That was on to the second leg of the triangle: it turned north towards the town of Vibraye but before it got there it veered into the forest, and more rough planking, in a tight dog-leg. It flowed north again to the town of La Ferté Bernard, and turned hard-hard left.

That was on to the third leg of the triangle: it flowed south but the road wriggled and bucked and twisted. One of the wriggles was through the town of Connerré where the road became a gully between the palisades with two corners, a right, a left. Montfort was shortly after Connerré.

These were 1906 roads, more like flattened, dusty tracks and dust meant you couldn't see where you were going. In an effort to beat this, the *ACF* treated the whole length with tar; and the cars' exhaust pipes had to be angled upwards so dust wasn't blown about, but the corners cut up so badly during practice that they had to be rolled and more tar was laid to try to seal them. This had agonising consequences and forced at least one driver to retire from the race because he couldn't bear any more pain. Thereby hangs a tale of what wasn't.

Long before, a Scot called John McAdam had worked out that if you raised the bed of a road and put drainage underneath, then covered it in small stones, the traffic would compact it until it was strong and smooth. Another pioneer used water stirred into stone dust – cement – to fill gaps between the stones. Later, a binding based on bitumen was laid on that: tarmacadam. The very first road made with this was in Paris in 1854, but clearly the technique had not reached Le Mans's countryside, 52 years later.

Instead, the roads guaranteed a plague of punctures. Three companies – Michelin, Dunlop and Continental – supplied tyres, another matrix: deploying innovation to gain an advantage. A puncture took about 15 minutes to repair because the tyre had to be levered off the rim and a new one levered on. Michelin produced a detachable rim, complete with tyre. The driver and mechanic undid eight nuts, lifted it off, lifted a new one into place and did the eight nuts up again. It took two minutes, but it came with its own penalty because each detachable wheel weighed 9kg, a real consideration with the car's maximum at 1,000kg. The Fiats carried four, other teams two, but some couldn't afford the extra weight at all. It would bring them constant back-breaking labour and cost them any chance in the race.

The cars were scrutineered and weighed inside a tall, broad tent in a field beside the track. As each car came, a crowd gathered to watch, and it was a crowd of its time, almost exclusively male, wearing suits, waistcoats, white panama hats, caps or boaters. Nobody was bare-headed. Some carried canes and used them to point to any interesting aspects of the cars. A woman in elegant white held the brim of her be-ribboned matching white hat in case it blew away. They all moved in a genteel, unhurried way, stopping to talk. The grass looked parched – and dusty.

Mechanics in dirty overalls pushed the cars on to the weighbridge in the tent, pushed them away again. The cars were squat and shaped like small railway engines, the driver and his mechanic sitting high up as if perched, unprotected, behind the engines. They favoured woollen or leather hats, or balaclavas. They all wore goggles.

The main grandstand, which held 2,000, spread along one side of the track and – in cream and gold, with an intricate canopy above it – looked like something from a fairground. Banners advertising Michelin ran along its frontage, hip high. This faced the 'pits' on the other side, a basic, stone-strewn working area inside the palisade with a counter on which the fuel churns and oil cans could be put.

The race was scheduled for a Tuesday. On the Sunday, people from all over France had begun to gather and…

Le Mans was *en fête*. Firework displays, running with bulls, banquets, singing and disturbances of the peace, nothing was missing. You got to bed late.[19]

The night before…

cars arrived ceaselessly, always coming in to the *Place de la Republique* [the main square] which swarmed with curious people, some grouped in front of the Stock Exchange's blazing windows where the *ACF* was holding a gala whose programme alternated between dancing and theatre. The café terraces overflowed. People bumped into each other, and bumped into each other again. The evening closed with the sensational arrival of a steam-driven omnibus which, leaving Paris in the morning, had energetically devoured the 207 kilometres without stopping.[20]

The cafés remained open until 4am, by which time the spectators needed to be on the move to reach the circuit. The roads would be closed at 5am so the race could start at the scheduled 6am. (*The Motor*'s correspondent stayed at a little inn, woke at 3.30 and was given 'coffee and the curious soapy sort of bread one gets in such a place.') Rain, likely to be heavy, had been feared, but the dawn broke blue and pure and clear, the sun burning off a little low-lying mist. By 4am a tide of vehicles and bicycles flowed towards the circuit and so many people tried to get on a train to a stop on the circuit that it appeared to be under assault. At the circuit…

among the hordes of cyclists and cars covered in dust, under the shade of the trees, in the fields, or in homemade tents held up by haphazard staves and draped by canvas or sheets, sat vast tables of drinkers, their ruddy faces happy, content.[21]

Soldiers cleared spectators off the course and tried to clear the journalists off it, too, but after 'heated discussion' the journalists stayed.

A man in a white boater and white overalls placed a tub of paint on the road and, using a long brush, set down the start-finish line with careful strokes, his back bowed.

The cars were driven from the field acting as a *parc fermé* into a passageway leading to the track and called one by one to the start, a white line across the road in front of the crowded grandstand. They halted there, waiting for the command to go. They were sent off at 90-second intervals and alternately, one car going from the left-hand side of the track, the next one already moving up to the line on the right. When that went, the next car on the left would have come up and be in place.

The grid, this first grid, was already as it would somehow always be, a mingling of cars, mechanics, officials, bystanders, officials with armbands and who knew who else?

A flat-faced Lorraine-Dietrich car,[22] its bonnet sloping to either side like a rooftop, its radiator painted with the race number 1A,[23] its driver and mechanic sitting far back over the rear axle and so high up they might have been enthroned, chugged up to the line, slowed, and stopped. At ground level in the grandstand, perhaps ten feet away, a clutch of women spectators, all in white with their matching white hats, watched. The sea of men all around them, still be-suited and be-hatted – an almost impossible formality in the open on a summer's day – watched, too. You could feel the intensity in their eyes. A knot of officials stood on the road beside 1A. The next starter, the Fiat of Vincenzo Lancia numbered 2A, must have been chugging up at that moment or perhaps it, too, had stopped and the two cars stood shoulder-to-shoulder, the drivers gazing down the long road ahead. There is no precision about these moments before it all began, no precise countdown, no photographic record. One of the officials held up a board illustrating what the flags round the circuit meant:

Blue = *beware*
Yellow = *stop*

The poignancy of the very final moment is that nobody knew because nobody could know, not least the devil-may-care Frenchman Fernand Gabriel who, at 25, was good enough to have survived the carnage on the 1903 Paris–Madrid killer – and been first to Bordeaux, winning it; nobody knew, as the official gave the signal and the Lorraine-Dietrich lurched forward creating a dust-storm behind, what had just been set in motion.

Nobody can conceivably have imagined, either, as the Lorraine-Dietrich crossed the line and accelerated away, its narrow tyres rutting the dry earth, the immensity of the future. Or even of the men who would be drawn into it, Nuvolari no doubt preparing to go to school in Castel d'Ario at this moment, Bernd Rosemeyer of mythical eyesight who'd be born in a little north German town three years on, Juan-Manuel Fangio who'd be born in an Argentinian town near the Atlantic five years on…or, two world wars later, that an Englishman called Stirling Moss would heat the blood, a quiet Scotsman called Jim Clark would redefine speed and simplicity, a rich Brazilian kid called Ayrton Senna would be touched by grace, another German from a small town,

Michael Schumacher, would reshape and rewrite everything...

There were already celebrated, heroic figures preparing to come forward to the white line. It was 6am – there is precision about this – on Tuesday, 26 June 1906. The driver of car 1A, Fernand Gabriel,[24] had been winning races since 1899 and it was he who had been in the lethal duel with Marcel Renault. He had a long-term contract with the Lorraine-Dietrich team and came to Le Mans as their leading driver. Now, as he headed down towards the turn into the first full leg of the triangle, he was the pathfinder and all others in Grand Prix history his followers.

Gabriel had gone at 06.00.00. Now decorously, while a sombre bearded official in dark hat and clothes noted the times, the others were waved on their way. Cars coughed and churned, their fumes wreathing the grid and making the people there suddenly ghostly, and then, like clouds, drifting towards the grandstand.

06.01:30: Vincenzo Lancia set off in a Fiat. He was from a small Piedmont village and his father had made money canning soup in Argentina. Young Vincenzo had an aptitude for numbers but machinery fascinated him, and the fascination lead all the way to here. He was 25.

06.03:00: François (Ferenc) Szisz set off in a Renault 90. He was from a large Hungarian family and his father practised faith healing. He'd been trained as a mechanic and to pursue that he went to Munich then Paris to join Renault and it had brought him all the way here. A shortish, strong man he had chiselled, swarthy features. He was 33.[25] The Renault had a sloping, aerodynamic bonnet which made it look unlike all the other cars. At the signal, Szisz corrected the front wheels, so they made a short jerking motion to be pointing straight ahead. It set off slowly, needing time and distance to gather pace. A small knot of people standing behind the white line gazed wistfully as it receded.

06:04.30: Hémery set off in a Darracq. He was a tempestuous, turbulent man and the year before had reportedly been banned from racing in Italy after he'd 'insulted his Italian rivals, snubbed the British and dismissed the Americans as mechanical peasants, unworthy of consideration.'[26] One time in America he aimed his powerful Darracq at a fellow competitor, and was disqualified.

06:06:00: Paul Baras set off in a Brasier. He'd been a 'tricycle champion and brilliantly fast with cumbersome cars.' More than that, he'd twice held the World Land Speed Record in 1904.[27]

06:07:30: Jenatzy set off in a Mercedes. He was known as the 'Red Devil'. An engineer by training, he adored speed, as he had proved on the road to Achères. He was 38. He was followed away by Louis Rigolly (Gobron-Brille).

06.10:30: Alessandro (Jacopo) Cagno set off in an Itala. He was a thin-faced, clean-shaven adventurer who had begun racing in 1902 and had come here from the Targa Florio. He was 23.

Ninety seconds later, George Heath, a Franco-American, set off in a Panhard-Levassor and so it went; Albert Clément in a Clément-Bayard at 06.18:00, Henri Rougier in a Lorraine-Dietrich at 06:19.30.

06:21.00: Nazzaro set off in a Fiat.[28] He was the son of a Turin coal merchant and had started in the motor trade with a small company as errand boy, mechanic, cleaner, apprentice at 15.[29] 'Tall, quiet, almost aristocratic in manner' he introduced the gentleman's way of driving, changing gears silently and treating his cars with respect.

These were the fast men – although that didn't prevent Nazzaro stalling, gentleman's style or not. The car was restarted without outside help, which would have disqualified him.

As they went, sometimes drivers saluted their mechanics or the crowd; some hunched forward and held the steering wheel tight, others sat rigid.

From a distance, the symmetry of the cars was mostly similar. The spectators, often in little groups behind the palisades or the solid barricades in the towns, saw the cars bounding and bouncing, and sometimes they slithered. The drivers looked as heroic as knights in armour had once done, galloping through. Trains had broadened the ordinary person's conception of speed but *this* cavalcade was coming round the corner into your main street at, to take the average of the fastest lap, 73.3mph. A primed racehorse will do barely half that and then only for a short time. The racing car, experienced in all its sound and fury, and from such close quarters, must have had a stunning impact all round the circuit. It still does. At one point, behind a tall palisade in a town, a group of nuns watched, captivated.

The crowds were in the country as well as the towns, standing at corners beneath tall trees while the cars fought their way round the bends, each trailing a plume of dust.

Gabriel got as far as St Calais when a mechanical failure made the car swerve 'violently in all directions, each swerve being checked by the driver ... it may have saved the lives of both in the car.'[30] Gabriel was out of the race.

A rough ride. On this first lap, one car ran off the planking at St Calais, bending a wheel. The car ran into a bank of loose earth built up against a palisade, burying its right rear wheel. While driver and mechanic struggled to repair it – that would take three hours, so they completed the first lap in just under 4 hours 20 minutes – an official positioned himself in the road and stood, hands behind his back, monitoring what was going on.

Three cars retired: engine failure, damaged radiator and a crash where the car overturned having taken a corner too fast. It was torn to pieces.

Szisz, with the advantage of two detachable rear wheels, moved into the lead on lap three of the six and would not lose it. The tar was worse than the dust. It melted in the heat, got behind the goggles and burnished the eyes. One Renault driver had broken goggles and on that lap and asked for them to be replaced but this was refused – it could only be done for the second day.

This was Edmond (initial J. – his first name does not seem to have survived) who pitted with his eyes swollen by the tar, and burning. Another driver offered to take his place, got in and was moving away when Louis Renault flagged it down by making big gestures. Renault knew the rules: you couldn't change a driver during the day. Edmond got back in and set off to a 'thunder of bravos' from the crowd. He slogged on but the pain overwhelmed him and he stopped briefly to recover, continued to the end of lap five when, his eyes on fire, he couldn't see the road any more and retired. Louis Renault, dapper in straw boater, waistcoat and suit, led him gently away, a cloth draped over his head to keep the sunlight from his eyes. Renault was everywhere, talking to officials, supervising the pit work.

Another driver was so exhausted his car got away from him at the Vibraye planking and he crashed. The exhaustion was partly the heat of the day, partly the incessant and laborious tyre changing – they were lasting only a lap or two – and partly because of the drivers' and mechanics' eyes.

The roof and rear of the main grandstand lacked ventilation, and when the temperature reached 120°F it was so hot inside that 60 people had to be treated for sunstroke. Spectators, too, had inflamed eyes from the dust the passing cars churned up. It had been a long morning and now, completing the six laps the crowd would know who led at half-distance ...

It was a quarter to twelve when, everyone being on the alert for the arrival of Szisz, a bugle call was heard in the distance, and as a car came over the brow of a hill a mile away, powerful binoculars showed that it was a Renault. At once a great yellow flag was held out, and amid a yell of delight Szisz roared past. [...] An official boarded the car when it stopped, and then it returned along the course between lines of cheering spectators to the enclosure, and there the car was run under the tent and barricaded round, not to be touched until next morning.[31]

Szisz said that from start to finish he hadn't had a moment's anxiety over anything mechanical. 'Once I got into the lead I didn't push. I only changed tyres every couple of laps as a precaution. Monsieur Renault told me to lap at 58 minutes. Now, I averaged 57 and a half minutes. That tells you what a pleasure it was to drive such a car.' When he came from his car, goggles up on his head, a well-wisher gripped his hand and shook it. Szisz looked at that moment like a warrior.

Seventeen cars survived this first day, with two and a half hours between the first of them, Szisz, and the last, a Lorraine-Dietrich. The leaderboard:

Szisz	5h 45m 30.4s
Clément	6h 11m 40.6s
Nazzaro	6h 26m 53.0s

The retirements included Hubert le Blon, whose wire wheels gave way on the planking at Vibraye, and Henri Tart, while 'replenishing his Panhard, was asked to look at the dumb iron[32] carrying the front spring. He looked, and found it broken, and, just like a Frenchman, he at once threw up his hands and commenced to sob.'[33]

Jenatzy and Lancia said they couldn't face another day like it. Other drivers 'smothered their ravaged faces with ointments and had their eyes treated by a doctor.'[34] Lancia's eyes were 'fearfully enflamed' and Jenatzy told *The Motor*'s correspondent he 'had never suffered such agony before. Goggles were no protection. The face became smothered with tarry emanations, and the vapour from this passed under the goggles and then set up inflammation of the pupil and cornea of the eyes.'

Like Szisz's Renault, the cars were taken to the *parc fermé* – some pushed by half a dozen men – to be guarded overnight and, as a further security precaution, the area was floodlit. Nobody was going to do any tampering, even with their own cars.

An ingenious method had been put in place for the second day's starting order. Cars were sent off *at* the time they'd done on the first day, so Szisz went first at 5.45am, Clément at 6.11, Nazzaro at 6.26 and so on down to the slowest, that Lorraine-Dietrich, at 8.15am. This meant their positions on the road were their actual positions, no adding and subtracting necessary...

> The cars were towed out of the 'park' by a horse[35] and brought to the starting line (and it was typical of the thoroughness with which the race details were carried out that yesterday afternoon the horse was continually practised in hauling a car out to the line, the engine being at once started, so as to accustom the horse to the noise, in case it should be on the line when the engine of a racing car was started this morning.[36]

The animal, white and clearly a carthorse, had a harness which trailed back to the front axle of the cars. One man guided the horse – the cars seemed to be of no great weight for it – while another walked alongside the car steering it.

Szisz and his mechanic did not mount their Renault, but on the order to '*Go!*' pushed it across to their pit, refuelled it and changed two wheels. This needed 11½ minutes and when it was done they set off to a tremendous cheer. Other competitors would do the same...

> A glance at the colossal grandstands showed them to be admirable, ravishing, built with so much taste. In the middle of a desert of sand and pine trees, under the blinding light of a ferocious sun, one saw – in the 'dress circle,' among the dyes of the white drapes, orange drapes and garlands of flowers – a dazzling bevy of deliciously pretty women, adorned in white, pink and blue. An incomparable ensemble of gaiety, radiance...[37]

The race had attracted celebrities and important people, another matrix: the Grand Duchess of Mecklenburg, the Duke of Parma, barons and marquises, the Minister of Public Work, several generals and the occasional viscount.

Lancia was due to go at 7.12 and this produced a moving scene. On the line his mechanic had cranked the engine into life, Lancia engaged the clutch and started. The mechanic didn't have time to get out of the way, grabbed hold of the bonnet and Lancia drove him the 200 yards to their pit. 'What anxiety! We thought the valiant boy had had it. He laughed.'[38] Meanwhile...

Shepard, who is an American and a cousin of the Vanderbilts, had made a good impression [...] and it was rather a pity that he should have had to spend half an hour in revictualling and tyre changing this morning. Hémery spent an hour in replacing defective inlet valves, and he earned the sympathy of the crowd over his many unavailing efforts to get the engine started, and went away with it missing rather badly.[39]

This was Elliot Shepard and before the race he had worn a cowboy hat. He was driving a Hotchkiss, a barrel-shaped car with wire wheels which set off in a great cloud of smoke and dust.

Jenatzy really couldn't face this second day and handed over to a giant of a man with a pseudonym, 'Burton', although he appears in *The Motor* as Alex Burton. Vincenzo Lancia had intended to hand the FIAT over to his reserve driver, but he wasn't around. Lancia had no time to go and change, and started in his ordinary clothes.

On the first lap a Panhard swerved so hard at a right-hander that the steering wheel was plucked from the driver's hand, the car lurched off the road into a gutter and overturned. It struck a tree, breaking the driver's leg.

Szisz completed the lap with eleven cars still waiting to go, and even the lap after that there were still four.

The corners had suffered a fearful pounding on the first day and were now strewn with stones and pebbles, the cars trying to navigate through. The punctures kept coming. Clément had one in a tight right-hander out in the country, the car slewing towards the edge of the track, a dust shroud pursuing it. Clément fought it, held it, straightened it, slowed it – then, with practised speed, he and the mechanic were out starting their work, lifting the spare from just behind their seats. Two gendarmes with obligatory moustaches came up to watch.

The planking at St Calais kept bringing problems, too. At one point an official signalled frantically to Shepard: *Slow! Corner!* waving his left arm up and down. Shepard didn't take the corner but went straight on down the road ahead, missing the turn for the banking completely. He vanished in a cloud of exhaust fumes, stopped, reversed in another cloud of fumes, drove on to the planking and stopped. He readied himself and proceeded, the car belching fumes like an industrial chimney. He didn't get far: a wire wheel failed, the car gouging into a bank beside a leafless sapling. He was out.

Szisz had held such a substantial lead that he only had to keep going to win and as he drove he raised a hand to acknowledge the cheering of the crowd. Behind him, a lively battle developed between Nazzaro's FIAT and Clément's Clément-Bayard. Szisz did keep going. On lap nine Nazzaro got past Clément and the order stayed like that. Szisz slowed to protect the car. He'd do his slowest lap of the race by three minutes, but that didn't matter any more. Finishing did. He sawed the big steering wheel round a last time on to the straight towards the pits and the grandstand. He moved towards the white line beside the time-keeper's hut and an official with a black flag, standing poised, dipped it as he passed. He had covered the twelve laps across the two days in 12 hours 14 minutes and 7 seconds, an average speed of 62.8mph. The crowd raised their hats high to him, some raised their arms and the ladies applauded politely.

Fernard Gabriel had been the first Grand Prix driver, François Szisz was now the first winner. Nuvolari and Rosemeyer, Fangio and Moss, Clark and Senna and Schumacher, were all his followers, too.

'The last lap was for me – despite the confidence I had in the car – a great anxiety,' he said. 'I feared something small which would take victory away at the moment when it had seemed to be won. Little by little, having gone through Saint-Calais, and Vibraye I came to Connerré. I drove carefully to avoid any problems and at last when we got to Belle-Inutile [just before the finish] my mechanic, who was so anxious he hadn't said a word all the lap, suddenly clapped me on the back. "Bravo, that's it!"'

Nazzaro came in at 12h 46m 26.4s, Clément more than three minutes behind...

> Albert Clément is a general favourite, and his father Adolphe Clément is one of those cheerful, short bearded men with no 'side,' always courteous and universally liked. When Clément fils was called up to be received by the Minister of Commerce he waited for his father to come along as he would not accept the honour or congratulations without him.[40]

When the race was done, Renault stood before one of the senior officials, the Minister of Transport, with his straw hat down over his face so that no-one would see his copious tears. In this moment of personal solitude, no doubt, he savoured the triumph and thought of his brother.[41]

One reflection was that, as a replacement for the Gordon Bennett races, the Grand Prix had left a great deal to be desired, and it had been decided by tyre choice, to use a modern idiom. Szisz changed 19 times while at least one car changed 14 times on this second day alone – but Szisz had the detachable wheels. The race had clearly been too long and, because of the nature of the circuit, no *dicing* seen, just lonely cars coming by and, at the end, only eleven of them. Szisz finished at midday, the last at 4.30pm.

Despite everything the race served its purpose. The matrix had been forged and it could be adapted to make it better and better.

Le Figaro's reporter caught a mood after Szisz came in...

One o'clock. Enthusiasm falls away, the stomachs speak, you rush to the buffets, for a small fortune you grab the exquisite champagne of G. H. Mumm to go with skinny little chicken, dusty slivers of ham which crunch in your teeth, warm drinks, stale bread and cheese, seasoned by the calls of those vending it.

The French Grand Prix was now poised to become, with the American Grand Prix, the core of motor racing. Up to the outbreak of the First World War in 1914, the French would be run six times and the American five. There were no other Grands Prix.

Of course there had been nationalism, as there always would be. That, too, seems very basic to human beings. However, 'over the years it is the magnificent machines and heroic drivers who have stirred the blood rather than the country that either have happened to originate from.'[42]

In November that year a poor blacksmith who also repaired bicycles in the small town of Komyo outside Tokyo had a son. Some miles away was a mill with a petrol-powered engine and the little lad used to be taken there by his grandfather so he could watch the engine working. It captivated him. He was called Soichiro Honda.

The *ACF* decided that their 1907 Grand Prix should be near the Channel port of Dieppe (perhaps to attract British entries), although it might have gone to Fontainebleau, the elegant and regal town south of Paris; but either way here was another matrix and the second staging post on the race's long journey through the years. Uniquely the *ACF*, in what seems to have been an enduring spirit of egalitarianism and accessibility, would take the race to many staging posts all over France – a total of 16 up to Magny-Cours in the present day. Although the 1908 and 1912 races were also at Dieppe, by 2005 they had also been run at Amiens, Lyon, Strasbourg, Tours, the banked Montlhéry circuit near Paris, Miramas, Cominges, Pau, Reims, Rouen, Clermont-Ferrand, Dijon, Paul Ricard and Magny-Cours. The people would come to the races, and the races would go to the people.

Dieppe in 1907 was significantly shorter than Le Mans, ten laps of 47 miles each against twelve laps of 64 miles, a total difference of almost 300 miles. That allowed adaptation, the race run on one day. The circuit was surprisingly similar to Le Mans in shape and feel, although several temporary bridges had been built. Palisades were erected in the towns and the whole circuit laid with tar again. First aid posts were connected to a telephone system; and to guard it all on race day the *ACF* had 700 policemen and 4,500 soldiers on hand.

Each car was allowed 231 litres of fuel, replacing the limit on the weight of the cars, and manufacturers could again enter three cars. That produced 24 French cars while six other countries entered 14, including Weigel[43] from Britain and the front-wheel drive Christie from the United States, the first time a car like that had ever raced in Europe.

Once Dieppe had been chosen several manufacturers went there to carry out trials, especially for fuel consumption on sections where they felt their rivals couldn't see them. The roads were not, of course, closed and the trials became very dangerous. Clément crashed outside a little village and was killed, a Darracq driver hit a cart and was killed. The outcry in the French Press was so intense that for a time the race came into question.

They'd race.

At scrutineering the day before, the fuel tanks were 'filled from the elaborate official apparatus and the balance of the fuel allowance was fed into cans, each of which was sealed and numbered. Cars and cans were then locked in individual wire pens for the night and placed under military guard.'[44] It had rained, and many worried what they would do to the course if it lingered to the morrow. It didn't.

The organisation of a Grand Prix was being refined. The police set out 17 articles governing how the race would be run, crowd controlled, and who could go where. Article 7 described places where the cars had to slow – round corners, through villages – and these were signalled by streamers stretched over the road…

Article 8. The signals will be 400 metres before the precise place where the slowing-down of the cars must be observed. The competitors must slow their speed to 40kmh. A bugler is to be positioned 200 metres before all built-up areas and will sound each approaching car.[45]

The race began at 6am again, but this time the cars went at 60-second intervals. To enable spectators to savour its scale special trains ran from Dieppe. Starting at 3.17 on race morning, there were eleven of them before 10.20, shuttling people up to Le Treport, a coastal town at the tip of the course and its neighbour Eu, where there was a hard, spectacular left-hander, the cars hugging it. The special trains also went across to the town of Envermeu, halfway down the first leg of the triangle. Those who preferred to stay in the start-finish area were reminded by the local paper that 'for the day of the Grand Prix, a popular terraced stand has been built. The entry is 2.0 francs and cold meals will be served at 3 francs 50.' Many would watch the race in the countryside, strung out along tree-lined roads in small groups standing on the grass verges or bordering fields as the big beasts fled by just before them.

As the cars left the *parc fermé* to make their way to the start over a pathway of duckboards, a band played. The start was laid with duckboards, too, and the crowd stretched away into the distance. A vast grandstand loomed and it was full of people. For the first time, pits had been dug at the side of the track so spares and tools could be stored there.

Lancia in the FIAT was sent off at 06.01, Szisz in his Renault at 06.09, Nazzaro in his FIAT at 06.18, Gabriel in his Lorraine-Dietrich two minutes later. Because of the fuel limitation, cars did not start their engines until just before they were due to go and that caused problems with some cutting out as they crossed the line. The mechanics got to work with the crank handles immediately.

Despite the tar, the road out in the country was so dusty the tracks each car's tyres cut were clearly visible to the little groups who'd gathered to watch. There was a downhill left-right (the first Grand Prix chicane?) flanked by high earthen banks with the crowd on top. It imposed great demands on the driver and produced its own catalogue of incidents. Drivers could drift – or try to drift – their cars through, the back end hanging out, slewing back in – or they could misjudge it, as a Lorraine-Dietrich driver did, skittering across the right-hander into the bank and thumping that hard. Driver and mechanic had to get out and push it to safety while an official stood at the mouth of the chicane with two flags preparing to warn oncoming cars of the danger. Another car did come through and three women in long dresses and bonnets, positioned to watch it enter the chicane, scampered along the banking to see it go through – or if it went through. Some got the mouth so wrong that they had to reverse. Some slithered on the edge of control. One, a Renault which may have been touched by another car, came in virtually sideways, whipped round and butted the banking, then rolled, throwing driver and mechanic out. The next car was too close to do anything except turn sharply away from the crash, towards the banking at the other side.

One driver stopped by the wreck on the right and, as it seems, enquired of the driver standing beside it, if he was OK, then sped off, the driver waving.

Lancia led but at half distance Arthur Duray (Lorraine-Dietrich) had got past him; Nazzaro third, Gabriel fourth and Szisz fifth – and all of them separated by under eight minutes.

Duray and Lancia duelled and they could see each other. Lancia regained the lead on lap six, Duray retook a lap later, but now Nazzaro made his move. He overhauled Lancia on the time stagger – Nazzaro had started 17 minutes later – and Szisz, consistently fast, was making *his* move in the scoop-nosed Renault.

Lap 7	*Lap 8*
Duray	Duray
Nazzaro	Nazzaro
Lancia	Szisz
Szisz	Lancia

Duray's gearbox failed, then Lancia's FIAT misfired so that on lap nine, with one lap to go after it, Duray was gone, Lancia had fallen away and the race lay between Nazzaro and Szisz. At lap nine Nazzaro led by more than five and a half minutes but the start times had to be factored in to that, Szisz off at 6.09am that morning, Nazzaro at 6.18. It meant in the most simple, direct way that nine minutes had to be subtracted from Szisz's 6h 13m 45s – making him 6h 4m 45s. On this last lap Szisz had to find almost three minutes and he couldn't. He did 39 minutes 25 seconds and crossed the line shortly after 1pm. He'd been driving for 6 hours 53 minutes and 10.6 seconds.

He knew that if Nazzaro appeared within those nine minutes the race had been plucked from him. While Szisz was driving away Nazzaro's red FIAT hoved into view as it crossed a low hill on the straight towards the finish. He crossed the line at 6 hours 46 minutes and 33 seconds, and he'd won it easily enough.

For 1908, the race stayed at Dieppe but the rules changed, the minimum weight raised to 1,100kg and with engine restrictions to try to make it safer.[46] It attracted a huge entry, 49, of which 48 started: as well as the usual FIATs, Renaults and Mercedes came three Austins, three Opels (one driven by Fritz von Opel), and three Benzs apart from the lovely, almost poetic, names of the era: Brasier, Porthos, Mors, Germain, Motobloc, Itala[47] and Thomas.

Jenatzy had of course driven a Mercedes at Dieppe in 1907 and waited to get his hands on one again now, but the company had selected a new generation of drivers. Mors had made a late entry of three hastily assembled cars and Jenatzy asked for one of them.

The race was scheduled for 7 July and, because these were public roads, all practice banned for five weeks and a 15kmh speed limit rigorously enforced in case any competitor tried to (this caught the occasional tourist unawares). To get round the ban some teams practised on similar strips of road nearby and an Austin driver, Dario Resta, ran into trouble twice. Resta…

who was born to drive but lacking in road experience, had a tendency to be reckless and was involved in two crashes, wrecking his car on both occasions. In the second he collided with a horse and cart ending up in a ditch with the car on top of him. He and his mechanic, having been rescued from this dangerous situation then became involved in an altercation with some locals who had come to the assistance of the driver of the cart. Finally, Resta was dragged off to prison and only released when his friend Mr Fry, whose Mercedes he had driven at Brooklands,[48] bailed him out in time for the weigh-in.[49]

An English enthusiast, Hall Watt, who had bought the 1906 winning Renault, was a non-competitor, but drove the course, crashed and died.

On Sunday, 5 July the *ACF* 'summoned drivers and mechanics to a lecture on the need to protect their faces.' Some of these drivers were staying in tents in a field near the start and so were spectators. A whole tented village had arisen.

On Monday 6 July there was a six-lap Voiturette[50] with 47 entries, and although the circuit's roads had had extensive work done on them, the Voiturettes dug this up.

On this race eve the local newspaper *La Vigie De Dieppe* wondered:

What speed will be reached? Nazzaro achieved an average speed of 113kmh last year and the fastest lap was covered by the same competitor in 38 minutes 16 seconds (120kmh). There are hopes of doing better this time and most of the drivers estimate that Nazzaro's total time will be beaten by several minutes. They believe themselves capable of doing a lap between 38 and 39 minutes and thus averaging between 115 and 120kmh.

For the Grand Prix some drivers wore only goggles and others 'added masks and helmets', but these offered minimal protection against the flying stones. Although there had been 'desperate clearing and patching through Monday night'[51] of the damaged corners huge numbers of stones remained to be thrown back by the car ahead.

On a cold morning a bitter wind, strong enough to keep blowing Monsieur Renault's straw hat off, raked the start at 6am. The start was given by a small cannon in grass beside the track. A nervous looking man in a dark suit borrowed a match and applied it – and was enveloped in a pall of smoke. The cars were sent off at one-minute intervals and Szisz in the Renault was soon travelling fast, leaving plumes of dust behind him as he moved out on to the narrow ribbon of road which undulated through the countryside, turning and twisting through the towns. The duel was resumed: Nazzaro's FIAT took the lead by lap two but now Christian Lautenschlager – a 31-year-old who had joined Daimler in 1899 as a mechanic, risen to foreman in the racing team by 1905 and was in his first major race – was threatening in his Mercedes.

Lautenschlager, from near Stuttgart and of poor parents, had been apprenticed at 14 as a locksmith. He travelled as a journeyman, and when he was 22 returned to Stuttgart and trained as a mechanic. Old Daimler liked the young man and he became a works driver. As he tackled Nazzaro's FIAT, he knew what he was about.

And, as is the way of motor racing so infuriatingly often, duels are destroyed by circumstance. On that lap two, Szisz had to swerve to miss a car which had misjudged the sharp triangular fork outside Dieppe, and Szisz did this so violently that his car threw a tyre and rim. He went some way on the iron bonding underneath but damaged that so badly that he couldn't fit another tyre. He limped to the Renault pit, spoke briefly, and retired. Some say the 'man fairly broke down under the blow.'[52] Nazzaro's engine broke on the next lap.

That left Lautenschlager clear. He drove calmly, shedding the square-jawed, youthful, determined Hémery (Benz), whose goggles had broken, but the circuit was full of perils. One car had to change tyres 19 times. Another suffered a puncture in a right-hand corner and the car twisted out of control, killing driver and mechanic.

Mercedes actually ran out of tyres. Lautenschlager had stopped ten times for new tyres, once when his right-front was completely shredded. He negotiated the last two laps with great care, using the engine's power whenever he judged the road surface safe, then picking a path through the damaged sections. He came in after 6 hours and 55 minutes to the consternation of the silent French. The band played the German national anthem, as it was obliged to do, but then moved immediately into the stirring French national rallying cry, the *Marseillaise*.

Hémery came next, another Benz third, and by now the band had fallen silent, too. Lautenschlager, a short, stocky man wearing a pullover, was escorted to the victory ceremony by an official in hat and armband who gripped him by the arm to steer him there. The podium was entirely German and *The Motor*'s correspondent wrote:

> The French have created for themselves a kind of Frankenstein's monster in motor racing. They have made of the mere winning of a race the essence of commercial success, and the natural corollary is that the losing of a race becomes a catastrophe.
>
> The horror, the chagrin and the humiliation of their defeat [...] filled the cup of the French to overflowing and, as a consequence, they lost their heads and took their beating very badly. In the paddock I saw notable Frenchmen livid with rage, stamping about and showing their bitter resentment.

It had been an endurance test again, with 25 retirements, although reportedly Lautenschlager proved to be 'exceedingly modest and free from self-consciousness. There was no posing, no straining after effect and one felt delighted to go up and congratulate' him.[53] The endurance element was captured in a single paragraph:

> At the end of the race some drivers were in a parlous state. Flying stones had smashed the glass of some of the goggles, Hémery for one being in agony for a couple of laps through a spicule [small, sharp piece] of glass working into his eye. He had to stop and be attended to by a doctor before he could finish the race. Resta had to stop twice [...] to get a doctor to wash his eyes out, so inflamed were they, and at the end they were dreadful to behold. Perhaps the most pitiful sight was Henry Fournier [Itala] who was so bad he could scarcely see to bring his car into the enclosure and he was completely blindfolded after medical treatment and had to be led away.[54]

Jenatzy finished 16th, lost in the pack. The career of the first great Grand Prix driver was over.

The race had proved that almost whatever regulations were in place the potential danger remained. At the left-hander at Eu, one driver either misjudged the corner completely or the car wouldn't turn in. It travelled at great speed to the protective wooden wall at the far side and struck it so hard it smashed a section. Later, another went directly into the wall, striking it so hard it brought down several sections and scattered the crowd behind. In a different left-hander, a car went straight on into an advertising hoarding, mincing the DU of DUNLOP.

Two months later, ten-year-old Enzo Ferrari and his father went to watch a race at Bologna, and there he saw Nazzaro and Lancia in their awesome FIATs. Ferrari had touched, and been touched by, motor racing for the first time. In due course, he would touch it and shape its very soul. He'd employ Nuvolari and their relationship would develop into an eternal question: what happens when an irresistible force meets an immovable object?

The French were livid and bitter. For 1909 a race had been tentatively set for Anjou and the *ACF* had drawn up regulations for a minimum of 40 cars but when only nine entered they cancelled it and didn't hold another until 1912, at Dieppe.

Pausing here, it is important to stress that the story of Grand Prix racing cannot be properly appreciated without considering the social context in which it happened. It was impossibly exclusive and although ordinary working folk may have thronged to watch, they were watching another world go by. Throughout this book I'm going to use various measures – comparing increases in speed (for example, at Monaco when we get there) – and three will be social in nature: the number of vehicles registered on Britain's roads from 1926, the first year it seems when we have accurate figures; the average weekly earnings of a Briton; the cost of the lowest priced Ford in their range.

In 1909, a Briton earned £1.50 a week. A Model T Ford cost £220. Saving all his money, the Briton would have taken 2 years 42 weeks to buy one. To chart one aspect of the rise in motoring, every decade I'm going to give the cost of an average small Ford and the ever-decreasing time the Briton took to buy it. For long decades, motoring was the province of the wealthy and motor racing the province of the even wealthier. Eventually, motoring was for everyone – which must be reflected in the enormous appeal of motor racing.

By 1912, the World Land Speed Record had been pushed to 141mph by an American in a Benz at Daytona.

The Grand Prix at Dieppe reverted to two days of ten laps each, and to safeguard against a small entry, it was opened up to Voiturettes as well, producing a total entry of 58. The Grand Prix drivers included Hémery (Lorraine-Dietrich), Louis Wagner (Fiat), newcomers Jules Goux (Peugeot), Georges Boillot (Peugeot) – a stern, rounded countenance, a decorative handlebar moustache – and two Americans, Ralph de Palma (Fiat) and David Bruce-Brown (Fiat).

Goux, a studious-looking, sharp-eyed Frenchman and de Palma, handsome in the open, clean-cut American way, were of a new generation whose careers would span the First World War. Goux, a Frenchman and then 39, competed in 150 races, winning several dozen including the Indianapolis 500. He'd actually drive in the 1926 French Grand Prix.

De Palma began in 1906 but on motorbikes. 'For Americans, he was a symbol of "up-by-the-bootstraps" industry; Italians considered him part of their folklore, even though he had left Italy as a nine-year-old and remembered little of the mother tongue. Sportsmanship and showmanship were wedded to his nature.'[55] He'd earn his fame with Mercedes, for whom he would win the Indianapolis 500. He didn't retire until 1933, and the number of his wins has been put at 2,557.

Boillot, who had a particularly fierce-looking moustache,[56] had also been racing since 1906. He and Goux helped build their own Peugeot, and in 1910, he won the Targa Florio with it. Boillot, who worked for Peugeot, was 'fully skilled as a mechanic and able to assist in the design of a racing car as well as in its preparation. Strong, square-built, determined […] very sure of himself, he would tackle anything.'[57]

Bruce-Brown was born to wealthy parents[58] and became a mechanic then a driver. In 1909 he was beating de Palma and in 1911 he drove a Fiat in the first Indianapolis 500. Because of the way he drove, the French nicknamed him the errant schoolboy. Of him, someone said: 'The instant I rested my eyes upon him, an utter stranger, I had a fairly accurate gauge of his character. He was the personification of fine, wholesome and splendid youth and upon him was an unmistakable stamp of good breeding. […] was a fellow of natural poise and courteous deportment, attired nattily yet inconspicuously and spoke in a soft, modulated voice. He introduced himself as David Bruce-Brown, a student at Yale, but he was too much the true gentleman to add that he was the scion of a very wealthy and socially prominent New York family. His code in fact did not tolerate *braggadocio* of any sort.'[59]

Several teams tested over the Dieppe course well before the race and six early-morning sessions had also been arranged. Boillot in his Peugeot – often described as the first modern Grand Prix car with its overhead camshafts – did successive laps of 41, 37 and 35 minutes while Bruce-Brown, who had arrived in Paris with de Palma the previous Wednesday, did 37. 'The roads were hastily patched and their surfaces were sprayed with a calcium chloride solution to keep down dust.'[60]

The arrangements to start the race, at 5.30am, were striking and very visual. A set of posts with numbered cards on them, were set down both sides of the track, even numbers to one side, odd numbers to the other. This was not like the original Le Mans alternation, cars arriving up one after another, because here, the cars drew up behind their respective numbers. They would however be sent off alternately. The grid, as it would seem, had been created.

The cars were in place by 5.15 and the track cleared. The starter marched to the head of the grid and at that moment the mechanics of the first few cars rushed to their starting-handles, the engines were fired and it sounded like a salvo of cannon fire. The starter signalled the cars away at 30-second intervals.

Bruce-Brown and his mechanic 'created a sensation by coming to the starting line in their American make-up, this comprising a grey cloth mask, through which peered a pair of ghostly-looking eyes.'[61]

On that first lap Hémery overtook ten cars and Boillot thirteen but Bruce-Brown had the lead on elapsed time (37m 18s), Boillot second (38m 40s). It was the story of the first day: Boillot *raced* Bruce-Brown and Wagner *raced* Boillot.

Bruce-Brown and Boillot pitted together to intense excitement, Bruce-Brown accelerated away but Boillot's Peugeot hesitated – to the anguish of the crowd. He 'wrestled' with the gear lever and he was away, too. Boillot was 'anxious to see' how Bruce-Brown would react to an attack and launched one in the V-shaped Dieppe corner. He went past and at speed but 'as I soon as I had pulled in to my side of the road again I glanced back. In a fraction of a second I was on the edge of a grassy bank. I had to cut out my ignition to save myself and, taking advantage of my error, Bruce-Brown roared past me.' This first day finished:

Bruce-Brown	6h 36m 37s
Boillot	6h 38m 40s
Wagner	7h 03m 12s

A French driver, Leon Collinet, put a wheel into a ditch trying to overtake a car in the Voiturette class and the car rolled, killing his mechanic.

Goux had been disqualified in extraordinary circumstances. A stone broke his petrol pipe and he soldered it at the roadside, but this cost so much time that he resumed at the rear of the field and, when he finished, the timekeepers told him he still had two laps to do. He protested and they reduced it to one. As he prepared to set off they realised he had done the ten rounds but then it emerged he had obtained petrol from 'outside sources', presumably to get back to the pits after the broken petrol pipe. It was illegal and he was out. De Palma was out, too, for the same offence.

Anyway...

soon after the winner had come in, a fox terrier escaped from the paddock on to the track, tearing down the course at top speed in a frantic endeavour to overtake a racing car. In the rear [John] Hancock was approaching on the Vauxhall. Evidently with the intention of removing all possibility of danger to himself and the other competitors, he made straight for the animal, hit it with his right front wheel, and killed it instantly.[62]

Drizzle melted into rain as the second day began and, under the regulations, no work could be done on the cars until they had been flagged away. Even when one mechanic tried to dry his car's steering wheel he was warned. A Rolland-Pilain had a problem with the plug leads and didn't move for an hour until Monsieur Pilain corrected the problem himself but, because he had physically touched the car, he had to take over the driving himself and supply his own mechanic. They finished eighth.

It was a fascinating sight to watch the drivers start up their cold motors and get away in the shortest possible time. Bruce-Brown rushed at his car in well-reasoned fury, but although there was a determined rage in all his actions there was never a false movement. After a few strokes on the pressure pump the big motor spluttered, the mechanic leaped on behind, and the car ran a few yards ahead to the pits, where, with the motor still running to warm it up and save time, tyres and petrol were taken. In an incredibly short space of time it was off, throwing up a cloud of water.[63]

The race was decided when Bruce-Brown's Fiat suffered a fuel pipe fracture – one report suggests he'd hit a dog – and to get back to the pits he had to borrow fuel. He was disqualified.

Wagner tracked Boillot and, on lap 18 of the 20, went past him near the small town of Londinieres. Boillot was stationary and trying, using a tyre lever, to repair the gearbox and other damage caused by a stone. When he had done that he had only second and fourth gears, and kept the Peugeot in fourth wherever possible because changing down was so difficult. He was good enough to maintain speed in spite of that and although Wagner came in first, on the time stagger Boillot won.

The pride of the French motor industry had been restored and the future of Grand Prix racing was safe.

Bruce-Brown was killed three months later, practising for the American Grand Prix at Milwaukee.

In 1913, the race went to its third staging post outside Amiens, a substantial town 90 miles north of Paris. It was in July again, so Goux came to it having won the Indianapolis 500 in May with a Peugeot – regarded as a tremendous feat because no European had won it before and, at pit stops during his 6 hours and 35 minutes of driving, he drank the equivalent of six bottles of Champagne.

The Amiens circuit formed the by-now traditional triangle with a long, straight outward side, a 90° turn to a much shorter second side, twisting right again in the village of Moreuil and then following curves and corners all the way back on the third side. There would be 29 laps of 19.6 miles, giving a race distance of 579 miles.

The rules had been changed to 800kg minimum weight, 1,100kg maximum and a 14mpg fuel consumption limit (20 litres per 100km). This effectively ruled out the big, heavy cars which had dominated the Grands Prix so far, but in any case, 'new companies were now building special cars for racing, and Peugeot remained in the ascendant.'[64]

Of the big manufactures, Mercedes and Fiat didn't enter. Goux and Boillot had Peugeots, Nazzaro an Itala, Adam Opel entered a single car but Sunbeam fielded four – Gustave Caillois, Resta, Jean Chassagne and Kenelm Lee Guinness, an Irishman of the brewing family with a wicked sense of humour. He was known as Bill.[65] Chassagne was known as 'Chass' and would become a leading European driver. 'Usually his attire is a model of neatness. He wears white kid gloves, and nothing can perturb him. He never makes a fuss, but if any expected or unexpected assistance can be given, he gives it.'[66]

There had been some testing on the circuit but it was opened to the public in May and the Itala team, who had come with one racing car, had to learn it in a tourer. They then travelled to Brooklands and practised there before returning to France and the old circuit at Dieppe. Early one morning Bigio, a company executive, went out with a mechanic for a run, and crashed. Both men died. Soon after, leading driver Paul Zuccarelli[67] was trying his Peugeot on a long straight. A farm kart emerged from a side turning and he hit it, killing himself.

Rationalising danger is always the hardest part of motorsport, and it is no easier when you're trying to recapture the mentality of eras long gone. It does seem that there is a constant all the way through: men prepared to measure their desires against the possible consequences. In that sense, Paul Zuccarelli was just like Jim Clark or Ayrton Senna although Zuccarelli *had* to know he was doing something very, very dangerous and with no safeguards. Too many have died, as we have seen, for him not to know – yet, until the *1960s,* they all accepted either no safeguards, or inadequate safeguards.

The Motor indulged in whimsy when it reported that the Sunbeam team were lodged in an old chateau near Moreuil which 'has a superb collection of ghosts'. One of the team said they 'disturb him in the early morning, and he dislikes being called early. Resta finds them distinctly companionable.' Caillois 'declares that the ghosts were guaranteed in the contract, and if they are not supplied before the day of the race he will protest.' The ladies were 'somewhat divided' – one thought she could face a French ghost, another that 'frankly she will not try.' *The Motor* added: 'It is worth noting that when night falls and the long, hollow corridors are plunged in obscurity and the big dining hall, with its oak ceiling bedecked with the fleur-de-lys, is dimly illuminated by candles, no proposal is ever made to wander far afield...'

At the weigh-in only the Itala cars were over the weight limit, and they made it by shedding parts.

'Who will win?' the local paper, *Le Progrès de la Somme,* wondered. 'The Italas have engines without exhaust valves. "That doesn't mean anything for the race!" a driver told me yesterday. One of the Italas is driven by Nazzaro, the famous Italian who is never very far from winning.'

Peugeot? The writer thought Boillot 'a bit fat, a bit heavy, certainly still affected by the loss of his friend Zuccarelli' and found Goux 'dry, agile, calm, marvellously fit.'

The start, due at 5am, had to be delayed by half an hour for fog. 'It was impossible to see a person in the field behind the tyre pits on the opposite side of the track, while the yellow advertising balloons presented mere dim outlines in the sky.'[68]

This did not deter an enormous crowd from coming and 'for miles down the fast stretch, the human road lining was continuous, the greater proportion of the crowd being of the poorer classes.' The race finally began when Caillios was sent off at 5.31, but the first lap was slow because of the fog and cold. Boillot led it. One car...

> stalled his motor on the first hill. The mechanic tired himself until he was no longer able to crank the engine, and the only means of getting away was by putting it in reverse gear and allowing the car to run backwards on the hill.[69]

The driver of an Itala lost control at the hairpin near the grandstands and his car slithered into the banking, flipping on to its side. Driver and mechanic managed to right it then the driver locked arms round the mechanic to hold him rigid while he cranked the engine and they set off again to loud applause. They had a damaged steering column, but wouldn't be deterred by anything so trivial.

As the fog cleared speeds increased. Near half distance, Albert Guyot (Delage), who had been given pit the instruction *attack,* was past Goux, Boillot running third. On lap 17 however Boillot went past the pits in the lead, Goux behind him – Guyot came in a long time after. He'd had to change two tyres out on the circuit and then a third blew.

> The mechanic [only referred to as Semos], in a desire to save time, vaulted out of the car before it had sufficiently slowed down. Instead of travelling at 15mph as the mechanic supposed, Guyot declared later that he must at the moment have been running at 30. The mechanic was knocked down, the car passing over him. No bones were broken, but he suffered flesh wounds, was injured in the head, and fainted with pain. It was necessary to wait a few minutes until the man regained consciousness, lift him into the car and drive round at a reduced speed to avoid shaking him. To have returned without the mechanic would have entailed disqualification.[70]

Guinness crashed on lap 15 when a front tyre on his Sunbeam let go at a village. He fought to keep control of the car but it struck the protective pailings on a bridge over a little river. The car flipped, hurling a spectator into the water. Guinness and his mechanic were thrown into the water, too, and suffered minor injuries, but the spectator was dead.

Boillot won it from Goux, giving Peugeot first and second places. Boillot drove the Peugeot into the winner's enclosure, a narrow path across grass between twin rows of wooden staves. He and his mechanic got off and posed for a photograph: Boillot round faced – almost cherubic – but that face was marked by grime. He wore leather boots and a stout jacket. His right hand was black, perhaps more grime, perhaps oil. The mechanic, stocky, swarthy and slightly shorter than Boillot, wore a leather jerkin which seems to have been completely coated by oil, and so had his face, and so had his hands. He wore a beret, his goggles hoisted up to rest on it. Both men were grinning, but they were tired grins. They had been in the car for 7 hours 53 minutes and 56.8 seconds, a margin of some 2½ minutes over Goux.

Not all the arrangements during the race had evidently proved satisfactory:

A car would come in to change a tyre, take in some oil or what not, and the mechanic or driver would ask for a drink. A couple of glasses of wine, beer or mineral water would be poured out and placed on the edge of the track. Driver and mechanic having completed their separate tasks, the former would spring into his seat, the latter would jump to the starting handle, both having entirely forgotten their desire for a drink, whilst the members of the pit staff who had filled the glasses would make no attempt to remind them, but, as the car moved off, would calmly step down and perhaps give the drinks to the pit attendants, or stand them on one side – to gather a surface of dust – for the next time round.[71]

In October, Jenatzy – who hadn't raced in Grands Prix since 1908 – was out with a party hunting wild boar in the wooded Ardennes. At nightfall, he left his hiding place, but the hunt wasn't over and, by a hideous irony, the friend who had invited him to the hunt mistook him for a boar and shot him. They carried him to his Mercedes and he died in it a few moments later.[72]

The 1914 American Grand Prix, in February, didn't attract the Europeans, although a Mercedes came fourth. The Indianapolis 500 at the end of May did. René Thomas, who had driven at Dieppe in 1912 and Amiens in 1913, won it in a Delage, Duray (Peugeot) second, Guyot (Delage) third, Goux (Peugeot) fourth. Boillot set a new track record in qualifying: 99.6mph in his Peugeot. Europeans wouldn't do anything like this again until 1966, when Graham Hill won from Jim Clark; Jackie Stewart sixth – Stewart had seemed certain to win but his car suffered an oil leak.

On 24 June 1914, a Briton called L. G. 'Cupid' Hornsted set a new World Land Speed Record at Brooklands of 124.0mph. Although considerably slower than the 1911 Daytona record this was the first 'two-way' run – a flying mile, turn, a flying mile back – and as such recognised by the governing body the *FIA*,[73] which had recently been formed.

Four days later Archduke Franz Ferdinand of Austria was assassinated in the Serbian town of Sarajevo, and it set in train the lock-step of events culminating in the First World War. One British newspaper spoke of a 'clap of thunder' over Europe.

This was the atmosphere surrounding the French Grand Prix at Lyon – the fourth staging post – the following Saturday. It produced a great race, some say *the* great race. Perhaps that was because the shadowland of war was moving across the landscape, perhaps it was because all the leading drivers and makes were there, including three Vauxhalls – de

Palma had one – while mighty Fiat returned and the entry of 37 *was* motor racing; perhaps it was because, at its heart, Peugeot was challenging Mercedes: France against Germany.

An estimated 300,000 came to see. They had to be spread round the circuit which remained triangular with a long, straight backbone, where in the fields, workmen would watch, some standing beside an old cart. A lot of twisting turns formed the rest of the circuit, including a U-shaped turn where cars slithered gloriously and the crowd thronged the hillocks all around it. There was a section like a ledge, with a rockface to one side and, beyond a stone parapet, a drop to the other. There was a tight uphill right-hander and, rounding it, the cars exhaled great, sudden, elongated plumes from their exhaust pipes. There was a narrow section through a town, under a temporary wooden bridge, and the crowds were dense everywhere you looked. Beyond the temporary bridge stood a railway viaduct and during the race trains would slip across it while beneath them the beasts roared and smoked.

Although the race had moved to central France for the first time, the roads were better than the previous circuits and a local grant improved them further, but it still had a corner called *le piege de la mort* – the trap of death. The engine capacity had been set at 4,500cc while the maximum weight was held at 1,100kg.

Initially, there wasn't any practice, although reports suggest some of the French drivers had covered some of the circuit in their racing cars. Then local authorities relented slightly and at 48 hours notice allowed the roads to be closed for two 90-minute practice periods. [...] The Indianapolis drivers [...] got back to France just in time to take advantage of these, many foreign drivers could not for one reason or another, and, in the eyes of some sections of the French press, officials inevitably "rested under the unpleasant odour of favouritism."'[74] One estimate suggests that half or more of the entrants hadn't been able to practice at all.

The local paper, *Le Progres,* caught the intoxication of the start:

> The drivers are in place, several wearing gaudy headgear but the most elegant are the Pic-Pic[75] whose hats and jerseys are well matched with the colours of the car. To facilitate the start, which is to be given simultaneously to cars in pairs, a long line had been whitewashed in the middle of the track [so the cars didn't run into each other]...Little by little the track was evacuated; the service personnel stand immobile, almost incrusted against their refuelling equipment. It is 8 o'clock. The course is entirely cleared and, ranged into two columns, odd numbers to the right,

even numbers to the left, the cars wait for the signal. Brusquely the starter lowers his flag and in a tremendous roar of engines, in a cloud of impenetrable smoke from the exhaust pipes, the competitors start, fly off and disappear round the corner.

This sense of anticipation and action was heightened because, going off in pairs at 30-second intervals, the 37 were all away by 8.10am. A little-known Mercedes driver, Max Sailer, made a tremendous start from the sixth 'row' and accelerated clean away from the Fiat paired with him.

Sailer led on elapsed time completing the opening lap – Boillot led 'on the road' – and by lap three Sailer had pulled a minute and a half away. Sailer was forcing the Mercedes hard – he set a new fastest lap on lap four – while the other four Mercedes drivers, including Lautenschlager, held back, watching and waiting. Or did they? 'There was, apparently, a good deal of rivalry between the veteran Lautenschlager and the dashing Sailer.'[76] At the end of lap five:

Sailer	1h 43m 16s
Boillot	1h 46m 00s
Duray	1h 46m 51s
Lautenschlager	1h 46m 57s

Soon after this a connecting rod in Sailer's engine failed so that into lap six Boillot led but Lautenschlager was up to second, a minute behind. Lautenschlager made his scheduled pit stop and resumed, stalking his distant prey. Boillot was 'flogging' his Peugeot, cornering as fast as he could – or dared – and forcing it to its maximum on the 'long switchback straight composing the third leg of the triangle.'[77]

At 15 laps, Lautenschlager was 2 minutes 28 seconds behind but, seeming to be able to pace himself, cut that by 23 seconds on lap 16, cut it further on lap 17. Boillot was driving like a man possessed, but the car had nothing more to give him. Lautenschlager led on the stagger (he'd started 5½ minutes after Boillot) by 33 seconds at the end of lap 18. As they crossed the line to begin the last lap Lautenschlager led by one minute and seven seconds.

The Peugeot sounded as if it was running on three cylinders. At the *virage de la Madelaine* (Madelaine Corner) a valve broke and Boillot stopped. 'In a moment which must have been of utter despair, in what was to be his last heroic race, he saw [because of the stagger] Christian Lautenschlager for the first time as the Mercedes swept past.'[78]

People asked what could have happened to Boillot: people murmured improbable noises like these – he'd gone into the canal at Givors, he'd killed himself at the *virage de la Madelaine*, he'd hit a barrier.[79]

As Lautenschlager crossed the line, the crowd were silent, but this wasn't like the bitterness of Dieppe in 1908. They were not anti-German, not showing disrespect, they were stunned, and further stunned when Louis Wagner's Mercedes came in second, Otto Salzer's Mercedes third. Goux brought his Peugeot in fourth – scant consolation, if any.

Three weeks later, Austria issued an ultimatum to Serbia. Within a week, Germany had declared war on Russia and France, and invaded Belgium; Britain had declared war on Germany. The unremitting slaughter would last until November 1918 and, although nobody knows exactly how many men died, 10,000,000 seems likely. It remains beyond imagining.

Some say as the vast crowd ebbed away from the circuit outside Lyon that the heroic days were over. The pioneering days certainly were and, in that sense, an era closed forever just before the guns played their deadly music across Europe.

It had been exactly 20 years since the Paris–Rouen reliability trial. The first World Land Speed Record, four years after that, was 39mph. Now, in 1914, it stood at 124mph. The fastest lap in the Le Mans Grand Prix averaged 73mph and although comparisons are elusive – regulations, different circuits – the fastest at Lyon, 4mph slower.

This wouldn't happen again.

And the end of heroic days? No, no. They were just beginning.

Notes

1. Daimler and Benz did not merge until 1926. 'The essential difference between the two great early pioneers was that Daimler was a visionary who dreamed of his engines serving mankind, while Benz only ever wanted to be a car-maker.' (*The Dawn of Motoring*, Mercedes-Benz).
2. James Watt, born in 1736, was trained as an instrument-maker. In 1763 he was sent a steam engine to repair and while he was doing that he 'discovered how he could make the engine more efficient. Watt worked on the idea for several months and eventually produced a steam engine that cooled the used steam in a condenser, separate from the main cylinder.' http://www.spartacus.schoolnet.co.uk/Scwatt.htm
3. The Michelin brothers André and Édouard were the first to use demountable pneumatic tyres on motor cars (1891). Michelin also

promoted motoring, putting milestones on French roads, producing road maps and, in 1900, a *Red Guide* with restaurant ratings.

4. *A Record of Grand Prix and Voiturette Racing, Volume 1,* Paul Sheldon.
5. *Great Racing Drivers,* edited by David Hodges.
6. *Enzo Ferrari,* Brock Yates.
7. *The Land Speed Record,* Peter J. R. Holthusen.
8. See http://www.8w.forix.com/gbt03.html
9. *The History of Motor Racing,* William Boddy.
10. René Panhard and Émile Levassor were French pioneers of the internal combustion engine, and built their own in 1876. They built their first car in 1890 with the engine under licence from Daimler. In 1891, they 'produced their second model and this vehicle is generally reckoned to be the first to establish the architecture of the modern motor car – front-mounted engine, clutch mounted between the engine and gearbox and driven rear axle.' The firm was bought by Citroën and stopped car manufacture in 1967. http://www.citroen.mb.ca/citroenet/html/p/panhard1.htm
11. Snoek-Bolide, a 10.6-litre four-cylinder Belgian car (bolide means racing car).
12. *The French Grand Prix,* David Hodges.
13. *The Motor,* 1906.
14. Ibid.
15. Before motor cars, even towns must have been quiet, or rather the sounds – people talking, shouting, laughing, church bells, the hum of markets, the lowing of cattle at auction, the barking of dogs – the same that had echoed down the centuries. The car did not immediately drown all this. As Brock Yates points out (in *Enzo Ferrari, The Man and The Machine)* there were no more than 27 private cars in Modena in 1903. Conversely, there's a photograph of Londinières' main street on race day 1908 (the circuit by-passed the town) and it is choked by cars, many parked neatly side-by-side outside the local hotel. I don't want to read too much into any of this – pedestrians are wandering the street, presumably in the way they did with horse-drawn carts and carriages – but high streets would not be reclaimed until the traffic-free zones of our own time.
16. Cagno was also a flying enthusiast, and he designed and tested aircraft, founding Italy's first flying school in Pordenone. He volunteered to fight in the war in Libya, and built the first bomber aircraft.
17. *The Motor.*
18. Ibid.
19. *Le Figaro.*
20. Ibid.
21. Ibid.

22. Lorraine-Dietrich made railway locomotives in Alsace-Lorraine, and then began to build cars under licence. Bugatti was one of their engineers. They changed their name to Lorraine-Deitrich in 1908 and specialised in big, heavy cars.

23. The cars were numbered by teams for ease of recognition rather than where they started. For example, at Lorraine-Dietrich, Gabriel had 1A, Rougier 1B, Arthur Duray 1C

24. Gabriel died in 1943 during a British night bombing raid on Paris. There is a memorial to him in the Museum of the Automobile at Le Mans.

25. Szisz became Louis Renault's riding mechanic, test driver and finally driver. He has been described as an unflustered and accomplished driver, with a wonderful handlebar moustache and a twinkle in his eye. He died in Hungary in 1970, at 97. See http://www.katylon.com/harisauto/x_archive/formula1/szisz/1stgp.htm

26. Quoted in *Speed on Sand* by William Tuthill (Ormand Beach Historic Trust, Florida, 1978).

27. *The French Grand Prix*, Hodges, op. cit.

28. Old race reports invariably describe a driver as 'on' a car rather than 'in' it. This is clearly because in the early days the driver did sit on it, high up.

29. *Great Racing Drivers*, Hodges, op. cit.

30. *The Motor.*

31. Ibid.

32. The side piece of a chassis, which joins it to the front springs.

33. *The Motor.*

34. *The French Grand Prix*, Hodges, op. cit.

35. *Figaro* said there were two horses 'hauling' the cars one by one. The reason for using the horse (or horses) was, presumably, to adhere strictly to the rule that driver and mechanic must not touch their car until it was on the line ready to re-start. Then 'the driver and his mechanic get on board; two aides start the engine. Will it go, will it not go? Agitation, anxiety. It goes. Hurrah!' (*Le Figaro*).

36. *The Motor.*

37. *Le Figaro.*

38. Ibid.

39. *The Motor.*

40. Ibid.

41. For a full portrait of Louis Renault see under Rhodes, Anthony in the Bibliography.

42. Sheldon, op. cit. On the matter of motor racing's international character you can see the logical conclusion in the early 2000s: Michael Schumacher of Germany driving for the iconic Italian team Ferrari under a French

director, Jean Todt, and a British race tactician, Ross Brawn, with a South African, Rory Byrne, designing the car and an Italian, Paolo Martinelli, designing the engine.

43. A London car manufacturer between 1907 and 1910.

44. *The French Grand Prix,* Hodges, op. cit.

45. *La Vigie de Dieppe.*

46. For the technical the cylinder bore was limited to 155mm for four-cylinder engines, 127mm for six cylinders.

47. Itala was a Turin-based company, formed in 1904 to build sporty cars with large engines. In 1907 an Itala won the Paris–Peking race. The company ceased production in 1934.

48. Brooklands was a banked track near London, holding race meetings from 1907 to 1939. It was a place where British society met, as they did at The Derby, the Henley Rowing Regatta and Lord's cricket ground.

49. *Grand Prix Racing 1906–1914,* Taso Mathieson.

50. This has been described as the 'little brother' to the Grands Prix racing and compared to the modern Formula 3000 or Indy light series. The cars had wonderful names – for example, in the 1906 race at Rambouillet you'd find (among others) a Civelli de Bosch, Sizaire-Naudin, Auto-Stand, Lion-Peugeot and a car driven by Henri Ballileau, built by Ballileau and called a Ballileau. Apart from that, presumably, Monsieur Ballileau had nothing to do with it at all…

51. *The French Grand Prix,* Hodges, op. cit.

52. *The Motor.*

53. Ibid.

54. Ibid.

55. *Great Racing Drivers,* Hodges, op. cit.

56. Boillot joined the (new) French Air Force when the First World War began and was killed in 1916 in a dogfight over Verdun. Several French streets and at least one school are named after him.

57. *Great Racing Drivers,* Hodges, op. cit.

58. At 18, Bruce-Brown bluffed his way into motor racing at Daytona in 1908. He was of wealthy stock but started humbly. He worked for FIAT and was evidently known as the millionaire mechanic. To try to stop him racing his mother threatened legal action against race organisers. It didn't work.

59. *Great Racing Drivers,* Hodges, op. cit.

60. *The French Grand Prix,* Hodges op. cit.

61. *The Motor.*

62. Ibid.

63. Ibid.

64. Boddy, op. cit.

65. Guinness brothers Algernon and Kenelm Lee scored international success in motor racing. Algernon, the older, did 117.7mph over a flying kilometre at the 1906 Ostend Speed Trials. He won notable races, too. Kenelm Lee was the first Irishman to 'win a major international motor race' when he won the 1914 TT on the Isle of Man. There's an example of Kenelm's sense of humour later in the book. (Adapted from *The Irish Times* website, 26 March 2003.)

66. *Full Throttle,* Tim Birkin.

67. Boillot's team was commissioned to develop a Grand Prix car for Peugeot, and they hired, among others, Zuccarelli. The result? The first modern racing engine. See http://www.grandprix.com/ft/ftjs006.html

68. *The Motor.*

69. Ibid.

70. Ibid.

71. Ibid.

72. *Great Racing Drivers,* Hodges, op. cit.

73. The original governing body was called *l'Association Internationale des Automobile Clubs Reconnus,* which in 1946 became the *Fédération Internationale de l'Automobile (FIA).*

74. *The French Grand Prix,* Hodges, op. cit.

75. Two wealthy Geneva sportsmen, Charles and Frederic Dufaux, wanted to build racing cars. For engines they went to Piccard & Pictet, who had a workshop. This may have inspired Lucien Pictet to make cars himself.

76. Mathieson, op. cit.

77. *The French Grand Prix,* Hodges, op. cit.

78. Ibid.

79. *Le Progres, Lyon.*

Chapter 2

THE CHAPS

When the First World War ended at 11am on the eleventh day of the eleventh month – November 1918 – the political map of Europe had become unrecognisable: the Bolsheviks poised to seize Mother Russia, the Austro-Hungarian empire dismembered, Germany humiliated and, for the first time, decisive military action had been undertaken by the United States on the European mainland.

None of this prevented ordinary folk from resuming those activities which pleased them and so there was continuity, however fractured. Many motor racing people had served, including Tazio Nuvolari, Enzo Ferrari and Antonio Ascari.

Motor racing continued in the United States until they entered the war in April 1917 and resumed there without delay, at the Indianapolis 500 in 1919 where de Palma finished sixth and at Daytona where, driving a Packard, he pushed the World Land Speed Record to 149mph. The United States and Europe were now much closer then than they ever would be again, and at Indianapolis 'Howdy' Wilcox, a studious-looking American, won in a Peugeot. René Thomas and Guyot were in cars manufactured by Édouard Ballot.[1]

In 1919, the average wage in Britain was £2 10s and a Model T Ford cost £170. Saving all his money, the Briton would have had to save for 1 year 28 weeks to buy one. (1910, £220 – 2 years 42 weeks).

The Land Speed Record ran like a backdrop down the years to come and it would be broken a further 28 times before the shadowlands of war moved across the landscape again. Here were new heroes, new heroism, and they interweaved in a way unthinkable now: of the seven Britons who held the record from 1919 to 1939 six also drove in Grands Prix; Kenelm Guinness, Malcolm Campbell, J. G. Parry Thomas, Ernest Eldridge, the elegant Sir Henry O'Neal de Hane Segrave, and Captain George Eyston. Money means freedom to do what you want and, like Gordon Bennett, they did.

Segrave came from an old Leicestershire family, although his mother was American and his father now lived in Ireland. He went to Eton but had left when war broke out and, at 18, became an infantry officer, serving in the trenches until 1915. He joined the Royal Flying Corps, 'was shot down by anti-aircraft fire, broke an ankle, and had to have several silver plates in his foot to be able to walk again. Invalided out of active service, he joined the executive side of the Air Ministry, went to the United States as attaché to an aviation mission.'[2] He'd come to racing through Bill Bruce-Brown, brother of David. They 'talked racing', Segrave did a little on Long Island then in England, headed for the Sunbeam-Talbot team.

Interesting. Years before, Enzo Ferrari gazed at a photograph of de Palma and vowed to become a racer himself. During the war he'd been called up by the Italian Army and given the job of putting shoes on mules for a mountain regiment. He fell ill, needed two operations and after discharge went to Turin to get into the motoring industry.

> He almost starved for lack of work until he found a job as a delivery driver. When the war ended, it emerged that Italy was suffering from a desperate shortage of transport vehicles: as a stopgap, Lancia military lorries were being turned into vans and buses, and it was Ferrari's job to drive the chassis from the Lancia plant to the workshops where the conversions were carried out.[3]

In 1919, he frequented 'the network of bars and restaurants along the Corse Vittorio Emanuele II where racing champion Felice Nazzaro and the equally prominent driver Pietro Bordino[4] ate and drank. The Bar del Nord, near the immense Porto Nuova railway station, was a centre of racing gossip and deal making.'[5] On one of his deliveries Ferrari met a 'brash, moustachioed former bicycle racer' – Ugo Sivocci, now the chief test driver for a car factory. He lived, Ferrari remembered, where there had once been a crime of passion.

Ferrari did a hill climb in October, in a car called a CMN which resembled a barrel on wire wheels with a seat, an enormous steering column and an equally enormous steering wheel which Ferrari, goggles perched on his forehead, sumo-wrestled. Even at 21, Ferrari had a distinctive demeanour, a Roman nose and the crowd, spread thin up the hillside and dressed decorously in their coats and hats, their collars and ties, all saw the Roman nose as the barrel bored its path in front of them climbing and climbing. There was fog, there was rain and 31-year-old Ascari won it.

Ferrari also drove in the Targa Florio. On the way down, wolves chased Ferrari and Sivocci's car in the mountains, but Ferrari held them off with an old Army revolver.

He retired on the third lap of the race although 12 others had already done that, including Ascari, whose Fiat plunged down a ravine and wasn't found for a long time.

A great passion held Ascari. His career began modestly in 1911 and during the war he worked on aeroplanes. When the war ended the passion which had been smouldering erupted in a volcanic way. He'd watched a race at Cremona which leading driver Giuseppe Campari won and immediately afterwards congratulated him.

Ascari: 'I can drive like that!'

Campari: 'maybe...'

Ascari established an agency selling cars made by the *Società Anonima Lombarda Fabbrici Automobili*, ALFA. He had a little, cherubic son, Alberto, and it seems certain that Alberto inherited the passion in full measure.

De Palma finished sixth in the 1920 Indianapolis 500, a place behind Jimmy Murphy in a Duesenberg. Murphy had been orphaned by the earthquake at San Francisco in 1906 and came into racing as a mechanic before driving. He crashed in his first race, but the Duesenberg brothers were impressed enough to offer him a car for a Californian race. He won.

Fred and August Duesenberg taught themselves engineering,[6] emigrated to the United States from Germany in 1885 and began building engines. They developed a straight eight engine[7] and now it delivered enough power for a one-eyed driver, Tommy Milton, to push the Land Speed Record to 156mph.

In Italy, Ferrari finished second in a swamp of a Targa Florio – rain fell for a week making the mudbath. Campari in an Alfa Romeo led the first lap but dropped out and Ferrari, driving a sports model Alfa Romeo, kept going for more than eight and a half hours. At the end, he, his mechanic and the car were completely caked in mud. A photographer advanced and Ferrari turned his head for the picture to be taken. He was bare-headed, his hair a dark thicket with one little curl hanging down on to his forehead. He looked severe in the composed Victorian way when confronted by a camera, and he would remain so all his life.

Campari liked good food and weighed nearly 16 stone (220lb). He was also an opera singer with a baritone voice, and sang arias to other drivers. Known as *Il Negher*, The Dark One, because of his swarthy complexion, he married a famous singer.[8]

Grand Prix racing came back to where it had begun, or rather nearby, and not much had changed. The French Grand Prix of 1921 become an ordinary story of several immigrants, an orphan, national pride, mild chaos, hiding behind bushes, elements of mystery, a shocking circuit, danger, and the heroes who hadn't disappeared.

The race, at Le Mans although not the 1906 circuit, provided yet another matrix. At 10.7 miles it would form, later, the basic contour of the 24-hour sports car race and although extensively re-directed remains like that today. In 1921, apart from round the pits, the surface – strewn with stones and small rocks – resembled a lunar landscape. An American writer said it was more like a pebble beach and added: 'It seems likely that no race before or since has been run on such a surface.'[9] The 30 laps (321 miles) stretched like an eternity.

Entries arrived from Britain and Italy but no Germans were welcome and wouldn't be for years. Ballot fielded four cars, for de Palma – who had driven one at Indianapolis – Chassagne, Wagner and Goux. These were old hands from pre-war days. Duesenberg entered late, and paid double because of that. They fielded four cars, for Guyot, Louis Inghibert – a wealthy, nattily-dressed sportsman – Boyer and Murphy. Inghibert, however, would be hurt in practice and his place taken by André Dubonnet, another nattily-*coiffured* sportsman, playboy and heir to the aperitif fortune bearing his name. Playboy? He'd also served in the artillery during the war before joining the French air force where he earned a citation for bravery.

The French didn't take the Duesenberg invasion particularly seriously because the cars were Indianapolis specialists with 'inadequate stopping power and three-speed gear-boxes' and, anyway, they hadn't even won Indianapolis. They competed in America 'with rear wheel brakes only, but for this race they were fitted with powerful hydraulic four-wheel brakes.' This was to be decisive.[10]

De Palma embarked for France the day after Indianapolis, leaving his nephew Peter de Paolo (the riding mechanic) and a couple of others to accompany the Ballot on a 'glorified tub' of a boat. When Peter arrived in Paris he found de Palma living in splendour at the Crillon Hotel, but he was directed to a grimy little place opposite a railway station. When Monsieur Ballot discovered guests in such unsatisfactory accommodation he felt the honour of France at stake and 'went wild in typical French fashion'.[11] Ballot was paying, so it couldn't have mattered to de Palma either way, but as Peter remembered: 'It conflicted with his ideas of discipline to have his mechanics stay at a place that offered too much luxury.'

They worked on the cars for a couple of weeks in Paris and decamped to the village of Ecommoy south of Le Mans, where they tuned them in an old barn they had made into a temporary workshop.

The team had a spare car they called 'the mule' – in modern Grand Prix racing, the French still call a spare car *un mulet* – and the drivers used it to learn the course during official practice at 5.0 and 6.0 in the morning when the roads were closed to ordinary traffic. This meant 'the Grand Prix entrants could be reasonably sure that the right of way would not be challenged by bands of sheep, parades of strutting geese, loads of hay and high-wheeled carts piled with produce.'

Fiat had labour problems at their factory, their car was delayed and they withdrew. The Sunbeam-Talbot-Darracq entry should have compensated for that with seven cars. However... 'many attempts have been made to unravel the mysteries of this conglomerate as, at the time, various names were used quite indiscriminately.'[12] The seven were described as two Talbots, two Sunbeams and three Talbot-Darracqs although they were 'all identical under their mildly old-fashioned skins, none of them remotely ready to race with ten days to go.'[13] Louis Coatalen, the great Sunbeam engineer who appreciated the importance of racing, surveyed the state of play and withdrew all seven entries. The drivers were unhappy about that and eventually all but two cars were re-entered.

This meant Segrave got the drive he cherished so much. He'd badgered Coatalen mercilessly but he had 'objected, time after time, that although I seemed to be able to drive a car fairly reasonably on the track I was woefully lacking in road experience and he made no bones about telling me that he did not believe I should be any good in a road race.'[14]

Finally Coatalen relented and offered an incentive. If Segrave finished within a time limit he might join the team on probation.

There were, Segrave judged, no 'really difficult corners... and the course was everywhere reasonably wide. On the other hand, the people responsible for it had evidently no ideas whatever of the wear and tear which a racing car can impose upon a road. After a few circuits [laps], the road, especially at the corners, was cut up in a shocking manner, and the number of loose stones was incredible.'[15]

The Duesenberg team walked the whole circuit making notes of the difficult parts and a photograph survives of them doing this. They stand in shadows beside a corner, tree trunks like sentinels behind them, and one man is clearly writing. The road in front of them does look like a pebble beach.

During practice, a group of the Ballot people were at the right-hander at Mulsanne village and heard a racing car approaching. They couldn't see which one because of a hump in the road but, by the engine noise, they knew it was coming fast and might be Murphy or one of the other immaculate white Duesenbergs, sensuously slender and streamlined, their chassis frames and numbers blue, the Stars and Stripes on their long graceful tails. They were wrong. When it crested the hump they saw their own 'mule' being driven by the reserve, Giulio Foresti, and he was travelling far too fast to take the corner.

De Palma: 'He'll never make it!'

Monsieur Ballot: 'He's crazy!'

Foresti went clean past the corner, went straight into Mulsanne village, went right through that and continued to Ecommoy. It was breakfast time.

Murphy crashed heavily during practice taking Inghibert round showing him where he could go faster. It may have been a loose horse or it may have been a brake seized. The car went through an earthen bank towards trees and seems to have somersaulted several times. Inghibert was thrown out, breaking three ribs and suffering concussion. Murphy had only bruising to his ribs. Both were taken to hospital. Dubonnet, due to drive one of the withdrawn Sunbeams, paid a considerable sum to replace him.

Goux was a passenger in a Delage which swerved into a ditch to avoid a dog cart but he, like Murphy, was able to start the race.

Ralph de Palma proved to be, according to nephew Peter, consistently faster than the other Ballot drivers despite the fact that, at the factory, his engine had been switched to make him the slowest. Monsieur Ballot couldn't understand this and neither could the other drivers – de Palma had moved the gear lever to the middle of the car so that, on command, young Peter as riding mechanic could change the gears and Ralph's hands didn't need to leave the steering wheel, an important time-saving device on stony tracks.

How Monsieur Ballot didn't notice this is not at all clear, but during final practice, he hid behind a bush to see what was going on. He saw. He howled in anguish. He said this won't do at all. He shouted that the driver had to change gear – the driver! The gear lever has to go back where it belongs!

Ah, thought Peter, *he wants a French driver to win…*

De Palma seemed dispirited by Ballot's lack of sportsmanship.

As the mechanics worked, the 'town of Le Mans slept not at all […] The sound of open exhausts rattled in the streets; big cars, little cars with bright lights and cars without any lights at all rushed merrily to and fro. In the cafés the people discussed the chances of the teams as they ate a meal that might have been anything between supper and breakfast. They spoke of the wonderful Duesenberg brakes, how the Ballots in their secret camp at Ecommoy had even better cars than ever for the event.'[16]

At that secret camp, the work on the gear lever finished at dawn and the mechanics climbed into the barn's loft to get whatever sleep they could.

Count Louis Zborowski, wealthy son of a Polish count and an American mother, suffered no such problems. He lived in splendour in a large country house near Canterbury 'where, with his engineer Captain Clive Gallop, he built three aero-engined cars, all called *Chitty Bang Bang*.'[17] He'd originally been invited to drive a Sunbeam and was now hastily summoned. However he found his car had no spare parts and he wouldn't be able to drive even a single practice lap. He said he'd prefer to watch, and did. Money meant freedom.

Race morning dawned misty. The thirteen runners were paired to go at 30-second intervals and they lined up each pair side by side. A crowd stood in a grandstand opposite a bare field with advertising hoardings on tall, skeletal wooden supports. Teams prepared to change to the equivalent of rain tyres – studded – but the Duesenbergs didn't have any and the team scanned the sky anxiously. The first pair, de Palma one of them, went at 9am, Segrave and Murphy as the fourth pair, a minute and a half later: Segrave had Jules Moriceau as his mechanic ('few better have ever lived. He had coolness, knowledge, a wonderful pair of hands, and a very quick imagination') while Murphy, one report says, had risen from his hospital bed and, heavily bandaged, had been helped into his car. Murphy in fact was 'taped from, his armpits to the waist to try and stabilise his chest because of the bruised ribs.'[18] He sat at the wheel, a boyish, slightly severe face while his riding mechanic, Ernie Olson, looked sombre in collar and tie. They must have sensed that a great ordeal was at hand, especially for Murphy.

Soon enough the stony surface savaged tyres and one Sunbeam changed seven times, another driver nine and Segrave fourteen. Amidst that a startling fact emerged: speeds had *visibly* increased. You could hurl cars at the corners and correct them without going off, you could accelerate hard out of corners and if the back of the car wobbled you could correct that, if your rear wheels dug dirt as you skimmed the rim of the road you didn't take your foot off the accelerator.

On the opening lap Wagner's Ballot stopped to change plugs and, as de Palma went by, Wagner raised a bottle of Champagne with the motion of drinking their health. Clearly chaps would take a bottle along for the ride, although not perhaps drink the equivalent of six à *la* Goux, Indianapolis, vintage 1913. Whatever, when they opened the bottle it must have been shaken enough to blow the cork over Le Mans town and into orbit.

Despite his name Wagner was French and, according to Peter, wanted de Palma to 'beat the other Frenchmen, especially Chassagne.'

De Palma remained angry after Ballot's treatment. Knowing Ballot would be watching intently and listening to the engine noise as he passed the pits de Palma shut the engine to 'get Ballot's goat' – Ballot thinking it had failed. The point made, de Palma switched it on again.

Completing that opening lap de Palma and Boyer's Duesenberg led on time – both did 8m 16s – with Murphy third and Chassagne fourth. There was some jostling and hustling on lap two, Murphy and Boyer both on 16m 13s, Chassagne only six seconds behind and de Palma close to Chassagne.

Segrave, running tenth, found himself in a nightmare. 'Quite soon after the start one of the wheels picked up a stone and hurled it at the oil tank,' fracturing it so badly that Segrave faced immediate retirement but Moriceau 'seized a large lump of cotton waste [wool], pushed it into the hole in the oil tank and, taking a hammer, caulked the hole by beating in the sides of the tank on the cotton waste.'

On lap three, the whole tempo of the race rising, Murphy pulled clear of Boyer and led by 15 seconds. The Americans had fully adjusted to road racing already and were enjoying themselves. Chassagne attacked Boyer hard, drawing level with him and lap after lap they slogged it out. On lap seven, Murphy did 7m 44s and led Boyer by almost two minutes, Chassagne still attacking.

Segrave's nightmare went on:

When following Murphy along one of the short pieces of straight, [Murphy's] car picked up a big stone off the road and hurled it back like a bullet. It was as though the Duesenberg was a sentient being and had determined to put us out of the race. The stone struck my car with such force that it went clean through the wire mesh stone guard which formed a sort of rudimentary wind-screen, through the moulded steel scoop which was intended to protect our eyes from the wind, struck the steering wheel, severing the cord wound round it and then hit Moriceau on the head, knocking him practically unconscious and cutting his head badly.[19]

They kept going.

Pit work was becoming more professional. Ballot gave their drivers lap times and positions by holding up a big blackboard (the first pit board?). Duesenberg waved flags of differing colours and the drivers could glance at a key on their dashboards. By contrast, the Sunbeam pits looked disorganised.

Chassagne passed Boyer on the ninth lap and set off towards Murphy and the lead. Murphy, meanwhile, had caught de Palma and, just after the right-hander at Pontlieue, made his attack, Olson gesturing for de Palma to move aside.

Murphy pitted a lap later to change his front wheels and did that fast enough to keep the lead – but Chassagne was a lot closer and stirred the crowd a lap later by taking Murphy at Arnage. This was then little more than a dirt track through the trees, but is now a celebrated landmark of the 24-hour race. Chassagne built a 27-second lead but there behind him panted *all* the Duesenbergs. Boyer found a way past Murphy but it was Chassagne who held the crowd and every time he came past the pits they shouted their approval.

De Palma and young Peter were into their own nightmare. 'Suddenly,' Peter said, 'I noticed a leak in our fuel tank that was directly under our seats. As we hit a bump, the rear end smacked down on the axle and opened a seam in the tank. I first had trouble keeping up the air pressure in the tank then I felt petrol on the seat of my pants.' It started burning skin 'but I didn't say a word about it to uncle for fear he would stop me at the pits and call it a day.' Finally they made a routine stop but Peter was 'very careful not to turn my back and give him a chance to see my petrol-soaked clothes. A good deal of my body was blistered […] and I must have appeared a bit nervous because I couldn't stand still.'

At half distance, 15 laps:

Chassagne	2h 0m 17s
Boyer	2h 0m 57s
Murphy	2h 1m 26s
Guyot	2h 1m 59s
De Palma	2h 8m 02s
Dubonnet	2h 10m 39s

The day was getting hotter, the sun high up in a clear blue sky. Segrave ran ninth but around now something on the ignition failed. 'It was necessary for Moriceau and myself to devote many valuable minutes, to say nothing of a lot of blistered skin, in retiming the engine, a job which is certainly not most appropriately accomplished by the roadside,' he said.

Only one car retired, with an engine problem on lap five, until Chassagne went out after 17 laps. He had led by a minute but a badly split fuel tank forced him into the pits. Boyer followed when a connecting rod broke, crippling his Duesenberg.

The Sunbeam tyre situation became so critical that Coatalen 'was borrowing tyres from other teams, Pirellis from Ballot, Oldfields from Duesenberg.'[20]

Now Murphy led, and that became secure when Guyot, second at lap 28, pitted for fuel and water and the car wouldn't restart. The riding mechanic pushed so hard that, in the heat, he virtually collapsed and staggered away. He had extensive facial lacerations from the flying stones, too. Arthur Duray, who had driven in the 1906 race and was now spectating, came forward and replaced the mechanic. The regulations allowed this and Duray managed to start the engine. He and Guyot set off but the clutch slipped and they pitted again. They finished sixth.

De Palma was now up into second although he, too, had had trouble restarting after his final pit stop.

Murphy came down the long straight towards the finish, the crowd strung back behind fencing, and came hard. The smooth dirt surface beneath him bore the weals of the whole race: the rod-straight lines all the wheels from the thirteen cars had cut lap after lap. These lines lay in a tight pattern across the middle of the track. Murphy took his right hand off the wheel, and raised his arm high in triumph. He'd averaged 78.10mph. He was booed as he crossed the line, de Palma and Goux were cheered in their made-in-France Ballots. Segrave battled in last more than an hour after Murphy.

The jagged stones, churned and flung back with such ferocity, had injured virtually every driver and mechanic.

Murphy	4h 7m 11.4s
De Palma	4h 22m 10.6s
Goux	4h 28m 38.2s

Murphy and Olson came down victory lane, a dusty track, with Olson sitting on the back of the car holding the bouquets and French soldiers in their tin hats standing guarding nothing at all. Murphy and Olson posed with Augie Duesenberg sitting on what seems to be their pit counter, a canvas awning above, the bouquets on their laps. Murphy's face was smeared with dust so that the part of his forehead covered by his driving skull cap was a band of perfect white. He looked very, very tired.

An American would win the French Grand Prix again, but at Rouen, 41 years later.

Young Peter de Palma claimed that French chauvinism dominated the banquet, 'humiliating' Murphy. The first toast was to Goux and this 'was more than Jimmy and his manager, the famous old-time racing champion George Robertson, could stand.' Murphy 'put down his glass and walked out, and, entering a side-street café, said to the waiter *bring us some ham and eggs!*'

The first non-French Grand Prix in Europe was run six weeks later, at Brescia. The Italian Grand Prix obeyed the matrix, a triangular road circuit and, surely by coincidence, 10.7 miles in length.

Duesenberg returned to America; Sunbeam and Itala sent entries and withdrew them and so at Brescia the Italian dynasty was born and delivered humbly by three Ballots (de Palma, Chassagne, Goux) and three Fiats (Wagner, Bordino, Sivocci).

Two Fiats broke down, de Palma broke down and Goux won it from Chassagne. Éduard Ballot, in a dark jacket, stood in front of the winning car in the 'pits' – a basic working counter under crude wooden roofing – and acknowledged the applause of the crowd by politely raising his homburg hat. By now, de Palma's relationship with him had deteriorated further. De Palma had asked for modifications on his car, Ballot said no and after the race de Palma said *that's why I didn't win.*

A week later, also at Brescia, a small crowd watched a lesser race, delightfully styled the Grand Prix of Gentlemen – the name Grand Prix was freely used over the years, presumably to give more minor races status. Only nine cars entered and a wiry young man did not complete a lap because the oil pump on his car broke. It was only the fifth event he had competed in and, lacking money, from now on he would concentrate on racing motorbikes because they were cheaper.

Tazio Nuvolari had been called up at the start of the war and driven a military ambulance which he crashed, no doubt exploring its maximum. He had a narrow, slightly bird-like face and, bowing to the fashion of the day, a moustache thin as a pencil.

In November, Benito Mussolini, son of a blacksmith, declared himself *Il Duce* – the leader – of the Italian Fascist party which was winning seats in the Italian parliament. He liked power. He intended to have a great deal more of it, and if that took violence he would use violence. He intended to promote Italy when he had that power and his roving eye would settle upon motorsport as, literally, a valuable vehicle.

The two 1921 Grands Prix were run under a 3-litre formula but that was now replaced in Europe by 2 litres and meant European cars rarely raced in America and American cars rarely raced in Europe. In essence, the interweaving ended. Ballot, meanwhile, now abandoned their racing programme in favour of passenger cars although adapted Ballots would still compete.

The same two Grands Prix were run in 1922, the French outside Strasbourg – its fifth staging post – and the Italian in the gentle, sculptured, tree-laden parkland of Monza, a small town outside Milan.

Monza stirred passion from its pre-birth because all Brescia exhaled outrage when they learnt the Grand Prix had been plucked from them and bestowed on this *unemotional* tract of controlled nature where people meandered with their dogs, a faded royal palace sank mute in its own distant splendour, and who the hell wanted a motor race in the middle of it?

The project was announced in February for a September race and enough land found. Work began to a tight timetable, 100 days and counting, in May after Nazzaro and Lancia enacted the ritual ceremony of turning the first sods. A workforce of 3,500, deploying 200 horse-drawn carts, 30 trucks and two small steam engines set to. A temporary railway was constructed to move the soil because they were constructing a modern-style racing track (the configuration the same to this day) and a banked oval. The ordinary and banked tracks interlocked, sharing the start-finish straight. The whole circuit guarded the atmosphere of its own setting with parts of the track wending between tall trees.

Nothing in Italy is straightforward, and almost immediately work halted because the local authority objected on 'artistic' grounds. Italian bureaucracy was doing its 'utmost to foil' the plans, 'vetting the cutting down of trees and the use of explosives, filtering plans through numerous obstructive authorities and even posting guards to ensure that no unauthorised work was carried out.'[21]

The workforce returned and started again.

Although Strasbourg had an immense straight and an equally immense grandstand along it – white-roofed and perhaps 300 yards long – it was an orthodox eight-mile triangle near the Bugatti factory.

It is all legend now, the man, the factory, the cars he made. By an irony, Ettore Bugatti was a native of Brescia and born into an artistic family. He studied fine arts in Milan but developed an intense interest in motor vehicles. This developed into a passion to manufacture his own and, in 1909, he found a disused dye plant at Molsheim, a small Alsatian town, and converted it. He ran this like an artist ruling a fiefdom, designing the factory layout and much of the working material inside.

For the French Grand Prix, Bugatti made four eight-cylinder cars shaped like armadillos. They were 'clothed in an ugly wind-cheating barrel-shaped body from which the top of horseshoe radiator poked shyly.'[22]

The leading drivers came: Nazzaro and Pietro Bordino in Fiats (plus Nazzaro's nephew Biagio), Guyot, Hémery and Wagner in Rolland-

Pilains,[23] Goux in an adapted Ballot, Segrave, Guinness and Chassagne in the Sunbeams. The Bugattis, however, were to be driven by newcomers. Zborowski had one of two Aston Martins.

Segrave and Guinness drove to the race from England. At one point they were about four miles apart through the countryside towards Strasbourg. Segrave reached some straight road and opened up. At the end of it…

> I swung round a corner and was amazed to see a long, straggling village ahead of me. It had been hidden by the hedges and I was into it before I knew where I was. All I saw as I flashed through was a kaleidoscope of houses and fleeing people and a blur of blue as the local Gendarmerie poured out screeching and yelling.[24]

Segrave wondered what they'd make of Guinness's arrival so he 'stalked' back on the far side of a hedge. 'Half the population was gathered gesticulating in the street, screaming as only Frenchmen can, and wondering what sort of a thunderbolt it was that had disturbed their rural peace.' When they heard Guinness in the far distance they ran to their houses to get their bicycles. They had time to lay them across the road in a barricade then scatter. Guinness saw the bikes and, braking desperately, stopped just in front of them. The residents re-emerged and 'piled their bikes against his bonnet' while the police bayed threatening noises. Guinness made the traditional British (Irish!) response to this, proffering incomprehension, and asked for directions. This diverted them, Guinness reversed – shedding the bikes – and sped off.

The Strasbourg circuit, mostly flanked by tall trees, was unusual in that it had two enormous straights which invited big speed and only passed through one village. There it turned right through 90° past a typically ornate Alsatian house with a temporary 'stand' cut into its tiled roof on one side, the crowd behind a wooden barrier on the other. There was a geometrical right-hand corner which deceived many drivers, who thundered straight on and vanished. It deceived others who battered themselves against the house just beyond the apex.

Segrave and Guinness practised hard, although Segrave had a fixation about his car being perfect and during the practice it got dirty and scratched. He sent it by lorry to a coach works at Kehl, over the border in Germany, and 'they made a very good job of it.' The Fiats were fastest, the Bugattis close to the pace, the Sunbeams – clean or dirty – off it.

Early on race morning Segrave and Guinness made their way to the circuit among the enormous crowds and a gendarme asked them where they thought they were going. *We're in the race!* He didn't believe them, then a mounted policeman came up and began asking questions. Guinness suddenly revved the engine so hard that the horse reared and they sped off again. Segrave 'fully expected a bullet in the back because the French gendarme does not hesitate to fire at you if he gets a little excited.'

A heavy storm the night before lingered as rain. The race had been due at 8am but the minutes ticked beyond that as the Mayor of Strasbourg 'marshalled the dignitaries gracing the event, careless of the tense and soaked drivers.'[25]

Segrave expressed irritation that 'various dignitaries connected with the organisation of the race, and others representing the government, turned up to the start a quarter of an hour late in Italian and American cars, and received a distinctly sarcastic ovation from one of the biggest crowds that has ever assembled to see car racing in Europe.'[26] The drivers milled about, hands in raincoat pockets, goggles on their heads looking bored and impatient.

Eighteen cars lined up for a rolling start, an important innovation because it ended the days of mental arithmetic calculating staggered times. The cars had to 'trundle' and 'at a very modest speed down the long tree-lined straight behind an official motorcyclist who, without much sign of warning, suddenly disappeared down a side bend.'[27] The cars threw showers of mud and spray as they accelerated towards a distant hairpin. When they reached it the surface was so treacherous at least two cars missed it.

Nazzaro led from the first lap, the circuit began to dry and the 18 ran in two bunches, but the pace of the Fiat imposed itself. Nazzaro still led from a Bugatti, Bordino moving up and Segrave fourth at the end of lap three. Segrave pitted for fuel but Moriceau 'bungled' it and…

> petrol was splashed over the seats, leaving a pool in the middle of my cushion. We could not afford time to attend to trifles of that kind, and instead of swabbing it up I jumped in, and relied on my clothes to absorb it almost immediately. I was in agony in a few minutes. Luckily, owing to valve trouble, the car broke down at approximately half the full distance. Even if there had been no mechanical trouble I could never have finished. Had I gone another two laps I would have fainted from petrol burns which are one of the most painful types of burn known. I spent the next three weeks in bandages.[28]

He was happy to escape the sheer misery of the race. As Nazzaro passed the timing hut at half distance, three laps later, the stopwatches froze: 3h

12m 55s. Bordino set a new fastest lap and was now a minute and a half behind, Biagio Nazzaro three minutes after that, a Ballot fourth then three Bugattis. These were the only cars still running – Goux had just crashed. At a right-hander out in the country his car demolished a wooden fence, sending planks flying, and even as the car ploughed on the mechanic was rising from his seat to get out and repair it. The car couldn't be repaired.

Biagio Nazzaro pitted and, with his mechanic, changed the whole fuel tank in a quarter of an hour, and came back out having lost only one place.

Felice Nazzaro made his single stop for fuel, and Bordino set a new fastest lap before he pitted but clearly Felice was going to win.

On lap 51, nine to go, Biagio travelled at maximum speed on the straight towards the hairpin. He did not know that part of the rear-axle had been wrongly cast. It gave way and a rear wheel sheared off, pitching the Fiat out of control. It hammered into a tree, went end over end, hammered into another tree, and Biagio was dead. The car had been battered into pieces. Seven laps later Bordino's Fiat lost a rear wheel for the same reason, but it happened just beyond where Goux's crashed car still stood. Goux's mechanic, who was working on the car, looked up startled as Bordino's left rear came clean off and the car beat against the fencing. The wheel spun and fell in front of the fence. Bordino's impetus carried him on like a ship beginning to sink and the car came to rest against palisades flanking a field. The mechanic wandered back, returned with the lost wheel – running it along the road with his hand like a hoop – laid it against the rear of the Fiat, and drank deeply from a bottle.

Felice Nazzaro won it by almost an hour from a brace of the Bugattis, a third Bugatti flagged off – *that's enough, sir, thank you* – because it still had three long laps to go all by itself. The Bugattis were reliable but awkward to handle in corners, where they lurched alarmingly.

Mud smeared Nazzaro's car but both he and his mechanic looked surprisingly fresh, their faces unsmeared. Subsequently, an examination revealed that Felice Nazzaro's rear axle had a developing crack…

Monza was completed on schedule in August and by then the race generated lively interest, not least because it carried substantial prize money. Although entries closed three months before, 39 had been received and they included just about every driver of note outside the United States. However after Fiat's dominance at Strasbourg many entries withdrew because they realised they'd have no chance.

Bugatti stayed in but when practice began they found the circuit so fast that their wheels and tyres couldn't take it and they were poised to withdraw, too, when Fiat lent them enough tyres for one car.

A German, Alfred Neubauer, ought to have driven an Austro-Daimler, a car made by a firm near Vienna under licence from Daimler, but during practice another of their drivers, Gregor Kuhn, was killed and the team withdrew. Neubauer, like Enzo Ferrari, would learn that his skills were not driving, but enabling others to drive.

It left eight: three Fiats (including cars for Nazzaro and Bordino), the Bugatti and a couple of Diattos, one for Alfieri Maserati.[29]

On a wet day, between 100,000 and 150,000 paid to watch Fiat romp the race. Bordino covered 80 laps in 5h 43m 13s, Nazzaro two laps down and the Bugatti two laps further down. Nobody else finished.

The following month, 24,000 of Mussolini's blackshirts marched from Naples to Rome and took the capital amid acclaim from cheering crowds. Mussolini stayed in Milan – which the blackshirts had seized in August – preparing to flee to Switzerland if the march failed. King Victor Emmanuel sent a special train for him but troops loyal to the outgoing government blew up the track and Mussolini completed the journey in an open top car, arriving just like a racing driver – covered in mud.

In January 1923 the Nazi Party, led by Hitler, held its first public congress in its natural home, Munich. That year inflation tore the fabric of Germany apart. On New Year's Day £1 bought 85,000 marks, by June 622,000, by the beginning of August 9,000,000, a week later, 15,000,000. Hitler watched and waited.

Grand Prix racing was not yet touched by this, and added the Spanish Grand Prix to the French and Italian.

Great technical changes were at hand, too, as modern – and technically very different cars – superseded the cars of the immediate post-war. The famous Fiat 805 and Alfa Romeo P.2 were the forerunners, the Fiat introduced this season, the Alfa Romeo in 1924.

The French race went to its sixth staging post, Tours. The 14.1-mile circuit there embraced two villages and two of France's national roads, which met at a V-shaped hairpin. One of the straights measured five miles. 'Much of the lap was intimidatingly lined with poplars and paling or plank fences,' Segrave said. He'd be driving a Sunbeam, along with Guinness and Frenchman Albert Divo. Segrave added, perhaps laconically, that he found the circuit 'unsurpassed for scenery.'

The Fiat 805s had superchargers and three of them were driven from the Turin factory over the Alps to Tours *by the drivers*. They 'literally crammed the petrol-air mixture into the engine instead of letting the engine suck it in, notably augmenting the power output. Its use in Grand Prix racing for the first time was the greatest technical sensation of a sensational race.'[30]

The arch of time. The Grand Prix century started at dawn on 26 June 1906, outside Le Mans. Here a Franco-American called George Heath is tenth away in his Panhard-Levassor (Grand Prix Racing 1906-1914, Connaisseur Automobile A.B. – Stockholm). It ended on the afternoon of 3 July 2005 outside Nevers when Fernando Alonso led the French Grand Prix – and won. (LAT)

They really did use a horse to pull the cars to the start. The Motor *magazine took the whole thing in its stride.*

The rudimentary Le Mans pits and there was trouble already: the nearest car, the Grégoire of Philippe Tavenaux, didn't start! (LAT)

In 1906 the roads were more like flattened, dusty tracks. To improve visibility the ACF treated the whole length of the route with tar. The drivers were fast men, however, with a magnificent disregard for safety. This is Ferenc Szisz on the way to victory in his Renault. (LAT)

Ferenc Szisz, aboard his Renault, is the centre of attention before the start. (LAT)

620D — Motor — July 3rd, 1906.

THE GRAND PRIX,

Fully Illustrated Description and Commentary on the Great French Race.

THE RESULT AT A GLANCE.

	Winner.	Second.	Third.	Fourth.	Fifth.	Sixth.	Seventh.	Eighth.	Ninth.	Tenth.	Eleventh.
	SZISZ.	Nazzaro.	Clement.	Barillier.	Lancia.	Heath.	Baras.	Duray.	Pierry.	Burton.	Mariaux.
	125h.p. Renault.	135h.p. Fiat.	125h.p. Bayard-Clement.	105h.p. Brasier.	135h.p. Fiat.	130h.p. Panhard.	105h.p. Brasier.	130h.p. Dietrich.	105h.p. Brasier.	125h.p. Mercédès.	125h.p. Mercédès.
	H. M. S.	H. M. S.	H. M. S.	H. M. S.	H. M. S.	H. M. S.	H. M. S.	H. M. S.	H. M. S.	H. M. S.	H. M. S.
First Day	5 45 30	6 26 53	6 11 40	6 31 48	7 12 9	6 48 12	7 41 43	7 58 46	7 59 5	8 7 20	7 39 31
Second Day ...	6 28 37	6 19 33	6 38 5	7 21 11	7 10 2	7 59 33	7 31 7	7 27 15	8 16 2	8 11 22	8 59 10
Total Time ...	12 14 7	12 46 26	12 49 46	13 53 0	14 22 11	14 47 45	15 15 50	15 26 1	16 15 7	16 18 42	16 38 41

* Jenatzy driving on first day.   NOTE.—Apparent inaccuracies are accounted for by the fact that fractions of seconds have been ignored.

Masters of their time: (top left) Felice Nazzaro, an Italian; (top right) the Hungarian Ferenc Szisz; (above) Frenchman Louis Renault, who gave up racing to concentrate on making cars; and (below), seen here at the 1906 race, the 'Red Devil', Belgian Camille Jenatzy, an early star of motor racing. (all LAT)

The arch of time: Felice Nazzaro (FIAT) is anxious about something in the 1907 race (Grand Prix Racing 1906–1914, Connaisseur Automobile A.B. – Stockholm) *and the same place today.* (Author)

Sigurd Hornsted in an Excelsior cornering in the village of Moreuil during the 1913 race (Grand Prix Racing 1906–1914, Connaisseur Automobile A.B. – Stockholm) *and the same place today.* (Author)

Georges Boillot drives his Peugeot at the 1914 race at Lyon. But this was not to be the great Frenchman's day – here he and his riding mechanic change a wheel. (LAT)

The Motor
The National Motor Journal.

VOL. XLIII. No. 1,125.   TUESDAY, JULY 10, 1923.   FOURPENCE.

ENGLAND WINS THE GRAND PRIX.
Sweeping Success of Sunbeams in Most Thrilling Contest Ever Run.
It Was Anyone's Race from Start to Finish.
Sunbeams were First, Second and Fourth. Bugatti Third.

English hero Henry Segrave, who triumphed in 1923 after Carlo Salamano's FIAT ran out of petrol and the riding mechanic ran to get more. The Motor magazine described the seven-hour race as 'a battle such as has never before been staged'. Three years later Segrave drove a Talbot in the first British Grand Prix at Brooklands. (LAT)

Antonio Ascari, like his son Alberto after him, was an outstanding racing driver who was plagued by superstitions. Each had a fatal accident at the age of 36. (LAT)

In 1929 nobody could quite believe a Grand Prix was going to be run at Monaco – but it was. 'Williams' wins in his Bugatti, and at least one spectator doffed his hat. The great Rudi Caracciola finished third in a Mercedes. (LAT)

Titans of the 1930s. The advanced machines and sheer professionalism of the Mercedes-Benz and Auto Union teams demonstrated Germany's technical dominance. (LAT)

Maestro. Nuvolari bends the mighty Auto Union to his will at Donington, 1938. (LAT)

The Bugatti provoked intense interest because it was shaped like a tank, with driver and mechanic inside and peering over. The car was also known variously as a tortoise, dish cover, beetle, or roller skate. At moments it resembled each of these and at speed all of them. Bugatti said it was aerodynamically efficient and the fact that a great cloud of dust didn't trail behind it proved that.

The Sunbeam team stayed in a hotel near Tours and indulged in a little horseplay – well, donkey-play – for a cameraman. Some of the racing mechanics grouped behind the car of Guinness and one sat on a donkey while Paul Dutoit, standing like a clown on a metal container, tweaked the donkey's ear. Dutoit, Segrave's own mechanic, was one of the strongest men Segrave had ever seen. They are all laughing (except the donkey).

In practice Bordino lapped the Fiat in 9m 54s, and that was 34 seconds faster than Segrave could do.[31]

The grid was arranged by entry number and at 8am on a clear, warm day the 17 cars went off to their rolling start with 50,000 watching. A touring car race had broken the surface, loosening stones. Bordino led, Guinness gamely trying to stay with him but the Fiats already looked formidable on the opening lap. Pierre de Vizcaya[32] in a Bugatti got the hairpin wrong and burst through the paling, killing one spectator and injuring many others.

After seven laps Bordino stopped because dust had been sucked into the supercharger and now Guinness led.

Segrave's creed – *start slowly, finish fast* – was to protect the car but soon his clutch began to 'slip badly, and lap after lap the car went more slowly.' He feared the clutch would fail completely and had no thoughts of finishing. He still moved comparatively fast, of course, and that created an 'amusing incident' on lap 12. He and Guinness came upon an amateur, Prince de Cystria in a Bugatti, while they were entering one of the two villages. The streets were narrow and overtaking impossible.

We, in turn, were being pressed by other cars following behind, so, to indicate to de Cystria that he should hurry a bit, Guinness put out his clutch and accelerated his engine violently several times. De Cystria looked wildly round, saw two enormous cars almost on top of him, swerved frantically from side to side of the road and crashed into the palisades. The last we saw of him was the tail of his car sticking pathetically out of the match-boarding, while planks, scaffolding, poles, and debris rained on his head. I think no one was hurt.[33]

Guinness suffered clutch problems, too, but it was a race of a different kind of suffering.

> Divo pulls up at the pits. His mechanic has succumbed to the terrible physical strain. Yells for Moriceau, his erstwhile team-mate. A white little figure bounces over the side of the pit, scrambles into the seat, and the green projectile shoots off again.[34]

Before half-distance, the Guinness problem developed into a slipping clutch and he tied rope round it so Perkins his riding mechanic...

> can hold it back to increase the pressure. The reverse catch of his gear lever is broken, the spare magneto carried on the footboard has come away and been sculling madly round the car, bruising driver and mechanic, and cutting their calves until blood comes through.[35]

At half distance an Italian, Carlo Salamano, led in a Fiat, Divo was second and Segrave third although...

> I actually stopped the car half way through the race to consult [...] whether it would be advisable to retire completely, and so not damage the car too seriously, or to continue as we were and chance some of the leading cars breaking down and thus allowing us to finish reasonably high up.[36]

Divo got past Salamano and led for four laps before he was re-passed. Guinness...

> comes in with Perkins absolutely exhausted. His place is taken by another one – Smith – and, his white overalls stained with oil and dust and blood, Perkins staggers over the pit side, the combined strain of holding back the clutch and the blows which his head has received in the cramped position he was forced to adopt having knocked him absolutely unconscious for over half a lap.[37]

Segrave struggled on, suddenly the clutch 'went in with a bang' and the car was fine again.

> After a few laps had been covered, I was signalled from our control station as lying third, close to Divo. From this instant things began to happen. Divo, realising that I was catching him up and having to stop to take on petrol, oil, and water, lost his head at the pits, and instead of loosening his

petrol filler cap to take it off, started to force it the reverse way. He struggled and struggled with it till suddenly he realised that he was tightening it instead of taking it off, and started to force it back the right way. Too late!

The cap had been forced too far and jammed up solid. [...] Finally they tried to cut the solid brass cap off with a cold chisel, but even this failed.[38]

That was lap 30 of the 35, and 18 minutes were wasted. Segrave, seeing Divo stationary, realised he'd moved up to second. Salamano was signalled to go flat out but with two laps left his Fiat stopped about a mile and a half from the pits. Salamano thought he had run out of petrol but he held a huge lead and still thought he could win. He despatched his riding mechanic, Feretti, to run to the pits and get some fuel.

The crowd in the grandstand at the finish watched and waited, not knowing Salamano had stopped although he should have come past by now.

The crowd, realising, bubbles up [...] All eyes turn towards the hilltop, watches are anxiously consulted. A man with field glasses yells: 'Salamano's mechanic!' Stumbling, sweating, almost too exhausted to walk, Feretti lurches towards the pits gasping for breath and demands petrol. The Fiat team manager tells another mechanic to take his place, handing him a big-spouted petrol can. The new man – fresh – starts to run up the course. The officials stop him. Boos and cries of derision from the crowd. Feretti, seizing a bicycle, vaults wearily over the pit side, snatches the can of petrol and, riding one handed, wobbles up the course. Once again the iron hand of officialdom. This is more than the crowd can stand. Rising as one man, they hiss and boo and whistle with scorn and shout cries of sympathy to the game-hearted Feretti who, forced to abandon his bicycle, starts staggering back to his car.[39]

Part of this outpouring may well have come from those who had backed Salamano to win. While this was going on Segrave drove as hard as he could...

but with no thought of winning, till suddenly – and I shall never forget the thrill – topping a rise in the road at about 116mph. I saw, a few hundred yards away, on the right-hand side of the road, a low red car.

One's mind works like lightning [...] and I had plenty of time to wonder whether it *could* be Salamano; immediately reason said: 'Ridiculous even to imagine such a thing! He's miles in front.'

Even passing the car I did not trust myself to glance momentarily at the number, so certain was I that it could not be! Yet it was, because no sooner had we shot by than Dutoit [the mechanic] letting go everything, and making a funnel of his hands close to my ear, shouted: *'C'est le quatorze qui est en panne! Nous sommes en tête.'* (It's number 14 who's broken down, we're in the lead').

I could scarcely believe my ears – for the first time in history an English car was leading in the Grand Prix with only one lap to go.

How can I ever forget those last few miles – every noise in the engine seemed magnified a hundredfold, every corner seemed impossible, my brain refused to work in complete co-ordination with my hands and feet.[40]

The finishing line lay directly in front of the packed grandstand. As Segrave crossed the line, the Sunbeam casting an elongated shadow across the road, he looked perfectly composed. He'd taken 6h 35m 19.6s, averaging 75mph over rough road. Divo came in second of the five finishers. Salamano hadn't run out of petrol: his car suffered the familiar problem of dirt in the supercharger.

Segrave and Dutoit wore white overalls and Segrave, under his, had a white shirt and tie. His hair was receding, his face ascetic. He was given a flute of champagne and drank it although, evidently, he didn't like champagne. As they strode towards the victory ceremony Segrave smiled in a wan sort of way but Dutoit, goggles on his head, kept on walking.

Meanwhile, all is sunbeams in the Sunbeam's box. Mrs Clegg is smiling. Mrs Coatelen, the imperturbable, alone is calm. Huntley Walker [a Sunbeam director] says racing is too exciting for his style of living, and pats the left side of his waistcoat affectionately. We adjust to the Sunbeam pit to help the shock absorber man out with his pailful of iced champagne. We […] see Segrave return to the pit behind a huge bouquet. More champagne.[41]

A party had travelled down with W. O. Bentley to see the race [see earlier Footnote] and one of them, A. F. C. Hillstead remembered[42] that 'after the race we had lunch in the marquee, as we intended starting back for Dieppe as soon as the crowd had got away. It was then I asked W. O. why he did not design a special car for the following year's race. A futile question, of course. But then I had yet to learn that true sport and commerce are as far apart as the two poles.' Bentley believed the Le

Mans 24-hour race, which he'd entered the year before and which his cars would dominate, offered much better commercial value than Grands Prix.

Enzo Ferrari, now working for Alfa Romeo, was not at Tours. He heard there had been 'a fight' at Fiat between Luigi Bazzi, expert technician and engine tuner, and chief engineer Guido Fornaca. When the team got back to Turin after Tours, Ferrari approached Bazzi about joining Alfa Romeo's racing department. They were developing a supercharged car for the Italian Grand Prix at Monza then seven weeks away. 'Using the seductive powers that would become legendary, Ferrari lured Bazzi, a quiet, steady, tough-minded native of Novara, to Alfa Romeo. It began a relationship that kept the two men together in the automotive trenches for sixty years.'[43]

Ferrari remained a driver and two weeks after Tours he took an Alfa Romeo to a race at Ravenna. He led every lap and afterwards met Count Enrico Baracca, the 'father of the man who had commanded the fighter squadron of the Italian Air Force in which Ferrari's own brother had served during the war. Major Francesco Baracca shot down 34 enemy aircraft before he too had been shot down and killed. His [plane] had carried the squadron badge, based on their own family crest of the black prancing horse of Ravenna.' The symbol was on the winning trophy and the Count thought Ferrari should adopt it as his own for luck.[44] He did. It is exactly this symbol which so many great drivers would carry to victory, climaxing in Michael Schumacher, from 2000 onwards.

Monza attracted a strong entry: Bordino and Nazzaro in Fiats, Jimmy Murphy and Zborowski in Millers,[45] a Benz, and three Alfas to be driven by Ascari, Campari and Sivocci. Ascari was 'known to be an energetic, enthusiastic gentleman-sportsman, a good businessman, simple, frank, open-minded – and above all a good friend, generous in the extreme. Behind the wheel he was a *garibaldino* driving with panache and great daring, always pushing engine and tyres to their limit. It was felt that it would only be a matter of time before he was victorious as well.'[46]

One early September day the team – Murphy, Olson and team manager Robertson – arrived at Milan railway station. They posed in a group for the camera, Murphy in a bow-tie and homburg hat, Olson and Robertson in collars and ties, wearing boaters. At the circuit, Murphy seems to have befriended a large dog and posed again, seated in the cockpit with the dog next to him, its paws on the bodywork.

During practice Sivocci was taking the Alfa through the Vialone[47] curve. The car lost balance and spun and Sivocci couldn't get it back. It slewed off, sideways, into trees and killed him. The other two Alfas were withdrawn, although some cynics whisper that they may have been influenced by the fact they were not competitive. Ascari would have to wait.

Two weeks before the race Bordino also crashed practising. He'd been driving the Fiat, with Enrico Giaccone – who had driven one in the 1922 race – in the mechanic's seat. The car went off and turned over, killing Giaccone and breaking Bordino's arm. He decided to race, using his one good arm and having the mechanic change gears. (What would Monsieur Ballot have said? *Mon Dieu!*)

Bordino led and sustained that for 45 laps of the 80 but pain and exhaustion forced him to stop. He stood disconsolate in the pits, left arm in a sling while people gazed at him in silence. Nazzaro inherited the lead but a leak dripped boiling oil onto his feet. He resisted that but did have to stop for water and Salamano went through to win it, Nazzaro 20 seconds behind, Murphy third – of four finishers.

Alfa Romeo 'drove the few miles back to the Portello works in shambles.' They'd lost a leading driver, the car needed re-engineering. 'Bazzi had a suggestion. There was a brilliant engineer on the Fiat staff who might be lured to defect. His name was Vittorio Jano,' a stocky man with a bushy, triangular moustache which dominated his face. 'The Alfa Romeo staff knew of the 33-year-old Torinese and were aware, through their Fiat contacts (some made by Ferrari), that the man was a legitimate genius with the new supercharged engines that were beginning to dominate the sport.'[48]

Jano said yes.

The Spanish Grand Prix was run on a 1.2-mile heavily banked circuit at Sitges, near Barcelona. It was the country's first proper track but the corners had been badly designed and it wasn't used again.

The Grand Prix formed part of a festival of speed which also featured a Voiturette race in which Nuvolari finished fourth after a typically hectic struggle against the opposition and mechanical problems.

Before the Grand Prix, Segrave went to a local bullring and reportedly berated the matadors for wounding young bullocks instead of fighting proper sized bulls. *All right,* one wiry matador challenged Segrave and some other drivers present, *take one on yourselves.* Segrave said *I will if you'll do two laps of the Lasarte circuit with me.* The matador said *hmmm, don't think so…*

Heavy rain threatened the Grand Prix, reducing it to 200 laps but the clouds parted and at 9am the seven cars sped away. Zborowski led but it developed into a furious battle with Divo which was only decided on lap

190 when Zborowski had to stop to change a wheel and Divo went by for the win.

In November, just a few days after the Spanish Grand Prix, a loaf of bread in Germany cost 201,000,000,000 marks. Hitler, leader of the Nazi party, still watched and waited.

For 1924 the format didn't change: France, this year at Lyon, a shorter circuit than 1914 despite incorporating some of the same sections; Spain, called the San Sebastian Grand Prix (there's an academic debate about whether it should be regarded as a proper Grand Prix); Italy now securely at Monza.

In May young Nuvolari went to Ravenno to race a 350cc bike and met Enzo Ferrari who had to race a car at the same meeting. They chatted before the start, Nuvolari earnest in balaclava and goggles, Ferrari dressed in overalls, sleeves rolled up, and wearing a flat cap. As he spoke he rested a hand on the car's door and smiled. The conversation is lost. Nuvolari retired with an unrecorded problem in his race and Ferrari won his.

Jano worked fast. His design for a new Alfa Romeo was 'no brilliantly unorthodox breakthrough in racing car engineering...that was not what he had been hired for.'[49] It was 'blunt-nosed, solid and purposeful.'[50] It has been described as a masterpiece, although not one Ferrari himself was able to exploit at Lyon. During practice he seems to have had a nervous breakdown because in short order he left the circuit, boarded a train and returned to Italy. That still left Campari, Ascari and wily veteran Wagner.

Twenty two cars entered, half supercharged. There were Sunbeams (Segrave, Resta) and Delages, Fiats (Nazzaro in one) and five Bugattis (including de Vizcaya and Chassagne), a Miller for Zborowski and they faced 35 laps: 503 miles.

Segrave described the circuit as:

a tricky one. It abounded in corners, and had one fairly long ascent of about three miles with a gradient of approximately one in twelve. This was also a twisty bit, rendered all the more formidable by the fact that if one did happen to go off the road whilst taking one of the sharp bends too fast, one would fall at least a couple of hundred feet sheer before hitting the ground. The circuit was, however, well chosen as a test for acceleration and braking.[51]

Something fundamental changed. The cars wouldn't be creating dust
storms – well, just one, see below – because they would be running over
roads with proper surfaces.

During practice a lesser Bugatti driver, an excitable Alsatian-Parisian
called Ernest Friedrich, went out to set a faster lap time than any of the
others had done. Segrave takes it up:

> All went well till he reached the beginning of the steep climb out of Givors.
> Here there is a sharp bend and on the apex of the bend a lamp-post.
>
> Against the lamp-post stood a girl, leaning carelessly. Friedrich saw the
> girl in the distance and, wishing to impress her, took the bend just ten
> miles an hour faster than it could be taken. He collected lamp-post and girl
> simultaneously and pulled up [...] When the dust subsided, no girl!
> However, this didn't worry Ernest, who set about straightening up his front
> axle with the help of the cross-bar of the lamp-post which had broken off.
> Meanwhile the wretched girl was struggling, wet and bedraggled, out of a
> reservoir about 80ft below the road! She was quite unhurt, except for
> bruises. She had been shot over the fence with the top of the lamp![52]

Just before the race, the Minister of the Interior and various French
officials arrived, preceded by a military Guard of Honour with mounted
police. Along each side of the road came a file of police, but Segrave,
standing facing the pits, didn't see them. Nor did he know that the road
was supposed to have been cleared of drivers and personnel while this
pomp and circumstance went by. Segrave found himself...

> elbowed off the road by a French gendarme. I caught my foot on the
> wooden side of the pits and fell headlong into them. Not appreciating this
> treatment I scrambled up, let drive at the gendarme and knocked him into
> a bunch of his friends. He, instead of arresting me, ran off as fast as he
> could screaming for assistance, and returned in a few minutes with an
> officer, complete with sword, and six more gendarmes who all screamed
> and gesticulated together, threatening me with immediate arrest. This did
> not have much effect, as it was a matter of complete indifference to me
> what they did.[53]

They calmed and ordered Segrave to go into his pit. He refused. They
moved along to Guinness who was standing there, too, minding his own
business. They ordered him off the road and he didn't take it well, either.
He walked up to the 'officer and pointing dramatically at his car he
shouted, *"Je refuse a bouger, ça, c'est mon voiture!"* ["I refuse to budge, that,

is my car."][54] The joke of it was that it was not his car at all – it was
Resta's.' The officer and men marched away 'discomfited'.

As the band began the *Marseillaise* Resta entered the fray by revving his
Sunbeam's engine and, 'face like a sphinx, solemnly accelerated and
decelerated his engine about forty times a minute, drowning the band in
a volley or roars and bangs.'

Soon after, all the cars lined up and the rolling start did create a dust
storm, Segrave into an immediate lead. He decided to reverse his creed.
He'd go for it. Completing the first lap he averaged 70.15mph with
Ascari behind him, then Guinness, Campari and Bordino. And Bordino
was coming like the wind: by lap three he led and Segrave was in the pits
having the plugs changed. The race evolved into duets, Ascari clinging to
Bordino, Campari clinging to Guinness. Campari set a new fastest lap,
and Ascari went through into the lead when Bordino overshot a corner.

Deep in to the race Segrave changed mechanics because his, unnamed, had been knocked out by a piece of flying tread from, ironically,
another Sunbeam. Ascari's engine failed with a lap to go – his mechanic
collapsed trying to push the car – and Campari had the win. Campari,
portly and with a flop of black hair hanging diagonally across his
forehead, wore a jersey with Alfa Romeo in flowing script over it and,
even holding a glass of champagne, guarded his severity for the camera.
Everyone around him smiled and smiled and smiled. Mind you, Campari
smiled too when two men in boaters presented him with a gift-wrapped
Lyon sausage about eight feet long and as thick as a man's thigh.

Three weeks before San Sebastian, Resta was killed at Brooklands. He
and Segrave were trying to set records and Resta, who wanted to go to
Eastbourne to see his wife, asked to do the shorter runs. At speed a rear
tyre blew and the car rammed a corrugated iron fence backwards – hard
enough to burst through it; Resta dead.

The entry for San Sebastian on Spain's north Atlantic coast included
two Mercedes. The circuit, at Lasarte just inland, formed a loop 10.7
miles long and passed through four places, including Lasarte itself. The
hazards included 'low walls, high walls, steep banks, tramlines,
excessive camber, ditches and a narrow archway under a town hall.[55]
Segrave, who had travelled down with Guinness again, found it:

> in an abominably dangerous condition. The corners were supposed to be
> sanded so as to give the tyres a reasonably good grip. But the Spanish
> workmen, true to their tradition of avoiding any unnecessary work,
> discovered that it was very much easier to dig clay out of a neighbouring
> field and sprinkle it on the road rather than go some little distance and get

the sand which they should have used. This nearly cost Guinness his life, and led to a crash in which his mechanic, Barratt, was instantly killed.[56]

Segrave reverted to his original creed, *watch and wait*, because the race had a strong entry and the course was so unfamiliar. Guinness favoured *full attack* from the start. It rained, making the dangerous track much more dangerous. That destroyed the creeds: completing the first lap, a Mercedes led, Segrave fourth, Guinness sixth.

By lap 11 three cars had crashed and now Guinness, who had just re-fuelled, lost control in a corner where the wet mud glistened like ice. The wheels may have been deflected by deep ruts in the clay. The Sunbeam skittered towards an incline at the side of the track, turning over twice. That brought it back across towards a railway cutting and telegraph poles. As the car turned a third time Guinness and Barratt were thrown out *over* the telegraph wires and down 50 feet. Guinness suffered serious injuries, his career over, Barratt lay dead. The car emerged battered but not savaged.

Segrave stopped to try to help but, powerless, drove on and 'had to pass the two stretchers carrying them to the field dressing-station, not knowing whether my friend was alive or dead.'

Segrave won it, and would remain the last Englishman to win a Grand Prix until 1938; and no other Englishman won after that until 1953.

In September, Jimmy Murphy was killed at Syracuse, New York, three days after his 30th birthday. Murphy drove on a dirt track there with cars because he found them unpredictable. He made a challenge for the lead deep into the race, couldn't get the Miller round a bend, ploughed into wooden fencing and a stave killed him.

The Italian Grand Prix was postponed in September and Fiat withdrew after Salamano and Bordino were injured in practice, Mercedes weren't ready, and it took place in October. Four Alfa Romeos were entered, including cars for Ascari and Campari, with four Mercedes, including cars for Neubauer, Werner and Zborowski.

Rudolf Caracciola, a young reserve driver with an Italian name who had worked in his father's hotel on the Rhine, was also to be given his chance.

Birkin described Caracciola poignantly:

Relying entirely on his mechanics for the preparation of his car, and knowing little of its inside himself, he is usually asleep two hours before the flag is due to fall, and arrives on the track a little before the start. He combines colossal speed with the most acute judgment, and I can recall no time at which he has been guilty of recklessness or inaccuracy. He is very brave, and one of the few men not subject to an attack of nerves before the race begins.'[57]

Two Rolland-Pilains and two Chiribiris completed the entry of twelve.[58]

The Mercedes was driven from Germany to Monza, which meant crossing the Alps.

This, Caracciola remembered, 'was no joy ride [...] across the Gotthard. The car was anything but curve-happy, and I had to work with both arms to steer the stubborn thing up and down over the rocky, narrow, dust-covered pass.'[59]

Neubauer accompanied him and said that on the way they would spend the night at a small inn at Sihlbrugg, a hamlet south of Zurich, 'because Werner always stayed there and the food must be good.' Neubauer summoned the waitress.

'Herr Werner, which wine does he drink when he stays here?'

'He never drinks anything but champagne!'

They arrived at Monza next evening exhausted and went to the Hotel Marchesi where they had rooms. It was in a lovely setting beside the park although Caracciola and Neubauer had to share because they couldn't get single rooms. That wasn't a problem but the mosquitoes were and although their room had thick curtains...

hordes of the bloodthirsty creatures got in and clung to the white walls. When it was time to go to bed, Neubauer and I sneaked into the room without turning on the lights. I rushed to the window and shut it. Neubauer, who waited at the door, turned the light on. And then we began, each with a slipper in hand, and swatted them on every wall. By standing on the bed we could even reach those on the ceiling. We must have slain at least sixty mosquitoes. The walls showed that previous guests had waged similar battles.[60]

Practice began five days before the race but during it Caracciola was unable to drive because the Mercedes cars needed so much work on them. He sat patiently and gazed in admiration at the Alfa Romeos and thought how much better they looked.

Zborowski was to drive one of the Mercedes. His father had been killed during a hill-climb in 1903 when, in a corner, the cuff-links on his sleeve caught the hand-throttle of his Mercedes and opened it. Louis, 'would show his close friends the gold cuff links' but swear that nothing would make him wear them. During 1924, while 'suffering from an extremely disturbing emotional entanglement with a woman', he joined Mercedes. He arrived at Monza with 'the cuffs of his black shirt held together by his father's ill-fated gold cuff links.'[61]

Caracciola watched the race from the roof over the Mercedes pit. He saw Ascari set off like a 'fire engine', Werner and Zborowski slower because their engines wouldn't fire. Ascari consolidated his lead, Werner far off the pace. He pitted for new spark plugs and one of the team called up to Caracciola to take over from him. The situation was so hopeless that Caracciola pretended not to hear.

On lap 44, Zborowski lost control at the Lesmo curve and hit a tree. Some say a tyre blew, others that oil smeared the track. Caracciola remembered people running, waving their arms. Zborowski was dead, his mechanic seriously injured. Mercedes withdrew, leaving six cars, the first four of them Alfa Romeos – and they kept increasing their pace.

Towards the end, race director Arturo Mercanti judged that Ascari was driving so fast at one corner – a wheel on the sand at the rim of the track – he represented danger. He sent a message to the Alfa Romeo pit: *If Ascari continues to take both large and small corners in a way dangerous to himself and others I shall be constrained to stop him.* Ascari kept his foot down and won by 16 minutes.

In December, Britain suffered its worst air crash. An Imperial Airways plane had just taken off from Croydon to Paris and went down into a housing estate, killing eight. The price of technology as well as its benefits was constantly revealing itself. The Land Speed Record had been broken five times during the year, the last of them by Malcolm Campbell, pioneer aviator and racing driver.

For 1925, riding mechanics were banned because of the deaths the previous autumn – mechanics were more likely to be thrown out than drivers, who had the steering wheel to hold on to.

Segrave did not like this. The mechanic's main duty, he said, consisted of keeping 'a constant watch behind for overtaking cars, and to warn his driver by a tap on the shoulder, in order that the latter may give way to a faster car. If there is no mechanic […] the driver is forced to look round himself – *the most fatal error that a racing driver can commit.*' (Segrave's italics).[62] Mirrors had to be installed but Segrave found this 'childish' because the vibration on the dashboard was so intense in a racing car that you couldn't read the instruments, never mind see a clear image in a mirror. At least some drivers were starting to wear crash helmets, which Segrave among others pioneered.

The riding mechanic is both an heroic and anonymous figure. The names of some of them have not come down to us at all, others were referred to simply by their surname, as we have seen, starting with Marteau. They deserve better and breaking the strict chronological sequence of this book, here is Wilkie Wilkinson, who had become a driver himself but acted as riding mechanic for George Eyston in one of the last races where there were riding mechanics. It wasn't a Grand Prix but the pleasure and the pain were exactly the same.

'The driver and the mechanic had to do all the work. At eight o'clock in the morning you'd run across the circuit' – the so-called Le Mans start, drivers sprinting across the track – 'jump in the car, get it started, go. We had to fill it up with petrol churns, five gallons at a time so before the race I'd made a big funnel which held five gallons and then go and get the other churn. Making this thing I cut my hand very badly and got lead poison in it. This was quite a tough job with pumping the pressure up all the time at 2.5lb per square inch. If you pumped too hard the carburettors would flood or go fluffy. If you didn't pump enough the carburettor would starve and the engine slow down. Halfway through the race it started thundering, terrible race it was. Eyston wore glasses all the time. The lenses of his racing glasses were the same so I had a spare pair in my overall pocket and a chamois leather. When we were on the straight he'd say "change!" I'd whip his glasses quickly off and put the other ones on, then clean them ready for the next change.

'My hand was terribly bad and then the car started jumping out of gear. He said "hold the bloody thing in gear" so I had to hold it with my bad hand in second gear. Unfortunately, the gearbox had no cover on the side so all the flesh on the inside of my foot was burnt off and on the other side it leaked petrol so all that was burnt. Honestly, I was in such a state that I didn't care if we won the race – didn't care when we were broadside on, because it was so wet. Finally, we finished fourth and by this time my hand had all swollen up, I had red streaks up my arm. He looked at me, we had a glass of champagne and he rushed me straight off to hospital. I had to stay there for three days to get the poison down.'[63]

The Grand Prix calendar broadened to four races with the addition of the Belgian at Spa, to begin the season in June. This was the old circuit, 9.3 miles long, and the matrix for every Grand Prix there until the 1960s, although the corners were much tighter and the road surface much rougher. It looked, and was, very rural. There is a wonderfully informal photograph of the practice. Ascari, an immensely strong man, sits on the rear wheel of the Alfa Romeo spooning his lunch out of a bowl on his lap while Campari, standing by the bonnet, scans the track. It's wonderful because it captures exactly how basic the whole thing was.

The road surface exacted a heavy toll and of the seven starters only two finished, Ascari winning it from Campari by 22 minutes. There's a photograph of Ascari making a pit stop, the front wheels jacked up to change the chewed tyres, Ascari holding a petrol churn over the bonnet, pouring it into the tank, a mechanic working on the rear of the car. An official in a colonial hat, jacket, collar and tie wanders hand on hips down the middle of the track towards the stationary car. Ascari did not hurry. He had no need.

Understandably, the crowd grew restless with only the two Alfa Romeos going round and more than twenty minutes apart. They booed and, in response, Jano had a table and chair brought to the front of the Alfa Romeo pit. He sat decorously down and proceeded to eat his lunch at his leisure. The crowd booed that, too.

The French Grand Prix at Montlhéry, south of Paris, on 26 July, was the first to be run in France on artificial roads – in other words, a custom-built circuit, complete with banked sections. The start-finish straight of this, the seventh staging post, was so broad it resembled an aerodrome. The part used for the race measured 7.6 miles and, with a race distance of 80 laps, this was the longest Grand Prix (621 miles) since Dieppe's 956 miles in 1912.

Segrave openly expressed criticism:

> The race from the driver's point of view, and probably also from the spectator's, was unpleasant, as it poured with rain the whole time. Another thing which reduced my own interest in it was the encroachments, as it were, of the track upon the road. It did not seem to me that a hybrid event of this kind was either as straightforward as an ordinary track event, or as good a test of driver and car as an out-and-out road race.[64]

A strong entry came, though Fiat had now withdrawn from racing: three Alfa Romeos, five Bugattis, four Delages, three Sunbeams.

Ascari lived prey to many superstitions. He left the family home on Lake Maggiore 'with an unexplainable, heavy sense of foreboding' to travel to Montlhéry for practice. When he got there he couldn't sleep for more than an hour or two each night, perhaps because, like Segrave, he didn't like the place.[65]

Specifically, Ascari didn't like 'a palisade, a wooden fence, about as high as a racing car, stretching right the way round the circuit made up of wooden stakes held together by wire.' The stakes were reinforced by posts hammered in to the ground. He requested that this palisade be taken down: they were a clear and present danger in the corners, particularly if you judged cornering as finely as he did.

The palisade stayed.

Ascari led from a rolling start and by lap five Campari had moved in behind him. On lap 11 Ascari set fastest lap and four laps after that came in for a scheduled pit stop. He had such command of the race that the team told him to slow down and keep calm. He replied that he was calmer than the people in the pits and wouldn't be holding back.

> While saying this, he munched a Zabaglione (an egg-flip with Marsala Wine), threw two bananas into the cockpit next to what he called his "Oriental Commodities" – Thermos of champagne and water, and a fire extinguisher – resting on the racing mechanic's empty seat. Then he climbed back in himself and, having lost only two minutes, resumed his lead! On his reappearance, even the French public appeared to cheer and applaud him again.[66]

On lap 20 rain fell and moving into lap 23 it fell more heavily. Through a fast left-hander Ascari reached between 110 and 120mph, and a wheel nudged one of the posts. The car went into a skid and began tearing up the palisade. It tore and tore it for more than fifty yards. The palisade under the car locked the wheels so it was completely out of control. It somersaulted twice, hurling Ascari out, and the car landed on him. It almost cut his right leg off and he was spread-eagled on the track, the other leg broken, an arm broken and bleeding profusely from a head wound. Eventually he was put in an ambulance for Paris but as it went through the small town of Linas, a couple of miles from the track, he shuddered convulsively, and died. The ambulance turned round and at funereal pace the body was taken back to Alfa Romeo's headquarters villa where a mortuary room had been made ready.

Robert Benoist and Albert Divo, sharing a Delage, won the race.

Benoist was born in a hamlet near the forest of Rambouillet in 1895 but he had a passion for mechanical things. 'As a child he knew little of town life, but he was an early student of nature, his perception became remarkably quick and even in his teens he was recognized as one of the best shots of the district.' Although cars were fairly common the family couldn't hope to afford one, but young Benoist won cycle races. When he left school he served an apprenticeship in a Versailles garage, and that's how it began.[67]

Now, in victory, he took his great, overflowing garland and laid it on what remained of Ascari's Alfa Romeo.

The death of Ascari shook the Alfa Romeo team profoundly. Ferrari had started a business as an Alfa Romeo concessionaire with a franchise in three districts and now he concentrated on that. He wouldn't drive at all the following year.

At Monza a month after Montlhéry, four Alfa Romeos were entered among the Delages, Bugattis and two Duesenbergs, one for Tommy Milton.[68] Ettore Bugatti attended, wearing a bowler hat and button-down collar and tie. He looked very much an important man doing something...important.

The Alfa Romeos were not to be caught – a Count, Gastone Brilli-Peri, winning it – although the Duesenbergs went well and Milton finished fourth. The Alfa Romeos did not go to San Sebastian, opening the way for the Delages which filled the first three places of only five finishers. Divo won it from Benoist.

By September 1925, Britain's Ministry of Transport decided to act to cut accidents. White lines were to be painted on roads to separate traffic at intersections or dangerous bends. In London, traffic lights were being considered for Piccadilly. This increase in traffic found graphic expression at the Motor Show, Olympia, where 500 stands showed the latest models from Europe and North America. The range was expressive, too, from a three-seater Citroën at £145 to a Rolls-Royce at £1,891. Many manufacturers claimed their cars would do 60mph.

Speeds rose constantly. In March 1926, the first rocket to be powered by liquid fuel was launched from a field in Massachusetts. The inventor said he believed that one day such rockets could take scientific instruments into space. In Britain, Segrave pushed the Land Speed Record to 149mph and a month later, Parry Thomas pushed that to 170mph.

The Grand Prix calendar expanded again, taking in Germany, but the sport was in chaos. A 1.5-litre rule (and a raising of the minimum weight to 700kg) had been brought in to combat the constant rise in speeds in the races, and Alfa Romeo and Sunbeam withdrew. 'The racing teams objected at having to throw away their investment in 2-litre engines and start all over again, but the organisers dug in their heels and deadlock gripped the sport. All these factors [in Alfa Romeo's view] provided a sound reason for withdrawing from the expense and uncertainty of Grand Prix racing.'[69]

The chaos reached the French Grand Prix at Miramas – the race's eighth staging post – on an autodrome near Marseilles which had been made by cementing over stones. Some of them protruded and gave racing tyres a pounding. The *ACF* neglected to put a clause in their rules allowing cancellation if too few entries were received. Only two had come by the February deadline and ultimately three Bugattis appeared, to cover the 100 laps. To heighten the sense of absurdity, the track was wide, the start-finish straight stretched far back and here, in a neat little row, the three Bugattis sat like dwarves. One of them retired with a piston failure after 45 laps, another had special fuel and could only go slowly, and that left Goux circling by himself for *hours*. Reportedly he tried to put on some sort of show for the crowd, cutting corners and churning dust.

By contrast, the organisers of the German Grand Prix at the AVUS circuit near Berlin – two six-mile parallel straights linked by a North Curve and a South Curve –[70] ignored the 1.5-litre rule and opened the event to what they called sports cars. It attracted an entry of 46, including Mercedes.

During practice two cars collided in the South Curve, the driver Gigi Platé badly hurt and his mechanic killed.

Caracciola in the Mercedes remembered driving past a minute afterwards. He saw Platé being carried away by ambulancemen while the mechanic lay where he had fallen. Caracciola went to this mechanic and gazed down at him because he'd never seen a dead person before. He would remember he was:

> sprawled out on his back, arms flung wide as if he were nailed to an invisible cross. His wide open eyes reflected the sky. The rain fell in long skeins and ran over his face. Presently, an ambulance man came with a piece of canvas and covered him. Only the feet in the white canvas shoes protruded from the covering.[71]

That night in his hotel, Caracciola tried to forget the image of the white canvas shoes. Race day dawned bright and sunny but threatening cloud – a greying wall of it – came over when the race began at 2pm. The cars were sent off in groups and Caracciola stalled.

He looked ahead at the track surface: 'black and smooth in the dim afternoon light.' He saw the cars vanish round the corner. He shouted to his mechanic *get out and push!* Still the motor wouldn't fire. The mechanic pushed on, and the last of the grid nosed past. Caracciola felt his hands moist. The cars ahead were creating such a downdraught that the grass at the side of the track waved in their wake. Still the mechanic pushed. Then the engine did fire, the mechanic jumped back on – much like a bike rider at the Isle of Man, after a push start – and they accelerated. The rest were certainly a minute ahead and out of sight. Caracciola felt a dreadful depression. He had no chance against his team-mate Adolf Rosenberger.

Soon rain was falling, light at first then so heavy it soaked the drivers and made the track surface very slippery. The raindrops danced along the circuit, stabbing at it. Caracciola's windscreen steamed up, the tyres cast watery plumes. Completing a lap, Caracciola saw a crowd at the pit and a couple of stationary cars. He thought *cars are dropping out, go slower.* He eased his speed back. *Better to finish last than not finish at all.*

On lap eight Caracciola saw, through all this, the timekeeper's hut at the North Curve and the sight hit him hard. Rosenberger, overtaking a slower car and doing about 90mph, skidded and went into the wooden hut sideways, smashing through it. Inside two students sat keeping times and a man handled the scoreboard. The students died immediately, the man died twelve hours after his crushed legs were amputated. Rosenberger's mechanic was seriously hurt. Caracciola saw 'glass splinters strewn around...twisted metal.' He saw a man lying, people running.

On the next lap Caracciola pitted for fuel and Ferdinand Porsche, working for Mercedes, confirmed it was Rosenberger and that he had been hurt. That only aroused Caracciola's suspicions after the impact he had witnessed: the car must have struck the little hut with terrible impact. Caracciola resumed and, passing the hut, saw a 'thick, black cluster' of people and an ambulance. Somebody was being loading on to a stretcher. Caracciola tried to concentrate on staying on the road. He peered at black asphalt streaming towards and under him and it looked 'like sealskin'.

Chassagne's Talbot went off in the South Curve and flipped, the mechanic knocked unconscious for several hours. A car slithered off into a petrol lorry. Another Talbot skated out of control as the driver braked for the North Curve and came across on to the other carriageway, went across Caracciola 'like a blue streak' and ploughed into spectators injuring three, one seriously.

Caracciola pitted for a new spark plug and was now, he estimated, one and a half minutes down. He drove fast, passing cars going slowly because, he assumed, of the accidents. He saw gesticulating from the pits: *faster!* The rain eased and patches of blue spread through the cloud. He felt on his own, disorientated, felt the race exacting a toll on his body. His legs and arms felt heavy, his eyes tired.

He saw the finish line coming towards him, crossed it and had no idea he'd won. He sat when he had halted, a thicket of dark hair, a spattered rounded face, a boyish grin. He would remember the German national anthem, remember an enormous wreath being placed over his head – and remember suddenly exploding in helpless laughter. The whole day had been as sad and mad as that.

From this moment, Rudolf Caracciola would be known as *regenmeister,* the rainmaster.

The European Grand Prix, at Lasarte, attracted only six starters and was run in great heat. Benoist, in a Delage, pitted so utterly exhausted that he was forbidden from going back out. Two drivers stopped with burnt feet and one of them had to be revived on grass behind the pits, his right foot bare and badly blistered. A couple of cars which had long been announced as retired resumed, one 16 laps down, and amid this tumult and torment Goux won it comfortably after driving steadily for nearly seven hours.

The organisers of the Spanish Grand Prix, at Lasarte a week after the European, couldn't forget Miramas and spent long, anxious days asking themselves how many of the 23 entries would come. Nor did a baking sun, a scorching wind and clouds of dust help.

Segrave found the circuit improved and faster but on lap six he saw the spectators 'behaving in a most unusual manner. They were shouting and waving and pointing.' He saw something wrong with the near-side front wheel of his car, which seemed to tilt. He slowed, but at 90mph the front axle sheared in two, the wheels folding in against the bonnet. The engine sank to the track surface gouging a path in a straight line for a hundred yards. Segrave couldn't steer the car at all.

Meo Costantini, later Bugatti team manager, won in a Bugatti from Goux in another.

Curiously, for a nation which would later exercise so much influence on Grand Prix racing, the first British Grand Prix was only now run for the first time. There were reasons. The Royal Automobile Club had been offered a Grand Prix opportunity in 1925 by the governing body, the *AIACR,* but to seal off public roads required an Act of Parliament except in the Isle of Man, where the Tourist Trophy course was considered too dangerous. Thoughts turned to Brooklands and to adapt it into a testing Grand Prix circuit, sandbanks – what would be chicanes today – were proposed, but rejected as too expensive, then adopted.

Two weeks after the Spanish race, nine cars started the first British Grand Prix, over 110 laps (287 miles), among them Segrave and Divo in Talbots, Malcolm Campbell in a Bugatti, Benoist and Wagner in Delages, George Eyston in an Aston Martin. Parry Thomas entered a car he had built himself, but it wasn't up to it and he withdrew.

Segrave found problems when the Talbots arrived. Under braking the front axle began to 'chatter', making the car awkward to steer as well as affecting the braking itself. 'It was a frightening thing to look at, because one saw the front wheels bouncing up. After a few practice laps […] I realised that the cars were not really in a fit state to be run, as they had no chance of winning even though they were much faster than the other runners.'[72]

Campbell didn't get his Bugatti until the day before the race – and the model had never been seen in Britain before. Campbell took it round but managed only eight or ten laps in the wet. He found the engine fine but the brakes suspect, so he drove it to Povey Cross, a village south of London where he lived, with a Bugatti mechanic. He and another mechanic worked on the problem through the night.

At Brooklands it was a glorious day. When the flag fell Divo seized the lead but Campbell's Bugatti stayed alongside him until the Railway Straight along the back of the circuit when Segrave 'swung' past, towing Benoist's Delage. Campbell ran fourth.

Suddenly, coming off the banking, the front axle on Moriceau's Talbot broke. Campbell estimated the Talbot, close behind, was covering almost two miles a minute. He glimpsed the Talbot as it skidded across the track but mercifully, it drew up before the edge of the concrete or it would have gone over.

Segrave judged it extraordinary that this should happen to Moriceau just as it had happened to him at San Sebastian but…

> the end of his axle was caught up in some way in the frame and did not dig into the ground as occurred in my case, and he was thus enabled to come to a gradual standstill on the side of the track. [...] He did not immediately apply his brakes as 99 out of a 100 other people would have done. Had he done so he would have killed himself. One or other of his front wheels would have locked.[73]

Divo had a misfire and Segrave led for six laps but he'd have a frustrating race because the 'dreadful' brakes were forcing him and Divo to brake earlier and earlier for the corners. 'It was pathetic to see [and] eventually we were applying them almost half a mile away. Even then we were in danger of overshooting the corner.' They struggled on until Divo retired with an oil leak and Segrave with a cracked supercharger.

Campbell watched the early 'dog fight' between Segrave and Benoist, and found it happening with such ferocity that he was in a race unlike anything he'd known before. That impression was reinforced on lap four when Campbell saw Wagner in the pits 'jumping with both feet into a shallow tub filled with water, which splashed over the concrete around.' Wagner's Delage foot pedals were being scorched by the exhaust. All the Delage drivers suffered this and bearded French driver Robert Senechal had holes burnt in the soles of his shoes. On one occasion an exhaust pipe was so hot it set fire to the bodywork.

Benoist led but towards the end his Delage belched smoke – Campbell saw marshals firing extinguishers at the engine – and Wagner, who had taken over Senechal's Delage, came through. Campbell was getting pit signals, *faster!* He couldn't make the car respond to them even though he rammed the accelerator pedal as far down as it would go.

Divo retired and Campbell ran third. Benoist, back out and second, was up ahead and Campbell saw him, chased him down, overtook him. Now Campbell was getting pit signals *you're second, faster!* Still he could not make the car respond and by now he felt tired. The 'jolting' of the car on Brooklands' uneven surface was taking its toll.

The Senechal/Wagner car finished in 4h 0m 56s, an average of 71mph; Campbell ten minutes behind.

Segrave cleaned himself up a bit and drove off to the garage where 'Alan Fenn, our racing manager, had arranged a marvellous champagne lunch to revive our spirits.' There Segrave found a 'tremendous row in progress.' Everyone was telling the Talbot designer what they thought of him and attempting to 'eat at the same time.' They tried to draw Segrave into giving his opinion but diplomatically, he preferred to watch. He thought that rows like this were interesting, but only if you were watching because…

the pandemonium which reigns, when you have a team of foreign mechanics, is truly remarkable. They let go completely. Everybody screams and gesticulates at the same time, and nobody listens to what anyone else is saying; consequently there are about fourteen different arguments in progress at the same time.

Divo was lamenting the fact that a driver of his repute should be so insulted as to be asked to drive a car which burst into a thousand pieces every time he put his foot on the loud pedal, or took it off to tread on the brakes – the result, he said, was the same in either case!

Moriceau was shouting that it was monstrous that an axle should be designed with such a low factor of safety, or if the design was sound, that it should be so indifferently made that it broke within three miles of the start.

[The designer] was leaning against the wall at the far end of the room paying not the slightest attention to anybody, picking his teeth with a piece of straw and waiting for the storm to calm down.[74]

Eventually, Segrave drove the designer, Moriceau, and Divo back to their London hotels, dropping them at St James's, and as he drove away he could hear the three of them still shouting at each other.

The Italian Grand Prix at Monza attracted few entries, but the Maserati brothers built their own cars, one for Ernesto and the other for Materassi. They didn't get far before engine problems halted them, Goux went out with an oil pressure problem and two cars finished, the first of them 'Sabipa' in a Bugatti. He was Jean Charavel, who would drive the Le Mans sports car race three times.

In October, a month later, a sea plane flew from London to Australia and back in 58 days, a record. Water, it seemed, might just be the future of aviation.

Notes

1. Ernest Ballot was a 'noted engine manufacturer' based in Paris (*The Racing Car*, Batsford) and built cars in 15 weeks for contesting the Indianapolis 500 in 1919.
2. *Great Racing Drivers*, Hodges.
3. *Alfa Romeo*, Owen.
4. Bordino was a stylist and leading Italian driver of the 1920s. Born in Turin in 1887, he was killed in a race at Alexandria in 1928 when a dog ran in front of his Bugatti.
5. *Enzo Ferrari*, Yates.
6. http://www.oldandsold.com/articles01/article826.shtml
7. An engine with all eight cylinders aligned in one row.
8. By Leif Snellman in http://8w.forix.com/monza33.html
9. In *Omnibus of Speed*, chapter on 1921 French Grand Prix by Rex Hays.
10. Ibid.
11. http://www.ddavid.com/formula1/french1921.htm
12. *A Record of Grand Prix and Voiturette Racing*, Volume 1, Sheldon.
13. *The French Grand Prix*, Hodges.
14. *The Lure of Speed*, Segrave.
15. Ibid
16. *The Motor.*
17. http://www.brooklandstrack.co.uk/Drivrlist/zborowsk.htm
18. *King of the Boards*, Gary D. Doyle.
19. Segrave op. cit.
20. *The French Grand Prix*, Hodges, op. cit.
21. *The Roaring Twenties*, Cyril Posthumus.
22. Sheldon, op. cit.

23. An old-established Tours firm.

24. Segrave, op. cit.

25. *The French Grand Prix,* Hodges, op. cit.

26. Segrave, op. cit.

27. Ibid

28. Ibid.

29. Diatto of Turin was an old company which was surviving financial difficulties but still developing cars.

30. *The Racing Car,* Batsford.

31. *Those Bentley Days,* Hillstead.

32. Baron D. Augustin de Vizcaya was a shareholder in the Darmastadt Bank which may have helped finance Bugatti to open the Molsheim factory. He raced Bugattis, as did Pierre and Ferdinand de Vizcaya, thought to be his sons. www.bugatti.co.uk/trust/nl17-3.html

33. Segrave, op. cit.

34. *The Motor.*

35. Ibid

36. Segrave, op. cit.

37. *The Motor.*

38. Segrave, op. cit.

39. *The Motor.*

40. Segrave, op. cit.

41. *The Motor.*

42. Hillstead, op. cit.

43. Yates, op. cit.

44. Owen, op. cit.

45. 'While never true Grand Prix machines, the American Millers were highly successful Indianapolis performers which did well on the fast Monza track. They were straight-eights.' (*The Racing Car,* op. cit.)

46. *The Man With Two Shadows,* Kevin Desmond.

47. Because Monza will figure so prominently in the narrative, here are the corners: at the end of the start-finish straight, the Variante Goodyear, into the sweeping right Curva Grande, into the kink-like Variante della Roggia, into the long horse-shoe right-right of the Curve di Lesmo, into the long-kink of Curva del Vialone and the Variante Ascari, along the Rettifilio Centrale to the tighter horse-shoe Curva Parabolica, sling-shotting round and flinging the cars onto the start-finish straight.

48. Yates, op. cit.

49. Owen, op. cit.

50. *The French Grand Prix,* Hodges, op. cit.

51. Segrave, op. cit.

52. Segrave, op. cit. Incidentally, it is difficult to imagine a more politically incorrect tale than this, or one more likely to enrage feminists – or indeed all other women.
53. Segrave, op. cit.
54. I've reproduced this as it appears in Segrave's book. My car in French is *ma voiture.*
55. *The Roaring Twenties,* Posthumus.
56. Segrave, op. cit.
57. *Full Throttle,* Birkin, op. cit.
58. Chiribiri, an Italian company founded before the first war (by Antonio Chiribiri) supplied aircraft parts before moving to car manufacture. It ceased in 1928.
59. *Racing Driver's World,* Caracciola.
60. Ibid.
61. *The Man with Two Shadows,* Desmond.
62. Segrave, op. cit.
63. *The Power and the Glory* (John Gau Productions for the BBC, 1991).
64. Segrave, op. cit.
65. Desmond, op. cit.
66. Ibid.
67. *Great Racing Drivers,* Hodges.
68. Milton was a leading American driver known for integrity and hard work. Despite being blind in his right eye and of less than perfect sight in the left, he became the first man to win the Indianapolis 500 twice.
69. Owen, op. cit.
70. AVUS derives from *Automobil Verkehrs und Übungs-Strasse* (car traffic and test road) and had originally been planned in 1907. During the First World War, Czarist Russian prisoners worked on it, and after the war a financier raised the money to complete it. By a great paradox, at the end of the Second World War Berlin was divided among the Allies and the AVUS was used as a normal road and ended at a checkpoint between the Western and the Soviet zones. The Russians had come back.
71. Caracciola, op. cit.
72. Segrave, op.cit.
73. Ibid.
74. Ibid.

Chapter 3

In Nuvolari's time

The Western world walked almost blindly into great and potentially deadly crisis. Soon enough, New York's Wall Street crashed, bringing a generation to the hopelessness of poverty and Hitler began to strut the Continent, real power almost within his grasp. Mussolini gripped Italy, Franco prepared to grip Spain. Stalin watched, brutal and greedy, from Moscow.

By a great paradox, motor racing assumed a settled state. The Targa Florio, the Mille Miglia, the Le Mans 24-hour race and the Indianapolis 500 occupied regular places on the annual calendar and, soon enough, the Grand Prix season did, too: Monaco in the spring, the cross-country of Spa in early July, itinerant France and the mighty Nürburgring in mid-summer, Monza in the autumn. Hitler, Mussolini, Franco and Stalin are long gone and hardly lamented. In its essences, the Grand Prix season has lasted until today.

Many of the drivers who would inhabit this landscape were already in place – Benoist, Caracciola, Campari – but the post-war generation was coming to maturity. There'd be the debonair Louis Chiron, a ladies' man deceived by a lady; Achille Varzi, an elegant, distant, chain-smoker who even smoked while the car was being refuelled; Jean-Pierre Wimille, son of affluent Parisian parents who had been born to race and, spectating at the 1922 Grand Prix at Strasbourg, realised it; urbane René Dreyfus who would end his days running a restaurant in New York, and Nuvolari. All, eventually, would be touched by the political crisis while others would lose their lives to it.

If we were doing something dangerous, they would say, *they were dangerous times.*

Nothing came to typify that more than the event which began on Saturday, 26 March 1927 in the stately, stone-arched streets of Brescia in northern Italy. They echoed to the sound of 78 cars being driven hard. As *The Autocar* pointed out, 'whereas in most European countries it has long been found necessary to restrict motor racing to special tracks or short, military-guarded circuits, the Mussolini Government permits speed contests from town to town.'

The Mille Miglia [1,000 miles] exercised ferocious and ultimately lethal fascination for another thirty years as it went down to Rome and back to Brescia. Eventually, half of Italy would line the route, more or less unprotected, as the cars passed at immense speeds just in front of them and the result, culminating in something approaching slaughter, became too much.

The driver of a square Bianchi Sport car in the 3,000cc class and bearing the number 89 would make the race his own but, this first time, his fifth place (in class) didn't rate even a mention in the Press coverage. Nuvolari hadn't raced a car for three years but now he would, more and more. So, on a modest level, would Enzo Ferrari during the season. Presumably the business of selling Alfa Romeos was going well enough to allow him the time off.

On the Tuesday after Brescia, Segrave pushed the Land Speed Record to 203mph at Daytona in response to Campbell's 174mph just a few weeks earlier at Pendine Sands in South Wales.

Meanwhile, Caracciola examined the possibilities for a Grand Prix drive, very much as modern drivers do. He concentrated on the four major manufacturers – Mercedes, Bugatti, Alfa Romeo, Maserati – and concluded that in character they were dissimilar. He noticed all the leading drivers were with one of these four. Delightfully he described Bugatti as created in the image of Ettore Bugatti himself. He 'bred cars as people breed horses; and he loved these cars, which he had himself designed down to the finest details, as if they were living creatures.' Even the factory resembled stables and Bugatti had called one of his cars *Pur Sang* – thoroughbred. 'He improvised everything – his inventions, the financing of his plant which he often, and with admirable skill, steered past the cliffs of financial ruin.'[1]

Caracciola doesn't seem to have been put off by the very Italian nature of Alfa Romeo. At various times they had run, among others, Nuvolari, Varzi and Campari. 'They were,' Birkin would judge:

> all very fine drivers, and one or two of them notoriously wild; capable of racing desperately against each other and breaking up their team. Only the very greatest of team managers could have controlled them, and only the very greatest of team managers did. His name was [Aldo] Giovannini; his position was that of an impresario producing an opera in which all the leading roles are taken by temperamental stars. Yet he contrived to satisfy every one and calm every storm. He had a deep insight into the qualities of men and of cars.[2]

Caracciola drove for Alfa Romeo as a 'semi-independent' at Monaco, and in the future the crowd would boo him mercilessly. Until then he'd driven Mercedes in a wide variety of events, and virtually nothing else.

In June, a month before the Grand Prix season began, Nuvolari took part in a major race at Rome, won it and *L'Auto Italiana* hailed the appearance of 'a great driver.' This might have been intended as mere verbal gesture, but it wasn't.

There would be five Grands Prix and Talbot had withdrawn, giving the season to Delage and Robert Benoist who dominated mediocre opposition.

The French Grand Prix, at Montlhéry, attracted few entries and no new cars except Eyston in a Halford Special.[3] A large crowd saluted the President of France, the guest of honour, but were startled when Bugatti withdrew just before the race – Ettore Bugatti didn't feel his cars were competitive – and the crowd taunted him, *you're frightened.* Seven cars started and Benoist began the domination, winning from another Delage by more than eight minutes. The vast saucer-like circuit with the feel of an aerodrome seemed curiously empty.

The Mille Miglia generated its own legend and mythology, and so did the Nürburgring, built to ease unemployment in the Eifel region of Germany, a rural area roughly at the centre of a triangle between Bonn, Koblenz and the Belgian border. Apart from racing, it offered the German motoring industry a permanent facility for experiment and testing – a clinical activity, by definition, and in absolute contrast to racing on it.

At 17.5 miles, the track contorted its way through the undulating wooded countryside like an immense, forbidding roller coaster. It had 88 left-hand and 84 right-hand corners. It had switchbacks, fast downhill sections, blind climbs, humpbacks. It had ravines, bridges, ditches, hedges, trees. Some drivers felt it was almost impossible to learn in detail, some adored its challenge. All, if one may risk a generalisation, knew intuitively that it must be paid respect or it would exact its own dues. Sometimes it exacted its dues even then.

The first Grand Prix there, two weeks after the French, was restricted to sports cars but attracted 75,000 (Brooklands was getting 15,000). This crowd walked, cycled, rode on motorbikes, drove and travelled in coaches to watch 21 cars set off on a cool, dry day, the seven Mercedes – Caracciola in one – drowning everything. Rosenberger led from the second row and Caracciola retired with an engine problem. Otto Merz, a bear of a man who reputedly could hammer six-inch nails into wooden tables with his hands, led when Rosenberg's engine failed, and won it.[4]

Benoist's Delage met 'vigorous and unexpected resistance from the daring Italian Emilio Materassi' – a wealthy Italian amateur – in a Bugatti during the Spanish Grand Prix at Lasarte. Benoist and Materassi duelled until, with nine laps left, Materassi used too much power and thumped a wall. Benoist, 'seeing only a thick cloud of dust ahead, spun under violent braking, lost all sense of direction, and resumed racing – the wrong way.'[5] Marshals waved and pointed, Benoist realised, spun the car again – and won it.

Delage sent only Benoist to the Italian Grand Prix to face a challenge which unexpectedly included the Indianapolis 500 winner George Souders in a Duesenberg. Souders, a 27-year-old rookie, looked older than his years with his heavy, jowelled face and furrowed forehead. Heavy rain, poor acceleration and inadequate brakes blunted the American effort. The car's wheels whipped whisps of water and the crowd crouched under umbrellas. Benoist, a handsome man with a striking face full of character and a curl of a smile, won by 22 minutes. A movie camera craned at him and he made a mock salute for it, then his lips curled into the smile.

Fiat now withdrew from racing to work on their aeroplane engine business.

Several privateers entered the British Grand Prix at Brooklands in October, one with the superb name of Prince Ghica-Cantacuzino.[6] Eyston and Campbell had Bugattis and would clearly be overwhelmed by the Delages. So would Chiron, whose father had been *maitre d'* at the Hotel de Paris in Monaco. Chiron, a socialite, raised money by being an escort to ladies. He was the 'smiling Frenchman,' Caracciola said, cheerful, full of jokes who had a pre-race ritual: he 'walked around his car, patted it, talked to it […] and then slid smiling behind the wheel.'[7]

A chill wind blew and the track glistened from earlier drizzle as the race approached. Campbell knew he needed to make a good start or the Delages *would* overwhelm his Bugatti. He did make a good start as the cars headed for the banked section – but Materassi roared by, flinging back spray from the puddles on the track. Materassi's Delage shivered under its own power as it went through the corner to the banking. On the banking, Campbell felt the wind gusting. What he described as squalls of rain fell and Eyston hemmed him from behind.

Materassi led but the car leaked water, and Ghica was most un-Princely when a mechanical failure stopped him. He seized a large hammer and began beating it on the pit counter. Meanwhile Campbell made a pit stop and, moving along the banking, noticed Count Carlos Conelli running alongside his Bugatti down by the infield pushing it towards the distant pits. Each time Campbell passed for the next few laps he saw Conelli still pushing it until eventually he reached his pit. Campbell now saw mechanics refuelling it. The push, of more than a mile, exhausted Conelli so much that his reserve driver – known simply as 'Williams'[8] – took over.

Benoist won it to become Champion of Europe and Delages filled the first three places, with Chiron in the Bugatti fourth.

In April 1928 an American, Ray Keech, pushed the Land Speed Record to 207mph, topping Campbell's 206mph set two months before.

The Grand Prix season followed the settled calendar, France, Germany, San Sebastian, Spain and Italy, but the racing had entered a wretched phase created by 'increasing gloom on the business front and a general tightening of purse-strings.'[9] There were no restrictions on engine size but cars had to weigh between 550kg and 600kg, and the minimum race distance was 375 miles (600km). No new cars were built and only one race, Monza, run under these regulations.

Only six entries were received for the French Grand Prix at Comminges, a road circuit near the Pyrenees, and the race's ninth staging post. A sports car race was substituted.

The sports cars again contested a steaming hot Nürburgring, the race run in three groups reflecting the different power of the cars. Almost 100,000 watched the Bugattis take on the Mercedes. Cars overheated, some boiled and the Nürburgring showed its murderous character as in places the tarmac melted.

One car went off, turned over and the driver died some days after the race. On lap five the Czech Viktor Junek in a Bugatti crashed on a twisting section at the far side of the circuit. He'd just taken over from his wife Elizabeth, one of the best women drivers of the time. The Bugatti overturned and Junek was crushed. Elizabeth did not race again.

Christian Werner damaged his shoulder wrestling the heavy, powerful Mercedes, pitted and handed over to reserve driver Willy Walb. A doctor was treating Werner when Caracciola pitted, overwhelmed by the heat. Caracciola collapsed and, partially revived, was helped into the shade. Werner, arm bandaged, clambered in and drove off.

Caracciola/Werner won it from Merz, 'the only Mercedes team-member to drive without relief, although his great hands were torn and bleeding from the merciless wracking of the wheel.'[10]

The San Sebastian Grand Prix at Lasarte was confined to nine Bugattis. Other manufacturers withdrew at the last minute, despite tempting start money. The race proved the fastest run at the circuit and attracted a huge crowd. Benoist led but Chiron caught him and broke the lap record, averaging 88mph – considered amazing on a circuit of so many bends and corners. Next lap Chiron passed Benoist which delighted the crowd and they were even more delighted when Benoist, who finished second, leapt from his car and embraced Chiron.

Chiron won the Spanish Grand Prix, a sports car event run to a handicap formula, at Lasarte four days later.

And now, at Monza, Nuvolari began his career as a Grand Prix driver and so did Varzi, who was significantly younger than Nuvolari (born in 1904). The son of a cotton magnate he started on motor bikes, like Nuvolari, in 1920 but could afford the best. He and Nuvolari rarely raced each other then. At the age of 19 Varzi won the Italian 350cc Championship and, years later, he'd say the first time he drove a racing car it felt quite natural. His style always reflected that. Of him, Caracciola would say he was 'seemingly soft, and certainly a little too soft with regard to women and the horde of his admiring camp followers. But the same man, whose kindness was often misrepresented and put down to weakness, was hard as steel the moment he got behind the steering wheel of his car.'[11]

This season he and Nuvolari joined forces to race Bugattis but the partnership was perhaps too volatile, too egocentric, too intense to survive long. For Monza, Varzi bought an Alfa Romeo.

Grand Prix racing had its first feud, although the relationship between the two men remains problematical and may well not have been as bad as it has been presented. Rivalry was endemic, the nature of the beast and its reason for being, but outright feuding – like Alain Prost and Ayrton Senna half a century later – would be surprisingly rare.

There's precious film of Nuvolari and Varzi before the start at Monza, 1928, Varzi bare-headed, nodding to someone just outside the cockpit, Nuvolari wearing a jumper and scarf smiling his toothy grin. He'd been in 'an extremely bad mood before the race because his car [the Bugatti, a private entry], which had been patched up as well as possible using pieces from two other cars, seemed unable to go fast.' In the fleeting moment of film he doesn't betray anything like that.[12]

A crowd of 120,000 stood fifty deep opposite the pits, their eyes ready to follow the 22 cars down the long straight and out into the woodland. They saw 'Williams' lead from Nuvolari's Bugatti, but by lap five Nuvolari had taken it from him, Varzi and Brilli-Peri (Talbot), a 35-year-old from Florence, chasing. After a lively scrap Brilli-Peri led and on lap 15 Varzi forced his Alfa Romeo past Nuvolari to a tremendous burst of applause. Gigione Arcangeli, another Italian, went past on lap 16, too.

Somewhere in all this ran Materassi's ex-works Talbot and, on the next lap, he was passing Foresti's Bugatti. His right front wheel brushed Foresti's left rear and Materassi veered off at 120mph. The Talbot struck a wall, vaulted a protective ditch and went into the crowd killing 23 and injuring around 40. Materassi got himself out of the car and walked a few steps trying to speak. He fell and died a few moments later, of a haemorrhage caused by a blow to the temple.

The race was not stopped.

Now Varzi led, Chiron's Bugatti a hundred yards from him, Nuvolari, almost magical in finding such pace in such a Bugatti, working and working in third. It finished like that.

The idea of a race through Monaco's streets had been conceived by Anthony Noghès, President of their Automobile Club, because it would be good for tourism. The notion seemed fanciful within the physical constrictions: too small, too cramped, too narrow and a built-up area. Noghés worked out that it was possible, although the whole idea evidently baffled *The Autocar:*

> They have the most astounding audacity in some parts of Europe. For instance, there is going to be a Grand Prix at Monaco – a Grand Prix, mark you, in a Principality which does not possess a single open road of any length, but only has ledges on the face of a cliff and the ordinary main thoroughfares that everyone who has been to the Casino knows so well.

This sense of disbelief echoed elsewhere, with the nature of the circuit expected to cause a chaos of crashes and breakdowns rendering the place where the beautiful lived into a breaker's yard.

Because it could be altered so little and because it endures in the same basic configuration today it can be used as a measure of progress. Year on year comparisons are possible which cannot be made elsewhere. In 1929 it was 1.97 miles and 70 years later, 2.05. In terms of longevity, only Monza stands comparison, but Monza has had many lives: 6.2 miles in 1923, 4.2 miles in 1930, rebuilt in 1948, a banked speedway section added in 1955, then the chicanes of today, themselves oft reshaped.

From here on after each Monaco Grand Prix I give the winner's time, average speed and from 1930, a comparison with the year before. I've included the Land Speed Record because so many of the holders competed in Grands Prix as well, and the Record is by definition a measure of increasing technology. After each decade, I've given the previous fastest laps – at decade intervals – and how many vehicles were registered in Britain.

In April 'the streets were barricaded with sandbags and hoardings, bridges were built across the streets for access to the all-important Casino and the tramways were stopped.'[13]

The Autocar softened towards the idea, writing that the race had 'received 23 entries, all of which the promoters appear anxious to start. This affair should be the nearest to a Roman chariot race that has been seen in recent years. Presumably the officials consider that the number of runners will be substantially reduced at the end of the first round.'

Only 16 of these entries started, many of them of the new generation – like Dreyfus and cheerful, unassuming Marcel Lehoux (Bugatti). Eight of the cars were Bugattis, and the drivers included 'Williams' and 'Pierre,' an assumed name used by Baron Henri de Rothschild to conceal his real identity because his father didn't approve of him racing. Caracciola had the only Mercedes and took his place on the last row. The Italian heavy-hitters weren't there at all.

As the cars accelerated towards *Ste Devote* corner they were already stretching out and bringing up gales of dust. They accelerated through *Ste Devote*, sweeping majestically round, spreading up the hill to Casino Square, Lehoux leading. Such a thing in such a place, so completely familiar now, had never been seen or even imagined before. By Casino, 'Williams' hustled past. In historical terms, the first lap was the most important because it proved the race's feasibility. Soon enough, when the cars had become a snake, they were fishtailing the cars through *Ste Devote*, were streaming into the darkness of the tunnel, and coming like a storm along the quayside.

Nobody retired until lap seven when Lehoux slid into sandbags at the quayside down from the tunnel, bending the Bugatti's wheels. Because the pits were further along the quayside, Lehoux walked there, picked up new wheels and, one at a time, bowled them back to the car. He fitted them and eventually rejoined for a couple of laps before the transmission failed.

While this slightly unreal performance went on Caracciola made a move. The Mercedes loomed vast and heavy and at the Station hairpin the spectators could see him leaning over battling the steering wheel, but his touch was so consummate that he made the Mercedes appear as nimble as a light car. At half distance he led but a long pit stop punished him. He was stationary for four and a half minutes while many cans of petrol were poured into the thirsty Mercedes. The race became a procession, 'Williams' winning it. He was a modest man sitting there, cap turned backwards. He had a face which was almost oval and large, looming eyes. He shook hands with someone who came up as he sat, said a few words, seemed embarrassed. There would be histrionics at Monaco, champagne spraying, tears of every sort, but not for many years. There were none on 14 April 1929 as the man with the pseudonym who had driven his rounded Bugatti to the kerbside, stopped and had his little chat with the man who shook his hand. He contented himself by pursing his lips briefly and exhaling as if to say to himself 'phew.'

The Monaco measure: 'Williams,' 100 laps, 3h 56m 11.0s, an average speed of 49.8mph.

The ultimate measure: the month before, Segrave pushed the Land Speed Record to 231mph.

Vehicles registered in Britain 2.2 million (1928, 2.0 million). A two-seater Ford cost £145 and a Briton earned on average £3.50 a week. Saving all his money, the Briton would have taken 41 weeks to buy one (1910, £220 – 2 years 42 weeks; 1919, £170 – 1 year 16 weeks).

The French Grand Prix at Le Mans and the Spanish at Lasarte were run to a fuel consumption formula, 85kg of petrol and oil. This seems to have been to prove motor racing was not profligate as the great financial depression continued. The French Grand Prix proved straightforward although a dispirited and dispiriting sort of occasion run partly in thundery showers. 'Williams' won it.

The Bugattis took on the Mercedes at the Nürburgring, an aristocratic gathering because as well as Baron de Rothschild, a Baron Sartorio drove an Alfa Romeo, a Count von Kalnein a Bugatti, a Count Arco in a Mercedes and the Marquis de Sterlich in a Maserati competed. Varzi, due to drive an Alfa Romeo, didn't make an appearance, the first intimation that he might be an unreliable loner.

Caracciola set an immense pace in his Mercedes to keep the buzzing Bugattis at bay but Chiron broke the lap record and came up to attack. Caracciola went as far as lap five when a connecting rod broke and Chiron brought the Bugatti home.

Chiron won in Spain, too, and Bugattis took all the first six places but the race was a strange, strangled event. Thirteen Bugattis, an Alfa Romeo and a Delage set off in heavy rain and only eight cars, all Bugattis, finished.

Nuvolari had a Talbot for the Italian Grand Prix at Monza where there were heats. Arcangeli won his from Nuvolari – Arthur Duray, the American, had overtaken both of them but a bearing seized. In the final Varzi and Alfieri Maserati (in a Maserati) fought for the lead but tyres were shredding, cars dropped out and Varzi won it from Nuvolari by a minute and a half.

Nuvolari once again showed himself to be a driver who admirably combines courage and cunning, calm and driving force, intelligence and character. When he got out of the car he rubbed his hands and smiled brightly. Thin, lean, excitable, bright dark eyes, eyebrows like two thick ink-strokes, dazzling white teeth: Nuvolari is a Saracen who happens to have been born in Mantova.[14]

Two days after Monza, a London couple called Moss – he a dentist who worked mainly in the poorer areas, she a keen horsewoman – had a son. Father wanted him called Hamish, mother wouldn't have that but she was a Scot and had connections with a town there. They agreed to give the lad the name of the town, Stirling.

Twelve days after that, Baconin Borzacchini drove a Maserati at almost 250kmh on the road outside Cremona. This had nothing to do with the Land Speed Record, now being set on sand, but was considered such a feat that it warranted a great celebration banquet. Enzo Ferrari was naturally among those invited and sat between a prominent industrialist, who had recently bought an Alfa Romeo from him, and a leading racing enthusiast. They had money, Ferrari had experience and connections. Some time during the evening the question came up *why don't we form a racing team?* There seemed no reason why not. The word *Scuderia* in Italian means stable in agricultural terms, but also a motor racing organisation. The name of the new team was no problem at all: *Scuderia Ferrari*.

Paradoxically, the depression was bearing away some of the Italian manufacturers, including Itala, Chiribiri and Diatto.

Ferrari stayed close to Alfa Romeo, securing technical assistance from them and 'then made similar deals with Bosch, Pirelli and Shell.' He ran amateur drivers who could pay and signed Campari.

'In his first year the *Scuderia Ferrari* could boast 50 full and part-time drivers!' The team 'caused a sensation. It was the largest team ever put together by one individual. None of the drivers was paid a salary but received a percentage of the prize money won.'[15]

On 29 October, Wall Street crashed. In one day, 13 million shares changed hands and in absolute panic people were selling at any price they could get. The shares which promised unlimited wealth and had been pushed grotesquely over their value from 1927 through 1928 to almost double in 1929 were all but worthless and riot police had to be called to Wall Street to control hysterical crowds.

Nobody understood on that long day what the consequences would be or where they would touch. Within ten months two million Britons were out of work.

Neubauer wrote that the crash 'set up a tidal wave that swept across Europe. *Sell, sell, sell!* ran the cry. Old-established banks closed their doors. There was a spate of suicides. In the midst of this economic chaos a new party gained thirteen seats in the election for the Berlin City parliament, and it was led by a certain Dr Joseph Goebbels. Motor racing was naturally hard hit by the crisis.'[16]

It hit so hard the 1930 German Grand Prix wasn't run.

The second Monaco Grand Prix, however, proved the race was not just viable but an adornment. Twenty cars came to the grid including Hans Stuck in an Austro-Daimler. Stuck, whose age was always a mystery, held dual Austrian and German nationality. He was a hill-climb specialist and an all-rounder, powerboat racing, skiing competitively and a six-handicap golfer.

Bugattis liked Monaco and Dreyfus had one, albeit as a privateer. During practice he watched the Bugatti team and concluded that to beat them he would need an advantage. Subsequently he wondered how the idea came to him and even thought if he had dreamed it: an extra fuel tank so he wouldn't have to stop. Initially the idea met with resistance, but a 30-litre tank was fitted.

Monaco presented itself as scenic and decorous. The cars started from back towards the Gasometer hairpin, three abreast. Directly ahead they could see the road curving stately towards *Ste Devote*. To their left sunlight fell across the rows of houses and the pavement – decorated, at its rim, by trees planted at tight intervals. The sunlight created wedges and patterns of shadow on the road itself. To their right, twin tram tracks then the pavement decorated by tall lamp standards about ten yards apart while behind that, trees were planted thick. A few people stood on the pavement there, unprotected and in the formal dress of the day, just as the racing cars were unprotected from the trees and the lamp standards.

They came in a great rush and a great roar bustling and hustling fast, still three abreast. The cars on the extreme left emerged from the wedge of shadow as they reached towards *Ste Devote*, 'Williams' squeezing the other two cars on the front row. The furthest, Borzacchini, went so far over to the right that he almost touched the lip of the pavement.

At *Ste Devote* the pavement protruded like an elbow and that broke up whatever symmetry remained from the grid so that as the cavalcade streamed up the hill the cars became a single file except, here and there, where they ran side-by-side. By the time they came round the harbourside on that first lap they were all single-file and Chiron led.

Chiron seemed to have the race won because at half distance he led Dreyfus by nearly two minutes, but Dreyfus took a minute out of that.

They traded fastest laps before Chiron had a slow pit stop and Dreyfus turned the little tap to let the 30-litres flow into his engine. It brought Dreyfus close enough to strike and he could see wisps of smoke, could smell petrol – Chiron in trouble. The people in the Dreyfus pit were wild with excitement, pointing to Chiron and telling Dreyfus *he's there, he's there!* Dreyfus went by on lap 85, broke the lap record and romped the race. An official in a light suit and homburg hat with a dark band round it stood by the crude white line painted across the road. He had one foot on the pavement, the other on the road itself and he held a small flag on a long stick which he waved twice as Dreyfus thundered towards him. Dreyfus's goggles were so dirty that all he could see was the road ahead to the finish and, in a blurred backdrop, the crowd. As Dreyfus passed, the official flailed and pumped his left arm towards the Bugatti signalling *yes! Yes! Yes!*

When Dreyfus stopped his gloved hands pushed the goggles down, undid the strap of his white balaclava then tugged at it to get it off. Somebody helped him and between them it did come off. His face was framed by dirt and he exhaled. He looked tired, perhaps very tired.

The Monaco measure: Dreyfus, 100 laps, 3h 41m 2.6s, an average speed of 53.6mph: 'Williams,' 1929, 49.8mph.

The ultimate comparison: The Land Speed Record wasn't improved but Segrave attempted the record on water. In June he'd been at Lake Windermere and on a third run his boat seems to have stuck a log, killing him – the ultimate price.

Vehicles registered in Britain 2.3 million (1929, 2.2 million).

Enzo Ferrari understood that amateur drivers, paying for their drives, were a necessary way forward, but if he was to become a serious player he'd need professionals – hence the original signing of Campari although that had been on a swop and return basis. Alfa Romeo would exercise priority for important races and during the spring Campari departed Ferrari who now approached Nuvolari. Both men 'possessed towering egos' and 'did not get along.'[17] Nevertheless, Nuvolari signed a contract in June 1930.

The depression touched hard. Bentley was 'allowed to die for the want of a few thousand pounds and Sunbeam sold off, together with Talbot. Stutz and Duesenberg were gone too, but other companies clung on. Mussolini did not permit this in Italy and new cars emerged from Maserati and Alfa Romeo.[18]

In July, 15 cars set off into the dangerous clutches of Spa's hills and dales. The Peugeot of Frenchman Henri Stoffel, who'd competed in the first Le Mans 24-hour sports car race in 1923, proved the only one capable of living with the Bugattis wielded by Chiron, Bouriat and Divo.

This trio led the opening twelve of the 40 laps but Stoffel clung on. Deep into the race Divo had a puncture and Stoffel, now running second – Chiron third – chased down Bouriat but the Peugeot coughed and stopped, out of petrol.

Bugatti's management had given strict instructions that if possible the race must be Chiron's but Bouriat was two and a half minutes up the road and uncatchable. The pits signalled him *Chiron to win!* and Bouriat obeyed with a flourish of defiance. He halted close to the line, awaited Chiron's arrival patiently, watched Chiron cross the line and precisely one minute later did it himself. *Visible* team orders with all their consequences would dog Grand Prix racing all down the coming years and reach a twin climax, if you can put it like that, when in the 1980s René Arnoux was ordered to slow by Renault so Prost could overtake him (and didn't), and in the 2000s when Rubens Barrichello was ordered to slow by Ferrari so Schumacher could overtake him (and did).

At Monza there were heats again and in the final Arcangeli led Nuvolari but Varzi went past him. On lap five Nuvolari re-took Varzi but was soon hobbled by tyre problems, and Varzi won it from Arcangeli.

The French Grand Prix, at Pau – the race's tenth staging post – should have been under the fuel consumption formula again but such a small entry arrived that the organisers postponed it until the autumn. Then, restricted to cars under 1,100cc, it proved a cracker in beautiful weather. A massive crowd watched round a pastoral circuit which undulated through the countryside.

Philippe Étancelin was an independent who had enjoyed a good 1930 season but decided that he wouldn't do well in such a prestigious international event and so didn't send in his application form. He had a business in Rouen – 'selling wool for mattresses [and] exporting the feathers and down of geese and ducks for pillows, bolsters and eiderdowns' – and needed to devote some time to that. His wife sent the application form in...

Étancelin went to Pau as one among 14 Bugattis but, too anxious to prove himself, drove the car so hard in practice that it was unraceable. He decided to load it up and take it back to Rouen. His wife and mechanic said *ring up the Bugatti factory and get spare parts.* Étancelin shrugged. They persisted, he rang the factory, pleaded and they flew them down. He was on the tarmac at Biarritz airport 'with a thumping heart' watching the plane land.

One Delage stalled at the start and the cars coming up swept round him while the driver got out to have a look. Amid the dust and jostling the crowd could see the Bentley of Birkin, an enormous vehicle, a whale among swordfish. It weighed two tons.

Lehoux's gearbox broke after a hundred yards and he strode back to the pits so enraged that he was unable to speak. Étancelin chose a big rear axle so it wouldn't break and as the race unfolded he noticed that the works Bugattis – he could tell them among all the other Bugatti drivers because they wore red scarves – had smaller axles. Étancelin followed them. As she always did, Étancelin's wife gave him a signal every lap telling him his position. When the works cars pitted he led, Chiron in pursuit after a tyre change.

Pau was almost a perfect triangle with a six-mile straight culminating in a complex of tight corners, some downhill. Chiron worried about his oil pressure and along the straight took the chance to investigate. Birkin came at him fast – Birkin knew that such a huge car would lose time in the corners and have to make it up on the straights. It proved difficult. Now he had the Bentley up to 135mph and into Chiron's wake and estimated he was travelling some five miles an hour faster than Chiron who:

> seemed to be having trouble of a sort. His head was continually ducking into the cockpit as if he wanted to find something. As I came up to the rear of his car, it began slowly to swerve across the road, until for an instant my left front wheel was between his two back wheels. He still had his head in the cockpit and there seemed no chance of avoiding a terrible crash. [...] I sounded the horn for all I was worth and then instinctively let out one of the loudest yells that can ever have been heard. It rose above the noise of my engine and it rose above the noise of his. He looked up as if he had been shot, and switched his car over to the right-hand side of the road. The Bentley just scraped past.
>
> It is the only mistake I have ever known Chiron make.[19]

On lap ten an even more horrific moment awaited Birkin. 'Sabipa' lost control of his Bugatti in a fast corner. The car went off, rolled back on and a Peugeot just missed it. Birkin arrived at 80mph. He saw the wrecked Bugatti while lying across the middle of the road...

> face downwards and arms stretched rigid by his side, was the driver with a pool of blood oozing from beneath his chin. I could not brake in time. If he was killed I would have to run over him, one death being better than two, but if he was not killed there seemed to be no room between him and the edge of the road to stop me tearing into a deep ditch. The crowd was quite

silent. No-one shouted to me to tell me what had happened. I did not dare assume that he was dead, so I went through, not daring to look at the wheels on the side of the ditch and I swear that the other wheels missed that man's head by less than two inches.[20]

Birkin kept on and next lap saw an ambulance moving away from the corner. He deduced that the driver was still alive and 'thanked my stars' he hadn't driven over him to save himself.

At lap 19 of the 25 he was up into second place, beginning a long thrust to try to catch Étancelin who, cap round the wrong way, sawed at the steering wheel as he took the Bugatti round the downhill corners, his hands constantly adjusting as if he played a musical instrument. Towards the end he held down his usual youthful impulsiveness and nursed his Bugatti into the last lap with the fuel low and the clutch requiring tender loving care. Somewhere behind him the mighty Bentley of Birkin panted along, straining hard and as Birkin thought, catching him.

Étancelin came down the straight, tall trees and the frontage of an old house within the trees to his right. An official stood holding a flag on two sticks to that it resembled a board. As Étancelin passed he lowered it, a group of four men shook their fists – in delight – and on the other side of the road a photographer in plus fours and alpine hat stepped quickly out to take a picture.

Étancelin had less than a litre of fuel left when he crossed the line. At that moment he was three and a half minutes in front of Birkin. As Étancelin made his way from the line the gearbox failed completely but that didn't matter now. He coasted to his pit just down the road, his wife in a tea-cosy hat so typical of the 1930s gave him a big kiss and he smiled broadly, shaking people's hands while he was still in the cockpit.

When Birkin crossed the line the official, the men and the photographer had all gone...

Birkin remembered this as the last big race to bring him success in the 'old green Bentley, and the most enjoyable' even though he'd finished second, and when he stopped found a trace of blood on his tyres, 'Sabipa's' blood that he'd run through.

Charles Faroux, doyen of French motor racing and intimately connected with the Le Mans 24-hour race which Bentleys had won from 1927 to 1930, said to Birkin: 'The crowd laugh at your Bentley, capitaine Birkin, but I tell them not to laugh. I have seen the Bentleys at Le Mans and I know. I am Faroux. I am not a bloody fool.'[21]

Next day 'Sabipa's' wife arrived at Birkin's hotel in Pau and asked to see him.

After thanking me with many tears, she told me that her husband had
been conscious the whole time, and saw quite clearly the wheels rushing at
his head and heard the hissing sound as they went past. He confirmed my
own belief that there were not two inches between them and himself.[22]

Birkin was the best British driver of the time, and an amateur although
the fame which racing brought must have helped the motoring business
he'd set up. Small, shy, 'not very approachable' he 'had a stammer but he
gave the impression of great physical strength and stamina. He wore
white trousers, a blue open-necked jersey with a BRDC [British Racing
Drivers' Club] badge on the breast-pocket and, always, around his neck
a blue and white polka dot scarf knotted at the back to allow the ends to
stream behind.'[23]

Étancelin's career had been gathering momentum for three or four
years. He was recognised for his courtesy behind the wheel, didn't crash
and didn't get involved in incidents. A 'broad shouldered, handsome,
smiling' man nicknamed Phi-Phi, he 'was one of the great French
drivers of the thirties. [...] He drove, in blue overalls buttoned at neck
and wrists and with a tweed cap worn back to front in the manner of the
early days of motoring, crouched close to his wheel, elbows flashing up
and down like pistons. Étancelin drove with great effort, in contrast to
the calm, debonair Chiron, who delicately changed gear with thumb and
two fingers and not gripping with his fist.'[24]

The Czech Grand Prix at Brno was added to the calendar and,
reflecting the era, two drivers with aristocratic names – Hermann zu
Leiningen and Heinrich-Joachim von Morgen – shared a Bugatti which
won it while Nuvolari had a typical race. Nuvolari and Borzacchini – 'shy,
boyish, little, never had much money'[25] – drove Alfa Romeos for *Scuderia
Ferrari*. Nuvolari locked into a fierce battle with Caracciola's Mercedes
but his clutch failed on lap five. Nuvolari took over Borzacchini's car and
attacked the leaders – on the final lap his water pump failed and he
finished the race at walking pace, third.

At San Sebastian in October, the final Grand Prix of the season, Varzi
won a hard race by 22 minutes in a Maserati. Étancelin's Bugatti
overturned when a wheel collapsed, another Bugatti caught fire and the
driver was seriously injured, a third crashed, but the driver was
unharmed.

The depression forced Caracciola to close down his elegant showrooms
on Berlin's most fashionable street. That wasn't the worst of it because
in November 1930 Mercedes wrote saying his contract had been
terminated. Caracciola and Neubauer found a way round this. They put

together a deal with Mercedes so that officially, Caracciola became a privateer with a tiny team, himself as driver, his wife Charly, a co-driver, and a mechanic with Neubauer to manage it.

In 1931, Grand Prix racing abandoned the fuel consumption formula and replaced it with minimal regulations. The minimum race distance was set at ten hours, requiring two drivers for each car. It produced 'mixed fields' of sports cars which had been stripped down, and proper racing cars.

Twenty eight cars entered Monaco but Alfa Romeo withdrew because they had a contract with an Italian tyre company and the tyres had been disappointing in the Mille Miglia the week before.

Grid positions were by ballot giving Dreyfus (Maserati) pole and putting 'Williams' (Bugatti) on the second row. 'Williams' led but retired on lap five with a valve problem. Varzi (Bugatti) and Caracciola (Mercedes) were moving up, and so was Chiron's Bugatti – but Varzi had a puncture and hit a kerb. Chiron led at half distance, Caracciola's clutch failed and Chiron won by nearly four minutes from Luigi Fagioli in a Maserati.

The Monaco measure: Chiron, 100 laps, 3h 39m 9.2s, an average speed of 54.0mph: Dreyfus, 1930, 53.6mph.

The ultimate measure: at Daytona in February Campbell pushed the Land Speed Record to 245mph.

Fagioli's career arched across the Second War and on into the modern world championship. He was 'short, stocky, swarthy, with close-cropped receding hair [...] his bullet head sat aggressively on an almost indiscernible neck. Broad shoulders and muscular, hairy arms told of great physical strength. He was indeed a man in the mould of the pioneer drivers who wrestled with the monster cars at the turn of the century. [...] He scowled more often than he laughed, he was taciturn and quick to fury. Like so many Italian racing men of his time he was a true tiger in action.'[26]

German driver Manfred von Brauchitsch said Fagioli was well known for his temperament. Another view was that Fagioli enraged teams he drove for by 'insubordination' to pit signals.

Unhappily, Fagioli was no believer in team work and held the opinion that if he could outdrive the other members of his team he should be allowed to benefit from his ability, but surrounding his unswerving determination to win was an irrepressible light-heartedness, and when he was not driving he was always clowning. His equally jovial wife would usually be in his pit, and they were often to be seen sitting together, Luigi in the blue overalls and white helmet that he rarely bothered to take off between races, simply pushing it up on his head as one might a bathing cap.[27]

The Italian Grand Prix at Monza attracted five Maseratis, four Alfa Romeos (Campari-Nuvolari) and a couple of Bugattis (Varzi-Chiron). Because of the ten-hour rule and holding it in May, the race started at 8 o'clock in the morning to maximise daylight time.

Nuvolari's Alfa Romeo broke down and he walked back to the pits. Then he lay down on a blanket on some grass, a towel for a pillow, his tartan cap resting on that. A masseur in a white coat held Nuvolari's right hand in both his hands and rubbed it hard, keeping the blood flowing, keeping it supple. Nuvolari smiled – perhaps embarrassment, because he was being filmed. Jano decided that when Campari pitted Nuvolari would replace him.

Varzi led into lap two and by lap five had stretched that to five minutes over Campari. Nuvolari took over on lap 43, fuelling the car himself, and was so dominant that he won by two laps. When he slowed and stopped a crowd gathered round the car and someone pinched his chin, a gesture of great affection. Nuvolari stood in the cockpit and, amid a sea of happy faces, took a heavy swig of what looked like champagne.

The French race, at Montlhéry, produced a typical mixed entry with three works teams, Alfa Romeo, Bugatti and Maserati, while Mercedes came back for the first time since the war.

Birkin met 'Sabipa' who shook him 'energetically by the hand' and thanked him for saving his life at Pau the year before. Birkin couldn't see 'that there was anything at work in his salvation except the very greatest of good fortune. I myself had had no time to weigh the pros and cons.'

The Alfa Romeos were favourites although they knew the Bugattis would be strong and Jano instructed his three drivers – Nuvolari, Borzacchini and Ferdinando Minoia – to proceed with caution, run at an even pace and let the Bugattis go. They had to do this until their first pit stops somewhere into the third hour of the race. Since it was over the ten hours and 1,000 kilometres there was time.

Birkin was partnered by Eyston:

The roads had become very slippery and every one was finding his seat almost intolerably uncomfortable; Varzi I think drove with a cushion at his back, and another driver called desperately for padding. I lost a large patch of skin which did not return for several weeks. But all of these were able to shield their discomfort with a screen of polite discretion; and, more important, the seat of their trousers. George Eyston was less fortunate: he lost the latter [...] We had stopped at the pits and he was bending over the engine in front of the grandstands when suddenly a roar of laughter rose from the ranks of Frenchmen. At first neither of us could understand the reason for it, and we looked up and down the course for a source of amusement. By their signs and cat-calls the delighted crowd soon betrayed George's disaster, but not until he himself had betrayed a liberal area of his person to them.[29]

The Alfa Romeos ran sixth, seventh and eighth, cars ahead began to drop out and Jano gave the instruction *attack!* Nuvolari responded and in the fifth hour was up to second but the Alfa Romeos had a weakness: brakes. Nuvolari's were beginning to feel soft and all three cars pitted to see what could be done. Nuvolari continued and drove the final hours with virtually no brakes at all. Chiron, sharing with Varzi, won it and that was received with polite applause. Varzi, in his white linen cap, goggles up on his forehead, stood in the cockpit, the garlands laid across the bonnet of the car. Even at such a moment he kept his face severe, unbending, remote. Then just for an instant as if he was saying *oh, all right then* he did smile, fleeting, stolen from an image of himself he didn't wish to portray.

At Spa, Varzi forced his Bugatti into the lead but Nuvolari thrust the Alfa Romeo up to him and 'it was immediately apparent that a desperate duel was to be fought between these two cars.'[28] Nuvolari burst by on this opening lap and for two hours it raged, ego against ego, will against will, skill against skill. During the second hour the lap record was broken twice. In the fury of this Chiron calmly brought his Bugatti up, joined the duel himself and broke the lap record again. Varzi dropped out (magneto) on lap 44 of the 88 and Chiron's Bugatti eventually gave up about two and a half miles from the pits. Chiron ran there for tools, and ran back, but couldn't repair the car in time. Nuvolari had to stop twice with an ignition problem letting 'Williams' in for the win.

The Nürburgring beckoned and 100,000 paid to watch even though the banks were closed because of the financial crisis gripping Germany. The crowd anticipated a struggle between the Bugattis of Varzi and Chiron, the Alfa Romeo of Nuvolari and the big Mercedes of Caracciola which weighed two tons, had an engine exceeding seven litres and had been described by one Italian journalist as 'a throwback to the cars built twenty years ago.'

Caracciola remembered the sky becoming darker and darker. As they went to the grid at 9.30 the rain began, fine initially – it reminded him of mist – but deepening into a downpour.[30] By then, the paddock had become a morass of yellowing mud.

Fagioli in the low red Maserati with the brass radiator was into the lead as they bunched for the first loop at the end of the straight, Caracciola behind him. Caracciola tried to pass but that wasn't easy. The rain smeared the windscreen, distorting Caracciola's vision, and if he lifted his head above it the rain smacked into his face. Fagioli's Maserati, too, flung back a wave of water. Caracciola edged up to him, pulled out at The Swallow's Tail (*Schwalbenschwanz*), a pronounced loop, and went by. He thought *I need to put some distance between us so I can pit for tyres.*

The white Mercedes went past the pits 'like a whining bullet'[31] and the crowd rose to Caracciola. Fagioli came though five second behind him, then a pack of cars with Varzi, Nuvolari and Chiron among them. By lap three Caracciola was averaging more than 60mph but behind him Nuvolari had caught Fagioli and on lap six took him. The track began to dry...

> Fagioli got tired of sitting on Nuvolari's tail, and was almost level with him as he passed the grandstand at the end of the seventh lap. In a desperate, although successful attempt to pass, he skidded right across in front of Nuvolari's car.[32]

Nuvolari responded instantly and in a loop passed him, sliding the Alfa Romeo, and that drew a great shout from the crowd. The rain came back, drifting cloud masked the castle on the hill and wily Louis Chiron was coming. On lap eight he was past Fagioli, on lap 11 past Nuvolari. Caracciola led by two minutes but pitted. They must have practised this because they changed the enormous rear wheels and refuelled in something over a minute. As Caracciola prepared to drive off, Neubauer, holding his stopwatch, barked 'record time!' for the pit stop.

The rain eased again and now Chiron held an advantage because, although the weight of the Mercedes had allowed Caracciola to exploit the wet track, the lighter, more nimble Bugatti liked the dry. Chiron was taking 15 seconds a lap from Caracciola but even that wasn't enough and, with the crowd in a frenzy, Caracciola crossed the line more than a minute ahead. When Caracciola stopped he was lifted from the car and saw 'hundreds of hands reaching out to me.' He glanced across to the pit and saw Charly standing at the back of it, tears of joy down her face.

Four days later, Britain, France and the United States agreed to renew their financial credits to Germany to prevent the currency collapsing completely. Confidence was so low that the banks, closed of course before the German Grand Prix, did not re-open for another three weeks.

The Czech Grand Prix became a freak event on lap two when Fagioli lost control of his Maserati and it skidded into the wooden posts which held up the public footbridge, bringing the whole thing down. Borzacchini, close behind, actually got his Alfa Romeo through *as* the bridge was coming down. Varzi and Nuvolari arrived side-by-side and at racing speed. They speared off in opposite directions, Varzi into a bank and Nuvolari into a ditch. Caracciola (Mercedes) and Chiron (Bugatti) arrived side-by-side, too. Caracciola went into the ditch and damaged his car but somehow Chiron ploughed along the ditch, emerged beyond the debris of the bridge and continued. Varzi gave Nuvolari a lift back to the pits and Caracciola, limping forward, hit a tree. Nuvolari took over Borazcchini's car but it wouldn't restart and thirty minutes were lost as they worked on it without realising the battery had gone flat. Lehoux chased Chiron for the lead and hit a tree, Chiron beating Stuck in another Mercedes by 14 minutes.

To the motor racing fraternity the depression was something to be ridden out, an irritant with unfortunate consequences, like making car manufacturers go broke. In the other world, times were getting tougher. Three days after Brno there was a day of heavy rioting in London in protest at the Government's austerity measures.

Approaching 1932, Grand Prix racing was low: Mercedes gone, Caracciola free to drive an Alfa Romeo and, apart from Italy, no factory team but Bugatti entered races. Mussolini, however, still actively encouraged motor racing for reasons of national virility. Birkin has described the extent, flavour and importance of it, beginning with the crowds.

> *'Avanti!'* they yell, *'Avanti! Coraggio!'*[33] and if [the driver] is driving without skill, they groan without restraint. There is always something to excite them even if they have to be content with mere speed. There is a crash and the noise that breaks out must be one of the loudest in the world. Every one has advice to offer: the crowds press forward to give assistance, enemies triumph and friends weep.
>
> But under this hysteria there is a profound and genuine enthusiasm for the sport. Signor Mussolini gives it active encouragement, and the drivers are presented to him after the race. He has made motor racing far more popular in Italy than horse racing, almost indeed substituted it. The public do not have to go to specialising newspapers for their information about races and technical improvements: the popular press segregates several columns for the subject, which hints at a popularity not enjoyed so largely in other countries. Every week-end from April to September there is a meeting on one or other of their courses.[34]

Monaco was in April and by now more than established, more than an adornment. It had become a centrepiece and everybody wanted to drive there. The race in 1932 *was* Grand Prix racing. Among the leading drivers…

Alfa Romeo: Nuvolari, making his debut there, Campari, Borzacchini, Caracciola as a semi-independent.

Maserati: Fagioli, Dreyfus.

Bugatti: Varzi, Chiron, 'Williams'.

In Saturday practice Chiron went quickest with 2m 4s but the grid was decided by a draw and Chiron drew a place on the second row.

Sunday dawned fine but clouded over before the race began. As a celebrity guest, Malcolm Campbell had been lent a Rolls-Royce to drive round the circuit. He was applauded warmly. At 1.30 the starter lowered his flag and 'Williams' led from Chiron up the hill towards Casino Square. Somewhere between Casino and the exit to the tunnel Chiron overtook 'Williams' and, going hard, was four seconds in front as he crossed the line into lap two. By lap nine Chiron had reached the back-markers and into lap ten led Nuvolari by 17 seconds, Varzi running fifth. The next lap, Varzi moved to third.

Jano signalled Nuvolari *attack now, Chiron has the back-markers.* Nuvolari responded and hammered the lap record, Chiron responded and they circled, equidistant, for ten laps. Varzi hammered Nuvolari's record. Nuvolari flung the Alfa Romeo at Monaco's narrow, unforgiving streets and by lap 25 was within five seconds of Chiron, by lap 29, three.

Next lap Chiron came up behind the Polish Count Czaikowski who didn't get out of the way, forcing Chiron to follow him through the tunnel. At the chicane Chiron's hubcap brushed a sandbag, destabilising the car. It swerved, hit the footpath and rolled three times, throwing Chiron out. He suffered a cut forehead and bruising. Nuvolari missed him…

A classic Monaco pursuit had been created, Varzi hunting Nuvolari and closing on him. At 30 laps the gap was six seconds, Borzacchini third, Caracciola fourth. Nuvolari destroyed the pursuit by driving so fast that at 40 laps he led by 28 seconds, and at half distance that had become 17. Caracciola caught Borzacchini and they grappled before Borzacchini pitted for a wheel change. Caracciola ran third, second when Varzi's rear axle broke.

Jano signalled Nuvolari *slow!* He, Caracciola and Borzacchini were all in Alfa Romeos and team orders applied – but Caracciola was semi-independent. At lap 60 Nuvolari led Caracciola by 30 seconds and Borzacchini by 38.

Caracciola accelerated. He'd describe the race as very difficult. He travelled at an 'almost murderous' speed within Monaco's constrictions. Caracciola knew about the unwritten rule that if two from the same team are clear they don't race each other, the driver leading at half-distance gets the race. Otherwise they risk straining and breaking their cars. Caracciola knew also that the unwritten rule was both time-honoured and regarded as etiquette *but* headstrong youngsters, fashioning their careers so urgently, sometimes declined the convention. Caracciola was catching Nuvolari's red Alfa Romeo...

At lap 70, Caracciola cut Nuvolari's lead to nine seconds. Still Caracciola attacked and across the next ten laps found a second – not easy to do against Nuvolari – then found more. Nuvolari's 'signs to his pit become increasingly agitated. The pit staff were somewhat perplexed, failing to realise that as the pace had not been accurately foreseen, Nuvolari's tanks were practically dry.'[35]

One report found the Rascasse hairpin an interesting place to watch because you could stand so close you could almost touch the cars.

> Nuvolari talks to himself. Naturally the words cannot be heard above the noise of the exhaust, but his lips can be seen moving, and one can imagine the full-throated words they are emitting.
>
> As the end of the race approaches he becomes excited, hitting the side of the car with his right hand, gesticulating – not to the spectators, because he is blind to all that is outside himself and his car. His fuel supply is very low. Perhaps he is beseeching Madonna that it may last to the end.[36]

With ten laps to go Nuvolari led by seven seconds but soon enough Caracciola had his car up so close – Nuvolari slowing slightly – that he could see into Nuvolari's car. Travelling side-by-side, Caracciola watched Nuvolari changing gears with 'nervous, hasty gestures.' Caracciola thought *I am not a works driver, the team rejected me, I don't owe them any conventions.* He'd overtake Nuvolari if he could. He glimpsed the grandstands, saw people on their feet – they seemed to be shouting – and then he saw the finishing line.[37]

Crossing it, Nuvolari won by two seconds. He stopped and was presented with a bouquet of flowers from the Rolls-Royce which Campbell had driven.

Caracciola halted and, stepping from his car, heard the sound of jeering and whistling coming from the grandstands in 'contempt' of him. They clearly thought Caracciola *had* obeyed the convention, robbing them of a dramatic finish. Caracciola walked over to the pits feeling miserable because, all else aside, he'd never been jeered before.

Caracciola's misery cannot have been mollified when Giovannini said 'that was decent of you' but this surely was when Giovannini asked if he would like to join the team.

The Monaco measure: Nuvolari, 100 laps, 3h 32m 25.3s, an average speed of 55.8mph; Chiron, 1931, 54.0mph.

The ultimate measure: in February at Daytona, Campbell pushed the Land Speed Record from 245 to 253mph.

The start at Monza was given by the Secretary General of the Italian Fascist Party. The race would run for five hours, the Alfa Romeo clearly superior although Fagioli led the first ten laps in his Maserati and set fastest lap. Chiron and Varzi were finding their Bugattis exhausting to handle and both retired with mechanical problems. 'The Bugatti and Alfa Romeo drivers changed cars among themselves, even driving other cars in the team for which they were not nominated as spare drivers. Nuvolari drove his car single-handed…'[38]

By now people were using the word master to describe Nuvolari, pointing out that he had won round the streets of Monaco, round the roads of Italy in the Mille Miglia and now round custom-built Monza.

The French Grand Prix was at Reims, the first time on this road circuit and the race's eleventh staging post. The talk inevitably centred on Alfa Romeo and Bugatti, the only two makes on the grid of 16 cars. Caracciola led, Varzi slowing with a gearbox problem and reportedly Nuvolari shook his fist at Caracciola as he went past him on lap 11. Nuvolari was in that mood and even at the end – when Jano signalled him to slow for a grandstand finish with team-mates Caracciola and Borzacchini – he kept on and won by a distance. Nuvolari did not enter motor races to go slowly in them.

At the Nürburgring only nine cars started, the absence of Mercedes keenly felt. A traditional contest, Alfa Romeos against Bugattis, soon dissolved into a milk run for the Alfa Romeos. Caracciola won it from Nuvolari and Borzacchini, Dreyfus in a Bugatti a long way back. Nobody else finished.

The Nazis doubled their seats in parliamentary elections to become the biggest party. Within days the President of Germany blocked Hitler's appointment as Chancellor. Hitler watched and waited.

The Czech Grand Prix at Brno attracted a strong entry, including Mercedes sports cars to be driven by Wagner and an aristocratic snob, von Brauchitsch. The Alfa Romeos of Nuvolari and Borzacchini had been fast in practice and they were confident they would win. In lashing rain they led but the race became chaotic on lap three when at least four cars retired – one on fire, Varzi with an eye injury. Borzacchini retired, too – brake problems – and Nuvolari's ignition wouldn't work properly so he was constantly in and out of the pits. Chiron won it from Fagioli's Maserati; Nuvolari half an hour from Chiron.

That was 4 September, the end of another season and the beginning of something which overshadowed everything else.

Notes

1. *Racing Driver's World,* Caracciola.
2. *Full Throttle,* Birkin.
3. A car produced by Major Frank Halford, later a well-known designer with the de Havilland aero company.
4. Merz was chauffeur to Archduke Ferdinand of Austria and was at Sarajevo when Ferdinand was assassinated, starting the First World War.
5. *The Roaring Twenties,* Posthumus.
6. As was the way of it, obscure people appeared in Grands Prix. There were two Ghica-Cantacuzinos, one Jean and the other simply G. They drove at Le Mans in 1928 and even the most authoritative histories of that race give him as G. The relationship between the two – brothers, cousins – is unclear or even whether both were Princes. Nor is it clear which of them drove at Brooklands.
7. Caracciola, op. cit.
8. Charles Frederick William Grover-Williams (1903–1945) had an English father and French mother. Born in Paris, he was fluent in both languages and soon fascinated by cars. He raced motorcycles and after the First World War got a job as a chauffeur before his career in racing cars began. In the Second World War, with France occupied, he came to England and joined the Royal Army Service Corps. Because of his command of French, he ended up in the French Resistance, was captured, taken to a concentration camp and did not survive.
   http://en.wikipedia.org/wiki/William_Grover-Williams
9. *Roaring Twenties.*
10. *The German Grand Prix,* Posthumus.
11. Caracciola, op. cit.
12. *L'Auto Italiana,* quoted in *When Nuvolari Raced.*
13. *Roaring Twenties.*
14. *When Nuvolari Raced.*
15. D. David, www.ddavid.com/formula1/
16. *Speed was my Life,* Neubauer.

17. *Enzo Ferrari,* Yates.

18. *Roaring Twenties.*

19. Birkin, op. cit.

20. Ibid.

21. Ibid.

22. Ibid.

23. *Great Racing Drivers,* Hodges.

24. Ibid.

25. Caracciola, op. cit.

26. *Great Racing Drivers.*

27. *Amateur Racing Driver,* Cholmondeley Tapper.

28. *The Motor.*

29. Birkin, op. cit.

30. Caracciola, op. cit.

31. *The Motor.*

32. Ibid.

33. *Forward! Forward! Courage!*

34. Birkin, op. cit.

35. *The Monaco Grand Prix,* Hodges.

36. *The Autocar.*

37. Caracciola, op. cit.

38. *The Motor.*

Chapter 4

END OF INNOCENCE

On 30 January 1933, a sharp, wintry Berlin day, Adolf Hitler became Chancellor of Germany. It happened at noon, and the darkness began to gather then. Within a short time he began to reshape the country in the image he wished for it: not just strength but strength through calculated brutality. Hitler encouraged the belief that Germany had been deceived and humiliated after the First World War. The strength was to demonstrate, inside and outside the country, that it could never happen again.

He would do this in many ways, and motor racing was one.

He moved quickly. Mercedes came to him with an idea to build a world-beating Grand Prix car for 1934, when a new formula was to be introduced. For several years there had been unease that the cars were becoming too fast so the new formula – maximum weight without fuel, oil, water or tyres of 750kg, and a minimum width of 850mm – aimed at standardisation.

Dropping phrases like 'world domination' into any conversation with Hitler seems to have had a soothing effect on him and by the spring of 1933 he had been to the AVUS where Bugattis won – a demonstration of motor racing's power – and made a speech at the Berlin Motor Show announcing a people's car would be built, a National Socialist Kraft Korps[1] formed to promote motoring and Grand Prix cars would be built. He'd given Mercedes the word: *go*, or rather he'd told them that any company making Grand Prix cars would be subsidised with 500,000 Marks.

'The justification was simple: the machine would showcase German technology to the European masses and thereby function as a powerful propaganda tool for the New Order.'[2]

Mercedes must have been surprised to learn they weren't alone. Auto Union – a company amalgamating Audi (cars), Horch (quality saloon cars), DKW (smaller cars and motorcycles) and Wanderer (bicycles and cars) – came in for their share of the subsidy. In 1931 Wanderer had commissioned a designer, Ferdinand Porsche, to draw a racing car and that now became part of Audi.

Following the Berlin Motor Show, Hitler met Porsche and a couple of Auto Union representatives. The subsidy would be divided between Auto Union and Mercedes: the two mighty companies had been set against each other. On 7 March a department at Auto Union's Zwickau plant was already working on the Grand Prix car.

For generations, racing cars had been painted in their national colours, yellow for Belgium, green for Britain, blue for France, red for Italy, silver for Germany. The cars coming from Stuttgart and Zwickau would follow that and as a consequence would always be known as the Silver Arrows.

We are in the land of giants, giants who made the earth tremble.

'Even as astute an observer of the racing scene as Enzo Ferrari could not have had the vaguest notion of the crushing blow that was about to be dealt to him and his now outdated [Alfa Romeo] P3s.'[3]

The year 1933, and the six Grands Prix (minimum distance 500 kilometres) run during it, could only be a time of waiting.

It opened quite normally at Monaco in April and of the 18 cars eight were Alfa Romeos, three Maseratis and the other seven Bugattis. It represented the old order, and it had only this year in waiting left to it.

For the first time grid positions were determined by best practice laps rather than ballot or entry number. Chiron and Caracciola had Alfa Romeos and they had formed a 'partnership' because Chiron, who had just left Bugatti, didn't know the cars. Chiron had been having an affair with Alice 'Baby' Hoffman-Trobeck, wife of Aldred ('Freddy') – a Swiss business magnate, heir to a pharmaceutical empire and racing enthusiast. Baby was a beautiful woman, spoke several languages and had an international pedigree. She was born in Hartford, Connecticut, her father German, her mother Swedish.

Years before, Alfred had met Chiron, thought him a promising young driver and championed him. By 1932 Baby travelled to the races with the Bugatti team, officially as Chiron's timekeeper, and everyone but Freddy knew the truth. To compound this, Meo Costantini, the Bugatti team manager, was flirting with Baby and that enraged Chiron.

To further compound this, Chiron made money at Bugatti and, according to Dreyfus, his 'head had become somewhat swollen.'[4] For the Grand Prix of Monza the previous autumn, Costantini booked the Bugatti team into a small Monza hotel but Chiron said it lacked the proper amenities and intended to stay in the luxurious Principe di Savoia in the Piazza della Repubblica, central Milan. Costantini threatened that if Chiron did that he wouldn't be driving for Bugatti in 1933. Chiron stayed at the Principe di Savoia...

Dreyfus replaced Chiron at Bugatti.

At Monaco, Caracciola would show Chiron the way round. On the opening day they both did 2m 3s (57.83mph), only a second from Varzi's lap record set the year before.

Nuvolari hit a barrier at *Ste Devote* damaging the car so badly that repairs took until the Sunday and, on the second day, Caracciola crashed heavily. On the way down to the quay he braked and the brakes failed, working on only one of the front wheels. That destabilised the car and he realised he couldn't take the corner onto the quayside. He estimated his speed as 60mph, possibly even more. He had a choice: ram a stone wall or plunge in to the sea. He rammed the wall.

Chiron, passing, called out 'I'll send the mechanics' but Caracciola was in agony. He felt his leg being 'slashed by hot, glowing knives.' He was carried in a chair to a tobacconist's, his face contorted by the pain. He'd smashed his thigh and would be out for more than a year. Chiron took provisional pole with his opening 2m 3s.

The third day proved 'more animated':

All the competitors were on the circuit except Étancelin, and I ask you to believe there were some beautiful struggles which make us think that tomorrow we will be attending an ardently disputed race. Varzi and Dreyfus, using the same car in relays, covered a total of thirty laps. It was Varzi who was fastest of all.[5]

He snatched pole with 2m 2s, Chiron alongside, Borzacchini next. Nuvolari, using someone else's car, managed 2m 4s.

The race started at 1.30 but by then 'thousands of people were peering down from the cliffs and from the windows of the houses on the terraces high above the course. It was a sunny, colourful scene.'[6] From the flag Varzi, accelerating hard, took the lead. The cars dug a dust storm as they accelerated away. Borzacchini moved across on Chiron to get behind Varzi, Nuvolari fourth. By lap three Nuvolari was into second place and on lap four, to a reverberating roar, Nuvolari – in what was described as a rather stained yellow jersey, overtook Varzi up to Casino Square.

The most intense struggle in motor racing history had begun. It drew together the two men of the feud and it did not release them for 95 laps. Nuvolari led for three laps, Varzi seized it and led two, Nuvolari seized it again. Sunlight fell across them, the cars casting fleeting, ever-changing shadows as they fled round nose-to-tail. In the corners the cars weaved under the pace being forced from them, the back-ends slithering. At moments, Nuvolari leant from the cockpit as if his body posture could help the Alfa Romeo round the corners. After ten laps:

Nuvolari	21m 12s
Varzi	21m 13s

Varzi retook the lead on lap 13 and held it for four, lost it, seized it again on lap 19, the two cars fleeing round sometimes nose-to-tail and never more than 20 yards apart. After 20 laps:

Varzi	42m 26s
Nuvolari	42m 27s

Nuvolari retook the lead three laps later and held it for six, lost it for two. *L'Equipe* reported that each lap was run 'with an unparalleled animation.' After 30 laps:

Varzi	1h 3m 23s
Nuvolari	1h 3m 24s

On lap 31 Nuvolari, Varzi – and Étancelin – did 2m 3s. Soon after, Varzi equalled the lap record on three successive laps and seized the lead again. Étancelin...

was driving magnificently, but just when it looked as if he might actually pass the two Italians he took the bend coming on to the quayside slightly too fast, turned completely round and hit the sandbags while at about the same time Nuvolari went over the pavement just after coming out of the tunnel.[7]

Étancelin's Alfa Romeo emerged undamaged, and he was temporarily out of contention. After 40 laps:

Nuvolari	1h 23m 57s
Varzi	1h 23m 58s

Étancelin recovered his pace, broke the lap record and moved up towards the duel again. At half distance:

Varzi	1h 44m 48s
Nuvolari	1h 44m 49s
Borzacchini	1h 45m 9s
Étancelin	1h 45m 18s

Étancelin found a way past Borzacchini on lap 55 but drew Borzacchini with him and now all four leading cars ran together. After 60 laps:

Nuvolari	2h 5m 39s
Varzi	2h 5m 40s
Étancelin	2h 5m 41s
Borzacchini	2h 5m 42s

Five laps later Varzi seized the lead again and Étancelin was attacking when his transmission failed. *The Autocar* captured that instant.

> The best place to watch this scrap is at the Gasworks hairpin. Here, on the footpath, behind the white-washed sandbags, one is so close to the drivers that it is possible to see their lips move and to read the words they are uttering.
>   Varzi, Nuvolari and Étancelin approach this bend in a compact group. […] Étancelin is three lengths behind. He swings his Alfa round the bend, grits his teeth in a manner which indicates 'now I am going to get these two,' accelerates, slips into third and – slows down. A differential shaft has broken! He free-wheels into the pits, only a short distance away, and after jumping out of the car finds that both his hands are a mass of blisters.

Borzacchini's engine sounded as if it had a problem and he fell away from the two leaders so that after 70 laps:

Nuvolari	2h 26m 3s
Varzi	2h 26m 4s

A great cheer went up when Varzi got past Nuvolari again. In front of the main stands they'd been hammering along side-by-side and gone wide to lap Freddy Zehender, a Sicilian who had 'a wonderfully unusual and mobile face'[8] decorated by bushy eyebrows and a vast grin. Zehender's Alfa Romeo was off the pace but overtaking him created a gap for Varzi. After 80 laps:

| Varzi | 2h 46m 47s |
| Nuvolari | 2h 46m 48s |

Nuvolari re-took Varzi two laps later and finally the destiny of the race appeared to have been decided because Nuvolari led to lap 90 of the 100. After 90 laps:

| Nuvolari | 3h 7m 23s |
| Varzi | 3h 7m 27s |

The decision appeared confirmed when a slower car baulked Varzi so that with only two laps to run…

> as Nuvolari and Varzi come into the hairpin, just as they had done for those preceding laps, Varzi, six inches astern, slips into second gear, presses on the accelerator, and shoots his Bugatti past the Alfa. But Nuvolari has slightly higher speed and on the hill to the Casino his car flashes past the Bugatti.[9]

That pitched them towards the final lap, Nuvolari still leading. They were both in third gear going up the hill to Casino, both risking engine explosions. By now the crowd, the journalists and the pit crews were near hysteria. Somewhere up the hill, or just into Casino, Varzi made his supreme, sublime move and went by. It was the 34th time he had taken the lead – and Nuvolari's car spat black smoke.

An oil pipe had given way and the oil fell on to the red-hot exhaust pipe. Into Casino, going past the imperious frontage of the Hotel de Paris, a signal flashed. *Nuvolari's on fire!* He drove on, down towards the Station hairpin, drove on into the tunnel.

> The crowd, not knowing of Nuvolari's misfortune, had their eyes glued on the exit from the tunnel. Who would appear first? A low blue car shot into view. 'Varzi!' But where was Nuvolari? He emerged from the tunnel slowly, and appeared to be sitting on the tail of the car with his feet on the seat and smoke was pouring from the bonnet.[10]

Nuvolari drove on down the incline to the quay. Marshals wielding fire extinguishers gesticulated to stop him to put it out but, standing so he wouldn't get burnt, Nuvolari ignored them. The engine failed and the car rolled gently to a halt. He sprang out and pushed. He 'smiled sadly, politely, at the crowd who acclaimed him and looked out for Borzacchini.

He smiled again at Varzi, who [came past] finishing his slowing down lap, a cigarette in his lips.'[11]

Nuvolari pushed on.[12]

He never made it.

On the victory rostrum, a temporary structure like a small marquee on a balcony, Varzi accepted the cup, waved politely and smiled the stolen smile because, clearly the occasion demanded it. To his left stood a cherubic nine-year-old lad, smartly dressed for the occasion and with a flop of dark hair hanging down his forehead. He had a wondrous name like a wave rippling into the harbour, Louis Henri Maxence Bertrand Grimaldi. He would become Prince Rainier and in the decades to come make a point of standing here. He'd know Fangio and Graham Hill and Senna and Schumacher...

The Monaco measure: Varzi, 100 laps, 3h 27m 49.4s, an average speed of 56.4mph; Nuvolari, 1932, 55.8mph.

The ultimate measure: at Daytona in February, Campbell pushed the Land Speed Record to 272mph.

Bugatti's latest car hadn't been completed in time for the French Grand Prix, at Montlhéry, on a cold, grey-tinged day, and a whole dimension of the race – Varzi against Nuvolari again – was gone.

Nuvolari took the lead with a clean, crisp start from the flag but his Alfa Romeo was by now outdated. The cars streamed onto the road circuit and some five minutes later streamed back round the vast, saucer-like banking, Nuvolari still leading. He retired with a transmission problem after six laps. Earl Howe[13] in a privately entered Bugatti retired when a stone shattered his visor and hurt an eye. Campari (Maserati) won it from Étancelin after a tremendous battle, Eyston third. Campari was intoxicated. As a crowd gathered round him he was so tall he loomed above them, the swarthy face smiling and smiling. Beneath his overalls he wore collar and tie. *I'm going to retire,* he'd say, *at the end of the season.*

Nuvolari was clearly unhappy with Alfa Romeo and a week before the Belgian Grand Prix he took part in a minor race at Reims, where the car broke down again. He reached a decision: *I'll take a Maserati to Spa* but exploring the powerful single-seater he felt the road holding wasn't satisfactory.

'Diagnosing the weak point, he wasted no time and transformed himself into a mechanical engineer: he dismantled the car, fitted a cross-member under the engine and reinforced the chassis side members using two robust bolted-on and welded liners. The car was ready on the Friday after 24 hours of uninterrupted work.'[14]

He started last but 'flew off like a dart,' led after the first lap – Spa is 9.2 miles long, of course – and won it from Varzi by more than three minutes.

Monza was touched hard by tragedy, although not in the Grand Prix where Nuvolari needed a wheel change with two laps to go – he'd gone down the straight 'gesticulating and pointing at his wheels' one lap, arrived at full speed at the pits next lap, 'so fast that the car skids slightly under braking, but Nuvolari manages to regain control.' He sat, anxious, consumed by impatience as the mechanic hammered the nut on the left rear wheel firm. Fagioli went by. Nuvolari glanced back a time or two, nervous like a bird. Deep in the pit Enzo Ferrari stood looking the stern supervisor. As the final hammer blow struck Nuvolari shifted the gearlever into first and was gone. An instant later, he took both hands off the wheel and raised them in the international gesture *nothing you can do against fate.*[15] Fagioli won it.

Dreyfus and Costantini were not at Monza because the Bugatti Type 59 wasn't ready. This car succeeded the Type 51, outpowered by its rivals. The Type 59 'was the last example of what is termed the classic Grand Prix car, with non-independent suspension and comparatively unstreamlined bodywork.'[16]

Instead they took lunch at the *Pur Sang*[17] – an inn which, according to Dreyfus, might have come from an enchanted fairy tale and looked as if it ought to be made of gingerbread – beside the Bugatti factory. They tried to listen to the commentary from Monza but reception was difficult.

During the first heat of a supporting race a Duesenberg shed oil on one of the banked curves.

For the second heat Campari helped push his car to the grid. By now he had grown into a portly man. Seeing the camera he grinned broadly. Campari told his mechanics to get a whole roast chicken ready for him because he'd be so hungry when he got back he'd eat it all. He and Borzacchini went out, both lost control on the oil, both overturned and both were killed. Campari's car lay belly up in foliage, a policeman guarding it. In the final, Count Czaikowski was also killed at the same place.

The running commentary suddenly stopped in the *Pur Sang* and in the silence Costantini turned to Dreyfus and said *there's been an accident.* Somehow Constantini sensed it. Dreyfus felt this was the saddest day of his time at Bugatti.

Nuvolari, deeply shocked, stayed away from the Czech Grand Prix which Chiron won. Chiron added the Spanish Grand Prix at San Sebastian a week later. Nuvolari, commanding that race, crashed on lap

21 of the 30 in a downpour. His Maserati struck a wall, throwing him out and he woke in hospital, a familiar environment.

In the background, work on the Mercedes progressed and Alfred Neubauer was putting together a team of drivers. He'd settled on von Brauchitsch, an awkward man with aristocratic pedigree but a brave, talented driver and had Fagioli, with all the rewards and problems the Italian would bring, in mind. For the third driver, Neubauer mused *Caracciola?* but had he recovered enough from the Monaco crash to drive? Would he ever drive again? In November, Neubauer travelled to Lugano, where Caracciola and Charly were staying, to find out. Neubauer has recounted[18] how he challenged Caracciola to walk. 'Without a word he got up and took several steps up and down the room. He laughed, but I could see the beads of sweat on his forehead and the twitch of pain round his mouth when he put his weight on the injured leg.'

Caracciola's leg 'hurt awfully, the plaster seemed to have loosened and I had the unpleasant feeling that Neubauer was following each step I took.'[19]

Mercedes and Auto Union wanted to make maximum impact on their debuts, and they selected the AVUS Grand Prix on May 27 for that. Neubauer offered Caracciola a contract, but with a stipulation. In practice for the AVUS he had to prove he could still handle a racing car. Neubauer left the next day.

In January 1934 Caracciola travelled to the Mercedes headquarters in Stuttgart to sign the contract. The journey put such strain on his leg that for a time he simply lay on his hotel bed. He wouldn't have signed the sort of contract on offer before his crash but now he had to be grateful for whatever he could get.

In February the Caracciolas were in their chalet at Arosa in the Swiss Alps. Charly went skiing with a party of friends and an avalanche hit them. Caracciola waited at the chalet in the dining room, lighting all the candles there. That night someone came. At first Caracciola thought it was Charly, but then saw the silhouette of a man. He went down, holding a candle and the man told him that she was dead. Caracciola went back to the dining room and put out all the candles except the one he held in his hand.

Caracciola retreated into a private world. Baby Hoffman-Trobeck nursed him out of it and Chiron brought him out of it when he arrived at the chalet without warning and asked if he would like to drive the lap of honour before the Monaco Grand Prix. Caracciola said no, Chiron persisted – 'You're still a young man, you can't retire just yet' – and Caracciola said yes.

The great career was reborn, and just in time to occupy the land of the giants.

The Mercedes, known as the W25, had a 3.3-litre engine and independent suspension: the wheels were 'sprung entirely independent of each other. The car was fitted with a thin-gauge light alloy body, with a streamlined nose piece over the radiator and front suspension, as well as a long headrest behind the driver.' The 'external appearance' was 'entirely new [...] and a complete break from the traditional single-seater racing car.'[20]

In February, Mercedes went to Monza to test the W25 with von Brauchitsch but he crashed and Fagioli was called in. At Monza, Fagioli showed what he could do and convinced Neubauer. He had of course been driving for Alfa Romeo and Enzo Ferrari was 'publicly furious over what he considered a traitorous act, but his histrionics surely veiled an understanding that Fagioli was a professional like himself and would race for the team – or the country – prepared to pay him the most money.'[21]

Auto Union unveiled their car on 6 March, exactly 365 days from work beginning on it. For the first time, the engine – 16 cylinders, initially giving 295 horsepower – was behind the driver. Stuck took it up and down the AVUS, breaking the track record. Stuck was an experienced driver, but the others in the team – zu Leiningen, Momberger and Wilhelm Sebastian – might have been a weak link. Manfred von Brauchitsch, firmly embedded in the Mercedes camp, looked carefully at this car made by the opposition and was 'not a little surprised' to see the engine at the back with the driver sitting over the front axle.

Alfa Romeo had produced a more powerful car and it raced under the name *Scuderia Ferrari*, with Varzi, Chiron and Guy Moll[22] driving it. Maserati provided cars for the privateers, including Nuvolari, although he would drive a Bugatti at Monaco and Alfa Romeos elsewhere.

At Monaco, in April, Caracciola did the lap of honour amid a conflict of emotions. He took care to go past the pits at reduced speed and there he saw the mechanics at work, heard the engines being fired. People waved. He reached the place where he'd crashed and drove past that, drove on to the shoreline at the harbour. He felt a breeze coming up from the water and thought *good weather for racing*. His leg ached and he manipulated the accelerator and brake pedals with his other foot. He completed the lap and by the time he had done that the grid had formed up, five rows, three deep. Caracciola stopped and gazed at the familiar faces. He saw Nuvolari's 'small, wiry toreador's figure,' Chiron 'in his light-blue racing suit with his red-and-white dotted scarf, Varzi 'with his precisely parted hair and his eternally smouldering cigarette,' Earl Howe 'with his shrewdly smiling eyes, this time without his grey umbrella.'[23]

Caracciola watched the start, watched Dreyfus take the lead and Chiron track him, poised to strike and take it for himself. Caracciola watched the cars scream up towards Casino then he turned round and walked away. The experience had shaken him because he understood that this was his home. *A man is a racing driver as another is a hunter.* He felt *it came from instinct, from an urge deeper than conscious thought.*[24]

The race turned on pit stops and only three drivers of the 15 starters didn't make one. Nuvolari suffered brake problems and a four-minute stop punished him. Chiron made a mistake with two laps to go and went into the sandbags at the Station hairpin, letting Moll through for the win.

The Monaco measure: Moll, 100 laps, 3h 31m 31.4s, an average speed of 56.0mph; Varzi, 1933, 56.4mph.

The ultimate measure: unchanged from Campbell's 272mph in 1933.

Nuvolari drove a Maserati at Alessandria between Monaco and the AVUS but in the wet it went off and rolled, trapping him. His left leg was broken and they took him to that familiar place, hospital. It gave him five weeks to recover before he would take a Maserati to the AVUS.

Caracciola travelled to Berlin and, staying at the same hotel as Neubauer, asked if he could make his first run early the next morning to avoid Press attention. Caracciola would remember a lovely May morning, the car a dream of a thing. He handled it and himself gently for a lap, the leg hurting, but bearable. He accelerated, and now the trees on either side of the track became a wall of grey and of green, the track itself became a white band and the wind rose and rose into a great whine.

He said to himself *I can still drive!*

The Mercedes cars suffered problems with their carburettors and made a tactical withdrawal. Nuvolari meanwhile made a tactical advance. He arrived at the AVUS with his leg in plaster and the Maserati modified so he could drive it using only his good foot. Violent rain delayed the start and Stuck led in the Auto Union, Chiron looming behind him out of rolling spray, Nuvolari third *on dry tyres*. Stuck forced the streamlined Auto Union so hard that it went out of sight. Smooth and sensuous, it seemed to skim the circuit rather than drive across it. However, Stuck retired with a failing clutch which opened the race to Moll in a streamlined Alfa Romeo, Momberger third, Nuvolari an extraordinary fifth. Moll, seated in the cockpit, had a vast, circular garland placed over him and almost submerged within it. One happy official in a military uniform, helping to hoist it over Moll's head, wore a swastika armband...

A week later at the Eifel race round the Nürburgring, von Brauchitsch won from Stuck, the Alfa Romeo of Chiron third, 5m 43s behind, the Alfa Romeo of a young German, Paul Pietsch, fourth, 16 minutes adrift. Everybody could see something profound had begun.

Both German teams went to the French Grand Prix at Montlhéry to launch their first concerted assault. The Mercedes, under Neubauer – already a portly, rotund figure – may even have had a sense of humour they were willing to show in public. On the cockpit of one car they put up a sign *Defense d'entrer* [No entry] in case, presumably, anyone wandered along and fancied having a go themselves. You can understand why Mercedes were anxious this did not happen. The engines developed over 300hp, all four wheels had independent springs and, to service their three cars, they had specialists in carburation, tyres and fuel.[25]

The Mercedes team hadn't raced in France since Lyon in 1914, when Lautenschlager won. The cars were potent propaganda – if they won – and Hitler watched closely.

Stuck equalled the lap record on his first flying lap and he'd never been to the circuit before. The record was soon tumbling, although the Italian cars were beating it, too, with Chiron going particularly fast in the Alfa Romeo. All this culminated in the record being beaten by 13 seconds.

A crowd of 80,000 watched as Chiron made a daring start from the third row, surging past all the German cars as they tried to get their power on. Caracciola was soon past him – the power coming on – but Chiron retook him. Stuck moved up and took the lead himself but both Mercedes and Auto Union showed fallibility. No German car finished and Stuck's Auto Union was so difficult to re-start after a pit stop that three mechanics had to link arms to swing the handle. The French crowd cheered when Stuck, the last German car running, finally dropped out on lap 32 of the 40 with a fuel system failure. This did not hide the truth. The Maseratis and Bugattis were clearly obsolete and, although Chiron won from Varzi – making Alfa Romeo 1 and 2 – the future lay elsewhere.

A crowd estimated at 200,000 trekked to the Nürburgring to cheer the German cars for quite another reason. Here was a symbol of a humiliated and battered nation gaining its dignity again with these prehensile, brutally powerful cars which represented *them*. The Nürburgring had always been an immense living panorama of an occasion and now

Germany made cars to compliment the immensity. This was so potent, so symbolic that German politicians – and German politics – could not resist exploiting it, and didn't.

In practice, von Brauchitsch crashed badly enough to break an arm and five ribs. 'Each racing driver will be caught out one time or another,' von Brauchitsch would say. 'After an accident he will always try to get back into the car as soon as possible. At the Nürburgring I had a particularly nasty one. I was blinded by the setting sun. I crashed and was bleeding from several wounds. I was unconscious on a stretcher. At the hospital they put me together again and on the Sunday I could hear the engines…'

It was a cool race day, clear and dry, and because grid positions had been drawn, the leading German car – Caracciola – took its place only on the third row. At such a circuit, and at such a race over 354 miles, that mattered nothing. Caracciola still wondered if his leg would last that distance. Chiron, from the second row, took his Alfa Romeo into an early lead but Stuck from two rows behind, gave the Auto Union its head, Caracciola following in the Mercedes. Chiron was quickly shed and Stuck covered the opening lap from a standing start at 76.0mph, a mere one and a half mph slower than Nuvolari's record of 1932 (no race in 1933, of course), and that had been a flying lap.

Caracciola urged his car up towards Stuck and they traded fast laps, Caracciola a 78mph, Stuck at 79.1 and 79.2, Caracciola at 79.2mph. They battled hard and at the Karusel, on lap 13 of the 25, Caracciola overtook Stuck on the outside. The crowd loved that, standing and cheering and roaring. Caracciola even accelerated, but next lap the engine let go.

Stuck stroked the Auto Union home, winning in 4h 38m 19.2s from Fagioli in the Mercedes, a couple of minutes behind. Chiron, third, came in more than eight minutes after Stuck, a distance of around ten miles. If Stuck and Fagioli were driving into the future, Chiron was driving from the past.

The Belgian customs decided the outcome of the Belgian Grand Prix by trying to charge both German teams duty on their alcohol-based fuel. The Germans refused and didn't go to Spa where only seven cars set off on the 40 laps in light rain. Chiron and Varzi were conducting an 'impassioned duel' trying to break each other, Dreyfus running third and Bugatti team-mate Tonino Brivio fourth. Chiron crashed near *Eau Rouge*, Varzi led but his engine blew and Dreyfus inherited the lead. He glanced in his mirror and saw that Brivio looked like a man possessed. Brivio was intent on overtaking, Dreyfus responded, Brivio responded to that. They went faster and faster. *Absurd,* Dreyfus thought, *for us to break each other.*

He signalled to Costantini, and Costantini signalled to Brivio *back off.* Dreyfus won it from Brivio by almost two minutes. The real drama happened just off the course. At the end, the spectator area over the pits collapsed and people fell onto the pits.

Von Brauchitsch, discharged from hospital, went to Bremgarten, a circuit west of Berne, for the first Swiss Grand Prix. He suffered constant pain, needing help to get into and out of the Mercedes and had a pillow to soften the juddering on his back.

A Voiturette race was run on race morning, in heavy rain, with two well-bred young Britons driving MG's, Dick Seaman and Hugh Hamilton. Seaman said the course was 'about five miles round. At first sight it appeared very slow, but later in practice we found it really fast, many of the corners that appeared to be quite sharp as you approached them turning out to be flat-out bends. This was due to the trees which bordered almost the entire course.'[26] Seaman worked into the lead and won it with the Grand Prix world watching.

Hamilton also competed in the Grand Prix, driving a Maserati. The rain was still heavy when the race began. Stuck led, Nuvolari in the Maserati doggedly after him for twenty laps. Eventually Nuvolari's ignition failed. Hamilton was far off the pace and Stuck had crossed the finishing line to win when news came through that he'd crashed. The Maserati went into a 'wild skid'[27] in a wooded section and hit a tree, killing Hamilton instantly. Seaman and the British Consul arranged the funeral, and Hamilton was buried in Berne.

Memories of Monza 1933, and the deaths there, lingered. The length of the track had been cut to 2.6 miles and chicanes added. Caracciola remembered how hot that autumn was, how they had to practise every day. He described the chicanes as 'an intricate system of various twists' and explained how you were changing gear the whole time. Another driver said *'Monza is a real mountain course minus the mountains.'*

Von Brauchitsch was back in hospital because he'd complained of a sore eye after Berne and tests revealed he had a fractured skull from the Nürburgring. Fagioli's mechanic, Hermann Lang, was given a chance because the brakes on that Mercedes needed bedding in. This was done after practice on the Milan autostrada. Fagioli's car, Lang remembered, 'hardly had any brakes left and could not have lasted the race.' Lang had strict instructions not to rev above 3,000 or 'you'll be bounced out of your seat.' Lang took this...

order calmly, but inwardly got quite excited as I had my own ideas about the forthcoming run! Secretly I put a set of 'hard' plugs into my pocket and drove the car as ordered up and down without exceeding 80mph and using the brakes from time to time to bed them in. This autostrada, lined with mulberry trees and passing through cornfields, runs from Milan to Lago Maggiore. My [fellow mechanics] had parked the lorry by a roadmender's hut. The autostrada was dead straight and flat. To-day, I promised myself, I would exceed 120mph in a racing car for the first time in my life. I stopped at the hut and told those two that the brakes were all right. They wanted to load the car into the transporter and were surprised when I kept my seat. Their faces dropped even more when I pulled the 'hard' plugs[28] from my pocket. […] After fitting the racing plugs I asked them to give me a push start. They refused at first and only relented after I swore at them in no mean fashion. After the car got going, I turned to see their long faces. As I opened the throttle, I realized quite well how high I could rev the engine. […] I did not exceed 3,000 revs in any gear. That already brought me to the exit road from the autostrada and I slowed to turn around. When the rev counter showed 3,000 in fourth gear (about 100mph) I quickly thought, should I or shouldn't I? 4,000 revs – 110mph, 5,000 revs – 130mph. For the first time in my life I had exceeded 120, it was wonderful! I was in a world of my own and the wind howled round my head and through my heart![29]

Nuvolari had the new Maserati but it was heavy and only just passed the 750kg weight restriction. One report suggests that as the cars and drivers paraded past the grandstands before the start the drivers gave a Fascist salute.

On a broiling day Stuck led from Fagioli, Varzi and Caracciola who moved up to second while 'in Nuvolari's magical hands the glorious Maserati ran wonderfully, even overcoming the Auto Unions. Nothing however could resist the progress of the Mercedes.'[30] Stuck led in the Auto Union from Caracciola at lap ten, Nuvolari's brakes fading. Stuck and Caracciola wrestled over the race. The heat was particularly oppressive and sweat stung Caracciola's eyes. To his dread he felt his leg beginning to hurt and asked himself *what if it gets worse?* He answered this by doing the only thing he knew, driving on.

Lap after lap as he passed the pits he saw Neubauer signal *Faster!*

All race long Caracciola tried to defy 'the hellish firebrand in my leg.' On lap 59 Stuck pitted because the radiator had burned his feet and zu Leiningen replaced him.

A lap later the pain overwhelmed Caracciola. He shouted to the mechanics not to waste time changing the wheels. *Fagioli to replace me!*

The mechanics lifted Caracciola out and Fagioli replaced him. Caracciola walked towards the rear of the pit trying, as best he could, to prevent the leg dragging. At unguarded moments, as he must have known, he just limped awkwardly.

Fagioli won it from the Stuck car, Nuvolari driving to the end without any brakes.

Stuck led Spain but an oil pipe failed after three laps, and Caracciola led now, from Wimille – a Parisian who has been described as aloof and lonely – in a Bugatti, Fagioli fourth. The Mercedes looked stronger and stronger, the Bugatti fell away and Caracciola seemed to have the race safe. Neubauer ordered him and Fagioli to *hold station* but that was just the kind of pit signal Fagioli disobeyed on principle. He caught and passed an exhausted Caracciola and they finished in that order.

Neubauer was not pleased. He'd describe Fagioli as a man with 'no sense of team-spirit and no time for team-discipline.' Fagioli's tactics in a race were 'to wait till the opposition had been worn down, and thinned out. Then, when I gave the signal to ease off, he would accelerate. That was how he won the race.' Neubauer 'tried to reason with him, pleaded and threatened – all to no purpose. Fagioli's invariable reply was that I did not want him to win because he was not a German.'[31] More than that, an intense rivalry burned between Caracciola and Fagioli. Neubauer put it another way: Caracciola's successes aroused in Fagioli an 'insane jealousy'.

At the Czech Grand Prix, the entry of the local driver, Josef Brazdil, became one of the strangest stories in all Grand Prix racing. He seems to have borrowed money to buy a Maserati and, unable to pay it back, went to prison. Some of the drivers appealed to the authorities to release him so he could take part in the Grand Prix, returning to prison after it. On his first practice lap Brazdil drove at a corner flat out and crashed into woods, destroying the car and killing himself. Inexperience or suicide? Nobody knew, and nobody knows.

By now the future was clearly visible. Fagioli in the Mercedes and Stuck in the Auto Union fought for the lead and Nuvolari urged his Maserati to stay with them. It couldn't. A pit stop towards the end cost Fagioli the race, Stuck streaming by and winning it by three minutes, Nuvolari almost a minute further back.

The future was German.

In 1935 there would be nine Grands Prix, from April at Monaco to Donington in England's Midlands in October, and weaved into that a European Championship.[32] If that has a modern feel, so too does the fact that the privateer – the inspired amateurs, sometimes titled, invariably rich – had been superseded. Only three teams mattered in 1935, Mercedes, Auto Union and Alfa Romeo. Of the nine Grands Prix, only once – in France – did any other make finish in the top three (Maserati, third) until Donington, when the Germans didn't go and a shoal of Bugattis helped themselves. Even then, an Alfa Romeo won.

Auto Union didn't enter Monaco and although the constrictions of the place prevented Mercedes from reaching maximum power they deployed enough of it. The front row became eloquent proof because it was decided by best practice times and the three Mercedes filled it, Caracciola (pole), von Brauchitsch and Fagioli. The next two rows were Alfa Romeos – Nuvolari on row two but nearly three seconds slower than Caracciola – and then an assortment of Maseratis and Earl Howe in a Bugatti.

Fagioli was in hungry form, leading and breaking the lap record, neither of the other Mercedes finished and he had a famous victory. Nuvolari indulged in a lively struggle for third place before his brakes began to fade. 'Nuvolari tried everything but he had to accept that it was useless, not to say dangerous, to fight on.'[33]

The Monaco measure: Fagioli, 100 laps, 3h 23m 49.8s, an average speed of 58.1mph: Moll, 1934, 56.0mph.

The ultimate measure: at Bonneville, USA in September, Campbell pushed the Land Speed Record to 301mph.

Although not a Grand Prix in the accepted sense of this book, the Eifel race at the Nürburgring a week before the French Grand Prix was instructive because a young German driver, Bernd Rosemeyer, had just been signed by Auto Union to race alongside Varzi. Rosemeyer made a striking impression on one of the English contestants who, having finished work on his car one evening, had a lift with him back to the hotel in the village of Adenau, where the drivers traditionally stayed.

This 26-year-old, impetuous German had achieved fame as a rider of motorcycles for DKW, part of the Auto Union combine [...] He had great capabilities, but in addition there was a strong streak of recklessness in his character, fully apparent on this occasion. He drove as fast as his car would go all the time, and his method of negotiating crossroads in the town was simply to charge straight over, leaving all other traffic to take care of itself. It was a brief drive, but long enough to make me feel thoroughly uncomfortable. As we drew up at the hotel in Adenau, Caracciola, the leading driver of Mercedes-Benz came walking along with the little wire-haired terrier that was his constant companion. He walked with a slight but unmistakable limp.[34]

Caracciola won the race from Rosemeyer, Lang fifth. Lang freely confessed that he could not keep up with the leaders but pointed out that nobody had expected him to and, anyway, as a reserve driver he couldn't expect the same sort of engines as the regular team-members. He was content with where he finished and here, quite suddenly, were two drivers who would dominate: Lang the humble mechanic, much derided for his peasant origins by the haughty von Brauchitsch; and Rosemeyer who stands alongside Nuvolari as among the greatest drivers who have ever lived. Some put Caracciola in with them, too.

The Auto Unions did go to Montlhéry where three chicanes had been incorporated to slow the cars. The Germans dominated the front of the grid (practice times gave grid placings) although Nuvolari wrung a 5m 23.6s from the Alfa Romeo, good enough for the middle of the front row.

Nuvolari led, which prompted one Italian journalist to wonder 'is the German superiority about to collapse?' and he answered his own question: 'no'. The Alfa Romeos retained their sit-up-and-beg body shapes and had new engines of almost four litres, but the expected happened. These engines, which developed at least 320hp, were fitted into the old chassis and they had too much power for them.

Von Brauchitsch had ambivalent feelings about the pit signals in general. 'They have to be followed under all circumstances,' he would say[35] – but long after he had retired! – 'and you just have to knuckle down, very often against your will, against what you want and sometimes against what you know you can really do. The driver does not have the time or the overall knowledge of what is happening everywhere and so he cannot think things through to their end. So he has to follow the signals. That's not always easy...sometimes it can even drive him to despair.'

Deep into the race Caracciola led with von Brauchitsch closing on him.

'I had to fight against myself when the pit signal was given and I had to let Caracciola have the victory.'

Nuvolari, whose transmission failed after 14 laps, set fastest lap but Zehender, in a Maserati, finished third, two laps down – 15½ miles.

The European Championship opened at Spa, although Auto Union felt their new engines weren't ready. After Lehoux stalled his Maserati and all the other nine cars got safely round him Caracciola led, von Brauchitsch fourth and moving up. Soon enough the Mercedes were first, second and third. Von Brauchitsch retired with a mechanical problem and Fagioli attacked Caracciola. The insane jealously gripped him and he brandished a fist when Caracciola wouldn't get out of the way. An intense anger gripped Neubauer, who signalled Fagioli *in!* For once, Fagioli obeyed.

Von Brauchitsch was out at the back of the pits having a glass of champagne and enjoying watching the race.

Fagioli shouted at Neubauer and Neubauer shouted at Fagioli.

Von Brauchitsch heard people calling his name and trotted through to the front of the pit. He heard Fagioli shouting, heard Neubauer order him to take over Fagioli's car. The mechanics changed the plugs and von Brauchitsch jumped into the car but the seat was 'far too wide for me. Fagioli's body was entirely different to mine and it had been made for him. I had to find room for my long legs somehow, which wasn't easy, but after a couple of kilometres I had done that.' He ran fourth, Dreyfus and Chiron between him and Caracciola. 'I raced like the devil and after a hard fight I was able to overtake Dreyfus. My whole body was streaming with sweat and my hands, arms and legs were terribly tired, but before I passed the great Chiron.'

That made von Brauchitsch second behind Caracciola at the end, and he felt completely exhausted. He lay on the pit floor but got up smartly when he heard the President of the Belgian Automobile Club had his cup for finishing second.[36]

The organisers of the German Grand Prix entertained no doubts that a German car would win it and be driven by a German. The winner's garland had been made large to fit that German, whoever he turned out to be. The only anthem available for the victory ceremony was the German. The three Auto Unions and five Mercedes would come across the outdated Alfa Romeos and Maseratis when they were lapping them, and even on a circuit of 14.1 miles that might happen several times. Nuvolari, poor Nuvolari, had an Alfa Romeo Tipo B 'P3'. Outdated? Jano was working on a new car but, at the Nürburgring, Nuvolari had to make do with 'the largest 3.8-litre version of the P3 engine.'[37] Nuvolari didn't want anyone to see the engine…

Pietsch, had joined Auto Union although he found the rear-engined car very difficult and he didn't care for it. He had another problem; his wife Ilse was having an affair with Varzi.

Neubauer[38] describes the Varzi-Ilse Pietsch love affair discreetly by giving Pietsch and Ilse pseudonyms, Lil and Peter.

The 'friendship' between Varzi and Lil was now a general subject of conversation, even among the mechanics. The only one who did not seem to realise what was going on, who was completely wrapped up in racing cars, was Peter. But the day soon came when he had his eyes opened.

Nor was this all, or anywhere near it. Baby Hoffman-Trobeck had left Freddy for Chiron, but the 'obsessively vain' Chiron wouldn't contemplate marriage to an older woman like her and she became known as 'Chiron's mattress'. She it was who helped console Caracciola after Charly's death in the avalanche, and they in turn began an affair – which Chiron didn't know about.[39]

The grid at the Nürburgring had many other dimensions than racing as the drivers prepared for the 22 laps.

The wear on tyres might prove crucial and when practice was over the chief technician of Continental, supplying Mercedes, had a look. He found Caracciola's quite normal but von Brauchitsch had worn his much more, especially the left rear which was down to the canvas inner-tubing. Von Brauchitsch would have to stop at least twice and even then his 'ruthless' driving style might bring danger.

An immense crowd streamed early towards the Nürburgring – start 11am – under fine drizzle and when they were there some, to amuse themselves, had sing-songs to harmonicas or watched the soldiers wearing swastikas march up and down.

Adolf Hühnlein, leading motorsport official and conduit to Hitler, was cheered when he arrived and Nuvolari, in an overcoat, goggles over his forehead, chatted to him.

An Englishman, Raymond Mays,[40] was on the fourth row in an ERA[41] with von Brauchitsch and Caracciola's Mercedes ahead and when all the German engines were fired up the noise was so violent it frightened him. Mercedes used special fuel and it 'acted like tear gas'. Mays called out to his mechanic – *handkerchief! handkerchief!* – because the tear gas made his eyes stream.[42]

The drizzle still fell, mist hung in the distant trees. The start was by lights, red, then yellow – *fifteen seconds!* – then green. Stuck's Auto Union stalled and his mechanics ran on to the grid as the cars were accelerating away. Varzi's rear wheel struck one of them, fracturing his skull. Varzi could seem cold, but under that he was sensitive, introverted, highly strung and the incident affected him so much that he drove badly after it.

'Caracciola's Mercedes just shoots clear of the pack, and Nuvolari with his Alfa is so close to Fagioli's Mercedes that the scarlet and silver wheels almost touch. Spray is flung high, and car after car hurtles past, while the crowds in the stand leap to their feet amid cries of *"Hinsitzen!"* ("Sit down!")'[43]

Caracciola completed the opening lap 12 seconds in front of Nuvolari and into lap two Rosemeyer devoured Fagioli and Nuvolari. The race assumed a turbulent shape. Nuvolari, outpowered on the straights, would do what he could, dancing his square-jawed Alfa Romeo up the hills and down the dales and gaining in the corners. Even that seemed only gesturing because he drifted back and, anyway, by lap six his was the only Alfa Romeo still running.

The turbulence went on. Rosemeyer's Auto Union struck a bank and he pitted, Nuvolari went past von Brauchitsch. At lap seven, Caracciola led Fagioli by 32.7s, Nuvolari at 48.0s, von Brauchitsch at 51.6s.

Von Brauchitsch re-took Nuvolari and a great impetus began to gather within the turbulence. Nuvolari went past von Brauchitsch again, Fagioli dropping back. The impetus tightened Nuvolari onto Caracciola, von Brauchitsch onto Nuvolari – and, astonishingly, Nuvolari set fastest lap. He'd remember all this in terms of a 'terrible battle' and during it the German drivers tried 'some amazing acrobatic feats, coming close to me on the grass and at the barriers. The track was strewn with earth and grass. Bits of gravel, thrown up by their rear wheels, were coming at me. Under a very dark sky I could hear the high pitched wail of their engines and see the flames coming out of the exhaust pipes.' Somewhere out there, Nuvolari got the Alfa Romeo up to and past Caracciola.

At lap ten, Nuvolari led Caracciola by 9.1s with Rosemeyer coming at them and von Brauchitsch fourth.

Von Brauchitsch's elbow bled from repeatedly hitting the Mercedes' bodywork, the palm of his hand bled from working the gearstick and the pedals were so hot they burned his feet.

The impetus broke the whole race order up, Rosemeyer passed Caracciola into second, Caracciola clinging, von Brauchitsch snapping at him and on a long dip going by. Into lap 11 the mechanics readied for pit stops – the first four cars would be stopping together.

'It is a sight for the gods as mechanics leap to the wheels, and others insert the gigantic funnels for the refills. The Germans are busy with their cars, like ants. Jacks go under, wheels are spun off, churns of fuel emptied in, while hubbub arises from the packed stands.'[44]

> Nuvolari jumps out of the car, runs to the pit, jumps into the car again, gets out again, puts a water bottle to his lips, shouts something to Chiron, goes to one of the mechanics, jumps into the car again. Under the excitement Chiron does knee-bends, with beseeching movements of his arms while Nuvolari urges the mechanics to hurry.[45]

Von Brauchitsch had a large towel draped over his head and shoulders to prevent spilt fuel running down his back. He was handed new goggles, handed a damp sponge for his face. Continental would be having a close look at the tyres which had just been taken off his Mercedes just as, each lap when he passed the pits, someone with binoculars monitored their condition. More than anywhere else except Spa, on the Nürburgring a tyre burst could kill.

Stop-watches clicked recording the length of the pit stops as the cars shrieked away.

Von Brauchitsch	47s
Caracciola	1m 7s
Rosemeyer	1m 15s

Nuvolari was stationary. The pressure pump which forced fuel into the tank had blocked and it had to be done using a funnel. Nuvolari swore, gesticulated for the mechanics to *Hurry! Hurry!* and in his frustration almost did a war dance.

Nuvolari	2m 14s

He emerged sixth and completing lap 12 ran almost a full minute behind von Brauchitsch, now leading after his swift pit stop. Nuvolari caught and passed Stuck, caught and passed Caracciola and there was Rosemeyer chugging towards the pits with a broken petrol pipe. Nuvolari went past him into second place but the impetus had borne von Brauchitsch far away. *As* Nuvolari went into second place he was 1m 9s behind. *As* von Brauchitsch passed the pits on lap 14, Neubauer made a gesture like closing a big suitcase: *calm down*. At lap 16 von Brauchitsch stretched the lead to 1m 16.9s but far from closing the suitcase Neubauer felt he was driving like a 'madman'.

It may be that after France von Brauchitsch was in no mood to obey pit signals like that.

In its totality, its 88 left-handed and 84 right-handed corners, its sudden pitches and rolls, the Nürburgring spread a feast of opportunities to find time – for the great driver. Von Brauchitsch had the power, Nuvolari had the greatness. At lap 17 he had found six seconds and a lap later, taking everything to the edge round the 14.1 miles, another 26.

Nuvolari worked to a tactic.

Von Brauchitsch, bearing family honour, the honour of Mercedes and the honour of Germany *had* to respond, although that risked his tyres. In practice, Nuvolari monitored von Brauchitsch, saw how brutally he used the brakes regardless of tyre wear. Nuvolari intended to push von

Brauchitsch so hard he'd have to stop for tyres twice *and I win the race.* Von Brauchitsch's response took the lead back out to 43.1s.

Nuvolari cut deep into that on lap 20, bringing it back in to 32.2s.

Von Brauchitsch responded to that, Neubauer pacing in front of the pit. Neubauer could see without binoculars that von Brauchitsch's left rear was wearing. Two laps to run, 28 miles at racing speed. Neubauer talked to the Continental people because if he brought von Brauchitsch in next lap the race was gone. Von Brauchitsch estimated that slowing for the pit, changing the tyre and accelerating out would cost him half a minute – and the race. Von Brauchitsch decided to conserve the tyres as best he could, especially in cornering. 'I braked as softly as possible although that is costing precious seconds.' He looked at the front tyres: fine. He looked at the rears, the left showed signs of wear and the right made 'the blood go to my head'. *It's only two more laps,* he told himself.

Neubauer decided the tyres would hold.

Von Brauchitsch and Nuvolari crossed the line into the final lap 35.1 seconds apart.

That final lap became a 'dance of death'. At the Flugplatz, a right-hander two and a half miles into it, Nuvolari cut five seconds. At Adenauerforst, a twisty four and a half miles into it, he'd cut another three. They ran towards the 13km mark – just over eight miles – and in the lonely, tree-lined corridors Nuvolari cut it so much that by the Karusel, just after that 13km mark, he could see von Brauchitsch maybe 200 yards away, maybe less. Between Adenauerforst and here, Tazio Nuvolari must have driven the Nürburgring as no man had ever done and no man would again until an Argentinian of similar gifts – in 1957.

Von Brauchitsch remembered thinking *the tyres are still holding – but I can see the binding on the left rear.* He'd remember 'through clenched teeth' saying to himself *if only the tyres, if only the tyres ...*

The Karusel: a left and right, a half-right then a horseshoe tightening right-right-right then a lunge to a left-left-left.

As von Brauchitsch went in Nuvolari closed.

'Von Brauchitsch is being closely followed by Nuvolari!' echoed over the loudspeakers.

Suddenly, von Brauchitsch heard a bang. The car bucked so violently that the steering wheel was almost plucked from his hands. The Mercedes slewed and suddenly Nuvolari was off the power: the Mercedes might veer anywhere.

'Von Brauchitsch has burst a tyre!'

It was the left rear and, as it churned, chunks of it were being flung away. Nuvolari saw 'something black fly into the air.'

The Mercedes 'tilted, swerved across the track'[46] to the other side, von Brauchitsch wrestling the steering wheel. He heard the 'high, metallic sound' of the rim running on the track surface. The car slewed again and he saw, all in the instant, the red Alfa Romeo go by. Nuvolari had barely had time to miss him.

The loudspeakers bayed *Nuvolari leads!*

Von Brauchitsch felt 'a wild energy comes over me. *I am not giving in!* On three tyres and one rim I drive stubbornly on at least at 140kmh' – nearly 90mph.

The crowd waited. The Alfa Romeo had to cover another three miles of the track's contortions before it reached the straight to the finish, and here it came, quite alone, alone in its immortality. It crossed the line to a tremendous, almost primitive shout from the crowd.

Stuck came through two minutes later, Caracciola a minute after, Rosemeyer nearly two minutes after, then von Brauchitsch who ran to the end on the metal rim of the wheel. He pulled up far beyond his pit so people wouldn't see him crying.

Eventually, the Italian flag was found and raised to what some say was polite applause and others the 'hush of dead women'. The Italian national anthem, the *Marcia Reale,* did not play – the organisers didn't have it. Nuvolari did. He took a gramophone record of it everywhere in his briefcase. A mechanic went to fetch that. Hühnlein made an improvised speech about Germany always recognising 'an honest and great performance' before placing the enormous garland over Nuvolari. Those around him gave the stiff-arm Nazi salute. Nuvolari crooked his arm upwards in uneasy compromise. They played the *Marcia Reale* – his *Marcia Reale* – to him.

No man could sustain this, especially at circuits which did not offer a feast of opportunities. What Nuvolari had done, all else aside, was give Alfa Romeo's P3 'the last and most brilliant' of its victories 'against the full might of the German challenge. After this the car would win, but only when the German teams missed an event. What was now overdue was a completely new car which could meet them on more equal terms.

'The successor to the P3 was in fact already almost ready to race. This time, given the new urgency and commitment backed by the Government's direct interest in Italian motor racing victories, Jano had at last been able to set to work on a new design to replace the brilliant stop-gaps of the past. The only way to catch up in the power race was to design and build an entirely new engine, and the only way to put the power gained by building a new engine to proper use was to design a completely new suspension system, using the ideas shown in the more advanced designs used by the opposition.'[47]

Caracciola won the Swiss Grand Prix from Fagioli, Rosemeyer third; Stuck won the Italian although Nuvolari, 'sharing' with Dreyfus, managed to force the new Alfa Romeo into second place. Nuvolari paced himself and when he was ready accelerated, overtaking Caracciola. He set fastest lap and during the pit stops actually led. When his engine blew he took over Dreyfus's car and finished two minutes after Stuck.

Caracciola won Spain from Fagioli and von Brauchitsch, and was declared European Champion; Rosemeyer won the Czech Grand Prix although, again, Nuvolari forced and cajoled the Alfa Romeo up to second place. He was never close enough to threaten.

A determined, earthy self-made man called Fred Craner had bought Donington Park in England's Midlands – a stately pile with extensive grounds – and built a track there. He started holding motorcycle meetings and broadened that to car racing. Now he held a Grand Prix. The RAC, the governing body, wouldn't allow anyone like Fred Craner to have the title British Grand Prix, and Fred Craner wouldn't allow anyone like the RAC to put him off. The race was called the Donington Grand Prix and it attracted 'an interesting, if not sensational, entry'[48] including a wealthy Frenchman, Raymond Sommer (Alfa Romeo), and Giuseppe 'Nino' Farina (Maserati), a doctor of law with a 'blunt, arrogant driving style which featured a chin-out Duce-like[49] pose with his arms extended far back from the steering wheel.'[50] He, although nobody could know it, was the bridge to the modern World Championship.

Richard 'Mad Jack' Shuttleworth, head bare, won the race in an Alfa Romeo from Earl Howe (Bugatti). Farina and Sommer both broke down.

Notes

1. NSKK: Nationalsozialistisches Kraftfahrkorps, or National Socialist Motoring Corps, which has been described as 'a semi comical home guard for motoring activities' headed by Hühnlein. It earned the sobriquet *no fighters, only drinkers*. It took over all German motor clubs in 1933 and, in 1939, was given responsibility for training drivers for the army.
2. *Enzo Ferrari*, Yates.
3. Ibid.
4. *My Two Lives*, Dreyfus.
5. *L'Equipe*.
6. *The Motor.*
7. Ibid.

8. Dreyfus, op. cit.

9. *The Autocar.*

10. *The Motor.*

11. *L'Equipe.*

12. There is a certain degree of uncertainty about this push: when it began and what happened next. The pits were on the quayside but the finishing line on the upward slope where today's Grand Prix grid is. What seems certain is that Nuvolari was able to push the Alfa Romeo as far as the pits but even he, with a tempest of adrenaline and frustration raging within him, couldn't push the car round the Gasworks hairpin and up to the finish; and didn't.

13. Edward Richard Assheton, Viscount Curzon, known as Earl Howe (1884–1956) began his racing career in his forties and competed widely. He won the Le Mans 24-hour race in 1931, partnering Birkin. He served in the Second World War as a naval officer.
http://www.brooklandstrack.co.uk/Drivrlist/howe.htm

14. *When Nuvolari Raced,* Moretti.

15. Ibid.

16. *The Racing Car,* Batsford.

17. *Pur Sang* = thoroughbred.

18. *Speed was my Life,* Neubauer.

19. *Racing Driver's World,* Caracciola.

20. Batsford, op. cit.

21. Yates, op. cit.

22. Guy Moll had a brief career – two years – but Enzo Ferrari rated him very highly. Moll was an Algerian, father French, mother Spanish. He died in the Coppa Acerbo in 1934.

23. Caracciola, op. cit.

24. Ibid.

25. *Shell History of Motor Sport.*

26. *Shooting Star,* Nixon.

27. *Dick Seaman,* Chula.

28. Hard racing plugs were made to tolerate great heat and cope with high speed.

29. *Grand Prix Driver,* Lang.

30. Moretti, op. cit.

31. Neubauer, op. cit.

32. *History of Grand Prix and Voiturette Racing,* Volume III, Sheldon.

33. *L'Auto Italiana,* quoted in Moretti.

34. *Amateur Racing Driver,* Cholmondeley Tapper.

35. *Kampf um Meter und Sekunden,* von Brauchitsch.

36. Ibid.

37. *Alfa Romeo,* Owen.

38. Neubauer, op. cit.

39. Yates, op. cit.

40. Raymond Mays (1899–1980) was the son of an early motorist and became known as driver then moving force behind two manufacturing ventures in racing, ERA and BRM.

41. ERA – English Racing Automobiles, founded in 1934 and manufacturer of many small racing cars.

42. *Split Seconds,* Mays.

43. *The Autocar.*

44. Ibid.

45. *Motor Revue,* Stuttgart.

46. *Nuvolari,* Lurani.

47. Owen, op. cit.

48. *The British Grand Prix 1926–1976,* Nye.

49. *Duce* – leader, commander.

50. Yates, op. cit.

Chapter 5

SHADOWLANDS

A t dawn on 3 October 1935, Mussolini invaded Abyssinia and on 22 October the League of Nations[1] imposed economic sanctions on Italy. Mussolini made several responses to this, including a boycott of motor races in France and Britain in 1936. The former was important, the latter in the nature of a gesture. There would be a Donington Grand Prix late in the season but it did not yet attract leading drivers or teams.

In February 1936, Hitler opened the first factory to make Volkswagens. Designed by Ferdinand Porsche, the cars were shaped like a beetle, had a rear engine and were intended to do for ordinary German people what Henry Ford had done for ordinary Americans. A month later Hitler entered the Rhineland, that part of Germany occupied by the French under the Versailles Treaty. It was a calculated risk but in response the French and British did nothing. Hitler would not forget.

On 4 March a son was born to James and Helen Clark, a farming family in Kilmany, Fife. They already had four daughters, Mattie, Susan, Isobel and Betty. They'd called the lad James after dad, but he would always be known as Jim.

As Alfa Romeo approached the 1936 season they felt they could be optimistic after Nuvolari's fastest lap in the Italian Grand Prix the season before, although a chassis failure in the Spanish Grand Prix was worrying. In fact, 'the old pattern re-established itself. If the German teams turned up, they won. If they didn't, the Alfa team usually took the honours. But by the start of the 1936 season, the Mercedes and Auto Unions were faster and more powerful than ever.'[2]

Lang drove one of those powerful Mercedes in early season practice at Monza. He was on a fast lap and reached the Lesmo curve when he felt a 'tremendous hit on my arm.' The shock was so severe that he almost passed out but, instinctively he got the car through and then brought it to a halt. He'd assumed the car had shredded a tyre and part of it had been flung at him but, instead, 'I saw a stone the size of a fist in the cockpit.' He…

remembered three young hooligans sitting on a wall where the track passes but 50 feet away. Neubauer glanced at my swollen arm, saw me into the care of [the doctor], and, accompanied by ten mechanics and Bianchi, the track guard, went in hot pursuit of the miscreants. He surrounded the place and after cross-examining some other boys, discovered the culprit in a nearby field. The boys had in fact been competing with each other for 'best shot.' The victor had been accurate enough to score a bull's-eye in spite of my speed of about 125mph.[3]

The Grand Prix season began in the rain at Monaco, sometimes hard as a storm, sometimes easing off. The cars were brought to the grid covered in tarpaulins. Chiron had a Mercedes and he had put it on pole from Nuvolari and Caracciola. At the start their wheels churned spray towards the sodden crowd. The surface glistened with treachery. His Mercedes twitching as the power came on, Caracciola led and towed Nuvolari with him. At the back, an Alfa Romeo had a broken oil pipe and oil bubbled down onto the wet track surface...

Caracciola and Nuvolari lapped this car but as it negotiated the chicane down from the tunnel a lot of oil bubbled down. Chiron scudded full on to it and slithered into the sandbags at the apex of the chicane. Farina (Maserati) hit the sandbags, too, and von Brauchitsch rammed the rear of Farina. Three other cars were involved but Rosemeyer, spinning wildly, somehow got his Auto Union through the gap.

That was lap two. On lap ten Nuvolari took Caracciola out of the tunnel but as the rain increased Caracciola's almost superhuman ability in the wet came into play. He re-took Nuvolari and at half distance led him by over a minute, although Varzi set fastest lap. Nuvolari slowed, a brake problem, and Caracciola won it from Varzi.

The Monaco measure: Caracciola, 100 laps, 3h 49m 20.4s, an average speed of 51.6mph; Fagioli, 1935, 58.1mph – the difference because 1936 was wet.

The ultimate measure: the Land Speed Record was not broken.

On 9 May, Mussolini announced in Rome that 'Italy at last has her empire' – Abyssinia beaten, Italian troops controlling the capital, Addis Ababa. The shadows of world war started to creep from the distant horizon.

Rosemeyer was emerging as a great driver and would become European Champion while one of those who might have challenged him, Auto Union team-mate Varzi, began a descent into living hell.

After Monaco there were four races – Tripoli, Tunis, Barcelona and the Eifel at the Nürburgring – before the next Championship round, the Hungarian at Budapest. During this, Varzi descended.

At Tripoli, Alfa Romeo had their new V12 engines but they were off the pace and the debut 'coincided with a grave and truly upsetting disadvantage caused by a series of tyre failures'[4] Varzi won Tripoli from Stuck but[5] politics were at work here. On orders from 'high up', because Fascist Italy and Nazi Germany were now soul-mates, an agreement had been reached that if possible Italians should win 'Italian' races and Libya was then an Italian protectorate. So Stuck, leading, was ordered to slow down and Varzi to speed up. Varzi won it on the final lap, much to Stuck's rage. At the celebration dinner, when a toast was being drunk to Stuck as the authentic victor, Varzi flew into a rage himself. It may be it was that night, in his hotel room with Ilse Pietsch, she introduced him to morphine for the first time.

In Tunis a week later, Varzi crashed heavily and that night took more morphine. It had a therapeutic effect, and he liked that.

At Barcelona, Varzi fell out with Auto Union and didn't drive. By now, industrial disputes spread in France and forced the cancellation of the Belgian Grand Prix. The Le Mans 24-hour race...

> could not be run because of the strikes which had paralysed all industries, and the automobile industry in particular. I was reporting in Barcelona at the time when, eight days before the race, the decision was made, and I still remember taking the last plane to leave for France, with Louis Chiron and Rudi Caracciola. The next day the Spanish Civil War broke out.[6]

This savage, unhappy conflict lasted until 1939, and Hitler exploited it for his own purposes. He backed the Fascist General Franco and used the town of Guernica to see what the mass bombing of civilians from the air would do. The Spanish Grand Prix became no more than a memory.

At the Eifel Grand Prix, Rosemeyer won in dense fog, a feat which remains inexplicable even today, Varzi seventh and a long way behind.

In Hungary, at a 3.1-mile Budapest circuit through public gardens, 100,000 watched Nuvolari take an early lead before Rosemeyer went past followed by the rest of the German phalanx. Caracciola led but had mechanical problems. Nuvolari overtook von Brauchitsch so closely he sent him spinning into a telegraph pole. Now Rosemeyer held a commanding lead but Nuvolari caught him, passed him and took the race by 14 seconds. *Motor Italia* wrote:

> Men like Nuvolari are, perhaps unknowingly, speculators in the best sense of the word. Speculators because they have a precise and lively sense of reality and of the varied possibilities that it contains. True realists, the great

motor racing aces give us some magnificent lessons. Nuvolari dares to challenge rivals with much more powerful machines and he won at Budapest as he has won on similar occasions.

The French Grand Prix, at Montlhéry, was for sports cars because the French didn't want another German humiliation and Wimille/Sommer won in a Bugatti. For the Milan Grand Prix on the same day – the term Grand Prix used freely – Varzi persuaded Auto Union to give him a car. Nuvolari took pole from him but Varzi exploited the Auto Union's sheer power to lead. Nuvolari drew up and by now the crowd, partisan, passionate, were in tumult. Nuvolari took Varzi, the tumult deepened and Nuvolari won it by eight seconds.

A different kind of emotion, more universal and less delirious, moved through Germany. The Olympic Games in Berlin would begin the week after the Grand Prix, as if the country was having a great sporting festival and the world was watching it.

A crowd of 350,000 came to the Nürburgring to witness, as they hoped, the five Mercedes and four Auto Unions take their revenge on Nuvolari for 1935. Down the grid, young Seaman took his place in a Maserati and Cholmondeley Tapper in another. He...

remembered something of the long and complicated circuit of the Nürburgring from the previous year, and soon worked up a good speed on the Maserati, thanks in part to the large signposts announcing each corner with its name. For instance, you would come to a corner hidden by the brow of a hill, see the signpost with the name of that corner, and stored in your memory would be whether it was a fast or slow one, to right or to left. As many of the corners were obscured, the good memory was at a premium.[7]

The grid was by ballot, Varzi missing. He simply hadn't arrived again. Lang lined up on the fourth row next to Seaman and immediately behind Rosemeyer. Lang 'wanted to put "reserve driver" behind me, and had a plan of campaign worked out. I was going to try to hang on to the tail of Rosemeyer. He was going to show me how to get out of this mêlée and get to the front.'

Cholmondeley Tapper wasn't 'surprised to see a crowd of mammoth proportions on the bright, cloudy morning of the race. All night long [the village of] Adenau had seemed in continual uproar, as thousands streamed through on their way to the course, and when I left my hotel a solid throng was moving slowly towards the Nürburgring.' There was...

a theatrical air about the pit area, with innumerable flags and bunting bright against the dark green pines, and officials resplendent in many-hued uniforms. My pit was conspicuously naive in equipment: a few cans of petrol, an odd spanner or two and my two spare wheels contrasted unfavourably with the high-powered efficiency of the big firms, but when eventually the twenty competing cars were lined up in front of the grandstand, and *Deutschland über Alles* ponderously echoed through the crowd, I was proud to see the Maserati, the only spot of English green amid a predominantly red and white field. Once again I endured an uncomfortable interlude while surging thousands gave the mechanically militant Nazi salute, and then we prepared our cars for the start.[8]

Lang followed his plan. Von Brauchitsch led, Rosemeyer after 'like a shadow' and Lang tucking in behind determined to stay there. Into the second lap Rosemeyer began to attack von Brauchitsch who stopped – by a great irony – at the Karusel to check his steering. He must have hit something. Rosemeyer and Lang went through but Lang suddenly...

noticed that my right hand was very painful and something was wrong with it. I looked down and saw that my little finger hung uselessly in my glove. Then I remembered having changed down somewhat hurriedly in a bend, I had hit the bodywork with my little finger and broken it. Damn the thing, I thought, I won't let it disturb me, and try to pretend that the pain does not exist. I pressed on like a madman behind Rosemeyer. I could not see anyone in my mirror, and drove on almost forgetting my finger in my joy.[9]

Rosemeyer broke the lap record on the lap three and led Lang by 23 seconds, Nuvolari hunting Lang. Rosemeyer pitted on lap seven for new rear tyres and Lang saw this pit board as he went past:

LAN–ROS–NUV.

He felt intoxicated to be leading a race for the first time in his life but the pain from the finger grew to the point where he could barely hold the wheel. When he pitted to refuel on lap nine he saw Caracciola ready to take over. Caracciola, senior member of the Mercedes team, had had a fuel pump problem with his own car, halting on lap four. Lang was 'not very pleased to hand over but reasoning told me that I could not have kept going with my broken finger.' He was also part of a team and needed to reject any 'false pride' which might jeopardise the effort of the whole.

The spectators were very displeased with me and whistled their disapproval [...] The public address announcer soon gave my reason for withdrawing, stating that I could not have continued with a broken finger. I do not know if the public judged me less severely after that. I looked for my fiancée but could not see her in the pits [...] she hated any form of limelight. She was always somewhere among the spectators.[10]

Rosemeyer led while Lang went to the doctor and had his finger bandaged. Now von Brauchitsch pitted and prepared to hand his car over to Zehender, the reserve driver, although why is something of a mystery. Lang felt he should have the car, Neubauer said he could and Lang emerged to a tremendous cheer.

After half distance Nuvolari moved to second behind Rosemeyer while supercharger trouble halted Caracciola – and Chiron, in another Mercedes, went off on the straight, burst through fencing and plunged down an embankment. He escaped with bruises. Nuvolari's Alfa Romeo broke down out in the country. Cholmondeley Tapper remembered:

it was odd that during this tremendous race I saw very few cars. The course is particularly long, and only occasionally I would be passed by the faster cars, or I myself would pass some competitors who had come to grief...I passed Nuvolari stranded by the side of the road with a broken back axle in his Alfa Romeo. He gave me a cheerful wave.

Sommer (Alfa Romeo) gave Nuvolari a lift back to the pits. Lang was in great pain. 'Every time I changed gear, the wooden splint on my finger touched the bodywork and I almost howled. However, it had been my choice, and I managed to finish.' Only ten cars did that, Rosemeyer winning it from Stuck, Lang seventh and Cholmondeley Tapper the last of them. He had covered 18 laps, 56 miles behind Rosemeyer.

Rosemeyer's wife Elly, an elegant, accomplished woman and pioneer aviator, remembered 'Bernd was almost torn apart by the crowds of well-wishers and the champagne flowed – how he would have enjoyed a glass of beer!'[11] Later she noticed that his hands were covered in blisters. 'Of course,' he replied. 'Do you think winning a Grand Prix is a picnic? You can't imagine how painful they are but everything will be all right by next Sunday.'

Mercedes had been so unsuccessful that they withdrew from racing to 'iron out design or construction difficulties.'[12] Specifically, they didn't enter the Milan Grand Prix – a street race round a park in central Milan – which Nuvolari won, did enter the Nürburgring (as we have just seen) but only two of their five cars finished – Fagioli/Caracciola fifth, von Brauchitsch/Lang seventh. They wouldn't go to the Italian Grand Prix.

At the Coppa Ciano, Varzi had an Auto Union but suffered brake problems. Two weeks later for the Coppa Acerbo he didn't show up again. Auto Union tracked him to a house in Rome but by now the morphine had changed his personality. In spite of that he went to the race and finished third.

One report suggests that while Varzi was practising for the Swiss Grand Prix at Bremgarten Auto Union's team manager, Dr Karl Feuereissen, went to his hotel room, confronted Ilse Pietsch, then found a syringe and morphine there. If Varzi was not yet an addict he was becoming one.

Mercedes sent four cars because they felt they had solved the problems.

Caracciola led from Rosemeyer, Nuvolari and Lang. Nuvolari's Alfa Romeo couldn't stand the pace (a magneto eventually failed) while Caracciola and Rosemeyer duelled. Caracciola blocked and this enraged Rosemeyer, who was not mollified when Caracciola was ordered to stop this or face a black flag – and not mollified when Caracciola retired with a rear axle problem and he won. After the race, Rosemeyer told Elly 'I shall have something to say to him when we meet, I can tell you. Racing is dangerous enough without having to take unnecessary risks, dammit!'[13]

The two drivers did meet – by chance – in the hotel lift that evening. Caracciola was with Baby Hoffman-Trobeck and Elly found herself trembling at what Rosemeyer would say to him.

Caracciola: 'Well, young man, you did well. May I add my congratulations?'

Rosemeyer: 'So you think I did well, do you? I would have done a lot better if you hadn't got in my way so long!'

When the lift stopped Elly escaped as quickly as she could while Rosemeyer and Caracciola argued on. The dispute lingered and festered for six months.

At the Italian Grand Prix there were now four chicanes, which did not prevent Elly driving some laps in Rosemeyer's Auto Union, taking care not to damage it. She seems to have been a very feminine feminist. That stood in odd contrast to the Auto Unions being wheeled past the grandstands towards the grid, preceded by three men in virgin white but bearing large flags adorned with the very masculine swastika.

Rosemeyer led from Stuck but Nuvolari got past Stuck on lap eight and that woke the crowd up all right. Varzi retired, an engine problem, and Stuck crashed in one of the chicanes. He missed the braking point, the car struck a tree, flipped and flung him out. He had to be helped away. Nuvolari 'raced like a champion. At the wheel of a clearly inferior car, whose small fuel tank necessitated several refuelling stops, he had hoped to make up ground on the corners as he could not hope to keep up with the faster and more powerful Auto Unions on the straights.'[14] Rosemeyer won it to complete his season of triumph.

The second Donington Grand Prix confirmed that the race was growing in stature. It attracted 24 entries, including an Alfa Romeo to be driven by a very self-confident Swiss, Hans Ruesch, and Seaman. Thereby hangs a curious (and to the English) very strange tale. Looking back on it, Ruesch says:

> If there was one country that cheated without any doubt it was England. They are famous for cheating – in sport, especially, but in everything, everything, everything. I knew it before ever getting to England from an Italian motor cycle rider who had won the Tourist Trophy – the biggest victory he could have – but they decided an Italian can't win so they took apart his motor cycle and measured everything. At that time you often had pit stops to change plugs because they got oily, he had a different brand of plug on the bike than he had declared before the race and they disqualified him.
>
> So this man said 'there's nothing to do in England, you can't win' and this was repeated to me by Seaman's manager. We spoke at various races and he said 'Seaman wants to win, he needs it because otherwise Birabongse[15] wins it and all of England would be offended if a Siamese does that. So', he said, 'I'll organise it for you so you will be a British entry with Seaman, and the moment you are a British entry, no problem.[16]

Ruesch led to lap 70 (of the 120) and handed the car to Seaman. Ruesch remembers:

> I felt sorry for him dangling his legs over the pit counter as if he thought I was not going to get out of the car. I could have stayed in, breaking up our agreement. He wanted absolutely to win that race.

The Seaman/Ruesch car did win, by more than three minutes and suddenly Seaman had a real reputation.

That October, a new formula was announced to take effect in 1938: maximum engine capacities of 4,500cc for normally aspirated and 3,000cc supercharged, and 400kg to 850kg minimum weight according to engine size.

That October, too, a 'two-seater racing car, its blue paintwork yet to be revealed by the dawn, travels along the dusty road that connects Tandil with Azul in the north-east of Argentina. Where Route 226 crosses 74, it will turn left. Its final destination: the town of Benito Juárez.' The driver of the converted 1929 Ford Model A taxi, was going to his first race. He'd go out to race 'in tremendous spirits. I felt like another person when I was at the wheel of a racing car. I felt ecstatic. I often used to sing to myself.'[17] It was the most modest of beginnings. Juan-Manuel Fangio never did complete the race because of an oil leak. Near the start a local driver had overtaken him, hit a culvert, cartwheeled and was killed. As Fangio embarked on the journey home he understood three things: motor racing was at the mercy of mechanical parts, it could be fatal, and he wanted to do it again.

The Mercedes to contest 1937 – the final year of the 750kg formula – had a mighty engine, developing 248bhp at only 2,000 revs, and 646bhp at 5,800rpm. In February Seaman had been given a draft contract by Mercedes, and when he signed it his life as well as his career altered. He would settle in Bavaria, marry an attractive, captivating German girl and find himself an Englishman far inside the Third Reich as the shadows crept closer and closer. The start of his career with Mercedes, however, wasn't anything like that. Because the 1937 car wasn't ready they took the 1936 to Monza for pre-season practice. Auto Union were there, too, and the teams watched each other carefully. Mercedes were so busy that they couldn't get to Milan for their mid-day meal[18] and had to make do with a cold collation put together by Mrs Neubauer. During one practice Seaman over-revved the car, lost control when the tail stepped out, and hit a tree. He was shaken up and fractured a knee-cap.

Von Brauchitsch was amused to learn how superstitious Seaman was.[19] 'He had a particular intolerance against Fridays and number 13. In Monza he was unlucky. From a training run he did not return. We found him later very near the burning car near the 13 kilometre mark. In his hotel he'd had the number 113 and on the evening before we were 13 to dinner. But he quickly recovered from this accident.'

The French Grand Prix was for sports cars again (Chiron won in a Talbot); the Belgian Grand Prix was run six days after the Vanderbilt Cup at Roosevelt Field, New York, which, in an era when the Atlantic was crossed only by sea, meant drivers couldn't compete in both. Caracciola, Rosemeyer, Seaman and Nuvolari went to America, Lang and von Brauchitsch to Spa along with four Auto Unions, a couple of Alfa Romeos and a Maserati. There's film of Caracciola en route to New York on the luxury liner *Bremen*, wearing a light jacket and walking to the edge of the deck, his limp very evident.

Von Brauchitsch crashed heavily in practice, his Mercedes somersaulting but landing upright in a field. He was only slightly hurt and took part in the race. The small grid, only eight cars, produced a furious race with Stuck leading from Lang and Hasse in pursuit. Attacking Spa's sinuous length, these three drew clear.

A dog, running in front of Christian Kautz's Mercedes, might have caused a very serious accident because he braked and the Mercedes spun through 360° heading directly towards a cameraman on the lip of the road, behind a tripod, and several dozen spectators on the other side of a small ditch. The photographer ran into the road, away from the car which smashed into the tripod while the crowd instinctively sprang backwards. Nobody was hurt.

There was real pace everywhere: Stuck hammered the lap record, von Brauchitsch hammered it, then Stuck again, then Lang on lap 18. The pace shredded tyres and the pit stops became a chaos of change but, with eleven laps to go, Rudi Hasse – a former bike rider who'd also been in rallies – had his Auto Union in a comfortable lead. Lang, who had just pitted for more tyres …

renewed the attack and got close to Hasse. Suddenly my car developed tail wag, which I guessed to be due to the back axle or shock absorbers. I managed to get past an apple tree and got back into the centre of the road. Trees lined the road and there was no ditch. I had to reduce speed as the car rolled all over the place and required the whole width of the road.[20]

This meant Hasse could win, and he did, his only Grand Prix victory. He clambered out and, with the winner's garland around his neck, waved to the crowd – but he was groggy, lurched, almost fell.

Ferrari sent three drivers to the German Grand Prix at the Nürburgring – Nuvolari, Farina and veteran Attilio Marinoni. The grid was decided by practice times, which hadn't happened here before, and it gave a front row of Rosemeyer, Lang with von Brauchitsch, Caracciola and Nuvolari on the second.

The start-finish straight was wide enough to accommodate cars three abreast easily and the surface had been repaired so often that it resembled a curious concrete mosaic. The grid stretched back 11 rows to accommodate the 26 cars and they were released by a violent cannon shot which sent a column of smoke towards the back of the grid before the breeze plucked it away. By then the cars were surging across the mosaic and as they reached into the great initial curve to the left they were already strung out.

Caracciola led but Lang and Rosemeyer went past him, Lang completing the opening lap clearly ahead. The speed of the cars propelled them towards the very edge of the track: in a tight right-left downhill section they skimmed within inches of the grassy knoll to one side, turned the cars hard and skimmed within inches of the grassy knoll on the other side – and they were gone, dissolving like a vision.

Rosemeyer's Auto Union hit a bank with the rear wheel, damaging the hubcap. On lap four, it came off in the South curve. Elly remembered that…

> not long after Bernd had gone by, an NSKK official appeared at our pits with a hubcap that had fallen off one of our cars. From my position in the pit I could see that Dr Feuereissen and the mechanics were looking anxious about something, but I didn't know what. Then Bernd failed to appear at the end of the fourth lap and I could see that the mechanics were no longer just anxious, they were very worried. Before I could discover just what was going on, however, Bernd came rolling in with a rear tyre in shreds and although the mechanics worked feverishly it was 2 minutes and 26 seconds before a furious Bernd could get back into the race.
>
> Once Bernd had left the pits, Ludwig Sebastian came to tell me about the missing hubcap and the mechanics' fear that he would lose the wheel and crash. Dr Feuereissen had telephoned several of the observer posts around the circuit in the hope that someone could warn Bernd of the danger, but to no avail. The first he knew of it was when the Auto Union had suddenly slid broadside for no apparent reason.[21]

Rosemeyer was tenth, a wall of Mercedes – Caracciola, von Brauchitsch, Lang, Seaman – setting the pace. Caracciola's sureness of touch revealed itself in the tightening loop of the Karusel where he kept the Mercedes perfectly placed on the inside, his hands constantly adjusting the wheel to do that in a sequence of small, taut, precise movements, and arms like short pistons. This was a master at work.

Ernst von Delius, however, managed to get his Auto Union up to Seaman. It was, initially, no more than another motor racing situation, but it obeyed many historical precedents. From the ordinariness came disaster.

The Autocar wrote: 'Delius, a fiery little fellow whom the German affectionately called *Kleiner* – Little One – was determined to be in front.' On lap seven, crossing a bridge, von Delius was slightly in front. 'As he landed he swerved to the outside – perhaps through landing crooked, perhaps because the cars touched – and just caught a fire-extinguisher post. This was sufficient to get him into a terrific skid. The Auto Union swerved right across Seaman's path, skidded all ways at scarcely reduced speed and, with a sickening leap, jumped the hedge on the left-hand side again. The flying car flattened a wire fence, was said by some to have cleared the heads of two Nazis, and slithered, mowing down the grass, into the main Koblenz road which runs parallel to the course. Seaman, seeing he was unable to accelerate through, braked hard, was squeezed into the right-hand hedge and, in his turn, skidded violently, was hurled out onto the road, his car finishing up through the hedge but on the right-hand side of the course. The two cars actually crashed at about 130mph.'

The loudspeakers announced that there had been an accident. Elly watched Rosemeyer go safely by and...

I ran to the circuit hospital to see if I could be of any help. I must admit that I found it difficult to tear myself away from the race just at that point: Bernd was driving absolutely flat out, lapping in under ten minutes, time and time again in his attempts to get to grips with the Mercedes once more.

At the hospital the news about Ernst was better than I had expected, likewise about Seaman. I breathed a sigh of relief. It appeared that Ernst had broken a leg, torn his mouth and was suffering from concussion but he was conscious and sent greetings to everyone! Seaman had a broken nose and flesh wounds – nothing more serious than that. All this was bad enough, but nonetheless much better than I had expected following the description of the crash. Clearly there was nothing I could do, so I returned – somewhat relieved – to the pits.[22]

In fact, von Delius had fatal injuries.

Rosemeyer mounted a tremendous charge and, while Elly was at the hospital, shattered the lap record but even that was not enough. Caracciola held the lead to the end, von Brauchitsch second, Rosemeyer reaching so hard that he finished only a minute behind Caracciola.

Caracciola took pole at Monaco from von Brauchitsch and Rosemeyer. Lang, suffering from 'flu, felt so terrible he stayed at home in bed.

Elly was amused that practice started at 6am, giving time to return to the hotel and bed again afterwards.

Although Rosemeyer was on that front row somehow the Auto Union team was not optimistic. Lang meanwhile listened to the commentary on the radio.

Huddled in bedclothes [...] when I heard the unleashed pack howling across the line, the longing to race made me go hot and cold all over. I think I even snapped at my wife when she spoke to me.[23]

Caracciola led but on the opening lap Hasse spun as he came out of the tunnel. The Auto Union slewed, just missing the tunnel wall, and came at tremendous pace backwards down the road. Hasse was thrown from his Auto Union. Elly remembered:

the whole Auto Union team was still suffering from the death of our friend von Delius and although news quickly arrived that Hasse was only slightly injured, none of us believed it until after the race. Then we were able to visit him and were delighted to find him quite chirpy in his hotel bed. Until then, however, the Auto Union pits were very gloomy indeed.[24]

On lap 19 Rosemeyer's steering seized and, helpless, he went into the sandbags at the Gasometer hairpin. He walked the short distance to the pits and sat with Elly.

Hans Stuck was now the only Auto Union driver left in the race and Bernd watched him like a hawk every time he came round. He was quick to see that Hans was in trouble. 'Look! There is something wrong with Hans's car, too. His brakes seem to be locking up. When he stops I shall ask him to let me take over. I can't stand about doing nothing while the race goes on!' And that is exactly what happened.[25]

Rosemeyer emerged and began to overtake cars in a long thrust round all these narrow streets. Way ahead von Brauchitsch led at half distance, Caracciola chasing. As Caracciola caught him the Mercedes team began signalling to von Brauchitsch *let him through! Caracciola is the number one driver!* Von Brauchitsch acknowledged these orders and studiously ignored them. A mechanic stood at the roadside waving his arm up and down in a gesture of anger, clapped both hands to his head – *what can you do?* – and turned away.

Lang's suffering increased:

I had a fit of rage when the few broadcast excerpts of the race were interrupted by music. [...] I let off steam by swearing at the radio and the people running it; this amused my wife, who said 'now you know what I feel when I listen to the radio or when I sit in the pits waiting for you whilst you race.'[26]

Caracciola forced his way through at *Ste Devote* but had to pit for fuel and tyres opening the race to von Brauchitsch who won it by nearly 15 seconds.

The Monaco measure: von Brauchitsch, 100 laps, 3h 7m 23.9s, an average speed of 63.2mph – the first over 100kmh (101.8); Caracciola, 1936 (wet), 51.6mph.

There wouldn't be another Grand Prix at Monaco until after the war, so here is the full span of the measure so far: 1929, 49.8mph against von Brauchitsch's 63.2.

The ultimate measure: in November at Bonneville, Eyston pushed the Land Speed Record to 311mph.

Vehicles registered in Britain 2.9m (1929, 2.2 million).

A Ford Prefect cost (in 1938) £150 and a Briton earned on average £4 a week. Saving all his money the Briton would have taken 37 weeks to buy one (1910, 2 years 42 weeks; 1919, 1 year 28 weeks; 1929, 41 weeks).

Nuvolari raced a new Alfa Romeo in the Coppa Acerbo and was so unhappy with it that he went to the Swiss Grand Prix a week after that and tried an Auto Union, but found the experience disconcerting because the rear-engined car was unlike anything else, and it demanded a new range of skills. He'd done ten laps; not long or far enough to assemble those skills. Lang, still weak after the 'flu, raced although a doctor prescribed consuming a lot of cream.

Caracciola took pole from Rosemeyer but on a wet track Stuck led and soon Rosemeyer crashed. That created a mix 'n' match race at Auto Union because understandably Nuvolari was signalled in to hand his car over to Rosemeyer, who of course knew all about how to drive it. Fagioli had a hip problem and brought his car in on lap 22, handing it to ... Nuvolari.

Caracciola overtook Stuck and Lang slogged forward running within himself. He knew that on this track and in these conditions there would be no catching Caracciola and he was right.

Lang completely recovered for the Italian Grand Prix at Livorno, a narrow road circuit where he recognised what today is a very common problem. 'The straight led along the sea front and the starting line was at one end. This straight was also the only place where overtaking would have been possible, but it was not very long, and the high speeds obtained along it made this practically impossible.' Elsewhere the cars threaded through the twisting streets. They'd go through a little square with a policeman standing in front of straw bales monitoring their progress. They'd lurch towards buildings clad with the bales. They'd be directed which way to go by bales laid out like marker barriers, and they'd corner fast enough to leave burnt rubber marks as they accelerated out of the corners.

Varzi appeared unannounced at Livorno and sought out Dr Feuereissen. He wanted a drive. Feuereissen was understandably reluctant and reminded Varzi of his behaviour the previous year, but Varzi proffered reassurance that he had come off the morphine and left Ilse. Rosemeyer spoke up for him and in the end Feuereissen said he could drive here and in the Czech Grand Prix at Brno, and at Donington.

Caracciola took pole, Varzi next – outqualifying Rosemeyer. It's easy to present Varzi as an enigma, an obsessive, an addict, easy to forget that he had profound, intuitive ability. Here it was again. Nuvolari struggled with an Alfa Romeo and although in the wet he set fastest time the car couldn't be made to replicate that in the dry.

Spectators poured on to the track aborting the start twice and an ambulance had to treat a spectator who'd fallen out of a tree. When the race did start Lang contradicted his own judgement of the track because on the opening lap 'I passed Rosemeyer and Varzi and later Caracciola. I was really back on form, but the pleasure was of short duration. Owing to the sharp bursts of speed, although the circuit was not a particularly fast one, I threw a tread and had to stop at the pits to change wheels.'

Nuvolari, 'performing indescribable prodigies and using all his talents'[27] hauled the Alfa Romeo past Varzi to a tremendous roar: a gesture only.

> For the first time, he was so disheartened he gave up before the end, handing his car over to his team-mate Farina [on lap 31]. It was almost the end of a glorious phase in Alfa-Romeo racing history, possibly the most brilliant and colourful years in the whole history of racing. But the series of failures on the track were viewed with displeasure in Government circles. What was the point of pouring cash into the company if it didn't deliver the prestige and publicity of racing victories?[28]

Lang tracked Caracciola but now the nature of the track worked against him. He couldn't get up to mount an overtaking move although it was a desperately tight finish, the cars 0.4 of a second apart. Varzi, sixth, was close to collapse and needed help to get out of the car.

Stuck was in disagreement with Auto Union and they fired him. They retained Varzi for Brno but his performance remains shrouded in the enigma of the man. He had two fingers of his right hand in a bandage but practised. On the first day he was slow and 'seemed distinctly nervous, claiming that the wounds on his fingers were very painful.'[29] He asked for changes to the car and then refused to drive it, left Brno and was not seen again until 1938.

Auto Union had only Rosemeyer and Hermann Müller, Hasse indisposed. Nuvolari and Lang, favoured by the ballot, filled the front row because Brno was so narrow that the grid couldn't be any wider. This was fortunate for Nuvolari – the Alfa Romeos arrived late giving him only a few laps. The ballot was constructed around teams, not drivers, so that the front row position went to Mercedes and after some arguing Lang got it as the fastest of the Mercedes drivers in practice.

Nuvolari 'took command of the race and held the lead until the end of the third lap, when he had to give way to Caracciola'[30] Nuvolari's left rear wheel threw its tread and he ran on the rim for a long way at a very respectable pace through the pretty villages and across cobbled streets. The crowd, gathered round the corners in the countryside or sitting in fields which sloped down towards the track pointed and gesticulated as Nuvolari went by but Brno was anything but idyllic.

In a dangerous era, with Spa and the Nürburgring as the centrepieces of that, it may have been more dangerous still. At 18.1 miles it was the longest on the Grand Prix calendar and run on a combination of national roads and rough country tracks. Over such a distance, and in a rural setting, crowd control proved all but impossible.

At a fast right-hander out in the woods the surface was tarmac but the corner had deep ditches on either side with a ribbon of earth and gravel in front of them. Some drivers, Lang would say, 'used this soft path adjoining the macadam to cut a sort of rut into which the car used to slide, thereby enabling the machine to be cornered faster.' It meant that the wheels dug stones and earth onto the tarmac, and made the tarmac into the equivalent of ice. Lang, approaching at speed on lap two, saw the road covered in this. He held the Mercedes on the correct line but once he saw the debris he knew he couldn't brake: if he skidded, braking might slither the car away from him.

He acted by reflex, trying to make the car describe a 'wide arc before it slid into the ditch.' For an instant he thought he'd got away with it but the left-front wheel hit a granite marker by the ditch. That impact twisted the Mercedes round and it somersaulted across the ditch where spectators sat, some even dangling their legs over the ditch. They shouldn't have been there, but they were.

The somersault caused the car to fall on its back in such a manner that the cockpit was over the ditch, and I fell out, albeit hitting my head on a stone; but the car's position upside down was only momentary, its momentum

carried it on into another lengthwise somersault to finish up on the edge of
the ditch on its wheels.

I was quite dazed and not sure where I was.[31]

Lang remembered a lot of people running and one man leading him
away by the arm. He couldn't see two people were dead and twelve
injured. The two men walked in silence through the woods, Lang
concussed. Lang felt something warm trickling down his neck. The man
eased Lang's helmet off and saw a deep head cut. They walked, Lang
thought, for 30 minutes to where the circuit went through a village with
a first aid post in a farm.

Lang estimated that the ambulance didn't come for about 45 minutes
and then, when he was in it, it continued to the accident to pick up two
injured spectators. Lang was recognised and...

the bystanders [...] started to insult me. Not knowing the language I
could not explain that I was hardly to blame; accidents did occur in
motor-racing and the spectators themselves were to blame for exposing
themselves to danger, against which they had been specifically warned.
I therefore kept quiet until the driver of the ambulance, a man of
Herculean physique, interfered, explaining the situation in Czech. To
me, he said briefly in German, 'Don't worry, nothing will happen to
you.'[32]

Lang was taken to hospital and only then did he learn the full extent of
the accident. Caracciola won from von Brauchitsch, late afternoon
sunlight cloaking the finishing line with a huge crowd on one side and
Caracciola easing the Mercedes to the pits at the other. He lifted his
goggles to his forehead, smiled through the grime on his face and gorged
avidly from a glass someone handed him.

The legal consequences of Lang's crash lingered for five years.

In October, the Silver Arrows came to Donington and caused a
genuine sensation. This is a much devalued word but here it's used in
the original, full-strength sense. The British, reared on their sit-up-and-
beg little racers in the hands of *good chaps,* suddenly found the
woodlands and straights of Donington echoing to mighty, rolling
thunder, and they had never even *imagined* anything like it before.[33]

Neubauer had asked Seaman to sound out Fred Craner about
Mercedes taking part, Craner (reluctantly) offered them £400 start
money and so, as one convoy of Mercedes arrived at Brno another was
setting off towards northern France and the crossing to England.

Those who came to Donington would see the full Mercedes team – von Brauchitsch, Lang, Seaman, Caracciola – and for good measure, the full Auto Union team, too: Rosemeyer, Hasse and Müller. Von Brauchitsch took pole but Lang led from Caracciola and a vast crowd – the ripple effect of traffic trying to get in to the circuit had flowed back to Derby – watched awestruck on a perfect autumnal day. The knowing among them kept one eye on Rosemeyer and understood that he was in no hurry. The race lasted 250 miles.

He ran third to lap 20 when the Mercedes pit stops began, then led; ran third again after his own pit stop; ran second to von Brauchitsch then led again when von Brauchitsch pitted. The race devolved into a struggle of wills between the two men and Rosemeyer won it. As he passed the pits he'd made a curious hand signal which nobody understood except his mechanic. It was 'tick-tack' they'd picked up the night before when they'd gone to a greyhound meeting – Rosemeyer hit himself in the neck and on the forehead – and it meant *I'm well, the car is well.*

To capture the full impact of the German cars...

The Donington measure: Rosemeyer averaging 82.6mph, Ruesch/Seaman, 1936, 69.1mph.

It was the master's final race. The rivalry between Auto Union and Mercedes extended to an annual record breaking *fest* on stretches of the autobahn. In January, between the Frankfurt and Darmstadt section, Caracciola raised the record speed set on a road to 271mph (436kmh) for Mercedes. Rosemeyer, responding in the Auto Union, reached 270mph, when something happened to the car, and he was found dead at the foot of some trees.

Something went from motor racing then. Many contemporaries tried to express that but could not. Like Jim Clark and Ayrton Senna it seemed more like the defining of an era than simply the death of a great driver, but with Rosemeyer that was, and remains, heightened further because in 1938 the shadows crept closer and closer. War is about death, Rosemeyer had been about being alive.

The European Championship had new rules, maximum engine capacity of 4,500cc for normally aspirated cars and 3,000cc supercharged, and minimum weights depending on engine size.

In February, Seaman was at the Berlin Motor Show as part of the Mercedes team and met Hitler for the first time. Hitler shook hands with the drivers and offered his congratulations. He and Goebbels made speeches declaring that 'the daring young race drivers present today fight their battles not for money, not for personal glory – but for the greater glory of the Fatherland!' This was greeted by a cheer although not, presumably, from Seaman.

The Mercedes was a very modern operation in scale, outlook, planning and perhaps psychology. The racing department consisted of 220 personnel, and that included two teams of 25 mechanics who 'were devoted entirely to the development and servicing of Mercedes racing cars. The Experimental Department did not manufacture any of the components but absolute priority was given to racing requirements. No expense was spared.'[34]

In March, to an ecstatic welcome, Hitler went to Vienna to receive Austria in to the German Reich. For many months he'd undermined the government while his supporters maintained a reign of terror. It had been heavy hitting but now, many hoped, he would be satisfied and the shadows recede.

The first big race, Pau in April, had lasting consequences. Auto Union, needing a replacement for Rosemeyer, contacted Nuvolari but as an Italian his first loyalty lay with Alfa Romeo who'd made an interim car for the new formula. It seemed to go well but Nuvolari didn't realise that 'the chassis was flexing under the cornering loads and causing the fuel tank, mounted just above his knees, to start to leak. In the race itself petrol seeped out and caught fire. Nuvolari had to steer the blazing car into the trees and bale out, narrowly escaping with his life. For the brave and unquenchable Tazio Nuvolari, it was the last straw. He swore never to drive an Alfa Romeo again, and he kept his promise until the day he died.'[35] In disgust, he announced his retirement.

Czechoslovakia had a significant German minority in the disputed Sudetenland (Neubauer had been born just over the border in Germany but after the war his village would become Czech). That spring Hitler turned his attention to the minority, and Britain and France gave a promise to defend Czechoslovakia against aggression and wanted to arrange a meeting with Hitler to explain that invading Czechoslovakia would mean war. Hitler had a Czech crisis to exploit. He knew what to do.

Nuvolari did not go to the French Grand Prix, run at Reims for the first time since 1932. It attracted only nine cars, including two Auto Unions which were having trouble taking the corners, and crashed in practice. Müller had to be taken to hospital and couldn't race. The Auto Unions were granted special additional practice on race morning.

The starter held the flag while, behind him, someone with a stopwatch tapped him rhythmically between the shoulder blades to count him down: five taps, one a second, and the flag fell. Far above the grandstand, flags fluttered in the wind – the swastika prominent.

Masters of their time: (from left, top) Rudi Caracciola and Dick Seaman; (below) Achille Varzi and Hermann Lang; and (bottom) Bernd Rosemeyer and Manfred von Brauchitsch. (all LAT)

Was this the race of the century? It was certainly dramatic, as described in The Autocar. *Nuvolari (right) in an Alfa Romeo took on Mercedes and Auto Union at the Nürburgring in 1935 — and won (LAT). Here's the grid (left) as it was handed to the Press on the day; Alfred Neubauer (top right), the Mercedes team manager, urges Manfred von Brauchitsch to be careful under Nuvolari's onslaught; von Brauchitsch's rear tyre shreds and this is what it looked like after the race.* (courtesy DaimlerChrysler)

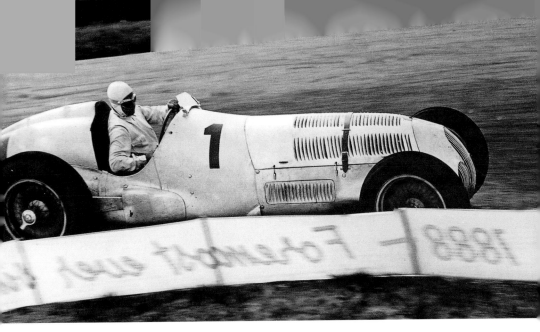

Rudi Caracciola, a driver touched with timeless skill, holds the mighty 1937 Mercedes monster hard with his left hand, lightly with his right. (LAT)

The matrix of the 1930s distilled into one evocative study. The Mercedes of Lang, Caracciola and Seaman leading, the sublime Rosemeyer in the Auto Union challenging. (LAT)

A new generation after the Second World War – at the 1953 French Grand Prix, the desperate finish between Mike Hawthorn's Ferrari (16) and Juan-Manuel Fangio's Maserati. (LAT)

Stirling Moss with the beautiful, mighty 1955 Mercedes W196, here at Spa where he finished second to Fangio. (courtesy BARC)

If Nuvolari drove the race of the century at the Nürburgring in 1935, Fangio (above) produced something almost as momentous two decades later. Below: Here he has his Maserati between the Ferraris of Mike Hawthorn and Peter Collins as the 1957 German Grand Prix reaches its unbearable climax. (LAT)

Maestro. Fangio has broken the Ferraris and the crowd surrender to him. (LAT)

September 1957. Motor Sport magazine, supreme master of understatement.

Masters of their time. Above: (with goggles)
Giuseppe Farina, the first World Champion,
alongside Alberto Ascari, who would become
the first-ever double World Champion (LAT).
Fangio (below) defined the 1950s
(Ludvigsen Library); and (right) Moss was
no stranger to Prince Rainier, Princess Grace
and the podium at Monaco. He won there in
1956, 1960 and 1961 (LAT).

The race existed in two dimensions, a titanic struggle for the lead and behind that a handful of cars scrabbling for whatever they could get. On the opening lap Hasse went off into a field and Müller's substitute driver hit a house in a village. With 61 laps left only five cars still ran. The three Mercedes gave an exhibition, Lang, Caracciola and von Brauchitsch trading lap records. Von Brauchitsch won it from Caracciola, Lang third a lap down and the next finisher, a Frenchman in a Talbot, *ten* laps down. As von Brauchitsch pulled into the pits to get out, half a dozen Germans rushed towards him, their arms stiff in the Nazi salute. One report says 'crowds of Nazis had come over to glory in humiliating the French.'

Auto Union lured Nuvolari out of his brief retirement and he'd have one for the German Grand Prix at the Nürburgring. Three Mercedes lined up on the front row, Caracciola in another on the second next to Nuvolari. Now that Nuvolari was with a German team, Hühnlein must have imagined he had some sort of authority over him, strode across the grid to where Nuvolari stood beside his car, shook his hand and gave the stiff arm salute. Nuvolari responded as he had done when he won in 1935, raising his arm crooked in a compromise.

The starting lights failed. Lang glanced across at Neubauer, Neubauer made some gesture – and Lang was gone into the lead, Nuvolari after him like a hare. Nuvolari spun off backwards trying to wipe oil from his goggles. A Nazi Obergruppenführer [Lieutenant-General], Irwin Krauss, presented himself at the Mercedes pit, said that the oil had come from a Mercedes car and ordered Neubauer to bring all his cars in to be checked for leaks. Neubauer refused, Krauss persisted and someone said Krauss must be doing this because he favoured the Auto Unions. Krauss 'stormed' off.

On lap 16 von Brauchitsch pitted for fuel and tyres. He complained to Neubauer that Seaman drove so close to him it was making him crazy, so close von Brauchitsch couldn't catch his breath.

Seaman pitted just for fuel – he hadn't been so hard on his tyres – and Neubauer told him to stay behind von Brauchitsch.

Meanwhile, 'the impatient von Brauchitsch slapped the sides of his Mercedes shouting: "Let's go, let's go!" Perhaps the refuelling mechanic was nervous. For whatever reason, he was a second late in shutting off the pump. In that one second five gallons of fuel shot from the mouth of the tank, drenching car and driver.'[36]

A mechanic was starting von Brauchitsch's car when a blowback from the exhaust produced a flash fire. 'I stayed in my seat because I knew the fire fighters knew what they were doing – our people absolutely knew how to handle these situations – but I felt the back of my head burning.

I tried as fast as I could to get out of the driving seat but I hadn't removed the steering wheel. I had to drop back down into the seat but I felt hands pulling at me.'[37] That was Neubauer who hauled him the rest of the way out. The crowd above the pits scattered. Von Brauchitsch fell and some reports say Neubauer fell onto him to smother the flames. Von Brauchitsch remembered 'wriggling' and rolling to put them out. The mechanics fired foam and it lay like a snow fall all around the car.

Now Seaman sat immobile in his car as the von Brauchitsch fire was put out. Neubauer went to Seaman and demanded to know why he hadn't gone back out. Seaman replied that he was obeying his instructions, waiting to follow von Brauchitsch...[38]

Seaman was ordered out immediately and, still on the ground, von Brauchitsch watched Seaman go. Once von Brauchitsch's car had been quickly checked, he went back out, too, his wheels cutting a path through the snowfall.

Seaman was leading the Grand Prix by more than two minutes from Lang. Von Brauchitsch got as far as *Flugplatz,* a right-hander, and went off into a ditch. He maintained the steering wheel hadn't been put back properly, a controversial claim which many felt was designed to conceal the fact that he'd simply made a mistake. He walked back holding the steering wheel and brandished it to the crowd. Hühnlein stood next to him, hands on hips, and did not look pleased. He had good reason.

Seaman – cheered all the way round by the crowd, thousands of hands waving him on – won the race, the first Briton to win a Grand Prix since Segrave at San Sebastian in 1924. Neubauer dipped into the cockpit and embraced him like a son.

Seaman's victory placed Hühnlein in a very delicate, unenviable position: he'd have to explain to the Fuehrer why an Englishman had won the Fuehrer's own trophy in the German Grand Prix in a German car in front of 400,000 Germans. The German newspapers faced a similar dilemma:[39]

Kissed and hugged by the joyful Neubauer, Seaman found himself lifted from his machine and escorted to the impressive awards platform. There, amid the swastika-laden trappings of Herr Hitler's political organization, he was congratulated by an embarrassed Hühnlein. 'On behalf of Chancellor Adolf Hitler,' said Hühnlein unenthusiastically, 'I present you with this trophy in honour of your victory.' A huge laurel wreath was draped across the youthful Englander's shoulders as he accepted the enormous trophy. The bands played first the German Anthem, then 'God

Save the King' and the mighty crowd roared its approval of Der
Englander's triumph.[40]

On the podium, a platform high up above the pits, Seaman faced an
awkward moment. To his right, Hühnlein gave a stiff-arm Nazi salute; to
his left von Brauchitsch did the same; behind him, a thicket of arms gave
the salute, too. Could he, as an Englishman, do that? He compromised,
lifting his arm halfway, almost exactly as Nuvolari had done. Hühnlein,
a stocky man, shook Seaman's hand, swastika prominent on the left arm
of his uniform. Other uniformed men stood nearby.

Krauss came back and virtually accused Neubauer of losing the race
for von Brauchitsch by send him back out with burnt brakes. Neubauer
pointed out that it was Hühnlein who had asked for the car to rejoin, no
doubt seeing with terribly clarity the dilemma he'd face if Seaman
won...

Seaman said privately he wished the winning car had been British.

A month later he led the Swiss Grand Prix at Bremgarten for eleven
laps in heavy rain but was baulked by back markers and Caracciola
surged through. Bremgarten lay shrouded by the rain, the tall trees
round its rural, undulating roads darkened by it, the track surface
glistening with it – and each passing car cutting in to that, churning it,
flinging it. They'd crest puddles and scatter the water there like little
cloudbursts. Did Caracciola have a sixth sense – a supernatural ability –
in the wet? His visor came off but he could *still see,* and see enough to
win it.

> The rain had softened the ground in the woods and rivulets ran to the road
> and flowed across the track. I watched like a lynx to catch any change in
> the surface of the road. Baby said I had the eyes of a seal because I could
> see so well in the rain. But on a slippery road you must have the right
> feeling for the car. The car wants to act like a wild horse on the
> cobblestones. I had to guess what it intended doing before it was done and
> then I had to control it with calm, gentle motions. It required not only the
> hands; the entire body was involved in feeling and controlling the car.[41]

Once he'd won it, he lost no time lighting a cigarette. Seaman, second,
had joined the leading drivers of the day because, as Caracciola said,
Seaman had matched him and in the wet that was the ultimate
compliment.

Hitler played the Czech crisis hard now. Three days before Monza, the
German minority held rallies and demanded union with Germany.

This political situation was coming to concern everyone, including the drivers. Caracciola remembered that at Monza we were 'met with some sympathy, but on the whole with outright hostility. War seemed inevitable. However... as yet we were still racing and the drivers of many nations participated.'

The Mercedes had been strong in practice but Hermann Müller, a former bike racer, forced his Auto Union into the lead, Lang chasing so hard that he overtook on the opening lap. On lap two Caracciola went off into straw bales and had to push the car back onto the circuit.

> It was as hot as only Italy can be in the autumn. It was hot in the cars, even hotter in mine because a gasket had burned out. The heat of the exhaust came directly through the openings of the gear and throttle pedals at my feet. In spite of asbestos lining, the throttle burned a hole through the leather sole, the asbestos inner sole, right to the sole of my foot. Brauchitsch took over from me for a few laps, then he had enough. I got in again, pressing down on the red-hot throttle with just the edge of my foot.[42]

The sun made the tall trees into shadows across the track, made the cars into symmetrical shadows turning and returning. Nuvolari had his Auto Union past Lang and into the lead by lap ten. Someone coined a lovely phrase to cover what Nuvolari was doing, *German engine, Italian heart*. The rear-engined Auto Unions were extremely difficult to tame and exploit, as we've seen, and there's enough cinematic evidence to illustrate that very graphically, the tail-ends twitching into corners, the cars weaving. Rosemeyer had had an advantage because he had never driven anything else and as a consequence did not have to make any adjustments of technique or even, perhaps, restructure an established technique altogether. Even Nuvolari, touched by genius, had taken this long to do the taming but, round Monza's parkland, he had done it.

The pace was so intense that Lang set fastest lap and blew his engine. Nuvolari won it, averaging more than 96mph, from Farina's Alfa Romeo, two laps down, Caracciola third three laps down – although that was enough to make him European Champion.

That only Caracciola of the Mercedes team finished prompted Neubauer to cancel a pre-planned victory celebration in Milan. Instead he set off with his wife to his favourite Milanese restaurant, but he'd been tricked because all the drivers came in and the Auto Union team, too. They did celebrate – Seaman's engagement to Erica Popp, the delightful daughter of the BMW president, and Neubauer paid the whole bill.

The Donington Grand Prix was scheduled for Sunday, 2 October, a comfortable three weeks after Monza. When the German teams arrived, British Prime Minister Neville Chamberlain was locked into negotiations with Hitler over the Czech crisis.

On Monday, 26 September, five days before Donington, Hitler said that if the Czechs had not agreed to his demands by the Wednesday they would have to take the consequences. That might well mean the start of a general European war – and the cars (and mechanics) of both teams were already at Donington, deep in the heart of England, the drivers in London preparing to go to a luncheon at the RAC Club in Pall Mall to celebrate Seaman's win at the Nürburgring.

Nobody knows who gave the order, but it came in the early hours of the Tuesday to both teams: *run for home*. The mechanics loaded everything as fast as they could and by breakfast two convoys of lorries – the Mercedes had ten – were lumbering out of the circuit towards the distant Channel ports. Mercedes had instructions that if an enraged English public stormed their convoy as it passed through any of the towns along they way they were to set fire to the racing cars to destroy them.

There was frantic activity between the team managements in London, the Mercedes and Auto Union headquarters, and Hühnlein in Berlin. He said that the cars must stay and race. The convoys were halted and turned round, and in those days it could be done by looking at a road map, working out the towns the convoys would go through, then ringing the police there with orders to intercept. Auto Union reached Market Harborough and a police sergeant flagged them down. They had a pleasant lunch at the Peacock Hotel before lumbering back. Mercedes reached Leicester and were drawn up outside the police headquarters. A team spokesman said that the decision to return to Donington meant there would be no war.

By Wednesday 28 September feverish horse-trading was going on in Germany. Hitler was taking it to the brink and was quite prepared to go over that brink.

In the mounting confusion neither German team could get through to Germany for further instructions and took the decision themselves: *run for home – again*. This time they did.

On Friday, 30 September Britain, France, Germany and Italy reached an agreement that the German-speaking area of Czechoslovakia was to be incorporated into Greater Germany by 10 October. Czechoslovakia, which had not even been present at these talks, was being dismembered. That same day Chamberlain flew back to London and, in front of a crowd rendered slightly hysterical by relief, waved a piece of paper which he and Hitler had signed. It represented 'peace in our time'.

The Germans came back and the Donington Grand Prix was run on 22 October. In practice, Nuvolari's Auto Union struck a deer and its head was stuffed, mounted and presented to him. Lang had pole from Nuvolari and an extraordinary race developed because one of the British cars dropped a large quantity of oil and the approaching cars, including Seaman, slithered off although Nuvolari got through by releasing the car to go where it wanted, not fighting or correcting it until it had done that. At 50 of the 80 laps, however, Lang led and Nuvolari ran third, 58 seconds behind. Nuvolari set off on a heroic chase and on lap 67 had caught him. A stone smashed Lang's windscreen and the onrushing air made breathing so difficult he felt he was swimming. He could barely hold the wheel.

On the long straight Nuvolari went cleanly by, and winning it by almost a minute and a half. That evening the world seemed a safer place, and Donington a warmer place because of Nuvolari. The Germans said at the banquet in Derby that of course they would be back again in 1939.

There'd be another Grand Prix at Donington, but with no German cars or engines and a single German driver, Michael Schumacher, on 11 April 1993.

Moving into 1939, the shadowlands became darker week by week. In February, plans were announced to provide British homes with bomb shelters; a month later Hitler crushed Czechoslovakia, and Britain and France said they would defend Poland's independence. However much motor racing people tried to ignore all this – and they did, some right to the end – they could not. Reality was going to assert itself over their closed world and there was already evidence of that because, as relations between France and Italy deteriorated, Mussolini forbade Italian teams to compete in French races.

Mercedes hadn't modified their 1938 car except for a system of supercharging, and Auto Union did the same.

In April, Mussolini occupied Albania and in May Italy and Germany signed a 'Pact of Steel'. The Axis had been forged.

The Championship began in Belgium on 26 June and perhaps Hermann Lang was typical of the desire to ignore the reality. He'd remember driving along the autobahn to Belgium, 'dance music on the car radio, and the car smooth in over-drive. We touched Aachen, then along the Rhine via *Malmédy* to Spa.'[43] Seaman and his young wife Erica checked in to the Palace Hotel there.

The ballot for grid places allowed Farina (Alfa Romeo) to be on the front row, and that had consequences because on the downhill start to *Eau Rouge* cars were apt to creep. Neubauer had frequently asked for the grid to be moved down to where the track flattened but, of course, the grandstands were facing the present grid. To avoid a false start Neubauer ordered lumps of chalk be put under the Mercedes' wheels like chocks. These prevented the creeping and when the cars set off they crushed the chalk, but didn't damage the tyres. Farina, Lang and Müller made up the front row, Seaman and Nuvolari the row after that.

On a wet afternoon Farina began to creep. Müller and Lang went past him but whenever Lang attacked, Müller positioned his Auto Union in the middle of the narrow track. Passing the pits Lang could see 'Neubauer raging against the officials … I had signalled to him, by means of my raised fist, that I was being baulked.'

Eau Rouge was the same fundamental shape as today, the left curving into the right and then up the hill. This day in 1939, the rim of the left was grass and, passing tight beside it, the cars ran through a puddle, their rear offside wheels spewing water. The cars powered through and set off again into the watery countryside.

On lap three Seaman went past Farina, too, and Lang signalled for him and Caracciola – both outstanding in the wet – to go by and attack Müller themselves. But Caracciola spun at *La Source,* got out and tried to push his Mercedes into the safety of the trees. When Neubauer heard Caracciola was out, he ordered a mechanic to take Caracciola's coat and cigarettes to him, and stay with the car.

Müller pitted, and now Seaman led. By lap 22 he had almost half a minute over Lang but the rain fell heavier. Trees lined whole tracts of the circuit and no barriers protected the cars from them. Each tree trunk bore a painted white mark, that was all. The trees were sodden, the track sodden, the spectators huddled under umbrellas. Lang remembered:

on a dangerous left-hand bend I was suddenly given the yellow danger flag. I slowed down at once, but was unable to find out straight away what was the matter. Coming out of the bend I saw that a racing car was positively glued to a tree, and on passing the spot I was horrified to recognise it as Seaman's. [...] The car had almost completely wrapped itself round the tree no doubt through the considerable force of impact, the fuel tank had burst, and, wedged in the seat like a stone statue, sat Seaman, surrounded by a sea of flames.[44]

It happened near *La Source*, Seaman losing control of the car at some 130mph. It seemed the primitive ambition of every racing driver had gripped him: he had wanted to demonstrate that he – not Caracciola – was *Der Regenmeister* now.

In the battered hulk of the Mercedes he sat trapped and unconscious, and when he was finally hauled from it he'd been badly burnt. Lang wanted to retire but was told to continue and won it from Hasse. Lang, distraught, managed a flicker of a smile when the garland was placed over his head, then the smile was gone. His eyelids blinked and blinked, his face locked into sombre posture. There were no celebrations that night as they all waited for medical bulletins on Seaman who had been taken to hospital in Spa and, astonishingly, regained consciousness. He died shortly before midnight.

He was buried in London and the Mercedes team attended before flying to Paris and travelling from there to Reims for the French Grand Prix.

Lang was in prime form and promptly broke the lap record when practice began. He had pole from Caracciola and Nuvolari.

> Everyone tried desperately to get into the lead, even at considerable personal risk. Even Caracciola wanted to take the first bend at such a speed that he got into a skid and split his fuel tank. The tussle became more determined, and tougher. I had quite a job to get out of the mêlées in which I was wedged, to follow the 'Flying Mantuan'. It took four laps to pass him. Even the straight [...] was too narrow and it was only on the corners that I caught up. [...] I had occasion to watch his superb driving style. How easily he handled the car on the bends, almost caressing the wheel! On a hairpin I got my car next to him and side by side we entered the straight, without either being able to gain an inch on the other. Occasionally I glanced over to him [...] the white teeth, leathery face and jutting chin. Then came a long fast right-hander. He had the inside and neither of us gave in. I kept my foot on the throttle and just got by the footpath. I could not have done more – it would have been fatal.[45]

Untypically, Nuvolari backed off, soon retired with a gearbox problem, Lang's engine failed and Müller won it.

By the German Grand Prix on 23 July, Hitler exploited the Danzig problem, the disputed Baltic port which provided Poland with a corridor to the sea. Britain said that if he used force to seize it that force would be resisted, meaning war.

Lang took pole again from von Brauchitsch and Caracciola, but showers fell when the race began and The Ring seemed to be brooding.

Into lap two Pietsch, now a privateer in a Maserati, came past in the lead, the Mercedes of Lang and von Brauchitsch crippled by the damp weather and needing new plugs. 'Loudspeakers braying excitedly at Pietsch's effrontery almost choked over this news.'[46] Nuvolari responded by going by and Pietsch had to pit for plugs. As the race developed, Caracciola got stronger and stronger. He'd remember how the rain teemed down but, on lap 12, he overtook Hasse and Müller and set off to build a cushion because he had to make a pit stop again. He stretched his lead over them to 39 seconds, then 44 and on lap 15 he saw Neubauer's pit signal – a flag – meaning *come in at the end of this lap*. He did that. He'd remember how fast the mechanics worked, putting in 60 litres of fuel in 17 seconds; remember how nobody spoke. He sensed the tension in the pit, sensed people looking for Müller coming. Caracciola got back out before that. 'I heard the high, singing, metallic sound of my car and I was driving on my beloved Nürburgring.'[47]

Lang had retired – engine – and wanted to take over reserve driver Heinz Brendel's car. Neubauer agreed and signalled Brendel in but Brendel missed the signal and halfway round the next lap saw Pietsch spinning. This seems to have distracted or unnerved him because he spun and the Mercedes went into a ditch. In the pits, Lang – unaware of this – waited for Brendel to appear and hand the car over. The pit phone rang. Brendel wanted someone to come and give him a lift back, Lang threw a cushion down in frustration while Neubauer spoke into the phone: *you can walk back.*

Caracciola won it from Müller.

Lang was 'still bad-tempered' that evening although he congratulated Caracciola on his victory at the Adler Hof hotel in Adenau. 'Here amongst my colleagues and friends my good humour returned and we spent a cheerful evening. Next day, almost as pleased as the winner, we returned home through the beautiful Eifel countryside, skirting the Rhine on the way.'

On 17 August, Hitler closed the border with Poland and on 20 August, the day of the Swiss Grand Prix, Poland sent troops to the border. Caracciola watched the political clouds darken and remembered how people couldn't contemplate another war. He applied it to the racing community which embraced so many nationalities and which now faced being 'made to hate each other from one day to the next.'[48]

On top of Mussolini's edict about racing in France, the Italians had been determined to enter only 1.5-litre events. To lure them to Bremgarten, the Swiss organisers created a bizarre solution of two heats, one for the 1.5 litre cars and the other for the Grand Prix cars, with the fastest meeting in a 'final'.

A wet race, and everyone murmured that it was made for Caracciola on such a cobbled track – demanding the utmost sensitivity in such conditions – but Lang, pole, wasn't worried about that. The 1.5-litre heat winner Farina (Alfa Romeo) ran sixth and was about to be a spoiler. Lang led but Farina got up behind him and none of the mighty German cars could get past. For the opening six laps Lang couldn't draw away from Farina any more than Caracciola could do anything about the Alfa Romeo. The rain stopped and Caracciola was past Farina, beginning a long pursuit of Lang. With 20 laps gone he was within 12 seconds and closing. 'The pit crew, the papers and the spectators said afterwards that it had been the most exciting tussle they had ever seen,' Lang wrote. He held Caracciola by three seconds at the end and was Champion of Europe. 'Caracciola asked me afterwards why we had driven like maniacs. "Yes – why?" There was nothing else I could reply.'

Three days later, Germany and the Soviet Union signed a Non-Aggression Pact. It left Hitler free to do what he wanted in the rest of Europe without a stab in the back from the east. Inside a week troops all over Europe were being mobilised.

The Yugoslavian Grand Prix in Belgrade was scheduled for 3 September. Hitler increased pressure on Poland hour by hour and only five cars went, two Mercedes (Lang, von Brauchitsch), two Auto Unions (Müller, Nuvolari) and a Bugatti for Bosko Milenkovic, a rich Viennese who'd lived in Belgrade for twenty years and indulged his passion for racing, moving from bikes to hill-climbs to a Bugatti.

On 25 August, the Mercedes convoy moved out of Stuttgart for the long haul to Belgrade. Louis Chiron was having his 40th birthday at his villa near Como and, Caracciola would say, 'asked us to come down with von Brauchitsch to celebrate. We remained together for quite a while. It seemed as if war might break out any day and we had so many things to tell each other. Before we parted we promised Chiron that we would phone him at once if we learned of such a catastrophe.' Von Brauchitsch 'left us with a heavy heart and gave us his luggage for safe-keeping.' He flew to Belgrade.

The circuit, in the city, was on roads round a park and had a rough surface cut through by tram lines. Some of the corners looked dangerously unprotected.

Both German teams could sense the political tension rising and Auto Union even decided to stay in their hotel in the evenings. The Mercedes team, however, went out strolling. As much as possible they didn't talk about the possibilities of war.

At 5.45am on 1 September, the Friday, Germany invaded Poland.

All the Germans in Belgrade faced the immediate question: *race or run for home?* One source claims Hühnlein 'ordered' them to stay because he 'wanted the race to be a frightening demonstration of German expertise.'

That day Lang went quickest in practice but von Brauchitsch took pole the day after. From this point on, accounts become confused, contradictory, slightly hysterical. On race morning, Neubauer would write: 'I could see that both Lang and Brauchitsch were oppressed by the worsening international situation and in no condition to drive their best. The evening before the race we were sitting in our hotel when the news came through that German troops had invaded Poland. We looked at one another in horrified silence.' But of course the invasion had been the day before that, and at dawn, not in the evening.

Britain declared war on Germany that race day morning, 3 September, and Lang says 'all of us lost every inclination to race but Neubauer returned from our Embassy with the news that we must keep calm and start. We owed this to our hosts.'

At some point in the confusion von Brauchitsch tried to fly home. Neubauer wrote that he – Neubauer – headed out to the airport, got onto the plane and confronted him. Von Brauchitsch gave an account confirming some details – Neubauer getting on to the plane, his hat at an angle as it always was when he was angry – but suggests it happened on the Friday, when news of the invasion of Poland came through. Von Brauchitsch raced.

It began at 3pm in front of some 50,000 spectators. The French ambassador to Yugoslavia had taken his seat in the grandstand, gazed at the four German cars, risen and left. France would not be at war with Germany for another two hours and it may be he was called away rather than registering his disgust.

Von Brauchitsch led immediately from Lang and they drove furiously for six laps before, as Lang remembered:

> suddenly something hit me and everything went dark before my eyes; with a tremendous effort, I tried to see again. Brauchitsch's car had thrown up a stone, which not only shattered my aeroscreen but also both glasses in my goggles. My eyes were full of splinters and when Dr Glaser [the Mercedes doctor] took out the last bits the short and furious race was over.[49]

Reserve driver Walter Bäumer took over, a lap down. Müller in second place, Nuvolari third. When Müller pitted Nuvolari attacked von Brauchitsch – and proud, perhaps arrogant, von Brauchitsch resisted to the point where Neubauer predicted a crash at any instant. Von Brauchitsch overtook Bäumer so brutally that he thrust the German reserve driver into the straw bales. Then, on lap 16, von Brauchitsch spun and Nuvolari was through. Von Brauchitsch couldn't catch him although, as a final flourish, he set joint fastest lap. That gesture distilled the spirit of the all motor racing, but it can stand particularly as the epitaph for the 1930s: *never say die.*

Auto Union started to pack there and then, buying sufficient fuel (they hoped) to get them back to Germany. Their convoy moved out next morning. Mercedes had brought extra fuel with them and, because there were ugly rumours about Hungary, they headed up Yugoslavia to cross into Austria, now of course a part of Germany.

> What awful, potholed, dusty roads! They led through endless maize fields and went on and on. We had to keep miles away from the main convoy and could recognize it by the enormous dust clouds in the distance. After passing the black, white and yellow frontier posts we felt at home again.[50]

When they reached Vienna it was blacked out. Neubauer distributed enough of the fuel to get them all back home, and they dispersed.

Lang remembered the 'melancholy' of realising that an era had suddenly ended and would never be coming back. Hitler was crushing Poland and, although ordinary people didn't know it, he would turn west to crush Holland, Belgium and France, turn east again for the great prize, Stalin's vast lair of the Soviet Union.

Lang was right.

Motor racing, which – distilled by the courage and skill of Bernd Rosemeyer – had been so wonderfully alive was one of the first deaths. There would be many, many more.

Notes

1. The League of Nations, set up in 1920 and headquartered in Geneva, was an early attempt at a body like the United Nations – which in essence it later became. The League proved powerless in reality.
2. *Alfa Romeo,* Owen.
3. *Grand Prix Driver,* Lang.
4. *When Nuvolari Raced,* Moretti.

5. *Racing the Silver Arrows,* Nixon.

6. *The Le Mans Story,* Fraichard.

7. *Amateur Racing Driver,* Cholmondeley Tapper.

8. Ibid.

9. Lang, op. cit.

10. Ibid.

11. *Rosemeyer!,* Elly Rosemeyer and Nixon.

12. *Complete History of Grand Prix Motor Racing,* Cimarosti.

13. *Racing the Silver Arrows,* Nixon.

14. Moretti, op. cit.

15. Prince Birabongse of Thailand, known as 'B. Bira.' He was an enthusiastic and wealthy amateur driver of the 1930s, mainly competing in Britain.

16. Interview with author.

17. *My Racing Life,* Fangio.

18. The idea of retreating to Milan ten miles away for lunch is a wonderful one to the modern team, with its enormous motor homes which dispense excellent food at circuits even during qualifying. The fare at Grands Prix are even more impressive. Renault, for example, say: 'About 2,000 meals are served every race weekend. The catering teams starts working in the kitchen at five in the morning – and everybody appreciates the quality of the service they provide. During the course of a Grand Prix meeting they provide 60kg of pasta, 200 chicken breasts, 7kg of salt and 15kg of sugar, among other things. A thousand bottles of water are consumed, while team guests enjoy up to 96 bottles of red wine and 72 bottles of white wine' – Renault F1 Team Press Office. Perhaps Mrs Neubauer didn't quite manage that.

19. *Kampf um Meter Und Sekunden,* von Brauchitsch.

20. Lang, op. cit.

21. *Rosemeyer!* op. cit. Karl Feureissen was Team Manager, Sebastian a mechanic.

22. Ibid.

23. Lang, op. cit.

24. *Rosemeyer!* op. cit.

25. Ibid.

26. Lang, op. cit.

27. Moretti, op. cit.

28. Owen, op. cit.

29. *Silver Arrows,* op. cit

30. Moretti, op. cit.

31. Lang, op. cit.

32. Ibid.

33. For a fuller description, see *Hitler's Grands Prix in England,* Hilton.

34. *Racing Mercedes* (Bill Mason Films Ltd, David Weguelin Productions)

35. Owen, op. cit.

36. *Omnibus of Speed,* eds Beaumont and Nolan.

37. Von Brauchitsch, op. cit.

38. Because this incident is so famous in motorsport history, some minutiae. Chris Nixon (*Shooting Star: the life of Richard Seaman*) has cast extreme doubt on whether all of these conversations happened and, if they did, on the way they have usually been presented. Neubauer's memoirs are unreliable (and sometimes outright invention) but have been used as a template by many. Nixon has studied film of the fire and concludes that although Neubauer did speak to von Brauchitsch, you can't tell if von Brauchitsch said anything back. Neubauer did trot to Seaman and speak briefly to him but returned to von Brauchitsch as the fire broke out; then Seaman drove on to the track with Neubauer trying – and failing – to speak to him again.

39. At this distance, it is impossible to say if the Berlin *Tageblatt* distorted its race report the following morning deliberately but it remains suggestive that Seaman is not mentioned in any headline and only appears in the final paragraph.

A MOVING GRAND PRIX

MERCEDES-BENZ AHEAD OF AUTO UNION
HARD FIGHTS
UNEXPECTED INCIDENTS

The second race in the fight regarding the European Championship for car racing, the German Grand Prix, has been decided and after the first two races – France three weeks ago and Germany yesterday – it already now possible to have a basic view of who the victor will be: Mercedes-Benz. We did not expect a different outcome and yet many things were so interesting. There were so many incidents that one didn't dare predict with any certainty, even one moment before the actual finish, what the outcome would be.

Looking first of all at the vehicles and their success: in terms of their racing car construction – the car came out in the spring and was adjudged a success – Mercedes-Benz were favourites. At the moment that vehicle cannot be beaten. The victories in Tripoli and Reims and now on the Nürburgring show this. The task of making a car according to the racing formula rules has succeeded. The racing tradition of the second Germany entry, Auto Union, is much more recent but one has to take into consideration the will to succeed of this firm. In January, just when the new construction was almost finished, Auto Union lost their best driver,

Rosemeyer, and naturally it was he who drove the project forward on and off the track. Thus by his death the work certainly was handicapped. Nevertheless, Auto Union had their car so far advanced that they could take the places behind Mercedes-Benz and showed, basically, they were far superior to their foreign competitors. The next meeting between Mercedes-Benz and Auto Union and hopefully the new Alfa Romeo will take place on 15 August in Pescara whilst Mercedes-Benz competes already eight days before that in Livorno.

The victory of Seaman on Mercedes-Benz, who also drove the fastest lap of the day with an average speed of 134.8kmh, was completely and utterly deserved. The young Englishman, who has been under contract to the Untertürkheim factory for some years, drove a considered and, from a technical point of view, extremely good race. After him came the second Mercedes-Benz with Lang.

40. *Omnibus, op. cit.*
41. *Racing Driver's World,* Caracciola.
42. Ibid.
43. Lang, op. cit.
44. Ibid.
45. Ibid.
46. *The German Grand Prix,* Posthumus.
47. Caracciola, op. cit.
48. Ibid.
49. Lang.
50. Ibid.

Chapter 6

IN FANGIO'S TIME

On 5 December 1940 – a raw, dark day – William Shirer, the resident CBS radio commentator who had daily tried to tell Americans what was happening in Germany, left Berlin because censorship was making his work meaningless. Towards the end of the war, when the greatest slaughter the human race has known was bleeding its way to the end, he prepared to go back.

By then the bombing of Britain had ended although there was still danger from the V2 rockets being fired from occupied France. They might strike anywhere in the greater London area, which put Hornsey, an anonymous northern suburb, as much at risk as anywhere else. That did not stop social life, which is how a 'blond 16-year-old with a shadow of a moustache, in baggy sports coat and ever baggier 1940s trousers' came to be dancing with a 'slim, dark-haired girl in casual sweater.'[1] He had little or no money but fancied himself as a racing driver. That wasn't his vocation, but he didn't know that yet. Colin Chapman would marry the dark haired girl, Hazel, and start a business in a lock-up garage owned by her father, who charged 10s (50p) a week rent. He didn't pay, of course.

On 30 October 1945, Shirer returned to Berlin and, approaching from the air, saw 'the great city demolished almost beyond recognition.'[2] Here, across the road from the Reich Chancellery, Hitler had inspected the Mercedes and Auto Unions while all around him stiff arm salutes cleaved the air and then became static. Alfred Neubauer did that. The drivers did that. The mechanics did that. Now the Chancellery was a broken tooth of a building, bombed, like whole swathes of the city, into stumps of buildings standing deep in rubble. The hotel which faced the Chancellery, the Kaiserhof, where Neubauer stayed during the war while he supervised aircraft repair workshops, was badly mauled.

Tom Wheatcroft, who'd been a spectator at Donington in 1938, served in the British Army and was passing Stuttgart. He went out of curiosity to see what had happened to the Mercedes factory. He'd remember the extent of the wreckage so vividly that half a century later he could still visualise it. Stuttgart had been bombed to devastation – every German city had.[3]

Europe was a bleeding continent, ravaged and exhausted. If the 10 million dead of 1914–1918 are beyond imagining, the Soviet Union alone had lost more than 20 million and the international total was so monstrous that even nightmares can't accommodate it.

Some drivers joined the French Resistance, including Robert Benoist – who'd pay with his life, as we shall see – and 'Williams', another who paid the same price. Jean-Pierre Wimille survived. Dreyfus, who had developed close ties with the United States, joined the American Army (and discovered real breakfasts. *Terrific,* he thought). In May 1944, as Dreyfus subsequently learned, his wife – who'd remained in France during the war – divorced him. Dreyfus was Jewish, and she gave that as one of the reasons. Dreyfus reflected that in Nazi-occupied France it was reason enough.[4]

Paris had been liberated in August 1944 after the German commander, General Dietrich von Cholitz, refused Hitler's order to physically destroy the city. Parisians fell upon collaborators, especially the women who had slept with Germans. In one instance the luxuries these women had been given – nylons, perfume and so on, all beyond price in wartime – were brought out onto a street. The crowd did not steal them, they trampled on them.

Neubauer wrote of being put into a prison camp for a couple of weeks and on release finding, as Wheatcroft had found, the Mercedes factory in ruins. Dr Porsche did two years and emerged with 'his health shattered.'[5] Lang did ten months, according to Neubauer, although he does not mention this himself. It was a time of many silences. Lang wrote that 'after the collapse [of Germany] one could not even talk of motorsport at a time when doctors had not enough fuel and tyres.'[6]

Whole tracts of Europe were the equivalent of wasteland, the roads choked by the wretchedness of millions of refugees; and then there were the Death Camps and the Six Million who wouldn't be coming back from them, the nuclear bombs on two Japanese cities, the Soviet army now seizing everything up into the middle of Germany, swallowing on the way Czechoslovakia and the deadly, primitive Brno circuit. Hungary and that decorous Budapest circuit in public gardens which Nuvolari had graced, was a memory.

The political division of Germany, which endured until 1989, was a compromise: eastern Germany given to Poland, the Soviet Union occupying part of middle Germany and the USA, Britain and France occupying the remainder. Berlin was divided along the same lines, although it fell within the Soviet Zone. To apply all this directly to motorsport, the AVUS circuit lay just inside the boundary of the US Sector with the Soviet Sector in Berlin, and was used as part of the autobahn system so that an ordinary motorist drove quite naturally along it, past grandstands, until he reached the eastern checkpoint beyond the other end of it where, soon enough, there would be wire fences, watchtowers and a death strip. Zwickau fell deep within the Soviet Zone. Some of the Auto Union racing cars were reportedly taken back to the Soviet Union and dismembered.

Italy was riven between Fascists and Communists, and much of the north badly battered by the advancing and retreating armies.

Enzo Ferrari spent the war ensuring his factory made machine tools (for, it seems, the Germans) – although the details are unclear – and making love to a gorgeous fair-haired woman who worked for him, Lina Lardi. She'd provide him with a son and heir, Dino. As the Germans retreated, Ferrari turned his thoughts to making cars and racing them. Italy would have to be rebuilt and that was an interesting thought to someone with a factory, although it had been hit by American bombers and would take some months to become operational again.[7]

Italian racing cars were 'among the few which had been saved from the bombing'[8] because Alfa Romeo hid some and 'numerous private owners' hid their Maseratis.

In July 1945, Ferrari invited Gioachino Colombo, a designer suspended by Alfa Romeo, for talks. Alfa Romeo was 'crippled and in political disarray'. Colombo drove down to Modena 'over shell-pocked roads and through bombed-out villages in a prewar car fuelled by black-market gasoline. The day was steamy and humid.'[9] The bridge over the River Po had been destroyed and the car crossed on a barge. At Modena, Ferrari said it bluntly: 'I want you to go back to making racing cars.'

When the shooting finally stopped, ordinary people felt a very deep desire for normality and, at the same time, escape from reality. To many that was represented by sport and even the most modest events drew immense crowds. Whether motor racing had ever represented normality is a subject for informed debate, but it certainly offered escape. One man and his machine confronting other men and their machines was even more intoxicating now, and that is how on 9 September 1945, just eleven months after the liberation and five months after all the shooting in Europe did stop, the other kind of noise started again in the Bois de Boulogne, Paris.[10]

'It was a park like Hyde Park with a lake and they cornered in front of it. Fortunately the pits and everything were very close to a tube station,'

Jabby Crombac, a leading French motor racing journalist, remembers. 'I didn't have a motor bike so I went by tube. It was like motor racing was for years: you could walk around the cars and mechanics and drivers. There was a big crowd – people were starved of attractions like that. What I remember most was the smell of racing fuel which was so pungent. The first race I'd ever seen was the 1936 Grand Prix at Montlhéry and I got exposed to this smell which was absolutely fantastic. I smelt it again now. I do remember also these engine were all very tired and old, didn't have new piston rings or anything. They were bellowing smoke in the biggest possible way, which was wonderful.'[11]

Hermann Lang turns a lovely general phrase for the rebirth which could apply anywhere and certainly applied here. 'The spell was broken' – the spell of five years of death and darkness.

The circuit measured 1.7 miles and by definition the cars were those which had survived the war. The first race was called the *Coupe Robert Benoist* in memory of the driver who had won four of the five Grands Prix in 1927, been parachuted into France from England and executed in Buchenwald concentration camp.

Seventeen cars started and Amédée Gordini in a Simca led throughout. He was presented with the winning cup by Benoist's daughter.

There were two other races, the *Coupe de la Libération* (The Liberation Cup) and the *Coupe des Prisonniers* (Prisoners' Cup), the highlight. Of the 16 starters, many were well known: Wimille, Sommer, Maurice Trintignant, Étancelin and one who would become extremely notorious, Pierre Levegh. Wimille was still in the French Army and a certain amount of influence had been wielded by friends to get him here, although he didn't arrive in time to practise and started down the grid.

Here were the music-makers again, the Bugattis, Talbots, Delahayes, an Alfa Romeo and a Maserati. The race was over 43 laps, Wimille up to ninth on the first of them and working his way into the lead. He won it in just over an hour by more than a minute from Sommer, the rest spread far back. That was of no importance. What Wimille said was: 'I have not lost my touch. I was rather afraid after such a long period of inactivity but after the first lap I knew all would be as before.' He praised his Bugatti for several reasons – and 'one must not forget it was Robert Benoist who concealed it from the Germans.'[12]

In many profound ways nothing could be as it was before although inevitably there was a sense of carry-over from the 1930s. The drivers in the Bois de Boulogne were those who'd had enough money to buy cars then and still had enough to race them now. Nobody knew, the moment the *Coupe Robert Benoist* was launched, that motor racing had begun a long journey away from the power of privilege, or that Grand Prix racing would come to reflect very accurately the direction in which Western Europe flowed. It had to remain exclusive in the practical sense because at any given moment there were so few teams, cars and drivers, but entry would be on merit, not the size of your inheritance.

Ken Tyrrell, a timber-merchant who'd spent the war in the RAF, received '£25 and a new suit for five and a half years' service. I set out to make my own way in life.' That would lead him to his own team and a multiple World Champion, Jackie Stewart, who on the day of Tyrrell's demob was a frisky little six-year-old in Dumbarton, Scotland.

It was the beginning of meritocracy.

Brooklands, of the right crowd and no crowding, had been requisitioned by the military, the banking partially dismantled to disguise it from enemy bombers. Now it was as much a memory as Budapest. Donington had been an enormous supply depot, Silverstone just another bomber base among so many lost in England's green and pleasant land. Nobody dreamed of racing cars there. Thruxton and Snetterton were air bases, too.

By the end of 1945 'it was possible to see the immediate future of motor racing. France was more than ready to organise events, the Italians had pre-war cars available, England had some cars available and plans were being made to start on new designs.'[13]

In February 1946 the international governing body was renamed the *Fédération Internationale de l'Automobile (FAI)* and it drew up a new formula (1,500cc for supercharged engines, 4,500cc unsupercharged). For the first time the expression 'Formula 1' became currency. Germany was not allowed to join – or rather re-join – the new body for political reasons.

In any case the sense of carry-over lingered because a new generation would take time to emerge. A race at Nice in April confirmed that. The entries included Chiron, Sommer, Étancelin and Villoresi, who won it in a Maserati. Piero Taruffi would write that 'Gigi's victory was hailed with tremendous enthusiasm in Italy, as an augury that our cars and drivers might once again come to the top after five years of inactivity.'[14] Villoresi was part of the carry-over because he'd been racing since 1931.

Nuvolari, who'd spent an unhappy war lodged in a valley in the north of Italy – he disliked both what the war was and what it represented – competed whenever he could, 13 times in 1946. He drove a Maserati at Marseille three weeks after Nice and the entry was so big, reflecting the hunger for normality, that two heats had to be run to sort out the runners for the final. Nuvolari set fastest lap in heat two but retired when a valve failed. Christian Kautz, who'd driven for Mercedes before the war, was a reserve driver. He was Swiss, and Switzerland had been neutral, so the German restriction did not apply.

On 30 May 1946 Wimille won the *Resistance Cup*, again in the Bois de Boulogne. Nuvolari dropped out on lap five with a gearbox problem. On 9 June there was a sprint race at St Cloud, between Versailles and Paris. Two works Alfettas[15] were entered 'exactly as they had been run prior to the war'[16] but neither won – a Maserati did (Sommer). Alfa Romeo could not develop a new racing car because the production cars had absolute priority so they overhauled what they had and did that so well they dominated the Grand Prix des Nations at Geneva on 21 July.

Taruffi competed in the Turin Grand Prix in September 1946, giving Cisitalia its debut.[17] He went in against Nuvolari, Sommer, Farina and Chiron among others.

> After a few laps a hydraulic pipeline broke, leaving me completely without brakes as I was slowing for a right-hand corner. I whistled past Sommer on the right at about 60mph. [...] and plunged full tilt into the straw bales, sending flying a fireman who had stationed himself on top to get a good view. He sailed into the air, all arms and legs, and by a miracle came down unhurt. The car pulled up twenty yards or so further on against some more straw bales, its wheels pointing outwards at a sad angle.[18]

Taruffi was another part of the carry-over because he'd begun competing in 1923. He describes how 'Nuvolari sent the crowd into ecstasies by driving without a steering wheel. Or to be exact, he drove a couple of laps frantically waving his steering wheel at the crowd while he steered by means of a single fixed spoke forming part of the column.'

Nuvolari remained touched by rarest charisma and still communicated it, but his face was narrower now, bark on an old tree, and in April 1946 his second son, Alberto, died. Nuvolari kept on racing because, as he said, he knew about nothing else and there was nothing else he could do.

The sense of carry-over lingered into the first post-war Grand Prix, the Swiss at Bremgarten in June 1947. The first six finishers were Wimille (Alfa Romeo), Varzi (Alfa Romeo), Trossi (Alfa Romeo), Sommer (Maserati), Sanesi (Alfa Romeo), Villoresi (Maserati). There'd be three further Grands Prix, at Spa (Wimille won), Milan (Trossi again) and Lyon (Chiron).

In the spring of 1948 Juan-Manuel Fangio, now in his late 30s, was still racing in Argentina although he thought he might be too old to have much of a future. The year before, the masterly Europeans – Varzi, who he'd remember as austere and monied, and Villoresi – had come to Argentina. Fangio watched and their 'elegant simplicity' of style surprised him.

Now they came back, Wimille with them. Fangio raced them despite being 'as nervous as I have ever been in my life' and Wimille, regarded as the best driver in the world, quickly recognised how good Fangio was. In one race Fangio overtook him, which provoked widespread incredulity. Wimille said that if one day Fangio had a 'car that is right for his temperament' he'd 'perform miracles.'[19]

He would.

The first major Grand Prix since the war, Monaco, had 19 cars on the grid. Eight finished and Farina won it from pole. Nuvolari was on the sixth row of the grid but the engine failed after 16 laps although that might be a diplomatic nicety. He was 'hardly recognisable and is weakening as the laps go by.' He was 'visibly' unwell and his career at Monaco 'ends in the most dramatic anonymity.'[20]

A young, strong, almost plump young Italian brought a Maserati home in fifth. Alberto Ascari was wracked by all manner of superstitions, as his father had been. He had already developed in three early races in 1948 'a religious horror of black cats'[21] – it started on 1 April when one got itself in front of his car on the way to a race. At Monaco his Maserati retired after gearbox and oil pump problems. Deep into the race he took over Villoresi's Maserati but smoke belched from that and it had only third gear. He nursed it to the finish three laps behind Farina.

The Monaco measure: Farina, 100 laps, 3h 18m 26.9s, an average speed of 59.7mph; von Brauchitsch, 1937, 63.2mph.

The measure of the decades: 1929, 49.8mph; 1937, 63.2mph; 1948, 59.7mph. Vehicles registered in Britain 3.7 million (1938, 2.9 million).

A Ford Anglia cost £326 and a Briton earned on average £7.13 (in 1949). Saving all his money, the Briton would have taken 45 weeks to buy one (1910, 2 years 42 weeks; 1919, 1 year 28 weeks; 1929, 41 weeks; 1938, 37 weeks).

The Argentine Auto Club found a way of getting Fangio to Europe, and he arrived on 25 May, eight days after Monaco. Soon enough he watched Ascari win a minor race at San Remo.

On 1 July, in practice for the Swiss Grand Prix at Bremgarten, Varzi was killed. Fangio remembered Varzi going out to try to beat the time set by Wimille, but Bremgarten was dangerous, everybody knew that.

There was a descent, and a downward sloping zigzag. Because of the rain, the road surface was very slippery. They had put planking against the wire fence, but where the planks were was only an earth bank. Varzi's car went into a spin, passed the planking and went into the earth. The car turned over rather slowly [...] and killed him.'[22]

Two weeks later, Fangio was at Reims driving in the French Grand Prix and a support race for small-capacity cars. In that he had a Simca-Gordini and qualified on the front row with Sommer's Ferrari but had to retire when he was sixth, the engine overheating.

The Grand Prix was over 64 laps. Nuvolari had come for the practice and covered a few laps in Villoresi's Maserati, a car they would share. Ascari qualified second, Fangio in a Maserati on the fifth row. Wimille, pole, led while Villoresi took his Maserati to lap 17 when, with only fourth gear left, he handed it over to Nuvolari. The old master sketched a final vignette matching the times Villoresi had set despite the gearbox and going through the corners faster than anybody except Wimille. On lap 28 he came in to hand it back. He clambered out and walked away from his Grand Prix career forever. Fangio went to lap 41 when the engine failed.

He felt he'd betrayed the confidence of the Argentine Auto Club and 'the next day's newspapers ignored me.'

His brief European trip was over.

Two races remained, the Italian at Turin – Wimille won there as he had won at Reims – and the British at Silverstone, used for racing since the year before although Grand Prix cars hadn't been there. 'Race day dawned sunny, and the spectacle-starved British public flocked [...] in their tens of thousands. Miles of traffic jams choked every approach as an enormous six-figure crowd assembled.'[23]

Chiron took pole but Villoresi won it in a new Maserati from Ascari in another. They'd started on the last row of the grid. The Maseratis indulged in some sliding at big speeds and once Villoresi went into the straw bales which were placed at strategic points round the circuit.

The Alfa Romeos had been so successful that the announcement they wouldn't contest the seven Grands Prix in 1949 came as a genuine shock.

The year began badly. Wimille, practising for a race in Buenos Aires, was killed and Fangio remembered: 'I can still see him, in clear blue overalls, getting into his Simca – also French racing blue – in the oblique rays of the sun filtering through the trees bordering the route.' He'd remember a great noise in the distance, Wimille's wife Christine holding a stopwatch and watching the last bend. Wimille never came through it.

'As Wimille drove along the tree-bordered circuit, a group of onlookers had edged too near the road. Seeing the danger, a mounted policeman spurred his horse towards them, forcing them back, but the horse's hooves raised a bit of dust. Lifted by the early morning breeze, the dust was wafted towards the exact spot which the little blue car was approaching. No-one ever knew exactly what happened. More than likely, blinded for a second by the barred sunlight shining through trees, Jean-Pierre roughly slammed on his brakes. Certain witnesses told me that his car overturned spectacularly before crashing into a tree.'[24]

It was a young tree but strong enough to fracture his skull and crush his chest against the steering wheel. Later, some of his Argentinian admirers took a knife and carved into it, in memoriam, three letters:

J

P

W

Villoresi once said: 'There are gentlemen in life who are not so in a race, but Wimille was a gentleman in a racing car also.'

Fangio returned to Europe and began to make a reputation in minor races although he said he wouldn't be happy until he'd won a major Grand Prix. He had already shown in South America that his abilities were so rare and refined they remain difficult to quantify. He was poised, as it seemed, permanently on the threshold of middle age. Perhaps that allowed him to make brutal racing cars perform with delicacy and precision: when he charged he did so from a perspective of age and experience.

Without the Alfa Romeos the Grand Prix season opened out: Emmanuel de Graffenried won Silverstone in a Maserati, Louis Rosier won Spa in a Lago-Talbot, Ascari won Bremgarten in a Ferrari, Chiron won Reims in a Lago-Talbot. Fangio drove a Maserati there but retired and then returned to Argentina. He'd won six races in Europe and although they were not of Grand Prix standing he received an astonishing welcome home from thousands and thousands of people. He was ushered onto a flag-draped balcony and they cheered him as if he'd won the World Championship.

Ascari won Monza in the Ferrari, Peter Whitehead won Brno in a Ferrari.[25] Whitehead took 2h 48m 41.0s to complete the 20 laps, more than half a minute in front of Étancelin. A driver called Dobry in a BMW finished eleventh and last. How long he took to do this is unclear because we have times for only the first three, with the next five a lap down and the driver after that two laps down. The final two – Dobry and someone called Jaroslav Vlcek, who came in tenth – have neither times nor laps.

This, in all its anonymity, ended the whole first era of Grand Prix racing which had begun at Le Mans in 1906.

The first World Championships for motorcycles were held in 1949, embracing 125cc, 250cc, 350cc, 500cc and sidecar categories. It was something of a revolutionary idea. There was no World Championships in any major sport except football (from 1930) and wouldn't be for many years: the cricket World Cup in 1973, athletics in 1983, Rugby Union in 1987. Some sports – golf, tennis, horse racing – had structures which did not lend themselves to competitors contesting a specific number of rounds to produce a champion. Motor car racing seemed like that, too, but in 1949, the *FIA* received a proposal from Count Antonio Brivio – the Automobile Club of Italy's representative and former Grand Prix driver – that a number of defined Grands Prix should become the World Championship.

The *FIA*, meeting in Paris, agreed and six Grands Prix were chosen for 1950: Britain, Monaco, Switzerland, Belgium, France and Italy. Argentina, Holland and Spain also wanted races but the *FIA* decided six would be enough with which to start. The American delegate, however, said that if you wanted a credible World Championship an American race, meaning the Indianapolis 500, would have to be included. This, too, was accepted because in theory, any American team or driver could be entered for the Grands Prix and any Grand Prix team or driver for the 500.

Points were awarded: 8 for a win, 6 for second, 4 for third, 3 for fourth, 2 for fifth and 1 for the fastest lap. Of the seven rounds a driver could count only his four best finishes, a device to minimise the risk of a dominant driver and car paralysing the championship. This best-finishes was a device which became a legacy and, in different combinations, it applied to every season until 1990.

Alfa Romeo came back and Fangio received a telegram from them...

The modern era began on a Wednesday at Silverstone when the transporters came in. Nobody knew that, of course, or even whether a World Championship would be a success.

We all breathed more freely when the big Alfa Romeo vans, 'Alfa Romeo, Gomme, Pirelli' on their flanks arrived with the four '158' Alfa Romeos, for the first time on English soil, accompanied by their attendant Alfa Romeo lorry full of tyres and equipment.

Even more imposing were the spotless and vast [...] Citroën vans, one towing a covered two-wheeled trailer, each containing two Talbots. They wore 'Dunlop' and the French flash and one had an identification lamp. Platé's Bianchi lorry, laden with many jerry-cans and Shell tins, brought the Maseratis; Étancelin drove up in a '203' Peugeot saloon. The Italian drivers used an Alfa Romeo saloon with 'Winner, 1000 Miglia, 1950' on its back-panel, and the big Fargo van of Écurie Belge, 'Specialité Voitures Course et Sport,' trundled into the pit-area.[26]

Meanwhile, 125 loudspeakers and seven miles of wiring were being tested. With the Royal Family coming and making a tour, the police rehearsed. *Motor Sport* reported that 'as well turned out as any of the Continental transports was Geoff Crossley's Chevrolet van, bearing the slogan "Alta-Sport, Brightwell Baldwin, England."' Crossley, 29, was a racing enthusiast who competed occasionally.

The British Grand Prix at Silverstone actually bore the title Grand Prix of Europe, an honorary thing and rarely used then. The Thursday was for practice and soon enough the big cars were wailing round with the Alfa Romeos clearly fast. They had four entries – Farina, Fagioli, Fangio, and Reg Parnell, the Derby man who'd competed before the war. Chiron drove a Maserati.

Farina, Fagioli and Fangio: they read like a line of poetry but the men themselves looked middle aged, hair receding.

Farina went fastest of all with a lap of 1m 50.8s and because nobody could improve on that next day the World Championship had its first pole position. The three other Alfa Romeos filled the front row of the grid (arranged 4–3–4–3–4–3).

The 21 drivers who assembled on it represent a lost era: Leslie Johnson (ERA, fourth row); David Murray (Maserati, fifth row, an accountant who would form the *Écurie Ecosse* racing team); Crossley the enthusiast; David Hampshire (Maserati, fifth row, a company director); Cuth Harrison (ERA, fifth row, an enthusiastic amateur); Joe Fry (Maserati, sixth row, a hill-climb specialist); Joe Kelly (Alta, sixth row, a Dublin motor dealer).

The Royal Family met the drivers, which Fangio considered his highlight of the day. 'I remember the King wore a dark-grey suit, and the Queen had a pleasant smile. The Princess Elizabeth showed lively curiosity about the motor racing world.' Lord Howe, who'd raced the Silver Arrows in a little ERA at Donington before the war, sat with them explaining what was going on and the Grenadier Guards band played.

As the flag fell Farina accelerated away and completed the opening lap in the lead becoming in the nature of it the first lap-leader of this modern era. As he crossed the line to do it, he was however, united with

Vincenzo Lancia, who had led the first lap of all at Le Mans that morning in 1906.

On lap two Farina did 1m 50.60s (94mph). That remained the fastest lap of the race, and consequently the first of those. He was united with Paul Baras, who'd done the very first of them at Le Mans.

The Alfa Romeos were simply too good to be challenged and, instead, staged a 'mock battle'[27] with the lead changing hands as the drivers decreed. Farina won it from Fagioli, and at that moment was united with Ferenc Szisz.

Motor Sport was unimpressed. 'The RAC *Grand Prix de L'Europe*, then, was no better than preceding races in the series, a sentiment with which we feel sure those who arrived late because of traffic congestion, those who spent four hours or so getting out of the car parks, those who received the wrong passes and those honorary club marshals who had to sleep the Friday night in old tents because RAC patrols had taken the beds in the huts, will readily concur.'

A week later they were in Monaco.

Froilan González, an Argentine known as 'the Bull of the Pampas,' had been in Europe the season before without much success. Now he made his Grand Prix debut in a Maserati. He was stout yet nimble enough to have played football in his youth. In a racing car he ignored finesse and punched it around the circuits, and that stood in odd contrast to his kindly nature. He was ten years younger than Fangio.

Enzo Ferrari noticed.

Ferrari had three cars at Monaco, for Sommer, Ascari and Villoresi. Their challenge to Alfa Romeo generated a context of its own: Alfa Romeo, a past Italian dynasty, pitted against a future Italian dynasty, Ferrari, who had been so intimate with them for so long.

The race at Monaco had always created a precise, almost mythological, image of itself. Here's an example. 'In the miniature fairy-tale realm of Prince Rainier, busy little men attach colourful posters to the stone balustrades of the quay, then they put them up between the palms and nail them on the wooden walls of the temporary grandstands which are being erected everywhere. An army of Monegasque workmen cover the corners and bends of the streets [...] with thick straw bales, and kindly police calmly direct surprised visitors to the nearest diversion roads. Soon the racing machines thunder through the elegant streets, the noise of their engines and the screaming of the tyres resounding even in the luxurious foyer of the Hotel de Paris. The old ladies who spend the evening of their lives there withdraw, shocked, to their apartments.'[28]

Fangio took pole from Farina but a high wind brought the sea cascading over the harbour wall. On the opening lap Farina spun on it at Tabac Corner and hammered the wall. His Alfa Romeo straddled the course and González ran full into it. The rest was like 'Chinese firecrackers.'[29] Fagioli brought his Alfa Romeo to a halt but across the course. Chiron found a way through but another car stopped and was rammed into Fagioli by a third. The firecrackers went off all over the place: ten cars out.

González pressed on but he didn't know the fuel tank had been damaged, and his Maserati caught fire. Fangio pieced together what had happened afterwards. González sprang out of the car while it was still moving, shirt on fire, and rolled over and over to douse the flames. Some spectators managed to get his shirt off and although he'd suffered burns he was alive.

As Fangio came from the tunnel towards the multi-crash he saw waved yellow flags. He slowed but a marshal ('he had evidently lost his head') waved to go right: no way through there. 'Reversing in a racing car is very difficult [and] would take too long.' Fangio climbed out and 'with my hands I began shoving on my rear tyres. The heat of the tyres penetrated my driving gloves but at last I managed to roll the car back a few yards, enough to manoeuvre and take the road again.'[30]

Officials poured on to the track to heave the wreckage out of the way. Seven or eight of them tugged at one car while the racers tip-toed round it. Fangio reached oil left by González. A spectator – presumably not realising – threw a lighted cigarette butt into the oil and Fangio braced himself 'for a wall of fire' but the oil didn't light.

Fangio won it.

The Monaco measure: Fangio, 100 laps, 3h 13m 18.7s, an average speed of 61.3mph: Farina, 1948, 59.7mph.

The ultimate measure: at Bonneville in September 1947, John Cobb had pushed the Land Speed Record to 394mph. It would remain there until 1960 and have only the most tenuous connection with Grand Prix racing after that – Donald Campbell, son of Malcolm, broke it in 1964. The days when any man could do both were gone, and so is its relevance to our story.

Farina won the Swiss (Fangio had mechanical problems), Fangio won Belgium and France, Farina won Italy, giving him 30 points against Fangio's 27.

So many aspects of Grand Prix racing are now so well documented but Giuseppe Farina remains a comparative stranger. What he thought is lost in silence, and so is why he did what he did, which was driving so hard he crashed repeatedly.

Born in Turin in 1908, his father was the oldest of brothers who'd founded a well-known coachbuilding business. 'A very handsome young man in his early twenties, Nino Farina was a brilliant cavalry officer during his military service (and many times was mistaken for the Prince of Piedmont, then Crown Prince and later King Umberto of Italy!). He already drove at nine years of age and proved to be a good cyclist, a good soccer player and a track athlete but his real love was to be motor racing even if he was also for many years a first class skier as well.'[31]

He was unpredictable and even Enzo Ferrari fretted about that. Ferrari likened him to a 'highstrung thoroughbred [...] capable of committing the most astonishing follies.' To compound all this, he'd a doctorate in political economy (whatever that is) from Turin University.

Fangio received another astonishing welcome when he returned to Argentina. President Juan Peron and his wife Eva embraced him at an official reception while thousands outside applauded. Someone had even written a song about him, and it was sung to triumphal music.

In the background Enzo Ferrari prepared his full assault. Ascari finished fifth in the 1950 table and would soon be in a position to challenge Fangio directly, while Villoresi and Taruffi ran well. Ascari, however, wouldn't be able to mount an immediate challenge because in a Formula 2 race at Genoa his car caught fire and, trying to get himself out of it, his foot caught in the steering wheel. 'While the flames licked him'[32] Ascari, helped by two others, struggled free but his right forearm was badly burnt.

The Swiss Grand Prix at Bremgarten was run in a rainstorm and Fangio, pole, reasoned that he had to make a clean, swift start and lead or he'd be lost in the others' spray.

It worked.

A young Englishman, Stirling Moss, qualified sixth in a HWM[33] and surveying the circuit regarded it as a terrific challenge.

The pain from Ascari's arm was so severe he let Taruffi through to try to attack the Alfa Romeos. Taruffi 'used goggles with a single curved glass in preference to the visors that most people wore. To keep the rain out I sealed the ventilation holes above the glass and enlarged the ones underneath and also put special anti-misting wax on the glass. This meant that I could close with other competitors and overtake without being blinded by spray.'[34]

This worked, too.

Moss 'initially ran eleventh amongst the 21 starters...suddenly my aeroscreen shattered into a cloud of flying splinters. My face was blistered with flying glass, and wind and rain nearly ripped off my visor and helmet. I had to hold my helmet down against the wind for the next thirty laps.'[35]

Fangio won.

Taruffi tracked Farina but even with the goggles found the spray difficult to penetrate, especially out in the wooded section. He caught and overtook him with one lap to go. Moss held seventh until 'only 300 yards from the finish I ran out of fuel.'

Farina won Belgium from Ascari.

Fangio led the French Grand Prix at Reims on a day so hot that breathing proved difficult and the tyres 'burned' through the corners sending choking, acrid smoke to the drivers. At one point, swerving to avoid another car, he spun completely round and his Alfa Romeo straddled the track. Rosier in a Talbot Lago braked frantically and stopped just short of him. It happened on a straight stretch of road with unprotected trees at regular intervals down both sides. Fangio executed a perfect three-point turn and continued on his way. He had magneto trouble, took over Fagioli's car and won.

González took pole at Silverstone but waiting for the race to start became more and more tense. He wandered 'in a daze,' as he'd say, and some fellow Argentinians there as spectators tried to calm him. He didn't hear them but he did hear his own voice talking to himself. A klaxon sounded – five minutes to go – and he fled to the toilet. Each further klaxon sound, at one-minute intervals, increased his tension. He got into his Ferrari and determined to keep it motionless to avoid a penalty for jumping the start. He felt his heart rate nearly out of control, he could barely breathe – and then he was off. The Alfa Romeos and Ferraris who filled the front row didn't make a good start and, passing the pits first time round, González noticed both team managers signalling – *forget the plans, go for the lead!*

González did that, took it and won from Fangio by 51 seconds. His wife and friends mobbed him and held him in such a strong embrace that years later he could still 'feel their warmth and the moisture of their tears mingling with mine.' He was presented to the Queen then taken towards the podium. 'From all sides I heard cries I did not understand. I saw hands trying to reach me and heard words in many languages but none in my own. It was strange music but very pleasing to the spirit.' On the rostrum, when the Argentine National Anthem began, the young country boy shed many more tears.[36]

'I have forgotten many races,' he'd say, 'but always fresh in my mind is 14 July 1951 and the British Grand Prix.'

Ken Tyrrell established a small timber business in Surrey and played as a robust centre-half for the local football club. The club got up a coach party to go to Silverstone and he went, although he had never seen a motor race and knew nothing about it. They threw some beer in the back and set off. At Silverstone they found themselves in the crowd at Stowe Corner and he watched, enchanted and entranced, as a support race for 500cc cars surged by, the cars in a nervous shoal. As that race settled, the leader, Moss, provoked hilarity in the crowd by taking his hands off the steering wheel and pointing to an aeroplane overhead.

Tyrrell noticed that one of the other drivers came from Guildford, not far away from the timber business. He'd go there and introduce himself to the driver because he, too, wanted to race. He was right about the enchantment and from 14 July 1951 it never left him.

The dynastic victory of González over the Alfa Romeos inspired Enzo Ferrari to some of his most 'mawkish prose' when he said he 'cried for joy [...] I thought today I had killed my mother.'[37]

The night before the German Grand Prix at the Nürburgring Ascari asked the famous Italian journalist Giovanni Canestrini to tell him about Nuvolari's 1935 victory and how you conquered such a circuit. Canestrini, who'd been there, explained the trick: *keep your tyres fresh for the final lap.* Ascari, leading, was unable to do that and with four laps left he passed the pits pointing to his rear tyres. It meant *coming in next time round for new tyres.* He did and kept the lead – the fresh tyres decisive.

Fangio came second and the championship tilted towards him with 28 points, Ascari 17, González 15, Farina 15. Italy and Spain remained. On the count-back four-finishes system (of the eight rounds) Fangio already dropped the point for fastest lap at Spa, Ascari and González had only three finishes, Farina four so he'd be dropping the point for fastest lap at Silverstone. Fangio began to feel, that hot September, 'some animosity due to national jealousy. I admit that, for weeks, I had been anxious to see the whole business come to an end.'[38]

At Monza six Ferraris took on four Alfa Romeos. Fangio's Alfa Romeo had pole but, the front row cars, four wide, jumped the start and Farina edged ahead. Fangio took him but Ascari's Ferrari went past on lap three. Fangio pitted on lap 14 with a flat left front tyre and that cost him 48 seconds. Eventually his engine failed and Ascari won it with only the González Ferrari on the same lap.

The wide avenues of Pedralbes, on the outskirts of Barcelona, became the decider. The circuit measured 3.9 miles and had a long start-finish straight, named after the dictator Franco.

Fangio's state of mind was uneasy as he came to the grid next to Ascari, on pole. In qualifying the Ferraris gave 'dazzling performances,'

Fangio said, and Ascari remained 'as dangerous as ever.' After qualifying Ascari sought Fangio out and said *a championship should not be a matter of life and death – the winner should buy his defeated rival dinner.*[39]

A cannon fired, *five minutes to go*. Farina was drinking water from a bottle over at the pits and sprinted towards his Alfa Romeo, clambered urgently in. Nineteen cars faced 70 laps and 274 miles. The drivers watched the red and yellow flag of Spain hoisted, watched it hover, descend. Franco's avenue – baroque lamp standards down the left-hand side, a lot of men in uniforms on the right – stretched so broad and so far that an instant after the cars set off they were already spread. Ascari thrust his Ferrari fractionally ahead of González, Farina and Fangio following.

Lap one: Ascari just leading from Farina and Fangio, González down to sixth.

Lap three: Fangio overtook Farina who'd have been told not to impede his team-mate, anyway. Ascari just ahead went 'like an arrow'. Fangio decided to stay with him but not challenge him, nursing the car. His main concern centred round losing time in the pits refuelling. By contrast, the Ferrari had extra tanks and could go further. That also meant the Ferraris were heavier, putting more pressure on their tyres.

Fangio overtook Ascari and held that to lap six. The crowd shouted and pointed to Taruffi's Ferrari as it limped towards the pits, nearside rear tyre in ribbons.

Lap seven: Villoresi limped to the pits, offside rear tyre in ribbons. When Fangio followed Ascari a little piece of rubber flew back and hit him in the face, and Fangio wondered about that.

Lap eight: Ascari signalled to the pits and next lap came in, tyres all but shredded. Ascari lost 32 seconds and never recovered. Fangio, imperious, continued to the end with González some 54 seconds behind him and Fangio had his first World Championship.

Somewhere amidst the presentations, the receptions and the speeches Juan-Manuel Fangio suddenly felt very tired. It was, he thought, a nervous reaction. He wouldn't race again in 1951.

Far in the background, the life of Manfred von Brauchitsch – last race Belgrade the day war broke out – was in typically self-imposed difficulties. He'd spent the war in a clerical position in Berlin because, after the beating his body had taken racing in the 1930s, he was in no state to do military service. When the war ended he tried to start motor bike racing in Germany (car racing was banned) and then, with the help of friends, set off for Argentina and a limitless future. After two months he hadn't found one, he'd upset a lot of people and returned embittered.

In 1951 he started to visit the Soviet Zone – Communist East Germany – and the West Germans watched him as a spy.

In 1952, Alfa Romeo withdrew from racing again. Fangio moved to Maserati and in one he crashed during a non-championship race at Monza, skidding across the track towards straw bales. He felt the car lift into shadows and trees, clung to the steering wheel but some sort of impact threw him forward and he thought *now I know what it's like to die in a racing car.* In that instant he found both life and death banal, 'almost derisive.' He saw a branch shaped into a fork come at him, hiss past him. He struck the ground and realised his shoes had come off.

He woke up in hospital with his neck injured so badly that he didn't compete in the championship. That weakened it, and it was already weak enough: Alfa Romeo gone, the Lago-Talbot organisation declined, the Simca-Gordini partnership disintegrated. It left Ferrari. Ascari had one and it proved enough. He plundered the season with a mid-summer ripple of races and wins, Belgium, France, Britain, Germany, Holland and Italy – from seven races. He missed the first, the Swiss – Taruffi won – because he was at Indianapolis.

That year the Monaco Grand Prix was restricted to sports cars.

Of Ascari, Ferrari would judge that he had a 'sure and precise style'[40] and, as a man, an 'impelling need to get into the lead at the very beginning.' If he did he was all but impossible to overtake. If he didn't he lacked 'the combative spirit'. This was for a strange reason. If he caught a driver in front and prepared to overtake he didn't have an inferiority complex, or anything like that, but he did go into a state of nerves. This hadn't been a factor in 1952: he led 35 of the 36 laps at Spa, all 76 in France, all 85 at Silverstone, all 18 in Germany, all 90 in Holland and 44 of the 80 at Monza.

A handsome young Englishman with straw-blond hair who sported a bow tie even when he drove and liked pretty ladies a great deal, qualified a Cooper-Bristol on the front row at Zandvoort. Mike Hawthorn had beaten Fangio in a race at the Goodwood circuit on the English south coast in 1952, a sensation, and knowing eyes were watching his progress, including Enzo Ferrari. Although he finished two laps down at Zandvoort he did finish. Enzo Ferrari noticed that.

Now in 1953 another dynasty, Maserati, began a struggle for supremacy with Ferrari. The championship lay between them – over the whole of it only one other car, a Gordini, scored any points at all – and they had the best drivers, too. Ascari led his title defence for Ferrari, backed by Farina, Villoresi…and Hawthorn. Maserati put Fangio against them with González as principal support.

Ascari struck early, winning Argentina where Fangio in an old Maserati came back after his injury at Monza but did not rediscover the joy of racing – his phrase. It was, perhaps, a necessary understatement. A vast crowd had come to watch, so many that the whole circuit was overwhelmed.

Hawthorn remembered the gathering atmosphere. Race day dawned hot and dry, and ordinary people who'd been 'harangued for days about the motor race from loudspeakers in the streets and squares of the city'[41] streamed towards the Autodrome on the outskirts of Buenos Aires hours before the four o'clock start. So many people went that the Autodrome was full and those inside resented the crowds trying to get in. The police struggled to control the situation but their task was made extra difficult because people used wire-cutters on the boundary fences letting even more in.

Peron was to attend and when he reached the Autodrome the police were jostling the people. Peron said, dangerously: *My children, my children! Let them in!* The Autodrome was called, after all, *El Autodromo 17 de Octobre* in honour of the day Peron took power in the name, he would certainly say, of the people.

Their numbers rose like a tide as the police obeyed Peron's order. To compound that, someone hooked a long section of the fencing to a lorry and hauled it down. That seems to have been like a damn releasing the tide completely: more and more poured through. Hawthorn claimed that they forced their way into the grandstand and forced the ticket-holders out by 'sticking lighted cigarettes into them.'[42]

The grid formed up but it resembled a gully between two walls of people. The organisers made reassuring noises – *everything's under control* – and the race started only four minutes late.

Ascari led. Farina ran down the field when, on lap 32, a spectator – some say a small boy – ran in front of his Ferrari. Farina swerved to miss him and slid helplessly into the wall of people. Many died as the Ferrari penetrated the crowd – the dead and dying were scattered all around. In the panic another child ran out and was killed.

The race continued.

Hawthorn claims that Farina was taken away in a 'state of collapse' and 'as I passed, every lap, the pile of mutilated bodies grew as helpers got to work'. Ambulances set off *the wrong way* round the course and one of them lost control, killing two more spectators. A mounted policeman used a stock whip to try and drive the crowd off the circuit but, enraged and wild, they hauled him down and kicked him to death.[43]

It is necessary to say in the context of our story that Ascari won and Fangio's universal joint failed – as if any of that mattered.

Holland was civilised and Ascari won. Spa was hot and dry and Ascari won. It gave him nine in succession which in the Grand Prix century remained an absolute record, Michael Schumacher nearest with six at the end of 2000 and the beginning of 2001, and seven in 2004.

The French Grand Prix went to Reims again and it brought this observation from Hawthorn: *going down an ordinary French road three abreast at 160 miles an hour it's a bit frightening when a hairpin corner's coming at you and you see the snout of another car ready to dice for it.*

The geometry of the hairpin, Thillois, assumed a critical importance. The straight stretched like an enormous backbone to the whole circuit, the hairpin forming a sharp V at the end of it. Through this V the finishing line lay some third of a mile ahead.

Ascari took pole, Fangio on the second row, Hawthorn on the third. A hot afternoon and cars overtook each other in profusion. At one stage Hawthorn went past Ascari who shrugged *can't go any faster!* but by lap 29 of the 60 Fangio led, Hawthorn shadowing him. That formed the classic, eternal confrontation which only motor racing gives: two men in the most powerful racing cars measuring their courage, skill and willpower against each other. Hawthorn and Fangio were united with Szisz and Nazzaro at Dieppe so long ago, Nuvolari and Varzi at Monaco, Nuvolari and von Brauchitsch at the Nürburgring.

Fangio led but Hawthorn got past him and, accelerating out of the hairpin, thought he'd lost him. Fangio seemed to have missed a gear. Hawthorn slowed for a back-marker and there was Fangio again, full in his wing mirrors. That was lap 32 and Hawthorn held the brittle, temporal lead to lap 34 when Fangio retook him. Fangio led to lap 36 and a pattern emerged amid the sound and the fury. Fangio could hold this lead from the pits all the way round to the backbone, all the way down the backbone to the hairpin, then Hawthorn – crouched in the cockpit to minimise wind resistance – would outbrake him.

At one point they grinned at each other, the cars so close Hawthorn could clearly see the rev counter on Fangio's dashboard. At another point Fangio braked earlier than Hawthorn anticipated at the hairpin and they bumped, kept on, flat out.

Hawthorn led laps 42–44, Fangio 45–47, Hawthorn 48, Fangio 49–53 – although it changed so fast Hawthorn thought *I can win this* – Hawthorn 54, Fangio 55–56…

The crowd responded.

Five laps to go and they came round with Fangio ahead by a fraction. Four laps to go and Hawthorn attacked, Fangio defended. Great drivers think on two levels simultaneously, controlling the present while examining the future. Hawthorn now made that separation. *How can I cross the line first?* It was a difficult dilemma and the V formed the pivot. If Fangio slipstreamed Hawthorn through getting a tow from the air pocket Hawthorn punched, he would power past on the run to the line. Fangio would be making separations in his own mind but he drove like a prisoner – of fading brakes.

Hawthorn led laps 57 and 58.

He had worked out his tactic, the only tactic. He had to get to the hairpin with enough of a lead to emerge from it and reach the line before Fangio could strike at him.

The commentators were gabbling.

As they went through the hairpin for the 59th time Hawthorn thought *Fangio hasn't changed down into first gear, must be having trouble with the gearbox*. Hawthorn had misread the situation because he didn't know about Fangio's brakes.

They fled into the final lap abreast, fled through the sequence of elongated corners to the straight and the long, long lunge to the hairpin which was hemmed by straw bales and fencing, the crowd in shirt sleeves standing behind.

They watched as Hawthorn positioned the Ferrari over to the left to turn in, watched as Fangio took the inside, the Maserati slewing slightly. He'd had to brake early and, worse, Hawthorn had braked late. Fangio thought *he'll never make it, he'll go off.*

Hawthorn slipped the Ferrari into first, shaved the apex of the hairpin, straightened the car and blasted the accelerator. The tyres gripped. He fled, alone now, towards the man in a jacket and hat holding the chequered flag. He reached him one second before Fangio, and the crowd watching here – behind garden fencing two or three deep, no bales at all – saw, suddenly and almost magically, González come from nowhere thrusting his Maserati towards Fangio – who held him by 0.4 of a second.

Hawthorn was concerned he'd bumped Fangio but as they cruised round on the slowing down lap Fangio pulled alongside and gestured that it was OK, a racing matter, forgotten.

Ascari won Silverstone from Fangio, Farina won Germany from Fangio.

That was 2 August. Nine days later Nuvolari, who had been ill for a long time, died. His last event was a hill-climb three years before. He'd been taken to hospital in June, 'knew he could not recover and told his friends that the man they had come to see was dead.'[44] He was taken home and died of thrombosis in his own bed.

Ascari made the championship safe in Switzerland where a man from memory, Hermann Lang, drove a Maserati because González was ill.

Farina led, Hawthorn second, Ascari third and the Ferrari pit signalled to these three drivers, as it traditionally did in such situations, *hold station*. Ascari responded by surging past Hawthorn and Farina to lead and win it by 13 seconds. Afterwards Farina sought Ascari out and heaped a torrent of abuse on him. The Ferrari management summoned Ascari and demanded to know why he had ignored the signal. No doubt putting on his best choirboy face, Ascari said the sun was so low it was in his eyes and he hadn't seen it ...

Lang finished fifth.

The Italian Grand Prix attracted 30 entrants, Ascari pole from Fangio, and a slipstreaming battle developed. Into Parabolica on the final lap Ascari and Farina ran abreast but Ascari spun. Farina twisted his Ferrari away on to the grass but Onofré Marimón, an Argentinian in a Maserati, rammed Ascari's car hard. Four men in shirtsleeves carried Ascari away, linking arms under his legs and shoulders. He looked concussed but talked to them as they went. Fangio went through for the win.

That close season Fangio received 'a very interesting proposition. Mercedes were perfecting a racing car which, judging by information leaking out of Germany, was something out of the ordinary.' The Mercedes racing department, reformed in 1950, felt its way back cautiously under Neubauer. Their car, designated the W196, had been designed for new rules in 1954 – unsupercharged 2,500cc cars – but they'd picked a highly competitive season to make their return. Ferrari and Maserati waited for them. Lancia returned, too, but not until the final race.

Fangio won Argentina in a Maserati, then Spa.

The Mercedes were ready and chose the French Grand Prix at Reims to launch their assault. No doubt by a complete coincidence Mercedes had chosen the French Grand Prix – at Montlhéry – to launch their previous assault, in 1934.

Fangio tested the car there and found himself helplessly reaching for extravagant phrases: magnificently streamlined ... sensational machine ... drivers dream about this all their lives ... perfect. He confided to Hawthorn that the Mercedes was 'quite fantastic'.

Mercedes fielded three drivers, Fangio, Hans Herrmann and Karl Kling. Fangio took pole with 2m 29.4s from Kling (2m 30.3s). Within a hundred yards of the starting flag the Mercedes, running almost abreast, were fifty yards clear. This was instant power and a deeply powerful image. Although Ascari was able to get close (2m 30.5s) his Maserati failed after a lap of the race. González spun on a corner, swerved onto grass where spectators and cameramen stood. He was able to stop the Ferrari before he reached them. The two leading Mercedes circled in splendid, and ominous, isolation.

Hawthorn in the Ferrari went to lap ten when he felt something fail at the high-speed curve after the pits. He estimated his speed at 150mph. His engine had blown and the car flicked round on its own oil, went into the escape road. Somehow Hawthorn seems to have been able to spin the Ferrari so that it was travelling forward – but towards a pole across the road, put there to stop traffic coming in. Hawthorn knew he couldn't get under it because, coming to the circuit and presumably regarding it as a short cut,[45] he'd tried. He glimpsed spectators to one side and tried to twist the car into a field but the steering wouldn't respond. He was frightened. Just then the car spun and stopped just short of the pole.[46]

Fangio beat Kling by a tenth of a second (Herrmann's engine failed), everybody else a lap and more behind.

The Mercedes domination spread across the season – after González won Silverstone in the Ferrari – and at the German Grand Prix they even entered a fourth car for Lang.

Marimón, in a works Maserati, was 'a lively young man, exuberant, loving a joke, laughing all the time'[47] who'd driven seven Grands Prix in the previous two years. In a very real sense Fangio regarded him as a protégé. During practice Fangio followed some way behind and saw him handling the Maserati in a 'clean, decided style.' The Maserati suddenly snapped out of control, moving in a 'terrible series of skids, slamming against everything in the way, brutally bouncing off obstacles.' It burst through a hedge, went down a slope and into a tree. When Fangio and González reached Marimon they could see his chest had been crushed and a priest recited a prayer in Latin. He had died instantly.

No death, Fangio subsequently wrote, moved him so deeply as this 'bitter loss'. He'd attempt a rationalisation. This 'cruel trick of fate' had taken a young man full of life and with so much to live for. Perhaps, Fangio thought, his own feelings were those 'we all feel when we lose someone who is young and dear to us; and in race driving, death is always waiting just around the next bend in the track, whether you are young or old.'[48]

Fangio took pole, beating Lang's record set in 1939 (Fangio 9m 50.1s, Lang 9m 52.2s), and won the race. Three weeks later he added the Swiss and that was the championship. For good measure he added the Italian at Monza and precious film clips of that, taken on one corner, offer a picture in two distinct dimensions. Fangio's Mercedes is broad, low, the bodywork smooth as rippling water. Ascari's Lancia, tucked in behind him, is narrow, vertical, almost extinct.

Hawthorn won the final race, the Spanish at Pedralbes, from Musso in a Maserati and Fangio. For once, the Mercedes suffered problems with brakes and a piston, and Fangio magnanimously said Hawthorn drove brilliantly.

Mercedes signed Moss in November 1954. He happened to be in New York, was told by telephone and couldn't sleep that night for excitement. He was right to be excited, despite a curious debut in Argentina. Sixteen driver substitutions were made during the race because of the great heat – ground temperatures reached 125°F – and at one point a Ferrari spent a lap in the pits because none of the five drivers was physically able to get in it. Moss, 'staggered' by the heat, went as far as lap 30 (of the 96) when an engine part failed. He got out 'groggy' although not in as bad a condition as the ambulancemen thought. They put him into the ambulance and he stayed there until an interpreter could be found. He walked to the pits, Neubauer signalled Herrmann to come in for Moss to take over. Moss finished fourth (or rather Herrmann/Kling/Moss finished fourth.) Fangio won, one of only two drivers who didn't need a co-driver, and even he was exhausted and dehydrated as he sat in President Peron's box afterwards.

Monaco was also curious and for two reasons: no Grand Prix had been held there since 1950 (except 1952 for sports cars) and the Mercedes showed fallibility.

The sky was azure and so was the sea. The front row was multi-coloured, the silver of Fangio on pole, the blood red of Ascari's Lancia, the silver of Moss. Castellotti sat in his blood red Lancia on the second row ready to put it into a gap. As they accelerated from the grid they created their own heat haze and these four reached Gasworks together – Fangio fractionally ahead. Four cars: classical Monaco. Fangio took his Mercedes safely round Station hairpin, then just a promitory of pavement with a couple of trees set into it and a handful of people standing watching. Moss took the entry wide enough for Castellotti to put the Lancia inside. Again, classical Monaco. Completing the first lap Fangio led from Castellotti, Moss and Ascari.

On lap five Moss went through and soon Ascari took Castellotti, too. Fangio and Moss had pulled away and were lapping the slower cars like scythes, swift and clinical in the hard sunlight of afternoon.

The fallibility? André Simon (an independent, replacing Herrmann who'd crashed in practice suffering severe internal injuries) went to lap 25 when the engine failed; Fangio's rear axle failed on lap 50, and Moss's engine failed on lap 81 and he came slowly to the pits, smoke wreathing the car. He parked the car near the line so that at the end he could push it over. His face was an extraordinary picture, darkened to black by the dirt except for the geometrical circle of the goggles, the skin there perfectly white. He look distracted, as if a Mercedes mechanical failure stretched credulity. He'd left oil on the track and Ascari approached the chicane on the harbour – and the oil.

The brakes on Ascari's Lancia may have been tired. The Lancia snapped away from him, struck kerbing, slithered on Moss's oil and charged the straw bales protecting drivers from the drop into the sea. The Lancia burst through, passing between two iron mooring bits and somersaulted an estimated fifty yards through the air before it hit the water. It submerged. Divers prepared to go to it but just then a 'blue helmet bobbed to the surface and Ascari's streaked face was seen beneath it. Alberto tore off the helmet but still holding it he struck out with a strong overarm until drivers had reached him and pulled him aboard their rescue boat.'[49]

Trintignant won in a Ferrari.

Moss did push his Mercedes across the line, to be classified ninth.

The Monaco measure: Trintignant, 100 laps, 2h 58m 9.8s, an average speed of 65.6mph; Fangio, 1950, 61.3mph.

That was 22 May. Ascari, taken to hospital bruised and shaken, stayed a day and although the doctors wanted him to stay longer he discharged himself. On May 26 he went to Monza to watch Eugenio Castellotti – 'dashing, handsome, very fast but wild and erratic'[50] – doing some testing. After lunch Ascari asked to have a go himself, perhaps because as a racing driver he knew it was the best way to recover from a crash. Somewhere near the Vialone curve the rasping sound of stressed engine and gearchanging was replaced by a metallic churning and then silence. Those who sprinted there found Ascari lying unconscious in a pool of blood and the car the wrong way up some distance away, savaged.

Nobody knew why it had happened.

Nobody knows now.

Hawthorn remembered him as 'barrel-chested with a plump, round face' and judged that he was faster than Fangio. Enzo Ferrari recalled how Ascari was one of the few drivers of his era who trained for the races and how although he was severe with his two children he always took them presents after a race. He explained the severity because he felt that one day he might not come back from a race and their suffering would be less.

Lancia announced the disbanding of their team and for the Belgian Grand Prix Castellotti entered one privately. He was fast enough to take pole but the gearbox failed in the race. Fangio won, beating Moss by eight seconds, Farina a distant 2m 40s behind.

Motor racing was a hard place and always had been, but whatever remained of its pre-war and post-war innocence perished a week later. Grand Prix drivers contested the Le Mans 24-hour sports car race quite normally and the drivers who had driven in Belgium – Hawthorn, Luigi Musso, Paul Frère, Trintignant, Fangio, Moss, Kling, Castellotti, Roberto Mières and Cesare Perdisa – went there. Only three did not.

The race developed into an intense struggle between Hawthorn's Jaguar and Fangio's Mercedes. Hawthorn was due to pit and approaching the pits pulled in front of an Austin-Healey which braked and spun. Fangio missed it but another Mercedes driver, Pierre Levegh – he'd competed at the Bois de Boulogne just after the war and nursed an obsession about winning Le Mans – did not. His car vaulted into the crowd. The engine and front axle, torn free, travelled like a monstrous scythe. More than 80 people died, Mercedes withdrew from the race and the future of motorsport came into open question.

The French, German, Swiss and Spanish Grands Prix were cancelled but the Dutch was run a week after Le Mans, the Zandvoort circuit considered safe after some modifications. Hawthorn, now returned to Ferrari having driven the British Vanwall, seems to have had no qualms about competing although Fangio spoke of an atmosphere of depression. In practice eleven drivers beat the lap record.

Fangio led from the line, Musso putting his Maserati in between him and Moss. Musso drove with spirit and managed to stay with the Mercedes for tracts of the race but Fangio won from Moss. He followed Fangio so closely that sand, a perennial hazard from the dunes circling the circuit, blew back into Moss's engine. As he has pointed out, in those days engines weren't removed and dismantled after every race. The sand had destroyed the engine.

Von Brauchitsch was due to stand trial in West Germany for spying. He'd been imprisoned for six months but released while a case was prepared against him. The trial was set for this June but von Brauchitsch fled to East Germany, 'leaving behind his distraught wife and a large unpaid tax demand.'[51] His wife committed suicide the following year.

In the wake of Le Mans the British Grand Prix had been questioned, but it too was run, at Aintree, the home of the Grand National horse race. A 31-year-old Australian, Jack Brabham, made his debut. He'd come to England early that year, made friends with manufacturer John Cooper and drove one of those cars.

Moss had pole from Fangio, Jean Behra in a Maserati completing the front row. As they waited for the flag to drop Neubauer, by now very portly indeed and slightly formal in jacket and hat – on this hot day, people all around him wore shirt sleeves – stabbed a finger towards his stopwatch, counting down to the start, then rotated his right arm in great, urgent circles: *Go!* The race was essentially settled after ten laps of the 90 and would be won by either Fangio or Moss: they'd already pulled clear.

George Eyston was there leaning on a straw bale resplendent on this summer's day in hat, collar and tie, jacket. He held a stopwatch and noted times on a piece of paper.

Fangio and Moss circled together as they would do so often this season that they were nicknamed The Train. Moss took the lead on lap 26 of the 90 and remembered making sure he put a back-marker between himself and Fangio approaching a corner so that he could pull away a little, which was all he could do; remembered Neubauer signalling *P1* – ['*Piano*', meaning *gently*, not 'position 1!']. Moss 'had to slow down. I still managed to slip in a quick 88th lap to break the record, but Fangio was now very close, and one lap later he was on my tail.'[52] Moss clung on and Fangio clung to him so that they crossed the line two-tenths of a second apart. Could Fangio have overtaken him on that rush to the line? Did he decide that a British driver ought to win the British Grand Prix and allowed that to happen? To this day, Stirling Moss does not know. All he and anybody else does know is that Fangio said the right man won on the day.

Only the Italian Grand Prix remained. Fangio won that and his third championship.

Mercedes withdrew from racing at the end of that season, leaving Maserati and Ferrari to dominate 1956. The very public career of Alfred Neubauer ended with a theatrical gesture when he drew a white sheet – a shroud – over the Mercedes racing cars and cried. He has repeatedly been described as the first great team manager although doubts about that linger. He was certainly a meticulous organiser, plotting and charting movements and material; he certainly worked the pit lane by making it a stage for his gestures. Here was Falstaff using the petrol churns and bit players as scenery and plot. He wore a black hat, buttoned up jacket straining to constrain the mountainous stomach and wielded a flag: he gave stage directions with it and the film clips of him from the 1930s to here in 1955 are unanimous in their imagery. He was acting out a great role – there are momentary images of him using the flag to drive a photographer off, others directing cars here and there, others of him simply gesticulating with it.

It may well be that engineer Rudolf Uhlenhaut, of an English mother and a German father, ran it all backstage. Neubauer sorted out the train timetables, Uhlenhaut created and sorted out the cars – he was a competent driver who could tell the engineers what the cars were and were not doing, but regarded as too valuable to risk putting him into races. You see him in an opposite guise to Neubauer in the clips: no gestures, no emotion just talking, listening and orchestrating.

Either way, it was gone.

The drivers' roundabout which, from this moment on, will become more and more of a familiar pre-season feature: Moss went to Maserati, Fangio to Ferrari where a young Englishman came to partner him. Like Hawthorn, Peter Collins was good looking and liked good-looking women. Hawthorn meanwhile could not agree terms with Ferrari and went back to Vanwall then BRM.

These three – Fangio, Moss, young Englishman Peter Collins – and Behra (Maserati), a tiger of a driver and heroic figure in France, shared the season: Fangio took Argentina, Moss took Monaco. In white helmet, white short-sleeved sweatshirt and hands working deftly, Moss wielded the Maserati with such precision that he led throughout. As he approached the line – on the harbour front – the Ferrari which Collins had handed to Fangio was 6.1 seconds away and not yet even in sight. Moss passed the man with the chequered flag and raised his right arm high, kept it there motionless as if he might have been saluting the crowd for their kind attention to his work.

The Monaco measure: Moss, 100 laps, 3h 0m 32.9s, an average speed of 64.9mph; Trintignant, 1955, 65.6mph.

Paul Frère was an aspiring motoring journalist as well as resolutely amateur driver and he'd decided not to compete in any Grands Prix this season, not even his home race at Spa. Musso broke an arm in a 1,000km event at the Nürburgring and Ferrari thought they'd run Hawthorn to replace him – but Maserati already had him. Ferrari approached Frère, who declined. The Ferrari team then 'bombarded' him for two days. He still said no and took care not to go near the circuit on the first practice day, Thursday. On the Friday he arrived as practice began and concentrated on writing a report about it.

The Ferrari still had no driver and it looked forlorn. Under pressure from friends and a desire to try the beautiful car Frère took it out towards the end of the session with the clear understanding that this did *not* mean he'd drive it in the Grand Prix. As he lapped, the Ferrari worked its magic.

Next day he did some serious laps but felt dismay that his best was only 4m 23.8s against the 4m 15.3s by Collins in the same car, never mind Fangio's pole of 4m 9.8s although that had been done in good weather on the Thursday.

Moss led initially in drizzle. From the flag he moved several car lengths ahead by the mouth of *Eau Rouge* and swept imperiously up the hill, Fangio fifth – he'd hesitated on the line – and further back Frère in a four-way struggle with two Vanwalls and a Maserati. A camera high up caught Moss into the S of *Eau Rouge* – left-right – as the race unfolded. He placed the Maserati far over to the pit lane wall so that he went through the S in almost a straight line, then soothing the car into the curve up the hill.

Castellotti's transmission failed and next lap – 11 – a rear wheel came off Moss's car. Frère saw Moss running away from the Maserati and now his pit signals were telling him he lay fourth. More than that each passing lap the signals told him that he was catching Behra. He saw Behra between *Stavelot* and *La Source*, tracked him and when they reached round to *Stavelot* again, Behra barely a hundred yards ahead, Frère saw Fangio's Ferrari parked, the transmission failed. Frère thought *this is for second place.* He came up to Behra and took him on the *Burnenville* curve. The track had dried and Frère concentrated on getting clear of Behra. Collins won it and Frère thought both he and Collins had driven the races of their lives.[53]

A month later Collins took France at Reims where Colin Chapman managed to get the third drive for Vanwall.[54] He was a competent driver but during practice his brakes locked and he rammed team-mate Hawthorn. Chapman's Grand Prix driving career began and ended all on the same day – in fact at that moment.

Fangio took Britain and Hawthorn driving the BRM went to lap 24 when an oil seal broke. He parked the car, clambered out and sat on its rear. Brooks had a throttle stick open and crashed heavily, the car bursting into flames. It was doused in foam and then, using a rope, half a dozen men tried to pull it off the circuit onto grass.

Fangio took Germany and when they reached the final race, the Italian, only Fangio or Collins could win the championship. A driver counted his best five finishes from the eight rounds and Fangio had 30 points from five, the lowest a couple of third places each worth four points. It meant he had to win or come second to increase his total. Moss had 19 from five finishes, lowest one point for fastest lap. He couldn't beat Fangio's total. Collins had 22 from four and could keep whatever he got: a win and fastest lap put him on 31. Behra also had 22 but from five finishes, lowest third, so he couldn't beat Fangio's total.

In simple terms it lay between Fangio and Collins and seemed decided when, on lap 19, Fangio pitted with the steering arm broken on his Ferrari. Moss led and Fangio watched, impotent, lap after lap. He was team leader and Luigi Musso, an Italian who Ferrari felt had the mark of greatness on him, got a pit signal to come in and hand Fangio his car. Musso ignored that and even when he pitted for tyres refused. Collins was signalled in for a tyre change and during it was asked if he would hand *his* car over – or, according to Fangio, 'saw me stuck there and, without being asked, got out of his car and offered it to me to finish in. My anxiety and misery gave way to joy, so much so that I threw my arms around him.'[55]

What Collins did has been described as one of the greatest, if not the greatest, acts of sportsmanship in motor racing history. Many accounts have described how Moss led and Fangio saw the championship slipping away – nonsense, of course, since Moss couldn't win it and, more significantly, Collins was lost now.

The moment Collins stepped out of his car Fangio became champion.

It would be unthinkable today and was a major news item then. What moved Collins to do this? In an age of deference he was showing that to Fangio, but he also understood, at 25, he was having the time of his life and the obligations of a World Championship would interfere with that. He'd add that Fangio deserved the championship, anyway.

Fangio called Collins 'the gentleman driver.'

It was one gentleman speaking about another.

The roundabout: Fangio left Ferrari for Maserati in 1957. 'The clash between the two men was more a matter of personal style. On the one hand, Fangio expected the same brand of intense, unemotional professionalism that had been the hallmark of the Mercedes-Benz effort. Ferrari, on the other hand, sought the kind of hysteria and mindless loyalty in his drivers that Fangio was simply unable to provide.'[56]

Fangio diplomatically said only that after considering all offers he was 'very pleased to be racing for Count Orsi and for his son Omar,[57] two great gentlemen whose correctness and courtesy could only be compared with the invariably proper attitude of the Mercedes and Alfa Romeo directors.' It might, or it might not, have been a discreet barb for Enzo Ferrari, who fielded Collins and Hawthorn.

Vanwall tempted Moss and it must have been in his thoughts that his best chance of beating Fangio was in an opposing team with different machinery. He'd be partnered by a quiet, pensive Englishman, Tony Brooks, who saw his motor racing career in its proper perspective and never equated it with the whole of life.

Moss, however, began the season in Argentina in a Maserati but Fangio won – Moss beset by mechanical problems. An 11-year-old living in São Paulo saw film clips of Fangio, saw his 'style of driving' and that became a great motivation for his own driving career. Emerson Fittipaldi had wanted to race from the age of six or seven. In his time, he'd race.

At Monaco in the Vanwall, Moss led from Fangio and Collins, but Collins rapidly overtook Fangio. On lap four Moss moved down the descent from the tunnel to the chicane and swears 'there was a system failure. The team said they could find no problem later, but I am adamant the front brakes had gone when I hit that pedal.' The car locked and 'my only course was to go straight on, smashing through a pole-and-sandbag barrier.'[58] Collins tried to avoid debris by swerving but crashed into the harbourside barrier. Fangio stole through. Brooks, braking, was hit by Hawthorn, whose Ferrari mounted that of Collins. Brooks was able to continue and finished second to Fangio.

The Monaco measure: Fangio, 105 laps, 3h 10m 12.8s, an average speed of 64.7mph: Moss, 1956, 100 laps, 64.9mph.

The Belgian and Dutch Grands Prix were cancelled because of financial disputes but Fangio won France before Moss struck back in Britain. He led but was halted again by a problem the team couldn't find. He stood and watched the race. On lap 26 Brooks, who'd been badly knocked about in a crash at Le Mans and wasn't fit enough to complete the Grand Prix, came in to hand Moss his car. Moss emerged ninth and, *willed* by the crowd, cut through the field. Retirements here and there helped clear the path and his charge gathered a great impetus to itself. Behra led but on lap 69 of the 90 the clutch on his Maserati failed. Hawthorn, second, punctured on debris. Moss came round leading, the whole of Aintree on their feet and cheering.

Fangio 25 points, Musso 13, Hawthorn 7, Moss 6.

The German Grand Prix was the fifth of the seven rounds and everything before it, even Aintree's emotional surrender, only a prelude. If Fangio won he had his fifth championship and as a step towards that he took pole from Hawthorn, Behra and Collins also on the front row. A hot day and, in an image which might have been plucked from the 1930s, the 24 cars lined up 4–3–4 on the broad grid radiating raw power as they waited for the signal. Hawthorn led from Collins, Fangio third but any race round The Ring might begin like this, cars and drivers settling. When he was ready Fangio pumped the Maserati past Collins and on the way down to Adenau pumped it past Hawthorn. He drew away but he knew he needed to do that because he'd be stopping for fuel and tyres, unlike the Ferraris. On lap three he led by five seconds and built on that to create a cushion when he did pit. That was lap 12, the cushion 31 seconds. He brought the Maserati in, a mechanic signalling him where to stop. Almost as the car drew to a halt he was preparing to get out

Hawthorn led Collins by a few yards and as they passed the pits they saw the crowd waving *you're in the lead*. Fangio must have stopped – but where? At 140mph neither Hawthorn nor Collins could see the Maserati in the bustling pitlane with mechanics, photographers and assorted other people gathered round it. As the two Ferraris disappeared Fangio stood impassive. The seconds melted. No one knows precisely how long the pit stop lasted because one source says 53.5 seconds, another 52.0, another 54.0 and a fourth 56.0. Fangio, doing mental arithmetic, worked out he'd lost the cushion *and* 48 seconds.

There's a haunting union between these seconds and this man standing within yards of where Nuvolari had stood 22 years before urging the mechanics to fill his Alfa Romeo while *his* seconds melted.

Marcello Giambertone, 'a wily agent' and 'general gadfly in the sport'[59] was in the Maserati pit preparing to lay a trap. 'Listen,' he said to Fangio, 'can you take it a bit easy for two laps and not go flat out until Guerino Bertocchi [the team manager] gives you a go-ahead signal?'

Giambertone remembered 'the old racing fox Juan caught on and was about to smile. I tightened my grip on his arm and whispered "don't smile. Look serious. Shake your head. You're being watched"' – the Ferrari pit was close by, and the Ferrari people surveyed every Maserati movement. 'Fangio played his part marvellously and behind his goggles his eyes sparkled with joy.'[60]

Fangio clambered back in to the cockpit, left leg in first, and as he began to sit down two burly mechanics were already pushing the car. Fangio moved back out, the Ferraris that 48 seconds ahead, and Collins hammered the lap record with 9m 28.9s. By contrast, Fangio's driving clearly indicated something wrong with his car. While he settled, the Ferraris' lead went out to 51 seconds. The crowd sensed Fangio's trouble and even one of the mechanics, who didn't know about the trap, shouted oaths and danced in frustration.

Ferrari held out a signal to Collins and Hawthorn: *Steady. Even pace. Fangio is losing seconds.*

On lap 14 the lead came down 48 seconds again. As Fangio passed the pits Bertocchi made a slight, discreet gesture and Fangio nodded. He'd bedded in the fresh tyres, re-found his rhythm and the petrol load was beginning to come down. Juan-Manuel Fangio sat poised to bend the Nürburgring to his will.

Hawthorn wondered whether Fangio had lost a gear or his engine was failing. He concluded that, regardless of what it was, one of the Ferraris would clearly win from the other. Hawthorn waved to Collins to draw up beside him and when Collins did Hawthorn jerked his thumb backwards indicating Fangio and downwards indicating *he's in trouble.*

Collins responded by a thumbs-up. *Message understood.* Then he raised one finger and pointed it towards Hawthorn, raised a second finger and pointed towards himself. *You win, I'll be second.*

A typically sporting gesture, Hawthorn thought. He wasn't aware that across lap 15 Fangio had cut seven seconds from the Ferraris and on lap 16, as Hawthorn acknowledged Collins's signal and eased ahead, the Ferrari pit were reduced to raw emotion. They held out a signal to both cars, *faster.*

'I knew the Nürburgring very well,' Fangio would say. 'It's one of those tracks where you lose touch with things. You think you're going fast and you're not going fast at all. I began to use higher gears for some of the faster curves – if you went in at the right angle you came out with the engine revving at a faster rate on the straight. It wasn't very comfortable feeling the lack of grip as the car went round but I began to take nearly all the bends in a higher gear than I would normally have used.'[61]

Hawthorn worked out that, with six laps left, Fangio still wouldn't be able to catch them.

Lap 17: Fangio 9m 28.5s. The tannoy bayed 'NEW RECORD!' The gap: 25.5s.

Brabham whose Cooper-Climax had broken down watched from the pits. 'Fangio,' he'd say almost breathlessly, 'threw that Maserati round the Nürburgring like no-one I've seen before or since.'[62]

Lap 18: Fangio 9m 25.3s. 'NEW RECORD!' The gap: 20s. He'd averaged 90mph on the lap and no man had ever inflicted that on the brooding, forbidding Nürburgring before, either.

Lap 19: A Ferrari mechanic held out a board with one word: *Flat.* Maximum speed regardless. As Hawthorn and Collins moved into the curve beyond the pit straight Fangio crossed the line: 9m 23.4s. 'NEW RECORD!' The gap: 13.5s.

The crowd, seized and transported, roared when they heard the time echoing from the loudspeakers, the announcer's voice shaking with excitement.

The Maserati pit signalled to Fangio *a Ferrari not far ahead*. He'd see 'a red blur disappearing round a bend among the trees.' He murmured to himself *I'll catch that one* and assumed it must be Collins. Hawthorn, Fangio reasoned, must be a long way up the road. On the descent to Adenau he glimpsed two red cars, one behind the other. Now he murmured to himself *I'll catch them both.*

The crowd heard the wail of engines growing ever louder, heard the wail rising along the immense straight from Schwalbenschwanz, the right-left-left-right which fed the straight, heard it rising and rising as the three cars moved towards the pits and the grandstand. There was Hawthorn, there was Collins perhaps three cars' length behind him, there was Fangio a hundred yards behind Collins. He came at them like a hound from hell, coming so fast that as the Ferraris passed the pits 'I was tailing them.'

Lap 20: The loudspeakers echoed. *'Achtung! Achtung!* NEW RECORD! NEW RECORD!' He'd done 9m 17.4s. The gap: 3.0s. The voice on the loudspeakers was lost as the crowd rose and roared again, flung a mass of hats in the air. It was probably the greatest lap ever driven.

Fangio would say that this August day he finally managed to master The Ring. 'It was as if I had screwed all the secrets out of it and got to know it once and for all. I was trying out new things during those last laps of the race, pushing myself further at many blind spots where I had never before had the courage to go to the limit. I was never a daredevil, never a spectacular driver. I would go just so fast and no faster. [...] Until that race I had demanded nothing more of myself or the cars.' Now he was making such demands on himself that he wouldn't be able to sleep for two days afterwards. He'd find himself shutting his eyes 'as if I were in the race again, making those leaps in the dark on those curves where I had never before had the courage to push things so far.'[63]

Two laps left and as they headed towards the first curve Fangio drew full up to Collins, then alongside, went in a fraction too fast and was wide coming out. Collins retook him and positioned the Ferrari for the next corner so that Fangio *had* to follow. At the Nordkehre, a bowl of a hard left-left-left just behind the pits, Fangio went through, two wheels on the grass and showering Collins with stones from the rim of the track. One shattered Collins' goggles.

Hawthorn watched in his mirrors, saw Collins drift into the corner, saw Fangio angle the Maserati to the outside and overtake. Hawthorn thought *yes, that's an old trick Fangio learnt in South American inter-city racing.*

Collins tried to stay with him.

Fangio remembered Hawthorn 'directly in front of me going down into a right-hand bend.' It was not the moment for the ultimate move. Fangio knew that. Fangio followed through corner after corner, *Hatzenbach* a mile out…

…Hawthorn at the Ferrari's absolute limit as they rushed through the endless tree-lined curves to the Hocheichen, a right-left two miles out, on to Quiddelbacher-Hohe, a straight two and a half miles out…then Flugplatz, a kinking right, *Schwedenkreuz*, a bending left three miles out…

Fangio did mental arithmetic again, calculating how many passing places remained on the lap. A short straight ended in a left-right…*Aremberg*, three and a half miles out. On the straight Fangio watched Hawthorn position the Ferrari over to the right, lining it up for the racing line through the beginning of *Aremberg*. Fangio saw a fleeting gap on the inside. It was the moment, one of Fangio's greatest and motor racing's greatest. He put the Maserati inside. 'Hawthorn must have seen a blur to his left because he suddenly pulled over as if startled.'

Hawthorn remembered how sharply – decisively – it was done, how forcefully it was done, Hawthorn's wheels on the grass and near the dirt beyond that. He remembered how Fangio, moving away, glanced back and might almost have been apologising. Hawthorn thought *my turn now* but as he prepared to attack they came upon a back-marker, the American Masten Gregory in a blue and white Maserati. Fangio went cleanly by but Hawthorn had to follow for precious instants.

From the commentary point at *Breidscheid* three miles from *Aremberg* the commentator bayed 'FANGIO LEADS! FANGIO LEADS!'

Hawthorn gained on the uphill sections but, approaching the immense start-finish straight – three miles of it – Fangio gunned the Maserati to *its* absolute maximum. 'I made a point of getting away from him before we reached the straight because there he might have been able to take advantage of my slipstream and pass me.'

The two cars crossed the line to begin the last lap but Fangio had siphoned out a little lead, enough so that Hawthorn couldn't get full up to him in the corners and position for overtaking coming out. All Hawthorn could do was drive a brave lap and watch for any semblance of a mistake. Fangio didn't make one. Hawthorn gained a bit here, lost a bit there but it was too late. Fangio crossed the line after 3h 30m 38.3s, Hawthorn 3.6s later.

That was when the crowd saw it, there beneath the heavy crash helmet of the man in the Maserati: the smile on the face of the master.

Notes

1. *Colin Chapman*, Crombac.
2. *End of a Berlin Diary*, William Shirer (Hamish Hamilton, London, 1947).
3. One of the few cities to escape the bombing and street fighting was the ancient town of Heidelberg, which became a favourite Formula 1 watering place during the German Grand Prix at Hockenheim just down the autobahn.
4. *My Two Lives*, Dreyfus.
5. *Speed was my Life*, Neubauer.
6. *Grand Prix Driver*, Lang.
7. There's a lovely anecdote about Harvey Postlethwaite's time at Modena as Ferrari designer. A barn was being renovated and some bullets from a fighter plane were discovered in the roof. Ferrari summoned Postlethwaite and said in faltering English: 'Yours, I believe, Mr Postlewhite!'
8. *When Nuvolari Raced*, Moretti.
9. *Enzo Ferrari*, Yates.
10. If you know Paris, the Bois de Boulogne is to the immediate west of the city, with the *Boulevard Peripherique* running along its edge. There's a lake with a road looping round. The circuit followed that and continued to the *Porte Dauphine* before doubling back to the *Porte de la Muette*.
11. Interview with the author.
12. On the website http://8w.forix.com/bdb.html
13. *The Racing Car*, Batsford.
14. *Works Driver*, Taruffi.
15. The name Alfetta came, evidently, from the Alfa Romeo Tipo B 158's nickname – and that was the car which took Farina to the World Championship in 1950.
16. *Alfa Romeo*, Owen.
17. Cisitalia (Consorzio Industriale Sportive Italia) had an extensive portfolio of interests, including banking, hotels and textiles. The man running it, Piero Dusio, drove as an amateur and decided to build racing cars for Grands Prix. www.carsfromitaly.com/others/cisitalia.html
18. Taruffi, op. cit.
19. *My Twenty Years of Racing*, Fangio.
20. Moretti, op. cit.
21. *The Man with two Shadows*, Desmond.
22. *My Racing Life*, Fangio.
23. *The British Grand Prix 1926–1976*, Nye.
24. *My Twenty Years of Racing*, Fangio.

25. Emmanuel de Graffenried, a Swiss who had raced before the war; Louis Rosier, a Frenchman who had started by racing bikes and owned a garage; Peter Whitehead, a wealthy Yorkshireman.

26. *Motor Sport.*

27. *The British Grand Prix,* Hamilton.

28. *Juan Manuel Fangio,* Molter.

29. *My Twenty Years of Racing,* Fangio.

30. Ibid.

31. *Great Racing Drivers,* Hodges.

32. Desmond, op. cit.

33. HWM – the Hersham and Walton Motors Garage near London, which started building cars using bought-in parts.

34. Taruffi, op. cit.

35. *My Cars, My career,* Moss.

36. *My Greatest Race,* Ball (editor).

37. Yates, op. cit.

38. *My Twenty Years of Racing,* Fangio.

39. The following winter, Fangio journeyed to Milan to buy Ascari (and Villoresi) dinner. In the restaurant Ascari presented Fangio with a silver plate commemorating his 1951 World Championship.

40. *The Enzo Ferrari Memoirs,* Ferrari.

41. *Challenge me the Race,* Hawthorn.

42. Ibid.

43. Ibid.

44. *Omnibus of Speed,* Beaumont.

45. However hard it is to believe today, racing drivers sometimes drove their racing cars to the circuit.

46. Hawthorn, op. cit.

47. *My Twenty Years of Racing,* Fangio.

48. Ibid.

49. Desmond, op. cit.

50. *The Grand Prix Who's Who,* Small.

51. *Racing the Silver Arrows,* Nixon.

52. Moss, op. cit.

53. *My Greatest Race,* Adrian Ball.

54. Vanwall – Vandervell Products Ltd. An industrialist, Tony Vandervell, tried to make a British Grand Prix car to beat the world, starting in 1954. By 1958 it was successful, but production ceased that year because of Vandervell's ill health.

55. *My Racing Life,* Fangio.

56. Yates, op. cit.

57. In 1936 the Maserati brothers sold their company to an industrialist, Omar Orsi, who took the business to Modena. The brothers remained for a decade and they went their own way. Eventually, Orsi began making Grand Touring cars as well as racers – much as Ferrari did. www.autoweek.com/article.cms?articleId=101037
58. Moss, op. cit.
59. Yates, op. cit.
60. *My Twenty Years of Racing*, Fangio.
61. *My Racing Life*, Fangio.
62. *When the Flag Drops*, Brabham.
63. *My Racing Life*, Fangio.

Chapter 7

IN CLARK'S TIME

A month after the Nürburgring, a shy 21-year-old farmer from the Scottish Borders took the Sunbeam Talbot which his father had given him to Charterhall, a two-mile circuit on a former airbase not far from where he lived. Jim Clark entered it for a sports car race, finished eighth and the era to follow Fangio began, however modestly. Eras in motor sport begin like that, and perhaps in everything else.

Two races remained in 1957, Pescara – a 15-mile triangular circuit on the Italian coast – and Monza. Moss won both.

Fangio drove a couple of Grands Prix in 1958 and went back to Argentina, his legend safe forever. With Fangio gone Moss ought finally to have won a championship. He and Brooks, who had now qualified as a medical student, drove Vanwalls, Hawthorn and Collins stayed at Ferrari. Maserati withdrew for financial reasons. The *CSI – Commission Sportive Internationale,* sporting subdivision of the *FIA* – permitted 'commercial petrol' and that led to the use of an aviation fuel, 'Avgas'. This created problems for some of the cars which had been designed for petrol.

For Moss it looked promising because he won Argentina (in a Cooper-Climax for this one race), Hawthorn third but only ten cars started because the trip was expensive. Moss felt the rear-engined Cooper was so small people took it 'as a bit of a joke' until qualifying. It wouldn't be a joke for long and Formula 1 would have to change to accommodate it.

The second race, Monaco, was a drawing together of different strands.

Two Englishmen, Roy Salvadori and Stuart Lewis-Evans, had been racing in New Zealand with Connaught cars[1] owned by Bernard Charles Ecclestone, a lively motor dealer from south London feeling his way into racing. He'd already done some racing himself on bikes but, Salvadori says, was a 'born dealer' who'd 'buy and sell almost anything.' Ecclestone did not yet know that these skills were to be much more important to motor racing than anything he could do holding the handlebars of a bike or the steering wheel of a racing car.

Salvadori remembered that Ecclestone bought the Connaughts to re-sell them, and New Zealand as good a place as any to do that. Ecclestone instructed Lewis-Evans, who 'was certainly no businessman,' to handle the sale but, Salvadori says, 'buyers seemed few and far between.' Lewis-Evans was 'delighted when he negotiated a deal with a foreigner who offered a stamp collection in exchange. I urged Stuart to do nothing until he had spoken to Bernie on the telephone and, of course, as soon as Bernie heard about it he scotched the deal. The cars were shipped back to England ...'[2]

Monaco teemed with entries, thirty of them including the same Bernard Charles Ecclestone in one of the Connaughts – and, for the first time, cars called Lotuses.

Colin Chapman entered Grand Prix racing with a design which looked like a Vanwall derivative. He had two drivers, Cliff Allison, an experienced north countryman, and Graham Hill, a former Lotus mechanic without money but with so much determination that that didn't matter.

Hill remembered driving down with his wife Bette in their Austin A35 and covering the distance between Calais and Monaco in 13 hours, a time he estimated as 'pretty good' in a small car like that.[3] Hawthorn remembered that Collins and Louise were living on their boat at Monaco. He wired and they met him at Nice airport. Louise allowed him to drive her little Vespa 400cc car and he delighted in 'throwing' it round the corners on the way back.

Two specific strands interwove in a curious similarity. Ecclestone failed to qualify the Connaught (and never tried again) and Louis Chiron failed to qualify a Maserati. He was 59 and had first competed in the Monaco Grand Prix in 1930. He'd prolonged his driving career after the war, taking part in various Grands Prix and now here was the end of it. Chiron had been born in 1899, Ecclestone would lead Grand Prix racing into the 2000s. Between them they spanned virtually the whole of *motoring*.

Another strand from qualifying: an Italian, Maria-Teresa de Filippis, had had a promising career in sports cars and finished fifth in the non-championship Formula 1 race at Syracuse in April. No woman had qualified for a Grand Prix in the World Championship and she tried, also in a Maserati. On the Friday she went 'quite well' but on the Saturday the car 'blew up and deposited oil on the circuit, causing several cars to do waltzing acts.'[4] She did not qualify.

Brooks took pole but Salvadori made a tremendous start then went wide at Gasworks and created chaos behind. Trintignant drove a Cooper for Rob Walker and took the lead on lap 46 when Hawthorn's fuel pump expired. Walking back Hawthorn espied a pretty girl leaning out of the window of one of the houses. He asked if she could give him a glass of water and she invited him in. As Moss says, there were pretty girls all over the place – he used to wave to one on the way to Mirabeau – and if you did stop it was natural for people to give you some sort or refreshment. Mind you, Moss adds, 'I bet Hawthorn chatted that girl up.'

Untypically, Rob Walker – a sanguine gentleman who, as he said, was supposed to be timekeeping – got so nervous with Trintignant leading and so far to go that he hid under the pit counter. Musso came fast and Walker's chief mechanic, Alf Francis, held out a yellow pit board:

+28
MUS

Trintignant saw that and accelerated, Musso accelerated, too, and in the end Trintignant won it by 20 seconds.

The Monaco measure: Trintignant, 100 laps, 2h 52m 27.9s, an average speed of 67.9mph; Fangio, 1957, 64.7mph.

The measure of the decades: 1929, 49.8mph; 1937, 63.2mph; 1948, 59.7mph.

Vehicles registered in Britain 8.0 million (1948, 3.7 million).

A Ford Popular (in 1959) cost £494 and a Briton earned on average £13.55 a week. Saving all his money, the Briton would have taken 26 weeks to buy one (1910, 2 years 42 weeks; 1919, 1 year 28 weeks; 1929, 41 weeks; 1938, 37 weeks; 1949, 45 weeks).

Trintignant drove a privately entered Cooper-Climax, of course. 'The Cooper designers had always been advocates of positioning the engine behind the driver, but in front of the rear axle.'[5] During this season, the Cooper was 'being watched by a number of designers but as yet no-one was taking it too seriously because Coventry-Climax[6] were only producing an engine of 2.2 litres with a little over 220bhp, not sufficient to challenge the Vanwalls or Ferraris on all occasions.'

On the same day as Monaco, Clark drove a Jaguar and a Porsche at Spa, his first foreign races. He'd say later that if he'd known what Spa was like he'd never have gone near the place. Jack Fairman, a veteran driver, took Clark round in a Volkswagen and 'kindly' pointed out among other things where, down the years, drivers had been killed. It made Clark feel miserable.[7]

He drove the Jaguar in the 'Grand Prix', for cars over 1,500cc, and the Porsche in the Grand Touring event. It started at 4pm and by then Clark had a 'good dose of the shakes.' They were about to get a great deal worse. Archie Scott-Brown, a fellow Scot, another veteran and something of a hero – his right arm was deformed – had won a host of national races in his career (although he only drove in one Grand Prix, the British, 1956.) Clark regarded him with something approaching awe and could scarcely believe he was on the same grid. In the race, Scott-Brown lost control of his Lister car[8] on a damp section of the track while, evidently, he diced with Masten Gregory. The car went into a field, caught fire and Scott-Brown died the following day.

Now Clark hated Spa, and always would.

A bitter season had begun.

Moss won Holland, Brooks won Belgium from Hawthorn, but three other aspects of that: Miss Filippis did qualify, with a time of 4m 31.0s (Hawthorn, pole, 3m 57.1s) and young Graham Hill, another newcomer to Spa, found approximately what Clark had found. Along one of the straights, which allowed the Lotus to go up to its maximum speed, he had the impression that the car was moving 'faster and faster,' the track becoming 'narrower and narrower.' It frightened him. He came in to the pits questioning whether he wanted to continue a career in this and briefly decided he didn't. When he reached the pits 'I decided I wasn't cut out to be a Grand Prix driver after all. I was pretty dejected about the whole thing.' He dug deep into his doggedness, went back out and soon found the speeds quite normal.[9]

Five laps into the race a tyre on Musso's Ferrari burst at 160mph at *Stavelot*. The car crashed and was wrecked, Musso unhurt. The bitter season had threatened to take Musso but released him – for three weeks.

Miss Filippis got the Maserati to the end, tenth and two laps behind the winner, Brooks.

In France – Reims – Hawthorn won from Moss, and Fangio drove a Grand Prix a final time. Hawthorn led from Collins and Musso, a lovely symmetry for the red cars before Collins took to an escape road. On lap ten Musso ran close behind Hawthorn on the long straight. Past the pits Hawthorn glanced in his mirrors to monitor if he'd pulled way from Musso but instead saw him slew across the track and spin, travelling backwards, saw a dust cloud.

The Ferrari somersaulted across a ditch in a cornfield, killing Musso instantly.

Next lap Hawthorn saw the medical helicopter – it carried a stretcher strapped to its outside – in the air. He saw see precisely where Musso left the track but the cornfield concealed the Ferrari.[10]

The last front-ranking Italian Grand Prix driver was gone.

Collins won the British Grand Prix from Hawthorn – Moss's engine blew. Four races remained and the championship lay between Hawthorn and Moss. Of the eleven rounds drivers could count their six best finishes. Hawthorn had 30 points from six (lowest 1 for Monaco fastest lap) and Moss 23 from only three.

Hawthorn took pole at the Nürburgring. A 21-year-old New Zealander, over in Europe on a racing scholarship, put his Formula 2 Cooper-Climax on the fourth row. The year before, to plump out the entry, Formula 2 cars had been allowed to enter although they competed for separate prizes. McLaren had 'set his heart' on getting into it.

> Bruce's entry had been placed as first reserve since the German organisers were probably not sure who he was, but John Cooper assured him that someone was bound to crash during practice so that his place at the head of the reserve list was as good as a guaranteed start. He borrowed passenger cars to try and form the horrors of 'The Ring' into some sort of order.[11]

From the flag Brooks forced his Vanwall into the lead but Moss went by, and soon enough Hawthorn and Collins went by, too. Moss retired (a magneto failure) and Brooks took on the Ferraris. That pushed the pace up and these three cars exchanged the lead. On lap 11 at the right-hander after Pflanzgarten Hawthorn watched Collins go round in the usual, ordinary way but, Hawthorn realised, slightly wide. That sliding motion took a rear wheel into a foot-high bank, hoisting the car so that both rear wheels rode the bank. Hawthorn thought they'd crash. Instead, he saw Collins' car turn over – like a whip – at ferocious speed and Collins flung from it.

Hawthorn intended to drive one more lap and pit for news because if he pitted immediately Collins' wife Louise would sense something dreadful must have happened. Hawthorn duly went past the pits and began the 12th lap but the clutch failed some three miles out into the country and about seven miles from where Collins crashed. By chance Hawthorn rolled to a halt beside a marshal's post – on a circuit of such length they were placed at intervals. Hawthorn asked the marshals to phone for news. Hawthorn was hellishly hot and a German gave him orange juice. He was virtually 'beside myself with anxiety' and accepted cigarettes from English spectators there. The news on the marshals' phone said Collins had bruising, nothing more.

After the race Hawthorn got a lift back to the pits but the long way round and he asked the driver to stop at the scene of the accident. He found the Ferrari upside down on the circuit's perimeter fence entangled in wire netting. Beside the car he found Collins's crash helmet, a shoe and a glove. The helmet had been pierced but Hawthorn saw no blood on it and that increased his sense of mistaken relief.[12]

Collins died in hospital.

Louise, Hawthorn and others, including racing manager Romolo Tavoni, went there. Tavoni remembered that 'the doctor pulled back the sheet and there was Peter, like he was asleep. Mike took one look, turned and went out into the corridor, where he leaned against the wall and slid down to the floor. He just sat there, saying nothing. I looked at Peter. There was a bruise on one arm and the skin at the back of his neck was red, but that was all.'[13]

Hawthorn reached for the only consolation: *he died doing what he wanted*. He reached further. *I will keep on doing it because that is what I want.*

McLaren won the Formula 2 race and finished fifth in the Grand Prix itself. This...

more than any other race that season, made Bruce's name and assured him of a Cooper drive the following season. [...] Although he might not have been aware of it at the time in the bustle to get back to England for a race at Brands Hatch the following day, he was on the threshold of a distinguished career as a Grand Prix driver and a racing car designer and builder.[14]

Hawthorn drove in the Portuguese Grand Prix, on the street circuit of Oporto, three weeks later. Moss won that and, for reasons of chivalry and integrity, gave Hawthorn the championship without knowing it. Hawthorn had the only Ferrari entered and it circled almost a lap down. As Moss crossed the line to win Hawthorn was embarking on his final lap. Moss moved into his slowing-down lap and coming round noticed Hawthorn had stalled and was trying to push-start the car in the direction of the track – uphill.

Moss shouted out: 'Push it downhill. You'll never start the bloody thing that way!' Hawthorn did and finished second, but was subsequently disqualified for taking the car against the direction of the race. Moss appeared on his behalf, pointing out that because Hawthorn pushed the car downhill it had been on the pavement, and therefore not part of the circuit. Hawthorn got off and kept the six points for second plus one for fastest lap. At season's end, these seven points were decisive.

At the Italian Grand Prix, Hawthorn and Moss duelled but Moss's gearbox failed. Brooks hunted Hawthorn and the Ferrari's clutch began to slip. Brooks took him in front of the grandstands with ten laps to go and now Hawthorn wondered if the car would last. Into the final lap Phil Hill in another Ferrari, came up to him and Hawthorn thought *I wonder if he realises it's me?* Hawthorn signalled for Hill, who had no interest in the championship – it was his first Grand Prix in a Ferrari – to slow and follow. Hill did, and explained afterwards that he hadn't realised it was Hawthorn until he saw the arm in its green overall come out. Then he knew. Hawthorn finished 24.4 seconds behind Brooks.

Hawthorn had 43 points but from eight finishes so he had to discard three points; anything lower than second place would be useless at the final race, at the unlikely venue of Morocco and the unlikely setting of Casablanca. Moss had 32 points but from only five finishes so he'd keep whatever he got. He *needed* to win, set fastest lap and for Vanwall team-mates Brooks or Lewis-Evans to hold Hawthorn in third place.

Hawthorn doesn't seem to have relished the prospect of Casablanca, perhaps because the year before there'd been a non-championship race and he'd endured a very uncomfortable flight down on Air France. He'd even remember the only food on board was cheese sandwiches. This time he flew down on a charter flight.

Race numbers were allocated race-by-race and at dinner on the Thursday he discovered he'd been given 2. This distressed him because Musso and Collins had both had it when they were killed. Tavoni told him he could have the 6 of his team-mate, Olivier Gendebien, who wasn't superstitious. The American Phil Hill, in a third Ferrari, carried 4.

Hawthorn took pole from Moss and Lewis-Evans, Brooks on the third row. Moss led from Phil Hill, who made a mistake and took to an escape road, letting Hawthorn and Jo Bonnier (BRM) through. Hill returned at speed, passed Bonnier and Hawthorn waved him through to attack Moss.

Order: Moss, Hill, Hawthorn, Bonnier.

Brooks was coming. On lap 12 he took Bonnier and on lap 19 took Hawthorn, breaking the championship open because Moss set fastest lap on lap 21. Hawthorn responded by attacking Brooks because he had to.

Order: Moss, Hill, Brooks, Hawthorn.

They swopped places several times and Hawthorn noticed some smoke from the Vanwall's engine. That proved initially deceptive because it was just a little oil. Brooks ran to lap 30, when the engine blew. Hill ran comfortably behind Moss some thirty seconds ahead of Hawthorn. A pit signal instructed him to slow and Hawthorn moved past him into the championship-winning place.

The bitter season was not over.

With 12 of the 53 laps to go, Lewis-Evans crashed when his Vanwall's engine blew and as the car ran off into the sand it caught fire. Lewis-

Evans managed to get out but his clothing was in flames and he had been so badly burned that he died six days later in England.

Moss won the Moroccan Grand Prix, Hawthorn 1m 24.7s behind. It was enough.

The bitter season was still not over. Three months later, on the Guildford by-pass, Hawthorn raced Rob Walker's Mercedes but his Jaguar went off the road and struck a tree. Walker found Hawthorn sitting in the back seat, dead.

Tony Vandervell suffered a heart-attack, perhaps induced by the death of Lewis-Evans, and withdrew from racing. The Vanwall team, which had carried the hopes of a nation, ceased to exist. Maserati had gone, too.

And the bitter season was over.

In November Clark was due to be best man at a wedding near London. Chapman was running a test session the day before at Brands Hatch in Kent, no real distance away, and Clark and his friend Ian Scott Watson went there: Scott Watson thought he might buy a Lotus. Peter Warr, who would one day run Lotus, attended and so did Keith Greene, who'd run teams at Le Mans, Graham Hill, Cliff Allison, Innes Ireland and Alan Stacey. They'd be doing some serious driving in, presumably, the Lotus Formula 1 car. The understanding was that others, like Clark, might have five-lap stints in the Formula 2 car.

Clark went last and he didn't feel comfortable in the cockpit. Approaching Paddock Hill Bend – the adverse-camber first corner – he couldn't even find the brakes and went off on to the grass. Instantaneously he thought *what if I destroy the car?* He settled and, lap after lap, went faster.

Chapman and Scott Watson stood together in what was virtually a hole in the ground near Paddock, positioned so drivers could see signals. Scott Watson clicked his stopwatch each time Clark went past, Chapman clicked, too, and soon Chapman realised Clark was going faster than Hill, faster than Allison (who'd driven the whole Grand Prix season in a Lotus), faster than Ireland (a very promising driver) and Stacey (who'd been driving for three years and made his debut at the 1958 British Grand Prix).

Chapman said to Scott Watson: 'God, but this bloke's quick.'

Scott Watson said: 'Yes, not bad for someone who's never been in a single-seater before and never been to Brands Hatch, either!'

Chapman said: 'Bring him in, for God's sake, he'll kill himself!'

Jim Clark would drive in 72 Grands Prix, winning 25 of them and two World Championships. He'd never drive for anyone but Chapman.

That didn't begin for two years.

The more immediate future belonged to the rear-engined Cooper in the hands of Jack Brabham. He'd say that 'to the bystander – and those very brave photographers who line the track – the back end breaking away in a Grand Prix car can be a very frightening sight. A lot of Grand Prix machinery just would not stand this sort of treatment. But a Cooper will.'[15]

The taciturn, almost monosyllabic Brabham, known as Black Jack because he was reputed to practice dark arts in the races, set about winning the 1959 championship partnered by McLaren.

Moss had Rob Walker's privateer Cooper and took pole at the first race, Monaco, but the rear axle failed in the race and Brabham won it from Brooks in the Ferrari.

The Monaco measure: Brabham, 100 laps, 2h 55m 51.3s, an average speed of 66.6mph: Trintignant, 1958, 67.9mph.

It was an open season, Bonnier (BRM) winning Holland on 31 May.

Far away on the Isle of Man, the motorcycling world prepared for its annual TT meeting, then the most important in the world. An entry had been received from a Japanese company, Honda, for the 125cc race. The little Japanese party consisted of a cook bringing their own rice and cooking equipment,[16] an American team-manager, Bill Hunt, and four Japanese riders. They were due, evidently, to sleep on mattresses north-south to observe their Shinto religion and folklore insists that Hunt, who rode as well, led whenever they went out on the circuit because, for reasons of honour, the Japanese riders would not overtake him. This was good, clean fun in terms of publicity and the presence of the Japanese, measuring themselves for the first time at a major event, was received with condescending good humour.

Soichiro Honda understood the value of racing and loved racing for itself, anyway. He knew, whatever anybody else thought, that the Isle of Man in June 1959 was a beginning.

Brooks won France on an extremely hot day while Moss lost the clutch on his BRM, stopped out in the country, took his helmet off and a spectator emptied a bottle of water over his head. He looked delighted – and refreshed.

Brabham won Britain, Brooks won Germany – although that was on the banked AVUS circuit in Berlin and in a sports car race there Jean Behra was killed – Moss won Portugal and Italy. The United States Grand Prix at Sebring remained and mental arithmetic was needed again. A driver could count his five best finishes of the nine rounds and Brabham had five: 31 points, lowest 4, Brooks 23 from three, Moss 25.5

but from five, lowest 1. For Moss here was the Casablanca conundrum again. He needed to win, set fastest lap and Brabham be no higher than third. Brooks remained an outside bet.

Caracciola died of a bone disease. He'd long resided in Lugano and drove after the war, even trying to qualify for the Indy 500 in 1946. He crashed. Neubauer insisted that of all the great drivers he had known, from Nuvolari to Fangio and Moss, Caracciola was the greatest. Another link to the 1930s was broken.

Sebring was flat, uneven, in the middle of nowhere in central Florida and the wrong place to launch Grand Prix racing in the United States, a problem which would recur. Brabham found it 'dull for spectators and drivers and had the appearance of being set up for a driving test in a rally.'[17]

Moss's team indulged in a little psychology on him. When he arrived they stuck a picture of Brabham on his rear view mirror, Brabham coming at him fast…

Moss took pole, Brabham next to him. Brabham intended to ask Masten Gregory, a wealthy man from Kansas and also in a Cooper-Climax, to go out and plunder fastest lap regardless of consequences so that, even if Gregory blew up afterwards, Moss could never dare risk going fast enough to take the fastest lap himself. Gregory; however, hurt himself before the Italian Grand Prix and wasn't driving at Sebring. Brabham did have McLaren there to help but didn't ask him to make the sacrifice.

Just before the race Harry Schell, who'd done the third best time in qualifying to be on the front row (three cars wide), was informed he'd been relegated to the second because the timekeepers didn't believe the time he'd done. Schell was an extrovert, a character and American. He was enraged, the timekeepers unrepentant.

Autosport reported that 'it looked exactly like a free-fight in a Glasgow dockside pub – only noisier. Then the majorettes started up, the band and the girls stamped their shapely legs. As if by magic the jostling and shouting ceased. Both Moss and Brabham were trying unsuccessfully to keep their faces straight.'

The start-finish straight was wide enough for a front row of nine cars so that the three on it – Moss, Brabham and Schell – looked lonely. On the far side, a roofless grandstand was half full; beyond that stretched the car park and some low buildings then, across the rim of the horizon, trees.

Brabham led but Moss came past him 'like a rocket.' Brabham thought like a champion: *let Moss go, his car will never stand that speed for a race.* Moss travelled hard towards the precious fastest lap and built a lead but just into lap six his gearbox failed. Had Moss overdone it? He'd say *no*.

Brabham came past where Moss spun and next time noted that Moss's car was still there. Brabham needed only a safe run home but after an incident early on Brooks launched a great attack. He could not sustain it and settled into fifth. Anyway, Brabham – leading – had McLaren as a shield behind him. Into the last lap Brabham nodded to John Cooper in the pits: *situation under full control, we're going to do it.* About a mile from the finishing line the engine began to make choking noises. He was running out of fuel, he coasted and McLaren drew alongside, he signalled McLaren to press on.

Brabham came to a halt about 500 yards from the line and wondered savagely *why must finishing straights be uphill?* He got out, took his helmet and goggles off and began to push. He'd remember Brooks going past and thinking *he's second in the championship, not Stirling.* As he pushed, his head down, all he could see was the track passing slowly beneath him. He was so exhausted he didn't know the crowd were in a frenzy or that motor bike policemen held them at bay. He worked his way slowly under the pedestrian bridge about a hundred yards from the line and the man with the chequered flag waved it to encourage him. Still Brabham worked his way forward and when he reached the line he collapsed by the side of the car. He'd remember drinking Coca-Cola handed to him by John Cooper and how it revived him. He'd remember shaking hands with people as he lay.

He was helped to an official caravan and lay down for a quarter of an hour. Then, quite suddenly, he thought *hey, I'm World Champion.*

He'd remember the rest as a 'bedlam' of Pressmen firing questions, newsreel men filming, photographers snapping, and when he got back to his hotel and sank into a warm bath the phone rang constantly. He didn't answer it although he did speak to his wife Betty, at home in Dorking, Surrey. She'd been there with some friends and a *News of the World* reporter, who'd been ringing one of the London press agencies for the latest news. These came in the form of 'snaps' at regular intervals, cabled from the reporter at the circuit to the newsroom in London. There was no other way to find out and the last 'snap' had been three laps before the end. He told Betty how it had finished.

For 1960 the point for fastest lap was dropped and the first six finishers in a Grand Prix were awarded points on the descending scale 8–6–4–3–2–1.

Chapman designed a rear-engined Lotus and Ferrari flirted with one but Cooper, retaining Brabham and McLaren, remained the team to beat despite an alarm at the first Grand Prix, Argentina. John Cooper remembered how quick Chapman was, how Chapman understood that you'd only be able to win races with engines at the rear. Cooper went to Buenos Aires with the previous year's cars but Chapman took an entirely new one, the Lotus 18, light and sophisticated.

Not that it was so simple. The boat bringing the Coopers from England was late and the Customs intervened when it did dock. The drivers waited impatiently at the circuit and Cooper decided to phone the Argentinian Automobile Club to see what was going on. A telephone, mounted on a wall, was so old it had a handle to wind it up. Cooper got through but he didn't speak Spanish and they didn't speak English. It culminated in Cooper, angry beyond endurance, tearing the whole thing from the wall and, as Brabham remembered, 'springs, bells and all kinds of bits and pieces' flying everywhere.

In the Lotus Innes Ireland qualified second (to Moss in a Cooper-Climax) and led. From the grid Brabham made a tremendous start and went down the inside but found a photographer standing in his path. The photographer did not move and Brabham, braking furiously, thought he brushed his trouser leg. Next lap, Ireland still leading, Brabham noticed the photographer lying on his stomach on the rim of the track holding the camera out onto the track itself. Ireland spun on oil – and later suffered mechanical problems – the photographer retreated.

McLaren won Argentina (Brabham's gearbox failed).

Ireland, Cooper said, nearly 'blew us away.' On the flight back Cooper, Brabham and McLaren said *we need a new car this season.* Brabham would describe it as Cooper's first 'really good' Grand Prix car.

Six weeks later, to the north in Brazil a wealthy São Paulo farmer and businessman had a son. He'd be christened using a combination of his father and mother's names: Ayrton Senna da Silva. There was no history of motorsport in the family.

Moss, in privateer Walker's Lotus, won Monaco from pole. Moss found the Lotus a 'more delicate instrument' than the Cooper, and it 'demanded precision.'[18] The car was a 'curious mixture of simplicity and sophistication which brought me quite a lot of success when it wasn't trying to kill me!' This was the first Grand Prix victory by a Lotus.

A strong-willed south Londoner made his debut, qualifying a Lotus on the fifth row but the transmission failed on lap 18. John Surtees understood all the undercurrents of speed and racing, because he'd been motorcycle World Champion at 500cc in 1956, 350cc and 500cc in 1958 and 1959, and would do it again this season of 1960, in between the Grand Prix car races.

He found Monaco something of an experience because he'd only run a few street races in the whole of his motor bike career. He'd capture the spirit of the times, about the absence of testing because Grand Prix teams lacked the sort of budgets you need for that. At the races, where Lotus fielded three cars there'd only be one spare engine between them.[19] Stacey only qualified 13th and retired with an engine mounting problem after 24 laps.

The Monaco measure: Moss, 100 laps, 2h 53m 45.5s, an average speed of 67.4mph: Brabham, 1959, 66.6mph.

Brabham won Holland, where Clark made his debut in a Lotus, but the gearbox failed when he was fifth.

At Spa, Stacey was evidently in the wrong frame of mind – afraid that if he didn't qualify fast Chapman would take the car off him and give it to Surtees. Perhaps Stacey was unused to moods like that because he seemed to be a very cheery, optimistic man. He needed to be. As Innes Ireland has pointed out, he had a metal leg but with a motorcycle twist-grip on the gear lever of his car he could do the equivalent of heeling-and-toeing, which he couldn't do in the orthodox way because the metal foot had no sensitivity. The drivers devised ruses to get him through medical checks before the races (if the leg had been discovered he'd have been out). For example, the reflex test where you put one leg over the other and the doctor taps the knee. His good leg done, one of the other drivers would knock over a chair or kick something. The doctor diverted, Stacey would cross his legs again making sure the real one stayed uppermost – and the doctor, having forgotten which knee he'd tapped, tapped the real one again. Ireland insists this never failed.

During Saturday morning practice Moss went into a long downhill sweeping corner when:

> I struck the hump in the middle of the curve and my car's left-rear wheel came off as the axle shaft broke.
>
>   All I knew at that instant was that the car had suddenly developed the most violent oversteer I had ever experienced. I hadn't a clue what had happened. I piled on full opposite lock and jammed on the brakes to scrub off speed – fast!
>
>   The car spun like a top, at which moment I saw the wheel bounding away on its own. I realised I was going to hit the steep left-side bank backwards, at around 90mph. I braced myself between wheel and seat-back – which fortunately spread the load as we did hit backwards – and then I can just remember my head being violently jerked back...

I next remember coming round, realising I was out of the car, crouching on my hands and knees, gasping for breath. The car was lying right-side up [...] and debris laid across the road. I felt terribly alone. I simply could not breathe. I remembered passing Bruce McLaren earlier on that lap and I couldn't think why he was taking so long to arrive. In fact, he stopped immediately, and ran to me. I begged him to give me artificial respiration, but he rightly refused in case I had broken ribs. Other drivers arrived, parked their cars, switched off and came to help. Then eventually marshals and an ambulance appeared.

The sun was blazing down so they held a blanket over me for shade. I had to fight for every breath. My nose was crushed. I knew my legs had suffered too. Somebody cut the elastic cuffs of my overalls and removed my watch. I could hear them speaking but my sight had gone – everything was blurred and dark. I was terrified I was going blind, and that a broken rib might puncture a lung – if it had not already. Then came some relief as I remembered that wheel bounding away. At least the accident had not been my fault...[20]

Meanwhile, news filtered in that Mike Taylor had gone off in another Lotus. The car hadn't taken a right-hander but gone straight on at big speed over a ditch uprooting a tree. Taylor sustained light injures but was taken to hospital and when Innes Ireland went to visit him there Taylor said the steering had broken. A check on their steering revealed that two of the three remaining Lotuses had cracks...

On lap 19 of the 36 young Londoner Chris Bristow lost control of his Cooper at *Burnenville,* the great carving right curve not far from where Moss crashed, went into catch fencing and was decapitated; a lap later Stacey, who'd been at Brands Hatch the day Clark first drove the Lotus Formula 2 car, was struck in the face by a bird. His Lotus hit a bank, throwing him to his death.

Spa remained a murderous place.

Ireland spun out, walked back to the pits and Chapman asked him to go and find out what had happened to Stacey. Ireland walked to the circuit medical room and watched an ambulance arrive, a priest shaking his head. Ireland had never seen a dead man before. He turned and ran and years later wouldn't remember where he ran to. He went back and saw, now, Stacey lying with a winner's laurel wreath lain over him. Ireland broke down.

Brabham won.

A new generation was coming which would no longer accept this. Its articulator was then a 21-year-old Scot, dyslexic, trying to qualify for the

British Olympic clay pigeon team and hadn't driven a racing car in his life.

Brabham won France, Britain and Portugal for his second championship and, in his taciturn way, said: '1960 was a good year for Coopers and for myself as a driver. It was much more satisfying than the previous year because we won more races and the car was much improved.'[21]

Phil Hill won Monza in a Ferrari. The race was run over the combined 10km road and banked circuit and the British teams boycotted it – regarding the banking as uneven and unsafe – which let Hill in for the win.

The Olympic Games were going on in Rome. Jackie Stewart, the 21-year-old Scotsman, narrowly failed to make the British team. He'd describe it as the biggest disappointment of his life. There was motor racing in the family – he'd often accompanied his brother Jimmy to hill-climbs.

Moss won the United States Grand Prix from Ireland.

A new formula was introduced in 1961 limiting engine capacity to 1,500cc, introducing minimum weights for the car and stipulating that commercial fuel be used. The British teams protested and were confident the new formula wouldn't be introduced but, cannily, Ferrari thought they might. The scoring was revised with a win becoming worth nine points, the descending order after that unchanged at 6–4–3–2–1.

'While the turbulence in his private life showed no signs of subsiding (nor did he want it to), Ferrari was at least able to look forward to the return of a modicum of stability on the Formula 1 front.' The technical team were 'making great strides with the new Tipo 156 Grand Prix car. It would finally be a rear-engined machine.'[22] The British had started late, Porsche had come in with a car which carried too much weight and too little power, but the new Ferraris 'were breathtaking. Their rakish bodywork featured a daring, twin-nostril front end and Ferrari's single refusal to part with tradition: Borrani wire wheels.'

The roundabout: Ferrari's campaign spearheaded by Phil Hill, Richie Ginther – another American – and Germany's popular Taffy von Trips; Graham Hill and Brooks with BRM; Brabham and McLaren with Cooper; Moss, Ireland and Clark with Lotus.

It opened on a warm, hazy day at Monaco. Clark, who hadn't driven the circuit before, learnt all about how much precision it demanded. In first practice he lost control at *Ste Devote* and clouted the barrier hard enough to throw the Lotus back full across the track. The car needed such extensive repairs it wasn't seen again until the race, and by then

Moss had pole in a year-old Lotus – Chapman wasn't about to let Rob Walker have the latest version. Before the crash Clark had done a time good enough for the front row, Ginther on it too and led from Clark and Moss as the cars jostled into Gasworks.

Clark pitted with a fuel pump problem and Moss chased Ginther, towing Bonnier with him. Moss was poised to drive what he considers the greatest race of his life. Through Casino Square, round the verdant, semi-tropical traffic island, he forced the Lotus up to the Ferrari. Moss understood pressure, understood the nuances of driver psychology and Moss knew his way round Monaco. On lap 14 he got past Ginther and moved away but a shark-pack of Ferraris were after him, Phil Hill, Ginther, von Trips. Their Ferrari had 20hp more. Hill surged into second place and Ginther followed into third, using the Ferrari's power to cut and carve into Moss's lead. At half distance it was less than ten seconds. Deep into the race, with the sharks close enough for Moss to see their jaws, he danced the little Lotus round Monaco at its limit, used all his race-craft to steal seconds lapping back markers – and still the Ferraris were there. One time into the Station hairpin he took an exquisite racing line, tightening as he went in, running tight round the lip of the pavement, easily on to the power – but *as* he began turning in, there they were looming into sight at Mirabeau. With 31 laps left Moss led by five seconds.

Ginther was signalled to move up past Phil Hill for a supreme attack on Moss. If Moss glanced back halfway up the hill to Casino he saw Ginther taking Hill, the attack already under way. In the last laps Moss ascended to a level nearing perfection, countering the attack by keeping his composure, keeping his lines clean and keeping control. At Station hairpin Trintignant, many laps down, ceded rites of passage and as Moss went inside him he raised a gloved hand in thanks, the calm gesture of a gentleman. Ginther hauled the gap down to three seconds, Moss forced it back to five with four laps left and perhaps that was the decisive moment.

In the end Moss won it from Ginther by 3.6 seconds. Just this once the unemotional man became emotional as the National Anthem played. Louis Chiron presented him with the trophy and he – Chiron – promptly strode off with it so he could present it to the next year's winner.

The Monaco measure: Moss, 100 laps, 2h 45m 50.1s, an average speed of 70.7mph: Moss, 1960, 67.4mph.

Across the season the strength of the Ferrari became an irresistible force. At Zandvoort, von Trips led Hill home. At Spa, where it was overcast but for once didn't rain, Phil Hill led four Ferraris home, Surtees in a Cooper, fifth. Reims was hot as the pavestones in hell and a crowd in summer dresses and shirt sleeves grouped all down the long, undulating straight as the red Ferraris seized the race. Moss had a brake problem and emerged from the car with sweat making his shirt cling to his back. He got back in after a long delay and by then the tarmac began to melt. That caught Phil Hill out in a corner and his Ferrari slewed, stopped. Moss could do nothing but ram him. Moss continued. Hill was stationary in the middle of the road and in short, taut gestures he waved his hands at each oncoming car. *Miss me! Miss me!* Then Hill got out and because the road sloped tried to push-start the car. He did that but it took two laps. Giancarlo Baghetti, a Milanese making his debut, kept cool for 2h 14m 17.50 seconds to win from Gurney's Porsche by 0.1 of a second. No man before, and no man since, has ever won his first Grand Prix.[23]

It did rain at Aintree for the British – von Trips won from Phil Hill – and it showered at the Nürburgring where Moss won from von Trips. Thereby hangs a tale. Dunlop had 'green spot' rain tyres – painted with this spot to identify them – which could chew up on a dry track and Moss decided to take the risk for the race but to conceal what they were up to from prying eyes the team painted the green spots black in the pits…

This was the opposite of Monaco and, in theory, the more powerful Ferrari ought to have been able to hunt him down because the Nürburgring was about power. Graham Hill went off on the second lap trying to overtake Hans Herrmann, who closed the door. Hill braked, skittered into Dan Gurney's Porsche – trying to sneak by on the other side of the road – and rode up a steep bank. He flew over a photographer's bag and, the car still travelling fast, plunged into long grass just missing one person while another tried to out-run the BRM and narrowly succeeded.

Moss waltzed the little Lotus round and towards the end, when the rain tyres had worn on the dry surface, it rained. The tyres appreciated that and he had the race by more than 20 seconds. As Rob Walker said, nobody could touch Stirling in the rain. Walker added he'd never forget that among the 300,000 German spectators were some members of the British Army in the grandstand and when the National Anthem played they held up a Union Jack. Patriotism was not something the British felt they had to hide then.

The championship could be decided at Monza. Of the eight rounds (the eighth, United States Grand Prix at Watkins Glen, still to come), a driver's five best finishes counted. Von Trips had 33 from five and needed at least third place to increase his total. Phil Hill had 29, again from five, and needed second to increase his total.

Hill 'got along fine with von Trips. He was happy-go-lucky, I didn't find him sort of serious enough. Maybe he was, but not in my way of being serious. Perhaps it was just a matter of degree although I did feel he was a little bit too light-hearted about everything. We were different, you know.'[24]

Von Trips took pole from the Mexican Ricardo Rodriguez, Phil Hill and Ginther on the second row. Monza was dry and very hot. Hill led the opening lap from Ginther, Clark fourth, von Trips fifth. Towards the end of the next lap von Trips got past Brabham and Clark, and now came hard into the Parabolica horseshoe. His Ferrari and the Lotus of Clark touched – it seems von Trips lost control. The Ferrari flipped, rotated three times in the air and, thrashing wildly, reared against some fencing, throwing von Trips out and killing 13 spectators. From there it rotated back on to the track.

Graham Hill, coming up hard, confronted a vast dust cloud and drove through blind, just missing the wrecked Ferrari.

Clark remembered nothing except helping pull the wrecked Ferrari off the track, seeing von Trip's body and feeling 'sick through and through.'

Phil Hill had the championship now. He came past the wrecked Ferrari but didn't know which one it was, and saw the Lotus, too. 'Any racing driver wants to get on, wants to pay attention to the things he is supposed to be paying attention to.' He won the race from Gurney and by then the Italian police actively sought Clark, who was nowhere to be seen. One report suggests he'd been spirited from Italy in Chapman's Piper Comanche, another implies he was in his hotel room until he could get on a commercial flight.

Phil Hill found himself in a strange situation, a championship gained, a team-mate lost. 'I had a feeling the world would recover from it but I felt a prisoner of the propriety of the whole thing.' He behaved with dignity.

A Scotsman with a rasping voice and firm views, Innes Ireland, won the final race at Watkins Glen for Lotus. It became a strange story. Ireland crashed at Monaco allowing a driver called Trevor Taylor, six years younger, to replace him in Holland. At the end of the season Chapman decided to keep Taylor and fired Ireland but did not give a reason, and Ireland went to his grave four decades later still wondering why.

One of these 1961 days a customer and family friend came into the Stewart family garage. He owned a Marcos sports car and offered to let wee Jackie do a couple of speed trials in it if he'd care to. Jackie's clay pigeon career was over and he cared to. His mother had already suffered agonies over brother Jimmy's racing so Jackie competed under the name A. N. Other. Throughout his career motor racing wasn't discussed at home and his mother didn't accept he was a driver even when his name rang round the world.

Phil Hill 'never received a word of thanks, much less formal acknowledgement of his achievement from Enzo Ferrari.'

Meanwhile at the factory a great 'blow up' raged between Ferrari and, ranged against him, Tavoni, chief designer Carlo Chiti, financial man Ermano Della Casa and Federico Giberti, a long-time employee who'd done various jobs. 'The blow up was, in typically Italian fashion, loud, profane and grandly operatic in scale. The dissidents met with Ferrari to pose a series of demands, with the threat of quitting employment as a lever. [...] Ferrari would not budge in the face of the billowing rhetoric [...] Finally the dissidents had no choice but to walk out.'[25]

In 1962, the Ferrari cars were not to be a force. Instead, Graham Hill (BRM), Clark and McLaren (still with Cooper) took the championship to the final race.

Before the season began Moss competed in a race at Goodwood. Nobody knows what happened, least of all Moss himself. His Lotus went off the circuit and smashed against banking, Moss badly battered, unconscious for one month and paralysed down his left side for six. His career as a serious, professional racing driver was over.

Reflecting on his career he'll say that 'it was more gentlemanly, because the consequences of doing silly things were so horrific. There was a lot of cut and thrust but it was still a sport, even though some people were paid to do it. People had sporting attitudes, much more than now. I mean, the last race at Monaco [2004] there is no doubt that what both the Schumachers did was appalling[26] but it's accepted. And they just stepped out of their cars. In the 1950s you might well not have stepped out.

'Then it was dangerous, and danger to me is an important ingredient of racing. If you make racing totally safe it's not the same as it was before it was safe although I don't think it could survive people getting hurt. We had three or four fatalities a year. Modern life would not allow that.

'Before everybody spoke English, we did have a language barrier: You might be able to exchange a few words with a driver like Farina. It was by the way you drove that you got the respect of other people. That might have been the respect of being fast, or the respect of being pretty dirty – as Farina was – or the respect of being slow. I remember a driver called Volonterio.[27] If you went really quickly you could go round the Nürburgring twice before he'd done one lap.

'These things were accepted. It was a relatively small band of people actually, whole teams were quite small. It started to change late '60s, I'd say, it certainly had changed by the time slick tyres came in.[28]

'The safety side started to try and come in when I was racing, too. I remember the GPDA's [Grand Prix Drivers' Association] first meeting. We said: "The safety of the drivers is up to the drivers. The one thing we have got to be careful of is marshals and spectators. Therefore we must be sure they are adequately protected. Drivers don't really matter." In other words, it's up to you. That was changed, mainly I think by Graham Hill and the Swiss Jo Bonnier – they were the first to really challenge that. I thought it was up to me to look after myself and that's what the others thought, too.

'Crash helmets didn't become mandatory until the early 1950s. When I started you didn't have to have one. The only reason I wore one was because my father said: "You must do it." I remember saying to him: "Dad, that's a bit cissy. None of the fast drivers – Sommer, Nuvolari – wear them."'

Stirling Moss was no cissy. None of them were.

Unusually, the 1962 championship started amid the dunes of Zandvoort, where Surtees (Lola-Climax) took pole but Graham Hill hustled the BRM home for his first victory. The car went 'beautifully' and the pace of progress was demonstrated in practice: the new formula cars, with 90 horsepower less than the cars of 1960, were already as fast. Hill remembered that there was a 'tremendous party' at the hotel where the drivers stayed. 'There is a lot of fun in the lounge and the bar and there's always a pretty good cabaret. I remember the hotel owners getting a bit upset when two or three drivers had a race to climb the columns in the lounge, which were about two storeys high.'[29]

It was the way it was, serious and sometimes deadly on the track, informal and slightly beery off it.

Graham Hill looked forward to Monaco because he'd never had a car before which might actually win it. Clark took pole but the start was messy and when it settled McLaren led from Hill, who got past but eventually had an oil pressure problem. McLaren won it from Phil Hill.

The Monaco measure: McLaren, 100 laps, 2h 46m 29.7s, an average speed of 70.4mph: Moss, 1961, 70.7mph.

Clark could only qualify on the fifth row at Spa but, on a warm, sunny afternoon, completed the opening lap fourth. Graham Hill led. On lap nine Clark was in the lead. Trevor Taylor and Willi Mairesse (Ferrari) locked into an intense struggle behind Clark – which culminated in them touching and going off, the Ferrari in flames. Although neither driver was hurt, Clark described it as a 'nasty moment and again I had those Spa qualms.' He won and was in such command that, rounding *La Source*, he took a hand off the wheel to wave to a photographer.[30]

The French Grand Prix went back to Rouen for the first time since 1957, graphically underlining the pace of progress. Clark did a lap of 2m 14.8s for pole, Musso had done 2m 22.7s in a Ferrari.

Gurney won – Clark had a front suspension problem – but Clark won the British at Aintree. Before it, he sat in the cockpit wearing a heavy, dark crash-hat – it looked like a military helmet – his face young as a choirboy. Chapman, very correct in jacket, collar and tie, looks young, too. He dipped his head towards Clark and spoke, Clark listened. He drove a beautiful race round Aintree's open spaces and beat Surtees by 49 seconds.

Graham Hill won round the Nürburgring. Surtees in the Lola was second there, as he had been at Aintree two weeks before. Cumulatively it showed how open the season was: the first six rounds produced four winners.

In practice at the Nürburgring Carel de Beaufort, a Dutchman and the last amateur to be a regular Grand Prix driver, was fast in a Porsche and, with a 16mm cine camera mounted on the rear of the car, doing some filming for a German television company. He reached Foxhole [Fuchsröhre], a downhill section which zigzagged. The camera broke from its mounting and was flung onto the track.

Hill was travelling at around 140mph and suddenly he saw a 'rather large black object' in front of him – the camera. Helplessly he ran over it and it tore off his oil cooler. The oil hit the rear wheels and the BRM snapped round, went down into a ditch 'like a giant mole,' ripping the car apart. When it came to rest Hill was sitting breathless on a bare chassis.[31]

Tony Maggs, a consistent South African in a Cooper, came rushing onto the oil and spun fiercely before charging a hedge and bouncing all over it. The Cooper was destroyed, Maggs unhurt. Hill saw Trintignant approaching in a Lotus and rushed down the track waving to warn him. It worked.

In 1961, Phil Hill had taken a Ferrari under the nine-minute barrier (8m 55.2s) but now the first four did it. Graham Hill won a wet race and the following month added the Italian Grand Prix at Monza. Clark led but the transmission failed after 13 laps and Hill found the long run for home comfortable. Clark, however, reasserted the pressure by winning Watkins Glen from Hill.

Something momentous happened there, but in the background. Professor Sid Watkins has recounted[32] how, working as a neurosurgeon at a hospital in Syracuse about 60 miles from Watkins Glen, he was asked to join the medical team at the United States Grand Prix. 'I thought "well if I'm going there and I've got some sort of responsibility, I'm not going to do it unprotected." So I took an anaesthetist with me, and an orthopaedic surgeon, and we went as a team. That was the concept and it had been foreign until that point. Until 1969 [when Hill broke both legs] that was the way I functioned at the Glen. We had a very primitive hut there – we used to have to sweep the flies out, and spray disinfectant around, to make it smell a bit clinical! And we took all of our own equipment.'

The racers went to East London, South Africa on 29 December for the decisive race. Again, the five best results of the nine rounds counted and Hill had 33 points from seven (lowest 1 and 3) so he needed to finish third or higher. Clark had 30 from only four. Hill's theoretical maximum was 42, if he won and Clark didn't finish. If Hill didn't finish, Clark need only be third.

The best-finish device may have kept the seasons alive but there was something particularly, perhaps damnably, artificial about it.

Clark found the long wait from Watkins Glen on 7 October 'terrible' because wherever he went people pestered him about how he thought he'd do. He had only one wish, to settle it once and for all. Porsche and Ferrari didn't go.

The circuit butted on to the Indian Ocean and winds battered against the cars moving them around in the two fast corners past the pits. Practice began on Boxing Day (traditionally, as Hill pointed out, a day of hangovers) and Clark was immediately so quick Hill thought he'd be powerless against him. Hill applied his doggedness and although Clark took pole he was alongside only 0.3 of a second slower. Hill also remembered how enthusiastic the crowd was and, although segregated into black and white, the blacks saw the whites 'busy patting us on the back and thought they'd do the same. They don't often get a chance to pat a white man on the back.'[33]

Clark led from Hill and, although they were within a second of each other after the opening lap, Clark drew away. Hill did what he was always going to do, wringing whatever he could out of the BRM. He knew he couldn't win unless something happened to Clark but *no surrender*. Clark's ability remains enigmatic, impossible to dissect, a thing of perfect, intuitive balance; of taking every aspect of the car, the circuit, the conditions and smoothing them into purity and harmony.

After 20 laps he'd drawn ten seconds from Hill but towards the end smoke ebbed from his car. He noticed it on lap 59 of the 82, blue smoke as he'd remember. He drove on for a couple of laps and pitted. He watched Hill go by into the lead and Hill relaxed because he could afford to retire himself and still be champion – but Hill did it properly winning the race from McLaren.

The world was a different place. Bette Hill, who'd only missed two races during the season, stayed at home in London – cost had to be considered in the days before drivers earned millions – and the only way she could find out what had happened was to telephone the Reuters news agency, who got the regular updates. That's how she learnt she was now the wife of the World Champion. She threw a party. Betty Brabham would understand.

There's no account of what Graham did in East London and we don't need that. He must have thrown a party, a hell of a party.

Clark bestrode 1963, although Monaco eluded him again. Villoresi, a man of studious dignity confirmed by receding snow-white hair, was an interested spectator, examining the cars and talking quietly about them. He, Étancelin, Chiron and Taruffi would take part in the parade of honour, Chiron waving a white hat vigorously to the crowd. Clark had pole but Hill led. Clark caught him, pressured him and overtook him on braking into Gasworks. He set a new lap record but the gearbox failed just round Gasworks. His first thought was that Hill, running second, would steam into his abandoned Lotus and he ran back to try and warn him. Hill won.

The Monaco measure: Graham Hill, 100 laps, 2h 41m 49.7s, an average speed of 72.4mph; McLaren, 1962, 70.4mph.

Four days later Clark was second at the Indianapolis 500. Belgium was wet and Clark drove well within his limits – his phrase. The limits existed within the harmony, of course, and were not the same as for other people.[34] Clark led immediately, Hill trailing, the rest shed on the opening lap. The gearbox problem struck again, this time the lever snapping out of top. This disturbed the harmony, and it was necessary to re-establish that. He had Hill coming up to press him and a completely unpredictable gearbox, which can only have been frightening on narrow, cambered ordinary roads. At the *Masta* kink, a left-right on the long straight in the country, Clark decided for reasons of prudence that he'd ease off by some 300 revs going through, although that still left his speed at around 150mph. Clark faced two problems approaching the kink at *Masta*: the gearbox, and the behaviour of the Lotus which drifted across the track in the kink. Clark restored the harmony by holding the gear lever rigid with his right hand – so it couldn't jump anywhere – while positioning his left hand at the bottom of the steering wheel so he had plenty of play to correct the slide. He did this to the end of the race.

At around half distance a storm broke over the circuit. Hill's gearbox seized and several cars spun off, including Belgian Lucien Bianchi. Clark came upon Bianchi standing in the middle of the track near *Masta* and 'groups of Belgians running about.' Clark missed them all then reduced his speed so drastically that from a fastest lap of 3m 58s he did 6m 41s. It allowed McLaren, running behind him, to unlap himself and Clark chose not to contest that. He won by more than five minutes, McLaren the only car on the same lap *and Spa measured 8.7 miles.*

Clark took pole at Zandvoort and lapped everybody in the race; pole at Reims and won by 1m 4s; pole at Silverstone and beat Surtees in the Ferrari by almost half a minute. This was a great driver at the height of his powers, every race at his mercy.

A famous and fabled bike rider, Mike Hailwood, made his debut in a Lotus at Silverstone and finished eighth. He imagined that racing cars would be a natural and effortless transition. Instead, financing himself, he found only expensive frustration. He seemed to himself to have become two people, the successful biker thoroughly enjoying life, the unsuccessful car driver going nowhere and 'miserable as sin.' He liked the matey, basic, unvarnished bike racing community, where he could get drunk, seduce women and nobody minded. (He was once glimpsed *in flagranto* in the back of a car before one of his races, and nobody thought that unusual. Just Mike, you know). He actively disliked the hangers-on at motor races who thought they were giving their lives importance by being close to the drivers.

Hailwood lingered a season or two, went back to the world he knew and, much later, came back to this world he didn't know.

Clark took pole at the Nürburgring but the engine kept cutting out on one cylinder so, to re-establish the harmony, he altered his style to seven cylinders and finished behind Surtees.

Clark went to Monza to win the championship but the Ferrari was much quicker, he was sure he couldn't hold Surtees and he felt 'dismal'. A slip-streaming battle developed but the Ferrari's engine failed on lap 17 and Clark won from Ginther (BRM). As the celebrations gathered pace he was told the Italian police wanted to interview him about the von Trips crash the year before. The police said he had to sign a document guaranteeing he'd appear in court the following morning. Eventually, he was allowed to leave provided he gave them the address of an Italian lawyer to act for him.

What ought to have been a party at the hotel to celebrate Clark's championship became very subdued and the only aspect of it he'd remember was a bun fight, Lotus versus Cooper.

A late-season ripple of races: Hill took pole at Watkins Glen and won, Clark third; Clark took pole in Mexico City and won from Brabham; Clark took pole and won South Africa. He'd won seven of the ten rounds with seven poles for 73 points (54 counting), Ginther (34, 29 counting) and Graham Hill (29) sharing second place.

Jackie Stewart had been club racing in England and winning consistently. Tyrrell was in Formula 3 and one of his drivers, American Tim Mayer, had been killed in a race in Tasmania at the end of February. Tyrrell needed a replacement and someone recommended Stewart. Tyrrell rang him at home in Dumbuck and invited him down to Goodwood for a test. Stewart, reflecting, says that represented a big door opening. He was immediately so fast that Tyrrell called him in and lectured him about dangerous driving. Stewart went out again and went faster...

Surtees, a man of trenchant opinions and self-assurance to a degree unusual even in a racing driver, ought to have treasured 1964 because he achieved something no man had done before, winning the World Championship to add to his seven motorcycle championships. He'd remember, however,[35] this year as more suitable for forgetting because so much which should have gone right went wrong, and it all could have been avoided. Surtees felt deep frustration.

Enzo Ferrari was strong-willed, John Surtees was strong-willed and Surtees insisted that the company was over-stretching itself by racing Grands Prix and sports cars. Surtees raised this with Enzo Ferrari in a frank discussion of views early on and was assured all would be well, but he soon found a preoccupation with the sports cars. When, finally, he did get into the new Formula 1 car, for the non-championship Syracuse Grand Prix, which he won. That convinced Ferrari they had a winning car and the necessary development, Surtees claimed, simply wasn't done.

Clark took pole at Monaco and led but the roll bar broke from its mounting and the pit stop to repair that pushed him far back. Graham Hill (BRM) won it from Ginther in another BRM, Clark fourth, Hailwood in a Lotus, sixth.

The Monaco measure: Graham Hill, 100 laps, 2h 41m 19.5s, an average speed of 72.6mph: Graham Hill, 1963, 72.4mph.

Unreliability pursued Surtees, although he finished second to Clark at Zandvoort: his engine failed on lap four at Spa (Clark won again), the engine failed on lap seven at Rouen (Gurney in the Brabham won, Graham Hill second); he was third at Brands Hatch (Clark won, Graham Hill second again). That was halfway through the season and Clark had 30 points, Graham Hill 26 and Surtees only 10.

At the Nürburgring Surtees took pole from Clark with a lap of 98.43mph, just a breath or two away from the 100mph barrier. Further down the pit lane a small group of men and an inexperienced Californian were about to broaden Grand Prix racing and, in time, energise and exasperate the very same John Surtees. Honda had come.

They'd hired Ronnie Bucknum, who looked like a US marine, to drive their tentative Formula 1 car with a V12 engine which produced something like 220bhp at 12,000 revs. Honda's original venture into bike racing at the Isle of Man grew into 'absolute superiority' which 'in 1961 electrified and stunned the European racing world.'[36] Of the 22 bike Grands Prix 125cc and 250cc races that season they won all but four.

Cars, however, were the big future and racing them held many advantages, not least in testing the personnel at race meetings; but the Nürburgring was a hell of a place to begin. They had to 'grapple with braking, handling and overheating troubles, culminating in an engine breakage on Saturday which meant a change to their only spare unit.'[37] The race organisers put on a brief extra qualifying session to accommodate this engine change, and that allowed the Honda to do the necessary five laps to get into the race. At one point the scrutineers pointed out that the car lacked an oil wastage system so Honda bored holes in a Coco-Cola can and used that.

The same day de Beaufort crashed heavily at *Bergwerk,* the right-hander about halfway round the circuit, while forcing his old Porsche to qualify. He had serious spinal injuries and died in hospital two days later.

Lorenzo Bandini, Surtees's team-mate, briefly led the race before Clark took him, Surtees close behind. It developed into a struggle between Clark and Surtees, passing and re-passing, but Clark suffered gearbox problems and fell away, leaving Gurney (Brabham) to come up and attack. Surtees described this as a 'really fine wheel-to-wheel battle' and during it Gurney forged ahead twice but Surtees sensed that he could find enough from the Ferrari to handle this. Both broke the lap record and Surtees broke it twice again, Gurney falling away because some newspaper blew into the Brabham's radiator. Surtees beat Graham Hill by more than a minute and a quarter.

In between that and the Austrian Grand Prix at Zeltweg, Hill did some testing at Snetterton and crashed heavily into banking, getting whiplash. He was taken to hospital in Norwich and analysis found he'd chipped a small neck bone. Any journey in any car became agonising.

A gangling Austrian prepared to make his debut in a Brabham-BRM Of him, Jackie Stewart would say that at this time he looked 'very

young, like a schoolboy, lost and somewhat out of place. His helmet
doesn't seem to fit him ...' At the airport local photographers tried to set
up pictures of the young man, Jochen Rindt, shaking hands with the
famous drivers like Clark and Hill, but Rindt 'was determined to avoid
being obtrusive; he didn't yet feel like master in his own home, but more
like a guest in his own country.'[38]

Zeltweg – nothing to do with the modern circuit there – was a military
base's perimeter road and very bumpy. Hill said the 'surface had a bad
ripple' and for someone with an injury like his, Zeltweg became a torture
chamber. In practice he covered a couple of laps and the pain proved too
much for him. He pitted and took codeine tablets, waited until they
worked – taking the sharp edge off the pain – then went out again. He
was not seeking Clark's harmony, just a way of being able to cope with
the car: in corners he'd use one hand to support his head, taking the
weight from the neck, and use the other hand to hold the steering wheel.
Hill took pole, the only driver under 1m 10s ...[39]

Rindt qualified 13th. Clark, Surtees and Hill didn't finish the race
(and neither did Rindt, a steering problem). Bandini won it.

The week before Monza Surtees crashed in a race at Goodwood, was
knocked unconscious and suffered whiplash. When he reached Monza
to practice, BRM protested his fitness on the grounds that he might be a
danger to others and he was allowed to compete only after further
checks. Typically, he won the Grand Prix. Clark's engine failed and the
championship tightened (six best finishes of the ten): Graham Hill 32
from six so he was now dropping points, Clark 30 from four, Surtees 28
from four.

The tightening became complexity at Watkins Glen, where Hill won
from Surtees – Clark fastest lap, the lead, fuel injection problems. Only
Mexico remained and, although the permutations were many, Surtees
knew that if he won the race he'd done it. Clark took pole, Surtees on the
second row, Hill on the third in what he described as a very tight,
contorting circuit decorated by 'lots of funny little bends in the middle.'
On the grid Hill's goggles fell onto his lap – a problem with the elastic.
He struggled to put them back as the race started and got away tenth.
The engine of Surtees's Ferrari cut and the grid surged past, including
Hill, then the engine fired again. Completing the opening lap Clark
clearly led, Hill still tenth and Surtees 13th.

As the race unfolded Hill worked his way up to third, Bandini's Ferrari
behind him, Surtees fifth. This was enough to give Hill the
championship but Bandini launched a series of challenges, making some
'wild attempts' at overtaking into the hairpin. They collided.

Subsequently people accused Bandini of reckless driving to take Hill out and open the way for Surtees. Surtees refuted the notion absolutely and Hill certainly didn't think Bandini had done it deliberately.

Hill's exhaust was damaged and he retreated to the pits, resumed at the back of the field. Clark still led, Gurney second while Bandini, undamaged, overtook Surtees for third. Seven laps remained and Clark began to lose oil. His engine seized going into the final lap. Race order: Gurney, Bandini, Surtees.

At that instant, Hill thought, *I've won the championship again* – the four points for third place gave Surtees 38 and Hill had 39. In the turmoil Hill must have forgotten that he'd be shedding two points because he'd finished seven races – working total 37. On that last lap Surtees overtook Bandini and later insisted Bandini had not been told to back off, although *Autosport* reported the Ferrari pit gave Bandini 'very agitated signals.'

Hill, running two laps down, didn't know Surtees was past Bandini but when he pulled into the BRM pits at the end the pit crew's expression told him everything.

That evening at the prize giving the President of Mexico presented Surtees with a gold Longines watch. Big John would always remember two things about that. British customs seized it and held it for a couple of months when he got home – and the watch was worth more than he got from the *FIA* for winning the championship. That was a diploma, and nowt else.

During this year, Milton da Silva gave son Ayrton a go-kart with a little engine to play around in. They lived in suburban São Paulo in a house on a hill and Ayrton went up and down that hill just as if it was a racetrack.

The whole 1965 season can be told in two words. Clark, Lotus. He took pole and won South Africa from Surtees; Jackie Stewart, making his debut in a BRM was sixth a couple of laps down. Stewart partnered Graham Hill and, despite his inexperience at Grand Prix level, often went quicker. Here was the classical racing situation, bringing all its inevitable tensions: a new generation, young and eager, challenging the accepted order and, whether consciously or not, intending to overthrow it.

Clark did not compete at Monaco – he prepared for the Indianapolis 500 the day after – and that let Graham Hill in for his third successive win there although Stewart led for five laps.

The Monaco measure: Hill, 100 laps, 2h 37m 39.6s, an average speed of 74.3mph: Hill, 1964, 72.4mph.

Coventry Climax announced that they were ceasing production and not going in to the new 3-litre formula, scheduled for 1966. This came as a particular shock to Colin Chapman who'd 'built up something of a special relationship'[40] with the company. Chapman approached Keith Duckworth, a former Lotus employee and co-founder of the Cosworth engineering firm, and asked if he could produce a new Grand Prix engine. Cosworth had been created by Mike *Cos*tin, engineer and successful racing driver, and Duck*worth*. They'd rise from being a small-time engineering concern working out of a workshop they didn't own to being, as one historian puts it, 'the outstanding race engine manufacturers of their day.' [41]

Chapman told Duckworth he'd find the finance and they agreed on a budget of £100,000. Eventually Chapman approached Walter Hayes of Ford. Hayes...

> had got to know Colin well by this time, and I sometimes used to go round to Colin's house in Hadley Wood, for dinner and a chat. On one occasion he said to me 'this is getting serious, I don't suppose you would do an engine, would you?' Now, every time I saw Colin, he would have nine or ten ideas to discuss, he wanted to work on all of them at once. So, at that point I only needed to say: 'Well, it's funny you should be saying that because I rather think that I would like to do an engine now. I think we've earned our spurs at the lower level of the sport. I've been thinking about ways that we might go further, but I've been uncertain as to which way to go.'
>
> In those days I was even considering trying to do a GP engine 'in house', but that would have been vastly expensive, and anyway at that time I didn't know that you needed a special kind of expertise to do a racing engine. Colin then said to me that he thought Keith could do it. I knew enough about Keith by then – the only ability I've ever really had was to be able to pick people.[42]

In great secrecy, Cosworth began to work on the design of the engine. It wouldn't appear for two full years but when it did proved more than a sensation: it became the backbone of Grand Prix racing, its workhorse and its saviour.

Hill took pole at Spa from Clark and Stewart by two seconds, which surprised even him. The race was run in heavy rain and Clark won his fourth successive victory at the circuit he disliked so much, from Stewart by 44 seconds.

At Clermont-Ferrand – the 13th staging post for the French Grand Prix – Clark took pole and gave a demonstration of car control. The circuit was sinuous and through an uphill curving left-right he seemed to caress the Lotus through constantly correcting tiny slides. He led throughout and won it from Stewart and Surtees; Clark took pole at Silverstone, led and towards the end, had a problem with his engine – and his oil pressure was falling. Clark re-established the harmony by switching the engine off at certain corners. Even so he beat Hill by three seconds.

Hill took pole in Holland but Clark led throughout, winning it from Stewart. Zandvoort, however, remains notorious because at one point a Dutch policeman, clearing the grid, didn't see that Colin Chapman wore his official armband on his belt and, assuming he had no right to be there, hustled him away. Chapman gave him a left hook and put him down. After the race a large number of Dutch policemen arrived at the Lotus pit to arrest Chapman. They grabbed him, he said: 'Come on, lads' to the mechanics and an international tug-o'-war began: the Dutch police pulling heads and arms, the mechanics pulling feet, while Hazel Chapman held a policeman by the hair.

Chapman was eventually marched off to spend a night in a cell. The Lotus team went to the police station and sang dirty songs outside to raise Chapman's spirits. They needn't have bothered. He was designing a new car on the back of the writ he'd been served.[43]

Clark could win the championship at the Nürburgring with three races to spare. He took pole and in practice all the first four – he, Stewart, Hill and Surtees – went through the 100mph barrier. Clark led the opening lap and, from a standing start, completed it two full seconds faster than Surtees's 1964 record, set on lap 11. In this mood Clark was not to be caught and won from Hill by 15.9s.

Stewart's astonishing progress in his debut season climaxed at Monza where Clark had a fuel pump problem, leaving Stewart to hold off Hill. Stewart described it as 'a tremendous thing' to have done that but in his canny, perceptive Scot's way rationalised that: Monza did not demand great finesse from a driver and consequently youngsters could be expected to do well there. Without the chicanes, which would be added in 1972 and 1976, Monza represented a straightforward, high-speed blast virtually all the way round.

One incident troubled Stewart. With a couple of laps to go he and Hill – team-mates at BRM of course – duelled and Hill ran a fraction wide at one point. It cost him the race and troubled Stewart that, as the newcomer, he might be seen as culpable. Hill assured Stewart he wasn't and it was confirmed when, at a party in Milan that night, the race was re-run on television and everyone could see Hill going fractionally wide.

Stewart found Hill's integrity touching.

Hill won Watkins Glen but in the background Honda had been making steady progress. They'd hired another American, Richie Ginther, to partner Bucknum which reflected a growing sense of confidence. A small, neat Californian, Ginther had been in Grand Prix racing since 1960 and his career was nearer the end than the beginning.

At Mexico, the final race, several drivers got lost on the way to the circuit, including Innes Ireland, who was driving for the Parnell team.[44] Ireland was dismissed and his car given to Bob Bondurant.

Ginther found the Honda 'just flat plain better' and led throughout. To make a Grand Prix car function reliably and faster than the others is a delicate, maddeningly frustrating activity. Engine manufacturer Brian Hart says: 'Most of the time it was very difficult to get the engine to run on 12 cylinders. It had these massive long exhaust pipes and it was tuned like 12 motor bikes. I mean, 12 exhaust pipes is very unusual. And the noise, the noise the thing made! Nobody had ever revved engines to 11,000 or 11,500 or 12,000rpm. When Ginther won in Mexico, he was running 12,500. The other engines were running about 10,500.'

Hill described Ginther's victory as 'a tremendous shock to the establishment.' It was also a tremendous delight to Honda as a company, and senior executive Nobuhiko Kawamoto said it 'gave us the necessary punch to forge ahead and continue to invest in the automobile industry.'

Mexico City, on the warm and sunny afternoon of 24 October 1965, was the end of the 1.5-litre Formula. From 1966, as we have seen, that would become 3-litres. Hill pointed out the 1.5-litre Formula would be unlamented and he even mused aloud about why it had ever been introduced. The bigger sports cars were by now lapping faster than Grand Prix cars.

They wouldn't be, any minute now.

That month, to end persistent rumours, Ford announced they were engaged in a joint project with Cosworth: the engine.

The future was coming fast.

Notes

1. Connaught Engineering was an English company founded by Kenneth McAlpine, a member of the construction family, in 1950. They started making racing cars in 1951.
2. *Racing Driver,* Salvadori.
3. *Life at the Limit,* Hill.
4. *Autosport.*
5. *The Racing Car,* Batsford.
6. Founded in 1903 as engine specialists, they achieved fame 'for supplying motors for the tractor used by Sir Ernest Shackleton's Antarctic Expedition

in 1914.' Their first racing engine was made in 1954, they were successful in Formula 2 and went into Formula 1 powering Cooper cars. http://www.grandprix.com/gpe/eng-coven.html

7. *Jim Clark at the Wheel*, Clark.
8. Lister, an English engineering company. In 1954 Brian Lister, the founder's grandson, decided to make racing cars.
9. Hill, op. cit.
10. *Champion Year*, Hawthorn.
11. *Bruce McLaren*, Young.
12. Hawthorn, op. cit.
13. *Mon Ami Mate*, Nixon.
14. Young, op. cit.
15. *Jack Brabham's Motor Racing Book*, Brabham.
16. *The Story of Honda Motor Cycles*, Carrick.
17. *When the Flag Drops*, Brabham.
18. *My Cars, My Career*, Moss.
19. *World Champion*, Surtees.
20. Moss, op. cit.
21. *When the Flag Drops*, Brabham.
22. *Enzo Ferrari*, Yates.
23. Baghetti is the only man to win his first Grand Prix, and more than that he won his first two non-championship Formula 1 races as well, making a unique hat-trick. In terms of the World Championship, inevitably 'firsts' were set in the initial race at Silverstone in 1950 so in the strict sense, Farina won his first, too.
24. Interview with the Author.
25. Yates, op. cit.
26. At Monaco in 2004, Ralf Schumacher was accused of ignoring blue flags and Fernando Alonso claimed he 'pushed me wide' at the tunnel. Michael crashed into Juan Pablo Montoya's Williams.
27. Ottorino Volonterio, a Swiss lawyer, has been described as 'usually slow or hopelessly slow' (*Grand Prix Who's Who*, Small.). He drove in three Grands Prix meetings but only qualified for one race.
28. Slick tyres were ungrooved, and aimed to get as much rubber in contact with the track surface as possible. The super sticky slicks used in qualifying in the 1980s – made to last one flying lap – gave astonishing adhesion. Today's grooved tyres in Grand Prix racing were designed to slow the cars and make braking for corners more challenging – in theory leading to overtaking chances for a car following.
29. Hill, op. cit.
30. Clark, op. cit.

31. Hill, op. cit.

32. Watkins interview with Nigel Roebuck, *Autosport,* 10 February 2005.

33. Hill, op. cit.

34. Brian Hart tells a revealing story about Clark. They were in a wet Formula 2 race and Clark came to up lap him. Hart thought *right, I'll follow him and see how it's done.* 'He vanished into the distance! Clearly his limit in the wet was completely different to mine. If I had followed him I'd have gone off.'

35. Surtees, op. cit.

36. Carrick, op. cit.

37. *The German Grand Prix,* Posthumus.

38. *Jochen Rindt*, Prüller.

39. Hill, op. cit.

40. *Cosworth,* Robson.

41. *History of the Grand Prix Car 1966–1991,* Nye.

42. Robson, op. cit.

43. *Colin Chapman,* Crombac.

44. Reg Parnell, who drove Grands Prix between 1950 and 1954, set up his own team but died suddenly in 1964. His son Tim, also a Grand Prix driver, had to take over. He became team manager of BRM.

Chapter 8

SAFETY FIRST

The dark green car, sleek and slightly prehensile, travelled towards the *Masta* kink on the opening lap of the Belgian Grand Prix. Rain had fallen. The driver, Stewart, was careful by nature, logical, precise but as he approached the *Masta* all that was plucked from him. His BRM ran full into water and aquaplaned out of control. It battered metal fencing and, bent and brutalised, came to rest in a ditch. Stewart sat semi-conscious and trapped.

These fleeting moments, etched in the grey rain of a drowning, dripping afternoon, were defining in the life of Stewart and Grand Prix racing. Nothing would ever be the same again.

The 1966 season promised something altogether different. The new 3-litre Formula, announced three years before, ought to have been a smooth transition – especially with so much warning – but the withdrawal of Coventry-Climax meant that British teams 'had to look elsewhere for engine supply with a very limited amount of time available.' As a result, 'solutions were many and varied indeed.'[1]

Tyres were now becoming a factor, and although this is a very technical aspect of the sport – and to the layman slightly mystifying – it had direct consequences on the racing. For many years Dunlop enjoyed something approaching a monopoly but Goodyear came in and when Ginther won Mexico he did so on Goodyears. Synthetic compounds allowed wider tyres, and smooth ('slick') and grooved tyres were available for dry or wet conditions. In 1966 Firestone came in against Goodyear and Dunlop, and a phrase was coined which would resonate down the years, *Tyre Wars*. In an activity like Formula 1, if you have superior tyres they can negate all sorts of technical advantages your opponents might have spent fortunes on, and that led to another resonating phrase, *there's time in the tyres.*

Initially: Lotus (Clark, Spence) had a modified 1965 Climax engine.
BRM (Stewart, Hill) made their own engines.
Ferrari (Surtees, Bandini) made their own, too.
Cooper (Rindt, Ginther, Bonnier, Ligier) had Maserati engines.
Eagle (Gurney), an American team, had a Climax engine.

Honda (Ginther, Bucknum) didn't appear until the Italian Grand Prix, with their own engine.

Brabham fielded four cars on the grid at the first race, Monaco: an Australian Repco engine for himself, Climax engines for Hulme and Londoner Bob Anderson, a Maserati engine for Bonnier.

Surtees was lucky to be there. He'd had a major crash practising for a race in Canada at the tail end of 1965. The car hit a barrier, somersaulted and came down on top of him. He spent the winter getting fit again and when he went back to the factory for the first time, on crutches, some of the mechanics were so moved they cried.[2]

He was fit for the pre-season races before Monaco but when he told a couple of team members about the 'gutless' V12 engine in the Grand Prix car they fell silent. Surtees approached Enzo Ferrari and said he wanted to take the previous year's car to Monaco but Ferrari shrugged that off. *You'll win it,* Ferrari said. Surtees gave a trenchant and entirely honest answer, *I can probably lead for a few laps but then the bloody gearbox will break because I'll have to drive the car so hard to hold that lead.*[3]

Clark took pole at Monaco, establishing continuity between the old Formula and the new, Surtees next to him. At the start, Clark's Lotus wouldn't come out of first gear and Surtees led from Stewart to lap 14 when he heard the ominous noise from the gearbox which he'd predicted. Stewart won it from Bandini, Hill third. Jack Brabham felt distinctly unwell – perhaps something he ate – and when his car's gearbox failed he decided to return to his hotel immediately. He walked up to the main street and caught a bus because, as he'd say, Monaco's so crowded it's the most efficient way to do it.

The Monaco measure: Stewart, 100 laps, 2h 33m 10.5s, an average speed of 76.5mph; Graham Hill, 1965, 74.3mph.

Surtees took pole at Spa, Stewart on the front row, Clark on the fourth after mechanical problems. As the 15 cars waited on the grid under dark, leaden cloud an announcement in the Press Box told the journalists rain fell at *Stavelot,* the corner on the far side of the circuit. One journalist wondered if the drivers knew and concluded they didn't.

At the *Masta* kink, about a mile from *Stavelot,* a farmer called Paul Dewalque prepared to watch the race from his front room because the farm butted on to the road. 'Every year I invited friends to come and watch with me. We'd stay inside the house for the first couple of laps because when the cars were racing close together it was too dangerous to go outside. Only when the cars were strung out did we do that.'

The 15 set off quite normally, the circuit perfectly dry down into *Eau Rouge.* Surtees got there first, Rindt and Brabham close behind. They moved into the country, the road rising and then angling down towards the long, carving right of *Burnenville*. As they travelled towards this Surtees saw spots of rain and thought clinically, *round* Burnenville *stay off the racing line because tyre rubber will have been laid there during practice and it'll be very, very slippery.*

Brabham remembered about halfway down the hill to *Burnenville* the drivers realised the conditions had changed absolutely. From nowhere he was in to 'a terrific slide' going sideways towards a house. As the car reached the rim of the road the slide stopped – he had no idea why – but he didn't hit the 'straw bales and concrete posts' there.[4]

Stewart just missed Brabham. 'I got through by a miracle. I remember giving a slight sigh of relief that I was clear.'[5]

Hill remembered how quickly the rain began because one moment he was handling the BRM in the dry quite normally, the next he was on a drenched track, visibility gone. He had a ghostly vision of cars spinning, seemingly everywhere. Bonnier's Cooper straddled a stone wall with a big drop the other side. Siffert and Spence crashed, too.

Hill picked a path through.

At *Malmédy*, a right-hander a little further on, two cars touched and went off.

Bonnier, Siffert and Spence took refuge in a barn doorway and watched the race from there.

The survivors moved along the straight to *Masta*, the left-right where farmer Dewalque and friends waited safe inside the solid farmhouse.

In these impossible conditions, Jochen Rindt overtook Brabham. Water flowed across the road at the kink and, although Surtees negotiated it safely, Brabham watched helplessly as Rindt lost control going in, described three complete rotations and continued straight ahead.

Stewart went headlong into a river of water flowing across the road and that's when he aquaplaned.

Hill, slightly further back, felt something didn't look right about the kink and, next instant, was on the river which had borne Stewart away. Hill spun wildly, too, and went backwards down the road fast. The car came to a stop at the side of the road with a rear wheel against a straw bale and the engine dead. As Hill fiddled for a gear to try to re-start he saw *there's a car down in that ditch* and thought *bugger me, Jackie's sitting in it.*

Stewart was in pain, looking 'terribly helpless.' Hill went and found him trapped by the steering wheel, the side of the BRM deformed. The fuel tank had split, soaking Stewart in petrol. Immediately Hill turned off the control switches in the cockpit to stop the fuel pump and looked round urgently for anything that might cause a spark. One spark could make the whole thing a bonfire. He saw the fuel was burning Stewart and he knew it could strip the skin off. He tried to lift Stewart out but couldn't because the steering wheel had jammed against Stewart's leg.

Bob Bondurant, an American in a BRM arrived at a canter. He'd crashed on the far side of the road and his car lay upturned there.

Stewart noticed Bondurant bleeding from the lips and wondered why he 'looked so sorry for himself.' After all, *I'm the one who's had the crash.* Stewart didn't know Bondurant had crashed, too. Hill sprinted off to find a marshal with a toolbox so the steering wheel could be removed. He couldn't find one but came across a spectator who had a car and a set of spanners in it. Hill sprinted back with them and got the steering wheel off, then he and Bondurant lifted Stewart and carried him to Dewalque's barn.

Of the 15 cars eight completed the first lap.

Stewart asked Hill to take off the overalls and Hill did that because they were soaked with fuel. Then Hill set off to telephone for an ambulance because one still hadn't appeared. While Hill was away, three nurses – nuns – ventured into the barn. Stewart, semi-delirious, wondered if they were real. When Hill returned, the ambulance – a converted bus – was arriving. He noticed that the nuns, seeing Stewart naked, had covered him up again with his petrol-soaked overalls and a lively discussion developed because Hill felt the nuns were more concerned about their embarrassment than Stewart's condition.

Jackie's wife Helen and Louis Stanley, the BRM chief, sat in the ambulance. They laid Stewart on the floor and he'd remember saying *Helen, this is very good experience for you.* He'd remember wondering how to address Stanley, who he habitually called Mr Stanley to his face and Big Lou in his absence. Stewart settled on Louis, to which Stanley said: 'Stewart! If you insist on calling me by my first name, call me Louie.'

The ambulance, heading for the town of Verviers and the hospital there, got lost.

Soon enough, the two men in the ambulance – patrician Stanley, perceptive Stewart – realised that this sort of thing could not go on. They'd do something about it.

Surtees won the race although Rindt had deep-grooved Dunlop all-weather tyres and Surtees contented himself following Rindt's wheel tracks which, of course, cut nicely through the rain and brushed it aside. That advantage was negated for Surtees because, in Rindt's spray, he drove blind and kept thinking *don't make a mistake, Rindt, don't make a mistake.*

After the race team manager Eugenio Dragoni – 'wealthy, headstrong, whose real business was perfume manufacturing in Milan'[6] – told Surtees he'd spent too long behind Rindt and Big John didn't appreciate that.

Eleven days after Spa, Keith Duckworth finally signed a contract with Ford for the engine although work on it had long been progressing, of course. Hayes thought Duckworth had never signed *any* contract before.

Surtees sensed something wrong when he received no congratulations from the Ferrari team management for winning Spa. They went to Le Mans testing for the 24-hour sports car race and Surtees fell into dispute with Dragoni, ostensibly over the running order within the team. Surtees felt he was the fastest of the three Ferrari drivers and found himself 'tired of being constantly sabotaged in my efforts to win by decisions that made no sense.'[7]

By the French Grand Prix, at Reims, he was no longer a Ferrari driver. He had a Cooper-Maserati instead.

Giuseppe Farina drove his Lotus Cortina from Italy towards Reims to watch the race but on slippery road at Chambery on the French side of the Alps he lost control, crashed and was killed. His place in history would always be secure as the first World Champion in 1950, although feelings about the man himself remained ambivalent. His courage had never been doubted but his temperament had. He was arguably the first of the modern drivers to exhibit naked ruthlessness.

During practice Clark hit a bird at speed and injured an eye so badly he didn't race. Bandini took pole from Surtees but both suffered mechanical problems and Jack Brabham won it. This was the first time a Grand Prix had been won in a car bearing the driver's own name.

As Stewart recovered – he only missed Reims – he began to work on plans to make Grand Prix racing safer. This was the re-energising of the Grand Prix Drivers' Association,[8] a body giving drivers a direct say. Initially some people viewed all this as cowardice and told Stewart so. He'd have to live with nonsense like that, and did. Louis Stanley set up the International Grand Prix Medical Service the following year featuring a mobile hospital and ambulance unit which went to the races with the capability of treating drivers immediately. In time, a leading driver evaluated the mobile hospital as 'fantastic' and added that it...

has marvellous equipment, a wonderful operating theatre, resuscitation facilities, everything. But some organisers are so jealous of it they won't allow it at their circuit, or they park it so far away from the centre of things that it is nearly useless. It seems the local doctors and hospitals get upset that anyone should think they are not adequate to cope with an accident...'

Ferrari stayed away from the British, at Brands Hatch, which Brabham won comfortably to lead the championship and, irked that the Press were calling him an old man at 40, he got his wife to buy him a false beard for the Dutch at Zandvoort. He appeared on the grid wearing it and using a jack handle as a walking stick. After a provocative performance like that, he felt he had to win it, and did.

At the Nürburgring, the Belgian son of a famous motor racing journalist put a Formula 2 Matra-Ford onto the fifth row of the grid. Jacky Ickx had been outstanding in motorcycle trials and now Ken Tyrrell saw his potential.

The race was wet and on the opening lap someone crashed into the Brabham of Leicester driver John Taylor. Taylor spun off and the Brabham burst into flames. Ickx went off trying to avoid this, and retired.

It developed into a battle between Brabham and Surtees. For once Brabham revealed his feelings in an uninhibited way. The race, he said, was 'shocking' and 'very dangerous.' The length of the Nürburgring, like Spa, meant that track conditions might not be uniform all round it and Brabham said they changed all the time: one lap this part dry, next lap wet. Without warning, you'd be into water flowing across or onto mud. He was sliding, Surtees was sliding.

Brabham judged this victory the most satisfying of his career.

Taylor died of his burns in a Koblenz hospital a month later.

Brabham had now won four consecutive races and that made him all but unbeatable in the championship. Although he didn't get a point at Monza – an oil leak halted him – of the chasers only Rindt in the Cooper-Maserati scored any points. Rindt finished fourth but a lap behind the winner, Ludovico Scarfiotti in a Ferrari. It made Brabham champion for the third time.

Honda finally had their new car ready for Monza but it proved too heavy. Ginther qualified it on the third row and got it up to second by lap 17 but the left rear tyre threw its tread and the car went into trees. It was destroyed, Ginther unhurt.

Clark won Watkins Glen, and Surtees won Mexico City. There, Yoshio Nakamura, running the Honda Grand Prix programme, approached him and explained that they were almost certainly withdrawing from racing but they'd stay if Surtees drove and ran the car 'on their behalf.'[10] Honda, in other words, offered him a sort of franchise.

Bucknum, who had driven the Honda that first time in Germany 1964, found Mexico 'bitter-sweet, because we knew we [he and Ginther] were leaving. I remember I was sitting on the pit lane wall and Surtees coming over to have a little chat. He spent a while in our pit having a look at the car.'

As the 1967 season began, the Cosworth engine was still very much in the background. Word of it leaked to the *Daily Mail* at a motor show on the Continent but that was all.

Chapman designed a new Lotus to take it and Hayes came into 'a bit of conflict' with him because Ford were paying for the engine and Hayes insisted Chapman...

> took on Graham Hill. With other teams, I had already observed that they had No. 1 drivers and No. 4 drivers, with nothing in between. I felt that this really meant that they produced one absolutely gorgeous car, and another that really was a lot less than gorgeous. I thought that if I could insist on two demanding drivers my engine could be in two first class cars. [...] Well of course there was conflict as to who actually *was* the No. 1 driver...[11]

The Cosworth wouldn't be ready until the third Grand Prix of the season, the Dutch at Zandvoort.

Pedro Rodriguez, a Mexican, won South Africa in a Cooper-Maserati, Surtees third in the Honda, Hulme in the Brabham-Repco fourth.

Jack Brabham started Monaco from pole but something wasn't right with the car and Bandini led, Hulme chasing him. Brabham struggled back to the pits and retired – engine – having unwittingly left a trail of oil all the way round the circuit. Marshals laid cement dust to soak up the oil and on lap two the cars churned the dust into clouds, causing confusion at the harbour chicane. Clark got through by going down the escape road and had to push the Lotus back, rejoining last. Hulme led from Stewart, Stewart led from Hulme but Stewart retired after 15 laps (crownwheel and pinion) and Bandini set off after Hulme. At half distance he had cut Hulme's lead to nine seconds and kept coming, but Hulme responded.

On lap 82 Bandini ran into the wooden barrier at the chicane, rolling the Ferrari which landed upside down and on fire among the bales. Hill remembered the crash as one of the worst things he'd ever seen in motor racing, remembered the intensity of the fire so you couldn't tell if Bandini was still in the car or not, remembered driving lap after lap through the smoke and foam.[12] Experienced *Daily Express* photographer

Vic Blackman took a picture – a morass of smoke and flames eating the carcass of the car – and immediately dashed to Nice where he could wire the picture to London. He had no idea Bandini was still alive.

Bandini, trapped for a long time, died three days later in hospital of burns. Hulme won the race.

The Monaco measure: Hulme, 100 laps, 2h 34m 34.3s, an average speed of 75.8mph; Stewart, 1966, 76.5mph.

At Zandvoort, a month after Monaco, the Cosworth DFV (Double Four Valve) engine came.

Duckworth had been...

> quite determined to control every aspect of the design. At one time he came dangerously close to damaging his health, and it was only a serious, though temporary, problem with his eyesight which caused him to back off a little. Perhaps Walter Hayes' memory has taken on a touch of hyperbole over the years, but he insists that: 'I think that obsessive is a dangerous word to use, because I think the last word I would apply to Keith is "obsessive", but the fact is that at one time the pressure on him caused him not to leave his drawing board for nearly ten days and nights. But I could see why he did this – it was his engine, and it was a masterpiece. It was really a piece of unique sculpture.'[13]

Before Zandvoort, Hill tested the Lotus and engine for a few laps at Snetterton and was impressed. The other car, for Clark, hadn't turned a wheel until it reached Zandvoort. There, Hill put his car on pole 4.2 seconds faster than the lap record and Clark, exploring the car, put his on the third row.

Hill led the race for ten laps from Brabham, Clark up to third. Hill's engine cut out – a camshaft problem – and he coasted to the pits. Brabham led five laps but now Clark was ready. He went past and controlled the race tightly, moving away from Brabham and winning by 23 seconds. Hayes remembered 'almost at once I began to think that we might destroy the sport. I realised that we had to widen the market for the DFV engine so that other teams could have access to it.' The only question for the rest of 1967 was whether the engine would be reliable.

Both Lotuses had problems at Spa where Gurney won in the Eagle-Weslake.

Neither finished the French Grand Prix on the Bugatti circuit at Le Mans using part of the 24-hour sports car circuit and a contorting section through car parks. Nobody liked it much and it wouldn't be used again. Jack Brabham won from Hulme; Clark won Silverstone from

Hulme by 12 seconds; neither finished at the Nürburgring where Hulme, a large, strong often gruff man, won from Jack Brabham.

Hulme 37 points, Jack Brabham 25, Clark 19.

Surtees came fourth in the Honda a long, long way off the pace. The push was on to design and build an entirely new car for the Italian Grand Prix five weeks away. Directly after the Nürburgring Nakamura flew to Japan to supervise that end of the push, taking with him the differential as hand luggage so there'd be no delay. Surtees remained at Slough, goading and forcing the thing through. He'd decreed 'we have got to save some weight, we have got to have a car which is more sensible than this one' because:

> we were carrying something like 300lb more than anybody else – not 50lb but 300. We agreed to undertake a joint venture with Eric Broadley, a good friend of mine with Lola. Honda sent over two young engineers and in our little factory in Slough we made that joint effort. Broadley designed the chassis and the Japanese engineers produced what you might call a compromise car – we didn't look at it as the car we would be using during the next season, it was just for the interim.
>
> It was done to prove to Japan that the car could go very much quicker if more effort was put into it. This was the way, also, for Nakamura to show Japan that given the tools we could do the job. So we got the engine modified in Tokyo and it had better fuel injection. We started work using, as a basis, an Indianapolis chassis. We made parts in Slough and they made parts in Japan. We put it all together in the factory and we finished it just about in time to get it on the truck for Monza.[14]

Honda missed Canada where Clark didn't finish and Hill was two laps down after a spin and a clutch problem. Brabham won from Hulme, keeping the championship alive.

At the Italian Grand Prix at Monza, Clark (of course) took pole, Surtees on the fourth row although grid positions were largely irrelevant where cars slip-streamed each other in packs and it was commonplace to have a host of leaders during a race: this year there'd be six.

With two laps to go Clark, leading, had a fuel pump problem. This was the culmination of an astonishing drive even by his standards because he'd led initially, had a puncture and lost a lap. At Monza, where finding time was considered almost impossible – the nature of the circuit allowed everybody to do big speeds – Clark *regained the lap* and regained the lead. Now that was over.

Surtees led, Jack Brabham hard on him and they were in the last lap approaching Parabolica – where Hill's Lotus had dumped oil ten laps before. Surtees:

> watched any car directly behind because all at once they'd pull out of your slipstream and nip away – especially on the final lap. I knew all about the oil going into the Parabolica. The normal place to position the car was on that very inside. It blocked anyone behind. That let you take the apex of the corner. That stopped anyone stealing the corner. Jack was there on my tail and we were coming up to the oil fast. I knew what he was thinking, 'Surtees will go to the inside and block me.' But there was no way I was going to take a chance on that oil. Obviously he was going to try and outbrake me because Jack was the last of the demon brakers. I took the orthodox line partially over to the left but not too much. If he did go inside me he'd have to put two wheels on the oil.[15]

Surtees never doubted that Brabham would go inside, risking everything to take the apex of the corner and the race. Surtees would brake as late as possible. Bluff, counter-bluff? Brabham 'knew' Surtees would 'go outside because of the oil but I decided I'd take the risk.'

Surtees positioned the Honda to the left.

Brabham saw him go left and 'I swerved to the inside.'

Surtees could not allow Brabham to follow him round the Parabolica. Brabham would get a tow then 'out-accelerate me once we'd come out and were going for the line. I had to rely on Jack having a go on the inside. And when I'd moved over he did see the option. Here he was alongside me and he'd hit the oil.'

Brabham knew that, if he could hold the inside, Surtees would 'never have been able to go all the way round the outside of me' but Brabham felt the car 'fishtailing' on the oil. He'd drawn level. At the end of the oil I was three metres in front of him but I'd started to drift. The oil didn't stop soon enough...'

Brabham slewed across the Honda and now the inside of the Parabolica opened to Surtees. He had the Honda in third gear. As he came out of the Parabolica he left it in third for the surge to the line, Brabham coming back at him. Surtees 'didn't dare try and change up. I let the revs go all the way to 12,000. I could see Jack had recovered. I knew that the time it would take me to snick up to fourth would be long enough for him to get past me.'

They fled towards the line and Brabham was coming, Brabham was coming. Surtees held the Honda in third and they crossed the line 0.2 of

Jack Brabham in a heat of the non-championship 1960 Brussels Grand Prix, driving a Cooper – the crowd was terrifyingly close. (courtesy BARC)

The start of the 1962 French Grand Prix at Rouen – the grid was incredibly narrow. Dan Gurney won in a Porsche. (courtesy BARC)

Maestro. Jim Clark, in absolute control, drives a Lotus 49 to win the 1967 Dutch Grand Prix from Jack Brabham. (courtesy Ford)

Lotus supremo Colin Chapman and Jim Clark formed one of the most successful partnerships Formula 1 has ever known. (LAT)

*New worlds. Honda launched its Grand Prix team at the 1964 German Grand Prix,
with American Ronnie Bucknum behind the wheel. There was much to discuss with
chief engineer Yoshio Nakamura. (LAT)*

*Bruce McLaren, the youngest ever driver to win a Grand Prix, started his own Grand Prix team
while in his 20s. Here, in 1969, he is talking to (from left) Denny Hulme, Phil Kerr, Tyler
Alexander and Teddy Mayer.* (Ludvigsen Library)

Left: *The spirit of the 1960s, Jackie Stewart, with trendy haircut and three World Championships.* (LAT)

Stewart would change Grand Prix racing by campaigning for safety after he crashed (right) at Spa during the 1966 Belgian Grand Prix (Eric della Faille photo – Alexis Callier collection). *He was carried to a barn, which stood where this one (below) stands now.* (Author)

Below: *The fantastic finish at the 1971 Italian Grand Prix. Peter Gethin (18, BRM) won from Ronnie Peterson (25, March) by 0.01 of a second, François Cevert (2, Tyrrell) by 0.09 and Mike Hailwood (9, Surtees) by 0.18 – Jo Bonnier (28, McLaren) is four laps down!* (LAT)

Above left: *Savage season. After a near riot Hunt won Brands Hatch, 1976, from Niki Lauda and was promptly disqualified.* (LAT)

Below left: *Lauda almost died at the 1976 German Grand Prix when his Ferrari crashed and caught fire on the treacherous Nürburgring. This is what the car looked like when they brought it back; Lauda, trapped in the burning wreckage, suffered terrible facial scarring.* (LAT)

Above: *James Hunt rode the storm at Fuji, Japan, on his way to the 1976 world title – and didn't realise he had clinched it.* (LAT)

Right: *Enzo Ferrari who, along with Bernie Ecclestone, was the most powerful and influential figure in all Grand Prix racing.* (LAT)

Masters of their time: (from left, top) John Surtees added the four-wheel World Championship to his bike titles; Graham Hill and a fed-up looking Damon; (above) Jack Brabham, who usually didn't say much; Jochen Rindt, the only posthumous champion; (below) Emerson Fittipaldi, who smiled a lot; and Mario Andretti, the quiet American. (all LAT)

a second apart. The crowd mobbed Big John, carried him shoulder high. Honda, clearly would win a lot more races – and been astounded if anybody had said the first of them wouldn't be for 17 years, driven by a Finn who, this summer of 1967, was a karter in his late teens yet to do his military service.

Clark won the United States Grand Prix at Watkins Glen from Hill, Hulme third a lap down, Siffert fourth two laps down. The Cosworth delivered that much power. It left Mexico City where Brabham had to win and Hulme finish no higher than fifth.

Clark won it from Brabham but Hulme safely in third, albeit – again – a lap down. Somehow the style of this championship suited the man, undemonstrative, understated but effective. Part of the prize-giving involved some of the drivers going to a bullring and fighting the bulls. There are sketchy reports of how good a matador Denny Hulme proved to be, although in that growl of a voice he insisted the bulls were calves, really, and probably more frightened of him than he was of them.

Ken Tyrrell, enticed by the possibilities of the Cosworth engine and having worked his team up through the junior formulae, felt ready for Grand Prix racing and he signed Stewart for 1968. That opened one era just as another was about to close forever. Tyrrell said 'why don't you come and drive for me?' and Stewart riposted 'I'd love to, but Ken, you don't have a car!' To which Tyrrell riposted 'what if I did have one...?' When he did, a Matra, Stewart said yes – a decision which surprised Tyrrell (who never asked him why he'd leave a big team like BRM for him.)

The season began in South Africa as anyone might have anticipated, Clark pole, fastest lap and victory over Hill by 25 seconds. That was 1 January. He flew to New Zealand and Australia for eight races, the last on 4 March. On 31 March he drove in a Formula 2 race at Barcelona where a young driver, Jacky Ickx, tried to overtake, braked too late and hit him. Icky apologised and Clark said 'OK, you're sorry, and that's OK one time – but not two times.'

Clark was now living in Paris as a tax exile and flew from there to Hockenheim for another Formula 2 race before flying on to Zandvoort for some Formula 1 testing. The Formula 2 race had little meaning and, anyway, both Clark and Hill might have been driving at Brands Hatch in a sports car event instead. Whether there was a mix-up with the Brands entries, or the authorities at Hockenheim said they'd fine the drivers if they failed to show up, is not clear but Clark and Hill went to Hockenheim. Chapman did not – he was on a family skiing holiday at St Moritz – but chief mechanic Jim Endruweit and mechanic Dave Sims did, Sims looking after Clark's car.

It was a dark, dank weekend and Clark thought he had a misfire. He even told Derek Bell, then a slightly star-struck beginner, to take care when he was lapping him because, with the misfire, the Lotus would be so slow.

The race was over two heats and in the first, on a wet track, Clark ran seventh, drifting back. Into lap five out in the country he almost certainly had a puncture at about 140mph. The car snaked, Clark catching it once, catching it again, losing it. The car went into trees at terrible speed.

Endruweit stood in the pits. 'Jimmy didn't come round and you thought "God, he's gone missing." Next thing there is a kerfuffle – an ambulance moving from the paddock area. You knew something had happened. There were a couple of young German ladies who had attached themselves to us for the weekend' – Endruweit used one as an interpreter. 'We went along to the organisers' place and I said: "What the hell's happened to Jimmy?" And they were very loath to say, they wouldn't say.'

Meanwhile Sims waited in the pits and 'you didn't have the communications then that you have now as soon as someone goes missing. No monitor, no radio, nothing. Then a Porsche came by – a road car, might have been the pace car. The guy in it said: "Come on, there's been an accident." "What's the problem?" "A Lotus has gone off, Jim Clark."

'They didn't stop the race and we went out onto the track in this Porsche, a bit scary in among all the racing cars, and I remember it was a bit dark. The racing cars didn't slow – no yellow flags. When we reached the scene there was nothing. So I asked myself *what's happened here?* Then I did see an ambulance parked in the shrubbery. You must remember I was fairly young then, 25.'

Sims asked *where is Clark, where is the car?* Someone said he was in the ambulance and Sims asked *is he having a check-up?* A voice said: 'I am afraid he is clinically dead.'

Sims imagined that this man, whoever he was, had 'got his German and English mixed up. Then I saw where the car was and I asked where the rest of it was, the engine and gearbox weren't there. "What have you done with them, what has happened here?" I could see the monocoque and it had gone a sort of banana shape when it hit the tree, but the force of hitting the tree ripped the engine and gearbox out. They went on in to the woods and sat there, 50 or 60 yards away. Then I started to realise. This man said: "I have to tell you again he is clinically dead but we are flying him to Mannheim." I didn't look in the ambulance. They had closed the doors.'

Someone pointed out where Clark's head had struck the tree 15 feet up.

'At that point I didn't know what to do. I hadn't got a phone, people were coming through the woods – spectators – people were picking up pieces. I said "first of all, don't let anybody touch anything, for goodness sake stop people pinching stuff. Get on to your people in the pits and tell them to give Graham the arrow to come in. You'd better get me back to the pits fast to speak to Graham to find out what we do now."'

The girl interpreter had found out where Clark was being taken. She and Endruweit got into her car, left everything and headed for Mannheim.

Sims was in shock by the time he got back to the pits. 'It's my fault the number one, the greatest driver has just been killed. What do I do? Run away? What do I do? Where is the chief mechanic, where is the Old Man? We got Graham in and I said "look, Jimmy is dead, they want somebody to go with him to Mannheim, what do I do?"'

Hill remembered hearing the words but not understanding what they meant.

'Without Graham,' Sims says, 'I don't know what would have happened, he was an absolute, unbelievable pillar of strength. He went and saw the organisers and told them we were going to take our truck out there and pick everything up.'

They did that.

Endruweit reached the hospital and 'I kept saying *what's happened, what's happened?* and they wouldn't tell me. Eventually, after a considerable time, they said: "Sit down, Mr Endruweit, have a drink" and I thought *hello, this is not good news.* Only then did they tell me that Jimmy had been killed. The only thing we'd assumed was that he'd been seriously injured and they were doing something fierce to him in the hospital. They asked me if I'd make a formal identification so we trolled off down and I did that. Jimmy wasn't marked. In essence he'd hit this modest tree, you know, four inch diameter, that sort of size, a young tree, and it had taken the rear suspension off. It was explained to me, in the hospital I think, that he had gone sideways into the tree and had a lower cranium fracture. In other words, the base of his skull – about the base of his crash hat – had taken the impact against the tree. And that was it.'

By now the truck had been driven back to the hotel.

Endruweit needed a phone 'and they took me to some vast room where there was one. I rang Chapman because I knew where he was. He'd left me a contact number at the something-hotel in the morning. I got through and I said: "Look, I need to speak to Colin Chapman" and they said he'd gone out for a walk. I snapped: "For Christ's sake go out and find him." They actually did go out and find him. I absolutely had to speak to Jimmy's father because it was the right thing to do, and by then obviously it was known about. This news, which I had been given quarter of an hour previously, had become common knowledge back in Britain. I broke it to his father with great difficulty. How do you do that? His dad took it in his dour Scots fashion, I suppose. I couldn't tell you whether he knew or not by the time I phoned him. All I was able to say was he'd been killed instantly, he wasn't damaged and things like that. Colin rang.'

Hazel Chapman remembered Chapman repeating everything Endruweit said.

Chapman got into his car and set off for Hockenheim fast. He arrived about one o'clock in the morning, looked at Sims and asked what the hell he'd done. Sims said he hadn't done anything. Chapman asked: 'What happened, what on earth happened? I can't believe this is going on.' Sims said none of them could. Chapman said 'Right, I want that truck out of here right now, get it to England now.'

Sims pointed out that the police had sealed it, left instructions not to move it and were returning at eight in the morning. Chapman said: 'You have got to go, but don't go through any borders whatever. Get out and do it and that is an order.'

As they walked to the truck Chapman asked again what had happened and concluded that 'something must have gone wrong with the car.'

Sims set off in the truck up the autobahn but 'we decided to get off that when we were up near Belgium and the Ardennes. We had a map and we found a track. It had a border post with just a swinging gate, nobody there. We went through and must have been across before 8 o'clock, before the police reached the hotel in Speyer. We drove through little villages and once we were on a farmer's track. Eventually we reached the main road and headed for Zeebrugge.'

A customs officer there proved difficult and wanted to take photographs of the car – or the truck didn't get on a ferry. Sims had to say yes. 'At this point we hadn't even got Jimmy's racing shoes out of the car, they were pinned behind the pedals. I mean, Jimmy's Rolex watch was still jammed beneath the master cylinder. We'd left Hockenheim so fast we hadn't had time to extract all that stuff.'

When they docked in Britain the police were waiting for them and escorted the truck to the Lotus factory but would not allow it to be taken inside for two days.[16]

By then, the motor racing world was beginning to understand that they would never see Clark's balletic car control ever again, never hear his soft voice, never wonder at his shyness, never ponder his harmonies. The motor racing world was beginning to understand, too, that if it could happen to Clark it could happen to anybody.

On 7 May an Englishman, Mike Spence, practised for the Indianapolis 500 in a Lotus. He'd driven for Lotus in Grands Prix in 1964 and 1965 but was now with BRM although Chapman took him to Indianapolis as a replacement for Clark. He struck a wall and the right front wheel swung back hitting his crash helmet. He died four and a half hours later.

Chapman was a hard man but there seems no doubt that these deaths, particularly Clark's, made him ask himself fundamental questions. He decided to continue but never allowed himself to get, or want to be, so close to any driver ever again. He certainly couldn't face going to the Spanish Grand Prix at Jarama, thus missing a revolution he had created and which would change Grand Prix racing even more than the Cosworth engine.

Esso had been a major sponsor but, unhappy that tyre manufacturers were being given more importance as sponsors, withdrew. The *Commission Sportive Internationale* feared other sponsors might follow and ended their restrictions on commercial sponsorship – cars ran with small, discreet logos or no logos at all. With the way clear Andrew Ferguson of Lotus – who'd had Esso – drew up a list of Britain's most important 200 companies and contacted them. As it happened a Lotus employee was looking for a sponsor for a couple of sports cars and came upon Imperial Tobacco. They, it transpired, were ready to spend lavishly to promote their Gold Leaf cigarettes.

In Spain the Lotus of Hill did not so much carry the Gold Leaf logo, it *was* Gold Leaf, red, white and gold livery replacing forever the old green and gold of Lotus.

This antagonised traditionalists who watched helpless as brash man Chapman vulgarised their corner of the world. Peter Warr, who worked for Chapman and later ran the team himself, once explained that Chapman's genius lay in seeing simple, original solutions to complex problems which nobody else had seen. These reshaped whole aspects of how Grand Prix racing worked. Soon enough the other teams followed Chapman and grids resembled advertising hoardings.

The big money had come.

Before Spain the Grand Prix Drivers' Association said they were unhappy about aspects of safety at the Jarama circuit and wouldn't race unless something was done about them. The GDPA was by definition an organisation of awkward, ego-propelled people who were solitary in what they did – the actual driving – and bred to fend for themselves. They performed cohesively only in times of communal danger and Jarama was that. The drivers didn't like the height of the guardrails, didn't like the loose gravel on the edge of the track and didn't like the rubber marker cones. The organisers worked hard to rectify this and the drivers drove.

In a feat of outstanding courage Hill won from Hulme. It proved that Lotus could survive the death of Clark, and Hill confirmed it by taking pole and winning at Monaco.

The Monaco measure: Hill, 80 laps, 2h 0m 32.3s, an average speed of 77.8mph; Hulme, 1967, 77.8mph.

The measure of the decades: 1929, 49.8mph; 1937, 63.2mph; 1948, 59.7mph; 1958, 67.9mph; 1968, 77.8mph.

Vehicles registered in Britain 14.4 million (1958, 8.0 million).

A Ford Escort Deluxe cost £635 and a Briton earned on average £25.40 a week. Saving all his money, the Briton would have taken 25 weeks to buy one (1910, 2 years 42 weeks; 1919, 1 year 28 weeks; 1929, 41 weeks; 1938, 37 weeks; 1949, 45 weeks; 1959, 26 weeks).

Stewart won Holland and confirmed the Tyrrell team had brought enormous potential with it.

Ickx won the French Grand Prix at Rouen in a Ferrari, Surtees in the Honda second but the race and its background remain like a spectre. Surtees worked out of the Slough factory developing a Honda numbered RA301. 'Suddenly' a 'new engine and car, the RA302, appeared at Slough without any advance warning. All the Honda engineers began to shake their heads apologetically.' Surtees tested it at Silverstone and concluded it was so bad 'there was no point in even talking about racing it.' It was stowed at the factory. 'Then one morning we arrived and it was gone. The previous night, representatives of Honda France had arrived and taken it away.'

The next time Surtees saw it was in the pit lane at Rouen, to be driven by Frenchman Jo Schlesser. Soichiro Honda was on a trade mission in France and it may be that for the most understandable of reasons he wanted to see the new car in the French Grand Prix with a Frenchman driving it. On a wet track during the third lap of the race Schlesser hit a bank, the Honda turning over and bursting into flames. The fire raged with such intensity that it covered the track and some spectators were lightly burnt. Schlesser lay dead.

Shortly afterwards Stewart pitted for new tyres and someone told him what had happened to Schlesser, the last thing to tell a racing driver about to go back out. Ken Tyrrell reacted with fury and virtually had the person thrown out of the pits. Stewart had never seen Tyrrell so 'wild'. Ickx won – from Surtees.

Siffert, driving a Lotus-Ford for Rob Walker, won the British Grand Prix at Brands Hatch.

For the Nürburgring Stewart flew up from Geneva in Graham Hill's Piper Aztec in the company of Bette Hill, Bonnier and Siffert. Rain began to fall as they unpacked their baggage and it never really stopped. The circuit was so shrouded in mist and rain that practice had to be extended to a session on Sunday morning. As Hill pointed out, because of the circuit's elevations they drove in mist and fog a lot of the time. You'd start from the pits in that but as the circuit descended you'd emerge and find the circuit only wet then climb back towards it again.[17]

That Sunday practice session Stewart judged the conditions to be so bad he'd stay in the pits. Tyrrell, for the only time in his life, ordered a driver – Stewart – to go out because it was the only way to find where the mud lay on the track, where and how deep the rivulets of water flowed across it. Stewart found the visibility so bad he was sure the flag marshals couldn't see each other. The start was delayed, the grid reshaped from the traditional 4–3–4 to 3–2–3 to reduce the risk of cars banging into each other. The GPDA met, but with 250,000 spectators waiting there wasn't much option but to race.

Ickx had pole, Stewart on the third row and convinced the idea of racing in this visibility was 'ill-advised'. That must be a mild choice of words. In the mounting uncertainty the signal to race was given only after the cars had been revving their engines for five minutes. Stewart saw engines boiling all round him and his own temperature gauge reached 100°C. From the start it resembled a 'powerboat race'[18] – rain falling, the mist lying like a shroud, roosters of spray behind each car, visibility a hundred yards. Into the first corner Hill led from Amon and Stewart who in the spray could see *nothing*.

Stewart moved up. On the run to Adenau he overtook Amon. Stewart was suddenly relieved to shed Amon's spray. In it, he had been more frightened than ever before in a racing car. Mid-way round the opening lap he ran second to Hill, overtook him at the Schwalbenschwanz after telling himself *I must get past before the straight, I must have no spray on the straight*. He crossed the line with a nine-second lead and increased that to 34 by the end of lap two. Tyrrell kept him informed by pit signals and he drove as fast as he could as slowly as he could. With three laps left the rain fell even harder and in an S bend he was into standing water, the car flicking from him. He headed towards a marshal who moved one way, moved the other and then froze in terror. Stewart was sure he'd hit him, but just before he did the tyres gripped.

He beat Hill by *four minutes*.

Hulme won Monza and, there, two American drivers – Mario Andretti and Indianapolis 500 winner Bobby Unser – ought to have made their Grand Prix debuts and even practiced. They were due to fly back to America for a race there the following day and return but this violated a *CSI* ruling about competing 24 hours before a Grand Prix and they were disqualified. Andretti, an immigrant from Trieste – an Italian city which became part of Yugoslavia, and therefore communist, after the war – arrived in the United States with his family when he was 15. He didn't look back.

Hulme won Canada and Stewart won the United States where Andretti did make his debut in a Lotus, putting it on pole. In the race the clutch failed.

The championship turned on Mexico. Hill went with 39 points, Stewart 36 and Hulme 33. It meant that if Stewart won and Hill came second they'd both have 45 but Stewart would get it on the most wins tie-break, 4–3. Hill decided on the direct tactics to cut through the permutations by winning the race himself. Stewart did the same.

Hill led but cars jostled and Stewart went through on lap five, thinking *this is going to be an epic*. On lap ten Hulme struck a guardrail, eliminating himself from the championship. Hill toyed with Stewart, pulling to one side threatening an overtaking move, pulling to the other side. Hill could see Stewart constantly glancing in his mirrors, reasoned Stewart must be thinking *where's the bugger now?* Stewart made a small mistake and Hill had him on the inside. Stewart's engine wouldn't pull properly at top speed and this became worse to the point where it cut out in corners. On one lap Stewart estimated he'd lost six or seven seconds and Hill 'just disappeared into the distance.'[19] So did the championship.

Sometime during this season a dark-haired little lad had his first race in a kart. He was eight and ought to have waited until he was 13 but people in a hurry don't. The grid was decided by drawing lots and he drew 1, giving him the first pole of his career. The other racers were naturally bigger and stronger – presumably they were at least 13 – but their weight slowed them against his lightness. With three laps to go another kart nudged him off. Years later, all this made Ayrton Senna smile his wan, slow smile as if the memories amused him. That's worth recording because from this moment on not winning races wouldn't amuse him at all – as Jackie Stewart, no less, would find out.

Honda finally withdrew from Grand Prix racing. Nakamura, visibly saddened, said quietly to Surtees, 'John-*san,* it is the end.'

On 3 January 1969 a house builder and his homely wife who lived in an anonymous German town had a son. As he grew, he'd have a dream to play in goal for Cologne because his namesake, Toni Schumacher, was doing that. About Grand Prix racing he never thought at all.

Rindt joined Hill at Lotus but Stewart, Tyrrell and their Matra car bestrode the season. It happens. Stewart led all 80 laps at Kyalami and that set the tone. He won in Spain at Montjuich Park although by now the use of giant mounted aerofoils was causing concern. The ones fitted to the Lotuses were so large that the downforce they generated snapped their supports.

Hill's snapped out of control at the first corner hairpin after the pits just beyond a hump which put maximum pressure on the aerofoil. The car battered the metal guardrails at both sides of the track and left a long trail of debris. Stewart, passing, saw Hill was all right and tried to signal that to the Lotus pit as he passed.[20]

Hill cleared the debris as best he could, putting it near the guardrail, examined his car and concluded the aerofoil had failed. Chapman sent Hill's mechanic, Dave, to see what had happened.

Rindt saw Hill and, each time he passed, tried to signal to him *am I in danger?* Hill doesn't seem to have seen these signals although he did watch Rindt intently and noticed a 'crease' appearing in the wing.

Hill despatched Dave back to the pits to tell Chapman *signal Rindt in, looks like the same thing's happening to him.* Hill then set off towards the hairpin because he reasoned the cars were going slowly enough through it for Rindt to see *Hill* gesticulating *danger.* Dave, it seems, lacked enough time to reach the pits.

Hill watched Rindt approaching, watched as the aerofoil collapsed, 'just folded in half.' The Lotus behaved as Rindt feared it would if an aerofoil failed: the whole rear of the car rose – for an instant threatened to go across the guardrail. The guardrail was just high enough to prevent it. Rindt had insisted some weeks before that the guardrails be raised.[21] The Lotus screamed down the guardrail into Hill's car, rode up and flipped.

Some of the crowd standing behind the guardrail vaulted over and with Hill organising them turned the car the right way up but getting Rindt out proved difficult. He was conscious although his face bled. He contented himself with an obscenity. Petrol ran everywhere – including down the gutters – and any cigarette end thrown carelessly by any member of the crowd would create an inferno. Hill stood on the car and hauled at the steering wheel, which had been forced down onto Rindt's lap. He prised it up enough for Rindt to be lifted out and placed on a stretcher.

Stewart of course had seen the aftermath of Hill's crash, seen Hill examining his Lotus. Stewart had seen the aftermath of Rindt's crash, Rindt trapped but at least moving. Stewart couldn't know if Hill was still examining his car when Rindt hammered into it. Now, as Stewart passed again, a marshal draw a finger across his throat. Why the marshal did this nobody knows, but Stewart drove the remainder of the race convinced Hill had been killed.

In hospital Rindt announced he'd finished with racing. He then asked Bernie Ecclestone, managing him: 'Did you get my start money?' and that gave Jackie Stewart his first laugh of the day.[22]

The next day noted Austrian journalist Heinz Prüller interviewed Rindt who could remember the crash in precise detail and explained that 'at the moment of impact one doesn't do anything.' You become detached, you become a spectator at your own misfortune. Rindt added that he'd always wondered what Jim Clark thought at that moment at Hockenheim and now he thought he knew. 'Nothing.'[23]

Rindt missed Monaco, where the aerofoils were banned. The car would now have more orthodox rear wings. Hill won for the fifth time, an absolute record until the little lad on the kart in São Paulo came along a generation later. An Englishman, Vic Elford, drove a Cooper but by now the company was troubled. They failed to find a big sponsor and didn't take part in another Grand Prix.

The Monaco measure: Hill, 80 laps, 1h 56m 59.4s, an average speed of 80.1mph; Hill, 1968, 77.8mph.

There's another measure, which is of a different kind of time. The 1960s live on as a self-contained era of great freedom the like of which ordinary people – suddenly with disposable incomes in their pocket – had never imagined before but motor racing moved along untouched by this. It did not reflect society, it reflected itself, the way it had always done. It continued from the 1950s to the 1970s on its own terms and at its own paces, existing constantly on the edge of change while being habitually resistant to change. Perhaps all life is so. It is true that girls in mini-skirts came to the races but they were everywhere, and hippy dressing, flower power, the first intoxication of the freedom did not reach to the drivers in hard hats searching out their own destinies. The big change to democratic values was coming but not quite yet.

Spa ought to have been next but the organisers and the GPDA could not agree on safety improvements, including a flexible start time in case of the usual bad weather. Stewart pointed out that apart from resurfacing and the elimination of one corner the circuit was the same as it had been in the 1930s. The Belgian government sealed the fate of the race when they insisted on unlimited cover for spectators at every sports event in the country and the insurers wouldn't touch the Grand Prix.

A mid-season ripple of races: Stewart won Holland, France and Britain, Ickx in a Brabham won Germany but with points counting from nine of the 11 rounds Stewart was virtually uncatchable. He'd been second at Nürburgring.

Stewart 51, Ickx 22, McLaren 21.

Stewart settled it at Monza and had only one moment of alarm when he ran over a hare and wondered if it had punctured a tyre. He kept an eye on the tyres for any sign of them changing shape. They didn't. In a great slip-streaming finish he got across the line 0.08 of a second before Rindt, 0.17 before Jean-Pierre Beltoise (Matra) and 0.19 before McLaren. The crowd came onto the track and invaded the pits. Stewart took refuge in a toilet and while the crowd hammered on its walls he sneaked out of the window at the back. On the podium his smile stretched so wide it might have been visible from Dumbuck. There, Stewart's mother still refused to accept Jackie was a racing driver. Brother Jimmy said to her *isn't that fantastic?* but she deflected that by asking what the weather was like.

Ickx won Canada and Rindt won Watkins Glen where Hill crashed, breaking both his legs.

Professor Watkins, who'd joined the medical team there in 1962, of course, remembers[24] that Hill was taken to Montour Falls hospital nearby and it was shut! He had to be taken to another one 40 or 50 miles away. Watkins recounted this as a graphic illustration of how far medical facilities have been improved since those days. It's a subject we shall be coming back to.

Hulme won Mexico City to round off the season.

Stewart was a very modern man in dress, appearance, presence and thinking, the first of the technocrats. He saw with clarity that the wholesale driver slaughter of the 1960s was no longer acceptable whatever anybody thought. He saw, too, that motor racing was beginning to draw to itself real money and the driver of yesterday might need to be the businessman of today. As a dyslexic he'd an astonishing spoken ability to distill situations into their simplicities after he'd thought them through. He understood there was serious money to be made from motor racing and joined IMG, an American company which promoted sportspeople. He understood the mechanisms of giving value for money to sponsors and was meticulous in preparation and delivery. He had this to such a degree that even as an individual he seemed to radiate his own corporate identity.

He was already firmly of the modern era in the sense that he offered himself for what he was, and it was done without guile. After all the mute people of the 1920s and '30s and the good chaps of the '50s and the subservient drivers of the early '60s, the articulator had come. Some would dismiss his message, some reject it but the logic demanded ultimate acceptance.

Chapman took the amateurism out of financing and running a team, Ecclestone would – soon enough – be taking the amateurism out of running the sport, Stewart was taking the amateurism out of being a driver.

Clark was an expression of romance in the Gallic soul, Stewart the perfect expression of Gallic pragmatism. Small wonder they were such close friends. Opposites attract.

The 1970 season belonged only to Jochen Rindt.

Matra and Tyrrell parted and Tyrrell went to a young British company, March, for a chassis. March had been founded the year before by among others Max Mosley, trained as a lawyer, and Robin Herd, who had designed cars at McLaren. Herd remembered 'we were full of the arrogance and naïveté of 25-year-olds and 29-year-olds, and had we not had that arrogance and naïveté – not knowing really what it's all about – we'd never have done it. It's actually a great advantage to have that.'

Mosley pointed out that in 1969 sometimes there'd only been 13 cars on the grid. 'If you had a car which was a Formula 1 car you could turn up and race. I mean, they'd pay you a little bit of money and you could have a go. There were only about six or seven even vaguely competitive cars. That all changed in 1970 when March came along and made so many cars.' He estimated that the company's first year budget was £113,000, and you'd have to multiply that by a factor of 200 to get a modern equivalent. (Note: the 1969 Ford Escort 1100 de Luxe cost £635, so the March budget was still a considerable amount of money.) March became popular very quickly and five of their cars lined up on the grid at the first race. The other main teams and main drivers:

Surtees (McLaren-Ford) – Surtees, Bell.
Ferrari – Ickx, Regazzoni.
Lotus (Lotus-Ford) – Rindt, Emerson Fittipaldi.
Walker (Lotus-Ford) – Hill.
McLaren (McLaren-Ford) – McLaren, Hulme.
Brabham (Brabham-Ford) – Brabham, Stommelen.
March (March-Ford) – Amon, Siffert.

There were others. Mario Andretti, looking astonishingly like The Fonz in the TV programme *Happy Days,* was in a March-Ford in the STP Corporation team.[25] Piers Courage, a wealthy Englishman, had a de Tomaso[26] run by Frank Williams, although the extent of Courage's wealth is open to question. For years, Williams had been a small-time operator surviving in the lesser formulae but became a 'presentable business' in the winter of 1967–68 when he 'found a small workshop, with a flat overhead, situated between a bingo hall and a pub at 361 Bath Road, Cippenham, near Slough.'[27] He and Courage went back a long way and now they'd go into Grand Prix racing.

And then there was Rindt. After the aerofoil collapse in Spain, he'd written to Chapman saying, in effect, he judged the Lotus unsafe and was losing confidence. Chapman thought his four-wheel-drive car was the way to go, and Rindt didn't. Approaching 1970, Rindt:

> had his choices. Brabham wanted him back, and Rindt was keen to return. Then there was March, in the process of being born. Jochen was in Robin Herd's mind from the start of the project, and at first was to be the team's only driver. When the new organisation showed signs of becoming unwieldy, however, he lost interest. And at the same time relations with Lotus began, by and by, to pick up. At the Nürburgring, Chapman and Rindt had a heart-to-heart, their first, and Colin promised Jochen a new two-wheel-drive car for 1970.[28]

Jack Brabham won South Africa, and Rindt had an engine failure. Stewart won Spain, and Rindt had an ignition problem. Rindt qualified on the fourth row at Monaco where a young, Swede, Ronnie Peterson, made his debut in a March. The received wisdom is that you can't win Monaco from row four and Rindt told his wife Nina he had no chance. She said: 'Don't be silly, you always have a chance' and Ecclestone, his manager, told him he had to keep going. 'Whatever you do, don't come into the pits – except on foot!'[29]

In the crowd sat a 15-year-old and his father, a furniture maker from a little-known town in central France. The Prosts were on a family holiday and this was just part of it, savouring what was available. Neither had any particular interest in motor racing beyond that and the teenager fully intended to become a footballer with St Etienne, his local big team. In the real world he'd probably follow his father and make furniture.

Stewart led from pole led to lap 27, Rindt by then sixth. Stewart's car suddenly started misfiring letting Brabham into the lead. Within a few laps Brabham estimated that lead as 'reasonable. I didn't really feel I had any problems after that.' Rindt was a man of moods, and nobody could predict which mood governed him at any given moment. Somewhere around half distance his mood changed and he launched a ferocious assault on Monaco. He hunted down Frenchman Henri Pescarolo (Matra-Simca), probed and prodded, and on lap 35 spectacularly outbraked him at the Gasworks hairpin.

Hulme was four seconds ahead, the gearbox on Hulme's McLaren misbehaving to the point where he had to hold first gear in. Rindt swept by on lap 40. Amon was 13 seconds ahead but fast and in twenty laps Rindt could only taken a couple of seconds out of him. Then Amon's suspension failed.

Brabham was 13 seconds ahead but felt with 29 laps left he had the situation under control. At lap 70 of the 80 he still led by 11 seconds and at the rate they were going Rindt wouldn't catch him. Rindt left his 'braking even later; the wheels locked; the front tyres smoked and screeched like they do in a touring car race.'[30] Rindt felt he'd never driven better and only once as fast.

With five laps to go he had the gap down to nine seconds and Brabham had a 'shocking run' of back-markers: he did lap 77 in 1m 29.3s, Rindt 1m 24.7s. Brabham came upon Siffert in the middle of the track after *Ste Devote* zigzagging the March because he'd run out of petrol and was trying to flush the dregs into re-starting the engine. Brabham had to wait until Siffert saw him. 'The flag marshals were going mad.' Brabham rode the pavement to go by.[31]

Into the last lap the gap was slightly over one second but even that should have been enough for Brabham. His shocking run went on. At the Tobacconist's corner he found three back-markers ambling forward and realised that in getting through them he'd be clearing the track for Rindt to get through them, too. The third of those back markers was Courage and Brabham reached him approaching the Gasworks hairpin. For an instant Brabham asked himself *take him on the inside or take him on the outside?* The instant took him beyond his braking point and with a little sand on the circuit he skated into the straw bales.

The Clerk of the Course, waiting on the finishing line out of sight, was so astonished to see Rindt coming and not Brabham that he forgot to drop the flag...

The Prosts had had a memorable day out, nothing more.

Now Rindt is holding the winner's silver bowl so slackly that it nestles limp against his waist. A vast garland encircles his neck and trails down so far that its fronds partially camouflage the bowl. Prince Rainier, a man of considerable and studious dignity, is positioned next to Rindt having just presented him with the bowl. Rainier's right hand clasps the tiny paw of a sweet five-year-old girl wearing a navy blue jacket all buttoned up and a pleated white skirt, her left hand is clasped by her mother, Princess Grace, who has simultaneously arranged herself to face the cameras. Always there would be cameras, particularly at moments like this. She had spent a lifetime knowing it and knowing how to arrange herself for them. The temporal smile remains immortally beautiful. And bless the little girl, she yawned. She would grow inevitably into a celebrity in her own right, a singer of pop songs, a model of fashions, a leggy creature of the Euro-culture of the born-rich trying to find themselves – members of the ancient House of Grimaldi would never do that, sing pop songs.[32]

She was called Stephanie and she would come to know Alain Prost well.

The Monaco measure: Rindt, 80 laps, 1h 54m 36.6s, an average speed of 81.8mph; Hill, 1969, 80.1mph.

On 2 June, Bruce McLaren was killed testing a Can-Am car at Goodwood. Any death in motor racing is shocking but this more so because of his renown as a safe driver. His legacy would be his name. The team which bore it did not contest the next race, the Belgian at Spa, out of respect, but returned at Holland and from then on began a growth which across three decades made them more successful even than Lotus.

Spa had been altered with Armco added at strategic points and a chicane at *Malmédy* to slow the cars. Rodriguez in a BRM won it from Amon by 1.1 seconds.

Tyrrell had a vacancy because Servoz-Gavin retired after Monaco where he didn't qualify and didn't seem to want to qualify. Elf, sponsoring Tyrrell, said they'd like another French driver and suggested François Cevert. Tyrrell knew a little about him and said he'd watch him in a Formula 2 race at Crystal Palace. After it they met and Tyrrell said he'd be in touch.

Cevert waited in his Paris flat day after day for the call and didn't venture out in case he missed it. He happened to be in the bath when the phone rang so his beautiful girlfriend answered. She knew nothing about motorsport and said it was someone called '*Tearelle*'. Cevert sprang out of the bath and stark naked grabbed the receiver.

He drove in the Dutch Grand Prix at Zandvoort.

On lap 23 of that race Courage crashed his de Tomaso in a 140mph corner. It scythed down 300 yards of wire fence, went into a sand dune which cut its speed from 130 to 25mph in three feet[33] and exploded in a fireball. Courage died immediately. Rindt won the race and found no comfort in that. Stewart, second, realised the death hit Frank Williams very, very hard and made sure Williams stayed with him 'all the time'. Rindt stood sombre on the podium, the garland round his neck, hands down by his sides and his craggy, hewn face dipped downwards.

Rindt won France at Clermont-Ferrand – some twisting sections protected by Armco, the rest a pastoral and unprotected run through the countryside – and won the British at Brands Hatch. There a Brazilian, Emerson Fittipaldi, made his debut. Fittipaldi had been testing a lot of Lotuses for the Components division of the company – not the Formula 1 cars, of course – at the Hethel test track which Chapman could see from his office. Evidently Chapman always carried a stopwatch, secretly timed Fittipaldi and invited him to test the Formula 1 car at Silverstone. When Fittipaldi came in after a fast lap he saw Chapman smiling and he knew.

Frank Williams approached him but Fittipaldi felt his career needed Lotus and he signed a contract. He went to Brands Hatch fully aware of all the things he did not know. He qualified on the last row and during the race 'had quite a good dice' with Cevert before finishing eighth nursing a gearbox problem.

Rindt won the German Grand Prix, run for the first time at Hockenheim because the drivers demanded certain safety improvements to the Nürburgring and the organisers wouldn't make them. Hockenheim was flat, it was a corridor through the tall, dark trees, it was a contorting complex before the pits, it was a saucer of stone-clad grandstands – and very, very fast despite the addition of two chicanes. It was clad in Armco, which it hadn't been when Clark crashed in 1968. Rindt averaged 124mph. Chapman didn't throw his cap in the air to celebrate – for once he wasn't wearing one – but as Rindt approached the line he raised both arms and threw his whole body in the air instead still waving his right hand, landed and *still* waved his arm, fist tightened – *yes! Yes! Yes!* Ickx in the Ferrari was 0.7 of a second behind.

Rindt's engine failed in Austria and Ickx won it. He went to Monza with 45 points and four races left. Brabham had 25, Ickx 19. Rindt could take the championship here and his mind was on that as a means of raising money to start a business. On the Friday he ran the Lotus without its triple rear wing and found it much faster, no downforce dragging him back, although when the wings were taken off the number 2 driver's car (John Miles) he found it twitching 'all over the place' and asked for them to be re-fitted.

The Lotus team had dinner on the Friday night and Warr remembered 'Jochen was telling everybody about his plans for using his name to build up a sports clothes company.' The conversation, however, kept coming back to the car and the question of wings.

On the Saturday, Rindt went out without the wings again. He moved into his fifth lap and Hulme, following, saw the Lotus snake in the braking area for the Parabolica then corkscrew hard left into the crash barrier. The car hit that with massive ferocity, ran down it, lifted the barrier out of the ground and went under it. The right wheel struck a substantial post. Warr said this post carried...

a public address loudspeaker, and [was] therefore somewhat stronger and heavier than the others. As a result, this tore the front bulkhead off the car, together with the suspension and the steering. The steering wheel itself was prised through the instrument panel and it was this that had torn the front bulkhead out of the car. Because he refused to wear the crotch straps of his seat harness, Jochen was forced down into the cockpit with his feet tangled up with the pedals and, in the process, his throat was cut by the harness.

My own feeling is that, considering the no-downforce configuration, he started to go quickly much too soon. Denny Hulme, who was actually behind him when the accident happened, said he couldn't believe it when he went past him. I believe that he was caught out because the tyres had not warmed up and the aerodynamic and brake balance was miles out due to having no rear wing. On the previous day they had been very slow to warm up. Also the Monza circuit then consisted almost entirely of right-hand corners, so the left-hand tyres would be the first to warm up. I think that the first time he hit the brakes really hard the car became totally out of balance and that was when the accident happened.[34]

Hulme went past his own pit and stopped at Lotus to tell Chapman and Ecclestone. Ecclestone set off running and when he reached the scene Rindt had been taken out of the car. Ecclestone picked up the white helmet, a shoe and, across at the far side of the track, a wheel.

People were trying to comfort Nina Rindt, assure her Jochen only had a broken foot. A priest came from the ambulance and murmured: 'Courage, Mrs Rindt.' There was nothing else to say.

Lotus withdrew.

There was an Italian Grand Prix and the Swiss Clay Regazzoni won it in a Ferrari, Stewart second. Ickx won Canada and, with the United States and Mexico left, could take the championship from Rindt. He needed to finish second at Watkins Glen but the Ferrari developed an oil leak and the pit stop for repairs lasted a long time. Ickx felt great relief. He'd not be taking the championship from a dead man.

Fittipaldi won in the Lotus – only his fourth Grand Prix – and when Ickx won Mexico two weeks later it didn't matter a damn.

Stewart, now at the summit of his powers, plundered 1971. Andretti won South Africa in a Ferrari but Stewart took Spain. He had pole at Monaco although in a wet qualifying Andretti didn't get into the race. Stewart led every lap, set fastest lap, beat Peterson (March) by 25.6 seconds.

The Monaco measure: Stewart, 80 laps, 1h 52m 21.3s, an average speed of 83.4mph; Rindt, 1970, 81.8mph.

Ickx took Holland, a wet race where Stewart was hampered by tyres, but Stewart took France at Paul Ricard – the 14th staging post – from pole. He led all 55 laps and set fastest lap along the way. Ricard, lost in the hills in the hinterland behind Marseille and Toulon, became a permanent home for the race and that lasted 14 years. It was a curious place, bleached by the Mediterranean sun, inaccessible because the approach roads were so narrow and tortuous yet not unpopular. Built by the drinks magnate whose name it bore it was modern in concept and facilities and featured a long straight called the Mistral after the wind which blows down the Rhône Valley. On the Mistral, Grand Prix cars were able to attain their absolute maximum speed. Because of the benevolent weather the circuit also became a stalwart for testing.

Ricard was significant for another reason. Slick tyres – ungrooved and giving enormous adhesion – were introduced for the first time.

A week after Ricard, Rodriguez was killed in a sports car race in Germany.

A mid-season ripple of races: Stewart won Britain and Germany although Siffert had pole from him in Austria.

A toothy young local of good breeding and completely crazy about motor racing sneaked a March-Ford onto the last row. Niki Lauda thoroughly enjoyed his schooldays because he took particular care 'not to let education get in the way [...] particularly once I reached twelve or so and started taking a real interest in cars.'[35] Siffert won from Fittipaldi (Stewart had a mechanical failure).

Peter Gethin, a perceptive and forceful Englishman, won the ultimate slip-streaming finish at Monza, Hailwood came back to car racing with the Surtees team and Stewart's engine failed. The Monza result is worth setting out because nothing like it was ever seen again anywhere.

Gethin	1h 18m 12.60s
Peterson	@ 0.01
Cevert	@ 0.09
Hailwood	@ 0.18
Ganley[36]	@ 0.61

Canada was wet and Stewart won it from Peterson after a long, tense duel which ended after thirty laps when a back-marker 'pushed' Peterson off the track. 'The engine in the March stopped and it took 14 seconds as long as hours before it started again. The car had also got a smashed nose in the hard contact with mother earth and wouldn't go straight forward.'[37]

Cevert won Watkins Glen, and it was described[38] as 'ringing out in France like a thunderclap. A bridge is thrown across time. Never, since Maurice Trintignant, victorious at Monaco in 1958, has a French driver 'lifted' a Grand Prix in the World Championship.' Cevert, of the angelic looks and captivating personality, seemed to be the future. Stewart thought so and groomed him for it. Stewart would remember particularly Cevert's light blue eyes and how deep they seemed, how he reminded Stewart of a fighting cock.

That winter Bernie Ecclestone bought the Brabham team. Whatever attention it attracted at the time, and beyond the Grand Prix racing fraternity and the specialist press, that may not have been much, it was arguably the most significant development in the sport since the war.

By 1972 sponsorship came in like a tide, Lotus in black and gold John Player Special livery, BRM in Marlboro red and white, and so on. The driver line-up remained essentially the same.

Argentina came back to the calendar after twelve years and a cattle rancher's son prepared to stun the Grand Prix community. Carlos Reutemann had been racing for seven years, mostly in saloon cars before sponsorship took him to Europe where he'd done well in Formula 2. Now with a quarter of an hour of practice left he took a Brabham-Ford round the 2.07 miles in 1m 12.46s to pole, a whisker faster than Stewart (1m 12.68s).

Stewart led but Reutemann pressured him for seven laps before falling back and Stewart won it from Hulme. Maybe it was going to be another of those seasons, especially when Stewart took pole in South Africa but his gearbox failed and Hulme won it from Fittipaldi.

Something stirred in the background during South Africa. FICA [the Formula 1 Constructors' Association] had for years done 'little more than oversee the co-ordination of transportation costs, particularly to transcontinental Grands Prix. It was a benign, low-key and loosely grouped organisation of no serious political intent.'[39] Ecclestone, as owner of Brabham, had become a member.

F1CA met at Kyalami and Ecclestone said how much money he could save on transportation. The teams, living in relative penury despite the sponsorship, agreed immediately. As payment for organising this Ecclestone would receive 2 per cent of the prize money – and he'd negotiate that prize money with the circuit organisers, something done race by race. In those days, when prize money wasn't great, 2 per cent may not have seemed much and, anyway, if Ecclestone negotiated bigger sums he was welcome to 2 per cent of them. The team owners were racing people who thought about racing and mostly only racing. The last thing they wanted was cutting deals about transportation or tackling circuit negotiations.

A central position was vacant and Ecclestone moved himself into it for two reasons: nobody else saw its enormous potential and, even if they had, nobody else wanted it. Ecclestone took the first step towards rationalising and modernising Grand Prix racing, and making himself one of the richest men in Britain.

When the European season began in Spain two months after Kyalami, Fittipaldi opened everything up. Ickx took pole but Hulme led a wet race from Stewart, Regazzoni third, Ickx fourth, Fittipaldi fifth. Hulme had a gearbox problem so that on lap five Stewart went through, Fittipaldi fourth. Next lap Hulme drifted back and Fittipaldi overtook Ickx. Now he was power-sliding the Lotus and on lap nine took a lead he didn't lose. He beat Ickx by more than 18 seconds.

Monaco measured the changes already in motion. A boycott was threatened when 'the organisers attempted to wriggle out of moving the pit area which had been one of the most dangerous parts of any race track in the world, openly inviting an accident which would have wiped out most of the Grand Prix entrants, team managers, mechanics, technicians, press and hangers-on. It was eventually moved from the narrow strip of road before the Gasworks hairpin to after the tunnel, which in turn meant moving the equally notorious chicane further down the road on the harbour front.'[40]

A further measure involved the number of cars in the race and it became a confrontation. In hindsight this was always going to be inevitable because F1CA challenged aspects of the *CSI*'s control.

The year before, 18 cars started. Now the organisers, the *Automobile Club de Monaco*, cut that to 16. Ecclestone and Max Mosley had met the newly-appointed president of the Club, Michel Boeri, during the Spanish Grand

Prix and he said he couldn't see any reason why 26 shouldn't start rather than 16. The teams travelled to Monaco on that assumption but when they arrived they discovered the *ACM*, probably encouraged by the *CSI*, had arbitrarily cut the 26 to 22, a 'political salvo'.[41] The teams met and issued an ultimatum, *26 cars or no cars*. The *ACM* responded by having the gates of the underground car park where the cars were, securely locked – the mechanics working on them didn't take that well – and patrolled by policemen. The teams responded by saying they wouldn't take part in the practice session, due to start immediately, even if the cars were released.

Boeri tried to be diplomatic, saying it could all be resolved after the session, but Ecclestone wasn't having any of that and a firm agreement was reached: *26* (in fact *25*, the full entry). The psychological impact of this clear victory for Ecclestone and the teams began a process of changing the power structure. It would last a decade and culminate in open civil war.

On race day at Monaco it rained and typically Hailwood (Surtees-Ford) said he might as well not bother going out. Smiling his broad smile he explained, almost giggling, that he was 'hopeless' in the wet and the best crasher there was.

Beltoise in a BRM seized his moment from the second row leading up the hill to Casino although round *Ste Devote* the whole car twitched. He rode the storm perfectly and at one point, lapping a slower car as Station hairpin was blocked and simply nudged the car – a Surtees – out of the way. Those in Beltoise's wake saw only ghostly outlines of cars around them in the rolling, dense spray. They floundered to such an extent that Ickx, renowned in the wet, finished 38 seconds behind him. Fittipaldi, third – he'd been up the escape road a time or two – disliked the whole thing so intensely that he wouldn't even speak to his biographer about it and kept changing the subject.[42]

The Monaco measure: Beltoise, 80 laps, 2h 26m 54.7s, an average speed of 63.8mph – but very wet; Stewart, 1971, 83.4mph.

Fittipaldi won the Belgian at Nivelles – a straightforward, 'flat and unpopular'[43] replacement for Spa, now considered too fast and dangerous – from pole.

A week later Bonnier, safety campaigner and president of the GPDA, was killed at Le Mans. His car vaulted a barrier and went in to trees. He died in a helicopter on the way to hospital. He'd been competing for 24 years and decided to retire at the end of the season to avoid further danger. 'Few people really came to know the remote, authoritative figure of Jo Bonnier, almost aristocratic with his military bearing and imposing beard. Those few who he elected to befriend found him utterly charming.'[44]

Stewart, who'd had an ulcer, won France at Clermont-Ferrand, Fittipaldi 27 seconds behind him. The Dutch Grand Prix had been cancelled because of safety concerns and Clermont-Ferrand only got their race because they'd installed double guardrails round virtually all the circuit.

Fittipaldi 34 points, Stewart 21, Hulme 19 and Ickx 16 – a driver's ten best finishes of the 12 rounds counted.

Ickx took pole at Brands Hatch but the Lotus felt so strong on full tanks that Fittipaldi didn't mind. In fact the Ferrari was nimble and fast round the undulations of the circuit and Ickx led while Fittipaldi missed a gear, letting Stewart pounce; and Stewart missed a gear, letting Fittipaldi pounce. Hill crashed while he was being lapped and said laconically: 'From a gentleman to a twit in a tenth of a second.' Ickx dropped out with an oil leak, Fittipaldi held on and won it by four seconds.

The Nürburgring disturbed the balance. Ickx led again and Fittipaldi needed five laps to get into second place. As he passed the pits he saw a commotion going on but he didn't know it was for him. Just round the South Loop, where the circuit moved out into the country, he glanced in his mirror and noticed that the Lotus was on fire. Fittipaldi emerged from it fast and he had a consolation because Regazzoni drifted wide in a corner, he and Stewart were side-by-side and Stewart slid into a guardrail. He finished a lap down and out of the points.

Austria, which Fittipaldi won from Hulme – Stewart seventh, with oversteer – set up Monza as the decider. Fittipaldi had 52 points, Stewart 27 and in real terms if Stewart didn't win there he'd lost the championship.

Monza had been slowed by two chicanes to break up the slip-streaming, the first just after the pits, the second by the Curva del Vialone, although they'd been constructed on the existing track simply narrowing it through the chicanes. Fittipaldi found them 'too narrow, stupid. I don't know why they did it that way.'[45] Even so he preferred it to the slip-streaming.

The chicanes did provide a sort of excitement on the Friday as the drivers tried to learn them. Fittipaldi got a tow behind Ickx, watched his braking points and in general assessed what the Ferrari was doing. Stewart went quickest but next day Ickx took pole from Amon (Matra-Simca), Stewart on the second row, Fittipaldi on the third. The handling wasn't right and Fittipaldi hadn't improved his Friday time.

It rained on the Sunday, dried. Fittipaldi was out-dragged by both Ferraris at the start but Stewart's Tyrrell had a clutch failure, the championship quite suddenly over. It happens. Fittipaldi chased Ickx and with 20 laps to go began to catch him. He had no need to do that but decided to become champion as a champion would by winning the race. He nursed his tyres for a final effort, estimating that they'd be good for four or five laps. He drew up and Ickx suddenly raised his arm. The Ferrari's electrics had failed. It happens, too.

At 25 years, 8 months and 29 days Fittipaldi was the youngest champion of all – so young that, when he'd been a karter in São Paulo, Ickx was his hero and he'd even painted the name on one of his kart engines. As he crossed the line Chapman had a cap, circled his right arm three times building up momentum and then launched it into orbit.

The celebrations and duties done, at 1 o'clock next morning Fittipaldi drove his Mercedes back to his home in Switzerland. He had a shower then he and his wife put cushions all over the telephone so he'd get some sleep when it started ringing early that same morning, as it would. He didn't take it off the hook for the simplest of reasons, as he explained himself. If you do that in Switzerland, they 'cut you off completely.'

Racing drivers notice details like that.

Stewart won Canada and Watkins Glen, Cevert second there. 'It was an excellent augury for the future. And of the podium at Watkins Glen, a marvellous image would remain: Helen and Jackie Stewart, Ken Tyrrell, François Cevert smiling hugely. Certainly, the garland which Stewart wore wasn't that of World Champion. But the Scot is a man with his mind at ease: he knows that a new stage in the progression of Cevert has begun.'[46]

At Watkins Glen a very self-confident young South Africa, Jody Scheckter, made his debut in a McLaren. He'd raced karts, motor bikes and a home-built Renault before arriving in England in 1971. He found it 'old, cold and grey' but now here he was at a Grand Prix, and he'd describe it with particular eloquence. He...

spent a lot of time just wandering round, soaking up the atmosphere. Hardly anybody knew who I was, so I could just put on my anorak and join the crowds without any of the hassle that most of the other drivers were getting. Denny [Hulme] kept a pretty close watch on me, introducing me to all his chums, and warning me all the time against talking to the Press, which seemed to be a particular phobia of his at the time.

My first five laps of practice very nearly convinced me that I should have stayed in Formula 2. At one stage, François Cevert passed me in his Tyrrell, and I remember thinking as he disappeared into the distance 'Christ, this is just no good for me – I'm definitely out of my depth in this game.' I went

> back to the pits and just sat in the car for a while, trying to think it all through and mentally adjust to what I had to do before trying another ten or twelve laps. I then reached the point where I could take the Esses flat out, and when I talked it over with Denny, I discovered that he was still lifting off slightly at that spot, although his lap times were about a second and a half quicker than mine. I think that really gave me the confidence I needed to have another go at cutting my times and after about thirty laps I found that it was suddenly becoming more comfortable.[47]

Scheckter qualified on the third row and ran third but rain fell. He spun, and finished a lap down.

Ecclestone negotiated agreements with individual organisers and in 1973, for the first time, the calendar had 15 races. More than that, from Belgium onwards, the cars retained the same numbers for all the races, and from here on the defending champion carried number 1. It was assuming its modern shape.

The roundabout: Peterson came to Lotus to join Fittipaldi; Scheckter would do five races with McLaren. With some backing from Marlboro Frank Williams entered cars under the name Iso[48] Marlboro for Ganley, Pescarolo and Italian Nanni Galli. Williams understood struggle because he had known virtually nothing else and the struggle continued. Financially deprived, the team managed only two points.

Fittipaldi began his championship defence at Argentina and on his own estimation ten thousand Brazilians travelled down to Buenos Aires to watch. That created pressure. The weather, steaming hot, created another. Rumours that a driver would be kidnapped by 'political gangsters' and the attendant security created a third. Cevert made a thrusting start to lead and Fittipaldi began a frustrating struggle to overtake Stewart for second place.

Fittipaldi selected the hairpin just after a fast right-hander to despatch Stewart and planned to slipstream Stewart into the right-hander and go past, making Stewart follow him through the hairpin. The Lotus became unstable whenever he got close to Stewart and lap after lap he followed him, sometimes brandishing a fist to say *you're holding me up!* He did get through on lap 76 when he decided to brake as late as humanly possible in the right-hander. Once past Stewart he set off towards Cevert and, working the Lotus very hard, caught him but couldn't get past at the same place because someone had dropped oil, forcing all the cars to take an inside line. For ten laps Cevert resisted but into the hairpin Fittipaldi drew up, forced the Lotus alongside – two wheels on the grass – and went through. He won by 4.69 seconds and judged because the front-running cars were so evenly matched that this was the most difficult race of his career.[49]

The Brazilian Grand Prix came on to the calendar and was run at Interlagos, São Paulo. On one of the practice days, Fittipaldi remembered, 'a boy is brought to see me by his father, a young Brazilian, and it is Ayrton.'

Race day was hot and sections of the large crowd used the fire engines and firemen as target practice for bottle throwing, and a fire engine turned its hose full on them. They adored the shower. Bare from the midriff up, the young men in the crowd danced up and down, waved their arms to the hoses *drench us again, it's beautiful!* Other sections began throwing bottles. *Hey, come and hose us down, too!* Fittipaldi won again from Stewart. That gave him 18 points, Stewart 10 and implied a two-pronged championship. Chapman only sent the black cap into low orbit. When Fittipaldi emerged from the car Chapman embraced him and said 'great!' Someone behind Fittipaldi tried to put a cap with a brand name on Fittipaldi's head. *No way,* Chapman said, and whipped it off him. The age of protecting your sponsor's image had come.

In South Africa three weeks after that, Regazzoni's BRM was involved in a multiple-crash on the third lap and burst into flames, Regazzoni trapped. Hailwood's Surtees was also on fire. Hailwood remembered that Dave Charlton, a South African, 'lost it on the first corner and I hit him. Consequently I spun and stalled in the middle of the track. Regazzoni came round, hit my car and the whole thing burst into flames. We disappeared to the edge of the track. I pressed my fire extinguisher and put my fire out, got out of my car and looked. Regga was unconscious in the car.' Hailwood went over, plunged his hands down and undid the seat belts. Hailwood tried to haul him out through the flames but it took five marshals to do that. Hailwood returned to the pits, said to his wife Pauline 'We're off' and they rode back to a friend's house on a motor bike. Pauline could see from his face that something had happened but he didn't say anything. She learnt about it when she saw the newspapers next morning.

Stewart won, Fittipaldi third.

When Fittipaldi took Spain from Cevert (Stewart's brakes failed) the championship looked to be tilting.

Fittipaldi 31, Stewart 19.

Warr felt that Fittipaldi, defending champion, was:

now assuming the attitude consistent with that high office. He was no longer the 'tiger' he had been when he first joined the team. Ronnie, on the other hand, was every man's dream of a 'racer.' He just breathed, walked

and talked motor racing the whole time. He was a marvellous guy to work
with, the only difficulty being that he was so good he was able to 'drive
around' any problems which arose with the car!

   We very quickly ran into a problem of a different sort when everywhere
we went Ronnie demonstrated that he was basically quicker than
Emerson. In some places he was staggeringly quicker, like at Barcelona
where he was 1.7 sec faster in practice than anybody else in the field, and
1.9 sec faster than his team-mate![50]

Peterson's problem was that his car kept breaking down and Fittipaldi's
didn't. Peterson took pole at Zolder but had a crash during the race and
Stewart won it from Cevert, Fittipaldi third. By now a great question had
been born: what happens when Peterson's car goes the distance?

   Monaco had been modified, the new tunnel in use. Stewart took pole
from Peterson (1m 27.5s against 1m 27.7s) while a blond, gangling ex-
public schoolboy put a Hesketh on the ninth row. James Hunt ought to
have been a medical student in the ordinary middle class way but chose
to race cars – who needs money? – instead. He was hired by Lord
Alexander Hesketh who'd formed a racing team to occupy the weekends
and concluded that rather than run at the back of Formula 2 grids it
would be much more fun to run at the back of Formula 1 grids. The
ensemble conformed to what a British pre-war team looked like, almost
a caricature of itself – the co-founder nicknamed Anthony 'Bubbles'
Horsley and everyone else had a nickname, too. They called Hunt
'Superstar' and the designer, Dr Harvey Postlethwaite, 'the Doc.'
Hesketh's mother, one eye in a patch, sold memorabilia from a stall at
Monaco quite naturally. You had to look hard underneath the bubbles to
see serious men at work, but they were.

   Peterson finished third behind Stewart and Fittipaldi, Hunt running
sixth when, with five laps to go, the engine failed.

   *The Monaco measure: Stewart, 78 laps, 1h 57m 44.3s, an average speed of
   80.9mph; Beltoise, 1972, 63.8mph – wet.*

   Peterson's moment seemed to have come at Anderstorp, the flat
Swedish circuit being used for the first time. From pole, and despite
feeling nervous, he led 78 of the 80 laps but a slow puncture let Hulme by.

   In France – Paul Ricard – the Lotus did hold together although on the
last lap Peterson 'heard the most peculiar noises from the engine and the
gearbox and for a while I thought the whole thing would fall apart.'[51]
Hunt, sixth, had his first Grand Prix point.

   Scheckter qualified on the third row for the British Grand Prix at
Silverstone and a soft-spoken, shy Ulsterman, John Watson, put a

Brabham-Ford on the ninth. It was the era of 'trendy' long hair. Stewart sat contemplating the race, his hair cascading down to his shoulders. Fittipaldi might have been wearing a thatch as he joked with Chapman on the grid – Chapman's hair a thicket of descending curls. Graham Hill stood like a Roman emperor, his face framed by his hair. Hunt's looked like a haystack after a storm. Somehow, in a process of unconscious and inexplicable osmosis, this suited the cars with their high airboxes set on curving, conical bodywork behind the driver. They were not unlike periscopes.

Scheckter was 'trying to make up places' when the race began, Stewart slicing past Peterson at Becketts for the lead. At Club Corner Stewart still led, his Tyrrell nicely balanced, Peterson chasing him. Approaching Woodcote Corner at 150mph Scheckter, now up to fourth, felt the McLaren get 'out of shape and run wide.' He 'couldn't avoid getting onto the grass on the outside of the corner, which spun the McLaren round and shot it back across the track into the pit wall, right in front of the bulk of the field.'[52]

The McLaren came from the pit wall backwards. One car went by, another as it came. A piece of bodywork was flung from the McLaren. Two more cars went by and the McLaren came to rest mid-track and across the track, Scheckter waving his arm, *miss me, miss me*. A gaggle of cars approached, some spearing round to one side of him, some to the other but one struck him a terrible blow.

Like a bomb burst, nine cars crashed and thrashed all across the track. Marshals and helpers ran frantically into the debris – scattered everywhere – but only one driver suffered real injury, breaking his ankle At the restart Peterson led again but American Peter Revson (McLaren) went through on lap 39 and won it. On the podium he quaffed champagne and shook the remainder all over the crowd. He wore an anorak, collar turned up, and a cap so you couldn't quite see his hair descending into kiss-curls at the back – but they were there...

Peterson was now driving the Lotus very, very fast. He took pole at Zandvoort and led but on lap eight the March of Roger Williamson, an affable and popular man from Leicester, went into the guardrail at a high speed corner – maybe puncture, maybe suspension failure. The guardrail bent backwards and that launched the car. It ran along the guardrail and was flung back across the track where it landed upside down on fire. David Purley, another Englishman, an adventurer and close friend of Williamson, stopped his car and ran to help.

A nightmare began. Purley tried to right the March but lacked the strength and marshals and firemen concentrated on pulling him away several times rather than helping Williamson. At this point the fire was small. Purley was quoted as saying he had to 'hit' one man holding a fire-extinguisher in order to get hold of it to try to do something himself. Because the race was being televised live many millions of people saw this. Spectators tried to help but police with dogs drove them back and all at once fire consumed the car.

Drivers passing the start-finish line signalled wildly for officials to stop the race and at one point Hulme drove close to the pit wall shaking his fist at them. The race continued and the millions on television watched incredulous as racing cars passed the inferno. The fire finally extinguished, the car was righted and a simple sheet laid over it, Williamson still inside.

Lauda was distressed that, afterwards, people who'd watched said he – Lauda – was 'ruthless', indifferent to the fate of a fellow driver. Lauda would explain that from a passing cockpit it looked as if the driver – Williamson – was trying to put out the fire. You simply couldn't tell, going past at speed, it was Purley trying to save Williamson. Lauda added that for the rest of his life he'd remember the 'crumpled figure' of Tom Wheatcroft – Donington owner, friend and backer of Williamson – 'tears streaming down his cheeks.'

Lauda described how many factors merged to create what had happened and he hammered out a list of them: 'woefully inadequate track marshals, cowardice, confusion, incompetent race administration, and drivers who totally misinterpreted the evidence of their own eyes.'[53]

Stewart won the race from Cevert, Hunt third.

A mid-season ripple of races: Stewart won Germany, Peterson won Austria but with Stewart second.

Stewart 66, Fittipaldi 42, Peterson 34.

There were internal strains at Lotus and they were about to tear at the fabric of the team. Because Fittipaldi had made such a strong start to the season Peterson would defer to him in order to secure the championship. In Austria Peterson gave the lead to him but Fittipaldi broke down.

At Monza Stewart had a puncture early on – a nail through the tyre – and the pit stop made him 20th. Classically he worked a path back through the field so that by lap 49 he ran fourth but by now Lotus had to make a decision. Peterson, pole, led with Fittipaldi behind him.

As Warr explained to Chapman, if Peterson – still in with a remote chance of the championship himself – had given this race to Fittipaldi he'd then have to give him the last two, Canada and the United States, to catch Stewart. On top of that, there'd been an original agreement about their national Grands Prix, Fittipaldi to win Brazil (Peterson helping him) and Peterson to win Sweden (Fittipaldi helping him). By the end of Watkins Glen, Peterson would have 'gifted' Fittipaldi a third of the whole calendar.

Chapman let the race unfold by itself. Peterson would say:

> Colin had asked me before the start if I would let Emerson past and I said yes. When I saw the signs from the pits that Jackie had come up to a fourth place after his run into the pits I just sat and waited for a sign to let Emerson past, but it never came. I thought that Emerson had lost the fight, but I had made a little miscalculation. There was still a chance for him [...] but nothing happened so we just drove and drove.[54]

Stewart, fourth, had his third championship and Fittipaldi was so angry he decided to leave Lotus.

Ferrari had had a terrible season. That autumn, Enzo Ferrari invited Lauda to test the car at the company's Fiorano track and give his impressions of it. Because Lauda did not then speak Italian Ferrari's son Piero translated.

Ferrari asked Lauda what he thought of the car.

A disaster, Lauda said.

Piero: 'You can't say that.'

Lauda: 'Why not? The car understeers and doesn't corner worth a damn. It's undriveable.'

Piero: 'No, you can't say that either.'[55]

Ferrari challenged Lauda to come back in a week and make the car go a second faster, which Lauda did...

In Canada, Scheckter and Cevert crashed, Cevert so incensed that he made for Scheckter and indulged in a boxing match before officials separated them. Because a breakdown truck went to the scene, for the first time a pace car came out and was supposed to position itself in front of the leader, the others forming an orderly queue behind – but there'd been a host of pit stops, and who was in the lead? More pit stops followed, the pace car pulled off and even when the race finished nobody was sure. Somebody suggested it should be given to Hunt – Hesketh would throw the best party...

The result wasn't announced until late in the evening, Revson from Fittipaldi.

The weather was fine at Watkins Glen for Saturday morning practice. Helen Stewart took her place with her stopwatch and towards the end of the session Cevert, preparing to go out again – he'd already set fourth fastest time – blew her a kiss before flipping his visor down. He went out. In the ferociously fast uphill Esses before the straight the Tyrrell swerved into the guardrail seemingly without reason and was flung across to the guardrail on the other side. Several drivers stopped including Stewart. Cevert had not been taken from the car because, as Stewart remembered, he was so obviously dead.

Word reached the pits. Warr of Lotus went urgently towards Chapman saying 'Cevert'. Chapman asked how bad it was. 'Very bad,' Warr said. Chapman turned towards the Tyrrell pits and murmured to himself 'bloody hell.' A camera tracked him but now he turned from that and walked along the pit lane. Suddenly he exhaled: a long, deep, profound sound which was for Cevert and all of them down these long, deadly years.

John Watson, an Ulsterman, was in his second Grand Prix, driving for Brabham.

> Bernie entered three cars and I was in the third. In practice Cevert was killed – a very unpleasant high speed accident, car just fell apart and he was…mutilated, let's put it that way. Jody Scheckter saw it all and that affected Jody a great deal, it made a seminal moment in his life.
>
> Suddenly there was this silence – the death silence – and you're into respect for a colleague. François was a very nice man. I knew him a little bit and talked to him. He was just one of those people who was a lovely guy. And suddenly he's dead. Anyway after a couple of hours the circuit was cleared up, the barriers replaced and the session continued. I was sitting there and Bernie said: 'What are you doing?' I'm already in the race and it's not right to go out, is it? He said: 'Let me tell you something. What's happened has happened, it's history now, François is not with us, he's dead. Up until that milli milli second when he had his accident he was doing the thing he wanted more than anything else and enjoying it at a level which only you guys understand. So don't feel you have to sit here out of respect for him. It's got nothing to do with that. You're a racing driver, he's a racing driver, he's dead, that's sad, go out and do your job.'
>
> I used that for the rest of my career and still do in a motor racing context. If you wanted to call it a mantra, it was my mantra.[56]

Tyrrell withdrew and that night in the hotel Stewart told Helen his career had ended. Shortly after that he announced it publicly. He'd been planning to do it anyway, pass the mantle on to Cevert.

Ten days after Watkins Glen the Arab oil states announced a 70 per cent increase in prices and a reduction in output as a direct protest against the United States for supporting Israel in the Yom Kippur War against Egypt and Syria. The decision on oil provoked panic, not least in

Europe where 80 per cent of the supplies were threatened. Motorsport was obviously vulnerable to the charge of squandering it while ordinary people held ration cards. To reinforce this, the Monte Carlo Rally was cancelled and Dutch people cycled on Sundays, keeping the day petrol free.

As Stewart's era ended it seemed for a perilous month or two that something much bigger might be ending, too.

Notes

1. *Grand Prix!*, Lang.
2. *World Champion*, Surtees.
3. Ibid.
4. *When the Flag Drops*, Brabham.
5. *The Day I Died*, Kahn.
6. *Enzo Ferrari*, Yates.
7. Surtees, op. cit.
8. The GPDA mentioned by Moss in the previous chapter.
9. *Flying on the Ground*, Fittipaldi.
10. Surtees, op. cit.
11. *Cosworth*, Robson.
12. *Life at the Limit*, Hill.
13. Robson, op. cit.
14. *Conquest of Formula 1*, Hilton.
15. Ibid.
16. This reconstruction of Clark's death is taken from *Champions* by Hilton and Blunsden.
17. Hill, op. cit.
18. Lang, op. cit.
19. *Faster!*, Stewart.
20. *Daily Express* photographer Vic Blackman was covering the race and worked out that a certain hump was where the action was most likely to be. He was looking completely the wrong way and never did get Hill's crash as it was happening. Blackman then thought that the odds against another crash happening at this same place were remote and left – missing Rindt.
21. *Jochen Rindt*, Prüller.
22. Ibid.
23. Ibid.
24. Watkins interview with Nigel Roebuck, *Autosport*, 10 February 2005.
25. American company Studebaker Test Products (STP) made racing boats and cars. Their STP Oil Treatment became popular and Indianapolis 500 cars used it. The Grand Prix effort seemed logical after that.

26. In 1959, Alejandro de Tomaso set up a car company near Modena. He made racing cars for a wide variety of formulae.

27. *Frank Williams,* Hamilton.

28. *Grand Prix Greats,* Roebuck.

29. Prüller.

30. Ibid.

31. Brabham, op. cit.

32. *Alain Prost,* Hilton.

33. Prüller.

34. *Colin Chapman,* Crombac.

35. *To Hell And Back,* Lauda.

36. Howden Ganley, a New Zealander who'd come to England with little money to become a racing driver, worked as a mechanic and eventually drove in 35 Grands Prix.

37. *The Viking Drivers,* Petersens.

38. *François Cevert,* Jean-Claude Hallé.

39. *Bernie's Game,* Lovell.

40. *Autocourse.*

41. Lovell, op. cit.

42. Fittipaldi, op. cit.

43. *Grand Prix Data Book,* Hayhoe.

44. *Autocourse.*

45. Fittipaldi, op. cit.

46. Hallé, op. cit.

47. *My Autobiography,* Scheckter.

48. An Italian company that had concentrated on mini-cars in the 1950s, moved to luxury Grand Tourers and then went racing.

49. *My Greatest Race,* Adrian Ball.

50. Crombac, op. cit.

51. Petersens, op. cit.

52. Scheckter, op. cit.

53. Lauda, op. cit.

54. Petersens, op. cit.

55. Lauda, op. cit.

56. Interview with author.

Chapter 9

MONEY MEN

By 1974 Philip Morris had been in Formula One for three years. They'd started with a budget of between $115,000 and $150,000, but it soon rose to $1.5 million and then $3 million. Their brand name, Marlboro, had been on the BRM in 1973 but in essence the company was just another sponsor. They decided to form a super team with much more direct involvement, chose McLaren, picked Fittipaldi as lead driver and paid him $250,000. Only a year before, Marlboro BRM drivers were getting $10,000.[1]

The revolution which Chapman started now altered the way Formula 1 regarded itself and conducted itself. John Watson says:

> In 1974, my first full season, a team's total complement at a race was around 12 people. By the time of my last full season, 1983, that had risen perhaps three-fold. By then you had turbo engines, which wasn't like running Cosworths. The engine manufacturers were sending their own people to races, so were the electronics people, so were the fuel people, and the PR side was expanding to reflect that.[2]

The cars on the grid in 1974 had had sponsors' logos and liveries all over them for years and this gradually impacted on everything because the more successful a team became the more attractive they were to major sponsors, and the money from that bought the best people and the best equipment, which brought more success, which brought more sponsorship.

From here on, with rare exceptions, only a handful of teams achieved this and they formed a shifting, largely self-perpetuating hierarchy. This restricted drivers' opportunities to get a winning car and eventually forced the leading teams to pay fortunes for drivers who could win – and often enough for drivers who couldn't. In 1974, however, the scale was still small by comparison.

The petrol situation calmed, largely because the whole sport acted together in pointing out how little fuel was actually consumed over a season.

Tyrrell signed Scheckter and Frenchman Patrick Depailler. Scheckter, who counted the whole workforce and found it was 32 – a leading team today would be well over 200 and counting – knew that:

> when I took the decision to join Elf Team Tyrrell at the beginning of 1974, a lot of people felt that I was making life unnecessarily hard for myself by following after Jackie Stewart and exposing myself to the natural comparisons that would be made between us. On the other hand, there were people who felt that I was in need of a good tight rein in Formula 1, and that Ken Tyrrell was just the man to control it. I suppose both views had some merit, but I had been influenced only by my wish to have a regular Grand Prix drive with a competitive team, where I could get down to doing something about my lousy finishing record.[3]

Ickx joined Lotus, partnering Peterson. Reutemann and Carlos Pace were at Brabham, Hunt stayed at Hesketh increasing the mythology day by day, Hulme partnered Fittipaldi at Marlboro Texaco McLaren – yes, that's what the world looked like now – and Frank Williams fielded four drivers. One of them, Arturo Merzario, was 'excitable and unpredictable',[4] as he proved by over-revving two engines in Argentina during the first Grand Prix meeting. This 'sheer exhibitionism' came at a time when Williams couldn't afford his engines destroyed. Lauda joined Ferrari, partnering Regazzoni.

Reutemann ought to have won Argentina but a variety of mechanical problems, culminating in the engine cutting out, slowed him at the end and Hulme went by, Lauda second. Fittipaldi won Brazil from Regazzoni.

In testing for the South African Grand Prix, Revson – who'd joined the Shadow team[5] – may have had a suspension failure. The car struck a guardrail and killed him. Reutemann won the race from Beltoise (BRM) so that, before the European season began in Spain, the three opening races produced three different winners and three different men in second place. The championship was going to be tight, right to the end, the hierarchy of the new money not yet established.

Lauda had other things on his mind, coming to terms with the mechanisms and demands of a leading team. That involved a learning process around losing in a car which should have won as distinct from 'ordinary losing' where you finish back down the field in an uncompetitive car. The unordinary losing was, he judged, the hardest kind and he pointed to South Africa where he'd taken the first pole of his career, led the race before the Ferrari broke down.[6]

Lauda took pole at Jarama and beat Regazzoni by 35 seconds, the first win of his career, so he was learning that as well.

Thirty-two entries came to Nivelles for the Belgian Grand Prix with the only stipulation that in qualifying they had to be within 110 per cent of the three fastest, and 31 were. The driver who wasn't should not be denied his footnote in history. Leo Kinnunen from Finland – he had to be aged 31, didn't he? and was – did 1m 28.77s; Lauda 1m 11.04 as third fastest.

This astonishing number of cars formed up two by two in the grid, stretching back 16 rows towards the German border a hundred kilometres away. Regazzoni and Scheckter formed the front row although whether Regazzoni *really* had taken pole became a subject of debate and disbelief. Even the Ferrari team felt he'd gone two seconds slower than the official timing, but the organisers wouldn't have it and Regazzoni had it.

The 31 set off, so many that they produced a motorway queuing effect at the first corner when the leaders braked and the cars at the back virtually halted.

Fittipaldi won from Lauda.

Lauda dominated practice at Monaco but Regazzoni led from the flag up the hill to Casino Square. Monaco ought to be processional and often can be, *but* Monaco's constrictions can, and often do, create highly dramatic situations from nowhere – as we have seen so often. On the opening lap up towards Casino Square eight cars resembled 'crashing surf in all directions.' Seven were out immediately.[7] Peterson thought it a 'miracle' he got through the wreckage and survived a spin. He was candid enough to say it was good luck, not skill.[8] By lap 11 another five cars crashed, leaving only 13 in motion.

Regazzoni spun, too, and Lauda led but the ignition failed on lap 33. Peterson won it from Scheckter.

The Monaco measure: Peterson, 78 laps, 1h 58m 3.7s, an average speed of 80.7mph; Stewart, 1973, 80.9mph.

Scheckter took Sweden, Peterson out with a drive-shaft failure. It angered him so much that when he got back to the pits he threw his crash helmet onto the ground. Still the season felt for its true shape.

A mid-season ripple of races: Lauda and Regazzoni dominated Holland, Peterson won France at Dijon – the race's 15th staging post – from Lauda, Scheckter won Britain from Fittipaldi, Regazzoni fourth, Lauda fifth.

Lauda 38 points, Fittipaldi 37, Scheckter and Regazzoni 35, Peterson 19.

Reflecting, Lauda felt that his learning season continued and he came to understand 'it is a curious fact that a lot of little things can add up to a great big zero.' He cited the Nürburgring where, before the start, the right-front tyre had been damaged and changed. He held pole from Regazzoni, Fittipaldi and Scheckter on the next row.

Ken Tyrrell checked with a local military base and they assured him the race day weather would be benign. Instead, light rain began as the cars set off on their lap round to the grid. Lauda's new tyre wasn't run in and he had a problem with the shock absorbers. Should they be changed? These decisions could only be distracting.

The German flag was hoisted, hung in the air for a time, cleaved the air and the two Ferraris moved in unison – but Regazzoni edged ahead and as they passed the pits Scheckter drew alongside Lauda, pulled in front.

First mistake, Lauda remembered, *bad start.*

Second mistake, too impatient, can't let Regazzoni get away.

They moved round the loop at the end of the pit straight, came back behind the pits and now the Ferrari's power brought Lauda alongside Scheckter

Third mistake, must take Scheckter now.

Lauda tried to do it by late braking and went into Scheckter, taking himself out. It was, Lauda judged, a combination of all the mistakes and that was the great big zero.[9]

On lap 13 Hailwood crashed in the McLaren-Ford, hitting the guardrail at 100mph at the Pflanzgarten. He'd say it happened where the cars are airborne and you have to land straight. He didn't. He felt he might have been tired but, in his customary honest way, dismissed notions of car failure. He put it down to his own brain fade. His leg and foot were badly damaged – his Grand Prix career over.

Regazzoni won the race, leading from start to finish.

Reutemann confused everything by taking Austria from Hulme, Hunt third. Peterson, who couldn't win the championship, confused it further by taking Monza although Fittipaldi came second. Drivers could count their 13 best finishes of the 15 rounds but, by a curiosity, approaching the North American finale, the top four – Regazzoni (46 points), Scheckter (45), Fittipaldi (43) and Lauda (38) – had all failed to finish enough times that they'd keep whatever they got.

Fittipaldi took pole at Mosport and won from Regazzoni. They went to Watkins Glen on 52 points apiece, Scheckter still in there on 45. Reutemann became the spoiler, taking pole from Hunt, Scheckter on the third row, Fittipaldi directly behind him on the fourth, Regazzoni on the fifth but in the other column.

Reutemann got away first when a cannon sounded, Hunt behind him, Scheckter, Fittipaldi and Regazzoni running 5–6–7. Regazzoni however found the handling of his Ferrari so bad he drifted back.

Helmuth Koinigg, a Viennese in his second Grand Prix, inexplicably went off on lap ten. The Surtees car penetrated three layers of catch fencing and struck a guardrail head on with such force it killed Koinigg instantly.

Pace kept a steady third place but Lauda dropped out, his Ferrari handling badly, too. Scheckter was fourth, Fittipaldi fifth. With 15 laps left Scheckter's engine cut, the fuel pipe broken. Fittipaldi had his second championship and after a season like that he'd earned his $250,000.

A mini-rotation of the roundabout: Hulme retired and Jochen Mass, a strong German with a twinkling sense of humour, replaced him at Marlboro McLaren for 1975 but all the other leading drivers stayed where they were. It made no difference. The year belonged to Lauda and his Ferrari, and so comprehensively that they 'held the entire racing world in our grasp.' Again it was a combination, but this time a successful one: best, most modern car, enough testing – as much, Lauda said, as all the other teams put together. Lauda won five of the 14 rounds, took nine poles, dominated the mid-season absolutely and overall Ferrari set entirely new standards for the sport.[10]

Lauda started comparatively slowly, Fittipaldi winning Argentina, Pace winning Brazil, Scheckter winning South Africa and Lauda taking no more than five points from these races. He got nothing from Spain either – a shambles of a meeting at Montjuich Park. On the Friday the drivers went on strike because guardrails were not properly secured and in some cases lacked bolts. This, they felt, was intolerable and they could cite immediate precedents. Koinigg's car, it seems, hit the guardrail at Watkins Glen at a point where it wasn't properly secured. Revson, it seems, had been a victim of guardrail failure at Kyalami, because the bottom rail came off and the top rail rammed his head and chest. Cevert was 'cut to pieces along with his car when the guardrail structure came apart and became so many knife edges'[11] at Watkins Glen. The drivers were having no more of it.

On the Saturday, despite overnight work, they remained unconvinced and only a threat by the organisers to impound the cars forced the team managers to send them out. 'It was not necessary to look around the paddock: at the oval stadium with its high walls and its pair of well-gated openings. The organisers had the entirety of Formula 1 at what could be literally gunpoint within seconds.'[12]

Lauda took pole and Fittipaldi went home to Switzerland, saying the circuit was still unsafe. A rugged Australian, Alan Jones, made his debut in a Hesketh, putting it towards the rear of the grid. He was, in his own words, a 'new boy' and 'tradition dictates that you snub new boys.'[13] Not everyone did that – Fittipaldi polite, Mass nice, Reutemann friendly – while others simply walked past him. He didn't blame them. He wasn't looking for favours or social graces, he was intent on his own career.

Lauda crashed on the opening lap, Fittipaldi's brother Wilson withdrew after one lap in a symbolic protest against the state of the circuit and more and more cars crashed so that on lap 25 of 75 only 11 still raced.

On lap 26, the rear wing on the Embassy Lola of Rolf Stommelen broke. He was doing about 150mph and the car snapped out of control. It hammered into the guardrail on the left and bounded back, causing Pace – just behind – to swerve into the guardrail himself. Stommelen's car mounted the guardrail, went along it and over it, killing three officials and a photographer. Stommelen emerged hurt, but alive.

The race wasn't stopped for four laps, and then half points were awarded giving Mass in the McLaren, the winner, 4.5. Lella Lombardi (March-Ford), a 32-year-old from near Alessandria, finished sixth – the only woman to score a World Championship point (or rather half a point).

Lauda spread his domination now. He won Monaco, leading every lap from pole – the grid was staggered for the first time to try and minimise crashing and bashing into *Ste Devote*. Jones just qualified the Hesketh and the team told him, respecting Monaco's constrictions which he hadn't encountered before, to *drive the race like an old woman*. Graham Hill didn't qualify his Embassy-Lola[14] and the great career drew to an end.

The Monaco measure: Lauda, 75 laps, 2h 1m 21.3s, an average speed of 75.5mph: Peterson, 1974, 80.7mph.

Lauda won Belgium, Sweden and was second to Hunt in Holland. Lauda pressured Hunt in the closing stages and Hunt handled it philosophically (or fatalistically): *what will be will be – I'll drive as fast as I can. If the Ferrari is faster on the straight and gets by, that's my tough luck.* As Hunt won it, arms outstretched, Hesketh stood on the edge of the track, an ample man, his hands raised in supplication before the fact. The legend of Hunt and the mythology of Hesketh fused heavily into that moment.

Lauda won the French at Paul Ricard and Fittipaldi the British at Silverstone after heavy, misty showers caught out a dozen drivers who speared off in all directions, stopping the race. Here, Graham Hill announced his retirement. He'd concentrate on running the Embassy team he'd set up in 1973 and had a young Englishman, Tony Brise, to drive the car. Hill thought of him as a future World Champion.

Reutemann won Germany, Frenchman Jacques Laffite in a Williams second, Lauda third.

During practice for the Austrian Grand Prix, American Mark Donohue, who'd trained as an engineer, had, as it seems, a puncture and his March-Ford[15] went wild. It pitched into catch fencing, spun, wrenched down 50 yards of fencing and the wire bunched under the car. That lifted it as it travelled, and it went over a guardrail, killing one marshal and injuring another. Donohue sat in what remained of the car unconscious. When he was extricated he came round and spoke lucidly, although he couldn't remember the accident at all. He was taken to hospital and had internal haemorrhaging. He died two days later.

Vittorio Brambilla (March), a fearless bear of a man, won the race in the wet, his only victory. Hunt came second – making him fourth in the championship – Lauda came sixth. Lauda's third place at Monza confirmed the championship (Regazzoni won the race), and Lauda rounded the season off by adding Watkins Glen.

A month later, Hill was flying his own plane back from a test session at Paul Ricard. In fog, approaching the little airport at Elstree, he hit a tree over a golf course and the plane crashed, killing Hill, Brise and four other team members.

There would always be divided opinions about Hill, who was renowned as an ambassador for the sport (and inevitably called Mr Monaco) but he had sharp and sometimes unattractive edges. However, there would never be doubt about his courage or the sheer willpower which enabled him both to overcome limited natural ability and sustain a career from the distant days of 1958 with two World Championships along the way.

If 1975 was straightforward, 1976 stretched like a minefield, each of the 16 rounds a detonation.

Hunt joined Marlboro McLaren, Mario Andretti joined Lotus and, spicing the whole thing, Tyrrell built a six-wheeler which provoked amazement, hilarity, incredulity and two questions, *will it work?* and *what if it does?* The car first appeared at the Spanish Grand Prix, the seventh detonation of the 16.[16]

Brazil, 25 January. Hunt took pole from Lauda (2m 32.50s against 2m 32.52s) and that was interesting because Hunt regarded Lauda very highly but, more than that, had so far in his career been the only driver at Hesketh (apart, briefly, from Jones) and so had no team-mate to measure himself against. He couldn't know if Hesketh had a terrific car and he was an average driver. The pole became the measure. Lauda won the race, Hunt had a freak accident. Part of the fuel injection fell and jammed the throttle open, sending him into the catch fencing. Lauda 9 points, Hunt 0.

South Africa, 6 March. The Grand Prix Drivers' Association was essentially disbanded, or rather incorporated into the FICA – whatever good work it had done, it could not overcome the drivers' natural habitat: loners with egos. Hunt took pole from Lauda (1m 16.10s against 1m 16.20s) but Lauda seized the lead with a decisive, powerful thrust from the line and held it throughout the race, Hunt tracking him and towards the end pressuring him. Lauda won it by 1.3 of a second. Lauda 18, Hunt 6.

United States West, 28 March. Long Beach, outside Los Angeles, was a street circuit, tight and bumpy. Before it Ferrari team manager Daniel Audetto suggested to Lauda that he allow Regazzoni to win. Lauda asked him if he'd gone mad and Audetto replied with a gesture which suggested the championship was over already in Lauda's favour. Regazzoni did win Long Beach but only because Lauda flat-spotted[17] his front tyres. Hunt claimed Depailler in the Tyrrell 'just moved over and pushed me off the track.' That displeased Master James. Lauda 24, Hunt 6.

Spain, 2 May. After Long Beach, Lauda went home to Salzburg and, working on a bank beside his swimming pool, driving a tractor, turned it over and trapped himself. He'd broken his ribs, blood everywhere. Spain was two weeks away and the injuries needed six weeks to heal. Lauda spent his time lying very still trying to breathe 'decently' while Ferrari – the Old Man and the team – exploded in the customary hysteria. Part of that involved putting a young Italian, Maurizio Flammini – doing well in Formula 2 – into Lauda's car in Spain. Lauda told a journalist that 'Italian drivers were good for nothing except driving round the church tower' and when that reached Italy the hysteria overwhelmed the hysteria already in place. 'All Italy howled with rage, but I didn't care. In my position I had to say something tough.' When Luca di Montezemolo, head of racing activities, rang to talk about Flammini for Spain Lauda said sarcastically that if it didn't 'interfere' with the team's plans he'd quite like to take part in the Spanish practice and whether he could drive or not would be revealed. If it did 'interfere with the team's plans', *You can go and stuff yourselves.*[18]

Hunt took pole – from Lauda (1m 18.52s against 1m 18.84). Lauda led but Hunt went through on lap 32 and so did Mass in the other McLaren. Meanwhile Depailler gave the six-wheeled Tyrrell its debut and put it on the second row (the brakes failed during the race). Mass's engine let go and Hunt crossed the line 30.97 seconds ahead of Lauda. Then the *CSI*, checking the McLaren, found it 18mm too wide. That evening, Hunt was told he'd been stripped of the win and McLaren lodged a protest the following day. Lauda 30 (33), Hunt 15 (6) pending the outcome.

Belgium, 16 May. Lauda took pole from Regazzoni, Hunt on the second row. Audetto again suggested Regazzoni should be given the win – and if Regazzoni made the better start a pit board would be held out instructing Lauda to follow him. Lauda said Audetto could hang out whatever pit board suited him, yellow, green or red, with plus and minus and double minus. He wouldn't be looking at it. Lauda led from start to finish, Regazzoni second, and Hunt's gearbox failed. Lauda (39) 42, Hunt 15 (6).

Monaco, 30 May. The circuit had been revised, with a chicane at *Ste Devote* and the corner at Rascasse tightened. Lauda took pole from Regazzoni, Hunt on the seventh row because the McLaren wasn't handling well. Lauda won and Hunt's engine failed. He drew on the fatalistic philosophy: *if you're going to have engine failures, better to have them when you're down the field.* Lauda 48 (51), Hunt 15 (6).

The Monaco measure: Lauda 78 laps, 1h 59m 51.4s, an average speed of 80.3mph; Lauda, 1975 (a wet-dry race), 75.5mph.

Sweden, 13 June. Scheckter put the six-wheel Tyrrell on pole, Depailler on the second row, Lauda on the third, Hunt on the fourth. The Tyrrells finished first and second, and very suddenly six-wheels threatened revolution. There was, however, an inherent problem with tyre wear because, by definition, the two small front wheels at either side rotated much faster than the two large rear wheels. The nature of the Anderstorp circuit disguised this. Lauda came third, Hunt fifth. Lauda 52 (55), Hunt 17 (8).

France, 4 July. Paul Ricard was hot. Lauda took pole from Hunt (1m 48.17s against 1m 47.89s) and led, but Hunt felt 'oil or water' coming from the Ferrari's rear, meaning Lauda would have a problem at some point, perhaps soon. For seven laps Lauda pulled away, sometimes by almost a second a lap but on lap nine Lauda's engine blew down the

Mistral straight. The rear wheels locked and Lauda had an instant to hold the car. He did. Regazzoni, tracking Hunt from second place, went as far as lap 18 when his engine blew, too, pitching him backwards into catch-fencing. Hunt went safely to the win although he had an upset stomach and felt sick. Lauda 52 (55), Depailler 26, Hunt 26 (17). The day after Paul Ricard, McLaren were fined by the *CSI* over Spain but the points were restored. Hunt returned to the hunt: Lauda 52, Hunt 26.

Britain, 18 July. Pole was as tight as it gets, Lauda 1m 19.35s against Hunt's 1m 19.41s. Brands Hatch boiled with passion, and soon enough boiled over. Lauda led into Paddock Hill Bend, Regazzoni up to him and trying to get the lead himself. Regazzoni touched Lauda and spun into the on-rush of cars. For an instant Hunt felt deep elation that both Ferraris were gone, taken themselves out. Next instant Hunt rode up over Regazzoni's wheel and went into the air. Cars darted like a shoal of startled fish, some on the grass. Hunt limped forward but the McLaren's steering suffered serious damage. The race was stopped.

Hunt and Regazzoni went to the grid for the restart in their spare cars although McLaren, sensing that switching to the spare at this point might mean trouble under the rules, worked on repairing the race car. Some teams protested and an announcement was made that only those cars which had completed the opening lap could take the restart. Hunt hadn't completed that lap. Ferrari, McLaren (and Jacques Laffite, Ligier) said they would not withdraw their spare cars and the crowd did boil over. No-one had ever seen a motor racing crowd in Britain do this and for a moment or two it might have become ugly. In the midst of it, the mechanics completed repairs on Hunt's race car and wheeled it to the grid, replacing the spare. Lauda led again with Hunt holding off Regazzoni and it developed like that. Halfway through the race Lauda's gearbox began to fail and Hunt drew up. He knew he'd got him. It was done with thrust and precision on the inside during the run up to the Druids horseshoe. Hunt closed his eyes and went for it. The crowd boiled over again – with delight. Hunt won it from Lauda. Then Ferrari, Tyrrell and the Fittipaldi teams protested the decision to let Hunt take the re-start. Ferrari persisted, their appeal was rejected and they took it to the *CSI*. Lauda 61 (58), Scheckter 30 (29), Depailler 26, Hunt 26 (35) pending the appeal.

Germany, 1 August. Niki Lauda started his career liking the Nürburgring, measuring himself against it, seeking out perfection. As he matured, as he saw drivers being killed, he judged the Nürburgring the most unsafe circuit. He based this on its length, which meant rescue teams – firefighters, ambulances – had to be spread out and might take too long to reach an accident.

Hunt took pole from Lauda (7m 6.5s against 7m 7.4s) but, on an overcast, threatening day word filtered back that rain fell on parts of the circuit. Lauda went for wet weather tyres. Hunt wanted dries but looked around, saw the others on wets and went that way, too. Regazzoni led, Hunt third, Lauda ninth and, when Regazzoni spun, Peterson moved in to the lead, Hunt second. Hunt and Lauda both pitted for dry tyres – Mass in the other McLaren started on dries and now led comfortably into lap two, but Hunt calculated that he could catch him by the end of the race. Just before *Bergwerk,* a fast right-hander, something happened to Lauda's Ferrari. It hit the concrete kerb, spun into catch-fencing, struck a bank and was catapulted back onto the track on fire. Three cars came hard-hard-hard at it. One missed it, the other two struck it glancing blows. A fourth car stopped and the drivers fought to lift Lauda from the flames. They got him out but he'd suffered cruel burns, his lungs damaged by inhaling toxic fumes.

Fourteen cars completed lap two: the 14 who had been in front of Lauda. The rest had to halt just before the accident. The initial word was that Lauda had superficial injuries only. The race restarted and Hunt won it from Scheckter. News of Lauda's real condition filtered through that evening and in Mannheim Hospital he fought for his life. Lauda 61 (58), Scheckter 36 (34), Hunt 35 (44).

Austria, 15 August. Lauda, given the Last Rites, remembered nothing of the crash. He lay in hospital with tubes going in to him and out of him, and he could hear people speaking to him. He understood 'my situation: accident, hospital, lungs.' On the Thursday they 'gave me a looking-glass. [...] My head is swollen to three times its normal size, it sits like a great melon on my shoulders. Neck and nose are hidden in the swelling.'[19] Enzo Ferrari, who felt he had been cheated of the wins in Spain and Brands Hatch, decided to withdraw from Grand Prix racing forever. This was widely disbelieved and may even have been an attempt to get the Austrian race cancelled – Regazzoni would be bringing thousands of Swiss supporters, the presence of Ferrari cars would bring more thousands from Italy, and all that on top of Lauda's absence. The race wasn't cancelled and Hunt took pole from John Watson (Penske) but could only finish fourth. A large stone damaged the underside of the car. Lauda 61 (58), Hunt 38 (47).

Holland, 29 August. By now Lauda was recovering and people wrote to him offering their skin, even their ears – his had been burnt off. Lauda found the Ferrari reaction 'partly moving and human, partly chaotic, and partly vile.' Ferrari, of course, came back in Holland but with only a single car, for Regazzoni. Peterson took pole from Hunt but in the race Peterson suffered understeer and Hunt won it from Regazzoni. Lauda 61 (58), Hunt 47 (56).

In between Holland the next Grand Prix, Italy, Hunt flew to Canada to take part in a celebrity Formula Atlantic[20] race at Trois-Rivières, Quebec (for $10,000). Jones, Brambilla and Depailler were among the others. Hunt partnered a local boy blessed with innocence, bravado and skill. It is not at all clear if Hunt had heard of Gilles Villeneuve before he reached Canada but he and everybody else had by the time he left. Villeneuve won the race consummately and when Hunt got back to England he started telling people, McLaren people.

Italy, 12 September. Lauda reported to the Ferrari factory 38 days after the crash. He was, as is his way, clear-thinking about it, logical about it, deadpan about it. He'd describe the Ferrari reaction as all underhand, like 'water polo.' Enzo Ferrari wouldn't say to Lauda *I do not want you to drive at Monza* but, Lauda sensed, what Ferrari really wanted was to proclaim *we lost the Championship with style, we are the moral victory – our man is lying helplessly in bed.* And here was Lauda, face disfigured, body battered, wanting to race.

He tested, covering forty laps of the test track at Fiorano. He could still drive, even though he needed foam rubber cushions so the helmet and the ear didn't hurt too much. He was unimpressed by being able to do the forty laps. He knew how easy they were on a placid day, alone, on your own test track.

It rained on the Friday at Monza, water on the track, and that frightened him. McLaren anticipated politics. After the Saturday session, fuel was taken to a laboratory for analysis and on Sunday morning announced to be above the maximum octane limit. Hunt would have to start from the back of the grid. Peterson won the race from Regazzoni, Hunt crashing and being jeered all the way back to the pits. Lauda's fourth place remains barely believable. Lauda 64 (61), Hunt 47 (56).

Canada, 3 October. The *CSI* announced Ferrari's appeal from Brands Hatch was upheld, and consequently Hunt lost the nine points while Lauda, retrospectively moving up from second place to first at Brands, gained three. Lauda 64, Hunt 47.

Ferrari were vulnerable, despite that: Regazzoni fired – not enough testing done since Lauda's accident (Lauda felt). At Mosport, Hunt took pole from Peterson, Lauda on the third row but in the race he had suspension problems and Hunt won it. A tourniquet had begun to tighten round Ferrari. Lauda 64, Hunt 56.

United States, 10 October. Hunt took pole from Scheckter, Lauda on the third row again. Scheckter led the race and after some ten laps Hunt told himself *you're driving like an old grandmother.* The McLaren oversteered and Hunt took another five laps to readjust his technique. Lauda was up to third and would remain there while, on lap 37 of the 59, Hunt drew up at the chicane before the long straight and, Scheckter slowed by a back-marker, powered through. Lauda 68, Hunt 65. We had, Lauda said, a 'demoralised team' who couldn't come to terms with Hunt.

Japan, 24 October. Mount Fuji, 3.05 in the afternoon. The arguments about whether the 25 drivers could – or would – start were over. The mist along the straight cleared, the torrential rain ceased although the track remained full of lurking dangers. Who really knew where the water lay or how deep? Hunt was on the front row with Andretti's Lotus, pole, Lauda on the second row. Lauda had already seen on the warm-up lap that 'you could hardly hold the car.' When the start was given and the cars moved Lauda would travel slowly. He did not intend to die and he did intend to minimise the danger from the cars around him. Already Hunt outdragged Andretti for the lead. The vast crowd spread up the hillsides watched intently, mist shrouded Mount Fuji and Hunt had gone clear: no spray blinding him, this spray which forced the others to stay back from him. Completing lap one, Hunt led from Watson, Lauda eleventh. On lap two, Hunt's McLaren wobbled alarmingly – aquaplaning – approaching the first turn and Watson coming hard had to go up the escape road to miss it, moving Andretti to second place.

Lauda pulled gently into the pits. He'd been concentrating entirely on not being hit by any other car, he'd been thinking *how stupid this race is.* He'd felt an unbearable tension that he would be hit. In the pits team manager Forghieri leant down and asked what'd happened. Lauda replied that to drive represented madness. He'd remember Forghieri saying quickly *OK, but we'll pretend you've got engine trouble.* Lauda would have none of that. He'd tell it like it was. He stood in the pits gazing at the track and after a while the rain began to stop. He did not reproach himself for his decision because he knew it was right. Hunt now had to finish third for the championship.

Burly Brambilla in a March forged his way through to Hunt, drew up alongside and spun off. On lap 14 of the 73, Hunt led from Andretti. Hunt drove a controlled race but, as the track dried, the wet-weather tyres became more and more overstressed. Could Hunt afford a pit stop?

> All the wet air was gone, the clouds had blown away from the circuit, some blue sky had appeared, and the lowering evening sun had begun to glow warmly over the scene. Mount Fuji began to loom through the clouds, showing hints of snow-covered slopes.[21]

The tyres began to shed little chunks as they disintegrated. Hunt slowed and Depailler swept by, Andretti swept by. Andretti overtook Depailler and Hunt began to move up towards the Frenchman. At the end of lap 64 one of Depailler's tyres finally let go and he had to limp the whole way round to the pits. Hunt's tyres were getting worse each yard he covered. He kept asking the pits *what do I do?* He didn't want to make the decision himself. The man running McLaren, Teddy Mayer, felt that *Hunt* should be the one making the decision because he could feel how good or bad the tyres were. On lap 62 the front left tyre shredded completely but he was not yet at the entrance to the pit lane. If he'd been past that, he'd have had to do another lap.

Instead, he angled into the pits and, when he stopped, the mechanics sprang onto the car but, with the tyre deflated, the chassis sank too low to get the jack underneath. A mechanic lifted the car with his bare hands while the jack was slipped into position. Hunt's pit stop lasted 27 seconds and during it Regazzoni had gone though into second place behind Andretti, Jones (Theodore) third. Depailler with new tyres ran strongly, too.

Hunt emerged with absolutely no idea where he was in the race but enraged by a terrible certainty: the championship had been taken from him because the team hadn't called him in. He was in fact fifth. Five laps remained and he vowed to overtake any car he could reach. On lap 70 he was still fifth but Regazzoni fell back. Hunt went past him on the outside, kept that line and went past Jones on the outside. He forced the McLaren towards Depailler and got to within 20, perhaps 30, yards of him by the finish. He came to his pit still certain he had lost. He roared abuse on a grand and terrible scale. Mayer and many others grinning hugely held their hands up, three fingers splayed. *Third! James, you were third!*

Lauda heard all this on his way to the airport, rang Enzo Ferrari and got a cold response. He would never forget that and perhaps never forgive it.

After such a season the realisation of the championship, Hunt would say, came to him slowly. Then he went off to get drunk on the same grand and terrible scale.

For the first time since 1965, no Grand Prix driver had been killed in any form of racing.

In December, two months after Fuji, Renault announced that they would be entering Grand Prix racing.

Lauda would win the 1977 championship in a Ferrari but, after Fuji, the relationship with the team was never the same. Reutemann replaced Regazzoni and the web of Ferrari politics was being spun in an attempt to make Lauda number two driver.

Roberto Nosetto, a long-time Ferrari employee and, according to Lauda, superstitious to the point of absolute obsession, replaced Audetto. Nosetto had to wear and be surrounded by things green; he couldn't ride in a car with the number 7 anywhere on it. If it was a hire car and had a 7 as part of its number-plate he covered it. To Lauda of the precise logic this did not bode well.

Scheckter joined the new Walter Wolf team.[22] Peterson moved to Tyrrell, tired of constant quarrelling with Chapman and 'afraid of the car which broke down every time we tested. If it wasn't a wing working loose then it was a wheel. There was only one thing to do and that was to leave Lotus.'[23] Andretti stayed at Lotus partnered by the young Swede Gunnar Nilsson, Regazzoni joined Ensign,[24] Hunt and Mass stayed at McLaren.

Scheckter won Argentina, Pace in the Brabham second. Forghieri had instructed Lauda to watch how Reutemann drove and learn from it. Lauda qualified on the second row...Reutemann the fourth. Lauda retired with a mechanical problem and Reutemann finished third. Reutemann, however, won Brazil.

Lauda decisively outqualified Reutemann at Kyalami and won the race from Scheckter, Reutemann eighth. On lap 23 quiet Welshman Tom Pryce, driving a Shadow came upon two fire marshals running across the track to reach a car which had stopped and briefly been alight. Pryce struck one of the marshals, struggling with a heavy fire extinguisher. The marshal was killed and the fire extinguisher struck Pryce's head, killing him. The Shadow's throttle jammed open and the car continued at full speed. Laffite (Ligier) reached it not knowing what had happened and the rudderless Shadow took them both off. Laffite was unhurt.

Lauda only learnt about Pryce at the prize-giving and found the twin emotions – the misery of that and the joy of winning – 'something indescribable.'

Pace, in his sixth year of Grand Prix racing and his third with Brabham, finished South Africa 13th. He went back to Brazil where he died in a light plane crash.

BRM had been taken over by Louis Stanley and now faded gently from Grand Prix racing.

Andretti loved the Lotus 78 from the start although it had a higher than anticipated drag factor, which meant that although it cornered beautifully its straight line speed wasn't competitive. By Long Beach, he had the car set up as he wanted it and put it on the front row, Lauda pole. At the start Reutemann was 'coming up like he wasn't stopping before he got to San Diego!'[25] and provoked a 'chain-reaction shunt' which Andretti wasn't involved in. Andretti won from Lauda.

In Spain during Saturday practice, Lauda felt a 'devilish pain' as if he was being sawn in half and heard a 'cracking sound' through one of the corners. He headed for the pits barely able to breathe. A rib, broken at the Nürburgring, had snapped. He could not contemplate racing. According to Lauda, Reutemann asked the mechanics *what's the matter with Lauda now? Will he drive, won't he drive?* Reutemann was told Lauda wouldn't be driving. He walked to the transporter where Lauda lay, saw Lauda white and immobile, smiled and walked off. Lauda had no doubt that Reutemann was pleased. It didn't trouble Lauda. In Grand Prix racing, Lauda would say, don't expect to get 'demonstrations of sympathy.'[26]

Andretti won Spain from Reutemann. Watson took pole at Monaco but Scheckter won it from Lauda, so that Scheckter led the Championship with 32 points, Lauda 25, Reutemann 23, Andretti 22.

The Monaco measure: Scheckter, 76 laps, 1h 57m 52.7s, an average speed of 79.6mph; Lauda, 1976, 80.3mph.

Nilsson won Belgium from Lauda. Andretti would say that:

Gunnar was getting better with every race, and that win really meant the world to him. At that point, of course, we knew nothing about his illness. But neither did he. It seems now that he knew something was a little wrong but figured he'd wait until the end of the season to have it investigated. There was no outward sign of any big problem, except that I used to think he got tired very easily for a guy of his age. Looking back on it now, I'm so glad that he won a Grand Prix. He got so much pleasure out of it.[27]

Laffite won Sweden (where before the start, Nosetto wanted to put a sprig of green in Lauda's cockpit and Lauda wanted to hit him), Andretti won France. That was the mid-point in the season, Scheckter still on 32 but Lauda up to 33, Reutemann 28 and Andretti 22.

Renault came to Silverstone for the British Grand Prix with a turbo engine[28] to be driven by Frenchman Jean-Pierre Jabouille. As a major manufacturer Renault were taking a distinct risk because they might be beaten by far smaller companies as turbo technology was an uncertain, awkward, unruly thing. Silverstone's broad acres ought to have embraced turbo power but Jabouille could only qualify 22nd. The Renaults had Michelin radial-ply tyres, another glimpse of the future. Six rows above Jabouille on the grid sat Gilles Villeneuve in a McLaren, poised to impress knowing people. Purley driving his own LEC car,[29] crashed at Becketts when the throttle stuck open. The car hit the bank cutting its speed from 108mph to 0 in a foot and a half, reportedly generating 179.8g, the highest ever G-force survived by a human being.

In the race, Jabouille's turbocharger failed after 17 laps. Hunt, who'd been having a wretched season with crashes, won but significantly from Lauda who now felt he had finally cured the Ferrari's handling problems. Lauda concluded immediately after Silverstone *the World Championship is in the bag.*

He put together a devastating run, winning Germany at Hockenheim and finishing second to Jones in Austria.

In the week between that and Holland, Teddy Mayer went to Mosport where Villeneuve was driving in a Can-Am race. Essentially, Mayer told Villeneuve he wouldn't be driving for McLaren again and if he got another Formula 1 offer for 1978 he should take it. Villeneuve went home depressed, with nothing on the horizon. Within a few days the phone rang and Villeneuve's wife Joann said a gentleman from Modena with an Italian accent wanted to speak to a Signor Villeneuve...

Lauda won Holland – Villeneuve arrived at the Ferrari factory the day after – and finished second to Andretti in Italy. Lauda needed a single point for the championship and fourth did nicely at Watkins Glen where Hunt won. Scheckter took Canada where Ferrari wanted to run three cars, for Lauda, Reutemann and Villeneuve. Lauda hadn't even met Villeneuve and anyway, he had gastric 'flu. There was no question of him driving.

Hunt won Fuji. During the race Villeneuve followed Peterson and in a right-hander struck the rear of his six-wheeled Tyrrell. The Ferrari launched and cartwheeled to where people were standing in a prohibited area. Two died instantly, one of them a marshal who'd evidently been trying to clear the area. Ten others were injured, seven seriously. Villeneuve did not feel responsible because the people shouldn't have been there, but he was badly shaken.

In 1978, the drivers' roundabout turned heavily. Peterson came back to Lotus, partnering Andretti, Nilsson joined Arrows. By then he knew he had cancer and he would never be well enough to drive the car. There is an almost unbearable pathos in a handsome man of 29, a competitive driver since the karting days and now a Grand Prix winner, being struck by this. He fought it all that summer, and he lost.

Patrick Tambay, an urbane Frenchman, replaced Mass at McLaren while Hunt stayed for a third season. Lauda joined Watson at Brabham and Jones joined Saudia Williams.

Frank Williams, his passion so strong for racing that he had survived all set-backs, was poised to become a serious player. He'd secured major sponsorship from Saudi Arabian Airlines and approached Jones at the end of 1977. Jones went to the factory and liked designer Patrick Head's approach and Williams liked Jones because he was a proper, feisty, no-nonsense racer. Jones said yes to £40,000.[30]

The Lotus 79 was one of the most aesthetically pleasing Formula 1 cars of recent years and people spoke of an Andretti championship already. The car, nicknamed The Black Beauty – the JPS livery was black and gold, of course – used what quickly became known as 'ground effects'. This was Chapman's way of using the air rushing at the car to generate downforce. The underside of the car was shaped to exert suction and this 'effectively reduced the air pressure under the car and consequently sucked it on to the ground.'[31] To control the air flow two skirts were placed down the sides of the car and maintained contact with the road. The air was channelled between them and, in its most extreme form, clawed the car to the road.

Andretti himself saw danger coming from Hunt, who'd finished 1977 so strongly, Lauda and Reutemann. Meanwhile Brabham's designer Gordon Murray, a lean South African who thought in original ways, worked on a device to give Grand Prix racing one of its periodic convulsions.

Renault, who'd done four races in 1977, prepared to contest the whole season. Whether a turbo engine could be made to work reliably and whether problems like turbo lag[32] could be overcome remained unproven.

Andretti took Argentina from Lauda, and took it so comprehensively it surprised even himself.

Peterson took pole from Hunt in Brazil, Jones on the fourth row. He'd outqualified Lauda and Scheckter. Goodyear, supplying the team and 'engaged in a fierce tyre war with Michelin,' decided that Williams must have the 'softer and faster rubber' which Lotus and McLaren enjoyed. After the long, lean years Williams found himself 'speechless' and had 'difficulty coping with the enormity of it.'³³

Reutemann won Brazil, Lauda third, Andretti fourth.

The Williams enormity grew in South Africa where Jones finished fourth. Peterson won, Andretti classified seventh – he'd run out of fuel. Chapman took three gallons out of the car before the start, assuring Andretti it wouldn't be a problem, to which Andretti said: 'If it does I'll have your hide!' Andretti was too much of a gentleman to say whether he ever did.

A combative Finn, Keke Rosberg, qualified on the second last row in a Theodore car. He'd drive for two other teams this season, ATS and Wolf, and appeared to be the archetypal journeyman with a career decorated by initials: ret, dnpq, dnq, dns = did not pre-qualify, did not qualify, did not start. He wouldn't even score a point until 1980.

At Long Beach, Jones forced the Williams up to second before the nose wing began to collapse. Reutemann won it from Andretti, and when Depailler took Monaco from Lauda the season still had an open feel to it.

Depailler 23 points, Reutemann and Andretti 18, Lauda 16, Peterson 14.

The Monaco measure: Depailler, 75 laps, 1h 55m 14.6s, an average speed of 80.3mph; Scheckter, 1977, 79.6mph.

The superiority of the Lotus began to assert itself and Andretti took Belgium – where an imp of a Frenchman, René Arnoux, made his debut in a Martini-Ford – and Spain from Peterson. In both races, the rest were a long way behind.

They went to Sweden.

That dry, warm June afternoon Lauda circled the Anderstorp circuit trying hard *not* to take pole for the Grand Prix the following day, team-mate Watson doing the same. Andretti had it with a lap of 1m 22.058s, a time set in the session the day before, Watson (1:22.737s) next and Lauda (1:22.78s) on the second row.

Gordon Murray had created something truly astonishing: a fan car. Murray was an unusual man. With his unkempt hair and slow South African accent he looked part guru, part visionary and might, at moments, have passed for a hippie. He liked fine wine and basic rock music. He once said: 'I'm not into boring people.'

He and his assistant David North struggled with a particular problem. The Brabham used the wide, low Alfa Romeo engine and how could you design a ground-effects car around that? They moved through the permutations even, evidently, considering mounting this engine in the front. They examined the regulations and noticed that an extractor fan was legal provided its 'primary function' was not aerodynamic. The fan was *only* supposed to cool the engine. If it also sucked up air from beneath the underbody, well, that was just coincidence...

The fan was no easy thing. A thermodynamics consultant had to work out the number of fan blades and the rotational speed. Plastic fans disintegrated and fans filled with glass-fibre disintegrated as well. Magnesium was used.

Lauda tested the car at Brands Hatch and found it 'unpleasant to drive. It understeered massively, all the more so when you took your foot off the accelerator. The fan was powered by the engine, with the result that the suction effect fell off when the revs dropped.' Watson, reflecting, says however: 'The beauty of the fan was that it operated at engine speed. The Lotus ground effects were conditional on the road speed, the fan conditional on engine speed so for example where cars are always handfuls at low speeds – because there is little downforce – the fan car was perfect. At 12,000rpm in *first gear* it produced the same amount of downforce as it did at 160mph in sixth gear.'

At Anderstorp the convulsions started on the Thursday morning at first practice. As the two cars were wheeled out, dustbin lids covered the fans.

After practice Andretti complained that, regardless of its legality the car would have to be banned on safety grounds. 'I spent a couple of laps behind the Brabham and my visor was covered in muck. If it rains it would be impossible to get past. I don't want anyone to get a bolt in the neck before anybody does anything about it. I think we have to stop this monster before it gets out of hand.' Chapman, the startling innovator, was so incensed he issued a long statement. He, Williams, Tyrrell and two other team principals lodged formal protests to the Swedish organisers before the race, but they were rejected.

By Friday qualifying the Brabham ran fine. Watson says that 'Anderstorp was a circuit which was good for it and Bernie didn't want the two Brabhams sitting on the front of the grid by about five seconds and everybody getting cheesed off so we ran the car with quite a lot of fuel on board.'

Andretti took the lead immediately with Lauda behind him. Watson spun avoiding another car, Lauda tracked Andretti and got past him on lap 39. Andretti's engine failed and young Riccardo Patrese in the Arrows finished second behind Lauda.

The fan car was banned within days on safety grounds.

This was the first race Professor Watkins attended as resident Formula 1 doctor. Bernie Ecclestone had met him, said there was a problem with medical facilities and would he take it over on a permanent basis? At

Anderstorp Watkins understood the problem – or rather the sort of problems – immediately. He had a caravan as the medical centre (room for one patient only) and a tent as an 'overflow'. There was no helicopter except on race day because, Watkins was told, *practice isn't dangerous.* During practice and the race itself he positioned himself at the foot of the control tower.[34]

By now Goodyear produced a whole array of qualifying tyres designed for one hot lap. That demanded judgement from the driver on precisely when to make his run – traffic could destroy it – and how to handle the wear. To broaden this, race tyres were available in various compounds and it became almost an art form choosing the right ones. Sometimes drivers exploited different combinations, and sometimes they got that wrong…

Andretti won France from Peterson, the ground effects devouring Paul Ricard. Andretti crossed the line and kept on at high speed towards where Chapman stood on the rim of the track. He'd already thrown his black hat into orbit and now saluted Andretti with both arms raised in a V. When Peterson passed him 2.93 seconds later he held just his right arm out, jerking the thumb up and down. Then he turned away and strode back towards the pit, the afternoon sun drawing a shadow from his chunky body. Lotus were big then.

Neither of Chapman's cars finished at Brands Hatch where Reutemann won from Lauda.

Andretti reasserted himself round Hockenheim from pole. A lean Brazilian with a face so young he might have been a teenager put an Ensign-Ford on the second last row of the grid. Nelson Souto Maior abandoned his studies to work in a garage and race karts. So his mother wouldn't know, he raced under the name of Piquet. He'd competed in European Formula 3 the year before this debut which ended when the engine failed.

Andretti 54 points, Peterson 36.

That closed in a wet Austria Grand Prix where Andretti claimed Reutemann moved over on him and he spun into the barrier. Peterson won it.

Andretti rectified that in Holland winning from Peterson which isolated them from the others. Nobody else could take the championship. Andretti evaluated the Dutch win as 'precious' and added 'I was getting edgy before it, no question.'[35]

Andretti took pole at Monza from Villeneuve, Peterson on the third row. That, in the theoretical world, meant Peterson had some work to do. In reality it meant something else altogether. Significantly, Jabouille in the Renault turbo was third quickest and Villeneuve said the car 'passed me on the straight like you can't believe. It must be 10kmh faster than anything else here.'

The signal to start was given while some at the back of the grid still trundled to their places. As Villeneuve's Ferrari sprang to life and leapt, as Andretti got onto the power, as Lauda was trying to outdrag Andretti, the grid bunched – and the cars travelled at widely different speeds.

Peterson made a bad start.

Where the track narrowed into a funnel at the old banking, someone – later to be named as Patrese – touched Hunt's McLaren and that in turn flung Peterson's Lotus into the guardrail where it exploded in fire. Seven other cars thrashed and crashed, the track covered in debris. Peterson sat trapped and the fire marshals came up while Hunt and Regazzoni ran to the Lotus. Hunt hesitated for an instant then plunged into the flames to try to get Peterson out. Nearby Brambilla sat in his Surtees unconscious, probably knocked out by one of his own wheels.

This accident, and its consequences, changed Grand Prix racing. Professor Watkins did not have a car to get to it and when he tried on foot the police, presumably having no idea who he was, barred the way. Watkins went to the medical centre and was there when Peterson was brought in. 'He was quite conscious and rational. We put a splint in his legs, and we put a drip up. That was all done correctly. There was no crowd control, though. While I was working on him, a photographer pointed a camera between my legs to get a picture of Ronnie. I kicked him.' Peterson had to be carried through the crowd to get to the helicopter.[36]

Peterson was flown to hospital in Milan and initial reports announced over the PA system at Monza said he'd broken both his legs but otherwise was fine.

The race eventually restarted over 40 laps with 19 cars. Villeneuve and Andretti were both penalised a minute for jumping the start and Lauda won it from Watson.

Peterson's condition deteriorated overnight – marrow was entering the bloodstream – and when Andretti arrived at the hospital Swedish journalist Fredrik af Petersens took him to one side and said Peterson had just died. Andretti drove on down the road and stopped. Journalists and photographers hemmed him but he didn't want to talk. He said only 'unhappily, motor racing is also this.'

Watkins remembers how 'appalled' Ecclestone was and how Ecclestone said that together they must take responsibility for circuit rescue. In future Watkins would have a medical car available to him that enabled him to follow the grid as it set off. During the race the car would be strategically placed for fast response. It meant that Watkins could be at any accident within a very short time and that might mean the difference between life and death.[37]

Reutemann won Watkins Glen, Villeneuve won Canada. 'Those last laps were torture. I could hear all kinds of noises in the car. And I didn't like it because I was having to drive like an old woman, shifting at 10,000 and being careful not to break anything.'[38]

Ends and beginnings, always ends and beginnings. Villeneuve's victory, on 8 October, created 'a sea of euphoria' and was the beginning of a legend, no less. Gunnar Nilsson died peacefully in a London hospital two weeks later.

For the second time in 40 days Colin Chapman's plane flew to Sweden with one of his drivers on it.

Ends and beginnings: that same October a Frenchman self-cloaked in great dignity, Jean-Marie Balestre, was elected president of the *CSI*, and immediately demanded that its name be changed to the *Fédération Internationale du Sport Automobile*, known as *FISA* Monsieur Balestre firmly intended to get hold of international motor sport and give it a shaking. That would involve getting hold of Mr Bernard Charles Ecclestone at FOCA. Mr Bernard Charles Ecclestone did not care for people getting hold of him, French or otherwise.

Scheckter joined Ferrari and was adamant that whilst he fully intended to become World Champion such a thing did not particularly interest Villeneuve who felt that if it came along, well, it came along.

Scheckter drove so consistently that by season's end he'd scored in twelve of the 15 rounds. The season was run in two halves and a driver could count only his four best finishes in each, so Scheckter had to drop four. Villeneuve ended up dropping a couple but his results tended to reflect his character: win or bust.

The roundabout: Regazzoni joined Jones at Williams; Piquet joined Lauda at Brabham; Reutemann joined Andretti at Lotus. Jabouille and Arnoux had the Renault turbos; and Watson departed Brabham for McLaren.

Laffite won Argentina for Ligier, and Balestre arrived for his first race. He made immediate attempts to impose himself. Watson and Scheckter collided on the first lap and five other cars were involved. Professor Watkins had been given a medical car but the organisers wouldn't allow him to use it trailing the grid on the first lap. When the race restarted, Watkins covered the initial part of the opening lap in an ambulance.[39]

Balestre, 'sartorially resplendent in white suit and matching shoes,'[40] intervened over the crash. The Stewards met, Watson was found guilty and fined 10,000 Swiss francs – a considerable sum which, one report suggests, equalled more than McLaren earned for Watson's third place.

In Brazil, Balestre said Watson would not be allowed to race unless he paid his fine. Ecclestone and Max Mosley met Balestre in a basement office at the Interlagos circuit and faced Balestre down. Watson raced (and finished eighth). Laffite won again, but these two victories proved a distraction because he'd only score points in one of the next seven races.

Some weeks after this, FOCA met at Maranello and Ecclestone announced that the basics of Grand Prix racing – car specifications, safety, race regulations, discipline – would be overseen by a FOCA committee. Balestre countered that the *FISA* was the governing body.

Battle had been joined.

Villeneuve won South Africa and Long Beach from Scheckter but when Depailler (Ligier) won Spain the season opened up: Villeneuve and Depailler 20 points, Laffite and Reutemann 18, Scheckter 16, Andretti 12.

Scheckter broke through in Belgium, winning from Laffite, and when he added Monaco to complete the first half of the season he had 30 points counting, Laffite 24, Villeneuve, Depailler and Reutemann 20. Hunt's Wolf failed after four laps and as he stepped out, someone noted, he had the look of a man who wasn't coming back. He wasn't.

The Monaco measure: Scheckter, 76 laps, 1h 55m 22.4s, an average speed of 81.3mph; Depailler, 1978, 80.3mph.

The measure of the decades: 1929, 49.8mph; 1937, 63.2mph; 1948, 59.7mph; 1958, 67.9mph; 1968, 77.8mph.

Vehicles registered in Britain 18.6 million (1958, 14.4 million).

A Ford Fiesta 957cc cost £1,856 and a Briton earned on average £89.60 a week. Saving all his money, the Briton would have taken 20 weeks to buy one (1910, 2 years 42 weeks; 1919, 1 year 28 weeks; 1929, 41 weeks; 1938, 37 weeks; 1949, 45 weeks; 1959, 36 weeks; 1969, 25 weeks).

Sweden was cancelled because of cash problems with sponsors. A Swedish oil company came forward at the last moment to rescue it and Ecclestone announced this. Balestre pointed out that such a re-instatement could not be a round of the World Championship or carry points unless it was approved by *FISA*, which couldn't meet in time. The race didn't happen.

Jabouille won France, the first time a car with a turbo-charged engine had done this. The race, at Dijon, ought to be remembered for that but it isn't. Instead, by lap 71 of the 80 Arnoux caught Villeneuve, second. They moved in among back-markers but with three laps left Arnoux scrambled by. There was a mood of devilment on both men, an exquisite expression of physical and mental combat, a distillation of everything pure racing cars could be made to do.

The mood grew, with each move and counter-move, into a powerful impetus feeding off itself.

In a right-hander they ran abreast, Arnoux on the inside. Into the right-left mini-complex Arnoux was through, the crowd on their feet: Renault 1–2. Arnoux crossed the line into the penultimate lap with Villeneuve directly behind him. Into the right-hander Villeneuve dived inside and locked his brakes, plumes of smoke from the Ferrari's wheels. Now he had the inside line, Arnoux running abreast on the outside. They went through the mini-complex, Arnoux following Villeneuve across the line into the last lap.

Now Arnoux probed over to the inside in the right-hander and Villeneuve twitched away from him, smoke from the wheels again. Villeneuve ran down the outside but ahead, and their wheels touched: no brake lights from either car. Into the next tight-right Villeneuve took Arnoux round the outside and they almost touched. Into the mini-complex they almost touched again and Arnoux slid wide, slid off. As he came back on the Renault swivelled to the other side of the track and Villeneuve was through. They banged wheels.

They banged wheels again in a right-hander, banged them so hard that the Renault was pitched semi-sideways. Arnoux caught the car by reflex – and the impact pushed the Ferrari wide. Arnoux was through, the Ferrari corkscrewing up the track behind him. They fled into another right. Villeneuve cut across the apex, Arnoux behind him. Arnoux followed and – finally, without any sense of anti-climax – they crossed the line in that order.

Frank Williams had been competing in the British Grand Prix since 1969. He was about to prove that everything does come to those who wait. Jones took pole at Silverstone (from Jabouille), Regazzoni on the second row. Jones led the race to lap 38, when the water pump failed, passing the lead to Regazzoni who won it. Understandably, Jones could not bear to stay and Neil Oatley, Regazzoni's engineer, would say:

it was not as emotional as I thought it would be. Frank is not one to show his emotion, not even on a day like this. Not in public. I think, also, with Alan retiring and then leaving the circuit, that put a bit of a dampener on things for Frank.[41]

A mid-season ripple of races: Jones won Germany from Regazzoni, won Austria from Villeneuve, won Holland from Scheckter. Superficially that made the championship interesting – Scheckter 44, Laffite 36, Jones 34, Villeneuve 32 – but it wasn't. Rather, the absurdity of the scoring system stood exposed because the instant Jones won Holland he lost all hope. Even if he won the final three races, by counting only his best four finishes in this second half he could total no more than 40.

Scheckter settled it at Monza, anyway. Laffite's engine failed on lap 42 of the 50, Scheckter leading and Villeneuve following.

> The only time I pushed the car after Laffite broke down was on the second last lap. I wanted to make sure that even if Gilles wanted to pass me he couldn't. I waited, pushed as hard as I could to make sure I didn't have to trust Gilles on the final lap. I couldn't leave it to anybody else, I had to do it. Even if he'd wanted to pass I made sure he couldn't.[42]

The *tifosi*, the emotional, unruly and passionate Italian supporters pouring their affection onto anything Ferrari, would not have believed anyone who dared to suggest that no other Ferrari driver would win the Championship until the year 2000, and the one who finally did would have no knowledge of, or great interest in, Ferrari's history.

A strange, low-key end of season: during practice in Canada Lauda suddenly decided to end his career. He got into the Brabham and suddenly it felt strange, boring, slow. He thought *I don't belong here anymore* and walked away from it, as he thought, forever. Jones won from Villeneuve, and Villeneuve won a wet Watkins Glen.

Jones bestrode 1980, creating, as he went, an uncomfortable legacy for all the Williams drivers to come after him. He spoke his mind if anything was wrong but otherwise just drove the car to its maximum, whatever condition it or he was in. Frank Williams liked and respected that.

The roundabout: Alain Prost joined Watson at McLaren; an elegant and versatile Italian, Elio de Angelis, joined Lotus from Shadow. All grids were now staggered.

Jones set the tone immediately, winning Argentina from Piquet, now beginning his second full season. Piquet, sometimes languid and sometimes fiery, carried natural speed with him. By 1980, he'd been competing for more than a decade, starting in karts at his hometown of Rio and in this championship he'd run Jones closer even than Reutemann – but Arnoux won Brazil.

In February, between Brazil and South Africa, seven Japanese, a Swiss (Jabby Crombac) and a photographer (Bernard Cahier) sat in the Prince of Wales Hotel, Paris having lunch. Honda were returning to racing and they wanted some advice. Crombac and Cahier had known them for a long time. They'd decided to develop an engine rather than build their own car, and decided it should be a Formula 2 engine. Crombac told them they'd better hurry because Formula 2 was 'almost dead' so they did hurry their engine to Jack Brabham, his designer Ron Tauranac and the RALT team.

The turbos were becoming a factor, especially on fast tracks. That's how Jabouille took pole again in South Africa, how Arnoux took the win again. At this point Arnoux led the Championship from Jones 18–13.

Jones was unhappy at Kyalami because he'd been slipping back and the gearbox failed. Before he left the circuit Frank Williams sent him to the Leyland hospitality tent – Leyland a major sponsor – and Jones did the right thing, had a beer or two, chatted. A drunk came up and said something rude, then took a lunge at Jones, which was not the thing to do whatever mood Jones happened to be in. Jones 'whacked' him and down he went.[43]

In the background Prost explored Grand Prix racing in his own rational way, taking the McLaren to sixth in Argentina and fifth in Brazil but at Kyalami two car failures, one breaking his wrist, made him sceptical about the safety of the car. He missed Long Beach.

Piquet led throughout from pole but on lap 51, approaching a hairpin on the 180mph straight, Regazzoni's brakes failed on the Ensign and he went up the escape road at full speed, striking a Brabham which had broken down long before. The Ensign flipped over a barrier and Regazzoni was trapped for 25 minutes. The crash was described at the time as one of the most violent in Grand Prix history.

Regazzoni never walked again.

Didier Pironi (Ligier), a handsome Parisian, won his first race in Belgium, Jones behind him. Sometime during practice Eddie Cheever, a young American and resident of Italy, struggled with an Osella-Ford and baulked Jones. When the session ended Jones came down the pit lane, overall tops undone and hanging down from his waist like a peeled banana. He lifted Cheever – a strong man – off the ground and explained the facts of life in the language of short, sharp words.[44]

By then Balestre and FOCA were at war on a much larger scale than Jones and Cheever. After Regazzoni's crash Balestre tried to say that it and others before it, including Prost's, now meant an 'accelerated' programme to strengthen 'cockpits plus the cars as a whole, as it has been sacrificed by certain constructors for the benefit of speed.' This provoked outrage, not least from Teddy Mayer at McLaren who described Balestre's Press statement as 'typically ill-considered and possibly libellous.'

In Belgium, FOCA took their revenge when they discovered that under supplementary regulations for the race, drivers did not have to attend pre-race briefings – which would defy a ruling introduced by Balestre when he took office. The teams made sure the drivers didn't go: Balestre fined each driver $2,000 and revoked their licences.

Reutemann won Monaco from Laffite, Jones out with a blown gearbox although he disliked Monaco's poseurs, yachts, constricted space and the 'bloody procession' of a race.

The Monaco measure: Reutemann, 76 laps, 1h 55m 34.3s, an average speed of 81.1mph; Scheckter, 1979, 81.3mph.

In Spain the political war brought chaos. Ecclestone held a meeting with the constructors in the paddock and although, the driver fines were not discussed, the immediate reinstatement of their licences was: *no reinstatement, no race.* The teams divided into 'loyalists' – Ferrari, Renault, Alfa Romeo and Osella inclined towards *FISA* – and 'rebels' (the rest) towards FOCA. The Spanish organisers pointed out that they had a contract with FOCA and the race would go ahead. Balestre countered that a race involving unlicensed drivers could not be a round of the World Championship. Ferrari, Renault and Alfa Romeo withdrew, and Jones won the race which never was. No points were awarded, so the nine he lost were a bitter blow.

Balestre was not about to interfere with the French Grand Prix and compromises were hammered out. Jones – in bellicose mood after the robbery in Spain – won it from Pironi. Standing on the podium he was surprised to see a horse being led up. The man leading it invited him to sit on it and he responded *not on yer life, mate.* Later, drinking a beer in the Williams motorhome, the same man came up and asked him where he wanted the horse put – Jones had no idea he had won it. (He shipped it back to Australia.)

This was the mid-point of the season. Ten best finishes out of the 14 rounds counted, five from each half.

Jones 28 points, Piquet 25, Pironi and Arnoux 23.

Jones won Brands Hatch after the Ligiers hit trouble and that launched him strongly into the second half, so strongly that eventually he'd have to drop his third place from the next race, Hockenheim, where Laffite won from Reutemann. An absent friend there: Depailler had been killed testing at the circuit a week before. His Alfa Romeo snapped out of control in the looping, fast Ostkurve and struck the barrier. This will do nicely as an obituary:

> The archetypal wiry Frenchman, a cigarette perpetually dangling from the corner of his mouth, Depailler was something of a free spirit – a throwback to an earlier age, who lived for the moment and raced accordingly.[45]

In Austria, an Englishman made his debut at the very back of the grid. Nigel Mansell saw his whole career in terms of struggle and that continued here. Driving a third Lotus the car wasn't right and he switched to that of de Angelis, and just made it. As the mechanics topped his car on the grid some petrol spilt and began burning him.

Jones consolidated his championship position in the race by running second – the turbo power enabled Jabouille to get past him so easily it seemed, as Jones said himself, as if he'd parked the Williams – while the petrol burnt Mansell mercilessly. The car failed on lap 41 and Mansell could barely walk away from it.

Six days later Alfred Neubauer, who'll always be remembered as Mercedes' team manager, died. He'd retired when Mercedes withdrew from racing at the end of 1955.

Piquet struck back in Holland where Jones was openly irritated by people saying *hello champ!* Jones knew that if he didn't finish the race, and Piquet won it, everything changed. Jones didn't finish, or rather did but three laps down after going off and damaging the skirts on the Williams.

Piquet maintained the pressure by winning Imola, the only time the Italian Grand Prix would be held there (from 1981, it was the San Marino Grand Prix) but Jones came in second and was satisfied.

Jones knew the combinations for the final two races, Canada and the United States, but they became irrelevant almost immediately. Piquet took pole, Jones alongside, in Canada, but as the race started they touched. 'Alan,' Piquet would say, 'pushed me into the wall.' Piquet's elbow had been badly bruised and he'd have to take the restart in the spare car.

He seized the lead and held it until lap 24 when the engine blew. 'One minute it was perfect, the next it went bang.' Brabham realised that only Pironi, running second, could keep Piquet's championship alive by catching and overtaking Jones. It didn't matter that Pironi, in a Ligier, had nothing to do with it. Brabham began hanging out a pit board to him with $ signs on it ...

Just then an announcement said Pironi was penalised a minute for jumping the start, and that of course removed him from the equation. After such a season, Jones didn't necessarily buy that on the strength of the pit signal Williams hung out to him. He raced on and only when the sign had been hung out for the third time – *and* he glimpsed Frank Williams nodding – did he relent.

Typically, he won Watkins Glen. As a man, and as the racer Williams treasured, that's what you did, every race everywhere except, perhaps, when you've had the nod that you're World Champion.

In 1981, Prost left McLaren and joined Renault, which meant breaking his contract. His confidence in the McLaren had finally been destroyed at Watkins Glen when the suspension failed. He was knocked out by the crash, withdrew from the race, packed his belongings and departed slamming the door behind him. He made clear to Mayer that if McLaren tried to hold him he'd leave the sport altogether.

Andrea de Cesaris, an Italian known to be wild but with powerful sponsorship connections, replaced Prost. Something else was moving, and had been since around 1980. At the insistence of Marlboro, McLaren were to become a blending of the original team and 'the ambitious, less experienced but highly talented Project Four team trio of Ron Dennis, Creighton Brown and engineer Barnard.'[46] Dennis, formerly a mechanic, was a gifted and meticulous organiser, John Barnard one of the greatest designers. Project Four served its apprenticeship in the lower formulae and was ready for something bigger. Mayer remained as joint managing director for a year.

Barnard introduced carbon-fibre moulded monocoques to Grand Prix racing. That is a semi-technical way of saying that carbon composites – put together in layers to give a material which was light, flexible and stronger than steel – changed everything. Initially, John Watson entertained doubts about just how strong it would be in an accident, and he'd get proof in the most direct way at Monza where he survived a crash of enormous impact.

Scheckter retired and Pironi replaced him at Ferrari.

Like a theme moving sporadically from background to foreground the power struggle between Balestre and FOCA continued. Balestre threatened that *FISA* would take over start and prize money, and Ecclestone threatened to set up a World Federation of Motor Sports to run the whole thing. Colin Chapman even wrote the Technical Regulations and explained:

> Formula 1 should be the pinnacle of motor racing. It should have the minimum of parameters controlling performance. There are only four parameters which control a racing car; one is the power from the engine; the second is the aerodynamical download it can produce; the third is the amount of grip which can be obtained by the tyres and the fourth is the weight. Then there should be some second category of regulations concerning the passive safety of the cars in the event of an accident. I think this should be controlled by some form of crash test rather than by myriads of little regulations which, in themselves, very rarely produce the objectives they were set up to achieve.[47]

There was also a lively controversy over skirts. Balestre wanted them banned because they were making cars too fast for the circuits. The faster a car went, the more the air forced under it – directed by the skirts rather than dissipated – gave adhesion. An intrinsic problem was that if a skirt broke and adhesion was lost the car could be launched like an aeroplane. Drivers' necks took tremendous strain in corners with the G-forces pulling the head; the G-forces were so extreme that drivers found their feet being forced away from the pedals. FOCA wanted skirts retained because the cars would have to be redesigned and, to achieve the same performance, fortunes would have to be spent on more powerful engines.

Balestre wanted new rules increasing the minimum weight of the cars – which suited Renault, who already had a heavy car – but would compel the other teams to have turbos themselves requiring daunting, perhaps fatal, amounts of money.

Far in the background, a thin, shy young man flew from São Paulo to London and then caught a train to Norwich station. He was met and taken for lunch at a hotel in the pleasant country town of Attleborough. There, Ayrton Senna da Silva talked terms with Ralph Firman, who ran van Diemen. They made 1,600cc cars, which was where youngsters began. For a karter who'd not yet even driven a racing car, da Silva drove a hard bargain. He'd been recommended to Firman by another Brazilian, Chico Serra, and now he'd come. Firman and da Silva agreed a deal for the season and soon after Senna did get in a car. Firman watched and thought *there's something about this young man*.

Firman was not wrong.

The championship ought to have opened at Kyalami in early February but only the FOCA teams went. They ran with skirts (Reutemann won from Piquet) and *FISA* wouldn't recognise the race. Formula 1 faced an abyss.

The future was now very grim. Sponsors were threatening to withdraw their support and the smaller teams were living from hand to mouth, dependent on start money to pay wages. Their very existence was now in jeopardy. Finally, FOCA realised they had lost the war and initiated talks with *FISA*.

This was well-timed, because Jean-Marie Balestre was not in a very strong position either. He knew that the FOCA members were feeling the pinch and his strategy should have been to cancel the first two or three GPs of the season and really have them crying out for mercy. However, it just so happened that the first championship race (after the South African fiasco) was scheduled to be [...] Long Beach. The American market was, of course, very important to Renault [...] When they realised that the race at Long Beach might not take place, Renault panicked and spread the word that, 'with or without Balestre, we shall be in Long Beach.'[48]

Only ten days before the race a 'Concorde Agreement' was hammered out to bring peace – but skirts were banned. The teams, who had already had to rebuild their cars when Chapman first introduced skirts, now faced having to do it again just two years later. The ban, too, was of crucial importance to Chapman who had a new Lotus, the 86, built and tested in absolute secrecy. It involved twin chassis, a simple idea, however complex in realisation: one chassis absorbed the shocks coming up off the track surface at high speed, leaving the other to cushion the driver. These had to be modified and the car was renumbered the 88.

Ferrari became the second team to run turbo engines. This was the future and soon enough any team without a turbo faced a crippling disadvantage.

The eleven best finishes of the 15 rounds counted and initially Williams looked very strong. Jones won Long Beach from Reutemann, while Chapman's Lotus 88 was black flagged in practice – Frank Williams said he'd withdraw his cars if it was passed legal.

Reutemann won Brazil from Jones. Between these two races, Mike Hailwood was killed in a car crash. He'd been taking his children to buy fish 'n' chips and a lorry did an illegal u-turn in front of him. He and his daughter died, his son survived. Like Gunnar Nilsson in another context, there is almost too much irony and pathos to bear.

Chapman, incandescent at the Lotus 88 ban in Argentina – the third race in a row – departed even before practice leaving a savage statement about 'cleaning up' Formula 1 before the sport ended up 'a quagmire of plagiarism, chicanery and petty rule interpretations forced by lobbies manipulated by people for whom the word sport has no meaning.' The race prised the whole season open. Jones made one of the best starts of his career. Piquet, almost sublimely fast here, swept imperiously by and, to a great roar, Reutemann went past Jones into second place.

Piquet won San Marino at Imola, the Lotus 88 was banned by the *FIA* Court of Appeal but so late that Chapman could not modify cars in time. The race provided an historical footnote as the first without a Lotus since 1958 when Graham Hill made his debut against such as Moss and Hawthorn at Monaco, and Ecclestone and Chiron hadn't qualified.

Brabham tested BMW turbos.

On the Friday afternoon at Zolder, a mechanic with the Osella team fell off the ledge along the pit wall just as Reutemann travelled slowly by. The mechanic was pitched against the wall and taken to hospital in critical condition. He died three days later. Reutemann, distraught, was able to compose himself enough to win the race from Laffite, and led the championship from Piquet 34–22, Jones third on 18.

At Monaco Piquet led to lap 54 but crashed at Tabac, Jones led by 12 seconds with seven laps to go and Villeneuve circled, hungry, a long way back. Then...

> on lap 67 Jones pulled into the pits, where fuel vaporization was diagnosed and he was sent out again with the problem unremedied. Gilles was now just six seconds behind him and began to lessen the interval, pushing ever harder and sending the attendant horde of Villeneuve fans into hysterics of screaming lungs, hooting air horns, wailing yacht sirens, and waving flags and banners. There was an explosion of joy as the Ferrari passed the Williams in front of the pits on lap 72 and an even greater one when Gilles acknowledged the chequered flag on the 76th lap.[49]

The Monaco measure: Villeneuve, 76 laps, 1h 54m 23.3s, an average speed of 82.0mph; Reutemann, 1980, 81.1mph.

Jones led Spain but locked his brakes and went off, and from that moment Villeneuve held the cumbersome, unwieldy Ferrari in front of a train of cars variously attacking him and each other. Villeneuve's tyres were going off. That made no difference. Reutemann constantly stabbed the Williams towards him. That made no difference. Laffite came up into second, thrust the Ligier alongside whenever he could. That made no difference. Villeneuve manipulated the Ferrari through the circuit's 16 corners, squeezed its power on the straights lap after lap, maintaining composure and concentration. He followed the racing line, as he was perfectly entitled to do, and afterwards even experienced observers mumbled in disbelief about controlling a race in *that* car. Crossing the finishing line:

Villeneuve	1h 46m 35.1s
Laffite	@ 0.21s
Watson	@ 0.57s
Reutemann	@ 1.00

A cloudburst stopped the French Grand Prix at Dijon after 58 laps and when it restarted Prost led. Watson almost forced a path past him and then Prost settled, hoping his slick tyres would survive the final 22 laps. They did. He became the fifth race winner of the season but, more important, described this first career victory as a 'passport to the future.'[50] He explained in his precise, thoughtful way the psychology: how it's a liberation from 'all the inhibitions and complexes' a driver must have on the way to it, how the instant you cross the line you've proved to yourself you're the equal of the others.

Chapman presented a revised version of the 88 at the British Grand Prix. The RAC Technical Commission, scrutineers for the race, earlier declared it legal. Balestre reacted by saying that, if it ran, the race would forfeit its championship status. The RAC reacted to that by saying it was running the Grand Prix. Balestre prevailed and Lotus had to run their 87 car. Watson won and years later would bask in the memory of the end when he could hear the vast crowd roaring their delight and suddenly realised it was for him.

Piquet won Germany, Laffite won Austria watched by Niki Lauda, commenting on Austrian television. Since his retirement Lauda worked on establishing an airline and didn't always watch races on his own television. If he did he felt nervous about crashes at the first corner. Like Caracciola so long ago in Monaco, coming back to the smells and sounds of racing exercised a powerful effect. Lauda felt a 'tingling' sensation and wasn't even nervous watching the wolf pack get to the first corner. Afterwards he went to see fitness guru Willy Dungl, made vague noises about the racing, and went on a regime to get fit.

Reutemann 45 points, Piquet 39, Laffite 34, Jones 27.

Prost led Holland, Jones chasing him. It moved Prost to describe Jones as the 'most fiery, the most powerful – I would even go so far as to say violent – driver that year.'[51] Prost felt Jones coming by on lap 23 but thought: *the driver doing that often thinks he has damaged your morale. His concentration can be affected.* Into the Tarzan horseshoe Prost drew alongside and retook Jones who, Prost felt, was so surprised he didn't respond. It settled the race.

Monza finished Prost-Jones, too,

Ron Dennis, becoming dominant at McLaren, kept in touch with Lauda and they talked during this Italian Grand Prix. Lauda explained to Dennis that something was gnawing at him: Lauda did not want to know if he should make a comeback, he needed to know if he was capable of it.

Three days later Lauda went to Donington for a secret test in the McLaren, Dennis supervising, Watson helping to set the car up. Much had changed, wings, ground effect, cornering speeds. Lauda was shocked that he couldn't drive three laps together because they required such extreme effort. Later in the day he did a couple of laps within a tenth of Watson and he knew the speed was still there.

Lauda went to Marlboro and asked for more money than any driver had ever been paid before. It provoked a 'deathly silence' and then they said yes, albeit offering a contract with get-out clauses in case Lauda proved an embarrassing failure.

Laffite won Canada from Watson. It made the finale, in a car park at Caesars Palace, Las Vegas, a mathematical morass trapping Reutemann (49 points), Piquet (48) and Laffite (43). The possible point totals:

	1st	2nd	3rd	4th	5th	6th
Reutemann	58	55	53	52	51	50
Piquet	57	54	52	51	50	49
Laffite	52	49	47	46	45	44

There was a possibility, however remote, that all three could finish on 52 and then Laffite won on the tie-break: he and Piquet would have the same number of wins but Laffite more second places. If Piquet didn't score, and Reutemann and Laffite finished on 49, Laffite got it again, on most third places.

Jones was eloquent about the circuit. 'It's like a goat track dragged down from the mountains and flattened out.' Reutemann took pole from Jones, Piquet on the second row, Laffite on the sixth. Jones made a crisp, decisive start but Reutemann didn't and Piquet didn't. They were running fifth and seventh. Piquet caught Reutemann and took him. Nobody knew that the Williams was having a gearbox problem, jumping out of fourth as the car rode the bumps on the circuit, or that he hadn't had time to bed in new brakes properly.

Piquet, neck sore after a practice crash, already felt exhausted. He was a slender, almost wan, man and looked too frail for anything like the 75 laps. With seven left Laffite got past Reutemann but that only made him seventh, Reutemann eighth. Both were a lap down, Piquet forcing himself forward in fifth place. It was enough. He had to be lifted from the car and on the podium was close to tears.

Alan Jones, about to retire, did not like Carlos Reutemann. 'Let's,' Reutemann said after the race, 'bury the hatchet' to which Jones responded 'yes, in your back.'

Like 1976, the 1982 season was complicated and each of the 16 rounds like a detonation.

The roundabout: Jones informed Frank Williams of his decision to retire at Monza, so late in the season that finding a top replacement for

1982 was now virtually impossible. Williams scanned the horizon and there glimpsed one Keijo Rosberg, a heavy-smoking Finn who'd driven 36 Grands Prix since 1978 for a variety of lowly teams and scored points only twice. To sign him might transport Williams back to the rent-a-driver days but at this stage Williams had to take what he could get and he could certainly get Rosberg. The team tested him at Paul Ricard, got him in the car at eight one morning, shod it with qualifying tyres, didn't warm it up and said *now show us what you can do*. He did.

Patrese joined Piquet at Brabham.

South Africa, 23 January. The turbos had come, Renault, Brabham-BMW, Ferrari and a young, small, homely team called Toleman running a Brian Hart engine. That wasn't the story. *FISA* worded the drivers' application for super-licences – which they had to have to compete – so that the driver was bound to his team. Lauda got his and saw all the dangers. He rang Pironi, President of the Grand Prix Drivers' Association, and said the drivers should come together to resist it. For once Balestre and Ecclestone were on the same side. The drivers, Lauda saw, had a choice: *accept or go to hell*. They went on strike.

Thursday: 30 drivers meet at the circuit entrance and board a coach to the Sunnyside Hotel, Johannesburg.

'Drivers' wives throw rolls and crockery at Balestre during dinner at the Kyalami Ranch,'[52] where the drivers usually stayed and would have been if they hadn't gone to Johannesburg.

Lauda remembered that the buoyant mood lasted through dinner at their hotel and then the manager was asked for a room big enough to take all the drivers. Lauda knew that if they had individual rooms the united front would be breached by morning. The drivers got a small suite used for banquets – a piano but no toilet. Sheets were laid on the floor.

Lauda remembered, too, that Mo Nunn, who ran the Ensign team, cunningly brought Roberto Guerrero's girlfriend. The love birds gazed at each other through the glass door, both crying. Lauda said: 'OK, you can go out to talk to her – but I'm coming.' The love birds whispered 'sweet nothings' and Guerrero said: 'I'm not going back in.' Lauda replied: 'Oh yes you are – and she can come in as well.'

Villeneuve played the piano (many drivers were astonished that he could play it at all, never mind this well) and de Angelis played it, too. There's a brief film of him playing a piano – not here during the strike, but that doesn't matter – and it seems to have come to him effortlessly.

Lauda remembered the man running the Arrows team, Jackie Oliver, arriving with a heavy minder and the police in an attempt to gain entry.

Lauda understood that if there was any sort of brawling the police would legitimately be able to use force so a tug o' war developed, with Oliver's army pushing one side of the door and Lauda's lieutenants pushing the other. Master tactician Lauda then used the piano to block the door.[53]

Friday: Negotiations go on from 8.30 in the morning. Teo Fabi of Toleman goes to the circuit prepared to drive. Jochen Mass (March), who hadn't joined the strike, does three laps and returns to the pits amid great applause.

Pironi rings Lauda from the circuit and Lauda tells the drivers *'We've got what we wanted.'* Drivers return to circuit and practice begins – only, now, one session. The race was on next day, the Saturday.

Arnoux took pole from Piquet but Prost won. He was leading but a tyre blew and he pitted, changed all four tyres, emerged eighth. The new tyres enabled him to drive so aggressively that 23 laps later he was in the lead again. He'd demonstrated, as he said himself, that if your pit crew was good enough and your car was good enough you could win from a pit stop – something Ecclestone and Murray at Brabham noticed.

Brazil, 21 March. Villeneuve led but under attack from Piquet went off into the guard-rail. Piquet won but was so exhausted he collapsed on the podium, Rosberg – second – virtually holding him up. Ferrari and Renault protested the Brabham and Williams under the loose minimum weight rule which gave rise to gamesmanship. Prost was particularly incensed by what he called the 'water-container ploy' – theoretically cars carried water to cool the brakes. When a race began the water was emptied so the cars ran 30–40kg [66–88lb] lighter and, after the race, were allowed to top up the water, so the car returned to its pre-race weight. The protests were later upheld, disqualifying Piquet and Rosberg – and Mr Rosberg expressing bitterness about it. 'The sport was at war again and I was disgusted.'[54]

United States West, 4 April. Reutemann suddenly announced his retirement, and Williams brought Mario Andretti in for this one race. De Cesaris (Alfa Romeo) took pole from Lauda, led the race but was baulked by a backmarker. De Cesaris shook his fist at this back marker and Lauda saw that, and thought *he should be changing gear with that hand now.* Lauda went by, keeping well clear of de Cesaris. In the last lap Lauda shouted and whistled in his delight then said to himself *don't be stupid, don't got into the wall.* Rosberg came second 14 seconds away.

San Marino, 25 April. Ten FOCA teams did not go to Imola because of Piquet and Rosberg's disqualifications. Tyrrell did, joining 12 other cars. Arnoux led from pole but his engine failed after 44 laps of the 60. Villeneuve led, Pironi behind him and the Ferrari team held out a SLOW sign which traditionally meant *hold station, run to the end in that order.* Villeneuve and Pironi put on a demonstration – or at least Villeneuve imagined they were – using the Ferraris to entertain the Italian crowd because for the final few laps only five cars remained. They swopped the lead to and fro, to and fro and Villeneuve assumed Pironi would tuck in behind before the end. Villeneuve had been leading at the SLOW sign and led again. He slowed and Pironi chopped him, won it. Villeneuve never spoke to him again.

Belgium, 9 May. With some 15 minutes of second qualifying left the Ferrari pit signalled Villeneuve in. He'd done three quick laps and his tyres were finished. Some drivers might have backed off completely, coasted round. Villeneuve didn't. He moved into the kink at a place called Terlamenbocht round at the back of the circuit. He came upon Jochen Mass travelling slowly. Mass saw Villeneuve and assumed he'd go by on the left. Mass shifted his March over to the right. In an instant he saw Villeneuve virtually on top of him. The Ferrari was pitched into the air and landed tearing itself to pieces in a series of savage cartwheels and impacts. Villeneuve, in his seat, was torn out and flung fifty yards. No man could have survived it and, for many people, Formula 1 would never be the same again. Villeneuve, open, almost naïve, totally natural in a racing car once said that that was the only place where he felt truly alive.

Arnoux led the race but Rosberg took him on lap five to lead a Grand Prix for the first time. Watson worked his way up to second and Rosberg, tyres badly worn, tried to get past a backmarker to hold Watson off, went wide and Watson was through.

Monaco, 23 May. Towards the end drizzle fell.

Prost led but with three laps to go the Renault suddenly flicked sideways into the guardrail, passing the lead to...

Patrese who lost control and the Brabham stalled beside the Loews Hotel, passing the lead to...

Pironi whose slick tyres glistening as they lapped at the wet track. Into the tunnel on the last lap the Ferrari slowed, stammered, stopped. Its electrics had failed, passing the lead to...

De Cesaris but the Alfa Romeo stopped out of fuel and de Cesaris stood nearby tears coursing down his face. Through his tears he passed the lead to...

Derek Daly in the second Williams who led but was stopping, crippled by a crash a couple of laps before, passing the lead back to...

Patrese who'd had had a push, his car in a dangerous position, and now came round unaware – like the man with the flag and the crowd – that he was about to win. Even after the race it took some time for the Brabham team to convince him he had.

The Monaco measure: Patrese, 76 laps, 1h 54m 11.2s, an average speed of 82.1mph; Villeneuve, 1981, 82.0mph.

United States, 6 June. Detroit, the home of the US automotive industry, seemed a logical place to have a Grand Prix but the reality proved quite different, a geometrical 2.4-mile circuit of streets, perfect 90° corners, concrete blocks, bumps and manhole covers. Initially the track wasn't ready and the drivers hung around bored until it was. Prost, who disliked the place, took pole from de Cesaris. Some crashing on lap seven stopped it and from the restart Watson, 13th, worked his way up to the lead. It was a consummate display drawing together patience, precision and the nerve to strike.

Watson 26 points, Pironi 20, Prost 18, Rosberg 17.

Canada, 13 June. Pironi took pole and broke down into sobbing. *We all know,* he said, *who would have been on pole if he had been here.* Pironi stalled at the start and the cars immediately behind weaved past but accelerating at full bore the Osella of rookie Riccardo Paletti – in third gear, doing 120mph – ran full into the Ferrari. The Osella burst into flames and many brave men, Pironi among them, did what they could. It took 28 minutes to get Paletti out and he was officially pronounced dead in hospital from extensive internal injuries. Piquet won a joyless victory from Patrese and Watson.

Holland, 3 July. Arnoux had a terrifying moment in practice when the Renault's left front wheel came off under braking for the Tarzan horseshoe and the car thumped a tyre barrier, riding up it. Arnoux was unhurt. Pironi dominated the race, Piquet second and Rosberg third.

Watson 30, Pironi 29, Rosberg 21.

Britain, 18 July. The problem for Rosberg and all the non-turbo runners had by now become plain: on fast tracks the turbos delivered too much power. The non-turbos might hold them at a place like Brands Hatch and Rosberg took pole, the first of his career. He had a good feeling but the Williams wouldn't start for the parade lap and when it did he took his place at the back of the grid. Brabham had been preparing the 'Prost ploy' from South Africa: would they bring Piquet in during the race for new tyres? Nobody found out because although he led a mechanical problem halted him and Lauda stroked the McLaren home, Pironi second and leading the championship.

France, 25 July. The French Grand Prix was always the centre-piece of any French team's efforts, especially for Renault – dispensing tax payer's money – so when Arnoux took pole from Prost great joy consumed the land although Prost lay joint fifth in the championship (19 points) and Arnoux joint 16th (4). The team boss, Gérard Larrousse, said before the race that if Arnoux led he should move aside and give it to Prost in the interests of the championship.

On lap 11 Mass and another car touched, Mass airborne across some catch fencing, a tyre wall and then through a further fence near the spectator area. Nobody was hurt.

From lap 24 to the end, lap 54, Arnoux led with Prost behind him. The Renault team repeatedly signalled to Arnoux but he wasn't having any of that. He'd say later that if it had been for the championship itself he might have considered helping Prost, and he might not. Arnoux won from Prost by 17 seconds. Prost has recounted how, driving home, he stopped to fill up the car and the attendant mistook him for Arnoux. The attendant congratulated him and said *that Prost had it coming to him.*[55]

Germany, 8 August. In a wet Saturday morning untimed session as he approached the Stadium complex Pironi came up to Daly, who was catching Prost. Daly overtook Prost by moving to the right. Through the spray Pironi *assumed* Daly did this to allow him through. Pironi couldn't see Prost within the spray and struck the Renault, the Ferrari flung into the air. When it came to rest Pironi sat trapped inside it, one leg terribly damaged and his Grand Prix career over.

Tambay won the race, although not before Piquet – who intended to adopt the 'Prost ploy' – crashed with a Colombian, Eliseo Salazar. Piquet sprang out, tried to kick Salazar in a very delicate place and then punched his face. *Not a problem,* Salazar would say, *I had my crash helmet on and like that he can punch me all day.*

Pironi 39, Watson 30, Rosberg 27, Prost 25, Lauda 24.

Austria, 15 August. Everything up to the final five laps – Piquet's pole, the three leaders who dropped out, Patrese finally using 'Prost's ploy' (24 gallons and new tyres in 15.6 seconds stationary) – served as a prelude. Now round the immense loops and descents of the Österreichring the black and gold Lotus of de Angelis held off the muscular Williams which Rosberg kept thrusting closer and closer to him. On the rush to the final corner, the carving downhill right, Rosberg mentally hesitated. Ordinarily he'd have gone to the inside, onto the kerbing, onto the *grass* but now he was thinking of the championship, and if de Angelis didn't give him room...

De Angelis went inside, forcing Rosberg to the outside – the long way round. Rosberg tucked in behind and now they rushed towards the line. Rosberg twisted the Williams out, gunning it as hard as it would go. He lost it by 0.050 of a second and there on the rim of the track stood Chapman and the black cap. It hadn't been in orbit since Holland, 1978, would be in just a moment and never would be again.

Pironi 39, Rosberg 33, Watson 30, Lauda 26.

Switzerland, 29 August. Rosberg thought the Dijon circuit might suit a non-turbo car although the turbos dominated qualifying. In the race Rosberg hustled up to third but de Cesaris, a lap down, wouldn't let him through for a long time. Rosberg came as near to losing control of himself in a race as he had ever done. At 170mph on the straight Rosberg 'banged him with my front wheel on his sideboards.' Eventually de Cesaris made a mistake, and Rosberg caught and overtook Arnoux. He moved on Prost and three laps from the end got him when Prost went wide. This was Rosberg's first win but he didn't care so much about that. He had eager eyes on the championship.

Rosberg 42, Pironi now out of it on 39, Prost 31, Watson and Lauda 30.

Italy, 12 September. Mario Andretti flew over to take the second Ferrari and put it on pole which lifted Monza to a magnificent frenzy, even by Monza's own tradition of frenzies. Rosberg on the fourth row kept a wary eye on Prost directly in front of him, Lauda on the row behind him and Watson on the row behind that. A drivers' eleven best finishes of the 16 rounds counted but by a curiosity that didn't affect any of the front-runners. Monza was a turbo track so Watson, Lauda and Rosberg were looking for salvage – Rosberg predicted he'd be seventh. Lauda suffered handling and brake problems and retired, Rosberg lost a wing and repairs meant he finished eighth. Watson came fourth behind the turbos of Arnoux, Tambay and Andretti. He sat in the McLaren motorhome and said life wasn't easy when the others had so many more *horses.*

Rosberg 42, Watson 33, Prost 31, Lauda 30.

Caesars Palace Grand Prix, 25 September. Lauda, third at Zolder, was disqualified because the McLaren had a weight infringement but an appeal about that was due. If Lauda got the points back he'd be on 34. Rosberg needed to be fifth for the championship: that took him beyond Watson's reach and, even with the points reinstated, Lauda couldn't reach Rosberg either.

Rosberg qualified sixth, Watson ninth, Lauda 13th. Ron Dennis asked Lauda to help Watson if possible, and Watson feels Lauda wasn't impressed by that. Watson thrived on street circuits and by character was more comfortable coming up through the field. A phrase followed him around: *burn from the stern.* He burnt the car park and by lap 20 lay third, Rosberg sixth. Watson's tyres had picked up rubber from the surface of the track and were going out of balance. Prost had the same problem and young Michele Alboreto in the Tyrrell went past him. Watson did, too. Rosberg was fifth…

He brought the Williams round the loop onto the start-finish straight a last time and it flickered across the empty white bays of the grid. He took it out into the bleached, level, geometrical looping which went on and on – corners with numbers but no names. As he positioned it on the rim of the track to the right, poised to turn through the first loop, Alboreto approached the finishing line behind him. That didn't matter. He turned through the next loop, a right, positioning the Williams close to red and white kerbing. Behind that three marshals in virgin white watched immobile. He ran alongside a low concrete wall, the car absolutely in his control. He ducked it over to another wall for the next loop, a left. Here and there the car skittered because the track surface wasn't perfectly level, but that didn't affect his control. He ran dwarfed by the backdrop, the cluster of skyscrapers and far beyond them low, barren mountains. Into the second to last loop his helmet buck-bounced, buck-bounced – the track surface again. Through the final loop he flickered over the empty bays again, a man waved the chequered flag as if he was a bullfighter with a cape – as theatrical as that – and both Rosberg's arms were out of the cockpit, went back to the wheel fast to get the car through the first loop, then the right arm was out, fist brandished in triumph.

Once the niceties were over, Rosberg concentrated his combative mind on capitalising on the World Championship. Forgive him. This time the year before, he'd been a nobody going nowhere.

In December Colin Chapman died of a heart attack. It's always tempting to attach eras, or rather the end of them, to such moments. In this case a convincing case could be constructed, not just on grounds of longevity or success but in constant innovation which sometimes drove the whole sport forward *at Chapman's pace.*

Arnoux joined Ferrari for 1983, Cheever replacing him at Renault. The driver they'd have to catch was Piquet armed with Gordon Murray's latest Brabham shaped like a dart. The design was so radical that at the first race – Brazil, at Rio – Murray wandered down the pit lane gazing at what the others had done and thought *have I gone too far this time?*

Rosberg took pole and led, running on half tanks – he'd be pitting. During it there was a flash fire, Rosberg sprang out, the fire was extinguished, he sprang in and continued but the car had to be push-started. Piquet won it and Rosberg, second, disqualified for the push.

At Long Beach, Watson qualified 22nd and Lauda 23rd almost four seconds from Tambay's pole time. McLaren were having a nightmare trying to set the cars up properly. For the race Watson went for a compromise tyre choice, like he'd used at Detroit the year before; Lauda went for Michelin's latest compound. The talk was not of that but Alan Jones, persuaded to drive an Arrows and now, so the rumour went, of such girth that they had to take the seat out and he sat on the chassis. The talk had also been of subsidence on the straight causing the cars to leave the ground. That was filled with quick-dry concrete overnight.

The race unfolded in two dimensions: a lot of crashing and retiring at the front – by lap 30, ten cars out – and Watson and Lauda running competitive lap-times. Imperceptibly they worked their path up and by that lap 30 Lauda was third, Watson fourth. Three laps later Watson overtook Lauda with pace and precision. Ahead lay Laffite, leading, and Patrese trying to pressure him but Patrese missed a braking point and went off up an escape road. Watson didn't see this and when he overtook Laffite was unaware he'd also taken the lead. Lauda finished second behind him.

Prost won France from Piquet.

Rolf Stommelen, who'd last driven a Grand Prix in 1978, continued his career in sports and GT cars. At Riverside, California he crashed fatally in an IMSA race.[56]

Patrese ought to have won Imola. On lap 52 of the 60 he went past Tambay's Ferrari for the lead, something greeted by silence in the crowd, enslaved by the Ferrari legend. Patrese was experiencing the opposite reaction: an Italian, he was going to win a Grand Prix in Italy. It proved too emotional for him and he went off, which was not greeted by silence in the crowd. Tambay won it from Prost.

Rosberg was brilliant round Monaco, taking Prost for the lead on lap two and never losing it.

The Monaco measure: Rosberg, 76 laps, 1h 56m 38.1s, an average speed of 80.4mph; Patrese, 1982, 82.1mph.

After 13 years Grand Prix racing went back to Spa and Grand Prix racing got as emotional as it ever gets about that. The old Spa, the 8.7-mile ribbon of unprotected road, had been unthinkable for a generation. Of the 17 drivers on the 1970 grid none was anywhere near still being a Grand Prix driver and Rindt, Ignazio Guinti, Rodriguez, Peterson, Siffert and Courage, now Stommelen were dead. The new Spa, 4.3 miles, kept the soul of the old, especially *La Source* hairpin and the majestic uphill sweep of *Eau Rouge*. Here, the drivers of 1983 were living again what their forefathers had known – the geography of challenge as well as the technology of it. Prost took pole from Tambay and won it – from Tambay.

Tyrrell still ran the trusty Cosworth engines and Detroit still repaid that if you survived the concrete walls for 60 laps and 150 miles. Alboreto, an elfin man with a sun-kissed smile, did that, winning it from Rosberg and (inevitably) Watson. The Tyrrell team continued until 1998 and never won another race. From the forefront of Grand Prix racing in the late 1960s they had from about 1976 drifted into the shadows while remaining part of the fabric of the sport. Grand Prix racing was always as much about the cars at the back of the grid, in their comparative anonymity, as the front-runners because without the lowly there is no way to measure the mighty.

Perhaps the Tyrrell team should be a symbol for the fabric itself, a symbol of all those – teams, drivers, everybody else – who loved and won, and then kept on loving when they were losing.

Arnoux dominated Canada.

Prost 30 points, Piquet and Tambay 27, Rosberg 25, Arnoux 17.

Arnoux took pole at Silverstone while, on the seventh row, a new car and a new driver were introducing a new era. Honda had enjoyed consistent success in Formula 2 and now supplied a group of bright youngsters called Spirit, founded by John Wickham and Gordon Coppuck. Honda produced a Formula 1 turbo engine and Spirit took it into Grand Prix racing with the Swede Stefan Johansson driving it. The engine made, Johansson would say, a truly glorious sound.

Two Ferraris on the front row, Prost next and he felt if he could push them hard their Goodyear tyres might not last but his Michelins would. The Ferraris led but Prost clung even as they waltzed so elegantly through the chicane before the pit lane straight. The Spirit broke, a fuel pump problem after five laps. Prost hunted down Arnoux and took him, slicing through on the inside at Copse; hunted down Tambay and took him, slicing down the inside at Copse. They called Prost The Professor and he habitually proved the adage that thinking is the best way to travel.

Arnoux dominated Germany and Piquet ought to have been second but, with three laps to run, the car caught fire. He parked it on the grass and was already half way out when it rolled to a halt.

Prost 42, Piquet 33, Tambay 31, Arnoux 28.

Rosberg clung on with 25 but you had to have a turbo. Williams and his designer Patrick Head gazed carefully at Spirit and their Honda.

The Williams team tested Ayrton Senna at Donington. He'd shown rarest, almost bewildering ability in Formula Ford 1600 and in Formula Ford 2000. Now in Formula 3 his head-to-head with the young Norfolk lad Martin Brundle reached a level of intensity attracting national attention. Senna hadn't handled a Formula 1 car and Frank Williams was happy to give him the chance. Senna went so fast on the Club circuit that Williams thought he might have frightened himself a bit. What Frank Williams did not think was *I must sign this man immediately.*

Prost won Austria from Arnoux, Piquet third. Prost was looking like the first French World Champion but in Holland he made a mistake: such a rarity it became a collector's piece. Piquet led and Prost knew his Renault could not stay with the Brabham on the straights but was more nimble in the corners. That made overtaking elusive and, Prost concluded, *I have to catch him off-guard.* Prost hustled, probing, feinting. Into the Tarzan horseshoe he went into clear space on the inside but the Renault twitched across into Piquet. Arnoux won it from Tambay.

McLaren brought a new car and a TAG[57] turbo engine at Zandvoort for Lauda. It was by now the only thing to do.

Prost went to the Italian Grand Prix with the two Ferraris directly behind him in the championship. Before it he received kidnap threats and Renault hired the French President's bodyguards – men who looked like Alps – to protect him at Monza. When word of that leaked, the *Tifosi* hated Prost even more. Somehow for Prost the mood was wrong and the turbo failed after 26 laps, leaving the win to Piquet from Arnoux. Prost 51, Arnoux 49, Piquet 46, Tambay 40.

De Angelis put the Lotus-Renault turbo on pole, Mansell third, for round 14, called the European Grand Prix, at Brands Hatch. They'd been team-mates since 1980, although by character and taste completely different men. When Chapman died Peter Warr came into an uneasy inheritance but was poised to sign a leading designer, Gérard Ducarouge, and make Lotus front-runners again.

Piquet won the race from Prost with Mansell third. Arnoux and Tambay both had problems. With only South Africa left, that took Tambay out of the championship and left Arnoux's chances problematical.

In one sense Piquet, Prost and Arnoux faced a simplicity, to win at Kyalami. The gathering began on Wednesday (a Saturday race, as usual). That day:

> Prost sat surrounded by Renault people locked into what was obviously deep conversation. He seemed vulnerable, still looked haunted. Only the day before he'd tried to relax by playing golf, a favourite pastime, but so many journalists and camera crews tracked him that he'd been forced to abandon it. Now he sat and Jean Sage [senior Renault team member] said: 'Please don't go near him. He bites people at the moment.' Prost gazed through glazed eyes and murmured, 'I'm OK.' Pause. 'I'm confident.' He looked anything but that. 'I think we are quicker than they are on the twisty sections.' End of interview.
>
> A couple of miles down the road at the Kyalami Ranch pretty girls frolicked round the swimming pool and a handful of drivers sunned themselves in deck chairs. Where was Piquet? 'Up there,' someone said, jerking a thumb towards the second floor of the hotel, 'up there in his bedroom, asleep.'
>
> It was a contrast you couldn't miss.[58]

During qualifying Arnoux's Ferrari stopped out on the circuit and he gesticulated for the marshals to push it to a safe place. As they did they pushed it over his foot. Arnoux would race. Tambay had pole from Piquet, Patrese and Arnoux on the second row, Prost on the third. Williams now had the Honda engine and Rosberg put it next to Prost.

Piquet, Murray and Brabham used 'Prost's ploy' – Piquet started with a fuel load so small he ought to be able to annihilate the opposition, pit and still lead handsomely. They put hard tyres on the car because Piquet would be punishing them. Piquet set off like a hare and on lap 28 pitted and rejoined still in the lead, an enormous thing because the others had yet to pit. Prost found the race 'absolute torture' and on lap 36 heard a sound from the engine which he recognised as a turbo failure. He pitted and watched helplessly as Piquet did not break down, gave Patrese the win and let de Cesaris through, too.

He moved into the last lap, sunlight glinting on the car. He took it down the long undulation to Crowthorne Corner, he threaded through the sweeping loops behind the pits and paddock heading out into the countryside and the climb to Wesbank Corner, he came poised and easy down the long, long incline back towards the elbow of a right-hander a hundred yards from the pits. A thicket of mechanics stood on the edge of the track, waiting. They watched Patrese go by, watched de Cesaris go by 21 seconds after Patrese, as Piquet reached them they spread across the track, brandishing their fists in triumph. He raised his left arm to acknowledge them. It was an act of communion in both directions.

Piquet had his second championship.

Senna won the Formula 3 Championship and tested for Toleman and Brabham. Other teams showed interest, but only Toleman made an offer. The Formula 1 roundabout: Renault fired Prost and he went to McLaren, replacing Watson whose career as a regular Grand Prix driver ended. Derek Warwick, Toleman's yeoman driver from Formula 2 days, replaced Prost at Renault, Tambay partnering him. Alboreto joined Arnoux at Ferrari. Senna caught the roundabout at Toleman, replacing Warwick. Brundle joined Tyrrell.

The man running Toleman, Alex Hawkridge, found negotiating with Senna disconcerting. Senna, Hawkridge began to realise, was uninterested in being another Grand Prix driver or even another Grand Prix winner. He intended to dominate it.

As Hawkridge sat in his office behind a plain English high street in the plain London suburb of Brentwood, he may have wondered about that: a wan, slender, soft-spoken Brazilian who had yet to drive a single Grand Prix. He wouldn't be wondering long. Neither would anybody else.

Notes

1. *Bernie's Game*, Lovell.
2. Interview with Author.
3. *Jody, An Autobiography*, Scheckter.
4. *Frank Williams*, Hamilton.
5. A team founded by American entrepreneur Don Nicholls which graduated from North American racing to Formula 1. It competed from 1973 to 1980.
6. *For the Record*, Lauda.
7. *Autocourse.*
8. *The Viking Drivers*, Petersens.
9. Lauda, op. cit.
10. Ibid.
11. *Autocourse.*
12. Ibid.
13. *Driving Ambition, Jones.*

14. Hill formed his own team in 1973 with Embassy the title sponsor.

15. Famed US businessman Roger Penske formed a team which was very successful in North America but moved to England to take on Formula 1 in 1974. They raced until 1977.

16. The car had orthodox-sized rear wheels, and two much smaller wheels at either side on the front. It was the brainchild of engineer Derek Gardner and based around a simple concept: if you reduced the lift at the front of the car you could corner quicker.

17. Flat spot: if you brake violently in a racing car, the wheels can lock and the part of the tyre in contract with the track at that instant is burnt flat. It doesn't make driving easy afterwards.

18. Lauda, op. cit.

19. Ibid.

20. Formula Atlantic was 'the top category of single-seater racing in Canada' – Donaldson.

21. *Autosport.*

22. Walter Wolf, a Canadian oil magnate, who came into Formula 1 and bought his way into the Williams team. The team raced under the Wolf name but he and Frank Williams parted company after a couple of years.

23. Petersens, op. cit.

24. Mo Nunn, a former driver and now important figure in North American racing, constructed Formula 3 cars before being asked by Rikky von Opel, a wealthy man from Liechtenstein, to make Formula 1 cars. They competed from 1973 to 1982.

25. *World Champion,* Andretti.

26. Lauda, op. cit.

27. Andretti, op. cit.

28. The turbocharger was 'a turbine fed by exhaust gases, connected to a compressor via a shaft that compresses intake air into the engine. More air in the cylinder means more fuel can be burnt per power stroke, more burnt fuel means more hot gas, more hot gas means more power – and more boost too.' http://www.turboclub.com/turbotech/TurboFun1.htm

29. LEC, a refrigeration business in southern England, set up by David Purley's father – *History of the Grand Prix Car,* Nye.

30. Hamilton, op. cit.

31. *Grand Prix!,* Lang.

32. Turbo lag was a disconcerting feature of the early turbo engines – the time between putting the power on and its delivery.

33. Hamilton, op. cit.

34. Watkins interview with Nigel Roebuck, *Autosport,* 10 February 2005.

35. Andretti, op. cit.

36. Watkins interview, op. cit.

37. Ibid.

38. *Villeneuve,* Donaldson.

39. Watkins interview, op. cit.

40. Lovell, op. cit.

41. Hamilton, op. cit.

42. *Grand Prix Showdown,* Hilton.

43. Jones, op. cit.

44. A tale recounted to the author with some relish by John MacDonald who ran the RAM Formula 1 team.

45. *The Grand Prix Who's Who,* Small.

46. Nye, op. cit.

47. In Crombac's *Colin Chapman.*

48. *Colin Chapman,* Crombac.

49. Donaldson, op. cit.

50. *Life in the Fast Lane,* Prost.

51. Ibid.

52. *To Hell and Back,* Lauda.

53. *Autosport.*

54. *Keke,* Rosberg.

55. Prost, op. cit.

56. IMSA, the International Motor Sports Association, organiser of series in North America.

57. TAG, *Techniques d'Avant Garde,* a company which helped to 'build and promote' McLaren's Porsche engine. (*McLaren: The Grand Prix, Can-Am and Indy Cars* by Doug Nye, Hazleton publishing, 1984).

58. *Grand Prix Showdown*, Hilton.

Chapter 10

IN SENNA'S TIME

Niki Lauda witnessed the arrival of Alain Prost at McLaren with a wary eye. When Prost said nice things about him, The Rat – as Lauda was known – wondered what the motive could be and watched closely. When Prost sought to establish a position within the team Lauda understood why but still watched closely. Lauda kept his antennae tuned for political intrigue and felt a sense of unease. It would take time for Lauda to realise that Prost was a straightforward fellow and, in a celebrated phrase, 'a fast son-of-a-bitch.'

The tension assumed a specific importance because the season belonged to McLaren, and with emotional dimensions: Lauda back from the dead these many years and, by a ferocious irony, the second last race scheduled for the Nürburgring, albeit a truncated and neutered version of the old widow. To win the championship again would represent a special kind of immortality.

For Prost, the championship meant a different kind of immortality. No matter that a Frenchman began the whole thing in France at 6am on Tuesday, 26 June 1906 when Fernand Gabriel headed his Lorraine-Dietrich down towards the turn into the first full leg of the giant Le Mans triangle; no matter that at Dieppe on 26 July 1912 Georges Boillot had used a tyre lever to repair the gearbox and other damage caused by a stone, then with only second and fourth gears nursed his Peugeot home to become the first French Grand Prix victor; no matter that France, the French automotive industry and generations of talented French drivers had been an essential part of the whole thing. No Frenchman had ever been champion.

Lauda, an Austrian, distrusted nationalism and felt it a dangerous distraction. Prost didn't necessarily share those sentiments. Any championship is a profound examination of how men respond to pressure, how they handle the unexpected, above all how they handle themselves, and when it devolves to two very different men in the same team all that is heightened, sometimes to an intolerable degree.

At Rio, de Angelis took pole from Alboreto, Warwick third in the Renault, then Prost half a second quicker than Lauda. That was another dimension, although Lauda did not understand it yet. Lauda could not hope to live with Prost in qualifying and would have to adjust mentally to that, wield his race-craft to compensate. He did that in Rio, getting up into the lead in twelve laps but an electrical fault stopped him and Prost – driving cautiously, still exploring the McLaren ('trying it for size, you might say')[1] – won it from Rosberg. It put Lauda on the defensive. You know what they say about cornered rats. The turbo boost failed on Senna's Toleman after eight laps so nobody knew yet what was coming.

Lauda won South Africa from Prost, although again, he'd been outqualified while Senna slogged to sixth and was so exhausted and dehydrated he had to be helped from the car. The Toleman team concluded that he was not fit enough, and by definition strong enough, for Grand Prix racing. Senna didn't need to be told twice.

Alboreto took pole at Zolder and was untouchable in the race, winning it from Warwick. It did seem at this stage that Warwick was growing into a leading role in a leading team, second in the championship to Prost 15–10. Prost however won Imola from Arnoux, Warwick fourth.

Lauda qualified ninth for the French Grand Prix at Dijon and felt he had to drive 'brutally' in case the leaders got away from him. Brutal? He added a second term, driving like a 'madman' and it carried him to third behind Tambay and Prost but Prost, approaching Pouas – the long, fast loop onto the straight – felt a shudder and felt a front wheel coming off. The car lurched about and he fought to control it, did that, got it to the pits. *A pity anything like that happened,* Lauda thought clinically, *he had no chance against me today, anyway.* Lauda did catch Tambay and laid pressure on him. *Maybe he'll get nervous.* Tambay, urbane, bilingual, handsome in a Hollywood way, didn't – yet. Lauda attacked here, attacked there, his normal calm gone. Under it Tambay drifted fractionally wide in a corner, Lauda through on the inside. Something went wrong with the McLaren signalling for Lauda to pit for tyres and eventually he came in himself, emerged second to Tambay – and angry. Lauda chose a single word to describe his driving, like a *maniac.* He retook Tambay.

Brundle crashed his Tyrrell heavily during qualifying for Monaco – he thought he knew where he was afterwards, and didn't really – while Mansell put the Lotus on the front row next to Prost, pole. Race day was wet, dripping-sodden.

Mansell led from Prost, and crashed. Senna started from the seventh row, which in the wet at Monaco – you can't see, can't afford any mistake – meant he had no chance. He saw only opportunities which he could take and the others couldn't. During these laps the power base of Formula 1 began moving towards Senna.

> Lap one: *ninth*. Lap two: *ninth*. Lap three: *eighth* (overtaking Laffite). Lap four: *eighth*. Lap five: *eighth*. Lap six: *eighth*. Lap seven: *seventh* (overtaking Manfred Winkelhock). Lap eight: *seventh*. Lap nine: *sixth* (Alboreto spun). Lap ten: *sixth*. Lap eleven: *sixth*. Lap twelve: *fifth* (overtaking Rosberg). Lap 13: *fifth*. Lap 14: *fourth* (overtaking Arnoux). Lap 15: *fourth*. Lap 16: *third* (Mansell crashed). Lap 17: *third*. Lap 18: *third*. Lap 19: *second* (overtaking Lauda).[2]

Senna was now 34.35 seconds behind Prost, he had the turbo boost turned down because the Toleman was more responsive like that, and he went after Prost who hated driving in the wet. The power base was moving quickly now, every lap and measurably so. This was more even than that, it spread itself round sodden Monaco as an astonishing pursuit, one of the greatest.

Lap	Prost	Senna	Gap
22	1:56.1	1:55.2	34.2
23	1:57.6	1:54.6	31.2
24	1:56.8	1:54.3	28.7
25	1:56.6	1:55.6	27.7
26	1:56.8	1:55.2	26.1
27	1:59.6	1:55.2	21.7
28	2:00.1	1:56.6	18.1
29	1:59.4	1:56.6	15.3
30	2:02.5	1:59.0	11.7
31	2:03.7	1:59.4	7.44

The race was stopped, a controversial decision because the weather didn't seem to have worsened – it hardly could – at the end of lap 32. Senna caught Prost so comprehensively that crossing the line he thought he'd won it. The final positions, however, were calculated from the end of the previous lap.

This was Senna's fifth Grand Prix (he hadn't qualified at Imola, Toleman in dispute with their tyre supplier, Pirelli) and with a small, fledgling team it was a performance born of the bravery of youth, the ambition of youth, the self-confidence of youth and car control of a sensitivity far beyond most Formula 1 drivers.

Ayrton Senna was not impressed by himself. Next morning at breakfast he happened to meet a Marlboro Press Relations man[3] who

naturally congratulated him and said what a big future he had. Senna
cried. Years later he'd outline his philosophy. *I am not designed to finish
second, third, fourth...*

More than that Stefan Bellof, who Ken Tyrrell felt would have been
Germany's first World Champion, finished third and he'd started last on
the grid. If Senna looked like the future, so did Bellof.

*The Monaco measure: Prost, 31 laps, 1h 1m 7.7s, an average speed of 62.6mph;
Rosberg, 1983, 80.4mph.*

A mid-season ripple of races: Piquet won Canada by a couple of
seconds from Lauda, Prost third; Piquet won the United States East at
Detroit from Brundle[4] who put together a wonderfully nimble, assured
drive. He looked like the future, too.

Two weeks later the United States Grand Prix at Dallas offered more
concrete canyons like Detroit. These were arranged through a place
called Fair Park, and Formula 1's long journey to find a real home in
America went on. Almost immediately it was an unhappy destination:
lack of run-off areas, a bumpy surface and, when temperatures reached
150°, the track began to break up. Mansell took pole, Senna on the third
row with Lauda. Senna made a run after the team-manager, Peter
Gethin, forbade it. One way and another Senna would not be staying at
Toleman beyond this season.

Race morning warm-up was brought forward to 7am because,
evidently, television schedules had decreed that the race start at 11am.
Laffite arrived in his pyjamas...

Of the 25 starters only eight cars were classified after the 67 laps.
Twelve of the others were *hit wall* and one *spun off*. Rosberg won from
Arnoux, the first Honda turbo victory. Nobuhiko Kawamoto, senior
executive and designer of the engine, was at Dallas.

> From the end of 1983 to 1984 was the hardest time for me. I thought we
> would never win, despite all our efforts. We had about 20 people in the
> team, three times as many as we had had before, but still we could not win.
> That is why I was so happy to win at Dallas. I remember former President
> Carter sitting behind me during the race and me thinking we wouldn't
> win. After the race I flew to Honda America in Los Angeles and we had a
> party at a Japanese restaurant. I called Mr [Tadashi] Kume [head of R&D]
> in Japan but he had his answering machine on so I had to record the news
> of our victory on it...[5]

All was not proceeding smoothly with the Honda engine, however, and
within three races Rosberg would be talking graphically about that.

Frank Williams took a decision from the beginning that whatever happened Japanese sensibilities would not be offended by the team blaming the engine. Honda had premises inside the Williams factory, although separate, and of the team only Frank himself and Patrick Head went in there. This was partly so that the Honda personnel wouldn't be distracted, partly because Williams sensed they wanted their privacy.

Lauda won the British at Brands Hatch, where Senna's team-mate at Toleman, Johnny Cecotto, crashed during practice and injured his legs so badly his Grand Prix career was over.

The championship tourniquet tightened.

With half points awarded at Monaco, Prost had 34.5, Lauda 33. Lauda said that the rivalry between them was under control and even tip-toed towards friendship, which was just as well because de Angelis led in Germany until a turbo failure then Prost and Lauda went head-to-head for the rest of the race – maybe a test of will-powers would be more accurate. Prost won it, and now Lauda was in deep – and divisive – contract talks with Ron Dennis. This, according to Lauda[6] had reached the point where, just before the Austrian Grand Prix, Dennis said he'd sign Rosberg for 1985. Lauda's riposte was typical. *OK, you sign Rosberg.* Meanwhile an Austrian with a boyish face was about to make his debut in an ATS. Gerhard Berger had started his career late – at 15, and unusually, not in karts – but he had believers in the Press and BMW, who were supplying ATS.

And Rosberg had troubles of his own.

> Everything felt soft. The engine was soft, the car was soft and the power was like an on-off switch. When the power came in, it was terrible. When we went to Austria, I just couldn't drive the car. It was impossible. I couldn't keep it on the road. It would twist and jump and do things which were totally unexpected. I had to stop. It was the only time in my career when I had to give up during a race.[7]

Lauda won from Piquet but only after applying his logic, race-craft and native cunning. Towards the end – Prost gone, spun out on oil, Piquet's tyres wearing – Lauda heard an explosion and the McLaren lost all power. *Differential gone,* he thought, and automatically held his hand up to warn approaching cars. He searched, equally automatically, for some grass to park the car on and then thought *it's a long walk back to the pits,* found third gear and set off for the pits in that. He accelerated, changed to fourth – nothing – and, again automatically, into fifth. It worked. His mind moved incisively: *continuing like this I'll lose five seconds a lap but I might still get a point or two.*

It is lap 44 of the 51 and from regular laps of 1m 34s, 1m 35s Lauda is now doing 1m 42s. His eyes scan the pit board and it tells him Piquet is 17 seconds behind so Piquet will be up with him in three more laps, maybe four. Next lap Lauda does another 1m 42 – and so does Piquet. *Piquet knows me,* Lauda double-thought, *knows I back off at the end to conserve the car, don't care by how little I win the races. Piquet will think: no point in flogging the tyres and getting up with Lauda, he'll only respond.*

Lauda coaxed the McLaren, Piquet ran at the same pace and in the last two laps backed off completely so that Lauda won it by 23 seconds.

Prost won Holland – from Lauda. At this meeting Lotus announced they'd signed Senna and would not be retaining Mansell. Toleman were incandescent, claiming that contractually Senna could not do this without informing them first and took the car off him at Monza, where Lauda won from Alboreto, Prost long gone with an engine failure. Lauda had prised the tourniquet open.

Lauda 63, Prost 53.5.

A driver could count his eleven best finishes of the 16 rounds but with only two left – the European at the Nürburgring, the Portuguese at Estoril – it didn't touch either man because both had only eight finishes.

Lauda was extremely phlegmatic about returning to the Nürburgring. 'I don't really have any bad feelings when I go there. It's over, really. I go there like I go to any other race.' Although the old castle still brooded on the hill the new circuit was not in any practical sense even a distant relative of the roller-coaster which Nuvolari and Fangio rode and which reached out in deadly embrace to Lauda.

Piquet took pole from Prost, Lauda 15th after a first day of endless problems and a second day trapped by rain. A win would give Lauda the championship whatever Prost did. Prost prepared to tighten the tourniquet again: he made a forceful start and led through the first corner. Into the race Lauda travelled up, selecting his moments, picking the other cars off in his own good time. By lap five he'd reached sixth and finished fourth, Prost leading throughout.

Lauda 66, Prost 62.5.

Lauda, thrown on the defensive, accepted Prost was driving beautifully but consoled himself that second place at Estoril would be enough. The fact that no Grand Prix had been run there before spiced everything. Set amid bleached hills, Estoril had a long straight as its backbone and uphill corners and curves round the back.

Qualifying went wrong, so wrong that Lauda described it as *like a second-rate movie.* He made mistakes, the car had niggling faults and he could go no faster than eleventh, Prost front row. Lauda demonstrated his mental discipline. *Everybody's nervous so I won't be. Do your best, ignore everything else because you can't affect that.* The moment Lauda caught sight of Prost he saw Prost was definitely not relaxed. Prost said he hasn't slept well and Lauda could see that, too.

Prost had to win and hope Lauda wasn't second.

An interviewer suggested to Lauda that all he had to do was follow Prost and he said: 'Yes, but first I have to catch him, that's the problem,' and grinned that toothy grin.

Rosberg hustled into the lead from Mansell and Prost – Lauda 13th. Prost took Mansell on lap 2, Lauda up to eleventh. Prost reeled in Rosberg while The Rat applied stealth, picking up places as he could. By the time Prost took Rosberg on lap nine – drawing up on the long drag to turn one, ducking inside – Lauda was ninth. Lauda came up to Johansson in the second Toleman and thought *he knows the TV cameras are on us, he's putting on a show, I'd do the same.* Johansson, meanwhile, had de Angelis in front of him and seemed more preoccupied with trying to get past him. Prost was 21 seconds up the road. Moment by moment the championship was ebbing away from Lauda, prisoner in seventh – the gap to Prost out to 29 seconds.

The race became a waltz, Lauda probing at Johansson down the drag but never close enough for a decisive strike, and they waltzed again while, so far away at the front, Mansell was long past Rosberg and trying to attack Prost. In swift succession Johansson made a mistake and Lauda was through, Alboreto seemed off the pace and Lauda steamed straight by. Fifth, he advanced on Rosberg, took him and advanced on Senna. They ran in that order for five laps before[8] Lauda dealt classically with him, fast onto the long drag, a tow, out from behind, inside through turn one. Lauda thought he'd just taken second place, didn't realise that Mansell was up ahead. Lauda ran 18 laps in third and Mansell suddenly lost his brakes, drifted into the pits.

The crowd were on their feet.

Late afternoon sunlight fell on Lauda's McLaren as he began the final lap, and this sunlight made geometrical shadows which licked the surface of the track. As the car wheeled and turned – through the right-hander at the end of the long start-finish straight, through the uphill loops out at the back – the shape of the shadow changed constantly. As he came round the long last loop Prost was already far down the start-finish straight 13 seconds ahead. McLaren mechanics were on the track saluting Lauda and Lauda responded as only Lauda could: he kept straight ahead because he had two cars immediately behind him, Piquet in one of them. He waited until they'd reached the first corner, gave Piquet room on the inside and as Piquet drew level Lauda inclined his head towards him, raised his right hand out of the cockpit – a little – and waved in taut, tight movements. Then he gave Piquet a good old fashioned thumbs up.

Prost had the race, Lauda had the championship by half a point. Afterwards Prost was warm about Lauda and Lauda was warm about Prost and, more than that, on the podium Lauda whispered to Prost *I'll help you win it next year*. Niki Lauda did not whisper such things carelessly.

In the close season Williams hired Mansell, although Rosberg said he didn't want him as a team-mate.

Prost launched his 1985 campaign immediately, winning Brazil – only he and Alboreto finished on the same lap – and summed it up neatly enough, *no problems*.

Ferrari fired Arnoux and replaced him with the affable Johansson who took the call in his London apartment and beat the World Land Speed Record getting to Maranello to sign the contract. He had to recount this so many times that even he grew tired of the repetition but repeat it he did.

Portugal was stormy wet, Senna caressing and smoothing the Lotus through two hours and 28 seconds of murk, mist and standing water. Seven drivers spun off, including Prost. This time only Senna and Alboreto finished on the same lap. The whole Lotus team *danced* with delight in the rain as Senna brought the Lotus back, led by Peter Warr, and designer Gérard Ducarouge described the moment Senna crossed the line as *orgasmic*. Were the great days back? They'd been a long time gone, de Angelis the last win before that in 1982, Andretti the last win before *that* in 1978.

The rule that a car could only have 220 litres for a race punished Johansson at Imola, traditionally a thirsty track. Prost encapsulated that by explaining you used 'rapid surges of acceleration and violent braking.'[9] Senna took pole and was proving himself stunning at the quick lap, something which brought deep satisfaction to the team mingled with a sense of mystery about how he could actually do it. They reached a consensus: *it comes from within himself*.

Senna led the race, de Angelis close to him, Prost hounding Alboreto for third. Alboreto was muscular as he and Prost dealt with de Angelis, and in the background Johansson made a long surge from 15th on the grid. On lap 23 Prost ducked right and went past Alboreto. He caught Senna and here was a tantalising glimpse of the bitter future because whatever Prost tried Senna countered.

Johansson was fourth then, taking de Angelis on the outside of a left-hander... third. Prost got a pit signal *watch your fuel* and backed off, saw

Johansson sweep by. That convulsed Imola, and was only a prelude because Senna slowed, out of fuel, and now Johansson in the Ferrari led in front of immense numbers of Ferrari faithful. Imola became a fevered festival of flag brandishing all the way round the circuit and every flag had the Prancing Horse on it.

Three laps to go and Johansson slowed, out of fuel, too. Prost won it and was disqualified, the McLaren two kilos under weight, elevating de Angelis in the Lotus to the victory. Were the great days really back?

Prost, downcast, was clinical at Monaco where Senna took pole from Mansell, Alboreto on the second row, Prost on the third. Prost applied his mind to that, reasoning that what he must do is make sure he didn't need to pit for new tyres. From the compression of the start Senna led, then Mansell, Alboreto and Prost. The Professor waited. The Professor was good at waiting. Alboreto went past Mansell and The Professor did, too. Senna's engine failed and three laps later Patrese (Alfa Romeo) crashed into Piquet on the start-finish straight. Alboreto slid off and, while he recovered, The Professor stole through.

De Angelis 20, Alboreto and Prost 18.

The Monaco measure: Prost, 78 laps, 1h 51m 58.0s, an average speed of 86.0mph; Prost, 1984, 62.6mph – wet.

Prost didn't like the circuit at Montreal ('ugly, congested, eminently forgettable') and finished third behind Alboreto and Johansson; Prost didn't like Detroit (nobody did) where Rosberg won.

Since the previous Monza Honda had realised their Formula 1 programme wasn't going anywhere and took it in hand, seeking to make the engine less brutal in its delivery of power. At Paul Ricard, Mansell crashed heavily in practice – a rear tyre exploded at 200mph – and flew home. The Williams was becoming a factor by this mid-summer, something confirmed along Ricard's generous straights. Rosberg finished second to Piquet's Brabham, holding Prost to third.

Round Silverstone, in qualifying for the British Grand Prix, Rosberg produced a lap of 160.92mph (with a slow puncture at the end!) and nobody had been through that barrier before. In 1950 Farina took pole with 93.8mph and the remorseless rise began, reaching 138.10mph in 1973. The new chicane at Woodcote cut the speed to 120.01mph in 1975, the next time the race was held there, but the remorseless rise began again and it reached all the way to Rosberg. Subsequent circuit alterations – the new Woodcote Corner in 1987, the new Complex in 1991 – left Rosberg's time safe. Perhaps this and Monza (as we shall see) as well as Monaco can be regarded as representative of what was and had always been happening everywhere all the time.

Mansell was fit but the clutch failed while Prost and Senna duelled again. Senna lost power and Prost went by, Senna regained power and got Prost at Stowe – and Prost re-took Senna into Copse: the fuel injection electronics were failing on the Lotus. Prost won it from Alboreto by a full lap.

Alboreto won Germany from Prost.

A week later Manfred Winkelhock – who, in a RAM, retired from the German Grand Prix with an engine problem – drove a Porsche at Mosport, Canada and inexplicably crashed. He died from head injuries. A strong, open man, Winkelhock had had a difficult Grand Prix career across four seasons with ATS, Brabham and now RAM. From his 47 races he'd taken two points for a fifth place in Brazil in 1982. It is with small variations the story of so many drivers and in this case the man was much bigger than his career.

Before Austria Lauda announced his retirement. Lauda told Ron Dennis some time before but Dennis asked him to delay any announcement because once it was made other teams would pressure their drivers to re-sign and Dennis wouldn't be able to get any of them. He did get Rosberg and now Lauda made the announcement. (Typically, when he told the Marlboro PR lady that he wanted to call a press conference and she asked why, he said: 'Maybe to tell them I'm pregnant...') In the race morning warm-up Prost's accelerator pedal jammed and the car almost flipped. After that, despite repairs, it never felt quite right but he won comfortably enough from Senna, Alboreto third.

Alboreto and Prost 50, de Angelis 28.

The Rat and The Professor: it ought to have been harmony now, The Rat leaving and as promised helping The Professor to the championship. Prost led Holland but Lauda, bullish, felt he could win from the fifth row. His car began to handle badly and the team tactics were that if he came in at this stage they'd fit soft tyres all round – which was what he wanted. Double-think: he came in without having signalled the lap before to warn the pit crew, giving them no time for second thoughts about the four softs...

As the others pitted Lauda led but, he'd claim the team gave him three softs and one hard, on the left rear – and Prost had four softs. Remorselessly Prost caught him and within the harmony Lauda should have moved courteously aside, graciously waved Prost through, blown him a kiss as he went by. The Rat didn't: wrong mood. The Rat saw here a last chance to do well, the old soldier who in his first Grand Prix – 1971 – had found himself among Surtees, Stewart, Cevert, Peterson and was now going to fire a final salvo. Prost hustled him but Lauda wouldn't let him through and it finished thus. Afterwards, grinning the toothy grin again, Lauda said Prost was too good a driver to need his help – but if he did he'd get it.

Between Holland and the Italian Grand Prix at Monza Bellof took part in the 1,000km race at Spa and driving a Porsche tried an ambitious overtaking move on Jacky Ickx. Bellof crashed and was killed. It seemed the heart and soul was being physically torn out of German motorsport. He had driven only 20 Grands Prix, all for Tyrrell, and whenever Ken Tyrrell spoke of Monaco 1984 he insisted that if the race had been allowed to run another couple of laps Senna would have taken the lead from Prost and Bellof would have taken the lead from Senna. As an epitaph to a motor racing career, that'll do nicely.

A mid-season ripple of races, proving Prost didn't need help: he won Monza and Alboreto's engine failed; Senna won Spa from Mansell – who'd never finished that high before – Prost third and Alboreto's clutch failed.

Prost 69, Alboreto 53.

At the European Grand Prix at Brands Hatch Prost needed to only finish two points ahead of Alboreto. Senna took pole from Piquet, Mansell and Rosberg on the second row, Prost on the third, Alboreto on the eighth. Rosberg made a hesitant start, forcing Prost on to the grass. As Prost worked his way up Senna led and was very robust in keeping Rosberg behind him. They touched and Rosberg retreated to the pits with a puncture, emerged just as Senna was coming along. Rosberg decided to give Senna a demonstration of what robust looked and felt like, and blocked him – pitching Mansell into the lead. The championship was essentially decided when Alboreto's engine caught fire and he toured to the pits, yellow flames licking the back of the car and smoke belching. Prost stroked the McLaren up to fourth, and that was enough.

Mansell won and vindicated his own beliefs about himself in front of 75,000 Britons, who were as emotional as a British crowd gets. That reduced him to tears during the slowing down lap and by then his wife Rosanne, in the pit lane, was crying, too.

Prost eased the McLaren through the adverse camber of Paddock Hill Bend a last time this autumn day under a blue sky and powder-puff clouds. He took it safely round the tree-fringed Druids horseshoe as precisely as he had done 74 times before, moved along Cooper Straight behind the paddock, went out into the country, out into the gully between the tall trees there. He was alone, Rosberg too far ahead, de

Angelis too far behind to keep him company. He came back round the loop onto the start-finish straight and he held the McLaren in mid-track, *precisely* there. As he crossed the line the McLaren team clasped each other and clapped with their hands above their heads.

Prost said on this lap his eyes 'misted over.'

As he crossed the line the long journey from Fernand Gabriel heading his Lorraine-Dietrich down towards the first turn at Le Mans triangle was finally over. France had her World Champion.

Mansell took pole in South Africa and won it from Rosberg, the Williams-Honda very strong now. Senna took pole at Adelaide, Mansell alongside him. Grand Prix racing had not been to Australia before and was warmed by the sincerity of the welcome. That melted on the track when Senna rudely punted Mansell off and forced his way through an altogether wild afternoon, culminating in an engine failure. Rosberg won.

Paradoxically, 1986 began with Mansell emerging after so many years of 'paying his dues,' as he put it. The apprenticeship had been long, although he'd only driven for major teams, Lotus and Williams. He'd be partnered by Piquet and together they'd push Prost hard. Senna was capable of pushing them all if the Lotus held together. This quartet made each race open, uncertain and that in turn made the championship a real tourniquet. The members of the quartet were so different that that made the championship multi-dimensional, too: Mansell seeing slights against himself everywhere, Piquet so laid back he liked nothing better than messing about on boats, Prost working everything out, Senna blessed with inexplicable talents and cursed by demons of obsession.

Just to stir this, Piquet from Rio did not like Senna from São Paulo and called him a taxi driver. Just to stir this further, Piquet set out to needle Mansell immediately. When they tested in Japan he, Mansell and Frank Williams were on the Bullet train and Mansell was suffering from a couple of cracked ribs. Piquet repeatedly 'prodded'[10] them, presumably, Mansell thought, to amuse Williams. Piquet only stopped when Mansell threatened to break a couple of his ribs.

In March, Williams flew to Paul Ricard where pre-season testing was going on. He'd be flying home the same evening because he was due to run in a half-marathon at Portsmouth the following day. Williams kept himself very, very fit. He had a hire car and gave Peter Windsor, the team's PR, a lift back to the airport. On the descent from Ricard, Williams lost control of the car and it went over a wall, landed upside down in a field. Williams was suspended by the seat-belts and in pain but thought *it shouldn't be hurting this much*. At that moment he began a long fight for his life. The half-marathon man would never take a single step again but, from a wheelchair, enable his team to make giant strides.

The team was strong enough to survive, and so was the man who had founded it.[11]

The season began in Brazil two weeks later and, there, Formula 1 came together as it rarely does with the team principals and many others gathered round a banner

DON'T WORRY FRANK
WE ARE MINDING THE STORE

There stood Warr and Ducarouge of Lotus; Larrousse of Ligier and Ron Dennis on their knees so that they didn't obstruct the message for the cameraman, Ken Tyrrell holding one end of it...

Senna took pole from Piquet, Mansell next (Prost the fifth row). The Williams chassis was excellent but, Prost wondered, what about the Honda engine and the new 195 litres of fuel maximum for a race? Hondas could be thirsty. Prost also wondered about the position at Lotus, where Senna vetoed the team hiring Warwick: Renault's Grand Prix team had been wound up but they were still supplying Lotus with engines. Senna reasoned that Lotus were not big enough to run two leading drivers. Prost questioned the wisdom of that decision.

At the start Piquet was hesitant, Senna away and Mansell behind him. Out into the sweepers of the Jacarapagua circuit they travelled, Mansell directly behind Senna and aggressive. In a long left Mansell tried the inside and Senna would not cede. Mansell went off into the Armco. Mansell thought *Senna's tactic is intimidation and I will not be intimidated next time*. On the third lap Piquet went past Senna for the lead – an instant in a civil war involving the whole country – and it finished like that. Prost's engine failed.

Spain distilled the truth that Mansell was not intimidated. Senna, pole (and Lotus's 100th), led early but Mansell took him, needed to pit for new tyres and then hunted him down. From lap 65 of the 72, this was classical Formula 1, strong car against strong car, strong man against strong man. It lasted to the desperate lunge for the line and the second tightest finish of any race from Le Mans 1906 (Italy 1971 closer, 0.010s). The last four laps, Mansell coming hard at Senna:

Lap	Senna	Mansell	Gap
69	1:31.3	1:32.4	+ 7.1
70	1:30.0	1:28.1	+ 5.3
71	1:32.1	1:28.4	+ 1.5
72	1:30.7	1:29.1	+ 0.014

Ford unveiled their turbo engine at Imola where Jones, with the fledgling Haas team[12] drove it. There was no suggestion that it would do to Formula 1 what the DFV had done at Zandvoort in 1967, and it didn't. Imola's thirst and the 195-litre ration reduced the San Marino Grand Prix to farce. Towards the end Patrese and Rosberg both ran out of fuel and Prost, weaving the McLaren to scour the last drop in his tank, limped over the line and stopped. Piquet finished second and young Berger, now with Benetton, third.

This win reinvigorated McLaren for Monaco and Prost won that clinically from pole, Rosberg bustling up to second, Senna third.

The Monaco measure: Prost, 78 laps, 1h 55m 41.0s, an average speed of 83.6mph; Prost, 1985, 86.0mph.

The week after that Elio de Angelis was killed testing the Brabham at Paul Ricard. The Brabham crashed at the fast S-bend beyond the pits and Prost, following, saw flames. The car somersaulted over the barrier and landed the wrong way up. There are dark stories of the lack of precautions, of drivers themselves trying to get de Angelis out, of a long delay until the helicopter came. He was pronounced dead in hospital and Grand Prix racing mourned the loss of a gentleman and friend. No driver had died in a Grand Prix car – Paletti, Montreal 1982 – for four years and none would again for eight; and it would never be a consolation.

Belgium, soon after, proved a sombre race, de Angelis still actively mourned. Mansell won it from Senna. The quartet created their own tourniquet and each took turns at the tightening. Mansell added Canada from Prost, Piquet, Rosberg and Senna – but inevitably Senna was fleet round Detroit's funnels and tunnels, winning the United States Grand Prix from Laffite and Prost.

Senna 36 points, Prost 33, Mansell 29, Piquet 19, Rosberg 14.

Mansell won France from Prost and Piquet so that only three points separated Prost, Mansell and Senna, Piquet still well within striking range.

Frank Williams came to Brands Hatch for the British Grand Prix, his first since the accident, and his presence provoked such an intensity of media interest that he gave a Press Conference. 'It was an emotional occasion, Frank struggling to articulate words due to his breathing difficulties. But his sheer determination shone through as he sat in his wheelchair, Mansell and Piquet on either side.'[13] By now Mansell's sheer pugnacity as well as his driving ability made him the equal of Piquet, always an awkward situation within a team. The contracts stipulated Piquet was No. 1 and he was No. 2.

Piquet took pole from Mansell and on race day a crowd of 120,000 made the circuit an amphitheatre. They saw Mansell make a confident start but almost immediately he had a driveshaft problem – it sounded like an explosion – and cruised, his race over already. He did not know that behind him the mid-grid had become something of a pin-ball machine, cars bouncing into each other culminating in Laffite ramming the barrier. The race was black flagged while Laffite was lifted from the Ligier, legs injured.

Mansell was able to take the spare car for the restart but it had been set up for Piquet. Worse, Mansell had driven it briefly and didn't rate it highly. Piquet led and Berger went past Mansell who, content to learn the car, wasn't concerned. When Mansell was ready he moved past Berger and from then to the end it was classical Formula 1 again but with many subtle differences.

If any championship is a profound examination of how men respond to pressure, how they handle the unexpected, above all how they handle themselves, so is every race and when it devolves to two very different men in the same team all that is heightened, too, sometimes to an intolerable degree. Here was a strong man against his own strong number 2, a strong car against his own strong spare car.

Mansell got past Piquet, who missed a gear, on lap 23 of the 75 and it turned on the pit stops. They went perfectly and for the final 40 laps it became a raw, macho struggle, Piquet trying to break Mansell, Mansell refusing to be broken. At no stage did Williams apply team orders because, as Frank said himself, *it's wrong to stand on a man's career* and, more than that, *it would have brought the sport into disrepute*. In the end Piquet backed off and Mansell won it by more than five seconds.

Mansell 47, Prost 43, Senna 36, Piquet 29.

Piquet took Germany from Senna and Mansell. Prost ran out of fuel and attempted to push the McLaren over the line as if to make the point *this fuel limit is absurd*. The same had happened to Rosberg.

Grand Prix racing, arguably the ultimate symbol of capitalist excess, now journeyed behind the Iron Curtain to the Hungaroring, a custom-built circuit in the countryside outside Budapest. Hungary grasped at Grand Prix racing (and gasped) and loved it. Grand Prix racing went to Hungary open-minded and was won over very quickly: immense crowds

Jean-Pierre Jabouille won the 1979 French Grand Prix at Dijon but the race will always be remembered for the wheel-banging duel between second-placed Gilles Villeneuve and René Arnoux. (LAT)

Moving towards the most amazing Monaco Grand Prix of all, in 1982, when even the victor, Riccardo Patrese, didn't know he'd won. Here the Brabham driver leads Alain Prost (Renault), Didier Pironi (Ferrari), Andrea de Cesaris (Alfa Romeo) and Michele Alboreto (Tyrrell). (LAT)

Above: *Nigel Mansell and Nelson Piquet, team-mates and bitter rivals.* (LAT)

Left: *Prost as a young man, preparing to conquer his world.* (LAT)

Prost conquering, at the 1986 Australian Grand Prix, Adelaide, when he took the second of his four World Championships. (LAT)

Ayrton Senna (left), with Prost at McLaren, intended to use his sublime gifts to destroy his team-mate. Here he wins his first world title in 1988. (LAT)

Nigel Mansell, seen here at the 1992 British Grand Prix, achieved a unique double which may never be repeated, winning the Formula 1 World Championship with Williams in 1992, then taking the IndyCar Championship with Newman-Haas in 1993. (LAT)

Passing dynasties. At the 1994 San Marino Grand Prix, Senna has only moments to live and, behind, young Benetton driver Michael Schumacher will suddenly have a tragic inheritance. (LAT)

Controversial champion. Schumacher took the 1994 title in Adelaide after he'd crashed his
Benetton into Damon Hill's Williams, raising a storm of protest about his tactics. It wouldn't
be the last time his sportsmanship was questioned. (LAT)

Quiet, pensive, almost shy, Mika Häkkinen took on and beat Michael Schumacher two
seasons running. (LAT)

Left: *Master of all he surveys. Schumacher takes his astonishing seventh championship in Belgium, 2004.* (LAT)

The men with power at century's end: (top left, clockwise) FIA President Max Mosley; Bernie Ecclestone, the ultimate entrepreneur; Frank Williams; Jean Todt of Ferrari; Ron Dennis of McLaren. (all LAT)

New generation for the second century: McLaren's Kimi Räikkönen and Juan Pablo Montoya who'd spend 2005 hunting Fernando Alonso in the Renault – here completing the actual first century as he crosses the line to win the French Grand Prix ... from Räikkönen. (both LAT)

thronged the circuit and savoured the excess. The Automobile Club of Hungary demonstrated their sense of history and occasion by unveiling a memorial plaque to Ferenc Szisz, inviting Jean Sage and Prost to attend. Prost read the plaque and was astonished to see that the 1906 race had been over two days. Like almost all modern drivers, Prost lived for today. How can he have known that, as we saw so long ago in our story:

> Szisz kept going, slowing to protect the car. He'd do his slowest lap of the race by three minutes but that didn't matter any more. Finishing did. He sawed the big steering wheel round a last time onto the straight towards the pits and the grandstand. He moved towards the white line beside the time-keeper's hut and an official with a black flag, standing poised, dipped it as he passed. He had covered the twelve laps across the two days in 12 hours 14 minutes and 7 seconds, an average speed of 62.8mph. The crowd raised their hats high to him, some raised their arms, and the ladies applauded politely.

Frank Williams went to the Hungaroring and had to listen to Piquet, tearful,[14] complaining about Mansell and Mansell, untearful, complaining about Piquet: the intolerable strains.

Piquet took the race from Senna and Mansell, Prost out when he crashed into Arnoux. In fact Arnoux had waved him through – a gesture which for historical reasons took Prost by so much surprise that helplessly he rammed him. Prost restored the shape of the championship in Austria where Alboreto came second in the Ferrari and Piquet, Mansell and Senna didn't finish.

Mansell 55, Prost 53, Senna 48, Piquet 47.

At Monza little Italian Teo Fabi took pole for Benetton from Prost but before the parade lap Fabi's car stalled and Prost's car suffered an alternator failure. Both started from the back of the grid, Prost then disqualified for switching to the spare car – the disqualification coming just at the moment when his engine blew. Piquet won from Mansell but Mansell won Portugal from Prost. Only two races remained, Mexico City and Australia.

Mansell 70, Piquet 60, Prost 59, Senna 51.

Hungary had been a journey into the unknown, Mexico, last used for a Grand Prix in 1970, was all too well known for its crowd which made Monza seem a model of restraint. In 1970, Regazzoni – who a year later would be pictured side-by-side with Frank Williams in their wheelchairs, this same Regazzoni who gave the Williams team their first victory – put his Ferrari on pole from Stewart in the Tyrrell. Stewart would remember how the crowd sat on the track, how they threw Coke bottles which shattered on the track, how Stewart thought any racing car going off could kill 200, 300 spectators and the organisers assured him it wouldn't be a problem; comprehensive insurance had been taken out.

Mansell, on the second row next to Berger, could take the championship. At the green light he thrust the Williams into first gear[15] but nothing happened and the cars behind flicked and ducked past him. He got the car moving and set himself to a long recovery drive. Berger had Pirelli tyres and didn't need to stop: Piquet, Prost and Senna had Goodyears and did. It corkscrewed the championship because Berger won from Prost, Senna and Piquet and the best-eleven-finishes rule began to cut deep.

Mansell 72 (70 counting), Prost 65 (64), Piquet 63.

Williams imposed no team orders for Adelaide while at McLaren Rosberg, preparing for the final race of his career, said he'd help Prost. To Prost and Piquet the tactic was win the race. There were permutations but the big currency remained the win.

Mansell led from the green light, Senna behind, Piquet behind him. At the geometrical right-hander Senna went inside, Mansell going so wide that Piquet stole through; and Rosberg hustled by on the outside into the next right-hander. Prost drew up behind Mansell. In time he'd go by and Mansell didn't mind that: fourth place was good enough.

On lap 32 of the 82 Rosberg led from Prost, Mansell third, Piquet fourth and Prost 'caught a kerb, punctured my right front tyre.' He pitted. The championship turned on that although Prost didn't know it and neither did anybody else. Goodyear examined Prost's tyres carefully, something entirely natural during a race, and concluded that anything could have caused the puncture. The wear-rate wasn't enough to prevent the other Goodyear runners going to the end without stopping. Barry Griffin of Goodyear remembered Frank Williams and Head asking *what are Prost's tyres like, what are Prost's tyres like?* Goodyear told them.

On lap 64 Rosberg heard a *brrrr* at the back of the McLaren and assumed the engine had failed. He pulled up at a little enclave in the track *to the right of the circuit.* He got out, gazed at the car and as Prost went by – level with Mansell – gave him a thumbs-up and a shrug: *sorry I can't help you any more.* Mansell saw Rosberg standing there but had no idea what had happened to the McLaren. What Rosberg heard was his *right* rear tyre, blown, flapping against the bodywork. Mansell and Prost couldn't see it because it was on the far side of the parked McLaren and Mansell would always wonder what might have been the difference if he had.

Griffin saw it on the TV monitor in the pits and realised that the same could happen to Mansell and Piquet at any instant. They had to be called in. Williams would do that at the end of the lap. Mansell was now on the long straight, the car eating the tarmac at 200mph. He came from behind a back marker and the left rear tyre exploded, flailing like a great black tentacle while the Williams bucked and danced and writhed as if a film had suddenly been flicked to fast forward. Mansell fought the car to the escape road using animal instincts and reactions – an utterly astonishing piece of sustained car control – and gently, almost apologetically, it bumped a wall.

Mansell was alive and Piquet was coming in to the pits.

Prost moved into his final lap and the championship, taking the McLaren carefully through the left and right after the pits, down to Westfield Corner, a geometrical right, the McLaren running over the ordinary street markings and, ironically, a solid white line here. He turned it onto the Brabham Straight, the rod-line backbone of the circuit through verdant, genteel Adelaide. There was a temporary grandstand to one side and a flutter of hands waved as he passed. He turned through the tightening Foster's Corner, moving from fifth gear to first. He could see the line when he emerged, flicked the gearbox up through second to third. The man with the chequered flag cleaved the air and Prost got both hands out of the cockpit instantly, punching the air. Then he stopped the car. For the last 25 laps, his fuel read-out had been showing him – *5 litres*. He never thought he'd make the finish.

Soichiro Honda had been at Adelaide to see the consummation of Honda's investment and achievement. What he did see was the two Williams drivers fighting each other, as they had done during the season, and Prost winning it. It may be Mr Honda was not pleased and it may even be that he felt his dignity affronted.[16]

There may have been even more: that the Honda company creed and psychology could not accept a quadriplegic in a wheelchair running a team.[17] It has never been publicly discussed. It is certain, however, that Mr Honda was deeply in thrall to Ayrton Senna and people who own successful multi-national companies are apt to get what they want.

The quartet became a troika in 1987 because Prost suffered abominable bad luck. Designer John Barnard went to Ferrari and was replaced by Gordon Murray who, initially, Prost of the precise logic wondered about. Prost learned all about Murray's qualities and felt, too, that the death of de Angelis – the only driver killed in a car designed by Murray – cut very deep.

The roundabout: Johansson left Ferrari to join Prost at McLaren, Berger joined Alboreto at Ferrari. Berger's interview with Enzo Ferrari revolved round their mutual passion, girls...

Senna stayed at Lotus because Gérard Ducarouge created an active suspension car[18] which, in the best Chapman tradition, promised to give an absolute advantage over all the others. If it did that and found elusive reliability Senna would take the championship in a great, irresistible sweep. If it didn't Piquet and Mansell would fight it out between themselves with all that that involved. They had Head's latest creation, the Williams FW11B, a strong development of the 1986 car and Honda's latest creation to propel it.

In Brazil Prost had an interesting day before practice had even begun. Marco Piccinini of Ferrari said Enzo would like him for 1988 and *would you care to sign a provisional agreement now?* And Honda's racing director came to Prost saying *Honda are desperate to have you, we will build a team round you if that is what you want.*[19] The Professor would not allow these potential developments to affect his driving.

Mansell put his marker down immediately with pole, Piquet alongside, Senna third but Piquet led then pitted because paper lodged in the car's radiators – Brazilians habitually did their equivalent of a Mexican wave on the opening lap of a Grand Prix, using shredded paper. Senna led, Mansell attacking but he, too, pitted with overheating. Prost drove a calculated, measured race protecting his tyres and from lap 21 to the end was not to be caught, Piquet second.

In Friday qualifying at Imola, Piquet went off at big speed. Teo Fabi in the Benetton saw it and stopped, used his on-board radio to tell his team to go down to Williams and tell them. Fabi said that Piquet was out of the car and lying beside it. Piquet was concussed, and lucky. He'd struck the concrete wall at a corner called Tamburello.

Prost, meanwhile, was expressing open delight with the McLaren. 'I can't ever remember a car that felt better in every way.' Mansell won the race from Senna, Prost halted early when the alternator failed.

Mansell took pole at Spa from Piquet but on race day that was momentarily forgotten when Moss toured the circuit in a Mercedes W196, and here almost magically was June 1955 when Moss had put just such a car on the front row round the fierce, forbidding and sometimes fatal long Spa. Moss 'howled' the car round, 'bare-headed and waving to an appreciative audience.'[20] Surtees drove a Mercedes W125 and here almost more magically was July 1937 when von Brauchitsch and Lang were on the front row.

Then, this dry, overcast day in May 1987 all the cars threaded through the eye of the needle at *La Source*, Senna leading, Mansell primed and full of running after him. Prost watched with detached interest, making sure he didn't touch anything and nothing touched him. Out at the back the

Lotus and Williams touched in one of those geometrical incidents where it is all but impossible to say which was where. Senna rotated off, Mansell continued to lap 17, pitted, sought Senna out deep inside the Lotus pit and grabbed him. The mechanics prised Mansell loose while Senna remained perfectly calm and, just over there the other side of the barrier The Professor sailed serenely by to equal Stewart's record number of victories, 27.

Senna won Monaco although Mansell took pole with what he'd describe as a 'perfect lap' and led it until he lost turbo boost. The Lotus active suspension liked Monaco's particular problems although, as someone observed, Senna was a little subdued on the victory rostrum because, across the breadth of the season, he knew the car could not live with the Williams.

The Monaco measure: Senna, 78 laps, 1h 57m 54.0s, an average speed of 82.0mph; Prost, 1986, 83.6mph.

The active Lotus liked Detroit's particular problems although Mansell led from pole again. Senna won it from Piquet, but Mansell bestrode Paul Ricard, a crackling pole and leading every lap, Piquet second.

Mansell was now riding high tide as an immense crowd flooded Silverstone bringing with them the sort of purblind nationalistic fervour motor racing in Britain hadn't experienced before. It created a sharp and enveloping atmosphere. Another atmosphere lived within the Williams team because by now Mansell and Piquet were not speaking any more, even professionally.

The race – exquisitely, deliciously, dramatically – devolved to these two men and these two men only. Piquet led and with 29 laps left Mansell pitted for fresh tyres. Piquet was 28 seconds distant and in a similar car. No-one ever disputed Mansell's bravery and now no-one disputed his ability to wring ultimate speed from a Grand Prix car. He attacked Silverstone and gained on Piquet *every* lap between 37 and 63 – two from the end – when he sold Piquet a dummy in the enormous rush of power to Stowe Corner, jinked the other way and detonated Silverstone.

Senna 31, Mansell and Piquet 30, Prost 26.

A mid-season ripple of races: Piquet, who – Mansell claimed[21] – felt Williams should have applied team orders at Silverstone, won Germany after Mansell had an engine failure; Mansell dominated Hungary but a wheel nut came loose and Piquet won from Prost.

The roundabout began to rotate already with a simple announcement, Piquet leaving Williams for Lotus in 1988, a deal done very swiftly. Senna, the catalyst, had been playing a poker game with Lotus and Warr felt he could wait no longer. Honda told Williams that they would not be supplying him with engines even though they were contracted to do so until the end of 1988. Williams might have kept the engines if they had been prepared to accept Japanese driver Satoru Nakajima, a good man, a pleasant man and at best a midfield runner. Williams hadn't been doing that since *Jonesey* strode purposefully towards the car in Argentina in 1978 to launch the whole success story. Senna went to McLaren and so did Honda.

In Austria Johansson hit a deer in qualifying and that frightened him. In the Sunday morning warm-up Prost went off at big speed, hit the barrier at the Bosch Kurve and that frightened him. He knew he was lucky to be alive. Others were frightened by the pit lane straight and the grid because it had Armco on both sides, no width to take avoiding action at the start.

The first time the lights went green the rear of the grid played dodgem cars, debris everywhere.

The second time Mansell's clutch failed and he coasted. Ten cars played dodgem cars, debris everywhere again.

The third time, at 4.10, six cars started from the pit lane and another restart, as one wit put it, might be a problem with darkness coming in. Mansell won it from Piquet.

Piquet 54, Senna 43, Mansell 39, Prost 31.

For Prost, the championship was all but gone and prudently McLaren adjusted their thinking towards 1988. They had a good deal to think about.

A week later Didier Pironi was killed in a powerboat crash. Despite Hockenheim in 1982, despite the crippling leg injury, it seems he could not live without speed or danger and he paid the price. He'd been competing in a round of the World Offshore Powerboat Championship on the English south coast and his powerboat ran onto the wash of another. It flipped at more than 100mph and two crew members on it were killed, too.

A late season ripple of races: Piquet won Monza from Senna; Prost won Portugal, Piquet third; Mansell won Spain from Prost.

Mansell won Mexico from Piquet.

Piquet 73, Mansell 61.

The day after that Hermann Lang, 82, died at his home near Stuttgart. After the war he'd begun competing again as soon as he could and even won the Le Mans sports car race in a Mercedes in 1952. He'd driven a Maserati in the 1953 Swiss Grand Prix and a Mercedes in the 1954 German Grand Prix. He didn't compete again but gave demonstration runs in the pre-war cars. They still hypnotised by their power, noise and prehensile shapes.

In Japan all Piquet had to do was win or, if Mansell didn't win, be second. There'd been no Japanese Grand Prix since Fuji in 1977 and of the present generation only Patrese had been there – itself irrelevant because this Grand Prix was at Suzuka.

Mansell settled quickly, fast in the introductory session on the Thursday, fast in the Friday during the morning untimed session. Piquet had a stomach disorder, said he didn't feel wonderful and didn't look wonderful either.

Into first qualifying Mansell made an early run culminating in a hot 1m 42.61s. Piquet did 1m 41.42s. Mansell went out again and on the pit lane wall Williams PR lady Ann Bradshaw watched the small monitor giving lap times. Piquet was in the pit watching a TV monitor on the wall. Mansell came round the right-hander at the back of the paddock and his pace carried him across towards the kerbing on the other side. He went a little wide and dug dust. That took the adhesion from the car and it snapped sideways, slewed. He was hard on the brakes and leaving rubber on the track. Backwards, at 140mph the car rammed a tyre wall breaking it apart and flinging tyres like an explosion. The car bounded back across the track and beached itself on kerbing.

Bradshaw heard a gasp from the pit and somebody said: 'Nigel's gone off.'

I went across and everybody was transfixed looking at the television screen. At that point they hadn't shown the replay. All I saw was Nigel in the car with his head back and looking in a lot of pain. Without the replay I didn't know how bad it was although he seemed to be in agony. Then they showed the replay. There was silence in the pit. Piquet went white, he drained. There have been all sorts of comments about what he said but I can tell you nobody said anything. Everybody had gone very quiet. There was nothing anybody could say. I don't think it had crossed Piquet's mind at that moment that he was World Champion.[22]

Mansell went to hospital, Berger won the race in the Ferrari and won Australia two weeks later. It seemed like the Ferrari revival might really be going to happen, seemed that Berger – an instinctive racer who had always known life was for living, a devil incarnate with practical jokes – might be the man to do it.

Nobody knew that a hurricane was coming out of an anonymous Surrey town called Woking and the McLaren factory there which would blow everybody away and scatter long-held Grand Prix records. Honda mastered the new rule limiting fuel to 150 litres (down from the

195 of the previous year), and new engine regulations absolutely. Their engine didn't break. Steve Nichols, an engaging American, soft spoken and with a nice sense of humour, designed a wonderful car to accommodate it. After its initial test at Imola rational people spoke of it winning all 16 races.

And then there was Senna.

He'd been at a health spa in Austria and met John Watson there. Watson, familiar with McLaren from the inside, counselled Senna to approach his new team quietly, patiently, prudently because Prost had been there so long. *It's Prost's team,* Watson concluded, *don't forget that.* Senna waved this away. *I'm going to beat him.*

As the season unfolded Senna praised Prost as the best driver in the world, and in Senna's logic once he'd beaten Prost he became that himself. Patience and prudence didn't figure in this but psychology certainly did and McLaren team co-ordinator Jo Ramirez has recounted how after one early grid session Prost gazed at the time sheets and murmured an expletive about how quick Senna had gone. Senna wasn't supposed to hear it but did and when Ramirez looked round winked at him. *I'm getting to him.* Any tensions between them were carefully concealed from the public gaze at this early stage, however.

The season can best be appreciated in tabulated form because so many of the races had a single plot: Prost or Senna, the rest playing minor roles.

Brazil: Senna pole, Prost 2nd row. Prost won, Senna disqualified.
San Marino: Senna pole from Prost. Senna won from Prost.
Monaco: Senna pole from Prost. Senna crashed while leading – a traumatic moment in his life and one which forced him to re-evaluate the way he thought about his driving. Prost won.

The Monaco measure: Prost, 78 laps, 1h 57m 17.0s, an average speed of 82.5mph; Senna, 1987, 82.0mph.

Mexico: Senna pole from Prost. Prost won from Senna.
Canada: Senna pole from Prost. Senna won from Prost.
USA: Senna pole, Prost 2nd row. Senna won from Prost.
France: Prost pole from Senna. Prost won from Senna.
Britain: Senna pole, Prost 2nd row. Senna won, Prost retired.
Germany: Senna pole from Prost. Senna won from Prost.
Hungary: Senna pole, Prost 4th row. Senna won from Prost.

Enzo Ferrari died, aged 90, on 14 August. All portraits of him in words, and perhaps even photographs, lean towards the caricature. He had been a bewildering series of contradictions, a semi-recluse and simultaneously one of the most recognised names in the world, a person who inspired half a century of intrigue around himself, a primitive man regarding women, coarse in word and deed, and yet a creator of genius who, as someone said, made cars which were so desirable that he could pick his own customers. He was, and remains, more of a presence than a human being and perhaps – the ultimate trick, the ultimate manipulation – he intended it to be so. His overall and direct impact on Grand Prix racing, and the sheer scale of it, would require another book in the telling and if anybody ever does try to gauge it with any accuracy they'll find it a very, very difficult thing to do. This was the man who hired Nuvolari...Ascari...Fangio...Lauda...Villeneuve...Mansell...

Belgium: Senna pole from Prost. Senna won from Prost.

Italy: Senna pole from Prost. The race demands an exploration because unlike all the others it was the opposite of straightforward. Senna led from Prost but, just this once, Prost's engine misfired and he sensed it must worsen. The championship, inevitably, had a knife-edge feel to it, Senna 75 points, Prost 72, and now Senna would be taking nine points, Prost none. The Professor applied his logic. Monza was a thirsty circuit, the 150 litres making it marginal. Senna did not know Prost had a misfire and so if Prost accelerated Senna would respond, maybe using more fuel that he could not afford later in the race.

They'd both been doing laps in the 1m 30s. Prost accelerated, Senna responded, Prost dropped out after 34 laps and, deep into the race, the Ferraris of Berger and Michele Alboreto were catching Senna. Was he conserving fuel? He came upon Jean-Louis Schlesser in a Williams, deputising for Mansell who was ill. In the chicane at the end of the start-finish straight Schlesser tried to get out of Senna's way and they collided. Was Senna low on fuel? He always insisted he wasn't but, whatever, Berger took the win, Alboreto second.

Portugal: Prost pole from Senna. Prost won, Senna 6th.

Spain: Senna pole from Prost. Prost won, Senna 4th.

That took them to Suzuka and the Japanese Grand Prix with Prost on 90 points (84 counting) and Senna on 79. Prost's consistency punished him so that if Senna won Suzuka he became champion.

At the green light Senna stalled and cars surged by but the grid sloped and the McLaren rolled forward. Senna let the clutch out and the engine fired. He was 14th, Prost leading. From this Senna constructed his monument: by lap three, fifth, by lap 11 third, by lap 20 second and, because Honda tested so much here, he knew fuel wouldn't be a problem. He went hard after Prost, caught him and on the start-finish straight Prost went wide to take a back marker, Senna even wider so that at big speed he ran down just in front of the pit wall. Senna had the momentum and pulled ahead, clinically, incisively. He ran for home across the next 23 laps and, near the end, light rain fell and he gestured for it to be stopped. It wasn't.

He threaded the McLaren through the chicane and took it round the graceful curve to the start-finish straight, an immense and crowded grandstand looking to his left. He took it hard down the straight into the horseshoe First Curve, took it cleanly through the unfolding snake bringing to the back of the paddock. He flowed to the cross-over – where the return leg of the track intersected – and round Spoon Curve. If emotion was to claim him it didn't yet because his eyes were everywhere searching for potential danger. He was out in the country, a bank and lush trees to one side, grassland to the other, another crowded grandstand looming. As he reached into the chicane his helmet was bouncing, the track slightly uneven and that coming up like shockwaves. As he emerged from the chicane he lifted his right hand and waved. He took the McLaren round the curve towards the flag and both hands were out now. Somewhere Brazilian flags waved.

Nobody except Ayrton Senna knew the full depths of his desire for this championship. When someone asked him if he'd relax as a person now, he burst into tears.

Australia: Senna pole from Prost, Prost won from Senna.

Turbo engines were now banned, ending a whole era which Renault pioneered so long ago. Cars had to run normal engines – technically called normally aspirated – of 3,500cc. The cars had to be a minimum 500kg and could carry as much fuel as they wanted. Pit stops for refuelling were banned.

Could the Prost-Senna partnership survive 1989? Mansell went to Ferrari and won Brazil, provoking the church bells to be rung in Modena and alarm bells to be rung elsewhere. A strong Ferrari might tilt the season away from McLaren and Honda – but in Brazil Prost came second not far behind Mansell.

A few externally innocent and ordinary moments at the next race, the San Marino at Imola, destroyed the Senna-Prost partnership so completely, and produced so much personal venom, that it was not healed until this same Imola five years later, when Senna had only one more day left to live. In many significant ways the core of Grand Prix racing between 23 April 1989 and 1 May 1994 was that. Other themes – people, cars, races, championships – arrived and departed but all revolved around this Senna-Prost core. Of the five championships the span covers they won four and barely spoke a word.

At Imola Senna took pole from Prost, Mansell on the second row and Berger in the other Ferrari on the third. Senna led, Prost behind him but on lap four Berger's car, entering Tamburello flat out, snapped from his control. He saw the wall round Tamburello rearing at him and thought *this is going to be a big one*. The Ferrari struck the wall at an angle and thrashed a path along it. Bits were plucked wildly from it and the car exploded in flames, its carcass seemingly consumed by it. The rescue services reacted with astonishing speed and professionalism. They got Berger out, laid him on the grass and Prof Watkins calmed him, got to work on him. Another of the team, Dr Domenico Salcito, would say: 'We had to lie on top of him to hold him to the ground and cut the strap of his crash helmet, then we had to cut a sleeve from his overalls to find a vein in his arm to begin anti-shock therapy.'[23]

Berger was taken to hospital.

At the restart Prost pulled away strongly but into *Tosa*, the downhill left, Senna outbraked him and went through. Anyone watching closely might have noticed that Prost, untypically, gave Senna room and time. Senna won the race, leading throughout, Prost second throughout and nobody else finished on the same lap.

Afterwards Prost was so incensed he refused to attend the (mandatory) Press Conference and subsequently said any co-operation between himself and Senna was over. The full explanation, when it emerged, had simple and complicated elements: the two drivers reached an agreement that rather than fight each other from the line with all the risks that that brought whichever made the better start would not be challenged by the other until they were through the tight corner called *Tosa* a third of the way round the lap. It worked the first time because Senna led and Prost followed him through, it didn't work the second because Senna violated it.

He'd explain that he felt Prost braked so early he had no option but to overtake him and in that circumstance was fully entitled to. The bitter seasons had come forming precisely the core around which all revolved. Monaco two weeks later proved that. Prost publicly accused Senna of dishonesty and said he wanted nothing more to do with him. On the track Senna took pole and won the race from Prost.

The Monaco measure: Senna, 77 laps, 1h 53m 33.2s, an average speed of 84.1mph; Prost, 1988, 82.5mph.

The measure of the decades: 1929, 49.8mph; 1937, 63.2mph; 1948, 59.7mph; 1958, 67.9mph; 1968, 77.8mph; 1979, 81.3mph.

Vehicles registered in Britain 24.2 million (1979, 18.6 million).

A Ford Fiesta Mk III cost £5,199 and a Briton earned on average £239.70 a week. Saving all his money, the Briton would have taken 21 weeks to buy one (1910, 2 years 42 weeks; 1919, 1 year 28 weeks; 1929, 41 weeks; 1938, 37 weeks; 1949, 45 weeks; 1959, 36 weeks; 1969, 25 weeks; 1979, 20 weeks).

A mid-season ripple of races: Senna won Mexico from Patrese's Williams; Prost won the United States Grand Prix at Phoenix from Patrese; neither Prost nor Senna left a soaking Canada with anything. Thierry Boutsen, a Belgian and one of those stalwarts who form the backbone of Formula 1, won it in a Williams, Patrese second again.

Prost announced at the French Grand Prix that he'd be leaving McLaren. Jean Alesi, a Frenchman of Sicilian origin, made his debut in a Tyrrell and during qualifying hampered Mansell, who demanded of Ken Tyrrell that this young man fresh from Formula 3000 apologise. Tyrrell explained to Alesi that it would be easier for all concerned if he said sorry and then forgot about it. Alesi thought for a long time and said *I don't think I want to do that.* And didn't. Prost won, Senna out immediately with a transmission problem, Alesi fourth (and during the pit stops had even run second).

Prost 38, Senna 27, Patrese 22, Mansell 15.

Senna had a gearbox problem at Silverstone, spun off and Prost romped it from Mansell. Berger would join McLaren in 1990 which prompted speculation that Prost might replace him at Ferrari.

By Germany Lotus were in crisis. They'd taken eight points so far despite running Piquet as well as Nakajima. Peter Warr left and so did Fred Bushell, the company's chairman – he'd been arrested by the Fraud Squad after the collapse, in dubious circumstances, of the Belfast-based DeLorean operation using public funding to build sports cars. The great days were suddenly further away than ever.[24] In the race Senna hunted down Prost and, near the end, Prost couldn't get sixth gear. Senna struck. The championship tilted heavily towards Prost, however.

Prost 53, Senna 36, Patrese and Mansell 25.

It tilted back a little way when Mansell won Hungary after overtaking Senna, something so rare nobody could remember when it had been done before, or where, or by whom. Mansell could be feisty, as the saying goes, in a racing car or out of it. Patrese led to lap 53 when he had a punctured water radiator, letting Senna into the lead with Mansell in pursuit. Mansell had already announced his mood by taking Prost for third and the dictum that the Hungaroring forbade overtaking provoked Mansell nicely. Mansell drew full up to Senna and rounding a tight-loop right-hander they came upon Johansson in an Onyx-Ford, limping over to the left with a gearbox problem.[25] Senna moved up behind preparing to pull out but Mansell had already corkscrewed the Ferrari to the right and, in a great slingshot, went through on the right-hand rim of the track, Senna stranded between Mansell and Johansson. It was a distillation of what Grand Prix racing can be, nerve, reaction, car control, seizing the moment and bravery. When people asked Mansell how he'd done it he'd distill that into a single word, instinct. He won it, Senna second, Prost fourth.

Neither Lotus qualified for the Belgian Grand Prix while, in the background, Joachim Luhti, the Swiss financier who'd bought Brabham, was arrested in Zurich on suspicion of embezzlement elsewhere, nothing to do with Brabham. Their great days were a long way away, too.

It rained which enabled Senna, from pole, to demonstrate his sensitivity. 'In conditions like these there is always a danger of pressing too hard. There is a tendency to want to press on faster than is perhaps prudent so the real key is to suppress your natural instincts slightly and keep well inside the limit. I always find myself wanting to push, push, push but you have to draw back.' He beat Prost by more than a minute.

Prost 62, Senna 51, Mansell 38.

Senna's engine failed at Monza, Prost won and was going to Ferrari. He unleashed an attack on Honda in the post-race Press Conference for the treatment they'd given him.

The roundabout: Piquet left Lotus for Benetton, Nakajima going to Tyrrell; Warwick and Ulsterman Martin Donnelly to be paired at Lotus.

Portugal brought controversy, strong words and amidst it all delight for Berger. McLaren, Honda and Prost issued a joint Press release trying to smooth their troubled waters. The strong words lay elsewhere because Mansell pitted, overshot it and reversed, which was illegal He emerged after the pit stop fourth, Berger leading Senna, Mansell soon up to third. Mansell was black flagged for three consecutive laps but claimed – as did Senna – that going down the pit straight at 170mph into the sun he couldn't see the flag. On the radio Ron Dennis was trying to tell Senna *ignore Mansell!* Senna couldn't hear it properly and next instant they crashed. Senna stood for a long time contemplating the lost points, contemplating Prost coming in second.

Prost 77 (75 counting), Senna 51.

The World Motor Sport Council[26] decided after Estoril that Mansell be suspended from the Spanish Grand Prix at Jerez. Mansell reacted forcefully by threatening to retire. The race needed him because Senna led every lap from pole, Berger second but unable to exert pressure, Prost running a tactical third.

Prost 81 (76 counting), Senna 60.

Japan and Australia remained and regardless of the eleven-finishes-counting Prost held a great advantage: Senna had to win at Suzuka. That gave The Professor an interesting array of weapons even when Senna took pole from him. Prost made the better start and led, forcing Senna to confront the imperative of overtaking him. Senna spent 46 of the 53 laps trying to resolve that. The two cars circled together but Prost covered all the crucial points on the track lap after lap and it seemed that the right-left chicane by the pits – an eye of the needle – offered Senna the only chance. Each time they reached it he'd probe but Prost covered that, too. On lap 47 Senna tried down the inside towards the mouth of the chicane and Prost remained on the racing line, which brought him across Senna. Unless Prost had been prepared to cede the corner there was never going to be enough room and Prost had, he felt, ceded too many corners in too many places to Senna in the past.

They both went down the escape road straight ahead and while Prost clambered out Senna urged marshals to give him a push. He restarted and rejoined from the escape road on the far side of the chicane, drove to the pits for wings and nose. Sandro Nannini in a Benetton led. Senna emerged and took Nannini into the chicane, Nannini ceding it...

Senna was excluded after the race on the grounds that he missed the chicane in the Prost incident, and McLaren lodged an appeal. Prost was scathing about Senna, saying he couldn't 'accept not to win and he can't accept that somebody will resist an overtaking manoeuvre.' Senna said Prost 'closed the door.'

McLaren's appeal was rejected and for days everybody seemed to be threatening everybody. Only, inexplicably, the United Nations remained uninvolved and probably would be soon but even they, now, could not take Prost's championship from him.

The threatening went on to the Australian Grand Prix at Adelaide where McLaren said they were not frightened by *FISA*'s assertion that the team might be banned from Grands Prix if they continued with a legal challenge over Senna's exclusion. Heavy rain drowned the circuit on race day, Prost said he wouldn't start and Senna punted Brundle's

Brabham hard – Senna unsighted by the spray – so Boutsen won it from Nannini and everybody went home. They were glad to.

Mansell did not know what to make of Prost because although he'd always had good relations with him they'd never been in the same team and that could change everything. Mansell claimed politics did not interest him but when you have two strong-willed men who both want the same thing – the championship – and are in the same team, politics become inevitable. We have been here before.

This was not the problem at McLaren where Berger set out to measure himself against Senna without losing himself as a human being. He felt that he learnt from Senna in the cockpit and Senna learnt from him outside the cockpit, which remains a lovely way of summing it up. No team-mate had survived with Senna long (Johnny Cecotto at Toleman, de Angelis, Dumfries and Nakajima at Lotus, Prost at McLaren) but none had been like Berger who, in temperament and general conduct, would have blended more easily into the 1960s: race hard, play hard.

He set out to humanise Senna by playing a series of diabolical practical jokes on him, Senna responded with some of his own, Dennis joined in and suddenly McLaren was a wonderfully dangerous place to be, or even be near.

The threats between Balestre, the World Motor Sport Council, Dennis, Senna and McLaren limped on into the close season with, at one point, Senna suspended from racing. 'It was,' Senna said with superb understatement, 'a complicated situation.' It culminated in the one thing nobody expected, sanity. Fines were paid, Superlicences to drive were granted, the United Nations still stayed away, and Senna raced.

Berger of the natural speed took pole at Phoenix but little Alesi in the Tyrrell, an imp of a man in an imp of a car, led and when mighty, imperious, intimidating Senna came up behind him and overtook him Alesi retook him instantly. It was, and remains, a great moment in a modern context, like Mansell in Hungary.

Balestre journeyed to Interlagos for the Brazilian Grand Prix with a bodyguard and taunted the crowd by blowing them kisses. That crowd, so passionately protective of Senna, reacted with fury and Balestre seemed to like that. Senna led but Nakajima lost control deep into the race, clouted Senna and said sorry afterwards. By then Prost had won it from Berger, Senna third.

Patrese broke up the symmetry by winning Imola in the Williams from Berger, Prost fourth, Senna spinning off.

Senna reasserted himself at Monaco where Alesi came second and neither Ferrari finished.

The Monaco measure: Senna, 78 laps, 1h 52m 46.98s, an average speed of 85.8mph; Senna, 1989, 84.1mph.

A mid-summer ripple of races: by Canada Mansell felt Prost had moved the centre of gravity within the team to himself and the 'ground was shifting fast underneath my feet.'[27] Senna won it comfortably; Prost won Mexico from Mansell; Prost won France from Ivan Capelli (Leyton House).

Senna 35, Prost 32, Berger 25.

At Silverstone Mansell would say,[28] his relationship with Ferrari reached a critical mass and he gave an example. His car for qualifying felt different and he demanded the truth from the mechanics. They said that, after his pole at Paul Ricard, Prost wanted his car and had now got it. Mansell responded to that by putting Prost's car on pole, from Senna, Prost himself on the third row.

Patrese became the first driver to compete in 200 races while Senna led and attacked Silverstone, trying to break Mansell behind him. Mansell wasn't in any mood to be broken. He'd do the breaking. He overtook Senna under the bridge in to the Complex but his impetus carried him wide and Senna stole back through. Mansell attacked again. This time under the bridge he moved earlier and held his line. He streaked away from the McLaren and Senna spun. Prost was coming...

A tumult of a race: Berger took Mansell, Mansell took Berger, Prost took Berger, Prost waited and took Mansell. On lap 55 of the 64 Mansell's gearbox failed, opening it to Prost, Boutsen second, Senna third. Mansell announced his retirement from racing.

Prost 41, Senna 39, Berger 25.

Impish Alesi wasn't impish at Hockenheim where, it transpired, he'd committed himself to Ferrari and Williams for 1991, not forgetting he had a binding contract with Tyrrell as well. Senna won the race cleanly although young Sandro Nannini pushed him hard and led when Senna pitted for tyres. Senna beat him by 6.5 seconds. At this point in his career Nannini showed big promise, barely reflected by his 13 points.

Senna 48, Prost 44, Berger 29.

Boutsen led throughout in Hungary but the compression behind him became a stark thing, Senna rudely punting off Nannini (who was in tears afterwards) for second place, Prost out early on with a transmission failure.

In Belgium the pressure began to grow on Mansell. He dropped out after 19 laps complaining of the Ferrari's handling and the team said they were not happy with his explanation. Senna won from Prost, and now the championship lay squarely between them, Senna 63, Prost 50.

At Monza, Warwick in the Lotus overturned on the start-finish straight on the opening lap. Like a drowning man he saw visions of 'my brother, my wife, my children, my mum, just lots of absolute millisecond pictures of people close to me.' He felt his crash helmet grinding along the track and, upside down at serious speed, thought *I've 220 litres of fuel on board, I have to turn the engine off.* He finally got out of the car and trotted back to the pits to get the spare, the crowd thundering their approval of his courage. He went to the Arrows pit – he'd driven for them for the previous three years – by instinct...[29]

Senna won from Prost, leading throughout, and at the Press Conference afterwards they declared peace between themselves, the first time they said this, and by no means the last.

In Portugal Ferrari confirmed Alesi would be Mansell's replacement at Ferrari in 1991. Mansell took pole from Prost but made a self-confessed bad start, squeezing Prost and letting Senna through. Mansell took Senna on lap 50 and won it from him, Prost third. Prost launched a bitter attack on Ferrari, 'a team without directive and without strategy.' He felt strongly that Mansell should have been told to move over and let him through

Mansell was talking to Williams.

In Spain during first qualifying, Donnelly's Lotus went into a barrier at 140mph in an impact so extreme it threw him out on to the track. Pierluigi Martini, following, positioned his Minardi so it shielded Donnelly's body until help came. Donnelly, terribly injured, survived. Prost won the race from Mansell, Senna out with a punctured radiator and the championship remained alive, Senna 76 points, Prost 69, Japan and Australia to come.

Mansell was confirmed at Williams.

Nannini's new helicopter crashed when he was trying to land it at his parents' home. It seems the ground under it gave way and, as it thrashed, threw Nannini out. The disintegrating rotor blade severed his arm below the elbow and although this was later re-attached using microsurgery his Grand Prix career ended. Perhaps active people, intrigued by technology and exploiting it, are more vulnerable. Perhaps we notice their deaths more because they are famous people. Perhaps it just happens – Hawthorn in his Jaguar on the Guildford by-pass, Hailwood taking his kids to buy fish 'n' chips, Pace in a light plane, Graham Hill landing in fog, David Purley doing aerobatics...

Roberto Moreno, for long a driver looking for a serious drive, replaced Nannini.

The imagery of Suzuka, or rather 15 seconds of it, remains too powerful to go away. Senna took pole from Prost and wanted that pole moved to the left side of the track where the surface was cleaner. This was refused and Senna took a fatalistic decision: *from the start I'll go for it and whatever happens happens.* It seems that he even managed to convince himself he would not be responsible for what did happen.

Prost made the better start and turned in to the first corner quite normally, Senna inside him but never level. Those were the 15 seconds. The cars touched, fled into the dusty embrace of the run-off area, disappeared into the dust. The World Championship had been decided in the most crude way, the whole sport – its awesome technology, its cultivated global image, its growing popularity – brought into disrepute.

Prost rounded on Senna, calling him a worthless human being and saying that if this sort of conduct went unpunished Grand Prix racing couldn't survive because crashing into people would become accepted practice. Senna called it a racing accident and said he didn't care what Prost thought about him or anything else.

Piquet in the Benetton won his first race for three years, Moreno second. Piquet won Australia to be third in the championship and on television Jackie Stewart had a strong confrontation with Senna over Suzuka. This proved poignant because whenever Stewart spoke of crashing – and by implication driver conduct and safety – everybody listened. They had had to ever since the nuns covered his modesty in the barn at *Masta*, 12 June 1966. The interview proved even more poignant when Senna made clear in trenchant language that he defended absolutely what he had done in the 15 seconds. Afterwards Stewart said: 'I think he honestly believes what he is saying, but then so did Hitler.'

And the bitter season was mercifully over, except for a bizarre postscript at Hyde Park Corner, London, when an Alfa Romeo road car collided with a London taxi one day in December. The driver, Bertrand Gachot, was on his way to meet Eddie Jordan. Instead, an altercation developed and he sprayed CS gas into the taxi driver's face. Gachot was charged with assault and possessing an offensive weapon.

For 1991, the points for a win were increased to ten, the rest of the descending scale unaltered: 6–4–3–2–1.

The power shifted from Ferrari to Williams where Mansell and Patrese formed a strong team. Patrese was no troublemaker but a quiet, highly competent driver and in his conduct a gentleman. He was unlikely to threaten Mansell on the track and certainly not off it. That allowed Mansell to free himself from a lifetime of conspiracy theories and concentrate on what he did so gloriously well: wring the balls off fast cars and, along the way, emerge as the only man strong enough in mind and body to tackle Senna.

This gathered across 1991 and reached a great climax in 1992. It was aided by Renault's philosophy. They'd come back as an engine supplier to Williams in 1989 after a three-year absence and fully intended to demonstrate that a European manufacturer could beat the Japanese, in this case Honda. That seemed an extremely difficult proposition because Senna won the United States Grand Prix at Phoenix, where a young, blond Finn, Mika Häkkinen, made his debut in a Lotus; Senna won Brazil, San Marino and Monaco. He had 40 points, Prost 11, Patrese and Mansell 6.

Senna understood, however, that something had begun to happen. It was only a moment at San Marino but it told him a great deal. Patrese had a mechanical problem, spent a long time in the pits and emerged to run as far as he could. Teams always learn from a lot of running. He tucked in behind Senna and they reached back markers. Senna got through them and thought *I won't be seeing Patrese again for a while,* glanced in his mirror and there Patrese was. Now Senna thought *what happens when that car is reliable?*

Senna urged everybody, including Honda, that they had to work harder although he conceded that, having won the first four races, persuading them was not easy. Just to spice that, Piquet won Canada from a bright young Italian, Stefano Modena, in a Tyrrell: Senna out with an electrical problem, Mansell leading towards the very end and waving to the crowd when his engine cut. He resented any suggestions that he'd switched the engine off by mistake and said that those who wrote he had gave a good example of 'how I am treated by those members of the Press who most resent my success.'[30]

A mid-season ripple of races: Patrese won Mexico from Mansell, Senna third and now going public with the need to improve; Mansell won France from Prost, Senna third – at Magny-Cours, the sixteenth staging post. Mansell won Britain from Berger; Mansell won Germany from Patrese.

Senna 51, Mansell 43, Patrese 28.

In Hungary Senna and Prost declared peace again and Senna won from Mansell.

Two days after this Gachot, due at Monza for tyre testing, appeared instead at Southwark Crown Court and was jailed over the affair of the taxi driver. This provoked outrage in Belgium, his adopted country, and meant the Belgian Grand Prix at the end of the following week could be no ordinary event. Eddie Jordan, constantly scanning the horizon for young talent, knew of a Mercedes sports car driver who, his sources assured him, was a bright and promising lad. A deal was put together because Mercedes wanted to see what the lad might do with a Formula 1 car.

And that's how Michael Schumacher came to Silverstone on the Tuesday before Belgium to drive the Jordan. He had never sat in a Formula 1 car before and impressed its designer, Gary Anderson, when he asked what were the car's good points – and bad points. He intended, Anderson realised, to *maximise the good bits, no point in trying to maximise the bad bits.*

Jordan was not then a rich team and Schumacher received strict instructions not to over-rev the Cosworth engine because it was due on the transporter for Spa directly after the test *and* Cosworth insisted over-revved engines were sent back to them. Jordan couldn't afford the money or the time it would take. Schumacher went out and, coming past where the little Jordan group stood, was going so fast they instinctively stepped backwards. They gave him three laps and called him in because they felt he was going too fast. They kept on about the over-revving but Schumacher didn't understand what the fuss was about. *No, I haven't been over-revving. Yes, I have been within myself.*

At Spa, where many drivers and spectators wore T-shirts with the legend GACHOT WHY? and GOD SAVE THE BRITISH AND GACHOT, Schumacher outqualified team-mate de Cesaris, who'd been competing since 1980, and in the Sunday morning warm-up went fourth overall, only Patrese, Mansell and Senna quicker.

At the start Schumacher burned the clutch and was out immediately, Mansell had a mechanical problem after 22 laps and Senna won it from Berger. That seemed important – Senna 71, Mansell 49, Patrese 34 – and suggested Mansell needed to win Monza or the championship had gone.

By Monza, Schumacher had joined Benetton after 'a tangled trail of complex negotiations, opportunistic manoeuvring and outraged indignation'[31] – and that was understatement. In short Jordan thought he had a contractual understanding and didn't, Benetton were given an opportunity and seized it. Schumacher finished the Grand Prix fifth, but that was no more than a sub-plot. Senna led from Mansell, Mansell signalled Patrese up and past for a full attack, Patrese did and took the lead, but the clutch failed. Now Mansell attacked himself and got through on lap 34 of the 53: Senna had a front tyre vibration. Mansell won it, Senna up to second by the end.

Mansell suffered cruelly in Portugal where, leading after a very robust move which displeased Senna, he pitted and was waved away, pit stop completed, with the right rear wheel not yet secured. The wheel was refitted in the acceleration lane, a violation of the rules leading to Mansell's disqualification. Patrese inherited the win but Senna had second place.

At the drivers' briefing in Spain Senna berated Mansell over the start in Portugal, Mansell berated Senna and Balestre, Piquet berated the whole thing – *how many times have I heard all this and nothing happens?* – and one team manager said it had been like 'a kindergarten full of millionaires.' Mansell went head-to-head with Senna in the race, pulling alongside on the main straight and at 180mph the cars flicked together until it seemed they must touch. It was a hypnotic, alarming, intoxicating moment.[32] Mansell ran second behind Berger who'd have engine problems, opening the way for Mansell to win it from Prost, Senna fifth.

Senna 85, Mansell 69.

Ten days later Max Mosley beat Balestre for the *FISA* Presidency, 43 votes to 29.

If 15 seconds settled the 1990 championship at Suzuka 17 minutes did it in 1991. Berger took pole from Senna, Mansell on the second row and McLaren's strategy became direct. Because Mansell had to win they'd send Berger off into the distance while Senna kept Mansell in third. Mansell moved up to attack Senna after nine laps but – maybe a problem with the brakes – ran wide and attacked the run-off area at 200mph instead. It was over.

Towards the very end Senna heard a radio message but couldn't make it out. He thought it said *slow, let Berger win* because Berger hadn't won in a McLaren yet. Senna knew if he told people he hadn't understood the message 'nobody would believe me' so he went slowly himself and did hear it clearly. Sunlight fell across his McLaren as he took it down the start-finish straight, through the unfolding snake at the back and – there, already – he had his right hand out waving. He skimmed the McLaren through Spoon, the Hairpin, the left-handed Degner curve. Shadows from the trees fell full across the circuit here and he ran easily across them: light and darkness. Cresting the little rise before the chicane Berger had come into view. Into the chicane Berger drew up, out of it Senna angled the McLaren across to the left opening the track and the victory to Berger.

Mansell stayed around to congratulate Senna who, after the race, lashed and savaged Balestre, explained why he'd done what he'd done at the 15-second Suzuka the year before and larded it all with four-letter words.

Australia was washed out after 14 laps (Senna won) and by then Ferrari had fired Prost.

And another bitter season was mercifully over.

Mansell's moment, or rather sequence of moments, had finally come in 1992 and they were overwhelming. He made the whole season a ripple of races: pole in South Africa and led every lap, same in Mexico, pole in Brazil and led the last 40 laps, pole and led every lap in Spain. The championship table presented a spectacle with only one dimension.

Mansell 40, Patrese 18, Schumacher – fourth in South Africa, third in Mexico and Brazil, second in Spain – 17. Any sport can only survive by constantly reinvigorating itself and here in the shape of a lean, angular German was the invigoration.

Mansell led every lap from pole in the San Marino Grand Prix and at this point seemed on the threshold of dominating *every* aspect of a season more completely than *any* man before him. He took pole at Monaco and led from Senna to lap 70 of the 78 but felt he had a puncture and pitted. He emerged behind Senna and exerted colossal pressure but Senna threaded the McLaren round on the racing line – the only line round most of Monaco – in perfect composure keeping Mansell in jail behind him.

The Monaco measure: Senna, 78 laps, 1h 50m 59.3s, an average speed of 87.1mph; Senna, 1991, 85.6mph.

Berger won Canada from Schumacher before the ripple of races continued: Mansell took pole in France and led the last 49 laps; pole and led every lap at Silverstone where he excited a huge crowd to the point where they invaded the track with the cars still going round.

One of those still going round, a quiet-spoken Englishman called Damon Hill, had a deeply uncompetitive Brabham and finished four laps down on Mansell. Fifteen other drivers lapped him, mostly several times, but he'd been mature enough to keep out of their way. Being the son of Graham cut both ways because it opened doors but excited expectations. When Graham died he left the family in straitened circumstances and Damon's journey to Silverstone had been long and difficult. He'd even worked as a dispatch rider to raise money. He was almost 32. Thus far into 1992, he had tried and failed to qualify the Brabham for Spain, San Marino, Monaco, Canada and France. During these cul-de-sac days Hill worked tirelessly in the background as the Williams test driver. He was good and if a vacancy ever did arise at the team he was available, knew the car, knew the team, didn't make trouble and wouldn't cost a fortune.

Mansell virtually locked up the championship in Germany, pole and leading every lap except for the pit stops, and did lock it up two weeks later in Hungary with second place behind Senna.

He'd been ticking the laps off and working out where he needed to finish to be sure. He'd been running third and now, into the last lap, was so emotional he couldn't work out where he did need to finish. He took the Williams down the start-finish straight and round the loop at the end, moved out into the countryside. The track cut through dried August grass. He wielded the Williams through the sequence of corners towards the sweeping loop onto the final straight, positioned it to mid-track to go cleanly round that.

He had vindicated all the struggles of his life in 1h 46m 59.35s.

Nobody had ever won a championship at this stage of a season – five races in hand – and perhaps nobody dreamed anybody ever would. In the time that the championship consisted of 16 rounds, beginning in 1976 (although not every year: 17 in '77, 15 in '79, 14 in '80, 15 in '81 and '83) it had not been done earlier than the 14th round – Prost at Brands Hatch in '85. Putting it another way Mansell needed only 68 per cent of the available races, Prost 87 per cent and even peering back across the whole championship from 1950 Clark was nearest on 70 per cent, winning both his championships at round seven of the ten.

Quietly, the Brabham team came to their end. They'd been struggling since Yamaha switched their engine supply to Jordan at the end of 1991 and now the company which owned them went into receivership. Since 1962, the team had competed in 394 races and won 35 of them. Whatever, Damon Hill was entirely free.

Schumacher won Belgium which, curiously, seems so early in a career but he'd already driven 18 races (Senna 16 for his first, Scheckter 13, Stewart 8 among many, many who'd done it quicker.) Of more significance, Schumacher was 22, virtually a decade younger than Senna, and he'd now scored points in eight of the rounds. A sense grew not just of reinvigoration but regime change, not immediately but one fine day soon.

Mansell announced his retirement at Monza, claiming Williams had been difficult in negotiations and gone back on their word. They said nothing. Damon Hill watched from afar and wondered. Senna won the race from Brundle (Benetton), Schumacher third and at Estoril Williams confirmed Prost for 1993. Mansell won from Berger, Patrese won Japan from Berger again and Berger won Australia from Schumacher. After the rigidity before Hungary it seemed loose, shapeless and delightful to behold because you didn't know what would happen next and neither did the drivers.

In Australia, Mansell and Senna collided on lap 18 and, almost as if it was a law of nature, they accused each other. Senna said Mansell gave him a brake test, Mansell raged that Senna could get away with anything and the Williams team weren't supporting him in his protest to the Stewards.

That apart, an *un*-bitter season had come to a close and hardly anybody could believe it.

The March team had also come to a close. They'd survived 1992 somehow although at one point the car ran with virtually no sponsorship, but they couldn't continue beyond that.

Denny Hulme suffered a heart attack while he drove in the Bathurst 1000 KM touring car race in Australia. Before he died he managed to pull the car safely off the circuit so that at the very final instant of his life he still thought and behaved like a racing driver.

Senna understandably coveted the drive which Prost now had – Senna even told James Hunt on the record he would drive for Williams without pay – and it did nothing to lead to another declaration of peace. Worse, for Senna, Honda withdrew leaving McLaren with Ford engines. Against Prost in the Williams-Renault he'd have no chance.

When the roundabout stopped the driver arrangement looked quite different: Senna and Michael Andretti, son of Mario, from IndyCars at McLaren; Prost and Hill at Williams; Schumacher and Patrese at Benetton; Alesi and Berger at Ferrari. This was not immutable, however, because Senna (reportedly wanting $16 million) and McLaren (reportedly offering $10 million) hadn't reached agreement and Senna proceeded on a race-by-race basis.

Prost took pole from Senna in South Africa and a chirpy Brazilian, Rubens Barrichello, put a Jordan on the seventh row of the grid. He was, as he'd tell people, very young – 20. Senna led but the Williams was just too strong and he conjured a second place. That seemed the matrix of the season already but Senna kept on conjuring. In Brazil it rained and Prost, leading from pole, skated off. Senna overcame a stop 'n' go penalty (for overtaking under yellow flags) and won it from Hill.

Now Senna conjured pure magic. Tom Wheatcroft, who owned Donington and made it into a modern track, had long been promised a Grand Prix and got one, the European. Some people in Grand Prix racing have an acute sense of history, most have no interest in it beyond the doings of their own era. How many who gathered in early April 1993 had heard of Rosemeyer or Nuvolari or knew that these great drivers passed just this way in 1937 and 1938? How many people knew that the stone house near the entrance had stood on the very rim of the pre-war track, protected by straw bales? How many knew that the downhill-uphill horseshoe section – where the Silver Arrows had been airborne – still existed, just over there out of sight? How many cared? Wheatcroft did because, as a lad, he'd attended the 1938 race.

If Nuvolari was the greatest of them all Senna was about to be united with him in 1h 50m 46.57s.

Prost took pole from Hill, then Schumacher, then Senna. Sega sponsored the race and clearly game over already. Then it rained...

Prost made a safe start, Hill near to him, Schumacher mid track, Karl Wendlinger, an affable Austrian in a Sauber, pulling alongside. Senna was forced over to the rim of the track by Schumacher. They reached into the mouth of the right-hander at the end of the straight – Redgate – and Senna corkscrewed the McLaren full across the track to the inside. As they rounded Redgate, Schumacher found himself marooned on the outside. They flowed downhill to the Craner Curves,[33] initially a left. With spray coming in plumes from the tyres Senna went round Wendlinger on the outside.

Wendlinger: 'I saw him in the mirrors and I could see the way he was driving. I knew his reputation in the wet and I knew precisely what he was going to do. I decided I'd better leave him some room. I didn't want to go out of the race there and then.'

The track snaked right, climbed and on the climb Senna put the McLaren up to Hill's rear, pulled out, powered past.

Hill: 'I made a bad start. I'd actually thought I could get ahead of Alain into Redgate. I was a bit peeved to be behind Alain, I couldn't really see...you can't see what's going on behind you: you certainly see there's a car behind, and you might just make it out as a red car or a white car or something. When he got past me I thought *for God's sake, Ayrton!*'

Senna hunted down Prost and at Melbourne hairpin went inside, the McLaren twitching under braking. He led and crossing the line was 0.7 of a second in front of Prost.

Perhaps we might ponder Nuvolari's final lap at the Nürburgring in 1935; add to that Rosemeyer's fastest lap at the Nürburgring in 1936 when he did 9m 56.6s, which would have been a competitive time in *1956* – front row of the grid; add to that Fangio's lap 20 at the Nürburgring in 1957 when he did 9m 17.4s, taking more than *24* seconds off his own record set the year before; and now add to that A. Senna, lap one, Donington, 1993, 1m 35.84s.

Jo Ramirez, the McLaren team co-ordinator, watched Senna go by completing that lap and wondered *how can he have that advantage? The Williamses must be on dry tyres.* Next lap, Senna more than three and a half seconds ahead, Ramirez thought *maybe I was mistaken about the tyres on the Williamses.* He ran back to the pit wall and *no mistake, wet tyres, same as us.*

The rest assumed surreal dimensions. The weather changed constantly and Williams changed tyres so many times in response that they eventually ran out of them. Senna meanwhile led at one stage by a complete lap and at the end only Hill was on the same lap. In Senna's time only Senna could have done this, and only Senna did.

In a car which could not compete he had 26 points, Prost 14, Hill 12. Only Senna could have done this, too, and only Senna did.

Prost reasserted himself at Imola although initially Hill led from Senna, Prost third. Hill spun off, Senna's hydraulics failed and Prost won it from Schumacher. Senna conjured a second place behind Prost in Spain and clung on.

Prost 34 points, Senna 32, Schumacher 14.

On the Saturday at Monaco, Hill's car had a suspension failure coming out of the tunnel at 170mph. 'That's the fastest part of the circuit,' he said. 'The back of the car just sat down, it spun and went down the escape road which my father went down X years ago. It went a long way.' That's another Monaco measure because when Graham did go down it, in 1965, he reckoned he was doing 120mph. Graham came upon a back marker and in missing him 'left some rare old skid marks.'[34]

Prost had pole from Schumacher, Senna and Hill on row two. Prost led securely, was given a stop 'n' go penalty for jumping the start and stalled twice in the pit lane. Schumacher led securely – but his hydraulics failed amid fire and smoke. Senna won it from Hill and led the championship again.

The Monaco measure: Senna, 78 laps, 1h 52m 10.9s, an average speed of 86.2mph; Senna, 1992, 87.1mph.

Ultimately the strength of the Williams and the Renault engine was not to be resisted. Prost created a mid-season tide rather than a ripple: he won Canada from Schumacher, won France from Hill, won Silverstone from Schumacher, won Germany from Schumacher.

For Prost the tide went out: in Hungary he stalled on the grid and had to start from the back. Hill won to become the first driver whose father had also won. While Hill was doing this Senna – throttle failed – stayed out on the circuit watching the Williams very, very closely. He had his reasons. Hill won Belgium from Schumacher, Prost third. Prost led Monza from pole but with five laps to go and the championship within touching distance the engine failed for the first time in the season.

At Estoril Senna announced he wouldn't be staying with McLaren in 1994, Prost announced he was retiring altogether, creating a vacancy at Williams, and you didn't have to be Einstein to work out what would happen next. By now an unhappy Andretti had gone back to America. He'd only finished six of the 13 rounds and been on the podium once, third at Monza. Andretti proved a charming and popular man but somehow Formula 1 didn't fit him and he didn't fit Formula 1. Häkkinen replaced him.

The Portuguese Grand Prix shook down to Schumacher leading and Prost tracking him, probing, constantly ready to seize on a mistake, constantly poised to administer the *coup de grâce*. He knew second was good enough and never did anything to jeopardise that but in this hour of genuine triumph – a fourth championship, and only Fangio with more – he did some real racing, too.

Into the last lap he was close to Schumacher and tracked him through the right-hander. In the snake at the back Prost drew up. Into turn six a back marker loomed at them, Prost poised to seize any Schumacher mistake. The back marker moved obediently aside and they went through. Suddenly, gloriously, Prost attacked in a right-hander, looking to one side, changing the line of attack to the other side but Schumacher accelerated away and Prost knew the moment had gone. He crossed the line 0.98 seconds behind.

Senna won Japan from Prost and then sought out young Eddie Irvine, an Ulsterman driving a Jordan – Senna said he'd been baulked by him – and larded upon him his full vocabulary of Anglo-Saxon. Some say he cuffed Irvine, who wasn't impressed by that, or impressed by Senna either.

Ramirez, long a close friend of Senna, said in Adelaide: 'I'll forgive you leaving us if you win the race!' Neither man trusted themselves to look at the other on the grid: 1h 43m 27.47s later Senna had won the Australian Grand Prix from Prost.

Schumacher was getting stronger and stronger.

That season Mansell, driving for the Newman-Haas team, won the IndyCar Championship and became the third dual champion after Mario Andretti (1978 in F1, 1965, 66, 69 and 84 in Indy) and Emerson Fittipaldi (1972, 1974 in F1, 1989 in Indy).

That season, too, James Hunt – acerbic BBC commentator in his later years – died of a heart attack. For a long time he left that most unusual of legacies for a racing driver: silence.

In December, Philippe Streiff organised a karting event at Bercy, near Paris. Streiff had had a fairly plain Grand Prix career and been paralysed since crashing in testing at Rio in 1989. After a long, sometimes hauntingly desolate struggle he was finding himself again. The karting was a charity event and he approached Senna who said he'd fly from Brazil specially. Streiff sent him a plane ticket which Senna never did use. He paid for himself and more than that competed against Prost. Streiff says that, to him, when Senna agreed to come it was a life-giving experience. Within five months that assumed a terrible poignancy.

For 1994 electronic aids were banned – traction control, fly-by-wire throttle mechanisms, active suspension. Senna, for one, felt that these neutralised a driver's skill but there was a wider point, a timeless tension about the effects of technology in a human activity *about technology.* Max Mosley postulated[35] the nightmare scenario, that technology would one day allow racing without drivers at all. A balance was constantly sought, however elusive, between returning the racing car to the purity of its driver's skills and giving him the most sophisticated piece of racing machinery human ingenuity could devise. Here, in 1994, was another reaching for the balance.

Refuelling stops had been imposed and many Formula 1 insiders wondered about the wisdom of that, if only on safety grounds. In reality it altered the nature of the sport, breaking up processional races and allowing chess-like strategies. It enlivened some races, left others open to the charge that in modern Formula 1 most of the overtaking was done with the cars stationary in the pits.

Approaching 1994 people spoke quite seriously about Senna winning all 16 races in the Williams-Renault and yet within the fabric of the first race – Brazil – came pressure from Schumacher. Senna took pole but Schumacher led 50 of the 71 laps and trying to overhaul him Senna spun off.

The Pacific Grand Prix, a handy title like the Grand Prix of Europe, was run at the Aida circuit, Japan, a remote location around 50 miles from Okayama City, itself 250 miles south of Tokyo, and Senna took pole again. Into the first corner of the race, however, Häkkinen bumped him and he spun out. Schumacher won it from Berger.

The real pressure had come now, Schumacher a perfect 20 points, Senna 0. The Williams was not as easy to handle as Senna anticipated and for the first time in his life a young pretender pushed him hard.

He'd fallen in love with a beautiful blonde, Adrianne Galisteu, as she had fallen in love with him. She was no decorative creature but a real person and he loved her for that. He was setting up a business empire and that would be the next chapter in his life. He had spoken with his sister, Viviane, about doing something to help the poor of Brazil.

All that provided the context for the San Marino Grand Prix at Imola.

A malevolence stalked the circuit. On the Friday Barrichello, driving the Jordan-Hart, lost control into the Variente Bassa, a 140mph right-left before the pit lane. The car hit the top of the tyre barrier and somersaulted. He emerged shaken but without any serious injuries. Senna, who regarded him as something of a protégé, was badly upset, went to the Medical Centre and Prof Watkins allowed him in to see for himself that Barrichello was joking about chasing nurses.

On the Saturday Roland Ratzenberger, went out in a Simtek.[36] This was his third Grand Prix meeting. In Brazil he'd failed to qualify and in Aida he'd finished eleventh. Now he worked the Simtek up to 180mph after Tamburello. Something happened to it – maybe bodywork came off – and it smashed itself into a concrete wall killing Ratzenberger and, in the same moment, pitching Formula 1 into mourning for the first time since de Angelis in 1986.

Death had been such a stranger to a Grand Prix that a generation of drivers, technicians, supporters and journalists had grown up since Paletti struck Pironi at Montreal 1982. They had not confronted it because they hadn't had to, and now here it was again.

This time Prof Watkins wouldn't let Senna into the Medical Centre but instead walked him to a little piece of grass and told him Ratzenberger was dead. Watkins, seeing the state Senna was in, said he should consider immediate retirement and, if he did that, Watkins would retire, too. They'd spend their time fishing in the Scottish Borders where Watkins had a house that Senna visited.

In the Sunday morning warm-up Senna sent a message via his on-board radio to Prost, commentating for French television: *Alain, we miss you*. This was the final declaration of peace.

Senna raced. He had pole and led from that but JJ Lehto stalled his Benetton, a Lotus struck the back of it and debris reached the spectators, injuring eight. The Safety Car came out and a crocodile, in race order, formed behind it, circling and circling while the track was cleaned up. The Safety Car pulled off at the end of lap five and Senna got onto the power very quickly, briefly shedding Schumacher but Schumacher came back at him and, completing lap six, Senna led by only 0.6. On that lap Schumacher noticed the Williams 'bottoming' into Tamburello.

Now they approached Tamburello again but instead of going round it the Williams continued towards the concrete wall. In the 1.8 seconds it took to reach that wall Senna clawed the speed from 192mph to 136mph. He struck the wall hard enough to gouge a chunk from it. Nobody knows why the Williams speared off and, it seems, nobody ever will. The one man who could tell us is forever silent.

A part of the suspension was driven back into his crash helmet, delivering a blow of unimaginable speed and strength. Ayrton Senna remained technically alive and was flown by helicopter to Maggiore Hospital in Bologna, but, treating him on the ground before he was put on the helicopter, Watkins thought *his soul has gone*.

Notes

1. *Life in the Fast Lane,* Prost.
2. *Hard Edge of Genius,* Hilton.
3. *Memories of Ayrton,* Hilton.
4. Tyrrell's points were taken away and the drivers' excluded retrospectively for an alleged fuel infringement, which Tyrrell vehemently denied. The exclusion of course meant the expunging of Bellof's superb drive at Monaco and Brundle's superb drive at Detroit.
5. *Honda, Conquerors of Formula 1,* Hilton.
6. *To Hell and Back,* Lauda.
7. Rosberg quoted in *Frank Williams,* Hamilton.
8. The context of Lauda and Estoril – Lauda the best known driver of his age to the world beyond, the return from the dead at the Nürburgring – placed many drivers in an awkward position. Dare they hold Lauda up as he reached them and needed to get past them or would they get smartly out of the way? Some quietly said they would, Senna for one said he wouldn't.
9. Prost, op. cit.
10. *My Autobiography,* Mansell.
11. There's a very moving account of Frank Williams' accident in *A Different Kind of Life,* Virginia Williams.
12. Carl Haas, legendary north American figure, tried Formula 1 with Lola and Cosworth engines. They competed in 19 Grands Prix in 1985 and 1986.
13. Hamilton, op. cit.
14. Ibid.
15. It was a contentious issue at the time. For Mansell's side of what happened, see his book *My Autobiography.*
16. Hamilton, op. cit.
17. Ibid.
18. Active suspension has been described (in an *Autocourse* 1987–88 feature by Doug Nye) as 'like an animal's muscular system. Whereas any steel spring and damper will deflect if you bounce on it, if somebody climbs on your shoulders your legs don't suddenly collapse under the extra load. Your muscles compensate and you maintain the same height under perhaps twice the load. [...] The secret is to teach the brain to recognise the load and to tell the muscles – or the hydraulic actuators – to compensate for it in the most relevant manner.' Nye was quoting Peter Wright, one of the instigators of the system at Lotus.
19. Prost, op. cit.
20. *Autosport.*
21. Mansell, op. cit.

22. *Grand Prix Showdown,* Hilton.
23. *Gerhard Berger: the Human Face of Formula 1,* Hilton.
24. John DeLorean, American entrepreneur who worked on the Pontiac GTO car in the 1960s, set up his own company to build gull-wing sports cars in Northern Ireland – a project Colin Chapman was involved in – and eventually went bankrupt.
25. Onyx, a Sussex-based team which, formed in 1979, competed in Formula 3000 then Formula 1 in 1989 and 1990.
26. The *FIA*'s World Motor Sport Council has responsibility for all aspects of motor sport. Like the World Council for Mobility and the Automobile, the elected members of the World Motor Sport Council come from all over the world. The Council's top priorities are: To promote continuously improving safety standards in all forms of motor sport. To administer international motor sport. To encourage and implement the adoption of common regulations for all forms of motorsports and series across the world. To encourage and develop all forms of motorsport, especially amongst the young and in developing countries. (*FIA* official website.)
27. Mansell, op. cit.
28. Ibid.
29. *Inside the Mind of the Grand Prix Driver,* Hilton.
30. Mansell, op. cit.
31. *Autocourse.*
32. Frank Williams was asked (by the author) if he wasn't a bit concerned when Mansell and Senna veered together at that speed. He replied: 'I wish all the races were like that!'
33. The Craner Curves are named for Fred Craner, who set up the Donington circuit in the 1930s and was instrumental in getting Mercedes and Auto Union to compete in the 1937 and 1938 Grands Prix there.
34. *Life at the Limit,* Hill.
35. Interview with author.
36. Simtek, established in 1989 to provide high-level technology in racing. Simtek decided to form their own team in 1993 and it competed in 1994.

Chapter 11

In Schumacher's time

The inheritance rested uneasy, as it would have to do. The San Marino Grand Prix was restarted but the malevolence lingered. Alboreto made a pit stop, a wheel wasn't fitted properly to his Minardi and, as he accelerated, it came off injuring four mechanics. Schumacher won from Nicola Larini[1] in a Ferrari and Häkkinen and they were as sombre about that as everyone at Imola was about everything else.

Senna's funeral at São Paulo the following week convulsed and consumed Brazil. As his body was transported from the airport to lie in state a million people – and maybe many, many more – lined the route. His true stature was revealed then and it would grow into a kind of enduring mystique. Good work would be done in his name, too, principally the *Ayrton Senna Foundation* feeding and educating the impoverished youth of Brazil on a considerable scale.

The malevolence of this spring 1994 had not played itself out, either. At Monaco in Thursday free practice, Wendlinger's Sauber crashed at the chicane after the tunnel, hammering the guardrail. He suffered serious head injuries and suddenly Grand Prix racing seemed terribly vulnerable, frighteningly brittle, every moment charged through with fragility.

That impression was reinforced because the week after Imola Mosley said that rushing through new safety regulations might create problems, but by Monaco the *FIA* 'had become the focal point of hysterical pressure from the French and Italian media.'[2] Mosley breached the Concorde Agreement he himself had drafted ten years before, stipulating no major changes without every team agreeing, in announcing that from the Spanish Grand Prix cars would have to run with less aerodynamic downforce; from the Canadian Grand Prix, cockpit protection would be improved and stronger front suspensions so wheels wouldn't hit drivers on the head; from the German Grand Prix, aerodynamic modifications – due in 1995 – to be introduced. For 1995, a raft of further measures were mandated: downforce reduced again, engine power reduced, a car's minimum weight increased.

Schumacher won Monaco from Brundle (McLaren).

The Monaco measure: Schumacher, 78 laps, 1h 49m 55.3s, an average speed of 88.0mph; Senna, 1993, 86.2mph.

The inheritance sat uneasy in Spain where the drivers – the Grand Prix Drivers' Association had been re-formed – strongly objected to one section of the track and an astonishing chicane of two tyre walls was constructed. Schumacher took his Benetton-Ford to pole, from Hill, and led but on lap 24 of the 65 his gearbox stuck in fifth.

From this moment the inheritance sat easier. Hill went by but Schumacher, adjusting to drive round the problem just as Jim Clark used to do, coaxed the car to second place, including a pit stop *which should not have been possible*. It required a tremendous shove by the mechanics to get the car up to enough speed that he could ease it away in fifth without stalling. Schumacher's performance was so astonishing that initially some journalists disbelieved it and Ford had to show them the telemetry.

Ford said the 'telemetry confirms that following the gearbox failure, the Zetec-R in Schumacher's car was required to pull from a minimum 5,200rpm on each remaining lap and rev to its maximum 14,500rpm for long periods on the straights. With his Benetton-Ford stuck in fifth gear Schumacher's best lap around the 2.95-mile Barcelona circuit was 1:26.17 seconds. There were only three other recorded laps better than that, one of those being Schumacher's own record-setting 1:25.15 seconds – with all gears operative [lap 18].'

Senna had been a giant. Here was his direct successor. Senna once said that if you are a front-runner the cameras are on you most of the time and whatever you do is always under scrutiny, with the consequence that accidents and incidents assume enormous proportions. Across the remainder of this season – and the next, and the one after that – Schumacher was to learn the truth of this, if he didn't know it already.

The historical connection in Spain, like an umbilical chord, did not end with Schumacher and Clark. Hill understood that his victory was important for himself – now cast into the role of number one driver – but also for the whole team. His father understood that when, four weeks after Clark's death he, too, won the Spanish Grand Prix – Jarama, not Cataluyna but that didn't matter – and what that meant to the whole of Lotus.

David Coulthard, a square-jawed, articulate Scot came in as number two at Williams and ran sixth in Spain until he had an electrical failure.

Schumacher won Canada from Hill, and on the way Hill had to surmount a psychological problem. Towards the end, when he'd given up hope of catching Schumacher, he felt as if he was 'choking'. He disconnected the pipe feeding liquid to his helmet and still he felt something tightening and tightening. He was close to panic. He 'detached my radio flex from the helmet and undid my overalls.' Within a couple of laps he felt better and concluded that the 'jarring' on the circuit had worked his clothing down his back, dragging the radio flex taut against his throat.[3]

Mansell replaced Coulthard for the French Grand Prix, generating a firestorm of publicity although Hill, having measured himself directly against Prost and Senna, regarded his arrival with equanimity. He was almost alone in this. Hill took pole from Mansell but Schumacher won it, Hill second, Mansell out with a transmission failure.

At Silverstone, Hill took pole from Schumacher but on the parade lap Schumacher clearly pulled ahead of Hill, violating the rule prohibiting that. On lap 13, Hill leading, Schumacher was given a five-second penalty but what precisely that meant wasn't explained to Benetton, who assumed it had to be added to Schumacher's final race time. Schumacher was black flagged but continued, and was eventually brought in for a five-second stop 'n' go and although he finished second was disqualified.

Hill described this as 'one of the greatest days of his life' and pointed out that it was a matter of family honour. Graham hadn't won it in '17 attempts.'[4] Damon's mother beamed at everyone, pointed to the Heavens and murmured 'somebody's having a party up there...'

Coulthard, reinstated, came sixth.

Before Hockenheim Schumacher, wearing a multi-coloured sports jacket went into the *FIA* headquarters, Place de la Concorde, Paris, on the Tuesday over the Silverstone debacle. He lost his six points from Silverstone and was given a two-race ban. If he accepted the ban he missed Hockenheim. If he appealed he could drive at Hockenheim but risked having the ban increased should the appeal fail. Leaving the Place de la Concorde, Schumacher 66 points, Hill 39.

It was easy, this mid-season, to overlook that Ferrari were getting podium finishes now, Berger three, Alesi three. The great, almost mythical Ferrari revival tantalised as it had done so often before, like a beautiful woman beckoning – but the closer you approached, the further away she seemed to be. Then, from the pine trees of Hockenheim, she beckoned again: Berger took pole from Alesi and led every lap with the Ligier pairing of Olivier Panis and Eric Bernard next. Schumacher had an engine failure, Hill punished by an early crash.

The image of Hockenheim, however, would always be of Jos Verstappen's Benetton at the pits refuelling and suddenly consumed by a fireball. It produced some of the most extraordinary photographs ever taken at a Grand Prix, principally of a mechanic's flame-proof overalls completely engulfed in yellow, molten, billowing flames. Equally extraordinary, nobody was hurt.

A strange impetus began to gather, and it would propel Schumacher across the remainder of this season, the whole of the next season and even the season after that. By (literally and figuratively) accident or design Schumacher gave Grand Prix racing regular convulsions in a way even Senna hadn't done. In fact nobody had. Senna's dictum about the eyes of the global audience constantly upon you was now moving into play in the starkest manner.

After Hockenheim the company which made the refuelling equipment, Intertechnique, gave a full report to the *FIA*, who issued a statement: 'The fuel spillage was caused by the fuel valve failing to close properly. The valve was slow to close due to the presence of a foreign body. The foreign body is believed to have reached the valve because a filter designed to eliminate the risk had been deliberately removed.'

One estimate was that, by removing the filter, fuel would have flowed in at 12.5 per cent faster, saving perhaps a second during the pit-stop. Saving seconds is Grand Prix racing's *only* currency.

Would the *FIA* banish Benetton from Formula 1? Would that be the end of Schumacher's championship? Benetton defended themselves vigorously. They'd held their own investigation. 'No evidence was seen, during the examination of scouring or of other effects, which could have resulted from debris fouling any of the moving parts. A study of the layout of the fuel path and of the evidence surrounding the incident did not suggest any way in which any feasible debris contamination from the fuel flow could have caused the failure of the nozzle to engage correctly.'

Schumacher won Hungary from Hill and would take some catching. Schumacher 76 points, Hill 45.

The World Motor Sport Council summoned Benetton to attend the Place de la Concorde on 19 October, before Japan and Australia. Schumacher was appealing against Silverstone, which might cost him more than missing two races. Benetton might be stripped of the championship *after* Schumacher had won it. Schumacher might win his appeal...

A dry race at Spa, Barrichello on pole leading, Schumacher behind. Barrichello could not hold him and now he led after Les Combes. Schumacher beat Hill by 13.66 seconds. Schumacher 86, Hill 51. However...the Stewards checked the Benetton and that evening announced the plank under it⁵ didn't conform to the regulations. Benetton and Schumacher forfeited their points. (The plank had to be 10mm deep with an allowance of 10 per cent wear during a race, meaning that it must measure a minimum 9mm afterwards. The Stewards claimed that in some places it measured only 7.4mm. In defence, Ross Brawn, the team's Technical Director, argued that Schumacher had spun during the race and that might have ground down the plank.) Benetton appealed. Schumacher 76, Hill 55.

On the Tuesday, Schumacher went to the Place de la Concorde and had his appeal over the two-race ban from Silverstone rejected. A reporter asked if he'd quit Formula 1 and he replied: 'I need a few days to think about a lot of things.'

The *FIA* abandoned 19 October to adjudicate on the fire and, instead of hearing the plank appeal on 5 September and the fire explanation on 7 September, did them all together on this Wednesday. They rejected the Spa appeal but decided to take no further action over the fire.

JJ Lehto joined Verstappen for Italy and Portugal, Schumacher's missing races, but they could do nothing about Hill. He won Monza and said it had been a team effort. He won Portugal, from Coulthard, and expressed relief.

Schumacher 76, Hill 75.

Before the European Grand Prix at Jerez Schumacher lambasted Hill. 'I don't think we would have been in this situation [in the championship] if Ayrton Senna had been in the car. Ayrton would have been driving circles around me. That shows what I think about Damon as a driver. He has been thrown into the No. 1 driver position but he never really was a No. 1 driver. With David Coulthard driving quicker than him after three races, it proves he is not a No. 1 driver. So the respect is certainly not as much as I have for other drivers.' And more, in the same vein.

The race turned on pit-stop strategy, Hill's refuelling rig malfunctioning and Schumacher beat him by 24.68 seconds.

Schumacher 86, Hill 81.

They went to Suzuka, chirpy Englishman Johnny Herbert replacing Verstappen. Schumacher took pole, Hill alongside and a storm fell all over the circuit. Schumacher led, Hill in behind, but cars spun off and the pace car came out for seven laps. They raced again but more cars spun off and the race had to be stopped. When it restarted the result would be decided on aggregate time, Schumacher enjoying a 6.8-second lead from the first part. Benetton's tactics went wrong – Schumacher pitted for fuel twice, Hill once so Hill led on the aggregate by 15 seconds.

Schumacher came at him but Hill resisted and won it by 3.36 seconds. 'I was on the radio every lap to keep myself informed of Michael's progress. There were about four people trying to get on the radio to tell me that I was P1 [Position, First], but there was so much interference that all I could hear was P-blah-blah. I had to tell everyone to calm down, shut up and tell me where I'd finished!'

Schumacher 92, Hill 91.

Mansell came back in the Williams for Adelaide and took pole from Schumacher, Hill next. At the green Mansell's Williams slithered under acceleration and Schumacher drew level, went through. Into the lap Hill stole inside Mansell and by lap two caught Schumacher. From then on they concertinaed round Adelaide's tree-fringed streets, gaining and losing, closing and separating. They pitted together, emerged together, concertinaed again. Hill sensed Schumacher felt the pressure.

On lap 36 of the 81 Schumacher wheeled the Benetton through a 90° right followed immediately by a 90° left. At the left, Schumacher would *say I got caught on a bump and the car went sideways*. It slithered over grass and slapped a wall, bouncing back onto the track diagonally. Hill saw none of this but now he found himself confronted by the Benetton. The next corner was a 90° right and Hill had a gap on the right, perfect for going round that. As he went there Schumacher began to turn in and they crashed, Schumacher pitched into the air. The Benetton punched a tyre wall when it landed.

Hill continued, Schumacher got out and waited to see if Hill came round again. The championship hung on that and fifth place would give it to Hill, who reached the pits with a wheel locked, a wishbone on the front suspension bent.

> He sat in the cockpit and the clock flickered, 7 seconds stationary, 8, 9, 10, 11, 12. At 12 he shook his head. He lifted the visor on his helmet and his eyes seemed enlarged, incredulous, saddened, resigned, perhaps embittered. The clock no longer held meaning. Mechanics, urgent uniformed figures flitting to and fro, gathered at the wishbone and felt it, probed it. A gloved hand, gentle as a caress, touched the wishbone where it had bent like a crease. Another gloved hand gripped it there, moved it up and down testing its strength – or its weakness.[6]

Worked stopped on the Williams. Hill sat motionless. Schumacher watched Mansell go by but no Hill, watched Mansell next time and still no Hill, and after the third time he understood the championship was his. Mansell won the race from Berger.

Hill said: 'I've a bit of an empty feeling but I gave him a good run for his money. He was certainly feeling the pressure because he ended up falling off the road. I saw the opportunity and I thought *I've got to go here.* I didn't make it. That's motor racing. I am not going to be drawn on the interpretation of what happened. I am very disappointed for my family as much as myself.'

Schumacher said: 'I have to say I did make some comments this year about Damon that I didn't have the kind of respect for him that maybe I had for somebody else [Senna], but I have to admit that I was wrong.' Next day Schumacher added 'I was still in front of Damon. I drove over his front wheel. It was still my corner...'

Lotus now faced bankruptcy after a long struggle for survival. They'd never really recovered from Chapman's death in 1982 although first Warr and then Australian Peter Collins – a long-time motorsport lover with, one way or another, a long association with Lotus – somehow kept the flame burning. It never burned again.

The 1995 season would be under new rules designed to bring the purity of racing back to racing, the eternal search for the balance between that and technology continuing. Engines were reduced from 3,500cc to 3,000cc, the cars had to weigh at least 595kg [1,311lb] with driver, refuelling was allowed and unlimited fuel loads, electronic driver aids were banned.

The roundabout: Herbert partnered Schumacher at Benetton, Williams kept Hill and hired Coulthard rather than Mansell, who went to McLaren partnering Häkkinen. Ferrari kept Berger and Alesi. Benetton had Renault engines, like Williams, and that promised an intense, perhaps torrid, confrontation between Schumacher and Hill. Yes, we have been here before.

Approaching the season McLaren admitted that Mansell wouldn't fit in their cockpit so he'd miss Brazil and Argentina.

In Brazil the drivers were weighed and it worked like this: the cars would be weighed again during the season but these drivers' weights be taken as a constant because they wouldn't vary by any significant amount. Schumacher weighed in at 77kg [12st 7lb] *but* at the same stage the season before he'd been 69kg [10st 8lb].

In Friday first qualifying he felt a 'little movement' from the car and in the next corner had no steering. The Benetton struck a tyre wall backwards and he said he wouldn't race unless the team found the cause. They found it. In second qualifying he went quickest, but not quick enough to dislodge Hill who'd taken provisional pole on the Friday. In the race Hill's gearbox seized, he spun off and Schumacher beat

Coulthard by eight seconds.

Schumacher was weighed again – a spot check – and the scales said 71.5kg. How could he have lost almost 12lb? If this spot check hadn't been carried out, the 77kg, not this 71.5kg, would have been added to the car during the season. One estimate translated that to 14 seconds over a race distance. A Schumacher spokesman explained that he'd been eating well, and was 'naturally losing between one and two kilos during the race.'

Meanwhile the *FIA* said Elf fuel samples from Benetton and Williams didn't match those previously submitted for approval. Schumacher and Coulthard were stripped of their points pending appeals, elevating Berger, third, to the win.

Schumacher holidayed on the Brazilian coast and eight miles off shore did some diving with three companions. When they surfaced, the boat had drifted out of sight. Schumacher swam for an hour until his fiancé Corinna Betsch, on the boat, saw him. The other three were rescued. Reflecting, Schumacher said: 'For the first time in my life, I thought that was it. For the first time I got scared, really scared.'

Grand Prix racing hadn't been to Argentina since 1981 for financial and political reasons. Hill won from Alesi, Schumacher third after three pit stops. He had problems with the tyres.

The *FIA* Appeals Committee met in Paris and reinstated the Brazilian points.

At Imola Mosley admonished Schumacher. 'I think it is unfortunate that the World Champion gets involved in a misunderstanding about how much he may or may not weigh at any time on a race weekend. It reflects poorly on the sport and shows lack of an adult attitude. It's not extraordinary that somebody should put on a stone over a year, particularly as weight no longer matters and they've been doing a lot of training and so on. What is extraordinary is that he should lose it in three days. It was a pity that it became a matter for public discussion, whether he drank a huge amount of water, didn't go to the loo or had a heavy helmet. It is just a pity he didn't take care that it didn't happen.'

Schumacher had pole for a wet race and made a powerful start, Berger following but after they'd pitted for dry tyres the Benetton spun and struck a wall then a tyre barrier. Hill won and had 20 points, Schumacher 14. Mansell finished tenth.

In Spain, Hill said he knew Schumacher had 'a certain amount of arrogance, but I don't believe he is impervious to criticism. At the weigh-in in Brazil he was pushing the regulations, and effectively stuck two fingers up at them. That is not the sort of behaviour you expect from a champion. He has been making mistakes, too, which is the sign of someone over-driving.' Schumacher took pole and led throughout the race ...

Mansell, running far down the field, stopped and would claim the McLaren was undriveable. He left the team, and Grand Prix racing, within days.

At Monaco Hill took pole, led, pitted for new tyres and fuel – the first of two stops. Schumacher now revealed a tactic which, with variations, would confound and mesmerise people inside and outside the sport. Lap after lap he did not come in. Instead he drove hard. Because he was stopping only once he established such a lead that when he pitted and emerged Hill would still be behind him – and Hill have to make another pit stop, too. The tactic could only work because Schumacher habitually drove within himself, giving him spare mental and physical capacity when he needed to summon it. That he had this spare capacity separated him from all the other drivers; that he had so much of it and could summon it so fast, sustain it for as long as he needed, was a thing of wonder. It enabled him to reshape races, reverse difficult situations, press home advantages – he won Monaco by 35 seconds, for example.

Schumacher 34, Hill 29.

The Monaco measure: Schumacher, 78 laps, 1h 53m 11.2s, an average speed of 85.5mph; Schumacher, 1994, 88.0mph.

For Hill, Canada was worse. The gearbox failed, and Alesi won it from Barrichello in the Jordan – Schumacher fifth after mechanical problems. France proved marginally better, Hill second to Schumacher, the British at Silverstone a lot worse. Hill tried to overtake Schumacher in the complex, a move Schumacher described variously as 'crazy' and 'stupid.' They both crashed out, opening the way for Herbert in the Benetton to win it and the crowd loved that. Germany was much worse for Hill: from pole he spun off at the start of lap two and Schumacher seized the race, never let it go.

Schumacher 56, Hill 35, Alesi 32.

This was Schumacher's fifth victory of 1995 and Ferrari offered him $20 million a year to do what so many had failed to do.

After Hockenheim Williams tested Jacques Villeneuve – son of Gilles – who'd been racing successfully in IndyCars and won the Indianapolis 500 in May. Like Hill, Jacques found the famous name help and hindrance. On the last lap of the 500, a journalist wondered: *Were you thinking about your father?* Jacques replied, as a racer would: *I was thinking 'I hope the car holds together.'* Jacques Villeneuve, chunky, unorthodox and an intellectual, was his own man and some driver, too.

Although Hill won Hungary, Schumacher put a strong race together winning Belgium (from Hill) before, at Monza, they crashed again amid the customary acrimony – Hill seems to have missed his braking point for the second chicane and punted the Benetton's rear. Herbert won from Häkkinen.

A trouble-free ripple of a run-in to the championship: Coulthard won Portugal from Schumacher and Hill; Schumacher won the European at the Nürburgring from Alesi, Hill crashing out.

At the Pacific Grand Prix at Aida, Schumacher became the youngest driver to win consecutive championships and only the sixth to do it at all. The lap chart told the story of a tactical triumph. Schumacher ran fifth at the start, fourth when he made his initial pit stop on lap 18 of the 83; ran second to Coulthard when others had pitted; led when Coulthard pitted a second time and – using the tactic again – drove so hard that he made his own third stop without sacrificing the lead.

He rounded the loop called, beautifully, Last Corner and took the Benetton down the start-finish straight radiating a subliminal message: *everything is in hand.* He went through the loop called, beautifully, First Corner. He held the car perfectly poised through the Moss S and the Attwood Curve which brought him onto a straight and the return leg. The Benetton was framed in sunlight, held against a backdrop of distant hillocks and rock faces. He swept round Hairpin Corner, swept on round the right-handed Piper Corner. Coulthard, nearly a quarter of a minute behind, was not yet in sight. Schumacher, quite alone, flowed down to the flag.

He added Japan from pole.

At Adelaide, Häkkinen survived an horrific crash in qualifying. His McLaren had a rear tyre deflate and smashed into a tyre wall. Two doctors, positioned there, performed a tracheotomy on him – putting a tube into his throat so he could breathe – and saved his life. In the race Schumacher and Alesi collided, Hill won from Olivier Panis (Ligier), Gianni Morbidelli (Footwork) third, Mark Blundell (McLaren) fourth, Mika Salo (Tyrrell) fifth, Pedro Lamy (Minardi) sixth.

Because this book covers so much terrain it would be unmanageable and unreadable if it embraced even fleetingly the immense host of drivers who constituted Grand Prix racing's backbone. Just this once it's good to be able to thrust some of them into the foreground. Perhaps we can regard them as representing the immense host. Consider the facts: well over 350 of them never even scored a point, at least eight had careers of less than a single lap, and one driver's career spanned six races, none of which he finished.

By now Schumacher *was* the foreground. At Ferrari he'd be partnered by Irvine, with significant rotations of the roundabout: Coulthard joining Häkkinen at McLaren, Villeneuve joining Hill at Williams, Alesi and Berger swopping Ferrari for Benetton.

At Maranello Schumacher found himself in a continuing and methodical Ferrari programme of revival. Luca di Montezemolo who ran the World soccer Cup in Italy in 1990 had been lured back years before. By 1993 he'd hired Jean Todt, former rally co-driver and arch organiser of Peugeot's rallying successes. Todt would fashion a team based on pragmatism, planning, attention to detail and, at the same time, trust in talented people to express themselves within the framework. Now Todt had Schumacher. Brawn, arch organiser at Benetton, would be coming soon.

John Barnard, Chief Designer at Ferrari, felt the 1995 car was 'actually quite nice, the 412 was a good little car, simple, basic. Alesi and Berger liked it. What we needed to do was improve the aerodynamic efficiency. One problem I had was that I kept being pushed by Montezemolo. "What are you going to do for us, what's new?" I shouldn't have succumbed to it but they wanted me to produce the miracle. "Where's the miracle?" They wanted something new, something different and I kept pushing to try and find it.'

Barnard remembers that everybody wanted Schumacher. 'He was thunderingly quick – but how do you get him? He was interested to work with me and we had programmes going at Ferrari. He went right above di Montezemolo, he went straight in up to Agnelli level [Gianni Agnelli, then head of Fiat, owning Ferrari]. He wasn't about to put himself in a situation where the President was changed after a year, which could happen very easily. He and his people made very sure about that.'

An immediate problem arose, however, because Barnard 'did not expect to be and did not want to be on track 100 per cent of the time looking after one driver.'

They tested at Estoril. 'I'd not spoken to Schumacher before, no, not really,' Barnard says. 'We had two cars at the test, the 12-cylinder – the one we'd been racing – and the first 10-cylinder "mule" [workhorse] that we'd put together. Schumacher came along and drove the 12-cylinder, and of course first thing he was immediately quicker than Alesi and Berger, he was on the pace with the current latest crop of other cars testing at Estoril. He said: "I like this, it's a good little car. If I'd had this I'd have won the championship easily." That's what he said. So we thought *bloody hell, this is a bit different.*

'Through all the 1995 season we'd been dealing with the 12-cylinder engine and it had a lot of internal friction in it. Our drivers were finding it difficult to drive smoothly because of this internal friction. Every time you lifted off the throttle you'd get a big reaction from the engine and it would tend to upset the car. We were always struggling with this. Schumacher, on the other hand, drove a car very differently and it was the first insight I'd had into seeing just how differently.

'In fact, Schumacher preferred the '12' because he drove it on the throttle and that's what I didn't understand until I was there. He had a front end that would turn into a corner like a go-kart: just flick it in and you're gone through the corner, react to the throttle. By this time [the Estoril test] we had already gone down the road for the 10-cylinder, which was the correct decision anyway.'

At Melbourne, the new venue for the Australian Grand Prix, Villeneuve took pole from Hill but Hill won it, Schumacher out with a brake failure. Brazil was wet and from the spray Hill won it from Alesi, Schumacher third. Argentina was dry and Hill won it from Villeneuve, Schumacher out with a rear wing failure. Hill 30 points, Villeneuve 12.

It's easy to compress three Grands Prix, with all their inherent dramas and uncertainties, into a single ripple-of-races paragraph but truth to tell some races are more interesting than others and some really are straightforward. The point here, however, is that even Schumacher could not implement the revival immediately, and Barnard was coming under pressure.

Villeneuve won the European at the Nürburgring from Schumacher, Hill won Imola from Schumacher so that the season assumed a shape. Hill now had 43 points, Villeneuve 22 and Schumacher 16. Hill would be very, very difficult to catch – but Panis won Monaco for Ligier from Coulthard and Herbert. Schumacher hit a wall on the opening lap and Hill's engine failed.

The Monaco measure: Panis, 75 laps, 2h 0m 45.6s, an average speed of 77.0mph – a wet race; Schumacher, 1995, 85.5mph.

Now, in torrential rain at Barcelona, Schumacher gave Ferrari the first of his masterpieces. He made a 'disaster' of the start. 'I went for the clutch and there was nothing. I nearly stalled, then tried it again. Now I know how it is to start a wet race from the back. You just can't see anything.' Quite possibly on this opening lap he overtook three cars, possibly four. He crossed the line in sixth position 6.25 seconds behind Villeneuve, leading. Irvine spun off, Hill spun off and came back but not before Berger and Schumacher had gone through. The gap was out to 8.476s, which is how it generally goes when the leader has the clear track and you're peering into the waterfall.

	Villeneuve	*Schumacher*	*Gain*
Lap 4	1m 52.26s	1m 52.14s	0.12s

Schumacher set fastest lap, moving cleanly past Berger to be third.

Lap 5	1m 52.59s	1m 50.56s	2.03s

He reeled in Alesi, who was running with Villeneuve. That took three laps but an inevitability hung over it.

Lap 6	1m 52.76s	1m 49.04s	3.71s
Lap 7	1m 52.35s	1m 51.14s	1.21s

Schumacher swarmed Alesi then left his braking late for a left-hander. Alesi didn't resist that and Schumacher moved on Villeneuve. He caught him, tracked him for four laps and out-braked him. He moved away into his own dimension and won the race from Alesi by 45 seconds.

Hill won Canada from Villeneuve and four days later Renault announced they'd be leaving Grand Prix racing at the end of 1997. Hill won France from Villeneuve – Schumacher's engine failed on the parade lap. Irvine reached lap five before his gearbox failed and Todt came under such pressure he offered to resign.

Hill 63, Villeneuve 38.

Hill took pole at Silverstone but a wheel bearing failed and he spun off, leaving the race to Villeneuve, Berger second. Schumacher had a hydraulic leak after three laps. Di Montezemolo, calming everything, said: 'We are extremely pleased with Schumacher and for me it is important that the driver is pleased with Ferrari. We both have the intention of going on together. I would rather pay $20 million for Schumacher than the same amount for two drivers.'

McLaren gave a test drive to Ralf Schumacher, younger brother of Michael. He said he hadn't spoken to Michael about it because he had to drive the car for himself. He enjoyed doing that.

Hill won Germany from Alesi, Villeneuve third, and Villeneuve won Hungary from Hill. That kept the championship alive – Hill 79, Villeneuve 62 – and it came further to life at Spa where Schumacher used the Ferrari's power to the full and the car went the distance, Villeneuve second, Hill fifth.

Hill 81, Villeneuve 68.

The week after, Williams announced they were terminating their negotiations with Hill for 1997. Frank Williams declined to say why and certainly Hill didn't know why. Heinz-Harald Frentzen, a promising German who'd been at Sauber, would replace him.

Frank Williams remained enigmatic, a favourite sportswriter's word [code: we don't understand him] but in this case it was accurate. In the Preface to her book *A Different Kind of Life*, his wife Virginia wrote: 'But by far the most important reason for writing the book is Frank himself. I'm sure that if I had asked him, he would have said he did not want me to write it. Yet I truly hope he reads it. His memory of the early days after his accident is blurred and vague, he has never asked me what it was like in France or in the London Hospital or what is has been like for me these past few years. Now he will know.'[7]

He appeared a hard sort, unsentimental, shorn of small talk, openly obsessive about motor racing. Formula 1 learnt to live with the paradox that one of its dominant figures – whose team made cars of immense speed and power – could propel his own wheelchair only with difficulty; that beyond Formula 1 his withdrawn face, forever locked into its own seriousness, was better known than almost all the drivers, and yet the man himself was not known at all. At moments of crisis, however they came, he always understood that the team was more important than the drivers and acted accordingly.

Schumacher won Monza, equivalent to The Second Coming and greeted as such. Alesi finished next, a different kind of second coming, and the vast crowd, always emotionally in resonance with him, adored that, too – Hill out after five laps when, leading and not under pressure, he spun off.

Villeneuve took Portugal from Hill, Schumacher third and for once a championship was being fought without bitterness, accusations and counter-accusations, protests, and assorted people tramping the well-beaten path to the Place de la Concorde. Perhaps that reflected Hill's personality.

Hill 87, Villeneuve 78.

Villeneuve had to win the final round, Japan, and hope Hill didn't get more than two points. Villeneuve took pole, Hill alongside, Villeneuve made a mess of the start and Hill led every lap to win his championship with an economy of style but plenty of effectiveness.

A bright, crisp day, the sunlight making the trees into the shadows carpeting the track which Senna had known. Hill came in a great swoop to the chicane, pushed the Williams through and as he began the final lap he took the Williams over towards the pit lane wall: *thanks, boys.* He skimmed round the right-hander and history rode with him. Graham's first Grand Prix was 38 years before, Graham's first championship was

34 years before so that now, in the sunlight, father and son made their own arch over time. An impetus carried Damon Hill through the snake behind the paddock, wheeling and turning, the same impetus which took him through Degner and the Hairpin. The Williams team created their own arch because at this moment the mechanics donned caps in the livery of the London Rowing Club – dark background, white stripes. Graham had had them on his crash helmet, Damon had them on his now. Sunlight held the whole car, refracting from it as it bathed the face of Georgie, Hill's wife, leaning over the pit wall waiting for him. She didn't have to wait long.

Ends and beginnings. There'd always been a certain English diffidence about him and now he'd join Arrows, a smaller team being run by rugged Scot Tom Walkinshaw, his career as a consistent front-line driver over.

By an irony Villeneuve took up the running. He'd lived with the legacy of his father's name in Formula 3 in Italy when everybody wanted him to *be* his father or at least his father reincarnated. He'd learnt to be himself. Like Hill he'd also learnt to speak about his father in sound bites because both he and Hill were sorely tried by people wanting this from them and often at all the wrong moments.

Two new teams entered in 1997, Prost and Stewart. Alain Prost bought Ligier, had good drivers in Panis and Jarno Trulli and the goodwill of all France behind him. That didn't guarantee anything. Jackie Stewart and son Paul had long run a team in the lesser formulae and been especially strong in Formula 3. They might have bought an existing team – Arrows was available when they first planned to go to Formula 1 – but decided to create it themselves although, for the first year, they wouldn't receive any FOCA money.

Barnard departed Ferrari and Rory Byrne, another of the Benetton boys, came in his place. Byrne had retired and gone to the far east to set up a scuba diving school. One day his landlady came rushing to the beach shouting: 'Telephone call! Telephone call!' He thought it must be bad news but when he picked the receiver up he heard a voice with a strong French accent saying: 'Jean Todt, calling from Maranello.'

The season began in a confusing way because Villeneuve and Frentzen shared the front row in Australia but Coulthard won from Schumacher – Frentzen drove strongly and ought to have been second but his brakes failed. Villeneuve asserted himself in Brazil, winning it from Berger, Panis third in the Prost. Villeneuve asserted himself again two weeks later in Argentina, winning this time from Irvine, Ralf Schumacher [hereafter only called Ralf] third in a Jordan.

Frentzen was strong, eager, pensive, sensitive. The son of an undertaker and a Spanish mother, he had genuine artistic ability and suggested that within a few weeks he'd be a leading Grand Prix driver, too. He won San Marino from Schumacher, took pole from Schumacher at Monaco and then it went wrong. Race day weather was uncertain, rain falling but the forecast for it to stop. Williams set Frentzen and Villeneuve up for that: dry tyres.

> In the pit lane Schumacher hesitated, weighing the case for and against. He had one Ferrari set up as the Williamses were, the other (the spare car) a compromise – intermediate. The decision could not long be postponed because he had to bring the chosen car to the grid. The decision on tyres, however, could wait until he was there.
>
> Todt watched carefully. 'Michael hesitated a great deal. Finally, 20 minutes before the start [five minutes before the pit lane closes] he alone took the decision and moved towards the car chassis number 175,' the intermediate.
>
> Schumacher was circumspect, almost matter-of-fact. 'I decided to jump into that one at the last possible moment.'
>
> On the grid he asked for more wing and selected intermediate tyres while at that moment Frentzen's car, alongside, was being fitted with dries. 'I was truly astonished,' Schumacher would say, 'and it perturbed me a bit.'[8]

On the formation lap the rain fell harder. At the green light Schumacher shed the Williamses instantly and so did Giancarlo Fisichella (Jordan, second row). By the tunnel Fisichella closed on him a little, after the tunnel Schumacher pulled away. The second masterpiece for Ferrari had begun. The Ferrari tugged and twitched as he imposed his will on it and when he crossed the line to complete this opening lap Fisichella was so far back he couldn't be seen. Fisichella reached the line 6.65 seconds afterwards.

Finding the context for this lap remains difficult because 6.65 is such an enormous margin. That feeling is increased because across lap two Schumacher gained a further 4.86 seconds making his lead 11.51. And he continued at this pace so that, like Senna at moments before him here, he appeared to be entirely in his own race, self-sufficient unto himself, moving in a different dimension. By lap five the lead had become 22.12 seconds and he won from Barrichello by 53 seconds.

The Monaco measure: Schumacher, 62 laps, 2h 0m 0s, an average speed of 64.7mph – a wet race; Panis, 1996, 77.0mph – a wet race.

Villeneuve won Spain to take the championship lead from Schumacher 30–27, Panis second in the race and third in the championship. That made the Prost team third in the constructors' table and suggested a very accomplished debut, but in Canada, where Schumacher won from Alesi – Villeuneuve spun off after a lap – Panis lost control at 145mph and his car hit a tyre barrier so hard it broke both his legs. Perhaps the decline and fall of Prost began then, perhaps other factors were already working through which would prove insurmountable.

Before the French Grand Prix Villeneuve said of the Panis crash: 'With the money we make, we know the risks we take. The risks are ten times less than they were a few years back and we make ten times more money, so we have nothing to complain about.' Villeneuve was trying to put the Panis crash into some sort of perspective: broken legs, but nothing worse. It was not politically correct to talk like that but Villeneuve was uninterested in political correctness. That made him interesting. He'd handle the championship his way although Schumacher was strong round Magny-Cours, winning it from Frentzen, Villeneuve fourth.

Now the championship tilted towards Schumacher because although Villeneuve won the British (from Alesi – Schumacher out when a wheel bearing failed) Schumacher came second to Berger in Germany, Villeneuve spinning off.

Schumacher 53, Villeneuve 43.

Hill ought to have won Hungary but at the very end his gearbox failed and Villeneuve nipped past him. Arrows, in its various guises, had been in existence since 1978 and this would have been their first victory.

We've already seen that the drivers forming Formula 1's backbone had their day at Adelaide in 1995. Now at the Hungaroring Hill took the Arrows as near the foreground as it would ever get. Perhaps that may be regarded as representing the backbone teams who never quite made it, AFM, AGS, Alta, Andrea Moda, ATS...

Schumacher 56, Villeneuve 53.

The weather at Spa proved to be authentic – wet-dry – and from that Schumacher inevitably drew another masterpiece. Villeneuve led from pole, Schumacher up past Alesi. Into *La Source* hairpin on lap five, the track drying, Schumacher took Villeneuve and was not seen again. He beat Fisichella by 26.75 seconds, Villeneuve fifth.

Schumacher 66, Villeneuve 55.

Coulthard shook the whole thing up by winning Monza, Villeneuve fifth and Schumacher sixth.

For the first time in a decade Grand Prix racing returned to the Österreichring or rather its sibling the A1-Ring. This was a mile shorter than the old circuit and shorn of the great, mind-expanding loops which made the old one so spectacular and dangerous. This sibling joined those at Spa and the Nürburgring in reflecting what had been and what had had to be done to what had been. Schumacher went through a difficult week-end for sixth place while Villeneuve won it from Coulthard.

Schumacher 68, Villeneuve 67.

It left Luxembourg (at the Nürburgring), a handy working title because following Japan the title European Grand Prix would be free for the finale at Jerez.

Häkkinen took pole from Villeneuve, Schumacher on the third row, Ralf on the fourth. At the green light the two Jordans – Ralf and Fisichella – engulfed Schumacher from either side. Into the right-loop at the end of the start-finish straight they ran three abreast and the Jordans squeezed each other then Ralf banged Schumacher – the Jordan's wheel rode up over the Ferrari – as they went into the dust-bowl of a run-off area. Schumacher completed two laps and retired, Villeneuve hunted down the two McLarens and won it from Alesi.

Villeneuve 77, Schumacher 68.

Schumacher drew deep on his diplomacy when he said: 'It's a shame that the incident happened with my brother, but I don't think anyone is to blame...because it was not a deliberate move.'

Japan proved simple and Japan proved complicated. Schumacher won it, Villeneuve fifth and disqualified. That was the complication. The Stewards excluded Villeneuve because, they said, he'd failed to slow during free practice for a waved yellow flag. He raced under appeal but Williams subsequently withdrew it so his two points for fifth had gone.

Schumacher 78, Villeneuve 77.

It brought them to Jerez, a place of inevitable tension which increased when Villeneuve took pole from Schumacher and increased a great deal further when Schumacher led (apart from pit stops) to lap 47 of the 69, Villeneuve hard onto him, poised to overtake for the lead and the championship. They ran together round the gentle undulations and loops and curves and corners, they reached down a straight towards the tight right-loop called *Dry Sack*. Villeneuve ducked to the inside and, in a manoeuvre of extraordinary crudity, Schumacher twisted the Ferrari into the flank of the Williams.

Villeneuve said: 'Trying the move was a big risk [for me] because I knew Michael was capable of just deciding to take me off, which he tried to do. So I wasn't really surprised when he finally decided to turn in on me.' Schumacher's on-board camera offered incriminating evidence.

Villeneuve's car could continue and, with Schumacher out, could allow the McLarens through. Third place would be ample.

Villeneuve came round the tight loop onto the start-finish straight leading, Häkkinen closing, into the right-left called Michelin but in the fast loop after that Villeneuve held the gap steady. Urgently in the background Coulthard was coming. Through Dry Sack and then the loops Häkkinen closed up, into the Senna chicane Villeneuve simply moved aside: Häkkinen through immediately. Into the final corner Villeneuve moved aside again: Coulthard through immediately. Third place was fine.

As an attempt at punishment, the World Motor Sport Council removed Schumacher from the championship but he escaped a ban or fine and was allowed to keep his season's points.

Had Schumacher missed his chance of becoming the first Ferrari champion since Scheckter in 1979? Someone posed that question and it seemed legitimate because Ferrari had made a supreme effort and failed. They'd lose themselves in the emotional wilderness for another generation, wouldn't they? The reality was completely different because, far from temperamental spasms – what Prost once described as crises of optimism – they were, under Todt, building on solid and pragmatic foundations.

In the background a full investigation into Senna's crash had been going on under a man called Maurizio Passarini, appointed State Prosecutor. Eventually Frank Williams, Patrick Head and designer Adrian Newey were charged with negligent manslaughter. The trial, in Imola, dragged on inconclusively amid suggestions that the Williams steering column had been welded and cracked. The car had been impounded and the Williams team given limited access to it. A feeling grew that the truth would never be known no matter how many sincere people tried to find it.

For 1998 another attempt to find the balance between speed and safety was made with the introduction of grooved tyres, which ought to have slowed the cars.

Hill joined Jordan, partnering Ralf, Alesi went to Sauber and, with Berger now retired, Benetton fielded Fisichella and the Austrian Alexander Wurz.

McLaren had been building, too. Häkkinen and Coulthard announced that in Melbourne where they filled the front row and finished the race in the same order, Schumacher out with an engine failure after five laps.

The McLarens repeated this in Brazil, Schumacher third but a full minute behind Häkkinen. A power shift was under way, the McLarens vaulting the Williamses to challenge, and beat, Ferrari. It happened quickly.

An early-season ripple of races: Coulthard led in Argentina but Schumacher elbowed him aside – the McLaren briefly airborne – and in a sprint finish held off Häkkinen; Coulthard won San Marino from Schumacher; Häkkinen won Spain from Coulthard.

Häkkinen 36, Coulthard 29, Schumacher 24.

By Monaco, Häkkinen winning from Fisichella, Schumacher tenth (after bumping Wurz) the quiet Finn with a mischievous sense of humour was driving like a man whose time has come.

The Monaco measure: Häkkinen, 78 laps, 1h 51m 23.5s, an average speed of 87.8mph; Schumacher, 1997, 64.7mph – a wet race.

Schumacher seized Canada, taking no prisoners. Coulthard led but retired on lap 19 with a throttle problem. Under the Safety Car – Salo's Arrows had crashed – Schumacher made his first pit stop. Emerging, he found Frentzen alongside and pushed him off into the gravel trap. He received a ten-second stop 'n' go penalty for that and *still* won. After the race Frank Williams sent a protest to the Stewards about the Frentzen incident and others Schumacher had been involved in. Williams did not expect the protest to be upheld but he did want to give vent to his feelings in public. 'I felt that Michael's behaviour was out of order.'

Schumacher won France from Irvine, Häkkinen third.

Häkkinen 50, Schumacher 44, Coulthard 30.

The British Grand Prix, at mid point in the season, became a proper Schumacher *event*. Häkkinen led him, Coulthard third, the track drying. On lap five Coulthard took him but rain fell. At lap 38 Coulthard spun off and the track became deluged. Then:

3.14 Schumacher lapped Wurz under a stationary yellow flag: *danger, no overtaking, slow down.* Neither saw the flag.

3.15 the Safety Car was out. The Stewards discussed Schumacher's offence but, under the rules, had to tell Ferrari of any infringement within 25 minutes of the offence being committed. The Stewards didn't record their decision to penalise Schumacher by ten seconds until **3.39.**

At **3.43,** 29 minutes after the offence, the Stewards told Ferrari: confusion in all directions, not least because Ferrari didn't know if the penalty was stop 'n' go – Schumacher slowing, serving it, accelerating out again – or the ten seconds being added to his race time at the end.

Because of the confusion Todt decided to bring Schumacher in. That was done at **3.47** and the last lap. To reach the Ferrari pit Schumacher had to cross the 'finishing line' as he went down the pit lane. He won the race stationary in his pit – a unique, surreal and absurd development – although after it he covered another couple of laps as insurance because the confusion hadn't gone away. Häkkinen, second, sat in his cockpit uncomprehending. He was not alone.

Before the Austrian Grand Prix Schumacher signed for four more years at Ferrari (at $32 million a year) but he couldn't celebrate in Austria, where Häkkinen won from Coulthard, Schumacher third.

Häkkinen 66 points, Schumacher 58, Coulthard 36.

He couldn't celebrate in Germany where Häkkinen won from Coulthard again, Schumacher fifth.

Schumacher prepared to respond to all this with another masterpiece, and in the most constricting of places – except Monaco: the straitjacket of the Hungaroring. Brawn, watching and scheming from the pit lane wall, saw a way to open the constrictions and Schumacher was able to execute it.

Ferrari and McLaren both planned to pit twice. The running order – Häkkinen, Coulthard, Schumacher – altered after the first of them because Schumacher came out behind Villeneuve and was a prisoner there in fourth place, no way to overtake in the constriction. Brawn said: 'Right, we'll switch to three stops' and when Schumacher heard that on the radio he thought *not sure it'll work.*

Villeneuve pitted and Schumacher drove so hard he pushed Coulthard up to Häkkinen, three seconds spanning them all. Schumacher made his second stop on lap 43 and with a light fuel load went so fast *instantly* that when Coulthard pitted next lap he emerged behind Schumacher; when Häkkinen pitted two laps later he emerged behind Schumacher, too.

Brawn came on the radio and announced matter-of-fact: 'You have 19 laps to build a 25-second lead to cover the third stop, Michael.' Schumacher, matter-of-fact, said: 'Thanks very much.' He drew the Hungaroring to himself and blitzed it.

	Schumacher	*Häkkinen*	*Gap*
Lap 48	1m 19.8s	1m 22.2s	2.4s
Lap 49	1m 20.6s	1m 22.2s	4.1s
Lap 50	1m 21.2s	1m 22.2s	5.0s
Lap 51	1m 20.3s	1m 22.8s	7.5s
Lap 52	1m 25.8s	1m 25.5s	7.3s

He was now pushing so hard the Ferrari went briefly off, returned, continued, the enormous impetus retained. It didn't matter that

Häkkinen had a handling problem or that Coulthard – past Häkkinen – had a rear tyre problem. Schumacher was in the dimension of his own again, man against circuit, man against time, man against himself. From Coulthard, successively he forced the gap from 13.89s through 15.71s to 15.96s. That was lap 56, the blitz gathering an astonishing pace: 18.54s, 21.08s, 22.77s. What followed stunned even Brawn: his own word, *stunned*.

	Schumacher	*Coulthard*	*Gap*
Lap 60	1m 19.2s	1m 21.2s	24.6s
Lap 61	1m 19.5s	1m 21.4s	26.6s

He pitted, the stop was quick and briskly efficient, and he won it by almost ten seconds. Some races in our long story have been won by heroism, some by technical innovation, some because one car proved faster than the others, some because the weather changed. This was quite different. This was a clinical exploitation of one man's unearthly talent in the modern context, and was overwhelming.

Häkkinen 77, Schumacher 70, Coulthard 48.

Belgium was filthy wet and Hill won it for Jordan, Ralf in the other Jordan second but plenty of action on the way to that. There'd been a thrashing, cascading multiple-accident at the start, more crashing at the restart – claiming, among others, Häkkinen. On lap 25 Schumacher, leading, came up to Coulthard but in the spray Coulthard could see nothing. Schumacher followed him, McLaren told Coulthard to let Schumacher through and Coulthard slowed, trying to do that. Schumacher ran into him.

Schumacher was enraged and sought Coulthard out. Coulthard said: 'Coming into the pits and asking me whether I was trying to kill him is totally unacceptable. I can't find words to describe how disappointed I am in Michael as a man that he could still have been in that state after driving back to the pits. It was disgusting behaviour.'

At autumn ripple of races took Schumacher to Japan: He won Monza, Häkkinen fourth but Häkkinen won Luxemburg at the Nürburgring.

Häkkinen 90, Schumacher 86.

At Suzuka Schumacher took pole from Häkkinen and on the grid Häkkinen shook his hand. Whatever tumults Schumacher had had they hadn't been with the Finn. Trulli in the Prost stalled aborting the first start. Six or seven minutes later Schumacher led the crocodile round and when they settled on the grid Schumacher's hand was up: *I can't move –* his engine stalled. Schumacher would be relegated to the back for the third start and from nowhere the four-point gap to Häkkinen became a chasm.

Schumacher switched to full attack because he could do nothing else. On the opening lap he swallowed *nine* back markers and by lap five ran seventh but, reaching the faster cars, progress slowed. He'd worked his tyres very, very hard, too. By lap 15 he ran fifth and after his pit stop third, but 26 seconds from Häkkinen. He spent ten laps in this third place and then at 170mph the right rear tyre disintegrated.

Into the final lap Häkkinen led Irvine comfortably and drove comfortably enough on an overcast day so that, just this once, virtually no dark shadow fell across the track. As the whole McLaren team swarmed to the pit lane wall Häkkinen handled the car so carefully it might have been an installation lap checking all systems functioned. He stayed away from the kerbs, stayed away from the rim of the track. He soothed the car through the chicane, held his left hand up, a finger distended into the number 1. He slowed and for a moment his gloved hand probed towards his eyes under the raised helmet visor.

Mopping tears?

When he came back and parked the car Schumacher went over to shake his hand.

Ends and beginnings. The Tyrrell team suffered a long, awkward season because they'd been bought out by British American Racing and Ken Tyrrell departed. From 1999 they'd be called BAR and the man to run it, Craig Pollock, fully intended to make changes. The Tyrrell story, stretching back over a quarter of a century, ended after 28 laps of the Japanese Grand Prix when their only driver in the race, Toranosuke Takagi, crashed.

And Tyrrell was gone, forever.

Todt set out the challenge for 1999: not just some wins but the championship and *we have to be on the pace immediately, we can't afford another start like last year when the McLarens ran away from us.*

Frentzen left Williams for Jordan, where E. Jordan Esq would apply interesting psychology. Frentzen's time at Williams had been fraught and reached the point where he doubted himself but arch driver psychologist Jordan intended to rectify that all right. Frentzen partnered Hill – Ralf had gone to Williams.

In Australia Häkkinen took pole and on the parade lap Schumacher couldn't engage first gear. He'd have to begin from the back, just like Japan. This became another Schumacher *event*. Häkkinen led until he had a throttle problem, Irvine led after that, Schumacher up to fourth despite gear selection problems. He went off, returned, had a puncture, pitted, set off last again then pitted to change the steering wheel. Irvine won it from Frentzen – Schumacher eighth...

Häkkinen won Brazil from Schumacher who expressed himself 'very satisfied. It was not what we expected after qualifying. I am not worried about the points situation because we are still at a very early stage in the season.'

A Ferrari hadn't won the San Marino Grand Prix since Tambay in 1983. At the end of lap 17 Häkkinen lost control in the corner onto the start-finish straight and the McLaren met the barrier. The barrier won. Coulthard led, Schumacher coming like the wind, but Coulthard held him and Brawn began his scheming on the pit lane wall. *If we make two stops, with a sprint in between, we might outrun Coulthard on his one stop.*

Schumacher took it on. He pitted on lap 31 and when Coulthard pitted the lead was down to 18.3 seconds. Coulthard came out into back markers and Schumacher put the hammer down. He pitted on lap 45 with a lead of 21.8 seconds, was stationary for 5.5 – the race decided.

He won Monaco remorselessly from Irvine, Häkkinen third so that Schumacher led the championship with 26 points, Irvine 18, Häkkinen 14.

The Monaco measure: Schumacher, 78 laps, 1h 49m 31.8s, an average speed of 89.3mph; Häkkinen, 1998, 87.8mph.

The measure of the decades: 1929, 49.8mph; 1937, 63.2mph; 1948, 59.7mph; 1958, 67.9mph; 1968, 77.8mph; 1979, 81.33mph; 1989, 84.13mph.

Vehicles registered in Britain 28.3 million (1989, 24.2 million).

A Ford Focus cost £7,350 and a Briton earned on average £400.10 a week. Saving all his money the Briton would have taken 18 weeks to buy one (1910, 2 years 42 weeks; 1919, 1 year 28 weeks; 1929, 41 weeks; 1938, 37 weeks; 1949, 45 weeks; 1959, 36 weeks; 1969, 25 weeks; 1979, 20 weeks; 1989, 21 weeks).

The tilt of the season moved away from Schumacher and towards Häkkinen, and the championship which Italy yearned and Ferrari were paying fortunes to grasp became a beautiful woman again, beckoning, receding.

A mid-season ripple of races: Häkkinen won a boring Spanish Grand Prix from Coulthard and Schumacher; Häkkinen won Canada, Schumacher out when 'I lost control of the car at the last chicane because I went off the racing line, got on the dirt and ended up in the wall'. Frentzen won France – dry, very wet – from Häkkinen, Schumacher fifth. The Jordan psychology was working.

Everything changed at Silverstone with shocking suddenness. Häkkinen led from pole, Irvine ahead of Schumacher but into Stowe Corner Schumacher went inside and straight ahead.

The brakes clawed the speed down. The *FIA* would describe what happened next graphically enough, once the Ferrari's black box had been downloaded. 'He first braked at 306kmh and achieved an initial deceleration of 3.1g. This fell to 2.1g. At 204kmh the front wheels locked.' He shrieked across in front of Irvine and smoke billowed from the tyres. He was onto the run-off area, a broad arc of gravel. The Ferrari buck-bounded across that [and] buried itself deep in the tyre wall.'

Schumacher suffered a double fracture of his leg requiring a 300mm steel pin. The race was restarted and Coulthard won it from Irvine.

Ferrari now faced a profound conundrum. Since Scheckter they'd spent perhaps $2 billion continuing their dynasty, or trying to. They'd constructed the present team around Schumacher and paid him a fortune to deliver the World Championship. They'd hired Irvine as supporting cast and bound him tight with a contract which meant he always deferred to Schumacher but now Irvine, after finishing second at Silverstone, was only eight points behind Häkkinen.

How would Ferrari look if Irvine took the championship? How would Ferrari look if, when Schumacher did return, he had to help Irvine? More immediately they hired Salo to deputise for Schumacher.

Irvine stoked everything by winning Austria from Coulthard; Häkkinen's championship lead cut to two. Salo, adjusting to the Ferrari, came in ninth but by Germany he'd adjusted so well that he led after Häkkinen crashed heavily when a rear tyre failed. Team orders applied almost instantly and Salo moved aside for Irvine to take the win; Frentzen third.

Irvine 52, Häkkinen 44, Frentzen 33.

Häkkinen led Hungary throughout, Coulthard second and Irvine third after losing control of the car on lap 63 and running wide. Salo, twelfth and two laps down, had a 'terrible race'.

Irvine 56, Häkkinen 54.

Schumacher recovered enough to do some testing. He'd miss Belgium but maybe make Monza. At Spa Irvine said: 'I assume that as I'm going for the championship and I am leading at the minute Ferrari will want to back me. At the start of the year Michael was the best chance the team had and it was logical to back him. Things have changed now. I've scored 30 points in four races. But it is Jean Todt's decision – I haven't asked. I work for the team and do what I'm told to do.' Coulthard, strong here, won from Häkkinen, Frentzen third and Irvine fourth.

Häkkinen 60, Irvine 59, Coulthard 46, Frentzen 40.

Schumacher tested at Monza, needed painkillers and missed the Italian Grand Prix. Frentzen won from Ralf, Coulthard fifth, Irvine sixth – Häkkinen spun off after a mistake changing gear.

The tourniquet tightened: Häkkinen and Irvine 60, Frentzen 50, Coulthard 48.

Ferrari announced that for 2000 Barrichello would replace Irvine, who'd be joining the new Jaguar team which had bought out Stewart.

Schumacher still wasn't fit for the European Grand Prix at the Nürburgring where, in mixed weather, Herbert mixed everything up by winning to give the Stewart team their only victory, Trulli second in a Prost, Barrichello in the other Stewart third.

That was after a race of many pressure points, Frentzen leading until his electrics failed, Coulthard leading until he spun off, Ralf leading until he had a puncture. That spread the race for Herbert. Irvine had a pit stop go wrong – the team couldn't find one of his tyres because Salo had just been in – and Häkkinen couldn't summon pace until near the end.

Häkkinen 62, Irvine 60, Frentzen 50, Coulthard 48.

At Maranello, di Montezemolo called a crisis meeting with the main team members. After two and a half hours he came out and said: 'We can still win the championship. It's not over.'

Schumacher came back for Malaysia, a new, custom-built track and challenging in the modern, technical way. Immediately he shook the closed world of Grand Prix racing by qualifying almost a second in front of Irvine and over a second quicker than both McLarens. He shook it further by moving so fast from the green light that after three laps he slowed and *waited* for Irvine to come up, let Irvine go and kept Häkkinen firmly behind him. Deep into the race – Coulthard out, fuel pressure – Schumacher led again, waited again, let Irvine through again and they finished in that order, Häkkinen third. Ferrari were then excluded because of an aerodynamic infringement of one centimetre, although that was overturned the week after the race.

Irvine 70, Häkkinen 66 but the tourniquet now so tight that Frentzen, 51, and Coulthard, 48, had been choked out of it.

There were permutations for Irvine and Häkkinen to ponder in Japan but in essence both had to think of winning the race because whoever did that had the championship. A Häkkinen win from Irvine gave them both 76 points, but Häkkinen got it on the most-wins tie-break, 5–4.

At the start Häkkinen was away fast, Schumacher slewing over towards him. By then Häkkinen led, the race decided because lap after lap Schumacher couldn't get close enough to mount an assault which he had to do if Irvine, running variously third and fourth, was to have any hope of the championship.

Beyond the halfway stage Coulthard went off, pitted for a new nosecone and emerged a lap down – but physically in front of Schumacher. Coulthard could help Häkkinen by hampering Schumacher, but if he saw waved blue flags, *someone's trying to overtake you*, he had to cede the position. Coulthard took his time doing that and Schumacher would vent his anger – not mentioning that Coulthard didn't take much time doing it (one report says three corners). This was the nearest to controversy anybody came.

Häkkinen flowed over the line to begin his final lap, Schumacher clearly in view some seven seconds behind. Häkkinen struck a balance between keeping the gap safe and not pushing too hard. At the hairpin he might have glanced back, and if he did he couldn't see Schumacher. He took the chicane circumspectly, showing it all respect, and an instant later he had his second consecutive championship.

During his lap of honour Schumacher returned to the pit lane.

Ron Dennis said: 'Michael, you're a great driver!'

Schumacher replied: 'Don't think I wasn't trying...'

The structure of this chapter from here differs from the rest of the book in one significant way. The task which so many had tried and failed to do – make Ferrari mighty again – was now to be accomplished so comprehensively that recounting it in detail must involve endless repetition. Races are interesting when a great deal happens, seasons are interesting for the same reason, but by the end of 2004 – and even in an activity so intrinsically uncertain as motor racing – the races came to resemble one another: the red Ferrari of Schumacher in the lead, the red Ferrari of Barrichello a discreet distance behind, then a void.

It was sometimes easy to forget that here was a master at work, and it was easy to forget because he made the maddening, demanding and dangerous business of marshalling a powerful machine look easy. The machine didn't break down, and for whole seasons that seemed the best chance the others had: to pass him when he was stationary at the side of the track – and you'd still look twice, just to be sure he wasn't toying with you and getting back in...

Nobody had ever dominated as he was doing. The conditions of cars and circuits before the First World War ruled out any form of sustained domination and did so through the 1920s. Nuvolari might have done something like this but at no stage did he have a dominant car for five consecutive years and in the end ran up against the Silver Arrows, who dominated collectively but – in terms of drivers – they had too much talent for one to emerge absolutely over the others. To emphasise this, Schumacher won 13 of the 18 rounds in 2004. In 1938, von Brauchitsch won France, Seaman won Germany, Caracciola won Switzerland, Nuvolari won Italy...

Perhaps Caracciola's four wins in eight rounds the year before might be a fairer comparison but the four are not and can never be the 13 out of 18.

This is not trying to construct a case for respective merits but rather an examination of scale. Fangio was mercenary in moving from team to team and his skills – so poorly served by surviving film – took him to the five championships. It also took him to an astonishing 24 wins from only 51 races in his Grand Prix career from 1950 to 1958. In three seasons, 2002 to 2004, Schumacher won 30. That's the scale which must be faced – and enjoyed.

When Chapman got the Lotus right Clark won everything but even Chapman had good years and not so good years. Senna might have done something similar with that McLaren and that Honda engine but he ran into (sometimes literally) Prost and Mansell and Piquet.

Schumacher was quite alone.

By 2000, when finally Ferrari had their champion – the first since Scheckter – Schumacher was not yet in a position to paralyse a whole season. He created an enormous start-of-season ripple: he won Australia from Barrichello, won Brazil from Coulthard (who was disqualified for an illegal front wing), won Imola from Häkkinen – and none of these from pole position. He was third at Silverstone (Coulthard won), fifth from pole in Spain (Häkkinen won), won the European at the Nürburgring – only he and Häkkinen on the same lap.

Schumacher 46 points, Häkkinen 28, Coulthard 24.

He led Monaco from pole to lap 56 when a pushrod broke, letting Coulthard in.

The Monaco measure: Coulthard, 78 laps, 1h 49m 28.2s, an average speed of 89.5mph; Schumacher, 1999, 89.3mph.

The ripple of races flowed on: he won Canada from pole, took pole at Magny-Cours but had an engine failure so that Coulthard, winning it, drew up to within twelve points. He crashed at the start in Austria, where Häkkinen won from Coulthard, and crashed at the start in Germany, where Barrichello won from Häkkinen and Coulthard. That took Coulthard to within two points. Häkkinen won Hungary, Schumacher second from pole, Coulthard third. Häkkinen won Belgium, Schumacher second, Coulthard fourth.

Häkkinen 74, Schumacher 68, Coulthard 61.

Schumacher won Monza from pole. The United States Grand Prix went to Indianapolis, an evocative name linking, inescapably, the race to the early days when European and American raced intertwined and, more obscurely, to the years from 1950 to 1960 when the championship included the Indianapolis 500. The circuit for the Grand Prix went the other way round, using one section of the oval with an infield section linked to that. Schumacher took pole and the race from Barrichello, Coulthard fifth; Häkkinen spun off.

Schumacher 88, Häkkinen 80, Coulthard 63.

All 17 rounds counted so that, with only Japan and Malaysia left, Schumacher could win it at Suzuka. He took pole from Häkkinen who led the race and it became a nervy, hard-pushing duel which at moments Schumacher thought he'd lost. He'd forced the pace up to his second pit stop and the championship turned on whether he got out before Häkkinen came round. Because of the pit wall Schumacher could see nothing as he flowed down towards the track.

Brawn, watching for Häkkinen, said into the radio *it's looking good.*

A moment later, and still no sign of Häkkinen *it's looking good.*

A moment after that *it's looking bloody good.*

He went fast into his final lap, Häkkinen 4.27 seconds behind him. He seemed to bend the circuit to his wishes, fast through the snake behind the paddock, licking a kerb here, caressing a kerb there – but still Häkkinen came, going even faster. Within sight of something Ferrari had worked so hard for and spent so much getting, Häkkinen was saying *I'm testing your nerve, Michael.* Häkkinen cut the gap to 2.03 seconds. Schumacher hustled the Ferrari through the chicane – *my nerve's holding, Mika, all right?* The track unfolded like a carpet before him, gently curving to the right and the line. He could have closed his eyes and made it easily.

He reached the chequered flag 1.83 seconds before Häkkinen did, and at that exact instant the 1.82 seconds was worth the $2 billion 20-year Ferrari investment to have this exact instant again.

Schumacher erupted, the Ferrari team erupted, Suzuka erupted, Italy erupted, Germany erupted. This, even if he did not realise it, was the blood red cars finally giving Grand Prix racing its life blood again. Perhaps, among so many thousand Japanese faces, few knew of Enzo starting it all in the 1920s, of Nuvolari and Varzi, of Ascari father and son, of Fangio and Hawthorn with the bow tie, of The Rat and Scheckter, but somehow they were all there on 8 October 2000.

Grand Prix racing had known its great moments but few greater than this.

Schumacher added Malaysia from pole just to keep everything neat and tidy. The 17 rounds comprised 1,074 laps and he'd led 548 of them which is as good a way of expressing dominance as any. It was only a prelude.

Autocourse wrote about his 'utterly unwavering and relentless focus' and added: 'More to the point, there has been precious little indication that his genius is peaking.' He'd won nine races, just as he had done in 1995, so in that sense he overtook Mansell's single nine in 1992. Up until this point in Grand Prix history that feat alone would have placed Schumacher statistically before all who had gone before. Without labouring the point, Graham Hill won only 14 of the 176 races in his career.

How could anyone, writing in 2000, foresee that four years later, in a supreme exhibition of what it's all really about, Schumacher would get to within one of Hill's total *in a single season* and far from peaking even then be full of running.

He was to move beyond reference points, beyond comparison, beyond virtually every record and ultimately his own dimension *was* one of scale. He was to mature from a determined, headstrong young man who sometimes behaved as if he was still driving go-karts to a balanced family man who dissected all aspects of Grand Prix racing which affected him, examined them minutely and then put them back together again as he wanted them to be.

He started 2001 by winning Australia from pole, added Malaysia, took pole in Brazil but came second to Coulthard. His brakes failed at Imola where Ralf won his first race but won Spain from pole, where Jacques Villeneuve got on to the podium in the BAR-Honda and Juan Pablo Montoya, a strong Colombian from IndyCars, came second in a Williams; was second to Coulthard from pole in Austria, won Monaco from Barrichello.

Schumacher 52 points, Coulthard 40, Barrichello 24.

It is simply no use talking about any of the others: they were nowhere. Of the 16 drivers who'd scored, Schumacher had more points than 11 of these drivers put together.

In the background the major manufacturers were talking of starting their own series. I'll mention it only briefly here because it involved the financial arrangements of the way the sport was run, specifically how much of a grip Ecclestone had on that and what little grip they had. It did not affect the racing.

The Monaco measure: Schumacher, 78 laps, 1h 47m 22.5s, an average speed of 91.2mph; Coulthard, 2000, 89.5mph.

He was erecting a monument, slab by slab. Here are the slabs:

Ralf won Canada from him.

He won the European from Montoya.

He won France from Ralf.

Schumacher 78, Coulthard 47.

Häkkinen won Silverstone from him.

In Germany the fuel pressure failed, Ralf winning it from Barrichello.

Schumacher 84 points, Coulthard 47.

In Hungary from pole he made two pit stops for tyres and fuel which is how, of the 77 laps, he led all but six. That was the final slab, that was the championship retained.

Faithful Barrichello followed him home and the podium became a Roman fountain of champagne. Jean Todt got a particularly spectacular jet. The champagne ran like a river down Barrichello's forearm which had locked round Schumacher in a team-mate's embrace and it cascaded from Schumacher's cap, and their delight knew no bounds.

Apart from Mansell nobody had ever won a championship this early. Schumacher said: 'I might be a good driver but I am not good at finding words to describe this. It had been a beautiful weekend and we have done everything we could. To be honest, I did not have such a good feeling when I came here, but now with the pole and the win it makes me equal with Alain Prost on 51 and the fourth championship, it is all too much for me. It is a great achievement for the team. They are wonderful guys and we have stuck together through the good and the bad times and I am really in love with all of them. They are such fun to work with. I cannot compare this title to the others: each one and each race win is different and special.'

Fangio's five championships now hoved into view, the five which had stood since 1957 and might ordinarily have stood until 2057.

Schumacher won Belgium to move past Prost.

Häkkinen announced his retirement at Monza and McLaren announced Kimi Räikkönen as his replacement. Montoya won the Italian Grand Prix from Barrichello, Schumacher fourth. That was on 16 September, the week of the terrorist attacks on the United States. Out of respect for the dead from the Twin Towers in New York, Ferrari removed all advertising logos from their cars and ran them with black nosecones.

Indianapolis, only two weeks later, brought a host of problems which Formula 1 rarely faces: personal security, showing sensitivity and showing it *about something else*. Perhaps Schumacher expressed it best. 'I never had any doubt about racing in the United States but of course, like anybody else, I wanted to wait and see if something might happen following the attacks. I very much hope that we can deliver a little moral support and maybe some courage to help the Americans overcome their despair.'

The race assumed symbolic proportions and Häkkinen won it from Schumacher, who in turn won Japan from pole – his third nine-wins-in-a-season.

The Prost team folded, proving a curious dictum: that great drivers do not necessarily make great team owners or managers. The men running Formula 1 at its apex – Ecclestone, Mosley, Todt, Williams, Dennis – had quite other abilities. And the drivers? Most understood they couldn't run teams and didn't try.

In 2001, the television viewing figures dropped by 3 billion, the first time this had happened since 1999. Inevitably, television coverage has moved in the background of our story although that does not diminish its importance. Only in 1978 did the BBC decide to cover every race in a season, and even then not all of them live. The growth in global terms had been almost exponential: for example in 1994, 150 countries were taking it and the total viewing figure stood at 45 billion – calculated over a year on people viewing any Formula 1 programme (so someone watching every qualifying session would register 16, thus explaining why the total annual figure is many times higher than the whole population of the planet). By 1997, 202 countries were taking the races and even the 3 billion drop in 2001 still left the total at 54 billion.

Like some of Einstein's equations, and the speed of light, it's slightly staggering and very difficult to grasp. More simply, advertising in Grand Prix racing reached this colossal audience – Senna's family had letters of condolence from as far as Afghanistan – and advertisers liked that, and the money came in, and the money kept coming in.

Schumacher, meanwhile, was just into his stride and now he could paralyse a whole season. Many races in 2002 barely require words to describe them.

Australia: Row 1, led 43 of the 58 laps, won.

Malaysia: Pole, third, Ralf winning.

Brazil: Row 1, led 63 of 71 laps (pit stops prevented him from leading all 71), won.

San Marino: Pole, led 61 of 62 laps (pit stop), won.

Spain: Pole, fastest lap, led all 65 laps, won.

The day after Spain Rob Walker died of pneumonia. His time had long gone and he could never escape the fact that he lived entirely by inherited wealth. He didn't try to. Some people have the arrogance of money, he had the money and no arrogance at all. A gentle, stooping soul, a reformed alcoholic, a benevolent vicar of a man, he might – with all that money – have done nothing with his life. Instead he coined the truly memorable phrase *if you want to have small fortune, go in to motor racing with a big fortune.* And ran Moss and others as front runners…

Austria: Row 2, fastest lap, led 2 laps of the 71, won. In reality, this race broke up the sequence because Barrichello, pole, dominated it but was ordered to move over at the very end and cede it to Schumacher. This enraged the crowd, bemused the global television audience and dug from those in the paddock the nearest to moral rectitude they get. Ferrari were quite entitled to decide what they wanted their employees to do but it seemed particularly crass because, going in, Schumacher had 44 points, Montoya 23, Ralf 20. On the podium Schumacher looked embarrassed and hustled Barrichello on to the top rung.

The assets of the Prost team were being auctioned. The first part, in Paris, consisted of the cars: the AP 03 Peugeot of 2000 (Jean Alesi), €265,833, AP 02 Peugeot 1999 (Jarno Trulli) €232,604, AP 01 Peugeot 1998 €99,687. Alesi's crash helmet, estimated at €4,500 went for €9,525.

The second part, in the team's headquarters at Guyancourt on the outskirts of Paris, attracted a crowd.

> They, in large numbers, went as they pleased into a factory now open to the four winds and to anybody who was curious. The passionate among them wandered here and there, eyes shining, touching with a finger the nameplates on the offices. The premises had stayed in working order since Thursday, 7 February 2002, the day of the official closure of Prost GP.
>
> In this fossilised world, you waited to see Alain Prost – and all those who had, with him, made the team blossom – suddenly appear but these sad mid-May days, bathed in sunlight, the technicians, now ex-Prost, are the only ones in any numbers.
>
> In the big hall, where the sale will last for three days, 260 chairs have been set out. It is not enough: each day there are three times as many people.[10]

Everything was to go. The neon sign *PROST GP* at the factory entrance – lot number 193 in the catalogue, under the section from the Marketing Department – was for sale at €600. Several people bid for it and the successful bidder explained afterwards: 'I was afraid it would go abroad.' This, too, may be symbolic of so many small teams who tried to navigate the stormy waters of Grand prix racing and ran onto rocks. When it goes away, it can go away fast and completely.

Monaco: Row 2, second to Coulthard. Montoya took pole but

Coulthard, alongside him, led immediately because the McLaren's electronic driver aid was better. As Coulthard said, I just took my finger off the button, kept my foot on the throttle and seconds later arrived at *Ste Devote*. It was nothing to do with me!'[11] Coulthard led throughout.

The Monaco measure: Coulthard, 78 laps, 1h 45m 39.0s, an average speed of 92.7mph; Schumacher, 2001, 91.2mph.

Canada: Row 1, led 32 of the 70 laps, won.

Europe (Nürburgring): Row 2, fastest lap, second to Barrichello.

Britain: Row 2, led 45 of the 60 laps, won.

Schumacher 86 points, Barrichello 32, Montoya 31.

He could make the championship mathematically certain by France in July – the championship continuing until October.

France: Row 1, led 14 of the 72 laps, won.

'Thank you is too small a word for what the team has done for me. I love and admire all of them for the work they do and for their motivation. I did not think about the championship this weekend.' Deep into the race Räikkönen led but with five laps to go and under severe Schumacher pressure he got on oil. Schumacher didn't. 'Once I was in the lead it was really the worst five laps of my life as I realised the championship was again in my pocket. I had a weight on my shoulders and felt enormous pressure not to make a mistake. Those laps went on forever. As I took the flag I felt an outburst of emotion and I realised how much it means and how much I love this sport.'

Into the final lap he danced the Ferrari into the great left of the Grande Courbe, danced it through the great right called Estoril. He went in to the Adelaide hairpin on a racing line born of prudence – keeping away from the oil – and fled through the sweepers, danced it through the chicane before the hard-right onto the finishing straight. He flung the Ferrari over to the pit lane wall in salute to his team there, flung it back across the track working the steering wheel so the car twitched left-right-left-right-left-right like frantic spasms of delight.

Fangio's five were equalled. Schumacher would insist he didn't think about things like that, as we shall see. Perhaps it's a modern trait to be uninterested in history, to be always moving forward. Perhaps some people are uninterested because they just are.

In a revealing interview,[12] Ecclestone spoke quite unconsciously for Grand Prix racing's psychology. Discussing the Suffolk village where he'd been born and why he'd never been back there he said: 'I have no curiosity about that. As far as I am concerned I cannot live yesterday again. So I never think about it.' This makes it all the stranger that at Silverstone in 2001 Schumacher drove a Ferrari described as a 'sister car' of the one in which González won the 1951 British Grand Prix. Ecclestone owned it. No doubt it is worth a great more now than when Ecclestone bought it but, even so, here was yesterday come to today...

Germany: Pole, fastest lap, led 62 of the 67 laps, won.

Hungary: Row 1, fastest lap, second to Barrichello.

Belgium: Pole, fastest lap, led 43 of the 44 laps (pit stop), won.

Italy: Row 1, led nine of the 53 laps, second to Barrichello.

USA: Pole, led 68 of the 73 laps, second to Barrichello.

Japan: Pole, fastest lap, led 52 of the 53 laps (pit stop), won.

He had 144 points, beating his own record of 123 the year before. He had 11 wins, beating his own and Mansell's nine. Of the 1,090 laps he had led 558. He'd finished every race, lowest position third. Cumulatively, nothing like this had ever been done before even by him. Barrichello scored 77 points, giving Ferrari 221 in the Constructors' Championship. And so it went. By now statistics were almost debased amidst so many totals, your mind numb with them, and some – most – of the races were difficult to recall because they merged into a great, red-tinged procession.

The boy was in his stride now, all right, and *still* full of running.

The background was almost incidental, almost unnoticed except as temporal phenomena: Ralf using Barrichello as a launching pad at the start of the Australian Grand Prix, Takuma Sato in a Jordan driving with a wonderful combination of judgement and lack of it, the Schumacher bros showing nothing familiar in pressure moments, the customary skirmishing about cutting costs to save the whole thing, the nightmare crash in Austria where Nick Heidfeld's Sauber snapped out of control and smashed into the side of Sato, an Aussie called Mark Webber saying and doing the right things in a Minardi, Räikkönen showing he wasn't afraid of anybody, young Briton Jenson Button in a Renault showing promise, Lauda lambasting Ferrari because Schumacher and Barrichello tried to stage a dead heat at Indianapolis – in the season's context, an awful lapse of judgement.

In 2003, one-shot qualifying was introduced. The cars had a session on Friday and their times determined the running order on the Saturday. The days of the late rush, the circuit suddenly teeming with cars, or drivers searching out a traffic-free lap had gone. Instead, on the Saturday a driver had a warm-up lap, the flying lap, a slowing down lap.

Räikkönen pushed Schumacher so hard that the championship went to the final race. Again it's more easily digested in tabulated form. Points were now awarded for the first eight finishers on the descending scale 10–8–6–5–4–3–2–1. That might at least keep the championship alive for longer because with only a two-point gap to whoever finished behind him Schumacher would have to take longer to win it.

A month before the season began Manfred von Brauchitsch died at the age of 97, severing one of the last chords with the Silver Arrows. He lived in East Germany, just outside Berlin and when the Berlin Wall came down attended motorsport functions at the invitation of Mercedes. He still watched the races on television, even into his final infirmity, but said his era and this were so different that comparisons couldn't be made.

Australia: Schumacher pole, Coulthard won from Montoya, Räikkönen third, Schumacher fourth.

Malaysia: Fernando Alonso (Renault) pole, Räikkönen winning from Barrichello, Schumacher sixth.

Brazil: Barrichello pole, Giancarlo Fisichella winning for Jordan from Räikkönen, Schumacher out – accident.

San Marino: Schumacher pole and the win, but from Räikkönen.

Spain: Schumacher pole and the win from Alonso, Räikkönen out immediately – a crash. Räikkönen 32, Schumacher 28.

Austria: Schumacher pole and the win from Räikkönen, now only two points between them.

Monaco: Ralf pole, Montoya winning from Räikkönen and Schumacher. That forced the gap back out to four points.

The Monaco measure: Montoya, 78 laps, 1h 42m 19.0s, an average speed of 94.9mph; Coulthard, 2002, 92.7mph.

Canada: Ralf pole, Schumacher winning from Ralf, Räikkönen sixth. Schumacher 54, Räikkönen 51.

Europe (Nürburgring): Räikkönen pole, the first of his career, Ralf winning from Montoya, Schumacher fifth, Räikkönen out – engine. Schumacher 58, Räikkönen 51.

France: Ralf pole and winning from Montoya, Schumacher third, Räikkönen fourth. Schumacher 64, Räikkönen 56, Ralf up to 53.

Britain: Barrichello pole and the win from Montoya, Räikkönen third, Schumacher fourth. Schumacher 69, Räikkönen 62.

Germany: Montoya pole, Montoya winning from Coulthard – Räikkönen out with a crash from the grid, Schumacher running second when he had a puncture, seventh.

Hungary: Alonso pole and the win from Räikkönen, Schumacher a fraught eighth after a slow pit stop. Schumacher 72, Montoya 71, Räikkönen 70.

Italy: Schumacher pole and winning it from Montoya, Räikkönen fourth. On lap 14 Schumacher went round in 1m 21.83s, an average speed of 158.35mph and a record for the circuit. Monza had always embraced raw speed and it gave quite a different measure than Monaco.[13] In 1958 Phil Hill did 201.1kmh (124.9mph), the first time anyone had gone through the 200kmh barrier. By 1971, it rose to 153mph and two chicanes were built to slow the cars. Despite that, four years later it was 138mph and rising. Two more chicanes were built and despite alterations to the Curva Grande and Lesmo it rose virtually every year to Schumacher's 158. Moreover, Schumacher's race average, 153.84mph, was an absolute record.

To relate this to everyday life is surprisingly easy and instructive. Several manufacturers with performance cars – Alfa Romeo, Audi, BMW,[14] Jaguar, Lexus, Mercedes, Saab, Volkswagen, Volvo – limit their top speed to 155mph (250kmh). Schumacher averaged within 1.2mph of that for 1h 14m 19s.[15] This gives some sort of authentic glimpse of the Grand Prix car's capabilities and also where the remorseless march of technology led to by 2003.

Schumacher 82, Montoya 79, Räikkönen 75.

United States: Räikkönen pole, but Schumacher winning from him, Montoya sixth. Schumacher 92, Räikkönen 83, Montoya 82 and out of the championship.

Villeneuve, unhappy at BAR and outdriven by Button, withdrew from the Japanese Grand Prix citing an absence of motivation. It demonstrated how easily a career can slip away, just as Damon Hill's had done. Since Villeneuve's championship in 1997 he'd scored 60 points – 21 less than in 1997 alone.

Japan: Räikkönen needed to win and hope Schumacher wasn't eighth. Qualifying shook that up, Räikkönen eighth and Schumacher, caught by rain, 14th. Schumacher said: 'It was a very interesting session' and expressed delight that Barrichello took pole – if Barrichello won, Schumacher had the championship, of course.

Montoya led initially from Barrichello, Räikkönen up to third by lap ten of the 53. By then Takuma Sato, who'd replaced Villeneuve at BAR, tangled with Schumacher at the chicane. Schumacher's pit stop for a new nosecone put him at the back of the field. After the first flurry of pit stops Barrichello led from Coulthard, Räikkönen third while Schumacher worked his way to tenth when he had to make a pit stop. He resumed twelfth but by then Barrichello commanded the race. Räikkönen found himself in a double bind, unable to catch Barrichello and, from lap 40 to the end, Schumacher ran eighth – enough, whatever Barrichello did. The world watched Barrichello, felt for Räikkönen. Barrichello crossed the line and ran slowly down the front of the pit lane wall, returning the gestures of the Ferrari mechanics who leant so far out they overhung him. Schumacher was out in the country easing the Ferrari round. As he crossed the line he made no gesture, just kept the car straight ahead.

Fangio's record of five championship had gone and perhaps no gesture could express that. Schumacher said: 'I have a lot of respect for what Fangio did but for me it's the team that's important. What we achieved today with the team has never happened before and the thing is that we have this mood – we've had so much success and still everybody is going in the same direction.'

In Fangio's time, as we have seen, teams and team-work were rudimentary and if you gave a great driver a good car he'd take care of the rest. Fangio did not concentrate on team building because teams didn't function like that. He kept his eye on the main chance, which was wherever the good car happened to be. He won his five championships in successively an Alfa Romeo, two Mercedes, a Ferrari and a Maserati.

In Fangio's time the world was like that, smaller and simpler.

In Schumacher's time the world found perfect expression in the words he spoke at Suzuka when the deed had been done. Inspired individuals couldn't do it any more and hadn't been able to for a couple of decades. Moreover, at Suzuka Schumacher expressed astonishment that reporters kept asking him if he'd be retiring. The subliminal message was clear. He might be leaving Fangio a long, long way behind.

In 2004 he extended the paralysis. Putting that another way, his grip on 2002 had been so complete that *no* driver since 1906, including Fangio, Clark and Senna, could offer anything approaching it. Again this is not an argument about respective merits but it is a statement that Schumacher won 144 points and Barrichello 77, Montoya 50 in 2002.

That's what he was poised to paralyse, all of it.

Of the first 13 rounds in 2004 he won 12.

Running lightly through the *career* records of some World Champions, Mario Andretti had 12 wins, Alberto Ascari 13, Giuseppe Farina 5, Emerson Fittipaldi 14, Mike Hawthorn 3, Graham Hill 14, Phil Hill 3, Denny Hulme 8, James Hunt 10, Alan Jones 12, Stirling Moss 16, Jochen Rindt 6, Keke Rosberg 5, John Surtees 6. As somebody said (in another context altogether) you need not build on this a monument – but you cannot ignore it.

The season's opening race, the Australian at Melbourne, was on 7 March, the 13th Hungary on 15 August. In that time Schumacher took Grand Prix racing to a place even he hadn't been able to take it to before. There's something fitting about that because when the white carthorse dragged the cars to the grid at Le Mans that very first time something with real impetus was launched and, in a great, century-long sweep of human endeavour and achievement, it kept on gathering all the way to here.

To deal with the season, shorthand is an improvement even on the tabulated form never mind ripples of races. He won Australia, Malaysia and Bahrain – a new circuit, bringing Formula 1 to the Middle East – from pole, won San Marino (Button pole), won Spain from pole and took pole at Monaco. There, Trulli led in the Renault. When he pitted on lap 43 Schumacher had that lead from him but the Safety Car was out. Montoya, a lap down, ran behind Schumacher and in the tunnel they collided. Montoya said they were both doing 'burn-outs' – Montoya accelerated just as Schumacher braked.

Schumacher said: 'The situation is that the race leader was knocked out after being hit by a back-marker. I am sure there was no deliberate intention on his part and I accept the Stewards' decision. I was accelerating and braking just as we do when we go to the grid and in the standard way when running behind the Safety Car. The tunnel was not even the first place I had done it as I had used the same procedure earlier in the lap.'

The Monaco measure: Jarno Trulli, 77 laps, 1h 45m 46.6s, an average speed of 90.4mph: Montoya, 2003, 94.9mph.

The sequence lay broken but not the spell it cast. Schumacher won Europe at the Nürburgring from pole, Canada (Ralf pole), the USA (Barrichello pole), France (Alonso pole), Britain (Räikkönen pole), Germany from pole, Hungary from pole. The point was that Schumacher repeatedly proved that he did not need pole. At this stage he had 120 points, Barrichello 82, Button 65 but because the season comprised 18 rounds he'd have to wait a little longer to make the championship mathematically certain. The two points difference between winning and coming second had provided a sort of tourniquet of its own.

Second place in Belgium behind Räikkönen did it nicely although the McLaren was getting stronger and stronger. That at least offered hope Schumacher wouldn't obliterate the remainder of the season.

Late afternoon sunlight for once at Spa, Räikkönen hard into the final lap, Schumacher within sight of him. Schumacher conceded it then, any further risks not worth taking. He melted away, ran the lap at his own pace but Räikkönen was in a combative, feisty mood and took the McLaren hard round. Schumacher finished 3.13 seconds behind and this seventh championship was a curiously dispassionate, implacable, overwhelming thing which compelled admiration but hardly emotional attachment. Even Brawn called it straightforward.

Barrichello took Monza from him but that still meant of a possible 150 points he'd got 136. It was more than the *career* totals of Boutsen, Farina, Hawthorn, de Angelis, Rindt, Ginther, Gilles Villeneuve, Tambay, Pironi...

The 16th round went to China, at Shanghai, a custom built facility. China emerged as a potentially giant economy and car imports flooded in, not forgetting China had its own automotive industry. A Grand Prix there made sense in many different ways and Schumacher anointed the circuit with one of his *events*, spinning in qualifying so with no time he had to start from the back of the grid. It suggested a race. Barrichello won it from pole, Schumacher setting off on his own Long March punctuated by a collision, later a spin, and later still a puncture. He finished twelfth.

To round it off he took Japan from pole and was seventh in Brazil (Montoya won) so that he had 148 points.

The background was almost incidental, almost unnoticed except as temporal phenomena: Button second four times and deserting BAR for Williams then, in an awful wrangle, staying; Jaguar and Jordan drifting into crisis so deep they'd be sold; another saga about cost-cutting to save Formula 1; Ralf's relations at Williams deteriorating – he was going to Toyota, anyway; Ralf suffering a crash at Indianapolis in the Grand Prix there when he struck a wall and took a 78g impact. A furore followed over how long the rescue teams took to get to him and that the race cars were passing through debris, with the risk of punctures; later, bubbling Sato got on the podium; Mosley resigned and withdrew it; another saga of whether the British Grand Prix would stay at Silverstone droned on; Trulli falling out with Flavio Briatore at Renault and departing, letting Villeneuve drive the car in the last three races; the threat of a typhoon cancelling one day at Suzuka; Trulli going to Toyota, who'd spent a fortune not getting very far since their entry in 2002.

This was the traditional fare, a microcosm of what it had been from the beginning, and ideal to take it into the year which would be its hundredth.

Notes

1. Nicola Larini, an Italian who spent long seasons with uncompetitive teams (Osella, Ligier, Modena) and drove four times for Ferrari – including Imola, where he deputised for Alesi, who was ill.
2. *Autocourse.*
3. *Grand Prix Year,* Damon Hill.
4. Ibid.

5. Stepped wooden planks had had to be fixed to the underbelly of the cars since the German Grand Prix to reduce downforce.

6. *Michael Schumacher,* Hilton.

7. *A Different Life,* Virginia Williams.

8. *Michael Schumacher: The Ferrari Years,* Hilton.

9. Ibid.

10. *Prost Grand Prix: vérités secrets.* De Laborderie.

11. Quoted in *Autocourse.*

12. Ecclestone interview in the *Observer,* London, 12 December 2004.

13. These statistics do not include the four races on the banked circuit (1955–56, 1960–61) which exist entirely by themselves. They do however demonstrate the speeds Grand Prix cars could do, with successive fastest laps of 134mph (215kmh), 135mph (217kmh), 136mph (220kmh) and 132mph (213kmh).

14. Except 3.2 SMG Coupé, 158mph.

15. I once asked John Barnard, then with McLaren, what the car's top speed was and he professed that he wasn't sure because, as he explained, the car is always set up to achieve its optimum in the context of circuits with their curves, corners, chicanes and so on. To find its true maximum you'd need to set it up for that and hire a runway – a long, straight runway.

Chapter 12

THE CENTURIONS

J ust when the world thought Ferrari had become – forgive me – an immovable object as well as an irresistible force, Renault imposed themselves in a way which, initially, was difficult to believe. Because Schumacher and Ferrari loomed as immensely as that. By the fourth race of 2005, San Marino, the believing was much easier. Renault had won all four races: Giancarlo Fisichella in Australia, and Fernando Alonso in Malaysia, Bahrain and around Imola's parkland. There, at last, Schumacher (from 13th on the grid) mounted a real challenge, which Alonso withstood. More than that, Kimi Räikkönen led from pole for nine laps until his McLaren halted with mechanical problems. These were psychological moments suggesting, as they did, that Grand Prix racing was doing what it had always done, reinvigorating itself by a constant infusion of new, brave, hungry young drivers.

Sometimes statistics are eloquent. Departing Imola the season before this, Schumacher had 40 points and Barrichello 24. Departing Imola in 2005, Alonso had 26 points, Trulli in the Toyota 18, Fisichella and Schumacher 10, Ralf Schumacher and Coulthard – now with Red Bull (formerly Jaguar) – 9, Barrichello and Montoya 8, Räikkönen and the Williams pair, Nick Heidfeld and Mark Webber, all on 7.

With 19 races on the calendar, engines having to last two Grands Prix and tyres a whole Grand Prix – never mind the qualifying, where the running order was based on the result of the previous race – suddenly the whole thing was no longer dormant.

To emphasise that, Räikkönen took Spain and led every lap at Monte Carlo from pole, beating Heidfeld by 15 seconds, Alonso fourth. Alonso knew that some you win, but at the ones you don't win you go canny and gather points. Räikkönen behaved more like a thoroughbred racer, taut, forever at his maximum, childlike (and naughty) outside the car, mighty within it. He spoke very softly, a whispering, monosyllabic sound. Like all the leading drivers as far back as you care to go, he didn't have to speak at all. His eloquence was motion.

The Monaco measure: Räikkönen, 78 laps, 1h 45m 15.5s, an average speed of 92.2mph; Trulli, 2004, 90.6mph.

The measure of the decades: 1929, 49.8mph; 1937, 63.2mph; 1948, 59.7mph; 1958, 67.9mph; 1968, 77.8mph; 1979, 81.3mph, 1989, 84.1mph; 1999, 89.3mph.

Vehicles registered 2003, 31.2m (1989, 24.2m). A Ford Ka cost £6,995 and a Briton earned on average £422.10. Saving all his money, the Briton would have taken 16 weeks to buy one (1910, two years 42 weeks; 1919, one year 28 weeks; 1929, 41 weeks; 1938, 37 weeks; 1948, 45 weeks; 1959, 36 weeks; 1969, 26 weeks; 1979, 20 weeks; 1989, 21 weeks; 1999, 18 weeks).

Alonso reasserted himself in the European GP at the Nürburgring, where Heidfeld took pole – although, truth to tell, pole positions were themselves becoming hard to believe in because drivers were carrying whatever fuel they had left after the session to the start of the race, and it was impossible knowing who'd fuelled 'light' to qualify fast, and who had fuelled 'heavy' for the race. Something else happened at the Nürburgring which offered an insight into Räikkönen. He was soon into the lead and stayed there but, lapping Jacques Villeneuve – back, with Sauber – he flat-spotted a front tyre. Every driver in modern times has known this. You brake so hard that the wheel locks, and the bit in contact with the track is burnished flat by the friction. For Räikkönen, every subsequent rotation of the wheel created a vibration so bad that it affected his vision, and brought danger. Alonso lurked in second place and the end of the race was nigh. Räikkönen had no thoughts of pitting – until, going into the final lap, his suspension failed.

Button took pole in Canada from Schumacher but Räikkönen took the race – Alonso hit the wall opposite the pits. That brought them to Indianapolis. It was the sixth year running that the United States Grand Prix was held there. After the nomadic decades – Sebring, Watkins Glen, Long Beach, Detroit, Dallas, Las Vegas, Phoenix – F1 had nestled into the spiritual home of American racing and was building a support base. Indianapolis gave the Canadians a chance to see two Grands Prix in the year, and many South Americans (notably Montoya followers from Colombia) and Central Americans (Mexicans) a chance to listen to the sounds and breathe the fumes by being there.

Nor could anyone doubt the primary importance of the vast US market to BMW (powering Williams), Mercedes (McLaren), Honda (BAR) and the three stand-alones, Ferrari, Renault and Toyota. It went deeper than commerce, however – if you can believe such a statement about Formula 1. Europeans had long sneered at the Baseball World Series because manifestly the world does not play baseball. Any red blooded Yank could have riposted *well, buddy, what's this Grand Prix World Championship of yours that goes to Bahrain and San Marino (which it doesn't even physically visit) but not the big one, the good ole US of A?* Answering that had previously been awkward but no longer. Formula 1 now had Indy – it's own Tranquillity Base – and was landed safely there.

In 2005, however, over three days of chaos and anger Formula 1 may well have destroyed the base. It began on the Friday when, in the banked right-hand Turn 13 – a place of maximum stress, and unlike other Formula 1 corners because of the banking – a left-rear tyre failed on Ralf Schumacher's Toyota. He struck the wall but emerged unhurt.

By the next day Michelin was advising the seven teams it supplied (all but Ferrari, Jordan and Minardi) not to race unless a chicane was built to cut speeds at Turn 13. The FIA refused. Max Mosley pointed out that Formula 1 ran to tight regulations and you couldn't just alter them to accommodate people who'd made mistakes – in this case Michelin, with the tyres they'd taken to Indianapolis. If you did, it would set a precedent leading to anarchy. Ecclestone tried 'a million things' and compromise hung briefly in the air: with a chicane, the Bridgestone runners could go to the front of the grid and they could have the points for the first six places *but the race had to go on.* In the mounting unreality, one suggestion was that the Michelin runners would be told to go through Turn 13 slowly, whatever that meant.

In the understandably lurid Press reporting there were very serious legal implications which didn't get the prominence they demanded. Michelin had in effect said their tyres were dangerous. Where did that leave team owners sending their drivers out if something went terribly wrong? What would insurance companies make of it? And what about Indiana State law which decreed that you can be deemed culpable if you do something when you've been warned it's dangerous – even if *nothing* happens?

And wasn't the good ole US of A densely packed with lawyers chasing ambulances because a potential client lay in every one? What would the ambulance chasers do if *anything* happened?

All the cars covered the parade lap but, as they came round, the Michelin runners peeled off into the pits never to return. It left a grid which wasn't a grid at all but, in context, a landscape from a nightmare:

_____

_____   _____

                                   _____
Schumacher
Barrichello   _____

_____   _____

_____   _____

_____   _____

_____   _____

_____
Monteiro   Albers
Karthikeyan   Friesacher

Nothing like this had ever been seen in Grand Prix racing before, nor surely imagined. Almost *everything* which had gone before – from the stony French roads before the First World War to the 14-strong 1982 Imola grid in the FISA-FOCA warfare, to Spa breaking up in 1985 – seemed more explicable than this. Schumacher 'won' the 'race' while sections of the crowd reacted with fury. For a time it looked ugly.

I've dwelt on the United States Grand Prix of 19 June 2005 for several reasons, but let's clear away the incongruous first. Tiago Monteiro of Portugal finished third in his Jordan, Narain Karthikeyan – Formula 1's first driver from India – fourth in the other Jordan, Christijan Albers of Holland fifth in one Minardi, Austrian Patrick Friesacher sixth in the other. For as long as people remain interested in Grand Prix racing – another hundred years, two hundred, whatever – these points will be as officially valid as any others scored.

Karthikeyan represented how broad the reach of Grand Prix racing had become, just as the 2005 calendar did by going to every continent except Africa and stopping at some unlikely places along the way. The appetite to stage races seemed insatiable and what role, in the fullness of time, would China's 1.3 billion citizens play? That's *double* the combined population of the USA, the European Union and Russia.

The Indianapolis debacle illustrated something else. Mechanised sports are inherently different from all other sports because of the endless technological possibilities. Brabham might show up in Sweden with their fan car, but no racehorse goes to post in the Derby with an aeroplane fan stuck on its rump. There is *nothing* like this that you can do in tennis (except the transition from wooden rackets to graphite), football or Rugby. Cricket's breathtaking moment of innovation came when Australian fast bowler Dennis Lillee made his way to the wicket with a metal bat. It was not illegal because nobody had thought of such a thing before, and that's as near as cricket got in a hundred and fifty years to what motorsport produces the whole time in bewildering permutations.

Drugs are another matter and any athlete who knowingly takes them is scarcely being innovative. They're cheating in a crude way, trying to advance themselves at the expense of the sport which gives them their living.

When swimmers shaved their body hair for aerodynamic reasons this was considered a revolution. Contrast that with Colin Chapman conjuring utterly original devices on a regular basis for two decades, including wooden strips down the underbellies of the cars which made them so fast they out-monstered the circuits. It would be the equivalent of swimmers swimming so fast they flung themselves clean out of the pool.

That's what makes the motor racing so damnably infuriating, a desperate thing to police in any ordinary sense and so damnably fascinating too. The FIA had to confront all those positions at Indianapolis, a brutal consequence of so much that had gone before.

It put great pressure on the French Grand Prix to produce normality and Alonso and Räikkönen did that. This would be no classic, palpitating race, no exploration of the outer reaches, but that didn't matter. There were the full complement of cars – 20 – on the grid, with Alonso on pole, the Ferraris lurking and Räikkönen relegated to 13th because his engine needed replacing (which cost him ten places). As the red lights blinked off, the contrast between the two columns of cars breaking up under their ferocious acceleration – flooding the width of the track, darting, thrusting, urging – and the stately square galleons of 1906 being released at 90-second intervals was in no sense irrelevant, because you needed the one to have evolved into the other.

By an irony, no Frenchman was on the grid at the 2005 race and that hadn't happened for 40 years. Alonso controlled it from the front while Räikkönen pushed hard and came up behind him. Montoya, Trulli, Schumacher and Barrichello played out sub-plots. In the end it was straightforward. Alonso won comfortably enough and, as a car manufacturer, Renault hadn't had a victory in their home Grand Prix for 22 years.

In the background Grand Prix racing was continuing to shift direction, as if a great wheel turned. The privateer drivers had long gone to the valley of the dinosaurs and the wealthy patrons – Rob Walker, Alexander Hesketh – with them. In their place the businessmen had come: Eddie Jordan sold out to one, Alex Shnaider, a Russian-Canadian, as we've seen; Dietrich Mateschitz bought Jaguar and renamed it Red Bull, after the soft drink which made him a billionaire. Mateschitz didn't say much in public. He didn't have to. Once upon a time, so the story goes, an Austrian magazine wanted to feature him and to prevent that he bought the magazine. We are a long way from Grand Prix people trying to get *into* magazines.

Of more significance, BMW bought out Peter Sauber because, as a global corporation, they wanted control over everything. With McLaren and Mercedes already wedded, this threatened to leave Frank Williams isolated although, in someone's memorable phrase, Formula 1 is so tightly packed with survivors that you don't ever count any of them out – especially him.

The direction had become clear: *very* large sums of money, major automotive companies, modern circuits and a global entertainment brand. Perhaps, in a curious sort of way, it was all inevitable since 6:00.00 on the misty morning of 26 June 1906 when Fernand Gabriel emerged from the billowing smoke which his Lorraine-Dietrich spread so artistically and set off as fast as he could make the car go. Perhaps all ages are innocent, and no ages really innocent – but, in broad sweep, progress always moves from the small to the large, the simple always moves to the sophisticated, the fast always moves to the faster.

It's the people who stay the same.

Ferenc Szisz and Fernando Alonso could sit together and find that they had much more in common than separated them, and in that they'd be joined by every man and woman who had ever eased themselves into a Grand Prix car, positioned themselves, steeled themselves and taken it on. This wouldn't just be the bearded, moustache-bearing pillars of racing before the First World War, or Nuvolari and Varzi, Rosemeyer and Caracciola, Fangio and Moss, Clark and Stewart, Prost, and Senna's tragic inheritance passed to Schumacher in the Benetton directly behind him. It would be the 20-odd drivers who scored a single point in their careers, and the forgotten host who didn't even manage that. It would be those who accepted, once they'd fired the engine and taken it on, that they might not be coming back and didn't come back. They're the ghost riders in the sky, and they're not forgotten.

Collectively, once they'd agreed the essentials of what they all were – and that would only take a moment – they'd have a hell of a lot to talk about.

They'd need a hundred years and more to do it.

THE MAJOR RECORDS
at 3 July 2005

THE DRIVERS

679 since 1950

Most championships

7	Michael Schumacher (94, 95, 00, 01, 02, 03, 04)	**5**	Juan-Manuel Fangio (51, 54, 55, 56, 57)
4	Alain Prost (85, 86, 89, 93)		

Most victories

84	Schumacher	**51**	Prost
41	Ayrton Senna		

Most Grands Prix

256	Riccardo Patrese	**223**	Schumacher
210	Gerhard Berger		

Pole positions

65	Senna	**63**	Schumacher
33	Jim Clark		

Fastest Laps

69	Schumacher	**41**	Prost
30	Nigel Mansell		

Most wins in season

13	Schumacher, 04	**11**	Schumacher, 02
9	Schumacher, 95, 00, 01 Mansell, 92		

Most points

1,226	Schumacher	**798.5**	Prost
614	Senna		

Youngest/oldest driver
19y 5m 29d – Mike Thackwell   **55y 9m 19d** – Louis Chiron

Youngest/oldest winner
22y 0m 26d – Fernando Alonso   **53y 0m 22d** – Luigi Fagioli

THE TEAMS

Most Grands Prix

714	Ferrari	**587**	McLaren
506	Williams		

Most Constructors' wins

14	Ferrari	**9**	Williams
8	McLaren		

Most race wins

183	Ferrari	**141**	McLaren
113	Williams		

THE CHAMPIONSHIP

741	races since 1950	**62**	circuits

Longest

15.8m	Pescara	**14.1m**	Nürburgring
8.7m	Spa		

Shortest

1.95m	Monaco	**1.97m**	Zeltweg (1964)
2.02m	Long Beach		

THE RACES

25	countries

Most races

80	Italy (inc. S. Marino)	**62**	Germany (inc. European, Lux.)
58	Britain (inc. European)		

ACKNOWLEDGEMENTS

Any work of this scope needs all the help it can get from all the directions it can get it. A glance at the Footnotes from any chapter demonstrates that, and rather than slog through them again here, I offer a sincere thanks to all those who wrote their books, gave their interviews, spoke their words to cameras.

Many people helped, and they have my gratitude. In no particular order: Sir Stirling Moss, John Watson, Jabby Crombac; John Nevill, Heritage Fleet Administrator, Public Affairs, Ford Motor Company; John Hallmark, Information Officer, Office for National Statistics; Noëlle Bouhanha, Bibliothèque Municipale de Lyon; Sylvie Blondel, Les Informations Dieppoises; Sandra, Service Documentation, Courrier Picard, Amiens; Bradley Lord, Press Officer, Renault F1 Team and Britta Roeske of the Press Office who put me safely in touch with Claud le Maitre of the *Societé d'Histoire du Groupe Renault* in Paris. He sent a wonderful packet full of priceless information about the 1906 Grand Prix. Barry Griffin, former Goodyear PR, also ferreted out priceless information. Vicky Mitchell of the BBC Commercial Agency for securing permission to quote from *The Power and The Glory;* Ann Bradshaw; the Ferrari Press Office for invaluable daily bulletins. Nigel Roebuck allowed me to raid his library and sought out relevant material. For that I am particularly grateful. Inge Donnell did her usual meticulous job on translating German into English.

For permission to quote: Brock Yates, *Enzo Ferrari, The Man and The Machine;* the late Chris Nixon, *Shooting Star, Racing the Silver Arrows, Mon Ami Mate, Rosemeyer!;* Kevin Desmond, *The Man with Two Shadows.*

I have leant heavily on *Autosport, The Motor* and *The Autocar* and several sources of reference were constantly at my elbow: *Autocourse, Marlboro Grand Prix Guide,* Hayhoe and Holland's *Grand Prix Data Book,* Steve Small's *The Grand Prix Who's Who,* Peter Higham's *Guinness Guide to International Motor Racing,* Mike Lang's three-volume *Grand Prix!* Doug Nye has written the definitive technical study, *The Autocourse History of the Grand Prix Car 1966–1991* (Hazleton Publishing, Richmond upon Thames,

Surrey). Some people need comfort food; I drew my comfort from having Nye's book at my elbow. Videos (and DVDs) have a particular relevance in bringing it all alive again so thanks in a broad way to the BBC and latterly ITV for the race coverage safely onto my videos. *Jackie Stewart, The Official DVD Biography* (a Mark Stewart Production) was illuminating and so was the Duke series of *Champion* drivers, on Moss and Clark. The Grand Prix series of videos on each season through the 1970s by Sports Seen gave precious glimpses. So did the *Shell History of Motor Racing* and *The Power and The Glory* (John Gau Productions for BBC Enterprises). *Racing Mercedes* (Bill Mason Films Ltd, David Weguelin Productions) is essential viewing for the 1930s.

The Internet is, simultaneously, a mine and a maze of information but no historian can afford to neglect it. I have used it extensively and cited the sources in the Footnotes. There are two outstanding sites and I pay particular thanks to them.

www.ddavid.com/formula1/
www.kolumbus.fi/leif.snellman/

Many, many races – major and minor – were called Grands Prix, a sort of verbal gesture. It leaves a question of definition: which ought to be legitimately included? Answering this is hampered by an absence of championships before 1950 except the European, between 1935 and 1939. I have used Peter Higham's *Guinness Guide to International Motor Racing* as the arbiter. Equally, I have simplified them to the country where they happened. For example, the Italian race of 1928 was also known as the Grand Prix of Europe, but it doesn't mean much and clutters the narrative.

BIBLIOGRAPHY

Audi. *A History of Progress*. Audi AG Public Relations, Ingolstadt, Germany, undated.

Ball, Adrian (editor). *My Greatest Race*. Hart-Davis, London, 1974.

Beaumont, Charles and Nolan, William F. (editors). *The Omnibus of Speed*. Stanley Paul, London, 1961.

Birkin, Sir Henry 'Tim.' *Full Throttle*. G. T. Foulis, London, 1943.

Boddy, Bill. *Brooklands Giants*. G. T. Foulis/Haynes, Sparkford, 1995.

— *The History of Motor Racing*. G. P. Putnam's Sons, New York, 1977.

Brabham, Jack. *When the Flag Drops*. William Kimber, London, 1971.

— *Jack Brabham's Motor Racing Book*. Frederick Muller Limited, London, 1962.

Caracciola, Rudolf. *A Racing Driver's World*. Motoraces Book Club, London, 1963.

Campbell, Sir Malcolm. *My Thirty Years of Speed*. Hutchinson & Co, London, undated.

Carrick, Peter. *The Story of Honda Motor Cycles*. Patrick Stephens, Cambridge, 1976.

Carter, Bruce. *Great Motor Races*. Weidenfeld and Nicholson, London, 1960.

Cholmondeley Tapper, T. P. *Amateur Racing Driver*. Motoraces Book Club, London, 1966.

Cimarosti, Adriano. *The Complete History of Grand Prix Motor Racing*. Aurum, London, 1997.

Clark, Jim. *Jim Clark at the Wheel*. Arthur Barker Limited, London, 1964.

Clutton, Cecil, Posthumus, Cyril and Jenkinson, Denis. *The Racing Car*. Batsford, London, 1962.

Crombac, Gerard. *Colin Chapman*. *The Man and his Cars*. Patrick Stephens, Wellingborough, 1986.

De Laborderie, Renaud. *Prost Grand Prix: vérités secrets*. Solar, Paris, 2003.

Desmond, Kevin. *The Man with Two Shadows*. Proteus books, London, 1981.

Donaldson, Gerald. *Gilles Villeneuve*. MRP, London, 1989.

— *James Hunt, The Biography*. Virgin Books, London, 2003.

Doyle, Gary D. *King of the Boards.* Gary Doyle, Sedona, Arizona, 2002.

Dreyfus, René with Beverly Rae Kimes. *My Two Lives.* Aztex Corporation, Tucson, Arizona, 1983.

Fangio, Jean-Manuel. *My Twenty years of Racing.* Temple Press, London, 1961.

— with Roberto Carozzo. *My Racing Life.* Patrick Stephens, Wellingborough, 1990.

Ferrari, Enzo. *The Enzo Ferrari Memoirs.* Hamish Hamilton, London, 1963.

Fittipaldi, Emerson with Hayward, Elizabeth. *Flying on the Ground.* William Kimber, London, 1973.

Hallè, Jean-Claude. *François Cevert: 'la mort dans mon contrat.'* Flammarion, Paris, 1974.

Hamilton, Maurice. *Frank Williams.* Macmillan, London, 1998.

— *British Grand Prix.* Crowood, Marlborough, Wiltshire, 1989.

Hawthorn, Mike. *Challenge me the Race.* William Kimber, London, 1958.

— *Champion Year.* William Kimber, London, 1959.

Hayhoe, David and Holland, David. *Grand Prix Data Book, 1997.* Duke, Isle of Man, 1996.

Higham, Peter. *The Guinness Guide to International Motor Racing.* Guinness Publishing, Enfield, London, 1995.

Hill, Damon. *Grand Prix Year.* Macmillan, London, 1994.

Hill, Graham. *Life at the Limit.* William Kimber, London, 1969.

Hillstead, AFC. *Those Bentley Days.* Faber and Faber, London, undated.

Hilton, Christopher. *Gerhard Berger, the Human Face of Formula 1.* Patrick Stephens/Haynes, Sparkford, 1995.

— *Alain Prost.* Partridge Press, London, 1992.

— with John Blunsden. *A Man Called Mike.* MRP, London, 1992.

— *Ayrton Senna: As Time Goes By.* Haynes, Sparkford, 2003.

— *Ayrton Senna: The Whole Story.* Haynes, Sparkford, 2004.

— *Grand Prix Showdown.* Haynes, Sparkford, 1992.

— *Gerhard Berger, The Human Face of Formula 1.* Patrick Stephens/Haynes, Sparkford, 1995.

— *Hitler's Grands Prix in England.* Haynes, Sparkford, 1999.

— *Honda, The Conquest of Formula 1.* Patrick Stephens, Wellingborough, 1989.

— *Ken Tyrrell.* Haynes, Sparkford, 2002.

— *Michael Schumacher.* Patrick Stephens, Sparkford, 1994.

— *Michael Schumacher: The Ferrari Years.* Haynes, Sparkford, 2001.

— *Michael Schumacher, The Greatest of All.* Haynes, Sparkford, 2003.

— *Nuvolari.* Breedon Books, Derby, 2003.

Hodges, David (editor). *Great Racing Drivers*. Temple Press Books, London, 1966.

— *The Monaco Grand Prix*. Temple Press Books, London, 1964.

— *The French Grand Prix*. Temple Press Books, London, 1967.

Holthusen, Peter J. R. *The Land Speed Record*. G. T. Foulis/Haynes, Sparkford, 1986.

Hotten, Russell. *Formula One*. Orion Business Books, London, 1999.

Ireland, Innes. *All Arms and Elbows*. Pelham Books, London, 1967.

Jones, Alan and Botsford, Keith. *Driving Ambition*. Stanley Paul, London, 1981.

Jones, Bruce. *The Official Formula 1 Season Review, 2004*. Haynes in association with Haymarket, Sparkford, 2004.

Kahn, Mark. *The Day I Died*. Gentry Books, London, 1974.

Lang, Hermann. *Grand Prix Driver*. G. T. Foulis, London, 1954.

Lang, Mike. *Grand Prix!* Haynes, Sparkford; three volumes 1981, 1982, 1983.

Lauda, Niki with Herbert Völker. *To Hell and Back*. Stanley Paul, London, 1986.

— *For The Record,* William Kimber, London.

Lurani, Count. *Nuvolari*. Cassel, London, 1959.

Lovell, Terry. *Bernie's Game*. Metro Publishing, London, 2003.

Mansell, Nigel with James Allen. *My Autobiography.* CollinsWillow, London, 1995.

Mathieson, Taso. *Grand Prix Racing, 1906–1914*. Connaisseur Automobile A.B., Stockholm, 1965.

Molter, Günter. *Juan Manuel Fangio*. G. T. Foulis, London, 2nd edition, undated.

Moretti, Valerio. *When Nuvolari Raced…* Veloce Publishing, Dorset, 1994.

Moss, Stirling with Doug Nye. *Mr Cars, My Career.* Patrick Stephens, Wellingborough, 1987.

— *All But My life* face to face with Ken Purdy. William Kimber, London, 1963.

Neubauer, Alfred. *Speed was my Life*. Barrie and Rockliff, London, 1960.

Nixon, Chris with Elly Beinhorn. *Rosemeyer!* Transport Bookman Publications, London, 1989.

— *Shooting Star: the life of Richard Seaman*. Transport Bookman Publications, London, 2000.

— *Mon Ami Mate*. Transport Bookman Publications, London, 1991.

— *Racing the Silver Arrows*. Osprey, London, 1986.

Nye, Doug. *The British Grand Prix 1926–1976*. Batsford, London, 1976.

— *History of the Grand Prix Car 1966–1991*. Hazleton Publishing, London, 1992.

Owen, David. *Alfa Romeo*. Patrick Stephens/Haynes, Sparkford, 1993.

Paris, Jean-Michel and Mearns, William D. *Jean-Pierre Wimille, à bientôt la revanche*. Editions Drivers, Toulouse, 2002.

Petersens, Fredrik af. *The Viking Drivers*. William Kimber, London, 1979.

Pritchard, Anthony. *Lotus, All the Cars*. Aston Publications Limited, Bourne End, Bucks, 1990.

— *A Century of Grand Prix Motor Racing*. MRP, London, 1998.

Prost, Alain with Jean-Louis Moncet. *Life in the Fast Lane*. Stanley Paul, London, 1989.

Prüller, Heinz. *Jochen Rindt*. William Kimber, London, 1970.

Posthumus, Cyril. *The Roaring Twenties*. Blandford Press, Poole, 1980.

— *The German Grand Prix*. Temple Press Books, London, 1966.

— *The Indianapolis Star. The 500, 1911 to 1990*. The Indianapolis Star, Indianapolis, 1990.

Rhodes, Anthony. *Louis Renault*. Cassell, London, 1969.

Robson, Graham. *Cosworth, the search for Power*. Patrick Stephens, Wellingborough, 1990.

Roebuck, Nigel. *Grand Prix Greats*. Patrick Stephens, Wellingborough, 1986.

— with Mario Andretti. *Mario Andretti, World Champion*. Hamlyn, London, 1979.

Rosberg, Keke and Botsford, Keith. *Keke. An Autobiography*. Stanley Paul, London, 1985.

Rosinski, José. *Depailler: La Course est un Combat*. Calmann-Lévy, Paris, 1978.

Salvadori, Roy and Pritchard, Anthony. *Roy Salvadori, Racing Driver*. Patrick Stephens, Wellingborough, 1985.

Sakiya, Tetso. *Honda Motor*. Kodansha International Ltd, Tokyo and New York, 1987.

Scheckter, Jody. *Jody, an Autobiography*. G. T. Foulis/Haynes, Sparkford,1976.

Schlegelmilch, Rainer. W. *Grand Prix: Fascination Formula 1*. Könemann, Cologne, 1993.

Segrave, H. O. D. *The Lure of Speed*. Hutchinson, London, 1928.

Sheldon, Paul. *A Record of Grand Prix and Voiturette Racing*. St Leonard's Press, Shipley, West Yorkshire, Vols 1, 2, 3, 4.

Small, Steve. *The Grand Prix Who's Who*. Guinness Publishing, Enfield, London, 2nd edition, 1996.

Stevenson, Peter. *Driving Forces*. Bentley Publishers, Cambridge, Massachusetts, 2000.

Stewart, Jackie (presenter). *François Cevert*. Solar, Paris 1973.

— and Eric Dymock. *World Champion*. Pelham Books, London, 1970.

— and Peter Manso. *Faster!* William Kimber, London, 1972.

Surtees, John. *World Champion*. Hazleton Publishing, London, 1991.

Taruffi, Piero. *Works Driver*. Temple Press Books, London, 1964.

Von Brauchitsch, Manfred. *Kampf um Meter und Sekunden*. Verlag der Nation, Berlin, 1955.

Williams, Virginia with Cockerill, Pamela. *A Different Kind of Life*. Doubleday, London, 1991.

Yates, Brock. *Enzo Ferrari, the Man and the Machine*. Bantam Edition, London, 1992.

Young, Eoin. *Bruce McLaren*. Patrick Stephens/Haynes, Sparkford, 1995.

— with James Hunt. *James Hunt, Against All Odds*. Hamlyn, London, 1977.

INDEX

Figures in italics refer to illustrations

AIACR 91
Argentine Auto Club 198–199, 241
Autocar magazine 97, 103–104, 127, 160, 170
Autocourse magazine 445
Automobile Club de France (ACF) 11–13, 15–16, 27–28, 31, 34, *67,* 88
Automobile Club of Hungary 385
Automobile Club of Italy 201
Automobile Club de Monaco (ACM) 300–301
Autosport magazine 239, 257
Ayrton Senna Foundation 416

BBC 411, 447
Belgian Automobile Club 141
Berlin Motor Show 123–124, 167
Bosch 106
Bridgestone 459
British Racing Drivers' Club (BRDC) 112

Can-Am 329
Concorde Agreement 344, 416
Continental tyres 17, 142, 144–145
CSI 230, 285, 288, 300–301, 320, 322, 324, 335

Daily Express 269, 311
Daily Mail 269
Dunlop tyres 17, 202, 246, 263, 266

Elf 295, 423
Embassy 360
Esso 285

FAI 196
FIA 41, 48, 201, 230, 257, *383,* 414, 416, 418–420, 423, 440, 459, 461
  Court of Appeal/Appeals Committee 344, 423
  World Motor Sport Council 398–399, 415, 419, 434
FISA 335–336, 340, 342–343, 348, 398, 405, 460
FOCA (F1CA) 299–300, 320, 335–336, 339–340, 342–343, 350, 430, 460
Formula Atlantic 324, 360
Formula Ford 357
Formula 2 205, 234–235, 268, 281, 295, 299, 303, 306, 338, 355
Formula 3 254, 333, 357, 359–360, 430
Formula 3000 47, 396, 415

Goodyear tyres 263, 330, 333, 356, 386
Grand Prix Drivers' Association (GPDA) 249, 267, 285, 287, 290, 301, 320, 348, 417

IMG 291
Imperial Tobacco 285
  Gold Leaf cigarettes 285
  John Player Special (JPS) 299, 330
IMSA 355, 361
IndyCars *380,* 408, 411, 424, 445, 459
Indy Lights series 47
International Grand Prix Medical Service 267
Intertechnique 419

La Figaro newspaper 27
La Vigie De Dieppe newspaper 31

L'Auto Italiana magazine
Le Progès de la Somme newspaper 39
Leyland 339
London Rowing Club 430

Marlboro 299, 304, 313, 342, 347, 364,
    371
Michelin 44
    tyres 11, 17, 329–330, 355–356, 459
Motor, The magazine 23, 25, 33, 38, *66, 71*
Motor Italia magazine 152
Motor Sport magazine *175*, 202–203
Museum of the Automobile, Le Mans 46

News of the World 240
NSKK 147, 160

Oldfield tyres 58

Philip Morris 313
Pirelli tyres 58, 106, 364, 386

Reuters 252
Royal Automobile Club (RAC) 91, 147,
    181, 203, 346
    Technical Commission 346

Saudi Arabian Airlines 330
Sega 409
Shell 106
Studebaker Test Products (STP) 311

World Federation of Motor Sports 342
World Land Speed Record 12–15, 20, 34,
    41, 44, 49, 51, 84, 88, 101, 103, 106,
    108, 113, 120, 129, 133, 139, 151,
    163, 204
World Offshore Powerboat
    Championship 390

CARS AND TEAMS
AFM 432
AGS 432
Alfa Romeo 51, 77–79, 81–88, 98–99,
    102, 105–106, 108, 112–120, 124,
    126, 129, 132–135, 139–141, 143,
    146–148, 150–152, 155–158, 163–165,

168, *170*, 180, 183, 186, 191, 194–195,
    197–198, 200–206, 208–209, 221,
    223, 331, 340, 349, 351, 370, *377*,
    402, 452–453
    158 Alfetta 197, 201, 227
    P.2 Model 64
    P3 Model124, 141, 146
Alta 202, 432
Andrea Moda 432
Arrows 329, 332, 348, 355, 401, 430,
    432, 435
Aston-Martin 61, 91
ATS 331, 366, 371, 432
Audi 123, 452
Austin 30–31
    A35 231
Austin-Healey 217
Austro-Daimler 64, 107
Auto-Stand 47
Auto Union *72*, 123–124, 131–135,
    137–143, 150–153, 156–159, 161–165,
    167–168, *170, 172*, 177, 180–182, 186,
    188, 190–192, 194

Ballileau 47
Ballot 52–56, 58–59, 61, 63
BAR 438, 452, 455, 458
BAR-Honda 445
Benetton 375, *380–381*, 385, 388,
    397–398, 402, 404, 407–408, 413,
    418–426, 430, 434, 462
Benetton-Ford 417
Bentley 108, 110–111
Benz 13, 30, 32, 34, 44, 77
Bianchi 98, 202
BMW 181, 200, 452, 462
Brabham 254–255, 264, 267, 292–293,
    299–300, 310, 314, 327, 330–332,
    335, 338–339, 341, 344, 348–349,
    351, 355, 357–359, 370–371, 375, *377*,
    397, 399, 406–407, 460
Brabham-BMW 348
Brabham-BRM 255
Brabham-Ford 292, 299, 306
Brabham-Repco 269
Brasier 20, 30
BRM 149, 219–220, 238, 244, 246,

248–249, 251, 253–254, 256–257, 259, 262–263, 265–266, *276*, 281, 285, 295, 299, 301, 313, 327

Bugatti 60–61, 63–64, *71*, 73, 79–80, 86, 88, 91–95, 98–105, 107, 109–110, 112–118, 120, 123–125, 129, 132, 134, 138–139, 147, 153, 186, 195
  Type 51 130
  Type 59 130

Chevrolet 202
Chiribiri 83, 96, 106
Chitty Bang Bang 55
Christie 28
Civelli de Bosch 47
Cistalia 197, 227
Citroën 45, 88, 201
Clément-Bayard 26
CMN 50
Connaught 230–231, 260
Cooper 235, 238, 240, 243–245, 248, 250, 253, 261, 263, 265, *273*, 290
Cooper-Bristol 209
Cooper-Climax 224, 230, 232, 234, 239, 241
Cooper-Maserati 267–269

Daimler 12, 32, 44–45, 64
Darracq 20, 28
de Lorean 396
de Tomaso 293, 295
Delage 40–41, 54, 79, 86–88, 92–93, 99–101, 109
Delahaye 195
Diatto 64, 106
DKW 123, 139
Duesenberg 51–59, 88, 100, 108, 130

Eagle 263
Eagle-Weslake 270
Écurie Belge 202
Écurie Ecosse 202
Elf Team Tyrrell 314
Embassy Lola 318
Ensign 327, 339, 348
Ensign-Ford 333
ERA 142, 149, 202

Excelsior *69*

Ferrari 7, 46, 106, 109, 112, 132, 159, *173–175*, 199–200, 207–209, 212, 214, 216–221, 223, 225–227, 229–230, 232–236, 238, 240, 245–251, 253, 256, 263, 267–268, *279*, 286, 292, 297–298, 302–303, 314–317, 320–324, 327, 329, 333, 335, 337–338, 340, 342, 344–345, 349, 351, 353, 355–356, 358, 370, *377*, *383*, 385, 387–388, 391, 393–395, 397, 399–402, 404, 408, 416, 418, 422, 424, 426–428, 430–431, 434–436, 439–444, 449–450, 452–453, 455, 457–459, 461
  156 Model 244

Fiat (FIAT) 12, 15, 19–21, 25, 29–30, 32, 34–35, 37–38, 42–43, 47, 51, 53, 59–64, *67*, *70*, 73–75, 77–79, 86, 99, 426
  805 Model 64

Footwork 425

Ford 34, 105, 258, 260, 331
  Anglia 198
  Escort Deluxe 286, 292
  Fiesta 336, 396
  Focus 439
  Ka 458
  Model A 158
  Model T 34, 49
  Popular 232
  Prefect 63

Germain 30
Gobron-Brille 21
Grégoire *66*

Haas 375
  Halford Special 99
Hesketh 306, 309, 314, 318–319
Hill 360
Honda 238, 255, 259–260, 264, 268–269, 271–272, *275*, 281, 286, 288, 338, 387, 394–395
  RA301 286
  RA302 286

Honda America 365
Honda France 286
Horch 123
Hotchkiss 25
HWM 205, 228

Iso Marlboro 304
Itala 15, 21, 30, 33, 38–39, 47, 59, 106

Jaguar 217, 232, 237, 401, 441, 452, 455, 457, 462
Jordan 404, 407–408, 411, 424, 430–432, 434, 437–439, 450, 455, 459–460
Jordan-Hart 412

Lago-Talbot 200, 206, 209
Lancia 50, 215–217
LEC 329, 360
Lexus 452
Leyton House 400
Ligier 322, 327, 335–336, 339–341, 345, 374, 376, 418, 425, 427, 429, 455
Lion-Peugeot 47
Lister 233, 261
Lola 250, 271, 318, 414
Lola-Climax 249
Lorraine-Dietrich 19, 21, 23, 29–30, 34, 46, 362, 373, 462
Lotus 231, 233, 237, 240–247, 250, 253, 257–259, 263–264, 269–270, 272, 274, 284–286, 288–289, 292–293, 296–299, 302, 304, 307, 310, 314, 325, 329–333, 335, 338, 341, 344, 353, 357, 363, 367, 370–371, 373–374, 388–389, 396–397, 399, 401, 403, 413–414, 417, 422, 443
　Cortina 267
　18 Model 241
　49 Model 274
　78 Model 328
　79 Model 330
　86 Model 344
　87 Model 346
　88 Model 344, 346
Lotus-Climax 248
Lotus-Ford 287, 292
Lotus-Renault 357

March 276, 292–293, 298, 307, 319, 325, 349, 408
March-Ford 292–293, 298, 318–319
Marcos 247
Marlboro Texaco McLaren 314, 317, 319
Martini-Ford 331
Maserati 98, 105–106, 108, 112–114, 116, 118, 120–121, 124, 129, 131, 133–134, 136–141, 147, 151, 153, 158, 173–174, 185, 194–200, 202, 204, 209–210, 212–215, 218–223, 225–226, 229–230, 303, 390, 453
Matra 281, 289, 291, 292
Matra-Ford 268
Matra-Simca 294, 302
McLaren 7, 275, 292, 294, 303, 307, 313–314, 317–327, 329–330, 334–335, 338–339, 342, 345, 352–355, 357, 359, 361–363, 366–368, 370, 372–373, 375–376, 379, 383–384, 386–387, 390–392, 394–400, 405, 408–410, 422, 424–426, 428, 433–439, 441, 443, 446, 454, 456–458, 462
McLaren-Ford 292
Mercedes-Benz 7–8, 15, 21, 30, 32, 35, 38, 41–44, 71–72, 81–84, 89–90, 98, 101, 104–105, 112–117, 120, 123–124, 131–135, 137–139, 141–146, 150, 153, 155–156, 158–161, 165–168, 170, 172, 177, 180, 183–186, 188, 190–192, 197, 213–218, 221, 237, 341, 390, 403, 415, 451–453, 462
　W25 132
　W125 388
　W196 173, 213
MG 136
Miller 77, 79, 82, 95
Minardi 401, 416, 425, 450, 459
Modena 455
Mors 30
Motobloc 30

Newman-Haas 380, 411

Onyx-Ford 397, 415
Opel 30
Osella 340, 345, 351, 455

Osella-Ford 339

Panhard 13–14, 23, 25
Panhard-Levassor 21, *65*
Parnell 260
Penske 323, 360
Peugeot 10–11, 34–42, 44, 49, *69*,
   108–110, 362, 417, 426
  203 Model 202
Piccard & Pictet 42, 48
Pontiac GTO 415
Porsche 232, 244, 246, 250–251, 255,
   273, 282, 371–372
Porthos 30
Project Four 342
Prost 430, 432, 441, 447–448

RALT 339
RAM 361, 371
Red Bull 457, 462
Renault 7–8, 20, 22–24, 29–32, *67*, 109,
   189, 303, 327–330, 333, 335, 337,
   340, 342–344, 348–352, 355,
   357–359, 362, 374, *377, 384*, 394,
   450–451, 454–455, 457–458, 461
  90 Model 20
Rolland-Pilain 37, 60–61, 83
Rolls-Royce 88, 118–119

Saab 452
Sauber 7, 409, 416, 429, 434, 450, 462
Saudia Williams 330
Shadow 314, 327, 338
Simca 195, 199
Simca-Gordini 199, 209
Simtek 413, 415
Sizaire-Naudin 47
Snoek-Bolide 13, 45
Spirit 356–357
Stewart 430, 441
STP Corporation 293
Stutz 108
Sunbeam 38–40, 53–54, 56, 58–59, 61,
   64, 73, 76, 81–82, 86, 88, 108
Sunbeam-Talbot 50, 230
Surtees *276*, 292, 298, 305, 317, 334
Surtees-Ford 301

Talbot 53, *70*, 90–93, 102–103, 108, 158,
   177, 195
  Special *70*
Talbot-Darracq 53
Theodore 326, 331
Thomas 30
Toleman 348–349, 359, 363–368, 399
Toyota 7, 455, 457–459
Tyrrell 254, *276*, 286, 289, 295, 302–303,
   307, 309–310, 314, 319–322, 327,
   329, 350, 354, 356, 359, 363, 372,
   377, 385, 396–397, 399–400, 403, 414,
   425, 438

van Diemen 343
Vanwall 217, 219–222, 228, 230–232,
   234, 236–237
Vauxhall 37, 41
Vespa 231
Volkswagen 150, 232, 452
Volvo 452

Walker 292
Wanderer 123
Weigel 28
Williams 7, 261, 318, 330–331, 335, 338,
   340–341, 344–345, 347–349, 352–353,
   357–358, 360, 366, 369–370,
   373–374, 376, *380–381*, 385–391, 393,
   396, 399–403, 406–410, 413, 417,
   421–423, 426, 428–431, 433–435,
   438, 455, 457–458
  FW11B 388
Williams-Honda 373
Williams-Renault 408, 412
Winton 13
Wolf 327, 331, 336, 360
Wolseley 14

ENGINES
Alfa Romeo 331
  P3 141
  V12 152
BMW 7, 344, 348, 366, 458
Cosworth 258, 260, 269, 281, 285, 313,
   356, 404, 414
  DFV 270, 375

Coventry-Climax 224, 230, 232, 234, 239, 241, 248–249, 257, 263–264
Daimler 10
Ford 267–269, 287, 292–293, 298–299, 306, 318–319, 331, 333, 339, 375, 397, 408, 417
  Zetec-R 417
Hart 348, 412
Honda 264, 356–357–358, 365–366, 370, 373–374, 389–391, 397, 403, 408, 443, 445, 458
Maserati 263–264, 267–269
Mercedes 7–8, 458
Peugeot 47, 448
Porsche 361
Renault 7, 357, 374, 403, 408, 410, 412, 422
Repco 264, 269
TAG 357, 361
Weslake 270
Yamaha 407

PERSONALITIES
Agnelli, Gianni 426
Albers, Christijan 460
Alboreto, Michele 354, 356, 359, 362–364, 367–372, *377,* 385, 387, 393, 416
Alesi, Jean 396, 399–401, 408, 418, 422–429, 432–434, 448, 455
Alexander, Tyler *275*
Allison, Cliff 231, 237
Alonso, Fernando 8, *65,* 261, 384, 451, 454, 457–458, 461–462
Amon, Chris 292, 294–295, 302
Anderson, Bob 264
Anderson, Gary 404
Andretti, Mario *280,* 288, 293, 298, 319, 325–336, 349, 353, 369, 408, 411, 453
Andretti, Michael 408, 410
Arcangeli, Gigione 102, 109
Arco, Count 105
Arnoux, René 109, 331, 335–340, 349–353, 355–359, 363–364, 369, *377,* 385
Ascari, Alberto 51, *71, 176,* 198–200, 203, 205–206, 210–213, 215–216, 228, 393, 444, 453

Ascari, Antonio 49–51, *71,* 77–79, 81–83, 85–87, *176,* 198, 444
Assheton, Richard 148
Audetto, Daniel 320–321

Baghetti, Giancarlo 246, 261
Balestre, Jean-Marie 335–336, 339–340, 342–344, 346, 348, 399, 405
Ballileau, Henri 47
Ballot, Édouard 49, 52, 54, 56, 59, 78
Ballot, Ernest 94
Bandini, Lorenzo 255–257, 263–264, 267, 269–270
Baracca, Count Enrico 77
Baracca, Major Francesco 77
Baras, Paul 20, 203
Barnard, John 342, 387, 426, 430, 456
Barratt (mechanic) 82
Barrichello, Rubens 109, 408, 412, 419, 424, 431, 441–446, 448–455, 457, 460–461
Bäumer, Walter 188
Bazzi, Luigi 77–78
Behra, Jean 218–222, 238
Bell, Derek 282, 292
Bellof, Stefan 365, 372, 414
Beltoise, Jean-Pierre 291, 301, 306, 314
Bennett, Gordon 10, 12, 49
Benoist, Robert 87–88, 91–93, 97, 99–102, 193, 195
Bentley, W. O. 76–77
Benz, Eugen 13
Benz, Karl 9–10, 13
Berger, Gerhard 366, 375–376, 386–387, 391, 393, 397–398, 400, 403–408, 412, 418, 421–423, 426–428, 430, 432, 434
Bernard, Eric 418
Bertocchi, Guerino 223
Bianchi, 151
Bianchi, Lucien 253
Bigio, 38
Birkin, Tim 82, 98, 110–112, 114, 117, 148
Blackman, Vic 270, 311
Blundell, Mark 425

Boeri, Michel 300–301

Boillot, Georges 34–37, 40–41, 43–44, 47–48, *69*, 362

Bondurant, Bob 260, 266

Bonnier, Jo 236, 238, 245, 249, 263–265, *276*, 287, 301

Bordino, Pietro 50, 59, 60, 62–64, 73, 77–78, 81–82, 94

Borzacchini, Baconin 106–107, 112, 114, 117–118, 120–121, 125, 127, 130

Bouriat, 108–109

Boutsen, Thierry 396, 399–400, 454

Boyer, 52, 56–57

Brabham, Betty 240, 252, 254

Brabham, Jack 217, 224, 238–244, 264–265, 267–272, *273–274, 280*, 281, 291–294, 296, 339

Bradshaw, Ann 391

Brambilla, Vittorio 319, 324–325, 334

Brawn, Ross 46, 420, 426, 436, 439, 454

Brazil, Josef 138

Brendel, Heinz 185

Briatore, Flavio 455

Brilli-Peri, Count Gastone 88, 102

Brise, Tony 318–319

Bristow, Chris 243

Brivio, Count Antonio 135–136, 201

Broadley, Eric 271

Brooks, Tony 220, 222, 230–231, 233–236, 238–240, 244

Brown, Creighton 342

Bruce-Brown, Bill 50

Bruce-Brown, David 34–37, 47, 50

Brundle, Martin 357, 359, 363, 365, 398, 407, 414, 417

Bucknam, Ronnie 255, 260, 264, 269, *275*

Bugatti, Ettore 35, 46, 60, 88, 98–99

Burton, Alex 25

Bushell, Fred 396

Button, Jenson 450, 452, 454–455, 458

Byrne, Rory 47, 430

Cagno, Alessandro (Jacopo) 15, 21, 45

Cahier, Bernard 338

Caillois, Gustave 38–39

Campari, Giuseppe 51, 77, 79, 81–82, 85–87, 97–98, 106, 108, 114, 118, 129–130

Campbell, Donald 204

Campbell, Malcolm 49, 84, 91–93, 98, 100–101, 113, 118–120, 129, 133, 139, 204

Canestrini, Giovanni 207

Capelli, Ivan 400

Caracciola, Charly 113, 116, 131, 142

Caracciola, Rudolf *71*, 82–84, 89–91, 97–99, 101–102, 104–105, 112–113, 115–120, 124–125, 131–143, 146–147, 151–152, 154–156, 158–167, *169, 172*, 177, 179–180, 183–186, 239, 346, 443, 462

Carter, Jimmy 365

Casa, Ermano Della 248

Castellotti, 215–217, 220

Cecotto, Johnny 366, 399

Cevert, François *276*, 295–296, 299, 303–306, 308–310, 317, 371

Chamberlain, Neville 181–182

Chapman, Colin 192, 220, 231, 237–238, 240–241, 243, 245, 247, 250, 258–259, 269, *274*, 281, 283–284, 292–293, 296–297, 303, 305, 307–308, 310, 313, 327, 330–333, 335, 342, 344, 346, 353, 355, 357, 388, 415, 422, 443, 461

Chapman, Hazel 192, 259, 284

Charavel, Jean 94

Charlton, Dave 305

Chassagne, Jean 38, 52, 56–57, 59, 61, 90

Chasseloup-Laubat, Count Gaston de 12

Cheever, Eddie 339, 355

Chevrolet, Louis 15

Chiron, Louis 97, 100, 102–103, 105, 107–110, 112–118, 120–121, 124–125, 130–135, 141–143, 151–152, 155, 158, 186, 196–197, 199–200, 202, 231, 245, 252, 344

Chiti, Carlo 248

Cholmondeley Tapper, T. P. 153, 155

Clark, Helen 150

Clark, James 150, 284

Clark, Jim 17, 26, 38, 41, 150, 167, 230, 232–233, 237, 242–245, 247–259, 262–263, 267–271, *274*, 282–285, 290, 292, 407, 417, 443, 453, 462

Clément, Adolphe 23–26, 28

Coatalen, Louis 53, 58

Cobb, John 204

Collinet, Leon 36

Collins, Louise 231, 234–235

Collins, Peter *174*, 219–225, 230, 233–236

Collins, Peter (Australian) 422

Colombo, Gioachino 194

Conelli, Count Carlos 100–101

Cooper, John 218, 234, 240–241

Coppuck, Gordon 356

Costantini. Meo 91, 124, 130, 136

Cosworth, Mike 258

Coulthard, David 417–418, 420, 422–423, 425–427, 430, 432, 434–437, 439–445, 448–449, 451, 457

Courage, Piers 293–296, 356

Craner, Fred 147, 166, 415

Crombac, Jabby 195, 338

Crossley, Geoff 202

Czaikowski, Count 118, 130

Daimler, Gottlieb 9–10, 32

da Silva, Milton 257

da Silva, Viviane 412

Daly, Derek 351–352

de Angelis, Elio 338, 341, 348, 353, 357, 362, 366, 369–373, 375, 387, 399, 413, 454

de Beaufort, Carel 250, 255

de Cesaris, Andrea 342, 349, 351, 358–359, *377*, 404

de Cysteria, Prince 73

de Filippis, Maria-Teresa 231, 233

de Graffenried, Emmanuel 200, 228

de Knyff, René 11

DeLorean, John 415

de Palma, Peter 54, 56–58

de Palma, Ralph 34–36, 42, 49–52, 54–59

de Paolo, Peter 52

de Rothschild, Baron Henri 'Pierre' 104–105

de Sterlich, Marquis 105

de Tomaso, Alejandro 312

de Vizcaya, Ferdinand 95

de Vizcaya, Pierre 73, 95

Dennis, Ron 342, 346, 354, 366, 371, 374, *383*, 397, 399, 442, 447

Depailler, Patrick 314, 320–322, 324, 326, 331, 336, 340

Dewalque, Paul 264–266

di Montezemolo, Luca 320, 426, 428, 441

Divo, Albert 64, 74–76, 79, 87–88, 91, 93–94, 108–109

Dobry, 200

Donnelly, Martin 397, 401

Donohue, Mark 319

Dragoni, Eugenio 267

Dreyfus, René 97, 104, 107–108, 113, 118, 120, 124–125, 130, 133, 135–136, 141, 147, 193

Dubonnet, André 52, 54, 57

Ducarouge, Gérard 357, 369, 374, 388

Duckworth, Keith 258, 267, 270

Duesenberg, August 51, 58

Duesenberg, Fred 51

Dufaux, Charles and Frederic 48

Dumfries, Johnny 399

Dungl, Willy 346

Duray, Arthur 30, 41, 43, 46, 58

Dusio, Piero 227

Dutoit, Paul 73, 76

Ecclestone, Bernie 230–231, *279*, 290, 292–293, 297, 299–301, 304, 310, 332, 334–336, 340, 342, 344, 348–349, *383*, 447, 449, 456, 459

Edmond, J. 22

Eldridge, Ernest 49

Elford, Vic 290

Endruweit, Jim 281–282, 284

Étancelin, Philippe 109–112, 125–127, 129, 195–196, 200, 252

Eyston, Capt George 49, 85, 91, 99, 114, 129, 163, 218

Fabi, Teo 349, 385, 388

Fagioli, Luigi 113, 116, 118, 121, 130–132, 135, 137–139, 141, 143, 147, 156, 163, 202, 204, 206

Fangio, Juan-Manuel 19, 26, 129, 158, *173–176*, 197–204, 206–220, 223–226, 228, 230, 232–233, 239, 367, 393, 409, 443–444, 446, 453, 462
Farina, Giuseppe 'Nino' 147, 151, 159, 164, *176*, 180, 183, 186, 197–198, 202–206, 208–210, 213, 217, 227, 248, 261, 267, 370, 453–454
Fairman, Jack 232
Farman, Maurice (Henry) 14
Faroux, Charles 111
Fenn, Alan 93
Ferdinand, Archduke Franz 41, 121
Feretti (mechanic) 75
Ferguson, Andrew 285
Ferrari, Dino 194
Ferrari, Enzo 12, 33–34, 49–51, 64, 77, 79, 87, 98, 106, 108, 124, 130, 132, 148, 194, 203, 205, 207, 209, 216, 248, 254, 264, *279*, 309, 323–324, 326, 387–388, 393, 444
Ferrari, Piero 309
Feuereissen, Dr Karl 156, 160, 164
Firman, Ralph 343
Fisichella, Giancarlo 431, 433–435, 451, 457
Fittipaldi, Emerson 222, *280*, 292, 296, 298–306, 308–309, 313–318, 322, 411, 453
Fittipaldi, Wilson 318
Flammini, Maurizio 320
Florio, Vincenzo 15
Ford, Henry 14, 150
Foresti, Giulio 54, 103
Forghieri, Mauro 325, 327
Fornaca, Guido 77
Fournier, Henry 33
Francis, Alf 232
Franco, General 97, 152
Frentzen, Heinz-Harald 429–432, 435, 438–441
Frère, Paul 217, 219–220
Friedrich, Ernest 80
Friesacher, Patrick 460
Fry, 31
Fry, Joe 202

Gabriel, Fernand 13, 20–22, 26, 29, 46, 362, 373, 462
Gachot, Bertrand 402–404
Galistea, Adrianne 412
Galli, Nanni 304
Gallop, Capt Clive 55
Ganley, Howden 299, 304, 312
Gardner, Derek 360
Gendebien, Olivier 236
Gethin, Peter *276*, 298–299, 365
Ghica-Cantacuzino, Princes Jean and G. 100, 121
Giaccone, Enrico 78
Giambertone, Marcello 223
Giberti, Federico 248
Ginther, Richie 244–245, 247, 253–254, 259–260, 263–264, 268, 454
Giovannini, Aldo 98, 120
Glaser, Dr 187
Goebbels, Dr Joseph 107, 167
González, Froilan 203–204, 206–209, 212–214, 449
Gordini, Amédée 195
Goux, Jules 34, 38–41, 44, 52, 58–59, 61, 63, 89, 91, 94
Grace, Princess *176*, 295
Greene, Keith 237
Gregory, Masten 226, 233, 239
Griffin, Barry 386
Grimaldi, Louis (see Rainer, Prince)
Grimaldi, Stephanie 295
Guerrero, Roberto 348
Guinness, Algernon 48
Guinness, Kenelm Lee 38, 40, 48–49, 61–62, 64, 73–74, 80–82
Guinti, Ignazio 356
Gurney, Dan 246–247, 250, 254–255, 257, 263, 270, *273*
Guyot, Albert 40, 49, 52, 57–58, 60

Haas, Carl 414
Hailwood, Mike 253–254, *276*, 298–299, 301, 305, 316, 344, 401
Hailwood, Pauline 305
Häkkinen, Mika *381*, 403, 410, 412, 416, 422, 425, 426, 433–444, 446–447
Halford, Major Frank 121

Hamilton, Hugh 136
Hampshire, David 202
Hancock, John 37
Harrison, Cuth 202
Hart, Brian 260, 262, 348
Hasse, Rudi 159, 162, 165, 167, 177, 184–185
Hawkridge, Alex 359
Hawthorn, Mike 173, 175, 209–211, 212–217, 219, 222–226, 230–237, 344, 401, 444, 453–454
Hayes, Walter 258, 267, 269–270
Head, Patrick 330, 357, 366, 386, 388, 434
Heath, George 21, 65
Heidfeld, Nick 450, 457–458
Hémery, Victor 14, 20, 32–34, 36, 60
Herbert, Johnny 420, 422, 424–425, 427, 441
Herd, Robin 292–293
Herrmann, Hans 213–215, 246
Hesketh, Lord Alexander 306, 318, 461
Hill, Bette 231, 252, 287
Hill, Damon 280, 381, 406–410, 417–427, 429–430, 432, 434, 437, 452
Hill, Georgie 430
Hill, Graham 41, 129, 231, 233, 237, 244, 246, 248–259, 263–266, 269–272, 280, 281, 283, 286–290, 292, 295, 302, 307, 311, 318–319, 344, 401, 406, 410, 418, 429–430, 438, 445, 453
Hill, Phil 236–237, 244–248, 451, 453
Hillstead, A. F. C. 76
Hitler, Adolf 64, 79, 97, 120, 123–124, 134, 150, 152, 167, 178–179, 181–182, 185–186, 188, 192–193
Hoffman-Trobeck, Alice 'Baby' 124, 131, 142, 156
Hoffman-Trobeck, Aldfred 'Freddy' 124, 142
Honda, Soichiro 27, 238, 286, 387
Hornsted, L. G. 'Cupid' 41, 69
Horsley Anthony 'Bubbles' 306
Howe, Earl (Lord) 129, 133, 139, 147–148, 202

Hühnlein, Adolf 142, 146–147, 177–179, 181
Hulme, Denny 264, 269–271, 275, 281, 286, 288, 291–292, 294, 297, 300, 302–304, 308, 314, 316–317, 408, 453
Hunt, Bill 238
Hunt, James 279, 306–309, 314, 316–326, 329–330, 334, 336, 408, 411, 453

Ickx, Jacky 268, 281, 286–287, 291, 297–298, 300–303, 314, 372
Inghibert, Louis 52, 54
Ireland, Innes 237, 241, 243–244, 247, 260
Irvine, Eddie 411, 426–427, 430, 435, 438–442

Jabouille, Jean-Pierre 328–329, 333, 335–337, 339, 341, 377
Jano, Vittorio 78–79, 86, 114–115, 118, 120, 141, 146
Jellinek, Emil 12
Jellinek, Mercedes 12
Jenatzy, Camille 7, 11–13, 21, 23, 25, 30, 33, 41, 68
Johansson, Stefan 356, 368–370, 387, 390, 397
Johnson, Leslie 202
Jones, Alan 318–319, 324, 326, 329–331, 335, 337–341, 344–346, 355, 375, 390, 453
Jordan, Eddie 402–403, 438, 462
Junek, Elizabeth 101
Junek, Viktor 101

Kalnein, Count von 105
Karthikeyan, Narain 460
Kautz, Chritstian 159, 197
Kawamoto, Nobuhiko 260, 365
Keech, Ray 101
Kelly, Joe 202
Kerr, Phil 275
Kinnunen, Leo
Kling, Karl 213–215, 217
Koinigg, Helmuth 317
Krauss, Irwin 177, 179

Kuhn, Gregor 64
Kume, Tadashi 365

Laffite, Jacques 318, 322, 327–328,
     335–338, 340, 345–347, 355, 365,
     375–376
Lamy, Pedro 425
Lancia, Vincenzo 14–15, 19–20, 23–25,
     29–30, 33, 60, 203
Lang, Hermann 136, 140, 150, 153–156,
     158–167, *169, 172*, 177–178, 180,
     182–187, 191, 193, 195, 213–214,
     388, 390
Lardi, Lina 194
Larini, Nicola 416, 455
Larrousse, Gérard 352, 374
Lauda, Niki *279*, 298, 308–309, 314–321,
     324–325, 327–335, 338, 346–349,
     352–355, 357, 362–369, 371–372,
     393, 414, 444, 450
Lautenschlager, Christian 32–33, 43–44,
     134
le Blon, Hubert 23
Lehoux, Macel 104, 110, 140
Lehto, JJ 413, 420
Levassor, Émile 45
Levegh, Pierre 195, 217
Lewis-Evans, Stuart 230–231, 236
Ligier, Guy 263
Lillee, Dennis 460
Lister, Brian 261
Lombardi, Lella 318
Luhti, Joachim 397

MacDonald, John 361
Maggs, Tony 250
Mairesse, Willi 249
Mansell, Nigel 341, 357–358, 363–365,
     367–376, *378, 380*, 385–391, 393–407,
     411, 414–415, 418, 421–424, 443,
     446, 450
Mansell, Rosanne 372
Marimón, Onofré 213–214
Marninoni, Attilio 159
Marteau (mechanic) 6, 85
Martinelli, Paolo 47
Martini, Pierluigi 401

Maserati, Alfieri 64, 105
Maserati, Ernesto 94
Mass, Jochen 317–318, 320, 323, 327,
     330, 349–350, 352
Materassi, Emilio 100, 103
Materassi, Ernest 94
Mateschitz, Dietrich 462
Mayer, Teddy *275*, 326, 329, 339, 342
Mayer, Tim 254
Mays, Raymond 142, 149
McAdam, John 17
McAlpine, Kenneth 260
McLaren, Bruce 234–235, 238–241,
     243–244, 248–249, 252–253, *275*,
     291–292, 295
Mecklenburg, Grand Duchess of 24
Mercanti, Arturo 84
Merz, Otto 99, 101, 121
Merzario, Arturo 314
Michelin, André 10, 44
Michelin, Édouard 10, 44
Mières, Roberto 217
Milenkovic, Bosko 186
Miles, John 296
Milton, Tommy 51, 88, 96
Minoia, Ferdinando 114
Moll, Guy 132–134, 139, 148
Modena, Stefano 403
Momberger, 132–133
Monteiro, Tiago 460
Montoya, Juan Pablo 261, *384,* 445–446,
     448–449, 451–455, 457–458, 461
Morbidelli, Gianni 425
Moreno, Roberto 401–402
Morgen, Heinrich-Joachim von 112
Moriceau, Jules 55–57, 62, 74, 92–94
Mosley, Max 292, 300, 335, *383*, 405,
     412, 416, 423, 447, 455, 459
Moss, Stirling 19, 26, 106, *173, 176*,
     205–207, 215–218, 220–221, 230,
     232–246, 249, 344, 388, 447, 453, 462
Müller, Hermann 165, 167–168, 177,
     180, 183, 185–186, 188
Murphy, Jimmy 51–58, 77–78, 82
Murray, David 202
Murray, Gordon 330–331, 349, 355, 358,
     387

Musso, Luigi 215, 217, 221–222,
    232–233, 236, 250
Mussolini, Benito 59, 64, 97–98, 117,
    150–151, 182

Nakajima, Satoru 390, 396–397, 399
Nakamura, Yoshio 268, 271, *275*, 288
Nannini, Sandro 398–400
Nazzaro, Biagio 60, 63
Nazzaro, Felice 14, 21, 23–25, 29–33,
    38–39, 51, 60, 62–63, *68–69*, 77–79,
    211
Neubauer, Alfred 64, 82–83, 107, 112–113,
    131–134, 137–138, 141, 144–145, 151,
    155, 166, *170*, 177–179, 183, 187, 190,
    192–193, 213, 215, 218–219, 236, 341
Newey, Adrian 434
Nicholls, Don 359
Nichols, Steve 392
Nilsson, Gunnar 327–329, 335, 344
Noghès, Anthony 103
North, David 331
Nosetto, Roberto 327–328
Nunn, Mo 348, 360
Nuvolari, Alberto 197
Nuvolari, Giuseppe 14
Nuvolari, Tazio 10, 14, 26, 34, 49, 59, *72,*
    78, 97–99, 103, 106, 108–109,
    114–119, 121, 125–130, 132–133,
    135–143, 146–148, 150–153, 155–159,
    163–165, 168, *170, 174,* 177, 179–180,
    182, 184–186, 188, 196–199, 207,
    211, 212, 223, 239, 249, 367,
    408–409, 442–444, 462

Oatley, Neil 337
Oliver, Jackie 348–349
Olson, Ernie 55, 57–58, 77
Opel, Adam 38
Opel, Fritz von 30
Opel, Rikky von 360
Orsi, Count 221
Orsi, Omar 221, 229

Pace, Carlos 314, 317–318, 327, 401
Paletti, Riccardo 351, 375, 413
Panhard, René 45

Panis, Olivier 418, 425, 427, 430–432
Parma, Duke of 24
Parnell, Reg 202, 262
Parnell, Tim 262
Parry Thomas, J. G. 49, 88, 91
Passarini, Maurizio 434
Patrese, Riccardo 332, 334, 348,
    350–351, 353, 355–356, 370, 375, *377,*
    391, 396–397, 399, 402–404, 408
Penske, Roger 360
Perdisa, Cesare 217
Perkins (mechanic) 74
Peron, Eva 205
Peron, Juan 205, 210, 215
Pescarolo, Henri 294, 304
Petersens, Fredrik af 334
Peterson, Ronnie *276,* 293, 298–299,
    304–309, 314–316, 318, 323–324,
    327, 329–330, 333–334, 371
Piccinini, Marco 388
Pictet, Lucien 48
Pietsch, Ilse 141, 152, 156
Pietsch, Paul 134, 141, 185
Pilain, 37
Piquet, Nelson 333, 335, 338–341,
    343–349, 352–353, 357–359, 365–370,
    372–376, *378,* 385–386, 388–391,
    402–403, 405, 443
Pironi, Didier 339–341, 348–353, *377,*
    390, 413, 454
Platé, Gigi 89, 202
Pollock, Craig 438
Popp, Erica 180, 183
Porsche, Dr Ferdinand 90, 123–124, 150,
    193
Postlethwaite, Dr Harvey 227, 306
Prost, Alain 109, 295, 338–339, 342,
    345–346, 349–354, 356–359, 362–369,
    371–375, *377–379,* 385–390, 392–403,
    405, 407–411, 413, 418, 430, 434,
    437, 443, 446, 448, 462
Prüller, Heinz 290
Pryce, Tom 327
Purley, David 307–308, 329, 360, 401

Räikkönen, Kimi 8, *384,* 446, 449–452,
    454, 457–458, 461

Rainier, Prince 129, *176*, 203
Ramirez, Jo 392, 409, 411
Ratzenberger, Roland 413
Regazzoni, Clay 292, 297, 300, 302, 305, 314–317, 319–324, 326–327, 334–335, 337, 339, 385
Renault, Louis 6–7, 22–23, 26, 32, 46, *68*
Renault, Marcel 7, 13, 20, 26
Resta, Dario 31, 33, 38–39, 79, 81
Reutemann, Carlos 299, 314, 316–318, 327, 329–331, 333–336, 340, 343–347, 349
Revson, Peter 307, 309, 314, 317
Rigolly, Louis 21
Rindt, Jochen 256, 263–268, *280*, 289–298, 311, 356, 453–454
Rindt, Nina 293, 297
Robertson, George 59, 77
Rodriguez, Pedro 269, 295, 298, 356
Rodriguez, Ricardo 247
Rolls, Hon Charles 11, 13–14
Rosberg, Keke 348–358, 363–366, 368–373, 375–376, 386, 453
Rosemeyer, Bernd 19, 26, 139–140, 142–143, 146–147, 151–163, 165, 167–168, *169*, *172*, 180, 188, 191, 408–409, 462
Rosemeyer, Elly 155–156, 160–162
Rosenberger, Adolf 89–90, 99
Rosier, Louis 200, 206, 228
Rougier, Henri 21, 46
Royce, Henry 14
Ruesch, Hans 157, 167

'Sabipa' 110–111, 114
Sage, Jean 358, 385
Sailer, Max 43
Salamano, Carlo *70*, 74–76, 78, 82
Salazar, Eliseo 352
Salcito, Dr Domenico 395
Salo, Mika 425, 435, 440–441
Salvadori, Roy 230–231
Salzer, Otto 44
Sanesi, 197
Sartrio, Baron 105
Sato, Takuma 450, 452, 455
Sauber, Peter 462

Scarfiotti, Ludovico 268
Scheckter, Jody 303–304, 306–307, 309–310, 314, 316, 321–323, 325, 327–331, 336, 338, 340, 342, 407, 434, 440, 443–444
Schell, Harry 239
Schlesser, Jean-Louis 393
Schlesser, Jo 286
Schumacher, Corinna (née Betsch) 423
Schumacher, Michael 6, 20, 26, 46, 77, 109, 129, 182, 211, 248, 261, *380–381*, *383*, 404, 406–413, 416–455, 457–458, 460–462
Schumacher, Ralf 248, 261, 428, 430, 433–434, 437–438, 441, 445–448, 450–451, 454–455, 457, 459
Schumacher, Toni 289
Scott-Brown, Archie 232
Seaman, Dick 136, 153, 157–158, 160–161, 166–168, *169*, *172*, 177, 179–181, 183–184, 190, 443
Sebastian, Wilhelm 132
Segrave, Sir Henry 49–50, 53, 55–58, 61–62, *70*, 73–76, 78–82, 84, 86, 88, 91–94, 96, 98, 105, 178
Semos (mechanic) 40
Senechal, Robert 92–93
Senna, Ayrton 17, 26, 38, 129, 167, 241, 257, 288, 305, 343, 357, 359, 363–376, *379–380*, 385–420, 422, 429, 434, 443, 447, 453, 462
Serra, Chico 343
Servoz-Gavin, Johnny 295
Shackleton, Sir Ernest 260
Shepard, Elliot 25
Shirer, William 192
Shnaider, Alex 462
Shuttleworth, Richard 147
Siffert, Jo 265, 281, 287, 292, 294, 298, 356
Simon, André 215
Sims, Dave 281–284
Sivocci, Ugo 50, 59, 77–78
Sommer, Raymond 147, 153, 155, 195–197, 199, 249
Souders, George 100
Spence, Mike 263, 265, 285

Stacey, Alan 237, 242
Stalin 97
Stanley, Louis 266–267, 327
Stephenson, Robert 9
Stewart, Helen 266, 303, 309–310
Stewart, Jackie 41, 196, 244, 247–248,
    254–255, 257–259, 263–267, 269–270,
    276, 281, 286–293, 296–306, 308–310,
    314–315, 371, 385–386, 389, 402,
    407, 430, 462
Stewart, Jimmy 244, 248, 291
Stewart, Paul 430
Stoffel, Henri 108–109
Stommelen, Rolf 292, 318, 355–356
Streiff, Philippe 411
Stuck, Hans 107, 117, 132–138, 142,
    144, 146–147, 155–157, 159, 162–164
Surtees, John 241–242, 245, 249–250,
    253–257, 259, 263–269, 271–272, *280*,
    281, 286, 292, 371, 388, 456
Szisz, Ferenc (François) 6–8, 20, 22–26,
    29–30, 32, 46, *67–68*, 203, 211, 385,
    462

Takagi, Toranosuke 438
Tambay, Patrick 330, 352–353, 355–359,
    363, 439, 454
Tart, Henri 23
Taruffi, Piero 196–197, 205–206, 208,
    252
Tauranac, Ron 339
Tavenaux, Philippe *66*
Tavoni, Romolo 235–236, 248
Taylor, John 268
Taylor, Mike 243
Taylor, Trevor 247, 249
Thomas, René 41, 49
Todt, Jean 46, *383*, 426, 430–431,
    434–435, 438, 440, 446–447
Trintignant, Maurice 195, 216–217, 219,
    231–232, 238, 245, 250, 299
Trossi, 197
Trulli, Jarno 430, 437, 441, 448,
    454–455, 457, 461
Tyrrell, Ken 196, 206–207, 268, 281,
    286–287, 303, 314, 316, 332, 365,
    372, 374, 396, 438

Uhlenhaut, Rudolf 219
Umberto, King of Italy 205
Unser, Bobby 288

Vanderbilt, William K. 13, 25
Vandervell, Tony 228, 237
Varzi, Achille 97–98, 102–103, 105, 109,
    113–118, 120–121, 125–130, 132–135,
    137, 139, 141, 151–153, 156, 164, *169*,
    197–198, 211, 444, 462
Verstappen, Jos 418, 420
Villeneuve, Gilles 324, 329, 333–336,
    338, 345, 348, 350, *377*, 393, 424, 454
Villeneuve, Jacques 424, 426–434, 436,
    445, 452, 455
Villeneuve, Joann 329
Villoresi, Luigi 196, 198–200, 203, 205,
    208–209, 228, 252
Vlcek, Jaroslav 201
Volonterio, Ottorino 248, 261
von Brauchitsch, Manfred 113, 120,
    131–132, 136, 139–143, 145–147,
    151–152, 154–156, 158–159, 162–163,
    166–167, *169–170*, 177–180, 184–188,
    190, 198, 208, 211, 217, 388, 443, 450
von Cholitz, Gen Dietrich 193
von Delius, Ernst 160–162
von Tripps, Taffy 244–247, 253

Wagner, Louis 34, 36, 44, 52, 55–56,
    59–60, 79, 91–93, 120
Walker, Huntley 76
Walker, Rob 231–232, 237, 241, 245–246,
    287, 447, 461
Walkinshaw, Tom 430
Warr, Peter 237, 285, 296–297, 305, 310,
    357, 369, 374, 387, 396, 422
Warwick, Derek 359, 362–363, 374, 397,
    401
Watkins, Prof Sid 250, 291, 332,
    334–335, 395, 412–413
Watson, John 306, 310, 323, 325,
    330–332, 334–335, 338, 342,
    345–347, 350–351, 353–356, 359, 392
Watson, Scott 237
Watt, Hall 31
Watt, James 9, 44

Webber, Mark 450, 457
Wendlinger, Karl 409, 416
Werner, Christian 82–84, 101
Wheatcroft, Tom 192–193, 308, 408
Whitehead, Peter 200, 228
Wickham, John 356
Wilcox, 'Howdy' 49
Wilkinson, Wilkie 85
'Williams' (Charles Grover-Williams) 71,
    101–102, 104–105, 107–108, 113,
    115, 118, 121, 193, 198
Williams, Frank 293, 296, 304, 314, 332,
    337–339, 341, 344, 347, 357, 360,
    366, 373, 375–376, 383, 385–386,
    414–415, 428–429, 434–435, 447, 462
Williams, Virginia 429
Williamson, Roger 307–308
Wimille, Christine 199
Wimille, Jean-Pierre 97, 138, 153, 193,
    195, 197, 199–200
Windsor, Peter 373
Winkelhock, Manfred 364, 371
Wolf, Walter 327, 360
Wright, Peter 414
Wurz, Alexander 434–435

Zborowski, Count Louis 55, 61, 77, 79,
    82–84
Zehender, 140, 155
zu Leiningen, Hermann 112, 132, 137
Zuccarelli, Paul 38–39, 48

RACES AND CIRCUITS

A1-Ring 433
Adelaide 373, 379, 381, 386–387, 398,
    411, 421, 425, 432
Aida 412–413, 425
Aintree 217, 222, 246, 250
Alessandria 133
American GP 27
  1912 37
  1914 41
Amiens 27, 38, 41
Anderstorp 306, 321, 331–332
Anjou 34
Argentine GP
  1950 201
  1952 210
  1953 213
  1956 219
  1957 222
  1958 230
  1960 241
  1972 299
  1973 304
  1974 314
  1977 327
  1978 330, 390
  1979 335
  1980 338–339
  1981 344, 423
  1995 422–423
  1996 427
  1998 435
Australian GP
  1986 379, 385
  1987 391
  1988 394
  1989 398
  1990 401
  1991 405
  1992 407
  1993 411
  1996 427
  1997 430
  1999 438
  2000 443
  2001 445
  2002 447
  2003 451
  2004 453–454
  2005 7, 457
Austrian GP
  1964 255
  1970 296
  1971 298
  1972 302
  1973 308
  1974 316
  1975 317, 319
  1976 323
  1977 329
  1978 333
  1979 337

1980 341
1981 346
1982 353
1983 357
1984 366
1985 371
1986 385
1987 390
1998 436
1999 440
2000 443
2001 445
2002 448
2003 451
AVUS 89, 96, 123, 131–133, 194, 238

Bahrain GP
 2004 454
 2005 7, 457
Barcelona 151–152, 207, 281, 417, 427
Bathurst 1000 KM 408
Belgian GP
 1925 85
 1933 129
 1934 135
 1936 152
 1937 158
 1949 204
 1950 201, 206
 1952 209
 1955 217
 1957 (cancelled) 222
 1958 233
 1963 252
 1966 263, *276*
 1972 301
 1974 315
 1976 321
 1978 331
 1979 336
 1980 339
 1982 350
 1986 375
 1988 393
 1989 397
 1990 400
 1991 403–404

1992 407
1993 410
1995 425
1998 437
1999 440
2000 443
2002 450
2004 *383*, 454
Belgrade 186, 208
Bonneville 139, 204
Brands Hatch 235, 237, 243, 254, 268,
    279, 281, 287, 296, 302, 322–324,
    332–333, 340, 352, 357, 366, 372,
    375, 407
Brazilian GP
 1973 308
 1974 314
 1975 317
 1976 319
 1977 327
 1978 330
 1979 335
 1980 338–339
 1981 344
 1982 349
 1983 355
 1985 369
 1986 374
 1987 388
 1988 392
 1989 394–395
 1990 399
 1991 403
 1993 408
 1994 412–413
 1995 422–423
 1996 427
 1997 430
 1998 435
 1999 439
 2000 443
 2001 445
 2002 447
 2003 451
 2004 455
Bremgarten 136, 156, 179, 185, 197–198,
    200, 205

Brescia 59, 97–98
  GP of Gentlemen 59
British GP 147, 455
  1923 *70*
  1926 *70*
  1927 100
  1948 199
  1949 (European) 202
  1950 201
  1951 206, 449
  1952 209
  1955 217–218
  1956 233
  1957 222
  1958 233, 237
  1959 239
  1962 250
  1966 268
  1968 287
  1969 291, 337
  1970 296
  1971 298
  1973 305–306
  1974 315
  1975 318
  1976 322
  1977 328
  1981 346
  1982 351
  1984 366
  1986 375
  1988 392
  1991 403
  1992 *380*
  1995 424
  1997 432
  1998 435
  2002 449
  2003 451
  2004 454
Brno 112, 120, 164–166, 193, 200
Brooklands 38, 41, 47, *70*, 81, 91–93,
  99–100, 121, 196
Brussels GP 1960 *273*
Budapest 151–152, 193, 196
Buenos Aires 199, 210, 241, 304

Caesars Palace GP
  1981 347
  1982 354
Canadian GP
  1967 271
  1968 288
  1969 291
  1970 297
  1971 299
  1972 303
  1973 309
  1976 324
  1977 29
  1978 334
  1979 338
  1980 341
  1982 351
  1983 356
  1984 365
  1985 370–371
  1988 392
  1989 396
  1990 400
  1991 403
  1992 406
  1993 410
  1994 416–417
  1995 424
  1996 428
  1997 432
  1998 435
  1999 439
  2000 443
  2001 446
  2002 449
  2003 451
  2004 454
  2005 7, 458
Casablanca 236, 239
Cataluyna 417
Charterhall circuit 230
Chinese GP 2004 455
Clermont-Ferrand 27, 258, 296, 302
Coppa Acerbo 148, 163
Coppa Ciano 156
Crystal Palace 295

Czech GP
  1930 112
  1931 116
  1932 120
  1933 130
  1934 138
  1935 147
  1937 164
  1938 68
Cominges 27
Cremona 51

Dallas 365, 458
Daytona 34, 41, 47, 49, 98, 113, 120, 129
Detroit 351, 355–356, 365, 375, 389, 414, 458
Dieppe 27, 30, 34–36, 38, 41, 44, 86, 211
Dijon 27, 315, 336, 345, 353, 363, *377*
Donington GP
  1936 147, 150, 167
  1937 157, 164, 166, 414
  1938 *72*, 181–182, 192, 414
Donington Park 138–139, 147, 167, 182, 196, 202, 308, 346, 357, 408–409, 414
Dutch GP (Holland)
  1950 201
  1952 209, 211
  1955 217
  1957 (cancelled) 222
  1958 233
  1960 242
  1961 247
  1966 268
  1967 269, *274*
  1968 286
  1969 291
  1970 295
  1971 298
  1972 303
  1974 315
  1975 318
  1976 323–324
  1977 329
  1978 333, 353
  1979 337
  1980 341
  1981 346

  1982 351
  1983 357
  1984 367
  1985 372

East London 251–252
Eifel GP 151–152
Estoril 367, 398, 407, 410, 414, 426
European GP
  1926 91
  1949 202–203
  1983 357
  1985 372
  1993 408
  1994 420
  1995 425
  1996 427
  1997 433
  1999 441
  2000 443–444
  2002 449
  2003 451
  2004 454
  2005 458

Fiorano test track 324
French GP 27, 97
  1906 6–7, 15–27, *65–66, 69*, 201, 203, 362, 374, 385, 453, 461–462
  1907 27–30, *69*
  1908 27, 30–34
  1909 (cancelled) 34
  1912 27, 34–37, 86
  1913 38–41, *67*
  1914 16, 41, *69*, 79
  1921 51, 59
  1922 60
  1923 64
  1924 79
  1925 86
  1926 34, 88
  1927 99
  1928 101
  1929 105
  1930 109
  1932 120
  1933 129

1934 134, 213
1935 139
1936 153, 195
1937 158
1938 168, 443
1939 184
1948 199
1949 204
1950 201, 206
1952 209, 211
1953 *173*
1955 (cancelled) 217
1956 220
1957 222, 250
1958 233
1959 238
1962 58, 250, *273*
1965 258
1966 267
1967 270
1968 286
1970 296
1971 298
1973 306
1974 315
1976 321
1978 333
1979 336, *377*
1980 340
1981 345
1982 352
1983 355
1984 363
1986 375
1988 392
1989 396
1990 400
1991 403
1992 406
1993 410
1994 418
1996 428
1997 432
1998 435
1999 439
2001 446
2002 449

2003 451
2004 454
2005 7, 27, *65*, 84, 461

Geneva, GP of Nations 197
Genoa 205
German GP 227
  1926 88–89
  1928 101
  1930 (cancelled) 107
  1931 116
  1935 141
  1937 159
  1938 177–178, 190, 443
  1939 184
  1951 207
  1952 209
  1953 212
  1954 214, 390
  1955 (cancelled) 217
  1957 *174*, 222
  1959 239
  1964 269
  1969 291
  1970 296
  1971 298
  1973 308
  1975 318
  1976 *279*, 322
  1977 329
  1979 337
  1981 346
  1982 352
  1983 357
  1984 366
  1985 371
  1986 376
  1987 389
  1988 392
  1991 403
  1992 406
  1993 410
  1994 416
  1996 428
  1997 432
  1998 436
  1999 440

2000 443
2001 446
2002 450
2003 451
2004 454
Goodwood 209, 248, 254, 256, 295
Gordon Bennett Trophy 13–15, 26

Hethel test track 296
Hockenheim 227, 281, 284, 290, 296,
    329, 333, 340, 390, 400, 418–419, 424
Hungarian GP
  1936 151–152
  1986 376
  1987 389
  1988 392
  1989 396
  1990 400
  1991 403
  1992 406
  1993 410
  1994 419
  1995 425
  1996 428
  1997 432
  1998 436
  1999 440
  2000 443
  2001 446
  2002 450
  2003 451
  2004 453–454
Hungaroring 376, 385, 397, 432

Imola 7, 341, 344, 350, 355, 364,
    369–370, 375, 388, 392, 395, 399,
    410, 412, 416, 427, 434, 443, 445,
    455, 457, 460
Indianapolis 444, 446, 450, 455, 458–461
Indianapolis 500 race 34–35, 38, 41, 49,
    51–52, 94–97, 199–200, 209, 239,
    252, 257, 285, 288, 424, 444
Interlagos 335, 399
Isle of Man TT 48, 91, 157, 238
Italian GP
  1921 59
  1922 60

1923 64, 77
1924 79, 82
1926 94
1927 100
1928 101
1929 105
1931 114
1935 147
1936 150
1937 156, 163
1938 443
1948 199
1949 204
1950 201
1951 207
1952 209
1953 213
1954 214
1955 218
1956 220
1958 235
1959 238
1962 250
1966 264
1967 271
1970 297
1971 *276*, 374
1976 324
1977 329
1980 341
1981 346
1982 353
1983 357
1985 372
1988 393
1994 420
1999 441
2001 446
2002 450
2003 451
Italian 350cc Championship 102

Jacarapagua 374
Japanese GP
  1976 325
  1977 391
  1987 391

1988 394
1989 398
1990 401
1992 407
1993 411
1995 425
1996 429
1997 433
1998 437–438
1999 441
2000 444
2002 450
2003 452
2004 455
Jarama 285–286, 315, 417
Jerez 398, 420, 433

Kyalami 289, 300, 317, 327, 339, 343, 358

Las Vegas 347, 354, 458
Lasarte 78, 81, 91, 100–102, 105
Le Mans 6–7, 15–16, 28, 35, 52, 54–55,
    65, 105, 121, 201, 203, 270, 362,
    373–374, 453
  Bugatti circuit 270
  24 hour race 52, 57, 77, 97, 108, 111,
    148, 152, 217, 222, 237, 301, 390
Livorno 163–164
Long Beach 320, 328, 331, 336, 339, 344,
    355, 458
Luxembourg GP
  1997 433
  1998 437
Lyon 27, 41, 44, 69, 79, 134, 197

Magny-Cours 7, 27, 403, 432, 443
Malaysian GP
  1999 441
  2000 444–445
  2001 445
  2002 447
  2003 451
  2004 454
  2005 7, 457
Marseille 196
Melbourne 7, 427, 434, 453
Mexico City 254, 268, 281, 291, 385

Mexico GP
  1964 256
  1966 263, 269
  1968 288
  1970 297–298, 385
  1986 385
  1987 390
  1988 392
  1989 396
  1990 400
  1991 403
  1992 406
Milan GP 153, 155, 197
Mille Miglia 97–99, 113, 120, 202
Milwaukee 37
Miramas 27, 88, 91
Monaco GP 97, 99, 176, 346
  1929 71, 103, 105, 163, 286
  1930 103, 107, 231
  1931 113, 120
  1932 118–120, 129
  1933 124–125, 129, 131, 133
  1934 131–133, 139
  1935 138–139
  1936 151, 163
  1937 161, 163, 198
  1948 198, 204, 286
  1949 203
  1950 201, 216
  1952 (sports cars) 209, 211
  1955 215–216, 219
  1956 219, 222
  1957 222, 232
  1958 230–232, 238, 286, 299, 344
  1959 238, 242
  1960 241–242, 245
  1961 245–247, 249
  1962 249, 252
  1963 252, 254
  1964 254, 257
  1965 257, 264
  1966 264, 270
  1967 269–270, 286
  1968 286, 290
  1969 290, 295
  1970 293–295, 298
  1971 298, 301

1972 300–301, 306
1973 306, 315
1974 315, 318
1975 318, 321
1976 321, 328
1977 328, 331
1978 331, 336
1979 336, 340
1980 340, 345
1981 345, 351
1982 350–351, 356, *377*
1983 356, 365
1984 363–366, 370, 372, 414
1985 370, 375
1986 375, 389
1987 389, 392
1988 392, 396
1989 396, 400
1990 399–400
1991 403, 406
1992 406, 410
1993 410, 417
1994 416–417, 424
1995 424, 427
1996 427, 431
1997 431, 435
1998 435–436, 439
1999 439, 443
2000 443, 445
2001 445, 449
2002 448–449, 451
2003 451, 454
2004 248, 261, 454, 458
2005 7, 457–458
Monte Carlo Rally 311
Montjuich 289, 317
Montlhéry 27, 86, 88, 99, 114, 129, 134,
    140, 153, 195, 213
Montreal 370, 375, 413
Monza 60, 63, 77, 79, 83–84, 88, 94–95,
    97, 102–103, 105–106, 109, 114, 120,
    124, 130, 132, 136, 150, 158, 179–181,
    200, 207, 209–210, 214, 216, 230,
    246–247, 250, 253, 256, 259, 268, 271,
    276, 288, 291, 296–298, 302, 308, 316,
    319, 324, 333, 338, 342, 346–347, 357,
    367, 370, 372, 385, 390, 393, 401,
    403–404, 410, 420, 425, 429, 432, 437,
    440–441, 444, 446, 451, 454
Moroccan GP 1958 236–237
Mosport 316, 324, 329, 371
Mount Fuji *279*, 325–327, 329, 391

Nevers *65*
Nice 196
    Speed Week, 1899 12
Nivelles 301, 315
Nürburgring 7, 97, 99, 101, 105, 115,
    120, 135–136, 139, 142, 144–145, 151,
    155–156, 159, 165, *170, 174,* 177, 181,
    184–185, 190, 207, 211, 219, 222,
    224–225, 230, 234, 248, 250, 253, 255,
    259, 268, 271, *279,* 291, 293, 296, 302,
    316, 322, 328, 362, 367, 409, 425, 427,
    433, 437, 441, 443, 449, 451 454, 458

Oporto 235
Österreichring 353, 433

Pacific GP
    1994 412
    1995 425
Paris-Amsterdam-Paris, 1898 11
Paris-Madrid 1903 13, 16
Paris-Marseilles-Paris, 1896 11
Paris-Rouen, 1894 10–11
Pau 27, 109–110, 113–114
Paul Ricard 27, 298, 306, 318–319,
    321–322, 333, 348, 373, 375, 389, 400
Pedralbes 215
Pendine Sands 98
Pescara circuit 230
Phoenix 396, 399, 403, 458
Portuguese GP
    1958 235
    1959 238
    1984 367
    1985 369
    1986 385
    1987 390
    1988 393
    1989 397
    1990 401
    1991 404–406